Business Rankings Annual

ISSN 1043-7908

2013

Business
Rankings
Annual

**Lists of Companies, Products, Services, and Activities
Compiled from a Variety of Published Sources.**

GALE
CENGAGE Learning®

Detroit • New York • San Francisco • New Haven, Conn • Waterville, Maine • London

GALE
CENGAGE Learning·

Business Rankings Annual, 2013

Deborah J. Draper

Project Editor: Hillary Hentschel

Product Management: Jenai Mynatt Drouillard

Editorial Support Services: Charles Beaumont

Composition and Electronic Prepress: Gary W. Leach

Manufacturing: Rita Wimberley

For product information and technology assistance, contact us at
Gale Customer Support, 1-800-877-4253.
For permission to use material from this text or product,
submit all requests online at **www.cengage.com/permissions.**
Further permissions questions can be emailed to
permissionrequest@cengage.com

Gale
27500 Drake Rd.
Farmington Hills, MI, 48331-3535

ISBN-13: 978-1-4144-5826-7
ISBN-10: 1-4144-5826-6
ISBN-13: 978-1-4144-5827-4 (4 volume set)
ISBN-10: 1-4144-5827-4
ISBN-13: 978-1-4144-5829-8 (Cumulative Index, 3 part set)
ISBN-10: 1-4144-5829-0
ISBN-13: 978-1-4144-9549-1 (Cumulative Index, part 1)
ISBN-10: 1-4144-9549-8
ISBN-13: 978-1-4144-9550-7 (Cumulative Index, part 2)
ISBN-10: 1-4144-9550-1
ISBN-13: 978-1-4144-9551-4 (Cumulative Index, part 3)
ISBN-10: 1-4144-9551-X

ISSN 1043-7908

Printed in Mexico
1 2 3 4 5 6 7 16 15 14 13 12

Contents

Business Rankings Annual is published in response to the number of requests librarians receive about ranking information. To provide quick answers to questions in the most frequently requested subject areas, Gale has researched and compiled nearly 5,000 relevant and timely rankings. The "top ten" from each of these rankings appears in this volume, grouped under standard subject headings for easy browsing.

Method of Compilation

The rankings have been researched and gathered from online and print sources. The lists that have been selected are those most in demand by business people, librarians, students, and the public; for each one, this volume typically provides at least the "top ten" on the list, along with important details about the ranking as described below. In order to represent as many publications as possible, sources of rankings are alternated from edition to edition. This volume draws most of its entries from serials and periodicals published between July, 2011 and June, 2012.

Arrangement

Business Rankings Annual presents the lists grouped by subject, and subjects are arranged alphabetically. Most headings are taken from the Library of Congress (LC) subject headings, for example: Banks and Banking; Banks and Banking, International. However, when LC did not offer an appropriate or sufficiently up-to-date heading, Wilson's *Business Periodicals Index* was consulted, and then the ABI/INFORM, a CD-ROM index from UMI, to find categories already in use in the field.

Broad subject categories like Advertising Agencies are subdivided. A primary method of subdivision is geographic; "International" indicates the category covers both U.S. and foreign aspects and "Foreign" indicates that the category excludes U.S. aspects. Some categories are further divided for individual U.S. states, foreign countries, and continents. Other subdivisions reflect different facets of an industry such as Advertising, Export, Import Trade, and Market Share. Cross-references have been included to help the user locate the exact subject term (for example: Building Contractors, *See* Contractors). All of these subject terms appear in the *Outline of Contents*, where it is possible to scan the list of headings quickly to determine the exact form of the subject term that has been used.

Bibliography

A complete listing of more than 300 original sources used to compile *Business Rankings Annual* is provided in the Bibliography. Information cited includes:

- Publication name
- Publisher
- Address, telephone, fax number and URL
- Frequency of publication
- Price
- ISSN, if applicable

Comprehensive Index

The reader can quickly locate all the rankings in which a given company, person, or product appears by consulting the *Index*. Under each citation, the subject code of the ranking is listed along with its book number. Thus, the *Index* provides an overview of the areas in which the companies, people, etc. are being ranked, and users can be more selective about looking up the entries that interest them. Every name in every list is indexed, not just those that are ranked first.

Available in Electronic Formats

The Directory is also available online as part of the *Gale Directory Library*. For more information, call 1-800-877-GALE.

Comments and Suggestions Welcome

Comments and suggestions are always welcome and can be addressed to the following:

Project Editor
Business Rankings Annual
Gale

27500 Drake Rd.

Farmington Hills, MI 48331-3535

Phone: (248) 699-4253

Free: (800) 347-4253

Fax: (248) 699-8070

E-mail: BusinessProducts@cengage.com

URL: www.gale.cengage.com

A sample entry describing the information contained in a typical listing is provided. Each numbered item is explained below in the paragraph with the same number.

Sample Entry

▪1▪■ 1281 ▪2▪ MOST ADMIRED COMPUTER SOFTWARE CORPORATIONS. 2009

▪3▪ **Ranked by:** Scores (1-10) derived from a survey of senior executives, outside directors, and securities analysts.

▪4▪ **Remarks:** Respondents rated companies in their own industry on eight attributes. Also notes previous uear's rank.

▪5▪ **Number listed:** 7

▪6▪ 1. Microsoft, with 8.26 points
2. Oracle Corp., 7.26
3. Computer Associates Interntional, 7.08
4. Computer Sciences, 6.97
5. Novell, 5.67
6. Sybase Inc., 5.63
7. Cognizant Corp., 5.60

▪7▪ Source: *Fortune*, America's Most Admired Corporations (annual), March 2, 2009 p. F-6

Description of Numbered Elements

▪1▪ Sequential entry number.

▪2▪ Ranking title: A descriptive phrase indentifying the contents of the list cited. The information for the titles is taken from the original source. In some instances, an asterisk will fllow the title year, indicating the year of the source rather than the actual year of the data.

▪3▪ Ranked by: Indicates the criteria that establishes the hierarchy, with specifics of date and units of measurement, if given.

▪4▪ Remarks: Provides additional details relating to the list from the source material.

▪5▪ Number listed: Notes the total number of listees that are contained in the original ranking source.

▪6▪ Top 10 items on the list: In many cases, the listing also includes data substantiating the rankings, as the scores in the above sample show.

▪7▪ Source: Gives complete bibliographic details. For periodicals, notes title, date, and page number. For serials, also gives frequency and publisher. For books, lists author/ editor and publisher, as well. For websites, lists URL.

AARP The Magazine
AARP
601 E St. NW
Washington DC 20049
Toll-free: 888-OUR-AARP
http://www.aarp.org/magazine
Monthly
Subscription Rate: Free for members
Special Issue:
International Innovative Employer
Awards (biennial)

ABA BANKING JOURNAL
American Bankers Association
20 S Clark St., Ste. 2450
Chicago, IL 60603
Toll-free: 800-BANKERS
Email: custserv@aba.com
http://www.ababj.com
Monthly
Subscription Rate: Free to qualified
ISSN: 0194-5947
Special Issues:
Top Performers: Part One (annual)
Top Performers: Part Two (annual)

ACCOUNTANCY
Wolters Kluwer UK Ltd.
145 London Rd.
Kingston Upon Thames, Surrey
United Kingdom
KT2 6SR
44 020 8247 1387
Fax: 44 020 8247 1424
Email: accountancynews@cch.co.uk
http://www.accountancymagazine.com
Monthly
Subscription Rate: £86.94 in U.K.; £99.60
in U.S.
Special Issue:
Top 60 League Table (annual)

ACCOUNTING TODAY
SourceMedia
1 State Street Plz., 27 Fl.
New York, NY 10004
(212)803-8200
Toll-free: 800-221-1809
http://www.accountingtoday.com

Monthly
Special Issues:
Best Accounting Firms to Work For
(annual)
Top 100 (annual)
VAR 100 (annual)

ADVERTISING AGE
Crain Communications Inc.
711 3rd Ave.
New York, NY 10017
(212)210-0100
Email: subs@crain.com
http://www.adage.com
Weekly
Subscription Rate: $99
ISSN: 0001-8899
Special Issues:
100 Leading Media Companies (an-
nual)
Agency A-List (annual)
Agency Report (annual)
America's Hottest Brands (annual)
Best Places to Work (annual)
Digital A-List (annual)
Digital Issue (annual)
Entertainment A-List (annual)
Hispanic Fact Pack (annual)
Leading National Advertisers (annual)
Magazine A-List (annual)
Top Global Marketers (annual)
World's Hottest Brands

AGRI MARKETING
Henderson Communications LLC
1422 Elbridge Payne Rd., Ste. 250
Chesterfield, MO 63017
(636)728-1428
Fax: (636)777-4178
Email: info@agrimarketing.com
http://www.agrimarketing.com
10x/yr.
Subscription Rate: Free to qualified
ISSN: 0002-1180
Special Issue:
Agency Update (annual)

AIR CARGO WORLD
UBM Aviation

Bldg. 200, Ste. 255
1080 Holcomb Bridge Rd.
Roswell, GA 30076
(770)642-9170
Fax: (770)642-9982
http://www.aircargoworld.com
Monthly
Subscription Rate: Free to qualified
Special Issue:
Top 50 Airports (annual)

AIR TRANSPORT WORLD
Penton Media, Inc.
The Blair Bldg., Ste. 700
8380 Colesville Rd.
Silver Spring, MD 20910
(301)755-0200
Fax: (913)514-3909
http://www.atwonline.com
Monthly
Subscription Rate: Free to qualified
ISSN: 0002-2543
Special Issue:
World Airline Report (annual)

ALBERTA VENTURE
Venture Publishing, Inc.
10259 105 St.
Edmonton, AB T5J 1E3
Canada
(780)990-0839
Toll-free: 866-227-4276
Fax: (780)425-4921
Email: admin@albertaventure.com
http://www.albertaventure.com
10x/yr.
Subscription Rate: C$21.95 in Canada
Special Issues:
Fast Growth 50 (annual)
Venture 100 (annual)

ALMANAC OF THE 50 STATES
Information Publications, Inc.
2995 Woodside Rd., Ste. 400-182
Woodside, CA 94062-2446
(650)568-6170
Toll-free: 877-544-INFO
Fax: (650)568-6150
Email: info@informationpublications.com

http://www.informationpublications.com
Annual
Copyright © 2010
ISBN: 978-0-929960-52-4

AMERICAN BANKER
SourceMedia
1 State Street Plz., 27 Fl.
New York, NY 10004
(212)803-8200
Toll-free: 800-221-1809
Fax: (212)843-9600
http://www.americanbanker.com
Daily
Subscription Rate: $895
   Special Issue:
   FinTech 100 (annual)

AMERICAN LAWYER
ALM Media Properties Inc.
120 Broadway, 5th Fl.
New York, NY 10271
(212)457-9400
Fax: (646)417-7705
http://www.law.com
Monthly
Subscription Rate: $445
   Special Issues:
   The A-List (annual)
   Am Law 100 (annual)
   Corporate Scoreboard (annual)
   Global 100 (annual)
   Pro Bono 100 (annual)

APPAREL
Edgell Communications
4 Middlebury Blvd.
Randolph, NJ 07869
(973)607-1300
Fax: (973)607-1395
Email: apparelmag@halldata.com
http://www.apparelmag.com
Monthly
Subscription Rate: Free to qualified
   Special Issues:
   Top 50 (annual)
   Top Innovators (annual)

ARABIAN BUSINESS
ITP Publishing Group Ltd.
PO Box 500024
Dubai, United Arab Emirates
971 4 444 3000
Fax: 971 4 444 3030
Email: info@itp.com
http://www.arabianbusiness.com
Monthly
   Special Issues:
   Expat Power 50 (annual)
   The Gulf's Most Efficient Bosses

ARCHITECT
Hanley-Wood, LLC
1 Thomas Circle NW, Ste. 600
Washington DC 20005
(202)452-0800

Toll-free: 800-829-9127
Fax: (202)785-1974
http://www.architectmagazine.com
Monthly
Subscription Rate: Free to qualified
   Special Issue:
   The Architect 50 (annual)

ARCHITECTURAL RECORD
McGraw-Hill Construction Information
   Group
2 Penn Plaza, 9th Fl.
New York, NY 10121
(212)904-2594
Toll-free: 800-525-5003
Fax: (212)904-4256
http://archrecord.construction.com
Monthly
Subscription Rate: $49
   Special Issue:
   Top 250 Firms (annual)

THE ARIZONA REPUBLIC
200 E Van Buren St., MC NM19
Phoenix, AZ 85004
(602)444-8000
800-331-9303
http://www.azcentral.com
Daily
Subscription Rate: $228.24
   Special Issue:
   Republic 100 (annual)

ASSEMBLY MAGAZINE
BNP Media
155 Pfingsten Rd., Ste. 205
Deerfield, IL 60015
(847)405-4000
Fax: (847)405-4100
http://www.assemblymag.com
Monthly
Subscription Rate: Free to qualified
   Special Issue:
   Top 50 (annual)

AUTOMOTIVE NEWS
Crain Communications Inc.
1155 Gratiot Ave.
Detroit, MI 48207-2997
(313)446-6000
Email: subs@crain.com
http://www.autonews.com
Weekly
Subscription Rate: $159
ISSN: 0005-1551
   Special Issues:
   Top 125 Dealership Groups (annual)
   Top OEM Parts Suppliers to North
      America (annual)

BACKBONE MAGAZINE
Publimedia Communications Inc.
1676 Wembury Rd.
Mississauga, ON L5J 4G3
Canada
(604)986-5344

Fax: (604)986-5309
Email: info@backbonemag.com
http://www.backbonemag.com
Bimonthly
Subscription Rate: C$29.06; U.S. $40.95
   Special Issue:
   Branham 300 (annual)

BACON'S NEWSPAPER DIRECTORY
Cision
332 S Michigan Ave.
Chicago, IL 60604
(866)639-5087
http://www.cision.com
Copyright © 2010
ISSN: 1088-9639

THE BANKER
Financial Times Ltd.
Number One Southwark Bridge
London SE1 9HL
United Kingdom
44 (0)20 7873 3000
Email: thebanker@ft.com
http://www.thebanker.com
Monthly
Subscription Rate: £525
ISSN: 0005-5395
   Special Issues:
   Top 25 Caricom Banks (annual)
   Top 75 Russian Banks (annual)
   Top 100 Arab Banks (annual)
   Top 100 Japanese Banks (annual)
   Top 100 Latin American Banks (an-
      nual)
   Top 300 EU Banks (annual)
   Top 500 Banking Brands (annual)
   Top 500 Islamic Financial Institutions
      (annual)
   Top Asia-Pacific Banks (annual)
   Top Central American Banks (annual)

BANKRUPTCYDATA.COM
New Generation Research, Inc.
225 Friend St., Ste. 801
Boston, MA 02114
(617)573-9550
Toll-free: 800-468-3810
Fax: (617)573-9554
Email: customersupport@bankruptcy data-
   .com
http://www.bankruptcydata.com
Subscription Rate: $750
   Special Annual Feature:
   Largest Public Company Bankruptcies

BARRON'S
Dow Jones & Co., Inc.
200 Liberty St., 9th Fl.
New York, NY 10281
(212)416-2000
Toll-free: 800-544-0422
Email: barrons.service@dowjones.com
http://www.barrons.com
Weekly

Subscription Rate: $149
ISSN: 1077-8039
Special Issues:
The 25 Best Givers
Barron's 500 (annual)
Best Mutual Fund Families (annual)
*The Corporate World's Most
  Respected (annual)*
Hedge Fund 100 (annual)
Most Respected CEOs (annual)
Review of Online Brokers (annual)
*Top 100 Independent Financial Advi-
  sors (annual)*
*Top 100 Women Financial Advisers
  (annual)*

BC BUSINESS
Canada Wide Media Ltd.
4180 Lougheed Hwy., 4th Fl.
Burnaby, B.C. V5C 6A7
Canada
(604)299-7311
Fax: (604)299-9188
Email: bcbsubscriptions@canadawide.com
http://www.bcbusinessonline.ca
Monthly
Subscription Rate: C$25.95; US$39.95
Special Issues:
Best Companies (annual)
Top 100 (annual)

BEAUTY PACKAGING
Rodman Publishing Corp.
70 Hilltop Rd.
Ramsey, NJ 07446
(201)825-2552
Fax: (201)825-0553
http://www.beautypackaging.com
Monthly
Subscription Rate: Free to qualified
Special Issue:
Top 20 (annual)

BELFAST TELEGRAPH
Independent News and Media (NI)
124-144 Royal Ave.
Belfast BT1 1EB
Northern Ireland
44 028 90 264000
Email: writeback@belfasttelegraph.co.uk
http://www.belfasttelegraph.co.uk
Daily
Special Issues:
*Northern Ireland's Richest People (an-
  nual)*
Top 100 Companies (annual)

BEST CHRISTIAN WORKPLACES
  INSTITUTE
9311 SE 36th St., Ste. 202
Mercer Island, WA 98040
(206)230-8111
Toll-free: 877-730-8111
Fax: (206)232-1036
http://www.bcwinstitute.com

Special Online Feature:
Best Christian Workplaces (annual)

BEST COMPANIES GROUP
1500 Paxton St.
Harrisburg, PA 17104
(717)909-1570
Toll-free: 877-455-2159
Fax: (717)236-6803
Email: info@bestcompaniesgroup.com
http://bestcompaniesgroup.com
Special Annual Online Features:
*Best Non-Profit Organizations to Work
  for*
Best Places to Work in Alabama
Best Places to Work in Collections
Best Places to Work in Connecticut
Best Places to Work in Illinois
Best Places to Work in Indiana
Best Places to Work in Kentucky
Best Places to Work in Los Angeles
Best Places to Work in Maine
Best Places to Work in New Jersey
Best Places to Work in New York
Best Places to Work in New York City
Best Places to Work in Oklahoma
Best Places to Work in Pennsylvania
Best Places to Work in Rhode Island
Best Places to Work in South Carolina
Best Places to Work in Texas
Best Places to Work in Vermont

BEST'S REVIEW
A.M. Best Co., Inc.
Ambest Rd.
Oldwick, NJ 08858
(908)439-2200
Fax: (908)439-3363
Email: customer_service@ambest.com
http://www.bestreview.com
Monthly
Subscription Rate: $55
ISSN: 1527-5914
Special Issues:
Asset Distribution (annual)
Leading Writers (annual)
Leading Writers, Life/Health (annual)
Top Auto Writers (annual)
Top Global Insurance Brokers (annual)
*Top Global Reinsurance Brokers (an-
  nual)*
*Top Global Reinsurance Groups (an-
  nual)*
*Top Marine, Fire, & Allied Writers (an-
  nual)*
Top P/C Writers by Line (annual)
World's Largest Insurers (annual)

BETTER INVESTING
National Association of Investors Corp.
PO Box 220
Royal Oak, MI 48068
(248)5836242
Tollfree: 8772756242
Fax: (248)5834880

Email: bi@betterinvesting.org
http://www.betterinvesting.org
Monthly
Subscription Rate: Free for members; $22
  nonmembers
Special Issue:
Top 100 Companies (annual)

BEVERAGE INDUSTRY
BNP Media
155 Pfingsten Rd., Ste. 205
Deerfield, IL 60015
(847)405-4000
Fax: (847)405-4100
http://www.bevindustry.com
Monthly
Subscription Rate: Free to qualified
Special Issues:
State of the Industry Report (annual)
*Top 100 Beverage Companies (an-
  nual)*

BEVERAGE WORLD
Ideal Media LLC
90 Broad St., Ste. 402
New York, NY 10004
(646)708-7300
Toll-free: 800-722-6658
Fax: (646)708-7399
Email: bw@halldata.com
http://www.beverageworld.com
Monthly
Subscription Rate: $89
Special Issues:
The Beverage World 100 (annual)
State of the Industry Report (annual)
Top 25 Beer Wholesalers (annual)
Top 25 Bottlers (annual)
Top Global Brands

BILLBOARD
Prometheus Global Media
770 Broadway, 7th Fl.
New York, NY 10003
(212)493-4100
Toll-free: 800-722-6658
http://www.billboard.com
Weekly
Subscription Rate: $149
Special Issue:
The Year in Music & Touring (annual)

BIZ(941)
Gulfshore Media LLC
330 S. Pineapple Ave., Ste. 205
Sarasota, FL 34236
(941)487-1100
Toll-free: 800-881-2394
http://www.biz941.com
Monthly
Subscription Rate: Free
Special Issue:
Top Companies (annual)

BLACK ENTERPRISE
Earl G. Graves, Ltd.

130 5th Ave., 10th Fl.
New York, NY 10011-4399
(212)242-8000
Email: customerservice@blackenter
prise.com
http://www.blackenterprise.com
Monthly
Subscription Rate: $14.95
ISSN: 0006-4165
Special Issues:
40 Best Companies for Diversity
40 Best Franchises for African
Americans
Annual Investment Guide
B. E. 100s (annual)
Most Powerful African-Americans in
Business
Top Executives in Diversity

BLOOMBERG BUSINESSWEEK
Bloomberg LP
731 Lexington Ave.
New York, NY 10022
(212)318-2000
Toll-free: 800-298-9867
Fax: (917)369-5000
http://www.businessweek.com
Weekly
Subscription Rate: $40
ISSN: 0007-7135
Special Issues:
The Best B-Schools (biennial)
Bloomberg Businessweek 50 (annual)
Stuck in Traffic
Taiwan's Best Global Brands (annual)
What's a Central Banker Worth?
The Year in Review (annual)

THE BOSTON GLOBE
The New York Times Co., Inc.
135 Morrissey Blvd.
PO Box 55819
Boston, MA 02205-5819
(617)929-2000
Email: circulationservices@globe.com
http://www.boston.com
Daily
Special Issues:
Globe 100 (annual)
Protobrand's Top 25 (annual)

BRAND POWER INDEX
CoreBrand LLC
122 W 27th St., 9th Fl.
New York, NY 10001
(212)329-3030
Fax: (212)329-3031
http://www.corebrand.com

BRANDWEEK
(ceased publication in 2011)

BROADBAND COMMUNITIES
Broadband Properties LLC
1909 Avenue G
Rosenberg, TX 77471

(281)342-9655
Toll-free: 877-588-1649
Fax: (281)342-1158
http://www.bbpmag.com
Monthly
Subscription Rate: Free to qualified
Special Issue:
Top 100 (annual)

BROADBAND PROPERTIES
(changed name to Broadband Communities)

BROADCASTING & CABLE
NewBay Media LLC
28 E 28th St., 12th Fl.
New York, NY 10016
(212)378-0400
Fax: (212)378-0470
http://www.broadcastingcable.com
Weekly
Subscription Rate: $199
Special Issue:
Top 25 TV Station Groups (annual)

BtoB
Crain Communications Inc.
711 3rd Ave.
New York, NY 10017
(212)210-0100
http://www.btobonline.com
Monthly
Subscription Rate: $59
ISSN: 1087-948X
Special Issues:
Media Power 50 (annual)
Top 100 B-to-B Advertisers (annual)
Vertical Insight: Construction (annual)
Vertical Insight: Electrical Engineering
(annual)
Vertical Insight: Government (annual)
Vertical Insight: Healthcare Manage-
ment (annual)
Vertical Insight: Information Technology
(annual)
Vertical Insight: Legal (annual)
Vertical Insight: Manufacturing (annual)
Vertical Insight: Small-Business (an-
nual)

BUILDER
Hanley-Wood, LLC
1 Thomas Circle NW, Ste. 600
Washington DC 20005
(202)452-0800
Toll-free: 800-829-9127
Fax: (202)785-1974
http://www.builderonline.com
Monthly
Subscription Rate: $29.95
ISSN: 0744-1193
Special Issue:
Builder 100 (annual)

BUILDING DESIGN & CONSTRUCTION
SGC Horizon LLC

3030 W. Salt Creek Ln., Ste. 201
Arlington Heights, IL 60005
(847)391-1000
Fax: (847)390-0408
http://www.bdcnetwork.com
Monthly
Subscription Rate: Free to qualified
Special Issue:
Giants 300 (annual)

BURRELLESLUCE
75 E. Northfield Rd.
Livingston, NJ 07039
(973)992-6600
Tollfree: 800-631-1160
Fax: (973)992-7675
http://www.burrellesluce.com
Annual Feature:
Top Media Outlets

BUSINESS INSURANCE
Crain Communications Inc.
711 3rd Ave.
New York, NY 10017
(212)210-0100
http://www.businessinsurance.com
Weekly
Subscription Rate: $149
ISSN: 0007-6864
Special Issues:
Captive Managers (annual)
Case Management Providers (annual)
Independent Safety Consultants (an-
nual)
Insurance Recovery Law Firms (an-
nual)
Largest Case Management Providers
(annual)
Largest Dental Plan Providers (annual)
Policy-Holder Facilities (annual)
Property Loss Control Specialists (an-
nual)
Reinsurance Brokers (annual)
Rent-A-Captive Facilities (annual)
Risk Management Consultants (an-
nual)
Surplus Lines Market Report (annual)
Third-Party Claims Administrators (an-
nual)
U.S. Health Insurers
U.S. Reinsurers
Wholesale Insurance Brokers (annual)
World's Largest Brokers (annual)
World's Largest Reinsurers (annual)

BUSINESS NORTH CAROLINA
Red Hand Media LLC
5605 77 Center Dr., Ste. 101
Charlotte, NC 28217
(704)523-6987
Fax: (704)523-4211
http://www.businessnc.com
Monthly
Subscription Rate: $30

Special Issues:
Top 75 (annual)
Top 100 Private Companies (annual)

BUSINESS RANKINGS
Dun & Bradstreet, Inc.
899 Eaton Ave.
Bethlehem, PA 18025-0001
Annual
Copyright © 2010
ISBN: 1-59274-511-3
ISSN: 0734-2845

CABINETMAKER + FDM
CCI Media LLC
2240 Country Club Pkwy. SE
Cedar Rapids, IA 52403
(319)651-5212
http://www.cabinetmakerfdm.com
Monthly
Subscription Rate: Free to qualified
Special Issue:
FDM 300 (annual)

CALIFORNIA CONSTRUCTION
(changed name to ENR California)

CALIFORNIA LAWYER
Daily Journal Corp.
44 Montgomery St., Ste. 250
San Francisco, CA 94104
(415)296-2400
Fax: (415)296-2440
http://www.callawyer.com
Monthly
Special Issue:
CA 50 (annual)

CANADA'S 50 BEST MANAGED COMPANIES
Deloitte Canada
2 Queen St. E., Ste. 1200
PO Box 8
Toronto, Ontario M5C 3G7
Canada
(416)874-3874
Fax: (416)874-3888
Email:
bestmanagedcompanies@deloitte.ca
http://www.canadas50best.com
Annual

CANADA'S TOP 100 EMPLOYERS
Mediacorp Canada Inc.
21 New St.
Toronto, Ontario M5R 1P7
Canada
(416)987-1464
Fax: (647)436-7186
Email: ct100@mediacorp.ca
http://www.canadastop100.com
Annual

CANADIAN BUSINESS
Rogers Media
1 Mount Pleasant Rd., 11th Fl.
Toronto, Ontario M4Y 2Y5

Canada
(416)764-1200
Toll-free: 800-465-0700
Fax: (416)764-1255
Email:
letters@canadianbusiness.rogers.com
http://www.canadianbusiness.com
22x/yr.
Subscription Rate: C$19.95
ISSN: 0008-3100
Special Issues:
Highest-Paid Chief Executives (annual)
Investor 500 (annual)
Rich 100 (annual)

CANADIAN MINING JOURNAL
Business Information Group
12 Concorde Pl., Ste. 800
Toronto, ON M3C 4J2
Canada
Toll-free: 800-387-0273
Fax: (416)510-5138
http://www.canadianminingjournal.com
Monthly
Subscription Rate: Free to qualified
Special Issue:
Canada's Top 40 (annual)

CANDY INDUSTRY
BNP Media
155 Pfingsten Rd., Ste. 205
Deerfield, IL 60015
(847)405-4000
Fax: (847)405-4100
http://www.candyindustry.com
Monthly
Subscription Rate: Free to qualified
ISSN: 0745-1032
Special Issue:
Global Top 100 (annual)

CAREERS & the disABLED
Equal Opportunity Publications Inc.
445 Broad Hollow Rd., Ste. 425
Melville, NY 11747
(631)421-9421
Fax: (631)421-1352
Email: info@eop.com
http://www.eop.com/mags-CD-
recruiting.php
3x/yr.
Subscription Rate: $11
Special Issue:
Top Employers (annual)

CE PRO
EH Publishing Inc.
111 Speen St., Ste. 200
PO Box 989
Framingham, MA 01701-2000
(508)663-1500
Fax: (508)663-1599
http://www.cepro.com
17x/yr.
Subscription Rate: Free to qualified

Special Issue:
CE Pro 100 (annual)

CHAIN STORE AGE
Lebhar-Friedman, Inc.
425 Park Ave.
New York, NY 10022
(212)756-5252
Toll-free: 800-216-7117
Fax: (212)756-5270
Email: mforseter@chainstoreage.com
http://www.chainstoreage.com
Monthly
Subscription Rate: Free to qualified
ISSN: 1087-0601
Special Issues:
Big Builders (annual)
Chain Store Age 100 (annual)

CHEMICAL & ENGINEERING NEWS
American Chemical Society
1155 16th St. NW
Washington DC 20036
(202)872-4600
Toll-free: 800-227-5558
Fax: (202)872-8727
Email: edit.cen@acs.org
http://pubs.acs.org/cen
Weekly
Subscription Rate: Free to members
ISSN: 0009-2347
Special Issue:
Global Top 50 (annual)

CHEMICAL WEEK
IHS Inc.
2 Grand Central Tower, 40th Fl.
140 E. 45th St.
New York, NY 10017
(212)884-9528
Fax: (212)884-9514
Email: clientservices@chemweek.com
http://www.chemweek.com
Weekly
Subscription Rate: $225.97
Special Issues:
Billion Dollar Club (annual)
Executive Compensation (annual)

CHIEF EXECUTIVE
Chief Executive Group LLC
1 Sound Shore Dr., Ste. 100
Greenwich, CT 06830
(203)930-2700
Fax: (201)930-2701
Email: info@chiefexecutive.net
http://www.chiefexecutive.net
8x/yr.
Subscription Rate: Free to members
Special Issues:
Best and Worst States for Business
(annual)

CHINA DAILY
China Daily Information Co.
No. 15 Huixin Dongjie

Chaoyang District
Beijing 100029
People's Republic of China
86 10 6499 5000
http://www.chinadaily.com.cn
Daily
Special Issue:
Annual Report of Listed Companies

CIO MAGAZINE
CXO Media Inc.
492 Old Connecticut Path
PO Box 9208
Framingham, MA 01701-9208
(508)872-0080
Fax: (508)879-7784
http://www.cio.com
23x/yr.
Subscription Rate: Free to qualified; $95
   others
Special Issue:
CIO 100 (annual)

**CLUB INDUSTRY'S FITNESS BUSINESS
   PRO**
Penton Media Inc.
9800 Metcalf Ave.
Overland Park, KS 66212
http://www.clubindustry.com
Monthly
Subscription Rate: Free to qualified
Special Issue:
Top 100 (annual)

COATINGS WORLD
Rodman Publishing Corp.
70 Hilltop Rd.
Ramsey, NJ 07446
(201)825-2552
Fax: (201)825-0553
Email: coatingsales@rodpub.com
http://www.coatingsworld.com
Monthly
Subscription Rate: Free to qualified
Special Issue:
Top Companies Report (annual)

COLLEGEGRAD.COM
CollegeGrad.com, Inc.
234 E. College Ave., Ste. 200
State College, PA 16801
(262)375-6700
http://www.collegegrad.com
Special Online Feature:
Top Entry Level Employers (annual)

COLORADOBIZ
WiesnerMedia LLC
6160 S. Syracuse Way, Ste. 300
Greenwood Village, CO 80111
(303)662-5200
Toll-free: 888-704-0059
Fax: (303)397-7619
http://www.cobizmag.com
Monthly
Subscription Rate: $23.97

ISSN: 0898-6363
Special Issues:
Best Large and Small Companies (an-
*   nual)*
Colorado's 25 Most Powerful (annual)
Public 100 (annual)
Top 50 Family-Owned Companies (an-
*   nual)*
Top 100 Women-Owned Businesses
*   (annual)*
Top 250 Private Companies (annual)
Top Minority-Owned Businesses (an-
*   nual)*
Top Professional Services (annual)

COMMERCIAL CARRIER JOURNAL
Randall-Reilly Publishing Co.
3200 Rice Mine Rd. NE
Tuscaloosa, AL 35406
(847)559-7303
Toll-free: 800-681-5829
http://www.ccjdigital.com
Monthly
Subscription Rate: Free to qualified
Special Issue:
The Top 250 (annual)

COMPUTERWORLD
International Data Group Inc.
492 Old Connecticut Path
PO Box 9171
Framingham, MA 01701
(508)879-0700
http://www.computerworld.com
Semimonthly
Subscription Rate: Free to qualified
Special Issue:
100 Best Places to Work in IT (annual)

CONCEIVE MAGAZINE
Bonnier Corp.
460 N Orlando Ave., Ste. 200
Winter Park, FL 32789
(407)628-4802
Fax: (407)628-7061
Email: comments@conceivemaga
   zine.com
http://www.conceiveonline.com
Quarterly
Subscription Rate: $11.20
Special Issue:
50 Best Companies (annual)

CONCRETE CONSTRUCTION
Hanley Wood LLC
8725 W. Higgins Rd., Ste. 600
Chicago, IL 60631
(773)824-2400
Fax: (773)824-2401
Email: cceditor@hanleywood.com
http://www.concreteconstruction.net
Monthly
Subscription Rate: $30
Special Issue:
CC 100 (annual)

THE CONCRETE PRODUCER
Hanley Wood LLC
8725 W. Higgins Rd., Ste. 600
Chicago, IL 60631
(773)824-2400
http://www.theconcreteproducer.com
Monthly
Subscription Rate: Free to qualified
Special Issue:
TCP 100 (annual)

CONNECTICUT MAGAZINE
Journal Register Co.
35 Nutmeg Dr.
Trumbull, CT 06611
(203)380-6600
Fax: (203)380-6610
http://www.connecticutmag.com
Monthly
Subscription Rate: $11.97
Special Issue:
Great Places to Work (annual)

**CONSENSUS ADVISORY SERVICES
   LLC**
73 Newbury St.
Boston, MA 02116
(617)651-2135
Fax: (617)437-6506
http://www.consensusadvisors.com
Special Online Feature:
Retailer Health Ratings

CONSULTING MAGAZINE
Kennedy Information LLC
1 Washington Park, Ste. 1300
Newark, NJ 07102
(212)563-1732
Fax: (212)564-0465
Email: consultingmag@kennedyinfo.com
http://www.consultingmag.com
Bimonthly
Subscription Rate: Free to qualified; $99
   others
Special Issues:
Best Firms to Work For (annual)
Top 25 Consultants (annual)

CONSUMER GOODS TECHNOLOGY
Edgell Communications
4 Middlebury Blvd.
Randolph, NJ 07869
(973)607-1300
Fax: (973)607-1395
http://www.consumergoods.com
Monthly
Subscription Rate: Free to qualified
Special Issue:
Consumer Goods Registry (annual)

CONTRACT PHARMA
Rodman Publishing Corp.
70 Hilltop Rd., Ste. 3000
Ramsey, NJ 07446
(201)825-2552
Fax: (201)825-0553

Email: info@contractpharma.com
http://www.contractpharma.com
Monthly
Subscription Rate: Free to qualified
   Special Issue:
   *Top 20 Pharmaceutical Companies
   (annual)*

CONTRACTOR
Penton Media Inc.
2700 S. River Rd., Ste. 109
Des Plaines, IL 60018
(847)299-3101
Fax: (847)299-3018
http://contractormag.com
Monthly
Subscription Rate: Free to qualified
   Special Issue:
   Book of Giants (annual)

CONTROL MAGAZINE
Putman Media, Inc.
555 W. Pierce Rd., Ste. 301
Itasca, IL 60143
(630)467-1300
Email: webmaster@putman.net
http://www.controlglobal.com
Monthly
Subscription Rate: Free to qualified
   Special Issue:
   Top 50 (annual)

CONVENIENCE STORE NEWS
Stagnito Media
570 Lake Cook Rd., Ste. 106
Deerfield, IL 60015
(224)632-8200
Fax: (224)632-8266
http://www.csnews.com
15x/yr.
Subscription Rate: Free to qualified
   Special Issues:
   Top 25 Wholesalers (annual)
   Top 100 (annual)

CORPORATE COUNSEL
ALM Media Properties Inc.
120 Broadway, 5th Fl.
New York, NY 10271
(212)457-9400
Fax: (646)417-7705
http://www.law.com/jsp/cc/index.jsp
Monthly
Subscription Rate: Free in the U.S.
   Special Issue:
   *Who Represents America's Biggest
   Companies (annual)*

CORPORATE EQUALITY INDEX
Human Rights Campaign
1640 Rhode Island Ave. NW
Washington DC 20036
(202)6284160
Toll-free: 800-777-4723
Fax: (202)3475323
Email: workplace@hrc.org

http://www.hrc.org/cei
Annual
Copyright © 2010
ISBN: 978-1-934765-18-0

CORPORATE KNIGHTS
Corporate Knights Inc.
147 Spadina Ave., Ste. 207
Toronto, ON M5V 2L7
Canada
(416)203-4674
Fax: (416)946-1770
Email: info@corporateknights.ca
http://www.corporateknights.ca
Quarterly
Subscription Rate: C$22; US$33
   Special Issues:
   Best 50 Corporate Citizens (annual)
   Cleantech 10 (annual)
   Global 100 (annual)
   Leadership Diversity Index (annual)

CORPORATE RESPONSIBILITY
SharedXpertise Media LLC
343 Thornall St., Ste. 515
Edison, NJ 08837
(732)476-6160
Fax: (732)476-6155
http://www.thecro.com
Bimonthly
Subscription Rate: $120
   Special Issue:
   100 Best Corporate Citizens (annual)

CRAIN'S CHICAGO BUSINESS
Crain Communications Inc.
360 N. Michigan Ave.
Chicago, IL 60601-3806
(312)649-5200
Fax: (312)280-3150
Email: subs@crain.com
http://www.chicagobusiness.com
Weekly
Subscription Rate: $97.95
   Special Issues:
   *Chicago's Fastest-Growing Companies
   (annual)*
   *Chicago's Largest Accounting Firms
   (annual)*
   Chicago's Largest Banks (annual)
   Chicago's Largest Employers (annual)
   Chicago's Largest Law Firms (annual)
   *Chicago's Largest Minority-Owned
   Firms (annual)*
   *Chicago's Largest Public Companies
   (annual)*
   Fortunate 100 (annual)
   Highest-Paid Non-CEOs (annual)
   *Largest Privately-Held Companies (an-
   nual)*
   Largest Women-Owned Firms (annual)

CRAIN'S NEW YORK BUSINESS
Crain Communications Inc.
711 3rd Ave.

New York, NY 10017
(212)210-0100
Email: customerservice@crainsnew
   york.com
http://www.crainsnewyork.com
Weekly
Subscription Rate: $29.95
   Special Issues:
   Fastest-Growing Companies (annual)
   Highest-Paid CEOs (annual)
   *Largest Minority-Owned Companies
   (annual)*
   *Largest Non-Profits in New York (an-
   nual)*
   Largest Private Companies (annual)
   Largest Public Companies (annual)
   *Largest Women-Owned Companies
   (annual)*
   Top Employers (annual)
   Top MBA Programs (annual)

THE CRB COMMODITY YEARBOOK
Commodity Research Bureau, Inc.
330 S. Wells St., Ste. 612
Chicago, IL 60606
(312)554-8456
Toll-free: 800-621-5271
Fax: (312)939-4135
Email: info@crbtrader.com
http://www.crbtrader.com
Annual
Copyright © 2010
ISBN: 978-0-470-57477-5

CREDIT UNION DIRECTORY
Callahan & Associates, Inc.
1001 Connecticut Ave. NW, Ste. 1001
Washington DC 20036
(202)223-3920
Toll-free: 800-446-7453
Fax: (202)223-1311
Email: directory@creditunions.com
http://www.creditunions.com
Annual
Copyright © 2010
ISBN: 1-934330-28-0
ISSN: 0888-8671

CREDIT UNION DIRECTORY
National Credit Union Administration
1775 Duke St.
Alexandria, VA 22314
Toll-free: 800-755-1030
http://www.ncua.gov
Annual

CRN
United Business Media LLC
600 Community Dr.
Manhasset, NY 11030
(516)562-5000
http://www.crn.com
Monthly
Subscription Rate: Free to qualified

Special Issues:
Fast Growth 100 (annual)
Tech Elite 250 (annual)
Top 100 Healthcare Vendors (annual)

CROPLIFE
CropLife Media Group
37733 Euclid Ave.
Willoughby, OH 44094
(440)942-2000
Email: cl.circ@meistermedia.com
http://www.croplife.com
Monthly
Subscription Rate: free for qualified
　Special Issue:
　CropLife 100 (annual)

DAIRY FOODS
BNP Media
755 W. Big Beaver, Ste. 1000
Troy, MI 48084
(248)362-3700
Fax: (248)362-0317
http://www.dairyfoods.com
Monthly
Subscription Rate: Free to qualified
ISSN: 0888-0050
　Special Issue:
　Dairy 100 (annual)

THE DALLAS MORNING NEWS
Belo Corp.
508 Young St.
Dallas, TX 75202
(214)977-8222
Toll-free: 800-925-1500
http://www.dallasnews.com
Daily
　Special Issues:
　D-FW Top 200 (annual)
　Fast Track (annual)

DEALERSCOPE
North American Publishing Co.
1500 Spring Garden St., 12th Fl.
Philadelphia, PA 19130
(215)238-5482
Toll-free: 800-777-8074
Fax: (215)238-5346
Email: customerservice@napco.com
http://www.dealerscope.com
Monthly
Subscription Rate: Free to qualified
　Special Issue:
　Top 101 CE Retailers (annual)

DELOITTE TOUCHE TOHMATSU
1633 Broadway
New York, NY 10019
(212)489-1600
Fax: (212)489-1687
http://www.deloitte.com
　Annual Features:
　Technology Fast 50 Australia
　Technology Fast 50 Canada
　Technology Fast 50 Central Europe

Technology Fast 50 Finland
Technology Fast 50 France
Technology Fast 50 Greater Philadelphia
Technology Fast 50 India
Technology Fast 50 Ireland
Technology Fast 50 Israel
Technology Fast 50 Japan
Technology Fast 50 New Zealand
Technology Fast 50 Turkey
Technology Fast 50 U.K.
Technology Fast 500 Asia Pacific
Technology Fast 500 EMEA
Technology Fast 500 North America

DENVER BUSINESS JOURNAL
American City Business Journals Inc.
1700 Broadway, Ste. 515
Denver, CO 80290
(303)803-9200
Fax: (303)803-9203
Email: denver@bizjournals.com
http://www.bizjournals.com/denver
Weekly
ISSN: 0893-7745
　Special Issue:
　Book of Lists (annual)

DIVERSITY INC MAGAZINE
DiversityInc Media LLC
570 Broad St., 15th Fl.
Newark, NJ 07102
(973)494-0500
Fax: (973)494-0525
Email: info@diversityinc.com
http://www.diversityinc.com
5x/yr.
Subscription Rate: $9.99
ISSN: 1540-1502

DIVERSITYBUSINESS.COM
200 Pequot Ave.
Southport, CT 06890
(203)255-8966
Fax: (203)255-8501
http://www.diversitybusiness.com
　Special Annual Feature:
　Div50 (annual)

DiversityMBA MAGAZINE
24 E 107th St.
Chicago, IL 60628
(773)660-1930
Fax: (773)660-1932
http://www.diversitymbamagazine.com
Quarterly
Subscription Rate: $27.97
　Special Issue:
　50 Out Front Companies for Diversity Leadership (annual)

EBOSS WATCH
http://www.ebosswatch.com
　Special Online Feature:
　America's Worst Bosses (annual)

EC & M MAGAZINE
Penton Business Media Inc.
9800 Metcalf Ave.
Overland, KS 66212
(913)967-1782
Fax: (913)514-6782
http://ecmweb.com
Monthly
Subscription Rate: Free to qualified; $48 others
　Special Issue:
　Top 50 Electrical Contractors (annual)

ECONTENT MAGAZINE
Information Today Inc.
48 S Main St., Ste. 3
Newtown, CT 06470
(203)761-1466
Toll-free: 800-248-8466
Fax: (203)304-9300
http://www.econtentmag.com
10x/yr.
Subscription Rate: $119
　Special Issue:
　EC 100 (annual)

EGG INDUSTRY
Watt Publishing Co.
303 N. Main St., Ste. 500
Rockford, IL 61101
(815)734-5617
Fax: (815)734-5649
http://www.wattagnet.com
Monthly
Subscription Rate: Free to qualified
　Special Issue:
　Egg Industry Survey (annual)

ELECTRIC LIGHT & POWER
PennWell Global Energy Group
1421 S. Sheridan Rd.
Tulsa, OK 74112
(918)831-9731
Fax: (918)831-9834
http://www.elp.com
Bimonthly
Subscription Rate: Free to qualified
　Special Issues:
　Utility Financial Rankings (annual)

ENR: ENGINEERING NEWS-RECORD
McGraw-Hill Construction Information Group
2 Penn Plaza, 9th Fl.
New York, NY 10121
(212)904-3507
Toll-free: 800-525-5003
Fax: (212)904-2820
http://enr.construction.com
36x/yr.
Subscription Rate: $82
ISSN: 0891-9526
　Special Issues:
　Top 100 Green Contractors (annual)
　Top 100 Green Designers (annual)

Top 200 Environmental Firms (annual)
Top 200 International Design Firms (annual)
Top 225 International Contractors (annual)
Top 400 Contractors (annual)
Top 500 Design Firms (annual)
Top 600 Specialty Contractors (annual)
Top CM Firms (annual)
Top Program Management Firms (annual)

ENR CALIFORNIA
McGraw-Hill Construction Information Group
160 Spear St., 6th Fl.
San Francisco, CA 94105
(415)357-8019
Fax: (415)357-8021
http://california.construction.com
Monthly
Subscription Rate: $82
Special Issues:
Top Design Firms (annual)
Top Specialty Contractors (annual)

ENR MIDWEST
McGraw-Hill Construction Information Group
130 E. Randolph St., Ste. 900
Chicago, IL 60601
(312)233-7492
http://midwest.construction.com
Monthly
Subscription Rate: $82
Special Issue:
Top Design Firms (annual)

ENR MOUNTAIN STATES
McGraw-Hill Construction Information Group
1114 W. 7th Ave., Ste. 100
Denver, CO 90204
(303)756-9995
Fax: (303)756-4465
http://mountainstates.construction.com
Monthly
Subscription Rate: $82
Special Issues:
Top Design Firms (annual)
Top Specialty Contractors (annual)

ENR NEW YORK
McGraw-Hill Construction Information Group
2 Penn Plaza, 9th Fl.
New York, NY 10121
(212)904-2334
http://newyork.construction.com
Monthly
Subscription Rate: $82
Special Issues:
Top Design Firms (annual)
Top "Green" Firms (annual)
Top Specialty Contractors (annual)

ENR SOUTHEAST
McGraw-Hill Construction Information Group
19239 N. Dale Mabry Hwy., Ste. 404
Lutz, FL 33548
(386)673-9887
Fax: (813)333-6716
http://southeast.construction.com
Monthly
Subscription Rate: $82
Special Issues:
Top Design-Build Contractors (annual)
Top Design Firms (annual)

ENR SOUTHWEST
McGraw-Hill Construction Information Group
4747 E. Elliot Rd. 29-339
Phoenix, AZ 85044
(480)656-7615
Fax: (480)656-7984
http://southwest.construction.com
Monthly
Subscription Rate: $82
Special Issues:
Top Design Firms (annual)
Top "Green" Design Firms (annual)

ENR TEXAS & LOUISIANA
McGraw-Hill Construction Information Group
9155 S. Sterling St., Ste. 160
Irving, TX 75063
(214)682-8229
Fax: (214)722-0552
http://texas.construction.com
Monthly
Subscription Rate: $82
Special Issues:
Top Design Firms (annual)
Top "Green" Design Firms (annual)
Top Specialty Contractors (annual)

ENTERTAINMENT WEEKLY
Time Inc.
1271 Avenue of the Americas
New York, NY 10020
(212)522-1212
Fax: (212)522-0602
http://www.ew.com
Weekly
Subscription Rate: $20
Special Issues:
40 Under 40 (annual)
The Power List (annual)
The Year in Charts (annual)

ENTREPRENEUR
Entrepreneur Media Inc.
2445 McCabe Way
Irvine, CA 92614
(949)261-2325
Toll-free: 800-274-6229
Fax: (949)261-0234
http://www.entrepreneur.com/magazine

Monthly
Subscription Rate: $11.97
ISSN: 0364-7218
Special Issues:
Fastest-Growing Franchises (annual)
Franchise 500 (annual)
Top Homebased Franchises (annual)

EQUAL OPPORTUNITY
Equal Opportunity Publications Inc.
445 Broad Hollow Rd., Ste. 425
Melville, NY 11747
(631)421-9421
Fax: (631)421-1352
Email: info@eop.com
http://www.eop.com/mags-EO.php
Quarterly
Subscription Rate: Free to qualified; $14 others
Special Issue:
Top Employers (annual)

ETHISPHERE MAGAZINE
Ethisphere Institute
1185 Avenue of the Americas, Ste. 1750
New York, NY 10036
Toll-free: 800-369-7583
http://ethisphere.com
Monthly
Subscription Rate: $59.95
Special Issues:
Most Influential People in Business Ethics (annual)
World's Most Ethical Companies (annual)

EUROPE'S 500
Zugspitzstrasse 15
Pullach/Munich, Germany D-82049
49 89 55277 106
Fax: 49 89 55277 299
Email: office@europes500.com
http://www.europes500.eu

EUROPE'S 15,000 LARGEST COMPANIES
ELC International
c/o Gap Books
Dephna House
24-26 Arcadia Ave.
London N3 2JU
United Kingdom
44 20 8349 7199
Fax: 44 20 8349 7198
Email: alan@gapbooks.com
http://www.gapbooks.com
Annual
Copyright © 2011
ISBN: 978-1-907128-06-6

FINANCIAL POST BUSINESS MAGAZINE
National Post
1450 Don Mills Rd., Ste. 300
Don Mills, Ontario M3B 3R5
Canada

(416)383-2300
Fax: (416)383-2305
http://www.financialpost.com/magazine
Monthly
Special Issue:
FP 500 (annual)

FINANCIAL TIMES
Financial Times Ltd.
One Southwark Bridge
London, SE1 9HL
United Kingdom
44 (020) 7873 3000
Fax: 44 (020) 7873 3922
http://www.ft.com
Daily, except Sundays/holidays
ISSN: 0884-6782
Special Issues:
EMBA Rankings (annual)
European Business School Rankings (annual)
FT 500 (annual)
Global Brands (annual)
Global MBA Rankings (annual)
Masters in Management Rankings (annual)
Top 50 Women in World Business (annual)

FLEET OWNER
Penton Media Inc.
11 River Bend Dr. S.
PO Box 4949
Stamford, CT 06907-0949
(203)358-9900
Fax: (203)358-5811
http://fleetowner.com
Monthly
Subscription Rate: Free to qualified
Special Issue:
Fleet Owner 500 (annual)

FLORIDA TREND
Trend Magazines Inc.
490 1st Ave. S., 8th Fl.
St. Petersburg, FL 33701
(727)821-5800
Fax: (727)822-5083
Email: custrelations@floridatrend.com
http://www.floridatrend.com
13x/yr.
Subscription Rate: $20 in Florida; $39.95 outside of Florida
Special Issues:
Best Companies to Work For (annual)
Florida Private 200 (annual)
Florida Public 150 (annual)
Largest Law Firms (annual)

FOOD & BEVERAGE PACKAGING
BNP Media
155 Pfingsten Rd., Ste. 205
Deerfield, IL 60015
(847)405-4000
Fax: (847)405-4100

http://www.foodandbeveragepackaging.com
Monthly
Subscription Rate: Free to qualified
Special Issue:
Top 100 Packagers (annual)

FOOD ENGINEERING
BNP Media II LLC
1050 IL Rte. 83, Ste. 200
Bensenville, IL 60106
http://www.foodengineeringmag.com
Monthly
Subscription Rate: Free to qualified
Special Issue:
Top 100 (annual)

FOOD PROCESSING
Putman Media, Inc.
555 W. Pierce Rd., Ste. 301
Itasca, IL 60143
(630)467-1300
Fax: (630)467-1179
Email: webmaster@putman.net
http://www.foodprocessing.com
Monthly
Subscription Rate: Free to qualified
Special Issues:
Capital Spending Report (annual)
Pacesetters (annual)
Top 100 Companies (annual)

FOODSERVICE EQUIPMENT & SUPPLIES
Zoomba Group Inc.
110 Schiller, Ste. 312
PO Box 156
Elmhurst, IL 60126
Toll-free: 800-630-4168
Fax: 800-630-4169
http://www.fesmag.com
Monthly
Subscription Rate: Free to qualified
Special Issue:
Distribution Giants (annual)

FORBES
Forbes Inc.
60 5th Ave.
New York, NY 10011
(212)620-2200
Fax: (212)620-2332
http://www.forbes.com
Biweekly
Subscription Rate: $29.99
ISSN: 0015-6914
Special Issues:
The 400 Richest Chinese (annual)
America's 200 Largest Charities (annual)
America's Best Colleges (annual)
America's Largest Private Companies (annual)
Asian Fab 50 (annual)
Asia's Best Under a Billion (annual)

Australia's 40 Richest (annual)
Baseball Team Valuations (annual)
Best Cities for an Active Retirement
Best Countries for Business (annual)
Best Places to Retire
Best Small Companies in America (annual)
Best States for Business (annual)
Best and Worst Bosses (annual)
The Celebrity 100 (annual)
Ethnic Enclaves
The Fast Tech List (annual)
Fictional 15 (annual)
Forbes 400 Richest in America (annual)
Forbes 2000 (annual)
The Global Billionaires (annual)
Highest-Paid NASCAR Drivers (annual)
Hong Kong's 40 Richest (annual)
India's Richest (annual)
Indonesia's 40 Richest (annual)
The Midas List (annual)
Most Expensive Zip Codes (annual)
The Most Powerful People on Earth
NASCAR Team Valuations (annual)
NBA Team Valuations (annual)
NFL Team Valuations (annual)
NHL Team Valuations (annual)
The Philippines' 40 Richest (annual)
Singapore's 40 Richest (annual)
Soccer Team Valuations (annual)
SportsMoney 50-50 (annual)
Thailand's 40 Richest (annual)
Top-Earning Dead Celebrities (annual)
Top-Earning Movies
World's Most Powerful Women (annual)
World's Most Valuable Brands (annual)

FORTUNE
Time, Inc.
Time & Life Building
Rockefeller Center
1271 Avenue of the Americas
New York, NY 10020-1393
(212)522-1212
Toll-free: 800-621-8000
Fax: (212)522-7686
http://www.fortune.com
20x/yr.
Subscription Rate: $19.99
ISSN: 0015-8259
Special Issues:
40 Under 40 (annual)
50 Most Powerful Women in Business (annual)
100 Best Companies to Work For (annual)
100 Fastest-Growing Companies (annual)
Asia's 25 Most Powerful (annual)
Businessperson of the Year (annual)
Fortune 500 (annual)

Global 500 (annual)
Global Outsourcing 100 (annual)
Top Employers for Women MBAs
World's Most Admired Companies (annual)

FOUNDATION CENTER
79 5th Ave. and 16th St.
New York, NY 10003-3076
(212)620-4230
Toll-free: 800-424-9836
Fax: (212)807-3677
E-mail: order@foundationcenter.org
http://foundationcenter.org
Special Annual Features:
Top 25 Community Foundations
Top 50 Corporate Foundations
Top 100 U.S. Foundations

FUTURES
Summit Business Media
222 S. Riverside Plz., Ste. 620
Chicago, IL 60606
(312)846-4600
Fax: (312)846-4638
http://www.futuresmag.com
Monthly
Subscription Rate: $78
Special Issue:
Top 50 Brokers (annual)

G.I. JOBS
PO Box 26
Sewickley, PA 15143
(412)269-1663
Fax: (412)291-3375
http://www.gijobs.com
Monthly
Subscription Rate: $19.95
Special Issue:
*Top 100 Military Friendly Employers
(annual)*

GLASS MAGAZINE
National Glass Association
8200 Greensboro Dr., Ste. 302
McLean, VA 22102-3881
866-DIAL-NGA
Fax: (703)442-0630
Email: nga@cambeywest.com
http://www.glassmagazine.net
Monthly
Subscription Rate: Free to qualified;
$34.95 others
Special Issue:
Glazier Survey (annual)

GLOBAL COMPETITIVENESS REPORT
World Economic Forum
91-93 route de la Capite
CH-1223 Cologny/Geneva
Switzerland
41 0 22 869 1212
Fax: 41 0 22 786 2744
Email: contact@weforum.org

http://www.weforum.org/en/initiatives/gcp/
index.htm
Annual
Copyright © 2010

GOVERNMENT EXECUTIVE
National Journal Group Inc.
600 New Hampshire Ave. NW, 4th Fl.
Washington DC 20037
(202)739-8500
Fax: (202)739-8511
Email: webmaster@govexec.com
http://www.govexec.com
Monthly
Subscription Rate: Free to qualified; $58
others
Special Issue:
Top 200 (annual)

GREAT PLACE TO WORK INSTITUTE INC.
222 Kearny St.
San Francisco, CA 94108
(415)503-1234
http://www.greatplacetowork.com
Special Annual Online Feature:
Best Places to Work in Australia
Best Places to Work in Austria
Best Places to Work in Belgium
Best Places to Work in Colombia
Best Places to Work in Denmark
Best Places to Work in Ecuador
Best Places to Work in Finland
Best Places to Work in France
Best Places to Work in Germany
Best Places to Work in India
Best Places to Work in Ireland
Best Places to Work in Italy
Best Places to Work in Japan
Best Places to Work in Norway
Best Places to Work in Paraguay
Best Places to Work in Peru
Best Places to Work in Portugal
Best Places to Work in the UAE
Best Places to Work in Uruguay
Best Places to Work in Venezuela

HAPPI: HOUSEHOLD & PERSONAL PRODUCTS INDUSTRY
Rodman Publishing Corp.
70 Hilltop Rd.
Ramsey, NJ 07446
(201)825-2552
Fax: (201)825-0553
http://www.happi.com
Monthly
Subscription Rate: Free to qualified
ISSN: 0090-8878
Special Issues:
International Top 30 (annual)
Top 50 (annual)

HARDWARE RETAILING
North American Retail Hardware Association

6325 Digital Way, Ste. 300
Indianapolis, IN 46278
(317)290-0338
Toll-free: 800-772-4424
Fax: (317)238-4354
Email: contact@nrha.org
http://www.nrha.org
Monthly
Subscription Rate: Free to qualified
Special Issue:
Annual Report

HAWAII BUSINESS
Aio Hawaii
1000 Bishop St., Ste. 405
PO Box 913
Honolulu, HI 96808-0913
(808)537-9500
Fax: (808)537-6455
Email: hawaii@hawaiibusiness.com
http://www.hawaiibusiness.com
Monthly
Subscription Rate: $29.95
Special Issues:
Best Places to Work in Hawaii (annual)
Top 250 (annual)

HEALTHCARE INFORMATICS
Vendome Group LLC
Medquest Communication Division
3800 Lakeside Ave., Ste. 201
Cleveland, OH 44114
(216)391-9100
Fax: (216)391-9200
Email: info@vendomegrp.com
http://www.healthcare-informatics.com
Monthly
Subscription Rate: Free to qualified
Special Issue:
Healthcare Informatics 100 (annual)

HFN: HOME FURNISHINGS NEWS
Macfadden Publications
333 7th Ave.
New York, NY 10001
(212)979-4800
Email: hfneditor@fairchildpub.com
http://www.hfnmag.com
Weekly
Subscription Rate: $69 for qualified; $109
others
ISSN: 1082-0310
Special Issues:
Top Home Suppliers (annual)
Top Retailers (annual)

HIGHLINE BANK & S&L QUARTERLY
Highline Financial LLC
807 Las Cimas Pky.
Austin, TX 78746
Toll-free: 877-305-6656
http://www.highlinedata.com
Quarterly
December 2010 ed.
Copyright © 2011

HISPANIC
Hispanic Publishing Associates LLC
6355 NW 36th St.
Miami, FL 33166
(305)774-3550
Toll-free: 800-251-2688
Fax: (305)774-3578
Email: custsvc_hispanic@fulcoinc.com
http://www.hispaniconline.com
Bimonthly
Subscription Rate: $12.95
ISSN: 0898-3097
   Special Issues:
   Top Colleges for Hispanics (annual)

HISPANIC BUSINESS
Hispanic Business, Inc.
425 Pine Ave.
Santa Barbara, CA 93117-3709
(805)964-4554
Toll-free: 888-447-7282
Fax: (805)964-5539
http://www.hispanicbusiness.com
10x/yr.
Subscription Rate: Free
ISSN: 0199-0349
   Special Issues:
   Boardroom Elite (annual)
   Corporate Elite (annual)
   Diversity Elite (annual)
   Diversity Supplier 25 (annual)
   Fastest-Growing 100 (annual)
   Hispanic Business 500 (annual)
   Nonprofit 25 (annual)
   Top 50 Exporters (annual)
   Top 100 Influentials (annual)
   Top Graduate Schools for Hispanics (annual)

HOME CHANNEL NEWS
Lebhar-Friedman Inc.
425 Park Ave.
New York, NY 10022
(212)756-5528
http://www.homechannelnews.com
16x/yr.
Subscription Rate: Free to qualified
   Special Issues:
   Top 150 Distribution Scoreboard (annual)
   Top 350 Pro Dealer Scoreboard (annual)
   Top 500 Retailers (annual)

HOOVER'S HANDBOOK OF EMERGING COMPANIES
Hoover's, Inc.
5800 Airport Blvd.
Austin, TX 78752
(512)374-4500
Fax: (512)374-4538
Email: orders@hoovers.com
http://www.hooversbooks.com
Annual
Price: $175

Copyright © 2010
ISBN: 978-1-57311-130-0
ISSN: 1069-7519

HOOVER'S HANDBOOK OF PRIVATE COMPANIES
Hoover's, Inc.
5800 Airport Blvd.
Austin, TX 78752
(512)374-4500
Fax: (512)374-4538
Email: orders@hoovers.com
http://www.hooversbooks.com
Annual
Price: $205
Copyright © 2010
ISBN: 978-1-57311-137-9
ISSN: 1073-6433

HOOVER'S INC.
5800 Airport Blvd.
Austin, TX 78752
(512)374-4500
Fax: (512)374-4538
http://www.hoovers.com
   Special Online Feature:
   IPO Scorecard (quarterly)

HOTEL MANAGEMENT
(previously entitled Hotel & Motel Management)
Questex Media Group Inc.
7500 Old Oak Blvd.
Cleveland, OH 44130-3343
(440)891-3105
Toll-free: 800-225-4569
Fax: (440)891-3120
http://www.hospitalityworldnetwork.com
15x/yr.
Subscription Rate: Free to qualified; $58.85 others
ISSN: 0018-6082
   Special Issues:
   Top Design Firms (annual)
   Top Hotel Companies (annual)
   Top Multi-unit Owners and Developers (annual)
   Top Third-Party Management Companies (annual)
   U.S. Hotel Brands Survey (annual)

ICIS CHEMICAL BUSINESS
Reed Business Information Ltd.
Quadrant House
The Quadrant, Sutton, Surrey SM2 5AS
United Kingdom
http://www.icis.com/v2/magazine/home.aspx
Weekly
Subscription Rate: $157.50 in U.S.
ISSN: 1092-0110
   Special Issues:
   Top 40 Power Players (annual)
   Top 50 Chemical 3PLs (annual)
   Top 100 Chemical Distributors (annual)

   Top 100 Global Chemical Companies, Part 1 (annual)
   Top 100 Global Chemical Companies, Part 2 (annual)

THE I.I.I. INSURANCE FACT BOOK
Insurance Information Institute
110 William St.
New York, NY 10038
(212)346-5500
Email: publications@iii.org
http://www.iii.org
Annual
Copyright © 2011
ISBN: 978-0-932387-55-4

IMPRESSIONS
Nielsen Business Media Inc.
1145 Sanctuary Pky., Ste. 355
Alpharetta, GA 30004
Toll-free: 800-241-9034
http://www.impressionsmag.com
8x/yr.
Subscription Rate: Free to qualified; $79 others
   Special Issue:
   Top Volume Decorators (annual)

INC.
Mansueto Ventures LLC
7 World Trade Ctr.
New York, NY 10007
(212)389-5377
Email: mail@inc.com
http://www.inc.com
10x/yr.
Subscription Rate: $12.97
ISSN: 0162-8968
   Special Issues:
   Best Industries for Starting a Business
   Best Small Company Workplaces
   Inc. 500 (annual)

INDEPENDENT PROCESSOR
BNP Media
155 Pfingsten Rd., Ste. 205
Deerfield, IL 60015
(847)405-4000
Fax: (847)405-4100
http://www.provisioneronline.com
Bimonthly
Subscription Rate: Free to qualified
   Special Issue:
   Top 75 (annual)

INDEX OF ECONOMIC FREEDOM
The Heritage Foundation/*The Wall Street Journal*
214 Massachusetts Ave. NE
Washington DC 20002-4999
(202)546-4400
Fax: (202)546-8328
http://www.heritage.org/index
Annual
ISSN: 1095-7308

INDIANAPOLIS BUSINESS JOURNAL
IBJ Media Corp.
41 E. Washington St., Ste. 200
Indianapolis, IN 46204-3592
(317)634-6200
Fax: (317)263-5060
Email: info-ibj@ibj.com
http://www.ibj.com
Weekly
Subscription Rate: $79
   Special Issues:
   Indiana 100 (annual)
   Largest Banks and Thrifts (annual)
   Top-Performing Indiana Stocks (annual)

INDUSTRIAL DISTRIBUTION
Advantage Business Media LLC
100 Enterprise Dr., Ste. 600
Rockaway, NJ 07866
(973)920-7000
http://www.inddist.com
Monthly
Subscription Rate: Free to qualified
   Special Issue:
   The Big 50 (annual)

INDUSTRY WEEK
Penton Media, Inc.
The Penton Media Bldg.
1300 E. 9th St.
Cleveland, OH 44114
(216)696-7000
Fax: (216)696-1752
Email: iwinfo@industryweek.com
http://www.industryweek.com
Monthly
Subscription Rate: Free to qualified
ISSN: 0039-0895
   Special Issues:
   50 Best Manufacturing Companies (annual)
   Best Plants (annual)
   IW 500 (annual)
   IW 1000 (annual)

INFORMATION WEEK
United Business Media LLC
600 Community Dr.
Manhasset, NY 11030
(516)562-5000
Fax: (516)562-5036
http://www.informationweek.com
Weekly
Subscription Rate: Free to qualified; $199 others
   Special Issue:
   InformationWeek 500 (annual)

INFOWORLD
InfoWorld Media Group
501 Second St.
San Francisco, CA 94107
(847)291-5217
Email: customerservice@infoworld.com
http://www.infoworld.com

Weekly
Subscription Rate: Free to qualified
   Special Issue:
   CTO 25 (annual)

INGRAM'S
Show-Me Publishing, Inc.
PO Box 411356
Kansas City, MO 64141-1356
(816)842-9994
Fax:(816)474-1111
Email: editorial@ingramsonline.com
http://www.ingramsonline.com
Monthly
   Special Issue:
   Corporate Report 100 (annual)

INK WORLD
Rodman Publishing Corp.
70 Hilltop Rd.
Ramsey, NJ 07446
(201)825-2552
Fax: (201)825-0553
Email: inksales@rodpub.com
http://www.inkworldmagazine.com
Monthly
Subscription Rate: Free to qualified
   Special Issues:
   North American Top 20 (annual)
   Top International Ink Companies (annual)

IN-PLANT GRAPHICS
North American Publishing Co.
1500 Spring Garden St., 12th Fl.
Philadelphia, PA 19130
(215)238-5300
Fax: (215)238-5270
http://www.ipgonline.com
Monthly
Subscription Rate: Free to qualified
   Special Issue:
   Industry Giants (annual)

INTELLECTUAL PROPERTY TODAY
381 W. Northwest Hwy.
Palatine, IL 60067
Toll-free: 800-232-8078
Fax: (847)705-7112
http://www.iptoday.com
Monthly
Subscription Rate: $96
   Special Issues:
   Corporate Patent Scoreboard (annual)
   Patent Scorecard: Aerospace & Defense (annual)
   Patent Scorecard: Automotive & Transportation (annual)
   Patent Scorecard: Electronics & Instruments (annual)
   Patent Scorecard: Financial Services (annual)
   Patent Scorecard: Government Agencies (annual)
   Patent Scorecard: Law Firms (annual)

   Patent Scorecard: Universities (annual)
   Top Patent Firms (annual)
   Top Trademark Firms (annual)

INTERBRAND
130 5th Ave.
New York, NY 10011
(212)798-7500
Fax: (212)798-7501
Email: inquiries@interbrand.com
http://www.interbrand.com
   Special Features:
   Best Brazilian Brands
   Best Global Brands
   Best Retail Brands
   Japan's Best Global Brands
   Most Valuable Swiss Bank Brands

INTERIOR DESIGN
Sandow Media LLC
360 Park Ave. S., 17th Fl.
New York, NY 10010
(646)746-6400
Fax: (646)746-7428
http://www.interiordesign.net
Monthly
Subscription Rate: $59.95
   Special Issue:
   Top 100 Design Giants (annual)

INTERNATIONAL LIVING
International Living Publishing Ltd.
Elysium House
Ballytruckle
Waterford, Ireland
011 353 51 304 557
Fax: 011 353 51 304 561
Email: customerservice@international living.com
http://www.internationalliving.com
Monthly
Subscription Rate: $49
   Special Annual Feature:
   Global Retirement Index

INTERNET RETAILER
Vertical Web Media
125 S. Wacker Dr., Ste. 2900
Chicago, IL 60606
(312)362-9527
http://www.internetretailer.com
Monthly
Subscription Rate: Free to qualified
   Special Issues:
   Europe 300 (annual)
   Hot 100 - Best Retail Web Sites (annual)
   Top 500 (annual)

INVESTOR'S BUSINESS DAILY
Investor's Business Daily Inc.
12655 Beatrice St.
Los Angeles, CA 90066
Tollfree: 8008312525
http://www.investors.com

Weekdays
Subscription Rate: $329
Special Issue:
The Year in Review (annual)

J. R. O'DWYER CO.
271 Madison Ave., Ste. 600
New York, NY 10016
(212)679-2471
Toll-free: 866-395-7710
http://www.odwyerpr.com
Special Annual Feature:
Top 100 Independent Firms

KANSAS CITY STAR
Knight Ridder, Inc.
1729 Grand Blvd.
Kansas City, MO 64108
(816)234-4636
Email: subscriptions@kcstar.com
http://www.kansascity.com
Daily
Special Issue:
The Star 50 (annual)

KIPLINGER'S PERSONAL FINANCE
Kiplinger Washington Editors Inc.
1729 H St. NW
Washington DC 20006
Toll-free: 888-544-0155
http://www.kiplinger.com/magazine
Monthly
Subscription Rate: $12
Special Issues:
Best Cities (annual)
Kiplinger 25 (annual)
Private College Rankings (annual)
Public College Rankings (annual)

KM WORLD
PO Box 1358
Camden, ME 04843
(207)236-8524
800-248-0588
Fax: (207)236-6452
http://www.kmworld.com
10x/yr.
Subscription Rate: Free to qualified
Special Issue:
*100 Companies That Matter in
Knowledge Management (annual)*

LANDSCAPE MANAGEMENT
Questex Media Group LLC
PO Box 1268
Skokie, IL 60076-8268
(847)763-9594
Fax: (847)763-9694
Email: landscapemanagement@hall
data.com
http://www.landscapemanagement.net
Monthly
Subscription Rate: $46
Special Issue:
LM 150 (annual)

THE LANE REPORT
Lane Communications Group
201 E. Main St., 14th Fl.
Lexington, KY 40507
(859)244-3500
http://www.lanereport.com
Subscription Rate: $29
Special Issues:
Highest-Paid CEOs (annual)
Largest Kentucky Banks (annual)
Stock Performance (annual)

LATIN TRADE
Miami Media LLC
1500 San Remo Ave., Ste. 249A
Coral Gables, FL 33146
(305)749-0880
Fax: (786)513-2407
Email: info@latintrade.com
http://www.latintrade.com
Monthly
Subscription Rate: $78
ISSN: 1087-0857
Special Issue:
LT 500 (annual)

LIBRARY JOURNAL
Media Source Inc.
160 Varick St., 11th Fl.
New York, NY 10013
(646)380-0700
Fax: (646)380-0756
Email: ljinfo@mediasourceinc.com
http://www.libraryjournal.com
20x/yr.
Subscription Rate: $157.99
Special Issue:
Best Business Books (annual)

LIGHT & MEDIUM TRUCK
American Trucking Associations Inc.
950 N. Glebe Rd., Ste. 210
Arlington, VA 22203
(703)838-1700
Fax: (703)548-3662
http://lmtruck.com
Monthly
Subscription Rate: Free to qualified
Special Issues:
Top 50 Utility & Telecom Fleets (annual)
Top 100 Commercial Fleets (annual)

LODGING HOSPITALITY
Penton Media, Inc.
The Penton Media Building
1300 E. 9th St.
Cleveland, OH 44114
(216)696-7000
Fax: (216)696-1752
http://lhonline.com
16x/yr.
Subscription Rate: Free to qualified
Special Issues:
Top Hotel Brands (annual)

*Top Third-Party Management
Companies (annual)*

LOGISTICS MANAGEMENT
EH Publishing Inc.
111 Speen St., Ste. 200
Framingham, MA 01701
(508)663-1500
Fax: 877-330-7427
http://www.logisticsmgmt.com
Monthly
Subscription Rate: Free to qualified
Special Issues:
Global Freight Forwarders
Top 3PLs (annual)
Top 30 Ocean Carriers (annual)
Top 50 Trucking Companies (annual)
Top U.S. Ports (annual)

LOS ANGELES BUSINESS JOURNAL
5700 Wilshire Blvd., Ste. 170
Los Angeles, CA 90036
(323)549-5225
Fax: (323)549-5255
http://www.labusinessjournal.com
Weekly
Subscription Rate: $99.95
Special Issues:
*Fastest-Growing Private Companies
(annual)*
Film Production Companies (annual)
L.A. County-Based Banks (annual)
L.A. County-Based Credit Unions (annual)
Largest Foreign Companies (annual)
Largest Franchises (annual)
Largest Law Firms (annual)
Largest Private Companies (annual)
*Largest Private Sector Companies
(annual)*
Largest Public Employers (annual)
Largest Talent Agencies (annual)
MBA Programs (annual)
Minority-Owned Businesses (annual)
Motion Picture Distributors (annual)
Women-Owned Businesses (annual)

LP/GAS MAGAZINE
Questex Media Group LLC
600 Superior Ave. E., Ste. 1100
Cleveland, OH 44114
(847)763-9594
Toll-free: 800-225-4569
Fax: (847)763-9694
http://www.lpgasmagazine.com
Monthly
Subscription Rate: Free to qualified
ISSN: 0024-7103
Special Issue:
Top 50 Propane Retailers (annual)

MACLEAN'S
Rogers Publishing Ltd.
1 Mount Pleasant Rd., 11th Fl.
Toronto, Ontario M4Y 2Y5

Canada
(416)764-1300
Toll-free: 800-268-9119
Fax: (416)764-1332
http://www.macleans.ca
Weekly
Subscription Rate: C$44.95
ISSN: 0024-9262
Special Issues:
50 Most Socially Responsible Corporations (annual)
Canada's Best Professional Schools (annual)
Canada's Top 100 Employers (annual)
University Rankings (annual)

MANAGEMENT TODAY
Haymarket Business Publications Ltd.
174 Hammersmith Rd.
London W6 7JP
United Kingdom
44 020 8267 4610
Fax: 44 020 8267 4966
Email: editorial@managementtoday.co.uk
http://www.managementtoday.co.uk
Monthly
Subscription Rate: £79
Special Issues:
Britain's Most Admired Companies (annual)
Britain's Top 100 Entrepreneurs (annual)

MARKETING
Haymarket Business Publications Ltd.
174 Hammersmith Rd.
London W6 7JP
United Kingdom
44 020 8267 5000
Fax: 44 020 8267 4268
Email: hpg@haymarketgroup.com
http://www.marketingmagazine.co.uk
Weekly
Subscription Rate: £155
Special Issues:
Top 100 Advertisers (annual)
Top 100 Direct Mailers (annual)
Top 100 Online Advertisers (annual)

MARKETING NEWS
American Marketing Association
311 S. Wacker Dr., Ste. 5800
Chicago, IL 60606
(312)542-9000
Toll-free: 800-AMA-1150
Fax: (312)542-9001
Email: info@ama.org
http://www.marketingpower.com
Biweekly
Subscription Rate: Free to members
ISSN: 0025-3790
Special Issues:
Honomichl Global 25 (annual)
Honomichl Top 50 (annual)

MEDICAL PRODUCT OUTSOURCING
Rodman Publishing
70 Hilltop Rd., 3rd Fl.
Ramsey, NJ 07446
(201)825-2552
Fax: (201)825-0553
Email: info@rodpub.com
http://www.mpo-mag.com
9x/yr.
Subscription Rate: Free to qualified
Special Issue:
Top Medical Device Manufacturers (annual)

METAL CENTER NEWS
Sackett Business Media, Inc.
1100 Jorie Blvd., Ste. 207
Oak Brook, IL 60523
(630)571-1067
Fax: (630)572-0689
Email: info@metalcenternews.com
http://www.metalcenternews.com
Monthly
Subscription Rate: Free to qualified; $109 others
Special Issue:
Top 50 (annual)

METAL CONSTRUCTION NEWS
Modern Trade Communications, Inc.
7450 Skokie Blvd.
Skokie, IL 60077
(847)674-2200
Fax: (847)674-3676
http://www.metalconstructionnews.com
Monthly
Subscription Rate: Free to qualified; $45 others
Special Issue:
Top Metal Roofers (annual)

METRO MAGAZINE
Bobit Business Media
3520 Challenger St.
Torrance, CA 90503
(310)533-2400
Fax: (310)533-2502
Email: info@metro-magazine.com
http://www.metro-magazine.com
9x/yr.
Subscription Rate: Free to qualified
Special Issues:
Motorcoach Top 50 (annual)
Top 50 Passenger Rail Projects (annual)
Top 100 Bus Fleets (annual)

MINORITY ENGINEER
Equal Opportunity Publications Inc.
445 Broad Hollow Rd., Ste. 425
Melville, NY 11747
(631)421-9421
Fax: (631)421-1352
Email: info@eop.com
http://www.eop.com/mags-ME.php

Quarterly
Subscription Rate: Free to qualified; $18 others
Special Issue:
Top Employers (annual)

MODERN HEALTHCARE
Crain Communications Inc.
360 N. Michigan Ave., 5th Fl.
Chicago, IL 60601
(312)649-5200
http://www.modernhealthcare.com
Weekly
Subscription Rate: $164
ISSN: 0160-7480
Special Issues:
Best Places to Work (annual)
Largest Biotechnology Companies (annual)
Largest Canadian Hospitals (annual)
Largest Children's Hospitals (annual)
Largest For-Profit Hospital Chains (annual)
Largest Group Practices (annual)
Largest Healthcare Executive Search Firms (annual)
Largest Healthcare Financing Companies (annual)
Largest Healthcare Foundations (annual)
Largest Healthcare Fraud Settlements (annual)
Largest Healthcare Outsourcing Companies (annual)
Largest Healthcare REITs (annual)
Largest Healthcare Unions (annual)
Largest Hospitals (annual)
Largest Management Consulting Firms (annual)
Largest Master's Programs (annual)
Largest Military Hospitals (annual)
Largest Nurse Staffing Firms (annual)
Largest Nursing Schools (annual)
Largest PAC Donations (annual)
Largest Pharmaceutical Companies (annual)
Largest Post-Acute-Care Companies (annual)
Largest Professional Liability Carriers (annual)
Largest Rehabilitation Providers (annual)
Largest Skilled-Nursing Companies (annual)
Most Profitable Critical-Access Hospitals (annual)
Thomson Reuters' Top 100 Hospitals (annual)
Thomson Reuters' Top Cardiovascular Hospitals (annual)
Top Business Graduate Schools for Physician-Executives (annual)
Uninsured Americans by State (annual)

MODERN MATERIALS HANDLING
EH Publishing Inc.
111 Speen St., Ste. 200
Framingham, MA 01701
(508)663-1500
Fax: 877-330-7427
http://www.mmh.com
Monthly
Subscription Rate: Free to qualified
   Special Issues:
   Top 20 ADC Suppliers (annual)
   Top 20 Materials Handling System
      Suppliers (annual)
   Top 20 Supply Chain Management
      Software Suppliers (annual)
   Warehouse Operators (annual)
   World's Top 20 Lift Truck Suppliers
      (annual)

MODERN TIRE DEALER
Bobit Business Media
3515 Massillon Rd., Ste. 350
Uniontown, OH 44685
(330)899-2200
Fax: (330)899-2209
Email: info@MTDealer.com
http://www.moderntiredealer.com
Monthly
Subscription Rate: Free to qualified
   Special Issues:
   Facts Issue (annual)
   MTD 100 (annual)
   Top 100 Tire Retreaders (annual)

MONEYSENSE
Rogers Publishing Ltd.
1 Mount Pleasant Rd., 11th Fl.
Toronto, Ontario M4Y 2Y5
Canada
(416)764-1400
Toll-free: 800-268-9119
Fax: (416)764-1376
Email: letters@moneysense.ca
http://www.moneysense.ca
7x/yr.
Subscription Rate: C$19.95
   Special Issues:
   The Charity 100 (annual)
   Retirement 100 (annual)
   Top 200 Stocks - Canada (annual)
   Top 500 Stocks - U.S. (annual)

MULTICHANNEL MERCHANT
Penton Media Inc.
11 River Bend Dr. S.
PO Box 4242
Stamford, CT 06907-0242
Fax: (203)358-5823
http://multichannelmerchant.com
Monthly
Subscription Rate: Free to qualified
   Special Issue:
   MultiChannel Merchant 100 (annual)

NATIONAL LAW JOURNAL
ALM Media Properties Inc.
120 Broadway, 5th Fl.
New York, NY 10271
(212)457-9400
Fax: (646)417-7705
http://www.law.com/jsp/nlj/index.jsp
Weekly
Subscription Rate: $299
   Special Issue:
   NLJ 250 (annual)

THE NATIONAL PROVISIONER
BNP Media
155 Pfingsten Rd., Ste. 205
Deerfield, IL 60015
(847)405-4000
Fax: (847)405-4100
http://www.provisioneronline.com
Monthly
Subscription Rate: Free to qualified
   Special Issues:
   State of the Industry (annual)
   Top 100 (annual)

NATIONAL REAL ESTATE INVESTOR
Penton Media, Inc.
6151 Powers Ferry Rd., Ste. 200
Atlanta, GA 30339
(770)955-2500
Fax: (770)618-0204
http://nreionline.com
16x/yr.
Subscription Rate: Free to qualified
ISSN: 0027-9994
   Special Issue:
   Best of the Best (annual)

NATIONAL UNDERWRITER, LIFE & HEALTH
Summit Business Media
33-41 Newark St., 2nd Fl.
Hoboken, NJ 07030
(201)526-1230
Fax: (201)526-1260
Email: bcoffin@sbmedia.com
http://www.lifeandhealthinsurance
   news.com
Weekly
   Special Issue:
   The NU 200 Industry Leaders (annual)

NATION'S RESTAURANT NEWS
Penton Media, Inc.
249 W 17th St.
New York, NY 10011
(212)204-4200
http://www.nrn.com
50x/yr.
Subscription Rate: $24.95
   Special Issue:
   Top 100 (annual)

NCB CO-OP 100
National Cooperative Bank
NCB Financial Group

2011 Crystal Dr., Ste. 800
Arlington, VA 22202
(703)302-8000
Toll-free: 800-955-9622
Fax: (703)647-3460
http://www.coop100.coop
Annual

NEVADA BUSINESS
Business Link LLC
375 N. Stephanie St., Bldg. 23
Henderson, NV 89014
(702)735-7003
Fax: (702)733-5953
http://www.nevadabusiness.com
Monthly
Subscription Rate: $44
   Special Issue:
   Best Companies to Work for in Nevada
      (annual)

NEW YORK LAW JOURNAL
ALM Media Properties Inc.
120 Broadway, 5th Fl.
New York, NY 10271
(212)457-9400
Fax: (646)417-7705
http://www.law.com/jsp/nylj/index.jsp
Daily
Subscription Rate: $395
   Special Issue:
   NYLJ 100 (annual)

NEWSWEEK
Newsweek Inc.
395 Hudson St.
New York, NY 10014
http://www.newsweek.com
Weekly
Subscription Rate: $39
   Special Issue:
   The Greenest Big Companies (annual)

THE NONPROFIT TIMES
201 Littleton Rd., 2nd Fl.
Morris Plains, NJ 07950
(973)401-0202
Fax: (973)401-0404
http://www.nptimes.com
17x/yr.
Subscription Rate: $49.95
   Special Issue:
   Power & Influence Top 50 (annual)

NONWOVENS INDUSTRY
Rodman Publishing Corp.
70 Hilltop Rd.
Ramsey, NJ 07446
(201)825-2552
Fax: (201)825-0553
http://www.nonwovens-industry.com
Monthly
Subscription Rate: Free to qualified
   Special Issue:
   Top 40 (annual)

NORTH BAY BUSINESS JOURNAL
427 Mendocino Ave.
Santa Rosa, CA 95401
(707)521-5270
Fax: (707)521-5269
http://www.northbaybusinessjournal.com
Monthly
Subscription Rate: $65
  Special Issues:
  Best Places to Work (annual)
  Highest-Paid Executives (annual)
  Largest Accounting Firms (annual)
  Largest Public Companies (annual)
  Private-Sector Employers: Marin
    County (annual)
  Private-Sector Employers: Napa
    County (annual)
  Private-Sector Employers: Solano
    County (annual)

NORTHWEST CONSTRUCTION
(ceased publication in 2011)

OIL & GAS JOURNAL
PennWell Publishing Co.
PO Box 2002
Tulsa, OK 74101-9957
(918)831-9423
Toll-free: 800-633-1656
Fax: (918)831-9482
http://www.ogj.com
Weekly
Subscription Rate: $69
ISSN: 0030-1388
  Special Issues:
  OGJ 100 (annual)
  OGJ 150 (annual)

ORANGE COUNTY BUSINESS JOURNAL
18500 Von Karman Ave., Ste. 150
Irvine, CA 92612
(949)833-8373
E-mail: cox@ocbj.com
http://www.ocbj.com
Weekly
Subscription Rate: $89
  Special Issues:
  Best Places to Work in Orange County
    (annual)
  Fastest-Growing Private Companies
    (annual)
  Fastest-Growing Public Companies
    (annual)
  Largest Accounting Firms (annual)
  Largest Employers (annual)
  Largest Law Firms (annual)
  Largest Public Companies (annual)
  Largest Women-Owned Businesses
    (annual)
  Minority-Owned Businesses (annual)
  Top Private Companies (annual)

OREGON BUSINESS
715 SW Morrison St., Ste. 800

Portland, OR 97205
(503)223-0304
Fax: (503)221-6544
Email: feedback@oregonbusiness.com
http://www.oregonbusiness.com
Monthly
Subscription Rate: Free to qualified;
  $24.95 others
  Special Issues:
  The 100 Best Companies to Work For
    in Oregon (annual)
  The 100 Best Green Companies (an-
    nual)
  The 100 Best Nonprofits (annual)

ORTHOPEDIC DESIGN & TECHNOL-OGY
Rodman Publishing Corp.
70 Hilltop Rd.
Ramsey, NJ 07446
(201)825-2552
Fax: (201)825-0553
http://www.odtmag.com
Bimonthly
Subscription Rate: Free to qualified
  Special Issue:
  Top 10 Orthopedic Device Manufactur-
    ers (annual)

PAINT & COATINGS INDUSTRY
BNP Media
2401 W. Big Beaver Rd., Ste. 700
Troy, MI 48084
(847)763-9534
Fax: (847)763-9538
http://www.pcimag.com
Monthly
Subscription Rate: Free to qualified
  Special Issue:
  PCI 25 (annual)

PENSIONS & INVESTMENTS
Crain Communications Inc.
711 3rd Ave.
New York, NY 10017-4036
(212)210-0100
Fax: (212)210-0117
http://www.pionline.com
26x/yr.
Subscription Rate: $279
  Special Issues:
  Mergers and Acquisitions (annual)
  P&I/Towers Watson World 300 (an-
    nual)
  P&I/Towers Watson World 500 (an-
    nual)

PEST CONTROL TECHNOLOGY
GIE Media Inc.
4020 Kinross Lakes Pky., Ste. 201
Richfield, OH 44286
Toll-free: 800-456-0707
Fax: (330)659-0823
http://www.pctonline.com
Monthly

Subscription Rate: $35
  Special Issue:
  Top 100 (annual)

PHARMACEUTICAL EXECUTIVE
Advanstar Communications, Inc.
641 Lexington Ave., 8th Fl.
New York, NY 10022
(212)951-6600
Fax: (212)951-6604
http://www.pharmexec.com
Monthly
Subscription Rate: Free to qualified
  Special Issues:
  Industry Audit (annual)
  Pharm Exec 50 (annual)

PIT & QUARRY
Questex Media Group Inc.
600 Superior Ave. E, Ste. 1100
Cleveland, OH 44114
(216)706-3700
Fax: (216)706-3710
E-mail: info@pitandquarry.com
http://www.pitandquarry.com
Monthly
Subscription Rate: Free to qualified
  Special Issue:
  MegaProducers (annual)

PITTSBURGH POST-GAZETTE
PG Publishing Co., Inc.
34 Blvd. of the Allies
Pittsburgh, PA 15222
(412)263-1100
Toll-free: 800-228-NEWS
http://www.post-gazette.com
Daily
Subscription Rate: $195
  Special Issue:
  Top 50 (annual)

PIZZA MARKETING QUARTERLY
PMQ Inc.
605 Edison St.
Oxford, MS 38655
(662)234-5481
Fax: (662)234-0665
Email: mail@pmq.com
http://www.pmq.com
Bimonthly
Subscription Rate: Free to qualified
  Special Issue:
  Pizza Power (annual)

PIZZA TODAY
MacFadden Protech LLC
908 S. 8th St., Ste. 200
Louisville, KY 40203
(502)736-9500
Toll-free: 800-489-8324
Fax: (502)736-9502
http://www.pizzatoday.com
Monthly
Subscription Rate: Free to qualified

Special Issues:
Hot 100 Independents (annual)
Top 100 Pizza Companies (annual)

THE PLAIN DEALER
The Plain Dealer Publishing Co.
Plain Dealer Plaza
1801 Superior Ave.
Cleveland, OH 44114
(216)999-5000
Toll-free: 800-362-0727
http://www.plaindealer.com
Daily
Special Issue:
Northeast Ohio's Top Workplaces (annual)

PLASTICS NEWS
Crain Communications Inc.
1725 Merriman Rd., Ste. 300
Akron, OH 44313
(330)836-9180
Toll-free: 800-678-9595
http://www.plasticsnews.com
Weekly
Subscription Rate: $84
Special Issues:
Highest-Paid Plastics Industry Executives (annual)
North American Blow Molders (annual)
North American Film and Sheet Manufacturers (annual)
North American Injection Molders (annual)
North American Plastics Recyclers and Brokers (annual)
North American Rotational Molders (annual)
North American Thermoformers (annual)
Top Mold Makers (annual)
Top Pipe, Profile, and Tubing Extruders (annual)

PLATTS
The McGraw-Hill Cos.
2 Penn Plz., 25th Fl.
New York, NY 10121-2298
(212)904-3070
Toll-free 800-PLATTS
http://www.platts.com
Special Annual Feature:
Top 250 Global Energy Company Rankings

PLUMBING & MECHANICAL
BNP Media
2401 W. Big Beaver Rd., Ste. 700
Troy, MI 48084
(248)362-3700
Fax: (248)362-0317
http://www.pmmag.com
Monthly
Subscription Rate: Free to qualified

Special Issue:
Pipe Trades Giants (annual)

PODER MAGAZINE
ET Publishing International Inc.
6355 NW 36th St.
Miami, FL 33166
(305)492-0070
http://www.poder360.com
Bimonthly
Subscription Rate: $12.95
Special Issues:
Top Business Schools for Hispanics (annual)
Top Companies for Supplier Diversity (annual)
Top Franchises for Hispanics (annual)
Top MBAs for Hispanics (annual)

POOL & SPA NEWS
Hanley Wood LLC
6222 Wilshire Blvd., Ste. 600
Los Angeles, CA 90048
(323)801-4903
http://www.poolspanews.com
24x/yr.
Subscription Rate: $19.97
Special Issue:
Top 50 Builders (annual)

PRINT SOLUTIONS
Print Services & Distribution Association
401 N. Michigan Ave., Ste. 2200
Chicago, IL 60611
(312)321-5120
800-230-0175
Fax: (312)673-6880
Email: contact@printsolutionsmag.com
http://www.printsolutionsmag.com
Monthly
Subscription Rate: Free to members; $99 others
Special Issues:
Top 100 Distributors (annual)
Top Trade Printers (annual)

PRINTING IMPRESSIONS
North American Publishing Co.
1500 Spring Garden St., Ste. 1200
Philadelphia, PA 19130
(215)238-5300
http://www.piworld.com
Monthly
Subscription Rate: Free to qualified
Special Issue:
PI 400 (annual)

PROFESSIONAL BUILDER
SGC Horizon LLC
3030 W. Salt Creek Ln., Ste. 201
Arlington Heights, IL 60005
(847)391-1000
Fax: (847)390-0408
http://www.housingzone.com
Monthly
Subscription Rate: Free to qualified

Special Issue:
Housing Giants (annual)

PROFIT
Rogers Media
1 Mount Pleasant Rd., 11th Fl.
Toronto, Ontario M4Y 2Y5
Canada
(416)764-1402
Fax: (416)764-1404
Email: profit@profit.rogers.com
http://www.profitguide.com
Bimonthly
Subscription Rate: Free to qualified
Special Issues:
Hot 100 (annual)
Profit 100 (annual)
W 100 (annual)

PROGRESS
Progress Media Group
Penthouse, Ste. 1202
1660 Hollis St.
Halifax, NS B3J 1V7
Canada
(902)494-0999
Fax: (902)494-0998
E-mail: progress@progressmedia.ca
http://www.progressmedia.ca
8x/yr.
Subscription Rate: Free to qualified
Special Issues:
Best Places to Work (annual)
Fastest-Growing Companies (annual)

PROGRESSIVE GROCER
Stagnito Media
570 Lake Cook Rd., Ste. 106
Deerfield, IL 60015
(224)632-8200
Fax: (224)632-8266
http://www.progressivegrocer.com
18x/yr.
Subscription Rate: Free to qualified
ISSN: 0033-0787
Special Issue:
The Super 50 (annual)

PROMO MAGAZINE
Penton Media, Inc.
11 River Bend Dr. S.
PO Box 4949
Stamford, CT 06907-0949
(203)358-9900
Fax: (203)358-5811
http://promomagazine.com
Monthly
Subscription Rate: Free to qualified
Special Issue:
PROMO 100 (annual)

PUBLISHERS WEEKLY
PWxyz LLC
71 W 23 St., Ste. 1608
New York, NY 10010
(212)377-5500

http://www.publishersweekly.com
Weekly
Subscription Rate: $249.99
ISSN: 0000-0019
    Special Issues:
    Bestsellers (annual)
    Facts & Figures (annual)

PULP AND PAPER INTERNATIONAL
RISI Inc.
4 Alfred Cir.
Bedford, MA 01730
(781)734-8900
Fax: (781)271-0337
Email: info@risiinfo.com
http://www.risiinfo.com
Monthly
Subscription Rate: Free to qualified
    Special Issue:
    Top 100 (annual)

QSR MAGAZINE
Journalistic, Inc.
4905 Pine Cone Dr., Ste. 2
Durham, NC 27707
(919)489-1916
Fax: (919)489-4767
http://www.qsrmagazine.com
Monthly
Subscription Rate: Free to qualified
    Special Issues:
    The Growth 40 (annual)
    The QSR 50 (annual)

QUALIFIED REMODELER
Cygnus Business Media
1233 Janesville Ave.
PO Box 803
Fort Atkinson, WI 53538-0803
(920)563-6388
Fax: (920)563-1704
http://www.qualifiedremodeler.com
Monthly
Subscription Rate: Free to qualified; $44
  others
    Special Issues:
    Specialty 200 (annual)
    Top 500 (annual)

QUICK PRINTING
Cygnus Business Media
1233 Janesville Ave.
Fort Atkinson, WI 53538
Toll-free: 877-382-9187
Email: circ.quickprinting@omeda.com
http://www.myprintresource.com/
  magazine/qp
Monthly
Subscription Rate: Free to qualified; $44
  others
    Special Issue:
    Top 100 (annual)

R & D MAGAZINE
Advantage Business Media
100 Enterprise Dr., Ste. 600

PO Box 912
Rockaway, NJ 07866-0912
(973)920-7000
http://www.rdmag.com
7x/yr.
Subscription Rate: Free to qualified; $63
  others
    Special Issue:
    R & D 100 (annual)

REALSCREEN
Brunico Communications Ltd.
500 - 366 Adelaide St. W.
Toronto, Ontario M5V 1R9
Canada
(416)408-2300
Fax: (416)408-0870
E-mail: realscreencustomercare@bruni
  co.com
http://www.realscreen.com
Monthly
Subscription Rate: $59; C$79
    Special Issue:
    Global 100 (annual)

REALTOR MAGAZINE
National Association of Realtors
430 N. Michigan Ave.
Chicago, IL 60611-4087
Toll-free: 800-874-6500
Fax: (312)329-5978
Email: narpubs@realtors.org
http://www.realtor.org/rmohome/home
Monthly
Subscription Rate: Free for members; $56
  for nonmembers
    Special Issue:
    Top 100 Companies (annual)

RED HERRING
Red Herring Inc.
1900 Alameda de las Pulgas, Ste. 112
San Mateo, CA 94403
(650)215-1520
Fax: (619)923-2792
http://www.redherring.com
Monthly
    Special Issues:
    Red Herring Asia (annual)
    Red Herring Europe (annual)
    Red Herring Global (annual)
    Red Herring North America (annual)

REFRIGERATED & FROZEN FOODS
BNP Media
155 Pfingsten Rd., Ste. 205
Deerfield, IL 60015
(847)405-4000
Fax: (847)405-4100
http://www.refrigeratedfrozenfood.com
Monthly
Subscription Rate: Free to qualified
    Special Issue:
    Top 150 Food Processors (annual)

REGISTERED REP.
Penton Media Inc.
PO Box 2100
Skokie, IL 60076-7800
(847)763-9504
Fax: (847)763-9682
Email: registeredrep@pbinews.com
http://registeredrep.com
Monthly
Subscription Rate: Free to qualified
    Special Issues:
    America's Top 100 RIAs (annual)
    America's Top 100 Wirehouse Advisors
      (annual)

REPORT ON BUSINESS MAGAZINE
The Globe and Mail Inc.
444 Front St. W.
Toronto, Ontario M5V 2S9
Canada
(416)585-5222
Toll-free: 800-387-5400
Fax: (416)585-5102
http://www.theglobeandmail.com/
  robmagazine
Monthly
    Special Issues:
    Online Broker Rankings (annual)
    Top 1000 Companies (annual)

RESTAURANT BUSINESS
CSP Information Group Inc.
90 Broad St., Ste. 1506
New York, NY 10004
(630)574-5075
Fax: (630)574-5175
Email: cspinquire@cspnet.com
http://www.monkeydish.com
Monthly
Subscription Rate: Free to qualified; $99
  others
ISSN: 0097-8043
    Special Issues:
    Future 50 (annual)
    Restaurant Growth Index (annual)
    Social Media 50

RETAIL ASIA
Retail Asia Publishing Pte. Ltd.
61 Tai Seng Ave.
05-01 UE Print Media Hub
Singapore 534167
65 6287 2025
Fax: 65 6287 2027
Email: info@retailasia.com.sg
http://www.retailasiaonline.com
Monthly
Subscription Rate: $170 in U.S.
    Special Issue:
    Retail Asia-Pacific Top 500 (annual)

RETAIL TRAFFIC
Penton Media Inc.
249 W. 17th St.
New York, NY 10011

(212)204-4200
Fax: (914)514-9050
http://retailtrafficmag.com
Bimonthly
Subscription Rate: Free to qualified
  Special Issues:
  Top 100 Managers (annual)
  Top 100 Owners (annual)
  Top Contractors (annual)

RETAILING TODAY
LebharFriedman, Inc.
425 Park Ave.
New York, NY 10022
(212)7565000
Tollfree: 8002167117
Fax: (212)7565125
http://www.retailingtoday.com
23x/yr.
Subscription Rate: Free to qualified
  Special Issue:
  Annual Brands Report

RV BUSINESS
RV Business/G & G Media Group LLC
2901 E. Bristol St., Ste. B
Elkhart, IN 46514
(574)266-7980
Toll-free: 800-831-1076
Fax: (574)266-7984
http://www.rvbusiness.com
Monthly
Subscription Rate: Free to qualified
  Special Issue:
  Top 50 Dealer Awards (annual)

SAN JOSE MERCURY NEWS
MediaNews Group
750 Ridder Park Dr.
San Jose, CA 95190
(408)920-5000
Fax: (408)288-8060
http://www.mercurynews.com
Daily
  Special Issue:
  Silicon Valley 150 (annual)

SASKATCHEWAN BUSINESS
Sunrise Publishing Ltd.
2213B Hanselman Ct.
Saskatoon, SK S7L 6A8
Canada
(306)244-5668
Toll-free: 800-247-5743
Fax: (306)244-5679
http://www.sunrisepublish.com/
  saskbusiness_magazine
9x/yr.
Subscription Rate: C$40
  Special Issue:
  Top 100 Companies (annual)

THE SAVINGS DIRECTORY
Accuity Inc.
1770 Breckinridge Pky., Ste. 500
Duluth, GA 30096

(770)381-2511
Fax: (770)564-8925
http://www.accuitysolutions.com
Annual
Copyright © 2010
ISBN: 978-1-56310-689-7

SC 25 FASTEST GROWING COMPANIES
The Capital Corp.
84 Villa Rd.
Greenville, SC 29615
(864)672-8400
800-259-0119
Fax: (864)542-1661
http://www.thecapitalcorp.com
Annual

SEAFOOD BUSINESS
Diversified Business Communications
121 Free St.
PO Box 7438
Portland, ME 04112-7438
(207)842-5500
Fax: (207)842-5503
Monthly
Subscription Rate: Free to qualified
http://www.seafoodbusiness.com
  Special Issue:
  North America's Top 20 Seafood Suppliers (annual)

THE SEATTLE TIMES
The Seattle Times Co.
1120 John St.
PO Box 70
Seattle, WA 98111
(206)464-2111
http://seattletimes.nwsource.com
Daily
  Special Issue:
  Northwest 100 (annual)

SECURITY DISTRIBUTING & MARKETING (SDM)
BNP Media
1050 IL Route 83, Ste. 200
Bensenville, IL 60106
(630)616-0200
Fax: (630)227-0214
Email: sdm@bnpmedia.com
http://www.sdmmag.com
13x/yr.
Subscription Rate: Free to qualified
ISSN: 0049-0016
  Special Issues:
  SDM 100 (annual)
  Top Systems Integrators (annual)

SITE SELECTION
Conway Data Inc.
6625 The Corners Pky., Ste. 200
Norcross, GA 30092
(770)446-6996
Toll-free: 800-554-5686
Fax: (770)263-8825

Email: editor@conway.com
http://www.siteselection.com
Bimonthly
Subscription Rate: Free to qualified; $95
  others
ISSN: 1080-7799
  Special Issues:
  Business Climate Rankings (annual)
  Canadian Rankings (annual)
  Emerging Logistics Hubs
  Europe's Best for Business (annual)
  Global Best to Invest Rankings (annual)
  The Governor's Cup (annual)
  Sustainability Rankings (annual)
  Top Competitive States (annual)
  Top Deals (annual)
  Top Global Projects (annual)
  Top Groups (annual)
  Top Industries (annual)
  Top Metros (annual)
  Top Micropolitans (annual)
  Top Utilities (annual)

SMALL BUSINESS SURVIVAL INDEX
Small Business & Entrepreneurship
  Council
2994 Hunter Mill Rd., Ste. 204
Oakton, VA 22124
(703)242-5840
Fax: (703)242-5841
http://www.sbecouncil.org
December 2010
Annual

SMALL BUSINESS TRENDS
Small Business Trends LLC
(330)242-1893
E-mail: sbtips@gmail.com
http://smallbiztrends.com
  Special Online Feature:
  Best Small Business Books (annual)

SMARTMONEY
Dow Jones & Co., Inc.
1755 Broadway, 2nd Fl.
New York, NY 10019
Toll-free: 800-444-4204
Email: editors@smartmoney.com
http://www.smartmoney.com/smartmoney-
  magazine
Monthly
Subscription Rate: $10
  Special Issue:
  Broker Survey (annual)

SNOHOMISH COUNTY BUSINESS JOURNAL
1213 California St.
Box 930
Everett, WA 98206
http://www.snohomishcountybusinessjour
  nal.com
Monthly
Subscription Rate: $22

Special Issue:
Market Facts (annual)

SNOW MAGAZINE
GIE Media Inc.
4020 Kinross Lakes Pky., Ste. 201
Richfield, OH 44286
Toll-free: 800-456-0707
Fax: (330)659-0823
http://www.snowmagazineonline.com
Bimonthly
Subscription Rate: Free to qualified
Special Issue:
Top 100 Contractors (annual)

SOFTWARE DEVELOPMENT TIMES
BZ Media LLC
7 High St., Ste. 407
Huntington, NY 11743
(631)421-4158
Fax: (631)421-4130
Email: info@bzmedia.com
http://www.sdtimes.com
Biweekly
Subscription Rate: Free to qualified
Special Issue:
SD Times 100 (annual)

SOFTWARE MAGAZINE
King Content Co.
233 Needham St., Ste. 300
Newton, MA 02464
(508)668-9928
Toll-free: 888-764-6614
http://www.softwaremag.com
Bimonthly
Subscription Rate: Free to qualified
Special Issue:
Software 500 (annual)

SOUTH CAROLINA BUSINESS
SC Biz News LLC
389 Johnnie Dodds Blvd., Ste. 200
Mount Pleasant, SC 29464
(843)849-3100
Fax: (843)849-3122
http://www.scbizmag.com
Quarterly
Subscription Rate: $43.50
Special Issue:
South Carolina 100 (annual)

SOUTH CENTRAL CONSTRUCTION
(ceased publication in 2011)

SPACE NEWS
Imaginova Corp.
6883 Commercial Dr.
Springfield, VA 22159
(703)658-8400
Fax: (703)750-8913
http://www.spacenews.com
Weekly
Subscription Rate: $199
Special Issues:
Top 50 (annual)

Top Fixed Satellite Service Operators
(annual)

SPECIAL EVENTS
Penton Media Inc.
17383 Sunset Blvd., Ste. A220
Pacific Palisades, CA 90272
(310)230-7160
Fax: (310)230-7168
http://specialevents.com
Bimonthly
Subscription Rate: Free to qualified
Special Issue:
25 Great, Big Caterers (annual)

SPORTING GOODS BUSINESS
2151 Hawkins St., Ste. 200
Charlotte, NC 28203
(704)987-3450
Fax: (704)987-3455
http://www.sportinggoodsbusiness.com
Monthly
Special Issues:
Brand Strength (annual)
Retail Top 100 (annual)

SPORTS ILLUSTRATED
Time Inc.
PO Box 30602
Tampa, FL 33630
http://www.si.com
Weekly
Subscription Rate: $48

STAR TRIBUNE
The StarTribune Media Co.
425 Portland Ave. S.
Minneapolis, MN 55488
(612)673-4000
Toll-free: 800-775-4344
http://www.startribune.com
Daily
Special Issue:
Star Tribune 100 (annual)

STORES
National Retail Federation
325 7th St. NW, Ste. 1100
Washington DC 20004
(202)783-7971
Toll-free: 800-NRF-HOW2
Fax: (202)737-2849
http://www.stores.org
Monthly
Subscription Rate: Free to qualified; $120
others
ISSN: 0039-1867
Special Issues:
Favorite 50 (annual)
Hot 100 (annual)
Top 100 Retailers (annual)
Top Global Retailers (annual)

SUCCESSFUL FARMING
Meredith Corp.
PO Box 37466

Boone, IA 50037-0466
(515)284-2845
Toll-free: 800-374-3276
http://www.agriculture.com/successful-
farming
Monthly
Subscription Rate: $15.95
Special Issue:
Pork Powerhouses (annual)

THE SUNDAY TIMES
Times Newspapers Ltd.
1 Pennington St.
London E98 1XY
United Kingdom
44 (0)20 7782 5000
Fax: 44 (0)20 7782 5046
Email: custserv@timesonline.co.uk
http://business.timesonline.co.uk
Weekly
Special Issue:
Rich List (annual)

SUPPLY CHAIN BRAIN
Keller Publishing LLC
150 Great Neck Rd., Ste. 400
Great Neck, NY 11021
(516)829-9210
Fax: (516)829-9722
http://www.supplychainbrain.com
Monthly
Subscription Rate: Free to qualified
Special Issue:
Supply Chain Top 100 (annual)

T & D MAGAZINE
American Society for Training & Develop-
ment
1640 King St.
Box 1443
Alexandria, VA 22313-1443
(703)683-8100
Fax: (703)683-8103
E-mail: customercare@astd.org
http://www.astd.org/TD
Monthly
Subscription Rate: Free for members;
$150 others
Special Issue:
Top 40 BEST Companies (annual)

TECHNOLOGY REVIEW
Massachusetts Institute of Technology
1 Main St., 13th Fl.
Cambridge, MA 02142
(617)475-8000
Fax: (617)475-8042
http://www.technologyreview.com
Monthly
Subscription Rate: $24.95
Special Issue:
TR 50 (annual)

TECHNOMIC INC.
300 S. Riverside Plaza, Ste. 1200
Chicago, IL 60606

(312)876-0004
Email: foodinfo@technomic.com
http://www.technomic.com
Special Feature:
Top 500

TECHNORATI INC.
360 Post St., Ste. 1100
San Francisco, CA 94108
(415)896-3000
http://www.technorati.com
Special Online Features:
Blog Directory
Top 100 (daily)

THE TIMES TOP 100 GRADUATE EMPLOYERS
High Fliers Publications Ltd.
10A Belmont St.
Camden Town
London NW1 8HH
United Kingdom
44 020 7428 9100
Fax: 44 020 7428 9111
Email: top100@highfliers.co.uk
http://www.top100graduateemployers.com
Annual

TODAY'S TRUCKING
Newcom Business Media Inc.
451 Attwell Dr.
Toronto, ON M9W 5C4
Canada
(416)614-2200
Fax: (416)614-8861
http://www.todaystrucking.com
10x/yr.
Subscription Rate: Free to qualified
Special Issue:
TT 100 (annual)

TOP RETIREMENTS.COM
(203)415-4792
http://www.topretirements.com
Special Online Feature:
Worst States to Retire

TRADE SHOW NEWS NETWORK
Tarsus Group plc
174 Concord St., Ste. 310
Peterborough, NH 03458
(603)925-1160
http://www.tsnn.com
Special Online Feature:
Top 250 Trade Shows

TRAINING
Lakewood Media Group
27020 Noble Rd.
PO Box 247
Excelsior, MN 55331
(847)559-7533
Fax: (847)291-4816
Email: ntrn@omeda.com
http://www.trainingmag.com
Bimonthly

Subscription Rate: Free to qualified
Special Issue:
The Top 125 (annual)

TRANSPORT TOPICS
American Trucking Associations, Inc.
2200 Mill Rd.
Alexandria, VA 22314
(703)838-1770
Fax: (703)548-3662
http://www.ttnews.com
Weekly
Subscription Rate: $109
ISSN: 0041-1558
Special Issue:
Transport Topics 100 (annual)

TRENCHLESS TECHNOLOGY
Benjamin Media Inc.
1770 Main St.
PO Box 190
Peninsula, OH 44264
(330)467-7588
Fax: (330)468-2289
Email: info@benjaminmedia.com
http://www.trenchlessonline.com
Monthly
Subscription Rate: Free in U.S.
Special Issue:
Top 50 Design Firms (annual)

TWIN CITIES BUSINESS
MSP Communications Inc.
220 S. 6th St., Ste. 500
Minneapolis, MN 55402
(612)339-7571
Fax: (612)336-9220
http://www.tcbmag.com
Monthly
Subscription Rate: $24.95
Special Issue:
The BIG Book (annual)

U.S. BANKER
SourceMedia Inc.
1 State Street Plaza, 27th Fl.
New York, NY 10004
(212)803-8200
http://www.americanbanker.com/usb
_issues
Monthly
Subscription Rate: $109
Special Issues:
25 Most Powerful Women in Banking (annual)
Top 200 Publicly Traded Community Banks (annual)

U.S. NEWS & WORLD REPORT
1050 Thomas Jefferson St. NW
Washington DC 20007
(202)955-2000
Fax: (202)955-2049
http://www.usnews.com
Weekly
Subscription Rate: $19.95

ISSN: 0041-5537
Special Issues:
America's Best Colleges (annual)
America's Best Hospitals (annual)
Best Children's Hospitals (annual)
Best Law Firms (annual)
Best Places to Retire (annual)
Top Health Insurance Companies (annual)
U.S. News & World Report

USAA MAGAZINE
USAA, the United Services Automobile Association
9800 Fredericksburg Rd.
San Antonio, TX 78288
Toll-free: 800-531-USAA
Email: usaamagazine@usaa.com
http://www.usaa.com/inet/pages/maga zines_USAA
Quarterly
Special Issue:
Best Places for Military Retirement (annual)

UTAH VALLEY BUSINESS MAGAZINE
Bennett Communications Inc.
PO Box 50142
Provo, UT 84605
(801)802-0200
http://www.uvmag.com
Bimonthly
Subscription Rate: $10
Special Issue:
UV 50 (annual)

VISION MONDAY
Jobson Healthcare Information LLC
100 Avenue of the Americas
New York, NY 10013
(212)274-7000
Fax: (212)431-0500
http://www.visionmonday.com
Weekly
Subscription Rate: Free to qualified
Special Issue:
Top 50 (annual)

VITRUE INC.
101 Marietta St., Ste. 1700
Atlanta, GA 30303
(404)478-8300
Fax: (404)478-8301
http://vitrue.com
Special Annual Feature:
Vitrue 100

THE WALL STREET JOURNAL
Dow Jones & Co., Inc.
200 Burnett Rd.
Chicopee, MA 01020
Toll-free: 800-JOURNAL
Fax: 800-975-8618
Email: wsj.service@dowjones.com
http://www.wsj.com
Weekdays

Subscription Rate: $119
Special Issues:
Airline Rankings
American Idle
Asia 200 (annual)
Best Executive MBA Programs (annual)
CEO Compensation Survey (annual)
College Survey (annual)
Top 10 Clean-Tech Companies
Top 50 Venture-Backed Companies (annual)
Year-End Review (annual)

THE WASHINGTON POST

The Washington Post Co.
1150 15th St. NW
Washington DC 20071
(202)3346000
Fax: (202)3344536
http://www.washingtonpost.com
Daily
Special Issue:
The Post 200 (annual)

WASHINGTON TECHNOLOGY

1105 Government Information Group
3141 Fairview Park Dr., Ste. 777
Falls Church, VA 22042
(703)876-5100
http://www.washingtontechnology.com
Semimonthly
Subscription Rate: Free to qualified
Special Issues:
Fast 50 (annual)
Top 25 8(a) Companies (annual)
Top 100 (annual)

WASTE AGE

Penton Media, Inc.
6151 Powers Ferry Rd., Ste. 200
Atlanta, GA 30339
(770)955-2500
Fax: (770)618-0204
http://waste360.com
Monthly
Subscription Rate: Free to qualified
Special Issue:
Waste Age 100 (annual)

WIDE-FORMAT IMAGING

Cygnus Business Media
3 Huntington Quadrangle, Ste. 301 N
Melville, NY 11747
Toll-free: 800-308-6397
Fax: (631)845-2741
http://www.wide-formatimaging.com
Monthly

Subscription Rate: Free to qualified
Special Issue:
Top Shops (annual)

WINDOW & DOOR

National Glass Association
8200 Greensboro Dr., Ste. 302
McLean, VA 22102-3881
866-DIAL-NGA
Fax: (703)442-0630
http://www.windowanddoor.com
11x/yr.
Subscription Rate: Free to qualified;
$29.95 others
Special Issue:
Top 100 Manufacturers (annual)

WINE BUSINESS MONTHLY

Wine Communications Group Inc.
110 W. Napa St.
Sonoma, CA 85476
(707)939-0822
Fax: (707)939-0833
Email: info@winebusiness.com
http://winebusinessmonthly.com
Monthly
Subscription Rate: $39
Special Issue:
WBM 30 (annual)

WOMAN ENGINEER

Equal Opportunity Publications Inc.
445 Broad Hollow Rd., Ste. 425
Melville, NY 11747
(631)421-9421
Fax: (631)421-1352
Email: info@eop.com
http://www.eop.com/mags-WE.php
Quarterly
Subscription Rate: Free to qualified; $18
others
Special Issue:
Top Employers (annual)

WOOD & WOOD PRODUCTS

Vance Publishing Corp.
PO Box 1400
Lincolnshire, IL 60069
(847)634-4347
Toll-free: 800-343-2016
Fax: (847)634-4374
Email: industrialinfo@vancepublishing.com
http://woodworkingnetwork.com
Monthly
Subscription Rate: Free to qualified
Special Issue:
Wood 100 (annual)

WORKFORCE DIVERSITY FOR ENGINEERING AND IT PROFESSIONALS

Equal Opportunity Publications Inc.
445 Broad Hollow Rd., Ste. 425
Melville, NY 11747
(631)421-9421
Fax: (631)421-1352
Email: info@eop.com
http://www.eop.com/mags-WD.php
Quarterly
Subscription Rate: Free to qualified; $18
others
Special Issue:
Top Employers (annual)

WORKFORCE MANAGEMENT

Crain Communications Inc.
360 N Michigan Ave.
Chicago, IL 60601
(312)649-5200
Email: mailroom@workforce.com
http://www.workforce.com
Semimonthly
Subscription Rate: $79
Special Issue:
The Hot List

WORKING MOTHER

Bonnier Corp.
2 Park Ave.
New York, NY 10016
(212)219-7470
http://www.workingmother.com
8x/yr.
Subscription Rate: $9.97
Special Issues:
100 Best Companies for Working Mothers (annual)
Best Companies for Hourly Workers (annual)
Best Companies for Multicultural Women (annual)
Best Companies for Women's Advancement (annual)

WORLD TRADE

BNP Media
2401 W. Big Beaver Rd., Ste. 700
Troy, MI 48084
(248)362-3700
Fax: (248)244-6439
http://www.worldtrademag.com
Monthly
Subscription Rate: Free to qualified
Special Issue:
World Trade 100 (annual)

Accounting Firms

1 ■ BEST LARGE ACCOUNTING FIRMS TO WORK FOR, 2011

Ranked by: Employee survey. **Remarks:** Scores not provided. Ranking covers firms with 250 or more employees. Also notes headquarters, website, number of employees, turnover rate, average number of training hours per employee, and chief executive. **Number listed:** 5

1. Kaufman, Rossin & Co.
2. WithumSmith + Brown
3. Kearney & Co.
4. The Bonadio Group
5. Anchin, Block & Anchin LLP

Source: *Accounting Today*, Best Accounting Firms to Work For (annual), December 2011, p. 36.

2 ■ BEST MIDSIZED ACCOUNTING FIRMS TO WORK FOR, 2011

Ranked by: Employee survey. **Remarks:** Scores not provided. Ranking covers firms with 50 to 249 employees. Also notes headquarters, website, number of employees, turnover rate, average number of training hours per employee, and chief executive. **Number listed:** 45

1. Lutz & Co.
2. Porter Keadle Moore
3. Wilkin & Guttenplan
4. Hemming Morse
5. Windham Brannon
6. Sisterson & Co.
7. RBZ
8. Gelman, Rosenberg & Freedman CPAs
9. Teal, Becker & Chiaramonte, CPAs
10. Boyer & Ritter CPAs & Consultants

Source: *Accounting Today*, Best Accounting Firms to Work For (annual), December 2011, p. 34-36.

3 ■ BEST SMALL ACCOUNTING FIRMS TO WORK FOR, 2011

Ranked by: Employee survey. **Remarks:** Scores not provided. Ranking covers firms with 15 to 49 employees. Also notes headquarters, website, number of employees, turnover rate, average number of training hours per employee, and chief executive. **Number listed:** 50

1. Johnson Jacobson Wilcox

2. Mowery & Schoenfeld
3. Santos, Ramos & Co.
4. Berlin, Ramos & Co.
5. LMGW Certified Public Accountants
6. Smith Leonard
7. Wessel & Co.
8. Ennis Pellum & Associates
9. BKM Sowan Horan
10. E. Cohen & Co.

Source: *Accounting Today*, Best Accounting Firms to Work For (annual), December 2011, p. 34.

4 ■ CHICAGO'S LARGEST ACCOUNTING FIRMS, 2011

Ranked by: Number of professional staff in the six-county Chicago area as of June 30, 2011. **Remarks:** Also notes contact information, managing partner in Chicago, figures for previous year, firmwide revenue, and breakdown of professional staff by practice emphasis. **Number listed:** 28

1. Deloitte LLP, with 3,142 staff
2. PricewaterhouseCoopers LLP, 2,206
3. Ernst & Young LLP, 1,913
4. KPMG LLP, 1,646
5. McGladrey LLP, 1,078

Source: *Crain's Chicago Business*, Chicago's Largest Accounting Firms (annual), http://www.chicagobusiness.com, October 17, 2011.

5 ■ FASTEST-GROWING ACCOUNTING FIRMS IN THE U.S., 2010-2011

Ranked by: Annual revenue growth, in percent. **Remarks:** Also notes headquarters, net revenue, and rank in the overall *Top 100*. **Number listed:** 12

1. Gallina LLP, with 31.3%
2. Kaufman Rossin Group, 22.5%
3. Blue & Co., 20.2%
4. SS & G Financial Services, 17%
5. RubinBrown LLP, 14%
6. Honkamp Krueger & Co., 13.9%
6. Argy, Wiltse & Robinson, 13.9%
8. Nigro Karlin Segal & Feldstein, 13.7%
9. Macias Gini & O'Connell, 13%
10. Citrin Cooperman, 11%

Source: *Public Accounting Report*, Top 100 (annual), October 24, 2011, p. 3.

6 ■ LARGEST ACCOUNTING FIRMS IN SOUTH CAROLINA, 2011

Ranked by: Number of certified public accountants. **Remarks:** Also notes contact information, number of employees, managing partner, services, and year founded. **Number listed:** 23

1. Elliott Davis LLC, with 162 CPAs
2. Dixon Hughes Goodman LLP, 130
3. PricewaterhouseCoopers LLP, 60
4. Ernst & Young LLP, 50
5. Cherry Bekaert & Holland LLP, 40
6. Grant Thornton LLP, 28
7. McGregor & Co., 27
8. Bauknight, Pietras & Stormer PA, 22
9. KPMG LLP, 21
10. Bradshaw Gordon & Clinkscales LLC, 20
10. McAbee Talbert Holliday & Co., 20
10. Moore Beauston & Woodham LLP, 20

Source: *South Carolina Business*, Book of Lists (annual), 2011, p. 22.

7 ■ LARGEST ACCOUNTING FIRMS IN THE U.S., 2010

Ranked by: U.S. net revenue, in dollars. **Remarks:** Also notes headquarters, fiscal year-end, annual revenue growth, number of partners and non-professionals, breakdown of revenue by type, and number of offices. **Number listed:** 100

1. Deloitte LLP, with $10,938,000,000
2. PricewaterhouseCoopers LLP, $8,034,000,000
3. Ernst & Young LLP, $7,100,000,000
4. KPMG LLP, $4,889,000,000
5. McGladrey & Pullen LLP, $1,378,867,000
6. Grant Thornton LLP, $1,086,000,000
7. CBIZ MHM LLC/Mayer Hoffman McCann PC, $590,600,000
8. BDO USA LLP, $585,000,000
9. Crowe Horwath LLP, $498,379,000
10. BKD LLP, $391,191,000

Source: *Public Accounting Report*, Top 100 (annual), October 24, 2011, p. 4-7.

8 ■ LARGEST COLORADO-BASED ACCOUNTING FIRMS, 2010

Ranked by: Number of employees. **Remarks:** Also notes contact information. **Number listed:** 10

1. Ehrardt Keefe Steiner & Hottman PC, with 398 employees
2. Hein & Associates LLP, 223
3. Dalby, Wendland & Co., 100
4. GHP Horwath PC, 98
5. Anton Collins Mitchell LLP, 85
6. JDS Professional Group LLC, 55
7. Brock & Co. CPAs PC, 51
8. Bauerle & Co., 48
9. Causey Demgen & Moore Inc., 47
10. Bondi & Co., 33

Source: *ColoradoBiz*, Top Professional Services (annual), December 2011, p. 46.

9 ■ LARGEST COMPANIES IN THE ENGINEERING, AC-COUNTING, RESEARCH, AND MANAGEMENT INDUSTRY BY EMPLOYEES, 2010

Ranked by: Total number of employees. **Remarks:** Also notes contact information for headquarters, number of employees at headquarters, revenue, rank by revenue, and primary SIC code. **Number listed:** 404

1. Sodexho Management Inc., with 110,000 employees
2. Ascension Health Inc., 106,000
3. Sodexho Operations LLC, 100,000
4. Golden Gate Private Equity Inc., 54,453
5. Mayo Foundation for Medical Education & Research, 52,700
6. Platinum Equity LLC, 48,808
7. Aecom Technology Corp., 48,100
8. Bechtel Group Inc., 47,000
8. URS Corp., 47,000
10. SAIC Inc., 46,200

Source: *Business Rankings*, (annual), Dun & Bradstreet Inc., 2011, p. VI.254+.

10 ■ LARGEST COMPANIES IN THE ENGINEERING, AC-COUNTING, RESEARCH, AND MANAGEMENT INDUSTRY BY SALES, 2010

Ranked by: Total revenue, in dollars. **Remarks:** Also notes contact information for headquarters, number of employees at headquarters and overall, rank by employees, and primary SIC code. **Number listed:** 406

1. Fluor Corp., with $20,849,349,000
2. Ascension Health Inc., $14,773,336,000
3. General Electric International Inc., $12,144,769,000
4. SAIC Inc., $10,846,000,000
5. Deloitte & Touche LLP, $10,722,000,000
5. Deloitte LLP, $10,722,000,000
7. Yellow Roadway Technologies Inc., $9,621,316,000
8. URS Corp., $9,177,051,000
9. The Shaw Group Inc., $7,000,779,000
10. Foster Wheeler Ltd., $6,854,290,000

Source: *Business Rankings*, (annual), Dun & Bradstreet Inc., 2011, p. V.228+.

11 ■ LARGEST U.S. ACCOUNTING FIRMS BY REVENUE, 2011

Ranked by: Revenue, in millions of dollars. **Remarks:** Also notes rank for previous year, headquarters, chief executive, year-end, annual growth in revenue, number of offices, fee split, and breakdown of personnel by type. **Number listed:** 100

1. Deloitte LLP, with $11,939 million
2. PricewaterhouseCoopers LLP, $8,844
3. Ernst & Young LLP, $7,500
4. KPMG LLP, $5,361
5. McGladrey & Pullen, $1,370.42
6. Grant Thornton LLP, $1,146.12
7. CBIZ/Mayer Hoffman McCann, $597.5
8. BDO USA, $572
9. Crowe Horwath, $529.71

10. BKD LLP, $391.2

Source: *Accounting Today*, Top 100 (annual), March 2012, p. 15+.

12 ■ TOP ACCOUNTING FIRMS IN ACCOUNTING & AUDITING, 2011

Ranked by: Revenue, in millions of dollars. **Remarks:** Also notes fee split. **Number listed:** 16

1. PricewaterhouseCoopers LLP, with $4,245.12 million
2. Deloitte LLP, $3,820.48
3. Ernst & Young LLP, $3,000
4. KPMG LLP, $2,305.23
5. McGladrey & Pullen, $586.77
6. Grant Thornton LLP, $515.75
7. BDO USA, $348.92
8. Crowe Horwath, $229.27
9. BKD LLP, $195.6
10. Moss Adams LLP, $164.73

Source: *Accounting Today*, Top 100 (annual), March 2012, p. 5.

13 ■ TOP ACCOUNTING FIRMS IN TAXATION, 2011

Ranked by: Revenue, in millions of dollars. **Remarks:** Also notes fee split. **Number listed:** 16

1. PricewaterhouseCoopers LLP, with $2,564.76 million
2. Deloitte LLP, $2,387.8
3. Ernst & Young LLP, $2,325
4. KPMG LLP, $1,393.86
5. McGladrey & Pullen, $491.84
6. Grant Thornton LLP, $332.37
7. CBIZ/Mayer Hoffman McCann, $161.33
8. BDO USA, $140.14
9. BKD LLP, $121.83
10. Crowe Horwath, $113.05

Source: *Accounting Today*, Top 100 (annual), March 2012, p. 5.

14 ■ TOP CPA FIRMS SERVING THE CREDIT UNION INDUSTRY, 2011

Ranked by: Number of credit unions (with assets over $40 million) served. **Remarks:** Also notes total assets audited and breakdown of number of credit unions by asset size. **Number listed:** 20

1. RSM McGladrey, with 144 credit unions
2. Orth, Chakler, Murnane & Co., CPAs, 124
3. LarsonAllen LLP, 123
4. Nearman, Maynard, Vallez CPAs, 111
5. Clifton Gunderson LLP, 77
6. Cindrich Mahalak & Co., 75
7. Turner, Warren, Hwang & Conrad, 65
8. Moss Adams LLP, 50
9. Petersen & Associates, 44
10. Financial Standards Group Inc., 42

Source: *Credit Union Directory*, (annual), Callahan & Associates Inc., 2012, p. 148.

15 ■ TOP LOCAL ACCOUNTING FIRMS IN THE CAPITAL REGION, 2011

Ranked by: Revenue, in millions of dollars. **Remarks:** Ranking covers firms in Delaware, Maryland, Virginia, Washington DC, and West Virginia. Also notes headquarters, annual growth in revenue, total number of employees, breakdown by type of employee, and fee split. **Number listed:** 16

1. Reznick Group, with $202.5 million
2. Kearney & Co., $79.78
3. Aronson, $52.15
4. Watkins Meegan, $50.2
5. Argy, Wiltse & Robinson, $50
6. SC & H Group, $49.62
7. Raffa, $33
8. Young, Hyde & Barbour, $23.86
9. Brown, Edward & Co., $23.85
10. Keiter, Stephens, Hurst, Gary & Shreavest, $21.04

Source: *Accounting Today*, Top 100 (annual), March 2012, p. 21.

16 ■ TOP LOCAL ACCOUNTING FIRMS IN THE GREAT LAKES REGION, 2011

Ranked by: Revenue, in millions of dollars. **Remarks:** Ranking covers firms in Illinois, Indiana, Michigan, Ohio, and Wisconsin. Also notes headquarters, annual growth in revenue, total number of employees, breakdown by type of employee, and fee split. **Number listed:** 20

1. Plante & Moran LLP, with $304.35 million
2. Baker Tilly Virchow Krause, $242
3. Wipfli, $142.17
4. Rehmann, $87
5. SS & G, $70.7
6. Schenck, $65.45
7. Sikich, $64.5
8. Blue & Co., $55.1
9. Blackman Kallick, $52
10. SVA CPAs, $47.09

Source: *Accounting Today*, Top 100 (annual), March 2012, p. 22.

17 ■ TOP LOCAL ACCOUNTING FIRMS IN THE GULF COAST, 2011

Ranked by: Revenue, in millions of dollars. **Remarks:** Ranking covers firms in Alabama, Florida, Louisiana, and Mississippi. Also notes headquarters, annual growth in revenue, total number of employees, breakdown by type of employee, and fee split. **Number listed:** 15

1. Carr, Riggs & Ingram, with $100.31 million
2. Warren Averett, $81.39
3. MBAF CPAs, $80
4. Horne, $56.77
5. Kaufman, Rossin & Co., $51.2
6. Berkowitz Dick Pollack & Brant, $38.56
7. Postlewaithe & Netterville, $38.54
8. Jackson Thornton & Co., $23.96
9. LaPorte Sehrt Romig Hand, $21.33
10. Sellers, Richardson, Holman & West, $15.05

Source: *Accounting Today*, Top 100 (annual), March 2012, p. 22.

18 ■ TOP LOCAL ACCOUNTING FIRMS IN THE MID-ATLANTIC REGION, 2011

Ranked by: Revenue, in millions of dollars. **Remarks:** Ranking covers firms in New Jersey, New York, and Pennsylvania. Also notes headquarters, annual growth in revenue, total number of employees, breakdown by type of employee, and fee split. **Number listed:** 24

1. Marcum, with $274.2 million
2. EisnerAmper, $254.6
3. J. H. Cohn, $243
4. Rothstein, Kass & Co., $179.5
5. ParenteBeard, $170
6. WeiserMazars, $124.5
7. Citrin Cooperman & Co., $115
8. Berden, $95
9. Anchin, Block & Anchin, $91.5
10. Marks Paneth & Shron, $67.36

Source: *Accounting Today*, Top 100 (annual), March 2012, p. 23.

19 ■ TOP LOCAL ACCOUNTING FIRMS IN THE MIDWEST, 2011

Ranked by: Revenue, in millions of dollars. **Remarks:** Ranking covers firms in Iowa, Kansas, Minnesota, Missouri, Nebraska, North Dakota, and South Dakota. Also notes headquarters, annual growth in revenue, total number of employees, breakdown by type of employee, and fee split. **Number listed:** 14

1. BKD LLP, with $391.2 million
2. Eide Bailly, $151.6
3. RubinBrown, $61.72
4. Lurie Besikoff Lapidus & Co. LLP, $34.2
5. Honkamp Krueger & Co., $33.62
6. Kennedy & Coe, $30.5
7. Brown Smith Wallace, $26
8. Brady, Martz & Associates, $23.66
9. Boulay, Heutmaker, Zibell & Co., $19.54
10. Lutz & Co., $19.39

Source: *Accounting Today*, Top 100 (annual), March 2012, p. 23.

20 ■ TOP LOCAL ACCOUNTING FIRMS IN THE MOUNTAIN REGION, 2011

Ranked by: Revenue, in millions of dollars. **Remarks:** Ranking covers firms in Colorado, Idaho, Montana, Utah, and Wyoming. Also notes headquarters, annual growth in revenue, total number of employees, breakdown by type of employee, and fee split. **Number listed:** 13

1. Ehrhardt Keefe Steiner & Hottman PC, with $58.47 million
2. Hein & Associates LLP, $45.28
3. Anderson ZurMuehlen & Co., $19.54
4. Galusha, Higgins & Galusha, $17.64
5. GHP Horwath, $16.7
6. Junkermier, Clark, Campanella, Stevens, $13.04
7. Tanner, $12.3
8. Dalby, Wendland & Co., $11.78
9. Squire & Co., $11.63
10. Anton Collins Mitchell, $9.75

Source: *Accounting Today*, Top 100 (annual), March 2012, p. 24.

21 ■ TOP LOCAL ACCOUNTING FIRMS IN NEW ENGLAND, 2011

Ranked by: Revenue, in millions of dollars. **Remarks:** Ranking covers firms in Connecticut, Maine, Massachusetts, New Hamp-

shire, Rhode Island, and Vermont. Also notes headquarters, annual growth in revenue, total number of employees, breakdown by type of employee, and fee split. **Number listed:** 14

1. Blum, Shapiro & Co., with $47.27 million
2. BerryDunn, $34.65
3. Kahn, Litwin, Renza & Co., $30.83
4. Baker Newman & Noyes, $28.3
5. Wolf & Co., $28.21
6. Feeley & Driscoll, $23.62
7. Braver, $19.35
8. DiCicco, Gulman & Co., $15.8
9. Whittlesey & Hadley, $13.8
10. Macdonald Page & Co., $12.25

Source: *Accounting Today*, Top 100 (annual), March 2012, p. 24.

22 ■ TOP LOCAL ACCOUNTING FIRMS IN THE SOUTHEAST, 2011

Ranked by: Revenue, in millions of dollars. **Remarks:** Ranking covers firms in Arkansas, Georgia, Kentucky, North Carolina, South Carolina, and Tennessee. Also notes headquarters, annual growth in revenue, total number of employees, breakdown by type of employee, and fee split. **Number listed:** 13

1. Dixon Hughes Goodman, with $295 million
2. Cherry Bekaert & Holland LLP, $111.18
3. Habif, Arogeti & Wynne, $58.14
4. Elliott Davis, $57.55
5. Lattimore Black Morgan & Cain PC, $57
6. Frazier & Deeter, $37.29
7. Joseph Decosimo & Co., $33.5
8. Mauldin & Jenkins, $31.8
9. Mountjoy Chilton Medley, $30.15
10. Bennett Thrasher, $23.22

Source: *Accounting Today*, Top 100 (annual), March 2012, p. 25.

23 ■ TOP LOCAL ACCOUNTING FIRMS IN THE SOUTHWEST, 2011

Ranked by: Revenue, in millions of dollars. **Remarks:** Ranking covers firms in Arizona, New Mexico, Oklahoma, and Texas. Also notes headquarters, annual growth in revenue, total number of employees, breakdown by type of employee, and fee split. **Number listed:** 15

1. Weaver, with $66.4 million
2. Whitley Penn, $37.5
3. Padgett, Stratemann & Co., $27.37
4. Gainer, Donnelly & Desroches, $20.53
5. PKF Texas, $19.93
6. Briggs & Veselka, $19.59
7. TravisWolff, $19.2
8. REDW, The Rogoff Firm, $19.08
9. Cain Watters & Associates, $18.1
9. Lane Gorman Trubitt, $18.1

Source: *Accounting Today*, Top 100 (annual), March 2012, p. 25.

24 ■ TOP LOCAL ACCOUNTING FIRMS IN THE WEST, 2011

Ranked by: Revenue, in millions of dollars. **Remarks:** Ranking covers firms in California, Nevada, Oregon, and Washington. Also notes headquarters, annual growth in revenue, total number of employees, breakdown by type of employee, and fee split. **Number listed:** 27

1. Moss Adams LLP, with $323 million
2. Armanio McKenna LLP, $84.2
3. Novogradac & Co., LLP, $72.06
4. Burr, Pilger & Mayer Inc., $70.2
5. Holthouse Carlin & Van Trigt LLP, $69
6. Frank, Rimerman & Co. LLP, $48.7
7. Nigro Karlin Segal & Feldstein, $44.76
8. SingerLewak, $40.2
9. Squar, Milner, Peterson, Miranda & Williamson, $37
10. Miller Kaplan Arase, $35

Source: *Accounting Today*, Top 100 (annual), March 2012, p. 26.

Accounting Firms, International

25 ■ LARGEST ACCOUNTING FIRMS IN THE U.K., 2011

Ranked by: Total staff. **Remarks:** Also notes fee income, fee/partner ratio, and breakdown by partners and female partners. **Number listed:** 60

1. PricewaterhouseCoopers LLP, with 14,973 employees
2. Deloitte LLP, 13,075
3. KPMG LLP, 10,150
4. Ernst & Young LLP, 9,239
5. Grant Thornton U.K. LLP, 3,685
6. RSM Tenon, 2,858
7. BDO LLP, 2,419
8. Baker Tilly LLP, 1,678
9. PKF (UK) LLP, 1,537
10. Moore Stephens U.K., 1,324

Source: *Accountancy*, Top 60 League Table (annual), January 2012, p. 20.

26 ■ TOP ACCOUNTING FIRMS IN THE U.K. BY AUDIT AND ACCOUNTING INCOME, 2011

Ranked by: Audit and accounting income, in millions of pounds sterling. **Remarks:** Also notes figures for previous year and percent change. **Number listed:** 20

1. PricewaterhouseCoopers LLP, with £909 million
2. Deloitte LLP, £652
3. KPMG LLP, £456
4. Ernst & Young LLP, £444
5. Grant Thornton U.K. LLP, £134.4
6. BDO LLP, £91.1
7. Baker Tilly LLP, £84
8. Mazars, £70
8. RSM Tenon, £70
10. Moore Stephens U.K., £60.6

Source: *Accountancy*, Top 60 League Table (annual), January 2012, p. 14.

27 ■ TOP ACCOUNTING FIRMS IN THE U.K. BY FEE INCOME, 2011

Ranked by: Fee income, in millions of pounds sterling. **Remarks:** Also notes rank and figures for previous year, percent change, number of U.K. offices, total number of partners, number of female partners, total number of professional staff, fees per partner, and fiscal year-end. **Number listed:** 60

1. PricewaterhouseCoopers LLP, with £2,461 million
2. Deloitte LLP, £2,098
3. KPMG LLP, £1,707
4. Ernst & Young LLP, £1,465
5. Grant Thornton U.K. LLP, £377
6. BDO LLP, £284.7
7. RSM Tenon, £249
8. Baker Tilly LLP, £182
9. Smith & Williamson Ltd., £171.4
10. PKF (UK) LLP, £140

Source: *Accountancy*, Top 60 League Table (annual), January 2012, p. 18.

28 ■ TOP ACCOUNTING FIRMS IN THE U.K. BY PROFITS, 2011

Ranked by: Pre-tax profits, in millions of pounds sterling. **Remarks:** Also notes overall rank in the *Top 60*, fee income, and number of partners. **Number listed:** 25

1. PricewaterhouseCoopers LLP, with £667 million
2. Deloitte LLP, £535
3. KPMG LLP, £396
4. Ernst & Young LLP, £350
5. Grant Thornton U.K. LLP, £75.2
6. BDO LLP, £62.2
7. RSM Tenon, £27
8. Smith & Williamson Ltd., £21.6
9. Begbies Traynor Group plc, £8.5
10. Crowe Clark Whitehill LLP, £1.4

Source: *Accountancy*, Top 60 League Table (annual), January 2012, p. 16.

29 ■ TOP ACCOUNTING FIRMS IN THE U.K. BY TAX INCOME, 2011

Ranked by: Tax income, in millions of pounds sterling. **Remarks:** Also notes figures for previous year and percent change. **Number listed:** 20

1. PricewaterhouseCoopers LLP, with £645 million
2. Deloitte LLP, £534
3. KPMG LLP, £392
4. Ernst & Young LLP, £372
5. Grant Thornton U.K. LLP, £91.7
6. BDO LLP, £80.5
7. RSM Tenon, £57
8. Baker Tilly LLP, £51
9. PKF (UK) LLP, £35.4
10. Smith & Williamson Ltd., £31.8

Source: *Accountancy*, Top 60 League Table (annual), January 2012, p. 15.

Actors/Actresses
See: **Entertainers**

Actuaries

30 ■ TOP ACTUARIAL FIRMS FOR THE INSURANCE INDUSTRY, 2010

Ranked by: Net premiums written for clients, in thousands of dollars. **Remarks:** Also notes market share and number of clients. **Number listed:** 35

1. PricewaterhouseCoopers LLP, with $75,147,923 thousand
2. KPMG LLP, $73,509,660
3. Milliman Inc., $48,087,613
4. Ernst & Young LLP, $24,688,383
5. Deloitte & Touche LLP, $23,841,509
6. Ingenix Consulting, $19,762,132
7. Towers Watson, $18,851,030
8. Lewis & Ellis Inc., $11,589,129
9. Beneficial Consultants LLC, $5,740,256
10. Eckler Ltd., $5,574,074

Source: *Best's Review*, Top Auditors & Actuaries (annual), January 2012, p. 46.

Adoption

31 ■ TOP LARGE U.S. ADOPTION-FRIENDLY WORKPLACES, 2011

Ranked by: Score based on financial reimbursement and fully or partially paid leave for adoption. **Remarks:** Scores not provided. Ranking covers companies with more than 1,000 employees. **Number listed:** 10

1. The Wendy's Co.
2. Hanesbrands Inc.
3. LSI Corp.
3. United Business Media LLC
5. Boston Scientific Corp.
6. Bloomberg LP
6. Putnam Investments
8. The Vanguard Group Inc.
9. BHP Billiton Ltd.
10. The Timberland Co.

Source: *Best Adoption-Friendly Workplaces*, (annual), Dave Thomas Foundation for Adoption, September 19, 2011.

32 ■ TOP MEDIUM-SIZED U.S. ADOPTION-FRIENDLY WORKPLACES, 2011

Ranked by: Score based on financial reimbursement and fully or partially paid leave for adoption. **Remarks:** Scores not provided. Ranking covers companies with 101 to 1,000 employees. **Number listed:** 10

1. Barilla America Inc.
2. Liquidnet Holdings Inc.
3. Subaru of America Inc.
4. Kao Brands Co.
5. American Academy of Pediatrics
5. Franklin International
5. Traylor Bros. Inc.
8. The Medicines Co.
8. Rodale Inc.
10. The Phoenix Cos., Inc.

Source: *Best Adoption-Friendly Workplaces*, (annual), Dave Thomas Foundation for Adoption, September 19, 2011.

33 ■ TOP SMALL U.S. ADOPTION-FRIENDLY WORKPLACES, 2011

Ranked by: Score based on financial reimbursement and fully or partially paid leave for adoption. **Remarks:** Scores not provided. Ranking covers companies with up to 100 employees. **Number listed:** 10

1. South Mountain Co.
2. Dave Thomas Foundation for Adoption
3. Municipal Securities Rulemaking Board
4. The Dallas Center for Sleep Disorders
5. Strata-G
6. Searcy Living Magazine
7. Foster Care Alumni of America
7. Leaf Software Solutions Inc.
9. eXude Benefits Group Inc.
10. Creative Lodging Solutions

Source: *Best Adoption-Friendly Workplaces*, (annual), Dave Thomas Foundation for Adoption, September 19, 2011.

34 ■ TOP U.S. ADOPTION-FRIENDLY WORKPLACES, 2011

Ranked by: Score based on financial reimbursement and fully or partially paid leave for adoption. **Remarks:** Scores not provided. **Number listed:** 100

1. The Wendy's Co.
2. Hanesbrands Inc.
3. Barilla America Inc.
4. Liquidnet Holdings Inc.
4. LSI Corp.
4. United Business Media LLC
7. Boston Scientific Corp.
8. Bloomberg LP
8. Putnam Investments
10. The Vanguard Group Inc.

Source: *Best Adoption-Friendly Workplaces*, (annual), Dave Thomas Foundation for Adoption, September 19, 2011.

Advertisements
See: **Advertising**

Advertisers

35 ■ TOP ADVERTISERS IN THE U.S., 2010

Ranked by: Total U.S. advertising expenditures, in millions of dollars. **Remarks:** Also notes rank and figures for previous year, headquarters, percent change from previous year, unmeasured spending, total measured media spending, and breakdown by medium. **Number listed:** 100

1. Procter & Gamble Co., with $4,614.7 million
2. AT&T Inc., $2,989
3. General Motors Co., $2,869
4. Verizon Communications Inc., $2,451
5. American Express Co., $2,222.6
6. Pfizer Inc., $2,124.1
7. Wal-Mart Stores Inc., $2,055.3
8. Time Warner Inc., $2,044.3
9. Johnson & Johnson, $2,026.5
10. L'Oreal SA, $1,978.8

Source: *Advertising Age*, Leading National Advertisers (annual), June 20, 2011, p. 10-14.

36 ■ TOP MARKETERS IN THE U.S., 2010

Ranked by: Advertising expenditures in country. **Remarks:** Specific figures not provided. **Number listed:** 5

1. Procter & Gamble Co.
2. General Motors Co.
3. AT&T Inc.
4. Verizon Communications Inc.
5. Comcast Corp.

Source: *Advertising Age*, Top Global Marketers (annual), December 5, 2011, p. 6.

Advertisers, International

37 ■ TOP MARKETERS IN BRAZIL, 2010

Ranked by: Advertising expenditures in country. **Remarks:** Specific figures not provided. **Number listed:** 5

1. Casas Bahia
2. Unilever
3. Hyundai Motor Co.
4. Anheuser-Busch InBev SA/NV
5. Lideranca Capitalizacao

Source: *Advertising Age*, Top Global Marketers (annual), December 5, 2011, p. 6.

38 ■ TOP MARKETERS IN CHINA, 2010

Ranked by: Advertising expenditures in country. **Remarks:** Specific figures not provided. **Number listed:** 5

1. Procter & Gamble Co.
2. L'Oreal SA
3. Unilever
4. Yum! Brands Inc.
5. The Coca-Cola Co.

Source: *Advertising Age*, Top Global Marketers (annual), December 5, 2011, p. 7.

39 ■ TOP MARKETERS IN INDIA, 2010

Ranked by: Advertising expenditures in country. **Remarks:** Specific figures not provided. **Number listed:** 5

1. Unilever
2. Reckitt Benckiser plc
3. Procter & Gamble Co.
4. Kraft Foods Inc.
5. ITC

Source: *Advertising Age*, Top Global Marketers (annual), December 5, 2011, p. 7.

40 ■ TOP MARKETERS IN INDONESIA, 2010

Ranked by: Advertising expenditures in country. **Remarks:** Specific figures not provided. **Number listed:** 5

1. Unilever
2. Telkomsel
3. Global TV
4. Nestle SA
5. Cakrawala Andalas Televisi

Source: *Advertising Age*, Top Global Marketers (annual), December 5, 2011, p. 7.

41 ■ TOP MARKETERS IN MEXICO, 2010

Ranked by: Advertising expenditures in country. **Remarks:** Specific figures not provided. **Number listed:** 5

1. Televisa Group
2. Genomma Lab
3. Grupos Salinas
4. Presidente de la Republica Mexico
5. Procter & Gamble Co.

Source: *Advertising Age*, Top Global Marketers (annual), December 5, 2011, p. 6.

42 ■ TOP MARKETERS IN RUSSIA, 2010

Ranked by: Advertising expenditures in country. **Remarks:** Specific figures not provided. **Number listed:** 5

1. Procter & Gamble Co.
2. L'Oreal SA
3. PepsiCo Inc.
4. Nestle SA
5. Mars Inc.

Source: *Advertising Age*, Top Global Marketers (annual), December 5, 2011, p. 7.

43 ■ TOP MARKETERS IN SOUTH KOREA, 2010

Ranked by: Advertising expenditures in country. **Remarks:** Specific figures not provided. **Number listed:** 5

1. Samsung Electronics Co.
2. Hyundai Motor Co.
3. LG Group
4. KT
5. SK Telecom

Source: *Advertising Age*, Top Global Marketers (annual), December 5, 2011, p. 7.

44 ■ TOP MARKETERS IN TURKEY, 2010

Ranked by: Advertising expenditures in country. **Remarks:** Specific figures not provided. **Number listed:** 5

1. Vodafone plc
2. Turkcell
3. Unilever
4. Procter & Gamble Co.
5. Reckitt Benckiser plc

Source: *Advertising Age*, Top Global Marketers (annual), December 5, 2011, p. 7.

Advertising

45 ■ TOP DIRECT MAIL ADVERTISING FRANCHISES, 2012

Ranked by: Cumulative score based on financial strength and stability, growth rate, size of the system, number of years in business, the length of time franchising, start-up costs, litigation, percentage of terminations, and whether the company provides financing. **Remarks:** Specific scores not provided. Also notes overall rank within the *Franchise 500*, contact information, description, year founded, year started franchising, states where registered, available U.S. regions, where seeking foreign expansion, number of franchised and company-owned units for past three years, start-up costs, franchise fees, royalty fees, and type of financing available. **Number listed:** 3

1. Money Mailer Franchise Corp.
2. Val-Pak Direct Marketing Systems Inc.

3. RSVP Publications

Source: *Entrepreneur*, Franchise 500 (annual), January 2012, p. 148-151.

46 ■ TOP MISCELLANEOUS ADVERTISING FRANCHISES, 2012

Ranked by: Cumulative score based on financial strength and stability, growth rate, size of the system, number of years in business, the length of time franchising, start-up costs, litigation, percentage of terminations, and whether the company provides financing. **Remarks:** Specific scores not provided. Also notes overall rank within the *Franchise 500,* contact information, description, year founded, year started franchising, states where registered, available U.S. regions, where seeking foreign expansion, number of franchised and company-owned units for past three years, start-up costs, franchise fees, royalty fees, and type of financing available. **Number listed:** 4

1. Billboard Connection Inc.
2. Mini Cities
3. Business Partner, One Stop Marketing
4. AArrow Advertising

Source: *Entrepreneur*, Franchise 500 (annual), January 2012, p. 150-151.

47 ■ TOP PUBLISHING ADVERTISING FRANCHISES, 2012

Ranked by: Cumulative score based on financial strength and stability, growth rate, size of the system, number of years in business, the length of time franchising, start-up costs, litigation, percentage of terminations, and whether the company provides financing. **Remarks:** Specific scores not provided. Also notes overall rank within the *Franchise 500,* contact information, description, year founded, year started franchising, states where registered, available U.S. regions, where seeking foreign expansion, number of franchised and company-owned units for past three years, start-up costs, franchise fees, royalty fees, and type of financing available. **Number listed:** 3

1. Coffee News
2. City Publications
3. Homes & Land Magazine

Source: *Entrepreneur*, Franchise 500 (annual), January 2012, p. 150-151.

Advertising Agencies

48 ■ BEST ADVERTISING AGENCIES, 2011

Ranked by: Score based on improvement to client's business, gain of new clients, innovation, and creativity. **Remarks:** Specific scores not provided. Also notes top executives, number of employees, key clients, and comments. **Number listed:** 10

1. McGarry Bowen
2. Droga5
3. BBDO
4. Razorfish
5. 72andSunny
6. Alma
7. Grey
8. Edelman
9. Huge
10. Arnold

Source: *Advertising Age*, Agency A-List (annual), January 23, 2012, p. 6-19.

49 ■ FASTEST-GROWING PRIVATE ADVERTISING AND MARKETING COMPANIES IN THE U.S., 2007-2010

Ranked by: Average annual sales growth over three years, in percent. **Remarks:** Also notes headquarters, revenue, and rank in the overall *Inc. 500*. To qualify, private companies must have had annual revenues of at least $100,000 in 2007 and $2 million in 2010. **Number listed:** 57

1. C2C Outdoor, with 17,744.3%
2. Show Media, 11,748.5%
3. CPAlead, 4,643.9%
4. Prodege, 4,460.9%
5. Leadnomics, 3,932.2%
6. Simplicity Consulting, 3,727.2%
7. Slingshot SEO, 3,596.8%
8. Millennial Media, 3,080.2%
9. Spongecell, 3,064.2%
10. Lead Research Group, 3,013.4%

Source: *Inc.*, Inc. 500 (annual), September 2011, p. 87-90.

50 ■ LARGEST COLORADO-BASED ADVERTISING, PUBLIC RELATIONS, AND MARKETING FIRMS, 2010

Ranked by: Number of employees. **Remarks:** Also notes contact information. **Number listed:** 10

1. Integer Group, Denver, with 565 employees
2. Sterling-Rice Group, 115
3. Factory Design Labs Inc., 88
4. Vladimir Jones, 75
5. Karsh & Hagan Communications, 60
6. Location3 Media Inc., 57
7. Blue Onion, 56
8. Cactus Marketing Communications, 42
9. 90octane LLC, 40
10. Linhart Public Relations, 24

Source: *ColoradoBiz*, Top Professional Services (annual), December 2011, p. 46.

51 ■ LARGEST U.S. ADVERTISING COMPANIES OVERALL, 2011

Ranked by: Score based on revenue, profits, assets, and market capitalization. **Remarks:** Specific scores not provided. Also notes overall rank in the *Forbes 2000* and figures for each criterion. **Number listed:** 2

1. Omnicom Group Inc.
2. The Interpublic Group of Companies Inc.

Source: *Forbes*, Forbes 2000 (annual), http://www.forbes.com, May 7, 2012.

52 ■ NEW YORK'S LARGEST ADVERTISING COMPANIES OVERALL, 2011

Ranked by: Score based on revenue, profits, assets, and market capitalization. **Remarks:** Specific scores not provided. Also notes overall rank in the *Forbes 2000* and figures for each criterion. **Number listed:** 2

1. Omnicom Group Inc.
2. The Interpublic Group of Companies Inc.

Source: *Forbes*, Forbes 2000 (annual), http://www.forbes.com, May 7, 2012.

53 ■ TOP *FORTUNE 500* COMPANIES IN ADVERTISING AND MARKETING, 2011

Ranked by: Revenue, in millions of dollars. **Remarks:** Also notes overall rank in the *Fortune 500;* profits; profits as a percentage of revenue; stockholders' equity; and rank by each criterion. **Number listed:** 2

1. Omnicom Group Inc., with $13,873 million
2. The Interpublic Group of Companies Inc., $7,015

Source: *Fortune*, Fortune 500 (annual), May 21, 2012, p. F-33.

Advertising Agencies, International

54 ■ JAPAN'S LARGEST ADVERTISING COMPANIES OVERALL, 2011

Ranked by: Score based on revenue, profits, assets, and market capitalization. **Remarks:** Specific scores not provided. Also notes overall rank in the *Forbes 2000* and figures for each criterion. **Number listed:** 2

1. Dentsu Inc.
2. Hakuhodo DY Holdings Inc.

Source: *Forbes*, Forbes 2000 (annual), http://www.forbes.com, May 7, 2012.

55 ■ LARGEST MEDIA AND ADVERTISING FIRMS IN EUROPE, 2010

Ranked by: Sales, in millions of U.S. dollars. **Remarks:** Also notes rank within country. **Number listed:** 100

1. Bertelsmann AG (Germany), with $22,849.3 million
2. Data Media & Research Ltd. (U.K.), $13,984.3
3. WPP plc (U.K.), $13,026.5
4. Lagardere SCA (France), $11,577.6
5. Reed Elsevier plc (U.K.), $9,106.5
6. British Sky Broadcasting Group plc (BSkyB, U.K.), $8,868
7. Pearson plc (U.K.), $8,436
8. British Sky Broadcasting Ltd. (U.K.), $6,721.5
9. Publicis Groupe SA (France), $6,630.3
10. Mediaset SpA (Italy), $5,992.9

Source: *Europe's 15,000 Largest Companies*, (annual), ELC International, 2011, p. 46.

56 ■ LARGEST U.K. ADVERTISING AGENCIES, 2011

Ranked by: Billings, in millions of pounds sterling. **Remarks:** Also notes rank and figures for previous year, percent change, and top clients. **Number listed:** 100

1. Abbott Mead Vickers BBDO, with £337.15 million
2. McCann Erickson, £309.39
3. Rainey Kelly Campbell Roalfe/Y&R, £264.02
4. Leo Burnett, £233.98
5. M&C Saatchi, £230.48
6. Bartle Bogle Hegarty, £215.27
7. DLKW Lowe, £208.04
8. WCRS, £190.02
9. Ogilvy & Mather, £185.67
10. VCCP, £184.74

Source: *Campaign*, Top 100 Agencies (annual), March 16, 2012, p. 17-18.

57 ■ TOP REGIONAL U.K. ADVERITISING AGENCIES, 2011

Ranked by: Billings, in millions of pounds sterling. **Remarks:** Also notes rank and figures for previous year, percent chane, and top clients. **Number listed:** 30

1. Gratterpalm, with £120.68 million
2. AV Browne, £44.25
3. Uber Agency, £39.99
4. TBWAManchester, £38.67
5. Big Communications, £33.88
6. Bray Leino, £29.84
7. Cravens Advertising, £24.24
8. Golley Slater Group, £20.04
9. Cheethambell JWT, £18.56
10. Designate, £16.41

Source: *Campaign*, Top 100 Agencies (annual), March 16, 2012, p. 20.

58 ■ TOP U.K. ADVERTISING HOLDING COMPANIES, 2011

Ranked by: Advertising billings, in millions of pounds sterling. **Remarks:** Also notes rank and figures for previous year, percent change, and key U.K. assets. **Number listed:** 5

1. WPP, with £851.7 million
2. Omnicom, £759.1
3. Publicis Group, £726.6
4. Interpublic, £556.9
5. Havas, £182.2

Source: *Campaign*, Top 100 Agencies (annual), March 16, 2012, p. 20.

59 ■ WORLD'S LARGEST ADVERTISING COMPANIES OVERALL, 2011

Ranked by: Score based on revenue, profits, assets, and market capitalization. **Remarks:** Specific scores not provided. Also notes country, overall rank in the *Forbes 2000,* and figures for each criterion. **Number listed:** 6

1. WPP Group plc
2. Omnicom Group Inc.
3. Publicis Groupe SA
4. Dentsu Inc.
5. The Interpublic Group of Companies Inc.
6. Hakuhodo DY Holdings Inc.

Source: *Forbes*, Forbes 2000 (annual), http://www.forbes.com, May 7, 2012.

60 ■ WORLD'S TOP ADVERTISING AGENCY BRANDS, 2011

Ranked by: Brand value, in millions of U.S. dollars. **Remarks:** Also notes rank and figures for previous year, country, and brand rating. **Number listed:** 50

1. Dentsu, with $1,375 million
2. Clear Media, $1,205
3. JC Decaux, $1,127
4. Teleperformance, $1,074
5. McCann Erickson Worldwide, $793

6. Ogilvy & Mather, $645
7. TBWA Worldwide, $560
8. IPSOS, $547
9. DDB Worldwide, $531
10. BBDO Worldwide, $517

Source: *Top 50 Advertising Agencies*, (annual), Brand Finance plc, 2011.

61 ■ WORLD'S TOP MARKETING ORGANIZATIONS BY REVENUE, 2011

Ranked by: Worldwide revenue, in millions of U.S. dollars. **Remarks:** Also notes rank for previous year, headquarters, U.S. revenue, figures for previous year, and percent change. **Number listed:** 50

1. WPP Group plc (Dublin), with $16,053 million
2. Omnicom Group Inc. (New York), $13,873
3. Publicis Groupe SA (Paris), $8,086
4. The Interpublic Group of Companies Inc. (New York), $7,015
5. Dentsu Inc. (Tokyo), $4,067
6. Havas Advertising (France), $2,291
7. Hakuhodo DY Holdings Inc. (Tokyo), $1,934
8. Aegis Group plc (London), $1,821
9. MDC Partners Inc. (New York), $943
10. Epsilon (Texas), $847

Source: *Advertising Age*, Agency Report (annual), April 30, 2012, p. 14.

Advertising Agencies—Public Relations Work

62 ■ TOP PUBLIC RELATIONS UNITS OF ADVERTISING AGENCIES, 2011

Ranked by: Net fees, in dollars. **Remarks:** Also notes percent change from previous year, number of employees, and headquarters. **Number listed:** 3

1. Godwin Advertising Agency, with $2,570,852
2. Luckie Strategic Public Relations, $1,436,675
3. MDi media group, $374,662

Source: *J. R. O'Dwyer Co.*, Top 100 Independent Firms (annual), http://www.odwyerpr.com, May 2012.

Advertising—Appeal to Hispanics

63 ■ TOP ADVERTISERS IN HISPANIC MAGAZINES, 2010

Ranked by: U.S. measured magazine advertising expenditures, in thousands of dollars. **Remarks:** Also notes figures for previous year and percent change. **Number listed:** 10

1. Procter & Gamble Co., with $25,221 thousand
2. L'Oreal SA, $16,324
3. General Motors Co., $8,529
4. Unilever, $4,476
5. Kimberly-Clark Corp., $3,392
6. U.S. government, $3,153
7. Estee Lauder Cos., $3,104
8. Mars Inc., $2,987
9. Time Warner Inc., $2,830

10. Ford Motor Co., $2,613

Source: *Advertising Age*, Hispanic Fact Pack (annual), July 25, 2011, p. 12.

64 ■ TOP ADVERTISERS IN HISPANIC MEDIA, 2010

Ranked by: Advertising expenditures, in thousands of dollars. **Remarks:** Also notes annual percent change. **Number listed:** 50

1. Procter & Gamble Co., with $197,717 thousand
2. Verizon Communications Inc., $137,966
3. AT&T Inc., $132,089
4. The DirecTV Group Inc., $128,911
5. McDonald's Corp., $117,269
6. General Motors Co., $102,471
7. Broadcasting Media Partners Inc., $100,479
8. Lexicon Marketing Corp., $98,620
9. General Mills Inc., $91,856
10. State Farm Mutual Automobile Insurance Co., $91,813

Source: *Advertising Age*, Hispanic Fact Pack (annual), July 25, 2011, p. 8-10.

65 ■ TOP ADVERTISERS ON HISPANIC NETWORK TV, 2010

Ranked by: U.S. measured advertising expenditures on broadcast and cable networks, in thousands of dollars. **Remarks:** Also notes figures for previous year and percent change. **Number listed:** 10

1. Procter & Gamble Co., with $165,763 thousand
2. The DirecTV Group Inc., $104,575
3. Lexicon Marketing Corp., $98,254
4. McDonald's Corp., $96,803
5. General Mills Inc., $88,825
6. Verizon Communications Inc., $86,259
7. State Farm Mutual Auto Insurance Co., $80,508
8. General Motors Co., $78,225
9. Dish Network Corp., $77,222
10. Deutsche Telekom AG, $77,199

Source: *Advertising Age*, Hispanic Fact Pack (annual), July 25, 2011, p. 14.

66 ■ TOP ADVERTISERS IN HISPANIC NEWSPAPERS, 2010

Ranked by: U.S. measured newspaper advertising expenditures, in thousands of dollars. **Remarks:** Also notes figures for previous year and percent change. **Number listed:** 10

1. News Corp., with $9,481 thousand
2. Interbond Corp. of America, $6,304
3. Valassis Communications, $5,797
4. Sears Holdings Corp., $5,086
5. U.S. government, $3,647
6. Target Corp., $3,565
7. Macy's Inc., $3,275
8. General Motors Co., $2,934
9. Best Buy Co., Inc., $2,854
10. Rooms To Go Inc., $2,648

Source: *Advertising Age*, Hispanic Fact Pack (annual), July 25, 2011, p. 12.

67 ■ TOP ADVERTISERS ON HISPANIC SPOT RADIO, 2010

Ranked by: U.S. spot radio advertising expenditures, in thousands of dollars. **Remarks:** Also notes figures for previous year and percent change. **Number listed:** 10

1. Broadcasting Media Partners Inc., with $21,213 thousand
2. AT&T Inc., $15,617
3. U.S. Government, $13,011
4. McDonald's Corp., $11,310
5. Verizon Communications Inc., $9,843
6. The Home Depot Inc., $9,091
7. Safeway Inc., $8,759
8. Comcast Corp., $8,631
9. General Motors Co., $8,461
10. J. C. Penney Co., Inc., $7,097

Source: *Advertising Age*, Hispanic Fact Pack (annual), July 25, 2011, p. 16.

68 ■ TOP ADVERTISERS ON HISPANIC SPOT TV, 2010

Ranked by: U.S. spot TV advertising expenditures, in thousands of dollars. **Remarks:** Also notes figures for previous year and percent change. **Number listed:** 10

1. AT&T Inc., with $61,943 thousand
2. Verizon Communications Inc., $45,557
3. Time Warner Cable Inc., $33,980
4. Broadcasting Media Partners Inc., $29,545
5. Comcast Corp., $28,384
6. The DirecTV Group Inc., $24,126
7. Cisneros Group of Cos., $18,602
8. McDonald's Corp., $17,316
9. Ford Motor Co., $17,172
10. Yum! Brands Inc., $14,076

Source: *Advertising Age*, Hispanic Fact Pack (annual), July 25, 2011, p. 14.

69 ■ TOP ADVERTISERS ON HISPANIC WEB SITES, 2010

Ranked by: Number of display ad impressions on Hispanic sites, in thousands. **Remarks:** Also notes share of Hispanic impressions, share of all ad impressions, and difference between the two. **Number listed:** 10

1. Verizon Communications Inc., with 575,962 thousand impressions
2. Procter & Gamble Co., 538,447
3. Ford Motor Co., 365,485
4. Sprint Nextel Corp., 360,090
5. Unilever, 286,958
6. Dish Network Corp., 271,954
7. Toyota Motor Corp. , 258,087
8. Allstate Corp., 216,646
9. Deutsche Telekom AG, 210,894
10. AT&T Inc., 183,237

Source: *Advertising Age*, Hispanic Fact Pack (annual), July 25, 2011, p. 16.

Advertising Expenditures

70 ■ MOST-ADVERTISED BRANDS, 2010

Ranked by: Measured U.S. advertising expenditures, in millions of dollars. **Remarks:** Also notes parent company, rank and figures for previous year, and percent change. **Number listed:** 50

1. AT&T, with $2,092.9 million
2. Verizon, $1,862.9
3. Chevrolet, $1,128.7
4. Ford, $889.4
5. Toyota, $888.3
6. McDonald's, $887.8
7. Wal-Mart, $873.8
8. Sprint, $855.2
9. Macy's, $808.4
10. Geico, $740.8

Source: *Advertising Age*, Leading National Advertisers (annual), June 20, 2011, p. 18.

Advertising, International

71 ■ TOP GLOBAL MARKETERS, 2010

Ranked by: Worldwide advertising expenditures, in billions of U.S. dollars. **Remarks:** Also notes headquarters, rank for previous year, and annual percent change. **Number listed:** 100

1. Procter & Gamble Co., with $11.43 billion
2. Unilever, $6.62
3. L'Oreal SA, $4.98
4. General Motors Co., $3.59
5. Nestle SA, $3.19
6. Toyota Motor Corp., $2.86
7. The Coca-Cola Co., $2.46
8. Reckitt Benckiser plc, $2.43
9. Kraft Foods Inc., $2.34
10. Johnson & Johnson, $2.32
10. McDonald's Corp., $2.32

Source: *Advertising Age*, Top Global Marketers (annual), December 5, 2011, p. 6-7.

72 ■ WORLD'S TOP CONSOLIDATED AGENCY NETWORKS, 2011

Ranked by: Worldwide revenue, in millions of U.S. dollars. **Remarks:** Also notes percent change from previous year and selected units. **Number listed:** 25

1. Dentsu (Japan), with $3,409 million
2. Young & Rubicam Group, $3,280
3. McCann Worldgroup, $2,920
4. DDB Worldwide Communications Group, $2,598
5. Ogilvy & Mather, $2,343
6. BBDO Worldwide, $2,323
7. TBWA Worldwide, $1,700
8. Publicis Worldwide, $1,400
8. DraftFCB, $1,400
10. Euro RSCG Worldwide, $1,328

Source: *Advertising Age*, Agency Report (annual), April 30, 2012, p. 15.

Advertising, Magazine

73 ■ TOP ADVERTISERS IN MAGAZINES, 2010

Ranked by: Measured advertising spending, in millions of dollars. **Remarks:** Also notes percent change from previous year. **Number listed:** 10

1. Procter & Gamble Co., with $1,096.9 million
2. L'Oreal SA, $566.1
3. General Motors Co., $409.6
4. Kraft Foods Inc., $347.3
5. Pfizer Inc., $333.3
6. Johnson & Johnson, $293.4
7. Nestle SA, $285.3
8. Time Warner Inc., $260.4
9. Merck & Co., Inc., $233.1
10. Unilever, $227.8

Source: *Advertising Age*, Leading National Advertisers (annual), June 20, 2011, p. 17.

Advertising, Newspaper

74 ■ TOP ADVERTISERS IN NATIONAL AND LOCAL NEWSPAPERS, 2010

Ranked by: Measured advertising spending, in millions of dollars. **Remarks:** Also notes percent change from previous year. **Number listed:** 10

1. Macy's Inc., with $470.5 million
2. Verizon Communications Inc., $291
3. General Motors Co., $245.6
4. News Corp., $235
5. Fry's Electronics Inc., $227.8
6. AT&T Inc., $214.9
7. Procter & Gamble Co., $202.7
8. Sears Holdings Corp., $157.4
9. Target Corp., $142.2
10. Comcast Corp., $131.8

Source: *Advertising Age*, Leading National Advertisers (annual), June 20, 2011, p. 17.

Advertising, Outdoor

75 ■ TOP OUTDOOR ADVERTISERS, 2010

Ranked by: Measured advertising spending, in millions of dollars. **Remarks:** Also notes percent change from previous year. **Number listed:** 10

1. Verizon Communications Inc., with $69.6 million
2. McDonald's Corp., $68.5
3. Time Warner Inc., $62.4
4. Comcast Corp., $53.9
5. AT&T Inc., $51.2
6. SABMiller plc, $39.5
7. J. P. Morgan Chase & Co., $36.3
7. Walt Disney Co., $36.3
9. Anheuser-Busch InBev SA/NV, $34.3
10. Apple Inc., $33.4

Source: *Advertising Age*, Leading National Advertisers (annual), June 20, 2011, p. 16-17.

Advertising, Radio
See: **Radio Advertising**

Advertising, Television
See: **Television Advertising**

Aerospace Industry
See also: **Defense Industry**

76 ■ LARGEST AEROSPACE AND ELECTRONICS COMPANIES IN EUROPE, 2010

Ranked by: Sales, in millions of U.S. dollars. **Remarks:** Also notes rank within country. **Number listed:** 100

1. Siemens AG (Germany), with $108,568.5 million
2. Nova Test 11 (Germany), $108,568.5
3. Nokia Oyj (Finland), $60,951.4
4. European Aeronautic Defense & Space Co. (EADS, Netherlands), $55,461.4
5. Koninklijke Philips Electronics NV (Royal Philips Electronics NV, Netherlands), $34,486.7
6. BAE Systems plc (U.K.), $30,561
7. Telefonaktiebolaget LM Ericsson (Sweden), $29,443.6
8. Alcatel-Lucent (France), $23,938.9
9. Finmeccanica SpA (Italy), $21,194.7
10. AB Electrolux (Sweden), $15,562.2

Source: *Europe's 15,000 Largest Companies*, (annual), ELC International, 2011, p. 34.

77 ■ WORLD'S LARGEST COMPANIES IN THE SPACE INDUSTRY, 2010

Ranked by: Space-related manufacturing and services revenue, in millions of dollars. **Remarks:** Also notes rank and figures for previous year, headquarters, total sales, and type of space business, which includes satellites, space and rocket components, launch services, launch vehicles, ground systems, and space and engineering services and software. **Number listed:** 50

1. Lockheed Martin Corp., with $11,037 million
2. Boeing Co., $9,455
3. European Aeronautic Defense & Space Co. (EADS), $6,630
4. Northrop Grumman Corp., $5,319
5. Raytheon Co., $4,463
6. Garmin Ltd., $2,690
7. Thales Alenia Space, $2,650
8. L-3 Communications Holdings Inc., $1,800
9. General Dynamics Corp., $1,752
10. EchoStar Corp., $1,470

Source: *Space News*, Top 50 (annual), August 1, 2011.

African American Business Enterprises

78 ■ BLACK-OWNED INDUSTRIAL/SERVICE COMPANIES WITH THE MOST EMPLOYEES, 2010

Ranked by: Total number of employees. **Remarks:** Also notes location, revenue, and employee-to-sales ratio. **Number listed:** 10

1. Manna Inc., with 11,500 employees
2. V & J Holding Cos., Inc., 4,500
3. Thompson Hospitality Corp., 3,700

4. Barden Cos., Inc., 3,200
5. The Gourmet Cos., 2,156
6. H. J. Russell & Co., 1,886
7. Manufacturers Industrial Group LLC, 1,462
8. Bridgewater Interiors LLC, 1,450
9. C. H. James Restaurant Holdings LLC, 1,412
10. UNIBAR Services Inc., 1,400

Source: *Black Enterprise*, B. E. 100s (annual), June 2011, p. 120.

79 ■ FASTEST-GROWING BLACK-OWNED INDUSTRIAL/ SERVICE COMPANIES, 2009-2010

Ranked by: One-year sales growth, in percent. **Remarks:** Also notes location and revenue for current and previous year. **Number listed:** 10

1. Urban Lending Solutions, with 130.91%
2. Millennium Steel Service LLC, 100%
3. B & S Electric Supply Co., Inc., 68.41%
4. Millennium Steel of Texas LP, 62.15%
5. World Wide Technology Inc., 51.64%
6. Facility Interiors Inc., 50.79%
7. Bridgewater Interiors LLC, 46.44%
8. Systems Electro Coating, 45.15%
9. Hightowers Petroleum Co., 41.39%
10. ACT-1 Group, 40.18%

Source: *Black Enterprise*, B. E. 100s (annual), June 2011, p. 120.

80 ■ FASTEST-GROWING PRIVATE BLACK-RUN COMPANIES IN THE U.S., 2007-2010

Ranked by: Average annual sales growth over three years, in percent. **Remarks:** Also notes overall rank in the *Inc. 5,000*, state, and revenue for current year. To qualify, private companies must have had annual revenues of at least $100,000 in 2007 and $2 million in 2010. **Number listed:** 87

1. ClearCorrect, with 8,625%
2. A. Harold & Associates, 5,509%
3. JMA Solutions, 4,317%
4. LinkVisum Consulting Group, 1,566%
5. Urban Lending Solutions, 1,529%
6. Network Solutions Provider, 1,102%
7. A10 Clinical Solutions, 1,011%
8. The Menkiti Group, 988%
9. Iris Data Services, 940%
10. SciMetrika, 921%

Source: *Inc.*, Inc. 500 (annual), http://www.inc.com, September 2011.

81 ■ LARGEST BLACK-OWNED ADVERTISING AGENCIES, 2010

Ranked by: Billings, in millions of dollars. **Remarks:** Also notes rank for previous year, location, chief executive, year founded, and staff. **Number listed:** 10

1. GlobalHue, with $82,965 million
2. Images USA, $31,168
3. UniWorld Group Inc., $21,175
4. Burrell Communications Group LLC, $21,000
5. Carol H. Williams Advertising, $17,850
6. Sanders Wingo Advertising Inc., $15,110

7. Prime Access Inc., $14,300
8. Walton Isaacson, $12,000
9. o2ideas Inc., $11,377
10. Fuse Inc., $8,365

Source: *Black Enterprise*, B. E. 100s (annual), June 2011, p. 157.

82 ■ LARGEST BLACK-OWNED ASSET MANAGERS, 2010

Ranked by: Assets under management, in billions of dollars. **Remarks:** Also notes rank for previous year, location, chief executive, year founded, and staff. **Number listed:** 15

1. American Beacon Advisors, with $44.051 billion
2. Rhumbline Advisers, $23.713
3. Earnest Partners LLC, $17.395
4. Progress Investment Management Co., $6.819
5. Advent Capital Management LLC, $5.8
6. Ariel Investments LLC, $5.467
7. Smith Graham & Co. Investment Advisors LP, $4.983
8. Piedmont Investment Advisors LLC, $3.449
9. Capri Capital Partners LLC, $3.4
10. Brown Capital Management LLC, $3.198

Source: *Black Enterprise*, B. E. 100s (annual), June 2011, p. 166.

83 ■ LARGEST BLACK-OWNED AUTOMOBILE DEALERS, 2010

Ranked by: Revenue, in millions of dollars. **Remarks:** Also notes rank for previous year, location, chief executive, year founded, staff, and type of business. **Number listed:** 60

1. RLJ McLarty Landers Automotive Holdings LLC, with $893,625 million
2. Prestige Automotive Group, $524,200
3. March/Hodge Automotive Group, $445,112
4. Boyland Auto Group, $315,601
5. Wade Ford Inc., $210,529
6. Winston Pittman Enterprise, $199,654
7. Martin Management Group, $176,238
8. Mills Auto Group, $150,509
9. Royal Oak Ford Sales Inc., $123,927
10. BMW of Sterling, $122,100

Source: *Black Enterprise*, B. E. 100s (annual), June 2011, p. 145-148.

84 ■ LARGEST BLACK-OWNED BANKS, 2010

Ranked by: Assets, in millions of dollars. **Remarks:** Also notes rank for previous year, location, chief executive, year founded, staff, capital, deposits, and loans. **Number listed:** 20

1. Carver Federal Savings Bank, with $744 million
2. OneUnited Bank, $522.899
3. Seaway Bank & Trust Co., $516.584
4. Broadway Federal Bank, $484.099
5. Liberty Bank & Trust Co., $463.847
6. Citizens Bancshares Inc., $387.731
7. City National Bank of New Jersey, $387.522
8. Industrial Bank NA, $382.063
9. Mechanics & Farmers Bank, $312.19
10. Capitol City Bank & Trust Co., $295.074

Source: *Black Enterprise*, B. E. 100s (annual), June 2011, p. 165.

85 ■ LARGEST BLACK-OWNED BUSINESSES IN DETROIT, 2010

Ranked by: Revenue, in millions of dollars. **Remarks:** Also notes contact information, majority owner, figures for previous year, and percent Black-owned. **Number listed:** 20

1. Bridgewater Interiors LLC, with $1,600 million
2. TAG Holdings LLC, $689
3. Prestige Automotive, $524.2
4. Global Automotive Alliance LLC, $389
5. Barden Cos., Inc., $385
6. Piston Automotive LLC, $324
7. SET Enterprises, $221
8. The Bartech Group Inc., $190
9. Briarwood Ford Inc., $124.2
10. Bill Perkins Automotive Group, $115.6

Source: *Crain's Detroit Business*, Book of Lists (annual), December 26, 2011, p. 42.

86 ■ LARGEST BLACK-OWNED INDUSTRIAL/SERVICE COMPANIES, 2010

Ranked by: Revenue, in millions of dollars. **Remarks:** Also notes rank for previous year, location, chief executive, year founded, staff, and type of business. **Number listed:** 100

1. World Wide Technology Inc., with $3,336,133 million
2. Bridgewater Interiors LLC, $1,600,000
3. Act-1 Group, $1,400,000
3. CAMAC International Corp., $1,400,000
5. TAG Holdings LLC, $675,000
6. RLJ Development LLC, $578,000
7. Manna Inc., $511,000
8. Anderson-DuBose Co., $395,036
9. Barden Cos., Inc., $385,000
10. Thompson Hospitality Corp., $373,000

Source: *Black Enterprise*, B. E. 100s (annual), June 2011, p. 131-136.

87 ■ LARGEST BLACK-OWNED INVESTMENT BANKS IN TAX-EXEMPT SECURITIES, 2010

Ranked by: Lead issues of taxable securities, in millions of dollars. **Remarks:** Also notes location, chief executive, staff, number of lead issues, value and number of co-lead issues, and value and number of total issues. **Number listed:** 5

1. Siebert Brandford Shank & Co. LLC, with $6,823.4 million
2. Loop Capital Markets LLC, $2,825.8
3. M. R. Beal & Co., $2,218.8
4. Rice Financial Products Co., $568
5. Grigsby & Associates Inc., $82.5

Source: *Black Enterprise*, B. E. 100s (annual), June 2011, p. 167.

88 ■ LARGEST BLACK-OWNED INVESTMENT BANKS IN TAXABLE SECURITIES, 2010

Ranked by: Lead issues of taxable securities, in millions of dollars. **Remarks:** Also notes location, chief executive, staff, number of lead issues, value and number of co-lead issues, and value and number of total issues. **Number listed:** 5

1. Loop Capital Markets LLC, with $29,027.9 million

2. Siebert Brandford Shank & Co. LLC, $8,109.4
3. CastleOak Securities LP, $3,586
4. The Williams Capital Group LP, $1,588.6
5. M. R. Beal & Co., $1,572

Source: *Black Enterprise*, B. E. 100s (annual), June 2011, p. 167.

89 ■ LARGEST BLACK-OWNED PRIVATE EQUITY FIRMS, 2010

Ranked by: Capital under management, in millions of dollars. **Remarks:** Also notes rank for previous year, location, chief executive, year founded, staff, number of funds, and total number of portfolio companies. **Number listed:** 15

1. Fairview Capital Partners Inc., with $3,100 million
2. Vista Equity Partners, $2,700
3. UrbanAmerica Principals III LLC, $1,027
4. GenNx360 Capital Partners, $600
4. Pharos Capital Group LLC, $600
6. ICV Capital Partners LLC, $440
7. Syncom Venture Partners, $410
8. Smith Whiley & Co., $300
9. RLJ Equity Partners LLC, $230
10. Inheritance Capital Group LLC, $200

Source: *Black Enterprise*, B. E. 100s (annual), June 2011, p. 168.

African Americans—Employment

90 ■ TOP U.S. COMPANIES FOR BLACK EMPLOYEES, 2011

Ranked by: Score based on mentoring, employee-resource groups, diversity training, communications, and demographics in the workplace. **Remarks:** Specific scores not provided. To qualify, companies must have more than 1,000 U.S. employees. **Number listed:** 10

1. AT&T Inc.
2. Cox Communications Inc.
3. Kaiser Permanente
4. Northrop Grumman Corp.
5. Marriott International Inc.
6. Southern Co.
7. Sodexo
8. McDonald's Corp.
9. Altria Group Inc.
10. The Coca-Cola Co.

Source: *DiversityInc*, Top 50 (annual), 2011, p. 94.

Aged—Care

91 ■ TOP SENIOR CARE FRANCHISES, 2012

Ranked by: Cumulative score based on financial strength and stability, growth rate, size of the system, number of years in business, the length of time franchising, start-up costs, litigation, percentage of terminations, and whether the company provides financing. **Remarks:** Specific scores not provided. Also notes overall rank within the *Franchise 500,* contact information, description, year founded, year started franchising, states where registered, available U.S. regions, where seeking foreign expansion, number of franchised and company-owned units for past three years, start-up costs, franchise fees, royalty fees, and type of financing available. **Number listed:** 24

1. Home Instead Senior Care
2. Comfort Keepers
3. Home Helpers/Direct Link
4. Visiting Angels
5. Interim Healthcare
6. BrightStar Care
7. Senior Helpers
8. Right at Home Inc.
9. Always Best Care Senior Services
10. Griswold Special Care

Source: *Entrepreneur*, Franchise 500 (annual), January 2012, p. 192-195.

Aged—Employment

92 ■ BEST EMPLOYERS FOR WORKERS OVER 50, 2011

Ranked by: Score based on human resources practices and policies that benefit all workers, especially those over the age of 50 years. **Remarks:** Specific scores not provided. **Number listed:** 50

1. Scripps Health
2. Cornell University
3. National Institutes of Health
4. First Horizon National Corp.
5. West Virginia University
6. YMCA of Greater Rochester
7. Atlantic Health System
8. Mercy Health System
9. Bon Secours Richmond Health System
10. The Aerospace Corp.

Source: *AARP Magazine*, Best Employers for Workers over 50 (biennial), September 2011.

93 ■ BEST NON-U.S. EMPLOYERS FOR WORKERS OVER AGE 50, 2011

Ranked by: Score based on innovative practices in employing workers over age 50. **Remarks:** Specific scores not provided; companies are listed alphabetically, not ranked. Also notes industry, location, website, number of employees, percentage of employees over age 50, and comments. **Number listed:** 15

1. Bundesagentur fur Arbeit (Germany)
2. Bayerische Motoren Werke AG (BMW, Germany)
3. Centrica plc (U.K.)
4. Daikin Industries Ltd. (Japan)
5. DB Services GmbH (Germany)
6. DSW21 (Germany)
7. Elkerliek Hospital (Netherlands)
8. Jena-Optronik GmbH (Germany)
9. Lam Soon Edible Oils Sdn. Bhd. (Malaysia)
10. Marks & Spencer plc (U.K.)

Source: *AARP Magazine*, International Innovative Employer Awards (biennial), http://www.aarpmagazine.com, September 2011.

Agents

94 ■ LARGEST TALENT AGENCIES IN LOS ANGELES COUNTY, 2010

Ranked by: Number of agents in Los Angeles County. **Remarks:** Also notes contact information, number of employees, types of agents and talent, notable clients, union affiliations, year founded, and top local executive. **Number listed:** 15

1. Creative Artists Agency, with 325 agents
2. WME Entertainment, 250
3. United Talent Agency, 121

Source: *Los Angeles Business Journal*, Largest Talent Agencies (annual), http://www.labusinessjournal.com, October 31, 2011.

Agricultural Cooperative Associations

95 ■ LARGEST AGRICULTURE COOPERATIVES, 2010

Ranked by: Revenue, in millions of dollars. **Remarks:** Also notes rank and figures for previous year, headquarters, type, and assets. **Number listed:** 99

1. CHS Inc., with $25,315 million
2. Land O'Lakes Inc., $11,146
3. Dairy Farmers of America, $9,872
4. GROWMARK Inc., $6,132
5. Ag Processing Inc., $3,302
6. California Dairies Inc., $2,987
7. Associated Milk Producers Inc., $1,709
8. United Sugars Corp., $1,700
9. Southern States Cooperative Inc., $1,695
10. Northwest Dairy Association, $1,650

Source: *Rural Cooperatives*, Top 100 (annual), 2012, p. 19-23.

Agricultural Industry—Advertising

96 ■ TOP ADVERTISING AGENCIES BY AGRIBUSINESS ADVERTISING, 2011

Ranked by: Income from agribusiness advertising, in thousands of dollars. **Number listed:** 5

1. Osborn & Barr Communications, with $12,320 thousand
2. McCormick Co., $10,008
3. Bader Rutter & Associates Inc., $7,926
4. Colle + McVoy, $5,238
5. AdFarm, $4,778

Source: *Agri Marketing*, Agency Update (annual), May 2012, p. 37.

97 ■ TOP ADVERTISING AGENCIES BY AGRIBUSINESS DIRECT MARKETING, 2011

Ranked by: Income from agribusiness direct marketing, in thousands of dollars. **Number listed:** 5

1. Bader Rutter & Associates Inc., with $5,144 thousand
2. LaTorra, Paul & McCann, $1,794
3. Woodruff Sweitzer, $1,688
4. McCormick Co., $1,535

5. Charleston | Orwig Inc., $1,427

Source: *Agri Marketing*, Agency Update (annual), May 2012, p. 37.

98 ■ TOP ADVERTISING AGENCIES BY AGRIBUSINESS INTERNET/ELECTRONIC MARKETING, 2011

Ranked by: Income from agribusiness web-based/electronic marketing, in thousands of dollars. **Number listed:** 5

1. Bader Rutter & Associates Inc., with $5,664 thousand
2. Colle + McVoy, $3,390
3. Woodruff Sweitzer, $3,047
4. Brighton, $1,792
5. Swanson Russell Associates, $1,770

Source: *Agri Marketing*, Agency Update (annual), May 2012, p. 37.

99 ■ TOP ADVERTISING AGENCIES BY AGRIBUSINESS PUBLIC RELATIONS, 2011

Ranked by: Income from agribusiness public relations, in thousands of dollars. **Number listed:** 5

1. Osborn & Barr Communications, with $11,221 thousand
2. Bader Rutter & Associates Inc., $8,762
3. Gibbs & Soell Inc., $7,675
4. McCormick Co., $3,792
5. AdFarm, $2,687

Source: *Agri Marketing*, Agency Update (annual), May 2012, p. 37.

100 ■ TOP ADVERTISING AGENCIES BY AGRIBUSINESS SALES PROMOTION, 2011

Ranked by: Income from agribusiness sales promotion, in thousands of dollars. **Number listed:** 5

1. LaTorra, Paul & McCann, with $1,794 thousand
2. Woodruff Sweitzer, $1,199
3. Farmer, Lumpe + McClelland, $900
4. Charleston | Orwig Inc., $725
5. AdFarm, $455

Source: *Agri Marketing*, Agency Update (annual), May 2012, p. 37.

101 ■ TOP ADVERTISING AGENCIES BY PRODUCER-FUNDED AGRIBUSINESS, 2011

Ranked by: Income from producer-funded accounts, in thousands of dollars. **Number listed:** 5

1. Osborn & Barr Communications, with $5,265 thousand
2. LaTorra, Paul + McCann, $4,485
3. Farmer, Lumpe + McClelland Advertising Agency Ltd., $2,700
4. Bader Rutter & Associates Inc., $2,348
5. AdFarm, $1,268

Source: *Agri Marketing*, Agency Update (annual), May 2012, p. 36.

102 ■ TOP ADVERTISING AGENCIES IN PROFESSIONAL AGRIBUSINESS PRODUCTS, 2011

Ranked by: Income from accounts for professional agribusiness products, in thousands of dollars. **Number listed:** 5

1. Colle + McVoy, with $6,500 thousand
2. Woodruff Sweitzer, $3,188
3. Swanson Russell Associates, $3,030
4. Bader Rutter & Associates Inc., $2,229
5. Exponent Public Relations, $766

Source: *Agri Marketing*, Agency Update (annual), May 2012, p. 36.

103 ■ TOP ADVERTISING AGENCIES IN RURAL LIFE-STYLE AGRIBUSINESS, 2011

Ranked by: Income from rural lifestyle accounts, in thousands of dollars. **Number listed:** 5

1. Bader Rutter & Associates Inc., with $2,593 thousand
2. Osborn & Barr Communications, $1,121
3. Swanson Russell Associates, $617
4. Paulsen Marketing Communications, $500
5. Colle + McVoy/Charleston | Orwig Inc., $122

Source: *Agri Marketing*, Agency Update (annual), May 2012, p. 36.

104 ■ TOP ADVERTISING AGENCIES BY TOTAL AGRIBUSINESS ACCOUNTS, 2011

Ranked by: Income from agribusiness accounts, in thousands of dollars. **Number listed:** 5

1. Bader Rutter & Associates Inc., with $20,405 thousand
2. Osborn & Barr Communications, $17,017
3. McCormick Co., $16,678
4. AdFarm, $9,098
5. Charleston | Orwig Inc., $7,736

Source: *Agri Marketing*, Agency Update (annual), May 2012, p. 36.

Agricultural Land
See: **Farms**

Agricultural Loans

105 ■ LARGEST U.S. BANKS BY AGRICULTURE LOANS, 2011

Ranked by: Total agriculture loans, in thousands of dollars. **Remarks:** Also notes city, state, and dollar and percent change from previous year. **Number listed:** 25

1. Wells Fargo Bank NA, with $9,364,000 thousand
2. Bank of the West, $3,150,511
3. Rabobank NA, $2,953,000
4. Bank of America NA, $2,257,532
5. U.S. Bank NA, $1,751,353
6. BMO Harris Bank NA, $1,216,783
7. Great Western Bank, $1,151,281
8. Regions Bank, $912,068
9. First National Bank of Omaha, $895,890
10. Keybank NA, $678,309

Source: *Highline Bank and S&L Quarterly, Dec. ed.*, 2011, p. I.48.

106 ■ LARGEST U.S. BANKS BY NONPERFORMING AGRICULTURAL LOANS, 2011

Ranked by: Total nonperforming agricultural loans, in thousands of dollars. **Remarks:** Also notes city, state, and dollar and percent change from previous year. **Number listed:** 25

1. Wells Fargo Bank NA, with $401,000 thousand
2. Bank of the West, $57,219
3. Fifth Third Bank, $37,034
4. Rabobank NA, $25,000
5. Citibank NA Inc., $21,000
6. Bank of America NA, $19,525
7. U.S. Bank NA, $12,195
8. Regions Bank, $12,023
9. Keybank NA, $9,397
10. Columbia State Bank, $8,316

Source: *Highline Bank and S&L Quarterly, Dec. ed.*, 2011, p. I.45.

Agricultural Machinery Industry

107 ■ TOP *FORTUNE 500* COMPANIES IN CONSTRUCTION AND FARM MACHINERY, 2011

Ranked by: Revenue, in millions of dollars. **Remarks:** Also notes overall rank in the *Fortune 500;* profits; profits as a percentage of revenue; stockholders' equity; and rank by each criterion. **Number listed:** 5

1. Caterpillar Inc., with $60,138 million
2. Deere & Co., $32,013
3. Cummins Inc., $18,048
4. AGCO Corp., $8,773
5. Terex Corp., $6,505

Source: *Fortune*, Fortune 500 (annual), May 21, 2012, p. F-34.

Agricultural Organizations

108 ■ LARGEST AGRICULTURAL RETAIL DEALERSHIPS AND COOPERATIVES IN THE U.S., 2010

Ranked by: Retail sales of fertilizer, crop protection, seed, and agricultural services, in millions of dollars. **Remarks:** Also notes headquarters, number of states served, number of retail outlets, and breakdown of sales by type. **Number listed:** 100

1. Agrium U.S. Retail, with $1,000+ million
1. GROWMARK Inc., $1,000+
1. Helena Chemical Co., $1,000+
1. Wilbur-Ellis Co., $1,000+
1. J. R. Simplot, $1,000+
1. CHS, $1,000+
7. Southern States Cooperative, $500-999
7. Jimmy Sanders Inc., $500-999
9. MFA Inc., $100-499
9. Tennessee Farmers Cooperative, $100-499

Source: *CropLife*, CropLife 100 (annual), http://www.croplife.com, December 2011.

Agriculture
See also: **Crops; Livestock**

109 ■ LARGEST U.S. RETAILERS IN AGRICULTURAL SERVICES, 2010

Ranked by: Agricultural services as a percentage of total revenue. **Number listed:** 100

1. Delta Growers Association, with 42%
2. Jay-Mar Inc., 21%
3. Watonwan Farm Service, 20%
4. Mott Grain & Agronomy, 15%
5. CPI, 14%
6. Sur-Gro Plant Food, 10%
6. Hintzsche Fertilizer Inc., 10%
8. Consumers Co-op Association, 9%
8. Willard Agri-Service, 9%
8. Cargill Inc., 9%
8. Woolsey Brothers Farm Supply Inc., 9%
8. Mid Kansas Coop, 9%

Source: *CropLife*, CropLife 100 (annual), http://www.croplife.com, December 2011.

Agriculture—Services

110 ■ LARGEST AGRICULTURAL SERVICES COMPANIES BY EMPLOYEES, 2010

Ranked by: Total number of employees. **Remarks:** Also notes contact information for headquarters, number of employees at headquarters, revenue, rank by revenue, and primary SIC code. **Number listed:** 159

1. PETsMART Inc., with 45,000 employees
2. ServiceMaster Holding Corp., 39,000
3. The ServiceMaster Co., 27,000
4. Bunge Ltd., 25,945
5. Asplundh Tree Expert Co., 24,120
6. Tru Green LP, 16,000
7. U.S. Premium Beef LLC, 8,900
8. VCA Antech Inc., 8,500
9. Medical Management International Inc., 7,000
10. Gruma Corp., 6,610

Source: *Business Rankings*, (annual), Dun & Bradstreet Inc., 2011, p. VI.7-VI.10.

111 ■ LARGEST AGRICULTURAL SERVICES COMPANIES BY SALES, 2010

Ranked by: Total revenue, in dollars. **Remarks:** Also notes contact information for headquarters, number of employees at headquarters and overall, rank by employees, and primary SIC code. **Number listed:** 160

1. Bunge Ltd., with $45,707,000,000
2. U.S. Premium Beef LLC, $5,807,929,000
3. PETsMART Inc., $5,336,392,000
4. Servicemaster Co., $3,240,079,000
5. Gruma Corp., $1,704,364,000
6. VCA Antech Inc., $1,381,468,000
7. Brickman Group Holdings Inc., $687,026,000
7. Brickman Group Ltd., $687,026,000
9. BG Holding LIC, $683,400,000
10. Davey Tree Expert Co., $591,732,000

Source: *Business Rankings*, (annual), Dun & Bradstreet Inc., 2011, p. V.7-V.10.

AIDS (Disease)

112 ■ COUNTRIES WITH THE HIGHEST BUSINESS COSTS OF HIV/AIDS, 2010

Ranked by: Score, on a scale of seven, based on the level of expected business costs associated with HIV/AIDS over the course of the next five years. **Number listed:** 142

1. Swaziland, with 1.9 points
2. Malawi, 2.3
2. Lesotho, 2.3
4. Zambia, 2.6
5. Chad, 2.7
6. Uganda, 2.8
7. Zimbabwe, 2.9
7. Botswana, 2.9
7. Mozambique, 2.9
10. Qatar, 3.0
10. South Africa, 3.0

Source: *Global Competitiveness Report*, (annual), World Economic Forum, 2011, p. 434.

Air Cargo
See: **Air Freight Service**

Air Conditioning Industry

113 ■ LARGEST HEATING, VENTILATION, AND AIR CONDITIONING (HVAC) CONTRACTORS, 2011

Ranked by: HVAC revenue, in millions of dollars. **Remarks:** Also notes headquarters and rank in the overall *Top 100*. **Number listed:** 10

1. Johnson Controls Inc., Building Efficiency Div., with $1,037.25 million
2. Comfort Systems USA Inc., $917.6
3. EMCOR Group Inc., $756.9
4. Service Experts division of Lennox Inc., $590.3
5. ARS/Rescue Rooter, $346.7
6. ACCO Engineered Systems Inc., $231.5
7. W. E. Bower Associates Inc., $216.25
8. APi Group Inc., $206.45
9. TDIndustries Ltd., $157.55
10. Southland Industries, $145

Source: *Contractor*, Book of Giants (annual), May 2012, p. 22.

114 ■ TOP BRANDS OF HOME HVAC/ENERGY MANAGEMENT SYSTEMS, 2010

Ranked by: Popularity among *CE Pro 100* companies, in percent. **Number listed:** 5

1. Crestron, with 47%
2. Control4, 31%
3. Aprilaire, 13%
4. HAI, 9%
5. AMX, 7%

Source: *CE Pro*, Brand Analysis (annual), June 2011, p. 59.

Air Couriers
See: **Air Freight Service**

Air Freight Service
See also: **Package Express Service**

115 ■ LARGEST FOR-HIRE AIR/EXPEDITED TRANSPORTATION COMPANIES, 2010

Ranked by: Revenue, in thousands of dollars. **Remarks:** Also notes figures for previous year and percent change. **Number listed:** 7

1. FedEx Custom Critical, with $329,000 thousand
2. Forward Air Inc., $321,702
3. Towne Air Freight, $226,000
4. Panther Expedited Services, $196,414
5. Express-1 Expedited Services, $141,866
6. UPS Express Critical, $132,000
7. Landstar Express America, $120,000

Source: *Transport Topics*, Top 100 For-Hire Carriers (annual), 2011, p. 26.

116 ■ LARGEST U.S. AIR COURIER COMPANIES OVERALL, 2011

Ranked by: Score based on revenue, profits, assets, and market capitalization. **Remarks:** Specific scores not provided. Also notes overall rank in the *Forbes 2000* and figures for each criterion. **Number listed:** 3

1. United Parcel Service Inc. (UPS)
2. FedEx Corp.
3. Expeditors International of Washington Inc.

Source: *Forbes*, Forbes 2000 (annual), http://www.forbes.com, May 7, 2012.

117 ■ WORLD'S LARGEST AIR COURIER COMPANIES OVERALL, 2011

Ranked by: Score based on revenue, profits, assets, and market capitalization. **Remarks:** Specific scores not provided. Also notes country, overall rank in the *Forbes 2000,* and figures for each criterion. **Number listed:** 6

1. United Parcel Service Inc. (UPS)
2. Deutsche Post AG (DHL)
3. FedEx Corp.
4. Expeditors International of Washington Inc.
5. Financiere de l'Odet
6. TNT Express NV

Source: *Forbes*, Forbes 2000 (annual), http://www.forbes.com, May 7, 2012.

Air Transport

118 ■ LARGEST AIR TRANSPORTATION COMPANIES BY EMPLOYEES, 2010

Ranked by: Total number of employees. **Remarks:** Also notes contact information for headquarters, number of employees at headquarters, revenue, rank by revenue, and primary SIC code. **Number listed:** 49

1. FedEx Corp., with 280,000 employees
2. Federal Express Corp., 141,000
3. Delta Air Lines Inc., 81,106
4. AMR Corp., 78,900
5. American Airlines Inc., 66,500
6. United Air Lines Inc., 47,000
6. United Continental Holdings Inc., 47,000
8. H Group Holding Inc., 42,000
9. Continental Airlines Inc., 41,300
10. US Airways Group Inc., 36,000
10. US Airways Inc., 36,000

Source: *Business Rankings*, (annual), Dun & Bradstreet Inc., 2011, p. VI.98-VI.99.

119 ■ LARGEST AIR TRANSPORTATION COMPANIES BY SALES, 2010

Ranked by: Total revenue, in dollars. **Remarks:** Also notes contact information for headquarters, number of employees at headquarters and overall, rank by employees, and primary SIC code. **Number listed:** 49

1. FedEx Corp., with $34,734,000,000
2. Delta Air Lines Inc., $31,755,000,000
3. United Continental Holdings Inc., $23,229,000,000
4. AMR Corp., $22,170,000,000
5. American Airlines Inc., $22,150,000,000
6. Federal Express Corp., $21,243,000,000
7. United Air Lines Inc., $19,682,000,000
8. Southwest Airlines Co., $12,104,000,000
9. US Airways Inc., $12,055,000,000
10. US Airways Group Inc., $11,908,000,000

Source: *Business Rankings*, (annual), Dun & Bradstreet Inc., 2011, p. V.98-V.99.

Airlines

120 ■ BEST MAJOR U.S. AIRLINES, 2011

Ranked by: Score based on flight cancellations, on-time flights, baggage handling, customer complaints, and history of bumping passengers. **Remarks:** Scores not provided. Also notes rank for each criterion. **Number listed:** 7

1. Alaska Air Group Inc.
2. Delta Air Lines Inc.
3. Southwest Airlines Co.
4. US Airways Group Inc.
5. JetBlue Airways Corp.
6. United Air Lines
7. American Airlines Inc.

Source: *The Wall Street Journal*, Airline Rankings (annual), January 5, 2012, p. D3.

121 ■ LARGEST U.S. AIRLINES OVERALL, 2011

Ranked by: Score based on revenue, profits, assets, and market capitalization. **Remarks:** Specific scores not provided. Also notes overall rank in the *Forbes 2000* and figures for each criterion. **Number listed:** 5

1. Delta Air Lines Inc.

2. United Continental Holdings Inc.
3. Southwest Airlines Co.
4. AMR Corp.
5. US Airways Group Inc.

Source: *Forbes*, Forbes 2000 (annual), http://www.forbes.com, May 7, 2012.

122 ■ TEXAS'S LARGEST AIRLINES OVERALL, 2011

Ranked by: Score based on revenue, profits, assets, and market capitalization. **Remarks:** Specific scores not provided. Also notes overall rank in the *Forbes 2000* and figures for each criterion. **Number listed:** 2

1. Southwest Airlines Co.
2. AMR Corp.

Source: *Forbes*, Forbes 2000 (annual), http://www.forbes.com, May 7, 2012.

123 ■ TOP *FORTUNE 500* AIRLINES, 2011

Ranked by: Revenue, in millions of dollars. **Remarks:** Also notes overall rank in the *Fortune 500;* profits; profits as a percentage of revenue; stockholders' equity; and rank by each criterion. **Number listed:** 5

1. United Continental Holdings Inc., with $37,110 million
2. Delta Air Lines Inc., $35,115
3. AMR Corp., $23,979
4. Southwest Airlines Co., $15,658
5. US Airways Group Inc., $13,055

Source: *Fortune*, Fortune 500 (annual), May 21, 2012, p. F-33.

124 ■ TOP U.S. AIRLINES, 2011

Ranked by: Score, on a scale of 100, based on consumer survey regarding cabin comfort, in-flight service, customer service, and value. **Number listed:** 10

1. Virgin America, with 86.76 points
2. JetBlue Airways, 81.60
3. Hawaiian Airlines, 78.58
4. Southwest Airlines, 78.53
5. Sun Country Airlines, 76.70
6. Alaska Airlines, 74.24
7. Frontier Airlines, 72.12
8. USA 3000 Airlines, 71.36
9. Allegiant Airlines, 69.65
10. Continental Airlines, 69.59

Source: *Travel + Leisure*, World's Best Awards (annual), August 2011.

125 ■ THE UNITED STATES' MOST VALUABLE AIRLINE BRANDS, 2011

Ranked by: Brand value, in millions of U.S. dollars. **Remarks:** Also notes rank within the *Global 500* for current and previous year, figures for current and previous year, and brand rating. Ranking is available online only. **Number listed:** 2

1. Delta, with $3,013 million
2. United, $2,763

Source: *Global 500*, (annual), Brand Finance plc, March 2012.

Airlines, Cargo

126 ■ WORLD'S LARGEST CARGO CARRIERS OVERALL, 2010

Ranked by: Scheduled freight-tonnes carried, in thousands. **Number listed:** 35

1. FedEx Corp., with 6,949 thousand tonnes
2. UPS Airlines, 4,509
3. Korean Air, 1,805
4. Emirates Airlines, 1,777
5. Cathay Pacific Airways, 1,579
6. United Airlines, 1,555
7. China Airlines, 1,347
8. Singapore Airlines, 1,149
9. China Eastern Airlines, 1,104
10. Air China, 1,069

Source: *Air Cargo World*, Top 50 Carriers (annual), October 2011, p. 42.

127 ■ WORLD'S LARGEST DOMESTIC CARGO CARRIERS, 2010

Ranked by: Scheduled freight-tonnes carried, in thousands. **Number listed:** 35

1. FedEx Corp., with 4,985 thousand tonnes
2. UPS Airlines, 2,929
3. China Southern Airlines, 833
4. Air China, 625
5. China Eastern Airlines, 527
6. Japan Airlines, 437
7. All Nippon Airways, 419
8. United Airlines, 257
9. Hainan Airlines, 250
10. Shenzhen Airlines, 222

Source: *Air Cargo World*, Top 50 Carriers (annual), October 2011, p. 42.

128 ■ WORLD'S LARGEST INTERNATIONAL CARGO CARRIERS, 2010

Ranked by: Scheduled freight-tonnes carried, in thousands. **Number listed:** 35

1. FedEx Corp., with 1,965 thousand tonnes
2. Emirates Airlines, 1,777
3. Korean Air, 1,661
4. UPS Airlines, 1,580
5. Cathay Pacific Airways, 1,579
6. China Airlines, 1,347
7. United Airlines, 1,298
8. Singapore Airlines, 1,149
9. Lufthansa, 1,037
10. EVA Air, 850

Source: *Air Cargo World*, Top 50 Carriers (annual), October 2011, p. 42.

Airlines, International

129 ■ CHINA'S LARGEST AIRLINES OVERALL, 2011

Ranked by: Score based on revenue, profits, assets, and market capitalization. **Remarks:** Specific scores not provided. Also notes overall rank in the *Forbes 2000* and figures for each criterion. **Number listed:** 3

1. China Southern Airlines Co., Ltd.
2. China Eastern Airlines Corp., Ltd.

3. Hainan Airlines Co., Ltd.

Source: *Forbes*, Forbes 2000 (annual), http://www.forbes.com, May 9, 2012.

130 ■ CHINA'S MOST VALUABLE AIRLINE BRANDS, 2011

Ranked by: Brand value, in millions of U.S. dollars. **Remarks:** Also notes rank within the *Global 500* for current and previous year, figures for current and previous year, and brand rating. Ranking is available online only. **Number listed:** 2

1. China Southern Airlines, with $2,765 million
2. Air China, $2,395

Source: *Global 500*, (annual), Brand Finance plc, March 2012.

131 ■ TOP AIRLINES IN AFRICA/MIDDLE EAST BY OPERATING REVENUE, 2010

Ranked by: Operating revenue, in thousands of U.S. dollars. **Remarks:** Also notes percent change from previous year, total operating expense, percent change in operating expense, operating profit/loss, net income/loss, and percent change from previous year. **Number listed:** 38

1. Emirates Air Lines, with $14,810,458 thousand
2. Saudi Arabian Airlines Corp., $5,333,333
3. South African Airways (Proprietary) Ltd., $3,021,580
4. Etihad Airways, $2,951,000
5. El Al Israel Airlines Ltd., $1,972,239
6. EgyptAir Holding Co. , $1,770,525
7. Pakistan International Airlines , $1,261,146
8. Ethiopian Airlines, $1,255,515
9. Kenya Airways Ltd., $1,043,244
10. Royal Jordanian Airlines Co., plc, $973,703

Source: *Air Transport World*, World Airline Report (annual), July 2011, p. 37.

132 ■ TOP AIRLINES IN AFRICA/MIDDLE EAST BY PASSENGERS, 2010

Ranked by: Number of passengers, in thousands. **Remarks:** Also notes percent change from previous year, revenue passenger kilometers (RPKs), freight tonne-kilometers (FTKs), and load factor. **Number listed:** 37

1. Emirates Air Lines, with 31,422 thousand passengers
2. Saudi Arabian Airlines Corp., 18,172
3. Qatar Airways, 12,392
4. EgyptAir Holding Co., 9,517
5. Etihad Airways, 7,100
6. South African Airways (Proprietary) Ltd., 6,634
7. Royal Air Maroc, 6,034
8. Gulf Air Co., 5,309
9. Air Arabia PJSC, 4,456
10. El Al Israel Airlines Ltd., 4,102

Source: *Air Transport World*, World Airline Report (annual), July 2011, p. 43.

133 ■ TOP AIRLINES IN ASIA/PACIFIC BY OPERATING REVENUE, 2010

Ranked by: Operating revenue, in thousands of U.S. dollars. **Remarks:** Also notes percent change from previous year, total operating expense, percent change in operating expense, operating profit/loss, net income/loss, and percent change from previous year. **Number listed:** 75

1. JAL Group, with $16,440,792 thousand
2. ANA Group, $16,384,902
3. Air China Ltd., $12,513,350
4. Qantas Airways Ltd., $11,801,200
5. China Southern Airlines Co., Ltd., $11,676,426
6. SIA Group, $11,509,350
7. Cathay Pacific Airways Ltd., $11,503,984
8. China Eastern Airlines Corp., Ltd., $11,295,855
9. Korean Air Lines Co., Ltd., $10,127,612
10. Thai Airways International Public Co., Ltd., $6,121,940

Source: *Air Transport World*, World Airline Report (annual), July 2011, p. 37-38.

134 ■ TOP AIRLINES IN ASIA/PACIFIC BY PASSENGERS, 2010

Ranked by: Number of passengers, in thousands. **Remarks:** Also notes percent change from previous year, revenue passenger kilometers (RPKs), freight tonne-kilometers (FTKs), and load factor. **Number listed:** 104

1. China Southern Airlines Co., Ltd., with 76,455 thousand passengers
2. China Eastern Airlines Corp., Ltd., 64,878
3. Air China Ltd., 46,241
4. All Nippon Airways Co., Ltd., 45,743
5. Japan Airlines Corp., 34,795
6. Cathay Pacific Airways Ltd., 26,796
7. Korean Air Lines Co., Ltd., 22,926
8. Qantas Airways Ltd., 22,540
9. Lion Air, 20,500
10. Virgin Australia, 19,009

Source: *Air Transport World*, World Airline Report (annual), July 2011, p. 43-45.

135 ■ TOP EUROPEAN AIRLINES BY OPERATING REVENUE, 2010

Ranked by: Operating revenue, in thousands of U.S. dollars. **Remarks:** Also notes percent change from previous year, total operating expense, percent change in operating expense, operating profit/loss, net income/loss, and percent change from previous year. **Number listed:** 107

1. Deutsche Lufthansa AG, with $36,190,728 thousand
2. Air France-KLM SA, $33,317,348
3. TUI Travel, $21,169,036
4. International Airlines Group, $19,609,600
5. British Airways plc, $10,345,201
6. TNT Express W. W., $9,341,722
7. Iberia Lineas Aereas de Espaetna SA, $6,317,881
8. SAS AB, $6,011,662
9. Ryanair, $5,119,182
10. Swiss International Air Lines AG, $5,073,326

Source: *Air Transport World*, World Airline Report (annual), July 2011, p. 38-40.

136 ■ TOP EUROPEAN AIRLINES BY PASSENGERS, 2010

Ranked by: Number of passengers, in thousands. **Remarks:** Also notes percent change from previous year, revenue passenger kilometers (RPKs), freight tonne-kilometers (FTKs), and load factor. **Number listed:** 159

1. Ryanair Holdings plc, with 72,100 thousand passengers
2. Air France-KLM SA, 71,320
3. Deutsche Lufthansa AG, 58,916
4. EasyJet plc, 48,800
5. Air Berlin plc, 33,593
6. Turkish Airlines Inc., 29,099
7. British Airways plc, 24,088
8. Alitalia, 23,355
9. SAS Scandinavian Airlines AB, 21,532
10. Swiss Air, 14,132

Source: *Air Transport World*, World Airline Report (annual), July 2011, p. 45-48.

137 ■ TOP LATIN AMERICA/CARIBBEAN AIRLINES BY OPERATING REVENUE, 2010

Ranked by: Operating revenue, in thousands of U.S. dollars. **Remarks:** Also notes percent change from previous year, total operating expense, percent change in operating expense, operating profit/loss, net income/loss, and percent change from previous year. **Number listed:** 9

1. TAM Linhas Aereas SA, with $6,829,952 thousand
2. LAN Airlines SA, $4,523,328
3. Gol Linhas Aereas Inteligentes SA, $4,189,344
4. AviancaTaca, $2,413,249
5. Aeromexico, $2,264,273
6. Copa Holdings SA, $1,414,806
7. Surinam Airways, $96,000
8. Pluna, $91,000
9. Vensecar International, $43,016

Source: *Air Transport World*, World Airline Report (annual), July 2011, p. 40.

138 ■ TOP LATIN AMERICA/CARIBBEAN AIRLINES BY PASSENGERS, 2010

Ranked by: Number of passengers, in thousands. **Remarks:** Also notes percent change from previous year, revenue passenger kilometers (RPKs), freight tonne-kilometers (FTKs), and load factor. **Number listed:** 60

1. TAM Linhas Aereas SA, with 34,553 thousand passengers
2. Gol Linhas Aereas Inteligentes SA, 32,122
3. AviancaTaca, 17,420
4. LAN Airlines SA, 17,293
5. Avianca, 11,663
6. AeroMexico, 6,500
7. Aerolineas Argentinas, 6,300
8. LAN Peru, 5,361
9. AeroMexico Connect, 4,891
10. Volaris, 4,203

Source: *Air Transport World*, World Airline Report (annual), July 2011, p. 48-49.

139 ■ TOP NON-U.S. AIRLINES, 2011

Ranked by: Score, on a scale of 100, based on consumer survey regarding cabin comfort, in-flight service, customer service, and value. **Number listed:** 10

1. Singapore Airlines, with 89.86 points
2. Emirates, 88.75
3. Etihad Airways, 87.58
4. Air New Zealand, 86.81
5. Virgin Atlantic Airways, 86.62
6. Cathay Pacific, 85.82
7. All Nippon Airways, 85.57
8. Korean Air, 85
9. Thai Airways International, 84.49
10. Qatar Airways, 84.15

Source: *Travel + Leisure*, World's Best Awards (annual), August 2011.

140 ■ TOP NORTH AMERICAN AIRLINES BY OPERATING REVENUE, 2010

Ranked by: Operating revenue, in thousands of U.S. dollars. **Remarks:** Also notes percent change from previous year, total operating expense, percent change in operating expense, operating profit/loss, net income/loss, and percent change from previous year. **Number listed:** 72

1. United Continental Holdings, with $34,013,000 thousand
2. Delta Air Lines Inc., $31,755,000
3. UAL Corp., $23,229,000
4. AMR Corp., $22,170,000
5. FedEx Express, $21,555,000
6. Southwest Airlines Co., $12,104,000
7. US Airways Group Inc., $11,908,000
8. Air Canada, $10,786,000
9. Continental Airlines Inc., $10,578,046
10. Alaska Air Group Inc., $3,832,300

Source: *Air Transport World*, World Airline Report (annual), July 2011, p. 40-41.

141 ■ TOP NORTH AMERICAN AIRLINES BY PASSENGERS, 2010

Ranked by: Number of passengers, in thousands. **Remarks:** Also notes percent change from previous year, revenue passenger kilometers (RPKs), freight tonne-kilometers (FTKs), and load factor. **Number listed:** 90

1. Delta Air Lines, with 162,615 thousand passengers
2. Southwest Airlines Co., 106,307
3. United Continental, 99,452
4. American Airlines Inc., 86,204
5. US Airways Group Inc., 51,853
6. AirTran Holdings Inc., 24,721
7. JetBlue Airways Corp., 24,254
8. Air Canada, 23,615
9. Alaska Airlines, 16,514
10. ExpressJet Airlines, 16,442

Source: *Air Transport World*, World Airline Report (annual), July 2011, p. 49-50.

142 ■ WORLD'S LARGEST AIRLINES OVERALL, 2011

Ranked by: Score based on revenue, profits, assets, and market capitalization. **Remarks:** Specific scores not provided. Also notes country, overall rank in the *Forbes 2000,* and figures for each criterion. **Number listed:** 19

1. Delta Air Lines Inc.
2. United Continental Holdings Inc.
3. Singapore Airlines Ltd.
4. Air France-KLM SA
5. International Consolidated Airlines Group SA
6. Cathay Pacific Airways Ltd.
7. China Southern Airlines Co., Ltd.
8. China Eastern Airlines Corp.
9. Deutsche Lufthansa AG
10. All Nippon Airways Co., Ltd.

Source: *Forbes*, Forbes 2000 (annual), http://www.forbes.com, May 7, 2012.

143 ■ WORLD'S LEADING LOW-COST CARRIERS BY LOAD FACTOR, 2010

Ranked by: Load factor, in percent. **Number listed:** 10

1. EasyJet plc, with 89.2%
2. Allegiant Air LLC, 87.5%
3. Jet2, 86.3%
4. Tiger Airways, 85.7%
5. IndiGo Airlines, 85.1%
6. Air Arabia PJSC, 83%
6. Ryanair Holdings plc, 83%
8. Spirit Airlines, 82.1%
9. Virgin America Inc., 81.5%
10. AirTran Airways, 81.4%

Source: *Air Transport World*, World Airline Report (annual), July 2011, p. 33.

144 ■ WORLD'S LEADING LOW-COST CARRIERS BY NET PROFIT, 2010

Ranked by: Net profit, in thousands of U.S. dollars. **Number listed:** 10

1. Ryanair Holdings plc, with $528,350 thousand
2. Southwest Airlines Co., $459,000
3. AirAsia Berhad, $346,501
4. EasyJet plc, $191,627
5. Cebu Pacific, $158,482
6. WestJet Airlines Ltd., $136,720
7. Gol Linhas Aereas Inteligentes SA, $128,570
8. IndiGo Airlines, $122,211
9. JetBlue Airways, $97,000
10. Air Arabia PJSC, $84,303

Source: *Air Transport World*, World Airline Report (annual), July 2011, p. 33.

145 ■ WORLD'S LEADING LOW-COST CARRIERS BY OPERATING FLEET, 2010

Ranked by: Number of aircraft in operating fleet. **Number listed:** 10

1. Southwest Airlines Co., with 550 aircraft
2. Ryanair Holdings plc, 269

3. EasyJet plc, 172
4. JetBlue Airways Corp., 164
5. AirTran Holdings Inc., 140
6. Gol Linhas Aereas Inteligentes SA, 97
7. WestJet Airlines Ltd., 95
8. Virgin Australia, 73
9. Jetstar, 59
10. Norwegian Air Shuttle ASA, 56

Source: *Air Transport World*, World Airline Report (annual), July 2011, p. 33.

146 ■ WORLD'S LEADING LOW-COST CARRIERS BY OPERATING PROFIT, 2010

Ranked by: Operating profit, in thousands of U.S. dollars. **Number listed:** 10

1. Southwest Airlines Co., with $988,000 thousand
2. Ryanair Holdings plc, $688,575
3. Gol Linhas Aereas Inteligentes SA, $418,845
4. AirAsia Berhad, $373,081
5. JetBlue Airways Corp., $333,000
6. EasyJet plc, $274,250
7. WestJet Airlines Ltd., $247,545
8. Cebu Pacific, $147,668
9. AirTran Holdings Inc., $128,191
10. Jetstar, $112,254

Source: *Air Transport World*, World Airline Report (annual), July 2011, p. 33.

147 ■ WORLD'S LEADING LOW-COST CARRIERS BY OPERATING REVENUE, 2010

Ranked by: Operating revenue, in thousands of U.S. dollars. **Number listed:** 10

1. Southwest Airlines Co., with $12,104,000 thousand
2. Ryanair Holdings plc, $5,119,182
3. EasyJet plc, $5,696,840
4. Gol Linhas Aereas Inteligentes SA, $4,189,344
5. JetBlue Airways Corp., $3,779,000
6. AirTran Holdings Inc., $2,619,172
7. WestJet Airlines Ltd., $2,609,261
8. Virgin Australia, $2,555,099
9. JetStar Inc., $1,882,605
10. Norwegian Air Shuttle ASA, $1,457,979

Source: *Air Transport World*, World Airline Report (annual), July 2011, p. 33.

148 ■ WORLD'S LEADING LOW-COST CARRIERS BY PASSENGERS, 2010

Ranked by: Number of passengers, in thousands. **Number listed:** 10

1. Southwest Airlines Co., with 106,307 thousand passengers
2. Ryanair Holdings plc, 72,100
3. EasyJet plc, 48,800
4. Gol Linhas Aereas Inteligentes SA, 32,122
5. AirTran Holdings Inc., 24,721

6. JetBlue Airways Corp., 24,254
7. Virgin Australia, 19,009
8. AirAsia Berhad, 16,055
9. WestJet Airlines Ltd., 15,174
10. Norwegian Air Shuttle ASA, 13,029

Source: *Air Transport World*, World Airline Report (annual), July 2011, p. 33.

149 ■ WORLD'S LEADING LOW-COST CARRIERS BY REVENUE PASSENGER KILOMETERS (RPKS), 2010

Ranked by: Revenue passenger kilometers (RPKs), in millions. **Number listed:** 10

1. Southwest Airlines Co., with 125,778 million RPKs
2. EasyJet plc, 56,128
3. JetBlue Airways Corp., 45,523
4. AirTran Holdings Inc., 31,515
5. Gol Linhas Aereas Inteligentes SA, 31,367
6. Virgin Australia, 28,824
7. WestJet Airlines Ltd., 25,127
8. JetStar Inc., 20,493
9. AirAsia Berhad, 18,500
10. Norwegian Air Shuttle ASA, 13,774

Source: *Air Transport World*, World Airline Report (annual), July 2011, p. 33.

150 ■ WORLD'S MOST ADMIRED AIRLINES, 2012

Ranked by: Score, on a scale of 10, based on a survey of executives, directors, and securities analysts of companies within their own industry on eight criteria: innovation, financial soundness, employee talent, use of corporate assets, long-term investment value, social responsibility, quality of management, and quality of products/services. **Remarks:** Specific scores not provided. Also notes rank for previous year. **Number listed:** 6

1. United Continental Holdings Inc.
2. Singapore Airlines Ltd.
3. Southwest Airlines Co.
4. Delta Air Lines Inc.
5. Deutsche Lufthansa AG
6. Air France-KLM SA

Source: *Fortune*, World's Most Admired Companies (annual), March 19, 2012, p. 150.

151 ■ WORLD'S TOP AIRLINE BRANDS, 2011

Ranked by: Brand value, in millions of U.S. dollars. **Remarks:** Also notes rank and figures for previous year, country, and brand rating. **Number listed:** 20

1. Lufthansa, with $3,801 million
2. Singapore Airlines, $3,757
3. Emirates Airlines, $3,622
4. Delta, $3,100
5. China Southern Airlines, $2,533
6. ANA, $2,448
7. Air China, $2,395
8. Cathay Pacific, $2,383
9. Air France, $2,382
10. United, $2,352

Source: *Top 20 Airline Brands*, (annual), Brand Finance plc, 2011.

152 ■ WORLD'S TOP AIRLINES BY FLEET SIZE, 2010

Ranked by: Total number of operating aircraft in fleet. **Number listed:** 25

1. Delta Air Lines Inc., with 719 aircraft
2. American Airlines Inc., 615
3. Southwest Airlines Co., 550
4. FedEx Express, 359
4. United Air Lines, 359
6. Air France-KLM SA, 358
7. China Southern Airlines Co., Ltd., 342
8. Continental Airlines Inc., 339
9. US Airways Group Inc., 338
10. Deutsche Lufthansa SA, 281

Source: *Air Transport World*, World Airline Report (annual), July 2011, p. 35.

153 ■ WORLD'S TOP AIRLINES BY FREIGHT TONNE-KILOMETERS (FTKS), 2010

Ranked by: Freight tonne-kilometers (FTKs), in millions. **Number listed:** 25

1. FedEx Express, with 15,943 million FTKs
2. Air France-KLM SA, 11,438
3. UPS Airlines, 10,523
4. Cathay Pacific Airways Ltd., 10,175
5. Korean Air Lines Co., Ltd., 9,670
6. Lufthansa Cargo, 8,905
7. SIA Cargo, 7,174
8. China Airlines, 6,674
9. Cargolux Airlines International SA, 5,284
10. EVA Air, 5,168

Source: *Air Transport World*, World Airline Report (annual), July 2011, p. 35.

154 ■ WORLD'S TOP AIRLINES BY NET PROFIT, 2010

Ranked by: Net profit, in thousands of U.S. dollars. **Number listed:** 25

1. Air China Ltd., with $1,871,359 thousand
2. Cathay Pacific Airways Ltd., $1,828,964
3. Deutsche Lufthansa AG, $1,498,013
4. Emirates Air Lines, $1,463,235
5. China Southern, $973,149
6. SIA Group, $865,293
7. Air France-KLM, $864,598
8. United Continental Holdings, $854,000
9. China Eastern, $801,626
10. Delta Air Lines, $593,000

Source: *Air Transport World*, World Airline Report (annual), July 2011, p. 35.

155 ■ WORLD'S TOP AIRLINES BY OPERATING PROFIT, 2010

Ranked by: Operating profit, in thousands of U.S. dollars. **Number listed:** 25

1. JAL Group, with $2,274,125 thousand
2. Delta Air Lines, $2,217,000
3. United Continental Holdings, $1,818,000

4. Air China Ltd., $1,657,767
5. Deutsche Lufthansa AG, $1,642,384
6. Emirates Air Lines, $1,481,754
7. Cathay Pacific Airways Ltd., $1,420,329
8. FedEx Express, $1,127,000
9. SIA Group, $1,007,369
10. Korean Air, $689,137

Source: *Air Transport World*, World Airline Report (annual), July 2011, p. 35.

156 ■ WORLD'S TOP AIRLINES BY OPERATING REVENUE, 2010

Ranked by: Operating revenue, in thousands of U.S. dollars. **Number listed:** 25

1. Deutsche Lufthansa AG, with $36,190,728 thousand
2. United Continental Holdings, $34,013,000
3. Air France-KLM SA, $33,317,348
4. Delta Air Lines Inc., $31,755,000
5. AMR Corp., $22,170,000
6. FedEx Express, $21,555,000
7. International Airlines Group, $19,609,600
8. JAL Group, $16,440,792
9. ANA Group, $16,384,902
10. Emirates Airline, $14,810,458

Source: *Air Transport World*, World Airline Report (annual), July 2011, p. 35.

157 ■ WORLD'S TOP AIRLINES BY PASSENGERS, 2010

Ranked by: Total number of passengers, in thousands. **Number listed:** 25

1. Delta Air Lines Inc., with 162,615 thousand passengers
2. Southwest Airlines Co., 106,307
3. United Continental, 99,452
4. American Airlines Inc., 86,204
5. China Southern Airlines Co., Ltd., 76,455
6. Ryanair Holdings plc, 72,100
7. Air France-KLM SA, 71,320
8. China Eastern Airlines, 64,878
9. Deutsche Lufthansa AG, 58,916
10. US Airways Group Inc., 51,853

Source: *Air Transport World*, World Airline Report (annual), July 2011, p. 35.

158 ■ WORLD'S TOP AIRLINES BY REVENUE PASSENGER KILOMETERS (RPKS), 2010

Ranked by: Revenue passenger kilometers (RPKs), in millions. **Number listed:** 25

1. Delta Air Lines Inc., with 310,956 million RPKs
2. United Continental, 297,129
3. Air France-KLM SA, 204,737
4. American Airlines Inc., 201,944
5. Emirates Air Lines, 146,134
6. Deutsche Lufthansa AG, 129,668
7. Southwest Airlines Co., 125,778
8. China Southern Airlines, 111,327

9. British Airways plc, 107,723

10. Cathay Pacific, 96,588

Source: *Air Transport World*, World Airline Report (annual), July 2011, p. 35.

Airport Duty Free Shops

159 ■ LARGEST TRAVEL RETAIL COMPANIES, 2010

Ranked by: Sales, in millions of euros. **Remarks:** Also notes sales by U.S. dollars and remarks. **Number listed:** 25

1. DFS Group, with €2,113 million
2. Dufry, €2,093
3. Lagardere Services Travel Retail, €2,000
4. Autogrill (travel retail and duty free segment), €1,676
5. Lotte Duty Free, €1,509
6. The Nuance Group, €1,467
7. Gebr Heinemann, €1,000
8. Dubai Duty Free, €958
9. Aer Rianta International, €954
10. The Shilla Duty Free, €830

Source: *The Moodie Report e-Zine*, Top 25 Travel Retail Companies, August 18, 2011, p. 17.

Airports

160 ■ WORLD'S TOP AIRPORTS BY MOVEMENTS, 2010

Ranked by: Total number of air movements. **Remarks:** Also notes airport code and percent change from previous year. **Number listed:** 50

1. Atlanta, GA, with 950,119 movements
2. Chicago, IL, 882,614
3. Dallas-Ft. Worth, TX, 652,61
4. Denver, CO, 630,089
5. Los Angeles, CA, 575,835
6. Houston, TX, 531,347
7. Charlotte, NC, 529,101
8. Beijing, China, 517,582
9. Las Vegas, NV, 505,591
10. Paris, France, 499,997

Source: *Air Transport World*, World Airline Report (annual), July 2011, p. 53.

161 ■ WORLD'S TOP AIRPORTS BY PASSENGERS, 2010

Ranked by: Total number of passengers. **Remarks:** Also notes airport code and percent change from previous year. **Number listed:** 50

1. Atlanta, GA, with 89,331,622 passengers
2. Beijing, China, 73,891,801
3. Chicago, IL, 66,665,390
4. London, England, 65,884,143
5. Tokyo, Japan, 64,069,098
6. Los Angeles, CA, 58,915,100
7. Paris, France, 58,167,062
8. Dallas-Ft. Worth, TX, 56,905,066
9. Frankfurt, Germany, 53,009,221

10. Denver, CO, 52,211,242

Source: *Air Transport World*, World Airline Report (annual), July 2011, p. 53.

Airports, Cargo

162 ■ ASIA-PACIFIC'S TOP CARGO AIRPORTS, 2010

Ranked by: Annual tonnage. **Remarks:** Also notes airport code and annual percent change in tonnage. **Number listed:** 27

1. Hong Kong, with 4,168,394 tons
2. Shanghai, China, 3,227,914
3. Incheon, South Korea, 2,684,500
4. Tokyo, Japan, 2,167,843
5. Singapore, 1,841,004
6. Taipei, Taiwan, 1,767,075
7. Beijing, Ching, 1,549,126
8. Bangkok, Thailand, 1,310,146
9. Guangzhou, China, 1,144,458
10. Shenzhen, China, 809,363

Source: *Air Cargo World*, Top 50 Airports (annual), September 2011, p. 36.

163 ■ EUROPE'S TOP CARGO AIRPORTS, 2010

Ranked by: Annual tonnage. **Remarks:** Also notes airport code and annual percent change in tonnage. **Number listed:** 19

1. Paris, France, with 2,399,067 tons
2. Frankfurt, Germany, 2,275,106
3. London, England, 1,551,405
4. Amsterdam, Netherlands, 1,538,135
5. Luxembourg, 705,370
6. Cologne, Germany, 644,029
7. Liege, Belgium, 639,669
8. Leipzig, Germany, 638,491
9. Brussels, Belgium, 441,442
10. Milan, Italy, 432,672

Source: *Air Cargo World*, Top 50 Airports (annual), September 2011, p. 37.

164 ■ LATIN AMERICA'S TOP CARGO AIRPORTS, 2010

Ranked by: Annual tonnage. **Remarks:** Also notes airport code and annual percent change in tonnage. **Number listed:** 10

1. Bogota, Colombia, with 526,844 tons
2. Sao Paulo, Brazil, 430,850
3. Mexico City, Mexico, 397,142
4. Santiago, Chile, 285,439
5. Lima, Peru, 271,794
6. Campinas, Brazil, 255,008
7. Buenos Aires, Argentina, 212,890
8. San Juan, Puerto Rico, 181,703
9. Quito, Ecuador, 164,104
10. Manaus, Brazil, 157,157

Source: *Air Cargo World*, Top 50 Airports (annual), September 2011, p. 39.

165 ■ NORTH AMERICA'S TOP CARGO AIRPORTS, 2010

Ranked by: Annual tonnage. **Remarks:** Also notes airport code and annual percent change in tonnage. **Number listed:** 30

1. Memphis, TN, with 3,916,937 tons
2. Anchorage, AK, 2,578,396
3. Louisville, KY, 2,166,226
4. Miami, FL, 1,835,793
5. Los Angeles, CA, 1,810,345
6. Chicago, IL, 1,424,077
7. New York, NY, 1,343,114
8. Indianapolis, IN, 947,279
9. Newark, NJ, 854,750
10. Atlanta, GA, 659,129

Source: *Air Cargo World*, Top 50 Airports (annual), September 2011, p. 38.

166 ■ TOP CARGO AIRPORTS IN THE MIDDLE EAST/ AFRICA, 2010

Ranked by: Annual tonnage. **Remarks:** Also notes airport code and annual percent change in tonnage. **Number listed:** 14

1. Dubai, United Arab Emirates, with 2,270,498 tons
2. Mumbai, India, 671,238
3. New Delhi, India, 594,496
4. Istanbul, Turkey, 466,553
5. Abu Dhabi, United Arab Emirates, 442,326
6. Sharjah, United Arab Emirates, 397,518
7. Madras, India, 385,726
8. Bahrain, 329,938
9. Tel-Aviv, Israel, 315,511
10. Johannesburg, South Africa, 311,032

Source: *Air Cargo World*, Top 50 Airports (annual), September 2011, p. 39.

167 ■ WORLD'S TOP CARGO AIRPORTS, 2010

Ranked by: Annual tonnage. **Remarks:** Also notes airport code and annual percent change in tonnage. **Number listed:** 50

1. Hong Kong, with 4,168,394 tons
2. Memphis, TN, 3,916,937
3. Shanghai, China, 3,227,914
4. Incheon, South Korea, 2,684,500
5. Anchorage, AK, 2,578,396
6. Paris, France, 2,399,067
7. Frankfurt, Germany, 2,275,106
8. Dubai, United Arab Emirates, 2,270,498
9. Tokyo, Japan, 2,167,843
10. Louisville, KY, 2,166,226

Source: *Air Cargo World*, Top 50 Airports (annual), September 2011, p. 40.

Alcoholic Beverages
See also: **Liquor Industry**

168 ■ TOP SPIRITS BRANDS IN THE U.S., 2011

Ranked by: Sales, in dollars. **Remarks:** Also notes percent change from previous year and case sales. **Number listed:** 10

1. Smirnoff Vodka, with $231,484,400
2. Jack Daniel's Tennessee Whiskey, $134,380,000

3. Captain Morgan Rum, $133,026,700
4. Bacardi Rum, $130,534,200
5. Crown Royal Canadian Whiskey, $102,299,700
6. Jose Cuervo Tequila, $86,595,980
7. Absolut Vodka, $74,043,500
8. Jim Beam Bourbon, $72,222,620
9. Jagermeister, $64,119,610
10. Skyy Vodka, $62,059,040

Source: *Beverage Industry*, State of the Industry Report (annual), July 2011, p. SOI-22.

169 ■ WORLD'S TOP ALCOHOL BRANDS, 2012

Ranked by: Brand value, in millions of U.S. dollars. **Remarks:** Also notes rank and figures for previous year, country, and brand rating. **Number listed:** 50

1. Johnnie Walker, with $2,432 million
2. Bacardi, $2,009
3. Hennessy, $1,917
4. Smirnoff, $1,718
5. Chivas Regal, $1,551
6. Moutai, $1,493
7. Wuliangye, $1,308
8. Baileys, $1,269
9. Moet, $1,252
10. Jack Daniels, $1,246

Source: *Top 50 Drinks Brands*, (annual), Brand Finance plc, 2012.

Aluminum Industry

170 ■ WORLD'S LARGEST ALUMINUM COMPANIES OVERALL, 2011

Ranked by: Score based on revenue, profits, assets, and market capitalization. **Remarks:** Specific scores not provided. Also notes country, overall rank in the *Forbes 2000,* and figures for each criterion. **Number listed:** 5

1. United Company RUSAL plc
2. Alcoa Inc.
3. Norsk Hydro ASA
4. Aluminum Corporation of China Ltd.
5. Hindalco Industries Ltd.

Source: *Forbes*, Forbes 2000 (annual), http://www.forbes.com, May 7, 2012.

Amphitheaters
See also: **Stadiums**

171 ■ WORLD'S TOP AMPHITHEATERS, 2011

Ranked by: Gross sales, in U.S. dollars. **Remarks:** Also notes venue capacity, total attendance, total capacity, number of shows, and number of sellouts. **Number listed:** 10

1. Comcast Center (Mansfield, MA), with $14,900,000
2. Shoreline Amphitheatre (Mountain View, CA), $14,600,000
3. Hollywood Bowl (Los Angeles, CA), $14,377,355
4. The Gorge (George, WA), $14,100,000

5. DTE Energy Music Center (Clarkston, MI), $14,057,087

6. Susquehanna Bank Center (Camden, NJ), $13,600,000

7. Molson Canadian Amphitheatre (Toronto, ON), $13,300,000

8. Cynthia Woods Mitchell Pavilion (The Woodlands, TX), $12,300,000

9. Greek Theatre (Los Angeles, CA), $11,966,397

10. PNC Bank Arts Center (Holmdel, NJ), $11,500,000

Source: *Billboard*, The Year in Music & Touring (annual), December 17, 2011, p. 100.

Amusement Industry
See also: **Entertainment Industry**

172 ■ LARGEST AMUSEMENT AND RECREATION COMPANIES BY EMPLOYEES, 2010

Ranked by: Total number of employees. **Remarks:** Also notes contact information for headquarters, number of employees at headquarters, revenue, rank by revenue, and primary SIC code. **Number listed:** 130

1. Walt Disney Parks & Resorts U.S. Inc., with 62,000 employees

2. Harrah's Operating Co., 30,000

3. Bally Total Fitness Holding Corp., 19,200

4. Equinox Holdings Inc., 18,000

5. Life Time Fitness Inc., 17,400

6. 24 Hour Fitness Worldwide Inc., 17,000

7. Concord Realty Inc., 16,000

8. Penn National Gaming Inc., 14,772

9. Universal City Development Partners Ltd., 13,850

10. Bally Total Fitness Corp., 12,340

Source: *Business Rankings*, (annual), Dun & Bradstreet Inc., 2011, p. VI.235-VI.237.

173 ■ LARGEST AMUSEMENT AND RECREATION COMPANIES BY SALES, 2010

Ranked by: Total revenue, in dollars. **Remarks:** Also notes contact information for headquarters, number of employees at headquarters and overall, rank by employees, and primary SIC code. **Number listed:** 129

1. Rogue Valley Manor, with $3,453,101,600

2. Penn National Gaming Inc., $2,459,111,000

3. Mohegan Tribal Gaming Authority, $1,455,117,000

4. Madison Square Garden Inc., $1,157,136,000

5. Universal City Development Partners Ltd., $1,128,475,000

6. Pinnacle Entertainment Inc., $1,098,380,000

7. Cedar Fair LP, $977,592,000

8. Dreamers Travels LLC, $975,000,000

9. St. John Health System Inc., $919,669,000

10. Six Flags Entertainment Corp., $912,861,000

Source: *Business Rankings*, (annual), Dun & Bradstreet Inc., 2011, p. V.209-V.211.

Apartment Houses

174 ■ LARGEST U.S. APARTMENT MANAGERS, 2010

Ranked by: Number of apartments with management interest. **Remarks:** Also notes headquarters and CEO. **Number listed:** 25

1. Greystar Real Estate Partners LLC, with 187,360 apartments

2. Riverstone Residential Group, 162,182

3. Pinnacle Family of Companies, 151,367

4. Lincoln Property Co., 133,425

5. Equity Residential, 129,604

6. AIMCO, 117,119

7. WinnCompanies, 84,817

8. Archstone, 81,613

9. Camden Property Trust, 63,498

10. Bell Partners, 60,182

Source: *National Real Estate Investor*, Best of the Best (annual), 2011, p. 51.

175 ■ LARGEST U.S. APARTMENT OWNERS, 2010

Ranked by: Number of apartments with ownership interest. **Remarks:** Also notes headquarters and CEO. **Number listed:** 25

1. Boston Capital Corp., with 158,947 apartments

2. Centerline Capital Group, 152,600

3. Boston Financial Investment Management LP, 145,454

4. SunAmerica Affordable Housing Partners Inc., 141,113

5. Equity Residential, 129,604

6. PNC Tax Credit Capital, 123,462

7. AIMCO, 110,946

8. National Equity Fund, 107,138

9. The Enterprise Community Investment Inc., 96,195

10. The Richman Group Affordable Housing Corp., 94,925

Source: *National Real Estate Investor*, Best of the Best (annual), 2011, p. 50.

Apparel Industry
See: **Clothing Industry**

Apparel Stores
See: **Clothing Stores**

Appliances, Household
See: **Household Appliances**

Architectural Firms

176 ■ LARGEST ARCHITECTURE COMPANIES, 2010

Ranked by: Architecture billings, in dollars. **Number listed:** 79

1. M. Arthur Gensler Jr. & Associates Inc., with $657,000,000

2. Perkins & Will Inc., $400,500,000

3. NBBJ, $193,800,000

4. ZGF Architects LLP, $124,593,079

5. Kohn Pedersen Fox Associates, $121,200,000

6. DLR Group, $116,000,000

7. Perkins Eastman Architects, $110,000,000

8. Populous, $99,000,000

9. Callison Architecture Inc., $90,000,000

10. HMC Architects, $88,041,517

Source: *Building Design & Construction*, Giants 300 (annual), July 2011, p. 43.

177 ■ LARGEST ARCHITECTURE/ENGINEERING COMPANIES, 2010

Ranked by: Architecture/engineering billings, in dollars. **Number listed:** 52

1. HOK Group Inc., with $473,848,779

2. HDR Architecture Inc., $320,055,000

3. Skidmore, Owings & Merrill LLP, $251,000,000

4. RTKL Associates Inc., $210,532,000

5. HKS Inc., $200,800,000

6. Cannon Design Inc., $192,700,000

7. SmithGroup, $179,672,000

8. Leo A. Daly Co., $154,706,644

9. Hammel, Green & Abrahamson, $121,628,877

10. KlingStubbins, $96,040,000

Source: *Building Design & Construction*, Giants 300 (annual), July 2011, p. 43.

178 ■ LARGEST COLORADO-BASED ARCHITECTURAL FIRMS, 2010

Ranked by: Number of licensed architects. **Remarks:** Also notes contact information and total number of employees. **Number listed:** 10

1. Fentress Architects, with 54 architects

2. RNL Design Inc., 46

3. OZ Architecture, 45

4. Davis Partnership Architects, 41

5. H & L Architecture, 29

6. Anderson Mason Dale Architects, 25

7. klipp, 18

8. Sink Combs Dethlefs PC, 17

9. 4240 Architecture Inc., 16

9. Merrick & Co., 16

Source: *ColoradoBiz*, Top Professional Services (annual), December 2011, p. 47.

179 ■ LARGEST U.S. ARCHITECTURAL FIRMS, 2010

Ranked by: Revenue for architectural services, in millions of dollars. **Remarks:** Also notes headquarters, type of firm, and breakdown of revenue by type. **Number listed:** 250

1. AECOM Technology Corp., with $666.4 million

2. M. Arthur Gensler Jr. & Associates Inc., $656.86

3. Perkins & Will Inc., $400.3

4. HDR Architecture Inc., $336.9

5. HOK Group Inc., $334.16

6. URS Corp., $282.8

7. NBBJ, $193.8

8. HKS Inc., $190.5

9. RTKL, $176

10. Skidmore, Owings & Merrill LLP, $169.9

Source: *Architectural Record*, Top 250 Firms (annual), http://www.archrecord.construction.com, July 2011.

Arenas
See: **Stadiums**

Art Dealers

180 ■ AMERICA'S MOST POWERFUL ART DEALERS, 2012

Ranked by: Score based on revenue and influence. **Remarks:** Scores not provided. Also notes age, gallery, number of locations, revenue, and comments. **Number listed:** 10

1. Larry Gagosian

2. David Zwirner

3. Arne Glimcher

4. Ursula Hauser and Iwan Wirth

5. Marian Goodman

6. Matthew Marks

7. Dominique Levy and Robert Mnuchin

8. Paula Cooper

9. Barbara Gladstone

10. William Acquavella

Source: *Forbes*, America's Most Powerful Art Dealers, May 21, 2012, p. 102.

Asian Americans in Business

181 ■ FASTEST-GROWING PRIVATE EAST ASIAN-RUN COMPANIES IN THE U.S., 2007-2010

Ranked by: Average annual sales growth over three years, in percent. **Remarks:** Also notes overall rank in the *Inc. 5,000*, state, and revenue for current year. To qualify, private companies must have had annual revenues of at least $100,000 in 2007 and $2 million in 2010. **Number listed:** 127

1. Vertiglo, with 4,928%

2. A10 Networks, 3,786%

3. Soft Tech Consulting, 2,138%

4. DiscoverOrg, 1,516%

5. Spark Revenue, 1,442%

6. Aztec Awards, 1,400%

7. LuxMobile Group, 1,358%

8. Pharmacare, 937%

9. BuddyTV, 932%

10. Nova Datacom, 893%

Source: *Inc.*, Inc. 500 (annual), http://www.inc.com, September 2011.

182 ■ FASTEST-GROWING PRIVATE SOUTH ASIAN-RUN COMPANIES IN THE U.S., 2007-2010

Ranked by: Average annual sales growth over three years, in percent. **Remarks:** Also notes overall rank in the *Inc. 5,000*, state, and revenue for current year. To qualify, private companies must have had annual revenues of at least $100,000 in 2007 and $2 million in 2010. **Number listed:** 248

1. I. T. Source, with 6,666%
2. WBPromotions, 6,199%
3. HappyBaby, 3,207%
4. Saxon-Global, 2,948%
5. KPaul, 2,795%
6. Product Movers, 2,659%
7. MyDailyMoment.com, 1,952%
8. Green Earth, 1,933%
9. MindPetal, 1,897%
10. Optimal Strategix Group, 1,878%

Source: *Inc.*, Inc. 500 (annual), http://www.inc.com, September 2011.

183 ■ LARGEST ASIAN-OWNED BUSINESSES IN DETROIT, 2010

Ranked by: Revenue, in millions of dollars. **Remarks:** Also notes contact information, majority owner, figures for previous year, percent change, number of local employees for current and previous year, percent Asian-owned, and type of business. **Number listed:** 10

1. Saturn Electronics & Engineering Inc., with $227.2 million
2. NYX Inc., $223
3. Acro Service Corp., $130
4. HTC Global Services Inc., $113
5. Synova Inc., $53.9
6. Rapid Global Business Solutions Inc., $35.5
7. Saturn Electronics Corp., $33.1
8. Ebinger Manufacturing/Jets Manufacturing Co., $21.6
9. Roy Smith Co., $20
10. Youngsoft Inc., $14.6

Source: *Crain's Detroit Business*, Book of Lists (annual), December 26, 2011, p. 40.

184 ■ TOP U.S. COMPANIES FOR ASIAN AMERICAN EMPLOYEES, 2011

Ranked by: Score based on mentoring, employee-resource groups, diversity training, communications, and demographics in the workplace. **Remarks:** Specific scores not provided. To qualify, companies must have more than 1,000 U.S. employees. **Number listed:** 10

1. Deloitte LLP
2. Starwood Hotels & Resorts Worldwide Inc.
3. Johnson & Johnson
4. International Business Machines Corp. (IBM)
5. PricewaterhouseCoopers LLP
6. Kaiser Permanente
7. Abbott Laboratories Inc.
8. American Express Co.
9. Procter & Gamble Co.
10. Wells Fargo & Co.

Source: *DiversityInc*, Top 50 (annual), 2011, p. 96.

Athletes

185 ■ MOST POWERFUL ATHLETES, 2011

Ranked by: Score based on earnings and such measures of popularity as Internet presence, press clippings, magazine cover

stories, and mentions on television and radio. **Remarks:** Specific scores not provided. Also notes overall rank in the *Celebrity 100*. **Number listed:** 19

1. Tiger Woods
2. LeBron James
3. Kobe Bryant
4. Roger Federer
5. David Beckham
6. Phil Mickelson
7. Cristiano Ronaldo
8. Rafael Nadal
9. Alex Rodriguez
10. Tom Brady

Source: *Forbes*, The Celebrity 100 (annual), http://www.forbes.com, June 6, 2011.

186 ■ WORLD'S MOST VALUABLE SPORTS BRANDS: ATHLETES

Ranked by: Brand value, in millions of dollars. **Number listed:** 10

1. Tiger Woods, with $55 million
2. Roger Federer, $26
3. Phil Mickelson, $24
4. David Beckham, $20
4. LeBron James, $20
6. Kobe Bryant, $14
7. Dale Earnhardt Jr., $9
7. Maria Sharapova, $9
9. Cristiano Ronaldo, $8
10. Shaun White, $7

Source: *Forbes*, Fab 40, http://www.forbes.com, October 3, 2011.

Athletes—Compensation

187 ■ HIGHEST-PAID BASEBALL PLAYERS, 2011

Ranked by: Salary and endorsements, in millions of dollars. **Number listed:** 10

1. Alex Rodriguez (NY Yankees), with $32 million
2. Joe Mauer (MN Twins), $27
3. Derek Jeter (NY Yankees), $25
4. Ichiro Suzuki (Seattle Mariners), $24.5
5. Johan Santana (NY Mets), $24.4
6. C. C. Sabathia (NY Yankees), $24
7. Prince Fielder (Detroit Tigers), $23.3
8. Mark Teixeira (NY Yankees), $22.8
9. Cliff Lee (Philadelphia Phillies), $21.8
10. Ryan Howard (Philadelphia Phillies), $21.5

Source: *Forbes*, Baseball Team Valuations (annual), April 9, 2012, p. 78-79.

188 ■ HIGHEST-PAID PLAYERS IN THE NATIONAL BASKETBALL ASSOCIATION, 2011

Ranked by: Earnings, in millions of dollars. **Remarks:** Also notes comments. **Number listed:** 10

1. Kobe Bryant (LA Lakers), with $53.2 million
2. LeBron James (Miami Heat), $49
3. Dwight Howard (Orlando Magic), $28.9

4. Dwyane Wade (Miami Heat), $27.7
5. Carmelo Anthony (NY Knicks), $26.5
6. Amar'e Stoudemire (NY Knicks), $26.2
6. Kevin Garnett (Boston Celtics), $26.2
8. Kevin Durant (OK City Thunder), $24.5
9. Tim Duncan (San Antonio Spurs), $23.3
10. Chris Paul (LA Clippers), $22.4

Source: *Forbes*, NBA Team Valuations (annual), February 13, 2012, p. 84-85.

189 ■ HIGHEST-PAID PLAYERS IN THE NATIONAL FOOTBALL LEAGUE, 2010

Ranked by: Salary, in millions of dollars. **Number listed:** 5

1. Peyton Manning (Indianapolis Colts), with $18 million
1. Tom Brady (New England Patriots), $18
3. Michael Vick (Philadelphia Eagles), $16.7
4. Eli Manning (New York Giants), $16.3
5. Philip Rivers (San Diego Chargers), $15.3

Source: *Forbes*, NFL Team Valuations (annual), September 26, 2011, p. 91.

190 ■ HIGHEST-PAID SOCCER PLAYERS, 2011

Ranked by: Earnings, in millions of U.S. dollars. **Remarks:** Also notes age and comments. **Number listed:** 10

1. David Beckham (LA Galaxy), with $46 million
2. Cristiano Ronaldo (Real Madrid), $42
3. Lionel Messi (Barcelona), $39
4. Wayne Rooney (Manchester United), $24
5. Kaka (Real Madrid), $21
6. John Terry (Chelsea), $18
6. Yaya Toure (Manchester City), $18
8. Fernando Torres (Chelsea), $17
9. Frank Lampard (Chelsea), $16
9. Steven Gerrard (Liverpool), $16

Source: *Forbes*, Soccer Team Valuations (annual), May 7, 2012, p. 22.

191 ■ WORLD'S HIGHEST-PAID TENNIS PLAYERS, 2010

Ranked by: Earnings, in millions of U.S. dollars. **Remarks:** Also notes age and comments. **Number listed:** 10

1. Roger Federer, with $47 million
2. Rafael Nadal, $31
3. Maria Sharapova, $25
4. Novak Djokovic, $18
5. Andy Murray, $13.5
6. Andy Roddick, $13
7. Caroline Wozniacki, $12.5
8. Venus Williams, $11.5
9. Kim Clijsters, $11
10. Serena Williams, $10.5

Source: *Forbes*, World's Highest-Paid Tennis Players, August 25, 2011.

Athletic Shoes
See: **Shoe Industry**

Audio and Video Equipment

192 ■ TOP BRANDS OF ACOUSTICAL TREATMENTS, 2010

Ranked by: Popularity among *CE Pro 100* companies, in percent. **Number listed:** 5

1. Acoustic Innovations, with 14%
2. Kinetics, 12%
3. Auralex, 10%
4. CinemaTech, 9%
4. RPG, 9%

Source: *CE Pro*, Brand Analysis (annual), June 2011, p. 56.

193 ■ TOP BRANDS OF ARCHITECTURAL SPEAKERS, 2010

Ranked by: Popularity among *CE Pro 100* companies, in percent. **Number listed:** 5

1. Sonance, with 43%
2. SpeakerCraft, 37%
3. Bowers & Wilkins, 29%
4. Triad, 22%
5. Klipsch, 21%

Source: *CE Pro*, Brand Analysis (annual), June 2011, p. 56.

194 ■ TOP BRANDS OF AUDIO PREAMPLIFIERS AND PROCESSORS, 2010

Ranked by: Popularity among *CE Pro 100* companies, in percent. **Number listed:** 5

1. Integra, with 45%
2. Marantz, 19%
3. Rotel, 17%
4. Anthem, 15%
5. McIntosh, 13%

Source: *CE Pro*, Brand Analysis (annual), June 2011, p. 56.

195 ■ TOP BRANDS OF AUDIO/VIDEO RECEIVERS, 2010

Ranked by: Popularity among *CE Pro 100* companies, in percent. **Number listed:** 5

1. Integra, with 61%
2. Marantz, 27%
3. Denon, 24%
4. Sony, 21%
5. Yamaha, 16%

Source: *CE Pro*, Brand Analysis (annual), June 2011, p. 56.

196 ■ TOP BRANDS OF AUDIO/VIDEO SOURCES, 2010

Ranked by: Popularity among *CE Pro 100* companies, in percent. **Number listed:** 6

1. AppleTV, with 25%
1. Sonos, 25%
3. Kaleidescape, 20%
4. Crestron, 19%
5. Sony, 18%
6. Control4, 14%

Source: *CE Pro*, Brand Analysis (annual), June 2011, p. 56.

197 ■ TOP BRANDS OF BLU-RAY DISC PLAYERS, 2010

Ranked by: Popularity among *CE Pro 100* companies, in percent.
Number listed: 5

1. Samsung, with 63%
2. Sony, 55%
3. Integra, 24%
4. LG, 17%
5. Panasonic, 13%

Source: *CE Pro*, Brand Analysis (annual), June 2011, p. 57.

198 ■ TOP BRANDS OF FLAT-PANEL TELEVISIONS, 2010

Ranked by: Popularity among *CE Pro 100* companies, in percent.
Number listed: 5

1. Samsung, with 81%
2. Sony, 57%
3. Panasonic, 34%
4. LG, 30%
5. Runco, 22%

Source: *CE Pro*, Brand Analysis (annual), June 2011, p. 57.

199 ■ TOP BRANDS OF FREESTANDING SPEAKERS, 2010

Ranked by: Popularity among *CE Pro 100* companies, in percent.
Number listed: 6

1. Bowers & Wilkins, with 30%
2. Klipsch, 23%
3. Paradigm, 22%
4. Triad, 12%
5. Monitor Audio, 11%
5. Revel, 11%

Source: *CE Pro*, Brand Analysis (annual), June 2011, p. 56.

200 ■ TOP BRANDS OF FRONT PROJECTORS, 2010

Ranked by: Popularity among *CE Pro 100* companies, in percent.
Number listed: 6

1. Runco, with 46%
2. Sony, 38%
3. Digital Projection, 34%
4. JVC, 30%
5. Epson, 24%
6. SIM2, 20%

Source: *CE Pro*, Brand Analysis (annual), June 2011, p. 57.

201 ■ TOP BRANDS OF HOME INFRARED (IR) DISTRIBUTION SYSTEMS, 2010

Ranked by: Popularity among *CE Pro 100* companies, in percent.
Number listed: 5

1. Xantech, with 30%
2. SpeakerCraft, 24%
3. Niles Audio, 21%
4. Sonance, 7%
5. Elan Home Systems, 6%

Source: *CE Pro*, Brand Analysis (annual), June 2011, p. 59.

202 ■ TOP BRANDS OF MEDIA SERVERS, 2010

Ranked by: Popularity among *CE Pro 100* companies, in percent.
Number listed: 5

1. Kaleidescape, with 59%
2. Apple, 31%
3. ReQuest, 19%
4. Crestron, 16%
5. Control4, 6%

Source: *CE Pro*, Brand Analysis (annual), June 2011, p. 56.

203 ■ TOP BRANDS OF OUTDOOR AUDIO/VIDEO SYSTEMS, 2010

Ranked by: Popularity among *CE Pro 100* companies, in percent.
Number listed: 5

1. SunBrite TV, with 33%
2. SpeakerCraft, 22%
3. Sonance, 21%
4. James, 17%
5. Klipsch, 12%

Source: *CE Pro*, Brand Analysis (annual), June 2011, p. 57.

204 ■ TOP BRANDS OF PROJECTION SCREENS, 2010

Ranked by: Popularity among *CE Pro 100* companies, in percent.
Number listed: 5

1. Stewart Filmscreen, with 78%
2. Da-Lite, 39%
3. Draper, 18%
4. Vutec, 16%
5. SnapAV, 10%

Source: *CE Pro*, Brand Analysis (annual), June 2011, p. 57.

205 ■ TOP BRANDS OF REMOTE CONTROLS/TABLETS, 2010

Ranked by: Popularity among *CE Pro 100* companies, in percent.
Number listed: 5

1. URC, with 79%
2. Crestron, 37%
3. Control4, 34%
4. RTI, 25%
5. Apple, 19%

Source: *CE Pro*, Brand Analysis (annual), June 2011, p. 59.

206 ■ TOP BRANDS OF SCALER/VIDEO PROCESSORS, 2010

Ranked by: Popularity among *CE Pro 100* companies, in percent.
Number listed: 5

1. Runco, with 14%
2. Crestron, 12%
3. DVDO, 8%
4. Key Digital, 7%
4. Lumagen, 7%

Source: *CE Pro*, Brand Analysis (annual), June 2011, p. 57.

207 ■ TOP BRANDS OF WHOLE-HOUSE AUDIO/VIDEO SYSTEMS, 2010

Ranked by: Popularity among *CE Pro 100* companies, in percent.
Number listed: 5

1. Crestron, with 61%
2. Control4, 46%

3. Savant, 17%

4. Niles Audio, 16%

5. Sonos, 15%

Source: *CE Pro*, Brand Analysis (annual), June 2011, p. 56.

Auditing

208 ■ COUNTRIES WITH THE BEST FINANCIAL AUDITING AND REPORTING STANDARDS, 2010

Ranked by: Score, on a scale of seven, based on financial auditing and reporting standards regarding company financial performance. **Number listed:** 142

1. South Africa, with 6.5 points

2. Sweden, 6.3

3. Singapore, 6.2

3. Canada, 6.2

5. New Zealand, 6.1

5. Bahrain, 6.1

5. Finland, 6.1

8. Qatar, 6.0

8. Norway, 6.0

8. Malta, 6.0

Source: *Global Competitiveness Report*, (annual), World Economic Forum, 2011, p. 407.

209 ■ COUNTRIES WITH THE WORST FINANCIAL AUDITING AND REPORTING STANDARDS, 2010

Ranked by: Score, on a scale of seven, based on financial auditing and reporting standards regarding company financial performance. **Number listed:** 142

1. Angola, with 2.6 points

2. Burundi, 2.7

3. Haiti, 3.0

4. Mauritania, 3.1

5. Timor-Leste, 3.2

5. Madagascar, 3.2

7. Benin, 3.3

7. Chad, 3.3

9. Cote d'Ivoire, 3.4

10. Ukraine, 3.5

10. Syria, 3.5

10. Kyrgyz Republic, 3.5

10. Algeria, 3.5

Source: *Global Competitiveness Report*, (annual), World Economic Forum, 2011, p. 407.

Auditing Services

210 ■ TOP AUDIT FIRMS FOR THE INSURANCE INDUSTRY, 2010

Ranked by: Net premiums written for clients, in thousands of dollars. **Remarks:** Also notes market share and number of clients. **Number listed:** 50

1. PricewaterhouseCoopers LLP, with $448,803,862 thousand

2. Deloitte & Touche LLP, $363,854,831

3. Ernst & Young LLP, $346,309,046

4. KPMG LLP, $248,891,150

5. McGladrey, $9,628,458

6. BDO LLP, $6,082,433

7. Eide Bailly LLP, $5,533,720

8. Baker Tilly Ltd., $3,727,214

9. Johnson Lambert & Co., LLP, $3,343,780

10. BKD LLP, $2,957,094

Source: *Best's Review*, Top Auditors & Actuaries (annual), January 2012, p. 45.

Authors

211 ■ MOST POWERFUL AUTHORS, 2011

Ranked by: Score based on earnings and such measures of popularity as Internet presence, press clippings, magazine cover stories, and mentions on television and radio. **Remarks:** Specific scores not provided. Also notes earnings. Ranking is available online only, not in print. **Number listed:** 4

1. James Patterson

2. Danielle Steel

3. Stephen King

4. Stephenie Meyer

Source: *Forbes*, The Celebrity 100 (annual), http://www.forbes.com, June 6, 2011.

Automobile Dealers

212 ■ LARGEST AUTOMOTIVE DEALERS AND GASOLINE SERVICE STATIONS BY EMPLOYEES, 2010

Ranked by: Total number of employees. **Remarks:** Also notes contact information for headquarters, number of employees at headquarters, revenue, rank by revenue, and primary SIC code. **Number listed:** 315

1. AutoZone Inc., with 63,000 employees

2. Advance Auto Parts Inc., 49,000

3. O'Reilly Automotive Inc., 44,822

4. Mobil Corp., 41,500

5. Advance Stores Co., 30,000

5. ConocoPhillips Co., 30,000

7. Genuine Parts Co., 29,000

8. Shell Oil Co., 24,008

9. Diamond Shamrock Refining & Marketing Co., 21,000

10. BP Co. North America Inc., 20,000

Source: *Business Rankings*, (annual), Dun & Bradstreet Inc., 2011, p. VI.137-VI.143.

213 ■ LARGEST AUTOMOTIVE DEALERS AND GASOLINE SERVICE STATIONS BY SALES, 2010

Ranked by: Total revenue, in dollars. **Remarks:** Also notes contact information for headquarters, number of employees at headquarters and overall, rank by employees, and primary SIC code. **Number listed:** 319

1. Sunoco Inc., with $37,489,000,000

2. AutoNation Inc., $12,461,000,000

3. Genuine Parts Co., $11,207,589,000

4. Penske Automotive Group Inc., $10,713,585,000
5. CarMax Inc., $7,470,193,000
6. AutoZone Inc., $7,362,618,000
7. Pantry Inc., $7,265,262,000
8. Sonic Automotive Inc., $6,880,844,000
9. TravelCenters of America LLC, $5,962,481,000
10. Advance Auto Parts Inc., $5,925,203,000

Source: *Business Rankings*, (annual), Dun & Bradstreet Inc., 2011, p. V.137-V.143.

214 ■ TOP AUTOMOBILE DEALER GROUPS IN THE U.S., 2011

Ranked by: Number of new retail vehicles sold. **Remarks:** Also notes contact information, top executive, number of used and fleet vehicles sold, total units sold, number of dealerships, group revenue, and rank for previous year. **Number listed:** 125

1. AutoNation Inc., with 224,034 vehicles
2. Penske Automotive Group Inc., 154,829
3. Sonic Automotive Inc., 114,132
4. Group 1 Automotive Inc., 102,022
5. Van Tuyl Group, 96,139
6. Hendrick Automotive Group, 69,676
7. Asbury Automotive Group Inc., 68,770
8. Staluppi Auto Group, 54,225
9. Lithia Motors Inc., 44,537
10. Larry H. Miller Group of Cos., 30,865

Source: *Automotive News*, Top 125 Dealership Groups (annual), March 19, 2012, p. insert.

215 ■ TOP DEALERS OF NEW VEHICLES BY DOLLAR SALES, 2009

Ranked by: Sales of new vehicles, in dollars. **Number listed:** 20

1. Fletcher Jones Motorcars, with $256,845,316
2. Dave Smith Motors, $195,283,721
3. Braman Motorcars, $190,243,824
4. Braman Motors, $185,534,125
5. Ancira Enterprises Inc., $171,786,597
6. Crevier BMW, $148,889,695
7. Classic Chevrolet Ltd., $144,429,731
8. Ray Catena Motorcars, $137,643,266
9. Fred Haas Toyota World, $137,418,069
10. South Bay BMW/Mini, $125,297,231

Source: *Ward's Automotive Yearbook*, (annual), 2011, p. 193.

216 ■ TOP DEALERS OF NEW VEHICLES BY PERCENT-AGE, 2009

Ranked by: New vehicles revenue as a percentage of total revenue. **Number listed:** 20

1. Atlantic Nissan, with 79.3%
2. Round Rock Honda, 78.1%
3. Ray Catena Lexus of Monmouth, 78
4. Galpin Honda, 77.5%
5. Atlantic Honda, 77.4%
6. Atlantic Hyundai, 77.1%
7. Suburban Chrysler Jeep Dodge Inc., 76.8%
8. Dave Smith Motors, 76.3%
9. Moroone Honda Hollywood, 75.6%
10. Suburban Imports of Troy, 75.5%
10. Royal Palm Toyota/Scion, 75.5%

Source: *Ward's Automotive Yearbook*, (annual), 2011, p. 193.

217 ■ TOP DEALERS OF NEW VEHICLES BY UNITS SOLD, 2009

Ranked by: Number of new vehicles sold. **Number listed:** 20

1. Ancira Enterprises Inc., with 5,837 units sold
2. Fred Haas Toyota World, 5,425
3. Dave Smith Motors, 5,124
4. Rick Case Honda, 4,699
5. Fletcher Jones Motorcars, 4,476
6. Classic Chevrolet Ltd., 4,181
7. Koons Tysons Toyota, 4,114
8. Galpin Ford, 4,055
9. Al Serra Auto Plaza, 4,035
10. Power Toyota Cerritos, 3,928

Source: *Ward's Automotive Yearbook*, (annual), 2011, p. 193.

218 ■ TOP DEALERS OF USED VEHICLES BY DOLLAR SALES, 2009

Ranked by: Sales of used vehicles, in dollars. **Number listed:** 20

1. Fletcher Jones Motorcars, with $73,216,468
2. Global Imports, $67,659,734
3. Braman Motorcars, $65,498,298
4. Ancira Enterprises Inc., $65,262,002
5. Momentum BMW/Mini, $63,128,910
6. Crevier BMW, $59,463,858
7. C & O Motors Inc., $56,055,655
8. Wilde Toyota, $54,865,341
9. Jack Maxton Chevrolet, $53,214,868
10. Momentum Jaguar Volvo, $52,136,551

Source: *Ward's Automotive Yearbook*, (annual), 2011, p. 193.

219 ■ TOP DEALERS OF USED VEHICLES BY PERCENT-AGE, 2009

Ranked by: Used vehicles revenue as a percentage of total revenue. **Number listed:** 20

1. Bonham Chrysler, with 55.4%
2. Jack Maxton Chevrolet, 48.4%
3. John L. Sullivan Chevrolet, 43%
4. Momentum BMW West, 42.7%
5. Harold Zeigler Lincoln Mercury BMW, 41.3%
6. United BMW Roswell, 40.6%
7. United BMW Gwinnett, 39.5%
8. Chrysler Jeep Dodge Bellevue, 39.1%
9. C & O Motors Inc., 38.9%
10. Roseville Toyota, 38%

Source: *Ward's Automotive Yearbook*, (annual), 2011, p. 193.

220 ■ TOP DEALERS OF USED VEHICLES BY UNITS SOLD, 2009

Ranked by: Number of used vehicles sold. **Number listed:** 20

1. Ancira Enterprises Inc., with 4,351 units sold

2. Wilde Toyota, 4,128
3. Jack Maxton Chevrolet, 3,989
4. C & O Motors Inc., 3,864
5. Rick Case Honda, 3,511
6. Al Serra Auto Plaza, 3,212
7. Joe Myers Toyota, 3,174
8. Bonham Chrysler, 2,845
9. Roseville Toyota, 2,786
10. Fred Haas Toyota World, 2,574

Source: *Ward's Automotive Yearbook*, (annual), 2011, p. 193.

Automobile Industry

221 ■ LARGEST U.S. AUTO AND TRUCK MANUFACTURERS OVERALL, 2011

Ranked by: Score based on revenue, profits, assets, and market capitalization. **Remarks:** Specific scores not provided. Also notes overall rank in the *Forbes 2000* and figures for each criterion. **Number listed:** 2

1. Ford Motor Co.
2. General Motors Co.

Source: *Forbes*, Forbes 2000 (annual), http://www.forbes.com, May 7, 2012.

222 ■ LARGEST U.S. MOTOR VEHICLE MANUFACTURERS, 2010

Ranked by: Revenue, in millions of dollars. **Remarks:** Also notes overall rank within the *IW 500,* revenue growth, and profit margin. **Number listed:** 7

1. General Motors Co., with $135,592 million
2. Ford Motor Co., $128,954
3. Navistar International Corp., $12,145
4. Paccar Inc., $9,871
5. Oshkosh Corp., $9,842
6. Harley-Davidson Inc., $4,859
7. Thor Industries Inc., $2,277

Source: *IndustryWeek*, IW 500 (annual), http://www.industryweek.com, July 2011.

223 ■ MICHIGAN'S LARGEST AUTO AND TRUCK MANUFACTURERS OVERALL, 2011

Ranked by: Score based on revenue, profits, assets, and market capitalization. **Remarks:** Specific scores not provided. Also notes overall rank in the *Forbes 2000* and figures for each criterion. **Number listed:** 2

1. Ford Motor Co.
2. General Motors Co.

Source: *Forbes*, Forbes 2000 (annual), http://www.forbes.com, May 7, 2012.

224 ■ MOST VALUABLE U.S. AUTOMOBILE AND PARTS COMPANIES, 2011

Ranked by: Market value as of March 2011, in millions of U.S. dollars. **Remarks:** Also notes rank within the *FT U.S. 500*, rank for previous year, country, revenue, net income, assets, number of employees, share price, price-to-earning ratio, dividend yield, and fiscal yearend. **Number listed:** 8

1. Ford Motor Co., with $56,400.2 million

2. General Motors Co., $48,429.8
3. Johnson Controls Inc., $28,157.3
4. Harley-Davidson Inc., $9,990.7
5. BorgWarner Inc., $8,907.1
6. Genuine Parts Co., $8,456.7
7. TRW Automotive Holdings Corp., $6,806.1
8. Autoliv Inc., $5,617.8

Source: *Financial Times*, FT 500 (annual), http://www.ft.com, June 24, 2011.

225 ■ TOP AUTOMAKERS BY MARKET SHARE, 2010

Ranked by: Market share, in percent. **Remarks:** Also notes figures for previous year and advertising expenditures for current and previous year. **Number listed:** 10

1. General Motors Co., with 19.1%
2. Ford Motor Co., 16.9%
3. Toyota Motor Corp., 15.2%
4. Honda Motor Co., Ltd., 10.6%
5. Fiat, 9.4%
6. Nissan Motor Co., Ltd., 7.8%
7. Hyundai Motor Co., 4.6%
8. Volkswagen AG, 3.11%
9. Kia Motors Corp., 3.07%
10. Bayerische Motoren Werke AG (BMW), 2.3%

Source: *Advertising Age*, Leading National Advertisers (annual), June 20, 2011, p. 20.

226 ■ TOP *FORTUNE 500* COMPANIES IN AUTOMOTIVE RETAILING/SERVICES, 2011

Ranked by: Revenue, in millions of dollars. **Remarks:** Also notes overall rank in the *Fortune 500;* profits; profits as a percentage of revenue; stockholders' equity; and rank by each criterion. **Number listed:** 7

1. AutoNation Inc., with $13,832 million
2. Penske Automotive Group Inc., $11,870
3. CarMax Inc., $9,402
4. Hertz Global Holdings Inc., $8,298
5. Sonic Automotive Inc., $7,871
6. Group 1 Automotive Inc., $6,080
7. Avis Budget Group Inc., $5,900

Source: *Fortune*, Fortune 500 (annual), May 21, 2012, p. F-33-F-34.

227 ■ TOP *FORTUNE 500* COMPANIES IN MOTOR VEHICLES AND PARTS, 2011

Ranked by: Revenue, in millions of dollars. **Remarks:** Also notes overall rank in the *Fortune 500;* profits; profits as a percentage of revenue; stockholders' equity; and rank by each criterion. **Number listed:** 16

1. General Motors Co., with $150,276 million
2. Ford Motor Co., $136,264
3. Johnson Controls Inc., $40,833
4. Goodyear Tire & Rubber Co., $22,767
5. Paccar Inc., $16,355
6. TRW Automotive Holdings Corp., $16,244
7. Lear Corp., $14,157
8. Navistar International Corp., $13,958
9. Icahn Enterprises, $11,855

10. Autoliv Inc., $8,232

Source: *Fortune*, Fortune 500 (annual), May 21, 2012, p. F-38.

228 ■ TOP MISCELLANEOUS AUTO PRODUCTS AND SERVICES FRANCHISES, 2012

Ranked by: Cumulative score based on financial strength and stability, growth rate, size of the system, number of years in business, the length of time franchising, start-up costs, litigation, percentage of terminations, and whether the company provides financing. **Remarks:** Specific scores not provided. Also notes overall rank within the *Franchise 500*, contact information, description, year founded, year started franchising, states where registered, available U.S. regions, where seeking foreign expansion, number of franchised and company-owned units for past three years, start-up costs, franchise fees, royalty fees, and type of financing available. **Number listed:** 5

1. Line-X Franchise Development Co.
2. J. D. Byrider.
3. Mighty Distribution System of America
4. RimTyme
5. Mr. Clean Carwash

Source: *Entrepreneur*, Franchise 500 (annual), January 2012, p. 148-149.

229 ■ THE UNITED STATES' MOST VALUABLE AUTOMOBILE MANUFACTURING BRANDS, 2011

Ranked by: Brand value, in millions of U.S. dollars. **Remarks:** Also notes rank within the *Global 500* for current and previous year, figures for current and previous year, and brand rating. Ranking is available online only. **Number listed:** 5

1. Ford, with $17,559 million
2. Chevrolet, $4,789
3. General Motors, $3,888
4. GMC, $3,209
5. Vauxhall, $2,485

Source: *Global 500*, (annual), Brand Finance plc, March 2012.

Automobile Industry, International

230 ■ CHINA'S LARGEST AUTO AND TRUCK MANUFACTURERS OVERALL, 2011

Ranked by: Score based on revenue, profits, assets, and market capitalization. **Remarks:** Specific scores not provided. Also notes overall rank in the *Forbes 2000* and figures for each criterion. **Number listed:** 6

1. SAIC Motor
2. Dongfeng Motor
3. Guangzhou Automobile
4. BYD
5. Great Wall Motor
6. Huayu Automotive

Source: *Forbes*, Forbes 2000 (annual), http://www.forbes.com, May 7, 2012.

231 ■ EUROPE'S MOST VALUABLE AUTOMOBILE AND PARTS COMPANIES, 2011

Ranked by: Market value as of March 2011, in millions of U.S. dollars. **Remarks:** Also notes rank within the *FT Europe 500*, rank for previous year, country, revenue, net income, assets, number of employees, share price, price-to-earning ratio, dividend yield, and fiscal yearend. **Number listed:** 12

1. Daimler AG, with $75,385.2 million
2. Volkswagen AG, $72,978.5
3. Bayerische Motoren Werke AG (BMW), $53,188.5
4. Continental AG, $18,130.8
5. Renault SA, $16,370.8
6. Compagnie Generale des Etablissements Michelin, $14,937.1
7. Fiat SpA, $11,265.5
8. Porsche Holding GmbH, $10,060.9
9. Peugeot SA, $9,260
10. Nokian Renkaat Holding Oy, $5,490.9

Source: *Financial Times*, FT 500 (annual), http://www.ft.com, June 24, 2011.

232 ■ FRANCE'S LARGEST AUTO AND TRUCK MANUFACTURERS OVERALL, 2011

Ranked by: Score based on revenue, profits, assets, and market capitalization. **Remarks:** Specific scores not provided. Also notes overall rank in the *Forbes 2000* and figures for each criterion. **Number listed:** 2

1. Renault SA
2. Peugeot SA

Source: *Forbes*, Forbes 2000 (annual), http://www.forbes.com, May 7, 2012.

233 ■ FRANCE'S MOST VALUABLE AUTOMOBILE MANUFACTURING BRANDS, 2011

Ranked by: Brand value, in millions of U.S. dollars. **Remarks:** Also notes rank within the *Global 500* for current and previous year, figures for current and previous year, and brand rating. Ranking is available online only. **Number listed:** 3

1. Renault, with $8,064 million
2. Peugeot, $7,976
3. Citroen, $4,175

Source: *Global 500*, (annual), Brand Finance plc, March 2012.

234 ■ GERMANY'S LARGEST AUTO AND TRUCK MANUFACTURERS OVERALL, 2011

Ranked by: Score based on revenue, profits, assets, and market capitalization. **Remarks:** Specific scores not provided. Also notes overall rank in the *Forbes 2000* and figures for each criterion. **Number listed:** 4

1. Volkswagen AG
2. Daimler AG
3. Bayerische Motoren Werke AG (BMW)
4. Porsche Automobil Holding SE

Source: *Forbes*, Forbes 2000 (annual), http://www.forbes.com, May 7, 2012.

235 ■ GERMANY'S MOST VALUABLE AUTOMOBILE MANUFACTURING BRANDS, 2011

Ranked by: Brand value, in millions of U.S. dollars. **Remarks:** Also notes rank within the *Global 500* for current and previous year, figures for current and previous year, and brand rating. Ranking is available online only. **Number listed:** 7

1. BMW, with $21,262 million
2. Mercedes-Benz, $19,762
3. Volkswagen, $17,758

4. Audi, $4,561

5. Daimler, $4,003

6. Skoda, $3,580

7. MINI, $2,654

Source: *Global 500*, (annual), Brand Finance plc, March 2012.

236 ■ INDIA'S LARGEST AUTO AND TRUCK MANUFACTURERS OVERALL, 2011

Ranked by: Score based on revenue, profits, assets, and market capitalization. **Remarks:** Specific scores not provided. Also notes overall rank in the *Forbes 2000* and figures for each criterion. **Number listed:** 2

1. Tata Motors Ltd.

2. Mahindra & Mahindra

Source: *Forbes*, Forbes 2000 (annual), http://www.forbes.com, May 7, 2012.

237 ■ JAPAN'S LARGEST AUTO AND TRUCK MANUFACTURERS OVERALL, 2011

Ranked by: Score based on revenue, profits, assets, and market capitalization. **Remarks:** Specific scores not provided. Also notes overall rank in the *Forbes 2000* and figures for each criterion. **Number listed:** 8

1. Toyota Motor Corp.

2. Honda Motor Co., Ltd.

3. Nissan Motor Co., Ltd.

4. Suzuki Motor Corp.

5. Isuzu Motors Ltd.

6. Fuji Heavy Industries Ltd.

7. Mitsubishi Motors Corp.

8. Mazda Motor Corp.

Source: *Forbes*, Forbes 2000 (annual), http://www.forbes.com, May 7, 2012.

238 ■ JAPAN'S MOST VALUABLE AUTOMOBILE MANUFACTURING BRANDS, 2011

Ranked by: Brand value, in millions of U.S. dollars. **Remarks:** Also notes rank within the *Global 500* for current and previous year, figures for current and previous year, and brand rating. Ranking is available online only. **Number listed:** 8

1. Toyota, with $24,461 million

2. Honda, $14,963

3. Nissan, $14,167

4. Suzuki, $4,433

5. Mazda, $3,325

6. Lexus, $2,725

7. Subaru, $2,566

8. Isuzu, $2,431

Source: *Global 500*, (annual), Brand Finance plc, March 2012.

239 ■ LARGEST AUTOMOTIVE AND TRANSPORT COMPANIES IN EUROPE, 2010

Ranked by: Sales, in millions of U.S. dollars. **Remarks:** Also notes rank within country. **Number listed:** 100

1. Volkswagen AG (Germany), with $145,890.5 million

2. Daimler AG (Germany), $117,375.8

3. Peugeot Citroen Automobile SA (France), $75,993.4

4. Bayerische Motoren Werke AG (BMW, Germany), $75,372.8

5. Robert Bosch GmbH (Germany), $56,772.4

6. Audi AG (Germany), $44,378

7. Renault SA (France), $38,740.3

8. AB Volvo (Sweden), $31,138.3

9. Continental AG (Germany), $29,886.3

10. Fiat Group Automobiles SpA (Italy), $27,357.5

Source: *Europe's 15,000 Largest Companies*, (annual), ELC International, 2011, p. 36.

240 ■ SOUTH KOREA'S LARGEST AUTOMOBILE AND TRUCK MANUFACTURERS OVERALL, 2011

Ranked by: Score based on revenue, profits, assets, and market capitalization. **Remarks:** Specific scores not provided. Also notes overall rank in the *Forbes 2000* and figures for each criterion. **Number listed:** 2

1. Hyundai Motor Co.

2. Kia Motors Corp.

Source: *Forbes*, Forbes 2000 (annual), http://www.forbes.com, May 7, 2012.

241 ■ SOUTH KOREA'S MOST VALUABLE AUTOMOBILE MANUFACTURING BRANDS, 2011

Ranked by: Brand value, in millions of U.S. dollars. **Remarks:** Also notes rank within the *Global 500* for current and previous year, figures for current and previous year, and brand rating. Ranking is available online only. **Number listed:** 2

1. Hyundai, with $13,098 million

2. Kia, $5,089

Source: *Global 500*, (annual), Brand Finance plc, March 2012.

242 ■ TOP CANADIAN AUTOMOTIVE COMPANIES, 2010

Ranked by: Revenue, in thousands of Canadian dollars (unless otherwise noted). **Remarks:** Also notes percent change from previous year. **Number listed:** 8

1. Magna International Inc. (U.S. dollars), with C$24,157,000 thousand

2. Ford Motor Co. of Canada (U.S. dollars), C$9,351,000

3. Honda Canada, C$8,646,000

4. Lear Canada (U.S. dollars), C$238,600

5. Wescast Industries, C$263,704

6. CVTech Group, C$260,013

7. Zongshen PEM Power Systems, C$142,587

8. Azure Dynamics, C$22,734

Source: *Report on Business Magazine*, Top 1000 Companies (annual), http://www.reportonbusiness.com, June 2011.

243 ■ WORLD'S LARGEST AUTO AND TRUCK MANUFACTURERS OVERALL, 2011

Ranked by: Score based on revenue, profits, assets, and market capitalization. **Remarks:** Specific scores not provided. Also notes country, overall rank in the *Forbes 2000*, and figures for each criterion. **Number listed:** 27

1. Volkswagen AG

2. Toyota Motor Corp.

3. Daimler AG

4. Ford Motor Co.

5. Honda Motor Co., Ltd.
6. Bayerische Motoren Werke AG (BMW)
7. General Motors Co.
8. Nissan Motor Co., Ltd.
9. Hyundai Motor Co.
10. Renault SA

Source: *Forbes*, Forbes 2000 (annual), http://www.forbes.com, May 7, 2012.

244 ■ WORLD'S LARGEST MOTOR VEHICLE MANUFACTURERS, 2010

Ranked by: Revenue, in millions of dollars. **Remarks:** Also notes rank for previous year, overall rank within the *IW 1000*, country, and revenue growth. **Number listed:** 38

1. Toyota Motor Corp., with $233,099 million
2. Volkswagen AG, $169,710
3. General Motors Co., $135,592
4. Daimler AG, $130,766
5. Ford Motor Co., $128,954
6. Honda Motor Co., Ltd., $105,525
7. Hyundai Motor Co., $101,332
8. Nissan Motor Co., Ltd., $92,463
9. Bayerische Motoren Werke AG (BMW), $81,168
10. Peugeot SA, $75,413

Source: *IndustryWeek*, IW 1000 (annual), http://www.industryweek.com, August 2011.

245 ■ WORLD'S MOST ADMIRED MOTOR VEHICLES COMPANIES, 2012

Ranked by: Score, on a scale of 10, based on a survey of executives, directors, and securities analysts of companies within their own industry on eight criteria: innovation, financial soundness, employee talent, use of corporate assets, long-term investment value, social responsibility, quality of management, and quality of products/services. **Remarks:** Specific scores not provided. Also notes rank for previous year. **Number listed:** 7

1. Volkswagen AG
2. Bayerische Motoren Werke AG (BMW)
3. Daimler AG
4. Toyota Motor Corp.
5. Ford Motor Co.
6. Hyundai Motor Co.
7. General Motors Co.

Source: *Fortune*, World's Most Admired Companies (annual), March 19, 2012, p. 150.

246 ■ WORLD'S MOST ETHICAL AUTOMOTIVE COMPANIES, 2012

Ranked by: Score based on five criteria: ethics and compliance program; reputation, leadership, and innovation; governance; corporate citizenship and responsibility; and culture of ethics. **Remarks:** Specific scores not provided; companies are listed alphabetically, not ranked. **Number listed:** 3

1. Cummins Inc. (U.S.)
2. Ford Motor Co. (U.S.)
3. Johnson Controls Inc. (U.S.)

Source: *Ethisphere Magazine*, World's Most Ethical Companies (annual), http://www.ethisphere.com, 2012.

247 ■ WORLD'S MOST VALUABLE AUTO MANUFACTURING BRANDS, 2011

Ranked by: Brand value, in millions of U.S. dollars. **Remarks:** Also notes rank within the *Global 500* for current and previous year, figures for current and previous year, country, and brand rating. Ranking is available online only. **Number listed:** 27

1. Toyota, with $24,461 million
2. BMW, $21,262
3. Mercedes-Benz, $19,762
4. Volkswagen, $17,758
5. Ford, $17,559
6. Honda, $14,963
7. Nissan, $14,167
8. Hyundai, $13,098
9. Renault, $8,064
10. Peugeot, $7,976

Source: *Global 500*, (annual), Brand Finance plc, March 2012.

248 ■ WORLD'S MOST VALUABLE AUTOMOBILE AND PARTS COMPANIES, 2011

Ranked by: Market value as of March 2011, in millions of U.S. dollars. **Remarks:** Also notes rank within the *FT 500*, rank for previous year, country, revenue, net income, assets, number of employees, share price, price-to-earning ratio, dividend yield, and fiscal year-end. **Number listed:** 15

1. Toyota Motor Corp., with $139,367.4 million
2. Daimler AG, $75,385.2
3. Volkswagen AG, $72,978.5
4. Honda Motor Co., Ltd., $68,300.1
5. Ford Motor Co., $56,400.2
6. Bayerische Motoren Werke AG (BMW), $53,188.5
7. General Motors Co., $48,429.8
8. Hyundai Motor Co., $40,764
9. Nissan Motor Co., Ltd., $40,254.4
10. Denso Corp., $29,440.5

Source: *Financial Times*, FT 500 (annual), http://www.ft.com, June 24, 2011.

249 ■ WORLD'S MOST VALUABLE CAR BRANDS, 2012

Ranked by: Brand value, a measure of a brand's earnings and contribution, in millions of U.S. dollars. **Remarks:** Also notes annual growth in brand value and rank by brand contribution and brand momentum. **Number listed:** 10

1. BMW, with $24,623 million
2. Toyota, $21,779
3. Mercedes-Benz, $16,111
4. Honda, $12,647
5. Nissan, $6,853
6. Volkswagen, $8,519
7. Ford, $7,025
8. Audi, $4,703
9. Hyundai, $3,598
10. Lexus, $3,392

Source: *Financial Times*, Global Brands (annual), http://www.ft.com, May 22, 2012.

Automobile Leasing and Renting

250 ■ LARGEST U.S. RENTAL AND LEASING COMPANIES OVERALL, 2011

Ranked by: Score based on revenue, profits, assets, and market capitalization. **Remarks:** Specific scores not provided. Also notes overall rank in the *Forbes 2000* and figures for each criterion. **Number listed:** 2

1. Hertz Global Holdings Inc.
2. Avis Budget Group Inc.

Source: *Forbes*, Forbes 2000 (annual), http://www.forbes.com, May 7, 2012.

251 ■ NEW JERSEY'S LARGEST RENTAL AND LEASING COMPANIES OVERALL, 2011

Ranked by: Score based on revenue, profits, assets, and market capitalization. **Remarks:** Specific scores not provided. Also notes overall rank in the *Forbes 2000* and figures for each criterion. **Number listed:** 2

1. Hertz Global Holdings Inc.
2. Avis Budget Group Inc.

Source: *Forbes*, Forbes 2000 (annual), http://www.forbes.com, May 7, 2012.

252 ■ WORLD'S TOP CAR RENTAL AGENCIES, 2011

Ranked by: Score, on a scale of 100, based on consumer survey regarding vehicle selection, vehicle availability, rental location, service, and value. **Number listed:** 10

1. ZipCar, with 82.05 points
2. Hertz, 80.18
3. Auto Europe, 79.43
4. National Car Rental, 78.45
5. Enterprise Rent-A-Car, 78.25
6. Sixt, 77.04
7. Avis, 76.40
8. Alamo Rent a Car, 75.26
9. Budget Rent a Car, 73.18
10. Europcar, 72.32

Source: *Travel + Leisure*, World's Best Awards (annual), August 2011.

Automobile Parts

253 ■ FRANCE'S LARGEST AUTO AND TRUCK PARTS COMPANIES OVERALL, 2011

Ranked by: Score based on revenue, profits, assets, and market capitalization. **Remarks:** Specific scores not provided. Also notes overall rank in the *Forbes 2000* and figures for each criterion. **Number listed:** 2

1. Compagnie Generale des Etablissements Michelin
2. Valeo SA

Source: *Forbes*, Forbes 2000 (annual), http://www.forbes.com, May 7, 2012.

254 ■ JAPAN'S LARGEST AUTO AND TRUCK PARTS COMPANIES OVERALL, 2011

Ranked by: Score based on revenue, profits, assets, and market capitalization. **Remarks:** Specific scores not provided. Also notes overall rank in the *Forbes 2000* and figures for each criterion. **Number listed:** 8

1. Denso Corp.
2. Bridgestone Corp.
3. Sumitomo Electric Industries Ltd.
4. Aisin Seiki Co., Ltd.
5. Toyota Industries Corp.
6. Sumitomo Rubber Industries Ltd.
7. JTEKT Corp.
8. Toyota Boshoku Corp.

Source: *Forbes*, Forbes 2000 (annual), http://www.forbes.com, May 7, 2012.

255 ■ JAPAN'S MOST VALUABLE AUTOMOBILE PARTS AND EQUIPMENT BRANDS, 2011

Ranked by: Brand value, in millions of U.S. dollars. **Remarks:** Also notes rank within the *Global 500* for current and previous year, figures for current and previous year, and brand rating. Ranking is available online only. **Number listed:** 2

1. Sumitomo, with $8,881 million
2. Bridgestone, $4,397

Source: *Global 500*, (annual), Brand Finance plc, March 2012.

256 ■ LARGEST U.S. AUTO AND TRUCK PARTS COMPANIES OVERALL, 2011

Ranked by: Score based on revenue, profits, assets, and market capitalization. **Remarks:** Specific scores not provided. Also notes overall rank in the *Forbes 2000* and figures for each criterion. **Number listed:** 5

1. Johnson Controls Inc.
2. TRW Automotive Holdings Corp.
3. Goodyear Tire & Rubber Co.
4. BorgWarner Inc.
5. Lear Corp.

Source: *Forbes*, Forbes 2000 (annual), http://www.forbes.com, May 7, 2012.

257 ■ LARGEST U.S. MOTOR VEHICLE PARTS MANUFACTURERS, 2010

Ranked by: Revenue, in millions of dollars. **Remarks:** Also notes overall rank within the *IW 500*, revenue growth, and profit margin. **Number listed:** 12

1. Johnson Controls Inc., with $34,305 million
2. TRW Automotive Holdings Corp., $14,383
3. Cummins Inc., $13,226
4. Lear Corp., $11,955
5. Visteon Corp., $6,685
6. Dana Holding Corp., $6,109
7. Tenneco Inc., $5,937
8. BorgWarner Inc., $5,653
9. Meritor Inc., $3,590
10. American Axle & Manufacturing Holdings Inc., $2,283

Source: *IndustryWeek*, IW 500 (annual), http://www.industryweek.com, July 2011.

258 ■ MICHIGAN'S LARGEST AUTO AND TRUCK PARTS COMPANIES OVERALL, 2011

Ranked by: Score based on revenue, profits, assets, and market capitalization. **Remarks:** Specific scores not provided. Also notes overall rank in the *Forbes 2000* and figures for each criterion. **Number listed:** 3

1. TRW Automotive Holdings Corp.
2. BorgWarner Inc.
3. Lear Corp.

Source: *Forbes*, Forbes 2000 (annual), http://www.forbes.com, May 7, 2012.

259 ■ SOUTH KOREA'S LARGEST AUTOMOBILE AND TRUCK PARTS COMPANIES OVERALL, 2011

Ranked by: Score based on revenue, profits, assets, and market capitalization. **Remarks:** Specific scores not provided. Also notes overall rank in the *Forbes 2000* and figures for each criterion. **Number listed:** 2

1. Hyundai Mobis Co., Ltd.
2. Hankook Tire Co., Ltd.

Source: *Forbes*, Forbes 2000 (annual), http://www.forbes.com, May 7, 2012.

260 ■ TOP OEM PARTS SUPPLIERS TO NORTH AMERICA, 2011

Ranked by: Total North American OEM automotive parts sales, in millions of U.S. dollars. **Remarks:** Also notes rank and figures for previous year. **Number listed:** 50

1. Magna International Inc., with $14,716 million
2. Johnson Controls Inc., $7,874
3. Continental AG, $5,799
4. Robert Bosch LLC, $5,565
5. Denso International America Inc., $5,464
6. Delphi Holding LLP, $5,133
7. Lear Corp., $4,955
8. Faurecia, $4,725
9. TRW Automotive Inc., $4,621
10. Cummins, $4,136

Source: *Automotive News*, Top OEM Parts Suppliers to North America (annual), May 21, 2012, p. 19.

261 ■ UNITED KINGDOM'S LARGEST AUTOMOBILE AND TRUCK PARTS COMPANIES OVERALL, 2011

Ranked by: Score based on revenue, profits, assets, and market capitalization. **Remarks:** Specific scores not provided. Also notes country, overall rank in the *Forbes 2000,* and figures for each criterion. **Number listed:** 2

1. Delphi Automotive plc
2. GKN plc

Source: *Forbes*, Forbes 2000 (annual), http://www.forbes.com, May 7, 2012.

262 ■ THE UNITED STATES' MOST VALUABLE AUTOMOBILE PARTS AND EQUIPMENT BRANDS, 2011

Ranked by: Brand value, in millions of U.S. dollars. **Remarks:** Also notes rank within the *Global 500* for current and previous year, figures for current and previous year, and brand rating. Ranking is available online only. **Number listed:** 2

1. Johnson Controls, with $3,748 million
2. Goodyear, $2,691

Source: *Global 500*, (annual), Brand Finance plc, March 2012.

263 ■ WORLD'S LARGEST AUTO AND TRUCK PARTS COMPANIES OVERALL, 2011

Ranked by: Score based on revenue, profits, assets, and market capitalization. **Remarks:** Specific scores not provided. Also notes country, overall rank in the *Forbes 2000,* and figures for each criterion. **Number listed:** 24

1. Denso Corp.
2. Johnson Controls Inc.
3. Continental AG
4. Bridgestone Corp.
5. Hyundai Mobis
6. Compagnie Generale des Etablissements Michelin
7. Sumitomo Electric Industries Ltd.
8. Aisin Seiki Co., Ltd.
9. Magna International Inc.
10. Toyota Industries Corp.

Source: *Forbes*, Forbes 2000 (annual), http://www.forbes.com, May 7, 2012.

264 ■ WORLD'S LARGEST MOTOR VEHICLE PARTS MANUFACTURERS, 2010

Ranked by: Revenue, in millions of dollars. **Remarks:** Also notes rank for previous year, overall rank within the *IW 1000,* country, and revenue growth. **Number listed:** 34

1. Denso Corp., with $36,614 million
2. Johnson Controls Inc., $34,305
3. Aisin Seiki Co., Ltd., $25,270
4. Magna International Inc., $24,102
5. Faurecia SA, $18,454
6. TRW Automotive Holdings Corp., $14,383
7. Cummins Inc., $13,226
8. Valeo SA, $12,884
9. Lear Corp., $11,955
10. Toyota Boshoku Corp., $11,731

Source: *IndustryWeek*, IW 1000 (annual), http://www.industryweek.com, August 2011.

265 ■ WORLD'S MOST ADMIRED MOTOR VEHICLE PARTS COMPANIES, 2012

Ranked by: Score, on a scale of 10, based on a survey of executives, directors, and securities analysts of companies within their own industry on eight criteria: innovation, financial soundness, employee talent, use of corporate assets, long-term investment value, social responsibility, quality of management, and quality of products/services. **Remarks:** Specific scores not provided. Also notes rank for previous year. **Number listed:** 8

1. Robert Bosch GmbH
2. Johnson Controls Inc.
3. Toyota Industries Corp.
4. Compagnie Generale des Etablissements Michelin
5. Navistar International Corp.
6. Bridgestone Corp.
7. Goodyear Tire & Rubber Co.
8. Denso Corp.

Source: *Fortune*, World's Most Admired Companies (annual), March 19, 2012, p. 150.

266 ■ WORLD'S MOST VALUABLE AUTOMOBILE PARTS AND EQUIPMENT BRANDS, 2011

Ranked by: Brand value, in millions of U.S. dollars. **Remarks:** Also notes rank within the *Global 500* for current and previous year, figures for current and previous year, country, and brand rating. Ranking is available online only. **Number listed:** 6

1. Sumitomo, with $8,881 million
2. Bridgestone, $4,397
3. Michelin, $3,886
4. Johnson Controls, $3,748
5. Continental, $3,118
6. Goodyear, $2,691

Source: *Global 500*, (annual), Brand Finance plc, March 2012.

Automobile Racing

267 ■ HIGHEST-PAID NASCAR DRIVERS, 2011

Ranked by: Earnings, in millions of dollars. **Remarks:** Also notes team name and comments. **Number listed:** 10

1. Dale Earnhardt Jr., with $28 million
2. Jeff Gordon, $24
3. Tony Stewart, $22
4. Jimmie Johnson, $21
5. Carl Edwards, $15.5
6. Kevin Harvick, $14
6. Kyle Busch, $14
8. Danica Patrick, $12
9. Matt Kenseth, $11.5
10. Kasey Kahne, $11

Source: *Forbes*, Highest-Paid NASCAR Drivers (annual), March 12, 2012, p. 102-103.

268 ■ MOST VALUABLE NASCAR TEAMS, 2011

Ranked by: Total value, in millions of dollars. **Remarks:** Also notes profits, annual growth in value, and comments. **Number listed:** 9

1. Hendrick Motorsports, with $350 million
2. Roush Fenway Racing, $185
3. Joe Gibbs Racing, $155
4. Richard Childress Racing, $147
5. Stewart-Haas Racing, $108
6. Penske Racing, $98
7. Michael Waltrip Racing, $90
8. Earnhardt Ganassi Racing, $76
9. Richard Petty Motorsports, $58

Source: *Forbes*, NASCAR Team Valuations (annual), March 12, 2012, p. 103.

Automobile Service Stations

269 ■ AMERICA'S LARGEST PRIVATE CONVENIENCE STORE AND GAS STATION COMPANIES, 2010

Ranked by: Revenue, in billions of dollars. **Remarks:** Also notes headquarters, number of employees, and overall rank in the *America's Largest Private Companies* list. Ranking is available online only, not in print. **Number listed:** 9

1. Love's Travel Stops & Country Stores Inc., with $24.4 billion
2. Pilot Flying J, $17.77
3. QuikTrip Corp., $8.77
4. Cumberland Farms Inc., $8.02
5. Wawa Inc., $6.99

6. RaceTrac Petroleum Inc., $5.75
7. Sheetz Inc., $5.23
8. Holiday Cos., $3.63
9. Kum & Go LC, $2.1

Source: *Forbes*, America's Largest Private Companies (annual), http://www.forbes.com, December 5, 2011.

270 ■ TOP OIL-CHANGE FRANCHISES, 2012

Ranked by: Cumulative score based on financial strength and stability, growth rate, size of the system, number of years in business, the length of time franchising, start-up costs, litigation, percentage of terminations, and whether the company provides financing. **Remarks:** Specific scores not provided. Also notes overall rank within the *Franchise 500,* contact information, description, year founded, year started franchising, states where registered, available U.S. regions, where seeking foreign expansion, number of franchised and company-owned units for past three years, start-up costs, franchise fees, royalty fees, and type of financing available. **Number listed:** 4

1. Jiffy Lube International Inc.
2. Express Oil Change
3. Grease Monkey Franchising LLC
4. Oil Can Henry's

Source: *Entrepreneur*, Franchise 500 (annual), January 2012, p. 148-149.

Automobile Supply Stores

271 ■ DIY/AUTO CHAINS ADDING THE MOST NEW STORES, 2011

Ranked by: Total number of new stores added during the year. **Remarks:** Also notes figures for previous year. **Number listed:** 5

1. AutoZone Inc., with 198 new stores
2. O'Reilly Automotive Inc., 170
3. Advance Auto Parts Inc., 140
4. Lowe's Companies Inc., 25
5. The Home Depot Inc., 10

Source: *Chain Store Age*, Big Builders (annual), December 2011, p. 37.

Automobiles

272 ■ TOP AUTO BRANDS BY MARKET SHARE, 2010

Ranked by: Market share, in percent. **Remarks:** Also notes figures for previous year and advertising expenditures for current and previous year. **Number listed:** 10

1. Ford, with 15.1%
2. Chevrolet, 13.5%
3. Toyota, 12.8%
4. Honda, 9.5%
5. Nissan, 6.9%
6. Hyundai, 4.6%
7. Dodge, 3.3%
8. Kia, 3.1%
9. GMC, 2.9%
10. Jeep, 2.5%

Source: *Advertising Age*, Leading National Advertisers (annual), June 20, 2011, p. 20.

273 ■ TOP AUTOMOTIVE APPEARANCE SERVICE FRANCHISES, 2012

Ranked by: Cumulative score based on financial strength and stability, growth rate, size of the system, number of years in business, the length of time franchising, start-up costs, litigation, percentage of terminations, and whether the company provides financing. **Remarks:** Specific scores not provided. Also notes overall rank within the *Franchise 500,* contact information, description, year founded, year started franchising, states where registered, available U.S. regions, where seeking foreign expansion, number of franchised and company-owned units for past three years, start-up costs, franchise fees, royalty fees, and type of financing available. **Number listed:** 4

1. Ziebart
2. Maaco Franchising Inc.
3. Interior Magic International
4. Colors on Parade

Source: *Entrepreneur,* Franchise 500 (annual), January 2011, p. 148-149.

274 ■ TOP-SELLING BRANDS OF AUTOMOBILES, 2009

Ranked by: Total average sales among dealership franchises, in dollars. **Remarks:** Also notes number of dealers, breakdown by new and used vehicles, fees and income, and sales by service, body shop, and parts and accessories. **Number listed:** 20

1. Hyundai, with $112,165,969
2. Mercedes-Benz, $105,626,825
3. BMW, $98,289,715
4. Lexus, $88,688,044
5. Toyota, $87,005,181
6. Chrysler, $73,464,807
7. Honda, $73,208,699
8. Chevrolet, $68,495,447
9. Ford, $66,385,947
10. Nissan, $58,089,472

Source: *Ward's Automotive Yearbook,* (annual), 2011, p. 193.

275 ■ TOP-SELLING CARS IN CANADA, 2010

Ranked by: Number of cars sold. **Number listed:** 10

1. Toyota Corolla/Matrix, with 57,773 cars
2. Honda Civic, 57,501
3. Mazda3, 47,740
4. Hyundai Elantra, 34,55
5. Chevrolet Cobalt, 25,957
6. Hyundai Accent, 24,017
7. Ford Focus, 23,452
8. Ford Fusion, 19,364
9. Volkswagen Golf, 15,868
10. Nissan Versa, 15,743

Source: *Ward's Automotive Yearbook,* (annual), 2011, p. 113.

276 ■ TOP-SELLING CARS IN MEXICO, 2010

Ranked by: Number of cars sold. **Number listed:** 10

1. Volkswagen Jetta/Bora, with 68,294 cars
2. Nissan Tsuru, 61,147
3. Chevrolet Chevy, 43,964
4. Nissan Tiida, 40,091
5. Chevrolet Aveo, 29,409

6. Volkswagen Gol, 24,294
7. Nissan Sentra, 19,836
8. Mazda3, 13,213
9. SEAT Ibiza, 11,243
10. Dodge Attitude, 10,989

Source: *Ward's Automotive Yearbook,* (annual), 2011, p. 129.

277 ■ TOP-SELLING CARS IN THE U.S., 2010

Ranked by: Number of cars sold. **Number listed:** 10

1. Toyota Camry, with 327,804 cars
2. Honda Accord, 282,530
3. Toyota Corolla/Matrix, 266,082
4. Honda Civic, 260,218
5. Nissan Altima, 229,263
6. Ford Fusion, 219,219
7. Chevrolet Malibu, 198,770
8. Hyundai Sonata, 196,623
9. Ford Focus, 172,421
10. Chevrolet Impala, 172,078

Source: *Ward's Automotive Yearbook,* (annual), 2011, p. 212.

Automobiles—Maintenance and Repair

278 ■ LARGEST AUTOMOTIVE REPAIR, SERVICE, AND PARKING COMPANIES BY EMPLOYEES, 2010

Ranked by: Total number of employees. **Remarks:** Also notes contact information for headquarters, number of employees at headquarters, revenue, rank by revenue, and primary SIC code. **Number listed:** 338

1. FirstGroup USA Inc., with 96,000 employees
2. Crawford Group Inc., 66,737
3. Enterprise Holdings Inc., 59,694
4. First Group Investment Partnership, 31,250
5. Ryder System Inc., 24,971
6. Hertz Global Holdings Inc., 23,138
7. Hertz Corp., 23,040
7. Hertz Investors Inc., 23,040
9. Avis Budget Group Inc., 22,700
10. Avis Group Holdings Inc., 19,500

Source: *Business Rankings,* (annual), Dun & Bradstreet Inc., 2011, p. VI.225-VI.232.

279 ■ LARGEST AUTOMOTIVE REPAIR, SERVICE, AND PARKING COMPANIES BY SALES, 2010

Ranked by: Total revenue, in dollars. **Remarks:** Also notes contact information for headquarters, number of employees at headquarters and overall, rank by employees, and primary SIC code. **Number listed:** 339

1. Hertz Corp., with $7,562,534,000
1. Hertz Global Holdings Inc., $7,562,534,000
3. Avis Budget Group Inc., $5,185,000,000
4. Ryder System Inc., $5,136,435,000
5. Amerco Inc., $2,002,005,000
6. U-Haul International Inc., $1,897,933,000
7. Dollar Thrifty Automotive Group Inc., $1,537,160,000

8. Benjamin Motors Inc., $750,000,000
9. Standard Parking Corp., $721,143,000
10. Monro Muffler Brake Inc., $564,639,000

Source: *Business Rankings*, (annual), Dun & Bradstreet Inc., 2011, p. V.199-V.206.

280 ■ TOP MISCELLANEOUS AUTOMOTIVE REPAIR AND MAINTENANCE FRANCHISES, 2012

Ranked by: Cumulative score based on financial strength and stability, growth rate, size of the system, number of years in business, the length of time franchising, start-up costs, litigation, percentage of terminations, and whether the company provides financing. **Remarks:** Specific scores not provided. Also notes overall rank within the *Franchise 500,* contact information, description, year founded, year started franchising, states where registered, available U.S. regions, where seeking foreign expansion, number of franchised and company-owned units for past three years, start-up costs, franchise fees, royalty fees, and type of financing available. **Number listed:** 5

1. Meineke Car Care Centers
2. Midas International Corp.
3. Precision Tune Auto Care
4. Christian Brothers Automotive Corp.
5. Tuffy Associates Corp./Car-X Associates Corp.

Source: *Entrepreneur*, Franchise 500 (annual), January 2012, p. 148-149.

281 ■ TOP TRANSMISSION REPAIR FRANCHISES, 2012

Ranked by: Cumulative score based on financial strength and stability, growth rate, size of the system, number of years in business, the length of time franchising, start-up costs, litigation, percentage of terminations, and whether the company provides financing. **Remarks:** Specific scores not provided. Also notes overall rank within the *Franchise 500,* contact information, description, year founded, year started franchising, states where registered, available U.S. regions, where seeking foreign expansion, number of franchised and company-owned units for past three years, start-up costs, franchise fees, royalty fees, and type of financing available. **Number listed:** 2

1. AAMCO Transmissions Inc.
2. Mr. Transmission/Transmission USA

Source: *Entrepreneur*, Franchise 500 (annual), January 2012, p. 148-149.

282 ■ TOP WINDSHIELD REPAIR FRANCHISES, 2012

Ranked by: Cumulative score based on financial strength and stability, growth rate, size of the system, number of years in business, the length of time franchising, start-up costs, litigation, percentage of terminations, and whether the company provides financing. **Remarks:** Specific scores not provided. Also notes overall rank within the *Franchise 500,* contact information, description, year founded, year started franchising, states where registered, available U.S. regions, where seeking foreign expansion, number of franchised and company-owned units for past three years, start-up costs, franchise fees, royalty fees, and type of financing available. **Number listed:** 2

1. Novus Glass
2. SuperGlass Windshield Repair

Source: *Entrepreneur*, Franchise 500 (annual), January 2012, p. 148-149.

Bacon

283 ■ TOP BRANDS OF REFRIGERATED BACON, 2011

Ranked by: Sales in supermarkets, drug stores, and mass merchandisers (excluding Wal-Mart), in dollars. **Remarks:** Also notes percent change from previous year, unit sales, and market share. **Number listed:** 10

1. Private label, with $579,377,100
2. Oscar Mayer, $463,496,400
3. Hormel Black Label, $144,510,100
4. Wright, $99,893,910
5. Farmland, $96,133,070
6. Smithfield, $80,230,340
7. Gwaltney, $72,485,380
8. Bar S, $72,396,180
9. Louis Rich Oscar Mayer, $63,350,860
10. Hormel, $63,110,240

Source: *The National Provisioner*, State of the Industry (annual), October 2011, p. 48.

Baked Goods

284 ■ TOP MISCELLANEOUS BAKED GOODS FRANCHISES, 2012

Ranked by: Cumulative score based on financial strength and stability, growth rate, size of the system, number of years in business, the length of time franchising, start-up costs, litigation, percentage of terminations, and whether the company provides financing. **Remarks:** Specific scores not provided. Also notes overall rank within the *Franchise 500,* contact information, description, year founded, year started franchising, states where registered, available U.S. regions, where seeking foreign expansion, number of franchised and company-owned units for past three years, start-up costs, franchise fees, royalty fees, and type of financing available. **Number listed:** 5

1. Cinnabon
2. Great Harvest Franchising Inc.
3. Gigi's Cupcakes
4. Big Apple Bagels
5. Breadsmith

Source: *Entrepreneur*, Franchise 500 (annual), January 2012, p. 162-163.

Bakers and Bakeries

285 ■ TOP PRETZEL FRANCHISES, 2012

Ranked by: Cumulative score based on financial strength and stability, growth rate, size of the system, number of years in business, the length of time franchising, start-up costs, litigation, percentage of terminations, and whether the company provides financing. **Remarks:** Specific scores not provided. Also notes overall rank within the *Franchise 500,* contact information, description, year founded, year started franchising, available U.S. regions, where seeking foreign expansion, number of franchised and company-owned units for past three years, start-up costs, franchise fees, royalty fees, and type of financing available. **Number listed:** 4

1. Auntie Anne's Hand-Rolled Soft Pretzels
2. Wetzel's Pretzels

3. Pretzelmaker
4. Philly Pretzel Factory

Source: *Entrepreneur*, Franchise 500 (annual), January 2012, p. 162-163.

Bank Credit Cards

286 ■ LARGEST U.S. BANKS BY CREDIT CARD LOANS, 2011

Ranked by: Total credit card loans, in thousands of dollars. **Remarks:** Also notes city, state, and dollar and percent change from previous year. **Number listed:** 25

1. Citibank NA Inc., with $150,914,000 thousand
2. FIA Card Services NA, $124,961,397
3. Chase Bank USA NA, $96,819,057
4. Capital One Bank (USA) NA, $53,038,976
5. Discover Bank, $47,773,150
6. J. P. Morgan Chase Bank NA, $27,317,000
7. Wells Fargo Bank NA, $23,419,000
8. HSBC Bank USA NA, $22,150,891
9. U.S. Bank NA, $19,774,939
10. Bank of America NA, $19,711,562

Source: *Highline Bank and S&L Quarterly, Dec. ed.*, 2011, p. I.51.

Bank Deposits

287 ■ LARGEST U.S. BANKS BY BROKERED DEPOSITS, 2011

Ranked by: Total brokered deposits, in thousands of dollars. **Remarks:** Also notes city, state, and dollar and percent change from previous year. **Number listed:** 25

1. Citibank NA Inc., with $64,351,000 thousand
2. Morgan Stanley Bank NA, $54,403,000
3. TD Bank NA, $48,111,677
4. Bank of America NA, $46,654,747
5. Goldman Sachs Bank USA, $20,084,000
6. Discover Bank, $16,616,996
7. FIA Card Services NA, $16,342,278
8. American Express Centurion, $16,026,988
9. Wells Fargo Bank NA, $15,279,000
10. TD Bank USA NA, $11,319,642

Source: *Highline Bank and S&L Quarterly, Dec. ed.*, 2011, p. I.50.

288 ■ LARGEST U.S. BANKS BY TIME DEPOSITS, 2011

Ranked by: Total time deposits of $100,000 or more, in thousands of dollars. **Remarks:** Also notes city, state, and dollar and percent change from previous year. **Number listed:** 25

1. J. P. Morgan Chase Bank NA, with $53,275,000 thousand
2. Bank of America NA, $50,817,584
3. Bank of New York Mellon Corp., $31,807,000
4. Wells Fargo Bank NA, $25,596,000
5. Chase Bank USA NA, $25,558,871
6. Branch Banking & Trust Co., $19,908,488
7. Citibank NA Inc., $17,089,000
8. U.S. Bank NA, $12,558,396

9. Ally Bank, $11,236,112
10. PNC Bank NA, $8,862,947

Source: *Highline Bank and S&L Quarterly, Dec. ed.*, 2011, p. I.51.

Bank Loans

289 ■ LARGEST U.S. BANKS BY CONSTRUCTION LOANS, 2011

Ranked by: Total construction loans, in thousands of dollars. **Remarks:** Also notes city, state, and dollar and percent change from previous year. **Number listed:** 25

1. Wells Fargo Bank NA, with $20,065,000 thousand
2. Bank of America NA, $16,416,425
3. U.S. Bank NA, $8,425,436
4. Branch Banking & Trust Co., $7,714,003
5. PNC Bank NA, $5,241,182
6. J. P. Morgan Chase Bank NA, $4,559,000
7. Manufacturers & Traders Trust Co., $4,285,614
8. Compass Bank, $3,873,982
9. Synovus Bank, $2,957,958
10. TD Bank NA, $2,933,340

Source: *Highline Bank and S&L Quarterly, Dec. ed.*, 2011, p. I.49.

290 ■ LARGEST U.S. BANKS BY FOREIGN LOANS, 2011

Ranked by: Total foreign loans, in thousands of dollars. **Remarks:** Also notes city, state, and dollar and percent change from previous year. **Number listed:** 25

1. Citibank NA Inc., with $247,112,000 thousand
2. J. P. Morgan Chase Bank NA, $96,947,000
3. Bank of America NA, $63,713,381
4. Wells Fargo Bank NA, $20,295,000
5. FIA Card Services NA, $17,485,071
6. Bank of New York Mellon Corp., $10,254,000
7. Capital One Bank (USA) NA, $8,817,794
8. HSBC Bank USA NA, $2,952,597
9. PNC Bank NA, $1,732,675
10. East West Bank, $1,083,031

Source: *Highline Bank and S&L Quarterly, Dec. ed.*, 2011, p. I.48.

291 ■ LARGEST U.S. BANKS BY NONPERFORMING CONSUMER LOANS, 2011

Ranked by: Total nonperforming consumer loans, in thousands of dollars. **Remarks:** Also notes city, state, and dollar and percent change from previous year. **Number listed:** 25

1. Citibank NA Inc., with $3,061,000 thousand
2. FIA Card Services NA, $2,762,731
3. Chase Bank USA NA, $1,335,235
4. Wells Fargo Bank NA, $1,147,000
5. J. P. Morgan Chase Bank NA, $1,077,000
6. Capital One Bank (USA) NA, $1,010,378
7. SunTrust Banks Inc., $912,482
8. Discover Bank, $770,601
9. U.S. Bank NA, $744,823
10. Wells Fargo Bank Northwest NA, $712,000

Source: *Highline Bank and S&L Quarterly, Dec. ed.*, 2011, p. I.44.

292 ■ LARGEST U.S. BANKS BY NONPERFORMING LOANS, 2011

Ranked by: Nonperforming loans, in thousands of dollars. **Remarks:** Also notes city, state, and dollar and percent change from previous year. **Number listed:** 25

1. Bank of America NA, with $54,345,015 thousand
2. Wells Fargo Bank NA, $47,947,000
3. J. P. Morgan Chase Bank NA, $35,412,000
4. Citibank NA Inc., $16,531,000
5. PNC Bank NA, $8,022,922
6. U.S. Bank NA, $7,622,342
7. SunTrust Banks Inc., $4,932,399
8. Branch Banking & Trust Co., $3,401,941
9. Regions Bank, $3,243,975
10. FIA Card Services NA, $2,970,274

Source: *Highline Bank and S&L Quarterly, Dec. ed.*, 2011, p. I.43.

293 ■ LARGEST U.S. BANKS BY NONPERFORMING REAL ESTATE LOANS, 2011

Ranked by: Total nonperforming real estate loans, in thousands of dollars. **Remarks:** Also notes city, state, and dollar and percent change from previous year. **Number listed:** 25

1. Bank of America NA, with $52,563,192 thousand
2. Wells Fargo Bank NA, $44,619,000
3. J. P. Morgan Chase Bank NA, $32,384,000
4. Citibank NA Inc., $10,492,000
5. PNC Bank NA, $7,009,408
6. U.S. Bank NA, $6,438,199
7. SunTrust Banks Inc., $3,901,721
8. Branch Banking & Trust Co., $3,193,194
9. Regions Bank, $2,768,776
10. BMO Harris Bank NA, $1,708,010

Source: *Highline Bank and S&L Quarterly, Dec. ed.*, 2011, p. I.44.

294 ■ LARGEST U.S. BANKS BY RESIDENTIAL REAL ESTATE LOANS, 2011

Ranked by: Total 1-4 family residential real estate loans, in thousands of dollars. **Remarks:** Also notes city, state, and dollar and percent change from previous year. **Number listed:** 25

1. Bank of America NA, with $359,351,076 thousand
2. Wells Fargo Bank NA, $310,507,000
3. J. P. Morgan Chase Bank NA, $214,455,000
4. Citibank NA Inc., $131,679,000
5. U.S. Bank NA, $66,431,549
6. PNC Bank NA, $49,316,613
7. SunTrust Banks Inc., $47,888,731
8. Branch Banking & Trust Co., $39,434,474
9. Wells Fargo Bank South Central, $34,007,000
10. RBS Citizens NA, $31,037,431

Source: *Highline Bank and S&L Quarterly, Dec. ed.*, 2011, p. I.52.

Bankruptcy

295 ■ LARGEST PUBLIC COMPANY BANKRUPTCIES IN THE U.S., 1980-2011

Ranked by: Pre-petition assets, in millions of dollars. **Remarks:** Also notes bankruptcy date and company description. **Number listed:** 20

1. Lehman Brothers Holdings Inc. (2008), with $691,063 million
2. Washington Mutual Inc. (2008), $327,913
3. WorldCom Inc. (2002), $103,914
4. General Motors Corp. (2009), $91,047
5. CIT Group Inc. (2009), $80,448
6. Enron Corp. (2001), $65,503
7. Conseco Inc. (2002), $61,392
8. MF Global Holdings Ltd. (2011), $40,541
9. Chrysler LLC (2009), $39,300
10. Thornburg Mortgage Inc. (2009), $36,521

Source: *BankruptcyData.com*, Largest Public Company Bankruptcies (annual), New Generation Research Inc., January 2012.

296 ■ LARGEST PUBLIC COMPANY BANKRUPTCIES IN THE U.S., 2011

Ranked by: Pre-petition assets, in millions of dollars. **Remarks:** Also notes bankruptcy date and company description. **Number listed:** 20

1. MF Global Holdings Ltd., with $40,541 million
2. AMR Corp., $25,088
3. Dynegy Holdings LLC, $9,949
4. The PMI Group Inc., $4,218
5. NewPage Corp., $3,512
6. First State Bancorporation, $2,744
7. Integra Bank Corp., $2,420
8. General Maritime Corp., $1,781
9. Borders Group Inc., $1,425
10. TerreStar Corp., $1,375

Source: *BankruptcyData.com*, Largest Public Company Bankruptcies (annual), New Generation Research Inc., January 2012.

297 ■ LARGEST PUBLIC COMPANY FINANCIAL BANKRUPTCIES IN THE U.S., 1980-2011

Ranked by: Pre-bankruptcy assets, in millions of dollars. **Remarks:** Also notes bankruptcy date and company description. **Number listed:** 20

1. Lehman Brothers Holdings Inc. (2008), with $691,063 million
2. Washington Mutual Inc. (2008), $327,913
3. CIT Group Inc. (2009), $80,448
4. Conseco Inc. (2002), $61,392
5. MF Global Holdings Ltd. (2011), $40,541
6. Thornburg Mortgage Inc. (2009), $36,521
7. Financial Corp. of America (1988), $33,864
8. Refco Inc. (2005), $33,333
9. IndyMac Bancorp Inc. (2008), $32,734
10. Bank of New England Corp. (1991), $29,773

Source: *BankruptcyData.com*, Largest Public Company Bankruptcies (annual), New Generation Research Inc., January 2012.

298 ■ LARGEST PUBLIC COMPANY NON-FINANCIAL BANKRUPTCIES IN THE U.S., 1980-2011

Ranked by: Pre-bankruptcy assets, in millions of dollars. **Remarks:** Also notes bankruptcy date and company description. **Number listed:** 20

1. WorldCom Inc. (2002), with $103,914 million
2. General Motors Corp. (2009), $91,047

3. Enron Corp. (2001), $65,503

4. Chrysler LLC (2009), $39,300

5. Pacific Gas & Electric Co. (PG & E, 2001), $36,152

6. Texaco Inc. (1987), $34,940

7. Global Crossing Ltd. (2002), $30,185

8. General Growth Properties Inc. (2009), $29,557

9. Lyondell Chemical Co. (2009), $27,392

10. Calpine Corp. (2005), $27,216

Source: *BankruptcyData.com*, Largest Public Company Bankruptcies (annual), New Generation Research Inc., January 2012.

299 ■ STATES WITH THE HIGHEST BUSINESS BANKRUPTCY RATE, 2009

Ranked by: Firms filing for bankruptcy as a percentage of employer firms in existence. **Number listed:** 51

1. Delaware, with 6.4%

2. Nevada, 1.7%

3. Georgia, 1.4%

4. Arizona, 1.3%

4. New Hampshire, 1.3%

6. Florida, 1.1%

6. Tennessee, 1.1%

8. Michigan, 1%

8. Texas, 1%

8. Utah, 1%

Source: *State Rankings*, (annual), CQ Press, 2011, p. 107.

Banks and Banking

---

300 ■ CALIFORNIA'S LARGEST REGIONAL BANKS OVERALL, 2011

Ranked by: Score based on revenue, profits, assets, and market capitalization. **Remarks:** Specific scores not provided. Also notes overall rank in the *Forbes 2000* and figures for each criterion. **Number listed:** 2

1. First Republic Bank CA

2. City National

Source: *Forbes*, Forbes 2000 (annual), http://www.forbes.com, May 7, 2012.

301 ■ CHICAGO'S LARGEST BANKS BY ASSETS, 2011

Ranked by: Total assets as of March 31, 2011, in millions of dollars. **Remarks:** Also notes contact information, earnings, percent change from previous year, breakdown by type of loan. **Number listed:** 25

1. Northern Trust Co., with $79,561.3 million

2. BMO Harris Bank NA, $49,886.5

3. PrivateBank & Trust Co., $12,465.6

4. MB Financial Bank NA, $10,016.1

5. First MidWest Bank NA, $7,892.1

Source: *Crain's Chicago Business*, Chicago's Largest Banks (annual), http://www.chicagobusiness.com, August 1, 2011.

302 ■ GEORGIA'S LARGEST REGIONAL BANKS OVERALL, 2011

Ranked by: Score based on revenue, profits, assets, and market capitalization. **Remarks:** Specific scores not provided. Also notes overall rank in the *Forbes 2000* and figures for each criterion. **Number listed:** 2

1. SunTrust Banks Inc.

2. Synovus Financial Corp.

Source: *Forbes*, Forbes 2000 (annual), http://www.forbes.com, May 7, 2012.

303 ■ LARGEST BANKS IN SOUTH CAROLINA, 2011

Ranked by: Statewide market share, in percent. **Remarks:** Also notes contact information, deposits, number of offices in state, top official, and year founded. **Number listed:** 22

1. Wells Fargo, with 16.64%

2. Bank of America NA, 11.82%

3. BB & T (Branch Banking & Trust Co.), 8.82%

4. First Citizens Bank & Trust Co., 8.34%

5. TD Bank, 7.24%

6. NBSC, 5.31%

7. First Federal, 3.12%

8. SCBT NA, 2.88%

9. SunTrust Bank, 2.78%

10. The Palmetto Bank, 1.7%

Source: *South Carolina Business*, Book of Lists (annual), 2011, p. 24.

304 ■ LARGEST COMMERCIAL BANKS IN THE TWIN CITIES, 2011

Ranked by: Assets, in thousands of dollars. **Remarks:** Also notes contact information, year founded, number of offices and employees, figures for previous year, percent change, deposits, equity, return on assets and equity, net loans, and net interest income. **Number listed:** 25

1. Bremer Bank, NA, with $2,629,837 thousand

2. KleinBank, $1,490,795

3. Anchor Bank, NA, $1,249,680

4. Stearns Bank, NA, $1,182,098

5. Frandsen Bank & Trust, $1,145,063

6. Merchants Bank, NA, $1,135,552

7. Central Bank, $769,629

8. American Bank of the North, $637,704

9. United Bankers' Bank, $624,606

10. Alliance Bank, $623,782

Source: *Twin Cities Business*, The BIG Book (annual), http://www.tcbmag.com, 2012.

305 ■ LARGEST COMMUNITY BANKS AND CREDIT UNIONS IN NEW MEXICO, 2011

Ranked by: Deposits, in millions of dollars. **Remarks:** Also notes contact information. **Number listed:** 25

1. Los Alamos National Bank, with $1,300 million

2. First National Bank of Santa Fe, $655

3. First American Bank, $606

4. Citizens Bank, $517

5. Century Bank, $441

Source: *New Mexico Business Weekly*, Top Community Banks and Credit Unions, March 23, 2012.

306 ■ LARGEST DEPOSITORY INSTITUTIONS BY EMPLOYEES, 2010

Ranked by: Total number of employees. **Remarks:** Also notes contact information for headquarters, number of employees at headquarters, revenue, rank by revenue, and primary SIC code. **Number listed:** 49

1. Bank of America Corp., with 284,000 employees
2. Citigroup Inc., 267,531
3. Wells Fargo & Co., 267,307
4. J. P. Morgan Chase & Co., 239,076
5. J. P. Morgan Chase Bank NA, 170,538
6. Bank of America NA, 170,158
7. Wells Fargo Corp., 158,880
8. Wachovia Corp., 121,970
9. Wachovia Bank NA, 120,000
10. Citibank N.A. Inc., 118,240

Source: *Business Rankings*, (annual), Dun & Bradstreet Inc., 2011, p. VI.176-VI.177.

307 ■ LARGEST KENTUCKY BANKS, 2011

Ranked by: Market share, in percent. **Remarks:** Also notes contact information, Kentucky deposits, and Kentucky officers. **Number listed:** 25

1. PNC Bank NA, with 9.32%
2. Fifth Third Bank, 7.13%
3. J. P. Morgan Chase Bank, 6.52%
4. Branch Banking & Trust Co., 5.62%
5. U.S. Bank, 4.95%
6. Community Trust Bank Inc., 3.42%
7. Republic Bank & Trust Co., 2.5%
8. Central Bank & Trust Co., 2.33%
9. PBI Bank, 2.1%
10. Bank of Kentucky Inc., 1.96%

Source: *The Lane Report*, Largest Kentucky Banks (annual), March 2012, p. 24.

308 ■ LARGEST LOS ANGELES COUNTY-BASED BANKS, 2011

Ranked by: Assets as of June 30, in millions of dollars. **Remarks:** Also notes contact information, deposits, net income, figures for previous year, percent change, capital ratios, non-current ratios, returns, number of employees and branches, year founded, and top executive. **Number listed:** 50

1. City National Bank, with $22,148 million
2. East West Bank, $21,862
3. Cathay Bank, $10,518

Source: *Los Angeles Business Journal*, L.A. County-Based Banks (annual), http://www.labusinessjournal.com, November 7, 2011.

309 ■ LARGEST U.S. BANKS BY ASSETS, 2011

Ranked by: Assets, in millions of dollars. **Remarks:** Also notes city, state, percent change from previous year, ratings, and measures of loan exposure, capital adequacy, asset quality, earnings, and liquidity. **Number listed:** 100

1. J. P. Morgan Chase Bank NA, with $1,811,678 million
2. Bank of America NA, $1,451,989
3. Citibank NA Inc., $1,288,658
4. Wells Fargo Bank NA, $1,161,490
5. U.S. Bank NA, $330,471
6. PNC Bank NA, $283,310
7. Bank of New York Mellon Corp., $256,205
8. State Street Bank & Trust Co., $212,293

9. HSBC Bank USA NA, $206,010
10. TD Bank NA, $188,913

Source: *Highline Bank and S&L Quarterly, Dec. ed.*, 2011, p. I.38-I.41.

310 ■ LARGEST U.S. BANKS BY FEE INCOME, 2011

Ranked by: Total fee income, excluding trading income, in thousands of dollars. **Remarks:** Also notes city, state, and dollar and percent change from previous year. **Number listed:** 25

1. J. P. Morgan Chase Bank NA, with $26,792,000 thousand
2. Wells Fargo Bank NA, $25,623,000
3. Bank of America NA, $23,785,006
4. Citibank NA Inc., $11,622,000
5. U.S. Bank NA, $8,243,769
6. Bank of New York Mellon Corp., $5,964,000
7. State Street Bank & Trust Co., $5,608,418
8. PNC Bank NA, $4,436,877
9. American Express Centurion, $3,900,441
10. Chase Bank USA NA, $3,707,938

Source: *Highline Bank and S&L Quarterly, Dec. ed.*, 2011, p. I.46.

311 ■ LARGEST U.S. BANKS BY FIDUCIARY INCOME, 2011

Ranked by: Total fiduciary income, in thousands of dollars. **Remarks:** Also notes city, state, and dollar and percent change from previous year. **Number listed:** 25

1. Bank of New York Mellon Corp., with $4,571,000 thousand
2. State Street Bank & Trust Co., $4,442,950
3. J. P. Morgan Chase Bank NA, $3,341,000
4. Northern Trust Corp., $2,034,590
5. Wells Fargo Bank NA, $1,792,000
6. Bank of America NA, $1,479,093
7. Citibank NA Inc., $1,432,000
8. Blackrock Institutional Trust Corp., $1,354,367
9. U.S. Bank NA, $919,649
10. PNC Bank NA, $628,217

Source: *Highline Bank and S&L Quarterly, Dec. ed.*, 2011, p. I.46.

312 ■ LARGEST U.S. BANKS BY INCOME, 2011

Ranked by: Income before extraordinary items, in thousands of dollars. **Remarks:** Also notes city, state, and dollar and percent change from previous year. **Number listed:** 25

1. Wells Fargo Bank NA, with $13,325,000 thousand
2. J. P. Morgan Chase Bank NA, $12,459,000
3. Citibank NA Inc., $10,391,000
4. Bank of America NA, $9,645,231
5. FIA Card Services NA, $5,838,301
6. U.S. Bank NA, $4,634,559
7. Chase Bank USA NA, $3,947,252
8. PNC Bank NA, $2,831,214
9. Capital One Bank (USA) NA, $2,456,532
10. Discover Bank, $2,153,957

Source: *Highline Bank and S&L Quarterly, Dec. ed.*, 2011, p. I.42.

313 ■ LARGEST U.S. BANKS BY NET CHARGE-OFFS, 2011

Ranked by: Net charge-offs, in thousands of dollars. **Remarks:** Also notes city, state, and dollar and percent change from previous year. **Number listed:** 25

1. Citibank NA Inc., with $17,646,000 thousand
2. FIA Card Services NA, $11,161,062
3. Bank of America NA, $9,482,332
4. Wells Fargo Bank NA, $9,366,000
5. J. P. Morgan Chase Bank NA, $6,311,000
6. Chase Bank USA NA, $4,382,089
7. Capital One Bank (USA) NA, $2,816,563
8. U.S. Bank NA, $2,725,047
9. HSBC Bank USA NA, $2,107,420
10. Suntrust Bank, $2,040,203

Source: *Highline Bank and S&L Quarterly, Dec. ed.*, 2011, p. I.43.

314 ■ LARGEST U.S. BANKS BY SALARY EXPENSE, 2011

Ranked by: Total salary expense, in thousands of dollars. **Remarks:** Also notes city, state, and dollar and percent change from previous year. **Number listed:** 25

1. J. P. Morgan Chase Bank NA, with $22,386,000 thousand
2. Wells Fargo Bank NA, $20,597,000
3. Bank of America NA, $18,912,530
4. Citibank NA Inc., $15,065,000
5. U.S. Bank NA, $4,681,982
6. PNC Bank NA, $3,528,906
7. Bank of New York Mellon Corp., $3,509,000
8. State Street Bank & Trust Co., $3,462,501
9. Capital One NA, $2,885,815
10. Branch Banking & Trust Co., $2,428,766

Source: *Highline Bank and S&L Quarterly, Dec. ed.*, 2011, p. I.47.

315 ■ LARGEST U.S. BANKS BY SERVICE CHARGE INCOME, 2011

Ranked by: Total service charge income, in thousands of dollars. **Remarks:** Also notes city, state, and dollar and percent change from previous year. **Number listed:** 25

1. Bank of America NA, with $5,438,512 thousand
2. J. P. Morgan Chase Bank NA, $4,728,000
3. Wells Fargo Bank NA, $4,290,000
4. U.S. Bank NA, $1,210,088
5. PNC Bank NA, $947,162
6. Regions Bank, $810,842
7. TD Bank NA, $742,100
8. SunTrust Banks Inc., $685,669
9. Citibank NA Inc., $596,000
10. Branch Banking & Trust Co., $564,563

Source: *Highline Bank and S&L Quarterly, Dec. ed.*, 2011, p. I.47.

316 ■ LARGEST U.S. MAJOR BANKS OVERALL, 2011

Ranked by: Score based on revenue, profits, assets, and market capitalization. **Remarks:** Specific scores not provided. Also notes overall rank in the *Forbes 2000* and figures for each criterion. **Number listed:** 6

1. J. P. Morgan Chase & Co.
2. Wells Fargo & Co.
3. Citigroup Inc.
4. Bank of America Corp.
5. U.S. Bancorp

6. Bank of New York Mellon Corp.

Source: *Forbes*, Forbes 2000 (annual), http://www.forbes.com, May 7, 2012.

317 ■ LARGEST U.S. REGIONAL BANKS OVERALL, 2011

Ranked by: Score based on revenue, profits, assets, and market capitalization. **Remarks:** Specific scores not provided. Also notes overall rank in the *Forbes 2000* and figures for each criterion. **Number listed:** 18

1. PNC Financial Services Group Inc.
2. BB & T Corp.
3. Fifth Third Bancorp
4. SunTrust Banks Inc.
5. M & T Bank
6. KeyCorp
7. Northern Trust Corp.
8. Regions Financial Corp.
9. Huntington Bancshares Inc.
10. Comerica Inc.

Source: *Forbes*, Forbes 2000 (annual), http://www.forbes.com, May 7, 2012.

318 ■ MOST VALUABLE U.S. BANKS, 2011

Ranked by: Market value as of March 2011, in millions of U.S. dollars. **Remarks:** Also notes rank within the *FT U.S. 500*, rank for previous year, country, revenue, net income, assets, number of employees, share price, price-to-earning ratio, dividend yield, and fiscal yearend. **Number listed:** 16

1. J. P. Morgan Chase & Co., with $183,639.7 million
2. Wells Fargo & Co., $157,415.9
3. Bank of America Corp., $134,914.9
4. Citigroup Inc., $128,703.9
5. U.S. Bancorp, $50,888.8
6. PNC Financial Services Group Inc., $33,101.8
7. BB & T Corp., $19,103.6
8. SunTrust Banks Inc., $15,449.3
9. Fifth Third Bancorp, $12,743.5
10. M & T Bank, $10,646.2

Source: *Financial Times*, FT 500 (annual), http://www.ft.com, June 24, 2011.

319 ■ NEW YORK'S LARGEST MAJOR BANKS OVERALL, 2011

Ranked by: Score based on revenue, profits, assets, and market capitalization. **Remarks:** Specific scores not provided. Also notes overall rank in the *Forbes 2000* and figures for each criterion. **Number listed:** 3

1. J. P. Morgan Chase & Co.
2. Citigroup Inc.
3. Bank of New York Mellon Corp.

Source: *Forbes*, Forbes 2000 (annual), http://www.forbes.com, May 7, 2012.

320 ■ OHIO'S LARGEST REGIONAL BANKS OVERALL, 2011

Ranked by: Score based on revenue, profits, assets, and market capitalization. **Remarks:** Specific scores not provided. Also notes overall rank in the *Forbes 2000* and figures for each criterion. **Number listed:** 3

1. Fifth Third Bancorp
2. KeyCorp
3. Huntington Bancshares

Source: *Forbes*, Forbes 2000 (annual), http://www.forbes.com, May 7, 2012.

321 ■ PUERTO RICO'S LARGEST BANKS BY CAPITAL, 2010

Ranked by: Tier one capital, in millions of U.S. dollars. **Remarks:** Also notes rank within the *Top 1000 World Banks,* fiscal year-end, percent change from previous year, assets, capital-assets ratio, pretax profits, real profits growth, profits-on-capital ratio, return on assets, cost-to-income ratio, BIS capital ratio, and non-performing loans as a percentage of total loans. **Number listed:** 6

1. Popular, with $3,734 million
2. First BanCorp, $1,277
3. Doral Financial Corp., $740
4. Oriental Financial Group, $699
5. Santander Bancorp, $687
6. BBVA PR Holding Corp., $364

Source: *The Banker*, Top 1000 World Banks (annual), July 2011, p. 244.

322 ■ TOP *FORTUNE 500* COMMERCIAL BANKS, 2011

Ranked by: Revenue, in millions of dollars. **Remarks:** Also notes overall rank in the *Fortune 500;* profits; profits as a percentage of revenue; stockholders' equity; and rank by each criterion. **Number listed:** 20

1. Bank of America Corp., with $115,074 million
2. J. P. Morgan Chase & Co., $110,838
3. Citigroup Inc., $102,939
4. Wells Fargo & Co., $87,597
5. Morgan Stanley, $39,376
6. Goldman Sachs Group Inc., $36,793
7. American Express Co., $32,282
8. U.S. Bancorp, $21,399
9. Capital One Financial Corp., $18,525
10. PNC Financial Services Group, $15,820

Source: *Fortune*, Fortune 500 (annual), May 21, 2012, p. F-34.

323 ■ TOP LARGE PRIVATE/FOREIGN BANKS IN THE U.S., 2011

Ranked by: Return on average equity of non-public commercial banks, thrifts, and bank holding companies with assets over $10 billion, in percent. **Remarks:** Also notes rank for previous year, location, total assets, and return on assets. **Number listed:** 5

1. USAA Federal Savings Bank, with 15.67%
2. BankWest Corp., 6.32%
3. Arvest Bank Group Inc., 6.09%
4. New York Private Bank & Trust Corp., 5.93%
5. EverBank, 5.03%

Source: *ABA Banking Journal*, Top Performers: Part One (annual), April 2012, p. 39.

324 ■ TOP LARGE U.S. BANKS BY RETURN ON EQUITY, 2011

Ranked by: Return on average equity of commercial banks, thrifts, and bank holding companies with assets over $10 billion, in percent. **Remarks:** Also notes rank for previous year, location, company type, total assets, return on assets, core return on aver-

age equity, non-interest income as a percentage of total revenue, price/earnings ratio, capital ratio, efficiency ratio, and nonperforming loans as a percentage of total loans. **Number listed:** 10

1. Bank of Hawaii Corp., with 15.69%
2. U.S. Bancorp, 14.71%
3. First Republic Bank, 14.54%
4. Signature Bank, 13.03%
5. Huntington Bancshares, 12.27%
6. Commerce Bancshares, 12.15%
7. First National of Nebraska Inc., 11.71%
8. Wells Fargo & Co., 11.56%
9. Capital One Financial Corp., 11.01%
10. East West Bancorp, 10.98%

Source: *ABA Banking Journal*, Top Performers: Part One (annual), April 2012, p. 37.

325 ■ THE UNITED STATES' LARGEST BANKS BY CAPITAL, 2010

Ranked by: Tier one capital, in millions of U.S. dollars. **Remarks:** Also notes rank within the *Top 1000 World Banks,* fiscal year-end, percent change from previous year, assets, capital-assets ratio, pretax profits, real profits growth, profits-on-capital ratio, return on assets, cost-to-income ratio, BIS capital ratio, and non-performing loans as a percentage of total loans. **Number listed:** 192

1. Bank of America Corp., with $163,626 million
2. J. P. Morgan Chase & Co., $142,450
3. Citigroup Inc., $126,193
4. Wells Fargo & Co., $109,353
5. Goldman Sachs Group Inc., $71,233
6. Morgan Stanley, $52,880
7. HSBC North America Holdings, $26,905
8. PNC Financial Services Group Inc., $26,092
9. U.S. Bancorp, $25,947
10. GMAC Inc., $22,189

Source: *The Banker*, Top 1000 World Banks (annual), July 2011, p. 254-258.

326 ■ THE UNITED STATES' MOST VALUABLE BANKING BRANDS, 2011

Ranked by: Brand value, in millions of U.S. dollars. **Remarks:** Also notes rank within the *Global 500* for current and previous year, figures for current and previous year, and brand rating. Ranking is available online only. **Number listed:** 13

1. Wells Fargo, with $23,229 million
2. Bank of America, $22,910
3. Chase, $18,964
4. Citi, $18,639
5. J. P. Morgan, $11,602
6. Goldman Sachs, $9,332
7. Morgan Stanley, $6,347
8. Capital One, $4,947
9. PNC, $4,845
10. U.S. Bank, $4,514

Source: *Global 500*, (annual), Brand Finance plc, March 2012.

Banks and Banking—Africa

327 ■ BENIN'S LARGEST BANKS BY CAPITAL, 2010

Ranked by: Tier one capital, in millions of U.S. dollars. **Remarks:** Also notes rank within the *Top African Banks,* fiscal year-end,

percent change from previous year, assets, capital-assets ratio, pretax profits, real profits growth, profits-on-capital ratio, return on assets, cost-to-income ratio, BIS capital ratio, and non-performing loans as a percentage of total loans. **Number listed:** 3

1. Bank of Africa Benin, with $80.02 million
2. Ecobank Benin, $34.73
3. Diamond Bank Benin, $30.35

Source: *The Banker*, Top 50 African Banks (annual), January 2012, p. 118.

328 ■ BURKINA FASO'S LARGEST BANKS BY CAPITAL, 2010

Ranked by: Tier one capital, in millions of U.S. dollars. **Remarks:** Also notes rank within the *Top African Banks*, fiscal year-end, percent change from previous year, assets, capital-assets ratio, pretax profits, real profits growth, profits-on-capital ratio, return on assets, cost-to-income ratio, BIS capital ratio, and non-performing loans as a percentage of total loans. **Number listed:** 3

1. Ecobank Burkina Faso, with $41.98 million
2. Societe Generale de Banque du Burkina, $33.32
3. Bank of Africa Burkina Faso, $29.06

Source: *The Banker*, Top 50 African Banks (annual), January 2012, p. 118.

329 ■ CAMEROON'S LARGEST BANKS BY CAPITAL, 2010

Ranked by: Tier one capital, in millions of U.S. dollars. **Remarks:** Also notes rank within the *Top African Banks*, fiscal year-end, percent change from previous year, assets, capital-assets ratio, pretax profits, real profits growth, profits-on-capital ratio, return on assets, cost-to-income ratio, BIS capital ratio, and non-performing loans as a percentage of total loans. **Number listed:** 4

1. Societe Generale de Banques au Cameroon, with $71.98 million
2. Banque Internationale du Cameroun pour l'Epargne et le Credit, $65.92
3. Afriland First Bank, $64.31
4. Ecobank Cameroon, $17.39

Source: *The Banker*, Top 50 African Banks (annual), January 2012, p. 118.

330 ■ COTE D'IVOIRE'S LARGEST BANKS BY CAPITAL, 2010

Ranked by: Tier one capital, in millions of U.S. dollars. **Remarks:** Also notes rank within the *Top African Banks*, fiscal year-end, percent change from previous year, assets, capital-assets ratio, pretax profits, real profits growth, profits-on-capital ratio, return on assets, cost-to-income ratio, BIS capital ratio, and non-performing loans as a percentage of total loans. **Number listed:** 5

1. Societe Generale de Banques en Cote d'Ivoire, with $145.79 million
2. Ecobank Cote d'Ivoire, $45.19
3. Banque Nationale d'Investissement, $45.02
4. Societe Ivoirienne de Banque, $38.25
5. Bank of Africa Cote d'Ivoire, $27.26

Source: *The Banker*, Top 50 African Banks (annual), January 2012, p. 118.

331 ■ GABON'S LARGEST BANKS BY CAPITAL, 2010

Ranked by: Tier one capital, in millions of U.S. dollars. **Remarks:** Also notes rank within the *Top African Banks*, fiscal year-end, percent change from previous year, assets, capital-assets ratio,

pretax profits, real profits growth, profits-on-capital ratio, return on assets, cost-to-income ratio, BIS capital ratio, and non-performing loans as a percentage of total loans. **Number listed:** 2

1. BGFI Bank, with $331.68 million
2. Banque Internationale pour le Commerce & l'Industrie du Gabon, $63.2

Source: *The Banker*, Top 50 African Banks (annual), January 2012, p. 119.

332 ■ GHANA'S LARGEST BANKS BY CAPITAL, 2010

Ranked by: Tier one capital, in millions of U.S. dollars. **Remarks:** Also notes rank within the *Top African Banks*, fiscal year-end, percent change from previous year, assets, capital-assets ratio, pretax profits, real profits growth, profits-on-capital ratio, return on assets, cost-to-income ratio, BIS capital ratio, and non-performing loans as a percentage of total loans. **Number listed:** 12

1. Barclays Bank Ghana, with $160.14 million
2. Ecobank Ghana, $141.72
3. Ghana Commercial Bank, $131.62
4. Standard Chartered Bank Ghana, $74.46
5. SG-SSB Bank, $71.44
6. Zenith Bank Ghana, $56.32
7. Stanbic Bank Ghana, $54.93
8. International Commercial Bank (Ghana), $46.05
9. Merchant Bank (Ghana), $43.11
10. Intercontinental Bank Ghana, $40.89

Source: *The Banker*, Top 50 African Banks (annual), January 2012, p. 119.

333 ■ LARGEST AFRICAN BANKS BY CAPITAL, 2010

Ranked by: Tier one capital, in millions of U.S. dollars. **Remarks:** Also notes consolidation level, fiscal year-end, and city. **Number listed:** 50

1. Standard Bank Group (South Africa), with $12,062.12 million
2. Absa Group (South Africa), $8,151.54
3. FirstRand Bank Holdings Ltd. (South Africa), $6,036.13
4. Nedbank Group Ltd. (South Africa), $5,715.92
5. Attijariwafabank (Morocco), $2,785.79
6. Libyan Foreign Bank (Libya), $2,573.11
7. Investec (South Africa), $2,518.88
8. Zenith Bank (Nigeria), $2,404.95
9. First Bank of Nigeria, $2,221.2
10. Groupe Banques Populaire (Morocco), $2,085.24

Source: *The Banker*, Top 50 African Banks (annual), January 2012, p. 115.

334 ■ LARGEST ALGERIAN BANKS BY CAPITAL, 2010

Ranked by: Tier one capital, in millions of U.S. dollars. **Remarks:** Also notes rank within the *Top African Banks*, fiscal year-end, percent change from previous year, assets, capital-assets ratio, pretax profits, real profits growth, profits-on-capital ratio, return on assets, cost-to-income ratio, BIS capital ratio, and non-performing loans as a percentage of total loans. **Number listed:** 3

1. Credit Populaire d'Algerie, with $773.99 million
2. Societe Generale Algerie, $183.36
3. Arab Banking Corp. Algeria, $153.67

Source: *The Banker*, Top 50 African Banks (annual), January 2012, p. 118.

335 ■ LARGEST ANGOLAN BANKS BY CAPITAL, 2010

Ranked by: Tier one capital, in millions of U.S. dollars. **Remarks:** Also notes rank within the *Top African Banks,* fiscal year-end, percent change from previous year, assets, capital-assets ratio, pretax profits, real profits growth, profits-on-capital ratio, return on assets, cost-to-income ratio, BIS capital ratio, and non-performing loans as a percentage of total loans. **Number listed:** 9

1. Banco African de Investimentos, with $638.8 million
2. Banco de Poupanca e Credito, $396.14
3. Banco de Fomento Angola, $395.77
4. Banco Espirito Santo Angola, $382.77
5. Banco BIC, $311.28
6. Banco Millenium Angola, $152.02
7. Banco Privado Atlantico, $96.17
8. Banco de Negocios International, $64.59
9. Banco Sol, $60.95

Source: *The Banker*, Top 50 African Banks (annual), January 2012, p. 118.

336 ■ LARGEST BOTSWANAN BANKS BY CAPITAL, 2010

Ranked by: Tier one capital, in millions of U.S. dollars. **Remarks:** Also notes rank within the *Top African Banks,* fiscal year-end, percent change from previous year, assets, capital-assets ratio, pretax profits, real profits growth, profits-on-capital ratio, return on assets, cost-to-income ratio, BIS capital ratio, and non-performing loans as a percentage of total loans. **Number listed:** 5

1. Barclays Bank Botswana, with $148.23 million
2. First National Bank of Botswana, $134.16
3. ABC Holdings, $67.98
4. Standard Chartered Bank Botswana, $53.79
5. Stanbic Bank Botswana, $51.62

Source: *The Banker*, Top 50 African Banks (annual), January 2012, p. 118.

337 ■ LARGEST ETHIOPIAN BANKS BY CAPITAL, 2010

Ranked by: Tier one capital, in millions of U.S. dollars. **Remarks:** Also notes rank within the *Top African Banks,* fiscal year-end, percent change from previous year, assets, capital-assets ratio, pretax profits, real profits growth, profits-on-capital ratio, return on assets, cost-to-income ratio, BIS capital ratio, and non-performing loans as a percentage of total loans. **Number listed:** 7

1. Commercial Bank of Ethiopia, with $446.17 million
2. Dashen Bank, $83.58
3. Wegagen Bank, $61.63
4. Awash International Bank, $58.25
5. NIB International Bank, $54.8
6. Bank of Abyssinia, $45.96
7. United Bank, $34.45

Source: *The Banker*, Top 50 African Banks (annual), January 2012, p. 119.

338 ■ LARGEST KENYAN BANKS BY CAPITAL, 2010

Ranked by: Tier one capital, in millions of U.S. dollars. **Remarks:** Also notes rank within the *Top African Banks,* fiscal year-end, percent change from previous year, assets, capital-assets ratio, pretax profits, real profits growth, profits-on-capital ratio, return on assets, cost-to-income ratio, BIS capital ratio, and non-performing loans as a percentage of total loans. **Number listed:** 17

1. Kenya Commercial Bank, with $436.16 million
2. Barclays Bank Kenya, $352.22
3. Equity Bank, $296.66
4. Co-operative Bank of Kenya, $222.55
5. Standard Chartered Bank Kenya, $141.1
6. Diamond Trust Bank Kenya, $119.34
7. National Bank of Kenya, $112.46
8. Investments & Mortgages Bank, $104.85
9. CfC Stanbic Bank, $98.02
10. National Industrial Credit Bank (NIC Bank), $91.26

Source: *The Banker*, Top 50 African Banks (annual), January 2012, p. 119-120.

339 ■ LARGEST LIBYAN BANKS BY CAPITAL, 2010

Ranked by: Tier one capital, in millions of U.S. dollars. **Remarks:** Also notes rank within the *Top African Banks,* fiscal year-end, percent change from previous year, assets, capital-assets ratio, pretax profits, real profits growth, profits-on-capital ratio, return on assets, cost-to-income ratio, BIS capital ratio, and non-performing loans as a percentage of total loans. **Number listed:** 4

1. Libyan Foreign Bank, with $2,573.11 million
2. National Commercial Bank, $453.39
3. Wahda Bank, $182.01
4. Bank of Commerce & Development, $81.22

Source: *The Banker*, Top 50 African Banks (annual), January 2012, p. 120.

340 ■ LARGEST SOUTH AFRICAN BANKS BY CAPITAL, 2010

Ranked by: Tier one capital, in millions of U.S. dollars. **Remarks:** Also notes rank within the *Top African Banks,* fiscal year-end, percent change from previous year, assets, capital-assets ratio, pretax profits, real profits growth, profits-on-capital ratio, return on assets, cost-to-income ratio, BIS capital ratio, and non-performing loans as a percentage of total loans. **Number listed:** 12

1. Standard Bank Group, with $12,062.12 million
2. Absa Group, $8,151.54
3. FirstRand Bank Holdings Ltd., $6,036.13
4. Nedbank Group Ltd., $5,715.92
5. Investec, $2,518.88
6. African Bank, $1,254.98
7. Capitec Bank, $196.11
8. Mercantile Bank Holdings, $192.46
9. Sasfin Holdings, $118.43
10. Bidvest Bank, $91.94

Source: *The Banker*, Top 50 African Banks (annual), January 2012, p. 122-123.

341 ■ MADAGASCAR'S LARGEST BANKS BY CAPITAL, 2010

Ranked by: Tier one capital, in millions of U.S. dollars. **Remarks:** Also notes rank within the *Top African Banks,* fiscal year-end, percent change from previous year, assets, capital-assets ratio, pretax profits, real profits growth, profits-on-capital ratio, return on assets, cost-to-income ratio, BIS capital ratio, and non-performing loans as a percentage of total loans. **Number listed:** 2

1. Bank of Africa Madagascar, with $49.8 million

2. BNI Madagascar, $33.67

Source: *The Banker,* Top 50 African Banks (annual), January 2012, p. 120.

342 ■ MALAWI'S LARGEST BANKS BY CAPITAL, 2010

Ranked by: Tier one capital, in millions of U.S. dollars. **Remarks:** Also notes rank within the *Top African Banks,* fiscal year-end, percent change from previous year, assets, capital-assets ratio, pretax profits, real profits growth, profits-on-capital ratio, return on assets, cost-to-income ratio, BIS capital ratio, and non-performing loans as a percentage of total loans. **Number listed:** 3

1. National Bank of Malawi, with $56.24 million
2. Standard Bank Malawi, $54.69
3. First Merchant Bank, $29.23

Source: *The Banker,* Top 50 African Banks (annual), January 2012, p. 120.

343 ■ MALI'S LARGEST BANKS BY CAPITAL, 2010

Ranked by: Tier one capital, in millions of U.S. dollars. **Remarks:** Also notes rank within the *Top African Banks,* fiscal year-end, percent change from previous year, assets, capital-assets ratio, pretax profits, real profits growth, profits-on-capital ratio, return on assets, cost-to-income ratio, BIS capital ratio, and non-performing loans as a percentage of total loans. **Number listed:** 2

1. Bank of Africa Group, with $410.52 million
2. Ecobank Mali, $28.46

Source: *The Banker,* Top 50 African Banks (annual), January 2012, p. 120.

344 ■ MAURITIUS'S LARGEST BANKS BY CAPITAL, 2010

Ranked by: Tier one capital, in millions of U.S. dollars. **Remarks:** Also notes rank within the *Top African Banks,* fiscal year-end, percent change from previous year, assets, capital-assets ratio, pretax profits, real profits growth, profits-on-capital ratio, return on assets, cost-to-income ratio, BIS capital ratio, and non-performing loans as a percentage of total loans. **Number listed:** 10

1. Mauritius Commercial Bank, with $591.35 million
2. State Bank of Mauritius, $309.61
3. Standard Chartered Bank Mauritius, $246.88
4. Investec Bank Mauritius, $228.35
5. Barclays Bank Mauritius, $208.91
6. HSBC Bank Mauritius, $179.37
7. SBI (Mauritius), $138.4
8. Standard Bank Mauritius, $48.06
9. Banque des Mascareignes, $40.11
10. Mauritius Post & Cooperative Bank, $22.04

Source: *The Banker,* Top 50 African Banks (annual), January 2012, p. 120.

345 ■ MOROCCO'S LARGEST REGIONAL BANKS OVERALL, 2011

Ranked by: Score based on revenue, profits, assets, and market capitalization. **Remarks:** Specific scores not provided. Also notes overall rank in the *Forbes 2000* and figures for each criterion. **Number listed:** 2

1. Attijariwafa Bank
2. Banque Centrale Populaire

Source: *Forbes,* Forbes 2000 (annual), http://www.forbes.com, May 7, 2012.

346 ■ MOZAMBIQUE'S LARGEST BANKS BY CAPITAL, 2010

Ranked by: Tier one capital, in millions of U.S. dollars. **Remarks:** Also notes rank within the *Top African Banks,* fiscal year-end, percent change from previous year, assets, capital-assets ratio, pretax profits, real profits growth, profits-on-capital ratio, return on assets, cost-to-income ratio, BIS capital ratio, and non-performing loans as a percentage of total loans. **Number listed:** 4

1. Millennium Banco Internacional de Mozambique, with $169.69 million
2. Banco de Desenvolvimento e Comercio de Mozambique, $69.18
3. BCI Fomento, $63.98
4. Standard Bank Mozambique, $46.72

Source: *The Banker,* Top 50 African Banks (annual), January 2012, p. 120-122.

347 ■ NAMIBIA'S LARGEST BANKS BY CAPITAL, 2010

Ranked by: Tier one capital, in millions of U.S. dollars. **Remarks:** Also notes rank within the *Top African Banks,* fiscal year-end, percent change from previous year, assets, capital-assets ratio, pretax profits, real profits growth, profits-on-capital ratio, return on assets, cost-to-income ratio, BIS capital ratio, and non-performing loans as a percentage of total loans. **Number listed:** 4

1. Standard Bank Namibia, with $219.55 million
2. First National Bank of Namibia, $189.32
3. Bank Windhoek, $148.86
4. Nedbank Namibia, $98.88

Source: *The Banker,* Top 50 African Banks (annual), January 2012, p. 122.

348 ■ NIGERIA'S LARGEST BANKS BY CAPITAL, 2010

Ranked by: Tier one capital, in millions of U.S. dollars. **Remarks:** Also notes rank within the *Top African Banks,* fiscal year-end, percent change from previous year, assets, capital-assets ratio, pretax profits, real profits growth, profits-on-capital ratio, return on assets, cost-to-income ratio, BIS capital ratio, and non-performing loans as a percentage of total loans. **Number listed:** 14

1. Zenith Bank, with $2,404.95 million
2. First Bank of Nigeria, $2,221.2
3. Guaranty Trust Bank, $1,361.91
4. Access Bank, $1,149.29
5. United Bank for Africa, $1,083.64
6. Fidelity Bank, $903.86
7. First City Monument Bank, $854.2
8. Diamond Bank, $704.57
9. Skye Bank, $694.77
10. Stanbic IBTC Bank, $555.26

Source: *The Banker,* Top 50 African Banks (annual), January 2012, p. 122.

349 ■ NIGER'S LARGEST BANKS BY CAPITAL, 2010

Ranked by: Tier one capital, in millions of U.S. dollars. **Remarks:** Also notes rank within the *Top African Banks,* fiscal year-end, percent change from previous year, assets, capital-assets ratio, pretax profits, real profits growth, profits-on-capital ratio, return on assets, cost-to-income ratio, BIS capital ratio, and non-performing loans as a percentage of total loans. **Number listed:** 2

1. Societe Nigerienne de Banque (SoniBank), with $25.17 million
2. Bank of Africa Niger, $24.28

Source: *The Banker*, Top 50 African Banks (annual), January 2012, p. 122.

350 ■ RWANDA'S LARGEST BANKS BY CAPITAL, 2010

Ranked by: Tier one capital, in millions of U.S. dollars. **Remarks:** Also notes rank within the *Top African Banks,* fiscal year-end, percent change from previous year, assets, capital-assets ratio, pretax profits, real profits growth, profits-on-capital ratio, return on assets, cost-to-income ratio, BIS capital ratio, and non-performing loans as a percentage of total loans. **Number listed:** 2

1. Banque de Kigali, with $41.58 million
2. Ecobank Rwanda, $14.98

Source: *The Banker*, Top 50 African Banks (annual), January 2012, p. 122.

351 ■ SENEGAL'S LARGEST BANKS BY CAPITAL, 2010

Ranked by: Tier one capital, in millions of U.S. dollars. **Remarks:** Also notes rank within the *Top African Banks,* fiscal year-end, percent change from previous year, assets, capital-assets ratio, pretax profits, real profits growth, profits-on-capital ratio, return on assets, cost-to-income ratio, BIS capital ratio, and non-performing loans as a percentage of total loans. **Number listed:** 6

1. CBAO-Groupe Attijariwafa Bank, with $139.04 million
2. Societe Generale de Banques au Senegal, $112.03
3. Banque de l'Habitat du Senegal, $55.32
4. Banque Internationale pour le Commerce & l'Industrie du Senegal, $46.33
5. Ecobank Senegal, $29.7
6. Bank of Africa Senegal, $15.27

Source: *The Banker*, Top 50 African Banks (annual), January 2012, p. 122.

352 ■ SOUTH AFRICA'S LARGEST MAJOR BANKS OVERALL, 2011

Ranked by: Score based on revenue, profits, assets, and market capitalization. **Remarks:** Specific scores not provided. Also notes overall rank in the *Forbes 2000* and figures for each criterion. **Number listed:** 2

1. Standard Bank Group (Stanbank)
2. FirstRand Ltd.

Source: *Forbes*, Forbes 2000 (annual), http://www.forbes.com, May 7, 2012.

353 ■ SUDAN'S LARGEST BANKS BY CAPITAL, 2010

Ranked by: Tier one capital, in millions of U.S. dollars. **Remarks:** Also notes rank within the *Top African Banks,* fiscal year-end, percent change from previous year, assets, capital-assets ratio, pretax profits, real profits growth, profits-on-capital ratio, return on assets, cost-to-income ratio, BIS capital ratio, and non-performing loans as a percentage of total loans. **Number listed:** 7

1. Omdurman National Bank, with $238.71 million
2. Bank of Khartoum, $197
3. Tadamon Islamic Bank, $70.86
4. Faisal Islamic Bank of Sudan, $60.75
5. Sudanese French Bank, $49.8
6. Al Baraka Bank Sudan, $38.32
7. Farmer's Commercial Bank, $37.33

Source: *The Banker*, Top 50 African Banks (annual), January 2012, p. 123.

354 ■ SWAZILAND'S LARGEST BANKS BY CAPITAL, 2010

Ranked by: Tier one capital, in millions of U.S. dollars. **Remarks:** Also notes rank within the *Top African Banks,* fiscal year-end, percent change from previous year, assets, capital-assets ratio, pretax profits, real profits growth, profits-on-capital ratio, return on assets, cost-to-income ratio, BIS capital ratio, and non-performing loans as a percentage of total loans. **Number listed:** 3

1. Swaziland Development & Savings Bank, with $42.89 million
2. Standard Bank Swaziland, $39.2
3. First National Bank of Swaziland, $38.47

Source: *The Banker*, Top 50 African Banks (annual), January 2012, p. 123.

355 ■ TANZANIA'S LARGEST BANKS BY CAPITAL, 2010

Ranked by: Tier one capital, in millions of U.S. dollars. **Remarks:** Also notes rank within the *Top African Banks,* fiscal year-end, percent change from previous year, assets, capital-assets ratio, pretax profits, real profits growth, profits-on-capital ratio, return on assets, cost-to-income ratio, BIS capital ratio, and non-performing loans as a percentage of total loans. **Number listed:** 6

1. National Microfinance Bank, with $155.06 million
2. CRDB Bank plc, $153.99
3. National Bank of Commerce, $100.68
4. Stanbic Bank Tanzania, $45.38
5. Exim Bank, $42.3
6. Diamond Trust Bank Tanzania, $15.39

Source: *The Banker*, Top 50 African Banks (annual), January 2012, p. 123.

356 ■ TUNISIA'S LARGEST BANKS BY CAPITAL, 2010

Ranked by: Tier one capital, in millions of U.S. dollars. **Remarks:** Also notes rank within the *Top African Banks,* fiscal year-end, percent change from previous year, assets, capital-assets ratio, pretax profits, real profits growth, profits-on-capital ratio, return on assets, cost-to-income ratio, BIS capital ratio, and non-performing loans as a percentage of total loans. **Number listed:** 9

1. Societe Tunisienne de Banque, with $357.75 million
2. Banque Nationale Agricole, $348.72
3. Banque Internationale Arabe de Tunisie, $334.73
4. Banque de Tunisie, $286.54
5. Amen Bank, $262.73
6. Arab Tunisian Bank, $248.03
7. Attijari Bank Tunisia, $188.88
8. Union Bancaire pour le Commerce et l'Industrie, $130.95
9. Al Baraka Bank Tunisia, $70.36

Source: *The Banker*, Top 50 African Banks (annual), January 2012, p. 123.

357 ■ UGANDA'S LARGEST BANKS BY CAPITAL, 2010

Ranked by: Tier one capital, in millions of U.S. dollars. **Remarks:** Also notes rank within the *Top African Banks,* fiscal year-end, percent change from previous year, assets, capital-assets ratio, pretax profits, real profits growth, profits-on-capital ratio, return on assets, cost-to-income ratio, BIS capital ratio, and non-performing loans as a percentage of total loans. **Number listed:** 4

1. Stanbic Bank Uganda, with $84.22 million

2. Crane Bank, $59.33

3. Centenary Bank, $34.24

4. Tropical Africa Bank, $22.15

Source: *The Banker*, Top 50 African Banks (annual), January 2012, p. 123.

358 ■ ZAMBIA'S LARGEST BANKS BY CAPITAL, 2010

Ranked by: Tier one capital, in millions of U.S. dollars. **Remarks:** Also notes rank within the *Top African Banks,* fiscal year-end, percent change from previous year, assets, capital-assets ratio, pretax profits, real profits growth, profits-on-capital ratio, return on assets, cost-to-income ratio, BIS capital ratio, and non-performing loans as a percentage of total loans. **Number listed:** 2

1. Zambia National Commercial Bank, with $74.63 million

2. Stanbic Bank Zambia, $28.63

Source: *The Banker*, Top 50 African Banks (annual), January 2012, p. 123.

359 ■ ZIMBABWE'S LARGEST BANKS BY CAPITAL, 2010

Ranked by: Tier one capital, in millions of U.S. dollars. **Remarks:** Also notes rank within the *Top African Banks,* fiscal year-end, percent change from previous year, assets, capital-assets ratio, pretax profits, real profits growth, profits-on-capital ratio, return on assets, cost-to-income ratio, BIS capital ratio, and non-performing loans as a percentage of total loans. **Number listed:** 3

1. CBZ Holdings, with $45.16 million

2. Barclays Bank Zimbabwe, $30.81

3. Stanbic Bank Zimbabwe, $26

Source: *The Banker*, Top 50 African Banks (annual), January 2012, p. 123.

Banks and Banking—Arab

360 ■ FASTEST-GROWING ARAB BANKS, 2009-2010

Ranked by: Annual growth in tier one capital, in percent. **Remarks:** Also notes overall rank in the *Top 100*, fiscal year-end, and tier one capital. **Number listed:** 10

1. BMCE Bank Group (Morocco), with 72.17%

2. Bank of Beirut, 45.32%

3. Al Ahli Bank of Kuwait, 44.77%

4. Arab Banking Corp., 43.69%

5. Jordan Islamic Bank, 38.01%

6. Burgan Bank, 33.48%

7. Byblos Bank, 32.88%

8. Rakbank, 31.04%

9. National Bank of Kuwait, 26.26%

10. Saudi British Bank, 24.13%

Source: *The Banker*, Top 100 Arab Banks (annual), October 2011, p. 84.

361 ■ LARGEST ARAB BANKS BY CAPITAL, 2010

Ranked by: Tier one capital, in millions of U.S. dollars. **Remarks:** Also notes fiscal year-end, assets, rank by assets, and percent change from previous year. **Number listed:** 100

1. National Commercial Bank (Saudi Arabia), with $8,313.18 million

2. Emirates NBD (UAE), $7,539.34

3. Riyad Bank (Saudi Arabia), $6,999.68

4. Samba Financial Group (Saudi Arabia), $6,820

5. National Bank of Abu Dhabi (UAE), $6,677.93

6. First Gulf Bank (UAE), $6,538.25

7. Al Rajhi Banking & Investment Corp. (Saudi Arabia), $6,279.19

8. National Bank of Kuwait, $5,246.58

9. Kuwait Finance House (Kuwait), $5,038.05

10. Arab Bank (Jordan), $4,888.91

Source: *The Banker*, Top 100 Arab Banks (annual), October 2011, p. 91.

362 ■ LARGEST EGYPTIAN BANKS BY CAPITAL, 2010

Ranked by: Tier one capital, in millions of U.S. dollars. **Remarks:** Also notes rank within the *Top 100 Arab Banks,* fiscal year-end, percent change from previous year, assets, capital-assets ratio, pretax profits, real profits growth, profits-on-capital ratio, return on assets, cost-to-income ratio, BIS capital ratio, and non-performing loans as a percentage of total loans. **Number listed:** 12

1. National Bank of Egypt, with $1,789.83 million

2. Commercial International Bank (Egypt), $1,103.57

3. Banque Misr, $1,036.65

4. National Societe Generale Bank, $840.24

5. Arab African International Bank, $551

6. Bank of Alexandria, $484.95

7. African Export-Import Bank, $456.68

8. Banque du Caire, $456.26

9. HSBC Bank Egypt, $448.13

10. Barclays Bank Egypt, $337.9

Source: *The Banker*, Top 100 Arab Banks (annual), October 2011, p. 86.

363 ■ LARGEST LEBANESE BANKS BY CAPITAL, 2010

Ranked by: Tier one capital, in millions of U.S. dollars. **Remarks:** Also notes rank within the *Top 100 Arab Banks,* fiscal year-end, percent change from previous year, assets, capital-assets ratio, pretax profits, real profits growth, profits-on-capital ratio, return on assets, cost-to-income ratio, BIS capital ratio, and non-performing loans as a percentage of total loans. **Number listed:** 9

1. Bank Audi SAL, with $1,866.42 million

2. Blom Bank, SAL, $1,828.35

3. Byblos Bank, $1,350.09

4. Fransabank, $796.56

5. Bank of Beirut, $744.01

6. BankMed, $687.26

7. Banque Libano-Francaise, $672.5

8. Credit Libanais, $389.14

9. Lebanese Canadian Bank, $334.29

Source: *The Banker*, Top 100 Arab Banks (annual), October 2011, p. 88.

364 ■ LARGEST MOROCCAN BANKS BY CAPITAL, 2010

Ranked by: Tier one capital, in millions of U.S. dollars. **Remarks:** Also notes rank within the *Top 100 Arab Banks,* fiscal year-end, percent change from previous year, assets, capital-assets ratio, pretax profits, real profits growth, profits-on-capital ratio, return on assets, cost-to-income ratio, BIS capital ratio, and non-performing loans as a percentage of total loans. **Number listed:** 6

1. Attijariwafabank, with $2,785.79 million

2. Groupe Banques Populaire, $2,085.24

3. BMCE Bank Group, $1,613.02

4. Societe Generale Marocaine de Banques, $908.22

5. Banque Marocaine pour le Commerce et l'Industrie, $545.73

6. Credit du Maroc, $357.2

Source: *The Banker*, Top 100 Arab Banks (annual), October 2011, p. 88.

365 ■ LARGEST SAUDI ARABIAN BANKS BY CAPITAL, 2010

Ranked by: Tier one capital, in millions of U.S. dollars. **Remarks:** Also notes rank within the *Top 100 Arab Banks,* fiscal year-end, percent change from previous year, assets, capital-assets ratio, pretax profits, real profits growth, profits-on-capital ratio, return on assets, cost-to-income ratio, BIS capital ratio, and non-performing loans as a percentage of total loans. **Number listed:** 10

1. National Commercial Bank, with $8,313.18 million

2. Riyad Bank, $6,999.68

3. Samba Financial Group, $6,820

4. Al Rajhi Banking & Investment Corp., $6,279.19

5. Banque Saudi Fransi, $4,340.83

6. Arab National Bank, $3,880.27

7. Saudi British Bank, $3,450.25

8. Saudi Hollandi Bank, $1,694.13

9. Bank Al-Jazira, $1,204.14

10. Bank Albilad, $802.84

Source: *The Banker*, Top 100 Arab Banks (annual), October 2011, p. 90.

366 ■ LARGEST TUNISIAN BANKS BY CAPITAL, 2010

Ranked by: Tier one capital, in millions of U.S. dollars. **Remarks:** Also notes rank within the *Top 100 Arab Banks,* fiscal year-end, percent change from previous year, assets, capital-assets ratio, pretax profits, real profits growth, profits-on-capital ratio, return on assets, cost-to-income ratio, BIS capital ratio, and non-performing loans as a percentage of total loans. **Number listed:** 4

1. Banque Internationale Arabe de Tunisie, with $329.01 million

2. Banque de Tunisie, $281.65

3. Amen Bank, $258.24

4. Arab Tunisian Bank, $243.79

Source: *The Banker*, Top 100 Arab Banks (annual), October 2011, p. 90.

367 ■ MOST POWERFUL ARABS IN BANKING AND FINANCE, 2012

Ranked by: Score based on scope of influence. **Remarks:** Specific scores not provided. Also notes rank in the overall *Power 500.* **Number listed:** 88

1. Prince Alwaleed bin Talal Al Saud

2. Sheikha Lubna Al Qasimi

3. Ahmad Al Sayed

4. Fahad Al Mubarak

5. Khaldoon Al Mubarak

6. Ibrahim Dabdoub

7. Ali Shareef Al Emadi

8. Lubna Olayan

9. Abdulaziz Al Ghurair

10. Abdel Hamid Shoman

Source: *Arab Business*, Power 500 (annual), June 4, 2012.

368 ■ MOST PROFITABLE ARAB BANKS, 2010

Ranked by: Pre-tax profits, in millions of U.S. dollars. **Remarks:** Also notes overall rank in the *Top 100 Arab Banks*, fiscal year-end, and annual growth in profits. **Number listed:** 10

1. Al Rajhi Banking & Investment Corp. (Saudi Arabia), with $1,805.55 million

2. Qatar National Bank, $1,570.8

3. National Commercial Bank (Saudi Arabia), $1,280.8

4. Samba Financial Group (Saudi Arabia), $1,182.67

5. National Bank of Kuwait, $1,137.29

6. National Bank of Abu Dhabi (UAE), $1,030.7

7. First Gulf Bank (UAE), $931.12

8. Attijariwafabank (Morocco), $843.21

9. Riyad Bank (Saudi Arabia), $753.23

10. Banque Saudi Fransi (Saudi Arabia), $747.01

Source: *The Banker*, Top 100 Arab Banks (annual), October 2011, p. 84.

369 ■ OMAN'S LARGEST BANKS BY CAPITAL, 2010

Ranked by: Tier one capital, in millions of U.S. dollars. **Remarks:** Also notes rank within the *Top 100 Arab Banks,* fiscal year-end, percent change from previous year, assets, capital-assets ratio, pretax profits, real profits growth, profits-on-capital ratio, return on assets, cost-to-income ratio, BIS capital ratio, and non-performing loans as a percentage of total loans. **Number listed:** 6

1. BankMuscat, with $1,753.77 million

2. National Bank of Oman, $632.68

3. Bank Dhofar, $546.8

4. Oman International Bank, $331.71

5. Oman Arab Bank, $323.35

6. Bank Sohar SAOG, $298.96

Source: *The Banker*, Top 100 Arab Banks (annual), October 2011, p. 88.

370 ■ QATAR'S LARGEST BANKS BY CAPITAL, 2010

Ranked by: Tier one capital, in millions of U.S. dollars. **Remarks:** Also notes rank within the *Top 100 Arab Banks,* fiscal year-end, percent change from previous year, assets, capital-assets ratio, pretax profits, real profits growth, profits-on-capital ratio, return on assets, cost-to-income ratio, BIS capital ratio, and non-performing loans as a percentage of total loans. **Number listed:** 7

1. Qatar National Bank, with $4.703.08 million

2. Commercial Bank of Qatar, $2.278.57

3. Qatar Islamic Bank, $1,790.66

4. Doha Bank, $1,268.65

5. Qatar International Islamic Bank, $824.81

6. International Bank of Qatar, $624.92

7. Ahli Bank, $448.08

Source: *The Banker*, Top 100 Arab Banks (annual), October 2011, p. 88-90.

371 ■ UNITED ARAB EMIRATES'S LARGEST BANKS BY CAPITAL, 2010

Ranked by: Tier one capital, in millions of U.S. dollars. **Remarks:** Also notes rank within the *Top 100 Arab Banks,* fiscal year-end,

percent change from previous year, assets, capital-assets ratio, pretax profits, real profits growth, profits-on-capital ratio, return on assets, cost-to-income ratio, BIS capital ratio, and non-performing loans as a percentage of total loans. **Number listed:** 16

1. Emirates NBD, with $7.539.34 million
2. National Bank of Abu Dhabi, $6,677.93
3. First Gulf Bank, $6,538.25
4. Abu Dhabi Commercial Bank, $4,414.95
5. MashreqBank PSC, $3,306.02
6. Union National Bank, $3,168.88
7. Dubai Islamic Bank, $2,823.22
8. Commercial Bank of Dubai, $1,478.21
9. Bank of Sharjah, $1,125.24
10. Sharjah Islamic Bank, $1,124.37

Source: *The Banker*, Top 100 Arab Banks (annual), October 2011, p. 90.

Banks and Banking—Asia

372 ■ ASEAN'S LARGEST BANKS BY CAPITAL, 2010

Ranked by: Tier one capital, in millions of U.S. dollars. **Remarks:** Ranking covers banks in the Association of South-East Asian Nations (ASEAN). Also notes rank within the *Top 1000 World Banks*. **Number listed:** 25

1. DBS Bank (Singapore), with $21,462 million
2. Oversea-Chinese Banking Corp. (Singapore), $13,314
3. United Overseas Bank (Singapore), $12,703
4. Malayan Banking Berhad (Malaysia), $9,281
5. Bangkok Bank (Thailand), $5,585
6. CIMB Group Holdings Berhad (Malaysia), $4,990
7. Public Bank (Malaysia), $4,882
8. Siam Commercial Bank (Thailand), $4,068
9. Krung Thai Bank (Thailand), $3,837
10. Kasikornbank (Thailand), $3,514

Source: *The Banker*, Top 1000 World Banks (annual), July 2011, p. 147.

373 ■ ASIA-PACIFIC'S (EXCLUDING CHINA AND JAPAN) FASTEST-GROWING BANKS, 2009-2010

Ranked by: Annual growth in tier one capital, in percent. **Remarks:** Also notes rank within the *Top 1000 World Banks* and total tier one capital. **Number listed:** 10

1. Bank Negara Indonesia, with 96.47%
2. IndusInd Bank (India), 78.27%
3. Bank Jabar Banten (Indonesia), 74.47%
4. Bank Islam Malaysia, 63.28%
5. Andhra Bank (India), 48.45%
6. Bank of Baroda (India), 47.68%
7. UCO Bank (India), 43.94%
8. Security Bank Corp. (Philippines), 43.76%
9. Oriental Bank of Commerce (India), 42.96%
10. Punjab & Sind Bank (India), 41.76%

Source: *The Banker*, Top 1000 World Banks (annual), July 2011, p. 147.

374 ■ ASIA-PACIFIC'S (EXCLUDING CHINA AND JAPAN) LARGEST BANKS BY CAPITAL, 2010

Ranked by: Tier one capital, in millions of U.S. dollars. **Remarks:** Also notes rank within the *Top 1000 World Banks*. **Number listed:** 25

1. National Australia Bank Ltd. (Australia), with $29,684 million
2. Australia & New Zealand Banking Group (ANZ, Australia), $25,813
3. Westpac Banking Corp. (Australia), $24,563
4. Commonwealth Bank Group (Australia), $22,678
5. DBS Bank (Singapore), $21,462
6. State Bank of India, $19,023
7. Woori Financial Group (S. Korea), $15,672
8. KB Financial Group (S. Korea), $15,610
9. Shinhan Financial Group (S. Korea), $14,502
10. Oversea-Chinese Banking Corp. (Singapore), $13,314

Source: *The Banker*, Top 1000 World Banks (annual), July 2011, p. 147.

375 ■ BANGLADESH'S LARGEST BANKS BY CAPITAL, 2010

Ranked by: Tier one capital, in millions of U.S. dollars. **Remarks:** Also notes rank within the *Top 300 Asia-Pacific Banks,* fiscal year-end, percent change from previous year, assets, capital-assets ratio, pretax profits, real profits growth, profits-on-capital ratio, return on assets, cost-to-income ratio, BIS capital ratio, and non-performing loans as a percentage of total loans. **Number listed:** 21

1. Sonali Bank, with $358.07 million
2. Islami Bank Bangladesh, $262.33
3. Prime Bank, $223.22
4. Pubali Bank, $203.25
5. National Bank, $200.75
6. SouthEast Bank, $197.79
7. Arab Bangladesh Bank, $179.44
8. Export Import Bank of Bangladesh, $175.91
9. Agrani Bank, $164.34
10. Janata Bank, $156.72

Source: *The Banker*, Top 300 Asia-Pacific Banks (annual), April 2012, p. 60.

376 ■ BRUNEI'S LARGEST BANKS BY CAPITAL, 2010

Ranked by: Tier one capital, in millions of U.S. dollars. **Remarks:** Also notes rank within the *Top 300 Asia-Pacific Banks,* fiscal year-end, percent change from previous year, assets, capital-assets ratio, pretax profits, real profits growth, profits-on-capital ratio, return on assets, cost-to-income ratio, BIS capital ratio, and non-performing loans as a percentage of total loans. **Number listed:** 2

1. Bank Islam Brunei Darussalam, with $675.89 million
2. Baiduri Bank, $156.02

Source: *The Banker*, Top 300 Asia-Pacific Banks (annual), April 2012, p. 60.

377 ■ CAMBODIA'S LARGEST BANKS BY CAPITAL, 2010

Ranked by: Tier one capital, in millions of U.S. dollars. **Remarks:** Also notes rank within the *Top 300 Asia-Pacific Banks,* fiscal year-end, percent change from previous year, assets, capital-assets ratio, pretax profits, real profits growth, profits-on-capital ratio, return on assets, cost-to-income ratio, BIS capital ratio, and non-performing loans as a percentage of total loans. **Number listed:** 3

1. Cambodian Public Bank, with $190.89 million

2. Canadia Bank, $130.7

3. Acleda Bank, $127.53

Source: *The Banker*, Top 300 Asia-Pacific Banks (annual), April 2012, p. 60.

378 ■ CHINA'S LARGEST MAJOR BANKS OVERALL, 2011

Ranked by: Score based on revenue, profits, assets, and market capitalization. **Remarks:** Specific scores not provided. Also notes overall rank in the *Forbes 2000* and figures for each criterion. **Number listed:** 4

1. Industrial & Commercial Bank of China (ICBC)

2. Bank of China

3. Bank of Communications

4. China Merchants Bank

Source: *Forbes*, Forbes 2000 (annual), http://www.forbes.com, May 7, 2012.

379 ■ CHINA'S LARGEST REGIONAL BANKS OVERALL, 2011

Ranked by: Score based on revenue, profits, assets, and market capitalization. **Remarks:** Specific scores not provided. Also notes overall rank in the *Forbes 2000* and figures for each criterion. **Number listed:** 13

1. China Construction Bank

2. Agricultural Bank of China

3. Shanghai Pudong Development Bank

4. China Citic Bank

5. China Minsheng Banking

6. Industrial Bank China

7. China Everbright Bank

8. Shenzhen Development Bank

9. Hua Xia Bank

10. Bank of Beijing

Source: *Forbes*, Forbes 2000 (annual), http://www.forbes.com, May 7, 2012.

380 ■ CHINA'S MOST VALUABLE BANKING BRANDS, 2011

Ranked by: Brand value, in millions of U.S. dollars. **Remarks:** Also notes rank within the *Global 500* for current and previous year, figures for current and previous year, and brand rating. Ranking is available online only. **Number listed:** 7

1. China Construction Bank, with $15,464 million

2. ICBC, $15,164

3. Bank of China, $12,857

4. Agricultural Bank of China, $9,929

5. Bank of Communications, $5,630

6. China Merchants Bank, $3,980

7. Shanghai Pudong Development Bank, $2,450

Source: *Global 500*, (annual), Brand Finance plc, March 2012.

381 ■ HONG KONG'S LARGEST BANKS BY CAPITAL, 2010

Ranked by: Tier one capital, in millions of U.S. dollars. **Remarks:** Also notes rank within the *Top 1000 World Banks,* fiscal year-end, percent change from previous year, assets, capital-assets ratio, pretax profits, real profits growth, profits-on-capital ratio, return on assets, cost-to-income ratio, BIS capital ratio, and non-performing loans as a percentage of total loans. **Number listed:** 16

1. Hongkong & Shanghai Banking Corp., with $24,359 million

2. Bank of China Hong Kong, $10,025

3. Hang Seng Bank, $4,360

4. Bank of East Asia, $4,309

5. Standard Chartered Bank Hong Kong, $4,135

6. DBS Bank (Hong Kong), $2,724

7. Industrial & Commercial Bank of China (Asia), $2,094

8. Shanghai Commercial Bank, $1,804

9. Citic Bank International Ltd., $1,544

10. Wing Hang Bank, $1,246

Source: *The Banker*, Top 1000 World Banks (annual), July 2011, p. 229.

382 ■ INDIA'S LARGEST BANKS BY CAPITAL, 2010

Ranked by: Tier one capital, in millions of U.S. dollars. **Remarks:** Also notes rank within the *Top 1000 World Banks,* fiscal year-end, percent change from previous year, assets, capital-assets ratio, pretax profits, real profits growth, profits-on-capital ratio, return on assets, cost-to-income ratio, BIS capital ratio, and non-performing loans as a percentage of total loans. **Number listed:** 35

1. State Bank of India, with $19,023 million

2. ICICI Bank, $10,073

3. HDFC Bank, $5,312

4. Punjab National Bank, $4,699

5. Bank of Baroda, $4,697

6. Canara Bank, $4,488

7. Axis Bank, $4,144

8. Bank of India, $3,872

9. IDBI, $3,125

10. Union Bank of India, $2,727

Source: *The Banker*, Top 1000 World Banks (annual), July 2011, p. 231.

383 ■ INDIA'S LARGEST MAJOR BANKS OVERALL, 2011

Ranked by: Score based on revenue, profits, assets, and market capitalization. **Remarks:** Specific scores not provided. Also notes overall rank in the *Forbes 2000* and figures for each criterion. **Number listed:** 2

1. Canara Bank

2. Indian Bank

Source: *Forbes*, Forbes 2000 (annual), http://www.forbes.com, May 7, 2012.

384 ■ INDIA'S LARGEST REGIONAL BANKS OVERALL, 2011

Ranked by: Score based on revenue, profits, assets, and market capitalization. **Remarks:** Specific scores not provided. Also notes overall rank in the *Forbes 2000* and figures for each criterion. **Number listed:** 18

1. State Bank of India Group

2. Icici Bank

3. HDFC Bank

4. Punjab National Bank

5. Bank of Baroda

6. Axis Bank

7. Bank of India

8. Union Bank of India

9. IDBI Bank
10. Kotak Mahindra Bank

Source: *Forbes*, Forbes 2000 (annual), http://www.forbes.com, May 7, 2012.

385 ■ INDONESIA'S LARGEST BANKS BY CAPITAL, 2010

Ranked by: Tier one capital, in millions of U.S. dollars. **Remarks:** Also notes rank within the *Top 1000 World Banks,* fiscal year-end, percent change from previous year, assets, capital-assets ratio, pretax profits, real profits growth, profits-on-capital ratio, return on assets, cost-to-income ratio, BIS capital ratio, and non-performing loans as a percentage of total loans. **Number listed:** 14

1. Bank Mandiri, with $3,119 million
2. Bank Negara Indonesia, $3,010
3. Bank Central Asia, $2,981
4. Bank Rakyat Indonesia, $2,518
5. Bank Danamon Indonesia, $1,623
6. Bank CIMB Niaga, $1,264
7. Panin Bank, $1,155
8. Bank Internasional Indonesia, $795
9. Bank UOB Buana, $713
10. Bank Permata, $676

Source: *The Banker*, Top 1000 World Banks (annual), July 2011, p. 231-233.

386 ■ INDONESIA'S LARGEST REGIONAL BANKS OVERALL, 2011

Ranked by: Score based on revenue, profits, assets, and market capitalization. **Remarks:** Specific scores not provided. Also notes overall rank in the *Forbes 2000* and figures for each criterion. **Number listed:** 5

1. Bank Rakyat Indonesia
2. Bank Mandiri
3. Bank Central Asia
4. Bank Negara Indonesia
5. Bank Danamon Indonesia

Source: *Forbes*, Forbes 2000 (annual), http://www.forbes.com, May 7, 2012.

387 ■ JAPAN'S LARGEST BANKS BY CAPITAL, 2010

Ranked by: Tier one capital, in millions of U.S. dollars. **Remarks:** Also notes rank within the *Top 1000 World Banks,* fiscal year-end, percent change from previous year, assets, capital-assets ratio, pretax profits, real profits growth, profits-on-capital ratio, return on assets, cost-to-income ratio, BIS capital ratio, and non-performing loans as a percentage of total loans. **Number listed:** 105

1. Mitsubishi UFJ Financial Group Inc., with $119,732 million
2. Sumitomo Mitsui Financial Group Inc., $76,074
3. Mizuho Financial Group, $74,224
4. Norinchukin Bank, $49,815
5. Nomura Holdings, $23,036
6. Resona Holdings, $17,068
7. Sumitomo Trust & Banking Co., $16,046
8. Shinkin Central Bank, $14,070
9. Shoko Chukin Bank, $8,946
10. Bank of Yokohama, $8,782

Source: *The Banker*, Top 1000 World Banks (annual), July 2011, p. 235-237.

388 ■ JAPAN'S LARGEST MAJOR BANKS OVERALL, 2011

Ranked by: Score based on revenue, profits, assets, and market capitalization. **Remarks:** Specific scores not provided. Also notes overall rank in the *Forbes 2000* and figures for each criterion. **Number listed:** 7

1. Mitsubishi UFJ Financial Group Inc.
2. Sumitomo Mitsui Financial Group Inc.
3. Mizuho Financial Group
4. Sumitomo Mitsui Trust
5. Bank of Yokohama
6. Chiba Bank
7. Aozora Bank

Source: *Forbes*, Forbes 2000 (annual), http://www.forbes.com, May 7, 2012.

389 ■ JAPAN'S LARGEST REGIONAL BANKS OVERALL, 2011

Ranked by: Score based on revenue, profits, assets, and market capitalization. **Remarks:** Specific scores not provided. Also notes overall rank in the *Forbes 2000* and figures for each criterion. **Number listed:** 55

1. Resona Holdings
2. Shizuoka Bank
3. Shinsei Bank
4. Nishi-Nippon City Bank
5. Tomony Holdings
6. Fukuoka Financial Group
7. Hokuhoku Financial Group
8. Yamaguchi Financial Group
9. Joyo Bank
10. Sapporo Hokuyo

Source: *Forbes*, Forbes 2000 (annual), http://www.forbes.com, May 7, 2012.

390 ■ LARGEST CHINESE BANKS BY CAPITAL, 2010

Ranked by: Tier one capital, in millions of U.S. dollars. **Remarks:** Also notes rank for previous year, city, percent change from previous year, assets, capital-assets ratio, pretax profits, profits-on-capital ratio, return on assets, BIS capital ratio, and non-performing loans as a percentage of total loans. **Number listed:** 100

1. Industrial Commercial Bank of China, with $113,393 million
2. China Construction Bank Corp., $95,834
3. Bank of China, $94,579
4. Agricultural Bank of China, $79,285
5. Bank of Communications, $34,321
6. China Merchants Bank, $19,324
7. Shanghai Pudong Development Bank, $18,222
8. China CITIC Bank, $17,994
9. China Minsheng Banking Corp., $15,626
10. Industrial Bank, $13,487

Source: *The Banker*, Top 100 Chinese Banks (annual), September 2011, p. 91-92.

391 ■ LARGEST JAPANESE BANKS BY CAPITAL, 2010

Ranked by: Tier one capital, in millions of U.S. dollars. **Remarks:** Also notes percent change from previous year, assets, capital-assets ratio, pretax profits, real profits growth, profits-on-capital ratio, return on assets, cost-to-income ratio, BIS capital ratio, and non-performing loans as a percentage of total loans. **Number listed:** 100

1. Mitsubishi UFJ Financial Group Inc., with $119,731.75 million
2. Sumitomo Mitsui Financial Group Inc., $76,073.62
3. Mizuho Financial Group, $74,223.51
4. Norinchukin Bank, $49,814.75
5. Nomura Holdings, $23,036.21
6. Resona Holdings, $17,068.45
7. Sumitomo Trust & Banking Co., $16,045.95
8. Shinkin Central Bank, $11,745.21
9. Shoko Chukin Bank, $10,173.87
10. Bank of Yokohama, $8,781.86

Source: *The Banker*, Top 100 Japanese Banks (annual), December 2011, p. 64+.

392 ■ MALAYSIA'S LARGEST BANKS BY CAPITAL, 2010

Ranked by: Tier one capital, in millions of U.S. dollars. **Remarks:** Also notes rank within the *Top 1000 World Banks,* fiscal year-end, percent change from previous year, assets, capital-assets ratio, pretax profits, real profits growth, profits-on-capital ratio, return on assets, cost-to-income ratio, BIS capital ratio, and non-performing loans as a percentage of total loans. **Number listed:** 17

1. Malayan Banking Berhad, with $9,281 million
2. CIMB Group Holdings Berhad, $4,990
3. Public Bank, $4,882
4. AMMB Holdings, $2,742
5. RHB Bank, $2,693
6. Hong Leong Bank, $1,924
7. Bank Kerjasama Rakyat Malaysia, $1,824
8. OCBC Bank (Malaysia), $1,453
9. EON Bank, $1,341
10. HSBC Bank Malaysia Berhad, $1,267

Source: *The Banker*, Top 1000 World Banks (annual), July 2011, p. 240.

393 ■ MALAYSIA'S LARGEST REGIONAL BANKS OVERALL, 2011

Ranked by: Score based on revenue, profits, assets, and market capitalization. **Remarks:** Specific scores not provided. Also notes overall rank in the *Forbes 2000* and figures for each criterion. **Number listed:** 4

1. CIMB Group Holdings
2. Public Bank
3. RHB Capital
4. AMMB Holdings

Source: *Forbes*, Forbes 2000 (annual), http://www.forbes.com, May 7, 2012.

394 ■ THE PHILIPPINES' LARGEST BANKS BY CAPITAL, 2010

Ranked by: Tier one capital, in millions of U.S. dollars. **Remarks:** Also notes rank within the *Top 1000 World Banks,* fiscal year-end, percent change from previous year, assets, capital-assets ratio, pretax profits, real profits growth, profits-on-capital ratio, return on assets, cost-to-income ratio, BIS capital ratio, and non-performing loans as a percentage of total loans. **Number listed:** 11

1. Banco de Oro Unibank, with $1,690 million

2. Bank of the Philippine Islands, $1,553
3. Metropolitan Bank & Trust Co., $1,542
4. Land Bank Philippines, $1,440
5. Rizal Commercial Banking Corp., $680
6. China Banking Corp., $661
7. Development Bank of the Philippines, $650
8. Philippine National Bank, $621
9. Security Bank Corp., $561
10. Allied Banking Corp., $479

Source: *The Banker*, Top 1000 World Banks (annual), July 2011, p. 242.

395 ■ THE PHILIPPINES' LARGEST REGIONAL BANKS OVERALL, 2011

Ranked by: Score based on revenue, profits, assets, and market capitalization. **Remarks:** Specific scores not provided. Also notes overall rank in the *Forbes 2000* and figures for each criterion. **Number listed:** 3

1. Bank Philippine Islands
2. Metropolitan Bank & Trust
3. BDO Unibank

Source: *Forbes*, Forbes 2000 (annual), http://www.forbes.com, May 7, 2012.

396 ■ SINGAPORE'S LARGEST BANKS BY CAPITAL, 2010

Ranked by: Tier one capital, in millions of U.S. dollars. **Remarks:** Also notes rank within the *Top 1000 World Banks,* fiscal year-end, percent change from previous year, assets, capital-assets ratio, pretax profits, real profits growth, profits-on-capital ratio, return on assets, cost-to-income ratio, BIS capital ratio, and non-performing loans as a percentage of total loans. **Number listed:** 3

1. DBS Bank, with $21,462 million
2. Oversea-Chinese Banking Corp., $13,314
3. United Overseas Bank, $12,703

Source: *The Banker*, Top 1000 World Banks (annual), July 2011, p. 247.

397 ■ SINGAPORE'S LARGEST MAJOR BANKS OVERALL, 2011

Ranked by: Score based on revenue, profits, assets, and market capitalization. **Remarks:** Specific scores not provided. Also notes overall rank in the *Forbes 2000* and figures for each criterion. **Number listed:** 2

1. DBS Group Holdings Ltd.
2. Overseas-Chinese Banking Corp.

Source: *Forbes*, Forbes 2000 (annual), http://www.forbes.com, May 7, 2012.

398 ■ SOUTH KOREA'S LARGEST BANKS BY CAPITAL, 2010

Ranked by: Tier one capital, in millions of U.S. dollars. **Remarks:** Also notes rank within the *Top 1000 World Banks,* fiscal year-end, percent change from previous year, assets, capital-assets ratio, pretax profits, real profits growth, profits-on-capital ratio, return on assets, cost-to-income ratio, BIS capital ratio, and non-performing loans as a percentage of total loans. **Number listed:** 11

1. Woori Financial Group, with $15,672 million
2. KB Financial Group, $15,610
3. Shinhan Financial Group, $14,502

4. National Agricultural Cooperative Federation, $11,158

5. Hana Financial Group, $9,383

6. Industrial Bank of Korea, $8,996

7. Korea Exchange Bank, $6,027

8. Citibank Korea, $4,704

9. Standard Chartered Bank Korea, $3,290

10. Daegu Bank, $2,000

Source: *The Banker*, Top 1000 World Banks (annual), July 2011, p. 247.

399 ■ SRI LANKA'S LARGEST BANKS BY CAPITAL, 2010

Ranked by: Tier one capital, in millions of U.S. dollars. **Remarks:** Also notes rank within the *Top 300 Asia-Pacific Banks,* fiscal year-end, percent change from previous year, assets, capital-assets ratio, pretax profits, real profits growth, profits-on-capital ratio, return on assets, cost-to-income ratio, BIS capital ratio, and non-performing loans as a percentage of total loans. **Number listed:** 8

1. Bank of Ceylon, with $271.99 million

2. Commercial Bank of Ceylon, $264.94

3. Hatton National Bank, $212.63

4. DFCC Bank, $183.92

5. People's Bank, $133.98

6. National Development Bank, $133.45

7. Sampath Bank, $123.49

8. Seylan Bank, $107.6

Source: *The Banker*, Top 300 Asia-Pacific Banks (annual), April 2012, p. 66.

400 ■ TAIWAN'S LARGEST BANKS BY CAPITAL, 2010

Ranked by: Tier one capital, in millions of U.S. dollars. **Remarks:** Also notes rank within the *Top 1000 World Banks,* fiscal year-end, percent change from previous year, assets, capital-assets ratio, pretax profits, real profits growth, profits-on-capital ratio, return on assets, cost-to-income ratio, BIS capital ratio, and non-performing loans as a percentage of total loans. **Number listed:** 23

1. Bank of Taiwan, with $6,067 million

2. Mega International Commercial Bank, $4,894

3. Chinatrust Commercial Bank, $4,174

4. Taiwan Cooperative Bank, $3,511

5. Hua Nan Financial Holdings, $3,351

6. Shanghai Commercial & Savings Bank, $3,213

7. Land Bank of Taiwan, $2,886

8. Cathay United Bank, $2,824

9. Chang Hwa Commercial Bank, $2,759

10. Taipei Fubon Bank, $2,692

Source: *The Banker*, Top 1000 World Banks (annual), July 2011, p. 250.

401 ■ TAIWAN'S LARGEST REGIONAL BANKS OVERALL, 2011

Ranked by: Score based on revenue, profits, assets, and market capitalization. **Remarks:** Specific scores not provided. Also notes overall rank in the *Forbes 2000* and figures for each criterion. **Number listed:** 2

1. Chang Hwa Bank

2. Taiwan Business Bank

Source: *Forbes*, Forbes 2000 (annual), http://www.forbes.com, May 7, 2012.

402 ■ THAILAND'S LARGEST BANKS BY CAPITAL, 2010

Ranked by: Tier one capital, in millions of U.S. dollars. **Remarks:** Also notes rank within the *Top 1000 World Banks,* fiscal year-end, percent change from previous year, assets, capital-assets ratio, pretax profits, real profits growth, profits-on-capital ratio, return on assets, cost-to-income ratio, BIS capital ratio, and non-performing loans as a percentage of total loans. **Number listed:** 15

1. Bangkok Bank, with $5,585 million

2. Siam Commercial Bank, $4,068

3. Krung Thai Bank, $3,837

4. Kasikornbank, $3,514

5. Bank of Ayudhya, $2,650

6. TMB Bank, $1,517

7. Siam City Bank, $1,248

8. Bank of Tokyo-Mitsubishi Thailand, $1,016

9. Standard Chartered Bank Thailand, $1,015

10. Kiatnakin Bank, $599

Source: *The Banker*, Top 1000 World Banks (annual), July 2011, p. 252.

403 ■ THAILAND'S LARGEST REGIONAL BANKS OVERALL, 2011

Ranked by: Score based on revenue, profits, assets, and market capitalization. **Remarks:** Specific scores not provided. Also notes overall rank in the *Forbes 2000* and figures for each criterion. **Number listed:** 5

1. Siam Commercial Bank

2. Bangkok Bank

3. Krung Thai Bank

4. Bank of Ayudhya

5. Thanachart Capital

Source: *Forbes*, Forbes 2000 (annual), http://www.forbes.com, May 7, 2012.

404 ■ VIETNAM'S LARGEST BANKS BY CAPITAL, 2010

Ranked by: Tier one capital, in millions of U.S. dollars. **Remarks:** Also notes rank within the *Top 1000 World Banks,* fiscal year-end, percent change from previous year, assets, capital-assets ratio, pretax profits, real profits growth, profits-on-capital ratio, return on assets, cost-to-income ratio, BIS capital ratio, and non-performing loans as a percentage of total loans. **Number listed:** 8

1. Vietnam Investment & Development Bank, with $1,068 million

2. Vietcombank, $1,001

3. VietinBank, $947

4. Vietnam Eximbank, $636

5. Saigon Thuong Tin Commercial Bank, $624

6. Asia Commercial Bank, $587

7. Techcombank, $340

8. DongA Commercial JSB, $279

Source: *The Banker*, Top 1000 World Banks (annual), July 2011, p. 258.

Banks and Banking—Caribbean

405 ■ BERMUDA'S LARGEST BANKS BY CAPITAL, 2010

Ranked by: Tier one capital, in millions of U.S. dollars. **Remarks:** Also notes rank within the *Top 1000 World Banks,* fiscal year-end, percent change from previous year, assets, capital-assets ratio, pretax profits, real profits growth, profits-on-capital ratio, return on assets, cost-to-income ratio, BIS capital ratio, and non-performing loans as a percentage of total loans. **Number listed:** 2

1. HSBC Bank Bermuda, with $1,624 million
2. Bank of NT Butterfield & Son, $773

Source: *The Banker*, Top 1000 World Banks (annual), July 2011, p. 217.

406 ■ LARGEST CARIBBEAN BANKS BY CAPITAL, 2010

Ranked by: Tier one capital, in millions of U.S. dollars. **Remarks:** Ranking covers banks in the Caribbean Community (Caricom). Also notes headquarters, fiscal year-end, percent change from previous year, assets, pretax profits, return on assets, BIS capital ratio, and non-performing loans as a percentage of total loans. **Number listed:** 20

1. RBC Financial Caribbean (Trinidad & Tobago), with $2,646.31 million
2. FirstCaribbean International Bank Group (Barbados), $1,229
3. Republic Bank (Trinidad & Tobago), $1,006.74
4. First Citizens Bank (Trinidad & Tobago), $577.41
5. Belize Bank Holdings, $402.7
6. Scotiabank Trinidad & Tobago, $320.62
7. Scotia Group Jamaica, $273.31
8. Scotiabank Barbados, $254.39
9. National Commercial Bank Jamaica, $232.53
10. Commonwealth Bank (Bahamas), $161.98

Source: *The Banker*, Top Caricom Banks (annual), August 2011, p. 58.

407 ■ TRINIDAD AND TOBAGO'S LARGEST BANKS BY CAPITAL, 2010

Ranked by: Tier one capital, in millions of U.S. dollars. **Remarks:** Also notes rank within the *Top 1000 World Banks,* fiscal year-end, percent change from previous year, assets, capital-assets ratio, pretax profits, real profits growth, profits-on-capital ratio, return on assets, cost-to-income ratio, BIS capital ratio, and non-performing loans as a percentage of total loans. **Number listed:** 4

1. RBC Financial (Caribbean), with $2,646 million
2. Republic Bank, $1,007
3. First Citizen Bank, $577
4. Scotiabank Trinidad & Tobago, $321

Source: *The Banker*, Top 1000 World Banks (annual), July 2011, p. 252.

Banks and Banking—Europe

408 ■ ANDORRA'S LARGEST BANKS BY CAPITAL, 2010

Ranked by: Tier one capital, in millions of U.S. dollars. **Remarks:** Also notes rank within the *Top 1000 World Banks,* fiscal year-end, percent change from previous year, assets, capital-assets ratio, pretax profits, real profits growth, profits-on-capital ratio, return on assets, cost-to-income ratio, BIS capital ratio, and non-performing loans as a percentage of total loans. **Number listed:** 3

1. Credit Andorra, with $675 million
2. Andbanc, $416
3. Banc International d'Andorra - Banca Mora, $387

Source: *The Banker*, Top 1000 World Banks (annual), July 2011, p. 216.

409 ■ AUSTRIA'S LARGEST BANKS BY CAPITAL, 2010

Ranked by: Tier one capital, in millions of U.S. dollars. **Remarks:** Also notes rank within the *Top 1000 World Banks,* fiscal year-end, percent change from previous year, assets, capital-assets ratio, pretax profits, real profits growth, profits-on-capital ratio, return on assets, cost-to-income ratio, BIS capital ratio, and non-performing loans as a percentage of total loans. **Number listed:** 15

1. Bank Austria, with $17,703 million
2. Erste Group, $16,336
3. Raiffeisen Bank International, $12,287
4. Osterreichische Volksbanken, $3,493
5. Raiffeisenlandesbank Niederosterriech-Wien, $3,186
6. Raiffeisen Landesbank Oberosterreich, $2,965
7. Bank fur Arbeit und Wirtschaft - PSK Group, $2,928
8. Hypo Alpe Adria (Group), $2,399
9. Oberbank, $1,375
10. Raiffeisen-Landesbank Steiermark, $1,261

Source: *The Banker*, Top 1000 World Banks (annual), July 2011, p. 216-217.

410 ■ AUSTRIA'S LARGEST MAJOR BANKS OVERALL, 2011

Ranked by: Score based on revenue, profits, assets, and market capitalization. **Remarks:** Specific scores not provided. Also notes overall rank in the *Forbes 2000* and figures for each criterion. **Number listed:** 2

1. Raiffeisen International Bank Holding
2. Erste Group Bank

Source: *Forbes*, Forbes 2000 (annual), http://www.forbes.com, May 7, 2012.

411 ■ BELARUS'S LARGEST BANKS BY CAPITAL, 2010

Ranked by: Tier one capital, in millions of U.S. dollars. **Remarks:** Also notes rank within the *Top 1000 World Banks,* fiscal year-end, percent change from previous year, assets, capital-assets ratio, pretax profits, real profits growth, profits-on-capital ratio, return on assets, cost-to-income ratio, BIS capital ratio, and non-performing loans as a percentage of total loans. **Number listed:** 3

1. Belagroprombank, with $2,049 million
2. Belarusbank, $1,380
3. Priorbank, $302

Source: *The Banker*, Top 1000 World Banks (annual), July 2011, p. 217.

412 ■ BELGIUM'S LARGEST BANKS BY CAPITAL, 2010

Ranked by: Tier one capital, in millions of U.S. dollars. **Remarks:** Also notes rank within the *Top 1000 World Banks,* fiscal year-end, percent change from previous year, assets, capital-assets ratio, pretax profits, real profits growth, profits-on-capital ratio, return on assets, cost-to-income ratio, BIS capital ratio, and non-performing loans as a percentage of total loans. **Number listed:** 6

1. BNP Paribas Fortis, with $26,287 million
2. Dexia, $24,632
3. KBC Group, $22,267
4. ING Belgium, $13,819
5. Axa Bank Europe, $1,287
6. Groupe Credit Agricole/Landbouwkrediet, $883

Source: *The Banker*, Top 1000 World Banks (annual), July 2011, p. 217.

413 ■ BELGIUM'S LARGEST MAJOR BANKS OVERALL, 2011

Ranked by: Score based on revenue, profits, assets, and market capitalization. **Remarks:** Specific scores not provided. Also notes overall rank in the *Forbes 2000* and figures for each criterion. **Number listed:** 3

1. KBC Group NV
2. Dexia Group
3. Banque Nationale de Belgique

Source: *Forbes*, Forbes 2000 (annual), http://www.forbes.com, May 7, 2012.

414 ■ BRITAIN'S MOST ADMIRED BANKS, 2011

Ranked by: Survey of peers and investment analysts based on nine criteria: quality of management, financial soundness, quality of goods/services, ability to attract and retain talent, value as long-term investment, innovation, marketing, community and environmental responsibility, and use of corporate assets. **Number listed:** 5

1. HSBC Holdings plc, with 60.3 points
2. Standard Chartered Bank plc, 57.6
3. Banco Santander SA, 55.3
4. Nationwide Building Society, 54.8
5. ING Direct, 54.1

Source: *Management Today*, Britain's Most Admired Companies (annual), December 2011, p. 43.

415 ■ BULGARIA'S LARGEST BANKS BY CAPITAL, 2010

Ranked by: Tier one capital, in millions of U.S. dollars. **Remarks:** Also notes rank within the *Top 1000 World Banks*, fiscal year-end, percent change from previous year, assets, capital-assets ratio, pretax profits, real profits growth, profits-on-capital ratio, return on assets, cost-to-income ratio, BIS capital ratio, and non-performing loans as a percentage of total loans. **Number listed:** 6

1. UniCredit Bulbank, with $981 million
2. DSK Bank, $749
3. Raiffeisenbank (Bulgaria), $540
4. Eurobank EFG Bulgaria, $357
5. Piraeus Bank, $314
6. First Investment Bank, $265

Source: *The Banker*, Top 1000 World Banks (annual), July 2011, p. 218.

416 ■ CROATIA'S LARGEST BANKS BY CAPITAL, 2010

Ranked by: Tier one capital, in millions of U.S. dollars. **Remarks:** Also notes rank within the *Top 1000 World Banks*, fiscal year-end, percent change from previous year, assets, capital-assets ratio, pretax profits, real profits growth, profits-on-capital ratio, return on assets, cost-to-income ratio, BIS capital ratio, and non-performing loans as a percentage of total loans. **Number listed:** 5

1. Zagrebacka Banka, with $2,463 million
2. Privredna Banka Zagreb, $1,959
3. Hypo Alpe-Aldria-Bank Croatia, $1,097
4. Erste & Steiermarkische Bank Rijeka, $982
5. Raiffeisenbank Austria Zagreb, $926

Source: *The Banker*, Top 1000 World Banks (annual), July 2011, p. 224.

417 ■ CYPRUS'S LARGEST BANKS BY CAPITAL, 2010

Ranked by: Tier one capital, in millions of U.S. dollars. **Remarks:** Also notes rank within the *Top 1000 World Banks*, fiscal year-end, percent change from previous year, assets, capital-assets ratio, pretax profits, real profits growth, profits-on-capital ratio, return on assets, cost-to-income ratio, BIS capital ratio, and non-performing loans as a percentage of total loans. **Number listed:** 3

1. Bank of Cyprus, with $3,858 million
2. Marfin Popular Bank Group, $3,680
3. Hellenic Bank, $857

Source: *The Banker*, Top 1000 World Banks (annual), July 2011, p. 224.

418 ■ THE CZECH REPUBLIC'S LARGEST BANKS BY CAPITAL, 2010

Ranked by: Tier one capital, in millions of U.S. dollars. **Remarks:** Also notes rank within the *Top 1000 World Banks*, fiscal year-end, percent change from previous year, assets, capital-assets ratio, pretax profits, real profits growth, profits-on-capital ratio, return on assets, cost-to-income ratio, BIS capital ratio, and non-performing loans as a percentage of total loans. **Number listed:** 6

1. Ceska Sporitelna, with $3,044 million
2. Komercni banka, $2,633
3. Ceskoslovenska Obchodni Banka, $2,431
4. UniCredit Czech Republic, $1,539
5. GE Money Bank, $1,150
6. Raiffeisenbank, $550

Source: *The Banker*, Top 1000 World Banks (annual), July 2011, p. 224.

419 ■ DENMARK'S LARGEST BANKS BY CAPITAL, 2010

Ranked by: Tier one capital, in millions of U.S. dollars. **Remarks:** Also notes rank within the *Top 1000 World Banks*, fiscal year-end, percent change from previous year, assets, capital-assets ratio, pretax profits, real profits growth, profits-on-capital ratio, return on assets, cost-to-income ratio, BIS capital ratio, and non-performing loans as a percentage of total loans. **Number listed:** 11

1. Danske Bank, with $22,241 million
2. Nykredit, $10,778
3. Nordea Bank Danmark, $4,857
4. Jyske Bank, $2,549
5. Sydbank, $1,881
6. FIH Ehrvevsbank, $1,810
7. Spar Nord Bank, $1,019
8. Arbejdernes Landsbank, $472
9. Ringkjobing Landbobank, $437
10. Alm. Brand Bank, $407

Source: *The Banker*, Top 1000 World Banks (annual), July 2011, p. 224-226.

420 ■ DENMARK'S LARGEST REGIONAL BANKS OVERALL, 2011

Ranked by: Score based on revenue, profits, assets, and market capitalization. **Remarks:** Specific scores not provided. Also notes overall rank in the *Forbes 2000* and figures for each criterion. **Number listed:** 2

1. Jyske Bank
2. Sydbank

Source: *Forbes*, Forbes 2000 (annual), http://www.forbes.com, May 7, 2012.

421 ■ ESTONIA'S LARGEST BANKS BY CAPITAL, 2010

Ranked by: Tier one capital, in millions of U.S. dollars. **Remarks:** Also notes rank within the *Top 1000 World Banks*, fiscal year-end,

percent change from previous year, assets, capital-assets ratio, pretax profits, real profits growth, profits-on-capital ratio, return on assets, cost-to-income ratio, BIS capital ratio, and non-performing loans as a percentage of total loans. **Number listed:** 2

1. Swedbank, with $2,260 million
2. SEB Pank, $636

Source: *The Banker,* Top 1000 World Banks (annual), July 2011, p. 226.

422 ■ EUROPE'S MOST VALUABLE BANKS, 2011

Ranked by: Market value as of March 2011, in millions of U.S. dollars. **Remarks:** Also notes rank within the *FT Europe 500,* rank for previous year, country, revenue, net income, assets, number of employees, share price, price-to-earning ratio, dividend yield, and fiscal yearend. **Number listed:** 55

1. HSBC Holdings plc, with $181,936.9 million
2. Banco Santander SA, $98,119.8
3. BNP Paribas, $87,789
4. Sberbank--Savings Bank of the Russian Federation, $83,576.6
5. UBS AG, $69,006.9
6. Lloyds Banking Group, $63,388.1
7. Standard Chartered Bank plc, $60,865.1
8. Deutsche Bank AG, $54,720.5
9. Banco Bilbao Vizcaya Argentaria SA (BBVA), $54,559.3
10. Barclays plc, $54,213.7

Source: *Financial Times,* FT 500 (annual), http://www.ft.com, June 24, 2011.

423 ■ FINLAND'S LARGEST BANKS BY CAPITAL, 2010

Ranked by: Tier one capital, in millions of U.S. dollars. **Remarks:** Also notes rank within the *Top 1000 World Banks,* fiscal year-end, percent change from previous year, assets, capital-assets ratio, pretax profits, real profits growth, profits-on-capital ratio, return on assets, cost-to-income ratio, BIS capital ratio, and non-performing loans as a percentage of total loans. **Number listed:** 4

1. Nordea Bank Finland, with $13,693 million
2. OP Pohjola Group, $7,291
3. Sampo Bank, $3,342
4. Aktia Savings Bank, $497

Source: *The Banker,* Top 1000 World Banks (annual), July 2011, p. 226.

424 ■ FRANCE'S LARGEST BANKS BY CAPITAL, 2010

Ranked by: Tier one capital, in millions of U.S. dollars. **Remarks:** Also notes rank within the *Top 1000 World Banks,* fiscal year-end, percent change from previous year, assets, capital-assets ratio, pretax profits, real profits growth, profits-on-capital ratio, return on assets, cost-to-income ratio, BIS capital ratio, and non-performing loans as a percentage of total loans. **Number listed:** 8

1. BNP Paribas SA, with $91,626 million
2. Credit Agricole SA, $77,406
3. Groupe BPCE, $54,836
4. Societe Generale SA, $47,277
5. Credit Mutuel, $36,917
6. HSBC France, $5,392
7. Electro Banque, $904
8. Compagnie Financiere E de Rothschild, $429

Source: *The Banker,* Top 1000 World Banks (annual), July 2011, p. 226.

425 ■ FRANCE'S LARGEST MAJOR BANKS OVERALL, 2011

Ranked by: Score based on revenue, profits, assets, and market capitalization. **Remarks:** Specific scores not provided. Also notes overall rank in the *Forbes 2000* and figures for each criterion. **Number listed:** 5

1. BNP Paribas
2. Societe Generale SA
3. Natixis
4. CIC Group
5. Credit Agricole SA

Source: *Forbes,* Forbes 2000 (annual), http://www.forbes.com, May 7, 2012.

426 ■ FRANCE'S MOST VALUABLE BANKING BRANDS, 2011

Ranked by: Brand value, in millions of U.S. dollars. **Remarks:** Also notes rank within the *Global 500* for current and previous year, figures for current and previous year, and brand rating. Ranking is available online only. **Number listed:** 3

1. BNP Paribas, with $16,809 million
2. Societe Generale, $4,734
3. Credit Agricole, $2,841

Source: *Global 500,* (annual), Brand Finance plc, March 2012.

427 ■ GERMANY'S LARGEST BANKS BY CAPITAL, 2010

Ranked by: Tier one capital, in millions of U.S. dollars. **Remarks:** Also notes rank within the *Top 1000 World Banks,* fiscal year-end, percent change from previous year, assets, capital-assets ratio, pretax profits, real profits growth, profits-on-capital ratio, return on assets, cost-to-income ratio, BIS capital ratio, and non-performing loans as a percentage of total loans. **Number listed:** 40

1. Deutsche Bank AG, with $56,905 million
2. Commerzbank AG, $42,416
3. HypoVereinsbank, $26,414
4. Bayerische Landesbank, $18,588
5. Landesbank Baden-Wurttemberg, $18,382
6. Deutsche Zentral-Genossenschaftsbank, $12,310
7. Nord/LB Norddeutsche Landesbank, $10,622
8. Hypo Real Estate Holding, $9,457
9. HSH Nordbank, $8,524
10. Helaba Landesbank Hessen-Thuringen Girozentrale, $7,684

Source: *The Banker,* Top 1000 World Banks (annual), July 2011, p. 227.

428 ■ GERMANY'S LARGEST MAJOR BANKS OVERALL, 2011

Ranked by: Score based on revenue, profits, assets, and market capitalization. **Remarks:** Specific scores not provided. Also notes overall rank in the *Forbes 2000* and figures for each criterion. **Number listed:** 3

1. Deutsche Bank AG
2. Commerzbank AG
3. Landesbank Berlin

Source: *Forbes,* Forbes 2000 (annual), http://www.forbes.com, May 7, 2012.

429 ■ GERMANY'S LARGEST REGIONAL BANKS OVERALL, 2011

Ranked by: Score based on revenue, profits, assets, and market capitalization. **Remarks:** Specific scores not provided. Also notes overall rank in the *Forbes 2000* and figures for each criterion. **Number listed:** 3

1. Aareal Bank
2. IKB Deutsche
3. DVB Bank

Source: *Forbes*, Forbes 2000 (annual), http://www.forbes.com, May 7, 2012.

430 ■ GERMANY'S MOST VALUABLE BANKING BRANDS, 2011

Ranked by: Brand value, in millions of U.S. dollars. **Remarks:** Also notes rank within the *Global 500* for current and previous year, figures for current and previous year, and brand rating. Ranking is available online only. **Number listed:** 2

1. Deutsche Bank, with $12,906 million
2. DZ Bank, $3,330

Source: *Global 500*, (annual), Brand Finance plc, March 2012.

431 ■ GREECE'S LARGEST BANKS BY CAPITAL, 2010

Ranked by: Tier one capital, in millions of U.S. dollars. **Remarks:** Also notes rank within the *Top 1000 World Banks,* fiscal year-end, percent change from previous year, assets, capital-assets ratio, pretax profits, real profits growth, profits-on-capital ratio, return on assets, cost-to-income ratio, BIS capital ratio, and non-performing loans as a percentage of total loans. **Number listed:** 11

1. National Bank of Greece, with $11,976 million
2. Alpha Bank, $7,801
3. EFG Eurobank Ergasias, $6,801
4. Piraeus Bank Group, $5,289
5. Emporiki Bank, $2,082
6. Hellenic Postbank, $1,635
7. Marfin Egnatia Bank, $1,382
8. Agricultural Bank of Greece, $1,241
9. Attica Bank, $727
10. Probank, $447

Source: *The Banker*, Top 1000 World Banks (annual), July 2011, p. 229.

432 ■ GREECE'S LARGEST MAJOR BANKS OVERALL, 2011

Ranked by: Score based on revenue, profits, assets, and market capitalization. **Remarks:** Specific scores not provided. Also notes overall rank in the *Forbes 2000* and figures for each criterion. **Number listed:** 2

1. National Bank of Greece
2. Bank of Greece

Source: *Forbes*, Forbes 2000 (annual), http://www.forbes.com, May 7, 2012.

433 ■ GREECE'S LARGEST REGIONAL BANKS OVERALL, 2011

Ranked by: Score based on revenue, profits, assets, and market capitalization. **Remarks:** Specific scores not provided. Also notes overall rank in the *Forbes 2000* and figures for each criterion. **Number listed:** 4

1. EFG Eurobank Ergasias SA
2. Alpha Bank
3. Piraeus Bank
4. ATEbank

Source: *Forbes*, Forbes 2000 (annual), http://www.forbes.com, May 7, 2012.

434 ■ HUNGARY'S LARGEST BANKS BY CAPITAL, 2010

Ranked by: Tier one capital, in millions of U.S. dollars. **Remarks:** Also notes rank within the *Top 1000 World Banks,* fiscal year-end, percent change from previous year, assets, capital-assets ratio, pretax profits, real profits growth, profits-on-capital ratio, return on assets, cost-to-income ratio, BIS capital ratio, and non-performing loans as a percentage of total loans. **Number listed:** 8

1. OTP Bank, with $4,999 million
2. CIB Bank, $1,035
3. Kereskedelmi es Hitelbank Bank, $930
4. MKB, $759
5. UniCredit Bank Hungary, $719
6. Erste Bank Hungary, $656
7. Raiffeisen Bank, $654
8. Budapest Bank, $515

Source: *The Banker*, Top 1000 World Banks (annual), July 2011, p. 229.

435 ■ ICELAND'S LARGEST BANKS BY CAPITAL, 2010

Ranked by: Tier one capital, in millions of U.S. dollars. **Remarks:** Also notes rank within the *Top 1000 World Banks,* fiscal year-end, percent change from previous year, assets, capital-assets ratio, pretax profits, real profits growth, profits-on-capital ratio, return on assets, cost-to-income ratio, BIS capital ratio, and non-performing loans as a percentage of total loans. **Number listed:** 2

1. Landsbankinn, with $1,552 million
2. Islandsbanki, $1,052

Source: *The Banker*, Top 1000 World Banks (annual), July 2011, p. 229.

436 ■ IRELAND'S LARGEST BANKS BY CAPITAL, 2010

Ranked by: Tier one capital, in millions of U.S. dollars. **Remarks:** Also notes rank within the *Top 1000 World Banks,* fiscal year-end, percent change from previous year, assets, capital-assets ratio, pretax profits, real profits growth, profits-on-capital ratio, return on assets, cost-to-income ratio, BIS capital ratio, and non-performing loans as a percentage of total loans. **Number listed:** 9

1. Bank of Ireland plc, with $10,262 million
2. Allied Irish Banks plc, $5,662
3. Anglo Irish Bank Corp., $5,337
4. Depfa Bank, $4,910
5. UniCredit Bank Ireland, $3,051
6. Irish Life & Permanent, $2,247
7. Wells Fargo Bank International, $1,574
8. Intesa Sanpaolo Bank, $1,206
9. KBC Bank Ireland, $1,031

Source: *The Banker*, Top 1000 World Banks (annual), July 2011, p. 233.

437 ■ ITALY'S LARGEST BANKS BY CAPITAL, 2010

Ranked by: Tier one capital, in millions of U.S. dollars. **Remarks:** Also notes rank within the *Top 1000 World Banks,* fiscal year-end, percent change from previous year, assets, capital-assets ratio, pretax profits, real profits growth, profits-on-capital ratio, return on assets, cost-to-income ratio, BIS capital ratio, and non-performing loans as a percentage of total loans. **Number listed:** 25

1. UniCredit SpA, with $57,536 million
2. Intesa Sanpaolo, $41,678
3. Banca Monte dei Paschi di Siena, $12,222
4. UBI Banca, $9,422

5. Banco Popolare, $9,082

6. Banca Nazionale del Lavoro, $7,411

7. Banca Popolare dell'Emilia Romagna, $4,306

8. Banca Popolare di Milano, $3,851

9. Cassa di Risparmio di Parma & Piacenza, $3,279

10. Banca Popolare di Vicenza, $2,883

Source: *The Banker*, Top 1000 World Banks (annual), July 2011, p. 233-235.

438 ■ ITALY'S LARGEST MAJOR BANKS OVERALL, 2011

Ranked by: Score based on revenue, profits, assets, and market capitalization. **Remarks:** Specific scores not provided. Also notes overall rank in the *Forbes 2000* and figures for each criterion. **Number listed:** 3

1. Intesa Sanpaolo SpA

2. UniCredit SpA

3. Banca MPS

Source: *Forbes*, Forbes 2000 (annual), http://www.forbes.com, May 7, 2012.

439 ■ ITALY'S LARGEST REGIONAL BANKS OVERALL, 2011

Ranked by: Score based on revenue, profits, assets, and market capitalization. **Remarks:** Specific scores not provided. Also notes overall rank in the *Forbes 2000* and figures for each criterion. **Number listed:** 9

1. Mediobanca Group

2. Banco Popolare

3. UBI Banca

4. Banca Popolare dell'Emilia Romagna

5. Banca Carige

6. Banca Popolare di Milano

7. Credito Emiliano

8. Banca Popolare di Sondrio

9. Credito Valtellinese

Source: *Forbes*, Forbes 2000 (annual), http://www.forbes.com, May 7, 2012.

440 ■ KAZAKHSTAN'S LARGEST BANKS BY CAPITAL, 2010

Ranked by: Tier one capital, in millions of U.S. dollars. **Remarks:** Also notes rank within the *Top 1000 World Banks,* fiscal year-end, percent change from previous year, assets, capital-assets ratio, pretax profits, real profits growth, profits-on-capital ratio, return on assets, cost-to-income ratio, BIS capital ratio, and non-performing loans as a percentage of total loans. **Number listed:** 5

1. Kazkommertsbank, with $2,838 million

2. Halyk Bank, $1,984

3. Bank CenterCredit, $570

4. Nurbank, $291

5. Kaspi Bank, $272

Source: *The Banker*, Top 1000 World Banks (annual), July 2011, p. 237-238.

441 ■ LARGEST BANKS IN EUROPE, 2010

Ranked by: Sales, in millions of U.S. dollars. **Remarks:** Also notes rank within country. **Number listed:** 100

1. Dexia Banque Belgique SA (Belgium), with $93,319.9 million

2. Barkleys plc (U.K.), $62,939.6

3. Banco Santander SA (Spain), $57,728.1

4. Societe Generale SA (France), $43,993.3

5. BNP Paribas (France), $38,586.5

6. ABN Amro Groenbank BV (Netherlands), $35,408.1

7. Banco Bilbao Vizcaya Argentaria SA (BBVA, Spain), $31,109.1

8. The Royal Bank of Scotland Group plc (U.K.), $30,207

9. HSH Nordbank AG (Germany), $27,922.7

10. Fonds de compensation de l'AVS (Switzerland), $26,872.1

Source: *Europe's 15,000 Largest Companies*, (annual), ELC International, 2011, p. 37.

442 ■ LARGEST BANKS IN THE EUROPEAN UNION BY CAPITAL, 2010

Ranked by: Tier one capital, in millions of U.S. dollars. **Remarks:** Also notes fiscal year-end, assets, and percent change from previous year. **Number listed:** 200

1. HSBC Holdings plc (U.K.), with $133,179 million

2. The Royal Bank of Scotland Group plc (U.K.), $94,091

3. BNP Paribas (France), $91,626

4. Barclays Bank plc (U.K.), $83,797

5. Banco Santander Central Hispano SA (Spain), $81,039

6. Credit Agricole SA (France), $77,406

7. Lloyds Banking Group (U.K.), $73,782

8. UniCredit SpA (Italy), $57,536

9. Deutsche Bank (Germany), $56,905

10. Groupe BPCE (France), $54,836

Source: *The Banker*, Top 200 EU Banks (annual), September 2011, p. 66-67.

443 ■ LARGEST RUSSIAN BANKS BY CAPITAL, 2010

Ranked by: Tier one capital, in millions of U.S. dollars. **Remarks:** Also notes rank for previous year, headquarters, fiscal year-end, percent change from previous year, assets, capital-assets ratio, pretax profits, real profits growth, profits-on-capital ratio, return on assets, cost-to-income ratio, BIS capital ratio, and non-performing loans as a percentage of total loans. **Number listed:** 100

1. Sberbank--Savings Bank of the Russian Federation, with $29,460.35 million

2. VTB Bank, $17,944.68

3. Gazprombank, $6,131.84

4. Russian Agricultural Bank, $3,794.63

5. Alfa Bank, $2,930

6. Rosbank, $2,557.73

7. Raiffeisenbank Russia, $2,452.3

8. MDM Bank, $1,972.21

9. Nomos-Bank, $1,857.61

10. UniCredit Bank Russia, $1,819.83

Source: *The Banker*, Top 100 Russian Banks (annual), February 2012, p. 82-84.

444 ■ LATVIA'S LARGEST BANKS BY CAPITAL, 2010

Ranked by: Tier one capital, in millions of U.S. dollars. **Remarks:** Also notes rank within the *Top 1000 World Banks,* fiscal year-end,

percent change from previous year, assets, capital-assets ratio, pretax profits, real profits growth, profits-on-capital ratio, return on assets, cost-to-income ratio, BIS capital ratio, and non-performing loans as a percentage of total loans. **Number listed:** 2

1. Swedbank, with $866 million
2. SEB banka, $418

Source: *The Banker*, Top 1000 World Banks (annual), July 2011, p. 238.

445 ■ LIECHTENSTEIN'S LARGEST BANKS BY CAPITAL, 2010

Ranked by: Tier one capital, in millions of U.S. dollars. **Remarks:** Also notes rank within the *Top 1000 World Banks,* fiscal year-end, percent change from previous year, assets, capital-assets ratio, pretax profits, real profits growth, profits-on-capital ratio, return on assets, cost-to-income ratio, BIS capital ratio, and non-performing loans as a percentage of total loans. **Number listed:** 3

1. LGT Group, with $2,586 million
2. Liechtensteinische Landesbank, $1,436
3. VP Bank Group, $850

Source: *The Banker*, Top 1000 World Banks (annual), July 2011, p. 238.

446 ■ LITHUANIA'S LARGEST BANKS BY CAPITAL, 2010

Ranked by: Tier one capital, in millions of U.S. dollars. **Remarks:** Also notes rank within the *Top 1000 World Banks,* fiscal year-end, percent change from previous year, assets, capital-assets ratio, pretax profits, real profits growth, profits-on-capital ratio, return on assets, cost-to-income ratio, BIS capital ratio, and non-performing loans as a percentage of total loans. **Number listed:** 3

1. Swedbank, with $680 million
2. SEB Bankas, $656
3. DnB Nord Bankas, $329

Source: *The Banker*, Top 1000 World Banks (annual), July 2011, p. 238.

447 ■ LUXEMBOURG'S LARGEST BANKS BY CAPITAL, 2010

Ranked by: Tier one capital, in millions of U.S. dollars. **Remarks:** Also notes rank within the *Top 1000 World Banks,* fiscal year-end, percent change from previous year, assets, capital-assets ratio, pretax profits, real profits growth, profits-on-capital ratio, return on assets, cost-to-income ratio, BIS capital ratio, and non-performing loans as a percentage of total loans. **Number listed:** 8

1. EFG Group, with $6,889 million
2. BGL BNP Paribas, $6,884
3. Dexia Banque Internationale a Luxembourg, $3,299
4. UniCredit Luxembourg, $2,371
5. Banque et Caisse d'Epargne de l'Etat Luxembourg, $1,866
6. Deutsche Postbank International, $1,021
7. Norddeutsche Landesbank Luxembourg, $904
8. DZ Bank International, $629

Source: *The Banker*, Top 1000 World Banks (annual), July 2011, p. 238-240.

448 ■ MALTA'S LARGEST BANKS BY CAPITAL, 2010

Ranked by: Tier one capital, in millions of U.S. dollars. **Remarks:** Also notes rank within the *Top 1000 World Banks,* fiscal year-end, percent change from previous year, assets, capital-assets ratio, pretax profits, real profits growth, profits-on-capital ratio, return on

assets, cost-to-income ratio, BIS capital ratio, and non-performing loans as a percentage of total loans. **Number listed:** 2

1. Raiffeisen Bank Malta, with $628 million
2. Bank of Valletta, $483

Source: *The Banker*, Top 1000 World Banks (annual), July 2011, p. 240.

449 ■ THE NETHERLANDS' LARGEST BANKS BY CAPITAL, 2010

Ranked by: Tier one capital, in millions of U.S. dollars. **Remarks:** Also notes rank within the *Top 1000 World Banks,* fiscal year-end, percent change from previous year, assets, capital-assets ratio, pretax profits, real profits growth, profits-on-capital ratio, return on assets, cost-to-income ratio, BIS capital ratio, and non-performing loans as a percentage of total loans. **Number listed:** 13

1. ING Bank, with $52,583 million
2. Rabobank Group, $46,071
3. ABN Amro Group, $19,832
4. SNS Bank, $3,176
5. Bank Nederlandse Gemeenten, $2,928
6. Van Lanschot, $1,869
7. Nederlandse Waterschapsbank, $1,405
8. Credit Europe Bank, $1,088
9. Home Credit, $938
10. Friesland Bank, $767

Source: *The Banker*, Top 1000 World Banks (annual), July 2011, p. 241.

450 ■ NORWAY'S LARGEST BANKS BY CAPITAL, 2010

Ranked by: Tier one capital, in millions of U.S. dollars. **Remarks:** Also notes rank within the *Top 1000 World Banks,* fiscal year-end, percent change from previous year, assets, capital-assets ratio, pretax profits, real profits growth, profits-on-capital ratio, return on assets, cost-to-income ratio, BIS capital ratio, and non-performing loans as a percentage of total loans. **Number listed:** 11

1. DnB NOR, with $17,640 million
2. Nordea Bank Norge, $4,475
3. SpareBank 1 SR-Bank, $1,611
4. SpareBank 1 SMN, $1,243
5. Sparebanken Vest, $1,013
6. Sparebank 1 Nord Norge, $998
7. Sparebanken Hedmark, $646
8. Sparebanken More, $587
9. Sparebanken Sor, $498
10. Sandnes Sparebank, $406

Source: *The Banker*, Top 1000 World Banks (annual), July 2011, p. 241-242.

451 ■ POLAND'S LARGEST BANKS BY CAPITAL, 2010

Ranked by: Tier one capital, in millions of U.S. dollars. **Remarks:** Also notes rank within the *Top 1000 World Banks,* fiscal year-end, percent change from previous year, assets, capital-assets ratio, pretax profits, real profits growth, profits-on-capital ratio, return on assets, cost-to-income ratio, BIS capital ratio, and non-performing loans as a percentage of total loans. **Number listed:** 15

1. Bank Pekao, with $5,675 million
2. PKO Bank Polski, $5,385
3. Bank Handlowy w Warszawie, $2,191
4. BRE Bank, $2,151
5. Bank Zachodni WBK, $1,844

6. ING Bank Slaski, $1,490
7. Bank Millennium, $1,319
8. Bank BPH, $1,080
9. Raiffisen Bank Polska, $873
10. Kredyt Bank, $860

Source: *The Banker,* Top 1000 World Banks (annual), July 2011, p. 242-244.

452 ■ PORTUGAL'S LARGEST BANKS BY CAPITAL, 2010

Ranked by: Tier one capital, in millions of U.S. dollars. **Remarks:** Also notes rank within the *Top 1000 World Banks,* fiscal year-end, percent change from previous year, assets, capital-assets ratio, pretax profits, real profits growth, profits-on-capital ratio, return on assets, cost-to-income ratio, BIS capital ratio, and non-performing loans as a percentage of total loans. **Number listed:** 7

1. Caixa Geral de Depositos, with $9,150 million
2. Banco Espirito Santo Group, $8,075
3. Millennium BCP, $7,293
4. Banco Santander Totta, $3,635
5. Banco BPI, $3,181
6. Banif-SPGS, $1,533
7. Banco Itau BBA International, $638

Source: *The Banker,* Top 1000 World Banks (annual), July 2011, p. 244.

453 ■ PORTUGAL'S LARGEST REGIONAL BANKS OVERALL, 2011

Ranked by: Score based on revenue, profits, assets, and market capitalization. **Remarks:** Specific scores not provided. Also notes overall rank in the *Forbes 2000* and figures for each criterion. **Number listed:** 2

1. Banco Com Portugues
2. Banco BPI

Source: *Forbes,* Forbes 2000 (annual), http://www.forbes.com, May 7, 2012.

454 ■ ROMANIA'S LARGEST BANKS BY CAPITAL, 2010

Ranked by: Tier one capital, in millions of U.S. dollars. **Remarks:** Also notes rank within the *Top 1000 World Banks,* fiscal year-end, percent change from previous year, assets, capital-assets ratio, pretax profits, real profits growth, profits-on-capital ratio, return on assets, cost-to-income ratio, BIS capital ratio, and non-performing loans as a percentage of total loans. **Number listed:** 5

1. Banca Comerciala Romana, with $2,081 million
2. BRD-Groupe Societe Generale, $1,219
3. Raiffeisen Bank, $579
4. UniCredit Tiriac Bank, $547
5. Banca Transilvania, $506

Source: *The Banker,* Top 1000 World Banks (annual), July 2011, p. 244.

455 ■ RUSSIA'S LARGEST BANKS BY CAPITAL, 2010

Ranked by: Tier one capital, in millions of U.S. dollars. **Remarks:** Also notes rank within the *Top 1000 World Banks,* fiscal year-end, percent change from previous year, assets, capital-assets ratio, pretax profits, real profits growth, profits-on-capital ratio, return on assets, cost-to-income ratio, BIS capital ratio, and non-performing loans as a percentage of total loans. **Number listed:** 31

1. Sberbank of Russia, with $29,460 million

2. VTB-Bank, $17,945
3. Gazprombank, $6,132
4. Russian Agricultural Bank, $3,795
5. Alfa Bank, $2,930
6. Rosbank, $2,558
7. Raiffeisenbank, $2,452
8. MDM Bank, $1,972
9. Nomos Bank, $1,858
10. UniCredit Bank Russia, $1,820

Source: *The Banker,* Top 1000 World Banks (annual), July 2011, p. 244-246.

456 ■ RUSSIA'S LARGEST REGIONAL BANKS OVERALL, 2011

Ranked by: Score based on revenue, profits, assets, and market capitalization. **Remarks:** Specific scores not provided. Also notes overall rank in the *Forbes 2000* and figures for each criterion. **Number listed:** 3

1. Sberbank
2. VTB Bank
3. Bank of Moscow

Source: *Forbes,* Forbes 2000 (annual), http://www.forbes.com, May 7, 2012.

457 ■ SERBIA'S LARGEST BANKS BY CAPITAL, 2010

Ranked by: Tier one capital, in millions of U.S. dollars. **Remarks:** Also notes rank within the *Top 1000 World Banks,* fiscal year-end, percent change from previous year, assets, capital-assets ratio, pretax profits, real profits growth, profits-on-capital ratio, return on assets, cost-to-income ratio, BIS capital ratio, and non-performing loans as a percentage of total loans. **Number listed:** 6

1. Banca Intesa Beograd, with $717 million
2. Raiffeisen banka, $557
3. Agroindustrijsko Komercijalna Banka, $486
4. Komercijalna Banka Beograd, $398
5. UniCredit Bank Srbija, $396
6. Hypo Alpe-Adria-Bank Beograd, $394

Source: *The Banker,* Top 1000 World Banks (annual), July 2011, p. 246.

458 ■ SLOVAKIA'S LARGEST BANKS BY CAPITAL, 2010

Ranked by: Tier one capital, in millions of U.S. dollars. **Remarks:** Also notes rank within the *Top 1000 World Banks,* fiscal year-end, percent change from previous year, assets, capital-assets ratio, pretax profits, real profits growth, profits-on-capital ratio, return on assets, cost-to-income ratio, BIS capital ratio, and non-performing loans as a percentage of total loans. **Number listed:** 3

1. Vseobecna uverova banka, with $1,156 million
2. Slovenska sporitel'na, $963
3. Tatra banka, $912

Source: *The Banker,* Top 1000 World Banks (annual), July 2011, p. 247.

459 ■ SLOVENIA'S LARGEST BANKS BY CAPITAL, 2010

Ranked by: Tier one capital, in millions of U.S. dollars. **Remarks:** Also notes rank within the *Top 1000 World Banks,* fiscal year-end, percent change from previous year, assets, capital-assets ratio, pretax profits, real profits growth, profits-on-capital ratio, return on assets, cost-to-income ratio, BIS capital ratio, and non-performing loans as a percentage of total loans. **Number listed:** 7

1. Nova Ljubljanska Banka, with $1,330 million
2. Abanka Vipa, $530
3. Gorenjska Banka, $466
4. Nova Kreditna banka Maribor, $421
5. SKB Banka, $348
6. Banka Koper, $320
7. Banka Celje, $295

Source: *The Banker,* Top 1000 World Banks (annual), July 2011, p. 247.

460 ■ SPAIN'S LARGEST BANKS BY CAPITAL, 2010

Ranked by: Tier one capital, in millions of U.S. dollars. **Remarks:** Also notes rank within the *Top 1000 World Banks,* fiscal year-end, percent change from previous year, assets, capital-assets ratio, pretax profits, real profits growth, profits-on-capital ratio, return on assets, cost-to-income ratio, BIS capital ratio, and non-performing loans as a percentage of total loans. **Number listed:** 26

1. Banco Santander SA, with $81,039 million
2. Banco Bilbao Vizcaya Argentaria SA (BBVA), $44,148
3. Banco Financiero y de Ahorros Group, $23,864
4. Caja de Ahorros y Pensiones de Barcelona - la Caixa, $21,710
5. Banco Popular Espanol, $12,126
6. Banco Sabadell, $7,571
7. Banco Base, $7,223
8. Grupo Banca Civica, $5,897
9. Group Banco Mare Nostrum, $5,896
10. Novacaixagalicia, $5,150

Source: *The Banker,* Top 1000 World Banks (annual), July 2011, p. 247-249.

461 ■ SPAIN'S LARGEST MAJOR BANKS OVERALL, 2011

Ranked by: Score based on revenue, profits, assets, and market capitalization. **Remarks:** Specific scores not provided. Also notes overall rank in the *Forbes 2000* and figures for each criterion. **Number listed:** 2

1. Banco Santander SA
2. Banco Bilbao Vizcaya Argentaria SA (BBVA)

Source: *Forbes,* Forbes 2000 (annual), http://www.forbes.com, May 7, 2012.

462 ■ SPAIN'S LARGEST REGIONAL BANKS OVERALL, 2011

Ranked by: Score based on revenue, profits, assets, and market capitalization. **Remarks:** Specific scores not provided. Also notes overall rank in the *Forbes 2000* and figures for each criterion. **Number listed:** 7

1. CaixaBank SA
2. Bankia
3. Banco Popular Espanol
4. Banco de Sabadell
5. Banco Civica
6. Bankinter
7. Banco de Valencia

Source: *Forbes,* Forbes 2000 (annual), http://www.forbes.com, May 7, 2012.

463 ■ SPAIN'S MOST VALUABLE BANKING BRANDS, 2011

Ranked by: Brand value, in millions of U.S. dollars. **Remarks:** Also notes rank within the *Global 500* for current and previous year, figures for current and previous year, and brand rating. Ranking is available online only. **Number listed:** 2

1. Santander, with $19,969 million
2. BBVA, $7,195

Source: *Global 500,* (annual), Brand Finance plc, March 2012.

464 ■ SWEDEN'S LARGEST BANKS BY CAPITAL, 2010

Ranked by: Tier one capital, in millions of U.S. dollars. **Remarks:** Also notes rank within the *Top 1000 World Banks,* fiscal year-end, percent change from previous year, assets, capital-assets ratio, pretax profits, real profits growth, profits-on-capital ratio, return on assets, cost-to-income ratio, BIS capital ratio, and non-performing loans as a percentage of total loans. **Number listed:** 6

1. Nordea Group, with $28,140 million
2. Skandinaviska Enskilda Banken Group, $14,776
3. Svenska Handelsbanken, $13,084
4. Swedbank, $12,278
5. Lansforsakringar Bank AB, $772
6. Sparbanken Oresund AB, $356

Source: *The Banker,* Top 1000 World Banks (annual), July 2011, p. 249.

465 ■ SWEDEN'S LARGEST MAJOR BANKS OVERALL, 2011

Ranked by: Score based on revenue, profits, assets, and market capitalization. **Remarks:** Specific scores not provided. Also notes overall rank in the *Forbes 2000* and figures for each criterion. **Number listed:** 3

1. Skandinaviska Enskilda Banken (SEB)
2. Svenska Handelsbanken AB
3. Swedbank

Source: *Forbes,* Forbes 2000 (annual), http://www.forbes.com, May 7, 2012.

466 ■ SWITZERLAND'S LARGEST BANKS BY CAPITAL, 2010

Ranked by: Tier one capital, in millions of U.S. dollars. **Remarks:** Also notes rank within the *Top 1000 World Banks,* fiscal year-end, percent change from previous year, assets, capital-assets ratio, pretax profits, real profits growth, profits-on-capital ratio, return on assets, cost-to-income ratio, BIS capital ratio, and non-performing loans as a percentage of total loans. **Number listed:** 37

1. Credit Suisse Group, with $40,133 million
2. UBS, $37,578
3. Schweizer Verband der Raiffeisenbanken, $9,547
4. Zurcher Kantonalbank, $8,193
5. HSBC Private Bank Holdings (Suisse), $5,326
6. Basler Kantonalbank, $3,059
7. Julius Baer Group, $3,057
8. Banque Cantonale Vaudoise, $3,044
9. BSI, $2,601
10. Berner Kantonalbank, $1,993

Source: *The Banker,* Top 1000 World Banks (annual), July 2011, p. 249-250.

467 ■ SWITZERLAND'S LARGEST REGIONAL BANKS OVERALL, 2011

Ranked by: Score based on revenue, profits, assets, and market capitalization. **Remarks:** Specific scores not provided. Also notes overall rank in the *Forbes 2000* and figures for each criterion. **Number listed:** 6

1. Banque Cantonale Vaudoise (BCV)
2. Basler Kantonalbank
3. BEKB-BCBE
4. Luzerner Kantonalbank
5. St. Galler Kantonalbank
6. Valiant Holding

Source: *Forbes*, Forbes 2000 (annual), http://www.forbes.com, May 7, 2012.

468 ■ SWITZERLAND'S MOST VALUABLE BANKING BRANDS, 2011

Ranked by: Brand value, in millions of U.S. dollars. **Remarks:** Also notes rank within the *Global 500* for current and previous year, figures for current and previous year, and brand rating. Ranking is available online only. **Number listed:** 2

1. Credit Suisse, with $8,368 million
2. UBS, $5,944

Source: *Global 500*, (annual), Brand Finance plc, March 2012.

469 ■ TURKEY'S LARGEST BANKS BY CAPITAL, 2010

Ranked by: Tier one capital, in millions of U.S. dollars. **Remarks:** Also notes rank within the *Top 1000 World Banks,* fiscal year-end, percent change from previous year, assets, capital-assets ratio, pretax profits, real profits growth, profits-on-capital ratio, return on assets, cost-to-income ratio, BIS capital ratio, and non-performing loans as a percentage of total loans. **Number listed:** 17

1. Turkiye Is Bankasi, with $11,669 million
2. Akbank, $10,494
3. Turkiye Garanti Bankasi, $7,527
4. TC Ziraat Bankasi, $6,324
5. Yapi ve Kredi Bankasi, $6,020
6. Turkiye Vakiflar Bankasi (VakifBank), $5,090
7. Finansbank, $3,269
8. Turkiye Halk Bankasi, $3,229
9. Denizbank, $2,401
10. Turk Ekonomi Bankasi, $1,266

Source: *The Banker*, Top 1000 World Banks (annual), July 2011, p. 252.

470 ■ TURKEY'S LARGEST REGIONAL BANKS OVERALL, 2011

Ranked by: Score based on revenue, profits, assets, and market capitalization. **Remarks:** Specific scores not provided. Also notes overall rank in the *Forbes 2000* and figures for each criterion. **Number listed:** 5

1. Turkiye Garanti Bankasi
2. Turkiye Is Bankasi AS (Isbank)
3. Akbank
4. Turkiye Halk Bankasi
5. VakifBank

Source: *Forbes*, Forbes 2000 (annual), http://www.forbes.com, May 7, 2012.

471 ■ THE UKRAINE'S LARGEST BANKS BY CAPITAL, 2010

Ranked by: Tier one capital, in millions of U.S. dollars. **Remarks:** Also notes rank within the *Top 1000 World Banks,* fiscal year-end, percent change from previous year, assets, capital-assets ratio, pretax profits, real profits growth, profits-on-capital ratio, return on

assets, cost-to-income ratio, BIS capital ratio, and non-performing loans as a percentage of total loans. **Number listed:** 8

1. State Export-Import Bank of Ukraine, with $2,034 million
2. State Savings Bank of Ukraine, $1,817
3. PrivatBank, $1,797
4. Raiffeisen Bank Aval, $759
5. UkrSibbank, $648
6. Prominvestbank, $577
7. Ukrsotsbank, $523
8. First Ukrainian International Bank, $269

Source: *The Banker*, Top 1000 World Banks (annual), July 2011, p. 253.

472 ■ THE UNITED KINGDOM'S LARGEST BANKS BY CAPITAL, 2010

Ranked by: Tier one capital, in millions of U.S. dollars. **Remarks:** Also notes rank within the *Top 1000 World Banks,* fiscal year-end, percent change from previous year, assets, capital-assets ratio, pretax profits, real profits growth, profits-on-capital ratio, return on assets, cost-to-income ratio, BIS capital ratio, and non-performing loans as a percentage of total loans. **Number listed:** 29

1. HSBC Holdings plc, with $133,179 million
2. The Royal Bank of Scotland Group plc, $94,094
3. Barclays plc, $83,797
4. Lloyds Banking Group plc, $73,782
5. Standard Chartered Bank plc, $34,313
6. Santander U.K., $17,042
7. Nationwide Building Society, $11,744
8. Clydesdale Bank, $4,107
9. FCE Bank, $3,676
10. The Co-operative Bank, $3,162

Source: *The Banker*, Top 1000 World Banks (annual), July 2011, p. 252-253.

473 ■ UNITED KINGDOM'S LARGEST MAJOR BANKS OVERALL, 2011

Ranked by: Score based on revenue, profits, assets, and market capitalization. **Remarks:** Specific scores not provided. Also notes overall rank in the *Forbes 2000* and figures for each criterion. **Number listed:** 5

1. HSBC Holdings plc
2. Barclays plc
3. Standard Chartered Bank plc
4. The Royal Bank of Scotland Group plc
5. Lloyds Banking Group plc

Source: *Forbes*, Forbes 2000 (annual), http://www.forbes.com, May 7, 2012.

474 ■ THE UNITED KINGDOM'S MOST VALUABLE BANKING BRANDS, 2011

Ranked by: Brand value, in millions of U.S. dollars. **Remarks:** Also notes rank within the *Global 500* for current and previous year, figures for current and previous year, and brand rating. Ranking is available online only. **Number listed:** 5

1. HSBC, with $27,597 million
2. Barclays, $13,552
3. Standard Chartered, $7,624

4. Royal Bank of Scotland, $4,056

5. Lloyds TSB, $2,701

Source: *Global 500*, (annual), Brand Finance plc, March 2012.

475 ■ WESTERN EUROPE'S FASTEST-GROWING BANKS, 2009-2010

Ranked by: Annual growth in tier one capital, in percent. **Remarks:** Also notes rank within the *Top 1000 World Banks* and total tier one capital. **Number listed:** 10

1. Caja de Ahorros y Monte de Piedad (Spain), with 116.33%

2. Dusseldorfer Hypothekenbank (Germany), 101.45%

3. West Bromwich Building Society (U.K.), 57.44%

4. Kreissparkasse Biberach (Germany), 53.23%

5. Islandsbanki (Iceland), 42.78%

6. Standard Chartered Bank plc (U.K.), 39.59%

7. TC Ziraat Bankasi (Turkey), 35.65%

8. Yorkshire Building Society (U.K.), 34.26%

9. Hellenic Bank (Cyprus), 33.65%

10. CatalunyaCaixa (Spain), 27.47%

Source: *The Banker*, Top 1000 World Banks (annual), July 2011, p. 139.

476 ■ WESTERN EUROPE'S LARGEST BANKS BY CAPITAL, 2010

Ranked by: Tier one capital, in millions of U.S. dollars. **Remarks:** Also notes rank within the *Top 1000 World Banks*. **Number listed:** 25

1. HSBC Holdings plc (U.K.), with $133,179 million

2. Royal Bank of Scotland plc (U.K.), $94,091

3. BNP Paribas SA (France), $91,626

4. Barclays plc (U.K.), $83,797

5. Banco Santander SA (Spain), $81,039

6. Credit Agricole SA (France), $77,406

7. Lloyds Banking Group plc (U.K.), $73,782

8. UniCredit SpA (Italy), $57,536

9. Deutsche Bank AG (Germany), $56,905

10. Groupe BPCE (France), $54,836

Source: *The Banker*, Top 1000 World Banks (annual), July 2011, p. 139.

Banks and Banking, Foreign

477 ■ AUSTRALIA'S LARGEST BANKS BY CAPITAL, 2010

Ranked by: Tier one capital, in millions of U.S. dollars. **Remarks:** Also notes rank within the *Top 1000 World Banks*, fiscal year-end, percent change from previous year, assets, capital-assets ratio, pretax profits, real profits growth, profits-on-capital ratio, return on assets, cost-to-income ratio, BIS capital ratio, and non-performing loans as a percentage of total loans. **Number listed:** 11

1. National Australia Bank Ltd., with $29,684 million

2. Australia & New Zealand Banking Group (ANZ), $25,813

3. Westpac Banking Corp., $24,563

4. Commonwealth Bank of Australia, $22,678

5. Macquarie Group Ltd., $6,130

6. Suncorp-Metway, $4,199

7. ING Bank Australia, $2,524

8. Bendigo & Adelaide Bank, $1,849

9. Bank of Queensland, $1,489

10. Members Equity Bank, $345

Source: *The Banker*, Top 1000 World Banks (annual), July 2011, p. 216.

478 ■ AUSTRALIA'S LARGEST MAJOR BANKS OVERALL, 2011

Ranked by: Score based on revenue, profits, assets, and market capitalization. **Remarks:** Specific scores not provided. Also notes overall rank in the *Forbes 2000* and figures for each criterion. **Number listed:** 4

1. Commonwealth Bank of Australia

2. Westpac Banking Corp.

3. National Australia Bank Ltd.

4. Australia & New Zealand Banking Group (ANZ)

Source: *Forbes*, Forbes 2000 (annual), http://www.forbes.com, May 7, 2012.

479 ■ AUSTRALIA'S LARGEST REGIONAL BANKS OVERALL, 2011

Ranked by: Score based on revenue, profits, assets, and market capitalization. **Remarks:** Specific scores not provided. Also notes overall rank in the *Forbes 2000* and figures for each criterion. **Number listed:** 2

1. Bendigo & Adelaide Bank

2. Bank of Queensland

Source: *Forbes*, Forbes 2000 (annual), http://www.forbes.com, May 7, 2012.

480 ■ AUSTRALIA'S MOST VALUABLE BANKING BRANDS, 2011

Ranked by: Brand value, in millions of U.S. dollars. **Remarks:** Also notes rank within the *Global 500* for current and previous year, figures for current and previous year, and brand rating. Ranking is available online only. **Number listed:** 4

1. Commonwealth Bank of Australia, with $4,244 million

2. NAB, $4,160

3. Westpac, $3,570

4. ANZ, $3,433

Source: *Global 500*, (annual), Brand Finance plc, March 2012.

481 ■ NEW ZEALAND'S LARGEST BANKS BY CAPITAL, 2010

Ranked by: Tier one capital, in millions of U.S. dollars. **Remarks:** Also notes rank within the *Top 1000 World Banks*, fiscal year-end, percent change from previous year, assets, capital-assets ratio, pretax profits, real profits growth, profits-on-capital ratio, return on assets, cost-to-income ratio, BIS capital ratio, and non-performing loans as a percentage of total loans. **Number listed:** 3

1. ANZ National Bank, with $4,901 million

2. Bank of New Zealand, $2,881

3. ASB Bank Ltd., $2,410

Source: *The Banker*, Top 1000 World Banks (annual), July 2011, p. 241.

Banks and Banking—Independent Banks

482 ■ TOP LARGE NON-SUBCHAPTER S COMMERCIAL BANKS, 2010

Ranked by: Return on average equity of commercial banks, thrifts, and bank holding companies with assets between $100 million and $3 billion, in percent. **Remarks:** Also notes rank for previous year, location, total assets, return on assets, non-interest income as a percentage of total revenue, efficiency ratio, nonperforming loans as a percentage of total loans, and leverage ratio. **Number listed:** 25

1. Eastern Federal Bank (Norwich, CT), with 38.77%
2. First Citizens Bank (Luverne, AL), 37.3%
3. First Michigan Bank (Troy, MI), 36.61%
4. Customers Bank (Phoenixville, PA), 31.78%
5. Crestmark Bank (Troy, MI), 28.58%
6. Northeast Bancorp (Lewiston, ME), 26.63%
7. Independence Bancshares (Owensboro, KY), 26.61%
8. Level One Bank (Farmington Hills, MI), 26.52%
9. Leader Bank NA (Arlington, MA), 25.26%
10. Eclipse Bank Inc. (Lousiville, KY), 24.84%

Source: *ABA Banking Journal*, Top Performers: Part Two (annual), June 2011, p. 40.

483 ■ TOP LARGE SUBCHAPTER S COMMERCIAL BANKS, 2010

Ranked by: Return on average equity of banks and thrifts with assets between $100 million and $3 billion, in percent. **Remarks:** Also notes rank for previous year, location, total assets, return on assets, non-interest income as a percentage of total revenue, efficiency ratio, nonperforming loans as a percentage of total loans, and leverage ratio. **Number listed:** 25

1. Continental Bank (Salt Lake City, UT), with 66.28%
2. Merchants Bank of Indiana (Lynn, IN), 52.63%
3. Live Oak Banking Co. (Wilmington, NC), 51.99%
4. Benchmark Bank (Plano, TX), 49.54%
5. Cenlar Federal Savings Bank (Ewing Twp., NJ), 45.16%
6. United National Corp. (Sioux Falls, SD), 44.99%
7. Roundbank (Waseca, MN), 34.36%
8. Charter Bank (Corpus Christi, TX), 32.55%
9. Community Bank (Longview, TX), 32.24%
10. First Financial Banc Corp. (El Dorado, AR), 31.93%

Source: *ABA Banking Journal*, Top Performers: Part Two (annual), June 2011, p. 42.

484 ■ TOP PUBLICLY TRADED COMMUNITY BANKS BY THREE-YEAR ROE, 2007-2010

Ranked by: Three-year average return on equity (ROE), in percent. **Remarks:** Also notes ticker symbol, market value, total assets, return on average equity, growth in earnings per share (EPS), diluted EPS, total capital ratio, and three-year median EPS growth, total risk based ratio, and price performance. **Number listed:** 200

1. HBancorporation Inc., with 28.74%

2. Guaranty Bancshares Inc., 23.24%
3. Tri-County Financial Group, 17.18%
4. Suffolk Bancorp, 16.85%
5. Citizens Financial Services, 16.43%
6. Minster Financial Corp., 16.31%
7. Commercial National Financial, 16.01%
8. Bridge Bancorp Inc., 15.72%
9. Arrow Financial Corp., 15.66%
10. Merchants Bancshares, 15.61%

Source: *U.S. Banker*, Top 200 Publicly Traded Community Banks (annual), June 2011, p. 20+.

485 ■ TOP SMALL NON-SUBCHAPTER S COMMERCIAL BANKS, 2010

Ranked by: Return on average equity of commercial banks, thrifts, and bank holding companies with assets under $100 million, in percent. **Remarks:** Also notes rank for previous year, location, total assets, return on assets, non-interest income as a percentage of total revenue, efficiency ratio, nonperforming loans as a percentage of total loans, and leverage ratio. **Number listed:** 25

1. Jefferson Bank (Fayette, MS), with 74.81%
2. State Bank of Paw Paw (Paw Paw, IL), 27.64%
3. Bank 2 (Oklahoma City, OK), 22.66%
4. American Trust Bank (Kirksville, MO), 21.75%
5. Hyperion Bank (Philadelphia, PA), 21.18%
6. Native American Bank NA (Denver, CO), 20.73%
7. Community Bank (Bristow, OK), 20.51%
8. First National Bank (Kinmundy, IL), 18.85%
9. State Bank (Schaller, IA), 18.18%
10. American Investors Bank & Mortgage (Eden Prairie, MN), 17.81%

Source: *ABA Banking Journal*, Top Performers: Part Two (annual), June 2011, p. 41.

486 ■ TOP SMALL SUBCHAPTER S COMMERCIAL BANKS, 2010

Ranked by: Return on average equity of banks and thrifts with assets under $100 million, in percent. **Remarks:** Also notes rank for previous year, location, total assets, return on assets, non-interest income as a percentage of total revenue, efficiency ratio, nonperforming loans as a percentage of total loans, and leverage ratio. **Number listed:** 25

1. Citizens State Bank (Clayton, WI), with 39.22%
2. Riverside Bank (Sparkman, AR), 35.29%
3. Wells Bank of Platte City (Platte City, MO), 33.7%
4. Bank of Buffalo (Buffalo, KY), 32.25%
5. Goodfield State Bank (Goodfield, IL), 31.98%
6. Heritage State Bank (Lawrenceville, IL), 31.3%
7. Priority Bank (Ozark, AR), 30.74%
8. Security State Bank (Sutherland, IA), 30.44%
9. Brunswick State Bank (Brunswick, NE), 28.93%
10. Mainland Bank (Texas City, TX), 28.88%

Source: *ABA Banking Journal*, Top Performers: Part Two (annual), June 2011, p. 43.

Banks and Banking, International

487 ■ COUNTRIES WITH THE LEAST SOUND BANKS, 2011

Ranked by: Score, on a scale of seven, based on the general health and financial soundness of banks. **Number listed:** 142

1. Ireland, with 1.4 points
2. Ukraine, 2.8
3. Iceland, 3.3
4. Burundi, 3.6
4. Algeria, 3.6
6. Yemen, 3.7
6. Nigeria, 3.7
7. Azerbaijan, 3.8
7. Mongolia, 3.8
7. Chad, 3.8
7. Mauritania, 3.8

Source: *Global Competitiveness Report*, (annual), World Economic Forum, 2011, p. 485.

488 ■ COUNTRIES WITH THE MOST SOUND BANKS, 2011

Ranked by: Score, on a scale of seven, based on the general health and financial soundness of banks. **Number listed:** 142

1. Canada, with 6.8 points
2. South Africa, 6.6
3. Panama, 6.5
3. Australia, 6.5
3. Singapore, 6.5
3. Chile, 6.5
3. New Zealand, 6.5
3. Finland, 6.5
9. Lebanon, 6.4
9. Hong Kong, 6.4
9. Barbados, 6.4
9. Malta, 6.4

Source: *Global Competitiveness Report*, (annual), World Economic Forum, 2011, p. 485.

489 ■ WORLD'S LARGEST BANKS BY CAPITAL, 2010

Ranked by: Tier one capital, in millions of U.S. dollars. **Remarks:** Also notes rank for previous year, fiscal year-end, percent change from previous year, assets, capital-assets ratio, pretax profits, profits-on-capital ratio, return on assets, BIS capital ratio, and non-performing loans as a percentage of total loans. **Number listed:** 1000

1. Bank of America Corp. (U.S.), with $163,626 million
2. J. P. Morgan Chase & Co. (U.S.), $142,450
3. HSBC Holdings plc (U.K.), $133,179
4. Citigroup Inc. (U.S.), $126,193
5. Mitsubishi UFJ Financial Group Inc. (Japan), $119,732
6. Industrial Commercial Bank of China, $113,393
7. Wells Fargo & Co. (U.S.), $109,353
8. China Construction Bank Corp. (China), $95,834

9. Bank of China, $94,579
10. The Royal Bank of Scotland Group plc (U.K.), $94,091

Source: *The Banker*, Top 1000 World Banks (annual), July 2011, p. 182+.

490 ■ WORLD'S LARGEST MAJOR BANKS OVERALL, 2011

Ranked by: Score based on revenue, profits, assets, and market capitalization. **Remarks:** Specific scores not provided. Also notes country, overall rank in the *Forbes 2000*, and figures for each criterion. **Number listed:** 78

1. J. P. Morgan Chase & Co.
2. Industrial & Commercial Bank of China (ICBC)
3. HSBC Holdings plc
4. Wells Fargo & Co.
5. Citigroup Inc.
5. BNP Paribas
7. Bank of China
8. Banco Santander SA
9. Itau Unibanco Holding SA
10. Mitsubishi UFJ Financial Group Inc.

Source: *Forbes*, Forbes 2000 (annual), http://www.forbes.com, May 7, 2012.

491 ■ WORLD'S LARGEST REGIONAL BANKS OVERALL, 2011

Ranked by: Score based on revenue, profits, assets, and market capitalization. **Remarks:** Specific scores not provided. Also notes country, overall rank in the *Forbes 2000*, and figures for each criterion. **Number listed:** 318

1. China Construction Bank
2. Agricultural Bank of China
3. Banco Bradesco
4. Sberbank
5. Nordea Bank
6. State Bank of India Group
7. Shanghai Pudong Development Bank
8. PNC Financial Services Group Inc.
9. China Citic Bank
10. China Minsheng Banking

Source: *Forbes*, Forbes 2000 (annual), http://www.forbes.com, May 7, 2012.

492 ■ WORLD'S MOST ADMIRED MEGABANKS, 2012

Ranked by: Score, on a scale of 10, based on a survey of executives, directors, and securities analysts of companies within their own industry on eight criteria: innovation, financial soundness, employee talent, use of corporate assets, long-term investment value, social responsibility, quality of management, and quality of products/services. **Remarks:** Specific scores not provided. Also notes rank for previous year. **Number listed:** 8

1. J. P. Morgan Chase & Co.
2. Goldman Sachs Group Inc.
3. Wells Fargo & Co.
4. HSBC Holdings plc
5. Barclays plc
6. Credit Suisse Group
7. Deutsche Bank AG

7. Morgan Stanley

Source: *Fortune*, World's Most Admired Companies (annual), March 19, 2012, p. 148.

493 ■ WORLD'S MOST ADMIRED SUPERREGIONAL BANKS, 2012

Ranked by: Score, on a scale of 10, based on a survey of executives, directors, and securities analysts of companies within their own industry on eight criteria: innovation, financial soundness, employee talent, use of corporate assets, long-term investment value, social responsibility, quality of management, and quality of products/services. **Remarks:** Specific scores not provided. Also notes rank for previous year. **Number listed:** 5

1. U.S. Bancorp
2. PNC Financial Services Group Inc.
3. Northern Trust Corp.
4. Bank of New York Mellon Corp.
5. State Street Corp.

Source: *Fortune*, World's Most Admired Companies (annual), March 19, 2012, p. 148.

494 ■ WORLD'S MOST ETHICAL BANKING COMPANIES, 2012

Ranked by: Score based on five criteria: ethics and compliance program; reputation, leadership, and innovation; governance; corporate citizenship and responsibility; and culture of ethics. **Remarks:** Specific scores not provided; companies are listed alphabetically, not ranked. **Number listed:** 5

1. National Australia Bank Ltd. (Australia)
2. Old National Bank (U.S.)
3. Rabobank Group (Netherlands)
4. Standard Chartered Bank plc (U.K.)
5. Westpac Banking Corp. (Australia)

Source: *Ethisphere Magazine*, World's Most Ethical Companies (annual), http://www.ethisphere.com, 2012.

495 ■ WORLD'S MOST PROFITABLE BANKS, 2010

Ranked by: Pre-tax profits, in millions of U.S. dollars. **Remarks:** Also notes tier one capital. **Number listed:** 25

1. Industrial Commercial Bank of China, with $32,528 million
2. China Construction Bank Corp., $26,448
3. J. P. Morgan Chase & Co. (U.S.), $24,859
4. Bank of China, $21,463
5. HSBC Holdings plc (U.K.), $19,037
6. Wells Fargo & Co. (U.S.), $18,700
7. Agricultural Bank of China, $18,230
8. BNP Paribas SA (France), $17,406
9. Banco Santander SA (Spain), $16,079
10. Goldman Sachs Group Inc. (U.S.), $12,892

Source: *The Banker*, Top 1000 World Banks (annual), July 2011, p. 128.

496 ■ WORLD'S MOST VALUABLE BANKING BRANDS, 2011

Ranked by: Brand value, in millions of U.S. dollars. **Remarks:** Also notes rank for previous year, country, brand rating, market capitalization, brand value as a percentage of market cap, and figures for previous year. **Number listed:** 500

1. HSBC, with $27,597 million

2. Wells Fago, $23,229
3. Bank of America, $22,910
4. Santander, $19,969
5. Chase, $18,964
6. Citi, $18,639
7. American Express, $18,231
8. BNP Paribas, $16,809
9. Bradesco, $15,692
10. China Construction Bank, $15,464

Source: *Banking 500*, (annual), Brand Finance plc, February 2012.

497 ■ WORLD'S MOST VALUABLE BANKS, 2011

Ranked by: Market value as of March 2011, in millions of U.S. dollars. **Remarks:** Also notes rank within the *FT 500*, rank for previous year, country, revenue, net income, assets, number of employees, share price, price-to-earning ratio, dividend yield, and fiscal year-end. **Number listed:** 75

1. Industrial & Commercial Bank of China, with $251,078.1 million
2. China Construction Bank, $232,608.6
3. J. P. Morgan Chase & Co., $183,639.7
4. HSBC Holdings plc, $181,936.9
5. Wells Fargo & Co., $157,415.9
6. Bank of China, $145,977.9
7. Agricultural Bank of China, $141,363.1
8. Bank of America Corp., $134,914.9
9. Citigroup Inc., $128,703.9
10. Itau Unibanco, $99,719.8

Source: *Financial Times*, FT 500 (annual), http://www.ft.com, June 24, 2011.

498 ■ WORLD'S TOP BANKING BRANDS, 2012

Ranked by: Brand value, in millions of U.S. dollars. **Remarks:** Also notes rank and figures for previous year, market capitalization, brand value as a portion of market value, and brand rating. **Number listed:** 500

1. HSBC Holdings plc (U.K.), with $27,597 million
2. Well Fargo (U.S.), $23,229
3. Bank of America (U.S.), $22,910
4. Santander (Spain), $19,969
5. Chase (U.S.), $18,964
6. Citi (U.S.), $18,639
7. American Express (U.S.), $18,231
8. BNP Paribas (France), $16,809
9. Bradesco (Brazil), $15,692
10. China Construction Bank (China), $15,464

Source: *The Banker*, Top 500 Banking Brands (annual), February 2012, p. 26-32.

499 ■ WORLD'S TOP BANKS BY ASSET GROWTH, 2009-2010

Ranked by: Annual growth in assets, in percent. **Remarks:** Also notes total assets and rank by assets. **Number listed:** 25

1. Kunlun Bank (China), with 294.22%
2. Members Equity Bank (Australia), 151.74%
3. Bohai Bank (China), 132.54%
4. Guangxi Beibu Gulf Bank (China), 123.34%
5. Bank of Guanzhou (China), 115.56%

6. First Southern Bancorp (U.S.), 112.19%

7. Caja Espana de Inversiones, Salamanca y Soria (Spain), 98.28%

8. Xiamen Bank (China), 92.84%

9. Zhanjiang City Commerical Bank (China), 90%

10. Nomos Bank (Russia), 89.82%

Source: *The Banker,* Top 1000 World Banks (annual), July 2011, p. 130.

500 ■ WORLD'S TOP BANKS BY CAPITAL GROWTH, 2009-2010

Ranked by: Annual growth in tier one capital, in percent. **Remarks:** Also notes total tier one capital and assets. **Number listed:** 25

1. First Southern Bancorp (U.S.), with 754.78%

2. Bank of Suzhou (China), 564.7%

3. Bank of Jining (China), 245.93%

4. Chongqing Rural Commercial Bank (China), 155.45%

5. Sterling Financial Corp. (U.S.), 153.52%

6. Capitec Bank (S. Africa), 128.16%

7. Bank of Ganzhou (China), 122.66%

8. West Coast Bancorp (U.S.), 119.26%

9. Bank of Jiujiang (China), 118.7%

10. Caja de Ahorros y Monte de Piedad (Spain), 116.33%

Source: *The Banker,* Top 1000 World Banks (annual), July 2011, p. 159.

Banks and Banking—Latin America

501 ■ ARGENTINA'S LARGEST BANKS BY CAPITAL, 2010

Ranked by: Tier one capital, in millions of U.S. dollars. **Remarks:** Also notes rank within the *Top 1000 World Banks,* fiscal year-end, percent change from previous year, assets, capital-assets ratio, pretax profits, real profits growth, profits-on-capital ratio, return on assets, cost-to-income ratio, BIS capital ratio, and non-performing loans as a percentage of total loans. **Number listed:** 11

1. Banco de la Nacion Argentina, with $1,949 million

2. Banco Macro, $1,050

3. Banco Santander Rio, $976

4. Banco Hipotecario, $702

5. BBVA Banco Frances, $644

6. HSBC Bank Argentina, $581

7. Banco de la Provincia de Buenos Aires, $547

8. Banco de Galicia y Buenos Aires, $538

9. Banco Patagonia, $494

10. Banco de la Ciudad de Buenos Aires, $401

Source: *The Banker,* Top 1000 World Banks (annual), July 2011, p. 216.

502 ■ BRAZIL'S LARGEST BANKS BY CAPITAL, 2010

Ranked by: Tier one capital, in millions of U.S. dollars. **Remarks:** Also notes rank within the *Top 1000 World Banks,* fiscal year-end, percent change from previous year, assets, capital-assets ratio, pretax profits, real profits growth, profits-on-capital ratio, return on assets, cost-to-income ratio, BIS capital ratio, and non-performing loans as a percentage of total loans. **Number listed:** 16

1. Itau Unibanco Holding, with $36,916 million

2. Banco do Brasil SA, $31,078

3. Banco Bradesco SA, $29,001

4. Santander Brasil, $26,622

5. Caixa Economica Federal, $10,037

6. HSBC Bank Brasil, $4,511

7. Banco Safra, $3,319

8. Citibank Brazil, $3,091

9. Banco do Estado do Rio Grande do Sul, $2,021

10. Banco do Nordeste do Brasil, $1,273

Source: *The Banker,* Top 1000 World Banks (annual), July 2011, p. 217-218.

503 ■ BRAZIL'S LARGEST MAJOR BANKS OVERALL, 2011

Ranked by: Score based on revenue, profits, assets, and market capitalization. **Remarks:** Specific scores not provided. Also notes rank in the overall *Forbes 2000* and figures for each criterion. **Number listed:** 2

1. Itau Unibanco Holding SA

2. Banco do Brasil SA

Source: *Forbes,* Forbes 2000 (annual), http://www.forbes.com, May 7, 2012.

504 ■ BRAZIL'S LARGEST REGIONAL BANKS OVERALL, 2011

Ranked by: Score based on revenue, profits, assets, and market capitalization. **Remarks:** Specific scores not provided. Also notes overall rank in the *Forbes 2000* and figures for each criterion. **Number listed:** 2

1. Banco Bradesco

2. Banrisul

Source: *Forbes,* Forbes 2000 (annual), http://www.forbes.com, May 7, 2012.

505 ■ BRAZIL'S MOST VALUABLE BANKING BRANDS, 2011

Ranked by: Brand value, in millions of U.S. dollars. **Remarks:** Also notes rank within the *Global 500* for current and previous year, figures for current and previous year, and brand rating. Ranking is available online only. **Number listed:** 3

1. Bradesco, with $15,692 million

2. Itau, $13,171

3. Banco do Brasil, $7,264

Source: *Global 500,* (annual), Brand Finance plc, March 2012.

506 ■ CHILE'S LARGEST BANKS BY CAPITAL, 2010

Ranked by: Tier one capital, in millions of U.S. dollars. **Remarks:** Also notes rank within the *Top 1000 World Banks,* fiscal year-end, percent change from previous year, assets, capital-assets ratio, pretax profits, real profits growth, profits-on-capital ratio, return on assets, cost-to-income ratio, BIS capital ratio, and non-performing loans as a percentage of total loans. **Number listed:** 9

1. Banco Santander Chile, with $3,911 million

2. Banco de Credito e Inversiones, $2,219

3. Banco de Chile, $2,190

4. Banco del Estado de Chile, $1,825

5. CorpBanca, $1,137

6. BBVA Chile, $961
7. Scotiabank Chile, $953
8. Banco BICE, $395
9. Banco Security, $369

Source: *The Banker*, Top 1000 World Banks (annual), July 2011, p. 218.

507 ■ COLOMBIA'S LARGEST BANKS BY CAPITAL, 2010

Ranked by: Tier one capital, in millions of U.S. dollars. **Remarks:** Also notes rank within the *Top 1000 World Banks*, fiscal year-end, percent change from previous year, assets, capital-assets ratio, pretax profits, real profits growth, profits-on-capital ratio, return on assets, cost-to-income ratio, BIS capital ratio, and non-performing loans as a percentage of total loans. **Number listed:** 6

1. Bancolombia, with $3,188 million
2. Banco de Bogota, $2,260
3. Banco Davivienda, $1,355
4. Banco de Occidente, $1,194
5. BBVA Colombia, $823
6. Banco Popular, $416

Source: *The Banker*, Top 1000 World Banks (annual), July 2011, p. 224.

508 ■ COLOMBIA'S LARGEST REGIONAL BANKS OVERALL, 2011

Ranked by: Score based on revenue, profits, assets, and market capitalization. **Remarks:** Specific scores not provided. Also notes overall rank in the *Forbes 2000* and figures for each criterion. **Number listed:** 2

1. BanColombia
2. Banco Davivienda

Source: *Forbes*, Forbes 2000 (annual), http://www.forbes.com, May 7, 2012.

509 ■ COSTA RICA'S LARGEST BANKS BY CAPITAL, 2010

Ranked by: Tier one capital, in millions of U.S. dollars. **Remarks:** Also notes rank within the *Top 1000 World Banks*, fiscal year-end, percent change from previous year, assets, capital-assets ratio, pretax profits, real profits growth, profits-on-capital ratio, return on assets, cost-to-income ratio, BIS capital ratio, and non-performing loans as a percentage of total loans. **Number listed:** 2

1. Banco de Costa Rica, with $547 million
2. Banco Nacional de Costa Rica, $399

Source: *The Banker*, Top 1000 World Banks (annual), July 2011, p. 224.

510 ■ LARGEST CENTRAL AMERICAN BANKS BY CAPITAL, 2010

Ranked by: Tier one capital, in millions of U.S. dollars. **Remarks:** Also notes consolidation level and fiscal year-end. **Number listed:** 100

1. HSBC Bank Panama, with $1,139.97 million
2. Banco General (Panama), $1,029.48
3. Banco de America Central Panama, $929.93
4. Banco Latinoamericano de Exportaciones (Panama), $701
5. Bancolombia Panama, $628.31
6. Banco de Costa Rica, $547.3
7. Banco Nacional de Panama, $528.65

8. Banco Agricola (El Salvador), $414.24
9. BCB Holdings (Belize), $402.7
10. Banco Nacional de Costa Rica, $398.6

Source: *The Banker*, Top Central American Banks (annual), March 2012, p. 86.

511 ■ LARGEST COSTA RICAN BANKS BY CAPITAL, 2010

Ranked by: Tier one capital, in millions of U.S. dollars. **Remarks:** Also notes percent change from previous year, assets, capital-assets ratio, pretax profits, return on assets, cost-to-income ratio, and BIS capital ratio. **Number listed:** 13

1. Banco de Costa Rica, with $547.3 million
2. Banco Nacional de Costa Rica, $398.6
3. Citibank Costa Rica, $207.93
4. Scotiabank de Costa Rica, $198.2
5. Banco de America Central San Jose, $175.04
6. HSBC Bank Costa Rica, $172.65
7. Corporacion BCT, $89.13
8. Banco Credito Agricola de Cartago, $70.54
9. Banco Improsa, $62.46
10. Banco Promerica Costa Rica, $41.06

Source: *The Banker*, Top Central American Banks (annual), March 2012, p. 87.

512 ■ LARGEST EL SALVADORIAN BANKS BY CAPITAL, 2010

Ranked by: Tier one capital, in millions of U.S. dollars. **Remarks:** Also notes percent change from previous year, assets, capital-assets ratio, pretax profits, return on assets, cost-to-income ratio, and BIS capital ratio. **Number listed:** 11

1. Banco Agricola, with $414.24 million
2. Citibank El Salvador, $268.14
3. HSBC Bank El Salvador, $226.8
4. Scotiabank El Salvador, $220.95
5. Banco de America Central, $110.92
6. Banco Hipotecario de El Salvador, $44.97
7. Banco Promerica, $33.79
8. Banco G & T Continental, $28.67
9. Banco de Fomento Agropecuario, $25.46
10. Banco ProCredit, $22.65

Source: *The Banker*, Top Central American Banks (annual), March 2012, p. 87.

513 ■ LARGEST GUATEMALAN BANKS BY CAPITAL, 2010

Ranked by: Tier one capital, in millions of U.S. dollars. **Remarks:** Also notes percent change from previous year, assets, capital-assets ratio, pretax profits, return on assets, cost-to-income ratio, and BIS capital ratio. **Number listed:** 12

1. Banco Industrial, with $384.06 million
2. Banco de Desarrollo Rural, $312.13
3. Banco G & T Continental, $279.57
4. Citibank Guatemala, $107.76
5. Banco Reformador, $87.01
6. Banco Agromercantil de Guatemala, $83.92
7. Banco de los Trabajadores, $66.73
8. Banco de America Central Guatemala, $50.28

9. Banco Internacional, $36.34

10. Credito Hipotecario Nacional de Guatemala, $25.96

Source: *The Banker*, Top Central American Banks (annual), March 2012, p. 87-88.

514 ■ LARGEST HONDURAN BANKS BY CAPITAL, 2010

Ranked by: Tier one capital, in millions of U.S. dollars. **Remarks:** Also notes percent change from previous year, assets, capital-assets ratio, pretax profits, return on assets, cost-to-income ratio, and BIS capital ratio. **Number listed:** 16

1. Banco Atlantida, with $187.7 million
2. Banco de Occidente Honduras, $141.2
3. Banco de America Central Honduras, $132.31
4. Banco Financiera Comercial Hondurena, $122.49
5. Banco del Pais, $107.86
6. HSBC Bank Honduras, $80.13
7. Banco Continental, $51.52
8. Banco Financiera Centroamericana, $34.5
9. Citibank Honduras, $31.19
10. Banco Lafise Honduras, $21.17

Source: *The Banker*, Top Central American Banks (annual), March 2012, p. 88.

515 ■ LARGEST NICARAGUAN BANKS BY CAPITAL, 2010

Ranked by: Tier one capital, in millions of U.S. dollars. **Remarks:** Also notes percent change from previous year, assets, capital-assets ratio, pretax profits, return on assets, cost-to-income ratio, and BIS capital ratio. **Number listed:** 6

1. Banco de la Produccion, with $93.38 million
2. Banco de America Centrale Nicaragua, $88.82
3. Banco Lafise Bancentro, $64.05
4. Citibank Nicaragua, $39.13
5. Banco de Finanzas, $35.55
6. Banco ProCredit Nicaragua, $19.07

Source: *The Banker*, Top Central American Banks (annual), March 2012, p. 88.

516 ■ LATIN AMERICA'S LARGEST BANKS, 2010

Ranked by: Tier one capital, in millions of U.S. dollars. **Remarks:** Also notes fiscal year-end, assets, and percent change from previous year. **Number listed:** 150

1. Itau Unibanco Holding (Brazil), with $36,915.78 million
2. Banco do Brasil (Brazil), $31,077.84
3. Banco Bradesco SA (Brazil), $29,001.19
4. Santander Brasil (Brazil), $26,621.58
5. Caixa Economica Federal (Brazil), $10,036.77
6. Grupo Financiero BBVA Bancomer (Mexico), $9,192.28
7. Grupo Financiero Banamex (Mexico), $8,576.43
8. Grupo Financiero Santander (Mexico), $5,353.56
9. HSBC Banco Brasil (Brazil), $4,510.86
10. Banco Santander Chile (Chile), $3,911.01

Source: *The Banker*, Top 150 Latin American Banks (annual), November 2011, p. 114-115.

517 ■ MEXICO'S LARGEST BANKS BY CAPITAL, 2010

Ranked by: Tier one capital, in millions of U.S. dollars. **Remarks:** Also notes rank within the *Top 1000 World Banks,* fiscal year-end, percent change from previous year, assets, capital-assets ratio, pretax profits, real profits growth, profits-on-capital ratio, return on assets, cost-to-income ratio, BIS capital ratio, and non-performing loans as a percentage of total loans. **Number listed:** 9

1. Grupo Financiero BBVA Bancomer, with $9,192 million
2. Grupo Financiero Banamex, $8,576
3. Grupo Financiero Santander, $5,354
4. Banco Inbursa, $3,192
5. Grupo Financiero Banorte, $3,186
6. Grupo Financiero HSBC, $2,771
7. Scotiabank Inverlat SA, $2,012
8. Banco Azteca, $351
9. JP Morgan Grupo Financiero, $333

Source: *The Banker*, Top 1000 World Banks (annual), July 2011, p. 240.

518 ■ PANAMA'S LARGEST BANKS BY CAPITAL, 2010

Ranked by: Tier one capital, in millions of U.S. dollars. **Remarks:** Also notes rank within the *Top 1000 World Banks,* fiscal year-end, percent change from previous year, assets, capital-assets ratio, pretax profits, real profits growth, profits-on-capital ratio, return on assets, cost-to-income ratio, BIS capital ratio, and non-performing loans as a percentage of total loans. **Number listed:** 6

1. HSBC Bank Panama, with $1,140 million
2. Banco General, $1,029
3. BAC International Bank, $930
4. Banco Latinoamericano de Exportaciones, $701
5. Bancolombia (Panama), $628
6. Banco Nacional de Panama, $529

Source: *The Banker*, Top 1000 World Banks (annual), July 2011, p. 242.

519 ■ PERU'S LARGEST BANKS BY CAPITAL, 2010

Ranked by: Tier one capital, in millions of U.S. dollars. **Remarks:** Also notes rank within the *Top 1000 World Banks,* fiscal year-end, percent change from previous year, assets, capital-assets ratio, pretax profits, real profits growth, profits-on-capital ratio, return on assets, cost-to-income ratio, BIS capital ratio, and non-performing loans as a percentage of total loans. **Number listed:** 3

1. Banco de Credito del Peru, with $1,559 million
2. BBVA Banco Continental, $846
3. Banco Internacional del Peru, $505

Source: *The Banker*, Top 1000 World Banks (annual), July 2011, p. 242.

520 ■ VENEZUELA'S LARGEST BANKS BY CAPITAL, 2010

Ranked by: Tier one capital, in millions of U.S. dollars. **Remarks:** Also notes rank within the *Top 1000 World Banks,* fiscal year-end, percent change from previous year, assets, capital-assets ratio, pretax profits, real profits growth, profits-on-capital ratio, return on assets, cost-to-income ratio, BIS capital ratio, and non-performing loans as a percentage of total loans. **Number listed:** 13

1. Mercantil Servicious Financieros, with $3,079 million
2. BBVA Banco Provincial - Banco Universal, $1,832

3. Banesco Banco Universal, $1,579

4. Banco de Venezuela, $1,273

5. Banco Bicentenario, $793

6. Banco Occidental de Descuento, $729

7. Banco Exterior, $495

8. Banco del Caribe, $437

9. CorpBanca, $376

10. Citibank Venezuela, $271

Source: *The Banker*, Top 1000 World Banks (annual), July 2011, p. 258.

Banks and Banking—Middle East

521 ■ BAHRAIN'S LARGEST BANKS BY CAPITAL, 2010

Ranked by: Tier one capital, in millions of U.S. dollars. **Remarks:** Also notes rank within the *Top 100 Arab Banks,* fiscal year-end, percent change from previous year, assets, capital-assets ratio, pretax profits, real profits growth, profits-on-capital ratio, return on assets, cost-to-income ratio, BIS capital ratio, and non-performing loans as a percentage of total loans. **Number listed:** 11

1. Arab Banking Corp., with $3,828 million

2. Ahli United Bank, $1,977.23

3. Gulf International Bank, $1,930

4. Al Baraka Banking Group BSC, $1,699

5. Bank of Bahrain & Kuwait, $623.05

6. National Bank of Bahrain, $620.47

7. Al Salam Bank, $459.5

8. United Gulf Bank, $414.5

9. Khaleeji Commercial Bank, $313.94

10. Future Bank, $226.74

Source: *The Banker*, Top 100 Arab Banks (annual), October 2011, p. 86.

522 ■ IRAN'S LARGEST BANKS BY CAPITAL, 2010

Ranked by: Tier one capital, in millions of U.S. dollars. **Remarks:** Also notes rank within the *Top 1000 World Banks,* fiscal year-end, percent change from previous year, assets, capital-assets ratio, pretax profits, real profits growth, profits-on-capital ratio, return on assets, cost-to-income ratio, BIS capital ratio, and non-performing loans as a percentage of total loans. **Number listed:** 10

1. Bank Saderat Iran, with $2,976 million

2. Export Development Bank of Iran, $2,077

3. Parsian Bank, $1,520

4. Bank Maskan, $1,288

5. Bank Mellat, $1,280

6. Bank Pasargad, $1,265

7. Bank Tejarat, $1,022

8. EN Bank (Bank Eghtesad Novin), $710

9. Bank Keshavarzi, $517

10. Karafarin Bank, $425

Source: *The Banker*, Top 1000 World Banks (annual), July 2011, p. 233.

523 ■ ISRAEL'S LARGEST BANKS BY CAPITAL, 2010

Ranked by: Tier one capital, in millions of U.S. dollars. **Remarks:** Also notes rank within the *Top 1000 World Banks,* fiscal year-end, percent change from previous year, assets, capital-assets ratio, pretax profits, real profits growth, profits-on-capital ratio, return on

assets, cost-to-income ratio, BIS capital ratio, and non-performing loans as a percentage of total loans. **Number listed:** 6

1. Bank Hapoalim, with $7,074 million

2. Bank Leumi le-Israel BM, $6,557

3. Israel Discount Bank, $3,410

4. Mizrahi Tefahot Bank, $2,061

5. First International Bank of Israel, $1,612

6. Union Bank of Israel, $555

Source: *The Banker*, Top 1000 World Banks (annual), July 2011, p. 233.

524 ■ ISRAEL'S LARGEST MAJOR BANKS OVERALL, 2011

Ranked by: Score based on revenue, profits, assets, and market capitalization. **Remarks:** Specific scores not provided. Also notes overall rank in the *Forbes 2000* and figures for each criterion. **Number listed:** 2

1. Bank Hapoalim

2. Bank Leumi

Source: *Forbes*, Forbes 2000 (annual), http://www.forbes.com, May 7, 2012.

525 ■ ISRAEL'S LARGEST REGIONAL BANKS OVERALL, 2011

Ranked by: Score based on revenue, profits, assets, and market capitalization. **Remarks:** Specific scores not provided. Also notes overall rank in the *Forbes 2000* and figures for each criterion. **Number listed:** 3

1. Israel Discount Bank

2. Mizrahi Tefahot Bank

3. FIBI Holding

Source: *Forbes*, Forbes 2000 (annual), http://www.forbes.com, May 7, 2012.

526 ■ JORDAN'S LARGEST BANKS BY CAPITAL, 2010

Ranked by: Tier one capital, in millions of U.S. dollars. **Remarks:** Also notes rank within the *Top 100 Arab Banks,* fiscal year-end, percent change from previous year, assets, capital-assets ratio, pretax profits, real profits growth, profits-on-capital ratio, return on assets, cost-to-income ratio, BIS capital ratio, and non-performing loans as a percentage of total loans. **Number listed:** 9

1. Arab Bank, with $4,888.91 million

2. The Housing Bank for Trade & Finance, $1,143.66

3. Jordan Kuwait Bank, $436.34

4. Union Bank, $331.25

5. Jordan Ahli Bank, $282.37

6. Jordan Islamic Bank, $246.48

7. Capital Bank of Jordan, $238.03

8. Bank of Jordan, $235.59

9. Cairo Amman Bank, $215.35

Source: *The Banker*, Top 100 Arab Banks (annual), October 2011, p. 86.

527 ■ KUWAIT'S LARGEST BANKS BY CAPITAL, 2010

Ranked by: Tier one capital, in millions of U.S. dollars. **Remarks:** Also notes rank within the *Top 100 Arab Banks,* fiscal year-end, percent change from previous year, assets, capital-assets ratio, pretax profits, real profits growth, profits-on-capital ratio, return on assets, cost-to-income ratio, BIS capital ratio, and non-performing loans as a percentage of total loans. **Number listed:** 9

1. National Bank of Kuwait, with $5,246.58 million
2. Kuwait Finance House, $5,038.05
3. Commonwealth Bank of Kuwait, $1,511.48
4. Al Ahli Bank of Kuwait, $1,483.12
5. Burgan Bank, $1,471.53
6. Gulf Bank, $1,342.35
7. Ahli United Bank KSC, $844.53
8. Boubyan Bank, $813.6
9. Kuwait International Bank, $597.5

Source: *The Banker*, Top 100 Arab Banks (annual), October 2011, p. 86-88.

528 ■ KUWAIT'S LARGEST REGIONAL BANKS OVERALL, 2011

Ranked by: Score based on revenue, profits, assets, and market capitalization. **Remarks:** Specific scores not provided. Also notes overall rank in the *Forbes 2000* and figures for each criterion. **Number listed:** 2

1. National Bank of Kuwait
2. Kuwait Finance House

Source: *Forbes*, Forbes 2000 (annual), http://www.forbes.com, May 7, 2012.

529 ■ LEBANON'S LARGEST REGIONAL BANKS OVERALL, 2011

Ranked by: Score based on revenue, profits, assets, and market capitalization. **Remarks:** Specific scores not provided. Also notes overall rank in the *Forbes 2000* and figures for each criterion. **Number listed:** 2

1. Bank Audi
2. Blom Bank

Source: *Forbes*, Forbes 2000 (annual), http://www.forbes.com, May 7, 2012.

530 ■ PAKISTAN'S LARGEST BANKS BY CAPITAL, 2010

Ranked by: Tier one capital, in millions of U.S. dollars. **Remarks:** Also notes rank within the *Top 1000 World Banks,* fiscal year-end, percent change from previous year, assets, capital-assets ratio, pretax profits, real profits growth, profits-on-capital ratio, return on assets, cost-to-income ratio, BIS capital ratio, and non-performing loans as a percentage of total loans. **Number listed:** 5

1. National Bank of Pakistan, with $1,089 million
2. Habib Bank, $913
3. MCB Bank, $799
4. United Bank, $638
5. Allied Bank Ltd., $361

Source: *The Banker*, Top 1000 World Banks (annual), July 2011, p. 242.

531 ■ QATAR'S LARGEST MAJOR BANKS OVERALL, 2011

Ranked by: Score based on revenue, profits, assets, and market capitalization. **Remarks:** Specific scores not provided. Also notes overall rank in the *Forbes 2000* and figures for each criterion. **Number listed:** 2

1. Qatar National Bank
2. Doha Bank

Source: *Forbes*, Forbes 2000 (annual), http://www.forbes.com, May 7, 2012.

532 ■ QATAR'S LARGEST REGIONAL BANKS OVERALL, 2011

Ranked by: Score based on revenue, profits, assets, and market capitalization. **Remarks:** Specific scores not provided. Also notes overall rank in the *Forbes 2000* and figures for each criterion. **Number listed:** 3

1. Commercial Bank of Qatar
2. Masraf Al Rayan
3. Qatar Islamic Bank

Source: *Forbes*, Forbes 2000 (annual), http://www.forbes.com, May 7, 2012.

533 ■ SAUDI ARABIA'S LARGEST REGIONAL BANKS OVERALL, 2011

Ranked by: Score based on revenue, profits, assets, and market capitalization. **Remarks:** Specific scores not provided. Also notes overall rank in the *Forbes 2000* and figures for each criterion. **Number listed:** 5

1. Al Rajhi Bank
2. Riyad Bank
3. Saudi British Bank
4. Banque Saudi Fransi
5. Arab National Bank

Source: *Forbes*, Forbes 2000 (annual), http://www.forbes.com, May 7, 2012.

534 ■ THE UAE'S BEST PERFORMING BANKS, 2010-2011

Ranked by: Annual share price growth, in percent. **Number listed:** 15

1. First Gulf Bank, with 24.55%
2. Abu Dhabi Commercial Bank, 12.59%
3. Commercial Bank International, 9.76%
4. Dubai Islamic Bank, 9.75%
5. National Bank of Umm Al Quwain, 8.99%
6. National Bank of Abu Dhabi, 8.8%
7. Abu Dhabi Islamic Bank, 8.65%
8. Union National Bank, 8.17%
9. Invest Bank, 7.64%
10. Ajman Bank, 4.7%

Source: *Arabian Business*, The UAE's Best Performing Banks, April 24, 2012.

535 ■ THE UNITED ARAB EMIRATES' LARGEST MAJOR BANKS OVERALL, 2011

Ranked by: Score based on revenue, profits, assets, and market capitalization. **Remarks:** Specific scores not provided. Also notes overall rank in the *Forbes 2000* and figures for each criterion. **Number listed:** 2

1. National Bank of Abu Dhabi
2. Mashreqbank

Source: *Forbes*, Forbes 2000 (annual), http://www.forbes.com, May 7, 2012.

536 ■ THE UNITED ARAB EMIRATES' LARGEST REGIONAL BANKS OVERALL, 2011

Ranked by: Score based on revenue, profits, assets, and market capitalization. **Remarks:** Specific scores not provided. Also notes overall rank in the *Forbes 2000* and figures for each criterion. **Number listed:** 6

1. First Gulf Bank
2. Emirates NBD
3. Abu Dhabi Commercial Bank
4. Union National Bank
5. Dubai Islamic Bank
6. Abu Dhabi Islamic Bank

Source: *Forbes*, Forbes 2000 (annual), http://www.forbes.com, May 7, 2012.

Banks and Banking—North America

537 ■ CANADA'S LARGEST BANKS BY CAPITAL, 2010

Ranked by: Tier one capital, in millions of U.S. dollars. **Remarks:** Also notes rank within the *Top 1000 World Banks,* fiscal year-end, percent change from previous year, assets, capital-assets ratio, pretax profits, real profits growth, profits-on-capital ratio, return on assets, cost-to-income ratio, BIS capital ratio, and non-performing loans as a percentage of total loans. **Number listed:** 11

1. Royal Bank of Canada, with $33,339 million
2. Bank of Nova Scotia (Scotiabank), $24,862
3. Toronto-Dominion Bank, $23,931
4. Bank of Montreal, $21,274
5. Canadian Imperial Bank of Commerce, $14,574
6. Desjardins Group, $12,021
7. National Bank of Canada, $6,840
8. HSBC Bank Canada, $4,539
9. Canadian Western Bank, $1,162
10. Laurentian Bank of Canada, $1,113

Source: *The Banker*, Top 1000 World Banks (annual), July 2011, p. 218.

538 ■ CANADA'S LARGEST MAJOR BANKS OVERALL, 2011

Ranked by: Score based on revenue, profits, assets, and market capitalization. **Remarks:** Specific scores not provided. Also notes overall rank in the *Forbes 2000* and figures for each criterion. **Number listed:** 6

1. Royal Bank of Canada
2. TD Bank Financial Group
3. Scotiabank--Bank of Nova Scotia
4. Bank of Montreal
5. Canadian Imperial Bank
6. National Bank of Canada

Source: *Forbes*, Forbes 2000 (annual), http://www.forbes.com, May 7, 2012.

539 ■ CANADA'S MOST VALUABLE BANKING BRANDS, 2011

Ranked by: Brand value, in millions of U.S. dollars. **Remarks:** Also notes rank within the *Global 500* for current and previous year, figures for current and previous year, and brand rating. Ranking is available online only. **Number listed:** 5

1. RBC, with $8,647 million
2. TD, $8,499
3. Scotiabank, $5,717
4. Bank of Montreal, $5,360
5. CIBC, $4,557

Source: *Global 500*, (annual), Brand Finance plc, March 2012.

540 ■ MEXICO'S LARGEST REGIONAL BANKS OVERALL, 2011

Ranked by: Score based on revenue, profits, assets, and market capitalization. **Remarks:** Specific scores not provided. Also notes overall rank in the *Forbes 2000* and figures for each criterion. **Number listed:** 2

1. Grupo Financiero Banorte, SAB de CV (GFNorte)
2. Grupo Financiero Inbursa, SAB de CV

Source: *Forbes*, Forbes 2000 (annual), http://www.forbes.com, May 7, 2012.

541 ■ NORTH AMERICA'S FASTEST-GROWING BANKS, 2009-2010

Ranked by: Annual growth in tier one capital, in percent. **Remarks:** Also notes rank within the *Top 1000 World Banks* and total tier one capital. **Number listed:** 10

1. First Southern Bancorp (U.S.), with 754.78%
2. Sterling Financial Corp. (U.S.), 153.52%
3. West Coast Bancorp (U.S.), 119.26%
4. Oriental Financial Group (Puerto Rico), 68.52%
5. EverBank (U.S.), 61.4%
6. First Niagara Financial Group (U.S.), 58.62%
7. Pacific Capital Bancorp (U.S.), 53.73%
8. Union Bankshares Corp. (U.S.), 46.2%
9. Popular (Puerto Rico), 45.63%
10. Iberiabank Corp. (U.S.), 45.24%

Source: *The Banker*, Top 1000 World Banks (annual), July 2011, p. 149.

542 ■ NORTH AMERICA'S LARGEST BANKS BY CAPITAL, 2010

Ranked by: Tier one capital, in millions of U.S. dollars. **Remarks:** Also notes rank within the *Top 1000 World Banks.* **Number listed:** 25

1. Bank of America Corp. (U.S.), with $163,626 million
2. J. P. Morgan Chase & Co. (U.S.), $142,450
3. Citigroup Inc. (U.S.), $126,193
4. Wells Fargo & Co. (U.S.), $109,353
5. Goldman Sachs Group Inc. (U.S.), $71,233
6. Morgan Stanley (U.S.), $52,880
7. Royal Bank of Canada, $33,339
8. PNC Financial Services Group Inc. (U.S.), $26,092
9. U.S. Bancorp (U.S.), $25,947
10. Bank of Nova Scotia (Scotiabank, Canada), $24,862

Source: *The Banker*, Top 1000 World Banks (annual), July 2011, p. 149.

543 ■ TOP CANADIAN BANKS, 2010

Ranked by: Revenue, in thousands of Canadian dollars (unless otherwise noted). **Remarks:** Also notes percent change from previous year. **Number listed:** 10

1. Royal Bank of Canada, with C$36,026,000 thousand
2. Toronto-Dominion Bank, C$25,409,000
3. Scotiabank--Bank of Nova Scotia, C$23,775,000

4. Bank of Montreal, C$15,453,000
5. Canadian Imperial Bank of Commerce, C$14,976,000
6. National Bank of Canada, C$5,259,000
7. HSBC Bank Canada, C$3,083,000
8. Laurentian Bank of Canada, C$1,188,248
9. Amex Bank of Canada, C$1,028,232
10. MBNA Canada Bank, C$1,017,424

Source: *Report on Business Magazine*, Top 1000 Companies (annual), http://www.reportonbusiness.com, June 2011.

Baseball

544 ■ MOST VALUABLE BASEBALL TEAMS, 2011

Ranked by: Value, based on current stadium deal without deduction for debt, in millions of dollars. **Remarks:** Also notes profit and comments. **Number listed:** 30

1. New York Yankees, with $1,850 million
2. Los Angeles Dodgers, $1,200
3. Boston Red Sox, $1,000
4. Chicago Cubs, $879
5. Philadelphia Phillies, $723
6. New York Mets, $719
7. Texas Rangers, $674
8. Los Angeles Angels of Anaheim, $656
9. San Francisco Giants, $643
10. Chicago White Sox, $600

Source: *Forbes*, Baseball Team Valuations (annual), April 9, 2012, p. 80-81.

Basketball

545 ■ HIGHEST-PAID COACHES IN THE NATIONAL BASKETBALL ASSOCIATION, 2011

Ranked by: Earnings, in millions of dollars. **Number listed:** 10

1. Doc Rivers (Celtics), with $7 million
2. Mike D'Antoni (Knicks), $6
2. Gregg Popovich (Spurs), $6
4. Nate McMillan (Trail Blazers), $5.5
5. Rick Adelman (Timberwolves), $5
6. Flip Saunders (Wizards), $4.8
7. Rick Carlisle (Mavericks), $4.5
7. Mike Brown (Lakers), $4.5
7. Stan Van Gundy (Magic), $4.5
7. Scott Skiles (Bucks), $4.5

Source: *Forbes*, NBA Team Valuations (annual), February 13, 2012, p. 85.

546 ■ MOST VALUABLE TEAMS IN THE NATIONAL BASKETBALL ASSOCIATION, 2011

Ranked by: Total value, in millions of dollars. **Remarks:** Also notes owner, year acquired, percent change in value from previous year, revenue, and operating income. **Number listed:** 30

1. Los Angeles Lakers, with $900 million
2. New York Knicks, $780
3. Chicago Bulls, $600

4. Dallas Mavericks, $497
5. Boston Celtics, $482
6. Miami Heat, $457
7. Houston Rockets, $453
8. Golden State Warriors, $450
9. San Antonio Spurs, $418
10. Phoenix Suns, $395

Source: *Forbes*, NBA Team Valuations (annual), February 13, 2012, p. 86-89.

547 ■ WEALTHIEST OWNERS OF NBA TEAMS, 2011

Ranked by: Wealth, in billions of dollars. **Number listed:** 10

1. Mikhail Prokhorov (Nets), with $18 billion
2. Paul Allen (Trail Blazers), $13.2
3. Philip Anschutz (Lakers), $7
4. Richard Devos (Magic), $5
5. Micky Arison (Heat), $4.2
6. Stanley Kroenke (Nuggets), $3.2
7. Tom Gores (Pistons), $2.5
8. Mark Cuban (Mavericks), $2.3
9. Glen Taylor (Timberwolves), $1.8
10. Herbert Simon (Pacers), $1.6

Source: *Forbes*, NBA Team Valuations (annual), February 13, 2012, p. 85.

Batteries

548 ■ TOP BATTERY RETAIL FRANCHISES, 2012

Ranked by: Cumulative score based on financial strength and stability, growth rate, size of the system, number of years in business, the length of time franchising, start-up costs, litigation, percentage of terminations, and whether the company provides financing. **Remarks:** Specific scores not provided. Also notes overall rank within the *Franchise 500*, contact information, description, year founded, year started franchising, states where registered, available U.S. regions, where seeking foreign expansion, number of franchised and company-owned units for past three years, start-up costs, franchise fees, royalty fees, and type of financing available. **Number listed:** 2

1. Batteries Plus
2. Interstate All Battery Center

Source: *Entrepreneur*, Franchise 500 (annual), January 2012, p. 198-199.

Beauty Products
See: **Personal Care Products**

Beer
See also: **Alcoholic Beverages; Liquor Industry**

549 ■ TOP BEER BRANDS BY SALES, 2011

Ranked by: Sales, in millions of dollars. **Remarks:** Also notes brewer/importer and annual growth. **Number listed:** 20

1. Bud Light, with $5,327.1 million
2. Budweiser, $2,072.4
3. Coors Light, $1,946.8

4. Miller Lite, $1,672.6

5. Natural Light, $1,089.7

6. Corona Extra, $965.1

7. Busch Light, $735.4

8. Busch, $684.5

9. Heineken, $577.5

10. Michelob Ultra, $518.1

Source: *Beverage World*, State of the Industry Report (annual), May 2012, p. 40.

550 ■ TOP BEER COMPANIES BY VOLUME, 2010

Ranked by: Market share of shipment volume, in percent. **Remarks:** Also notes parent company, measured media expenditures, and figures for previous year. **Number listed:** 10

1. Anheuser-Busch InBev SA/NV, with 47.9%

2. MillerCoors, 28.9%

3. Crown Imports, 5.3%

4. Heineken NV, 4%

5. Pabst Brewing Co., 2.7%

6. Diageo, 1.3%

7. North American Breweries, 1.2%

8. Boston Beer Co., 1.1%

9. D. G. Yuengling & Son, 1%

10. Mark Anthony Group, 0.6%

Source: *Advertising Age*, Leading National Advertisers (annual), June 20, 2011, p. 22.

551 ■ TOP BEER WHOLESALERS IN THE U.S., 2010

Ranked by: Case volume, in millions. **Remarks:** Also notes dollar sales, contact information, key executives, number of employees, additional sites, leading suppliers/brands, and comments. **Number listed:** 20

1. Reyes Beverage Group, with 93 million cases

2. Silver Eagle Distributors LP, 45.6

3. Ben E. Keith Beverages, 38.7

4. Columbia Distributing, 33.5

5. Manhattan Beer Distributors LLC, 32.1

6. Goldring/Moffett Holdings, 30.8

7. Andrews Distributing Cos., 27.5

8. Gold Coast Beverage Distributors Inc., 25.9

9. JJ Taylor Cos., Inc., 25

10. Topa Equities Ltd., 24.4

Source: *Beverage Executive*, Distribution 20 (annual), October 2011, p. 39+.

552 ■ TOP DOMESTIC BEER BRANDS, 2011

Ranked by: Sales, in dollars. **Remarks:** Also notes percent change from previous year and case sales. **Number listed:** 10

1. Bud Light, with $5,291,023,000

2. Budweiser, $2,086,417,000

3. Coors Light, $1,898,200,000

4. Miller Lite, $1,683,484,000

5. Natural Light, $1,105,459,000

6. Busch Light, $732,388,400

7. Busch, $676,409,000

8. Miller High Life, $497,994,100

9. Keystone Light, $489,566,500

10. Natural Ice, $352,004,900

Source: *Beverage Industry*, State of the Industry Report (annual), July 2011, p. SOI-20.

553 ■ WORLD'S MOST VALUABLE BEER BRANDS, 2012

Ranked by: Brand value, a measure of a brand's earnings and contribution, in millions of U.S. dollars. **Remarks:** Also notes annual growth in brand value and rank by brand contribution and brand momentum. **Number listed:** 10

1. Bud Light, with $8,368 million

2. Budweiser, $7,514

3. Heineken, $6,058

4. Corona, $5,114

5. Skol, $4,698

6. Stella Artois, $4,529

7. Guinness, $4,044

8. Brahma, $2,359

9. Miller Lite, $2,313

10. Beck's, $1,554

Source: *Financial Times*, Global Brands (annual), http://www.ft.com, May 22, 2012.

Beer Industry—Export/Import Trade

554 ■ TOP IMPORTED BEER BRANDS IN THE U.S., 2011

Ranked by: Sales, in dollars. **Remarks:** Also notes percent change from previous year and case sales. **Number listed:** 10

1. Corona Extra, with $916,551,000

2. Heineken, $565,347,300

3. Modelo Especial, $292,687,700

4. Corona Light, $165,675,500

5. Tecate, $159,479,800

6. Labatt Blue, $116,525,600

7. Dos Equis XX Lager Especial, $107,457,200

8. Labatt Blue Light, $105,300,900

9. Stella Artois Lager, $95,537,540

10. Newcastle Brown Ale, $79,169,860

Source: *Beverage Industry*, State of the Industry Report (annual), July 2011, p. SOI-20.

Benefits
See: **Employee Benefits**

Best Sellers

555 ■ BESTSELLING ADULT AND JUVENILE FICTION, 2011

Ranked by: Sales. **Remarks:** Figures not provided. Also notes author. **Number listed:** 10

1. *The Help* (paperback)

2. *The Hunger Games*

3. *Cabin Fever*

4. *The Help* (movie tie-in)

5. *Catching Fire*

6. *Mockingjay*

7. *Inheritance*
8. *Water for Elephants*
9. *The Son of Neptune*
10. *The Throne of Fire*

Source: *People*, Tops of 2011, December 26, 2011, p. 52.

556 ■ LONGEST-RUNNING FICTION HARDCOVER BEST-SELLERS, 2011

Ranked by: Number of weeks appearing on Publishers Weekly's bestsellers charts during the year. **Remarks:** Also notes author, publisher, and number of weeks it appeared on the bestsellers charts in the previous year. **Number listed:** 4

1. *The Girl Who Kicked the Hornet's Nest*, with 39 weeks
2. *The Paris Wife*, 23
3. *A Dance with Dragons: A Song of Fire & Ice*, Book 5, 19
4. *The Help*, 18

Source: *Publishers Weekly*, Bestsellers (annual), January 9, 2012, p. 19.

557 ■ LONGEST-RUNNING MASS MARKET PAPERBACK BESTSELLERS, 2011

Ranked by: Number of weeks appearing on Publishers Weekly's bestsellers charts during the year. **Remarks:** Also notes author, publisher, and number of weeks it appeared on the bestsellers charts in the previous year. **Number listed:** 6

1. *A Game of Thrones*, with 36 weeks
2. *The Girl with the Dragon Tattoo*, 28
3. *A Storm of Swords*, 25
4. *A Clash of Kings*, 23
5. *The Girl Who Played with Fire*, 19
6. *A Feast for Crows*, 15

Source: *Publishers Weekly*, Bestsellers (annual), January 9, 2012, p. 19.

558 ■ LONGEST-RUNNING NONFICTION HARDCOVER BESTSELLERS, 2011

Ranked by: Number of weeks appearing on Publishers Weekly's bestsellers charts during the year. **Remarks:** Also notes author, publisher, and number of weeks it appeared on the bestsellers charts in the previous year. **Number listed:** 8

1. *Unbroken*, with 50 weeks
2. *The 17 Day Diet*, 27
3. *Bossypants*, 23
4. *The Dukan Diet*, 21
5. *In the Garden of the Beasts*, 22
6. *Go the F**k to Sleep*, 20
7. *The 4-Hour Body*, 19
8. *The Greater Journey*, 15

Source: *Publishers Weekly*, Bestsellers (annual), January 9, 2012, p. 19.

559 ■ LONGEST-RUNNING TRADE PAPERBACK BEST-SELLERS, 2011

Ranked by: Number of weeks appearing on Publishers Weekly's bestsellers charts during the year. **Remarks:** Also notes author, publisher, and number of weeks it appeared on the bestsellers charts in the previous year. **Number listed:** 14

1. *Heaven Is for Real*, with 49 weeks
2. *The Art of Racing in the Rain*, 44
3. *The Immortal Life of Henrietta Lacks*, 40
4. *Water for Elephants*, 37
5. *The Help*, 36
6. *Room*, 27
7. *Sarah's Key*, 25
8. *The Girl with the Dragon Tattoo*, 23
8. *Outliers*, 23
10. *Inside of a Dog*, 20
10. *The Glass Castle*, 20

Source: *Publishers Weekly*, Bestsellers (annual), January 9, 2012, p. 19.

560 ■ TOP CHILDREN'S E-BOOK BESTSELLERS, 2011

Ranked by: Number of electronic books sold during the year. **Remarks:** Also notes author and publisher. **Number listed:** 286

1. *The Hunger Games*, with 1,093,091 copies
2. *Hunger Games No. 2: Catching Fire*, 849,957
3. *Hunger Games No. 3: Mockingjay*, 782,445
4. *The Twilight Saga No. 4: Breaking Dawn*, 296,366
5. *Inheritance Cycle No. 4: Inheritance*, n/a
6. *Heroes of Olympus No. 2: The Son of Neptune*, 204,500
7. *Twilight*, 174,672
8. *I Am Number Four*, 158,552
9. *Kane Chronicles No. 2: The Throne of Fire*, 137,917
10. *The Twilight Saga No. 3: Eclipse*, 137,164

Source: *Publishers Weekly*, Facts & Figures (annual), March 19, 2012, p. 55-59.

561 ■ TOP CHILDREN'S HARDCOVER BACKLIST BEST-SELLERS, 2011

Ranked by: Number of books sold during the year. **Remarks:** Also notes author and publisher. **Number listed:** 70

1. *Hunger Games No. 2: Catching Fire*, with 1,671,902 copies
2. *Hunger Games No. 3: Mockingjay*, 1,450,207
3. *Diary of a Wimpy Kid No. 2: Rodrick Rules*, 741,944
4. *Diary of a Wimpy Kid No. 5: The Ugly Truth*, 696,518
5. *Diary of a Wimpy Kid No. 3: The Last Straw*, 632,534
6. *Diary of a Wimpy Kid*, 622,871
7. *The Hunger Games*, 594,562
8. *Diary of a Wimpy Kid No. 4: Dog Days*, 582,729
9. *Green Eggs & Ham*, 569,371
10. *Goodnight Moon* (board book), 557,602

Source: *Publishers Weekly*, Facts & Figures (annual), March 19, 2012, p. 50-51.

562 ■ TOP CHILDREN'S HARDCOVER FRONTLIST BEST-SELLERS, 2011

Ranked by: Number of books sold during the year. **Remarks:** Also notes author and publisher. **Number listed:** 93

1. *Diary of a Wimpy Kid No. 6: Cabin Fever*, with 3,321,388 copies
2. *Inheritance Cycle No. 4: Inheritance*, 1,811,022
3. *The Heroes of Olympus No. 2: The Son of Neptune*, 1,781,189
4. *The Kane Chronicles No. 2: The Throne of Fire*, 1,187,604
5. *House of Night No. 9: Destined*, 625,000
6. *Middle School, the Worst Years of My Life*, 543,254
7. *Every Thing on It*, 511,389
8. *If You Give a Dog a Donut*, 508,884
9. *Mortal Instruments No. 4: City of Fallen Angels*, 495,766
10. *Dork Diaries No. 3: Tales from a Not-So-Talented Pop Star*, 492,32

Source: *Publishers Weekly*, Facts & Figures (annual), March 19, 2012, p. 48-50.

563 ■ TOP CHILDREN'S PAPERBACK BACKLIST BEST-SELLERS, 2011

Ranked by: Number of books sold during the year. **Remarks:** Also notes author and publisher. **Number listed:** 134

1. *The Hunger Games*, with 2,696,707 copies
2. *Harry Potter & the Sorcerer's Stone*, 452,076
3. *The Giver*, 435,710
4. *Love You Forever*, 381,347
5. *Harry Potter & the Deathly Hallows*, 371,873
6. *Percy Jackson & the Olympians: Book One: The Lightning Thief*, 358,706
7. *Magic Tree House No. 1: Dinosaurs Before Dark*, 345,220
8. *Harry Potter & the Chamber of Secrets*, 343,735
9. *Harry Potter & the Prisoner of Azkaban*, 309,458
10. *Harry Potter & the Order of the Phoenix*, 296,849

Source: *Publishers Weekly*, Facts & Figures (annual), March 19, 2012, p. 52-55.

564 ■ TOP CHILDREN'S PAPERBACK FRONTLIST BEST-SELLERS, 2011

Ranked by: Number of books sold during the year. **Remarks:** Also notes author and publisher. **Number listed:** 66

1. *The Twilight Saga No. 4: Breaking Dawn*, with 753,888 copies
2. *Witch & Wizard*, 656,665
3. *Phineas & Ferb: Across the 2nd Dimension*, 516,007
4. *Pinkalicious: Pinkie Promise*, 457,416
5. *Percy Jackson & the Olympians No. 5: The Last Olympian*, 448,672
6. *Phineas & Ferb: Agent P's Top-Secret Joke Book*, 403,950
7. *Disney/Pixar Cars 2: Race Around the World*, 356,822
8. *Maximum Ride No. 6: Fang*, 330,806
9. *African Cats: A Lion's Pride*, 296,077
10. *Beastly*, 276,033

Source: *Publishers Weekly*, Facts & Figures (annual), March 19, 2012, p. 51-52.

565 ■ TOP E-BOOK BESTSELLERS, 2011

Ranked by: Number of copies sold in electronic book format during the year. **Remarks:** Also notes author and publisher. **Number listed:** 340

1. *The Help*, with 1,950,000 copies
2. *Heaven is for Real*, 958,837
3. *Unbroken: A World War II Story of Survival, Resilence, and Redemption*, 789,998
4. *Steve Jobs*, 624,595
5. *The Lincoln Lawyer*, 481,985
6. *Explosive Eighteen*, 477,474
7. *Stolen Life*, 457,724
8. *Bossypants*, 431,117
9. *Now You See Her*, 411,827
10. *Something Borrowed*, 351,993

Source: *Publishers Weekly*, Facts & Figures (annual), March 19, 2012, p. 43-47.

566 ■ TOP HARDCOVER FICTION BESTSELLERS, 2011

Ranked by: Number of books sold during the year. **Remarks:** Also notes author, publisher, and publication date. **Number listed:** 110

1. *The Litigators*, with 1,100,000 copies
2. *11/23/1963*, 919,524
3. *The Best of Me*, 850,653
4. *Smokin' Seventeen*, 751,899
5. *A Dance with Dragons*, 750,000
6. *Explosive Eighteen*, 744,029
7. *Kill Alex Cross*, 619,406
8. *Micro*, 537,835
9. *Dead Reakoning*, 500,000
10. *Locked On*, 450,000

Source: *Publishers Weekly*, Facts & Figures (annual), March 19, 2012, p. 34-36.

567 ■ TOP HARDCOVER NON-FICTION BESTSELLERS, 2011

Ranked by: Number of books sold during the year. **Remarks:** Also notes author, publisher, and publication date. **Number listed:** 78

1. *Unbroken: A World War II Story of Survival, Resilence, and Redemption*, with 1,100,000 copies
2. *Killing Lincoln*, 990,000
3. *The 17 Day Diet*, 833,847
4. *Bossypants*, 671,106
5. *Go the F**k to Sleep*, 550,000
6. *Every Day a Friday*, 513,681
7. *Gabby: A Story of Courage and Hope*, 479,618
8. *In the Garden of Beasts*, 476,121
9. *Through My Eyes*, 448,190
10. *Inside of a Dog*, 421,123

Source: *Publishers Weekly*, Facts & Figures (annual), March 19, 2012, p. 36-37.

568 ■ TOP MASS MARKET FICTION PAPERBACK BEST-SELLERS, 2011

Ranked by: Number of books sold during the year. **Remarks:** Also notes author and publisher. **Number listed:** 47

1. *A Feast for Crows*, with 1,632,878 copies
2. *The Confession*, 1,576,834
3. *A Game of Thrones*, 1,539,783
4. *A Clash of Kings*, 1,204,723
5. *A Storm of Swords*, 1,136,075
6. *The Search*, 1,039,005
7. *Sizzling Sixteen*, 900,000
8. *Worth Dying For*, 862,852
9. *Big Girl*, 848,608
10. *Smokin' Seventeen*, 833,763

Source: *Publishers Weekly*, Facts & Figures (annual), March 19, 2012, p. 39-40.

569 ■ TOP TRADE PAPERBACK BESTSELLERS, 2011

Ranked by: Number of books sold during the year. **Remarks:** Also notes author and publisher. **Number listed:** 117

1. *Heaven Is for Real*, with 4,679,793 copies
2. *The Help*, n/a
3. *The Help* (movie tie-in), n/a
4. *The Girl with the Dragon Tattoo* (movie tie-in), 1,100,000
5. *Water for Elephants*, 723,249
6. *The Next Always*, n/a
7. *Sarah's Key*, 600,000
8. *Water for Elephants* (movie tie-in), 540,000
9. *Cutting for Stone*, 496,000
9. *One Day*, 496,000

Source: *Publishers Weekly*, Facts & Figures (annual), March 19, 2012, p. 40-42.

Beverage Industry

570 ■ BRITAIN'S MOST ADMIRED BEVERAGE COMPANIES, 2011

Ranked by: Survey of peers and investment analysts based on nine criteria: quality of management, financial soundness, quality of goods/services, ability to attract and retain talent, value as long-term investment, innovation, marketing, community and environmental responsibility, and use of corporate assets. **Number listed:** 5

1. Diageo, with 72.3 points
2. SABMiller plc, 67.2
3. Coca-Cola GB, 65.8
4. InBev (U.K.), 64.4
5. Britvic, 63.3

Source: *Management Today*, Britain's Most Admired Companies (annual), December 2011, p. 43.

571 ■ CHINA'S LARGEST BEVERAGE COMPANIES OVERALL, 2011

Ranked by: Score based on revenue, profits, assets, and market capitalization. **Remarks:** Specific scores not provided. Also notes overall rank in the *Forbes 2000* and figures for each criterion. **Number listed:** 4

1. Kweichow Moutai
2. Wiliangye Yibin
3. Jiangsu Yanghe Brewery

4. Luzhou Laojiao

Source: *Forbes*, Forbes 2000 (annual), http://www.forbes.com, May 7, 2012.

572 ■ EUROPE'S MOST VALUABLE BEVERAGE COMPANIES, 2011

Ranked by: Market value as of March 2011, in millions of U.S. dollars. **Remarks:** Also notes rank within the *FT Europe 500*, rank for previous year, country, revenue, net income, assets, number of employees, share price, price-to-earning ratio, dividend yield, and fiscal yearend. **Number listed:** 10

1. Anheuser-Busch InBev SA/NV, with $91,560.1 million
2. SABMiller plc, $56,154.2
3. Diageo plc, $47,541.2
4. Heineken Holding NV, $31,514.8
5. Pernod Ricard SA, $24,710.5
6. Carlsberg A/S, $16,512.9
7. Heineken NV, $13,864.5
8. Coca-Cola Hellenic Bottling Co. SA, $9,855.6
9. OAO Baltika Breweries, $7,096.2
10. Anadolu Efes, $6,368.7

Source: *Financial Times*, FT 500 (annual), http://www.ft.com, June 24, 2011.

573 ■ FASTEST-GROWING BEVERAGE COMPANIES, 2008-2011

Ranked by: Score based on three-year growth in revenue and earnings, and three-year total return to investors. **Remarks:** Specific scores not provided. To qualify for list, companies must have revenues of at least $50 million, net income of at least $10 million, market capitalization of at least $250 million, and stock price of at least $5. Int'l companies are eligible if they trade on a U.S. exchange and file quarterly reports. **Number listed:** 2

1. Green Mountain Coffee Roasters Inc.
2. Medifast

Source: *Fortune*, 100 Fastest-Growing Companies (annual), http://www.fortune.com, September 26, 2011.

574 ■ GEORGIA'S LARGEST BEVERAGE COMPANIES OVERALL, 2011

Ranked by: Score based on revenue, profits, assets, and market capitalization. **Remarks:** Specific scores not provided. Also notes overall rank in the *Forbes 2000* and figures for each criterion. **Number listed:** 2

1. The Coca-Cola Co.
2. Coca-Cola Enterprises Inc.

Source: *Forbes*, Forbes 2000 (annual), http://www.forbes.com, May 7, 2012.

575 ■ JAPAN'S LARGEST BEVERAGE COMPANIES OVERALL, 2011

Ranked by: Score based on revenue, profits, assets, and market capitalization. **Remarks:** Specific scores not provided. Also notes overall rank in the *Forbes 2000* and figures for each criterion. **Number listed:** 2

1. Asahi Group Holdings Ltd.
2. Kirin Holdings Co., Ltd.

Source: *Forbes*, Forbes 2000 (annual), http://www.forbes.com, May 7, 2012.

576 ■ LARGEST FOOD, BEVERAGE, AND TOBACCO COMPANIES IN EUROPE, 2010

Ranked by: Sales, in millions of U.S. dollars. **Remarks:** Also notes rank within country. **Number listed:** 100

1. Nestle SA (Switzerland), with $105,973.4 million
2. Unilever NV (Netherlands), $59,224.8
3. Imperial Tobacco Group plc (U.K.), $39,775.5
4. Anheuser-Busch InBev SA/NV (Belgium), $36,758
5. SABMiller plc (U.K.), $27,030
6. Heineken NV (Netherlands), $21,863.3
7. British American Tobacco plc (U.K.), $21,312
8. Groupe Danone SA (France), $21,452.6
9. Caledonian Brewery Ltd. (U.K.), $18,000
10. Diageo plc (U.K.), $14,670

Source: *Europe's 15,000 Largest Companies*, (annual), ELC International, 2011, p. 42.

577 ■ LARGEST U.S. BEVERAGE COMPANIES OVERALL, 2011

Ranked by: Score based on revenue, profits, assets, and market capitalization. **Remarks:** Specific scores not provided. Also notes overall rank in the *Forbes 2000* and figures for each criterion. **Number listed:** 10

1. The Coca-Cola Co.
2. PepsiCo Inc.
3. Coca-Cola Enterprises Inc.
4. Dr Pepper Snapple Group Inc.
5. Molson Coors Brewing Co.
6. Beam Inc.
7. Brown-Forman Corp.
8. Monster Beverage Corp.
9. Constellation Brands Inc.
10. Green Mountain Coffee Roasters Inc.

Source: *Forbes*, Forbes 2000 (annual), http://www.forbes.com, May 7, 2012.

578 ■ LARGEST U.S. BEVERAGE MANUFACTURERS, 2010

Ranked by: Revenue, in millions of dollars. **Remarks:** Also notes overall rank within the *IW 500,* revenue growth, and profit margin. **Number listed:** 10

1. PepsiCo Inc., with $57,838 million
2. The Coca-Cola Co., $35,119
3. Coca-Cola Enterprises Inc., $6,714
4. Dr Pepper Snapple Group Inc., $5,636
5. Constellation Brands Inc., $3,365
6. Molson Coors Brewing Co., $3,254
7. Mead Johnson Nutrition Co.., $3,142
8. Brown-Forman Corp., $2,469
9. Coca-Cola Bottling Co. Consolidated, $1,515
10. Hansen Natural Corp., $1,304

Source: *IndustryWeek*, IW 500 (annual), http://www.industryweek.com, July 2011.

579 ■ MEXICO'S LARGEST BEVERAGE COMPANIES OVERALL, 2011

Ranked by: Score based on revenue, profits, assets, and market capitalization. **Remarks:** Specific scores not provided. Also notes overall rank in the *Forbes 2000* and figures for each criterion. **Number listed:** 2

1. Fomento Economico Mexicano, SA de CV (FEMSA)
2. Grupo Modelo, SAB de CV

Source: *Forbes*, Forbes 2000 (annual), http://www.forbes.com, May 7, 2012.

580 ■ MOST VALUABLE U.S. BEVERAGE COMPANIES, 2011

Ranked by: Market value as of March 2011, in millions of U.S. dollars. **Remarks:** Also notes rank within the *FT U.S. 500*, rank for previous year, country, revenue, net income, assets, number of employees, share price, price-to-earning ratio, dividend yield, and fiscal yearend. **Number listed:** 6

1. The Coca-Cola Co., with $152,258.8 million
2. PepsiCo Inc., $103,085.3
3. Coca-Cola Enterprises Inc., $9,013.6
4. Dr Pepper Snapple Group Inc., $8,224.3
5. Molson Coors Brewing Co., $7,598.1
6. Brown-Forman Corp., $5,052.3

Source: *Financial Times*, FT 500 (annual), http://www.ft.com, June 24, 2011.

581 ■ NEW YORK'S LARGEST BEVERAGE COMPANIES OVERALL, 2011

Ranked by: Score based on revenue, profits, assets, and market capitalization. **Remarks:** Specific scores not provided. Also notes overall rank in the *Forbes 2000* and figures for each criterion. **Number listed:** 2

1. PepsiCo Inc.
2. Constellation Brands

Source: *Forbes*, Forbes 2000 (annual), http://www.forbes.com, May 7, 2012.

582 ■ TOP *FORTUNE 500* COMPANIES IN BEVERAGES, 2011

Ranked by: Revenue, in millions of dollars. **Remarks:** Also notes overall rank in the *Fortune 500;* profits; profits as a percentage of revenue; stockholders' equity; and rank by each criterion. **Number listed:** 3

1. The Coca-Cola Co., with $46,542 million
2. Coca-Cola Enterprises Inc., $7,939
3. Dr Pepper Snapple Group Inc., $5,903

Source: *Fortune*, Fortune 500 (annual), May 21, 2012, p. F-34.

583 ■ UNITED KINGDOM'S LARGEST BEVERAGE COMPANIES OVERALL, 2011

Ranked by: Score based on revenue, profits, assets, and market capitalization. **Remarks:** Specific scores not provided. Also notes overall rank in the *Forbes 2000* and figures for each criterion. **Number listed:** 2

1. SABMiller plc
2. Diageo plc

Source: *Forbes*, Forbes 2000 (annual), http://www.forbes.com, May 7, 2012.

584 ■ WORLD'S LARGEST BEVERAGE COMPANIES, 2010

Ranked by: Beverage sales, in millions of U.S. dollars. **Remarks:** Also notes headquarters, website, chief executive, primary market segment, and comments. **Number listed:** 100

1. Anheuser-Busch InBev SA/NV, with $36,297 million
2. The Coca-Cola Co., $35,119
3. Nestle SA, $33,589
4. SABMiller plc, $28,311
5. PepsiCo Inc., $21,400
6. Heineken NV, $21,378.6
7. Diageo, $20,470.8
8. Suntory Holdings Ltd., $19,629.8
9. Kirin Holdings Co., Ltd., $17,236
10. Asahi Group Holdings Ltd., $16,289.3

Source: *Beverage Executive*, Worldwide 100 (annual), October 2011, p. 44+.

585 ■ WORLD'S LARGEST BEVERAGE COMPANIES OVERALL, 2011

Ranked by: Score based on revenue, profits, assets, and market capitalization. **Remarks:** Specific scores not provided. Also notes country, overall rank in the *Forbes 2000,* and figures for each criterion. **Number listed:** 28

1. The Coca-Cola Co.
2. PepsiCo Inc.
3. Anheuser-Busch InBev SA/NV
4. SABMiller plc
5. Diageo plc
6. Pernod Ricard SA
7. Heineken Holding NV
8. Fomento Economico Mexicano, SA de CV (FEMSA)
9. Carlsberg A/S
10. Asahi Group Holdings Ltd.

Source: *Forbes*, Forbes 2000 (annual), http://www.forbes.com, May 7, 2012.

586 ■ WORLD'S LARGEST BEVERAGE MANUFACTURERS, 2010

Ranked by: Revenue, in millions of dollars. **Remarks:** Also notes rank for previous year, overall rank within the *IW 1000,* country, and revenue growth. **Number listed:** 23

1. PepsiCo Inc., with $57,838 million
2. Anheuser-Busch InBev SA/NV, $36,782
3. The Coca-Cola Co., $35,119
4. Kirin Holdings Co., Ltd., $26,787
5. Heineken NV, $21,899
6. SABMiller plc, $18,299
7. Companhia de Bebidas das Americas, $15,564
8. Diageo plc, $15,267
9. Fomento Economico Mexicano, SA de CV (FEMSA), $13,747
10. Carlsberg A/S, $10,862

Source: *IndustryWeek*, IW 1000 (annual), http://www.industryweek.com, August 2011.

587 ■ WORLD'S MOST ADMIRED BEVERAGE COMPANIES, 2012

Ranked by: Score, on a scale of 10, based on a survey of executives, directors, and securities analysts of companies within their own industry on eight criteria: innovation, financial soundness, employee talent, use of corporate assets, long-term investment value, social responsibility, quality of management, and quality of

products/services. **Remarks:** Specific scores not provided. Also notes rank for previous year. **Number listed:** 6

1. The Coca-Cola Co.
2. Anheuser-Busch InBev SA/NV
3. SABMiller plc
4. Coca-Cola Enterprises Inc.
5. Fomento Economico Mexicano, SA de CV (FEMSA)
6. Diageo plc

Source: *Fortune*, World's Most Admired Companies (annual), March 19, 2012, p. 147.

588 ■ WORLD'S MOST VALUABLE BEVERAGE COMPANIES, 2011

Ranked by: Market value as of March 2011, in millions of U.S. dollars. **Remarks:** Also notes rank within the *FT 500*, rank for previous year, country, revenue, net income, assets, number of employees, share price, price-to-earning ratio, dividend yield, and fiscal year-end. **Number listed:** 9

1. The Coca-Cola Co., with $152,258.8 million
2. PepsiCo Inc., $103,085.3
3. Anheuser-Busch InBev SA/NV, $91,560.1
4. Companhia de Bebidas das Americas (AmBev), $79,604.2
5. SABMiller plc, $56,154.2
6. Diageo plc, $47,541.2
7. Heineken Holding NV, $31,514.8
8. Kweichow Moutal, $25,920.7
9. Pernod Ricard SA, $24,710.5

Source: *Financial Times*, FT 500 (annual), http://www.ft.com, June 24, 2011.

589 ■ WORLD'S TOP BEVERAGE COMPANIES BY CAPITAL SPENDING, 2010

Ranked by: Capital expenditures, in millions of U.S. dollars. **Number listed:** 10

1. Nestle SA, with $4,576 million
2. Groupo Modelo SA, $3,969
3. PepsiCo Inc., $3,253
4. The Coca-Cola Co., $2,215
5. Anheuser-Busch InBev SA/NV, $2,123
6. Unilever, $1,701
7. Kraft Foods Inc., $1,661
8. SABMiller plc, $1,436
9. Groupe Danone, $1,345
10. MHD Moet Hennessy Diageo SAS, $1,327

Source: *Beverage Industry*, Top 100 Beverage Companies (annual), June 2011, p. 34.

590 ■ WORLD'S TOP BEVERAGE COMPANIES BY EMPLOYEES, 2010

Ranked by: Number of employees. **Number listed:** 10

1. PepsiCo Inc., with 294,000 employees
2. Nestle SA, 281,000
3. Unilever, 165,000
4. The Coca-Cola Co., 139,600
5. Starbucks Corp., 137,000
6. Kraft Foods Inc., 127,000

7. Dr Pepper Snapple Group Inc., 120,000
8. Anheuser-Busch InBev SA/NV, 114,000
9. Groupe Danone, 100,995
10. MHD Moet Hennessy Diageo SAS, 83,542

Source: *Beverage Industry*, Top 100 Beverage Companies (annual), June 2011, p. 36.

591 ■ WORLD'S TOP BEVERAGE COMPANIES BY SALES, 2010

Ranked by: Sales, in millions of U.S. dollars. **Remarks:** Also notes location and product mix. **Number listed:** 100

1. Anheuser-Busch InBev SA/NV, with $36,297 million
2. The Coca-Cola Co., $35,119
3. Nestle SA, $30,369
4. PepsiCo Inc., $29,297
5. Heineken NV, $21,595
6. SABMiller plc, $18,020
7. Diageo plc, $15,269
8. Starbucks Corp., $10,707
9. Pernod Ricard SA, $9,478
10. Kraft Foods Inc., $8,800

Source: *Beverage Industry*, Top 100 Beverage Companies (annual), June 2011, p. 28-36.

Beverage Industry—Advertising

592 ■ WORLD'S TOP BEVERAGE COMPANIES BY ADVERTISING, 2010

Ranked by: Advertising expenditures, in thousands of U.S. dollars. **Number listed:** 10

1. The Coca-Cola Co., with $377,557.7 thousand
2. PepsiCo Inc., $313,223
3. Dr Pepper Snapple Group Inc., $180,545.4
4. Kraft Foods Inc., $123,866.5
5. Innovation Vendors LLC, $91,082.4
6. Nestle SA, $90,391.5
7. Campbell Soup Co., $76,714
8. The J. M. Smucker Co., $70,054.2
9. Starbucks Corp., $49,914.3
10. Ocean Spray, $43,389.8

Source: *Beverage Industry*, Top 100 Beverage Companies (annual), June 2011, p. 35.

Beverages

593 ■ TOP ENERGY SHOT BRANDS IN THE U.S., 2011

Ranked by: Sales, in dollars. **Remarks:** Also notes percent change from previous year and market share. **Number listed:** 10

1. 5 Hour Energy, with $885,257,700
2. Stacker2 6 Hour Power, $29,779,970
3. Red Bull, $25,366,220
4. 5 Hour Energy Extra Strength, $11,717,890
5. private label, $10,212,980
6. Monster Hitman, $9,638,077

7. Stacker2, $3,918,653
8. Nitro 2 Go, $3,413,823
9. VPX Redline Power Rush, $3,234,767
10. Vital 4U Screamin Energy, $3,148,175

Source: *Beverage Industry*, State of the Industry Report (annual), July 2011, p. SIO-6.

594 ■ TOP NON-ALCOHOLIC BEVERAGES BY MARKET SHARE, 2010

Ranked by: Market share, in percent. **Remarks:** Also notes parent company, figures for previous year, and advertising expenditures for current and previous year. **Number listed:** 10

1. Coke, with 15%
2. Pepsi, 8.3%
3. Mountain Dew, 4.6%
4. Dr Pepper, 4.1%
5. Gatorade, 3.2%
6. Sprite, 3%
7. Nestle Pure Life, 2.8%
8. Poland Spring, 2.2%
9. Tropicana, 1.9%
10. Dasani, 1.6%

Source: *Advertising Age*, Leading National Advertisers (annual), June 20, 2011, p. 22.

595 ■ TOP NON-ASEPTIC ENERGY DRINK BRANDS IN THE U.S., 2011

Ranked by: Sales, in dollars. **Remarks:** Also notes percent change from previous year and market share. **Number listed:** 10

1. Red Bull, with $2,337,445,000
2. Monster Energy, $1,220,415,000
3. Rockstar, $436,116,200
4. NOS, $220,540,700
5. Monster Mega Energy, $179,469,600
6. Java Monster, $173,869,100
7. Amp, $139,591,600
8. Full Throttle, $104,086,400
9. Rockstar Recovery, $88,220,340
10. Monster Energy XXL, $88,117,680

Source: *Beverage Industry*, State of the Industry Report (annual), July 2011, p. SIO-6.

596 ■ WORLD'S MOST VALUABLE BEVERAGES BRANDS, 2011

Ranked by: Brand value, in millions of U.S. dollars. **Remarks:** Also notes rank within the *Global 500* for current and previous year, figures for current and previous year, country, and brand rating. Ranking is available online only. **Number listed:** 14

1. Coca-Cola, with $31,082 million
2. Pepsi, $17,096
3. Budweiser, $5,607
4. Sprite, $3,882
5. Heineken, $3,867
6. Mountain Dew, $3,487
7. Asahi, $3,202
8. Nestle Pure Life, $3,144
9. Green Mountain Coffee, $3,124

10. Corona Extra, $2,886

Source: *Global 500*, (annual), Brand Finance plc, March 2012.

597 ■ WORLD'S TOP BEVERAGE BRANDS, 2010

Ranked by: Brand value, in millions of U.S. dollars. **Number listed:** 10

1. Coca-Cola, with $25,807 million
2. Pepsi, $19,514
3. Heineken, $11,108
4. Starbucks, $5,462
5. Nescafe, $4,927
6. Budweiser, $4,304
7. Mountain Dew, $3,882
8. Carlsberg, $3,646
9. Gatorade, $3,505
10. Amstel, $3,263

Source: *Beverage Industry*, Top 100 Beverage Companies (annual), June 2011, p. 30.

598 ■ WORLD'S TOP BEVERAGE BRANDS ON FACEBOOK, 2011

Ranked by: Number of users that "like" the brand, as of May 13, 2011. **Number listed:** 10

1. Coca-Cola, with 26,696,800 users
2. Starbucks, 21,853,700
3. Red Bull, 18,520,600
4. Dr Pepper, 8,953,700
5. Starbucks' Frappuccino, 6,442,300
6. Mountain Dew, 5,081,900
7. Pepsi, 3,929,900
8. Gatorade, 3,438,300
9. Sprite, 3,410,500
10. Slurpee, 3,333,300

Source: *Beverage Industry*, Top 100 Beverage Companies (annual), June 2011, p. 31.

Bicycles

599 ■ TOP BICYCLE RETAILERS, 2011

Ranked by: Score based on market share, community outreach, and store appearance. **Remarks:** Scores not provided; retailers are listed alphabetically, not ranked. Also notes headquarters, number of locations, years in business, square footage, number of employees, owner(s), and comments. **Number listed:** 100

1. Absolute Bikes
2. Agee's Bicycle
3. Atlanta Cycling
4. Bay Area Bicycles
5. Benidorm Bikes
6. Bicycle Center
7. Bicycle Garage Indy
8. Bicycle Habitat
9. Bicycle One Inc.
10. Bicycle Trip

Source: *Bicycle Retailer*, Top 100 Retailers (annual), November 1, 2011, p. 10-23.

Billionaires
See: **Wealth**

Biopharmaceutics

600 ■ TOP BIOPHARMACEUTICAL COMPANIES BY REVENUE, 2010

Ranked by: Biopharmaceutical revenue, in millions of dollars. **Number listed:** 10

1. Roche Group, with $35,629 million
2. Amgen Inc., $15,053
3. Novo Nordisk A/S, $10,835
4. Merck Serono SA, $7,641
5. Baxter BioScience, $5,640
6. Biogen Idec Inc., $4,547
7. CSL Ltd., $3,930
8. Genzyme Corp., $3,417
9. Allergan Inc., $1,419
10. Alexion Pharmaceuticals Inc., $541

Source: *Contract Pharma*, Top 20 Pharmaceutical Companies (annual), http://www.contractpharma.com, 2011.

Biotechnology Industry

601 ■ CALIFORNIA'S LARGEST BIOTECHNOLOGY COMPANIES OVERALL, 2011

Ranked by: Score based on revenue, profits, assets, and market capitalization. **Remarks:** Specific scores not provided. Also notes overall rank in the *Forbes 2000* and figures for each criterion. **Number listed:** 3

1. Amgen Inc.
2. Gilead Sciences Inc.
3. Life Technologies Corp.

Source: *Forbes*, Forbes 2000 (annual), http://www.forbes.com, May 7, 2012.

602 ■ LARGEST BIOTECHNOLOGY COMPANIES, 2010

Ranked by: Worldwide revenue, in millions of U.S. dollars. **Remarks:** Also notes location, market capitalization, and Web site. **Number listed:** 20

1. Amgen Inc., with $15,053 million
2. Genentech Inc., $11,724
3. Biogen Idec Inc., $4,716.4
4. Genzyme Corp., $4,000
5. Celgene Corp., $3,625.7
6. Life Technologies Corp., $3,588.1
7. Cephalon Inc., $2,811
8. Amylin Pharmaceuticals, $668.8
9. Cubist Pharmaceuticals, $636.5
10. United Therapeutics Corp., $603.8

Source: *Modern Healthcare*, Largest Biotechnology Companies (annual), August 1, 2011, p. 33.

603 ■ LARGEST TECHNOLOGY/BIOTECHNOLOGY COMPANIES IN BRITISH COLUMBIA, 2010

Ranked by: Revenue, in thousands of Canadian dollars. **Remarks:** Also notes figures for previous year. **Number listed:** 10

1. Telus Corp., with C$9,779,000 thousand
2. MacDonald, Dettwiler & Associates Ltd., C$689,030
3. Sierra Wireless Inc., C$669,812
4. PMC-Sierra Inc., C$654,114
5. Glentel Inc., C$412,307
6. Angiotech Pharmaceuticals Inc., C$253,614
7. Peer 1 Network Enterprises Inc., C$100,855
8. Ballard Power Systems Inc., C$66,966
9. Cardiome Pharma Corp., C$66,064
10. Absolute Software Corp., C$64,076

Source: *BCBusiness*, Top 100 (annual), July 2011, p. 135.

604 ■ LARGEST U.S. BIOTECHNOLOGY COMPANIES OVERALL, 2011

Ranked by: Score based on revenue, profits, assets, and market capitalization. **Remarks:** Specific scores not provided. Also notes overall rank in the *Forbes 2000* and figures for each criterion. **Number listed:** 7

1. Amgen Inc.
2. Gilead Sciences Inc.
3. Celgene Corp.
4. Biogen Idec Inc.
5. Life Technologies Corp.
6. Alexion Pharmaceuticals Inc.
7. Regeneron Pharmaceuticals Inc.

Source: *Forbes*, Forbes 2000 (annual), http://www.forbes.com, May 7, 2012.

605 ■ WORLD'S LARGEST BIOTECHNOLOGY COMPANIES OVERALL, 2011

Ranked by: Score based on revenue, profits, assets, and market capitalization. **Remarks:** Specific scores not provided. Also notes country, overall rank in the *Forbes 2000,* and figures for each criterion. **Number listed:** 9

1. Amgen Inc.
2. Gilead Sciences Inc.
3. Celgene Corp.
4. Biogen Idec Inc.
5. CSL Ltd.
6. Life Technologies Corp.
7. Alexion Pharmaceuticals Inc.
8. Novozymes A/S
9. Regeneron Pharmaceuticals Inc.

Source: *Forbes*, Forbes 2000 (annual), http://www.forbes.com, May 7, 2012.

606 ■ WORLD'S MOST INNOVATIVE BIOMEDICINE COMPANIES - PRIVATE, 2012

Ranked by: Editorial determination. **Remarks:** Companies are listed alphabetically, not ranked. Also notes comments. **Number listed:** 5

1. Cellular Dynamics International
2. Foundation Medicine
3. Healthpoint Services
4. Integrated Diagnostics
5. PatientsLikeMe

Source: *Technology Review*, TR 50 (annual), http://www.technologyreview.com, 2012.

607 ■ WORLD'S MOST INNOVATIVE BIOMEDICINE COMPANIES - PUBLIC, 2012

Ranked by: Editorial determination. **Remarks:** Companies are listed alphabetically, not ranked. Also notes comments. **Number listed:** 5

1. Athenahealth
2. Complete Genomics Inc.
3. Life Technologies
4. Organovo
5. Roche Group

Source: *Technology Review*, TR 50 (annual), http://www.technologyreview.com, 2012.

Black Business Enterprises
See: **African American Business Enterprises**

Blogs

608 ■ TOP BUSINESS BLOGS IN THE UNITED STATES, 2012

Ranked by: Score, on a scale of 1000, based on a site's standing and influence in the blogosphere over a short, finite period of time. **Remarks:** Also notes URL and recent blog topics. **Number listed:** 32094

1. Mashable!, with 892 points
2. Business Insider, 870
3. TechCrunch, 865
4. zero hedge, 846
5. VentureBeat, 841
5. Felix Salmon, 841
7. SEOmoz Daily SEO Blog, 811
8. One Cent at a Time, 808
9. Calculated Risk, 805
10. GigaOM, 799

Source: *Blog Directory*, (daily), Technorati Inc., June 4, 2012.

609 ■ TOP FINANCE BLOGS IN THE UNITED STATES, 2012

Ranked by: Score, on a scale of 1000, based on a site's standing and influence in the blogosphere over a short, finite period of time. **Remarks:** Also notes URL and recent blog topics. **Number listed:** 10100

1. Boomer & Echo, with 911 points
2. Good Financial Cents, 886
3. One Cent at a Time, 884
4. 20s Finances, 875
5. Balance Junkie, 857
6. Free From Broke, 856
7. blogs maverick, 843
8. My University Money, 834
8. Rewards Cards Canada, 834
10. Financial Highway, 822

Source: *Blog Directory*, (daily), Technorati Inc., June 4, 2012.

610 ■ TOP SMALL BUSINESS BLOGS IN THE UNITED STATES, 2012

Ranked by: Score, on a scale of 1000, based on a site's standing and influence in the blogosphere over a short, finite period of time. **Remarks:** Also notes URL and recent blog topics. **Number listed:** 21628

1. Mashable!, with 892 points
2. Business Insider, 870
3. TechCrunch, 865
4. ZeroHedge, 846
5. VentureBeat, 841
5. Felix Salmon, 841
7. SEOmoz Daily SEO Blog, 811
8. One Cent at a Time, 808
9. Calculated Risk, 805
10. GigaOM, 799

Source: *Blog Directory*, (daily), Technorati Inc., June 4, 2012.

Blow Molders

611 ■ LARGEST BLOW MOLDERS IN NORTH AMERICA, 2010

Ranked by: Blow molding sales, in millions of dollars. **Remarks:** Also notes headquarters and top blow molding official. **Number listed:** 140

1. Amcor Rigid Plastics, with $2,600 million
2. Graham Packaging Co., LP, $2,177.5
3. Plastipak Packaging Inc., $1,514
4. Alpla Inc., $822.7
5. Consolidated Container Co., LLC, $737
6. Southeastern Container Inc., $700
7. Inergy Automotive Systems LLC, $670
8. ABC Group Inc., $620
9. Silgan Plastics Corp., $588.6
10. Kautex Textron GmbH, $560

Source: *Plastics News*, North American Blow Molders (annual), http://www.plasticsnews.com, November 7, 2011.

Boards of Directors
See: **Corporate Directors**

Bond Funds
See also: **Junk Bonds; Mutual Funds; Stock Funds**

612 ■ BEST TAX-EXEMPT BOND FUND FAMILIES, 2011

Ranked by: Score based on asset size and relative importance in the Lipper fund universe. **Number listed:** 5

1. TIAA-CREF, with 4.31 points
2. Affiliated Managers Group, 4.25
3. USAA Investment Management, 3.97
4. Legg Mason, 3.88
5. Oppenheimer Funds, 3.86

Source: *Barron's*, Best Mutual Fund Families (annual), February 6, 2012, p. 30.

613 ■ BEST TAXABLE BOND FUND FAMILIES, 2011

Ranked by: Score based on asset size and relative importance in the Lipper fund universe. **Number listed:** 5

1. GE Asset Management, with 25.25 points
2. State Farm Investment Management, 25.17

3. Vanguard Group, 22.4
4. Lord Abbett, 20.89
5. Ivy Investment Management, 20.31

Source: *Barron's*, Best Mutual Fund Families (annual), February 6, 2012, p. 30.

614 ■ TOP BOND FUNDS, 2012

Ranked by: Score based on long-term performance, management experience, risk, expenses, assets, and integrity. **Remarks:** Specific scores not provided; funds are listed alphabetically, not ranked. Also notes ticker symbol, expense ratio, toll-free number, and one-, three-, and five-year return. **Number listed:** 6

1. DoubleLine Total Return
2. Fidelity Intermediate Municipal Income
3. Fidelity New Markets Income
4. Harbor Bond
5. Loomis Sayles Bond
6. Vanguard Short-Term Investment-Grade

Source: *Kiplinger's Personal Finance*, Kiplinger 25 (annual), May 2012, p. 31.

615 ■ TOP PERFORMING BOND FUNDS, 2010-2011

Ranked by: Annual change in share price, in percent. **Remarks:** Also notes ticker symbol, 36-month performance rating, three-month share price change, five-year average share price change, and 10-year average share price change. **Number listed:** 50

1. PIMCO Extended Duration Institutional, with 55.33%
2. Vanguard Extended Duration Treasury Index Institutional, 55.24%
3. ProFunds U.S. Government Plus Investment, 43.72%
4. Rydex Government Long Bond 1.2x Strategy Investment, 42.58%
5. Wasatch-Holsington U.S. Treasury, 40.53%
6. American Century Zero Coupon 2025 Investment, 34.87%
7. Direxion Monthly 10-Year Note Bull 2X, 29.82%
8. Fidelity Spartan Long-Term Trust Bond Index Investment, 29.26%
9. Vanguard Long-Term Treasury Investment, 28.95%
10. Dreyfus U.S. Treasury Long-Term, 28.86%

Source: *Investor's Business Daily*, The Year in Review (annual), January 3, 2012, p. A15.

616 ■ WORST TAX-EXEMPT BOND FUND FAMILIES, 2011

Ranked by: Score based on asset size and relative importance in the Lipper fund universe. **Number listed:** 5

1. Highmark Capital Management, with 0.19 points
2. Frost Investment Advisors, 0.22
3. Manning & Napier Advisors, 0.31
4. Calvert Funds, 0.35
5. PIMCO/Allianz, 0.49

Source: *Barron's*, Best Mutual Fund Families (annual), February 6, 2012, p. 30.

617 ■ WORST TAXABLE BOND FUND FAMILIES, 2011

Ranked by: Score based on asset size and relative importance in the Lipper fund universe. **Number listed:** 5

1. Victory Capital Management, with 1.33 points
2. Franklin Templeton, 4.29
3. Putnam Investment Management, 4.36
4. Calvert Funds, 4.43
5. Frost Investment Advisors, 4.61

Source: *Barron's*, Best Mutual Fund Families (annual), February 6, 2012, p. 30.

Bond Traders
See: **Security Dealers**

Books

618 ■ BEST SMALL BUSINESS BOOKS, 2011

Ranked by: Determination by readers as to the originality, quality of writing, and usefulness of the book for the widest range of small business people, entrepreneurs, and the self-employed. **Remarks:** Specific scores not provided. Also notes author. **Number listed:** 10

1. *Problogging Action Plan*
2. *Acclerate!*
3. *Export Now*
4. *MBA Preferred*
5. *Paper Flow*
6. *Managing with a Conscience*, 2nd edition
7. *Big Wave Surfing*
8. *The Botty Rules*
9. *The Lemonade Stand*
10. *Appetite for Acquisition*

Source: *Small Business Trends*, Best Small Business Books (annual), http://www.smallbiztrends.com, February 27, 2012.

619 ■ BEST SMALL BUSINESS BOOKS: ECONOMICS, 2011

Ranked by: Determination by readers as to the originality, quality of writing, and usefulness of the book for the widest range of small business people, entrepreneurs, and the self-employed. **Remarks:** Specific scores not provided. Also notes author. **Number listed:** 5

1. *The Other Side of Wall Street*
2. *The WSJ Guide to the 50 Economic Indicators That Really Matter*
3. *J.K. Lasser's Small Business Taxes 2012*
4. *Turning Myths into Money*
5. *Locavesting*

Source: *Small Business Trends*, Best Small Business Books (annual), http://www.smallbiztrends.com, February 27, 2012.

620 ■ BEST SMALL BUSINESS BOOKS: MANAGEMENT, 2011

Ranked by: Determination by readers as to the originality, quality of writing, and usefulness of the book for the widest range of small business people, entrepreneurs, and the self-employed. **Remarks:** Specific scores not provided. Also notes author. **Number listed:** 5

1. *Shifting the Monkey*
2. *Impact Your Business*
3. *Co-Active Coaching*
4. *Mastering Uncertainty*

5. *Fulfilling the Potential of Your Business*

Source: *Small Business Trends*, Best Small Business Books (annual), http://www.smallbiztrends.com, February 27, 2012.

621 ■ BEST SMALL BUSINESS BOOKS: MARKETING, 2011

Ranked by: Determination by readers as to the originality, quality of writing, and usefulness of the book for the widest range of small business people, entrepreneurs, and the self-employed. **Remarks:** Specific scores not provided. Also notes author. **Number listed:** 5

1. *31 Days to Network Marketing Mastery*
2. *FT Guide to Business Networking*
3. *31 Days to Write Better Copy*
4. *Brand Against the Machine*
5. *Free Marketing*

Source: *Small Business Trends*, Best Small Business Books (annual), http://www.smallbiztrends.com, February 27, 2012.

622 ■ BEST SMALL BUSINESS BOOKS: SOCIAL MEDIA, 2011

Ranked by: Determination by readers as to the originality, quality of writing, and usefulness of the book for the widest range of small business people, entrepreneurs, and the self-employed. **Remarks:** Specific scores not provided. Also notes author. **Number listed:** 5

1. *The Step by Step Guide to Facebook for Business*
2. *Facebook Marketing All-in-One for Dummies*
3. *Engagement from Scratch!*
4. *Marketing Shortcuts for the Self-Employed*
5. *Likeable Social Media*

Source: *Small Business Trends*, Best Small Business Books (annual), http://www.smallbiztrends.com, February 27, 2012.

623 ■ BEST SMALL BUSINESS BOOKS: START-UP, 2011

Ranked by: Determination by readers as to the originality, quality of writing, and usefulness of the book for the widest range of small business people, entrepreneurs, and the self-employed. **Remarks:** Specific scores not provided. Also notes author. **Number listed:** 5

1. *The Right-Brain Business Plan*
2. *Small Business, Big Vision*
3. *From Idea to Exit*
4. *Starting Your Own Business*
5. *Starting an eBay Business for Dummies*

Source: *Small Business Trends*, Best Small Business Books (annual), http://www.smallbiztrends.com, February 27, 2012.

624 ■ BEST SMALL BUSINESS BOOKS: TECHNOLOGY, 2011

Ranked by: Determination by readers as to the originality, quality of writing, and usefulness of the book for the widest range of small business people, entrepreneurs, and the self-employed. **Remarks:** Specific scores not provided. Also notes author. **Number listed:** 5

1. *The Official Joomla! Book*
2. *Joomla! 1.7 - Beginner's Guide*
3. *The Plugged in Manager*
4. *Joomla! Development*
5. *Provoke*

Source: *Small Business Trends*, Best Small Business Books (annual), http://www.smallbiztrends.com, February 27, 2012.

625 ■ THE YEAR'S BEST BUSINESS BOOKS, 2011

Ranked by: Editorial determination. **Remarks:** Specific scores not provided; books are listed alphabetically by author, not ranked. Also notes author, publisher, ISBN, and price. **Number listed:** 9

1. *Poor Economics: A Radical Rethinking of the Way to Fight Global Poverty*
2. *Money & Power: How Goldman Sachs Came to Rule the World*
3. *Locavesting: The Revolution in Local Investing & How to Profit from It*
4. *Oil's Endless Bid: Taming the Unreliable Price of Oil to Secure Our Economy*
5. *Enchantment: The Art of Changing Hearts, Minds, & Actions*
6. *The Velocity Manifesto: Harnessing Technology, Vision & Culture to Future-Proof Your Organization*
7. *In the Plex: How Google Thinks, Works, & Shapes Our Lives*
8. *The Deal from Hell: How Moguls & Wall Street Plunderred Great American Newspapers*
9. *Good Strategy, Bad Strategy: The Difference & Why It Matters*

Source: *Library Journal*, Best Books of the Year (annual), http://www.libraryjournal.com, December 1, 2011.

Booksellers and Bookselling

626 ■ TOP ADULT HARDCOVER DIVISIONS/IMPRINTS ON THE BESTSELLER CHARTS, 2011

Ranked by: Total number of adult hardcovers listed on Publishers Weekly's bestsellers charts during the year. **Remarks:** Also notes number of weeks on charts. **Number listed:** 100

1. Putnam, with 29 hardcovers
2. Grand Central, 25
3. Crown, 22
3. Little, Brown, 22
5. Knopf, 16
5. St. Martin's, 16
5. Morrow, 16
8. Simon & Schuster, 15
9. Random House, 14
9. HarperCollins, 14

Source: *Publishers Weekly*, Bestsellers (annual), January 9, 2012, p. 20.

627 ■ TOP HARDCOVER PUBLISHERS ON THE BEST-SELLER CHARTS, 2011

Ranked by: Total number of hardcovers listed on Publishers Weekly's bestsellers charts during the year. **Remarks:** Also notes number of weeks on charts, market share, and percent change from previous year. **Number listed:** 11

1. Random House Inc., with 106 hardcovers
2. Penguin USA, 86
3. Hachette Book Group USA, 56
4. Simon & Schuster, 46
5. HarperCollins Publishers Inc., 43
6. Macmillan, 40
7. Hyperion, 9

8. Tyndale, 3
9. Harlequin, 2
10. Kensington, 1

Source: *Publishers Weekly*, Bestsellers (annual), January 9, 2012, p. 18.

628 ■ TOP MASS MARKET PAPERBACK DIVISIONS/IMPRINTS ON THE BESTSELLER CHARTS, 2011

Ranked by: Total number of mass market paperbacks listed on Publishers Weekly's bestsellers charts during the year. **Remarks:** Also notes number of weeks on charts. **Number listed:** 35

1. Putnam, with 29 paperbacks
2. Grand Central, 25
3. Crown, 22
3. Little, Brown, 22
5. Berkeley, 23
6. Signet, 22
7. Mira, 17
8. Knopf , 16
9. Bantam, 13
9. St. Martin's, 13
9. Avon, 13

Source: *Publishers Weekly*, Bestsellers (annual), January 9, 2012, p. 20.

629 ■ TOP PAPERBACK PUBLISHERS ON THE BEST-SELLER CHARTS, 2011

Ranked by: Total number paperbacks listed on Publishers Weekly's bestsellers charts during the year. **Remarks:** Also notes number of weeks on charts, market share, and percent change from previous year. **Number listed:** 11

1. Penguin USA, with 74 paperbacks
2. Random House Inc., 54
3. Hachette Book Group USA, 37
4. Harlequin, 34
5. Simon & Schuster, 33
6. Macmillan, 29
7. HarperCollins Publishers Inc., 27
8. Kensington, 9
9. Workman/Algonquin, 3
10. Hyperion, 2

Source: *Publishers Weekly*, Bestsellers (annual), January 9, 2012, p. 18.

630 ■ TOP TRADE PAPERBACK DIVISIONS/IMPRINTS ON THE BESTSELLER CHARTS, 2011

Ranked by: Total number of trade paperbacks listed on Publishers Weekly's bestsellers charts during the year. **Remarks:** Also notes number of weeks on charts. **Number listed:** 48

1. Grand Central, with 13 paperbacks
2. Vintage, 8
2. Little, Brown/Back Bay, 8
4. St. Martin's/Griffin, 7
5. Berkley, 5
5. Scribner, 5
7. Harper, 3
7. Anchor, 3
7. Penguin Press, 3

7. Zondervan, 3

Source: *Publishers Weekly*, Bestsellers (annual), January 9, 2012, p. 20.

Bottled Water

631 ■ TOP CONVENIENCE/STILL BOTTLED WATER BRANDS IN THE U.S., 2011

Ranked by: Sales, in dollars. **Remarks:** Also notes percent change from previous year and market share. **Number listed:** 10

1. private label, with $993,905,600
2. Aquafina, $705,308,200
3. Glaceau Vitaminwater, $687,748,600
4. Dasani, $626,157,100
5. Poland Spring, $392,077,400
6. Nestle Pure Life, $339,850,500
7. Glaceau Smartwater, $308,392,100
8. Deer Park, $236,007,800
9. Arrowhead, $197,723,600
10. SoBe Lifewater, $196,034,200

Source: *Beverage Industry*, State of the Industry Report (annual), July 2011, p. SOI-8.

632 ■ TOP SPARKLING WATER BRANDS IN THE U.S., 2011

Ranked by: Sales, in dollars. **Remarks:** Also notes percent change from previous year and market share. **Number listed:** 10

1. private label, with $106,831,800
2. Perrier, $81,219,460
3. San Pellegrino, $70,544,850
4. La Croix, $35,348,470
5. Poland Spring, $20,583,740
6. Topo Chico, $18,248,910
7. Arrowhead, $15,306,590
8. Cascade Ice, $12,125,440
9. Crystal Geyser, $9,129,889
10. Sparkling Ice, $4,344,327

Source: *Beverage Industry*, State of the Industry Report (annual), July 2011, p. SIO-8.

633 ■ TOP U.S. BOTTLED WATER BRANDS BY SALES, 2011

Ranked by: Sales, in millions of dollars. **Remarks:** Also notes annual growth. **Number listed:** 10

1. Private label, with $1,030.1 million
2. Aquafina, $686.1
3. Glaceau Vitaminwater, $651.1
4. Dasani, $645.2
5. Poland Spring, $388.1
6. Nestle Pure Life, $380.2
7. Glaceau Smartwater, $348.6
8. Deer Park, $237.3
9. Glaceau Vitaminwater Zero, $207.7
10. Ozarka, $195.5

Source: *Beverage World*, State of the Industry Report (annual), May 2012, p. 32.

Bottling

634 ■ LARGEST BOTTLERS IN THE U.S., 2010

Ranked by: Net sales, in millions of dollars. **Remarks:** Also notes contact information, case sales, number of employees, key executives, facilities, territories, and comments. **Number listed:** 20

1. Coca-Cola Refreshments, with $15,000 million
2. Pepsi Beverages Co., $14,000
3. Dr Pepper Snapple Bottling Group Inc., $3,300
4. Coca-Cola Bottling Co. Consolidated, $1,500
5. Honickman Affiliates, $1,300
6. Pepsi Bottling Ventures LLC, $782
7. Coca-Cola Bottling Co. United Inc., $712
8. Buffalo Rock Co., $550
9. Swire Coca-Cola USA, $480
10. G & J Pepsi-Cola Bottlers Inc., $426.4

Source: *Beverage Executive*, Soft Drink 20 (annual), September 2011, p. 38+.

Brand Choice

635 ■ BRANDS CONSUMERS ARE MOST ATTACHED TO, 2011

Ranked by: Score based on consumers' emotional attachment to brands. **Remarks:** Also notes percent change from previous year. **Number listed:** 100

1. iPod, with 63.8%
2. iPhone, 59.9%
3. Google Search, 55.7%
4. Disney Parks, 55.5%
5. Google, 55.4%
6. Microsoft Office Suite, 53.8%
7. Apple, 53.7%
8. Sony Play Station, 52.3%
9. Android, 52%
10. Audi, 51.5%

Source: *Advertising Age*, The Leap Index (annual), October 17, 2011, p. 38.

Brand Loyalty
See: **Brand Choice**

Brand Name Products

636 ■ AMERICA'S HOTTEST BRANDS, 2011

Ranked by: Score based on brand impact and potential for growth. **Remarks:** Scores not provided; brands are listed alphabetically, not ranked. Also notes key executive or advertising director, as well as comments. **Number listed:** 25

1. Arizona Tea
2. Chegg

3. Chevy Cruze
4. CND Shellac
5. Crossfit
6. DC Comics
7. Dove
8. Finish
9. Forever 21
10. Honey Badger

Source: *Advertising Age*, America's Hottest Brands (annual), November 28, 2011, p. 36+.

637 ■ MOST POWERFUL U.S. CORPORATE BRANDS, 2011

Ranked by: Score based on market reputation and awareness. **Remarks:** Specific scores not provided. Also notes rank for previous two years. **Number listed:** 790

1. Coca-Cola
2. Hershey
3. Harley-Davidson
4. Campbell Soup
5. Kellogg
6. Johnson & Johnson
7. Bayer
8. Hallmark Cards
9. UPS
10. Colgate-Palmolive

Source: *Brand Power Index*, (annual), CoreBrand, 2011.

638 ■ MOST VALUABLE U.S. RETAIL BRANDS, 2012

Ranked by: Brand value, in millions of U.S. dollars. **Number listed:** 50

1. Wal-Mart, with $139,190 million
2. Target, $23,444
3. Home Depot, $22,020
4. CVS/pharmacy, $17,343
5. Best Buy, $16,755
6. Walgreens, $15,018
7. Coach, $13,442
8. Sam's Club, $12,854
9. Amazon.com, $12,758
10. eBay, $9,805

Source: *Interbrand*, Best Retail Brands (annual), http://www.interbrand.com, February 21, 2012.

639 ■ NEW ENGLAND'S MOST POWERFUL CONSUMER BRANDS, 2011

Ranked by: Score based on 10 criteria: brand momentum, cultural power, distinctiveness, uniqueness, quality, loyalty, admiration, responsibility, "New Englandness," and whether experience working with the brand enhances a marketing professional's resume. **Remarks:** Scores not provided. Also notes rank for previous year, headquarters, revenue, number of Twitter followers, and comments. **Number listed:** 25

1. ESPN
2. Subway
3. GE

4. Dunkin' Donuts
5. Ben & Jerry's
6. L. L. Bean
7. Samuel Adams
8. Bose
9. Gillette
10. Fidelity Investments

Source: *Protobrand*, New England's Most Powerful Brands (annual), June 2011.

640 ■ THE UNITED STATES' MOST VALUABLE BRANDS, 2011

Ranked by: Brand value, in millions of U.S. dollars. **Remarks:** Also notes rank within the *Global 500* for current and previous year, figures for current and previous year, and brand rating. Ranking is available online only. **Number listed:** 180

1. Apple, with $70,605 million
2. Google, $47,463
3. Microsoft, $45,812
4. IBM, $39,135
5. Wal-Mart, $38,320
6. GE, $33,214
7. Coca-Cola, $31,082
8. Amazon, $28,665
9. AT&T, $28,379
10. Verizon, $27,616

Source: *Global 500*, (annual), Brand Finance plc, March 2012.

Brand Name Products, International

641 ■ AUSTRALIA'S MOST VALUABLE BRANDS, 2011

Ranked by: Brand value, in millions of U.S. dollars. **Remarks:** Also notes rank within the *Global 500* for current and previous year, figures for current and previous year, and brand rating. Ranking is available online only. **Number listed:** 8

1. Woolworths, with $7,299 million
2. Telstra, $5,283
3. Coles, $4,873
4. Commonwealth Bank of Australia, $4,244
5. NAB, $4,160
6. Westpac, $3,570
7. ANZ, $3,433
8. Optus, $2,529

Source: *Global 500*, (annual), Brand Finance plc, March 2012.

642 ■ AUSTRIA'S MOST VALUABLE BRANDS, 2011

Ranked by: Brand value, in millions of U.S. dollars. **Remarks:** Also notes rank within the *Global 500* for current and previous year, figures for current and previous year, and brand rating. Ranking is available online only. **Number listed:** 2

1. OMB, with $3,504 million
2. Erste, $2,476

Source: *Global 500*, (annual), Brand Finance plc, March 2012.

643 ■ BEST GLOBAL GREEN BRANDS, 2011

Ranked by: Score based on brand value as well as public perception of environmental sustainability ("green") performance. **Number listed:** 50

1. Toyota, with 64.19 points
2. 3M, 63.33
3. Siemens, 63.08
4. Johnson & Johnson, 59.41
5. HP, 59.06
6. VW, 58.9
7. Honda, 58.85
8. Dell, 58.81
9. Cisco, 57.66
10. Panasonic, 57.32

Source: *Interbrand*, Best Global Green Brands (annual), http://www.interbrand.com, July 26, 2011.

644 ▪ BRAZIL'S MOST VALUABLE BRANDS, 2011

Ranked by: Brand value, in millions of U.S. dollars. Remarks: Also notes rank within the *Global 500* for current and previous year, figures for current and previous year, and brand rating. Ranking is available online only. Number listed: 10

1. Bradesco, with $15,692 million
2. Itau, $13,171
3. TIM, $7,859
4. Banco do Brasil, $7,264
5. Petrobras, $5,511
6. Vivo, $4,316
7. Vale, $3,942
8. Pao de Acucar, $3,361
9. Oi, $2,782
10. Sadia, $2,370

Source: *Global 500*, (annual), Brand Finance plc, March 2012.

645 ▪ CANADA'S MOST VALUABLE BRANDS, 2011

Ranked by: Brand value, in millions of U.S. dollars. Remarks: Also notes rank within the *Global 500* for current and previous year, figures for current and previous year, and brand rating. Ranking is available online only. Number listed: 14

1. RBC, with $8,647 million
2. TD, $8,499
3. Scotiabank, $5,717
4. Bank of Montreal, $5,360
5. Bell, $5,258
6. CIBC, $4,557
7. Bombardier, $4,199
8. Rogers, $4,087
9. BlackBerry, $3,293
10. Manulife Financial, $3,261

Source: *Global 500*, (annual), Brand Finance plc, March 2012.

646 ▪ CHINA'S BEST BRANDS, 2011

Ranked by: Brand value, in millions of renminbi. Remarks: Also notes industry and percent change from previous year. Number listed: 50

1. China Mobile, with 208,980 million renminbi
2. China Life, 104,031
3. China Construction Bank, 100,822
4. ICBC, 88,489
5. Bank of China, 72,855
6. Ping An, 59,995

7. Tencent, 40,320
8. Moutai, 29,546
9. China Merchant's Bank, 27,561
10. CPIC, 21,383

Source: *Interbrand*, Best China Brands (annual), http://www.interbrand.com, September 15, 2011.

647 ▪ DENMARK'S MOST VALUABLE BRANDS, 2011

Ranked by: Brand value, in millions of U.S. dollars. Remarks: Also notes rank within the *Global 500* for current and previous year, figures for current and previous year, and brand rating. Ranking is available online only. Number listed: 2

1. Danske Bank, with $2,792 million
2. Maersk, $2,725

Source: *Global 500*, (annual), Brand Finance plc, March 2012.

648 ▪ FRANCE'S MOST VALUABLE BRANDS, 2011

Ranked by: Brand value, in millions of U.S. dollars. Remarks: Also notes rank within the *Global 500* for current and previous year, figures for current and previous year, and brand rating. Ranking is available online only. Number listed: 34

1. Orange, with $18,557 million
2. BNP Paribas, $16,809
3. GDF Suez, $16,598
4. AXA, $13,406
5. Total, $12,968
6. Carrefour, $8,812
7. Renault, $8,064
8. Peugeot, $7,976
9. L'Oreal, $7,744
10. EDF, $7,690

Source: *Global 500*, (annual), Brand Finance plc, March 2012.

649 ▪ GERMANY'S MOST VALUABLE BRANDS, 2011

Ranked by: Brand value, in millions of U.S. dollars. Remarks: Also notes rank within the *Global 500* for current and previous year, figures for current and previous year, and brand rating. Ranking is available online only. Number listed: 33

1. BMW, with $21,262 million
2. Mercedes-Benz, $19,762
3. Volkswagen, $17,758
4. Siemens, $16,320
5. Deutsche Bank, $12,906
6. T-Mobile, $12,046
7. Allianz, $10,951
8. E.On, $9,695
9. SAP, $9,042
10. DHL, $8,169

Source: *Global 500*, (annual), Brand Finance plc, March 2012.

650 ▪ HONG KONG'S MOST VALUABLE BRANDS, 2011

Ranked by: Brand value, in millions of U.S. dollars. Remarks: Also notes rank within the *Global 500* for current and previous year, figures for current and previous year, and brand rating. Ranking is available online only. Number listed: 3

1. China Mobile, with $17,919 million
2. China Unicom, $7,944

3. Jardines, $5,246

Source: *Global 500*, (annual), Brand Finance plc, March 2012.

651 ■ INDIA'S MOST VALUABLE BRANDS, 2011

Ranked by: Brand value, in millions of U.S. dollars. **Remarks:** Also notes rank within the *Global 500* for current and previous year, figures for current and previous year, and brand rating. Ranking is available online only. **Number listed:** 6

1. Tata, with $16,343 million
2. Airtel, $5,221
3. State Bank of India, $4,687
4. Reliance, $4,367
5. Indian Oil, $3,666
6. Infosys, $3,628

Source: *Global 500*, (annual), Brand Finance plc, March 2012.

652 ■ ITALY'S MOST VALUABLE BRANDS, 2011

Ranked by: Brand value, in millions of U.S. dollars. **Remarks:** Also notes rank within the *Global 500* for current and previous year, figures for current and previous year, and brand rating. Ranking is available online only. **Number listed:** 6

1. Generali, with $11,168 million
2. Eni, $6,295
3. Enel, $6,009
4. Fiat, $4,350
5. UniCredit, $4,140
6. Prada, $3,346

Source: *Global 500*, (annual), Brand Finance plc, March 2012.

653 ■ JAPAN'S BEST DOMESTIC BRANDS, 2012

Ranked by: Brand value, in millions of U.S. dollars. **Remarks:** Also notes sector and ratio of overseas sales. **Number listed:** 30

1. NTT DoCoMo, with $10,850 million
2. MUFG, $5,677
3. Softbank, $4,419
4. SMFG, $3,733
5. au, $3,234
6. Uniqlo, $2,949
7. Mizuho, $2,660
8. Kirin, $1,798
9. Kao, $1,681
10. Rakuten, $1,554

Source: *Interbrand*, Japan's Best Global Brands (annual), http://www.interbrand.com, February 14, 2012.

654 ■ JAPAN'S BEST GLOBAL BRANDS, 2012

Ranked by: Brand value, in millions of U.S. dollars. **Remarks:** Also notes rank for previous year, sector, annual growth in brand value, and ratio of overseas sales. **Number listed:** 30

1. Toyota, with $27,764 million
2. Honda, $19,431
3. Canon, $11,715
4. Sony, $9,880
5. Nintendo, $7,731
6. Panasonic, $5,047
7. Nissan, $3,819
8. Lexus, $2,554

9. Toshiba, $2,325
10. Komatsu, $2,317

Source: *Interbrand*, Japan's Best Global Brands (annual), http://www.interbrand.com, February 14, 2012.

655 ■ JAPAN'S MOST VALUABLE BRANDS, 2011

Ranked by: Brand value, in millions of U.S. dollars. **Remarks:** Also notes rank within the *Global 500* for current and previous year, figures for current and previous year, and brand rating. Ranking is available online only. **Number listed:** 52

1. NTT Group, with $26,324 million
2. Toyota, $24,461
3. Mitsubishi, $19,488
4. Hitachi, $16,391
5. Mitsui, $15,405
6. Honda, $14,963
7. Toshiba, $14,185
8. Nissan, $14,167
9. Sony, $12,358
10. Canon, $9,293

Source: *Global 500*, (annual), Brand Finance plc, March 2012.

656 ■ MALAYSIA'S MOST VALUABLE BRANDS, 2011

Ranked by: Brand value, in millions of U.S. dollars. **Remarks:** Also notes rank within the *Global 500* for current and previous year, figures for current and previous year, and brand rating. Ranking is available online only. **Number listed:** 2

1. Petronas, with $5,796 million
2. Genting, $2,825

Source: *Global 500*, (annual), Brand Finance plc, March 2012.

657 ■ MEXICO'S MOST VALUABLE BRANDS, 2011

Ranked by: Brand value, in millions of U.S. dollars. **Remarks:** Also notes rank within the *Global 500* for current and previous year, figures for current and previous year, and brand rating. Ranking is available online only. **Number listed:** 4

1. Claro, with $5,721 million
2. Telcel, $3,756
3. Corona Extra, $2,886
4. Grupo Bimbo, $2,634

Source: *Global 500*, (annual), Brand Finance plc, March 2012.

658 ■ MOST VALUABLE ASIAN BRANDS, 2012

Ranked by: Brand value, a measure of a brand's earnings and contribution, in millions of U.S. dollars. **Remarks:** Also notes rank by brand contribution and brand momentum. **Number listed:** 10

1. China Mobile, with $47,041 million
2. ICBC, $41,518
3. China Construction Bank, $24,517
4. Baidu, $24,326
5. Toyota, $21,779
6. Tencent/QQ, $17,992
7. Agricultural Bank of China, $17,867
8. NTT DoCoMo, $15,981
9. China Life Insurance, $14,587
10. Samsung, $14,164

Source: *Financial Times*, Global Brands (annual), May 22, 2012, p. 3.

659 ■ MOST VALUABLE ASIAN-PACIFIC RETAIL BRANDS, 2012

Ranked by: Brand value, in millions of U.S. dollars. **Number listed:** 15

1. Woolworths, with $4,203 million
2. Uniqlo, $2,949
3. Harvey Norman, $873
4. Myer, $599
5. David Jones, $562
6. Suning, $493
7. Muji, $355
8. Belle, $310
9. Nitori, $275
10. Yamada Denki, $202

Source: *Interbrand*, Best Retail Brands (annual), http://www.interbrand.com, February 21, 2012.

660 ■ MOST VALUABLE CHINESE BRANDS, 2011

Ranked by: Brand value, in millions of U.S. dollars. **Remarks:** Also notes industry, annual growth in value, and brand contribution. **Number listed:** 50

1. China Mobile, with $53,607 million
2. ICBC, $43,910
3. China Construction Bank, $21,981
4. Bank of China, $18,643
5. Agricultural Bank of China, $17,329
6. Baidu, $16,256
7. China Life, $15,253
8. Sinopec, $13,791
9. PetroChina, $13,755
10. Tencent, $12,624

Source: *BrandZ Top 50 Most Valuable Chinese Brands*, (annual), Millward Brown, December 12, 2011.

661 ■ MOST VALUABLE CONTINENTAL EUROPEAN BRANDS, 2012

Ranked by: Brand value, a measure of a brand's earnings and contribution, in millions of U.S. dollars. **Remarks:** Also notes rank by brand contribution and brand momentum. **Number listed:** 10

1. Deutsche Telekom, with $26,837 million
2. Louis Vuitton, $25,920
3. SAP, $25,715
4. BMW, $24,623
5. Hermes, $19,161
6. Movistar, $17,113
7. Mercedes-Benz, $16,111
8. Orange, $15,351
9. L'Oreal, $13,773
10. H & M, $13,485

Source: *Financial Times*, Global Brands (annual), May 22, 2012, p. 4.

662 ■ MOST VALUABLE FRENCH RETAIL BRANDS, 2012

Ranked by: Brand value, in millions of U.S. dollars. **Number listed:** 10

1. Carrefour, with $11,076 million
2. Auchan, $3,155
3. Leroy Merlin, $1,930
4. Sephora, $1,549
5. L'Occitane, $1,475
6. Conforama, $1,087
7. Decathlon, $908
8. Darty, $892
9. FNAC, $523
10. Casino, $467

Source: *Interbrand*, Best Retail Brands (annual), http://www.interbrand.com, February 21, 2012.

663 ■ MOST VALUABLE GERMAN RETAIL BRANDS, 2012

Ranked by: Brand value, in millions of U.S. dollars. **Number listed:** 10

1. Aldi, with $3,152 million
2. Edeka, $1,433
3. Lidl, $1,414
4. MediaMarkt, $1,340
5. Kaufland, $538
6. Rewe, $439
7. dm, $409
8. Schlecker, $320
9. OBI, $278
10. Netto Marken-Discount, $276

Source: *Interbrand*, Best Retail Brands (annual), http://www.interbrand.com, February 21, 2012.

664 ■ MOST VALUABLE GLOBAL BRANDS, 2011

Ranked by: Brand value, in millions of dollars. **Remarks:** Also notes rank for previous year, industry, country, brand rating, enterprise value, brand value as a percentage of enterprise value, and figures for previous year. **Number listed:** 500

1. Apple, with $70,605 million
2. Google, $47,463
3. Microsoft, $45,812
4. IBM, $39,135
5. Walmart, $38,319
6. Samsung, $38,197
7. General Electric, $33,214
8. Coca-Cola, $31,082
9. Vodafone, $30,044
10. Amazon, $28,665

Source: *Global 500*, (annual), Brand Finance plc, March 2012, p. 63-82.

665 ■ MOST VALUABLE LATIN AMERICAN BRANDS, 2012

Ranked by: Brand value, a measure of a brand's earnings and contribution, in millions of U.S. dollars. **Remarks:** Also notes rank by brand contribution and brand momentum. **Number listed:** 8

1. Petrobras, with $10,560 million
2. Telcel, $8,449
3. Falabella, $5,263
4. Corona, $5,114
5. Skol, $4,698
6. Sodimac, $3,318

7. Natura, $3,307

8. Brahma, $2,359

Source: *Financial Times*, Global Brands (annual), May 22, 2012, p. 4.

666 ■ MOST VALUABLE NATION BRANDS, 2011

Ranked by: Brand value, in millions of U.S. dollars. **Remarks:** Brand value is calculated based on infrastructure and efficiency, brand equity, and economic performance, as well as such factors as the quality of a country's workforce, the ability to attract foreign talent, perceptions of is quality of life, and its projected growth in gross domestic product. Also notes rank for previous year, growth in brand value, brand rating, and figures for previous year. **Number listed:** 100

1. United States, with $11,370 million

2. Germany, $3,146

3. China, $3,001

4. Japan, $1,940

5. United Kingdom, $1,849

6. France, $1,673

7. Italy, $1,515

8. Canada, $1,309

9. India, $1,266

10. Brazil, $959

Source: *Nation Brands 100*, (annual), Brand Finance plc, November 2011.

667 ■ MOST VALUABLE NORTH AMERICAN BRANDS, 2012

Ranked by: Brand value, a measure of a brand's earnings and contribution, in millions of U.S. dollars. **Remarks:** Also notes rank by brand contribution and brand momentum. **Number listed:** 10

1. Apple, with $182,951 million

2. IBM, $115,985

3. Google, $107,857

4. McDonald's, $95,188

5. Microsoft, $76,651

6. Coca-Cola, $74,286

7. Marlboro, $73,612

8. AT&T, $68,870

9. Verizon, $49,151

10. GE, $45,810

Source: *Financial Times*, Global Brands (annual), May 22, 2012, p. 4.

668 ■ MOST VALUABLE SPANISH RETAIL BRANDS, 2012

Ranked by: Brand value, in millions of U.S. dollars. **Number listed:** 5

1. Zara, with $8,065 million

2. El Corte Ingles, $1,827

3. Mango, $1,199

4. Bershka, $873

5. Mercadona, $844

Source: *Interbrand*, Best Retail Brands (annual), http://www.interbrand.com, February 21, 2012.

669 ■ MOST VALUABLE U.K. BRANDS, 2012

Ranked by: Brand value, a measure of a brand's earnings and contribution, in millions of U.S. dollars. **Remarks:** Also notes rank by brand contribution and brand momentum. **Number listed:** 10

1. Vodafone, with $43,033 million

2. HSBC, $19,313

3. Tesco, $18,007

4. Shell, $17,781

5. BP, $10,424

6. Standard Chartered Bank, $10,064

7. O2, $8,562

8. Barclays, $5,961

9. Dove, $4,696

10. M & S, $4,327

Source: *Financial Times*, Global Brands (annual), May 22, 2012, p. 4.

670 ■ MOST VALUABLE U.K. RETAIL BRANDS, 2012

Ranked by: Brand value, in millions of U.S. dollars. **Number listed:** 10

1. Tesco, with $11,011 million

2. Marks & Spencer, $6,256

3. Boots, $2,852

4. Asda, $1,576

5. Next, $1,319

6. Sainsbury's, $976

7. Argos, $876

8. Morrisons, $438

9. Waitrose, $382

10. Debenhams, $288

Source: *Interbrand*, Best Retail Brands (annual), http://www.interbrand.com, February 21, 2012.

671 ■ THE NETHERLANDS' MOST VALUABLE BRANDS, 2011

Ranked by: Brand value, in millions of U.S. dollars. **Remarks:** Also notes rank within the *Global 500* for current and previous year, figures for current and previous year, and brand rating. Ranking is available online only. **Number listed:** 10

1. Shell, with $22,021 million

2. KPMG, $10,555

3. Rabobank, $7,328

4. ING, $7,054

5. Philips, $6,730

6. Randstad, $5,321

7. Airbus, $4,755

8. Heineken, $3,867

9. Aegon, $3,460

10. KPN, $2,653

Source: *Global 500*, (annual), Brand Finance plc, March 2012.

672 ■ NORWAY'S MOST VALUABLE BRANDS, 2011

Ranked by: Brand value, in millions of U.S. dollars. **Remarks:** Also notes rank within the *Global 500* for current and previous year, figures for current and previous year, and brand rating. Ranking is available online only. **Number listed:** 3

1. StatoilHydro, with $4,693 million

2. Telenor, $4,533

3. DnB, $2,395

Source: *Global 500*, (annual), Brand Finance plc, March 2012.

673 ■ THE RUSSIAN FEDERATION'S MOST VALUABLE BRANDS, 2011

Ranked by: Brand value, in millions of U.S. dollars. **Remarks:** Also notes rank within the *Global 500* for current and previous

year, figures for current and previous year, and brand rating. Ranking is available online only. **Number listed:** 8

1. Sberbank, with $10,772 million
2. Gazprom, $6,407
3. Beeline, $4,707
4. Rostelecom, $4,510
5. Lukoil, $3,809
6. MTS, $3,491
7. Rosneft, $3,324
8. Magnit, $2,613

Source: *Global 500*, (annual), Brand Finance plc, March 2012.

674 ■ SOUTH KOREA'S MOST VALUABLE BRANDS, 2011

Ranked by: Brand value, in millions of U.S. dollars. **Remarks:** Also notes rank within the *Global 500* for current and previous year, figures for current and previous year, and brand rating. Ranking is available online only. **Number listed:** 11

1. Samsung, with $38,197 million
2. Hyundai, $13,098
3. LG Electronics, $9,809
4. Kia, $5,089
5. Daewoo, $4,136
6. SK Telecom, $2,834
7. KT, $3,624
8. Korea Electric Power, $3,302
9. Shinhan Financial, $2,746
10. Korea Gas, $2,590

Source: *Global 500*, (annual), Brand Finance plc, March 2012.

675 ■ SPAIN'S MOST VALUABLE BRANDS, 2011

Ranked by: Brand value, in millions of U.S. dollars. **Remarks:** Also notes rank within the *Global 500* for current and previous year, figures for current and previous year, and brand rating. Ranking is available online only. **Number listed:** 10

1. Santander, with $19,969 million
2. Movistar, $14,412
3. Iberdrola, $7,468
4. BBVA, $7,195
5. O2, $6,773
6. Zara, $4,732
7. ACS, $3,978
8. Endesa, $3,300
9. Ferrovial, $2,905
10. Mapfre, $2,634

Source: *Global 500*, (annual), Brand Finance plc, March 2012.

676 ■ SWEDEN'S MOST VALUABLE BRANDS, 2011

Ranked by: Brand value, in millions of U.S. dollars. **Remarks:** Also notes rank within the *Global 500* for current and previous year, figures for current and previous year, and brand rating. Ranking is available online only. **Number listed:** 5

1. IKEA, with $15,211 million
2. H & M, $8,596
3. Ericsson, $6,735
4. Nordea, $5,253
5. Telia, $2,648

Source: *Global 500*, (annual), Brand Finance plc, March 2012.

677 ■ SWITZERLAND'S MOST VALUABLE BRANDS, 2011

Ranked by: Brand value, in millions of U.S. dollars. **Remarks:** Also notes rank within the *Global 500* for current and previous year, figures for current and previous year, and brand rating. Ranking is available online only. **Number listed:** 20

1. Nestle, with $16,661 million
2. Credit Suisse, $8,368
3. UBS, $5,944
4. Zurich, $5,381
5. Nescafe, $4,150
6. Purina, $4,118
7. ABB, $3,666
8. Swiss Re, $3,661
9. Swisscom, $3,465
10. KitKat, $3,279

Source: *Global 500*, (annual), Brand Finance plc, March 2012.

678 ■ TAIWAN'S BEST GLOBAL BRANDS, 2011

Ranked by: Brand value, in millions of U.S. dollars. **Remarks:** Also notes logo and comments. **Number listed:** 20

1. HTC, with $3,605 million
2. Acer, $1,940
3. ASUS, $1,637
4. TrendMicro, $1,217
5. MasterKong, $1,190
6. Want-Want, $739
7. Giant, $337
8. Maxxis, $335
9. Synnex, $317
10. Advantech, $241

Source: *Bloomberg Businessweek*, Taiwan's Best Global Brands (annual), October 24, 2011, p. 56.

679 ■ TAIWAN'S MOST VALUABLE BRANDS, 2011

Ranked by: Brand value, in millions of U.S. dollars. **Remarks:** Also notes rank within the *Global 500* for current and previous year, figures for current and previous year, and brand rating. Ranking is available online only. **Number listed:** 2

1. HTC, with $4,106 million
2. Chunghwa Telecom, $2,418

Source: *Global 500*, (annual), Brand Finance plc, March 2012.

680 ■ TOP BRANDS IN BAHRAIN, 2011

Ranked by: Brand value, in millions of U.S. dollars. **Remarks:** Also notes industry sector, brand rating, enterprise value, brand value as a percentage of enterprise value, and figures for previous year. **Number listed:** 3

1. Ahli United Bank, with $366 million
2. Batelco, $292
3. Arab Banking Corp., $220

Source: *Gulf Marketing Review*, Top 50 Corporate GCC Brands (annual), October 2011, p. 42.

681 ■ TOP BRANDS IN KUWAIT, 2011

Ranked by: Brand value, in millions of U.S. dollars. **Remarks:** Also notes industry sector, brand rating, enterprise value, brand value as a percentage of enterprise value, and figures for previous year. **Number listed:** 6

1. Zain, with $2,293 million
2. NBK, $743
3. Agility, $462
4. Kuwait Finance House, $326
5. Americana, $324
6. Burgan Bank, $203

Source: *Gulf Marketing Review*, Top 50 Corporate GCC Brands (annual), October 2011, p. 42.

682 ■ TOP BRANDS IN OMAN, 2011

Ranked by: Brand value, in millions of U.S. dollars. **Remarks:** Also notes industry sector, brand rating, enterprise value, brand value as a percentage of enterprise value, and figures for previous year. **Number listed:** 2

1. Omantel, with $323 million
2. BankMuscat, $300

Source: *Gulf Marketing Review*, Top 50 Corporate GCC Brands (annual), October 2011, p. 44.

683 ■ TOP BRANDS IN QATAR, 2011

Ranked by: Brand value, in millions of U.S. dollars. **Remarks:** Also notes industry sector, brand rating, enterprise value, brand value as a percentage of enterprise value, and figures for previous year. **Number listed:** 7

1. Qtel, with $2,949 million
2. QNB, $703
3. Industries Qatar, $629
4. QIB, $368
5. Commercialbank, $342
6. Woqod, $256
7. Doha Bank, $224

Source: *Gulf Marketing Review*, Top 50 Corporate GCC Brands (annual), October 2011, p. 44.

684 ■ TOP BRANDS IN SAUDI ARABIA, 2011

Ranked by: Brand value, in millions of U.S. dollars. **Remarks:** Also notes industry sector, brand rating, enterprise value, brand value as a percentage of enterprise value, and figures for previous year. **Number listed:** 15

1. STC, with $2,616 million
2. Al Rajhi Bank, $1,504
3. Mobily, $1,423
4. Samba Financial Group, $792
5. Sabic, $791
6. Riyad Bank, $751
7. Almarai, $738
8. Saudi Electricity Co., $650
9. Banque Saudi Fransi, $507
10. SABB, $476

Source: *Gulf Marketing Review*, Top 50 Corporate GCC Brands (annual), October 2011, p. 44.

685 ■ TOP BRANDS IN THE UNITED ARAB EMIRATES, 2011

Ranked by: Brand value, in millions of U.S. dollars. **Remarks:** Also notes industry sector, brand rating, enterprise value, brand value as a percentage of enterprise value, and figures for previous year. **Number listed:** 16

1. Emirates, with $3,622 million

2. Etisalat, $3,390
3. Emirates NBD, $1,238
4. National Bank of Abut Dhabi, $1,142
5. DP World, $942
6. First Gulf Bank, $750
7. ADCB, $584
8. Du, $524
9. TAQA, $449
10. Mashreq, $425

Source: *Gulf Marketing Review*, Top 50 Corporate GCC Brands (annual), October 2011, p. 42.

686 ■ TOP CANADIAN BRANDS, 2011

Ranked by: Score, on a scale of 100, based on corporate governance, citizenship, innovation, workplace, leadership, performance, and products and services, as well as consumer trust, esteem, and goodwill toward brand. **Remarks:** Also notes rank for previous year and annual change in score. **Number listed:** 50

1. Jean Coutu Group, with 78.95 points
2. Tim Hortons, 78.24
3. Shoppers Drug Mart, 75.73
4. WestJet, 75.38
5. Research in Motion, 75.17
6. Bombardier, 74.42
7. Yellow Pages, 73.37
8. Alimentation Couche-Tard, 72.2
9. Canadian Tire, 71.23
10. Saputo, 71.16

Source: *Canadian Business*, Top Brands (annual), June 13, 2011, p. 38-39.

687 ■ TOP CHINESE BRANDS, 2011

Ranked by: Brand value, in millions of U.S. dollars. **Remarks:** Also notes rank and figures for previous year, and brand rating. **Number listed:** 100

1. China Mobile, with $19,317 million
2. ICBC, $17,194
3. China Construction Bank, $17,092
4. Bank of China, $13,257
5. Agricultural Bank of China, $9,283
6. China Life Insurance, $9,212
7. PetroChina, $8,031
8. China Telecom, $7,261
9. Sinopec, $7,135
10. China Unicom, $6,315

Source: *China 100*, (annual), Brand Finance plc, 2011.

688 ■ TOP KENYAN BRANDS, 2011

Ranked by: Brand value, in millions of U.S. dollars. **Remarks:** Also notes rank and figures for previous year, and brand rating. **Number listed:** 40

1. Safaricom, with $286 million
2. East African Breweries, $247
3. Kenya Commercial Bank, $151
4. Equity Bank, $129
5. Barclays Bank of Kenya, $110

6. Kenya Airways, $107
7. Kenya Power, $87
8. Bamburi Cement, $80
9. Standard Chartered Bank Kenya, $75
10. Co-op Bank, $73

Source: *Kenya 40*, (annual), Brand Finance plc, 2011.

689 ■ TOP MIDDLE EASTERN BRANDS, 2011

Ranked by: Brand value, in millions of U.S. dollars. **Remarks:** Also notes rank for previous year, industry sector, country, brand rating, and enterprise value. **Number listed:** 50

1. Emirates, with $3,622 million
2. Etisalat, $3,390
3. Qtel, $2,949
4. STC, $2,616
5. Zain, $2,293
6. Al Rajhi Bank, $1,504
7. Mobily, $1,423
8. Emirates NBD, $1,238
9. National Bank of Abu Dhabi, $1,142
10. DP World, $942

Source: *Gulf Marketing Review*, Top 50 Corporate GCC Brands (annual), October 2011, p. 40.

690 ■ TOP SINGAPORE BRANDS, 2011

Ranked by: Brand value, in millions of U.S. dollars. **Remarks:** Also notes rank and figures for previous year, and brand rating. **Number listed:** 50

1. Singapore Airlines, with $3,757 million
2. Wilmar, $3,101
3. DBS, $2,041
4. Astra International, $1,771
5. SingTel, $1,357
6. Keppel, $1,350
7. United Overseas Bank, $1,277
8. Flextronics, $1,176
9. Great Eastern, $1,150
10. OCBC Bank, $1,032

Source: *Singapore 50*, (annual), Brand Finance plc, 2011.

691 ■ TOP TURKISH BRANDS, 2011

Ranked by: Brand value, in millions of U.S. dollars. **Remarks:** Also notes rank and figures for previous year, country, and brand rating. **Number listed:** 100

1. Turk Telekom, with $2,389 million
2. Isbank, $2,280
3. Turkcell, $1,898
4. Akbank, $1,780
5. Garanti, $1,754
6. Turk Hava Yollari, $1,662
7. Efes Bira, $1,565
8. Yapi Kredi, $1,395
9. Arcelik, $1,204
10. Bim, $1,182

Source: *Turkey 100*, (annual), Brand Finance plc, 2011.

692 ■ TOP UNITED KINGDOM BRANDS, 2011

Ranked by: Brand value, in millions of U.S. dollars. **Remarks:** Also notes rank and figures for previous year, and brand rating. **Number listed:** 50

1. Vodafone, with $30,674 million
2. HSBC, $27,632
3. Tesco, $21,129
4. Orange, $18,622
5. Shell, $18,605
6. Barclays, $17,358
7. PwC, $11,445
8. ASDA, $10,689
9. KPMG, $10,160
10. BT, $9,061

Source: *UK Top 50*, (annual), Brand Finance plc, 2011.

693 ■ THE UNITED ARAB EMIRATES' MOST VALUABLE BRANDS, 2011

Ranked by: Brand value, in millions of U.S. dollars. **Remarks:** Also notes rank within the *Global 500* for current and previous year, figures for current and previous year, and brand rating. Ranking is available online only. **Number listed:** 3

1. Emirates Airlines, with $3,700 million
2. Etisalat, $3,117
3. VTB Bank, $2,437

Source: *Global 500*, (annual), Brand Finance plc, March 2012.

694 ■ WORLD'S BEST GLOBAL BRANDS, 2011

Ranked by: Brand value, in millions of U.S. dollars. **Remarks:** Also notes rank and figures for previous year, sector, and percent change. **Number listed:** 100

1. Coca-Cola, with $71,861 million
2. IBM, $69,905
3. Microsoft, $59,087
4. Google, $55,317
5. GE, $42,808
6. McDonald's, $35,593
7. Intel, $35,217
8. Apple, $33,492
9. Disney, $29,018
10. HP, $28,479

Source: *Interbrand*, Best Global Brands (annual), http://www.interbrand.com, October 4, 2011.

695 ■ WORLD'S FASTEST-GROWING BRANDS, 2011-2012

Ranked by: Growth in brand value, in percent. **Number listed:** 20

1. Facebook, with 74%
2. Hermes, 61%
3. MasterCard, 53%
4. Ralph Lauren, 51%
5. Starbucks, 43%
5. Clinique, 43%
7. Rolex, 36%
8. Visa, 34%
9. Hugo Boss, 33%
10. The Home Depot, 31%

Source: *Financial Times*, Global Brands (annual), May 22, 2012, p. 2.

696 ■ WORLD'S MOST VALUABLE BRANDS, 2012

Ranked by: Brand value, a measure of a brand's earnings and contribution, in millions of U.S. dollars. **Remarks:** Also notes

figures for previous two years, brand contribution, brand momentum, annual change in rank, and annual change in brand value.
Number listed: 100

1. Apple, with $182,951 million
2. IBM, $115,985
3. Google, $107,857
4. McDonald's, $95,188
5. Microsoft, $76,651
6. Coca-Cola, $74,286
7. Marlboro, $73,612
8. AT&T, $68,870
9. Verizon, $49,151
10. China Mobile, $47,041

Source: *Financial Times*, Global Brands (annual), May 22, 2012, p. 2.

Brewing Industry

697 ■ TOP U.S. CRAFT BEER BREWERS, 2011

Ranked by: Volume, in barrels **Remarks:** Also notes location. **Number listed:** 10

1. Boston Beer Co., with 2,500,000 barrels
2. Sierra Nevada Brewing Co., 860,000
3. New Belgium Brewing Co., 712,816
4. The Gambrinus Co., 450,000
5. Deschutes Brewery, 220,000
6. Matt Brewing Co., 190,000
7. Bell's Brewery Inc., 180,536
8. Harpoon Brewery Inc., 175,000
9. Lagunitas Brewing Co., 160,000
10. Boulevard Brewing Co., 157,277

Source: *Beverage World*, State of the Industry Report (annual), May 2012, p. 41.

Broadband Communication Systems

698 ■ TOP BRANDS OF HIGH-SPEED INTERNET DEVICES (BROADBAND), 2010

Ranked by: Popularity among *CE Pro 100* companies, in percent. **Number listed:** 6

1. Cisco/Linksys, with 58%
2. Netgear, 23%
3. Pakedge, 19%
4. D-Link, 15%
5. Apple, 10%
5. Ruckus, 10%

Source: *CE Pro*, Brand Analysis (annual), June 2011, p. 60.

699 ■ TOP BROADBAND COMPANIES, 2011

Ranked by: Editorial determination. **Remarks:** Companies are listed alphabetically, not ranked. Also notes Web site, phone number, and description. **Number listed:** 100

1. 3M Co.
2. Actiontec Electronics
3. A-D Technologies
4. ADTRAN

5. ADVA Optical Networking
6. Advanced Media Technologies
7. AFL Telecommunications LLC
8. Alcatel-Lucent
9. Allied Fiber
10. Allied Telesis

Source: *Broadband Communities*, Top 100 (annual), July 2011, p. 39+.

700 ■ TOP VIDEO/BROADBAND COMPANIES IN THE U.S., 2010

Ranked by: Net U.S. revenue, in millions of dollars. **Remarks:** Also notes rank and figures for previous year, annual growth in, and top system. **Number listed:** 10

1. Comcast Corp., with $30,334 million
2. The DirecTV Group Inc., $20,268
3. Time Warner Cable Inc., $16,836
4. Dish Network Corp., $12,544
5. Cox Enterprises Inc., $9,061
6. AT&T Inc., $8,777
7. Verizon Communications Inc., $6,800
8. Charter Communications Inc., $6,236
9. Cablevision Systems Corp., $5,349
10. Advance Publications Inc., $2,958

Source: *Advertising Age*, 100 Leading Media Companies (annual), October 3, 2011, p. 52.

Broadcasting Industry

701 ■ CALIFORNIA'S LARGEST BROADCASTING AND CABLE COMPANIES OVERALL, 2011

Ranked by: Score based on revenue, profits, assets, and market capitalization. **Remarks:** Specific scores not provided. Also notes overall rank in the *Forbes 2000* and figures for each criterion. **Number listed:** 2

1. Walt Disney Co.
2. The DirecTV Group Inc.

Source: *Forbes*, Forbes 2000 (annual), http://www.forbes.com, May 7, 2012.

702 ■ COLORADO'S LARGEST BROADCASTING AND CABLE COMPANIES OVERALL, 2011

Ranked by: Score based on revenue, profits, assets, and market capitalization. **Remarks:** Specific scores not provided. Also notes overall rank in the *Forbes 2000* and figures for each criterion. **Number listed:** 3

1. Dish Network Corp.
2. Liberty Global Inc.
3. Liberty Media Corp.

Source: *Forbes*, Forbes 2000 (annual), http://www.forbes.com, May 7, 2012.

703 ■ FRANCE'S LARGEST BROADCASTING AND CABLE COMPANIES OVERALL, 2011

Ranked by: Score based on revenue, profits, assets, and market capitalization. **Remarks:** Specific scores not provided. Also notes overall rank in the *Forbes 2000* and figures for each criterion. **Number listed:** 2

1. Vivendi SA
2. Eutelsat Communications

Source: *Forbes*, Forbes 2000 (annual), http://www.forbes.com, May 7, 2012.

704 ■ LARGEST U.S. BROADCASTING AND CABLE COMPANIES OVERALL, 2011

Ranked by: Score based on revenue, profits, assets, and market capitalization. **Remarks:** Specific scores not provided. Also notes overall rank in the *Forbes 2000* and figures for each criterion. **Number listed:** 16

1. Comcast Corp.
2. Walt Disney Co.
3. News Corp.
4. Time Warner Inc.
5. Time Warner Cable Inc.
6. The DirecTV Group Inc.
7. Viacom Inc.
8. CBS Corp.
9. Dish Network Corp.
10. Liberty Global Inc.

Source: *Forbes*, Forbes 2000 (annual), http://www.forbes.com, May 7, 2012.

705 ■ LUXEMBOURG'S LARGEST BROADCASTING AND CABLE COMPANIES OVERALL, 2011

Ranked by: Score based on revenue, profits, assets, and market capitalization. **Remarks:** Specific scores not provided. Also notes overall rank in the *Forbes 2000* and figures for each criterion. **Number listed:** 2

1. RTL Group
2. SES SA

Source: *Forbes*, Forbes 2000 (annual), http://www.forbes.com, May 7, 2012.

706 ■ NEW YORK'S LARGEST BROADCASTING AND CABLE COMPANIES OVERALL, 2011

Ranked by: Score based on revenue, profits, assets, and market capitalization. **Remarks:** Specific scores not provided. Also notes overall rank in the *Forbes 2000* and figures for each criterion. **Number listed:** 6

1. News Corp.
2. Time Warner Inc.
3. Time Warner Cable Inc.
4. Viacom Inc.
5. CBS Corp.
6. Sirius XM Radio

Source: *Forbes*, Forbes 2000 (annual), http://www.forbes.com, May 6, 2012.

707 ■ TOP CANADIAN MEDIA, BROADCASTING, AND CABLE COMPANIES, 2010

Ranked by: Revenue, in thousands of Canadian dollars (unless otherwise noted). **Remarks:** Also notes percent change from previous year. **Number listed:** 10

1. Rogers Communications Inc., with C$12,190,000 thousand
2. Quebecor Media, C$4,071,800
3. Shaw Communications Inc., C$3,858,946

4. Bell Media (U.S. Dollars), C$1,752,150
5. Videotron Ltee., C$2,209,000
6. Bell ExpressVu, C$1,749,000
7. Cogeco Inc., C$1,322,682
8. Canadian Broadcasting Corp., C$589,247
9. TVA Group, C$448,381
10. Newfoundland Capital Corp., C$117,836

Source: *Report on Business Magazine*, Top 1000 Companies (annual), http://www.reportonbusiness.com, June 2011.

708 ■ WORLD'S LARGEST BROADCASTING AND CABLE COMPANIES OVERALL, 2011

Ranked by: Score based on revenue, profits, assets, and market capitalization. **Remarks:** Specific scores not provided. Also notes country, overall rank in the *Forbes 2000,* and figures for each criterion. **Number listed:** 27

1. Comcast Corp.
2. Walt Disney Co.
3. News Corp.
4. Time Warner Inc.
5. Vivendi SA
6. Time Warner Cable Inc.
7. The DirecTV Group Inc.
8. Viacom Inc.
9. CBS Corp.
10. Dish Network Corp.

Source: *Forbes*, Forbes 2000 (annual), http://www.forbes.com, May 7, 2012.

Brokers
See also: **Discount Brokers; Insurance Brokers**

709 ■ BEST FULL-SERVICE BROKERS, 2011

Ranked by: Score based on 246 criteria in the areas of customer service, the account-opening process, website, trading mechanism, and account statements and 1099s. **Remarks:** Specific scores not provided. Also notes number of brokers and branches, web site, categories of high and low points, and comments. **Number listed:** 6

1. Raymond James Financial Inc.
2. Edward Jones
3. Wells Fargo Advisors
4. UBS AG
5. Merrill Lynch & Co., Inc.
6. Morgan Stanley Smith Barney

Source: *SmartMoney*, Broker Survey (annual), June 2011, p. 60-61.

Brokers—Internet

710 ■ BEST ONLINE BROKERS FOR FREQUENT TRADERS, 2012

Ranked by: Score based on trade execution, trade technology, usability, range of offerings, research amenities, portfolio analysis and reports, customer access and help, and costs. **Number listed:** 5

1. TradeStation Securities, with 4.5 points

1. Interactive Brokers Group LLC, 4.5
1. MB Trading, 4.5
1. Lightspeed Trading, 4.5
5. TD Ameritrade (thinkorswim), 4

Source: *Barron's*, Best Online Brokers (annual), March 12, 2012, p. 30.

711 ■ BEST ONLINE BROKERS FOR INTERNATIONAL TRADERS, 2012

Ranked by: Score based on trade execution, trade technology, usability, range of offerings, research amenities, portfolio analysis and reports, customer access and help, and costs. Number listed: 5

1. Interactive Brokers Group LLC, with 4.5 points
1. TradeStation Securities, 4.5
3. ChoiceTrade, 4
3. Fidelity, 4
3. MB Trading (foreign exchange), 4

Source: *Barron's*, Best Online Brokers (annual), March 12, 2012, p. 30.

712 ■ BEST ONLINE BROKERS FOR LONG-TERM INVESTING, 2012

Ranked by: Score based on trade execution, trade technology, usability, range of offerings, research amenities, portfolio analysis and reports, customer access and help, and costs. Number listed: 5

1. Fidelity Investments, with 4.5 points
1. TD Ameritrade, 4.5
3. The Charles Schwab Corp., 4
3. E*Trade, 4
3. TradeKing, 4

Source: *Barron's*, Best Online Brokers (annual), March 12, 2012, p. 30.

713 ■ BEST ONLINE BROKERS FOR OPTIONS TRAD-ERS, 2012

Ranked by: Score based on trade execution, trade technology, usability, range of offerings, research amenities, portfolio analysis and reports, customer access and help, and costs. Number listed: 5

1. tradeMonster, with 4.5 points
1. OptionsHouse, 4.5
1. TD Ameritrade, 4.5
4. optionsXpress Inc., 4
4. TradeKing, 4

Source: *Barron's*, Best Online Brokers (annual), March 12, 2012, p. 30.

714 ■ BEST ONLINE BROKERS OVERALL, 2012

Ranked by: Score based on trade execution, trade technology, usability, range of offerings, research amenities, portfolio analysis and reports, customer access and help, and costs. Remarks: Also notes score for each criterion. Number listed: 27

1. Interactive Brokers Group LLC, with 4.5 points
1. MB Trading, 4.5
1. tradeMonster, 4.5
1. TradeStation Securities, 4.5
5. OptionsHouse, 4

5. TD Ameritrade, 4
5. optionsXpress Inc., 4
5. TradeKing, 4
5. Place Trade, 4
5. E*Trade, 4
5. Fidelity Investments, 4

Source: *Barron's*, Best Online Brokers (annual), March 12, 2012, p. 28.

715 ■ CANADA'S BEST ONLINE BROKERAGES, 2011

Ranked by: Score based on cost, trading, tools, account information, customer satisfaction, and Web site. Remarks: Also notes score for previous year and for each criterion. Number listed: 12

1. Qtrade Investor, with 77 points
2. Virtual Brokers, 71
3. BMO InvestorLine, 68
4. Scotia iTrade, 67.5
5. RBC Direct Investing, 66.5
6. Credential Direct, 66
7. TD Waterhouse, 60.5
8. CIBC Investor's Edge, 57
9. Disnat, 55.5
10. Questrade, 55.5

Source: *The Globe and Mail*, Online Broker Rankings (annual), November 14, 2011.

716 ■ ONLINE BROKERS WITH THE HIGHEST FEES FOR FREQUENT TRADERS, 2012

Ranked by: Monthly broker costs, in dollars. Remarks: Frequent traders are defined as making 100 stock trades and 100 options trades per month, and having $30,000 in margin debt. Number listed: 3

1. ING Direct, with $3,420
2. TD Ameritrade, $2,960
3. Scottrade Inc., $2,831

Source: *Barron's*, Best Online Brokers (annual), March 12, 2012, p. 32.

717 ■ ONLINE BROKERS WITH THE HIGHEST FEES FOR OCCASIONAL TRADERS, 2012

Ranked by: Monthly broker costs, in dollars. Remarks: Occasional traders are defined as making six stock trades and two options trades per month. Number listed: 3

1. ING Direct, with $104.60
2. TD Ameritrade, $94.92
2. E*Trade, $94.92

Source: *Barron's*, Best Online Brokers (annual), March 12, 2012, p. 32.

718 ■ ONLINE BROKERS WITH THE LOWEST FEES FOR FREQUENT TRADERS, 2012

Ranked by: Monthly broker costs, in dollars. Remarks: Frequent traders are defined as making 100 stock trades and 100 options trades per month, and having $30,000 in margin debt. Number listed: 4

1. eOption, with $825
2. Lightspeed Trading, $975
3. ChoiceTrade, $986

4. Interactive Brokers Group LLC, $990

Source: *Barron's*, Best Online Brokers (annual), March 12, 2012, p. 32.

719 ■ ONLINE BROKERS WITH THE LOWEST FEES FOR OCCASIONAL TRADERS, 2012

Ranked by: Monthly broker costs, in dollars. **Remarks:** Occasional traders are defined as making six stock trades and two options trades per month. **Number listed:** 4

1. eOption, with $26
2. Merrill Edge, $29
2. Interactive Brokers Group LLC, $29
4. Lightspeed/Just2Trade, $30

Source: *Barron's*, Best Online Brokers (annual), March 12, 2012, p. 32.

Building Cleaning Industry

720 ■ TOP MISCELLANEOUS MAINTENANCE PRODUCTS AND SERVICES FRANCHISES, 2012

Ranked by: Cumulative score based on financial strength and stability, growth rate, size of the system, number of years in business, the length of time franchising, start-up costs, litigation, percentage of terminations, and whether the company provides financing. **Remarks:** Specific scores not provided. Also notes overall rank within the *Franchise 500,* contact information, description, year founded, year started franchising, states where registered, available U.S. regions, where seeking foreign expansion, number of franchised and company-owned units for past three years, start-up costs, franchise fees, royalty fees, and type of financing available. **Number listed:** 11

1. American Leak Detection
2. Aire Serv Heating & Air Conditioning
3. AdvantaClean
4. Mr. Electric
5. Critter Control Inc.
6. Ductz International Inc.
7. Dryer Vent Wizard International
8. America's Swimming Pool Co. (ASP)
9. Jet-Black International
10. Chemstation

Source: *Entrepreneur*, Franchise 500 (annual), January 2012, p. 188-189.

721 ■ TOP RESIDENTIAL CLEANING FRANCHISES, 2012

Ranked by: Cumulative score based on financial strength and stability, growth rate, size of the system, number of years in business, the length of time franchising, start-up costs, litigation, percentage of terminations, and whether the company provides financing. **Remarks:** Specific scores not provided. Also notes overall rank within the *Franchise 500,* contact information, description, year founded, year started franchising, states where registered, available U.S. regions, where seeking foreign expansion, number of franchised and company-owned units for past three years, start-up costs, franchise fees, royalty fees, and type of financing available. **Number listed:** 7

1. The Maids
2. Merry Maids
3. Maid Brigade
4. Molly Maid Inc.
5. MaidPro

6. Maid To Perfection Corp.
7. The Cleaning Authority

Source: *Entrepreneur*, Franchise 500 (annual), January 2012, p. 186-187.

722 ■ TOP RESTROOM MAINTENANCE FRANCHISES, 2012

Ranked by: Cumulative score based on financial strength and stability, growth rate, size of the system, number of years in business, the length of time franchising, start-up costs, litigation, percentage of terminations, and whether the company provides financing. **Remarks:** Specific scores not provided. Also notes overall rank within the *Franchise 500,* contact information, description, year founded, year started franchising, states where registered, available U.S. regions, where seeking foreign expansion, number of franchised and company-owned units for past three years, start-up costs, franchise fees, royalty fees, and type of financing available. **Number listed:** 2

1. Aerowest/Westair Deodorizing Services
2. Aire-Master of America Inc.

Source: *Entrepreneur*, Franchise 500 (annual), January 2012, p. 186-187.

Building Contractors
See: **Contractors**

Building Management
See: **Real Estate Management**

Building Materials Industry

723 ■ LARGEST COMPANIES IN THE BUILDING MATERIALS, HARDWARE, GARDEN SUPPLY, AND MOBILE HOME INDUSTRY BY EMPLOYEES, 2010

Ranked by: Total number of employees. **Remarks:** Also notes contact information for headquarters, number of employees at headquarters, revenue, rank by revenue, and primary SIC code. **Number listed:** 139

1. The Home Depot Inc., with 317,000 employees
2. Lowe's Companies Inc., 239,000
3. Lowe's Home Centers Inc., 209,850
4. Home Depot International Inc., 140,000
4. Home Depot USA Inc., 140,000
6. Menard Inc., 32,000
7. CMH Capital Inc., 11,000
8. Saturn Acquisition Holdings LLC, 9,100
8. Stock Building Supply Holdings Inc., 9,100
10. Laird Norton Co., 7,500

Source: *Business Rankings*, (annual), Dun & Bradstreet Inc., 2011, p. VI.126-VI.128.

724 ■ LARGEST COMPANIES IN THE BUILDING MATERIALS, HARDWARE, GARDEN SUPPLY, AND MOBILE HOME INDUSTRY BY SALES, 2010

Ranked by: Total revenue, in dollars. **Remarks:** Also notes contact information for headquarters, number of employees at headquarters and overall, rank by employees, and primary SIC code. **Number listed:** 140

1. The Home Depot Inc., with $66,176,000,000
2. Lowe's Companies Inc., $47,220,000,000
3. Ace Hardware Corp., $3,457,182,000
4. Signature Custom Woodworking Inc., $950,000,000
5. Lumber Liquidators Holdings Inc., $620,281,000
6. Carter-Jones Cos., $583,136,000
7. Precoat Metal, $350,000,000
8. Carter-Jones Lumber Co., $314,441,997
9. Atwood Distributing LP, $275,831,312
10. Central Carolina Farm & Mower Inc., $260,000,000

Source: *Business Rankings*, (annual), Dun & Bradstreet Inc., 2011, p. V.126-V.128.

725 ■ TOP U.S. LUMBER AND BUILDING MATERIALS DEALERS, 2010

Ranked by: Total sales, in millions of dollars. **Remarks:** Also notes headquarters, figures for previous year, percent change, and number of units. **Number listed:** 200

1. ProBuild Holdings Inc., with $3,500 million
2. 84 Lumber Co., $1,458
3. Stock Building Supply Holdings Inc., $861
4. Builders FirstSource, $700.3
5. Carter Lumber, $652
6. BMC Select Inc., $600
7. McCoy's Building Supply, $515.1
8. MarJam Supply, $405
9. E. C. Barton & Co., $312.2
10. U.S. LBM Holdings, $275

Source: *Home Channel News*, Top 200 Pro Dealer Scoreboard (annual), July 2011.

726 ■ WORLD'S LARGEST MANUFACTURERS OF STONE, CLAY, GLASS, AND CONCRETE PRODUCTS, 2010

Ranked by: Revenue, in millions of dollars. **Remarks:** Also notes rank for previous year, overall rank within the *IW 1000*, country, and revenue growth. **Number listed:** 28

1. Cie. de Saint Gobain SA, with $53,780 million
2. Holcim Ltd., $23,181
3. CRH plc, $22,999
4. Lafarge SA, $21,667
5. HeidelbergCement AG, $16,135
6. Asahi Glass Co., Ltd., $15,854
7. Cemex SAB de CV, $14,440
8. The Siam Cement Public Co., Ltd., $10,247
9. Taiheiyo Cement Corp., $8,962
10. Nippon Sheet Glass Co., Ltd., $7,237

Source: *IndustryWeek*, IW 1000 (annual), http://www.industryweek.com, August 2011.

727 ■ WORLD'S MOST VALUABLE BUILDING MATERIALS BRANDS, 2011

Ranked by: Brand value, in millions of U.S. dollars. **Remarks:** Also notes rank within the *Global 500* for current and previous year, figures for current and previous year, country, and brand rating. Ranking is available online only. **Number listed:** 2

1. Saint Gobain, with $6,623 million
2. Holcim, $2,587

Source: *Global 500*, (annual), Brand Finance plc, March 2012.

Buses

728 ■ LARGEST MOTOR COACH OPERATORS, 2011

Ranked by: Total number of buses and coaches in fleet. **Remarks:** Also notes headquarters, rank for previous year, and breakdown of fleet by type of bus. **Number listed:** 50

1. FirstGroup America, with 13,375 buses/coaches
2. Coach USA Inc. and Coach Canada, 1,642
3. Academy Express LLC, 674
4. Pacific Western Group of Companies, 506
5. Royal Hyway Tours Inc., 419
6. Peter Pan Bus Lines Inc., 330
7. Easton Coach Co., 314
8. Horizon Coach Lines, 260
9. Mears Transportation, 222
10. Arrow Stage Lines, 212

Source: *Metro Magazine*, Motorcoach Top 50 (annual), January 2012, p. 14+.

729 ■ LARGEST TRANSIT BUS FLEETS, 2011

Ranked by: Number of vehicles in fleet. **Remarks:** Also notes rank for previous year, location, percent change, and breakdown of fleet by vehicle type. **Number listed:** 200

1. MTA New York City Transit, with 4,336 vehicles
2. Los Angeles Metropolitan Transportation Authority, 2,515
3. New Jersey Transit Corp., 2,371
4. Toronto Transit Commission, 2,066
5. Coast Mountain Bus Co., 1,891
6. King County Metro Transit, 1,870
7. Pace Suburban Bus, 1,856
8. Montreal Urban Transit, 1,782
9. Chicago Transit Authority, 1,781
10. Washington Metropolitan Area Transit Authority, 1,492

Source: *Metro Magazine*, Top 200 Bus Fleets (annual), 2011, p. 24+.

Business Conditions

730 ■ METRO AREAS WITH THE HIGHEST COST OF DOING BUSINESS, 2011

Ranked by: Cost of business as a percentage above the national average. **Number listed:** 5

1. New York, NY, with 50.7%
2. Boston, MA, 38.3%
3. Cambridge, MA, 32.5%
4. San Francisco, CA, 23%
4. Southern Connecticut, 23%

Source: *Forbes*, Best Places for Business and Careers (annual), July 18, 2011, p. 76.

731 ■ METRO AREAS WITH THE LOWEST COST OF DO-ING BUSINESS, 2011

Ranked by: Cost of business as a percentage below the national average. **Number listed:** 5

1. Shreveport, LA, with 25.7%
2. Fort Smith, AR, 24.6%
3. Eugene, OR, 23.8%
4. Greensboro, NC, 23.5%
5. El Paso, TX, 23.4%

Source: *Forbes*, Best Places for Business and Careers (annual), July 18, 2011, p. 76.

Business Consultants

732 ■ TOP BUSINESS COACHING/CONSULTING/BROKERAGE FRANCHISES, 2012

Ranked by: Cumulative score based on financial strength and stability, growth rate, size of the system, number of years in business, the length of time franchising, start-up costs, litigation, percentage of terminations, and whether the company provides financing. **Remarks:** Specific scores not provided. Also notes overall rank within the *Franchise 500*, contact information, description, year founded, year started franchising, states where registered, available U.S. regions, where seeking foreign expansion, number of franchised and company-owned units for past three years, start-up costs, franchise fees, royalty fees, and type of financing available. **Number listed:** 8

1. ActionCoach
2. The Entrepreneur's Source
3. The Growth Coach
4. AdviCoach
5. Transworld Business Advisors
6. CEO Focus
7. The Alternative Board (TAB)
8. Murphy Business & Financial Corp.

Source: *Entrepreneur*, Franchise 500 (annual), January 2012, p. 150-153.

Business Ethics

733 ■ COUNTRIES WITH THE HIGHEST CORPORATE ETHICS, 2010

Ranked by: Score, on a scale of seven, based on corporate ethical behavior in interactions with public officials, politicians, and other enterprises. **Number listed:** 142

1. Denmark, with 6.7 points
1. New Zealand, 6.7
3. Sweden, 6.6
3. Singapore, 6.6
3. Finland, 6.6
6. Switzerland, 6.5
6. Canada, 6.5
8. Netherlands, 6.4
9. Norway, 6.3
10. Luxembourg, 6.2

Source: *Global Competitiveness Report*, (annual), World Economic Forum, 2011, p. 406.

734 ■ COUNTRIES WITH THE LOWEST CORPORATE ETHICS, 2010

Ranked by: Score, on a scale of seven, based on corporate ethical behavior in interactions with public officials, politicians, and other enterprises. **Number listed:** 139

1. Angola, with 2.4 points
2. Yemen, 2.6
3. Haiti, 2.8
4. Kyrgyz Republic, 2.9
4. Chad, 2.9
4. Mauritania, 2.9
4. Burundi, 2.9
4. Timor-Leste, 2.9
9. Bosnia & Herzegovina, 3.0
9. Madagascar, 3.0
9. Paraguay, 3.0
9. Venezuela, 3.0
9. Serbia, 3.0

Source: *Global Competitiveness Report*, (annual), World Economic Forum, 2011, p. 406.

735 ■ WORLD'S MOST INFLUENTIAL PEOPLE IN BUSINESS ETHICS, 2012

Ranked by: Score based on impact in one or more of eight categories: government and regulatory, business leadership, non-government organizations, design and sustainability, media and whistleblowers, thought leadership, corporate culture, investment and research, and philanthropy. **Remarks:** Specific scores not provided. Also notes category and comments. **Number listed:** 100

1. Anna Hazare (Indian anti-corruption activist)
2. Jed Rakoff (U.S. District judge)
3. Alexei Navalny (blogger)
4. Irving Picard (trustee, Madoff estate)
5. Joaquin Almunia (European Competition Commission)
6. Lanny Breuer (Asst. Attorney General)
7. Preet Bharara (U.S. Attorney, Southern District of NY)
8. Richard Alderman (Serious Fraud Office)
9. Mary Schapiro (SEC)
10. Nick Davies (reporter, The Guardian)

Source: *Ethisphere Magazine*, Most Influential People in Business Ethics (annual), http://www.ethisphere.com, January 19, 2012.

Business Failures

736 ■ STATES WITH THE FEWEST FIRM CESSATIONS, 2008

Ranked by: Number of employer firms that cease business. **Remarks:** Also notes share of national total. **Number listed:** 51

1. South Dakota, with 2,311 firms
2. North Dakota, 2,344
3. Vermont, 2,555
4. Wyoming, 2,703
5. Washington DC, 2,765
6. Alaska, 2,879
7. Delaware, 3,698

8. Hawaii, 3,973

9. Rhode Island, 4,459

10. West Virginia, 4,644

Source: *State Rankings*, (annual), CQ Press, 2011, p. 113.

737 ■ STATES WITH THE HIGHEST RATE OF FIRM CESSATION, 2008

Ranked by: Firms ceasing operations during the year as a percentage of total firms in existence. **Number listed:** 51

1. Washington, with 18.7%

2. Nevada, 17.9%

3. Colorado, 17.2%

4. Alaska, 16.7%

5. Tennessee, 16.1%

6. Arizona, 15.9%

7. Michigan, 15.3%

8. Missouri, 15.2%

9. Maryland, 14.9%

10. Pennsylvania, 14.6%

Source: *State Rankings*, (annual), CQ Press, 2011, p. 114.

738 ■ STATES WITH THE LOWEST RATE OF FIRM CESSATION, 2008

Ranked by: Firms ceasing operations during the year as a percentage of total firms in existence. **Number listed:** 51

1. Louisiana, with 7.5%

2. Texas, 8.1%

3. South Dakota, 9.2%

4. Minnesota, 9.3%

4. Ohio, 9.3%

6. Oklahoma, 9.6%

7. Wisconsin, 9.7%

8. Washington DC, 9.9%

9. Kentucky, 10.2%

10. Iowa, 10.7%

10. Kansas, 10.7%

Source: *State Rankings*, (annual), CQ Press, 2011, p. 114.

739 ■ STATES WITH THE MOST FIRM CESSATIONS, 2008

Ranked by: Number of employer firms that cease business. **Remarks:** Also notes share of national total. **Number listed:** 51

1. California, with 150,314 firms

2. Florida, 72,003

3. New York, 69,267

4. Pennsylvania, 42,318

5. Washington, 37,955

6. Texas, 36,108

7. Illinois, 35,689

8. Michigan, 34,272

9. New Jersey, 31,167

10. Georgia, 29,945

Source: *State Rankings*, (annual), CQ Press, 2011, p. 113.

Business Leaders

740 ■ TOP BUSINESS LEADERS UNDER 40, 2011

Ranked by: Editorial determination. **Remarks:** Also notes age, title, industry, and comments. **Number listed:** 40

1. Mark Zuckerberg (Facebook)

2. Larry Page (Google)

3. Greg Jensen (Bridgewater Associates)

4. Aditya Mittal (ArcelorMittal)

5. John Arnold (Centaurus Energy)

6. Brian Deese (Nat'l Economic Council)

7. Daniel Ammann (General Motors)

8. Jack Dorsey (Twitter and Square)

9. Jeff George (Sandoz and Novartis)

10. Sid Sankaran (AIG)

Source: *Fortune*, 40 Under 40 (annual), November 7, 2010, p. 131+.

741 ■ TOP PEOPLE IN BUSINESS, 2011

Ranked by: Score based on financial results, stock performance, influence, customer base, strategic initiatives and alliance, and sheer muscle. **Remarks:** Specific scores not provided. Also notes title and comments. **Number listed:** 50

1. Howard Schultz (Starbucks)

2. Jeffrey Bezos (Amazon)

3. John Watson (Chevron)

4. Reid Hoffman (LinkedIn and Greylock)

5. James Skinner (McDonald's)

6. Mark Zuckerberg (Facebook)

7. Irene Rosenfeld (Kraft Foods)

8. Tim Cook (Apple)

9. Muhtar Kent (Coca-Cola)

10. Samuel Palmisano (IBM)

Source: *Fortune*, Businessperson of the Year (annual), December 12, 2011, p. 88-96.

Business Loans

742 ■ COUNTRIES WITH THE HIGHEST ACCESS TO BUSINESS LOANS, 2011

Ranked by: Score, on a scale of seven, based on the level of ease in obtaining a bank loan with only a good business plan and no collateral. **Number listed:** 142

1. Qatar, with 5.3 points

2. Bahrain, 5.0

3. Singapore, 4.6

3. Norway, 4.6

3. Saudi Arabia, 4.6

6. Sweden, 4.5

6. Finland, 4.5

6. Malaysia, 4.5

9. Luxembourg, 4.4

10. United Arab Emirates , 4.3

Source: *Global Competitiveness Report*, (annual), World Economic Forum, 2011, p. 483.

743 ■ COUNTRIES WITH THE LOWEST ACCESS TO BUSINESS LOANS, 2011

Ranked by: Score, on a scale of seven, based on the level of ease in obtaining a bank loan with only a good business plan and no collateral. **Number listed:** 142

1. Yemen, with 1.2 points

2. Burundi, 1.3
3. Haiti, 1.5
4. Burkina Faso, 1.6
4. Cote d'Ivoire, 1.6
6. Iran, 1.7
6. Mongolia, 1.7
6. Mauritania, 1.7
9. Argentina, 1.8
10. Ethiopia, 1.9
10. Ireland, 1.9
10. Kyrgyz Republic, 1.9
10. Angola, 1.9

Source: *Global Competitiveness Report*, (annual), World Economic Forum, 2011, p. 483.

Business Losses

744 ■ LARGEST PROPERTY LOSS CONTROL CONSULTANTS BY CLIENTS, 2010

Ranked by: Number of unbundled clients. **Number listed:** 10

1. ABSG Consulting Inc., with 1,665 clients
2. Aon Global Risk Consulting, 1,500
2. Marsh-Risk Consulting, 1,500
4. Global Risk Consultants Corp., 1,014
5. Arup, 900
6. Regional Reporting Inc., 300
7. Hughes Associates Inc., 250
8. XL Global Asset Protection Services LLC, 240
9. Gallagher Bassett Services Inc., 200
10. AXA Matrix Risk Consultants, 165

Source: *Business Insurance*, Property Loss Control Specialists (annual), August 15, 2011, p. 10.

745 ■ LARGEST PROPERTY LOSS CONTROL SPECIALISTS BY REVENUE, 2010

Ranked by: Gross revenue from unbundled property loss control consulting, in dollars. **Remarks:** Also notes contact information, property loss control as a percentage of total revenue, professional property loss control staff, branch offices, unbundled clients, and principal officer. **Number listed:** 10

1. ABSG Consulting Inc., with $205,400,00
2. Arup, $58,280,000
3. Global Risk Consultants Corp., $57,904,700
4. Aon Global Risk Consulting, $53,175,000
5. Marsh Risk Consulting, $51,000,000
6. Hughes Associates Inc., $30,000,000
7. XL Global Asset Protection Services LLC, $27,900,000
8. AXA Matrix Risk Consultants, $20,500,000
9. EFI Global Inc., $12,990,000
10. Regional Reporting Inc., $9,000,000

Source: *Business Insurance*, Property Loss Control Specialists (annual), August 15, 2011, p. 10.

746 ■ LARGEST PROPERTY LOSS CONTROL SPECIALISTS BY STAFF, 2010

Ranked by: Number of professional property loss control staff. **Number listed:** 10

1. ABSG Consulting Inc., with 700 employees
2. Arup, 400
3. Global Risk Consultants Corp., 349
4. Aon Global Risk Consulting, 320
5. EFI Global Inc., 253
6. Marsh-Risk Consulting, 250
6. Regional Reporting Inc., 250
8. XL Global Asset Protection Services LLC, 194
9. Zurich Services Corp., 175
10. AXA Matrix Risk Consultants, 140

Source: *Business Insurance*, Property Loss Control Specialists (annual), August 15, 2011, p. 10.

Business Machines
See: **Office Equipment Industry**

Business Schools and Colleges

747 ■ BEST CUSTOM EXECUTIVE EDUCATION PROGRAMS, 2011

Ranked by: Score based on survey of client companies. **Remarks:** Scores not provided. Also notes previous rank. **Number listed:** 10

1. Duke Corporate Education
2. INSEAD
3. IESE Business School
4. Harvard University
5. IE Business School
6. IMD
7. ESADE
8. University of Pennsylvania, Wharton School
9. Center for Creative Leadership
10. Columbia University

Source: *Bloomberg Businessweek*, The Best B-Schools: Part-Time and EMBA (biennial), November 14, 2011, p. 64.

748 ■ BEST EXECUTIVE MBA PROGRAMS, 2011

Ranked by: Score based on surveys of Executive MBA graduates and directors. **Remarks:** Scores not provided. Also notes previous rank and financial and academic figures. **Number listed:** 25

1. University of Chicago, Booth School of Business
2. Columbia University
3. Northwestern University, Kellogg School of Management
4. IE Business School
5. University of California-Los Angeles, Anderson School of Management
6. University of Michigan, Ross School of Business
7. Southwest Methodist University, Cox School of Business
8. University of Southern California, Marshall School of Business
9. University of Pennsylvania, Wharton School
10. Duke University, Fuqua School of Business

Source: *Bloomberg Businessweek*, The Best B-Schools: Part-Time and EMBA (biennial), November 14, 2011, p. 66.

749 ■ BEST OPEN ENROLLMENT EXECUTIVE EDUCATION PROGRAMS, 2011

Ranked by: Score based on survey of client companies. **Remarks:** Scores not provided. Also notes previous rank. **Number listed:** 10

1. Harvard University
2. IESE Business School
3. INSEAD
4. Columbia University
5. ESADE
6. Center for Creative Leadership
7. University of Pennsylvania, Wharton School
8. Stanford University
9. Duke University, Fuqua School of Business
10. IE Business School

Source: *Bloomberg Businessweek*, The Best B-Schools: Part-Time and EMBA (biennial), November 14, 2011, p. 64.

750 ■ BEST PART-TIME BUSINESS SCHOOLS, 2011

Ranked by: Score based on student satisfaction, academic quality, and post-graduation outcome. **Remarks:** Scores not provided. Also notes previous rank, regional rank, and financial and academic figures. **Number listed:** 25

1. Elon University, Love School of Business
2. University of California-Los Angeles, Anderson School of Management
3. Carnegie Mellon University, Tepper School of Business
4. University of Nevada-Reno
5. University of California-Berkeley, Haas School of Business
6. Rice University, Jones Graduate School of Business
7. Southwest Methodist University, Cox School of Business
8. Worcester Polytechnic Institute
9. University of Michigan, Ross School of Business
10. University of Washington, Foster School of Business

Source: *Bloomberg Businessweek*, The Best B-Schools: Part-Time and EMBA (biennial), November 14, 2011, p. 63.

751 ■ LARGEST MBA PROGRAMS IN CONNECTICUT, 2010

Ranked by: Autumn enrollment. **Remarks:** Also notes contact information, number of MBAs conferred during the year, average age of students, breakdown by full- and part-time enrollment, costs, whether offers an executive MBA program, specialties, principal contacts, and date founded locally. **Number listed:** 3

1. University of New Haven, with 493 students
2. University of Connecticut, 492
3. University of Bridgeport, 455

Source: *Hartford Business Journal*, Largest MBA Programs (annual), http://www.hartfordbusiness.com, July 25, 2011.

752 ■ LARGEST MBA PROGRAMS IN LOS ANGELES COUNTY, 2011

Ranked by: Number of graduates at Los Angeles County campuses. **Remarks:** Also notes contact information, figures for previous year, enrollment, types of programs offered, number of campuses and faculty, profile, and top local administrator. **Number listed:** 20

1. University of Southern California, Marshall School of Business, with 728 graduates
2. University of California-Los Angeles, Anderson School of Management, 702
3. Pepperdine University, Graziadio School of Business & Management, 517

Source: *Los Angeles Business Journal*, MBA Programs (annual), http://www.labusinessjournal.com, September 12, 2011.

753 ■ LARGEST MBA PROGRAMS IN THE TWIN CITIES, 2010

Ranked by: Enrollment in the fall semester. **Remarks:** Also notes contact information, year founded, breakdown by full- and part-time students, tuition, length, average age of student, number of faculty, dean, business-related accreditations, and degrees offered. **Number listed:** 19

1. Capella University, with 1,858 students
2. University of Minnesota-Twin Cities, Carlson School of Management, 1,729
3. Walden University, 1,480
4. University of St. Thomas, Opus College of Business, 1,172
5. Hamline University, 433
6. National American University, 400
7. St. Mary's University of Minnesota, 307
8. St. Cloud State University, G. R. Herberger College of Business, 230
9. The College of St. Scholastica, 220
10. Bethel University, 202

Source: *Twin Cities Business*, The BIG Book (annual), http://www.tcbmag.com, 2012.

754 ■ TOP BUSINESS SCHOOLS FOR HISPANIC STUDENTS, 2011

Ranked by: Score based on total Hispanic enrollment, Hispanic faculty, and programs aimed at increasing enrollment of Hispanic students. **Remarks:** Specific scores not provided. Also notes contact information, figures for each criterion, and additional figures. **Number listed:** 10

1. University of Texas-El Paso
2. University of Texas-Austin, McCombs School of Business
3. University of Texas-San Antonio
4. New York University, Leonard N. Stern School of Business
5. University of Miami
6. University of Virginia, Darden School of Business
7. University of New Mexico, Anderson School of Management
8. Stanford University
9. Yale University
10. Florida International University, Alvah H. Chapman Jr. Graduate School of Business

Source: *Hispanic Business*, Top Graduate Schools for Hispanics (annual), September 2011, p. 50+.

755 ■ TOP MBA PROGRAMS IN NEW YORK, 2011

Ranked by: Total enrollment. **Remarks:** Also notes contact information, dean, breakdown by full- and part-time enrollment, tuition and fees, number of MBA applications, acceptance rate, percentage of graduates employed at graduation, average starting salary, and student demographics. **Number listed:** 20

1. New York University, Stern School of Business, with 2,890 students
2. Baruch College, Zicklin School of Business, 1,664
3. Columbia University, 1,298

Source: *Crain's New York Business*, Top MBA Programs (annual), http://www.crainsnewyork.com, April 23, 2012.

756 ■ TOP U.S. BUSINESS SCHOOLS, 2012

Ranked by: Score based on value for money, career progress, aim achievement, and placement success. **Remarks:** Specific scores not provided. Also notes overall rank in the *Global MBA Rankings*, three-year rank, salary of graduates, and percentage of salary increase. **Number listed:** 52

1. Stanford University
2. Harvard University
3. University of Pennsylvania, Wharton School of Business
4. Columbia University
5. Massachusetts Institute of Technology, Sloan School of Business
6. University of Chicago, Booth School of Business
7. University of California, Berkeley, Haas School of Business
8. Duke University, Fuqua School of Business
9. Northwestern University, Kellogg School of Business
10. New York University, Stern School of Business

Source: *Financial Times*, Global MBA Rankings (annual), http://www.ft.com, January 30, 2012.

Business Schools and Colleges, Foreign

757 ■ AUSTRALIA'S TOP BUSINESS SCHOOLS, 2012

Ranked by: Score based on value for money, career progress, aim achievement, and placement success. **Remarks:** Specific scores not provided. Also notes overall rank in the *Global MBA Rankings*, three-year rank, salary of graduates, and percentage of salary increase. **Number listed:** 2

1. Australian School of Business
2. Melbourne Business School

Source: *Financial Times*, Global MBA Rankings (annual), http://www.ft.com, January 30, 2012.

758 ■ CANADA'S TOP BUSINESS SCHOOLS, 2012

Ranked by: Score based on value for money, career progress, aim achievement, and placement success. **Remarks:** Specific scores not provided. Also notes overall rank in the *Global MBA Rankings*, three-year rank, salary of graduates, and percentage of salary increase. **Number listed:** 5

1. University of Toronto, Rotman School of Business
2. York University, Schulich Business School
3. McGill University, Desautels Faculty of Management
4. University of Western Ontario, Ivey School of Business

5. University of British Columbia, Sauder Business School

Source: *Financial Times*, Global MBA Rankings (annual), http://www.ft.com, January 30, 2012.

759 ■ CHINA'S TOP BUSINESS SCHOOLS, 2012

Ranked by: Score based on value for money, career progress, aim achievement, and placement success. **Remarks:** Specific scores not provided. Also notes overall rank in the *Global MBA Rankings*, three-year rank, salary of graduates, and percentage of salary increase. **Number listed:** 5

1. Hong Kong University of Science & Technology
2. China Europe International Business School (CEIBS)
3. Chinese University of Hong Kong
4. University of Hong Kong
5. Peking University, Guanghu School of Business

Source: *Financial Times*, Global MBA Rankings (annual), http://www.ft.com, January 30, 2012.

760 ■ EUROPE'S TOP BUSINESS SCHOOLS, 2011

Ranked by: Score based on value for money, career progress, aim achievement, and placement success. **Remarks:** Specific scores not provided. Also notes rank for previous two years, three-year average rank, salaries of MBA and EMBA graduates, and executive programs. **Number listed:** 75

1. HEC Paris (France)
2. INSEAD (France/Singapore)
3. London Business School (U.K.)
4. Iese Business School (Spain)
5. IMD International (Switzerland)
6. Instituto de Empresa (Spain)
7. Erasmus University, Rotterdam School of Management (Netherlands)
8. Esade Business School (Spain)
9. SDA Bocconi (Italy)
10. Essec Business School (France)

Source: *Financial Times*, European Business School Rankings (annual), http://www.ft.com, December 5, 2011.

761 ■ FRANCE'S TOP BUSINESS SCHOOLS, 2012

Ranked by: Score based on value for money, career progress, aim achievement, and placement success. **Remarks:** Specific scores not provided. Also notes overall rank in the *Global MBA Rankings*, three-year rank, salary of graduates, and percentage of salary increase. **Number listed:** 2

1. INSEAD (France/Singapore)
2. Ecole des Hautes Etudes Commerciales de Paris (HEC Paris)

Source: *Financial Times*, Global MBA Rankings (annual), http://www.ft.com, January 30, 2012.

762 ■ INDIA'S TOP BUSINESS SCHOOLS, 2012

Ranked by: Score based on value for money, career progress, aim achievement, and placement success. **Remarks:** Specific scores not provided. Also notes overall rank in the *Global MBA Rankings*, three-year rank, salary of graduates, and percentage of salary increase. **Number listed:** 2

1. Indian Institute of Management, Ahmedabad (IIMA)

2. Indian School of Business

Source: *Financial Times*, Global MBA Rankings (annual), http://www.ft.com, January 30, 2012.

763 ■ SINGAPORE'S TOP BUSINESS SCHOOLS, 2012

Ranked by: Score based on value for money, career progress, aim achievement, and placement success. **Remarks:** Specific scores not provided. Also notes overall rank in the *Global MBA Rankings*, three-year rank, salary of graduates, and percentage of salary increase. **Number listed:** 2

1. National University of Singapore, School of Business
2. Nanyang Business School

Source: *Financial Times*, Global MBA Rankings (annual), http://www.ft.com, January 30, 2012.

764 ■ SPAIN'S TOP BUSINESS SCHOOLS, 2012

Ranked by: Score based on value for money, career progress, aim achievement, and placement success. **Remarks:** Specific scores not provided. Also notes overall rank in the *Global MBA Rankings*, three-year rank, salary of graduates, and percentage of salary increase. **Number listed:** 3

1. Instituto de Empresa
2. Iese Business School
3. Esade Business School

Source: *Financial Times*, Global MBA Rankings (annual), http://www.ft.com, January 30, 2012.

765 ■ SWITZERLAND'S TOP BUSINESS SCHOOLS, 2012

Ranked by: Score based on value for money, career progress, aim achievement, and placement success. **Remarks:** Specific scores not provided. Also notes overall rank in the *Global MBA Rankings*, three-year rank, salary of graduates, and percentage of salary increase. **Number listed:** 2

1. IMD
2. Universitat St. Gallen

Source: *Financial Times*, Global MBA Rankings (annual), http://www.ft.com, January 30, 2012.

766 ■ THE UNITED KINGDOM'S TOP BUSINESS SCHOOLS, 2012

Ranked by: Score based on value for money, career progress, aim achievement, and placement success. **Remarks:** Specific scores not provided. Also notes overall rank in the *Global MBA Rankings*, three-year rank, salary of graduates, and percentage of salary increase. **Number listed:** 14

1. London Business School
2. Oxford University, Said Business School
3. Cambridge University, Judge Business School
4. Warwick Business School
5. Manchester Business School
6. Cranfield School of Management
7. City University, Cass Business School
8. Imperial College Business School
9. Lancaster University Management School
10. University of Edinburgh Business School

Source: *Financial Times*, Global MBA Rankings (annual), http://www.ft.com, January 30, 2012.

Business Schools and Colleges, International

767 ■ COUNTRIES WITH THE BEST MANAGEMENT SCHOOLS, 2010

Ranked by: Score, on a scale of seven, based on the quality of management or business schools. **Number listed:** 142

1. Belgium, with 6.1 points
2. United Kingdom, 6.0
2. Switzerland, 6.0
4. Canada, 5.8
5. France, 5.7
5. Spain, 5.7
5. Qatar, 5.7
8. Singapore, 5.6
9. Sweden, 5.5
9. Netherlands, 5.5
9. Iceland, 5.5

Source: *Global Competitiveness Report*, (annual), World Economic Forum, 2011, p. 446.

768 ■ COUNTRIES WITH THE WORST MANAGEMENT SCHOOLS, 2010

Ranked by: Score, on a scale of seven, based on the quality of management or business schools. **Number listed:** 142

1. Angola, with 1.8 points
2. Timor-Leste, 2.1
3. Yemen, 2.4
4. Mauritania, 2.5
5. Swaziland, 2.6
5. Burundi, 2.6
7. Haiti, 2.7
8. Mongolia, 2.8
9. Lesotho, 2.9
10. Egypt, 3.0
10. Kyrgyz Republic, 3.0

Source: *Global Competitiveness Report*, (annual), World Economic Forum, 2011, p. 446.

769 ■ WORLD'S TOP BUSINESS SCHOOLS, 2012

Ranked by: Score based on value for money, career progress, aim achievement, and placement success. **Remarks:** Specific scores not provided. Also notes rank for previous two years, three-year average rank, salary of graduates, rank by each criterion, and characteristics of student body and faculty. **Number listed:** 100

1. Stanford University (U.S.)
2. Harvard University (U.S.)
3. University of Pennsylvania, Wharton School of Business (U.S.)
4. London Business School (U.K.)
5. Columbia University (U.S.)
6. INSEAD (France/Singapore)
7. Massachusetts Institute of Technology, Sloan School of Business (U.S.)
8. Instituto de Empresa (Spain)
9. Iese Business School (Spain)
10. Hong Kong University of Science & Technology (China)

Source: *Financial Times*, Global MBA Rankings (annual), http://www.ft.com, January 30, 2012.

770 ■ WORLD'S TOP SCHOOLS OF BUSINESS FOR AN EXECUTIVE MBA, 2011

Ranked by: Score based on value for money, career progress, aim achievement, and placement success. **Remarks:** Specific scores not provided. Also notes program name, rank for previous two years, three-year average rank, salary of graduates, rank by each criterion, and breakdown of faculty, students, and board. **Number listed:** 100

1. Kellogg/Hong Kong University of Science & Technology (China)
2. TRIUM: HEC Paris (France), London School of Economics & Political Science (U.K.), and New York University, Stern School of Business
3. Columbia University/London School of Business (U.S./U.K.)
4. INSEAD (France/Singapore/UAE)
5. University of Chicago, Booth School of Business (U.S.)
6. Duke University, Fuqua School of Business (U.S.)
7. University of Pennsylvania, Wharton School of Business (U.S.)
8. Instituto de Empresa (Spain)
9. University of California, Los Angeles/National University of Singapore (U.S./Singapore)
10. London School of Business (U.K./UAE)

Source: *Financial Times*, EMBA Rankings (annual), http://www.ft.com, October 24, 2011.

771 ■ WORLD'S TOP SCHOOLS FOR A MASTERS DEGREE IN MANAGEMENT, 2011

Ranked by: Score based on value for money, career progress, aim achievement, placement success, international mobility, and international course experience. **Remarks:** Specific scores not provided. Also notes program name, rank for previous two years, three-year average rank, salary of graduates, rank by each criterion, and breakdown of faculty, students, and board. **Number listed:** 65

1. Universitat St. Gallen (Switzerland)
2. CEMS (various locations)
3. ESCP Europe (France, UK, Germany, Spain, Italy)
4. HEC Paris (France)
5. EM Lyon Business School (France)
6. WHU - Otto Beisheim School of Management (Germany)
7. Indian Institute of Management, Ahmedabad (IIMA)
8. Essec Business School (France)
9. Grenoble Graduate School of Business (France, Singapore)
10. Rotterdam School of Management (Netherlands)

Source: *Financial Times*, Masters in Management Rankings (annual), http://www.ft.com, September 19, 2011.

Business Services

772 ■ AMERICA'S LARGEST PRIVATE BUSINESS SERVICE AND SUPPLY COMPANIES, 2010

Ranked by: Revenue, in billions of dollars. **Remarks:** Also notes headquarters, number of employees, and overall rank in the *America's Largest Private Companies* list. Ranking is available online only, not in print. **Number listed:** 15

1. PricewaterhouseCoopers LLP, with $29.2 billion

2. Ernst & Young LLP, $22.88
3. ARAMARK Corp., $13
4. Gavilon Group LLC, $12.6
5. First Data Corp., $10.38
6. Bloomberg LP, $7
6. McKinsey & Co. , $7
8. Allegis Group Inc., $6.4
9. The ServiceMaster Co., $3.37
10. The Boston Consulting Group Inc., $3.05

Source: *Forbes*, America's Largest Private Companies (annual), http://www.forbes.com, December 5, 2011.

773 ■ BEST PROFESSIONAL SERVICES AND COMMUNICATIONS COMPANIES TO WORK FOR IN BRITISH COLUMBIA, 2010

Ranked by: Editorial determination. **Remarks:** Specific scores not provided. **Number listed:** 5

1. 6S Marketing Inc.
2. Habanero Consulting Group Inc.
3. Chemistry Consulting Group Inc.
4. Benefits by Design Inc.
5. Cobra Integrated Systems Ltd.

Source: *BCBusiness*, Best Companies (annual), http://www.bcbusinessonline.ca, December 2011.

774 ■ BEST SMALL BUSINESS SERVICES AND SUPPLIES COMPANIES IN AMERICA, 2011

Ranked by: Score based on revenue, profits, and return on equity for the past 12 months and five years. **Remarks:** Specific scores not provided. Also notes rank in the overall *100 Best Small Companies in America*. To qualify, companies must have revenues between $5 million and $1 billion, a net margin above five percent, and share price above $5. List is available online only. **Number listed:** 13

1. American Public Education Inc.
2. Grand Canyon Education
3. Wright Express
4. Strayer Education
5. Capella Education
6. Industrial Services of America
7. ExlService Holdings
8. Portfolio Recovery Associates
9. Multi-Color
10. Team

Source: *Forbes*, Best Small Companies in America (annual), November 7, 2011.

775 ■ BRITAIN'S MOST ADMIRED SUPPORT SERVICE COMPANIES, 2011

Ranked by: Survey of peers and investment analysts based on nine criteria: quality of management, financial soundness, quality of goods/services, ability to attract and retain talent, value as long-term investment, innovation, marketing, community and environmental responsibility, and use of corporate assets. **Number listed:** 5

1. Aggreko plc, with 71.2 points
2. Experian plc, 66.2
3. Babcock International Group plc, 65.6
4. Bunzl plc, 65.2

5. Intertek, 63.8

Source: *Management Today*, Britain's Most Admired Companies (annual), December 2011, p. 43.

776 ■ FASTEST-GROWING PRIVATE BUSINESS SERVICES COMPANIES IN THE U.S., 2007-2010

Ranked by: Average annual sales growth over three years, in percent. **Remarks:** Also notes headquarters, revenue, and rank in the overall *Inc. 500*. To qualify, private companies must have had annual revenues of at least $100,000 in 2007 and $2 million in 2010. **Number listed:** 37

1. I. T. Source, with 6,665.9%
2. WBPromotion, 6,199.4%
3. Square Peg Packaging & Printing, 5,985.9%
4. MAG Trucks, 2,932.2%
5. Classroom Essentials Online, 2,749.5%
6. Avondale Consulting, 2,705.9%
7. Software Advice, 2,077.4%
8. The Trademark Co., 2,034.3%
9. Green Earth, 1,933.4%
10. Warehouse Solutions, 1,869.8%

Source: *Inc.*, Inc. 500 (annual), September 2011, p. 94-96.

777 ■ FLORIDA'S LARGEST BUSINESS AND PERSONAL SERVICES COMPANIES OVERALL, 2011

Ranked by: Score based on revenue, profits, assets, and market capitalization. **Remarks:** Specific scores not provided. Also notes overall rank in the *Forbes 2000* and figures for each criterion. **Number listed:** 2

1. Fidelity National Information Services Inc.
2. World Fuel Services Corp.

Source: *Forbes*, Forbes 2000 (annual), http://www.forbes.com, May 7, 2012.

778 ■ LARGEST BUSINESS SERVICE COMPANIES BY EMPLOYEES, 2010

Ranked by: Total number of employees. **Remarks:** Also notes contact information for headquarters, number of employees at headquarters, revenue, rank by revenue, and primary SIC code. **Number listed:** 487

1. International Business Machines Corp. (IBM), with 399,409 employees
2. Express Services Inc., 357,735
3. Securitas Holdings Inc., 250,000
4. United Parcel Service Inc. (UPS), 204,986
5. SFN Group Inc., 161,000
6. HP Enterprise Services LLC, 139,500
7. Administaff Inc., 107,025
8. Oracle Corp., 105,000
9. Securitas Security Services USA Inc., 98,600
10. ABM Industries Inc., 96,000

Source: *Business Rankings*, (annual), Dun & Bradstreet Inc., 2011, p. VI.214-VI.224.

779 ■ LARGEST BUSINESS SERVICE COMPANIES BY SALES, 2010

Ranked by: Total revenue, in dollars. **Remarks:** Also notes contact information for headquarters, number of employees at headquarters and overall, rank by employees, and primary SIC code. **Number listed:** 495

1. International Business Machines Corp. (IBM), with $99,870,000,000
2. Microsoft Corp., $62,484,000,000
3. Google Inc., $29,321,000,000
4. Oracle Corp., $26,820,000,000
5. FIA Card Services NA, $25,752,912,000
6. Manpower Inc., $18,866,500,000
7. Computer Sciences Corp., $16,128,000,000
8. Omnicom Group Inc., $12,542,500,000
9. Automatic Data Processing Inc., $8,927,700,000
10. Visa Inc., $8,065,000,000

Source: *Business Rankings*, (annual), Dun & Bradstreet Inc., 2011, p. V.188-V.198.

780 ■ LARGEST U.S. BUSINESS AND PERSONAL SERVICES COMPANIES OVERALL, 2011

Ranked by: Score based on revenue, profits, assets, and market capitalization. **Remarks:** Specific scores not provided. Also notes overall rank in the *Forbes 2000* and figures for each criterion. **Number listed:** 9

1. Automatic Data Processing Inc.
2. Priceline.com Inc.
3. Fidelity National Information Services Inc.
4. Paychex Inc.
5. Moody's Corp.
6. World Fuel Services Corp.
7. Manpower Inc.
8. Apollo Group Inc.
9. Alliance Data Systems Corp.

Source: *Forbes*, Forbes 2000 (annual), http://www.forbes.com, May 7, 2012.

781 ■ THE NETHERLANDS' MOST VALUABLE COMMERCIAL SERVICE BRANDS, 2011

Ranked by: Brand value, in millions of U.S. dollars. **Remarks:** Also notes rank within the *Global 500* for current and previous year, figures for current and previous year, and brand rating. Ranking is available online only. **Number listed:** 2

1. KPMG, with $10,555 million
2. Randstad, $5,321

Source: *Global 500*, (annual), Brand Finance plc, March 2012.

782 ■ NEW YORK'S LARGEST BUSINESS AND PERSONAL SERVICES COMPANIES OVERALL, 2011

Ranked by: Score based on revenue, profits, assets, and market capitalization. **Remarks:** Specific scores not provided. Also notes overall rank in the *Forbes 2000* and figures for each criterion. **Number listed:** 2

1. Paychex Inc.
2. Moody's Corp.

Source: *Forbes*, Forbes 2000 (annual), http://www.forbes.com, May 7, 2012.

783 ■ SWITZERLAND'S LARGEST BUSINESS AND PERSONAL SERVICES COMPANIES OVERALL, 2011

Ranked by: Score based on revenue, profits, assets, and market capitalization. **Remarks:** Specific scores not provided. Also notes overall rank in the *Forbes 2000* and figures for each criterion. **Number listed:** 2

1. Adecco SA
2. SGS SA

Source: *Forbes*, Forbes 2000 (annual), http://www.forbes.com, May 7, 2012.

784 ■ TOP MISCELLANEOUS BUSINESS SERVICES FRANCHISES, 2012

Ranked by: Cumulative score based on financial strength and stability, growth rate, size of the system, number of years in business, the length of time franchising, start-up costs, litigation, percentage of terminations, and whether the company provides financing. **Remarks:** Specific scores not provided. Also notes overall rank within the *Franchise 500,* contact information, description, year founded, year started franchising, states where registered, available U.S. regions, where seeking foreign expansion, number of franchised and company-owned units for past three years, start-up costs, franchise fees, royalty fees, and type of financing available. **Number listed:** 5

1. ProForma
2. Real Property Management
3. Bevintel
4. Cybertary
5. Intelligent Office

Source: *Entrepreneur*, Franchise 500 (annual), January 2012, p. 154-155.

785 ■ UNITED KINGDOM'S LARGEST BUSINESS AND PERSONAL SERVICES COMPANIES OVERALL, 2011

Ranked by: Score based on revenue, profits, assets, and market capitalization. **Remarks:** Specific scores not provided. Also notes overall rank in the *Forbes 2000* and figures for each criterion. **Number listed:** 4

1. Thomas Cook Group plc
2. Aggreko plc
3. The Capita Group plc
4. Bunzl plc

Source: *Forbes*, Forbes 2000 (annual), http://www.forbes.com, May 7, 2012.

786 ■ THE UNITED STATES' MOST VALUABLE COMMERCIAL SERVICE BRANDS, 2011

Ranked by: Brand value, in millions of U.S. dollars. **Remarks:** Also notes rank within the *Global 500* for current and previous year, figures for current and previous year, and brand rating. Ranking is available online only. **Number listed:** 7

1. PwC, with $14,296 million
2. Deloitte, $9,660
3. Ernst & Young, $8,538
4. Visa, $7,087
5. MasterCard, $5,177
6. Hertz, $2,719
7. McKinsey, $2,578

Source: *Global 500*, (annual), Brand Finance plc, March 2012.

787 ■ WORLD'S LARGEST BUSINESS AND PERSONAL SERVICES COMPANIES OVERALL, 2011

Ranked by: Score based on revenue, profits, assets, and market capitalization. **Remarks:** Specific scores not provided. Also notes country, overall rank in the *Forbes 2000,* and figures for each criterion. **Number listed:** 23

1. Automatic Data Processing Inc.

2. Sodexho SA
3. Adecco SA
4. SECOM Co., Ltd.
5. Priceline.com Inc.
6. Fidelity National Information Services Inc.
7. Cielo SA
8. SGS SA
9. Experian plc
10. TUI AG

Source: *Forbes*, Forbes 2000 (annual), http://www.forbes.com, May 7, 2012.

788 ■ WORLD'S MOST ETHICAL BUSINESS SERVICES COMPANIES, 2012

Ranked by: Score based on five criteria: ethics and compliance program; reputation, leadership, and innovation; governance; corporate citizenship and responsibility; and culture of ethics. **Remarks:** Specific scores not provided; companies are listed alphabetically, not ranked. **Number listed:** 5

1. Accenture Ltd. (Ireland)
2. The Dun & Bradstreet Corp. (U.S.)
3. Noblis Inc. (U.S.)
4. Paychex Inc. (U.S.)
5. William E. Connor & Associates Ltd. (Hong Kong)

Source: *Ethisphere Magazine*, World's Most Ethical Companies (annual), http://www.ethisphere.com, 2012.

789 ■ WORLD'S MOST ETHICAL PROFESSIONAL, SCIENTIFIC, AND TECHNICAL SERVICES COMPANIES, 2012

Ranked by: Score based on five criteria: ethics and compliance program; reputation, leadership, and innovation; governance; corporate citizenship and responsibility; and culture of ethics. **Remarks:** Specific scores not provided; companies are listed alphabetically, not ranked. **Number listed:** 2

1. Concurrent Technologies Corp. (U.S.)
2. SRA International Inc. (U.S.)

Source: *Ethisphere Magazine*, World's Most Ethical Companies (annual), http://www.ethisphere.com, 2012.

790 ■ WORLD'S MOST VALUABLE COMMERCIAL SERVICES BRANDS, 2011

Ranked by: Brand value, in millions of U.S. dollars. **Remarks:** Also notes rank within the *Global 500* for current and previous year, figures for current and previous year, country, and brand rating. Ranking is available online only. **Number listed:** 10

1. PwC, with $14,296 million
2. KPMG, $10,555
3. Deloitte, $9,660
4. Ernst & Young, $8,538
5. Visa, $7,087
6. Randstad, $5,321
7. MasterCard, $5,177
8. Adecco, $2,998
9. Hertz, $2,719
10. McKinsey, $2,578

Source: *Global 500*, (annual), Brand Finance plc, March 2012.

Business Supplies

791 ■ CONNECTICUT'S LARGEST BUSINESS PRODUCTS AND SUPPLIES COMPANIES OVERALL, 2011

Ranked by: Score based on revenue, profits, assets, and market capitalization. **Remarks:** Specific scores not provided. Also notes overall rank in the *Forbes 2000* and figures for each criterion. **Number listed:** 2

1. Xerox Corp.
2. Pitney Bowes

Source: *Forbes*, Forbes 2000 (annual), http://www.forbes.com, May 7, 2012.

792 ■ JAPAN'S LARGEST BUSINESS PRODUCTS AND SUPPLIES COMPANIES OVERALL, 2011

Ranked by: Score based on revenue, profits, assets, and market capitalization. **Remarks:** Specific scores not provided. Also notes overall rank in the *Forbes 2000* and figures for each criterion. **Number listed:** 3

1. Canon Inc.
2. Ricoh Co., Ltd.
3. Seiko Epson Corp.

Source: *Forbes*, Forbes 2000 (annual), http://www.forbes.com, May 7, 2012.

793 ■ LARGEST U.S. BUSINESS PRODUCTS AND SUPPLIES COMPANIES OVERALL, 2011

Ranked by: Score based on revenue, profits, assets, and market capitalization. **Remarks:** Specific scores not provided. Also notes overall rank in the *Forbes 2000* and figures for each criterion. **Number listed:** 2

1. Xerox Corp.
2. Pitney Bowes Inc.

Source: *Forbes*, Forbes 2000 (annual), http://www.forbes.com, May 7, 2012.

794 ■ WORLD'S LARGEST BUSINESS PRODUCTS AND SUPPLIES COMPANIES OVERALL, 2011

Ranked by: Score based on revenue, profits, assets, and market capitalization. **Remarks:** Specific scores not provided. Also notes country, overall rank in the *Forbes 2000,* and figures for each criterion. **Number listed:** 5

1. Canon Inc.
2. Xerox Corp.
3. Ricoh Co., Ltd.
4. Pitney Bowes Inc.
5. Seiko Epson Corp.

Source: *Forbes*, Forbes 2000 (annual), http://www.forbes.com, May 7, 2012.

Business-to-Business Advertising

795 ■ BEST BUSINESS NEWS OUTLETS FOR BUSINESS-TO-BUSINESS ADVERTISING, 2012

Ranked by: Editorial score based on advertising revenue and audience, as well as determination of the power of the venue for b-to-b advertising. **Remarks:** Specific score not provided; publications are listed alphabetically, not ranked. Also notes phone number, website, circulation, advertising revenue, ad rate, and comments. **Number listed:** 13

1. *Barron's*/Barrons.com
2. Bloomberg.com
3. *Bloomberg Businessweek*/Businessweek.com
4. Business.com
5. BusinessInsider.com
6. *The Economist*/Economist.com
7. *Entrepreneur*/Entrepreneur.com
8. *Financial Times*/FT.com
9. *Forbes*/Forbes.com
10. *Fortune*/CNNMoney.com

Source: *BtoB*, Media Power 50 (annual), May 14, 2012, p. 42.

796 ■ BEST GENERAL NEWS OUTLETS FOR BUSINESS-TO-BUSINESS ADVERTISING, 2012

Ranked by: Editorial score based on advertising revenue and audience, as well as determination of the power of the venue for b-to-b advertising. **Remarks:** Specific score not provided; newspapers are listed alphabetically, not ranked. Also notes phone number, website, circulation, advertising revenue, ad rate, and comments. **Number listed:** 4

1. CNN
2. MSNBC.com
3. *The New York Times*/NYTimes.com
4. *USA Today*/USAToday.com

Source: *BtoB*, Media Power 50 (annual), May 14, 2012, p. 42.

797 ■ BEST INFORMATION TECHNOLOGY OUTLETS FOR BUSINESS-TO-BUSINESS ADVERTISING, 2012

Ranked by: Editorial score based on advertising revenue and audience, as well as determination of the power of the venue for b-to-b advertising. **Remarks:** Specific score not provided; magazines are listed alphabetically, not ranked. Also notes phone number, website, circulation, advertising revenue, ad rate, and comments. **Number listed:** 8

1. *CIO*/CIO.com
2. *Computerworld*/Computerworld.com
3. *CRN*/CRN.com
4. *EE Times*/EETimes.com
5. *Federal Computer Week*/FCW.com
6. *InformationWeek*/Informationweek.com
7. TechTarget
8. ZDnet.com

Source: *BtoB*, Media Power 50 (annual), May 14, 2012, p. 43-44.

798 ■ BEST ONLINE PORTALS FOR BUSINESS-TO-BUSINESS ADVERTISING, 2012

Ranked by: Editorial score based on advertising revenue and audience, as well as determination of the power of the venue for b-to-b advertising. **Remarks:** Specific score not provided; Internet sites are listed alphabetically, not ranked. Also notes phone number, website, traffic, advertising revenue, ad rate, and comments. **Number listed:** 3

1. Google.com
2. Manta.com
3. Weather.com

Source: *BtoB*, Media Power 50 (annual), May 14, 2012, p. 42-43.

799 ■ BEST OUT-OF-HOME OUTLETS FOR BUSINESS-TO-BUSINESS ADVERTISING, 2012

Ranked by: Editorial score based on advertising revenue and audience, as well as determination of the power of the venue for b-to-b advertising. **Remarks:** Specific score not provided; outlets are listed alphabetically, not ranked. Also notes phone number, website, circulation, advertising revenue, ad rate, and comments. **Number listed:** 3

1. Billboards at O'Hare International Airport (Chicago, IL)
2. Captivate Network
3. The Wall Street Journal Office Network

Source: *BtoB*, Media Power 50 (annual), May 14, 2012, p. 44.

800 ■ BEST SOCIAL MEDIA OUTLETS FOR BUSINESS-TO-BUSINESS ADVERTISING, 2012

Ranked by: Editorial score based on advertising revenue and audience, as well as determination of the power of the venue for b-to-b advertising. **Remarks:** Specific score not provided; Internet sites are listed alphabetically, not ranked. Also notes phone number, website, traffic, advertising revenue, ad rate, and comments. **Number listed:** 3

1. Facebook
2. LinkedIn
3. Twitter

Source: *BtoB*, Media Power 50 (annual), May 14, 2012, p. 43.

801 ■ BEST TELEVISION AND RADIO OUTLETS FOR BUSINESS-TO-BUSINESS ADVERTISING, 2012

Ranked by: Editorial score based on advertising revenue and audience, as well as determination of the power of the venue for b-to-b advertising. **Remarks:** Specific score not provided; broadcast venues are listed, not ranked. Also notes phone number, website, audience, advertising revenue, ad rate, and comments. **Number listed:** 7

1. "Squawk Box" (CNBC)
2. "Fox News Sunday" (Fox News)
3. "Meet the Press" (NBC)
4. National Football League
5. PGA Tour
6. NCAA Men's Basketball Tournament
7. CBS Radio

Source: *BtoB*, Media Power 50 (annual), May 14, 2012, p. 43.

802 ■ BEST VENUES FOR BUSINESS-TO-BUSINESS ADVERTISING, 2012

Ranked by: Editorial score based on advertising revenue and audience, as well as determination of the power of the venue for b-to-b advertising. **Remarks:** Specific score not provided. Also notes phone number, website, circulation/traffic/audience, advertising revenue, ad rate, and comments. **Number listed:** 10

1. *The Wall Street Journal*
2. Google
3. National Football League
4. *Bloomberg Businessweek*
5. *Financial Times*
6. CNN
7. LinkedIn
8. Facebook
9. PGA Tour
10. *Forbes*

Source: *BtoB*, Media Power 50 (annual), May 14, 2012, p. 37-41.

803 ■ BEST VERTICAL BUSINESS INFORMATION OUTLETS FOR BUSINESS-TO-BUSINESS ADVERTISING, 2012

Ranked by: Editorial score based on advertising revenue and audience, as well as determination of the power of the venue for

b-to-b advertising. **Remarks:** Specific score not provided; outlets are listed alphabetically, not ranked. Also notes phone number, website, circulation, advertising revenue, ad rate, and comments. **Number listed:** 9

1. *American Banker*
2. *Architectural Record*
3. *Automotive News*
4. *CFO*/CFO.com
5. GlobalSpec
6. *Meetings & Conventions*
7. *TWICE*
8. *Wired*
9. *WWD*/WWD.com

Source: *BtoB*, Media Power 50 (annual), May 14, 2012, p. 44.

Business Travel

804 ■ TOP COMPANIES IN BUSINESS AIR TRAVEL, 2010

Ranked by: Volume of airline tickets purchased for business travel, in million of dollars. **Number listed:** 100

1. International Business Machines Corp. (IBM), with $545 million
2. General Electric Co., $285.7
3. Boeing Co., $263.2
4. Deloitte LLP, $263
5. General Dynamics Corp., $256
6. Accenture Ltd., $240
7. Lockheed Martin Corp., $221
8. Exxon Mobil Corp., $220
9. World Bank, $195
10. Bank of America Corp., $182

Source: *Business Travel News*, Corporate Travel 100 (annual), September 26, 2011, p. 12.

Business Women
See: **Women Executives**

Cable Networks

805 ■ TOP CABLE NETWORK OWNERS IN THE U.S., 2010

Ranked by: Net U.S. cable network revenue, in millions of dollars. **Remarks:** Also notes rank and figures for previous year, percent change, and top broadcast property. **Number listed:** 10

1. Walt Disney Co., with $10,059 million
2. Time Warner Inc., $9,419
3. Viacom Inc., $6,476
4. Comcast Corp., $6,253
5. News Corp., $5,829
6. A & E Television Networks, $2,774
7. Discovery Communications Inc., $2,363
8. Scripps Networks Interactive, $1,867
9. CBS Corp., $1,475
10. Liberty Media Corp., $1,247

Source: *Advertising Age*, 100 Leading Media Companies (annual), October 3, 2011, p. 52.

Cable Television Industry—Advertising

806 ■ TOP ADVERTISERS ON CABLE TELEVISION NETWORKS, 2010

Ranked by: Measured advertising spending, in millions of dollars. **Remarks:** Also notes percent change from previous year. **Number listed:** 10

1. Procter & Gamble Co., with $893.4 million
2. Johnson & Johnson, $313.1
3. General Mills Inc., $313
4. AT&T Inc., $308.3
5. General Motors Co., $293.6
6. Berkshire Hathaway Inc., $274.1
7. Yum! Brands Inc., $257.6
8. Walt Disney Co., $234.5
9. Sony Corp., $218.1
10. Time Warner Inc., $210.4

Source: *Advertising Age*, Leading National Advertisers (annual), June 20, 2011, p. 16.

Cafeterias
See: **Restaurants**

Candy Industry

807 ■ TOP CANDY STORE FRANCHISES, 2012

Ranked by: Cumulative score based on financial strength and stability, growth rate, size of the system, number of years in business, the length of time franchising, start-up costs, litigation, percentage of terminations, and whether the company provides financing. **Remarks:** Specific scores not provided. Also notes overall rank within the *Franchise 500*, contact information, description, year founded, year started franchising, states where registered, available U.S. regions, where seeking foreign expansion, number of franchised and company-owned units for past three years, start-up costs, franchise fees, royalty fees, and type of financing available. **Number listed:** 3

1. Kilwin's Chocolates Franchise
2. Rocky Mountain Chocolate Factory
3. Fuzziwig's Candy Factory

Source: *Entrepreneur*, Franchise 500 (annual), January 2012, p. 174-175.

808 ■ WORLD'S LARGEST CANDY COMPANIES, 2011

Ranked by: Net sales, in millions of U.S. dollars. **Remarks:** Also notes headquarters, number of plants and employees, chief officer, and types of products manufactured. **Number listed:** 100

1. Kraft Foods Inc. (U.S.), with $19,965 million
2. Mars Inc. (U.S.), $16,200
3. Nestle SA (Switzerland), $12,808
4. Ferrero SpA (Italy), $9,612
5. Hershey Foods Corp. (U.S.), $6,112
6. Perfetti Van Melle SpA (Italy/Netherlands), $3,333
7. Haribo GmbH & Co. (Switzerland), $2,885
8. Chocoladefabriken Lindt & Sprungli AG (Switzerland), $2,796

9. August Storck KG (Germany), $2,205
10. Yildiz Holding (Turkey), $2,095

Source: *Candy Industry*, Global Top 100 (annual), January 2012, p. 52+.

Capital Equipment Industry
See: **Industrial Equipment Industry**

Capital Goods

809 ■ AMERICA'S LARGEST PRIVATE CAPITAL GOODS COMPANIES, 2010

Ranked by: Revenue, in billions of dollars. **Remarks:** Also notes headquarters, number of employees, and overall rank in the *America's Largest Private Companies* list. Ranking is available online only, not in print. **Number listed:** 5

1. Graybar Electric Co., Inc., with $4.62 billion
2. Southwire Co., $4.3
3. McJunkin Red Man Holding Corp., $3.85
4. Consolidated Electrical Distributors Inc., $3.80
5. Heico Cos., $2.3

Source: *Forbes*, America's Largest Private Companies (annual), http://www.forbes.com, December 5, 2011.

810 ■ BEST SMALL CAPITAL GOODS COMPANIES IN AMERICA, 2011

Ranked by: Score based on revenue, profits, and return on equity for the past 12 months and five years. **Remarks:** Specific scores not provided. Also notes rank in the overall *100 Best Small Companies in America*. To qualify, companies must have revenues between $5 million and $1 billion, a net margin above five percent, and share price above $5. List is available online only. **Number listed:** 6

1. Lindsay
2. Middleby
3. Raven Industries
4. Preformed Line Products
5. Chart Industries
6. Altra Holdings

Source: *Forbes*, Best Small Companies in America (annual), November 7, 2011.

Capital Spending

811 ■ COMPANIES WITH THE BIGGEST CAPITAL INVESTMENT IN CORPORATE FACILITY PROJECTS OUTSIDE THE U.S., 2011

Ranked by: Total capital investment in new and expanded facilities located outside the U.S., in millions of U.S. dollars. **Remarks:** Also notes city, country, type of facility, and product line. **Number listed:** 5

1. Chevron Corp./Kuwait Foreign Petroleum Exploration/Shell, with $29,000 million
2. Canadian Natural Resources Ltd., $4,000
3. Rio Tinto Alcan, $3,600
4. Daimler AG/Beijing Automotive Industry Corp., $2,700
5. SK Global Chemical Co., $2,400

812 ■ COMPANIES GENERATING THE MOST JOBS IN CORPORATE FACILITY PROJECTS OUTSIDE THE U.S., 2011

Ranked by: Total number of new jobs created in new and expanded facilities located outside the U.S. **Remarks:** Also notes city, country, type of facility, and product line. **Number listed:** 6

1. Ford Motor Co., with 5,000 jobs
2. Infosys Technologies, 4,000
3. Amazon.com Inc., 3,300
4. Honda de Mexico, 3,200
5. International Business Machines Corp. (IBM), 3,000
5. Mazda/Sumitomo Corp., 3,000

813 ■ COMPANIES WITH THE LARGEST CORPORATE FACILITY PROJECTS OUTSIDE THE U.S., 2011

Ranked by: Total size of new and expanded facilities located outside the U.S., in thousands of square feet. **Remarks:** Also notes city, country, type of facility, and product line. **Number listed:** 5

1. IBM/Range Technology Development Co., with 6,673 thousand sq.ft.
2. Hankook Tire Co., 6,400
3. BEFUT International, 3,229
4. Henkel KgaA, 1,614
5. Anheuser-Busch InBev SA/NV, 1,463

Carbon

814 ■ AUSTRALIA'S BEST COMPANIES IN CARBON EMISSIONS, 2011

Ranked by: Number of Scope 3 emission categories disclosed. Within ties, companies are then ranked by combined emissions intensity across all three Scopes. **Remarks:** Also notes data for Scopes 1 and 2. **Number listed:** 5

1. Westpac Banking Corp., with 5 categories
2. National Australia Bank Ltd., 5
3. Transurban Group, 5
4. Telstra Corp., Ltd., 4
5. Wesfarmers Ltd., 4

815 ■ AUSTRALIA'S WORST COMPANIES IN CARBON EMISSIONS, 2011

Ranked by: Number of Scope 3 emission categories disclosed. Within ties, companies are then ranked by combined emissions intensity across all three Scopes. **Remarks:** Also notes data for Scopes 1 and 2. **Number listed:** 5

1. WorleyParsons Ltd., with 0 categories
2. AMP Ltd., 0
2. Westfield Retail Trust, 0

2. ASX Ltd., 0
5. Origin Energy Ltd., 0

816 ■ BEST ASIA-PACIFIC COMPANIES IN CARBON EMISSIONS, 2011

Ranked by: Number of Scope 3 emission categories disclosed. Within ties, companies are then ranked by combined emissions intensity across all three Scopes. **Remarks:** Also notes data for Scopes 1 and 2. **Number listed:** 5

1. Westpac Banking Corp., with 5 categories
2. National Australia Bank Ltd., 5
3. Transurban Group, 5
4. Telstra Corp., Ltd., 4
5. Wesfarmers Ltd., 4

817 ■ BEST BRICS COMPANIES IN CARBON EMISSIONS, 2011

Ranked by: Number of Scope 3 emission categories disclosed. Within ties, companies are then ranked by combined emissions intensity across all three Scopes. **Remarks:** BRICS is an acronym referring to the countries Brazil, Russia, India, China, and South Africa. Also notes data for Scopes 1 and 2. **Number listed:** 5

1. Gold Fields Ltd., with 8 categories
2. Banco Santander (Brasil) SA, 6
3. Vale SA, 6
4. Itau Unibanco Holding, 5
5. Infrastructure Development Finance Co., Ltd., 4

818 ■ BEST U.S. COMPANIES IN CARBON EMISSIONS, 2011

Ranked by: Number of Scope 3 emission categories disclosed. Within ties, companies are then ranked by combined emissions intensity across all three Scopes. **Remarks:** Also notes data for Scopes 1 and 2. **Number listed:** 5

1. Baxter International Inc., with 6 categories
2. United Parcel Service Inc. (UPS), 5
3. Praxair Inc., 5
4. Bank of America Corp., 4
5. E. I. du Pont de Nemours & Co., 4

819 ■ BRAZIL'S BEST COMPANIES IN CARBON EMISSIONS, 2011

Ranked by: Number of Scope 3 emission categories disclosed. Within ties, companies are then ranked by combined emissions intensity across all three Scopes. **Remarks:** Also notes rank within the overall *Top 300* and data for Scopes 1 and 2. **Number listed:** 5

1. Banco Santander (Brasil) SA, with 6 categories
2. Vale SA, 6
3. Itau Unibanco Holding, 5
4. Redecard S/A, 3

5. Companhia Energetica de Minas Gerais (Ce-mig), 3

Source: *ET BRICS 300*, (annual), Environmental Investment Organisation, 2011.

820 ■ BRAZIL'S WORST COMPANIES IN CARBON EMISSIONS, 2011

Ranked by: Number of Scope 3 emission categories disclosed. Within ties, companies are then ranked by combined emissions intensity across all three Scopes. **Remarks:** Also notes rank within the overall *Top 300* and data for Scopes 1 and 2. **Number listed:** 5

1. Companhia de Saneamento Basico do Estado de Sao Paulo (SABESP), with 0 categories
2. OGX Petroleo, 0
2. HRT Petroleo, 0
4. Companhia Siderurgica Nacional, 0
4. Gerdau PN, 0

Source: *ET BRICS 300*, (annual), Environmental Investment Organisation, 2011.

821 ■ CANADA'S BEST COMPANIES IN CARBON EMISSIONS, 2011

Ranked by: Number of Scope 3 emission categories disclosed. Within ties, companies are then ranked by combined emissions intensity across all three Scopes. **Remarks:** Also notes data for Scopes 1 and 2. **Number listed:** 5

1. BCE Inc., with 1 categories
2. Telus Corp., 1
3. Toronto-Dominion Bank, 1
4. Talisman Engineering, 0
5. Barrick Gold Corp., 0

Source: *ET North America 300*, (annual), Environmental Investment Organisation, 2011.

822 ■ CANADA'S WORST COMPANIES IN CARBON EMISSIONS, 2011

Ranked by: Number of Scope 3 emission categories disclosed. Within ties, companies are then ranked by combined emissions intensity across all three Scopes. **Remarks:** Also notes data for Scopes 1 and 2. **Number listed:** 5

1. Silver Wheaton Corp., with 0 categories
1. Eldorado Gold Corp., 0
3. Crescent Point Energy, 0
3. Canadian Oil Sands Ltd., 0
5. Thomson Reuters Corp., 0

Source: *ET North America 300*, (annual), Environmental Investment Organisation, 2011.

823 ■ CHINA'S BEST COMPANIES IN CARBON EMISSIONS, 2011

Ranked by: Number of Scope 3 emission categories disclosed. Within ties, companies are then ranked by combined emissions intensity across all three Scopes. **Remarks:** Also notes data for Scopes 1 and 2. **Number listed:** 5

1. China Telecommunications Corp., with 0 categories
2. China Coal Energy Co., Ltd., 0
3. China Minsheng Banking Corp., 0
3. PICC Property and Casualty Co., Ltd., 0

3. China CITIC Bank, 0

Source: *ET BRICS 300*, (annual), Environmental Investment Organisation, 2011.

824 ■ CHINA'S WORST COMPANIES IN CARBON EMISSIONS, 2011

Ranked by: Number of Scope 3 emission categories disclosed. Within ties, companies are then ranked by combined emissions intensity across all three Scopes. **Remarks:** Also notes data for Scopes 1 and 2. **Number listed:** 5

1. Anhui Conch Cement Co., Ltd., with 0 categories
1. China National Building Material Co., Ltd., 0
1. China Communications Construction Group Ltd., 0
4. China Shenhua Energy Co., Ltd., 0
4. Yanzhou Coal Mining Co., 0

Source: *ET BRICS 300*, (annual), Environmental Investment Organisation, 2011.

825 ■ EUROPE'S BEST COMPANIES IN CARBON EMISSIONS, 2011

Ranked by: Number of Scope 3 emission categories disclosed. Within ties, companies are then ranked by combined emissions intensity across all three Scopes. **Remarks:** Also notes data for Scopes 1 and 2. **Number listed:** 5

1. BASF SE, with 15 categories
2. Anglo American plc, 8
3. Alcatel-Lucent, 7
4. Commerzbank AG, 5
5. Xstrata plc, 5

Source: *ET Europe 300*, (annual), Environmental Investment Organisation, 2011.

826 ■ EUROPE'S WORST COMPANIES IN CARBON EMISSIONS, 2011

Ranked by: Number of Scope 3 emission categories disclosed. Within ties, companies are then ranked by combined emissions intensity across all three Scopes. **Remarks:** Also notes data for Scopes 1 and 2. **Number listed:** 5

1. Pkagrupa Energetycna, with 0 categories
2. Bouygues SA, 0
3. JSW, 0
4. KGHM, 0
5. Aggreko plc, 0

Source: *ET Europe 300*, (annual), Environmental Investment Organisation, 2011.

827 ■ FRANCE'S BEST COMPANIES IN CARBON EMISSIONS, 2011

Ranked by: Number of Scope 3 emission categories disclosed. Within ties, companies are then ranked by combined emissions intensity across all three Scopes. **Remarks:** Also notes data for Scopes 1 and 2. **Number listed:** 5

1. Alcatel-Lucent, with 7 categories
2. Vallourec SA, 4
3. LVMH Moet Hennessy Louis Vuitton SA, 2
4. PPR SA, 2
5. Lafarge SA, 2

Source: *ET Europe 300*, (annual), Environmental Investment Organisation, 2011.

828 ■ FRANCE'S WORST COMPANIES IN CARBON EMISSIONS, 2011

Ranked by: Number of Scope 3 emission categories disclosed. Within ties, companies are then ranked by combined emissions intensity across all three Scopes. **Remarks:** Also notes data for Scopes 1 and 2. **Number listed:** 5

1. Bouygues SA, with 0 categories
2. Sodexo, 0
3. Safran SA, 0
4. Eutelsat Communications, 0
5. Hermes International, 0

Source: *ET Europe 300*, (annual), Environmental Investment Organisation, 2011.

829 ■ GERMANY'S BEST COMPANIES IN CARBON EMISSIONS, 2011

Ranked by: Number of Scope 3 emission categories disclosed. Within ties, companies are then ranked by combined emissions intensity across all three Scopes. **Remarks:** Also notes data for Scopes 1 and 2. **Number listed:** 5

1. BASF SE, with 15 categories
2. Commerzbank AG, 5
3. SAP AG, 3
4. RWE AG, 3
5. Deutsche Post AG, 2

Source: *ET Europe 300*, (annual), Environmental Investment Organisation, 2011.

830 ■ GERMANY'S WORST COMPANIES IN CARBON EMISSIONS, 2011

Ranked by: Number of Scope 3 emission categories disclosed. Within ties, companies are then ranked by combined emissions intensity across all three Scopes. **Remarks:** Also notes data for Scopes 1 and 2. **Number listed:** 5

1. GEA Group AG, with 0 categories
2. Kabel Deutschland, 0
3. Infineon Technologies AG, 0
4. Fresenius Medical Care AG, 0
4. Fresenius SE, 0

Source: *ET Europe 300*, (annual), Environmental Investment Organisation, 2011.

831 ■ HONG KONG'S BEST COMPANIES IN CARBON EMISSIONS, 2011

Ranked by: Number of Scope 3 emission categories disclosed. Within ties, companies are then ranked by combined emissions intensity across all three Scopes. **Remarks:** Also notes data for Scopes 1 and 2. **Number listed:** 5

1. CLP Holdings Ltd., with 0 categories
2. Swire Pacific Ltd., 0
3. Power Assets Holdings Ltd., 0
4. Lenovo Group Ltd., 0
5. Hysan Development Co., Ltd., 0

Source: *ET BRICS 300*, (annual), Environmental Investment Organisation, 2011.

832 ■ HONG KONG'S WORST COMPANIES IN CARBON EMISSIONS, 2011

Ranked by: Number of Scope 3 emission categories disclosed. Within ties, companies are then ranked by combined emissions intensity across all three Scopes. **Remarks:** Also notes data for Scopes 1 and 2. **Number listed:** 5

1. ENN Energy Holdings Ltd., with 0 categories
2. Cheung Kong Infrastructure Holdings Ltd., 0
2. China Resource Power Holdings Co., Ltd., 0
2. GCL-Poly Energy Holdings Ltd., 0
5. NWS Holdings Ltd., 0

Source: *ET BRICS 300*, (annual), Environmental Investment Organisation, 2011.

833 ■ INDIA'S BEST COMPANIES IN CARBON EMISSIONS, 2011

Ranked by: Number of Scope 3 emission categories disclosed. Within ties, companies are then ranked by combined emissions intensity across all three Scopes. **Remarks:** Also notes data for Scopes 1 and 2. **Number listed:** 5

1. Infrastructure Development Finance Co., Ltd., with 4 categories
2. Larsen & Toubro Ltd., 2
3. Bharat Petroleum Corp., 0
4. Reliance Industries Ltd., 0
5. Tata Power Co., Ltd., 0

Source: *ET BRICS 300*, (annual), Environmental Investment Organisation, 2011.

834 ■ INDIA'S WORST COMPANIES IN CARBON EMISSIONS, 2011

Ranked by: Number of Scope 3 emission categories disclosed. Within ties, companies are then ranked by combined emissions intensity across all three Scopes. **Remarks:** Also notes data for Scopes 1 and 2. **Number listed:** 5

1. NTPC Ltd., with 0 categories
1. Power Grid Corporation of India Ltd., 0
3. Asian Paints, 0
3. Grasim Industries Ltd., 0
3. Jaiprakash Associates Ltd., 0

Source: *ET BRICS 300*, (annual), Environmental Investment Organisation, 2011.

835 ■ INDONESIA'S BEST COMPANIES IN CARBON EMISSIONS, 2011

Ranked by: Number of Scope 3 emission categories disclosed. Within ties, companies are then ranked by combined emissions intensity across all three Scopes. **Remarks:** Also notes data for Scopes 1 and 2. **Number listed:** 5

1. PT Astra International Tbk, with 0 categories
2. PT Telekomunikasi Indonesia Tbk, 0
3. Bank Rakyat Indonesia, 0
3. Bank Mandiri, 0
3. Bank Central Asia, 0

Source: *ET Asia-Pacific 300*, (annual), Environmental Investment Organisation, 2011.

836 ■ INDONESIA'S WORST COMPANIES IN CARBON EMISSIONS, 2011

Ranked by: Number of Scope 3 emission categories disclosed. Within ties, companies are then ranked by combined emissions intensity across all three Scopes. **Remarks:** Also notes data for Scopes 1 and 2. **Number listed:** 3

1. Adaro Energy, with 0 categories

1. Bumi Resources, 0
3. United Tractors, 0

Source: *ET Asia-Pacific 300*, (annual), Environmental Investment Organisation, 2011.

837 ■ ITALY'S BEST COMPANIES IN CARBON EMISSIONS, 2011

Ranked by: Number of Scope 3 emission categories disclosed. Within ties, companies are then ranked by combined emissions intensity across all three Scopes. **Remarks:** Also notes data for Scopes 1 and 2. **Number listed:** 5

1. Fiat SpA, with 3 categories
2. UniCredit SpA, 2
3. Terna, 2
4. Enel SpA, 2
5. ENI SpA, 2

Source: *ET Europe 300*, (annual), Environmental Investment Organisation, 2011.

838 ■ ITALY'S WORST COMPANIES IN CARBON EMISSIONS, 2011

Ranked by: Number of Scope 3 emission categories disclosed. Within ties, companies are then ranked by combined emissions intensity across all three Scopes. **Remarks:** Also notes data for Scopes 1 and 2. **Number listed:** 5

1. Luxottica Group SpA, with 0 categories
2. Mediobanca, 0
3. Saipem SpA, 0
4. Fiat Industrial SpA, 0
5. Atlantia SpA, 0

Source: *ET Europe 300*, (annual), Environmental Investment Organisation, 2011.

839 ■ JAPAN'S BEST COMPANIES IN CARBON EMISSIONS, 2011

Ranked by: Number of Scope 3 emission categories disclosed. Within ties, companies are then ranked by combined emissions intensity across all three Scopes. **Remarks:** Also notes data for Scopes 1 and 2. **Number listed:** 5

1. Sony Corp., with 3 categories
2. Sharp Corp., 2
3. Toshiba Corp., 2
4. Panasonic, 1
5. Sumitomo Electric Industries Ltd., 1

Source: *ET Asia-Pacific 300*, (annual), Environmental Investment Organisation, 2011.

840 ■ JAPAN'S WORST COMPANIES IN CARBON EMISSIONS, 2011

Ranked by: Number of Scope 3 emission categories disclosed. Within ties, companies are then ranked by combined emissions intensity across all three Scopes. **Remarks:** Also notes data for Scopes 1 and 2. **Number listed:** 5

1. Shikoku Electric Power, with 0 categories
2. Daito Trust Construction, 0
3. Secom, 0
4. Kintetsu, 0
4. Odakyu Electric, 0

Source: *ET Asia-Pacific 300*, (annual), Environmental Investment Organisation, 2011.

841 ■ MALAYSIA'S BEST COMPANIES IN CARBON EMISSIONS, 2011

Ranked by: Number of Scope 3 emission categories disclosed. Within ties, companies are then ranked by combined emissions intensity across all three Scopes. **Remarks:** Also notes data for Scopes 1 and 2. **Number listed:** 5

1. Malayan Banking, with 0 categories
1. CIMB Group Holdings Bhd., 0
1. Public Bank, 0
4. Axiata, 0
5. Petronas Chemicals Group, 0

Source: *ET Asia-Pacific 300*, (annual), Environmental Investment Organisation, 2011.

842 ■ MALAYSIA'S WORST COMPANIES IN CARBON EMISSIONS, 2011

Ranked by: Number of Scope 3 emission categories disclosed. Within ties, companies are then ranked by combined emissions intensity across all three Scopes. **Remarks:** Also notes data for Scopes 1 and 2. **Number listed:** 3

1. Sime Darby, with 0 categories
2. Genting, 0
3. Tenaga Nasional, 0

Source: *ET Asia-Pacific 300*, (annual), Environmental Investment Organisation, 2011.

843 ■ MEXICO'S BEST COMPANIES IN CARBON EMISSIONS, 2011

Ranked by: Number of Scope 3 emission categories disclosed. Within ties, companies are then ranked by combined emissions intensity across all three Scopes. **Remarks:** Also notes data for Scopes 1 and 2. **Number listed:** 5

1. Fomento Economico Mexicano, SA de CV (FEMSA), with 0 categories
2. Grupo Mexico SA de CV, 0
3. Walmart de Mexico y Centroamerica, 0
4. America Movil, SA de CV, 0
5. Grupo Financiero Inbursa, SAB de CV, 0

Source: *ET North America 300*, (annual), Environmental Investment Organisation, 2011.

844 ■ THE NETHERLANDS' BEST COMPANIES IN CARBON EMISSIONS, 2011

Ranked by: Number of Scope 3 emission categories disclosed. Within ties, companies are then ranked by combined emissions intensity across all three Scopes. **Remarks:** Also notes data for Scopes 1 and 2. **Number listed:** 5

1. Koninklijke KPN NV (Royal KPN NV), with 2 categories
2. Koninklijke Philips Electronics NV (Royal Philips Electronics NV), 2
3. AEGON NV, 1
4. Royal Dutch Shell plc, 1
5. Akzo Nobel NV, 1

Source: *ET Europe 300*, (annual), Environmental Investment Organisation, 2011.

845 ■ THE NETHERLANDS' WORST COMPANIES IN CARBON EMISSIONS, 2011

Ranked by: Number of Scope 3 emission categories disclosed. Within ties, companies are then ranked by combined emissions intensity across all three Scopes. **Remarks:** Also notes data for Scopes 1 and 2. **Number listed:** 5

1. Wolters Kluwer NV, with 0 categories
2. ING Groep NV, 0
3. ArcelorMittal, 0
4. Koninklijke DSM NV (Royal DSM NV), 0
5. Koninklijke Ahold NV (Royal Ahold NV), 0

Source: *ET Europe 300*, (annual), Environmental Investment Organisation, 2011.

846 ■ NORTH AMERICA'S BEST COMPANIES IN CARBON EMISSIONS, 2011

Ranked by: Number of Scope 3 emission categories disclosed. Within ties, companies are then ranked by combined emissions intensity across all three Scopes. **Remarks:** Also notes data for Scopes 1 and 2. **Number listed:** 5

1. Baxter International Inc., with 6 categories
2. United Parcel Service Inc. (UPS), 5
3. Praxair Inc., 5
4. Bank of America Corp., 4
5. E. I. du Pont de Nemours & Co., 4

Source: *ET North America 300*, (annual), Environmental Investment Organisation, 2011.

847 ■ NORTH AMERICA'S WORST COMPANIES IN CARBON EMISSIONS, 2011

Ranked by: Number of Scope 3 emission categories disclosed. Within ties, companies are then ranked by combined emissions intensity across all three Scopes. **Remarks:** Also notes data for Scopes 1 and 2. **Number listed:** 5

1. FirstEnergy Corp., with 0 categories
1. Edison International, 0
1. Entergy Corp., 0
4. Honeywell International Inc., 0
4. Silver Wheaton Corp., 0

Source: *ET North America 300*, (annual), Environmental Investment Organisation, 2011.

848 ■ THE PHILIPPINE'S BEST COMPANIES IN CARBON EMISSIONS, 2011

Ranked by: Number of Scope 3 emission categories disclosed. Within ties, companies are then ranked by combined emissions intensity across all three Scopes. **Remarks:** Also notes data for Scopes 1 and 2. **Number listed:** 4

1. Ayala Land, with 0 categories
2. Aboitiz Power, 0
3. Philippines Long Distance Telephone, 0
4. Aboitiz Equity Ventures, 0

Source: *ET Asia-Pacific 300*, (annual), Environmental Investment Organisation, 2011.

849 ■ RUSSIA'S BEST COMPANIES IN CARBON EMISSIONS, 2011

Ranked by: Number of Scope 3 emission categories disclosed. Within ties, companies are then ranked by combined emissions intensity across all three Scopes. **Remarks:** Also notes rank within the overall *Top 300* and data for Scopes 1 and 2. **Number listed:** 5

1. OAO TNK-BP Holding, with 0 categories
2. RusHydro JSC, 0

2. Novolipetsk Steel, 0
4. OJSC Novolipetsk, 0
5. OAO Tatneft, 0

Source: *ET BRICS 300*, (annual), Environmental Investment Organisation, 2011.

850 ■ RUSSIA'S WORST COMPANIES IN CARBON EMISSIONS, 2011

Ranked by: Number of Scope 3 emission categories disclosed. Within ties, companies are then ranked by combined emissions intensity across all three Scopes. **Remarks:** Also notes rank within the overall *Top 300* and data for Scopes 1 and 2. **Number listed:** 5

1. Federal Grid Co., with 0 categories
1. JSC Inter RAO UES, 0
3. LSR Group, 0
4. Polyus Gold, 0
4. OJSC Polyus Gold, 0

Source: *ET BRICS 300*, (annual), Environmental Investment Organisation, 2011.

851 ■ SINGAPORE'S BEST COMPANIES IN CARBON EMISSIONS, 2011

Ranked by: Number of Scope 3 emission categories disclosed. Within ties, companies are then ranked by combined emissions intensity across all three Scopes. **Remarks:** Also notes data for Scopes 1 and 2. **Number listed:** 5

1. Singapore Telecommunications Ltd., with 1 categories
2. Singapore Exchange Ltd., 0
2. CapitaLand Ltd., 0
4. Keppel Corp., Ltd., 0
5. Singapore Airlines Ltd., 0

Source: *ET Asia-Pacific 300*, (annual), Environmental Investment Organisation, 2011.

852 ■ SINGAPORE'S WORST COMPANIES IN CARBON EMISSIONS, 2011

Ranked by: Number of Scope 3 emission categories disclosed. Within ties, companies are then ranked by combined emissions intensity across all three Scopes. **Remarks:** Also notes data for Scopes 1 and 2. **Number listed:** 5

1. Jardine Strategic Holdings Ltd., with 0 categories
1. Jardine Matheson Holdings Ltd., 0
1. Nobel Group, 0
1. Fraser & Neave Ltd., 0
5. Wilmar International Ltd., 0

Source: *ET Asia-Pacific 300*, (annual), Environmental Investment Organisation, 2011.

853 ■ SOUTH AFRICA'S BEST COMPANIES IN CARBON EMISSIONS, 2011

Ranked by: Number of Scope 3 emission categories disclosed. Within ties, companies are then ranked by combined emissions intensity across all three Scopes. **Remarks:** Also notes data for Scopes 1 and 2. **Number listed:** 5

1. Gold Fields Ltd., with 8 categories
2. Woolworths Holdings Ltd., 4
3. Standard Bank Group, 2

4. Sasol Ltd., 1

5. ABSA Group, 0

Source: *ET BRICS 300*, (annual), Environmental Investment Organisation, 2011.

854 ■ SOUTH AFRICA'S WORST COMPANIES IN CARBON EMISSIONS, 2011

Ranked by: Number of Scope 3 emission categories disclosed. Within ties, companies are then ranked by combined emissions intensity across all three Scopes. **Remarks:** Also notes data for Scopes 1 and 2. **Number listed:** 5

1. Remgro Ltd., with 0 categories

2. Tiger Brands Ltd., 0

2. Pioneer Food Group Ltd., 0

2. Shoprite, 0

2. SPAR Group Inc., 0

Source: *ET BRICS 300*, (annual), Environmental Investment Organisation, 2011.

855 ■ SOUTH KOREA'S BEST COMPANIES IN CARBON EMISSIONS, 2011

Ranked by: Number of Scope 3 emission categories disclosed. Within ties, companies are then ranked by combined emissions intensity across all three Scopes. **Remarks:** Also notes data for Scopes 1 and 2. **Number listed:** 5

1. Pohang Iron & Steel Co., Ltd. (POSCO), with 3 categories

2. LG Electronics Inc., 2

3. LG Corp., 2

4. LG Household & Health Care, 1

5. Samsung C & T Corp., 1

Source: *ET Asia-Pacific 300*, (annual), Environmental Investment Organisation, 2011.

856 ■ SOUTH KOREA'S WORST COMPANIES IN CARBON EMISSIONS, 2011

Ranked by: Number of Scope 3 emission categories disclosed. Within ties, companies are then ranked by combined emissions intensity across all three Scopes. **Remarks:** Also notes data for Scopes 1 and 2. **Number listed:** 5

1. Samsung Engineering Co., Ltd., with 0 categories

1. Daewoo Engineering & Construction Co., Ltd., 0

3. Honam Petrochemical Corp., 0

4. SK Innovation Co., Ltd., 0

4. GS Holdings Co., Ltd., 0

Source: *ET Asia-Pacific 300*, (annual), Environmental Investment Organisation, 2011.

857 ■ SPAIN'S BEST COMPANIES IN CARBON EMISSIONS, 2011

Ranked by: Number of Scope 3 emission categories disclosed. Within ties, companies are then ranked by combined emissions intensity across all three Scopes. **Remarks:** Also notes data for Scopes 1 and 2. **Number listed:** 5

1. Banco Popular Espanol, with 2 categories

2. Iberdrola SA, 2

3. Telefonica SA, 1

4. Industria de Diseno Textil SA (Inditex), 1

5. Gas Natural SDG SA, 1

Source: *ET Europe 300*, (annual), Environmental Investment Organisation, 2011.

858 ■ SPAIN'S WORST COMPANIES IN CARBON EMISSIONS, 2011

Ranked by: Number of Scope 3 emission categories disclosed. Within ties, companies are then ranked by combined emissions intensity across all three Scopes. **Remarks:** Also notes data for Scopes 1 and 2. **Number listed:** 5

1. Red Electric Corp., with 0 categories

2. Amadeus IT Holding, 0

3. Banco Santander SA, 0

3. Banco Bilbao Vizcaya Argentaria SA (BBVA), 0

5. Banco de Sabadell, 0

Source: *ET Europe 300*, (annual), Environmental Investment Organisation, 2011.

859 ■ SWEDEN'S BEST COMPANIES IN CARBON EMISSIONS, 2011

Ranked by: Number of Scope 3 emission categories disclosed. Within ties, companies are then ranked by combined emissions intensity across all three Scopes. **Remarks:** Also notes data for Scopes 1 and 2. **Number listed:** 5

1. Telefonaktiebolaget LM Ericsson, with 3 categories

2. SKF AB, 2

3. SCA, 0

4. Sandvik AB, 0

5. TeliaSonera AB, 0

Source: *ET Europe 300*, (annual), Environmental Investment Organisation, 2011.

860 ■ SWEDEN'S WORST COMPANIES IN CARBON EMISSIONS, 2011

Ranked by: Number of Scope 3 emission categories disclosed. Within ties, companies are then ranked by combined emissions intensity across all three Scopes. **Remarks:** Also notes data for Scopes 1 and 2. **Number listed:** 5

1. Investor AB, with 0 categories

1. Svenska Handelsbanken AB, 0

1. Swedbank, 0

4. Getinge, 0

5. Assa Abloy AB, 0

Source: *ET Europe 300*, (annual), Environmental Investment Organisation, 2011.

861 ■ SWITZERLAND'S BEST COMPANIES IN CARBON EMISSIONS, 2011

Ranked by: Number of Scope 3 emission categories disclosed. Within ties, companies are then ranked by combined emissions intensity across all three Scopes. **Remarks:** Also notes data for Scopes 1 and 2. **Number listed:** 5

1. UBS AG, with 3 categories

2. Syngenta AG, 2

3. Roche Holding Ltd., 1

4. Compagnie Financiere Richemont SA, 1

5. ABB Ltd., 1

Source: *ET Europe 300*, (annual), Environmental Investment Organisation, 2011.

862 ■ SWITZERLAND'S WORST COMPANIES IN CARBON EMISSIONS, 2011

Ranked by: Number of Scope 3 emission categories disclosed. Within ties, companies are then ranked by combined emissions intensity across all three Scopes. **Remarks:** Also notes data for Scopes 1 and 2. **Number listed:** 5

1. The Swatch Group Ltd., with 0 categories
2. Swiss Prime Site, 0
3. Actelion, 0
4. Synthes Inc., 0
5. Adecco SA, 0

Source: *ET Europe 300*, (annual), Environmental Investment Organisation, 2011.

863 ■ TAIWAN'S BEST COMPANIES IN CARBON EMISSIONS, 2011

Ranked by: Number of Scope 3 emission categories disclosed. Within ties, companies are then ranked by combined emissions intensity across all three Scopes. **Remarks:** Also notes data for Scopes 1 and 2. **Number listed:** 5

1. Asustek Computer Inc., with 1 categories
2. Advanced Semiconductor Engineering Inc., 0
3. Taiwan Semiconductor Manufacturing Co., Ltd., 0
4. United Microelectronics Corp., 0
5. Delta Electronics Inc., 0

Source: *ET Asia-Pacific 300*, (annual), Environmental Investment Organisation, 2011.

864 ■ TAIWAN'S WORST COMPANIES IN CARBON EMISSIONS, 2011

Ranked by: Number of Scope 3 emission categories disclosed. Within ties, companies are then ranked by combined emissions intensity across all three Scopes. **Remarks:** Also notes data for Scopes 1 and 2. **Number listed:** 5

1. Taiwan Cement Co., Ltd., with 0 categories
2. Formosa Plastics Corp., 0
2. Nan Ya Plastics Corp., 0
2. Formosa Chemicals & Fiber Corp., 0
5. Formosa Petrochemical Corp., 0

Source: *ET Asia-Pacific 300*, (annual), Environmental Investment Organisation, 2011.

865 ■ THAILAND'S BEST COMPANIES IN CARBON EMISSIONS, 2011

Ranked by: Number of Scope 3 emission categories disclosed. Within ties, companies are then ranked by combined emissions intensity across all three Scopes. **Remarks:** Also notes data for Scopes 1 and 2. **Number listed:** 5

1. PTT Exploration & Production Public Co., Ltd., with 0 categories
2. The Siam Cement Public Co., Ltd., 0
3. Advanced Info Service plc, 0
4. Bangkok Bank, 0
4. Kasikornbank, 0

Source: *ET Asia-Pacific 300*, (annual), Environmental Investment Organisation, 2011.

866 ■ THAILAND'S WORST COMPANIES IN CARBON EMISSIONS, 2011

Ranked by: Number of Scope 3 emission categories disclosed. Within ties, companies are then ranked by combined emissions

intensity across all three Scopes. **Remarks:** Also notes data for Scopes 1 and 2. **Number listed:** 4

1. Banpu, with 0 categories
2. PTT Public Co., Ltd., 0
3. Caroen Pokphand Foods, 0
4. Siam Commercial Bank, 0

Source: *ET Asia-Pacific 300*, (annual), Environmental Investment Organisation, 2012.

867 ■ THE UNITED KINGDOM'S BEST COMPANIES IN CARBON EMISSIONS, 2011

Ranked by: Number of Scope 3 emission categories disclosed. Within ties, companies are then ranked by combined emissions intensity across all three Scopes. **Remarks:** Also notes data for Scopes 1 and 2. **Number listed:** 5

1. Anglo American plc, with 8 categories
2. Xstrata plc, 5
3. British Land plc, 4
4. Reckitt Benckiser plc, 4
5. Centrica plc, 4

Source: *ET Europe 300*, (annual), Environmental Investment Organisation, 2011.

868 ■ THE UNITED KINGDOM'S WORST COMPANIES IN CARBON EMISSIONS, 2011

Ranked by: Number of Scope 3 emission categories disclosed. Within ties, companies are then ranked by combined emissions intensity across all three Scopes. **Remarks:** Also notes data for Scopes 1 and 2. **Number listed:** 5

1. Aggreko plc, with 0 categories
1. Intertek Group plc, 0
3. Genting Singapore, 0
3. International Consolidated Airlines Group SA, 0
5. Ensco plc, 0

Source: *ET Europe 300*, (annual), Environmental Investment Organisation, 2011.

869 ■ WORLD'S BEST BASIC MATERIALS COMPANIES IN CARBON EMISSIONS, 2011

Ranked by: Number of Scope 3 emission categories disclosed. Within ties, companies are then ranked by combined emissions intensity across all three Scopes. **Remarks:** Also notes data for Scopes 1 and 2. **Number listed:** 3

1. BASE SE, with 15 categories
2. Anglo American plc, 8
3. Gold Fields Ltd., 8

Source: *ET Global 800*, (annual), Environmental Investment Organisation, 2011.

870 ■ WORLD'S BEST COMPANIES IN CARBON EMISSIONS, 2011

Ranked by: Number of Scope 3 emission categories disclosed. Within ties, companies are then ranked by combined emissions intensity across all three Scopes. **Remarks:** Also notes data for Scopes 1 and 2. **Number listed:** 800

1. BASF SE, with 15 categories
2. Anglo American plc, 8
3. Gold Fields Ltd., 8
4. Alcatel-Lucent, 7

5. Banco Santander (Brasil) SA, 6
6. Baxter International Inc., 6
7. Vale SA, 6
8. Westpac Banking Corp., 5
9. Commerzbank AG, 5
10. National Australia Bank Ltd., 5

Source: *ET Global 800*, (annual), Environmental Investment Organisation, 2011.

871 ■ WORLD'S BEST CONSUMER GOODS COMPANIES IN CARBON EMISSIONS, 2011

Ranked by: Number of Scope 3 emission categories disclosed. Within ties, companies are then ranked by combined emissions intensity across all three Scopes. **Remarks:** Also notes data for Scopes 1 and 2. **Number listed:** 3

1. Reckitt Benckiser plc, with 4 categories
2. Sony Corp., 3
3. LVMH Moet Hennessy Louis Vuitton SA, 2

Source: *ET Global 800*, (annual), Environmental Investment Organisation, 2011.

872 ■ WORLD'S BEST CONSUMER SERVICES COMPANIES IN CARBON EMISSIONS, 2011

Ranked by: Number of Scope 3 emission categories disclosed. Within ties, companies are then ranked by combined emissions intensity across all three Scopes. **Remarks:** Also notes data for Scopes 1 and 2. **Number listed:** 3

1. Wesfarmers Ltd., with 4 categories
2. Kingfisher plc, 3
3. Woolworths Ltd., 3

Source: *ET Global 800*, (annual), Environmental Investment Organisation, 2011.

873 ■ WORLD'S BEST FINANCIALS COMPANIES IN CARBON EMISSIONS, 2011

Ranked by: Number of Scope 3 emission categories disclosed. Within ties, companies are then ranked by combined emissions intensity across all three Scopes. **Remarks:** Also notes data for Scopes 1 and 2. **Number listed:** 3

1. Banco Santander (Brasil) SA, with 6 categories
2. Westpac Banking Corp., 5
3. Commerzbank AG, 5

Source: *ET Global 800*, (annual), Environmental Investment Organisation, 2011.

874 ■ WORLD'S BEST HEALTHCARE COMPANIES IN CARBON EMISSIONS, 2011

Ranked by: Number of Scope 3 emission categories disclosed. Within ties, companies are then ranked by combined emissions intensity across all three Scopes. **Remarks:** Also notes data for Scopes 1 and 2. **Number listed:** 3

1. Baxter International Inc., with 6 categories
2. AstraZeneca plc, 2
3. Roche Holding Ltd., 1

Source: *ET Global 800*, (annual), Environmental Investment Organisation, 2011.

875 ■ WORLD'S BEST INDUSTRIALS COMPANIES IN CARBON EMISSIONS, 2011

Ranked by: Number of Scope 3 emission categories disclosed. Within ties, companies are then ranked by combined emissions

intensity across all three Scopes. **Remarks:** Also notes data for Scopes 1 and 2. **Number listed:** 3

1. United Parcel Service Inc. (UPS), with 5 categories
2. Vallourec SA, 4
3. Toshiba Corp., 2

Source: *ET Global 800*, (annual), Environmental Investment Organisation, 2011.

876 ■ WORLD'S BEST OIL AND GAS COMPANIES IN CARBON EMISSIONS, 2011

Ranked by: Number of Scope 3 emission categories disclosed. Within ties, companies are then ranked by combined emissions intensity across all three Scopes. **Remarks:** Also notes data for Scopes 1 and 2. **Number listed:** 3

1. Hess Corp., with 3 categories
2. ENI SpA, 2
3. Royal Dutch Shell plc, 1

Source: *ET Global 800*, (annual), Environmental Investment Organisation, 2011.

877 ■ WORLD'S BEST TECHNOLOGY COMPANIES IN CARBON EMISSIONS, 2011

Ranked by: Number of Scope 3 emission categories disclosed. Within ties, companies are then ranked by combined emissions intensity across all three Scopes. **Remarks:** Also notes data for Scopes 1 and 2. **Number listed:** 3

1. Nokia Corp., with 4 categories
2. Telefonaktiebolaget LM Ericsson, 3
3. SAP AG, 3

Source: *ET Global 800*, (annual), Environmental Investment Organisation, 2011.

878 ■ WORLD'S BEST TELECOMMUNICATIONS COMPANIES IN CARBON EMISSIONS, 2011

Ranked by: Number of Scope 3 emission categories disclosed. Within ties, companies are then ranked by combined emissions intensity across all three Scopes. **Remarks:** Also notes data for Scopes 1 and 2. **Number listed:** 3

1. Telstra Corp., Ltd., with 4 categories
2. Koninklijke KPN NV (Royal KPN NV), 2
3. BT Group plc, 2

Source: *ET Global 800*, (annual), Environmental Investment Organisation, 2011.

879 ■ WORLD'S BEST UTILITIES COMPANIES IN CARBON EMISSIONS, 2011

Ranked by: Number of Scope 3 emission categories disclosed. Within ties, companies are then ranked by combined emissions intensity across all three Scopes. **Remarks:** Also notes data for Scopes 1 and 2. **Number listed:** 3

1. Centrica plc, with 4 categories
2. RWE AG, 3
3. Fortum Oyj, 3

Source: *ET Global 800*, (annual), Environmental Investment Organisation, 2011.

880 ■ WORLD'S WORST COMPANIES IN CARBON EMISSIONS, 2011

Ranked by: Number of Scope 3 emission categories disclosed. Within ties, companies are then ranked by combined emissions intensity across all three Scopes. **Remarks:** Also notes data for Scopes 1 and 2. **Number listed:** 800

1. FirstEnergy Corp., with 0 categories
1. Edison International, 0
1. Entergy Corp., 0
1. JSC Inter RAO UES, 0
5. Fluor Corp., 0
5. Fortune Brands Inc., 0
7. Hutchison Whampoa Ltd., 0
7. Honeywell International Inc., 0
7. Jardine Strategic Holdings Ltd., 0
7. Jardine Matheson Holdings Ltd., 0

Source: *ET Global 800*, (annual), Environmental Investment Organisation, 2011.

881 ■ WORST ASIA-PACIFIC COMPANIES IN CARBON EMISSIONS, 2011

Ranked by: Number of Scope 3 emission categories disclosed. Within ties, companies are then ranked by combined emissions intensity across all three Scopes. **Remarks:** Also notes data for Scopes 1 and 2. **Number listed:** 5

1. Shikoku Electric Power Co., with 0 categories
2. Samsung Engineering Co., Ltd., 0
2. Daito Trust Construction Co., Ltd., 0
2. Taiwan Cement Co., Ltd., 0
2. Daewoo Engineering & Construction Co., Ltd., 0

Source: *ET Asia-Pacific 300*, (annual), Environmental Investment Organisation, 2011.

882 ■ WORST BRICS COMPANIES IN CARBON EMISSIONS, 2011

Ranked by: Number of Scope 3 emission categories disclosed. Within ties, companies are then ranked by combined emissions intensity across all three Scopes. **Remarks:** BRICS is an acronym referring to the countries Brazil, Russia, India, China, and South Africa. Also notes data for Scopes 1 and 2. **Number listed:** 5

1. Companhia de Saneamento Basico do Estado de Sao Paulo (SABESP), with 0 categories
1. ENN Energy Holdings Ltd., 0
3. NTPC Ltd., 0
3. Cheung Kong (Holdings) Ltd., 0
3. Federal Grid Co., 0

Source: *ET BRICS 300*, (annual), Environmental Investment Organisation, 2011.

883 ■ WORST U.S. COMPANIES IN CARBON EMISSIONS, 2011

Ranked by: Number of Scope 3 emission categories disclosed. Within ties, companies are then ranked by combined emissions intensity across all three Scopes. **Remarks:** Also notes data for Scopes 1 and 2. **Number listed:** 5

1. FirstEnergy Corp., with 0 categories
1. Edison International, 0
1. Entergy Corp., 0
4. Honeywell International Inc., 0
5. CF Industries Holdings Inc., 0

Source: *ET North America 300*, (annual), Environmental Investment Organisation, 2011.

Carbonated Beverages
See: **Beer; Soft Drink Industry**

Cars
See: **Automobiles**

Casinos

884 ■ HONG KONG'S LARGEST CASINOS AND GAMING COMPANIES OVERALL, 2011

Ranked by: Score based on revenue, profits, assets, and market capitalization. **Remarks:** Specific scores not provided. Also notes overall rank in the *Forbes 2000* and figures for each criterion. **Number listed:** 3

1. SJM Holdings Ltd.
2. Galaxy Entertainment Group Ltd.
3. Melco Crown Entertainment Ltd.

Source: *Forbes*, Forbes 2000 (annual), http://www.forbes.com, May 7, 2012.

885 ■ LARGEST CASINOS AND CARD CLUBS IN THE TWIN CITIES, 2011

Ranked by: Total number of games. **Remarks:** Also notes contact information, year founded, breakdown of games by electronic and table, square feet of gaming space, manager, number of employees, number of restaurants, number of rooms and suites, tribe affiliation, miles from the Twin Cities, and amenities. **Number listed:** 20

1. Mystic Lake Casino Hotel, with 3,892 games
2. Treasure Island Resort & Casino, 2,559
3. Grand Casino Hinckley, 2,503
4. Black Bear Casino Resort, 2,012
5. Grand Casino Mille Lacs, 1,924
6. Jackpot Junction Casino Hotel, 1,278
7. Shooting Star Casino, Hotel & Event Center, 1,040
8. Northern Lights Casino, Hotel & Event Center, 950
9. Prairie's Edge Casino Resort, 910
10. Fortune Bay Resort Casino, 819

Source: *Twin Cities Business*, The BIG Book (annual), http://www.tcbmag.com, 2012.

886 ■ LARGEST U.S. CASINOS AND GAMING COMPANIES OVERALL, 2011

Ranked by: Score based on revenue, profits, assets, and market capitalization. **Remarks:** Specific scores not provided. Also notes overall rank in the *Forbes 2000* and figures for each criterion. **Number listed:** 4

1. Las Vegas Sands Corp.
2. MGM Mirage Inc.
3. Wynn Resorts Ltd.
4. Caesars Entertainment Corp.

Source: *Forbes*, Forbes 2000 (annual), http://www.forbes.com, May 7, 2012.

887 ■ NEVADA'S LARGEST CASINOS AND GAMING COMPANIES OVERALL, 2011

Ranked by: Score based on revenue, profits, assets, and market capitalization. **Remarks:** Specific scores not provided. Also notes overall rank in the *Forbes 2000* and figures for each criterion. **Number listed:** 4

1. Las Vegas Sands Corp.
2. MGM Mirage Inc.
3. Wynn Resorts Ltd.
4. Caesars Entertainment

Source: *Forbes*, Forbes 2000 (annual), http://www.forbes.com, May 7, 2012.

888 ■ TOP *FORTUNE 500* HOTELS, CASINOS, AND RESORTS, 2011

Ranked by: Revenue, in millions of dollars. **Remarks:** Also notes overall rank in the *Fortune 500;* profits; profits as a percentage of revenue; stockholders' equity; and rank by each criterion. **Number listed:** 6

1. Marriott International Inc., with $12,317 million
2. Las Vegas Sands Corp., $9,411
3. Caesars Entertainment Corp., $8,835
4. MGM Resorts International, $7,849
5. Starwood Hotels & Resorts Worldwide Inc., $5,624
6. Wynn Resorts, $5,270

Source: *Fortune*, Fortune 500 (annual), May 21, 2012, p. F-36.

889 ■ WORLD'S LARGEST CASINOS AND GAMING COMPANIES OVERALL, 2011

Ranked by: Score based on revenue, profits, assets, and market capitalization. **Remarks:** Specific scores not provided. Also notes country, overall rank in the *Forbes 2000,* and figures for each criterion. **Number listed:** 10

1. Las Vegas Sands Corp.
2. MGM Mirage Inc.
3. Genting Bhd.
4. SJM Holdings Ltd.
5. Wynn Resorts Ltd.
6. Caesars Entertainment Corp.
7. Galaxy Entertainment Group Ltd.
8. OPAP SA
9. Crown Ltd.
10. Melco Crown Entertainment Ltd.

Source: *Forbes*, Forbes 2000 (annual), http://www.forbes.com, May 7, 2012.

Catalogs

---

890 ■ TOP CHILDREN'S APPAREL CATALOGERS, 2010

Ranked by: Direct sales, in millions of dollars. **Number listed:** 5

1. Hanna Andersson, with $57.6 million
2. Chasing Fireflies, $31.8
3. CWD, $18.9
4. French Toast, $13
5. Tea Collection, $8.8

Source: *MultiChannel Merchant*, MultiChannel Merchant 100 (annual), September 2011, p. 29.

891 ■ TOP COMPUTER/HIGH-TECH CATALOGERS, 2010

Ranked by: Direct sales, in millions of dollars. **Number listed:** 10

1. Dell Inc., with $52,161.4 million

2. International Business Machines Corp. (IBM), $10,496
3. CDW Corp., $8,800
4. Hewlett-Packard Co., $3,671
5. Systemax, $3,590
6. PC Connection, $1,970
7. Crutchfield Corp., $270
8. Wayside Technology, $206.7
9. Black Box Corp., $188.9
10. PC Mall, $136

Source: *MultiChannel Merchant*, MultiChannel Merchant 100 (annual), September 2011, p. 33.

892 ■ TOP ELECTRONICS/COMPONENTS CATALOGERS, 2010

Ranked by: Direct sales, in millions of dollars. **Number listed:** 5

1. Digi-Key Corp., with $1,000 million
2. Premier Farnell, $612.6
3. Ingram Micro Consumer Electronics, $409.5
4. Allied Electronics, $388
5. Mouser Electronics, $344

Source: *MultiChannel Merchant*, MultiChannel Merchant 100 (annual), September 2011, p. 33.

893 ■ TOP FOOD CATALOGERS, 2010

Ranked by: Direct sales, in millions of dollars. **Number listed:** 10

1. Omaha Steaks, with $327 million
2. Harry & David Holdings, $280.4
3. Green Mountain Coffee Roasters, $188
4. Figi's, $100
5. The Swiss Colony, $65
6. Southern Fulfillment Services, $39
7. Hickory Farms, $35.6
8. HoneyBaked Ham, $33.6
9. Godiva Chocolatier, $15.5
10. Dean & Deluca, $12.3

Source: *MultiChannel Merchant*, MultiChannel Merchant 100 (annual), September 2011, p. 35.

894 ■ TOP GENERAL MERCHANDISE CATALOGERS, 2010

Ranked by: Direct sales, in millions of dollars. **Number listed:** 10

1. Sears Holding Corp., with $3,107 million
2. HSNi, $1,500
3. J. C. Penney Co., Inc., $1,500
4. L. L. Bean, $1,440
5. Redcats USA, $1,250
6. Orchard Brands, $1,100
7. Colony Brands, $612
8. Bluestem Brands, $435
9. LTD Commodities, $420
10. Sierra Trading Post, $250

Source: *MultiChannel Merchant*, MultiChannel Merchant 100 (annual), September 2011, p. 26-27.

895 ■ TOP GIFTS CATALOGERS, 2010

Ranked by: Direct sales, in millions of dollars. **Number listed:** 10

1. Oriental Trading Co., with $505 million
2. 1-800-Flowers.com, $500
3. Provide Commerce, $406.3
4. Potpourri Group, $295
5. Collections Etc., $237.1
6. Blyth, $159.9
7. Tiffany & Co., $152.7
8. Evergreen Enterprises, $120
9. Ross-Simons, $119.5
10. Harriet Carter, $107.9

Source: *MultiChannel Merchant*, MultiChannel Merchant 100 (annual), September 2011, p. 31.

896 ■ TOP HOME DECOR/FURNISHINGS CATALOGERS, 2010

Ranked by: Direct sales, in millions of dollars. **Number listed:** 10

1. Williams-Sonoma, with $1,454.2 million
2. Home Depot (Home Decorator's Collection), $610
3. Crate & Barrel, $331.3
4. Restoration Hardware, $328
5. Lamps Plus, $117.2
6. Ikea, $63.5
7. Country Curtains, $38.3
8. Touch of Class, $36.5
9. Design Within Reach, $35.7
10. Wisteria, $22.4

Source: *MultiChannel Merchant*, MultiChannel Merchant 100 (annual), September 2011, p. 31.

897 ■ TOP INDUSTRIAL/MAINTENANCE, REPAIR, OPERATIONS (MRO) CATALOGERS, 2010

Ranked by: Direct sales, in millions of dollars. **Number listed:** 10

1. Wesco International, with $5,060 million
2. VWR International, $3,600
3. Patterson Cos., $3,420
4. W. W. Grainger, $1,800
5. MSC Industrial Direct Co., $1,652
6. Interline Brands, $655
7. HD Supply, $580.4
8. Takkt America, $443
9. Newport Corp., $121.8
10. Production Tool Supply, $117.1

Source: *MultiChannel Merchant*, MultiChannel Merchant 100 (annual), September 2011, p. 33.

898 ■ TOP MIXED GENDER APPAREL CATALOGERS, 2010

Ranked by: Direct sales, in millions of dollars. **Number listed:** 10

1. The Gap Inc., with $1,300 million
2. Nordstrom, $841
3. Neiman Marcus Group, $700.8
4. J. Crew Group, $490.6
5. Urban Outfitters, $433.8
6. Foot Locker, $432
7. Saks Inc., $350
8. Hanesbrands, $183.5
9. Boden USA, $134.4
10. Brooks Brothers, $120

Source: *MultiChannel Merchant*, MultiChannel Merchant 100 (annual), September 2011, p. 29.

899 ■ TOP PET SUPPLIES CATALOGERS, 2010

Ranked by: Direct sales, in millions of dollars. **Number listed:** 10

1. Doctors Foster and Smith, with $280 million
2. PetMed Express, $231.6
3. Dover Saddlery, $52.1
4. Jeffers, $50
5. Valley Vet Supply, $39.5
6. SmartPak, $20.2
7. PetEdge, $17.3
8. State Line Tack, $14.2
9. Heartland Vet Supply, $9.6
10. American Livestock & Pet Supply, $8.4

Source: *MultiChannel Merchant*, MultiChannel Merchant 100 (annual), September 2011, p. 32.

900 ■ TOP SEEDS AND PLANTS CATALOGERS, 2010

Ranked by: Direct sales, in millions of dollars. **Number listed:** 5

1. Gardens Alive!, with $100.6 million
2. Park Seed/Jackson & Perkins, $24.8
3. Burpee, $15.9
4. Aerogrow, $9
5. Jung Seed Co., $8.1

Source: *MultiChannel Merchant*, MultiChannel Merchant 100 (annual), September 2011, p. 31.

901 ■ TOP SHOE CATALOGERS, 2010

Ranked by: Direct sales, in millions of dollars. **Number listed:** 5

1. Benchmark Brands, with $144.2 million
2. Mason Shoes, $120
3. Masseys Footwear, $60
4. Maryland Square, $51.4
5. Aerosoles, $34.7

Source: *MultiChannel Merchant*, MultiChannel Merchant 100 (annual), September 2011, p. 30.

902 ■ TOP SPORTING GOODS/LEISURE CATALOGERS, 2010

Ranked by: Direct sales, in millions of dollars. **Number listed:** 10

1. Cabela's, with $999.8 million
2. Bass Pro Shops, $299.6
3. REI, $290
4. Sport Supply Group, $250.2
5. Dick's Sporting Goods, $185
6. Gander Mountain, $125
7. Golfsmith, $79
8. Road Runner Sports, $74
9. Campmor, $45.6
10. Moosejaw, $44

Source: *MultiChannel Merchant*, MultiChannel Merchant 100 (annual), September 2011, p. 30.

903 ■ TOP U.S. CATALOGERS OVERALL, 2010

Ranked by: Direct sales, in millions of dollars. **Remarks:** Also notes contact information, figures for previous year, and market segment. **Number listed:** 100

1. Dell Inc., with $52,161.4 million
2. Thermo Fisher Scientific Inc., $10,790
3. International Business Machines Corp. (IBM), $10,496
4. Staples Inc., $9,849.2
5. CDW Corp., $8,800
6. Henry Schein Inc., $7,530
7. WESCO International Inc., $5,060
8. United Stationers Inc., $4,830
9. OfficeMax Inc., $3,766
10. Hewlett-Packard Co., $3,671

Source: *MultiChannel Merchant*, MultiChannel Merchant 100 (annual), September 2011, p. 26-32.

904 ■ TOP VITAMINS/SUPPLEMENTS CATALOGERS, 2010

Ranked by: Direct sales, in millions of dollars. **Number listed:** 5

1. NBTY, with $246 million
2. Vitacost.com, $220.7
3. Swanson Health Products, $102
4. Vitamin Shoppe, $83.5
5. Indiana Botanic Gardens, $20

Source: *MultiChannel Merchant*, MultiChannel Merchant 100 (annual), September 2011, p. 32.

905 ■ TOP WOMEN'S APPAREL CATALOGERS, 2010

Ranked by: Direct sales, in millions of dollars. **Number listed:** 10

1. Limited Brands (Victoria's Secret), with $1,500 million
2. Coldwater Creek, $248.6
3. Talbots, $222
4. Boston Apparel Group, $174.8
5. Boston Proper, $168
6. Signature Styles, $119.9
7. Chico's, $108.7
8. Delia's, $98.2
9. J. Jill, $98
10. Soft Surroundings, $89.3

Source: *MultiChannel Merchant*, MultiChannel Merchant 100 (annual), September 2011, p. 29.

Celebrities

906 ■ MOST POWERFUL ARABS IN ARTS AND ENTERTAINMENT, 2012

Ranked by: Score based on scope of influence. **Remarks:** Specific scores not provided. Also notes rank in the overall *Power 500*. **Number listed:** 72

1. Fairouz
2. Khaled Samawi

3. Amr Diab
4. Bassam Kousa
5. Nadine Labaki
6. Al Laith Hajo
7. Ghassan Bin Jiddu
8. Safwan Dahoul
9. Nancy Ajram
10. Ziad Rahbani

Source: *Arabian Business*, Power 500 (annual), June 4, 2012.

907 ■ TOP-EARNING DEAD CELEBRITIES, 2011

Ranked by: Annual earnings of celebrities' estates, in millions of dollars. **Remarks:** Also notes occupation, date and cause of death, age, and comments. **Number listed:** 15

1. Michael Jackson, with $170 million
2. Elvis Presley, $55
3. Marilyn Monroe, $27
4. Charles M. Schulz, $25
5. John Lennon, $12
5. Elizabeth Taylor, $12
7. Albert Einstein, $10
8. Theodor Geisel (Dr. Seuss), $9
9. Jimi Hendrix, $7
9. Stieg Larsson, $7
9. Steve McQueen, $7
9. Richard Rodgers, $7

Source: *Forbes*, Top-Earning Dead Celebrities (annual), http://www.forbes.com, October 25, 2011.

Chain and Franchise Operations

908 ■ BEST FRANCHISES TO START, 2012

Ranked by: Score based on five criteria: average initial investment, total number of locations, closure rate, three-year growth in U.S. locations, and the number of training hours as a perdentage of start-up cost. **Remarks:** Scores not provided. Also notes headquarters, comments, and figures for each criterion. **Number listed:** 10

1. Snap-On Inc.
2. 7-Eleven Inc.
3. Aaron's
4. Panera Bread Co.
5. Servpro
6. McDonald's Corp.
7. Liberty Tax Service
8. Merry Maids
9. The Maids International
10. Jimmy John's Gourmet Sandwiches

Source: *Forbes*, Proven Path, February 27, 2012, p. 70-72.

909 ■ FASTEST-GROWING FRANCHISES, 2010-2011

Ranked by: Number of new franchise units added in the U.S. and Canada between July 2010 and July 2011. **Remarks:** Also notes rank within the *Franchise 500*, total number of franchises, industry category, and contact information. **Number listed:** 108

1. Stratus Building Solutions, with 1,625 new units
2. Subway, 1,024

3. CleanNet USA Inc., 518

4. Vanguard Cleaning Systems, 305

5. H & R Block Inc., 297

6. Dunkin' Donuts, 280

7. Chester's, 256

8. Liberty Tax Service, 239

9. 7-Eleven, 208

10. Anytime Fitness, 189

Source: *Entrepreneur*, Fastest-Growing Franchises (annual), February 2012, p. 90+.

910 ■ LARGEST COLORADO-BASED FRANCHISERS, 2010

Ranked by: Total number of units in operation. **Remarks:** Also notes contact information, rank for previous year, number of Colorado and company-owned locations, business description, franchise fee, top local executive, owner, ticker symbol, and headquarters. **Number listed:** 23

1. Re/Max LLC, with 6,275 units

2. Watermill Express LLC, 1,301

3. Maui Wowi Hawaiian Coffees & Smoothies, 575

4. Qdoba Restaurant Corp., 536

5. Pak Mail Centers of America Inc., 465

6. Red Robin Gourmet Burgers Inc., 451

7. Fitness Together Holdings Inc., 394

8. Bark Busters Home Dog Training, 363

9. PostNet International Franchise Corp., 347

10. Noodles & Co., 256

Source: *Denver Business Journal*, Book of Lists (annual), December 16, 2011, p. 52.

911 ■ LARGEST FRANCHISES IN LOS ANGELES COUNTY, 2011

Ranked by: Total number of franchises in Los Angeles County. **Remarks:** Also notes contact information, number of company-owned locations, description of franchise, franchise costs, contact information, and top local executive. **Number listed:** 25

1. DineEquity Inc., with 3,286 franchises

2. International Coffee & Tea LLC, 535

3. Mathnasium Learning Centers, 324

Source: *Los Angeles Business Journal*, Largest Franchises (annual), http://www.labusinessjournal.com, January 9, 2012.

912 ■ TOP FRANCHISE SYSTEMS, 2012

Ranked by: Cumulative score based on financial strength and stability, growth rate, size of the system, number of years in business, the length of time franchising, start-up costs, litigation, percentage of terminations, and whether the company provides financing. **Remarks:** Specific scores not provided. Also notes comments. **Number listed:** 10

1. Hampton Hotels

2. Subway

3. 7-Eleven Inc.

4. Servpro

5. Days Inn

6. McDonald's Corp.

7. Denny's Inc.

8. H & R Block

9. Dunkin' Donuts

10. Pizza Hut

Source: *Entrepreneur*, Franchise 500 (annual), January 2012, p. 84-95.

913 ■ TOP MISCELLANEOUS CHILDREN'S FRANCHISES, 2012

Ranked by: Cumulative score based on financial strength and stability, growth rate, size of the system, number of years in business, the length of time franchising, start-up costs, litigation, percentage of terminations, and whether the company provides financing. **Remarks:** Specific scores not provided. Also notes overall rank within the *Franchise 500*, contact information, description, year founded, year started franchising, states where registered, available U.S. regions, where seeking foreign expansion, number of franchised and company-owned units for past three years, start-up costs, franchise fees, royalty fees, and type of financing available. **Number listed:** 4

1. Pump It Up

2. The GameTruck Licensing

3. Monkey Joe's Parties & Play

4. Games2U Franchising LLC

Source: *Entrepreneur*, Franchise 500 (annual), January 2012, p. 160-161.

Chain Stores

914 ■ FASTEST-GROWING HARDGOODS STORE CHAINS, 2009-2010

Ranked by: Annual gain in basis points. **Remarks:** To qualify, chains must have annual revenues of at least $100 million. Also notes sales and market share for current and previous year. **Number listed:** 14

1. Apple, with 368 points

2. Bed Bath & Beyond, 109

3. HHGregg, 89

4. RadioShack, 87

5. O'Reilly Automotive, 63

6. Tractor Supply Co., 54

7. Advance Auto Parts, 52

8. AutoZone, 29

9. GameStop, 26

10. TJX, 17

10. Williams-Sonoma, 17

Source: *Stores*, Hot 100 (annual), August 2011, p. s10.

915 ■ MOST PRODUCTIVE U.S. RETAILERS, 2010

Ranked by: Average net income per store, in dollars. **Number listed:** 10

1. Coach Inc., with $5,698,630

2. Nordstrom Inc., $3,004,901

3. Costco Wholesale Corp., $2,277,900

4. Wal-Mart Stores Inc., $1,827,000

5. Target Corp., $1,668,500

6. Tiffany & Co., $1,581,129

7. The Home Depot Inc., $1,485,000

8. Publix Super Markets Inc., $1,294,000

9. Lowe's Companies Inc., $1,149,000

10. Kohl's Corp., $1,022,956

Source: *Chain Store Age*, Chain Store Age 100 (annual), 2011, p. 31A.

916 ■ RETAIL CHAINS WITH THE FASTEST-GROWING REVENUE, 2009-2010

Ranked by: Annual revenue growth, in percent. **Remarks:** To qualify, chains must have annual revenues of at least $100 million. Also notes headquarters; revenue, earnings, and number of units for current and previous year; and annual growth in earnings and number of units. **Number listed:** 100

1. Ascena Retail Group, with 58.9%
2. Amazon.com, 46.2%
3. Fresh & Easy Neighborhood Market, 37.8%
4. HHGregg, 36.3%
5. Tops Friendly Markets, 33.1%
6. Bodega Latina, 32.5%
7. Apple Stores/iTunes, 32.3%
8. Netflix, 29.5%
9. H & M, 29.3%
10. Overstock.com, 23.8%

Source: *Stores*, Hot 100 (annual), August 2011, p. s7-s13.

917 ■ RETAILERS ADDING THE MOST NEW SQUARE FOOTAGE, 2011

Ranked by: Total square footage added during the year. **Remarks:** Also notes figures for previous year. **Number listed:** 20

1. Wal-Mart Stores Inc., with 12,000,000 sq.ft.
2. The TJX Companies Inc., 5,849,000
3. Dollar General Corp., 5,625,000
4. CVS Caremark Corp., 3,987,500
5. Costco Wholesale Corp., 3,892,000
6. Dollar Tree Stores Inc., 3,825,000
7. Walgreen Co., 3,683,000
8. Target Corp., 3,163,000
9. Kohl's Corp., 3,000,000
10. Lowe's Companies Inc., 2,825,000

Source: *Chain Store Age*, Big Builders (annual), December 2011, p. 33.

918 ■ RETAILERS ADDING THE MOST NEW STORES, 2011

Ranked by: Total number of new stores added during the year. **Remarks:** Also notes figures for previous year. **Number listed:** 20

1. Dollar General Corp., with 625 new stores
2. GameStop Corp., 300
2. Dollar Tree Stores Inc., 300
2. Family Dollar Stores Inc., 300
5. CVS Caremark Corp., 275
6. Walgreen Co., 254
7. AutoZone Inc., 198
8. The TJX Companies Inc., 196
9. Best Buy Co., Inc., 175
10. O'Reilly Automotive Inc., 170

Source: *Chain Store Age*, Big Builders (annual), December 2011, p. 32.

919 ■ RETAILERS INVESTING THE MOST ON CONSTRUCTION PROJECTS, 2011

Ranked by: Capital investment, in thousands of dollars. **Remarks:** Also notes figures for previous year. **Number listed:** 20

1. Wal-Mart Stores Inc., with $8,000,000 thousand
2. Target Corp., $2,500,000
3. CVS Caremark Corp., $2,000,000
4. The Kroger Co., $1,900,000
5. Lowe's Companies Inc., $1,800,000
6. Costco Wholesale Corp., $1,600,000
7. Walgreen Co., $1,400,000
8. The Home Depot Inc., $1,350,000
9. Safeway Inc., $1,000,000
9. Kohl's Corp., $1,000,000

Source: *Chain Store Age*, Big Builders (annual), December 2011, p. 32.

920 ■ TOP U.S. RETAILERS BY NET INCOME, 2010

Ranked by: Net income, in thousands of dollars. **Remarks:** Also notes figures for previous year and two-year total. **Number listed:** 20

1. Wal-Mart Stores Inc., with $16,389,000 thousand
2. CVS Caremark Corp., $4,537,000
3. The Home Depot Inc., $3,338,000
4. Target Corp., $2,920,000
5. Walgreen Co., $2,091,000
6. Lowe's Companies Inc., $2,010,000
7. eBay Inc., $1,800,961
8. Publix Super Markets Inc., $1,338,147
9. Costco Wholesale Corp., $1,303,000
10. The TJX Companies Inc., $1,300,000

Source: *Chain Store Age*, Chain Store Age 100 (annual), 2011, p. 31A.

921 ■ TOP U.S. RETAILERS BY REVENUE, 2010

Ranked by: Revenue, in thousands of dollars. **Remarks:** Also notes headquarters, fiscal year-end, net income, number of stores, comments, and figures for previous year. **Number listed:** 100

1. Wal-Mart Stores Inc., with $418,952,000 thousand
2. The Kroger Co., $81,189,000
3. Costco Wholesale Corp., $76,255,000
4. The Home Depot Inc., $67,997,000
5. Walgreen Co., $67,420,000
6. Target Corp., $67,390,000
7. CVS Caremark Corp., $57,345,000
8. Best Buy Co., Inc., $50,272,000
9. Lowe's Companies Inc., $48,815,000
10. Sears Holdings Corp., $43,326,000

Source: *Chain Store Age*, Chain Store Age 100 (annual), 2011, p. 20A+.

922 ■ TOP U.S. RETAILERS BY STORE COUNT, 2010

Ranked by: Total number of stores. **Number listed:** 20

1. Dollar General Corp., with 9,372 stores
2. Walgreen Co., 8,046
3. Starbucks Corp., 7,506
4. CVS Caremark Corp., 7,182
5. Family Dollar Stores Inc., 6,785

6. 7-Eleven Inc., 6,610
7. Wal-Mart Stores Inc., 6,468
8. Alimentation Couche-Tard Inc., 5,795
9. GameStop Corp., 4,881
10. Luxottica Group SpA, 4,733

Source: *Chain Store Age*, Chain Store Age 100 (annual), 2011, p. 30A.

Chain Stores, Apparel
See: **Clothing Stores**

Chain Stores, Electronics
See: **Electronics Stores**

Check Cashing Services

923 ■ TOP CHECK CASHING FRANCHISES, 2012

Ranked by: Cumulative score based on financial strength and stability, growth rate, size of the system, number of years in business, the length of time franchising, start-up costs, litigation, percentage of terminations, and whether the company provides financing. **Remarks:** Specific scores not provided. Also notes overall rank within the *Franchise 500*, contact information, description, year founded, year started franchising, states where registered, available U.S. regions, where seeking foreign expansion, number of franchised and company-owned units for past three years, start-up costs, franchise fees, royalty fees, and type of financing available. **Number listed:** 2

1. Mr. Payroll Corp.
2. United Check Cashing

Source: *Entrepreneur*, Franchise 500 (annual), January 2012, p. 160-161.

Chemical Industry

924 ■ AMERICA'S LARGEST PRIVATE CHEMICAL COMPANIES, 2010

Ranked by: Revenue, in billions of dollars. **Remarks:** Also notes headquarters, number of employees, and overall rank in the *America's Largest Private Companies* list. Ranking is available online only, not in print. **Number listed:** 4

1. Momentive Performance Materials Holdings, with $7.41 billion
2. The InterTech Group Inc., $3.6
3. ICC Industries Inc., $2.6
4. Wilbur-Ellis Co., $2.34

Source: *Forbes*, America's Largest Private Companies (annual), http://www.forbes.com, December 5, 2011.

925 ■ BEST SMALL CHEMICAL COMPANIES IN AMERICA, 2011

Ranked by: Score based on revenue, profits, and return on equity for the past 12 months and five years. **Remarks:** Specific scores not provided. Also notes rank in the overall *100 Best Small Companies in America*. To qualify, companies must have revenues between $5 million and $1 billion, a net margin above five percent, and share price above $5. List is available online only. **Number listed:** 5

1. LSB Industries
2. FutureFuel
3. Balchem
4. KMG Chemicals
5. Hawkins

Source: *Forbes*, Best Small Companies in America (annual), November 7, 2011.

926 ■ LARGEST CHEMICALS COMPANIES BY EMPLOYEES, 2010

Ranked by: Total number of employees. **Remarks:** Also notes contact information for headquarters, number of employees at headquarters, revenue, rank by revenue, and primary SIC code. **Number listed:** 49

1. Pfizer Inc., with 119,149 employees
2. Merck & Co., Inc., 100,000
3. Abbott Laboratories Inc., 73,000
4. E. I. du Pont de Nemours & Co., 60,000
5. Merck Sharp & Dohme Corp., 55,625
6. Dow Chemical Co., 55,095
7. Baxter International Inc., 49,700
8. Wyeth LLC, 47,426
9. America Air Liquide Holdings Inc., 42,500
10. Air Liquide Electronics U.S. LP, 42,300

Source: *Business Rankings*, (annual), Dun & Bradstreet Inc., 2011, p. VI.63-VI.64.

927 ■ LARGEST CHEMICALS COMPANIES BY SALES, 2010

Ranked by: Total revenue, in dollars. **Remarks:** Also notes contact information for headquarters, number of employees at headquarters and overall, rank by employees, and primary SIC code. **Number listed:** 49

1. Pfizer Inc., with $67,809,000,000
2. Dow Chemical Co., $53,674,000,000
3. Merck & Co., Inc., $45,987,000,000
4. Abbott Laboratories Inc., $35,166,721,000
5. E. I. du Pont de Nemours & Co., $32,733,000,000
6. Merck Sharp & Dohme Corp., $23,643,200,000
7. Eli Lilly & Co., $23,076,000,000
8. Bristol-Myers Squibb Co., $19,484,000,000
9. Roche Holdings Inc., $17,098,000,000
10. Colgate-Palmolive Co., $15,564,000,000

Source: *Business Rankings*, (annual), Dun & Bradstreet Inc., 2011, p. V.63-V.64.

928 ■ LARGEST U.S. CHEMICAL MANUFACTURERS, 2010

Ranked by: Revenue, in millions of dollars. **Remarks:** Also notes overall rank within the *IW 500*, revenue growth, and profit margin. **Number listed:** 58

1. Procter & Gamble Co., with $78,938 million
2. Dow Chemical Co., $53,674
3. E. I. du Pont de Nemours & Co., $32,554
4. 3M Co., $26,662
5. Colgate-Palmolive Co., $15,564
6. PPG Industries Inc., $13,423

7. Avon Products Inc., $10,863

8. Monsanto Co., $10,502

9. Praxair Inc., $10,116

10. Air Products & Chemicals Inc., $9,026

Source: *IndustryWeek*, IW 500 (annual), http://www.industryweek.com, July 2011.

929 ■ LARGEST U.S. DIVERSIFIED CHEMICAL COMPANIES OVERALL, 2011

Ranked by: Score based on revenue, profits, assets, and market capitalization. **Remarks:** Specific scores not provided. Also notes overall rank in the *Forbes 2000* and figures for each criterion. **Number listed:** 5

1. Dow Chemical Co.

2. E. I. du Pont de Nemours & Co.

3. PPG Industries Inc.

4. Celanese Corp.

5. Huntsman Corp.

Source: *Forbes*, Forbes 2000 (annual), http://www.forbes.com, May 7, 2012.

930 ■ MOST VALUABLE U.S. CHEMICAL COMPANIES, 2011

Ranked by: Market value as of March 2011, in millions of U.S. dollars. **Remarks:** Also notes rank within the *FT U.S. 500*, rank for previous year, country, revenue, net income, assets, number of employees, share price, price-to-earning ratio, dividend yield, and fiscal yearend. **Number listed:** 13

1. E. I. du Pont de Nemours & Co., with $50,922.7 million

2. Dow Chemical Co., $44,290.1

3. The Mosaic Co., $35,134.2

4. Praxair Inc., $30,845.8

5. Air Products & Chemicals Inc., $19,381.5

6. PPG Industries Inc., $15,327.4

7. Ecolab Inc., $11,838.6

8. CF Industries Holdings Inc., $9,752.8

9. Lubrizol Corp., $8,583.7

10. Sigma-Aldrich Corp., $7,751.5

Source: *Financial Times*, FT 500 (annual), http://www.ft.com, June 24, 2011.

931 ■ TOP CHEMICALS/PHARMACEUTICALS COMPANIES IN CORPORATE FACILITY PROJECTS, 2011

Ranked by: Investment in new or expanded facilities, in millions of dollars. **Remarks:** Also notes location, product line, and whether facility is new or expanded. **Number listed:** 10

1. Chevron Corp., with $2,005 million

2. OCI, $1,600

3. Merck & Co., Inc., $1,500

4. BASF SE, $1,200

5. Delaware City Refinery, $1,000

5. SABIC Corp./China Petroleum & Chemical Corp. (Sinopec), $1,000

7. Evonik, $653

8. Lafarge Canada, $600

9. E. I. du Pont de Nemours & Co., $500

9. Trimex Group, $500

Source: *Site Selection*, Top Industries (annual), March 2012, p. 121.

932 ■ TOP *FORTUNE 500* COMPANIES IN CHEMICALS, 2011

Ranked by: Revenue, in millions of dollars. **Remarks:** Also notes overall rank in the *Fortune 500;* profits; profits as a percentage of revenue; stockholders' equity; and rank by each criterion. **Number listed:** 16

1. Dow Chemical Co., with $59,985 million

2. E. I. du Pont de Nemours & Co., $38,719

3. PPG Industries Inc., $14,885

4. Monsanto Co., $11,822

5. Huntsman Corp., $11,259

6. Praxair Inc., $11,252

7. Air Products & Chemicals Inc., $10,082

8. The Mosaic Co., $9,938

9. The Sherwin-Williams Co., $8,766

10. Ashland Inc., $8,370

Source: *Fortune*, Fortune 500 (annual), May 21, 2012, p. F-34.

Chemical Industry—Distributors

933 ■ ASIA'S LARGEST CHEMICAL DISTRIBUTORS, 2010

Ranked by: Sales, in millions of U.S. dollars. **Number listed:** 23

1. Helm, with $1,056 million

2. ICC Chemical, $815

3. Connell Brother, $731.5

4. Dovechem Group, $331

5. Brenntag, $287

6. Petrochem Middle East, $266

7. IMCD, $179

8. Biesterfeld Spezialchemie, $88.8

9. Union Petrochemical, $83.7

10. Caldic, $45

Source: *ICIS Chemical Business*, Top 100 Chemical Distributors (annual), July 18, 2011, p. 58.

934 ■ EUROPE'S LARGEST CHEMICAL DISTRIBUTORS, 2010

Ranked by: Sales, in millions of U.S. dollars. **Number listed:** 44

1. Brenntag, with $5,210 million

2. Helm, $2,946

3. Univar, $1,900

4. IMCD, $1,150

5. Biesterfeld Spezialchemie, $876

6. Barentz Europe, $742

7. Caldic, $707

8. TER Group, $570

9. Stockmeier Chemie, $490

10. ICC Chemical, $440

Source: *ICIS Chemical Business*, Top 100 Chemical Distributors (annual), July 18, 2011, p. 54.

935 ■ LARGEST CHEMICAL DISTRIBUTORS IN THE MIDDLE EAST AND AFRICA, 2010

Ranked by: Sales, in millions of U.S. dollars. **Number listed:** 16

1. Protea Chemicals, with $596 million
2. Petrochem Middle East, $301
3. REDA Chemicals, $272
4. ICC Chemical, $175
5. Helm, $111
6. Campi y Jove, $54.5
7. Multisol, $44.2
8. Arpadis Chemicals, $39.9
9. Biesterfeld Spezialchemie, $33
10. Atlantic Chemicals Trading, $11.5

Source: *ICIS Chemical Business*, Top 100 Chemical Distributors (annual), July 18, 2011, p. 60.

936 ■ LATIN AMERICA'S LARGEST CHEMICAL DISTRIBUTORS, 2010

Ranked by: Sales, in millions of U.S. dollars. **Number listed:** 20

1. Brenntag, with $960 million
2. quantiQ, $418.5
3. M. Cassab, $358.6
4. Sasil, $297.5
5. Bandeirante Brazmo, $192.1
6. Indukern, $152
7. Biesterfeld Spezialchemie, $111
8. Makeni Chemicals, $90.1
9. ICC Chemical, $80
10. T. Z. Group, $38

Source: *ICIS Chemical Business*, Top 100 Chemical Distributors (annual), July 18, 2011, p. 56.

937 ■ NORTH AMERICA'S LARGEST CHEMICAL DISTRIBUTORS, 2010

Ranked by: Sales, in millions of U.S. dollars. **Number listed:** 99

1. Univar, with $5,800 million
2. Nexeo Solutions, $3,400
3. Brenntag, $3,230
4. Helm, $1,440
5. Hydrite Chemical, $370
6. Quadra Chemicals, $303.7
7. Canada Colors & Chemicals, $267
8. EMCO Chemical Distributors, $257.7
9. Interstate Chemical, $241
10. L. V. Lomas, $231

Source: *ICIS Chemical Business*, Top 100 Chemical Distributors (annual), July 18, 2011, p. 53.

938 ■ WORLD'S LARGEST CHEMICAL DISTRIBUTORS, 2010

Ranked by: Sales, in millions of U.S. dollars. **Remarks:** Also notes sales in home currency, headquarters, website, CEO, products, services, and assets. **Number listed:** 162

1. Brenntag Group, with $10,100 million
2. Univar, $7,200
3. Helm, $5,560

4. Nexeo Solutions, $3,400
5. ICC Chemical, $1,700
6. Azelis, $1,550
7. IMCD Group, $1,350
8. Biesterfeld, $1,210
9. DKSH, $796
10. Connell Brothers, $770

Source: *ICIS Chemical Business*, Top 100 Chemical Distributors (annual), July 18, 2011, p. 53+.

939 ■ WORLD'S LARGEST THIRD-PARTY LOGISTICS CHEMICAL PROVIDERS, 2010

Ranked by: Sales, in millions of U.S. dollars. **Remarks:** Specific figures not provided; companies are listed alphabetically, not ranked. Also notes headquarters, website, key executive, total sales, chemical sales. geographic area served, and comments. **Number listed:** 50

1. Agility
2. Ahlers
3. A. N. Deringer
4. Alfred Talke Logistic Services
5. APL Logistics
6. Baltransa
7. Barrett Distribution Centers
8. BDP International
9. Bertschi
10. Bowker Group

Source: *ICIS Chemical Business*, Top 50 Chemical 3PLs (annual), May 7, 2012, p. 26-31.

Chemical Industry, International

940 ■ BRITAIN'S MOST ADMIRED CHEMICAL COMPANIES, 2011

Ranked by: Survey of peers and investment analysts based on nine criteria: quality of management, financial soundness, quality of goods/services, ability to attract and retain talent, value as long-term investment, innovation, marketing, community and environmental responsibility, and use of corporate assets. **Number listed:** 5

1. BASF AG (UK & Ireland), with 67.8 points
2. Victrex plc, 66.1
3. Croda International plc, 64.5
4. Johnson Matthey plc, 64.2
5. Syngenta AG, 62.6

Source: *Management Today*, Britain's Most Admired Companies (annual), December 2011, p. 43.

941 ■ EUROPE'S MOST VALUABLE CHEMICAL COMPANIES, 2011

Ranked by: Market value as of March 2011, in millions of U.S. dollars. **Remarks:** Also notes rank within the *FT Europe 500*, rank for previous year, country, revenue, net income, assets, number of employees, share price, price-to-earning ratio, dividend yield, and fiscal yearend. **Number listed:** 20

1. BASF AG, with $79,546.8 million
2. Bayer AG, $64,120.8
3. L'Air Liquide SA, $37,817.3
4. Syngenta AG, $30,865.4

5. Linde AG, $26,933.7
6. OJSC Uralkali, $17,562.5
7. Akzo Nobel NV, $15,937.9
8. Yara International ASA, $14,630.2
9. K + S, $14,531.3
10. Wacker Chemie AG, $11,745.3

Source: *Financial Times*, FT 500 (annual), http://www.ft.com, June 24, 2011.

942 ■ GERMANY'S LARGEST DIVERSIFIED CHEMICAL COMPANIES OVERALL, 2011

Ranked by: Score based on revenue, profits, assets, and market capitalization. **Remarks:** Specific scores not provided. Also notes overall rank in the *Forbes 2000* and figures for each criterion. **Number listed:** 6

1. BASF SE
2. Bayer AG
3. Linde AG
4. K + S AG
5. Lanxess
6. Wacker Chemie AG

Source: *Forbes*, Forbes 2000 (annual), http://www.forbes.com, May 7, 2012.

943 ■ JAPAN'S LARGEST DIVERSIFIED CHEMICAL COMPANIES OVERALL, 2011

Ranked by: Score based on revenue, profits, assets, and market capitalization. **Remarks:** Specific scores not provided. Also notes overall rank in the *Forbes 2000* and figures for each criterion. **Number listed:** 10

1. Shin-Etsu Chemical Co., Ltd.
2. Mitsubishi Chemical Holdings Corp.
3. Toray Industries Inc.
4. Asahi Kasei Corp.
5. Sumitomo Chemical Co., Ltd.
6. Nitto Denko
7. Showa Denko
8. Teijin
9. Tosoh
10. DIC

Source: *Forbes*, Forbes 2000 (annual), http://www.forbes.com, May 7, 2012.

944 ■ LARGEST ASIAN CHEMICAL COMPANIES, 2010

Ranked by: Sales, in millions of U.S. dollars. **Remarks:** Also notes figures for previous year, operating profit for current and previous year, and net profit for current and previous year. **Number listed:** 10

1. China Petroleum & Chemical Corp. (Sinopec), with $48,725 million
2. Mitsubishi Chemical, $38,241
3. Sumitomo Chemical, $23,939
4. Toray, $18,593
5. Mitsui Chemicals, $16,806
6. LG Chem Ltd., $15,053
7. SK Energy Corp., $14,279
8. Reliance Industries Ltd., $14,058
9. Asahi Kasei, $12,955

10. Shin-Etsu, $12,779

Source: *ICIS Chemical Business*, Top 100 Global Chemical Companies, Part 2 (annual), September 19, 2011, p. 33.

945 ■ LARGEST ASIAN CHEMICAL COMPANIES BY SALES, 2010

Ranked by: Chemical sales, in millions of U.S. dollars. **Remarks:** Also notes overall rank in the *Billion Dollar Club*. **Number listed:** 30

1. Sinochem International Co., Ltd. (China), with $49,876 million
2. China Petroleum & Chemical Corp. (Sinopec, China), $44,282
3. Mitsubishi Chemical Corp. (Japan), $27,520
4. PetroChina Co., Ltd. (China), $23,681
5. China National Offshore Oil Corp. (China), $21,259
6. Sumitomo Chemical Co., Ltd. (Japan), $19,441
7. Formosa Plastics Corp. (Taiwan), $16,913
8. Mitsui Chemicals Inc. (Japan), $16,737
9. Reliance Industries Ltd. (India), $15,185
10. LG Chem Ltd. (S. Korea), $12,971

Source: *Chemical Week*, Billion Dollar Club (annual), September 5, 2011, p. 31.

946 ■ LARGEST CHEMICAL COMPANIES IN THE MIDDLE EAST/AFRICA, 2010

Ranked by: Sales, in millions of U.S. dollars. **Remarks:** Also notes percent change from previous year, operating profit for current and previous year, and net profit for current and previous year. **Number listed:** 10

1. Saudi Basic Industries Corp. (SABIC), with $40,525 million
2. National Petrochemical Co. (Iran), $9,810
3. Sasol Ltd., $8,572
4. Israel Chemical Ltd., $5,692
5. TASNEE, $2,630
6. Makhteshim-Agan, $2,362
7. PIC, $2,206
8. Industries Qatar, $2,087
9. AECI, $1,756
10. Oil Refineries, $1,576

Source: *ICIS Chemical Business*, Top 100 Global Chemical Companies, Part 2 (annual), September 19, 2011, p. 37.

947 ■ LARGEST EUROPEAN CHEMICAL COMPANIES, 2010

Ranked by: Sales, in millions of U.S. dollars. **Remarks:** Also notes figures for previous year, operating profit for current and previous year, and net profit for current and previous year. **Number listed:** 10

1. BASF AG, with $84,651 million
2. LyondellBasell Industries, $41,151
3. Shell Chemicals Ltd., $39,629
4. Ineos Group Ltd., $34,561
5. Total SA, $24,480
6. Bayer AG, $23,983
7. Akzo Nobel, $19,402
8. L'Air Liquide SA, $17,876

9. Linde, $17,054
10. Evonik, $17,053

Source: *ICIS Chemical Business*, Top 100 Global Chemical Companies, Part 2 (annual), September 19, 2011, p. 31.

948 ■ LARGEST EUROPEAN/MIDDLE EASTERN/ AFRICAN CHEMICAL COMPANIES BY SALES, 2010

Ranked by: Chemical sales, in millions of U.S. dollars. **Remarks:** Also notes overall rank in the *Billion Dollar Club*. **Number listed:** 30

1. BASF AG (Germany), with $63,221 million
2. Saudi Basic Industries Corp. (Sabic, Saudi Arabia), $46,588
3. Royal Dutch Shell plc (Netherlands), $39,629
4. E. I. du Pont de Nemours & Co. (U.S.), $31,505
5. LyondellBasell Industries (Netherlands), $31,262
6. Ineos Group Ltd. (U.K.), $28,400
7. Total SA (France), $23,437
8. Bayer AG (Germany), $22,759
9. Akzo Nobel NV (Netherlands), $19,618
10. L'Air Liquide SA (France), $18,074

Source: *Chemical Week*, Billion Dollar Club (annual), September 5, 2011, p. 31.

949 ■ LARGEST LATIN AMERICAN CHEMICAL COMPANIES, 2010

Ranked by: Sales, in millions of U.S. dollars. **Remarks:** Also notes figures for previous year, percent change, operating profit for current and previous year, and net profit for current and previous year. **Number listed:** 10

1. Braskem SA, with $19,004 million
2. Alpek, $4,957
3. Pemex Petroquimica, $3,348
4. Mexichem, $2,955
5. SQM, $1,830
6. Vale Fertilizantes, $1,603
7. Oxiteno, $1,247
8. Unigel, $1,212
9. Petrobras Argentina, $881
10. Propilco, $664

Source: *ICIS Chemical Business*, Top 100 Global Chemical Companies, Part 2 (annual), September 19, 2011, p. 35.

950 ■ LARGEST NORTH AMERICAN CHEMICAL COMPANIES, 2010

Ranked by: Sales, in millions of U.S. dollars. **Remarks:** Also notes net profit, operating profit, capital spending, research and development expenditures, total assets, number of employees, and percent change from previous year. **Number listed:** 10

1. Dow Chemical Co., with $53,674 million
2. ExxonMobil Chemical Co., $53,636
3. E. I. du Pont de Nemours & Co., $31,505
4. PPG Industries, $11,297
5. Chevron Phillips Chemicals, $11,204
6. Praxair, $10,116
7. Mosaic, $9,938
8. Huntsman, $9,049

9. Air Products, $9,026
10. Sherwin-Williams, $7,776

Source: *ICIS Chemical Business*, Top 100 Global Chemical Companies, Part 2 (annual), September 19, 2011, p. 30.

951 ■ LARGEST NORTH AND SOUTH AMERICAN CHEMICAL COMPANIES BY SALES, 2010

Ranked by: Chemical sales, in millions of U.S. dollars. **Remarks:** Also notes overall rank in the *Billion Dollar Club*. **Number listed:** 30

1. Dow Chemical Co. (U.S.), with $53,674 million
2. Exxon Mobil Corp. (U.S.), $53,600
3. Braskem SA (Brazil), $15,942
4. PPG Industries Inc. (U.S.), $12,438
5. Chevron Phillips Chemical Co. (U.S.), $11,204
6. Agrium Inc. (Canada), $10,520
7. Monsanto Co. (U.S.), $10,502
8. Praxair Inc. (U.S.), $10,116
9. The Mosaic Co. (U.S.), $9,938
10. Huntsman (U.S.), $9,049

Source: *Chemical Week*, Billion Dollar Club (annual), September 5, 2011, p. 31.

952 ■ THE NETHERLANDS' LARGEST DIVERSIFIED CHEMICAL COMPANIES OVERALL, 2011

Ranked by: Score based on revenue, profits, assets, and market capitalization. **Remarks:** Specific scores not provided. Also notes overall rank in the *Forbes 2000* and figures for each criterion. **Number listed:** 3

1. LyondellBasell Industries NV
2. Akzo Nobel NV
3. Koninklijke DSM NV (Royal DSM NV)

Source: *Forbes*, Forbes 2000 (annual), http://www.forbes.com, May 7, 2012.

953 ■ SAUDI ARABIA'S LARGEST DIVERSIFIED CHEMICAL COMPANIES OVERALL, 2011

Ranked by: Score based on revenue, profits, assets, and market capitalization. **Remarks:** Specific scores not provided. Also notes overall rank in the *Forbes 2000* and figures for each criterion. **Number listed:** 3

1. Saudi Basic Industries Corp. (Sabic)
2. Petro Rabigh
3. Saudi Kayan Petrochemical

Source: *Forbes*, Forbes 2000 (annual), http://www.forbes.com, May 7, 2012.

954 ■ SOUTH KOREA'S LARGEST DIVERSIFIED CHEMICAL COMPANIES OVERALL, 2011

Ranked by: Score based on revenue, profits, assets, and market capitalization. **Remarks:** Specific scores not provided. Also notes overall rank in the *Forbes 2000* and figures for each criterion. **Number listed:** 3

1. OCI Co.
2. Kumho Petro Chemical
3. Hanwha Chemical Corp.

Source: *Forbes*, Forbes 2000 (annual), http://www.forbes.com, May 7, 2012.

955 ■ TAIWAN'S LARGEST DIVERSIFIED CHEMICALS COMPANIES OVERALL, 2011

Ranked by: Score based on revenue, profits, assets, and market capitalization. **Remarks:** Specific scores not provided. Also notes overall rank in the *Forbes 2000* and figures for each criterion. **Number listed:** 2

1. Nan Ya Plastics Corp.
2. Far Eastern New Century

Source: *Forbes*, Forbes 2000 (annual), http://www.forbes.com, May 7, 2012.

956 ■ TOP CANADIAN CHEMICAL COMPANIES, 2010

Ranked by: Revenue, in thousands of Canadian dollars (unless otherwise noted). **Remarks:** Also notes percent change from previous year. **Number listed:** 10

1. Agrium Inc. (U.S. dollars), with C$10,829,000 thousand
2. Potash Corp. of Saskatchewan (U.S. dollars), C$6,883,200
3. Nova Chemicals (U.S. dollars), C$4,582,000
4. Dow Chemical Canada, C$4,272,000
5. Methanex Corp. (U.S. dollars), C$1,991,585
6. DuPont Canada, C$1,000,000
7. BASF Canada, C$912,973
8. PPG Canada (U.S. dollars), C$625,000
9. Chemtrade Logistics IF, C$558,070
10. Canexus LP, C$504,761

Source: *Report on Business Magazine*, Top 1000 Companies (annual), http://www.reportonbusiness.com, June 2011.

957 ■ WORLD'S LARGEST CHEMICAL COMPANIES BY CAPITAL EXPENDITURES, 2010

Ranked by: Chemical spending as a percentage of chemical sales. **Number listed:** 50

1. Potash Corp. of Saskatchewan Inc. (Canada), with 30%
2. PetroChina Co., Ltd. (China), 18%
3. Air Products & Chemicals Inc. (U.S.), 14%
3. Tokuyama (Japan), 14%
3. Praxair Inc. (U.S.), 14%
6. Wacker Chemie AG (Germany), 13%
6. The Mosaic Co. (U.S.), 13%
8. Shin-Etsu Chemical Co., Ltd. (Japan), 11%
8. Lonza (Switzerland), 11%
10. Ineos (Switzerland), 10%
10. Petroleos Mexicanos (PEMEX, Mexico), 10%

Source: *Chemical Week*, Billion Dollar Club (annual), September 5, 2011, p. 29.

958 ■ WORLD'S LARGEST CHEMICAL COMPANIES BY OPERATING PROFIT, 2010

Ranked by: Chemical profits as a percentage of chemical sales. **Number listed:** 50

1. Potash Corp. of Saskatchewan Inc. (Canada), with 40%
2. Linde AG (Germany), 27%
2. The Mosaic Co. (U.S.), 27%
4. Petroliam Nasional Berhad (Petronas, Malaysia), 25%

5. Sigma-Aldrich Corp. (U.S.), 24%
6. Israel Chemicals Ltd. (Israel), 23%
6. CF Industries (U.S.), 23%
8. 3M Co. (U.S.), 21%
8. Tasnee Petrochemical (Saudi Arabia), 21%
8. Praxair Inc. (U.S.), 21%

Source: *Chemical Week*, Billion Dollar Club (annual), September 5, 2011, p. 28.

959 ■ WORLD'S LARGEST CHEMICAL COMPANIES BY RESEARCH & DEVELOPMENT EXPENDITURES, 2010

Ranked by: Research and development expenditures as a percentage of chemical sales. **Number listed:** 50

1. Monsanto Co. (U.S.), with 11%
2. Syngenta AG (Switzerland), 9%
3. International Flavors & Fragrances Inc. (U.S.), 8%
4. Symrise GmbH (Germany), 7%
4. Merck KGaA (Germany), 7%
6. Altana (Germany), 5%
6. Sud Chemie (Germany), 5%
6. E. I. du Pont de Nemours & Co. (U.S.), 5%
6. DSM (Netherlands), 5%
6. JSR (Japan), 5%
6. Givaudan (Switzerland), 5%

Source: *Chemical Week*, Billion Dollar Club (annual), September 5, 2011, p. 29.

960 ■ WORLD'S LARGEST CHEMICAL COMPANIES BY REVENUE, 2010

Ranked by: Sales, in millions of U.S. dollars. **Remarks:** Also notes net profit, operating profit, capital spending, research and development expenditures, total assets, number of employees, and percent change from previous year. **Number listed:** 100

1. BASF AG, with $84,651 million
2. Dow Chemical Co., $53,674
3. ExxonMobil Chemical Co., $53,636
4. China Petroleum & Chemical Corp. (Sinopec), $48,725
5. LyondellBasell Industries, $41,151
6. Saudi Basic Industries Corp. (SABIC), $40,525
7. Shell Chemicals Ltd., $39,629
8. Mitsubishi Chemical Corp., $38,241
9. Ineos Group Ltd., $34,561
10. E. I. du Pont de Nemours & Co., $31,505

Source: *ICIS Chemical Business*, Top 100 Global Chemical Companies, Part 1 (annual), September 12, 2011, p. 32+.

961 ■ WORLD'S LARGEST CHEMICAL COMPANIES BY SALES, 2010

Ranked by: Chemical sales, in millions of U.S. dollars. **Remarks:** Also notes rank for previous year, annual change in rank, total sales, chemical capital spending, chemical operating profit, chemical research and development expenditures, number of employees, chemical sales per employee, and percent change from previous year. **Number listed:** 133

1. BASF AG (Germany), with $63,221 million
2. Dow Chemical Co. (U.S.), $53,674
3. Exxon Mobil Corp. (U.S.), $53,600

4. Saudi Basic Industries Corp. (Sabic, Saudi Arabia), $46,588
5. China Petroleum & Chemical Corp. (Sinopec, China), $43,681
6. Royal Dutch Shell plc (U.S./Netherlands), $39,629
7. E. I. du Pont de Nemours & Co. (U.S.), $31,505
8. LyondellBasell Industries (Netherlands), $31,262
9. Ineos Group Ltd. (U.K.), $28,400
10. Mitsubishi Chemical (Japan), $27,520

Source: *Chemical Week*, Billion Dollar Club (annual), September 5, 2011, p. 22-27.

962 ■ WORLD'S LARGEST CHEMICAL MANUFACTURERS, 2010

Ranked by: Revenue, in millions of dollars. **Remarks:** Also notes rank for previous year, overall rank within the *IW 1000,* country, and revenue growth. **Number listed:** 103

1. BASF SE, with $86,726 million
2. Procter & Gamble Co., $78,938
3. Dow Chemical Co., $53,674
4. Wesfarmers Ltd., $53,155
5. Bayer AG, $47,671
6. Saudi Basic Industries Corp. (Sabic), $40,531
7. E. I. du Pont de Nemours & Co., $32,554
8. Mitsubishi Chemical Holdings Corp., $30,936
9. LyondellBasell Industries NV, $30,828
10. 3M Co., $26,662

Source: *IndustryWeek*, IW 1000 (annual), http://www.industryweek.com, August 2011.

963 ■ WORLD'S LARGEST DIVERSIFIED CHEMICAL COMPANIES OVERALL, 2011

Ranked by: Score based on revenue, profits, assets, and market capitalization. **Remarks:** Specific scores not provided. Also notes country, overall rank in the *Forbes 2000,* and figures for each criterion. **Number listed:** 36

1. BASF SE
2. Saudi Basic Industries Corp. (Sabic)
3. Bayer AG
4. Dow Chemical Co.
5. E. I. du Pont de Nemours & Co.
6. Linde AG
7. LyondellBasell Industries NV
8. Shin-Etsu Chemical Co., Ltd.
9. Mitsubishi Chemical Holdings Corp.
10. Nan Ya Plastics Corp.

Source: *Forbes*, Forbes 2000 (annual), http://www.forbes.com, May 7, 2012.

964 ■ WORLD'S MOST ADMIRED CHEMICALS COMPANIES, 2012

Ranked by: Score, on a scale of 10, based on a survey of executives, directors, and securities analysts of companies within their own industry on eight criteria: innovation, financial soundness, employee talent, use of corporate assets, long-term investment value, social responsibility, quality of management, and quality of products/services. **Remarks:** Specific scores not provided. Also notes rank for previous year. **Number listed:** 8

1. E. I. du Pont de Nemours & Co.
2. BASF SE
3. PPG Industries Inc.
4. Bayer Corp.
5. Dow Chemical Co.
6. L'Air Liquide SA
7. Linde AG
8. Akzo Nobel NV

Source: *Fortune*, World's Most Admired Companies (annual), March 19, 2012, p. 148.

965 ■ WORLD'S MOST ETHICAL CHEMICAL COMPANIES, 2012

Ranked by: Score based on five criteria: ethics and compliance program; reputation, leadership, and innovation; governance; corporate citizenship and responsibility; and culture of ethics. **Remarks:** Specific scores not provided; companies are listed alphabetically, not ranked. **Number listed:** 2

1. Ecolab Inc. (U.S.)
2. Pantheon Enterprises (U.S.)

Source: *Ethisphere Magazine*, World's Most Ethical Companies (annual), http://www.ethisphere.com, 2012.

966 ■ WORLD'S MOST POWERFUL PEOPLE IN THE CHEMICAL INDUSTRY, 2011

Ranked by: Score based on influence and achievements. **Remarks:** Scores not provided. Also notes title and comments. **Number listed:** 40

1. James Gallogly (LyondellBasell)
2. Andrew Liveris (Dow Chemical)
3. Ben Van Beurden (Shell)
4. Jim Ratcliffe (Ineos)
5. Ellen Kullman (DuPont)
6. Khalid Al-Falih (Saudi Aramco)
7. Fu Chengyu (Sinopec)
8. Khadem Al-Qubaisi (IPIC)
9. Stephen Pryor (ExxonMobil)
10. Yoshimitsu Kobayashi (Mitsubishi Chemical)

Source: *ICIS Chemical Business*, Top 40 Power Players (annual), December 5, 2011, p. 29+.

967 ■ WORLD'S MOST PRODUCTIVE CHEMICAL COMPANIES, 2010

Ranked by: Chemical sales per chemical employee, in millions of dollars. **Number listed:** 50

1. Texas Petrochemical (U.S.), with $3.54 million
2. Ineos (Switzerland), $1.83
3. Westlake Chemical Corp. (U.S.), $1.69
4. Kaneka (Japan), $1.66
5. CF Industries (U.S.), $1.59
6. Yara International ASA (Norway), $1.53
7. Eni SpA, $1.38
8. Bayer AG (Germany), $1.23
9. Potash Corp. of Saskatchewan Inc. (Canada), $1.19
10. Dow Chemical Co. (U.S.), $1.08

Source: *Chemical Week*, Billion Dollar Club (annual), September 5, 2011, p. 29.

968 ■ WORLD'S MOST VALUABLE CHEMICAL COMPANIES, 2011

Ranked by: Market value as of March 2011, in millions of U.S. dollars. **Remarks:** Also notes rank within the *FT 500*, rank for previous year, country, revenue, net income, assets, number of employees, share price, price-to-earning ratio, dividend yield, and fiscal year-end. **Number listed:** 18

1. Saudi Basic Industries Corp. (Sabic), with $84,196.6 million
2. BASF AG, $79,546.8
3. Bayer AG, $54,120.8
4. E. I. du Pont de Nemours & Co., $50,922.7
5. Potash Corp. of Saskatchewan Inc., $50,224.6
6. Dow Chemical Co., $44,290.1
7. L'Air Liquide SA, $37,817.3
8. The Mosaic Co., $35,134.2
9. Syngenta AG, $30,865.4
10. Praxair Inc., $30,845.8

Source: *Financial Times*, FT 500 (annual), http://www.ft.com, June 24, 2011.

969 ■ WORLD'S TOP CHEMICAL COMPANIES, 2010

Ranked by: Chemical sales, in millions of U.S. dollars. **Remarks:** Also notes rank for previous year, annual percent change, chemicals as a percentage of total sales, chemical operating profits, chemical operating profits as a percentage of total operating profits, operating profit margin, identifiable chemical assets, chemical assets as a percentage of total assets, and operating return on chemical assets. **Number listed:** 50

1. BASF AG (Germany), with $70,391 million
2. Dow Chemical Co. (U.S.), $53,674
3. China Petroleum & Chemical Corp. (Sinopec, China), $47,444
4. Exxon Mobil Corp. (U.S.), $35,521
5. Royal Dutch Shell plc (Netherlands), $35,277
6. Formosa Plastics Corp. (Taiwan), $34,663
7. Saudi Basic Industries Corp. (Sabic, Saudi Arabia), $33,712
8. E. I. du Pont de Nemours & Co. (U.S.), $31,312
9. LyondellBasell Industries (Netherlands), $27,682
10. Mitsubishi Chemical (Japan), $26,021

Source: *Chemical & Engineering News*, Global Top 50 (annual), July 25, 2011.

Chemicals

970 ■ GERMANY'S MOST VALUABLE CHEMICAL BRANDS, 2011

Ranked by: Brand value, in millions of U.S. dollars. **Remarks:** Also notes rank within the *Global 500* for current and previous year, figures for current and previous year, and brand rating. Ranking is available online only. **Number listed:** 2

1. BASF, with $5,415 million
2. Bayer, $3,401

Source: *Global 500*, (annual), Brand Finance plc, March 2012.

971 ■ WORLD'S MOST VALUABLE CHEMICAL BRANDS, 2011

Ranked by: Brand value, in millions of U.S. dollars. **Remarks:** Also notes rank within the *Global 500* for current and previous

year, figures for current and previous year, country, and brand rating. Ranking is available online only. **Number listed:** 3

1. BASF, with $5,415 million
2. Bayer, $3,401
3. Du Pont, $2,638

Source: *Global 500*, (annual), Brand Finance plc, March 2012.

Chemicals, Specialty

972 ■ CANADA'S LARGEST SPECIALIZED CHEMICAL COMPANIES OVERALL, 2011

Ranked by: Score based on revenue, profits, assets, and market capitalization. **Remarks:** Specific scores not provided. Also notes overall rank in the *Forbes 2000* and figures for each criterion. **Number listed:** 2

1. Potash Corp. of Saskatchewan Inc.
2. Agrium Inc.

Source: *Forbes*, Forbes 2000 (annual), http://www.forbes.com, May 7, 2012.

973 ■ JAPAN'S LARGEST SPECIALIZED CHEMICALS COMPANIES OVERALL, 2011

Ranked by: Score based on revenue, profits, assets, and market capitalization. **Remarks:** Specific scores not provided. Also notes overall rank in the *Forbes 2000* and figures for each criterion. **Number listed:** 2

1. Mitsui Chemicals Inc.
2. Kuraray Co., Ltd.

Source: *Forbes*, Forbes 2000 (annual), http://www.forbes.com, May 7, 2012.

974 ■ LARGEST U.S. SPECIALIZED CHEMICAL COMPANIES OVERALL, 2011

Ranked by: Score based on revenue, profits, assets, and market capitalization. **Remarks:** Specific scores not provided. Also notes overall rank in the *Forbes 2000* and figures for each criterion. **Number listed:** 12

1. Monsanto Co.
2. Praxair Inc.
3. The Mosaic Co.
4. Air Products & Chemicals Inc.
5. Ecolab Inc.
6. CF Industries Holdings Inc.
7. Eastman Chemical Co.
8. Ashland Inc.
9. Sigma-Aldrich Corp.
10. FMC Corp.

Source: *Forbes*, Forbes 2000 (annual), http://www.forbes.com, May 7, 2012.

975 ■ MINNESOTA'S LARGEST SPECIALIZED CHEMICAL COMPANIES OVERALL, 2011

Ranked by: Score based on revenue, profits, assets, and market capitalization. **Remarks:** Specific scores not provided. Also notes overall rank in the *Forbes 2000* and figures for each criterion. **Number listed:** 2

1. The Mosaic Co.
2. Ecolab Inc.

Source: *Forbes*, Forbes 2000 (annual), http://www.forbes.com, May 7, 2012.

976 ■ MISSOURI'S LARGEST SPECIALIZED CHEMICAL COMPANIES OVERALL, 2011

Ranked by: Score based on revenue, profits, assets, and market capitalization. **Remarks:** Specific scores not provided. Also notes overall rank in the *Forbes 2000* and figures for each criterion. **Number listed:** 2

1. Monsanto Co.
2. Sigma-Aldrich Corp.

Source: *Forbes*, Forbes 2000 (annual), http://www.forbes.com, May 7, 2012.

977 ■ PENNSYLVANIA'S LARGEST SPECIALTY CHEMICAL COMPANIES OVERALL, 2011

Ranked by: Score based on revenue, profits, assets, and market capitalization. **Remarks:** Specific scores not provided. Also notes overall rank in the *Forbes 2000* and figures for each criterion. **Number listed:** 3

1. Air Products & Chemicals Inc.
2. FMC Corp.
3. Airgas Inc.

Source: *Forbes*, Forbes 2000 (annual), http://www.forbes.com, May 7, 2012.

978 ■ SOUTH KOREA'S LARGEST SPECIALIZED CHEMICAL COMPANIES OVERALL, 2011

Ranked by: Score based on revenue, profits, assets, and market capitalization. **Remarks:** Specific scores not provided. Also notes overall rank in the *Forbes 2000* and figures for each criterion. **Number listed:** 2

1. LG Chem Ltd.
2. Honam Petrochemical

Source: *Forbes*, Forbes 2000 (annual), http://www.forbes.com, May 7, 2012.

979 ■ SWITZERLAND'S LARGEST SPECIALIZED CHEMICAL COMPANIES OVERALL, 2011

Ranked by: Score based on revenue, profits, assets, and market capitalization. **Remarks:** Specific scores not provided. Also notes overall rank in the *Forbes 2000* and figures for each criterion. **Number listed:** 3

1. Syngenta AG
2. Clariant
3. Givaudan

Source: *Forbes*, Forbes 2000 (annual), http://www.forbes.com, May 7, 2012.

980 ■ TAIWAN'S LARGEST SPECIALIZED CHEMICAL COMPANIES OVERALL, 2011

Ranked by: Score based on revenue, profits, assets, and market capitalization. **Remarks:** Specific scores not provided. Also notes overall rank in the *Forbes 2000* and figures for each criterion. **Number listed:** 2

1. Formosa Chemicals & Fiber Corp.
2. Formosa Plastics Corp.

Source: *Forbes*, Forbes 2000 (annual), http://www.forbes.com, May 7, 2012.

981 ■ THAILAND'S LARGEST SPECIALIZED CHEMICAL COMPANIES OVERALL, 2011

Ranked by: Score based on revenue, profits, assets, and market capitalization. **Remarks:** Specific scores not provided. Also notes overall rank in the *Forbes 2000* and figures for each criterion. **Number listed:** 2

1. PTT Global Chemical Public Co., Ltd.
2. Indorama Ventures

Source: *Forbes*, Forbes 2000 (annual), http://www.forbes.com, May 7, 2012.

982 ■ WORLD'S LARGEST SPECIALIZED CHEMICAL COMPANIES OVERALL, 2011

Ranked by: Score based on revenue, profits, assets, and market capitalization. **Remarks:** Specific scores not provided. Also notes country, overall rank in the *Forbes 2000,* and figures for each criterion. **Number listed:** 34

1. L'Air Liquide SA
2. Monsanto Co.
3. LG Chem Ltd.
4. Potash Corp. of Saskatchewan Inc.
5. Praxair Inc.
6. Syngenta AG
7. The Mosaic Co.
8. Formosa Chemicals & Fiber Corp.
9. Agrium Inc.
10. Air Products & Chemicals Inc.

Source: *Forbes*, Forbes 2000 (annual), http://www.forbes.com, May 7, 2012.

Chief Executive Officers

983 ■ BEST-PERFORMING U.S. CHIEF EXECUTIVES, 2011

Ranked by: Efficiency score, which is based on annualized stock performance during tenure, stock performance relative to the S&P 500 and industry peers during tenure, and total compensation. **Remarks:** Specific scores not provided. Also notes annualized return and compensation. To qualify, persons must have served at least six years as chief executive and have a six-year pay history. **Number listed:** 10

1. Jeffrey P. Bezos (Amazon)
2. Marc Benioff (Salesforce.com)
3. Bob Sasser (Dollar Tree)
4. Neal Patterson (Cerner)
5. Leonard Bell (Alexion Pharma)
6. Steve Ells (Chipotle Mexican Grill)
7. William Rhodes III (Autozone)
8. Stephen Wilson (CF Industries)
9. Willard Oberton (Fastenal)
10. Gregory Henslee (O'Reilly Automotive)

Source: *Forbes*, Best and Worst Bosses (annual), April 23, 2012, p. 96.

984 ■ WORLD'S BEST CEOS, 2012

Ranked by: Editorial determination based, in part, on earnings growth during tenure, leadership strength, industry stature, and competitive challenges. **Remarks:** Specific scores not provided; CEOs are listed alphabetically, not ranked. Also notes year appointed CEO, one- and five-year returns, percent change in return during tenure, earnings per share, five-year growth in earnings per share, and comments. **Number listed:** 30

1. Marc Benioff (Salesforce.com)
2. Jeffrey P. Bezos (Amazon)
3. Jeffrey Boyd (Priceline)

4. Carlos Brito (Anheuser-Busch InBev)
5. Warren Edward Buffett (Berkshire Hathaway)
6. Ed Clark (TD Bank)
7. Jamie Dimon (JPMorgan Chase)
8. Lawrence Ellison (Oracle)
9. Larry Fink (BlackRock)
10. Lew Frankfort (Coach)

Source: *Barron's*, World's Best CEOs (annual), March 26, 2012, p. s5-s19.

985 ■ WORST-PERFORMING U.S. CHIEF EXECUTIVES, 2011

Ranked by: Efficiency score, which is based on annualized stock performance during tenure, stock performance relative to the S&P 500 and industry peers during tenure, and total compensation. **Remarks:** Specific scores not provided. Also notes six-year average pay. To qualify, persons must have served at least six years as chief executive and have a six-year pay history. **Number listed:** 5

1. Mel Karmazin (Sirius XM)
2. Michael Fraizer (Genworth Fin'l)
3. Wiliam Klesse (Valero Energy)
4. Gregory Boyce (Peabody Energy)
5. Wendell Weeks (Corning)

Source: *Forbes*, Best and Worst Bosses (annual), April 23, 2012, p. 96.

Chief Executive Officers—Compensation

986 ■ HIGHEST-PAID CEOS OF COLORADO PUBLIC COMPANIES, 2010

Ranked by: Total compensation, in dollars. **Remarks:** Also notes age, year made officer, ticker symbol, and breakdown of compensation by type. **Number listed:** 25

1. Richard M. Weil (Janus Capital), with $20,337,868
2. Kent J. Thiry (DaVita), $14,121,043
3. Steve Ells (Chipotle Mexican Grill), $14,095,870
4. Monty Moran (Chipotle Mexican Grill), $13,449,506
5. Richard T. O'Brien (Newmont Mining), $12,506,131
6. Michael T. Fries (Liberty Global), $12,315,033
7. R. David Hoover (Ball), $10,469,602
8. Larissa L. Herda (TW Telecom), $9,262,996
9. Larry A. Mizel (MDC), $9,206,403
10. Thomas W. Toomey (UDR), $8,651,734

Source: *Denver Business Journal*, Book of Lists (annual), December 16, 2011, p. 44.

987 ■ HIGHEST-PAID CEOS IN NEW YORK CITY, 2010

Ranked by: Total compensation, in thousands of dollars. **Remarks:** Also notes age, company ticker symbol, revenue, one-year return, and breakdown of compensation by type. **Number listed:** 100

1. Philippe P. Dauman (Viacom), with $84,469.5 thousand
2. Leslie Moonves (CBS), $56,859.2

3. Mario J. Gabelli (Gamco Investors), $56,608.7

Source: *Crain's New York Business*, Highest-Paid CEOs (annual), http://www.crainsnewyork.com, June 20, 2011.

988 ■ HIGHEST-PAID KANSAS CITY CHIEF EXECUTIVES, 2011

Ranked by: Total compensation, in dollars. **Remarks:** Also notes figures for previous year, percent change, and overall rank in the *Star 50*. **Number listed:** 48

1. Daniel R. Hesse (Sprint Nextel), with $11,882,651
2. Matthew E. Rubel (Collective Brands), $9,320,598
3. Hank Hermann (Waddell & Reed), $6,668,705
4. David S. Haffner (Leggett & Platt), $5,982,756
5. William B. Moore (Westar), $5,758,073
6. Alan M. Bennett (H&R Block), $5,673,640
7. Neal L. Patterson (Cerner), $5,595,390
8. Thomas A. McDonnell (DST), $5,494,966
9. Tom W. Olofson (Epiq), $5,237,278
10. Steven J. Bresky (Seaboard), $5,190,668

Source: *Kansas City Star*, The Star 50 (annual), http://www.kansascity.com, May 7, 2012.

989 ■ HIGHEST-PAID U.S. CHIEF EXECUTIVES, 2011

Ranked by: Total annual compensation, in millions of dollars. **Remarks:** Only the top 5 are published; the remainder of the list is available online. **Number listed:** 500

1. John Hammergren (McKesson), with $131.2 million
2. Ralph Lauren (Ralph Lauren), $66.7
3. Michael Fascitelli (Vornado Realty), $64.4
4. Richard Kinder (Kinder Morgan), $60.9
5. David Cote (Honeywell), $55.8
6. George Paz (Express Scripts), $51.5
7. Jeffery H. Boyd (Priceline.com), $50.2
8. Stephen J. Hemsley (UnitedHealth), $48.8
9. Clarence P. Cazalot Jr. (Marathon Oil), $43.7
10. John C. Martin (Gilead Sciences), $43.2

Source: *Forbes*, Best and Worst Bosses (annual), April 23, 2012, p. 96.

Child Care

990 ■ AMERICA'S BEST COMPANIES IN CHILD CARE BENEFITS, 2012

Ranked by: Monthly rate for onsite child care center, in dollars. **Remarks:** Also notes overall rank in the *100 Best Companies to Work For*. **Number listed:** 10

1. Publix Super Markets Inc., with $130
2. SAS Institute Inc., $410
3. Bright Horizons Family Solutions Inc., $485
4. AFLAC Inc., $490
5. Chesapeake Energy, $560
6. The Men's Wearhouse Inc., $600
7. Meridian Health, $632
8. Baptist Health South Florida Inc., $672

9. USAA, $680

10. Atlantic Health System Inc., $756

Source: *Fortune*, 100 Best Companies to Work For (annual), http://www.fortune.com, February 6, 2012.

991 ■ TOP CHILDREN'S IDENTIFICATION SERVICE FRANCHISES, 2012

Ranked by: Cumulative score based on financial strength and stability, growth rate, size of the system, number of years in business, the length of time franchising, start-up costs, litigation, percentage of terminations, and whether the company provides financing. **Remarks:** Specific scores not provided. Also notes overall rank within the *Franchise 500,* contact information, description, year founded, year started franchising, states where registered, available U.S. regions, where seeking foreign expansion, number of franchised and company-owned units for past three years, start-up costs, franchise fees, royalty fees, and type of financing available. **Number listed:** 2

1. Guard-A-Kid
2. Ident-A-Kid Franchise Corp.

Source: *Entrepreneur*, Franchise 500 (annual), January 2012, p. 158-159.

Child Care Centers

992 ■ TOP CHILD CARE FRANCHISES, 2012

Ranked by: Cumulative score based on financial strength and stability, growth rate, size of the system, number of years in business, the length of time franchising, start-up costs, litigation, percentage of terminations, and whether the company provides financing. **Remarks:** Specific scores not provided. Also notes overall rank within the *Franchise 500,* contact information, description, year founded, year started franchising, states where registered, available U.S. regions, where seeking foreign expansion, number of franchised and company-owned units for past three years, start-up costs, franchise fees, royalty fees, and type of financing available. **Number listed:** 6

1. Goddard Systems Inc.
2. Primrose School Franchising Co.
3. The Learning Experience
4. SeekingSitters Franchise System Inc.
5. Kiddie Academy Child Care Learning Centers
6. Discovery Point Franchising Inc.

Source: *Entrepreneur*, Franchise 500 (annual), January 2012, p. 154-155.

Cigarette Industry
See: **Tobacco Industry**

Closely Held Corporations
See: **Private Companies**

Clothing and Dress—Children

993 ■ TOP CHILDREN'S RETAILING FRANCHISES

Ranked by: Cumulative score based on financial strength and stability, growth rate, size of the system, number of years in business, the length of time franchising, start-up costs, litigation, percentage of terminations, and whether the company provides financing. **Remarks:** Specific scores not provided. Also notes

overall rank within the *Franchise 500,* contact information, description, year founded, year started franchising, states where registered, available U.S. regions, where seeking foreign expansion, number of franchised and company-owned units for past three years, start-up costs, franchise fees, royalty fees, and type of financing available. **Number listed:** 4

1. Once Upon A Child
2. Just Between Friends Franchise Systems
3. Kid to Kid
4. Learning Express

Source: *Entrepreneur*, Franchise 500 (annual), January 2012, p. 158-159.

Clothing Industry

994 ■ LARGEST COMPANIES IN THE APPAREL AND OTHER FABRIC PRODUCTS INDUSTRY BY EMPLOYEES, 2010

Ranked by: Total number of employees. **Remarks:** Also notes contact information for headquarters, number of employees at headquarters, revenue, rank by revenue, and primary SIC code. **Number listed:** 49

1. VF Corp., with 45,700 employees
2. Polo Ralph Lauren Corp., 19,000
3. Levi Strauss & Co., 16,200
4. VF Jeanswear LP, 15,000
5. Guess? Inc., 12,700
6. Liz Claiborne Inc., 11,500
7. Phillips-Van Heusen Corp., 10,800
8. Vanity Fair Brands LP, 10,303
9. Lee Apparel Co., 10,300
10. American Apparel Inc., 10,000
10. Bali LLC, 10,000

Source: *Business Rankings*, (annual), Dun & Bradstreet Inc., 2011, p. VI.52-VI.53.

995 ■ LARGEST COMPANIES IN THE APPAREL AND OTHER FABRIC PRODUCTS INDUSTRY BY SALES, 2010

Ranked by: Total revenue, in dollars. **Remarks:** Also notes contact information for headquarters, number of employees at headquarters and overall, rank by employees, and primary SIC code. **Number listed:** 50

1. VF Corp., with $7,702,589,000
2. Polo Ralph Lauren Corp., $4,978,900,000
3. Levi Strauss & Co., $4,410,649,000
4. Jones Group Inc., $3,642,700,000
5. Liz Claiborne Inc., $2,500,072,000
6. Phillips-Van Heusen Corp., $2,398,731,000
7. Warnaco Group Inc., $2,295,751,000
8. Guess? Inc., $2,128,466,000
9. Quiksilver Inc., $1,837,620,000
10. Carters Inc., $1,749,256,000

Source: *Business Rankings*, (annual), Dun & Bradstreet Inc., 2011, p. V.52-V.53.

996 ■ LARGEST U.S. APPAREL AND ACCESSORIES COMPANIES OVERALL, 2011

Ranked by: Score based on revenue, profits, assets, and market capitalization. **Remarks:** Specific scores not provided. Also notes overall rank in the *Forbes 2000* and figures for each criterion. **Number listed:** 5

1. Nike Inc.
2. VF Corp.
3. Ralph Lauren Corp.
4. Coach Inc.
5. PVH Corp.

Source: *Forbes,* Forbes 2000 (annual), http://www.forbes.com, May 7, 2012.

997 ■ LARGEST U.S. APPAREL MANUFACTURERS, 2010

Ranked by: Revenue, in millions of dollars. **Remarks:** Also notes overall rank within the *IW 500,* revenue growth, and profit margin. **Number listed:** 17

1. Nike Inc., with $19,014 million
2. VF Corp., $7,703
3. Phillips-Van Heusen Corp., $4,637
4. Coach Inc., $3,608
5. Cintas Corp., $3,547
6. Liz Claiborne Inc., $2,500
7. Guess? Inc., $2,487
8. Warnaco Group Inc., $2,296
9. Fossil Inc., $2,031
10. Quiksilver Inc., $1,838

Source: *IndustryWeek,* IW 500 (annual), http://www.industryweek.com, July 2011.

998 ■ MOST POPULAR APPAREL COMPANIES ON FACEBOOK, 2011

Ranked by: Number of Facebook fans as of July. **Remarks:** Also notes rank and figures for previous year, and percent change. **Number listed:** 50

1. Limited Brands, with 14,477,665 fans
2. Nike Inc., 8,490,521
3. Levi Strauss, 6,134,759
4. Abercrombie & Fitch, 5,082,227
5. American Eagle Outfitters, 4,882,966
6. Aeropostale, 4,877,891
7. Polo Ralph Lauren, 3,450,956
8. Hanesbrands, 1,748,925
9. Wet Seal, 1,578,258
10. The Gap Inc., 1,568,513

Source: *Apparel,* Rankings by Socia Media Popularity (annual), August 2011, p. 7.

999 ■ NEW YORK'S LARGEST APPAREL AND ACCESSORIES COMPANIES OVERALL, 2011

Ranked by: Score based on revenue, profits, assets, and market capitalization. **Remarks:** Specific scores not provided. Also notes overall rank in the *Forbes 2000* and figures for each criterion. **Number listed:** 3

1. Ralph Lauren Corp.
2. Coach Inc.
3. PVH Corp.

Source: *Forbes,* Forbes 2000 (annual), http://www.forbes.com, May 7, 2012.

1000 ■ TOP *FORTUNE 500* COMPANIES IN APPAREL, 2011

Ranked by: Revenue, in millions of dollars. **Remarks:** Also notes overall rank in the *Fortune 500;* profits; profits as a percentage of revenue; stockholders' equity; and rank by each criterion. **Number listed:** 4

1. Nike Inc., with $20,862 million
2. VF Corp., $9,459
3. PVH Corp., $5,891
4. Ralph Lauren Corp., $5,660

Source: *Fortune,* Fortune 500 (annual), May 21, 2012, p. F-33.

1001 ■ TOP U.S. APPAREL COMPANIES BY PROFIT MARGIN, 2010

Ranked by: Profit margin, in percent. **Remarks:** Ranking covers publicly traded apparel companies (not including department stores) with at least $100 million in annual sales. Also notes rank and figures for previous year, fiscal year-end, sales for current and previous year, net income for current and previous year, and annual growth. **Number listed:** 48

1. lululemon athletica inc., with 17.11%
2. The Buckle Inc., 14.18%
3. Oxford Industries, 13.03%
4. Urban Outfitters Inc., 12%
5. True Religion Apparel Inc., 11.96%
6. Guess? Inc., 11.64%
7. Nike Inc., 10.03%
7. Polo Ralph Lauren Corp., 10.03%
9. Jos. A. Bank Clothiers Inc., 10%
9. Aeropostale Inc., 9.64%

Source: *Apparel,* Top 50 (annual), July 2011, p. 6.

1002 ■ THE UNITED STATES' MOST VALUABLE APPAREL BRANDS, 2011

Ranked by: Brand value, in millions of U.S. dollars. **Remarks:** Also notes rank within the *Global 500* for current and previous year, figures for current and previous year, and brand rating. Ranking is available online only. **Number listed:** 4

1. Nike, with $18,619 million
2. Polo Ralph Lauren, $3,367
3. Coach, $3,134
4. Champion, $2,963

Source: *Global 500,* (annual), Brand Finance plc, March 2012.

Clothing Industry, International

1003 ■ FRANCE'S LARGEST APPAREL AND ACCESSORIES COMPANIES OVERALL, 2011

Ranked by: Score based on revenue, profits, assets, and market capitalization. **Remarks:** Specific scores not provided. Also notes overall rank in the *Forbes 2000* and figures for each criterion. **Number listed:** 2

1. Christian Dior SA
2. Hermes International

Source: *Forbes,* Forbes 2000 (annual), http://www.forbes.com, May 7, 2012.

1004 ■ GERMANY'S LARGEST APPAREL AND ACCESSORIES COMPANIES OVERALL, 2011

Ranked by: Score based on revenue, profits, assets, and market capitalization. **Remarks:** Specific scores not provided. Also notes overall rank in the *Forbes 2000* and figures for each criterion. **Number listed:** 2

1. adidas AG

2. Hugo Boss AG

Source: *Forbes*, Forbes 2000 (annual), http://www.forbes.com, May 7, 2012.

1005 ■ WORLD'S LARGEST APPAREL AND ACCESSORIES COMPANIES OVERALL, 2011

Ranked by: Score based on revenue, profits, assets, and market capitalization. **Remarks:** Specific scores not provided. Also notes country, overall rank in the *Forbes 2000,* and figures for each criterion. **Number listed:** 12

1. Christian Dior SA
2. Nike Inc.
3. adidas AG
4. The Swatch Group Ltd.
5. VF Corp.
6. Ralph Lauren Corp.
7. Coach Inc.
8. Hermes International
9. Prada SpA
10. Burberry Group plc

Source: *Forbes*, Forbes 2000 (annual), http://www.forbes.com, May 7, 2012.

1006 ■ WORLD'S LARGEST APPAREL MANUFACTURERS, 2010

Ranked by: Revenue, in millions of dollars. **Remarks:** Also notes rank for previous year, overall rank within the *IW 1000,* country, and revenue growth. **Number listed:** 15

1. Christian Dior SA, with $28,254 million
2. Nike Inc., $19,014
3. Industria de Diseno Textil SA, $16,751
4. adidas AG, $16,297
5. VF Corp., $7,703
6. Pou Chen Corp., $6,625
7. Yue Yuen Industrial Holdings Ltd., $5,912
8. Phillips-Van Heusen Corp., $4,637
9. Puma AG Rudolf Dassler Sport, $3,646
10. Coach Inc., $3,608

Source: *IndustryWeek*, IW 1000 (annual), http://www.industryweek.com, August 2011.

1007 ■ WORLD'S LARGEST CONSUMER FOOTWEAR, APPAREL, AND ACCESSORY COMPANIES, 2010

Ranked by: Sales, in millions of U.S. dollars. **Remarks:** Also notes brands and annual sales growth. **Number listed:** 20

1. LVMH Moet Hennessy Louis Vuitton SA, with $28,210 million
2. PPR SA, $20,049
3. Nike Inc., $19,014
4. adidas AG, $16,646
5. VF Corp., $7,703
6. Compagnie Financiere Richemont SA, $7,186
7. Polo Ralph Lauren Corp., $5,000
8. PVH Corp., $4,636
9. Esprit Co., $4,335
10. Hanesbrands Inc., $4,327

Source: *Consumer Goods Technology*, Consumer Goods Registry (annual), http://www.consumergoods.com, December 2011.

1008 ■ WORLD'S MOST ADMIRED APPAREL COMPANIES, 2012

Ranked by: Score, on a scale of 10, based on a survey of executives, directors, and securities analysts of companies within their own industry on eight criteria: innovation, financial soundness, employee talent, use of corporate assets, long-term investment value, social responsibility, quality of management, and quality of products/services. **Remarks:** Specific scores not provided. Also notes rank for previous year. **Number listed:** 8

1. Ralph Lauren Corp.
2. Nike Inc.
3. VF Corp.
4. Coach Inc.
5. PVH Corp.
6. adidas AG
7. Compagnie Financiere Richemont SA
8. PPR SA

Source: *Fortune*, World's Most Admired Companies (annual), March 19, 2012, p. 147.

1009 ■ WORLD'S MOST ETHICAL APPAREL COMPANIES, 2012

Ranked by: Score based on five criteria: ethics and compliance program; reputation, leadership, and innovation; governance; corporate citizenship and responsibility; and culture of ethics. **Remarks:** Specific scores not provided; companies are listed alphabetically, not ranked. **Number listed:** 4

1. Comme Il Faut (Israel)
2. The Gap Inc. (U.S.)
3. Patagonia Inc. (U.S.)
4. The Timberland Co. (U.S.)

Source: *Ethisphere Magazine*, World's Most Ethical Companies (annual), http://www.ethisphere.com, 2012.

1010 ■ WORLD'S MOST INNOVATIVE APPAREL COMPANIES, 2012

Ranked by: Editorial determination. **Remarks:** Companies are listed alphabetically, not ranked. **Number listed:** 33

1. Ash City
2. Betsy & Adam
3. Castlewood Apparel
4. Chef Works
5. Columbia Sportswear
6. Dao Chloe Dao
7. Duluth Trading Co.
8. Fruit of the Loom
9. Grupo Cortefiel
10. Guess

Source: *Apparel*, Top Innovators (annual), May 2012, p. 15-54.

1011 ■ WORLD'S MOST VALUABLE APPAREL BRANDS, 2011

Ranked by: Brand value, in millions of U.S. dollars. **Remarks:** Also notes rank within the *Global 500* for current and previous year, figures for current and previous year, country, and brand rating. Ranking is available online only. **Number listed:** 6

1. Nike, with $18,619 million
2. adidas, $7,150
3. Hermes, $3,430

4. Polo Ralph Lauren, $3,367
5. Coach, $3,134
6. Champion, $2,963

Source: *Global 500*, (annual), Brand Finance plc, March 2012.

1012 ■ WORLD'S MOST VALUABLE APPAREL BRANDS, 2012

Ranked by: Brand value, a measure of a brand's earnings and contribution, in millions of U.S. dollars. **Remarks:** Also notes annual growth in brand value and rank by brand contribution and brand momentum. **Number listed:** 10

1. Nike, with $16,255 million
2. H & M, $13,485
3. Zara, $12,616
4. Ralph Lauren, $5,086
5. adidas, $3,863
6. Uniqlo, $3,689
7. Hugo Boss, $3,257
8. Next, $2,973
9. MetersBonwe, $1,395
10. Calvin Klein, $1,183

Source: *Financial Times*, Global Brands (annual), http://www.ft.com, May 22, 2012.

Clothing Stores

1013 ■ CALIFORNIA'S LARGEST APPAREL AND FOOTWEAR RETAILERS OVERALL, 2011

Ranked by: Score based on revenue, profits, assets, and market capitalization. **Remarks:** Specific scores not provided. Also notes overall rank in the *Forbes 2000* and figures for each criterion. **Number listed:** 2

1. The Gap Inc.
2. Ross Stores Inc.

Source: *Forbes*, Forbes 2000 (annual), http://www.forbes.com, May 7, 2012.

1014 ■ FASTEST-GROWING SOFTGOODS CHAINS, 2009-2010

Ranked by: Annual gain in basis points. **Remarks:** To qualify, chains must have annual revenues of at least $100 million. Also notes sales and market share for current and previous year. **Number listed:** 11

1. Ascena Retail Group, with 454 points
2. Nordstrom, 247
3. Limited Brands, 174
4. TJX, 146
5. Kohl's, 142
6. Macy's, 124
7. Polo Ralph Lauren, 118
8. H & M, 95
9. Ross Stores, 65
10. DSW, 62

Source: *Stores*, Hot 100 (annual), August 2011, p. s8.

1015 ■ LARGEST APPAREL AND ACCESSORY STORES BY EMPLOYEES, 2010

Ranked by: Total number of employees. **Remarks:** Also notes contact information for headquarters, number of employees at headquarters, revenue, rank by revenue, and primary SIC code. **Number listed:** 189

1. The TJX Companies Inc., with 154,000 employees
2. The Gap Inc., 135,000
3. Limited Brands Inc., 92,100
4. Abercrombie & Fitch Co., 80,000
5. Nordstrom Inc., 48,000
6. Ross Stores Inc., 45,600
7. American Eagle Outfitters Inc., 39,400
8. Foot Locker Inc., 38,764
9. Ascena Retail Group Inc., 30,000
9. Collective Brands Inc., 30,000
9. Dress Barn Inc., 30,000
9. Foot Locker Retail Inc., 30,000

Source: *Business Rankings*, (annual), Dun & Bradstreet Inc., 2011, p. VI.144-VI.148.

1016 ■ LARGEST APPAREL AND ACCESSORY STORES BY SALES, 2010

Ranked by: Total revenue, in dollars. **Remarks:** Also notes contact information for headquarters, number of employees at headquarters and overall, rank by employees, and primary SIC code. **Number listed:** 190

1. The TJX Companies Inc., with $20,288,444,000
2. The Gap Inc., $14,197,000,000
3. Limited Brands Inc., $8,632,000,000
4. Nordstrom Inc., $8,627,000,000
5. Ross Stores Inc., $7,184,213,000
6. Foot Locker Inc., $4,854,000,000
7. Burlington Coat Factory Warehouse Corp., $3,390,000,000
8. Collective Brands Inc., $3,307,900,000
9. American Eagle Outfitters Inc., $2,967,559,000
10. Abercrombie & Fitch Co., $2,928,626,000

Source: *Business Rankings*, (annual), Dun & Bradstreet Inc., 2011, p. V.144-V.148.

1017 ■ LARGEST ASIA-PACIFIC CLOTHING, FOOTWEAR, AND ACCESSORIES RETAILERS, 2010

Ranked by: Sales, in millions of U.S. dollars. **Remarks:** Also notes country, fascias/brands, number of outlets, sales in national currency, sales area, sales per square meter, and figures for previous year. **Number listed:** 10

1. Fast Retailing Co., with $7,729 million
2. Shimamura, $4,379
3. World, $3,405
4. Belle International Holdings, $3,156
5. Aoyama Trading, $1,859
6. Louis Vuitton Japan, $1,826
7. Aeon Group, $1,404
8. Li Ning Co., Ltd., $1,271
9. Sanyo Shokai, $1,267
10. Right-On Inc., $1,043

Source: *Retail Asia*, Retail Asia-Pacific Top 500 (annual), July 2011, p. 64-64a.

1018 ■ LARGEST U.S. APPAREL AND FOOTWEAR RETAILERS OVERALL, 2011

Ranked by: Score based on revenue, profits, assets, and market capitalization. **Remarks:** Specific scores not provided. Also notes overall rank in the *Forbes 2000* and figures for each criterion. **Number listed:** 3

1. The Gap Inc.
2. Limited Brands Inc.
3. Ross Stores Inc.

Source: *Forbes*, Forbes 2000 (annual), http://www.forbes.com, May 7, 2012.

1019 ■ TOP APPAREL AND ACCESSORIES RETAIL FRANCHISES, 2012

Ranked by: Cumulative score based on financial strength and stability, growth rate, size of the system, number of years in business, the length of time franchising, start-up costs, litigation, percentage of terminations, and whether the company provides financing. Remarks: Specific scores not provided. Also notes overall rank within the *Franchise 500,* contact information, description, year founded, year started franchising, states where registered, available U.S. regions, where seeking foreign expansion, number of franchised and company-owned units for past three years, start-up costs, franchise fees, royalty fees, and type of financing available. Number listed: 4

1. Plato's Closet
2. Flip Flop Shops
3. Clothes Mentor
4. Apricot Lane

Source: *Entrepreneur*, Franchise 500 (annual), January 2012, p. 198-199.

1020 ■ TOP U.S. APPAREL DEPARTMENT STORES BY PROFIT MARGIN, 2010

Ranked by: Profit margin, in percent. Remarks: Ranking covers publicly traded department stores with at least $100 million in annual sales. Also notes rank and figures for previous year, fiscal year-end, sales for current and previous year, net income for current and previous year, and annual growth. Number listed: 10

1. Kohl's, with 6.06%
2. Belk, 3.63%
3. Macy's, 3.39%
4. Dillards, 2.93%
5. J. C. Penney Co., Inc., 2.19%
6. Saks, 1.72%
7. Burlington Coat Factory, 0.84%
8. The Bon-Ton Stores, 0.72%
9. Sears Holdings, 0.35%
10. Neiman Marcus, -0.05%

Source: *Apparel*, Top 50 (annual), July 2011, p. 9.

1021 ■ TOP U.S. APPAREL RETAILERS BY SALES, 2010

Ranked by: Sales volume, in thousands of dollars. Remarks: Also notes comparable-store sales and sales per store. Number listed: 26

1. The TJX Companies Inc., with $14,820,000 thousand
2. The Gap Inc., $11,718,000
3. Ross Stores Inc., $7,860,000
4. Limited Brands Inc., $5,507,000
5. Burlington Coat Factory Warehouse Corp., $3,660,000
6. Foot Locker, $3,577,000
7. Abercrombie & Fitch Co., $2,846,000
8. Dress Barn, $2,724,000
9. American Eagle Outfitters Inc., $2,676,000

10. Collective Brands, $2,287,000

Source: *Stores*, Top 100 Retailers (annual), July 2011, p. s6.

1022 ■ WORLD'S LARGEST APPAREL AND FOOTWEAR RETAILERS OVERALL, 2011

Ranked by: Score based on revenue, profits, assets, and market capitalization. Remarks: Specific scores not provided. Also notes country, overall rank in the *Forbes 2000,* and figures for each criterion. Number listed: 8

1. Inditex SA
2. Hennes & Mauritz AB
3. Fast Retailing Co.
4. The Gap Inc.
5. Limited Brands Inc.
6. Ross Stores Inc.
7. Belle International Holdings Ltd.
8. Next Inc.

Source: *Forbes*, Forbes 2000 (annual), http://www.forbes.com, May 7, 2012.

Coal Industry

1023 ■ LARGEST U.S. PETROLEUM AND COAL PRODUCT MANUFACTURERS, 2010

Ranked by: Revenue, in millions of dollars. Remarks: Also notes overall rank within the *IW 500,* revenue growth, and profit margin. Number listed: 52

1. Exxon Mobil Corp., with $372,544 million
2. Chevron Corp., $199,291
3. ConocoPhillips, $195,522
4. Valero Energy Corp., $82,233
5. Marathon Oil Corp., $73,207
6. Sunoco Inc., $37,461
7. Hess Corp., $35,135
8. Enterprise Products Partners LP, $33,739
9. Murphy Oil Corp., $23,345
10. Tesoro Corp., $20,583

Source: *IndustryWeek*, IW 500 (annual), http://www.industryweek.com, July 2011.

1024 ■ TOP COAL AND CONSUMABLE FUEL COMPANIES, 2010

Ranked by: Score based on asset worth, revenue, profits, earnings per share, and return on invested capital. Remarks: Specific scores not provided. Also notes rank in the overall *Top 250.* Number listed: 12

1. China Shenhua Energy Co., Ltd.
2. Coal India
3. China Coal Energy Co., Ltd.
4. Yanzhou Coal Mining Co.
5. Peabody Energy Corp.
6. Banpu Pcl
7. Shanxi Lu'an Environmental
8. Consol Energy Inc.
9. Shanxi Xishan Coal
10. Cameco Corp.

Source: *Platts*, Top 250 Global Energy Company Rankings (annual), http://www.platts.com/top250, November 2, 2011.

1025 ■ WORLD'S LARGEST PETROLEUM AND COAL PRODUCT MANUFACTURERS, 2010

Ranked by: Revenue, in millions of dollars. **Remarks:** Also notes rank for previous year, overall rank within the *IW 1000*, country, and revenue growth. **Number listed:** 116

1. Exxon Mobil Corp., with $372,544 million
2. Royal Dutch Shell plc, $372,199
3. BP plc, $302,545
4. China Petroleum & Chemical Corp. (Sinopec), $290,039
5. PetroChina Co., Ltd., $222,157
6. Chevron Corp., $199,291
7. ConocoPhillips, $195,522
8. Total SA, $187,903
9. ENI SpA, $133,064
10. Petroleo Brasileiro SA (Petrobras), $120,052

Source: *IndustryWeek*, IW 1000 (annual), http://www.industryweek.com, August 2011.

Coal Mines and Mining

1026 ■ LARGEST COAL MINING COMPANIES BY EMPLOYEES, 2010

Ranked by: Total number of employees. **Remarks:** Also notes contact information for headquarters, number of employees at headquarters, revenue, rank by revenue, and primary SIC code. **Number listed:** 49

1. Cyprus Amax Minerals Co., with 13,500 employees
2. Florida Progress Corp., 9,100
3. Consol Energy Inc., 8,630
4. Peabody Energy Corp., 7,300
5. Alpha Natural Resources Inc., 6,400
6. Massey Energy Co., 5,851
7. A. T. Massey Coal Co., 5,407
8. Arch Coal Inc., 4,601
9. Peabody Holding Co., 4,500
10. Leslie Resources Inc., 3,991

Source: *Business Rankings*, (annual), Dun & Bradstreet Inc., 2011, p. VI.17-VI.18.

1027 ■ LARGEST COAL MINING COMPANIES BY SALES, 2010

Ranked by: Total revenue, in dollars. **Remarks:** Also notes contact information for headquarters, number of employees at headquarters and overall, rank by employees, and primary SIC code. **Number listed:** 50

1. Peabody Energy Corp., with $6,860,000,000
2. Consol Energy Inc., $5,236,021,000
3. Alpha Natural Resources Inc., $3,917,156,000
4. Consol Pennsylvania Coal Co., $3,700,000,000
5. Arch Coal Inc., $3,186,268,000
6. Massey Energy Co., $3,038,974,000
7. Arch Western Resources LLC, $1,651,389,000
8. Alliance Resource Partners LP, $1,610,065,000
9. Alliance Holdings GP LP, $1,609,743,000
10. Cloud Peak Energy Inc., $1,370,761,000

10. Cloud Peak Energy Resouces LLC, $1,370,761,000

Source: *Business Rankings*, (annual), Dun & Bradstreet Inc., 2011, p. V.17-V.18.

Coatings
See also: **Paint Industry**

1028 ■ WORLD'S LARGEST PAINT, COATINGS, ADHESIVES, AND SEALANTS COMPANIES, 2010

Ranked by: Sales of paint, coatings, adhesives, and sealants, in billions of U.S. dollars. **Remarks:** Also notes Web site, number of employees, year established, and total revenue. **Number listed:** 86

1. Akzo Nobel NV (Netherlands), with $13 billion
2. PPG Industries Inc. (U.S.), $10
3. Henkel KgaA (Germany), $9.7
4. The Sherwin-Williams Co. (U.S.), $6.5
5. E. I. du Pont de Nemours & Co. (U.S.), $3.8
6. BASF AG (Germany), $3.42
7. RPM International Inc. (U.S.), $3.41
8. Valspar Corp. (U.S.), $3
9. Kansai Paint Co. (Japan), $2.8
10. Nippon Paint Co., Ltd. (Japan), $2.5

Source: *Coatings World*, Top Companies Report (annual), http://www.coatingsworld.com, July 2011.

Coffee

1029 ■ TOP GROUND COFFEE BRANDS IN THE U.S., 2011

Ranked by: Sales, in dollars. **Remarks:** Also notes percent change from previous year and market share. **Number listed:** 10

1. Folger's, with $743,330,400
2. Maxwell House, $429,048,400
3. private label, $273,151,400
4. Starbucks, $249,081,700
5. Dunkin' Donuts, $174,697,100
6. Eight O'Clock, $67,127,570
7. Peet's Coffee, $66,358,960
8. Chock Full O'Nuts, $53,706,730
9. Yuban, $48,323,430
10. Seattle's Best, $43,739,120

Source: *Beverage Industry*, State of the Industry Report (annual), July 2011, p. SIO-14.

1030 ■ TOP READY-TO-DRINK COFFEE BRANDS IN THE U.S., 2011

Ranked by: Sales, in dollars. **Remarks:** Also notes percent change from previous year and market share. **Number listed:** 10

1. Frappuccino, with $544,829,600
2. Doubleshot, $245,049,600
3. Doubleshot Light, $9,618,175
4. private label, $5,289,082
5. Seattle's Best, $7,819,626
6. Illy Issimo, $1,444,609

7. Emmi, $1,178,551
8. PomX, $655,873
9. Cinnabon, $650,357
10. Community, $385,998

Source: *Beverage Industry*, State of the Industry Report (annual), July 2011, p. SIO-14.

Coffee Shops

1031 ■ TOP COFFEE FRANCHISES, 2012

Ranked by: Cumulative score based on financial strength and stability, growth rate, size of the system, number of years in business, the length of time franchising, start-up costs, litigation, percentage of terminations, and whether the company provides financing. **Remarks:** Specific scores not provided. Also notes overall rank within the *Franchise 500*, contact information, description, year founded, year started franchising, states where registered, available U.S. regions, where seeking foreign expansion, number of franchised and company-owned units for past three years, start-up costs, franchise fees, royalty fees, and type of financing available. **Number listed:** 6

1. Dunkin' Donuts
2. Biggby Coffee
3. Mountain Mudd Espresso
4. Maui Wowi Hawaiian Coffees & Smoothies
5. Dunn Bros. Coffee
6. The Human Bean Drive Thru

Source: *Entrepreneur*, Franchise 500 (annual), January 2012, p. 164-165.

Collection Agencies

1032 ■ BEST LARGE PLACES TO WORK IN THE COLLECTIONS INDUSTRY, 2011

Ranked by: Score based on employee surveys. **Remarks:** Specific scores not provided. Ranking covers companies with 250 or more employees. To qualify, companies must be collection agencies, collection law firms, or vendors to the collections industry. **Number listed:** 3

1. Williams & Fudge Inc.
2. National Patient Account Services
3. Professional Account Services Inc.

Source: *Best Companies Group*, Best Places to Work in Collections (annual), http://www.bestplacestoworkcollections.com, October 2011.

1033 ■ BEST MEDIUM-SIZED PLACES TO WORK IN THE COLLECTIONS INDUSTRY, 2011

Ranked by: Score based on employee surveys. **Remarks:** Specific scores not provided. Ranking covers companies with 75 to 249 employees. To qualify, companies must be collection agencies, collection law firms, or vendors to the collections industry. **Number listed:** 9

1. Account Recovery Specialists Inc.
2. F. H. Cann & Associates Inc.
3. DCM Services LLC
4. Phillips & Cohen Associates Ltd.
5. Asset Recovery Solutions LLC
6. RMB Inc.

7. American Coradius International LLC
8. Credit Management Services Inc.
9. Collection Technology Inc.

Source: *Best Companies Group*, Best Places to Work in Collections (annual), http://www.bestplacestoworkcollections.com, October 2011.

1034 ■ BEST SMALL PLACES TO WORK IN THE COLLECTIONS INDUSTRY, 2011

Ranked by: Score based on employee surveys. **Remarks:** Specific scores not provided. Ranking covers companies with 15 to 74 employees. To qualify, companies must be collection agencies, collection law firms, or vendors to the collections industry. **Number listed:** 18

1. KeyBridge Medical Revenue Management
2. Tucker, Albin & Associates Inc.
3. GB Collects
4. Receivable Recovery Partners LLC
5. J & L Teamworks
6. Agency of Credit Control Inc.
7. Americollect Inc.
8. Meade & Associates Inc.
9. Alliance Collection Service Inc.
10. National Recovery Services LLC

Source: *Best Companies Group*, Best Places to Work in Collections (annual), http://www.bestplacestoworkcollections.com, October 2011.

College Graduates

1035 ■ TOP EMPLOYERS FOR GRADUATES IN THE U.K., 2011-2012

Ranked by: Survey of final-year U.K. students as to the perceived opportunities offered by potential employers. **Remarks:** Specific scores not provided. Also notes rank for previous year. **Number listed:** 100

1. PricewaterhouseCoopers LLP
2. Deloitte LLP
3. KPMG LLP
4. Aldi Group
5. NHS
6. British Broadcasting Corp. (BBC)
7. Teach First
8. Civil service
9. Accenture Ltd.
10. Ernst & Young LLP

Source: *The Times Top 100 Graduate Employers*, (annual), High Fliers Publications Ltd., 2011.

1036 ■ TOP ENTRY LEVEL EMPLOYERS, 2011

Ranked by: Number of entry-level positions expected to be filled during the year. **Remarks:** Also notes industry. **Number listed:** 93

1. Enterprise Rent-A-Car Co., with 8,500 positions
2. Teach For America Inc., 4,925
3. Verizon Wireless, 4,250
4. Hertz Corp., 4,000
5. PricewaterhouseCoopers LLP, 3,938
6. KPMG LLP, 2,300

7. Target Corp., 2,200
8. Ernst & Young LLP, 2,000
9. City Year, 1,700
10. Aerotek, 900
10. Total Quality Logistics, 900

Source: *CollegeGrad.com*, Top Entry Level Employers (annual), http://www.collegegrad.com, June 13, 2011.

1037 ■ TOP INTERN EMPLOYERS, 2011

Ranked by: Number of internship positions expected to be filled during the year. **Remarks:** Also notes industry. **Number listed:** 78

1. PricewaterhouseCoopers LLP, with 3,125 positions
2. The Southwestern Co., 3,000
3. Ernst & Young LLP, 2,000
4. KPMG LLP, 1,800
5. Enterprise Rent-A-Car Co., 1,500
6. Target Corp., 1,400
7. University Directories LLC, 600
8. Northrop Grumman Corp., 585
9. Liberty Mutual, 550
10. Kohl's Corp., 500

Source: *CollegeGrad.com*, Top Entry Level Employers (annual), http://www.collegegrad.com, June 13, 2011.

1038 ■ TOP MASTER'S LEVEL EMPLOYERS, 2011

Ranked by: Number of Master's-level positions expected to be filled during the year. **Remarks:** Also notes industry. **Number listed:** 63

1. Ernst & Young LLP, with 800 positions
2. Target Corp., 400
3. Teach for America Inc., 370
4. Principal Financial Group Inc., 150
5. Verizon Wireless, 125
6. PricewaterhouseCoopers LLP, 113
7. Aerotek, 100
7. Bechtel Corp., 100
9. Mattress Firm, 80
10. AT&T Inc., 66

Source: *CollegeGrad.com*, Top Entry Level Employers (annual), http://www.collegegrad.com, June 13, 2011.

Commercial Loans

1039 ■ LARGEST S & LS BY COMMERCIAL LOANS, 2011

Ranked by: Total commercial loans, in thousands of dollars. **Remarks:** Also notes city, state, association type, and dollar and percent change from previous year. **Number listed:** 25

1. American Express Bank, FSB, with $15,605,552 thousand
2. Sovereign Bank NA, $11,819,612
3. People's United Bank, $7,373,832
4. Flagstar Bank, FSB, $1,615,805
5. GE Capital Retail Bank, $1,083,330
6. Raymond James Bank, FSB, $909,658
7. Everbank, $743,568

8. American Savings Bank, FSB, $714,565
9. Wilmington Savings Fund Society, $543,551
10. Midfirst Bank, $531,810

Source: *Highline Bank and S&L Quarterly, Dec. ed.*, 2011, p. V.59.

1040 ■ LARGEST S & LS BY NONPERFORMING COMMERCIAL LOANS, 2011

Ranked by: Nonperforming commercial loans, in thousands of dollars. **Remarks:** Also notes city, state, association type, and dollar and percent change from previous year. **Number listed:** 25

1. Sovereign Bank NA, with $245,974 thousand
2. American Express Bank, FSB, $233,753
3. People's United Bank, $151,951
4. Everbank, $22,992
5. North Shore Bank, FSB, $22,476
6. American Savings Bank, FSB, $17,974
7. NCB FSB, $14,696
8. GE Capital Retail Bank, $14,023
9. Liberty Bank, FSB, $12,360
10. AnchorBank, FSB, $10,744

Source: *Highline Bank and S&L Quarterly, Dec. ed.*, 2011, p. V.54.

1041 ■ LARGEST U.S. BANKS BY COMMERCIAL REAL ESTATE LOANS, 2011

Ranked by: Total commercial real estate loans, in thousands of dollars. **Remarks:** Also notes city, state, and dollar and percent change from previous year. **Number listed:** 25

1. Wells Fargo Bank NA, with $103,719,000 thousand
2. J. P. Morgan Chase Bank NA, $57,873,000
3. Bank of America NA, $45,488,570
4. U.S. Bank NA, $30,130,119
5. Branch Banking & Trust Co., $24,882,641
6. New York Community Bank, $23,244,997
7. PNC Bank NA, $21,468,972
8. Manufacturers & Traders Trust Co., $19,981,316
9. Regions Bank, $19,515,723
10. TD Bank NA, $19,323,302

Source: *Highline Bank and S&L Quarterly, Dec. ed.*, 2011, p. I.49.

1042 ■ LARGEST U.S. BANKS BY NONPERFORMING COMMERCIAL AND OTHER LOANS, 2011

Ranked by: Total nonperforming commercial loans and all loans other than real estate, consumer, and agricultural, in thousands of dollars. **Remarks:** Also notes city, state, and dollar and percent change from previous year. **Number listed:** 25

1. Citibank NA Inc., with $2,978,000 thousand
2. Wells Fargo Bank NA, $2,181,000
3. J. P. Morgan Chase Bank NA, $1,951,000
4. Bank of America NA, $1,326,331
5. PNC Bank NA, $570,487
6. Regions Bank, $454,547
7. Fifth Third Bank, $445,670
8. U.S. Bank NA, $439,320
9. Comerica NA, $258,648

10. TD Bank NA, $247,464

Source: *Highline Bank and S&L Quarterly, Dec. ed.*, 2011, p. I.45.

Commodities Exchanges

1043 ■ TOP U.S. EXCHANGES FOR COMMODITY FUTURES, 2010

Ranked by: Number of contracts traded. **Remarks:** Also notes exchange abbreviation, percent share, and rank and figures for previous year. **Number listed:** 8

1. Chicago Mercantile Exchange, with 238,174,901 contracts
2. Chicago Board of Trade, 123,666,496
3. New York Mercantile Exchange, 80,574,639
4. ICE Futures U.S., 14,654,805
5. Kansas City Board of Trade, 148,032
6. Chicago Climate Futures Exchange, 79,951
7. Minneapolis Grain Exchange, 32,290
8. NYSE Liffe U.S., 5,736

Source: *The CRB Commodity Yearbook*, (annual), Commodity Research Bureau, 2011, p. 43T.

1044 ■ TOP U.S. FUTURES EXCHANGES FOR COMMODITY OPTIONS, 2010

Ranked by: Number of contracts traded. **Remarks:** Also notes percent share, and rank and figures for previous year. **Number listed:** 11

1. Chicago Mercantile Exchange, with 1,418,240,658 contracts
2. Chicago Board of Trade, 799,926,808
3. New York Mercantile Exchange, 419,908,616
4. ICE Futures U.S., 92,520,026
5. ELX Futures, 13,142,541
6. Kansas City Board of Trade, 5,549,842
7. OneChicago, 4,971,160
8. CBOE Futures Exchange, 4,402,616
9. NYSE Liffe U.S., 4,064,780
10. Minneapolis Grain Exchange, 1,690,207

Source: *The CRB Commodity Yearbook*, (annual), Commodity Research Bureau, 2011, p. 32T.

1045 ■ TOP U.S. SECURITIES EXCHANGES FOR COMMODITY OPTIONS, 2010

Ranked by: Number of contracts traded. **Remarks:** Also notes percent share, and rank and figures for previous year. **Number listed:** 9

1. Chicago Board of Options Exchange, with 1,115,491,922 contracts
2. NASDAQ OMX PHLX, 846,895,365
3. International Securities Exchange, 745,176,328
4. NYSE-ARCA, 488,093,760
5. NYSE-AMEX, 440,021,234
6. NASDAQ Options Market, 142,922,225
7. Boston Options Exchange, 91,754,121
8. BATS Exchange, 25,103,245
9. C2 Exchange, 3,610,470

Source: *The CRB Commodity Yearbook*, (annual), Commodity Research Bureau, 2011, p. 43T.

Commodity Brokers
See: **Brokers**

Communication Equipment Industry

1046 ■ CALIFORNIA'S LARGEST COMMUNICATIONS EQUIPMENT COMPANIES OVERALL, 2011

Ranked by: Score based on revenue, profits, assets, and market capitalization. **Remarks:** Specific scores not provided. Also notes overall rank in the *Forbes 2000* and figures for each criterion. **Number listed:** 3

1. Cisco Systems Inc.
2. QUALCOMM Inc.
3. Juniper Networks Inc.

Source: *Forbes*, Forbes 2000 (annual), http://www.forbes.com, May 7, 2012.

1047 ■ ILLINOIS'S LARGEST COMMUNICATIONS EQUIPMENT COMPANIES OVERALL, 2011

Ranked by: Score based on revenue, profits, assets, and market capitalization. **Remarks:** Specific scores not provided. Also notes overall rank in the *Forbes 2000* and figures for each criterion. **Number listed:** 2

1. Motorola Solutions Inc.
2. Motorola Mobility Holdings Inc.

Source: *Forbes*, Forbes 2000 (annual), http://www.forbes.com, May 7, 2012.

1048 ■ LARGEST U.S. COMMUNICATIONS EQUIPMENT COMPANIES OVERALL, 2011

Ranked by: Score based on revenue, profits, assets, and market capitalization. **Remarks:** Specific scores not provided. Also notes overall rank in the *Forbes 2000* and figures for each criterion. **Number listed:** 7

1. Cisco Systems Inc.
2. QUALCOMM Inc.
3. Corning Inc.
4. Motorola Solutions Inc.
5. Motorola Mobility Holdings Inc.
6. Juniper Networks Inc.
7. Harris Corp.

Source: *Forbes*, Forbes 2000 (annual), http://www.forbes.com, May 7, 2012.

1049 ■ LARGEST U.S. COMMUNICATIONS EQUIPMENT MANUFACTURERS, 2010

Ranked by: Revenue, in millions of dollars. **Remarks:** Also notes overall rank within the *IW 500*, revenue growth, and profit margin. **Number listed:** 9

1. Motorola Solutions Inc., with $19,282 million
2. L-3 Communications Holdings Inc., $15,680
3. QUALCOMM Inc., $10,991
4. Corning Inc., $6,632
5. Harris Corp., $5,206
6. Rockwell Collins Inc., $4,665
7. Tellabs Inc., $1,642
8. Ciena Corp., $1,237

9. NETGEAR Inc., $902

Source: *IndustryWeek*, IW 500 (annual), http://www.industryweek.com, July 2011.

1050 ■ TOP *FORTUNE 500* COMPANIES IN NETWORK AND OTHER COMMUNICATIONS EQUIPMENT, 2011

Ranked by: Revenue, in millions of dollars. **Remarks:** Also notes overall rank in the *Fortune 500;* profits; profits as a percentage of revenue; stockholders' equity; and rank by each criterion. **Number listed:** 7

1. Cisco Systems Inc., with $43,218 million
2. QUALCOMM Inc., $14,962
3. Motorola Mobility Holdings, $13,064
4. Motorola Solutions Inc., $9,549
5. Corning Inc., $7,890
6. Harris Corp., $5,925
7. Avaya Inc., $5,547

Source: *Fortune*, Fortune 500 (annual), May 21, 2012, p. F-38.

1051 ■ WORLD'S LARGEST COMMUNICATIONS EQUIP-MENT COMPANIES OVERALL, 2011

Ranked by: Score based on revenue, profits, assets, and market capitalization. **Remarks:** Specific scores not provided. Also notes country, overall rank in the *Forbes 2000,* and figures for each criterion. **Number listed:** 15

1. Cisco Systems Inc.
2. QUALCOMM Inc.
3. Telefonaktiebolaget LM Ericsson
4. Corning Inc.
5. Nokia Corp.
6. Alcatel-Lucent
7. Research in Motion Ltd.
8. HTC Corp.
9. Motorola Solutions Inc.
10. ZTE Corp.

Source: *Forbes*, Forbes 2000 (annual), http://www.forbes.com, May 7, 2012.

1052 ■ WORLD'S LARGEST COMMUNICATIONS EQUIP-MENT MANUFACTURERS, 2010

Ranked by: Revenue, in millions of dollars. **Remarks:** Also notes rank for previous year, overall rank within the *IW 1000,* country, and revenue growth. **Number listed:** 20

1. France Telecom SA, with $62,063 million
2. Nokia Corp., $57,413
3. Telefonaktiebolaget LM Ericsson, $30,480
4. Alcatel-Lucent, $21,396
5. Research in Motion Ltd., $19,907
6. Motorola Solutions Inc., $19,282
7. L-3 Communications Holdings Inc., $15,680
8. Safran SA, $15,286
9. LS Corp., $15,282
10. QUALCOMM Inc., $10,991

Source: *IndustryWeek*, IW 1000 (annual), http://www.industryweek.com, August 2011.

Communication Industry

1053 ■ ASIA'S LEADING PRIVATE COMMUNICATIONS COMPANIES, 2011

Ranked by: Editorial determination based on market impact and technological innovation. **Remarks:** Specific figures not provided; companies are listed alphabetically, not ranked. **Number listed:** 100

1. A1 Future Technologies
2. AaramShop Private Ltd.
3. Alpha Cloud Labs
4. Apostrophe Digital
5. ArcusIT
6. ArrayShield Technologies Private Ltd.
7. Augen Software Group
8. Beehive Strategy
9. cacaFly International Media
10. CapitalVia Global Research Ltd.

Source: *Red Herring*, Red Herring Asia (annual), http://www.redherring.com, November 19, 2011.

1054 ■ EUROPE'S LEADING PRIVATE COMMUNICA-TIONS COMPANIES, 2012

Ranked by: Editorial determination based on market impact and technological innovation. **Remarks:** Specific figures not provided; companies are listed alphabetically, not ranked. Also notes industry and country. **Number listed:** 100

1. Abionic SA
2. Acronis GmbH
3. AlertMe.com Ltd.
4. Almira Labs
5. AlphaSIP
6. Analytics SEO Ltd.
7. AQUAFADAS
8. ATG Media
9. Atosho
10. Avangate Holding

Source: *Red Herring*, Red Herring Europe (annual), http://www.redherring.com, April 30, 2012.

1055 ■ LARGEST COMMUNICATIONS COMPANIES BY EMPLOYEES, 2010

Ranked by: Total number of employees. **Remarks:** Also notes contact information for headquarters, number of employees at headquarters, revenue, rank by revenue, and primary SIC code. **Number listed:** 49

1. AT&T Inc., with 278,519 employees
2. Verizon Communications Inc., 222,900
3. Walt Disney Co., 149,000
4. GTE Corp., 111,285
5. Comcast Corp., 107,000
6. Cellco Partnership, 70,599
7. Cox Enterprises Inc., 66,000
8. SBC Teleholdings Inc., 65,345
9. BellSouth Corp., 63,000
10. Southwestern Bell Telephone LP, 50,700

Source: *Business Rankings*, (annual), Dun & Bradstreet Inc., 2011, p. VI.104-VI.105.

1056 ■ LARGEST COMMUNICATIONS COMPANIES BY SALES, 2010

Ranked by: Total revenue, in dollars. **Remarks:** Also notes contact information for headquarters, number of employees at headquarters and overall, rank by employees, and primary SIC code. **Number listed:** 50

1. AT&T Inc., with $124,280,000,000
2. Verizon Communications Inc., $106,565,000,000
3. Cellco Partnership, $62,131,000,000
4. Notiont Inc., $50,000,000,000
5. Walt Disney Co., $38,063,000,000
6. Comcast Corp., $37,937,000,000
7. Sprint Nextel Corp., $32,563,000,000
8. Time Warner Inc., $26,888,000,000
9. DirecTV, $24,102,000,000
10. DirecTV Holdings LLC, $20,268,000,000

Source: *Business Rankings*, (annual), Dun & Bradstreet Inc., 2011, p. V.104-V.105.

1057 ■ NORTH AMERICA'S LEADING PRIVATE COMMUNICATIONS COMPANIES, 2011

Ranked by: Editorial determination based on market impact and technological innovation. **Remarks:** Specific figures not provided; companies are listed alphabetically, not ranked. **Number listed:** 100

1. Acumatica
2. Adaptik Corp.
3. AgigA Tech Inc.
4. Airclic
5. Antenna Software
6. Apprion Inc.
7. Aquantia
8. ASSIA
9. aTyr Pharma
10. Automation Anywhere

Source: *Red Herring*, Red Herring North America (annual), http://www.redherring.com, June 15, 2011.

1058 ■ WORLD'S LEADING PRIVATE COMMUNICATIONS COMPANIES, 2011

Ranked by: Editorial determination based on market impact and technological innovation. **Remarks:** Specific figures not provided; companies are listed alphabetically, not ranked. **Number listed:** 100

1. AaramShop
2. ActivNetworks
3. Acumatica
4. Allinea Software
5. Antenna Software
6. ASSIA
7. ATEME
8. Axioma Inc.
9. Beneq Oy
10. Bitswoven Technologies

Source: *Red Herring*, Red Herring Global (annual), http://www.redherring.com, December 12, 2011.

Communications Satellites

1059 ■ WORLD'S TOP FIXED SATELLITE SERVICE OPERATORS, 2010

Ranked by: Revenue for fixed satellite services (defined as leasing transponders for video, data, or voice communications), in millions of U.S. dollars. **Remarks:** Also notes figures for previous year, number of satellites in orbit, number of satellites on order, and comments. **Number listed:** 25

1. Intelsat Ltd. (Luxembourg), with $2,540 million
2. SES SA (Luxembourg), $2,300
3. Eutelsat Communications (France), $1,480
4. Telesat Holding Inc. (Canada), $821
5. Sky Perfect JSal Corp. (Japan), $391.3
6. Star One (Brazil), $319.2
7. SingTel Optus (Singapore/Australia), $286.5
8. Hispasat (Spain), $240.2
9. Russian Satellite Communications Co. (Russia), $227
10. Arabsat (Saudi Arabia), $202

Source: *Space News*, Top Fixed Satellite Service Operators (annual), July 4, 2011, p. 11.

Commuter Airlines
See: **Airlines**

Commuter Railroads

1060 ■ LARGEST PASSENGER RAIL FLEETS IN THE U.S. AND CANADA, 2010

Ranked by: Total number of railcars. **Number listed:** 10

1. MTA New York City Transit, with 6,745 railcars
2. Amtrak, 1,530
3. Chicago Transit Authority, 1,190
4. New Jersey Transit Corp., 1,160
5. MTA Metro-North Railroad, 1,150
6. MTA Long Island Railroad, 1,140
7. Washington Metropolitan Area Transit Authority, 1,128
8. Massachusetts Bay Area Transportation Authority, 1,080
9. Metra, 1,010
10. Toronto Transit Commission, 954

Source: *Metro Magazine*, Top 50 Passenger Rail Projects (annual), June 2011, p. 25.

1061 ■ LARGEST PASSENGER RAIL PROJECTS IN THE U.S. AND CANADA, 2010

Ranked by: Cost of projects, in millions of U.S. dollars. **Remarks:** Also notes rank for previous year and breakdown of project by type. **Number listed:** 50

1. Toronto Transit Commission, with $14,000 million
2. MTA New York City Transit, $9,400
3. Regional Transportation District (Denver, CO), $6,700

4. City & County of Honolulu Department of Transportation, Rapid Transit Div., $5,300

5. TriMet (Portland, OR), $5,000

6. Sound Transit (Seattle, WA), $4,362

7. Metropolitan Transit Authority (Houston, TX), $4,000

8. Massachusetts Bay Transportation Authority, $3,104

9. Utah Transit Authority, $2,850

10. Los Angeles County Metropolitan Transportation Authority, $2,675

Source: *Metro Magazine*, Top 50 Passenger Rail Projects (annual), June 2011, p. 26+.

Companies
See: **Corporations**

Compensation

1062 ■ AMERICA'S BEST COMPANIES WITH THE HIGHEST HOURLY PAY, 2012

Ranked by: Average annual pay of hourly employees, in dollars. **Remarks:** Also notes most common job title and overall rank in the *100 Best Companies to Work For*. **Number listed:** 89

1. Hitachi Data Systems, with $132,341

2. Scripps Health, $108,483

3. QUALCOMM Inc., $99,000

4. Adobe Systems Inc., $92,792

5. Cisco Systems, $91,791

6. Atlantic Health System Inc., $90,422

7. NuStar Energy LP, $88,564

8. Methodist Hospital, $83,377

9. OhioHealth, $83,084

10. Meridian Health, $81,593

Source: *Fortune*, 100 Best Companies to Work For (annual), http://www.fortune.com, February 6, 2012.

1063 ■ AMERICA'S BEST COMPANIES WITH THE HIGHEST SALARIES, 2012

Ranked by: Average annual pay of salaried employees, in dollars. **Remarks:** Also notes most common job title and overall rank in the *100 Best Companies to Work For*. **Number listed:** 88

1. Southern Ohio Medical Center, with $490,647

2. Bingham McCutchen LLP, $228,851

3. Alston & Bird LLP, $201,233

4. Perkins Cole LLP, $189,409

5. EOG Resources Inc., $188,662

6. Devon Energy Corp., $178,305

7. Ultimate Software, $166,000

8. Hitachi Data Systems, $163,694

9. The Boston Consulting Group Inc., $154,543

10. Autodesk, $150,500

Source: *Fortune*, 100 Best Companies to Work For (annual), http://www.fortune.com, February 6, 2012.

1064 ■ STATES WITH THE HIGHEST ANNUAL PAY, 2009

Ranked by: Average annual pay, in dollars. **Number listed:** 51

1. Washington DC, with $77,483

2. Connecticut, $57,771

3. New York, $57,739

4. Massachusetts, $56,267

5. New Jersey, $55,168

6. California, $51,566

7. Maryland, $50,579

8. Illinois, $48,358

9. Virginia, $48,239

10. Delaware, $47,770

Source: *State Rankings*, (annual), CQ Press, 2011, p. 167.

1065 ■ STATES WITH THE HIGHEST HOURLY PAY, 2010

Ranked by: Average hourly earnings of production workers on manufacturing payrolls, in dollars. **Number listed:** 51

1. Alaska, with $24.63

2. Connecticut, $24.60

3. Washington, $23.65

4. Colorado, $22.43

5. Michigan, $21.88

6. Idaho, $21.31

7. Wyoming, $20.90

8. Louisiana, $20.78

9. Maryland, $20.40

10. Maine, $20.16

Source: *State Rankings*, (annual), CQ Press, 2011, p. 172.

1066 ■ STATES WITH THE LOWEST HOURLY PAY, 2010

Ranked by: Median hourly pay, in dollars. **Number listed:** 50

1. Arkansas, with $14.10

2. Oklahoma, $14.49

3. Mississippi, $14.84

4. Rhode Island, $14.85

5. South Dakota, $15.38

6. Nevada, $15.56

7. North Dakota, $15.71

8. North Carolina, $15.87

9. Alabama, $15.90

9. Tennessee, $15.90

Source: *State Rankings*, (annual), CQ Press, 2011, p. 172.

Competition, International

1067 ■ COUNTRIES WITH THE LEAST EFFECTIVE ANTI-MONOPOLY POLICY, 2010

Ranked by: Score, on a scale of seven, based on the level of that the anti-monopoly policy is effective and promotes competition. **Number listed:** 142

1. Angola, with 2.3 points

2. Yemen, 2.5

2. Venezuela, 2.5

4. Haiti, 2.6

5. Armenia, 2.8

5. Serbia, 2.8

5. Ukraine, 2.8

8. Georgia, 2.9

8. Burundi, 2.9

8. Suriname, 2.9

Source: *Global Competitiveness Report*, (annual), World Economic Forum, 2011, p. 454.

1068 ■ COUNTRIES WITH THE LEAST INTENSE LOCAL COMPETITION, 2010

Ranked by: Score, on a scale of seven, based on the level of competition in the local market. **Number listed:** 142

1. Angola, with 3.2 points

1. Chad, 3.2

3. Venezuela, 3.3

4. Armenia, 3.4

4. Timor-Leste, 3.4

4. Mauritania, 3.4

7. Serbia, 3.6

8. Haiti, 3.7

9. Bolivia, 3.8

9. Azerbaijan, 3.8

9. Bosnia & Herzegovina, 3.8

Source: *Global Competitiveness Report*, (annual), World Economic Forum, 2011, p. 452.

1069 ■ COUNTRIES WITH THE MOST EFFECTIVE ANTI-MONOPOLY POLICY, 2010

Ranked by: Score, on a scale of seven, based on the level of that the anti-monopoly policy is effective and promotes competition. **Number listed:** 142

1. Netherlands, with 5.8 points

1. Sweden, 5.8

3. Denmark, 5.5

3. Finland, 5.5

3. United Kingdom, 5.5

6. New Zealand, 5.4

7. Bahrain, 5.3

7. South Africa, 5.3

9. Canada, 5.2

9. France, 5.2

9. Japan, 5.2

9. Singapore, 5.2

Source: *Global Competitiveness Report*, (annual), World Economic Forum, 2011, p. 454.

1070 ■ COUNTRIES WITH THE MOST INTENSE LOCAL COMPETITION, 2010

Ranked by: Score, on a scale of seven, based on the level of competition in the local market. **Number listed:** 142

1. Taiwan, with 6.1 points

2. Belgium, 6.0

3. United Kingdom, 5.9

3. Japan, 5.9

3. Qatar, 5.9

3. Netherlands, 5.9

3. Australia, 5.9

8. Austria, 5.8

8. Germany, 5.8

8. Sweden, 5.8

Source: *Global Competitiveness Report*, (annual), World Economic Forum, 2011, p. 452.

1071 ■ LEAST COMPETITIVE COUNTRIES, 2011

Ranked by: Score based on global competitiveness. **Remarks:** Also notes rank for previous year. **Number listed:** 142

1. Chad, with 2.87 points

2. Haiti, 2.90

3. Burundi, 2.95

4. Angola, 2.96

5. Yemen, 3.06

6. Mauritania, 3.20

7. Burkina Faso, 3.25

8. Lesotho, 3.26

9. Swaziland, 3.30

10. Mozambique, 3.31

Source: *Global Competitiveness Report*, (annual), World Economic Forum, 2011, p. 15.

1072 ■ MOST COMPETITIVE COUNTRIES, 2011

Ranked by: Score based on global competitiveness. **Remarks:** Also notes rank for previous year. **Number listed:** 142

1. Switzerland, with 5.74 points

2. Singapore, 5.63

3. Sweden, 5.61

4. Finland, 5.47

5. United States, 5.43

6. Germany, 5.41

6. Netherlands, 5.41

8. Denmark, 5.40

8. Japan, 5.40

10. United Kingdom, 5.39

Source: *Global Competitiveness Report*, (annual), World Economic Forum, 2011, p. 15.

Computer Industry
See also: **Personal Computers**

1073 ■ CALIFORNIA'S LARGEST COMPUTER HARDWARE COMPANIES OVERALL, 2011

Ranked by: Score based on revenue, profits, assets, and market capitalization. **Remarks:** Specific scores not provided. Also notes overall rank in the *Forbes 2000* and figures for each criterion. **Number listed:** 2

1. Apple Inc.

2. Hewlett-Packard Co.

Source: *Forbes*, Forbes 2000 (annual), http://www.forbes.com, May 7, 2012.

1074 ■ CALIFORNIA'S LARGEST COMPUTER SERVICES COMPANIES OVERALL, 2011

Ranked by: Score based on revenue, profits, assets, and market capitalization. **Remarks:** Specific scores not provided. Also notes overall rank in the *Forbes 2000* and figures for each criterion. **Number listed:** 2

1. Google Inc.
2. Yahoo! Inc.

Source: *Forbes*, Forbes 2000 (annual), http://www.forbes.com, May 7, 2012.

1075 ■ CHINA'S LARGEST COMPUTER SERVICES COMPANIES OVERALL, 2011

Ranked by: Score based on revenue, profits, assets, and market capitalization. **Remarks:** Specific scores not provided. Also notes overall rank in the *Forbes 2000* and figures for each criterion. **Number listed:** 3

1. Tencent Holdings Ltd.
2. Baidu
3. Netease.com

Source: *Forbes*, Forbes 2000 (annual), http://www.forbes.com, May 7, 2012.

1076 ■ FASTEST-GROWING PRIVATE COMPUTER HARDWARE COMPANIES IN THE U.S., 2007-2010

Ranked by: Average annual sales growth over three years, in percent. **Remarks:** Also notes headquarters, revenue, and rank in the overall *Inc. 500*. To qualify, private companies must have had annual revenues of at least $100,000 in 2007 and $2 million in 2010. **Number listed:** 2

1. A10 Networks, with 3,785.5%
2. Cosemi Technologies, 806.3%

Source: *Inc.*, Inc. 500 (annual), September 2011, p. 100.

1077 ■ FRANCE'S LARGEST COMPUTER SERVICES COMPANIES OVERALL, 2011

Ranked by: Score based on revenue, profits, assets, and market capitalization. **Remarks:** Specific scores not provided. Also notes overall rank in the *Forbes 2000* and figures for each criterion. **Number listed:** 3

1. Capgemini
2. Atos
3. Iliad

Source: *Forbes*, Forbes 2000 (annual), http://www.forbes.com, May 7, 2012.

1078 ■ INDIA'S LARGEST COMPUTER SERVICES COMPANIES OVERALL, 2011

Ranked by: Score based on revenue, profits, assets, and market capitalization. **Remarks:** Specific scores not provided. Also notes overall rank in the *Forbes 2000* and figures for each criterion. **Number listed:** 3

1. Tata Consultancy Services Ltd.
2. Infosys Technologies Ltd.
3. Wipro Ltd.

Source: *Forbes*, Forbes 2000 (annual), http://www.forbes.com, May 7, 2012.

1079 ■ LARGEST U.S. COMPUTER HARDWARE COMPANIES OVERALL, 2011

Ranked by: Score based on revenue, profits, assets, and market capitalization. **Remarks:** Specific scores not provided. Also notes overall rank in the *Forbes 2000* and figures for each criterion. **Number listed:** 3

1. Apple Inc.
2. Hewlett-Packard Co.

3. Dell Inc.

Source: *Forbes*, Forbes 2000 (annual), http://www.forbes.com, May 7, 2012.

1080 ■ LARGEST U.S. COMPUTER AND OTHER ELECTRONIC PRODUCT MANUFACTURERS, 2010

Ranked by: Revenue, in millions of dollars. **Remarks:** Also notes overall rank within the *IW 500*, revenue growth, and profit margin. **Number listed:** 61

1. Hewlett-Packard Co., with $126,033 million
2. International Business Machines Corp. (IBM), $99,870
3. Apple Inc., $65,225
4. Microsoft Corp., $62,484
5. Dell Inc., $61,494
6. Intel Corp., $43,623
7. Cisco Systems Inc., $40,040
8. Oracle Corp., $26,820
9. Texas Instruments Inc., $13,966
10. Jabil Circuit Inc., $13,409

Source: *IndustryWeek*, IW 500 (annual), http://www.industryweek.com, July 2011.

1081 ■ LARGEST U.S. COMPUTER SERVICES COMPANIES OVERALL, 2011

Ranked by: Score based on revenue, profits, assets, and market capitalization. **Remarks:** Specific scores not provided. Also notes overall rank in the *Forbes 2000* and figures for each criterion. **Number listed:** 8

1. International Business Machines Corp. (IBM)
2. Google Inc.
3. Yahoo! Inc.
4. Cognizant Technology Solutions Corp.
5. Computer Sciences Corp.
6. Fiserv Inc.
7. Teradata Corp.
8. F5 Networks Inc.

Source: *Forbes*, Forbes 2000 (annual), http://www.forbes.com, May 7, 2012.

1082 ■ TAIWAN'S LARGEST COMPUTER HARDWARE COMPANIES OVERALL, 2011

Ranked by: Score based on revenue, profits, assets, and market capitalization. **Remarks:** Specific scores not provided. Also notes overall rank in the *Forbes 2000* and figures for each criterion. **Number listed:** 7

1. Quanta Computer Inc.
2. Compal Electronics Inc.
3. Asustek Computer Inc.
4. Chimei Innolux
5. Wistron Corp.
6. Acer Inc.
7. Inventec Corp.

Source: *Forbes*, Forbes 2000 (annual), http://www.forbes.com, May 7, 2012.

1083 ■ TOP *FORTUNE 500* COMPANIES IN COMPUTERS AND OFFICE EQUIPMENT, 2011

Ranked by: Revenue, in millions of dollars. **Remarks:** Also notes overall rank in the *Fortune 500;* profits; profits as a percentage of revenue; stockholders' equity; and rank by each criterion. **Number listed:** 6

1. Hewlett-Packard Co., with $127,245 million
2. Apple Inc., $108,249
3. Dell Inc., $62,071
4. Xerox Corp., $22,626
5. NCR Corp., $5,443
6. Pitney Bowes Inc., $5,278

Source: *Fortune*, Fortune 500 (annual), May 21, 2012, p. F-34.

1084 ■ TOP SOLUTION PROVIDER ORGANIZATIONS IN NORTH AMERICA, 2010

Ranked by: Revenue, in dollars. **Remarks:** Also notes contact information and CEO. **Number listed:** 500

1. IBM Global Services, with $56,424,000,000
2. Hewlett-Packard (Services)/EDS, $34,935,000,000
3. Accenture Ltd., $21,551,000,000
4. Computer Sciences Corp., $16,500,000,000
5. Xerox Services, $13,739,000,000
6. Cap Gemini SA, $12,240,000,000
7. Dell Inc. (Services), $11,492,000,000
8. CDW Corp., $8,801,000,000
9. Atos Origin Inc., $6,650,000,000
10. Insight Enterprises Inc., $4,800,000,000

Source: *CRN*, VAR 500 (annual), http://www.crn.com, June 2011.

1085 ■ WORLD'S LARGEST COMPUTER HARDWARE COMPANIES OVERALL, 2011

Ranked by: Score based on revenue, profits, assets, and market capitalization. **Remarks:** Specific scores not provided. Also notes country, overall rank in the *Forbes 2000*, and figures for each criterion. **Number listed:** 12

1. Apple Inc.
2. Hewlett-Packard Co.
3. Dell Inc.
4. Fujitsu Ltd.
5. Quanta Computer Inc.
6. Compal Electronics Inc.
7. Lenovo Group Ltd.
8. Asustek Computer Inc.
9. Chimei InnoLux Corp.
10. Wistron Corp.

Source: *Forbes*, Forbes 2000 (annual), http://www.forbes.com, May 7, 2012.

1086 ■ WORLD'S LARGEST COMPUTER AND OTHER ELECTRONIC PRODUCT MANUFACTURERS, 2010

Ranked by: Revenue, in millions of dollars. **Remarks:** Also notes rank for previous year, overall rank within the *IW 1000*, country, and revenue growth. **Number listed:** 105

1. Samsung Electronics Co., Ltd., with $139,169 million
2. Hewlett-Packard Co., $126,033
3. Hitachi Ltd., $110,314
4. Hon Hai Precision Industry Co., Ltd., $102,806
5. Siemens AG, $102,211
6. International Business Machines Corp. (IBM), $99,871
7. Panasonic Corp., $91,242

8. LG Electronics Inc., $51,988
9. Canon Inc., $45,595
10. NEC Corp., $44,073

Source: *IndustryWeek*, IW 1000 (annual), http://www.industryweek.com, August 2011.

1087 ■ WORLD'S LARGEST COMPUTER SERVICES COMPANIES OVERALL, 2011

Ranked by: Score based on revenue, profits, assets, and market capitalization. **Remarks:** Specific scores not provided. Also notes country, overall rank in the *Forbes 2000,* and figures for each criterion. **Number listed:** 20

1. International Business Machines Corp. (IBM)
2. Google Inc.
3. Accenture plc
4. Tata Consultancy Services Ltd.
5. Yahoo! Inc.
6. Infosys Technologies Ltd.
7. Wipro Ltd.
8. Tencent Holdings Ltd.
9. Cognizant Technology Solutions Corp.
10. Capgemini

Source: *Forbes*, Forbes 2000 (annual), http://www.forbes.com, May 7, 2012.

1088 ■ WORLD'S MOST ADMIRED COMPUTER COMPANIES, 2012

Ranked by: Score, on a scale of 10, based on a survey of executives, directors, and securities analysts of companies within their own industry on nine criteria: innovation, financial soundness, employee talent, use of corporate assets, long-term investment value, social responsibility, quality of management, quality of products/services, and globalness. **Remarks:** Specific scores not provided. Also notes rank for previous year. **Number listed:** 8

1. Apple Inc.
2. EMC Corp.
3. Xerox Corp.
4. Dell Inc.
5. Canon Inc.
6. Hewlett-Packard Co.
7. Seagate Technology Inc.
8. Western Digital Corp.

Source: *Fortune*, World's Most Admired Companies (annual), March 19, 2012, p. 147.

1089 ■ WORLD'S MOST ETHICAL COMPUTER HARDWARE COMPANIES, 2012

Ranked by: Score based on five criteria: ethics and compliance program; reputation, leadership, and innovation; governance; corporate citizenship and responsibility; and culture of ethics. **Remarks:** Specific scores not provided; companies are listed alphabetically, not ranked. **Number listed:** 2

1. Hitachi Data Systems
2. Intel Corp.

Source: *Ethisphere Magazine*, World's Most Ethical Companies (annual), http://www.ethisphere.com, 2012.

1090 ■ WORLD'S MOST TECHNOLOGICALLY INNOVATIVE COMPUTING AND COMMUNICATIONS COMPANIES - PRIVATE, 2012

Ranked by: Editorial determination. **Remarks:** Companies are listed alphabetically, not ranked. Also notes comments. **Number listed:** 5

1. Nicira
2. Palantir Technologies
3. Skybox Imaging
4. Square
5. Tabula

Source: *Technology Review*, TR 50 (annual), http://www.technologyreview.com, 2012.

1091 ■ WORLD'S MOST TECHNOLOGICALLY INNOVATIVE COMPUTING AND COMMUNICATIONS COMPANIES - PUBLIC, 2012

Ranked by: Editorial determination. **Remarks:** Companies are listed alphabetically, not ranked. Also notes comments. **Number listed:** 8

1. Alcatel-Lucent
2. Apple Inc.
3. ARM Holdings plc
4. Dreamworks Animation
5. International Business Machines Corp. (IBM)
6. QUALCOMM Inc.
7. Samsung
8. Taiwan Semiconductor

Source: *Technology Review*, TR 50 (annual), http://www.technologyreview.com, 2012.

Computer Peripherals Equipment Industry

1092 ■ LARGEST SUPPLIERS OF AUTOMATIC DATA CAPTURE SYSTEMS, 2010

Ranked by: Global revenue, in millions of dollars, for such automatic data capture systems as scanning systems, laser bar code scanners, and thermal bar code printers. **Remarks:** Also notes website. **Number listed:** 20

1. Motorola Inc., with $1,227.9 million
2. Zebra Technologies Corp., $526.5
3. Datalogic, $403.5
4. Honeywell International Inc., $380
5. Intermec Technologies Corp., $377.5
6. Sato Corp., $234.7
7. TEC, $181.4
8. Avery Dennison Corp., $151.2
9. Psion Teklogix, $143.7
10. Hewlett-Packard Co., $136.4

Source: *Modern Materials Handling*, Top 20 ADC Suppliers (annual), October 2011, p. 32.

1093 ■ TOP *FORTUNE 500* COMPANIES IN COMPUTER PERIPHERALS, 2011

Ranked by: Revenue, in millions of dollars. **Remarks:** Also notes overall rank in the *Fortune 500;* profits; profits as a percentage of revenue; stockholders' equity; and rank by each criterion. **Number listed:** 3

1. EMC Corp., with $20,008 million
2. Western Digital Corp., $9,526
3. NetApp Inc., $5,123

Source: *Fortune*, Fortune 500 (annual), May 21, 2012, p. F-34.

Computer Software Industry

1094 ■ AMERICA'S LARGEST PRIVATE COMPUTER SOFTWARE AND SERVICE COMPANIES, 2010

Ranked by: Revenue, in billions of dollars. **Remarks:** Also notes headquarters, number of employees, and overall rank in the *America's Largest Private Companies* list. Ranking is available online only, not in print. **Number listed:** 2

1. SunGard Data Systems Inc., with $4.99 billion
2. SAS Institute Inc., $2.43

Source: *Forbes*, America's Largest Private Companies (annual), http://www.forbes.com, December 5, 2011.

1095 ■ BEST SMALL SOFTWARE AND SERVICES COMPANIES IN AMERICA, 2011

Ranked by: Score based on revenue, profits, and return on equity for the past 12 months and five years. **Remarks:** Specific scores not provided. Also notes rank in the overall *100 Best Small Companies in America*. To qualify, companies must have revenues between $5 million and $1 billion, a net margin above five percent, and share price above $5. List is available online only. **Number listed:** 15

1. SolarWinds
2. Interactive Intelligence
3. Quality Systems
4. NIC
5. Virtusa Corp.
6. CommVault Systems
7. Syntel
8. Rackspace Hosting
9. Opnet Technologies
10. HealthStream

Source: *Forbes*, Best Small Companies in America (annual), November 7, 2011.

1096 ■ CALIFORNIA'S LARGEST COMPUTER SOFTWARE AND PROGRAMMING COMPANIES OVERALL, 2011

Ranked by: Score based on revenue, profits, assets, and market capitalization. **Remarks:** Specific scores not provided. Also notes overall rank in the *Forbes 2000* and figures for each criterion. **Number listed:** 7

1. Oracle Corp.
2. Symantec Corp.
3. VMware
4. Adobe Systems Inc.
5. Intuit Inc.
6. Salesforce.com Inc.
7. Autodesk

Source: *Forbes*, Forbes 2000 (annual), http://www.forbes.com, May 7, 2012.

1097 ■ FASTEST-GROWING PRIVATE SOFTWARE COMPANIES IN THE U.S., 2007-2010

Ranked by: Average annual sales growth over three years, in percent. **Remarks:** Also notes headquarters, revenue, and rank in the overall *Inc. 500*. To qualify, private companies must have had annual revenues of at least $100,000 in 2007 and $2 million in 2010. **Number listed:** 47

1. Vertiglo, with 8,648.3%
2. HubSpot, 6,015.3%
3. Agiliance, 4,909.1%
4. Intelligent Integration Systems, 3,893.4%
5. FastSpring, 3,850.7%
6. Rivet Software, 3,466.5%
7. AppAssure Software, 3,449.6%
8. Black Mountain Systems, 3,445.8%
9. NextDocs, 3,213.4%
10. AutoLoop, 3,159%

Source: *Inc.*, Inc. 500 (annual), September 2011, p. 192-198.

1098 ■ LARGEST U.S. COMPUTER SOFTWARE AND PROGRAMMING COMPANIES OVERALL, 2011

Ranked by: Score based on revenue, profits, assets, and market capitalization. **Remarks:** Specific scores not provided. Also notes overall rank in the *Forbes 2000* and figures for each criterion. **Number listed:** 11

1. Microsoft Corp.
2. Oracle Corp.
3. Symantec Corp.
4. CA Inc.
5. VMware Inc.
6. Adobe Systems Inc.
7. Intuit Inc.
8. Citrix Systems Inc.
9. Salesforce.com Inc.
. BMC Software Inc.

Source: *Forbes*, Forbes 2000 (annual), http://www.forbes.com, May 7, 2012.

1099 ■ LARGEST U.S. SOFTWARE MANUFACTURERS, 2010

Ranked by: Revenue, in millions of dollars. **Remarks:** Also notes overall rank within the *IW 500*, revenue growth, and profit margin. **Number listed:** 4

1. Citrix Systems Inc., with $1,875 million
2. Parametric Technology Corp., $1,010
3. THQ Inc., $899
4. Scientific Games Corp., $882

Source: *IndustryWeek*, IW 500 (annual), http://www.industryweek.com, July 2011.

1100 ■ MOST VALUABLE U.S. SOFTWARE AND COMPUTER SERVICES COMPANIES, 2011

Ranked by: Market value as of March 2011, in millions of U.S. dollars. **Remarks:** Also notes rank within the *FT U.S. 500*, rank for previous year, country, revenue, net income, assets, number of employees, share price, price-to-earning ratio, dividend yield, and fiscal yearend. **Number listed:** 25

1. Microsoft Corp., with $213,336.4 million
2. International Business Machines Corp. (IBM), $198,869.8
3. Oracle Corp., $169,185.6
4. Google Inc., $147,199.8
5. Cognizant Technology Solutions Corp., $24,763.1
6. Yahoo! Inc., $21,841

7. Salesforce.com Inc., $17,752.8
8. Adobe Systems Inc., $15,782.7
9. Intuit Inc., $15,070.1
10. Symantec Corp., $14,150.6

Source: *Financial Times*, FT 500 (annual), http://www.ft.com, June 24, 2011.

1101 ■ TOP BRANDS OF HOME BACK-OFFICE SOFTWARE, 2010

Ranked by: Popularity among *CE Pro 100* companies, in percent. **Number listed:** 6

1. D-Tools, with 28%
2. AutoCAD, 8%
3. QuickBooks, 7%
3. SRS, 7%
5. Excel, 6%
5. Horizon, 6%

Source: *CE Pro*, Brand Analysis (annual), June 2011, p. 60.

1102 ■ TOP *FORTUNE 500* COMPANIES IN COMPUTER SOFTWARE, 2011

Ranked by: Revenue, in millions of dollars. **Remarks:** Also notes overall rank in the *Fortune 500;* profits; profits as a percentage of revenue; stockholders' equity; and rank by each criterion. **Number listed:** 3

1. Microsoft Corp., with $69,943 million
2. Oracle Corp., $35,622
3. Symantec Corp., $6,190

Source: *Fortune*, Fortune 500 (annual), May 21, 2012, p. F-34.

1103 ■ THE UNITED STATES' MOST VALUABLE SOFTWARE BRANDS, 2011

Ranked by: Brand value, in millions of U.S. dollars. **Remarks:** Also notes rank within the *Global 500* for current and previous year, figures for current and previous year, and brand rating. Ranking is available online only. **Number listed:** 6

1. Microsoft, with $45,812 million
2. Oracle, $17,031
3. Xbox, $4,897
4. Adobe, $2,900
5. Activision Blizzard, $2,892
6. Electronic Arts (EA), $2,628

Source: *Global 500*, (annual), Brand Finance plc, March 2012.

Computer Software Industry, International

1104 ■ BRITAIN'S MOST ADMIRED SOFTWARE AND COMPUTER SERVICE COMPANIES, 2011

Ranked by: Survey of peers and investment analysts based on nine criteria: quality of management, financial soundness, quality of goods/services, ability to attract and retain talent, value as long-term investment, innovation, marketing, community and environmental responsibility, and use of corporate assets. **Number listed:** 5

1. IBM U.K., with 66.4 points
2. Telecity Group, 66
3. Autonomy Corp. plc, 64.4
4. The Sage Group plc, 61.8

5. Fidessa, 60.1

Source: *Management Today*, Britain's Most Admired Companies (annual), December 2011, p. 49.

1105 ■ EUROPE'S MOST VALUABLE SOFTWARE AND COMPUTER SERVICES COMPANIES, 2011

Ranked by: Market value as of March 2011, in millions of U.S. dollars. **Remarks:** Also notes rank within the *FT Europe 500*, rank for previous year, country, revenue, net income, assets, number of employees, share price, price-to-earning ratio, dividend yield, and fiscal yearend. **Number listed:** 8

1. SAP AG, with $75,209.9 million
2. Dassault Systemes, $9,113.8
3. Cap Gemini, $9,059.8
4. Iliad, $6,553
5. Autonomy Corp. plc, $6,185.4
6. The Sage Group plc, $5,890.1
7. Software AG, $4,772.3
8. Invensys plc, $4,480.1

Source: *Financial Times*, FT 500 (annual), http://www.ft.com, June 24, 2011.

1106 ■ FASTEST-GROWING SOFTWARE AND SERVICES SUPPLIERS OVER $1 BILLION IN REVENUE, 2009-2010

Ranked by: Annual growth in software/services revenue of companies over $1 billion in revenue, in percent. **Remarks:** Also notes overall rank in the *Top 500* and software/services revenue for the current year. **Number listed:** 10

1. Research in Motion Ltd., with 46.1%
2. Google Inc., 42.4%
2. Sykes Enterprises Inc., 42.4%
4. Fidelity National Information Services Inc., 42%
5. VMware Inc., 41.2%
6. Cognizant Technology Solutions Corp., 40.1%
7. Tata Consultancy, 29.6%
8. Adobe Systems Inc., 29%
9. ManTech International Corp., 28.9%
10. HCL Technologies Ltd., 28%

Source: *Software Magazine*, Software 500 (annual), 2011, p. 24.

1107 ■ FASTEST-GROWING SOFTWARE AND SERVICES SUPPLIERS, 2009-2010

Ranked by: Annual growth in software/services revenue, in percent. **Remarks:** Also notes overall rank in the *Top 500* and software/services revenue for the current year. **Number listed:** 10

1. BackWeb Technologies, with 470%
2. Cortex Business Solutions Inc., 279.7%
3. NetQin Mobile Inc., 204.5%
4. SXC Health Solutions Corp., 157.6%
5. Support.com Inc., 152.5%
6. CyberDefender Corp., 141.8%
7. Roadnet Technologies, 141.2%
8. Merge Healthcare Inc., 109.9%
9. Tableau Software, 109.6%
10. Kofax plc, 100.3%

Source: *Software Magazine*, Software 500 (annual), 2011, p. 26.

1108 ■ FASTEST-GROWING SOFTWARE AND SERVICES SUPPLIERS BELOW $10 MILLION IN REVENUE, 2009-2010

Ranked by: Annual growth in software/services revenue of companies below $10 million in revenue, in percent. **Remarks:**

Also notes overall rank in the *Top 500* and software/services revenue for the current year. **Number listed:** 10

1. Cortex Business Solutions Inc., with 279.7%
2. Route1 Inc., 96.6%
3. Make Technologies Inc., 74.6%
4. DatamanUSA LLC, 71%
5. 3C Software, 66.4%
6. Tiempo Development LLC, 60%
7. Nitro PDF Inc., 44.9%
8. TDCI Inc., 41%
9. Computer Solutions & Software International, 40.7%
10. CSI Software, 34.6%

Source: *Software Magazine*, Software 500 (annual), 2011, p. 26.

1109 ■ FASTEST-GROWING SOFTWARE AND SERVICES SUPPLIERS BETWEEN $10 MILLION AND $30 MILLION IN REVENUE, 2009-2010

Ranked by: Annual growth in software/services revenue of companies between $10 million and $30 million in revenue, in percent. **Remarks:** Also notes overall rank in the *Top 500* and software/services revenue for the current year. **Number listed:** 10

1. BackWeb Technologies, with 470%
2. NetQin Mobile Inc., 204.5%
3. Trunkbow International Holdings Ltd., 84.5%
4. Park City Group Inc., 82.3%
5. Bronto Software, 68.8%
6. QHR Technologies Inc., 52.1%
7. Blackline Systems, 49.6%
8. Foliage, 47.6%
9. SmartDraw.com, 45.5%
10. Covario Inc., 45.1%

Source: *Software Magazine*, Software 500 (annual), 2011, p. 26.

1110 ■ FASTEST-GROWING SOFTWARE AND SERVICES SUPPLIERS BETWEEN $100 MILLION AND $1 BILLION IN REVENUE, 2009-2010

Ranked by: Annual growth in software/services revenue of companies between $100 million and $1 billion in revenue, in percent. **Remarks:** Also notes overall rank in the *Top 500* and software/services revenue for the current year. **Number listed:** 10

1. SXC Health Solutions Corp., with 157.6%
2. Merge Healthcare Inc., 109.9%
3. Kofax plc, 100.3%
4. Longtop Financial Technologies Ltd., 88.8%
5. Datalink Corp., 64.9%
6. AsiaInfo-Linkage Inc., 63.2%
7. MicroTech, 60.8%
8. JDA Software Group Inc., 60%
9. Micro Focus International plc, 57.5%
10. Syntel Inc., 55.4%

Source: *Software Magazine*, Software 500 (annual), 2011, p. 24.

1111 ■ FASTEST-GROWING SOFTWARE AND SERVICES SUPPLIERS BETWEEN $30 MILLION AND $50 MILLION IN REVENUE, 2009-2010

Ranked by: Annual growth in software/services revenue of companies between $30 million and $50 million in revenue, in percent. **Remarks:** Also notes overall rank in the *Top 500* and software/services revenue for the current year. **Number listed:** 10

1. Support.com Inc., with 152.5%
2. CyberDefender Corp., 141.8%
3. Roadnet Technologies, 141.2%
4. Tableau Software, 109.6%
5. CriticalControl Solutions, 88.7%
6. Xoriant Corp., 63.3%
7. Cornerstone OnDemand Inc., 49.1%
8. NetSol Technologies Inc., 39.1%
9. Opera Software ASA, 35.6%
10. Allocate Software plc, 33.6%

Source: *Software Magazine*, Software 500 (annual), 2011, p. 24.

1112 ■ FASTEST-GROWING SOFTWARE AND SERVICES SUPPLIERS BETWEEN $50 MILLION AND $100 MILLION IN REVENUE, 2009-2010

Ranked by: Annual growth in software/services revenue of companies between $50 million and $100 million in revenue, in percent. **Remarks:** Also notes overall rank in the *Top 500* and software/services revenue for the current year. **Number listed:** 10

1. Edgewater Technology Inc., with 76.8%
2. Magic Software Enterprises, 60%
3. BSQUARE Corp., 50.3%
4. Helios & Matheson IT Ltd., 44.7%
5. Emailvision, 43.9%
6. BroadSoft Inc., 38.8%
7. AppLabs, 38.3%
8. Enghouse Systems Ltd., 37.4%
9. Merced Systems Inc., 34%
10. Absolute Software Corp., 32%

Source: *Software Magazine*, Software 500 (annual), 2011, p. 24.

1113 ■ TOP SOFTWARE COMPANIES IN CANADA, 2011

Ranked by: Revenue, in thousands of Canadian dollars. **Remarks:** Specific figures not provided. Also notes rank for previous year and overall rank in the *Branham 300*. **Number listed:** 25

1. Open Text Corp.
2. Constellation Software Inc.
3. Mitel Networks Corp.
4. Algorithmics
5. Points.com
6. Enghouse Systems
7. VendTek Systems
8. Descartes Systems Group
9. MKS
10. Logibec Groupe Informatique

Source: *Backbone Magazine*, Branham 300 (annual), 2012, p. 34.

1114 ■ WORLD'S LARGEST COMPUTER SOFTWARE AND PROGRAMMING COMPANIES OVERALL, 2011

Ranked by: Score based on revenue, profits, assets, and market capitalization. **Remarks:** Specific scores not provided. Also notes country, overall rank in the *Forbes 2000,* and figures for each criterion. **Number listed:** 16

1. Microsoft Corp.
2. Oracle Corp.

3. SAP AG
4. Symantec Corp.
5. CA Inc.
6. VMware Inc.
7. Adobe Systems Inc.
8. Intuit Inc.
9. Amadeus IT Holdings SA
10. Check Point Software Technologies Ltd.

Source: *Forbes*, Forbes 2000 (annual), http://www.forbes.com, May 7, 2012.

1115 ■ WORLD'S LARGEST SOFTWARE AND SERVICES SUPPLIERS, 2010

Ranked by: Software/services revenue, in millions of U.S. dollars. **Remarks:** Also notes headquarters, website, software/services revenue growth, total revenue, total revenue growth, software/services as a percentage of total revenue, research and development as a percentage of total revenue, number of employees, and software business sector. **Number listed:** 500

1. International Business Machines Corp. (IBM), with $78,659 million
2. Microsoft Corp., $54,426
3. Hewlett-Packard Co., $38,521
4. Oracle Corp., $24,530
5. Accenture Ltd., $21,550.6
6. EMC Corp., $17,015.1
7. SAP AG, $16,539
8. Computer Sciences Corp., $16,128
9. NTT Data Corp., $12,289.7
10. Hitachi Ltd., $12,253.8

Source: *Software Magazine*, Software 500 (annual), 2011, p. 33-55.

1116 ■ WORLD'S LEADING SOFTWARE COMPANIES IN CLOUD COMPUTING, 2011

Ranked by: Editorial determination of companies' reputation, products, and industry influence. **Remarks:** Specific figures not provided; companies are listed alphabetically, not ranked. **Number listed:** 10

1. Amazon.com Inc.
2. Cloudera
3. Engine Yard
4. GitHub
5. Gizmox
6. Google Inc.
7. Hadoop Project
8. OpenStack
9. Salesforce.com Inc.
10. VMware

Source: *Software Development Times*, SD Times 100 (annual), June 2011.

1117 ■ WORLD'S LEADING SOFTWARE COMPANIES IN COMPONENTS, 2011

Ranked by: Editorial determination of companies' reputation, products, and industry influence. **Remarks:** Specific figures not provided; companies are listed alphabetically, not ranked. **Number listed:** 17

1. Amyuni

2. Aspose
3. Atalasoft
4. ComponentArt
5. ComponentOne LLC
6. DevExpress
7. Dundas
8. Grape City
9. Infragistics Inc.
10. Intersoft Solutions

Source: *Software Development Times*, SD Times 100 (annual), June 2011.

1118 ■ WORLD'S LEADING SOFTWARE COMPANIES IN DATABASE AND INTEGRATION SYSTEMS, 2011

Ranked by: Editorial determination of companies' reputation, products, and industry influence. **Remarks:** Specific figures not provided; companies are listed alphabetically, not ranked. **Number listed:** 16

1. Couchbase
2. Embarcadero
3. International Business Machines Corp. (IBM)
4. Ingres
5. InterSystems
6. Magic Software
7. Micro Focus
8. Microsoft Corp.
9. MuleSoft
10. Oracle Corp.

Source: *Software Development Times*, SD Times 100 (annual), June 2011.

1119 ■ WORLD'S LEADING SOFTWARE COMPANIES IN LIFE-CYCLE MANAGEMENT, 2011

Ranked by: Editorial determination of companies' reputation, products, and industry influence. **Remarks:** Specific figures not provided; companies are listed alphabetically, not ranked. **Number listed:** 20

1. AccuRev
2. Aldon
3. CollabNet
4. Electric Cloud
5. Git
6. Hudson/Jenkins
7. International Business Machines Corp. (IBM)
8. Mercurial
9. Microsoft Corp.
10. MKS

Source: *Software Development Times*, SD Times 100 (annual), June 2011.

1120 ■ WORLD'S LEADING SOFTWARE COMPANIES IN MOBILE TECHNOLOGY, 2011

Ranked by: Editorial determination of companies' reputation, products, and industry influence. **Remarks:** Specific figures not provided; companies are listed alphabetically, not ranked. **Number listed:** 6

1. Android Project
2. Apple Inc.

3. EffectiveUI
4. Google Inc.
5. Mono Project
6. Motorola

Source: *Software Development Times*, SD Times 100 (annual), June 2011.

1121 ■ WORLD'S LEADING SOFTWARE COMPANIES IN SECURITY AND QUALITY ASSURANCE, 2011

Ranked by: Editorial determination of companies' reputation, products, and industry influence. **Remarks:** Specific figures not provided; companies are listed alphabetically, not ranked. **Number listed:** 13

1. dynaTrace
2. Hewlett-Packard Co.
3. International Business Machines Corp. (IBM)
4. Klocwork Inc.
5. Mu Dynamics
6. Parasoft
7. PreEmptive Solutions
8. Progress
9. SafeNet
10. Sauce Labs

Source: *Software Development Times*, SD Times 100 (annual), June 2011.

1122 ■ WORLD'S LEADING SOFTWARE COMPANIES IN TOOLS AND FRAMEWORKS, 2011

Ranked by: Editorial determination of companies' reputation, products, and industry influence. **Remarks:** Specific figures not provided; companies are listed alphabetically, not ranked. **Number listed:** 18

1. ActiveState
2. Apigee
3. Atlassian
4. Black Duck
5. CUDA Project
6. Django
7. Embarcadero
8. JackBe
9. JRuby
10. Mashery

Source: *Software Development Times*, SD Times 100 (annual), June 2011.

1123 ■ WORLD'S MOST ADMIRED COMPUTER SOFTWARE COMPANIES, 2012

Ranked by: Score, on a scale of 10, based on a survey of executives, directors, and securities analysts of companies within their own industry on eight criteria: innovation, financial soundness, employee talent, use of corporate assets, long-term investment value, social responsibility, quality of management, and quality of products/services. **Remarks:** Specific scores not provided. Also notes rank for previous year. **Number listed:** 6

1. Intuit Inc.
2. Adobe Systems Inc.
3. Symantec Corp.
4. Oracle Corp.
5. Microsoft Corp.

6. Autodesk Inc.

Source: *Fortune*, World's Most Admired Companies (annual), March 19, 2012, p. 147.

1124 ■ WORLD'S MOST ETHICAL COMPUTER SOFTWARE COMPANIES, 2012

Ranked by: Score based on five criteria: ethics and compliance program; reputation, leadership, and innovation; governance; corporate citizenship and responsibility; and culture of ethics. **Remarks:** Specific scores not provided; companies are listed alphabetically, not ranked. **Number listed:** 6

1. Adobe Systems Inc. (U.S.)
2. Microsoft Corp. (U.S.)
3. Salesforce.com Inc. (U.S.)
4. Symantec Corp. (U.S.)
5. Teradata Corp. (U.S.)
6. Wipro Ltd. (India)

Source: *Ethisphere Magazine*, World's Most Ethical Companies (annual), http://www.ethisphere.com, 2012.

1125 ■ WORLD'S MOST INFLUENTIAL SOFTWARE COMPANIES, 2011

Ranked by: Editorial determination of industry influence. **Remarks:** Specific figures not provided; companies are listed alphabetically, not ranked. **Number listed:** 13

1. Agile Alliance
2. The Apache Foundation
3. Apple Inc.
4. Eclipse Foundation
5. Free Software Foundation
6. Google Inc.
7. HTML5 Project
8. International Business Machines Corp. (IBM)
9. Intel Corp.
10. Linux Foundation

Source: *Software Development Times*, SD Times 100 (annual), June 2011.

1126 ■ WORLD'S MOST PRODUCTIVE SOFTWARE AND SERVICES SUPPLIERS, 2010

Ranked by: Software/services revenue per employee, in U.S. dollars. **Remarks:** Also notes overall rank in the *Top 500*, number of employees, and total software/services revenue. **Number listed:** 10

1. Vendtek Systems Inc., with $3,985,000
2. SYNNEX Corp., $1,155,640
3. Innodata Isogen Inc., $1,025,217
4. Datalink Corp., $982,204
5. Network Engines Inc., $980,619
6. Peerless Systems Corp., $968,600
7. Check Point Software Technology Ltd., $946,438
8. Technology Integration Group, $743,644
9. CSP Inc., $683,583
10. MicroTech, $639,755

Source: *Software Magazine*, Software 500 (annual), 2011, p. 28.

1127 ■ WORLD'S MOST VALUABLE SOFTWARE BRANDS, 2011

Ranked by: Brand value, in millions of U.S. dollars. **Remarks:** Also notes rank within the *Global 500* for current and previous year, figures for current and previous year, country, and brand rating. Ranking is available online only. **Number listed:** 7

1. Microsoft, with $45,812 million
2. Oracle, $17,031
3. SAP, $9,042
4. Xbox, $4,897
5. Adobe, $2,900
6. Activision Blizzard, $2,892
7. Electronic Arts (EA), $2,628

Source: *Global 500*, (annual), Brand Finance plc, March 2012.

1128 ■ WORLD'S MOST VALUABLE SOFTWARE AND COMPUTER SERVICES COMPANIES, 2011

Ranked by: Market value as of March 2011, in millions of U.S. dollars. **Remarks:** Also notes rank within the *FT 500*, rank for previous year, country, revenue, net income, assets, number of employees, share price, price-to-earning ratio, dividend yield, and fiscal year-end. **Number listed:** 12

1. Microsoft Corp., with $213,336.4 million
2. International Business Machines Corp. (IBM), $198,869.8
3. Oracle Corp., $169,185.6
4. Google Inc., $147,199.8
5. SAP AG, $75,209.9
6. Tata Consultancy Services Ltd., $51,898.5
7. Tencent Holdings Ltd., $44,747.2
8. Infosys Technologies Ltd., $41,465.2
9. Wipro Ltd., $26,317.4
10. Cognizant Technology Solutions Corp., $24,763.1

Source: *Financial Times*, FT 500 (annual), http://www.ft.com, June 24, 2011.

1129 ■ WORLD'S TOP SOFTWARE AND SERVICES SUPPLIERS BY EMPLOYEES, 2010

Ranked by: Number of employees. **Remarks:** Also notes overall rank in the *Top 500*. **Number listed:** 10

1. International Business Machines Corp. (IBM), with 463,869 employees
2. Hitachi Ltd., 359,746
3. Hewlett-Packard Co., 324,000
4. Accenture Ltd., 204,000
5. Tata Consultancy Services Ltd., 160,429
6. Lockheed Martin Corp., 132,000
7. Emerson Electric Co., 127,700
8. Infosys Technologies Ltd., 113,800
9. Capgemini, 108,698
10. Wipro Ltd., 108,000

Source: *Software Magazine*, Software 500 (annual), 2011.

1130 ■ WORLD'S TOP SOFTWARE AND SERVICES SUPPLIERS IN RESEARCH AND DEVELOPMENT, 2010

Ranked by: Research and development expenditures as a percentage of total revenue. **Remarks:** Also notes overall rank in the *Top 500*, corporate revenue, and research and development expenditures. **Number listed:** 10

1. Macadamian Technologies Inc., with 73%
2. Nucleus Software Exports Ltd., 67.7%

3. Polaris Software Lab Ltd., 64.3%
4. Zylog Systems Ltd., 63.9%
5. Diversinet Corp., 63.1%
6. MindTree Ltd., 61.6%
7. ANTs Software Inc., 53.7%
8. TigerLogic Corp., 44.1%
9. DemandTec Inc., 40.8%
10. Cadence Design Systems Inc., 40.2%

Source: *Software Magazine*, Software 500 (annual), 2011, p. 26.

Computer Software Publishers
See: **Computer Software Industry**

Computer Storage Devices

1131 ■ CALIFORNIA'S LARGEST COMPUTER STORAGE DEVICE COMPANIES OVERALL, 2011

Ranked by: Score based on revenue, profits, assets, and market capitalization. **Remarks:** Specific scores not provided. Also notes overall rank in the *Forbes 2000* and figures for each criterion. **Number listed:** 3

1. SanDisk Corp.
2. NetApp Inc.
3. Western Digital Corp.

Source: *Forbes*, Forbes 2000 (annual), http://www.forbes.com, May 7, 2012.

1132 ■ LARGEST U.S. COMPUTER STORAGE DEVICE COMPANIES OVERALL, 2011

Ranked by: Score based on revenue, profits, assets, and market capitalization. **Remarks:** Specific scores not provided. Also notes overall rank in the *Forbes 2000* and figures for each criterion. **Number listed:** 4

1. EMC Corp.
2. SanDisk Corp.
3. NetApp Inc.
4. Western Digital Corp.

Source: *Forbes*, Forbes 2000 (annual), http://www.forbes.com, May 7, 2012.

1133 ■ WORLD'S LARGEST COMPUTER STORAGE DEVICE COMPANIES OVERALL, 2011

Ranked by: Score based on revenue, profits, assets, and market capitalization. **Remarks:** Specific scores not provided. Also notes country, overall rank in the *Forbes 2000,* and figures for each criterion. **Number listed:** 7

1. EMC Corp.
2. Seagate Technology Inc.
3. SanDisk Corp.
4. NetApp Inc.
5. Western Digital Corp.
6. Lite-On Technology Corp.
7. TPV Technology Ltd.

Source: *Forbes*, Forbes 2000 (annual), http://www.forbes.com, May 7, 2012.

Computers

1134 ■ THE UNITED STATES' MOST VALUABLE COMPUTER BRANDS, 2011

Ranked by: Brand value, in millions of U.S. dollars. **Remarks:** Also notes rank within the *Global 500* for current and previous year, figures for current and previous year, and brand rating. Ranking is available online only. **Number listed:** 4

1. Apple, with $70,605 million
2. Dell, $11,605
3. EMC, $4,699
4. Sandisk, $2,782

Source: *Global 500*, (annual), Brand Finance plc, March 2012.

1135 ■ WORLD'S MOST VALUABLE COMPUTER BRANDS, 2011

Ranked by: Brand value, in millions of U.S. dollars. **Remarks:** Also notes rank within the *Global 500* for current and previous year, figures for current and previous year, country, and brand rating. Ranking is available online only. **Number listed:** 6

1. Apple, with $70,605 million
2. Dell, $11,605
3. Fujitsu, $5,349
4. EMC, $4,699
5. BlackBerry, $3,293
6. Sandisk, $2,782

Source: *Global 500*, (annual), Brand Finance plc, March 2012.

Concerts

1136 ■ TOP CONCERT PROMOTERS, 2011

Ranked by: Total gross, in dollars. **Remarks:** Also notes total attendance, total capacity, number of shows, and number of sell-outs. **Number listed:** 25

1. Live Nation, with $1,302,619,696
2. AEG Live, $797,969,654
3. SJM Concerts, $206,328,377
4. T4F: Time For Fun, $191,213,322
5. Dainty Group, $147,168,146
6. Evenpro/Water Brother/XYZ, $118,617,450
7. Michael Coppel Presents, $117,358,359
8. MCD, $110,593,518
9. Frontier Touring, $109,070,597
10. Evenko, $91,266,177

Source: *Billboard*, The Year in Music & Touring (annual), December 17, 2011, p. 114.

1137 ■ WORLD'S TOP CONCERT TOURS, 2011

Ranked by: Gross sales, in U.S. dollars. **Remarks:** Also notes total attendance, total capacity, number of shows, and number of sell-outs. **Number listed:** 25

1. U2, with $293,281,487
2. Bon Jovi, $192,947,951
3. Take That, $185,175,360
4. Roger Waters, $149,904,965
5. Taylor Swift, $97,368,416

6. Kenny Chesney, $84,576,917
7. Usher, $74,954,681
8. Lady Gaga, $71,900,434
9. Andre Rieu, $67,104,756
10. Sade, $53,178,550

Source: *Billboard*, The Year in Music & Touring (annual), December 17, 2011, p. 96.

1138 ■ WORLD'S TOP CONCERTS, 2011

Ranked by: Gross sales, in U.S. dollars. **Remarks:** Also notes ticket prices, venues, location, dates, attendance, number of sell-outs, and promoters. **Number listed:** 25

1. Take That (London), with $61,713,184
2. Take That (Manchester, England), $44,183,145
3. U2/Muse (Sao Paulo, Brazil), $32,754,065
4. Coachella Valley Music & Arts Festival, $24,993,698
5. U2/Snow Patrol, $22,866,542
6. Take That (Sunderland, England), $21,600,077
7. Oxegen, $21,113,100
8. U2/Muse (Buenos Aires, Argentina), $20,550,302
9. Lollapalooza, $19,902,224
10. Take That (Dublin, Ireland), $18,217,500

Source: *Billboard*, The Year in Music & Touring (annual), December 17, 2011, p. 96.

1139 ■ WORLD'S TOP INTIMATE CONCERT VENUES, 2011

Ranked by: Gross sales, in U.S. dollars. **Remarks:** Ranking covers venues with capacities below 5,000. Also notes venue capacity, total attendance, total capacity, number of shows, and number of sell-outs. **Number listed:** 10

1. The Colosseum at Caesars Palace (Las Vegas, NV), with $76,400,771
2. Fox Theatre (Atlanta, GA), $29,450,162
3. Beacon Theatre (New York, NY), $22,096,139
4. Broward Center for the Performing Arts (Ft. Lauderdale, FL), $18,524,444
5. Princess Theatre (Melbourne, Australia), $18,113,800
6. David A. Straz Jr. Center for the Performing Arts (Tampa, FL), $14,194,573
7. Chicago Theatre (Chicago, IL), $13,682,387
8. Citi Wang Theatre (Boston, MA), $13,420,787
9. Teatro Abril (Sao Paulo, Brazil), $11,588,931
10. Bob Carr Performing Arts Centre (Orlando, FL), $11,410,798

Source: *Billboard*, The Year in Music & Touring (annual), December 17, 2011, p. 111.

1140 ■ WORLD'S TOP LARGE CONCERT VENUES, 2011

Ranked by: Gross sales, in U.S. dollars. **Remarks:** Ranking covers venues with capacities of 15,001 and more. Also notes venue capacity, total attendance, total capacity, number of shows, and number of sell-outs. **Number listed:** 10

1. O2 Arena (London), with $136,531,810
2. Rod Laver Arena (Melbourne, Australia), $91,038,061

3. Allphones Arena (Sydney, Australia), $81,830,193
4. Manchester Evening News Arena (Manchester, England), $72,058,698
5. Staples Center (Los Angeles), $60,872,868
6. Madison Square Garden (New York City), $58,269,143
7. Air Canada Centre (Toronto, Canada), $51,029,449
8. Sportpaleis (Antwerp, Belgium), $45,946,315
9. Bell Centre (Montreal, Canada), $45,568,731
10. Wells Fargo Center (Philadelphia, PA), $37,974,905

Source: *Billboard*, The Year in Music & Touring (annual), December 17, 2011, p. 102.

1141 ■ WORLD'S TOP MEDIUM-SIZED CONCERT VENUES, 2011

Ranked by: Gross sales, in U.S. dollars. **Remarks:** Ranking covers venues with capacities between 10,001 and 15,000. Also notes venue capacity, total attendance, total capacity, number of shows, and number of sell-outs. **Number listed:** 10

1. Brisbane Entertainment Centre (Brisbane, Australia), with $68,205,019
2. Sydney Entertainment Centre (Sydney, Australia), $29,642,714
3. The O2 (Dublin, Ireland), $29,548,826
4. O2 World (Hamburg, Germany), $29,540,633
5. O2 World (Berlin, Germany), $29,517,778
6. Adelaide Entertainment Center (Adelaide, Australia), $17,301,694
7. 1st Mariner Arena (Baltimore, MD), $15,983,649
8. Atlantic City Boardwalk Hall (Atlantic City, NJ), $14,699,593
9. Valley View Casino Center (San Diego, CA), $13,646,952
10. Van Andel Arena (Grand Rapids, MI), $12,904,833

Source: *Billboard*, The Year in Music & Touring (annual), December 17, 2011, p. 102.

1142 ■ WORLD'S TOP MUSIC FESTIVALS, 2011

Ranked by: Gross sales, in U.S. dollars. **Remarks:** Also notes ticket prices, venue, location, dates, attendance, number of sell-outs, and promoters. **Number listed:** 10

1. Coachella Valley Music & Arts Festival, with $24,993,698
2. Oxegen, $21,113,100
3. Lollapalooza, $19,902,224
4. Austin City Limits Music Festival, $15,446,113
5. Outside Lands Music & Arts Festival, $12,914,990
6. Stagecoach: California's Country Music Festival, $9,195,415
7. Z Festival, $7,937,520
8. L.A. Rising, $4,886,555
9. Corona Capital, $4,076,130
10. Tennent's Vital, $3,839,920

Source: *Billboard*, The Year in Music & Touring (annual), December 17, 2011, p. 113.

1143 ■ WORLD'S TOP SMALL CONCERT VENUES, 2011

Ranked by: Gross sales, in U.S. dollars. **Remarks:** Ranking covers venues with capacities between 5,001 and 10,000. Also notes venue capacity, total attendance, total capacity, number of shows, and number of sell-outs. **Number listed:** 10

1. Radio City Music Hall (New York City), with $126,909,370
2. Auditorio Nacional (Mexico City, Mexico), $48,120,818
3. The Theater at Madison Square Garden (New York City), $21,318,622
4. Nokia Theatre L.A. Live (Los Angeles, CA), $21,244,346
5. Mohegan Sun Arena (Uncasville, CT), $20,869,750
6. Credicard Hall (Sao Paulo, Brazil), $19,453,544
7. Verizon Theatre (Grand Prairie, TX), $14,311,864
8. Newcastle Entertainment Centre (Newcastle, Australia), $13,083,114
9. Citibank Hall (Rio de Janeiro, Brazil), $11,254,127
10. Hordern Pavilion (Sydney, Australia), $10,254,042

Source: *Billboard*, The Year in Music & Touring (annual), December 17, 2011, p. 110.

Conglomerate Corporations
See: **Diversified Corporations**

Construction Industry

1144 ■ AMERICA'S LARGEST PRIVATE CONSTRUCTION COMPANIES, 2010

Ranked by: Revenue, in billions of dollars. **Remarks:** Also notes headquarters, number of employees, and overall rank in the *America's Largest Private Companies* list. Ranking is available online only, not in print. **Number listed:** 21

1. Bechtel Group Inc., with $27.9 billion
2. Kiewit Corp., $9.94
3. CH2M Hill Cos., Ltd., $5.42
4. Guardian Industries Corp., $4.9
5. Clark Enterprises Inc., $4.7
6. Kohler Co., $4.68
7. Gilbane Inc., $4.3
8. ABC Supply Co., $4.07
9. ProBuild Holdings Inc., $3.5
10. Walsh Group Ltd., $3.46

Source: *Forbes*, America's Largest Private Companies (annual), http://www.forbes.com, December 5, 2011.

1145 ■ BEST SMALL CONSTRUCTION COMPANIES IN AMERICA, 2011

Ranked by: Score based on revenue, profits, and return on equity for the past 12 months and five years. **Remarks:** Specific scores not provided. Also notes rank in the overall *100 Best Small Companies in America*. To qualify, companies must have revenues between $5 million and $1 billion, a net margin above five percent, and share price above $5. List is available online only. **Number listed:** 2

1. Ameresco
2. Carbo Ceramics

Source: *Forbes*, Best Small Companies in America (annual), November 7, 2011.

1146 ■ FASTEST-GROWING PRIVATE CONSTRUCTION COMPANIES IN THE U.S., 2007-2010

Ranked by: Average annual sales growth over three years, in percent. **Remarks:** Also notes headquarters, revenue, and rank in the overall *Inc. 500*. To qualify, private companies must have had annual revenues of at least $100,000 in 2007 and $2 million in 2010. **Number listed:** 17

1. MZI Group, with 3,874%
2. Cadillac Stone Works, 2,677%
3. Property Masters, 2,114%
4. Build Group, 2,104.4%
5. Landmark Retail, 1,825%
6. Decision Distribution, 1,334.6%
7. QSS International, 1,291.6%
8. Stellar Development, 1,255.3%
9. Daytner Construction Group, 1,194.3%
10. New South Equipment Mats, 1,191.6%

Source: *Inc.*, Inc. 500 (annual), September 2011, p. 100-102.

1147 ■ LARGEST ARCHITECTURAL AND ENGINEERING DESIGN FIRMS IN TEXAS AND LOUISIANA, 2010

Ranked by: Revenue from projects in Texas and Louisiana, in millions of dollars. **Remarks:** Also notes rank for previous year, location, and market sectors. **Number listed:** 72

1. AECOM Technology Corp., with $239.17 million
2. Jacobs Engineering Group Inc., $236.93
3. CH2M Hill Cos., Ltd., $163.15
4. Parsons Brinckerhoff Inc., $141.41
5. HNTB Corp., $139.99
6. HDR Inc., $132.68
7. M. Arthur Gensler Jr. & Associates Inc., $99.4
8. Arcadis, $86.64
9. Atkins North America, $81
10. Freese & Nichols Inc., $78.49

Source: *ENR Texas & Louisiana*, Top Design Firms (annual), http://www.texas.construction.com, October 2011.

1148 ■ LARGEST BUILDING CONTRACTORS BY EMPLOYEES, 2010

Ranked by: Total number of employees. **Remarks:** Also notes contact information for headquarters, number of employees at headquarters, revenue, rank by revenue, and primary SIC code. **Number listed:** 438

1. Zachry Holdings Inc., with 15,134 employees
2. Zachry Industrial Inc., 13,819
3. Kiewit Corp., 10,441
4. Skanska USA Inc., 10,000
5. Kiewit Infrastructure Co., 9,000
6. Centex International Inc., 7,750
7. Tutor Perini Corp., 7,100
8. Yates Cos., Inc., 7,000
9. Austin Industries Inc. (Delaware), 6,500
10. BE & K Construction Co., 6,000

10. Hochtief USA Inc., 6,000

10. Selectbuild Construction Inc., 6,000

Source: *Business Rankings*, (annual), Dun & Bradstreet Inc., 2011, p. VI.23-VI.32.

1149 ■ LARGEST BUILDING CONTRACTORS BY SALES, 2010

Ranked by: Total revenue, in dollars. **Remarks:** Also notes contact information for headquarters, number of employees at headquarters and overall, rank by employees, and primary SIC code. **Number listed:** 438

1. Kiewit Corp., with $9,973,000,000

2. Turner Corp., $7,413,961,000

3. Turner Construction Co., $7,403,125,000

4. Skanska USA Inc., $5,850,653,000

5. PulteGroup Inc., $4,569,290,000

6. D. R. Horton Inc., $4,309,700,000

7. Balfour Beatty LLC, $4,119,158,000

8. The Whiting-Turner Contracting Co., $3,504,116,039

9. Walsh Group Ltd., $3,316,006,121

10. Tutor Perini Corp., $3,199,210,000

Source: *Business Rankings*, (annual), Dun & Bradstreet Inc., 2011, p. V.23-V.32.

1150 ■ LARGEST "GREEN" CONTRACTORS, 2010

Ranked by: "Green" revenue, in dollars. **Number listed:** 25

1. The Turner Corp., with $4,212,000,000

2. Gilbane Building Co., $2,621,020,740

3. The Clark Construction Group Inc., $2,396,763,200

4. Hensel Phelps Construction Co., $2,027,008,000

5. Tutor Perini Corp., $1,533,831,066

6. The Whiting-Turner Contracting Co., $1,478,966,372

7. Skanska USA, $1,268,548,000

8. Holder Construction Co., $1,176,030,000

9. Balfour Beatty U.S., $1,001,437,272

10. Mortenson Construction, $885,420,000

Source: *Building Design & Construction*, Giants 300 (annual), July 2011, p. 49.

1151 ■ LARGEST SPECIALTY CONTRACTORS IN CALIFORNIA, 2010

Ranked by: Regional revenue, in millions of dollars. **Remarks:** Also notes rank for previous year, contact information, and specialties. **Number listed:** 70

1. EMCOR Group Inc., with $744.41 million

2. ACCO Engineered Systems Inc., $457

3. Rosendin Electric Inc., $434

4. Cupertino Electric Inc., $276

5. Bergelectric Corp., $234.3

6. Helix Electric Inc., $176

7. Redwood City Electric Inc., $163

8. Southland Industries, $130

9. KHS & S Contractors, $118.3

10. ISEC Inc., $115.55

Source: *ENR California*, Top Specialty Contractors (annual), October 10, 2011.

1152 ■ LARGEST TRENCHLESS CONSTRUCTION DESIGN FIRMS, 2010

Ranked by: Trenchless revenue, in millions of dollars. **Remarks:** Also notes total revenue, trenchless as a percentage of total billings, number of trenchless specialists, number of projects, and rank for previous year. **Number listed:** 50

1. CH2M Hill Cos., Ltd., with $95.3 million

2. Hatch Mott MacDonald Inc., $87.1

3. Camp Dresser & McKee Inc. (CDM), $61.4

4. Jacobs Engineering Group Inc., $60.7

5. Black & Veatch Holding Co., $49.32

6. MWH Global Inc., $45.4

7. Cardno TBE, $27.327

8. Brown & Caldwell, $27.1

9. Parsons Brinckerhoff, $21.5

10. Lockwood, Andrews & Newnam Inc., $20.47

Source: *Trenchless Technology*, Top 50 Design Firms (annual), December 2011, p. 31.

1153 ■ LARGEST U.S. CONSTRUCTION SERVICES COMPANIES OVERALL, 2011

Ranked by: Score based on revenue, profits, assets, and market capitalization. **Remarks:** Specific scores not provided. Also notes overall rank in the *Forbes 2000* and figures for each criterion. **Number listed:** 3

1. Fluor Corp.

2. KBR Inc.

3. Jacobs Engineering Group Inc.

Source: *Forbes*, Forbes 2000 (annual), http://www.forbes.com, May 7, 2012.

1154 ■ MOST VALUABLE U.S. CONSTRUCTION AND BUILDING MATERIALS COMPANIES, 2011

Ranked by: Market value as of March 2011, in millions of U.S. dollars. **Remarks:** Also notes rank within the *FT U.S. 500*, rank for previous year, country, revenue, net income, assets, number of employees, share price, price-to-earning ratio, dividend yield, and fiscal yearend. **Number listed:** 5

1. Fluor Corp., with $13,025.3 million

2. Fortune Brands Inc., $9,509.2

3. The Sherwin-Williams Co., $9,007.4

4. Jacobs Engineering Group Inc., $5,499.9

5. Vulcan Materials Co., $5,885

Source: *Financial Times*, FT 500 (annual), http://www.ft.com, June 24, 2011.

1155 ■ STATES WITH THE FEWEST EMPLOYEES IN CONSTRUCTION, 2010

Ranked by: Number of employees in the construction industry. **Remarks:** Also notes share of national total **Number listed:** 51

1. Washington DC, with 11,100 employees

2. Vermont, 11,800

3. Alaska, 14,700

4. Rhode Island, 15,700

5. Delaware, 19,100

6. North Dakota, 19,600

7. South Dakota, 20,400

8. Montana, 20,500

9. Wyoming, 22,200

10. New Hampshire, 22,800

Source: *State Rankings*, (annual), CQ Press, 2011, p. 190.

1156 ■ STATES WITH THE HIGHEST RATE OF EMPLOYEES IN CONSTRUCTION, 2010

Ranked by: Percentage of nonfarm employees in the construction industry. **Number listed:** 51

1. Wyoming, with 7.8%

2. Louisiana, 6.7%

3. Maryland, 5.9%

4. Texas, 5.6%

4. Utah, 5.6%

6. New Mexico, 5.5%

7. North Dakota, 5.3%

8. Nevada, 5.2%

9. Colorado, 5.1%

9. Hawaii, 5.1%

Source: *State Rankings*, (annual), CQ Press, 2011, p. 191.

1157 ■ STATES WITH THE LOWEST RATE OF EMPLOYEES IN CONSTRUCTION, 2010

Ranked by: Percentage of nonfarm employees in the construction industry. **Number listed:** 51

1. Washington DC, with 1.5%

2. Connecticut, 3.1%

2. Michigan, 3.1%

2. Minnesota, 3.1%

5. New Jersey, 3.3%

5. Ohio, 3.3%

5. Wisconsin, 3.3%

8. Massachusetts, 3.4%

9. Kentucky, 3.5%

9. Rhode Island, 3.5%

Source: *State Rankings*, (annual), CQ Press, 2011, p. 191.

1158 ■ STATES WITH THE MOST EMPLOYEES IN CONSTRUCTION, 2010

Ranked by: Number of employees in the construction industry. **Remarks:** Also notes share of national total. **Number listed:** 51

1. Texas, with 586,300 employees

2. California, 535,600

3. Florida, 338,400

4. New York, 305,800

5. Pennsylvania, 216,200

6. Illinois, 201,200

7. Virginia, 176,600

8. North Carolina, 166,400

9. Ohio, 163,900

10. Maryland, 148,400

Source: *State Rankings*, (annual), CQ Press, 2011, p. 190.

1159 ■ TEXAS'S LARGEST CONSTRUCTION SERVICES COMPANIES OVERALL, 2011

Ranked by: Score based on revenue, profits, assets, and market capitalization. **Remarks:** Specific scores not provided. Also notes overall rank in the *Forbes 2000* and figures for each criterion. **Number listed:** 2

1. Fluor Corp.

2. KBR Inc.

Source: *Forbes*, Forbes 2000 (annual), http://www.forbes.com, May 7, 2012.

Construction Industry, International

1160 ■ BEST MANUFACTURING, CONSTRUCTION, AND DISTRIBUTION COMPANIES TO WORK FOR IN BRITISH COLUMBIA, 2010

Ranked by: Editorial determination. **Remarks:** Specific scores not provided. **Number listed:** 5

1. Kryton International Inc.

2. Waterplay Solutions Corp.

3. Great Little Box Co., Ltd.

4. Sequel Natural Ltd.

5. Maxem Eyewear Corp.

Source: *BCBusiness*, Best Companies (annual), http://www.bcbusinessonline.ca, December 2011.

1161 ■ BRITAIN'S MOST ADMIRED HEAVY CONSTRUCTION COMPANIES, 2011

Ranked by: Survey of peers and investment analysts based on nine criteria: quality of management, financial soundness, quality of goods/services, ability to attract and retain talent, value as long-term investment, innovation, marketing, community and environmental responsibility, and use of corporate assets. **Number listed:** 5

1. Balfour Beatty plc, with 65.2 points

2. Carillion, 59.2

3. Kier Group, 57.9

4. Costain Group, 55.2

5. Keller Group, 52.8

Source: *Management Today*, Britain's Most Admired Companies (annual), December 2011, p. 43.

1162 ■ BRITAIN'S MOST ADMIRED HOME CONSTRUCTION COMPANIES, 2011

Ranked by: Survey of peers and investment analysts based on nine criteria: quality of management, financial soundness, quality of goods/services, ability to attract and retain talent, value as long-term investment, innovation, marketing, community and environmental responsibility, and use of corporate assets. **Number listed:** 5

1. The Berkeley Group Holdings plc, with 73 points

2. Persimmon plc, 63.3

3. Bellway, 59.5

4. Bovis Homes, 58.9

5. Barrett Developments, 56.5

Source: *Management Today*, Britain's Most Admired Companies (annual), December 2011, p. 43.

1163 ■ CHINA'S LARGEST CONSTRUCTION SERVICES COMPANIES OVERALL, 2011

Ranked by: Score based on revenue, profits, assets, and market capitalization. **Remarks:** Specific scores not provided. Also notes overall rank in the *Forbes 2000* and figures for each criterion. **Number listed:** 7

1. China Communications Construction Group Ltd.
2. China State Construction Engineering Corp.
3. China Railway Group Ltd.
4. China Railway Construction Corp.
5. Metallurgical Corporation of China Ltd. (MCC)
6. Sinohydro Group
7. Shanghai Construction

Source: *Forbes*, Forbes 2000 (annual), http://www.forbes.com, May 7, 2012.

1164 ■ CHINA'S MOST VALUABLE ENGINEERING AND CONSTRUCTION BRANDS, 2011

Ranked by: Brand value, in millions of U.S. dollars. **Remarks:** Also notes rank within the *Global 500* for current and previous year, figures for current and previous year, and brand rating. Ranking is available online only. **Number listed:** 3

1. China State Construction, with $5,375 million
2. Metallurgical Corp. of China, $3,268
3. CCCC, $2,600

Source: *Global 500*, (annual), Brand Finance plc, March 2012.

1165 ■ EUROPE'S MOST VALUABLE CONSTRUCTION AND BUILDING MATERIALS COMPANIES, 2011

Ranked by: Market value as of March 2011, in millions of U.S. dollars. **Remarks:** Also notes rank within the *FT Europe 500*, rank for previous year, country, revenue, net income, assets, number of employees, share price, price-to-earning ratio, dividend yield, and fiscal yearend. **Number listed:** 23

1. VINCI, with $34,790.7 million
2. Cie. de Saint Gobain SA, $32,546.5
3. Holcim Ltd., $24,740.4
4. Lafarge SA, $17,892.2
5. Bouygues SA, $17,592.8
6. CRH plc, $16,287.3
7. Actividades de Construccion y Servicios SA (ACS), $14,771.5
8. Heidelbergcement, $13,140.3
9. Assa Abloy AB, $10,028.4
10. Grupo Ferrovial SA, $9,212.1

Source: *Financial Times*, FT 500 (annual), http://www.ft.com, June 24, 2011.

1166 ■ FRANCE'S LARGEST CONSTRUCTION SERVICES COMPANIES OVERALL, 2011

Ranked by: Score based on revenue, profits, assets, and market capitalization. **Remarks:** Specific scores not provided. Also notes overall rank in the *Forbes 2000* and figures for each criterion. **Number listed:** 3

1. VINCI
2. Bouygues SA
3. Eiffage

Source: *Forbes*, Forbes 2000 (annual), http://www.forbes.com, May 7, 2012.

1167 ■ FRANCE'S MOST VALUABLE ENGINEERING AND CONSTRUCTION BRANDS, 2011

Ranked by: Brand value, in millions of U.S. dollars. **Remarks:** Also notes rank within the *Global 500* for current and previous

year, figures for current and previous year, and brand rating. Ranking is available online only. **Number listed:** 2

1. Vinci, with $6,181 million
2. Bouygues, $3,590

Source: *Global 500*, (annual), Brand Finance plc, March 2012.

1168 ■ GERMANY'S LARGEST CONSTRUCTION SERVICES COMPANIES OVERALL, 2011

Ranked by: Score based on revenue, profits, assets, and market capitalization. **Remarks:** Specific scores not provided. Also notes overall rank in the *Forbes 2000* and figures for each criterion. **Number listed:** 2

1. Hochtief AG
2. Bilfinger Berger SE

Source: *Forbes*, Forbes 2000 (annual), http://www.forbes.com, May 7, 2012.

1169 ■ INDIA'S LARGEST CONSTRUCTION SERVICES COMPANIES OVERALL, 2011

Ranked by: Score based on revenue, profits, assets, and market capitalization. **Remarks:** Specific scores not provided. Also notes overall rank in the *Forbes 2000* and figures for each criterion. **Number listed:** 2

1. Larsen & Toubro Ltd.
2. Jaiprakash Associates Ltd.

Source: *Forbes*, Forbes 2000 (annual), http://www.forbes.com, May 7, 2012.

1170 ■ JAPAN'S LARGEST CONSTRUCTION SERVICES COMPANIES OVERALL, 2011

Ranked by: Score based on revenue, profits, assets, and market capitalization. **Remarks:** Specific scores not provided. Also notes overall rank in the *Forbes 2000* and figures for each criterion. **Number listed:** 9

1. Daiwa House Industry
2. Sekisui House
3. Daito Trust Construction
4. Kajima
5. Shimizu
6. Obayashi
7. Taisei
8. Sekisui Chemical
9. JGC

Source: *Forbes*, Forbes 2000 (annual), http://www.forbes.com, May 7, 2012.

1171 ■ LARGEST CONSTRUCTION COMPANIES IN EUROPE, 2010

Ranked by: Sales, in millions of U.S. dollars. **Remarks:** Also notes rank within country. **Number listed:** 100

1. VINCI (France), with $48,129.4 million
2. Bouygues SA (France), $44,935.1
3. Fonciere Euris (France), $35,385.5
4. A. Hak Pijpleidingen BV (Netherlands), $32,757.4
5. Actividades de Construccion y Servicios SA (ACS, Spain), $22,566.1
6. Holcim Ltd. (Switzerland), $20,806.7
7. Grupo Ferrovial SA (Spain), $19,910.6

8. Skanska AB (Sweden), $19,508.1
9. Eiffage SA (France), $18,736.5
10. Strabag SE (Austria), $18,667.2

Source: *Europe's 15,000 Largest Companies*, (annual), ELC International, 2011, p. 39.

1172 ■ LARGEST REAL ESTATE/CONSTRUCTION COMPANIES IN BRITISH COLUMBIA, 2010

Ranked by: Revenue, in thousands of Canadian dollars. **Remarks:** Also notes figures for previous year. **Number listed:** 10

1. Ledcor Group of Cos., with C$2,300,000 thousand
2. Colliers Macaulay Nicolls, C$861,916
3. Charlwood Pacific Group, C$700,000
4. Northland Properties Corp., C$611,000
5. Polygon Homes Ltd., C$450,000
6. Shato Holdings Ltd., C$425,000
7. Bosa Properties Inc., C$300,000
8. Aquilini Investment Group, C$250,000
9. Whistler Blackcomb Holdings Inc., C$224,673
10. ITC Construction Group, C$224,000

Source: *BCBusiness*, Top 100 (annual), July 2011, p. 135.

1173 ■ MOST POWERFUL ARABS IN CONSTRUCTION, 2012

Ranked by: Score based on scope of influence. **Remarks:** Specific scores not provided. Also notes rank in the overall *Power 500*. **Number listed:** 74

1. Mohamed Alabbar
2. Khalid Al Falih
3. Matty Moroun
4. Moafaq Al Gaddah
5. Fahd Al Rasheed
6. Munib Al Masri
7. Anas Kouzbari
8. Mohammed Al Mady
9. Bakr Bin Ladin
10. Riad Kamal

Source: *Arab Business*, Power 500 (annual), June 4, 2012.

1174 ■ SOUTH KOREA'S LARGEST CONSTRUCTION SERVICES COMPANIES OVERALL, 2011

Ranked by: Score based on revenue, profits, assets, and market capitalization. **Remarks:** Specific scores not provided. Also notes overall rank in the *Forbes 2000* and figures for each criterion. **Number listed:** 5

1. Hyundai Engineering & Construction Co., Ltd.
2. Samsung Engineering Co., Ltd.
3. GS Engineering & Construction Corp.
4. Daelim Industrial Co., Ltd.
5. Kumho Industrial Co., Ltd.

Source: *Forbes*, Forbes 2000 (annual), http://www.forbes.com, May 7, 2012.

1175 ■ SPAIN'S LARGEST CONSTRUCTION SERVICES COMPANIES OVERALL, 2011

Ranked by: Score based on revenue, profits, assets, and market capitalization. **Remarks:** Specific scores not provided. Also notes overall rank in the *Forbes 2000* and figures for each criterion. **Number listed:** 6

1. Actividades de Construccion y Servicios SA (ACS)
2. Fomento de Construcciones y Contratas SA (FCC)
3. Abengoa SA
4. Acciona SA
5. Obrascon Huarte Lain SA (OHL)
6. Sacyr Vallehermoso SA

Source: *Forbes*, Forbes 2000 (annual), http://www.forbes.com, May 7, 2012.

1176 ■ SPAIN'S MOST VALUABLE ENGINEERING AND CONSTRUCTION BRANDS, 2011

Ranked by: Brand value, in millions of U.S. dollars. **Remarks:** Also notes rank within the *Global 500* for current and previous year, figures for current and previous year, and brand rating. Ranking is available online only. **Number listed:** 2

1. ACS, with $3,978 million
2. Ferrovial, $2,905

Source: *Global 500*, (annual), Brand Finance plc, March 2012.

1177 ■ WORLD'S LARGEST CONSTRUCTION SERVICES COMPANIES OVERALL, 2011

Ranked by: Score based on revenue, profits, assets, and market capitalization. **Remarks:** Specific scores not provided. Also notes country, overall rank in the *Forbes 2000*, and figures for each criterion. **Number listed:** 47

1. VINCI
2. China Communications Construction Group Ltd.
3. China State Construction Engineering Corp.
4. Bouygues SA
5. China Railway Group Ltd.
6. Actividades de Construccion y Servicios SA (ACS)
7. China Railway Construction Corp.
8. Metallurgical Corporation of China Ltd. (MCC)
9. Larsen & Toubro Ltd.
10. Skanska AB

Source: *Forbes*, Forbes 2000 (annual), http://www.forbes.com, May 7, 2012.

1178 ■ WORLD'S MOST ADMIRED ENGINEERING AND CONSTRUCTION COMPANIES, 2012

Ranked by: Score, on a scale of 10, based on a survey of executives, directors, and securities analysts of companies within their own industry on eight criteria: innovation, financial soundness, employee talent, use of corporate assets, long-term investment value, social responsibility, quality of management, and quality of products/services. **Remarks:** Specific scores not provided. Also notes rank for previous year. **Number listed:** 8

1. Fluor Corp.
2. Jacobs Engineering Group Inc.
3. Peter Kiewit Sons' Inc.
4. Skanska AB
5. EMCOR Group Inc.
6. Grupo Ferrovial SA
7. VINCI
8. Hochtief AG

Source: *Fortune*, World's Most Admired Companies (annual), March 19, 2012, p. 149.

1179 ▪ WORLD'S MOST ETHICAL CONSTRUCTION COMPANIES, 2012

Ranked by: Score based on five criteria: ethics and compliance program; reputation, leadership, and innovation; governance; corporate citizenship and responsibility; and culture of ethics. **Remarks:** Specific scores not provided; companies are listed alphabetically, not ranked. **Number listed:** 2

1. CRH plc (Ireland)
2. Granite Construction Co. (U.S.)

Source: *Ethisphere Magazine*, World's Most Ethical Companies (annual), http://www.ethisphere.com, 2012.

1180 ▪ WORLD'S MOST VALUABLE CONSTRUCTION AND BUILDING MATERIALS COMPANIES, 2011

Ranked by: Market value as of March 2011, in millions of U.S. dollars. **Remarks:** Also notes rank within the *FT 500*, rank for previous year, country, revenue, net income, assets, number of employees, share price, price-to-earning ratio, dividend yield, and fiscal year-end. **Number listed:** 5

1. VINCI, with $34,790.7 million
2. Cie. de Saint Gobain SA, $32,546.5
3. Holcim Ltd., $24,740.4
4. Larsen & Toubro Ltd., $22,571.7
5. Anhui Conch Cement Co., Ltd., $21,918.2

Source: *Financial Times*, FT 500 (annual), http://www.ft.com, June 24, 2011.

1181 ▪ WORLD'S MOST VALUABLE ENGINEERING AND CONSTRUCTION BRANDS, 2011

Ranked by: Brand value, in millions of U.S. dollars. **Remarks:** Also notes rank within the *Global 500* for current and previous year, figures for current and previous year, country, and brand rating. Ranking is available online only. **Number listed:** 8

1. Vinci, with $6,181 million
2. China State Construction, $5,375
3. ACS, $3,978
4. ABB, $3,666
5. Bouygues, $3,590
6. Metallurgical Corp. of China, $3,268
7. Ferrovial, $2,905
8. CCCC, $2,600

Source: *Global 500*, (annual), Brand Finance plc, March 2012.

Construction Industry, Nonresidential

1182 ▪ LARGEST HEAVY CONSTRUCTION CONTRACTORS BY EMPLOYEES, 2010

Ranked by: Total number of employees. **Remarks:** Also notes contact information for headquarters, number of employees at headquarters, revenue, rank by revenue, and primary SIC code. **Number listed:** 68

1. Halliburton Delaware Inc., with 57,300 employees
2. KBR Inc., 51,160
3. Jacobs Engineering Group Inc., 38,500
4. McDermott International Inc., 29,000
5. URS Energy & Construction Inc., 23,000

6. KBR Holdings LLC, 20,010
6. Kellogg Brown & Root LLC, 20,010
8. Zachry Consolidated Inc., 15,000
9. Peter Kiewit Sons' Inc., 14,700
10. McDermott Inc., 11,400

Source: *Business Rankings*, (annual), Dun & Bradstreet Inc., 2011, p. VI.33-VI.34.

1183 ▪ LARGEST HEAVY CONSTRUCTION CONTRACTORS BY SALES, 2010

Ranked by: Total revenue, in dollars. **Remarks:** Also notes contact information for headquarters, number of employees at headquarters and overall, rank by employees, and primary SIC code. **Number listed:** 70

1. KBR Inc., with $10,099,000,000
2. Peter Kiewit Sons Inc., $9,985,000,000
3. Jacobs Engineering Group Inc., $9,915,517,000
4. McDermott International Inc., $2,403,743,000
5. MasTec Inc., $2,308,031,000
6. Granite Construction Co., $2,268,333,000
7. Colas Inc., $1,875,864,000
8. Granite Construction Inc., $1,762,965,000
9. Eagle Rock Pipeline GP LLC, $1,743,321,000
10. Skanska USA Civil Inc., $1,707,545,000

Source: *Business Rankings*, (annual), Dun & Bradstreet Inc., 2011, p. V.33-V.34.

Construction Industry, Residential

1184 ▪ LARGEST HOME BUILDERS BY REVENUE, 2011

Ranked by: Total new residential revenue, in dollars. **Remarks:** Also notes rank for previous year, headquarters, key executive, website, year founded, number of new residential closings, other revenue, and housing types. **Number listed:** 235

1. PulteGroup Inc., with $3,950,743,000
2. D. R. Horton Inc., $3,665,523,000
3. Lennar Corp., $2,624,785,000
4. NVR Inc., $2,611,195,000
5. Toll Brothers Inc., $1,475,882,000
6. KB Home, $1,305,299,000
7. Hovnanian Enterprises Inc., $1,244,817,000
8. Standard Pacific Corp., $895,943,773
9. The Ryland Group, $890,733,000
10. Meritage Homes Corp., $860,884,000

Source: *Professional Builder*, Housing Giants (annual), May 2012, p. 12-28.

1185 ▪ LARGEST RESIDENTIAL BUILDERS IN THE U.S. BY CLOSINGS, 2011

Ranked by: Number of U.S. closings. **Remarks:** Also notes rank for previous year, contact information, CEO, gross revenue, percent change from previous year, breakdown of units by type, and regions of operation. **Number listed:** 100

1. D. R. Horton Inc., with 17,176 closings
2. PulteGroup Inc., 15,275
3. Lennar Corp., 10,845
4. NVR Inc., 8,487

5. KB Home, 5,812
6. Habitat for Humanity International, 4,970
7. Hovnanian Enterprises Inc., 4,216
8. The Ryland Group Inc., 3,664
9. Beazer Homes USA Inc., 3,597
10. Meritage Homes Corp., 3,268

Source: *Builder*, Builder 100 (annual), May 2012, p. 72-82.

1186 ■ U.S. RESIDENTIAL BUILDERS WITH THE FASTEST-GROWING CLOSINGS, 2010-2011

Ranked by: Annual growth in the number of U.S. closings, in percent. **Remarks:** Also notes rank in the overall *Builder 100*. **Number listed:** 10

1. DSLD, with 89%
2. Grayhawk Homes, 68%
3. Chesmar Homes, 49%
4. Landon Homes, 47%
5. HHHunt Corp., 45%
6. LGI Homes, 43%
7. Neal Communities, 41%
8. Orleans Homebuilders, 32%
9. S & A Homes, 31%
10. Westin Homes, 25%

Source: *Builder*, Builder 100 (annual), May 2012, p. 71.

1187 ■ U.S. RESIDENTIAL BUILDERS WITH THE FASTEST-GROWING REVENUE, 2010-2011

Ranked by: Annual growth in revenue, in percent. **Remarks:** Also notes rank in the overall *Builder 100*. **Number listed:** 10

1. DSLD, with 97%
2. Grayhawk Homes, 70%
3. Landon Homes, 64%
4. Chesmar Homes, 57%
5. LGI Homes, 49%
5. Neal Communities, 49%
7. The Villages of Lake-Sumter, 49%
8. The Related Group, 45%
9. Lombardo Homes, 33%
10. HHHunt Corp., 28%

Source: *Builder*, Builder 100 (annual), May 2012, p. 71.

Construction Machinery

1188 ■ TOP *FORTUNE 500* COMPANIES IN CONSTRUCTION AND FARM MACHINERY, 2011

Ranked by: Revenue, in millions of dollars. **Remarks:** Also notes overall rank in the *Fortune 500;* profits; profits as a percentage of revenue; stockholders' equity; and rank by each criterion. **Number listed:** 5

1. Caterpillar Inc., with $60,138 million
2. Deere & Co., $32,013
3. Cummins Inc., $18,048
4. AGCO Corp., $8,773
5. Terex Corp., $6,505

Source: *Fortune*, Fortune 500 (annual), May 21, 2012, p. F-34.

1189 ■ WORLD'S MOST VALUABLE CONSTRUCTION AND MINING MACHINERY BRANDS, 2011

Ranked by: Brand value, in millions of U.S. dollars. **Remarks:** Also notes rank within the *Global 500* for current and previous year, figures for current and previous year, country, and brand rating. Ranking is available online only. **Number listed:** 2

1. Caterpillar, with $8,253 million
2. Komatsu, $2,575

Source: *Global 500*, (annual), Brand Finance plc, March 2012.

Construction Materials

1190 ■ CHINA'S LARGEST CONSTRUCTION MATERIALS COMPANIES OVERALL, 2011

Ranked by: Score based on revenue, profits, assets, and market capitalization. **Remarks:** Specific scores not provided. Also notes overall rank in the *Forbes 2000* and figures for each criterion. **Number listed:** 3

1. Anhui Conch Cement Co., Ltd.
2. China National Building
3. BBMG

Source: *Forbes*, Forbes 2000 (annual), http://www.forbes.com, May 7, 2012.

1191 ■ FRANCE'S LARGEST CONSTRUCTION MATERIALS COMPANIES OVERALL, 2011

Ranked by: Score based on revenue, profits, assets, and market capitalization. **Remarks:** Specific scores not provided. Also notes overall rank in the *Forbes 2000* and figures for each criterion. **Number listed:** 2

1. Cie. de Saint Gobain SA
2. Lafarge SA

Source: *Forbes*, Forbes 2000 (annual), http://www.forbes.com, May 7, 2012.

1192 ■ JAPAN'S LARGEST CONSTRUCTION MATERIALS COMPANIES OVERALL, 2011

Ranked by: Score based on revenue, profits, assets, and market capitalization. **Remarks:** Specific scores not provided. Also notes overall rank in the *Forbes 2000* and figures for each criterion. **Number listed:** 5

1. Asahi Glass Co., Ltd.
2. Daikin Industries Ltd.
3. JS Group
4. Taiheiyo Cement
5. Nippon Sheet Glass

Source: *Forbes*, Forbes 2000 (annual), http://www.forbes.com, May 7, 2012.

1193 ■ SWITZERLAND'S LARGEST CONSTRUCTION MATERIALS COMPANIES OVERALL, 2011

Ranked by: Score based on revenue, profits, assets, and market capitalization. **Remarks:** Specific scores not provided. Also notes overall rank in the *Forbes 2000* and figures for each criterion. **Number listed:** 3

1. Holcim Ltd.
2. Wolseley plc
3. Geberit AG

Source: *Forbes*, Forbes 2000 (annual), http://www.forbes.com, May 7, 2012.

1194 ■ WORLD'S LARGEST CONSTRUCTION MATERIALS COMPANIES OVERALL, 2011

Ranked by: Score based on revenue, profits, assets, and market capitalization. **Remarks:** Specific scores not provided. Also notes country, overall rank in the *Forbes 2000,* and figures for each criterion. **Number listed:** 22

1. Cie. de Saint Gobain SA
2. Lafarge SA
3. CRH plc
4. HeidelbergCement AG
5. Asahi Glass Co., Ltd.
6. Holcim Ltd.
7. The Siam Cement Public Co., Ltd.
8. Wolseley plc
9. Cemex, SA de CV
10. Anhui Conch Cement Co., Ltd.

Source: *Forbes*, Forbes 2000 (annual), http://www.forbes.com, May 7, 2012.

Construction Project Management

1195 ■ LARGEST CONSTRUCTION MANAGERS, 2010

Ranked by: Construction management revenue, in dollars. **Number listed:** 25

1. Gilbane Building Co., with $4,598,282,000
2. Skanska USA, $2,617,150,000
3. Lend Lease, $2,434,652,534
4. Hensel Phelps Construction, $2,027,008,000
5. The Whiting-Turner Contracting Co., $1,864,243,326
6. Suffolk Construction, $1,670,000,000
7. Structure Tone Inc., $1,456,377,000
8. Jacobs Engineering Group Inc., $1,299,450,000
9. Flintco, $1,240,000,000
10. The Yates Cos., $888,108,000

Source: *Building Design & Construction*, Giants 300 (annual), July 2011, p. 47.

1196 ■ TOP CONSTRUCTION MANAGEMENT-FOR-FEE FIRMS, 2010

Ranked by: Total revenue, in millions of dollars. **Remarks:** Also notes rank for previous year, headquarters, and international revenue. **Number listed:** 100

1. Bechtel Group Inc., with $3,941 million
2. CH2M Hill Cos., Ltd., $1,866.7
3. Jacobs Engineering Group Inc., $1,797
4. URS Corp., $1,599.7
5. AECOM Technology Corp., $1,491.1
6. Parsons Corp., $846.5
7. Parsons Brinckerhoff Inc., $724.8
8. Hill International Inc., $451.8
9. Science Applications International Corp. (SAIC), $445.8
10. KBR Inc., $440.8

Source: *ENR: Engineering News-Record*, Top Professional Service Firms (annual), June 13, 2011, p. 43.

1197 ■ TOP CONSTRUCTION PROGRAM-MANAGEMENT FIRMS, 2010

Ranked by: Total revenue from combined design and construction management/project management services, in millions of dollars. **Remarks:** Also notes headquarters and breakdown of revenue by type. **Number listed:** 20

1. AECOM Technology Corp., with $7,410.9 million
2. URS Corp., $6,638.5
3. Jacobs Engineering Group Inc., $6,545.4
4. Bechtel Group Inc., $6,111
5. CH2M Hill Cos., Ltd., $5,469.4
6. Fluor Corp., $3,134.2
7. AMEC plc, $2,456.3
8. KBR Inc., $2,451.1
9. Parsons Brinckerhoff Inc., $2,286.3
10. Tetra Tech Inc., $2,285

Source: *ENR: Engineering News-Record*, Top Professional Service Firms (annual), June 13, 2011, p. 38.

Consultants

1198 ■ BEST CONSULTING FIRMS TO WORK FOR BASED ON CAREER DEVELOPMENT, 2011

Ranked by: Score based on career development. **Remarks:** Specific scores not provided. **Number listed:** 10

1. Bain & Co.
2. The Boston Consulting Group Inc.
3. North Highland
4. McKinsey & Co.
5. PricewaterhouseCoopers LLP
6. Ernst & Young LLP
7. Deloitte Consulting LLP
8. Booz Allen Hamilton Inc.
9. Accenture Ltd.
10. Slalom Consulting

Source: *Consulting Magazine*, Best Firms to Work For (annual), http://www.consultingmag.com, September 2011.

1199 ■ BEST CONSULTING FIRMS TO WORK FOR BASED ON CLIENT ENGAGEMENT, 2011

Ranked by: Score based on client engagement. **Remarks:** Specific scores not provided. **Number listed:** 10

1. Bain & Co.
2. The Boston Consulting Group Inc.
3. North Highland
4. Point B
5. A. T. Kearney Inc.
6. Oliver Wyman Group
7. Alix Partners
8. Deloitte Consulting LLP
9. Kurt Salmon Associates
10. PRTM

Source: *Consulting Magazine*, Best Firms to Work For (annual), http://www.consultingmag.com, September 2011.

1200 ■ BEST CONSULTING FIRMS TO WORK FOR BASED ON COMPENSATION SATISFACTION, 2011

Ranked by: Score based on satisfaction with compensation and benefits. **Remarks:** Specific scores not provided. **Number listed:** 10

1. Bain & Co.
2. The Boston Consulting Group Inc.

3. McKinsey & Co.
4. Deloitte Consulting
5. North Highland
6. Booz & Co.
7. Slalom Consulting
8. Point B
9. Booz Allen Hamilton Inc.
10. Alvarez & Marsal

Source: *Consulting Magazine*, Best Firms to Work For (annual), http://www.consultingmag.com, September 2011.

1201 ■ BEST CONSULTING FIRMS TO WORK FOR BASED ON FIRM CULTURE, 2011

Ranked by: Score based on firm culture. **Remarks:** Specific scores not provided. **Number listed:** 10

1. Bain & Co.
2. North Highland
3. The Boston Consulting Group Inc.
4. Point B
5. Deloitte Consulting LLP
6. Monitor
7. Slalom Consulting
8. Capgemini
9. PricewaterhouseCoopers LLP
10. McKinsey & Co.

Source: *Consulting Magazine*, Best Firms to Work For (annual), http://www.consultingmag.com, September 2011.

1202 ■ BEST CONSULTING FIRMS TO WORK FOR BASED ON LEADERSHIP, 2011

Ranked by: Score based on satisfaction with firm leadership. **Remarks:** Specific scores not provided. **Number listed:** 10

1. Bain & Co.
2. The Boston Consulting Group Inc.
3. Point B
4. North Highland
5. Slalom Consulting
6. Monitor
7. Oliver Wyman Group
8. AlixPartners
9. A. T Kearney Inc.
10. PricewaterhouseCoopers LLP

Source: *Consulting Magazine*, Best Firms to Work For (annual), http://www.consultingmag.com, September 2011.

1203 ■ BEST CONSULTING FIRMS TO WORK FOR BASED ON WORK/LIFE BALANCE, 2011

Ranked by: Score based on work/life balance. **Remarks:** Specific scores not provided. **Number listed:** 10

1. Point B
2. North Highland
3. Slalom Consulting
4. Bain & Co.
5. Crowe Horwath
6. Booz & Co.
7. Deloitte Consulting LLP
8. The Boston Consulting Group Inc.

9. PricewaterhouseCoopers LLP
10. Grant Thornton LLP

Source: *Consulting Magazine*, Best Firms to Work For (annual), http://www.consultingmag.com, September 2011.

1204 ■ BEST CONSULTING FIRMS TO WORK FOR IN THE FIELD OF FINANCIAL ADVISORY SERVICES, 2011

Ranked by: Score based on compensation, work/life balance, career development, job experience, firm leadership, and firm culture. **Remarks:** Specific scores not provided. **Number listed:** 5

1. Huron Consulting Group
2. Crowe Haworth
3. Alvarez & Marsel
4. Grant Thornton LLP
5. Proliviti

Source: *Consulting Magazine*, Best Firms to Work For (annual), http://www.consultingmag.com, September 2011.

1205 ■ BEST CONSULTING FIRMS TO WORK FOR IN THE FIELD OF INFORMATION TECHNOLOGY, 2011

Ranked by: Score based on compensation, work/life balance, career development, job experience, firm leadership, and firm culture. **Remarks:** Specific scores not provided. **Number listed:** 5

1. SunGard
2. SAP Business Transformation Services
3. Infosys Consulting
4. Wipro Ltd.
5. Capgemini

Source: *Consulting Magazine*, Best Firms to Work For (annual), http://www.consultingmag.com, September 2011.

1206 ■ BEST CONSULTING FIRMS TO WORK FOR IN THE FIELD OF MULTI-SERVICE CONSULTING, 2011

Ranked by: Score based on compensation, work/life balance, career development, job experience, firm leadership, and firm culture. **Remarks:** Specific scores not provided. **Number listed:** 5

1. Deloitte Consulting LLP
2. PricewaterhouseCoopers LLP
3. Ernst & Young LLP
4. Accenture Ltd.
5. Monitor

Source: *Consulting Magazine*, Best Firms to Work For (annual), http://www.consultingmag.com, September 2011.

1207 ■ BEST CONSULTING FIRMS TO WORK FOR IN THE FIELD OF OPERATIONS MANAGEMENT, 2011

Ranked by: Score based on compensation, work/life balance, career development, job experience, firm leadership, and firm culture. **Remarks:** Specific scores not provided. **Number listed:** 5

1. Point B
2. A. T. Kearney Inc.
3. Oliver Wyman Group
4. Kurt Salmon Associates
5. PRTM

Source: *Consulting Magazine*, Best Firms to Work For (annual), http://www.consultingmag.com, September 2011.

1208 ■ BEST CONSULTING FIRMS TO WORK FOR IN THE FIELD OF STRATEGY, 2011

Ranked by: Score based on compensation, work/life balance, career development, job experience, firm leadership, and firm culture. **Remarks:** Specific scores not provided. **Number listed:** 6

1. Bain & Co.
2. The Boston Consulting Group Inc.
3. North Highland
4. Slalom Consulting
5. McKinsey & Co.
6. Booz Allen Hamilton Inc.

Source: *Consulting Magazine*, Best Firms to Work For (annual), http://www.consultingmag.com, September 2011.

1209 ■ BEST LARGE CONSULTING FIRMS TO WORK FOR, 2011

Ranked by: Score based on compensation, work/life balance, career development, job experience, firm leadership, and firm culture. **Remarks:** Specific scores not provided. Also notes rank for previous year and for each criterion. To qualify, firms must have at least 200 billable consultants. **Number listed:** 15

1. Bain & Co.
2. The Boston Consulting Group Inc.
3. North Highland
4. Point B
5. Deloitte Consulting LLP
6. Slalom Consulting
7. McKinsey & Co.
8. PricewaterhouseCoopers LLP
9. Booz Allen Hamilton Inc.
10. Huron Consulting Group

Source: *Consulting Magazine*, Best Firms to Work For (annual), http://www.consultingmag.com, September 2011.

1210 ■ BEST SMALL CONSULTING FIRMS TO WORK FOR, 2011

Ranked by: Score based on compensation, work/life balance, career development, job experience, firm leadership, and firm culture. **Remarks:** Specific scores not provided. Also notes rank for previous year and for each criterion. To qualify, firms must have fewer than 200 billable consultants. **Number listed:** 15

1. Stroud Consulting
2. Impact Advisors
3. Cask
4. Vynamic
5. Infinitive
6. Fitzgerald Analytics
7. Leneti
8. Jabian Consulting
9. PeopleFirm
10. HiSoft

Source: *Consulting Magazine*, Best Firms to Work For (annual), http://www.consultingmag.com, September 2011.

1211 ■ TOP U.S. CONSULTANTS, 2012

Ranked by: Editorial determination. **Remarks:** Specific scores not provided; consultants are listed alphabetically, not ranked. **Number listed:** 25

1. Jim Armetta (Protiviti)
2. Chris Bierly (Bain & Co.)
3. Jon Caforio (McGladrey)
4. Michael Carberry (North Highland)
5. Michael Cirafesi (CSC)

6. Matthew Cohn (Capco)
7. Dave Cutler (Slalom Consulting)
8. John Distefano (Ernst & Young)
9. Lynne Doughtie (KPMG)
10. Jack Dunn (FTI Consulting)

Source: *Consulting*, Top 25 Consultants (annual), May 2012, p. 12.

Consumer Electronics
See: **Home Electronics**

Consumer Goods

1212 ■ AMERICA'S LARGEST PRIVATE CONSUMER DU-RABLES COMPANIES, 2010

Ranked by: Revenue, in billions of dollars. **Remarks:** Also notes headquarters, number of employees, and overall rank in the *America's Largest Private Companies* list. Ranking is available online only, not in print. **Number listed:** 5

1. JM Family Enterprises Inc., with $9.3 billion
2. Gulf States Toyota Inc., $5.1
3. International Automotive Components Group North America LLC, $3.7
4. General Parts Inc., $2.87
5. Flex-N-Gate, $2.57

Source: *Forbes*, America's Largest Private Companies (annual), http://www.forbes.com, December 5, 2011.

1213 ■ BEST SMALL CONSUMER DURABLES COMPANIES IN AMERICA, 2011

Ranked by: Score based on revenue, profits, and return on equity for the past 12 months and five years. **Remarks:** Specific scores not provided. Also notes rank in the overall *100 Best Small Companies in America*. To qualify, companies must have revenues between $5 million and $1 billion, a net margin above five percent, and share price above $5. List is available online only. **Number listed:** 2

1. iRobot
2. Dorman Products

Source: *Forbes*, Best Small Companies in America (annual), November 7, 2011.

1214 ■ FASTEST-GROWING PRIVATE CONSUMER PRODUCTS COMPANIES IN THE U.S., 2007-2010

Ranked by: Average annual sales growth over three years, in percent. **Remarks:** Also notes headquarters, revenue, and rank in the overall *Inc. 500*. To qualify, private companies must have had annual revenues of at least $100,000 in 2007 and $2 million in 2010. **Number listed:** 30

1. Contour, with 11,662.7%
2. Gold & Silver Buyers, 11,430.3%
3. Astro Gaming, 9,178.6%
4. Gazelle, 5,753.4%
5. OtterBox, 3,179.1%
6. Southern Tide, 3,121.4%
7. European Wax Center, 2,924.4%
8. ING Solutions, 2,920.7%
9. Scentsy, 2,904.4%

10. International Inspirations, 2,743.5%

Source: *Inc.*, Inc. 500 (annual), September 2011, p. 102-112.

1215 ■ LARGEST CONSUMER PRODUCTS COMPANIES IN EUROPE, 2010

Ranked by: Sales, in millions of U.S. dollars. **Remarks:** Also notes rank within country. **Number listed:** 100

1. Christian Dior SA (France), with $25,382.9 million
2. Adidas AG (Germany), $15,438.6
3. Hennes & Mauritz AB (Sweden), $14,549.9
4. Stora Enso Oyj (Finland), $13,303.2
5. Smurfit Kappa Group plc (Ireland), $9,008
6. Sony Europe Ltd. (U.K.), $8,238.3
7. Luxottica Group SpA (Italy), $7,331.7
8. Compagnie Financiere Richemont SA (Switzerland), $7,076.1
9. Freudenberg Household Products BV (Netherlands), $6,473.7
10. SCA Hygiene Products SE (Germany), $5,404.5

Source: *Europe's 15,000 Largest Companies*, (annual), ELC International, 2011, p. 40.

1216 ■ MOST PROFITABLE CANADIAN CONSUMER DISCRETIONARY COMPANIES, 2011

Ranked by: Profits, in millions of Canadian dollars. **Number listed:** 6

1. Magna International Inc., with C$1,018 million
2. Canadian Tire Corp., C$467
3. Shaw Communications Inc., C$454
4. Tim Hortons Inc., C$383
5. Gildan Activewear Inc., C$240
6. Torstar Corp., C$218

Source: *Canadian Business*, Investor 500 (annual), 2012, p. 55.

1217 ■ MOST PROFITABLE CANADIAN CONSUMER STAPLES COMPANIES, 2011

Ranked by: Profits, in millions of Canadian dollars. **Number listed:** 6

1. Loblaw Cos., with C$769 million
2. George Weston Ltd., C$635
3. Shoppers Drug Mart Corp., C$613.9
4. Saputo Inc., C$451.1
5. Metro Inc., C$386.3
6. Alimentation Couche-Tard Inc., C$370.1

Source: *Canadian Business*, Investor 500 (annual), 2012, p. 55.

1218 ■ WORLD'S LARGEST CONSUMER GOODS COMPANIES, 2010

Ranked by: Sales, in millions of U.S. dollars. **Number listed:** 100

1. Nestle SA, with $118,940 million
2. Procter & Gamble Co., $82,900
3. British American Tobacco plc, $70,609
4. Philip Morris International Inc., $67,713
5. Japan Tobacco Inc., $65,936
6. Unilever plc, $60,000

7. PepsiCo Inc., $57,838
8. Kraft Foods Inc., $49,207
9. Imperial Tobacco Group plc, $45,360
10. Anheuser-Busch InBev SA/NV, $36,297

Source: *Consumer Goods Technology*, Consumer Goods Registry (annual), http://www.consumergoods.com, December 2011.

1219 ■ WORLD'S LARGEST CONSUMER PACKAGED GOODS COMPANIES, 2010

Ranked by: Sales, in millions of U.S. dollars. **Remarks:** Also notes brands and annual sales growth. **Number listed:** 20

1. Procter & Gamble Co., with $82,900 million
2. Unilever plc, $60,000
3. 3M Co., $26,700
4. Henkel KgaA, $20,389
5. Kimberly-Clark Corp., $19,746
6. Svenska Cellulosa AB (SCA), $16,016
7. Colgate-Palmolive Co., $15,564
8. Kao Corp., $14,273
9. Reckitt Benckiser plc, $13,150
10. Newell Rubbermaid Inc., $5,800

Source: *Consumer Goods Technology*, Consumer Goods Registry (annual), http://www.consumergoods.com, December 2011.

1220 ■ WORLD'S MOST ETHICAL CONSUMER PRODUCTS COMPANIES, 2012

Ranked by: Score based on five criteria: ethics and compliance program; reputation, leadership, and innovation; governance; corporate citizenship and responsibility; and culture of ethics. **Remarks:** Specific scores not provided; companies are listed alphabetically, not ranked. **Number listed:** 5

1. Colgate-Palmolive Co. (U.S.)
2. Hasbro Inc. (U.S.)
3. Henkel AG (Germany)
4. Kao Corp. (Japan)
5. Kimberly-Clark Corp. (U.S.)

Source: *Ethisphere Magazine*, World's Most Ethical Companies (annual), http://www.ethisphere.com, 2012.

Consumer Products
See: **Consumer Goods**

Container Industry

1221 ■ LARGEST U.S. CONTAINERS AND PACKAGING COMPANIES OVERALL, 2011

Ranked by: Score based on revenue, profits, assets, and market capitalization. **Remarks:** Specific scores not provided. Also notes overall rank in the *Forbes 2000* and figures for each criterion. **Number listed:** 3

1. Ball Corp.
2. Crown Holdings Inc.
3. Rock-Tenn Co.

Source: *Forbes*, Forbes 2000 (annual), http://www.forbes.com, May 7, 2012.

1222 ■ TOP *FORTUNE 500* COMPANIES IN PACKAGING AND CONTAINERS, 2011

Ranked by: Revenue, in millions of dollars. **Remarks:** Also notes overall rank in the *Fortune 500;* profits; profits as a percentage of revenue; stockholders' equity; and rank by each criterion. **Number listed:** 7

1. Crown Holdings Inc., with $8,644 million
2. Ball Corp., $8,631
3. Owens-Illinois Inc., $7,358
4. MeadWestvaco Corp., $6,079
5. Sealed Air Corp., $5,641
6. Rock-Tenn Co., $5,400
7. Bemis Co., Inc., $5,323

Source: *Fortune*, Fortune 500 (annual), May 21, 2012, p. F-38.

1223 ■ WORLD'S LARGEST CONTAINERS AND PACKAGING COMPANIES OVERALL, 2011

Ranked by: Score based on revenue, profits, assets, and market capitalization. **Remarks:** Specific scores not provided. Also notes country, overall rank in the *Forbes 2000,* and figures for each criterion. **Number listed:** 6

1. Amcor Ltd.
2. Rexam plc
3. Ball Corp.
4. Crown Holdings Inc.
5. Rock-Tenn Co.
6. Toyo Seikan Kaisha Ltd.

Source: *Forbes*, Forbes 2000 (annual), http://www.forbes.com, May 7, 2012.

1224 ■ WORLD'S MOST ADMIRED PACKAGING AND CONTAINERS COMPANIES, 2012

Ranked by: Score, on a scale of 10, based on a survey of executives, directors, and securities analysts of companies within their own industry on eight criteria: innovation, financial soundness, employee talent, use of corporate assets, long-term investment value, social responsibility, quality of management, and quality of products/services. **Remarks:** Specific scores not provided. Also notes rank for previous year. **Number listed:** 5

1. Sealed Air Corp.
2. Bemis Co., Inc.
2. Ball Corp.
4. Sonoco Products Co.
5. MeadWestvaco Corp.

Source: *Fortune*, World's Most Admired Companies (annual), March 19, 2012, p. 149.

Contract Logistics Services

1225 ■ LARGEST U.S. THIRD-PARTY LOGISTICS PROVIDERS, 2010

Ranked by: Gross logistics revenue, in millions of U.S. dollars. **Number listed:** 30

1. C. H. Robinson Worldwide Inc., with $9,274 million
2. UPS Supply Chain Solutions, $8,923
3. Expeditors International of Washington Inc., $5,968
4. UTi Worldwide Inc., $4,550
5. Exel (DHL Supply Chain, Americas), $4,200
6. DB Schenker Americas, $4,072
7. Kuehne + Nagel Inc. (The Americas), $3,831
8. Caterpillar Logistics Services Inc., $3,465
9. GENCO ATC, $3,096

10. CEVA Logistics (The Americas), $2,756

Source: *Logistics Management*, Top 3PLs (annual), June 2011, p. 50s.

1226 ■ WORLD'S LARGEST THIRD-PARTY LOGISTICS PROVIDERS, 2010

Ranked by: Gross logistics revenue, in millions of U.S. dollars. **Number listed:** 50

1. DHL Supply Chain & Global Forwarding, with $30,486 million
2. Kuehne + Nagel Inc., $19,476
3. DB Schenker Logistics, $18,999
4. Nippon Express Co., Ltd., $18,450
5. C. H. Robinson Worldwide Inc., $9,274
6. CEVA Logistics, $9,091
7. UPS Supply Chain Solutions, $8,923
8. DSV A/S, $7,587
9. Panalpina World Transport (Holding) Ltd., $6,887
10. Glovis Co., Ltd., $6,303

Source: *Logistics Management*, Top 3PLs (annual), June 2011, p. 48s.

Contractors

1227 ■ LARGEST COLORADO-BASED GENERAL CONTRACTORS, 2010

Ranked by: Number of Colorado employees. **Remarks:** Also notes contact information and total number of employees. **Number listed:** 10

1. G. H. Phipps Construction Cos., with 350 employees
2. Hensel Phelps Construction Co., 302
3. Saunders Construction Inc., 300
3. G. E. Johnson Construction, 300
5. FCI Constructors, 170
6. PCL Construction Enterprises Inc., 163
7. Shaw Construction, 93
8. Roche Constructors Inc., 74
9. Calcon Constructors Inc., 65
10. Palace Construction, 64

Source: *ColoradoBiz*, Top Professional Services (annual), December 2011, p. 47.

1228 ■ LARGEST COLORADO SPECIALTY CONTRACTORS, 2010

Ranked by: Revenue, in millions of dollars. **Remarks:** Also notes rank for previous year, contact information, largest project, and top market sectors. **Number listed:** 44

1. Sturgeon Electric Co., with $137.68 million
2. RK Mechanical Inc., $124.25
3. EMCOR Group Inc., $84.83
4. MasTec Inc., $76.46
5. U.S. Engineering Co., $74.4
6. Ludvik Electric Co., $52.95
7. Fiore & Sons Inc., $50.95

8. Douglass Colony Group Inc., $43.6
9. Murphy Co., $42.28
10. E Light Electric Services Inc., $39.53

Source: *ENR Mountain States*, Colorado's Top Specialty Contractors (annual), http://www.mountainstates.construction.com, December 19, 2011.

1229 ■ LARGEST COMMERCIAL CONCRETE CONTRACTORS, 2010

Ranked by: Commercial concrete revenue, in millions of dollars. **Remarks:** Also notes rank in the overall *Top 100*. **Number listed:** 20

1. Baker Concrete Construction Inc., with $639.8 million
2. Gulf Shores C & A LLC, $539
3. CECO Concrete Construction Corp., $353.2
4. Capform, $99.3
5. Keystone Concrete Placement, $93
6. S & F Concrete Construction, $63.4
7. Southland Concrete, $61.1
8. JT Wimsatt Contracting, $58
9. Bomel Construction, $56
10. Vee-Jay Cement, $51.4

Source: *Concrete Construction*, CC 100 (annual), July 2011.

1230 ■ LARGEST CONCRETE CONTRACTORS BY TOTAL CONCRETE REVENUE, 2010

Ranked by: Concrete revenue, in millions of dollars. **Remarks:** Also notes rank for previous year, headquarters, CEO, percentage of work that is concrete, gross revenue, annual growth in revenue, number of projects, regions working in, number of employees, and breakdown of concrete work by type. **Number listed:** 100

1. Baker Concrete Construction Inc., with $744 million
2. Gulf Shores C & A LLC, $718.6
3. The Walsh Group, $517.3
4. Structural Group Inc., $394.1
5. CECO Concrete Construction Corp., $353.2
6. Interstate Highway Construction, $180
7. McCarthy Holdings, $173.8
8. Keystone Concrete Placement, $169
9. Webcor Concrete, $149.3
10. Griffin Cement LLC, $120

Source: *Concrete Construction*, CC 100 (annual), July 2011, p. 32+.

1231 ■ LARGEST CONTRACTORS IN CALIFORNIA, 2010

Ranked by: Regional revenue, in millions of dollars. **Remarks:** Also notes rank for previous year, headquarters, and top market sectors. **Number listed:** 52

1. Turner Construction Co., with $1,385.17 million
2. McCarthy Building Cos., $1,358
3. Swinerton Inc., $800.4
4. DPR Construction Inc., $758.8
5. Webcor Builders Inc., $708.88
6. PCL Construction, $705.4
7. Rudolph & Sletten Inc., $650
8. The Clark Construction Group Inc., $606.75

9. Kiewit Corp., $594.81
10. Balfour Beatty U.S., $572.13

Source: *ENR California*, Top Contractors (annual), August 2011.

1232 ■ LARGEST CONTRACTORS IN THE MIDWEST, 2010

Ranked by: Revenue from projects in Illinois, Indiana, Wisconsin, and eastern Missouri, in millions of dollars. **Remarks:** Also notes rank for previous year, contact information, and top market sectors. **Number listed:** 50

1. Walsh Construction Co., with $1,003.51 million
2. Clayco Inc., $880
3. Pepper Construction Group, $720.35
4. Turner Construction Co., $551.58
5. Mortenson Construction, $546.17
6. Gilbane Building Co., $539.6
7. Power Construction Co., $518.3
8. F. H. Paschen, S. N. Nielsen, $397.4
9. Miron Construction Co., $381.5
10. Strand Associates Inc., $381

Source: *ENR Midwest*, Top Contractors (annual), July 25, 2011.

1233 ■ LARGEST CONTRACTORS IN THE SOUTHEASTERN U.S., 2010

Ranked by: Revenue from projects in Florida, Georgia, North Carolina, and South Carolina, in millions of dollars. **Remarks:** Also notes rank for previous year, location, and top market sectors. **Number listed:** 110

1. Brasfield & Gorrie LLC, with $1,034.08 million
2. Balfour Beatty U.S., $986.34
3. Turner Construction Co., $809.86
4. BE & K Building Group, $683.74
5. Archer Western Contractors Ltd., $665.47
6. Skanska USA Inc., $602.4
7. Holder Construction Co., $536
8. The Clark Construction Group LLC, $410.33
9. Hunt Construction Group, $385.3
10. Choate Construction Co., $369.43

Source: *ENR Southeast*, Top Contractors (annual), http://www.southeast.construction.com, July 4, 2011.

1234 ■ LARGEST CONTRACTORS IN TEXAS AND LOUISIANA, 2010

Ranked by: Revenue, in millions of dollars. **Remarks:** Also notes location and key market sectors. **Number listed:** 120

1. Turner Industries Group, with $1,561.35 million
2. Kiewit Corp., $1,519.31
3. Balfour Beatty plc, $1,010.48
4. Austin Industries, $928.9
5. The Shaw Group, $715.43
6. The Clark Construction Group Inc., $654
7. Gilbane Building Co., $625.41
8. Webber, $599.18
9. Zachry Holdings Inc., $579.99
10. Archer Western Contractors Ltd., $566.14

Source: *ENR Texas & Louisiana*, Top Contractors (annual), http://www.texas.construction.com, August 15, 2011.

1235 ■ LARGEST CONTRACTORS BY TOTAL REVENUE, 2010

Ranked by: Total contracting revenue, in dollars. **Number listed:** 81

1. The Turner Corp., with $7,800,000,000
2. The Clark Construction Group Inc., $3,929,120,000
3. Tutor Perini Corp., $2,894,020,880
4. Mortenson Construction, $2,459,500,000
5. McCarthy Holdings Inc., $2,189,000,000
6. J. E. Dunn Construction Group, $1,923,750,000
7. The Walsh Group, $1,661,675,412
8. Holder Construction, $1,611,000,000
9. Brasfield & Gorrie, $1,563,938,616
10. DPR Construction, $1,431,687,000

Source: *Building Design & Construction*, Giants 300 (annual), July 2011, p. 47.

1236 ■ LARGEST CONTRACTORS IN THE U.S. MOUNTAIN STATES, 2010

Ranked by: Revenue from projects in Colorado, Idaho, Montana, Utah, and Wyoming, in millions of dollars. **Remarks:** Also notes rank for previous year, contact information, largest project, and top market sectors. **Number listed:** 34

1. Layton Construction Co., with $430.4 million
2. Okland Construction Co., $427.3
3. Kiewit Corp., $404.45
4. Jacobsen Construction Co., $342.52
5. Staker Parson Cos., $251.86
6. Big-D Construction Corp., $186.44
7. Ralph L. Wadsworth Construction Co., $184.01
8. Hogan & Associates Construction, $173
9. Wadsworth Brothers Construction, $107
10. Engineered Structures Inc., $82.7

Source: *ENR Mountain States*, Intermountain Top Contractors (annual), August 29, 2011.

1237 ■ LARGEST DECORATIVE CONCRETE CONTRACTORS, 2010

Ranked by: Decorative concrete revenue, in millions of dollars. **Remarks:** Also notes rank in the overall *Top 100*. **Number listed:** 8

1. Griffin Cement LLC, with $24 million
2. T. B. Penick & Sons, $20.3
3. Trademark Concrete Systems, $8.5
4. Colorado Hardscapes, $4.9
5. Greystone Masonry, $2.5
6. Urata & Sons Cement, $2.4
7. Stephens & Smith Construction, $2
8. Groninger Construction, $0.6

Source: *Concrete Construction*, CC 100 (annual), July 2011.

1238 ■ LARGEST DOMESTIC HEAVY CONTRACTORS, 2011

Ranked by: Total revenue, in millions of dollars. **Remarks:** Also notes breakdown by market. **Number listed:** 50

1. Kiewit Corp., with $3,287 million
2. The Walsh Group Ltd., $2,409.9
3. Fluor Corp., $1,976.1
4. Bechtel Group Inc., $1,645
5. Tutor Perini Corp., $1,633.8
6. Skanska USA Inc., $1,606.7
7. Granite Construction Inc., $1,558
8. Colas USA, $1,410
9. The Shaw Group Inc., $1,225.1
10. The Lane Construction Corp., $1,187.3

Source: *ENR: Engineering News-Record*, Top 400 Contractors (annual), May 14, 2012, p. 87.

1239 ■ LARGEST FIRE PROTECTION CONTRACTORS, 2011

Ranked by: Fire protection revenue, in millions of dollars. **Remarks:** Also notes headquarters and rank in the overall *Top 100*. **Number listed:** 10

1. EMCOR Group Inc., with $208.8 million
2. APi Group Inc., $206.45
3. VSC Fire & Security, $13.12
4. Fire & Life Safety America Holdings Inc., $86.7
5. J. F. Ahern Co., $61.24
6. Par Plumbing Co., $46.32
7. J. C. Cannistraro, $39.17
8. John W. Danforth Co., $27.21
9. Mechanical Systems & Services Inc., $22.67
10. Great Lakes Plumbing & Heating Co., $20.67

Source: *Contractor*, Book of Giants (annual), May 2012, p. 22.

1240 ■ LARGEST GENERAL CONTRACTORS BY DOMESTIC REVENUE, 2011

Ranked by: Domestic general building revenue, in millions of dollars. **Number listed:** 50

1. The Turner Corp., with $6,666.7 million
2. The Clark Construction Group Inc., $3,428
3. The Whiting-Turner Contracting Co., $3,351.1
4. Balfour Beatty U.S., $2,908.8
5. Gilbane Building Co., $2,707.2
6. Skanska USA Inc., $2,553.3
7. Tutor Perini Corp., $2,414.3
8. McCarthy Holdings Inc., $1,998
9. Structure Tone Inc., $1,963.9
10. J.E. Dunn Construction Group, $1,825.8

Source: *ENR: Engineering News-Record*, Top 400 Contractors (annual), May 14, 2012, p. 88.

1241 ■ LARGEST GENERAL CONTRACTORS BY FOREIGN REVENUE, 2011

Ranked by: Revenue from projects outside of the U.S., in millions of dollars. **Number listed:** 50

1. Bechtel Group Inc., with $16,700 million
2. Fluor Corp., $13,526.8
3. KBR, $5,382.5
4. PCL Construction Enterprises Inc., $3,939.2
5. Foster Wheeler AG, $3,710.7
6. McDermott International Inc., $2,944
7. CB & I Constructors Inc., $2,930.4

8. Kiewit Corp., $2,533
9. Jacobs Engineering Group Inc., $1,586.3
10. Contrack International Inc., $600.7

Source: *ENR: Engineering News-Record*, Top 400 Contractors (annual), May 14, 2012, p. 85.

1242 ■ LARGEST GENERAL CONTRACTORS IN HAZARDOUS WASTE, 2011

Ranked by: Revenue from hazardous waste projects. **Remarks:** Specific figures not provided. Also notes rank for previous year. **Number listed:** 20

1. Bechtel Group Inc.
2. The Shaw Group Inc.
3. Fluor Corp.
4. Parsons Corp.
5. Sevenson Environmental Services Inc.
6. Kiewit Corp.
7. URS Corp.
8. Weston Solutions Inc.
9. Jacobs Engineering Group Inc.
10. Remedial Construction Services LP

Source: *ENR: Engineering News-Record*, Top 400 Contractors (annual), May 14, 2012, p. 81.

1243 ■ LARGEST GENERAL CONTRACTORS IN INDUSTRIAL PROCESSES, 2011

Ranked by: Revenue from industrial processes projects. **Remarks:** Specific figures not provided. Also notes rank for previous year. **Number listed:** 20

1. Bechtel Group Inc.
2. Fluor Corp.
3. The Turner Corp.
4. KBR
5. Jacobs Engineering Group Inc.
6. Haskell
7. DPR Construction Inc.
8. Stellar
9. Kiewit Corp.
10. CCC Group Inc.

Source: *ENR: Engineering News-Record*, Top 400 Contractors (annual), May 14, 2012, p. 81.

1244 ■ LARGEST GENERAL CONTRACTORS BY NEW CONTRACTS, 2011

Ranked by: Value of new contracts, in millions of dollars. **Number listed:** 100

1. Bechtel Group Inc., with $47,216 million
2. Fluor Corp., $26,900
3. KBR, $10,128.4
4. Kiewit Corp., $9,249
5. The Turner Corp., $9,005.7
6. PCL Construction Enterprises Inc., $7,925.1
7. CB & I, $6,807.7
8. Skanska USA Inc., $6,327.8
9. Gilbane Building Co., $5,251.6
10. Balfour Beatty U.S., $4,298

Source: *ENR: Engineering News-Record*, Top 400 Contractors (annual), May 14, 2012, p. 82.

1245 ■ LARGEST GENERAL CONTRACTORS IN PETROLEUM, 2011

Ranked by: Revenue from petroleum projects. **Remarks:** Specific figures not provided. Also notes rank for previous year. **Number listed:** 20

1. Bechtel Group Inc.
2. Fluor Corp.
3. CB & I Constructors Inc.
4. Foster Wheeler AG
5. KBR
6. McDermott International Inc.
7. Jacobs Engineering Group Inc.
8. Kiewit Corp.
9. Turner Industries Group LLC
10. PCL Construction Enterprises Inc.

Source: *ENR: Engineering News-Record*, Top 400 Contractors (annual), May 14, 2012, p. 78.

1246 ■ LARGEST GENERAL CONTRACTORS IN POWER, 2011

Ranked by: Revenue from power projects. **Remarks:** Specific figures not provided. Also notes rank for previous year. **Number listed:** 20

1. Bechtel Group Inc.
2. The Shaw Group Inc.
3. Kiewit Corp.
4. The Day & Zimmermann Group Inc.
5. First Solar Inc.
6. The Babcock & Wilcox Co.
7. Foster Wheeler AG
8. URS Corp.
9. Fluor Corp.
10. Mortenson Construction

Source: *ENR: Engineering News-Record*, Top 400 Contractors (annual), May 14, 2012, p. 78.

1247 ■ LARGEST GENERAL CONTRACTORS IN TELECOMMUNICATIONS, 2011

Ranked by: Revenue from telecommunications projects. **Remarks:** Specific figures not provided. Also notes rank for previous year. **Number listed:** 20

1. Holder Construction Co.
2. DPR Construction Inc.
3. Balfour Beatty U.S.
4. Black & Veatch
5. The Turner Corp.
6. Bechtel Group Inc.
7. Skanska USA Inc.
8. Mortenson Construction
9. Fluor Corp.
10. Structure Tone Inc.

Source: *ENR: Engineering News-Record*, Top 400 Contractors (annual), May 14, 2012, p. 81.

1248 ■ LARGEST GENERAL CONTRACTORS BY TOTAL REVENUE, 2011

Ranked by: Total revenue, in millions of dollars. **Remarks:** Also notes rank for previous year, headquarters, international revenue, number of new contracts, and breakdown of revenue by market. **Number listed:** 400

1. Bechtel Group Inc., with $25,005 million
2. Fluor Corp., $18,684.7
3. Kiewit Corp., $8,477
4. The Turner Corp., $8,014.7
5. KBR, $7,071.5
6. PCL Construction Enterprises Inc., $5,607.7
7. Skanska USA Inc., $5,307.8
8. Foster Wheeler AG, $4,480.7
9. Tutor Perini Corp., $4,404
10. The Clark Construction Group Inc., $4,276.9

Source: *ENR: Engineering News-Record*, Top 400 Contractors (annual), May 14, 2012, p. 93-106.

1249 ■ LARGEST GENERAL CONTRACTORS IN TRANSPORTATION, 2011

Ranked by: Revenue from transportation projects. **Remarks:** Specific figures not provided. Also notes rank for previous year. **Number listed:** 20

1. Bechtel Group Inc.
2. Kiewit Corp.
3. Fluor Corp.
4. The Walsh Group Ltd.
5. Granite Construction Inc.
6. Tutor Perini Corp.
7. Colas USA
8. The Lane Construction Corp.
9. Skanska USA Inc.
10. Flatiron Construction Corp.

Source: *ENR: Engineering News-Record*, Top 400 Contractors (annual), May 14, 2012, p. 78.

1250 ■ LARGEST MECHANICAL CONTRACTORS IN THE MIDWEST, 2011

Ranked by: Revenue, in millions of dollars. **Remarks:** Also notes headquarters and rank in the overall *Top 100*. **Number listed:** 10

1. Johnson Controls Inc., Building Efficiency Div., with $2,305 million
2. APi Group Inc., $1,238.7
3. Roto-Rooter Services Co., $369.7
4. John E. Green Co., $300
4. Waldinger Corp., $300
6. BMW Constructors, $269
7. Hill Mechanical Group, $225.22
8. U.S. Engineering, $210.03
9. Harris Cos., $193
10. J. F. Ahern Co., $180.13

Source: *Contractor*, Book of Giants (annual), May 2012, p. 14.

1251 ■ LARGEST MECHANICAL CONTRACTORS IN THE NORTHEASTERN U.S., 2011

Ranked by: Revenue, in millions of dollars. **Remarks:** Also notes headquarters and rank in the overall *Top 100*. **Number listed:** 10

1. EMCOR Group Inc., with $2,610 million
2. W. E. Bowers Associates Inc., $432.5
3. Limbach Facility Services LLC, $296.1
4. Nooter Construction, $256.3
5. Durr Mechanical, $153

6. J. J. White Inc., $147
7. Sauer Inc., $146.1
8. McCarl's, $42
9. Par Plumbing Co., $138.96
10. John W. Danforth Co., $136.05

Source: *Contractor*, Book of Giants (annual), May 2012, p. 14.

1252 ■ LARGEST MECHANICAL CONTRACTORS IN THE SOUTHERN U.S., 2011

Ranked by: Revenue, in millions of dollars. **Remarks:** Also notes headquarters and rank in the overall *Top 100*. **Number listed:** 10

1. Comfort Systems USA Inc., with $1,240 million
2. ARS/Rescue Rooter, $693.4
3. Service Experts division of Lennox Industries, $590.3
4. TDIndustries Ltd., $315.1
5. McKenney's Inc., $200
6. Ivey Mechanical Co., $181
7. Titan Contracting & Leasing/The Horn Cos., $171.1
8. Trinity Mechanical Systems Inc., $150
9. Brandt Engineering Co., $141.6
10. Coastal Mechanical Services, $133.44

Source: *Contractor*, Book of Giants (annual), May 2012, p. 14.

1253 ■ LARGEST MECHANICAL CONTRACTORS IN THE U.S., 2011

Ranked by: Revenue, in millions of dollars. **Remarks:** Also notes rank for previous year, location, and breakdown by type. **Number listed:** 100

1. EMCOR Group Inc., with $2,610 million
2. Johnson Controls Inc., Building Efficiency Div., $2,305
3. Comfort Systems USA Inc., $1,240
4. APi Group Inc., $1,238.7
5. ARS/Rescue Rooter, $693.4
6. Service Experts division of Lennox Inc., $590.3
7. ACCO Engineered Systems Inc., $463
8. Southland Industries, $435
9. W. E. Brown Associates Inc., $432.5
10. McKinstry Co., $400

Source: *Contractor*, Book of Giants (annual), May 2012, p. 16-21.

1254 ■ LARGEST MECHANICAL CONTRACTORS IN THE WESTERN U.S., 2011

Ranked by: Revenue, in millions of dollars. **Remarks:** Also notes headquarters and rank in the overall *Top 100*. **Number listed:** 10

1. ACCO Engineered Systems Inc., with $463 million
2. Southland Industries, $435
3. McKinstry Co., $400
4. JH Kelly Holdings LLC, $260
5. Harder Mechanical Contractors Inc., $190
6. Critchfield Mechanical Inc., $159.3
7. Kinetics Systems Inc., $146.1
8. Apollo Mechanical Contractors, $139
9. Elkhorn Construction, $135

10. Therma Corp., $120.7

Source: *Contractor*, Book of Giants (annual), May 2012, p. 14.

1255 ■ LARGEST PIPING CONTRACTORS, 2011

Ranked by: Piping revenue, in millions of dollars. **Remarks:** Also notes headquarters and rank in the overall *Top 100*. **Number listed:** 10

1. EMCOR Group Inc., with $261 million
2. W. E. Bowers Associates Inc., $216.25
3. APi Group inc., $206.45
4. Nooter Construction, $205.04
5. BMW Constructors, $161.4
6. Southland Industries, $145
7. Sterling Boiler & Mechanical Inc., $113.92
8. U.S. Engineering Co., $111.32
9. Joule Industrial Contractors, $109.2
10. Titan Contracting & Leasing/The Horn Cos., $101.64

Source: *Contractor*, Book of Giants (annual), May 2012, p. 22.

1256 ■ LARGEST SHEET METAL CONTRACTORS, 2011

Ranked by: Sheet metal revenue, in millions of dollars. **Remarks:** Also notes headquarters and rank in the overall *Top 100*. **Number listed:** 10

1. APi Group Inc., with $206.45 million
2. EMCOR Group Inc., $182.7
3. Johnson Controls, $115.25
4. Waldinger Corp., $100
5. McKinstry Co., $80
6. Hill Mechanical Group, $78.83
7. ACCO Engineered Systems Inc., $77.17
8. Limbach Facility Services LLC, $76
9. McKenney's Inc., $40
10. Kinetic Systems Inc., $36.53

Source: *Contractor*, Book of Giants (annual), May 2012, p. 22.

1257 ■ LARGEST SPECIAL TRADE CONTRACTORS BY EMPLOYEES, 2010

Ranked by: Total number of employees. **Remarks:** Also notes contact information for headquarters, number of employees at headquarters, revenue, rank by revenue, and primary SIC code. **Number listed:** 498

1. Encompass Services Corp., with 30,000 employees
2. EMCOR Group Inc., 26,083
3. Brock Group Inc., 15,666
4. Quanta Services Inc., 14,673
5. Chemed Corp., 12,308
6. Brock Holdings II Inc., 11,219
6. Brock Holdings III Inc., 11,219
8. Brock Services Holdings LLC, 9,477
8. Brock Services Ltd., 9,477
10. Builder Services Group Inc., 8,210

Source: *Business Rankings*, (annual), Dun & Bradstreet Inc., 2011, p. VI.35-VI.45.

1258 ■ LARGEST SPECIAL TRADE CONTRACTORS BY SALES, 2010

Ranked by: Total revenue, in dollars. **Remarks:** Also notes contact information for headquarters, number of employees at headquarters and overall, rank by employees, and primary SIC code. **Number listed:** 497

1. Debra-Kuempel Inc., with $5,547,942,000
2. EMCOR Group Inc., $5,121,285,000
3. Quanta Services Inc., $3,931,218,000
4. API Group Inc., $1,358,338,000
5. Building Materials Holding Corp., $1,324,679,000
6. Chemed Corp., $1,280,545,000
7. Comfort Systems USA Inc., $1,108,282,000
8. Ultra Resources Inc., $979,386,000
9. Atlas Roofing, $962,588,047
10. Baker Concrete Construction Inc., $960,000,000

Source: *Business Rankings*, (annual), Dun & Bradstreet Inc., 2011, p. V.35-V.45.

1259 ■ LARGEST SPECIALTY CONTRACTORS IN COLORADO AND WYOMING, 2010

Ranked by: Regional revenue, in millions of dollars. **Remarks:** Also notes rank for previous year, headquarters, and top market sectors. **Number listed:** 48

1. Kiewit Corp., with $417.12 million
2. Saunders Construction Inc., $349.4
3. Mortenson Construction, $284.07
4. Adolfson & Peterson Construction, $273
5. PCL Construction Services Inc., $256.46
6. GE Johnson Construction Co., $250.53
7. FCI Constructors Inc., $208.96
8. Haselden Construction, $165.15
9. J. E. Dunn Construction Co., $137.97
10. Hensel Phelps Construction Co., $120.27

Source: *ENR Mountain States*, Colorado/Wyoming Top Contractors (annual), August 29, 2011.

1260 ■ LARGEST SPECIALTY CONTRACTORS IN THE MIDWEST, 2010

Ranked by: Regional revenue, in millions of dollars. **Remarks:** Also notes rank for previous year, contact information, and specialities. **Number listed:** 50

1. EMCOR Group Inc., with $482.74 million
2. The Hill Group, $193.69
3. BMW Constructors Inc., $184.3
4. J. F. Ahern Co., $180.81
5. Faith Technologies Inc., $143.86
6. Bowen Engineering Corp., $136.65
7. Mechanical Inc., $136.08
8. Guarantee Electrical Co., $112.21
9. Gaylor Inc., $106.66
10. Murphy Co., $105.78

Source: *ENR Midwest*, Top Specialty Contractors (annual), September 26, 2011.

1261 ■ LARGEST SPECIALTY CONTRACTORS IN NY, NJ, AND CT, 2010

Ranked by: Revenue from projects in New York, New Jersey, and Connecticut, in millions of dollars. **Remarks:** Also notes rank for previous year, headquarters, and top market sectors. **Number listed:** 50

1. EMCOR Group Inc., with $762.7 million

2. GreenStar Services Corp., $520.31
3. E-J Electric Installation Co., $167.5
4. Unity International Group, $150.51
5. Durr Mechanical Construction Inc., $141.71
6. Donaldson Interiors Inc., $126.45
7. Fresh Meadow Mechanical Corp., $110
7. W & W Glass LLC, $110
9. Northeast Remsco Construction Inc., $104.56
10. O'Connell Electric Co., $101.68

Source: *ENR New York*, Top Specialty Contractors (annual), http://www.newyork.construction.com, August 2011.

1262 ■ LARGEST SPECIALTY CONTRACTORS IN THE SOUTHEASTERN U.S., 2010

Ranked by: Regional revenue, in millions of dollars. **Remarks:** Also notes rank for previous year, location, and key market sectors. **Number listed:** 110

1. MasTec Inc., with $759.86 million
2. EMCOR Group Inc., $265.7
3. Quinco Electrical, $177
4. Coastal Mechanical Services Group, $149.44
5. SteelFab Inc., $148.57
6. Miller Electric Co., $129.04
7. Inglett & Stubbs LLC, $127.35
8. Cleveland Electric Co., $125.39
9. Acousti Engineering Co. of Florida, $120
10. Precision Walls Inc., $119.38

Source: *ENR Southeast*, Top Specialty Contractors (annual), http://www.southeast.construction.com, September 12, 2011.

1263 ■ LARGEST SPECIALTY CONTRACTORS IN TEXAS AND LOUISIANA, 2010

Ranked by: Revenue from projects in Texas and Louisiana, in millions of dollars. **Remarks:** Also notes rank for previous year, location, and top specialties. **Number listed:** 108

1. The Brock Group, with $653.05 million
2. MasTec Inc., $394.16
3. Orion Marine Group Inc., $353.14
4. Brandt Engineering Co., $340
5. TD Industries, $290.7
6. Facility Solutions Group, $260.64
7. Fisk, $209.58
8. MMR Group, $20
9. The Newtron Group, $199.74
10. ISC, $198

Source: *ENR Texas & Louisiana*, Top Specialty Contractors (annual), http://www.texas.construction.com, October 17, 2011.

1264 ■ LARGEST SPECIALTY CONTRACTORS IN THE U.S. MOUNTAIN STATES, 2010

Ranked by: Revenue from projects in Colorado, Idaho, Montana, Utah, and Wyoming, in millions of dollars. **Remarks:** Also notes rank for previous year, contact information, largest project, and top market sectors. **Number listed:** 28

1. Cache Valley Electric Co., with $140.3 million
2. CCI Mechanical Inc., $85.84
3. EMCOR Group Inc., $83.1
4. SME Steel Contractors Inc., $59.24

5. Taylor Electric Inc., $35.39
6. A & B Mechanical Contractors Inc., $26.75
7. ACI Northwest Inc., $24
8. Daw Construction Group LLC, $23.11
9. Sure Steel Inc., $20.2
10. Pacific Coast Steel, $19.76

Source: *ENR Mountain States*, Intermountain Top Specialty Contractors (annual), http://www.mountainstates.construction.com, December 19, 2011.

1265 ■ LARGEST TILT-UP CONCRETE CONTRACTORS, 2010

Ranked by: Tilt-up concrete revenue, in millions of dollars. **Remarks:** Also notes rank in the overall *Top 100*. **Number listed:** 10

1. Keystone Concrete Placement, with $67.6 million
2. Seretta Construction, $32
3. Concrete Strategies, $17.5
4. Builders Plus, $14
5. Suntec Concrete, $10.7
6. Woodland Construction, $8.6
7. Cantera Concrete Co., $5
8. Kent Cos., $4.5
9. Danko Concrete Construction, $4.4
10. MK Concrete Construction, $4.1

Source: *Concrete Construction*, CC 100 (annual), July 2011.

1266 ■ LARGEST WATER/WASTEWATER TREATMENT CONTRACTORS, 2011

Ranked by: Water/wastewater treatment revenue, in millions of dollars. **Remarks:** Also notes headquarters and rank in the overall *Top 100*. **Number listed:** 10

1. EMCOR Group Inc., with $208.8 million
2. John E. Green Co., $45
3. McCarl's Inc., $29.82
4. Worth & Co., $29.5
5. J. F. Ahern Co., $28.82
6. Durr Mechanical, $27.12
7. Corval Group Inc., $23
8. Sauer Inc., $18.26
9. BMW Constructors, $13.45
10. University Mechanical Contractors Inc., $11.5

Source: *Contractor*, Book of Giants (annual), May 2012, p. 22.

1267 ■ TOP ASBESTOS ABATEMENT CONTRACTORS, 2010

Ranked by: Asbestos abatement revenue, in millions of dollars. **Remarks:** Also notes percentage change from previous year. **Number listed:** 20

1. LVI Services Inc., with $147.7 million
2. NCM, $71.5
3. IREX Contracting Group, $39.1
4. Precision Environmental Co., Inc., $34.2
5. Performance Contracting Group Inc., $27.9
6. Pal Environmental Services, $24.1
7. Environmental Remediation Services Inc., $22.2

7. ERSI, $22.2
9. Midwest Service Group, $19.4
10. Environmental Holdings Group LLC, $18.4

Source: *ENR: Engineering News-Record*, Top 600 Specialty Contractors (annual), October 17, 2011, p. 64.

1268 ■ TOP CONCRETE CONTRACTORS, 2010

Ranked by: Concrete revenue, in millions of dollars. Remarks: Also notes percentage change from previous year. Number listed: 20

1. Baker Concrete Construction Inc., with $744 million
2. Structural Group, $394
3. Ceco Concrete Construction Corp., $182.6
4. Gate Precast Co., $139
5. TAS Commercial Concrete Construction LLC, $115.1
6. United Forming Inc., $106.7
7. High Concrete Group LLC, $105
8. Capform Inc., $104.5
9. Schuster Concrete Construction, $94.4
10. S & F Concrete Contractors Inc., $91.5

Source: *ENR: Engineering News-Record*, Top 600 Specialty Contractors (annual), October 17, 2011, p. 62.

1269 ■ TOP CONTRACTORS IN NEW YORK, 2010

Ranked by: Regional revenue, in millions of dollars. Remarks: Also notes rank for previous year, location, and markets served. Number listed: 50

1. Skanska USA Inc., with $1,955 million
2. Turner Construction Co., $1,910.45
3. Structure Tone Organization, $1,345.26
4. Lend Lease Inc., $813.01
5. Hunter Roberts Construction Group, $536.52
6. Gilbane Building Co., $535.2
7. Greenstar Services Corp., $520.31
8. Tutor Perini Corp., $482.58
9. LeChase Construction Services LLC, $467.18
10. Tishman Construction Corp., $447.66

Source: *ENR New York*, Top Contractors (annual), http://www.newyork.construction.com, July 25, 2011.

1270 ■ TOP CONTRACTORS IN THE SOUTHWESTERN U.S., 2010

Ranked by: Revenue from projects in Arizona, Nevada, and New Mexico, in millions of dollars. Remarks: Also notes rank for previous year, headquarters, and key market sectors. Number listed: 90

1. Perini Building Co., with $1,247.97 million
2. McCarthy Building Cos., $446.35
3. Sundt Construction Inc., $396.51
4. Las Vegas Paving Corp., $306
5. Skanska USA Inc., $246.76
6. Kitchell, $244.28
7. The Whiting Turner Contracting Co., $203.32
8. Kiewit Corp., $190.82
9. Clark Construction Group LLC, $189.13
10. M. A. Mortenson Co., $188.89

Source: *ENR Southwest*, Top Contractors (annual), http://www.southwest.construction.com, July 2011.

1271 ■ TOP DEMOLITION/WRECKING CONTRACTORS, 2010

Ranked by: Demolition/wrecking revenue, in millions of dollars. Remarks: Also notes location and percentage change from previous year. Number listed: 20

1. Penhall Co., with $158 million
2. Brandenburg Industrial Service Co., $132.6
3. NCM, $124.7
4. LVI Services Inc., $102.7
5. D. H. Griffin Wrecking Co., Inc., $99
6. Bierlein Demolition & Dismantling, $74.2
7. NASDI LLC, $60
8. North American Dismantling Corp., $37.7
9. Cleveland Wrecking Co., $34.3
10. Cherry Demolition, $28.1

Source: *ENR: Engineering News-Record*, Top 600 Specialty Contractors (annual), October 17, 2011, p. 64.

1272 ■ TOP ELECTRICAL CONTRACTORS, 2010

Ranked by: Sales, in dollars. Remarks: Also notes rank for previous year, headquarters, and annual percent change. Number listed: 50

1. EMCOR Group Inc., with $1,167,724,026
2. M. C. Dean Inc., $820,000,000
3. Rosendin Electric Inc., $727,000,000
4. MYR Group Inc., $597,100,000
5. Integrated Electrical Services Inc., $460,600,000
6. Henkels & McCoy Inc., $427,000,000
7. Bergelectric Corp., $403,500,000
8. MMR Group, $365,000,000
9. Truland Group of Cos., $342,000,000
10. Cupertino Electric Inc., $338,000,000

Source: *EC & M Magazine*, Top 50 Electrical Contractors (annual), http://www.ecmweb.com, September 2011.

1273 ■ TOP ELECTRICAL CONTRACTORS, 2010

Ranked by: Electrical revenue, in millions of dollars. Remarks: Also notes percentage change from previous year. Number listed: 50

1. Quanta Services Inc., with $2,044.2 million
2. EMCOR Group Inc., $1,638.5
3. M. C. Dean Inc., $810.1
4. Rosendin Electric Inc., $727
5. MYR Group Inc., $597.1
6. Pike Electric Corp., $485.1
7. Integrated Electrical Services Inc., $460.6
8. Bergelectric Corp., $403.5
9. MMR Group Inc., $367
10. Truland Group of Cos., $342

Source: *ENR: Engineering News-Record*, Top 600 Specialty Contractors (annual), October 17, 2011, p. 60.

1274 ■ TOP EXCAVATION/FOUNDATION CONTRACTORS, 2010

Ranked by: Excavation/foundation revenue, in millions of dollars. Remarks: Also notes percentage change from previous year. Number listed: 20

1. Hayward Baker Inc., with $298 million
2. Malcolm Drilling Co., Inc., $162.1
3. Morgan Corp., $160
4. Nicholson Construction Co., $129.4
5. Treviicos, $126.6
6. Berkel & Co. Contractors Inc., $120
7. Beaver Excavating Co., $114
8. E. S. Wagner Co., $100.9
9. McKinney Drilling Co., $98.6
10. MasTec Inc., $92.3

Source: *ENR: Engineering News-Record*, Top 600 Specialty Contractors (annual), October 17, 2011, p. 63.

1275 ■ TOP "GREEN" CONTRACTORS BY REVENUE, 2010

Ranked by: Revenue from projects that were either registered with or certified by a third-party organization that set standards for measuring a building's or facility's environmental impact, energy efficiency, or carbon footprint, in millions of dollars. **Remarks:** Also notes headquarters, "green" revenue as a percentage of total revenue, accredited staff, and breakdown of revenue by market. **Number listed:** 100

1. The Turner Corp., with $4,229.1 million
2. Gilbane Building Co., $2,541.7
3. The Clark Construction Group Inc., $2,408.9
4. Hensel Phelps Construction Co., $2,026.2
5. Tutor Perini Corp., $1,678
6. PCL Construction Enterprises Inc., $1,507.1
7. The Whiting-Turner Contracting Co., $1,478.8
8. Skanska USA Inc., $1,305.2
9. Holder Construction Co., $1,179
10. Balfour Beatty U.S., $1,001.4

Source: *ENR: Engineering News-Record*, Top 100 Green Contractors (annual), September 19, 2011, p. 67+.

1276 ■ TOP MASONRY CONTRACTORS, 2010

Ranked by: Masonry revenue, in millions of dollars. **Remarks:** Also notes percentage change from previous year. **Number listed:** 20

1. Western Construction Group, with $74.3 million
2. Wilks Masonry Corp., $47.3
3. McGee Brothers Co., Inc., $46.2
4. Seedorff Masonry Inc., $38.2
5. C. A. Lindman Cos., $36.8
6. Wasco Inc., $26.7
7. Sun Valley Masonry Inc., $26.3
8. Otto Baum Co., $22.2
9. Old North State Masonry LLC, $20
10. Dee Brown Inc., $19.8

Source: *ENR: Engineering News-Record*, Top 600 Specialty Contractors (annual), October 17, 2011, p. 62.

1277 ■ TOP MECHANICAL CONTRACTORS, 2010

Ranked by: Mechanical revenue, in millions of dollars. **Remarks:** Also notes percentage change from previous year. **Number listed:** 50

1. EMCOR Group Inc., with $1,997 million
2. Comfort Systems USA Inc., $842.3

3. Acco Engineered Systems Inc., $463
4. Southland Industries, $435
5. W. E. Bowers, $432.5
6. TDIndustries Ltd., $308
7. API Group Inc., $261.2
8. Nooter Construction Co., $256.3
9. Limbach Facility Services LLC, $242.7
10. John E. Green Co., $234.9

Source: *ENR: Engineering News-Record*, Top 600 Specialty Contractors (annual), October 17, 2011, p. 61.

1278 ■ TOP PAINTING CONTRACTORS, 2010

Ranked by: Painting revenue, in millions of dollars. **Remarks:** Also notes percentage change from previous year. **Number listed:** 20

1. The Brock Group, with $264 million
2. Techno Coatings Inc., $49.7
3. K2 Industrial Services Inc., $48.1
4. Avalotis Corp., $46.1
5. North American Coatings LLC, $37.3
6. FD Thomas Inc., $36.2
7. Thomas Industrial Coatings Inc., $36.1
8. Dunkin & Bush Inc., $33.2
9. Hartman Walsh Painting Co., $28.8
10. Swanson & Youngdale Inc., $28.3

Source: *ENR: Engineering News-Record*, Top 600 Specialty Contractors (annual), October 17, 2011, p. 63.

1279 ■ TOP SHEET METAL CONTRACTORS, 2010

Ranked by: Sheet metal revenue, in millions of dollars. **Remarks:** Also notes percentage change from previous year. **Number listed:** 20

1. Crown Corr Inc., with $73 million
2. Hill Mechanical Group, $61.7
3. Superior Air Handling Corp., $44.6
4. Dee Cramer Inc., $38.9
5. Kinetics, $30.9
6. B. T. Mancini Co., Inc., $26.9
7. MMC Corp., $25.3
8. Kovach Inc., $21.3
9. Mechanical Inc., $20.4
10. Greenwood Industries Inc., $18

Source: *ENR: Engineering News-Record*, Top 600 Specialty Contractors (annual), October 17, 2011, p. 64.

1280 ■ TOP SPECIALTY CONTRACTORS, 2010

Ranked by: Specialty prime or subcontracting construction revenue, in millions of dollars. **Remarks:** Also notes location, type of firm, value of new contracts, breakdown by market, and rank for previous year. **Number listed:** 600

1. EMCOR Group Inc., with $5,120.4 million
2. Quanta Services Inc., $3,931.2
3. MasTec Inc., $2,308
4. Brand Energy & Infrastructure Services Inc., $1,510
5. The Brock Group, $1,200.1
6. API Group Inc., $1,135.7

7. Comfort Systems USA Inc., $1,108.3
8. Henkels & McCoy Inc., $1,030.5
9. M. C. Dean Inc., $810.1
10. Baker Concrete Construction Inc., $744

Source: *ENR: Engineering News-Record*, Top 600 Specialty Contractors (annual), October 17, 2011, p. 67+.

1281 ■ TOP STEEL ERECTION CONTRACTORS, 2010

Ranked by: Steel erection revenue, in millions of dollars. **Remarks:** Also notes percentage change from previous year. **Number listed:** 20

1. Schuff International Inc., with $287.6 million
2. Midwest Steel Inc., $126
3. The Williams Group, $63.1
4. Area Erectors Inc., $51.7
5. Sure Steel Inc., $48.5
6. Century Steel Erectors, $37.1
7. National Steel City LLC, $37
8. Basden Steel Corp., $36.1
9. Buckner Cos., $33.5
10. L. P. R. Construction Co., $30.2

Source: *ENR: Engineering News-Record*, Top 600 Specialty Contractors (annual), October 17, 2011, p. 64.

1282 ■ TOP UTILITY CONTRACTORS, 2010

Ranked by: Utility construction revenue, in millions of dollars. **Remarks:** Also notes percentage change from previous year. **Number listed:** 20

1. Quanta Services Inc., with $1,415.2 million
2. Henkels & McCoy Inc., $989.2
3. MasTec Inc., $830.9
4. Miller Pipeline Corp., $235.6
5. Team Fishel, $120.1
6. West Valley Construction Co., $78.7
7. Sak Construction LLC, $70.4
8. W. A. Chester LLC, $52
9. Brent Scarbrough & Co., $46.6
10. C. J. Hughes Construction Co., Inc., $45

Source: *ENR: Engineering News-Record*, Top 600 Specialty Contractors (annual), October 17, 2011, p. 62.

1283 ■ TOP WALL/CEILING CONTRACTORS, 2010

Ranked by: Wall/ceiling revenue, in millions of dollars. **Remarks:** Also notes percentage change from previous year. **Number listed:** 20

1. Performance Contracting Group Inc., with $341.6 million
2. KHS & S Contractors, $269.2
3. Standard Drywall Inc., $132.7
4. Acousti Engineering Co. of Florida Inc., $120
5. Precision Walls Inc., $119.4
6. BakerTriangle, $117
7. National Construction Enterprises Inc., $92.2
8. Midwest Drywall Co., Inc., $81
9. Group Builders Inc., $60.4
10. California Drywall Co., $50

Source: *ENR: Engineering News-Record*, Top 600 Specialty Contractors (annual), October 17, 2011, p. 62.

Contractors, Foreign

1284 ■ TOP FOREIGN CONTRACTORS IN AFRICA, 2010

Ranked by: Construction revenue generated by companies based outside region. **Remarks:** Specific figures not provided. Also notes rank for previous year. **Number listed:** 10

1. Saipem SpA
2. CITIC Construction Co., Ltd.
3. China Communications Construction Group Ltd.
4. VINCI
5. Sinohydro Corp.
6. China State Construction Engineering Corp.
7. Bechtel Group Inc.
8. Bouygues SA
9. KBR
10. China Railway Construction Corp.

Source: *ENR: Engineering News-Record*, Top 225 International Contractors (annual), August 29, 2011, p. 48.

1285 ■ TOP FOREIGN CONTRACTORS IN ASIA/ AUSTRALIA, 2010

Ranked by: Construction revenue generated by companies based outside region. **Remarks:** Specific figures not provided. Also notes rank for previous year. **Number listed:** 10

1. Hochtief AG
2. Fluor Corp.
3. China Communications Construction Group Ltd.
4. Leighton Holdings Ltd.
5. Bechtel
6. Foster Wheeler AG
7. Bouygues
8. China State Construction Engineering Corp.
9. Saipem SpA
10. Polimeks Insaat Taahhut Ve San Tic A/S

Source: *ENR: Engineering News-Record*, Top 225 International Contractors (annual), August 29, 2011, p. 48.

1286 ■ TOP FOREIGN CONTRACTORS IN CANADA, 2010

Ranked by: Construction revenue generated by companies based outside country. **Remarks:** Specific figures not provided. **Number listed:** 10

1. Bechtel Group Inc.
2. Fluor Corp.
3. Kiewit Corp.
4. Bouygues SA
5. VINCI
6. Hochtief AG
7. CB & I
8. Jacobs Engineering Group Inc.
9. KBR
10. Acciona Infraestructuras

Source: *ENR: Engineering News-Record*, Top 225 International Contractors (annual), August 29, 2011, p. 48.

1287 ■ TOP FOREIGN CONTRACTORS IN EUROPE, 2010

Ranked by: Construction revenue generated by companies based outside region. **Remarks:** Specific figures not provided. Also notes rank for previous year. **Number listed:** 10

1. VINCI
2. Strabag SE
3. Skanska AB
4. Fomento de Construcciones y Contratas SA
5. Bouygues SA
6. Royal Bam Groep NV
7. Bilfinger Berger AG
8. Eiffage SA
9. Ferrovial Agroman SA
10. Fluor Corp.

Source: *ENR: Engineering News-Record*, Top 225 International Contractors (annual), August 29, 2011, p. 48.

1288 ■ TOP FOREIGN CONTRACTORS IN LATIN AMERICA/CARIBBEAN, 2010

Ranked by: Construction revenue generated by companies based outside region. Remarks: Specific figures not provided. Number listed: 10

1. Construtora Norberto Odebrecht SA
2. Grupo ACS
3. OHL
4. Abeinsa SA
5. Techint Group
6. China Railway Group Ltd.
7. Fluor Corp.
8. Grupo Isolux Corsan SA
9. Maire Tecnimont SpA
10. Bechtel

Source: *ENR: Engineering News-Record*, Top 225 International Contractors (annual), August 29, 2011, p. 48.

1289 ■ TOP FOREIGN CONTRACTORS IN THE MIDDLE EAST, 2010

Ranked by: Construction revenue generated by companies based outside region. Remarks: Specific figures not provided. Also notes rank for previous year. Number listed: 10

1. Consolidated Contractors International Co. SAL
2. KBR
3. Hyundai Engineering & Construction Co., Ltd.
4. Fluor Corp.
5. Bechtel Group Inc.
6. Daelim Industrial Co., Ltd.
7. Petrofac Ltd.
8. Tecnicas Reunidas SA
9. Saipem SpA
10. JGC Corp.

Source: *ENR: Engineering News-Record*, Top 225 International Contractors (annual), August 29, 2011, p. 48.

1290 ■ TOP FOREIGN CONTRACTORS IN THE U.S., 2010

Ranked by: Construction revenue generated by companies based outside country. Remarks: Specific figures not provided. Also notes rank for previous year. Number listed: 10

1. Hochtief AG
2. Skanska AB
3. Lend Lease Group
4. Balfour Beatty plc

5. Bouygues SA
6. PCL Construction Enterprises Inc.
7. Grupo ACS
8. Ferrovial Agroman SA
9. Obayashi Corp.
10. Kajaima Corp.

Source: *ENR: Engineering News-Record*, Top 225 International Contractors (annual), August 29, 2011, p. 48.

1291 ■ TOP NON-U.S. CONTRACTORS IN INTERNATIONAL MANAGEMENT FEES, 2010

Ranked by: Construction management and program management fees derived from outside home country, in millions of U.S. dollars. Remarks: Also notes headquarters and breakdown by construction management and program management fees. Number listed: 20

1. Lend Lease Group, with $863 million
2. Balfour Beatty plc, $669.3
3. Dar Al-Handasah Consultants, $484.2
4. Hochtief AG, $237.6
5. WorleyParsons Ltd., $237.4
6. Arcadis NV, $223
7. Turner & Townsend plc, $177.8
8. Hatch Group, $171.2
9. Ausenco, $156.4
10. KEO International Consultants, $122.6

Source: *ENR: Engineering News-Record*, Top 225 International Contractors (annual), August 29, 2011, p. 50.

1292 ■ TOP NON-U.S. CONTRACTORS IN TOTAL MANAGEMENT FEES, 2010

Ranked by: Total construction management and program management fees, in millions of U.S. dollars. Remarks: Also notes headquarters and breakdown by construction management and program management fees. Number listed: 20

1. Hochtief AG, with $1,005.2 million
2. Balfour Beatty plc, $885.7
3. Lend Lease Group, $863.1
4. Leighton Holdings Ltd., $829
5. Dar Al-Handasah Consultants, $486.2
6. China Power Engineering Consulting Group Co., $382.9
7. Atkins, $354.1
8. Turner & Townsend plc, $316.7
9. Hatch Group, $259.7
10. Arcadis NV, $258

Source: *ENR: Engineering News-Record*, Top 225 International Contractors (annual), August 29, 2011, p. 50.

Contractors, International

1293 ■ TOP GLOBAL CONTRACTORS, 2010

Ranked by: Total construction contracting revenue, in millions of U.S. dollars. Remarks: Also notes headquarters, international revenue, new contracts, breakdown by market, and rank for previous year. Number listed: 225

1. China Railway Construction Corp. (China), with $76,206 million

2. China Railway Group Ltd. (China), $73,012.1
3. China State Construction Engineering Corp. (China), $48,868
4. VINCI (France), $45,110
5. China Communications Construction Group Ltd. (China), $40,418.7
6. Bouygues SA (France), $30,671
7. China Metallurgical Group Corp. (China), $29,905.1
8. Hochtief AG (Germany), $28,979.7
9. Grupo ACS (Spain), $20,631.8
10. Bechtel Group Inc. (U.S.), $19,714

Source: *ENR: Engineering News-Record*, Top 225 International Contractors (annual), August 29, 2011, p. 61-65.

1294 ■ TOP INTERNATIONAL CONTRACTORS, 2010

Ranked by: Construction revenue derived from projects outside home country, in millions of U.S. dollars. **Remarks:** Also notes headquarters, total revenue, new contracts, breakdown by market, and rank for previous year. **Number listed:** 225

1. Hochtief AG (Germany), with $27,424.7 million
2. VINCI (France), $16,557.6
3. Bechtel Group Inc. (U.S.), $12,500
4. Bouygues SA (France), $12,432
5. Skanska AB (Sweden), $11,632.3
6. Saipem SpA (Italy), $11,604.9
7. Fluor Corp. (U.S.), $11,585.6
8. Strabag SE (Austria), $10,870
9. Technip (France), $7,940
10. Fomento de Construcciones y Contratas SA (Spain), $7,457.8

Source: *ENR: Engineering News-Record*, Top 225 International Contractors (annual), August 29, 2011, p. 53-57.

1295 ■ TOP INTERNATIONAL CONTRACTORS IN BUILDING PROJECTS, 2010

Ranked by: Construction revenue derived from projects outside home country. **Remarks:** Specific figures not provided. Also notes rank for previous year. **Number listed:** 10

1. Hochtief AG
2. Skanska AB
3. Lend Lease Group
4. China State Construction Engineering Corp.
5. Bouygues SA
6. Balfour Beatty plc
7. Royal Bam Groep NV
8. Fomento de Construcciones y Contratas SA
9. Strabag SE
10. VINCI

Source: *ENR: Engineering News-Record*, Top 225 International Contractors (annual), August 29, 2011, p. 49.

1296 ■ TOP INTERNATIONAL CONTRACTORS IN HAZARDOUS WASTE PROJECTS, 2010

Ranked by: Construction revenue derived from projects outside home country. **Remarks:** Specific figures not provided. **Number listed:** 10

1. VINCI

2. China Communications Construction Group Ltd.
3. Shanghai Urban Construction (Group) Corp.
4. Hochtief AG
5. Bouygues SA
6. PCL Construction Enterprises Inc.
7. Fomento de Construcciones y Contratas SA
8. Leighton Holdings Ltd.
9. ECC
10. Abeinsa SA

Source: *ENR: Engineering News-Record*, Top 225 International Contractors (annual), August 29, 2011, p. 49.

1297 ■ TOP INTERNATIONAL CONTRACTORS IN INDUSTRIAL PROJECTS, 2010

Ranked by: Construction revenue derived from projects outside home country. **Remarks:** Specific figures not provided. Also notes rank for previous year. **Number listed:** 10

1. Fluor Corp.
2. Bechtel
3. Danieli & C SpA
4. Bilfinger Berger SE
5. Techint Group
6. Grupo ACS
7. VINCI
8. China Metallurgical Group Corp.
9. Strabag SE
10. Taikisha Ltd.

Source: *ENR: Engineering News-Record*, Top 225 International Contractors (annual), August 29, 2011, p. 49.

1298 ■ TOP INTERNATIONAL CONTRACTORS IN MANUFACTURING PROJECTS, 2010

Ranked by: Construction revenue derived from projects outside home country. **Remarks:** Specific figures not provided. Also notes rank for previous year. **Number listed:** 10

1. Takenaka Corp.
2. Eiffage SA
3. Samsung C & T Corp.
4. Skanska AB
5. Kajima Corp.
6. Taikisha Ltd.
7. Renaissance Construction
8. Fomento de Construcciones y Contratas SA
9. Hochtief AG
10. Shimizu Corp.

Source: *ENR: Engineering News-Record*, Top 225 International Contractors (annual), August 29, 2011, p. 49.

1299 ■ TOP INTERNATIONAL CONTRACTORS IN PETROLEUM PROJECTS, 2010

Ranked by: Construction revenue derived from projects outside home country. **Remarks:** Specific figures not provided. Also notes rank for previous year. **Number listed:** 10

1. Saipem SpA
2. Technip
3. Bechtel Group Inc.
4. Petrofac Ltd.

5. Fluor Corp.
6. China Petroleum Engineering & Construction
7. JGC Corp.
8. Samsung Engineering Co., Ltd.
9. Foster Wheeler AG
10. Tecnicas Reunidas

Source: *ENR: Engineering News-Record*, Top 225 International Contractors (annual), August 29, 2011, p. 49.

1300 ■ TOP INTERNATIONAL CONTRACTORS IN POWER PROJECTS, 2010

Ranked by: Construction revenue derived from projects outside home country. Remarks: Specific figures not provided. Number listed: 10

1. Abeinsa SA
2. Grupo ACS
3. Sinohydro Corp.
4. China National Machinery Industrial Corp.
5. Hyundai Engineering & Construction Co., Ltd.
6. SEPCO Electric Power Construction Corp.
7. VINCI
8. Maire Tecnimont SpA
9. Iberdola Ingenieria y Construccion
10. Grupo Isolux Corsan SA

Source: *ENR: Engineering News-Record*, Top 225 International Contractors (annual), August 29, 2011, p. 49.

1301 ■ TOP INTERNATIONAL CONTRACTORS IN SEWER/WASTE PROJECTS, 2010

Ranked by: Construction revenue derived from projects outside home country. Remarks: Specific figures not provided. Also notes rank for previous year. Number listed: 10

1. Hochtief AG
2. Daewoo Engineering & Construction Co., Ltd.
3. Skanska AB
4. Grupo ACS
5. Strabag SE
6. Fomento de Construcciones y Contratas SA
7. China Gezhouba Group Co., Ltd.
8. Ferrovial Agroman SA
9. IMPREGILO SpA
10. Kharafi National KSCC

Source: *ENR: Engineering News-Record*, Top 225 International Contractors (annual), August 29, 2011, p. 49.

1302 ■ TOP INTERNATIONAL CONTRACTORS IN TRANSPORTATION PROJECTS, 2010

Ranked by: Construction revenue derived from projects outside home country. Remarks: Specific figures not provided. Also notes rank for previous year. Number listed: 10

1. VINCI
2. Bouygues SA
3. Hochtief AG
4. China Communications Construction Group Ltd.
5. Strabag SE
6. Fomento de Construcciones y Contratas SA
7. OHL

8. Skanska AB
9. Construtora Norberto Odebrecht
10. Bechtel Group Inc.

Source: *ENR: Engineering News-Record*, Top 225 International Contractors (annual), August 29, 2011, p. 49.

1303 ■ TOP INTERNATIONAL CONTRACTORS IN WATER PROJECTS, 2010

Ranked by: Construction revenue derived from projects outside home country. Remarks: Specific figures not provided. Also notes rank for previous year. Number listed: 10

1. Hochtief AG
2. Consolidated Contractors International Co. SAL
3. IMPREGILO SpA
4. Construtora Norberto Odebrecht SA
5. VINCI
6. SNC-Lavalin International Inc.
7. Salini Costruttori SpA
8. Skanska AB
9. Strabag SE
10. Mapa Insaat Ve Ticaret

Source: *ENR: Engineering News-Record*, Top 225 International Contractors (annual), August 29, 2011, p. 49.

Contracts, Government
See also: **Defense Contracts**

1304 ■ FASTEST-GROWING PRIVATE GOVERNMENT SERVICES COMPANIES IN THE U.S., 2007-2010

Ranked by: Average annual sales growth over three years, in percent. Remarks: Also notes headquarters, revenue, and rank in the overall *Inc. 500*. To qualify, private companies must have had annual revenues of at least $100,000 in 2007 and $2 million in 2010. Number listed: 62

1. Crystal Clear Technologies, with 16,048.1%
2. Connected Logistics, 10,112.3%
3. Trillacorpe Construction, 7,736.8%
4. Integrated Medical Solutions, 6,610.9%
5. A. Harold & Associates, 5,508.7%
6. Integrity Management Consulting, 4,460%
7. JMA Solutions, 4,316.7%
8. The Cybrix Group, 3,758.9%
9. Cask, 3,713.9%
10. Rhythm Engineering, 3,389%

Source: *Inc.*, Inc. 500 (annual), September 2011, p. 140-150.

1305 ■ FASTEST-GROWING SMALL GOVERNMENT CONTRACTORS, 2006-2010

Ranked by: Four-year compound annual growth in revenue from government contracts, in percent. Remarks: Also notes rank for previous year. Number listed: 50

1. Sava Workforce Solutions LLC, with 326.05%
2. Octo Consulting Group, 227.75%
3. VAE Inc., 211.4%
4. Insignia Technology Services LLC, 199.76%
5. MicroTech LLC, 196.09%
6. FedSys Inc., 189.59%

7. Integrity Management Consulting Inc., 188.18%
8. Next Tier Concepts Inc., 176.34%
9. Axom Technologies Inc., 167.87%
10. Centuria Corp., 155.98%

Source: *Washington Technology*, Fast 50 (annual), http://www.washingtontechnology.com, August 2011.

1306 ■ FEDERAL PRIME CONTRACTORS WITH THE HIGHEST MARKET VALUE, 2010

Ranked by: Market valuation, in millions of dollars. **Remarks:** Also notes rank in the overall *Top 100*. **Number listed:** 49

1. General Electric Co., with $194,875 million
2. International Business Machines Corp. (IBM), $182,329
3. AT&T Inc., $173,636
4. Oracle Corp., $158,141
5. Verizon Communications Inc., $101,142
6. Hewlett-Packard Co., $92,217
7. United Technologies Corp., $72,691
8. Boeing Co., $47,873
9. Honeywell International Inc., $41,474
10. Accenture Ltd., $31,064

Source: *Washington Technology*, Top 100 (annual), http://www.washingtontechnology.com, June 2011.

1307 ■ TOP CONSULTING CONTRACTORS FOR THE FEDERAL GOVERNMENT, 2010

Ranked by: Value of federal contracts, in dollars. **Remarks:** Also notes rank in the overall *Top 100* and for previous year. **Number listed:** 2

1. Deloitte LLP, with $1,190,904,000
2. Booz Allen Hamilton Inc., $3,718,644,000

Source: *Washington Technology*, Top 100 (annual), http://www.washingtontechnology.com, June 2011.

1308 ■ TOP ENGINEERING SERVICE CONTRACTORS FOR THE FEDERAL GOVERNMENT, 2010

Ranked by: Value of federal contracts, in dollars. **Remarks:** Also notes rank in the overall *Top 100* and for previous year. **Number listed:** 16

1. Fluor Corp., with $1,804,871,000
2. United Technologies Corp., $1,465,147,000
3. URS Corp., $1,133,733,000
4. General Atomics International, $634,573,000
5. Alion Science & Technology Corp., $478,236,000
6. VSE Corp., $443,919,000
7. Arctic Slope Regional Corp., $405,373,000
8. Cubic Corp., $277,846,000
9. Scientific Research Corp., $235,710,000
10. Babcock International Group plc, $229,421,000

Source: *Washington Technology*, Top 100 (annual), http://www.washingtontechnology.com, June 2011.

1309 ■ TOP FEDERAL PRIME CONTRACTORS BY CIVILIAN REVENUE, 2010

Ranked by: Civilian revenue, in dollars. **Remarks:** Also notes rank in the overall *Top 100*. **Number listed:** 100

1. Lockheed Martin Corp., with $6,455,480,000
2. Boeing Co., $3,348,131,000
3. Northrop Grumman Corp., $2,587,562,000
4. Raytheon Co., $2,111,206,000
5. Science Applications International Corp. (SAIC), $1,878,759,000
6. Computer Sciences Corp., $1,704,114,000
7. Hewlett-Packard Co., $1,487,195,000
8. International Business Machines Corp. (IBM), $1,300,953,000
9. Verizon Communications Inc., $1,106,672,000
10. Battelle Memorial Institute, $1,020,909,000

Source: *Washington Technology*, Top 100 (annual), http://www.washingtontechnology.com, June 2011.

1310 ■ TOP FEDERAL PRIME CONTRACTORS BY PRICE-TO-EARNINGS RATIO, 2010

Ranked by: Price-to-earnings ratio. **Remarks:** Also notes rank in the overall *Top 100*. **Number listed:** 49

1. SRA International Inc., with 64.4
2. Verizon Communications Inc., 39.7
3. Fluor Corp., 33
4. Booz Allen Hamilton Inc., 29.9
5. Xerox Corp., 26.1
6. Jacobs Engineering Group Inc., 23.8
7. Oracle Corp., 23.2
8. Orbital Sciences Corp., 21
9. Honeywell International Inc., 20.3
10. Tetra Tech Inc., 20

Source: *Washington Technology*, Top 100 (annual), http://www.washingtontechnology.com, June 2011.

1311 ■ TOP FEDERAL PRIME CONTRACTORS BY RETURN ON INVESTMENT, 2010

Ranked by: Return on investment, in percent. **Remarks:** Also notes rank in the overall *Top 100*. **Number listed:** 49

1. KBR Inc., with 61.4%
2. Fluor Corp., 48.2%
3. Honeywell International Inc., 38.7%
4. Xerox Corp., 38.2%
5. Qwest Communications International Inc., 35.5%
6. Ball Corp., 32.4%
7. Oracle Corp., 28.4%
8. Cubic Corp., 26.9%
9. Dynamics Research Corp., 26.3%
10. General Electric Co., 23.9%

Source: *Washington Technology*, Top 100 (annual), http://www.washingtontechnology.com, June 2011.

1312 ■ TOP FEDERAL PRIME CONTRACTORS BY REVENUE GROWTH, 2009-2010

Ranked by: Annual growth in revenue, in percent. **Remarks:** Also notes rank in the overall *Top 100* and revenue for current and previous year. **Number listed:** 100

1. Xerox Corp., with 42.5%
2. Qwest Communications International Inc., 41.6%

3. Oracle Corp., 37.8%

4. ManTech International Corp., 28.9%

5. Booz Allen Hamilton Inc., 25.3%

6. NCI Inc., 24%

7. Cubic Corp., 20.1%

8. Dell Inc., 18%

9. Orbital Sciences Corp., 15%

10. CACI International Inc., 14.2%

Source: *Washington Technology*, Top 100 (annual), http://www.washingtontechnology.com, June 2011.

1313 ■ TOP FEDERAL PRIME CONTRACTORS BY VALUE OF CONTRACTS, 2010

Ranked by: Total value of federal contracts, in dollars. **Remarks:** Also notes rank for previous year. **Number listed:** 100

1. Lockheed Martin Corp., with $17,344,113,000

2. Northrop Grumman Corp., $10,800,453,000

3. Boeing Co., $8,400,115,000

4. Raytheon Co., $6,206,515,000

5. General Dynamics Corp., $5,493,414,000

6. Science Applications International Corp. (SAIC), $5,159,739,000

7. Hewlett-Packard Co., $3,831,520,000

8. L-3 Communications Corp., $3,815,873,000

9. Booz Allen Hamilton Inc., $3,718,644,000

10. KBR Inc., $3,546,605,000

Source: *Washington Technology*, Top 100 (annual), http://www.washingtontechnology.com, June 2011.

1314 ■ TOP HARDWARE CONTRACTORS FOR THE FEDERAL GOVERNMENT, 2010

Ranked by: Value of federal contracts, in dollars. **Remarks:** Also notes rank in the overall *Top 100* and for previous year. **Number listed:** 3

1. Dell Inc., with $2,180,421,000

2. General Electric Co., $813,760,000

3. Xerox Corp., $427,916,000

Source: *Washington Technology*, Top 100 (annual), http://www.washingtontechnology.com, June 2011.

1315 ■ TOP INTERNATIONAL DEVELOPMENT CONTRACTORS FOR THE FEDERAL GOVERNMENT, 2010

Ranked by: Value of federal contracts, in dollars. **Remarks:** Also notes rank in the overall *Top 100* and for previous year. **Number listed:** 4

1. Development Alternatives Inc., with $455,721,000

2. Chemonics International Inc., $454,521,000

3. Creative Associates International Inc., $267,518,000

4. Louis Berger Group Inc., $181,740,000

Source: *Washington Technology*, Top 100 (annual), http://www.washingtontechnology.com, June 2011.

1316 ■ TOP IT CONTRACTORS IN THE SMALL BUSINESS ADMINISTRATION'S 8(A) PROGRAM, 2010

Ranked by: Prime contract information technology revenue, in dollars. **Remarks:** Also notes rank for previous year. The Small Business Administration's 8(a) program is designed to help small,

minority-owned businesses through preferential contracting opportunities with the federal government. Ranking excludes Alaska Native corporations and tribally-owned companies. **Number listed:** 25

1. MicroTech LLC, with $273,867,000

2. ActioNet Inc., $132,557,000

3. Neany Inc., $97,479,000

4. USfalcon Inc., $79,398,000

5. Digital Management Inc., $71,152,000

6. Alon Inc., $54,135,000

7. 2020 Co. LLC, $45,161,000

8. Harrington, Moran, Barksdale Inc., $40,814,000

9. Haynes Inc., $35,479,000

10. Paragon Technology Group Inc., $34,640,000

Source: *Washington Technology*, Top 25 8(a) Companies (annual), http://www.washingtontechnology.com, November 2011.

1317 ■ TOP IT SERVICES CONTRACTORS FOR THE FEDERAL GOVERNMENT, 2010

Ranked by: Value of federal contracts, in dollars. **Remarks:** Also notes rank in the overall *Top 100* and for previous year. **Number listed:** 11

1. Apptis Inc., with $826,280,000

2. Wyle Laboratories Inc., $772,933,000

3. Vangent Inc., $529,059,000

4. NCI Inc., $492,477,000

5. SGT Inc., $338,665,000

6. Artel Inc., $284,749,000

7. Microtech LLC, $273,857,000

8. Telos Corp., $273,575,000

9. Eyak Technology LLC, $239,986,000

10. Energy Enterprise Solutions Ltd., $230,353,000

Source: *Washington Technology*, Top 100 (annual), http://www.washingtontechnology.com, June 2011.

1318 ■ TOP PRIVATE FEDERAL PRIME CONTRACTORS BY VALUE OF CONTRACTS, 2010

Ranked by: Total value of federal contracts, in dollars. **Remarks:** Also notes rank in the overall *Top 100* and for previous year. **Number listed:** 51

1. DynCorp International Inc., with $3,047,513,000

2. United Technologies Corp., $1,465,147,000

3. Battelle Memorial Institute, $1,330,333,000

4. Deloitte LLP, $1,190,904,000

5. Aerospace Corp., $842,638,000

6. Apptis Inc., $826,280,000

7. Bechtel Marine Propulsion Corp., $793,298,000

8. Wyle Laboratories Inc., $772,933,000

9. DRS Technologies Inc., $767,390,000

10. Mission Essential Personnel LLC, $681,304,000

Source: *Washington Technology*, Top 100 (annual), http://www.washingtontechnology.com, June 2011.

1319 ■ TOP PROFESSIONAL SERVICES CONTRACTORS FOR THE FEDERAL GOVERNMENT, 2010

Ranked by: Value of federal contracts, in dollars. **Remarks:** Also notes rank in the overall *Top 100* and for previous year. **Number listed:** 11

1. KBR Inc., with $3,546,605,000
2. Battelle Memorial Institute, $1,330,333,000
3. Aerospace Corp., $842,638,000
4. Bechtel Marine Propulson Corp., $793,298,000
5. Mission Essential Personnel LLC, $681,304,000
6. Nana Regional Corp., $401,781,000
7. U.S. Investigation Services Inc., $356,150,000
8. Chenega Corp., $309,457,000
9. Alutiiq LLC, $299,640,000
10. Navmar Applied Sciences Corp., $233,034,000

Source: *Washington Technology*, Top 100 (annual), http://www.washingtontechnology.com, June 2011.

1320 ■ TOP PUBLICLY-TRADED FEDERAL PRIME CONTRACTORS BY VALUE OF CONTRACTS, 2010

Ranked by: Total value of federal contracts, in dollars. **Remarks:** Also notes rank in the overall *Top 100* and for previous year. **Number listed:** 49

1. Lockheed Martin Corp., with $17,344,113,000
2. Northrop Grumman Corp., $10,800,453,000
3. Boeing Co., $8,400,115,000
4. Raytheon Co., $6,206,515,000
5. General Dynamics Corp., $5,493,414,000
6. Science Applications International Corp. (SAIC), $5,159,739,000
7. Hewlett-Packard Co., $3,831,520,000
8. L-3 Communications Corp., $3,815,873,000
9. Booz Allen Hamilton Inc., $3,718,644,000
10. KBR Inc., $3,546,605,000

Source: *Washington Technology*, Top 100 (annual), http://www.washingtontechnology.com, June 2011.

1321 ■ TOP RESEARCH CONTRACTORS FOR THE FEDERAL GOVERNMENT, 2010

Ranked by: Value of federal contracts, in dollars. **Remarks:** Also notes rank in the overall *Top 100* and for previous year. **Number listed:** 4

1. RTI International, with $402,469,000
2. Westat Inc., $361,987,000
3. ABT Associates Inc., $226,404,000
4. SRA International, $181,032,000

Source: *Washington Technology*, Top 100 (annual), http://www.washingtontechnology.com, June 2011.

1322 ■ TOP SMALL FEDERAL PRIME CONTRACTORS BY VALUE OF CONTRACTS, 2010

Ranked by: Total value of federal contracts, in dollars. **Remarks:** Also notes rank in the overall *Top 100* and for previous year. **Number listed:** 14

1. Arctic Slope Regional Corp., with $405,373,000
2. SGT Inc., $338,665,000
3. Chenega Corp., $309,457,000
4. ImmixGroup Inc., $306,840,000
5. Alutiiq LLC, $299,640,000
6. Artel Inc., $284,749,000
7. Microtech LLC, $273,857,000
8. Telos Corp., $273,575,000

9. Carahsoft Technology Corp., $246,375,000
10. Eyak Technology LLC, $239,986,000

Source: *Washington Technology*, Top 100 (annual), http://www.washingtontechnology.com, June 2011.

1323 ■ TOP SYSTEMS INTEGRATION CONTRACTORS FOR THE FEDERAL GOVERNMENT, 2010

Ranked by: Value of federal contracts, in dollars. **Remarks:** Also notes rank in the overall *Top 100* and for previous year. **Number listed:** 19

1. Science Applications International Corp. (SAIC), with $5,159,739,000
2. Hewlett-Packard Co., $3,831,520,000
3. Computer Sciences Corp., $3,532,784,000
4. Harris Corp., $2,893,847,000
5. CACI International Inc., $2,517,616,000
6. International Business Machines Corp. (IBM), $1,594,165,000
7. ManTech International Corp., $1,467,181,00
8. Serco Inc., $992,211,000
9. SRA International Inc., $936,812,000
10. Accenture Ltd., $837,671,000

Source: *Washington Technology*, Top 100 (annual), http://www.washingtontechnology.com, June 2011.

1324 ■ TOP TELECOMMUNICATIONS CONTRACTORS FOR THE FEDERAL GOVERNMENT, 2010

Ranked by: Value of federal contracts, in dollars. **Remarks:** Also notes rank in the overall *Top 100* and for previous year. **Number listed:** 4

1. Verizon Communications Inc., with $1,844,453,000
2. Sprint Corp., $820,557,000
3. AT&T Inc., $664,057,000
4. Qwest Communications International Inc., $435,395,000

Source: *Washington Technology*, Top 100 (annual), http://www.washingtontechnology.com, June 2011.

1325 ■ TOP VALUE-ADDED RESELLER CONTRACTORS FOR THE FEDERAL GOVERNMENT, 2010

Ranked by: Value of federal contracts, in dollars. **Remarks:** Also notes rank in the overall *Top 100* and for previous year. **Number listed:** 7

1. World Wide Technology Inc., with $557,693,000
2. CDW Government Inc., $506,229,000
3. ImmixGroup Inc., $306,840,000
4. GTSI Corp., $287,668,000
5. Carahsoft Technology Corp., $246,375,000
6. Mythics Inc., $197,639,000
7. DLT Solutions Inc., $190,121,000

Source: *Washington Technology*, Top 100 (annual), http://www.washingtontechnology.com, June 2011.

Convenience Stores

1326 ■ AMERICA'S LARGEST PRIVATE CONVENIENCE STORE AND GAS STATION COMPANIES, 2010

Ranked by: Revenue, in billions of dollars. **Remarks:** Also notes headquarters, number of employees, and overall rank in the *Ameri-*

ca's *Largest Private Companies* list. Ranking is available online only, not in print. **Number listed:** 9

1. Love's Travel Stops & Country Stores Inc., with $24.4 billion
2. Pilot Flying J, $17.77
3. QuikTrip Corp., $8.77
4. Cumberland Farms Inc., $8.02
5. Wawa Inc., $6.99
6. RaceTrac Petroleum Inc., $5.75
7. Sheetz Inc., $5.23
8. Holiday Cos., $3.63
9. Kum & Go LC, $2.1

Source: *Forbes*, America's Largest Private Companies (annual), http://www.forbes.com, December 5, 2011.

1327 ■ FASTEST-GROWING CONVENIENCE STORE CHAINS, 2010-2011

Ranked by: Number of new stores added during the year. **Remarks:** Also notes total store count and percentage growth. **Number listed:** 21

1. 7-Eleven Inc., with 523 new stores
2. Shell Oil/Motiva Enterprises LLC, 167
3. Sunoco Inc., 122
4. Casey's General Stores Inc., 107
5. Marathon Petroleum Corp., 106
6. Alimentation Couche-Tard Inc., 100
7. Chevron Corp., 81
8. Valero Energy Corp., 76
9. Military, 74
10. Fikes Wholesale Inc., 72

Source: *Convenience Store News*, Top 20 Growth Chains (annual), March 1, 2012, p. 21.

1328 ■ LARGEST ASIA-PACIFIC CONVENIENCE STORE COMPANIES, 2010

Ranked by: Sales, in millions of U.S. dollars. **Remarks:** Also notes country, fascias/brands, number of outlets, sales in national currency, sales area, sales per square meter, and figures for previous year. **Number listed:** 10

1. Seven & I Holdings Co., Ltd., with $31,064 million
2. Lawson, $20,974
3. Family Mart, $15,992
4. Uny, $12,651
5. Daily Yamazaki, $8,446
6. CP All, $5,076
7. President Chain Store Corp., $2,994
8. Aeon Group, $2,928
9. Bokwang Family Mart, $1,868
10. GS Holdings, $1,862

Source: *Retail Asia*, Retail Asia-Pacific Top 500 (annual), July 2011, p. 64-64a.

1329 ■ LARGEST COMPANY-OPERATED CONVENIENCE STORE CHAINS, 2011

Ranked by: Number of company-operated stores. **Remarks:** Also notes share of total stores. **Number listed:** 20

1. Alimentation Couche-Tard Inc., with 3,049 stores

2. Casey's General Stores Inc., 1,692
3. The Pantry Inc., 1,614
4. Marathon Petroleum Corp./Speedway LLC, 1,372
5. Hess Corp., 1,084
6. Valero Energy Corp., 1,000
7. The Kroger Co., 811
8. Cumberland Gulf Group, 603
9. Wawa Inc., 599
10. QuikTrip Corp., 597

Source: *Convenience Store News*, Top 100 (annual), May 21, 2012, p. 24.

1330 ■ LARGEST CONVENIENCE STORE COMPANIES, 2011

Ranked by: Total store count. **Remarks:** Also notes rank for previous year, headquarters, company-operated stores, franchised stores, annual financials, and store names. **Number listed:** 100

1. 7-Eleven Inc., with 7,341 stores
2. Shell Oil Products U.S./Motiva Enterprises LLC, 4,934
3. BP North America, 4,691
4. Chevron Corp., 4,057
5. Alimentation Couche-Tard Inc., 3,585
6. Exxon Mobil Corp., 3,446
7. Marathon Petroleum Corp./Speedway LLC, 2,670
8. Sunoco Inc., 1,987
9. Valero Energy Corp., 1,786
10. CITGO Petroleum Corp., 1,722

Source: *Convenience Store News*, Top 100 (annual), May 21, 2012, p. 26-30.

1331 ■ LARGEST FRANCHISEE/LICENSEE CONVENIENCE STORE CHAINS, 2011

Ranked by: Number of franchisee/licensee-operated stores. **Remarks:** Also notes share of total stores. **Number listed:** 20

1. 7-Eleven Inc., with 7,157 stores
2. Shell Oil Products U.S./Motiva Enterprises LLC, 4,896
3. BP North America, 4,688
4. Chevron Corp., 3,642
5. Exxon Mobil Corp., 3,433
6. CITGO Petroleum Corp., 1,722
7. Sunoco Inc., 1,615
8. Marathon Petroleum Corp./Speedway LLC, 1,298
9. ConocoPhillips Inc., 1,281
10. Getty Petroleum Corp., 1,141

Source: *Convenience Store News*, Top 100 (annual), May 21, 2012, p. 31.

1332 ■ LARGEST WHOLESALERS TO CONVENIENCE STORES BY LOCATIONS, 2010

Ranked by: Number of retail locations served. **Number listed:** 10

1. McLane Co., with 37,560 locations
2. Core-Mark Holding Co., Inc., 28,000
3. Eby-Brown Co., 20,000

3. H. T. Hackney Co., 20,000
5. Harold Levinson Associates Inc., 13,000
6. Farner-Bocken Co., 12,000
7. GSC Enterprises Inc., 8,000
8. Amcon Distributing Co., 5,000
9. Consumer Product Distributors Inc., 4,560
10. Stephenson Wholesale Co., Inc., 3,572

Source: *Convenience Store News*, Top 25 Wholesalers (annual), October 3, 2011, p. 66.

1333 ■ LARGEST WHOLESALERS TO CONVENIENCE STORES BY SALES, 2010

Ranked by: Estimated sales, in millions of dollars. **Remarks:** Also notes rank and figures for previous year, percent change, headquarters, trading area, sales from chain and single stores, number and total area of warehouses, and number of employees. **Number listed:** 25

1. McLane Co., with $27,300 million
2. Core-Mark Holding Co., Inc., $7,267
3. Eby-Brown Co., $4,500
4. H. T. Hackney Co., $3,600
5. GSC Enterprises Inc., $1,200
6. Amcon Distributing Co., $1,170
7. Harold Levinson Associates Inc., $1,105
8. S. Abraham & Sons Inc., $994
9. Imperial/Harrison Super Regional, $900
10. Consumer Product Distributors Inc., $884

Source: *Convenience Store News*, Top 25 Wholesalers (annual), October 3, 2011, p. 64-65.

1334 ■ LARGEST WHOLESALERS TO CONVENIENCE STORES BY SALES PER LOCATION, 2010

Ranked by: Sales per retail location served, in dollars. **Number listed:** 10

1. McLane Co., with $726,837
2. Imperial/Harrison Super Regional, $382,979
3. Liberty USA Inc., $350,000
4. Garber Bros. Inc., $342,500
5. J. T. Davenport & Sons Inc., $340,000
5. Cooper-Booth Wholesale Co., $340,000
7. S. Abraham & Sons Inc., $327,297
8. Core-Mark Holding Co., Inc., $259,536
9. Southco Distributing Co., $251,538
10. Amcon Distributing Co., $234,000

Source: *Convenience Store News*, Top 25 Wholesalers (annual), October 3, 2011, p. 62.

1335 ■ TOP CONVENIENCE STORE CHAINS BY SALES PER UNIT, 2010

Ranked by: Sales per unit, in thousands of dollars. **Remarks:** Also notes rank for previous year, fiscal year-end, and figures for previous two years. **Number listed:** 3

1. Wawa, with $891.4 thousand
2. 7-Eleven, $273
3. Circle K, $130.6

Source: *Nation's Restaurant News*, Top 100 (annual), June 27, 2011, p. 38.

1336 ■ TOP CONVENIENCE STORE FRANCHISES, 2012

Ranked by: Cumulative score based on financial strength and stability, growth rate, size of the system, number of years in busi-ness, the length of time franchising, start-up costs, litigation, percentage of terminations, and whether the company provides financing. **Remarks:** Specific scores not provided. Also notes overall rank within the *Franchise 500*, contact information, description, year founded, year started franchising, states where registered, available U.S. regions, where seeking foreign expansion, number of franchised and company-owned units for past three years, start-up costs, franchise fees, royalty fees, and type of financing available. **Number listed:** 3

1. 7-Eleven Inc.
2. am/pm Mini Market
3. Circle K

Source: *Entrepreneur*, Franchise 500 (annual), January 2012, p. 198-199.

1337 ■ TOP WHOLESALERS TO CONVENIENCE STORES BY SALES PER DELIVERY, 2010

Ranked by: Sales per delivery, in dollars. **Number listed:** 10

1. McLane Co., with $10,581
2. Harold Levinson Associates Inc., $8,340
3. Liberty USA Inc., $8,005
4. Cooper-Booth Wholesale Co., $6,873
5. Richmond-Master Distributors Inc., $6,872
6. Imperial/Harrison Super Regional, $6,531
7. J. T. Davenport & Sons Inc., $6,097
8. S. Abraham & Sons Inc., $5,817
9. Garber Bros. Inc., $4,971
10. Harbor Wholesale Foods, $4,792

Source: *Convenience Store News*, Top 25 Wholesalers (annual), October 3, 2011, p. 68.

1338 ■ TOP WHOLESALERS TO CONVENIENCE STORES BY SALES PER EMPLOYEE, 2010

Ranked by: Sales per full-time employee, in millions of dollars. **Number listed:** 10

1. Allen Brothers Wholesale Distribution Inc., with $2,805 million
2. Liberty USA Inc., $2,800
3. Cooper-Booth Wholesale Co., $2,684
4. Chambers & Owen Inc., $2,530
5. Harold Levinson Associates Inc., $2,455
6. Atlantic Dominion Distributors, $2,394
7. Garber Bros. Inc., $2,386
8. Imperial/Harrison Super Regional, $2,368
9. Eby-Brown Co., $2,250
10. J. T. Davenport & Sons Inc., $2,225

Source: *Convenience Store News*, Top 25 Wholesalers (annual), October 3, 2011, p. 66.

1339 ■ TOP WHOLESALERS TO CONVENIENCE STORES BY SALES PER WAREHOUSE SQUARE FOOT, 2010

Ranked by: Sales per square foot of warehouse, in dollars. **Number listed:** 10

1. Liberty USA Inc., with $4,667
2. Cooper-Booth Wholesale Co., $4,636
3. Garber Bros. Inc., $3,425
4. Allen Brothers Wholesale Distribution Inc., $3,108
5. J. T. Davenport & Sons Inc., $2,985

6. Imperial/Harrison Super Regional, $2,866
7. Chambers & Owen Inc., $2,864
8. Core-Mark Holding Co., Inc., $2,750
9. Atlantic Dominion Distributors, $2,594
10. McLane Co., $2,557

Source: *Convenience Store News*, Top 25 Wholesalers (annual), October 3, 2011, p. 68.

1340 ■ TOP WHOLESALERS TO CONVENIENCE STORES BY SKUS, 2010

Ranked by: Number of stock-keeping units (SKUs) handled. **Number listed:** 10

1. McLane Co., with 45,724 SKUs
2. Core-Mark Holding Co., Inc., 43,000
3. H. T. Hackney Co., 25,000
4. Stephenson Wholesale Co., Inc., 15,000
5. Amcon Distributing Co., 14,000
5. Harold Levinson Associates Inc., 14,000
7. Eby-Brown Co., 12,000
7. Chambers & Owen Inc., 12,000
7. Garber Bros. Inc., 12,000
10. S. Abraham & Sons Inc., 11,549

Source: *Convenience Store News*, Top 25 Wholesalers (annual), October 3, 2011, p. 68.

Cookies and Crackers

1341 ■ TOP BRANDS OF CRACKERS, 2011

Ranked by: Sales for the 52 weeks ending March 20, 2011, in millions of dollars. **Remarks:** Also notes annual growth, dollar share, and unit sales. **Number listed:** 10

1. Sunshine Cheez-It, with $342.4 million
2. Nabisco Ritz, $299.4
3. Nabisco Wheat Thins, $264.2
4. Nabisco Triscuit, $245.4
5. Pepperidge Farm Goldfish, $240.7
6. Private label, $147.2
7. Keebler Club, $131.2
8. Stacy's Pita Chips, $97.5
9. Keebler Townhouse, $92.3
10. Pepperidge Farm Flavor-Blasted Goldfish, $69.8

Source: *Snack Food & Wholesale Bakery*, State of the Industry (annual), July 2011, p. 40.

1342 ■ TOP COOKIE FRANCHISES, 2012

Ranked by: Cumulative score based on financial strength and stability, growth rate, size of the system, number of years in business, the length of time franchising, start-up costs, litigation, percentage of terminations, and whether the company provides financing. **Remarks:** Specific scores not provided. Also notes overall rank within the *Franchise 500,* contact information, description, year founded, year started franchising, states where registered, available U.S. regions, where seeking foreign expansion, number of franchised and company-owned units for past three years, start-up costs, franchise fees, royalty fees, and type of financing available. **Number listed:** 2

1. Great American Cookie Co. Franchising LLC

2. Nestle Toll House Cafe by Chip

Source: *Entrepreneur*, Franchise 500 (annual), January 2012, p. 162-163.

Cooperatives

1343 ■ LARGEST FINANCIAL CANADIAN COOPERATIVES, 2010

Ranked by: Revenue, in thousands of Canadian dollars (unless otherwise noted). **Remarks:** Also notes rank change from previous year. **Number listed:** 10

1. Desjardins Group, with C$13,481,000 thousand
2. Co-operators Group, C$3,530,507
3. Vancouver City Savings Credit Union, C$638,932
4. Groupe Promutuel, C$523,000
5. Servus Credit Union, C$499,659
6. Coast Capital Savings Credit Union, C$476,952
7. Central 1 Credit Union, C$310,717
8. First West Credit Union, C$292,863
9. Meridian Credit Union, C$256,788
10. Credit Union Central Saskatchewan, C$240,611

Source: *Report on Business Magazine*, Top 1000 Companies (annual), http://www.reportonbusiness.com, June 2011.

1344 ■ LARGEST NON-FINANCIAL CANADIAN COOPERATIVES, 2010

Ranked by: Revenue, in thousands of Canadian dollars (unless otherwise noted). **Remarks:** Also notes rank change from previous year. **Number listed:** 10

1. Federated Co-operatives, with C$7,130,031 thousand
2. La Coop Federee de Quebec, C$3,954,691
3. Agropur Cooperative, C$3,345,995
4. United Farmers of Alberta Co-operative, C$1,746,533
5. Calgary Co-operative Association, C$1,064,445
6. Co-op Atlantic, C$613,794
7. Exceldor Cooperative Avicole, C$394,900
8. Red River Cooperative, C$390,784
9. Hensall District Co-op, C$308,208
10. Nutrinor, Coop Agroalimentaire, C$286,397

Source: *Report on Business Magazine*, Top 1000 Companies (annual), http://www.reportonbusiness.com, June 2011.

1345 ■ TOP COOPERATIVES IN THE U.S. BY REVENUE, 2010

Ranked by: Revenue, in millions of dollars. **Remarks:** Also notes Web site, total assets, rank and figures for previous year, industry, and key executive. **Number listed:** 100

1. CHS Inc., with $25,268 million
2. Land O'Lakes Inc., $11,146
3. TOPCO Associates LLC, $10,405
4. Dairy Farmers of America Inc., $9,880
5. Wakefern Food Corp., $9,458
6. Associated Wholesale Grocers Inc., $7,252

7. GROWMARK Inc., $6,132
8. Agribank FCB, $3,975
9. Unified Grocers Inc., $3,921
10. HealthPartners Inc., $3,578

Source: *National Cooperative Bank*, NCB Co-op 100 (annual), http://www.coop100.coop, October 18, 2011.

Corporate Acquisition and Merger Services

1346 ■ WORLD'S TOP MERGER ADVISERS BY TOTAL VALUE, 2011

Ranked by: Total value of merger transactions, in billions of U.S. dollars. **Remarks:** Also notes number of deals, and rank and figures for previous year. **Number listed:** 10

1. Goldman Sachs Group Inc., with $676.6 billion
2. J. P. Morgan Chase & Co., $524.5
3. Morgan Stanley, $453.6
4. Credit Suisse Group, $402.4
5. Bank of America Corp./Merrill Lynch, $385.1
6. Citigroup Inc., $362.4
7. Barclays Capital Inc., $356.8
8. Deutsche Bank AG, $289.7
9. UBS AG, $288.1
10. Lazard LLC, $255.5

Source: *The Wall Street Journal*, Year-End Review (annual), January 3, 2012, p. R19.

Corporate Directors

1347 ■ COUNTRIES WITH THE HIGHEST EFFICACY OF CORPORATE BOARDS, 2010

Ranked by: Score, on a scale of seven, based on the accountability of investors and boards of directors. **Number listed:** 142

1. Sweden, with 5.9 points
2. South Africa, 5.8
2. Australia, 5.8
4. Canada, 5.6
4. Singapore, 5.6
6. Finland, 5.5
6. New Zealand, 5.5
6. Norway, 5.5
9. Malaysia, 5.3
9. Switzerland, 5.3
9. United Kingdom, 5.3
9. Denmark, 5.3
9. Puerto Rico, 5.3

Source: *Global Competitiveness Report*, (annual), World Economic Forum, 2011, p. 408.

1348 ■ COUNTRIES WITH THE LOWEST EFFICACY OF CORPORATE BOARDS, 2010

Ranked by: Score, on a scale of seven, based on corporate governance by investors and boards of directors. **Number listed:** 142

1. Yemen, with 2.5 points
2. Angola, 3.2

3. Chad, 3.4
3. Timor-Leste, 3.4
5. Mauritania, 3.5
6. Bolivia, 3.7
6. Serbia, 3.7
6. Mongolia, 3.7
6. Greece, 3.7
10. Algeria, 3.8
10. Kuwait, 3.8
10. Croatia, 3.8
10. Nepal, 3.8

Source: *Global Competitiveness Report*, (annual), World Economic Forum, 2011, p. 408.

1349 ■ TOP CANADIAN COMPANIES IN FEMALE REPRESENTATION ON BOARDS, 2011

Ranked by: Representation on the board of directors by women, in percent. **Number listed:** 20

1. Vancouver City Savings Credit Union, with 67%
1. Mountain Equipment Co-op, 67%
3. Corus Entertainment Inc., 50%
4. Shoppers Drug Mart Corp., 40%
5. Jean Coutu Group Inc., 33%
6. Hydro-Quebec, 31%
7. ING Direct Canada, 30%
7. British Columbia Hydro & Power Authority (BC Hydro), 30%
9. Mouvement des caisses Desjardins, 29%
9. Imperial Oil Ltd., 29%

Source: *Corporate Knights*, Diversity Index (annual), http://www.corporateknights.ca, 2011.

1350 ■ TOP CANADIAN COMPANIES IN MINORITY/ ABORIGINAL REPRESENTATION ON BOARDS, 2011

Ranked by: Representation on the board of directors by minorities or aboriginals, in percent. **Number listed:** 20

1. Husky Energy Inc., with 47%
2. Sears Canada, 25%
3. Teck Resources Ltd., 21%
4. SaskTel, 17%
5. CI Financial Corp., 14%
5. Scotiabank, Bank of Nova Scotia, 14%
5. Thomson Reuters Corp., 14%
8. Westport Innovations Inc., 13%
8. Ballard Power Systems Inc., 13%
8. HSBC Bank Canada, 13%

Source: *Corporate Knights*, Diversity Index (annual), http://www.corporateknights.ca, 2011.

Corporate Growth
See: **Growth Companies**

Corporate Image

1351 ■ AMERICA'S BEST CORPORATE CITIZENS, 2012

Ranked by: Score based on financials as well as policies and actions in six areas: environment, climate change, human rights, employee relations, corporate governance, philanthropy, and finances. **Remarks:** The lower the score, the higher the rank. Also notes ticker symbol and scores for each criterion. **Number listed:** 100

1. Bristol-Myers Squibb Co., with 49.815 points
2. International Business Machines Corp. (IBM), 52.15
3. Intel Corp., 54.565
4. Microsoft Corp., 67.815
5. Johnson Controls Inc., 70.045
6. Accenture plc, 73.88
7. Spectra Energy Corp., 76.185
8. Campbell Soup Co., 76.5
9. Nike Inc., 80.21
10. Freeport-McMoRan Copper & Gold Inc., 82.41

Source: *Corporate Responsibility*, 100 Best Corporate Citizens (annual), http://www.thecro.com, 2012.

1352 ■ AMERICA'S TOP CORPORATE BRANDS, 2011

Ranked by: Survey of consumer based on 12 attributes, including honesty and trustworthiness, innovation, and dedication to making communities better places. **Remarks:** Scores not provided. Only the top 5 are printed; the entire list is available online. **Number listed:** 100

1. Johnson & Johnson
2. General Mills
3. Google
4. Kraft Foods
5. Hershey
6. Apple
7. Kellogg
8. Home Depot
9. Clorox
10. Amazon.com

Source: *Forbes*, Corporate Approval Ratings, October 24, 2011, p. 33.

1353 ■ AMERICA'S WORST CORPORATE BRANDS, 2011

Ranked by: Survey of consumer based on 12 attributes, including honesty and trustworthiness, innovation, and dedication to making communities better places. **Remarks:** Scores not provided. Only the bottom 5 are printed; the entire list is available online. **Number listed:** 100

1. Fannie Mae
2. BP
3. Goldman Sachs
4. Capital One Financial
5. ExxonMobil
6. Citigroup
7. Bank of America
8. ConocoPhillips
9. JP Morgan Chase
10. Chevron

Source: *Forbes*, Corporate Approval Ratings, October 24, 2011, p. 33.

Corporate Reputation
See: **Corporate Image**

Corporate Social Responsibility

1354 ■ CANADA'S MOST SOCIALLY RESPONSIBLE CORPORATIONS, 2011

Ranked by: Score based on performance across a broad range of environmental, social, and governance indicators. **Remarks:** Specific scores not provided; companies are listed alphabetically, not ranked. Also notes comments. To qualify, companies must be Canadian-listed or wholly-owned subsidiaries of foreign-listed companies with significant operations or brand presence in Canada. **Number listed:** 50

1. 3M Co.
2. adidas AG
3. Bank of Montreal
4. BCE Inc.
5. Best Buy Co., Inc.
6. BMW Canada Inc.
7. Bombardier Inc.
8. Brookfield Office Properties Inc.
9. Campbell Soup Co.
10. Canadian National Railway Co.

Source: *Maclean's*, Top 50 Socially Responsible Corporations (annual), June 20, 2011, p. 46+.

1355 ■ WORLD'S MOST SUSTAINABLE LARGE CORPORATIONS, 2011

Ranked by: Score based on corporate responsibility. **Remarks:** Also notes country, industry group, carbon productivity, energy productivity, water productivity, waste productivity, percentage tax paid, leadership diversity, clean capitalism pay link, CEO/average worker pay ratio, safety productivity, employee turnover, and innovation capacity. **Number listed:** 100

1. Novo Nordisk A/S, with 74.37 points
2. Natura Cosmeticos SA, 67.09
3. Statoil ASA, 65.73
4. Novozymes A/S, 64.81
5. ASML Holding NV, 64.79
6. BG Group plc, 63.24
7. Vivendi SA, 59.53
8. Umicore SA, 58.44
9. Norsk Hydro ASA, 58.29
10. Atlas Copco AB, 54.19

Source: *Corporate Knights*, Global 100 (annual), http://www.corporateknights.ca, February 2012.

Corporations
See also: **Growth Companies**

1356 ■ AMERICA'S BEST COMPANIES WITH THE HIGHEST ACTUAL JOB GROWTH, 2012

Ranked by: Number of employees hired. **Remarks:** Also notes total number of employees and overall rank in the *100 Best Companies to Work For*. **Number listed:** 10

1. Google Inc., with 7,020 new employees
2. Darden Restaurants Inc., 5,137
3. Novo Nordisk, 3,957
4. Marriott International, 2,951
5. Whole Foods Market Inc., 2,699

6. Deloitte, 2,630
7. Accenture Ltd., 2,600
8. Cisco Systems Inc., 2,486
9. PricewaterhouseCoopers, 2,468
10. Stryker, 1,981

Source: *Fortune*, 100 Best Companies to Work For (annual), http://www.fortune.com, February 6, 2012.

1357 ■ AMERICA'S BEST COMPANIES TO WORK FOR, 2012

Ranked by: Score based on employee surveys as well as evaluation of companies' credibility, respect, fairness, and pride/camaraderie. **Remarks:** Specific scores not provided. Also notes rank for previous year, headquarters, number of employees, whether or not company is hiring, and comments. **Number listed:** 100

1. Google Inc.
2. The Boston Consulting Group Inc.
3. SAS Institute Inc.
4. Wegmans Food Markets Inc.
5. Edward Jones
6. NetApp Inc.
7. Camden Property Trust
8. Recreational Equipment Inc. (REI)
9. CHG Healthcare Services
10. Quicken Loans

Source: *Fortune*, 100 Best Companies to Work For (annual), February 2, 2012, p. 118+.

1358 ■ AMERICA'S BEST LARGE COMPANIES TO WORK FOR, 2012

Ranked by: Score based on employee surveys as well as evaluation of companies' credibility, respect, fairness, and pride/camaraderie. **Remarks:** Specific scores not provided. Ranking includes companies that have more than 10,000 employees. Also notes number of employees and overall rank in the *100 Best Companies to Work For*. **Number listed:** 38

1. Google Inc.
2. Wegmans Food Markets Inc.
3. Edward Jones
4. Recreational Equipment Inc. (REI)
5. Chesapeake Energy
6. United Services Automobile Association (USAA)
7. QUALCOMM Inc.
8. Whole Foods Market Inc.
9. Baptist Health South Florida
10. Intel Corp.

Source: *Fortune*, 100 Best Companies to Work For (annual), http://www.fortune.com, February 6, 2012.

1359 ■ AMERICA'S BEST MID-SIZED COMPANIES TO WORK FOR, 2012

Ranked by: Score based on employee surveys as well as evaluation of companies' credibility, respect, fairness, and pride/camaraderie. **Remarks:** Specific scores not provided. Ranking includes companies that have 2,500 to 10,000 employees. Also notes number of employees and overall rank in the *100 Best Companies to Work For*. **Number listed:** 29

1. SAS Institute Inc.

2. NetApp Inc.
3. Quicken Loans Inc.
4. Zappos.com Inc.
5. Kimpton Hotels & Restaurants
6. JM Family Enterprises Inc.
7. Intuit
8. Robert W. Baird & Co.
9. The Container Store
10. Burns & McDonnell

Source: *Fortune*, 100 Best Companies to Work For (annual), http://www.fortune.com, February 6, 2012.

1360 ■ AMERICA'S BEST SMALL COMPANIES TO WORK FOR, 2012

Ranked by: Score based on employee surveys as well as evaluation of companies' credibility, respect, fairness, and pride/camaraderie. **Remarks:** Specific scores not provided. Ranking includes companies that have fewer than 2,500 employees. Also notes number of employees and overall rank in the *100 Best Companies to Work For*. **Number listed:** 32

1. The Boston Consulting Group Inc.
2. Camden Property Trust
3. CHG Healthcare Services
4. Mercedes-Benz USA
5. DPR Construction Inc.
6. DreamWorks Animation SKG Inc.
7. NuStar Energy
8. Alston & Bird LLP
9. Ultimate Software
10. PCL Construction

Source: *Fortune*, 100 Best Companies to Work For (annual), http://www.fortune.com, February 6, 2012.

1361 ■ FASTEST-DECLINING U.S. COMPANIES, 2010-2011

Ranked by: Annual change in rank in the Forbes 2000. **Number listed:** 5

1. Tenet Healthcare, with -905 rank positions
2. SAIC, -799
3. Computer Sciences Corp., -695
4. Hudson City Bancorp, -664
5. Micron Technology, -588

Source: *Forbes*, Forbes 2000 (annual), May 7, 2012, p. 122.

1362 ■ FASTEST-GROWING COMPANIES BY FIVE-YEAR PROFIT GROWTH, 2006-2011

Ranked by: Five-year growth in earnings per share, in percent. **Remarks:** Also notes overall rank in the *Fortune 500*. **Number listed:** 20

1. Mastercard, with 109.3%
2. CF Industries Holdings, 105.5%
3. Celgene, 73.7%
4. Apple Inc., 64.9%
5. Biogen Idec Inc., 51.6%
6. Pitney Bowes, 45.4%
7. Navistar International, 40.6%
8. TRW Automotive Holdings, 38.8%
9. Symantec, 38.3%

10. INTL FCStone, 36.7%

Source: *Fortune*, Fortune 500 (annual), May 21, 2012, p. F-30.

1363 ■ FASTEST-GROWING COMPANIES BY FIVE-YEAR REVENUE GROWTH, 2006-2011

Ranked by: Five-year growth in revenue, in percent. **Remarks:** Also notes overall rank in the *Fortune 500*. **Number listed:** 20

1. INTL FCStone, with 274.3%
2. Icahn Enterprises LP, 51.7%
3. CenturyLink, 44.4%
4. Apple Inc., 41.2%
5. Mylan Inc., 37.3%
6. Amazon.com Inc., 35%
7. BlackRock, 34.1%
8. Cognizant Technology Solutions Corp., 33.9%
9. Las Vegas Sands Corp., 33.3%
10. Catalyst Health Solutions, 33.2%

Source: *Fortune*, Fortune 500 (annual), May 21, 2012, p. F-30.

1364 ■ FASTEST-GROWING COMPANIES BY ONE-YEAR PROFIT GROWTH, 2010-2011

Ranked by: Annual growth in earnings per share, in percent. **Remarks:** Also notes overall rank in the *Fortune 500*. **Number listed:** 20

1. Allergan, with 158,321.1%
2. Susser Holdings, 5,260%
3. CVR Energy, 2,362.5%
4. Con-Way, 2,157.1%
5. Huntsman, 827.3%
6. Pepco Holdings, 714.3%
7. Navistar International, 642.3%
8. Merck & Co., Inc., 621.4%
9. AES, 600%
10. HollyFrontier, 561.9%

Source: *Fortune*, Fortune 500 (annual), May 21, 2012, p. F-30.

1365 ■ FASTEST-GROWING COMPANIES BY ONE-YEAR REVENUE GROWTH, 2010-2011

Ranked by: Annual growth in revenue, in percent. **Remarks:** Also notes overall rank in the *Fortune 500*. **Number listed:** 20

1. CenturyLink, with 118%
2. Global Partners, 90.2%
3. HollyFrontier, 85.5%
4. Alpha Natural Resources, 81.5%
5. World Fuel Services, 81%
6. Rock-Tenn, 79.9%
7. EOG Resources, 66%
7. Apple Inc., 66%
9. INTL FCStone, 60.8%
10. United Continental Holdings, 59.8%

Source: *Fortune*, Fortune 500 (annual), May 21, 2012, p. F-30.

1366 ■ FASTEST-GROWING COMPANIES BY TEN-YEAR PROFIT GROWTH, 2001-2011

Ranked by: Ten-year growth in earnings per share, in percent. **Remarks:** Also notes overall rank in the *Fortune 500*. **Number listed:** 20

1. Steel Dynamics, with 52.9%
2. Gilead Sciences, 49.2%
3. Advance Auto Parts, 44.4%
4. Ingram Micro, 44%
5. Avnet, 42%
6. Cognizant Technology Solutions Corp., 41.1%
6. Devon Energy, 41.1%
8. eBay Inc., 40.9%
9. Harris Corp., 39.9%
10. Fluor Corp., 39.1%

Source: *Fortune*, Fortune 500 (annual), May 21, 2012, p. F-30.

1367 ■ FASTEST-GROWING COMPANIES BY TEN-YEAR REVENUE GROWTH, 2001-2011

Ranked by: Ten-year growth in revenue, in percent. **Remarks:** Also notes overall rank in the *Fortune 500*. **Number listed:** 20

1. World Fuel Services Corp., with 36.6%
2. Apple Inc., 35.1%
3. eBay Inc., 31.6%
4. Amazon.com Inc., 31.5%
5. Enterprise Products Partners LP, 30.1%
6. HollyFrontier, 29.8%
7. Freeport-McMoRan Copper & Gold Inc., 27.5%
8. ConocoPhillips, 25.7%
9. National Oilwell Varco Inc., 23.7%
10. Valero Energy, 23.6%

Source: *Fortune*, Fortune 500 (annual), May 21, 2012, p. F-30.

1368 ■ FASTEST-GROWING U.S. COMPANIES, 2010-2011

Ranked by: Annual change in rank in the Forbes 2000. **Number listed:** 5

1. American Capital Agency, with 993 rank positions
2. Ventas, 855
3. MGM Mirage, 666
4. Continental Resources, 593
5. Concho Resources, 584

Source: *Forbes*, Forbes 2000 (annual), May 7, 2012, p. 122.

1369 ■ LARGEST COMPANIES IN THE U.S. BY EMPLOYEES, 2010

Ranked by: Total number of employees. **Remarks:** Also notes contact information for headquarters, number of employees at headquarters, revenue, rank by revenue, and primary SIC code. **Number listed:** 5000

1. Wal-Mart Stores Inc., with 2,100,000 employees
2. United Parcel Service Inc. (UPS), 414,500
3. International Business Machines Corp. (IBM), 399,409
4. McDonald's Restaurant Operations Inc., 390,000
4. McDonald's USA LLC, 390,000
6. McDonald's Corp., 385,000
7. Yum! Brands Inc., 378,000
8. Compass Group USA Investments LLP, 360,000
9. Express Services Inc., 357,735

10. Target Corp., 351,000

Source: *Business Rankings*, (annual), Dun & Bradstreet Inc., 2011, p. II.1+.

1370 ■ LARGEST COMPANIES IN THE U.S. BY SALES, 2010

Ranked by: Revenue, in dollars. **Remarks:** Also notes contact information for headquarters, number of employees at headquarters and overall, rank by employees, and primary SIC code. **Number listed:** 5000

1. Wal-Mart Stores Inc., with $408,214,000,000
2. Chevron Corp., $204,928,000,000
3. ConocoPhillips, $198,655,000,000
4. General Motors Co., $135,592,000,000
5. Ford Motor Co., $128,954,000,000
6. Hewlett-Packard Co., $126,033,000,000
7. AT&T Inc., $124,280,000,000
8. McKesson Corp., $108,702,000,000
9. Verizon Communications Inc., $106,565,000,000
10. International Business Machines Corp. (IBM), $99,870,000,000

Source: *Business Rankings*, (annual), Dun & Bradstreet Inc., 2011, p. I.1+.

1371 ■ LARGEST CORPORATIONS IN THE U.S. BY REVENUE, 2010

Ranked by: Revenue, in millions of U.S. dollars. **Remarks:** Also notes headquarters city and overall rank in the *Global 500*. Ranking is available online only, not in print. **Number listed:** 133

1. Wal-Mart Stores Inc., with $421,849 million
2. Exxon Mobil Corp., $354,674
3. Chevron Corp., $196,337
4. ConocoPhillips, $184,966
5. Fannie Mae, $153,825
6. General Electric Co., $151,628
7. Berkshire Hathaway Inc., $136,185
8. General Motors Co., $135,592
9. Bank of America Corp., $134,194
10. Ford Motor Co., $128,954

Source: *Fortune*, Global 500 (annual), http://www.fortune.com, July 25, 2011.

1372 ■ LARGEST PUBLIC COMPANIES IN THE U.S. BY EMPLOYEES, 2010

Ranked by: Total number of employees. **Remarks:** Also notes contact information for headquarters, number of employees at headquarters, revenue, rank by revenue, and primary SIC code. **Number listed:** 5000

1. Wal-Mart Stores Inc., with 2,100,000 employees
2. United Parcel Service Inc. (UPS), 414,500
3. International Business Machines Corp. (IBM), 399,409
4. McDonald's Corp., 385,000
5. Yum! Brands Inc., 378,000
6. Target Corp., 351,000
7. The Kroger Co., 334,000
8. Hewlett-Packard Co., 324,600

9. The Home Depot Inc., 317,000
10. General Electric Co., 306,304

Source: *Business Rankings*, (annual), Dun & Bradstreet Inc., 2011, p. VIII.1+.

1373 ■ LARGEST PUBLIC COMPANIES IN THE U.S. BY SALES, 2010

Ranked by: Revenue, in dollars. **Remarks:** Also notes contact information for headquarters, number of employees at headquarters and overall, rank by employees, and primary SIC code. **Number listed:** 4204

1. Wal-Mart Stores Inc., with $408,214,000,000
2. Chevron Corp., $204,928,000,000
3. ConocoPhillips, $198,655,000,000
4. Ford Motor Co., $128,954,000,000
5. Hewlett-Packard Co., $126,033,000,000
6. AT&T Inc., $124,280,000,000
7. McKesson Corp., $108,702,000,000
8. Verizon Communications Inc., $106,565,000,000
9. International Business Machines Corp. (IBM), $99,870,000,000
10. Cardinal Health Inc., $98,502,800,000

Source: *Business Rankings*, (annual), Dun & Bradstreet Inc., 2011, p. VII.1+.

1374 ■ LARGEST U.S. COMPANIES BY ASSETS, 2011

Ranked by: Assets, in millions of dollars. **Number listed:** 100

1. Fannie Mae, with $3,221,972 million
2. Bank of America Corp., $2,264,909
3. Freddie Mac, $2,261,780
4. J. P. Morgan Chase & Co., $2,117,605
5. Citigroup Inc., $1,913,902
6. Wells Fargo & Co., $1,258,128
7. Goldman Sachs Group Inc., $911,332
8. Morgan Stanley, $807,698
9. General Electric Co., $751,216
10. MetLife Inc., $730,906

Source: *Hoover's Handbook of American Business*, (annual), Hoover's Inc., 2012.

1375 ■ LARGEST U.S. COMPANIES BY EMPLOYEES, 2011

Ranked by: Number of employees. **Number listed:** 300

1. Wal-Mart Stores Inc., with 2,100,000 employees
2. U.S. Postal Service, 583,908
3. Kelly Services Inc., 538,000
4. International Business Machines Corp. (IBM), 426,751
5. United Parcel Service Inc. (UPS), 400,600
6. McDonald's Corp., 400,000
7. Yum! Brands Inc., 378,000
8. Target Corp., 355,000
9. The Kroger Co., 338,000
10. Hewlett-Packard Co., 324,600

Source: *Hoover's Handbook of American Business*, (annual), Hoover's Inc., 2012, p. 8a-9a.

1376 ■ LARGEST U.S. COMPANIES OVERALL, 2011

Ranked by: Score based on revenue, profits, assets, and market capitalization. **Remarks:** Specific scores not provided. Also notes rank in the overall *Forbes 2000* and figures for each criterion. **Number listed:** 524

1. Exxon Mobil Corp.
2. J. P. Morgan Chase & Co.
3. General Electric Co.
4. Berkshire Hathaway Inc.
5. Wells Fargo & Co.
6. Chevron Corp.
7. Citigroup Inc.
8. Wal-Mart Stores Inc.
9. Apple Inc.
10. ConocoPhillips

Source: *Forbes*, Forbes 2000 (annual), http://www.forbes.com, May 7, 2012.

1377 ■ LARGEST U.S. COMPANIES BY SALES, 2011

Ranked by: Sales, in millions of dollars. **Number listed:** 300

1. Wal-Mart Stores Inc., with $421,849 million
2. Exxon Mobil Corp., $383,221
3. Chevron Corp., $204,928
4. ConocoPhillips, $198,655
5. Fannie Mae, $153,825
6. General Electric Co., $150,211
7. Berkshire Hathaway Inc., $136,185
8. General Motors Corp., $135,592
9. Bank of America Corp., $134,194
10. Ford Motor Co., $128,954

Source: *Hoover's Handbook of American Business*, (annual), Hoover's Inc., 2012, p. 2a-3a.

1378 ■ LARGEST U.S. CORPORATIONS BY REVENUE, 2011

Ranked by: Revenue, in millions of dollars. **Remarks:** Also notes location; rank for previous year; profits; profit growth; assets; stockholders' equity; market value; earnings per share; return to investors; profits as a percentage of revenue, assets, and stockholders' equity; and rank by each criterion. Only the first 500 companies are included in the print magazine; the remaining 500 (known together as the *Fortune 1,000*) are avail **Number listed:** 500

1. Exxon Mobil Corp., with $452,926 million
2. Wal-Mart Stores Inc., $446,950
3. Chevron Corp., $245,621
4. ConocoPhillips, $237,272
5. General Motors Co., $150,276
6. General Electric Co., $147,616
7. Berkshire Hathaway Inc., $143,688
8. Fannie Mae, $137,451
9. Ford Motor Co., $136,264
10. Hewlett-Packard Co., $127,245

Source: *Fortune*, Fortune 500 (annual), May 21, 2012, p. F-1-F-26.

1379 ■ MOST ADMIRED COMPANIES IN THE UNITED STATES, 2012

Ranked by: Score based on a survey of executives, directors, and securities analysts of companies within their own industry.

Remarks: List is available online only, not in print. Also notes headquarters. **Number listed:** 251

1. Apple Inc., with 8.42 points
2. McDonald's Corp., 8.27
3. Philip Morris International, 8.25
4. Walt Disney Co., 8.14
5. Procter & Gamble Co., 8.10
6. Chevron Corp., 7.93
7. Caterpillar, 7.89
8. Exxon Mobil Corp., 7.87
9. Starbucks, 7.85
10. Intel Corp., 7.80

Source: *Fortune*, World's Most Admired Companies (annual), http://www.fortune.com, March 19, 2012.

1380 ■ MOST PROFITABLE COMPANIES BY RETURN ON REVENUE, 2011

Ranked by: Profits as a percentage of revenue. **Remarks:** Also notes overall rank in the *Fortune 500*. **Number listed:** 20

1. Devon Energy Corp., with 40.9%
2. Visa Inc., 39.7%
2. MGM Resorts International, 39.7%
4. Corning Inc., 35.6%
5. Gilead Sciences Inc., 33.4%
6. Microsoft Corp., 33.1%
7. QUALCOMM Inc., 28.5%
8. MasterCard Inc., 28.4%
9. Occidental Petroleum, 28%
10. eBay Inc., 27.7%

Source: *Fortune*, Fortune 500 (annual), May 21, 2012, p. F-31.

1381 ■ MOST PROFITABLE COMPANIES BY RETURN ON SHAREHOLDERS' EQUITY, 2011

Ranked by: Profits as a percentage of shareholders' equity. **Remarks:** Also notes overall rank in the *Fortune 500*. **Number listed:** 20

1. Philip Morris International Inc., with 3,751.5%
2. Limited Brands, 620.5%
3. Energy Transfer Equity LP, 579.3%
4. Lockheed Martin Corp., 265.2%
5. Ford Motor Co., 134.5%
6. The Western Union Co., 130.2%
7. Boeing Co., 114.3%
8. Colgate-Palmolive Co., 102.4%
9. Altria Group Inc., 92.1%
10. International Business Machines Corp. (IBM), 78.7%

Source: *Fortune*, Fortune 500 (annual), May 21, 2012, p. F-31.

1382 ■ MOST PROFITABLE COMPANIES BY TOTAL PROFITS, 2011

Ranked by: Profits, in millions of dollars. **Remarks:** Also notes overall rank in the *Fortune 500*. **Number listed:** 20

1. Exxon Mobil Corp., with $41,060 million
2. Chevron Corp., $26,895
3. Apple Inc., $25,922
4. Microsoft Corp., $23,150

5. Ford Motor Co., $20,213
6. J. P. Morgan Chase & Co., $18,976
7. American International Group, $17,798
8. Wells Fargo, $15,869
9. International Business Machines Corp. (IBM), $15,855
10. Wal-Mart Stores Inc., $15,699

Source: *Fortune*, Fortune 500 (annual), May 21, 2012, p. F-31.

1383 ■ MOST PROFITABLE U.S. COMPANIES, 2011

Ranked by: Net income, in millions of dollars. **Number listed:** 300

1. Exxon Mobil Corp., with $30,460 million
2. Apple Inc., $25,922
3. Microsoft Corp., $23,150
4. AT&T Inc., $19,864
5. Chevron Corp., $19,024
6. J. P. Morgan Chase & Co., $17,370
7. Wal-Mart Stores Inc., $16,389
8. International Business Machines Corp. (IBM), $14,833
9. Johnson & Johnson, $13,334
10. Berkshire Hathaway Inc., $12,967

Source: *Hoover's Handbook of American Business*, (annual), Hoover's Inc., 2012, p. 4a-5a.

1384 ■ MOST VALUABLE U.S. COMPANIES, 2011

Ranked by: Market value as of March 2011, in millions of U.S. dollars. **Remarks:** Also notes rank for previous year, sector, revenue, net income, assets, number of employees, share price, price-to-earning ratio, dividend yield, and fiscal year-end. **Number listed:** 500

1. Exxon Mobil Corp., with $417,166.7 million
2. Apple Inc., $321,072.1
3. Chevron Corp., $215,780.6
4. Microsoft Corp., $213,336.4
5. General Electric Co., $212,917.8
6. Berkshire Hathaway Inc., $206,671.3
7. International Business Machines Corp. (IBM), $198,869.8
8. J. P. Morgan Chase & Co., $183,639.7
9. Wal-Mart Stores Inc., $181,716.7
10. AT&T Inc., $180,948.8

Source: *Financial Times*, FT 500 (annual), http://www.ft.com, June 24, 2011.

1385 ■ MOST VALUABLE U.S. COMPANIES, 2011

Ranked by: Market value, in millions of dollars. **Number listed:** 240

1. Exxon Mobil Corp., with $364,064 million
2. Apple Inc., $354,352
3. Microsoft Corp., $217,776
4. Berkshire Hathaway Inc., $197,672
5. Wal-Mart Stores Inc., $197,142
6. General Electric Co., $194,155
7. Google Inc., $188,747
8. Chevron Corp., $183,183

9. International Business Machines Corp. (IBM), $180,220
10. Procter & Gamble Co., $175,816

Source: *Hoover's Handbook of American Business*, (annual), Hoover's Inc., 2012, p. 6a-7a.

1386 ■ STATES WITH THE FEWEST FIRMS, 2009

Ranked by: Number of employer firms. **Remarks:** Also notes share of national total. **Number listed:** 51

1. Alaska, with 17,306 firms
2. North Dakota, 20,560
3. Wyoming, 21,861
4. Vermont, 21,863
5. South Dakota, 25,515
6. Delaware, 25,980
7. Washington DC, 28,633
8. Hawaii, 31,242
9. Rhode Island, 33,024
10. West Virginia, 35,895

Source: *State Rankings*, (annual), CQ Press, 2011, p. 110.

1387 ■ STATES WITH THE MOST FIRMS, 2009

Ranked by: Number of employer firms. **Number listed:** 51

1. California, with 1,219,760 firms
2. New York, 494,607
3. Florida, 464,190
4. Texas, 449,677
5. Illinois, 302,293
6. Pennsylvania, 285,010
7. New Jersey, 235,184
8. Ohio, 227,429
9. Georgia, 211,334
10. Michigan, 206,883

Source: *State Rankings*, (annual), CQ Press, 2011, p. 110.

1388 ■ TOP COMPANIES BY FIVE-YEAR RETURN TO SHAREHOLDERS, 2006-2011

Ranked by: Five-year total return to shareholders, in percent. **Remarks:** Also notes overall rank in the *Fortune 500*. **Number listed:** 20

1. CF Industries Holdings, with 42%
2. Apple Inc., 36.7%
3. Amazon.com Inc., 34.4%
4. Dollar Tree Stores Inc., 32.9%
5. MasterCard, 30.9%
6. FMC Technologies, 29%
7. Ross Stores, 28.1%
8. Cummins Inc., 26.2%
9. Goodrich, 24.1%
10. W. W. Grainger, 24%

Source: *Fortune*, Fortune 500 (annual), May 21, 2012, p. F-32.

1389 ■ TOP COMPANIES BY ONE-YEAR RETURN TO SHAREHOLDERS, 2010-2011

Ranked by: Annual total return to shareholders, in percent. **Remarks:** Also notes overall rank in the *Fortune 500*. **Number listed:** 20

1. El Paso Corp., with 93.6%
2. Wellcare Health Plans, 73.7%
3. MasterCard, 66.7%
4. Biogen Idec, 64.1%
5. Susser Holdings, 63.3%
6. Oneok, 61.3%
7. Humana, 61.1%
8. Dish Network, 56.6%
9. Centene, 56.2%
10. Targa Resources, 56.1%

Source: *Fortune*, Fortune 500 (annual), May 21, 2012, p. F-32.

1390 ■ TOP COMPANIES BY TEN-YEAR RETURN TO SHAREHOLDERS, 2001-2011

Ranked by: Ten-year total return to shareholders, in percent. **Remarks:** Also notes overall rank in the *Fortune 500*. **Number listed:** 20

1. INTL FCStone, with 43.9%
2. Apple Inc., 43.5%
3. Cliffs Natural Resources Inc., 40.1%
4. Cognizant Technology Solutions Corp., 34.1%
5. Amazon.com Inc., 31.9%
6. Tenneco Inc., 30.7%
7. FMC Technologies, 29.6%
8. Crown Holdings, 29.5%
9. Precision Castparts, 28.1%
10. HollyFrontier, 28%

Source: *Fortune*, Fortune 500 (annual), May 21, 2012, p. F-32.

1391 ■ TOP MISCELLANEOUS *FORTUNE 500* COMPANIES, 2011

Ranked by: Revenue, in millions of dollars. **Remarks:** Also notes overall rank in the *Fortune 500;* profits; profits as a percentage of revenue; stockholders' equity; and rank by each criterion. **Number listed:** 6

1. 3M Co., with $29,611 million
2. Spectrum Group International Inc., $7,203
3. Mattel Inc., $6,266
4. Mohawk Industries Inc., $5,642
5. Owens Corning, $5,335
6. Harley-Davidson Inc., $5,312

Source: *Fortune*, Fortune 500 (annual), May 21, 2012, p. F-40.

1392 ■ TOP U.S. CORPORATIONS BY EMPLOYEES, 2011

Ranked by: Total number of employees. **Remarks:** Also notes overall rank in the *Fortune 500*. **Number listed:** 20

1. Wal-Mart Stores Inc., with 2,200,000 employees
2. International Business Machines Corp. (IBM), 433,362
3. McDonald's Corp., 420,000
4. Target Corp., 365,000
5. Hewlett-Packard Co., 349,600
6. The Kroger Co., 339,000
7. United Parcel Service Inc. (UPS), 310,010
8. General Electric Co., 301,000
9. PepsiCo Inc., 297,000

10. Sears Holdings Corp., 293,000

Source: *Fortune*, Fortune 500 (annual), May 21, 2012, p. F-32.

1393 ■ TOP U.S. CORPORATIONS BY EQUITY, 2011

Ranked by: Equity, in millions of dollars. **Remarks:** Also notes overall rank in the *Fortune 500*. **Number listed:** 20

1. Bank of America Corp., with $230,101 million
2. J. P. Morgan Chase & Co., $183,573
3. Citigroup Inc., $177,806
4. Berkshire Hathaway Inc., $164,850
5. Exxon Mobil Corp., $154,396
6. Wells Fargo & Co., $140,241
7. Chevron Corp., $121,382
8. General Electric Co., $116,438
9. AT&T Inc., $105,534
10. American International Group, $104,951

Source: *Fortune*, Fortune 500 (annual), May 21, 2012, p. F-32.

1394 ■ TOP U.S. CORPORATIONS BY MARKET VALUE, 2012

Ranked by: Market capitalization, in millions of dollars, as of March 2012. **Remarks:** Also notes overall rank in the *Fortune 500*. **Number listed:** 20

1. Apple Inc., with $568,615.1 million
2. Exxon Mobil Corp., $405,714.1
3. Microsoft Corp., $269,511.6
4. International Business Machines Corp. (IBM), $241,314.5
5. Chevron Corp., $211,238.9
6. General Electric Co., $211,096.1
7. Google Inc., $210,835
8. Wal-Mart Stores Inc., $207,064
9. Berkshire Hathaway Inc., $202,095.1
10. AT&T Inc., $185,036.3

Source: *Fortune*, Fortune 500 (annual), May 21, 2012, p. F-32.

1395 ■ TOP U.S. CORPORATIONS BY REVENUE PER ASSET DOLLAR, 2011

Ranked by: Revenue per dollar of assets, in dollars. **Remarks:** Also notes overall rank in the *Fortune 500*. **Number listed:** 20

1. INTL FCStone, with $28.60
2. Spectrum Group International Inc., $19.40
3. World Fuel Services Corp., $9.40
4. Global Partners LP, $7.90
5. TravelCenters of America LLC, $7.80
6. Core-Mark Holding Co., $7.10
7. AmerisourceBergen Corp., $5.40
8. C. H. Robinson Worldwide, $4.80
9. Tech Data, $4.60
10. Cardinal Health Inc., $4.50
10. Nash Finch Co., $4.50

Source: *Fortune*, Fortune 500 (annual), May 21, 2012, p. F-31.

1396 ■ TOP U.S. CORPORATIONS BY REVENUE PER EMPLOYEE, 2011

Ranked by: Revenue per employee, in millions of dollars. **Remarks:** Also notes overall rank in the *Fortune 500*. **Number listed:** 20

1. INTL FCStone, with $83.5 million
2. Global Partners LP, $56.2
3. Spectrum Group International Inc., $40.7
4. Host Hotels & Resorts Inc., $22.8
5. Fannie Mae, $19.6
6. World Fuel Services Corp., $19.3
7. Freddie Mac, $18.1
8. Plains All American Pipeline LP, $9
9. AmerisourceBergen Corp., $8.1
10. ConocoPhillips, $8

Source: *Fortune*, Fortune 500 (annual), May 21, 2012, p. F-31.

1397 ■ TOP U.S. CORPORATIONS BY REVENUE PER EQUITY DOLLAR, 2011

Ranked by: Revenue per dollar of equity, in dollars. **Remarks:** Also notes overall rank in the *Fortune 500*. **Number listed:** 20

1. INTL FCStone, with $254.80
2. Energy Transfer Equity LP, $154.10
3. Philip Morris International, $135.80
4. First Data, $110.90
5. US Airways Group Inc., $87
6. Spectrum Group International Inc., $78.90
7. Limited Brands, $75.60
8. Sunoco, $51.20
9. Global Partners LP, $47.10
10. Lockheed Martin Corp., $46.60

Source: *Fortune*, Fortune 500 (annual), May 21, 2012, p. F-31.

Corporations—Alabama

1398 ■ ALABAMA'S LARGEST COMPANIES OVERALL, 2011

Ranked by: Score based on revenue, profits, assets, and market capitalization. **Remarks:** Specific scores not provided. Also notes overall rank in the *Forbes 2000* and figures for each criterion. **Number listed:** 2

1. Regions Financial Corp.
2. Protective Life Corp.

Source: *Forbes*, Forbes 2000 (annual), http://www.forbes.com, May 7, 2012.

1399 ■ ALABAMA'S LARGEST PRIVATE COMPANIES, 2010

Ranked by: Revenue, in billions of dollars. **Remarks:** Also notes business segment, number of employees, and overall rank in the *America's Largest Private Companies* list. Ranking is available online only, not in print. **Number listed:** 2

1. Drummond Co., with $3.03 billion
2. Ebsco Industries Inc., $2.26

Source: *Forbes*, America's Largest Private Companies (annual), http://www.forbes.com, December 5, 2011.

1400 ■ BEST LARGE COMPANIES TO WORK FOR IN ALABAMA, 2011

Ranked by: Score based on employee surveys. **Remarks:** Specific scores not provided. To qualify, companies must have at least 250 employees. **Number listed:** 5

1. Baker Donelson
2. Edward Jones
3. Alacare Home Health & Hospice
4. America's First Federal Credit Union
5. Baptist Health System Inc.

Source: *Best Companies Group*, Best Places to Work in Alabama (annual), http://www.bestcompaniesal.com, August 2011.

1401 ■ BEST MEDIUM-SIZED COMPANIES TO WORK FOR IN ALABAMA, 2011

Ranked by: Score based on employee surveys. **Remarks:** Specific scores not provided. To qualify, companies must have between 50 and 249 employees. **Number listed:** 5

1. CTS Inc.
2. Wilson Price Barranco Blankenship & Billingsley PC
3. Luckie & Co.
4. Premier Bank of the South
5. Medseek Inc.

Source: *Best Companies Group*, Best Places to Work in Alabama (annual), http://www.bestcompaniesal.com, August 2011.

1402 ■ BEST SMALL COMPANIES TO WORK FOR IN ALABAMA, 2011

Ranked by: Score based on employee surveys. **Remarks:** Specific scores not provided. To qualify, companies must have between 15 and 49 employees. **Number listed:** 4

1. Proventix
2. RealtyBid International
3. ITAC Solutions
4. AlaCOMP/Business Insurance Group

Source: *Best Companies Group*, Best Places to Work in Alabama (annual), http://www.bestcompaniesal.com, August 2011.

1403 ■ LARGEST COMPANIES IN ALABAMA BY EMPLOYEES, 2010

Ranked by: Number of employees at headquarters. **Remarks:** Also notes contact information for headquarters, total number of employees, revenue, rank by revenue, and primary SIC code. **Number listed:** 119

1. BE & K Construction Co., with 6,000 employees
2. Health Care Authority of the City of Huntsville, 3,500
3. DCH Healthcare Authority, 3,167
4. Mobile Infirmary Association, 2,938
5. Infirmary Health System Inc., 2,900
6. Children's Hospital of Alabama, 2,400
7. Honda Manufacturing of Alabama LLC, 2,300
7. Houston County Healthcare Authority, 2,300
9. Blue Cross & Blue Shield of Alabama, 2,273
10. SCI Enclosures LLC, 2,000

Source: *Business Rankings*, (annual), Dun & Bradstreet Inc., 2011, p. IV.1-IV.3.

1404 ■ LARGEST COMPANIES IN ALABAMA BY SALES, 2010

Ranked by: Revenue, in dollars. **Remarks:** Also notes contact information for headquarters, number of employees at headquarters and overall, rank by employees, and primary SIC code. **Number listed:** 129

1. Alabama Power Co., with $5,976,000,000
2. Triangle Aggregates LLC, $3,000,000,000
3. Vulcan Materials Co. , $2,558,862,000
4. HealthSouth Corp., $1,999,300,000
5. Energen Corp., $1,578,534,000
6. American Cancer Socity Mid-South Division Inc., $956,159,000
7. Piggly Wiggly Alabama Distributing Co., $837,661,349
8. Wolverine Tube Inc., $815,801,000
9. Alabama Department of Mental Health, $700,000,000
10. Caddell Construction Co., $690,934,154

Source: *Business Rankings*, (annual), Dun & Bradstreet Inc., 2011, p. III.1-III.3.

Corporations—Alaska

1405 ■ LARGEST COMPANIES IN ALASKA BY EMPLOYEES, 2010

Ranked by: Number of employees at headquarters. **Remarks:** Also notes contact information for headquarters, total number of employees, revenue, rank by revenue, and primary SIC code. **Number listed:** 48

1. Alaskan Professional Employers, with 1,420 employees
2. USPHS Alaska Native Medical Center, 1,200
3. Banner Health System, 1,000
4. Wells Fargo Bank Alaska NA, 954
5. BP Transportation (Alaska) Inc., 830
6. Nabors Alaska Drilling Inc., 800
7. Coeur Alaska Inc., 767
8. Doyon Universal Services LLC, 730
9. Ketchikan General Hospital Foundation, 700
10. Veco Corp., 698

Source: *Business Rankings*, (annual), Dun & Bradstreet Inc., 2011, p. IV.4-IV.5.

1406 ■ LARGEST COMPANIES IN ALASKA BY SALES, 2010

Ranked by: Revenue, in dollars. **Remarks:** Also notes contact information for headquarters, number of employees at headquarters and overall, rank by employees, and primary SIC code. **Number listed:** 50

1. Bristol Bay Native Corp., with $1,294,854,000
2. Nana Regional Corp., $1,257,803,772
3. Chugach Alaska Corp., $1,105,264,921
4. Petro Star Inc., $992,067,000
5. General Communication Inc., $651,250,000
6. GCI Communication Corp., $440,000,000
7. Chugach Government Services Inc., $364,736,247
8. Alaska Communications Systems Group Inc., $341,524,000
9. Chugach Electric Association Inc., $290,247,308
10. Chugach Management Services Inc., $274,336,106

Source: *Business Rankings*, (annual), Dun & Bradstreet Inc., 2011, p. III.4-III.5.

Corporations—Argentina

1407 ■ BEST COMPANIES TO WORK FOR IN ARGENTINA, 2011

Ranked by: Score based on the relationships between employees and management, employees and their jobs/company, and employees and coworkers. **Remarks:** Specific scores not provided. **Number listed:** 14

1. Tarjeta Naranja
2. Santander Rio
3. Movistar
4. Fiat Argentina
5. Citibank Argentina
6. Atento Argentina
7. Arcos Dorados Argentina
8. Dow Argentina
9. Sodimac
10. Nextel Argentina

Source: *Great Place to Work Institute Inc.*, Best Places to Work in Argentina (annual), 2011.

Corporations—Arizona

1408 ■ ARIZONA'S LARGEST COMPANIES OVERALL, 2011

Ranked by: Score based on revenue, profits, assets, and market capitalization. **Remarks:** Specific scores not provided. Also notes overall rank in the *Forbes 2000* and figures for each criterion. **Number listed:** 8

1. Freeport-McMoRan Copper & Gold Inc.
2. Republic Services Inc.
3. Avnet Inc.
4. PETsMART Inc.
5. Apollo Group Inc.
6. Pinnacle West Capital Corp.
7. US Airways Group Inc.
8. Microchip Technology Inc.

Source: *Forbes*, Forbes 2000 (annual), http://www.forbes.com, May 7, 2012.

1409 ■ ARIZONA'S LARGEST EMPLOYERS, 2011

Ranked by: Number of Arizona employees. **Remarks:** Also notes type of company. **Number listed:** 100

1. Wal-Mart Stores Inc., with 31,637 employees
2. Banner Health, 28,993
3. Wells Fargo & Co., 13,859
4. Bank of America Corp., 13,000
5. McDonald's Corp., 12,770
6. Raytheon Co., 12,000
7. J. P. Morgan Chase & Co., 11,600
8. Apollo Group Inc., 11,031
9. Intel Corp., 11,000
10. The Kroger Co., 10,767

Source: *The Arizona Republic*, Republic 100 (annual), http://www.azcentral.com, April 16, 2012.

1410 ■ ARIZONA'S LARGEST PRIVATE COMPANIES, 2010

Ranked by: Revenue, in billions of dollars. **Remarks:** Also notes business segment, number of employees, and overall rank in the

America's Largest Private Companies list. Ranking is available online only, not in print. **Number listed:** 2

1. Discount Tire Co., with $3 billion
2. Services Group of America Inc., $2.6

Source: *Forbes*, America's Largest Private Companies (annual), http://www.forbes.com, December 5, 2011.

1411 ■ LARGEST COMPANIES IN ARIZONA BY EMPLOYEES, 2010

Ranked by: Number of employees at headquarters. **Remarks:** Also notes contact information for headquarters, total number of employees, revenue, rank by revenue, and primary SIC code. **Number listed:** 139

1. General Dynamics C4 Systems Inc., with 3,400 employees
2. Paramount Building Solutions LLC, 3,200
3. Tucson Medical Center, 2,926
4. Avnet Inc., 2,800
5. Swift Transportation Co., Inc., 2,700
6. Phoenix Virginia Health Care System PLLC, 2,500
6. TMC Healthcare, 2,500
8. Chase Bankcard Services Inc., 2,300
9. Swift Transportation Corp., 2,200
10. Insight Direct USA Inc., 2,000
10. Northern Arizona Healthcare Corp., 2,000
10. Scottsdale Healthcare Corp., 2,000
10. TriWest Healthcare Alliance Corp., 2,000

Source: *Business Rankings*, (annual), Dun & Bradstreet Inc., 2011, p. IV.6-IV.8.

1412 ■ LARGEST COMPANIES IN ARIZONA BY SALES, 2010

Ranked by: Revenue, in dollars. **Remarks:** Also notes contact information for headquarters, number of employees at headquarters and overall, rank by employees, and primary SIC code. **Number listed:** 138

1. Avnet Inc., with $19,160,172,000
2. Freeport-McMoRan Copper & Gold Inc., $18,982,000,000
3. US Airways Inc., $12,055,000,000
4. US Airways Group Inc., $11,908,000,000
5. Republic Services Inc., $8,106,600,000
6. PETsMART Inc., $5,336,392,000
7. Southern Copper Corp., $5,149,500,000
8. Insight Enterprises Inc., $4,809,930,000
9. Banner Health, $4,676,707,000
10. Polymicro Technologies LLC, $4,000,000,000

Source: *Business Rankings*, (annual), Dun & Bradstreet Inc., 2011, p. III.6-III.8.

1413 ■ TOP *FORTUNE 500* COMPANIES IN ARIZONA, 2011

Ranked by: Revenue, in millions of dollars. **Remarks:** Also notes overall rank in the *Fortune 500*, headquarters, and number of employees. **Number listed:** 6

1. Avnet Inc., with $26,534.4 million
2. Freeport-McMoRan Copper & Gold Inc., $20,880

3. US Airways Group Inc., $13,055
4. Republic Services Inc., $8,192.9
5. PETsMART Inc., $6,113.3
6. Insight Enterprises Inc., $5,287.2

Source: *Fortune*, Fortune 500 (annual), May 21, 2012, p. F41.

Corporations—Arkansas

1414 ■ ARKANSAS' LARGEST MANUFACTURERS, 2011

Ranked by: Number of employees in Arkansas. **Remarks:** Also notes figures for previous year, contact information, Arkansas locations, top executive, and business description. **Number listed:** 20

1. Tyson Foods Inc., with 23,300 employees
2. Simmons Foods Inc., 3,238
3. O. K. Industries Inc., 2,970
4. Baldor Electric Co., 2,500
4. Georgia-Pacific LLC, 2,500
6. George's Inc., 2,300
7. Pilgrim's Pride Corp., 2,175
8. ConAgra Foods Inc., 1,970
9. Cooper Tire & Rubber Co., 1,731
10. Dassault Falcon Jet Corp., 1,700

Source: *Arkansas Business*, Largest Manufacturers, February 20, 2012.

1415 ■ ARKANSAS' LARGEST PRIVATE COMPANIES, 2011

Ranked by: Revenue, in millions of dollars. **Remarks:** Also notes rank and figures for previous year, percent change, contact information, top executive, number of employees, year established, and business description. **Number listed:** 75

1. Truman Arnold Cos., with $3,023 million
2. Stephens Inc., $1,835
3. Mountaire Corp., $1,388
4. Arkansas Blue Cross & Blue Shield, $1,273.2
5. Simmons Foods Inc., $1,252
6. Riceland Foods Inc., $1,107.8
7. Stephen LaFrance Pharmacy Inc., $1,080
8. Flash Market Inc., $1,058.7
9. RLJ McLarty Landers Automotive Holdings LLC, $1,033.5
10. Baptist Health, $962.3

Source: *Arkansas Business*, Largest 75 Private Companies (annual), May 21, 2012.

1416 ■ ARKANSAS'S LARGEST COMPANIES OVERALL, 2011

Ranked by: Score based on revenue, profits, assets, and market capitalization. **Remarks:** Specific scores not provided. Also notes overall rank in the *Forbes 2000* and figures for each criterion. **Number listed:** 5

1. Wal-Mart Stores Inc.
2. Murphy Oil Corp.
3. Tyson Foods Inc.
4. Windstream Corp.
5. Dillard's

Source: *Forbes*, Forbes 2000 (annual), http://www.forbes.com, May 7, 2012.

1417 ■ LARGEST COMPANIES IN ARKANSAS BY EMPLOYEES, 2010

Ranked by: Number of employees at headquarters. **Remarks:** Also notes contact information for headquarters, total number of employees, revenue, rank by revenue, and primary SIC code. **Number listed:** 77

1. Wal-Mart Stores Inc., with 11,700 employees
2. Mountaire Farms Inc., 4,384
3. St. Vincent Health Services Inc., 3,200
4. Fidelity Information Services Inc., 3,000
4. St. Vincent Health System, 3,000
6. Tyson Foods Inc., 2,850
7. Baptist Health, 2,800
8. J. B. Hunt Transport Inc., 2,500
9. J. B. Hunt Transport Inc. (subsidiary), 2,400
10. Arkansas Children's Hospital Research Institute Inc., 2,100

Source: *Business Rankings*, (annual), Dun & Bradstreet Inc., 2011, p. IV.9-IV.10.

1418 ■ LARGEST COMPANIES IN ARKANSAS BY SALES, 2010

Ranked by: Revenue, in dollars. **Remarks:** Also notes contact information for headquarters, number of employees at headquarters and overall, rank by employees, and primary SIC code. **Number listed:** 80

1. Wal-Mart Stores Inc., with $408,214,000,000
2. Tyson Foods Inc., $28,430,000,000
3. Murphy Oil Corp., $23,345,071,000
4. Murphy Oil USA Inc., $13,292,055,000
5. Dillard's Inc., $6,094,948,000
6. J. B. Hunt Transport Services Inc., $3,793,485,000
7. Windstream Corp., $3,712,000,000
8. J. B. Hunt Transport Inc., $3,500,000,000
9. Valor Telecommunications LLC, $3,033,300,000
10. Southwestern Energy Pipeline Co., $2,145,779,000

Source: *Business Rankings*, (annual), Dun & Bradstreet Inc., 2011, p. III.9-III.10.

1419 ■ TOP *FORTUNE 500* COMPANIES IN ARKANSAS, 2011

Ranked by: Revenue, in millions of dollars. **Remarks:** Also notes overall rank in the *Fortune 500,* headquarters, and number of employees. **Number listed:** 4

1. Wal-Mart Stores Inc., with $446,950 million
2. Tyson Foods Inc., $32,266
3. Murphy Oil Corp., $31,446.3
4. Dillard's Inc., $6,399.8

Source: *Fortune*, Fortune 500 (annual), May 21, 2012, p. F-41.

Corporations—Asia

1420 ■ LARGEST CORPORATIONS IN ASIA BY REVENUE, 2010

Ranked by: Revenue, in millions of U.S. dollars. **Remarks:** Also notes city and overall rank in the *Global 500*. Ranking is available online only, not in print. **Number listed:** 50

1. China Petroleum & Chemical Corp. (Sinopec), with $273,422 million
2. China National Petroleum Co., $240,192
3. State Grid Corp. of China, $226,294
4. Toyota Motor Corp., $221,760
5. Japan Post Holdings Co., Ltd., $203,958
6. Samsung Electronics Co., Ltd., $133,781
7. Nippon Telegraph & Telephone Corp. (NTT), $120,316
8. Hitachi Ltd., $108,766
9. Honda Motor Co., Ltd., $104,342
10. Nissan Motor Co., Ltd., $102,430

Source: *Fortune*, Global 500 (annual), http://www.fortune.com, July 25, 2011.

1421 ■ MOST PROFITABLE SMALL ASIAN COMPANIES, 2010

Ranked by: Net income, in millions of U.S. dollars. **Remarks:** To qualify for list, which is available online only, companies must have under US$1 billion in annual revenue and positive earnings growth over the past five years. **Number listed:** 200

1. Netease.com (China & Hong Kong), with $331 million
2. Mount Gibson Iron (Australia), $256
3. Polyplex (India), $237
4. Alibaba.com (China & Hong Kong), $223
5. China Dongxiang Group (China & Hong Kong), $222
6. Yantai Changyu Pioneer Wine (China & Hong Kong), $218
7. Guizhou Panjian Refined Coal (China & Hong Kong), $204
8. Wiefu High-Technology (China & Hong Kong), $203
9. 361 Degrees International (China & Hong Kong), $185
10. Zhaojin Mining Industry (China & Hong Kong), $182

Source: *Forbes Asia*, Asia's Best Under a Billion (annual), September 12, 2011.

1422 ■ MOST VALUABLE SMALL ASIAN COMPANIES, 2010

Ranked by: Market value, in millions of U.S. dollars. **Remarks:** To qualify for list, which is available online only, companies must have under US$1 billion in annual revenue and positive earnings growth over the past five years. **Number listed:** 200

1. New Oriental Education & Technology Group (China & Hong Kong), with $17,092 million
2. Zhaojin Mining Industry (China & Hong Kong), $13,096
3. Yantai Changyu Pioneer Wine (China & Hong Kong), $9,443
4. GoerTek (China & Hong Kong), $6,348
5. Alibaba.com (China & Hong Kong), $5,580
6. Netease.com (China & Hong Kong), $5,543
7. Ctrip.com International (China & Hong Kong), $5,527
8. Guizhou Panjian Refined Coal (China & Hong Kong), $5,247
9. Shandong Dong-E E-Jiao (China & Hong Kong), $4,795

10. Golden Eagle Retail (China & Hong Kong), $4,500

Source: *Forbes Asia*, Asia's Best Under a Billion (annual), September 12, 2011.

1423 ■ TOP ASIAN COMPANIES, 2011

Ranked by: Score based on profits, sales and earnings growth, and projected earnings and stock-price gains. **Remarks:** Specific scores not provided; companies are listed alphabetically, not ranked. Also notes market value, revenue, and industry. To quality, companies must be publicly traded with revenues or market capitalization of at least US$3 billion. Ranking is available online only, not in print. **Number listed:** 50

1. Adaro Energy
2. Agile Property Holdings
3. Anhui Conch Cement Co., Ltd.
4. Asia Pacific Breweries
5. Asian Paints
6. Axiata Group
7. Bank Central Asia
8. Belle International Holdings
9. Bharti Airtel Ltd.
10. Changsha Zoomlion Heavy Industry

Source: *Forbes*, Asian Fab 50 (annual), September 13, 2011.

Corporations—Asia Pacific

1424 ■ BEST SMALL ASIAN COMPANIES BY REVENUE, 2010

Ranked by: Revenue, in millions of U.S. dollars. **Remarks:** Also notes net income, market value, and industry. To qualify for list, which is available online only, companies must have under US$1 billion in annual revenue and positive earnings growth over the past five years. **Number listed:** 200

1. Fufeng Group (China/Hong Kong), with $974 million
2. Gintech Energy (Taiwan), $966
3. Changchun FAWAY Automobile Components (China/Hong Kong), $938
4. 361 Degrees International (China/Hong Kong), $845
5. Alibaba.com (China/Hong Kong), $843
6. Guizhou Panjiang Refined Coal (China/Hong Kong), $830
7. Netease.com (China/Hong Kong), $815
7. Weifu High-Technology (China/Hong Kong), $815
9. Texhong Textile Group (China/Hong Kong), $809
10. Sino-American Silicon Products (Taiwan), $773

Source: *Forbes Asia*, Asia's Best Under a Billion (annual), http://www.forbes.com, September 12, 2011.

1425 ■ FASTEST-DECLINING ASIA-PACIFIC COMPANIES, 2010-2011

Ranked by: Annual change in rank in the Forbes 2000. **Number listed:** 5

1. Acer, with -827 rank positions
2. Hanwha Corp., -800

3. Tokyo Electric Power, -679
4. Olympus, -642
5. Samsung Electromechanics, -606

Source: *Forbes*, Forbes 2000 (annual), May 7, 2012, p. 128.

1426 ■ FASTEST-GROWING ASIA-PACIFIC COMPANIES, 2010-2011

Ranked by: Annual change in rank in the Forbes 2000. **Number listed:** 5

1. Longfor Properties, with 782 rank positions
2. Tokyo Electron, 721
3. Zoomlion Heavy Industry, 676
4. SMC, 609
5. Korea Zinc, 574

Source: *Forbes*, Forbes 2000 (annual), May 7, 2012, p. 128.

1427 ■ MOST ADMIRED COMPANIES IN THE ASIA PACIFIC, 2012

Ranked by: Survey of top executives, directors, and securities analysts regarding the Fortune 1,000 companies that they admire the most, regardless of industry. **Remarks:** Specific scores not provided. List is available online only, not in print. **Number listed:** 53

1. Toyota Motor Corp.
2. Canon Inc.
3. Samsung Electronics Co., Ltd.
4. Sony Corp.
5. Honda Motor Co., Ltd.
6. Singapore Airlines Ltd.
7. Panasonic Corp.
8. Huawei Technologies
9. China Mobile Communications Corp.
10. LG Electronics Inc.

Source: *Fortune*, World's Most Admired Companies (annual), http://www.fortune.com, March 19, 2012.

Corporations—Australia

1428 ■ AUSTRALIA'S LARGEST COMPANIES OVERALL, 2011

Ranked by: Score based on revenue, profits, assets, and market capitalization. **Remarks:** Specific scores not provided. Also notes rank in the overall *Forbes 2000* and figures for each criterion. **Number listed:** 44

1. Commonwealth Bank of Australia
2. BHP Billiton Ltd.
3. Westpac Banking Corp.
4. National Australia Bank Ltd.
5. Australia & New Zealand Banking Group (ANZ)
6. Wesfarmers Ltd.
7. Telstra Corp., Ltd.
8. Woolworths Ltd.
9. QBE Insurance Group Ltd.
10. Macquarie Group Ltd.

Source: *Forbes*, Forbes 2000 (annual), http://www.forbes.com, May 7, 2012.

1429 ■ BEST COMPANIES TO WORK FOR IN AUSTRALIA, 2011

Ranked by: Score based on the relationships between employees and management, employees and their jobs/company, and employees and coworkers. **Remarks:** Specific scores not provided. **Number listed:** 50

1. Google Australia Pty., Ltd.
2. E-Web Marketing
3. NetApp Australia Pty., Ltd.
4. Juniper Networks
5. Atlassian Pty., Ltd.
6. Davidson Recruitment
7. OBS
8. Ikon Communications
9. MRWED Group
10. Altis Consulting

Source: *Great Place to Work Institute Inc.*, Best Places to Work in Australia (annual), http://www.greatplacetowork.com, June 2011.

1430 ■ BEST SMALL AUSTRALIAN COMPANIES, 2010

Ranked by: Score based on sales, net income, and market value. **Remarks:** Specific scores not provided; companies are listed alphabetically, not ranked. Also notes sales, net income, market value, and industry. To qualify for list, which is available online only, companies must have under US$1 billion in annual revenue and positive earnings growth over the past five years. **Number listed:** 12

1. ARB
2. AstiVita Renewables
3. carsales.com
4. Finbar Group
5. Medusa Mining
6. Mineral Resources
7. Mount Gibson Iron
8. Navitas
9. REA Group
10. Technology One

Source: *Forbes Asia*, Asia's Best Under a Billion (annual), http://www.forbes.com, September 12, 2011.

1431 ■ LARGEST CORPORATIONS IN AUSTRALIA BY REVENUE, 2010

Ranked by: Revenue, in millions of U.S. dollars. **Remarks:** Also notes headquarters city and overall rank in the *Global 500*. Ranking is available online only, not in print. **Number listed:** 8

1. BHP Billiton Ltd., with $52,798 million
2. Wesfarmers Ltd., $45,659
3. Woolworths Ltd., $45,622
4. Commonwealth Bank of Australia, $35,710
5. Westpac Banking Corp., $35,282
6. National Australia Bank Ltd., $34,350
7. Australia & New Zealand Banking Group (ANZ), $28,275
8. Telstra Corp., Ltd., $22,050

Source: *Fortune*, Global 500 (annual), http://www.fortune.com, July 25, 2011.

1432 ■ TOP AUSTRALIAN COMPANIES, 2011

Ranked by: Score based on profits, sales and earnings growth, and projected earnings and stock-price gains. **Remarks:** Specific

scores not provided; companies are listed alphabetically, not ranked. Also notes market value, revenue, and industry. To quality, companies must be publicly traded with revenues or market capitalization of at least US$3 billion. Ranking is available online only, not in print. **Number listed:** 3

1. Newcrest Mining Ltd.
2. Wesfarmers Ltd.
3. WorleyParsons Ltd.

Source: *Forbes*, Asian Fab 50 (annual), September 13, 2011.

Corporations—Austria

1433 ■ AUSTRIA'S LARGEST COMPANIES OVERALL, 2011

Ranked by: Score based on revenue, profits, assets, and market capitalization. **Remarks:** Specific scores not provided. Also notes rank in the overall *Forbes 2000* and figures for each criterion. **Number listed:** 12

1. OMV Group
2. Raiffeisen International Bank Holding
3. Erste Bank
4. Vienna Insurance Group
5. voestalpine
6. Verbund AG
7. UNIQA Versicherungen AG
8. Strabag SE
9. Immofinanz
10. Volksbank

Source: *Forbes*, Forbes 2000 (annual), http://www.forbes.com, May 7, 2012.

1434 ■ LARGEST COMPANIES IN AUSTRIA, 2010

Ranked by: Sales, in millions of U.S. dollars. **Remarks:** Also notes city; industrial code; percent change in sales; profits; profit as a percentage of sales, assets, and equity; number of employees; sales per employee; assets; equity capital; equity capital as a percentage of assets; year established; and figures for previous year. **Number listed:** 500

1. OMV AG, with $26,646.6 million
2. Strabag SE, $18,667.2
3. Voestalpine AG, $14,940.8
4. Porsche Holding GmbH, $13,609.5
5. Gazprom Neft Trading GmbH, $11,426.9
6. Erste Group Bank AG, $9,865
7. OMV Refining & Marketing GmbH, $9,396
8. UniCredit Bank Austria AG, $9,051.5
9. Osterreichische Bundesbahnen-Holding AG, $7,180
10. Telekom Austria AG, $7,141.5

Source: *Europe's 15,000 Largest Companies*, (annual), ELC International, 2011, p. 52+.

Corporations—Belgium

1435 ■ BELGIUM'S LARGEST COMPANIES OVERALL, 2011

Ranked by: Score based on revenue, profits, assets, and market capitalization. **Remarks:** Specific scores not provided. Also notes rank in the overall *Forbes 2000* and figures for each criterion. **Number listed:** 12

1. Anheuser-Busch InBev SA/NV
2. KBC Group NV
3. Delhaize Group
4. Belgacom SA
5. Solvay SA
6. Ageas NV
7. Dexia Group
8. Banque Nationale de Belgique
9. Umicore SA
10. Groep Colruyt

Source: *Forbes*, Forbes 2000 (annual), http://www.forbes.com, May 7, 2012.

1436 ■ BEST LARGE COMPANIES TO WORK FOR IN BELGIUM, 2012

Ranked by: Score based on the relationships between employees and management, employees and their jobs/company, and employees and coworkers. **Remarks:** Specific scores not provided. Ranking covers companies with more than 500 employees. **Number listed:** 10

1. Schoenen Torfs L NV
2. Accent Jobs
3. Care
4. McDonald's Belgium
5. Randstad Group Belgium NV
6. Genzyme
7. FedEx Express
8. KBC Groep
9. Accenture
10. Partena Ziekenfonds & Partners

Source: *Great Place to Work Institute Inc.*, Best Places to Work in Belgium (annual), http://www.greatplacetowork.com, February 2012.

1437 ■ BEST SMALL COMPANIES TO WORK FOR IN BELGIUM, 2012

Ranked by: Score based on the relationships between employees and management, employees and their jobs/company, and employees and coworkers. **Remarks:** Specific scores not provided. Ranking covers companies with fewer than 500 employees. **Number listed:** 10

1. SAS Institute NV/SA
2. Microsoft Belgium
3. AE
4. Mars Belgium SA
5. Ormit
6. Handson & Partners
7. Bank van Breda
8. Boss Paints
9. Abbott
10. Grunenthal

Source: *Great Place to Work Institute Inc.*, Best Places to Work in Belgium (annual), http://www.greatplacetowork.com, February 2012.

1438 ■ LARGEST COMPANIES IN BELGIUM, 2010

Ranked by: Sales, in millions of U.S. dollars. **Remarks:** Also notes city; industrial code; percent change in sales; profits; profit as a percentage of sales, assets, and equity; number of employ-

ees; sales per employee; assets; equity capital; equity capital as a percentage of assets; year established; and figures for previous year. **Number listed:** 700

1. Dexia Banque Belgique SA, with $93,319.9 million
2. Anheuser-Busch InBev SA/NV, $36,758
3. ExxonMobil Petroleum & Chemical BVBA, $29,697.1
4. Delhaize Group SA/NV, $26,814.3
5. Toyota Motor Europe SA, $21,723.9
6. PetroFina SA, $21,488.5
7. Electrabel SA, $21,029
8. Solvay SA/NV, $13,376.2
9. Fortis Banque SA, $13,172.5
10. KBC Group NV, $13,137.9

Source: *Europe's 15,000 Largest Companies*, (annual), ELC International, 2011, p. 74+.

1439 ■ LARGEST CORPORATIONS IN BELGIUM BY REVENUE, 2010

Ranked by: Revenue, in millions of U.S. dollars. **Remarks:** Also notes headquarters city and overall rank in the *Global 500*. Ranking is available online only, not in print. **Number listed:** 5

1. Dexia NV/SA, with $69,491 million
2. Anheuser-Busch InBev SA/NV, $36,297
3. Delhaize Group, $27,615
4. KBC Group NV, $24,473
5. Compagnie Nationale a Portefeuille SA, $20,373

Source: *Fortune*, Global 500 (annual), http://www.fortune.com, July 25, 2011.

Corporations—Bolivia

1440 ■ BEST COMPANIES TO WORK FOR IN BOLIVIA, 2011

Ranked by: Score based on the relationships between employees and management, employees and their jobs/company, and employees and coworkers. **Remarks:** Specific scores not provided. **Number listed:** 5

1. Kimberly-Clark Bolivia
2. Belcorp
3. Cotas
4. Tigo
5. Cargill Bolivia

Source: *Great Place to Work Institute Inc.*, Best Places to Work in Bolivia (annual), 2011.

Corporations—Brazil

1441 ■ BEST COMPANIES TO WORK FOR IN BRAZIL, 2011

Ranked by: Score based on the relationships between employees and management, employees and their jobs/company, and employees and coworkers. **Remarks:** Specific scores not provided. **Number listed:** 17

1. Google Brasil
2. Caterpillar Brasil

3. Kimberly-Clark Brasil
4. Laboratorio Sabin
5. GAZIN
6. Magazine Luiza
7. SAS Brasil
8. TICKET
9. J. W. Marriot
10. Accor Brasil

Source: *Great Place to Work Institute Inc.*, Best Places to Work in Brazil (annual), 2011.

1442 ■ BRAZIL'S LARGEST COMPANIES OVERALL, 2011

Ranked by: Score based on revenue, profits, assets, and market capitalization. **Remarks:** Specific scores not provided. Also notes rank in the overall *Forbes 2000* and figures for each criterion. **Number listed:** 33

1. Petroleo Brasileiro SA (Petrobras)
2. Itau Unibanco Holding SA
3. Banco Bradesco SA
4. Banco do Brasil SA
5. Vale SA
6. Investimentos Itau SA (Itausa)
7. Centrais Eletricas Brasileiras SA (Eletrobras)
8. Companhia Siderurgica Nacional (CSN)
9. Companhia Energetica de Minas Gerais (Cemig)
10. Tele Norte Leste Participacoes SA

Source: *Forbes*, Forbes 2000 (annual), http://www.forbes.com, May 7, 2012.

1443 ■ LARGEST CORPORATIONS IN BRAZIL BY REVENUE, 2010

Ranked by: Revenue, in millions of U.S. dollars. **Remarks:** Also notes headquarters city and overall rank in the *Global 500*. Ranking is available online only, not in print. **Number listed:** 7

1. Petroleo Brasileiro SA (Petrobras), with $120,052 million
2. Banco do Brasil SA, $62,891
3. Banco Bradesco SA, $53,010
4. Vale SA, $45,293
5. JBS SA, $31,279
6. Investimentos Itau SA (Itausa), $26,982
7. Ultrapar Holdings, $24,135

Source: *Fortune*, Global 500 (annual), http://www.fortune.com, July 25, 2011.

1444 ■ MOST ADMIRED COMPANIES IN BRAZIL, 2012

Ranked by: Score based on a survey of executives, directors, and securities analysts of companies within their own industry. **Remarks:** List is available online only, not in print. Also notes headquarters. **Number listed:** 2

1. Ultrapar Holdings, with 7.35 points
2. Petroleo Brasileiro SA (Petrobras), 6.73

Source: *Fortune*, World's Most Admired Companies (annual), http://www.fortune.com, March 19, 2012.

Corporations—Bulgaria

1445 ■ LARGEST COMPANIES IN BULGARIA, 2010

Ranked by: Sales, in millions of U.S. dollars. **Remarks:** Also notes city; industrial code; percent change in sales; profits; profit

as a percentage of sales, assets, and equity; number of employees; sales per employee; assets; equity capital; equity capital as a percentage of assets; year established; and figures for previous year. **Number listed:** 100

1. Lukoil Neftochim Bourgas AD, with $2,414 million
2. Natsionalna Elektricheska Kompania EAD, $1,642.4
3. Petrol AD, $978.2
4. Mobiltel EAD, $857.4
5. Bulgarian Telecommunications Co., $762.9
6. Kremikovtzi AD, $677.5
7. KCM AD, $406.8
8. Dsk Bank EAD, $379.9
9. Unicredit Bulbank AD, $310.3
10. Chimimport AD, $309.1

Source: *Europe's 15,000 Largest Companies*, (annual), ELC International, 2011, p. 104+.

Corporations—California

1446 ■ BEST EXTRA-LARGE PLACES TO WORK IN THE NORTH BAY, 2010

Ranked by: Score, on a scale of 5, based on employee survey. **Remarks:** Ranking covers companies with 251-500 employees in the California counties of Sonoma, Napa, and Marin. Also notes contact information, number of North Bay employee, number of years on ranking, comments, and top local executive. **Number listed:** 4

1. Bradley Real Estate, with 4.76 points
2. Redwood Credit Union, 4.55
3. Exchange Bank, 4.52
4. Becoming Independent, 4.25

Source: *North Bay Business Journal*, Best Places to Work (annual), http://www.northbaybusinessjournal.com, September 26, 2011.

1447 ■ BEST LARGE COMPANIES TO WORK FOR IN LOS ANGELES, 2011

Ranked by: Score based on employee surveys. **Remarks:** Specific scores not provided. To qualify, companies must have 250 or more employees. **Number listed:** 32

1. Point B
2. North Highland
3. Equity Office
4. Bryan Cave LLP
5. PCL Construction Services Inc.
6. Cresa Partners
7. Slalom Consulting
8. Bingham McCutchen LLP
9. Bentley Prince Street Inc.
10. Ryan LLC

Source: *Best Companies Group*, Best Places to Work in Los Angeles (annual), http://www.bestplacestoworkla.com, August 2011.

1448 ■ BEST LARGE COMPANIES TO WORK FOR IN ORANGE COUNTY, CALIFORNIA, 2011

Ranked by: Score based on employee surveys. **Remarks:** Specific scores not provided. Also notes contact information, number of employees, turnover rate, average salary, benefits, company description, unique perks, and top local official. To qualify, companies must have at least 250 employees. **Number listed:** 27

1. Kforce Inc.
2. Stream Realty Partners LP
3. Edgewood Partners Insurance Center
4. Jeffer Mangels Butler & Mitchell LLP
5. Aerotek
6. Bingham McCutchen LLP
7. Moss Adams LLP
8. McCarthy Building Cos.
9. The Paradies Shops
10. Alpine Mortgage Planning

Source: *Orange County Business Journal*, Best Places to Work in Orange County (annual), http://www.ocbj.com, September 2011.

1449 ■ BEST LARGE PLACES TO WORK IN THE NORTH BAY, 2010

Ranked by: Score, on a scale of 5, based on employee survey. **Remarks:** Ranking covers companies with 101-250 employees in the California counties of Sonoma, Napa, and Marin. Also notes contact information, number of North Bay employee, number of years on ranking, comments, and top local executive. **Number listed:** 12

1. Embassy Suites San Rafael, with 4.79 points
2. Sonicnet, 4.69
3. Petaluma Health Center, 4.53
4. Collotype Labels USA, 4.50
5. Nova Group, 4.49
6. REACH Air Medical Services, 4.45
7. W. Bradley Electric, 4.29
8. Cagwin & Dorward, 4.25
9. Idex Health & Science, 4.18
10. Bank of Marin, 4.08

Source: *North Bay Business Journal*, Best Places to Work (annual), http://www.northbaybusinessjournal.com, September 26, 2011.

1450 ■ BEST MEDIUM-SIZED COMPANIES TO WORK FOR IN LOS ANGELES, 2011

Ranked by: Score based on employee surveys. **Remarks:** Specific scores not provided. To qualify, companies must have between 50 and 249 employees. **Number listed:** 28

1. Walker Financial Partners LLC
2. NSBN LLP
3. New Horizons Computer Learning Centers of Southern California
4. True Partners Consulting
5. uSamp
6. Wpromote Inc.
7. RBZ LLP
8. Wong, Doody, Crandall, Wiener
9. Morley Builders
10. GNW-Evergreen Insurance Services LLC

Source: *Best Companies Group*, Best Places to Work in Los Angeles (annual), http://www.bestplacestoworkla.com, August 2011.

1451 ■ BEST MEDIUM-SIZED COMPANIES TO WORK FOR IN ORANGE COUNTY, CALIFORNIA, 2011

Ranked by: Score based on employee surveys. **Remarks:** Specific scores not provided. Also notes contact information, number

of employees, turnover rate, average salary, benefits, company description, unique perks, and top local official. To qualify, companies must have between 50 and 249 employees. **Number listed:** 14

1. Trace3 Inc.
2. New Horizons Computer Learning Centers of Southern California
3. Motorcycle Industry Council
4. Aspen Medical Products
5. CyberCoders
6. Telogis
7. Windes & McClaughry Accountancy Corp.
8. Precept
9. Kimco Staffing Services Inc.
10. Green Street Advisors

Source: *Orange County Business Journal*, Best Places to Work in Orange County (annual), http://www.ocbj.com, September 2011.

1452 ■ BEST MEDIUM-SIZED PLACES TO WORK IN THE NORTH BAY, 2010

Ranked by: Score, on a scale of 5, based on employee survey. **Remarks:** Ranking covers companies with 51-100 employees in the California counties of Sonoma, Napa, and Marin. Also notes contact information, number of North Bay employee, number of years on ranking, comments, and top local executive. **Number listed:** 16

1. Golden Living Center of Petaluma, with 4.98 points
2. Moss Adams LLP, 4.8
3. Sonoma Technology, 4.79
4. Summit State Bank, 4.77
5. St. Francis Winery & Vineyards, 4.66
6. Sequoia Senior Solutions, 4.56
7. Costeaux French Bakery, 4.54
7. First Community Bank, 4.54
7. Umpqua Bank, 4.54
10. Wells Fargo Insurance Services USA, 4.51

Source: *North Bay Business Journal*, Best Places to Work (annual), http://www.northbaybusinessjournal.com, September 26, 2011.

1453 ■ BEST SMALL COMPANIES IN CALIFORNIA, 2011

Ranked by: Score based on revenue, profits, and return on equity for the past 12 months and five years. **Remarks:** Specific scores not provided. Also notes rank in the overall *100 Best Small Companies in America*. To qualify, companies must have revenues between $5 million and $1 billion, a net margin above five percent, and share price above $5. List is available online only. **Number listed:** 17

1. Questcor Pharmaceuticals
2. Quality Systems
3. Synaptics
4. Masimo
5. True Religion Apparel
6. Ensign Group
7. Dolby Laboratories
8. j2 Global Communications
9. Alliance Fiber Optic Products
10. Exponent

Source: *Forbes*, Best Small Companies in America (annual), November 7, 2011.

1454 ■ BEST SMALL COMPANIES TO WORK FOR IN LOS ANGELES, 2011

Ranked by: Score based on employee surveys. **Remarks:** Specific scores not provided. To qualify, companies must have between 15 and 49 employees. **Number listed:** 15

1. VACO Los Angeles LLC
2. Dawson Co.
3. The 1st Movement LLC
4. Mansour Travel Co.
5. Onisko & Scholz, Certified Public Accountants
6. Financial Finesse Inc.
7. FPA Technology Services Inc.
8. GlobalWide Media
9. Murphy O'Brien Public Relations
10. Palmer, Lombardi & Donohue LLP

Source: *Best Companies Group*, Best Places to Work in Los Angeles (annual), http://www.bestplacestoworkla.com, August 2011.

1455 ■ BEST SMALL COMPANIES TO WORK FOR IN ORANGE COUNTY, CALIFORNIA, 2011

Ranked by: Score based on employee surveys. **Remarks:** Specific scores not provided. Also notes contact information, number of employees, turnover rate, average salary, benefits, company description, unique perks, and top local official. To qualify, companies must have between 15 and 49 employees. **Number listed:** 19

1. Burnham Benefits Insurance Services
2. HBA Inc.
3. Express Systems Inc.
4. Wright Ford Young & Co.
5. Lexipol LLC
6. Benefits Resource LLC
7. Mattson Resources
8. Beacon Pointe Advisors LLC
9. e3 Financial Inc.
10. The Bascom Group

Source: *Orange County Business Journal*, Best Places to Work in Orange County (annual), http://www.ocbj.com, September 2011.

1456 ■ BEST SMALL PLACES TO WORK IN THE NORTH BAY, 2010

Ranked by: Score, on a scale of 5, based on employee survey. **Remarks:** Ranking covers companies with 20-50 employees in the California counties of Sonoma, Napa, and Marin. Also notes contact information, number of North Bay employee, number of years on ranking, comments, and top local executive. **Number listed:** 32

1. Innovative Business Solutions, with 4.86 points
1. Metier, 4.86
3. Codding Enterprises, 4.84
4. O'Brien Watters & Davis, 4.83
5. Smith Dollar, 4.76
6. Bank of Napa, 4.73
7. Private Ocean, 4.70
7. Quattrocchi Kwok Architects, 4.70
9. Friedemann Goldberg, 4.67
9. Ghirardo CPA, 4.67

Source: *North Bay Business Journal*, Best Places to Work (annual), http://www.northbaybusinessjournal.com, September 26, 2011.

1457 ■ CALIFORNIA'S BEST COMPANIES TO WORK FOR, 2012

Ranked by: Score based on employee surveys as well as evaluation of companies' credibility, respect, fairness, and pride/camaraderie. **Remarks:** Specific scores not provided; companies are listed alphabetically, not ranked. Available online only, not in print. **Number listed:** 18

1. Adobe Systems Inc.
2. Autodesk
3. Cisco Systems Inc.
4. DPR Construction Inc.
5. DreamWorks Animation SKG Inc.
6. Genentech Inc.
7. Google Inc.
8. Hitachi Data Systems
9. Intel Corp.
10. Intuit Inc.

Source: *Fortune*, 100 Best Companies to Work For (annual), http://www.fortune.com, February 6, 2012.

1458 ■ CALIFORNIA'S LARGEST COMPANIES OVERALL, 2011

Ranked by: Score based on revenue, profits, assets, and market capitalization. **Remarks:** Specific scores not provided. Also notes overall rank in the *Forbes 2000* and figures for each criterion. **Number listed:** 63

1. Wells Fargo & Co.
2. Chevron Corp.
3. Apple Inc.
4. Hewlett-Packard Co.
5. Intel Corp.
6. Cisco Systems Inc.
7. Google Inc.
8. Oracle Corp.
9. Walt Disney Co.
10. Occidental Petroleum Corp.

Source: *Forbes*, Forbes 2000 (annual), http://www.forbes.com, May 7, 2012.

1459 ■ CALIFORNIA'S LARGEST PRIVATE COMPANIES, 2010

Ranked by: Revenue, in billions of dollars. **Remarks:** Also notes business segment, number of employees, and overall rank in the *America's Largest Private Companies* list. Ranking is available online only, not in print. **Number listed:** 24

1. Bechtel Group Inc., with $27.9 billion
2. Platinum Equity LLC, $10.4
3. Capital Group Companies Inc., $7.5
4. Kingston Technology Co., $6.48
5. Save Mart Supermarkets Inc., $4.8
6. Golden State Foods Corp., $4.6
7. J. D. Heiskell & Co., $4.58
8. Levi Strauss & Co., $4.41
9. Consolidated Electrical Distributors Inc., $3.8
10. Stater Bros. Holdings Inc., $3.67

Source: *Forbes*, America's Largest Private Companies (annual), http://www.forbes.com, December 5, 2011.

1460 ■ FASTEST-GROWING PRIVATE COMPANIES IN LOS ANGELES COUNTY, 2008-2010

Ranked by: Three-year growth in revenue, in percent. **Remarks:** Also notes rank for previous year, contact information, revenue for each year, number of offices and employees, year founded, company description, and top local executive. **Number listed:** 100

1. RateSpecial Interactive, with 7,257.6%
2. LT Source Corp., 1,604.4%
3. Prodege LLC/Swagbucks.com, 896.6%

Source: *Los Angeles Business Journal*, Fastest-Growing Private Companies (annual), http://www.labusinessjournal.com, November 21, 2011.

1461 ■ FASTEST-GROWING PRIVATE COMPANIES IN ORANGE COUNTY, CALIFORNIA, 2009-2011

Ranked by: Two-year growth in revenue, in percent. **Remarks:** Also notes contact information, revenue for current and previous year, number of employees, business description, and top local executive. **Number listed:** 100

1. ymarketing LLC, with 2,037.3%
2. First Fuel Inc., 1,530%
3. BookPal LLC, 1,025%
4. Meritus Payment Solutions, 707.6%
5. U.S. Lighting Technologies, 624%
6. U.S. Alliance Group Inc., 561.1%
7. ePropertySites LLC, 555.3%
8. eGumBall Inc., 516.1%
9. Oleumtech Corp., 473.7%
10. Purple Platypus, 392.1%

Source: *Orange County Business Journal*, Fastest-Growing Private Companies (annual), October 3, 2011, p. 41+.

1462 ■ FASTEST-GROWING PUBLIC COMPANIES IN ORANGE COUNTY, CALIFORNIA, 2009-2011

Ranked by: Two-year growth in revenue, in percent. **Remarks:** Also notes contact information, revenue, net income, number of employees, business description, and top local executive. **Number listed:** 44

1. Seychelle Environmental Technologies Inc., with 289.9%
2. Patient Safety Technologies Inc., 257.9%
3. Identive Group Inc., 206%
4. Viaspace Inc., 199.5%
5. Acacia Research Corp., 197.8%
6. Sunwest Bank, 192.9%
7. TTM Technologies Inc., 129.5%
8. Clean Energy Fuels Corp., 119%
9. Liquidmetal Technologies Inc., 90.1%
10. Ista Pharmaceuticals Inc., 77.4%

Source: *Orange County Business Journal*, Fastest-Growing Public Companies (annual), October 17, 2011, p. 32-34.

1463 ■ LARGEST COMPANIES IN CALIFORNIA BY EMPLOYEES, 2010

Ranked by: Number of employees at headquarters. **Remarks:** Also notes contact information for headquarters, total number of employees, revenue, rank by revenue, and primary SIC code. **Number listed:** 1134

1. UCLA Medical Group, with 8,000 employees
2. Menlo Worldwide Forwarding Inc., 6,500
3. Disney Enterprises Inc., 6,000
3. Shaw Environmental & Infrastructure, 6,000
3. Walt Disney Co., 6,000

3. Wells Fargo Bank NA, 6,000
7. Prolease Pacific Inc., 5,930
8. Intel Corp., 5,700
9. Cypress Semiconductor International Inc., 5,000
9. KSL Recreation Management Operations LLC, 5,000
9. Stanford Hospital & Clinics, 5,000
9. Warner Bros. Entertainment inc., 5,000

Source: *Business Rankings*, (annual), Dun & Bradstreet Inc., 2011, p. IV.11-IV.35.

1464 ■ LARGEST COMPANIES IN CALIFORNIA BY SALES, 2010

Ranked by: Revenue, in dollars. **Remarks:** Also notes contact information for headquarters, number of employees at headquarters and overall, rank by employees, and primary SIC code. **Number listed:** 1142

1. Chevron Corp., with $204,928,000,000
2. Hewlett-Packard Co., $126,033,000,000
3. McKesson Corp., $108,702,000,000
4. Apple Inc., $65,225,000,000
5. NotionT Inc., $50,000,000,000
6. Intel Corp., $43,623,000,000
7. Safeway Inc., $41,050,000,000
8. Cisco Systems Inc., $40,040,000,000
9. Walt Disney Co., $38,063,000,000
10. Northrop Grumman Corp., $34,757,000,000

Source: *Business Rankings*, (annual), Dun & Bradstreet Inc., 2011, p. III.11-III.35.

1465 ■ LARGEST COMPANIES IN THE SILICON VALLEY BY REVENUE, 2011

Ranked by: Revenue, in millions of dollars. **Remarks:** Also notes business description, rank for previous year, percent change, and figures for and rank by profits, profitability, and market capitalization. Ranking includes companies headquartered in Santa Clara, Santa Cruz, southern San Mateo, and southern Alameda counties, in California. **Number listed:** 150

1. Apple Inc., with $127,841 million
2. Hewlett-Packard Co., $124,979
3. Intel Corp., $53,999
4. Cisco Systems Inc., $44,844
5. Google Inc., $37,905
6. Oracle Corp., $36,980
7. eBay Inc., $11,652
8. SYNNEX Corp., $10,370
9. Applied Materials Inc., $10,020
10. Gilead Sciences Inc., $8,385

Source: *San Jose Mercury News*, Silicon Valley 150 (annual), http://www.siliconvalley.com, April 21, 2012.

1466 ■ LARGEST EMPLOYERS IN ORANGE COUNTY, CALIFORNIA, 2010

Ranked by: Number of Orange County employees. **Remarks:** Also notes rank for previous year, companywide employees, annual growth in employees, and operations in Orange County. **Number listed:** 50

1. Walt Disney Co., with 22,000 employees

2. University of California-Irvine, 21,291
3. St. Joseph Health System, 12,048
4. Boeing Co., 7,700
5. Bank of America Corp., 6,300
5. Yum! Brands Inc., 6,300
7. Kaiser Permanente, 5,968
8. Target Corp., 5,527
9. Cedar Fair LP, 5,200
10. California State University, Fullerton, 5,173

Source: *Orange County Business Journal*, Largest Employers (annual), November 28, 2011, p. 10+.

1467 ■ LARGEST NORTH BAY PUBLIC COMPANIES, 2010

Ranked by: Revenue, in thousands of dollars. **Remarks:** Ranking covers companies in the California counties of Sonoma, Napa, and Marin. Also notes rank for previous year, contact information, net income, growth in revenue and net income, market capitalization, assets, nature of business, trading symbol, stock exchange, fiscal year-end, and CEO. **Number listed:** 16

1. Autodesk Inc., with $1,951,800 thousand
2. BioMarin Pharmaceutical Inc., $376,267
3. Calix Inc., $287,043
4. Westamerica Bancorp, $282,609
5. Redwood Trust, $230,000
6. Willis Lease Finance Corp., $148,302
7. Exchange Bank, $96,498
8. Bank of Marin, $66,878
9. Mendocino Brewing Co., $35,000
10. Summit State Bank, $20,149

Source: *North Bay Business Journal*, Largest Public Companies (annual), http://www.northbaybusinessjournal.com, September 5, 2011.

1468 ■ LARGEST PRIVATE COMPANIES IN LOS ANGELES COUNTY, 2010

Ranked by: Revenue, in millions of dollars. **Remarks:** Also notes contact information, figures for previous year, number of offices and employees, year founded, company description, controlling stakeholder, and top local executive. **Number listed:** 150

1. Platinum Equity LLC, with $10,400 million
2. Trader Joe's Co., $9,000
3. Capital Group Cos., $7,300

Source: *Los Angeles Business Journal*, Largest Private Companies (annual), http://www.labusinessjournal.com, October 24, 2011.

1469 ■ LARGEST PRIVATE COMPANIES IN ORANGE COUNTY, 2010

Ranked by: Revenue, in millions of dollars. **Remarks:** Also notes rank for previous year, contact information, annual growth, number of employees, business description, and top local executive. **Number listed:** 75

1. Kingston Technology Co., with $6,500 million
2. Pacific Mutual Holding Co., $5,800
3. Golden State Foods Corp., $4,632
4. Automobile Club of Southern California, $4,060
5. Vizio Inc., $2,900
6. Young's Market Co., $2,250
7. Irvine Co., $2,100

7. Ventura Foods LLC, $2,100
9. Apria Healthcare Group Inc., $2,080
10. LA Fitness International LLC, $1,300

Source: *Orange County Business Journal*, Top Private Companies (annual), May 9, 2011, p. 24+.

1470 ■ LARGEST PRIVATE SECTOR COMPANIES IN LOS ANGELES COUNTY, 2011

Ranked by: Number of employees in Los Angeles County. **Remarks:** Also notes contact information, figures for previous year, total number of employees, description, headquarters, and top local executive. **Number listed:** 25

1. Kaiser Permanente, with 33,600 employees
2. Northrop Grumman Corp., 21,000
3. University of Southern California, 16,180

Source: *Los Angeles Business Journal*, Largest Private Sector Companies (annual), http://www.labusinessjournal.com, September 5, 2011.

1471 ■ LARGEST PRIVATE-SECTOR EMPLOYERS IN MARIN COUNTY, 2010

Ranked by: Number of employees in Marin County, California. **Remarks:** Also notes rank for previous year, contact information, number of locations in county, nature of business, job positions most in demand, healthcare insurance providers, and top local executive. **Number listed:** 27

1. Kaiser Permanente, with 1,803 employees
2. Marin General Hospital, 1,100
3. Fireman's Fund Insurance, 950
4. Autodesk Inc., 878
5. BioMarin Pharmaceutical Inc., 871
6. Safeway Inc., 840
7. Comcast Corp., 620
8. Macy's Inc., 380
9. Bradley Real Estate, 376
10. MHN, 350

Source: *North Bay Business Journal*, Private-Sector Employers: Marin County (annual), http://www.northbaybusinessjournal.com, June 6, 2011.

1472 ■ LARGEST PRIVATE-SECTOR EMPLOYERS IN NAPA COUNTY, 2010

Ranked by: Number of employees in Napa County, California. **Remarks:** Also notes rank for previous year, contact information, number of locations in county, nature of business, job positions most in demand, healthcare insurance providers, and top local executive. **Number listed:** 24

1. Queen of the Valley Medical Center, with 1,500 employees
2. Treasury Wine Estates, 600
3. Trinchero Family Estates, 575
4. St. Helena Hospital, 510
5. Silverado Resort, 500
6. Boral Stone Products, 347
7. Meadowood Napa Valley, 300
7. Pacific Union College, 300
9. Villagio Inn & Spa/Vintage Inn, 299
10. Wal-Mart Stores Inc., 261

Source: *North Bay Business Journal*, Private-Sector Employers: Napa County (annual), http://www.northbaybusinessjournal.com, August 29, 2011.

1473 ■ LARGEST PRIVATE-SECTOR EMPLOYERS IN SOLANO COUNTY, 2010

Ranked by: Number of employees in Solano County, California. **Remarks:** Also notes rank for previous year, contact information, number of locations in county, nature of business, job positions most in demand, healthcare insurance providers, and top local executive. **Number listed:** 25

1. Kaiser Permanente, with 3,030 employees
2. North Bay Health Care, 1,750
3. Six Flags Discovery Kingdom, 1,600
4. Wal-Mart Stores Inc., 875
5. Genentech Inc., 850
6. The Home Depot Inc., 675
7. Sutter Solano Medical Center, 650
8. Alza Corp., 535
9. Safeway Inc., 530
10. Valero Benicia Refinery, 516

Source: *North Bay Business Journal*, Private-Sector Employers: Solano County (annual), http://www.northbaybusinessjournal.com, August 15, 2011.

1474 ■ LARGEST PRIVATE-SECTOR EMPLOYERS IN SONOMA COUNTY, 2010

Ranked by: Number of employees in Sonoma County, California. **Remarks:** Also notes rank for previous year, contact information, number of locations in county, nature of business, job positions most in demand, healthcare insurance providers, and top local executive. **Number listed:** 26

1. Kaiser Permanente, with 2,812 employees
2. St. Joseph Health System, 2,489
3. Sutter Medical Cnter of Santa Rosa, 1,497
4. Safeway Inc., 1,200
5. Agilent Technologies, 1,150
6. Amy's Kitchen, 900
7. Medtronic CardioVascular, 840
8. Wal-Mart Stores Inc., 650
9. Kendall-Jackson Wine Estates, 640
10. AT&T Inc., 600

Source: *North Bay Business Journal*, Private-Sector Employers: Sonoma County (annual), http://www.northbaybusinessjournal.com, October 17, 2011.

1475 ■ LARGEST PUBLIC COMPANIES IN ORANGE COUNTY, 2011

Ranked by: Revenue, in millions of dollars. **Remarks:** Also notes rank for previous year, contact information, annual growth, net income, market capitalization, assets, ticker symbol, stock exchange, number of employees, business description, and top local executive. **Number listed:** 100

1. Ingram Micro Inc., with $36,328.7 million
2. Western Digital Corp., $9,344
3. Spectrum Group International Inc., $8,381.7
4. Broadcom Corp., $7,389
5. Allergan Inc., $5,419.1
6. First American Financial Corp., $3,820.6
7. Quiksilver Inc., $1,953.1
8. Sun Healthcare Group Inc., $1,930.3
9. Corinthian Colleges Inc., $1,716.2
10. Edwards Lifesciences Corp., $1,678.6

Source: *Orange County Business Journal*, Largest Public Companies (annual), April 9, 2012, p. 12-22.

1476 ■ MOST ADMIRED COMPANIES IN CALIFORNIA, 2012

Ranked by: Survey of top executives, directors, and securities analysts regarding the Fortune 1,000 companies that they admire the most, regardless of industry. **Remarks:** Also notes city and industry rank. List is available online only, not in print. **Number listed:** 31

1. Apple Inc., with 8.42 points
2. Walt Disney Co., 8.14
3. Chevron Corp., 7.93
4. Intel Corp., 7.8
5. Google Inc., 7.74
6. QUALCOMM Inc., 7.71
7. Occidental Petroleum Corp., 7.54
8. Visa Corp., 7.46
9. Robert Half International, 7.38
10. Cisco Systems, 7.19

Source: *Fortune*, World's Most Admired Companies (annual), http://www.fortune.com, March 19, 2012.

1477 ■ MOST PROFITABLE COMPANIES IN THE SILICON VALLEY, 2011

Ranked by: Net profits, in millions of dollars. **Remarks:** Also notes overall rank and annual growth in profits. Ranking includes companies headquartered in Santa Clara, Santa Cruz, southern San Mateo, and southern Alameda counties, in California. **Number listed:** 10

1. Apple Inc., with $32.98 million
2. Intel Corp., $12.94
3. Oracle Corp., $9.74
3. Google Inc., $9.74
5. Cisco Systems Inc., $7
6. Hewlett-Packard Co., $5.94
7. eBay Inc., $3.23
8. Gilead Sciences Inc., $2.8
9. Applied Materials Inc., $1.54
10. Agilent Technologies, $1.05

Source: *San Jose Mercury News*, Silicon Valley 150 (annual), http://www.siliconvalley.com, April 21, 2012.

1478 ■ MOST VALUABLE COMPANIES IN THE SILICON VALLEY, 2011

Ranked by: Market value, in billions of dollars. **Remarks:** Also notes overall rank and annual growth in market value. Ranking includes companies headquartered in Santa Clara, Santa Cruz, southern San Mateo, and southern Alameda counties, in California. **Number listed:** 10

1. Apple Inc., with $558.93 billion
2. Google Inc., $207.69
3. Oracle Corp., $145.07
4. Intel Corp., $140.44
5. Cisco Systems Inc., $113.91
6. eBay Inc., $47.47
7. VMware, $47.44
8. Hewlett-Packard Co., $47.12
9. Gilead Sciences Inc., $37.03

10. Intuitive Surgical, $21.47

Source: *San Jose Mercury News*, Silicon Valley 150 (annual), http://www.siliconvalley.com, April 21, 2012.

1479 ■ MOST VALUABLE PUBLIC COMPANIES IN LOS ANGELES COUNTY, 2011

Ranked by: Market capitalization as of June, in millions of dollars. **Remarks:** Also notes contact information, revenue, net income, figures for previous year, ticker symbol, number of employees, business description, and top executive. **Number listed:** 180

1. Occidental Petroleum Corp., with $84,571.5 million
2. Walt Disney Co., $73,791.6
3. Amgen Inc., $54,249.8

Source: *Los Angeles Business Journal*, Largest Public Employers (annual), http://www.labusinessjournal.com, July 25, 2011.

1480 ■ TOP *FORTUNE 500* COMPANIES IN CALIFORNIA, 2011

Ranked by: Revenue, in millions of dollars. **Remarks:** Also notes overall rank in the *Fortune 500,* headquarters, and number of employees. **Number listed:** 53

1. Chevron Corp., with $245,621 million
2. Hewlett-Packard Co., $127,245
3. McKesson Corp., $112,084
4. Apple Inc., $108,249
5. Wells Fargo & Co., $87,597
6. Intel Corp., $53,999
7. Safeway Inc., $43,630.2
8. Cisco Systems Inc., $43,218
9. Walt Disney Co., $40,893
10. Google Inc., $37,905

Source: *Fortune*, Fortune 500 (annual), May 21, 2012, p. F-41-F-42.

Corporations—Canada

1481 ■ ALBERTA'S FASTEST-GROWING LARGE COMPANIES, 2008-2011

Ranked by: Score based on three-year growth in revenue and assets, as well as profits, employees, product development, incentive programs, investment in research and development, capital expenditures, marketing, and exports. **Remarks:** Specific scores not provided. Ranking includes companies with sales over $20 million. Also notes gross sales, sales growth, total assets, asset increase, pretax profit, industry, location, public/private ownership, CEO/president, website, year founded, and business description. **Number listed:** 50

1. Dynamic Manufacturing Solutions
2. Rocking Horse Energy Services
3. Yardstick Technologies
4. Western Energy Services
5. Poynt
6. Fabulous Furballs
7. ClearMotive Marketing
8. DevFacto Technologies Inc.
9. CAN Telematicsw
10. FourQuest Energy

Source: *Alberta Venture*, Fast Growth 50 (annual), http://www.albertaventure.com, January 2012.

1482 ■ ALBERTA'S TOP EMPLOYERS, 2012

Ranked by: Score based on eight criteria: physical workplace; work atmosphere; health, financial, and family benefits; vacation and time off; employee communications; performance management; training and skills development; and community involvement. **Remarks:** Scores not provided; companies are listed alphabetically, not ranked. **Number listed:** 55

1. Agriculture Financial Services Corp.
2. Agrium Inc.
3. Alberta Blue Cross
4. Alberta School Employee Benefit Plan
5. Alberta Utilities Commission
6. Alberta-Pacific Forest Industries Inc.
7. AltaGas Ltd.
8. ATB Financial
9. Athabasca University
10. Bayer CropScience Canada Inc.

Source: *Canada's Top 100 Employers*, (annual), http://www.canadastop100.com, February 1, 2012.

1483 ■ ATLANTIC CANADA'S TOP EMPLOYERS, 2012

Ranked by: Score based on eight criteria: physical workplace; work atmosphere; health, financial, and family benefits; vacation and time off; employee communications; performance management; training and skills development; and community involvement. **Remarks:** Scores not provided; companies are listed alphabetically, not ranked. **Number listed:** 25

1. Admiral Insurance Services Inc.
2. Alcool NB Liquor
3. Annapolis Valley District Health Authority
4. Cape Breton District Health Authority
5. Capital District Health Authority
6. CBCL Ltd.
7. Clearwater Seafoods LP
8. College of Physicians & Surgeons of Nova Scotia
9. Dalhousie University
10. DeltaWare Systems Inc.

Source: *Canada's Top 100 Employers*, (annual), http://www.canadastop100.com, January 2012.

1484 ■ BEST CANADIAN EMPLOYERS, 2011

Ranked by: Survey results based on the quality of workplace culture. **Remarks:** Specific scores not provided; companies are listed alphabetically, not ranked. Also notes location, business description, and notable perks. **Number listed:** 50

1. Accor/Novotel Canada
2. Aecon Group Inc.
3. ATB Financial
4. Banque Nationale Groupe Financier
5. BBA Inc.
6. BC Biomedical Laboratories Ltd.
7. Bennett Jones LLP
8. Birchwood Automotive Group
9. British Columbia Automobile Association
10. La Capitale Groupe Financier Inc.

Source: *Maclean's*, The Best Employers (annual), October 31, 2011, p. 60+.

1485 ■ BEST EMPLOYERS FOR NEW CANADIANS, 2012

Ranked by: Score based on programs and initiatives that assist employees who are recent immigrants to Canada. **Remarks:** Scores not provided; companies are listed alphabetically, not ranked. **Number listed:** 40

1. AltaGas Ltd.
2. BC Hydro
3. BMO Financial Group
4. Bombardier Aerospace
5. Business Development Bank of Canada
6. Canadian Imperial Bank of Canada
7. CH2M Hill Canada Ltd.
8. COM DEV International Ltd.
9. Deloitte & Touche LLP
10. Energy Resources Conservation Board

Source: *Canada's Top 100 Employers*, (annual), http://www.canadastop100.com, March 14, 2012.

1486 ■ BEST LARGE COMPANIES TO WORK FOR IN BRITISH COLUMBIA, 2010

Ranked by: Editorial determination. **Remarks:** Specific scores not provided. Ranking covers companies with more than 100 employees. **Number listed:** 11

1. Chemistry Consulting Group Inc.
2. 1-800-Got-Junk?
3. Nurse Next Door Home Healthcare Services Inc.
4. Cactus Restaurants Ltd.
5. Joe Fortes & Goldfish Restaurants
6. Accent Inns Inc.
7. Slant Six Games Inc.
8. Great Little Box Co., Ltd.
9. Para Space Landscaping Inc.
10. Flight Centre Canada

Source: *BCBusiness*, Best Companies (annual), http://www.bcbusinessonline.ca, December 2011.

1487 ■ BEST PLACES TO WORK IN ATLANTIC CANADA, 2011

Ranked by: Score based on employee surveys. **Remarks:** Specific scores not provided. Also notes industry, number of employees, key executive, head office, website, and comments. **Number listed:** 29

1. Molson Coors Moncton Brewery
2. AC Dockrill Horwich Rossieter
3. Wilson Insurance Ltd.
4. Institute for Human Services Education
5. Assumption Life
6. Omista Credit Union
7. Servant Dunbrack McKenzie & MacDonald Ltd.
8. Bergengren Credit Union
9. Premiere Executive Suites
10. Directors' Choice

Source: *Progress*, Best Places to Work (annual), June 2011, p. 49+.

1488 ■ BEST SMALL COMPANIES TO WORK FOR IN BRITISH COLUMBIA, 2010

Ranked by: Editorial determination. **Remarks:** Ranking covers companies with 100 employees or fewer. Specific scores not provided. **Number listed:** 11

1. Strangeloop Networks Inc.
2. Kardium Inc.
3. Kryton International Inc.
4. 6S Marketing Inc.
5. Habanero Consulting Group Inc.
6. Summerland & District Credit Union
7. Schill Insurance Brokers Ltd.
8. Tourism Victoria
9. Benefits by Design Inc.
10. Adrena Line Adventure Tours Ltd.

Source: *BCBusiness*, Best Companies (annual), http://www.bcbusinessonline.ca, December 2011.

1489 ■ BRITISH COLUMBIA'S TOP EMPLOYERS, 2012

Ranked by: Score based on eight criteria: physical workplace; work atmosphere; health, financial, and family benefits; vacation and time off; employee communications; performance management; training and skills development; and community involvement. **Remarks:** Scores not provided; companies are listed alphabetically, not ranked. **Number listed:** 60

1. 6S Marketing Inc.
2. AbeBooks Inc.
3. airG Inc.
4. ArcTeryx Equipment Inc.
5. BC Assessment
6. BC Housing Management Commission
7. BC Hydro
8. BC Public Service
9. Best Buy Canada Ltd.
10. British Columbia Institute of Technology

Source: *Canada's Top 100 Employers*, (annual), http://www.canadastop100.com, February 3, 2012.

1490 ■ CANADA'S BEST MANAGED COMPANIES, 2011

Ranked by: Score based on corporate strategy, capability, commitment, and financial performance. **Remarks:** Specific scores not provided; companies are listed alphabetically, not ranked. Also notes city and website. **Number listed:** 50

1. Airline Hotels Ltd.
2. ALPHA Assurances Auto et Habitation
3. Avison Young
4. Blackjack Investments Ltd.
5. Burnbrae Farms Ltd.
6. CarProof
7. CARSTAR Automotive Canada Inc.
8. Cruickshank Construction Ltd.
9. Da-Lee Dust Control
10. David Aplin Group

Source: *Canada's 50 Best Managed Companies*, (annual), http://www.canadas50best.com, February 21, 2012.

1491 ■ CANADA'S GREENEST EMPLOYERS, 2012

Ranked by: Score based on earth-friendly programs and initiatives, and success in attracting people due to environmental leadership. **Remarks:** Scores not provided; companies are listed alphabetically, not ranked. **Number listed:** 55

1. Bayer Inc.
2. BC Hydro
3. BC Public Service
4. Calgary Laboratory Services
5. Certified General Accountants Association of Canada
6. Compass Group Canada
7. Corus Entertainment Inc.
8. Enbridge Inc.
9. ENMAX Corp.
10. Fairmont Hotels & Resorts

Source: *Canada's Top 100 Employers*, (annual), http://www.canadastop100.com, April 20, 2012.

1492 ■ CANADA'S LARGEST COMPANIES OVERALL, 2011

Ranked by: Score based on revenue, profits, assets, and market capitalization. **Remarks:** Specific scores not provided. Also notes rank in the overall *Forbes 2000* and figures for each criterion. **Number listed:** 66

1. Royal Bank of Canada
2. TD Bank Financial Group
3. Scotiabank--Bank of Nova Scotia
4. Suncor Energy Inc.
5. Bank of Montreal
6. Canadian Imperial Bank of Commerce
7. Barrick Gold Corp.
8. Brookfield Asset Management Inc.
9. BCE Inc.
10. Canadian Natural Resources Ltd.

Source: *Forbes*, Forbes 2000 (annual), http://www.forbes.com, May 7, 2012.

1493 ■ CANADA'S LARGEST CORPORATIONS BY REVENUE, 2010

Ranked by: Revenue, in thousands of Canadian dollars. **Remarks:** Also notes rank for previous year, headquarters, industry, annual growth in revenue, percentage of sales outside Canada, assets, annual growth in assets, rank by assets, profit, annual growth in profits, rank by profits, earnings per share, profits as a percentage of revenue, profits as a percentage of assets, profits as a percentage of equity, five-year profit growth, one- and five-year **Number listed:** 500

1. Manulife Financial Corp., with C$37,633,000 thousand
2. Royal Bank of Canada, C$36,026,000
3. Suncor Energy Inc., C$33,961,000
4. Power Corporation of Canada, C$32,896,000
5. George Weston Ltd., C$32,008,000
6. Toronto-Dominion Bank, C$25,409,000
7. Imperial Oil Ltd., C$24,946,000
8. Magna International Inc., C$24,825,060
9. Sun Life Financial Inc., C$26,640,000
10. Onex Corp., C$24,366,000

Source: *Financial Post Business Magazine*, FP 500 (annual), http://www.financialpost.com, June 2011.

1494 ■ CANADA'S LARGEST EMPLOYERS, 2010

Ranked by: Number of employees. **Remarks:** Also notes head office, revenue per employee, and profits per employee. **Number listed:** 50

1. Onex Corp., with 238,000 employees
2. George Weston Ltd., 155,000
3. Magna International, 96,600
4. Empire Co., 90,000
5. Royal Bank of Canada, 72,126
6. Scotiabank--Bank of Nova Scotia, 70,772
7. Toronto-Dominion Bank, 68,725
8. Bombardier Inc., 65,370
9. Metro Inc., 65,000
10. Canadian Tire Corp., 56,900

Source: *Report on Business Magazine*, Top 1000 Companies (annual), http://www.reportonbusiness.com, June 2011.

1495 ■ CANADA'S LARGEST FOREIGN-CONTROLLED CORPORATIONS, 2010

Ranked by: Revenue, in thousands of Canadian dollars. **Remarks:** Also notes percentage of foreign ownership, parent company, headquarters, and rank in the overall *FP 500*. **Number listed:** 100

1. Imperial Oil Ltd., with C$24,946,000 thousand
2. Wal-Mart Canada Corp., C$22,000,000
3. Husky Energy Inc., C$18,178,000
4. Costco Wholesale Canada Ltd., C$12,029,668
5. Ford Motor Co. of Canada Ltd., C$9,631,530
6. Direct Energy Marketing Ltd., C$9,478,027
7. Novelis Inc., C$9,462,243
8. Honda Canada Inc., C$8,800,000
9. Ultramar Ltd., C$8,411,012
10. Toyota Motor Manufacturing Canada Inc., C$7,900,000

Source: *Financial Post Business Magazine*, FP 500 (annual), http://www.financialpost.com, June 2011.

1496 ■ CANADA'S TOP CORPORATIONS BY ONE-YEAR PROFIT MARGIN, 2009-2010

Ranked by: One-year profit margin, in percent. **Remarks:** Also notes figures for previous year and rank in the overall *FP 500*. **Number listed:** 50

1. Central Fund of Canada Ltd., with 99%
2. EnerVest Diversified Income Trust, 92.9%
3. Fonds de Solidarite des Trav. du Quebec, 81.4%
4. Silver Wheaton Corp., 68.5%
5. AbitibiBowater Inc., 55.1%
6. Canadian REIT, 50.1%
7. Ultra Petroleum Corp., 47.4%
8. Genworth MI Canada Inc., 43.4%
9. Goldcorp Inc., 41.4%
10. Centerra Gold Inc., 38.1%

Source: *Financial Post Business Magazine*, FP 500 (annual), http://www.financialpost.com, June 2011.

1497 ■ CANADA'S TOP EMPLOYERS, 2012

Ranked by: Score based on eight criteria: physical workplace; work atmosphere; health, financial, and family benefits; vacation and time off; employee communications; performance management; training and skills development; and community involvement. **Remarks:** Scores not provided; companies are listed alphabetically, not ranked. **Number listed:** 100

1. Accenture Inc.
2. Adobe Systems Canada Inc.
3. Agriculture Financial Services Corp.
4. Agrium Inc.
5. Alberta-Pacific Forest Industries Inc.
6. AMEC Americas Ltd.
7. Bank of Canada
8. Bayer Inc.
9. BC Public Service
10. Bennett Jones LLP

Source: *Canada's Top 100 Employers*, (annual), http://www.canadastop100.com, October 7, 2011.

1498 ■ CANADIAN COMPANIES WITH THE BEST CORPORATE CITIZENSHIP, 2011

Ranked by: Score based on a company's connection and responsibility to the people and places it employs, affects, and serves, including such criteria as pension health, cash tax payments, and long-term shareholder value. **Remarks:** Also notes rank for previous year, sector, revenue, number of employees, pension assets, pension fund surplus, tax gap, sustainable development board committee, salary ratio, and diversity. **Number listed:** 50

1. The Co-operators Group Ltd., with 85.96 points
2. Mountain Equipment Co-op, 82.86
3. Domtar Corp., 80.39
4. Loblaw Cos., 79.87
5. BC Hydro & Power Authority, 79.39
6. Vancouver City Savings Credit Union, 79.23
7. Cascades Inc., 79.15
8. Enmax, 78.89
9. Nexen Inc., 77.73
10. Enbridge Inc., 77.1

Source: *Corporate Knights*, Best 50 Corporate Citizens (annual), http://www.corporateknights.ca, June 2, 2011.

1499 ■ CANADIAN COMPANIES WITH THE BEST FIVE-YEAR RETURN, 2007-2012

Ranked by: Five-year annualized return, in percent. **Number listed:** 15

1. Rio Alto Mining Ltd., with 1,574.1%
2. Orbite Aluminae Inc., 1,194.4%
3. Tag Oil Ltd., 903.1%
4. Rare Element Resources Ltd., 825.4%
5. Canadian Energy Services & Technology, 744.2%
6. Pacific Rubiales Energy Corp., 696.2%
7. Atac Resources Ltd., 655.9%
8. SXC Health Solutions Corp., 580.3%
9. Westport Innovations Inc., 558.7%
10. Black Diamond Group Ltd., 520.8%

Source: *Canadian Business*, Investor 500 (annual), 2012, p. 54.

1500 ■ CANADIAN COMPANIES WITH THE HIGHEST MARKET CAPITALIZATION, 2012

Ranked by: Market capitalization, in millions of Canadian dollars. **Number listed:** 15

1. Royal Bank of Canada, with C$80,583 million

2. Toronto-Dominion Bank, C$74,226
3. Scotiabank--Bank of Nova Scotia, C$61,487
4. Suncor Energy Inc., C$47,479
5. Barrick Gold Corp., C$41,508
6. Imperial Oil Ltd., C$36,999
7. Bank of Montreal, C$36,937
8. Potash Corp. of Saskatchewan Inc., C$36,670
9. Canadian Natural Resources Ltd., C$35,111
10. Canadian National Railway Co., C$34,562

Source: *Canadian Business*, Investor 500 (annual), 2012, p. 54.

1501 ■ CANADIAN COMPANIES WITH THE HIGHEST REVENUE, 2011

Ranked by: Revenue, in millions of Canadian dollars. **Number listed:** 15

1. Manulife Financial Corp., with C$49,982 million
2. Suncor Energy Inc., C$39,337
3. Power Corporation of Canada, C$32,912
4. Power Financial Corp., C$32,400
5. George Weston Ltd., C$32,376
6. Loblaw Cos. Ltd., C$31,250
7. Great-West Lifeco Inc., C$29,898
8. Imperial Oil Ltd., C$29,154
9. Magna International Inc., C$28,440
10. Onex Corp., C$24,378

Source: *Canadian Business*, Investor 500 (annual), 2012, p. 54.

1502 ■ GREATER TORONTO'S TOP EMPLOYERS, 2012

Ranked by: Score based on eight criteria: physical workplace; work atmosphere; health, financial, and family benefits; vacation and time off; employee communications; performance management; training and skills development; and community involvement. **Remarks:** Scores not provided; companies are listed alphabetically, not ranked. **Number listed:** 95

1. Accenture Inc.
2. Agfa HealthCare Inc.
3. Agnico-Eagle Mines Ltd.
4. AMEC Americas Ltd.
5. Amex Canada Inc.
6. Amgen Canada Inc.
7. AMAPCEO
8. Bayer Inc.
9. BD Canada Inc.
10. Blake, Cassels & Graydon LLP

Source: *Canada's Top 100 Employers*, (annual), http://www.canadastop100.com, November 16, 2011.

1503 ■ LARGEST CANADIAN COMPANIES BY MARKET CAPITALIZATION, 2011

Ranked by: Market capitalization as of May, in millions of Canadian dollars (unless otherwise noted). **Remarks:** Also notes figures for previous two years. **Number listed:** 100

1. Royal Bank of Canada, with C$83,125 million
2. Toronto-Dominion Bank, C$72,714
3. Suncor Energy, C$61,539
4. Scotiabank--Bank of Nova Scotia, C$60,360
5. Canadian Natural Resources, C$43,896

6. Barrick Gold (U.S. dollars), C$43,754

7. Potash Corp. of Saskatchewan (U.S. dollars), C$42,827

8. Imperial Oil, C$38,667

9. Goldcorp Inc. (U.S. dollars), C$36,765

10. Bank of Montreal, C$34,526

Source: *Report on Business Magazine*, Top 1000 Companies (annual), http://www.reportonbusiness.com, June 2011.

1504 ■ LARGEST CANADIAN COMPANIES BY RETURN ON EQUITY, 2010

Ranked by: One-year return on common equity (ROCE), in percent. **Remarks:** Also notes five-year ROCE. **Number listed:** 100

1. General Donlee Canada, with 163.9%

2. Heritage Oil, 161.7%

3. Craig Wireless Systems, 144.6%

4. Athabasca Oil Sands, 134.1%

5. Wellpoint Systems, 129.6%

6. Cardiome Pharma, 118.7%

7. Sprott Inc., 90.6%

8. Carfinco Income Fund, 77.2%

9. High Arctic Energy Services, 69.2%

10. Boyd Group Income Fund, 63.5%

10. CMP Gold Trust, 63.5%

Source: *Report on Business Magazine*, Top 1000 Companies (annual), http://www.reportonbusiness.com, June 2011.

1505 ■ LARGEST CANADIAN COMPANIES BY REVENUE, 2010

Ranked by: Revenue, in thousands of Canadian dollars (unless otherwise noted). **Remarks:** Also notes percent change from previous year. **Number listed:** 100

1. Manulife Financial, with C$37,856,000 thousand

2. Suncor Energy, C$36,820,000

3. Royal Bank of Canada, C$36,026,000

4. Power Corp. of Canada, C$33,013,000

5. George Weston Ltd., C$32,030,000

6. Loblaw Cos., C$31,005,000

7. Toronto-Dominion Bank, C$25,409,000

8. Imperial Oil, C$25,092,000

9. Magna International (U.S. dollars), C$24,157,000

10. Sun Life Financial, C$24,686,000

Source: *Report on Business Magazine*, Top 1000 Companies (annual), http://www.reportonbusiness.com, June 2011.

1506 ■ LARGEST CANADIAN CROWN CORPORATIONS, 2010

Ranked by: Revenue, in thousands of Canadian dollars. **Remarks:** Also notes rank for previous year, headquarters, industry, revenue growth, assets, asset growth, profits, profit growth, earnings per share, and number of employees. **Number listed:** 40

1. Caisse de depot et placement du Quebec, with C$18,002,000 thousand

2. Hydro-Quebec, C$12,338,000

3. Canada Mortgage & Housing Corp., C$10,551,000

4. Canada Post Corp., C$7,312,000

5. Ontario Lottery & Gaming Corp., C$6,279,019

6. Ontario Power Generation Inc., C$5,375,000

7. Canadian Wheat Board, C$5,150,987

8. Crown Investment Corp. of Saskatchewan, C$4,589,291

9. Liquor Control Board of Ontario, C$4,344,099

10. Workplace Safety & Insurance Board, C$4,227,000

Source: *Financial Post Business Magazine*, FP 500 (annual), http://www.financialpost.com, June 2011.

1507 ■ LARGEST CANADIAN SUBSIDIARIES, 2010

Ranked by: Revenue, in thousands of Canadian dollars. **Remarks:** Also notes rank for previous year, headquarters, industry, revenue growth, assets, asset growth, profits, profit growth, earnings per share, number of employees, ticker symbol, stock exchange, and major voting interests. **Number listed:** 100

1. The Manufacturers Life Insurance Co., with $36,569,620 thousand

2. Power Financial Corp., $32,427,000

3. Loblaw Cos. Ltd., $30,997,000

4. Great-West Lifeco Inc., $29,998,000

5. Sun Life Assurance Co. of Canada, $20,018,000

6. Bell Canada, $15,245,000

7. Sobeys Inc., $15,243,000

8. Canada Life Financial Corp., $10,373,000

9. CIBC Retail Markets, $9,688,000

10. Telus Communications Inc., $9,553,000

Source: *Financial Post Business Magazine*, FP 500 (annual), http://www.financialpost.com, June 2011.

1508 ■ LARGEST COMPANIES IN ALBERTA BY MARKET CAPITALIZATION, 2010

Ranked by: Market capitalization, in thousands of Canadian dollars. **Remarks:** Also notes ticker symbol, head office, share price, and overall rank in the *Venture 100*. **Number listed:** 5

1. Suncor Energy Inc., with C$59,346,000 thousand

2. Canadian Natural Resources Ltd., C$44,068,700

3. Imperial Oil Ltd., C$38,226,760

4. TransCanada Corp., C$29,645,000

5. Cenovus Energy Inc., C$27,391,000

Source: *Alberta Venture*, Venture 100 (annual), http://www.albertaventure.com, September 2011.

1509 ■ LARGEST COMPANIES IN ALBERTA BY REVENUE, 2010

Ranked by: Revenue, in thousands of Canadian dollars. **Remarks:** Also notes head office, rank and figures for previous year, percent change, net income, assets, employees, and senior executive. **Number listed:** 200

1. Suncor Energy Inc., with C$34,350,000 thousand

2. Imperial Oil Ltd., C$24,900,000

3. Husky Energy Inc., C$18,178,000

4. Enbridge Inc., C$15,127,000

5. Cenovus Energy Inc., C$12,973,000

6. Canadian Natural Resources Ltd., C$12,901,000
7. Agrium Inc., C$10,463,192
8. Syncrude Canada Ltd., C$8,655,416
9. EnCana Corp., C$8,613,657
10. TransCanada Corp., C$8,064,000

Source: *Alberta Venture*, Venture 100 (annual), http://www.albertaventure.com, September 2011.

1510 ■ LARGEST COMPANIES IN SASKATCHEWAN, 2011

Ranked by: Gross sales, in Canadian dollars. **Remarks:** Specific figures not provided. Also notes rank for previous year, location, CEO/President, number of local employees, and major shareholders. **Number listed:** 100

1. Viterra Inc.
2. Federated Co-operatives Ltd.
3. Potash Corp. of Saskatchewan Inc.
4. Canpotex Ltd.
5. Mosaic Potash ULC
6. Cameco Corp.
7. Saskatchewan Power Corp.
8. SGI Canada
9. Co-operators Life Insurance Co.
10. SaskTel

Source: *SaskBusiness, the Saskatchewan Business Magazine*, Top 100 Companies (annual), September 2011, p. 15+.

1511 ■ LARGEST CORPORATIONS IN CANADA BY REVENUE, 2010

Ranked by: Revenue, in millions of U.S. dollars. **Remarks:** Also notes headquarters city and overall rank in the *Global 500*. Ranking is available online only, not in print. **Number listed:** 11

1. Manulife Financial Corp., with $36,534 million
2. Royal Bank of Canada, $34,716
3. Suncor Energy Inc., $34,251
4. Power Corp. of Canada, $32,023
5. George Weston Ltd., $31,073
6. Toronto-Dominion Bank, $24,485
7. Magna International Inc., $24,102
8. Sun Life Financial Inc., $23,920
9. Onex Corp., $23,654
10. Scotiabank--Bank of Nova Scotia, $22,911

Source: *Fortune*, Global 500 (annual), http://www.fortune.com, July 25, 2011.

1512 ■ LARGEST PRIVATE CANADIAN COMPANIES, 2010

Ranked by: Revenue, in thousands of Canadian dollars (unless otherwise noted). **Remarks:** Also notes fiscal year-end and major shareholders. **Number listed:** 350

1. The Manufacturers Life Insurance Co., with C$37,080,000 thousand
2. Suncor Energy Products, C$21,092,000
3. Sun Life Assurance of Canada, C$20,018,000
4. Bombardier Aerospace (U.S. dollars), C$17,712,000
5. Rio Tinto Alcan Inc. (U.S. dollars), C$15,206,100

6. Bell Canada, C$15,425,000
7. Sobeys Inc., C$15,246,400
8. Costco Wholesale Canada, C$12,026,668
9. Canada Life Assurace Co., C$10,372,000
10. McKesson Canada (U.S. dollars), C$9,784,000

Source: *Report on Business Magazine*, Top 1000 Companies (annual), http://www.reportonbusiness.com, June 2011.

1513 ■ LARGEST PRIVATE, PUBLIC AND CROWN CORPORATIONS IN BRITISH COLUMBIA, 2010

Ranked by: Revenue, in thousands of Canadian dollars. **Remarks:** Also notes rank and figures for previous year, percent change, type of company, net income, assets, CEO, industry, and major shareholders. **Number listed:** 100

1. Telus Corp., with C$9,779,000 thousand
2. Teck Resources Ltd., C$9,300,000
3. Jim Pattison Group, C$7,200,000
4. Best Buy Canada Ltd., C$5,551,000
5. Finning International Inc., C$4,641,302
6. H. Y. Louie Co., Ltd., C$4,500,000
7. Goldcorp Inc., C$3,913,562
8. BC Hydro & Power Authority, C$3,822,000
9. Insurance Corporation of British Columbia, C$3,721,952
10. Westcoast Energy Inc., C$3,387,000

Source: *BCBusiness*, Top 100 (annual), July 2011, p. 118-121.

1514 ■ LARGEST PUBLIC CORPORATIONS IN BRITISH COLUMBIA, 2010

Ranked by: Revenue, in thousands of Canadian dollars. **Remarks:** Also notes rank and figures for previous year, percent change, income, earnings per share, shareholder equity, return on equity, assets, CEO, industry, and major shareholders. **Number listed:** 100

1. Telus Corp., with C$9,779,000 thousand
2. Teck Resources Ltd., C$9,300,000
3. Finning International Inc., C$4,641,302
4. Goldcorp Inc., C$3,913,562
5. Westcoast Energy Inc., C$3,387,000
6. West Fraser Timber Co., Ltd., C$2,885,900
7. First Quantum Minerals Ltd., C$2,449,401
8. Canfor Corp., C$2,430,400
9. Teekay Corp., C$2,130,818
10. Methanex Corp., C$2,025,461

Source: *BCBusiness*, Top 100 (annual), July 2011, p. 126-129.

1515 ■ MANITOBA'S TOP EMPLOYERS, 2012

Ranked by: Score based on eight criteria: physical workplace; work atmosphere; health, financial, and family benefits; vacation and time off; employee communications; performance management; training and skills development; and community involvement. **Remarks:** Scores not provided; companies are listed alphabetically, not ranked. **Number listed:** 25

1. Aboriginal Peoples Television Network Inc.
2. Boeing Canada Operations Ltd.
3. Brandon Regional Health Authority Inc.
4. Calm Air International LP
5. Canad Inns
6. Canadian Wheat Board

7. Cargill Ltd.
8. Ceridian Canada Ltd.
9. Manitoba Blue Cross
10. Manitoba Civil Service Commission

Source: *Canada's Top 100 Employers*, (annual), http://www.canadastop100.com, November 19, 2011.

1516 ■ MONTREAL'S TOP EMPLOYERS, 2012

Ranked by: Score based on eight criteria: physical workplace; work atmosphere; health, financial, and family benefits; vacation and time off; employee communications; performance management; training and skills development; and community involvement. **Remarks:** Scores not provided; companies are listed alphabetically, not ranked. **Number listed:** 20

1. Aeroplan LP
2. Bombardier Aerospace
3. Business Development Bank of Canada
4. C & D Aerospace Canada Co.
5. Centre de sante et de services sociaux de la Montagne
6. Fednay Ltd.
7. Genetec Inc.
8. L'Oreal Canada Inc.
9. Lundbeck Canada Inc.
10. McGill University

Source: *Canada's Top 100 Employers*, (annual), http://www.canadastop100.com, February 1, 2012.

1517 ■ MOST ADMIRED COMPANIES IN CANADA, 2012

Ranked by: Score based on a survey of executives, directors, and securities analysts of companies within their own industry. **Remarks:** List is available online only, not in print. Also notes headquarters. **Number listed:** 2

1. Thomson Reuters Corp., with 6.83 points
2. EnCana Corp., 5.75

Source: *Fortune*, World's Most Admired Companies (annual), http://www.fortune.com, March 19, 2012.

1518 ■ MOST PROFITABLE CANADIAN COMPANIES, 2010

Ranked by: After-tax profits, in thousands of Canadian dollars (unless otherwise noted). **Remarks:** Also notes rank change from previous year, fiscal year-end, revenue, and percent change from previous year. **Number listed:** 1000

1. Royal Bank of Canada, with C$5,223,000 thousand
2. Toronto-Dominion Bank, C$4,644,000
3. Scotiabank--Bank of Nova Scotia, C$4,239,000
4. Suncor Energy, C$3,571,000
5. Research in Motion Ltd. (U.S. dollars), C$3,411,000
6. Barrick Gold (U.S. dollars), C$3,274,000
7. Bank of Montreal, C$2,810,000
8. Canadian Imperial Bank of Commerce, C$2,452,000
9. BCE Inc., C$2,277,000
10. Imperial Oil, C$2,210,000

Source: *Report on Business Magazine*, Top 1000 Companies (annual), http://www.reportonbusiness.com, June 2011.

1519 ■ MOST PROFITABLE CANADIAN COMPANIES, 2011

Ranked by: Profits, in millions of Canadian dollars. **Number listed:** 15

1. Toronto-Dominion Bank, with C$5,889 million
2. Scotiabank--Bank of Nova Scotia, C$5,175
3. Royal Bank of Canada, C$4,852
4. Barrick Gold Corp., C$4,484
5. Suncor Energy Inc., C$4,304
6. Imperial Oil Ltd., C$3,371
7. Bank of Montreal, C$3,266
8. Potash Corp. of Saskatchewan Inc., C$3,081
9. Canadian Imperial Bank of Commerce, C$3,079
10. Teck Resources Ltd., C$2,668

Source: *Canadian Business*, Investor 500 (annual), 2012, p. 54.

1520 ■ MOST PROFITABLE COMPANIES IN BRITISH COLUMBIA, 2010

Ranked by: Income as a percentage of revenue. **Remarks:** Also notes revenue and income. **Number listed:** 10

1. Silver Standard Resources Inc., with 308.4%
2. Canfor Pulp Products Inc., 102.1%
3. Scorpio Mining Corp., 95%
4. Silver Wheaton Corp., 68.5%
5. Cardiome Pharma, 53.7%
6. Taseko Mines Ltd., 53.4%
7. A & W Revenue Royalties Income Fund, 51.4%
8. Callinan Mines Ltd., 51%
9. Goldcorp Inc., 41.2%
10. QLT Inc., 39.2%

Source: *BCBusiness*, Top 100 (annual), July 2011.

1521 ■ NOVA SCOTIA'S TOP EMPLOYERS, 2012

Ranked by: Score based on eight criteria: physical workplace; work atmosphere; health, financial, and family benefits; vacation and time off; employee communications; performance management; training and skills development; and community involvement. **Remarks:** Scores not provided; companies are listed alphabetically, not ranked. **Number listed:** 15

1. Admiral Insurance Services Inc.
2. Annapolis Valley District Health Authority
3. Cape Breton District Health Authority
4. Capital District Health Authority
5. CBCL Ltd.
6. College of Physicians & Surgeons of Nova Scotia
7. Dalhousie University
8. High Liner Foods Inc.
9. IMP Group Ltd.
10. Jazz Aviation LP

Source: *Canada's Top 100 Employers*, (annual), http://www.canadastop100.com, November 19, 2011.

1522 ■ SASKATCHEWAN'S TOP EMPLOYERS, 2012

Ranked by: Score based on eight criteria: physical workplace; work atmosphere; health, financial, and family benefits; vacation and time off; employee communications; performance management; training and skills development; and community involvement. **Remarks:** Scores not provided; companies are listed alphabetically, not ranked. **Number listed:** 20

1. Access Communications Co-operative Ltd.
2. Cameco Corp.
3. Co-operators Life Insurance Co.
4. Group Medical Services
5. Information Services Corp. of Saskatchewan
6. ISM Canada
7. Magna Electric Corp.
8. Prince Albert Parkland Health Region
9. Ranch Ehrio Society
10. Regina Police Service

Source: *Canada's Top 100 Employers*, (annual), http://www.canadastop100.com, February 1, 2012.

1523 ■ TOP EMPLOYERS IN CANADA'S NATIONAL CAPITAL REGION, 2012

Ranked by: Score based on eight criteria: physical workplace; work atmosphere; health, financial, and family benefits; vacation and time off; employee communications; performance management; training and skills development; and community involvement. **Remarks:** Scores not provided; companies are listed alphabetically, not ranked. **Number listed:** 30

1. Aboriginal Affairs & Northern Development Canada
2. Accreditation Canada
3. Adobe Systems Canada Inc.
4. Andrew Fleck Child Care Services
5. Bank of Canada
6. Canada Mortgage & Housing Corp.
7. Canada Science & Technology Museums Corp.
8. Canadian Food Inspection Agency
9. Canadian Institutes of Health Research
10. Canadian Nuclear Safety Commission

Source: *Canada's Top 100 Employers*, (annual), http://www.canadastop100.com, February 7, 2012.

1524 ■ TOP EMPLOYERS FOR CANADIANS OVER AGE 40, 2012

Ranked by: Score based on programs and initiatives for employees over 40 years of age as well as success in attracting older workers. **Remarks:** Scores not provided; companies are listed alphabetically, not ranked. **Number listed:** 15

1. Agriculture Financial Services Corp.
2. BMO Financial Group
3. British Columbia Lottery Corp.
4. Business Development Bank of Canada
5. Cameco Corp.
6. Canadian Security Intelligence Service
7. EllisDon Corp.
8. Gay Lea Foods Co-operative Ltd.
9. Office of the Auditor General of Canada
10. Ontario Public Service

Source: *Canada's Top 100 Employers*, (annual), http://www.canadastop100.com, June 7, 2011.

1525 ■ TOP EMPLOYERS IN THE HAMILTON-NIAGARA REGION, 2012

Ranked by: Score based on eight criteria: physical workplace; work atmosphere; health, financial, and family benefits; vacation

and time off; employee communications; performance management; training and skills development; and community involvement. **Remarks:** Scores not provided; companies are listed alphabetically, not ranked. **Number listed:** 10

1. Brant Community Healthcare System
2. Hamilton Utilities Corp.
3. IKEA Canada LP
4. Niagara Fallsview Casino Resort
5. O. C. Tanner Recognition Co., Ltd.
6. Roxul Inc.
7. Siemens Canada Ltd.
8. Sodexo Canada Ltd.
9. St. Joseph's Healthcare Hamilton
10. Stryker Canada Inc.

Source: *Canada's Top 100 Employers*, (annual), http://www.canadastop100.com, November 23, 2011.

1526 ■ TOP EMPLOYERS IN THE KITCHENER-WATERLOO AND GUELPH REGION, 2012

Ranked by: Score based on eight criteria: physical workplace; work atmosphere; health, financial, and family benefits; vacation and time off; employee communications; performance management; training and skills development; and community involvement. **Remarks:** Scores not provided; companies are listed alphabetically, not ranked. **Number listed:** 15

1. COM DEV International Ltd.
2. Crawford & Company (Canada) Inc.
3. Desire2Learn Inc.
4. The Economical Mutual Insurance Co.
5. Equitable Life Insurance Company of Canada
6. George Morris Center for Agri-Food Research & Education
7. Geosyntec Consultants International Inc.
8. Gore Mutual Insurance Co.
9. OpenText Corp.
10. Perimeter Institute for Theoretical Physics

Source: *Canada's Top 100 Employers*, (annual), http://www.canadastop100.com, November 26, 2011.

1527 ■ TOP EMPLOYERS FOR YOUNG CANADIANS, 2012

Ranked by: Score based on success in attracting and retaining younger employees. **Remarks:** Scores not provided; companies are listed alphabetically, not ranked. **Number listed:** 55

1. Alberta Blue Cross
2. AltaGas Ltd.
3. ATB Financial
4. Bayer CropScience Canada Inc.
5. Bayer Inc.
6. Cactus Restaurants Ltd.
7. Canad Inns
8. Capital One Bank
9. Cargill Ltd.
10. City of Mississauga, Ontario

Source: *Canada's Top 100 Employers*, (annual), http://www.canadastop100.com, September 19, 2011.

1528 ■ TOP LARGE-CAP CANADIAN COMPANIES BY ONE-YEAR RETURN, 2011-2012

Ranked by: One-year return, in percent. **Remarks:** Also notes rank for previous year, rank in the overall *Investor 500*, industry sector, headquarters, ticker symbol, five-year return, stock price, dividend yield, market capitalization, price-to-earnings ratio, price-to-sales ratio, price-to-book ratio, revenue, revenue growth, earnings per share, earnings per share growth, operating margin, profit margin, return on equity, and re **Number listed:** 50

1. Enbridge Inc., with 32.6%
2. Canadian Utilities Ltd., 28.1%
3. Yamana Gold Inc., 27.9%
3. Canadian Pacific Railway Ltd., 27.9%
5. Telus Corp., 23.9%
6. BCE Inc., 17.8%
7. Rogers Communications Inc., 17.7%
8. Canadian National Railway Co., 13.9%
9. TransCanada Corp., 12.2%
10. Shoppers Drug Mart Corp., 7.8%

Source: *Canadian Business*, Investor 500 (annual), 2012, p. 78-79.

1529 ■ TOP MID-CAP CANADIAN COMPANIES BY ONE-YEAR RETURN, 2011-2012

Ranked by: One-year return, in percent. **Remarks:** Also notes rank for previous year, rank in the overall *Investor 500*, industry sector, headquarters, ticker symbol, five-year return, stock price, dividend yield, market capitalization, price-to-earnings ratio, price-to-sales ratio, price-to-book ratio, revenue, revenue growth, earnings per share, earnings per share growth, operating margin, profit margin, return on equity, and re **Number listed:** 150

1. Dollarama Inc., with 74%
2. Flint Energy Services Ltd., 62.8%
3. Pretium Resources Inc., 61.2%
4. Imperial Metals Corp., 57.8%
5. Westport Innovations Inc., 53.8%
6. SXC Health Solutions Corp., 50.6%
7. Morguard Corp., 50.4%
8. Viterra Inc., 41.9%
9. Jean Coutu Group PJC Inc., 39.3%
10. Pembina Pipeline Corp., 37.4%

Source: *Canadian Business*, Investor 500 (annual), 2012, p. 80-85.

1530 ■ TOP PUBLIC COMPANIES IN BRITISH COLUMBIA BY PROFIT GROWTH, 2009-2010

Ranked by: Annual growth in profits, in percent. **Remarks:** Also notes CEO and profit for current and previous year. **Number listed:** 10

1. Methanex Corp., with 12,332.5%
2. Taiga Building Products Ltd., 6,139.6%
3. CIBT Education Group Inc., 3,181.2%
4. Fortuna Silver Mines Inc., 1,775.4%
5. Cardiome Pharma Corp., 1,408%
6. Taseko Mines Ltd., 1,307%
7. Canfor Pulp Products Inc., 898.4%
8. Amerigo Resources Ltd., 636.9%
9. Goldcorp Inc., 488%
10. First Majestic Silver Corp., 472.2%

Source: *BCBusiness*, Top 100 (annual), July 2011.

1531 ■ TOP PUBLIC COMPANIES IN BRITISH COLUMBIA BY REVENUE GROWTH, 2009-2010

Ranked by: Annual revenue growth, in percent. **Remarks:** Also notes revenue for current and previous year. **Number listed:** 25

1. Silver Standard Resources Inc., with 1,760.4%
2. Canfor Pulp Products Inc., 1,234.2%
3. Yukon-Nevada Gold Corp., 549.3%
4. IND DairyTech Ltd., 299%
5. Great Basin Gold Ltd., 195.5%
6. Day4 Energy Inc., 177.6%
7. CanWel Building Materials Group Ltd., 152.9%
8. Finning International Inc., 133.9%
9. Energold Drilling Corp., 130.2%
10. SouthGobi Resources Ltd., 121.7%

Source: *BCBusiness*, Top 100 (annual), July 2011.

1532 ■ TOP SMALL-CAP CANADIAN COMPANIES BY ONE-YEAR RETURN, 2011-2012

Ranked by: One-year return, in percent. **Remarks:** Also notes rank for previous year, rank in the overall *Investor 500*, industry sector, headquarters, ticker symbol, five-year return, stock price, dividend yield, market capitalization, price-to-earnings ratio, price-to-sales ratio, price-to-book ratio, revenue, revenue growth, earnings per share, earnings per share growth, operating margin, profit margin, return on equity, and re **Number listed:** 300

1. Intertape Polymer Group Inc., with 291.5%
2. Pershimco Resources Inc., 235%
3. Trimel Pharmaceuticals Corp., 152.8%
4. Rio Alto Mining Ltd., 126%
5. Lumina Copper Corp., 124.7%
6. Africa Oil Corp., 106.9%
7. Absolute Software Corp., 97.6%
8. Miranda Technologies Inc., 87.6%
9. Banro Corp., 77.4%
10. Canadian Helicopters Group Inc., 74%

Source: *Canadian Business*, Investor 500 (annual), 2012, p. 86-91.

Corporations—Caribbean

1533 ■ BERMUDA'S LARGEST COMPANIES OVERALL, 2011

Ranked by: Score based on revenue, profits, assets, and market capitalization. **Remarks:** Specific scores not provided. Also notes rank in the overall *Forbes 2000* and figures for each criterion. **Number listed:** 10

1. Bunge Corp.
2. Seadrill Ltd.
3. Invesco
4. Assured Guaranty Ltd.
5. Marvell Technology Group Ltd.
6. Arch Capital Group Ltd.
7. White Mountains Insurance Group Ltd.
8. Nabors Industries Ltd.
9. PartnerRe Ltd.
10. Everest Re Group Ltd.

Source: *Forbes*, Forbes 2000 (annual), http://www.forbes.com, May 7, 2012.

1534 ■ BEST COMPANIES TO WORK FOR IN THE CARIBBEAN, 2012

Ranked by: Score based on the relationships between employees and management, employees and their jobs/company, and employees and coworkers. **Remarks:** Specific scores not provided. **Number listed:** 15

1. Kimberly-Clark Republica Dominicana
2. Scotiabank Republica Dominicana
3. Kimberly-Clark Puerto Rico y Jamaica
4. Atento Puerto Rico
5. Oracle Caribbean Inc. Puerto Rico
6. Hotel Catalonia Royal Republica Dominicana
7. Hotel Catalonia Bavaro Republica Dominicana
8. AES Dominicana Republica Dominicana
9. Odebrecht Republica Dominicana
10. Grupo Universal Republica Dominicana

Source: *Great Place to Work Institute Inc.*, Best Places to Work in Central America & the Caribbean (annual), 2012.

Corporations—Central America

1535 ■ BEST LARGE COMPANIES TO WORK FOR IN CENTRAL AMERICA, 2012

Ranked by: Score based on the relationships between employees and management, employees and their jobs/company, and employees and coworkers. **Remarks:** Specific scores not provided. To qualify, companies must have more than 1,000 employees. **Number listed:** 12

1. Atento El Salvador
2. Arcos Dorados Panama
3. Kimberly-Clark Costa Rica
4. Scotiabank Guatemala
5. Cementos Progreso Guatemala
6. Atento Guatemala
7. Scotiabank Costa Rica
8. Scotiabank El Salvador
9. Dell Panama
10. Grupo Ficohsa Honduras

Source: *Great Place to Work Institute Inc.*, Best Places to Work in Central America (annual), 2012.

1536 ■ BEST MULTINATIONAL COMPANIES TO WORK FOR IN CENTRAL AMERICA, 2012

Ranked by: Score based on the relationships between employees and management, employees and their jobs/company, and employees and coworkers. **Remarks:** Specific scores not provided. **Number listed:** 18

1. Kimberly-Clark Corp.
2. S. C. Johnson de Centroamerica
3. Atento
4. FedEx Corp.
5. Telefonica SA
6. Scotiabank, the Bank of Nova Scotia
7. Grupo :Progreso
8. Autofacil
9. Arcos Dorados
10. British American Tobacco plc

Source: *Great Place to Work Institute Inc.*, Best Places to Work in Central America (annual), 2012.

1537 ■ BEST SMALL COMPANIES TO WORK FOR IN CENTRAL AMERICA, 2012

Ranked by: Score based on the relationships between employees and management, employees and their jobs/company, and

employees and coworkers. **Remarks:** Specific scores not provided. To qualify, companies must have fewer than 1,000 employees. **Number listed:** 18

1. Kimberly-Clark Honduras
2. Kimberly-Clark El Salvador
3. FedEx Guatemala
4. Kimberly-Clark Nicaragua
5. Telefonica Nicaragua
6. Kimberly-Clark Guatemala
7. Telefonica Panama
8. S. C. Johnson de Centroamerica
9. Sacos del Atlantico Guatemala
10. Kimberly-Clark Panama

Source: *Great Place to Work Institute Inc.*, Best Places to Work in Central America (annual), 2012.

Corporations—Chile

1538 ■ BEST COMPANIES TO WORK FOR IN CHILE, 2011

Ranked by: Score based on the relationships between employees and management, employees and their jobs/company, and employees and coworkers. **Remarks:** Specific scores not provided. **Number listed:** 35

1. Kimberly-Clark Chile
2. Transbank
3. Coca-Cola de Chile
4. Telefonica SA
5. BancoEstado MicroEmpresas
6. VTR
7. S. C. Johnson & Son Chile
8. Microsoft Chile
9. Banchile Inversiones
10. Mars Chile

Source: *Great Place to Work Institute Inc.*, Best Places to Work in Chile (annual), 2011.

1539 ■ CHILE'S LARGEST COMPANIES OVERALL, 2011

Ranked by: Score based on revenue, profits, assets, and market capitalization. **Remarks:** Specific scores not provided. Also notes rank in the overall *Forbes 2000* and figures for each criterion. **Number listed:** 9

1. SACI Falabella
2. Cencosud SA
3. Antarchile
4. Banco de Credito e Inversiones SA (BCI)
5. Empresas CMPC SA
6. Quinenco SA
7. Sociedad Quimica y Minera de Chile SA (SQM)
8. LAN Airlines SA
9. CAP SA

Source: *Forbes*, Forbes 2000 (annual), http://www.forbes.com, May 7, 2012.

Corporations—China

1540 ■ BEST SMALL CHINESE/HONG KONG COMPANIES, 2010

Ranked by: Score based on sales, net income, and market value. **Remarks:** Specific scores not provided; companies are listed alphabetically, not ranked. Also notes sales, net income, market value, and industry. To qualify for list, which is available online only, companies must have under US$1 billion in annual revenue and positive earnings growth over the past five years. **Number listed:** 65

1. 361 Degrees International
2. AAC Acoustic Technologies
3. Alibaba.com
4. Anhui Gujing Distillery
5. Anhui Jiangnan Chemical Industry
6. Anhui Zhongding Sealing Parts
7. Anxin Trust & Investment
8. APAC Resources
9. Beijing Shiji Information Technology
10. Beijing SL Pharmaceutical

Source: *Forbes Asia*, Asia's Best Under a Billion (annual), http://www.forbes.com, September 12, 2011.

1541 ■ CHINA'S LARGEST COMPANIES OVERALL, 2011

Ranked by: Score based on revenue, profits, assets, and market capitalization. **Remarks:** Specific scores not provided. Also notes rank in the overall *Forbes 2000* and figures for each criterion. **Number listed:** 136

1. Industrial & Commercial Bank of China
2. PetroChina Co., Ltd.
3. China Construction Bank
4. Agricultural Bank of China
5. Bank of China
6. China Petroleum & Chemical Corp. (Sinopec)
7. China Life Insurance Co., Ltd.
8. Ping An Insurance (Group) Company of China Ltd.
9. Bank of Communications
10. China Shenhua Energy Co., Ltd.

Source: *Forbes*, Forbes 2000 (annual), http://www.forbes.com, May 7, 2012.

1542 ■ LARGEST CORPORATIONS IN CHINA BY REVENUE, 2010

Ranked by: Revenue, in millions of U.S. dollars. **Remarks:** Also notes headquarters city and overall rank in the *Global 500*. Ranking is available online only, not in print. **Number listed:** 61

1. China Petroleum & Chemical Corp. (Sinopec), with $273,422 million
2. China National Petroleum Co., $240,192
3. State Grid Corp. of China, $226,294
4. Industrial & Commercial Bank of China, $80,501
5. China Mobile Communications Corp., $76,673
6. China Railway Group Ltd., $69,973
7. China Railway Construction Corp., $67,414
8. China Construction Bank, $67,081
9. China Life Insurance Co., Ltd., $64,635
10. Agricultural Bank of China, $60,536

Source: *Fortune*, Global 500 (annual), http://www.fortune.com, July 25, 2011.

1543 ■ MOST ADMIRED COMPANIES IN CHINA, 2012

Ranked by: Score based on a survey of executives, directors, and securities analysts of companies within their own industry. **Remarks:** List is available online only, not in print. Also notes headquarters. **Number listed:** 2

1. Baosteel Group Corp., with 6.44 points
2. China National Offshore Oil, 5.77

Source: *Fortune*, World's Most Admired Companies (annual), http://www.fortune.com, March 19, 2012.

1544 ■ TOP CHINESE COMPANIES, 2011

Ranked by: Score based on profits, sales and earnings growth, and projected earnings and stock-price gains. **Remarks:** Specific scores not provided; companies are listed alphabetically, not ranked. Also notes market value, revenue, and industry. To quality, companies must be publicly traded with revenues or market capitalization of at least US$3 billion. Ranking is available online only, not in print. **Number listed:** 23

1. Agile Property Holdings
2. Anhui Conch Cement Co., Ltd.
3. Belle International Holdings
4. Changsha Zoomlion Heavy Industry
5. China Mengniu Dairy
6. China Merchants Bank
7. Country Garden Holdings
8. Digital China Holdings
9. Dongfang Motor Group
10. GD Midea Holding

Source: *Forbes*, Asian Fab 50 (annual), September 13, 2011.

Corporations—Colombia

1545 ■ BEST COMPANIES TO WORK FOR IN COLOMBIA, 2011

Ranked by: Score based on the relationships between employees and management, employees and their jobs/company, and employees and coworkers. **Remarks:** Specific scores not provided. **Number listed:** 25

1. Seguros Bolivar SA
2. Seguridad Atlas Ltda.
3. Seguros Generales Suramericana SA/Seguros de Vida Suramericana SA
4. Eps y Medicina Prepagada Suramericana
5. Colombia Telecomunicaciones SA/Telefonica Moviles Colombia SA
6. Branch of Microsoft Colombia Inc.
7. Seguros de Riesgos Profesionales Suramericana SA
8. Diageo Colombia SA
9. Camara de Comercio de Medellin para Antioquia
10. Arcos Dorados de Colombia SA

Source: *Great Place to Work Institute Inc.*, Best Places to Work in Colombia (annual), http://www.greatplacetowork.com, December 2011.

1546 ■ COLOMBIA'S LARGEST COMPANIES OVERALL, 2011

Ranked by: Score based on revenue, profits, assets, and market capitalization. **Remarks:** Specific scores not provided. Also notes rank in the overall *Forbes 2000* and figures for each criterion. **Number listed:** 6

1. Ecopetrol SA
2. BanColombia

3. Grupo Aval Acciones y Valores SA
4. Banco Davivienda
5. Interconexion Electrica
6. Energia de Bogota

Source: *Forbes*, Forbes 2000 (annual), http://www.forbes.com, May 7, 2012.

Corporations—Colorado

1547 ■ BEST LARGE COLORADO COMPANIES TO WORK FOR, 2011

Ranked by: Score based on employee surveys. **Remarks:** Specific scores not provided. Ranking covers companies with 250 or more employees. Also notes contact information, year founded, location, CEO, number of Colorado employees, rank for previous year, and comments. **Number listed:** 10

1. Edward Jones
2. Alpine Bank
3. PricewaterhouseCoopers LLP
4. Mercury Payment Systems
5. Omni Interlocken Resort
6. Hospice & Palliative Care of Western Colorado
7. Cheyenne Mountain Resort
8. The Progressive Group of Insurance Cos.
9. DaVita Inc.
10. CoBank

Source: *ColoradoBiz*, Best Companies to Work for in Colorado (annual), August 2011, p. 30-34.

1548 ■ BEST LARGE DENVER-AREA PLACES TO WORK, 2010

Ranked by: Score, on a scale of 100, based on employee survey of workplace culture. **Remarks:** Ranking includes companies with 251 to 750 employees. Also notes contact information, number of local employees, business description, and top local executive. **Number listed:** 10

1. Grand Hyatt Denver, with 92.98 points
2. Allied/Nationwide Insurance, 89.63
3. PricewaterhouseCoopers LLP, 87.97
4. RK Mechanical Inc., 86.55
5. Holland & Hart LLP, 86.12
6. Mental Health Center of Denver, 86.05
7. Accenture, 85.62
8. DCP Midstream LLC, 85.45
9. Re/Max LLC, 84.59
10. Ashford University, 83.6

Source: *Denver Business Journal*, Book of Lists (annual), December 16, 2011, p. 60.

1549 ■ BEST MEDIUM-SIZED COLORADO COMPANIES TO WORK FOR, 2011

Ranked by: Score based on employee surveys. **Remarks:** Specific scores not provided. Ranking covers companies with 100 to 249 employees. Also notes contact information, year founded, location, CEO, number of Colorado employees, rank for previous year, and comments. **Number listed:** 10

1. ReadyTalk
2. Rally Software Development Corp.

3. PCL Construction Enterprises Inc.
4. Return Path Inc.
5. Executive Resorts LLC
6. Blu Sky Restoration Contractors Inc.
7. Encompass Home Health
8. DataLogix
9. Bona USA Inc.
10. Wind Crest

Source: *ColoradoBiz*, Best Companies to Work for in Colorado (annual), August 2011, p. 38-43.

1550 ■ BEST MEDIUM-SIZED DENVER-AREA PLACES TO WORK, 2010

Ranked by: Score, on a scale of 100, based on employee survey of workplace culture. **Remarks:** Ranking includes companies with 51 to 250 employees. Also notes contact information, number of local employees, business description, and top local executive. **Number listed:** 10

1. Point B Inc., with 98.92 points
2. Wealth Concepts LLC, 96.15
3. Wheeler Trigg O'Donnell LLP, 95.09
4. PCL Construction Enterprises Inc., 93.69
5. GHP Horwath PC, 93.44
6. Partner Credit Union/Eagle Legacy Credit Union, 93.39
7. Clinic Service Corp., 92.55
8. Haynes Mechanical Systems Inc., 91.64
9. ReadyTalk, 91.58
10. Location3 Media, 90.18

Source: *Denver Business Journal*, Book of Lists (annual), December 16, 2011, p. 60.

1551 ■ BEST MEGA DENVER-AREA PLACES TO WORK, 2010

Ranked by: Score, on a scale of 100, based on employee survey of workplace culture. **Remarks:** Ranking includes companies with 751 or more employees. Also notes contact information, number of local employees, business description, and top local executive. **Number listed:** 4

1. Comcast Cable, with 88.64 points
2. Chipotle Mexican Grill Inc., 88.23
3. DaVita Inc., 85.73
4. OppenheimerFunds, 82.32

Source: *Denver Business Journal*, Book of Lists (annual), December 16, 2011, p. 60.

1552 ■ BEST SMALL COLORADO COMPANIES TO WORK FOR, 2011

Ranked by: Score based on employee surveys. **Remarks:** Specific scores not provided. Ranking covers companies with 25 to 99 employees. Also notes contact information, year founded, location, CEO, number of Colorado employees, rank for previous year, and comments. **Number listed:** 10

1. IP5280 Communications
2. Rothstein Kass
3. Odell Brewing Co.
4. R. A. Nelson & Associates Inc.
5. Anton Collins Mitchell LLP
6. Crestone Capital Advisors LLC

7. Insperity
8. Applied Control Equipment LLLP
9. Maptek
10. Adperio

Source: *ColoradoBiz*, Best Companies to Work for in Colorado (annual), August 2011, p. 46-48.

1553 ■ BEST SMALL COMPANIES IN COLORADO, 2011

Ranked by: Score based on revenue, profits, and return on equity for the past 12 months and five years. **Remarks:** Specific scores not provided. Also notes rank in the overall *100 Best Small Companies in America*. To qualify, companies must have revenues between $5 million and $1 billion, a net margin above five percent, and share price above $5. List is available online only. **Number listed:** 2

1. Air Methods
2. Royal Gold

Source: *Forbes*, Best Small Companies in America (annual), November 7, 2011.

1554 ■ BEST SMALL DENVER-AREA PLACES TO WORK, 2010

Ranked by: Score, on a scale of 100, based on employee survey of workplace culture. **Remarks:** Ranking includes companies with 10 to 50 employees. Also notes contact information, number of local employees, business description, and top local executive. **Number listed:** 10

1. Kendall, Koenig & Oelsner PC, with 100 points
2. Razor Technical Staffing, 99.72
3. Catapult Systems, 98.82
4. Entasis Group LLC, 98.64
5. Verus Global Inc., 98.13
6. Management Recruiters of Colorado Inc., 97.77
7. Protiviti Inc., 97.54
8. Total Quality Logistics, 97.12
9. Tom James Co., 96.99
10. GroundFloor Media Inc., 96.49

Source: *Denver Business Journal*, Book of Lists (annual), December 16, 2011, p. 60.

1555 ■ COLORADO'S FASTEST-GROWING PUBLIC COMPANIES, 2008-2010

Ranked by: Two-year net income growth, in percent. **Remarks:** Also notes business description, ticker symbol, and net income for 2008 and 2010. **Number listed:** 16

1. National CineMedia Inc., with 2,820%
2. Zynex Inc., 215.5%
3. Newmont Mining Corp., 174%
4. Hallador Petroleum Co., 151.4%
5. Air Methods Corp., 128.9%
5. Chipotle Mexican Grill Inc., 128.9%
7. Molson Coors Brewing Co., 86.9%
8. Evolving Systems Inc., 82.8%
9. Emergency Medical Services Corp., 55.2%
10. Ball Corp., 46.5%

Source: *Denver Business Journal*, Book of Lists (annual), December 16, 2011, p. 49.

1556 ■ COLORADO'S LARGEST COMPANIES OVERALL, 2011

Ranked by: Score based on revenue, profits, assets, and market capitalization. **Remarks:** Specific scores not provided. Also notes overall rank in the *Forbes 2000* and figures for each criterion. **Number listed:** 14

1. Dish Network Corp.
2. Newmont Mining Corp.
3. Liberty Interactive Corp.
4. Liberty Global Inc.
5. The Western Union Co.
6. Arrow Electronics
7. DaVita Inc.
8. Molson Coors Brewing Co.
9. Liberty Media Corp.
10. Ball Corp.

Source: *Forbes*, Forbes 2000 (annual), http://www.forbes.com, May 7, 2012.

1557 ■ COLORADO'S LARGEST PRIVATE COMPANIES, 2010

Ranked by: Revenue, in billions of dollars. **Remarks:** Also notes business segment, number of employees, and overall rank in the *America's Largest Private Companies* list. Ranking is available on-line only, not in print. **Number listed:** 6

1. TransMontaigne Inc., with $12 billion
2. CH2M Hill Cos., Ltd., $5.42
3. Pro-Build Holdings Inc., $3.5
4. The Sports Authority Inc., $3.2
5. Leprino Foods Co., $2.6
6. Hensel Phelps Construction Co., $2.5

Source: *Forbes*, America's Largest Private Companies (annual), http://www.forbes.com, December 5, 2011.

1558 ■ COLORADO'S LARGEST PUBLIC COMPANIES BY MARKET CAPITALIZATION, 2011

Ranked by: Market capitalization as of August 5, in millions of dollars. **Remarks:** Also notes contact information, website, rank for previous year, ticker symbol, net income and revenue for previous three years, high and low stock prices, business description, top local executive, and year founded. **Number listed:** 100

1. Newmont Mining Corp., with $26,890 million
2. Liberty Media Corp. (Starz, LSTZB), $19,770
3. Liberty Media Corp. (LINTB), $18,680
4. Liberty Media Corp. (Capital, LCAPB), $17,470
5. The Western Union Co., $11,200
6. Dish Network LLC, $11,170
7. Liberty Global Inc. (LBTYB), $11,110
8. Liberty Global Inc. (LBTYA), $10,520
9. Chipotle Mexican Grill Inc., $9,760
10. Liberty Media Corp. (LINTA), $8,360

Source: *Denver Business Journal*, Book of Lists (annual), December 16, 2011, p. 45+.

1559 ■ COLORADO'S LARGEST PUBLIC COMPANIES BY NET INCOME, 2010

Ranked by: Net income, in millions of dollars. **Remarks:** Also notes rank and figures for previous two years, business description, and ticker symbol. **Number listed:** 50

1. Newmont Mining Corp., with $2,277 million
2. Dish Network LLC, $984.7
3. The Western Union Co., $909.9
4. Liberty Media Corp. (LINTA/LINTB), $871
5. Liberty Media Corp. (LCAPA/LCAPB), $815

6. Molson Coors Brewing Co., $707.7
7. Cimarex Energy Co., $574.8
8. Ball Corp., $468
9. DaVita Inc., $405.7
10. Liberty Global Inc. (LBTYA/LBTYB), $388.2

Source: *Denver Business Journal*, Book of Lists (annual), December 16, 2011, p. 49.

1560 ■ COLORADO'S LARGEST PUBLIC COMPANIES BY NUMBER OF EMPLOYEES, 2010

Ranked by: Number of employees. **Remarks:** Also notes rank and figures for previous year, business description, ticker symbol, and one-year employee growth. **Number listed:** 100

1. TeleTech Holdings Inc., with 45,500 employees
2. Pilgrim's Pride Corp., 42,300
3. DaVita Inc., 36,500
4. Qwest Communications International Inc./ CenturyLink Inc., 28,343
5. Chipotle Mexican Grill Inc., 26,500
6. Red Robin Gourmet Burgers Inc., 23,198
7. Dish Network LLC, 22,000
8. Liberty Global Inc., 20,000
9. Liberty Media Corp., 19,070
10. Emergency Medical Services Corp., 17,500

Source: *Denver Business Journal*, Book of Lists (annual), December 16, 2011, p. 50.

1561 ■ COLORADO'S LARGEST PUBLIC COMPANIES BY SALES, 2010

Ranked by: Sales, in millions of dollars. **Remarks:** Also notes rank for previous year, business description, ticker symbol, and sales for previous two years. **Number listed:** 100

1. Dish Network LLC, with $12,640.7 million
2. Qwest Communications International Inc./ CenturyLink Inc., $11,730
3. Newmont Mining Corp., $9,540
4. Liberty Global Inc., $9,016.9
5. Liberty Media Corp., $8,932
6. Ball Corp., $7,630
7. Pilgrim's Pride Corp., $6,881.6
8. DaVita Inc., $6,447.4
9. The Western Union Co., $5,192.7
10. Level 3 Communications Inc., $3,651

Source: *Denver Business Journal*, Book of Lists (annual), December 16, 2011, p. 51.

1562 ■ COLORADO'S TOP PRIVATE COMPANIES, 2010

Ranked by: Gross revenue, in thousands of dollars. **Remarks:** Also notes business description, rank and figures for previous year, percent change, number of employees, and number of years in business. **Number listed:** 250

1. CH2M Hill Cos., Ltd., with $6,300,000 thousand
2. PCL Construction Enterprises Inc., $4,984,868
3. Hensel Phelps Construction Co., $2,021,000
4. MWH Global Inc., $1,139,165
5. Flatiron Construction Corp., $1,033,556
6. Global Technology Resources Inc., $307,153

7. American Furniture Warehouse Co., $307,000
8. Xanterra Parks & Resorts Inc., $305,353
9. FCI Constructors Inc., $252,327
10. Mike Shaw Automotive Group, $252,088

Source: *ColoradoBiz*, Top 250 Private Companies (annual), October 2011, p. 47+.

1563 ■ FASTEST-GROWING COMPANIES IN COLORADO, 2008-2011

Ranked by: Score based on three-year growth in revenue and earnings, and three-year total return to investors. **Remarks:** Specific scores not provided. To qualify for list, companies must have revenues of at least $50 million, net income of at least $10 million, market capitalization of at least $250 million, and stock price of at least $5. Int'l companies are eligible if they trade on a U.S. exchange and file quarterly reports. **Number listed:** 2

1. Chipotle Mexican Grill Inc.
2. Newmont Mining

Source: *Fortune*, 100 Fastest-Growing Companies (annual), http://www.fortune.com, September 26, 2011.

1564 ■ LARGEST COLORADO-BASED PUBLIC COMPANIES, 2010

Ranked by: Revenue, in thousands of dollars. **Remarks:** Also notes ticker symbol, business description, figures for previous year, percent change, net income, and number of employees. **Number listed:** 100

1. Dish Network Corp., with $12,640,744 thousand
2. Qwest Communications International Inc., $11,730,000
3. Newmont Mining Corp., $9,540,000
4. Liberty Global Inc., $9,016,900
5. Ball Corp., $7,630,000
6. DaVita Inc., $6,447,391
7. The Western Union Co., $5,192,700
8. Level 3 Communications Inc., $3,651,000
9. Molson Coors Brewing Co., $3,254,400
10. Emergency Medical Services Corp., $2,859,322

Source: *ColoradoBiz*, Public 100 (annual), June 2011, p. 68-69.

1565 ■ LARGEST COLORADO PRIVATE COMPANIES, 2007

Ranked by: Revenue, in dollars. **Remarks:** Also notes contact information, rank for previous year, figures for previous two years, number of employees and locations locally and nationally, business description, top local executive, owner, headquarters, and year founded locally. **Number listed:** 100

1. DCP Midstream LLC, with $8,597,000,000
2. CH2M Hill Cos., Ltd., $6,303,018,000
3. PCL Construction Enterprises Inc., $5,428,640,638
4. ProBuild Holdings Inc., $3,200,000,000
5. Hensel Phelps Construction Co., $3,024,757,000
6. Clarion Mortgage Capital Inc., $1,500,000,000
7. MWH Global Inc., $1,188,200,000
8. Saunders Construction Inc., $339,597,554
9. American Furniture Warehouse Co., $300,000,000

10. HealthTrans LLC, $268,813,000

Source: *Denver Business Journal*, Book of Lists (annual), December 17, 2010, p. 93+.

1566 ■ LARGEST COMPANIES IN COLORADO BY EMPLOYEES, 2010

Ranked by: Number of employees at headquarters. **Remarks:** Also notes contact information for headquarters, total number of employees, revenue, rank by revenue, and primary SIC code. **Number listed:** 177

1. Dish Network Corp., with 6,500 employees
2. Gart Bros. Sporting Goods Co., 5,600
3. Medical Center of the Rockies, 4,000
4. Strasburg Telephone Co., 3,700
5. Western Union Financial Services Inc., 3,200
6. Noodles & Co., 2,916
7. TW Telecom Holdings Inc., 2,800
8. Alpine Access Inc., 2,600
9. University of Colorado Hospital Authority, 2,595
10. Memorial Health System, 2,408

Source: *Business Rankings*, (annual), Dun & Bradstreet Inc., 2011, p. IV.36-IV.39.

1567 ■ LARGEST COMPANIES IN COLORADO BY SALES, 2010

Ranked by: Revenue, in dollars. **Remarks:** Also notes contact information for headquarters, number of employees at headquarters and overall, rank by employees, and primary SIC code. **Number listed:** 174

1. Catholic Health Initiatives, with $13,360,714,000
2. Dish Network Corp., $12,640,744,000
3. Dish DBS Corp., $12,635,737,000
4. Qwest Communications International Inc., $11,730,000,000
5. Liberty Media Corp., $10,982,000,000
6. Liberty Media LLC, $10,084,000,000
7. Newmont Mining Corp., $9,540,000,000
8. Qwest Corp., $9,271,000,000
9. Liberty Global Inc., $9,016,900,000
10. Jacor Broadcasting of Colorado Inc., $8,000,000,000

Source: *Business Rankings*, (annual), Dun & Bradstreet Inc., 2011, p. III.36-III.39.

1568 ■ MOST ADMIRED COMPANIES IN COLORADO, 2012

Ranked by: Survey of top executives, directors, and securities analysts regarding the Fortune 1,000 companies that they admire the most, regardless of industry. **Remarks:** Also notes city and industry rank. List is available online only, not in print. **Number listed:** 4

1. Arrow Electronics, with 6.88 points
2. Ball Corp., 6.69
3. Chipotle Mexican Grill, 6.63
4. DaVita Inc., 5.68

Source: *Fortune*, World's Most Admired Companies (annual), http://www.fortune.com, March 19, 2012.

1569 ■ TOP *FORTUNE 500* COMPANIES IN COLORADO, 2011

Ranked by: Revenue, in millions of dollars. **Remarks:** Also notes overall rank in the *Fortune 500*, headquarters, and number of employees. **Number listed:** 9

1. Arrow Electronics, with $21,390.3 million
2. Dish Network Corp., $14,048.4
3. Liberty Interactive Corp., $11,624
4. Newmont Mining Corp., $10,358
5. Liberty Global Inc., $10,246.5
6. Ball Corp., $8,630.9
7. DaVita Inc., $6,998.9
8. CH2M Hill Cos., Ltd., $5,555.2
9. The Western Union Co., $5,491.4

Source: *Fortune*, Fortune 500 (annual), May 21, 2012, p. F-42.

Corporations—Connecticut

1570 ■ BEST LARGE COMPANIES TO WORK FOR IN CONNECTICUT, 2011

Ranked by: Score based on employee surveys. **Remarks:** Specific scores not provided. To qualify, companies must have at least 200 employees. Also notes contact information, number of Connecticut office and employees, business description, top executive, and year founded. **Number listed:** 18

1. Bingham McCutchen LLP
2. Edward Jones
3. FactSet Research Systems Inc.
4. Bearingstar Insurance
5. Digitas
6. Burns & McDonnell
7. Citrin Cooperman & Co.
8. American Eagle Federal Credit Union
9. Kforce Inc.
10. Comcast Cable

Source: *Hartford Business Journal*, Best Places to Work in Connecticut (annual), http://www.hartfordbusiness.com, March 26, 2012.

1571 ■ BEST SMALL COMPANIES IN CONNECTICUT, 2011

Ranked by: Score based on revenue, profits, and return on equity for the past 12 months and five years. **Remarks:** Specific scores not provided. Also notes rank in the overall *100 Best Small Companies in America*. To qualify, companies must have revenues between $5 million and $1 billion, a net margin above five percent, and share price above $5. List is available online only. **Number listed:** 2

1. Sturm, Ruger & Co., Inc.
2. FactSet Research Systems

Source: *Forbes*, Best Small Companies in America (annual), November 7, 2011.

1572 ■ BEST SMALL/MEDIUM COMPANIES TO WORK FOR IN CONNECTICUT, 2011

Ranked by: Score based on employee surveys. **Remarks:** Specific scores not provided. To qualify, companies must have between 15 and 199 employees. Also notes contact information, number of Connecticut office and employees, business description, top executive, and year founded. **Number listed:** 12

1. Pullman & Comley LLC
2. Tauck
3. Turnpike Motors Auto Body
4. Acsys Interactive

5. VLink Inc.
6. NBC Connecticut
7. ICON International
8. Fiduciary Investment Advisors LLC
9. Pyramid Time Systems
10. Rib-X Pharmaceuticals

Source: *Hartford Business Journal*, Best Places to Work in Connecticut (annual), http://www.hartfordbusiness.com, March 26, 2012.

1573 ■ CONNECTICUT'S LARGEST COMPANIES OVERALL, 2011

Ranked by: Score based on revenue, profits, assets, and market capitalization. **Remarks:** Specific scores not provided. Also notes overall rank in the *Forbes 2000* and figures for each criterion. **Number listed:** 17

1. General Electric Co.
2. United Technologies Corp.
3. Aetna Inc.
4. Cigna Corp.
5. The Hartford Financial Services Group Inc.
6. Xerox Corp.
7. Praxair Inc.
8. Stanley Black & Decker Inc.
9. Priceline.com Inc.
10. Starwood Hotels

Source: *Forbes*, Forbes 2000 (annual), http://www.forbes.com, May 7, 2012.

1574 ■ CONNECTICUT'S LARGEST EMPLOYERS, 2011

Ranked by: Number of Connecticut employees. **Remarks:** Also notes contact information, total employees, figures for previous year, number of Connecticut locations, type of business, key executive, and year founded. **Number listed:** 5

1. State of Connecticut, with 63,000 employees
2. United Technologies Corp., 26,900
3. Hartford Healthcare, 15,216
4. Yale University, 13,615
5. Pratt & Whitney, 10,500

Source: *Hartford Business Journal*, Connecticut's Largest Employers (annual), http://www.hartfordbusiness.com, August 31, 2011.

1575 ■ FASTEST-GROWING COMPANIES IN CONNECTICUT, 2008-2011

Ranked by: Score based on three-year growth in revenue and earnings, and three-year total return to investors. **Remarks:** Specific scores not provided. To qualify for list, companies must have revenues of at least $50 million, net income of at least $10 million, market capitalization of at least $250 million, and stock price of at least $5. Int'l companies are eligible if they trade on a U.S. exchange and file quarterly reports. **Number listed:** 3

1. Alexion Pharmaceuticals
2. Sturm, Ruger & Co.
3. Priceline.com Inc.

Source: *Fortune*, 100 Fastest-Growing Companies (annual), http://www.fortune.com, September 26, 2011.

1576 ■ LARGEST COMPANIES IN CONNECTICUT BY EMPLOYEES, 2010

Ranked by: Number of employees at headquarters. **Remarks:** Also notes contact information for headquarters, total number of employees, revenue, rank by revenue, and primary SIC code. **Number listed:** 173

1. Electric Boat Corp., with 7,900 employees
2. Aetna Inc., 7,800
3. Carters Retail Inc., 6,547
4. Connecticut General Corp., 6,476
5. Sikorsky Aircraft Corp., 6,000
6. Travelers Home & Marine Insurance Co., 5,999
7. Hartford Hospital Inc., 5,000
7. Hartford Insurance Co. of Illinois, 5,000
7. Southern New England Telephone Co., 5,000
7. University of Connecticut Research & Development Corp., 5,000

Source: *Business Rankings*, (annual), Dun & Bradstreet Inc., 2011, p. IV.40-IV.43.

1577 ■ LARGEST COMPANIES IN CONNECTICUT BY SALES, 2010

Ranked by: Revenue, in dollars. **Remarks:** Also notes contact information for headquarters, number of employees at headquarters and overall, rank by employees, and primary SIC code. **Number listed:** 179

1. United Technologies Corp., with $54,326,000,000
2. Xerox Corp., $21,633,000,000
3. General Electric International Inc., $12,144,769,000
4. Praxair Inc., $10,116,000,000
5. Stanley Black & Decker Inc., $8,409,600,000
6. Statoil Marketing & Trading U.S. Inc., $5,608,448,000
7. Pitney Bowes Inc., $5,425,254,000
8. Emcor Group Inc., $5,121,285,000
9. Terex Corp., $4,418,200,000
10. Frontier Communications Corp., $3,797,675,000

Source: *Business Rankings*, (annual), Dun & Bradstreet Inc., 2011, p. III.40-III.43.

1578 ■ LARGEST WOMEN-OWNED BUSINESSES IN HARTFORD, CONNECTICUT, 2012

Ranked by: Number of employees in the Hartford region. **Remarks:** Also notes contact information, total number of employees, number of offices, type of business, owner and percentage owned, and year founded. **Number listed:** 5

1. Companions & Homemakers, with 1,310 employees
2. Nursing Services Inc., 110
3. Companions for Living LLC, 107
4. DeMarco Management Corp., 100
5. Theis Precision Steel Corp., 90

Source: *Hartford Business Journal*, Largest Women-Owned Businesses (annual), http://www.hartfordbusiness.com, April 2, 2012.

1579 ■ MOST ADMIRED COMPANIES IN CONNECTICUT, 2012

Ranked by: Survey of top executives, directors, and securities analysts regarding the Fortune 1,000 companies that they admire the most, regardless of industry. **Remarks:** Also notes city and industry rank. List is available online only, not in print. **Number listed:** 8

1. Starwood Hotels & Resorts, with 7.45 points

2. United Technologies Corp., 7.43

3. General Electric Co., 6.82

4. EMCOR Group Inc., 6.43

5. Xerox Corp., 6.33

6. Aetna Inc., 6.25

7. Stanley Black & Decker Inc., 6.04

8. Cigna, 5.15

Source: *Fortune*, World's Most Admired Companies (annual), http://www.fortune.com, March 19, 2012.

1580 ■ TOP *FORTUNE 500* COMPANIES IN CONNECTICUT, 2011

Ranked by: Revenue, in millions of dollars. **Remarks:** Also notes overall rank in the *Fortune 500,* headquarters, and number of employees. **Number listed:** 14

1. General Electric Co., with $147,616 million

2. United Technologies Corp., $58,190

3. Aetna Inc., $33,779.8

4. Xerox Corp., $22,626

5. CIGNA Corp., $21,998

6. The Hartford Financial Services Group Inc., $21,918

7. Praxair Inc., $11,252

8. Stanley Black & Decker Inc., $10,437.6

9. Terex Corp., $6,504.6

10. EMCOR Group Inc., $5,731.7

Source: *Fortune*, Fortune 500 (annual), May 21, 2012, p. F-42.

1581 ■ TOP PUBLICLY TRADED COMPANIES IN CONNECTICUT, 2011

Ranked by: Market value, in billions of dollars. **Remarks:** Also notes ticker symbol, contact information, stock price, revenue, net income, figures for previous year, and chief executive officer. **Number listed:** 3

1. General Electric Co., with $177.87 billion

2. AT & T Inc., $173.1

3. Pfizer Inc., $147.38

Source: *Hartford Business Journal*, Top Publicly Traded Companies (annual), http://www.hartfordbusiness.com, October 31, 2011.

Corporations—Costa Rica

1582 ■ BEST COMPANIES TO WORK FOR IN COSTA RICA, 2012

Ranked by: Score based on the relationships between employees and management, employees and their jobs/company, and employees and coworkers. **Remarks:** Specific scores not provided. **Number listed:** 15

1. S. C. Johnson de Centroamerica

2. Kimberly-Clark Costa Rica

3. FedEx Costa Rica

4. Scotiabank Costa Rica

5. Amba Research Costa Rica

6. Concesonaria SAM SA Costa Rica

7. BN Valores Puesto de Bolsa SA Costa Rica

8. Grupo Roble Corporativo y Administracion Costa Rica

9. Vitec Videocom Ltda. Costa Rica

10. British American Tobacco Costa Rica

Source: *Great Place to Work Institute Inc.*, Best Places to Work in Central America & the Caribbean (annual), 2012.

Corporations—Cyprus

1583 ■ LARGEST COMPANIES IN CYPRUS, 2010

Ranked by: Sales, in millions of U.S. dollars. **Remarks:** Also notes city; industrial code; percent change in sales; profits; profit as a percentage of sales, assets, and equity; number of employees; sales per employee; assets; equity capital; equity capital as a percentage of assets; year established; and figures for previous year. **Number listed:** 50

1. J & S Service & Investment Ltd., with $60,129.9 million

2. Mercuria Energy Group Ltd., $46,906.9

3. G1 Investments Ltd., $39,197.2

3. Ahimsa Development Ltd., $39,197.2

5. Societe Generale Bank Cyprus Ltd., $32,316.9

6. Honeywell Controls International Ltd., $30,908

7. Tamoil Overseas Ltd., $15,740.7

8. Norilsk Nickel (Cyprus) Ltd., $13,980

9. National Bank of Greece (Cyprus) Ltd., $12,876.3

10. Aker Solutions Cyprus Ltd., $9,501.3

Source: *Europe's 15,000 Largest Companies*, (annual), ELC International, 2011, p. 110+.

Corporations—Czech Republic

1584 ■ LARGEST COMPANIES IN THE CZECH REPUBLIC, 2010

Ranked by: Sales, in millions of U.S. dollars. **Remarks:** Also notes city; industrial code; percent change in sales; profits; profit as a percentage of sales, assets, and equity; number of employees; sales per employee; assets; equity capital; equity capital as a percentage of assets; year established; and figures for previous year. **Number listed:** 300

1. Skoda Auto as, with $10,324.8 million

2. CEZ as, $7,332.6

3. Unipetrol as, $4,566.6

4. Foxconn CZ sro, $4,117.5

5. Conseq Finance as, $3,599.9

6. Telefonica O2 Czech Republic as, $3,425.8

7. Panasonic AVC Networks Czech sro, $3,051.6

8. Ceska sporitelna as, $2,790.1

9. CEPRO as, $2,708.1

10. Barum Continental spol sro, $2,490.3

Source: *Europe's 15,000 Largest Companies*, (annual), ELC International, 2011, p. 114+.

Corporations—Delaware

1585 ■ DELAWARE'S LARGEST COMPANIES OVERALL, 2011

Ranked by: Score based on revenue, profits, assets, and market capitalization. **Remarks:** Specific scores not provided. Also notes overall rank in the *Forbes 2000* and figures for each criterion. **Number listed:** 2

1. E. I. du Pont de Nemours & Co.
2. SLM Corp.

Source: *Forbes*, Forbes 2000 (annual), http://www.forbes.com, May 7, 2012.

1586 ■ LARGEST COMPANIES IN DELAWARE BY EMPLOYEES, 2010

Ranked by: Number of employees at headquarters. **Remarks:** Also notes contact information for headquarters, total number of employees, revenue, rank by revenue, and primary SIC code. **Number listed:** 49

1. E. I. du Pont de Nemours & Co., with 6,000 employees
2. AstraZeneca Pharmaceuticals LP, 4,000
3. MBNA America Delaware NA, 3,855
4. MBNA Consumer Services Inc., 3,009
5. DuPont Hospital for Children, 2,568
6. AstraZeneca LP, 2,500
6. International Specialty Holdings Inc., 2,500
8. J. P. Morgan Chase & Co., 2,400
9. RBC Insurance Holding Inc., 2,024
10. DuPont Foreign Sales Corp., 2,000

Source: *Business Rankings*, (annual), Dun & Bradstreet Inc., 2011, p. IV.44-IV.45.

1587 ■ LARGEST COMPANIES IN DELAWARE BY SALES, 2010

Ranked by: Revenue, in dollars. **Remarks:** Also notes contact information for headquarters, number of employees at headquarters and overall, rank by employees, and primary SIC code. **Number listed:** 50

1. E. I. du Pont de Nemours & Co., with $32,733,000,000
2. FIA Card Services NA, $25,752,912,000
3. Balfour Beatty LLC, $4,119,158,000
4. Barclays Bank Delaware, $1,687,806,000
5. Conectiv, $1,539,000,000
6. Atlantic City Electric Co., $1,430,000,000
7. Delmarva Power & Light Co., $1,400,000,000
8. Christiana Care Health Services Inc., $1,097,515,177
9. International Specialty Holdings Inc., $845,297,303
10. DuPont Hospital for Children, $706,573,024

Source: *Business Rankings*, (annual), Dun & Bradstreet Inc., 2011, p. III.44-III.45.

1588 ■ TOP *FORTUNE 500* COMPANIES IN DELAWARE, 2011

Ranked by: Revenue, in millions of dollars. **Remarks:** Also notes overall rank in the *Fortune 500,* headquarters, and number of employees. **Number listed:** 2

1. E. I. du Pont de Nemours & Co., with $38,719 million
2. SLM Corp., $5,756

Source: *Fortune*, Fortune 500 (annual), May 21, 2012, p. F-42.

Corporations—Denmark

1589 ■ BEST LARGE COMPANIES TO WORK FOR IN DENMARK, 2011

Ranked by: Score based on the relationships between employees and management, employees and their jobs/company, and employees and coworkers. **Remarks:** Specific scores not provided. To qualify, companies must have more than 500 employees. **Number listed:** 10

1. McDonald's Darmark
2. Nordea Liv & Pension
3. Tivoli
4. Energi Midt
5. Irma
6. Novozymes A/S
7. Syd Energi
8. Beierholm
9. Alka Forsikring
10. Atea

Source: *Great Place to Work Institute Inc.*, Best Places to Work in Denmark (annual), http://www.greatplacetowork.com, 2011.

1590 ■ BEST SMALL COMPANIES TO WORK FOR IN DENMARK, 2011

Ranked by: Score based on the relationships between employees and management, employees and their jobs/company, and employees and coworkers. **Remarks:** Specific scores not provided. To qualify, companies must have between 50 and 499 employees. **Number listed:** 35

1. Abbott Laboratories Inc.
2. Fros Herreds Sparekasse
3. Hartmanns
4. Roche Pharmaceuticals
5. Middelfart Sparekasse
6. NetDesign
7. Boehringer Ingelheim
8. Electrolux Home Products Denmark
9. Mjolner Informatics
10. Kyocera Unimerco

Source: *Great Place to Work Institute Inc.*, Best Places to Work in Denmark (annual), http://www.greatplacetowork.com, 2011.

1591 ■ DENMARK'S LARGEST COMPANIES OVERALL, 2011

Ranked by: Score based on revenue, profits, assets, and market capitalization. **Remarks:** Specific scores not provided. Also notes rank in the overall *Forbes 2000* and figures for each criterion. **Number listed:** 10

1. A. P. Moller-Maersk A/S
2. Novo Nordisk A/S
3. Danske Bank A/S
4. Carlsberg A/S
5. TDC A/S
6. Jyske Bank
7. Novozymes A/S
8. Sydbank
9. Coloplast
10. Vestas Wind Systems A/S

Source: *Forbes*, Forbes 2000 (annual), http://www.forbes.com, May 7, 2012.

1592 ■ LARGEST COMPANIES IN DENMARK, 2010

Ranked by: Sales, in millions of U.S. dollars. **Remarks:** Also notes city; industrial code; percent change in sales; profits; profit as a percentage of sales, assets, and equity; number of employees; sales per employee; assets; equity capital; equity capital as a percentage of assets; year established; and figures for previous year. **Number listed:** 500

1. Carlsberg A/S, with $11,420 million
2. A. P. Moller-Maersk A/S, $9,813.5
3. Danske Bank A/S, $8,498.8
4. Nyk Group Danmark, $8,196
5. Fluor Daniel Construction Co., $7,424.7
5. Nordea, $7,424.7
7. Nike Retail Denmark, $7,352.3
8. ISS Global A/S, $7,159.3
9. Swedbank, $7,031.5
10. General Electric International Inc., $6,743.3

Source: *Europe's 15,000 Largest Companies*, (annual), ELC International, 2011, p. 128+.

1593 ■ LARGEST CORPORATIONS IN DENMARK BY REVENUE, 2010

Ranked by: Revenue, in millions of U.S. dollars. **Remarks:** Also notes headquarters city and overall rank in the *Global 500*. Ranking is available online only, not in print. **Number listed:** 2

1. A. P. Moller-Maersk A/S, with $56,177 million
2. Danske Bank A/S, $21,425

Source: *Fortune*, Global 500 (annual), http://www.fortune.com, July 25, 2011.

Corporations—Directors
See: **Corporate Directors**

Corporations—Dominican Republic

1594 ■ BEST COMPANIES TO WORK FOR IN THE DOMINICAN REPUBLIC, 2012

Ranked by: Score based on the relationships between employees and management, employees and their jobs/company, and employees and coworkers. **Remarks:** Specific scores not provided. **Number listed:** 11

1. Kimberly-Clark Republica Dominicana
2. Scotiabank Republica Dominicana
3. Hotel Catalonia Royal Republica Dominicana
4. Hotel Catalonia Bavaro Republica Dominicana
5. AES Dominicana Republica Dominicana
6. Odebrecht Republica Dominicana
7. Grupo Universal Republica Dominicana
8. British American Tobacco Republica Dominicana
9. Hotel Catalonia Gran Dominicus Republica Dominicana
10. Pfizer Republica Dominicana

Source: *Great Place to Work Institute Inc.*, Best Places to Work in Central America & the Caribbean (annual), 2012.

Corporations—Ecuador

1595 ■ BEST COMPANIES TO WORK FOR IN ECUADOR, 2011

Ranked by: Score based on the relationships between employees and management, employees and their jobs/company, and employees and coworkers. **Remarks:** Specific scores not provided. **Number listed:** 31

1. ASEVIG
2. Telefonica Ecuador
3. Aseguradora del Sur
4. Banco General Ruminahui SA
5. Citibank Ecuador
6. ACE Seguros SA
7. Kimberly-Clark Ecuador SA
8. Quality Serivices SA
9. Floreloy SA
10. Yanbal Ecuador SA

Source: *Great Place to Work Institute Inc.*, Best Places to Work in Ecuador (annual), http://www.greatplacetowork.com, November 2011.

Corporations—El Salvador

1596 ■ BEST COMPANIES TO WORK FOR IN EL SALVADOR, 2012

Ranked by: Score based on the relationships between employees and management, employees and their jobs/company, and employees and coworkers. **Remarks:** Specific scores not provided. **Number listed:** 14

1. Kimberly-Clark El Salvador
2. Atento El Salvador
3. Aseguradora Agricola Comercial SA El Salvador
4. Scotiabank El Salvador
5. Aseguradora Suiza Salvadorena SA El Salvador
6. Autofacil El Salvador
7. Telefonica El Salvador
8. AFP Crecer El Salvador
9. Grupo Roble Corporativo y Administracion El Salvador
10. Division Hotelera de Grupo Agrisal Hotel Holiday Inn y Crowne Plaza El Salvador

Source: *Great Place to Work Institute Inc.*, Best Places to Work in Central America & the Caribbean (annual), 2012.

Corporations—Estonia

1597 ■ LARGEST COMPANIES IN ESTONIA, 2010

Ranked by: Sales, in millions of U.S. dollars. **Remarks:** Also notes city; industrial code; percent change in sales; profits; profit as a percentage of sales, assets, and equity; number of employees; sales per employee; assets; equity capital; equity capital as a percentage of assets; year established; and figures for previous year. **Number listed:** 50

1. Baltic International Trading Ou, with $760.9 million
2. AS Eesti Telekom, $550.7
3. Tallink Grupp AS, $508.6
4. Rimi Eesti Food AS, $454.8
5. A-Selver AS, $387.6
6. Eesti Energia Narva Elektrijaamad AS, $362.9
7. Mazeikiu Nafta Trading House Ou, $356.8
8. Eesti Gaas AS, $302.9
9. Eesti Statoil AS, $294.1

10. Lavesta AS, $277.6

Source: *Europe's 15,000 Largest Companies*, (annual), ELC International, 2011, p. 150+.

Corporations—Europe

1598 ■ BEST LARGE COMPANIES TO WORK FOR IN EUROPE, 2011

Ranked by: Score based on the relationships between employees and management, employees and their jobs/company, and employees and coworkers. **Remarks:** Specific scores not provided. **Number listed:** 25

1. Elica SpA (Italy)
2. ATP (Denmark)
3. EMC Corp. (Ireland, Poland)
4. DIS AG (Germany)
5. Domino-World TM (Germany)
6. Nordea Liv & Pension (Denmark)
7. Heilingenfed Kliniken (Germany)
8. NetDesign (Denmark)
9. SMA Solar Technology (Germany)
10. Energi Midt (Denmark)

Source: *Great Place to Work Institute Inc.*, Best Places to Work in Europe (annual), 2011.

1599 ■ BEST MULTINATIONAL COMPANIES TO WORK FOR IN EUROPE, 2011

Ranked by: Score based on the relationships between employees and management, employees and their jobs/company, and employees and coworkers. **Remarks:** Specific scores not provided. **Number listed:** 25

1. Microsoft Corp.
2. Amgen Inc.
3. Mars Inc.
4. Cisco Systems Inc.
5. 3M Co.
6. NetApp Inc.
7. McDonald's Corp.
8. SAS Institute Inc.
9. W. L. Gore & Associates Inc.
10. Kellogg Co.

Source: *Great Place to Work Institute Inc.*, Best Places to Work in Europe (annual), 2011.

1600 ■ BEST SMALL AND MEDIUM-SIZED COMPANIES TO WORK FOR IN EUROPE, 2011

Ranked by: Score based on the relationships between employees and management, employees and their jobs/company, and employees and coworkers. **Remarks:** Specific scores not provided. **Number listed:** 50

1. Fros Herreds Sparekasse (Denmark)
2. Reaktor (Finland)
3. Creativ Co. (Denmark)
4. Noventum Consulting (Germany)
5. Middelfart Sparekasse (Denmark)
6. Atrias PersonalManagement (Germany)
7. Baringa Partners (UK)
8. Euro Car Parks (Ireland)

9. Bain & Co. Iberica (Spain)
10. Jones Lang LaSalle Ireland

Source: *Great Place to Work Institute Inc.*, Best Places to Work in Europe (annual), 2011.

1601 ■ EUROPE'S LARGEST COMPANIES BY PROFITS, 2010

Ranked by: Profits, in millions of U.S. dollars. **Number listed:** 500

1. BP plc (U.K.), with $37,686 million
2. BHP Billiton plc (U.K.), $29,358
3. Delhaize Group SA/NV (Belgium), $27,842.4
4. Citigroup Global Markets Ltd. (Switzerland), $21,540
5. Stichting Pensioenfonds Zorg en Welzijn (Netherlands), $19,509.1
6. AstraZeneca plc (U.K.), $16,210.5
7. DPA (Holding) SA (Switzerland), $15,344.8
8. BP Holdings North America Ltd. (U.K.), $14,311.2
9. Stichting Pensioenfonds Alliance Nederland (Netherlands), $14,232.7
10. Solvay SA (Belgium), $13,804.3

Source: *Europe's 15,000 Largest Companies*, (annual), ELC International, 2011, p. 12+.

1602 ■ EUROPE'S LARGEST COMPANIES BY SALES, 2010

Ranked by: Sales, in millions of U.S. dollars. **Number listed:** 500

1. BP plc (U.K.), with $358,908 million
2. Royal Dutch Shell plc (Netherlands), $278,190
3. Cargill Holdings (U.K.), $237,963
4. Vitol Holding BV (Netherlands), $191,165.4
5. Volkswagen AG (Germany), $145,890.5
6. Carrefour SA (France), $125,360
7. E.On AG (Germany), $121,678.2
8. Hewlett-Packard The Hague BV (Netherlands), $121,083.1
9. EDF Trading Ltd. (U.K.), $120,114
10. Daimler AG (Germany), $117,375.8

Source: *Europe's 15,000 Largest Companies*, (annual), ELC International, 2011, p. 2+.

1603 ■ EUROPE'S LARGEST EMPLOYERS, 2010

Ranked by: Total number of employees. **Number listed:** 500

1. Deutsche Post AG (Germany), with 447,626 employees
2. Siemens AG (Germany), 405,000
3. Compass Group plc (U.K.), 386,170
4. Volkswagen AG (Germany), 369,928
5. DPA (Holding) SA (Switzerland), 283,000
6. Robert Bosch GmbH (Germany), 281,717
7. Metro AG (Germany), 281,455
8. Daimler AG (Germany), 273,218
9. Tesco Stores Ltd. (U.K.), 257,293
10. PPR SA (France), 253,000

Source: *Europe's 15,000 Largest Companies*, (annual), ELC International, 2011, p. 22+.

1604 ■ LARGEST CORPORATIONS IN EUROPE BY REVENUE, 2010

Ranked by: Revenue, in millions of U.S. dollars. **Remarks:** Also notes city and overall rank in the *Global 500*. Ranking is available online only, not in print. **Number listed:** 50

1. Royal Dutch Shell plc, with $378,152 million
2. BP plc, $308,928
3. Total SA, $186,055
4. Volkswagen AG, $168,041
5. AXA, $162,236
6. ING Groep NV, $147,052
7. Glencore International, $144,978
8. ENI SpA, $131,756
9. Daimler AG, $129,481
10. BNP Paribas, $128,726

Source: *Fortune*, Global 500 (annual), http://www.fortune.com, July 25, 2011.

1605 ■ MOST ADMIRED COMPANIES IN EUROPE, 2012

Ranked by: Survey of top executives, directors, and securities analysts regarding the Fortune 1,000 companies that they admire the most, regardless of industry. **Remarks:** Specific scores not provided. List is available online only, not in print. **Number listed:** 20

1. Bayerische Motoren Werke AG (BMW)
2. Nestle SA
3. Volkswagen AG
4. Siemens AG
5. Daimler AG
6. Deutsche Lufthansa AG
7. L'Oreal SA
8. Unilever
9. BASF SE
10. Novartis AG

Source: *Fortune*, World's Most Admired Companies (annual), http://www.fortune.com, March 19, 2012.

1606 ■ MOST VALUABLE EUROPEAN COMPANIES, 2011

Ranked by: Market value as of March 2011, in millions of U.S. dollars. **Remarks:** Also notes rank for previous year, sector, revenue, net income, assets, number of employees, share price, price-to-earning ratio, dividend yield, and fiscal year-end. **Number listed:** 500

1. Royal Dutch Shell plc (U.K.), with $228,128.7 million
2. Nestle SA (Switzerland), $199,406.6
3. OAO Gazprom (Russia), $190,829.1
4. HSBC Holdings plc (U.K.), $181,936.9
5. Vodafone Group plc (U.K.), $145,923.3
6. Novartis AG (Switzerland), $143,633
7. Total SA (France), $143,227.1
8. BP plc (U.K.), $136,848
9. Roche Group (Switzerland), $127,055.6
10. Siemens AG (Germany), $125,465.5

Source: *Financial Times*, FT 500 (annual), http://www.ft.com, June 24, 2011.

Corporations—Finland

1607 ■ BEST LARGE COMPANIES TO WORK FOR IN FINLAND, 2012

Ranked by: Score based on the relationships between employees and management, employees and their jobs/company, and employees and coworkers. **Remarks:** Specific scores not provided. Ranking covers companies with at least 500 employees. **Number listed:** 5

1. Ikea
2. Diacor Terveyspalvelut Oy
3. Ilmarinen
4. Fujitsu Finland
5. Yliopiston Apteekki

Source: *Great Place to Work Institute Inc.*, Best Places to Work in Finland (annual), http://www.greatplacetowork.com, February 2012.

1608 ■ BEST MEDIUM-SIZED COMPANIES TO WORK FOR IN FINLAND, 2012

Ranked by: Score based on the relationships between employees and management, employees and their jobs/company, and employees and coworkers. **Remarks:** Specific scores not provided. Ranking covers companies with 50 to 499 employees. **Number listed:** 30

1. Futurice Oy
2. Tutoris
3. Fondia Oy
4. Microsoft Oy
5. Novia Finland Oy
6. Vincit
7. Bonnier Publications
8. Mars Finland Oy
9. Novo Nordisk Farma
10. 3 Step IT

Source: *Great Place to Work Institute Inc.*, Best Places to Work in Finland (annual), http://www.greatplacetowork.com, February 2012.

1609 ■ BEST SMALL COMPANIES TO WORK FOR IN FINLAND, 2012

Ranked by: Score based on the relationships between employees and management, employees and their jobs/company, and employees and coworkers. **Remarks:** Specific scores not provided. Ranking covers companies with 15 to 49 employees. **Number listed:** 15

1. Bitwise Oy
2. SICK Oy
3. Frami Oy
4. Kartanokylpyla Kaisankoti
5. WWF Suomi
6. Fudeco Oy
7. Borenius & Co.
8. Meltwater Group
9. Visma Severa
10. Communicea

Source: *Great Place to Work Institute Inc.*, Best Places to Work in Finland (annual), http://www.greatplacetowork.com, February 2012.

1610 ■ FINLAND'S LARGEST COMPANIES OVERALL, 2011

Ranked by: Score based on revenue, profits, assets, and market capitalization. **Remarks:** Specific scores not provided. Also notes rank in the overall *Forbes 2000* and figures for each criterion. **Number listed:** 12

1. Fortum Oyj
2. Sampo Oyj
3. Nokia Corp.
4. UPM-Kymmene Oyj
5. Stora Enso Oyj
6. KONE Corp.
7. Metso Corp.
8. Pohjola Bank
9. Neste Oil Oyj
10. Wartsila Corp.

Source: *Forbes*, Forbes 2000 (annual), http://www.forbes.com, May 7, 2012.

1611 ■ LARGEST COMPANIES IN FINLAND, 2010

Ranked by: Sales, in millions of U.S. dollars. **Remarks:** Also notes city; industrial code; percent change in sales; profits; profit as a percentage of sales, assets, and equity; number of employees; sales per employee; assets; equity capital; equity capital as a percentage of assets; year established; and figures for previous year. **Number listed:** 400

1. Nokia Oyj, with $60,951.4 million
2. Neste Oil Oyj, $14,330.7
3. Stora Enso Oyj, $13,303.2
4. Kesko Oyj, $12,562.1
5. Nokia Siemens Networks Oy, $10,376.4
6. Suomen Osuuskauppojen Keskuskunta, $9,207.8
7. Metsaeliitto Osuuskunta, $9,068.7
8. Fortum Oyj, $8,082.9
9. Tamro Oyj, $7,477
10. Metso Oyj, $7,459.8

Source: *Europe's 15,000 Largest Companies*, (annual), ELC International, 2011, p. 154+.

Corporations—Florida

1612 ■ BEST LARGE COMPANIES TO WORK FOR IN FLORIDA, 2011

Ranked by: Score based on employee surveys. **Remarks:** Specific scores not provided. Also notes headquarters and industry. To qualify, companies must have 250 or more employees. **Number listed:** 31

1. North Highland
2. Edward Jones
3. Duke Realty
4. RCI
5. Shared Technologies Inc.
6. DPR Construction
7. Balfour Beatty Construction LLC
8. FCCI Insurance Group
9. Skanska USA Building Inc.
10. PCL Civil Constructors (Tampa) and PCL Construction Services (Orlando)

Source: *Florida Trend*, Best Companies to Work For (annual), http://www.floridatrend.com, August 2011.

1613 ■ BEST MIDSIZED COMPANIES TO WORK FOR IN FLORIDA, 2011

Ranked by: Score based on employee surveys. **Remarks:** Specific scores not provided. Also notes headquarters and industry. To qualify, companies must have between 50 and 249 employees. **Number listed:** 38

1. WilsonHCG
2. Cross, Fernandez & Riley LLP
3. Foley & Mansfield
4. True Partners Consulting LLC
5. Veredus Corp.
6. BGT Partners
7. AppRiver
8. Trenam Kemker
9. Brightway Insurance
10. Alltrust Insurance

Source: *Florida Trend*, Best Companies to Work For (annual), http://www.floridatrend.com, August 2011.

1614 ■ BEST SMALL COMPANIES TO WORK FOR IN FLORIDA, 2011

Ranked by: Score based on employee surveys. **Remarks:** Specific scores not provided. Also notes headquarters and industry. To qualify, companies must have between 15 and 49 employees. **Number listed:** 31

1. Law Offices of Jill S. Schwartz & Associates
2. Incepture Inc.
3. Benefit Advisors Inc.
4. ChappellRoberts
5. Moore Consulting Group
6. Fintech
7. Bit-Wizards Custom Software Solutions Inc.
8. Vaco Orlando LLC
9. Brunet-Garcia Advertising
10. AgileThought Inc.

Source: *Florida Trend*, Best Companies to Work For (annual), http://www.floridatrend.com, August 2011.

1615 ■ FLORIDA'S BEST COMPANIES TO WORK FOR, 2012

Ranked by: Score based on employee surveys as well as evaluation of companies' credibility, respect, fairness, and pride/camaraderie. **Remarks:** Specific scores not provided; companies are listed alphabetically, not ranked. Available online only, not in print. **Number listed:** 5

1. Baptist Health South Florida Inc.
2. Darden Restaurants Inc.
3. JM Family Enterprises Inc.
4. Publix Super Markets Inc.
5. Ultimate Software

Source: *Fortune*, 100 Best Companies to Work For (annual), http://www.fortune.com, February 6, 2012.

1616 ■ FLORIDA'S LARGEST COMPANIES OVERALL, 2011

Ranked by: Score based on revenue, profits, assets, and market capitalization. **Remarks:** Specific scores not provided. Also notes overall rank in the *Forbes 2000* and figures for each criterion. **Number listed:** 13

1. NextEra Energy Inc.
2. CSX Corp.
3. Fidelity National Information Services Inc.
4. Jabil Circuit Inc.
5. Darden Restaurants Inc.
6. Citrix Systems Inc.
7. Harris Corp.
8. AutoNation Inc.
9. Roper Industries
10. World Fuel Services Corp.

Source: *Forbes*, Forbes 2000 (annual), http://www.forbes.com, May 7, 2012.

1617 ■ FLORIDA'S LARGEST PRIVATE COMPANIES, 2010

Ranked by: Revenue, in billions of dollars. **Remarks:** Also notes business segment, number of employees, and overall rank in the *America's Largest Private Companies* list. Ranking is available online only, not in print. **Number listed:** 7

1. Publix Super Markets Inc., with $25.13 billion
2. JM Family Enterprises Inc., $9.3
3. Southern Wine & Spirits of America Inc., $9
4. Brightstar Corp., $4.61
5. Oxbow Corp., $4
6. OSI Restaurant Partners LLC, $3.63
7. Burger King Holdings Inc., $2.33

Source: *Forbes*, America's Largest Private Companies (annual), http://www.forbes.com, December 5, 2011.

1618 ■ FLORIDA'S LARGEST PUBLIC COMPANIES, 2010

Ranked by: Revenue, in thousands of dollars. **Remarks:** Also notes rank for previous year, stock exchange, ticker symbol, contact information, income, number of employees, line of business, and senior executive. **Number listed:** 150

1. International Assets Holding Corp., with $46,709,200 thousand
2. Tech Data Corp., $24,375,973
3. World Fuel Services Corp., $19,131,147
4. Florida Power & Light Co., $15,317,000
5. Carnival Corp., $14,469,000

Source: *Florida Trend*, Florida Public 150 (annual), http://www.floridatrend.com, June 2011.

1619 ■ LARGEST COMPANIES IN FLORIDA BY EMPLOYEES, 2010

Ranked by: Number of employees at headquarters. **Remarks:** Also notes contact information for headquarters, total number of employees, revenue, rank by revenue, and primary SIC code. **Number listed:** 473

1. Landrum Professional Employer Services Inc., with 11,000 employees
2. Hughes Supply Inc., 9,319
3. Florida Hospital Medical Center Inc., 7,200
4. Baptist Health South Florida Inc., 7,169
5. Administrative Concept Inc., 7,000
6. Orlando Health Inc., 6,000
7. Mayo Clinic Jacksonville Corp., 5,214
8. Baptist Health System Inc., 5,000
8. Blue Cross & Blue Shield of Florida Inc., 5,000

8. United Space Alliance LLC, 5,000
8. Universal City Florida Partners, 5,000

Source: *Business Rankings*, (annual), Dun & Bradstreet Inc., 2011, p. IV.48-IV.58.

1620 ■ LARGEST COMPANIES IN FLORIDA BY SALES, 2010

Ranked by: Revenue, in dollars. **Remarks:** Also notes contact information for headquarters, number of employees at headquarters and overall, rank by employees, and primary SIC code. **Number listed:** 474

1. Publix Super Markets Inc., with $25,328,054,000
2. Tech Data Corp., $22,099,876,000
3. World Fuel Services Corp., $19,131,147,000
4. Nextera Energy Inc., $15,317,000,000
5. Carnival Corp., $14,469,000,000
6. Jabil Circuit Inc., $13,409,411,000
7. AutoNation Inc., $12,461,000,000
8. Office Depot Inc., $11,633,094,000
9. CSX Corp., $10,636,000,000
10. Florida Power & Light Co., $10,485,000,000

Source: *Business Rankings*, (annual), Dun & Bradstreet Inc., 2011, p. III.48-III.58.

1621 ■ LARGEST COMPANIES IN SARASOTA AND MANATEE, FLORIDA, 2010

Ranked by: Revenue, in millions of dollars. **Remarks:** Also notes rank and figures for previous year, chief executive, number of employees locally and globally, year founded, website, and comments. **Number listed:** 58

1. Vengroff Williams & Associates Inc., with $2,800 million
2. Roper, $2,400
3. Bealls, $1,200
4. Boar's Head Provisions Co., $864
5. Manatee Memorial Hospital, $831
6. Intertape Polymer Group, $720.5
7. FCCI Insurance Group, $461
8. Progressive Employer Services, $397.3
9. Gettel Automotive, $319
10. Administrative Concepts Corp., $312

Source: *Biz(941)*, Top Companies (annual), http://www.biz941.com, July 2011.

1622 ■ LARGEST FLORIDA PRIVATE COMPANIES, 2010

Ranked by: Revenue, in thousands of dollars. **Remarks:** Also notes rank for previous year, contact information, annual growth in revenue, number of employees, line of business, and senior executive. **Number listed:** 200

1. Sun Capital Partners Inc., with $40,000,000 thousand
2. Publix Super Markets Inc., $25,328,054
3. JM Family Enterprises Inc., $9,300,000
4. Southern Wine & Spirits of America Inc., $9,000,000
5. H. L. G. Capital Management, $8,500,000

Source: *Florida Trend*, Florida Private 200 (annual), http://www.floridatrend.com, June 2011.

1623 ■ MOST ADMIRED COMPANIES IN FLORIDA, 2012

Ranked by: Survey of top executives, directors, and securities analysts regarding the Fortune 1,000 companies that they admire the most, regardless of industry. **Remarks:** Also notes city and industry rank. List is available online only, not in print. **Number listed:** 10

1. NextEra Energy Inc., with 6.89 points
2. Tech Data Corp., 6.62
3. Publix Super Markets Inc., 6.55
4. Tupperware Brands Corp., 6.43
5. Harris Corp., 6.22
6. CSX Corp., 5.98
7. Raymond James Financial Inc., 5.93
8. Darden Restaurants Inc., 5.84
9. Health Management Associates, 5.81
10. Jabil Circuit, 5.45

Source: *Fortune*, World's Most Admired Companies (annual), http://www.fortune.com, March 19, 2012.

1624 ■ TOP *FORTUNE 500* COMPANIES IN FLORIDA, 2011

Ranked by: Revenue, in millions of dollars. **Remarks:** Also notes overall rank in the *Fortune 500,* headquarters, and number of employees. **Number listed:** 16

1. World Fuel Services Corp., with $34,622.9 million
2. Publix Super Markets Inc., $27,178.8
3. Tech Data Corp., $26,488.1
4. Jabil Circuit Inc., $16,518.8
5. NextEra Energy Inc., $15,341
6. AutoNation Inc., $13,832.4
7. CSX Corp., $11,743
8. Office Depot Inc., $11,489.5
9. Darden Restaurants Inc., $7,500.2
10. Winn-Dixie Stores Inc., $6,929.9

Source: *Fortune*, Fortune 500 (annual), May 21, 2012, p. F-42.

Corporations, Foreign
See also: **Corporations, International**

1625 ■ COUNTRIES WITH THE HIGHEST PREVALENCE OF FOREIGN OWNERSHIP, 2010

Ranked by: Score, on a scale of seven, based on the level of foreign ownership of companies. **Number listed:** 142

1. Luxembourg, with 6.5 points
2. Singapore, 6.2
2. United Kingdom, 6.2
4. Slovak Republic, 6.1
5. Sweden, 6.0
5. New Zealand, 6.0
7. Uruguay, 5.9
7. Chile, 5.9
7. Hong Kong, 5.9
10. Australia, 5.8
10. Panama, 5.8
10. France, 5.8

Source: *Global Competitiveness Report*, (annual), World Economic Forum, 2011, p. 462.

1626 ■ COUNTRIES WITH THE LOWEST PREVALENCE OF FOREIGN OWNERSHIP, 2010

Ranked by: Score, on a scale of seven, based on the level of foreign ownership of companies. **Number listed:** 142

1. Yemen, with 2.0 points
2. Iran, 2.3
3. Mauritania, 2.6
3. Burundi, 2.6
5. Haiti, 2.8
5. Syria, 2.8
7. Nepal, 3.0
8. Kuwait, 3.1
9. Iceland, 3.2
10. Chad, 3.3
10. Kyrgyz Republic, 3.3

Source: *Global Competitiveness Report*, (annual), World Economic Forum, 2011, p. 462.

1627 ■ FASTEST-DECLINING COMPANIES IN THE AMERICAS (NOT U.S.), 2010-2011

Ranked by: Annual change in rank in the Forbes 2000. **Number listed:** 5

1. Partnerre, with -701 rank positions
2. Usiminas, -625
3. Kinross Gold, -550
4. Everest Re Group, -528
5. Embraer, -437

Source: *Forbes*, Forbes 2000 (annual), May 7, 2012, p. 136.

1628 ■ FASTEST-DECLINING COMPANIES IN EUROPE, THE MIDDLE EAST, AND AFRICA, 2010-2011

Ranked by: Annual change in rank in the Forbes 2000. **Number listed:** 5

1. Ezdan Real Estate, with -765 rank positions
2. Mediaset, -736
3. Investor, -664
4. Telekom Austria, -624
5. Sacyr Vallehermoso, -607

Source: *Forbes*, Forbes 2000 (annual), May 7, 2012, p. 114.

1629 ■ FASTEST-GROWING COMPANIES IN THE AMERICAS (NOT U.S.), 2010-2011

Ranked by: Annual change in rank in the Forbes 2000. **Number listed:** 5

1. Grupo Elektra, with 746 rank positions
2. Onex, 413
3. Centrais Eletricas Brasileiras SA (Eletrobras), 294
4. Penn West Petroleum, 281
5. Brasil Foods, 273

Source: *Forbes*, Forbes 2000 (annual), May 7, 2012, p. 136.

1630 ■ FASTEST-GROWING COMPANIES IN EUROPE, THE MIDDLE EAST, AND AFRICA, 2010-2011

Ranked by: Annual change in rank in the Forbes 2000. **Number listed:** 5

1. Pirelli & C., with 689 rank positions
2. Subsea 7, 625
3. Abu Dhabi Commercial, 598
4. GEA Group, 580
5. RMB Holdings, 481

Source: *Forbes*, Forbes 2000 (annual), May 7, 2012, p. 114.

1631 ■ FASTEST-GROWING FOREIGN COMPANIES LISTED IN THE U.S., 2008-2011

Ranked by: Score based on three-year growth in revenue and earnings, and three-year total return to investors. **Remarks:** Specific scores not provided. To qualify for list, companies must have revenues of at least $50 million, net income of at least $10 million, market capitalization of at least $250 million, and stock price of at least $5. Int'l companies are eligible if they trade on a U.S. exchange and file quarterly reports. **Number listed:** 22

1. Baidu
2. Home Inns & Hotel Management
3. Lululemon Athletica
4. MercadoLibre
5. Silver Wheaton
6. Trina Solar
7. IAMGOLD Corp.
8. Maiden Holdings
9. Eldorado Gold Corp.
10. VanceInfo Technologies

Source: *Fortune*, 100 Fastest-Growing Companies (annual), http://www.fortune.com, September 26, 2011.

1632 ■ LARGEST FOREIGN COMPANIES WITH U.S. HEADQUARTERS IN LOS ANGELES COUNTY, 2010

Ranked by: Parent company revenue, in millions of dollars. **Remarks:** Also notes contact information, figures for previous year, description of operations, parent company, location, and top local executive. **Number listed:** 20

1. American Honda Motor Co., Inc., with $107.5 million
2. Nestle USA Inc., $105
3. Fresh & Easy, $99.1

Source: *Los Angeles Business Journal*, Largest Foreign Companies (annual), http://www.labusinessjournal.com, June 20, 2011.

1633 ■ LARGEST FOREIGN-OWNED COMPANIES WITH U.S. HEADQUARTERS IN COLORADO, 2010

Ranked by: Number of U.S. employees. **Remarks:** Also notes rank for previous year, contact information, number of Colorado employees, total number of employees, business description, top local executive, ticker symbol, owner, and foreign headquarters. **Number listed:** 10

1. Gates Corp., with 4,199 employees
2. PCL Construction Enterprises Inc., 3,915
3. Arcadis U.S. Inc., 3,724
4. Great West Life & Annuity Insurance Co., 2,917
5. EnCana Oil & Gas (USA) Inc., 1,712
6. Norgren USA, 1,500
7. Swisslog Healthcare Solutions, 400
8. Bona U.S., 104
9. Intermap Technologies Inc., 85

10. Maptek, 63

Source: *Denver Business Journal*, Book of Lists (annual), December 16, 2011, p. 53.

1634 ■ LARGEST NON-U.S. COMPANIES BY EMPLOYEES, 2011

Ranked by: Number of employees. **Number listed:** 100

1. U.K. National Health Service, with 1,400,000 employees
2. Randstad Holding NV, 546,980
3. Deutsche Post AG, 477,280
4. ISS A/S, 472,800
5. Carrefour SA, 471,755
6. Compass Group plc, 428,202
7. Siemens AG, 405,000
8. Volkswagen AG, 399,381
9. Tata Group, 395,000
10. Tesco plc, 384,389

Source: *Hoover's Handbook of World Business*, (annual), Hoover's Inc., 2012, p. 4a.

1635 ■ LARGEST NON-U.S. COMPANIES BY SALES, 2011

Ranked by: Sales, in millions of U.S. dollars. **Number listed:** 100

1. Royal Dutch Shell plc, with $378,152 million
2. BP plc, $302,545
3. Toyota Motor Corp., $229,197
4. Total SA, $186,159
5. Volkswagen AG, $168,135
6. AXA, $162,326
7. E.On AG, $144,993
8. ING Groep NV, $144,848
9. ENI SpA, $131,830
10. Daimler AG, $129,553

Source: *Hoover's Handbook of World Business*, (annual), Hoover's Inc., 2012, p. 2a.

1636 ■ LARGEST PRIVATE OR FOREIGN-OWNED COMPANIES IN THE U.S. BY EMPLOYEES, 2010

Ranked by: Total number of employees. **Remarks:** Also notes contact information for headquarters, number of employees at headquarters, revenue, rank by revenue, and primary SIC code. **Number listed:** 5000

1. Compass Group USA Investments Inc., with 360,000 employees
2. Express Services Inc., 357,735
3. ARAMARK Holdings Corp., 260,000
4. ARAMARK Intermediate Holdco Corp., 255,000
5. Securitas Holdings Inc., 250,000
6. General Motors Co., 244,500
6. General Motors Holdings LLC, 244,500
6. General Motors LLC, 244,500
9. American Drug Stores Inc., 200,000
10. Hercules Holding II LLC, 194,100

Source: *Business Rankings*, (annual), Dun & Bradstreet Inc., 2011, p. X.1+.

1637 ■ LARGEST PRIVATE OR FOREIGN-OWNED COMPANIES IN THE U.S. BY SALES, 2010

Ranked by: Revenue, in dollars. **Remarks:** Also notes contact information for headquarters, number of employees at headquarters and overall, rank by employees, and primary SIC code. **Number listed:** 5000

1. General Motors Co., with $135,592,000,000
2. BP America Inc., $83,982,000,000
3. NotionT Inc., $50,000,000,000
4. HCA Holdings Inc., $30,683,000,000
4. HCA Inc., $30,683,000,000
6. Methodist Healthcare Memphis Hospitals, $27,000,000,000
7. Veolia Water North America Northeast LLC, $23,000,000,000
8. Atlantic Trading & Marketing Inc., $19,000,000,000
9. DPH Holdings Corp., $18,060,000,000
10. Roche Holdings Inc., $17,098,000,000

Source: *Business Rankings*, (annual), Dun & Bradstreet Inc., 2011, p. IX.1+.

1638 ■ MOST ADMIRED COMPANIES IN THE AMERICAS (EXCLUDING U.S.), 2012

Ranked by: Survey of top executives, directors, and securities analysts regarding the Fortune 1,000 companies that they admire the most, regardless of industry. **Remarks:** Specific scores not provided. List is available online only, not in print. **Number listed:** 17

1. Thomson Reuters Corp.
2. Bombardier Inc.
3. Petroleo Brasileiro SA (Petrobras)
4. Schlumberger Ltd.
5. Vale SA
6. Bunge Corp.
7. Research in Motion Ltd.
8. Magna International Inc.
8. Seagate Technology Inc.
10. America Movil, SA de CV

Source: *Fortune*, World's Most Admired Companies (annual), http://www.fortune.com, March 19, 2012.

1639 ■ MOST PROFITABLE NON-U.S. COMPANIES, 2011

Ranked by: Net income, in millions of U.S. dollars. **Number listed:** 100

1. Nestle SA, with $36,386 million
2. OAO Gazprom, $31,792
3. BHP Billiton Ltd., $23,648
4. Royal Dutch Shell plc, $20,127
5. Petroleo Brasileiro SA (Petrobras), $19,184
6. Vale SA, $17,264
7. Bank of China, $16,585
8. Rio Tinto Ltd., $14,324
9. Total SA, $14,009
10. Telefonica SA, $13,473

Source: *Hoover's Handbook of World Business*, (annual), Hoover's Inc., 2012, p. 3a.

1640 ■ MOST VALUABLE NON-U.S. COMPANIES, 2011

Ranked by: Market value, in millions of U.S. dollars. **Number listed:** 100

1. Nordea Bank AB, with $391,922 million
2. A. P. Moller-Maersk A/S, $275,134
3. BHP Billiton Ltd., $251,837
4. Petroleo Brasileiro SA (Petrobras), $246,802
5. Vodafone plc, $237,731
6. Royal Dutch Shell plc, $205,489
7. Nestle SA, $203,627
8. Vale SA, $185,479
9. HSBC plc, $180,540
10. Bank of China, $173,049

Source: *Hoover's Handbook of World Business*, (annual), Hoover's Inc., 2012, p. 7a.

Corporations—France

1641 ■ BEST LARGE COMPANIES TO WORK FOR IN FRANCE, 2012

Ranked by: Score based on the relationships between employees and management, employees and their jobs/company, and employees and coworkers. **Remarks:** Specific scores not provided. To qualify, companies must have more than 500 employees. **Number listed:** 12

1. PepsiCo France
2. Microsoft France
3. Mars Petcare & Food France
4. Davidson Consulting
5. Leroy Merlin France
6. Procter & Gamble France
7. EMC2
8. Ferrero France
9. McDonald's France
10. Decathlon France

Source: *Great Place to Work Institute Inc.*, Best Places to Work in France (annual), http://www.greatplacetowork.com, March 2012.

1642 ■ BEST SMALL COMPANIES TO WORK FOR IN FRANCE, 2012

Ranked by: Score based on the relationships between employees and management, employees and their jobs/company, and employees and coworkers. **Remarks:** Specific scores not provided. To qualify, companies must have fewer than 500 employees. **Number listed:** 34

1. OCTO
2. NetApp France
3. Accuracy
4. W. L. Gore & Associates Inc.
5. Nexteer Automotive France
6. National Instruments France
7. SAS France
8. Leboncoin.fr
9. Webhelp SAS
10. Bio 3G

Source: *Great Place to Work Institute Inc.*, Best Places to Work in France (annual), http://www.greatplacetowork.com, March 2012.

1643 ■ FRANCE'S LARGEST COMPANIES OVERALL, 2011

Ranked by: Score based on revenue, profits, assets, and market capitalization. **Remarks:** Specific scores not provided. Also notes rank in the overall *Forbes 2000* and figures for each criterion. **Number listed:** 63

1. Total SA
2. BNP Paribas
3. AXA
4. GDF Suez
5. Electricite de France
6. Sanofi SA
7. Societe Generale SA
8. France Telecom SA
9. Vinci
10. Vivendi SA

Source: *Forbes*, Forbes 2000 (annual), http://www.forbes.com, May 7, 2012.

1644 ■ LARGEST COMPANIES IN FRANCE, 2010

Ranked by: Sales, in millions of U.S. dollars. **Remarks:** Also notes city; industrial code; percent change in sales; profits; profit as a percentage of sales, assets, and equity; number of employees; sales per employee; assets; equity capital; equity capital as a percentage of assets; year established; and figures for previous year. **Number listed:** 1700

1. Carrefour SA, with $125,360 million
2. Peugeot Citroen Automobile SA, $75,993.4
3. Electricite de France, $57,844.6
4. Veolia Environnement SA, $51,031.7
5. VINCI, $48,129.4
6. Total Raffinage Marketing, $45,114.1
7. Bouygues SA, $44,935.1
8. Societe Generale SA, $43,993.3
9. Finatis, $41,020
10. Renault SA, $38,740.3

Source: *Europe's 15,000 Largest Companies*, (annual), ELC International, 2011, p. 172+.

1645 ■ LARGEST CORPORATIONS IN FRANCE BY REVENUE, 2010

Ranked by: Revenue, in millions of U.S. dollars. **Remarks:** Also notes headquarters city and overall rank in the *Global 500*. Ranking is available online only, not in print. **Number listed:** 35

1. Total SA, with $186,055 million
2. AXA, $162,236
3. BNP Paribas, $128,726
4. Carrefour SA, $120,297
5. GDF Suez, $111,888
6. Credit Agricole SA, $105,003
7. Electricite de France, $86,309
8. Societe Generale SA, $84,350
9. Peugeot SA, $74,251
10. Groupe BPCE, $69,297

Source: *Fortune*, Global 500 (annual), http://www.fortune.com, July 25, 2011.

1646 ■ MOST ADMIRED COMPANIES IN FRANCE, 2012

Ranked by: Score based on a survey of executives, directors, and securities analysts of companies within their own industry. **Remarks:** List is available online only, not in print. Also notes headquarters. **Number listed:** 13

1. L'Oreal SA, with 7.45 points
2. GDF Suez, 7.33

3. Total SA, 6.62
4. Groupe Danone, 6.55
5. PPR SA, 6.49
6. Compagnie Generale des Etablissements Michelin, 6.41
7. Rexel, 6.13
8. VINCI, 6.01
9. Air France-KLM SA, 5.85
10. Sodexo, 5.84

Source: *Fortune*, World's Most Admired Companies (annual), http://www.fortune.com, March 19, 2012.

Corporations—Georgia

1647 ■ BEST LARGE ATLANTA WORKPLACES, 2012

Ranked by: Score based on employee survey. **Remarks:** Scores not provided. Ranking covers companies with 500 or more employees. **Number listed:** 20

1. Woodward Academy Inc.
2. Alston & Bird LLP
3. FedEx Corp.
4. Ernst & Young LLP
5. InterContinental Hotels Group plc
6. Children's Healthcare of Atlanta
7. Resurgens Orthopaedics
8. Sprint Corp.
9. Federal Reserve Bank of Atlanta
10. RaceTrac Petroleum Inc.

Source: *Atlanta Journal-Constitution*, Top 100 Workplaces (annual), April 20, 2012.

1648 ■ BEST MID-SIZED ATLANTA WORKPLACES, 2012

Ranked by: Score based on employee survey. **Remarks:** Scores not provided. Ranking covers companies with 150 to 499 employees. **Number listed:** 30

1. AutomationDirect.com
2. Dorsey Alston, Realtors
3. North Point Ministries
4. Oglethorpe Power Corp.
5. Edward Jones
6. LeasePlan USA
7. NASCO
8. Post Properties Inc.
9. Larson-Juhl Inc.
10. PBD Worldwide

Source: *Atlanta Journal-Constitution*, Top 100 Workplaces (annual), April 20, 2012.

1649 ■ BEST SMALL ATLANTA WORKPLACES, 2012

Ranked by: Score based on employee survey. **Remarks:** Scores not provided. Ranking covers companies with 149 or fewer employees. **Number listed:** 50

1. Pardot
2. Peachtree Planning Corp.
3. The Schenck School
4. DPR Construction

5. Meadows & Ohly
6. Premier Elevator
7. Hire Dynamics
8. Transwestern Commercial Services
9. eVestment Alliance
10. Contact At Once LLC

Source: *Atlanta Journal-Constitution*, Top 100 Workplaces (annual), April 20, 2012.

1650 ■ GEORGIA'S BEST COMPANIES TO WORK FOR, 2012

Ranked by: Score based on employee surveys as well as evaluation of companies' credibility, respect, fairness, and pride/camaraderie. **Remarks:** Specific scores not provided; companies are listed alphabetically, not ranked. Available online only, not in print. **Number listed:** 4

1. AFLAC Inc.
2. Alston & Bird LLP
3. Children's Healthcare of Atlanta
4. Intercontinental Hotels Group

Source: *Fortune*, 100 Best Companies to Work For (annual), http://www.fortune.com, February 6, 2012.

1651 ■ GEORGIA'S LARGEST COMPANIES OVERALL, 2011

Ranked by: Score based on revenue, profits, assets, and market capitalization. **Remarks:** Specific scores not provided. Also notes overall rank in the *Forbes 2000* and figures for each criterion. **Number listed:** 13

1. The Coca-Cola Co.
2. The Home Depot Inc.
3. United Parcel Service Inc. (UPS)
4. AFLAC Inc.
5. Southern Co.
6. Delta Air Lines Inc.
7. SunTrust Banks Inc.
8. IntercontinentalExchange Inc.
9. Coca-Cola Enterprises Inc.
10. Genuine Parts Co.

Source: *Forbes*, Forbes 2000 (annual), http://www.forbes.com, May 7, 2012.

1652 ■ GEORGIA'S LARGEST PRIVATE COMPANIES, 2010

Ranked by: Revenue, in billions of dollars. **Remarks:** Also notes business segment, number of employees, and overall rank in the *America's Largest Private Companies* list. Ranking is available online only, not in print. **Number listed:** 7

1. Cox Enterprises Inc., with $14.6 billion
2. First Data Corp., $10.38
3. Mansfield Oil Co., Inc., $6.5
4. RaceTrac Petroleum Inc., $5.75
5. Colonial Group Inc., $5.2
6. Southwire Co., $4.3
7. Unisource Worldwide Inc., $4.2

Source: *Forbes*, America's Largest Private Companies (annual), http://www.forbes.com, December 5, 2011.

1653 ■ LARGEST COMPANIES IN GEORGIA BY EMPLOYEES, 2010

Ranked by: Number of employees at headquarters. **Remarks:** Also notes contact information for headquarters, total number of employees, revenue, rank by revenue, and primary SIC code. **Number listed:** 205

1. Delta Air Lines Inc., with 27,100 employees
2. DT Express LLC, 8,020
3. The Coca-Cola Co., 8,000
4. Lockheed Martin Aeronautical Co., 7,600
5. Georgia Health Sciences University Foundation Inc., 6,500
6. Hospitality Staffing Solutions, 5,000
7. Avondale Mills Inc., 4,999
8. Fulton Dekalb Hospital Authority, 4,800
9. The Home Depot Inc., 4,600
10. Total System Services Inc., 4,400

Source: *Business Rankings*, (annual), Dun & Bradstreet Inc., 2011, p. IV.59-IV.63.

1654 ■ LARGEST COMPANIES IN GEORGIA BY SALES, 2010

Ranked by: Revenue, in dollars. **Remarks:** Also notes contact information for headquarters, number of employees at headquarters and overall, rank by employees, and primary SIC code. **Number listed:** 208

1. The Home Depot Inc., with $66,176,000,000
2. United Parcel Service Inc. (UPS), $49,545,000,000
3. The Coca-Cola Co., $35,119,000,000
4. Delta Air Lines Inc., $31,755,000,000
5. Southern Co., $17,456,000,000
6. Cox Enterprises Inc., $14,700,000,000
7. Genuine Parts Co., $11,207,589,000
8. Novelis Corp., $8,673,000,000
9. Georgia Power Co., $8,349,000,000
10. H. D. Supply Inc., $7,418,000,000

Source: *Business Rankings*, (annual), Dun & Bradstreet Inc., 2011, p. III.59-III.63.

1655 ■ MOST ADMIRED COMPANIES IN GEORGIA, 2012

Ranked by: Survey of top executives, directors, and securities analysts regarding the Fortune 1,000 companies that they admire the most, regardless of industry. **Remarks:** Also notes city and industry rank. List is available online only, not in print. **Number listed:** 9

1. United Parcel Service Inc. (UPS), with 7.42 points
2. The Coca-Cola Co., 6.69
3. Southern Co., 6.57
4. The Home Depot Inc., 6.39
5. AFLAC Inc., 6.24
6. Delta Air Lines Inc., 6.01
7. Equifax, 5.88
8. Coca-Cola Enterprises Inc., 5.83
9. Global Payments, 5.53

Source: *Fortune*, World's Most Admired Companies (annual), http://www.fortune.com, March 19, 2012.

1656 ■ **TOP** *FORTUNE 500* **COMPANIES IN GEORGIA, 2011**

Ranked by: Revenue, in millions of dollars. **Remarks:** Also notes overall rank in the *Fortune 500,* headquarters, and number of employees. **Number listed:** 15

1. The Home Depot Inc., with $70,395 million
2. United Parcel Service Inc. (UPS), $53,105
3. The Coca-Cola Co., $46,542
4. Delta Air Lines Inc., $35,115
5. AFLAC Inc., $22,171
6. Southern Co., $17,657
7. Genuine Parts Co., $12,458.9
8. First Data Corp., $10,713.6
9. SunTrust Banks Inc., $9,602
10. AGCO Corp., $8,773.2

Source: *Fortune*, Fortune 500 (annual), May 21, 2012, p. F-42.

Corporations—Germany

1657 ■ **BEST EXTRA-LARGE COMPANIES TO WORK FOR IN GERMANY, 2012**

Ranked by: Score based on the relationships between employees and management, employees and their jobs/company, and employees and coworkers. **Remarks:** Specific scores not provided. Ranking covers companies with 5,001 to 10,000 employees. **Number listed:** 3

1. SMA Solar Technology AG
2. Techniker Krankenkasse
3. Telefonica Germany GmbH

Source: *Great Place to Work Institute Inc.*, Best Places to Work in Germany (annual), http://www.greatplacetowork.com, 2012.

1658 ■ **BEST LARGE COMPANIES TO WORK FOR IN GERMANY, 2012**

Ranked by: Score based on the relationships between employees and management, employees and their jobs/company, and employees and coworkers. **Remarks:** Specific scores not provided. Ranking covers companies with 2,001 to 5,000 employees. **Number listed:** 3

1. Volkswagen Financial Services AG
2. Tegut Gutberlet Stiftung & Co.
3. SICK AG

Source: *Great Place to Work Institute Inc.*, Best Places to Work in Germany (annual), http://www.greatplacetowork.com, 2012.

1659 ■ **BEST MEDIUM-SIZED COMPANIES TO WORK FOR IN GERMANY, 2012**

Ranked by: Score based on the relationships between employees and management, employees and their jobs/company, and employees and coworkers. **Remarks:** Specific scores not provided. Ranking covers companies with 501 to 2,000 employees. **Number listed:** 3

1. DIS AG
2. NetApp Deutschland GmbH
3. W. L. Gore & Associates GmbH

Source: *Great Place to Work Institute Inc.*, Best Places to Work in Germany (annual), http://www.greatplacetowork.com, 2012.

1660 ■ **BEST SMALL COMPANIES TO WORK FOR IN GERMANY, 2012**

Ranked by: Score based on the relationships between employees and management, employees and their jobs/company, and

employees and coworkers. **Remarks:** Specific scores not provided. Ranking covers companies with 50 to 500 employees. **Number listed:** 3

1. noventum consulting GmbH
2. astrias personalmanagement gmbh
3. LEGO GmbH

Source: *Great Place to Work Institute Inc.*, Best Places to Work in Germany (annual), http://www.greatplacetowork.com, 2012.

1661 ■ **GERMANY'S LARGEST COMPANIES OVERALL, 2011**

Ranked by: Score based on revenue, profits, assets, and market capitalization. **Remarks:** Specific scores not provided. Also notes rank in the overall *Forbes 2000* and figures for each criterion. **Number listed:** 53

1. Volkswagen AG
2. Daimler AG
3. Allianz AG
4. Siemens AG
5. Deutsche Bank AG
6. Bayerische Motoren Werke AG (BMW)
7. BASF SE
8. Bayer AG
9. RWE AG
10. Munchener Ruckversicherungs Gesellschaft AG (Munich Re)

Source: *Forbes*, Forbes 2000 (annual), http://www.forbes.com, May 7, 2012.

1662 ■ **LARGEST COMPANIES IN GERMANY, 2010**

Ranked by: Sales, in millions of U.S. dollars. **Remarks:** Also notes city; industrial code; percent change in sales; profits; profit as a percentage of sales, assets, and equity; number of employees; sales per employee; assets; equity capital; equity capital as a percentage of assets; year established; and figures for previous year. **Number listed:** 2000

1. Volkswagen AG, with $145,890.5 million
2. E.On AG, $121,678.2
3. Daimler AG, $117,375.8
4. Nova Test 11, $108,568.5
4. Siemens AG, $108,568.5
6. Metro AG, $97,454.7
7. Deutsche Telekom AG, $96,076.1
8. E.On Energy Trading SE, $91,734.1
9. BASF SE, $75,390.6
10. Bayerische Motoren Werke AG (BMW), $75,372.8

Source: *Europe's 15,000 Largest Companies*, (annual), ELC International, 2011, p. 242+.

1663 ■ **LARGEST CORPORATIONS IN GERMANY BY REVENUE, 2010**

Ranked by: Revenue, in millions of U.S. dollars. **Remarks:** Also notes headquarters city and overall rank in the *Global 500.* Ranking is available online only, not in print. **Number listed:** 34

1. Volkswagen AG, with $168,041 million
2. Daimler AG, $129,481
3. Allianz AG, $127,379
4. E.On AG, $125,064

5. Siemens AG, $102,657
6. Metro AG, $89,081
7. BASF SE, $84,597
8. Deutsche Telekom AG, $82,674
9. Bayerische Motoren Werke AG (BMW), $80,099
10. Munchener Ruckversicherungs-Gesellschaft AG (Munich Re), $76,220

Source: *Fortune*, Global 500 (annual), http://www.fortune.com, July 25, 2011.

1664 ■ MOST ADMIRED COMPANIES IN GERMANY, 2012

Ranked by: Score based on a survey of executives, directors, and securities analysts of companies within their own industry. **Remarks:** List is available online only, not in print. Also notes headquarters. **Number listed:** 21

1. RWE AG, with 7.5 points
2. Marquard & Bahls, 7.21
3. Volkswagen A, 7.13
4. Bayerische Motoren Werke AG (BMW), 7.12
5. Robert Bosch Corp.Henkel KgaA, 6.84
6. Daimler, 6.75
7. adidas AG, 6.64
8. BASF SE, 6.60
9. ThyssenKrupp AG, 6.53
10. Siemens, 6.3

Source: *Fortune*, World's Most Admired Companies (annual), http://www.fortune.com, March 19, 2012.

Corporations—Greece

1665 ■ BEST LARGE COMPANIES TO WORK FOR IN GREECE, 2012

Ranked by: Score based on the relationships between employees and management, employees and their jobs/company, and employees and coworkers. **Remarks:** Specific scores not provided. Ranking covers companies with more than 250 employees. **Number listed:** 10

1. Athenian Brewery
2. Elais - Unilever Hellas
3. Tasty Foods
4. Ygeia Hospital
5. Media Strom
6. Pharmathen
7. Leroy Merlin
8. Wurth Hellas
9. Vivechrom
10. Accenture Ltd.

Source: *Great Place to Work Institute Inc.*, Best Places to Work in Greece (annual), 2011.

1666 ■ BEST SMALL COMPANIES TO WORK FOR IN GREECE, 2012

Ranked by: Score based on the relationships between employees and management, employees and their jobs/company, and employees and coworkers. **Remarks:** Specific scores not provided. Ranking covers companies with 50 to 250 employees. **Number listed:** 10

1. Xerox Hellas
2. Kri-Kri, Milk Industry
3. Imperial Tobacco Hellas
4. Medtronic Hellas
5. Genesis Pharma
6. Data Communication
7. 3M Co.
8. Melissa Kikizas
9. Amgen Hellas
10. British American Tobacco Hellas

Source: *Great Place to Work Institute Inc.*, Best Places to Work in Greece (annual), 2011.

1667 ■ GREECE'S LARGEST COMPANIES OVERALL, 2011

Ranked by: Score based on revenue, profits, assets, and market capitalization. **Remarks:** Specific scores not provided. Also notes rank in the overall *Forbes 2000* and figures for each criterion. **Number listed:** 11

1. National Bank of Greece
2. Public Power
3. Coca-Cola Hellenic Bottling Co. SA
4. EFG Eurobank Ergasias SA
5. Alpha Bank
6. Bank of Greece
7. Piraeus Bank
8. OPAP SA
9. Hellenic Petroleum SA
10. ATEbank

Source: *Forbes*, Forbes 2000 (annual), http://www.forbes.com, May 7, 2012.

1668 ■ LARGEST COMPANIES IN GREECE, 2010

Ranked by: Sales, in millions of U.S. dollars. **Remarks:** Also notes city; industrial code; percent change in sales; profits; profit as a percentage of sales, assets, and equity; number of employees; sales per employee; assets; equity capital; equity capital as a percentage of assets; year established; and figures for previous year. **Number listed:** 200

1. Coca-Cola Hellenic Bottling Co. SA, with $9,839.3 million
2. Hellenic Petroleum SA, $8,846.6
3. Hellenic Telecommunications Organization SA, $8,576.4
4. OPAP SA, $7,779.9
5. Public Power Corp. SA, $7,547.9
6. National Bank of Greece SA, $6,976.6
7. Alpha Bank Group, $5,768.2
8. Hellenic Transmission System Operator SA, $5,102.9
9. EFG Eurobank Ergasias SA, $4,578.1
10. Aegean Marine Petroleum Network Inc., $2,778

Source: *Europe's 15,000 Largest Companies*, (annual), ELC International, 2011, p. 324+.

Corporations—Guatemala

1669 ■ BEST COMPANIES TO WORK FOR IN GUATEMALA, 2012

Ranked by: Score based on the relationships between employees and management, employees and their jobs/company, and employees and coworkers. **Remarks:** Specific scores not provided. **Number listed:** 15

1. FedEx Guatemala
2. Kimberly-Clark Guatemala
3. Sacos del Atlantico (Grupo Progreso) Guatemala
4. Centro de Servicios Corporativos (Grupo Progreso) Guatemala
5. Scotiabank Guatemala
6. Cementos Progreso (Grupo Progreso) Guatemala
7. Atento Guatemala
8. Mixto Listo (Grupo Progreso) Guatemala
9. British American Tobacco CA (Guatemala)
10. Monsanto Guatemala

Source: *Great Place to Work Institute Inc.*, Best Places to Work in Central America & the Caribbean (annual), 2012.

Corporations—Hawaii

1670 ■ BEST LARGE COMPANIES TO WORK FOR IN HAWAII, 2012

Ranked by: Score based on surveys of employers and employees. **Remarks:** Specific scores not provided. Ranking covers companies with 250 to 999 U.S. employees. Also notes headquarters, website, number of employees, average annual pay, number of vacation and sick days granted annually, and comments. **Number listed:** 3

1. SVC Management Hawaii LLC
2. Hawaii USA Federal Credit Union
3. Castle Medical Center

Source: *Hawaii Business*, Best Places to Work in Hawaii (annual), April 2012, p. 51-52.

1671 ■ BEST MEDIUM-SIZED COMPANIES TO WORK FOR IN HAWAII, 2012

Ranked by: Score based on surveys of employers and employees. **Remarks:** Specific scores not provided. Ranking covers companies with 50 to 249 U.S. employees. Also notes headquarters, website, number of employees, average annual pay, number of vacation and sick days granted annually, and comments. **Number listed:** 3

1. Bowers + Kubota Consulting
2. PKF Pacific Hawaii LLP
3. N & K CPAs Inc.

Source: *Hawaii Business*, Best Places to Work in Hawaii (annual), April 2012, p. 57-58.

1672 ■ BEST SMALL COMPANIES TO WORK FOR IN HAWAII, 2012

Ranked by: Score based on surveys of employers and employees. **Remarks:** Specific scores not provided. Ranking covers companies with 15 to 49 U.S. employees. Also notes headquarters, web-

site, number of employees, average annual pay, number of vacation and sick days granted annually, and comments. **Number listed:** 3

1. Hawaii Information Consortium LLC
2. Hawaii Human Resources (HiHR)
3. Wealth Strategy Partners LLC

Source: *Hawaii Business*, Best Places to Work in Hawaii (annual), April 2012, p. 65-66.

1673 ■ BEST VERY LARGE COMPANIES TO WORK FOR IN HAWAII, 2012

Ranked by: Score based on surveys of employers and employees. **Remarks:** Specific scores not provided. Ranking covers companies with 1,000 or more U.S. employees. Also notes headquarters, website, number of employees, average annual pay, number of vacation and sick days granted annually, and comments. **Number listed:** 3

1. New York Life
2. Edward Jones
3. University of Phoenix, Hawaii Campus

Source: *Hawaii Business*, Best Places to Work in Hawaii (annual), April 2012, p. 45-46.

1674 ■ FASTEST-GROWING COMPANIES IN THE STATE OF HAWAII, 2009-2010

Ranked by: Annual increase in revenue, in percent. **Remarks:** Also notes revenue for current year. **Number listed:** 25

1. RevoluSun/DEP, with 1,042.6%
2. University of Hawaii Foundation, 388.8%
3. Hawaii Human Resources Inc., 350.6%
4. Sunetric, 98.5%
5. Kuhio Auto Group, 76.2%
6. Aloha Auto Group Ltd., 67.9%
7. PEMCO Ltd., 45.4%
8. Honolulu Community Action Program Inc., 43.3%
9. Hawaii Medical Assurance Association, 42.6%
10. Swinerton Builders, 41.6%

Source: *Hawaii Business*, Top 250 (annual), August 2011, p. 126.

1675 ■ LARGE HAWAIIAN COMPANIES WITH THE HEALTHIEST WORKPLACE, 2012

Ranked by: Score based on surveys of employers and employees. **Remarks:** Specific scores not provided. Ranking covers companies with 250 to 999 employees. **Number listed:** 3

1. Castle Medical Center
2. HawaiiUSA Federal Credit Union
3. SVC Hawaii Management Inc.

Source: *Hawaii Business*, Best Places to Work in Hawaii (annual), April 2012, p. 42.

1676 ■ LARGEST COMPANIES IN HAWAII BY EMPLOYEES, 2010

Ranked by: Number of employees at headquarters. **Remarks:** Also notes contact information for headquarters, total number of employees, revenue, rank by revenue, and primary SIC code. **Number listed:** 49

1. Marriott Kauai Ownership Resorts Inc., with 5,000 employees
2. Kyo-Ya Hotels & Resorts LP, 3,276

3. Hawaii Pacific Health, 2,300

4. St. Francis Healthcare System of Hawaii, 1,350

5. Hawaii Medical Service Association, 1,300

6. Hawaii Medical Center West LLC, 1,250

7. Polynesian Cultural Center Inc., 1,100

7. Polynesian Culture Center, 1,100

9. First Hawaiian Bank, 1,000

9. Oahu Transit Services Inc., 1,000

Source: *Business Rankings*, (annual), Dun & Bradstreet Inc., 2011, p. IV.64-IV.65.

1677 ■ LARGEST COMPANIES IN HAWAII BY SALES, 2010

Ranked by: Revenue, in dollars. **Remarks:** Also notes contact information for headquarters, number of employees at headquarters and overall, rank by employees, and primary SIC code. **Number listed:** 50

1. Hawaiian Electric Industries Inc., with $2,664,982,000

2. Hawaiian Electric Co., $2,026,672,000

3. Alexander & Baldwin Inc., $1,646,000,000

4. Nordic PCL Construction Inc., $1,616,776,802

5. Hawaiian Holdings Inc., $1,310,093,000

6. Hawaii Pacific Health, $812,344,756

7. Servco Pacific Inc., $699,395,000

8. Ambulatory Services Inc., $425,000,000

9. Hawaiian Telcom Holdco Inc., $408,595,000

10. Hawaiian Dredging Construction Co., $345,294,092

Source: *Business Rankings*, (annual), Dun & Bradstreet Inc., 2011, p. III.64-III.65.

1678 ■ LARGEST COMPANIES ON THE ISLAND OF HAWAII, 2010

Ranked by: Revenue, in millions of dollars. **Remarks:** Also notes rank in the overall *Top 250*. **Number listed:** 15

1. Puna Plantation Hawaii Ltd., with $125 million

2. Fairmont Hotels & Resorts Hawaii, $113.3

3. North Hawaii Community Hospital, $101.9

4. Hawaii Petroleum Inc., $76.2

5. Suisan Group Inc., $73.9

6. Isemoto Contracting Co., Ltd., $71.9

7. David S. De Luz Sr. Enterprises Inc., $54.5

8. I. Kitagawa & Co., Ltd., $49.8

9. Mauna Lani Resort (Operation) Inc., $37.6

10. Inter Pacific Motors Inc., $24

Source: *Hawaii Business*, Top 250 (annual), August 2011, p. 144.

1679 ■ LARGEST COMPANIES ON THE ISLAND OF KAUAI, 2010

Ranked by: Revenue, in millions of dollars. **Remarks:** Also notes rank in the overall *Top 250*. **Number listed:** 6

1. Kauai Island Utility Cooperative, with $155.3 million

2. King Auto Center Inc., $76.5

3. Kawailoa Development LLP, $68

4. Koa Properties, Land & Homes LLC, $56.8

5. Kuhio Auto Group, $37

6. Kauai Community Federal Credit Union, $16

Source: *Hawaii Business*, Top 250 (annual), August 2011, p. 144.

1680 ■ LARGEST COMPANIES ON THE ISLAND OF MAUI, 2010

Ranked by: Revenue, in millions of dollars. **Remarks:** Also notes rank in the overall *Top 250*. **Number listed:** 14

1. Jim Falk Automotive Group, with $196.4 million

2. Grand Wailea, $163

3. Dorvin D. Leis Co., Inc., $90

4. VIP Foodservice, $66

5. Minit Stop Stores, $50

6. Maui Petroleum Inc., $48.5

7. Maui Land & Pineapple Co., Inc., $42

8. Hale Makua Health Services, $36.1

9. Maui Medical Group Inc., $33.3

10. Cheeseburger Restaurants, $28.6

Source: *Hawaii Business*, Top 250 (annual), August 2011, p. 144.

1681 ■ LARGEST COMPANIES IN THE STATE OF HAWAII, 2010

Ranked by: Revenue, in millions of dollars. **Remarks:** Also notes rank and figures for previous two years, percent change, line of business, website, parent company, chief executives, number of employees, and employee growth. **Number listed:** 250

1. Hawaiian Electric Industries Inc., with $2,665 million

2. Hawaii Medical Service Association, $2,473

3. Alexander & Baldwin Inc., $1,646.2

4. University of Hawaii, $1,462.8

5. Hawaiian Airlines Inc., $1,310.1

6. Kaiser Permanente Hawaii, $1,000

7. Hawaii Pacific Health, $852

8. The Queen's Health Systems, $789.6

9. Bank of Hawaii Corp., $720.5

10. First Hawaiian Bank, $716.5

Source: *Hawaii Business*, Top 250 (annual), August 2011, p. 76+.

1682 ■ LARGEST HAWAIIAN COMPANIES WITH CANADIAN PARENT COMPANIES, 2010

Ranked by: Revenue, in millions of dollars. **Remarks:** Specific figures not provided; companies are listed alphabetically, not ranked. Also notes rank in the overall *Top 250*. **Number listed:** 2

1. Nordic PCL Construction Inc.

2. Fairmont Hotels & Resorts Hawaii

Source: *Hawaii Business*, Top 250 (annual), August 2011, p. 142.

1683 ■ LARGEST HAWAIIAN COMPANIES WITH JAPANESE PARENT COMPANIES, 2010

Ranked by: Revenue, in millions of dollars. **Remarks:** Specific figures not provided; companies are listed alphabetically, not ranked. Also notes rank in the overall *Top 250*. **Number listed:** 11

1. Alaka'i Mechanical Corp.

2. First Insurance Co. of Hawaii Ltd.

3. Jalpak International Hawaii Inc.

4. Japan Airlines International Co.

5. JTB Hawaii Inc.

6. Kyo-ya Co., Ltd.
7. Marukai Corp.
8. Mauna Lani Resort (Operation) Inc.
9. Pacific Guardian Life Insurance Co., Ltd.
10. R & C Hawaii Tours Inc.

Source: *Hawaii Business*, Top 250 (annual), August 2011, p. 142.

1684 ■ MEDIUM-SIZED HAWAIIAN COMPANIES WITH THE HEALTHIEST WORKPLACE, 2012

Ranked by: Score based on surveys of employers and employees. **Remarks:** Specific scores not provided. Ranking covers companies with 50 to 249 employees. **Number listed:** 3

1. Bowers + Kubota Consulting
2. Aloha Pacific Federal Credit Union
3. Hickam Communities LLC

Source: *Hawaii Business*, Best Places to Work in Hawaii (annual), April 2012, p. 42.

1685 ■ MOST FAMILY-FRIENDLY LARGE HAWAIIAN COMPANIES, 2012

Ranked by: Score based on surveys of employers and employees. **Remarks:** Specific scores not provided. Ranking covers companies with 250 to 999 employees. **Number listed:** 3

1. Servo Pacific Inc.
2. Castle Medical Center
3. Expedia Local Expert

Source: *Hawaii Business*, Best Places to Work in Hawaii (annual), April 2012, p. 42.

1686 ■ MOST FAMILY-FRIENDLY MEDIUM-SIZED HAWAIIAN COMPANIES, 2012

Ranked by: Score based on surveys of employers and employees. **Remarks:** Specific scores not provided. Ranking covers companies with 50 to 249 employees. **Number listed:** 3

1. Y&M Radiology
2. Bowers + Kubota Consulting
3. Island Insurance Co., Ltd.

Source: *Hawaii Business*, Best Places to Work in Hawaii (annual), April 2012, p. 42.

1687 ■ MOST FAMILY-FRIENDLY SMALL HAWAIIAN COMPANIES, 2012

Ranked by: Score based on surveys of employers and employees. **Remarks:** Specific scores not provided. Ranking covers companies with 15 to 49 employees. **Number listed:** 3

1. Gregory House Programs
2. Pacific Administrators Inc.
3. Maui Family Support Services Inc.

Source: *Hawaii Business*, Best Places to Work in Hawaii (annual), April 2012, p. 42.

1688 ■ MOST FAMILY-FRIENDLY VERY LARGE HAWAIIAN COMPANIES, 2012

Ranked by: Score based on surveys of employers and employees. **Remarks:** Specific scores not provided. Ranking covers companies with 1,000 or more employees. **Number listed:** 3

1. Kiewit Infrastructure West Co.
2. UBS Financial Services Inc.
3. Booz Allen Hamilton Inc.

Source: *Hawaii Business*, Best Places to Work in Hawaii (annual), April 2012, p. 42.

1689 ■ SMALL HAWAIIAN COMPANIES WITH THE HEALTHIEST WORKPLACE, 2012

Ranked by: Score based on surveys of employers and employees. **Remarks:** Specific scores not provided. Ranking covers companies with 15 to 49 employees. **Number listed:** 3

1. Hawaii Information Consortium LLC
2. Wakelight Technologies Inc.
3. Pacific Administrators Inc.

Source: *Hawaii Business*, Best Places to Work in Hawaii (annual), April 2012, p. 42.

1690 ■ VERY LARGE HAWAIIAN COMPANIES WITH THE HEALTHIEST WORKPLACE, 2012

Ranked by: Score based on surveys of employers and employees. **Remarks:** Specific scores not provided. Ranking covers companies with at least 1,000 employees. **Number listed:** 3

1. Kiewit Infrastructure West Co.
2. UBS Financial Services Inc.
3. Booz Allen Hamilton Inc.

Source: *Hawaii Business*, Best Places to Work in Hawaii (annual), April 2012, p. 42.

Corporations—Honduras

1691 ■ BEST COMPANIES TO WORK FOR IN HONDURAS, 2012

Ranked by: Score based on the relationships between employees and management, employees and their jobs/company, and employees and coworkers. **Remarks:** Specific scores not provided. **Number listed:** 6

1. Kimberly-Clark Honduras
2. Autofacil Honduras
3. British American Tobacco Honduras
4. Grupo Roble Corporativo y Administracion Honduras
5. Grupo Ficohsa Honduras
6. Pfizer Honduras

Source: *Great Place to Work Institute Inc.*, Best Places to Work in Central America & the Caribbean (annual), 2012.

Corporations—Hong Kong

1692 ■ HONG KONG'S LARGEST COMPANIES OVERALL, 2011

Ranked by: Score based on revenue, profits, assets, and market capitalization. **Remarks:** Specific scores not provided. Also notes rank in the overall *Forbes 2000* and figures for each criterion. **Number listed:** 48

1. China Mobile Ltd.
2. CNOOC Ltd.
3. Hutchison Whampoa Ltd.
4. Jardine Matheson Holdings Ltd.
5. AIA Group Ltd.
6. Sun Hung Kai Properties Ltd.
7. China Unicom Ltd.

8. CLP Holdings Ltd.

9. Swire Pacific Ltd.

10. Cheung Kong (Holdings) Ltd.

Source: *Forbes*, Forbes 2000 (annual), http://www.forbes.com, May 7, 2012.

Corporations—Hungary

1693 ■ HUNGARY'S LARGEST COMPANIES OVERALL, 2011

Ranked by: Score based on revenue, profits, assets, and market capitalization. **Remarks:** Specific scores not provided. Also notes rank in the overall *Forbes 2000* and figures for each criterion. **Number listed:** 2

1. MOL Magyar Olaj-es Gazipari Nyrt

2. OTP Bank

Source: *Forbes*, Forbes 2000 (annual), http://www.forbes.com, May 7, 2012.

1694 ■ LARGEST COMPANIES IN HUNGARY, 2010

Ranked by: Sales, in millions of U.S. dollars. **Remarks:** Also notes city; industrial code; percent change in sales; profits; profit as a percentage of sales, assets, and equity; number of employees; sales per employee; assets; equity capital; equity capital as a percentage of assets; year established; and figures for previous year. **Number listed:** 200

1. Erste Leasing Autofinanszirozasi Penzugyi, with $17,991.2 million

2. MOL Magyar Olaj- Es Gazipari Nyrt, $10,024

3. OTP Bank, $8,370

4. Edison Trading SPA, $7,844

5. Nokia Komarom Kft, $5,905.5

6. Audi Hungaria Motor Kft, $5,752.6

7. E.ON Foeldgas Trade Zrt, $4,295.9

8. Samsung Electronics Magyar Zrt, $4,224.2

9. Philips Industries Magyarorszag, $3,108.2

10. Szatmar Butorgyar Kft, $3,096.2

Source: *Europe's 15,000 Largest Companies*, (annual), ELC International, 2011, p. 334+.

Corporations—Iceland

1695 ■ LARGEST COMPANIES IN ICELAND, 2010

Ranked by: Sales, in millions of U.S. dollars. **Remarks:** Also notes city; industrial code; percent change in sales; profits; profit as a percentage of sales, assets, and equity; number of employees; sales per employee; assets; equity capital; equity capital as a percentage of assets; year established; and figures for previous year. **Number listed:** 100

1. Bakkavoer Group hf, with $2,628.4 million

2. Actavis Group hf, $2,084.7

3. Icelandic Group hf, $2,037.7

4. Islandsbanki hf, $1,226.1

5. Alfesca hf, $1,022.2

6. Promens hf, $959.1

7. Hf. Eimskipafelag Islands, $938.3

8. New Landsbanki Islands hf, $915.9

9. Icelandair hf, $868.1

10. Alcoa Fjardaal sf, $780.7

Source: *Europe's 15,000 Largest Companies*, (annual), ELC International, 2011, p. 344+.

Corporations—Idaho

1696 ■ IDAHO'S LARGEST EMPLOYERS, 2010

Ranked by: Number of full-time employees in Idaho. **Remarks:** Also notes contact information, key executive, revenue, and type of business. **Number listed:** 5

1. St. Luke's Health System, with 9,400 employees

2. Micron Technology Inc., 5,000

3. Saint Alphonsus Health System, 4,300

4. J. R. Simplot Co., 3,150

5. Albertson's LLC, 2,292

Source: *Idaho Business Review*, Largest Employers (annual), August 26, 2011.

1697 ■ IDAHO'S LARGEST PRIVATE COMPANIES, 2010

Ranked by: Revenue, in billions of dollars. **Remarks:** Also notes business segment, number of employees, and overall rank in the *America's Largest Private Companies* list. Ranking is available online only, not in print. **Number listed:** 3

1. J. R. Simplot Co., with $4.9 billion

2. WinCo Foods Inc., $4.73

3. Boise Cascade, $2.24

Source: *Forbes*, America's Largest Private Companies (annual), http://www.forbes.com, December 5, 2011.

1698 ■ LARGEST COMPANIES IN IDAHO BY EMPLOYEES, 2010

Ranked by: Number of employees at headquarters. **Remarks:** Also notes contact information for headquarters, total number of employees, revenue, rank by revenue, and primary SIC code. **Number listed:** 58

1. St. Lukes Health System Ltd., with 7,891 employees

2. Micron Technology Inc., 5,000

3. St. Lukes Regional Medical Center Ltd., 4,000

4. St. Alphonsus Regional Medical Center Inc., 2,700

5. First Call Jewel Inc., 2,527

6. Coldwater Creek Outlet Stores Inc., 2,500

7. American Drug Stores Inc., 1,500

7. Eastern Idaho Regional Medical Center Auxiliary Inc., 1,500

7. Jewel Food Stores Inc., 1,500

10. Kootenai Hospital District, 1,450

Source: *Business Rankings*, (annual), Dun & Bradstreet Inc., 2011, p. IV.66-IV.67.

1699 ■ LARGEST COMPANIES IN IDAHO BY SALES, 2010

Ranked by: Revenue, in dollars. **Remarks:** Also notes contact information for headquarters, number of employees at headquarters and overall, rank by employees, and primary SIC code. **Number listed:** 59

1. Micron Technology Inc., with $8,482,000,000

2. WinCo Holdings Inc., $4,104,467,640
3. WinCo Foods LLC, $4,100,000,000
4. Boise Cascade LLC, $2,977,498,000
5. Boise Inc., $2,093,777,000
6. Building Materials Holding Corp., $1,324,679,000
7. MWI Veterinary Supply Inc., $1,229,342,000
8. Coldwater Creek Inc., $1,038,581,000
9. Idacorp Inc., $1,036,029,000
10. Idaho Power Co., $1,033,052,000

Source: *Business Rankings*, (annual), Dun & Bradstreet Inc., 2011, p. III.66-III.67.

Corporations—Illinois

1700 ■ BEST LARGE COMPANIES TO WORK FOR IN ILLINOIS, 2011

Ranked by: Score based on employee surveys. **Remarks:** Specific scores not provided. To qualify, companies must have at least 250 employees. **Number listed:** 15

1. Ryan LLC
2. Edward Jones
3. Lockton Cos.
4. Shared Technologies Inc.
5. National Futures Association
6. Digitas
7. Ice Miller LLP
8. Burns & McDonnell
9. Starcom
10. ATI Physical Therapy

Source: *Best Companies Group*, Best Places to Work in Illinois (annual), http://www.bestplacestoworkinil.com, June 2011.

1701 ■ BEST SMALL COMPANIES IN ILLINOIS, 2011

Ranked by: Score based on revenue, profits, and return on equity for the past 12 months and five years. **Remarks:** Specific scores not provided. Also notes rank in the overall *100 Best Small Companies in America*. To qualify, companies must have revenues between $5 million and $1 billion, a net margin above five percent, and share price above $5. List is available online only. **Number listed:** 5

1. KapStone Paper & Packaging
2. Neutral Tandem
3. Middleby
4. Morningstar
5. Heritage-Crystal Clean

Source: *Forbes*, Best Small Companies in America (annual), November 7, 2011.

1702 ■ BEST SMALL/MEDIUM COMPANIES TO WORK FOR IN ILLINOIS, 2011

Ranked by: Score based on employee surveys. **Remarks:** Specific scores not provided. To qualify, companies must have between 15 and 249 employees. **Number listed:** 24

1. Assurance
2. Radio Flyer Inc.
3. Laurus Strategies
4. Tasty Catering

5. TRIS3CT LLC
6. Skender Construction
7. Balasa Dinverno Foltz LLC
8. Adage Technologies
9. Black Diamond Plumbing & Mechanical Inc.
10. Geneca LLC

Source: *Best Companies Group*, Best Places to Work in Illinois (annual), http://www.bestplacestoworkinil.com, June 2011.

1703 ■ CHICAGO'S FASTEST-GROWING COMPANIES, 2005-2010

Ranked by: Five-year growth in revenue, in percent. **Remarks:** Also notes contact information, top executive, revenue for 2005 and 2010, number of employees, year founded, type of business, and whether public or private. **Number listed:** 50

1. AlphaMetrix Group LLC, with 8,030.4%
2. Echo Global Logistics Inc., 5,723.5%
3. SXC Health Solutions Corp., 3,499.9%
4. Lime Energy Co., 1,871.6%
5. One Stop Mailing LLC, 1,829.8%

Source: *Crain's Chicago Business*, Chicago's Fastest-Growing Companies (annual), http://www.chicagobusiness.com, June 6, 2011.

1704 ■ CHICAGO'S LARGEST EMPLOYERS, 2011

Ranked by: Number of local full-time employees. **Remarks:** Also notes contact information, head of Chicago office, number of employees worldwide, annual revenue, and revenue growth. **Number listed:** 25

1. U.S. Government, with 55,183 employees
2. Chicago Public Schools, 39,667
3. City of Chicago, 31,307
4. Cook County, IL, 21,785
5. Advocate Health Care, 18,485

Source: *Crain's Chicago Business*, Chicago's Largest Employers (annual), http://www.chicagobusiness.com, January 16, 2012.

1705 ■ CHICAGO'S LARGEST PUBLIC COMPANIES, 2011

Ranked by: Revenue, in millions of dollars. **Remarks:** Also notes stock symbol, contact information, top executive, net profits, percent change from previous year, market capitalization, number of employees, and company description. **Number listed:** 139

1. Archer Daniels Midland Co., with $80,676 million
2. Walgreen Co., $72,184
3. Boeing Co., $68,735
4. Caterpillar Inc., $60,138
5. Kraft Foods Inc., $54,365

Source: *Crain's Chicago Business*, Chicago's Largest Public Companies (annual), http://www.chicagobusiness.com, May 21, 2012.

1706 ■ FASTEST-GROWING COMPANIES IN ILLINOIS, 2008-2011

Ranked by: Score based on three-year growth in revenue and earnings, and three-year total return to investors. **Remarks:** Specific scores not provided. To qualify for list, companies must have revenues of at least $50 million, net income of at least $10 million, market capitalization of at least $250 million, and stock price of at least $5. Int'l companies are eligible if they trade on a U.S. exchange and file quarterly reports. **Number listed:** 5

1. SXC Health Solutions Corp.
2. KapStone Paper & Packaging Corp.
3. Neutral Tandem
4. DeVry Inc.
5. Ulta Salon, Cosmetics & Fragrance

Source: *Fortune*, 100 Fastest-Growing Companies (annual), http://www.fortune.com, September 26, 2011.

1707 ■ ILLINOIS'S LARGEST COMPANIES OVERALL, 2011

Ranked by: Score based on revenue, profits, assets, and market capitalization. **Remarks:** Specific scores not provided. Also notes overall rank in the *Forbes 2000* and figures for each criterion. **Number listed:** 34

1. Caterpillar Inc.
2. Boeing Co.
3. Kraft Foods Inc.
4. Abbott Laboratories Inc.
5. McDonald's Corp.
6. Deere & Co.
7. Walgreen Co.
8. Exelon Corp.
9. Archer Daniels Midland Co.
10. The Allstate Corp.

Source: *Forbes*, Forbes 2000 (annual), http://www.forbes.com, May 7, 2012.

1708 ■ ILLINOIS'S LARGEST PRIVATE COMPANIES, 2010

Ranked by: Revenue, in billions of dollars. **Remarks:** Also notes business segment, number of employees, and overall rank in the *America's Largest Private Companies* list. Ranking is available online only, not in print. **Number listed:** 13

1. U.S. Foods Inc., with $18.86 billion
2. Reyes Holdings LLC, $14
3. CDW Corp., $8.8
4. Eby-Brown Co., LLC, $4.5
5. Medline Industries Inc., $4.01
6. Dot Foods Inc., $3.6
7. The Walsh Group Ltd., $3.46
8. Tribune Co., $3.22
9. OSI Group LLC, $3
10. Follett Corp., $2.72

Source: *Forbes*, America's Largest Private Companies (annual), http://www.forbes.com, December 5, 2011.

1709 ■ LARGEST COMPANIES IN ILLINOIS BY EMPLOYEES, 2010

Ranked by: Number of employees at headquarters. **Remarks:** Also notes contact information for headquarters, total number of employees, revenue, rank by revenue, and primary SIC code. **Number listed:** 457

1. Abbott Laboratories Inc., with 12,284 employees
2. SCC Holding Co., 8,000
3. ConAgra Grocery Products Co., 7,000
4. Solo Cup Co., 6,799
5. Aon Hewitt LLC, 6,600
6. Aon Services Inc., 6,000

6. Loyola University Health System, 6,000
8. Recycle America Alliance LLC, 5,500
9. Northwestern Memorial Hospital, 5,300
10. Allstate Corp., 5,000

Source: *Business Rankings*, (annual), Dun & Bradstreet Inc., 2011, p. IV.68-IV.77.

1710 ■ LARGEST COMPANIES IN ILLINOIS BY SALES, 2010

Ranked by: Revenue, in dollars. **Remarks:** Also notes contact information for headquarters, number of employees at headquarters and overall, rank by employees, and primary SIC code. **Number listed:** 464

1. BP America Inc., with $83,982,000,000
2. Walgreen Co., $67,420,000,000
3. Boeing Co., $64,306,000,000
4. Archer Daniels Midland Co., $61,682,000,000
5. Kraft Foods Inc., $49,207,000,000
6. Sears Holdings Corp., $43,326,000,000
7. Caterpillar Inc., $42,588,000,000
8. Abbott Laboratories Inc., $35,166,721,000
9. Deere & Co., $26,004,600,000
10. McDonald's Corp., $24,074,600,000

Source: *Business Rankings*, (annual), Dun & Bradstreet Inc., 2011, p. III.68-III.77.

1711 ■ LARGEST PRIVATE COMPANIES IN CHICAGO, 2011

Ranked by: Revenue, in millions of dollars. **Remarks:** Also notes contact information, top executive, percent change from previous year, number of fulltime employees in Chicago and worldwide, type of businesses, and year founded. **Number listed:** 5

1. State Farm Mutual Automobile Insurance Co., with $64,300 million
2. Health Care Service Corp., $49,000
3. US Foods, $20,344.9
4. Reyes Holdings LLC, $14,300
5. Topco Associates LLC, $11,600

Source: *Crain's Chicago Business*, Largest Privately-Held Companies (annual), http://www.chicagobusiness.com, April 16, 2012.

1712 ■ MOST ADMIRED COMPANIES IN ILLINOIS, 2012

Ranked by: Survey of top executives, directors, and securities analysts regarding the Fortune 1,000 companies that they admire the most, regardless of industry. **Remarks:** Also notes city and industry rank. List is available online only, not in print. **Number listed:** 22

1. McDonald's Corp., with 8.27 points
2. Caterpillar, 7.89
3. Deere & Co., 7.65
4. W. W. Grainger, 7.37
5. Hyatt Hotels Corp., 7.30
6. Illinois Tool Works, 6.98
7. Northern Trust Corp., 6.85
8. Boeing Co., 6.81
9. Archer Daniels Midland Co., 6.77
10. Baxter International, 6.76

Source: *Fortune*, World's Most Admired Companies (annual), http://www.fortune.com, March 19, 2012.

1713 ■ TOP *FORTUNE 500* COMPANIES IN ILLINOIS, 2011

Ranked by: Revenue, in millions of dollars. **Remarks:** Also notes overall rank in the *Fortune 500*, headquarters, and number of employees. **Number listed:** 32

1. Archer Daniels Midland Co., with $80,676 million
2. Walgreen Co., $72,184
3. Boeing Co., $68,735
4. State Farm Insurance Companies, $64,305.1
5. Caterpillar Inc., $60,138
6. Kraft Foods Inc., $54,365
7. Sears Holdings Corp., $41,567
8. Abbott Laboratories Inc., $38,851.3
9. United Continental Holdings, $37,110
10. The Allstate Corp., $32,654

Source: *Fortune*, Fortune 500 (annual), May 21, 2012, p. F-43.

1714 ■ TOP PRIVATE SECTOR EMPLOYERS IN ILLINOIS, 2011

Ranked by: Number of employees. **Remarks:** Also notes city and industry. **Number listed:** 25

1. Wal-Mart Stores Inc., with 46,500 employees
2. Jewel-Osco, 25,600
3. Advocate Health Care, 22,000
4. Caterpillar Inc., 20,500
5. Target Corp., 15,700
6. State Farm Insurance, 15,500
7. United Parcel Service, 15,000
8. Resurrection Health Care, 13,600
9. Walgreen Co., 13,280
10. Abbott Laboratories, 13,000
10. United Continental Holdings Inc., 13,000

Source: *Daily Herald Business Ledger*, Top Private Sector Employers (annual), December 26, 2011, p. 18.

Corporations—India

1715 ■ BEST COMPANIES TO WORK FOR IN INDIA, 2011

Ranked by: Score based on the relationships between employees and management, employees and their jobs/company, and employees and coworkers. **Remarks:** Specific scores not provided. **Number listed:** 50

1. Google India Pvt. Ltd.
2. Intel Technology India Pvt. Ltd.
3. MakeMyTrip (India) Pvt. Ltd.
4. American Express India Pvt. Ltd.
5. Marriott Hotels India Pvt. Ltd.
6. Classic Stripes Pvt. Ltd.
7. Scope International Pvt. Ltd.
8. Agilent Technologies
9. Claris Lifesciences Ltd.
10. NetApp India Pvt. Ltd.

Source: *Great Place to Work Institute Inc.*, Best Places to Work in India (annual), http://www.greatplacetowork.com, 2011.

1716 ■ BEST SMALL INDIAN COMPANIES, 2010

Ranked by: Score based on sales, net income, and market value. **Remarks:** Specific scores not provided; companies are listed alphabetically, not ranked. Also notes sales, net income, market value, and industry. To qualify for list, which is available online only, companies must have under US$1 billion in annual revenue and positive earnings growth over the past five years. **Number listed:** 31

1. A. K. Capital Services
2. Ador Fontech
3. Arihant Capital Markets
4. Ashiana Housing
5. Banco Products
6. Camson Bio Technologies
7. Delta Corp.
8. Dhanuka Agritech
9. eClerx Services
10. EdServ Softsystems

Source: *Forbes Asia*, Asia's Best Under a Billion (annual), http://www.forbes.com, September 12, 2011.

1717 ■ INDIA'S LARGEST COMPANIES OVERALL, 2011

Ranked by: Score based on revenue, profits, assets, and market capitalization. **Remarks:** Specific scores not provided. Also notes rank in the overall *Forbes 2000* and figures for each criterion. **Number listed:** 62

1. Reliance Industries Ltd.
2. State Bank of India Group
3. Oil & Natural Gas Corp., Ltd.
4. Indian Oil Corp.
5. Icici Bank
6. NTPC Ltd.
7. Tata Motors Ltd.
8. Bharti Airtel Ltd.
9. Coal India Ltd.
10. Tata Steel Ltd.

Source: *Forbes*, Forbes 2000 (annual), http://www.forbes.com, May 7, 2012.

1718 ■ LARGEST CORPORATIONS IN INDIA BY REVENUE, 2010

Ranked by: Revenue, in millions of U.S. dollars. **Remarks:** Also notes headquarters city and overall rank in the *Global 500*. Ranking is available online only, not in print. **Number listed:** 8

1. Indian Oil Corp., with $68,837 million
2. Reliance Industries Ltd., $58,900
3. Bharat Petroleum Corp., $34,102
4. State Bank of India, $32,450
5. Hindustan Petroleum Corp., $28,593
6. Tata Motors Ltd., $27,046
7. Oil & Natural Gas Corp., Ltd., $26,945
8. Tata Steel Ltd., $26,065

Source: *Fortune*, Global 500 (annual), http://www.fortune.com, July 25, 2011.

1719 ■ MOST ADMIRED COMPANIES IN INDIA, 2012

Ranked by: Score based on a survey of executives, directors, and securities analysts of companies within their own industry. **Remarks:** List is available online only, not in print. Also notes headquarters. **Number listed:** 2

1. Tata Steel, with 6.46 points
2. Oil & Natural Gas, 5.86

Source: *Fortune*, World's Most Admired Companies (annual), http://www.fortune.com, March 19, 2012.

1720 ■ TOP INDIAN COMPANIES, 2011

Ranked by: Score based on profits, sales and earnings growth, and projected earnings and stock-price gains. **Remarks:** Specific scores not provided; companies are listed alphabetically, not ranked. Also notes market value, revenue, and industry. To quality, companies must be publicly traded with revenues or market capitalization of at least US$3 billion. Ranking is available online only, not in print. **Number listed:** 7

1. Asian Paints
2. Bharti Airtel Ltd.
3. HCL Technologies
4. ITC
5. Kotak Mahindra Bank
6. Mahindra & Mahindra
7. Tata Consultancy Services Ltd.

Source: *Forbes*, Asian Fab 50 (annual), September 13, 2011.

Corporations—Indiana

1721 ■ BEST LARGE COMPANIES TO WORK FOR IN INDIANA, 2012

Ranked by: Score based on employee surveys. **Remarks:** Specific scores not provided. Also notes primary Indiana location. To qualify, companies must have at least 250 employees. **Number listed:** 31

1. Microsoft Corp.
2. ExactTarget
3. Edward Jones
4. Centier Bank
5. Brotherhood Mutual Insurance Co.
6. Ogletree Deakins Law Firm
7. Sogeti USA
8. Interactive Intelligence Group Inc.
9. Heartland Payment Systems
10. Shiel Sexton Co.

Source: *Best Companies Group*, Best Places to Work in Indiana (annual), http://www.bestplacestoworkin.com, May 3, 2012.

1722 ■ BEST SMALL/MEDIUM COMPANIES TO WORK FOR IN INDIANA, 2012

Ranked by: Score based on employee surveys. **Remarks:** Specific scores not provided. Also notes primary Indiana location. To qualify, companies must have between 15 and 249 employees. **Number listed:** 39

1. Hollingsworth & Zivitz PC
2. E-gineering LLC
3. Indiana CPA Society
4. SEP
5. Purdue Federal Credit Union
6. Lawson-Fisher Associates PC
7. Somerset CPAs
8. Harding Poorman Group Inc.
9. Slingshot SEO Inc.

10. Delivra

Source: *Best Companies Group*, Best Places to Work in Indiana (annual), http://www.bestplacestoworkin.com, May 3, 2012.

1723 ■ INDIANA'S LARGEST COMPANIES OVERALL, 2011

Ranked by: Score based on revenue, profits, assets, and market capitalization. **Remarks:** Specific scores not provided. Also notes overall rank in the *Forbes 2000* and figures for each criterion. **Number listed:** 7

1. WellPoint Inc.
2. Eli Lilly & Co.
3. Cummins Inc.
4. Simon Property Group Inc.
5. Zimmer Holdings Inc.
6. NiSource Inc.
7. CNO Financial Group Inc.

Source: *Forbes*, Forbes 2000 (annual), http://www.forbes.com, May 7, 2012.

1724 ■ INDIANA'S LARGEST PRIVATE COMPANIES, 2010

Ranked by: Revenue, in billions of dollars. **Remarks:** Also notes business segment, number of employees, and overall rank in the *America's Largest Private Companies* list. Ranking is available on-line only, not in print. **Number listed:** 2

1. Berry Plastics Corp., with $4.44 billion
2. Biomet Inc., $2.73

Source: *Forbes*, America's Largest Private Companies (annual), http://www.forbes.com, December 5, 2011.

1725 ■ LARGEST COMPANIES IN INDIANA BY EMPLOYEES, 2010

Ranked by: Number of employees at headquarters. **Remarks:** Also notes contact information for headquarters, total number of employees, revenue, rank by revenue, and primary SIC code. **Number listed:** 196

1. Methodist Hospital, with 6,000 employees
1. St. Vincent Hospital & Health Care Center Inc., 6,000
3. Quality Dining Inc., 5,000
4. Rolls-Royce Corp., 4,600
5. Parkview Hospital Inc., 4,500
6. Eli Lilly & Co., 4,000
7. Lincoln National Risk Management Inc., 3,650
8. Conseco Variable Insurance Co., 3,500
9. Allison Transmission Inc., 3,300
10. Community Hospitals of Indiana Inc., 3,000
10. St. Margaret Mercy Healthcare Center, 3,000

Source: *Business Rankings*, (annual), Dun & Bradstreet Inc., 2011, p. IV.78-IV.82.

1726 ■ LARGEST COMPANIES IN INDIANA BY SALES, 2010

Ranked by: Revenue, in dollars. **Remarks:** Also notes contact information for headquarters, number of employees at headquarters and overall, rank by employees, and primary SIC code. **Number listed:** 198

1. Eli Lilly & Co., with $23,076,000,000
2. Cummins Inc., $13,226,000,000

3. MPI Holdings Inc., $11,579,400,000

4. NiSource Inc., $6,422,000,000

5. Steel Dynamics Inc., $6,300,887,000

6. Berry Plastics Corp., $4,257,000,000

7. Zimmer Holdings Inc., $4,220,200,000

8. Brightpoint Inc., $3,593,239,000

9. Proliance Energy LLC, $3,000,000,000

10. Biomet Inc., $2,698,000,000

Source: *Business Rankings*, (annual), Dun & Bradstreet Inc., 2011, p. III.78-III.82.

1727 ■ LARGEST INDIANA EMPLOYERS, 2011

Ranked by: Number of full-time employees in Indiana. **Remarks:** Also notes rank and figures for previous year, contact information, plants or divisions in Indiana, and three largest division locations in Indiana. **Number listed:** 25

1. Wal-Mart Stores Inc., with 39,246 employees

2. U.S. government, 38,800

3. State of Indiana, 27,821

4. Indiana University Health, 24,447

5. Indiana University, 18,317

Source: *Indianapolis Business Journal*, Largest Employers (annual), http://www.ibj.cm, December 5, 2011.

1728 ■ LARGEST INDIANA PRIVATE COMPANIES, 2010

Ranked by: Revenue, in billions of dollars. **Remarks:** Also notes rank and figures for previous year, contact information, number of employees, and products and services **Number listed:** 50

1. Biomet Inc., with $2.7 billion

2. Do It Best Corp., $2.4

3. Cook Group Inc., $1.8

3. Petroleum Traders Corp., $1.8

3. Hunt Construction Group Inc., $1.8

6. One America Financial Partners Inc., $1.3

7. CountryMark, $1.1

7. Marsh Supermarkets Inc., $1.1

7. Remy International, $1.1

10. LDI Ltd. LLC, $0.906

Source: *Indianapolis Business Journal*, Largest Private Companies (annual), http://www.ibj.com, June 20, 2011.

1729 ■ MOST ADMIRED COMPANIES IN INDIANA, 2012

Ranked by: Survey of top executives, directors, and securities analysts regarding the Fortune 1,000 companies that they admire the most, regardless of industry. **Remarks:** Also notes city and industry rank. List is available online only, not in print. **Number listed:** 3

1. Cummins Inc., with 6.91 points

2. Simon Property Group Inc., 6.66

3. WellPoint Inc., 6.03

Source: *Fortune*, World's Most Admired Companies (annual), http://www.fortune.com, March 19, 2012.

1730 ■ TOP *FORTUNE 500* COMPANIES IN INDIANA, 2011

Ranked by: Revenue, in millions of dollars. **Remarks:** Also notes overall rank in the *Fortune 500,* headquarters, and number of employees. **Number listed:** 6

1. WellPoint Inc., with $60,710.7 million

2. Eli Lilly & Co., $24,286.5

3. Cummins Inc., $18,048

4. Steel Dynamics Inc., $7,997.5

5. NiSource Inc., $6,019.1

6. Brightpoint Inc., $5,244.4

Source: *Fortune*, Fortune 500 (annual), May 21, 2012, p. F-43.

1731 ■ TOP-PERFORMING INDIANA STOCKS, 2011

Ranked by: Return, in percent. **Remarks:** Also notes contact information, closing price for current and previous year, and high and low prices within the current year. **Number listed:** 25

1. Patrick Industries Inc., with 115.8%

2. NiSource Inc., 35.1%

3. Haynes International Inc., 30.5%

4. Simon Property Group Inc., 29.6%

5. 1st Source Corp., 25.1%

6. Angie's List, 23.8%

7. BrightPoint, 23.3%

8. Lakeland Financial Corp., 20.5%

9. Vectren Corp., 19.1%

10. Eli Lilly & Co., 18.6%

Source: *Indianapolis Business Journal*, Top-Performing Indiana Stocks (annual), http://www.ibj.com, January 30, 2012.

Corporations—Indonesia

1732 ■ BEST SMALL INDONESIAN COMPANIES, 2010

Ranked by: Score based on sales, net income, and market value. **Remarks:** Specific scores not provided; companies are listed alphabetically, not ranked. Also notes sales, net income, market value, and industry. To qualify for list, which is available online only, companies must have under US$1 billion in annual revenue and positive earnings growth over the past five years. **Number listed:** 3

1. Jasuindo Tiga Perkasa

2. Nippon Indosari Corpindo

3. Panin Sekuritas

Source: *Forbes Asia*, Asia's Best Under a Billion (annual), http://www.forbes.com, September 12, 2011.

1733 ■ INDONESIA'S LARGEST COMPANIES OVERALL, 2011

Ranked by: Score based on revenue, profits, assets, and market capitalization. **Remarks:** Specific scores not provided. Also notes rank in the overall *Forbes 2000* and figures for each criterion. **Number listed:** 10

1. Bank Rakyat Indonesia

2. Bank Mandiri

3. Bank Central Asia

4. Telekom Indonesia

5. Bank Negara Indonesia

6. PGN

7. PT Gudang Garam TBK

8. Bank Danamon Indonesia

9. Semen Gresik

10. Bumi Resources

Source: *Forbes*, Forbes 2000 (annual), http://www.forbes.com, May 7, 2012.

1734 ■ TOP INDONESIAN COMPANIES, 2011

Ranked by: Score based on profits, sales and earnings growth, and projected earnings and stock-price gains. **Remarks:** Specific scores not provided; companies are listed alphabetically, not ranked. Also notes market value, revenue, and industry. To quality, companies must be publicly traded with revenues or market capitalization of at least US$3 billion. Ranking is available online only, not in print. **Number listed:** 2

1. Adaro Energy
2. Bank Central Asia

Source: *Forbes*, Asian Fab 50 (annual), September 13, 2011.

Corporations, International

1735 ■ WORLD'S COMPANIES WITH THE HIGHEST REPUTATION FOR FINANCIAL SOUNDNESS, 2012

Ranked by: Score based on a survey of executives, directors, and securities analysts of companies within their own industry. **Remarks:** Specific scores not provided. Ranking is available online only, not in print. Also notes rank within industry. **Number listed:** 10

1. Apple Inc.
2. McDonald's Corp.
3. Exxon Mobil Corp.
4. Philip Morris International
5. Intel Corp.
6. Google Inc.
7. GDF Suez
8. Procter & Gamble
9. Wal-Mart Stores Inc.
10. Altria Group

Source: *Fortune*, World's Most Admired Companies (annual), http://www.fortune.com, March 19, 2012.

1736 ■ WORLD'S COMPANIES WITH THE HIGHEST REPUTATION FOR GLOBAL COMPETITIVENESS, 2012

Ranked by: Score based on a survey of executives, directors, and securities analysts of companies within their own industry. **Remarks:** Specific scores not provided. Ranking is available online only, not in print. Also notes rank within industry. **Number listed:** 10

1. Gas Natural Fenosa
2. McDonald's Corp.
3. Nestle SA
4. Apple Inc.
4. International Business Machines Corp. (IBM)
6. Procter & Gamble
7. Philip Morris International
8. Yum! Brands Inc.
9. Caterpillar
10. RWE

Source: *Fortune*, World's Most Admired Companies (annual), http://www.fortune.com, March 19, 2012.

1737 ■ WORLD'S COMPANIES WITH THE HIGHEST REPUTATION FOR INNOVATION, 2012

Ranked by: Score based on a survey of executives, directors, and securities analysts of companies within their own industry.

Remarks: Specific scores not provided. Ranking is available online only, not in print. Also notes rank within industry. **Number listed:** 10

1. Apple Inc.
2. Sistema
3. GDF Suez
4. Limited Brands
5. QUALCOMM
6. Enterprise Products Partners
6. Koc Holding
8. Amazon.com Inc.
9. Sealed Air Corp.
10. Nike Inc.

Source: *Fortune*, World's Most Admired Companies (annual), http://www.fortune.com, March 19, 2012.

1738 ■ WORLD'S COMPANIES WITH THE HIGHEST REPUTATION FOR LONG-TERM INVESTMENT VALUE, 2012

Ranked by: Score based on a survey of executives, directors, and securities analysts of companies within their own industry. **Remarks:** Specific scores not provided. Ranking is available online only, not in print. Also notes rank within industry. **Number listed:** 10

1. Koc Holding
2. Sistema
3. Philip Morris International
4. McDonald's Corp.
5. Exxon Mobil Corp.
6. Walt Disney Co.
7. Chevron Corp.
8. Nestle SA
8. Procter & Gamble
10. Amazon.com Inc.

Source: *Fortune*, World's Most Admired Companies (annual), http://www.fortune.com, March 19, 2012.

1739 ■ WORLD'S COMPANIES WITH THE HIGHEST REPUTATION FOR PEOPLE MANAGEMENT, 2012

Ranked by: Score based on a survey of executives, directors, and securities analysts of companies within their own industry. **Remarks:** Specific scores not provided. Ranking is available online only, not in print. Also notes rank within industry. **Number listed:** 10

1. Apple Inc.
2. Google Inc.
3. Goldman Sachs Group Inc.
4. McDonald's Corp.
5. Philip Morris International
6. Chevron Corp.
7. Procter & Gamble Co.
8. Sysco
9. Exxon Mobil Corp.
9. Walt Disney Co.

Source: *Fortune*, World's Most Admired Companies (annual), http://www.fortune.com, March 19, 2012.

1740 ■ WORLD'S COMPANIES WITH THE HIGHEST REPUTATION FOR QUALITY OF MANAGEMENT, 2012

Ranked by: Score based on a survey of executives, directors, and securities analysts of companies within their own industry.

Remarks: Specific scores not provided. Ranking is available on-line only, not in print. Also notes rank within industry. **Number listed:** 10

1. Koc Holding
2. McDonald's Corp.
3. Apple Inc.
3. Philip Morris International
5. Costco Wholesale Corp.
6. J. P. Morgan Chase
7. Wyndham Worldwide
8. Sysco
9. Walt Disney Co.
10. TJX

Source: *Fortune*, World's Most Admired Companies (annual), http://www.fortune.com, March 19, 2012.

1741 ■ WORLD'S COMPANIES WITH THE HIGHEST REPUTATION FOR QUALITY OF PRODUCTS/SERVICES, 2012

Ranked by: Score based on a survey of executives, directors, and securities analysts of companies within their own industry. **Remarks:** Specific scores not provided. Ranking is available on-line only, not in print. Also notes rank within industry. **Number listed:** 10

1. Koc Holding
2. Apple Inc.
3. Nordstrom Inc.
4. RWE
5. Amazon.com Inc.
6. Nieman Marcus
6. Walt Disney Co.
8. Wynn Resorts
9. Caterpillar
10. Whole Foods Market Inc.

Source: *Fortune*, World's Most Admired Companies (annual), http://www.fortune.com, March 19, 2012.

1742 ■ WORLD'S COMPANIES WITH THE HIGHEST REPUTATION FOR SOCIAL RESPONSIBILITY, 2012

Ranked by: Score based on a survey of executives, directors, and securities analysts of companies within their own industry. **Remarks:** Specific scores not provided. Ranking is available on-line only, not in print. Also notes rank within industry. **Number listed:** 10

1. GDF Suez
2. Marquard & Bahls
3. RWE
4. Altria Group
5. Starbucks
6. Walt Disney Co.
7. United Natural Foods
8. Sealed Air Corp.
9. Chevron Corp.
9. Whole Foods Market Inc.

Source: *Fortune*, World's Most Admired Companies (annual), http://www.fortune.com, March 19, 2012.

1743 ■ WORLD'S COMPANIES WITH THE HIGHEST REPUTATION FOR USE OF CORPORATE ASSETS, 2012

Ranked by: Score based on a survey of executives, directors, and securities analysts of companies within their own industry.

Remarks: Specific scores not provided. Ranking is available on-line only, not in print. Also notes rank within industry. **Number listed:** 10

1. McDonald's Corp.
2. Koc Holding
2. RWE
4. Enterprise Products Partners
5. Philip Morris International
6. Gas Natural Fenosa
6. Plains All American Pipelines
6. Wyndham Worldwide
9. Chevron Corp.
10. Exxon Mobil Corp.

Source: *Fortune*, World's Most Admired Companies (annual), http://www.fortune.com, March 19, 2012.

1744 ■ WORLD'S COMPANIES WITH THE LOWEST REPUTATION FOR FINANCIAL SOUNDNESS, 2012

Ranked by: Score based on a survey of executives, directors, and securities analysts of companies within their own industry. **Remarks:** Specific scores not provided. Ranking is available on-line only, not in print. Also notes rank within industry. **Number listed:** 12

1. AMR Corp.
2. YRC Worldwide Inc.
3. U.S. Postal Service
4. AbitibiBowater Inc.
5. MF Global Holdings
6. General Growth Properties Inc.
7. Advanced Micro Devices
8. AREVA Group
9. NewPage Holding
10. Burger King Holdings
10. Regions Financial
10. Sears Holdings

Source: *Fortune*, World's Most Admired Companies (annual), http://www.fortune.com, March 19, 2012.

1745 ■ WORLD'S COMPANIES WITH THE LOWEST REPUTATION FOR GLOBAL COMPETITIVENESS, 2012

Ranked by: Score based on a survey of executives, directors, and securities analysts of companies within their own industry. **Remarks:** Specific scores not provided. Ranking is available on-line only, not in print. Also notes rank within industry. **Number listed:** 10

1. WellCare Health Plans
2. Universal American
3. Coventry Health Care
4. Amerigroup
5. China South Industries Group
6. Health Net
7. Cracker Barrel Old Country Store
8. Jack in the Box
9. China FAW Group
10. Dongfeng Motor

Source: *Fortune*, World's Most Admired Companies (annual), http://www.fortune.com, March 19, 2012.

1746 ■ WORLD'S COMPANIES WITH THE LOWEST REPUTATION FOR INNOVATION, 2012

Ranked by: Score based on a survey of executives, directors, and securities analysts of companies within their own industry.

Remarks: Specific scores not provided. Ranking is available online only, not in print. Also notes rank within industry. **Number listed:** 10

1. China South Industries Group Corp.
2. China FAW Group Corp.
3. Dongfeng Motor
4. Sears Holdings
5. China North Industries
5. Shanghai Automotive Industry Corp.
7. AMR Corp.
7. MF Global Holdings
9. Burger King Holdings
10. AbitibiBowater Inc.

Source: *Fortune*, World's Most Admired Companies (annual), http://www.fortune.com, March 9, 2012.

1747 ■ WORLD'S COMPANIES WITH THE LOWEST REPUTATION FOR LONG-TERM INVESTMENT VALUE, 2012

Ranked by: Score based on a survey of executives, directors, and securities analysts of companies within their own industry. **Remarks:** Specific scores not provided. Ranking is available online only, not in print. Also notes rank within industry. **Number listed:** 10

1. AMR Corp.
2. Sears Holdings
3. U.S. Postal Service
4. Burger King Holdings
5. MF Global Holdings
6. YRC Worldwide Inc.
7. NewPage Holding Corp.
8. Regions Financial
9. AbitibiBowater Inc.
10. Best Buy

Source: *Fortune*, World's Most Admired Companies (annual), http://www.fortune.com, March 19, 2012.

1748 ■ WORLD'S COMPANIES WITH THE LOWEST REPUTATION FOR PEOPLE MANAGEMENT, 2012

Ranked by: Score based on a survey of executives, directors, and securities analysts of companies within their own industry. **Remarks:** Specific scores not provided. Ranking is available online only, not in print. Also notes rank within industry. **Number listed:** 10

1. Burger King Holdings
2. NewPage Holding
3. MF Global Holdings
4. YRC Worldwide Inc.
5. AbitibiBowater Inc.
6. Dongfeng Motor
7. Yahoo! Inc.
8. Sanmina-SCI
9. OfficeMax
10. AMR Corp.

Source: *Fortune*, World's Most Admired Companies (annual), http://www.fortune.com, March 19, 2012.

1749 ■ WORLD'S COMPANIES WITH THE LOWEST REPUTATION FOR QUALITY OF MANAGEMENT, 2012

Ranked by: Score based on a survey of executives, directors, and securities analysts of companies within their own industry.

Remarks: Specific scores not provided. Ranking is available online only, not in print. Also notes rank within industry. **Number listed:** 10

1. Sears Holdings
2. China South Industries Group Corp.
2. MF Global Holdings
4. NewPage Holding
5. Gas Natural Fenosa
6. Yahoo! Inc.
7. AMR Corp.
8. GDF Suez
9. Dongfeng Motor
10. China FAW Group Corp.

Source: *Fortune*, World's Most Admired Companies (annual), http://www.fortune.com, March 19, 2012.

1750 ■ WORLD'S COMPANIES WITH THE LOWEST REPUTATION FOR QUALITY OF PRODUCTS/SERVICES, 2012

Ranked by: Score based on a survey of executives, directors, and securities analysts of companies within their own industry. **Remarks:** Specific scores not provided. Ranking is available online only, not in print. Also notes rank within industry. **Number listed:** 10

1. China South Industries Group Corp.
2. China FAW Group Corp.
3. Dongfeng Motor
4. MF Global Holdings
5. Shanghai Automotive Industry Corp.
6. China North Industries
7. AMR Corp.
8. US Airways Group Inc.
9. China Post Group
10. Aviation Industry Corp. of China

Source: *Fortune*, World's Most Admired Companies (annual), http://www.fortune.com, March 19, 2012.

1751 ■ WORLD'S COMPANIES WITH THE LOWEST REPUTATION FOR SOCIAL RESPONSIBILITY, 2012

Ranked by: Score based on a survey of executives, directors, and securities analysts of companies within their own industry. **Remarks:** Specific scores not provided. Ranking is available online only, not in print. Also notes rank within industry. **Number listed:** 10

1. China Railway Group
2. China Railway Construction
3. China State Construction Engineering
4. China South Industries Group Corp.
5. China FAW Group Corp.
6. Aviation Industry Corp. of China
7. Dongfeng Motor
8. MF Global Holdings
9. China North Industries Group Corp.
10. Hon Hai Precision Industry

Source: *Fortune*, World's Most Admired Companies (annual), http://www.fortune.com, March 19, 2012.

1752 ■ WORLD'S COMPANIES WITH THE LOWEST REPUTATION FOR USE OF CORPORATE ASSETS, 2012

Ranked by: Score based on a survey of executives, directors, and securities analysts of companies within their own industry.

Remarks: Specific scores not provided. Ranking is available on-line only, not in print. Also notes rank within industry. **Number listed:** 10

1. China Railway Construction
2. MF Global Holdings
3. China Railway Group
4. AMR Corp.
5. GasTerra
6. Sears Holdings
7. China State Construction Engineering
8. Burger King Holdings
9. YRC Worldwide Inc.
10. China North Industries

Source: *Fortune*, World's Most Admired Companies (annual), http://www.fortune.com, March 19, 2012.

1753 ■ WORLD'S FASTEST-GROWING CORPORATIONS BY PROFITS, 2009-2010

Ranked by: Annual growth in profits, in percent. **Remarks:** Also notes revenue for current year and overall rank in the *Global 500*. Ranking is available online only, not in print. **Number listed:** 50

1. Bridgestone Corp., with 10,014.6%
2. Franz Haniel, 4,966.2%
3. Adecco Group, 4,938.4%
4. Flextronics International Ltd., 3,106.5%
5. ArcelorMittal, 2,371.2%
6. The Kroger Co., 1,494.7%
7. Bayerische Motoren Werke AG (BMW), 1,403.1%
8. FedEx Corp., 1,108.2%
9. Idemitsu Kosan, 1,000.6%
10. Compagnie Generale des Etablissements Michelin, 842.1%

Source: *Fortune*, Global 500 (annual), http://www.fortune.com, July 25, 2011.

1754 ■ WORLD'S FASTEST-GROWING CORPORATIONS BY REVENUE, 2009-2010

Ranked by: Annual growth in revenue, in percent. **Remarks:** Also notes revenue for current year and overall rank in the *Global 500*. Ranking is available online only, not in print. **Number listed:** 50

1. Fannie Mae, with 429.2%
2. Jizhong Energy Group, 176.3%
3. Freddie Mac, 161.5%
4. Vale SA, 94.3%
5. China Electronics, 89%
6. MS & AD Insurance Group Holdings Inc., 88.1%
7. JX Holdings, 86.7%
8. JBS, 82.3%
9. Noble Group, 81.8%
9. Express Scripts, 81.8%

Source: *Fortune*, Global 500 (annual), http://www.fortune.com, July 25, 2011.

1755 ■ WORLD'S LARGEST COMPANIES BY ASSETS, 2011

Ranked by: Assets, in millions of U.S. dollars. **Number listed:** 25

1. Fannie Mae (U.S.), with $3,211,484 million

2. Deutsche Bank AG (Germany), $2,809,429
3. HSBC Holdings plc (U.K.), $2,549,994
4. BNP Paribas (France), $2,539,104
5. Mitsubishi UFJ Financial Group Inc. (Japan), $2,478,846
6. Barclays plc (U.K.), $2,425,200
7. The Royal Bank of Scotland Group plc (Scotland), $2,335,795
8. J.P. Morgan Chase (U.S.), $2,265,792
9. Credit Agricole SA (France), $2,237,570
10. Freddie Mac (U.S.), $2,147,216

Source: *Forbes*, Forbes 2000 (annual), May 7, 2012, p. 101.

1756 ■ WORLD'S LARGEST COMPANIES BY MARKET CAPITALIZATION, 2011

Ranked by: Market capitalization, in millions of U.S. dollars. **Number listed:** 25

1. Apple Inc. (U.S.), with $545,968 million
2. Exxon Mobil Corp. (U.S.), $407,411
3. PetroChina Co., Ltd. (China), $294,726
4. Microsoft Corp. (U.S.), $273,539
5. International Business Machines Corp. (IBM, U.S.), $238,696
6. Industrial & Commercial Bank of China (China), $237,401
7. Royal Dutch Shell plc (Netherlands), $227,597
8. Chevron Corp. (U.S.), $218,020
9. China Mobile (Hong Kong), $216,510
10. General Electric Co. (U.S.), $213,741

Source: *Forbes*, Forbes 2000 (annual), May 7, 2012, p. 102.

1757 ■ WORLD'S LARGEST COMPANIES OVERALL, 2011

Ranked by: Score based on revenue, profits, assets, and market capitalization. **Remarks:** Specific scores not provided. **Number listed:** 2000

1. Exxon Mobil Corp. (U.S.)
2. J. P. Morgan Chase & Co. (U.S.)
3. General Electric Co. (U.S.)
4. Royal Dutch Shell plc (Netherlands)
5. Industrial & Commercial Bank of China (China)
6. HSBC Holdings plc (U.K.)
7. PetroChina Co., Ltd. (China)
8. Berkshire Hathaway Inc. (U.S.)
8. Wells Fargo (U.S.)
10. Petroleo Brasileiro SA (Petrobras, Brazil)

Source: *Forbes*, Forbes 2000 (annual), http://www.forbes.com, May 7, 2012.

1758 ■ WORLD'S LARGEST COMPANIES BY REVENUE, 2011

Ranked by: Revenue, in millions of U.S. dollars. **Number listed:** 25

1. Royal Dutch Shell plc (Netherlands), with $470,171 million
2. Wal-Mart Stores Inc. (U.S.), $446,950
3. Exxon Mobil Corp. (U.S.), $433,526

4. China Petroleum & Chemical Corp. (Sinopec, China), $391,447
5. BP plc (U.K.), $375,517
6. PetroChina Co., Ltd. (China), $310,090
7. Chevron Corp. (U.S.), $236,286
8. ConocoPhillips (U.S.), $230,859
9. Toyota Motor Corp. (Japan), $228,494
10. Volkswagen AG (Germany), $221,862

Source: *Forbes*, Forbes 2000 (annual), May 7, 2012, p. 99.

1759 ■ WORLD'S LARGEST CORPORATIONS BY REVENUE, 2010

Ranked by: Revenue, in millions of U.S. dollars. **Remarks:** Also notes country, rank for previous year, and percent change from previous year. **Number listed:** 500

1. Wal-Mart Stores Inc., with $421,849 million
2. Royal Dutch Shell plc, $378,152
3. Exxon Mobil Corp., $354,674
4. BP plc, $308,928
5. China Petroleum & Chemical Corp. (Sinopec), $273,421.9
6. China National Petroleum Co., $240,192.4
7. State Grid Corp. of China, $226,294
8. Toyota Motor Corp., $221,760.2
9. Japan Post Holdings Co., Ltd., $203,958.1
10. Chevron Corp., $196,337

Source: *Fortune*, Global 500 (annual), July 25, 2011, p. F-1-F-5.

1760 ■ WORLD'S LARGEST EMPLOYERS, 2010

Ranked by: Number of employees. **Remarks:** Also notes overall rank in the *Global 500*. **Number listed:** 50

1. Wal-Mart Stores Inc., with 2,100,000 employees
2. China National Petroleum Co., 1,674,541
3. State Grid Corp. of China, 1,564,000
4. China Post Group, 860,200
5. Hon Hai Precision Industry Co., Ltd., 836,000
6. China Petroleum & Chemical Corp. (Sinopec), 640,535
7. U. S. Postal Service, 627,798
8. China Telecommunications Corp., 493,919
9. Carrefour SA, 471,755
10. Agricultural Bank of China, 444,447

Source: *Fortune*, Global 500 (annual), July 25, 2011, p. F-6.

1761 ■ WORLD'S MOST ADMIRED COMPANIES, 2012

Ranked by: Survey of top executives, directors, and securities analysts regarding the large companies that they admire the most. **Remarks:** Specific scores not provided. Also notes rank for previous year and industry. Only the top 50 appear in print; the rest of the list is available online. **Number listed:** 50

1. Apple Inc. (U.S.)
2. Google Inc. (U.S.)
3. Amazon.com Inc. (U.S.)
4. The Coca-Cola Co. (U.S.)
5. International Business Machines Corp. (IBM, U.S.)
6. FedEx Corp. (U.S.)
7. Berkshire Hathaway Inc. (U.S.)
8. Starbucks (U.S.)
9. Procter & Gamble Co. (U.S.)
10. Southwest Airlines Co. (U.S.)

Source: *Fortune*, World's Most Admired Companies (annual), March 19, 2012, p. 140.

1762 ■ WORLD'S MOST INNOVATIVE COMPANIES, 2011

Ranked by: Innovative premium, a measure of projected income and comparison of net present value from existing businesses to current market capitalization. **Remarks:** Also notes country, sales, income growth, and the "big idea." **Number listed:** 50

1. Salesforce.com Inc., with 78.7%
2. Amazon.com Inc., 58.9%
3. Intuitive Surgical Inc., 57.6%
4. Tencent Holdings Ltd., 52.3%
5. Apple Inc., 48.2%
6. Hindustan Unilever, 47.7%
7. Google Inc., 44.9%
8. Natura Cosmeticos SA, 44.5%
9. Bharat Heavy Electricals Ltd., 43.6%
10. Monsanto Co., 42.6%

Source: *Forbes*, The Nifty 50, August 8, 2011, p. 76+.

1763 ■ WORLD'S MOST PROFITABLE COMPANIES, 2011

Ranked by: Profits, in millions of U.S. dollars. **Number listed:** 25

1. Exxon Mobil Corp. (U.S.), with $41,060 million
2. Apple Inc. (U.S.), $32,982
3. OAO Gazprom (Russia), $31,672
4. Royal Dutch Shell plc (Netherlands), $30,918
5. Chevron Corp. (U.S.), $26,895
6. BP plc (U.K.), $25,700
7. Industrial & Commercial Bank of China (China), $25,057
8. BHP Billiton (Australia, U.K.), $23,648
9. Microsoft Corp. (U.S.), $23,468
10. Volkswagen AG (Germany), $21,456

Source: *Forbes*, Forbes 2000 (annual), May 7, 2012, p. 100.

1764 ■ WORLD'S MOST PROFITABLE CORPORATIONS, 2010

Ranked by: Profits, in millions of U.S. dollars. **Remarks:** Also notes annual growth in profits and overall rank in the *Global 500*. Ranking is available online only, not in print. **Number listed:** 50

1. Nestle SA, with $32,843 million
2. OAO Gazprom, $31,894.5
3. Exxon Mobil Corp., $30,460
4. Industrial & Commercial Bank of China, $24,398.2
5. Royal Dutch Shell plc, $20,127
6. China Construction Bank, $19,920.3
7. AT&T Inc., $19,864
8. Petroleo Brasileiro SA (Petrobras), $19,184
9. Chevron Corp., $19,024
10. Microsoft Corp., $18,760

Source: *Fortune*, Global 500 (annual), http://www.fortune.com, July 25, 2011.

1765 ▪ WORLD'S MOST VALUABLE COMPANIES, 2011

Ranked by: Market value as of March 2011, in millions of U.S. dollars. **Remarks:** Also notes rank for previous year, sector, revenue, net income, assets, number of employees, share price, price-to-earning ratio, dividend yield, and fiscal year-end. **Number listed:** 500

1. Exxon Mobil Corp. (U.S.), with $417,166.7 million
2. PetroChina Co., Ltd. (China), $326,199.2
3. Apple Inc. (U.S.), $321,072.1
4. Industrial & Commercial Bank of China (China), $251,078.1
5. Petroleo Brasileiro SA (Petrobras, Brazil), $247,417.6
6. BHP Billiton Ltd. (Australia/U.K.), $247,079.5
7. China Construction Bank (China), $232,608.6
8. Royal Dutch Shell plc (U.K.), $228,128.7
9. Chevron Corp. (U.S.), $215,780.5
10. Microsoft Corp. (U.S.), $213,336.4

Source: *Financial Times*, FT 500 (annual), http://www.ft.com, June 24, 2011.

Corporations—Iowa

1766 ▪ FASTEST-GROWING COMPANIES IN IOWA, 2008-2011

Ranked by: Score based on three-year growth in revenue and earnings, and three-year total return to investors. **Remarks:** Specific scores not provided. To qualify for list, companies must have revenues of at least $50 million, net income of at least $10 million, market capitalization of at least $250 million, and stock price of at least $5. Int'l companies are eligible if they trade on a U.S. exchange and file quarterly reports. **Number listed:** 2

1. American Equity Investment Life Holding
2. FBL Financial Group

Source: *Fortune*, 100 Fastest-Growing Companies (annual), http://www.fortune.com, September 26, 2011.

1767 ▪ IOWA'S LARGEST COMPANIES OVERALL, 2011

Ranked by: Score based on revenue, profits, assets, and market capitalization. **Remarks:** Specific scores not provided. Also notes overall rank in the *Forbes 2000* and figures for each criterion. **Number listed:** 3

1. Principal Financial Group Inc.
2. Rockwell Collins Inc.
3. American Equity Investment Life Holding Co.

Source: *Forbes*, Forbes 2000 (annual), http://www.forbes.com, May 7, 2012.

1768 ▪ IOWA'S LARGEST PRIVATE COMPANIES, 2010

Ranked by: Revenue, in billions of dollars. **Remarks:** Also notes business segment, number of employees, and overall rank in the *America's Largest Private Companies* list. Ranking is available online only, not in print. **Number listed:** 2

1. Hy-Vee Inc., with $6.9 billion
2. Kum & Go LC, $2.1

Source: *Forbes*, America's Largest Private Companies (annual), http://www.forbes.com, December 5, 2011.

1769 ▪ LARGEST COMPANIES IN IOWA BY EMPLOYEES, 2010

Ranked by: Number of employees at headquarters. **Remarks:** Also notes contact information for headquarters, total number of employees, revenue, rank by revenue, and primary SIC code. **Number listed:** 157

1. Rockwell Collins Inc., with 9,000 employees
2. Iowa Health System, 4,110
3. Chi-Iowa Corp., 3,700
4. Central Iowa Hospital Corp., 3,300
5. Goodman Co., 3,000
5. Trinity Medical Center, 3,000
7. Amco Insurance Co., 2,850
8. Cadet Holding Corp., 2,700
9. Data Link Solutions LLC, 2,500
10. Mercy Medical Center Foundation in Iowa, 2,100

Source: *Business Rankings*, (annual), Dun & Bradstreet Inc., 2011, p. IV.83-IV.86.

1770 ▪ LARGEST COMPANIES IN IOWA BY SALES, 2010

Ranked by: Revenue, in dollars. **Remarks:** Also notes contact information for headquarters, number of employees at headquarters and overall, rank by employees, and primary SIC code. **Number listed:** 158

1. MidAmerican Energy Holdings Co., with $11,127,000,000
2. Hy-Vee Inc., $6,894,397,000
3. Rockwell Collins Inc., $4,665,000,000
4. Casey's General Stores Inc., $4,637,087,000
5. MidAmerican Funding LLC, $3,815,000,000
6. MidAmerican Energy Co., $3,810,000,000
7. HNI Corp., $1,686,728,000
8. Sauer-Danfoss Inc., $1,640,583,000
9. Meredith Corp., $1,387,730,000
10. Krause Holdings Inc., $1,000,000,000

Source: *Business Rankings*, (annual), Dun & Bradstreet Inc., 2011, p. III.83-III.86.

1771 ▪ TOP *FORTUNE 500* COMPANIES IN IOWA, 2011

Ranked by: Revenue, in millions of dollars. **Remarks:** Also notes overall rank in the *Fortune 500,* headquarters, and number of employees. **Number listed:** 3

1. Principal Financial Group Inc., with $8,709.6 million
2. Casey's General Stores Inc., $5,140.2
3. Rockwell Collins Inc., $4,825

Source: *Fortune*, Fortune 500 (annual), May 21, 2012, p. F-43.

Corporations—Ireland

1772 ▪ BEST LARGE COMPANIES TO WORK FOR IN IRELAND, 2012

Ranked by: Score based on the relationships between employees and management, employees and their jobs/company, and employees and coworkers. **Remarks:** Specific scores not provided. Ranking covers companies with more than 250 employees. **Number listed:** 18

1. Microsoft Corp.
2. Google Ireland
3. PepsiCo Ireland
4. EMC Information Systems Ireland
5. McDonald's Restaurants of Ireland
6. Telefonica Ireland

7. Dell Ireland

8. Boots Retail (Ireland) Ltd.

9. Diageo Demand

10. Kellogg Ireland

Source: *Great Place to Work Institute Inc.*, Best Places to Work in Ireland (annual), http://www.greatplacetowork.com, 2012.

1773 ■ BEST MEDIUM-SIZED COMPANIES TO WORK FOR IN IRELAND, 2012

Ranked by: Score based on the relationships between employees and management, employees and their jobs/company, and employees and coworkers. **Remarks:** Specific scores not provided. Ranking covers companies with 50 to 250 employees. **Number listed:** 21

1. Jones Lang LaSalle (Ireland) Ltd.

2. Mars Ireland

3. Morgan McKinley

4. MSD Ireland (Human Health) Ltd.

5. Euro Car Parks

6. FedEx Express

7. The Westin Dublin

8. Core Media

9. Whirlpool SSC Ltd.

10. Tourism Ireland

Source: *Great Place to Work Institute Inc.*, Best Places to Work in Ireland (annual), http://www.greatplacetowork.com, 2012.

1774 ■ BEST SMALL COMPANIES TO WORK FOR IN IRELAND, 2012

Ranked by: Score based on the relationships between employees and management, employees and their jobs/company, and employees and coworkers. **Remarks:** Specific scores not provided. Ranking covers companies with 20 to 49 employees. **Number listed:** 6

1. Hilti Fastening Systems

2. Ecclesiastical Insurance

3. Grunenthal Pharma Ltd.

4. Merlin Group

5. Precision Construction Ltd.

6. Vayu

Source: *Great Place to Work Institute Inc.*, Best Places to Work in Ireland (annual), http://www.greatplacetowork.com, 2012.

1775 ■ IRELAND'S LARGEST COMPANIES OVERALL, 2011

Ranked by: Score based on revenue, profits, assets, and market capitalization. **Remarks:** Specific scores not provided. Also notes rank in the overall *Forbes 2000* and figures for each criterion. **Number listed:** 18

1. Accenture Ltd.

2. WPP Group plc

3. Covidien plc

4. CRH plc

5. Allied Irish Banks plc

6. Ingersoll-Rand plc

7. Seagate Technology Inc.

8. Bank of Ireland plc

9. XL Group plc

10. Shire plc

Source: *Forbes*, Forbes 2000 (annual), http://www.forbes.com, May 7, 2012.

1776 ■ LARGEST COMPANIES IN IRELAND, 2010

Ranked by: Sales, in millions of U.S. dollars. **Remarks:** Also notes city; industrial code; percent change in sales; profits; profit as a percentage of sales, assets, and equity; number of employees; sales per employee; assets; equity capital; equity capital as a percentage of assets; year established; and figures for previous year. **Number listed:** 400

1. Pfizer Service Co. Ireland, with $27,888.7 million

2. CRH plc, $25,837.1

3. CMR Holdings Ltd., $21,365

4. Agricultural Limestone Ltd., $16,943.2

5. Dursey Investment Co., $15,950.6

5. Irish Cement (Sales) Ltd., $15,950.6

7. Intervet (Ireland) Ltd., $15,040

8. Microsoft Ireland Operations Ltd., $14,746.1

9. Dell Products, $14,341.9

10. UDV Operations Ireland Ltd., $13,596.1

Source: *Europe's 15,000 Largest Companies*, (annual), ELC International, 2011, p. 350+.

1777 ■ LARGEST CORPORATIONS IN IRELAND BY REVENUE, 2010

Ranked by: Revenue, in millions of U.S. dollars. **Remarks:** Also notes headquarters city and overall rank in the *Global 500*. Ranking is available online only, not in print. **Number listed:** 2

1. Accenture Ltd., with $23,094 million

2. CRH plc, $22,745

Source: *Fortune*, Global 500 (annual), http://www.fortune.com, July 25, 2011.

Corporations—Israel

1778 ■ ISRAEL'S LARGEST COMPANIES OVERALL, 2011

Ranked by: Score based on revenue, profits, assets, and market capitalization. **Remarks:** Specific scores not provided. Also notes rank in the overall *Forbes 2000* and figures for each criterion. **Number listed:** 11

1. Teva Pharmaceutical Industries Ltd.

2. Delek Group

3. Bank Hapoalim

4. Bank Leumi le-Israel

5. Israel Corp.

6. IDB Holding Corp., Ltd.

7. Check Point Software Technologies Ltd.

8. Israel Discount Bank

9. Mizrahi Tefahot Bank

10. FIBI Holding

Source: *Forbes*, Forbes 2000 (annual), http://www.forbes.com, May 7, 2012.

Corporations—Italy

1779 ■ BEST LARGE COMPANIES TO WORK FOR IN ITALY, 2011

Ranked by: Score based on the relationships between employees and management, employees and their jobs/company, and employees and coworkers. **Remarks:** Specific scores not provided. **Number listed:** 10

1. Elica SpA
2. Fater
3. FexEx Express
4. Unilever Italia
5. McDonald's Italia
6. Eli Lilly Italia
7. Leroy Merlin Italia
8. Decathlon Italia
9. Unieuro
10. Carglass

Source: *Great Place to Work Institute Inc.*, Best Places to Work in Italy (annual), http://www.greatplacetowork.com, 2011.

1780 ■ BEST SMALL AND MEDIUM-SIZED COMPANIES TO WORK FOR IN ITALY, 2011

Ranked by: Score based on the relationships between employees and management, employees and their jobs/company, and employees and coworkers. **Remarks:** Specific scores not provided. **Number listed:** 25

1. Tetra Pak Packaging Solutions
2. Cisco Systems Italia
3. Microsoft Italia
4. Nissan Italia
5. W. L. Gore & Associati Srl
6. National Instruments Italia
7. PepsiCo Italia
8. ConTe.it - Admiral Group
9. Gruppo Quintiles
10. Medtronic Italia

Source: *Great Place to Work Institute Inc.*, Best Places to Work in Italy (annual), http://www.greatplacetowork.com, 2011.

1781 ■ ITALY'S LARGEST COMPANIES OVERALL, 2011

Ranked by: Score based on revenue, profits, assets, and market capitalization. **Remarks:** Specific scores not provided. Also notes rank in the overall *Forbes 2000* and figures for each criterion. **Number listed:** 34

1. ENI SpA
2. Enel SpA
3. Intesa Sanpaolo SpA
4. UniCredit SpA
5. Assicurazioni Generali SpA
6. Telecom Italia SpA
7. Fiat SpA
8. Fiat Industrial SpA
9. Banca MPS
10. Finmeccanica SpA

Source: *Forbes*, Forbes 2000 (annual), http://www.forbes.com, May 7, 2012.

1782 ■ LARGEST COMPANIES IN ITALY, 2010

Ranked by: Sales, in millions of U.S. dollars. **Remarks:** Also notes city; industrial code; percent change in sales; profits; profit as a percentage of sales, assets, and equity; number of employees; sales per employee; assets; equity capital; equity capital as a percentage of assets; year established; and figures for previous year. **Number listed:** 900

1. ENI SpA, with $48,798.6 million

2. ENI Trading & Shipping SpA, $33,573.5
3. Telecom Italia SpA, $31,423
4. PetroFina SA, $30,448.8
5. Fiat Group Automobiles SpA, $27,357.5
6. Gestore Del Mercato Elettrico SpA, $26,628.3
7. Enel Trade SpA, $21,454.6
8. Finmeccanica SpA, $21,194.7
9. Fondiaria-Sai SpA, $18,007.1
10. Esso Italiana Srl, $17,433.3

Source: *Europe's 15,000 Largest Companies*, (annual), ELC International, 2011, p. 368+.

1783 ■ LARGEST CORPORATIONS IN ITALY BY REVENUE, 2010

Ranked by: Revenue, in millions of U.S. dollars. **Remarks:** Also notes headquarters city and overall rank in the *Global 500*. Ranking is available online only, not in print. **Number listed:** 10

1. ENI SpA, with $131,756 million
2. Assicurazioni Generali SpA, $120,234
3. Enel SpA, $97,185
4. EXOR Group, $78,123
5. UniCredit SpA, $53,338
6. Intesa Sanpaolo SpA, $44,285
7. Telecom Italia SpA, $36,855
8. Poste Italiane SpA, $28,922
9. Finmeccanica SpA, $25,591
10. Premafin Finanziaria SpA, $19,750

Source: *Fortune*, Global 500 (annual), http://www.fortune.com, July 25, 2011.

1784 ■ MOST ADMIRED COMPANIES IN ITALY, 2012

Ranked by: Score based on a survey of executives, directors, and securities analysts of companies within their own industry. **Remarks:** List is available online only, not in print. Also notes headquarters. **Number listed:** 2

1. ENI SpA, with 5.73 points
2. Poste Italiane, 5.26

Source: *Fortune*, World's Most Admired Companies (annual), http://www.fortune.com, March 19, 2012.

Corporations—Japan

1785 ■ BEST LARGE COMPANIES TO WORK FOR IN JAPAN, 2012

Ranked by: Score based on the relationships between employees and management, employees and their jobs/company, and employees and coworkers. **Remarks:** Specific scores not provided. Ranking covers companies with more than 250 employees. **Number listed:** 30

1. Google Japan Inc.
2. Works Applications Co., Ltd.
3. Plan Do See Inc.
4. CyberAgent Inc.
5. American Express Co.
6. Microsoft Co., Ltd.
7. Disco Corp.
8. Trend Micro

9. Morgan Stanley

10. Asahi Breweries Ltd.

Source: *Great Place to Work Institute Inc.*, Best Places to Work in Japan (annual), http://www.greatplacetowork.com, February 2012.

1786 ■ BEST SMALL COMPANIES TO WORK FOR IN JAPAN, 2012

Ranked by: Score based on the relationships between employees and management, employees and their jobs/company, and employees and coworkers. **Remarks:** Specific scores not provided. Ranking covers companies with fewer than 250 employees. **Number listed:** 10

1. Cold Stone Creamery Japan Co., Ltd.
2. NetApp Inc.
3. National Instruments Japan Corp.
4. NOAH Indoor Stage
5. ZIGEXN Co., Ltd.
6. LifeNet Insurance Co.
7. GaiaX Co., Ltd.
8. Florence
9. TripleGood
10. Upgarage Corp.

Source: *Great Place to Work Institute Inc.*, Best Places to Work in Japan (annual), http://www.greatplacetowork.com, 2012.

1787 ■ JAPAN'S LARGEST COMPANIES OVERALL, 2011

Ranked by: Score based on revenue, profits, assets, and market capitalization. **Remarks:** Specific scores not provided. Also notes rank in the overall *Forbes 2000* and figures for each criterion. **Number listed:** 258

1. Toyota Motor Corp.
2. Mitsubishi UFJ Financial Group Inc.
3. Nippon Telegraph & Telephone Corp. (NTT)
4. Honda Motor Co., Ltd.
5. Sumitomo Mitsui Financial Group Inc.
6. Nissan Motor Co., Ltd.
7. Mitsubishi Corp.
8. Mizuho Financial Group
9. Hitachi Ltd.
10. Mitsui & Co., Ltd.

Source: *Forbes*, Forbes 2000 (annual), http://www.forbes.com, May 7, 2012.

1788 ■ LARGEST CORPORATIONS IN JAPAN BY REVENUE, 2010

Ranked by: Revenue, in millions of U.S. dollars. **Remarks:** Also notes headquarters city and overall rank in the *Global 500*. Ranking is available online only, not in print. **Number listed:** 68

1. Toyota Motor Corp., with $221,760 million
2. Japan Post Holdings Co., Ltd., $203,958
3. Nippon Telegraph & Telephone Corp. (NTT), $120,316
4. Hitachi Ltd., $108,766
5. Honda Motor Co., Ltd., $104,342
6. Nissan Motor Co., Ltd., $102,430
7. Panasonic Corp., $101,491
8. JX Holdings, $95,964
9. Sony Corp., $83,845

10. Nippon Life Insurance Co., $78,571

Source: *Fortune*, Global 500 (annual), http://www.fortune.com, July 25, 2011.

1789 ■ MOST ADMIRED COMPANIES IN JAPAN, 2012

Ranked by: Score based on a survey of executives, directors, and securities analysts of companies within their own industry. **Remarks:** List is available online only, not in print. Also notes headquarters. **Number listed:** 15

1. Nippon Steel Corp., with 6.84 points
2. Toyota Industries Corp., 6.49
3. Komatsu, 6.48
4. Nippon Telegraph & Telephone Corp. (NTT), 6.18
5. Toyota Motor Corp., 6.04
6. Canon Inc., 6.01
7. Sony Corp., 5.98
8. KDDI, 5.89
9. Tokio Marine Holdings Inc., 5.64
10. Bridgestone Corp., 5.48
10. Panasonic Corp., 5.48

Source: *Fortune*, World's Most Admired Companies (annual), http://www.fortune.com, March 19, 2012.

1790 ■ MOST VALUABLE JAPANESE COMPANIES, 2011

Ranked by: Market value as of March 2011, in millions of U.S. dollars. **Remarks:** Also notes rank for previous year, sector, revenue, net income, assets, number of employees, share price, price-to-earning ratio, dividend yield, and fiscal year-end. **Number listed:** 500

1. Toyota Motor Corp., with $139,367.4 million
2. NTT DoCoMo Inc., $76,998.4
3. Honda Motor Co., Ltd., $68,300.1
4. Mitsubishi UFJ Financial Group Inc., $65,563.9
5. Nippon Telegraph & Telephone Corp. (NTT), $65,284
6. Canon Inc., $58,255.5
7. Mitsubishi Corp., $47,282.3
8. Sumitomo Mitsui Financial Group Inc., $44,120.9
9. Softbank Corp., $43,363.8
10. Nissan Motor Co., Ltd., $40,254.4

Source: *Financial Times*, FT 500 (annual), http://www.ft.com, June 24, 2011.

Corporations—Kansas

1791 ■ FASTEST-GROWING COMPANIES IN KANSAS CITY, 2007-2010

Ranked by: Three-year growth in revenue, in percent. **Remarks:** Also notes revenue for 2007 and 2010, number of full-time employees, and comments. **Number listed:** 100

1. Rhythm Engineering, with 3,388.96%
2. Nextaff, 1,167.49%
3. Adknowledge, 767.44%
4. TruckMovers, 435.17%
5. Gragg Advertising Inc., 302.54%
6. LynxSpring, 253.43%

7. Platinum Realty, 240.62%
8. Intouch Solutions, 222.37%
9. Technology Group Solutions, 207.76%
10. Arsalon Technologies LLC, 198.26%

Source: *Ingram's*, Corporate Report 100 (annual), http://www.ingramsonline.com, July 2011.

1792 ■ KANSAS CITY COMPANIES WITH THE HIGHEST MARKET VALUE, 2011

Ranked by: Market capitalization, in millions of dollars. **Remarks:** Also notes rank for previous year, headquarters, percent change from previous year, and overall rank and score in the Top 50. **Number listed:** 48

1. Cerner Corp., with $10,385.91 million
2. O'Reilly Automotive Inc., $10,168.02
3. Garmin Ltd., $7,749.52
4. Kansas City Southern, $7,475.04
5. Sprint Nextel Corp., $7,010.64
6. H & R Block Inc., $4,793.9
7. Westar Energy Inc., $3,617.6
8. Commerce Bancshares Inc., $3,394.95
9. Leggett & Platt Inc., $3,211.78
10. Inergy LP, $3,211.45

Source: *Kansas City Star*, The Star 50 (annual), http://www.kansascity.com, May 7, 2012.

1793 ■ KANSAS CITY COMPANIES WITH THE HIGHEST PROFITS, 2011

Ranked by: Profits, in millions of dollars. **Remarks:** Also notes rank for previous year, headquarters, percent change from previous year, and overall rank and score in the Top 50. **Number listed:** 48

1. Garmin Ltd., with $520.9 million
2. O'Reilly Automotive Inc., $507.67
3. Seaboard Corp., $345.85
4. H & R Block Inc., $338.39
5. Kansas City Southern, $330.3
6. Cerner Corp., $306.63
7. Commerce Bancshares Inc., $256.34
8. Westar Energy Inc., $230.24
9. Spirit AeroSystems Holdings Inc., $192.4
10. DST Systems Inc., $183.1

Source: *Kansas City Star*, The Star 50 (annual), http://www.kansascity.com, May 7, 2012.

1794 ■ KANSAS CITY COMPANIES WITH THE HIGHEST REVENUE, 2011

Ranked by: Revenue, in millions of dollars. **Remarks:** Also notes rank for previous year, headquarters, percent change from previous year, and overall rank and score in the Top 50. **Number listed:** 48

1. Sprint Nextel Corp., with $33,679 million
2. O'Reilly Automotive Inc., $5,788.82
3. Seaboard Corp., $5,746.9
4. YRC Worldwide Inc., $4,868.84
5. Spirit AeroSystems Holdings Inc., $4,863.8
6. Leggett & Platt Inc., $3,636
7. Collective Brands Inc., $3,461.7

8. H & R Block Inc., $3,385.56
9. Garmin Ltd., $2,758.57
10. Ferrellgas Partners LP, $2,549.73

Source: *Kansas City Star*, The Star 50 (annual), http://www.kansascity.com, May 7, 2012.

1795 ■ KANSAS'S LARGEST PRIVATE COMPANIES, 2010

Ranked by: Revenue, in billions of dollars. **Remarks:** Also notes business segment, number of employees, and overall rank in the *America's Largest Private Companies* list. Ranking is available online only, not in print. **Number listed:** 2

1. Koch Industries Inc., with $100 billion
2. Black & Veatch Holding Co., $2.27

Source: *Forbes*, America's Largest Private Companies (annual), http://www.forbes.com, December 5, 2011.

1796 ■ LARGEST COMPANIES IN KANSAS BY EMPLOYEES, 2010

Ranked by: Number of employees at headquarters. **Remarks:** Also notes contact information for headquarters, total number of employees, revenue, rank by revenue, and primary SIC code. **Number listed:** 118

1. Cessna Aircraft Co., with 6,200 employees
2. Embarq Corp., 5,000
3. B & V-Baker Guam JV, 4,500
4. Sprint/United Management Co., 4,000
4. Via Christi Regional Medical Center Inc., 4,000
6. Performance Contracting Inc., 2,900
7. Stormont-Vail Healthcare Inc., 2,871
8. University of Kansas Hospital Authority, 2,750
9. Black & Veatch Corp., 2,552
10. HCA Hospital Services of San Diego, 2,500

Source: *Business Rankings*, (annual), Dun & Bradstreet Inc., 2011, p. IV.87-IV.89.

1797 ■ LARGEST COMPANIES IN KANSAS BY SALES, 2010

Ranked by: Revenue, in dollars. **Remarks:** Also notes contact information for headquarters, number of employees at headquarters and overall, rank by employees, and primary SIC code. **Number listed:** 118

1. Sprint Nextel Corp., with $32,563,000,000
2. Yellow Roadway Technologies Inc., $9,621,316,000
3. Associated Wholesale Grocers Inc., $7,057,036,000
4. Seaboard Corp., $4,385,702,000
5. YRC Worldwide Inc., $4,334,640,000
6. Collective Brands Inc., $3,307,900,000
7. Hawker Beechcraft Corp., $3,200,000,000
8. Lansing Trade Group LLC, $3,000,000,000
9. National Cooperative Refinery Association, $2,810,339,000
10. Hawker Beechcraft Acquisition Co., $2,804,700,000

Source: *Business Rankings*, (annual), Dun & Bradstreet Inc., 2011, p. III.87-III.89.

1798 ■ TOP *FORTUNE 500* COMPANIES IN KANSAS, 2011

Ranked by: Revenue, in millions of dollars. **Remarks:** Also notes overall rank in the *Fortune 500,* headquarters, and number of employees. **Number listed:** 3

1. Sprint Nextel Corp., with $33,679 million
2. Seaboard Corp., $5,746.9
3. YRC Worldwide Inc., $4,868.8

Source: *Fortune*, Fortune 500 (annual), May 21, 2012, p. F-43.

1799 ■ TOP KANSAS CITY COMPANIES OVERALL, 2011

Ranked by: Score based on revenue, revenue growth, earnings, earnings growth, market value, and market value growth. **Remarks:** The lower the score, the better the rank; a perfect score is 1 point. Also notes rank for previous year, headquarters, business, and figures for and rank by each criterion. **Number listed:** 48

1. Cerner Corp., with 7.5 points
2. Kansas City Southern, 7.83
3. Seaboard Corp., 9.17
4. O'Reilly Automotive Inc., 9.33
5. Spirit AeroSystems Holdings Inc., 14
5. Garmin Ltd., 14
7. Westar Energy Inc., 14.33
8. Euronet Worldwide Inc., 16
9. H & R Block Inc., 16.17
10. Leggett & Platt Inc., 17.67

Source: *Kansas City Star*, The Star 50 (annual), http://www.kansascity.com, May 7, 2012.

Corporations—Kazakhstan

1800 ■ KAZAKHSTAN'S LARGEST COMPANIES OVERALL, 2011

Ranked by: Score based on revenue, profits, assets, and market capitalization. **Remarks:** Specific scores not provided. Also notes overall rank in the *Forbes 2000* and figures for each criterion. **Number listed:** 2

1. KazMunaiGas Exploration
2. BTA Bank

Source: *Forbes*, Forbes 2000 (annual), http://www.forbes.com, May 7, 2012.

Corporations—Kentucky

1801 ■ BEST LARGE COMPANIES TO WORK FOR IN KENTUCKY, 2012

Ranked by: Score based on employee surveys. **Remarks:** Specific scores not provided; companies are listed alphabetically, not ranked. To qualify, companies must have at least 250 employees. **Number listed:** 37

1. Appriss Inc.
2. Baptist Hospital East
3. Baptist Hospital Northeast
4. Blue & Co.
5. Booz Allen Hamilton Inc.
6. C. A. Jones Management Group LLC
7. Central Bank & Trust
8. Central Baptist Hospital
9. Corning Inc.
10. Crowe Horwath LLP

Source: *Best Companies Group*, Best Places to Work in Kentucky (annual), http://www.bestplacestoworkky.com, January 19, 2012.

1802 ■ BEST SMALL/MEDIUM COMPANIES TO WORK FOR IN KENTUCKY, 2012

Ranked by: Score based on employee surveys. **Remarks:** Specific scores not provided; companies are listed alphabetically, not ranked. To qualify, companies must have between 25 and 249 employees. **Number listed:** 28

1. Air Hydro Power
2. Alure Salon & Day Spa
3. ARGI Financial Group
4. Benefit Insurance Marketing
5. Big Ass Fans
6. Bowling Green Technical College
7. Connected Nation
8. Creative Lodging Solutions
9. Dean Dorton Allen Ford PLLC
10. Farmers Bank & Capital Trust Co.

Source: *Best Companies Group*, Best Places to Work in Kentucky (annual), http://www.bestplacestoworkky.com, January 19, 2012.

1803 ■ KENTUCKY CORPORATIONS WITH THE FASTEST-GROWING STOCK, 2010-2011

Ranked by: Annual growth in stock price, in percent. **Remarks:** Also notes ticker symbol, stock price for May 2010 and 2011, and 52-week range. **Number listed:** 25

1. Tempur-Pedic International Inc., with 95.9%
2. Humana Inc., 74.9%
3. Kindred Healthcare, 58.2%
4. Bank of Kentucky, 55.5%
5. Yum! Brands, 35.1%
6. General Cable, 34%
7. Papa John's International, 33.4%
8. Computer Services Inc., 33.3%
9. Churchill Downs, 30.3%
10. Ashland Inc., 27.5%
10. Brown-Forman, 27.5%

Source: *The Lane Report*, Stock Performance (annual), June 2011, p. 38.

1804 ■ KENTUCKY'S LARGEST COMPANIES OVERALL, 2011

Ranked by: Score based on revenue, profits, assets, and market capitalization. **Remarks:** Specific scores not provided. Also notes overall rank in the *Forbes 2000* and figures for each criterion. **Number listed:** 4

1. Humana Inc.
2. Yum! Brands Inc.
3. Ashland Inc.
4. Brown-Forman Corp.

Source: *Forbes*, Forbes 2000 (annual), http://www.forbes.com, May 7, 2012.

1805 ■ LARGEST COMPANIES IN KENTUCKY BY EMPLOYEES, 2010

Ranked by: Number of employees at headquarters. **Remarks:** Also notes contact information for headquarters, total number of employees, revenue, rank by revenue, and primary SIC code. **Number listed:** 123

1. Norton Hospitals Foundation Inc., with 9,000 employees
2. Russell Brands LLC, 7,000
3. Toyota Motor Manufacturing Kentucky Inc., 6,500
4. Lexmark International Inc., 4,200
5. Thomas & King of Arizona Inc., 4,000
6. California Square LP, 3,900
7. Jewish Hospital & St. Mary's Healthcare Inc., 3,450
8. Brown-Forman Worldwide Corp., 3,000
8. Corporex Cos., LLC, 3,000
8. Directech of Kentucky Inc., 3,000

Source: *Business Rankings*, (annual), Dun & Bradstreet Inc., 2011, p. IV.90-IV.92.

1806 ■ LARGEST COMPANIES IN KENTUCKY BY SALES, 2010

Ranked by: Revenue, in dollars. **Remarks:** Also notes contact information for headquarters, number of employees at headquarters and overall, rank by employees, and primary SIC code. **Number listed:** 126

1. Yum! Brands Inc., with $11,343,000,000
2. Ashland Inc., $9,012,000,000
3. Omnicare Inc., $6,146,212,000
4. General Cable Corp., $4,864,900,000
5. Kindred Healthcare Inc., $4,359,697,000
6. Lexmark International Inc., $4,199,700,000
7. Brown-Forman Corp., $3,226,000,000
8. Houchens Industries Inc., $2,666,868,000
9. Pharmerica Corp., $1,847,300,000
10. Baptist Healthcare System Inc., $1,448,062,000

Source: *Business Rankings*, (annual), Dun & Bradstreet Inc., 2011, p. III.90-III.92.

1807 ■ MOST ADMIRED COMPANIES IN KENTUCKY, 2012

Ranked by: Survey of top executives, directors, and securities analysts regarding the Fortune 1,000 companies that they admire the most, regardless of industry. **Remarks:** Also notes city and industry rank. List is available online only, not in print. **Number listed:** 3

1. Yum! Brands Inc., with 6.96 points
2. Humana Inc., 6.23
3. Kindred Healthcare Inc., 5.23

Source: *Fortune*, World's Most Admired Companies (annual), http://www.fortune.com, March 19, 2012.

1808 ■ TOP *FORTUNE 500* COMPANIES IN KENTUCKY, 2011

Ranked by: Revenue, in millions of dollars. **Remarks:** Also notes overall rank in the *Fortune 500*, headquarters, and number of employees. **Number listed:** 6

1. Humana Inc., with $36,832 million
2. Yum! Brands Inc., $12,626
3. Ashland Inc., $8,370
4. Omnicare Inc., $6,239.9
5. General Cable Corp., $5,866.7

6. Kindred Healthcare Inc., $5,523.3

Source: *Fortune*, Fortune 500 (annual), May 21, 2012, p. F-43.

Corporations—Kuwait

1809 ■ KUWAIT'S LARGEST COMPANIES OVERALL, 2011

Ranked by: Score based on revenue, profits, assets, and market capitalization. **Remarks:** Specific scores not provided. Also notes rank in the overall *Forbes 2000* and figures for each criterion. **Number listed:** 3

1. National Bank of Kuwait
2. Zain Group
3. Kuwait Finance House

Source: *Forbes*, Forbes 2000 (annual), http://www.forbes.com, May 7, 2012.

Corporations—Latin America

1810 ■ BEST COMPANIES TO WORK FOR IN LATIN AMERICA, 2011

Ranked by: Score based on the relationships between employees and management, employees and their jobs/company, and employees and coworkers. **Remarks:** Specific scores not provided. **Number listed:** 50

1. Asesoria, Seguridad y Vigilancia (Ecuador)
2. Seguros Bolivar (Colombia)
3. Gases de Occidente (Colombia)
4. Floreloy (Ecuador)
5. Interseguro (Peru)
6. Banco de Occidente (Colombia)
7. J & V Resguardo (Peru)
8. Transbank (Chile)
9. Banco General Ruminahui (Ecuador)
10. Laboratorio Sabin (Brazil)

Source: *Great Place to Work Institute Inc.*, Best Places to Work in Latin America (annual), 2011.

1811 ■ BEST MULTINATIONAL COMPANIES TO WORK FOR IN LATIN AMERICA, 2011

Ranked by: Score based on the relationships between employees and management, employees and their jobs/company, and employees and coworkers. **Remarks:** Specific scores not provided. **Number listed:** 50

1. Kimberly-Clark Corp.
2. Telefonica SA
3. Renault-Sofasa
4. Quala
5. Google Inc.
6. Caterpillar Inc.
7. International Business Machines Corp. (IBM)
8. ACE Seguros SA
9. Sodimac
10. Accor SA

Source: *Great Place to Work Institute Inc.*, Best Places to Work in Latin America (annual), 2011.

Corporations—Latvia

1812 ■ LARGEST COMPANIES IN LATVIA, 2010

Ranked by: Sales, in millions of U.S. dollars. **Remarks:** Also notes city; industrial code; percent change in sales; profits; profit as a percentage of sales, assets, and equity; number of employees; sales per employee; assets; equity capital; equity capital as a percentage of assets; year established; and figures for previous year. **Number listed:** 50

1. A/S Latvenergo, with $847.4 million
2. A/S Elko Group, $831.7
3. SIA Rimi Latvia, $823.6
4. LG Electronics Latvia Sia, $740.6
5. Norvik Banka AS, $732.6
6. Greis Sia, $721.7
7. Swedbank AS, $659.4
8. A/S Latvijas Gaze, $634.2
9. Latvija Statoil Sia, $592.8
10. Rietumu Banka AS, $492

Source: *Europe's 15,000 Largest Companies*, (annual), ELC International, 2011, p. 408+.

Corporations—Lebanon

1813 ■ LEBANON'S LARGEST COMPANIES OVERALL, 2011

Ranked by: Score based on revenue, profits, assets, and market capitalization. **Remarks:** Specific scores not provided. Also notes rank in the overall *Forbes 2000* and figures for each criterion. **Number listed:** 2

1. Bank Audi
2. Blom Bank

Source: *Forbes*, Forbes 2000 (annual), http://www.forbes.com, May 7, 2012.

Corporations—Lithuania

1814 ■ LARGEST COMPANIES IN LITHUANIA, 2010

Ranked by: Sales, in millions of U.S. dollars. **Remarks:** Also notes city; industrial code; percent change in sales; profits; profit as a percentage of sales, assets, and equity; number of employees; sales per employee; assets; equity capital; equity capital as a percentage of assets; year established; and figures for previous year. **Number listed:** 50

1. Orlen Lietuva AB, with $4,422.9 million
2. Maxima Lt UAB, $2,042.6
3. Lukoil Baltija UAB, $870.8
4. Palink UAB, $769
5. Achema AB, $766.9
6. Lietuvos Gelezinkelai AB, $599.3
7. Senuku Prekybos Centras UAB, $572.7
8. Norfos Mazmena UAB, $548.8
9. Lietuva Statoil UAB, $508.8
10. Lietuvos Energija AB, $472.2

Source: *Europe's 15,000 Largest Companies*, (annual), ELC International, 2011, p. 412+.

Corporations—Louisiana

1815 ■ BEST LARGE PLACES TO WORK IN NEW ORLEANS, 2011

Ranked by: Score based on employee survey. **Remarks:** Scores not provided. Only the top three companies are ranked; the remainder are listed alphabetically. To qualify, companies must have 50 or more employees. **Number listed:** 35

1. Eagan Insurance Agency
2. First NBC Bank
3. Fair Grounds Race Couse & Slots

Source: *New Orleans CityBusiness*, Best Places to Work (annual), 2011.

1816 ■ BEST SMALL PLACES TO WORK IN NEW ORLEANS, 2011

Ranked by: Score based on employee survey. **Remarks:** Scores not provided. Only the top three companies are ranked; the remainder are listed alphabetically. To qualify, companies must have fewer than 50 employees. **Number listed:** 15

1. Zehnder Communications
2. Ericksen, Krentel & LaPorte
3. Blitch Knevel Architects

Source: *New Orleans CityBusiness*, Best Places to Work (annual), 2011.

1817 ■ LARGEST COMPANIES IN LOUISIANA BY EMPLOYEES, 2010

Ranked by: Number of employees at headquarters. **Remarks:** Also notes contact information for headquarters, total number of employees, revenue, rank by revenue, and primary SIC code. **Number listed:** 140

1. Avondale Industries of New York Inc., with 5,400 employees
2. General Health System Management Inc., 4,000
2. Ochsner Foundation Hospital, 4,000
4. ABMB-HNTB JV LLC, 3,500
4. Our Lady of the Lake Hospital Inc., 3,500
6. East Jefferson Hospital, 3,428
7. Alton Ochsner Medical Foundation, 3,000
7. Capital One NA, 3,000
7. Mid City Medical Center, 3,000
7. Ochsner Clinic Foundation, 3,000

Source: *Business Rankings*, (annual), Dun & Bradstreet Inc., 2011, p. IV.93-IV.95.

1818 ■ LARGEST COMPANIES IN LOUISIANA BY SALES, 2010

Ranked by: Revenue, in dollars. **Remarks:** Also notes contact information for headquarters, number of employees at headquarters and overall, rank by employees, and primary SIC code. **Number listed:** 140

1. Entergy Corp., with $11,487,577,000
2. CenturyLink Inc., $7,041,534,000
3. The Shaw Group Inc., $7,000,779,000
4. Zen-Noh Grain Corp., $5,988,204,000
5. Chalmette Refining LLC, $5,647,787,000
6. CGB Enterprises Inc., $4,157,938,220

7. PT Freeport Indonesia Co., $3,412,281,000

8. Entergy Louisiana LLC, $2,538,766,000

9. Albemarle Corp., $2,362,764,000

10. Entergy Gulf States Louisiana LLC, $2,097,021,000

Source: *Business Rankings*, (annual), Dun & Bradstreet Inc., 2011, p. III.93-III.95.

1819 ■ LOUISIANA'S LARGEST COMPANIES OVERALL, 2011

Ranked by: Score based on revenue, profits, assets, and market capitalization. **Remarks:** Specific scores not provided. Also notes overall rank in the *Forbes 2000* and figures for each criterion. **Number listed:** 3

1. CenturyTel Inc.

2. Entergy Corp.

3. Albemarle

Source: *Forbes*, Forbes 2000 (annual), http://www.forbes.com, May 7, 2012.

1820 ■ TOP *FORTUNE 500* COMPANIES IN LOUISIANA, 2011

Ranked by: Revenue, in millions of dollars. **Remarks:** Also notes overall rank in the *Fortune 500,* headquarters, and number of employees. **Number listed:** 3

1. CenturyLink Inc., with $15,351 million

2. Entergy Corp., $11,229.1

3. The Shaw Group Inc., $5,937.7

Source: *Fortune*, Fortune 500 (annual), May 21, 2012, p. F-43.

Corporations—Luxembourg

1821 ■ LARGEST COMPANIES IN LUXEMBOURG, 2010

Ranked by: Sales, in millions of U.S. dollars. **Remarks:** Also notes city; industrial code; percent change in sales; profits; profit as a percentage of sales, assets, and equity; number of employees; sales per employee; assets; equity capital; equity capital as a percentage of assets; year established; and figures for previous year. **Number listed:** 100

1. ArcelorMittal Fiat Carbon Europe SA, with $28,295.7 million

2. Evraz Group SA, $20,380

3. Tenaris SA, $12,131.8

4. ArcelorMittal Sourcing SCA, $8,771.2

5. Ternium SA, $8,464.9

6. RTL Group, $8,010

7. Millicom International Cellular SA, $3,412.4

8. Espirito Santo Financial Group SA, $2,855.6

9. SES SA, $2,438.7

10. Pfizer Enterprises SARL, $2,421

Source: *Europe's 15,000 Largest Companies*, (annual), ELC International, 2011, p. 416+.

1822 ■ LUXEMBOURG'S LARGEST COMPANIES OVERALL, 2011

Ranked by: Score based on revenue, profits, assets, and market capitalization. **Remarks:** Specific scores not provided. Also notes rank in the overall *Forbes 2000* and figures for each criterion. **Number listed:** 7

1. ArcelorMittal

2. Tenaris SA

3. RTL Group

4. SES SA

5. Ternium

6. Espirito Santo Financial

7. Millicom International Cellular

Source: *Forbes*, Forbes 2000 (annual), http://www.forbes.com, May 7, 2012.

Corporations—Maine

1823 ■ BEST LARGE COMPANIES TO WORK FOR IN MAINE, 2011

Ranked by: Score based on employee surveys. **Remarks:** Specific scores not provided. To qualify, companies must have at least 250 employees. **Number listed:** 12

1. Consigli Construction Co.

2. Edward Jones

3. Unum

4. Bangor Savings Bank

5. athenahealth Inc.

6. Cianbro

7. EMHS

8. New Balance Athletic Shoe Inc.

9. Tyler Technologies

10. L. L. Bean Inc.

Source: *Best Companies Group*, Best Places to Work in Maine (annual), http://www.bestplacestoworkinme.com, October 2011.

1824 ■ BEST SMALL/MEDIUM COMPANIES TO WORK FOR IN MAINE, 2011

Ranked by: Score based on employee surveys. **Remarks:** Specific scores not provided. To qualify, companies must have between 15 and 249 employees. **Number listed:** 28

1. Burgess Advertising & Marketing

2. Garrand

3. Skowhegan Savings Bank

4. MMG Insurance Co.

5. Kepware Technologies

6. Maine Savings Federal Credit Union

7. Turner Barker Insurance

8. FISC Solutions

9. Nurse Anesthesia of Maine

10. Machias Savings Bank

Source: *Best Companies Group*, Best Places to Work in Maine (annual), http://www.bestplacestoworkinme.com, October 2011.

1825 ■ LARGEST COMPANIES IN MAINE BY EMPLOYEES, 2010

Ranked by: Number of employees at headquarters. **Remarks:** Also notes contact information for headquarters, total number of employees, revenue, rank by revenue, and primary SIC code. **Number listed:** 67

1. Hannaford Bros. Co., with 5,000 employees

2. Maine Medical Center Inc., 4,200

3. Midcoast Seamless Gutters, 1,986

4. St. Marys Health System, 1,600
5. Hannaford Bros. Co. (subsidiary), 1,262
6. Jackson Laboratory, 1,250
7. Rumford Paper Co., 1,200
7. Unum Life Insurance Co. of America, 1,200
9. Central Maine Medical Center Inc., 1,190
10. Mercy Hospital, 1,032

Source: *Business Rankings*, (annual), Dun & Bradstreet Inc., 2011, p. IV.96-IV.97.

1826 ■ LARGEST COMPANIES IN MAINE BY SALES, 2010

Ranked by: Revenue, in dollars. **Remarks:** Also notes contact information for headquarters, number of employees at headquarters and overall, rank by employees, and primary SIC code. **Number listed:** 67

1. Iberdrola USA Inc., with $4,361,641,000
2. Fairchild Semiconductor International Inc., $1,599,700,000
3. Idexx Laboratories Inc., $1,103,392,000
4. Miles Health Care Inc., $1,042,978,000
5. Maine Medical Center, $685,625,944
6. Cedar Ridge Nursing Home, $641,208,900
7. Hibbard Nursing Home Inc., $627,589,800
8. Central Maine Power Co., $524,969,000
9. Wright Express Corp., $390,406,000
10. MaineGeneral Health, $378,591,688

Source: *Business Rankings*, (annual), Dun & Bradstreet Inc., 2011, p. III.96-III.97.

1827 ■ MAINE'S LARGEST PRIVATE EMPLOYERS, 2010

Ranked by: Average monthly employment range. **Remarks:** Also notes contact information, principal location in Maine, and industry. **Number listed:** 50

1. Hannaford Bros. Co., with 8,001-9,000 employees
2. Wal-Mart Stores Inc., 7,001-8,000
3. Maine Medical Center, 6,001-7,000

Source: *MaineBiz*, Largest Private Employers (annual), http://www.mainebiz.biz, July 25, 2011.

Corporations—Malaysia

1828 ■ BEST SMALL MALAYSIAN COMPANIES, 2010

Ranked by: Score based on sales, net income, and market value. **Remarks:** Specific scores not provided; companies are listed alphabetically, not ranked. Also notes sales, net income, market value, and industry. To qualify for list, which is available online only, companies must have under US$1 billion in annual revenue and positive earnings growth over the past five years. **Number listed:** 14

1. Coastal Contracts Bhd
2. EA Holdings
3. Hartalega Holdings
4. HELP International
5. Hirotako Holdings
6. Hock Seng Lee
7. KKB Engineering

8. Latexx Partners
9. Masterskill Education
10. Mudajaya Group

Source: *Forbes Asia*, Asia's Best Under a Billion (annual), http://www.forbes.com, September 12, 2011.

1829 ■ MALAYSIA'S LARGEST COMPANIES OVERALL, 2011

Ranked by: Score based on revenue, profits, assets, and market capitalization. **Remarks:** Specific scores not provided. Also notes rank in the overall *Forbes 2000* and figures for each criterion. **Number listed:** 18

1. Maybank
2. CIMB Group Holdings
3. Sime Darby
4. Public Bank
5. Genting Bhd.
6. Axiata Group Bhd.
7. Tenaga Nasional
8. Petronas Chemicals
9. IOI Group
10. RHB Capital

Source: *Forbes*, Forbes 2000 (annual), http://www.forbes.com, May 7, 2012.

Corporations—Malta

1830 ■ LARGEST COMPANIES IN MALTA, 2010

Ranked by: Sales, in millions of U.S. dollars. **Remarks:** Also notes city; industrial code; percent change in sales; profits; profit as a percentage of sales, assets, and equity; number of employees; sales per employee; assets; equity capital; equity capital as a percentage of assets; year established; and figures for previous year. **Number listed:** 50

1. Water Services Corp., with $3,7392.6 million
2. STMicroelectronics (Malta) Ltd., $1,224.1
3. Norasia Container Lines Ltd., $961.6
4. Samchrome Ltd., $658.4
5. Expekt Corn Co., $567.1
6. HC Trading Malta Ltd., $473.7
7. Air Malta plc, $439.8
8. Chempetrol Overseas Ltd., $430.6
9. Enemalta Corp., $269.8
10. Palmali Holding Co., Ltd., $212.4

Source: *Europe's 15,000 Largest Companies*, (annual), ELC International, 2011, p. 422+.

Corporations—Maryland

1831 ■ BEST SMALL COMPANIES IN MARYLAND, 2011

Ranked by: Score based on revenue, profits, and return on equity for the past 12 months and five years. **Remarks:** Specific scores not provided. Also notes rank in the overall *100 Best Small Companies in America*. To qualify, companies must have revenues between $5 million and $1 billion, a net margin above five percent, and share price above $5. List is available online only. **Number listed:** 4

1. Medifast

2. Opnet Technologies
3. Emergent Biosolutions
4. Jos. A. Bank Clothiers

Source: *Forbes*, Best Small Companies in America (annual), November 7, 2011.

1832 ■ FASTEST-GROWING COMPANIES IN MARYLAND, 2008-2011

Ranked by: Score based on three-year growth in revenue and earnings, and three-year total return to investors. **Remarks:** Specific scores not provided. To qualify for list, companies must have revenues of at least $50 million, net income of at least $10 million, market capitalization of at least $250 million, and stock price of at least $5. Int'l companies are eligible if they trade on a U.S. exchange and file quarterly reports. **Number listed:** 4

1. Medifast Inc.
2. Discovery Communications
3. United Therapeutics
4. Catalyst Health Solutions Inc.

Source: *Fortune*, 100 Fastest-Growing Companies (annual), http://www.fortune.com, September 26, 2011.

1833 ■ LARGEST COMPANIES IN MARYLAND BY EMPLOYEES, 2010

Ranked by: Number of employees at headquarters. **Remarks:** Also notes contact information for headquarters, total number of employees, revenue, rank by revenue, and primary SIC code. **Number listed:** 179

1. Johns Hopkins Medicine International LLC, with 6,900 employees
2. Adventist Healthcare Inc., 4,119
3. Childrens National Medical Center, 4,000
4. Simmons Investigative & Security Agency, 3,500
5. Johns Hopkins Bayview Medical Center Inc., 3,000
5. Marriott International Inc., 3,000
5. Marriott Worldwide Sales & Marketing Inc., 3,000
8. Greater Baltimore Medical Center Inc., 2,900
9. St. Joseph Medical Center Inc., 2,700
10. Carefirst Inc., 2,500
10. E2 Acquisition Corp., 2,500
10. Ritz Camera & Image LLC, 2,500

Source: *Business Rankings*, (annual), Dun & Bradstreet Inc., 2011, p. IV.98-IV.101.

1834 ■ LARGEST COMPANIES IN MARYLAND BY SALES, 2010

Ranked by: Revenue, in dollars. **Remarks:** Also notes contact information for headquarters, number of employees at headquarters and overall, rank by employees, and primary SIC code. **Number listed:** 177

1. Lockheed Martin Corp., with $45,803,000,000
2. Constellation Energy Group Inc., $14,340,000,000
3. Marriott International Inc., $11,691,000,000
4. North Bethesda Hotel LLC, $9,000,000
5. Allegis Group Inc., $4,880,924,600
6. Catalyst Health Solutions Inc., $3,764,092,000

7. MedStar Health Inc., $3,678,000,000
8. Discovery Communications Inc., $3,516,000,000
9. Maryland Department of Transportation, $3,506,266,000
10. The Whiting-Turner Contracting Co., $3,504,116,039

Source: *Business Rankings*, (annual), Dun & Bradstreet Inc., 2011, p. III.98-III.101.

1835 ■ MARYLAND'S LARGEST COMPANIES OVERALL, 2011

Ranked by: Score based on revenue, profits, assets, and market capitalization. **Remarks:** Specific scores not provided. Also notes overall rank in the *Forbes 2000* and figures for each criterion. **Number listed:** 8

1. Lockheed Martin Corp.
2. American Capital Agency Corp.
3. Discovery Communications Inc.
4. T. Rowe Price Group Inc.
5. Coventry Health Care Inc.
6. Marriott International Inc.
7. Host Hotels & Resorts Inc.
8. McCormick & Co.

Source: *Forbes*, Forbes 2000 (annual), http://www.forbes.com, May 7, 2012.

1836 ■ MARYLAND'S LARGEST PRIVATE COMPANIES, 2010

Ranked by: Revenue, in billions of dollars. **Remarks:** Also notes business segment, number of employees, and overall rank in the *America's Largest Private Companies* list. Ranking is available online only, not in print. **Number listed:** 4

1. Allegis Group Inc., with $6.4 billion
2. Clark Enterprises Inc., $4.7
3. Perdue Farms Inc., $4.6
4. The Whiting-Turner Contracting Co., $3.23

Source: *Forbes*, America's Largest Private Companies (annual), http://www.forbes.com, December 5, 2011.

1837 ■ MOST ADMIRED COMPANIES IN MARYLAND, 2012

Ranked by: Survey of top executives, directors, and securities analysts regarding the Fortune 1,000 companies that they admire the most, regardless of industry. **Remarks:** Also notes city and industry rank. List is available online only, not in print. **Number listed:** 6

1. Marriott International Inc., with 7.2 points
2. Discovery Communications Inc., 6.94
3. Lockheed Martin Corp., 6.90
4. T. Rowe Price Group Inc., 6.82
5. Host Hotels & Resorts Inc., 6.35
6. Catalyst Health Solutions, 5.81

Source: *Fortune*, World's Most Admired Companies (annual), http://www.fortune.com, March 19, 2012.

1838 ■ TOP *FORTUNE 500* COMPANIES IN MARYLAND, 2011

Ranked by: Revenue, in millions of dollars. **Remarks:** Also notes overall rank in the *Fortune 500*, headquarters, and number of employees. **Number listed:** 6

1. Lockheed Martin Corp., with $46,692 million
2. Constellation Energy Group Inc., $13,758.2
3. Marriott International Inc., $12,317
4. Coventry Health Care Inc., $12,186.7
5. Catalyst Health Solutions Inc., $5,329.6
6. Host Hotels & Resorts Inc., $5,003

Source: *Fortune*, Fortune 500 (annual), May 21, 2012, p. F-43.

Corporations—Massachusetts

1839 ■ BEST SMALL COMPANIES IN MASSACHUSETTS, 2011

Ranked by: Score based on revenue, profits, and return on equity for the past 12 months and five years. **Remarks:** Specific scores not provided. Also notes rank in the overall *100 Best Small Companies in America*. To qualify, companies must have revenues between $5 million and $1 billion, a net margin above five percent, and share price above $5. List is available online only. **Number listed:** 10

1. IPG Photonics
2. Virtusa Corp.
3. Hittite Microwave
4. Boston Beer
5. iRobot
6. Ameresco
7. UFP Technologies
8. Zoll Medical
9. Altra Holdings
10. Atlantic Tele-Network

Source: *Forbes*, Best Small Companies in America (annual), November 7, 2011.

1840 ■ FASTEST-GROWING COMPANIES IN MASSACHUSETTS, 2008-2011

Ranked by: Score based on three-year growth in revenue and earnings, and three-year total return to investors. **Remarks:** Specific scores not provided. To qualify for list, companies must have revenues of at least $50 million, net income of at least $10 million, market capitalization of at least $250 million, and stock price of at least $5. Int'l companies are eligible if they trade on a U.S. exchange and file quarterly reports. **Number listed:** 4

1. Acme Packet
2. Cubist Pharmaceuticals Inc.
3. NetScout Systems Inc.
4. American Science & Engineering

Source: *Fortune*, 100 Fastest-Growing Companies (annual), http://www.fortune.com, September 26, 2011.

1841 ■ LARGEST COMPANIES IN MASSACHUSETTS BY EMPLOYEES, 2010

Ranked by: Number of employees at headquarters. **Remarks:** Also notes contact information for headquarters, total number of employees, revenue, rank by revenue, and primary SIC code. **Number listed:** 283

1. UMASS Memorial Hospitals Inc., with 8,683 employees
2. John Hancock Corporate Tax Credit Fund I LP, 8,000
3. State Street Bank & Trust Co., 7,619

4. Lahey Clinic Foundation Inc., 5,000
5. Baystate Health Systems Health Services Inc., 4,900
6. UMASS Memorial Health Care Inc., 4,800
7. Baystate Medical Center Inc., 4,400
8. Worcester Episcopal Housing Co., 3,900
9. Massachusetts General Hospital, 3,647
10. Tufts Medical Center Parent Inc., 3,620

Source: *Business Rankings*, (annual), Dun & Bradstreet Inc., 2011, p. IV.102-IV.108.

1842 ■ LARGEST COMPANIES IN MASSACHUSETTS BY SALES, 2010

Ranked by: Revenue, in dollars. **Remarks:** Also notes contact information for headquarters, number of employees at headquarters and overall, rank by employees, and primary SIC code. **Number listed:** 289

1. Raytheon Co., with $25,183,000,000
2. Staples Inc., $24,545,113,000
3. The TJX Companies Inc., $20,288,444,000
4. EMC Corp., $17,015,126,000
5. Thermo Fisher Scientific Inc., $10,788,700,000
6. BJ's Wholesale Club Inc., $10,186,981,000
7. Boston Scientific Corp., $7,806,000,000
8. Global Partners LP, $7,801,559,000
9. Fresenius Medical Care Holdings Inc., $7,515,711,000
10. Northeast Utilities, $4,898,167,000

Source: *Business Rankings*, (annual), Dun & Bradstreet Inc., 2011, p. III.102-III.108.

1843 ■ MASSACHUSETTS'S BEST COMPANIES TO WORK FOR, 2012

Ranked by: Score based on employee surveys as well as evaluation of companies' credibility, respect, fairness, and pride/camaraderie. **Remarks:** Specific scores not provided; companies are listed alphabetically, not ranked. Available online only, not in print. **Number listed:** 4

1. Bingham McCutchen LLP
2. The Boston Consulting Group Inc.
3. Bright Horizons Family Solutions Inc.
4. Millennium: The Takeda Oncology Co.

Source: *Fortune*, 100 Best Companies to Work For (annual), http://www.fortune.com, February 6, 2012.

1844 ■ MASSACHUSETTS'S LARGEST COMPANIES OVERALL, 2011

Ranked by: Score based on revenue, profits, assets, and market capitalization. **Remarks:** Specific scores not provided. Also notes overall rank in the *Forbes 2000* and figures for each criterion. **Number listed:** 14

1. EMC Corp.
2. State Street Corp.
3. Raytheon Co.
4. Thermo Fisher Scientific Inc.
5. The TJX Companies Inc.
6. Staples Inc.
7. Biogen Idec Inc.
8. Boston Scientific Corp.

9. American Tower Corp.
10. Analog Devices

Source: *Forbes*, Forbes 2000 (annual), http://www.forbes.com, May 7, 2012.

1845 ■ MASSACHUSETTS'S LARGEST PRIVATE COMPANIES, 2010

Ranked by: Revenue, in billions of dollars. **Remarks:** Also notes business segment, number of employees, and overall rank in the *America's Largest Private Companies* list. Ranking is available online only, not in print. **Number listed:** 7

1. Fidelity Investments, with $12.26 billion
2. Cumberland Farms Inc., $8.02
3. International Data Group Inc., $3.24
4. Demoulas Super Markets Inc., $3.20
5. The Boston Consulting Group Inc., $3.05
6. HP Hood LLC, $2.4
7. Bose Corp., $2.28

Source: *Forbes*, America's Largest Private Companies (annual), http://www.forbes.com, December 5, 2011.

1846 ■ MOST ADMIRED COMPANIES IN MASSACHUSETTS, 2012

Ranked by: Survey of top executives, directors, and securities analysts regarding the Fortune 1,000 companies that they admire the most, regardless of industry. **Remarks:** Also notes city and industry rank. List is available online only, not in print. **Number listed:** 8

1. The TJX Companies Inc., with 6.85 points
2. EMC Corp., 6.78
3. Staples Inc., 6.69
4. Raytheon Co., 6.51
5. State Street Corp., 6.23
6. Iron Mountain Inc., 6.04
7. Massachusetts Mutual Life Insurance Co., 5.69
8. Liberty Mutual Insurance Group, 5.56

Source: *Fortune*, World's Most Admired Companies (annual), http://www.fortune.com, March 19, 2012.

1847 ■ TOP *FORTUNE 500* COMPANIES IN MASSACHUSETTS, 2011

Ranked by: Revenue, in millions of dollars. **Remarks:** Also notes overall rank in the *Fortune 500,* headquarters, and number of employees. **Number listed:** 11

1. Liberty Mutual Insurance Companies, with $34,671 million
2. Staples Inc., $25,022.2
3. Raytheon Co., $24,857
4. Massachusetts Mutual Life Insurance Co., $24,226.4
5. The TJX Companies Inc., $23,191.5
6. EMC Corp., $20,007.6
7. Global Partners LP, $14,835.7
8. Thermo Fisher Scientific Inc., $11,780.2
9. State Street Corp., $10,207
10. Boston Scientific Corp., $7,622

Source: *Fortune*, Fortune 500 (annual), May 21, 2012, p. F-43.

1848 ■ TOP MASSACHUSETTS COMPANIES, 2011

Ranked by: Score based on revenue, return on equity, and growth in revenue and profits. **Remarks:** The lower the score, the higher

the rank. Also notes rank for previous year, headquarters, industry, and figures for each criterion. **Number listed:** 100

1. Momenta Pharmaceuticals, with 80 points
2. IPG Photonics Corp., 87
3. Altra Holdings, 106
4. Sapient Corp., 107
5. Parametric Technology Corp., 108
6. Beacon Roofing Supply, 116
7. EMC Corp., 119
8. Skyworks Solutions, 123
9. Kadant, 124
10. Five Star Quality Care, 125

Source: *Boston Globe*, Globe 100 (annual), http://www.boston.com/business/globe, May 20, 2012.

Corporations—Mexico

1849 ■ BEST LARGE COMPANIES TO WORK FOR IN MEXICO, 2012

Ranked by: Score based on the relationships between employees and management, employees and their jobs/company, and employees and coworkers. **Remarks:** Specific scores not provided. Ranking covers companies with more than 5,000 employees. **Number listed:** 11

1. Compartamos Banco
2. Atento
3. McDonald's Mexico
4. Scotiabank Mexico
5. BBVA Bancomer Mexico
6. Gruma Mexico
7. Supermercados S-MART
8. Grupo Vidanta
9. Liverpool
10. Nextel de Mexico

Source: *Great Place to Work Institute Inc.*, Best Places to Work in Mexico (annual), 2011.

1850 ■ BEST MEDIUM-SIZED COMPANIES TO WORK FOR IN MEXICO, 2012

Ranked by: Score based on the relationships between employees and management, employees and their jobs/company, and employees and coworkers. **Remarks:** Specific scores not provided. Ranking covers companies with 500 to 5,000 employees. **Number listed:** 100

1. Plantronics Mexico
2. DJ Orthopedics de Mexico
3. Diageo Mexico
4. Terra Mexico
5. Cisco
6. Infonavit
7. FedEx Express
8. Mayan Resorts Riviera Maya
9. S. C. Johnson & Son Mexico
10. Central

Source: *Great Place to Work Institute Inc.*, Best Places to Work in Mexico (annual), 2011.

1851 ■ BEST SMALL COMPANIES TO WORK FOR IN MEXICO, 2012

Ranked by: Score based on the relationships between employees and management, employees and their jobs/company, and employees and coworkers. **Remarks:** Specific scores not provided. Ranking covers companies with 50 to 500 employees. **Number listed:** 60

1. Human Kind
2. CONTPAQ i
3. Interproteccion, Agente de Seguros y de Fianzas
4. Christus Muguerza Hospital Sur
5. Mayan Resorts Puerto Penasco
6. Grupo Prom
7. Mayan Resorts Los Cabos
8. Nearsoft
9. CompuSoluciones
10. Gasored

Source: *Great Place to Work Institute Inc.*, Best Places to Work in Mexico (annual), 2011.

1852 ■ LARGEST CORPORATIONS IN MEXICO BY REVENUE, 2010

Ranked by: Revenue, in millions of U.S. dollars. **Remarks:** Also notes headquarters city and overall rank in the *Global 500*. Ranking is available online only, not in print. **Number listed:** 3

1. Petroleos Mexicanos (PEMEX), with $101,506 million
2. America Movil, SA de CV, $48,127
3. Comision Federal de Electricidad (CFE), $20,143

Source: *Fortune*, Global 500 (annual), http://www.fortune.com, July 25, 2011.

1853 ■ MEXICO'S LARGEST COMPANIES OVERALL, 2011

Ranked by: Score based on revenue, profits, assets, and market capitalization. **Remarks:** Specific scores not provided. Also notes rank in the overall *Forbes 2000* and figures for each criterion. **Number listed:** 15

1. America Movil, SA de CV
2. Fomento Economico Mexicano, SA de CV (FEMSA)
3. Grupo Mexico, SA de CV
4. Grupo Financiero Banorte, SAB de CV (GFNorte)
5. Grupo Elektra, SA de CV
6. Grupo Modelo, SA de CV
7. Industrias Penoles, SAB de CV
8. Cemex, SA de CV
9. Grupo Financiero Inbursa, SAB de CV
10. Grupo Bimbo, SAB de CV

Source: *Forbes*, Forbes 2000 (annual), http://www.forbes.com, May 7, 2012.

1854 ■ MOST ADMIRED COMPANIES IN MEXICO, 2012

Ranked by: Score based on a survey of executives, directors, and securities analysts of companies within their own industry. **Remarks:** List is available online only, not in print. Also notes headquarters. **Number listed:** 2

1. America Movil, with 6 points
2. FEMSA, 5.55

Source: *Fortune*, World's Most Admired Companies (annual), http://www.fortune.com, March 19, 2012.

Corporations—Michigan

1855 ■ DETROIT'S FASTEST-GROWING COMPANIES, 2009-2010

Ranked by: Annual revenue growth, in percent. **Remarks:** Also notes contact information, top executive, revenue for each year, and reason for increase. **Number listed:** 20

1. Lakeshore TolTest Corp., with 149.6%
2. Chrysler Group LLC, 136.8%
3. Vision Information Technologies Inc., 127.7%
4. Aristeo Construction Co., 100%
5. Rapid Global Business Solutions Inc., 91.9%
6. Amerigon Inc., 84.5%
7. Trillacorpe/Bk LLC, 83.9%
8. Global Automotive Alliance LLC, 75.2%
9. Benlee Inc., 68%
10. MPS Trading LLC, 67.1%

Source: *Crain's Detroit Business*, Book of Lists (annual), December 26, 2011, p. 25.

1856 ■ DETROIT'S LARGEST PRIVATE COMPANIES, 2010

Ranked by: Revenue, in millions of dollars. **Remarks:** Also notes contact information, top executives, figures for previous year, percent change, number of employees locally and worldwide, and type of business. **Number listed:** 200

1. Chrysler Group LLC, with $41,946 million
2. Penske Corp., $18,125
3. Guardian Automotive Products Inc., $5,000
4. IAC Group, $3,700
5. TI Automotive Ltd., $2,500
6. Ilitch Companies, $2,200
7. Affinia Group Inc., $1,991
8. Plastipak Holdings Inc., $1,941.8
9. Soave Enterprises LLC, $1,734
10. Atlas Oil Co., $1,614.8

Source: *Crain's Detroit Business*, Book of Lists (annual), December 26, 2011, p. 11+.

1857 ■ DETROIT'S LARGEST PUBLICLY HELD COMPANIES, 2010

Ranked by: Revenue, in millions of dollars. **Remarks:** Also notes fiscal year end, contact information, top executives, figures for previous year, percent change, net income, stock exchange, ticker symbol, high and low stock prices, and type of industry. **Number listed:** 35

1. General Motors Co., with $135,600 million
2. Ford Motor Co., $128,954
3. TRW Automotive Holding Corp., $14,400
4. Delphi Automotive plc, $13,817
5. Lear Corp., $11,954.6
6. Penske Automotive Group Inc., $10,713.6
7. DTE Energy Co., $8,557
8. Masco Corp., $7,592
9. Visteon Corp., $7,466
10. Federal-Mogul Corp., $6,219

Source: *Crain's Detroit Business*, Book of Lists (annual), December 26, 2011, p. 22.

1858 ■ FASTEST-GROWING COMPANIES IN MICHIGAN, 2008-2011

Ranked by: Score based on three-year growth in revenue and earnings, and three-year total return to investors. **Remarks:** Specific scores not provided. To qualify for list, companies must have revenues of at least $50 million, net income of at least $10 million, market capitalization of at least $250 million, and stock price of at least $5. Int'l companies are eligible if they trade on a U.S. exchange and file quarterly reports. **Number listed:** 2

1. Credit Acceptance Corp.
2. Perrigo Co.

Source: *Fortune*, 100 Fastest-Growing Companies (annual), http://www.fortune.com, September 26, 2011.

1859 ■ LARGEST COMPANIES IN MICHIGAN BY EMPLOYEES, 2010

Ranked by: Number of employees at headquarters. **Remarks:** Also notes contact information for headquarters, total number of employees, revenue, rank by revenue, and primary SIC code. **Number listed:** 384

1. Chrysler Group LLC, with 10,000 employees
1. General Motors LLC, 10,000
3. DPH-DAS LLC, 9,300
4. Alticor Inc., 5,000
5. Eagle Ottawa LLC, 4,203
6. St. Joseph Mercy Oakland Foundation, 4,000
7. Suntree-Oxford Associated Ltd., Dividend Housing Association, 3,900
8. Employees Only Inc., 3,500
8. Oakwood Healthcare Inc., 3,500
10. AutoAlliance Management Co., 3,200

Source: *Business Rankings*, (annual), Dun & Bradstreet Inc., 2011, p. IV.109-IV.117.

1860 ■ LARGEST COMPANIES IN MICHIGAN BY SALES, 2010

Ranked by: Revenue, in dollars. **Remarks:** Also notes contact information for headquarters, number of employees at headquarters and overall, rank by employees, and primary SIC code. **Number listed:** 186

1. General Motors Co., with $135,592,000,000
2. Ford Motor Co., $128,954,000,000
3. Dow Chemical Co., $53,674,000,000
4. Whirlpool Corp., $18,366,000,000
5. DPH Holdings Corp., $18,060,000,000
6. TRW Automotive Holdings Corp., $14,383,000,000
7. Kellogg Co., $12,397,000,000
8. Lear Corp., $11,954,600,000
9. Penske Automotive Group Inc., $10,713,585,000
10. DTE Energy Co., $8,557,000,000

Source: *Business Rankings*, (annual), Dun & Bradstreet Inc., 2011, p. III.109-III.117.

1861 ■ LARGEST EMPLOYERS IN METRO DETROIT, 2011

Ranked by: Number of employees in metropolitan Detroit. **Remarks:** Also notes contact information, top local executives, worldwide employee, figures for previous year, and type of business. **Number listed:** 25

1. Ford Motor Co., with 38,000 employees
2. University of Michigan, 27,754
3. General Motors Co., 24,867
4. Chrysler Group LLC, 21,927
5. Henry Ford Health System, 19,951
6. U.S. government, 18,900
7. Trinity Health, 13,123
8. St. John Providence Health System, 13,004
9. Beaumont Health System, 12,437
10. Detroit Medical Center, 12,121

Source: *Crain's Detroit Business*, Book of Lists (annual), December 26, 2011, p. 33.

1862 ■ MICHIGAN'S BEST COMPANIES TO WORK FOR, 2012

Ranked by: Score based on employee surveys as well as evaluation of companies' credibility, respect, fairness, and pride/camaraderie. **Remarks:** Specific scores not provided; companies are listed alphabetically, not ranked. Available online only, not in print. **Number listed:** 3

1. Plante & Moran LLP
2. Quicken Loans Inc.
3. Stryker Corp.

Source: *Fortune*, 100 Best Companies to Work For (annual), http://www.fortune.com, February 6, 2012.

1863 ■ MICHIGAN'S LARGEST COMPANIES OVERALL, 2011

Ranked by: Score based on revenue, profits, assets, and market capitalization. **Remarks:** Specific scores not provided. Also notes overall rank in the *Forbes 2000* and figures for each criterion. **Number listed:** 13

1. Ford Motor Co.
2. General Motors Co.
3. Dow Chemical Co.
4. Kellogg Co.
5. Stryker Corp.
6. DTE Energy Co.
7. TRW Automotive Holdings Corp.
8. Whirlpool Corp.
9. BorgWarner Inc.
10. CMS Energy Corp.

Source: *Forbes*, Forbes 2000 (annual), http://www.forbes.com, May 7, 2012.

1864 ■ MICHIGAN'S LARGEST PRIVATE COMPANIES, 2010

Ranked by: Revenue, in billions of dollars. **Remarks:** Also notes business segment, number of employees, and overall rank in the *America's Largest Private Companies* list. Ranking is available online only, not in print. **Number listed:** 5

1. Meijer Inc., with $14.63 billion
2. Amway Corp., $9.2
3. Gordon Food Service Inc., $7.7
4. Guardian Industries Corp., $4.9
5. International Automotive Components Group North America LLC, $3.7

Source: *Forbes*, America's Largest Private Companies (annual), http://www.forbes.com, December 5, 2011.

1865 ■ MOST ADMIRED COMPANIES IN MICHIGAN, 2012

Ranked by: Survey of top executives, directors, and securities analysts regarding the Fortune 1,000 companies that they admire the most, regardless of industry. **Remarks:** Specific scores not provided. Also notes city and industry rank. List is available online only, not in print. **Number listed:** 8

1. Stryker Corp., with 7.02 points
2. Whirlpool Corp., 6.46
3. Kellogg Co., 6.26
4. Steelcase, 5.95
5. Ford Motor Co., 5.88
6. General Motors Co., 5.86
7. Dow Chemical Co., 5.67
8. Spartan Stores, 5.66

Source: *Fortune*, World's Most Admired Companies (annual), http://www.fortune.com, March 19, 2012.

1866 ■ TOP *FORTUNE 500* COMPANIES IN MICHIGAN, 2011

Ranked by: Revenue, in millions of dollars. **Remarks:** Also notes overall rank in the *Fortune 500,* headquarters, and number of employees. **Number listed:** 20

1. General Motors Co., with $150,276 million
2. Ford Motor Co., $136,264
3. Dow Chemical Co., $59,985
4. Whirlpool Corp., $18,666
5. TRW Automotive Holdings Corp., $16,244
6. Lear Corp., $14,156.5
7. Ally Financial Inc., $13,642
8. Kellogg Co., $13,198
9. Penske Automotive Group Inc., $11,869.5
10. DTE Energy Co., $8,897

Source: *Fortune*, Fortune 500 (annual), May 21, 2012, p. F-43.

Corporations—Minnesota

1867 ■ BEST SMALL COMPANIES IN MINNESOTA, 2011

Ranked by: Score based on revenue, profits, and return on equity for the past 12 months and five years. **Remarks:** Specific scores not provided. Also notes rank in the overall *100 Best Small Companies in America*. To qualify, companies must have revenues between $5 million and $1 billion, a net margin above five percent, and share price above $5. List is available online only. **Number listed:** 6

1. Winmark
2. NVE
3. Capella Education
4. Buffalo Wild Wings
5. Hickory Tech
6. Hawkins

Source: *Forbes*, Best Small Companies in America (annual), November 7, 2011.

1868 ■ LARGEST COMPANIES IN MINNESOTA BY EMPLOYEES, 2010

Ranked by: Number of employees at headquarters. **Remarks:** Also notes contact information for headquarters, total number of employees, revenue, rank by revenue, and primary SIC code. **Number listed:** 193

1. Mayo Foundation for Medical Education & Research, with 29,186 employees
2. 3M Co., 10,000
3. Thomson Legal & Regulatory Inc., 8,000
3. West Publishing Corp., 8,000
5. Bethesda Healthy Rehabilitation Hospital, 6,700
6. St. Paul Fire & Marine Insurance Co., 6,347
7. St. Mary's Duluth Clinic Health System Hospice & Palliative Care, 6,000
8. Rosemount-Apple Valley & Eagan, 5,981
9. Avery Weigh-Tronix LLC, 5,288
10. Best Buy Purchasing LLC, 5,000

Source: *Business Rankings*, (annual), Dun & Bradstreet Inc., 2011, p. IV.118-IV.122.

1869 ■ LARGEST COMPANIES IN MINNESOTA BY SALES, 2010

Ranked by: Revenue, in dollars. **Remarks:** Also notes contact information for headquarters, number of employees at headquarters and overall, rank by employees, and primary SIC code. **Number listed:** 197

1. Target Corp., with $67,390,000,000
2. Best Buy Co., Inc., $49,694,000,000
3. SuperValu Inc., $40,597,000,000
4. 3M Co., $26,662,000,000
5. CHS Inc., $25,267,931,000
6. Medtronic Inc., $15,817,000,000
7. General Mills Inc., $14,796,500,000
8. Xcel Energy Inc., $10,310,947,000
9. C. H. Robinson Worldwide Inc., $9,274,305,000
10. Hormel Foods Corp., $7,220,719,000

Source: *Business Rankings*, (annual), Dun & Bradstreet Inc., 2011, p. III.118-III.122.

1870 ■ LARGEST EMPLOYERS IN MINNESOTA, 2011

Ranked by: Number of Minnesota employees. **Remarks:** Also notes contact information, year founded, headquarters, figures for previous year, number of employees worldwide, top executive, fiscal year-end, total revenue, and business description. **Number listed:** 25

1. State of Minnesota, with 55,668 employees
2. Mayo Clinic, 38,626
3. U.S. federal government, 34,000
4. Target Corp., 30,525
5. University of Minnesota, 25,307
6. Allina Hospitals & Clinics, 23,302
7. Wal-Mart Stores Inc., 20,434
8. Fairview Health Services, 20,178
9. Wells Fargo Minnesota, 20,000
10. 3M Co., 15,000

Source: *Twin Cities Business*, The BIG Book (annual), http://www.tcbmag.com, 2012.

1871 ■ LARGEST PRIVATE COMPANIES BASED IN MINNESOTA, 2011

Ranked by: Revenue, in dollars. **Remarks:** Also notes contact information, year founded, headquarters, figures for previous year, number of employees, key executives, and nature of business. **Number listed:** 25

1. Cargill Inc., with $119,500,000,000
2. Thrivent Financial for Lutherans, $7,533,000,000
3. Carlson Cos., Inc., $4,130,000,000
4. Schwan Food Co., $3,670,000,000
5. Holiday Cos., $3,630,000,000
6. Securian Financial Group Inc., $3,100,000,000
7. Rosen's Diversified Inc., $2,500,000,000
8. Mortenson Construction, $2,459,000,000
9. Andersen Corp., $2,160,000,000
10. AgriBank FCB, $1,654,321,000

Source: *Twin Cities Business*, The BIG Book (annual), http://www.tcbmag.com, 2012.

1872 ■ LARGEST PUBLIC COMPANIES BASED IN THE TWIN CITIES, 2011

Ranked by: Revenue, in thousands of dollars. **Remarks:** Also notes contact information, year founded, number of employees, figures for previous year, percent change, basic earnings, assets, ticker symbol, high and low stock prices, and key executives. **Number listed:** 100

1. UnitedHealth Group Inc., with $94,160,000 thousand
2. Target Corp., $67,390,000
3. Best Buy Co., Inc., $50,300,000
4. SuperValu Inc., $37,534,000
5. 3M Co., $26,662,000
6. U.S. Bancorp, $18,148,000
7. Medtronic Inc., $15,933,000
8. General Mills Inc., $14,880,200
9. Xcel Energy Inc., $10,310,947
10. The Mosaic Co., $9,937,800

Source: *Twin Cities Business*, The BIG Book (annual), http://www.tcbmag.com, 2012.

1873 ■ MINNESOTA'S BEST COMPANIES TO WORK FOR, 2012

Ranked by: Score based on employee surveys as well as evaluation of companies' credibility, respect, fairness, and pride/camaraderie. **Remarks:** Specific scores not provided; companies are listed alphabetically, not ranked. Available online only, not in print. **Number listed:** 3

1. Allianz Life Insurance
2. General Mills Inc.
3. Mayo Clinic

Source: *Fortune*, 100 Best Companies to Work For (annual), http://www.fortune.com, February 6, 2012.

1874 ■ MINNESOTA'S LARGEST COMPANIES OVERALL, 2011

Ranked by: Score based on revenue, profits, assets, and market capitalization. **Remarks:** Specific scores not provided. Also notes overall rank in the *Forbes 2000* and figures for each criterion. **Number listed:** 16

1. UnitedHealth Group Inc.
2. U.S. Bancorp
3. Target Corp.
4. 3M Co.
5. Medtronic Inc.

6. General Mills Inc.
7. Ameriprise Financial Inc.
8. The Mosaic Co.
9. Best Buy Co., Inc.
10. Xcel Energy Inc.

Source: *Forbes*, Forbes 2000 (annual), http://www.forbes.com, May 7, 2012.

1875 ■ MINNESOTA'S LARGEST PRIVATE COMPANIES, 2010

Ranked by: Revenue, in billions of dollars. **Remarks:** Also notes business segment, number of employees, and overall rank in the *America's Largest Private Companies* list. Ranking is available online only, not in print. **Number listed:** 7

1. Cargill Inc., with $109.56 billion
2. Carlson Cos., Inc., $4.13
3. Schwan Food Co., $3.67
4. Holiday Cos., $3.63
5. Rosen's Diversified Inc., $2.66
6. M. A. Mortenson Co., $2.46
7. Andersen Corp., $2.16

Source: *Forbes*, America's Largest Private Companies (annual), http://www.forbes.com, December 5, 2011.

1876 ■ MINNESOTA'S LARGEST PUBLICLY-HELD COMPANIES BY ASSETS, 2011

Ranked by: Assets, in millions of dollars. **Remarks:** Also notes rank for previous year, ticker symbol, fiscal year-end, profits, revenue, market capitalization, employment, annual growth in each, and returns on equity, assets, and revenue. **Number listed:** 100

1. U.S. Bancorp, with $340,122 million
2. Ameriprise Financial Inc., $133,986
3. UnitedHealth Group Inc., $67,889
4. Target Corp., $46,630
5. Medtronic Inc., $31,911
6. 3M Co., $31,616
7. Xcel Energy Inc., $29,497.3
8. General Mills Inc., $21,466.8
9. TCF Financial Corp., $18,979.4
10. Ecolab Inc., $18,240.8

Source: *Star Tribune*, Star Tribune 100 (annual), http://www.startribune.com, May 6, 2012.

1877 ■ MINNESOTA'S LARGEST PUBLICLY-HELD COMPANIES BY EMPLOYEES, 2012

Ranked by: Number of employees. **Remarks:** Also notes ticker symbol, figures for previous year, and percent change. **Number listed:** 100

1. Target Corp., with 365,000 employees
2. Best Buy Co., Inc., 167,000
3. SuperValu Inc., 135,000
4. UnitedHealth Group Inc., 99,000
5. 3M Co., 84,000
6. U.S. Bancorp, 64,000
7. Regis Corp., 54,000
8. Medtronic Inc., 45,000
9. Ecolab Inc., 40,200

10. General Mills Inc., 35,000

Source: *Star Tribune*, Star Tribune 100 (annual), http://www.startribune.com, May 6, 2012.

1878 ■ MINNESOTA'S LARGEST PUBLICLY-HELD COMPANIES BY MARKET VALUE, 2011

Ranked by: Market capitalization, in millions of dollars. **Remarks:** Also notes rank for previous year, ticker symbol, fiscal year-end, profits, assets, revenue, employment, annual growth in each, and returns on equity, assets, and revenue. **Number listed:** 100

1. UnitedHealth Group Inc., with $60,660.2 million
2. 3M Co., $59,515.5
3. U.S. Bancorp, $59,047.7
4. Medtronic Inc., $39,032.6
5. Target Corp., $38,391.2
6. General Mills Inc., $25,050.9
7. The Mosaic Co., $21,372.7
8. Ecolab Inc., $17,978.3
9. Fastenal Co., $14,406.7
10. Xcel Energy Inc., $12,667.3

Source: *Star Tribune*, Star Tribune 100 (annual), http://www.startribune.com, May 6, 2012.

1879 ■ MINNESOTA'S LARGEST PUBLICLY-HELD COMPANIES BY PROFITS, 2011

Ranked by: Profits, in millions of dollars. **Remarks:** Also notes rank for previous year, ticker symbol, fiscal year-end, revenue, assets, market capitalization, employment, annual growth in each, and returns on equity, assets, and revenue. **Number listed:** 100

1. UnitedHealth Group Inc., with $5,142 million
2. U.S. Bancorp, $4,872
3. 3M Co., $4,283
4. Medtronic Inc., $3,597
5. Target Corp., $3,018
6. The Mosaic Co., $2,340.9
7. General Mills Inc., $1,564.1
8. Best Buy Co., Inc., $1,432
9. Ameriprise Financial Inc., $1,232
10. Xcel Energy Inc., $841.4

Source: *Star Tribune*, Star Tribune 100 (annual), http://www.startribune.com, May 6, 2012.

1880 ■ MINNESOTA'S LARGEST PUBLICLY-HELD COMPANIES BY REVENUE, 2011

Ranked by: Revenue, in millions of dollars. **Remarks:** Also notes rank for previous year, ticker symbol, fiscal year-end, profits, assets, market capitalization, employment, annual growth in each, and returns on equity, assets, and revenue. **Number listed:** 100

1. UnitedHealth Group Inc., with $101,862 million
2. Target Corp., $69,865
3. Best Buy Co., Inc., $50,705
4. SuperValu Inc., $36,529
5. 3M Co., $29,611
6. U.S. Bancorp, $19,108
7. Medtronic Inc., $16,506
8. General Mills Inc., $15,751.9
9. The Mosaic Co., $11,172.5
10. Xcel Energy Inc., $10,654.8

Source: *Star Tribune*, Star Tribune 100 (annual), http://www.startribune.com, May 6, 2012.

1881 ■ MOST ADMIRED COMPANIES IN MINNESOTA, 2012

Ranked by: Survey of top executives, directors, and securities analysts regarding the Fortune 1,000 companies that they admire the most, regardless of industry. **Remarks:** Also notes city and industry rank. List is available online only, not in print. **Number listed:** 8

1. Target Corp., with 7.2 points
2. UnitedHealth Group Inc., 7.15
3. U.S. Bancorp, 7.12
4. St. Jude Medical Inc., 7.02
5. Medtronic, 6.5
6. C. H. Robinson Worldwide Inc., 6.42
7. General Mills Inc., 6.24
8. 3M Co., n/a

Source: *Fortune*, World's Most Admired Companies (annual), http://www.fortune.com, March 19, 2012.

1882 ■ TOP *FORTUNE 500* COMPANIES IN MINNESOTA, 2011

Ranked by: Revenue, in millions of dollars. **Remarks:** Also notes overall rank in the *Fortune 500,* headquarters, and number of employees. **Number listed:** 19

1. UnitedHealth Group Inc., with $101,862 million
2. Target Corp., $69,865
3. Best Buy Co., Inc., $50,272
4. SuperValu Inc., $37,534
5. CHS Inc., $36,915.8
6. 3M Co., $29,611
7. U.S. Bancorp, $21,399
8. Medtronic Inc., $15,933
9. General Mills Inc., $14,880.2
10. Land O'Lakes Inc., $12,849.3

Source: *Fortune*, Fortune 500 (annual), May 21, 2012, p. F-44.

1883 ■ TOP LARGE COMPANIES TO WORK FOR IN MINNESOTA, 2012

Ranked by: Score based on surveys. **Remarks:** Specific scores not provided; companies are listed alphabetically, not ranked. Also notes website, industry, and number of Minnesota employees. **Number listed:** 11

1. Accenture Ltd.
2. American Engineering Testing Inc.
3. Amerilab Technologies Inc.
4. Loffler Cos.
5. Mall of America
6. Merchant & Gould
7. Minnesota Twins LLC/Twins Ballpark LLC
8. Reliable Property Services
9. Space150
10. The Nerdery

Source: *Minnesota Business*, 100 Best Companies to Work For (annual), June 2012, p. 49.

1884 ■ TOP MIDSIZED COMPANIES TO WORK FOR IN MINNESOTA, 2012

Ranked by: Score based on surveys. **Remarks:** Specific scores not provided; companies are listed alphabetically, not ranked. Also notes website, industry, and number of Minnesota employees. **Number listed:** 36

1. Abetech
2. Apex Print Technologies LLC
3. Bassford Remele
4. Biomedix
5. Bowman Tool & Machining
6. Brenny Transportation Inc.
7. Broadhead
8. Certes Financial Pros
9. David Martin Agency Inc.
10. Duluth Entertainment Convention Center

Source: *Minnesota Business*, 100 Best Companies to Work For (annual), June 2012, p. 46-49.

1885 ■ TOP SMALL COMPANIES TO WORK FOR IN MINNESOTA, 2012

Ranked by: Score based on surveys. **Remarks:** Specific scores not provided; companies are listed alphabetically, not ranked. Also notes website, industry, and number of Minnesota employees. **Number listed:** 37

1. A & K Material Handling Systems
2. ACoupleOfGurus
3. Advantage Billing Concepts Inc.
4. The Bailey Group
5. Ciceron
6. Crossroads Properties
7. Deerwood Technologies Inc.
8. Dynamic Solutions Group, the Fax Guys
9. Ergodyne
10. Evantage Consulting

Source: *Minnesota Business*, 100 Best Companies to Work For (annual), June 2012, p. 44-46.

Corporations—Mississippi

1886 ■ LARGEST COMPANIES IN MISSISSIPPI BY EMPLOYEES, 2010

Ranked by: Number of employees at headquarters. **Remarks:** Also notes contact information for headquarters, total number of employees, revenue, rank by revenue, and primary SIC code. **Number listed:** 78

1. North Mississippi Health Services Inc., with 4,000 employees
2. North Mississippi Medical Center Inc., 3,944
3. Forrest County General Hospital, 3,130
4. B. L. Development Corp., 3,000
4. Robinson Property Group LP, 3,000
6. Mississippi Baptist Health Systems Inc., 2,800
7. Gulfport Memorial Hospital EMR, 2,400
8. St. Dominic-Jackson Memorial Hospital, 2,200
9. Rush Health Systems Inc., 1,980
10. Memorial Hospial Auxiliary Inc., 1,850

Source: *Business Rankings*, (annual), Dun & Bradstreet Inc., 2011, p. IV.123-IV.124.

1887 ■ LARGEST COMPANIES IN MISSISSIPPI BY SALES, 2010

Ranked by: Revenue, in dollars. **Remarks:** Also notes contact information for headquarters, number of employees at headquarters and overall, rank by employees, and primary SIC code. **Number listed:** 79

1. Sanderson Farms Inc., with $1,925,445,000
2. Yates Cos., Inc., $1,317,462,000
3. McLane/Southern Inc., $1,281,105,192
4. Entergy Mississippi Inc., $1,230,185,000
5. CLC of Biloxi LLC, $1,169,241,500
6. Mississippi Power Co., $1,143,068,000
7. Sanderson Farms Inc. (Processing), $1,000,000,000
8. W. G. Yates & Sons Construction Co., $968,152,000
9. Cal-Maine Foods Inc., $910,143,000
10. Waverley Group Inc., $836,597,900

Source: *Business Rankings*, (annual), Dun & Bradstreet Inc., 2011, p. III.123-III.124.

Corporations—Missouri

1888 ■ FASTEST-GROWING COMPANIES IN MISSOURI, 2008-2011

Ranked by: Score based on three-year growth in revenue and earnings, and three-year total return to investors. **Remarks:** Specific scores not provided. To qualify for list, companies must have revenues of at least $50 million, net income of at least $10 million, market capitalization of at least $250 million, and stock price of at least $5. Int'l companies are eligible if they trade on a U.S. exchange and file quarterly reports. **Number listed:** 2

1. O'Reilly Automotive Inc.
2. Insituform Technologies

Source: *Fortune*, 100 Fastest-Growing Companies (annual), http://www.fortune.com, September 26, 2011.

1889 ■ LARGEST COMPANIES IN MISSOURI BY EMPLOYEES, 2010

Ranked by: Number of employees at headquarters. **Remarks:** Also notes contact information for headquarters, total number of employees, revenue, rank by revenue, and primary SIC code. **Number listed:** 193

1. Cox Health Systems, with 6,000 employees
1. HCA Midwest, 6,000
3. Barnes Hospital, 5,358
4. University Physicians Hospital , 5,000
4. Wells Fargo Advisors LLC, 5,000
6. St. John's Mercy Health System, 4,541
7. St. John's Health System Inc., 4,000
7. St. John's Regional Health Center, 4,000
9. Union Electric Development Corp., 3,200
10. North Kansas City Hospital, 3,100

Source: *Business Rankings*, (annual), Dun & Bradstreet Inc., 2011, p. IV.125-IV.129.

1890 ■ LARGEST COMPANIES IN MISSOURI BY SALES, 2010

Ranked by: Revenue, in dollars. **Remarks:** Also notes contact information for headquarters, number of employees at headquarters and overall, rank by employees, and primary SIC code. **Number listed:** 197

1. Express Scripts Inc., with $44,973,200,000
2. Emerson Electric Co., $21,039,000,000
3. Ascension Health Inc., $14,773,336,000

4. Dairy Farmers of America Inc., $12,000,000,000

5. Monsanto Co., $10,502,000,000

6. Ameren Corp., $7,638,000,000

7. Charter Communications Inc., $7,059,000,000

8. Peabody Energy Corp., $6,860,000,000

9. Charter Communications Holdings LLC, $6,479,000,000

10. National Beef Packing Co., $5,807,929,000

Source: *Business Rankings*, (annual), Dun & Bradstreet Inc., 2011, p. III.125-III.129.

1891 ■ MISSOURI'S BEST COMPANIES TO WORK FOR, 2012

Ranked by: Score based on employee surveys as well as evaluation of companies' credibility, respect, fairness, and pride/camaraderie. Remarks: Specific scores not provided; companies are listed alphabetically, not ranked. Available online only, not in print. Number listed: 5

1. Build-A-Bear Workshop Inc.

2. Burns & McDonnell

3. Edward Jones

4. Scottrade Inc.

5. World Wide Technology

Source: *Fortune*, 100 Best Companies to Work For (annual), http://www.fortune.com, February 6, 2012.

1892 ■ MISSOURI'S LARGEST COMPANIES OVERALL, 2011

Ranked by: Score based on revenue, profits, assets, and market capitalization. Remarks: Specific scores not provided. Also notes overall rank in the *Forbes 2000* and figures for each criterion. Number listed: 12

1. Emerson Electric Co.

2. Express Scripts Inc.

3. Monsanto Co.

4. Peabody Energy Corp.

5. Ameren Corp.

6. Reinsurance Group of America Inc.

7. O'Reilly Automotive Inc.

8. Charter Communications Inc.

9. Sigma-Aldrich Corp.

10. Cerner Corp.

Source: *Forbes*, Forbes 2000 (annual), http://www.forbes.com, May 7, 2012.

1893 ■ MISSOURI'S LARGEST PRIVATE COMPANIES, 2010

Ranked by: Revenue, in billions of dollars. Remarks: Also notes business segment, number of employees, and overall rank in the *America's Largest Private Companies* list. Ranking is available online only, not in print. Number listed: 10

1. Enterprise Rent-A-Car Co., with $14.1 billion

2. Graybar Electric Co., Inc., $4.62

3. Apex Oil Co., $4.26

4. Edward Jones, $4.16

5. Bass Pro Shops Inc., $3.83

6. Hallmark Cards Inc., $3.81

7. World Wide Technology Inc., $3

8. Schnuck Markets Inc., $2.6

9. McCarthy Holdings Inc., $2.45

10. AMC Entertainment Inc., $2.42

Source: *Forbes*, America's Largest Private Companies (annual), http://www.forbes.com, December 5, 2011.

1894 ■ MOST ADMIRED COMPANIES IN MISSOURI, 2012

Ranked by: Survey of top executives, directors, and securities analysts regarding the Fortune 1,000 companies that they admire the most, regardless of industry. Remarks: Also notes city and industry rank. List is available online only, not in print. Number listed: 5

1. Express Scripts Inc., with 6.65 points

2. Graybar Electric Co., Inc., 6.33

3. Cerner Corp., 5.67

4. Emerson Electric Co., 5.56

5. Jones Financial, 5.47

Source: *Fortune*, World's Most Admired Companies (annual), http://www.fortune.com, March 19, 2012.

1895 ■ TOP *FORTUNE 500* COMPANIES IN MISSOURI, 2011

Ranked by: Revenue, in millions of dollars. Remarks: Also notes overall rank in the *Fortune 500*, headquarters, and number of employees. Number listed: 10

1. Express Scripts Holding, with $46,128.3 million

2. Emerson Electric Co., $24,234

3. Monsanto Co., $11,822

4. Reinsurance Group of America Inc., $8,829.5

5. Peabody Energy Corp., $8,096

6. Ameren Corp., $7,531

7. Charter Communications Inc., $7,204

8. O'Reilly Automotive Inc., $5,788.8

9. Graybar Electric Co., Inc., $5,374.8

10. Centene Corp., $5,340.6

Source: *Fortune*, Fortune 500 (annual), May 21, 2012, p. F-44.

Corporations—Montana

1896 ■ LARGEST COMPANIES IN MONTANA BY EMPLOYEES, 2010

Ranked by: Number of employees at headquarters. Remarks: Also notes contact information for headquarters, total number of employees, revenue, rank by revenue, and primary SIC code. Number listed: 50

1. Billings Clinic, with 3,000 employees

2. Benefis Healthcare System, 1,672

3. St. Patrick Hospital & Health Sciences Center, 1,600

4. St. Vincent Healthcare Foundation Inc., 1,407

5. St. Patrick Hospital Corp., 1,341

6. Nightingale Nursing Service, 1,000

7. St. Peters Hospital, 800

8. Clark Fork Organics LLC, 723

9. Watkins & Shepard Trucking Inc., 666

10. Bozeman Deaconess Health Services, 661

Source: *Business Rankings*, (annual), Dun & Bradstreet Inc., 2011, p. IV.130-IV.131.

1897 ■ LARGEST COMPANIES IN MONTANA BY SALES, 2010

Ranked by: Revenue, in dollars. **Remarks:** Also notes contact information for headquarters, number of employees at headquarters and overall, rank by employees, and primary SIC code. **Number listed:** 50

1. CityServiceValcon LLC, with $625,064,168
2. Stillwater Mining Co., $555,878,000
3. Billings Clinic, $494,500,654
4. Cooney Convalescent Home, $455,124,900
5. Tobacco Root Mountains Care Center, $395,511,900
6. Sports Inc., $363,200,163
7. Sletten Inc., $247,282,805
8. Benefis Healthcare System, $243,537,249
9. Pacific Hide & Fur Depot Corp., $241,446,286
10. St. Patrick Hospital Corp., $191,572,725

Source: *Business Rankings*, (annual), Dun & Bradstreet Inc., 2011, p. III.130-III.131.

Corporations—Morocco

1898 ■ MOROCCO'S LARGEST COMPANIES OVERALL, 2011

Ranked by: Score based on revenue, profits, assets, and market capitalization. **Remarks:** Specific scores not provided. Also notes rank in the overall *Forbes 2000* and figures for each criterion. **Number listed:** 2

1. Attijariwafa Bank
2. Banque Centrale Populaire

Source: *Forbes*, Forbes 2000 (annual), http://www.forbes.com, May 7, 2012.

Corporations—Nebraska

1899 ■ BEST SMALL COMPANIES IN NEBRASKA, 2011

Ranked by: Score based on revenue, profits, and return on equity for the past 12 months and five years. **Remarks:** Specific scores not provided. Also notes rank in the overall *100 Best Small Companies in America*. To qualify, companies must have revenues between $5 million and $1 billion, a net margin above five percent, and share price above $5. List is available online only. **Number listed:** 2

1. Buckle
2. Lindsay

Source: *Forbes*, Best Small Companies in America (annual), November 7, 2011.

1900 ■ LARGEST COMPANIES IN NEBRASKA BY EMPLOYEES, 2010

Ranked by: Number of employees at headquarters. **Remarks:** Also notes contact information for headquarters, total number of employees, revenue, rank by revenue, and primary SIC code. **Number listed:** 79

1. Drivers Management LLC, with 9,500 employees
2. Valmont Industries Inc., 6,029
3. Mutual of Omaha Insurance Co., 4,200
4. Nebraska Medical Center, 4,100
5. First Data Resources Inc., 4,000
6. Bryanlgh Medical Center, 3,800
7. Leo A. Daly/Burns & McConnell JV, 3,000
8. Archbishop Bergan Mercy Hospital, 2,500
9. Kiewit Offshore Services Ltd., 2,368
10. Alegent Health-Immanuel Medical Center, 2,000
10. Cabela's Inc., 2,000

Source: *Business Rankings*, (annual), Dun & Bradstreet Inc., 2011, p. IV.132-IV.133.

1901 ■ LARGEST COMPANIES IN NEBRASKA BY SALES, 2010

Ranked by: Revenue, in dollars. **Remarks:** Also notes contact information for headquarters, number of employees at headquarters and overall, rank by employees, and primary SIC code. **Number listed:** 80

1. Union Pacific Corp., with $16,965,000,000
2. ConAgra Foods Inc., $12,079,400,000
3. Peter Kiewit Sons' Inc., $9,985,000,000
4. Kiewit Corp., $9,973,000,000
5. Kiewit Infrastructure Co., $3,162,370,000
6. Cabela's Inc., $2,663,242,000
7. West Corp., $2,388,211,000
8. Green Plains Renewable Energy Inc., $2,132,968,000
9. Valmont Industries Inc., $1,975,505,000
10. Werner Enterprises Inc., $1,815,020,000

Source: *Business Rankings*, (annual), Dun & Bradstreet Inc., 2011, p. III.132-III.133.

1902 ■ MOST ADMIRED COMPANIES IN NEBRASKA, 2012

Ranked by: Survey of top executives, directors, and securities analysts regarding the Fortune 1,000 companies that they admire the most, regardless of industry. **Remarks:** Also notes city and industry rank. List is available online only, not in print. **Number listed:** 4

1. Berkshire Hathaway Inc., with 7.34 points
2. Union Pacific Corp., 6.60
3. Peter Kiewit Sons', 6.54
4. TD Ameritrade, 5.71

Source: *Fortune*, World's Most Admired Companies (annual), http://www.fortune.com, March 19, 2012.

1903 ■ NEBRASKA'S LARGEST COMPANIES OVERALL, 2011

Ranked by: Score based on revenue, profits, assets, and market capitalization. **Remarks:** Specific scores not provided. Also notes overall rank in the *Forbes 2000* and figures for each criterion. **Number listed:** 5

1. Berkshire Hathaway Inc.
2. Union Pacific Corp.
3. ConAgra Foods Inc.
4. TD Ameritrade Holding Corp.
5. Nelnet Inc.

Source: *Forbes*, Forbes 2000 (annual), http://www.forbes.com, May 7, 2012.

1904 ■ NEBRASKA'S LARGEST PRIVATE COMPANIES, 2010

Ranked by: Revenue, in billions of dollars. **Remarks:** Also notes business segment, number of employees, and overall rank in the

America's Largest Private Companies list. Ranking is available online only, not in print. **Number listed:** 5

1. Gavilon Group LLC, with $12.6 billion
2. Tenaska Energy Inc., $9.95
3. Kiewit Corp., $9.94
4. The Scoular Co., $4.9
5. West Corp., $2.39

Source: *Forbes*, America's Largest Private Companies (annual), http://www.forbes.com, December 5, 2011.

1905 ■ TOP *FORTUNE 500* COMPANIES IN NEBRASKA, 2011

Ranked by: Revenue, in millions of dollars. **Remarks:** Also notes overall rank in the *Fortune 500,* headquarters, and number of employees. **Number listed:** 5

1. Berkshire Hathaway Inc., with $143,688 million
2. Union Pacific Corp., $19,557
3. ConAgra Foods Inc., $12,395.5
4. Peter Kiewit Sons' Inc., $10,381
5. Mutual of Omaha Insurance Co., $5,974.1

Source: *Fortune*, Fortune 500 (annual), May 21, 2012, p. F-44.

Corporations—Netherlands

1906 ■ LARGEST COMPANIES IN THE NETHERLANDS, 2010

Ranked by: Sales, in millions of U.S. dollars. **Remarks:** Also notes city; industrial code; percent change in sales; profits; profit as a percentage of sales, assets, and equity; number of employees; sales per employee; assets; equity capital; equity capital as a percentage of assets; year established; and figures for previous year. **Number listed:** 1000

1. Royal Dutch Shell plc, with $278,190 million
2. Vitol Holding BV, $191,165.4
3. Hewlett-Packard The Hague BV, $121,083.1
4. ING Groep NV, $68,030.4
5. Nokia Nederland BV, $65,005.1
6. Unilever NV, $59,224.8
7. European Aeronautic Defense & Space Co. (EADS), $55,461.4
8. Naamlooze Vennootschap Elma, $51,946.4
9. Louis Dreyfus Holding BV, $50,441.7
10. Trafigura Beheer BV, $47,269.4

Source: *Europe's 15,000 Largest Companies*, (annual), ELC International, 2011, p. 426+.

1907 ■ LARGEST CORPORATIONS IN THE NETHERLANDS BY REVENUE, 2010

Ranked by: Revenue, in millions of U.S. dollars. **Remarks:** Also notes headquarters city and overall rank in the *Global 500*. Ranking is available online only, not in print. **Number listed:** 12

1. Royal Dutch Shell plc, with $378,152 million
2. ING Groep NV, $147,052
3. AEGON NV, $65,136
4. European Aeronautic Defense & Space Co. (EADS), $60,597
5. LyondellBasell Industries, $41,151
6. Koninklijke Ahold NV (Royal Ahold NV), $39,111

7. Koninklijke Philips Electronics NV (Royal Philips Electronics NV), $33,667
8. Rabobank Group, $32,672
9. GasTerra BV, $24,313
10. Heineken Holding NV, $21,684

Source: *Fortune*, Global 500 (annual), http://www.fortune.com, July 25, 2011.

1908 ■ MOST ADMIRED COMPANIES IN THE NETHERLANDS, 2012

Ranked by: Score based on a survey of executives, directors, and securities analysts of companies within their own industry. **Remarks:** List is available online only, not in print. Also notes headquarters. **Number listed:** 4

1. Royal Dutch Shell plc, with 7.55 points
2. Randstad Holding, 6.15
3. Koninklijke Philips Electronics NV (Royal Philips Electronics NV), 5.53
4. Akzo Nobel NV, 4.99

Source: *Fortune*, World's Most Admired Companies (annual), http://www.fortune.com, March 19, 2012.

1909 ■ THE NETHERLANDS' LARGEST COMPANIES OVERALL, 2011

Ranked by: Score based on revenue, profits, assets, and market capitalization. **Remarks:** Specific scores not provided. Also notes rank in the overall *Forbes 2000* and figures for each criterion. **Number listed:** 24

1. Royal Dutch Shell plc
2. ING Groep NV
3. Unilever
4. Schlumberger Ltd.
5. European Aeronautic Defense & Space Co. (EADS)
6. LyondellBasell Industries NV
7. Koninklijke KPN NV (Royal KPN NV)
8. Koninklijke Ahold NV (Royal Ahold NV)
9. Heineken Holding NV
10. VimpelCom Ltd.

Source: *Forbes*, Forbes 2000 (annual), http://www.forbes.com, May 7, 2012.

Corporations—Nevada

1910 ■ LARGEST COMPANIES IN NEVADA BY EMPLOYEES, 2010

Ranked by: Number of employees at headquarters. **Remarks:** Also notes contact information for headquarters, total number of employees, revenue, rank by revenue, and primary SIC code. **Number listed:** 50

1. Venetian Casino Resort LLC, with 8,500 employees
2. E-T-T LLC, 5,000
2. Las Vegas Sands Corp., 5,000
4. New Castle Corp., 4,200
5. Paris Hotel Casino Resort, 4,000
6. Primm Valley Resort & Casino, 3,000
7. Sunrise Hospital & Medical Center LLC, 2,882
8. Barrick Gaming Operations LLC, 2,500

8. FHR Corp., 2,500

8. Sam-Will Inc., 2,500

Source: Business Rankings, (annual), Dun & Bradstreet Inc., 2011, p. IV.134-IV.135.

1911 ■ LARGEST COMPANIES IN NEVADA BY SALES, 2010

Ranked by: Revenue, in dollars. **Remarks:** Also notes contact information for headquarters, number of employees at headquarters and overall, rank by employees, and primary SIC code. **Number listed:** 50

1. Nevada Bell Telephone Co., with $16,000,000,000

2. Caesars Entertainment Corp., $8,818,600,000

3. Las Vegas Sands Corp., $6,853,182,000

4. MGM Resorts International, $6,019,233,000

5. Wynn Resorts Ltd., $4,184,698,000

6. NV Energy Inc., $3,280,222,000

7. Nevada Power Co., $2,252,377,000

8. Boyd Gaming Corp., $2,140,899,000

9. Amerco Inc., $2,002,005,000

10. International Game Technology Inc., $1,987,200,000

Source: Business Rankings, (annual), Dun & Bradstreet Inc., 2011, p. III.134-III.135.

1912 ■ NEVADA'S LARGEST COMPANIES OVERALL, 2011

Ranked by: Score based on revenue, profits, assets, and market capitalization. **Remarks:** Specific scores not provided. Also notes overall rank in the *Forbes 2000* and figures for each criterion. **Number listed:** 4

1. Las Vegas Sands Corp.

2. MGM Mirage Inc.

3. Wynn Resorts Ltd.

4. Caesars Entertainment

Source: Forbes, Forbes 2000 (annual), http://www.forbes.com, May 7, 2012.

1913 ■ TOP *FORTUNE 500* COMPANIES IN NEVADA, 2011

Ranked by: Revenue, in millions of dollars. **Remarks:** Also notes overall rank in the *Fortune 500,* headquarters, and number of employees. **Number listed:** 4

1. Las Vegas Sands Corp., with $9,410.7 million

2. Caesars Entertainment Corp., $8,834.5

3. MGM Resorts International, $7,849.3

4. Wynn Resorts, $5,269.8

Source: Fortune, Fortune 500 (annual), May 21, 2012, p. F-44.

Corporations—New Hampshire

1914 ■ LARGEST COMPANIES IN NEW HAMPSHIRE BY EMPLOYEES, 2010

Ranked by: Number of employees at headquarters. **Remarks:** Also notes contact information for headquarters, total number of employees, revenue, rank by revenue, and primary SIC code. **Number listed:** 69

1. Dartmouth-Hitchcock Medical Center, with 7,500 employees

2. Dartmouth-Hitchcock Obligated Group, 5,000

3. Hollis Telephone Co., 2,700

3. Union Telephone Co., 2,700

5. Elliot Hospital of the City of Manchester, 1,937

6. Catholic Medical Center, 1,536

7. Don Henry Jr. & Sons, 1,520

8. Wentworth-Douglass Hospital, 1,500

9. Catholic Medical Center Physician Practice Association, 1,400

9. Fitz, Vogt & Associates Ltd., 1,400

Source: Business Rankings, (annual), Dun & Bradstreet Inc., 2011, p. IV.136-IV.137.

1915 ■ LARGEST COMPANIES IN NEW HAMPSHIRE BY SALES, 2010

Ranked by: Revenue, in dollars. **Remarks:** Also notes contact information for headquarters, number of employees at headquarters and overall, rank by employees, and primary SIC code. **Number listed:** 68

1. PC Connection Inc., with $1,974,198,000

2. The Timberland Co., $1,429,484,000

3. Dartmouth-Hitchcock Obligated Group, $1,212,028,000

4. Edgewood Manor Inc., $1,200,561,000

5. Public Service Co. of New Hampshire, $1,033,439,000

6. Standex International Corp., $578,454,000

7. GT Solar International Inc., $544,245,000

8. Brookstone Inc., $496,745,000

9. Morrison Hospital Association, $491,281,500

10. Amphenol Printed Circuits Inc., $450,000,000

Source: Business Rankings, (annual), Dun & Bradstreet Inc., 2011, p. III.136-III.137.

Corporations—New Jersey

1916 ■ BEST LARGE COMPANIES TO WORK FOR IN NEW JERSEY, 2012

Ranked by: Score based on employee surveys. **Remarks:** Specific scores not provided. To qualify, companies must have at least 250 employees. **Number listed:** 48

1. The North Highland Co.

2. Patton Boggs LLP

3. WithumSmith + Brown PC

4. Novo Nordisk Inc.

5. Wakefern Food Corp.

6. NuVasive Inc.

7. Edward Jones

8. Mercedes-Benz USA LLC

9. Resources Global Professionals

10. Friedman LLP

Source: Best Companies Group, Best Places to Work in New Jersey (annual), http://www.bestplacestoworknj.com, April 2012.

1917 ■ BEST SMALL COMPANIES IN NEW JERSEY, 2011

Ranked by: Score based on revenue, profits, and return on equity for the past 12 months and five years. **Remarks:** Specific scores not provided. Also notes rank in the overall *100 Best Small Companies in America*. To qualify, companies must have revenues between $5 million and $1 billion, a net margin above five percent, and share price above $5. List is available online only. **Number listed:** 3

1. CommVault Systems
2. Bio-Reference Laboratories
3. B & G Foods

Source: *Forbes*, Best Small Companies in America (annual), November 7, 2011.

1918 ■ BEST SMALL/MEDIUM COMPANIES TO WORK FOR IN NEW JERSEY, 2012

Ranked by: Score based on employee surveys. **Remarks:** Specific scores not provided. To qualify, companies must have between 15 and 249 employees. **Number listed:** 52

1. Red Nucleus
2. Coordinated Family Care
3. SGA Group PC
4. Teknicks
5. Rue Insurance
6. Wilkin & Guttenplan PC
7. Pharmalink Consulting
8. Sharpe, Kawam, Carmosino & Co. LLC
9. RAMPS International Inc.
10. Profit Sense Innovations

Source: *Best Companies Group*, Best Places to Work in New Jersey (annual), http://www.bestplacestoworknj.com, April 2012.

1919 ■ FASTEST-GROWING COMPANIES IN NEW JERSEY, 2008-2011

Ranked by: Score based on three-year growth in revenue and earnings, and three-year total return to investors. **Remarks:** Specific scores not provided. To qualify for list, companies must have revenues of at least $50 million, net income of at least $10 million, market capitalization of at least $250 million, and stock price of at least $5. Int'l companies are eligible if they trade on a U.S. exchange and file quarterly reports. **Number listed:** 3

1. Lincoln Educational Services Corp.
2. Celgene Corp.
3. Cognizant Technology Solutions Corp.

Source: *Fortune*, 100 Fastest-Growing Companies (annual), http://www.fortune.com, September 26, 2011.

1920 ■ LARGEST COMPANIES IN NEW JERSEY BY EMPLOYEES, 2010

Ranked by: Number of employees at headquarters. **Remarks:** Also notes contact information for headquarters, total number of employees, revenue, rank by revenue, and primary SIC code. **Number listed:** 324

1. On Time Staffing LLC, with 10,000 employees
2. Marina District Development Co., 7,000
3. Trump Taj Mahal Inc., 6,000
4. JFK Johnson Rehabilitation Institute, 5,000
4. Prudential Insurance Company of America, 5,000
4. Solaris Health System Inc., 5,000
7. Novartis Pharmaceuticals Corp., 4,600
8. Cooper Health Care, 4,500
9. Trump Plaza Associates New Jersey Group, 4,488

10. Prudential Financial Inc., 4,350

Source: *Business Rankings*, (annual), Dun & Bradstreet Inc., 2011, p. IV.138-IV.145.

1921 ■ LARGEST COMPANIES IN NEW JERSEY BY SALES, 2010

Ranked by: Revenue, in dollars. **Remarks:** Also notes contact information for headquarters, number of employees at headquarters and overall, rank by employees, and primary SIC code. **Number listed:** 324

1. Medco Health Solutions Inc., with $65,968,300,000
2. Cellco Partnership, $62,131,000,000
3. Johnson & Johnson, $61,587,000,000
4. Merck & Co., Inc., $45,987,000,000
5. Honeywell International Inc., $33,370,000,000
6. Merck Sharp & Dohme Corp., $23,643,200,000
7. Roche Holdings Inc., $17,098,000,000
8. Toys "R" Us Inc., $13,568,000,000
9. Public Service Enterprise Group Inc., $11,793,000,000
10. LG Electronics USA Inc., $10,365,966,717

Source: *Business Rankings*, (annual), Dun & Bradstreet Inc., 2011, p. III.138-III.144.

1922 ■ MOST ADMIRED COMPANIES IN NEW JERSEY, 2012

Ranked by: Survey of top executives, directors, and securities analysts regarding the Fortune 1,000 companies that they admire the most, regardless of industry. **Remarks:** Also notes city and industry rank. List is available online only, not in print. **Number listed:** 14

1. Wyndham Worldwid, with 7.77 points
2. Sealed Air Corp., 7.38
3. Medco Health Solutions Inc., 6.85
4. Becton, Dickinson & Co., 6.62
5. Automatic Data Processing Inc., 6.5
6. Honeywell International Inc., 6.45
7. Cognizant Technology Solutions, 6.31
8. Prudential Financial Inc., 6.27
9. Public Service Enterprise Group Inc., 6.22
10. Merck & Co., Inc., 6.16

Source: *Fortune*, World's Most Admired Companies (annual), http://www.fortune.com, March 19, 2012.

1923 ■ NEW JERSEY'S BEST COMPANIES TO WORK FOR, 2012

Ranked by: Score based on employee surveys as well as evaluation of companies' credibility, respect, fairness, and pride/camaraderie. **Remarks:** Specific scores not provided; companies are listed alphabetically, not ranked. Available online only, not in print. **Number listed:** 4

1. Atlantic Health System Inc.
2. Mercedes-Benz USA
3. Meridian Health
4. Novo Nordisk Inc.

Source: *Fortune*, 100 Best Companies to Work For (annual), http://www.fortune.com, February 6, 2012.

1924 ■ NEW JERSEY'S LARGEST COMPANIES OVERALL, 2011

Ranked by: Score based on revenue, profits, assets, and market capitalization. **Remarks:** Specific scores not provided. Also notes overall rank in the *Forbes 2000* and figures for each criterion. **Number listed:** 21

1. Johnson & Johnson
2. Merck & Co., Inc.
3. Prudential Financial Inc.
4. Honeywell International Inc.
5. The Chubb Corp.
6. Automatic Data Processing Inc.
7. Public Service Enterprise Group Inc.
8. Becton, Dickinson & Co.
9. Celgene Corp.
10. Bed Bath & Beyond

Source: *Forbes*, Forbes 2000 (annual), http://www.forbes.com, May 7, 2012.

1925 ■ NEW JERSEY'S LARGEST PRIVATE COMPANIES, 2010

Ranked by: Revenue, in billions of dollars. **Remarks:** Also notes business segment, number of employees, and overall rank in the *America's Largest Private Companies* list. Ranking is available online only, not in print. **Number listed:** 6

1. Toys "R" Us Inc., with $13.86 billion
2. Avaya Inc., $5.3
3. Burlington Coat Factory Warehouse Corp., $3.67
4. SHI International Corp., $3
5. G-I Holdings Inc., $2.87
6. Conair Corp., $2.01

Source: *Forbes*, America's Largest Private Companies (annual), http://www.forbes.com, December 5, 2011.

1926 ■ NEW JERSEY'S LARGEST PUBLIC COMPANIES, 2010

Ranked by: Revenue, in billions of dollars. **Remarks:** Also notes rank and figures for previous year, percent change, contact information, ticker symbol, and senior executive. **Number listed:** 130

1. Johnson & Johnson, with $61.59 billion
2. Merck & Co., Inc., $45.99
3. Prudential Financial Inc., $38.41
4. Honeywell, $33.37
5. The Chubb Corp., $13.32
6. Public Service Enterprise Group Inc., $11.79
7. Automatic Data Processing, $8.93
8. NRG Energy Inc., $8.85
9. The Great Atlantic & Pacific Tea Co., $8.08
10. Bed Bath & Beyond, $7.83

Source: *NJBiz*, Top Public Companies (annual), http://www.njbiz.com, July 4, 2011.

1927 ■ NEW JERSEY'S TOP PRIVATE COMPANIES, 2010

Ranked by: Revenue, in billions of dollars. **Remarks:** Also notes rank for previous year, contact information, year founded, senior executives, type of business, and number of New Jersey employees. **Number listed:** 313

1. Wakefern Food Corp., with $11.8 billion
2. Realogy, $4.09
3. Burlington Coat Factory Warehouse Corp., $3.7
4. SHI International Corp., $3.04
5. GAF, $2.6
6. Alpha Industries, $2.1
7. Conair Corp., $2
8. New Jersey Manufacturers Insurance Co., $1.44
9. Inserra Supermarkets Inc., $1.1
10. NFI, $0.9

Source: *NJBiz*, Top Private Companies (annual), http://www.njbiz.com, August 22, 2011.

1928 ■ TOP *FORTUNE 500* COMPANIES IN NEW JERSEY, 2011

Ranked by: Revenue, in millions of dollars. **Remarks:** Also notes overall rank in the *Fortune 500,* headquarters, and number of employees. **Number listed:** 21

1. Medco Health Solutions Inc., with $70,063.3 million
2. Johnson & Johnson, $65,030
3. Prudential Financial Inc., $49,045
4. Merck & Co., Inc., $48,047
5. Honeywell International Inc., $37,059
6. Toys "R" Us Inc., $13,909
7. The Chubb Corp., $13,585
8. Public Service Enterprise Group Inc., $11,191
9. Automatic Data Processing Inc., $9,879.5
10. NRG Energy Inc., $9,079

Source: *Fortune*, Fortune 500 (annual), May 21, 2012, p. F-44.

Corporations—New Mexico

1929 ■ LARGEST COMPANIES IN NEW MEXICO BY EMPLOYEES, 2010

Ranked by: Number of employees at headquarters. **Remarks:** Also notes contact information for headquarters, total number of employees, revenue, rank by revenue, and primary SIC code. **Number listed:** 69

1. Sandia Corp., with 7,200 employees
2. Next Phase Inc., 2,400
3. St. Vincent Hospital, 1,555
4. Memorial Medical Center Inc., 1,350
5. Navajo Agricultural Products Industry, 1,200
6. San Juan Regional Medical Center Inc., 1,100
7. Psitronics Group Systems International, 1,016
8. KSL Services Joint Venture, 1,000
8. Mediplex of Massachusetts Inc., 1,000
8. PHC Las Cruces Inc., 1,000

Source: *Business Rankings*, (annual), Dun & Bradstreet Inc., 2011, p. IV.146-IV.147.

1930 ■ LARGEST COMPANIES IN NEW MEXICO BY SALES, 2010

Ranked by: Revenue, in dollars. **Remarks:** Also notes contact information for headquarters, number of employees at headquarters and overall, rank by employees, and primary SIC code. **Number listed:** 69

1. Sandia Corp., with $2,230,564,735
2. Presbyterian Healthcare Services, $2,014,311,000
3. PNM Resources Inc., $1,673,517,000
4. Public Service Co. of New Mexico, $1,017,128,000
5. Akal Security Inc., $490,718,226
6. Jaynes Corp., $344,836,718
7. South Valley Care Center, $338,225,300
8. Descalero Care Center, $308,505,900
9. Summit Electric Supply Co., $301,000,000
10. San Juan Regional Medical Center Inc., $259,750,299

Source: *Business Rankings*, (annual), Dun & Bradstreet Inc., 2011, p. III.145-III.146.

Corporations—New York

1931 ■ BEST COMPANIES TO WORK FOR IN NEW YORK CITY, 2011

Ranked by: Score based on employee surveys. **Remarks:** Specific scores not provided. **Number listed:** 50

1. North Highland
2. Mr. Youth LLC
3. Conductor Inc.
4. Hunton & Williams LLP
5. Interclick
6. NetApp Inc.
7. Text 100
8. RightsFlow
9. Bingham McCutchen LLP
10. ZocDoc Inc.

Source: *Best Companies Group*, Best Places to Work in New York City (annual), http://www.bestplacestoworknyc.com, December 2011.

1932 ■ BEST LARGE COMPANIES TO WORK FOR IN NEW YORK, 2012

Ranked by: Score based on employee surveys. **Remarks:** Specific scores not provided. To qualify, companies must have at least 250 employees. **Number listed:** 24

1. Sybase Inc.
2. Edward Jones
3. Arrow S3
4. Discovery Communications
5. iProspect
6. Rothstein Kass
7. Acorda Therapeutics Inc.
8. Capital District Physicians' Health Plan Inc.
9. Independent Health
10. Globecomm

Source: *Best Companies Group*, Best Places to Work in New York (annual), http://www.bestcompaniesny.com, May 1, 2012.

1933 ■ BEST SMALL COMPANIES IN NEW YORK, 2011

Ranked by: Score based on revenue, profits, and return on equity for the past 12 months and five years. **Remarks:** Specific scores not provided. Also notes rank in the overall *100 Best Small*

Companies in America. To qualify, companies must have revenues between $5 million and $1 billion, a net margin above five percent, and share price above $5. List is available online only. **Number listed:** 9

1. IEC Electronics
2. Sirona Dental Systems
3. Balchem
4. HMS Holdings
5. Coffee Holding
6. ExlService Holdings
7. AboveNet
8. Steven Madden Ltd.
9. Iconix Brand Group

Source: *Forbes*, Best Small Companies in America (annual), November 7, 2011.

1934 ■ BEST SMALL/MEDIUM COMPANIES TO WORK FOR IN NEW YORK, 2012

Ranked by: Score based on employee surveys. **Remarks:** Specific scores not provided. To qualify, companies must have between 15 and 249 employees. **Number listed:** 26

1. First American Equipment Finance
2. Nigel Frank International
3. MAC Source Communications
4. Conductor Inc.
5. HR Works Inc.
6. Ambrose Employer Group LLC
7. Grassi & Co.
8. Veramark Technologies Inc.
9. SeaComm Federal Credit Union
10. MBMS Inc.

Source: *Best Companies Group*, Best Places to Work in New York (annual), http://www.bestcompaniesny.com, May 1, 2012.

1935 ■ FASTEST-GROWING COMPANIES IN NEW YORK, 2008-2011

Ranked by: Score based on three-year growth in revenue and earnings, and three-year total return to investors. **Remarks:** Specific scores not provided. To qualify for list, companies must have revenues of at least $50 million, net income of at least $10 million, market capitalization of at least $250 million, and stock price of at least $5. Int'l companies are eligible if they trade on a U.S. exchange and file quarterly reports. **Number listed:** 9

1. Hi-Tech Pharmacal
2. Ares Capital
3. AboveNet
4. MarketAxess Holdings
5. HMS Holdings Corp.
6. LivePerson
7. Steven Madden Ltd.
8. Signature Bank
9. Epoch Holding

Source: *Fortune*, 100 Fastest-Growing Companies (annual), http://www.fortune.com, September 26, 2011.

1936 ■ FASTEST-GROWING COMPANIES IN THE NEW YORK AREA, 2007-2010

Ranked by: Score based on three-year growth in revenue, net income, and share price. **Remarks:** Specific scores not provided. Also notes contact information, ticker symbol, revenue and net income for current year, share price, industry, number of employees, and three-year growth in revenue, net income, and share price. **Number listed:** 100

1. HMS Holdings Corp.
2. Cognizant Technology Solutions Corp.
3. AboveNet Inc.

Source: *Crain's New York Business*, Fastest-Growing Companies (annual), http://www.crainsnewyork.com, October 17, 2011.

1937 ■ LARGEST COMPANIES IN NEW YORK BY EMPLOYEES, 2010

Ranked by: Number of employees at headquarters. **Remarks:** Also notes contact information for headquarters, total number of employees, revenue, rank by revenue, and primary SIC code. **Number listed:** 784

1. Merrill Lynch & Co., Inc., with 10,000 employees
2. Eastman Kodak Co., 8,200
3. Patriarch Partners LLC, 8,112
4. Paramount Communications Acquisition Corp., 8,000
5. Mount Sinai Hospital, 7,869
6. American Express Co., 7,000
6. New York & Presbyterian Hospital, 7,000
8. Corning Inc., 6,300
9. Long Island Rail Road Co., 6,030
10. Albany Medical Center, 6,000

Source: *Business Rankings*, (annual), Dun & Bradstreet Inc., 2011, p. IV.148-IV.164.

1938 ■ LARGEST COMPANIES IN NEW YORK BY SALES, 2010

Ranked by: Revenue, in dollars. **Remarks:** Also notes contact information for headquarters, number of employees at headquarters and overall, rank by employees, and primary SIC code. **Number listed:** 795

1. Verizon Communications Inc., with $106,565,000,000
2. International Business Machines Corp. (IBM), $99,870,000,000
3. Pfizer Inc., $67,809,000,000
4. Philip Morris International Inc., $67,713,000,000
5. PepsiCo Inc., $57,838,000,000
6. Bunge Ltd., $45,707,000,000
7. Hess Corp., $34,613,000,000
8. News Corp., $32,778,000,000
9. Time Warner Inc., $26,888,000,000
10. Alcoa Inc., $21,013,000,000

Source: *Business Rankings*, (annual), Dun & Bradstreet Inc., 2011, p. III.147-III.163.

1939 ■ LARGEST EMPLOYERS IN NEW YORK CITY, 2011

Ranked by: Number of employees in New York City. **Remarks:** Also notes contact information, top executive, figures for previous year, percent change, number of employees company-wide, company-wide revenue, and selected subsidiaries or system members operating in New York City. **Number listed:** 25

1. City of New York, NY, with 148,898 employees
2. New York City Department of Education, 119,410

3. Metropolitan Transportation Authority, 66,804

Source: *Crain's New York Business*, Top Employers (annual), http://www.crainsnewyork.com, April 9, 2012.

1940 ■ LARGEST PRIVATE COMPANIES IN THE NEW YORK AREA, 2010

Ranked by: Revenue, in millions of dollars. **Remarks:** Also notes contact information, top executive, annual growth, projected figures for upcoming year, total number of employees, and nature of business. **Number listed:** 125

1. The Trump Organization, with $9,200 million
2. Transammonia Inc., $8,414.7
3. Advance Publications Inc., $7,160
4. Bloomberg LP, $6,900
5. Renco Group Inc., $6,000

Source: *Crain's New York Business*, Largest Private Companies (annual), http://www.crainsnewyork.com, November 21, 2011.

1941 ■ LARGEST PUBLIC COMPANIES IN THE NEW YORK AREA, 2011

Ranked by: Revenue, in millions of dollars. **Remarks:** Also notes contact information, ticker symbol, net income, percent change from previous year, total number of employees, and nature of business. **Number listed:** 250

1. Verizon Communications Inc., with $110,875 million
2. J. P. Morgan Chase & Co., $110,838
3. International Business Machines Corp. (IBM), $106,916
4. Citigroup Inc., $102,587
5. Philip Morris International Inc., $76,346

Source: *Crain's New York Business*, Largest Public Companies (annual), http://www.crainsnewyork.com, May 21, 2012.

1942 ■ MOST ADMIRED COMPANIES IN NEW YORK, 2012

Ranked by: Survey of top executives, directors, and securities analysts regarding the Fortune 1,000 companies that they admire the most, regardless of industry. **Remarks:** Also notes city and industry rank. List is available online only, not in print. **Number listed:** 31

1. Philip Morris International, with 8.25 points
2. International Business Machines Corp. (IBM), 7.79
3. Ralph Lauren Corp., 7.77
4. Colgate-Palmolive, 7.51
5. Viacom, 7.41
6. American Express Co., 7.38
7. Estee Lauder, 7.33
8. J. P. Morgan Chase, 7.23
9. MasterCard Inc., 7.22
10. Time Warner, 7.18

Source: *Fortune*, World's Most Admired Companies (annual), http://www.fortune.com, March 19, 2012.

1943 ■ NEW YORK'S BEST COMPANIES TO WORK FOR, 2012

Ranked by: Score based on employee surveys as well as evaluation of companies' credibility, respect, fairness, and pride/

camaraderie. **Remarks:** Specific scores not provided; companies are listed alphabetically, not ranked. Available online only, not in print. **Number listed:** 10

1. Accenture Ltd.
2. American Express Co.
3. Deloitte LLP
4. Ernst & Young LLP
5. Goldman Sachs Group Inc.
6. KPMG LLP
7. PricewaterhouseCoopers LLP
8. SRC Inc.
9. Teach For America Inc.
10. Wegmans Food Markets

Source: *Fortune*, 100 Best Companies to Work For (annual), http://www.fortune.com, February 6, 2012.

1944 ■ NEW YORK'S LARGEST COMPANIES OVERALL, 2011

Ranked by: Score based on revenue, profits, assets, and market capitalization. **Remarks:** Specific scores not provided. Also notes overall rank in the *Forbes 2000* and figures for each criterion. **Number listed:** 66

1. J. P. Morgan Chase & Co.
2. Citigroup Inc.
3. International Business Machines Corp. (IBM)
4. Pfizer Inc.
5. American International Group Inc.
6. MetLife Inc.
7. Verizon Communications Inc.
8. Goldman Sachs Group Inc.
9. PepsiCo Inc.
10. Morgan Stanley

Source: *Forbes*, Forbes 2000 (annual), http://www.forbes.com, May 7, 2012.

1945 ■ NEW YORK'S LARGEST PRIVATE COMPANIES, 2010

Ranked by: Revenue, in billions of dollars. **Remarks:** Also notes business segment, number of employees, and overall rank in the *America's Largest Private Companies* list. Ranking is available on-line only, not in print. **Number listed:** 26

1. PricewaterhouseCoopers LLP, with $29.2 billion
2. Ernst & Young LLP, $22.88
3. Transammonia Inc., $8.42
4. The Renco Group Inc., $7.75
5. Bloomberg LP, $7
5. McKinsey & Co., $7
7. Advance Publications Inc., $6.55
8. Wegmans Food Markets Inc., $5.6
9. Charmer Sunbelt Group, $3.83
10. Hearst Corp., $3.80
10. Red Apple Group Inc., $3.80

Source: *Forbes*, America's Largest Private Companies (annual), http://www.forbes.com, December 5, 2011.

1946 ■ TOP *FORTUNE 500* COMPANIES IN NEW YORK, 2011

Ranked by: Revenue, in millions of dollars. **Remarks:** Also notes overall rank in the *Fortune 500,* headquarters, and number of employees. **Number listed:** 50

1. Verizon Communications Inc., with $110,875 million
2. J. P. Morgan Chase & Co., $110,838
3. International Business Machines Corp. (IBM), $106,916
4. Citigroup Inc., $102,939
5. INTL FCStone, $75,497.6
6. American International Group Inc., $71,730
7. MetLife Inc., $70,641
8. Pfizer Inc., $67,932
9. PepsiCo Inc., $66,504
10. Morgan Stanley, $39,376

Source: *Fortune*, Fortune 500 (annual), May 21, 2012, p. F-44-F-45.

1947 ■ TOP PRIVATE COMPANIES IN THE ROCHESTER AREA, 2008-2010

Ranked by: Revenue growth over the past three years. **Remarks:** Specific figures not provided. Ranking covers companies with at least $1 million in revenue. Also notes company description, number of employees, website, and number of years on the list. **Number listed:** 100

1. Manning & Napier Advisors LLC
2. RailComm
3. Real Lease Inc.
4. Fibertech Networks LLC
5. Pictometry International Corp.
6. Systems Management/Planning Inc.
7. Leveraging Technology Solutions LLC
8. Soleo Communications Inc.
9. Videk Inc.
10. MaeTec Power

Source: *Rochester Democrat & Chronicle*, Top 100 (annual), October 30, 2011.

Corporations—Nicaragua

1948 ■ BEST COMPANIES TO WORK FOR IN NICARAGUA, 2012

Ranked by: Score based on the relationships between employees and management, employees and their jobs/company, and employees and coworkers. **Remarks:** Specific scores not provided. **Number listed:** 4

1. Kimberly-Clark Nicaragua
2. Telefonica Nicaragua
3. British American Tobacco Nicaragua
4. Excel Automotriz Nicaragua

Source: *Great Place to Work Institute Inc.*, Best Places to Work in Central America & the Caribbean (annual), 2012.

Corporations—Nigeria

1949 ■ BEST COMPANIES TO WORK FOR IN NIGERIA, 2012

Ranked by: Score based on the relationships between employees and management, employees and their jobs/company, and employees and coworkers. **Remarks:** Specific scores not provided. **Number listed:** 10

1. Guinness Nigeria plc
2. First Bank of Nigeria plc
3. Guaranty Trust Assurance plc
4. Accenture Nigeria
5. Fidelity Bank plc
6. Lagos Business School
7. Financial Institutions Training Center
8. Total Nigeria
9. Access Bank plc
10. GlaxoSmithKline Consumer

Source: *Great Place to Work Institute Inc.*, Best Places to Work in Nigeria (annual), April 19, 2012.

1950 ■ NIGERIA'S LARGEST COMPANIES OVERALL, 2011

Ranked by: Score based on revenue, profits, assets, and market capitalization. **Remarks:** Specific scores not provided. Also notes overall rank in the *Forbes 2000* and figures for each criterion. **Number listed:** 2

1. Dangote Cement
2. Union Bank of Nigeria

Source: *Forbes*, Forbes 2000 (annual), http://www.forbes.com, May 7, 2012.

Corporations—North Carolina

1951 ■ LARGEST COMPANIES IN NORTH CAROLINA BY EMPLOYEES, 2010

Ranked by: Number of employees at headquarters. **Remarks:** Also notes contact information for headquarters, total number of employees, revenue, rank by revenue, and primary SIC code. **Number listed:** 235

1. Duke University Health System, with 33,000 employees
2. Duke University Health System Inc., 18,000
3. Wake Forest University Baptist Medical Center, 11,000
4. Wachovia Corp., 8,849
5. University Health Systems of Eastern Carolina Inc., 8,373
6. Merchandising Solutions Group Inc., 8,300
7. Bank of America NA, 8,000
8. Carlisle Companies Inc., 7,500
9. Zen Hro Inc., 7,000
10. Duke Energy Business Services LLC, 6,884

Source: *Business Rankings*, (annual), Dun & Bradstreet Inc., 2011, p. IV.165-IV.170.

1952 ■ LARGEST COMPANIES IN NORTH CAROLINA BY SALES, 2010

Ranked by: Revenue, in dollars. **Remarks:** Also notes contact information for headquarters, number of employees at headquarters and overall, rank by employees, and primary SIC code. **Number listed:** 236

1. Lowe's Companies Inc., with $47,220,000,000
2. Nucor Corp., $15,844,627,000
3. Duke Energy Corp., $14,272,000,000
4. Progress Energy Inc., $10,190,000,000

5. Reynolds American Inc., $8,551,000,000
6. Family Dollar Stores Inc., $7,866,971,000
7. VF Corp., $7,702,589,000
8. The Pantry Inc., $7,265,262,000
9. Goodrich Corp., $6,966,900,000
10. Sonic Automotive Inc., $6,880,844,000

Source: *Business Rankings*, (annual), Dun & Bradstreet Inc., 2011, p. III.164-III.168.

1953 ■ MOST ADMIRED COMPANIES IN NORTH CAROLINA, 2012

Ranked by: Survey of top executives, directors, and securities analysts regarding the Fortune 1,000 companies that they admire the most, regardless of industry. **Remarks:** Also notes city and industry rank. List is available online only, not in print. **Number listed:** 3

1. VF Corp., with 7.53 points
2. Nucor Corp., 6.52
3. Lowe's Companies Inc., 6.12

Source: *Fortune*, World's Most Admired Companies (annual), http://www.fortune.com, March 19, 2012.

1954 ■ NORTH CAROLINA'S LARGEST COMPANIES OVERALL, 2011

Ranked by: Score based on revenue, profits, assets, and market capitalization. **Remarks:** Specific scores not provided. Also notes overall rank in the *Forbes 2000* and figures for each criterion. **Number listed:** 13

1. Bank of America Corp.
2. Lowe's Companies Inc.
3. Duke Energy Corp.
4. BB & T Corp.
5. Reynolds American Inc.
6. Nucor Corp.
7. Progress Energy Inc.
8. VF Corp.
9. Goodrich Corp.
10. Lorillard Inc.

Source: *Forbes*, Forbes 2000 (annual), http://www.forbes.com, May 7, 2012.

1955 ■ NORTH CAROLINA'S LARGEST PRIVATE COMPANIES, 2010

Ranked by: Revenue, in billions of dollars. **Remarks:** Also notes business segment, number of employees, and overall rank in the *America's Largest Private Companies* list. Ranking is available online only, not in print. **Number listed:** 7

1. MBM Corp., with $6.3 billion
2. Belk Inc., $3.51
3. Alex Lee Inc., $3.1
4. Quintiles Transnational Corp., $3
5. General Parts Inc., $2.87
6. American Tire Distributors Holdings Inc., $2.46
7. SAS Institute Inc., $2.43

Source: *Forbes*, America's Largest Private Companies (annual), http://www.forbes.com, December 5, 2011.

1956 ■ NORTH CAROLINA'S TOP COMPANIES BY MARKET CAPITALIZATION, 2011

Ranked by: Market capitalization, in millions of dollars. **Remarks:** Also notes rank for previous year, location, stock exchange, ticker symbol, industry, percent change from previous year, and stock price and earnings data. **Number listed:** 75

1. Bank of America Corp., with $111,057.3 million
2. Lowe's Companies Inc., $30,351.2
3. Duke Energy Corp., $25,069
4. Reynolds American Inc., $21,596
5. BB & T Corp., $18,693.2
6. Lorillard Inc., $15,645.2
7. Progress Energy Inc., $14,140.3
8. Nucor Corp., $13,028.1
9. Goodrich Corp., $11,925.1
10. VF Corp., $11,876.3

Source: *Business North Carolina*, Top 75 (annual), http://www.businessnc.com, October 2011.

1957 ■ TOP *FORTUNE 500* COMPANIES IN NORTH CAROLINA, 2011

Ranked by: Revenue, in millions of dollars. **Remarks:** Also notes overall rank in the *Fortune 500,* headquarters, and number of employees. **Number listed:** 14

1. Bank of America Corp., with $115,074 million
2. Lowe's Companies Inc., $50,208
3. Nucor Corp., $20,023.6
4. Duke Energy Corp., $14,529
5. BB & T Corp., $9,998
6. VF Corp., $9,459.2
7. Progress Energy Inc., $8,907
8. Family Dollar Stores Inc., $8,547.8
9. Reynolds American Inc., $8,541
10. Goodrich Corp., $8,074.9

Source: *Fortune*, Fortune 500 (annual), May 21, 2012, p. F-45.

1958 ■ TOP PRIVATE COMPANIES IN NORTH CAROLINA, 2010

Ranked by: Revenue. **Remarks:** Specific figures not provided. Also notes rank for previous year, headquarters, CEO, number of employees, and business description. **Number listed:** 100

1. Belk Inc.
2. General Parts International Inc.
3. SAS Institute Inc.
4. Baker & Taylor Inc.
5. House of Raeford Farms Inc.
6. VPS C-Store Holding LLC
7. New NGC Inc.
8. Lord Corp.
9. J. T. Davenport & Sons Inc.
10. New Breed Logistics Inc.

Source: *Business North Carolina*, Top 100 Private Companies (annual), http://www.businessnc.com, October 2011.

Corporations—North Dakota

1959 ■ LARGEST COMPANIES IN NORTH DAKOTA BY EMPLOYEES, 2010

Ranked by: Number of employees at headquarters. **Remarks:** Also notes contact information for headquarters, total number of employees, revenue, rank by revenue, and primary SIC code. **Number listed:** 50

1. Altru Health System, with 3,100 employees
2. Medcenter One Inc., 2,781
3. Sanford Clinic North, 2,500
4. Sanford Medical Center Fargo, 2,000
5. St. Alexius Medical Center, 1,800
6. Essentia Health LLC, 1,500
7. Trinity Health, 1,200
8. Sanford North, 1,000
9. Wanzek Construction Inc., 800
10. Noridian Mutual Insurance Co., 755

Source: *Business Rankings*, (annual), Dun & Bradstreet Inc., 2011, p. IV.171-IV.172.

1960 ■ LARGEST COMPANIES IN NORTH DAKOTA BY SALES, 2010

Ranked by: Revenue, in dollars. **Remarks:** Also notes contact information for headquarters, number of employees at headquarters and overall, rank by employees, and primary SIC code. **Number listed:** 50

1. MDU Resources Group Inc., with $3,909,695,000
2. RDO Equipment Co., $870,288,000
3. Basin Electric Power Cooperative, $853,950,000
4. Titan Machinery Inc., $838,781,000
5. SPF Energy Inc., $772,794,546
6. Sanford North, $677,409,657
7. Dakota Gasification Co., $566,750,000
8. Lake Region Lutheran Home Inc., $563,067,400
9. Farstad Oil Inc., $476,561,224
10. Meritcare Medical Group, $431,785,668

Source: *Business Rankings*, (annual), Dun & Bradstreet Inc., 2011, p. III.169-III.170.

Corporations—Norway

1961 ■ LARGEST COMPANIES IN NORWAY, 2010

Ranked by: Sales, in millions of U.S. dollars. **Remarks:** Also notes city; industrial code; percent change in sales; profits; profit as a percentage of sales, assets, and equity; number of employees; sales per employee; assets; equity capital; equity capital as a percentage of assets; year established; and figures for previous year. **Number listed:** 400

1. Statoil ASA, with $60,024.4 million
2. Bilfinger Berger AG, $14,297.9
3. Yara International ASA, $12,579.4
4. General Electric International Inc., $11,675.3
5. Helse Sor-Ost RHF, $9,353.8
6. Orkla ASA, $9,059.9
7. Total E & P Norge AS, $7,304
8. Esso Norge AS, $6,900.1
9. ExxonMobil Exploration & Production Norway AS, $6,298.7
10. Hydro Aluminium AS, $6,075.9

Source: *Europe's 15,000 Largest Companies*, (annual), ELC International, 2011, p. 468+.

1962 ■ NORWAY'S LARGEST COMPANIES OVERALL, 2011

Ranked by: Score based on revenue, profits, assets, and market capitalization. **Remarks:** Specific scores not provided. Also notes rank in the overall *Forbes 2000* and figures for each criterion. **Number listed:** 9

1. Statoil
2. DnB NOR ASA
3. Telenor ASA
4. Norsk Hydro ASA
5. Yara International ASA
6. Orkla ASA
7. Storebrand ASA
8. Aker Solutions ASA
9. Gjensidige Forsikring ASA

Source: *Forbes*, Forbes 2000 (annual), http://www.forbes.com, May 7, 2012.

Corporations—Ohio

1963 ■ BEST LARGE COMPANIES TO WORK FOR IN OHIO, 2012

Ranked by: Score based on employee surveys. **Remarks:** Specific scores not provided. To qualify, companies must have at least 250 employees. **Number listed:** 19

1. SRC Inc.
2. Edward Jones
3. Stress Engineering Services inc.
4. Employment Plus Inc.
5. Teradata Corp.
6. Sheetz Inc.
7. Glimcher
8. Hilliard Lyons
9. Catholic Health Partners
10. Blue & Co.

Source: *Best Companies Group*, Best Places to Work in Ohio (annual), May 2012.

1964 ■ BEST SMALL COMPANIES IN OHIO, 2011

Ranked by: Score based on revenue, profits, and return on equity for the past 12 months and five years. **Remarks:** Specific scores not provided. Also notes rank in the overall *100 Best Small Companies in America*. To qualify, companies must have revenues between $5 million and $1 billion, a net margin above five percent, and share price above $5. List is available online only. **Number listed:** 3

1. Performed Line Products
2. Multi-Color
3. Chart Industries

Source: *Forbes*, Best Small Companies in America (annual), November 7, 2011.

1965 ■ BEST SMALL/MEDIUM COMPANIES TO WORK FOR IN OHIO, 2012

Ranked by: Score based on employee surveys. **Remarks:** Specific scores not provided. To qualify, companies must have between 15 and 249 employees. **Number listed:** 16

1. Fusion Alliance Inc.

2. Certified Angus Beef LLC
3. Cohen & Co./Cohen Fund Audit Services
4. Quandel Construction Group Inc.
5. Stout Risius Ross Inc.
6. BCG & Co.
7. Realeflow LLC
8. BMI Federal Credit Union
9. FRCH Design Worldwide
10. EWI

Source: *Best Companies Group*, Best Places to Work in Ohio (annual), May 2012.

1966 ■ LARGEST COMPANIES IN OHIO BY EMPLOYEES, 2010

Ranked by: Number of employees at headquarters. **Remarks:** Also notes contact information for headquarters, total number of employees, revenue, rank by revenue, and primary SIC code. **Number listed:** 372

1. Procter & Gamble Co., with 14,500 employees
2. Limited Brands Inc., 10,000
3. University Hospitals of Cleveland, 7,000
4. Nationwide Mutual Insurance Co., 6,953
5. American Greetings Corp., 6,000
5. Children's Hospital Medical Center, 6,000
7. Akron General Health System, 5,010
8. Nationwide Children's Hospital, 5,000
9. Toledo Hospital, 4,900
10. Timken Co., 4,800

Source: *Business Rankings*, (annual), Dun & Bradstreet Inc., 2011, p. IV.173-IV.181.

1967 ■ LARGEST COMPANIES IN OHIO BY SALES, 2010

Ranked by: Revenue, in dollars. **Remarks:** Also notes contact information for headquarters, number of employees at headquarters and overall, rank by employees, and primary SIC code. **Number listed:** 375

1. Cardinal Health Inc., with $98,502,800,000
2. Procter & Gamble Co., $78,938,000,000
3. The Kroger Co., $76,733,000,000
4. Macy's Inc., $23,489,000,000
5. Goodyear Tire & Rubber Co., $18,832,000,000
6. American Electric Power Co., Inc., $14,427,000,000
7. Eaton Corp., $13,715,000,000
8. FirstEnergy Corp., $13,339,000,000
9. Parker Hannifin Corp., $9,993,166,000
10. Limited Brands Inc., $8,632,000,000

Source: *Business Rankings*, (annual), Dun & Bradstreet Inc., 2011, p. III.171-III.178.

1968 ■ MOST ADMIRED COMPANIES IN OHIO, 2012

Ranked by: Survey of top executives, directors, and securities analysts regarding the Fortune 1,000 companies that they admire the most, regardless of industry. **Remarks:** Also notes city and industry rank. List is available online only, not in print. **Number listed:** 11

1. Procter & Gamble Co., with 8.1 points
2. Limited Brands Inc., 7.31

3. Parker Hannifin Corp., 6.9

4. Eaton Corp., 6.87

5. The Kroger Co., 6.55

6. Chiquita Brands International Inc., 6.16

7. Abercrombie & Fitch, 6.14

8. Cardinal Health Inc., 5.8

9. Macy's, 5.79

10. Cintas Corp., 5.78

Source: *Fortune*, World's Most Admired Companies (annual), http://www.fortune.com, March 19, 2012.

1969 ■ OHIO'S BEST COMPANIES TO WORK FOR, 2012

Ranked by: Score based on employee surveys as well as evaluation of companies' credibility, respect, fairness, and pride/camaraderie. **Remarks:** Specific scores not provided; companies are listed alphabetically, not ranked. Available online only, not in print. **Number listed:** 2

1. OhioHealth

2. Southern Ohio Medical Center

Source: *Fortune*, 100 Best Companies to Work For (annual), http://www.fortune.com, February 6, 2012.

1970 ■ OHIO'S LARGEST COMPANIES OVERALL, 2011

Ranked by: Score based on revenue, profits, assets, and market capitalization. **Remarks:** Specific scores not provided. Also notes overall rank in the *Forbes 2000* and figures for each criterion. **Number listed:** 24

1. Procter & Gamble Co.

2. Marathon Petroleum Corp.

3. American Electric Power Co., Inc.

4. FirstEnergy Corp.

5. Cardinal Health Inc.

6. Macy's Inc.

7. Eaton Corp.

8. The Kroger Co.

9. Fifth Third Bancorp

10. The Progressive Corp.

Source: *Forbes*, Forbes 2000 (annual), http://www.forbes.com, May 7, 2012.

1971 ■ OHIO'S LARGEST PRIVATE COMPANIES, 2010

Ranked by: Revenue, in billions of dollars. **Remarks:** Also notes business segment, number of employees, and overall rank in the *America's Largest Private Companies* list. Ranking is available online only, not in print. **Number listed:** 4

1. Momentive Performance Materials Holdings, with $7.41 billion

2. HCR ManorCare , $4.5

3. Aleris International Inc., $4.12

4. NewPage Holding Corp., $3.6

Source: *Forbes*, America's Largest Private Companies (annual), http://www.forbes.com, December 5, 2011.

1972 ■ TOP *FORTUNE 500* COMPANIES IN OHIO, 2011

Ranked by: Revenue, in millions of dollars. **Remarks:** Also notes overall rank in the *Fortune 500,* headquarters, and number of employees. **Number listed:** 28

1. Cardinal Health Inc., with $102,644.2 million

2. The Kroger Co., $90,374

3. Procter & Gamble Co., $82,559

4. Marathon Petroleum, $73,645

5. Nationwide, $30,697.8

6. Macy's Inc., $26,405

7. Goodyear Tire & Rubber Co., $22,767

8. FirstEnergy Corp., $16,258

9. Eaton Corp., $16,049

10. The Progressive Corp., $15,508.1

Source: *Fortune*, Fortune 500 (annual), May 21, 2012, p. F-45.

1973 ■ TOP LARGE COMPANIES TO WORK FOR IN NORTHEAST OHIO, 2011

Ranked by: Score based on employee survey. **Remarks:** Scores not provided. Ranking covers companies with 500 or more local employees. **Number listed:** 28

1. Keller Williams Realty

2. Third Federal Savings & Loan

3. Hyland Software Inc.

4. The Lubrizol Corp.

5. Automated Packaging Systems

6. InfoCision Management Corp.

7. Medical Mutual of Ohio

8. Avon Lake City School District

9. Invacare Corp.

10. Cuyahoga County Board of Developmental Disabilities

Source: *The Plain Dealer*, Northeast Ohio's Top Workplaces (annual), http://www.plaindealer.com, June 19, 2011.

1974 ■ TOP MIDSIZED COMPANIES TO WORK FOR IN NORTHEAST OHIO, 2011

Ranked by: Score based on employee survey. **Remarks:** Scores not provided. Ranking covers companies with 150 to 499 local employees. **Number listed:** 44

1. Tucker Ellis & West LLP

2. Gardiner Trane

3. Collection Auto Group

4. Quicken Loans

5. Edward Jones

6. Cliffs Natural Resources Inc.

7. Cohen & Co.

8. New York Life Insurance Co., General Office

9. Reminger Co. LPA

10. Laurel School

Source: *The Plain Dealer*, Northeast Ohio's Top Workplaces (annual), http://www.plaindealer.com, June 19, 2011.

1975 ■ TOP SMALL COMPANIES TO WORK FOR IN NORTHEAST OHIO, 2011

Ranked by: Score based on employee survey. **Remarks:** Scores not provided. Ranking covers companies with 50 to 149 local employees. **Number listed:** 60

1. Skylight Financial Group/MassMutual

2. WideOpenWest Cleveland LLC

3. Cargill Salt

4. Software Answers Inc.

5. Metrics Marketing Group, A Precision Dialogue Co.

6. EnviroScience Inc.
7. Aero-Instruments Co.
8. Fathom SEO
9. Cornucopia Inc.
10. Marcus Thomas LLC

Source: *The Plain Dealer*, Northeast Ohio's Top Workplaces (annual), http://www.plaindealer.com, June 19, 2011.

Corporations—Oklahoma

1976 ■ BEST LARGE COMPANIES TO WORK FOR IN OKLAHOMA, 2011

Ranked by: Score based on employee surveys. **Remarks:** Specific scores not provided. To qualify, companies must have at least 250 employees. **Number listed:** 10

1. Edward Jones
2. Capital One Auto Finance
3. Cancer Treatment Centers of America
4. Encompass Home Health
5. Diagnostic Laboratory of Oklahoma
6. Eide Bailly LLP
7. The Hartford
8. University of Phoenix
9. First United Bank
10. Cintas Corp.

Source: *Best Companies Group*, Best Places to Work in Oklahoma (annual), http://www.bestplacestoworkok.com, June 2011.

1977 ■ BEST SMALL/MEDIUM COMPANIES TO WORK FOR IN OKLAHOMA, 2011

Ranked by: Score based on employee surveys. **Remarks:** Specific scores not provided. To qualify, companies must have between 25 and 249 employees **Number listed:** 20

1. Wymer Brownlee
2. GableGotwals
3. Insurica
4. QuiBids
5. InterWorks Inc.
6. Coppermark Bank
7. GMX Resources
8. HoganTaylor LLP
9. Tri County Technology Center
10. Ideal Homes of Norman LP

Source: *Best Companies Group*, Best Places to Work in Oklahoma (annual), http://www.bestplacestoworkok.com, June 2011.

1978 ■ LARGEST COMPANIES IN OKLAHOMA BY EMPLOYEES, 2010

Ranked by: Number of employees at headquarters. **Remarks:** Also notes contact information for headquarters, total number of employees, revenue, rank by revenue, and primary SIC code. **Number listed:** 145

1. St. John Health System Inc., with 3,675 employees
2. St. Francis Hospital Inc., 3,095
3. Caprock Pipeline Co., 3,000
3. Chesapeake Energy Corp., 3,000

5. Everett Hospital, 2,800
6. Integris Baptist Medical Center Inc., 2,600
7. Cherokee Nation Enterprises LLC, 2,500
8. Devon OEI Operating Inc., 2,000
8. Tronox LLC, 2,000
10. Chesapeake Operating Inc., 1,800

Source: *Business Rankings*, (annual), Dun & Bradstreet Inc., 2011, p. IV.182-IV.185.

1979 ■ LARGEST COMPANIES IN OKLAHOMA BY SALES, 2010

Ranked by: Revenue, in dollars. **Remarks:** Also notes contact information for headquarters, number of employees at headquarters and overall, rank by employees, and primary SIC code. **Number listed:** 150

1. ONEOK Inc., with $13,030,051,000
2. Enterprise Crude Oil LLC, $12,000,000,000
3. Devon Energy Corp., $9,940,000,000
4. Chesapeake Energy Corp., $9,366,000,000
5. ONEOK Partners LP, $8,675,900,000
6. Williams Partners LP, $5,715,000,000
7. Love's Travel Stops & Country Stores Inc., $5,450,237,000
8. Musket Corp., $5,000,000,000
9. OGE Energy Corp., $3,716,900,000
10. Oklahoma Gas & Electric Co., $2,109,900,000

Source: *Business Rankings*, (annual), Dun & Bradstreet Inc., 2011, p. III.179-III.182.

1980 ■ OKLAHOMA'S BEST COMPANIES TO WORK FOR, 2012

Ranked by: Score based on employee surveys as well as evaluation of companies' credibility, respect, fairness, and pride/camaraderie. **Remarks:** Specific scores not provided; companies are listed alphabetically, not ranked. Available online only, not in print. **Number listed:** 4

1. American Fidelity Assurance Co.
2. Chesapeake Energy Corp.
3. Devon Energy Corp.
4. QuikTrip Corp.

Source: *Fortune*, 100 Best Companies to Work For (annual), http://www.fortune.com, February 6, 2012.

1981 ■ OKLAHOMA'S LARGEST COMPANIES OVERALL, 2011

Ranked by: Score based on revenue, profits, assets, and market capitalization. **Remarks:** Specific scores not provided. Also notes overall rank in the *Forbes 2000* and figures for each criterion. **Number listed:** 8

1. Devon Energy Corp.
2. Chesapeake Energy Corp.
3. The Williams Companies Inc.
4. ONEOK Inc.
5. Continental Resources Inc.
6. BOK Financial Corp.
7. Helmerich & Payne Inc.
8. OGE Energy Corp.

Source: *Forbes*, Forbes 2000 (annual), http://www.forbes.com, May 7, 2012.

1982 ■ OKLAHOMA'S LARGEST PRIVATE COMPANIES, 2010

Ranked by: Revenue, in billions of dollars. **Remarks:** Also notes business segment, number of employees, and overall rank in the *America's Largest Private Companies* list. Ranking is available online only, not in print. **Number listed:** 3

1. Love's Travel Stops & Country Stores Inc., with $24.4 billion
2. QuikTrip Corp., $8.77
3. Hobby Lobby Stores Inc., $2.28

Source: *Forbes*, America's Largest Private Companies (annual), http://www.forbes.com, December 5, 2011.

1983 ■ TOP *FORTUNE 500* COMPANIES IN OKLAHOMA, 2011

Ranked by: Revenue, in millions of dollars. **Remarks:** Also notes overall rank in the *Fortune 500,* headquarters, and number of employees. **Number listed:** 4

1. ONEOK Partners LP, with $15,119.2 million
2. Chesapeake Energy Corp., $11,635
3. Devon Energy Corp., $11,497
4. The Williams Companies Inc., $7,930

Source: *Fortune*, Fortune 500 (annual), May 21, 2012, p. F-45.

Corporations—Oregon

1984 ■ BEST GREEN COMPANIES IN OREGON, 2011

Ranked by: Score based on employee satisfaction and importance related to sustainable practices. **Remarks:** To qualify, companies must employ at least 15 Oregon workers. Also notes rank for previous year, Web site, city, and company description. **Number listed:** 100

1. Redside, with 297.8 points
2. Standing Stone Brewing Co., 292.67
3. SERA Architects, 291.8
4. Hummingbird Wholesale, 291.07
5. Sokol Blosser Winery, 290.83
6. Kimpton Hotel & Restaurant Group LLC Portland, 289.33
7. Rose City Mortgage, 288.12
8. Research Into Action Inc., 287.33
9. Neil Kelly Co., 283.4
10. Neil Kelly Co., 282.2

Source: *Oregon Business*, The 100 Best Green Companies (annual), http://www.oregonbusiness.com, June 2011.

1985 ■ BEST LARGE COMPANIES TO WORK FOR IN OREGON, 2012

Ranked by: Score, on a scale of 600, based on 50 specific workplace conditions in the areas of compensation; working environment; decision-making and trust; performance management; career development and learning; and employee benefits. **Remarks:** Large companies are defined as having 100 or more employees in Oregon. Also notes rank for previous year, headquarters, senior Oregon executive, number of employees, business classification, and employee and employer survey scores. **Number listed:** 33

1. Perkins Cole LLP, with 531.37 points
2. Walsh Construction Co., 528.27

3. PricewaterhouseCoopers, 523.77
4. Kimpton Hotel & Restaurant Group LLC, Portland, 519.04
5. Levi Strauss & Co., 513.72
6. Oregon Research Institute, 512.43
7. Unitus Community Credit Union, 510.35
8. U.S. Cellular, 508.93
9. McKinstry, 507.51
10. Digimarc Corp., 507.06

Source: *Oregon Business*, The 100 Best Companies to Work For in Oregon (annual), http://www.oregonbusiness.com, March 2012.

1986 ■ BEST MEDIUM-SIZED COMPANIES TO WORK FOR IN OREGON, 2012

Ranked by: Score, on a scale of 600, based on 50 specific workplace conditions in the areas of compensation; working environment; decision-making and trust; performance management; career development and learning; and employee benefits. **Remarks:** Medium-sized companies are defined as having 35 to 99 employees in Oregon. Also notes rank for previous year, headquarters, website, business classification, and score for each criterion. **Number listed:** 34

1. Slalom Consulting, with 556.91 points
2. Microsoft Corp., 538.54
3. Ruby Receptionists, 537.53
4. Jibe Consulting, 520.46
5. Urban Airship, 520.45
6. Grant Thornton, 520.42
7. Cardinal Services, 520.29
8. Western States Insurance Agency, 520.14
9. Kidder Mathews, 519.53
10. Smart Wireless, 518.79

Source: *Oregon Business*, The 100 Best Companies to Work For in Oregon (annual), http://www.oregonbusiness.com, March 2012.

1987 ■ BEST SMALL COMPANIES TO WORK FOR IN OREGON, 2012

Ranked by: Score, on a scale of 600, based on 50 specific workplace conditions in the areas of compensation; working environment; decision-making and trust; performance management; career development and learning; and employee benefits. **Remarks:** Small companies are defined as having 15 to 34 employees in Oregon. Also notes rank for previous year, headquarters, website, business classification, and score for each criterion. **Number listed:** 33

1. Rose City Mortgage, with 542.7 points
2. Boly: Welch Recruiting & Consulting, 536.21
3. Point B, 535.31
4. Aim High Academy of Martial Arts, 532.32
5. Evergreen Consulting Group, 530.6
6. Sterling Communications, 527.84
7. Cascade Employers Association, 527.64
8. Isler Northwest LLC, 526.83
9. Barran Liebman LLP, 524.92
10. Mortgage Trust, 524.8

Source: *Oregon Business*, The 100 Best Companies to Work For in Oregon (annual), http://www.oregonbusiness.com, March 2012.

1988 ■ LARGEST COMPANIES IN OREGON BY EMPLOYEES, 2010

Ranked by: Number of employees at headquarters. **Remarks:** Also notes contact information for headquarters, total number of employees, revenue, rank by revenue, and primary SIC code. **Number listed:** 145

1. Nike Inc., with 6,000 employees
2. Hermiston Foods Inc., 4,000
3. Coho Distributing LLC, 2,600
4. PCC Structurals Inc., 2,000
4. Shilo Management Corp., 2,000
6. St. Charles Health System Inc., 1,962
7. Legacy-Emanuel Hospital & Health Center, 1,953
8. Portland Adventist Medical Center, 1,900
9. Con-Way Enterprise Services Inc., 1,600
10. Esco Corp., 1,500
10. Spirit Mountain Gaming Inc., 1,500

Source: *Business Rankings*, (annual), Dun & Bradstreet Inc., 2011, p. IV.186-IV.189.

1989 ■ LARGEST COMPANIES IN OREGON BY SALES, 2010

Ranked by: Revenue, in dollars. **Remarks:** Also notes contact information for headquarters, number of employees at headquarters and overall, rank by employees, and primary SIC code. **Number listed:** 146

1. Nike Inc., with $19,014,000,000
2. Precision Castparts Corp., $5,486,600,000
3. PacifiCorp, $4,432,000,000
4. Rogue Valley Manor, $3,453,101,600
5. NMHG Holding Co., $2,719,700,000
6. Schnitzer Steel Industries Inc., $2,301,240,000
7. Lithia Motors Inc., $2,131,598,000
8. Portland General Electric Co., $1,783,000,000
9. Columbia Sportswear Co., $1,483,524,000
10. Epic Aviation LLC, $1,439,267,000

Source: *Business Rankings*, (annual), Dun & Bradstreet Inc., 2011, p. III.183-III.186.

1990 ■ OREGON'S LARGEST COMPANIES OVERALL, 2011

Ranked by: Score based on revenue, profits, assets, and market capitalization. **Remarks:** Specific scores not provided. Also notes overall rank in the *Forbes 2000* and figures for each criterion. **Number listed:** 2

1. Nike Inc.
2. Precision Castparts Corp.

Source: *Forbes*, Forbes 2000 (annual), http://www.forbes.com, May 7, 2012.

1991 ■ TOP *FORTUNE 500* COMPANIES IN OREGON, 2011

Ranked by: Revenue, in millions of dollars. **Remarks:** Also notes overall rank in the *Fortune 500*, headquarters, and number of employees. **Number listed:** 2

1. Nike Inc., with $20,862 million
2. Precision Castparts Corp., $6,267.2

Source: *Fortune*, Fortune 500 (annual), May 21, 2012, p. F-45.

Corporations—Pakistan

1992 ■ BEST SMALL PAKISTANI COMPANIES, 2010

Ranked by: Score based on sales, net income, and market value. **Remarks:** Specific scores not provided; companies are listed alphabetically, not ranked. Also notes sales, net income, market value, and industry. To qualify for list, which is available online only, companies must have under US$1 billion in annual revenue and positive earnings growth over the past five years. **Number listed:** 2

1. Millat Tractors
2. Netsol Technologies

Source: *Forbes Asia*, Asia's Best Under a Billion (annual), http://www.forbes.com, September 12, 2011.

Corporations—Panama

1993 ■ BEST COMPANIES TO WORK FOR IN PANAMA, 2012

Ranked by: Score based on the relationships between employees and management, employees and their jobs/company, and employees and coworkers. **Remarks:** Specific scores not provided. **Number listed:** 14

1. Telefonica Panama
2. Arcos Dorados Panama
3. Kimberly-Clark Panama
4. British American Tobacco Panama
5. ENSA Panama
6. Scotiabank Panama
7. Dell Panama
8. Excel Automotriz Panama
9. FedEx Panama
10. AES Panama

Source: *Great Place to Work Institute Inc.*, Best Places to Work in Central America & the Caribbean (annual), 2012.

Corporations—Paraguay

1994 ■ BEST COMPANIES TO WORK FOR IN PARAGUAY, 2011

Ranked by: Score based on the relationships between employees and management, employees and their jobs/company, and employees and coworkers. **Remarks:** Specific scores not provided. **Number listed:** 5

1. DHL
2. British American Tobacco Paraguay
3. Botica Magistral
4. Grupo Luminotecnia
5. Tigo Paraguay

Source: *Great Place to Work Institute Inc.*, Best Places to Work in Paraguay (annual), http://www.greatplacetowork.com, 2011.

Corporations—Pennsylvania

1995 ■ BEST LARGE COMPANIES TO WORK FOR IN PENNSYLVANIA, 2011

Ranked by: Score based on employee surveys. **Remarks:** Specific scores not provided; companies are listed alphabetically by primary city. To qualify, companies must have at least 251 employees. **Number listed:** 35

1. Sheetz Inc.
2. Philadelphia Insurance Cos.

3. The Jones Group Inc.
4. Holy Spirit Health System
5. F & M Trust
6. NPC Inc.
7. Quest Diagnostics Inc.
8. Shared Technologies Inc.
9. Gettysburg College
10. Maris Grove by Erickson Living

Source: *Best Companies Group*, Best Places to Work in Pennsylvania (annual), http://www.bestplacestoworkinpa.com, September 19, 2011.

1996 ■ BEST SMALL COMPANIES IN PENNSYLVANIA, 2011

Ranked by: Score based on revenue, profits, and return on equity for the past 12 months and five years. **Remarks:** Specific scores not provided. Also notes rank in the overall *100 Best Small Companies in America*. To qualify, companies must have revenues between $5 million and $1 billion, a net margin above five percent, and share price above $5. List is available online only. **Number listed:** 4

1. Rue21
2. II-VI
3. Ansys
4. Dorman Products

Source: *Forbes*, Best Small Companies in America (annual), November 7, 2011.

1997 ■ BEST SMALL/MEDIUM-SIZED COMPANIES TO WORK FOR IN PENNSYLVANIA, 2011

Ranked by: Score based on employee surveys. **Remarks:** Specific scores not provided; companies are listed alphabetically by primary city. To qualify, companies must have between 25 and 249 employees. **Number listed:** 65

1. Penn State Federal Credit Union
2. Adaptik Corp.
3. Pentec Health
4. DVL Inc.
5. Boyer & Ritter CPAs & Consultants
6. Brown Schultz Sheridan & Fritz
7. Gunn Mowery LLC
8. McKonly & Asbury
9. Momentum Inc.
10. Fitzpatrick Lentz & Bubba PC

Source: *Best Companies Group*, Best Places to Work in Pennsylvania (annual), http://www.bestplacestoworkinpa.com, September 19, 2011.

1998 ■ LARGEST COMPANIES IN PENNSYLVANIA BY EMPLOYEES, 2010

Ranked by: Number of employees at headquarters. **Remarks:** Also notes contact information for headquarters, total number of employees, revenue, rank by revenue, and primary SIC code. **Number listed:** 456

1. Comcast Holdings Corp., with 22,000 employees
2. The Vanguard Group Inc., 9,500
3. Einstein Community Health Associates Inc., 6,000
4. Hershey Entertainment & Resorts Co., 5,500

5. FedEx Ground Package System Inc., 5,000
5. PNC Bank NA, 5,000
5. St. Luke's Hospital & Health Network, 5,000
8. Allegheny General Hospital Inc., 4,864
9. Westinghouse Electric Co., 4,500
10. York Hospital, 4,500

Source: *Business Rankings*, (annual), Dun & Bradstreet Inc., 2011, p. IV.190-IV.199.

1999 ■ LARGEST COMPANIES IN PENNSYLVANIA BY SALES, 2010

Ranked by: Revenue, in dollars. **Remarks:** Also notes contact information for headquarters, number of employees at headquarters and overall, rank by employees, and primary SIC code. **Number listed:** 461

1. AmerisourceBergen Corp., with $77,953,979,000
2. Comcast Corp., $37,937,000,000
3. Sunoco Inc., $37,489,000,000
4. Rite Aid Corp., $25,669,117,000
5. United States Steel Corp., $17,374,000,000
6. PPG Industries Inc., $13,423,000,000
7. H. J. Heinz Co., $10,494,983,000
8. Air Products & Chemicals Inc., $9,026,000,000
9. PPL Corp., $8,521,000,000
10. University of Pittsburgh Medical Center, $8,046,467,000
10. UPMC Presbyterian, $8,046,467,000

Source: *Business Rankings*, (annual), Dun & Bradstreet Inc., 2011, p. III.187-III.196.

2000 ■ LARGEST PITTSBURGH COMPANIES OVERALL, 2011

Ranked by: Score based on revenue, net income, stock price change, return on equity, market value, and growth in revenue and net income. **Remarks:** Specific scores not provided. Also notes headquarters. **Number listed:** 50

1. Lanxess
2. GlaxoSmithKline
3. Verizon
4. Siemens AG
5. Kennametal
6. Comcast
7. Fidelity Bancorp
8. AmeriServ Financial
9. TMS International
10. McKesson

Source: *Pittsburgh Post-Gazette*, Top 50 (annual), http://www.post-gazette.com, March 20, 2012.

2001 ■ LARGEST PRIVATE COMPANIES IN THE PITTSBURGH AREA, 2011

Ranked by: Revenue, in millions of dollars. **Number listed:** 33

1. Giant Eagle Inc., with $9,300 million
2. Westinghouse Electric Co., $5,200
3. Genco ATC, $1,550
4. Gateway Health Plan, $1,460
5. 84 Lumber Co., $1,430

6. K & L Gates LLP, $1,060
7. Reed Smith, $993.19
8. P. J. Dick, $616
9. Hunter Truck Sales & Service, $534.5
10. Centimark, $462.8

Source: *Pittsburgh Post-Gazette*, Top 50 (annual), http://www.post-gazette.com, March 20, 2012.

2002 ■ LARGEST PUBLIC COMPANIES IN CENTRAL PENNSYLVANIA, 2010

Ranked by: Revenue, in billions of dollars. **Remarks:** Also notes contact information, rank and figures for previous year, percent growth, total local executive, earnings for current and previous year, stock exchange, ticker symbol, number of full-time employees, number of locations, year founded, and type of business. **Number listed:** 24

1. Rite Aid Corp., with $25.67 billion
2. The Hershey Co., $5.67
3. Harsco Corp., $3.04
4. Bon Ton Stores Inc., $2.98
5. Armstrong World Industries Inc., $2.77
6. Weis Markets Inc., $2.62
7. Penn National Gaming Inc., $2.46
8. Select Medical Holdings Corp., $2.39
9. Dentsply International Inc., $2.22
10. P. H. Glatfelter Co., dba Glatfelter, $1.47

Source: *Central Penn Business Journal*, Largest Public Companies (annual), June 24, 2011.

2003 ■ MOST ADMIRED COMPANIES IN PENNSYLVANIA, 2012

Ranked by: Survey of top executives, directors, and securities analysts regarding the Fortune 1,000 companies that they admire the most, regardless of industry. **Remarks:** Also notes city and industry rank. List is available online only, not in print. **Number listed:** 8

1. PNC Financial Services Group Inc., with 6.92 points
2. Airgas Inc., 6.16
3. ARAMARK Corp., 6.11
4. PPG Industries Inc., 6.05
5. Comcast Corp., 6.03
6. SunGard Data Systems, 5.83
7. AmerisourceBergen, 5.82
8. Universal Health Services Inc., 5.6

Source: *Fortune*, World's Most Admired Companies (annual), http://www.fortune.com, March 19, 2012.

2004 ■ PENNSYLVANIA'S LARGEST COMPANIES OVERALL, 2011

Ranked by: Score based on revenue, profits, assets, and market capitalization. **Remarks:** Specific scores not provided. Also notes overall rank in the *Forbes 2000* and figures for each criterion. **Number listed:** 20

1. Comcast Corp.
2. PNC Financial Services Group Inc.
3. PPL Corp.
4. AmerisourceBergen Corp.
5. PPG Industries Inc.

6. Air Products & Chemicals Inc.
7. H. J. Heinz Co.
8. Lincoln National Corp.
9. Mylan Inc.
10. Consol Energy Inc.

Source: *Forbes*, Forbes 2000 (annual), http://www.forbes.com, May 7, 2012.

2005 ■ PENNSYLVANIA'S LARGEST PRIVATE COMPANIES, 2010

Ranked by: Revenue, in billions of dollars. **Remarks:** Also notes business segment, number of employees, and overall rank in the *America's Largest Private Companies* list. Ranking is available online only, not in print. **Number listed:** 10

1. ARAMARK Corp., with $13 billion
2. Giant Eagle Inc., $8.2
3. Wawa Inc., $6.99
4. Sheetz Inc., $5.23
5. SunGard Data Systems Inc., $4.99
6. VWR Funding Inc., $3.64
7. D & H Distributing Co., $2.61
8. Genesis HealthCare Corp., $2.55
9. Asplundh Tree Expert Co., $2.49
10. The Day & Zimmermann Group Inc., $2.39

Source: *Forbes*, America's Largest Private Companies (annual), http://www.forbes.com, December 5, 2011.

2006 ■ PITTSBURGH COMPANIES WITH THE FASTEST-GROWING PROFITS, 2010-2011

Ranked by: Annual growth in net income, in percent. **Remarks:** Also notes headquarters. **Number listed:** 50

1. Lanxess, with 847.5%
2. AmeriServ Financial, 409.9%
3. Kennametal Inc., 394.9%
4. Fidelity Bancorp, 319.8%
5. GlaxoSmithKline, 234.6%
6. WVS Financial, 229.6%
7. TMS International, 211.5%
8. Allegheny Technologies, 203.1%
9. Alcoa, 140.6%
10. Mylan Inc., 140.1%

Source: *Pittsburgh Post-Gazette*, Top 50 (annual), http://www.post-gazette.com, March 20, 2012.

2007 ■ PITTSBURGH COMPANIES WITH THE HIGHEST PROFITS, 2011

Ranked by: Net income, in millions of dollars. **Remarks:** Also notes headquarters. **Number listed:** 50

1. Verizon, with $10,198 million
2. GlaxoSmithKline, $8,471
3. Siemens AG, $8,462.2
4. Comcast, $4,160
5. Bayer, $3,201.6
6. PNC Financial Services Group Inc., $2,998
7. Bank of New York Mellon Corp., $2,516
8. Emerson Electric, $2,480
9. FedEx Corp., $1,452

10. Eaton, $1,350

Source: *Pittsburgh Post-Gazette*, Top 50 (annual), http://www.post-gazette.com, March 20, 2012.

2008 ■ PITTSBURGH COMPANIES WITH THE HIGHEST REVENUE, 2011

Ranked by: Revenue, in millions of dollars. **Remarks:** Also notes headquarters. **Number listed:** 50

1. McKesson, with $112,084 million
2. Verizon, $110,875
3. Siemens AG, $98,417.6
4. Comcast, $55,842
5. Bayer, $47,309.3
6. GlaxoSmithKline, $44,093
7. Royal Bank of Scotland, $43,183.6
8. FedEx Corp., $39,304
9. Supervalu, $37,534
10. Koninklijke Philips Electronics NV (Royal Philips Electronics NV), $29,243.2

Source: *Pittsburgh Post-Gazette*, Top 50 (annual), http://www.post-gazette.com, March 20, 2012.

2009 ■ TOP *FORTUNE 500* COMPANIES IN PENNSYLVANIA, 2011

Ranked by: Revenue, in millions of dollars. **Remarks:** Also notes overall rank in the *Fortune 500,* headquarters, and number of employees. **Number listed:** 23

1. AmerisourceBergen Corp., with $80,217.6 million
2. Comcast Corp., $55,842
3. Sunoco Inc., $45,765
4. Rite Aid Corp., $25,214.9
5. United States Steel Corp., $19,884
6. PNC Financial Services Group Inc., $15,820
7. PPG Industries Inc., $14,885
8. ARAMARK Corp., $13,244.7
9. PPL Corp., $12,756
10. H. J. Heinz Co., $10,706.6

Source: *Fortune*, Fortune 500 (annual), May 21, 2012, p. F-45.

2010 ■ TOP PITTSBURGH COMPANIES BY MARKET VALUE, 2011

Ranked by: Market capitalization, in millions of dollars. **Remarks:** Also notes headquarters. **Number listed:** 50

1. GlaxoSmithKline, with $115,194 million
2. Verizon, $113,583.4
3. Siemens AG, $87,407
4. Comcast, $65,987.5
5. Royal Bank of Scotland, $60,816
6. Bayer, $52,971.7
7. Emerson Electric, $34,256.5
8. PNC Financial Services Group Inc., $30,340.9
9. FedEx Corp., $26,262.6
10. Bank of New York Mellon Corp., $24,143.5

Source: *Pittsburgh Post-Gazette*, Top 50 (annual), http://www.post-gazette.com, March 20, 2012.

2011 ■ TOP PITTSBURGH COMPANIES BY RETURN ON EQUITY, 2011

Ranked by: Return on equity, in percent. **Remarks:** Also notes headquarters. **Number listed:** 50

1. GlaxoSmithKline, with 58.8%
2. Koppers Holdings Inc., 40.2%
3. H. J. Heinz Co., 39.6%
4. Joy Global, 37%
5. TMS International, 33%
6. PPG Industries Inc., 31.8%
7. rue21 Inc., 31.2%
8. Emerson Electric, 24.2%
9. Lanxess, 23.6%
10. Bombardier, 20.6%
10. Siemens AG, 20.6%

Source: *Pittsburgh Post-Gazette*, Top 50 (annual), http://www.post-gazette.com, March 20, 2012.

Corporations—Peru

2012 ■ BEST LARGE COMPANIES TO WORK FOR IN PERU, 2011

Ranked by: Score based on the relationships between employees and management, employees and their jobs/company, and employees and coworkers. **Remarks:** Specific scores not provided. Ranking covers companies with more than 1,000 employees. **Number listed:** 17

1. Kimberly-Clark Peru
2. Sodimac Peru
3. J & V Resguardo
4. Supermercados Peruanos
5. CinePlanet
6. Interbank
7. Nextel
8. Scotiabank Peru
9. Atento Peru
10. Saga Falabella

Source: *Great Place to Work Institute Inc.*, Best Places to Work in Peru (annual), http://www.greatplacetowork.com, November 2011.

2013 ■ BEST MEDIUM-SIZED COMPANIES TO WORK FOR IN PERU, 2011

Ranked by: Score based on the relationships between employees and management, employees and their jobs/company, and employees and coworkers. **Remarks:** Specific scores not provided. Ranking covers companies with 251 to 1,000 employees. **Number listed:** 18

1. JW Marriott Lima
2. IBM del Peru
3. Centro Ceramica Las Flores
4. Casa Andina
5. Interseguro
6. DHL Express Peru
7. McDonald's Corp.
8. Pamolsa
9. British American Tobacco Peru
10. Telefonica Servicios Comerciales

Source: *Great Place to Work Institute Inc.*, Best Places to Work in Peru (annual), http://www.greatplacetowork.com, November 2011.

2014 ■ BEST SMALL COMPANIES TO WORK FOR IN PERU, 2011

Ranked by: Score based on the relationships between employees and management, employees and their jobs/company, and employees and coworkers. **Remarks:** Specific scores not provided. Ranking covers companies with 50 to 250 employees. **Number listed:** 10

1. Corporacion Radial del Peru
2. Inteligo SAB
3. Pinturas Aurora
4. Intralot de Peru
5. Terra Networks Peru
6. VisaNet Peru
7. Coca-Cola Servicios de Peru
8. Accor
9. GMV
10. Lima Tours

Source: *Great Place to Work Institute Inc.*, Best Places to Work in Peru (annual), http://www.greatplacetowork.com, November 2011.

2015 ■ PERU'S LARGEST COMPANIES OVERALL, 2011

Ranked by: Score based on revenue, profits, assets, and market capitalization. **Remarks:** Specific scores not provided. Also notes rank in the overall *Forbes 2000* and figures for each criterion. **Number listed:** 2

1. Credicorp
2. Buenaventura

Source: *Forbes*, Forbes 2000 (annual), http://www.forbes.com, May 7, 2012.

Corporations—Philippines

2016 ■ BEST SMALL PHILIPPINE COMPANIES, 2010

Ranked by: Score based on sales, net income, and market value. **Remarks:** Specific scores not provided; companies are listed alphabetically, not ranked. Also notes sales, net income, market value, and industry. To qualify for list, which is available online only, companies must have under US$1 billion in annual revenue and positive earnings growth over the past five years. **Number listed:** 2

1. Pacific Online Systems
2. Philweb

Source: *Forbes Asia*, Asia's Best Under a Billion (annual), http://www.forbes.com, September 12, 2011.

2017 ■ THE PHILIPPINES' LARGEST COMPANIES OVERALL, 2011

Ranked by: Score based on revenue, profits, assets, and market capitalization. **Remarks:** Specific scores not provided. Also notes rank in the overall *Forbes 2000* and figures for each criterion. **Number listed:** 8

1. San Miguel Corp.
2. Philippine LDT
3. SM Investments
4. Bank Philippine Islands
5. Aboitiz Equity Ventures
6. Metropolitan Bank & Trust
7. Manila Electric
8. BDO Unibank

Source: *Forbes*, Forbes 2000 (annual), http://www.forbes.com, May 7, 2012.

Corporations—Poland

2018 ■ LARGEST COMPANIES IN POLAND, 2010

Ranked by: Sales, in millions of U.S. dollars. **Remarks:** Also notes city; industrial code; percent change in sales; profits; profit as a percentage of sales, assets, and equity; number of employees; sales per employee; assets; equity capital; equity capital as a percentage of assets; year established; and figures for previous year. **Number listed:** 400

1. Narodowy Fundusz Zdrowia, with $17,969.1 million
2. Polski Koncern Naftowy Orlen SA (PKN Orlen), $85,18.9
3. Fiat Auto Poland SA, $6,840.4
4. Tesco (Polska) Sp Zoo, $6,036.6
5. PKO Bank Polski, $4,510
6. Powszechny Zaklad Ubezpieczen Na Zycie SA, $4,498.9
7. Jeronimo Martins Dystrybucja SA, $4,413.5
8. Kompania Weglowa SA, $3,637.7
9. Lotos Paliwa Sp Zoo, $3,617.3
10. Polskie Gornictwo Naftowe i Gazownictwo SA, $3,150.2

Source: *Europe's 15,000 Largest Companies*, (annual), ELC International, 2011, p. 486+.

2019 ■ POLAND'S LARGEST COMPANIES OVERALL, 2011

Ranked by: Score based on revenue, profits, assets, and market capitalization. **Remarks:** Specific scores not provided. Also notes rank in the overall *Forbes 2000* and figures for each criterion. **Number listed:** 7

1. PGE Polska Grupa
2. PKO Bank Polski
3. Polski Koncern Naftowy Orlen SA (PKN Orlen)
4. KGMH Polska Miedz
5. Powszechny Zaklad Ubezpieczen SA (PZU SA)
6. Polskie Gornictwo Naftowe i Gazownictwo SA (PGNiG SA)
7. JSW Group

Source: *Forbes*, Forbes 2000 (annual), http://www.forbes.com, May 7, 2012.

Corporations—Portugal

2020 ■ LARGEST COMPANIES IN PORTUGAL, 2010

Ranked by: Sales, in millions of U.S. dollars. **Remarks:** Also notes city; industrial code; percent change in sales; profits; profit as a percentage of sales, assets, and equity; number of employees; sales per employee; assets; equity capital; equity capital as a percentage of assets; year established; and figures for previous year. **Number listed:** 400

1. Petroleos de Portugal SA (Petrogal), with $9,736.3 million
2. Jeronimo Martins SGPS SA, $9,718.7
3. Portugal Telecom SGPS SA, $9,492
4. Sonae SGPS SA, $7,545.2
5. Modelo Continente SGPS SA, $4,530.7
6. Pingo Doce - Distribuio Alimentar SA, $3,981.4
7. Banco Comercial Portugues SA, $3,546.8
8. Transportes Areos Portugueses SA, $2,809.8
9. CIMPOR - Cimentos de Portugal SGPS SA, $2,793.1
10. Wainfleet - Alumina, Sociedade Unipessoal Lda, $2,706.3

Source: *Europe's 15,000 Largest Companies*, (annual), ELC International, 2011, p. 504+.

2021 ■ PORTUGAL'S LARGEST COMPANIES OVERALL, 2011

Ranked by: Score based on revenue, profits, assets, and market capitalization. **Remarks:** Specific scores not provided. Also notes rank in the overall *Forbes 2000* and figures for each criterion. **Number listed:** 7

1. Energias de Portugal SA (EDP)
2. Galp Energia SGPS
3. Portugal Telecom SA
4. Jeronimo Martins SGPS SA
5. Banco Com Portugues
6. Banco BPI
7. Sonae SGPS

Source: *Forbes*, Forbes 2000 (annual), http://www.forbes.com, May 7, 2012.

Corporations—Puerto Rico

2022 ■ BEST COMPANIES TO WORK FOR IN PUERTO RICO, 2012

Ranked by: Score based on the relationships between employees and management, employees and their jobs/company, and employees and coworkers. **Remarks:** Specific scores not provided. **Number listed:** 4

1. Kimberly-Clark Puerto Rico
2. Atento Puerto Rico
3. Oracle Caribbean Inc. Puerto Rico
4. Scotiabank Puerto Rico

Source: *Great Place to Work Institute Inc.*, Best Places to Work in Central America & the Caribbean (annual), 2012.

Corporations—Qatar

2023 ■ QATAR'S LARGEST COMPANIES OVERALL, 2011

Ranked by: Score based on revenue, profits, assets, and market capitalization. **Remarks:** Specific scores not provided. Also notes rank in the overall *Forbes 2000* and figures for each criterion. **Number listed:** 10

1. Qatar National Bank
2. Qatar Telecom
3. Industries Qatar QSC
4. Commercial Bank of Qatar
5. Masraf Al Rayan
6. Qatar Islamic Bank
7. Ezdan Real Estate
8. Barwa Real Estate
9. United Development Co. PSC
10. Doha Bank

Source: *Forbes*, Forbes 2000 (annual), http://www.forbes.com, May 7, 2012.

Corporations—Rhode Island

2024 ■ BEST LARGE COMPANIES TO WORK FOR IN RHODE ISLAND, 2011

Ranked by: Score based on employee surveys. **Remarks:** Specific scores not provided. To qualify, companies must have at least 150 employees. **Number listed:** 15

1. Pawtucket Credit Union
2. SEA Corp.
3. AIPSO
4. BankNewport
5. Collette Vacations
6. Atrion Networking Corp.
7. University Medicine Foundation Inc.
8. The Washington Trust Co.
9. Amgen Inc.
10. Embrace Home Loans

Source: *Best Companies Group*, Best Places to Work in Rhode Island (annual), http://www.bestplacestoworkri.com, June 2011.

2025 ■ BEST MEDIUM-SIZED COMPANIES TO WORK FOR IN RHODE ISLAND, 2011

Ranked by: Score based on employee surveys. **Remarks:** Specific scores not provided. To qualify, companies must have between 50 and 149 employees. **Number listed:** 11

1. Highlander Charter School
2. Hinckley, Allen & Synder LLP
3. Oceanstate Financial Services
4. A Child's University
5. Accutrust Mortgage Inc.
6. Partridge Snow & Hahn LLP
7. Kahn, Litwin, Renza & Co.
8. Tides Family Services Inc.
9. Barnum Financial Group
10. Koch Eye Associates

Source: *Best Companies Group*, Best Places to Work in Rhode Island (annual), http://www.bestplacestoworkri.com, June 2011.

2026 ■ BEST SMALL COMPANIES TO WORK FOR IN RHODE ISLAND, 2011

Ranked by: Score based on employee surveys. **Remarks:** Specific scores not provided. To qualify, companies must have between 15 and 49 employees. **Number listed:** 14

1. Taylor Duane Barton & Gilman LLP
2. Provider Insurance Group Inc.
3. Edward Jones
4. Tele-Consultants Inc.
5. Province Mortgage Associates Inc.
6. Kforce Inc.
7. ShapeUp
8. Darrow Everett LLP
9. Embolden
10. Envision Technology Advisors LLC

Source: *Best Companies Group*, Best Places to Work in Rhode Island (annual), http://www.bestplacestoworkri.com, June 2011.

2027 ■ LARGEST COMPANIES IN RHODE ISLAND BY EMPLOYEES, 2010

Ranked by: Number of employees at headquarters. **Remarks:** Also notes contact information for headquarters, total number of employees, revenue, rank by revenue, and primary SIC code. **Number listed:** 47

1. Hasbro Managerial Services Inc., with 5,000 employees
2. Rhode Island Hospital Inc., 4,200

3. A & M Special Purchasing Inc., 4,000

4. Hasbro Inc., 2,000

5. Kent County Memorial Hospital, 1,840

6. Women & Infants Hospital of Rhode Island, 1,800

7. Southeastern Healthcare System Inc., 1,653

8. The Memorial Hospital, 1,564

9. CVS Pharmacy Inc., 1,500

10. Roger Williams Medical Center, 1,470

Source: *Business Rankings*, (annual), Dun & Bradstreet Inc., 2011, p. IV.200-IV.201.

2028 ■ LARGEST COMPANIES IN RHODE ISLAND BY SALES, 2010

Ranked by: Revenue, in dollars. **Remarks:** Also notes contact information for headquarters, number of employees at headquarters and overall, rank by employees, and primary SIC code. **Number listed:** 50

1. CVS Caremark Corp., with $96,413,000,000

2. Textron Inc., $10,525,000,000

3. Hasbro Inc., $4,002,161,000

4. United Natural Foods Inc., $3,757,139,000

5. Gilbane Building Co., $3,060,357,000

6. NTK Holdings Inc., $2,269,700,000

7. Rhode Island Hospital, $918,618,000

8. Green Valley Oil LLC, $700,000,000

9. Teknor Apex Co., $647,895,000

10. Lin Television Corp., $420,047,000

10. Lin TV Corp., $420,047,000

Source: *Business Rankings*, (annual), Dun & Bradstreet Inc., 2011, p. III.197-III.198.

2029 ■ LARGEST EMPLOYERS IN RHODE ISLAND, 2011

Ranked by: Number of local employees. **Remarks:** Also notes rank and figures for previous year, contact information, president/CEO, type of business, and year founded. **Number listed:** 24

1. State of Rhode Island, with 13,207 employees

2. Lifespan Corp., 12,330.3

3. Care New England, 6,711.4

4. CVS Caremark Corp., 6,200

5. Citizens Financial Group Inc., 5,400

Source: *Providence Business News*, Rhode Island Employers (annual), May 21, 2012.

2030 ■ LARGEST PUBLIC COMPANIES IN RHODE ISLAND, 2011

Ranked by: Number of local employees. **Remarks:** Also notes rank for previous year, contact information, CEO, top local executive, type of business, and financial data. **Number listed:** 21

1. CVS Caremark Corp., with 6,200 employees

2. Citizens Bank, 5,350

3. Bank of America Corp., 3,000

4. Electric Boat Corp., 2,300

5. Wal-Mart Stores Inc., 2,188

Source: *Providence Business News*, Public Companies (annual), January 9, 2012.

2031 ■ MOST ADMIRED COMPANIES IN RHODE ISLAND, 2012

Ranked by: Survey of top executives, directors, and securities analysts regarding the Fortune 1,000 companies that they admire

the most, regardless of industry **Remarks:** Also notes city and industry rank. List is available online only, not in print. **Number listed:** 2

1. United Natural Foods, with 6.91 points

2. CVS Caremark, 6.27

Source: *Fortune*, World's Most Admired Companies (annual), http://www.fortune.com, March 19, 2012.

2032 ■ RHODE ISLAND'S LARGEST COMPANIES OVERALL, 2011

Ranked by: Score based on revenue, profits, assets, and market capitalization. **Remarks:** Specific scores not provided. Also notes overall rank in the *Forbes 2000* and figures for each criterion. **Number listed:** 2

1. CVS Caremark Corp.

2. Textron Inc.

Source: *Forbes*, Forbes 2000 (annual), http://www.forbes.com, May 7, 2012.

2033 ■ TOP *FORTUNE 500* COMPANIES IN RHODE ISLAND, 2011

Ranked by: Revenue, in millions of dollars. **Remarks:** Also notes overall rank in the *Fortune 500,* headquarters, and number of employees. **Number listed:** 2

1. CVS Caremark Corp., with $107,750 million

2. Textron Inc., $11,275

Source: *Fortune*, Fortune 500 (annual), May 21, 2012, p. F-45.

Corporations—Romania

2034 ■ LARGEST COMPANIES IN ROMANIA, 2010

Ranked by: Sales, in millions of U.S. dollars. **Remarks:** Also notes city; industrial code; percent change in sales; profits; profit as a percentage of sales, assets, and equity; number of employees; sales per employee; assets; equity capital; equity capital as a percentage of assets; year established; and figures for previous year. **Number listed:** 100

1. BRD - Groupe Societe Generale SA, with $6,047.7 million

2. OMV Petrom SA, $4,439.6

3. Dacia Group, $2,978.3

4. Banca Comerciala Romana SA, $2,965.3

5. Rompetrol Rafinare SA, $2,331.4

6. Lukoil Romania SA, $1,755.4

7. Rompetrol Downstream SRL, $1,748.9

8. Banca Transilvania SA, $1,467.9

9. Porsche Romania SRL, $1,434.3

10. GDF Suez Energy Romania SA, $1,380.6

Source: *Europe's 15,000 Largest Companies*, (annual), ELC International, 2011, p. 522+.

Corporations—Russia

2035 ■ LARGEST CORPORATIONS IN RUSSIA BY REVENUE, 2010

Ranked by: Revenue, in millions of U.S. dollars. **Remarks:** Also notes headquarters city and overall rank in the *Global 500*. Ranking is available online only, not in print. **Number listed:** 7

1. OAO Gazprom, with $118,657 million
2. OAO Lukoil, $86,078
3. OAO Rosneft Oil Co., $46,304
4. TNK-BP International, $36,881
5. Sberbank--Savings Bank of the Russian Federation, $32,066
6. JSFC Sistema, $28,099
7. OJSC Surgutneftegas, $19,656

Source: *Fortune*, Global 500 (annual), http://www.fortune.com, July 25, 2011.

2036 ■ RUSSIA'S LARGEST COMPANIES OVERALL, 2011

Ranked by: Score based on revenue, profits, assets, and market capitalization. **Remarks:** Specific scores not provided. Also notes rank in the overall *Forbes 2000* and figures for each criterion. **Number listed:** 27

1. OAO Gazprom
2. OAO Lukoil
3. OAO Rosneft Oil Co.
4. Sberbank--Savings Bank of the Russian Federation
5. TNK-BP Holding
6. OJSC Surgutneftegas
7. VTB Bank
8. OJSC Mining & Metallurgical Company Norilsk Nickel
9. Sistema JSFC
10. United Company RUSAL plc

Source: *Forbes*, Forbes 2000 (annual), http://www.forbes.com, May 7, 2012.

Corporations—Saudi Arabia

2037 ■ SAUDI ARABIA'S LARGEST COMPANIES OVERALL, 2011

Ranked by: Score based on revenue, profits, assets, and market capitalization. **Remarks:** Specific scores not provided. Also notes rank in the overall *Forbes 2000* and figures for each criterion. **Number listed:** 16

1. Saudi Basic Industries Corp. (Sabic)
2. Saudi Telecom Co.
3. Saudi Electricity Co.
4. Al Jajhi Bank
5. Samba Financial Group
6. Riyad Bank
7. Saudi British Bank
8. Mobily
9. Banque Saudi Fransi
10. Arab National Bank

Source: *Forbes*, Forbes 2000 (annual), http://www.forbes.com, May 7, 2012.

Corporations—Singapore

2038 ■ BEST SMALL SINGAPORE COMPANIES, 2010

Ranked by: Score based on sales, net income, and market value. **Remarks:** Specific scores not provided; companies are listed alphabetically, not ranked. Also notes sales, net income, market value, and industry. To qualify for list, which is available online only, companies must have under US$1 billion in annual revenue and positive earnings growth over the past five years. **Number listed:** 6

1. ARA Asset Management
2. CWT
3. Ezion Holdings
4. Leader Environmental Technologies
5. Miclyn Express Offshore
6. PEC

Source: *Forbes Asia*, Asia's Best Under a Billion (annual), http://www.forbes.com, September 12, 2011.

2039 ■ LARGEST CORPORATIONS IN SINGAPORE BY REVENUE, 2010

Ranked by: Revenue, in millions of U.S. dollars. **Remarks:** Also notes headquarters city and overall rank in the *Global 500*. Ranking is available online only, not in print. **Number listed:** 2

1. Wilmar International Ltd., with $30,378 million
2. Flextronics International Ltd., $28,680

Source: *Fortune*, Global 500 (annual), http://www.fortune.com, July 25, 2011.

2040 ■ MOST ADMIRED COMPANIES IN SINGAPORE, 2012

Ranked by: Score based on a survey of executives, directors, and securities analysts of companies within their own industry. **Remarks:** List is available online only, not in print. Also notes headquarters. **Number listed:** 2

1. Wilmar International Ltd., with 7.01 points
2. Singapore Airlines Ltd., 6.28

Source: *Fortune*, World's Most Admired Companies (annual), http://www.fortune.com, March 19, 2012.

2041 ■ SINGAPORE'S LARGEST COMPANIES OVERALL, 2011

Ranked by: Score based on revenue, profits, assets, and market capitalization. **Remarks:** Specific scores not provided. Also notes rank in the overall *Forbes 2000* and figures for each criterion. **Number listed:** 18

1. Wilmar International Ltd.
2. Singapore Telecommunications Ltd.
3. DBS Group Holdings Ltd.
4. Overseas-Chinese Banking Corp.
5. United Overseas Bank
6. Keppel Corp., Ltd.
7. Singapore Airlines Ltd.
8. CapitaLand Ltd.
9. Flextronics International Ltd.
10. Golden Agri-Resources Ltd.

Source: *Forbes*, Forbes 2000 (annual), http://www.forbes.com, May 7, 2012.

Corporations—Slovakia

2042 ■ LARGEST COMPANIES IN SLOVAKIA, 2010

Ranked by: Sales, in millions of U.S. dollars. **Remarks:** Also notes city; industrial code; percent change in sales; profits; profit as a percentage of sales, assets, and equity; number of employees; sales per employee; assets; equity capital; equity capital as a percentage of assets; year established; and figures for previous year. **Number listed:** 100

1. Volkswagen Slovakia AS, with $6,876.4 million
2. Samsung Electronics Slovakia sro, $6,119.1
3. Slovnaft as, $5,197
4. Kia Motors Slovakia SRO, $4,882.9
5. Coal Energy AS, $4,086.6
6. Euronics Trencin SRO, $3,891.3
7. PCA Slovakia SRO, $3,628.6
8. Slovensky plynarensky pnemysel as, $2,647
9. Slovenske elektrame as, $2,612
10. Agromepa SRO, $1,865.4

Source: *Europe's 15,000 Largest Companies*, (annual), ELC International, 2011, p. 528+.

Corporations—Slovenia

2043 ■ LARGEST COMPANIES IN SLOVENIA, 2010

Ranked by: Sales, in millions of U.S. dollars. **Remarks:** Also notes city; industrial code; percent change in sales; profits; profit as a percentage of sales, assets, and equity; number of employees; sales per employee; assets; equity capital; equity capital as a percentage of assets; year established; and figures for previous year. **Number listed:** 50

1. Gorenje, Gospodnijski Aparati dd, with $1,663.9 million
2. Revoz, Podjetje Za Proizvodnjo Novo Mesto, $1,839
3. Merkur dd, $1,319.1
4. Zavarovalnica Triglav dd, $1,078.9
5. Krka dd Novo mesto, $1,004.6
6. LEK dd, $949.9
7. Slovenska Industrija Jekla dd, $873.3
8. Ach, Druzba Za Gospodarjenje z Nalozabmi, $809.1
9. SPAR Slovenija doo, $791.3
10. Impol 2000 dd, $625

Source: *Europe's 15,000 Largest Companies*, (annual), ELC International, 2011, p. 534+.

Corporations—South Africa

2044 ■ SOUTH AFRICA'S LARGEST COMPANIES OVERALL, 2011

Ranked by: Score based on revenue, profits, assets, and market capitalization. **Remarks:** Specific scores not provided. Also notes rank in the overall *Forbes 2000* and figures for each criterion. **Number listed:** 20

1. Standard Bank Group (Stanbank)
2. Sasol Ltd.
3. FirstRand Ltd.
4. MTN Group Ltd.
5. Sanlam Ltd.
6. AngloGold Ashanti
7. Naspers Ltd.
8. Impala Platinum Holdings Ltd.

9. Steinhoff International
10. Gold Fields Ltd.

Source: *Forbes*, Forbes 2000 (annual), http://www.forbes.com, May 7, 2012.

Corporations—South Carolina

2045 ■ FASTEST-GROWING SOUTH CAROLINA COMPANIES, 2011

Ranked by: Score based on growth in revenue and employment. **Remarks:** Specific scores not provided. Also notes year founded, headquarters, top executive, description, and industry. To qualify, companies must have been in operation for at least three years and have a minimum of $3 million in annual revenue. **Number listed:** 25

1. Barling Bay
2. Southern Tide
3. Levelwing Media
4. Select Health of South Carolina
5. Thomas Glover Associates Inc.
6. Pegasus Steel LLC
7. Human Technologies Inc.
8. Returnable Packaging Resource Inc.
9. SCRA
10. Dennis Corp.

Source: *South Carolina Business*, 25 Fastest-Growing Companies (annual), 2011, p. 75-76.

2046 ■ LARGEST COMPANIES IN SOUTH CAROLINA BY EMPLOYEES, 2010

Ranked by: Number of employees at headquarters. **Remarks:** Also notes contact information for headquarters, total number of employees, revenue, rank by revenue, and primary SIC code. **Number listed:** 108

1. BMW Manufacturing Co. LLC, with 5,000 employees
2. Greenville Hospital System Inc., 4,000
2. Medical University Hospital Authority, 4,000
2. Medical University of South Carolina, 4,000
5. Palmetto-Richland Memorial Hospital, 3,900
6. Spartanburg Regional Health Services District Inc., 3,444
7. Lockheed Martin Logistics Management Inc., 3,200
8. Blue Cross & Blue Shield of South Carolina, 2,500
9. Delta Apparel Inc., 2,460
10. Anmed Health, 2,420

Source: *Business Rankings*, (annual), Dun & Bradstreet Inc., 2011, p. IV.202-IV.204.

2047 ■ LARGEST COMPANIES IN SOUTH CAROLINA BY SALES, 2010

Ranked by: Revenue, in dollars. **Remarks:** Also notes contact information for headquarters, number of employees at headquarters and overall, rank by employees, and primary SIC code. **Number listed:** 105

1. Scana Corp., with $4,601,000,000
2. Sonoco Products Co., $4,124,121,000

3. South Carolina Electric & Gas Co., $2,815,000,000
4. Lexmed Inc., $2,416,696,700
5. J. M. Smith Corp., $2,367,091,815
6. Scansource Inc., $2,114,979,000
7. South Carolina Public Service Authority, $1,702,001,000
8. AVX Corp., $1,304,966,000
9. Palmetto Health, $1,275,785,000
10. Scana Energy Marketing Inc., $1,200,000,000

Source: *Business Rankings*, (annual), Dun & Bradstreet Inc., 2011, p. III.199-III.201.

2048 ■ SOUTH CAROLINA'S LARGEST PRIVATE COMPANIES, 2010

Ranked by: Revenue, in billions of dollars. Remarks: Also notes business segment, number of employees, and overall rank in the *America's Largest Private Companies* list. Ranking is available online only, not in print. Number listed: 3

1. The InterTech Group Inc., with $3.6 billion
2. J. M. Smith Corp., $2.43
3. Bi-Lo Holdings, $2.2

Source: *Forbes*, America's Largest Private Companies (annual), http://www.forbes.com, December 5, 2011.

Corporations—South Dakota

2049 ■ LARGEST COMPANIES IN SOUTH DAKOTA BY EMPLOYEES, 2010

Ranked by: Number of employees at headquarters. Remarks: Also notes contact information for headquarters, total number of employees, revenue, rank by revenue, and primary SIC code. Number listed: 49

1. Citibank South Dakota N.A., with 3,200 employees
2. Premier Bankcard Inc., 2,889
3. Rapid City Regional Hospital Inc., 2,565
4. Tyson Fresh Meats Inc., 2,100
5. Avera McKennan Hospital & University Center, 1,500
6. Evangelical Lutheran Good Samaritan Society, 1,200
7. Lodgenet Interactive Corp., 825
8. Larson Manufacturing Co. of South Dakota Inc., 750
8. Sacred Heart Health Services, 750
10. Gehl Power Products Inc., 716

Source: *Business Rankings*, (annual), Dun & Bradstreet Inc., 2011, p. IV.205-IV.206.

2050 ■ LARGEST COMPANIES IN SOUTH DAKOTA BY SALES, 2010

Ranked by: Revenue, in dollars. Remarks: Also notes contact information for headquarters, number of employees at headquarters and overall, rank by employees, and primary SIC code. Number listed: 49

1. Black Hills Corp., with $1,307,251,000
2. NorthWestern Corp., $1,110,720,000
3. Evangelical Lutheran Good Samaritan Society, $891,210,000

4. Jenkins Living Center Inc., $853,531,500
5. Verasun Energy Corp., $848,281,000
6. Avera McKennan, $562,063,787
7. Black Hills Utility Holdings Inc., $553,576,111
8. North Central Farmers Elevator, $454,267,189
9. Lodgenet Interactive Corp., $452,172,000
10. Daktronics Inc., $393,185,000

Source: *Business Rankings*, (annual), Dun & Bradstreet Inc., 2011, p. III.202-III.203.

2051 ■ LARGEST EMPLOYERS IN SIOUX FALLS, SOUTH DAKOTA, 2011

Ranked by: Number of employees in the Sioux Falls region. Remarks: Also notes rank for previous year, contact information, total number of employees, number of locations regionally and systemwide, revenue, net income, type of business, year founded, year founded locally, owner or parent company, and top local executive. Number listed: 10

1. Sanford Health, with 8,200 employees
2. Avera Health, 5,905
3. John Morrell & Co., 3,300
4. Wells Fargo & Co., 2,900
4. Citibank NA, 2,900
6. Hy-Vee Inc., 2,733
7. Wal-Mart Stores Inc./Sam's Club, 1,250
8. The Evangelical Lutheran Good Samaritan Society, 1,215
9. First Premier Bank/Premier Bankcard, 1,040
10. Raven Industries Inc./Aerostar International Inc., 936

Source: *Sioux Falls Business Journal*, Top Employers, February 22, 2012, p. 14.

2052 ■ LARGEST PUBLIC COMPANIES IN SIOUX FALLS, SOUTH DAKOTA, 2010

Ranked by: Number of employees in the Sioux Falls region. Remarks: Also notes rank for previous year, contact information, total number of employees, revenue, net income, type of business, year founded, year first publicly traded, stock exchange, ticker symbol, and top local executive. Number listed: 5

1. Raven Industries Inc., with 740 employees
2. LodgeNet Interactive Corp., 500
3. HF Financial Corp., 272
4. NorthWestern Energy, 40
5. Summit Hotel Properties Inc., 13

Source: *Sioux Falls Business Journal*, Publicly Traded Companies, June 29, 2011, p. 17.

Corporations—South Korea

2053 ■ BEST SMALL SOUTH KOREAN COMPANIES, 2010

Ranked by: Score based on sales, net income, and market value. Remarks: Specific scores not provided; companies are listed alphabetically, not ranked. Also notes sales, net income, market value, and industry. To qualify for list, which is available online only, companies must have under US$1 billion in annual revenue and positive earnings growth over the past five years. Number listed: 16

1. Daum Communications

2. EO Technics
3. ESTec
4. ESTsoft
5. Eugene Technology
6. Geumhwa
7. Global Standard Technology
8. INFOvine
9. InterPark
10. Koh Young Technology

Source: *Forbes Asia*, Asia's Best Under a Billion (annual), http://www.forbes.com, September 12, 2011.

2054 ■ LARGEST CORPORATIONS IN SOUTH KOREA BY REVENUE, 2010

Ranked by: Revenue, in millions of U.S. dollars. **Remarks:** Also notes headquarters city and overall rank in the *Global 500*. Ranking is available online only, not in print. **Number listed:** 14

1. Samsung Electronics Co., Ltd., with $133,781 million
2. Hyundai Motor Co., $97,408
3. SK Holdings Co., Ltd., $78,435
4. Pohang Iron & Steel Co., Ltd. (POSCO), $52,462
5. LG Electronics Inc., $48,236
6. Hyundai Heavy Industries Co., Ltd., $38,996
7. GS Holdings Co., Ltd., $36,570
8. Korea Electric Power Co., $34,110
9. Hanwha Chemical Corp., $30,041
10. Samsung Life Insurance Co., $28,773

Source: *Fortune*, Global 500 (annual), http://www.fortune.com, July 25, 2011.

2055 ■ MOST ADMIRED COMPANIES IN SOUTH KOREA, 2012

Ranked by: Score based on a survey of executives, directors, and securities analysts of companies within their own industry. **Remarks:** List is available online only, not in print. Also notes headquarters. **Number listed:** 3

1. Pohang Iron & Steel Co., Ltd. (POSCO), with 6.93 points
2. Samsung Electronics Co., Ltd., 6.5
3. Hyundai Motor Co., 5.87

Source: *Fortune*, World's Most Admired Companies (annual), http://www.fortune.com, March 19, 2012.

2056 ■ SOUTH KOREA'S LARGEST COMPANIES OVERALL, 2011

Ranked by: Score based on revenue, profits, assets, and market capitalization. **Remarks:** Specific scores not provided. Also notes rank in the overall *Forbes 2000* and figures for each criterion. **Number listed:** 68

1. Samsung Electronics Co., Ltd.
2. Hyundai Motor Co.
3. Pohang Iron & Steel Co., Ltd. (POSCO)
4. Shinhan Financial Group Co., Ltd.
5. Hyundai Heavy Industries Co., Ltd.
6. Samsung Life Insurance Co., Ltd.
7. Kia Motors Corp.
8. KB Financial Group

9. SK Innovation
10. Woori Finance Holdings Co., Ltd.

Source: *Forbes*, Forbes 2000 (annual), http://www.forbes.com, May 7, 2012.

2057 ■ TOP SOUTH KOREAN COMPANIES, 2011

Ranked by: Score based on profits, sales and earnings growth, and projected earnings and stock-price gains. **Remarks:** Specific scores not provided; companies are listed alphabetically, not ranked. Also notes market value, revenue, and industry. To quality, companies must be publicly traded with revenues or market capitalization of at least US$3 billion. Ranking is available online only, not in print. **Number listed:** 8

1. CJ CheilJedang
2. Dongbu Insurance
3. Halla Engineering & Construction
4. Hyundai Glovis
5. Hyundai Mobis
6. LG Household & Health Care
7. NHN
8. Samsung Engineering

Source: *Forbes*, Asian Fab 50 (annual), September 13, 2011.

Corporations—Spain

2058 ■ BEST EXTRA-LARGE COMPANIES TO WORK FOR IN SPAIN, 2012

Ranked by: Score based on the relationships between employees and management, employees and their jobs/company, and employees and coworkers. **Remarks:** Specific scores not provided. Ranking covers companies with more than 1,000 employees. **Number listed:** 10

1. Atento Spain
2. Novartis Spain
3. Ikea Iberica
4. Vodafone Spain
5. Mutua Madrilena
6. Wolters Kluwer Espana
7. Bankinter
8. Lilly
9. Everis
10. Aki Bricolaje Espana

Source: *Great Place to Work Institute Inc.*, Best Places to Work in Spain (annual), 2011.

2059 ■ BEST LARGE COMPANIES TO WORK FOR IN SPAIN, 2012

Ranked by: Score based on the relationships between employees and management, employees and their jobs/company, and employees and coworkers. **Remarks:** Specific scores not provided. Ranking covers companies with 500 to 1,000 employees. **Number listed:** 6

1. Microsoft Spain
2. Janssen
3. DKV Seguros
4. Baxter
5. Philips Iberica
6. 3M Espana

Source: *Great Place to Work Institute Inc.*, Best Places to Work in Spain (annual), 2011.

2060 ■ BEST MEDIUM-SIZED COMPANIES TO WORK FOR IN SPAIN, 2012

Ranked by: Score based on the relationships between employees and management, employees and their jobs/company, and employees and coworkers. **Remarks:** Specific scores not provided. Ranking covers companies with 250 to 500 employees. **Number listed:** 18

1. Cisco Systems Spain
2. Medtronic Spain
3. Amgen Spain
4. Synthon Hispania
5. Quintiles Commercial
6. Grupo Intercom
7. Wrigley Espana
8. Telefonica Internacional
9. Telefonica International Wholesale Services
10. Astellas Pharma

Source: *Great Place to Work Institute Inc.*, Best Places to Work in Spain (annual), 2011.

2061 ■ BEST MICRO-SIZED COMPANIES TO WORK FOR IN SPAIN, 2011

Ranked by: Score based on the relationships between employees and management, employees and their jobs/company, and employees and coworkers. **Remarks:** Specific scores not provided. To qualify, companies must have between 50 and 100 employees. **Number listed:** 4

1. Bain & Co. Iberica
2. Grupo Visual MS
3. Emagister.com
4. Trovit

Source: *Great Place to Work Institute Inc.*, Best Places to Work in Spain (annual), 2011.

2062 ■ BEST SMALL COMPANIES TO WORK FOR IN SPAIN, 2011

Ranked by: Score based on the relationships between employees and management, employees and their jobs/company, and employees and coworkers. **Remarks:** Specific scores not provided. To qualify, companies must have between 100 and 250 employees. **Number listed:** 12

1. Softonic.com
2. Eurofirms ETT
3. Kellogg Espana
4. Coca-Cola Espana
5. Proclinic
6. Royal Canin
7. Mars Espana
8. R
9. Infojobs
10. Admiral Seguros - Balumba

Source: *Great Place to Work Institute Inc.*, Best Places to Work in Spain (annual), 2011.

2063 ■ LARGEST COMPANIES IN SPAIN, 2010

Ranked by: Sales, in millions of U.S. dollars. **Remarks:** Also notes city; industrial code; percent change in sales; profits; profit as a percentage of sales, assets, and equity; number of employ-ees; sales per employee; assets; equity capital; equity capital as a percentage of assets; year established; and figures for previous year. **Number listed:** 800

1. Banco Santander SA, with $57,728.1 million
2. Banco Bilbao Vizcaya Argentaria SA (BBVA), $31,109.1
3. Repsol Petroleo SA, $23,864.6
4. Actividades de Construccion y Servicios SA (ACS), $22,566.1
5. MAPFRE SA, $21,475.2
6. Mercadona SA, $21,419.2
7. Compania Espanola de Petroleos SA (Cepsa), $21,010.9
8. Grupo Ferrovial SA, $19,910.6
9. Repsol Comercial de Productos Petroliferos SA, $18,989.5
10. Telefonica de Espana SA, $16,727.5

Source: *Europe's 15,000 Largest Companies*, (annual), ELC International, 2011, p. 538+.

2064 ■ LARGEST CORPORATIONS IN SPAIN BY REVENUE, 2010

Ranked by: Revenue, in millions of U.S. dollars. **Remarks:** Also notes headquarters city and overall rank in the *Global 500*. Ranking is available online only, not in print. **Number listed:** 9

1. Banco Santander SA, with $100,350 million
2. Telefonica SA, $80,444
3. Repsol YPF, SA, $70,456
4. Banco Bilbao Vizcaya Argentaria SA (BBVA), $43,465
5. Iberdrola SA, $40,305
6. Compania Espanola de Petroleos SA (Cepsa), $26,150
7. Gas Natural Fenosa, $25,999
8. MAPFRE SA, $24,387
9. Actividades de Construccion y Servicios SA (ACS), $21,558

Source: *Fortune*, Global 500 (annual), http://www.fortune.com, July 25, 2011.

2065 ■ MOST ADMIRED COMPANIES IN SPAIN, 2012

Ranked by: Score based on a survey of executives, directors, and securities analysts of companies within their own industry. **Remarks:** List is available online only, not in print. Also notes headquarters. **Number listed:** 2

1. Telefonica SA, with 6.36 points
2. Grupo Ferrovial SA, 6.17

Source: *Fortune*, World's Most Admired Companies (annual), http://www.fortune.com, March 19, 2012.

2066 ■ SPAIN'S LARGEST COMPANIES OVERALL, 2011

Ranked by: Score based on revenue, profits, assets, and market capitalization. **Remarks:** Specific scores not provided. Also notes rank in the overall *Forbes 2000* and figures for each criterion. **Number listed:** 28

1. Banco Santander SA
2. Telefonica SA
3. Banco Bilbao Vizcaya Argentaria SA (BBVA)
4. Repsol YPF, SA
5. Iberdrola SA

6. Gas Natural SDG SA
7. CaixaBank SA
8. MAPFRE SA
9. Industria de Diseno Textil SA (Inditex SA)
10. Actividades de Construccion y Servicios SA (ACS)

Source: *Forbes*, Forbes 2000 (annual), http://www.forbes.com, May 7, 2012.

Corporations—Sri Lanka

2067 ■ BEST SMALL SRI LANKAN COMPANIES, 2010

Ranked by: Score based on sales, net income, and market value. **Remarks:** Specific scores not provided; companies are listed alphabetically, not ranked. Also notes sales, net income, market value, and industry. To qualify for list, which is available online only, companies must have under US$1 billion in annual revenue and positive earnings growth over the past five years. **Number listed:** 4

1. Asian Alliance Insurance
2. Bairaha Farms
3. Ceylon Investment
4. Renuka Holdings

Source: *Forbes Asia*, Asia's Best Under a Billion (annual), http://www.forbes.com, September 12, 2011.

Corporations—Sweden

2068 ■ BEST LARGE COMPANIES TO WORK FOR IN SWEDEN, 2012

Ranked by: Score based on the relationships between employees and management, employees and their jobs/company, and employees and coworkers. **Remarks:** Specific scores not provided. Ranking covers companies with at least 250 employees. **Number listed:** 10

1. Microsoft Sweden
2. Accenture Sweden
3. Enfo Sweden
4. Rejler
5. Klarna
6. Hilti
7. Adecco Sweden
8. IFS
9. QlikTech
10. McDonald's Sweden

Source: *Great Place to Work Institute Inc.*, Best Places to Work in Sweden (annual), March 15, 2012.

2069 ■ BEST MEDIUM-SIZED COMPANIES TO WORK FOR IN SWEDEN, 2012

Ranked by: Score based on the relationships between employees and management, employees and their jobs/company, and employees and coworkers. **Remarks:** Specific scores not provided. Ranking covers companies with 50 to 249 employees. **Number listed:** 15

1. SAS Institute Sweden
2. Kungsleden
3. Centiro Solutions

4. Diversify Consulting Group AB
5. Stretch
6. Newsec
7. Cinnobar Financial Technology AB
8. DGC
9. Frontit AB
10. Aleris Geriatrik Nacka

Source: *Great Place to Work Institute Inc.*, Best Places to Work in Sweden (annual), March 15, 2012.

2070 ■ BEST SMALL COMPANIES TO WORK FOR IN SWEDEN, 2012

Ranked by: Score based on the relationships between employees and management, employees and their jobs/company, and employees and coworkers. **Remarks:** Specific scores not provided. Ranking covers companies with 20 to 49 employees. **Number listed:** 10

1. W. L. Gore & Associates Scandinavia
2. Tenant & Partner
3. Elicit
4. JSC IT-Partner AB
5. Navigio Rekrytering & Ledarskap
6. Transcendent Group
7. Trygghetsstifelsen
8. Concrete IT
9. Bouvet
10. Devoteam

Source: *Great Place to Work Institute Inc.*, Best Places to Work in Sweden (annual), March 15, 2012.

2071 ■ LARGEST COMPANIES IN SWEDEN, 2010

Ranked by: Sales, in millions of U.S. dollars. **Remarks:** Also notes city; industrial code; percent change in sales; profits; profit as a percentage of sales, assets, and equity; number of employees; sales per employee; assets; equity capital; equity capital as a percentage of assets; year established; and figures for previous year. **Number listed:** 700

1. AB Volvo, with $31,138.3 million
2. Telefonaktiebolaget LM Ericsson, $29,443.6
3. Vattenfall AB, $29,291
4. Skandinaviska Enskilda Banken AB, $24,870.1
5. Nordea Bank AB, $21,161
6. Skanska AB, $19,508.1
7. Svenska Cellulosa AB (SCA), $15,808.2
8. TeliaSonera AB, $15,566.4
9. AB Electrolux, $15,562.2
10. Hennes & Mauritz AB, $14,549.9

Source: *Europe's 15,000 Largest Companies*, (annual), ELC International, 2011, p. 572+.

2072 ■ LARGEST CORPORATIONS IN SWEDEN BY REVENUE, 2010

Ranked by: Revenue, in millions of U.S. dollars. **Remarks:** Also notes headquarters city and overall rank in the *Global 500*. Ranking is available online only, not in print. **Number listed:** 3

1. AB Volvo, with $36,749 million
2. Vattenfall AB, $29,645
3. Telefonaktiebolaget LM Ericsson, $28,226

Source: *Fortune*, Global 500 (annual), http://www.fortune.com, July 25, 2011.

2073 ■ MOST ADMIRED COMPANIES IN SWEDEN, 2012

Ranked by: Score based on a survey of executives, directors, and securities analysts of companies within their own industry. **Remarks:** List is available online only, not in print. Also notes headquarters. **Number listed:** 4

1. Telefonaktiebolaget LM Ericsson, with 6.53 points
2. Skanska AB, 6.50
3. Svenska Cellulosa AB (SCA), 6.07
4. AB Electrolux, 6.05

Source: *Fortune*, World's Most Admired Companies (annual), http://www.fortune.com, March 19, 2012.

2074 ■ SWEDEN'S LARGEST COMPANIES OVERALL, 2011

Ranked by: Score based on revenue, profits, assets, and market capitalization. **Remarks:** Specific scores not provided. Also notes rank in the overall *Forbes 2000* and figures for each criterion. **Number listed:** 25

1. Nordea Bank AB
2. AB Volvo
3. Telefonaktiebolaget LM Ericsson
4. Skandinaviska Enskilda Banken (SEB)
5. Svenska Handelsbanken AB
6. TeliaSonera AB
7. Swedbank
8. Hennes & Mauritz AB
9. Atlas Copco AB
10. Sandvik AB

Source: *Forbes*, Forbes 2000 (annual), http://www.forbes.com, May 7, 2012.

Corporations—Switzerland

2075 ■ BEST COMPANIES TO WORK FOR IN SWITZERLAND, 2011

Ranked by: Score based on the relationships between employees and management, employees and their jobs/company, and employees and coworkers. **Remarks:** Specific scores not provided. **Number listed:** 20

1. Cisco Systems (Switzerland) GmbH
2. NetApp Switzerland GmbH
3. Hilti AG
4. Microsoft Schweiz
5. Mundipharma Medical Co.
6. Innovation Process Technology AG
7. Federal Express Europe Inc.
8. Pini Associati
9. Novo Nordisk
10. Accenture Ltd.

Source: *Great Place to Work Institute Inc.*, Best Places to Work in Switzerland (annual), 2011.

2076 ■ LARGEST COMPANIES IN SWITZERLAND, 2010

Ranked by: Sales, in millions of U.S. dollars. **Remarks:** Also notes city; industrial code; percent change in sales; profits; profit as a percentage of sales, assets, and equity; number of employees; sales per employee; assets; equity capital; equity capital as a percentage of assets; year established; and figures for previous year. **Number listed:** 700

1. Glencore Holding AG, with $106,360 million
2. Nestle SA, $105,973.4
3. DPA (Holding) SA, $93,489.4
4. Citigroup Global Markets Ltd., $89,620
5. Zurich Financial Services AG, $70,270
6. Roche Holding AG, $48,299.5
7. Novartis AG, $44,270
8. Schweizerische Ruckversicherung GmbH, $32,869.3
9. Credit Suisse Group AG, $32,780.7
10. Swiss Reinsurance Co., $32,618.7

Source: *Europe's 15,000 Largest Companies*, (annual), ELC International, 2011, p. 602+.

2077 ■ LARGEST CORPORATIONS IN SWITZERLAND BY REVENUE, 2010

Ranked by: Revenue, in millions of U.S. dollars. **Remarks:** Also notes headquarters city and overall rank in the *Global 500*. Ranking is available online only, not in print. **Number listed:** 15

1. Glencore International, with $144,978 million
2. Nestle SA, $105,267
3. Zurich Financial Services, $67,850
4. Novartis AG, $51,561
5. Credit Suisse Group, $48,314
6. Roche Group, $47,171
7. UBS AG, $44,811
8. Alliance Boots GmbH, $31,998
9. ABB Ltd., $31,589
10. Xstrata, $30,499

Source: *Fortune*, Global 500 (annual), http://www.fortune.com, July 25, 2011.

2078 ■ MOST ADMIRED COMPANIES IN SWITZERLAND, 2012

Ranked by: Score based on a survey of executives, directors, and securities analysts of companies within their own industry. **Remarks:** List is available online only, not in print. Also notes headquarters. **Number listed:** 7

1. Nestle SA, with 7.93 points
2. ABB Ltd., 6.87
3. Compagnie Financiere Richemont SA, 6.6
4. Novartis AG, 6.56
5. Zurich Financial Services, 6.39
6. Roche Group, 6.05
7. Credit Suisse Group, 5.65

Source: *Fortune*, World's Most Admired Companies (annual), http://www.fortune.com, March 19, 2012.

2079 ■ SWITZERLAND'S LARGEST COMPANIES OVERALL, 2011

Ranked by: Score based on revenue, profits, assets, and market capitalization. **Remarks:** Specific scores not provided. Also notes rank in the overall *Forbes 2000* and figures for each criterion. **Number listed:** 45

1. Nestle SA
2. Novartis AG
3. UBS AG
4. Zurich Financial Services AG

5. Glencore International plc
6. Roche Holding Ltd.
7. Credit Suisse Group AG
8. Xstrata plc
9. Swiss Reinsurance Co.
10. ABB Ltd.

Source: *Forbes*, Forbes 2000 (annual), http://www.forbes.com, May 7, 2012.

Corporations—Taiwan

2080 ■ BEST SMALL TAIWANESE COMPANIES, 2010

Ranked by: Score based on sales, net income, and market value. **Remarks:** Specific scores not provided; companies are listed alphabetically, not ranked. Also notes sales, net income, market value, and industry. To qualify for list, which is available online only, companies must have under US$1 billion in annual revenue and positive earnings growth over the past five years. **Number listed:** 25

1. Advanced Ceramic X
2. Chuwa Wool Industry
3. Edison Opto
4. Elite Advanced Laser
5. eMemory Technology
6. Entire Technology
7. Feedback Technology
8. Genmont Biotech
9. Gintech Energy
10. Grand Plastic Technology

Source: *Forbes Asia*, Asia's Best Under a Billion (annual), http://www.forbes.com, September 12, 2011.

2081 ■ LARGEST CORPORATIONS IN TAIWAN BY REVENUE, 2010

Ranked by: Revenue, in millions of U.S. dollars. **Remarks:** Also notes headquarters city and overall rank in the *Global 500*. Ranking is available online only, not in print. **Number listed:** 8

1. Hon Hai Precision Industry Co., Ltd., with $95,191 million
2. Quanta Computer Inc., $35,721
3. Cathay Life Insurance Co., Ltd., $34,796
4. Compal Electronics Inc., $28,171
5. Chinese Petroleum Corp., $27,570
6. Formosa Petrochemical Corp., $23,734
7. Acer Inc., $19,979
8. Wistron Corp., $19,538

Source: *Fortune*, Global 500 (annual), http://www.fortune.com, July 25, 2011.

2082 ■ TAIWAN'S LARGEST COMPANIES OVERALL, 2011

Ranked by: Score based on revenue, profits, assets, and market capitalization. **Remarks:** Specific scores not provided. Also notes rank in the overall *Forbes 2000* and figures for each criterion. **Number listed:** 42

1. Hon Hai Precision Industry Co., Ltd.
2. Taiwan Semiconductor Manufacturing Co., Ltd.
3. Formosa Petrochemical Corp.

4. Fubon Financial Holding Co., Ltd.
5. Nan Ya Plastics Corp.
6. Formosa Chemicals & Fiber Corp.
7. China Steel Corp.
8. Chunghwa Telecom Co.
9. Quanta Computer Inc.
10. HTC Corp.

Source: *Forbes*, Forbes 2000 (annual), http://www.forbes.com, May 7, 2012.

Corporations—Tennessee

2083 ■ LARGEST COMPANIES IN TENNESSEE BY EMPLOYEES, 2010

Ranked by: Number of employees at headquarters. **Remarks:** Also notes contact information for headquarters, total number of employees, revenue, rank by revenue, and primary SIC code. **Number listed:** 167

1. Southern Tennessee Medical Center LLC, with 9,300 employees
2. ARS Investment Holdings LLC, 7,700
3. Eastman Chemical Co., 7,000
4. Southeast Service Corp., 6,000
5. Davidson Hotel Co., 5,000
6. Vanderbilt University, 4,200
7. Blue Cross Blue Shield of Tennessee Inc., 4,167
8. Baptist Memorial Hospital of Memphis, 4,000
8. Gaylord Opryland USA Inc., 4,000
8. Lockheed Martin Energy Research Corp., 4,000
8. UT-Battelle LLC, 4,000

Source: *Business Rankings*, (annual), Dun & Bradstreet Inc., 2011, p. IV.207-IV.210.

2084 ■ LARGEST COMPANIES IN TENNESSEE BY SALES, 2010

Ranked by: Revenue, in dollars. **Remarks:** Also notes contact information for headquarters, number of employees at headquarters and overall, rank by employees, and primary SIC code. **Number listed:** 168

1. FedEx Corp., with $34,734,000,000
2. HCA Holdings Inc., $30,683,000,000
2. HCA Inc., $30,683,000,000
4. Methodist Healthcare Memphis Hospitals, $27,000,000,000
5. International Paper Co., $25,179,000,000
6. Federal Express Corp., $21,243,000,000
7. Community Health Systems Inc., $12,986,500,000
8. Dollar General Corp., $11,796,380,000
9. Tennessee Valley Authority, $10,874,000,000
10. AutoZone Inc., $7,362,618,000

Source: *Business Rankings*, (annual), Dun & Bradstreet Inc., 2011, p. III.204-III.207.

2085 ■ MOST ADMIRED COMPANIES IN TENNESSEE, 2012

Ranked by: Survey of top executives, directors, and securities analysts regarding the Fortune 1,000 companies that they admire the most, regardless of industry. **Remarks:** Also notes city and industry rank. List is available online only, not in print. **Number listed:** 4

1. FedEx Corp., with 7.31 points
2. International Paper Co., 6.2
3. HCA Inc., 5.94
4. The ServiceMaster Co., 5.83

Source: *Fortune*, World's Most Admired Companies (annual), http://www.fortune.com, March 19, 2012.

2086 ■ TENNESSEE'S BEST COMPANIES TO WORK FOR, 2012

Ranked by: Score based on employee surveys as well as evaluation of companies' credibility, respect, fairness, and pride/camaraderie. **Remarks:** Specific scores not provided; companies are listed alphabetically, not ranked. Available online only, not in print. **Number listed:** 2

1. Baker, Donelson, Bearman, Caldwell & Berkowitz PC
2. St. Jude Children's Research Hospital

Source: *Fortune*, 100 Best Companies to Work For (annual), http://www.fortune.com, February 6, 2012.

2087 ■ TENNESSEE'S LARGEST COMPANIES OVERALL, 2011

Ranked by: Score based on revenue, profits, assets, and market capitalization. **Remarks:** Specific scores not provided. Also notes overall rank in the *Forbes 2000* and figures for each criterion. **Number listed:** 9

1. FedEx Corp.
2. HCA Holdings Inc.
3. International Paper Co.
4. Dollar General Corp.
5. AutoZone Inc.
6. Unum Group
7. Eastman Chemical Co.
8. Community Health Systems Inc.
9. First Horizon National Corp.

Source: *Forbes*, Forbes 2000 (annual), http://www.forbes.com, May 7, 2012.

2088 ■ TENNESSEE'S LARGEST PRIVATE COMPANIES, 2010

Ranked by: Revenue, in billions of dollars. **Remarks:** Also notes business segment, number of employees, and overall rank in the *America's Largest Private Companies* list. Ranking is available online only, not in print. **Number listed:** 5

1. Pilot Flying J, with $17.77 billion
2. H. T. Hackney Co., $3.6
3. The ServiceMaster Co., $3.37
4. Iasis Healthcare LLC, $2.76
5. Life Care Centers of America, $2.65

Source: *Forbes*, America's Largest Private Companies (annual), http://www.forbes.com, December 5, 2011.

2089 ■ TOP *FORTUNE 500* COMPANIES IN TENNESSEE, 2011

Ranked by: Revenue, in millions of dollars. **Remarks:** Also notes overall rank in the *Fortune 500,* headquarters, and number of employees. **Number listed:** 9

1. FedEx Corp., with $39,304 million
2. HCA Holdings Inc., $32,506
3. International Paper Co., $26,034
4. Dollar General Corp., $14,807.2
5. Community Health Systems Inc., $13,817
6. Unum Group, $10,278
7. AutoZone Inc., $8,073
8. Eastman Chemical Co., $7,283
9. Vanguard Health Systems, $4,895.9

Source: *Fortune*, Fortune 500 (annual), May 21, 2012, p. F-46.

Corporations—Texas

2090 ■ BEST LARGE COMPANIES TO WORK FOR IN TEXAS, 2012

Ranked by: Score based on employee surveys. **Remarks:** Specific scores not provided. Ranking covers companies with 500 or more employees. **Number listed:** 30

1. Medical City Dallas Hospital
2. North Highland Consulting
3. UMC Health System
4. Flintco LLC
5. Transwestern
6. Duke Realty
7. Edward Jones
8. Rothstein Kass
9. SRC Inc.
10. Cirrus Logic Inc.

Source: *Best Companies Group*, Best Places to Work in Texas (annual), http://www.bestcompaniestx.com, February 2012.

2091 ■ BEST MEDIUM-SIZED COMPANIES TO WORK FOR IN TEXAS, 2012

Ranked by: Score based on employee surveys. **Remarks:** Specific scores not provided. To qualify, companies must have 100 and 499 employees. **Number listed:** 38

1. SOS Staffing Services Inc.
2. iProspect
3. Pariveda Solutions Inc.
4. Texas Health Harris Methodist Hospital Southlake
5. Improving Enterprises
6. Advancial
7. Northstar Bank of Texas
8. Coppermark Bank
9. Decypher
10. Apex Capital Corp.

Source: *Best Companies Group*, Best Places to Work in Texas (annual), http://www.bestcompaniestx.com, February 2012.

2092 ■ BEST SMALL COMPANIES IN TEXAS, 2011

Ranked by: Score based on revenue, profits, and return on equity for the past 12 months and five years. **Remarks:** Specific scores not provided. Also notes rank in the overall *100 Best Small Companies in America*. To qualify, companies must have revenues between $5 million and $1 billion, a net margin above five percent, and share price above $5. List is available online only. **Number listed:** 11

1. SolarWinds
2. Atwood Oceanics
3. Cirrus Logic
4. Rackspace Hosting
5. AZZ
6. DG
7. KMG Chemicals
8. GeoResources
9. Team
10. Carbo Ceramics

Source: *Forbes*, Best Small Companies in America (annual), November 7, 2011.

2093 ■ BEST SMALL COMPANIES TO WORK FOR IN TEXAS, 2012

Ranked by: Score based on employee surveys. **Remarks:** Specific scores not provided. To qualify, companies must have between 15 and 99 employees. **Number listed:** 32

1. LiquidAgents Healthcare LLC
2. The Starr Conspiracy
3. Longnecker & Associates
4. GDSX Ltd.
5. Debt Education & Certification Foundation
6. Award Solutions Inc.
7. Vintage IT Services
8. University Title Co.
9. Patrick Henry Creative Promotions
10. The Steam Team

Source: *Best Companies Group*, Best Places to Work in Texas (annual), http://www.bestcompaniestx.com, February 2012.

2094 ■ FASTEST-GROWING COMPANIES IN TEXAS, 2008-2011

Ranked by: Score based on three-year growth in revenue and earnings, and three-year total return to investors. **Remarks:** Specific scores not provided. To qualify for list, companies must have revenues of at least $50 million, net income of at least $10 million, market capitalization of at least $250 million, and stock price of at least $5. Int'l companies are eligible if they trade on a U.S. exchange and file quarterly reports. **Number listed:** 6

1. Cirrus Logic
2. Concho Resources
3. DG FastChannel Inc.
4. EZCORP Inc.
5. Cyberonics
6. First Cash Financial Services

Source: *Fortune*, 100 Fastest-Growing Companies (annual), http://www.fortune.com, September 26, 2011.

2095 ■ FASTEST-GROWING DALLAS/FT. WORTH COMPANIES, 2009-2010

Ranked by: Score based on sales growth, operating income growth, total stock return, and return on assets. **Remarks:** The lower the points, the higher the rank. **Number listed:** 122

1. Zix Corp., with 41 points
2. Fossil Inc., 50
3. Dorchester Minerals LP, 75
4. Texas Instruments Inc., 86

5. Pioneer Natural Resources Co., 89
6. Diodes Inc., 91
7. Holly Corp., 98
8. First Cash Financial Services Inc., 115
9. Holly Energy Partners LP, 125
10. Westwood Holdings Group Inc., 128

Source: *Dallas Morning News*, Fast Track (annual), http://www.dallasnews.com, June 5, 2011.

2096 ■ LARGEST COMPANIES IN TEXAS BY EMPLOYEES, 2010

Ranked by: Number of employees at headquarters. **Remarks:** Also notes contact information for headquarters, total number of employees, revenue, rank by revenue, and primary SIC code. **Number listed:** 685

1. United Services Automobile Association, with 14,802 employees
2. HP Enterprise Services LLC, 11,118
3. Texas Instruments Inc., 9,800
4. AEI Services LLC, 8,300
5. Gunze Electronics USA Corp., 8,000
6. Methodist Hospital, 7,999
7. Romanos Macaroni Grill Inc., 7,500
8. AMR Corp., 6,500
9. SFG Management LLC, 6,000
10. Parkland Health & Hospital System, 5,700

Source: *Business Rankings*, (annual), Dun & Bradstreet Inc., 2011, p. IV.211-IV.225.

2097 ■ LARGEST COMPANIES IN TEXAS BY SALES, 2010

Ranked by: Revenue, in dollars. **Remarks:** Also notes contact information for headquarters, number of employees at headquarters and overall, rank by employees, and primary SIC code. **Number listed:** 689

1. ConocoPhillips, with $198,655,000,000
2. AT&T Inc., $124,280,000,000
3. Valero Energy Corp., $82,233,000,000
4. Marathon Oil Corp., $73,621,000,000
5. Dell Inc., $61,494,000,000
6. Sysco Corp., $37,243,495,000
7. Enterprise Products Partners LP, $33,739,300,000
8. McLane Co., $31,133,614,952
9. Plains All American Pipeline LP, $25,893,000,000
10. Veolia Water North America-Northeast LLC, $23,000,000,000

Source: *Business Rankings*, (annual), Dun & Bradstreet Inc., 2011, p. III.208-III.222.

2098 ■ MOST ADMIRED COMPANIES IN TEXAS, 2012

Ranked by: Survey of top executives, directors, and securities analysts regarding the Fortune 1,000 companies that they admire the most, regardless of industry. **Remarks:** Also notes city and industry rank. List is available online only, not in print. **Number listed:** 19

1. Exxon Mobil Corp., with 7.87 points
2. FMC Technologies, 7.75

3. Schlumberger, 7.69
4. National Oilwell Varco, 7.65
5. Sysco Corp., 7.56
6. Enterprise Products Partners, 7.49
7. Texas Instruments Inc., 7.38
8. Halliburton, 7.27
9. Fluor Corp., 7.25
10. Whole Foods Market Inc., 7.18

Source: *Fortune*, World's Most Admired Companies (annual), http://www.fortune.com, March 19, 2012.

2099 ■ PUBLIC DALLAS/FT. WORTH COMPANIES WITH THE HIGHEST REVENUE, 2011

Ranked by: Revenue, in billions of dollars. **Remarks:** Specific figures not provided. Also notes CEO and net income. **Number listed:** 150

1. Exxon Mobil Corp.
2. AT&T Inc.
3. AMR Corp.
4. Fluor Corp.
5. Kimberly-Clark Corp.
6. J. C. Penney Co., Inc.
7. Southwest Airlines Co.
8. HollyFrontier Corp.
9. Texas Instruments Inc.
10. Dean Foods Co.

Source: *Dallas Morning News*, D-FW Top 150 (annual), http://www.dallasnews.com, June 10, 2012.

2100 ■ TEXAS'S BEST COMPANIES TO WORK FOR, 2012

Ranked by: Score based on employee surveys as well as evaluation of companies' credibility, respect, fairness, and pride/camaraderie. **Remarks:** Specific scores not provided; companies are listed alphabetically, not ranked. Available online only, not in print. **Number listed:** 12

1. Balfour Beatty Construction LLC
2. Camden Property Trust
3. The Container Store
4. EOG Resources Inc.
5. The Men's Wearhouse Inc.
6. Methodist Hospital
7. National Instruments Corp.
8. NuStar Energy LP
9. Rackspace Hosting Inc.
10. TDIndustries Ltd.

Source: *Fortune*, 100 Best Companies to Work For (annual), http://www.fortune.com, February 6, 2012.

2101 ■ TEXAS'S LARGEST COMPANIES OVERALL, 2011

Ranked by: Score based on revenue, profits, assets, and market capitalization. **Remarks:** Specific scores not provided. Also notes overall rank in the *Forbes 2000* and figures for each criterion. **Number listed:** 52

1. Exxon Mobil Corp.
2. ConocoPhillips
3. AT & T Inc.
4. Dell Inc.

5. Apache Corp.
6. Valero Energy Corp.
7. Halliburton Co.
8. Marathon Oil Corp.
9. National Oilwell Varco Inc.
10. Baker Hughes Inc.

Source: *Forbes*, Forbes 2000 (annual), http://www.forbes.com, May 7, 2012.

2102 ■ TEXAS'S LARGEST PRIVATE COMPANIES, 2010

Ranked by: Revenue, in billions of dollars. **Remarks:** Also notes business segment, number of employees, and overall rank in the *America's Largest Private Companies* list. Ranking is available online only, not in print. **Number listed:** 18

1. H. E. Butt Grocery Co., with $15.6 billion
2. Energy Future Holdings Corp., $8.24
3. Gulf States Toyota Inc., $5.1
4. Republic National Distributing Co., $4.58
5. Michaels Stores Inc., $4.03
6. Neiman Marcus Group Inc., $4
6. Hunt Consolidated Inc./Hunt Oil Co., $4
8. McJunkin Red Man Holding Corp., $3.85
9. Grocers Supply Co., $3.3
9. Sammons Enterprises Inc., $3.3

Source: *Forbes*, America's Largest Private Companies (annual), http://www.forbes.com, December 5, 2011.

2103 ■ TOP *FORTUNE 500* COMPANIES IN TEXAS, 2011

Ranked by: Revenue, in millions of dollars. **Remarks:** Also notes overall rank in the *Fortune 500,* headquarters, and number of employees. **Number listed:** 52

1. Exxon Mobil Corp., with $452,926 million
2. ConocoPhillips, $237,272
3. AT&T Inc., $126,723
4. Valero Energy Corp., $125,095
5. Dell Inc., $62,071
6. Enterprise Products Partners LP, $44,313
7. Sysco Corp., $39,323.5
8. Plains All American Pipeline LP, $34,275
9. Tesoro Corp., $29,927
10. Halliburton Co., $24,829

Source: *Fortune*, Fortune 500 (annual), May 21, 2012, p. F-46.

Corporations—Thailand

2104 ■ BEST SMALL THAI COMPANIES, 2010

Ranked by: Score based on sales, net income, and market value. **Remarks:** Specific scores not provided; companies are listed alphabetically, not ranked. Also notes sales, net income, market value, and industry. To qualify for list, which is available online only, companies must have under US$1 billion in annual revenue and positive earnings growth over the past five years. **Number listed:** 5

1. Advanced Information Technology
2. Brooker Group
3. Bualuang Securities
4. Polyplex

5. Robinson Department Store

Source: *Forbes Asia*, Asia's Best Under a Billion (annual), http://www.forbes.com, September 12, 2011.

2105 ▪ THAILAND'S LARGEST COMPANIES OVERALL, 2011

Ranked by: Score based on revenue, profits, assets, and market capitalization. **Remarks:** Specific scores not provided. Also notes rank in the overall *Forbes 2000* and figures for each criterion. **Number listed:** 17

1. PTT Public Co., Ltd.
2. Siam Commercial Bank
3. PTT Global Chemical Public Co., Ltd.
4. Kasikornbank Public Co., Ltd.
5. The Siam Cement Public Co., Ltd.
6. Bangkok Bank
7. Krung Thai Bank
8. Advanced Information Service
9. Charoen Pokphand Foods
10. Thai Oil Co., Ltd.

Source: *Forbes*, Forbes 2000 (annual), http://www.forbes.com, May 7, 2012.

2106 ▪ TOP THAI COMPANIES, 2011

Ranked by: Score based on profits, sales and earnings growth, and projected earnings and stock-price gains. **Remarks:** Specific scores not provided; companies are listed alphabetically, not ranked. Also notes market value, revenue, and industry. To quality, companies must be publicly traded with revenues or market capitalization of at least US$3 billion. Ranking is available online only, not in print. **Number listed:** 2

1. CP All
2. PTT Chemical

Source: *Forbes*, Asian Fab 50 (annual), September 13, 2011.

Corporations—Turkey

2107 ▪ TURKEY'S LARGEST COMPANIES OVERALL, 2011

Ranked by: Score based on revenue, profits, assets, and market capitalization. **Remarks:** Specific scores not provided. Also notes rank in the overall *Forbes 2000* and figures for each criterion. **Number listed:** 11

1. Turkiye Garanti Bankasi
2. Koc Holding AS
3. Turkiye Is Bankasi AS (Isbank)
4. Haci Omer Sabanci Holding AS
5. Akbank
6. Turkiye Halk Bankasi
7. Turk Telekomunikasyon AS
8. VakifBank
9. Turkcell Iletisim Hizmetleri AS
10. Enka

Source: *Forbes*, Forbes 2000 (annual), http://www.forbes.com, May 7, 2012.

Corporations—United Arab Emirates

2108 ▪ TOP UAE COMPANIES BY MARKET CAPITALIZATION, 2011

Ranked by: Market capitalization, in billions of UAE Dirhams. **Number listed:** 50

1. Etisalat, with 75.5 billion
2. DP World, 34.4
3. National Bank of Abu Dhabi, 31.57
4. First Gulf Bank, 27.45
5. Emaar, 18.58
6. Abu Dhabi Commercial Bank, 16.89
7. Emirates NBD, 16.73
8. Mashreq Bank, 15.46
9. Du, 13.7
10. Dubai Islamic Bank, 8.53

Source: *Arabian Business*, Top 50 UAE Companies, February 27, 2012.

2109 ▪ THE UNITED ARAB EMIRATES' LARGEST COMPANIES OVERALL, 2011

Ranked by: Score based on revenue, profits, assets, and market capitalization. **Remarks:** Specific scores not provided. Also notes rank in the overall *Forbes 2000* and figures for each criterion. **Number listed:** 13

1. Emirates Telecommunictions Corp. (Etisalat)
2. National Bank of Abu Dhabi
3. First Gulf Bank
4. Emirates NBD
5. Abu Dhabi Commercial Bank
6. DP World
7. Emaar Properties
8. Abu Dhabi National Energy Co. (TAQA)
9. Union National Bank
10. Dubai Islamic Bank

Source: *Forbes*, Forbes 2000 (annual), http://www.forbes.com, May 7, 2012.

Corporations—United Kingdom

2110 ▪ BEST COMPANIES TO WORK FOR IN THE UNITED KINGDOM, 2011

Ranked by: Score based on the relationships between employees and management, employees and their jobs/company, and employees and coworkers. **Remarks:** Specific scores not provided. **Number listed:** 50

1. Baringa Partners
2. NetApp U.K. Ltd.
3. Twinings - U.K. & Ireland
4. Bacardi Brown-Forman Brands
5. Taff Housing Association
6. Danone Ltd.
7. Chiswick Park Enjoy-Work
8. Dow Corning Corp.
9. Admiral Group plc
10. Ketchum Pleon

Source: *Great Place to Work Institute Inc.*, Best Places to Work in the United Kingdom (annual), 2011.

2111 ▪ BRITISH COMPANIES WITH THE HIGHEST REPUTATION FOR ATTRACTING, DEVELOPING, AND RETAINING TOP TALENT, 2011

Ranked by: Score, on a scale of 10, based on a survey of peers and investment analysts. **Number listed:** 10

1. Marks & Spencer plc, with 8.33 points
2. Berkeley Group, 8.2
3. Diageo, 8.14
4. Aggreko, 8.05
5. Paddy Power, 8
5. Derwent London, 8
7. John Lewis Partnership, 7.89
8. Balfour Beatty, 7.81
9. Shaftesbury, 7.80
10. Rolls-Royce plc, 7.75
10. Tesco plc, 7.75

Source: *Management Today*, Britain's Most Admired Companies (annual), December 2011, p. 41.

2112 ■ BRITISH COMPANIES WITH THE HIGHEST REPUTATION FOR CAPACITY TO INNOVATE, 2011

Ranked by: Score, on a scale of 10, based on a survey of peers and investment analysts. **Number listed:** 10

1. Paddy Power, with 8.14 points
2. Rotork, 8
2. Royal Dutch Shell plc, 8
4. Experian Group, 7.83
5. Derwent London, 7.80
5. Ocado, 7.80
7. Rolls-Royce plc, 7.75
7. Betfair, 7.75
9. Diageo, 7.71
10. Homeserve, 7.67
10. British Sky Broadcasting Group plc (BSkyB), 7.67

Source: *Management Today*, Britain's Most Admired Companies (annual), December 2011, p. 41.

2113 ■ BRITISH COMPANIES WITH THE HIGHEST REPUTATION FOR COMMUNITY AND ENVIRONMENTAL RESPONSIBILITY, 2011

Ranked by: Score, on a scale of 10, based on a survey of peers and investment analysts. **Number listed:** 10

1. Diageo, with 8.08 points
2. British Land Co., 7.94
3. Marks & Spencer plc, 7.83
4. Land Securities, 7.80
5. Co-operative Group, 7.7
6. Coca-Cola GB, 7.67
7. Croda International, 7.58
8. Unilever, 7.57
9. J Sainsbury plc, 7.55
10. BASF (U.K.), 7.50

Source: *Management Today*, Britain's Most Admired Companies (annual), December 2011, p. 41.

2114 ■ BRITISH COMPANIES WITH THE HIGHEST REPUTATION FOR FINANCIAL SOUNDNESS, 2011

Ranked by: Score, on a scale of 10, based on a survey of peers and investment analysts. **Number listed:** 10

1. Royal Dutch Shell plc, with 9.11 points
2. BASF (U.K.), 9.10

2. The Berkeley Group Holdings plc, 9.10
4. Betfair, 9
4. Diageo, 9
6. Paddy Power, 8.71
7. Aggreko, 8.70
8. ASDA Group Ltd., 8.64
9. InterContinental Hotels, 8.5
10. Bwin.Party Digital Entertainment plc, 8.43

Source: *Management Today*, Britain's Most Admired Companies (annual), December 2011, p. 41.

2115 ■ BRITISH COMPANIES WITH THE HIGHEST REPUTATION FOR LONG-TERM INVESTMENT VALUE, 2011

Ranked by: Score, on a scale of 10, based on a survey of peers and investment analysts. **Number listed:** 10

1. Rotork, with 8.4 points
2. Unilever, 8.29
3. Aggreko plc, 8.20
3. Telecity Group, 8.20
5. Paddy Power, 8.14
6. BG Group plc, 8.13
7. Royal Dutch Shell plc, 8.11
8. Derwent London, 8.08
9. Spirax Sarco Engineering, 8
9. Weir Group, 8

Source: *Management Today*, Britain's Most Admired Companies (annual), December 2011, p. 41.

2116 ■ BRITISH COMPANIES WITH THE HIGHEST REPUTATION FOR QUALITY OF GOODS/SERVICES, 2011

Ranked by: Score, on a scale of 10, based on a survey of peers and investment analysts. **Number listed:** 10

1. Rotork, with 9.2 points
2. Aggreko plc, 8.85
3. John Lewis Partnership plc, 8.44
3. Diageo, 8.43
5. Rolls-Royce plc, 8.38
5. Berkeley Group, 8.30
7. Victrex, 8.25
8. Spirax Sarce Engineering, 8.20
9. Derwent London, 8.08
10. Experian plc, 8
10. Royal Dutch Shell plc, 8
10. Croda International, 8
10. British Broadcasting Corp. (BBC), 8

Source: *Management Today*, Britain's Most Admired Companies (annual), December 2011, p. 41.

2117 ■ BRITISH COMPANIES WITH THE HIGHEST REPUTATION FOR QUALITY OF MANAGEMENT, 2011

Ranked by: Score, on a scale of 10, based on a survey of peers and investment analysts. **Number listed:** 10

1. The Berkeley Group Holdings plc, with 9 points
2. Aggreko plc, 8.8
3. Rotork, 8.6
4. Derwent London, 8.58

5. Great Portland Estates, 8.55

6. IG Group, 8.5

6. Stagecoach Group plc, 8.5

8. Paddy Power, 8.43

9. Vodafone plc, 8.22

9. Royal Dutch Shell plc, 8.22

Source: *Management Today*, Britain's Most Admired Companies (annual), December 2011, p. 41.

2118 ■ BRITISH COMPANIES WITH THE HIGHEST REPUTATION FOR QUALITY OF MARKETING, 2011

Ranked by: Score, on a scale of 10, based on a survey of peers and investment analysts. **Number listed:** 10

1. Paddy Power, with 8.57 points

2. Berkeley Group, 8.25

3. Unilever, 8.14

4. McDonald's Restaurants U.K., 8.08

5. Telefonica O2, 8

5. Centrica plc, 8

5. British Sky Broadcasting Group plc (BSkyB), 8

8. Diageo, 7.92

9. Carphone Warehouse, 7.9

9. Derwent London, 7.9

Source: *Management Today*, Britain's Most Admired Companies (annual), December 2011, p. 41.

2119 ■ BRITISH COMPANIES WITH THE HIGHEST REPUTATION FOR USE OF CORPORATE ASSETS, 2011

Ranked by: Score, on a scale of 10, based on a survey of peers and investment analysts. **Number listed:** 10

1. Aggreko plc, with 8.45 points

2. Shaftesbury, 8.2

3. The Berkeley Group Holdings plc, 8.1

4. Bunzl plc, 8

4. Melrose, 8

4. Telecity Group, 8

7. Derwent London, 7.92

7. Diageo, 7.92

9. Admiral plc, 7.81

10. Aldi, 7.80

Source: *Management Today*, Britain's Most Admired Companies (annual), December 2011, p. 41.

2120 ■ THE CHANNEL ISLANDS' LARGEST COMPANIES OVERALL, 2011

Ranked by: Score based on revenue, profits, assets, and market capitalization. **Remarks:** Specific scores not provided. Also notes overall rank in the *Forbes 2000* and figures for each criterion. **Number listed:** 2

1. Randgold Resources Ltd.

2. Heritage Oil plc

Source: *Forbes*, Forbes 2000 (annual), http://www.forbes.com, May 7, 2012.

2121 ■ LARGEST COMPANIES IN THE UNITED KINGDOM, 2010

Ranked by: Sales, in millions of U.S. dollars. **Remarks:** Also notes city; industrial code; percent change in sales; profits; profit as a percentage of sales, assets, and equity; number of employees; sales per employee; assets; equity capital; equity capital as a percentage of assets; year established; and figures for previous year. **Number listed:** 2000

1. BP plc, with $358,908 million

2. Cargill Holdings, $237,963

3. EDF Trading Ltd., $120,114

4. Tesco plc, $85,365

5. BHP Billiton plc, $79,197

6. The Chef & Brewer Group Ltd., $77,632.2

7. Shell Trading International Ltd., $76,376

8. Partstripe Ltd., $75,859.7

9. Richardson Projects Holdings Ltd., $72,097.6

10. Vodafone Group plc, $66,708

Source: *Europe's 15,000 Largest Companies*, (annual), ELC International, 2011, p. 632+.

2122 ■ LARGEST CORPORATIONS IN BRITAIN BY REVENUE, 2010

Ranked by: Revenue, in millions of U.S. dollars. **Remarks:** Also notes headquarters city and overall rank in the *Global 500*. Ranking is available online only, not in print. **Number listed:** 30

1. BP plc, with $308,928 million

2. HSBC Holdings plc, $102,680

3. Lloyds Banking Group plc, $95,682

4. Tesco plc, $94,185

5. Aviva plc, $90,211

6. Prudential plc, $73,598

7. Vodafone Group plc, $71,344

8. The Royal Bank of Scotland Group plc, $68,088

9. Barclays plc, $63,661

10. Legal & General Group plc, $59,377

Source: *Fortune*, Global 500 (annual), http://www.fortune.com, July 25, 2011.

2123 ■ LARGEST EMPLOYERS IN NORTHERN IRELAND, 2011

Ranked by: Number of employees in Northern Ireland. **Remarks:** Also notes rank for previous year, turnover, profits, figures for previous year, and percent change. To qualify, companies must employ at least 100 people and post turnover of at least 15 million pounds sterling. **Number listed:** 100

1. Moy Park Ltd., with 10,594 employees

2. Tesco plc, 8,597

3. Bombardier Aerospace, 4,975

4. ASDA Group Ltd., 4,496

5. Four Seasons Healthcare, 4,461

6. Translink/NITHC, 4,042

7. Quinn Group, 3,865

8. Royal Mail Group, 3,326

9. Dunbia, 3,069

10. Almac Group, 3,034

Source: *Belfast Telegraph*, Top 100 Companies (annual), April 3, 2012, p. 18+.

2124 ■ LEAST ADMIRED BRITISH COMPANIES OVERALL, 2011

Ranked by: Survey of peers and investment analysts based on nine criteria: quality of management, financial soundness, quality of goods/services, ability to attract and retain talent, value as long-term investment, innovation, marketing, community and environmental responsibility, and use of corporate assets. **Number listed:** 10

1. Thomas Cook Group, with 33.8 points
2. Millennium & Copthorne, 34.3
3. Enterprise Inns, 34.4
4. Cable & Wireless Communications, 35.7
5. Royal Mall Group, 35.9
6. Gala Coral, 36.4
7. Premier Foods, 37.1
8. Tote plc, 37.7
9. Punch Taverns, 38.4
10. Charter plc, 38.6

Source: *Management Today*, Britain's Most Admired Companies (annual), December 2011, p. 50.

2125 ■ MOST ADMIRED BRITISH COMPANIES OVERALL, 2011

Ranked by: Survey of peers and investment analysts based on nine criteria: quality of management, financial soundness, quality of goods/services, ability to attract and retain talent, value as long-term investment, innovation, marketing, community and environmental responsibility, and use of corporate assets. **Remarks:** Also notes rank for previous year. **Number listed:** 238

1. Berkeley Group, with 72.95 points
2. Diageo, 72.35
3. Rotork, 71.6
4. Aggreko plc, 71.2
5. Derwent London, 70.9
6. Paddy Power, 70.29
7. Royal Dutch Shell plc, 70.24
8. Unilever, 69.29
9. Rolls-Royce plc, 68.35
10. Shaftesbury, 68.2

Source: *Management Today*, Britain's Most Admired Companies (annual), December 2011, p. 38+.

2126 ■ MOST ADMIRED COMPANIES IN BRITAIN, 2012

Ranked by: Score based on a survey of executives, directors, and securities analysts of companies within their own industry. **Remarks:** List is available online only, not in print. Also notes headquarters. **Number listed:** 11

1. British American Tobacco plc, with 7.76 points
2. Reckitt Benckiser plc, 7.07
3. Imperial Tobacco, 6.83
4. Vodafone Group plc, 6.33
5. Rolls-Royce plc, 6.18
6. HSBC Holdings plc, 6.07
7. GlaxoSmithKline plc, 5.97
8. SABMiller, 5.86
9. Barclays plc, 5.75
10. BG Group plc, 5.54

Source: *Fortune*, World's Most Admired Companies (annual), http://www.fortune.com, March 19, 2012.

2127 ■ MOST VALUABLE U.K. COMPANIES, 2011

Ranked by: Market value as of March 2011, in millions of British pounds. **Remarks:** Also notes rank for previous year, sector,

revenue, net income, assets, number of employees, share price, price-to-earning ratio, dividend yield, and fiscal year-end. **Number listed:** 500

1. Royal Dutch Shell plc, with £142,318.1 million
2. HSBC Holdings plc, £113,501.4
3. Vodafone Group plc, £91,034.3
4. BP plc, £85,372.6
5. Rio Tinto Ltd., £66,287.4
6. GlaxoSmithKline plc, £61,511.7
7. BHP Billiton Ltd., £53,328.2
8. BG Group plc, £52,546.9
9. British American Tobacco plc, £49,848.1
10. Xstrata plc, £43,195.6

Source: *Financial Times*, FT 500 (annual), http://www.ft.com, June 24, 2011.

2128 ■ UNITED KINGDOM'S LARGEST COMPANIES OVERALL, 2011

Ranked by: Score based on revenue, profits, assets, and market capitalization. **Remarks:** Specific scores not provided. Also notes rank in the overall *Forbes 2000* and figures for each criterion. **Number listed:** 90

1. HSBC Holdings plc
2. BP plc
3. Vodafone Group plc
4. Barclays plc
5. Rio Tinto Ltd.
6. Standard Chartered Bank plc
7. Tesco plc
8. GlaxoSmithKline plc
9. Prudential plc
10. Anglo American plc

Source: *Forbes*, Forbes 2000 (annual), http://www.forbes.com, May 7, 2012.

Corporations—Uruguay

2129 ■ BEST COMPANIES TO WORK FOR IN URUGUAY, 2011

Ranked by: Score based on the relationships between employees and management, employees and their jobs/company, and employees and coworkers. **Remarks:** Specific scores not provided. **Number listed:** 5

1. Movistar
2. Deloitte LLP
3. Atento
4. Pronto!
5. McDonald's Corp.

Source: *Great Place to Work Institute Inc.*, Best Places to Work in Uruguay (annual), http://www.greatplacetowork.com, 2011.

Corporations—Utah

2130 ■ FASTEST-GROWING COMPANIES IN THE UTAH VALLEY, 2008-2011

Ranked by: Three-year revenue growth, in percent. **Remarks:** Also notes revenue for current year, year founded, headquarters, number of employees, industry, Web site, founder, and comments. **Number listed:** 30

1. 2GIG Technologies, with 1,426%
2. Complete Merchant Solutions, 691%
3. Four Foods Group, 420%
4. Latter Day Products, 409%
5. Sub Zero Ice Cream, 279%
6. Mommy Bear Media, 258%
7. Goodwin Media, 228%
8. Property Solutions International, 169%
9. One on One Marketing LLC, 155%
10. Simply Mac, 145%

Source: *Utah Valley Business Quarterly*, UV 50 (annual), 2012, p. 22-29.

2131 ■ LARGEST COMPANIES IN UTAH BY EMPLOYEES, 2010

Ranked by: Number of employees at headquarters. **Remarks:** Also notes contact information for headquarters, total number of employees, revenue, rank by revenue, and primary SIC code. **Number listed:** 68

1. World Financial Capital Bank, with 7,392 employees
2. ATK Launch Systems Inc., 3,800
3. University of Utah Hospitals & Clinics, 3,200
4. Icon Health & Fitness Inc., 3,000
5. Marketstar Corp., 2,500
6. Kennecott Corp., 2,300
7. ARUP Laboratories Inc., 2,100
8. About Time Technologies LLC, 2,000
8. Western Wats Center Inc., 2,000
10. Brush Resources Inc., 1,862

Source: *Business Rankings*, (annual), Dun & Bradstreet Inc., 2011, p. IV.226-IV.227.

2132 ■ LARGEST COMPANIES IN UTAH BY SALES, 2010

Ranked by: Revenue, in dollars. **Remarks:** Also notes contact information for headquarters, number of employees at headquarters and overall, rank by employees, and primary SIC code. **Number listed:** 66

1. Huntsman Corp., with $9,250,000,000
1. Huntsman International LLC, $9,250,000,000
3. Sinclair Cos., $7,753,458,000
4. Autoliv Inc., $7,170,600,000
5. Intermountain Health Care Inc., $3,568,200,000
6. IHC Health Services Inc., $3,324,700,000
7. Big Oil West LLC, $3,053,269,000
8. Skywest Inc., $2,765,145,000
9. Associated Food Stores Inc., $1,785,595,008
10. EnergySolutions Inc., $1,623,893,000

Source: *Business Rankings*, (annual), Dun & Bradstreet Inc., 2011, p. III.223-III.224.

2133 ■ LARGEST COMPANIES IN THE UTAH VALLEY, 2011

Ranked by: Revenue, in dollars. **Remarks:** Also notes year founded, headquarters, number of employees, industry, Web site, founder, and comments. **Number listed:** 10

1. Nu Skin Enterprises Inc., with $1,740,000,000

2. Novell, $1,100,000,000
3. Ancestry.com, $399,700,000
4. Vivint Inc., $317,465,705
5. Employer Solutions Group, $254,427,074
6. Young Living Essential Oils, $188,891,642
7. 2GIG Technologies, $131,267,230
8. One on One Marketing LLC, $56,432,403
9. Certiport, $48,478,000
10. Bank of American Fork, $45,877,000

Source: *Utah Valley Business Quarterly*, UV 50 (annual), 2012, p. 36-38.

2134 ■ UTAH'S LARGEST COMPANIES OVERALL, 2011

Ranked by: Score based on revenue, profits, assets, and market capitalization. **Remarks:** Specific scores not provided. Also notes overall rank in the *Forbes 2000* and figures for each criterion. **Number listed:** 2

1. Zions Bancorp
2. Huntsman Corp.

Source: *Forbes*, Forbes 2000 (annual), http://www.forbes.com, May 7, 2012.

Corporations—Venezuela

2135 ■ BEST COMPANIES TO WORK FOR IN VENEZUELA, 2012

Ranked by: Score based on the relationships between employees and management, employees and their jobs/company, and employees and coworkers. **Remarks:** Specific scores not provided. **Number listed:** 16

1. Telefonica Venezuela
2. S. C. Johnson & Son de Venezuela SCA
3. Ron Santa Teresa
4. McDonald's de Venezuela SA
5. 3M Co.
6. Banco Exterior CA
7. Diageo Venezuela SA
8. Tolon Fashion Mall
9. Novartis de Venezuela SA
10. Cestaticket Services CA

Source: *Great Place to Work Institute Inc.*, Best Places to Work in Venezuela (annual), http://www.greatplacetowork.com, 2012.

Corporations—Vermont

2136 ■ BEST LARGE COMPANIES TO WORK FOR IN VERMONT, 2012

Ranked by: Score based on employee surveys. **Remarks:** Specific scores not provided. To qualify, companies must have at least 150 employees. **Number listed:** 9

1. Edward Jones
2. BioTek Instruments Inc.
3. Entergy Vermont Yankee
4. The King Arthur Flour Co.
5. Merchants Bank
6. Green Mountain Coffee Roasters Inc.

7. Vermont Energy Investment Corp.

8. Comcast Cable

9. Country Home Products

Source: *Best Companies Group*, Best Places to Work in Vermont (annual), http://www.bestplacestoworkvt.com, April 2012.

2137 ■ BEST SMALL/MEDIUM COMPANIES TO WORK FOR IN VERMONT, 2012

Ranked by: Score based on employee surveys. **Remarks:** Specific scores not provided. To qualify, companies must have between 15 and 149 employees. **Number listed:** 13

1. Resource Systems Group Inc.
2. Instrumart
3. Fuse Marketing
4. Heritage Aviation
5. Hickok & Boardman Financial Planning & Group Benefits Inc.
6. ASIC North Inc.
7. Wells River Savings Bank
8. Wild Apple Graphics Ltd.
9. Liquid Measurement Systems Inc.
10. Gallagher, Flynn & Co.

Source: *Best Companies Group*, Best Places to Work in Vermont (annual), http://www.bestplacestoworkvt.com, April 2012.

2138 ■ LARGEST COMPANIES IN VERMONT BY EMPLOYEES, 2010

Ranked by: Number of employees at headquarters. **Remarks:** Also notes contact information for headquarters, total number of employees, revenue, rank by revenue, and primary SIC code. **Number listed:** 50

1. Fletcher Allen Health Ventures Inc., with 4,200 employees
2. Fletcher Allen Health Care Inc., 4,000
3. Rutland Hospital Inc., 1,348
4. Central Vermont Medical Center Inc., 1,200
4. Southwestern Vermont Health Care Corp., 1,200
6. Rutland Regional Health Services Inc., 1,000
7. Southwestern Vermont Medical Center Inc., 750
8. NLV Financial Corp., 718
9. Simmonds Precision Products Inc., 650
9. Visiting Nurse Association Inc., 650

Source: *Business Rankings*, (annual), Dun & Bradstreet Inc., 2011, p. IV.228-IV.229.

2139 ■ LARGEST COMPANIES IN VERMONT BY SALES, 2010

Ranked by: Revenue, in dollars. **Remarks:** Also notes contact information for headquarters, number of employees at headquarters and overall, rank by employees, and primary SIC code. **Number listed:** 50

1. Green Mountain Coffee Roasters Inc., with $1,356,775,000
2. Casella Waste Systems Inc., $552,328,000
3. Velan Valve Corp., $465,945,000
4. Central Vermont Public Service Corp., $342,098,000

5. Cabot Creamery Cooperative Inc., $300,000,000
6. St. Albans Co-operative Creamery Inc., $293,049,507
7. Southwestern Vermont Medical Center Inc., $227,698,231
8. SB Collins Inc., $200,000,000
9. Rutland Regional Health Services Inc., $188,876,653
10. Vermont Yankee Nuclear Power Corp., $183,411,000

Source: *Business Rankings*, (annual), Dun & Bradstreet Inc., 2011, p. III.225-III.226.

Corporations—Vietnam

2140 ■ BEST SMALL VIETNAMESE COMPANIES, 2010

Ranked by: Score based on sales, net income, and market value. **Remarks:** Specific scores not provided; companies are listed alphabetically, not ranked. Also notes sales, net income, market value, and industry. To qualify for list, which is available online only, companies must have under US$1 billion in annual revenue and positive earnings growth over the past five years. **Number listed:** 10

1. DHG Pharmaceutical
2. Dinh Vu Port Investment & Development
3. Doan Xa Port
4. Dong Phu Rubber
5. Long An Food Processing Export
6. Nari Hamico Minerals
7. Ninh Hoa Sugar
8. Petroleum Equipment Assembly & Metal Structure
9. PetroVietNam Low Pressure Gas Distribution
10. Vietnam Container Shipping

Source: *Forbes Asia*, Asia's Best Under a Billion (annual), http://www.forbes.com, September 12, 2011.

Corporations—Virginia

2141 ■ BEST LARGE COMPANIES TO WORK FOR IN VIRGINIA, 2012

Ranked by: Employee survey. **Remarks:** Specific scores not provided. To qualify, companies must have 250 or more employees. **Number listed:** 20

1. Edward Jones
2. Brandywine Realty Trust
3. Health Diagnostic Laboratory Inc.
4. Commonwealth Financial Partners LC
5. Kearney & Co.
6. CARFAX Vehicle History Reports
7. WRSystems Ltd.
8. MBP
9. Capital One
10. Spectrum

Source: *Virginia Business*, Best Places to Work (annual), February 2012.

2142 ■ BEST MIDSIZED COMPANIES TO WORK FOR IN VIRGINIA, 2012

Ranked by: Employee survey. **Remarks:** Specific scores not provided. To qualify, companies must have between 100 and 249 employees. **Number listed:** 18

1. SNVC LC
2. Valkyrie Enterprises LLC
3. Damuth Trane
4. Base Technologies
5. ProSol
6. Vandeventer Black LLP
7. Consumer Electronics Association
8. Valley Bank
9. JBM
10. Member One Federal Credit Union

Source: *Virginia Business*, Best Places to Work (annual), February 2012.

2143 ■ BEST SMALL COMPANIES IN VIRGINIA, 2011

Ranked by: Score based on revenue, profits, and return on equity for the past 12 months and five years. **Remarks:** Specific scores not provided. Also notes rank in the overall *100 Best Small Companies in America*. To qualify, companies must have revenues between $5 million and $1 billion, a net margin above five percent, and share price above $5. List is available online only. **Number listed:** 3

1. Strayer Education
2. Portfolio Recovery Associates
3. ICF International

Source: *Forbes*, Best Small Companies in America (annual), November 7, 2011.

2144 ■ BEST SMALL COMPANIES TO WORK FOR IN VIRGINIA, 2012

Ranked by: Employee survey. **Remarks:** Specific scores not provided. To qualify, companies must have between 15 and 99 employees. **Number listed:** 32

1. Knight Point Systems LLC
2. C2 Solutions Group Inc.
3. Homeland Contracting Corp.
4. Veris Consulting Inc.
5. n-tieractive Inc.
6. Vaco Richmond LLC
7. Kinsale Insurance Co.
8. Virginia Society of Certified Public Accountants
9. Cassaday & Co.
10. Wells, Coleman & Co. LLP

Source: *Virginia Business*, Best Places to Work (annual), February 2012.

2145 ■ LARGEST COMPANIES IN VIRGINIA BY EMPLOYEES, 2010

Ranked by: Number of employees at headquarters. **Remarks:** Also notes contact information for headquarters, total number of employees, revenue, rank by revenue, and primary SIC code. **Number listed:** 198

1. Virginia Department of Transportation, with 9,000 employees
2. Carmax Auto Superstores inc., 7,800

2. Dominion Resources Inc., 7,800
4. Dominion Resources Services Inc., 6,000
5. Smithfield Packing Co., 4,636
6. University of Virginia Medical Center, 4,248
7. VF Imagewear (East) Inc., 4,180
8. S. I. International Zen Technology Inc., 4,000
8. Verizon Business Global LLC, 4,000
10. City Line Apartments, 3,900

Source: *Business Rankings*, (annual), Dun & Bradstreet Inc., 2011, p. IV.230-IV.234.

2146 ■ LARGEST COMPANIES IN VIRGINIA BY SALES, 2010

Ranked by: Revenue, in dollars. **Remarks:** Also notes contact information for headquarters, number of employees at headquarters and overall, rank by employees, and primary SIC code. **Number listed:** 196

1. General Dynamics Corp., with $32,466,000,000
2. Altria Group Inc., $24,363,000,000
3. Computer Sciences Corp., $16,128,000,000
4. Dominion Resources Inc., $15,197,000,000
5. AES Corp., $14,119,000,000
6. Smithfield Foods Inc., $11,202,600,000
7. SAIC Inc., $10,846,000,000
8. Norfolk Southern Corp., $9,516,000,000
9. Owens & Minor Inc., $8,123,608,000
10. Ferguson Enterprises Inc., $8,123,159,000

Source: *Business Rankings*, (annual), Dun & Bradstreet Inc., 2011, p. III.227-III.231.

2147 ■ LARGEST PRIVATE EMPLOYERS IN RICHMOND, VIRGINIA, 2011

Ranked by: Number of local employees. **Remarks:** Also notes sales/assets and profits. **Number listed:** 50

1. Capital One Financial Corp., with 9,995 employees
2. Virginia Commonwealth University Health System, 7,935
3. HCA Virginia Health System, 7,236
4. Bon Secours Richmond Health System, 5,991
5. Wal-Mart Stores Inc., 5,462
6. Dominion Resources Inc., 5,378
7. Altria Group Inc., 4,110
8. SunTrust Banks Inc., 4,100
9. E. I. du Pont de Nemours & Co., 3,084
10. Wells Fargo & Co., 2,851

Source: *Richmond Times-Dispatch*, Top 50 Area Employers (annual), April 23, 2012.

2148 ■ MOST ADMIRED COMPANIES IN VIRGINIA, 2012

Ranked by: Survey of top executives, directors, and securities analysts regarding the Fortune 1,000 companies that they admire the most, regardless of industry. **Remarks:** Also notes city and industry rank. List is available online only, not in print. **Number listed:** 10

1. Altria Group Inc., with 7.52 points
2. Universal, 6.97
3. Booz Allen Hamilton Holding, 6.89

4. Dominion Resources Inc., 6.83

5. Northrop Grumman, 6.64

6. General Dynamics Corp., 6.57

7. CACI International, 6.18

8. Capital One Financial Corp., 6.13

9. Norfolk Southern Corp., 6.10

10. MeadWestvaco, 5.69

Source: *Fortune*, World's Most Admired Companies (annual), http://www.fortune.com, March 19, 2012.

2149 ■ TOP *FORTUNE 500* COMPANIES IN VIRGINIA, 2011

Ranked by: Revenue, in millions of dollars. **Remarks:** Also notes overall rank in the *Fortune 500,* headquarters, and number of employees. **Number listed:** 24

1. Freddie Mac, with $88,262 million

2. General Dynamics Corp., $32,677

3. Northrop Grumman Corp., $28,058

4. Capital One Financial Corp., $18,525

5. The AES Corp., $17,759

6. Altria Group Inc., $16,619

7. Computer Sciences Corp., $16,144

8. Dominion Resources Inc., $14,379

9. Smithfield Foods Inc., $12,202.7

10. Norfolk Southern Corp., $11,172

Source: *Fortune*, Fortune 500 (annual), May 21, 2012, p. F-46.

2150 ■ VIRGINIA'S BEST COMPANIES TO WORK FOR, 2012

Ranked by: Score based on employee surveys as well as evaluation of companies' credibility, respect, fairness, and pride/camaraderie. **Remarks:** Specific scores not provided; companies are listed alphabetically, not ranked. Available online only, not in print. **Number listed:** 4

1. Booz Allen Hamilton Inc.

2. Capital One

3. CarMax Inc.

4. Navy Federal Credit Union

Source: *Fortune*, 100 Best Companies to Work For (annual), http://www.fortune.com, February 6, 2012.

2151 ■ VIRGINIA'S LARGEST COMPANIES OVERALL, 2011

Ranked by: Score based on revenue, profits, assets, and market capitalization. **Remarks:** Specific scores not provided. Also notes overall rank in the *Forbes 2000* and figures for each criterion. **Number listed:** 20

1. Capital One Financial Corp.

2. Altria Group Inc.

3. General Dynamics Corp.

4. Dominion Resources Inc.

5. Northrop Grumman Corp.

6. Norfolk Southern Corp.

7. Sprint Nextel Corp.

8. The AES Corp.

9. Freddie Mac

10. Genworth Financial Inc.

Source: *Forbes*, Forbes 2000 (annual), http://www.forbes.com, May 7, 2012.

2152 ■ VIRGINIA'S LARGEST PRIVATE COMPANIES, 2010

Ranked by: Revenue, in billions of dollars. **Remarks:** Also notes business segment, number of employees, and overall rank in the *America's Largest Private Companies* list. Ranking is available online only, not in print. **Number listed:** 3

1. Mars Inc., with $30 billion

2. Performance Food Group Co., $10.6

3. Hilton Worldwide Inc., $8

Source: *Forbes*, America's Largest Private Companies (annual), http://www.forbes.com, December 5, 2011.

2153 ■ VIRGINIA'S TOP PRIVATE COMPANIES, 2011

Ranked by: Revenue, in millions of dollars. **Remarks:** Also notes contact information, top executive, and number of employees. **Number listed:** 3

1. Mars Inc., with $30 million

2. Performance Food Group, $11

3. Hilton Worldwide, $8

Source: *Virginia Business*, Top Private Companies (annual), March 2012.

2154 ■ VIRGINIA'S TOP PUBLIC COMPANIES, 2011

Ranked by: Revenue, in thousands of dollars. **Remarks:** Also notes contact information, CEO, and net income. **Number listed:** 3

1. General Dynamics, with $32,677,000 thousand

2. Northrop Grumman Corp., $26,412,000

3. Altria Group, $23,800,000

Source: *Virginia Business*, Top Public Companies (annual), March 2012.

Corporations—Washington

2155 ■ BEST LARGE COMPANIES IN THE SEATTLE AREA, 2011

Ranked by: Score based on surveys. **Remarks:** Specific scores not provided. Ranking covers companies with 500 or more employees. Also notes website, industry, number of Washington employees, and top executive in Washington. **Number listed:** 6

1. The Everett Clinic

2. F5 Networks Inc.

3. McKinstry Co.

3. Columbia Bank

5. PAML

6. Proliance Surgeons

Source: *Seattle Business*, The 100 Best Companies (annual), July 2011, p. 42.

2156 ■ BEST LARGE COMPANIES IN THE SEATTLE AREA HEADQUARTERED OUTSIDE OF WASHINGTON, 2011

Ranked by: Score based on surveys. **Remarks:** Specific scores not provided. Ranking covers companies with fewer than 100 employees. Also notes website, industry, number of Washington employees, and top executive in Washington. **Number listed:** 3

1. West Monroe Partners

2. Weber Shandwick

3. Grant Thornton LLP

Source: *Seattle Business*, The 100 Best Companies (annual), July 2011, p. 42.

2157 ■ BEST MID-SIZED COMPANIES IN THE SEATTLE AREA, 2011

Ranked by: Score based on surveys. **Remarks:** Specific scores not provided. Ranking covers companies with 100 to 499 employees. Also notes website, industry, number of Washington employees, and top executive in Washington. **Number listed:** 27

1. MoneyTree
2. Baker Boyer National Bank
3. The Legacy Group
4. Apptio
5. Sprague Pest Solutions
6. Allyis
7. Concur Technologies
8. Slalom Consulting
9. ING Direct
10. Family Home Care & Hospice

Source: *Seattle Business*, The 100 Best Companies (annual), July 2011, p. 40-42.

2158 ■ BEST NONPROFITS IN THE SEATTLE AREA, 2011

Ranked by: Score based on surveys. **Remarks:** Specific scores not provided. Also notes website, industry, number of Washington employees, and top executive in Washington. **Number listed:** 6

1. Valley Medical Center
2. Career Path Services
3. Pacific Medical Centers
4. Washington Technology Industry Association
5. Housing Resources Group
6. United Way of King County

Source: *Seattle Business*, The 100 Best Companies (annual), July 2011, p. 39.

2159 ■ BEST SMALL COMPANIES IN THE SEATTLE AREA, 2011

Ranked by: Score based on surveys. **Remarks:** Specific scores not provided. Ranking covers companies with fewer than 100 employees. Also notes website, industry, number of Washington employees, and top executive in Washington. **Number listed:** 59

1. The CashLINQ Group
2. Buckland & Taylor Ltd.
3. Brightlight Consulting
4. Exclaim
5. Modern Dental Laboratory USA
6. Cook Security Group
7. Resultrix
8. GreenRubino
9. Ubermind
10. Arryve

Source: *Seattle Business*, The 100 Best Companies (annual), July 2011, p. 39-40.

2160 ■ FASTEST-GROWING COMPANIES IN WASHINGTON, 2008-2011

Ranked by: Score based on three-year growth in revenue and earnings, and three-year total return to investors. **Remarks:** Spe-

cific scores not provided. To qualify for list, companies must have revenues of at least $50 million, net income of at least $10 million, market capitalization of at least $250 million, and stock price of at least $5. Int'l companies are eligible if they trade on a U.S. exchange and file quarterly reports. **Number listed:** 3

1. Coinstar Inc.
2. Amazon.com Inc.
3. F5 Networks Inc.

Source: *Fortune*, 100 Fastest-Growing Companies (annual), http://www.fortune.com, September 26, 2011.

2161 ■ LARGEST COMPANIES IN WASHINGTON BY EMPLOYEES, 2010

Ranked by: Number of employees at headquarters. **Remarks:** Also notes contact information for headquarters, total number of employees, revenue, rank by revenue, and primary SIC code. **Number listed:** 216

1. T-Mobile USA Inc., with 30,500 employees
2. Microsoft Corp., 28,000
3. Swedish Health Services, 4,400
4. Battelle Memorial Institute, 4,000
4. Harborview Medical Center, 4,000
4. SNC-Lavalin Constructors Inc., 4,000
7. Sacred Heart Medical Center, 3,700
8. Southwest Washington Hospital Inc., 3,400
9. King County Public Hospital District 2, 2,800
9. Virginia Mason Medical Center, 2,800

Source: *Business Rankings*, (annual), Dun & Bradstreet Inc., 2011, p. IV.235-IV.239.

2162 ■ LARGEST COMPANIES IN WASHINGTON BY SALES, 2010

Ranked by: Revenue, in dollars. **Remarks:** Also notes contact information for headquarters, number of employees at headquarters and overall, rank by employees, and primary SIC code. **Number listed:** 220

1. Costco Wholesale Corp., with $77,946,000,000
2. Microsoft Corp., $62,484,000,000
3. Amazon.com Inc., $34,204,000,000
4. Starbucks Corp., $10,707,400,000
5. Paccar Inc., $9,325,100,000
6. Nordstrom Inc., $8,627,000,000
7. Providence Health & Services, $7,026,141,000
8. Weyerhaeuser Co., $6,552,000,000
9. Expeditors International of Washington Inc., $5,967,573,000
10. Alaska Air Group Inc., $3,832,300,000

Source: *Business Rankings*, (annual), Dun & Bradstreet Inc., 2011, p. III.232-III.236.

2163 ■ LARGEST EMPLOYERS IN ISLAND COUNTY, WASHINGTON, 2011

Ranked by: Number of employees. **Number listed:** 19

1. NAS Whidbey, with 10,000+ employees
2. Whidbey General Hospital, 700
3. Oak Harbor School District, 612
4. Whidbey Island Bank, 464
5. Island County, 450
6. Navy Exchange, 250

7. Coupeville School District, 234
8. Wal-Mart Stores Inc., 210
9. South Whidbey School District, 205
10. Nichols Broths Boat Builders, 189

Source: *Northwest Business Journal*, Top Employers, February 2012, p. 21.

2164 ■ LARGEST EMPLOYERS IN SKAGIT COUNTY, WASHINGTON, 2011

Ranked by: Number of employees. **Number listed:** 20

1. Skagit Valley Hospital, with 1,700+ employees
2. Skagit Valley College, 900-1,100
3. Mount Vernon School District, 800-1,000
4. Skagit County, 684
5. Janicki Machines, 526
6. Sedro-Woolley School District, 525
7. Burlington-Edison School District, 486-600
8. Regence Blue Shield, 472
9. Draper Valley Farms, 403
10. Wal-Mart Stores Inc., 400+

Source: *Northwest Business Journal*, Top Employers, February 2012, p. 21.

2165 ■ LARGEST EMPLOYERS IN WHATCOM COUNTY, WASHINGTON, 2011

Ranked by: Number of employees. **Number listed:** 22

1. PeaceHealth St. Joseph Medical Center, with 2,721 employees
2. Western Washington University, 2,255
3. Bellingham School District, 1,500
4. BP Cherry Point, 850
5. City of Bellingham, 809
6. Whatcom County, 804
7. Haggen, 760
7. Heath Tecna, 760
9. Lummi Indian Business Council, 750-800
10. Ferndale School District, 660-670

Source: *Northwest Business Journal*, Top Employers, February 2012, p. 21.

2166 ■ LARGEST PRIVATE COMPANIES IN NORTHWEST WASHINGTON, 2010

Ranked by: Revenue range, in millions of dollars. **Remarks:** Ranking covers companies based in Whatcom, Skagit, Island, and San Juan counties. Also notes business description, location, year founded, number of regional employees, total number of employees, and top executive. **Number listed:** 100

1. Haggen Inc., with $600+ million
2. The Markets LLC, $200+
3. Snelson Cos., $150+
4. Saar's Inc., $150+
5. Grizzley Industrial, $110+
6. Fisher & Sons/Fisher Construction, $110+
7. Dawson Construction, $80+
8. LTI, $80+
9. IMCO General Construction, $70+
10. Ryzex, $70+

Source: *Northwest Business Monthly*, Private 100 (annual), December 2011, p. 36-43.

2167 ■ LARGEST PRIVATE EMPLOYERS IN SNOHOMISH COUNTY, WASHINGTON, 2011

Ranked by: Number of full-time-equivalent employees located within Snohomish County. **Remarks:** Also notes company type and website. **Number listed:** 18

1. Boeing Co., with 39,000 employees
2. Providence Regional Medical Center, Everett, 3,500
3. Tulalp Tribes Enterprises, 3,100
4. Premera Blue Cross, 2,400
5. The Everett Clinic, 2,100
6. Philips Medical Systems, 2,000
7. Swedish/Edmonds Hospital, 1,700
8. Fluke Corp., 1,100
9. Aviation Technical Services LLC, 1,000
10. CEMEX, 850

Source: *Snohomish County Business Journal*, Market Facts (annual), 2012, p. 50.

2168 ■ LARGEST PUBLIC EMPLOYERS IN SNOHOMISH COUNTY, WASHINGTON, 2011

Ranked by: Number of full-time-equivalent employees located within Snohomish County. **Remarks:** Also notes company type and website. **Number listed:** 13

1. Naval Station Everett, with 6,000 employees
1. Washington State, 6,000
3. Snohomish County Government, 2,500
4. Edmonds School District, 2,000
5. Everett School District, 1,900
6. City of Everett, 1,200
7. Marysville School District, 1,200
8. Monroe Correctional Complex, 1,000
9. Snohomish County Public Utility Department, 950
10. Community Transit, 650

Source: *Snohomish County Business Journal*, Market Facts (annual), 2012, p. 50.

2169 ■ MOST ADMIRED COMPANIES IN WASHINGTON, 2012

Ranked by: Survey of top executives, directors, and securities analysts regarding the Fortune 1,000 companies that they admire the most, regardless of industry. **Remarks:** Also notes city and industry rank. List is available online only, not in print. **Number listed:** 8

1. Starbucks Corp., with 7.85 points
2. Amazon.com Inc., 7.45
3. Nordstrom Inc., 7.15
4. Costco Wholesale Corp., 6.95
5. Microsoft Corp., 6.48
6. Expedia Inc., 6.08
7. Expeditors International of Washington Inc., 5.97
8. Weyerhaeuser Co., 5.66

Source: *Fortune*, World's Most Admired Companies (annual), http://www.fortune.com, March 19, 2012.

2170 ■ MOST PRODUCTIVE PACIFIC NORTHWEST COMPANIES, 2010

Ranked by: Revenue per employee, in dollars. **Remarks:** Ranking covers companies located in Washington, Oregon, and Idaho. **Number listed:** 82

1. Blue Nile Inc., with $1,742,874
2. InfoSpace Inc., $1,418,592
3. MWI Veterinary Supply Inc., $1,266,058
4. Amazon.com Inc., $1,014,955
5. Plum Creek Timber Co., $990,017
6. Jewett-Cameron Trading Co., Ltd., $903,746
7. StanCorp Financial Group Inc., $894,565
8. SeaBright Insurance Holdings, $891,104
9. Barrett Business Services, $805,673
10. Northwest Natural Gas Co., $775,650

Source: *The Seattle Times*, Best of the Northwest (annual), http://www.seattletimes.nwsource.com, June 17, 2011.

2171 ■ MOST PROFITABLE PACIFIC NORTHWEST COMPANIES, 2010

Ranked by: Profits, in thousands of dollars. **Remarks:** Ranking covers companies located in Washington, Oregon, and Idaho. **Number listed:** 82

1. Microsoft Corp., with $18,760,000 thousand
2. Nike Inc., $1,906,700
3. Micron Technology Inc., $1,850,000
4. Costco Wholesale Corp., $1,303,000
5. Weyerhaeuser Co., $1,281,000
6. Amazon.com Inc., $1,152,000
7. Starbucks Corp., $945,600
8. Precision Castparts Corp., $921,800
9. Nordstrom Inc., $613,000
10. Paccar Inc., $457,600

Source: *The Seattle Times*, Best of the Northwest (annual), http://www.seattletimes.nwsource.com, June 17, 2011.

2172 ■ PACIFIC NORTHWEST COMPANIES WITH THE FASTEST-GROWING PROFITS, 2009-2010

Ranked by: Annual growth in profits, in percent. **Remarks:** Ranking covers companies located in Washington, Oregon, and Idaho. **Number listed:** 82

1. Heritage Financial, with 2,198.5%
2. Washington Banking, 311.5%
3. Paccar Inc., 308.9%
4. SonoSite, 203.7%
5. Zumiez, 165.1%
6. Washington Federal, 146.3%
7. Starbucks Corp., 142%
8. FEI Co., 136.5%
9. TrueBlue, 125.5%
10. Alaska Air Group Inc., 106.5%

Source: *The Seattle Times*, Best of the Northwest (annual), http://www.seattletimes.nwsource.com, June 17, 2011.

2173 ■ PACIFIC NORTHWEST COMPANIES WITH THE HIGHEST MARKET CAPITALIZATION, 2010

Ranked by: Market value, in millions of dollars. **Remarks:** Ranking covers companies located in Washington, Oregon, and Idaho. **Number listed:** 82

1. Microsoft Corp., with $238,785 million
2. Amazon.com Inc., $80,791
3. Nike Inc., $40,820
4. Costco Wholesale Corp., $31,521
5. Starbucks Corp., $23,812
6. Paccar Inc., $20,912
7. Precision Castparts Corp., $19,854
8. Expeditors International of Washington Inc., $11,595
9. F5 Networks Inc., $10,523
10. Weyerhaeuser Co., $10,145

Source: *The Seattle Times*, Best of the Northwest (annual), http://www.seattletimes.nwsource.com, June 17, 2011.

2174 ■ PACIFIC NORTHWEST COMPANIES WITH THE HIGHEST OPERATING INCOME, 2010

Ranked by: Operating income, in thousands of dollars. **Remarks:** Ranking covers companies located in Washington, Oregon, and Idaho. **Number listed:** 82

1. Microsoft Corp., with $24,157,000 thousand
2. Nike Inc., $2,474,000
3. Costco Wholesale Corp., $2,085,000
4. Micron Technology Inc., $1,579,000
5. Precision Castparts Corp., $1,422,400
6. Amazon.com Inc., $1,406,000
7. Starbucks Corp., $1,324,300
8. Nordstrom Inc., $1,118,000
9. Expedia Inc., $737,457
10. Paccar Inc., $648,500

Source: *The Seattle Times*, Best of the Northwest (annual), http://www.seattletimes.nwsource.com, June 17, 2011.

2175 ■ PACIFIC NORTHWEST COMPANIES WITH THE HIGHEST PRICE-TO-EARNINGS RATIO, 2010

Ranked by: Price-to-earnings ratio. **Remarks:** Ranking covers companies located in Washington, Oregon, and Idaho. **Number listed:** 82

1. Rentrak, with 135
2. Concur Technologies Inc., 127
3. Umpqua Holdings, 81
4. Amazon.com Inc., 71
5. Blue Nile Inc., 61
6. F5 Networks Inc., 6
7. Digimarc, 55
8. Pope Resources LP, 53
9. InfoSpace Inc., 49
10. Williams Controls, 48

Source: *The Seattle Times*, Best of the Northwest (annual), http://www.seattletimes.nwsource.com, June 17, 2011.

2176 ■ PACIFIC NORTHWEST COMPANIES WITH THE HIGHEST RETURN ON ASSETS, 2010

Ranked by: Return on assets, in percent. **Remarks:** Ranking covers companies located in Washington, Oregon, and Idaho. **Number listed:** 82

1. Microsoft Corp., with 22.9%
2. Starbucks Corp., 15.8%
3. Flir Systems Inc., 14.8%

4. Micro Technology Inc., 14.1%

5. Nike Inc., 13.8%

5. Expeditors International of Washington Inc., 13.8%

7. Precision Castparts Corp., 12.8%

8. F5 Networks Inc., 12.4%

9. Data I/O, 11%

10. Blue Nile Inc., 10%

Source: *The Seattle Times*, Best of the Northwest (annual), http://www.seattletimes.nwsource.com, June 17, 2011.

2177 ■ PACIFIC NORTHWEST COMPANIES WITH THE HIGHEST RETURN ON EQUITY, 2010

Ranked by: Return on equity, in percent. **Remarks:** Ranking covers companies located in Washington, Oregon, and Idaho. **Number listed:** 82

1. Nordstrom Inc., with 43.8%

2. Microsoft Corp., 34.1%

3. Blue Nile Inc., 30.6%

4. Weyerhaeuser Co., 29.6%

5. Micron Technology Inc., 28.5%

6. Starbucks Corp., 28.1%

7. Alaska Air Group Inc., 25.4%

8. Expeditors International of Washington Inc., 20.9%

9. Nike Inc., 20.7%

10. Amazon.com Inc., 19%

Source: *The Seattle Times*, Best of the Northwest (annual), http://www.seattletimes.nwsource.com, June 17, 2011.

2178 ■ PACIFIC NORTHWEST COMPANIES WITH THE HIGHEST REVENUE, 2010

Ranked by: Revenue, in millions of dollars. **Remarks:** Ranking covers companies located in Washington, Oregon, and Idaho. **Number listed:** 10

1. Costco Wholesale Corp., with $77,946 million

2. Microsoft Corp., $62,484

3. Amazon.com Inc., $34,204

4. Nike Inc., $19,014

5. Starbucks Corp., $10,707

6. Paccar Inc., $10,293

7. Nordstrom Inc., $9,700

8. Micron Technology Inc., $8,482

9. Weyerhaeuser Co., $6,552

10. Expeditors International of Washington Inc., $5,968

Source: *The Seattle Times*, Best of the Northwest (annual), http://www.seattletimes.nwsource.com, June 17, 2011.

2179 ■ PACIFIC NORTHWEST COMPANIES WITH THE MOST EMPLOYEES, 2010

Ranked by: Number of employees. **Remarks:** Ranking covers companies located in Washington, Oregon, and Idaho. **Number listed:** 82

1. Costco Wholesale Corp., with 147,000 employees

2. Starbucks Corp., 137,000

3. Microsoft Corp., 89,000

4. Nordstrom Inc., 54,000

5. Nike Inc., 34,400

6. Amazon.com Inc., 33,700

7. Micron Technology Inc., 25,900

8. Emeritus Corp., 20,000

9. Precision Castparts Corp., 18,100

10. Paccar Inc., 17,700

Source: *The Seattle Times*, Best of the Northwest (annual), http://www.seattletimes.nwsource.com, June 17, 2011.

2180 ■ TOP *FORTUNE 500* COMPANIES IN WASHINGTON, 2011

Ranked by: Revenue, in millions of dollars. **Remarks:** Also notes overall rank in the *Fortune 500,* headquarters, and number of employees. **Number listed:** 8

1. Costco Wholesale Corp., with $88,915 million

2. Microsoft Corp., $69,943

3. Amazon.com Inc., $48,077

4. Paccar Inc., $16,355.2

5. Starbucks Corp., $11,700.4

6. Nordstrom Inc., $10,877

7. Weyerhaeuser Co., $6,618

8. Expeditors International of Washington Inc., $6,150.5

Source: *Fortune*, Fortune 500 (annual), May 21, 2012, p. F-46.

2181 ■ TOP PACIFIC NORTHWEST COMPANIES OVERALL, 2010

Ranked by: Score based on a variety of financial data. **Remarks:** Scores not provided. Ranking covers companies located in Washington, Oregon, and Idaho. **Number listed:** 82

1. Starbucks Corp.

2. Alaska Air Group Inc.

3. F5 Networks Inc.

4. Amazon.com Inc.

5. Coinstar Inc.

6. Nordstrom Inc.

7. MWI Veterinary Supply Inc.

8. Blue Nile Inc.

9. Todd Shipyards

10. Clearwater Paper

Source: *The Seattle Times*, Best of the Northwest (annual), http://www.seattletimes.nwsource.com, June 17, 2011.

2182 ■ WASHINGTON'S BEST COMPANIES TO WORK FOR, 2012

Ranked by: Score based on employee surveys as well as evaluation of companies' credibility, respect, fairness, and pride/camaraderie. **Remarks:** Specific scores not provided; companies are listed alphabetically, not ranked. Available online only, not in print. **Number listed:** 7

1. The Everett Clinic

2. Microsoft Corp.

3. Nordstrom Inc.

4. Perkins Cole LLP

5. Recreational Equipment Inc. (REI)

6. Schweitzer Engineering Labs

7. Starbucks Corp.

Source: *Fortune*, 100 Best Companies to Work For (annual), http://www.fortune.com, February 6, 2012.

2183 ■ WASHINGTON'S LARGEST COMPANIES OVERALL, 2011

Ranked by: Score based on revenue, profits, assets, and market capitalization. **Remarks:** Specific scores not provided. Also notes overall rank in the *Forbes 2000* and figures for each criterion. **Number listed:** 10

1. Microsoft Corp.
2. Costco Wholesale Corp.
3. Amazon.com Inc.
4. Paccar Inc.
5. Starbucks Corp.
6. Nordstrom Inc.
7. Weyerhaeuser Co.
8. Expeditors International of Washington Inc.
9. Symetra Financial Corp.
10. F5 Networks Inc.

Source: *Forbes*, Forbes 2000 (annual), http://www.forbes.com, May 7, 2012.

Corporations—Washington DC

2184 ■ LARGEST COMPANIES IN THE DISTRICT OF COLUMBIA BY EMPLOYEES, 2010

Ranked by: Number of employees at headquarters. **Remarks:** Also notes contact information for headquarters, total number of employees, revenue, rank by revenue, and primary SIC code. **Number listed:** 49

1. International Bank for Reconstruction & Development Inc., with 6,000 employees
2. Medstar-Georgetown Medical Center Inc., 3,700
3. Universities Research Association Inc., 3,200
4. The Washington Post Co., 2,800
5. Childrens Hospital, 2,757
6. Washington Metropolitan Area Transit Authority, 2,691
7. International Monetary Fund, 2,600
8. Federal National Mortgage Association, 2,500
8. Geico Corp., 2,500
10. Federal Deposit Insurance Corp., 2,242

Source: *Business Rankings*, (annual), Dun & Bradstreet Inc., 2011, p. IV.46-IV.47.

2185 ■ LARGEST COMPANIES IN THE DISTRICT OF COLUMBIA BY SALES, 2010

Ranked by: Revenue, in dollars. **Remarks:** Also notes contact information for headquarters, number of employees at headquarters and overall, rank by employees, and primary SIC code. **Number listed:** 48

1. Danaher Corp., with $13,202,602,000
2. Pepco Holdings Inc., $7,039,000,000
3. The Washington Post Co., $4,723,573,000
4. WGL Holdings Inc., $2,708,876,000
5. Potomac Electric Power Co., $2,288,000,000
6. Washington Gas Light Co., $1,321,521,000

7. XM Satellite Radio Holdings Inc., $1,297,341,000
7. XM Satellite Radio Inc., $1,297,341,000
9. Intelsat Corp., $1,128,136,000
10. Federal Prison Industries Inc., $983,227,000

Source: *Business Rankings*, (annual), Dun & Bradstreet Inc., 2011, p. III.46-III.47.

2186 ■ LARGEST EMPLOYERS IN THE WASHINGTON DC AREA, 2011

Ranked by: Number of area employees. **Remarks:** Companies headquartered in Washington DC or parts of Maryland and Virginia are eligible for ranking. **Number listed:** 11

1. MedStar Health, with 15,559 employees
2. Inova Health System, 15,534
3. Northrop Grumman, 15,053
4. Science Applications International Corp., 15,000
5. McDonald's Corp., 14,980
6. Booz Allen Hamilton, 14,000
7. Marriott International, 13,330
8. Verizon Communications Inc., 13,100
9. FedEx Corp., 12,800
10. Safeway Inc., 10,700

Source: *Washington Post*, The Post 200 (annual), http://www.washingtonpost.com, December 15, 2011.

2187 ■ TOP *FORTUNE 500* COMPANIES IN WASHINGTON DC, 2011

Ranked by: Revenue, in millions of dollars. **Remarks:** Also notes overall rank in the *Fortune 500,* headquarters, and number of employees. **Number listed:** 3

1. Fannie Mae, with $137,451 million
2. Danaher Corp., $16,476.4
3. Pepco Holdings Inc., $5,920

Source: *Fortune*, Fortune 500 (annual), May 21, 2012, p. F-42.

2188 ■ WASHINGTON DC'S LARGEST COMPANIES OVERALL, 2011

Ranked by: Score based on revenue, profits, assets, and market capitalization. **Remarks:** Specific scores not provided. Also notes overall rank in the *Forbes 2000* and figures for each criterion. **Number listed:** 3

1. Danaher Corp.
2. Fannie Mae
3. Pepco Holdings Inc.

Source: *Forbes*, Forbes 2000 (annual), http://www.forbes.com, May 7, 2012.

Corporations—West Virginia

2189 ■ LARGEST COMPANIES IN WEST VIRGINIA BY EMPLOYEES, 2010

Ranked by: Number of employees at headquarters. **Remarks:** Also notes contact information for headquarters, total number of employees, revenue, rank by revenue, and primary SIC code. **Number listed:** 58

1. CAMC Health System Inc., with 2,500 employees

1. Charleston Area Medical Center Inc., 2,500
3. West Virginia University Hospitals, 2,250
4. St. Mary's Medical Center Inc., 2,000
5. Ohio Valley Health Services & Education Corp., 1,825
6. Mountaineer Park Inc., 1,700
6. Oglebay Resort Conference Center, 1,700
8. Snowshoe Mountain Inc., 1,400
9. H. J. Thomas Memorial Hospital Inc., 1,200
10. Huntington Alloys Corp., 1,153

Source: *Business Rankings*, (annual), Dun & Bradstreet Inc., 2011, p. IV.240-IV.241.

2190 ■ LARGEST COMPANIES IN WEST VIRGINIA BY SALES, 2010

Ranked by: Revenue, in dollars. **Remarks:** Also notes contact information for headquarters, number of employees at headquarters and overall, rank by employees, and primary SIC code. **Number listed:** 58

1. McJunkin Red Man Corp., with $3,659,622,000
2. International Coal Group Inc., $1,166,471,000
3. Hilltop Health Care Center Inc., $1,028,963,900
4. CAMC Health System Inc., $878,793,000
5. Charleston Area Medical Center Inc., $833,241,917
6. Community Health Systems Inc., $646,949,000
7. West Virginia University Hospitals, $529,510,342
8. MTR Gaming Group Inc., $424,891,000
9. Monongalia County General Hospital Co., $368,057,206
10. Gabriel Brothers Inc., $361,919,824

Source: *Business Rankings*, (annual), Dun & Bradstreet Inc., 2011, p. III.237-III.238.

Corporations—Wisconsin

2191 ■ LARGEST COMPANIES IN WISCONSIN BY EMPLOYEES, 2010

Ranked by: Number of employees at headquarters. **Remarks:** Also notes contact information for headquarters, total number of employees, revenue, rank by revenue, and primary SIC code. **Number listed:** 213

1. Cathedral Square Pharmacy, with 5,000 employees
1. University of Wisconsin Hospital & Clinics, 5,000
3. Rexnord Corp., 4,700
4. Wisconsin Energy Corp., 4,321
5. Wisconsin Bell Inc., 4,080
6. Gunderson Clinic Ltd., 4,000
6. Gunderson Lutheran Medical Center Inc., 4,000
6. IDSC Holdings LLC, 4,000
6. Thedacare Inc., 4,000
10. Ashley Furniture Industries Inc., 3,800
10. Schneider National Inc., 3,800

Source: *Business Rankings*, (annual), Dun & Bradstreet Inc., 2011, p. IV.242-IV.246.

2192 ■ LARGEST COMPANIES IN WISCONSIN BY SALES, 2010

Ranked by: Revenue, in dollars. **Remarks:** Also notes contact information for headquarters, number of employees at headquarters and overall, rank by employees, and primary SIC code. **Number listed:** 213

1. Johnson Controls Inc., with $34,305,000,000
2. Manpower Inc., $18,866,500,000
3. Kohl's Corp., $17,178,000,000
4. Oshkosh Corp., $9,842,400,000
5. Pierce Manufacturing Inc., $7,100,000,000
6. Thermo Noran Inc., $5,000,000,000
7. Harley-Davidson Inc., $4,859,336,000
8. Rockwell Automation Inc., $4,857,000,000
9. Remis Co., $4,835,042,000
10. Wisconsin Energy Corp., $4,202,500,000

Source: *Business Rankings*, (annual), Dun & Bradstreet Inc., 2011, p. III.239-III.243.

2193 ■ MOST ADMIRED COMPANIES IN WISCONSIN, 2012

Ranked by: Survey of top executives, directors, and securities analysts regarding the Fortune 1,000 companies that they admire the most, regardless of industry. **Remarks:** Also notes city and industry rank. List is available online only, not in print. **Number listed:** 6

1. Manpower Inc., with 7.27 point
2. Bemis Co., Inc., 6.74
3. Johnson Controls Inc., 6.62
4. Northwestern Mutual Life Insurance Co., 5.89
5. Fiserv, 5.87
6. Kohl's Corp., 5.7

Source: *Fortune*, World's Most Admired Companies (annual), http://www.fortune.com, March 19, 2012.

2194 ■ TOP *FORTUNE 500* COMPANIES IN WISCONSIN, 2011

Ranked by: Revenue, in millions of dollars. **Remarks:** Also notes overall rank in the *Fortune 500,* headquarters, and number of employees. **Number listed:** 9

1. Johnson Controls Inc., with $40,833 million
2. Northwestern Mutual Life Insurance Co., $24,861
3. Manpower Inc., $22,006
4. Kohl's Corp., $18,804
5. Oshkosh Corp., $7,584.7
6. American Family Insurance Group, $6,400.2
7. Rockwell Automation Inc., $6,000.4
8. Bemis Co., Inc., $5,322.7
9. Harley-Davidson Inc., $5,311.7

Source: *Fortune*, Fortune 500 (annual), May 21, 2012, p. F-46.

2195 ■ WISCONSIN'S LARGEST COMPANIES OVERALL, 2011

Ranked by: Score based on revenue, profits, assets, and market capitalization. **Remarks:** Specific scores not provided. Also notes overall rank in the *Forbes 2000* and figures for each criterion. **Number listed:** 8

1. Johnson Controls Inc.

2. Kohl's Corp.
3. Rockwell Automation Inc.
4. Wisconsin Energy Corp.
5. Harley-Davidson Inc.
6. Joy Global Inc.
7. Fiserv Inc.
8. Manpower Inc.

Source: *Forbes*, Forbes 2000 (annual), http://www.forbes.com, May 7, 2012.

2196 ■ WISCONSIN'S LARGEST PRIVATE COMPANIES, 2010

Ranked by: Revenue, in billions of dollars. **Remarks:** Also notes business segment, number of employees, and overall rank in the *America's Largest Private Companies* list. Ranking is available on-line only, not in print. **Number listed:** 9

1. S. C. Johnson & Son Inc., with $9 billion
2. Menard Inc., $7.17
3. Kohler Co., $4.68
4. ABC Supply Co., $4.07
5. Roundys Supermarkets Inc., $3.8
6. Schreiber Foods Inc., $3.5
7. Schneider National Inc., $3.1
8. Ashley Furniture Industries Inc., $2.9
9. ShopKo Properties Inc., $2.2

Source: *Forbes*, America's Largest Private Companies (annual), http://www.forbes.com, December 5, 2011.

Corporations—Wyoming

2197 ■ LARGEST COMPANIES IN WYOMING BY EMPLOYEES, 2010

Ranked by: Number of employees at headquarters. **Remarks:** Also notes contact information for headquarters, total number of employees, revenue, rank by revenue, and primary SIC code. **Number listed:** 50

1. Wyoming Medical Center Inc., with 1,018 employees
2. FMC Wyoming Corp., 875
3. Memorial Hospital of Laramie County, 830
4. Cyclone Drilling Inc., 600
5. Sierra Trading Post Inc., 565
6. Cordero Rojo Mining Co., 550
7. Cordero Mining Holdings LLC, 500
7. Grand Teton Lodge Co., 500
9. Albany County Hospital District, 490
10. Teton County Hospital District, 444

Source: *Business Rankings*, (annual), Dun & Bradstreet Inc., 2011, p. IV.247-IV.248.

2198 ■ LARGEST COMPANIES IN WYOMING BY SALES, 2010

Ranked by: Revenue, in dollars. **Remarks:** Also notes contact information for headquarters, number of employees at headquarters and overall, rank by employees, and primary SIC code. **Number listed:** 50

1. Power Integration & Systems, with $1,500,000,000

2. Cloud Peak Energy Inc., $1,370,761,000
2. Cloud Peak Energy Resources LLC, $1,370,761,000
4. Maverik Inc., $1,274,407,000
5. OCI Wyoming LP, $300,000,000
6. Wyoming Medical Center Inc., $204,223,035
7. Powder River Energy Corp., $165,967,558
8. Great Lakes Aviation Ltd., $121,844,631
9. Kussy Inc., $116,262,000
10. J. W. Williams Inc., $106,444,713

Source: *Business Rankings*, (annual), Dun & Bradstreet Inc., 2011, p. III.244-III.245.

Cosmetics Industry
See also: **Personal Care Products**

2199 ■ WORLD'S TOP COSMETICS BRANDS, 2011

Ranked by: Brand value, in millions of U.S. dollars. **Remarks:** Also notes rank and figures for previous year, country, and brand rating. **Number listed:** 50

1. Olay, with $11,066 million
2. Avon, $10,171
3. Gillette, $7,784
4. L'Oreal, $7,630
5. Nivea, $6,569
6. Neutrogena, $6,350
7. Lancome, $5,685
8. Dove, $4,517
9. Estee Lauder, $3,037
10. Biore, $3,014

Source: *Top 50 Cosmetics Brands*, (annual), Brand Finance plc, 2011.

Credit Cards
See also: **Bank Credit Cards**

2200 ■ TOP U.S. CREDIT CARD ISSUERS, 2010

Ranked by: Market share of purchase volume, in percent. **Remarks:** Also notes measured media spending and figures for previous year. **Number listed:** 5

1. American Express Co., with 24.6%
2. Chase, 17.7%
3. Bank of America Corp., 12.7%
4. Citigroup, 10.3%
5. Capital One Financial Corp., 5.3%

Source: *Advertising Age*, Leading National Advertisers (annual), June 20, 2011, p. 21.

2201 ■ WORLD'S MOST ADMIRED CONSUMER CREDIT CARD COMPANIES, 2012

Ranked by: Score, on a scale of 10, based on a survey of executives, directors, and securities analysts of companies within their own industry on eight criteria: innovation, financial soundness, employee talent, use of corporate assets, long-term investment value, social responsibility, quality of management, and quality of products/services. **Remarks:** Specific scores not provided. Also notes rank for previous year. **Number listed:** 6

1. Visa Inc.
2. American Express Co.
3. MasterCard Inc.
4. Capital One Financial Corp.
5. Discover Financial Services
6. Global Payments Inc.

Source: *Fortune*, World's Most Admired Companies (annual), March 19, 2012, p. 148.

Credit Institutions

2202 ■ LARGEST NONDEPOSITORY CREDIT INSTITU-TIONS BY EMPLOYEES, 2010

Ranked by: Total number of employees. **Remarks:** Also notes contact information for headquarters, number of employees at headquarters, revenue, rank by revenue, and primary SIC code. **Number listed:** 46

1. General Electric Co., with 306,304 employees
2. General Electric Capital Corp., 73,000
2. General Electric Capital Services Inc., 73,000
4. Countrywide Financial Corp., 50,600
5. Associates First Capital Corp., 31,706
6. BAC Home Loans Servicing LP, 21,500
7. Citicorp Banking Corp., 19,100
8. CitiFinancial Credit Co., 19,000
9. Associates Corp. of North America, 18,000
10. Bank of New York Inc., 7,302

Source: *Business Rankings*, (annual), Dun & Bradstreet Inc., 2011, p. VI.178-VI.179.

Credit Unions

2203 ■ LARGEST BRIDGE CORPORATE CREDIT UNIONS, 2011

Ranked by: Total assets, in dollars. **Remarks:** Also notes total capital, capital ratio, total investments, total shares, annual share growth, total loans, annual loan growth, and return on investments. **Number listed:** 4

1. WesCorp Credit Union (CA), with $12,990,153,939
2. Members United Corporate Credit Union (IL), $8,030,642,291
3. U.S. Central Credit Union (KS), $7,666,402,669
4. Southwest Corporate Credit Union (TX), $7,359,720,982

Source: *Credit Union Directory*, (annual), National Credit Union Administration, 2012, p. 133.

2204 ■ LARGEST CREDIT UNIONS IN THE TWIN CITIES, 2011

Ranked by: Assets, in dollars. **Remarks:** Also notes contact information, year founded, number of employees, loans and leases, investments, net income, shares and deposits, principal officer, number of members and branches, and membership requirements. **Number listed:** 25

1. Wings Financial Federal Credit Union, with $3,198,150,691
2. Affinity Plus Federal Credit Union, $1,357,709,711

3. U.S. Federal Credit Union, $826,800,884
4. Hiway Federal Credit Union, $819,760,998
5. Trustone Financial Credit Union, $675,505,895
6. Central Minnesota Credit Union, $577,385,220
7. Spire Federal Credit Union, $533,513,172
8. Postal Credit Union, $504,450,737
9. Mayo Employees Federal Credit Union, $491,154,902
10. City-County Credit Union, $353,802,022

Source: *Twin Cities Business*, The BIG Book (annual), http://www.tcbmag.com, 2012.

2205 ■ LARGEST LOS ANGELES COUNTY-BASED CREDIT UNIONS, 2011

Ranked by: Assets as of June 30, in millions of dollars. **Remarks:** Also notes contact information, deposits, net income, figures for previous year, percent change, number of members, number of employees and branches, year founded, and top executive. **Number listed:** 25

1. Kinecta Federal Credit Union, with $3,434 million
2. Lockheed Federal Credit Union, $3,056
3. Wescom Credit Union, $2,529

Source: *Los Angeles Business Journal*, L.A. County-Based Credit Unions (annual), http://www.labusinessjournal.com, November 14, 2011.

2206 ■ LARGEST NON-BRIDGE CORPORATE CREDIT UNIONS, 2011

Ranked by: Total assets, in dollars. **Remarks:** Also notes total capital, capital ratio, total investments, total shares, growth in shares, total loans, growth in loans, and return on investments. **Number listed:** 22

1. Mid-Atlantic Corporate Credit Union (PA), with $3,432,131,903
2. Corporate America Credit Union (AL), $3,347,964,803
3. Corporate One Credit Union (OH), $2,839,977,224
4. Southeast Corporate Credit Union (FL), $2,248,006,893
5. CenCorp Credit Union (MI), $2,027,942,840
6. Georgia Corporate Credit Union (GA), $1,770,808,538
7. Corporate Central Credit Union (WI), $1,746,430,305
8. Suncorp Credit Union (CO), $1,604,474,712
9. First Carolina Corporate Credit Union (NC), $1,535,103,527
10. Volunteer Corporate Credit Union (TN), $1,341,952,441

Source: *Credit Union Directory*, (annual), Callahan & Associates Inc., 2012, p. 133.

2207 ■ TOP CREDIT UNIONS IN ALABAMA, 2011

Ranked by: Total assets, in thousands of dollars. **Remarks:** Also notes percentage of state's total assets as well as various financial, productivity, and member service ratios. **Number listed:** 50

1. Redstone Credit Union, with $3,094,362 thousand
2. APCO Employees Credit Union, $2,065,660

3. America's First Credit Union, $1,176,510
4. Army Aviation Center Credit Union, $999,163
5. Max, Your Community Credit Union, $884,401
6. Alabama One Credit Union, $595,317
7. Alabama Telco Credit Union, $556,166
8. Listerhill Credit Union, $525,832
9. Alabama Credit Union, $456,810
10. Family Security Credit Union, $456,676

Source: *Credit Union Directory*, (annual), Callahan & Associates Inc., 2012, p. 177.

2208 ■ TOP CREDIT UNIONS IN ALASKA, 2011

Ranked by: Total assets, in thousands of dollars. **Remarks:** Also notes percentage of state's total assets as well as various financial, productivity, and member service ratios. **Number listed:** 12

1. Alaska USA Credit Union, with $4,401,536 thousand
2. Credit Union 1, $750,706
3. Denali Alaskan Credit Union, $443,625
4. Matanuska Valley Credit Union, $345,035
5. Spirit of Alaska Credit Union, $123,756
6. True North Credit Union, $108,896
7. Military & Civilian Credit Union, $87,081
8. Northern Skies Credit Union, $53,804
9. Tongass Credit Union, $53,657
10. Alps Credit Union, $38,850

Source: *Credit Union Directory*, (annual), Callahan & Associates Inc., 2012, p. 181.

2209 ■ TOP CREDIT UNIONS IN ARIZONA, 2011

Ranked by: Total assets, in thousands of dollars. **Remarks:** Also notes percentage of state's total assets as well as various financial, productivity, and member service ratios. **Number listed:** 50

1. Desert Schools Credit Union, with $2,836,681 thousand
2. Arizona State Savings & Credit Union, $1,263,424
3. Arizona Credit Union, $1,252,735
4. Vantage West Credit Union, $1,089,759
5. Truwest Credit Union, $760,942
6. Hughes Credit Union, $546,428
7. Credit Union West, $438,300
8. First Credit Union , $418,042
9. Arizona Central Credit Union, $404,182
10. Pima Credit Union, $354,092

Source: *Credit Union Directory*, (annual), Callahan & Associates Inc., 2012, p. 183.

2210 ■ TOP CREDIT UNIONS IN ARKANSAS, 2011

Ranked by: Total assets, in thousands of dollars. **Remarks:** Also notes percentage of state's total assets as well as various financial, productivity, and member service ratios. **Number listed:** 50

1. Arkansas Credit Union, with $820,338 thousand
2. Telcoe Credit Union, $288,993
3. Mil-Way Credit Union, $102,873
4. Arkansas Best Credit Union, $102,871
5. Northeast Arkansas Credit Union, $96,915

6. Timberline Credit Union, $84,296
7. Fairfield Credit Union, $79,023
8. Arkansas Superior Credit Union, $61,355
9. Pine Bluff Cotton Belt Credit Union, $59,531
10. Diamond Lakes Credit Union, $57,736

Source: *Credit Union Directory*, (annual), Callahan & Associates Inc., 2012, p. 185.

2211 ■ TOP CREDIT UNIONS BY ASSETS PER EMPLOYEE, 2011

Ranked by: Assets per full-time employee, in dollars. **Remarks:** Also notes total number of full-time employees and total assets. **Number listed:** 50

1. Merck Employees Credit Union (NJ), with $63,394,483
2. NCPD Credit Union (NY), $34,446,454
3. Star One Credit Union (CA), $34,026,444
4. Lufthansa Employees Credit Union (NY), $27,902,903
5. Air Line Pilots Association Credit Union (IL), $26,525,188
6. State Farm Credit Union (IL), $25,975,459
7. APCO Employees Credit Union (AL), $25,820,755
8. Alliant Credit Union (IL), $24,901,613
9. Connecticut State Employees Credit Union (CT), $23,967,521
10. Equitable Resources Employees Credit Union (PA), $23,737,997

Source: *Credit Union Directory*, (annual), Callahan & Associates Inc., 2012, p. 108.

2212 ■ TOP CREDIT UNIONS BY AUTO LOAN PENETRA-TION, 2011

Ranked by: Percentage of members with automobile loans. **Remarks:** Also notes total auto loans, auto loans as a percentage of total loans, one-year growth in auto loans, and indirect loans outstanding. **Number listed:** 50

1. Citizens Community Credit Union (IA), with 84.76%
2. California Adventist Credit Union (CA), 80.77%
3. Nikkei Credit Union (CA), 75.57%
4. Tulare County Credit Union (CA), 65.33%
5. Kings Credit Union (CA), 64.33%
6. Hanin Credit Union (CA), 61.7%
7. USAgencies Credit Union (OR), 57.61%
8. Atlanta Postal Credit Union (GA), 56.93%
9. Hawaii Schools Credit Union (HI), 56.54%
10. CSC Employees Credit Union (CA), 55.31%

Source: *Credit Union Directory*, (annual), Callahan & Associates Inc., 2012, p. 48.

2213 ■ TOP CREDIT UNIONS BY AVERAGE LOAN BAL-ANCE, 2011

Ranked by: Average loan balance, in dollars. **Remarks:** Also notes total value of loans. **Number listed:** 100

1. California Lithuanian Credit Union (CA), with $295,233
2. Evangelical Christian Credit Union (CA), $291,461

3. Melrose Credit Union (NY), $243,173
4. Progressive Credit Union (NY), $188,260
5. Montauk Credit Union (NY), $185,200
6. League of Mutual Taxi Owners Credit Union (NY), $157,716
7. Industrial Credit Union (MA), $126,241
8. Self Reliance New York Credit Union (NY), $101,780
9. Ukranian SelfReliance Credit Union (PA), $99,303
10. Whitefish Credit Union (MT), $86,144

Source: *Credit Union Directory*, (annual), Callahan & Associates Inc., 2012, p. 38.

2214 ■ TOP CREDIT UNIONS BY BRANCHES AND ATMS, 2011

Ranked by: Combined number of branches and automated teller machines (ATMs). Remarks: Also notes number of branches, number of wholly-owned ATMs, members per branch, and total assets. Number listed: 50

1. State Employees' Credit Union (NC), with 1,214 branches/ATMs
2. Navy Credit Union (VA), 550
3. The Golden 1 Credit Union (CA), 357
4. Schools First Credit Union (CA), 293
5. Suncoast Schools Credit Union (FL), 236
6. Wescom Credit Union (CA), 206
7. Actors Credit Union (NY), 204
8. Boeing Employees Credit Union (WA), 193
9. New Mexico Educators Credit Union (NM), 188
10. Alaska USA Credit Union (AK), 183

Source: *Credit Union Directory*, (annual), Callahan & Associates Inc., 2012, p. 114.

2215 ■ TOP CREDIT UNIONS BY BUSINESS LOANS, 2011

Ranked by: Total member business loans outstanding, in dollars. Remarks: Also notes growth in member business loans outstanding, member business loans as a percentage of total loans, and total assets. Number listed: 50

1. Melrose Credit Union (NY), with $1,184,799,121
2. Evangelical Christian Credit Union (CA), $887,599,736
3. Progressive Credit Union (NY), $461,478,416
4. Royal Credit Union (WI), $440,367,909
5. San Diego County Credit Union (CA), $423,180,062
6. Citizens Equity First Credit Union (IL), $401,450,790
7. Digital Credit Union (MA), $399,808,236
8. State Employees' Credit Union (NC), $373,992,393
9. Beacon Credit Union (IN), $338,164,016
10. Central Minnesota Credit Union (MN), $326,708,610

Source: *Credit Union Directory*, (annual), Callahan & Associates Inc., 2012, p. 79.

2216 ■ TOP CREDIT UNIONS IN CALIFORNIA, 2011

Ranked by: Total assets, in thousands of dollars. Remarks: Also notes percentage of state's total assets as well as various financial, productivity, and member service ratios. Number listed: 50

1. Schools First Credit Union, with $8,820,543 thousand
2. The Golden 1 Credit Union, $7,458,123
3. Star One Credit Union, $5,665,403
4. San Diego County Credit Union, $5,228,245
5. First Tech Credit Union, $4,909,019
6. Patelco Credit Union, $3,592,836
7. Kinecta Credit Union, $3,434,439
8. Lockheed Credit Union, $3,055,675
9. Wescom Central Credit Union, $2,528,542
10. Mission Credit Union, $2,112,072

Source: *Credit Union Directory*, (annual), Callahan & Associates Inc., 2012, p. 188.

2217 ■ TOP CREDIT UNIONS IN COLORADO, 2011

Ranked by: Total assets, in thousands of dollars. Remarks: Also notes percentage of state's total assets as well as various financial, productivity, and member service ratios. Number listed: 50

1. ENT Credit Union, with $3,225,457 thousand
2. Bellco Credit Union, $1,937,798
3. Westerra Credit Union, $1,171,079
4. Public Service Employees Credit Union, $1,048,414
5. Elevations Credit Union, $966,303
6. Credit Union of Colorado, $929,771
7. Credit Union of Denver, $517,267
8. Air Academy Credit Union, $405,710
9. Premier Members Credit Union, $392,756
10. Sooper Credit Union, $240,928

Source: *Credit Union Directory*, (annual), Callahan & Associates Inc., 2012, p. 198.

2218 ■ TOP CREDIT UNIONS IN CONNECTICUT, 2011

Ranked by: Total assets, in thousands of dollars. Remarks: Also notes percentage of state's total assets as well as various financial, productivity, and member service ratios. Number listed: 50

1. Connecticut State Employees Credit Union, with $1,617,808 thousand
2. American Eagle Credit Union, $1,365,454
3. Charter Oak Credit Union, $688,278
4. Sikorsky Financial Credit Union, $634,681
5. Connex Credit Union, $372,970
6. Nutmeg State Federal Credit Union, $332,497
7. Mutual Security Credit Union, $237,693
8. Waterbury Connecticut Teachers Credit Union, $218,095
9. Ledge Light Credit Union, $216,015
10. 360 Credit Union, $198,703

Source: *Credit Union Directory*, (annual), Callahan & Associates Inc., 2012, p. 201.

2219 ■ TOP CREDIT UNIONS BY CREDIT CARD LOAN BALANCE, 2011

Ranked by: Average credit card loan balance, in dollars. Remarks: Also notes credit card loans outstanding, number of credit card loans, growth in credit card loans outstanding, and total assets. Number listed: 50

1. Fort Financial Credit Union (IN), with $7,247

2. Boeing Helicopters Credit Union (PA), $6,434
3. PEF Credit Union (OH), $5,540
4. First Financial Credit Union (NJ), $5,349
5. Compass Credit Union (NY), $5,315
6. Navy Credit Union (VA), $5,303
7. Suncoast Schools Credit Union (FL), $5,216
8. School Employees Credit Union of Washington (WA), $5,202
9. Chicago Municipal Employees Credit Union (IL), $5,191
10. Pocatello Railroad Credit Union (ID), $5,084

Source: *Credit Union Directory*, (annual), Callahan & Associates Inc., 2012, p. 70.

2220 ■ TOP CREDIT UNIONS BY CREDIT CARD PENETRATION, 2011

Ranked by: Percentage of members with credit cards. Remarks: Also notes credit card loans as a percentage of total loans, average credit card balance, credit card growth rate, and total assets. Number listed: 50

1. School Employees of Lorain County Credit Union (OH), with 56.92%
2. Pentago Credit Union (VA), 56.39%
3. San Diego Firefighters Credit Union (CA), 53.88%
4. O. A. S. Staff Credit Union (DC), 52.86%
5. Napus Credit Union (VA), 52.31%
6. Entrust Credit Union (VA), 52.26%
7. Saginaw Medical Credit Union (MI), 51.47%
8. Acme Continental Credit Union (IL), 50.05%
9. Houston Texas Fire Fighters Credit Union (TX), 49.44%
10. Schlumberger Employees Credit Union (TX), 48.42%

Source: *Credit Union Directory*, (annual), Callahan & Associates Inc., 2012, p. 74.

2221 ■ TOP CREDIT UNIONS IN DELAWARE, 2011

Ranked by: Total assets, in thousands of dollars. Remarks: Also notes percentage of state's total assets as well as various financial, productivity, and member service ratios. Number listed: 26

1. Dover Credit Union, with $329,633 thousand
2. Del-One Credit Union, $276,170
3. Sussex County Credit Union, $222,256
4. Louviers Credit Union, $211,800
5. Dexsta Credit Union, $178,580
6. Delaware State Police Credit Union, $117,723
7. Community Powered Credit Union, $114,864
8. Chestnut Run Credit Union, $60,162
9. American Spirit Credit Union, $57,693
10. New Castle County School Employees Credit Union, $38,982

Source: *Credit Union Directory*, (annual), Callahan & Associates Inc., 2012, p. 205.

2222 ■ TOP CREDIT UNIONS IN THE DISTRICT OF COLUMBIA, 2011

Ranked by: Total assets, in thousands of dollars. Remarks: Also notes percentage of D.C.'s total assets as well as various financial, productivity, and member service ratios. Number listed: 50

1. Bank-Fund Staff Credit Union, with $3,140,255 thousand
2. Congressional Credit Union, $675,200
3. United States Senate Credit Union, $511,031
4. IDB-IIC Credit Union, $388,569
5. Department of Commerce Credit Union, $257,687
6. Library of Congress Credit Union, $207,638
7. PAHO/WHO Credit Union, $187,145
8. Transportation Credit Union, $174,341
9. Treasury Department Credit Union, $163,578
10. HEW Credit Union, $148,984

Source: *Credit Union Directory*, (annual), Callahan & Associates Inc., 2012, p. 207.

2223 ■ TOP CREDIT UNIONS BY FIRST MORTGAGE ORIGINATIONS, 2011

Ranked by: Value of first mortgage originations, in dollars. Remarks: Also notes first mortgage originations as a percentage of total loan originations, real estate loans as a percentage of total loans, real estate loan outstanding, and total assets. Number listed: 50

1. Navy Credit Union (VA), with $1,811,204,744
2. Pentagon Credit Union (VA), $1,552,544,261
3. State Employees' Credit Union (NC), $1,011,319,802
4. Kinecta Credit Union (CA), $808,022,495
5. Boeing Employees Credit Union (WA), $579,139,973
6. Alliant Credit Union (IL), $509,699,811
7. Alaska USA Credit Union (AK), $487,830,567
8. Bethpage Credit Union (NY), $442,384,198
9. First Tech Credit Union (CA), $371,603,708
10. Digital Credit Union (MA), $337,145,102

Source: *Credit Union Directory*, (annual), Callahan & Associates Inc., 2012, p. 58.

2224 ■ TOP CREDIT UNIONS IN FLORIDA, 2011

Ranked by: Total assets, in thousands of dollars. Remarks: Also notes percentage of state's total assets as well as various financial, productivity, and member service ratios. Number listed: 50

1. Suncoast Schools Credit Union, with $5,003,546 thousand
2. Vystar Credit Union, $4,245,587
3. Space Coast Credit Union, $3,087,710
4. Grow Financial Credit Union, $1,697,637
5. Mid-Florida Credit Union, $1,615,155
6. Fairwinds Credit Union, $1,553,046
7. GTE Credit Union, $1,436,713
8. Eglin Credit Union, $1,341,431
9. Central Florida Educators Credit Union, $1,238,000
10. Community First Credit Union of Florida, $1,145,217

Source: *Credit Union Directory*, (annual), Callahan & Associates Inc., 2012, p. 209.

2225 ■ TOP CREDIT UNIONS IN GEORGIA, 2011

Ranked by: Total assets, in thousands of dollars. Remarks: Also notes percentage of state's total assets as well as various financial, productivity, and member service ratios. Number listed: 50

1. Delta Community Credit Union, with $4,030,987 thousand
2. Atlanta Postal Credit Union, $1,967,357
3. Georgia's Own Credit Union, $1,675,257
4. Robins Credit Union, $1,526,490
5. Associated Credit Union, $1,182,393
6. Georgia United Credit Union, $876,048
7. LGE Community Credit Union, $814,737
8. The Southern Credit Union, $283,732
9. TIC Credit Union, $237,109
10. CDC Credit Union, $228,329

Source: *Credit Union Directory*, (annual), Callahan & Associates Inc., 2012, p. 214.

2226 ■ TOP CREDIT UNIONS IN GUAM, 2011

Ranked by: Total assets, in thousands of U.S. dollars. **Remarks:** Also notes percentage of Guam's total assets as well as various financial, productivity, and member service ratios. **Number listed:** 2

1. Coast360 Credit Union, with $279,255 thousand
2. Community First Guam Credit Union, $87,404

Source: *Credit Union Directory*, (annual), Callahan & Associates Inc., 2012, p. 395.

2227 ■ TOP CREDIT UNIONS IN HAWAII, 2011

Ranked by: Total assets, in thousands of dollars. **Remarks:** Also notes percentage of state's total assets as well as various financial, productivity, and member service ratios. **Number listed:** 50

1. HawaiiUSA Credit Union, with $1,258,556 thousand
2. Hawaii State Credit Union, $1,229,746
3. Aloha Pacific Credit Union, $710,571
4. University of Hawaii Credit Union, $513,699
5. Hawaiian Telephone Employees Credit Union, $504,900
6. Hickam Credit Union, $504,490
7. HFS Credit Union, $429,706
8. Pearl Harbor Credit Union, $349,336
9. Hawaii Community Credit Union, $340,655
10. Kauai Community Credit Union, $309,266

Source: *Credit Union Directory*, (annual), Callahan & Associates Inc., 2012, p. 218.

2228 ■ TOP CREDIT UNIONS IN IDAHO, 2011

Ranked by: Total assets, in thousands of dollars. **Remarks:** Also notes percentage of state's total assets as well as various financial, productivity, and member service ratios. **Number listed:** 50

1. Idaho Central Credit Union, with $930,859 thousand
2. Potlatch No. 1 Credit Union, $465,414
3. Westmark Credit Union, $455,316
4. Pioneer Federal Credit Union, $302,236
5. Capital Educators Credit Union, $277,964
6. East Idaho Credit Union, $244,264
7. TruGrocer Credit Union, $226,278
8. Beehive Credit Union, $158,215
9. Icon Credit Union, $138,279

10. Idaho State University Credit Union, $113,656

Source: *Credit Union Directory*, (annual), Callahan & Associates Inc., 2012, p. 221.

2229 ■ TOP CREDIT UNIONS IN ILLINOIS, 2011

Ranked by: Total assets, in thousands of dollars. **Remarks:** Also notes percentage of state's total assets as well as various financial, productivity, and member service ratios. **Number listed:** 50

1. Alliant Credit Union, with $7,856,459 thousand
2. Citizens Equity First Credit Union, $4,628,257
3. State Farm Credit Union, $3,688,515
4. Baxter Credit Union, $1,487,192
5. I. H. Mississippi Valley Credit Union, $842,531
6. Motorola Employees Credit Union, $796,394
7. Scott Credit Union, $754,590
8. Credit Union 1, $649,067
9. Abbott Laboratories Credit Union, $586,182
10. Corporate America Family Credit Union, $552,056

Source: *Credit Union Directory*, (annual), Callahan & Associates Inc., 2012, p. 224.

2230 ■ TOP CREDIT UNIONS IN INDIANA, 2011

Ranked by: Total assets, in thousands of dollars. **Remarks:** Also notes percentage of state's total assets as well as various financial, productivity, and member service ratios. **Number listed:** 50

1. Teachers Credit Union, with $2,067,524 thousand
2. Indiana Members Credit Union, $1,311,448
3. Eli Lilly Credit Union, $987,544
4. Centra Credit Union, $952,613
5. Forum Credit Union, $939,010
6. Beacon Credit Union, $890,374
7. Evansville Teachers Credit Union, $813,602
8. Indiana University Employees Credit Union, $668,291
9. Purdue Employees Credit Union, $663,591
10. Three Rivers Credit Union, $658,562

Source: *Credit Union Directory*, (annual), Callahan & Associates Inc., 2012, p. 233.

2231 ■ TOP CREDIT UNIONS IN IOWA, 2011

Ranked by: Total assets, in thousands of dollars. **Remarks:** Also notes percentage of state's total assets as well as various financial, productivity, and member service ratios. **Number listed:** 50

1. Veridian Credit Union, with $1,875,730 thousand
2. University of Iowa Community Credit Union, $1,285,643
3. Dupaco Community Credit Union, $941,643
4. Collins Community Credit Union, $651,018
5. Du Trac Community Credit Union, $508,614
6. Community 1st Credit Union, $352,969
7. Community Choice Credit Union, $321,104
8. Greater Iowa Credit Union, $273,678
9. Linn Area Credit Union, $265,084
10. Ascentra Credit Union, $246,040

Source: *Credit Union Directory*, (annual), Callahan & Associates Inc., 2012, p. 238.

2232 ■ TOP CREDIT UNIONS IN KANSAS, 2011

Ranked by: Total assets, in thousands of dollars. **Remarks:** Also notes percentage of state's total assets as well as various financial, productivity, and member service ratios. **Number listed:** 50

1. Meritrust Credit Union, with $710,684 thousand
2. Credit Union of America, $385,744
3. Golden Plains Credit Union, $352,471
4. Mainstreet Credit Union, $291,804
5. Quest Credit Union, $244,785
6. Envista Credit Union, $213,603
7. Cessna Employees Credit Union, $200,679
8. Hutchinson Credit Union, $170,595
9. Mid American Credit Union, $167,272
10. Educational Credit Union, $146,687

Source: *Credit Union Directory*, (annual), Callahan & Associates Inc., 2012, p. 242.

2233 ■ TOP CREDIT UNIONS IN KENTUCKY, 2011

Ranked by: Total assets, in thousands of dollars. **Remarks:** Also notes percentage of state's total assets as well as various financial, productivity, and member service ratios. **Number listed:** 50

1. Fort Knox Credit Union, with $981,012 thousand
2. Commonwealth Credit Union, $893,183
3. L & N Credit Union, $698,584
4. Park Community Credit Union, $469,232
5. University of Kentucky Credit Union, $403,360
6. Members Heritage Credit Union, $302,960
7. Kentucky Telco Credit Union, $283,072
8. Paducah Credit Union, $191,897
9. Ashland Credit Union, $175,797
10. ClassAct Credit Union, $153,787

Source: *Credit Union Directory*, (annual), Callahan & Associates Inc., 2012, p. 245.

2234 ■ TOP CREDIT UNIONS IN LOUISIANA, 2011

Ranked by: Total assets, in thousands of dollars. **Remarks:** Also notes percentage of state's total assets as well as various financial, productivity, and member service ratios. **Number listed:** 50

1. Barksdale Credit Union, with $1,028,668 thousand
2. Neighbors Credit Union, $492,387
3. Campus Credit Union, $447,816
4. LA Capitol Credit Union, $404,821
5. ASI Credit Union, $302,302
6. C. S. E. Credit Union, $269,600
7. E Federal Credit Union, $259,928
8. Dow Louisiana Credit Union, $247,335
9. Jefferson Financial Credit Union, $246,613
10. Carter Credit Union, $199,786

Source: *Credit Union Directory*, (annual), Callahan & Associates Inc., 2012, p. 248.

2235 ■ TOP CREDIT UNIONS IN MAINE, 2011

Ranked by: Total assets, in thousands of dollars. **Remarks:** Also notes percentage of state's total assets as well as various financial, productivity, and member service ratios. **Number listed:** 50

1. Maine State Employees Credit Union, with $331,509 thousand

2. Infinity Credit Union, $264,322
3. Atlantic Regional Credit Union, $245,249
4. Maine Savings Credit Union, $224,758
5. Town & Country Credit Union, $209,346
6. Evergreen Credit Union, $207,754
7. University Credit Union, $201,343
8. York County Credit Union, $197,305
9. Five County Credit Union, $187,236
10. The County Credit Union, $164,535

Source: *Credit Union Directory*, (annual), Callahan & Associates Inc., 2012, p. 254.

2236 ■ TOP CREDIT UNIONS IN MARYLAND, 2011

Ranked by: Total assets, in thousands of dollars. **Remarks:** Also notes percentage of state's total assets as well as various financial, productivity, and member service ratios. **Number listed:** 50

1. Tower Credit Union, with $2,382,971 thousand
2. State Employees Credit Union of Maryland, $2,231,262
3. NASA Credit Union, $1,127,948
4. Municipal Employees Credit Union of Baltimore, $1,123,136
5. First Financial of Maryland Credit Union, $914,262
6. Aberdeen Proving Ground Credit Union, $873,446
7. Andrews Credit Union, $815,000
8. Point Breeze Credit Union, $702,186
9. National Institutes of Health Credit Union, $538,115
10. NRL Credit Union, $465,546

Source: *Credit Union Directory*, (annual), Callahan & Associates Inc., 2012, p. 257.

2237 ■ TOP CREDIT UNIONS IN MASSACHUSETTS, 2011

Ranked by: Total assets, in thousands of dollars. **Remarks:** Also notes percentage of state's total assets as well as various financial, productivity, and member service ratios. **Number listed:** 50

1. Digital Credit Union, with $3,833,247 thousand
2. HarborOne Credit Union, $1,837,276
3. Greylock Credit Union, $1,210,812
4. Rockland Credit Union, $1,064,809
5. Hanscom Credit Union, $919,486
6. Jeanne d'Arc Credit Union, $913,427
7. Metropolitan Credit Union, $897,071
8. Workers' Credit Union, $794,217
9. St. Anne's of Fall River Credit Union, $764,454
10. RTN Credit Union, $705,840

Source: *Credit Union Directory*, (annual), Callahan & Associates Inc., 2012, p. 261.

2238 ■ TOP CREDIT UNIONS BY MEMBERS PER BRANCH, 2011

Ranked by: Number of members per branch. **Remarks:** Also notes number of members, number of branches, members per employee, and total assets. **Number listed:** 50

1. Greenwood Credit Union (RI), with 56,481 members

2. Dow Chemical Employees Credit Union (MI), 55,816

3. Utilities Employees Credit Union (PA), 44,465

4. F & A Credit Union (CA), 41,037

5. School Employees Credit Union of Washington (WA), 39,917

6. Pentagon Credit Union (VA), 37,171

7. Napus Credit Union (VA), 35,303

8. Direct Credit Union (MA), 31,261

9. 1199 SEIU Credit Union (NY), 30,455

10. Los Angeles Firemen's Credit Union (CA), 28,931

Source: *Credit Union Directory*, (annual), Callahan & Associates Inc., 2012, p. 115.

2239 ■ TOP CREDIT UNIONS BY MEMBERS PER EMPLOYEE, 2011

Ranked by: Number of members per full-time employee. **Remarks:** Also notes total number of members, total number of full-time employees, and total assets. **Number listed:** 50

1. Good Samaritan Credit Union (SD), with 2,940 members

2. Omaha Public Power District Employees Credit Union (NE), 1,655

3. 1199 SEIU Credit Union (NY), 1,646

4. B & V Credit Union (KS), 1,628

5. Aflac Credit Union (GA), 1,613

6. Elektra Credit Union (NY), 1,487

7. Jersey Trades Credit Union (NJ), 1,397

8. Children's Medical Center Credit Union (OH), 1,340

9. Dowell Credit Union (OK), 1,291

10. Wiremens Credit Union (OH), 1,254

Source: *Credit Union Directory*, (annual), Callahan & Associates Inc., 2012, p. 109.

2240 ■ TOP CREDIT UNIONS IN MICHIGAN, 2011

Ranked by: Total assets, in thousands of dollars. **Remarks:** Also notes percentage of state's total assets as well as various financial, productivity, and member service ratios. **Number listed:** 50

1. DFCU Financial Credit Union, with $3,054,200 thousand

2. Lake Michigan Credit Union, $2,289,129

3. Michigan State University Credit Union, $2,063,226

4. Lake Trust Credit Union, $1,583,024

5. Dow Chemical Employees' Credit Union, $1,405,209

6. Genisys Credit Union, $1,351,564

7. United Credit Union, $1,285,078

8. Michigan Schools & Government Credit Union, $1,089,316

9. Credit Union One, $739,180

10. First Community Credit Union, $651,506

Source: *Credit Union Directory*, (annual), Callahan & Associates Inc., 2012, p. 267.

2241 ■ TOP CREDIT UNIONS IN MINNESOTA, 2011

Ranked by: Total assets, in thousands of dollars. **Remarks:** Also notes percentage of state's total assets as well as various financial, productivity, and member service ratios. **Number listed:** 50

1. Wings Financial Credit Union, with $3,198,151 thousand

2. Affinity Plus Credit Union, $1,357,710

3. U.S. Credit Union, $826,801

4. Hiway Credit Union, $819,761

5. Trustone Financial Credit Union, $675,506

6. Central Minnesota Credit Union, $577,385

7. Spire Credit Union, $533,513

8. Postal Employees Credit Union, $504,451

9. Mayo Employees Credit Union, $491,155

10. City & County Credit Union, $353,802

Source: *Credit Union Directory*, (annual), Callahan & Associates Inc., 2012, p. 275.

2242 ■ TOP CREDIT UNIONS IN MISSISSIPPI, 2011

Ranked by: Total assets, in thousands of dollars. **Remarks:** Also notes percentage of state's total assets as well as various financial, productivity, and member service ratios. **Number listed:** 50

1. Keesler Credit Union, with $1,931,225 thousand

2. Navigator Credit Union, $243,005

3. Central Sunbelt Credit Union, $171,569

4. Singing River Credit Union, $153,422

5. Mutual Credit Union, $153,295

6. Mississippi Telco Credit Union, $149,162

7. Hope Community Credit Union, $136,561

8. Magnolia Credit Union, $110,541

9. Statewide Credit Union, $83,883

10. Mississippi Credit Union, $72,433

Source: *Credit Union Directory*, (annual), Callahan & Associates Inc., 2012, p. 279.

2243 ■ TOP CREDIT UNIONS IN MISSOURI, 2011

Ranked by: Total assets, in thousands of dollars. **Remarks:** Also notes percentage of state's total assets as well as various financial, productivity, and member service ratios. **Number listed:** 50

1. Community America Credit Union, with $1,796,812 thousand

2. First Community Credit Union, $1,731,070

3. Anheuser-Busch Employees Credit Union, $1,306,024

4. Vantage Credit Union, $672,751

5. Mazuma Credit Union, $454,564

6. Great Plains Credit Union, $287,817

7. Neighbors Credit Union, $276,763

8. 1st Financial Credit Union, $219,943

9. Missouri Credit Union, $217,149

10. St. Louis Community Credit Union, $206,347

Source: *Credit Union Directory*, (annual), Callahan & Associates Inc., 2012, p. 282.

2244 ■ TOP CREDIT UNIONS IN MONTANA, 2011

Ranked by: Total assets, in thousands of dollars. **Remarks:** Also notes percentage of state's total assets as well as various financial, productivity, and member service ratios. **Number listed:** 50

1. Whitefish Credit Union, with $1,214,040 thousand

2. Missoula Credit Union, $346,818

3. Altana Credit Union, $203,626

4. Montana Federal Credit Union, $172,617

5. Valley Federal Credit Union of Montana, $168,493

6. 1st Liberty Credit Union, $139,174

7. Helena Community Credit Union, $135,693

8. Rocky Mountain Credit Union, $119,096

9. Park Side Credit Union, $116,880

10. Southwest Montana Community Credit Union, $102,244

Source: *Credit Union Directory*, (annual), Callahan & Associates Inc., 2012, p. 286.

2245 ■ TOP CREDIT UNIONS IN NEBRASKA, 2011

Ranked by: Total assets, in thousands of dollars. **Remarks:** Also notes percentage of state's total assets as well as various financial, productivity, and member service ratios. **Number listed:** 50

1. SAC Federal Credit Union, with $516,767 thousand

2. Centris Credit Union, $447,159

3. Nebraska Energy Credit Union, $237,618

4. Metro Health Services Credit Union, $181,637

5. Liberty First Credit Union, $144,544

6. Siouxland Credit Union, $141,121

7. Four Points Credit Union, $119,799

8. Mutual First Federal Credit Union, $107,463

9. First Nebraska Educators & Employee Groups Credit Union, $85,025

10. MembersOwn Credit Union, $80,382

Source: *Credit Union Directory*, (annual), Callahan & Associates Inc., 2012, p. 289.

2246 ■ TOP CREDIT UNIONS IN NEVADA, 2011

Ranked by: Total assets, in thousands of dollars. **Remarks:** Also notes percentage of state's total assets as well as various financial, productivity, and member service ratios. **Number listed:** 23

1. Silver State Schools Family Credit Union, with $711,867 thousand

2. One Nevada Credit Union, $677,544

3. Clark County Credit Union, $480,202

4. Boulder Dam Credit Union, $460,859

5. Greater Nevada Credit Union, $443,719

6. Weststar Credit Union, $135,747

7. Financial Horizons Credit Union, $131,793

8. Great Basin Credit Union, $102,488

9. Elko Credit Union, $101,307

10. Plus Credit Union, $89,923

Source: *Credit Union Directory*, (annual), Callahan & Associates Inc., 2012, p. 292.

2247 ■ TOP CREDIT UNIONS IN NEW HAMPSHIRE, 2011

Ranked by: Total assets, in thousands of dollars. **Remarks:** Also notes percentage of state's total assets as well as various financial, productivity, and member service ratios. **Number listed:** 23

1. Service Credit Union, with $1,880,904 thousand

2. St. Mary's Bank Credit Union, $710,132

3. Northeast Credit Union, $702,763

4. Triangle Credit Union, $472,593

5. Bellwether Community Credit Union, $349,552

6. Granite State Credit Union, $283,541

7. New Hampshire Credit Union, $240,590

8. Holy Rosary Regional Credit Union, $168,115

9. Members First Credit Union of New Hampshire, $133,434

10. Woodlands Credit Union, $90,812

Source: *Credit Union Directory*, (annual), Callahan & Associates Inc., 2012, p. 294.

2248 ■ TOP CREDIT UNIONS IN NEW JERSEY, 2011

Ranked by: Total assets, in thousands of dollars. **Remarks:** Also notes percentage of state's total assets as well as various financial, productivity, and member service ratios. **Number listed:** 50

1. Affinity Credit Union, with $2,055,668 thousand

2. Merck Employees Credit Union, $1,648,257

3. Proponent Credit Union, $507,093

4. Financial Resources Credit Union, $398,479

5. Paragon Credit Union, $324,298

6. South Jersey Credit Union, $307,483

7. Credit Union of New Jersey, $306,081

8. United Teletech Financial Credit Union, $291,234

9. Picatinny Credit Union, $279,254

10. The Atlantic Credit Union, $277,068

Source: *Credit Union Directory*, (annual), Callahan & Associates Inc., 2012, p. 296.

2249 ■ TOP CREDIT UNIONS IN NEW MEXICO, 2011

Ranked by: Total assets, in thousands of dollars. **Remarks:** Also notes percentage of state's total assets as well as various financial, productivity, and member service ratios. **Number listed:** 50

1. Sandia Laboratory Credit Union, with $1,665,781 thousand

2. New Mexico Educators Credit Union, $1,097,861

3. U.S. New Mexico Credit Union, $662,675

4. Kirtland Credit Union, $579,301

5. Sandia Area Credit Union, $393,307

6. Del Norte Credit Union, $388,290

7. First Financial Credit Union, $267,078

8. State Employees Credit Union, $296,032

9. Otero Credit Union, $240,904

10. White Sands Credit Union, $237,503

Source: *Credit Union Directory*, (annual), Callahan & Associates Inc., 2012, p. 302.

2250 ■ TOP CREDIT UNIONS IN NEW YORK, 2011

Ranked by: Total assets, in thousands of dollars. **Remarks:** Also notes percentage of state's total assets as well as various financial, productivity, and member service ratios. **Number listed:** 50

1. Bethpage Credit Union, with $4,226,338 thousand

2. Teachers Credit Union, $4,153,802

3. ESL Credit Union, $4,000,085

4. United Nations Credit Union, $3,422,083

5. Hudson Valley Credit Union, $3,189,209

6. Visions Credit Union, $2,662,513
7. State Employees Credit Union, $2,272,918
8. Nassau Educators Credit Union, $1,693,268
9. Municipal Credit Union, $1,674,847
10. Melrose Credit Union, $1,502,698

Source: *Credit Union Directory*, (annual), Callahan & Associates Inc., 2012, p. 304.

2251 ■ TOP CREDIT UNIONS IN NORTH CAROLINA, 2011

Ranked by: Total assets, in thousands of dollars. **Remarks:** Also notes percentage of state's total assets as well as various financial, productivity, and member service ratios. **Number listed:** 50

1. State Employees' Credit Union, with $23,061,183 thousand
2. Coastal Credit Union, $1,995,149
3. Truliant Federal Credit Union, $1,471,201
4. Local Government Employees Credit Union, $1,151,808
5. Allegacy Credit Union, $928,134
6. Marine Credit Union, $682,232
7. Self-Help Credit Union, $539,094
8. Self-Help Credit Union, $390,142
9. Fort Bragg Credit Union, $362,622
10. Carolinas Telco Credit Union, $357,279

Source: *Credit Union Directory*, (annual), Callahan & Associates Inc., 2012, p. 314.

2252 ■ TOP CREDIT UNIONS IN NORTH DAKOTA, 2011

Ranked by: Total assets, in thousands of dollars. **Remarks:** Also notes percentage of state's total assets as well as various financial, productivity, and member service ratios. **Number listed:** 45

1. First Community Credit Union, with $355,753 thousand
2. Capital Credit Union, $257,225
3. Town & Country Credit Union, $255,305
4. Western Cooperative Credit Union, $250,827
5. Community Credit Union, $143,653
6. Dakota West Credit Union, $133,414
7. Citizens Community Credit Union, $123,937
8. North Star Community Credit Union, $123,655
9. Northern Tier Credit Union, $85,821
10. Prairie Credit Union, $82,381

Source: *Credit Union Directory*, (annual), Callahan & Associates Inc., 2012, p. 317.

2253 ■ TOP CREDIT UNIONS IN OHIO, 2011

Ranked by: Total assets, in thousands of dollars. **Remarks:** Also notes percentage of state's total assets as well as various financial, productivity, and member service ratios. **Number listed:** 50

1. Wright-Patt Credit Union, with $2,140,518 thousand
2. General Electric Credit Union, $1,259,875
3. Seven Seventeen Credit Union, $775,990
4. Kemba Financial Credit Union, $617,458
5. Directions Credit Union, $548,788
6. Kemba Credit Union, $477,457
7. Telhio Credit Union, $442,044
8. Sun Federal Credit Union, $401,858

9. BMI Credit Union, $356,562
10. Superior Credit Union, $354,664

Source: *Credit Union Directory*, (annual), Callahan & Associates Inc., 2012, p. 319.

2254 ■ TOP CREDIT UNIONS IN OKLAHOMA, 2011

Ranked by: Total assets, in thousands of dollars. **Remarks:** Also notes percentage of state's total assets as well as various financial, productivity, and member service ratios. **Number listed:** 50

1. Tinker Credit Union, with $2,509,062 thousand
2. Tulsa Teachers Credit Union, $1,051,893
3. Communication Federal Credit Union, $821,638
4. Weokie Credit Union, $796,953
5. 66 Credit Union, $599,845
6. Tulsa Federal Employees Credit Union, $584,302
7. Federal Aviation Administration Employees Credit Union, $502,413
8. Oklahoma Central Credit Union, $428,118
9. Oklahoma Employees Credit Union, $352,999
10. Fort Sill Credit Union, $228,776

Source: *Credit Union Directory*, (annual), Callahan & Associates Inc., 2012, p. 328.

2255 ■ TOP CREDIT UNIONS BY ONE-YEAR MEMBER GROWTH, 2010-2011

Ranked by: Annual growth in number of members, in percent. **Remarks:** Also notes assets and number of members. **Number listed:** 50

1. Realtors Credit Union (MD), with 24.57%
2. Meridian Credit Union (IA), 20.67%
3. Central Florida Postal Credit Union (FL), 16.06%
4. Northeast Arkansas Credit Union (AR), 15.99%
5. Lufthansa Employees Credit Union (NY), 15.94%
6. Coral Community Credit Union (FL), 15.81%
7. Marin County Credit Union (CA), 15.63%
8. Alliance Blackstone Valley Credit Union (RI), 14.82%
9. River City Credit Union (TX), 14.73%
10. Bank-Fund Staff Credit Union (DC), 14.62%

Source: *Credit Union Directory*, (annual), Callahan & Associates Inc., 2012, p. 28.

2256 ■ TOP CREDIT UNIONS BY ONLINE BANKING, 2011

Ranked by: Online banking penetration, in percent. **Remarks:** Also notes number of members using online banking, total number of members, and total assets. **Number listed:** 50

1. Realtors Credit Union (MD), with 100%
2. Palmetto Health Credit Union (SC), 98.01%
3. Idaho State University Credit Union (ID), 96.72%
4. Cutting Edge Credit Union (OR), 94.63%
5. IDB-IIC Credit Union (DC), 93.05%
6. Spirit of Alaska Credit Union (AK), 92.62%
7. National 1st Credit Union (CA), 91.83%
8. Fairfax County Credit Union (VA), 91.54%

9. Kemba Charleston Credit Union (WV), 91.3%

10. A.C.P.E. Credit Union (WY), 90.19%

Source: *Credit Union Directory*, (annual), Callahan & Associates Inc., 2012, p. 116.

2257 ■ TOP CREDIT UNIONS IN OREGON, 2011

Ranked by: Total assets, in thousands of dollars. **Remarks:** Also notes percentage of state's total assets as well as various financial, productivity, and member service ratios. **Number listed:** 50

1. Onpoint Community Credit Union, with $2,934,002 thousand
2. Oregon Community Credit Union, $983,689
3. Selco Community Credit Union, $893,702
4. Unitus Community Credit Union, $833,859
5. Advantis Credit Union, $810,007
6. OSU Federal Credit Union, $693,434
7. Northwest Community Credit Union, $661,061
8. Rivermark Community Credit Union, $517,598
9. Rogue Credit Union, $515,985
10. Oregon First Community Credit Union, $414,860

Source: *Credit Union Directory*, (annual), Callahan & Associates Inc., 2012, p. 331.

2258 ■ TOP CREDIT UNIONS IN PENNSYLVANIA, 2011

Ranked by: Total assets, in thousands of dollars. **Remarks:** Also notes percentage of state's total assets as well as various financial, productivity, and member service ratios. **Number listed:** 50

1. Police & Fire Credit Union, with $3,913,718 thousand
2. Pennsylvania State Employees Credit Union, $3,757,660
3. Members 1st Credit Union, $1,994,507
4. Citadel Credit Union, $1,627,799
5. Trumark Financial Credit Union, $1,358,759
6. American Heritage Credit Union, $1,083,374
7. Utilities Employees Credit Union, $983,898
8. Philadelphia Federal Credit Union, $816,778
9. Clearview Credit Union, $728,905
10. Franklin Mint Credit Union, $699,292

Source: *Credit Union Directory*, (annual), Callahan & Associates Inc., 2012, p. 334.

2259 ■ TOP CREDIT UNIONS IN PUERTO RICO, 2011

Ranked by: Total assets, in thousands of U.S. dollars. **Remarks:** Also notes percentage of Puerto Rico's total assets as well as various financial, productivity, and member service ratios. **Number listed:** 12

1. Caribe Credit Union, with $219,185 thousand
2. VAPR Credit Union, $152,362
3. Puerto Rico Credit Union, $109,926
4. Borinquen Community Credit Union, $20,911
5. Universal Co-op Credit Union, $16,977
6. Borinquen Sur Credit Union, $8,927
7. Philcore Credit Union, $5,406
8. Glamour Community Credit Union, $2,806
9. Banco de Santander Credit Union, $1,856
10. V. Suarez Employees Credit Union, $410

Source: *Credit Union Directory*, (annual), Callahan & Associates Inc., 2012, p. 395.

2260 ■ TOP CREDIT UNIONS BY REVENUE PER EMPLOYEE, 2011

Ranked by: Revenue per full-time employee, in dollars. **Remarks:** Also notes total number of full-time employees and total assets. **Number listed:** 50

1. Merck Employees Credit Union (NJ), with $1,796,988
2. Progressive Credit Union (NY), $1,429,511
3. NCPD Credit Union (NY), $1,241,940
4. Melrose Credit Union (NY), $1,219,467
5. Star One Credit Union (CA), $1,026,697
6. Montauk Credit Union (NY), $907,194
7. Mead Coated Board Credit Union (AL), $893,039
8. San Joaquin Power Employees Credit Union (CA), $819,233
9. Equitable Resources Employees Credit Union (PA), $812,110
10. Lufthansa Employees Credit Union (NY), $804,077

Source: *Credit Union Directory*, (annual), Callahan & Associates Inc., 2012, p. 110.

2261 ■ TOP CREDIT UNIONS IN RHODE ISLAND, 2011

Ranked by: Total assets, in thousands of dollars. **Remarks:** Also notes percentage of state's total assets as well as various financial, productivity, and member service ratios. **Number listed:** 23

1. Pawtucket Credit Union, with $1,268,018 thousand
2. Navigant Credit Union, $1,239,725
3. The Peoples Credit Union, $369,830
4. Greenwood Credit Union, $306,793
5. Coventry Credit Union, $258,793
6. Rhode Island Credit Union, $226,138
7. Westerly Community Credit Union, $214,160
8. Dexter Credit Union, $124,185
9. Wave Credit Union, $111,505
10. Columbus Credit Union, $66,293

Source: *Credit Union Directory*, (annual), Callahan & Associates Inc., 2012, p. 346.

2262 ■ TOP CREDIT UNIONS BY SBA LOANS, 2011

Ranked by: Total Small Business Administration (SBA) loans outstanding, in dollars. **Remarks:** Also notes SBA loans as a percentage of total member business loans, average SBA loan balance outstanding, and total assets. **Number listed:** 50

1. Mountain America Credit Union (UT), with $94,442,636
2. Redwood Credit Union (CA), $49,743,823
3. Navy Credit Union (VA), $34,641,671
4. Northwest Credit Union (VA), $22,779,137
5. Telesis Community Credit Union (CA), $21,978,117
6. Randolph-Brooks Credit Union (TX), $18,254,911
7. Redstone Credit Union (AL), $17,538,294
8. Vision One Credit Union (CA), $16,724,556

9. Greylock Credit Union (MA), $11,971,291

10. Safe Credit Union (UT), $10,910,905

Source: *Credit Union Directory*, (annual), Callahan & Associates Inc., 2012, p. 80.

2263 ■ TOP CREDIT UNIONS IN SOUTH CAROLINA, 2011

Ranked by: Total assets, in thousands of dollars. **Remarks:** Also notes percentage of state's total assets as well as various financial, productivity, and member service ratios. **Number listed:** 50

1. Founders Credit Union, with $1,595,940 thousand
2. South Carolina Credit Union, $1,271,116
3. Sharonview Credit Union, $964,288
4. Safe Credit Union, $719,721
5. Allsouth Credit Union, $638,065
6. Savannah River Plant Credit Union, $593,102
7. South Carolina State Credit Union, $520,387
8. Palmetto Citizens Credit Union, $488,498
9. Heritage Trust Credit Union, $426,125
10. Family Trust Credit Union, $265,601

Source: *Credit Union Directory*, (annual), Callahan & Associates Inc., 2012, p. 348.

2264 ■ TOP CREDIT UNIONS IN SOUTH DAKOTA, 2011

Ranked by: Total assets, in thousands of dollars. **Remarks:** Also notes percentage of state's total assets as well as various financial, productivity, and member service ratios. **Number listed:** 50

1. Black Hills Credit Union, with $884,654 thousand
2. Dakotaland Credit Union, $163,961
3. Sioux Falls Credit Union, $159,506
4. Service First Credit Union, $122,262
5. Aberdeen Credit Union, $90,227
6. Highmark Credit Union, $80,058
7. Sioux Empire Credit Union, $67,180
8. Sentinel Credit Union, $55,979
9. Rapid City Telco Credit Union, $44,773
10. Northern Hills Credit Union, $44,095

Source: *Credit Union Directory*, (annual), Callahan & Associates Inc., 2012, p. 351.

2265 ■ TOP CREDIT UNIONS IN TENNESSEE, 2011

Ranked by: Total assets, in thousands of dollars. **Remarks:** Also notes percentage of state's total assets as well as various financial, productivity, and member service ratios. **Number listed:** 50

1. Eastman Credit Union, with $2,503,450 thousand
2. Ascend Credit Union, $1,456,840
3. ORNL Credit Union, $1,312,665
4. Knoxville TVA Employees Credit Union, $969,254
5. Tennessee Valley Credit Union, $793,284
6. Y-12 Credit Union, $588,082
7. Orion Credit Union, $535,383
8. Fort Campbell Credit Union, $427,410
9. Southeast Financial Credit Union, $424,904
10. First South Financial Credit Union, $385,347

Source: *Credit Union Directory*, (annual), Callahan & Associates Inc., 2012, p. 353.

2266 ■ TOP CREDIT UNIONS IN TEXAS, 2011

Ranked by: Total assets, in thousands of dollars. **Remarks:** Also notes percentage of state's total assets as well as various financial, productivity, and member service ratios. **Number listed:** 50

1. Security Service Credit Union, with $6,505,532 thousand
2. American Airlines Credit Union, $5,418,171
3. Randolph-Brooks Credit Union, $4,388,037
4. San Antonio Credit Union, $2,943,777
5. Government Employees Credit Union of El Paso, $1,779,152
6. Texas Dow Employees Credit Union, $1,679,568
7. Texans Credit Union, $1,497,712
8. JSC Federal Credit Union, $1,495,461
9. University Credit Union, $1,367,805
10. EECU, $1,266,311

Source: *Credit Union Directory*, (annual), Callahan & Associates Inc., 2012, p. 358.

2267 ■ TOP CREDIT UNIONS BY TOTAL ASSETS, 2011

Ranked by: Total assets, in dollars. **Remarks:** Also notes rank for previous year. **Number listed:** 200

1. Navy Credit Union (VA), with $44,423,206,637
2. State Employees' Credit Union (NC), $23,061,183,256
3. Pentagon Credit Union (VA), $15,14,500,672
4. Boeing Employees Credit Union (WA), $9,498,504,417
5. Schools First Credit Union (CA), $8,820,542,812
6. Alliant Credit Union (IL), $7,856,458,982
7. The Golden 1 Credit Union (CA), $7,458,123,465
8. Security Service Credit Union (TX), $6,505,531,844
9. Star One Credit Union (CA), $5,665,402,998
10. American Airlines Credit Union (TX), $5,418,170,543

Source: *Credit Union Directory*, (annual), Callahan & Associates Inc., 2012, p. 18-20.

2268 ■ TOP CREDIT UNIONS BY TOTAL MEMBERS, 2011

Ranked by: Number of members. **Remarks:** Also notes assets and average share balance. **Number listed:** 200

1. Navy Credit Union (VA), with 3,724,421 members
2. State Employees' Credit Union (NC), 1,680,041
3. Pentagon Credit Union (VA), 1,040,784
4. Security Service Credit Union (TX), 854,810
5. Boeing Employees Credit Union (WA), 702,737
6. The Golden 1 Credit Union (CA), 591,620
7. America First Credit Union (UT), 548,808
8. Suncoast Schools Credit Union (FL), 506,861
9. Schools First Credit Union (CA), 481,360
10. Alaska USA Credit Union (FL), 427,059

Source: *Credit Union Directory*, (annual), Callahan & Associates Inc., 2012, p. 26-27.

2269 ■ TOP CREDIT UNIONS IN THE U.S. VIRGIN ISLANDS, 2011

Ranked by: Total assets, in thousands of U.S. dollars. **Remarks:** Also notes percentage of the Virgin Islands' total assets as well as various financial, productivity, and member service ratios. **Number listed:** 5

1. St. Thomas Credit Union, with $45,006 thousand
2. Christiansted Credit Union, $18,467
3. Frederiksted Credit Union, $11,378
4. Mid-Island Credit Union, $9,805
5. Vitelco Employees Credit Union, $2,340

Source: *Credit Union Directory*, (annual), Callahan & Associates Inc., 2012, p. 395.

2270 ■ TOP CREDIT UNIONS IN UTAH, 2011

Ranked by: Total assets, in thousands of dollars. **Remarks:** Also notes percentage of state's total assets as well as various financial, productivity, and member service ratios. **Number listed:** 50

1. America First Credit Union, with $5,062,711 thousand
2. Mountain America Credit Union, $2,868,720
3. Goldenwest Credit Union, $777,119
4. Utah Community Credit Union, $745,324
5. Cyprus Credit Union, $569,285
6. University First Credit Union, $567,485
7. Deseret First Credit Union, $423,807
8. Utah Power & Light Employees Credit Union, $417,820
9. Granite Credit Union, $336,401
10. Utah First Credit Union, $236,508

Source: *Credit Union Directory*, (annual), Callahan & Associates Inc., 2012, p. 370.

2271 ■ TOP CREDIT UNIONS IN VERMONT, 2011

Ranked by: Total assets, in thousands of dollars. **Remarks:** Also notes percentage of state's total assets as well as various financial, productivity, and member service ratios. **Number listed:** 27

1. New England Federal Credit Union, with $843,168 thousand
2. Vermont State Employees Credit Union, $559,697
3. Northcountry Credit Union, $327,938
4. Vermont Credit Union, $319,341
5. Heritage Family Credit Union, $269,739
6. One Credit Union, $120,206
7. Members Advantage Community Credit Union, $70,145
8. River Valley Credit Union, $65,044
9. Opportunities Credit Union, $33,222
10. Granite Hills Credit Union, $32,756

Source: *Credit Union Directory*, (annual), Callahan & Associates Inc., 2012, p. 373.

2272 ■ TOP CREDIT UNIONS IN VIRGINIA, 2011

Ranked by: Total assets, in thousands of dollars. **Remarks:** Also notes percentage of state's total assets as well as various financial, productivity, and member service ratios. **Number listed:** 50

1. Navy Credit Union, with $44,423,207 thousand

2. Pentagon Credit Union, $15,104,501
3. Virginia Credit Union Inc., $2,164,278
4. Northwest Credit Union, $2,023,103
5. Chartway Credit Union, $1,895,624
6. Langley Credit Union, $1,622,984
7. State Department Credit Union, $1,384,935
8. Apple Credit Union, $1,349,682
9. Bayport Credit Union, $1,166,564
10. Du Pont Community Credit Union, $764,737

Source: *Credit Union Directory*, (annual), Callahan & Associates Inc., 2012, p. 375.

2273 ■ TOP CREDIT UNIONS IN WASHINGTON, 2011

Ranked by: Total assets, in thousands of dollars. **Remarks:** Also notes percentage of state's total assets as well as various financial, productivity, and member service ratios. **Number listed:** 50

1. Boeing Employees Credit Union, with $9,498,504 thousand
2. Washington State Employees Credit Union, $1,598,596
3. Spokane Teachers Credit Union, $1,526,252
4. Numerica Credit Union, $1,107,646
5. GESA Credit Union, $1,070,503
6. Hapo Community Credit Union, $923,704
7. Kitsap Community Credit Union, $840,597
8. School Employees Credit Union of Washington, $829,762
9. Columbia Credit Union, $769,120
10. Twinstar Credit Union, $750,370

Source: *Credit Union Directory*, (annual), Callahan & Associates Inc., 2012, p. 380.

2274 ■ TOP CREDIT UNIONS IN WEST VIRGINIA, 2011

Ranked by: Total assets, in thousands of dollars. **Remarks:** Also notes percentage of state's total assets as well as various financial, productivity, and member service ratios. **Number listed:** 50

1. First Choice America Community Credit Union, with $344,675 thousand
2. Bayer Heritage Credit Union, $262,608
3. Fairmont Credit Union, $254,311
4. West Virginia Credit Union, $165,173
5. Star USA Credit Union, $159,097
6. Pioneer West Virginia Credit Union, $139,453
7. West Virginia Central Credit Union, $90,942
8. People's Credit Union, $84,535
9. Members Choice West Virginia Credit Union, $82,838
10. Universal Credit Union, $61,611

Source: *Credit Union Directory*, (annual), Callahan & Associates Inc., 2012, p. 384.

2275 ■ TOP CREDIT UNIONS IN WISCONSIN, 2011

Ranked by: Total assets, in thousands of dollars. **Remarks:** Also notes percentage of state's total assets as well as various financial, productivity, and member service ratios. **Number listed:** 50

1. Summit Credit Union, with $1,671,453 thousand
2. Landmark Credit Union, $1,624,923

3. Community First Credit Union, $1,537,762
4. University of Wisconsin Credit Union, $1,370,286
5. Educators Credit Union, $1,366,286
6. Royal Credit Union, $1,235,066
7. Covantage Credit Union, $906,937
8. Altra Credit Union, $832,476
9. Fox Communities Credit Union, $795,160
10. Westconsin Credit Union, $727,519

Source: *Credit Union Directory*, (annual), Callahan & Associates Inc., 2012, p. 387.

2276 ■ TOP CREDIT UNIONS IN WYOMING, 2011

Ranked by: Total assets, in thousands of dollars. **Remarks:** Also notes percentage of state's total assets as well as various financial, productivity, and member service ratios. **Number listed:** 29

1. Warren Credit Union, with $381,241 thousand
2. Meridian Trust Credit Union, $238,508
3. Uniwyo Credit Union, $214,953
4. WYHY Credit Union, $169,130
5. Trona Valley Community Credit Union, $136,698
6. Western Vista Credit Union, $116,652
7. Atlantic City Credit Union, $90,511
8. Sunlight Federal Credit Union, $87,746
9. Reliant Credit Union, $86,427
10. Campco Credit Union, $62,321

Source: *Credit Union Directory*, (annual), Callahan & Associates Inc., 2012, p. 393.

Crime and Criminals

2277 ■ COUNTRIES WITH THE HIGHEST BUSINESS COSTS OF CRIME AND VIOLENCE, 2010

Ranked by: Score, on a scale of seven, based on the level of business costs associated with crime and violence. **Number listed:** 142

1. Guatemala, with 1.7 points
2. El Salvador, 1.9
2. Jamaica, 1.9
4. Venezuela, 2.1
5. Haiti, 2.4
6. Honduras, 2.5
6. South Africa, 2.5
6. Trinidad & Tobago, 2.5
9. Mexico, 2.7
10. Colombia, 2.8
10. Belize, 2.8

Source: *Global Competitiveness Report*, (annual), World Economic Forum, 2011, p. 403.

2278 ■ COUNTRIES WITH THE HIGHEST BUSINESS COSTS OF ORGANIZED CRIME, 2010

Ranked by: Score, on a scale of seven, based on the level of business costs associated with organized crime. **Number listed:** 142

1. El Salvador, with 1.9 points
2. Guatemala, 2.0
3. Venezuela, 2.5
4. Mexico, 2.7
4. Colombia, 2.7
6. Honduras, 3.0
7. Haiti, 3.1
7. Jamaica , 3.1
9. Cote d'Ivoire, 3.3
10. Argentina, 3.5
10. Italy, 3.5
10. Pakistan, 3.5

Source: *Global Competitiveness Report*, (annual), World Economic Forum, 2011, p. 404.

2279 ■ COUNTRIES WITH THE LOWEST BUSINESS COSTS OF CRIME AND VIOLENCE, 2010

Ranked by: Score, on a scale of seven, based on the level of business costs associated with crime and violence. **Number listed:** 142

1. Syria, with 6.6 points
2. Saudi Arabia, 6.5
3. United Arab Emirates, 6.4
3. Iceland, 6.4
5. Finland, 6.3
5. Oman, 6.3
7. Denmark, 6.2
8. Hong Kong, 6.1
8. Switzerland, 6.1
8. Qatar, 6.1
8. Slovenia, 6.1

Source: *Global Competitiveness Report*, (annual), World Economic Forum, 2011, p. 403.

2280 ■ COUNTRIES WITH THE LOWEST BUSINESS COSTS OF ORGANIZED CRIME, 2010

Ranked by: Score, on a scale of seven, based on the level of business costs associated with organized crime. **Number listed:** 142

1. Denmark, with 6.8 points
1. Egypt, 6.8
1. Iceland, 6.8
1. Saudi Arabia, 6.8
5. Luxembourg, 6.7
5. Singapore, 6.7
5. Syria, 6.7
5. United Arab Emirates, 6.7
9. Malta, 6.6
9. Oman, 6.6
9. Estonia, 6.6
9. Sweden, 6.6
9. Finland, 6.6

Source: *Global Competitiveness Report*, (annual), World Economic Forum, 2011, p. 404.

Crops
See also: Agriculture

2281 ■ LARGEST CROP PRODUCTION COMPANIES BY EMPLOYEES, 2010

Ranked by: Total number of employees. **Remarks:** Also notes contact information for headquarters, number of employees at headquarters, revenue, rank by revenue, and primary SIC code. **Number listed:** 148

1. DHM Holding Co., Inc., with 75,000 employees
2. Dole Holding Co., LLC, 59,000
3. Dole Food Co., Inc., 39,100
4. Chiquita Brands International Inc., 21,000
5. Chiquita Brands LLC, 20,900
6. Yasheng Group, 15,000
7. Ball Horticultural Co., 3,000
7. Fanjul Corp., 3,000
7. Giumarra Vineyards Corp., 3,000
7. Mike Jackson, 3,000
7. Monterey Mushrooms Inc., 3,000

Source: *Business Rankings*, (annual), Dun & Bradstreet Inc., 2011, p. VI.1-VI.4.

2282 ■ LARGEST CROP PRODUCTION COMPANIES BY SALES, 2010

Ranked by: Total revenue, in dollars. **Remarks:** Also notes contact information for headquarters, number of employees at headquarters and overall, rank by employees, and primary SIC code. **Number listed:** 150

1. Dole Food Co., Inc., with $6,892,614,000
2. Chiquita Brands International Inc., $3,227,432,000
3. Yasheng Group, $739,630,043
4. Cavendish Farms Operations Inc., $500,000,000
5. A. Duda & Sons Inc., $425,033,000
6. Duda Farm Fresh Foods Inc., $352,000,000
7. E. Ritter & Co., $199,790,285
8. Sun World International LLC, $152,910,000
9. Pacific Tomato Growers Ltd., $151,553,140
10. Agro Power Development Inc., $150,000,000

Source: *Business Rankings*, (annual), Dun & Bradstreet Inc., 2011, p. V.1-V.4.

2283 ■ LARGEST U.S. RETAILERS IN CROP PROTECTION, 2010

Ranked by: Crop protection as a percentage of total revenue. **Number listed:** 100

1. T. H. Agri-Chemicals Inc., with 95%
2. Asmus Farm Supply Inc., 91%
3. Sims Fertilizer & Chemical, 86%
4. Northwest Ag Supply LLC, 84%
5. G. S. Long Co., 79%
6. Maine Potato Growers, 72%
7. Gar Tootelian Inc., 69%
8. Hefty Seed Co., 67%
9. East Kansas Chemical Co., 56%

10. Mid Valley Ag Service Inc., 53%

Source: *CropLife*, CropLife 100 (annual), http://www.croplife.com, December 2011.

2284 ■ STATES WITH THE HIGHEST FARM INCOME FROM CROPS, 2009

Ranked by: Farm income from crops, in dollars. **Remarks:** Also notes share of national total. **Number listed:** 50

1. California, with $27,026,641,000
2. Illinois, $12,696,303,000
3. Iowa, $12,492,972,000
4. Minnesota, $8,422,873,000
5. Nebraska, $8,025,772,000
6. Indiana, $6,388,823,000
7. Florida, $5,997,750,000
8. Texas, $5,932,189,000
9. Kansas, $5,733,270,000
10. North Dakota, $5,580,563,000

Source: *State Rankings*, (annual), CQ Press, 2011, p. 12.

Crown Corporations
See: Government Ownership

Cruise Lines

2285 ■ WORLD'S TOP LARGE-SHIP CRUISE LINES, 2011

Ranked by: Score, on a scale of 100, based on consumer survey regarding cabins, food, service, itineraries/destinations, activities, and value. **Number listed:** 10

1. Crystal Cruises, with 92.45 points
2. Regent Seven Seas, 90.14
3. Oceania Cruises, 86.42
4. Disney Cruise Lines, 85.70
5. Cunard Line, 84.27
6. Azamara Club Cruises, 82.51
7. Celebrity Cruises, 81.92
8. Holland America Line, 81.29
9. Royal Caribbean International, 80.28
10. Princess Cruises, 79.81

Source: *Travel + Leisure*, World's Best Awards (annual), August 2011.

2286 ■ WORLD'S TOP RIVER CRUISE LINES, 2011

Ranked by: Score, on a scale of 100, based on consumer survey regarding cabins, food, service, itineraries/destinations, activities, and value. **Number listed:** 5

1. Tauck, with 90.06 points
2. Uniworld Boutique River Cruise Collection, 88.70
3. Viking River Cruises, 86.76
4. AmaWaterways, 85.23
5. Avalon Waterways, 84.27

Source: *Travel + Leisure*, World's Best Awards (annual), August 2011.

2287 ■ WORLD'S TOP SMALL-SHIP CRUISE LINES, 2011

Ranked by: Score, on a scale of 100, based on consumer survey regarding cabins, food, service, itineraries/destinations, activities, and value. **Number listed:** 4

1. Seabourn, with 93.30 point

2. Silversea Cruises, 90.03
3. SeaDream Yacht Club, 88.33
4. Windstar Cruises, 85.63

Source: *Travel + Leisure*, World's Best Awards (annual), August 2011.

Customer Service

2288 ■ COUNTRIES WITH THE BEST CUSTOMER SERVICE, 2010

Ranked by: Score, on a scale of seven, based on the level of companies' customer orientation. **Number listed:** 142

1. Japan, with 6.4 points
2. Sweden, 6
2. Switzerland, 6
4. Austria, 5.9
5. Belgium, 5.7
6. Canada, 5.6
6. New Zealand, 5.6
6. Iceland, 5.6
6. Taiwan, 5.6
6. Denmark, 5.6

Source: *Global Competitiveness Report*, (annual), World Economic Forum, 2011, p. 466.

2289 ■ COUNTRIES WITH THE WORST CUSTOMER SERVICE, 2010

Ranked by: Score, on a scale of seven, based on the level of companies' customer orientation. **Number listed:** 142

1. Angola, with 2.5 points
2. Chad, 3.2
2. Burundi, 3.2
4. Venezuela, 3.3
4. Haiti, 3.3
6. Mauritania, 3.4
7. Russian Federation, 3.5
7. Trinidad & Tobago, 3.5
7. Timor-Leste, 3.5
7. Cape Verde, 3.5

Source: *Global Competitiveness Report*, (annual), World Economic Forum, 2011, p. 466.

Dairy Industry

2290 ■ TOP U.S. AND CANADIAN DAIRY COMPANIES, 2010

Ranked by: Revenue, in millions of U.S. dollars. **Remarks:** Also notes headquarters, dairy executive, type of company, parent company and subsidiaries, fiscal year-end, figures for previous year, brands, products, and plants. **Number listed:** 100

1. Dean Foods Co., with $12,123 million
2. Nestle USA, $10,400
3. Saputo Inc., $5,506
4. Kraft Foods Global Inc., $4,000
5. Land O'Lakes Inc., $3,708
6. Schreiber Foods Inc., $3,600

7. Agropur Cooperative, $3,490
8. Leprino Foods Co., $3,000
9. Prairie Farms Dairy Inc., $2,500
10. HP Hood LLC, $2,400

Source: *Dairy Foods*, Dairy 100 (annual), August 2011, p. 66+.

Dairy Products
See: **Milk Products**

Day Care Centers
See: **Child Care Centers**

Debt

2291 ■ WORLD'S MOST INDEBTED DEVELOPED COUNTRIES, 2011

Ranked by: Debt as a percentage of gross domestic product. **Remarks:** Also note size of debt in billions of dollars. **Number listed:** 10

1. Japan, with 234%
2. Greece, 139%
3. Italy, 120%
4. Iceland, 108%
5. Belgium, 103%
6. Ireland, 102%
7. United States, 99%
8. Singapore, 95%
9. France, 88%
10. Portugal, 87%

Source: *Fortune*, Who's Most in Debt?, August 15, 2011.

Debt Financing

2292 ■ TOP GLOBAL DEBT ISSUES, 2011

Ranked by: Amount, in billions of dollars. **Remarks:** Also notes issue date. **Number listed:** 10

1. Sanofi-Aventis SA, with $7 billion
2. Verizon Communications Inc., $6.3
3. Panasonic Corp., $6.1
4. General Electric Capital, $6
4. Petrobras International Finance, $6
4. Amgen Inc., $6
7. Wal-Mart Stores Inc., $5
7. Hewlett-Packard Co., $5
7. HCA Inc., $5
7. AT&T Inc., $5

Source: *The Wall Street Journal*, Year-End Review (annual), January 3, 2012, p. R9.

2293 ■ TOP UNDERWRITERS OF GLOBAL DEBT, 2011

Ranked by: Amount, in billions of U.S. dollars. **Remarks:** Also notes market share for current and previous year. **Number listed:** 10

1. J. P. Morgan Chase & Co., with $387.8 billion

2. Barclays Capital Inc., $376.5

3. Deutsche Bank AG, $365.8

4. Bank of America Corp./Merrill Lynch, $314

5. Citigroup Inc., $310.9

6. UBS AG, $253.5

7. Goldman Sachs Group Inc., $250.8

8. Morgan Stanley, $237.3

9. BNP Paribas SA, $236.6

10. Credit Suisse Group, $228.1

Source: *The Wall Street Journal*, Year-End Review (annual), January 3, 2012, p. R9.

Defense Contracts
See also: **Contracts, Government**

2294 ■ TOP DEFENSE CONTRACTORS FOR THE FEDERAL GOVERNMENT, 2010

Ranked by: Value of federal contracts, in dollars. **Remarks:** Also notes rank in the overall *Top 100* and for previous year. **Number listed:** 16

1. Lockheed Martin Corp., with $17,344,113,000

2. Northrop Grumman Corp., $10,800,453,000

3. Boeing Co., $8,400,115,000

4. Raytheon Co., $6,206,515,000

5. General Dynamics Corp., $5,493,414,000

6. DynCorp International Inc., $3,047,513,000

7. ITT Corp., $2,061,343,000

8. BAE Systems Inc., $1,986,983,000

9. Jacobs Engineering Group Inc., $1,703,308,00

10. Honeywell International Inc., $1,143,030,000

Source: *Washington Technology*, Top 100 (annual), http://www.washingtontechnology.com, June 2011.

2295 ■ TOP FEDERAL PRIME CONTRACTORS BY DEFENSE REVENUE, 2010

Ranked by: Defense revenue, in dollars. **Remarks:** Also notes rank in the overall *Top 100*. **Number listed:** 100

1. Lockheed Martin Corp., with $10,888,633,000

2. Northrop Grumman Corp., $8,212,891,000

3. Boeing Co., $5,051,984,000

4. General Dynamics Corp., $4,576,415,000

5. Raytheon Co., $4,095,309,000

6. KBR Inc., $3,546,554,000

7. L-3 Communications Corp., $3,332,433,000

8. Science Applications International Corp. (SAIC), $3,280,980,000

9. DynCorp International Inc., $2,398,874,000

10. Hewlett-Packard Co., $2,344,325,000

Source: *Washington Technology*, Top 100 (annual), http://www.washingtontechnology.com, June 2011.

Defense Industry
See also: **Aerospace Industry**

2296 ■ BEST SMALL AEROSPACE AND DEFENSE COMPANIES IN AMERICA, 2011

Ranked by: Score based on revenue, profits, and return on equity for the past 12 months and five years. **Remarks:** Specific scores not provided. Also notes rank in the overall *100 Best Small Companies in America*. To qualify, companies must have revenues between $5 million and $1 billion, a net margin above five percent, and share price above $5. List is available online only. **Number listed:** 2

1. Heico

2. National Presto Industries

Source: *Forbes*, Best Small Companies in America (annual), November 7, 2011.

2297 ■ BRITAIN'S MOST ADMIRED AEROSPACE AND DEFENSE ENGINEERING COMPANIES, 2011

Ranked by: Survey of peers and investment analysts based on nine criteria: quality of management, financial soundness, quality of goods/services, ability to attract and retain talent, value as long-term investment, innovation, marketing, community and environmental responsibility, and use of corporate assets. **Number listed:** 5

1. Rolls-Royce plc, with 68.3 points

2. Ultra Electronics Holdings plc, 62

3. Senior plc, 58.4

4. Meggitt, 57.2

5. Chemring Group, 57.1

Source: *Management Today*, Britain's Most Admired Companies (annual), December 2011, p. 45.

2298 ■ EUROPE'S MOST VALUABLE AEROSPACE AND DEFENSE COMPANIES, 2011

Ranked by: Market value as of March 2011, in millions of U.S. dollars. **Remarks:** Also notes rank within the *FT Europe 500*, rank for previous year, country, revenue, net income, assets, number of employees, share price, price-to-earning ratio, dividend yield, and fiscal yearend. **Number listed:** 6

1. European Aeronautic Defense & Space Co. (EADS), with $23,809.2 million

2. Rolls Royce Group plc, $18,576.3

3. BAE Systems plc, $17,794.6

4. Safran SA, $14,759.5

5. Thales SA, $7,951.4

6. Finmeccanica SpA, $7,285.6

Source: *Financial Times*, FT 500 (annual), http://www.ft.com, June 24, 2011.

2299 ■ FRANCE'S LARGEST AEROSPACE AND DEFENSE COMPANIES OVERALL, 2011

Ranked by: Score based on revenue, profits, assets, and market capitalization. **Remarks:** Specific scores not provided. Also notes overall rank in the *Forbes 2000* and figures for each criterion. **Number listed:** 3

1. Safran SA

2. Thales SA

3. Dassault Aviation

Source: *Forbes*, Forbes 2000 (annual), http://www.forbes.com, May 7, 2012.

2300 ■ LARGEST U.S. AEROSPACE AND DEFENSE COMPANIES OVERALL, 2011

Ranked by: Score based on revenue, profits, assets, and market capitalization. **Remarks:** Specific scores not provided. Also notes overall rank in the *Forbes 2000* and figures for each criterion. **Number listed:** 10

1. Boeing Co.
2. Lockheed Martin Corp.
3. General Dynamics Corp.
4. Raytheon Co.
5. Northrop Grumman Corp.
6. Precision Castparts Corp.
7. L-3 Communications Holdings Inc.
8. Goodrich Corp.
9. Rockwell Collins Inc.
10. SAIC Inc.

Source: *Forbes,* Forbes 2000 (annual), http://www.forbes.com, May 7, 2012.

2301 ■ LARGEST U.S. AEROSPACE AND DEFENSE MANUFACTURERS, 2010

Ranked by: Revenue, in millions of dollars. **Remarks:** Also notes overall rank within the *IW 500,* revenue growth, and profit margin. **Number listed:** 11

1. Boeing Co., with $64,306 million
2. United Technologies Corp., $54,326
3. Lockheed Martin Corp., $45,803
4. Northrop Grumman Corp., $34,757
5. Raytheon Co., $25,183
6. Textron Inc., $10,525
7. Goodrich Corp., $6,967
8. Alliant Techsystems Inc., $4,808
9. Spirit AeroSystems Holdings Inc., $4,172
10. BE Aerospace Inc., $1,984

Source: *IndustryWeek,* IW 500 (annual), http://www.industryweek.com, July 2011.

2302 ■ MOST VALUABLE U.S. AEROSPACE AND DEFENSE COMPANIES, 2011

Ranked by: Market value as of March 2011, in millions of U.S. dollars. **Remarks:** Also notes rank within the *FT U.S. 500,* rank for previous year, country, revenue, net income, assets, number of employees, share price, price-to-earning ratio, dividend yield, and fiscal yearend. **Number listed:** 11

1. United Technologies Corp., with $77,979 million
2. Boeing Co., $54,491.7
3. General Dynamics Corp., $28,584.3
4. Lockheed Martin Corp., $28,101.6
5. Precision Castparts Corp., $21,113.1
6. Raytheon Co., $18,297.6
7. Northrop Grumman Corp., $18,268.2
8. Goodrich Corp., $10,704.6
9. Rockwell Collins Inc., $10,033.1
10. L-3 Communications Holdings Inc., $9,060.6

Source: *Financial Times,* FT 500 (annual), http://www.ft.com, June 24, 2011.

2303 ■ TOP *FORTUNE 500* COMPANIES IN AEROSPACE AND DEFENSE, 2011

Ranked by: Revenue, in millions of dollars. **Remarks:** Also notes overall rank in the *Fortune 500;* profits; profits as a percentage of revenue; stockholders' equity; and rank by each criterion. **Number listed:** 14

1. Boeing Co., with $68,735 million

2. United Technologies Corp., $58,190
3. Lockheed Martin Corp., $46,692
4. Honeywell International Inc., $37,059
5. General Dynamics Corp., $32,677
6. Northrop Grumman Corp., $28,058
7. Raytheon Co., $24,857
8. L-3 Communications Holdings Inc., $15,169
9. Textron Inc., $11,275
10. Goodrich Corp., $8,075

Source: *Fortune,* Fortune 500 (annual), May 21, 2012, p. F-33.

2304 ■ UNITED KINGDOM'S LARGEST AEROSPACE AND DEFENSE COMPANIES OVERALL, 2011

Ranked by: Score based on revenue, profits, assets, and market capitalization. **Remarks:** Specific scores not provided. Also notes overall rank in the *Forbes 2000* and figures for each criterion. **Number listed:** 2

1. BAE Systems plc
2. Rolls-Royce plc

Source: *Forbes,* Forbes 2000 (annual), http://www.forbes.com, May 7, 2012.

2305 ■ THE UNITED KINGDOM'S MOST VALUABLE AEROSPACE AND DEFENSE BRANDS, 2011

Ranked by: Brand value, in millions of U.S. dollars. **Remarks:** Also notes rank within the *Global 500* for current and previous year, figures for current and previous year, and brand rating. Ranking is available online only. **Number listed:** 2

1. BAE Systems, with $3,899 million
2. Rolls-Royce, $3,175

Source: *Global 500,* (annual), Brand Finance plc, March 2012.

2306 ■ THE UNITED STATES' MOST VALUABLE AEROSPACE AND DEFENSE BRANDS, 2011

Ranked by: Brand value, in millions of U.S. dollars. **Remarks:** Also notes rank within the *Global 500* for current and previous year, figures for current and previous year, and brand rating. Ranking is available online only. **Number listed:** 4

1. Boeing, with $9,022 million
2. Raytheon, $3,856
3. General Dynamics, $3,330
4. Lockheed Martin, $2,884

Source: *Global 500,* (annual), Brand Finance plc, March 2012.

2307 ■ VIRGINIA'S LARGEST AEROSPACE AND DEFENSE COMPANIES OVERALL, 2011

Ranked by: Score based on revenue, profits, assets, and market capitalization. **Remarks:** Specific scores not provided. Also notes overall rank in the *Forbes 2000* and figures for each criterion. **Number listed:** 3

1. General Dynamics Corp.
2. Northrop Grumman Corp.
3. SAIC Inc.

Source: *Forbes,* Forbes 2000 (annual), http://www.forbes.com, May 7, 2012.

2308 ■ WORLD'S LARGEST AEROSPACE AND DEFENSE COMPANIES OVERALL, 2011

Ranked by: Score based on revenue, profits, assets, and market capitalization. **Remarks:** Specific scores not provided. Also notes country, overall rank in the *Forbes 2000,* and figures for each criterion. **Number listed:** 20

1. Boeing Co.
2. European Aeronautic Defense & Space Co. (EADS)
3. Lockheed Martin Corp.
4. General Dynamics Corp.
5. BAE Systems plc
6. Raytheon Co.
7. Northrop Grumman Corp.
8. Rolls-Royce plc
9. Safran SA
10. Thales SA

Source: *Forbes*, Forbes 2000 (annual), http://www.forbes.com, May 7, 2012.

2309 ■ WORLD'S LARGEST AEROSPACE AND DEFENSE MANUFACTURERS, 2010

Ranked by: Revenue, in millions of dollars. **Remarks:** Also notes rank for previous year, overall rank within the *IW 1000*, country, and revenue growth. **Number listed:** 22

1. Boeing Co., with $64,306 million
2. EADS NV, $61,217
3. United Technologies Corp., $54,326
4. Lockheed Martin Corp., $45,803
5. Northrop Grumman Corp., $34,757
6. BAE Systems plc, $33,160
7. Finmeccanica SpA, $25,610
8. Raytheon Co., $25,183
9. Rolls Royce Holdings plc, $17,452
10. Textron Inc., $10,525

Source: *IndustryWeek*, IW 1000 (annual), http://www.industryweek.com, August 2011.

2310 ■ WORLD'S MOST ADMIRED AEROSPACE AND DEFENSE COMPANIES, 2012

Ranked by: Score, on a scale of 10, based on a survey of executives, directors, and securities analysts of companies within their own industry on eight criteria: innovation, financial soundness, employee talent, use of corporate assets, long-term investment value, social responsibility, quality of management, and quality of products/services. **Remarks:** Specific scores not provided. Also notes rank for previous year. **Number listed:** 8

1. United Technologies Corp.
2. Lockheed Martin Corp.
3. Boeing Co.
4. Northrop Grumman Corp.
5. General Dynamics Corp.
6. Raytheon Co.
7. Honeywell International Inc.
8. Rolls-Royce plc

Source: *Fortune*, World's Most Admired Companies (annual), March 19, 2012, p. 150.

2311 ■ WORLD'S MOST ETHICAL AEROSPACE AND DEFENSE COMPANIES, 2012

Ranked by: Score based on five criteria: ethics and compliance program; reputation, leadership, and innovation; governance; corporate citizenship and responsibility; and culture of ethics. **Remarks:** Specific scores not provided; companies are listed alphabetically, not ranked. **Number listed:** 2

1. Rockwell Collins Inc. (U.S.)
2. The Aerospace Corp. (U.S.)

Source: *Ethisphere Magazine*, World's Most Ethical Companies (annual), http://www.ethisphere.com, 2012.

2312 ■ WORLD'S MOST VALUABLE AEROSPACE AND DEFENSE BRANDS, 2011

Ranked by: Brand value, in millions of U.S. dollars. **Remarks:** Also notes rank within the *Global 500* for current and previous year, figures for current and previous year, country, and brand rating. Ranking is available online only. **Number listed:** 7

1. Boeing, with $9,022 million
2. Airbus, $4,755
3. BAE Systems, $3,899
4. Raytheon, $3,856
5. General Dynamics, $3,330
6. Rolls-Royce, $3,175
7. Lockheed Martin, $2,884

Source: *Global 500*, (annual), Brand Finance plc, March 2012.

2313 ■ WORLD'S MOST VALUABLE AEROSPACE AND DEFENSE COMPANIES, 2011

Ranked by: Market value as of March 2011, in millions of U.S. dollars. **Remarks:** Also notes rank within the *FT 500*, rank for previous year, country, revenue, net income, assets, number of employees, share price, price-to-earning ratio, dividend yield, and fiscal year-end. **Number listed:** 6

1. United Technologies Corp., with $77,979 million
2. Boeing Co., $54,491.7
3. General Dynamics Corp., $28,584.3
4. Lockheed Martin Corp., $28,101.6
5. European Aeronautic Defense & Space Co. (EADS), $23,809.2
6. Precision Castparts Corp., $21,113.1

Source: *Financial Times*, FT 500 (annual), http://www.ft.com, June 24, 2011.

Defined Benefit Plans
See: Pension Fund Investments

Defined Contribution Plans
See: Pension Fund Investments

Dental Care Products

2314 ■ TOP DENTAL HANDPIECE REPAIR FRANCHISES, 2012

Ranked by: Cumulative score based on financial strength and stability, growth rate, size of the system, number of years in business, the length of time franchising, start-up costs, litigation, percentage of terminations, and whether the company provides financing. **Remarks:** Specific scores not provided. Also notes overall rank within the *Franchise 500,* contact information, description, year founded, year started franchising, available U.S. regions, where seeking foreign expansion, number of franchised and company-owned units for past three years, start-up costs, franchise fees, royalty fees, and type of financing available. **Number listed:** 2

1. The Dentist's Choice
2. Hayes Handpiece Franchises

Source: *Entrepreneur*, Franchise 500 (annual), January 2012, p. 202-203.

Dental Clinics

2315 ■ STATES WITH THE HIGHEST RATE OF DENTISTS, 2009

Ranked by: Number of dentists per 100,000 in population. **Number listed:** 51

1. Washington DC, with 107 dentists
2. Massachusetts, 83
3. Hawaii, 81
4. New Jersey, 80
5. New York, 77
6. California, 76
7. Connecticut, 75
8. Alaska, 73
8. Maryland, 73
10. Washington, 70

Source: *State Rankings*, (annual), CQ Press, 2011, p. 389.

2316 ■ STATES WITH THE LOWEST RATE OF DENTISTS, 2009

Ranked by: Number of dentists per 100,000 in population. **Number listed:** 51

1. Arkansas, with 39 dentists
1. Mississippi, 39
3. Alabama, 43
4. Georgia, 44
5. North Carolina, 45
5. Texas, 45
7. Delaware, 46
7. Louisiana, 46
7. New Mexico, 46
7. South Carolina, 46

Source: *State Rankings*, (annual), CQ Press, 2011, p. 389.

Department Stores

2317 ■ DEPARTMENT RETAILERS ADDING THE MOST NEW STORES, 2011

Ranked by: Total number of new stores added during the year. **Remarks:** Also notes figures for previous year. **Number listed:** 8

1. Kohl's Corp., with 40 new stores
2. Nordstrom Inc., 20
3. J. C. Penney Co., Inc., 13
4. Saks Inc., 5
4. Stein Mart Inc., 5
6. Macy's Inc., 3
7. Neiman Marcus Group Inc., 2
8. Belk Inc., 1

Source: *Chain Store Age*, Big Builders (annual), December 2011, p. 36.

2318 ■ JAPAN'S LARGEST DEPARTMENT STORE COMPANIES OVERALL, 2011

Ranked by: Score based on revenue, profits, assets, and market capitalization. **Remarks:** Specific scores not provided. Also notes overall rank in the *Forbes 2000* and figures for each criterion. **Number listed:** 5

1. Aeon Co., Ltd.
2. Isetan Mitsukoshi Holdings
3. J Front Retailing
4. Takashimaya
5. Daiei

Source: *Forbes*, Forbes 2000 (annual), http://www.forbes.com, May 7, 2012.

2319 ■ LARGEST ASIA-PACIFIC DEPARTMENT STORE COMPANIES, 2010

Ranked by: Sales, in millions of U.S. dollars. **Remarks:** Also notes country, fascias/brands, number of outlets, sales in national currency, sales area, sales per square meter, and figures for previous year. **Number listed:** 10

1. Aeon Group, with $26,501 million
2. Seven & I Holdings Co., Ltd., $24,426
3. Isetan Mitsukoshi Holdings, $10,561
4. Takashimaya, $8,318
5. Lotte Shopping Co., Ltd., $8,174
6. J Front Retailing, $7,656
7. Wesfarmers Ltd., $7,022
8. The Daiei, $6,078
9. Uny, $5,916
10. Wal-Mart Stores Inc., $4,956

Source: *Retail Asia*, Retail Asia-Pacific Top 500 (annual), July 2011, p. 64-64a.

2320 ■ LARGEST U.S. DEPARTMENT STORE COMPANIES OVERALL, 2011

Ranked by: Score based on revenue, profits, assets, and market capitalization. **Remarks:** Specific scores not provided. Also notes overall rank in the *Forbes 2000* and figures for each criterion. **Number listed:** 7

1. Macy's Inc.
2. The TJX Companies Inc.
3. Kohl's Corp.
4. Sears Holdings Corp.
5. Nordstrom Inc.
6. J. C. Penney Co., Inc.
7. Dillard's Inc.

Source: *Forbes*, Forbes 2000 (annual), http://www.forbes.com, May 7, 2012.

2321 ■ TOP U.S. DEPARTMENT STORES BY SALES, 2010

Ranked by: Sales volume, in thousands of dollars. **Remarks:** Also notes comparable-store sales and sales per store. **Number listed:** 9

1. Macy's Inc., with $24,834,000 thousand
2. Kohl's Corp., $18,391,000
3. J. C. Penney Co., Inc., $17,659,000
4. Sears Holdings Corp., $16,353,000
5. Nordstrom Inc., $7,745,000

6. Dillard's Inc., $6,020,000

7. Belk Inc., $3,513,000

8. Neiman Marcus Group Inc., $3,326,000

9. The Bon-Ton Stores Inc., $2,980,000

Source: *Stores*, Top 100 Retailers (annual), July 2011, p. s12.

2322 ■ UNITED KINGDOM'S LARGEST DEPARTMENT STORE COMPANIES OVERALL, 2011

Ranked by: Score based on revenue, profits, assets, and market capitalization. **Remarks:** Specific scores not provided. Also notes overall rank in the *Forbes 2000* and figures for each criterion. **Number listed:** 2

1. Marks & Spencer plc

2. Home Retail Group plc

Source: *Forbes*, Forbes 2000 (annual), http://www.forbes.com, May 7, 2012.

2323 ■ WORLD'S LARGEST DEPARTMENT STORE COMPANIES OVERALL, 2011

Ranked by: Score based on revenue, profits, assets, and market capitalization. **Remarks:** Specific scores not provided. Also notes country, overall rank in the *Forbes 2000,* and figures for each criterion. **Number listed:** 20

1. PPR SA

2. Macy's Inc.

3. Aeon Co., Ltd.

4. Lotte Shopping Co., Ltd.

5. The TJX Companies Inc.

6. Kohl's Corp.

6. SACI Falabella

8. Marks & Spencer plc

9. Sears Holdings Corp.

10. Nordstrom Inc.

Source: *Forbes*, Forbes 2000 (annual), http://www.forbes.com, May 7, 2012.

Design, Building
See: **Engineering Design**

Dietary Supplements
See: **Vitamins**

Direct Mail Advertising

2324 ■ TOP DIRECT MAIL ADVERTISERS IN THE UNITED KINGDOM, 2011

Ranked by: Direct mail advertising expenditures, in millions of pounds sterling. **Remarks:** Also notes rank for previous year, volume of mailings, annual percent change in spending, breakdown by prospect and current customers, and direct mail as a percentage of total advertising budget. **Number listed:** 100

1. Virgin Media Inc., with £29.24 million

2. JD Williams & Co., £28.51

3. BT Group plc, £27.56

4. British Sky Broadcasting Group plc (BSkyB), £23.52

5. Saga Services, £23.24

6. Beaconsfield Footwear, £23.20

7. Tesco plc, £19.47

8. MBNA Europe Bank, £18.63

9. Healthspan Direct, £16.89

10. Chums, £16.13

Source: *Marketing*, Top 100 Direct Mailers (annual), October 26, 2011, p. 5+.

Direct Marketing Agencies

2325 ■ TOP DIRECT MARKETING AND SALES PROMOTION AGENCIES IN THE U.K., 2011

Ranked by: Gross profit, in millions of pounds sterling. **Remarks:** Also notes rank and figurs for previous year, percent change, turnover, and number of staff and creatives. **Number listed:** 100

1. Gyro, with £48.5 million

2. Iris Worldwide, £47.6

3. 20:20 Agency, £36

4. Wunderman, £28.8

5. CHI & Partners, £28.6

6. Tangible, £23

7. Tullo Marshall Warren, £20.4

8. G2 Joshua, £19.2

9. BD Network, £16.9

10. Billington Cartmell, £16

Source: *Marketing*, Top Direct Marketing & Sales Promotion Agencies (annual), March 28, 2012, p. 35-37.

Direct Selling

2326 ■ TOP ASIA-PACIFIC DIRECT-SELLING COMPANIES, 2011

Ranked by: Net sales. **Remarks:** Specific figures not provided. **Number listed:** 5

1. AmorePacific (S. Korea)

2. New Era (Japan)

3. Menard Japan Cosmetics (Japan)

4. Cosway (Malaysia)

5. DXN Holdings Berhad (Malaysia)

Source: *DirectSelling News*, Global 100 (annual), June 2012.

2327 ■ TOP EUROPEAN DIRECT-SELLING COMPANIES, 2011

Ranked by: Net sales. **Remarks:** Specific figures not provided. **Number listed:** 5

1. Vorwerk & Co. KG (Germany)

2. Oriflame Cosmetics SA (Luxembourg)

3. Telecom Plus (U.K.)

4. WIV Wein International (Germany)

5. LR Health & Beauty Systems (Germany)

Source: *DirectSelling News*, Global 100 (annual), June 2012.

2328 ■ TOP SOUTH AMERICAN DIRECT-SELLING COMPANIES, 2011

Ranked by: Net sales. **Remarks:** Specific figures not provided. **Number listed:** 3

1. Natura Cosmeticos SA (Brazil)
2. Belcorp (Peru)
3. Yanbal International (Peru)

Source: *DirectSelling News*, Global 100 (annual), June 2012.

2329 ■ TOP U.S. DIRECT-SELLING COMPANIES, 2011

Ranked by: Net sales. **Remarks:** Specific figures not provided. **Number listed:** 5

1. Avon Products Inc.
2. Amway Corp.
3. Herbalife Ltd.
4. Mary Kay Inc.
5. Tupperware Brands Corp.

Source: *DirectSelling News*, Global 100 (annual), June 2012.

2330 ■ WORLD'S TOP DIRECT-SELLING COMPANIES, 2011

Ranked by: Net sales, in billions of U.S. dollars. **Remarks:** Also notes sales method, compensation structure, products, markets, number of salespeople, number of employees, headquarters, key executive, year founded, stock exchange, and ticker symbol. **Number listed:** 100

1. Avon Products Inc., with $11.3 billion
2. Amway Corp., $10.9
3. Herbalife Ltd., $3.5
4. Natura Cosmeticos SA, $3.01
5. Vorwerk & Co. KG, $3
6. Mary Kay Inc., $2.9
7. Tupperware Brands Corp., $2.6
8. Oriflame Cosmetics SA, $2.1
9. NuSkin Enterprises inc., $1.7
10. Belcorp, $1.6

Source: *DirectSelling News*, Global 100 (annual), June 2012.

2331 ■ WORLD'S TOP DIRECT-SELLING COMPANIES IN BEAUTY/PERSONAL CARE PRODUCTS, 2011

Ranked by: Net sales. **Remarks:** Specific figures not provided. **Number listed:** 5

1. Avon Products Inc.
2. Amway Corp.
3. Natura Cosmeticos SA
4. Mary Kay Inc.
5. Oriflame Cosmetics SA

Source: *DirectSelling News*, Global 100 (annual), June 2012.

2332 ■ WORLD'S TOP DIRECT-SELLING COMPANIES BY DOLLAR GROWTH, 2010-2011

Ranked by: Annual sales growth, in millions of U.S. dollars. **Number listed:** 6

1. Amway Corp., with $1,700 million
2. Herbalife Ltd., $800
3. Avon Products Inc., $400
3. Mary Kay Inc., $400
5. Tupperware Brands Corp., $300
5. Belcorp, $300

Source: *DirectSelling News*, Global 100 (annual), June 2012.

2333 ■ WORLD'S TOP DIRECT-SELLING COMPANIES IN HEALTH AND WELLNESS PRODUCTS, 2011

Ranked by: Net sales. **Remarks:** Specific figures not provided. **Number listed:** 5

1. Amway Corp. (Nutrilite)
2. Herbalife Ltd.
3. NuSkin Enterprises inc.
4. USANA
5. Shaklee Corp.

Source: *DirectSelling News*, Global 100 (annual), June 2012.

2334 ■ WORLD'S TOP DIRECT-SELLING COMPANIES IN JEWELRY AND ACCESSORIES, 2011

Ranked by: Net sales. **Remarks:** Specific figures not provided. **Number listed:** 2

1. Avon Products Inc. (Silpada Designs)
2. Thirty-One Gifts

Source: *DirectSelling News*, Global 100 (annual), June 2012.

2335 ■ WORLD'S TOP DIRECT-SELLING COMPANIES BY PERCENTAGE GROWTH, 2010-2011

Ranked by: Annual sales growth, in percent. **Number listed:** 7

1. ViSalus, with 579%
2. Thirty-One Gifts, 382%
3. Viridian Energy, 300%
4. Organo Gold, 200%
4. LifeVantage, 200%
6. Ambit Energy, 60%
7. AdvoCare International, 55%

Source: *DirectSelling News*, Global 100 (annual), June 2012.

2336 ■ WORLD'S TOP DIRECT-SELLING COMPANIES IN SERVICES, 2011

Ranked by: Net sales. **Remarks:** Specific figures not provided. **Number listed:** 5

1. Primerica (financial svcs.)
2. Ignite (energy)
3. Telecom Plus (telecommunications)
4. Ambit Energy (energy)
5. ACN (telecommunications)

Source: *DirectSelling News*, Global 100 (annual), June 2012.

2337 ■ WORLD'S TOP PARTY PLAN DIRECT-SELLING COMPANIES, 2011

Ranked by: Net sales. **Remarks:** Specific figures not provided. **Number listed:** 5

1. Mary Kay Inc.
2. Tupperware Brands Corp.
3. Belcorp
4. The Pampered Chef
5. PartyLite

Source: *DirectSelling News*, Global 100 (annual), June 2012.

2338 ■ WORLD'S TOP PUBLIC DIRECT-SELLING COMPANIES, 2011

Ranked by: Net sales. **Remarks:** Figures not provided. **Number listed:** 5

1. Avon Products Inc.
2. Herbalife Ltd.
3. Natura Cosmeticos SA
4. Tupperware Brands Corp.
5. Oriflame Cosmetics SA

Source: *DirectSelling News*, Global 100 (annual), June 2012.

Directors
See: **Corporate Directors**

Discount Brokers
See also: **Brokers**

2339 ■ BEST DISCOUNT BROKERS, 2011

Ranked by: Score based on 246 criteria in the areas of customer service, the account-opening process, website, trading mechanism, and account statements and 1099s. **Remarks:** Specific scores not provided. Also notes website, comments, standard commission, default rate on cash, and scores for customer service, mutual funds, trading tools, research, investment products, and banking amenities. **Number listed:** 10

1. Fidelity Investments
2. TD Ameritrade Holding Corp.
3. Scottrade Inc.
4. TradeKing
5. The Charles Schwab Corp.
6. E*Trade Financial Corp.
7. Vanguard
8. Merrill Edge
9. OptionsXpress
10. ShareBuilder

Source: *SmartMoney*, Broker Survey (annual), June 2011, p. 56.

Discount Stores

2340 ■ DISCOUNT RETAILERS ADDING THE MOST NEW STORES, 2011

Ranked by: Total number of new stores added during the year. **Remarks:** Also notes figures for previous year. **Number listed:** 11

1. Dollar General Corp., with 625 new stores
2. Dollar Tree Stores Inc., 300
2. Family Dollar Stores Inc., 300
4. The TJX Companies Inc., 196
5. Wal-Mart Stores Inc., 160
6. Big Lots Inc., 90
7. Ross Dress for Less, 80
8. Five Below, 50
9. Costco Wholesale Corp., 28
10. Target Corp., 21

Source: *Chain Store Age*, Big Builders (annual), December 2011, p. 36.

2341 ■ LARGEST U.S. DISCOUNT STORE COMPANIES OVERALL, 2011

Ranked by: Score based on revenue, profits, assets, and market capitalization. **Remarks:** Specific scores not provided. Also notes overall rank in the *Forbes 2000* and figures for each criterion. **Number listed:** 6

1. Wal-Mart Stores Inc.
2. Target Corp.
3. Costco Wholesale Corp.
4. Dollar General Corp.
5. Dollar Tree Stores Inc.
6. Family Dollar Stores Inc.

Source: *Forbes*, Forbes 2000 (annual), http://www.forbes.com, May 7, 2012.

2342 ■ WORLD'S LARGEST DISCOUNT STORE COMPANIES OVERALL, 2011

Ranked by: Score based on revenue, profits, assets, and market capitalization. **Remarks:** Specific scores not provided. Also notes country, overall rank in the *Forbes 2000,* and figures for each criterion. **Number listed:** 9

1. Wal-Mart Stores Inc.
2. Target Corp.
3. Costco Wholesale Corp.
4. Dollar General Corp.
5. Dollar Tree Stores Inc.
6. Family Dollar Stores Inc.
7. E-Mart Co., Ltd.
8. Lojas Americanas SA
9. Distribuidora Internacional de Alimentacion SA (DIA)

Source: *Forbes*, Forbes 2000 (annual), http://www.forbes.com, May 7, 2012.

Diseases

2343 ■ COUNTRIES WITH THE HIGHEST BUSINESS COSTS OF MALARIA, 2010

Ranked by: Score, on a scale of seven, based on the level of expected business costs associated with malaria over the course of the next five years. **Number listed:** 72

1. Angola, with 1.8 points
2. Mali, 2.2
2. Timor-Leste, 2.2
2. Malawi, 2.2
5. Chad, 2.3
6. Uganda, 2.5
7. Zambia, 2.7
7. Burundi, 2.7
7. Nigeria, 2.7
10. Tanzania, 2.8

Source: *Global Competitiveness Report*, (annual), World Economic Forum, 2011, p. 430.

2344 ■ COUNTRIES WITH THE HIGHEST BUSINESS COSTS OF TUBERCULOSIS, 2010

Ranked by: Score, on a scale of seven, based on the level of expected business costs associated with tuberculosis over the course of the next five years. **Number listed:** 142

1. Swaziland, with 2.2 points
2. Lesotho, 2.5
3. Timor-Leste, 2.6

4. Malawi, 2.8

5. Zambia, 3.0

5. Chad, 3.0

7. Mozambique, 3.4

7. South Africa, 3.4

9. Angola, 3.5

9. Zimbabwe, 3.5

Source: *Global Competitiveness Report*, (annual), World Economic Forum, 2011, p. 432.

Distilling Industry
See: **Liquor Industry**

Distribution of Goods

2345 ■ JAPAN'S MOST VALUABLE DISTRIBUTION/ WHOLESALE BRANDS, 2011

Ranked by: Brand value, in millions of U.S. dollars. **Remarks:** Also notes rank within the *Global 500* for current and previous year, figures for current and previous year, and brand rating. Ranking is available online only. **Number listed:** 3

1. Mitsubishi, with $19,488 million

2. Mitsui, $15,405

3. Marubeni, $4,298

Source: *Global 500*, (annual), Brand Finance plc, March 2012.

2346 ■ WORLD'S MOST VALUABLE DISTRIBUTION/ WHOLESALE BRANDS, 2011

Ranked by: Brand value, in millions of U.S. dollars. **Remarks:** Also notes rank within the *Global 500* for current and previous year, figures for current and previous year, country, and brand rating. Ranking is available online only. **Number listed:** 4

1. Mitsubishi, with $19,488 million

2. Mitsui, $15,405

3. Marubeni, $4,298

4. Daewoo, $4,136

Source: *Global 500*, (annual), Brand Finance plc, March 2012.

Diversified Corporations

2347 ■ AMERICA'S LARGEST PRIVATE CONGLOMER-ATES, 2010

Ranked by: Revenue, in billions of dollars. **Remarks:** Also notes headquarters, number of employees, and overall rank in the *America's Largest Private Companies* list. Ranking is available online only, not in print. **Number listed:** 8

1. Koch Industries Inc., with $100 billion

2. Platinum Equity LLC, $10.4

3. Tenaska Energy Inc., $9.95

4. VWR Funding Inc., $3.64

5. Sammons Enterprises Inc., $3.3

6. Roll Global LLC, $2.4

7. Arctic Slope Regional Corp., $2.33

8. Ebsco Industries Inc., $2.26

Source: *Forbes*, America's Largest Private Companies (annual), http://www.forbes.com, December 5, 2011.

2348 ■ CONNECTICUT'S LARGEST CONGLOMERATES OVERALL, 2011

Ranked by: Score based on revenue, profits, assets, and market capitalization. **Remarks:** Specific scores not provided. Also notes overall rank in the *Forbes 2000* and figures for each criterion. **Number listed:** 2

1. General Electric Co.

2. United Technologies Corp.

Source: *Forbes*, Forbes 2000 (annual), http://www.forbes.com, May 7, 2012.

2349 ■ GERMANY'S LARGEST CONGLOMERATES OVERALL, 2011

Ranked by: Score based on revenue, profits, assets, and market capitalization. **Remarks:** Specific scores not provided. Also notes overall rank in the *Forbes 2000* and figures for each criterion. **Number listed:** 3

1. Siemens AG

2. ThyssenKrupp AG

3. GEA Group AG

Source: *Forbes*, Forbes 2000 (annual), http://www.forbes.com, May 7, 2012.

2350 ■ HONG KONG'S LARGEST CONGLOMERATES OVERALL, 2011

Ranked by: Score based on revenue, profits, assets, and market capitalization. **Remarks:** Specific scores not provided. Also notes overall rank in the *Forbes 2000* and figures for each criterion. **Number listed:** 5

1. Hutchison Whampoa Ltd.

2. Jardine Matheson Holdings Ltd.

3. Swire Pacific Ltd.

4. The Wharf (Holdings) Ltd.

5. Noble Group Ltd.

Source: *Forbes*, Forbes 2000 (annual), http://www.forbes.com, May 7, 2012.

2351 ■ IRELAND'S LARGEST CONGLOMERATES OVERALL, 2011

Ranked by: Score based on revenue, profits, assets, and market capitalization. **Remarks:** Specific scores not provided. Also notes overall rank in the *Forbes 2000* and figures for each criterion. **Number listed:** 2

1. Ingersoll-Rand plc

2. DCC

Source: *Forbes*, Forbes 2000 (annual), http://www.forbes.com, May 7, 2012.

2352 ■ LARGEST U.S. CONGLOMERATES OVERALL, 2011

Ranked by: Score based on revenue, profits, assets, and market capitalization. **Remarks:** Specific scores not provided. Also notes overall rank in the *Forbes 2000* and figures for each criterion. **Number listed:** 7

1. General Electric Co.

2. United Technologies Corp.

3. 3M Co.

4. Honeywell International Inc.

5. Danaher Corp.

6. Dover Corp.

7. Textron Inc.

Source: *Forbes*, Forbes 2000 (annual), http://www.forbes.com, May 7, 2012.

2353 ■ MEXICO'S LARGEST CONGLOMERATES OVERALL, 2011

Ranked by: Score based on revenue, profits, assets, and market capitalization. **Remarks:** Specific scores not provided. Also notes overall rank in the *Forbes 2000* and figures for each criterion. **Number listed:** 2

1. Alfa, SA de CV

2. Grupo Carso, SA de CV

Source: *Forbes*, Forbes 2000 (annual), http://www.forbes.com, May 7, 2012.

2354 ■ SINGAPORE'S LARGEST CONGLOMERATES OVERALL, 2011

Ranked by: Score based on revenue, profits, assets, and market capitalization. **Remarks:** Specific scores not provided. Also notes overall rank in the *Forbes 2000* and figures for each criterion. **Number listed:** 2

1. Keppel

2. Fraser & Neave

Source: *Forbes*, Forbes 2000 (annual), http://www.forbes.com, May 7, 2012.

2355 ■ SOUTH AFRICA'S LARGEST CONGLOMERATES OVERALL, 2011

Ranked by: Score based on revenue, profits, assets, and market capitalization. **Remarks:** Specific scores not provided. Also notes overall rank in the *Forbes 2000* and figures for each criterion. **Number listed:** 2

1. Bidvest Group Ltd.

2. Remgro

Source: *Forbes*, Forbes 2000 (annual), http://www.forbes.com, May 7, 2012.

2356 ■ TURKEY'S LARGEST CONGLOMERATES OVERALL, 2011

Ranked by: Score based on revenue, profits, assets, and market capitalization. **Remarks:** Specific scores not provided. Also notes overall rank in the *Forbes 2000* and figures for each criterion. **Number listed:** 2

1. Koc Holding AS

2. Haci Omer Sabanci Holding AS

Source: *Forbes*, Forbes 2000 (annual), http://www.forbes.com, May 7, 2012.

2357 ■ WORLD'S LARGEST CONGLOMERATES OVERALL, 2011

Ranked by: Score based on revenue, profits, assets, and market capitalization. **Remarks:** Specific scores not provided. Also notes country, overall rank in the *Forbes 2000,* and figures for each criterion. **Number listed:** 33

1. General Electric Co.

2. Siemens AG

3. United Technologies Corp.

4. Investimentos Itau SA (Itausa)

5. Hutchison Whampoa Ltd.

6. Jardine Matheson Holdings Ltd.

7. 3M Co.

8. Honeywell International Inc.

9. Danaher Corp.

10. Koc Holding AS

Source: *Forbes*, Forbes 2000 (annual), http://www.forbes.com, May 7, 2012.

Diversity

2358 ■ AMERICA'S BEST COMPANIES WITH THE GREATEST DIVERSITY, 2012

Ranked by: Percentage of employees that are minorities. **Remarks:** Also notes number of employees and overall rank in the *100 Best Companies to Work For.* **Number listed:** 96

1. Baptist Health South Florida Inc., with 72%

2. Methodist Hospital, 66%

3. Intercontinental Hotels Group, 65%

4. Four Seasons Hotels & Resorts, 62%

4. Marriott International Inc., 62%

4. Kimpton Hotel & Restaurant Group LLC, 62%

7. Scripps Health, 53%

7. QUALCOMM Inc., 53%

9. The Men's Wearhouse Inc., 52%

9. Cisco Systems, 49%

Source: *Fortune*, 100 Best Companies to Work For (annual), http://www.fortune.com, February 6, 2012.

2359 ■ BEST COMPANIES FOR DIVERSITY, 2011

Ranked by: Score based on activities related to the participation of African Americans and other ethnic minority groups in the areas of senior management, board of directors, employee base, and supplier diversity. **Remarks:** Scores not provided; companies are listed alphabetically, not ranked. Also notes headquarters, Web site, type of business, areas of opportunity, and strengths. **Number listed:** 40

1. Aetna Inc.

2. AFLAC Inc.

3. Allstate Corp.

4. American Express Co.

5. AT&T Inc.

6. Bank of America Corp.

7. Comerica Inc.

8. Darden Restaurants Inc.

9. Exelon Corp.

10. Fannie Mae

Source: *Black Enterprise*, 40 Best Companies for Diversity, July 2011, p. 86+.

2360 ■ CANADA'S BEST DIVERSITY EMPLOYERS, 2012

Ranked by: Score based on diversity initiatives covering five major employee groups: women; members of visible minorities; persons with disabilities; Aboriginal people; and lesbian, gay, bisexual, and transgendered/transsexual people. **Remarks:** Scores not provided; companies are listed alphabetically, not ranked. **Number listed:** 50

1. Agrium Inc.
2. Amex Canada Inc.
3. BC Hydro
4. Boeing Canada Operations Ltd.
5. Bombardier Aerospace
6. Business Development Bank of Canada
7. Cameco Corp.
8. Canadian Imperial Bank of Commerce
9. Capital District Health Authority
10. Centre for Addiction & Mental Health

Source: *Canada's Top 100 Employers*, (annual), http://www.canadastop100.com, February 21, 2012.

2361 ■ TOP CORPORATIONS FOR SUPPLIER DIVERSITY, 2012

Ranked by: Score, on a scale of 30, based on management involvement in supplier diversity, procurement from minority suppliers, and outreach efforts to minority suppliers. **Remarks:** Also notes score for each criterion. **Number listed:** 25

1. PG & E Corp., with 20.4 points
2. Comerica Bank, 20.04
3. AT&T Inc., 17.38
4. Freddie Mac, 15.47
5. Consolidated Edison Co. of New York, 15.35
6. Wal-Mart Stores Inc., 15
7. Bank of America Corp., 14.65
8. Verizon Communications Inc., 13.96
9. Southern California Edison Co., 13.77
10. Marriott International Inc., 13.01

Source: *Hispanic Business*, Diversity Supplier 25 (annual), March 2012, p. 20.

2362 ■ TOP REGIONAL U.S. COMPANIES FOR DIVERSITY, 2011

Ranked by: Score based on strength in four areas: CEO commitment to diversity, human capital, corporate and organizational communications, and supplier diversity. **Remarks:** Specific scores not provided. To qualify, companies must have more than 1,000 U.S. employees. **Number listed:** 10

1. Comerica Inc.
2. Blue Cross & Blue Shield of Florida
3. Blue Cross Blue Shield of Michigan
4. KeyCorp
5. BlueCross BlueShield of North Carolina
6. Blue Cross Blue Shield of Rhode Island
7. Horizon Blue Cross Blue Shield of New Jersey
8. AAA Northern California, Nevada & Utah
9. Independence Blue Cross
10. Union Bank

Source: *DiversityInc*, Top 50 (annual), 2011, p. 100.

2363 ■ TOP U.S. COMPANIES FOR DIVERSITY, 2011

Ranked by: Score based on strength in four areas: CEO commitment to diversity, human capital, corporate and organizational communications, and supplier diversity. **Remarks:** Specific scores not provided. To qualify, companies must have more than 1,000 U.S. employees. **Number listed:** 50

1. Kaiser Permanente

2. Sodexo
3. PricewaterhouseCoopers LLP
4. AT&T Inc.
5. Ernst & Young LLP
6. Johnson & Johnson
7. International Business Machines Corp. (IBM)
8. Deloitte LLP
9. Kraft Foods Inc.
10. Colgate-Palmolive Co.

Source: *DiversityInc*, Top 50 (annual), 2011, p. 28.

2364 ■ TOP U.S. COMPANIES FOR DIVERSITY IN RECRUITMENT AND RETENTION, 2011

Ranked by: Score based on progress in attracting new talent that is diverse, in retaining that talent, and in promoting people of all races/ethnicities, genders, orientations, and physical abilities. **Remarks:** Specific scores not provided. To qualify, companies must have more than 1,000 U.S. employees. **Number listed:** 10

1. PricewaterhouseCoopers LLP
2. Ernst & Young LLP
3. AT&T Inc.
4. Kaiser Permanente
5. Sodexo
6. Johnson & Johnson
7. Bank of America Corp.
8. Novartis Pharmaceuticals Corp.
9. Procter & Gamble Co.
10. Marriott International Inc.

Source: *DiversityInc*, Top 50 (annual), 2011, p. 94.

2365 ■ TOP U.S. COMPANIES FOR GLOBAL DIVERSITY, 2011

Ranked by: Score based on commitment to employees and their families who work in countries outside of the United States. **Remarks:** Specific scores not provided. To qualify, companies must have more than 1,000 U.S. employees. **Number listed:** 10

1. International Business Machines Corp. (IBM)
2. Ernst & Young LLP
3. PricewaterhouseCoopers LLP
4. Sodexo
5. Deloitte LLP
6. KPMG LLP
7. Merck & Co., Inc.
8. Procter & Gamble Co.
9. American Express Co.
10. Colgate-Palmolive Co.

Source: *DiversityInc*, Top 50 (annual), 2011, p. 98.

2366 ■ TOP U.S. COMPANIES FOR SUPPLIER DIVERSITY, 2011

Ranked by: Score based on commitment to minority-owned, women-owned, homosexual-owned, and disabilityowned vendors. **Remarks:** Specific scores not provided. To qualify, companies must have more than 1,000 U.S. employees. **Number listed:** 10

1. Marriott International Inc.
2. AT&T Inc.
3. Sodexo
4. KeyCorp

5. Hewlett-Packard Co.
6. CSX Corp.
7. Cox Communications Inc.
8. Pacific Gas & Electric Co. (PG & E)
9. Bank of America Corp.
10. Merck & Co., Inc.

Source: *DiversityInc*, Top 50 (annual), 2011, p. 94.

Drug Industry
See: **Pharmaceutical Industry**

Drug Stores

2367 ■ LARGEST PHARMACY RETAILERS, 2011

Ranked by: Pharmacy sales, in millions of dollars. **Remarks:** Also notes total corporate sales, total number of stores, and number of store with pharmacies. **Number listed:** 50

1. Walgreen Co., with $46,700 million
2. CVS Caremark Corp., $40,700
3. Rite Aid Corp., $17,800
4. Wal-Mart Stores Inc., $15,900
5. Cardinal Health Inc., $13,700
6. The Kroger Co., $7,200
6. Good Neighbor Pharmacy, $7,200
8. Health Mart, $5,900
9. Safeway Inc., $3,900
10. American Associated Pharmacies, $3,500

Source: *Drug Store News*, Top 50 Power Players (annual), April 2012.

2368 ■ LARGEST REGIONAL DRUG STORE CHAINS, 2011

Ranked by: Pharmacy sales, in millions of dollars. **Remarks:** Also notes number of stores, region, and comments. **Number listed:** 25

1. Publix Super Markets Inc., with $1,500 million
2. H. E. Butt Grocery Co., $1,200
3. Giant Eagle Inc., $1,100
4. Hy-Vee Inc., $942
5. Fred's Inc., $628
6. Kinney Drugs, $602
7. Meijer Inc., $435
8. Winn-Dixie Stores Inc., $434
9. Hannaford Bros. Co., $396
10. USA Drug, $390

Source: *Drug Store News*, Regional Chain Report (annual), January 2012.

2369 ■ LARGEST U.S. DRUG RETAILERS OVERALL, 2011

Ranked by: Score based on revenue, profits, assets, and market capitalization. **Remarks:** Specific scores not provided. Also notes overall rank in the *Forbes 2000* and figures for each criterion. **Number listed:** 3

1. CVS Caremark Corp.
2. Walgreen Co.

3. Rite Aid Corp.

Source: *Forbes*, Forbes 2000 (annual), http://www.forbes.com, May 7, 2012.

2370 ■ MOST VALUABLE U.S. FOOD AND DRUG RETAILERS, 2011

Ranked by: Market value as of March 2011, in millions of U.S. dollars. **Remarks:** Also notes rank within the *FT U.S. 500*, rank for previous year, country, revenue, net income, assets, number of employees, share price, price-to-earning ratio, dividend yield, and fiscal yearend. **Number listed:** 9

1. CVS Caremark Corp., with $46,886.8 million
2. Walgreen Co., $37,025.8
3. McKesson Corp., $20,099.3
4. Sysco Corp., $15,141
5. The Kroger Co., $14,876.6
6. Cardinal Health Inc., $14,385.2
7. Whole Foods Market Inc., $11,437.9
8. AmerisourceBergen Corp., $10,843.2
9. Safeway Inc., $8,667.4

Source: *Financial Times*, FT 500 (annual), http://www.ft.com, June 24, 2011.

2371 ■ TOP *FORTUNE 500* FOOD AND DRUG STORES, 2011

Ranked by: Revenue, in millions of dollars. **Remarks:** Also notes overall rank in the *Fortune 500;* profits; profits as a percentage of revenue; stockholders' equity; and rank by each criterion. **Number listed:** 10

1. CVS Caremark Corp., with $107,750 million
2. The Kroger Co., $90,374
3. Walgreen Co., $72,184
4. Safeway Inc., $43,630
5. SuperValu Inc., $37,534
6. Publix Super Markets Inc., $27,179
7. Rite Aid Corp., $25,216
8. Whole Foods Market Inc., $10,108
9. The Great Atlantic & Pacific Tea Co., Inc., $8,078
10. Winn-Dixie Stores Inc., $6,930

Source: *Fortune*, Fortune 500 (annual), May 21, 2012, p. F-35.

2372 ■ TOP U.S. DRUG STORES BY SALES, 2010

Ranked by: Sales volume, in thousands of dollars. **Remarks:** Also notes comparable-store sales and sales per store. **Number listed:** 3

1. Walgreen Co., with $61,240,000 thousand
2. CVS Caremark Corp., $57,464,000
3. Rite Aid Corp., $25,196,000

Source: *Stores*, Top 100 Retailers (annual), July 2011, p. s12.

2373 ■ WORLD'S LARGEST DRUG RETAILERS OVERALL, 2011

Ranked by: Score based on revenue, profits, assets, and market capitalization. **Remarks:** Specific scores not provided. Also notes country, overall rank in the *Forbes 2000,* and figures for each criterion. **Number listed:** 4

1. CVS Caremark Corp.
2. Walgreen Co.

3. Shoppers Drug Mart Corp.

4. Rite Aid Corp.

Source: *Forbes*, Forbes 2000 (annual), http://www.forbes.com, May 7, 2012.

2374 ■ WORLD'S MOST ADMIRED FOOD AND DRUG STORES, 2012

Ranked by: Score, on a scale of 10, based on a survey of executives, directors, and securities analysts of companies within their own industry on eight criteria: innovation, financial soundness, employee talent, use of corporate assets, long-term investment value, social responsibility, quality of management, and quality of products/services. **Remarks:** Specific scores not provided. Also notes rank for previous year. **Number listed:** 5

1. Whole Foods Market Inc.
2. Publix Super Markets Inc.
3. The Kroger Co.
4. Walgreen Co.
5. CVS Caremark Corp.

Source: *Fortune*, World's Most Admired Companies (annual), March 19, 2012, p. 149-150.

2375 ■ WORLD'S MOST VALUABLE FOOD AND DRUG RETAILERS, 2011

Ranked by: Market value as of March 2011, in millions of U.S. dollars. **Remarks:** Also notes rank within the *FT 500*, rank for previous year, country, revenue, net income, assets, number of employees, share price, price-to-earning ratio, dividend yield, and fiscal year-end. **Number listed:** 7

1. Tesco plc, with $49,141.7 million
2. CVS Caremark Corp., $46,886.8
3. Walgreen Co., $37,025.8
4. Woolworths Ltd., $33,716.2
5. Carrefour SA, $30,116.6
6. Metro AG, $22,176.1
7. McKesson Corp., $20,099.3

Source: *Financial Times*, FT 500 (annual), http://www.ft.com, June 24, 2011.

Drugs
See also: **Pharmaceutical Industry**

2376 ■ TOP U.S. DRUGS BY SALES, 2011

Ranked by: U.S. sales, in billions of U.S. dollars. **Remarks:** Also notes figures for previous year and annual sales growth. **Number listed:** 25

1. Lipitor, with $7.7 billion
2. Plavix, $6.8
3. Nexium, $6.2
4. Abilify, $5.2
5. Advair Diskus, $4.6
5. Seroquel, $4.6
5. Singulair, $4.6
8. Crestor, $4.4
9. Cymbalta, $3.7
10. Humira, $3.5
10. Enbrel, $3.5
10. Remicade, $3.5

Source: *Pharmaceutical Executive*, Pharm Exec 50 (annual), May 5012, p. 32.

2377 ■ WORLD'S TOP DRUGS BY SALES, 2011

Ranked by: Global sales, in billions of U.S. dollars. **Remarks:** Also notes annual sales growth. **Number listed:** 20

1. Lipitor, with $12.5 billion
2. Plavix, $9.3
3. Seretide, $8.7
4. Crestor, $8
5. Nexium, $7.9
6. Seroquel, $7.6
7. Humira, $7.3
8. Enbrel, $6.8
8. Remicade, $6.8
10. Abilify, $6.3

Source: *Pharmaceutical Executive*, Pharm Exec 50 (annual), May 2012, p. 25.

Drugs, Prescription

2378 ■ TOP PRESCRIPTION DRUGS BY MARKET SHARE, 2010

Ranked by: Market share, in percent. **Remarks:** Also notes parent company, figures for previous year, and advertising expenditures for current and previous year. **Number listed:** 10

1. Lipitor, with 2.3%
2. Nexium, 2.0%
2. Plavix, 2.0%
4. Advair Diskus, 1.5%
4. Abilify, 1.5%
6. Seroquel, 1.4%
7. Singulair, 1.3%
8. Crestor, 1.2%
8. Actos, 1.1%
8. Epogen, 1.1%

Source: *Advertising Age*, Leading National Advertisers (annual), June 20, 2011, p. 21.

Drugstores
See: **Drug Stores**

Dry Cleaning

2379 ■ TOP DRY CLEANING AND DELIVERY SERVICE FRANCHISES, 2012

Ranked by: Cumulative score based on financial strength and stability, growth rate, size of the system, number of years in business, the length of time franchising, start-up costs, litigation, percentage of terminations, and whether the company provides financing. **Remarks:** Specific scores not provided. Also notes overall rank within the *Franchise 500,* contact information, description, year founded, year started franchising, states where registered, available U.S. regions, where seeking foreign expansion, number of franchised and company-owned units for past three years, start-up costs, franchise fees, royalty fees, and type of financing available. **Number listed:** 8

1. Martinizing Dry Cleaning

2. Zips Dry Cleaners
3. FRSTeam
4. Comet Cleaners
5. Certified Restoration DryCleaning Network
6. 1-800-DryClean
7. Dryclean USA
8. Pressed4Time Inc.

Source: *Entrepreneur*, Franchise 500 (annual), January 2012, p. 202-203.

E-Commerce
See: **Electronic Commerce**

Economic Development

2380 ■ TOP ECONOMIC DEVELOPMENT PROJECTS OUTSIDE NORTH AMERICA, 2011

Ranked by: Score based on capital investment, number and value of jobs created, regional economic impact, creativity of deal, role of incentives, competition by other locations, and speed to market.
Remarks: Specific scores not provided; groups are listed alphabetically, not ranked. Also notes investment, number of jobs created, and comments. **Number listed:** 10

1. Amazon.com Inc. (India)
2. Audi (Hungary)
3. Caracol Industrial Park (Haiti)
4. China Motor Corp. (S. Africa)
5. Ford Motor Co. (India)
6. GCL-Poly (China)
7. General Electric Co. (Saudi Arabia)
8. International Business Machines Corp. (IBM; Malaysia)
9. Infosys Technologies (China)
10. Nissan (Brazil)

Source: *Site Selection*, Top Deals (annual), May 2012, p. 76-78.

2381 ■ TOP ECONOMIC DEVELOPMENT PROJECTS IN NORTH AMERICA, 2011

Ranked by: Score based on capital investment, number and value of jobs created, regional economic impact, creativity of deal, role of incentives, competition by other locations, and speed to market.
Remarks: Specific scores not provided; groups are listed alphabetically, not ranked. Also notes investment, number of jobs created, and comments. **Number listed:** 10

1. Amazon.com Inc. (various cities in TN)
2. Continental Tire the Americas (Sumter Co., SC)
3. eBay Inc. (Draper, UT)
4. GE Transportation (Ft. Worth, TX)
5. Honda (Mexico)
6. Intel Corp. (Chandler, AZ)
7. The Jackson Laboratory (Farmington, CT)
8. Navistar International Corp. (Muscle Shoals, AL)
9. Pratt & Whitney Canada (multiple locations)
10. Sasol (Westlake, LA)

Source: *Site Selection*, Top Deals (annual), May 2012, p. 74-76.

Economy

2382 ■ ASIA AND PACIFIC COUNTRIES WITH THE LEAST ECONOMIC FREEDOM, 2012

Ranked by: Score based on 50 variables in 10 areas: business freedom, trade freedom, fiscal freedom, government size, monetary freedom, investment freedom, financial freedom, property rights, freedom from corruption, and labor freedom.
Remarks: Also notes worldwide rank and score for each criterion.
Number listed: 41

1. North Korea, with 1 points
2. Burma, 38.7
3. Timor-Leste, 43.3
4. Turkmenistan, 43.8
5. Uzbekistan, 45.8
6. Solomon Islands, 46.2
7. Kiribati, 46.9
8. Maldives, 49.2
9. Laos, 50
10. Nepal, 50.2

Source: *Index of Economic Freedom*, (annual), The Heritage Foundation/The Wall Street Journal, 2012, p. 38-39.

2383 ■ ASIA AND PACIFIC COUNTRIES WITH THE MOST ECONOMIC FREEDOM, 2012

Ranked by: Score based on 50 variables in 10 areas: business freedom, trade freedom, fiscal freedom, government size, monetary freedom, investment freedom, financial freedom, property rights, freedom from corruption, and labor freedom.
Remarks: Also notes worldwide rank and score for each criterion.
Number listed: 41

1. Hong Kong, with 89.9 points
2. Singapore, 87.5
3. Australia, 83.1
4. New Zealand, 82.1
5. Taiwan, 71.9
6. Macau, 71.8
7. Japan, 71.6
8. South Korea, 69.9
9. Malaysia, 66.4
10. Thailand, 64.9

Source: *Index of Economic Freedom*, (annual), The Heritage Foundation/The Wall Street Journal, 2012, p. 38-39.

2384 ■ COUNTRIES WITH THE LEAST ECONOMIC FREEDOM, 2012

Ranked by: Score based on 50 variables in 10 areas: business freedom, trade freedom, fiscal freedom, government size, monetary freedom, investment freedom, financial freedom, property rights, freedom from corruption, and labor freedom.
Remarks: Also notes score for each criterion. **Number listed:** 179

1. North Korea, with 1 points
2. Zimbabwe, 26.3
3. Cuba, 28.3
4. Libya, 35.9
5. Eritrea, 36.2
6. Venezuela, 38.1
7. Burma, 38.7

8. Democratic Republic of Congo, 41.1

9. Iran, 42.3

10. Equatorial Guinea, 42.8

Source: *Index of Economic Freedom*, (annual), The Heritage Foundation/The Wall Street Journal, 2012, p. 8-12.

2385 ■ COUNTRIES WITH THE MOST ECONOMIC FREEDOM, 2012

Ranked by: Score based on 50 variables in 10 areas: business freedom, trade freedom, fiscal freedom, government size, monetary freedom, investment freedom, financial freedom, property rights, freedom from corruption, and labor freedom. **Remarks:** Also notes score for each criterion. **Number listed:** 179

1. Hong Kong, with 89.9 points

2. Singapore, 87.5

3. Australia, 83.1

4. New Zealand, 82.1

5. Switzerland, 81.1

6. Canada, 79.9

7. Chile, 78.3

8. Mauritius, 77

9. Ireland, 76.9

10. United States, 76.3

Source: *Index of Economic Freedom*, (annual), The Heritage Foundation/The Wall Street Journal, 2012, p. 8-12.

2386 ■ COUNTRIES IN SOUTH AMERICA, CENTRAL AMERICA, AND THE CARIBBEAN WITH THE LEAST ECONOMIC FREEDOM, 2012

Ranked by: Score based on 50 variables in 10 areas: business freedom, trade freedom, fiscal freedom, government size, monetary freedom, investment freedom, financial freedom, property rights, freedom from corruption, and labor freedom. **Remarks:** Also notes worldwide rank and score for each criterion. **Number listed:** 29

1. Cuba, with 28.3 points

2. Venezuela, 38.1

3. Argentina, 48

4. Ecuador, 48.3

5. Bolivia, 50.2

6. Haiti, 50.7

7. Guyana, 51.3

8. Suriname, 52.6

9. Nicaragua, 57.9

9. Brazil, 57.9

Source: *Index of Economic Freedom*, (annual), The Heritage Foundation/The Wall Street Journal, 2012, p. 33.

2387 ■ COUNTRIES IN SOUTH AMERICA, CENTRAL AMERICA, AND THE CARIBBEAN WITH THE MOST ECONOMIC FREEDOM, 2012

Ranked by: Score based on 50 variables in 10 areas: business freedom, trade freedom, fiscal freedom, government size, monetary freedom, investment freedom, financial freedom, property rights, freedom from corruption, and labor freedom. **Remarks:** Also notes worldwide rank and score for each criterion. **Number listed:** 29

1. Chile, with 78.3 points

2. St. Lucia, 71.3

3. Uruguay, 69.9

4. Barbados, 69

5. El Salvador, 68.7

5. Peru, 68.7

7. Costa Rica, 68

7. Colombia, 68

7. Bahamas, 68

10. St. Vincent and the Grenadines, 66.5

Source: *Index of Economic Freedom*, (annual), The Heritage Foundation/The Wall Street Journal, 2012, p. 33.

2388 ■ EUROPEAN COUNTRIES WITH THE LEAST ECONOMIC FREEDOM, 2012

Ranked by: Score based on 50 variables in 10 areas: business freedom, trade freedom, fiscal freedom, government size, monetary freedom, investment freedom, financial freedom, property rights, freedom from corruption, and labor freedom. **Remarks:** Also notes worldwide rank and score for each criterion. **Number listed:** 43

1. Ukraine, with 46.1 points

2. Belarus, 49

3. Russia, 50.5

4. Moldova, 54.4

5. Greece, 55.4

6. Bosnia & Herzegovina, 57.3

7. Serbia, 58

7. Italy, 58.8

9. Croatia, 60.9

10. Montenegro, 62.5

10. Turkey, 62.5

Source: *Index of Economic Freedom*, (annual), The Heritage Foundation/The Wall Street Journal, 2012, p. 30-31.

2389 ■ EUROPEAN COUNTRIES WITH THE MOST ECONOMIC FREEDOM, 2012

Ranked by: Score based on 50 variables in 10 areas: business freedom, trade freedom, fiscal freedom, government size, monetary freedom, investment freedom, financial freedom, property rights, freedom from corruption, and labor freedom. **Remarks:** Also notes worldwide rank and score for each criterion. **Number listed:** 43

1. Switzerland, with 81.1 points

2. Ireland, 76.9

3. Denmark, 76.2

4. Luxembourg, 74.5

5. United Kingdom, 74.1

6. Netherlands, 73.3

7. Estonia, 73.2

8. Finland, 72.3

9. Cyprus, 71.8

10. Sweden, 71.7

Source: *Index of Economic Freedom*, (annual), The Heritage Foundation/The Wall Street Journal, 2012, p. 30-31.

2390 ■ NORTH AFRICAN AND MIDDLE EAST COUNTRIES WITH THE MOST ECONOMIC FREEDOM, 2012

Ranked by: Score based on 50 variables in 10 areas: business freedom, trade freedom, fiscal freedom, government size, monetary freedom, investment freedom, financial freedom, property rights, freedom from corruption, and labor freedom. **Remarks:** Also notes worldwide rank and score for each criterion. **Number listed:** 17

1. Bahrain, with 75.2 points
2. Qatar, 71.3
3. Jordan, 69.9
4. United Arab Emirates, 69.3
5. Oman, 67.9
6. Israel, 67.8
7. Kuwait, 62.5
7. Saudi Arabia, 62.5
9. Morocco, 60.2
10. Lebanon, 60.1

Source: *Index of Economic Freedom*, (annual), The Heritage Foundation/The Wall Street Journal, 2012, p. 36.

2391 ■ NORTH AMERICAN COUNTRIES WITH THE MOST ECONOMIC FREEDOM, 2012

Ranked by: Score based on 50 variables in 10 areas: business freedom, trade freedom, fiscal freedom, government size, monetary freedom, investment freedom, financial freedom, property rights, freedom from corruption, and labor freedom. **Remarks:** Also notes worldwide rank and score for each criterion. **Number listed:** 3

1. Canada, with 79.9 points
2. United States, 76.3
3. Mexico, 65.3

Source: *Index of Economic Freedom*, (annual), The Heritage Foundation/The Wall Street Journal, 2012, p. 28.

2392 ■ SUB-SAHARA AFRICAN COUNTRIES WITH THE LEAST ECONOMIC FREEDOM, 2012

Ranked by: Score based on 50 variables in 10 areas: business freedom, trade freedom, fiscal freedom, government size, monetary freedom, investment freedom, financial freedom, property rights, freedom from corruption, and labor freedom. **Remarks:** Also notes worldwide rank and score for each criterion. **Number listed:** 46

1. Zimbabwe, with 26.3 points
2. Eritrea, 36.2
3. Democratic Republic of Congo, 41.1
4. Equatorial Guinea, 42.8
5. Republic of Congo, 43.8
6. Chad, 44.8
7. Comoros, 45.7
8. Lesotho, 46.6
9. Angola, 46.7
10. Burundi, 48.1

Source: *Index of Economic Freedom*, (annual), The Heritage Foundation/The Wall Street Journal, 2012, p. 42-43.

2393 ■ SUB-SAHARA AFRICAN COUNTRIES WITH THE MOST ECONOMIC FREEDOM, 2012

Ranked by: Score based on 50 variables in 10 areas: business freedom, trade freedom, fiscal freedom, government size, monetary freedom, investment freedom, financial freedom, property rights, freedom from corruption, and labor freedom. **Remarks:** Also notes worldwide rank and score for each criterion. **Number listed:** 46

1. Mauritius, with 77 points

2. Botswana, 69.6
3. Rwanda, 64.9
4. Cape Verde, 63.5
5. South Africa, 62.7
5. Madagascar, 62.4
7. Namibia, 61.9
7. Uganda, 61.9
9. Ghana, 60.7
10. Burkina Faso, 60.6

Source: *Index of Economic Freedom*, (annual), The Heritage Foundation/The Wall Street Journal, 2012, p. 42-43.

Education

2394 ■ FASTEST-GROWING EDUCATION COMPANIES, 2008-2011

Ranked by: Score based on three-year growth in revenue and earnings, and three-year total return to investors. **Remarks:** Specific scores not provided. To qualify for list, companies must have revenues of at least $50 million, net income of at least $10 million, market capitalization of at least $250 million, and stock price of at least $5. Int'l companies are eligible if they trade on a U.S. exchange and file quarterly reports. **Number listed:** 5

1. Lincoln Educational Services Corp.
2. American Public Education
3. New Oriental Education & Technology Group Inc.
4. DeVry Inc.
5. ITT Educational Services

Source: *Fortune*, 100 Fastest-Growing Companies (annual), http://www.fortune.com, September 26, 2011.

2395 ■ FASTEST-GROWING PRIVATE EDUCATIONAL SERVICES/SUPPLIES COMPANIES IN THE U.S., 2007-2010

Ranked by: Average annual sales growth over three years, in percent. **Remarks:** Also notes headquarters, revenue, and rank in the overall *Inc. 500*. To qualify, private companies must have had annual revenues of at least $100,000 in 2007 and $2 million in 2010. **Number listed:** 6

1. The Armando Montelongo Co., with 8,160.6%
2. Charfen Institute, 8,007%
3. FortuneBuilders, 2,628.7%
4. Bach to Rock, 1,000%
5. Group Excellence, 773.4%
6. Trade the Markets, 772.6%

Source: *Inc.*, Inc. 500 (annual), September 2011, p. 112-114.

2396 ■ STATES WITH THE HIGHEST RATE OF EMPLOYEES IN EDUCATION AND HEALTH SERVICES, 2010

Ranked by: Percentage of nonfarm employees that are employed in the education and health services industries. **Number listed:** 51

1. Rhode Island, with 22.5%
2. Massachusetts, 21%
3. Vermont, 20.7%
4. Pennsylvania, 20.4%
5. Maine, 20.3%

6. New York, 20.1%
7. Connecticut, 19.2%
8. Minnesota, 17.5%
9. New Hampshire, 17.2%
10. Ohio, 16.8%

Source: *State Rankings*, (annual), CQ Press, 2011, p. 193.

2397 ■ STATES WITH THE LOWEST RATE OF EMPLOYEES IN EDUCATION AND HEALTH SERVICES, 2010

Ranked by: Percentage of nonfarm employees in the education and health services industries. **Number listed:** 49

1. Nevada, with 9.1%
2. Alabama, 11.5%
3. South Carolina, 11.6%
4. Colorado, 12.2%
5. Mississippi, 12.5%
6. California, 12.8%
6. Virginia, 12.8%
8. Georgia, 12.9%
9. Alaska, 13%
9. Hawaii, 13%

Source: *State Rankings*, (annual), CQ Press, 2011, p. 193.

2398 ■ TOP CHILDREN'S ENRICHMENT PROGRAM FRANCHISES, 2012

Ranked by: Cumulative score based on financial strength and stability, growth rate, size of the system, number of years in business, the length of time franchising, start-up costs, litigation, percentage of terminations, and whether the company provides financing. **Remarks:** Specific scores not provided. Also notes overall rank within the *Franchise 500*, contact information, description, year founded, year started franchising, states where registered, available U.S. regions, where seeking foreign expansion, number of franchised and company-owned units for past three years, start-up costs, franchise fees, royalty fees, and type of financing available. **Number listed:** 7

1. LearningRx
2. Young Rembrandts Franchise
3. School of Rock
4. FasTracKids International Ltd.
5. Kidville
6. The Mad Science Group
7. CompuChild

Source: *Entrepreneur*, Franchise 500 (annual), January 2012, p. 154-157.

2399 ■ TOP CHILDREN'S TUTORING FRANCHISES, 2012

Ranked by: Cumulative score based on financial strength and stability, growth rate, size of the system, number of years in business, the length of time franchising, start-up costs, litigation, percentage of terminations, and whether the company provides financing. **Remarks:** Specific scores not provided. Also notes overall rank within the *Franchise 500*, contact information, description, year founded, year started franchising, states where registered, available U.S. regions, where seeking foreign expansion, number of franchised and company-owned units for past three years, start-up costs, franchise fees, royalty fees, and type of financing available. **Number listed:** 10

1. Kumon Math & Reading Centers
2. Sylvan Learning Centers

3. E.nopi
4. Mathnasium Learning Centers
5. Tutor Doctor
6. College Nannies & Tutors
7. Club Z! In-Home Tutoring Services
8. Chyten Educational Services
9. Tutoring Club LLC
10. Huntington Learning Centers Inc.

Source: *Entrepreneur*, Franchise 500 (annual), January 2012, p. 158-159.

Eggs

2400 ■ LARGEST EGG PRODUCTION COMPANIES, 2011

Ranked by: Number of layers in production. **Number listed:** 57

1. Cal-Maine Foods, with 28,000,000 layers
2. Rose Acre Farms, 23,700,000
3. Moark LLC, 15,700,000
4. Sparboe Farms, 13,500,000
5. Rembrandt Enterprises, 12,000,000
6. Hillandale Farms of PA, 11,000,000
7. Michael Foods Inc., 10,636,000
8. Daybreak Foods, 9,500,000
9. Center Fresh Egg Group, 8,400,000
10. Midwest Poultry Services, 7,600,000

Source: *Egg Industry*, Egg Industry Survey (annual), February 2012, p. 17.

Electric Appliances, Domestic
See: **Household Appliances**

Electric Equipment

2401 ■ FRANCE'S LARGEST ELECTRICAL EQUIPMENT COMPANIES OVERALL, 2011

Ranked by: Score based on revenue, profits, assets, and market capitalization. **Remarks:** Specific scores not provided. Also notes overall rank in the *Forbes 2000* and figures for each criterion. **Number listed:** 2

1. Schneider Electric SA
2. Legrand Holding SA

Source: *Forbes*, Forbes 2000 (annual), http://www.forbes.com, May 7, 2012.

2402 ■ JAPAN'S LARGEST ELECTRICAL EQUIPMENT COMPANIES OVERALL, 2011

Ranked by: Score based on revenue, profits, assets, and market capitalization. **Remarks:** Specific scores not provided. Also notes overall rank in the *Forbes 2000* and figures for each criterion. **Number listed:** 4

1. Mitsubishi Electric Corp.
2. Nidec Corp.
3. Furukawa Electric Co., Ltd.
4. Fuji Electric Holdings Co., Ltd.

Source: *Forbes*, Forbes 2000 (annual), http://www.forbes.com, May 7, 2012.

2403 ■ JAPAN'S MOST VALUABLE ELECTRICAL COMPONENTS AND EQUIPMENT BRANDS, 2011

Ranked by: Brand value, in millions of U.S. dollars. **Remarks:** Also notes rank within the *Global 500* for current and previous year, figures for current and previous year, and brand rating. Ranking is available online only. **Number listed:** 2

1. Hitachi, with $16,391 million
2. Sanyo, $4,069

Source: *Global 500*, (annual), Brand Finance plc, March 2012.

2404 ■ LARGEST U.S. ELECTRICAL EQUIPMENT AND APPLIANCE MANUFACTURERS, 2010

Ranked by: Revenue, in millions of dollars. **Remarks:** Also notes overall rank within the *IW 500*, revenue growth, and profit margin. **Number listed:** 23

1. General Electric Co., with $150,211 million
2. Emerson Electronic Co., $21,039
3. Whirlpool Corp., $18,366
4. Eaton Corp., $13,715
5. Rockwell Automation Inc., $4,857
6. Energizer Holdings Inc., $4,248
7. Lennox International Inc., $3,096
8. Diebold Inc., $2,824
9. Exide Technologies, $2,686
10. Spectrum Brands Holdings Inc., $2,567

Source: *IndustryWeek*, IW 500 (annual), http://www.industryweek.com, July 2011.

2405 ■ LARGEST U.S. ELECTRICAL EQUIPMENT COMPANIES OVERALL, 2011

Ranked by: Score based on revenue, profits, assets, and market capitalization. **Remarks:** Specific scores not provided. Also notes overall rank in the *Forbes 2000* and figures for each criterion. **Number listed:** 3

1. Emerson Electric Co.
2. W. W. Grainger Inc.
3. Ametek Inc.

Source: *Forbes*, Forbes 2000 (annual), http://www.forbes.com, May 7, 2012.

2406 ■ TOP *FORTUNE 500* COMPANIES IN ELECTRON-ICS AND ELECTRICAL EQUIPMENT, 2011

Ranked by: Revenue, in millions of dollars. **Remarks:** Also notes overall rank in the *Fortune 500;* profits; profits as a percentage of revenue; stockholders' equity; and rank by each criterion. **Number listed:** 4

1. Emerson Electric Co., with $24,234 million
2. Whirlpool Corp., $18,666
3. Rockwell Automation Inc., $6,000
4. General Cable Corp., $5,867

Source: *Fortune*, Fortune 500 (annual), May 21, 2012, p. F-35.

2407 ■ WORLD'S LARGEST ELECTRICAL EQUIPMENT AND APPLIANCE MANUFACTURERS, 2010

Ranked by: Revenue, in millions of dollars. **Remarks:** Also notes rank for previous year, overall rank within the *IW 1000*, country, and revenue growth. **Number listed:** 28

1. General Electric Co., with $150,211 million
2. Mitsubishi Electric Corp., $41,246

3. Schneider Electric SA, $26,201
4. Emerson Electronic Co., $21,039
5. Whirlpool Corp., $18,366
6. Panasonic Electric Works Co., Ltd., $17,927
7. AB Electrolux, $15,800
8. Eaton Corp., $13,715
9. Furukawa Electric Co., Ltd., $9,959
10. Qingdao Haier Co., Ltd., $9,225

Source: *IndustryWeek*, IW 1000 (annual), http://www.industryweek.com, August 2011.

2408 ■ WORLD'S LARGEST ELECTRICAL EQUIPMENT COMPANIES OVERALL, 2011

Ranked by: Score based on revenue, profits, assets, and market capitalization. **Remarks:** Specific scores not provided. Also notes country, overall rank in the *Forbes 2000*, and figures for each criterion. **Number listed:** 15

1. ABB Ltd.
2. Schneider Electric SA
3. Mitsubishi Electric Corp.
4. Emerson Electric Co.
5. Bharat Heavy Electricals Ltd.
6. Nidec Corp.
7. W. W. Grainger Inc.
8. Cooper Industries plc
9. Legrand Holding SA
10. Dongfang Electric Corp., Ltd.

Source: *Forbes*, Forbes 2000 (annual), http://www.forbes.com, May 7, 2012.

2409 ■ WORLD'S MOST VALUABLE ELECTRICAL COMPONENTS AND EQUIPMENT BRANDS, 2011

Ranked by: Brand value, in millions of U.S. dollars. **Remarks:** Also notes rank within the *Global 500* for current and previous year, figures for current and previous year, country, and brand rating. Ranking is available online only. **Number listed:** 5

1. Hitachi, with $16,391 million
2. LG Electronics, $9,809
3. Sanyo, $4,069
4. Schneider Electric, $3,550
5. Emerson, $3,042

Source: *Global 500*, (annual), Brand Finance plc, March 2012.

2410 ■ WORLD'S MOST VALUABLE ELECTRONIC AND ELECTRIC EQUIPMENT COMPANIES, 2011

Ranked by: Market value as of March 2011, in millions of U.S. dollars. **Remarks:** Also notes rank within the *FT 500*, rank for previous year, country, revenue, net income, assets, number of employees, share price, price-to-earning ratio, dividend yield, and fiscal year-end. **Number listed:** 6

1. Schneider Electric SA, with $46,543.7 million
2. Emerson Electric Co., $44,062.8
3. Danaher Corp., $34,211.5
4. Hon Hai Precision Industry Co., Ltd., $33,839.7
5. Hitachi Ltd., $23,608.1
6. Kyocera Corp., $19,458.7

Source: *Financial Times*, FT 500 (annual), http://www.ft.com, June 24, 2011.

Electric Utilities
See also: **Gas Utilities**

2411 ■ AMERICA'S LARGEST PRIVATE UTILITIES, 2010

Ranked by: Revenue, in billions of dollars. **Remarks:** Also notes headquarters, number of employees, and overall rank in the *America's Largest Private Companies* list. Ranking is available online only, not in print. **Number listed:** 3

1. Energy Future Holdings Corp., with $8.24 billion
2. Oxbow Corp., $4
3. Drummond Co., $3.03

Source: *Forbes*, America's Largest Private Companies (annual), http://www.forbes.com, December 5, 2011.

2412 ■ CALIFORNIA'S LARGEST ELECTRIC UTILITIES OVERALL, 2011

Ranked by: Score based on revenue, profits, assets, and market capitalization. **Remarks:** Specific scores not provided. Also notes overall rank in the *Forbes 2000* and figures for each criterion. **Number listed:** 2

1. Pacific Gas & Electric Co. (PG & E)
2. Edison International

Source: *Forbes*, Forbes 2000 (annual), http://www.forbes.com, May 7, 2012.

2413 ■ LARGEST ELECTRIC, GAS, AND SANITARY SERVICES COMPANIES BY EMPLOYEES, 2010

Ranked by: Total number of employees. **Remarks:** Also notes contact information for headquarters, number of employees at headquarters, revenue, rank by revenue, and primary SIC code. **Number listed:** 49

1. Waste Management Inc., with 43,530 employees
2. Republic Services Inc., 31,000
3. AES Corp., 27,000
4. Southern Co., 26,112
5. Puget Holding Co., 22,860
6. American Electric Power Co., Inc., 21,673
7. Progress Energy Inc., 20,500
8. PG & E Corp., 19,425
9. Pacific Gas & Electric Co., 19,401
10. Edison International, 19,244

Source: *Business Rankings*, (annual), Dun & Bradstreet Inc., 2011, p. VI.106-VI.107.

2414 ■ LARGEST ELECTRIC, GAS, AND SANITARY SERVICES COMPANIES BY SALES, 2010

Ranked by: Total revenue, in dollars. **Remarks:** Also notes contact information for headquarters, number of employees at headquarters and overall, rank by employees, and primary SIC code. **Number listed:** 50

1. Enterprise Products Partners LP, with $33,739,300,000
2. Veolia Water North America Northeast LLC, $23,000,000,000
3. Exelon Corp., $18,644,000,000
4. Southern Co., $17,456,000,000
5. Nextera Energy Inc., $15,317,000,000

6. Dominion Resources Inc., $15,197,000,000
7. American Electric Power Co., Inc., $14,427,000,000
8. Constellation Energy Group Inc., $14,340,000,000
9. Duke Energy Corp., $14,272,000,000
10. AES Corp., $14,119,000,000

Source: *Business Rankings*, (annual), Dun & Bradstreet Inc., 2011, p. V.106-V.107.

2415 ■ LARGEST U.S. ELECTRIC UTILITIES OVERALL, 2011

Ranked by: Score based on revenue, profits, assets, and market capitalization. **Remarks:** Specific scores not provided. Also notes overall rank in the *Forbes 2000* and figures for each criterion. **Number listed:** 27

1. Southern Co.
2. Exelon Corp.
3. NextEra Energy Inc.
4. Duke Energy Corp.
5. Dominion Resources Inc.
6. American Electric Power Co., Inc.
7. FirstEnergy Corp.
8. PPL Corp.
9. Pacific Gas & Electric Co. (PG & E)
10. Consolidated Edison Inc.

Source: *Forbes*, Forbes 2000 (annual), http://www.forbes.com, May 7, 2012.

2416 ■ MICHIGAN'S LARGEST ELECTRIC UTILITIES OVERALL, 2011

Ranked by: Score based on revenue, profits, assets, and market capitalization. **Remarks:** Specific scores not provided. Also notes overall rank in the *Forbes 2000* and figures for each criterion. **Number listed:** 2

1. DTE Energy Co.
2. CMS Energy Corp.

Source: *Forbes*, Forbes 2000 (annual), http://www.forbes.com, May 7, 2012.

2417 ■ MOST VALUABLE U.S. ELECTRICITY COMPANIES, 2011

Ranked by: Market value as of March 2011, in millions of U.S. dollars. **Remarks:** Also notes rank within the *FT U.S. 500*, rank for previous year, country, revenue, net income, assets, number of employees, share price, price-to-earning ratio, dividend yield, and fiscal yearend. **Number listed:** 19

1. Southern Co., with $32,226.4 million
2. Exelon Corp., $27,309.7
3. Dominion Resources Inc., $25,906.6
4. FPL Group Inc., $23,202.9
5. PG & E Corp., $17,530.1
6. American Electric Power Co., Inc., $15,906
7. Public Service Enterprise Group Inc., $15,945.3
8. FirstEnergy Corp., $15,511.3
9. Consolidated Edison Inc., $14,808.7
10. Progress Energy Inc., $13,555.7

Source: *Financial Times*, FT 500 (annual), http://www.ft.com, June 24, 2011.

2418 ■ NEW JERSEY'S LARGEST ELECTRIC UTILITIES COMPANIES OVERALL, 2011

Ranked by: Score based on revenue, profits, assets, and market capitalization. **Remarks:** Specific scores not provided. Also notes overall rank in the *Forbes 2000* and figures for each criterion. **Number listed:** 2

1. Public Service Enterprise Group Inc.
2. NRG Energy Inc.

Source: *Forbes*, Forbes 2000 (annual), http://www.forbes.com, May 7, 2012.

2419 ■ NORTH CAROLINA'S LARGEST ELECTRIC UTILITIES COMPANIES OVERALL, 2011

Ranked by: Score based on revenue, profits, assets, and market capitalization. **Remarks:** Specific scores not provided. Also notes overall rank in the *Forbes 2000* and figures for each criterion. **Number listed:** 2

1. Duke Energy Corp.
2. Progress Energy Inc.

Source: *Forbes*, Forbes 2000 (annual), http://www.forbes.com, May 7, 2012.

2420 ■ OHIO'S LARGEST ELECTRIC UTILITIES OVERALL, 2011

Ranked by: Score based on revenue, profits, assets, and market capitalization. **Remarks:** Specific scores not provided. Also notes overall rank in the *Forbes 2000* and figures for each criterion. **Number listed:** 2

1. American Electric Power Co., Inc.
2. FirstEnergy Corp.

Source: *Forbes*, Forbes 2000 (annual), http://www.forbes.com, May 7, 2012.

2421 ■ STATES WITH THE HIGHEST ELECTRIC UTILITY COSTS, 2011

Ranked by: Index of state average revenue per kilowatt hour for electricity utilities relative to the U.S. average. **Number listed:** 51

1. Hawaii, with 3.02
2. Connecticut, 1.65
3. Alaska, 1.61
4. New York, 1.60
5. New Hampshire, 1.49
6. New Jersey, 1.45
7. Massachusetts, 1.43
8. Vermont, 1.38
9. California, 1.37
10. Rhode Island, 1.35

Source: *Small Business Survival Index*, (annual), Small Business & Entrepreneurship Council, November 2011, p. 50.

2422 ■ STATES WITH THE LOWEST ELECTRIC UTILITY COSTS, 2011

Ranked by: Index of state average revenue per kilowatt hour for electricity utilities relative to the U.S. average. **Number listed:** 51

1. Wyoming, with 0.65
2. Idaho, 0.67
3. Utah, 0.70
3. Washington, 0.70
5. Kentucky, 0.72

6. Arkansas, 0.73
6. North Dakota, 0.73
8. Iowa, 0.76
9. Louisiana, 0.77
9. Oklahoma, 0.77

Source: *Small Business Survival Index*, (annual), Small Business & Entrepreneurship Council, November 2011, p. 50.

2423 ■ TOP *FORTUNE 500* GAS AND ELECTRIC UTILITIES, 2011

Ranked by: Revenue, in millions of dollars. **Remarks:** Also notes overall rank in the *Fortune 500;* profits; profits as a percentage of revenue; stockholders' equity; and rank by each criterion. **Number listed:** 22

1. Exelon Corp., with $18,924 million
2. AES Corp., $17,759
3. Southern Co., $17,657
4. FirstEnergy Corp., $16,258
5. NextEra Energy Inc., $15,341
6. PG & E Corp., $14,956
7. Duke Energy Corp., $14,529
8. Dominion Resources Inc., $14,379
9. Consolidated Edison Inc., $12,938
10. Edison International, $12,760

Source: *Fortune*, Fortune 500 (annual), May 21, 2012, p. F-40.

2424 ■ TOP REGIONAL UTILITIES FOR DIVERSITY, 2011

Ranked by: Score based on strength in four areas: CEO commitment to diversity, human capital, corporate and organizational communications, and supplier diversity. **Remarks:** Specific scores not provided. To qualify, companies must have more than 1,000 U.S. employees. **Number listed:** 5

1. Southern California Edison Co.
2. Pacific Gas & Electric Co. (PG & E)
3. Consolidated Edison Co. of New York
4. Sempra Energy
5. Ameren Corp.

Source: *DiversityInc*, Top 50 (annual), 2011, p. 100.

2425 ■ TOP UTILITY COMPANIES IN ECONOMIC DEVELOPMENT, 2011

Ranked by: Score based on economic development performance, including job creation, capital investment, and innovation. **Remarks:** Specific scores not provided; companies are listed alphabetically, not ranked. Also notes headquarters, website, and comments. **Number listed:** 10

1. Alabama Power Co.
2. Ameren
3. Duke Energy Corp.
4. Entergy Corp.
5. FirstEnergy
6. Georgia Power Co.
7. Hoosier Energy
8. Hydro-Quebec
9. Progress Energy
10. Tennessee Valley Authority

Source: *Site Selection*, Top Utilities (annual), September 2011, p. 719-723.

2426 ■ THE UNITED STATES' MOST VALUABLE ELECTRIC BRANDS, 2011

Ranked by: Brand value, in millions of U.S. dollars. **Remarks:** Also notes rank within the *Global 500* for current and previous year, figures for current and previous year, and brand rating. Ranking is available online only. **Number listed:** 2

1. Southern, with $3,518 million
2. PSEG, $2,463

Source: *Global 500*, (annual), Brand Finance plc, March 2012.

2427 ■ VIRGINIA'S LARGEST ELECTRIC UTILITIES OVERALL, 2011

Ranked by: Score based on revenue, profits, assets, and market capitalization. **Remarks:** Specific scores not provided. Also notes overall rank in the *Forbes 2000* and figures for each criterion. **Number listed:** 2

1. Dominion Resources Inc.
2. The AES Corp.

Source: *Forbes*, Forbes 2000 (annual), http://www.forbes.com, May 7, 2012.

Electric Utilities, International

2428 ■ AUSTRALIA'S LARGEST ELECTRIC UTILITIES COMPANIES OVERALL, 2011

Ranked by: Score based on revenue, profits, assets, and market capitalization. **Remarks:** Specific scores not provided. Also notes overall rank in the *Forbes 2000* and figures for each criterion. **Number listed:** 2

1. Origin Energy Ltd.
2. AGL Energy Ltd.

Source: *Forbes*, Forbes 2000 (annual), http://www.forbes.com, May 7, 2012.

2429 ■ BRAZIL'S LARGEST ELECTRIC UTILITIES OVERALL, 2011

Ranked by: Score based on revenue, profits, assets, and market capitalization. **Remarks:** Specific scores not provided. Also notes overall rank in the *Forbes 2000* and figures for each criterion. **Number listed:** 4

1. Centrais Eletricas Brasileiras SA (Eletrobras)
2. Companhia Energetica de Minas Gerais (Cemig)
3. CPFL Energia
4. Copel

Source: *Forbes*, Forbes 2000 (annual), http://www.forbes.com, May 7, 2012.

2430 ■ BRITAIN'S MOST ADMIRED UTILITIES, 2011

Ranked by: Survey of peers and investment analysts based on nine criteria: quality of management, financial soundness, quality of goods/services, ability to attract and retain talent, value as long-term investment, innovation, marketing, community and environmental responsibility, and use of corporate assets. **Number listed:** 5

1. Centrica plc, with 62 points
2. Pennon Group, 61.2
3. National Grid plc, 58.7
4. Scottish & Southern Energy plc, 55.7

5. EDF Energy plc, 52.6

Source: *Management Today*, Britain's Most Admired Companies (annual), December 2011, p. 49.

2431 ■ CHINA'S LARGEST DIVERSIFIED UTILITIES COMPANIES OVERALL, 2011

Ranked by: Score based on revenue, profits, assets, and market capitalization. **Remarks:** Specific scores not provided. Also notes overall rank in the *Forbes 2000* and figures for each criterion. **Number listed:** 2

1. China Longyuan Power
2. Sinovel Wind Group

Source: *Forbes*, Forbes 2000 (annual), http://www.forbes.com, May 7, 2012.

2432 ■ CHINA'S LARGEST ELECTRIC UTILITIES COMPANIES OVERALL, 2011

Ranked by: Score based on revenue, profits, assets, and market capitalization. **Remarks:** Specific scores not provided. Also notes overall rank in the *Forbes 2000* and figures for each criterion. **Number listed:** 5

1. Huaneng Power International
2. China Yangtze Power
3. Datang International Power
4. GD Power Development
5. Huadian Power International

Source: *Forbes*, Forbes 2000 (annual), http://www.forbes.com, May 7, 2012.

2433 ■ COLOMBIA'S LARGEST ELECTRIC UTILITIES OVERALL, 2011

Ranked by: Score based on revenue, profits, assets, and market capitalization. **Remarks:** Specific scores not provided. Also notes overall rank in the *Forbes 2000* and figures for each criterion. **Number listed:** 2

1. Interconexion Electrica
2. Energia de Bogota

Source: *Forbes*, Forbes 2000 (annual), http://www.forbes.com, May 7, 2012.

2434 ■ EUROPE'S MOST VALUABLE ELECTRICITY COMPANIES, 2011

Ranked by: Market value as of March 2011, in millions of U.S. dollars. **Remarks:** Also notes rank within the *FT Europe 500*, rank for previous year, country, revenue, net income, assets, number of employees, share price, price-to-earning ratio, dividend yield, and fiscal yearend. **Number listed:** 20

1. Electricite de France, with $76,664.7 million
2. Enel SpA, $59,355.1
3. Iberdrola SA, $50,697
4. Fortum Oyj, $30,205.7
5. CEZ AS, $27,507.3
6. Scottish & Southern Energy plc, $18,938.2
7. Iberdrola Renovables SA, $18,252.7
8. Federal Grid Co., $17,665.7
9. Polska Grupa Energetyczna, $15,078.8
10. Rushydro, $14,531.3

Source: *Financial Times*, FT 500 (annual), http://www.ft.com, June 24, 2011.

2435 ■ FRANCE'S LARGEST DIVERSIFIED UTILITIES COMPANIES OVERALL, 2011

Ranked by: Score based on revenue, profits, assets, and market capitalization. **Remarks:** Specific scores not provided. Also notes overall rank in the *Forbes 2000* and figures for each criterion. **Number listed:** 2

1. Veolia Environnement SA
2. AREVA

Source: *Forbes*, Forbes 2000 (annual), http://www.forbes.com, May 7, 2012.

2436 ■ FRANCE'S LARGEST ELECTRIC UTILITIES OVERALL, 2011

Ranked by: Score based on revenue, profits, assets, and market capitalization. **Remarks:** Specific scores not provided. Also notes overall rank in the *Forbes 2000* and figures for each criterion. **Number listed:** 2

1. GDF Suez
2. Electricite de France

Source: *Forbes*, Forbes 2000 (annual), http://www.forbes.com, May 7, 2012.

2437 ■ GERMANY'S LARGEST ELECTRIC UTILITIES OVERALL, 2011

Ranked by: Score based on revenue, profits, assets, and market capitalization. **Remarks:** Specific scores not provided. Also notes overall rank in the *Forbes 2000* and figures for each criterion. **Number listed:** 3

1. RWE AG
2. E.On AG
3. Energie Baden-Wurttemberg AG

Source: *Forbes*, Forbes 2000 (annual), http://www.forbes.com, May 7, 2012.

2438 ■ GERMANY'S MOST VALUABLE ELECTRIC BRANDS, 2011

Ranked by: Brand value, in millions of U.S. dollars. **Remarks:** Also notes rank within the *Global 500* for current and previous year, figures for current and previous year, and brand rating. Ranking is available online only. **Number listed:** 3

1. E.On, with $9,695 million
2. RWE, $4,396
3. ENBW, $3,008

Source: *Global 500*, (annual), Brand Finance plc, March 2012.

2439 ■ HONG KONG'S LARGEST ELECTRIC UTILITIES OVERALL, 2011

Ranked by: Score based on revenue, profits, assets, and market capitalization. **Remarks:** Specific scores not provided. Also notes overall rank in the *Forbes 2000* and figures for each criterion. **Number listed:** 3

1. CLP Holdings Ltd.
2. China Resources Power Holdings
3. Power Assets Holdings Ltd.

Source: *Forbes*, Forbes 2000 (annual), http://www.forbes.com, May 7, 2012.

2440 ■ INDIA'S LARGEST ELECTRIC UTILITIES OVERALL, 2011

Ranked by: Score based on revenue, profits, assets, and market capitalization. **Remarks:** Specific scores not provided. Also notes overall rank in the *Forbes 2000* and figures for each criterion. **Number listed:** 4

1. NTPC Ltd.
2. Power Grid of India
3. NHPC Ltd.
4. Tata Power Co., Ltd.

Source: *Forbes*, Forbes 2000 (annual), http://www.forbes.com, May 7, 2012.

2441 ■ ITALY'S LARGEST ELECTRIC UTILITIES OVERALL, 2011

Ranked by: Score based on revenue, profits, assets, and market capitalization. **Remarks:** Specific scores not provided. Also notes overall rank in the *Forbes 2000* and figures for each criterion. **Number listed:** 4

1. Enel SpA
2. Edison SpA
3. Terna
4. A2A

Source: *Forbes*, Forbes 2000 (annual), http://www.forbes.com, May 7, 2012.

2442 ■ JAPAN'S LARGEST ELECTRIC UTILITIES OVERALL, 2011

Ranked by: Score based on revenue, profits, assets, and market capitalization. **Remarks:** Specific scores not provided. Also notes overall rank in the *Forbes 2000* and figures for each criterion. **Number listed:** 10

1. The Kansai Electric Power Co., Inc.
2. Chubu Electric Power
3. Kyushu Electric Power
4. Tokyo Electric Power Co., Inc.
5. Tohoku Electric Power
6. Chugoku Electric Power
7. Shikoku Electric Power
8. Electric Power Development
9. Hokkaido Electric Power
10. Hokuriku Electric Power

Source: *Forbes*, Forbes 2000 (annual), http://www.forbes.com, May 7, 2012.

2443 ■ JAPAN'S MOST VALUABLE ELECTRIC BRANDS, 2011

Ranked by: Brand value, in millions of U.S. dollars. **Remarks:** Also notes rank within the *Global 500* for current and previous year, figures for current and previous year, and brand rating. Ranking is available online only. **Number listed:** 3

1. TEPCO, with $3,479 million
2. Chubu Electric Power, $3,090
3. Kansai Electric Power, $2,377

Source: *Global 500*, (annual), Brand Finance plc, March 2012.

2444 ■ MOST PROFITABLE CANADIAN UTILITIES, 2011

Ranked by: Profits, in millions of Canadian dollars. **Number listed:** 6

1. Just Energy Group Inc., with C$515.4 million
2. Canadian Utilities Ltd., C$515
3. Fortis Inc., C$347
4. ATCO Ltd., C$327
5. TransAlta Corp., C$305

6. Emera Inc., C$247.7

Source: *Canadian Business*, Investor 500 (annual), 2012, p. 55.

2445 ■ RUSSIA'S LARGEST ELECTRIC UTILITIES OVERALL, 2011

Ranked by: Score based on revenue, profits, assets, and market capitalization. **Remarks:** Specific scores not provided. Also notes overall rank in the *Forbes 2000* and figures for each criterion. **Number listed:** 4

1. IDGC Holding
2. RusHydro
3. Federal Grid
4. Inter Rao

Source: *Forbes*, Forbes 2000 (annual), http://www.forbes.com, May 7, 2012.

2446 ■ SPAIN'S LARGEST ELECTRIC UTILITIES OVERALL, 2011

Ranked by: Score based on revenue, profits, assets, and market capitalization. **Remarks:** Specific scores not provided. Also notes overall rank in the *Forbes 2000* and figures for each criterion. **Number listed:** 2

1. Iberdrola SA
2. Red Electrica

Source: *Forbes*, Forbes 2000 (annual), http://www.forbes.com, May 7, 2012.

2447 ■ SPAIN'S MOST VALUABLE ELECTRIC BRANDS, 2011

Ranked by: Brand value, in millions of U.S. dollars. **Remarks:** Also notes rank within the *Global 500* for current and previous year, figures for current and previous year, and brand rating. Ranking is available online only. **Number listed:** 2

1. Iberdrola, with $7,468 million
2. Endesa, $3,300

Source: *Global 500*, (annual), Brand Finance plc, March 2012.

2448 ■ TOP CANADIAN GAS AND ELECTRICAL UTILITIES, 2010

Ranked by: Revenue, in thousands of Canadian dollars (unless otherwise noted). **Remarks:** Also notes percent change from previous year. **Number listed:** 10

1. Hydro-Quebec, with C$12,536,000 thousand
2. Direct Energy Marketing Ltd., C$9,480,000
3. Ontario Power Generation Inc., C$6,046,000
4. British Columbia Hydro & Power Authority, C$3,952,000
5. Fortis Inc., C$3,664,000
6. TransAlta Corp., C$2,846,000
7. Canadian Utilities, C$2,716,200
8. Toronto Hydro Corp., C$2,621,213
9. Enbridge Gas Distribution, C$2,538,000
10. ENMAX Corp., C$2,404,200

Source: *Report on Business Magazine*, Top 1000 Companies (annual), http://www.reportonbusiness.com, June 2011.

2449 ■ TOP DIVERSIFIED UTILITY COMPANIES, 2010

Ranked by: Score based on asset worth, revenue, profits, earnings per share, and return on invested capital. **Remarks:** Specific scores not provided. Also notes rank in the overall *Top 250.* **Number listed:** 33

1. RWE AG
2. Centrica plc
3. GDF Suez
4. National Grid plc
5. Dominion Resources Inc.
6. Public Service Enterprise Group Inc.
7. Veolia Environnement SA
8. PG & E Corp.
9. Consolidated Edison Inc.
10. Midamerican Energy

Source: *Platts*, Top 250 Global Energy Company Rankings (annual), http://www.platts.com/top250, November 2, 2011.

2450 ■ TOP ELECTRIC UTILITY COMPANIES, 2010

Ranked by: Score based on asset worth, revenue, profits, earnings per share, and return on invested capital. **Remarks:** Specific scores not provided. Also notes rank in the overall *Top 250.* **Number listed:** 71

1. E.On AG
2. Endesa SA
3. Scottish & Southern Energy plc
4. Exelon Corp.
5. Enel SpA
6. Iberdrola SA
7. Energie Baden-Wurttemberg AG
8. CEZ AS
9. Vattenfall AB
10. Southern Co.

Source: *Platts*, Top 250 Global Energy Company Rankings (annual), http://www.platts.com/top250, November 2, 2011.

2451 ■ UNITED KINGDOM'S LARGEST DIVERSIFIED UTILITIES COMPANIES OVERALL, 2011

Ranked by: Score based on revenue, profits, assets, and market capitalization. **Remarks:** Specific scores not provided. Also notes overall rank in the *Forbes 2000* and figures for each criterion. **Number listed:** 2

1. United Utilities Group plc
2. Severn Trent plc

Source: *Forbes*, Forbes 2000 (annual), http://www.forbes.com, May 7, 2012.

2452 ■ UNITED KINGDOM'S LARGEST ELECTRIC UTILITIES OVERALL, 2011

Ranked by: Score based on revenue, profits, assets, and market capitalization. **Remarks:** Specific scores not provided. Also notes country, overall rank in the *Forbes 2000,* and figures for each criterion. **Number listed:** 2

1. SSE plc
2. Drax Group plc

Source: *Forbes*, Forbes 2000 (annual), http://www.forbes.com, May 7, 2012.

2453 ■ THE UNITED KINGDOM'S MOST VALUABLE ELECTRIC BRANDS, 2011

Ranked by: Brand value, in millions of U.S. dollars. **Remarks:** Also notes rank within the *Global 500* for current and previous year, figures for current and previous year, and brand rating. Ranking is available online only. **Number listed:** 3

1. National Grid, with $3,401 million
2. Scottish & Southern Energy, $2,990
3. International Power, $2,462

Source: *Global 500*, (annual), Brand Finance plc, March 2012.

2454 ■ WORLD'S LARGEST DIVERSIFIED UTILITIES COMPANIES OVERALL, 2011

Ranked by: Score based on revenue, profits, assets, and market capitalization. **Remarks:** Specific scores not provided. Also notes country, overall rank in the *Forbes 2000,* and figures for each criterion. **Number listed:** 10

1. Veolia Environnement SA
2. AREVA
3. Companhia de Saneamento Basico do Estado de Sao Paulo (SABESP)
4. United Utilities Group plc
5. YTL Corporation Bhd.
6. Severn Trust plc
7. American Water Works Co.
8. China Longyuan Power Group Ltd.
9. GCL-Poly Energy Holdings Ltd.
10. Sinovel Wind Group Co., Ltd.

Source: *Forbes*, Forbes 2000 (annual), http://www.forbes.com, May 7, 2012.

2455 ■ WORLD'S LARGEST ELECTRIC UTILITIES OVERALL, 2011

Ranked by: Score based on revenue, profits, assets, and market capitalization. **Remarks:** Specific scores not provided. Also notes country, overall rank in the *Forbes 2000,* and figures for each criterion. **Number listed:** 86

1. GDF Suez
2. Electricite de France
3. Enel SpA
4. Iberdrola SA
5. RWE AG
6. Southern Co.
7. Exelon Corp.
8. SSE plc
9. The Kansai Electric Power Co., Inc.
10. NextEra Energy Inc.

Source: *Forbes*, Forbes 2000 (annual), http://www.forbes.com, May 7, 2012.

2456 ■ WORLD'S MOST ADMIRED ELECTRIC AND GAS UTILITIES, 2012

Ranked by: Score, on a scale of 10, based on a survey of executives, directors, and securities analysts of companies within their own industry on eight criteria: innovation, financial soundness, employee talent, use of corporate assets, long-term investment value, social responsibility, quality of management, and quality of products/services. **Remarks:** Specific scores not provided. Also notes rank for previous year. **Number listed:** 5

1. NextEra Energy Inc.
1. Dominion Resources Inc.
3. Southern Co.
4. Public Service Enterprise Group Inc.
5. Exelon Corp.

Source: *Fortune*, World's Most Admired Companies (annual), March 19, 2012, p. 149.

2457 ■ WORLD'S MOST ETHICAL ELECTRIC UTILITIES, 2012

Ranked by: Score based on five criteria: ethics and compliance program; reputation, leadership, and innovation; governance; corporate citizenship and responsibility; and culture of ethics. **Remarks:** Specific scores not provided; companies are listed alphabetically, not ranked. **Number listed:** 3

1. Energias de Portugal SA (EDP; Portugal)
2. ENMAX Corp. (Canada)
3. National Grid plc (U.K./U.S.)

Source: *Ethisphere Magazine*, World's Most Ethical Companies (annual), http://www.ethisphere.com, 2012.

2458 ■ WORLD'S MOST VALUABLE ELECTRIC BRANDS, 2011

Ranked by: Brand value, in millions of U.S. dollars. **Remarks:** Also notes rank within the *Global 500* for current and previous year, figures for current and previous year, country, and brand rating. Ranking is available online only. **Number listed:** 17

1. E.On, with $9,695 million
2. EDF, $7,690
3. Iberdrola, $7,468
4. Enel, $6,009
5. RWE, $4,396
6. Southern Co., $3,518
7. TEPCO, $3,479
8. National Grid, $3,401
9. Korea Electric, $3,302
10. Endesa, $3,300

Source: *Global 500*, (annual), Brand Finance plc, March 2012.

2459 ■ WORLD'S MOST VALUABLE ELECTRICITY COMPANIES, 2011

Ranked by: Market value as of March 2011, in millions of U.S. dollars. **Remarks:** Also notes rank within the *FT 500*, rank for previous year, country, revenue, net income, assets, number of employees, share price, price-to-earning ratio, dividend yield, and fiscal year-end. **Number listed:** 14

1. Electricite de France, with $76,654.7 million
2. Enel SpA, $59,355.1
3. Iberdrola SA, $50,697
4. National Thermal Power Corp., $35,685
5. Southern Co., $32,226.4
6. Fortum Oyj, $30,205.7
7. CEZ AS, $27,507.3
8. Exelon Corp., $27,309.7
9. Dominion Resources Inc., $25,906.6
10. FPL Group Inc., $23,202.9

Source: *Financial Times*, FT 500 (annual), http://www.ft.com, June 24, 2011.

Electronic Commerce

2460 ■ FASTEST-GROWING ONLINE RETAILERS, 2009-2010

Ranked by: Annual gain in basis points. **Remarks:** To qualify, chains must have annual revenues of at least $100 million. Also notes sales and market share for current and previous year. **Number listed:** 9

1. Amazon.com, with 2,343 points
2. Apple, 558
3. Wal-Mart, 360
4. Liz Claiborne, 298
5. L. L. Bean, 98
6. Macy's, 94
7. Kohl's, 89
8. Target, 66
9. Overstock.com, 47

Source: *Stores*, Hot 100 (annual), August 2011, p. s14.

2461 ■ LARGEST U.S. INTERNET AND CATALOG RETAILERS OVERALL, 2011

Ranked by: Score based on revenue, profits, assets, and market capitalization. **Remarks:** Specific scores not provided. Also notes overall rank in the *Forbes 2000* and figures for each criterion. **Number listed:** 4

1. eBay Inc.
2. Amazon.com Inc.
3. Liberty Interactive Corp.
4. Groupon Inc.

Source: *Forbes*, Forbes 2000 (annual), http://www.forbes.com, May 7, 2012.

2462 ■ MOST POPULAR ONLINE RETAILERS, 2011

Ranked by: Score based on consumer preferences. **Remarks:** Specific scores not provided. Also notes headquarters, main product, and comments. **Number listed:** 50

1. Amazon.com Inc.
2. Wal-Mart.com
3. eBay.com
4. BestBuy.com
5. JCPenney.com
6. Kohls.com
7. Target.com
8. Macys.com
9. Sears.com
10. Google.com

Source: *Stores*, Favorite 50 (annual), http://www.stores.org, September 2011.

2463 ■ TOP EUROPEAN RETAILERS IN E-COMMERCE, 2012

Ranked by: Online sales. **Remarks:** Specific figures not provided. **Number listed:** 400

1. Amazon.com Inc.
2. Otto Group
3. Tesco Stores
4. Staples Inc.
5. PPR SA
6. Home Retail Group
7. Shop Direct Group
8. Apple Inc.
9. CDiscount.com
10. 3 Suisses

Source: *Internet Retailer*, Europe 400 (annual), http://www.internetretailer.com, 2012.

2464 ■ TOP *FORTUNE 500* COMPANIES IN INTERNET SERVICES AND RETAILING, 2011

Ranked by: Revenue, in millions of dollars. **Remarks:** Also notes overall rank in the *Fortune 500;* profits; profits as a percentage of revenue; stockholders' equity; and rank by each criterion. **Number listed:** 5

1. Amazon.com Inc., with $48,077 million
2. Google Inc., $37,905
3. eBay Inc., $11,652
4. Liberty Interactive Corp., $11,624
5. Yahoo! Inc., $4,984

Source: *Fortune*, Fortune 500 (annual), May 21, 2012, p. F-37.

2465 ■ TOP U.S. AND CANADIAN RETAILERS IN E-COMMERCE, 2011

Ranked by: Online sales. **Remarks:** Specific figures not provided. **Number listed:** 500

1. Amazon.com Inc.
2. Staples Inc.
3. Apple Inc.
4. Dell Inc.
5. Office Depot Inc.
6. Walmart.com
7. Sears Holdings Corp.
8. Liberty Media Corp.
9. OfficeMax Inc.
10. CDW Corp.

Source: *Internet Retailer*, Top 500 (annual), http://www.internetretailer.com, 2011.

2466 ■ TOP WEBSITES OF APPAREL AND ACCESSORIES SPECIALTY STORES, 2011

Ranked by: Score based on successful utilization of the Internet to achieve a strategic goal and to showcase best practices. **Remarks:** Specific scores not provided; companies are listed alphabetically, not ranked. Also includes profile and comments. **Number listed:** 28

1. Abercrombie.com
2. AE.com
3. AnnTaylor.com
4. Ariat.com
5. Coach.com
6. Customink.com
7. Eshakti.com
8. Express.com
9. Eyefly.com
10. FreshPair.com

Source: *Internet Retailer*, Hot 100 - Best Retail Web Sites (annual), http://www.internetretailer.com, December 2011.

2467 ■ TOP WEBSITES FOR FOOD AND DRUG RETAILING, 2011

Ranked by: Score based on successful utilization of the Internet to achieve a strategic goal and to showcase best practices. **Remarks:** Specific scores not provided; companies are listed alphabetically, not ranked. Also includes profile and comments. **Number listed:** 9

1. AbesMarket.com
2. CellarThief.com

3. EdibleArrangements.com
4. FamousCookies.com
5. KingArthurFlour.com
6. MyExtraGum.com
7. OldTimeCandy.com
8. RepublicOfTea.com
9. StarbuckStore.com

Source: *Internet Retailer*, Hot 100 - Best Retail Web Sites (annual), http://www.internetretailer.com, December 2011.

2468 ■ TOP WEBSITES FOR HEALTH AND BEAUTY RETAILING, 2011

Ranked by: Score based on successful utilization of the Internet to achieve a strategic goal and to showcase best practices.
Remarks: Specific scores not provided; companies are listed alphabetically, not ranked. Also includes profile and comments.
Number listed: 7

1. 1800Contacts.com
2. BenefitCosmetics.com
3. Clinique.com
4. H2OPlus.com
5. MacCosmetics.com
6. Smashbox.com
7. StockNGo.com

Source: *Internet Retailer*, Hot 100 - Best Retail Web Sites (annual), http://www.internetretailer.com, December 2011.

2469 ■ TOP WEBSITES OF MASS MERCHANTS AND DEPARTMENT STORES, 2011

Ranked by: Score based on successful utilization of the Internet to achieve a strategic goal and to showcase best practices.
Remarks: Specific scores not provided; companies are listed alphabetically, not ranked. Also includes profile and comments.
Number listed: 5

1. Amazon.com
2. Buy.com
3. HSN.com
4. Kohls.com
5. Overstock.com

Source: *Internet Retailer*, Hot 100 - Best Retail Web Sites (annual), http://www.internetretailer.com, December 2011.

2470 ■ TOP WEBSITES FOR MOBILE COMMERCE, 2011

Ranked by: Score based on successful utilization of the Internet to achieve a strategic goal and to showcase best practices.
Remarks: Specific scores not provided; companies are listed alphabetically, not ranked. Also includes profile and comments.
Number listed: 10

1. Bluefly.com
2. eBay.com
3. Gap.com
4. JCP.com
5. OfficeDepot.com
6. PacSun.com
7. RedCats.com
8. Sephora.com
9. SwimOutlet.com
10. Threadless.com

Source: *Internet Retailer*, Hot 100 - Best Retail Web Sites (annual), http://www.internetretailer.com, December 2011.

2471 ■ TOP WEBSITES OF NON-APPAREL SPECIALTY STORES, 2011

Ranked by: Score based on successful utilization of the Internet to achieve a strategic goal and to showcase best practices.
Remarks: Specific scores not provided; companies are listed alphabetically, not ranked. Also includes profile and comments.
Number listed: 11

1. 3FlOz.com
2. Art.com
3. BabiesRUs.com
4. Babybot.com
5. Case-Mate.com
6. Groupon.com
7. LivingSocial.com
8. Redoxx.com
9. SkinIt.com
10. SkyMall.com

Source: *Internet Retailer*, Hot 100 - Best Retail Web Sites (annual), http://www.internetretailer.com, December 2011.

2472 ■ TOP WEBSITES FOR THE RETAILING OF BOOKS, FILM, AND MUSIC, 2011

Ranked by: Score based on successful utilization of the Internet to achieve a strategic goal and to showcase best practices.
Remarks: Specific scores not provided; companies are listed alphabetically, not ranked. Also includes profile and comments.
Number listed: 6

1. BarnesandNoble.com
2. BetterWorldBooks.com
3. Fandango.com
4. GameFly.com
5. Netflix.com
6. Samash.com

Source: *Internet Retailer*, Hot 100 - Best Retail Web Sites (annual), http://www.internetretailer.com, December 2011.

2473 ■ TOP WEBSITES FOR THE RETAILING OF COMPUTERS AND ELECTRONICS, 2011

Ranked by: Score based on successful utilization of the Internet to achieve a strategic goal and to showcase best practices.
Remarks: Specific scores not provided; companies are listed alphabetically, not ranked. Also includes profile and comments.
Number listed: 5

1. Apple.com
2. BestBuy.com
3. GoHastings.com
4. JayBirdGear.com
5. RadioShack.com

Source: *Internet Retailer*, Hot 100 - Best Retail Web Sites (annual), http://www.internetretailer.com, December 2011.

2474 ■ TOP WEBSITES FOR THE RETAILING OF FLOWERS, GIFTS, AND JEWELRY, 2011

Ranked by: Score based on successful utilization of the Internet to achieve a strategic goal and to showcase best practices.
Remarks: Specific scores not provided; companies are listed alphabetically, not ranked. Also includes profile and comments.
Number listed: 9

1. 1800Flowers.com
2. AmericanGreetings.com
3. BaubleBar.com
4. BlueNile.com
5. Gemvara.com
6. Hallmark.com
7. Ice.com
8. UncommonGoods.com
9. VermontTeddyBear.com

Source: *Internet Retailer*, Hot 100 - Best Retail Web Sites (annual), http://www.internetretailer.com, December 2011.

2475 ■ TOP WEBSITES FOR THE RETAILING OF HOUSE-WARES, HARDWARE, AND HOME FURNISHINGS, 2011

Ranked by: Score based on successful utilization of the Internet to achieve a strategic goal and to showcase best practices. **Remarks:** Specific scores not provided; companies are listed alphabetically, not ranked. Also includes profile and comments. **Number listed:** 8

1. Fab.com
2. OverstockArt.com
3. RoomAndBoard.com
4. RugsDirect.com
5. SurLaTable.com
6. Tempurpedic.com
7. TheGardenGates.com
8. Williams-Sonoma.com

Source: *Internet Retailer*, Hot 100 - Best Retail Web Sites (annual), http://www.internetretailer.com, December 2011.

2476 ■ TOP WEBSITES FOR THE RETAILING OF OFFICE SUPPLIES, 2011

Ranked by: Score based on successful utilization of the Internet to achieve a strategic goal and to showcase best practices. **Remarks:** Specific scores not provided; companies are listed alphabetically, not ranked. Also includes profile and comments. **Number listed:** 4

1. OfficeMax.com
2. ParadisePen.com
3. Staples.com
4. UltOffice.com

Source: *Internet Retailer*, Hot 100 - Best Retail Web Sites (annual), http://www.internetretailer.com, December 2011.

2477 ■ TOP WEBSITES FOR THE RETAILING OF TOYS, HOBBIES, AND SPORTING GOODS, 2011

Ranked by: Score based on successful utilization of the Internet to achieve a strategic goal and to showcase best practices. **Remarks:** Specific scores not provided; companies are listed alphabetically, not ranked. Also includes profile and comments. **Number listed:** 8

1. Burton.com
2. Cabelas.com
3. ChainLove.com
4. Evo.com
5. FatBrainToys.com
6. Lego.com
7. Puma.com
8. SaltLife.com

Source: *Internet Retailer*, Hot 100 - Best Retail Web Sites (annual), http://www.internetretailer.com, December 2011.

2478 ■ WORLD'S LARGEST INTERNET AND CATALOG RETAILERS OVERALL, 2011

Ranked by: Score based on revenue, profits, assets, and market capitalization. **Remarks:** Specific scores not provided. Also notes country, overall rank in the *Forbes 2000,* and figures for each criterion. **Number listed:** 5

1. eBay Inc.
2. Amazon.com Inc.
3. Liberty Interactive Corp.
4. Rakuten Inc.
5. Groupon Inc.

Source: *Forbes*, Forbes 2000 (annual), http://www.forbes.com, May 7, 2012.

Electronic Commerce—Advertising

2479 ■ TOP ADVERTISERS ON THE INTERNET, 2010

Ranked by: Measured advertising spending, in millions of dollars. **Remarks:** Also notes percent change from previous year. **Number listed:** 10

1. TD Ameritrade Holding Corp., with $262.9 million
2. Experian Group, $250.4
3. FMR Corp., $242.6
4. Sprint Nextel Corp., $241.1
5. General Motors Co., $240
6. E*Trade Financial Corp., $191.2
7. Walt Disney Co., $186.9
8. Scottrade, $181.8
9. Netflix Inc., $177.6
10. Verizon Communications Inc., $169.2

Source: *Advertising Age*, Leading National Advertisers (annual), June 20, 2011, p. 16-17.

2480 ■ TOP DIGITAL AD NETWORKS, 2011

Ranked by: Number of unique visitors reached during the month of December, in millions. **Number listed:** 6

1. Google Ad Network, with 204.8 million visitors
2. Yahoo! Network Plus, 187.1
3. AOL Advertising, 185.4
4. AT&T AdWorks, 182.7
5. ValueClick Networks, 181
6. Specific Media, 180.6

Source: *Advertising Age*, Digital Issue (annual), February 27, 2012, p. 16.

2481 ■ TOP PLAYERS IN THE DIGITAL WORLD, 2012

Ranked by: Score based on impact of change in digital media and marketing. **Remarks:** Specific scores not provided. **Number listed:** 10

1. Louis C. K.
2. Unilever
3. HBO GO
4. Pinterest
5. Windows phone

6. Sopa protesters
7. YouTube
8. Wal-Mart Stores Inc.
9. B-Reel
10. Buzzfeed

Source: *Advertising Age*, Digital A-List (annual), February 27, 2012, p. 29-40.

Electronic Communications
See: **Communication Industry**

Electronic Data Processing
See: **Computer Industry**

Electronic Industry
See also: **Home Electronics**

2482 ■ CALIFORNIA'S LARGEST ELECTRONICS COMPANIES OVERALL, 2011

Ranked by: Score based on revenue, profits, assets, and market capitalization. **Remarks:** Specific scores not provided. Also notes overall rank in the *Forbes 2000* and figures for each criterion. **Number listed:** 2

1. Agilent Technologies Inc.
2. Ingram Micro Inc.

Source: *Forbes*, Forbes 2000 (annual), http://www.forbes.com, May 7, 2012.

2483 ■ EUROPE'S MOST VALUABLE ELECTRONIC AND ELECTRIC EQUIPMENT COMPANIES, 2011

Ranked by: Market value as of March 2011, in millions of U.S. dollars. **Remarks:** Also notes rank within the *FT Europe 500*, rank for previous year, country, revenue, net income, assets, number of employees, share price, price-to-earning ratio, dividend yield, and fiscal yearend. **Number listed:** 6

1. Schneider Electric SA, with $46,543.7 million
2. Legrand Holding SA, $10,967.6
3. Hexagon, $8,081
4. Rexel, $6,573.8
5. Prysmian, $4,600.2
6. Gemalto, $4,334.7

Source: *Financial Times*, FT 500 (annual), http://www.ft.com, June 24, 2011.

2484 ■ FLORIDA'S LARGEST ELECTRONICS COMPANIES OVERALL, 2011

Ranked by: Score based on revenue, profits, assets, and market capitalization. **Remarks:** Specific scores not provided. Also notes overall rank in the *Forbes 2000* and figures for each criterion. **Number listed:** 2

1. Jabil Circuit Inc.
2. Tech Data Corp.

Source: *Forbes*, Forbes 2000 (annual), http://www.forbes.com, May 7, 2012.

2485 ■ JAPAN'S LARGEST ELECTRONICS COMPANIES OVERALL, 2011

Ranked by: Score based on revenue, profits, assets, and market capitalization. **Remarks:** Specific scores not provided. Also notes overall rank in the *Forbes 2000* and figures for each criterion. **Number listed:** 10

1. Hitachi Ltd.
2. Toshiba Corp.
3. Kyocera Corp.
4. Murata Manufacturing
5. NEC Corp.
6. TDK
7. Hoya
8. Keyence
9. Nippon Electric Glass
10. Omron

Source: *Forbes*, Forbes 2000 (annual), http://www.forbes.com, May 7, 2012.

2486 ■ JAPAN'S MOST VALUABLE ELECTRONICS BRANDS, 2011

Ranked by: Brand value, in millions of U.S. dollars. **Remarks:** Also notes rank within the *Global 500* for current and previous year, figures for current and previous year, and brand rating. Ranking is available online only. **Number listed:** 3

1. Toshiba, with $14,185 million
2. NEC, $3,599
3. Kyocera, $2,407

Source: *Global 500*, (annual), Brand Finance plc, March 2012.

2487 ■ LARGEST AEROSPACE AND ELECTRONICS COMPANIES IN EUROPE, 2010

Ranked by: Sales, in millions of U.S. dollars. **Remarks:** Also notes rank within country. **Number listed:** 100

1. Siemens AG (Germany), with $108,568.5 million
2. Nova Test 11 (Germany), $108,568.5
3. Nokia Oyj (Finland), $60,951.4
4. European Aeronautic Defense & Space Co. (EADS, Netherlands), $55,461.4
5. Koninklijke Philips Electronics NV (Royal Philips Electronics NV, Netherlands), $34,486.7
6. BAE Systems plc (U.K.), $30,561
7. Telefonaktiebolaget LM Ericsson (Sweden), $29,443.6
8. Alcatel-Lucent (France), $23,938.9
9. Finmeccanica SpA (Italy), $21,194.7
10. AB Electrolux (Sweden), $15,562.2

Source: *Europe's 15,000 Largest Companies*, (annual), ELC International, 2011, p. 34.

2488 ■ LARGEST COMPANIES IN THE ELECTRONIC/ ELECTRICAL EQUIPMENT AND COMPONENTS INDUSTRY BY EMPLOYEES, 2010

Ranked by: Total number of employees. **Remarks:** Also notes contact information for headquarters, number of employees at headquarters, revenue, rank by revenue, and primary SIC code. **Number listed:** 48

1. Intel Corp., with 79,800 employees
2. Tyco Electronics Corp., 75,000
3. Raytheon Intelligence & Information Systems Inc., 72,115
4. Whirlpool Corp., 70,758
5. Eaton Corp., 70,155
6. Jabil Circuit Inc., 69,000

7. L-3 Communications Holdings Inc., 67,074
8. L-3 Communications Corp., 66,145
9. Maytag Corp., 60,000
10. Motorola Solutions Inc., 53,000

Source: *Business Rankings*, (annual), Dun & Bradstreet Inc., 2011, p. VI.80-VI.81.

2489 ■ LARGEST COMPANIES IN THE ELECTRONIC/ ELECTRICAL EQUIPMENT AND COMPONENTS INDUSTRY BY SALES, 2010

Ranked by: Total revenue, in dollars, for companies outside the computer equipment industry. **Remarks:** Also notes contact information for headquarters, number of employees at headquarters and overall, rank by employees, and primary SIC code. **Number listed:** 50

1. Intel Corp., with $43,623,000,000
2. Motorola Solutions Inc., $19,282,000,000
3. Whirlpool Corp., $18,366,000,000
4. L-3 Communications Holdings Inc., $15,680,000,000
5. Texas Instruments Inc., $13,966,000,000
6. Eaton Corp., $13,715,000,000
7. Jabil Circuit Inc., $13,409,411,000
8. Sony Broadband Entertainment Corp., $11,500,000,000
9. ITT Corp., $10,995,000,000
10. QUALCOMM Inc., $10,991,000,000

Source: *Business Rankings*, (annual), Dun & Bradstreet Inc., 2011, p. V.80-V.81.

2490 ■ LARGEST U.S. ELECTRONICS COMPANIES OVERALL, 2011

Ranked by: Score based on revenue, profits, assets, and market capitalization. **Remarks:** Specific scores not provided. Also notes overall rank in the *Forbes 2000* and figures for each criterion. **Number listed:** 7

1. Agilent Technologies Inc.
2. Avnet Inc.
3. Arrow Electronics Inc.
4. Jabil Circuit Inc.
5. Ingram Micro Inc.
6. Amphenol Corp.
7. Tech Data Corp.

Source: *Forbes*, Forbes 2000 (annual), http://www.forbes.com, May 7, 2012.

2491 ■ MOST VALUABLE U.S. ELECTRONIC AND ELECTRIC EQUIPMENT COMPANIES, 2011

Ranked by: Market value as of March 2011, in millions of U.S. dollars. **Remarks:** Also notes rank within the *FT U.S. 500*, rank for previous year, country, revenue, net income, assets, number of employees, share price, price-to-earning ratio, dividend yield, and fiscal yearend. **Number listed:** 9

1. Emerson Electric Co., with $44,062.8 million
2. Danaher Corp., $34,211.5
3. TE Connectivity Ltd., $15,511.7
4. Agilent Technologies Inc., $15,454.6
5. Cooper Industries Ltd., $10,700.3
6. Amphenol Corp., $9,569

7. Roper Industries Inc., $8,242.8
8. Ametek Inc., $7,056.4
9. Trimble Navigation Ltd., $5,188.6

Source: *Financial Times*, FT 500 (annual), http://www.ft.com, June 24, 2011.

2492 ■ SOUTH KOREA'S LARGEST ELECTRONICS COMPANIES OVERALL, 2011

Ranked by: Score based on revenue, profits, assets, and market capitalization. **Remarks:** Specific scores not provided. Also notes overall rank in the *Forbes 2000* and figures for each criterion. **Number listed:** 2

1. LG Display Co., Ltd.
2. Samsung Electro-Mechanics Co., Ltd.

Source: *Forbes*, Forbes 2000 (annual), http://www.forbes.com, May 7, 2012.

2493 ■ TAIWAN'S LARGEST ELECTRONICS COMPANIES OVERALL, 2011

Ranked by: Score based on revenue, profits, assets, and market capitalization. **Remarks:** Specific scores not provided. Also notes overall rank in the *Forbes 2000* and figures for each criterion. **Number listed:** 5

1. Hon Hai Precision Industry Co., Ltd.
2. AU Optronics Corp.
3. Delta Electronics
4. Pegatron
5. WPG Holdings

Source: *Forbes*, Forbes 2000 (annual), http://www.forbes.com, May 7, 2012.

2494 ■ TOP ELECTRONICS COMPANIES IN CORPORATE FACILITY PROJECTS, 2011

Ranked by: Investment in new or expanded facilities, in millions of dollars. **Remarks:** Also notes location, product line, and whether facility is new or expanded. **Number listed:** 10

1. Intel Corp. (U.S.), with $5,000 million
2. IM Flash Technologies, $1,500
3. MEMC Electronic Materials/Samsung Group, $1,000
3. Qatar Solar Technologies, $1,000
5. Robert Bosch GmbH, $722
6. Bosch Solar Energy AG, $701
6. Panasonic Corp., $651
8. Intel Corp. (Ireland), $500
9. AQT Solar, $460
10. LG Chem, $455

Source: *Site Selection*, Top Industries (annual), March 2012, p. 121.

2495 ■ TOP *FORTUNE 500* COMPANIES IN ELECTRONICS AND ELECTRICAL EQUIPMENT, 2011

Ranked by: Revenue, in millions of dollars. **Remarks:** Also notes overall rank in the *Fortune 500;* profits; profits as a percentage of revenue; stockholders' equity; and rank by each criterion. **Number listed:** 4

1. Emerson Electric Co., with $24,234 million
2. Whirlpool Corp., $18,666
3. Rockwell Automation Inc., $6,000

4. General Cable Corp., $5,867

Source: *Fortune*, Fortune 500 (annual), May 21, 2012, p. F-35.

2496 ■ WORLD'S LARGEST ELECTRONICS COMPANIES OVERALL, 2011

Ranked by: Score based on revenue, profits, assets, and market capitalization. Remarks: Specific scores not provided. Also notes country, overall rank in the *Forbes 2000,* and figures for each criterion. Number listed: 26

1. Hitachi Ltd.
2. Hon Hai Precision Industry Co., Ltd.
3. Toshiba Corp.
4. Kyocera Corp.
5. TE Connectivity Ltd.
6. Agilent Technologies Inc.
7. Murata Manufacturing Co., Ltd.
8. LG Display Co., Ltd.
9. Avnet Inc.
10. NEC Corp.

Source: *Forbes*, Forbes 2000 (annual), http://www.forbes.com, May 7, 2012.

2497 ■ WORLD'S MOST ADMIRED ELECTRONICS COMPANIES, 2012

Ranked by: Score, on a scale of 10, based on a survey of executives, directors, and securities analysts of companies within their own industry on eight criteria: innovation, financial soundness, employee talent, use of corporate assets, long-term investment value, social responsibility, quality of management, and quality of products/services. Remarks: Specific scores not provided. Also notes rank for previous year. Number listed: 8

1. General Electric Co.
2. Samsung Electronics Co., Ltd.
3. Siemens AG
4. Sony Corp.
5. Emerson Electric Co.
6. Koninklijke Philips Electronics NV (Royal Philips Electronics NV)
7. Panasonic Corp.
8. Toshiba Corp.

Source: *Fortune*, World's Most Admired Companies (annual), March 19, 2012, p. 149.

2498 ■ WORLD'S MOST ETHICAL ELECTRONICS AND SEMICONDUCTOR COMPANIES, 2012

Ranked by: Score based on five criteria: ethics and compliance program; reputation, leadership, and innovation; governance; corporate citizenship and responsibility; and culture of ethics. Remarks: Specific scores not provided; companies are listed alphabetically, not ranked. Number listed: 4

1. Applied Materials Inc. (U.S.)
2. Freescale Semiconductor Inc. (U.S.)
3. Premier Farnell plc (U.K.)
4. Rockwell Automation (U.S.)

Source: *Ethisphere Magazine*, World's Most Ethical Companies (annual), http://www.ethisphere.com, 2012.

2499 ■ WORLD'S MOST VALUABLE ELECTRONIC AND ELECTRIC EQUIPMENT COMPANIES, 2011

Ranked by: Market value as of March 2011, in millions of U.S. dollars. Remarks: Also notes rank within the *FT 500*, rank for

previous year, country, revenue, net income, assets, number of employees, share price, price-to-earning ratio, dividend yield, and fiscal year-end. Number listed: 6

1. Schneider Electric SA, with $46,543.7 million
2. Emerson Electric Co., $44,062.8
3. Danaher Corp., $34,211.5
4. Hon Hai Precision Industry Co., Ltd., $33,839.7
5. Hitachi Ltd., $23,608.1
6. Kyocera Corp., $19,458.7

Source: *Financial Times*, FT 500 (annual), http://www.ft.com, June 24, 2011.

2500 ■ WORLD'S MOST VALUABLE ELECTRONICS BRANDS, 2011

Ranked by: Brand value, in millions of U.S. dollars. Remarks: Also notes rank within the *Global 500* for current and previous year, figures for current and previous year, country, and brand rating. Ranking is available online only. Number listed: 4

1. Toshiba, with $14,185 million
2. Philips, $6,730
3. NEC, $3,599
4. Kyocera, $2,407

Source: *Global 500*, (annual), Brand Finance plc, March 2012.

Electronic Industry—Distributors

2501 ■ LARGEST ELECTRICAL DISTRIBUTORS, 2010

Ranked by: Revenue, in dollars. Remarks: Also notes headquarters, number of electrical employees, number of U.S. locations, and senio executive. Number listed: 200

1. Sonepar North America, with $5,238,000,000
2. WESCO International Inc., $4,880,835,000
3. Rexel, $4,793,000,000
4. Graybar Electric Co., $4,616,377,000
5. Anixter International, $3,889,400,000
6. Consolidated Electrical Distributors, $n/a
7. Border States Industries Inc., $1,025,000,000
8. W. W. Grainger Inc., $n/a
9. HD Supply, $n/a
10. Crescent Electric Supply Co., $768,882,644

Source: *Electrical Wholesaling*, The Top 200 (annual), June 2011.

Electronics Stores

2502 ■ JAPAN'S LARGEST COMPUTER AND ELECTRONICS RETAILERS OVERALL, 2011

Ranked by: Score based on revenue, profits, assets, and market capitalization. Remarks: Specific scores not provided. Also notes overall rank in the *Forbes 2000* and figures for each criterion. Number listed: 3

1. Yamada Denki Co., Ltd.
2. K's Holdings Corp.
3. Edion Corp.

Source: *Forbes*, Forbes 2000 (annual), http://www.forbes.com, May 7, 2012.

2503 ■ LARGEST ASIA-PACIFIC HARDLINE RETAILERS, 2010

Ranked by: Sales, in millions of U.S. dollars. Remarks: Also notes country, fascias/brands, number of outlets, sales in national currency, sales area, sales per square meter, and figures for previous year. Number listed: 10

1. Yamada Denki Co., Ltd., with $13,668 million
2. Gome Electrical Appliances Holding, $11,674
3. Suning Appliance Chain Store, $10,467
4. Edion Corp., $9,316
5. Yodobashi Camera, $7,846
6. Bic Camera, $7,812
7. K's Holdings Corp., $7,763
8. Wesfarmers Ltd., $5,498
9. Harvey Norman Holdings, $5,047
10. Cainz, $4,991

Source: *Retail Asia*, Retail Asia-Pacific Top 500 (annual), July 2011, p. 65-65a.

2504 ■ LARGEST U.S. COMPUTER AND ELECTRONICS RETAILERS OVERALL, 2011

Ranked by: Score based on revenue, profits, assets, and market capitalization. **Remarks:** Specific scores not provided. Also notes overall rank in the *Forbes 2000* and figures for each criterion. **Number listed:** 2

1. Best Buy Co., Inc.
2. GameStop Corp.

Source: *Forbes*, Forbes 2000 (annual), http://www.forbes.com, May 7, 2012.

2505 ■ TOP ELECTRONICS RETAIL FRANCHISES, 2012

Ranked by: Cumulative score based on financial strength and stability, growth rate, size of the system, number of years in business, the length of time franchising, start-up costs, litigation, percentage of terminations, and whether the company provides financing. **Remarks:** Specific scores not provided. Also notes overall rank within the *Franchise 500,* contact information, description, year founded, year started franchising, states where registered, available U.S. regions, where seeking foreign expansion, number of franchised and company-owned units for past three years, start-up costs, franchise fees, royalty fees, and type of financing available. **Number listed:** 2

1. RadioShack
2. Wireless Zone

Source: *Entrepreneur*, Franchise 500 (annual), January 2012, p. 198-201.

2506 ■ TOP U.S. ELECTRONICS AND ENTERTAINMENT RETAILERS BY SALES, 2010

Ranked by: Sales volume, in thousands of dollars. **Remarks:** Also notes comparable-store sales and sales per store. **Number listed:** 10

1. Best Buy Co., Inc., with $36,667,000 thousand
2. Amazon.com Inc., $18,526,000
3. Apple Inc./iTunes, $18,064,000
4. Verizon Wireless, $8,021,000
5. GameStop Corp., $6,611,000
6. Barnes & Noble Inc., $5,715,000
7. QVC Inc., $5,236,000
8. AT&T Wireless, $4,990,000
9. Dell Inc., $4,946,000
10. RadioShack, $4,615,000

Source: *Stores*, Top 100 Retailers (annual), July 2011, p. s8.

2507 ■ WORLD'S LARGEST COMPUTER AND ELECTRONICS RETAILERS OVERALL, 2011

Ranked by: Score based on revenue, profits, assets, and market capitalization. **Remarks:** Specific scores not provided. Also notes country, overall rank in the *Forbes 2000,* and figures for each criterion. **Number listed:** 8

1. Best Buy Co., Inc.
2. Yamada Denki Co., Ltd.
3. Grupo Elektra, SA de CV
4. Suning Appliance Co., Ltd.
5. GameStop Corp.
6. Dixons Retail plc
7. K's Holdings Corp.
8. Edion Corp.

Source: *Forbes*, Forbes 2000 (annual), http://www.forbes.com, May 7, 2012.

Employee Benefits

2508 ■ AMERICA'S BEST COMPANIES IN HEALTH CARE BENEFITS, 2012

Ranked by: Companies among the 100 Best Companies to Work For that pay 100% of their employees' healthcare premiums; companies are ranked in order of their overall rank in the 100 Best Companies to Work For. **Number listed:** 14

1. The Boston Consulting Group Inc.
2. Zappos.com Inc.
3. NuStar Energy LP
4. QUALCOMM Inc.
5. Ultimate Software
6. Whole Foods Market Inc.
7. Nugget Market Inc.
8. Perkins Cole LLP
9. Umpqua Bank
10. EOG Resources

Source: *Fortune*, 100 Best Companies to Work For (annual), http://www.fortune.com, February 6, 2012.

2509 ■ AMERICA'S BEST COMPANIES FOR SAB-BATICALS, 2012

Ranked by: Companies that offer employees fully paid sabbaticals. **Remarks:** Also notes overall rank in the *100 Best Companies to Work For.* **Number listed:** 23

1. The Boston Consulting Group Inc.
2. Recreational Equipment Inc. (REI)
3. DPR Construction Inc.
4. DreamWorks Animation SKG Inc.
5. Kimpton Hotels & Restaurants
6. The Container Store
7. Alston & Bird LLP
8. Plante & Moran LLP
9. St. Jude Children's Research Hospital
10. Adobe

Source: *Fortune*, 100 Best Companies to Work For (annual), http://www.fortune.com, February 6, 2012.

2510 ■ AMERICA'S BEST COMPANIES FOR UNUSUAL PERKS, 2012

Ranked by: Companies that offer employees unusual benefits and perks. **Remarks:** Also notes overall rank in the *100 Best Companies to Work For.* **Number listed:** 12

1. Google Inc.
2. Wegmans Food Markets

3. NetApp
4. Zappos.com Inc.
5. Alston & Bird LLP
6. Southern Ohio Medical Center
7. PricewaterhouseCoopers
8. Autodesk
9. FactSet Research Systems
10. Four Seasons Hotels & Resorts

Source: *Fortune*, 100 Best Companies to Work For (annual), http://www.fortune.com, February 6, 2012.

2511 ■ AMERICA'S BEST COMPANIES IN WORK-LIFE BALANCE, 2012

Ranked by: Companies where employees feel "encouraged to balance their work and personal life." **Remarks:** Specific scores not provided. Also notes overall rank in the *100 Best Companies to Work For*. **Number listed:** 10

1. SAS Institute Inc.
2. Edward Jones
3. Camden Property Trust
4. Recreational Equipment Inc. (REI)
5. Kimpton Hotels & Restaurants
6. DPR Construction Inc.
7. Southern Ohio Medical Center
8. Wegmans Food Markets Inc.
9. Ultimate Software
10. CHG Healthcare Services

Source: *Fortune*, 100 Best Companies to Work For (annual), http://www.fortune.com, February 6, 2012.

Employee Retention

2512 ■ AMERICA'S BEST COMPANIES WITH THE LOWEST TURNOVER, 2011-2012

Ranked by: Percentage of employees who voluntarily left the company during a 12-month period. **Remarks:** Also notes overall rank in the *100 Best Companies to Work For*. **Number listed:** 12

1. SAS Institute Inc., with 2%
1. Intel Corp., 2%
3. NuStar Energy LP, 2%
3. Atlantic Health System Inc., 2%
3. General Mills Inc., 2%
3. Hasbro Inc., 2%
3. Mercedes-Benz USA, 2%
3. DPR Construction Inc., 2%
3. W. L. Gore & Associates Inc., 3%
3. PCL Construction, 3%
3. Publix Super Markets, 3%
3. Darden Restaurants, 3%

Source: *Fortune*, 100 Best Companies to Work For (annual), http://www.fortune.com, February 6, 2012.

Employee Training

2513 ■ COUNTRIES WITH THE BEST CORPORATE TRAINING, 2010

Ranked by: Score, on a scale of seven, based on the level of corporate investment in the attraction, training, and retention of employees. **Number listed:** 142

1. Switzerland, with 5.6 points
2. Sweden, 5.5
2. Denmark, 5.5
4. Singapore, 5.4
4. Norway, 5.4
6. Japan, 5.3
6. Luxembourg, 5.3
6. Finland, 5.3
9. Malaysia, 5.2
10. Netherlands, 5.1

Source: *Global Competitiveness Report*, (annual), World Economic Forum, 2011, p. 449.

2514 ■ COUNTRIES WITH THE WORST CORPORATE TRAINING, 2010

Ranked by: Score, on a scale of seven, based on the level of corporate investment in the attraction, training, and retention of employees. **Number listed:** 142

1. Haiti, with 2.3 points
2. Mauritania, 2.4
3. Syria, 2.6
3. Burundi, 2.6
5. Burkina Faso, 2.7
5. Bosnia & Herzegovina, 2.7
7. Nepal, 2.9
7. Yemen, 2.9
7. Ethiopia, 2.9
7. Iran, 2.9
7. Serbia, 2.9

Source: *Global Competitiveness Report*, (annual), World Economic Forum, 2011, p. 449.

Employment

2515 ■ LARGEST DENVER-AREA PRIVATE-SECTOR EMPLOYERS, 2010

Ranked by: Number of Colorado employees. **Remarks:** Also notes contact information, rank for previous year, number of offices in Colorado, total revenue and number of employees, business description, top local executive, owner, ticker symbol, and headquarters. **Number listed:** 25

1. Wal-Mart Stores Inc., with 24,900 employees
2. Safeway Inc., 9,500
3. HCA-HealthOne LLC, 8,700
4. Qwest Communications International Inc./ CenturyLink Inc., 7,900
5. Wells Fargo & Co., 6,313
6. Exempla Healthcare, 6,282
7. Kaiser Foundation Health Plan of Colorado, 6,000
8. University of Denver, 5,902
9. Dish Network LLC, 5,000
10. The Children's Hospital, 4,348

Source: *Denver Business Journal*, Book of Lists (annual), December 16, 2011, p. 57.

2516 ■ LARGEST DENVER-AREA PUBLIC SECTOR EMPLOYERS, 2010

Ranked by: Number of Colorado employees. **Remarks:** Also notes contact information, rank for previous year, number of offices, budget for current and previous year, top elected official, and human resources administrator. **Number listed:** 17

1. U.S. Government, with 39,983 employees
2. State of Colorado, 33,515
3. University of Colorado System, 16,131
4. Denver Public Schools, 13,087
5. City & County of Denver, 10,851
6. Denver Health, 5,508
7. Adams 12 Five Star Schools, 5,017
8. Aurora Public Schools, 5,000
9. Boulder Valley School District RE-2, 4,000
10. Jefferson County, CO, 2,826

Source: *Denver Business Journal*, Book of Lists (annual), December 16, 2011, p. 58.

2517 ■ STATES WITH THE HIGHEST EMPLOYMENT RATE, 2010

Ranked by: Percentage of population aged 16 years and older that is employed. **Number listed:** 51

1. North Dakota, with $68.3%
2. Nebraska, $66.7%
3. South Dakota, $66.6%
4. Minnesota, $66.2%
5. Iowa, $66%
5. Vermont, $66%
7. New Hampshire, $65.9%
8. Wyoming, $64.2%
9. Kansas, $63.9%
10. Utah, $62.7%
10. Wisconsin, $62.7%

Source: *State Rankings*, (annual), CQ Press, 2011, p. 181.

2518 ■ STATES WITH THE LARGEST CIVILIAN LABOR FORCE, 2010

Ranked by: Number of civilian employees. **Remarks:** Also notes share of national total. **Number listed:** 51

1. California, with 18,214,800 employees
2. Texas, 12,210,500
3. New York, 9,630,400
4. Florida, 9,245,400
5. Illinois, 6,687,500
6. Pennsylvania, 6,357,700
7. Ohio, 5,906,500
8. Michigan, 4,763,100
9. Georgia, 4,672,500
10. New Jersey, 4,487,000

Source: *State Rankings*, (annual), CQ Press, 2011, p. 179.

2519 ■ STATES WITH THE LARGEST LABOR FORCE, 2010

Ranked by: Number of employed workers in the civilian labor force. **Remarks:** Also notes share of national total. **Number listed:** 51

1. California, with 15,945,500 workers
2. Texas, 11,202,400
3. New York, 8,837,600
4. Florida, 8,137,100

5. Illinois, 6,066,900
6. Pennsylvania, 5,819,400
7. Ohio, 5,339,900
8. Michigan, 4,207,800
9. Georgia, 4,193,700
10. New Jersey, 4,079,200

Source: *State Rankings*, (annual), CQ Press, 2011, p. 180.

2520 ■ STATES WITH THE LOWEST EMPLOYMENT RATE, 2010

Ranked by: Percentage of population 16 years and older that is employed. **Number listed:** 51

1. West Virginia, with 47.6%
2. Alabama, 52.2%
3. Mississippi, 52.3%
4. Michigan, 53.2%
5. South Carolina, 53.5%
6. Florida, 54.4%
7. North Carolina, 54.8%
8. Kentucky, 54.9%
9. Delaware, 55.1%
10. Arkansas, 55.3%

Source: *State Rankings*, (annual), CQ Press, 2011, p. 181.

2521 ■ STATES WITH THE SMALLEST CIVILIAN LABOR FORCE, 2010

Ranked by: Number of civilian employees. **Remarks:** Also notes share of national total. **Number listed:** 51

1. Wyoming, with 293,100 employees
2. Washington DC, 332,300
3. Vermont, 358,600
4. Alaska, 363,300
5. North Dakota, 369,000
6. Delaware, 422,600
7. South Dakota, 443,700
8. Montana, 494,700
9. Rhode Island, 573,200
10. Hawaii, 633,600

Source: *State Rankings*, (annual), CQ Press, 2011, p. 179.

2522 ■ STATES WITH THE SMALLEST LABOR FORCE, 2010

Ranked by: Number of employed workers in the civilian labor force. **Remarks:** Also notes share of national total. **Number listed:** 51

1. Wyoming, with 274,300 workers
2. Washington DC, 300,100
3. Alaska, 334,000
4. Vermont, 337,900
5. North Dakota, 355,000
6. Delaware, 386,700
7. South Dakota, 423,300
8. Montana, 459,000
9. Rhode Island, 507,200
10. Hawaii, 593,300

Source: *State Rankings*, (annual), CQ Press, 2011, p. 180.

2523 ■ TOP STATES FOR INSOURCING EMPLOYMENT, 2011

Ranked by: Employment insourced. **Number listed:** 20

1. California, with 594,100 jobs
2. Texas, 439,400
3. New York, 417,000
4. Illinois, 273,300
5. Pennsylvania, 263,500
6. Florida, 254,000
7. Ohio, 231,600
8. New Jersey, 230,000
9. North Carolina, 206,700
10. Massachusetts, 188,900

Source: *Site Selection*, November 2011, p. 917.

Energy Industry

2524 ■ EUROPE'S MOST VALUABLE ALTERNATIVE ENERGY COMPANIES, 2011

Ranked by: Market value as of March 2011, in millions of U.S. dollars. **Remarks:** Also notes rank within the *FT Europe 500*, rank for previous year, country, revenue, net income, assets, number of employees, share price, price-to-earning ratio, dividend yield, and fiscal yearend. **Number listed:** 2

1. Vestas Wind Systems A/S, with $8,847.4 million
2. SMA Solar Technology AG, $4,355

Source: *Financial Times*, FT 500 (annual), http://www.ft.com, June 24, 2011.

2525 ■ FASTEST-GROWING ASIAN ENERGY COMPANIES, 2007-2010

Ranked by: Three-year revenue growth, in percent. **Remarks:** Also notes industry and rank in the overall *Top 250*. **Number listed:** 20

1. Cairn India Ltd. (India), with 116.5%
2. PTT Aromatics & Refining plc (Thailand), 49.6%
3. YTL Power International Bhd. (Malaysia), 48.9%
4. China Resource Power Holdings Co., Ltd. (Hong Kong), 42.4%
5. YTL Corp. Bhd., 40%
6. China Yangtze Power Co., Ltd. (China), 35.8
7. GD Power Development Co., Ltd. (China), 32.7%
8. Shanxi Xishan Coal & Electricity Power (China), 29.5%
9. Shanxi Lu'an Environmental Energy Development (China), 29.1%
10. Reliance Infrastructure Ltd. (India), 28.8%

Source: *Platts*, Top 250 Global Energy Company Rankings (annual), http://www.platts.com/top250, November 2, 2011.

2526 ■ FASTEST-GROWING ENERGY COMPANIES, 2008-2011

Ranked by: Score based on three-year growth in revenue and earnings, and three-year total return to investors. **Remarks:** Specific scores not provided. To qualify for list, companies must have

revenues of at least $50 million, net income of at least $10 million, market capitalization of at least $250 million, and stock price of at least $5. Int'l companies are eligible if they trade on a U.S. exchange and file quarterly reports. **Number listed:** 6

1. Green Plains Renewable Energy
2. Concho Resources
3. Trina Solar Ltd.
4. First Solar Inc.
5. TransGlobe Energy
6. Walter Energy

Source: *Fortune*, 100 Fastest-Growing Companies (annual), http://www.fortune.com, September 26, 2011.

2527 ■ FASTEST-GROWING ENERGY COMPANIES IN THE AMERICAS, 2007-2010

Ranked by: Three-year revenue growth, in percent. **Remarks:** Also notes location and rank in the overall *Top 250*. **Number listed:** 10

1. El Paso Pipeline Partners LP (U.S.), with 130.3%
2. Ultrapar Participacoes SA (Brazil), 28.7%
3. Southwestern Energy Co. (U.S.), 27.7%
4. Suncor Energy Inc. (Canada), 27.5%
5. Empresa de Energia de Bogota SA (Colombia), 27.2%
6. Ecopetrol SA (Colombia), 23.4%
7. Companhia de Transmissao de Energia Eletrica Paulista (Brazil), 20.2%
8. YPF SA (Argentina), 14.9%
9. Peabody Energy Corp. (U.S.), 14.5%
10. Light SA (Brazil), 14.3%

Source: *Platts*, Top 250 Global Energy Company Rankings (annual), http://www.platts.com/top250, November 2, 2011.

2528 ■ FASTEST-GROWING EUROPEAN, MIDDLE EASTERN, AND AFRICAN ENERGY COMPANIES, 2007-2010

Ranked by: Three-year revenue growth, in percent. **Remarks:** Also notes industry and rank in the overall *Top 250*. **Number listed:** 10

1. Essar Energy plc (U.K.), with 199.5%
2. Rabigh Refining & Petrochemical Co. (Saudi Arabia), 167.5%
3. RusHydro JSC (Russian Fed.), 106.1%
4. Bashneft OJSC (Russian Fed.), 57.9%
5. Moscow United Electric Power (Russian Fed.), 42.4%
6. Abu Dhabi National Energy Co. (UAE), 35.8%
7. Iberdrola Renovables SA (Spain), 33%
8. Gas Natural SDG SA (Spain), 24.8%
8. SNAM Rete Gas SpA (Italy), 24.8%
10. Novatek OAO (Russian Fed.), 23.6%

Source: *Platts*, Top 250 Global Energy Company Rankings (annual), http://www.platts.com/top250, November 2, 2011.

2529 ■ FASTEST-GROWING PRIVATE ENERGY COMPANIES IN THE U.S., 2007-2010

Ranked by: Average annual sales growth over three years, in percent. **Remarks:** Also notes headquarters, revenue, and rank in the overall *Inc. 500*. To qualify, private companies must have had annual revenues of at least $100,000 in 2007 and $2 million in 2010. **Number listed:** 16

1. Greenspring Energy, with 8,730%
2. re2g, 7,493.4%
3. SunDurance Energy, 5,126.2%
4. OnForce Solar, 4,492.5%
5. FLS Energy, 4,303%
6. K2 Energy Solutions, 2,984%
7. Check-6, 2,661.2%
8. Standard Solar, 1,686%
9. Clean Currents, 1,548.2%
10. Realgy, 1,146.7%

Source: *Inc.*, Inc. 500 (annual), September 2011, p. 114-118.

2530 ■ LARGEST ENERGY AND UTILITIES COMPANIES IN EUROPE, 2010

Ranked by: Sales, in millions of U.S. dollars. **Remarks:** Also notes rank within country. **Number listed:** 100

1. E.On AG (Germany), with $121,678.2 million
2. RWE AG (Germany), $68,695.3
3. Electricite de France (France), $57,844.6
4. Veolia Environnement SA (France), $51,031.7
5. BP Europe SE (Germany), $48,130.1
6. Accord Energy Ltd. (U.K.), $40,039
7. GDF Suez (France), $37,022.4
8. Centrica plc (U.K.), $32,944.5
9. Scottish & Southern Energy plc (U.K.), $32,325.6
10. Vattenfall AB (Sweden), $29,291

Source: *Europe's 15,000 Largest Companies*, (annual), ELC International, 2011, p. 41.

2531 ■ MOST POWERFUL ARABS IN ENERGY, 2012

Ranked by: Score based on scope of influence. **Remarks:** Specific scores not provided. Also notes rank in the overall *Power 500*. **Number listed:** 2

1. Ayman Asfari
2. Farouq Al Zanki

Source: *Arabian Business*, Power 500 (annual), June 4, 2012.

2532 ■ MOST PROFITABLE CANADIAN ENERGY COMPANIES, 2011

Ranked by: Profits, in millions of Canadian dollars. **Number listed:** 6

1. Suncor Energy Inc., with C$4,304 million
2. Imperial Oil Ltd., C$3,371
3. Canadian Natural Resources Ltd., C$2,643
4. Husky Energy Inc., C$2,224
5. TransCanada Corp., C$1,582
6. Cenovus Energy Inc., C$1,478

Source: *Canadian Business*, Investor 500 (annual), 2012, p. 55.

2533 ■ TOP ENERGY COMPANIES IN THE AMERICAS, 2010

Ranked by: Score based on asset worth, revenue, profits, earnings per share, and return on invested capital. **Remarks:** Specific scores not provided. Also notes rank in the overall *Top 250*. **Number listed:** 101

1. Exxon Mobil Corp.

2. Chevron Corp.
3. ConocoPhillips
4. Petroleo Brasileiro SA (Petrobras)
5. Empresa Colombiana de Petroleos SA (Ecopetrol SA)
6. Occidental Petroleum Corp.
7. Marathon Oil Co.
8. Exelon Corp.
9. Hess Corp.
10. Dominion Resources Inc.

Source: *Platts*, Top 250 Global Energy Company Rankings (annual), http://www.platts.com/top250, November 2, 2011.

2534 ■ TOP ENERGY COMPANIES IN ASIA AND THE PACIFIC RIM, 2010

Ranked by: Score based on asset worth, revenue, profits, earnings per share, and return on invested capital. **Remarks:** Specific scores not provided. Also notes rank in the overall *Top 250*. **Number listed:** 70

1. PetroChina Co., Ltd.
2. China Petroleum & Chemical Corp. (Sinopec)
3. CNOOC Ltd.
4. JX Holdings Inc.
5. Oil & Natural Gas Corp., Ltd.
6. China Shenhua Energy Co.
7. Reliance Industries Ltd.
8. PTT plc
9. Indian Oil Corp.
10. Coal India

Source: *Platts*, Top 250 Global Energy Company Rankings (annual), http://www.platts.com/top250, November 2, 2011.

2535 ■ TOP ENERGY COMPANIES IN EUROPE, THE MIDDLE EAST, AND AFRICA, 2010

Ranked by: Score based on asset worth, revenue, profits, earnings per share, and return on invested capital. **Remarks:** Specific scores not provided. Also notes rank in the overall *Top 250*. **Number listed:** 79

1. OAO Gazprom
2. Total SA
3. Royal Dutch Shell plc
4. OJSC Rosneft
5. OAO Lukoil
6. Statoil ASA
7. E.On AG
8. Repsol YPF SA
9. ENI SpA
10. RWE AG

Source: *Platts*, Top 250 Global Energy Company Rankings (annual), http://www.platts.com/top250, November 2, 2011.

2536 ■ TOP *FORTUNE 500* COMPANIES IN ENERGY, 2011

Ranked by: Revenue, in millions of dollars. **Remarks:** Also notes overall rank in the *Fortune 500*; profits; profits as a percentage of revenue; stockholders' equity; and rank by each criterion. **Number listed:** 7

1. American Electric Power Co., Inc., with $15,116 million

2. Constellation Energy Group Inc., $13,758

3. NRG Energy Inc., $9,079

4. The Williams Companies Inc., $7,930

5. Energy Future Holdings Corp., $7,040

6. Calpine Corp., $6,800

7. UGI Corp., $6,091

Source: *Fortune*, Fortune 500 (annual), May 21, 2012, p. F-35.

2537 ■ TOP INDEPENDENT POWER PRODUCERS, 2010

Ranked by: Score based on asset worth, revenue, profits, earnings per share, and return on invested capital. **Remarks:** Specific scores not provided. Also notes rank in the overall *Top 250*. **Number listed:** 17

1. NTPC Ltd.

2. Empresa Nacional de Electricidad

3. China Yangtze Power Co.

4. Huaneng Power International Inc.

5. Tractebel Energia SA

6. China Resource Power Holdings Co., Ltd.

7. NRG Energy Inc.

8. Datang Power

9. The AES Corp.

10. Enel Green Power SpA

Source: *Platts*, Top 250 Global Energy Company Rankings (annual), http://www.platts.com/top250, November 2, 2011.

2538 ■ WORLD'S FASTEST-GROWING ENERGY COMPANIES, 2007-2010

Ranked by: Three-year revenue growth, in percent. **Remarks:** Also notes industry and rank in the overall *Top 250*. **Number listed:** 50

1. Essar Energy plc (U.K.), with 199.5%

2. Rabigh Refining & Petrochemical Co. (Saudi Arabia), 167.5%

3. El Paso Pipeline Partners LP (U.S.), 130.3%

4. Cairn India Ltd. (India), 116.5%

5. RusHydro JSC (Russian Fed.), 106.1%

6. Bashneft OJSC (Russian Fed.), 57.9%

7. PTT Aromatics & Refining plc (Thailand), 49.6%

8. YTL Power International Bhd. (Malaysia), 48.9%

9. Moscow United Electric Power (Russian Fed.), 42.4%

9. China Resource Power Holdings Co., Ltd. (Hong Kong), 42.4%

Source: *Platts*, Top 250 Global Energy Company Rankings (annual), http://www.platts.com/top250, November 2, 2011.

2539 ■ WORLD'S MOST ADMIRED ENERGY COMPANIES, 2012

Ranked by: Score, on a scale of 10, based on a survey of executives, directors, and securities analysts of companies within their own industry on eight criteria: innovation, financial soundness, employee talent, use of corporate assets, long-term investment value, social responsibility, quality of management, and quality of products/services. **Remarks:** Specific scores not provided. Also notes rank for previous year. **Number listed:** 8

1. Koc Holding A.S.

2. JSFC Sistema

3. RWE AG

4. Enterprise Products Partners LP

5. Ultrapar Holdings

6. GDF Suez

7. Marquard & Bahls AG

8. Plains All American Pipeline LP

Source: *Fortune*, World's Most Admired Companies (annual), March 19, 2012, p. 149.

2540 ■ WORLD'S MOST TECHNOLOGICALLY INNOVATIVE ENERGY COMPANIES - PRIVATE, 2012

Ranked by: Editorial determination. **Remarks:** Companies are listed alphabetically, not ranked. Also notes comments. **Number listed:** 3

1. Alta Devices

2. LanzaTech

3. Sakti3

Source: *Technology Review*, TR 50 (annual), http://www.technologyreview.com, 2012.

2541 ■ WORLD'S MOST TECHNOLOGICALLY INNOVATIVE ENERGY COMPANIES - PUBLIC, 2012

Ranked by: Editorial determination. **Remarks:** Companies are listed alphabetically, not ranked. Also notes comments. **Number listed:** 7

1. Babcock & Wilcox

2. First Solar Inc.

3. General Electric Co.

4. Goldwind Science & Technology

5. Shell

6. Siemens AG

7. Suntech

Source: *Technology Review*, TR 50 (annual), http://www.technologyreview.com, 2012.

2542 ■ WORLD'S MOST VALUABLE ENERGY COMPANIES IN ALTERNATIVE TECHNOLOGIES, 2011

Ranked by: Market capitalization, in billions of U.S. dollars. **Remarks:** Also notes rank for previous year, annual growth in share price, price/earnings ratio, debt/capital ratio, headquarters country, ticker symbol, and stock exchange. **Number listed:** 15

1. GCL-Poly Energy Holdings, with $4.3 billion

2. Acciona Energy, $4.2

3. Xinjiang Goldwind, $3.6

4. Cosan, $3.1

5. First Solar Inc., $2.9

6. Vestas Wind Systems A/S, $2.6

7. Abengoa, $2

8. SMA Solar Technology, $1.8

9. Sunpower, $1

10. Gamesa, $1

Source: *PFC Energy 50*, (annual), PFC Energy, January 23, 2012.

2543 ■ WORLD'S MOST VALUABLE ENERGY COMPANIES IN EQUIPMENT, ENGINEERING, AND CONSTRUCTION, 2011

Ranked by: Market capitalization, in billions of U.S. dollars. **Remarks:** Also notes rank for previous year, annual growth in share price, price/earnings ratio, debt/capital ratio, headquarters country, ticker symbol, and stock exchange. **Number listed:** 15

1. National Oilwell Varco Inc., with $28.8 billion
2. Tenaris SA, $21.9
3. Saipem SpA, $18.8
4. Keppel Corp., Ltd., $12.8
5. FMC Technologies Inc., $12.4
6. Cameron International Corp., $12.1
7. Technip, $10.4
8. Fluor Corp., $8.5
9. Petrofac Ltd., $7.7
10. Samsung Engineering, $7

Source: *PFC Energy 50*, (annual), PFC Energy, January 23, 2012.

2544 ■ WORLD'S MOST VALUABLE ENERGY COMPANIES IN EXPLORATION AND PRODUCTION, 2011

Ranked by: Market capitalization, in billions of U.S. dollars. **Remarks:** Also notes rank for previous year, annual growth in share price, price/earnings ratio, debt/capital ratio, headquarters country, ticker symbol, and stock exchange. **Number listed:** 15

1. Occidental Petroleum Corp., with $76.1 billion
2. Canadian Natural Resources Ltd., $41.1
3. Anadarko Petroleum Corp., $38
4. Novatek OAO, $37.2
5. BHP Billiton Ltd., $n/a
6. Apache Corp., $34.8
7. EOG Resources Inc., $26.5
8. Woodside Petroleum Ltd., $25.3
9. Devon Energy Corp., $25
10. OGX, $23.6

Source: *PFC Energy 50*, (annual), PFC Energy, January 23, 2012.

2545 ■ WORLD'S MOST VALUABLE ENERGY COMPANIES IN MIDSTREAM/INFRASTRUCTURE, 2011

Ranked by: Market capitalization, in billions of U.S. dollars. **Remarks:** Also notes rank for previous year, annual growth in share price, price/earnings ratio, debt/capital ratio, headquarters country, ticker symbol, and stock exchange. **Number listed:** 15

1. Enterprise GP Holdings LP, with $41.1 billion
2. TransCanada Corp., $29.5
3. Enbridge Inc., $28.1
4. Kinder Morgan Energy LP, $27.1
5. El Paso Corp., $20
6. The Williams Companies Inc., $17.4
7. Snam Rete Gas SpA, $15.8
8. ONEOK Inc., $11.8
9. Plains All American Pipeline LP, $11.2
10. Energy Transfer Partners LP, $10.6

Source: *PFC Energy 50*, (annual), PFC Energy, January 23, 2012.

2546 ■ WORLD'S MOST VALUABLE ENERGY COMPANIES IN OILFIELD AND DRILLING SERVICES, 2011

Ranked by: Market capitalization, in billions of U.S. dollars. **Remarks:** Also notes rank for previous year, annual growth in share price, price/earnings ratio, debt/capital ratio, headquarters country, ticker symbol, and stock exchange. **Number listed:** 15

1. Schlumberger Ltd., with $91.7 billion
2. Halliburton Co., $31.8

3. Baker Hughes Inc., $21.2
4. Seadrill Ltd., $15.7
5. Transocean Inc., $14
6. Weatherford International Ltd., $11
7. Ensco International, $10.8
8. China Oilfield Services, $9.2
9. Diamond Offshore Drilling Inc., $7.7
10. Noble Corp., $7.6

Source: *PFC Energy 50*, (annual), PFC Energy, January 23, 2012.

2547 ■ WORLD'S MOST VALUABLE ENERGY COMPANIES OVERALL, 2011

Ranked by: Market capitalization, in billions of U.S. dollars. **Remarks:** Also notes rank for previous year, annual growth in share price, primary business, ticker symbol, and stock exchange. **Number listed:** 50

1. Exxon Mobil Corp. (U.S.), with $406.3 billion
2. PetroChina Co., Ltd. (China), $276.6
3. Royal Dutch Shell plc (Netherlands), $234.6
4. Chevron Corp. (U.S.), $211.9
5. Petroleo Brasileiro SA (Petrobras, Brazil), $156.3
6. BP plc (U.K.), $135.5
7. OAO Gazprom (Russia), $122.6
8. Total SA (France), $121
9. China Petroleum & Chemical Corp. (Sinopec, China), $97.4
10. ConocoPhillips (U.S.), $96.8

Source: *PFC Energy 50*, (annual), PFC Energy, January 23, 2012.

2548 ■ WORLD'S MOST VALUABLE ENERGY COMPANIES IN REFINING AND MARKETING, 2011

Ranked by: Market capitalization, in billions of U.S. dollars. **Remarks:** Also notes rank for previous year, annual growth in share price, price/earnings ratio, debt/capital ratio, headquarters country, ticker symbol, and stock exchange. **Number listed:** 15

1. Reliance Industries Ltd., with $42.7 billion
2. Formosa Petrochemical Corp., $29.5
3. Marathon Petroleum Co., $11.8
3. Valero Energy Corp., $11.8
5. Indian Oil Corp., $11.6
6. SK Energy Co., Ltd., $11.4
7. S-Oil, $9.7
8. Tonengen Sekiyu, $6.2
9. Turkish Petroleum Refineries Corp. (Tupras), $5.3
10. OMV Petrom SA, $4.9

Source: *PFC Energy 50*, (annual), PFC Energy, January 23, 2012.

2549 ■ WORLD'S TOP ENERGY COMPANIES, 2010

Ranked by: Score based on asset worth, revenue, profits, earnings per share, and return on invested capital. **Remarks:** Specific scores not provided. **Number listed:** 250

1. Exxon Mobil Corp.
2. Chevron Corp.
3. OAO Gazprom
4. PetroChina Co., Ltd.
5. Total SA

6. Royal Dutch Shell plc
7. ConocoPhillips
8. China Petroleum & Chemical Corp. (Sinopec)
9. OJSC Rosneft
10. OAO Lukoil

Source: *Platts*, Top 250 Global Energy Company Rankings (annual), http://www.platts.com/top250, November 2, 2011.

Engineering

2550 ■ BRITAIN'S MOST ADMIRED ENGINEERING AND MACHINERY COMPANIES, 2011

Ranked by: Survey of peers and investment analysts based on nine criteria: quality of management, financial soundness, quality of goods/services, ability to attract and retain talent, value as long-term investment, innovation, marketing, community and environmental responsibility, and use of corporate assets. **Number listed:** 5

1. Rotork, with 71.6 points
2. Spirax Sarco Engineering, 64.8
3. Weir Group, 64.4
4. Melrose plc, 59.8
5. IMI plc, 56.5

Source: *Management Today*, Britain's Most Admired Companies (annual), December 2011, p. 45.

Engineering Construction Companies

2551 ■ TOP *FORTUNE 500* COMPANIES IN ENGINEERING AND CONSTRUCTION, 2011

Ranked by: Revenue, in millions of dollars. **Remarks:** Also notes overall rank in the *Fortune 500;* profits; profits as a percentage of revenue; stockholders' equity; and rank by each criterion. **Number listed:** 9

1. Fluor Corp., with $23,381 million
2. Jacobs Engineering Group Inc., $10,382
3. Peter Kiewit Sons' Inc., $10,381
4. URS Corp., $9,545
5. KBR Inc., $9,261
6. AECOM Technology Corp., $8,037
7. The Shaw Group Inc., $5,938
8. EMCOR Group Inc., $5,732
9. CH2M Hill Cos., Ltd., $5,555

Source: *Fortune*, Fortune 500 (annual), May 21, 2012, p. F-35.

Engineering Design

2552 ■ LARGEST ARCHITECTURAL AND ENGINEERING DESIGN FIRMS IN COLORADO AND WYOMING, 2010

Ranked by: Billings for design work in Colorado and Wyoming, in millions of dollars. **Remarks:** Also notes rank for previous year, contact information, and top market sectors. **Number listed:** 50

1. CH2M Hill Cos., Ltd., with $327.94 million
2. HDR Inc., $103.28
3. AECOM Technology Corp., $71.99
4. Merrick & Co., $59.6

5. Jacobs Engineering Group Inc., $53.56
6. Arcadis, $42.06
7. H + L Architecture, $23.07
8. Martin/Martin Inc., $20.64
9. Terracon Consultants Inc., $18.22
10. RNL, $17.88

Source: *ENR Mountain States*, Colorado/Wyoming Top Design Firms (annual), June 27, 2011.

2553 ■ LARGEST ARCHITECTURAL AND ENGINEERING DESIGN FIRMS IN THE MIDWEST, 2010

Ranked by: Revenue from projects in Illinois, Indiana, Wisconsin, and eastern Missouri, in millions of dollars. **Remarks:** Also notes rank for previous year, contact information, and top market sectors. **Number listed:** 80

1. AECOM Technology Corp., with $177.9 million
2. CH2M Hill Cos., Ltd., $129.63
3. HNTB Corp., $119.75
4. Jacobs Engineering Group Inc., $115.55
5. Trow Global Holdings Inc., $90.8
6. Parsons Brinckerhoff Inc., $71.53
7. Arcadis, $64.33
8. American Structurepoint Inc., $52.6
9. HOK Group Inc., $46.83
10. Strand Associates Inc., $41.59

Source: *ENR Midwest*, Top Design Firms (annual), http://www.midwest.construction.com, October 2011.

2554 ■ LARGEST ARCHITECTURAL AND ENGINEERING DESIGN FIRMS BY NY, NJ, AND CT REVENUE, 2010

Ranked by: Revenue from projects in New York, New Jersey, and Connecticut, in millions of dollars. **Remarks:** Also notes rank for previous year, headquarters, and top market sectors. **Number listed:** 95

1. AECOM Technology Corp., with $803.35 million
2. Arcadis/Malcolm Pirnie, $288.65
3. STV, $176.48
4. Parsons Brinckerhoff Inc., $166.07
5. HDR Inc., $119.02
6. Stantec Inc., $104.91
7. Jacobs Engineering Group Inc., $97.61
8. Greenman-Pedersen, $93.7
9. Arup, $92.91
10. M. Arthur Gensler Jr. & Associates Inc., $82.59

Source: *ENR New York*, Top Design Firms (annual), http://www.newyork.construction.com, October 2011.

2555 ■ LARGEST ARCHITECTURAL AND ENGINEERING DESIGN FIRMS IN THE SOUTHEASTERN U.S., 2010

Ranked by: Revenue from projects in Florida, Georgia, North Carolina, and South Carolina, in millions of dollars. **Remarks:** Also notes rank for previous year, contact information, and breakdown of work by type. **Number listed:** 90

1. CH2M Hill Cos., Ltd., with $257.31 million
2. Atkins North America, $230.71
3. AECOM Technology Corp., $222.21
4. Jacobs Engineering Group Inc., $172.8
5. Arcadis U.S., $171.88

6. HDR Inc., $132.24

7. HNTB Corp., $118.22

8. Reynolds, Smith & Hills Inc., $107.7

9. Parsons Brinckerhoff Inc., $86.19

10. Perkins & Will Inc., $52.4

Source: *ENR Southeast*, Top Design Firms (annual), http://www.southeast.construction.com, November 2011.

2556 ■ LARGEST ARCHITECTURAL AND ENGINEERING DESIGN FIRMS IN THE SOUTHWESTERN U.S., 2010

Ranked by: Revenue from projects in Arizona, Nevada, and New Mexico, in millions of dollars. **Remarks:** Also notes rank for previous year, contact information, and market sectors. **Number listed:** 53

1. CH2M Hill Cos., Ltd., with $183.46 million

2. AECOM Technology Corp., $89.03

3. HDR Inc., $86.13

4. AMEC plc, $66.87

5. Jacobs Engineering Group Inc., $50.12

6. Stantec Consulting Services Inc., $36.06

7. M. Arthur Gensler Jr. & Associates Inc., $33.01

8. Parsons Brinckerhoff Inc., $32.4

9. Michael Baker Jr. Inc., $29.89

10. AZTEC Engineering Group Inc., $29.27

Source: *ENR Southwest*, Top Design Firms (annual), http://www.southwest.construction.com, October 2011.

2557 ■ LARGEST ARCHITECTURAL AND ENGINEERING DESIGN FIRMS IN THE U.S. MOUNTAIN STATES, 2010

Ranked by: Billings for design work in Colorado, Idaho, Montana, Utah, and Wyoming, in millions of dollars. **Remarks:** Also notes rank for previous year, contact information, and top market sectors. **Number listed:** 35

1. HDR Inc., with $139.01 million

2. CH2M Hill Cos., Ltd., $112.58

3. Stanley Consultants, $26.66

4. Horrocks Engineers Inc., $24.65

5. Morrison-Maierle Inc., $24.54

6. MWH Americas Inc., $23.97

7. Parsons Brinckerhoff Inc., $23

8. HNTB Corp., $20.87

9. Jacobs Engineering Group Inc., $15.62

10. DOWL HKM, $13.9

Source: *ENR Mountain States*, Intermountain Top Design Firms (annual), http://www.mountainstates.construction.com, June 27, 2011.

2558 ■ LARGEST "GREEN" DESIGN FIRMS, 2010

Ranked by: "Green" design revenue, in dollars. **Number listed:** 25

1. M. Arthur Gensler Jr. & Associates Inc., with $394,200,000

2. M + W U.S., $241,651,491

3. URS Corp., $202,617,600

4. Perkins & Will Inc., $172,215,000

5. HOK Group Inc., $156,370,097

6. Skidmore, Owings & Merrill, $150,600,000

7. AECOM Technology Corp., $150,600,000

8. Stantec, $115,650,000

9. HKS Inc., $108,432,000

10. Science Applications International Corp. (SAIC), $100,012,000

Source: *Building Design & Construction*, Giants 300 (annual), July 2011, p. 49.

2559 ■ TOP ALL-DESIGN FIRMS, 2011

Ranked by: Revenue from design work, which represents 100% of the company's revenue. **Remarks:** Specific figures not provided. Also notes type of firm. **Number listed:** 100

1. AECOM Technology Corp.

2. Parsons Brinckerhoff Inc.

3. Arcadis U.S./RTKL/Rise

4. WorleyParsons Group Inc.

5. HNTB Cos.

6. Wood Group Mustang

7. M. Arthur Gensler Jr. & Associates Inc.

8. Stantec Inc.

9. The Louis Berger Group Inc.

10. Michael Baker Corp.

Source: *ENR: Engineering News-Record*, Top 500 Design Firms (annual), April 23, 2012, p. 61.

2560 ■ TOP DESIGN FIRMS IN GENERAL BUILDING, 2011

Ranked by: Revenue for design services. **Remarks:** Specific figures not provided. Also notes rank for previous year. **Number listed:** 20

1. AECOM Technology Corp.

2. M. Arthur Gensler Jr. & Associates Inc.

3. URS Corp.

4. Jacobs Engineering Group Inc.

5. HOK Group Inc.

6. HDR Inc.

7. Perkins & Will Inc.

8. AMEC

9. Parsons Brinckerhoff Inc.

10. Cannon Design

Source: *ENR: Engineering News-Record*, Top 500 Design Firms (annual), April 23, 2012, p. 54.

2561 ■ TOP DESIGN FIRMS IN HAZARDOUS WASTE, 2011

Ranked by: Revenue for design services. **Remarks:** Specific figures not provided. Also notes rank for previous year. **Number listed:** 20

1. URS Corp.

2. Arcadis U.S./RTKL/Rise

3. AECOM Technology Corp.

4. CH2M Hill Cos., Ltd.

5. Tetra Tech Inc.

6. Bechtel Group Inc.

7. Conestoga-Rovers & Associates

8. Fluor Corp.

9. The Shaw Group Inc.

10. Parsons Corp.

Source: *ENR: Engineering News-Record*, Top 500 Design Firms (annual), April 23, 2012, p. 55.

2562 ■ TOP DESIGN FIRMS IN INDUSTRIAL PROCESS/ PETROLEUM, 2011

Ranked by: Revenue for design services. **Remarks:** Specific figures not provided. Also notes rank for previous year. **Number listed:** 20

1. Fluor Corp.
2. Jacobs Engineering Group Inc.
3. KBR
4. Bechtel Group Inc.
5. AMEC plc
6. URS Corp.
7. Wood Group Mustang
8. CB & I Constructors Inc.
9. WorleyParsons Group Inc.
10. CH2M Hill Cos., Ltd.

Source: *ENR: Engineering News-Record*, Top 500 Design Firms (annual), April 23, 2012, p. 54.

2563 ■ TOP DESIGN FIRMS IN MANUFACTURING, 2011

Ranked by: Revenue for design services. **Remarks:** Specific figures not provided. Also notes rank for previous year. **Number listed:** 20

1. Jacobs Engineering Group Inc.
2. CH2M Hill Cos., Ltd.
3. URS Corp.
4. Foth Cos.
5. Tetra Tech Inc.
6. M+W U.S. Inc.
7. Ghafari Associates LLC
8. Bureau Veritas
9. SSOE Group
10. AMEC plc

Source: *ENR: Engineering News-Record*, Top 500 Design Firms (annual), April 23, 2012, p. 56.

2564 ■ TOP DESIGN FIRMS IN POWER, 2011

Ranked by: Revenue for design services. **Remarks:** Specific figures not provided. Also notes rank for previous year. **Number listed:** 20

1. The Shaw Group Inc.
2. Black & Veatch
3. Sargent & Lundy LLC
4. AECOM Technology Corp.
5. Bechtel Group Inc.
6. Burns & McDonnell Engineering Co.
7. Tetra Tech Inc.
8. CH2M Hill Cos., Ltd.
9. Parsons Brinckerhoff Inc.
10. URS Corp.

Source: *ENR: Engineering News-Record*, Top 500 Design Firms (annual), April 23, 2012, p. 55.

2565 ■ TOP DESIGN FIRMS IN SEWER AND WASTE, 2011

Ranked by: Revenue for design services. **Remarks:** Specific figures not provided. Also notes rank for previous year. **Number listed:** 20

1. CH2M Hill Cos., Ltd.
2. AECOM Technology Corp.
3. MWH Global Inc.
4. CDM Smith
5. URS Corp.
6. Tetra Tech Inc.
7. HDR Inc.
8. Black & Veatch
9. Arcadis U.S./RTKL/Rise
10. Brown & Caldwell

Source: *ENR: Engineering News-Record*, Top 500 Design Firms (annual), April 23, 2012, p. 56.

2566 ■ TOP DESIGN FIRMS IN TELECOMMUNICATIONS, 2011

Ranked by: Revenue for design services. **Remarks:** Specific figures not provided. Also notes rank for previous year. **Number listed:** 20

1. Black & Veatch
2. Bechtel Group Inc.
3. Jacobs Engineering Group Inc.
4. Parsons Corp.
5. Syska Hennessy Group
6. EXP Global Inc.
7. Morrison Hershfield
8. Corgan Associates Inc.
9. CDI Corp.
10. Gensler

Source: *ENR: Engineering News-Record*, Top 500 Design Firms (annual), April 23, 2012, p. 56.

2567 ■ TOP DESIGN FIRMS IN TRANSPORTATION, 2011

Ranked by: Revenue for design services. **Remarks:** Specific figures not provided. Also notes rank for previous year. **Number listed:** 20

1. AECOM Technology Corp.
2. URS Corp.
3. Parsons Brinckerhoff Inc.
4. CH2M Hill Cos., Ltd.
5. HNTB Cos.
6. Jacobs Engineering Group Inc.
7. HDR Inc.
8. Parsons Corp.
9. STV Group Inc.
10. The Louis Berger Group Inc.

Source: *ENR: Engineering News-Record*, Top 500 Design Firms (annual), April 23, 2012, p. 54.

2568 ■ TOP DESIGN FIRMS IN THE U.S., 2011

Ranked by: Total revenue for design services, in millions of dollars. **Remarks:** Also notes headquarters, rank for previous year, type of firm, international revenue, and breakdown by market. **Number listed:** 500

1. AECOM Technology Corp., with $6,875.2 million
2. URS Corp., $5,334
3. Jacobs Engineering Group Inc., $5,222.7
4. Fluor Corp., $4,029.4

5. CH2M Hill Cos., Ltd., $3,903
6. Bechtel Group Inc., $2,587
7. AMEC plc, $2,573.7
8. Tetra Tech Inc., $2,510
9. KBR, $2,189.6
10. Parsons Brinckerhoff Inc., $1,681.9

Source: *ENR: Engineering News-Record*, Top 500 Design Firms (annual), April 23, 2012, p. 67-81.

2569 ■ TOP DESIGN FIRMS IN WATER, 2011

Ranked by: Revenue for design services. **Remarks:** Specific figures not provided. Also notes rank for previous year. **Number listed:** 20

1. Tetra Tech Inc.
2. CH2M Hill Cos., Ltd.
3. AECOM Technology Corp.
4. MWH Global Inc.
5. URS Corp.
6. HDR Inc.
7. Black & Veatch
8. CDM Smith
9. Arcadis U.S./RTKL/Rise
10. AMEC plc

Source: *ENR: Engineering News-Record*, Top 500 Design Firms (annual), April 23, 2012, p. 55.

2570 ■ TOP "GREEN" DESIGN FIRMS BY REVENUE, 2010

Ranked by: Revenue from projects that were either registered with or certified by a third-party organization that set standards for measuring a building's or facility's environmental impact, energy efficiency, or carbon footprint, in millions of dollars. **Remarks:** Also notes headquarters, "green" revenue as a percentage of total revenue, number of accredited employees, and breakdown of revenue by market. **Number listed:** 100

1. URS Corp., with $333.2 million
2. M. Arthur Gensler Jr. & Associates Inc., $321.5
3. AECOM Technology Corp., $192.5
4. Perkins & Will Inc., $171.5
5. HOK Group Inc., $158.2
6. Tetra Tech Inc., $158
7. CH2M Hill Cos., Ltd., $140.6
8. HDR Inc., $122.4
9. NBBJ, $109.4
10. HKS Inc., $100

Source: *ENR: Engineering News-Record*, Top 100 Green Designers (annual), July 4, 2011, p. 41+.

2571 ■ TOP INTERNATIONAL DESIGN FIRMS IN THE U.S., 2010

Ranked by: Revenue for design services performed by companies based outside of the U.S. **Remarks:** Specific figures not provided. **Number listed:** 10

1. ARCADIS NV
2. Balfour Beatty plc
3. Stantec Inc.
4. WorleyParsons Ltd.
5. Fugro NV
6. Dar Al-Handasah Consultants

7. WS Atkins plc
8. Cardno Ltd.
9. Mott MacDonald Group Ltd.
10. Golder Associates Corp.

Source: *ENR: Engineering News-Record*, Top 200 International Design Firms (annual), July 25, 2011, p. 40.

Engineering Design, International

2572 ■ TOP GLOBAL DESIGN FIRMS, 2010

Ranked by: Revenue for design services performed both inside and outside of home country, in millions of U.S. dollars. **Remarks:** Also notes headquarters, type of firm, international as a percentage of total design revenue, rank for previous year, and breakdown by market. **Number listed:** 150

1. AECOM Technology Corp. (U.S.), with $5,919.8 million
2. URS Corp. (U.S.), $5,038.8
3. Jacobs Engineering Group Inc. (U.S.), $4,748.4
4. WorleyParsons Ltd. (Australia), $3,650.5
5. CH2M Hill Cos., Ltd. (U.S.), $3,602.7
6. AMEC plc (U.K.), $3,399
7. Fluor Corp. (U.S.), $3,127.5
8. Fugro NV (Netherlands), $3,001
9. SNC-Lavalin International Inc. (Canada), $2,848.5
10. ARCADIS NV (Netherlands), $2,653

Source: *ENR: Engineering News-Record*, Top 200 International Design Firms (annual), July 25, 2011, p. 46+.

2573 ■ TOP INTERNATIONAL DESIGN FIRMS, 2010

Ranked by: Revenue for design services performed outside of home country, in millions of U.S. dollars. **Remarks:** Also notes headquarters, type of firm, international as a percentage of total design revenue, rank for previous year, and breakdown by market. **Number listed:** 200

1. WorleyParsons Ltd. (Australia), with $2,850.6 million
2. Fugro NV (Netherlands), $2,826
3. AECOM Technology Corp. (U.S.), $2,629
4. AMEC plc (U.K.), $2,456
5. Jacobs Engineering Group Inc. (U.S.), $2,256.3
6. ARCADIS NV (Netherlands), $2,122
7. Fluor Corp. (U.S.), $2,057.6
8. Dar Al-Handasah Consultants (Shair & Partners, Egypt), $1,776.6
9. KBR Inc. (U.S.), $1,737.9
10. SNC-Lavalin International Inc. (Canada), $1,670.9

Source: *ENR: Engineering News-Record*, Top 200 International Design Firms (annual), July 25, 2011, p. 42+.

2574 ■ TOP INTERNATIONAL DESIGN FIRMS IN AFRICA, 2010

Ranked by: Revenue for design services performed by companies based outside of the region. **Remarks:** Specific figures not provided. **Number listed:** 10

1. SNC-Lavalin International Inc.
2. KBR Inc.
3. Aurecon
4. Dar Al-Handasah Consultants
5. Egis
6. AMEC plc
7. Mott MacDonald Group Ltd.
8. Anhui Foreign Economic Construction Group
9. Hatch Group
10. DHV Group

Source: *ENR: Engineering News-Record*, Top 200 International Design Firms (annual), July 25, 2011, p. 40.

2575 ■ TOP INTERNATIONAL DESIGN FIRMS IN ASIA, 2010

Ranked by: Revenue for design services performed by companies based outside of the region. Remarks: Specific figures not provided. Number listed: 10

1. AECOM Technology Corp.
2. KBR Inc.
3. Fluor Corp.
4. Aurecon
5. Bechtel Group Inc.
6. Balfour Beatty plc
7. Arup Group Ltd.
8. Fugro NV
9. URS Corp.
10. China Chengda Engineering Co., Ltd.

Source: *ENR: Engineering News-Record*, Top 200 International Design Firms (annual), July 25, 2011, p. 40.

2576 ■ TOP INTERNATIONAL DESIGN FIRMS IN CANADA, 2010

Ranked by: Revenue for design services performed by companies based outside of Canada. Remarks: Specific figures not provided. Number listed: 10

1. AMEC plc
2. WorleyParsons Ltd.
3. Jacobs Engineering Group Inc.
4. AECOM Technology Corp.
5. CH2M Hill Cos., Ltd.
6. Bechtel Group Inc.
7. Fluor Corp.
8. Tetra Tech Inc.
9. Mott MacDonald Group Ltd.
10. URS Corp.

Source: *ENR: Engineering News-Record*, Top 200 International Design Firms (annual), July 25, 2011, p. 40.

2577 ■ TOP INTERNATIONAL DESIGN FIRMS IN EUROPE, 2010

Ranked by: Revenue for design services performed by companies based outside of the region. Remarks: Specific figures not provided. Number listed: 10

1. Fugro NV
2. Jacobs Engineering Group Inc.
3. Grontimij NV

4. Ramboll Gruppen A/S
5. AECOM Technology Corp.
6. Fluor Corp.
7. Poyry
8. ARCADIS NV
9. Tecnicas Reunidas SA
10. WSP Group plc

Source: *ENR: Engineering News-Record*, Top 200 International Design Firms (annual), July 25, 2011, p. 40.

2578 ■ TOP INTERNATIONAL DESIGN FIRMS IN GENERAL BUILDING CONSTRUCTION, 2010

Ranked by: Revenue for design services performed outside of home country. Remarks: Specific figures not provided. Number listed: 10

1. Dar Al-Handasah Consultants
2. AECOM Technology Corp.
3. Arup Group Ltd.
4. WSP Group plc
5. ARCADIS NV
6. Fugro NV
7. WS Atkins plc
8. Ramboll Gruppen A/S
9. Grontmij NV
10. Aedas

Source: *ENR: Engineering News-Record*, Top 200 International Design Firms (annual), July 25, 2011, p. 39.

2579 ■ TOP INTERNATIONAL DESIGN FIRMS IN HAZARDOUS WASTE STRUCTURE CONSTRUCTION, 2010

Ranked by: Revenue for design services performed outside of home country. Remarks: Specific figures not provided. Number listed: 10

1. ARCADIS NV
2. AECOM Technology Corp.
3. URS Corp.
4. Stantec Inc.
5. CH2M Hill Cos., Ltd.
6. Tetra Tech Inc.
7. Cardno
8. AMEC plc
9. Conestoga-Rovers & Associates
10. WS Atkins plc

Source: *ENR: Engineering News-Record*, Top 200 International Design Firms (annual), July 25, 2011, p. 39.

2580 ■ TOP INTERNATIONAL DESIGN FIRMS IN INDUSTRIAL STRUCTURE CONSTRUCTION, 2010

Ranked by: Revenue for design services performed outside of home country. Remarks: Specific figures not provided. Number listed: 10

1. Fluor Corp.
2. SNC-Lavalin International Inc.
3. Jacobs Engineering Group Inc.
4. Hatch Group
5. Bechtel Group Inc.
6. Poyry

7. Aurecon
8. AMEC plc
9. ARCADIS NV
10. WSP Group plc

Source: *ENR: Engineering News-Record*, Top 200 International Design Firms (annual), July 25, 2011, p. 39.

2581 ■ TOP INTERNATIONAL DESIGN FIRMS IN LATIN AMERICA AND THE CARIBBEAN, 2010

Ranked by: Revenue for design services performed by companies based outside of the region. **Remarks:** Specific figures not provided. **Number listed:** 10

1. SNC-Lavalin International Inc.
2. Fluor Corp.
3. ARCADIS NV
4. China Railway Group Ltd.
5. Fugro NV
6. Technip
7. Bechtel Group Inc.
8. AMEC plc
9. WorleyParsons Ltd.
10. Maire Tecnimont SpA

Source: *ENR: Engineering News-Record*, Top 200 International Design Firms (annual), July 25, 2011, p. 40.

2582 ■ TOP INTERNATIONAL DESIGN FIRMS IN MANUFACTURING STRUCTURE CONSTRUCTION, 2010

Ranked by: Revenue for design services performed outside of home country. **Remarks:** Specific figures not provided. **Number listed:** 10

1. Golder Associates Corp.
2. Arup Group Ltd.
3. URS Corp.
4. ARCADIS NV
5. CH2M Hill Cos., Ltd.
6. Sumitomo Mitsui Construction Co., Ltd.
7. Larsen & Toubro Ltd.
8. Tebodin Consultants & Engineers
9. Aurecon
10. Setec

Source: *ENR: Engineering News-Record*, Top 200 International Design Firms (annual), July 25, 2011, p. 39.

2583 ■ TOP INTERNATIONAL DESIGN FIRMS IN THE MIDDLE EAST, 2010

Ranked by: Revenue for design services performed by companies based outside of the region. **Remarks:** Specific figures not provided. **Number listed:** 10

1. Dar Al-Handasah Consultants
2. Tecnicas Reunidas SA
3. WorleyParsons Ltd.
4. JGC Corp.
5. AECOM Technology Corp.
6. Sinopec Engineering Inc.
7. KBR Inc.
8. SNC-Lavalin International Inc.
9. Mott MacDonald Group Ltd.

10. Fluor Corp.

Source: *ENR: Engineering News-Record*, Top 200 International Design Firms (annual), July 25, 2011, p. 40.

2584 ■ TOP INTERNATIONAL DESIGN FIRMS IN PETROLEUM STRUCTURE CONSTRUCTION, 2010

Ranked by: Revenue for design services performed outside of home country. **Remarks:** Specific figures not provided. **Number listed:** 10

1. WorleyParsons Ltd.
2. Fugro NV
3. KBR Inc.
4. AMEC plc
5. Tecnicas Reunidas SA
6. Fluor Corp.
7. Jacobs Engineering Group Inc.
8. Technip
9. Bechtel Group Inc.
10. JGC Corp.

Source: *ENR: Engineering News-Record*, Top 200 International Design Firms (annual), July 25, 2011, p. 39.

2585 ■ TOP INTERNATIONAL DESIGN FIRMS IN POWER STRUCTURE CONSTRUCTION, 2010

Ranked by: Revenue for design services performed outside of home country. **Remarks:** Specific figures not provided. **Number listed:** 10

1. WorleyParsons Ltd.
2. AMEC plc
3. China Chengda Engineering Co., Ltd.
4. SNC-Lavalin International Inc.
5. Jacobs Engineering Group Inc.
6. Poyry
7. AF AB
8. AECOM Technology Corp.
9. Black & Veatch
10. Balfour Beatty plc

Source: *ENR: Engineering News-Record*, Top 200 International Design Firms (annual), July 25, 2011, p. 39.

2586 ■ TOP INTERNATIONAL DESIGN FIRMS IN SEWER/ WASTE STRUCTURE CONSTRUCTION, 2010

Ranked by: Revenue for design services performed outside of home country. **Remarks:** Specific figures not provided. **Number listed:** 10

1. AECOM Technology Corp.
2. MWH Global Inc.
3. CH2M Hill Cos., Ltd.
4. Mott MacDonald Group Ltd.
5. Golder Associates Corp.
6. ARCADIS NV
7. The Louis Berger Group Inc.
8. GHD Pty., Ltd.
9. Black & Veatch
10. Stantec Inc.

Source: *ENR: Engineering News-Record*, Top 200 International Design Firms (annual), July 25, 2011, p. 39.

2587 ■ TOP INTERNATIONAL DESIGN FIRMS IN TRANSPORTATION STRUCTURE CONSTRUCTION, 2010

Ranked by: Revenue for design services performed outside of home country. **Remarks:** Specific figures not provided. **Number listed:** 10

1. Balfour Beatty plc
2. AECOM Technology Corp.
3. The Louis Berger Group Inc.
4. Dar Al-Handasah Consultants
5. EGIS
6. Arup Group Ltd.
7. Mott MacDonald Group Ltd.
8. WS Atkins plc
9. COWI A/S
10. SYSTRA

Source: *ENR: Engineering News-Record*, Top 200 International Design Firms (annual), July 25, 2011, p. 39.

2588 ■ TOP INTERNATIONAL DESIGN FIRMS IN WATER STRUCTURE CONSTRUCTION, 2010

Ranked by: Revenue for design services performed outside of home country. **Remarks:** Specific figures not provided. **Number listed:** 10

1. ARCADIS NV
2. Grontimij NV
3. MWH Global Inc.
4. AECOM Technology Corp.
5. SNC-Lavalin International Inc.
6. Mott MacDonald Group Ltd.
7. Balfour Beatty plc
8. Stantec Inc.
9. The Louis Berger Group Inc.
10. Tetra Tech Inc.

Source: *ENR: Engineering News-Record*, Top 200 International Design Firms (annual), July 25, 2011, p. 39.

2589 ■ TOP U.S. DESIGN FIRMS IN INTERNATIONAL MARKETS, 2011

Ranked by: International revenue. **Remarks:** Specific figures not provided. Also notes rank for previous year. **Number listed:** 50

1. Fluor Corp.
2. AECOM Technology Corp.
3. Jacobs Engineering Group Inc.
4. KBR
5. AMEC plc
6. Bechtel Group Inc.
7. CH2M Hill Cos., Ltd.
8. URS Corp.
9. Parsons Brinckerhoff Inc.
10. CB & I

Source: *ENR: Engineering News-Record*, Top 500 Design Firms (annual), April 23, 2012, p. 58.

2590 ■ WORLD'S MOST ETHICAL ENGINEERING AND DESIGN COMPANIES, 2012

Ranked by: Score based on five criteria: ethics and compliance program; reputation, leadership, and innovation; governance; corporate citizenship and responsibility; and culture of ethics. **Remarks:** Specific scores not provided; companies are listed alphabetically, not ranked. **Number listed:** 4

1. AECOM Technology Corp. (U.S.)
2. CH2M Hill Cos., Ltd. (U.S.)
3. Fluor Corp. (U.S.)
4. Parsons Corp. (U.S.)

Source: *Ethisphere Magazine*, World's Most Ethical Companies (annual), http://www.ethisphere.com, 2012.

Engineering Firms

2591 ■ LARGEST COLORADO-BASED ENGINEERING FIRMS, 2010

Ranked by: Number of engineers. **Remarks:** Also notes contact information and number of employees. **Number listed:** 10

1. CH2M Hill Cos., Ltd., with 3,716 engineers
2. MWH Global Inc., 2,851
3. ARCADIS, 1,188
4. Merrick & Co., 128
5. Martin/Martin, 88
6. M-E Engineers Inc., 75,
7. CTL Thompson, 51
8. Felburg Holt & Ullevig, 42
9. Samuel Engineering, 25
10. MKK Consulting Engineers Inc., 22

Source: *ColoradoBiz*, Top Professional Services (annual), December 2011, p. 47.

2592 ■ LARGEST ENGINEERING/ARCHITECTURE COMPANIES, 2010

Ranked by: Engineering/architecture revenue, in dollars. **Number listed:** 42

1. Jacobs Engineering Group Inc., with $3,032,050,000
2. AECOM Technology Corp., $1,502,576,000
3. M + W U.S., $423,949,985
4. URS Corp., $422,120,000
5. Stantec Inc., $257,000,000
6. Parsons Brinckerhoff Inc., $219,900,000
7. Science Applications International Corp. (SAIC), $200,024,000
8. Burns & McDonnell, $131,850,000
9. Arup, $124,340,604
10. STV Group, $120,960,000

Source: *Building Design & Construction*, Giants 300 (annual), July 2011, p. 45.

2593 ■ LARGEST ENGINEERING COMPANIES, 2010

Ranked by: Engineering billings, in dollars. **Number listed:** 58

1. Fluor Corp., with $2,657,929,000
2. Syska Hennessy Group, $94,868,000
3. Affiliated Engineers Inc., $86,516,430
4. WSP Flack-Kurtz, $78,235,251
5. KPFF Consulting Engineers, $69,000,000
6. Smith Seckman Reid, $61,900,000
7. TMAD Taylor & Gaines, $61,196,592

8. AKF Group, $59,000,000
9. Henderson Engineers, $56,300,000
10. R. G. Vanderweil Engineers, $46,260,000

Source: *Building Design & Construction*, Giants 300 (annual), July 2011, p. 45.

Engineering Services

2594 ■ FASTEST-GROWING PRIVATE ENGINEERING COMPANIES IN THE U.S., 2007-2010

Ranked by: Average annual sales growth over three years, in percent. **Remarks:** Also notes headquarters, revenue, and rank in the overall *Inc. 500.* To qualify, private companies must have had annual revenues of at least $100,000 in 2007 and $2 million in 2010. **Number listed:** 4

1. Bridger Photonis, with 1,795.6%
2. CORE Consulting, 860%
3. Celestech, 787.1%
4. Photon Machine, 713.5%

Source: *Inc.*, Inc. 500 (annual), September 2011, p. 118.

2595 ■ LARGEST COMPANIES IN THE ENGINEERING, ACCOUNTING, RESEARCH, AND MANAGEMENT INDUSTRY BY EMPLOYEES, 2010

Ranked by: Total number of employees. **Remarks:** Also notes contact information for headquarters, number of employees at headquarters, revenue, rank by revenue, and primary SIC code. **Number listed:** 404

1. Sodexho Management Inc., with 110,000 employees
2. Ascension Health Inc., 106,000
3. Sodexho Operations LLC, 100,000
4. Golden Gate Private Equity Inc., 54,453
5. Mayo Foundation for Medical Education & Research, 52,700
6. Platinum Equity LLC, 48,808
7. Aecom Technology Corp., 48,100
8. Bechtel Group Inc., 47,000
8. URS Corp., 47,000
10. SAIC Inc., 46,200

Source: *Business Rankings*, (annual), Dun & Bradstreet Inc., 2011, p. VI.254+.

2596 ■ LARGEST COMPANIES IN THE ENGINEERING, ACCOUNTING, RESEARCH, AND MANAGEMENT INDUSTRY BY SALES, 2010

Ranked by: Total revenue, in dollars. **Remarks:** Also notes contact information for headquarters, number of employees at headquarters and overall, rank by employees, and primary SIC code. **Number listed:** 406

1. Fluor Corp., with $20,849,349,000
2. Ascension Health Inc., $14,773,336,000
3. General Electric International Inc., $12,144,769,000
4. SAIC Inc., $10,846,000,000
5. Deloitte & Touche LLP, $10,722,000,000
5. Deloitte LLP, $10,722,000,000
7. Yellow Roadway Technologies Inc., $9,621,316,000

8. URS Corp., $9,177,051,000
9. The Shaw Group Inc., $7,000,779,000
10. Foster Wheeler Ltd., $6,854,290,000

Source: *Business Rankings*, (annual), Dun & Bradstreet Inc., 2011, p. V.228+.

Entertainers

2597 ■ MOST POWERFUL ACTORS, 2011

Ranked by: Score based on earnings and such measures of popularity as Internet presence, press clippings, magazine cover stories, and mentions on television and radio. **Remarks:** Specific scores not provided. Also notes overall rank in the *Celebrity 100.* **Number listed:** 10

1. Johnny Depp
2. Leonardo DiCaprio
3. Adam Sandler
4. Brad Pitt
5. Robert Pattinson
6. Tom Hanks
7. Will Smith
8. Robert Downey Jr.
9. Ben Stiller
10. Mark Wahlberg

Source: *Forbes*, The Celebrity 100 (annual), http://www.forbes.com, June 6, 2011.

2598 ■ MOST POWERFUL ACTRESSES, 2011

Ranked by: Score based on earnings and such measures of popularity as Internet presence, press clippings, magazine cover stories, and mentions on television and radio. **Remarks:** Specific scores not provided. Also notes overall rank in the *Celebrity 100.* **Number listed:** 10

1. Angelina Jolie
2. Jennifer Aniston
3. Sandra Bullock
4. Kristen Stewart
5. Reese Witherspoon
6. Julia Roberts
7. Sarah Jessica Parker
8. Natalie Portman
9. Cameron Diaz
10. Katherine Heigl

Source: *Forbes*, The Celebrity 100 (annual), http://www.forbes.com, June 6, 2011.

2599 ■ MOST POWERFUL CELEBRITIES, 2011

Ranked by: Score based on earnings and such measures of popularity as Internet presence, press clippings, magazine cover stories, and mentions on television and radio. **Remarks:** Specific scores not provided. Also notes earnings. **Number listed:** 100

1. Lady Gaga
2. Oprah Winfrey
3. Justin Bieber
4. U2
5. Elton John
6. Tiger Woods

7. Taylor Swift
8. Bon Jovi
9. Simon Cowell
10. LeBron James

Source: *Forbes*, The Celebrity 100 (annual), June 6, 2011, p. 76-86.

2600 ■ MOST POWERFUL COMEDIANS, 2011

Ranked by: Score based on earnings and such measures of popularity as Internet presence, press clippings, magazine cover stories, and mentions on television and radio. **Remarks:** Specific scores not provided. Also notes overall rank in the *Celebrity 100*. **Number listed:** 4

1. Jerry Seinfeld
2. Jeff Dunham
3. Larry the Cable Guy

Source: *Forbes*, The Celebrity 100 (annual), http://www.forbes.com, June 6, 2011.

2601 ■ MOST POWERFUL DIRECTORS/PRODUCERS, 2011

Ranked by: Score based on earnings and such measures of popularity as Internet presence, press clippings, magazine cover stories, and mentions on television and radio. **Remarks:** Specific scores not provided. Also notes overall rank in the *Celebrity 100*. **Number listed:** 8

1. Tyler Perry
2. Steven Spielberg
3. James Cameron
4. Jerry Bruckheimer
5. Christopher Nolan
6. Dick Wolf
7. Mark Burnett
8. Chuck Lorre

Source: *Forbes*, The Celebrity 100 (annual), http://www.forbes.com, June 6, 2011.

2602 ■ MOST POWERFUL HIP-HOP IMPRESARIOS, 2011

Ranked by: Score based on earnings and such measures of popularity as Internet presence, press clippings, magazine cover stories, and mentions on television and radio. **Remarks:** Specific scores not provided. Also notes overall rank in the *Celebrity 100*. **Number listed:** 5

1. Jay-Z
2. Sean (Diddy) Combs
3. Eminem
4. Kanye West
5. Lil Wayne

Source: *Forbes*, The Celebrity 100 (annual), http://www.forbes.com, June 6, 2011.

2603 ■ MOST POWERFUL MUSICIANS, 2011

Ranked by: Score based on earnings and such measures of popularity as Internet presence, press clippings. magazine cover stories, and mentions on television and radio. **Remarks:** Specific scores not provided. Also notes overall rank in the *Celebrity 100*. **Number listed:** 15

1. Lady Gaga
2. Justin Bieber
3. U2

4. Elton John
5. Taylor Swift
6. Bon Jovi
7. Katy Perry
8. Black Eyed Peas
9. Paul McCartney
10. Beyonce Knowles

Source: *Forbes*, The Celebrity 100 (annual), http://www.forbes.com, June 6, 2011.

2604 ■ MOST POWERFUL PERSONALITIES, 2011

Ranked by: Score based on earnings and such measures of popularity as Internet presence, press clippings, magazine cover stories, and mentions on television and radio. **Remarks:** Specific scores not provided. Also notes earnings. Ranking is available online only, not in print. **Number listed:** 13

1. Oprah Winfrey
2. Simon Cowell
3. Donald Trump
4. Dr. Phil McGraw
5. Rush Limbaugh
6. Ryan Seacrest
7. Howard Stern
8. Glenn Beck
9. Ellen DeGeneres
10. David Letterman

Source: *Forbes*, The Celebrity 100 (annual), http://www.forbes.com, June 6, 2011.

2605 ■ MOST POWERFUL TV ACTORS, 2011

Ranked by: Score based on earnings and such measures of popularity as Internet presence, press clippings, magazine cover stories, and mentions on television and radio. **Remarks:** Specific scores not provided. Also notes overall rank in the *Celebrity 100*. **Number listed:** 5

1. Charlie Sheen
2. Steve Carell
3. Ray Romano
4. Hugh Laurie
5. Mark Harmon

Source: *Forbes*, The Celebrity 100 (annual), http://www.forbes.com, June 6, 2011.

2606 ■ MOST POWERFUL TV ACTRESSES, 2011

Ranked by: Score based on earnings and such measures of popularity as Internet presence, press clippings, magazine cover stories, and mentions on television and radio. **Remarks:** Specific scores not provided. Also notes overall rank in the *Celebrity 100*. **Number listed:** 5

1. Eva Longoria
2. Tina Fey
3. Courteney Cox
4. Teri Hatcher
5. Mariska Hargitay

Source: *Forbes*, The Celebrity 100 (annual), http://www.forbes.com, June 6, 2011.

Entertainers—Compensation

2607 ■ HIGHEST-PAID CELEBRITIES, 2011

Ranked by: Annual earnings, in millions of dollars. **Number listed:** 100

1. Oprah Winfrey, with $290 million
2. U2, $195
3. Tyler Perry, $130
4. Bon Jovi, $125
5. Jerry Bruckheimer, $113
6. Steven Spielberg, $107
7. Elton John, $100
8. Lady Gaga, $90
8. Simon Cowell, $90
10. James Patterson, $84

Source: *Forbes*, The Celebrity 100 (annual), http://www.forbes.com, June 6, 2011.

Entertainment Industry
See also: **Amusement Industry**

2608 ■ FASTEST-GROWING ENTERTAINMENT COMPANIES, 2008-2011

Ranked by: Score based on three-year growth in revenue and earnings, and three-year total return to investors. **Remarks:** Specific scores not provided. To qualify for list, companies must have revenues of at least $50 million, net income of at least $10 million, market capitalization of at least $250 million, and stock price of at least $5. Int'l companies are eligible if they trade on a U.S. exchange and file quarterly reports. **Number listed:** 2

1. Discovery Communications
2. DG FastChannel Inc.

Source: *Fortune*, 100 Fastest-Growing Companies (annual), http://www.fortune.com, September 26, 2011.

2609 ■ TOP *FORTUNE 500* COMPANIES IN ENTERTAIN-MENT, 2011

Ranked by: Revenue, in millions of dollars. **Remarks:** Also notes overall rank in the *Fortune 500;* profits; profits as a percentage of revenue; stockholders' equity; and rank by each criterion. **Number listed:** 7

1. Walt Disney Co., with $40,893 million
2. News Corp., $33,405
3. Time Warner Inc., $28,974
4. Viacom Inc., $14,963
5. CBS Corp., $14,245
6. CC Media Holdings Inc., $6,161
7. Live Nation Entertainment Inc., $5,384

Source: *Fortune*, Fortune 500 (annual), May 21, 2012, p. F-35.

2610 ■ WORLD'S MOST ADMIRED ENTERTAINMENT COMPANIES, 2012

Ranked by: Score, on a scale of 10, based on a survey of executives, directors, and securities analysts of companies within their own industry on eight criteria: innovation, financial soundness, employee talent, use of corporate assets, long-term investment value, social responsibility, quality of management, and quality of products/services. **Remarks:** Specific scores not provided. Also notes rank for previous year. **Number listed:** 6

1. Walt Disney Co.
2. Viacom Inc.
3. Time Warner Inc.
4. Discovery Communications Inc.
5. Bertelsmann AG

6. CBS Corp.

Source: *Fortune*, World's Most Admired Companies (annual), March 19, 2012, p. 148.

Entrepreneurs
See: **Small Business**

Environmental Protection

2611 ■ THE "GREENEST" BIG COMPANIES IN AMERICA, 2011

Ranked by: Score based on environmental impact, policies, and reputation. **Remarks:** Also notes industry and score for each criterion. **Number listed:** 500

1. International Business Machines Corp. (IBM), with 82.5 points
2. Hewlett-Packard Co., 75.8
3. Sprint Nextel Corp., 75.6
4. Baxter, 74.9
5. Dell Inc., 74.7
6. Johnson & Johnson, 74.6
7. Accenture Ltd., 74
8. Office Depot Inc., 73.6
9. CA Technologies, 72.6
10. NVIDIA Corp., 71.9

Source: *Newsweek*, The Greenest Big Companies (annual), http://www.newsweek.com, October 16, 2011.

2612 ■ THE LEAST "GREEN" BIG COMPANIES IN AMERICA, 2011

Ranked by: Score based on environmental impact, policies, and reputation. **Remarks:** Scores not provided. **Number listed:** 20

1. T. Rowe Price Group
2. BlackRock
3. Monsanto Co.
4. Invesco
5. CONSOL Energy
6. Archer Daniels Midland Co.
7. Ameren
8. Bunge Ltd.
9. Peabody Energy
10. Ralcorp Holdings

Source: *Newsweek*, The Greenest Big Companies (annual), http://www.newsweek.com, October 16, 2011.

2613 ■ THE WORLD'S "GREENEST" BIG COMPANIES, 2011

Ranked by: Score based on environmental impact, policies, and reputation. **Remarks:** Also notes industry and score for each criterion. **Number listed:** 100

1. Munchener Ruckversicherungs Gesellschaft AG (Munich Re), with 83.6 points
2. International Business Machines Corp. (IBM), 82.5
3. National Australia Bank, 82.2
3. Banco Bradesco SA, 82.2

5. Australia & New Zealand Banking Group (ANZ), 80.9
6. BT Group, 80.4
7. Tata Consultancy Services, 79.1
8. Infosys, 77.3
9. Koninklijke Philips Electronics NV (Royal Philips Electronics NV), 77.2
10. Swisscom, 77

Source: *Newsweek*, The Greenest Big Companies (annual), http://www.newsweek.com, October 16, 2011.

2614 ■ WORLD'S TOP RETAILERS IN SEAFOOD SUSTAINABILITY, 2011

Ranked by: Score, on a scale of 10, based on policy to avoid supporting destructive fishing and aquaculture practices, to promote seafood sustainability and ocean conservation outside of the grocery industry, and to adopt transparency in providing relevant information about the seafood supply chain to consumers and other interested parties. **Number listed:** 20

1. Safeway Inc., with 7.1 points
2. Whole Foods Market Inc., 7
3. Wegmans Food Markets Inc., 6.6
4. Harris Teeter Inc., 6.5
5. Target Corp., 6.4
6. Aldi Group, 6
7. Koninklijke Ahold NV (Royal Ahold NV), 5.9
8. Delhaize Group, 5.5
9. A & P, 5.4
10. H. E. Butt Grocery Co., 5.1
10. Price Chopper Operating Co., Inc., 5.1

Source: *Carting Away the Oceans*, (annual), Greenpeace, April 2012.

Environmental Services Firms

2615 ■ FASTEST-GROWING PRIVATE ENVIRONMENTAL SERVICES COMPANIES IN THE U.S., 2007-2010

Ranked by: Average annual sales growth over three years, in percent. **Remarks:** Also notes headquarters, revenue, and rank in the overall *Inc. 500*. To qualify, private companies must have had annual revenues of at least $100,000 in 2007 and $2 million in 2010. **Number listed:** 3

1. CleanScapes, with 1,023.4%
2. Resource Environmental Solutions, 855.8%
3. Resource Solutions Group, 850.3%

Source: *Inc.*, Inc. 500 (annual), September 2011, p. 118.

2616 ■ TOP ENVIRONMENTAL CONTRACTORS IN AIR POLLUTION CONTROL, 2010

Ranked by: Relevant revenue, in millions of dollars. **Number listed:** 10

1. URS Corp., with $504.3 million
2. Bechtel Corp., $464..3
3. Fluor Corp., $383.1
4. CH2M Hill Cos., Ltd., $149.6
5. Parsons Corp., $135.2
6. WorleyParsons Ltd., $100.2
7. Casey Industrial Inc., $98.3

8. Golder Associates Corp., $87.7
9. Tetra Tech Inc., $82
10. Black & Veatch, $69.2

Source: *ENR: Engineering News-Record*, Top 200 Environmental Firms (annual), August 1, 2011, p. 54.

2617 ■ TOP ENVIRONMENTAL CONTRACTORS IN CONSTRUCTION/REMEDIATION, 2010

Ranked by: Relevant revenue, in millions of dollars. **Number listed:** 20

1. Bechtel Corp., with $1,747.9 million
2. The Shaw Group Inc., $1,013.4
3. Fluor Corp., $963.8
4. Layne Christensen Co., $654.9
5. Skanska USA Inc., $608.4
6. Insituform Technologies Inc., $532.7
7. The Walsh Group Ltd., $526.
8. Kiewit Corp., $491.8
9. Alberici Corp., $480
10. CH2M Hill Cos., Ltd., $421.9

Source: *ENR: Engineering News-Record*, Top 200 Environmental Firms (annual), August 1, 2011, p. 57.

2618 ■ TOP ENVIRONMENTAL CONTRACTORS IN CONSULTING/STUDIES, 2010

Ranked by: Relevant revenue, in millions of dollars. **Number listed:** 10

1. CH2M Hill Cos., Ltd., with $1,265.6 million
2. URS Corp., $1,143.1
3. Tetra Tech Inc., $697
4. AECOM Technology Corp., $424.2
5. Environmental Resources Management Ltd. (ERM Group), $420.9
6. Golder Associates Corp., $406.7
7. Arcadis/Malcolm Pirnie, $365.8
8. Science Applications International Corp. (SAIC), $307.7
9. Stantec Inc., $277.2
10. Cardno Ltd., $231.6

Source: *ENR: Engineering News-Record*, Top 200 Environmental Firms (annual), August 1, 2011, p. 57.

2619 ■ TOP ENVIRONMENTAL CONTRACTORS IN DESIGN/ENGINEERING, 2010

Ranked by: Relevant revenue, in millions of dollars. **Number listed:** 10

1. CH2M Hill Cos., Ltd., with $1,303.9 million
2. MWH Global Inc., $894.9
3. Tetra Tech Inc., $861
4. AECOM Technology Corp., $742.4
5. Bechtel Corp., $710.1
6. Camp Dresser & McKee Inc. (CDM), $447.1
7. URS Corp., $437.1
8. Black & Veatch, $389.2
9. Parsons Brinckerhoff Inc., $313.3
10. HDR Inc., $282

Source: *ENR: Engineering News-Record*, Top 200 Environmental Firms (annual), August 1, 2011, p. 57.

2620 ■ TOP ENVIRONMENTAL CONTRACTORS IN ENVIRONMENTAL MANAGEMENT, 2010

Ranked by: Relevant revenue, in millions of dollars. **Number listed:** 10

1. Tetra Tech Inc., with $369 million
2. URS Corp., $269
3. Environmental Resources Management Ltd. (ERM Group), $235
4. AECOM Technology Corp., $233.9
5. Golder Associates Corp., $215.3
6. EQ, the Environmental Quality Co., $135
7. Science Applications International Corp. (SAIC), $118.9
8. Camp Dresser & McKee Inc. (CDM), $94.4
9. The Shaw Group Inc., $93.5
10. Parsons Corp., $92.8

Source: *ENR: Engineering News-Record*, Top 200 Environmental Firms (annual), August 1, 2011, p. 54.

2621 ■ TOP ENVIRONMENTAL CONTRACTORS IN ENVIRONMENTAL SCIENCE, 2010

Ranked by: Relevant revenue, in millions of dollars. **Number listed:** 10

1. URS Corp., with $403.4 million
2. Veolia Environnement SA, $395.3
3. Tetra Tech Inc., $369
4. Golder Associates Corp., $287.1
5. CH2M Hill Cos., Ltd., $230.1
6. Cardno Ltd., $210.8
7. HDR Inc., $207.8
8. Stantec Inc., $187
9. Battelle Memorial Institute, $183.5
10. Science Applications International Corp. (SAIC), $153.9

Source: *ENR: Engineering News-Record*, Top 200 Environmental Firms (annual), August 1, 2011, p. 54.

2622 ■ TOP ENVIRONMENTAL CONTRACTORS BY FEDERAL CLIENTS, 2010

Ranked by: Total revenue from federal government clients, in millions of dollars. **Number listed:** 10

1. CH2M Hill Cos., Ltd., with $1,844.6 million
2. Bechtel Corp., $1,720.6
3. URS Corp., $1,647.4
4. The Shaw Group Inc., $1,091.3
5. Battelle Memorial Institute, $978.9
6. Fluor Corp., $852.6
7. Tetra Tech Inc., $779
8. Kiewit Corp., $580.3
9. Science Applications International Corp. (SAIC), $573.5
10. Alberici Corp., $364.8

Source: *ENR: Engineering News-Record*, Top 200 Environmental Firms (annual), August 1, 2011, p. 57.

2623 ■ TOP ENVIRONMENTAL CONTRACTORS IN HAZARDOUS WASTE CLEANUP, 2010

Ranked by: Relevant revenue, in millions of dollars. **Number listed:** 20

1. Veolia Environnement SA, with $1,811.7 million
2. CH2M Hill Cos., Ltd., $667.3
3. Arcadis/Malcolm Pirnie, $651.5
4. The Shaw Group Inc., $561.2
5. AECOM Technology Corp., $555.9
6. URS Corp., $470.7
7. Bechtel Corp., $464.3
8. Sevenson Environmental Services Inc., $322.3
9. Science Applications International Corp. (SAIC), $307.7
10. Parsons Corp., $305.4

Source: *ENR: Engineering News-Record*, Top 200 Environmental Firms (annual), August 1, 2011, p. 54.

2624 ■ TOP ENVIRONMENTAL CONTRACTORS BY NEW CONTRACTS, 2010

Ranked by: Total value of new contracts awarded during the year, in millions of dollars. **Number listed:** 30

1. CH2M Hill Cos., Ltd., with $2,525 million
2. URS Corp., $2,310.5
3. Tetra Tech Inc., $2,250
4. AECOM Technology Corp., $1,928.8
5. The Shaw Group Inc., $1,389.6
6. Arcadis/Malcolm Pirnie, $1,206
7. Camp Dresser & McKee Inc. (CDM), $1,163.4
8. Veolia Environnement SA, $1,159
9. Battelle Memorial Institute, $1,019.8
10. EnergySolutions Inc., $1,000

Source: *ENR: Engineering News-Record*, Top 200 Environmental Firms (annual), August 1, 2011, p. 60.

2625 ■ TOP ENVIRONMENTAL CONTRACTORS BY NON-U.S. WORK, 2010

Ranked by: Total revenue from work based outside the U.S., in millions of dollars. **Number listed:** 20

1. CH2M Hill Cos., Ltd., with $1,112.2 million
2. EnergySolutions Inc., $1,014.4
3. Tetra Tech Inc., $820
4. AECOM Technology Corp., $813.1
5. Golder Associates Corp., $638
6. Bechtel Corp., $600.8
7. MWH Global Inc., $475.1
8. Black & Veatch, $467.1
9. URS Corp., $403.4
10. Environmental Resources Management Ltd. (ERM Group), $364

Source: *ENR: Engineering News-Record*, Top 200 Environmental Firms (annual), August 1, 2011, p. 58.

2626 ■ TOP ENVIRONMENTAL CONTRACTORS IN NUCLEAR WASTE CLEANUP, 2010

Ranked by: Relevant revenue, in millions of dollars. **Number listed:** 10

1. EnergySolutions Inc., with $1,752 million
2. Bechtel Corp., $1,310.9
3. URS Corp., $1,210.3
4. CH2M Hill Cos., Ltd., $916.6

5. Fluor Corp., $852.6

6. The Shaw Group Inc., $810.7

7. Battelle Memorial Institute, $764.7

8. Portage Inc., $240.6

9. Los Alamos Technical Associates Inc., $228.1

10. The S. M. Stoller Corp., $123.3

Source: *ENR: Engineering News-Record*, Top 200 Environmental Firms (annual), August 1, 2011, p. 54.

2627 ■ TOP ENVIRONMENTAL CONTRACTORS BY PRIVATE CLIENTS, 2010

Ranked by: Total revenue from clients in the private sector, in millions of dollars. **Number listed:** 10

1. Veolia Environnement SA, with $2,207 million

2. EnergySolutions Inc., $1,408.6

3. URS Corp., $1,378.4

4. Bechtel Corp., $1,010.5

5. Tetra Tech Inc., $1,004.5

6. CH2M Hill Cos., Ltd., $832.2

7. Golder Associates Corp., $661.9

8. AECOM Technology Corp., $655.8

9. Arcadis/Malcolm Pirnie, $651.5

10. Environmental Resources Management Ltd. (ERM Group), $622.6

Source: *ENR: Engineering News-Record*, Top 200 Environmental Firms (annual), August 1, 2011, p. 57.

2628 ■ TOP ENVIRONMENTAL CONTRACTORS BY REVENUE, 2010

Ranked by: Revenue from environmental work, including hazardous waste, nuclear waste, solid waste, air quality, water quality, wastewater treatment, environmental management/compliance, and environmental science/planning, in millions of dollars. **Remarks:** Also notes rank for previous year, headquarters, environmental revenue as a percentage of total revenue, number of non-U.S. firms, breakdown of revenue by market, and breakdown of clients by private, federal, and state/local sources. **Number listed:** 200

1. CH2M Hill Cos., Ltd., with $3,835 million

2. URS Corp., $3,362

3. Veolia Environnement SA, $3,294

4. Bechtel Corp., $2,731.1

5. Tetra Tech Inc., $2,050

6. AECOM Technology Corp., $1,767.7

7. EnergySolutions Inc., $1,752

8. The Shaw Group Inc., $1,559

9. Fluor Corp., $1,235.7

10. Kiewit Corp., $1,160.6

Source: *ENR: Engineering News-Record*, Top 200 Environmental Firms (annual), August 1, 2011, p. 61+.

2629 ■ TOP ENVIRONMENTAL CONTRACTORS BY STATE/LOCAL CLIENTS, 2010

Ranked by: Total revenue from state/local government clients, in millions of dollars. **Number listed:** 10

1. CH2M Hill Cos., Ltd., with $1,158.2 million

2. Veolia Environnement SA, $1,054.1

3. AECOM Technology Corp., $797.2

4. Camp Dresser & McKee Inc. (CDM), $665.7

5. MWH Global Inc., $629.7

6. The Walsh Group Ltd., $625.5

7. Insituform Technologies Inc., $527.4

8. Skanska USA Inc., $517.1

9. Kiewit Corp., $499.1

10. Parsons Corp., $434.3

Source: *ENR: Engineering News-Record*, Top 200 Environmental Firms (annual), August 1, 2011, p. 57.

2630 ■ TOP ENVIRONMENTAL CONTRACTORS IN WASTEWATER TREATMENT, 2010

Ranked by: Relevant revenue, in millions of dollars. **Number listed:** 20

1. CH2M Hill Cos., Ltd., with $939.6 million

2. Veolia Environnement SA, $691.7

3. Insituform Technologies Inc., $523.1

4. AECOM Technology Corp., $480.8

5. Kiewit Corp., $450.4

6. MWH Global Inc., $441.9

7. Camp Dresser & McKee Inc. (CDM), $367.6

8. Black & Veatch, $302.7

9. Layne Christensen Co., $291.9

10. URS Corp., $269

Source: *ENR: Engineering News-Record*, Top 200 Environmental Firms (annual), August 1, 2011, p. 54.

2631 ■ TOP ENVIRONMENTAL CONTRACTORS IN WATER SUPPLY/TREATMENT, 2010

Ranked by: Relevant revenue, in millions of dollars. **Number listed:** 20

1. Tetra Tech Inc., with $1,025 million

2. CH2M Hill Cos., Ltd., $931.9

3. Kiewit Corp., $707.8

4. MWH Global Inc., $530.3

5. The Walsh Group Ltd., $460.9

6. Black & Veatch, $432.5

7. AECOM Technology Corp., $422.8

8. Layne Christensen Co., $412.9

9. Skanska USA Inc., $352.9

10. Alberici Corp., $350.4

Source: *ENR: Engineering News-Record*, Top 200 Environmental Firms (annual), August 1, 2011, p. 54.

Equity Funds
See also: Bond Funds; Mutual Funds; Stock Funds

2632 ■ BEST MIXED EQUITY FUND FAMILIES, 2011

Ranked by: Score based on asset size and relative importance in the Lipper fund universe. **Number listed:** 5

1. Northern Trust Investment, with 16.75 points

2. Neuberger Berman Management, 16.48

3. American Funds, 15.86

4. First Investors Management, 15.63

5. Calvert Funds, 14.86

Source: *Barron's*, Best Mutual Fund Families (annual), February 6, 2012, p. 30.

2633 ■ BEST U.S. EQUITY FUND FAMILIES, 2011

Ranked by: Score based on asset size and relative importance in the Lipper fund universe. **Number listed:** 5

1. State Street Bank & Trust, with 37.08 points
2. Delaware Management, 31.79
3. PNC Funds, 30.29
4. First Investors Management, 29.56
5. HighMark Capital Management, 28.95

Source: *Barron's*, Best Mutual Fund Families (annual), February 6, 2012, p. 30.

2634 ■ WORST MIXED EQUITY FUND FAMILIES, 2011

Ranked by: Score based on asset size and relative importance in the Lipper fund universe. **Number listed:** 5

1. AllianceBernstein, with 3.36 points
2. Russell Investment Group, 3.44
3. Dimensional Fund Advisors, 3.73
4. Pyxis Capital, 3.99
5. Thrivent Financial, 4

Source: *Barron's*, Best Mutual Fund Families (annual), February 6, 2012, p. 30.

2635 ■ WORST U.S. EQUITY FUND FAMILIES, 2011

Ranked by: Score based on asset size and relative importance in the Lipper fund universe. **Number listed:** 5

1. Hartford, with 6.34 points
2. Manning & Napier Advisors, 7.51
3. Thrivent Financial, 9.43
4. RidgeWorth Funds, 10.13
5. Putnam Investment Management, 10.73

Source: *Barron's*, Best Mutual Fund Families (annual), February 6, 2012, p. 30.

Eurobond Market
See: **Security Underwriting**

Executives—Compensation
See also: **Chief Executive Officers**

2636 ■ CHEMICAL EXECUTIVES WITH THE HIGHEST OVERALL COMPENSATION, 2010

Ranked by: Total compensation, in dollars. **Number listed:** 20

1. James Gallogly (LyondellBasell), with $77,061,964
2. George W. Buckley (3M), $23,709,094
3. Andrew N. Liveris (Dow Chemical), $21,337,757
4. John E. McGlade (Air Products), $16,918,012
5. Stephen F. Angel (Praxair), $15,326,642
6. Ellen J. Kullman (DuPont), $14,796,974
7. Hugh Grant (Monsanto), $13,172,341
8. Seifi Ghasemi (Rockwood), $13,158,331
9. Charles Bunch (PPG Industries), $12,386,000
10. Pierre Brondeau (FMC), $9,762,101

Source: *Chemical Week*, Executive Compensation (annual), August 15, 2011, p. 57.

2637 ■ HIGHEST-PAID CEOS IN KENTUCKY, 2010

Ranked by: Annual compensation, in dollars. **Remarks:** Also notes ticker symbol and total compensation. **Number listed:** 25

1. David Novak (Yum! Brands), with $6,470,000
2. Paul Varga (Brown-Forman), $4,690,000
3. John Figueroa (Omnicare), $n/a
4. James O'Brien (Ashland), $3,120,000
5. Michael McCallister (Humana), $3,080,000
6. Paul Rooke (Lexmark Int'l), $2,580,000
7. Mark Sarvary (Tempur-Pedic), $2,200,000
8. Paul Diaz (Kindred Healthcare), $1,340,000
9. Gregory Kenny (General Cable), $825,000
10. Greg Weishar (PharMerica), $736,174

Source: *The Lane Report*, Highest-Paid CEOs (annual), June 2011, p. 38.

2638 ■ HIGHEST-PAID EXECUTIVES OF NORTH BAY PUBLIC COMPANIES, 2010

Ranked by: Total compensation, in dollars. **Remarks:** Ranking covers companies in the California counties of Sonoma, Napa, and Marin. Also notes rank for previous year, contact information, title, age, nature of business, salary and bonus, number of shares held, percentage of voting power, revenues, and fiscal year-end. **Number listed:** 27

1. Carl Bass (Autodesk), with $2,355,953
2. Charles Willis IV (Willis Lease Finance), $1,830,290
3. Martin Hughes (Redwood Trust), $1,819,789
4. George Bado (Autodesk), $1,662,484
5. Jean-Jacques Bienaime (BioMarin Pharm.), $1,492,266
6. Brett Nicholas (Redwood Trust), $1,401,819
7. Mark Hawkins (Autodesk), $960,001
8. George Bull III (Redwood Trust), $893,706
9. John Isbrandtsen (Redwood Trust), $888,970
9. Fred Matera (Redwood Trust), $888,970

Source: *North Bay Business Journal*, Highest-Paid Executives (annual), http://www.northbaybusinessjournal.com, November 28, 2011.

Export/Import Trade

2639 ■ COUNTRIES WITH THE FEWEST EXPORTS, 2010

Ranked by: Exports of goods and services as a percentage of gross domestic product. **Number listed:** 142

1. Burundi, with 5.0%
2. Rwanda, 8.5%
3. Timor-Leste, 9.9%
4. Ethiopia, 10.2%
5. Nepal, 10.6%
6. Brazil, 11.1%
7. Burkina Faso, 11.6%
8. Gambia, 12.1%
9. United States, 12.2%
10. Haiti, 13.8%

Source: *Global Competitiveness Report*, (annual), World Economic Forum, 2011, p. 501.

2640 ■ COUNTRIES WITH THE FEWEST IMPORTS, 2010

Ranked by: Imports of goods and services as a percentage of gross domestic product. **Number listed:** 142

1. Brazil, with 12%
2. Japan, 15.5%
3. United States, 15.9%
4. Qatar, 17%
5. Colombia, 17.1%
6. Venezuela, 17.5%
7. Argentina, 18.9%
8. Azerbaijan, 19.4%
9. Australia, 20.4%
10. Iran, 21.1%

Source: *Global Competitiveness Report*, (annual), World Economic Forum, 2011, p. 465.

2641 ■ COUNTRIES WITH THE HIGHEST LEVEL OF TRADE BARRIERS, 2010

Ranked by: Score, on a scale of seven, based on the level in which tariff and non-tariff barriers significantly reduce the ability of imported goods to compete in the domestic market. **Number listed:** 142

1. Argentina, with 2.5 points
2. Ecuador, 3.1
2. Venezuela, 3.1
4. Belize, 3.3
4. Ukraine, 3.3
6. Iran, 3.4
6. Burundi, 3.4
8. Chad, 3.5
8. Russian Federation, 3.5
8. Haiti, 3.5

Source: *Global Competitiveness Report*, (annual), World Economic Forum, 2011, p. 460.

2642 ■ COUNTRIES WITH THE HIGHEST TRADE-WEIGHTED TARIFF RATE, 2010

Ranked by: Average rate of duty per imported value unit, in percent. **Number listed:** 140

1. Iran, with 23.3%
2. Zimbabwe, 20.5%
3. Gambia, 17.3%
3. Barbados, 17.3%
5. Pakistan, 16.8%
6. Morocco, 16.3%
7. Nepal, 16.2%
8. Tunisia, 15.8%
9. Egypt, 14.7%
10. Algeria, 13.8%

Source: *Global Competitiveness Report*, (annual), World Economic Forum, 2011, p. 461.

2643 ■ COUNTRIES WITH THE LARGEST FOREIGN MARKET SIZE, 2010

Ranked by: Score, on a scale of seven, based on the value of exports of goods and services. **Number listed:** 142

1. China, with 7 points

2. United States, 6.7
3. Germany, 6.5
4. India, 6.2
4. South Korea, 6.2
6. Hong Kong, 6.1
6. Japan, 6.1
6. Russian Federation, 6.1
9. France, 6
9. Netherlands, 6
9. Singapore, 6
9. Taiwan, 6
9. United Kingdom, 6

Source: *Global Competitiveness Report*, (annual), World Economic Forum, 2011, p. 499.

2644 ■ COUNTRIES WITH THE LOWEST LEVEL OF TRADE BARRIERS, 2010

Ranked by: Score, on a scale of seven, based on the level in which tariff and non-tariff barriers significantly reduce the ability of imported goods to compete in the domestic market. **Number listed:** 142

1. New Zealand, with 6.4 points
2. Sweden, 6.1
2. Singapore, 6.1
2. Finland, 6.1
5. Chile, 6.0
5. Luxembourg, 6.0
5. Qatar, 6.0
5. Bahrain, 6.0
5. Hong Kong, 6.0
10. Ireland, 5.7

Source: *Global Competitiveness Report*, (annual), World Economic Forum, 2011, p. 460.

2645 ■ COUNTRIES WITH THE LOWEST TRADE-WEIGHTED TARIFF RATE, 2010

Ranked by: Average rate of duty per imported value unit, in percent. **Number listed:** 140

1. Hong Kong, with 0.0%
1. Singapore, 0.0%
3. Georgia, 0.7%
4. Austria, 0.8%
4. Belgium, 0.8%
4. Bulgaria, 0.8%
4. Cyprus, 0.8%
4. Czech Republic, 0.8%
4. Denmark, 0.8%
4. Estonia, 0.8%
4. Finland, 0.8%
4. France, 0.8%
4. Germany, 0.8%

Source: *Global Competitiveness Report*, (annual), World Economic Forum, 2011, p. 461.

2646 ■ COUNTRIES WITH THE MOST EXPORTS, 2010

Ranked by: Exports of goods and services as a percentage of gross domestic product. **Number listed:** 142

1. Hong Kong, with 226.2%
2. Singapore, 208.2%
3. Luxembourg, 159.1%
4. Puerto Rico, 118.5%
5. Belgium, 105.7%
6. Ireland, 103.9%
7. Malaysia, 97.2%
8. Hungary, 88.3%
9. Netherlands, 87.2%
10. Slovak Republic, 81%

Source: *Global Competitiveness Report*, (annual), World Economic Forum, 2011, p. 501.

2647 ■ **COUNTRIES WITH THE MOST IMPORTS, 2010**

Ranked by: Imports of goods and services as a percentage of gross domestic product. **Number listed:** 142

1. Hong Kong, with 219.2%
2. Singapore, 182.7%
3. Timor-Leste, 152.4%
4. Puerto Rico, 140.4%
5. Lesotho, 118.6%
6. Luxembourg, 113.3%
7. Belgium, 100%
8. Kyrgyz Republic, 90.5%
9. Vietnam, 90%
10. Lebanon, 88.4%

Source: *Global Competitiveness Report*, (annual), World Economic Forum, 2011, p. 465.

2648 ■ **COUNTRIES WITH THE SMALLEST FOREIGN MARKET SIZE, 2010**

Ranked by: Score, on a scale of seven, based on the value of exports of goods and services. **Number listed:** 142

1. Burundi, with 1 points
2. Timor-Leste, 1.4
3. Gambia, 1.6
4. Cape Verde, 1.8
5. Rwanda, 2.1
6. Belize, 2.2
7. Lesotho, 2.3
8. Haiti, 2.4
9. Burkina Faso, 2.6
9. Montenegro, 2.6
9. Guyana, 2.6

Source: *Global Competitiveness Report*, (annual), World Economic Forum, 2011, p. 499.

Family-Friendly Benefits

2649 ■ **CANADA'S TOP FAMILY-FRIENDLY EMPLOYERS, 2012**

Ranked by: Score based on programs and initiatives that assist employees with young families. **Remarks:** Scores not provided; companies are listed alphabetically, not ranked. **Number listed:** 20

1. Catholic Children's Aid Society of Toronto

2. Dalhousie University
3. Desjardins, Mouvement des caisses
4. Georgian College
5. HP Advanced Solutions Inc.
6. Human Resources & Skills Development Canada
7. ISM Canada
8. Johnson Inc.
9. Manitoba Hydro
10. National Energy Board

Source: *Canada's Top 100 Employers*, (annual), http://www.canadastop100.com, December 8, 2011.

Family-Owned Corporations

2650 ■ **IDAHO'S LARGEST FAMILY-OWNED BUSINESSES, 2010**

Ranked by: Number of employees. **Remarks:** Also notes contact information, key executive, and organization goals. **Number listed:** 5

1. J. R. Simplot Co., with 3,147 employees
2. Scentsy, 920
3. Knipe Land Co., Inc., 510
4. Owyhee Plaza Hotel, 100
5. The Caxton Printers, 48

Source: *Idaho Business Review*, Largest Family-Owned Businesses (annual), August 5, 2011.

2651 ■ **LARGEST FAMILY-OWNED BUSINESSES IN DETROIT, 2010**

Ranked by: Revenue, in millions of dollars. **Remarks:** Also notes contact information, year founded, first generation owner, figures for previous year, and family members in management that have a relation to the first-generation owner. **Number listed:** 20

1. Guardian Automotive Products Inc., with $5,000 million
2. Kelly Services Inc., $4,950.3
3. Ilitch Companies, $2,200
4. Plastipak Holdings Inc., $1,941.8
5. Sherwood Food Distributors LLC, $1,271.3
6. Barton Malow Co., $1,122.3
7. The Suburban Collection, $1,054.8
8. Walbridge Aldinger, $1,001.5
9. Wolverine Packing Co., $934
10. H. W. Kaufman Financial Group Inc./Burns & Wilcox Ltd., $900

Source: *Crain's Detroit Business*, Book of Lists (annual), December 26, 2011, p. 43.

2652 ■ **LARGEST FAMILY-OWNED BUSINESSES IN NEW JERSEY, 2011**

Ranked by: Number of New Jersey employees. **Remarks:** Also notes rank for previous year, contact information, year founded, senior executive, number of generation involved in business, and business description. **Number listed:** 187

1. Bayada Home Health Care, with 5,100 employees
2. Inserra Supermarkets Inc., 3,100

3. Quick Chek Food Stores, 3,000
4. The Shevell Group, 2,900
5. Crystal Springs Resort, 2,000
6. Holman Enterprises, 1,700
7. Mars Global Chocolate, 1,500
8. Food Circus Supermarkets, 1,200
9. North Jersey Media Group, 1,129
10. J. Fletcher Creamer & Son, 956

Source: *NJBiz*, Top Family-Owned Businesses (annual), http://www.njbiz.com, September 26, 2011.

2653 ■ TOP FAMILY-OWNED COMPANIES IN COLORADO, 2011

Ranked by: Number of employees. **Remarks:** Also notes rank for previous year, business type, revenue for current and previous year, revenue growth, number of relatives and family generations with company, and number of years family-owned. **Number listed:** 50

1. American Furniture Warehouse Co., with 1,528 employees
2. Vitamin Cottage Natural Food Markets Inc., 1,300
3. RE/MAX Alliance, 840
4. RK Mechanical Inc., 718
5. C & D Enterprises Inc., 660
6. Brakes Plus Inc., 509
7. Ralph Schomp Automotive Inc., 469
8. Mike Shaw Automotive Group, 371
9. OtterBox, 367
10. Publication Printers Corp., 357

Source: *ColoradoBiz*, Top 50 Family-Owned Companies (annual), February 2012, p. 26-27.

Farm Machinery Industry
See: **Agricultural Machinery Industry**

Farms

2654 ■ STATES WITH THE HIGHEST FARM INCOME PER ACRE, 2009

Ranked by: Net farm income per acre, in dollars. **Number listed:** 50

1. New Jersey, with $404
2. Delaware, $394
3. California, $346
4. North Carolina, $319
5. Connecticut, $291
6. Georgia, $229
7. Massachusetts, $207
8. Rhode Island, $194
9. Indiana, $172
10. Iowa, $163

Source: *State Rankings*, (annual), CQ Press, 2011, p. 10.

2655 ■ STATES WITH THE HIGHEST NET FARM INCOME, 2009

Ranked by: Net farm income, in dollars. **Remarks:** Also notes share of national total. **Number listed:** 50

1. California, with $8,782,066,032
2. Iowa, $5,012,848,577
3. Illinois, $3,641,424,489
4. Nebraska, $3,275,706,662
5. Minnesota, $3,020,138,942
6. North Carolina, $2,739,163,485
7. Indiana, $2,539,974,056
8. South Dakota, $2,376,051,657
9. Kansas, $2,368,809,057
10. Georgia, $2,359,381,109

Source: *State Rankings*, (annual), CQ Press, 2011, p. 8.

2656 ■ STATES WITH THE HIGHEST NET FARM INCOME PER OPERATION, 2009

Ranked by: Net farm income per operation, in dollars. **Remarks:** Also notes share of national total. **Number listed:** 50

1. California, with $107,755
2. Delaware, $77,922
3. South Dakota, $75,430
4. Nebraska, $69,401
5. North Dakota, $60,498
6. Iowa, $54,134
7. North Carolina, $52,274
8. Georgia, $49,567
9. Illinois, $48,040
10. Indiana, $41,300

Source: *State Rankings*, (annual), CQ Press, 2011, p. 9.

2657 ■ STATES WITH THE MOST ACRES PER FARM, 2009

Ranked by: Average number of acres per farm. **Number listed:** 50

1. Wyoming, with 2,745 acres
2. New Mexico, 2,098
3. Montana, 2,040
4. Nevada, 1,916
5. Arizona, 1,684
6. South Dakota, 1,387
7. Alaska, 1,294
8. North Dakota, 1,238
9. Nebraska, 966
10. Colorado, 865

Source: *State Rankings*, (annual), CQ Press, 2011, p. 5.

2658 ■ STATES WITH THE MOST FARMS, 2009

Ranked by: Total number of farms. **Remarks:** Also notes share of national total. **Number listed:** 50

1. Texas, with 247,500 farms
2. Missouri, 108,000
3. Iowa, 72,600
4. Oklahoma, 86,500
5. Kentucky, 85,500
6. California, 81,500
7. Minnesota, 81,000
8. Tennessee, 78,700
9. Wisconsin, 78,000

10. Illinois, 75,800

Source: *State Rankings*, (annual), CQ Press, 2011, p. 3.

Fast Food

2659 ■ WORLD'S MOST VALUABLE FAST FOOD BRANDS, 2012

Ranked by: Brand value, a measure of a brand's earnings and contribution, in millions of U.S. dollars. **Remarks:** Also notes annual growth in brand value and rank by brand contribution and brand momentum. **Number listed:** 10

1. McDonald's, with $95,188 million
2. Starbucks, $17,072
3. Subway, $14,843
4. KFC, $8,852
5. Pizza Hut, $5,397
6. Tim Hortons, $3,346
7. Taco Bell, $2,045
8. Wendy's, $1,722
9. Domino's, $797
10. Arby's, $344

Source: *Financial Times*, Global Brands (annual), http://www.ft.com, May 22, 2012.

Fast Food Restaurants

2660 ■ LARGEST BURGER FAST-FOOD CHAINS BY SALES, 2010

Ranked by: Systemwide sales, in millions of dollars. **Remarks:** Also notes average sales per unit, number of franchised and company-owned units, total number of units, and overall rank in the *The QSR 50*. **Number listed:** 16

1. McDonald's, with $32,395 million
2. Burger King, $8,600
3. Wendy's, $8,340
4. Sonic Drive-In, $3,619.9
5. Jack in the Box, $2,934.8
6. Dairy Queen, $2,660
7. Hardee's, $1,695
8. Carl's Jr., $1,310
9. Whataburger, $1,225.7
10. Steak 'n Shake, $786.6

Source: *QSR Magazine*, The QSR 50 (annual), http://www.qsrmagazine.com, August 2011.

2661 ■ LARGEST CHICKEN FAST-FOOD CHAINS BY SALES, 2010

Ranked by: Systemwide sales, in millions of dollars. **Remarks:** Also notes average sales per unit, number of franchised and company-owned units, total number of units, and overall rank in the *The QSR 50*. **Number listed:** 8

1. KFC, with $4,700 million
2. Chick-fil-A, $3,582.5
3. Popeyes, $1,635
4. Church's Chicken, $872.7
5. Zaxby's, $777.6
6. Bojangle's Famous Chicken 'n Biscuits, $712.8

7. El Pollo Loco, $557
8. Boston Market, $513

Source: *QSR Magazine*, The QSR 50 (annual), http://www.qsrmagazine.com, August 2011.

2662 ■ LARGEST FAST-FOOD CHAINS BY SALES, 2010

Ranked by: Systemwide sales, in millions of dollars. **Remarks:** Also notes rank for previous year, restaurant segment, sales for previous two years, percent change, sales per unit, number of franchised and company-owned units, total units, and comments. **Number listed:** 50

1. McDonald's, with $32,395 million
2. Subway, $10,600
3. Burger King, $8,600
4. Wendy's, $8,340
5. Starbucks, $7,560
6. Taco Bell, $6,900
7. Dunkin' Donuts, $6,000
8. Pizza Hut, $5,400
9. KFC, $4,700
10. Sonic Drive-In, $3,619.9

Source: *QSR Magazine*, The QSR 50 (annual), http://www.qsrmagazine.com, August 2011.

2663 ■ LARGEST FAST-FOOD CHAINS BY UNITS, 2010

Ranked by: Total number of units. **Remarks:** Also notes segment, breakdown by franchised and company-owned units, and rank in the overall *QSR 50*. **Number listed:** 50

1. Subway's, with 23,850 units
2. McDonald's, 14,027
3. Starbucks, 11,131
4. Pizza Hut, 7,542
5. Burger King, 7,253
6. Dunkin' Donuts, 6,772
7. Wendy's, 6,576
8. Taco Bell, 5,634
9. KFC, 5,055
10. Domino's Pizza, 4,929

Source: *QSR Magazine*, The QSR 50 (annual), http://www.qsrmagazine.com, August 2011.

2664 ■ LARGEST MEXICAN FAST-FOOD CHAINS BY SALES, 2010

Ranked by: Systemwide sales, in millions of dollars. **Remarks:** Also notes average sales per unit, number of franchised and company-owned units, total number of units, and overall rank in the *The QSR 50*. **Number listed:** 4

1. Taco Bell, with $6,900 million
2. Chipotle Mexican Grill, $1,840
3. Del Taco, $579
4. Qdoba Mexican Grill, $480.8

Source: *QSR Magazine*, The QSR 50 (annual), http://www.qsrmagazine.com, August 8011.

2665 ■ LARGEST PIZZA AND PASTA FAST-FOOD CHAINS BY SALES, 2010

Ranked by: Systemwide sales, in millions of dollars. **Remarks:** Also notes average sales per unit, number of franchised and company-owned units, total number of units, and overall rank in the *The QSR 50*. **Number listed:** 7

1. Pizza Hut, with $5,400 million
2. Domino's Pizza, $3,305.6
3. Papa John's Pizza, $2,081.8
4. Little Caesars Pizza, $1,253
5. Papa Murphy's Pizza, $648.8
6. CiCi's Pizza, $545
7. Sbarro's Italian Eatery, $501.5

Source: *QSR Magazine*, The QSR 50 (annual), http://www.qsrmagazine.com, August 2011.

2666 ■ LARGEST SEAFOOD FAST-FOOD CHAINS BY SALES, 2010

Ranked by: Systemwide sales, in millions of dollars. **Remarks:** Also notes average sales per unit, number of franchised and company-owned units, total number of units, and overall rank in the *The QSR 50*. **Number listed:** 2

1. Long John Silver's, with $700 million
2. Captain D's Seafood Kitchen, $436.2

Source: *QSR Magazine*, The QSR 50 (annual), http://www.qsrmagazine.com, August 2011.

2667 ■ LARGEST SNACK FAST-FOOD CHAINS BY SALES, 2010

Ranked by: Systemwide sales, in millions of dollars. **Remarks:** Also notes average sales per unit, number of franchised and company-owned units, total number of units, and overall rank in the *The QSR 50*. **Number listed:** 5

1. Starbucks, with $7,560 million
2. Dunkin' Donuts, $6,000
3. Baskin-Robbins, $565
4. Tim Hortons, $439.2
5. Cold Stone Creamery, $385.7

Source: *QSR Magazine*, The QSR 50 (annual), http://www.qsrmagazine.com, August 2011.

2668 ■ TOP CHICKEN WING FRANCHISES, 2012

Ranked by: Cumulative score based on financial strength and stability, growth rate, size of the system, number of years in business, the length of time franchising, start-up costs, litigation, percentage of terminations, and whether the company provides financing. **Remarks:** Specific scores not provided. Also notes overall rank within the *Franchise 500*, contact information, description, year founded, year started franchising, states where registered, available U.S. regions, where seeking foreign expansion, number of franchised and company-owned units for past three years, start-up costs, franchise fees, royalty fees, and type of financing available. **Number listed:** 3

1. Buffalo Wild Wings
2. Wingstop Restaurants Inc.
3. Hurricane Grill & Wings

Source: *Entrepreneur*, Franchise 500 (annual), January 2012, p. 164-165.

2669 ■ TOP HAMBURGER FAST-FOOD FRANCHISES, 2012

Ranked by: Cumulative score based on financial strength and stability, growth rate, size of the system, number of years in business, the length of time franchising, start-up costs, litigation, percentage of terminations, and whether the company provides financing. **Remarks:** Specific scores not provided. Also notes

overall rank within the *Franchise 500*, contact information, description, year founded, year started franchising, states where registered, available U.S. regions, where seeking foreign expansion, number of franchised and company-owned units for past three years, start-up costs, franchise fees, royalty fees, and type of financing available. **Number listed:** 10

1. McDonald's Corp.
2. Hardee's
3. Carl's Jr. Restaurants
4. Sonic Drive-In Restaurants
5. Checkers Drive-In Restaurants Inc.
6. A & W Restaurants Inc.
7. Smashburger Franchising
8. Mooyah Franchise
9. Boardwalk Fresh Burgers & Fries
10. Elevation Burger

Source: *Entrepreneur*, Franchise 500 (annual), January 2012, p. 164-167.

2670 ■ TOP MARKETS FOR FAST FOOD RESTAURANTS, 2012

Ranked by: Score based on fast food competition and Growth Index, a measure of change in unemployment, disposable income, retail sales, and home prices. **Remarks:** Specific scores not provided. Also notes number of fast food units, population per unit, Growth Index, projected population, projected number of households, and median household income. **Number listed:** 10

1. Orlando, FL
2. Seattle, WA
3. Portland, OR
4. Riverside, CA
5. Austin, TX
6. Las Vegas, NV
7. Washington DC
8. Miami, FL
9. Minneapolis, MN
10. Denver, CO

Source: *QSR Magazine*, The Growth 40 (annual), http://www.qsrmagazine.com, January 2012.

2671 ■ TOP MEXICAN FAST-FOOD FRANCHISES, 2012

Ranked by: Cumulative score based on financial strength and stability, growth rate, size of the system, number of years in business, the length of time franchising, start-up costs, litigation, percentage of terminations, and whether the company provides financing. **Remarks:** Specific scores not provided. Also notes overall rank within the *Franchise 500*, contact information, description, year founded, year started franchising, states where registered, available U.S. regions, where seeking foreign expansion, number of franchised and company-owned units for past three years, start-up costs, franchise fees, royalty fees, and type of financing available. **Number listed:** 6

1. Taco Bell Corp.
2. Moe's Southwest Grill
3. Qdoba Mexican Grill
4. TacoTime
5. Taco John's Internationsl
6. Salsarita's Fresh Cantina

Source: *Entrepreneur*, Franchise 500 (annual), January 2012, p. 168-169.

2672 ■ TOP MISCELLANEOUS CHICKEN FAST-FOOD FRANCHISES, 2012

Ranked by: Cumulative score based on financial strength and stability, growth rate, size of the system, number of years in business, the length of time franchising, start-up costs, litigation, percentage of terminations, and whether the company provides financing. **Remarks:** Specific scores not provided. Also notes overall rank within the *Franchise 500,* contact information, description, year founded, year started franchising, states where registered, available U.S. regions, where seeking foreign expansion, number of franchised and company-owned units for past three years, start-up costs, franchise fees, royalty fees, and type of financing available. **Number listed:** 5

1. KFC Corp.
2. Church's Chicken
3. Bojangles' Restaurants Inc.
4. Chester's International
5. Golden Chick

Source: *Entrepreneur,* Franchise 500 (annual), January 2012, p. 164-165.

2673 ■ TOP MISCELLANEOUS FAST-FOOD FRANCHISES, 2012

Ranked by: Cumulative score based on financial strength and stability, growth rate, size of the system, number of years in business, the length of time franchising, start-up costs, litigation, percentage of terminations, and whether the company provides financing. **Remarks:** Specific scores not provided. Also notes overall rank within the *Franchise 500,* contact information, description, year founded, year started franchising, states where registered, available U.S. regions, where seeking foreign expansion, number of franchised and company-owned units for past three years, start-up costs, franchise fees, royalty fees, and type of financing available. **Number listed:** 9

1. Long John Silver's Restaurants Inc.
2. Nathan's Famous Inc.
3. Zoup! Systems LLC
4. VooDoo BBQ & Grill
5. L & L Hawaiian Barbecue
6. Golden Krust Franchising Inc.
7. Saladworks
8. Hot Stuff Foods LLC
9. Nature's Table Cafe

Source: *Entrepreneur,* Franchise 500 (annual), January 2012, p. 172-173.

Fertilizer Industry

2674 ■ LARGEST U.S. RETAILERS IN FERTILIZER, 2010

Ranked by: Fertilizer as a percentage of total revenue. **Number listed:** 100

1. Abell Corp., with 99%
2. El Dorado Chemical Co., 90%
3. Eldon C. Stutsman Inc., 89%
4. Warner Fertilizer Co., 87%
5. Growers Fertilizer Corp., 86%
6. Verdegaal Brothers Inc., 80%
7. Griffin Fertilizer Co., 77%
7. Mountain View Cooperative, 77%
9. The Andersons Inc., 76%

10. Wisconsin River Cooperative, 75%
10. Centennial Ag Supply, 75%

Source: *CropLife,* CropLife 100 (annual), http://www.croplife.com, December 2011.

Filling Stations
See: **Automobile Service Stations**

Film Production

2675 ■ LARGEST FILM PRODUCTION COMPANIES IN LOS ANGELES COUNTY, 2011

Ranked by: Number of permitted days on location in Los Angeles County. **Remarks:** Also notes contact information, figures for previous year, top filming shows, and top production executive. **Number listed:** 10

1. ABC Studios, with 833 days
2. Twentieth Century Fox Television, 670
3. Universal Media Studios/Open 4 Business, 628

Source: *Los Angeles Business Journal,* Film Production Companies (annual), http://www.labusinessjournal.com, January 30, 2012.

2676 ■ TOP CANADIAN PRODUCTION COMPANIES IN NON-FICTION FILM AND TELEVISION, 2011

Ranked by: Editorial determination. **Remarks:** Specific scores not provided; companies are listed alphabetically. Also notes head office, web site, number of employees, number of hours, most recent titles, upcoming projects, and comments. **Number listed:** 12

1. Anaid Productions
2. Cineflix Productions
3. Clearwater Documentary
4. Cream Productions
5. Force Four Entertainment
6. Frantic Films
7. Handel Productions
8. Insight Productions
9. National Film Board of Canada
10. Omni Film

Source: *realscreen,* Global 100 (annual), 2012, p. 33-34.

2677 ■ TOP INTERNATIONAL PRODUCTION COMPANIES IN NON-FICTION FILM AND TELEVISION, 2011

Ranked by: Editorial determination. **Remarks:** Ranking covers companies headquartered outside of Canada, the United Kingdom, and the United States. Specific scores not provided; companies are listed alphabetically. Also notes head office, web site, number of employees, number of hours, most recent titles, upcoming projects, and comments. **Number listed:** 9

1. Beyond Productions
2. Cordell Jigsaw
3. Clarke, Costelle & Co.
4. Endemol
5. Essential Media & Entertainment
6. Gruppe 5 Filmproduktion
7. Heymann Brothers Films
8. NHNZ
9. Off the Fence

Source: *realscreen,* Global 100 (annual), 2012, p. 47.

2678 ■ TOP U.K. PRODUCTION COMPANIES IN NON-FICTION FILM AND TELEVISION, 2011

Ranked by: Editorial determination. **Remarks:** Specific scores not provided; companies are listed alphabetically. Also notes head office, web site, number of employees, number of hours, most recent titles, upcoming projects, and comments. **Number listed:** 33

1. Atlantic Productions
2. Brink Films
3. Darlow Smithson
4. Dragonfly Productions
5. Firecracker Films
6. FremantleMedia
7. The Garden
8. Icon Films
9. Impossible Pictures
10. KEO Films

Source: *realscreen*, Global 100 (annual), 2012, p. 40-42.

2679 ■ TOP U.S. PRODUCTION COMPANIES IN NON-FICTION FILM AND TELEVISION, 2011

Ranked by: Editorial determination. **Remarks:** Specific scores not provided; companies are listed alphabetically. Also notes head office, web site, number of employees, number of hours, most recent titles, upcoming projects, and comments. **Number listed:** 44

1. 3Ball Productions
2. 495 Productions
3. Asylum Entertainment
4. Atlas Media Corp.
5. Authentic Entertainment
6. Base Productions
7. Big Fish Productions
8. Bunim/Murray Productions
9. Collins Avenue
10. Embassy Row

Source: *realscreen*, Global 100 (annual), 2012, p. 44-47.

Finance Companies

2680 ■ AMERICA'S LARGEST PRIVATE DIVERSIFIED FINANCIAL COMPANIES, 2010

Ranked by: Revenue, in billions of dollars. **Remarks:** Also notes headquarters, number of employees, and overall rank in the *America's Largest Private Companies* list. Ranking is available online only, not in print. **Number listed:** 3

1. Fidelity Investments, with $12.26 billion
2. Capital Group Companies Inc., $7.5
3. Edward Jones, $4.16

Source: *Forbes*, America's Largest Private Companies (annual), http://www.forbes.com, December 5, 2011.

2681 ■ BRITAIN'S MOST ADMIRED SPECIALTY AND OTHER FINANCE COMPANIES, 2011

Ranked by: Survey of peers and investment analysts based on nine criteria: quality of management, financial soundness, quality of goods/services, ability to attract and retain talent, value as long-term investment, innovation, marketing, community and environmental responsibility, and use of corporate assets. **Number listed:** 5

1. IG Group Holdings plc, with 63.8 points
2. Hargreaves Lansdown plc, 60.9
3. Schroders plc, 60.6
4. Aberdeen Asset Management, 58.1
5. Ashmore Group, 56.1

Source: *Management Today*, Britain's Most Admired Companies (annual), December 2011, p. 49.

2682 ■ MOST PROFITABLE CANADIAN FINANCIAL COMPANIES, 2011

Ranked by: Profits, in millions of Canadian dollars. **Number listed:** 6

1. Toronto-Dominion Bank, with C$5,889 million
2. Scotiabank--Bank of Nova Scotia, C$5,175
3. Royal Bank of Canada, C$4,852
4. Bank of Montreal, C$3,266
5. Canadian Imperial Bank of Commerce, C$3,079
6. Great-West Lifeco Inc., C$2,118

Source: *Canadian Business*, Investor 500 (annual), 2012, p. 55.

Financial Companies
See: **Financial Institutions**

Financial Executives

2683 ■ MOST POWERFUL AFRICAN AMERICANS ON WALL STREET, 2011

Ranked by: Score based on influence within their company and throughout the financial services industry. **Remarks:** Scores not provided; individual are listed alphabetically, not ranked. Also notes title and comments. **Number listed:** 75

1. Bernard Beal (M.R. Beal & Co.)
2. Ronald Blaylock (GenNx 360)
3. Cedric Bobo (The Carlyle Group)
4. D. Steve Boland (Bank of America Merrill Lynch)
5. Francisco Borges (Landmark Partners)
6. Napoleon Brandford III (Siebert Brandford Shank & Co.)
7. Eddie Brown (Brown Caital Mgmt.)
8. Tina Byles-Williams (FIS Group)
9. Edith Cooper (Goldman Sachs)
10. T. Troy Dixon (Deutsche Bank Securities)

Source: *Black Enterprise*, Most Powerful Blacks on Wall Street, October 2011, p. 78+.

Financial Institutions

2684 ■ TOP *FORTUNE 500* COMPANIES IN DIVERSIFIED FINANCIALS, 2011

Ranked by: Revenue, in millions of dollars. **Remarks:** Also notes overall rank in the *Fortune 500;* profits; profits as a percentage of revenue; stockholders' equity; and rank by each criterion. **Number listed:** 8

1. General Electric Co., with $147,616 million

2. Fannie Mae, $137,451
3. Freddie Mac, $88,262
4. INTL FCStone, $75,498
5. Marsh & McLennan Companies Inc., $11,526
6. Aon Corp., $11,287
7. Ameriprise Financial Inc., $10,621
8. SLM Corp., $5,756

Source: *Fortune*, Fortune 500 (annual), May 21, 2012, p. F-34.

2685 ■ WORLD'S MOST VALUABLE FINANCIAL INSTITUTION BRANDS, 2012

Ranked by: Brand value, a measure of a brand's earnings and contribution, in millions of U.S. dollars. **Remarks:** Also notes rank by brand contribution and brand momentum, annual growth in brand value, and two-year compound annual growth rate. **Number listed:** 20

1. ICBC, with $41,518 million
2. Wells Fargo, $39,754
3. Visa, $38,284
4. China Construction Bank, $24,517
5. MasterCard, $20,759
6. American Express, $20,198
7. HSBC, $19,313
8. Agricultural Bank of China, $17,867
9. RBC, $17,225
10. TD, $14,561

Source: *Financial Times*, Global Brands (annual), May 22, 212, p. 4.

Financial Services

2686 ■ BEST FINANCIAL SERVICES COMPANIES TO WORK FOR IN BRITISH COLUMBIA, 2010

Ranked by: Editorial determination. **Remarks:** Specific scores not provided. **Number listed:** 5

1. Summerland & District Credit Union
2. Schill Insurance Brokers Ltd.
3. Davidson & Co.
4. Optimum West Insurance Co.
5. First Group of Companies Realty Holdings Ltd.

Source: *BCBusiness*, Best Companies (annual), http://www.bcbusinessonline.ca, December 2011.

2687 ■ COUNTRIES WITH THE HIGHEST VARIETY OF FINANCIAL SERVICES, 2011

Ranked by: Score, on a scale of seven, based on the level of variety of financial products and services for businesses. **Number listed:** 142

1. Switzerland, with 6.6 points
2. Luxembourg, 6.3
2. South Africa, 6.3
2. United Kingdom, 6.3
2. Canada, 6.3
2. Sweden, 6.3
7. Panama, 6.2
7. Hong Kong, 6.2
9. Belgium, 6.1

9. Netherlands, 6.1
9. Bahrain, 6.1

Source: *Global Competitiveness Report*, (annual), World Economic Forum, 2011, p. 480.

2688 ■ COUNTRIES WITH THE LEAST AFFORDABLE FINANCIAL SERVICES, 2011

Ranked by: Score, on a scale of seven, based on the level of competition among providers of financial services to ensure the provision of financial services at affordable prices. **Number listed:** 142

1. Algeria, with 2.3 points
2. Yemen, 2.5
3. Haiti, 2.6
3. Timor-Leste, 2.6
5. Angola, 2.8
5. Burundi, 2.8
5. Chad, 2.8
5. Kyrgyz Republic, 2.8
9. Mauritania, 2.9
10. Burkina Faso, 3.0
10. Madagascar, 3.0

Source: *Global Competitiveness Report*, (annual), World Economic Forum, 2011, p. 481.

2689 ■ COUNTRIES WITH THE LOWEST VARIETY OF FINANCIAL SERVICES, 2011

Ranked by: Score, on a scale of seven, based on the level of variety of financial products and services for businesses. **Number listed:** 142

1. Timor-Leste, with 2.6 points
1. Yemen, 2.6
3. Chad, 2.7
3. Algeria, 2.7
5. Angola, 2.8
5. Burundi, 2.8
7. Haiti, 2.9
7. Mauritania, 2.9
9. Iran, 3.1
10. Kyrgyz Republic, 3.2
10. Ethiopia, 3.2

Source: *Global Competitiveness Report*, (annual), World Economic Forum, 2011, p. 480.

2690 ■ COUNTRIES WITH THE MOST AFFORDABLE FINANCIAL SERVICES, 2011

Ranked by: Score, on a scale of seven, based on the level of competition among providers of financial services to ensure the provision of financial services at affordable prices. **Number listed:** 142

1. Taiwan, with 6 points
2. Switzerland, 5.9
3. Hong Kong, 5.8
3. Panama, 5.8
5. Bahrain, 5.8
5. Luxembourg, 5.7
5. Singapore, 5.7
8. Finland, 5.6

8. Qatar, 5.6

8. Sweden, 5.6

Source: *Global Competitiveness Report*, (annual), World Economic Forum, 2011, p. 481.

2691 ■ EUROPE'S MOST VALUABLE FINANCIAL SERVICES COMPANIES, 2011

Ranked by: Market value as of March 2011, in millions of U.S. dollars. **Remarks:** Also notes rank within the *FT Europe 500*, rank for previous year, country, revenue, net income, assets, number of employees, share price, price-to-earning ratio, dividend yield, and fiscal yearend. **Number listed:** 21

1. Criteria CaixaCorp, with $23,751.5 million

2. Investor, $18,453

3. GBL, $15,087.6

4. Deutsche Boerse, $14,873.8

5. Koc Holding A.S., $11,232

6. Haci Omer Sabanci, $9,489.2

7. Hal Trust, $9,328.5

8. Schroders plc, $7,620.7

9. Compagnie Nationale a Portefeuille SA, $7,444.7

10. Pargesa, $7,427.1

Source: *Financial Times*, FT 500 (annual), http://www.ft.com, June 24, 2011.

2692 ■ FASTEST-GROWING FINANCIAL SERVICES COMPANIES, 2008-2011

Ranked by: Score based on three-year growth in revenue and earnings, and three-year total return to investors. **Remarks:** Specific scores not provided. To qualify for list, companies must have revenues of at least $50 million, net income of at least $10 million, market capitalization of at least $250 million, and stock price of at least $5. Int'l companies are eligible if they trade on a U.S. exchange and file quarterly reports. **Number listed:** 10

1. Ares Capital

2. Maiden Holdings

3. Credit Acceptance Corp.

4. First Financial Bancorp

5. MarketAxess Holdings

6. Cninsure

7. Signature Bank

8. American Equity Investment Life Holding

9. FBL Financial Group

10. Enstar Group

Source: *Fortune*, 100 Fastest-Growing Companies (annual), http://www.fortune.com, September 26, 2011.

2693 ■ FASTEST-GROWING PRIVATE FINANCIAL SERVICES COMPANIES IN THE U.S., 2007-2010

Ranked by: Average annual sales growth over three years, in percent. **Remarks:** Also notes headquarters, revenue, and rank in the overall *Inc. 500*. To qualify, private companies must have had annual revenues of at least $100,000 in 2007 and $2 million in 2010. **Number listed:** 23

1. PaymentMax, with 10,057.8%

2. Century Payments, 9,257.9%

3. Entrust Bankcard, 8,416.9%

4. AdVentures, 6,533.9%

5. Electronic Cash Systems, 6,132.7%

6. Braintree, 4,199.9%

7. ECS, 3,188.4%

8. 1st Merchant Funding, 2,717.1%

9. Aurum Advisors, 2,425%

10. Stonegate Mortgage, 2,011.1%

Source: *Inc.*, Inc. 500 (annual), September 2011, p. 118-123.

2694 ■ JAPAN'S LARGEST CONSUMER FINANCIAL SERVICES COMPANIES OVERALL, 2011

Ranked by: Score based on revenue, profits, assets, and market capitalization. **Remarks:** Specific scores not provided. Also notes overall rank in the *Forbes 2000* and figures for each criterion. **Number listed:** 4

1. ORIX Corp.

2. Orient

3. Jaccs

4. Credit Saison

Source: *Forbes*, Forbes 2000 (annual), http://www.forbes.com, May 7, 2012.

2695 ■ JAPAN'S MOST VALUABLE DIVERSIFIED FINANCIAL SERVICE BRANDS, 2011

Ranked by: Brand value, in millions of U.S. dollars. **Remarks:** Also notes rank within the *Global 500* for current and previous year, figures for current and previous year, and brand rating. Ranking is available online only. **Number listed:** 2

1. Mizuho Securities, with $3,377 million

2. Nomura, $2,841

Source: *Global 500*, (annual), Brand Finance plc, March 2012.

2696 ■ LARGEST ENTERPRISE TECHNOLOGY COMPANIES, 2010

Ranked by: Financial technology revenue, in millions of dollars. **Remarks:** Ranking covers horizontal technology companies that sell and support multiple industries. Also notes rank for previous year, headquarters, total revenue, and financial technology revenue as a percentage of total revenue. **Number listed:** 25

1. International Business Machines Corp. (IBM), with $29,291 million

2. Hewlett-Packard Co., $13,987

3. Dell Inc., $7,994

4. Fujitsu Ltd., $6,910

5. Cisco Systems Inc., $5,507

6. Microsoft Corp., $5,335

7. Accenture Ltd., $5,177

8. Oracle Corp., $4,479

9. Hitachi Ltd., $4,096

10. Intel Corp., $3,926

Source: *Bank Technology News*, FinTech 100 (annual), October 2011.

2697 ■ LARGEST FINANCIAL SERVICES COMPANIES IN BRITISH COLUMBIA, 2010

Ranked by: Revenue, in thousands of Canadian dollars. **Remarks:** Also notes figures for previous year. **Number listed:** 10

1. HSBC Bank Canada, with C$2,493,000 thousand

2. Industrial Alliance Pacific Insurance & Financial Inc., C$927,272

3. Canaccord Financial Inc., C$577,537
4. Vancouver City Savings Credit Union, C$424,014
5. Coast Capital Savings Credit Union, C$318,460
6. First West Credit Union, C$292,863
7. Raymond James Ltd., C$265,668
8. Central 1 Credit Union, C$169,517
9. British Columbia Investment Management Corp., C$129,192
10. Westminster Savings Credit Union, C$101,379

Source: *BCBusiness*, Top 100 (annual), July 2011, p. 135.

2698 ■ LARGEST FINANCIAL TECHNOLOGY COMPANIES, 2010

Ranked by: Financial technology revenue, in millions of dollars. **Remarks:** Ranking covers companies that derive more than one-third of their total revenue from the financial services industry. Also notes rank for previous year, headquarters, type of ownership, total revenue, and financial technology revenue as a percentage of total revenue. **Number listed:** 100

1. Fidelity Information Services Inc., with $4,426 million
2. Fiserv Inc., $3,926
3. Tata Consultancy Services Ltd., $3,456
4. SunGard Data Systems Inc., $3,102
5. NCR Corp., $2,651
6. Diebold Inc., $2,552
7. Lender Processing Services, $2,334
8. First Data Corp., $2,281
9. Nomura Research Institute, $2,181
10. Infosys Ltd., $2,031

Source: *Bank Technology News*, FinTech 100 (annual), October 2011.

2699 ■ LARGEST U.S. CONSUMER FINANCIAL SERVICES COMPANIES OVERALL, 2011

Ranked by: Score based on revenue, profits, assets, and market capitalization. **Remarks:** Specific scores not provided. Also notes overall rank in the *Forbes 2000* and figures for each criterion. **Number listed:** 10

1. American Express Co.
2. Capital One Financial Corp.
3. Visa Inc.
4. Discover Financial Services
5. MasterCard Inc.
6. SLM Corp.
7. The Western Union Co.
8. CIT Group Inc.
9. The First Marblehead Corp.
10. Nelnet Inc.

Source: *Forbes*, Forbes 2000 (annual), http://www.forbes.com, May 7, 2012.

2700 ■ MOST VALUABLE U.S. FINANCIAL SERVICES COMPANIES, 2011

Ranked by: Market value as of March 2011, in millions of U.S. dollars. **Remarks:** Also notes rank within the *FT U.S. 500*, rank for previous year, country, revenue, net income, assets, number of

employees, share price, price-to-earning ratio, dividend yield, and fiscal yearend. **Number listed:** 24

1. Goldman Sachs Group Inc., with $82,552.4 million
2. American Express Co., $54,348.8
3. Morgan Stanley, $42,226.6
4. BlackRock Inc., $38,547.7
5. Bank of New York Mellon Corp., $37,096.7
6. Visa Inc., $36,417.8
7. MasterCard Inc., $31,126.7
8. Franklin Resources Inc., $27,901
9. Capital One Financial Corp., $23,832.2
10. State Street Corp., $22,568.4

Source: *Financial Times*, FT 500 (annual), http://www.ft.com, June 24, 2011.

2701 ■ NEW YORK'S LARGEST CONSUMER FINANCIAL SERVICES COMPANIES OVERALL, 2011

Ranked by: Score based on revenue, profits, assets, and market capitalization. **Remarks:** Specific scores not provided. Also notes overall rank in the *Forbes 2000* and figures for each criterion. **Number listed:** 3

1. American Express Co.
2. MasterCard Inc.
3. CIT Group Inc.

Source: *Forbes*, Forbes 2000 (annual), http://www.forbes.com, May 7, 2012.

2702 ■ SOUTH KOREA'S LARGEST CONSUMER FINANCIAL SERVICES COMPANIES OVERALL, 2011

Ranked by: Score based on revenue, profits, assets, and market capitalization. **Remarks:** Specific scores not provided. Also notes overall rank in the *Forbes 2000* and figures for each criterion. **Number listed:** 3

1. Hana Financial Group
2. Samsung Card
3. DGB Financial Group

Source: *Forbes*, Forbes 2000 (annual), http://www.forbes.com, May 7, 2012.

2703 ■ STATES WITH THE HIGHEST RATE OF EMPLOYEES IN FINANCIAL ACTIVITIES, 2010

Ranked by: Percentage of nonfarm employees in the financial industry. **Number listed:** 50

1. Delaware, with 10.4%
2. Connecticut, 8.3%
3. New York, 7.9%
4. Nebraska, 7.1%
5. South Dakota, 7%
6. Iowa, 6.8%
7. Arizona, 6.7%
7. Rhode Island, 6.7%
9. Massachusetts, 6.6%
9. New Jersey, 6.6%

Source: *State Rankings*, (annual), CQ Press, 2011, p. 195.

2704 ■ STATES WITH THE LOWEST RATE OF EMPLOYEES IN FINANCIAL ACTIVITIES, 2010

Ranked by: Percentage of employees in the financial industry. **Number listed:** 50

1. Washington DC, with 3.6%
1. West Virginia, 3.6%
3. Wyoming, 3.9%
4. New Mexico, 4%
5. Vermont, 4.3%
6. Arkansas, 4.4%
7. Alaska, 4.6%
7. Hawaii, 4.6%
7. Louisiana, 4.6%
9. Indiana, 4.7%
9. Nevada, 4.7%

Source: *State Rankings*, (annual), CQ Press, 2011, p. 195.

2705 ■ TAIWAN'S LARGEST CONSUMER FINANCIAL SERVICES COMPANIES OVERALL, 2011

Ranked by: Score based on revenue, profits, assets, and market capitalization. **Remarks:** Specific scores not provided. Also notes overall rank in the *Forbes 2000* and figures for each criterion. **Number listed:** 5

1. Chinatrust Financial
2. Hua Nan Financial
3. Taiwan Cooperative Bank
4. SinoPac Financial Holdings
5. E.Sun Financial

Source: *Forbes*, Forbes 2000 (annual), http://www.forbes.com, May 7, 2012.

2706 ■ TOP BUSINESS FINANCIAL SERVICE FRANCHISES, 2012

Ranked by: Cumulative score based on financial strength and stability, growth rate, size of the system, number of years in business, the length of time franchising, start-up costs, litigation, percentage of terminations, and whether the company provides financing. **Remarks:** Specific scores not provided. Also notes overall rank within the *Franchise 500,* contact information, description, year founded, year started franchising, states where registered, available U.S. regions, where seeking foreign expansion, number of franchised and company-owned units for past three years, start-up costs, franchise fees, royalty fees, and type of financing available. **Number listed:** 5

1. Padgett Business Services
2. Interface Financial Corp.
3. Express Reduction Analysts Inc.
4. Expense Reduction Consulting
5. BookKeeping Express

Source: *Entrepreneur*, Franchise 500 (annual), January 2012, p. 160-161.

2707 ■ TOP MISCELLANEOUS FINANCIAL SERVICE FRANCHISES, 2012

Ranked by: Cumulative score based on financial strength and stability, growth rate, size of the system, number of years in business, the length of time franchising, start-up costs, litigation, percentage of terminations, and whether the company provides financing. **Remarks:** Specific scores not provided. Also notes overall rank within the *Franchise 500,* contact information, description, year founded, year started franchising, states where registered, available U.S. regions, where seeking foreign expansion, number of franchised and company-owned units for past three years, start-up costs, franchise fees, royalty fees, and type of financing available. **Number listed:** 2

1. Fiesta Insurance Franchise Corp.

2. The ATM Franchise Business

Source: *Entrepreneur*, Franchise 500 (annual), January 2012, p. 162-163.

2708 ■ THE UNITED STATES' MOST VALUABLE DIVERSIFIED FINANCIAL SERVICE BRANDS, 2011

Ranked by: Brand value, in millions of U.S. dollars. **Remarks:** Also notes rank within the *Global 500* for current and previous year, figures for current and previous year, and brand rating. Ranking is available online only. **Number listed:** 2

1. American Express, with $18,231 million
2. BlackRock, $2,433

Source: *Global 500*, (annual), Brand Finance plc, March 2012.

2709 ■ WORLD'S LARGEST CONSUMER FINANCIAL SERVICES COMPANIES OVERALL, 2011

Ranked by: Score based on revenue, profits, assets, and market capitalization. **Remarks:** Specific scores not provided. Also notes country, overall rank in the *Forbes 2000,* and figures for each criterion. **Number listed:** 24

1. American Express Co.
2. Capital One Financial Corp.
3. Visa Inc.
4. Discover Financial Services
5. ORIX Corp.
6. Hana Financial Group Inc.
7. Housing Development Finance Corp. Ltd. (HDFC)
8. MasterCard Inc.
9. SLM Corp.
10. The Western Union Co.

Source: *Forbes*, Forbes 2000 (annual), http://www.forbes.com, May 7, 2012.

2710 ■ WORLD'S MOST ADMIRED FINANCIAL DATA SERVICES, 2012

Ranked by: Score, on a scale of 10, based on a survey of executives, directors, and securities analysts of companies within their own industry on eight criteria: innovation, financial soundness, employee talent, use of corporate assets, long-term investment value, social responsibility, quality of management, and quality of products/services. **Remarks:** Specific scores not provided. Also notes rank for previous year. **Number listed:** 6

1. Thomson Reuters Corp.
2. Automatic Data Processing Inc.
3. Paychex Inc.
4. Equifax Inc.
5. Fiserv Inc.
6. SunGard Data Systems Inc.

Source: *Fortune*, World's Most Admired Companies (annual), March 19, 2012, p. 148.

2711 ■ WORLD'S MOST ETHICAL FINANCIAL SERVICES COMPANIES, 2012

Ranked by: Score based on five criteria: ethics and compliance program; reputation, leadership, and innovation; governance; corporate citizenship and responsibility; and culture of ethics. **Remarks:** Specific scores not provided; companies are listed alphabetically, not ranked. **Number listed:** 5

1. American Express Co. (U.S.)

2. NYSE Euronext Inc. (U.S./Netherlands)
3. The Hartford Financial Services Group Inc. (U.S.)
4. Thrivent Financial for Lutherans (U.S.)
5. TeleCommunication Systems Inc. (TSYS; U.S.)

Source: *Ethisphere Magazine*, World's Most Ethical Companies (annual), http://www.ethisphere.com, 2012.

2712 ■ WORLD'S MOST VALUABLE DIVERSIFIED FINANCIAL SERVICE BRANDS, 2011

Ranked by: Brand value, in millions of U.S. dollars. **Remarks:** Also notes rank within the *Global 500* for current and previous year, figures for current and previous year, country, and brand rating. Ranking is available online only. **Number listed:** 5

1. American Express, with $18,231 million
2. Mizuho Securities, $3,377
3. Nomura, $2,841
4. Shinhan Financial, $2,746
5. BlackRock, $2,433

Source: *Global 500*, (annual), Brand Finance plc, March 2012.

2713 ■ WORLD'S MOST VALUABLE FINANCIAL SERVICES COMPANIES, 2011

Ranked by: Market value as of March 2011, in millions of U.S. dollars. **Remarks:** Also notes rank within the *FT 500*, rank for previous year, country, revenue, net income, assets, number of employees, share price, price-to-earning ratio, dividend yield, and fiscal year-end. **Number listed:** 18

1. Goldman Sachs Group Inc., with $82,552.4 million
2. American Express Co., $54,348.8
3. Morgan Stanley, $42,226.6
4. BlackRock Inc., $38,547.7
5. Bank of New York Mellon Corp., $37,096.7
6. Visa Inc., $36,417.8
7. Investimentos Itau SA (Itausa), $33,943.5
8. MasterCard Inc., $31,126.7
9. Franklin Resources Inc., $27,901
10. Capital One Financial Corp., $23,832.2

Source: *Financial Times*, FT 500 (annual), http://www.ft.com, June 24, 2011.

Fixtures
See: **Store Fixtures**

Food Distribution

2714 ■ LARGEST FOOD DISTRIBUTION COMPANIES BY REVENUE, 2011

Ranked by: Revenue, in millions of dollars. **Remarks:** Also notes location, rank and figures for previous year, product types, number of sales people, buying group, and Web site. **Number listed:** 102

1. Edward Don & Co., with $594 million
2. TriMark USA Inc., $560
3. The Wasserstrom Co., $478
4. Strategic Equipment & Supply Co., $228.38
5. The Boelter Cos., $186

6. Singer Equipment Co., $171.3
7. Clark Associates, $158.5
8. Bargreen-Ellingson Inc., $158.2
9. Hubert Co., $153
10. Stafford-Smith Inc., $105

Source: *Foodservice Equipment & Supplies*, Distribution Giants (annual), April 2012, p. 30-36.

Food Industry

2715 ■ AMERICA'S LARGEST PRIVATE FOOD, DRINK, AND TOBACCO COMPANIES, 2010

Ranked by: Revenue, in billions of dollars. **Remarks:** Also notes headquarters, number of employees, and overall rank in the *America's Largest Private Companies* list. Ranking is available online only, not in print. **Number listed:** 40

1. Cargill Inc., with $109.56 billion
2. Mars Inc., $30
3. C & S Wholesale Grocers Inc., $20.4
4. U.S. Foods Inc., $18.86
5. Reyes Holdings LLC, $14
6. Performance Food Group Co., $10.6
7. Southern Wine & Spirits of America Inc., $9
8. Gordon Food Service Inc., $7.7
9. MBM Corp., $6.3
10. The Scoular Co., $4.9
10. J. R. Simplot Co., $4.9

Source: *Forbes*, America's Largest Private Companies (annual), http://www.forbes.com, December 5, 2011.

2716 ■ BEST SMALL FOOD, DRINK, AND TOBACCO COMPANIES IN AMERICA, 2011

Ranked by: Score based on revenue, profits, and return on equity for the past 12 months and five years. **Remarks:** Specific scores not provided. Also notes rank in the overall *100 Best Small Companies in America*. To qualify, companies must have revenues between $5 million and $1 billion, a net margin above five percent, and share price above $5. List is available online only. **Number listed:** 4

1. Coffee Holding
2. Boston Beer
3. B & G Foods
4. Calavo Growers

Source: *Forbes*, Best Small Companies in America (annual), November 7, 2011.

2717 ■ FASTEST-GROWING PRIVATE FOOD AND BEVERAGE COMPANIES IN THE U.S., 2007-2010

Ranked by: Average annual sales growth over three years, in percent. **Remarks:** Also notes headquarters, revenue, and rank in the overall *Inc. 500*. To qualify, private companies must have had annual revenues of at least $100,000 in 2007 and $2 million in 2010. **Number listed:** 15

1. Big Night Entertainment Group, with 16,093.4%
2. HappyBaby, 3,206.7%
3. Nest Collective, 3,054%
4. Smashburger, 2,676.3%
5. Signature Foods, 2,648%
6. Tradavo, 1,578.2%

7.   VeeV Acai Spirit, 1,316.2%
8.   GrubHub, 1,308.1%
9.   Revolution Foods, 1,218.5%
10. The Fresh Diet, 1,156.2%

Source: *Inc.*, Inc. 500 (annual), September 2011, p. 126-127.

2718 ■ LARGEST FOOD COMPANIES BY EMPLOYEES, 2010

Ranked by: Total number of employees. **Remarks:** Also notes contact information for headquarters, number of employees at headquarters, revenue, rank by revenue, and primary SIC code. **Number listed:** 47

1.   PepsiCo Inc., with 203,000 employees
2.   Tyson Foods Inc., 115,000
3.   Pepsi-Cola Metropolitan Bottling Co., 112,050
4.   Kraft Foods Inc., 97,000
5.   The Coca-Cola Co., 92,800
6.   Bottling Group LLC, 66,800
7.   Mars Inc., 65,000
8.   Smithfield Foods Inc., 48,000
9.   Tyson Fresh Meats Inc., 41,000
10. Pilgrima Pride Corp., 40,700

Source: *Business Rankings*, (annual), Dun & Bradstreet Inc., 2011, p. VI.46-VI.47.

2719 ■ LARGEST FOOD COMPANIES BY SALES, 2010

Ranked by: Total revenue, in dollars. **Remarks:** Also notes contact information for headquarters, number of employees at headquarters and overall, rank by employees, and primary SIC code. **Number listed:** 50

1.   Archer Daniels Midland Co., with $61,682,000,000
2.   PepsiCo Inc., $57,838,000,000
3.   Kraft Foods Inc., $49,207,000,000
4.   The Coca-Cola Co., $35,119,000,000
5.   Tyson Foods Inc., $28,430,000,000
6.   General Mills Inc., $14,796,500,000
7.   Bottling Group LLC, $13,219,000,000
8.   Kellogg Co., $12,397,000,000
9.   Dean Foods Co., $12,122,887,000
10. ConAgra Foods Inc., $12,079,400,000

Source: *Business Rankings*, (annual), Dun & Bradstreet Inc., 2011, p. V.46-V.47.

2720 ■ LARGEST U.S. FOOD PRODUCT MANUFACTURERS, 2010

Ranked by: Revenue, in millions of dollars. **Remarks:** Also notes overall rank within the *IW 500*, revenue growth, and profit margin. **Number listed:** 29

1.   Archer Daniels Midland Co., with $61,682 million
2.   Kraft Foods Inc., $49,207
3.   Tyson Foods Inc., $28,430
4.   General Mills Inc., $14,797
5.   Kellogg Co., $12,397
6.   Dean Foods Co., $12,123
7.   ConAgra Foods Inc., $12,079
8.   Smithfield Foods Inc., $11,203

9.   Sara Lee Corp., $10,793
10. H. J. Heinz Co., $10,495

Source: *IndustryWeek*, IW 500 (annual), http://www.industryweek.com, July 2011.

2721 ■ MOST VALUABLE U.S. FOOD PRODUCTION COMPANIES, 2011

Ranked by: Market value as of March 2011, in millions of U.S. dollars. **Remarks:** Also notes rank within the *FT U.S. 500*, rank for previous year, country, revenue, net income, assets, number of employees, share price, price-to-earning ratio, dividend yield, and fiscal yearend. **Number listed:** 17

1.   Kraft Foods Inc., with $54,946.3 million
2.   Monsanto Co., $38,782
3.   General Mills Inc., $23,333.7
4.   Archer Daniels Midland Co., $22,949.3
5.   Kellogg Co., $19,797.1
6.   H. J. Heinz Co., $15,711.3
7.   Mead Johnson Nutrition Co., $11,839.2
8.   Sara Lee Corp., $10,998.6
9.   Bunge Corp., $10,621.2
10. Campbell Soup Co., $10,602.8

Source: *Financial Times*, FT 500 (annual), http://www.ft.com, June 24, 2011.

2722 ■ TOP *FORTUNE 500* COMPANIES IN FOOD CONSUMER PRODUCTS, 2011

Ranked by: Revenue, in millions of dollars. **Remarks:** Also notes overall rank in the *Fortune 500;* profits; profits as a percentage of revenue; stockholders' equity; and rank by each criterion. **Number listed:** 14

1.   PepsiCo Inc., with $66,504 million
2.   Kraft Foods Inc., $54,365
3.   General Mills Inc., $14,880
4.   Kellogg Co., $13,198
5.   Dean Foods Co., $13,055
6.   Land O'Lakes Inc., $12,849
7.   ConAgra Foods Inc., $12,396
8.   Sara Lee Corp., $12,103
9.   H. J. Heinz Co., $10,707
10. Hormel Foods, $7,895

Source: *Fortune*, Fortune 500 (annual), May 21, 2012, p. F-35.

2723 ■ TOP *FORTUNE 500* COMPANIES IN FOOD PRODUCTION, 2011

Ranked by: Revenue, in millions of dollars. **Remarks:** Also notes overall rank in the *Fortune 500;* profits; profits as a percentage of revenue; stockholders' equity; and rank by each criterion. **Number listed:** 5

1.   Archer Daniels Midland Co., with $80,676 million
2.   Tyson Foods Inc., $32,266
3.   Smithfield Foods Inc., $12,203
4.   Corn Products International, $6,219
5.   Seaboard Corp., $5,747

Source: *Fortune*, Fortune 500 (annual), May 21, 2012, p. F-35.

2724 ■ TOP THIRD-PARTY LOGISTICS AND COLD STORAGE PROVIDERS TO THE FOOD INDUSTRY, 2011

Ranked by: Editorial determination. **Remarks:** Companies are listed alphabetically, not ranked. Also notes headquarters, website, area served, whether asset based, types of transportation services, and types of warehousing services. **Number listed:** 100

1. Allen Lund Co.
2. Alliance Shippers Inc.
3. Americold
4. A. N. Deringer Inc.
5. ArrowStream Inc.
6. Aspen Logistics Inc.
7. Atlanta Bonded Warehouse Corp.
8. Burris Logistics
9. Cardinal Logistics Management Corp.
10. CaseStack Inc.

Source: *Food Logistics*, Top 100 3PL Providers (annual), 2011, p. 30-46.

2725 ■ THE UNITED STATES' MOST VALUABLE FOOD BRANDS, 2011

Ranked by: Brand value, in millions of U.S. dollars. **Remarks:** Also notes rank within the *Global 500* for current and previous year, figures for current and previous year, and brand rating. Ranking is available online only. **Number listed:** 9

1. Kellogg, with $7,955 million
2. Heinz, $5,373
3. Kraft, $5,029
4. Kroger, $4,561
5. Publix, $4,470
6. Safeway, $3,947
7. Cadbury, $3,550
8. Hershey's, $3,053
9. Whole Foods, $2,947

Source: *Global 500*, (annual), Brand Finance plc, March 2012.

Food Industry, International

2726 ■ BRAZIL'S MOST VALUABLE FOOD BRANDS, 2011

Ranked by: Brand value, in millions of U.S. dollars. **Remarks:** Also notes rank within the *Global 500* for current and previous year, figures for current and previous year, and brand rating. Ranking is available online only. **Number listed:** 2

1. Pao de Acucar, with $3,361 million
2. Sadia, $2,370

Source: *Global 500*, (annual), Brand Finance plc, March 2012.

2727 ■ BRITAIN'S MOST ADMIRED FOOD PRODUCTION AND PROCESSING COMPANIES, 2011

Ranked by: Survey of peers and investment analysts based on nine criteria: quality of management, financial soundness, quality of goods/services, ability to attract and retain talent, value as long-term investment, innovation, marketing, community and environmental responsibility, and use of corporate assets. **Number listed:** 5

1. Unilever, with 69.3 points
2. Associated British Foods plc, 63.4
3. Kerry Group plc, 62.7
4. Tate & Lyle plc, 58.2
5. Glanbia plc, 57.6

Source: *Management Today*, Britain's Most Admired Companies (annual), December 2011, p. 45.

2728 ■ EUROPE'S MOST VALUABLE FOOD PRODUCTION COMPANIES, 2011

Ranked by: Market value as of March 2011, in millions of U.S. dollars. **Remarks:** Also notes rank within the *FT Europe 500*, rank for previous year, country, revenue, net income, assets, number of employees, share price, price-to-earning ratio, dividend yield, and fiscal yearend. **Number listed:** 13

1. Nestle SA, with $199,406.6 million
2. Unilever, $87,303.4
3. Groupe Danone, $42,382.5
4. Associated British Foods plc, $12,588.6
5. Orkla ASA, $9,969.9
6. Chocoladefabriken Lindt & Sprungli AG, $7,198.9
7. Kerry Group plc, $6,547.7
8. Danisco A/S, $6,027.4
9. Wimms-Bill-Dann Foods, $5,869.4
10. Parmalat, $5,830.3

Source: *Financial Times*, FT 500 (annual), http://www.ft.com, June 24, 2011.

2729 ■ FRANCE'S MOST VALUABLE FOOD BRANDS, 2011

Ranked by: Brand value, in millions of U.S. dollars. **Remarks:** Also notes rank within the *Global 500* for current and previous year, figures for current and previous year, and brand rating. Ranking is available online only. **Number listed:** 3

1. Carrefour, with $8,812 million
2. Danone, $7,241
3. Casino, $3,712

Source: *Global 500*, (annual), Brand Finance plc, March 2012.

2730 ■ GERMANY'S MOST VALUABLE FOOD BRANDS, 2011

Ranked by: Brand value, in millions of U.S. dollars. **Remarks:** Also notes rank within the *Global 500* for current and previous year, figures for current and previous year, and brand rating. Ranking is available online only. **Number listed:** 2

1. Metro Cash & Carry, with $5,296 million
2. Media Markt & Saturn, $4,202

Source: *Global 500*, (annual), Brand Finance plc, March 2012.

2731 ■ LARGEST FOOD, BEVERAGE, AND TOBACCO COMPANIES IN EUROPE, 2010

Ranked by: Sales, in millions of U.S. dollars. **Remarks:** Also notes rank within country. **Number listed:** 100

1. Nestle SA (Switzerland), with $105,973.4 million
2. Unilever NV (Netherlands), $59,224.8
3. Imperial Tobacco Group plc (U.K.), $39,775.5
4. Anheuser-Busch InBev SA/NV (Belgium), $36,758
5. SABMiller plc (U.K.), $27,030
6. Heineken NV (Netherlands), $21,863.3
7. British American Tobacco plc (U.K.), $21,312
8. Groupe Danone SA (France), $21,452.6
9. Caledonian Brewery Ltd. (U.K.), $18,000

10. Diageo plc (U.K.), $14,670

Source: *Europe's 15,000 Largest Companies*, (annual), ELC International, 2011, p. 42.

2732 ■ SWITZERLAND'S MOST VALUABLE FOOD BRANDS, 2011

Ranked by: Brand value, in millions of U.S. dollars. **Remarks:** Also notes rank within the *Global 500* for current and previous year, figures for current and previous year, and brand rating. Ranking is available online only. **Number listed:** 4

1. Nestle, with $16,661 million
2. Nescafe, $4,150
3. Purina, $4,118
4. KitKat, $3,279

Source: *Global 500*, (annual), Brand Finance plc, March 2012.

2733 ■ THE UNITED KINGDOM'S MOST VALUABLE FOOD BRANDS, 2011

Ranked by: Brand value, in millions of U.S. dollars. **Remarks:** Also notes rank within the *Global 500* for current and previous year, figures for current and previous year, and brand rating. Ranking is available online only. **Number listed:** 5

1. Tesco, with $20,051 million
2. Morrisons, $6,274
3. Sainsbury's, $5,849
4. Dove, $5,045
5. Lipton, $2,461

Source: *Global 500*, (annual), Brand Finance plc, March 2012.

2734 ■ WORLD'S LARGEST CONSUMER BEVERAGES COMPANIES, 2010

Ranked by: Sales, in millions of U.S. dollars. **Remarks:** Also notes brands and annual sales growth. **Number listed:** 20

1. PepsiCo Inc., with $57,838 million
2. Anheuser-Busch InBev SA/NV, $36,297
3. The Coca-Cola Co., $35,119
4. Kirin Holdings Co., Ltd., $28,301
5. SABMiller plc, $26,350
6. Heineken NV, $22,052
7. Asahi Breweries Ltd., $18,277
8. Diageo plc, $15,370
9. Fomento Economico Mexicano, SA de CV (FEMSA), $13,705
10. Carlsberg A/S, $11,026

Source: *Consumer Goods Technology*, Consumer Goods Registry (annual), http://www.consumergoods.com, December 2011.

2735 ■ WORLD'S LARGEST CONSUMER FOODS COMPANIES, 2010

Ranked by: Sales, in millions of U.S. dollars. **Remarks:** Also notes brands and annual sales growth. **Number listed:** 20

1. Nestle SA, with $118,940 million
2. Kraft Foods Inc., $49,207
3. JBS SA, $29,925
4. Tyson Foods Inc., $28,430
5. Groupe Danone, $22,704
6. General Mills Inc., $14,800
7. Brasil Foods SA, $12,905

8. Nippon Meat Packers Inc., $12,426
9. Kellogg Co., $12,397
10. Dean Foods Co., $12,123

Source: *Consumer Goods Technology*, Consumer Goods Registry (annual), http://www.consumergoods.com, December 2011.

2736 ■ WORLD'S LARGEST FOOD PRODUCT MANUFACTURERS, 2011

Ranked by: Revenue, in millions of dollars. **Remarks:** Also notes rank for previous year, overall rank within the *IW 1000*, country, and revenue growth. **Number listed:** 83

1. Nestle SA, with $117,463 million
2. Archer Daniels Midland Co., $61,682
3. Unilever, $59,205
4. Kraft Foods Inc., $49,207
5. Bunge Ltd., $45,707
6. George Weston Ltd., $32,217
7. Tyson Foods Inc., $28,430
8. Onex Corp., $24,525
9. Groupe Danone, $22,753
10. Associated British Foods plc, $15,871

Source: *IndustryWeek*, IW 1000 (annual), http://www.industryweek.com, August 2011.

2737 ■ WORLD'S MOST ADMIRED CONSUMER FOOD PRODUCTS COMPANIES, 2012

Ranked by: Score, on a scale of 10, based on a survey of executives, directors, and securities analysts of companies within their own industry on eight criteria: innovation, financial soundness, employee talent, use of corporate assets, long-term investment value, social responsibility, quality of management, and quality of products/services. **Remarks:** Specific scores not provided. Also notes rank for previous year. **Number listed:** 7

1. Nestle SA
2. PepsiCo Inc.
3. Unilever
4. Groupe Danone
5. Kellogg Co.
6. General Mills Inc.
7. Kraft Foods Inc.

Source: *Fortune*, World's Most Admired Companies (annual), March 19, 2012, p. 147.

2738 ■ WORLD'S MOST ADMIRED FOOD PRODUCTION COMPANIES, 2012

Ranked by: Score, on a scale of 10, based on a survey of executives, directors, and securities analysts of companies within their own industry on eight criteria: innovation, financial soundness, employee talent, use of corporate assets, long-term investment value, social responsibility, quality of management, and quality of products/services. **Remarks:** Specific scores not provided. Also notes rank for previous year. **Number listed:** 5

1. Wilmar International Ltd.
2. Archer Daniels Midland Co.
3. Bunge Corp.
4. Corn Products International Inc.
5. Chiquita Brands International Inc.

Source: *Fortune*, World's Most Admired Companies (annual), March 19, 2012, p. 148.

2739 ■ WORLD'S MOST ETHICAL FOOD AND BEVERAGE COMPANIES, 2012

Ranked by: Score based on five criteria: ethics and compliance program; reputation, leadership, and innovation; governance; corporate citizenship and responsibility; and culture of ethics. **Remarks:** Specific scores not provided; companies are listed alphabetically, not ranked. **Number listed:** 4

1. Kellogg Co. (U.S.)
2. PepsiCo Inc. (U.S.)
3. Solae LLC (U.S.)
4. Stonyfield Farm Inc. (U.S.)

Source: *Ethisphere Magazine*, World's Most Ethical Companies (annual), http://www.ethisphere.com, 2012.

2740 ■ WORLD'S MOST VALUABLE FOOD BRANDS, 2011

Ranked by: Brand value, in millions of U.S. dollars. **Remarks:** Also notes rank within the *Global 500* for current and previous year, figures for current and previous year, country, and brand rating. Ranking is available online only. **Number listed:** 28

1. Tesco, with $20,051 million
2. Nestle, $16,661
3. Carrefour, $8,812
4. Kellogg, $7,955
5. Woolworths, $7,299
6. Danone, $7,241
7. Morrisons, $6,274
8. Sainsbury's, $5,849
9. Heinz, $5,373
10. Metro Cash & Carry, $5,296

Source: *Global 500*, (annual), Brand Finance plc, March 2012.

2741 ■ WORLD'S MOST VALUABLE FOOD PRODUCTION COMPANIES, 2011

Ranked by: Market value as of March 2011, in millions of U.S. dollars. **Remarks:** Also notes rank within the *FT 500*, rank for previous year, country, revenue, net income, assets, number of employees, share price, price-to-earning ratio, dividend yield, and fiscal year-end. **Number listed:** 9

1. Nestle SA, with $199,406.6 million
2. Unilever, $87,303.4
3. Kraft Foods Inc., $54,846.3
4. Groupe Danone, $42,382.5
5. Monsanto Co., $38,782
6. Wilmar International Ltd., $27,720.6
7. General Mills Inc., $23,333.7
8. Archer Daniels Midland Co., $22,949.3
9. Kellogg Co., $19,797.1

Source: *Financial Times*, FT 500 (annual), http://www.ft.com, June 24, 2011.

2742 ■ WORLD'S TOP FOOD AND BEVERAGE COMPANIES, 2010

Ranked by: Food sales, in millions of U.S. dollars. **Number listed:** 100

1. Nestle SA, with $99,733 million
2. PepsiCo Inc., $57,838
3. Kraft Foods Inc., $49,207
4. Anheuser-Busch InBev SA/NV, $36,297

5. The Coca-Cola Co., $35,119
6. JBS SA, $31,285
7. Archer Daniels Midland Co., $31,000
8. Unilever, $30,160
9. Mars Inc., $30,000
10. Tyson Foods Inc., $28,430

Source: *Food Engineering*, Top 100 (annual), September 2011, p. 66.

Food Packages

2743 ■ LARGEST PACKAGERS OF FOOD PRODUCTS, 2010

Ranked by: Total revenue, in billions of dollars. **Remarks:** Also notes headquarters, number of plants, chief packaging officer, and selected brands. **Number listed:** 50

1. Nestle SA, with $63.1 billion
2. Kraft Foods Inc., $39.37
3. Mars Inc., $30
4. Tyson Foods Inc., $28.43
5. PepsiCo Inc., $28.34
6. Groupe Danone, $19.85
7. Unilever plc, $18.47
8. JBS USA, $16.06
9. Cargill Meat Solutions, $15
10. General Mills Inc., $14.8

Source: *Food & Beverage Packaging*, Top 50 Packagers (annual), 2011, p. 32-34.

Food Processing

2744 ■ BRAZIL'S LARGEST FOOD PROCESSING COMPANIES OVERALL, 2011

Ranked by: Score based on revenue, profits, assets, and market capitalization. **Remarks:** Specific scores not provided. Also notes overall rank in the *Forbes 2000* and figures for each criterion. **Number listed:** 4

1. BRF-Brasil Foods
2. JBS
3. Cosan
4. Marfrig Group

Source: *Forbes*, Forbes 2000 (annual), http://www.forbes.com, May 7, 2012.

2745 ■ CANADA'S LARGEST FOOD PROCESSING COMPANIES OVERALL, 2011

Ranked by: Score based on revenue, profits, assets, and market capitalization. **Remarks:** Specific scores not provided. Also notes overall rank in the *Forbes 2000* and figures for each criterion. **Number listed:** 2

1. Saputo
2. Viterra

Source: *Forbes*, Forbes 2000 (annual), http://www.forbes.com, May 7, 2012.

2746 ■ CHINA'S LARGEST FOOD PROCESSING COMPANIES OVERALL, 2011

Ranked by: Score based on revenue, profits, assets, and market capitalization. **Remarks:** Specific scores not provided. Also notes overall rank in the *Forbes 2000* and figures for each criterion. **Number listed:** 4

1. Tingyi Holding
2. Want Want China
3. Inner Mongolia Yili
4. Henan Shuanghui Investment

Source: *Forbes*, Forbes 2000 (annual), http://www.forbes.com, May 7, 2012.

2747 ■ ILLINOIS'S LARGEST FOOD PROCESSING COMPANIES OVERALL, 2011

Ranked by: Score based on revenue, profits, assets, and market capitalization. **Remarks:** Specific scores not provided. Also notes overall rank in the *Forbes 2000* and figures for each criterion. **Number listed:** 4

1. Kraft Foods Inc.
2. Archer Daniels Midland Co.
3. Sara Lee Corp.
4. Corn Products International

Source: *Forbes*, Forbes 2000 (annual), http://www.forbes.com, May 7, 2012.

2748 ■ JAPAN'S LARGEST FOOD PROCESSING COMPANIES OVERALL, 2011

Ranked by: Score based on revenue, profits, assets, and market capitalization. **Remarks:** Specific scores not provided. Also notes overall rank in the *Forbes 2000* and figures for each criterion. **Number listed:** 4

1. Ajinomoto
2. Meiji Holdings
3. Yamazaki Baking
4. Nippon Meat Packers

Source: *Forbes*, Forbes 2000 (annual), http://www.forbes.com, May 7, 2012.

2749 ■ LARGEST FOOD PROCESSING COMPANIES, 2010

Ranked by: Food sales, in millions of U.S. dollars. **Remarks:** Also notes rank for previous year, total sales, net income, and figures for previous year. **Number listed:** 100

1. PepsiCo Inc., with $35,600 million
2. Nestle SA (U.S. & Canada), $29,600
3. Kraft Foods Inc., $29,524
4. Tyson Foods Inc., $27,293
5. Anheuser-Busch InBev SA/NV, $15,296
6. JBS USA Holdings Inc., $13,342
7. General Mills Inc., $12,005
8. Dean Foods Co., $11,758
9. Mars Inc., $10,500
10. Smithfield Foods Inc., $10,264

Source: *Food Processing*, Top 100 Companies (annual), August 2011, p. 38+.

2750 ■ LARGEST U.S. FOOD PROCESSING COMPANIES OVERALL, 2011

Ranked by: Score based on revenue, profits, assets, and market capitalization. **Remarks:** Specific scores not provided. Also notes overall rank in the *Forbes 2000* and figures for each criterion. **Number listed:** 16

1. Kraft Foods Inc.
2. Archer Daniels Midland Co.

3. General Mills Inc.
4. Kellogg Co.
5. H. J. Heinz Co.
6. ConAgra Foods Inc.
7. Tyson Foods Inc.
8. Sara Lee Corp.
9. Campbell Soup Co.
10. Hershey Foods Corp.

Source: *Forbes*, Forbes 2000 (annual), http://www.forbes.com, May 7, 2012.

2751 ■ MALAYSIA'S LARGEST FOOD PROCESSING COMPANIES OVERALL, 2011

Ranked by: Score based on revenue, profits, assets, and market capitalization. **Remarks:** Specific scores not provided. Also notes overall rank in the *Forbes 2000* and figures for each criterion. **Number listed:** 2

1. IOI Group
2. Kuala Lumpur Kepong

Source: *Forbes*, Forbes 2000 (annual), http://www.forbes.com, May 7, 2012.

2752 ■ MINNESOTA'S LARGEST FOOD PROCESSING COMPANIES OVERALL, 2011

Ranked by: Score based on revenue, profits, assets, and market capitalization. **Remarks:** Specific scores not provided. Also notes overall rank in the *Forbes 2000* and figures for each criterion. **Number listed:** 2

1. General Mills Inc.
2. Hormel Foods Corp.

Source: *Forbes*, Forbes 2000 (annual), http://www.forbes.com, May 7, 2012.

2753 ■ PENNSYLVANIA'S LARGEST FOOD PROCESSING COMPANIES OVERALL, 2011

Ranked by: Score based on revenue, profits, assets, and market capitalization. **Remarks:** Specific scores not provided. Also notes overall rank in the *Forbes 2000* and figures for each criterion. **Number listed:** 2

1. H. J. Heinz Co.
2. Hershey Foods Corp.

Source: *Forbes*, Forbes 2000 (annual), http://www.forbes.com, May 7, 2012.

2754 ■ SINGAPORE'S LARGEST FOOD PROCESSING COMPANIES OVERALL, 2011

Ranked by: Score based on revenue, profits, assets, and market capitalization. **Remarks:** Specific scores not provided. Also notes overall rank in the *Forbes 2000* and figures for each criterion. **Number listed:** 3

1. Wilmar International Ltd.
2. Golden Agri-Resources Ltd.
3. Olam International Ltd.

Source: *Forbes*, Forbes 2000 (annual), http://www.forbes.com, May 7, 2012.

2755 ■ SWITZERLAND'S LARGEST FOOD PROCESSING COMPANIES OVERALL, 2011

Ranked by: Score based on revenue, profits, assets, and market capitalization. **Remarks:** Specific scores not provided. Also notes overall rank in the *Forbes 2000* and figures for each criterion. **Number listed:** 2

1. Nestle SA
2. Aryzta

Source: *Forbes*, Forbes 2000 (annual), http://www.forbes.com, May 7, 2012.

2756 ■ WORLD'S LARGEST FOOD PROCESSING COMPANIES OVERALL, 2011

Ranked by: Score based on revenue, profits, assets, and market capitalization. **Remarks:** Specific scores not provided. Also notes country, overall rank in the *Forbes 2000,* and figures for each criterion. **Number listed:** 48

1. Nestle SA
2. Unilever
3. Kraft Foods Inc.
4. Groupe Danone
5. Archer Daniels Midland Co.
6. Wilmar International Ltd.
7. General Mills Inc.
8. Bunge Ltd.
9. Associated British Foods plc
10. Kellogg Co.

Source: *Forbes*, Forbes 2000 (annual), http://www.forbes.com, May 7, 2012.

Food Processors

2757 ■ TOP FOOD PROCESSING COMPANIES IN CAPITAL SPENDING, 2012

Ranked by: Budget, in millions of U.S. dollars. **Remarks:** Also notes percent change from previous year, overall rank in the *Top 100*, and actual spending for two previous years. **Number listed:** 36

1. Anheuser-Busch InBev SA/NV, with $3,200 million
2. The Coca-Cola Co., $3,100
3. PepsiCo Inc., $3,000
4. Kraft Foods Inc., $2,000
5. Tyson Foods Inc., $825
6. General Mills Inc., $670
7. Kellogg Co., $625
8. ConAgra Foods Inc., $475
9. H. J. Heinz, $432
10. Sara Lee Corp., $370

Source: *Food Processing*, Capital Spending Report (annual), April 2012, p. 29.

Food Service Industry

2758 ■ LARGEST FOODS MANAGEMENT COMPANIES, 2010

Ranked by: Revenue, in millions of dollars. **Remarks:** Also notes headquarters, website, figures for previous two years, number of locations, segments served, and comments. **Number listed:** 50

1. Compass Group North America, with $9,900 million
2. Aramark Corp., $8,605
3. Sodexo Inc., $8,000

4. Delaware North Cos., $1,900
5. Centerplate, $750
6. Thompson Hospitality, $351
7. Guckenheimer Enterprises Inc., $350
7. Guest Services Inc., $350
9. Ovations Food Services, $200
10. Valley Services Inc., $189

Source: *Food Management*, Top 50 (annual), September 2011.

2759 ■ TOP FOODSERVICE COMPANIES BY GROWTH IN U.S. REVENUE, 2009-2010

Ranked by: Annual growth in U.S. foodservice revenue, in percent. **Remarks:** Also notes rank for previous year, fiscal year-end, and figures for previous year. **Number listed:** 100

1. Apollo Global Management LLC, with 119.34%
2. Pilot Flying J, 67.72%
3. Golden Gate Capital Group LLC, 52.69%
4. Fidelity Newport Holdings LLC, 22.2%
5. Chipotle Mexican Grill Inc., 20.7%
6. BJ's Restaurants Inc., 20.44%
7. Delaware North Cos., Inc., 19.45%
8. Sun Capital Partners Inc., 18.14%
9. Kohlberg & Co. LLP, 16.62%
10. Blackstone Group LP, 14.25%

Source: *Nation's Restaurant News*, Top 100 (annual), June 27, 2011, p. 34.

2760 ■ TOP FOODSERVICE COMPANIES BY U.S. REVENUE, 2010

Ranked by: U.S. food and beverage revenue, in millions of dollars. **Remarks:** Also notes rank for previous year, headquarters, chains and divisions, fiscal year-end, and sales for previous two years. **Number listed:** 100

1. Compass Group plc, with $8,150 million
2. Darden Restaurants Inc., $7,385
3. Starbucks Corp., $6,582
4. ARAMARK Holdings Corp., $6,454
5. Sodexho Inc., $5,759
6. McDonald's Corp., $5,362.3
7. Yum! Brands Inc., $4,120
8. Bain Capital LLC, $3,323.5
9. Wendy's/Arby's Group Inc., $3,129
10. Brinker International Inc., $2,798

Source: *Nation's Restaurant News*, Top 100 (annual), June 27, 2011, p. 28+.

2761 ■ TOP FOODSERVICE CONTRACT CHAINS BY GROWTH IN CONTRACT VENUES, 2009-2010

Ranked by: Annual growth in number of U.S. venues served, in percent. **Remarks:** Also notes rank for previous year, fiscal year-end, and figures for previous year. **Number listed:** 20

1. Centerplate, with 80.45%
2. HMSHost (airports), 8.33%
3. Delaware North Cos. Sportservice, 8%
4. Aramark Healthcare, 7.02%
5. Levy Restaurants (sports concessions), 4.35%
6. Sodexo School Services, 4.01%

7. Sodexo Campus Services, 3.57%
8. Aramark Sports, Entertainment & Conference Centers, 2.03%
9. Sodexo Health Care Services, 1.34%
10. Bon Appetit Management Co., 1.14%

Source: *Nation's Restaurant News*, Top 100 (annual), June 27, 2011, p. 66.

2762 ■ TOP FOODSERVICE CONTRACT CHAINS BY GROWTH IN SALES, 2009-2010

Ranked by: Annual growth in systemwide sales, in percent. **Remarks:** Also notes rank for previous year, fiscal year-end, and figures for previous year. **Number listed:** 20

1. Delaware North Cos. Sportservice, with 32.53%
2. Levy Restaurants sports concessions, 18.85%
3. Bon Appetit Management Co., 14.52%
4. Chartwells, 13.19%
5. LSG Sky Chefs, 10.94%
6. Aramark Higher Education, 8.13%
7. Centerplate, 7.96%
8. Morrison Management Specialists, 7.17%
9. Gate Gourmet, 6.73%
10. Aramark Healthcare, 6.33%

Source: *Nation's Restaurant News*, Top 100 (annual), June 27, 2011, p. 66.

2763 ■ TOP FOODSERVICE CONTRACT CHAINS BY U.S. CONTRACT VENUES, 2010

Ranked by: Total number of U.S. venues served. **Remarks:** Also notes rank for previous year, fiscal year-end, and figures for previous two years. **Number listed:** 20

1. Canteen Services, with 18,125 venues
2. Aramark Business & Corrections, 2,000
3. Sodexo Health Care Services, 1,666
4. Eurest Dining Services, 1,210
5. Sodexo Corporate Services, 1,110
6. Chartwells, 1,072
7. Sodexo Campus Services, 957
8. Morrison Management Specialists, 860
9. Aramark Healthcare, 503
10. Sodexo School Services, 493

Source: *Nation's Restaurant News*, Top 100 (annual), June 27, 2011, p. 66.

2764 ■ TOP FOODSERVICE CONTRACT CHAINS BY U.S. SYSTEMWIDE SALES, 2010

Ranked by: U.S. systemwide foodservice sales, in millions of dollars. **Remarks:** Also notes rank for previous year, fiscal year-end, and figures for previous two years. **Number listed:** 20

1. Sodexo Health Care Services, with $1,893 million
2. Sodexo Campus Services, $1,836
3. Canteen Services, $1,825
4. Aramark Sports, Entertainment & Conference Centers, $1,820
5. Aramark Business & Corrections, $1,617
6. Chartwells, $1,545

7. Morrison Management Specialists, $1,495
8. HMSHost, $1,469
9. Sodexo Corporate Services, $1,328
10. Aramark Healthcare, $1,143

Source: *Nation's Restaurant News*, Top 100 (annual), June 27, 2011, p. 66.

2765 ■ TOP *FORTUNE 500* COMPANIES IN FOOD SERVICES, 2011

Ranked by: Revenue, in millions of dollars. **Remarks:** Also notes overall rank in the *Fortune 500;* profits; profits as a percentage of revenue; stockholders' equity; and rank by each criterion. **Number listed:** 4

1. McDonald's Corp., with $27,006 million
2. Yum! Brands Inc., $12,626
3. Starbucks Corp., $11,700
4. Darden Restaurants Inc., $7,500

Source: *Fortune*, Fortune 500 (annual), May 21, 2012, p. F-35.

2766 ■ WORLD'S MOST ADMIRED FOOD SERVICES COMPANIES, 2012

Ranked by: Score, on a scale of 10, based on a survey of executives, directors, and securities analysts of companies within their own industry on eight criteria: innovation, financial soundness, employee talent, use of corporate assets, long-term investment value, social responsibility, quality of management, and quality of products/services. **Remarks:** Specific scores not provided. Also notes rank for previous year. **Number listed:** 5

1. McDonald's Corp.
2. Starbucks Corp.
3. Yum! Brands Inc.
4. Chipotle Mexican Grill Inc.
5. Darden Restaurants Inc.

Source: *Fortune*, World's Most Admired Companies (annual), March 19, 2012, p. 149-150.

Football

2767 ■ RICHEST NFL TEAMS, 2010

Ranked by: Value of team, based on current stadium deal, in millions of dollars. **Remarks:** Also notes principal owners, year acquired, growth in value, debt-to-value ratio, total revenue, and total operating income. **Number listed:** 32

1. Dallas Cowboys, with $1,850 million
2. Washington Redskins, $1,560
3. New England Patriots, $1,400
4. New York Giants, $1,300
5. New York Jets, $1,220
6. Houston Texans, $1,200
7. Philadelphia Eagles, $1,160
8. Chicago Bears, $1,090
8. Green Bay Packers, $1,090
8. Baltimore Ravens, $1,090

Source: *Forbes*, NFL Team Valuations (annual), September 26, 2011, p. 92-97.

2768 ■ WEALTHIEST OWNERS OF NFL TEAMS, 2010

Ranked by: Worth, in billions of dollars. **Number listed:** 5

1. Paul Allen (Seattle Seahawks), with $13 billion
2. Stephen M. Ross (Miami Dolphins), $3.1
3. Malcolm Glazer (Tampa Bay Buccaneers), $2.6
3. Stanley Kroenke (St. Louis Rams), $2.6
5. Jerry Jones (Dallas Cowboys), $2

Source: *Forbes*, NFL Team Valuations (annual), September 26, 2011, p. 91.

Forest Products Industry
See also: **Paper Industry**

2769 ■ EUROPE'S MOST VALUABLE FORESTRY AND PAPER COMPANIES, 2011

Ranked by: Market value as of March 2011, in millions of U.S. dollars. **Remarks:** Also notes rank within the *FT Europe 500*, rank for previous year, country, revenue, net income, assets, number of employees, share price, price-to-earning ratio, dividend yield, and fiscal yearend. **Number listed:** 2

1. UPM-Kymmene Oyj, with $11,009.2 million
2. Stora Enso Oyj, $9,456.2

Source: *Financial Times*, FT 500 (annual), http://www.ft.com, June 24, 2011.

2770 ■ LARGEST FORESTRY COMPANIES IN BRITISH COLUMBIA, 2010

Ranked by: Revenue, in thousands of Canadian dollars. **Remarks:** Also notes figures for previous year. **Number listed:** 10

1. West Fraser Timber Co., Ltd., with C$2,885,900 thousand
2. Canfor Corp., C$2,430,400
3. Futura Corp., C$1,300,000
4. Mercer International Inc., C$1,230,222
5. Catalyst Paper Corp., C$1,228,600
6. CanWel Building Materials Group Ltd., C$1,032,347
7. Taiga Building Products Ltd., C$931,514
8. Tolko Industries Ltd., C$900,000
9. Western Forest Products Inc., C$667,900
10. International Forest Products Ltd., C$625,618

Source: *BCBusiness*, Top 100 (annual), July 2011, p. 135.

2771 ■ TOP *FORTUNE 500* COMPANIES IN FOREST AND PAPER PRODUCTS, 2011

Ranked by: Revenue, in millions of dollars. **Remarks:** Also notes overall rank in the *Fortune 500*; profits; profits as a percentage of revenue; stockholders' equity; and rank by each criterion. **Number listed:** 3

1. International Paper Co., with $26,034 million
2. Weyerhaeuser Co., $6,618
3. Domtar Inc., $5,612

Source: *Fortune*, Fortune 500 (annual), May 21, 2012, p. F-35.

Forestry

2772 ■ LARGEST FORESTRY COMPANIES BY EMPLOYEES, 2010

Ranked by: Total number of employees. **Remarks:** Also notes contact information for headquarters, number of employees at headquarters, revenue, rank by revenue, and primary SIC code. **Number listed:** 50

1. Weyerhaeuser Co., with 14,900 employees
2. Interfor Pacific Inc., 3,000
3. Rayonier Forest Resources LP, 1,400
4. Roy O. Martin Lumber Co., 1,200
5. Potlatch Corp., 945
5. Potlatch Land & Lumber LLC, 945
7. Boething Treeland Farms Inc., 700
8. Westervelt Co., 650
9. AFA Forest Products (USA) Inc., 600
9. Aviagen Inc., 600

Source: *Business Rankings*, (annual), Dun & Bradstreet Inc., 2011, p. VI.11-VI.12.

2773 ■ LARGEST FORESTRY COMPANIES BY SALES, 2010

Ranked by: Total revenue, in dollars. **Remarks:** Also notes contact information for headquarters, number of employees at headquarters and overall, rank by employees, and primary SIC code. **Number listed:** 50

1. Weyerhaeuser Co., with $6,552,000,000
2. Potlatch Corp., $539,447,000
3. Deltic Timber Corp., $141,623,000
4. Lake County Forest Preserve District, $67,295,500
5. Continental Heavy Haul Inc., $60,000,000
6. Menasha Forest Products Corp., $58,549,483
7. Hal Hays Construction Inc., $32,631,578
8. Pope Resources Delaware LP, $31,192,000
9. Pennhill Farms Inc., $31,000,000
10. AFA Forest Products (USA) Inc., $26,500,000

Source: *Business Rankings*, (annual), Dun & Bradstreet Inc., 2011, p. V.11-V.12.

Fraud

2774 ■ LARGEST HEALTHCARE FRAUD SETTLEMENTS, 2010

Ranked by: Settlement amount agreed to pay under the federal False Claims Act, in millions of dollars. **Remarks:** Also notes amount recovered, date of settlement, and allegations. **Number listed:** 14

1. Allergan, with $600 million
2. AstraZeneca plc and AstraZeneca Pharmaceuticals, $520
3. Novartis Pharmaceuticals Corp., $422.5
4. Forest Laboratories and Forest Pharmaceuticals, $313
5. Elan Corp. and Elan Pharmaceuticals, $214.5
6. Teva Pharmaceuticals, $169
7. WellCare Health Plans, $137.5
8. Health Alliance of Greater Cincinnati, $108
9. Ortho-McNeil Pharmaceutical and Ortho-McNeil-Janssen Pharmaceuticals, $81
10. Novartis Vaccines & Diagnostics and Novartis Pharmaceuticals Corp., $72.5

Source: *Modern Healthcare*, Largest Healthcare Fraud Settlements (annual), June 6, 2011, p. 34.

Freight and Freightage

2775 ■ LARGEST COMPANIES IN THE MOTOR FREIGHT TRANSPORTATION/WAREHOUSING INDUSTRY BY EMPLOYEES, 2010

Ranked by: Total number of employees. **Remarks:** Also notes contact information for headquarters, number of employees at headquarters, revenue, rank by revenue, and primary SIC code. **Number listed:** 168

1. United Parcel Service Inc. (UPS), with 414,500 employees
2. United Parcel Service of New York Inc., 75,000
3. Roadway LLC, 46,000
3. YRC Inc., 46,000
5. YRC Worldwide Inc., 36,000
6. Con-Way Inc., 27,900
7. FedEx Freight Corp., 26,828
8. Schneider National Inc., 22,000
9. Saint Corp., 21,900
10. USF Corp., 21,000

Source: *Business Rankings*, (annual), Dun & Bradstreet Inc., 2011, p. VI.92-VI.95.

2776 ■ LARGEST COMPANIES IN THE MOTOR FREIGHT TRANSPORTATION/WAREHOUSING INDUSTRY BY SALES, 2010

Ranked by: Total revenue, in dollars. **Remarks:** Also notes contact information for headquarters, number of employees at headquarters and overall, rank by employees, and primary SIC code. **Number listed:** 170

1. United Parcel Service Inc. (UPS), with $49,545,000,000
2. Con-Way Inc., $4,952,000,000
3. Advance Logistics Services Inc., $4,500,000,000
4. YRC Worldwide Inc., $4,334,640,000
5. J. B. Hunt Transport Services Inc., $3,793,485,000
6. J. B. Hunt Transport Inc., $3,500,000,000
7. Iron Mountain Inc., $3,127,549,000
8. Iron Mountain Information Management Inc., $3,000,000,000
9. Landstar System Holdings Inc., $2,900,000,000
10. Con-Way Freight Inc., $2,600,000,000

Source: *Business Rankings*, (annual), Dun & Bradstreet Inc., 2011, p. V.92-V.95.

2777 ■ TOP GLOBAL FREIGHT FORWARDERS, 2010

Ranked by: Score based on gross revenue and freight forwarding volumes. **Remarks:** Scores not provided. Also notes net revenue, gross revenue, ocean volumes, and airfreight volume. **Number listed:** 25

1. DHL Supply Chain & Global Forwarding
2. Kuehne + Nagel Inc.
3. DB Schenker Logistics
4. Panalpina World Transport (Holding) Ltd.
5. UPS Supply Chain Solutions
6. CEVA Logistics
7. Sinotrans Ltd.

8. Expeditors International of Washington Inc.
9. Bollore/SDV Logistics
10. DSV A/S

Source: *Logistics Management*, Top 25 Freight Forwarders, September 2011, p. 68s.

2778 ■ TOP WORLDWIDE FREIGHT FORWARDERS, 2010

Ranked by: Airfreight tonnage. **Remarks:** Also notes figures for previous year. **Number listed:** 25

1. DHL Supply Chain & Global Forwarding, with 4,435,000 tonnes
2. DB Schenker Logistics, 1,125,000
3. Kuehne + Nagel Inc., 948,000
4. Panalpina World Transport (Holding) Ltd., 892,000
5. Kintetsu World Express Inc., 869,225
6. UPS Supply Chain Solutions, 862,000
7. Nippon Express Co., Ltd., 855,400
8. Expeditors International of Washington Inc., 807,211
9. CEVA Logistics, 536,000
10. Hellmann Worldwide Logistics GmbH, 513,278

Source: *Air Cargo World*, Top 25 Worldwide Freight Forwarders (annual), July 2011, p. 32.

Frozen Pizza

2779 ■ TOP BRANDS OF FROZEN PIZZA, 2011

Ranked by: Sales, in millions of dollars. **Remarks:** Also notes unit sales and annual growth. **Number listed:** 5

1. DiGiorno, with $622.7 million
2. Private label, $271.3
3. Red Baron, $266.2
4. Tombstone, $246.6
5. Totino's, $160.9

Source: *Refrigerated & Frozen Foods*, State of the Industry (annual), July 2011, p. 36.

Fruit Drinks

2780 ■ TOP BOTTLED FRUIT DRINK BRANDS IN THE U.S., 2011

Ranked by: Sales, in dollars. **Remarks:** Also notes percent change from previous year and market share. **Number listed:** 10

1. Hawaiian Punch, with $183,391,900
2. V8 Splash, $113,908,200
3. Tampico, $90,766,480
4. Bug Juice, $78,699,500
5. Snapple, $64,131,300
6. Fuze Slenderize, $62,933,100
7. private label, $62,911,200
8. Lipton Brisk, $60,054,940
9. Kool Aid Bursts, $54,153,280
10. Tum-E Yummies, $48,783,290

Source: *Beverage Industry*, State of the Industry Report (annual), July 2011, p. SIO-16.

Furniture Industry

2781 ■ LARGEST FURNITURE AND CABINET MANUFACTURERS, 2011

Ranked by: Annual sales, in billions of dollars. **Remarks:** Also notes main location, annual sales, total employees, and website. **Number listed:** 300

1. Steelcase Inc., with $2.44 billion
2. Herman Miller Inc., $1.649
3. HNI Corp., $1.55
4. MasterBrand Cabinets Inc., $1.275
5. Masco Corp., $1.265
6. Haworth Inc., $1.21
7. Andersen Corp., $1.20
8. Ashley Furniture Industries Inc., $1.1
9. La-Z-Boy Inc., $1.069
10. Furniture Brands International Inc., $1.05

Source: *CabinetMaker+FDM*, FDM 300 (annual), February 2012, p. 36+.

2782 ■ LARGEST FURNITURE AND FIXTURES COMPANIES BY EMPLOYEES, 2010

Ranked by: Total number of employees. **Remarks:** Also notes contact information for headquarters, number of employees at headquarters, revenue, rank by revenue, and primary SIC code. **Number listed:** 50

1. Johnson Controls Inc., with 137,000 employees
2. Lear Corp., 75,000
3. Leggett & Platt Inc., 18,500
4. Ashley Furniture Industries Inc., 16,300
5. Universal Furniture Ltd., 12,000
6. Steelcase Inc., 11,000
7. HNI Corp., 8,700
8. Hunter Douglas Inc., 8,625
9. Furniture Brands International Inc., 8,500
10. La-Z-Boy Inc., 8,290

Source: *Business Rankings*, (annual), Dun & Bradstreet Inc., 2011, p. VI.56-VI.57.

2783 ■ LARGEST FURNITURE AND FIXTURES COMPANIES BY SALES, 2010

Ranked by: Total revenue, in dollars. **Remarks:** Also notes contact information for headquarters, number of employees at headquarters and overall, rank by employees, and primary SIC code. **Number listed:** 50

1. Johnson Controls Inc., with $34,305,000,000
2. Lear Corp., $11,954,600,000
3. Leggett & Platt Inc., $3,359,100,000
4. Steelcase Inc., $2,291,700,000
5. Kinetic Concepts Inc., $2,017,752,000
6. BE Aerospace Inc., $1,984,200,000
7. HNI Corp., $1,686,728,000
8. Hill-Rom Holdings Inc., $1,469,600,000
9. Herman Miller Inc., $1,318,800,000
10. Sealy Corp., $1,219,471,000

Source: *Business Rankings*, (annual), Dun & Bradstreet Inc., 2011, p. V.56-V.57.

2784 ■ LARGEST U.S. FURNITURE AND FIXTURE MANUFACTURERS, 2010

Ranked by: Revenue, in millions of dollars. **Remarks:** Also notes overall rank within the *IW 500*, revenue growth, and profit margin. **Number listed:** 9

1. Masco Corp., with $7,592 million
2. Leggett & Platt Inc., $3,359
3. Steelcase Inc., $2,292
4. HNI Corp., $1,687
5. Herman Miller Inc., $1,319
6. La-Z-Boy Inc., $1,179
7. Furniture Brands International Inc., $1,160
8. Kimball International Inc., $1,123
9. Tempur-Pedic International Inc., $1,105

Source: *IndustryWeek*, IW 500 (annual), http://www.industryweek.com, July 2011.

2785 ■ NORTH AMERICA'S LARGEST CONTRACT WOOD FURNITURE COMPANIES, 2010

Ranked by: Revenue, in dollars. **Remarks:** Also notes headquarters and percent change from previous year. **Number listed:** 24

1. Steelcase Inc., with $2,291,000,000
2. HNI Corp., $1,686,728,000
3. Herman Miller Inc., $1,318,800,000
4. Haworth Inc., $1,210,000,000
5. Knoll Inc., $809,500,000
6. Global Group, $750,000,000
7. KI, $700,000,000
8. Teknion Corp., $500,000,000
9. Sauder Woodworking, $450,000,000
10. Kimball International Inc., $415,439,000

Source: *Wood & Wood Products*, Wood 100 (annual), September 2011, p. 52.

2786 ■ NORTH AMERICA'S LARGEST RESIDENTIAL WOOD FURNITURE COMPANIES, 2010

Ranked by: Revenue, in dollars. **Remarks:** Also notes headquarters and percent change from previous year. **Number listed:** 15

1. Ashley Furniture Industries Inc., with $2,130,000,000
2. La-Z-Boy Inc., $1,180,000,000
3. Furniture Brands International Inc., $1,159,934,000
4. Dorel Industries Inc., $507,790,000
5. Klaussner Furniture Industries, $400,000,000
6. Ethan Allen Interiors Inc., $362,500,000
7. Flexsteel Industries Inc., $326,400,000
8. Hooker Furniture Corp., $203,300,000
9. Berkline/BenchCraft Holdings, $200,000,000
9. Bernhardt Furniture, $200,000,000

Source: *Wood & Wood Products*, Wood 100 (annual), September 2011, p. 52.

2787 ■ TOP BRANDS OF AUDIO/VIDEO FURNITURE, 2010

Ranked by: Popularity among *CE Pro 100* companies, in percent. **Number listed:** 5

1. Salamander, with 32%

2. BDI, 21%

2. Sanus, 21%

4. OmniMount, 7%

4. Bell'O, 7%

Source: *CE Pro*, Brand Analysis (annual), June 2011, p. 58.

2788 ■ TOP BRANDS OF AUDIO/VIDEO SEATING, 2010

Ranked by: Popularity among *CE Pro 100* companies, in percent. **Number listed:** 5

1. CinemaTech, with 17%

2. Berkline, 15%

3. Fortress, 13%

4. Salamander, 11%

5. Acoustic Innovations, 9%

Source: *CE Pro*, Brand Analysis (annual), June 2011, p. 58.

2789 ■ WORLD'S LARGEST FURNITURE AND FIXTURE MANUFACTURERS, 2010

Ranked by: Revenue, in millions of dollars. **Remarks:** Also notes rank for previous year, overall rank within the *IW 1000,* country, and revenue growth. **Number listed:** 3

1. Masco Corp., with $7,592 million

2. Steinhoff International Holdings Ltd., $7,452

3. Leggett & Platt Inc., $3,359

Source: *IndustryWeek*, IW 1000 (annual), http://www.industryweek.com, August 2011.

Furniture Stores

2790 ■ LARGEST CONVENTIONAL FURNITURE STORES, 2011

Ranked by: Estimated sales of furniture, bedding, and accessories, in millions of dollars. **Remarks:** Also notes rank in the overall *Top 100*, figures for previous year, percent change, and number of units. **Number listed:** 10

1. Ashley Furniture HomeStores, with $2,686 million

2. Rooms To Go Inc., $1,500

3. Berkshire Hathaway Inc., furniture division, $1,208.2

4. Raymour & Flanigan, $1,008.8

5. American Signature, $965.8

6. Ethan Allen Interiors Inc., $695.1

7. Bob's Discount Furniture, $638.8

8. Havertys, $620.9

9. Art Van, $470

10. Slumberland, $383.7

Source: *Furniture Today*, Top 100 (annual), May 21, 2012, p. 30.

2791 ■ LARGEST SINGLE-SOURCE FURNITURE STORE NETWORKS, 2011

Ranked by: Estimated sales of furniture, bedding, and accessories, in millions of dollars. **Remarks:** Also notes rank in the overall *Top 100*, figures for previous year, percent change, and number of units. **Number listed:** 7

1. Ashley Furniture HomeStores, with $2,686 million

2. La-Z-Boy Furniture Galleries, $820

3. Select Comfort, $713.5

4. Ethan Allen Interiors Inc., $695.1

5. America's Mattress, $275.5

6. Bassett Home Furnishings, $267.9

7. Thomasville Home Furnishings Stores, $240

Source: *Furniture Today*, Top 100 (annual), May 21, 2012, p. 34.

2792 ■ LARGEST SPECIALTY FURNITURE STORES, 2011

Ranked by: Estimated sales of furniture, bedding, and accessories, in millions of dollars. **Remarks:** Also notes rank in the overall *Top 100*, figures for previous year, percent change, and number of units. **Number listed:** 10

1. Ikea, with $2,280 million

2. Williams-Sonoma Inc., $1,480

3. Pier 1 Imports Inc., $956.8

4. Sleepy's, $846

5. Mattress Firm, $831.2

6. La-Z-Boy Furniture Galleries, $820

7. Crate & Barrel, $717.6

8. Select Comfort, $713.5

9. Restoration Hardware, $515

10. Sleep Train, $371.8

Source: *Furniture Today*, Top 100 (annual), May 21, 2012, p. 30.

2793 ■ LARGEST U.S. FURNITURE STORES, 2011

Ranked by: Estimated sales of furniture, bedding, and accessories, in millions of dollars. **Remarks:** Also notes rank and figures for previous year, percent change, headquarters, number of units, total selling space, average sales per square foot, and comments. **Number listed:** 100

1. Ashley Furniture HomeStores, with $2,686 million

2. Ikea, $2,280

3. Rooms To Go Inc., $1,500

4. Williams-Sonoma Inc., $1,480

5. Berkshire Hathaway Inc., furniture division, $1,208.2

6. Raymour & Flanigan, $972.3

7. American Signature, $965.8

8. Pier 1 Imports Inc., $956.8

9. Sleepy's, $846

10. Mattress Firm, $831.2

Source: *Furniture Today*, Top 100 (annual), May 21, 2012, p. 38-62.

Futures Contracts

2794 ■ TOP COMMODITY FUTURES TRADED IN THE U.S., 2010

Ranked by: Number of contracts traded. **Remarks:** Also notes percent share and figures and rank for previous year. **Number listed:** 50

1. E Mini S & P 500 Index, with 556,314,143 contracts

2. Eurodollars, 3-month, 437,585,193

3. T-Notes, 10-year, 189,852,019

4. Oil, crude, 137,428,494

5. T-Notes, 5-year, 98,391,120

6. E Mini NASDAQ 100, 77,972,143

7. T-Bonds, 30-year, 62,232,671

8. Euro FX, 54,393,644

9. Corn, 50,948,804

10. T-Notes, 2-year, 48,158,948

Source: *The CRB Commodity Yearbook*, (annual), Commodity Research Bureau, 2011, p. 32T.

2795 ■ TOP FUTURES COMMISSION MERCHANTS (BROKERS), 2011

Ranked by: U.S. customer equity, in millions of dollars. **Remarks:** Also notes figures and rank for previous year, secured amount, adjusted net capital, non-U.S. customer equity, global clearing volume, details about type of brokers, and stock markets covered. **Number listed:** 50

1. Goldman Sachs & Co., with $21,218.01 million

2. Newedge USA LLC, $20,455.38

3. J. P. Morgan Securities LLC, $19,543.63

4. Deutsche Bank Securities Inc., $15,085.17

5. UBS Securities LLC, $10,990.73

6. Merrill Lynch Pierce Fenner & Smith, $10,599.79

7. Citigroup Global Markets Inc., $10,457.45

8. Credit Suisse Securities (USA) LLC, $6,467.64

9. Morgan Stanley, $6,026.95

10. Barclays Capital Inc., $5,412.44

Source: *Futures*, Top 50 Brokers (annual), December 2011, p. 50.

Gambling

2796 ■ BRITAIN'S MOST ADMIRED GAMING COMPANIES, 2011

Ranked by: Survey of peers and investment analysts based on nine criteria: quality of management, financial soundness, quality of goods/services, ability to attract and retain talent, value as long-term investment, innovation, marketing, community and environmental responsibility, and use of corporate assets. **Number listed:** 5

1. Paddy Power, with 70.3 points

2. William Hill Organization Ltd., 59.3

3. Bwin.Party Digital Entertainment plc, 59

4. Betfair, 58.6

5. Sportingbet, 55.6

Source: *Management Today*, Britain's Most Admired Companies (annual), December 2011, p. 45.

Games
See: **Video Games**

Garden Centers

2797 ■ LARGEST INDEPENDENT GARDEN CENTERS, 2011

Ranked by: Sales, in millions of dollars. **Remarks:** Also notes rank for previous year, annual growth in sales, total number of stores, website, and locations. **Number listed:** 100

1. Armstrong Garden Centers/Pike Nurseries, with $125 million

2. Stein Gardens & Gifts, $74.1

3. Houston Garden Centers, $66.7

4. Star Nursery, $57.8

5. Meadows Farms Nurseries, $49.9

6. Calloway's Nursery, $46.5

7. Petitti Garden Centers, $44.3

8. Green Thumb-Green Arrow, $36

9. Gertens, $35

10. The Bruce Co. of Wisconsin, $34.1

Source: *IGC Retailer*, IGC 100 (annual), 2012, p. 33-35.

Gas Industry
See: **Natural Gas**

Gas Producers

2798 ■ TOP U.S. OIL COMPANIES BY U.S. GAS PRODUCTION, 2010

Ranked by: U.S. gas production, in billions of cubic feet (bcf). **Number listed:** 20

1. Exxon Mobil Corp., with 1,057 bcf

2. Anadarko Petroleum Corp., 829

3. Chesapeake Energy Corp., 775

4. ConocoPhillips, 764

5. Devon Energy Corp., 716

6. Chevron Corp., 479

7. EOG Resources Inc., 422.6

8. The Williams Companies Inc., 420

9. Southwestern Energy Co., 403.6

10. Apache Corp., 266.8

Source: *Oil & Gas Journal*, OGJ 150 (annual), October 3, 2011, p. 34.

2799 ■ TOP U.S. OIL COMPANIES BY WORLDWIDE GAS PRODUCTION, 2010

Ranked by: Worldwide gas production, in billions of cubic feet (bcf). **Number listed:** 20

1. Exxon Mobil Corp., with 2,920 bcf

2. Chevron Corp., 1,839

3. ConocoPhillips, 1,794

4. Devon Energy Corp., 930

5. Anadarko Petroleum Corp., 829

6. Chesapeake Energy Corp., 775

7. Apache Corp., 689.4

8. EOG Resources Inc., 633.4

9. Occidental Petroleum Corp., 431

10. The Williams Companies Inc., 420

Source: *Oil & Gas Journal*, OGJ 150 (annual), October 3, 2011, p. 34.

Gas Stations
See: **Automobile Service Stations**

Gas Utilities
See also: Electric Utilities

2800 ■ AMERICA'S LARGEST PRIVATE UTILITIES, 2010

Ranked by: Revenue, in billions of dollars. **Remarks:** Also notes headquarters, number of employees, and overall rank in the *America's Largest Private Companies* list. Ranking is available online only, not in print. **Number listed:** 3

1. Energy Future Holdings Corp., with $8.24 billion
2. Oxbow Corp., $4
3. Drummond Co., $3.03

Source: *Forbes*, America's Largest Private Companies (annual), http://www.forbes.com, December 5, 2011.

2801 ■ EUROPE'S MOST VALUABLE GAS, WATER, AND MULTIUTILITIES COMPANIES, 2011

Ranked by: Market value as of March 2011, in millions of U.S. dollars. **Remarks:** Also notes rank within the *FT Europe 500*, rank for previous year, country, revenue, net income, assets, number of employees, share price, price-to-earning ratio, dividend yield, and fiscal yearend. **Number listed:** 13

1. GDF Suez, with $91,809.4 million
2. E.On AG, $61,193.3
3. RWE AG, $35,754.8
4. National Grid Transco plc, $33,402.3
5. Centrica plc, $26,876
6. International Power plc, $25,143.2
7. Snam Rete Gas SpA, $20,097.9
8. Gas Natural SDG SA, $17,338.3
9. Veolia Environnement SA, $15,540.2
10. Suez Environnement, $10,145.9

Source: *Financial Times*, FT 500 (annual), http://www.ft.com, June 24, 2011.

2802 ■ JAPAN'S LARGEST NATURAL GAS UTILITIES OVERALL, 2011

Ranked by: Score based on revenue, profits, assets, and market capitalization. **Remarks:** Specific scores not provided. Also notes overall rank in the *Forbes 2000* and figures for each criterion. **Number listed:** 2

1. Tokyo Gas Co.
2. Osaka Gas Co.

Source: *Forbes*, Forbes 2000 (annual), http://www.forbes.com, May 7, 2012.

2803 ■ LARGEST ELECTRIC, GAS, AND SANITARY SERVICES COMPANIES BY EMPLOYEES, 2010

Ranked by: Total number of employees. **Remarks:** Also notes contact information for headquarters, number of employees at headquarters, revenue, rank by revenue, and primary SIC code. **Number listed:** 49

1. Waste Management Inc., with 43,530 employees
2. Republic Services Inc., 31,000
3. AES Corp., 27,000
4. Southern Co., 26,112
5. Puget Holding Co., 22,860
6. American Electric Power Co., Inc., 21,673

7. Progress Energy Inc., 20,500
8. PG & E Corp., 19,425
9. Pacific Gas & Electric Co., 19,401
10. Edison International, 19,244

Source: *Business Rankings*, (annual), Dun & Bradstreet Inc., 2011, p. VI.106-VI.107.

2804 ■ LARGEST ELECTRIC, GAS, AND SANITARY SERVICES COMPANIES BY SALES, 2010

Ranked by: Total revenue, in dollars. **Remarks:** Also notes contact information for headquarters, number of employees at headquarters and overall, rank by employees, and primary SIC code. **Number listed:** 50

1. Enterprise Products Partners LP, with $33,739,300,000
2. Veolia Water North America Northeast LLC, $23,000,000,000
3. Exelon Corp., $18,644,000,000
4. Southern Co., $17,456,000,000
5. Nextera Energy Inc., $15,317,000,000
6. Dominion Resources Inc., $15,197,000,000
7. American Electric Power Co., Inc., $14,427,000,000
8. Constellation Energy Group Inc., $14,340,000,000
9. Duke Energy Corp., $14,272,000,000
10. AES Corp., $14,119,000,000

Source: *Business Rankings*, (annual), Dun & Bradstreet Inc., 2011, p. V.106-V.107.

2805 ■ LARGEST U.S. NATURAL GAS UTILITIES OVERALL, 2011

Ranked by: Score based on revenue, profits, assets, and market capitalization. **Remarks:** Specific scores not provided. Also notes overall rank in the *Forbes 2000* and figures for each criterion. **Number listed:** 3

1. Sempra Energy
2. CenterPoint Energy Inc.
3. NiSource Inc.

Source: *Forbes*, Forbes 2000 (annual), http://www.forbes.com, May 7, 2012.

2806 ■ MOST PROFITABLE CANADIAN UTILITIES, 2011

Ranked by: Profits, in millions of Canadian dollars. **Number listed:** 6

1. Just Energy Group Inc., with C$515.4 million
2. Canadian Utilities Ltd., C$515
3. Fortis Inc., C$347
4. ATCO Ltd., C$327
5. TransAlta Corp., C$305
6. Emera Inc., C$247.7

Source: *Canadian Business*, Investor 500 (annual), 2012, p. 55.

2807 ■ MOST VALUABLE U.S. GAS, WATER, AND MULTIUTILITIES COMPANIES, 2011

Ranked by: Market value as of March 2011, in millions of U.S. dollars. **Remarks:** Also notes rank within the *FT U.S. 500*, rank for previous year, country, revenue, net income, assets, number of employees, share price, price-to-earning ratio, dividend yield, and fiscal yearend. **Number listed:** 8

1. Duke Energy Corp., with $24,159.2 million
2. Spectra Energy Corp., $17,644.8
3. Sempra Energy, $12,902.9
4. CenterPoint Energy Inc., $7,462.9
5. ONEOK Partners LP, $7,157.6
6. Wisconsin Energy Corp., $7,129.3
7. Ameren Corp., $5,755.1
8. National Fuel Gas Co., $5,093.6

Source: *Financial Times*, FT 500 (annual), http://www.ft.com, June 24, 2011.

2808 ■ SPAIN'S LARGEST NATURAL GAS UTILITIES OVERALL, 2011

Ranked by: Score based on revenue, profits, assets, and market capitalization. **Remarks:** Specific scores not provided. Also notes overall rank in the *Forbes 2000* and figures for each criterion. **Number listed:** 2

1. Gas Natural SDG SA
2. Enagas SA

Source: *Forbes*, Forbes 2000 (annual), http://www.forbes.com, May 7, 2012.

2809 ■ TOP CANADIAN GAS AND ELECTRICAL UTILITIES, 2010

Ranked by: Revenue, in thousands of Canadian dollars (unless otherwise noted). **Remarks:** Also notes percent change from previous year. **Number listed:** 10

1. Hydro-Quebec, with C$12,536,000 thousand
2. Direct Energy Marketing Ltd., C$9,480,000
3. Ontario Power Generation Inc., C$6,046,000
4. British Columbia Hydro & Power Authority, C$3,952,000
5. Fortis Inc., C$3,664,000
6. TransAlta Corp., C$2,846,000
7. Canadian Utilities, C$2,716,200
8. Toronto Hydro Corp., C$2,621,213
9. Enbridge Gas Distribution, C$2,538,000
10. ENMAX Corp., C$2,404,200

Source: *Report on Business Magazine*, Top 1000 Companies (annual), http://www.reportonbusiness.com, June 2011.

2810 ■ TOP DIVERSIFIED UTILITY COMPANIES, 2010

Ranked by: Score based on asset worth, revenue, profits, earnings per share, and return on invested capital. **Remarks:** Specific scores not provided. Also notes rank in the overall *Top 250*. **Number listed:** 33

1. RWE AG
2. Centrica plc
3. GDF Suez
4. National Grid plc
5. Dominion Resources Inc.
6. Public Service Enterprise Group Inc.
7. Veolia Environnement SA
8. PG & E Corp.
9. Consolidated Edison Inc.
10. Midamerican Energy

Source: *Platts*, Top 250 Global Energy Company Rankings (annual), http://www.platts.com/top250, November 2, 2011.

2811 ■ TOP *FORTUNE 500* GAS AND ELECTRIC UTILITIES, 2011

Ranked by: Revenue, in millions of dollars. **Remarks:** Also notes overall rank in the *Fortune 500;* profits; profits as a percentage of revenue; stockholders' equity; and rank by each criterion. **Number listed:** 22

1. Exelon Corp., with $18,924 million
2. AES Corp., $17,759
3. Southern Co., $17,657
4. FirstEnergy Corp., $16,258
5. NextEra Energy Inc., $15,341
6. PG & E Corp., $14,956
7. Duke Energy Corp., $14,529
8. Dominion Resources Inc., $14,379
9. Consolidated Edison Inc., $12,938
10. Edison International, $12,760

Source: *Fortune*, Fortune 500 (annual), May 21, 2012, p. F-40.

2812 ■ TOP GAS UTILITY COMPANIES, 2010

Ranked by: Score based on asset worth, revenue, profits, earnings per share, and return on invested capital. **Remarks:** Specific scores not provided. Also notes rank in the overall *Top 250*. **Number listed:** 14

1. Gas Natural SDG SA
2. Tokyo Gas Co.
3. Snam Rete Gas SpA
4. GAIL (India) Ltd.
5. Osaka Gas Co.
6. Hong Kong & China Gas Co.
7. ONEOK Inc.
8. Korea Gas Corp.
9. NV Nederlandse Gasunie
10. Empresa de Energia de Bogota SA

Source: *Platts*, Top 250 Global Energy Company Rankings (annual), http://www.platts.com/top250, November 2, 2011.

2813 ■ TOP REGIONAL UTILITIES FOR DIVERSITY, 2011

Ranked by: Score based on strength in four areas: CEO commitment to diversity, human capital, corporate and organizational communications, and supplier diversity. **Remarks:** Specific scores not provided. To qualify, companies must have more than 1,000 U.S. employees. **Number listed:** 5

1. Southern California Edison Co.
2. Pacific Gas & Electric Co. (PG & E)
3. Consolidated Edison Co. of New York
4. Sempra Energy
5. Ameren Corp.

Source: *DiversityInc*, Top 50 (annual), 2011, p. 100.

2814 ■ UNITED KINGDOM'S LARGEST DIVERSIFIED UTILITIES COMPANIES OVERALL, 2011

Ranked by: Score based on revenue, profits, assets, and market capitalization. **Remarks:** Specific scores not provided. Also notes overall rank in the *Forbes 2000* and figures for each criterion. **Number listed:** 2

1. United Utilities Group plc
2. Severn Trent plc

Source: *Forbes*, Forbes 2000 (annual), http://www.forbes.com, May 7, 2012.

2815 ■ UNITED KINGDOM'S LARGEST NATURAL GAS UTILITIES OVERALL, 2011

Ranked by: Score based on revenue, profits, assets, and market capitalization. **Remarks:** Specific scores not provided. Also notes overall rank in the *Forbes 2000* and figures for each criterion. **Number listed:** 2

1. National Grid plc
2. Centrica plc

Source: *Forbes*, Forbes 2000 (annual), http://www.forbes.com, May 7, 2012.

2816 ■ WORLD'S LARGEST DIVERSIFIED UTILITIES COMPANIES OVERALL, 2011

Ranked by: Score based on revenue, profits, assets, and market capitalization. **Remarks:** Specific scores not provided. Also notes country, overall rank in the *Forbes 2000,* and figures for each criterion. **Number listed:** 10

1. Veolia Environnement SA
2. AREVA
3. Companhia de Saneamento Basico do Estado de Sao Paulo (SABESP)
4. United Utilities Group plc
5. YTL Corporation Bhd.
6. Severn Trust plc
7. American Water Works Co.
8. China Longyuan Power Group Ltd.
9. GCL-Poly Energy Holdings Ltd.
10. Sinovel Wind Group Co., Ltd.

Source: *Forbes*, Forbes 2000 (annual), http://www.forbes.com, May 7, 2012.

2817 ■ WORLD'S LARGEST NATURAL GAS UTILITIES OVERALL, 2011

Ranked by: Score based on revenue, profits, assets, and market capitalization. **Remarks:** Specific scores not provided. Also notes country, overall rank in the *Forbes 2000,* and figures for each criterion. **Number listed:** 15

1. National Grid plc
2. Gas Natural SDG SA
3. Centrica plc
4. Sempra Energy
5. Tokyo Gas Co.
6. CenterPoint Energy Inc.
7. Osaka Gas Co.
8. GAIL (India) Ltd.
9. Hong Kong & China Gas Co.
10. Korea Gas Corp.

Source: *Forbes*, Forbes 2000 (annual), http://www.forbes.com, May 7, 2012.

2818 ■ WORLD'S MOST ADMIRED ELECTRIC AND GAS UTILITIES, 2012

Ranked by: Score, on a scale of 10, based on a survey of executives, directors, and securities analysts of companies within their own industry on eight criteria: innovation, financial soundness, employee talent, use of corporate assets, long-term investment value, social responsibility, quality of management, and quality of products/services. **Remarks:** Specific scores not provided. Also notes rank for previous year. **Number listed:** 5

1. NextEra Energy Inc.

1. Dominion Resources Inc.
3. Southern Co.
4. Public Service Enterprise Group Inc.
5. Exelon Corp.

Source: *Fortune*, World's Most Admired Companies (annual), March 19, 2012, p. 149.

2819 ■ WORLD'S MOST VALUABLE GAS BRANDS, 2011

Ranked by: Brand value, in millions of U.S. dollars. **Remarks:** Also notes rank within the *Global 500* for current and previous year, figures for current and previous year, country, and brand rating. Ranking is available online only. **Number listed:** 3

1. GDF Suez, with $16,598 million
2. British Gas, $3,562
3. Korea Gas, $2,590

Source: *Global 500*, (annual), Brand Finance plc, March 2012.

2820 ■ WORLD'S MOST VALUABLE GAS UTILITY COMPANIES, 2011

Ranked by: Market capitalization, in billions of U.S. dollars. **Remarks:** Also notes rank for previous year, annual growth in share price, price/earnings ratio, debt/capital ratio, headquarters country, ticker symbol, and stock exchange. **Number listed:** 15

1. GDF Suez, with $61.7 billion
2. E.On AG, $43.2
3. Centrica plc, $23.2
4. RWE AG, $21.5
5. Hong Kong & China Gas Co., $18.3
6. Gas Natural SDG SA, $17
7. Origin Energy Ltd., $14.9
8. Sempra Energy, $13.2
9. Tokyo Gas Co., $11.9
10. Petronas Gas, $9.5

Source: *PFC Energy 50*, (annual), PFC Energy, January 23, 2012.

2821 ■ WORLD'S MOST VALUABLE GAS, WATER, AND MULTIUTILITIES COMPANIES, 2011

Ranked by: Market value as of March 2011, in millions of U.S. dollars. **Remarks:** Also notes rank within the *FT 500*, rank for previous year, country, revenue, net income, assets, number of employees, share price, price-to-earning ratio, dividend yield, and fiscal year-end. **Number listed:** 9

1. GDF Suez, with $91,809.4 million
2. E.On AG, $61,193.3
3. RWE AG, $35,754.8
4. National Grid Transco plc, $33,402.3
5. Centrica plc, $26,876
6. International Power plc, $25,143.2
7. Duke Energy Corp., $24,159.2
8. Snam Rete Gas SpA, $20,097.9
9. Origin Energy Ltd., $19,569

Source: *Financial Times*, FT 500 (annual), http://www.ft.com, June 24, 2011.

General Merchandise
See: **Retail Industry**

Glass

2822 ■ LARGEST GLASS FABRICATORS, 2010

Ranked by: Gross sales, in millions of dollars. **Remarks:** Sales are provided in ranges, not exact figures. When tied, companies are listed alphabetically. **Number listed:** 45

1. Viracon, with $250-500 million
2. Tecnoglass SA, $150-200
3. Hartung Glass Industries, $100-150
4. Glasswerks LA Inc., $50-100
4. Prelco, $50-100
6. Cristacurva Glass, $35-50
6. Northwestern Industries, $35-50
8. Dlubak Corp., $20-35
8. Gardner Glass Products, $20-35
8. Garibaldi Glass Industries Inc., $20-35
8. General Glass International, $20-35
8. Glaz-Tech Industries Inc., $20-35
8. Goldray Industries Ltd., $20-35

Source: *Glass Magazine*, Top Glass Fabricators (annual), December 2011.

Glazing

2823 ■ LARGEST CONTRACT GLAZING COMPANIES, 2010

Ranked by: Gross sales, in millions of dollars. **Remarks:** Sales are provided in ranges, not exact figures. Also notes headquarters, Web site, number of employees, and comments. **Number listed:** 50

1. Permasteelisa North America, with $100-300 million
2. Benson Industries LLC, $100-300
3. Trainor Glass Co., $100-300
4. Enclos Corp., $100-300
5. Harmon Inc., $100-300
6. Walters & Wolf, $100-300
7. W & W Glass LLC, $100-300
8. ASI Ltd., $50-100
9. Continental Glass Systems, $50-100
10. Admiral Glass & Mirror, $50-100

Source: *Glass Magazine*, Glazier Survey (annual), June 2011.

2824 ■ TOP GLAZING/CURTAIN WALL CONTRACTORS, 2010

Ranked by: Glazing/curtain wall revenue, in millions of dollars. **Remarks:** Also notes percentage change from previous year. **Number listed:** 20

1. Enclos Corp., with $164.4 million
2. Walters & Wolf, $158.9
3. W & W Glass LLC, $110
4. Architectural Glass & Aluminum Co., $62.5
5. Gamma USA Inc., $53.8
6. CBO Glass Inc., $48
7. Tower Glass Inc., $40.1
8. Karas & Karas Glass Co., $34.6

9. Giroux Glass Inc., $33
10. Ajay Glass & Mirror Co., $28.2

Source: *ENR: Engineering News-Record*, Top 600 Specialty Contractors (annual), October 17, 2011, p. 63.

Gold Mines and Mining

2825 ■ TOP CANADIAN GOLD AND DIAMOND COMPANIES, 2010

Ranked by: Revenue, in thousands of Canadian dollars (unless otherwise noted). **Remarks:** Also notes percent change from previous year. **Number listed:** 10

1. Barrick Gold Corp. (U.S. dollars), with C$11,068,000 thousand
2. Goldcorp Inc. (U.S. dollars), C$3,799,800
3. Kinross Gold (U.S. dollars), C$3,349,300
4. Yamana Gold (U.S. dollars), C$1,721,312
5. Agnico-Eagle Mines (U.S. dollars), C$1,517,400
6. Iamgold Corp. (U.S. dollars), C$1,210,688
7. Centerra Gold (U.S. dollars), C$847,158
8. Eldorado Gold (U.S. dollars), C$811,276
9. Pan American Silver (U.S. dollars), C$648,946
10. Harry Winston Diamond (U.S. dollars), C$624,449

Source: *Report on Business Magazine*, Top 1000 Companies (annual), http://www.reportonbusiness.com, June 2011.

Government Contracts
See: **Contracts, Government**

Government Ownership

2826 ■ LARGEST FEDERAL CANADIAN CROWN CORPORATIONS, 2010

Ranked by: Revenue, in thousands of Canadian dollars. **Remarks:** Also notes fiscal year-end, group type, percent change from previous year, return on capital, profits, assets, and number of employees. **Number listed:** 10

1. Canada Mortgage & Housing, with C$13,164,000 thousand
2. Canada Post, C$7,341,000
3. Canadian Commercial, C$1,579,296
4. Export Development Canada, C$1,499,000
5. Farm Credit Canada, C$827,778
6. Business Development Bank of Canada, C$680,607
7. Atomic Energy of Canada, C$599,126
8. Canadian Broadcasting Corp., C$589,247
9. Canadian Air Transport Security, C$583,575
10. Via Rail Canada, C$277,924

Source: *Report on Business Magazine*, Top 1000 Companies (annual), http://www.reportonbusiness.com, June 2011.

2827 ■ LARGEST PROVINCIAL CANADIAN CROWN CORPORATIONS, 2010

Ranked by: Revenue, in thousands of Canadian dollars. **Remarks:** Also notes fiscal year-end, business type, percent change from previous year, return on capital, profits, assets, and number of employees. **Number listed:** 10

1. Caisse de depot et placement, with C$21,075,000 thousand
2. Hydro-Quebec, C$12,536,000
3. Ontario Power Generation Inc., C$6,046,000
4. Hydro One Inc., C$5,137,000
5. Insurance Corp. of British Columbia, C$4,241,309
6. British Columbia Hydro & Power Authority, C$4,228,000
7. Manitoba Hydro-Electric Board, C$2,102,000
8. Alberta Heritage Savings, C$2,077,000
9. Saskatchewan Power Corp., C$1,795,000
10. ATB Financial, C$1,251,895

Source: *Report on Business Magazine*, Top 1000 Companies (annual), http://www.reportonbusiness.com, June 2011.

Grocery Industry
See: **Supermarkets**

Gross Domestic Product

2828 ■ COUNTRIES WITH THE HIGHEST GROSS DOMESTIC PRODUCT, 2010

Ranked by: Gross domestic product, in billions of U.S. dollars. **Number listed:** 142

1. United States, with $14,657.8 billion
2. China, $5,878.3
3. Japan, $5,468.9
4. Germany, $3,315.6
5. France, $2,582.5
6. United Kingdom, $2,247.5
7. Brazil, $2,090.3
8. Italy, $2,055.1
9. Canada, $1,574.1
10. India, $1,538

Source: *Global Competitiveness Report*, (annual), World Economic Forum, 2011, p. 384.

2829 ■ COUNTRIES WITH THE HIGHEST GROSS DOMESTIC PRODUCT PER CAPITA, 2010

Ranked by: Gross domestic product per capita, in U.S. dollars. **Number listed:** 142

1. Luxembourg, with $108,832
2. Norway, $84,444
3. Qatar, $76,168
4. Switzerland, $67,246
5. United Arab Emirates, $59,717
6. Denmark, $56,147
7. Australia, $55,590
8. Sweden, $48,875
9. United States, $47,284
10. Netherlands, $47,172

Source: *Global Competitiveness Report*, (annual), World Economic Forum, 2011, p. 386.

2830 ■ COUNTRIES WITH THE LOWEST GROSS DOMESTIC PRODUCT, 2010

Ranked by: Gross domestic product, in billions of U.S. dollars. **Number listed:** 142

1. Timor-Leste, with $0.6 billion
2. Gambia, $1.1
3. Belize, $1.4
4. Burundi, $1.5
5. Cape Verde, $1.7
6. Lesotho, $2.1
7. Guyana, $2.2
8. Swaziland, $3.6
9. Suriname, $3.7
10. Mauritania, $3.8

Source: *Global Competitiveness Report*, (annual), World Economic Forum, 2011, p. 384.

2831 ■ COUNTRIES WITH THE LOWEST GROSS DOMESTIC PRODUCT PER CAPITA, 2010

Ranked by: Gross domestic product per capita, in U.S. dollars. **Number listed:** 142

1. Burundi, with $180
2. Malawi, $322
3. Ethiopia, $350
4. Madagascar, $392
5. Mozambique, $458
6. Uganda, $501
7. Tanzania, $548
8. Nepal, $462
8. Rwanda, $462
10. Timor-Leste, $488

Source: *Global Competitiveness Report*, (annual), World Economic Forum, 2011, p. 386.

2832 ■ STATES WITH THE HIGHEST GROWTH IN GROSS DOMESTIC PRODUCT, 2005-2009

Ranked by: Growth in gross domestic product, in percent. **Number listed:** 51

1. Wyoming, with 25.6%
2. North Dakota, 19%
3. Oklahoma, 18.1%
4. Utah, 12.6%
5. South Dakota, 12.4%
6. Oregon, 12%
7. Washington, 10.6%
8. Alaska, 10.1%
9. Iowa, 9.2%
10. Kansas, 9%
10. Nebraska, 9%

Source: *State Rankings*, (annual), CQ Press, 2011, p. 94.

2833 ■ STATES WITH THE HIGHEST PER CAPITA GROSS DOMESTIC PRODUCT, 2009

Ranked by: Gross domestic product per capita, in dollars. **Number listed:** 51

1. Washington DC, with $165,310
2. Wyoming, $68,980

3. Delaware, $68,452
4. Alaska, $65,441
5. Connecticut, $64,635
6. New York, $55,944
7. New Jersey, $55,464
8. Massachusetts, $55,384
9. Virginia, $51,816
10. Hawaii, $51,291

Source: *State Rankings*, (annual), CQ Press, 2011, p. 96.

2834 ■ STATES WITH THE LOWEST GROWTH IN GROSS DOMESTIC PRODUCT, 2005-2009

Ranked by: Growth in gross domestic product, in percent. **Number listed:** 51

1. Michigan, with -9.3%
2. Louisiana, -4.7%
3. Ohio, -3.4%
4. Rhode Island, -2.2%
5. Nevada, -2%
6. Florida, -1.7%
7. Georgia, -0.7%
8. Tennessee, 0%
9. Illinois, 0.3%
9. Minnesota, 0.3%

Source: *State Rankings*, (annual), CQ Press, 2011, p. 94.

2835 ■ STATES WITH THE LOWEST PER CAPITA GROSS DOMESTIC PRODUCT, 2009

Ranked by: Gross domestic product per capita, in dollars. **Number listed:** 51

1. Mississippi, with $32,488
2. West Virginia, $34,809
3. Idaho, $34,937
4. South Carolina, $35,001
5. Arkansas, $35,238
6. Alabama, $36,073
7. Kentucky, $36,289
8. Montana, $36,876
9. Michigan, $36,952
10. New Mexico, $37,221

Source: *State Rankings*, (annual), CQ Press, 2011, p. 96.

Group Medical Practice

2836 ■ LARGEST PHYSICIAN GROUP PRACTICES, 2011

Ranked by: Total number of full-time physicians. **Remarks:** Also notes headquarters and Web site. **Number listed:** 15

1. Permanente Medical Group, with 7,000 physicians
2. Partners HealthCare System, 6,000
3. Southern California Permanente Medical Group, 5,500
4. New York City Health & Hospitals Corp., 5,000
5. Johns Hopkins University, 3,939
6. Advocate Physician Partners, 3,800
7. Mayo Clinic, 3,700

8. University of Medicine & Dentistry of New Jersey, 2,936
9. Yeshiva University, Albert Einstein College of Medicine, 2,775
10. University of Pittsburgh Medical Center, 2,700

Source: *Modern Healthcare*, Largest Group Practices (annual), September 26, 2011, p. 34.

Growth Companies

2837 ■ AMERICA'S MOST PROMISING COMPANIES, 2011

Ranked by: Score based on overall corporate health, annual revenue, number of employees, size of market, strength of competitors, experience of management team, significant customers and strategic partnerships, and capital raised. **Remarks:** Scores not provided. To qualify, companies must be privately held, for-profit, stand-alone businesses. Also notes industry, CEO, and sales. Only the top 10 are published; the remainder of the list is available online. **Number listed:** 100

1. Smashburger
2. Boku
3. Digital Broadcasting Group
4. Popchips
5. Implantable Provider Group
6. Virtual Instruments
7. Allonhill LLC
8. SecondMarket
9. ServiceNow
10. Opower

Source: *Forbes*, America's Most Promising Companies, December 19, 2011, p. 110.

2838 ■ CANADA'S FASTEST-GROWING COMPANIES, 2005-2010

Ranked by: Five-year revenue growth, in percent. **Remarks:** Also notes ticker symbol, revenue for 2005 and 2010, profit margin, number of employees, and exports as a percentage of sales. **Number listed:** 200

1. Mood Media Corp., with 72,384%
2. Pacific Mortgage Group Inc., 24,065%
3. Avigilon Corp., 16,042%
4. Varicent Software Inc., 12,562%
5. Marport Deep Sea Technologies Inc., 5,016%
6. GuestLogix Inc., 4,938%
7. Dependable Mechanical Systems Inc., 4,765%
8. Globeways Canada Inc., 4,021%
9. PrecisionERP Inc., 4,009%
10. Timbercreek Asset Management Inc., 3,852%

Source: *Profit*, Profit 200 (annual), http://www.profitguide.com, June 2011.

2839 ■ CANADA'S TOP EMERGING COMPANIES, 2008-2010

Ranked by: Two-year revenue growth, in percent. **Remarks:** Also notes ticker symbol, revenue and number of employees for 2008 and 2010, profit margin, and exports as a percentage of sales. To qualify for ranking, companies must be headquartered in Canada, be Canadian-owned, and have a minimum of $50,000 gross revenue. **Number listed:** 50

1. Contingent Workforce Solutions Inc., with 10,330%

2. Morega Systems Inc., 7,919%
3. Lions Bay Media Inc., 7,451%
4. Innovative Residential Investment Inc., 4,826%
5. Source 44 Consulting Inc., 3,365%
6. Great Circle Works Inc./Zipfy Inc., 1,268%
7. VonKids Inc., 1,107%
8. Brave Control Solutions Inc., 1,082%
9. Syncapse Corp., 1,020%
10. HR Downloads Inc., 1,012%

Source: *Profit*, Hot 50 (annual), http://www.profitguide.com, October 2011.

2840 ■ EMERGING COMPANIES WITH THE HIGHEST PRICE/EARNINGS RATIO, 2010

Ranked by: Price/earnings ratio. **Remarks:** To qualify for ranking, companies must be public U.S. companies with revenue between $10 million and $2.5 billion, and have had sustained annualized sales growth of more than 7 percent during a three-year period. **Number listed:** 40

1. Human Genome Sciences, with 785
2. American Apparel, 697
3. Taleo Corp., 638
4. DuPont Fabros Technology, 459
5. SunLink Health Systems, 452
6. Alere Inc., 339
7. Verint Systems, 323
8. NuVasive Inc., 300
9. Riverbed Technology, 260
10. Global Traffic Network, 213

Source: *Hoover's Handbook of Emerging Companies*, (annual), Hoover's Inc., 2011, p. 9.

2841 ■ EMERGING COMPANIES WITH THE LOWEST PRICE/EARNINGS RATIO, 2010

Ranked by: Price/earnings ratio. **Remarks:** To qualify for ranking, companies must be public U.S. companies with revenue between $10 million and $2.5 billion, and have had sustained annualized sales growth of more than 7 percent during a three-year period. **Number listed:** 40

1. Synta Pharmaceuticals, with 1
1. Hallwood Group, 1
1. Joe's Jeans, 1
1. LecTec Corp., 1
1. Zalicus Inc., 1
1. Great Lakes Aviation, 1
1. Franklin Wireless, 1
1. FBL Financial Group, 1
1. Providence Service, 1
1. APAC Customer Services, 1
1. AeroCentury Corp., 1
1. Coffee Holding Co., 1
1. First Financial Bancorp, 1

Source: *Hoover's Handbook of Emerging Companies*, (annual), Hoover's Inc., 2011, p. 9.

2842 ■ FASTEST-GROWING COMPANIES IN THE U.S., 2008-2011

Ranked by: Score based on three-year growth in revenue and earnings, and three-year total return to investors. **Remarks:** Spe-

cific scores not provided. To qualify for list, companies must have revenues of at least $50 million, net income of at least $10 million, market capitalization of at least $250 million, and stock price of at least $5. Int'l companies are eligible if they trade on a U.S. exchange and file quarterly reports. Also notes rank for previous year, headquarters, and financials. **Number listed:** 100

1. SXC Health Solutions Corp.
2. Green Mountain Coffee Roasters Inc.
3. Hi-Tech Pharmacal
4. Baidu
5. Medifast
6. Alexion Pharmaceuticals
7. Discovery Communications
8. Green Plains Renewable Energy
9. Home Inns & Hotel Management
10. Sturm, Ruger & Co.

Source: *Fortune*, 100 Fastest-Growing Companies (annual), September 26, 2011, p. 125-133.

2843 ■ TOP EMERGING COMPANIES BY FIVE-YEAR EMPLOYMENT GROWTH, 2005-2010

Ranked by: Five-year growth in number of employees, in percent. **Remarks:** To qualify for ranking, companies must be public U.S. companies with revenue between $10 million and $2.5 billion, and have had sustained annualized sales growth of more than 7 percent during a three-year period. **Number listed:** 100

1. Green Plains Renewable Energy, with 196%
2. Summer Infant, 177.5%
3. Eagle Bulk Shipping Inc., 169.4%
4. Internet Capital Group, 100.5%
5. Homeland Security Capital, 94.7%
6. True Religion Apparel Inc., 93.2%
7. AboveNet Inc., 90.1%
8. Northfield Bancorp, 88.5%
9. Homeowners Choice, 87.9%
10. DineEquity Inc., 78.9%

Source: *Hoover's Handbook of Emerging Companies*, (annual), Hoover's Inc., 2011, p. 6.

2844 ■ TOP EMERGING COMPANIES BY FIVE-YEAR PROFIT GROWTH, 2005-2010

Ranked by: Five-year growth in sales, in percent. **Remarks:** To qualify for ranking, companies must be public U.S. companies with revenue between $10 million and $2.5 billion, and have had sustained annualized sales growth of at least 7 percent during a three-year period. **Number listed:** 100

1. Ellington Financial, with 432%
2. TC PipeLines, 302.8%
3. Douglas Dynamics, 265.9%
4. InterDigital Inc., 237.3%
5. Iconix Brand Group, 227.3%
6. Genco Shipping & Trading Ltd., 177.7%
7. Edwards Lifesciences, 166.6%
8. Higher One Holdings, 148.5%
9. Limelight Networks, 133.8%
10. ITC Holdings Corp., 119%

Source: *Hoover's Handbook of Emerging Companies*, (annual), Hoover's Inc., 2011, p. 4.

2845 ■ TOP EMERGING COMPANIES BY FIVE-YEAR SALES GROWTH, 2005-2010

Ranked by: Five-year growth in sales, in percent. **Remarks:** To qualify for ranking, companies must be public U.S. companies with revenue between $10 million and $2.5 billion, and have had sustained annualized sales growth of at least 7 percent during a three-year period. **Number listed:** 100

1. Aircastle Ltd., with 464%
2. Solera Holdings, 401%
3. AboveNet Inc., 347.8%
4. MaxLinear Inc., 340.5%
5. TC PipeLines, 284.1%
6. Summer Infant, 261.4%
7. Hercules Technology Growth Capital, 226.6%
8. Franklin Wireless, 220.8%
9. Genoptix Inc., 204.9%
10. Homeland Security Capital, 200.4%

Source: *Hoover's Handbook of Emerging Companies*, (annual), Hoover's Inc., 2011, p. 2.

2846 ■ TOP EMERGING COMPANIES BY FIVE-YEAR STOCK APPRECIATION, 2005-2010

Ranked by: Five-year annualized stock appreciation, in percent. **Remarks:** To qualify for ranking, companies must be public U.S. companies with revenue between $10 million and $2.5 billion, and have had sustained annualized sales growth of more than 7 percent during a three-year period. **Number listed:** 40

1. Rackspace Hosting Inc., with 287.5%
2. IPC, The Hospitalist Co., 97.6%
3. Sourcefire Inc., 79.1%
4. Lumber Liquidators, 72.7%
5. First Solar Inc., 65.6%
6. Green Mountain Coffee Roasters Inc., 64.6%
7. Pioneer Southwest Energy Partners, 63.9%
8. Ebix Inc., 57.7%
9. Priceline.com Inc., 56.1%
10. SXC Health Solutions, 55.3%

Source: *Hoover's Handbook of Emerging Companies*, (annual), Hoover's Inc., 2011, p. 7.

2847 ■ TOP EMERGING COMPANIES BY MARKET VALUE, 2010

Ranked by: Market value, in millions of dollars. **Remarks:** To qualify for ranking, companies must be public U.S. companies with revenue between $10 million and $2.5 billion, and have had sustained annualized sales growth of more than 7 percent during a three-year period. **Number listed:** 40

1. VMware Inc., with $17,562 million
2. American Tower, $17,244
3. Intuitive Surgical Inc., $11,923
4. First Solar Inc., $11,606
5. Priceline.com Inc., $10,723
6. F5 Networks Inc., $8,393
7. Salesforce.com Inc., $8,350
8. IntercontinentalExchange Inc., $8,215
9. Citrix Systems, $7,813
10. Cree Inc., $6,511

Source: *Hoover's Handbook of Emerging Companies*, (annual), Hoover's Inc., 2011, p. 7.

2848 ■ TOP EMERGING COMPANIES BY ONE-YEAR PROFIT GROWTH, 2009-2010

Ranked by: One-year growth in net income, in percent. **Remarks:** To qualify for ranking, companies must be public U.S. companies

with revenue between $10 million and $2.5 billion, and have had sustained annualized sales growth of more than 7 percent during a three-year period. **Number listed:** 100

1. Archipelago Learning, with 2,133.3%
2. APAC Customer Services, 1,836.7%
3. SciQuest inc., 1,663.6%
4. STEC Inc., 1,588.4%
5. Immunomedics Inc., 1,508.7%
6. Tessera Technologies, 1,417.4%
7. Hallwood Group, 1,121.4%
8. Accretive Health, 1,116.7%
9. Cirrus Logic, 997.1%
10. First Financial Bancorp, 971.7%

Source: *Hoover's Handbook of Emerging Companies*, (annual), Hoover's Inc., 2011, p. 5.

2849 ■ TOP EMERGING COMPANIES BY ONE-YEAR SALES GROWTH, 2009-2010

Ranked by: One-year growth in sales, in percent. **Remarks:** To qualify for ranking, companies must be public U.S. companies with revenue between $10 million and $2.5 billion, and have had sustained annualized sales growth of at least 7 percent during a three-year period. **Number listed:** 100

1. LecTec Corp., with 24,800%
2. BioDelivery Sciences International, 20,833.3%
3. Synta Pharmaceuticals, 5,446.2%
4. Cheniere Energy Partners, 2,678.7%
5. Keryx Biopharmaceuticals, 1,838.5%
6. Green Plains Renewable Energy, 590.8%
7. Cytokinetics Inc., 557.3%
8. Human Genome Sciences, 469.6%
9. Syntroleum Corp., 459.2%
10. Osiris Therapeutics, 345%

Source: *Hoover's Handbook of Emerging Companies*, (annual), Hoover's Inc., 2011, p. 3.

2850 ■ TOP EMERGING COMPANIES BY PROFIT MARGIN, 2010

Ranked by: Profit margin, in percent. **Remarks:** To qualify for ranking, companies must be public U.S. companies with revenue between $10 million and $2.5 billion, and have had sustained annualized sales growth of more than 7 percent during a three-year period. **Number listed:** 40

1. Insmed Inc., with 1,137.5%
2. Ellington Financial, 180.7%
3. Isis Pharmaceuticals, 123.9%
4. NuStar GP Holdings, 103.8%
5. Zalicus Inc., 89%
6. AboveNet Inc., 78.2%
7. Alexion Pharmaceuticals, 76.3%
8. Spectra Energy Partners LP, 76%
9. TC PipeLines, 63.4%
10. Immonomedics Inc., 60.8%

Source: *Hoover's Handbook of Emerging Companies*, (annual), Hoover's Inc., 2011, p. 8.

2851 ■ TOP EMERGING COMPANIES BY RETURN ON EQUITY, 2010

Ranked by: Return on equity, in percent. **Remarks:** To qualify for ranking, companies must be public U.S. companies with revenue between $10 million and $2.5 billion, and have had sustained annualized sales growth of more than 7 percent during a three-year period. **Number listed:** 40

1. Osiris Therapeutics, with 387.3%
2. Radiant Logistics, 271.5%
3. LecTec Corp., 263.8%
4. Overstock.com Inc., 197.1%
5. Insmed Inc., 195.4%
6. DineEquity Inc., 175.8%
7. ITT Educational Services, 174.4%
8. Immunomedics Inc., 173.3%
9. Vector Group, 171.5%
10. SolarWinds Inc., 145.6%

Source: *Hoover's Handbook of Emerging Companies*, (annual), Hoover's Inc., 2011, p. 8.

Hair Salons

2852 ■ TOP HAIR CARE FRANCHISES, 2012

Ranked by: Cumulative score based on financial strength and stability, growth rate, size of the system, number of years in business, the length of time franchising, start-up costs, litigation, percentage of terminations, and whether the company provides financing. **Remarks:** Specific scores not provided. Also notes overall rank within the *Franchise 500,* contact information, description, year founded, year started franchising, states where registered, available U.S. regions, where seeking foreign expansion, number of franchised and company-owned units for past three years, start-up costs, franchise fees, royalty fees, and type of financing available. **Number listed:** 10

1. Supercuts
2. Great Clips Inc.
3. Fantastic Sams Hair Salons
4. Sport Clips
5. Cost Cutters Family Hair Care
6. First Choice Haircutters
7. Magicuts
8. Roosters Men's Grooming Center
9. Pro-Cuts Classic
10. Snip-Its

Source: *Entrepreneur*, Franchise 500 (annual), January 2012, p. 190-193.

Handicapped—Employment

2853 ■ BEST COMPANIES FOR DISABLED EMPLOYEES, 2012

Ranked by: Survey based on how progressive the work environment is for people with disabilities. **Remarks:** Specific scores not provided. **Number listed:** 50

1. AT&T Inc.
2. Motorola Solutions Inc.
3. Deere & Co.
4. Boeing Co.
5. Lockheed Martin Corp.
6. Apple Inc.
7. Raytheon Co.
8. General Dynamics Corp.

9. Intel Corp.
10. Microsoft Corp.

Source: *Careers & the disAbled*, Top Employers (annual), http://www.eop.com/mags-CD.php, 2011.

2854 ■ BEST GOVERNMENT AGENCIES FOR DISABLED EMPLOYEES, 2012

Ranked by: Survey based on how progressive the work environment is for people with disabilities. **Remarks:** Specific scores not provided. **Number listed:** 20

1. National Aeronautics & Space Administration (NASA)
2. U.S. Department of Defense
3. Social Security Administration
4. Internal Revenue Service
5. Library of Congress
6. Federal Aviation Administration
7. U.S. Department of Veterans Affairs
8. U.S. Department of Education
9. U.S. Navy
10. U.S. Department of State

Source: *Careers & the disAbled*, Top Employers (annual), http://www.eop.com/mags-CD.php, 2011.

2855 ■ TOP U.S. COMPANIES FOR PEOPLE WITH DISABILITIES, 2011

Ranked by: Score based on recruitment practices, work/life and other accommodation benefits, diversityawareness training, employee-resource groups, and communications that feature employees with disabilities. **Remarks:** Specific scores not provided. To qualify, companies must have more than 1,000 U.S. employees. **Number listed:** 10

1. International Business Machines Corp. (IBM)
2. KPMG LLP
3. Kaiser Permanente
4. Aetna Inc.
5. Ernst & Young LLP
6. Procter & Gamble Co.
7. Merck & Co., Inc.
8. Deloitte LLP
9. Sodexo
10. Starwood Hotels & Resorts Worldwide Inc.

Source: *DiversityInc*, Top 50 (annual), 2011, p. 98.

Hardware Stores

2856 ■ LARGEST COMPANIES IN THE BUILDING MATERIALS, HARDWARE, GARDEN SUPPLY, AND MOBILE HOME INDUSTRY BY EMPLOYEES, 2010

Ranked by: Total number of employees. **Remarks:** Also notes contact information for headquarters, number of employees at headquarters, revenue, rank by revenue, and primary SIC code. **Number listed:** 139

1. The Home Depot Inc., with 317,000 employees
2. Lowe's Companies Inc., 239,000
3. Lowe's Home Centers Inc., 209,850
4. Home Depot International Inc., 140,000
4. Home Depot USA Inc., 140,000

6. Menard Inc., 32,000
7. CMH Capital Inc., 11,000
8. Saturn Acquisition Holdings LLC, 9,100
8. Stock Building Supply Holdings Inc., 9,100
10. Laird Norton Co., 7,500

Source: *Business Rankings*, (annual), Dun & Bradstreet Inc., 2011, p. VI.126-VI.128.

2857 ■ LARGEST COMPANIES IN THE BUILDING MATERIALS, HARDWARE, GARDEN SUPPLY, AND MOBILE HOME INDUSTRY BY SALES, 2010

Ranked by: Total revenue, in dollars. Remarks: Also notes contact information for headquarters, number of employees at headquarters and overall, rank by employees, and primary SIC code. Number listed: 140

1. The Home Depot Inc., with $66,176,000,000
2. Lowe's Companies Inc., $47,220,000,000
3. Ace Hardware Corp., $3,457,182,000
4. Signature Custom Woodworking Inc., $950,000,000
5. Lumber Liquidators Holdings Inc., $620,281,000
6. Carter-Jones Cos., $583,136,000
7. Precoat Metal, $350,000,000
8. Carter-Jones Lumber Co., $314,441,997
9. Atwood Distributing LP, $275,831,312
10. Central Carolina Farm & Mower Inc., $260,000,000

Source: *Business Rankings*, (annual), Dun & Bradstreet Inc., 2011, p. V.126-V.128.

2858 ■ TOP TOOLS DISTRIBUTION FRANCHISES, 2012

Ranked by: Cumulative score based on financial strength and stability, growth rate, size of the system, number of years in business, the length of time franchising, start-up costs, litigation, percentage of terminations, and whether the company provides financing. Remarks: Specific scores not provided. Also notes overall rank within the *Franchise 500*, contact information, description, year founded, year started franchising, states where registered, available U.S. regions, where seeking foreign expansion, number of franchised and company-owned units for past three years, start-up costs, franchise fees, royalty fees, and type of financing available. Number listed: 2

1. Matco Tools
2. Snap-on Tools

Source: *Entrepreneur*, Franchise 500 (annual), January 2012, p. 200-201.

Health And Beauty Aid Products
See: **Personal Care Products**

Health Care Financing

2859 ■ LARGEST HEALTHCARE FINANCING COMPANIES, 2010

Ranked by: Value of loans in the healthcare sector underwritten, in millions of dollars. Remarks: Also notes market share, number of loans, and Web site. Number listed: 20

1. J. P. Morgan Chase & Co., with $21,824 million

2. Bank of America Merrill Lynch, $20,621
3. Citigroup Inc., $12,104
4. Goldman Sachs Group Inc., $5,595
5. Deutsche Bank AG, $4,994
6. U.S. Bancorp, $4,859
7. Credit Suisse Group, $4,591
8. Wells Fargo Securities, $3,375
9. Barclays Capital Inc., $3,095
10. Morgan Stanley, $2,831

Source: *Modern Healthcare*, Largest Healthcare Financing Companies (annual), November 21, 2011, p. 34.

Health Care Industry

2860 ■ AMERICA'S LARGEST PRIVATE HEALTHCARE EQUIPMENT AND SERVICES COMPANIES, 2010

Ranked by: Revenue, in billions of dollars. Remarks: Also notes headquarters, number of employees, and overall rank in the *America's Largest Private Companies* list. Ranking is available online only, not in print. Number listed: 11

1. HCA ManorCare, with $4.5 billion
2. Medline Industries Inc., $4.01
3. Quintiles Transnational Corp., $3
4. Quality King Distributors Inc., $2.85
5. Iasis Healthcare LLC, $2.76
6. Biomet Inc., $2.73
6. Golden Living, $2.73
8. Life Care Centers of America, $2.65
9. Bausch & Lomb Inc., $2.60
10. Genesis HealthCare Corp., $2.55

Source: *Forbes*, America's Largest Private Companies (annual), http://www.forbes.com, December 5, 2011.

2861 ■ BEST LARGE PLACES TO WORK IN HEALTH-CARE, 2011

Ranked by: Score based on workplace culture, benefits, and salaries. Remarks: Specific scores not provided. To qualify, companies must have 1,000 or more employees. Also notes overall rank in the Top 100. Number listed: 31

1. Kootenai Health
2. Valley Medical Center
3. Premier
4. Roper St. Francis Healthcare
5. Pikeville Medical Center
6. Memorial Healthcare System
7. Southern Ohio Medical Center
8. EMP Management Group
9. Holy Name Medical Center
10. Baptist Health South Florida

Source: *Modern Healthcare*, Best Places to Work (annual), October 24, 2011, p. 36.

2862 ■ BEST MEDIUM-SIZED PLACES TO WORK IN HEALTHCARE, 2011

Ranked by: Score based on workplace culture, benefits, and salaries. Remarks: Specific scores not provided. To qualify, companies must have 100 to 999 employees. Also notes overall rank in the Top 100. Number listed: 51

1. Weatherby Healthcare
2. CompHealth
3. Doctors Hospital of Sarasota
4. Texas Health Harris Methodist Hospital
5. ZocDoc
6. The Women's Hospital
7. Baptist Memorial Hospital (Union City, TN)
8. Lovelace Women's Hospital
9. Jacksonville Medical Center
10. Beacon Partners

Source: *Modern Healthcare*, Best Places to Work (annual), October 24, 2011, p. 32.

2863 ■ BEST PLACES TO WORK IN HEALTHCARE, 2011

Ranked by: Score based on workplace culture, benefits, and salaries. **Remarks:** Specific scores not provided. Also notes rank for previous year, location, number of employees, average annual salary for exempt and non-exempt employees, healthcare category, tenure of the current CEO, voluntary turnover rate, and web site. **Number listed:** 100

1. Weatherby Healthcare
2. LiquidAgents Healthcare
3. Impact Advisors
4. CompHealth
5. Doctors Hospital of Sarasota
6. Texas Health Harris Methodist Hospital (Southlake, TX)
7. ZocDoc
8. The Women's Hospital (Newburgh, IN)
9. Baptist Memorial Hospital (Union City, TN)
10. Hayes Management Consulting

Source: *Modern Healthcare*, Best Places to Work (annual), October 24, 2011, p. 18+.

2864 ■ BEST SMALL HEALTHCARE EQUIPMENT AND SERVICES COMPANIES IN AMERICA, 2011

Ranked by: Score based on revenue, profits, and return on equity for the past 12 months and five years. **Remarks:** Specific scores not provided. Also notes rank in the overall *100 Best Small Companies in America*. To qualify, companies must have revenues between $5 million and $1 billion, a net margin above five percent, and share price above $5. List is available online only. **Number listed:** 8

1. Masimo
2. II-VI
3. Sirona Dental Systems
4. HMS Holdings
5. Bio-Reference Laboratories
6. Ensign Group
7. LHC Group
8. Zoll Medical

Source: *Forbes*, Best Small Companies in America (annual), November 7, 2011.

2865 ■ BEST SMALL PLACES TO WORK IN HEALTH-CARE, 2011

Ranked by: Score based on workplace culture, benefits, and salaries. **Remarks:** Specific scores not provided. To qualify, companies must have 25 to 99 employees. Also notes overall rank in the Top 100. **Number listed:** 18

1. LiquidAgents Healthcare
2. Impact Advisors
3. Hayes Management Consulting
4. Wamego City Hospital
5. HHA Services
6. Aspen Advisors
7. Contegra Physician Care
8. South Broward Endoscopy
9. IMA Consulting
10. AllBetterCare Urgent Care Center

Source: *Modern Healthcare*, Best Places to Work (annual), October 24, 2011, p. 28.

2866 ■ EUROPE'S MOST VALUABLE HEALTHCARE EQUIPMENT AND SERVICES COMPANIES, 2011

Ranked by: Market value as of March 2011, in millions of U.S. dollars. **Remarks:** Also notes rank within the *FT Europe 500*, rank for previous year, country, revenue, net income, assets, number of employees, share price, price-to-earning ratio, dividend yield, and fiscal yearend. **Number listed:** 9

1. Fresenius Medical Care AG, with $19,889.2 million
2. Synthes Inc., $16,124.7
3. Essilor International SA, $15,738.8
4. Fresenius SE, $11,920.9
5. Smith & Nephew plc, $10,053.8
6. Coloplast, $6,004.2
7. Sonova Holding AG, $5,930.6
8. Getinge, $5,492.3
9. William Demant, $5,059.7

Source: *Financial Times*, FT 500 (annual), http://www.ft.com, June 24, 2011.

2867 ■ FASTEST-GROWING HEALTHCARE COMPANIES, 2008-2011

Ranked by: Score based on three-year growth in revenue and earnings, and three-year total return to investors. **Remarks:** Specific scores not provided. To qualify for list, companies must have revenues of at least $50 million, net income of at least $10 million, market capitalization of at least $250 million, and stock price of at least $5. Int'l companies are eligible if they trade on a U.S. exchange and file quarterly reports. **Number listed:** 19

1. SXC Health Solutions Corp.
2. Hi-Tech Pharmacal
3. Alexion Pharmaceuticals
4. Illumina Inc.
5. HMS Holdings Corp.
6. United Therapeutics
7. Cubist Pharmaceuticals Inc.
8. Celgene Corp.
9. Thoratec Corp.
10. HealthSpring

Source: *Fortune*, 100 Fastest-Growing Companies (annual), http://www.fortune.com, September 26, 2011.

2868 ■ FASTEST-GROWING PRIVATE HEALTH COMPANIES IN THE U.S., 2007-2010

Ranked by: Average annual sales growth over three years, in percent. **Remarks:** Also notes headquarters, revenue, and rank in

the overall *Inc. 500*. To qualify, private companies must have had annual revenues of at least $100,000 in 2007 and $2 million in 2010. **Number listed:** 31

1. ClearCorrect, with 8,625%
2. PruGen Pharmaceuticals, 6,412.2%
3. PetRays, 3,249.1%
4. SightLine Health, 2,868.4%
5. PureFormulas.com, 2,678.8%
6. EndoChoice, 2,645.6%
7. TFSupplements, 2,231.1%
8. Vitals, 2,213%
9. InGenesis Diversified Healthcare Solutions, 2,176.5%
10. Arcadia Solutions, 2,116.9%

Source: *Inc.*, Inc. 500 (annual), September 2011, p. 150-156.

2869 ■ LARGEST HEALTH SERVICES COMPANIES BY EMPLOYEES, 2010

Ranked by: Total number of employees. **Remarks:** Also notes contact information for headquarters, number of employees at headquarters, revenue, rank by revenue, and primary SIC code. **Number listed:** 493

1. Hercules Holding II LLC, with 194,100 employees
2. HCA Inc., 190,000
3. HCA-Hospital Corp. of America, 134,000
4. Community Health Systems Inc., 79,214
5. Catholic Health Initiatives, 68,000
6. Mayo Clinic, 67,000
7. Universal Health Services Inc., 62,900
8. Tenet Healthcare Corp., 57,613
9. Kindred Healthcare Inc., 54,100
10. University of Pittsburgh Medical Center, 53,159

Source: *Business Rankings*, (annual), Dun & Bradstreet Inc., 2011, p. VI.238-VI.248.

2870 ■ LARGEST HEALTH SERVICES COMPANIES BY SALES, 2010

Ranked by: Total revenue, in dollars. **Remarks:** Also notes contact information for headquarters, number of employees at headquarters and overall, rank by employees, and primary SIC code. **Number listed:** 489

1. HCA Holdings Inc., with $30,683,000,000
1. HCA Inc., $30,683,000,000
3. Methodist Healthcare Memphis Hospitals, $27,000,000,000
4. Catholic Health Initiatives, $13,360,714,000
5. Community Health Systems Inc., $12,986,500,000
6. Catholic Healthcare West, $9,430,414,000
7. Tenet Healthcare Corp., $9,205,000,000
8. Sutter Health, $8,772,000,000
9. University of Pittsburgh Medical Center, $8,046,467,000
9. UPMC Presbyterian, $8,046,467,000

Source: *Business Rankings*, (annual), Dun & Bradstreet Inc., 2011, p. V.212-V.222.

2871 ■ LARGEST HEALTHCARE MANAGEMENT CONSULTING FIRMS, 2010

Ranked by: Total provider revenue, in millions of dollars. **Remarks:** Also notes headquarters, type of ownership, total contracts, total provider contracts, total revenue, and Web site. **Number listed:** 20

1. Deloitte Consulting, with $372 million
2. Advisory Board Co., $276.4
3. Huron Healthcare, $261.7
4. Dell Services, $196.9
5. Navigant Consulting, $151.9
6. ACS, a Xerox Co., $125.9
7. Quorum Health Resources, $115
8. Ernst & Young LLP, $102
9. FTI Consulting, $98.2
10. GE Healthcare, $95

Source: *Modern Healthcare*, Largest Management Consulting Firms (annual), August 29, 2011, p. 34.

2872 ■ LARGEST POST-ACUTE-CARE COMPANIES, 2010

Ranked by: Net revenue, in millions of dollars. **Remarks:** Also notes type of ownership, type of company, fiscal year-end, net income, number of facilities, and figures for previous year. **Number listed:** 25

1. Kindred Healthcare Inc., with $4,359.7 million
2. Golden Living, $2,725
3. Genesis HealthCare Corp., $2,500
4. Select Medical Holdings Corp., $2,390.3
5. Brookdale Senior Living, $2,213.3
6. Sun Healthcare Group, $1,906.9
7. Amedisys, $1,634.3
8. Sunrise Senior Living, $1,406.7
9. Extendicare Health Services, $1,347.6
10. Meridian Health, $1,324

Source: *Modern Healthcare*, Largest Post-Acute-Care Companies (annual), September 12, 2011, p. 32.

2873 ■ LARGEST U.S. HEALTHCARE SERVICES COMPANIES OVERALL, 2011

Ranked by: Score based on revenue, profits, assets, and market capitalization. **Remarks:** Specific scores not provided. Also notes overall rank in the *Forbes 2000* and figures for each criterion. **Number listed:** 9

1. HCA Holdings Inc.
2. Express Scripts Inc.
3. Quest Diagnostics Inc.
4. DaVita Inc.
5. Laboratory Corp. of America Holdings Inc. (LabCorp)
6. Community Health Systems Inc.
7. Universal Health Services Inc.
8. Cerner Corp.
9. Tenet Healthcare Corp.

Source: *Forbes*, Forbes 2000 (annual), http://www.forbes.com, May 7, 2012.

2874 ■ MISSOURI'S LARGEST HEALTHCARE SERVICES COMPANIES OVERALL, 2011

Ranked by: Score based on revenue, profits, assets, and market capitalization. **Remarks:** Specific scores not provided. Also notes overall rank in the *Forbes 2000* and figures for each criterion. **Number listed:** 2

1. Express Scripts Inc.
2. Cerner Corp.

Source: *Forbes*, Forbes 2000 (annual), http://www.forbes.com, May 7, 2012.

2875 ■ MOST PROFITABLE CANADIAN HEALTHCARE COMPANIES, 2011

Ranked by: Profits, in millions of Canadian dollars. **Number listed:** 6

1. Valent Pharmaceuticals International Inc., with C$159.6 million
2. SXC Health Solutions Corp., C$92
3. CML HealthCare Inc., C$59.9
4. Paladin Labs Inc., C$50.2
5. Nordion Inc., C$16.9
6. Amica Mature Lifestyles Inc., C$11.4

Source: *Canadian Business*, Investor 500 (annual), 2012, p. 55.

2876 ■ MOST VALUABLE U.S. HEALTHCARE EQUIP-MENT AND SERVICES COMPANIES, 2011

Ranked by: Market value as of March 2011, in millions of U.S. dollars. **Remarks:** Also notes rank within the *FT U.S. 500*, rank for previous year, country, revenue, net income, assets, number of employees, share price, price-to-earning ratio, dividend yield, and fiscal yearend. **Number listed:** 30

1. Alcon Inc., with $50,048.6 million
2. UnitedHealth Group Inc., $49,435
3. Medtronic Inc., $42,080
4. Baxter International Inc., $30,852.2
5. Express Scripts Inc., $29,424.4
6. WellPoint Inc., $26,206.9
7. Covidien Ltd., $25,650.5
8. Stryker Corp., $23,643.8
9. Medco Health Solutions Inc., $22,714.3
10. Thermo Fisher Scientific Inc., $21,698.2

Source: *Financial Times*, FT 500 (annual), http://www.ft.com, June 24, 2011.

2877 ■ TENNESSEE'S LARGEST HEALTHCARE SERVICES COMPANIES OVERALL, 2011

Ranked by: Score based on revenue, profits, assets, and market capitalization. **Remarks:** Specific scores not provided. Also notes overall rank in the *Forbes 2000* and figures for each criterion. **Number listed:** 2

1. HCA Holdings Inc.
2. Community Health Systems Inc.

Source: *Forbes*, Forbes 2000 (annual), http://www.forbes.com, May 7, 2012.

2878 ■ TOP *FORTUNE 500* COMPANIES IN PHARMACY AND OTHER HEALTH SERVICES, 2011

Ranked by: Revenue, in millions of dollars. **Remarks:** Also notes overall rank in the *Fortune 500;* profits; profits as a percentage of revenue; stockholders' equity; and rank by each criterion. **Number listed:** 6

1. Medco Health Solutions Inc., with $70,063 million
2. Express Scripts Holding, $46,128
3. Quest Diagnostics Inc., $7,510

4. Omnicare Inc., $6,240
5. Laboratory Corp. of America, $5,542
6. Catalyst Health Solutions, $5,330

Source: *Fortune*, Fortune 500 (annual), May 21, 2012, p. F-36.

2879 ■ TOP HEALTH SERVICES FRANCHISES, 2012

Ranked by: Cumulative score based on financial strength and stability, growth rate, size of the system, number of years in business, the length of time franchising, start-up costs, litigation, percentage of terminations, and whether the company provides financing. **Remarks:** Specific scores not provided. Also notes overall rank within the *Franchise 500,* contact information, description, year founded, year started franchising, states where registered, available U.S. regions, where seeking foreign expansion, number of franchised and company-owned units for past three years, start-up costs, franchise fees, royalty fees, and type of financing available. **Number listed:** 3

1. HealthSource Chiropractic & Progressive Rehab
2. Passport Health
3. ApexNetwork Physical Therapy

Source: *Entrepreneur*, Franchise 500 (annual), January 2012, p. 176-177.

2880 ■ TOP INFORMATION TECHNOLOGY COMPANIES BY HEALTHCARE REVENUE, 2010

Ranked by: Healthcare revenue, in dollars. **Remarks:** Also notes contact information, rank for previous year, figures for previous two years, number of employees, type of company, year founded, healthcare as a percentage of total revenue, executives, and comments. **Number listed:** 98

1. McKesson Technology Solutions, with $3,124,000,000
2. Dell Inc., $2,625,000,000
3. CareFusion, $2,600,000,000
4. Philips Healthcare, $2,400,000,000
5. Cerner Corp., $1,850,222,000
6. Siemens Healthcare, $1,600,000,000
7. Keane, an NTT Data Co., $1,400,000,000
8. Computer Sciences Corp., $1,334,000,000
9. Pulse Systems Inc., $1,200,000,000
10. Cognizant Technology Solutions Corp., $1,177,085,193

Source: *Healthcare Informatics*, Healthcare Informatics 100 (annual), June 2011, p. 12-40.

2881 ■ THE UNITED STATES' MOST VALUABLE HEALTHCARE PRODUCTS BRANDS, 2011

Ranked by: Brand value, in millions of U.S. dollars. **Remarks:** Also notes rank within the *Global 500* for current and previous year, figures for current and previous year, and brand rating. Ranking is available online only. **Number listed:** 3

1. Johnson & Johnson, with $7,329 million
2. Medtronic, $4,424
3. Covidien, $2,568

Source: *Global 500*, (annual), Brand Finance plc, March 2012.

2882 ■ THE UNITED STATES' MOST VALUABLE HEALTHCARE SERVICES BRANDS, 2011

Ranked by: Brand value, in millions of U.S. dollars. **Remarks:** Also notes rank within the *Global 500* for current and previous

year, figures for current and previous year, and brand rating. Ranking is available online only. **Number listed:** 4

1. UnitedHealth, with $9,920 million
2. Aetna, $3,689
3. WellPoint, $3,460
4. Cigna, $3,271

Source: *Global 500*, (annual), Brand Finance plc, March 2012.

2883 ■ WORLD'S LARGEST HEALTHCARE SERVICES COMPANIES OVERALL, 2011

Ranked by: Score based on revenue, profits, assets, and market capitalization. **Remarks:** Specific scores not provided. Also notes country, overall rank in the *Forbes 2000,* and figures for each criterion. **Number listed:** 10

1. HCA Holdings Inc.
2. Express Scripts Inc.
3. Quest Diagnostics Inc.
4. DaVita Inc.
5. Celesio AG
6. Community Health Systems Inc.
7. Laboratory Corp. of America Holdings Inc. (LabCorp)
8. Universal Health Services Inc.
9. Cerner Corp.
10. Tenet Healthcare Corp.

Source: *Forbes*, Forbes 2000 (annual), http://www.forbes.com, May 7, 2012.

2884 ■ WORLD'S MOST ETHICAL HEALTHCARE SERVICES COMPANIES, 2012

Ranked by: Score based on five criteria: ethics and compliance program; reputation, leadership, and innovation; governance; corporate citizenship and responsibility; and culture of ethics. **Remarks:** Specific scores not provided; companies are listed alphabetically, not ranked. **Number listed:** 5

1. Baptist Health South Florida (U.S.)
2. Hospital Corp. of America (U.S.)
3. Novation (U.S.)
4. Premier Inc. (U.S.)
5. University Hospitals (U.S.)

Source: *Ethisphere Magazine*, World's Most Ethical Companies (annual), http://www.ethisphere.com, 2012.

2885 ■ WORLD'S MOST VALUABLE HEALTHCARE EQUIPMENT AND SERVICES COMPANIES, 2011

Ranked by: Market value as of March 2011, in millions of U.S. dollars. **Remarks:** Also notes rank within the *FT 500*, rank for previous year, country, revenue, net income, assets, number of employees, share price, price-to-earning ratio, dividend yield, and fiscal year-end. **Number listed:** 11

1. Alcon Inc., with $50,048.6 million
2. UnitedHealth Group Inc., $49,435
3. Medtronic Inc., $42,080
4. Baxter International Inc., $30,852.2
5. Express Scripts Inc., $29,424.4
6. WellPoint Inc., $26,206.9
7. Covidien Ltd., $25,650.5
8. Stryker Corp., $23,643.8
9. Medco Health Solutions Inc., $22,714.3

10. Thermo Fisher Scientific Inc., $21,698.2

Source: *Financial Times*, FT 500 (annual), http://www.ft.com, June 24, 2011.

2886 ■ WORLD'S MOST VALUABLE HEALTHCARE PRODUCT BRANDS, 2011

Ranked by: Brand value, in millions of U.S. dollars. **Remarks:** Also notes rank within the *Global 500* for current and previous year, figures for current and previous year, country, and brand rating. Ranking is available online only. **Number listed:** 3

1. Johnson & Johnson, with $7,329 million
2. Medtronic, $4,424
3. Covidien, $2,568

Source: *Global 500*, (annual), Brand Finance plc, March 2012.

2887 ■ WORLD'S MOST VALUABLE HEALTHCARE SERVICES BRANDS, 2011

Ranked by: Brand value, in millions of U.S. dollars. **Remarks:** Also notes rank within the *Global 500* for current and previous year, figures for current and previous year, country, and brand rating. Ranking is available online only. **Number listed:** 5

1. UnitedHealth, with $9,920 million
2. Fresenius Medical Care, $3,894
3. Aetna, $3,689
4. WellPoint, $3,460
5. Cigna, $3,271

Source: *Global 500*, (annual), Brand Finance plc, March 2012.

Health Care Institutions
See: **Health Facilities**

Health Clubs

2888 ■ LARGEST HEALTH CLUB CHAINS, 2010

Ranked by: Corporate revenue, in millions of dollars. **Remarks:** Also notes contact information, annual revenue growth, number of sites, number of states of operation, year founded, number of employees, number of clubs to open or acquire next year, and company profile. **Number listed:** 100

1. 24 Hour Fitness Worldwide Inc., with $1,352 million
2. L. A. Fitness International, $1,000
3. LifeTime Fitness Inc., $912.8
4. Club Corp., $812
5. Bally Total Fitness, $550
6. Town Sports International Inc., $462.4
7. Planet Fitness, $157.1
8. Capital Fitness Inc., $142
9. Western Athletic Clubs, $121
10. Lifestyle Family Fitness Inc., $102.4

Source: *Club Industry's Fitness Business Pro*, Top 100 (annual), July 2011, p. 26+.

Health Facilities

2889 ■ TOP *FORTUNE 500* COMPANIES IN MEDICAL FACILITIES, 2011

Ranked by: Revenue, in millions of dollars. **Remarks:** Also notes overall rank in the *Fortune 500;* profits; profits as a percentage of revenue; stockholders' equity; and rank by each criterion. **Number listed:** 8

1. HCA Holdings Inc., with $32,506 million
2. Community Health Systems Inc., $13,817
3. Tenet Healthcare Corp., $9,601
4. Universal Health Services Inc., $7,534
5. DaVita Inc., $6,999
6. Health Management Associates Inc., $5,822
7. Kindred Healthcare, $5,523
8. Vanguard Health Systems, $4,896

Source: *Fortune*, Fortune 500 (annual), May 21, 2012, p. F-36.

Health Food Industry
See: **Food Industry**

Health Maintenance Organizations

2890 ■ LARGEST COLORADO-BASED SMALL-GROUP HEALTHCARE CARRIERS, 2010

Ranked by: Number of Colorado individuals covered. **Remarks:** Also notes contact information. **Number listed:** 10

1. UnitedHealthcare Insurance Co., with 92,538 individuals
2. Rocky Mountain Hospital & Medical Service Inc., 62,782
3. Kaiser Foundation Health Plan of Colorado, 61,575
4. Humana Insurance Co., 17,682
5. Humana Health Plan Inc., 16,406
6. Rocky Mountain HMO Inc., 14,522
7. Rocky Mountain HealthCare Options Inc., 14,297
8. Aetna Life Insurance Co., 3,808
9. Colorado Choice Health Plan, 2,121
10. HMO Colorado Inc., 721

Source: *ColoradoBiz*, Top Professional Services (annual), December 2011, p. 48.

Healthcare Systems
See: **Multihospital Systems**

Heating And Cooling Industry
See: **Air Conditioning Industry**

Heating Pads
See: **Household Appliances**

Hedge Funds
See also: **Mutual Funds**

2891 ■ HIGHEST-EARNING HEDGE FUND MANAGERS, 2011

Ranked by: Earnings, in millions of dollars. **Remarks:** Also notes company, location, and comments. **Number listed:** 40

1. Raymond Dalio, with $3,000 million

2. James Simons, $2,100
3. Carl Icahn, $2,000
4. Steve Cohen, $600
5. David Shaw, $580
6. Charles Coleman III, $500
7. Kenneth Griffin, $400
7. Alan Howard, $400
9. John Arnold, $360
10. Bruce Kovner, $210

Source: *Forbes*, Hedge Funds: Top Earners, April 9, 2012, p. 86+.

2892 ■ WORLD'S BEST HEDGE FUNDS, 2008-2011

Ranked by: Three-year annualized return, in percent. **Remarks:** Also notes rank for previous year, fund assets, strategy, return for latest year, company name and location, and total firm assets. **Number listed:** 100

1. Zais Opportunity Ltd. Class B, with 78.49%
2. Metacapital Mortgage Opportunities Ltd., 61.99%
3. SPM Structured Servicing Holdings LP, 61.84%
4. SPM Directional Mortgage Prepay, 50.73%
5. Marwyn Value Investors LP, 50.3%
6. ECF Value LP, 45.5%
7. Providence MBS Ltd., 45.04%
8. Barnegat Ltd. Series B, 44.16%
9. VR Global Partners LP, 44.13%
10. Palomino Ltd., 41.49%

Source: *Barron's*, Hedge Fund 100 (annual), May 21, 2012, p. P28-P29.

High Technology Industry
See also: **Information Technology**

2893 ■ BEST DIGITAL TECHNOLOGY AND TECHNOLOGY SERVICES COMPANIES TO WORK FOR IN BRITISH COLUMBIA, 2010

Ranked by: Editorial determination. **Remarks:** Specific scores not provided. **Number listed:** 5

1. Strangeloop Networks Inc.
2. Vineyard Networks Inc.
3. Vivonet Canada Inc.
4. Tasktop Technologies
5. Clevest Solutions Inc.

Source: *BCBusiness*, Best Companies (annual), http://www.bcbusinessonline.ca, December 2011.

2894 ■ BEST SMALL TECHNOLOGY HARDWARE AND EQUIPMENT COMPANIES IN AMERICA, 2011

Ranked by: Score based on revenue, profits, and return on equity for the past 12 months and five years. **Remarks:** Specific scores not provided. Also notes rank in the overall *100 Best Small Companies in America*. To qualify, companies must have revenues between $5 million and $1 billion, a net margin above five percent, and share price above $5. List is available online only. **Number listed:** 3

1. IEC Electronics
2. Synaptics
3. AZZ

Source: *Forbes*, Best Small Companies in America (annual), November 7, 2011.

2895 ■ CANADA'S FASTEST-GROWING TECHNOLOGY COMPANIES, 2010-2011

Ranked by: Annual growth in revenue, in percent. **Remarks:** Also notes overall rank in the *Branham 300* for each year. **Number listed:** 10

1. Virtutone Networks, with 239%
2. Amaya Gaming Group, 202%
3. Novra Technologies, 186%
4. Architech, 171%
5. DevFacto Technologies, 168%
6. DataWind, 150%
7. CoreTech Staffing & Professional Services, 134%
8. WiLAN, 114%
9. Enflick, 110%
10. Silanis, 105%

Source: *Backbone Magazine*, Branham 300 (annual), 2012, p. 35.

2896 ■ CANADA'S TOP TECHNOLOGY COMPANIES, 2011

Ranked by: Revenue, in thousands of Canadian dollars. **Remarks:** Also notes rank for previous year and annual growth in revenue. **Number listed:** 250

1. Research in Motion Ltd., with C$20,245,419 thousand
2. BCE Inc., C$9,050,900
3. Rogers Communications Inc., C$7,989,760
4. TELUS Corp., C$7,980,657
5. Celestica Inc., C$7,335,621
6. CGI Group Inc., C$4,323,237
7. Shaw Communications Inc., C$2,586,520
8. CAE Inc., C$1,629,000
9. Open Text Corp., C$1,050,869
10. Softchoice Corp., C$1,022,113

Source: *Backbone Magazine*, Branham 300 (annual), 2012, p. 30-32.

2897 ■ EUROPE'S MOST VALUABLE TECHNOLOGY HARDWARE AND EQUIPMENT COMPANIES, 2011

Ranked by: Market value as of March 2011, in millions of U.S. dollars. **Remarks:** Also notes rank within the *FT Europe 500*, rank for previous year, country, revenue, net income, assets, number of employees, share price, price-to-earning ratio, dividend yield, and fiscal yearend. **Number listed:** 8

1. Telefonaktiebolaget LM Ericsson, with $42,148.2 million
2. Nokia Corp., $32,072.6
3. ASML Holding NV, $19,034.1
4. Alcatel-Lucent, $13,327.8
5. ARM Holdings plc, $12,397.6
6. STMicroelectronics NV, $11,291
7. Infineon Technologies AG, $11,190.1
8. Aixtron, $4,408

Source: *Financial Times*, FT 500 (annual), http://www.ft.com, June 24, 2011.

2898 ■ FASTEST-GROWING ASIAN-PACIFIC TECHNOLOGY FIRMS, 2008-2010

Ranked by: Three-year revenue growth, in percent. **Remarks:** Also notes industry sector. **Number listed:** 500

1. The Store Corp. (China), with 19,217.976%
2. Silicon Mitus Inc. (S. Korea), 9,335.657%
3. Tendyron Corp. (China), 9,150.048%
4. Jiaxing Mbaobao Network Technology Co., Ltd. (China), 6,287.871%
5. Giga Solar Materials Corp. (Taiwan), 5,560.336%
6. Powershop NZ Ltd. (New Zealand), 5,280.410%
7. Two Degrees Mobile Ltd. (New Zealand), 3,761.766%
8. Brightek Optoelectronic Co., Ltd. (Taiwan), 3,754.886%
9. 3-D Matrix Ltd. (Japan), 3,582.951%
10. Sinsung Solar Energy Corp. (S. Korea), 3,560.124%

Source: *Technology Fast 500 Asia Pacific*, (annual), Deloitte LLP, 2011.

2899 ■ FASTEST-GROWING TECHNOLOGY FIRMS IN AUSTRALIA, 2008-2010

Ranked by: Three-year revenue growth, in percent. **Remarks:** Also notes sector, CEO, website, and state. **Number listed:** 50

1. Anittel Ltd., with 1,022.22%
2. Observatory Crest Australia Pty. Ltd., 869.93%
3. BizCover Pty. Ltd., 792.03%
4. SurfStitch Pty. Ltd., 573.66%
5. Vocus Communications Ltd., 505.79%
6. Energy Matters Pty. Ltd., 379.86%
7. catchoftheday.com.au, 327.17%
8. Switched on Media Pty. Ltd., 287%
9. SportingPulse Pty. Ltd., 280.86%
10. Hotels Combined Pty. Ltd., 261.58%

Source: *Technology Fast 50 Australia*, (annual), Deloitte LLP, 2011.

2900 ■ FASTEST-GROWING TECHNOLOGY FIRMS IN CANADA, 2006-2010

Ranked by: Five-year revenue growth, in percent. **Remarks:** Also notes headquarters and website. **Number listed:** 50

1. Accedian Networks, with 50,136%
2. RTI Cryogenics, 46,278%
3. Avigilon, 38,796%
4. NexJ Systems, 29,161%
5. Real Matters, 28,265%
6. ARISE Technologies, 10,017%
7. Clevest Solutions, 7,976%
8. Dominion Voting Systems, 3,539%
9. Acquisio, 2,622%
10. GuestLogix Inc., 2,322%

Source: *Backbone Magazine*, The Fast 50 (annual), October 2011, p. 22.

2901 ■ FASTEST-GROWING TECHNOLOGY FIRMS IN CENTRAL EUROPE, 2006-2010

Ranked by: Five-year revenue growth, in percent. **Remarks:** Also notes industry sector. Ranking covers companies from 17 Central European countries: Albania, Bosnia & Herzegovina, Bulgaria, Croatia, Czech Republic, Estonia, Hungary, Latvia, Lithuania,

Macedonia, Moldova, Poland, Romania, Serbia, Montenegro, Slovakia, and Slovenia. **Number listed:** 50

1. Vola.ro Student Adventure SRL (Romania), with 6,219%
2. LiveSport SRO (Czech Republic), 5,820%
3. Internet Shop SRO (Czech Republic), 3,995%
4. Netmedia SA (Poland), 3,640%
5. Inwestycje.pl SA (Poland), 2,719%
6. TeamNet International SA (Romania), 2,136%
7. Datera SA (Poland), 2,011%
8. Kompan.pl SP (Poland), 1,584%
9. Technitel Polska SJ (Poland), 1,526%
10. Ideo SP (Poland), 1,423%

Source: *Technology Fast 50 Central Europe*, (annual), Deloitte LLP, 2011.

2902 ■ FASTEST-GROWING TECHNOLOGY FIRMS IN CHINA, 2008-2010

Ranked by: Three-year revenue growth, in percent. **Remarks:** Also notes headquarters and industry sector. **Number listed:** 50

1. The Store Corp., with 19,218%
2. Tendyron Corp., 9,150%
3. Jiaxing Mbaobao Network Technology Co., Ltd., 6,288%
4. ganji.com, 2,186%
5. Shanghai Greenbox Internet Technology Co., Ltd., 1,955%
6. Wuhan Guoce Nordic New Energy Co., Ltd., 1,799%
7. Lattice Power Corp., 1,547%
8. Aesthetic Technology (Beijing) Ltd., 1,328%
9. Borqs Hong Kong Ltd., 1,054%
10. Zhejiang Yutian Technology Co., Ltd., 846%

Source: *Technology Fast 50 China*, (annual), Deloitte LLP, 2011.

2903 ■ FASTEST-GROWING TECHNOLOGY FIRMS IN EUROPE, THE MIDDLE EAST, AND AFRICA, 2006-2010

Ranked by: Five-year revenue growth, in percent. **Remarks:** Also notes business sector. **Number listed:** 500

1. Logic Bilisim (Turkey), with 28,617%
2. Fixnetix (UK), 24,557%
3. LeadPoint U.K., 21,801%
4. GPEG International Ltd. (UK), 17,716%
5. PKR (UK), 9,314%
6. RatedPeople.com (UK), 8,144%
7. Populis Ireland Ltd. (Ireland), 7,982%
8. Sacoin GmbH (Germany), 7,850%
9. Elkotek (Turkey), 7,093%
10. Software Asset Management Ltd. (Ireland), 6,899%

Source: *Technology Fast 500 EMEA*, (annual), Deloitte LLP, 2011.

2904 ■ FASTEST-GROWING TECHNOLOGY FIRMS IN FINLAND, 2006-2010

Ranked by: Five-year revenue growth, in percent. **Remarks:** Also notes rank in the *Technology Fast 500 EMEA*. **Number listed:** 50

1. Eniram Oy, with 6,209%
2. SLM Finland Oy, 5,146%

3. Analyse, 2,630%
4. Retail Logistics Excellence - RELEX Oy, 2,015%
5. Klikkicom Oy, 1,826%
6. Priorite Oy, 1,707%
7. Endero Oy, 1,106%
8. Confidex Oy, 1,083%
9. Sympa Oy, 1,010%
10. Hibox Systems Oy, 923%

Source: *Technology Fast 50 Finland*, (annual), Deloitte LLP, 2011.

2905 ■ FASTEST-GROWING TECHNOLOGY FIRMS IN FRANCE, 2006-2010

Ranked by: Five-year revenue growth, in percent. **Remarks:** Also notes headquarters and financial data. **Number listed:** 50

1. Bioalliance Pharma, with 4,800%
2. Aquafadas, 3,231%
3. Ikos Group, 2,667%
4. Bookeen, 2,537%
5. Mexel Industries, 2,288%
6. Robopolis, 2,279%
7. Intersec, 2,108%
8. Prowebce, 1,994%
9. Groupe Consoursmania, 1,953%
10. STS Group, 1,783%

Source: *Technology Fast 50 France*, (annual), Deloitte LLP, 2011.

2906 ■ FASTEST-GROWING TECHNOLOGY FIRMS IN GREATER PHILADELPHIA, 2006-2010

Ranked by: Five-year revenue growth, in percent. **Remarks:** Also notes headquarters and industry. Ranking covers Pennsylvania east of Harrisburg, New Jersey south of Princeton, and Delaware. **Number listed:** 50

1. myYearbook, with 6,918%
2. SevOne Inc., 5,075%
3. Knowland Group Inc., 1,387%
4. SkillSurvey Inc., 919%
5. Transcend United Technologies, 566%
6. QlikTech Inc., 412%
7. iPipeline, 396%
8. Education Management Solutions Inc., 277%
9. AppLabs, 255%
10. CardioNet Inc., 254%

Source: *Technology Fast 50 Greater Philadelphia*, (annual), Deloitte LLP, 2011.

2907 ■ FASTEST-GROWING TECHNOLOGY FIRMS IN INDIA, 2006-2010

Ranked by: Five-year revenue growth, in percent. **Remarks:** Also notes industry. **Number listed:** 50

1. Ubona Technologies Pvt. Ltd., with 1,353%
2. Aujas Networks Pvt. Ltd., 1,010%
3. Prizm Payment Services Pvt. Ltd., 792%
4. Webaroo Technology India Pvt. Ltd., 780%
5. Edusys Services Pvt. Ltd., 614%
6. Telibrahma Convergent Communications Pvt. Ltd., 434%

7. Nitor Infotech Pvt. Ltd., 428%
8. Pilani Soft Labs Pvt. Ltd., 412%
9. Omnesys Technologies Pvt. Ltd., 350%
10. Prodapt Solutions Pvt. Ltd., 342%

Source: *Technology Fast 50 India*, (annual), Deloitte LLP, 2011.

2908 ■ FASTEST-GROWING TECHNOLOGY FIRMS IN IRELAND, 2006-2010

Ranked by: Five-year revenue growth, in percent. **Remarks:** Specific figures not provided. **Number listed:** 50

1. Populis Ireland Ltd.
2. Software Asset Management Ireland Ltd.
3. H2 Compliance
4. Lincor Solutions Ltd.
5. iSite
6. Learning Pool
7. Impedans Ltd.
8. Altobridge Ltd.
9. Creme Software Ltd.
10. CarTrawler

Source: *Technology Fast 50 Ireland*, (annual), Deloitte LLP, 2011.

2909 ■ FASTEST-GROWING TECHNOLOGY FIRMS IN ISRAEL, 2006-2010

Ranked by: Five-year revenue growth, in percent. **Remarks:** Also notes business description. **Number listed:** 50

1. Tufin, with 6,343%
2. WebsPlanet, 6,041%
3. Kenshoo, 5,926%
4. MyThings, 3,982%
5. Mazor Robotics, 3,168%
6. Pontis, 2,990%
7. Promisec, 1,629%
8. Telmap, 1,573%
9. Syneron Dental Lasers, 1,244%
10. AlgoSec, 1,158%

Source: *Technology Fast 50 Israel*, (annual), Deloitte LLP, 2011.

2910 ■ FASTEST-GROWING TECHNOLOGY FIRMS IN THE NETHERLANDS, 2006-2010

Ranked by: Five-year revenue growth, in percent. **Remarks:** Also notes headquarters and website. **Number listed:** 50

1. Voiceworks BV, with 2,768%
2. drukwerkdeal.nl, 2,750%
3. YourSurprise.com BV, 2,681%
4. Paylogic, 2,590%
5. Clansman BV, 2,269%
6. OYPO, 2,238%
7. Blue Billywig, 1,791%
8. Digimo Media, 1,549%
9. Conclusion FIT, 1,491%
10. Service2Media BV, 1,425%

Source: *Technology Fast 50 Netherlands*, (annual), Deloitte LLP, 2011.

2911 ■ FASTEST-GROWING TECHNOLOGY FIRMS IN NORTH AMERICA, 2006-2010

Ranked by: Five-year revenue growth, in percent. **Remarks:** Also notes primary industry, headquarters, and CEO. **Number listed:** 500

1. MAKO Surgical Corp. (U.S.), with 70,211%
2. Accedian Networks (Canada), 50,136%
3. RTI Cryogenics Inc. (Canada), 46,278%
4. Avigilon (Canada), 38,796%
5. ServiceNow (U.S.), 32,048%
6. NexJ Systems Inc. (Canada), 29,161%
7. Real Matters (Canada), 28,265%
8. HubSpot (U.S.), 27,746%
9. AVI BioPharma Inc. (U.S.), 25,483%
10. ARIAD Pharmaceuticals Inc. (U.S.), 19,875%

Source: *Technology Fast 500 North America*, (annual), Deloitte LLP, 2011.

2912 ■ FASTEST-GROWING TECHNOLOGY FIRMS IN TURKEY, 2006-2010

Ranked by: Five-year revenue growth, in percent. **Remarks:** Also notes type of business. **Number listed:** 50

1. Logic Bilisim Sistemleri ve Danismanlik Ltd. Sti., with 28,617%
2. Elkotek Iletisim, 7,093%
3. Erguvan Bilisim, 3,380%
4. P. I. Works, 2,940%
5. Medianova, 2,637%
6. MCD Telekom, 2,004%
7. Bilginet Information Technologies, 1,847%
8. KodA, 1,727%
9. BTT Bilgi Teknoloji, 1,175%
10. Ericom Telekomunikasyon, 1,046%

Source: *Technology Fast 50 Turkey*, (annual), Deloitte LLP, 2011.

2913 ■ FASTEST-GROWING TECHNOLOGY FIRMS IN THE UNITED KINGDOM, 2006-2010

Ranked by: Five-year revenue growth, in percent. **Remarks:** Also notes type of business. **Number listed:** 50

1. Fixnetix, with 24,557%
2. LeadPoint UK, 21,801%
3. GPEG International Ltd., 17,716%
4. PKR, 9,314%
5. RatedPeople.com, 8,144%
6. Nujira, 4,487%
7. Mimecast Ltd., 3,102%
8. notonthehighstreet.com, 2,720%
9. Voice 2 Voice Ltd., 2,610%
10. Quickstart Global, 2,481%

Source: *Technology Fast 50 U.K.*, (annual), Deloitte LLP, 2011.

2914 ■ LARGEST TECHNOLOGY/BIOTECHNOLOGY COMPANIES IN BRITISH COLUMBIA, 2010

Ranked by: Revenue, in thousands of Canadian dollars. **Remarks:** Also notes figures for previous year. **Number listed:** 10

1. Telus Corp., with C$9,779,000 thousand
2. MacDonald, Dettwiler & Associates Ltd., C$689,030
3. Sierra Wireless Inc., C$669,812
4. PMC-Sierra Inc., C$654,114
5. Glentel Inc., C$412,307
6. Angiotech Pharmaceuticals Inc., C$253,614

7. Peer 1 Network Enterprises Inc., C$100,855
8. Ballard Power Systems Inc., C$66,966
9. Cardiome Pharma Corp., C$66,064
10. Absolute Software Corp., C$64,076

Source: *BCBusiness*, Top 100 (annual), July 2011, p. 135.

2915 ■ MOST VALUABLE U.S. TECHNOLOGY HARDWARE AND EQUIPMENT COMPANIES, 2011

Ranked by: Market value as of March 2011, in millions of U.S. dollars. **Remarks:** Also notes rank within the *FT U.S. 500*, rank for previous year, country, revenue, net income, assets, number of employees, share price, price-to-earning ratio, dividend yield, and fiscal yearend. **Number listed:** 38

1. Apple Inc., with $321,072.1 million
2. Intel Corp., $110,747.8
3. Cisco Systems Inc., $94,805.1
4. QUALCOMM Inc., $90,126.6
5. Hewlett-Packard Co., $88,656.2
6. EMC Corp., $54,787.1
7. Texas Instruments Inc., $40,400.7
8. Corning Inc., $32,302.3
9. Dell Inc., $27,666.9
10. Juniper Networks Inc., $22,509.5

Source: *Financial Times*, FT 500 (annual), http://www.ft.com, June 24, 2011.

2916 ■ TOP CANADIAN IT INFRASTRUCTURE AND HARDWARE COMPANIES, 2011

Ranked by: Revenue, in thousands of Canadian dollars. **Remarks:** Specific figures not provided. Also notes rank for previous year and overall rank in the *Branham 300*. **Number listed:** 25

1. Research in Motion Ltd.
2. Celestica Inc.
3. CAE Inc.
4. SMART Technologies
5. Aastra Technologies Ltd.
6. Sierra Wireless Inc.
7. Pason Systems
8. Evertz Microsystems
9. EXFO
10. Zarlink Semiconductor

Source: *Backbone Magazine*, Branham 300 (annual), 2012, p. 34.

2917 ■ TOP CANADIAN TECHNOLOGY COMPANIES, 2010

Ranked by: Revenue, in thousands of Canadian dollars (unless otherwise noted). **Remarks:** Also notes percent change from previous year. **Number listed:** 10

1. Research in Motion Ltd. (U.S. dollars), with C$19,915,000 thousand
2. Bombardier Inc. (U.S. dollars), C$17,887,000
3. IBM Canada, C$7,919,000
4. Rogers Wireless, C$6,968,000
5. Celestica Inc. (U.S. dollars), C$6,530,700
6. Bell Mobility, C$4,934,000
7. CGI Group, C$3,736,873
8. Siemens Canada, C$2,759,000
9. Linamar Corp., C$2,232,662

10. Apple Canada, C$2,158,454

Source: *Report on Business Magazine*, Top 1000 Companies (annual), http://www.reportonbusiness.com, June 2011.

2918 ■ TOP CANADIAN TECHNOLOGY COMPANIES IN RESOURCE EFFICIENCY AND ENVIRONMENTAL IMPACT, 2011

Ranked by: Score based on purity, quality, and finances. **Remarks:** Scores not provided. Also notes location, industry, ticker symbol, comments, and number of years appearing in ranking. To qualify, companies must be listed on the Toronto Stock Exchange. **Number listed:** 10

1. Westport Innovations Inc.
2. RuggedCom
3. WaterFurnace Renewable Energy
4. 5N Plus
5. GLV Inc.
6. Pure Technologies Ltd.
7. ATS Automation
8. Innergex Renewable Energy
9. Ecosynthetix
10. TSO3

Source: *Corporate Knights*, Cleantech 10 (annual), http://www.corporateknights.ca, 2011.

2919 ■ TOP MULTINATIONAL TECHNOLOGY COMPANIES IN CANADA, 2011

Ranked by: Revenue, in thousands of Canadian dollars. **Remarks:** Also notes rank for previous year, percentage change, year established in Canada, business specialties, and number of employees in Canada. **Number listed:** 25

1. IBM Canada Ltd., with C$5,746,050 thousand
2. Hewlett-Packard (Canada) Ltd., C$4,645,858
3. Cisco Systems Canada Co., C$1,642,455
4. Microsoft Canada Co., C$1,627,200
5. Xerox Canada Inc., C$1,236,000
6. Honeywell Canada, C$1,230,000
7. Oracle Canada, C$1,193,958
8. Ericsson Canada Inc., C$1,055,000
9. SAP Canada, C$965,798
10. Wipro Technologies, C$797,525

Source: *Backbone Magazine*, Branham 300 (annual), 2012, p. 33.

2920 ■ TOP TECHNOLOGY SERVICES COMPANIES IN CANADA, 2011

Ranked by: Revenue, in thousands of Canadian dollars. **Remarks:** Specific figures not provided. Also notes rank for previous year and overall rank in the *Branham 300*. **Number listed:** 25

1. CGI Group
2. Softchoice Corp.
3. MacDonald, Dettwiler & Associates Ltd.
4. Procom Consultants Group
5. Hartco
6. Compugen
7. Teranet
8. OnX Enterprise Solutions
9. Calian Technologies
10. S.i. Systems

Source: *Backbone Magazine*, Branham 300 (annual), 2012, p. 35.

2921 ■ WORLD'S MOST VALUABLE TECHNOLOGY BRANDS, 2012

Ranked by: Brand value, a measure of a brand's earnings and contribution, in millions of U.S. dollars. **Remarks:** Also notes annual growth in brand value and rank by brand contribution and brand momentum. **Number listed:** 20

1. Apple, with $182,951 million
2. IBM, $115,985
3. Google, $107,857
4. Microsoft, $76,651
5. Facebook, $33,233
6. SAP, $25,715
7. Baidu, $24,326
8. HP, $22,898
9. Oracle, $22,529
10. Tencent/QQ, $17,992

Source: *Financial Times*, Global Brands (annual), http://www.ft.com, May 22, 2012.

2922 ■ WORLD'S MOST VALUABLE TECHNOLOGY HARDWARE AND EQUIPMENT COMPANIES, 2011

Ranked by: Market value as of March 2011, in millions of U.S. dollars. **Remarks:** Also notes rank within the *FT 500*, rank for previous year, country, revenue, net income, assets, number of employees, share price, price-to-earning ratio, dividend yield, and fiscal year-end. **Number listed:** 19

1. Apple Inc., with $321,072.1 million
2. Samsung Electronics Co., Ltd., $138,159.2
3. Intel Corp., $110,747.8
4. Cisco Systems Inc., $94,805.1
5. QUALCOMM Inc., $90,126.6
6. Hewlett-Packard Co., $88,656.2
7. Taiwan Semiconductor Manufacturing Co., Ltd., $62,212
8. Canon Inc., $58,255.5
9. EMC Corp., $54,787.1
10. Telefonaktiebolaget LM Ericsson, $42,148.2

Source: *Financial Times*, FT 500 (annual), http://www.ft.com, June 24, 2011.

Hispanic American Business Enterprises

2923 ■ BEST FRANCHISES FOR HISPANICS, 2011

Ranked by: Score based on financial performance, brand identification, franchisee satisfaction, training, ongoing support, financial stability, Hispanic ownership, overall minority representation, and Hispanics in top management. **Remarks:** Scores not provided; companies are listed alphabetically, not ranked. Also notes number of units, total investment, franchise fee and royalty, employees needed, projected number of new units in next 12 months, and business description. **Number listed:** 25

1. Anytime Fitness
2. Burger King
3. Church's Chicken
4. Coverall Health-Based Cleaning System
5. CruiseOne
6. Denny's Inc.
7. El Pollo Loco
8. Estrella Insurance

9. Fantastic Sams
10. Fast-Fix Jewelry & Watch Repairs

Source: *PODER Hispanic Magazine*, Top Franchises for Hispanics (annual), 2011, p. 68+.

2924 ■ FASTEST-GROWING HISPANIC EXPORTERS, 2009-2010

Ranked by: Annual growth in export sales, in percent. **Remarks:** Also notes export sales for current and previous year. **Number listed:** 10

1. CAPE Inc., with 287.7%
2. Amtec Sales Inc., 224.1%
3. SolvChem Inc., 204.4%
4. Everglades Steel Corp. and Medley Steel Corp., 201.8%
5. The Plaza Group Inc., 134.8%
6. Nital Trading Co., 108.3%
7. Gonzales Group, 100%
8. Sweetlake Chemicals Ltd., 88.9%
9. Lopez Foods Inc., 75.7%
10. Information & Computing Services Inc., 74.8%

Source: *Hispanic Business*, Top 50 Exporters (annual), 2011, p. 40.

2925 ■ FASTEST-GROWING HISPANIC-OWNED COMPANIES BY PERCENT GROWTH, 2006-2010

Ranked by: Five-year growth in revenue, in percent. **Remarks:** Also notes location, business classification, compound annual growth rate, and revenue, profit range, and number of employees for 2006 and 2010. **Number listed:** 100

1. MicroTech LLC, with 7,585.7%
2. Link America Inc., 4,443.3%
3. Alliance Drywall & Acoustical Inc., 3,150%
4. P3S Corp., 2,757.1%
5. Genesis Networks Enterprises LLC, 2,260.6%
6. InGenesis Inc., 1,574.7%
7. SBG Technology Solutions Inc., 1,334.9%
8. VisionIT, 931.4%
9. Intuitive Research & Technology Corp., 685.3%
10. GenQuest Inc., 416.4%

Source: *Hispanic Business*, Fastest-Growing 100 (annual), 2011, p. 29+.

2926 ■ FASTEST-GROWING PRIVATE HISPANIC/LATINO-RUN COMPANIES IN THE U.S., 2007-2010

Ranked by: Average annual sales growth over three years, in percent. **Remarks:** Also notes overall rank in the *Inc. 5,000*, state, and revenue for current year. To qualify, private companies must have had annual revenues of at least $100,000 in 2007 and $2 million in 2010. **Number listed:** 100

1. Contour, with 11,663%
2. The Armando Montelongo Co., 8,161%
3. BrokersWeb.com, 8,127%
4. Charfen Institute, 8,007%
5. MZI Group, 3,874%
6. HomeInsurance.com, 3,458%
7. Link America, 3,224%
8. PureFormulas.com, 2,679%

9. MicroTech, 2,579%

10. Provideo Management, 2,465%

Source: *Inc.*, Inc. 500 (annual), http://www.inc.com, September 2011.

2927 ■ LARGEST HISPANIC AUTOMOTIVE COMPANIES, 2010

Ranked by: Revenue, in dollars. **Remarks:** Also notes figures for previous year, percent change, and primary products and services. **Number listed:** 10

1. Greenway Ford Inc., with $579,030,642

2. Ancira Enterprises Inc., $462,835,000

3. Mike Shaw Automotive, $217,198,539

4. Cable-Dahmer Chevrolet Inc., $166,629,508

5. Elder Automotive Group, $165,066,874

6. Headquarter Toyota, $162,648,650

7. Allan Vigil Ford Lincoln Inc., $120,335,492

8. Miami Automotive Retail Inc., $97,613,900

9. Gus Machado Ford Inc., $92,450,000

10. Paul Young Co., $80,460,239

Source: *Hispanic Business*, Hispanic Business 500 (annual), June 2011.

2928 ■ LARGEST HISPANIC COMPANIES, 2010

Ranked by: Revenue, in millions of dollars. **Remarks:** Also notes rank for previous year, location, CEO, type of business, and number of employees. **Number listed:** 500

1. Brightstar Corp., with $4,600 million

2. MasTec Inc., $2,308.03

3. The Related Group of Florida, $960.93

4. International Bancshares Corp., $677.55

5. Quirch Foods Co., $612.22

6. Greenway Ford Inc., $579.03

7. The Diaz Group, $557

8. Ruiz Foods Inc., $525

9. Group O Inc., $515.1

10. Genesis Networks Enterprises LLC, $485.21

Source: *Hispanic Business*, Hispanic Business 500 (annual), June 2011, p. 36+.

2929 ■ LARGEST HISPANIC CONSTRUCTION COMPANIES, 2010

Ranked by: Revenue, in dollars. **Remarks:** Also notes figures for previous year, percent change, and primary products and services. **Number listed:** 10

1. MasTec Inc., with $2,308,031,000

2. The Related Group of Florida, $960,927,911

3. Crossland Construction Co., $424,813,017

4. Thos. S. Byrne Ltd., $150,000,000

5. MCM, $128,475,000

6. CAPE Inc., $123,244,000

7. Northeast Remsco Construction Inc., $121,100,000

8. Azteca-Omega Group, $114,669,000

9. Bay Cities Paving & Grading Inc., $98,210,359

10. J2 Engineering Inc., $75,000,000

Source: *Hispanic Business*, Hispanic Business 500 (annual), June 2011, p. 56.

2930 ■ LARGEST HISPANIC ENERGY COMPANIES, 2010

Ranked by: Revenue, in dollars. **Remarks:** Also notes figures for previous year, percent change, and primary products and services. **Number listed:** 10

1. Venoco Inc., with $295,292,000

2. Petro Amigos Supply Inc., $253,000,000

3. The Plaza Group Inc., $198,000,000

4. PS Energy Group Inc., $132,870,078

5. Delta Fuel Co., $55,742,236

6. Protec Inc., $15,700,000

7. Michigan Pipe & Valve, $7,383,000

8. PAZ Resources LLC, $4,668,553

9. Malaco International Inc., $4,500,000

10. Source Technologies LLC, $2,445,000

Source: *Hispanic Business*, Hispanic Business 500 (annual), June 2011, p. 55.

2931 ■ LARGEST HISPANIC FINANCE COMPANIES, 2010

Ranked by: Revenue, in dollars. **Remarks:** Also notes figures for previous year, percent change, and primary products and services. **Number listed:** 10

1. International Bancshares Corp., with $677,553,000

2. Pan-American Life Insurance Co., $455,000,000

3. Fred Loya Insurance, $433,671,907

4. BMI Financial Group Inc., $227,200,000

5. First Equity Mortgage Bankers Inc., $194,657,000

6. Bankers Healthcare Group Inc., $130,682,928

7. TELACU Industries Inc., $130,000,000

8. Manuel Lujan Insurance Inc., $105,046,048

9. Jules & Associates Inc., $95,600,000

10. Falcon International Bank, $52,480,000

Source: *Hispanic Business*, Hispanic Business 500 (annual), June 2011, p. 55.

2932 ■ LARGEST HISPANIC MANUFACTURING COMPANIES, 2010

Ranked by: Revenue, in dollars. **Remarks:** Also notes figures for previous year, percent change, and primary products and services. **Number listed:** 10

1. The Diez Group, with $557,000,000

2. Ruiz Foods Inc., $525,000,000

3. Lopez Foods Inc., $359,086,000

4. HUSCO International Inc., $250,000,000

5. Gusto Packing Co., $235,000,000

6. Ole Mexican Foods Inc., $194,000,000

7. The Ideal Group Inc., $141,472,115

8. Dynaric Inc., $122,000,000

9. Roses Southwest Papers Inc., $91,000,000

10. La Tortilla Factory Inc., $48,000,000

Source: *Hispanic Business*, Hispanic Business 500 (annual), June 2011, p. 56.

2933 ■ LARGEST HISPANIC-OWNED BUSINESSES IN DETROIT, 2010

Ranked by: Revenue, in millions of dollars. **Remarks:** Also notes contact information, majority owner, figures for previous year, percent change, number of local employees for current and previous year, percent Hispanic-owned, and type of business. **Number listed:** 11

1. The Diez Group, with $557 million
2. Troy Motors Inc., $376.6
3. Vision Information Technologies Inc., $230
4. The Ideal Group Inc., $97.1
5. Gonzalez Design Group, $78
6. PMA Consultants LLC, $34.7
7. Industrial Control Repair Inc., $28
8. ASG Renaissance LLC, $22.9
9. Aztec Manufacturing Corp., $22
10. Alliance Technology Solutions LLC, $17.7

Source: *Crain's Detroit Business*, Book of Lists (annual), December 26, 2011, p. 41.

2934 ■ LARGEST HISPANIC-OWNED BUSINESSES IN SUBURBAN CHICAGO, 2010

Ranked by: Revenue, in millions of dollars. **Remarks:** Also notes location, CEO, number of employees, and type of business. **Number listed:** 34

1. Group O Inc., with $515.1 million
2. Gusto Packing Co., $235
3. Cardenas Marketing Network, $48.49
4. United Building Maintenance Inc., $42.62
5. La Bodega Ltd., $23.3
6. La Hacienda Brands Inc., $23
7. Cano Container Corp., $22
8. A.L.L. Masonry Construction Co., $18.53
9. Primera Engineers Ltd., $18.2
10. 7Search.com, $18.15

Source: *Daily Herald Business Ledger*, Top Suburan Hispanic-Owned Businesses (annual), August 22, 2011, p. 18.

2935 ■ LARGEST HISPANIC-OWNED COMPANIES IN NEW MEXICO, 2010

Ranked by: Revenue, in millions of dollars. **Remarks:** Also notes rank in the overall *Hispanic 500*. **Number listed:** 20

1. Manuel Lujan Insurance Inc., with $105.05 million
2. Roses Southwest Papers Inc., $91
3. Holman's Inc., $48.25
4. David Montoya Construction inc., $45
5. Abba Technologies Inc., $41.5
6. A-Tech Corp., $40.24
7. L & M Technologies Inc., $34.5
8. Star Paving Co., $28.12
9. Integrated Control Systems Inc., $21.5
10. Service Electric Co., $15

Source: *Hispanic Business*, Top 20 Hispanic-Owned Companies in New Mexico, 2012, p. 6.

2936 ■ LARGEST HISPANIC-OWNED COMPANIES IN VIRGINIA, 2011

Ranked by: Revenue, in millions of dollars. **Remarks:** Also notes rank in the overall *Hispanic 500*. **Number listed:** 15

1. MicroTech LLC, with $331.11 million
2. MVM Inc., $214.55

3. The Centech Group Inc., $152.31
4. Dynaric Inc., $122
5. Geologics Corp., $58
6. Knowledge Information Solutions Inc., $50
7. Computing Technologies Inc., $48.82
8. SCI Consulting Services Inc., $47
9. Engineering Services Network Inc., $36.79
10. Priority One Services Inc., $33.4

Source: *Hispanic Business*, Top 15 Hispanic-Owned Companies in Virginia, March 2012, p. 8.

2937 ■ LARGEST HISPANIC RETAIL COMPANIES, 2010

Ranked by: Revenue, in dollars. **Remarks:** Also notes figures for previous year, percent change, and primary products and services. **Number listed:** 10

1. Navarro Discount Pharmacies, with $319,500,000
2. Mid-Atlantic Petroleum Properties LLC, $247,500,000
3. Sterling Computers Corp., $156,576,013
4. Norsan Group, $120,000,000
5. Holman's Inc., $48,249,000
6. Cuellar LLC, $43,765,000
7. Puente Enterprises Inc., $34,618,867
8. Everglades Steel Corp. and Medley Steel Corp., $31,927,904
9. Camiceria 3 Hermanos Inc., $29,700,000
10. Office Solutions Business Products & Services Inc., $25,200,000

Source: *Hispanic Business*, Hispanic Business 500 (annual), June 2011, p. 58.

2938 ■ LARGEST HISPANIC SERVICE COMPANIES, 2010

Ranked by: Revenue, in dollars. **Remarks:** Also notes figures for previous year, percent change, and primary products and services. **Number listed:** 10

1. Genesis Networks Enterprises LLC, with $485,212,327
2. G & A Partners, $410,001,621
3. MicroTech LLC, $331,107,229
4. SDI International Corp., $260,000,000
5. VisionIT, $230,000,000
6. MVM Inc., $214,551,000
7. Pinnacle Technical Resources, $187,000,000
8. MEI Technologies Inc., $152,933,035
9. The Centech Group Inc., $152,306,000
10. COLSA Corp., $149,893,990

Source: *Hispanic Business*, Hispanic Business 500 (annual), June 2011, p. 59.

2939 ■ LARGEST HISPANIC TRANSPORTATION COMPANIES, 2010

Ranked by: Revenue, in dollars. **Remarks:** Also notes figures for previous year, percent change, and primary products and services. **Number listed:** 10

1. Public Special Commodities Inc., with $28,000,000
2. Pan American Express Inc., $27,157,998
3. La Rosa Del Monte Express Inc., $27,000,000

4. J. L. Patterson & Associates, $19,600,000
5. Three Star Trucking Co., $12,342,327
6. Time Definite Services Inc., $11,800,000
7. LB Transportation Group & Omni Warehouse, $10,300,000
8. Golden Gate Air Freight Inc., $10,055,928
9. Leticia Inc., $9,720,000
10. Jess Diaz Trucking Inc., $9,640,000

Source: *Hispanic Business*, Hispanic Business 500 (annual), June 2011, p. 58.

2940 ■ LARGEST HISPANIC WHOLESALE COMPANIES, 2010

Ranked by: Revenue, in dollars. **Remarks:** Also notes figures for previous year, percent change, and primary products and services. **Number listed:** 10

1. Brightstar Corp., with $4,600,000,000
2. Quirch Foods Co., $612,223,000
3. Group O Inc., $515,100,000
4. OneSource Distributors Inc., $385,000,000
5. Blackstone Calling Card Inc., $249,296,775
6. Precision Trading Corp., $170,000,000
7. Bartlett Dairy Inc., $142,852,000
8. Refricenter of Miami Inc., $114,198,798
9. SolvChem Inc., $112,400,000
10. TriNet Communications Inc., $87,293,904

Source: *Hispanic Business*, Hispanic Business 500 (annual), June 2011, p. 59.

2941 ■ TOP HISPANIC EXPORTERS, 2010

Ranked by: Export sales, in millions of dollars. **Remarks:** Also notes location, CEO, number of employees, revenue, and percent of revenue from exports. **Number listed:** 50

1. Quirch Foods Co., with $210 million
2. Precision Trading Corp., $120
3. HUSCO International Inc., $112.5
4. Tire Group International, $54
5. Lucy's Tire Inc., $50
6. Andes Chemical Corp., $43.4
7. Century Metal & Supplies Inc., $32
8. The Plaza Group Inc., $29
9. The Intermarket Group, $27.6
10. CAPE Inc., $25.2

Source: *Hispanic Business*, Top 50 Exporters (annual), 2011, p. 42+.

2942 ■ TOP HISPANIC NONPROFIT ORGANIZATIONS IN THE U.S., 2011

Ranked by: Expenditures, in dollars. **Remarks:** Also notes principal executive, annual percent change in expenditures, and revenue. **Number listed:** 25

1. AltaMed Health Services Corp., with $188,512,873
2. Acacia Network, $96,000,000
3. The Aspira Association, $94,096,901
4. Chicanos Por La Causa Inc., $91,226,576
5. Southwest Key Programs, $74,113,465

6. Mexican American Opportunity Foundation, $71,668,017
7. La Clinica de la Raza, $71,408,169
8. Clinica Sierra Vista, $69,000,000
9. San Ysidro Health Center, $63,655,624
10. AVANCE Inc., $53,226,190

Source: *Hispanic Business*, Nonprofit 25 (annual), May 2012.

2943 ■ TOP U.S. HISPANIC ADVERTISING AGENCIES, 2010

Ranked by: Revenue, in thousands of dollars. **Remarks:** Also notes holding company affiliation, Web site, key officer, headquarters, and percent change from previous year. **Number listed:** 50

1. Dieste, with $37,000 thousand
2. GlobalHue, $34,148
3. Bravo Group, $30,000
4. Lopez Negrete Communications, $24,090
5. Vidal Partnership, $21,600
6. LatinWorks, $21,170
7. Conill, $19,710
8. Alma DDB, $19,044
9. Zubi Advertising Services, $18,500
10. De la Cruz Group, $15,713

Source: *Advertising Age*, Hispanic Fact Pack (annual), July 25, 2011, p. 54-57.

2944 ■ TOP U.S. HISPANIC MEDIA AGENCIES, 2010

Ranked by: Revenue from Hispanic media activities, in thousands of dollars. **Remarks:** Also notes parent company, network, Web site, key officer, and headquarters. **Number listed:** 15

1. Tapestry, with $16,995 thousand
2. MV42, $13,680
3. GlobalHue, $7,664
4. MEC Bravo, $7,650
5. OMD Latino, $5,700
6. Mindshare Multicultural, $5,600
7. Bromley Communications, $4,500
8. Conill, $4,025
9. Vidal Partnership, $3,931
10. LatinWorks, $3,900

Source: *Advertising Age*, Hispanic Fact Pack (annual), July 25, 2011, p. 58.

Hispanic Market

2945 ■ TOP ENGLISH-LANGUAGE CABLE TV PROGRAMS AMONG HISPANICS, 2011

Ranked by: Percentage of Hispanic TV households that tuned into program during the month of May. **Remarks:** Also notes network and average number of Hispanic households and viewers. **Number listed:** 10

1. "WWE," with 3.9%
2. "A.N.T. Farm," 3.8%
3. "NBA Playoffs" (conf. finals), 3.7%
4. "iCarly Movie: Shelby Marx," 3.6%
5. "The Boy Who Cried Werewolf," 3.3%
5. "Big Time Rish," 3.3%

7. "Victorious," 3.2%

7. "The Amazing World of Gumball," 3.2%

7. "NBA Playoffs," 3.2%

10. "High School Musical 2," 3%

Source: *Advertising Age*, Hispanic Fact Pack (annual), 2011, p. 22.

2946 ■ TOP ENGLISH-LANGUAGE PRIMETIME NETWORK TV PROGRAMS AMONG HISPANICS, 2011

Ranked by: Percentage of Hispanic TV households that tuned into program during the month of May. **Remarks:** Also notes network and average number of Hispanic households and viewers. **Number listed:** 10

1. "American Idol" (Wed.), with 8.1%

2. "American Idol" (Thurs.), 7.4%

2. "Dancing with the Stars," 7.4%

4. "Dancing with the Stars" (Results), 6.7%

5. "Glee," 5%

6. "The Voice," 4.9%

7. "Modern Family, 4.6%

8. "Dancing with the Stars" (Tue.), 4.4%

9. "So You Think You Can Dance," 4.3%

10. " Grey's Anatomy," 4.1%

Source: *Advertising Age*, Hispanic Fact Pack (annual), 2011, p. 20.

2947 ■ TOP HISPANIC LOCAL TV MARKETS, 2010

Ranked by: Number of Hispanic television households. **Remarks:** Also notes total number of households, and Hispanic as a percentage of total households. **Number listed:** 10

1. Los Angeles, CA, with 1,893,810 households

2. New York, NY, 1,276,130

3. Miami-Fort Lauderdale, FL, 690,640

4. Houston, TX, 586,120

5. Dallas-Fort Worth, TX, 526,760

6. Chicago, IL, 501,090

7. San Antonio, TX, 400,710

8. Phoenix, AZ, 398,750

9. San Francisco-Oakland, CA, 393,530

10. Harlingen, TX, 297,250

Source: *Advertising Age*, Hispanic Fact Pack (annual), 2011, p. 18.

2948 ■ TOP HISPANIC MAGAZINES, 2010

Ranked by: Measured advertising expenditures, in thousands of dollars. **Remarks:** Also notes parent company and annual percent change. **Number listed:** 10

1. *People en Espanol*, with $47,444 thousand

2. *Latina*, $27,888

3. *Ser Padres*, $15,061

4. *TV y Novelas*, $14,190

5. *Vanidades*, $12,807

6. *Siempre Mujer*, $11,994

7. *TV Notas*, $8,236

8. *Ser Padres Espera*, $4,514

9. *Hispanic Business*, $4,256

10. *Cosmopolitan en Espanol*, $3,304

Source: *Advertising Age*, Hispanic Fact Pack (annual), 2011, p. 26.

2949 ■ TOP HISPANIC NEWSPAPERS, 2010

Ranked by: Measured advertising expenditures, in thousands of dollars. **Remarks:** Also notes annual percent change. **Number listed:** 10

1. *El Nuevo Herald* (Miami), with $56,528 thousand

2. *El Diario La Prensa* (New York), $25,174

3. *Chicago Hoy*, $25,118

4. *La Opinion* (Los Angeles), $24,943

5. *El Diario* (Mexico), $23,048

6. *Washington Hispanic*, $8,263

7. *El Norte* (El Paso, TX), $8,009

8. *La Raza* (Chicago), $7,793

9. *El Sentinel* (Miami-Ft. Lauderdale), $7,765

10. *Al Dia* (Dallas), $6,742

Source: *Advertising Age*, Hispanic Fact Pack (annual), 2011, p. 27.

2950 ■ TOP HISPANIC TV NETWORKS, 2011

Ranked by: Percentage of Hispanic TV households that tuned into network during the period from April 25, 2011 to May 29, 2011. **Remarks:** Also notes number of Hispanic households and viewers. **Number listed:** 12

1. Univision, with 15%

2. Telemundo, 6.3%

3. Fox, 3.3%

4. ABC, 3.2%

5. TeleFutura, 2.4%

6. CBS, 2.1%

7. NBC, 1.9%

8. CW, 1.3%

9. Azteca America, 1.1%

10. Estrella TV, 1%

Source: *Advertising Age*, Hispanic Fact Pack (annual), 2011, p. 24.

2951 ■ TOP SOCIAL NETWORKING SITES AMONG HISPANIC USERS, 2011

Ranked by: Number of unique visitors, in thousands. **Remarks:** Also notes percent reach and Hispanic composition. **Number listed:** 10

1. Facebook, with 22,772 thousand visitors

2. MySpace, 5,582

3. Windows Live Profile, 3,540

4. Twitter, 3,387

5. LinkedIn, 2,964

6. Yahoo! Pulse, 2,179

7. DeviantArt, 1,418

8. MyLife, 1,369

9. Tumblr, 1,031

10. Badoo, 745

Source: *Advertising Age*, Hispanic Fact Pack (annual), July 25, 2011, p. 32.

2952 ■ TOP SPANISH-FORMATTED RADIO STATIONS, 2010

Ranked by: Average number of listeners per quarter-hour. **Remarks:** Also notes format, owner, and weekly time spent listening. **Number listed:** 10

1. WSKQ-FM (New York), with 55,900 listeners
2. KLVE-FM (Los Angeles), 43,500
3. WPAT-FM (New York), 40,200
4. WXNY-FM (New York), 38,200
5. KSCA-FM (Los Angeles), 36,200
6. KLAX-FM (Los Angeles), 33,100
7. KBUE-FM (Los Angeles), 30,400
8. KLNO-FM (Dallas-Ft. Worth, TX), 28,800
9. KLYY-FM (Riverside, CA), 27,800
10. KRCD-FM (Inglewood, CA), 27,700

Source: *Advertising Age*, Hispanic Fact Pack (annual), 2011, p. 28.

2953 ■ TOP SPANISH-LANGUAGE CABLE NETWORKS, 2011

Ranked by: Cable TV coverage as a percent of all Hispanic TV households. **Remarks:** Also notes parent company and share as a percent of Hispanic cable households. **Number listed:** 7

1. Galavision, with 71.3%
2. MTV Tr3s, 46.1%
3. Mun2, 53.3%
4. Fox Deportes, 44.6%
5. ESPN Deportes, 39%
6. Discovery en Espanol, 30.1%
7. Gol TV, 24.2%

Source: *Advertising Age*, Hispanic Fact Pack (annual), 2011, p. 24.

2954 ■ TOP SPANISH-LANGUAGE CABLE TV PROGRAMS AMONG HISPANICS, 2011

Ranked by: Percentage of Hispanic TV households that tuned into program during the month of May. **Remarks:** Also notes network and average number of Hispanic households and viewers. **Number listed:** 10

1. "UEFA Champions League" (Final), with 6.2%
2. "UEFA Champions League" (Match 3), 3.1%
3. "UEFA Champions League" (Match 2), 3%
4. "El Chavo del Ocho" (6:30 p.m.), 2.6%
5. "El Chavo del Ocho" (6:00 p.m.), 2.4%
6. "UEFA Champions League" (Match 4), 2%
7. "El Chavo del Ocho" (7:30 p.m.), 1.9%
8. "UEFA Champions League" (Final Preview), 1.8%
8. "Copa Libertadores" (Game 9), 1.8%
8. "Copa Libertadores" (Game 4), 1.8%

Source: *Advertising Age*, Hispanic Fact Pack (annual), 2011, p. 22.

2955 ■ TOP SPANISH-LANGUAGE PRIMETIME NETWORK TV PROGRAMS AMONG HISPANICS, 2011

Ranked by: Percentage of Hispanic TV households that tuned into program during the month of May. **Remarks:** Also notes network and average number of Hispanic households and viewers. **Number listed:** 10

1. "Triunfo del Amor" (Thurs.), with 21.4%
2. "Triunfo del Amor" (Mon.), 21.2%
3. "Triunfo del Amor" (Wed.), 20.8%
3. "Triunfo del Amor" (Tue.), 20.8%

5. "Triunfo del Amor" (Fri.), 18.9%
6. "Teresa" (Wed.), 18.3%
7. "Teresa" (Thurs.), 18%
8. "Teresa" (Mon.), 17.6%
9. "Nuestra Belleza Latina" (Sun.), 17.5%
10. "Teresa" (Tue.), 17.3%

Source: *Advertising Age*, Hispanic Fact Pack (annual), 2011, p. 20.

2956 ■ TOP WEB PROPERTIES AMONG HISPANIC USERS, 2011

Ranked by: Number of unique visitors, in thousands. **Remarks:** Also notes percent reach and Hispanic composition. **Number listed:** 10

1. Univision Communications, with 3,340 thousand visitors
2. Yahoo! en Espanol, 1,916
3. Terra - Telefonica, 1,906
4. MSN Latino, 1,704
5. Televisa Interactive Media, 963
6. AOL Latino, 723
7. Orange sites, 636
8. Batanga, 581
9. Musica.com, 580
10. ImpreMedia Network, 392

Source: *Advertising Age*, Hispanic Fact Pack (annual), July 25, 2011, p. 34.

Hispanics
See also: **Hispanic Market**

2957 ■ MOST INFLUENTIAL HISPANIC DIRECTORS, 2012

Ranked by: Ranking lists Hispanic individuals who serve as board members of Fortune 500 companies. **Remarks:** Specific scores not included; directors are listed alphabetically, not ranked. Also notes board(s). To qualify, individuals must be a U.S. citizen of Hispanic descent who sits on the board of directors of a *Fortune 500* company. **Number listed:** 95

1. Arcilia C. Acosta
2. Fernando Aguirre
3. Humberto Alfonso
4. Donna M. Alvarado
5. Linda G. Alvarado
6. Aida Alvarez
7. Jose Alvarez
8. Ralph Alvarez
9. Dan Arvizu
10. Mario L. Baeza

Source: *Hispanic Business*, Boardroom Elite (annual), 2012, p. 33+.

2958 ■ MOST INFLUENTIAL HISPANIC EXECUTIVES, 2012

Ranked by: Score based on impact and influence. **Remarks:** Specific scores not included; executives are listed, not ranked. Also notes title and comments. **Number listed:** 25

1. Armando Olivera (Florida Power & Light)
2. Grace Lieblein (GM do Brasil)

3. Darren Rebelez (7-Eleven)
4. Robert Rodriguez (Denny's Corp.)
5. Toby Redshaw (American Express)
6. Geisha Williams (Pacific Gas & Electric)
7. Daniel Ayala (Wells Fargo)
8. Mike Garcia (Omni Hotels)
9. Grace Puma (PepsiCo)
10. Patrick Apodaca (PNM Resources)

Source: *Hispanic Business*, Corporate Elite (annual), 2012, p. 26-31.

2959 ■ MOST INFLUENTIAL HISPANICS IN DIVERSITY, 2011

Ranked by: Score for Hispanics of U.S. citizenship that have had recent impact in promoting diversity in business operations. **Remarks:** Scores not provided; individuals are listed alphabetically, not ranked. Also notes title and comments. **Number listed:** 31

1. Luisa Acosta-Franco (Farmers Insurance)
2. Maria Arias (Comcast)
3. Raymond Arroyo (Aetna)
4. Theresa Barrera (Wal-Mart)
5. Lorraine Cortes-Vazquez (AARP)
6. Monica Diaz (Microsoft)
7. Ana Duarte McCarthy (Citi)
8. Emilio Egea (Prudential Financial)
9. Mike Escobar (Allstate)
10. Grace Figueredo (Hartford Financial Services Group)

Source: *Hispanic Business*, Top 100 Influentials (annual), October 2011, p. 20-28.

2960 ■ MOST INFLUENTIAL HISPANICS IN U.S. ACADEMICS, 2011

Ranked by: Score for Hispanics of U.S. citizenship that have had recent and national impact and whose achievement inspire other Hispanics to similar endeavors. **Remarks:** Scores not provided; individuals are listed alphabetically, not ranked. Also notes title and comments. **Number listed:** 8

1. Alfredo Artiles (Arizona State U)
2. Luis Fraga (U of Washington)
3. Patricia Gandara (UCLA)
4. Laura Gomez (UCLA School of Law)
5. Carmen Heredia-Lopez (Chicago Public Schools)
6. Darline Robles (U of Southern CA)
7. Carlos Santiago (Hispanic College Fund)
8. Zuleyma Tang-Martinez (U of Missouri, St. Louis

Source: *Hispanic Business*, Top 100 Influentials (annual), October 2011, p. 28+.

2961 ■ MOST INFLUENTIAL HISPANICS IN U.S. ARTS AND ENTERTAINMENT, 2011

Ranked by: Score for Hispanics of U.S. citizenship that have had recent and national impact and whose achievement inspire other Hispanics to similar endeavors. **Remarks:** Scores not provided; individuals are listed alphabetically, not ranked. Also notes title and comments. **Number listed:** 6

1. Joaquin Alvardo (American Public Media/ Minnesota Public Radio)

2. Lino Garcia (ESPN Deportes
3. Fernando Garibay (Interscope Records)
4. Sofia Ioannou (Viacom)
5. Alex Meruelo (owner, Atlanta Hawks)
6. Jose Tillan (Tr3s: MTV musica y Mas)

Source: *Hispanic Business*, Top 100 Influentials (annual), October 2011, p. 30+.

2962 ■ MOST INFLUENTIAL HISPANICS IN THE U.S. CORPORATE WORLD, 2011

Ranked by: Score for Hispanics of U.S. citizenship that have had recent and national impact and whose achievement inspire other Hispanics to similar endeavors. **Remarks:** Scores not provided; individuals are listed alphabetically, not ranked. Also notes title and comments. **Number listed:** 30

1. Benny Agosto Jr. (Watkins, Nichols, et al)
2. Fernando Aguirre (Chiquita)
3. Jose Armario (McDonald's)
4. Alex Cabanas (Benchmark Hospitality)
5. William Candelaria (Colt & Mosle)
6. Nelson Diaz (Dilworth Paxson)
7. Christina Estrada (Aramark)
8. Henry Fernandez (USA Funds)
9. Michael Fernandez (Cargill)
10. Rosanna Fiske (Public Relations Society of America)

Source: *Hispanic Business*, Top 100 Influentials (annual), October 2011, p. 32+.

2963 ■ MOST INFLUENTIAL HISPANICS IN U.S. GOVERNMENT, 2011

Ranked by: Score for Hispanics of U.S. citizenship that have had recent and national impact and whose achievement inspire other Hispanics to similar endeavors. **Remarks:** Scores not provided; individuals are listed alphabetically, not ranked. Also notes title and comments. **Number listed:** 20

1. Mayra Elvarez (US Dept. of Health & Human Svcs.)
2. Xavier Becerra (CA representative)
3. Marty Castro (US Commission on Civil Rights)
4. Edward Davila (US District Court judge)
5. Manny Diaz (former mayor, Miami)
6. Carmen Espinosa (Appellate Court judge)
7. Juan Carcia III (Asst. Secretary of the Navy)
8. Arlene Gonzalez-Sanchez (NY state Office of Alcoholism & Substance Abuse Services)
9. Carmen Lomellin (Org. of American States)
10. P. David Lopez (US Equal Employment Opportunity Commission

Source: *Hispanic Business*, Top 100 Influentials (annual), October 2011, p. 38+.

Hispanics—Employment

2964 ■ TOP U.S. COMPANIES FOR LATINOS, 2011

Ranked by: Score based on mentoring, employee-resource groups, diversity training, communications, and demographics in the workplace. **Remarks:** Specific scores not provided. To qualify, companies must have more than 1,000 U.S. employees. **Number listed:** 10

1. Colgate-Palmolive Co.
2. Kaiser Permanente
3. Sodexo
4. Automatic Data Processing Inc.
5. Procter & Gamble Co.
6. AT&T Inc.
7. J. C. Penney Co., Inc.
8. Deloitte LLP
9. Pacific Gas & Electric Co. (PG & E)
10. Ernst & Young LLP

Source: *DiversityInc*, Top 50 (annual), 2011, p. 96.

Hockey

2965 ■ MOST VALUABLE TEAMS IN THE NATIONAL HOCKEY LEAGUE, 2010-2011

Ranked by: Total value during the season, in millions of dollars. **Remarks:** Also notes operating income and percent change in value from previous year. **Number listed:** 30

1. Toronto Maple Leafs, with $521 million
2. New York Rangers, $507
3. Montreal Canadiens, $445
4. Detroit Red Wings, $336
5. Boston Bruins, $325
6. Chicago Blackhawks, $306
7. Vancouver Canucks, $300
8. Philadelphia Flyers, $290
9. Pittsburgh Penguins, $264
10. Los Angeles Kings, $232

Source: *Forbes*, NHL Team Valuations (annual), December 19, 2011, p. 26.

2966 ■ WEALTHIEST OWNERS OF NHL TEAMS, 2010-2011

Ranked by: Wealth, in billions of dollars. **Number listed:** 3

1. Philip Anschutz (LA Kings), with $7 billion
2. Stan Kroenke (CO Avalanche), $3.2
2. Ron Burkle (Pittsburgh Penguins), $3.2

Source: *Forbes*, NHL Team Valuations (annual), December 19, 2011, p. 26.

Holding Companies

2967 ■ FRANCE'S MOST VALUABLE DIVERSIFIED HOLDING COMPANY BRANDS, 2011

Ranked by: Brand value, in millions of U.S. dollars. **Remarks:** Also notes rank within the *Global 500* for current and previous year, figures for current and previous year, and brand rating. Ranking is available online only. **Number listed:** 2

1. Louis Vuitton, with $4,961 million
2. Dior, $2,540

Source: *Global 500*, (annual), Brand Finance plc, March 2012.

2968 ■ LARGEST HOLDING AND INVESTMENT OFFICE BY EMPLOYEES, 2010

Ranked by: Total number of employees. **Remarks:** Also notes contact information for headquarters, number of employees at headquarters, revenue, rank by revenue, and primary SIC code. **Number listed:** 96

1. Buck Holdings LP, with 79,801 employees
2. Sun Capital Partners Inc., 74,977
3. Willis Stein & Partners Management III LLC, 54,896
4. MacAndrews & Forbes Holdings Inc., 52,200
5. Bain Capital LLC, 49,000
6. 3G Capital Inc., 41,325
7. Kohlberg & Co., 36,060
8. FC-GEN Acquisition Inc., 35,000
9. Fortress Investment Group LLC, 32,063
10. KPLT Holdings Inc., 29,060

Source: *Business Rankings*, (annual), Dun & Bradstreet Inc., 2011, p. VI.199-VI.201.

2969 ■ TOP CANADIAN MANAGEMENT COMPANIES, 2010

Ranked by: Revenue, in thousands of Canadian dollars (unless otherwise noted). **Remarks:** Also notes percent change from previous year. **Number listed:** 10

1. Power Corp. of Canada, with C$33,013,000 thousand
2. Onex Corp., C$24,311,000
3. Brookfield Asset Management Inc., C$13,796,000
4. TransCanada Corp., C$8,158,000
5. Jim Pattison Group, C$7,200,000
6. ATCO Ltd., C$3,483,700
7. Emera Inc., C$1,593,300
8. Avenir Energy, C$886,429
9. Stratos Global, C$648,553
10. SGF Mines, Materials, Energy & Environment, C$475,317

Source: *Report on Business Magazine*, Top 1000 Companies (annual), http://www.reportonbusiness.com, June 2011.

2970 ■ WORLD'S MOST VALUABLE DIVERSIFIED HOLDING COMPANY BRANDS, 2011

Ranked by: Brand value, in millions of U.S. dollars. **Remarks:** Also notes rank within the *Global 500* for current and previous year, figures for current and previous year, country, and brand rating. Ranking is available online only. **Number listed:** 3

1. Jardines, with $5,246 million
2. Louis Vuitton, $4,961
3. Dior, $2,540

Source: *Global 500*, (annual), Brand Finance plc, March 2012.

Home Automation

2971 ■ TOP BRANDS OF WHOLE-HOUSE AUTOMATION SYSTEMS, 2010

Ranked by: Popularity among *CE Pro 100* companies, in percent. **Number listed:** 5

1. Crestron, with 64%
2. Control4, 55%
3. Savant, 24%
4. AMX, 19%
5. Elan Home Systems, 12%

Source: *CE Pro*, Brand Analysis (annual), June 2011, p. 59.

Home-Based Businesses

2972 ■ TOP HOMEBASED FRANCHISES, 2011

Ranked by: Cumulative score, for systems that can be run from home, based on financial strength and stability, growth rate, size of the system, number of years in business, the length of time franchising, start-up costs, litigation, percentage of terminations, and whether the company provides financing. **Remarks:** Specific scores not provided. Also notes rank in the *Franchise 500*, type of business, start-up costs, number of franchised and company-owned units, and contact information. **Number listed:** 101

1. Vanguard Cleaning Systems
2. Servpro
3. Jan-Pro Franchising International Inc.
4. Jazzercise Inc.
5. Matco Tools
6. Stratus Building Solutions
7. Snap-on Tools
8. CleanNet USA Inc.
9. Bonus Building Care
10. System4

Source: *Entrepreneur*, Top Homebased Franchises (annual), June 2011, p. 109+.

Home Electronics

2973 ■ CHINA'S LARGEST CONSUMER ELECTRONICS COMPANIES OVERALL, 2011

Ranked by: Score based on revenue, profits, assets, and market capitalization. **Remarks:** Specific scores not provided. Also notes overall rank in the *Forbes 2000* and figures for each criterion. **Number listed:** 2

1. TCL Corp.
2. Great Wall Technology

Source: *Forbes*, Forbes 2000 (annual), http://www.forbes.com, May 7, 2012.

2974 ■ JAPAN'S LARGEST CONSUMER ELECTRONICS COMPANIES OVERALL, 2011

Ranked by: Score based on revenue, profits, assets, and market capitalization. **Remarks:** Specific scores not provided. Also notes overall rank in the *Forbes 2000* and figures for each criterion. **Number listed:** 8

1. Panasonic Corp.
2. Fujifilm Holdings Corp.
3. Sony Corp.
4. Nintendo Co., Ltd.
5. Sharp Corp.
6. Nikon Corp.
7. Konica Minolta Holdings Inc.
8. Olympus Corp.

Source: *Forbes*, Forbes 2000 (annual), http://www.forbes.com, May 7, 2012.

2975 ■ TOP BRANDS OF CONSUMER ELECTRONICS MOUNTS, 2010

Ranked by: Popularity among *CE Pro 100* companies, in percent. **Number listed:** 5

1. Chief, with 63%
2. OmniMount, 37%
3. Sanus, 35%
4. Peerless, 21%
5. SnapAV, 15%

Source: *CE Pro*, Brand Analysis (annual), June 2011, p. 58.

2976 ■ TOP BRANDS OF HOME ELECTRONICS LIFTS, 2010

Ranked by: Popularity among *CE Pro 100* companies, in percent. **Number listed:** 5

1. Auton, with 26%
2. Chief, 24%
3. Inca, 14%
4. Nexus 21, 11%
5. Electro Kinetics, 8%

Source: *CE Pro*, Brand Analysis (annual), June 2011, p. 58.

2977 ■ TOP BRANDS OF HOME ELECTRONICS POWER CONDITIONERS, 2010

Ranked by: Popularity among *CE Pro 100* companies, in percent. **Number listed:** 7

1. Furman, with 68%
1. Panamax, 68%
3. APC, 30%
4. Monster, 17%
5. Richard Gray's, 7%
6. Crestron, 6%
6. Tripp Lite, 6%

Source: *CE Pro*, Brand Analysis (annual), June 2011, p. 58.

2978 ■ TOP BRANDS OF HOME ELECTRONICS RACKS, 2010

Ranked by: Popularity among *CE Pro 100* companies, in percent. **Number listed:** 4

1. Middle Atlantic, with 86%
2. OmniMount, 16%
2. Sanus, 16%
4. SnapAV, 12%

Source: *CE Pro*, Brand Analysis (annual), June 2011, p. 58.

2979 ■ TOP BRANDS OF HOME REMOTE DIAGNOSTICS SYSTEMS, 2010

Ranked by: Popularity among *CE Pro 100* companies, in percent. **Number listed:** 4

1. Panamax/Furman, with 15%
2. Control4, 11%
2. Crestron, 11%
4. Ihiji, 6%

Source: *CE Pro*, Brand Analysis (annual), June 2011, p. 59.

2980 ■ TOP BRANDS OF INTERCOM SYSTEMS, 2010

Ranked by: Popularity among *CE Pro 100* companies, in percent. **Number listed:** 5

1. Legrand, with 20%
2. Panasonic, 16%

3. Crestron, 12%

4. Control4, 8%

5. M & S, 7%

Source: *CE Pro*, Brand Analysis (annual), June 2011, p. 58.

2981 ▪ TOP CONSUMER ELECTRONICS RETAILERS IN THE U.S. AND CANADA, 2011

Ranked by: Consumer electronics sales, in billions of U.S. dollars. **Remarks:** Also notes contact information, key personnel, whether company is public or private, rank and figures for previous year, percent change, total sales, number of stores, and comments. **Number listed:** 101

1. Dell Inc., with $35.35 billion

2. Hewlett-Packard Co., $32.16

3. Best Buy Co., Inc., $33.08

4. Wal-Mart Stores Inc., $20.2

5. Apple Computer Retail Stores, $13.2

6. Amazon.com Inc., $13.03

7. CDW Corp., $9.6

8. Staples Inc., $7.86

9. GameStop Corp., $7.24

10. Target Corp., $6.8

Source: *Dealerscope*, Top 101 CE Retailers (annual), March 2012, p. 70+.

2982 ▪ TOP CUSTOM ELECTRONICS INSTALLERS, 2011

Ranked by: Custom residential revenues, in dollars. **Remarks:** Also notes headquarters, number of installations, revenue per installation, number of employees, revenue per employee, number of years in business, outlook, and buying group. **Number listed:** 100

1. Best Buy/Geek Squad/Magnolia/AudioVisions, with $680,000,000

2. ADT Security Services, $162,500,000

3. Vivint, $51,140,000

4. Abt Electronics, $31,000,000

5. Guardian Protection Services, $26,397,806

6. Just One Touch/Video & Audio Center, $26,370,926

7. MODIA, $23,665,048

8. Audio Command Systems Inc., $21,500,000

9. Audio Video Systems, $16,989,450

10. Vision Systems Automation, $14,000,000

Source: *CE Pro*, CE Pro 100 (annual), May 2012, p. 44+.

2983 ▪ TOP CUSTOM ELECTRONICS RETAILERS, 2011

Ranked by: Installation revenue. **Remarks:** Specific figures not provided. **Number listed:** 6

1. Best Buy/Geek Squad/Magnolia/AudioVisions

2. Abt Electronics

3. Just One Touch/Video & Audio Center

4. MODIA

5. Hifi House

6. World Wide Stereo

Source: *CE Pro*, CE Pro 100 (annual), May 2012, p. 42.

2984 ▪ TOP RETAILERS OF CONSUMER ELECTRONICS AND MAJOR APPLIANCES, 2010

Ranked by: Sales of consumer electronics and major appliances, in millions of dollars. **Remarks:** Also notes breakdown by consumer electronics and major appliances, figures for previous year, and comments. **Number listed:** 100

1. Best Buy Co., Inc., with $34,363 million

2. Wal-Mart Stores Inc., $20,291

3. Sears Holdings Corp., $9,993

4. Apple Retail Stores, $8,655

5. Amazon.com Inc., $7,992

6. Target Corp., $6,678

7. Lowe's Companies Inc., $5,386

8. Costco Wholesale Corp., $5,178

9. GameStop Corp., $4,939

10. Dell Inc., $4,260

Source: *TWICE: This Week in Consumer Electronics*, Top 100 Retailers (annual), August 25, 2011, p. 2-10.

2985 ▪ TOP TRADITIONAL CUSTOM AUDIO/VIDEO INTEGRATORS, 2011

Ranked by: Revenue. **Remarks:** Specific figures not provided. **Number listed:** 10

1. Audio Command Systems Inc.

2. Audio Video Systems

3. Vision Systems Automation

4. Engineered Environments

5. Audio Interiors

6. Cyber Sound

7. DSI Entertainment Systems

8. Performance Imaging

9. Intech

10. ETC

Source: *CE Pro*, CE Pro 100 (annual), May 2012, p. 42.

2986 ▪ WORLD'S LARGEST CONSUMER ELECTRONICS COMPANIES OVERALL, 2011

Ranked by: Score based on revenue, profits, assets, and market capitalization. **Remarks:** Specific scores not provided. Also notes country, overall rank in the *Forbes 2000,* and figures for each criterion. **Number listed:** 12

1. Panasonic Corp.

2. Fujifilm Holdings Corp.

3. Sony Corp.

4. Nintendo Co., Ltd.

5. LG Electronics Inc.

6. Sharp Corp.

7. Nikon Corp.

8. Konica Minolta Holdings Inc.

9. Garmin Ltd.

10. Olympus Corp.

Source: *Forbes*, Forbes 2000 (annual), http://www.forbes.com, May 7, 2012.

2987 ▪ WORLD'S MOST ETHICAL CONSUMER ELECTRONICS COMPANIES, 2012

Ranked by: Score based on five criteria: ethics and compliance program; reputation, leadership, and innovation; governance; corporate citizenship and responsibility; and culture of ethics. **Remarks:** Specific scores not provided; companies are listed alphabetically, not ranked. **Number listed:** 4

1. AB Electrolux (Sweden)

2. Ricoh Corp. (Japan)

3. Texas Instruments (U.S.)

4. Xerox Corp. (U.S.)

Source: *Ethisphere Magazine*, World's Most Ethical Companies (annual), http://www.ethisphere.com, 2012.

Home Equity Loans

2988 ■ LARGEST S & LS BY HOME EQUITY LOANS, 2011

Ranked by: Total home equity loans, in thousands of dollars. **Remarks:** Also notes city, state, association type, and dollar and percent change from previous year. **Number listed:** 25

1. USAA FSB, with $7,186,730 thousand

2. Sovereign Bank NA, $5,384,873

3. E*Trade Bank, $4,006,571

4. Charles Schwab Bank, $3,508,807

5. Third Federal Savings & Loan Association of Cleveland, $2,207,259

6. People's United Bank, $1,848,931

7. OneWest Bank FSB, $1,741,892

8. State Farm Bank, FSB, $1,384,342

9. Ameriprise Bank, FSB, $1,081,649

10. BankAtlantic, $545,504

Source: *Highline Bank and S&L Quarterly, Dec. ed.*, 2011, p. V.60.

2989 ■ LARGEST U.S. BANKS BY HOME EQUITY LOANS, 2011

Ranked by: Total home equity loans, in thousands of dollars. **Remarks:** Also notes city, state, and dollar and percent change from previous year. **Number listed:** 25

1. Bank of America NA, with $100,934,352 thousand

2. Wells Fargo Bank NA, $95,198,000

3. J. P. Morgan Chase Bank NA, $77,976,000

4. Citibank NA Inc., $27,369,000

5. PNC Bank NA, $22,490,822

6. U.S. Bank NA, $16,217,905

7. SunTrust Banks Inc., $14,318,344

8. RBS Citizens NA, $14,032,182

9. Regions Bank, $11,723,205

10. Fifth Third Bank, $9,449,998

Source: *Highline Bank and S&L Quarterly, Dec. ed.*, 2011, p. I.52.

Home Furnishings

2990 ■ JAPAN'S MOST VALUABLE HOME FURNISHING BRANDS, 2011

Ranked by: Brand value, in millions of U.S. dollars. **Remarks:** Also notes rank within the *Global 500* for current and previous year, figures for current and previous year, and brand rating. Ranking is available online only. **Number listed:** 4

1. Sony, with $12,358 million

2. Panasonic, $9,233

3. Sharp, $5,584

4. PlayStation, $3,695

Source: *Global 500*, (annual), Brand Finance plc, March 2012.

2991 ■ WORLD'S MOST VALUABLE HOME FURNISHING BRANDS, 2011

Ranked by: Brand value, in millions of U.S. dollars. **Remarks:** Also notes rank within the *Global 500* for current and previous year, figures for current and previous year, country, and brand rating. Ranking is available online only. **Number listed:** 5

1. Sony, with $12,358 million

2. Panasonic, $9,233

3. Sharp, $5,584

4. PlayStation, $3,695

5. Haier, $2,428

Source: *Global 500*, (annual), Brand Finance plc, March 2012.

Home Furnishings Industry

2992 ■ TOP *FORTUNE 500* COMPANIES IN HOME EQUIPMENT AND FURNISHINGS, 2011

Ranked by: Revenue, in millions of dollars. **Remarks:** Also notes overall rank in the *Fortune 500;* profits; profits as a percentage of revenue; stockholders' equity; and rank by each criterion. **Number listed:** 4

1. Stanley Black & Decker Inc., with $10,438 million

2. Masco Corp., $7,560

3. Jarden Corp., $6,680

4. Newell Rubbermaid Inc., $5,923

Source: *Fortune*, Fortune 500 (annual), May 21, 2012, p. F-36.

2993 ■ TOP HOME FURNISHINGS VENDORS, 2010

Ranked by: Revenue, in millions of dollars. **Remarks:** Also notes rank and figures for previous year, percent change, and types of products. **Number listed:** 20

1. Whirlpool Corp., with $9,734 million

2. AB Electrolux, $4,696

3. Newell Rubbermaid Inc., $2,018

4. Jarden Corp., $1,321

5. Furniture Brands International Inc., $1,160

6. La-Z-Boy Inc., $1,159

7. Hunter Douglas, $955

8. Sealy Corp., $951

9. Tempur-Pedic International Inc., $772

10. NACCO Housewares Group, $735

Source: *HFN: Home Furnishings News*, Top Vendors (annual), June 2011, p. 21.

2994 ■ TOP WINDOW AND FLOOR COVERING FRANCHISES, 2012

Ranked by: Cumulative score based on financial strength and stability, growth rate, size of the system, number of years in business, the length of time franchising, start-up costs, litigation, percentage of terminations, and whether the company provides financing. **Remarks:** Specific scores not provided. Also notes overall rank within the *Franchise 500,* contact information, description, year founded, year started franchising, states where registered, available U.S. regions, where seeking foreign expansion, number of franchised and company-owned units for past three years, start-up costs, franchise fees, royalty fees, and type of financing available. **Number listed:** 2

1. Budget Blinds Inc.
2. Floor Coverings International

Source: *Entrepreneur*, Franchise 500 (annual), January 2012, p. 178-179.

2995 ■ WORLD'S MOST ADMIRED HOME EQUIPMENT AND FURNISHINGS COMPANIES, 2012

Ranked by: Score, on a scale of 10, based on a survey of executives, directors, and securities analysts of companies within their own industry on eight criteria: innovation, financial soundness, employee talent, use of corporate assets, long-term investment value, social responsibility, quality of management, and quality of products/services. **Remarks:** Specific scores not provided. Also notes rank for previous year. **Number listed:** 6

1. Whirlpool Corp.
2. Tupperware Brands Corp.
3. Fortune Brands Home & Security
4. AB Electrolux
5. Stanley Black & Decker Inc.
6. Steelcase Inc.

Source: *Fortune*, World's Most Admired Companies (annual), March 19, 2012, p. 148.

Home Furnishings Stores

2996 ■ LARGEST HOME FURNITURE, FURNISHINGS, AND EQUIPMENT STORES BY EMPLOYEES, 2010

Ranked by: Total number of employees. **Remarks:** Also notes contact information for headquarters, number of employees at headquarters, revenue, rank by revenue, and primary SIC code. **Number listed:** 239

1. Best Buy Co., Inc., with 180,000 employees
2. Bed Bath & Beyond Inc., 41,000
3. RadioShack Corp., 36,700
4. Williams-Sonoma Inc., 26,000
5. Hollywood Entertainment Corp., 19,000
6. Linens Investors LLC, 17,501
7. Pier 1 Imports Inc., 16,200
8. Pier 1 Licensing Inc., 13,500
9. Pier 1 Imports (U.S.) Inc., 12,571
10. Bealls Inc., 10,400

Source: *Business Rankings*, (annual), Dun & Bradstreet Inc., 2011, p. VI.149-VI.154.

2997 ■ LARGEST HOME FURNITURE, FURNISHINGS, AND EQUIPMENT STORES BY SALES, 2010

Ranked by: Total revenue, in dollars. **Remarks:** Also notes contact information for headquarters, number of employees at headquarters and overall, rank by employees, and primary SIC code. **Number listed:** 239

1. Best Buy Co., Inc., with $49,694,000,000
2. Bed Bath & Beyond Inc., $7,828,793,000
3. RadioShack Corp., $4,472,700,000
4. Williams-Sonoma Inc., $3,102,704,000
5. Newegg Inc., $2,289,839,000
6. HHGregg Inc., $1,534,253,000
7. A. J. Richard & Sons Inc., $1,500,000,000

8. Pier 1 Imports Inc., $1,290,852,000
9. PC Mall Inc., $1,138,061,000
10. Beall's Inc., $1,132,675,000

Source: *Business Rankings*, (annual), Dun & Bradstreet Inc., 2011, p. V.149-V.154.

2998 ■ TOP HOME FURNISHINGS RETAILERS, 2010

Ranked by: Home furnishings revenue, in millions of dollars. **Remarks:** Also notes rank for previous year, headquarters, type of retailer, percent change from previous year, total retail revenue, home furnishings as a percent of total revenue, and number of stores. **Number listed:** 50

1. Wal-Mart Stores Inc., with $23,709.16 million
2. Target Corp., $12,804.1
3. Sears Holdings Corp., $10,628.29
4. Lowe's Companies Inc., $10,089.45
5. The Home Depot Inc., $8,796.03
6. Bed Bath & Beyond Inc., $8,758.5
7. CCA Global Partners, $4,940
8. The TJX Companies Inc., $4,223.87
9. Costco Wholesale Corp., $3,976.73
10. Macy's Inc., $3,600.43

Source: *HFN: Home Furnishings News*, Top Retailers (annual), August 2011, p. 12+.

Home Improvement Centers

2999 ■ LARGEST U.S. HOME IMPROVEMENT RETAILERS OVERALL, 2011

Ranked by: Score based on revenue, profits, assets, and market capitalization. **Remarks:** Specific scores not provided. Also notes overall rank in the *Forbes 2000* and figures for each criterion. **Number listed:** 4

1. The Home Depot Inc.
2. Lowe's Companies Inc.
3. The Sherwin-Williams Co.
4. Fastenal Co.

Source: *Forbes*, Forbes 2000 (annual), http://www.forbes.com, May 7, 2012.

3000 ■ TOP HOME IMPROVEMENT CHAINS, 2010

Ranked by: Sales, in billions of dollars. **Remarks:** Also notes headquarters and number of stores. **Number listed:** 10

1. The Home Depot Inc., with $68 billion
2. Lowe's Companies Inc., $49
3. ABC Supply Co., $4.1
4. Pro-Build Holdings Inc., $3.5
5. Menard Inc., $2.2
6. 84 Lumber Co., $1.5
7. Stock Building Supply Inc., $0.9
8. Sears Hardware Stores, $0.7
8. Sutherland Lumber Co., $0.7
8. Orchard Supply Hardware, $0.7

Source: *Hardware Retailing*, Annual Report, November 2011, p. 34.

3001 ■ TOP HOME MERCHANDISE RETAILERS, 2010

Ranked by: Total sales, in millions of dollars. **Remarks:** Also notes headquarters, type of retailer, figures for previous year, percent change, do-it-yourself market share, and number of units. **Number listed:** 300

1. The Home Depot Inc., with $67,997 million
2. Lowe's Companies Inc., $48,815
3. CCA Global Partners, $10,100
4. Menard Inc., $8,300
5. The Sherwin-Williams Co., $4,381.2
6. Tractor Supply Co., $3,638.3
7. Pro-Build Holdings Inc., $3,500
8. Fastenal Co., $2,269.5
9. Abbey Carpet & Floor, $2,100
10. Dal-Tile, $1,922.7

Source: *Home Channel News*, Top 300 Retailers (annual), June 2011.

3002 ■ TOP U.S. HOME IMPROVEMENT RETAILERS BY SALES, 2010

Ranked by: Sales volume, in thousands of dollars. **Remarks:** Also notes comparable-store sales and sales per store. **Number listed:** 5

1. The Home Depot Inc., with $60,194,000 thousand
2. Lowe's Companies Inc., $48,175,000
3. True Value, $16,738,000
4. Ace Hardware, $9,101,000
5. Menard Inc., $8,032,000

Source: *Stores*, Top 100 Retailers (annual), July 2011, p. s14.

3003 ■ UNITED KINGDOM'S LARGEST HOME IMPROVEMENT RETAILERS OVERALL, 2011

Ranked by: Score based on revenue, profits, assets, and market capitalization. **Remarks:** Specific scores not provided. Also notes country, overall rank in the *Forbes 2000,* and figures for each criterion. **Number listed:** 2

1. Kingfisher plc
2. Travis Perkins plc

Source: *Forbes*, Forbes 2000 (annual), http://www.forbes.com, May 7, 2012.

3004 ■ WORLD'S LARGEST HOME IMPROVEMENT RETAILERS OVERALL, 2011

Ranked by: Score based on revenue, profits, assets, and market capitalization. **Remarks:** Specific scores not provided. Also notes country, overall rank in the *Forbes 2000,* and figures for each criterion. **Number listed:** 6

1. The Home Depot Inc.
2. Lowe's Companies Inc.
3. Kingfisher plc
4. The Sherwin-Williams Co.
5. Fastenal Co.
6. Travis Perkins plc

Source: *Forbes*, Forbes 2000 (annual), http://www.forbes.com, May 7, 2012.

Home Improvement Industry

3005 ■ LARGEST EXTERIOR REMODELING COMPANIES, 2010

Ranked by: Sales from roofing, siding, windows, sunrooms, and decks, in dollars. **Remarks:** Also notes location, website, key executive, website, number of jobs, and breakdown by type of service. **Number listed:** 200

1. Window World Inc., with $371,728,092
2. Champion Window Manufacturing & Supply Co., $316,970,124
3. Power Home Remodeling Group, $129,279,367
4. ABC Inc., dba ABC Seamless, $61,000,000
5. Castle, the Window People Inc., $55,627,892
6. Thompson Creek Window Co., $47,885,820
7. 1-800-Hansons, $46,159,920
8. United States Seamless, $39,086,736
9. True Home Value Inc., $38,005,036
10. Window World of Baton Rouge, $35,321,682

Source: *Qualified Remodeler*, Exterior 200 (annual), November 2011, p. 40+.

3006 ■ TOP MISCELLANEOUS HOME IMPROVEMENT FRANCHISES, 2012

Ranked by: Cumulative score based on financial strength and stability, growth rate, size of the system, number of years in business, the length of time franchising, start-up costs, litigation, percentage of terminations, and whether the company provides financing. **Remarks:** Specific scores not provided. Also notes overall rank within the *Franchise 500,* contact information, description, year founded, year started franchising, states where registered, available U.S. regions, where seeking foreign expansion, number of franchised and company-owned units for past three years, start-up costs, franchise fees, royalty fees, and type of financing available. **Number listed:** 6

1. Mr. Sandless Inc.
2. N-Hance
3. ShelfGenie Franchise Systems LLC
4. USA Insulation
5. Nite Time Decor Inc.
6. California Closets

Source: *Entrepreneur*, Franchise 500 (annual), January 2012, p. 180-181.

Home Inspection

3007 ■ TOP HOME INSPECTION FRANCHISES, 2012

Ranked by: Cumulative score based on financial strength and stability, growth rate, size of the system, number of years in business, the length of time franchising, start-up costs, litigation, percentage of terminations, and whether the company provides financing. **Remarks:** Specific scores not provided. Also notes overall rank within the *Franchise 500,* contact information, description, year founded, year started franchising, states where registered, available U.S. regions, where seeking foreign expansion, number of franchised and company-owned units for past three years, start-up costs, franchise fees, royalty fees, and type of financing available. **Number listed:** 5

1. AmeriSpec Home Inspection Services
2. Pillar To Post Inspection Services
3. HouseMaster Home Inspections
4. WIN Home Inspection
5. National Property Inspections

Source: *Entrepreneur*, Franchise 500 (annual), January 2012, p. 202-203.

Homosexuals—Employment

3008 ■ BEST ADVERTISING AND MARKETING COMPANIES FOR GAY AND LESBIAN EMPLOYEES, 2011

Ranked by: Score, on a scale of 100, based on how lesbian, gay, bisexual, and transgender (LGBT) employees are treated. Criteria include the equal employment opportunity policy, employment benefits, organizational LGBT competency, public engagement, and responsible citizenship. **Remarks:** In the event of ties, companies are listed alphabetically. Also notes headquarters, rank for previous year, score for each criterion, and rank among the *Fortune 1000* and *AmLaw 200.* **Number listed:** 6

1. Publicis Inc., with 90 points
1. WPP Group USA, 90
3. The Interpublic Group of Companies Inc., 85
3. Starcom MediaVest Group, 85
5. Valassis Communications Inc., 75
6. Omnicom Group Inc., 65

Source: *Human Rights Campaign,* Corporate Equality Index (annual), 2011, p. 68.

3009 ■ BEST AEROSPACE AND DEFENSE COMPANIES FOR GAY AND LESBIAN EMPLOYEES, 2011

Ranked by: Score, on a scale of 100, based on how lesbian, gay, bisexual, and transgender (LGBT) employees are treated. Criteria include the equal employment opportunity policy, employment benefits, organizational LGBT competency, public engagement, and responsible citizenship. **Remarks:** In the event of ties, companies are listed alphabetically. Also notes headquarters, rank for previous year, score for each criterion, and rank among the *Fortune 1000* and *AmLaw 200.* **Number listed:** 8

1. Lockheed Martin Corp., with 100 points
2. Raytheon Co., 100
3. Boeing Co., 85
3. General Dynamics Corp., 85
3. Honeywell International Inc., 85
6. Northrup Grumman Corp., 75
6. Rockwell Collins Inc., 75
8. Alliant Techsystems Inc., 35

Source: *Human Rights Campaign,* Corporate Equality Index (annual), 2011, p. 68.

3010 ■ BEST AIRLINE COMPANIES FOR GAY AND LESBIAN EMPLOYEES, 2011

Ranked by: Score, on a scale of 100, based on how lesbian, gay, bisexual, and transgender (LGBT) employees are treated. Criteria include the equal employment opportunity policy, employment benefits, organizational LGBT competency, public engagement, and responsible citizenship. **Remarks:** In the event of ties, companies are listed alphabetically. Also notes headquarters, rank for previous year, score for each criterion, and rank among the *Fortune 1000* and *AmLaw 200.* **Number listed:** 8

1. AMR Corp., with 100 points
1. United Continental Holdings Inc., 100
3. Alaska Air Group Inc., 90
3. Delta Air Lines Inc., 90
3. JetBlue Airways Corp., 90
3. Southwest Airlines Co., 90
3. Virgin America, 90
8. US Airways Group Inc., 85

Source: *Human Rights Campaign,* Corporate Equality Index (annual), 2011, p. 68.

3011 ■ BEST APPAREL, FASHION, TEXTILES, AND DEPARTMENT STORE COMPANIES FOR GAY AND LESBIAN EMPLOYEES, 2011

Ranked by: Score, on a scale of 100, based on how lesbian, gay, bisexual, and transgender (LGBT) employees are treated. Criteria include the equal employment opportunity policy, employment benefits, organizational LGBT competency, public engagement, and responsible citizenship. **Remarks:** In the event of ties, companies are listed alphabetically. Also notes headquarters, rank for previous year, score for each criterion, and rank among the *Fortune 1000* and *AmLaw 200.* **Number listed:** 7

1. Levi Strauss & Co., with 100 points
1. Nike Inc., 100
3. Kenneth Cole Productions Inc., 90
3. Macy's Inc., 90
5. Jones Apparel Group Inc., 70
6. L. L. Bean Inc., 65
7. Hanesbrands Inc., 60

Source: *Human Rights Campaign,* Corporate Equality Index (annual), 2011, p. 68.

3012 ■ BEST AUTOMOTIVE COMPANIES FOR GAY AND LESBIAN EMPLOYEES, 2011

Ranked by: Score, on a scale of 100, based on how lesbian, gay, bisexual, and transgender (LGBT) employees are treated. Criteria include the equal employment opportunity policy, employment benefits, organizational LGBT competency, public engagement, and responsible citizenship. **Remarks:** In the event of ties, companies are listed alphabetically. Also notes headquarters, rank for previous year, score for each criterion, and rank among the *Fortune 1000* and *AmLaw 200.* **Number listed:** 14

1. Chrysler LLC, with 100 points
1. Ford Motor Co., 100
1. Toyota Motor Sales USA Inc., 100
4. Volkswagen Group of America Inc., 90
5. Subaru of America Inc., 85
5. Visteon Corp., 85
5. General Motors Co., 85
8. Bridgestone Americas Holding Inc., 70
9. Hertz Global Holdings Inc., 65
10. Nissan North America Inc., 30

Source: *Human Rights Campaign,* Corporate Equality Index (annual), 2011, p. 68-69.

3013 ■ BEST BANKING AND FINANCIAL SERVICES COMPANIES FOR GAY AND LESBIAN EMPLOYEES, 2011

Ranked by: Score, on a scale of 100, based on how lesbian, gay, bisexual, and transgender (LGBT) employees are treated. Criteria include the equal employment opportunity policy, employment benefits, organizational LGBT competency, public engagement, and responsible citizenship. **Remarks:** In the event of ties, companies are listed alphabetically. Also notes headquarters, rank for previous year, score for each criterion, and rank among the *Fortune 1000* and *AmLaw 200.* **Number listed:** 55

1. American Express Co., with 100 points
1. Ameriprise Financial Inc., 100
1. Bank of America Corp., 100
1. Bank of New York Mellon Corp., 100
1. Barclays Capital Inc., 100

1. BMO Bankcorp Inc., 100

1. Capital One Financial Corp., 100

1. The Charles Schwab Corp., 100

1. Citigroup Inc., 100

1. Credit Suisse USA Inc., 100

1. Deutsche Bank AG, 100

1. Freddie Mac, 100

1. Goldman Sachs Group Inc., 100

Source: *Human Rights Campaign*, Corporate Equality Index (annual), 2011, p. 69-70.

3014 ■ BEST CHEMICALS AND BIOTECHNOLOGY COMPANIES FOR GAY AND LESBIAN EMPLOYEES, 2011

Ranked by: Score, on a scale of 100, based on how lesbian, gay, bisexual, and transgender (LGBT) employees are treated. Criteria include the equal employment opportunity policy, employment benefits, organizational LGBT competency, public engagement, and responsible citizenship. **Remarks:** In the event of ties, companies are listed alphabetically. Also notes headquarters, rank for previous year, score for each criterion, and rank among the *Fortune 1000*and *AmLaw 200*. **Number listed:** 10

1. Dow Chemical Co., with 100 points

1. E. I. du Pont de Nemours & Co., 100

1. Genentech Inc., 100

4. BASF Corp., 90

4. Bayer Corp., 90

4. Ecolab Inc., 90

7. Air Products & Chemicals Inc., 80

7. Monsanto Co., 80

9. PPG Industries Inc., 60

10. Praxair Inc., 50

Source: *Human Rights Campaign*, Corporate Equality Index (annual), 2011, p. 70-71.

3015 ■ BEST COMPANIES FOR GAY AND LESBIAN EMPLOYEES, 2011

Ranked by: Score, on a scale of 100, based on how lesbian, gay, bisexual, and transgender (LGBT) employees are treated. Criteria include the equal employment opportunity policy, employment benefits, organizational LGBT competency, public engagement, and responsible citizenship. **Remarks:** In the event of ties, companies are listed alphabetically. Also notes headquarters, rank for previous year, score for each criterion, and rank among the *Fortune 1000* and *AmLaw 200*. **Number listed:** 636

1. 3M Co., with 100 points

1. A. T. Kearney Inc., 100

1. AAA Northern California, Nevada, & Utah Insurance Exchange, 100

1. Abercrombie & Fitch Co., 100

1. Accenture Ltd., 100

1. Aetna Inc., 100

1. Akin, Gump, Strauss, Hauer & Feld LLP, 100

1. Alcatel-Lucent, 100

1. Alcoa Inc., 100

1. Alston & Bird LLP, 100

1. American Express Co., 100

1. Ameriprise Financial Inc., 100

1. AMR Corp., 100

Source: *Human Rights Campaign*, Corporate Equality Index (annual), 2011, p. 43-46.

3016 ■ BEST COMPANIES IN MISCELLANEOUS INDUSTRIES FOR GAY AND LESBIAN EMPLOYEES, 2011

Ranked by: Score, on a scale of 100, based on how lesbian, gay, bisexual, and transgender (LGBT) employees are treated. Criteria include the equal employment opportunity policy, employment benefits, organizational LGBT competency, public engagement, and responsible citizenship. **Remarks:** In the event of ties, companies are listed alphabetically. Also notes headquarters, rank for previous year, score for each criterion, and rank among the *Fortune 1000*and *AmLaw 200*. **Number listed:** 2

1. 3M Co., with 100 points

2. Imation Corp., 70

Source: *Human Rights Campaign*, Corporate Equality Index (annual), 2011, p. 83.

3017 ■ BEST COMPUTER AND DATA SERVICES COMPANIES FOR GAY AND LESBIAN EMPLOYEES, 2011

Ranked by: Score, on a scale of 100, based on how lesbian, gay, bisexual, and transgender (LGBT) employees are treated. Criteria include the equal employment opportunity policy, employment benefits, organizational LGBT competency, public engagement, and responsible citizenship. **Remarks:** Score, on a scale of 100, based on how lesbian, gay, bisexual, and transgender (LGBT) employees are treated. Criteria include the equal employment opportunity policy, employment benefits, organizational LGBT competency, public engagement, and responsible citizenship. **Number listed:** 10

1. Automatic Data Processing Inc., with 100 points

1. EMC Corp., 100

1. Hewlett-Packard Co., 100

4. Broadridge Financial Solutions Inc., 90

4. LexisNexis Group, 90

6. Computer Sciences Corp., 85

7. SRA International Inc., 45

8. Affiliated Computer Services Inc., 40

8. Unisys Corp., 40

10. Keane Inc., 25

Source: *Human Rights Campaign*, Corporate Equality Index (annual), 2011, p. 71.

3018 ■ BEST COMPUTER HARDWARE AND OFFICE EQUIPMENT COMPANIES FOR GAY AND LESBIAN EMPLOYEES, 2011

Ranked by: Score, on a scale of 100, based on how lesbian, gay, bisexual, and transgender (LGBT) employees are treated. Criteria include the equal employment opportunity policy, employment benefits, organizational LGBT competency, public engagement, and responsible citizenship. **Remarks:** In the event of ties, companies are listed alphabetically. Also notes headquarters, rank for previous year, score for each criterion, and rank among the *Fortune 1000*and *AmLaw 200*. **Number listed:** 15

1. Apple Inc., with 100 points

1. Cisco Systems Inc., 100

1. Dell Inc., 100

1. Tech Data Corp., 100

1. Xerox Corp., 100

6. CDW Corp., 90

6. Lexmark International Inc., 90

6. NetApp Inc., 90

9. NCR Corp., 80

10. Ingram Micro Inc., 60

Source: *Human Rights Campaign*, Corporate Equality Index (annual), 2011, p. 71.

3019 ■ BEST COMPUTER SOFTWARE COMPANIES FOR GAY AND LESBIAN EMPLOYEES, 2011

Ranked by: Score, on a scale of 100, based on how lesbian, gay, bisexual, and transgender (LGBT) employees are treated. Criteria include the equal employment opportunity policy, employment benefits, organizational LGBT competency, public engagement, and responsible citizenship. **Remarks:** In the event of ties, companies are listed alphabetically. Also notes headquarters, rank for previous year, score for each criterion, and rank among the *Fortune 1000* and *AmLaw 200*. **Number listed:** 14

1. Intuit Inc., with 100 points
1. Microsoft Corp., 100
1. Oracle Corp., 100
1. Symantec Corp., 100
5. Adobe Systems Inc., 90
5. Electronic Arts Inc., 90
5. SAP America Inc., 90
8. BMC Software Inc., 80
8. CA Inc., 80
8. Software AG USA Inc., 80

Source: *Human Rights Campaign*, Corporate Equality Index (annual), 2011, p. 72.

3020 ■ BEST CONSULTING AND BUSINESS SERVICES COMPANIES FOR GAY AND LESBIAN EMPLOYEES, 2011

Ranked by: Score, on a scale of 100, based on how lesbian, gay, bisexual, and transgender (LGBT) employees are treated. Criteria include the equal employment opportunity policy, employment benefits, organizational LGBT competency, public engagement, and responsible citizenship. **Remarks:** In the event of ties, companies are listed alphabetically. Also notes headquarters, rank for previous year, score for each criterion, and rank among the *Fortune 1000* and *AmLaw 200*. **Number listed:** 23

1. A. T. Kearney Inc., with 100 points
1. Accenture Ltd., 100
1. Aon Corp., 100
1. Bain & Co., Inc., 100
1. Booz Allen Hamilton Inc., 100
1. The Boston Consulting Group Inc., 100
1. Deloitte LLP, 100
1. Ernst & Young LLP, 100
1. International Business Machines Corp. (IBM), 100
1. KPMG LLP, 100
1. Marsh & McLennan Companies Inc., 100
1. McKinsey & Co., 100
1. Navigant Consulting Inc., 100

Source: *Human Rights Campaign*, Corporate Equality Index (annual), 2011, p. 72.

3021 ■ BEST ENERGY AND UTILITIES COMPANIES FOR GAY AND LESBIAN EMPLOYEES, 2011

Ranked by: Score, on a scale of 100, based on how lesbian, gay, bisexual, and transgender (LGBT) employees are treated. Criteria include the equal employment opportunity policy, employment benefits, organizational LGBT competency, public engagement, and responsible citizenship. **Remarks:** In the event of ties, companies are listed alphabetically. Also notes headquarters, rank for previous year, score for each criterion, and rank among the *Fortune 1000* and *AmLaw 200*. **Number listed:** 33

1. Exelon Corp., with 100 points
1. PG & E Corp., 100
1. Sempra Energy, 100
1. Southern California Edison Co., 100
5. Consolidated Edison Co., 90
5. Constellation Energy Group Inc., 90
5. Entergy Corp., 90
5. National Grid USA, 90
5. Portland General Electric Co., 90
10. Dominion Resources Inc., 85
10. Public Service Enterprise Group Inc., 85

Source: *Human Rights Campaign*, Corporate Equality Index (annual), 2011, p. 72-73.

3022 ■ BEST ENGINEERING AND CONSTRUCTION COMPANIES FOR GAY AND LESBIAN EMPLOYEES, 2011

Ranked by: Score, on a scale of 100, based on how lesbian, gay, bisexual, and transgender (LGBT) employees are treated. Criteria include the equal employment opportunity policy, employment benefits, organizational LGBT competency, public engagement, and responsible citizenship. **Remarks:** In the event of ties, companies are listed alphabetically. Also notes headquarters, rank for previous year, score for each criterion, and rank among the *Fortune 1000* and *AmLaw 200*. **Number listed:** 6

1. AECOM Technology Corp., with 85 points
1. CH2M Hill Cos., Ltd., 85
3. Jacobs Engineering Group Inc., 50
3. KB Home, 50
5. Perkins & Will Inc., 45
6. The Ryland Group Inc., 20

Source: *Human Rights Campaign*, Corporate Equality Index (annual), 2011, p. 74.

3023 ■ BEST ENTERTAINMENT AND ELECTRONIC MEDIA COMPANIES FOR GAY AND LESBIAN EMPLOYEES, 2011

Ranked by: Score, on a scale of 100, based on how lesbian, gay, bisexual, and transgender (LGBT) employees are treated. Criteria include the equal employment opportunity policy, employment benefits, organizational LGBT competency, public engagement, and responsible citizenship. **Remarks:** In the event of ties, companies are listed alphabetically. Also notes headquarters, rank for previous year, score for each criterion, and rank among the *Fortune 1000* and *AmLaw 200*. **Number listed:** 12

1. Time Warner Inc., with 100 points
1. Walt Disney Co., 100
3. AMC Entertainment Inc., 90
3. CBS Corp., 90
3. Cox Enterprises Inc., 90
3. Thomson Reuters Corp., 90
3. Viacom Inc., 90
8. Comcast Corp., 90
9. CC Media Holdings Inc., 75
9. SIRIUS XM Radio Inc., 75

Source: *Human Rights Campaign*, Corporate Equality Index (annual), 2011, p. 74.

3024 ■ BEST FOOD, BEVERAGE, AND GROCERY COMPANIES FOR GAY AND LESBIAN EMPLOYEES, 2011

Ranked by: Score, on a scale of 100, based on how lesbian, gay, bisexual, and transgender (LGBT) employees are treated. Criteria include the equal employment opportunity policy, employment benefits, organizational LGBT competency, public engagement, and responsible citizenship. **Remarks:** In the event of ties, companies are listed alphabetically. Also notes headquarters, rank for previous year, score for each criterion, and rank among the *Fortune 1000*and *AmLaw 200*. **Number listed:** 48

1. Brown-Forman Corp., with 100 points
1. Campbell Soup Co., 100
1. Cargill Inc., 100
1. The Coca-Cola Co., 100
1. Delhaize America Inc., 100
1. Diageo North America Inc., 100
1. General Mills Inc., 100
1. Kellogg Co., 100
1. Kraft Foods Inc., 100
1. MillerCoors LLC, 100
1. Sodexo Inc., 100
1. SuperValu Inc., 100

Source: *Human Rights Campaign*, Corporate Equality Index (annual), 2011, p. 74-75.

3025 ■ BEST FOREST AND PAPER PRODUCTS COMPANIES FOR GAY AND LESBIAN EMPLOYEES, 2011

Ranked by: Score, on a scale of 100, based on how lesbian, gay, bisexual, and transgender (LGBT) employees are treated. Criteria include the equal employment opportunity policy, employment benefits, organizational LGBT competency, public engagement, and responsible citizenship. **Remarks:** In the event of ties, companies are listed alphabetically. Also notes headquarters, rank for previous year, score for each criterion, and rank among the *Fortune 1000*and *AmLaw 200*. **Number listed:** 2

1. Weyerhauser Co., with 60 points
2. International Paper Co., 45

Source: *Human Rights Campaign*, Corporate Equality Index (annual), 2011, p. 76.

3026 ■ BEST HEALTHCARE/HEALTH INSURANCE COMPANIES FOR GAY AND LESBIAN EMPLOYEES, 2011

Ranked by: Score, on a scale of 100, based on how lesbian, gay, bisexual, and transgender (LGBT) employees are treated. Criteria include the equal employment opportunity policy, employment benefits, organizational LGBT competency, public engagement, and responsible citizenship. **Remarks:** In the event of ties, companies are listed alphabetically. Also notes headquarters, rank for previous year, score for each criterion, and rank among the *Fortune 1000*and *AmLaw 200*. **Number listed:** 27

1. Aetna Inc., with 100 points
1. Blue Cross Blue Shield of Florida Inc., 100
1. Blue Cross Blue Shield of Minnesota, 100
1. Cardinal Health Inc., 100
1. Group Health Cooperative, 100
1. UnitedHealth Group Inc., 100
7. CareFusion Corp., 90
7. CIGNA Corp., 90
7. Excellus Health Plan Inc., 90
7. Humana Inc., 90
7. Group Health Permanente, 90
7. Kaiser Permanente, 90

Source: *Human Rights Campaign*, Corporate Equality Index (annual), 2011, p. 76.

3027 ■ BEST HIGH-TECH/PHOTO/SCIENCE EQUIPMENT COMPANIES FOR GAY AND LESBIAN EMPLOYEES, 2011

Ranked by: Score, on a scale of 100, based on how lesbian, gay, bisexual, and transgender (LGBT) employees are treated. Criteria include the equal employment opportunity policy, employment benefits, organizational LGBT competency, public engagement, and responsible citizenship. **Remarks:** In the event of ties, companies are listed alphabetically. Also notes headquarters, rank for previous year, score for each criterion, and rank among the *Fortune 1000*and *AmLaw 200*. **Number listed:** 15

1. Eastman Kodak Co., with 100 points
1. Medtronic Inc., 100
3. Intel Corp., 95
4. Rockwell Automation Inc., 90
4. Texas Instruments Inc., 90
6. Applied Materials Inc., 85
7. Agilent Technologies Inc., 75
7. ITT Corp., 75
9. Advanced Micro Devices Inc., 70
9. Nokia Corp., 70

Source: *Human Rights Campaign*, Corporate Equality Index (annual), 2011, p. 77.

3028 ■ BEST HOTEL, RESORT, AND CASINO COMPANIES FOR GAY AND LESBIAN EMPLOYEES, 2011

Ranked by: Score, on a scale of 100, based on how lesbian, gay, bisexual, and transgender (LGBT) employees are treated. Criteria include the equal employment opportunity policy, employment benefits, organizational LGBT competency, public engagement, and responsible citizenship. **Remarks:** In the event of ties, companies are listed alphabetically. Also notes headquarters, rank for previous year, score for each criterion, and rank among the *Fortune 1000*and *AmLaw 200*. **Number listed:** 13

1. Caesars Entertainment Corp., with 100 points
1. Choice Hotels International Inc., 100
1. Hyatt Hotels Corp., 100
1. Kimpton Hotel & Restaurant Group Inc., 100
1. Starwood Hotels & Resorts Worldwide Inc., 100
6. Marriott International Inc., 90
6. MGM Resorts International, 90
6. Wyndham Worldwide Corp., 90
6. Wynn Resorts Ltd., 90
10. Carlson Cos., Inc., 85

Source: *Human Rights Campaign*, Corporate Equality Index (annual), 2011, p. 77-78.

3029 ■ BEST INSURANCE COMPANIES FOR GAY AND LESBIAN EMPLOYEES, 2011

Ranked by: Score, on a scale of 100, based on how lesbian, gay, bisexual, and transgender (LGBT) employees are treated. Criteria include the equal employment opportunity policy, employment benefits, organizational LGBT competency, public engagement, and responsible citizenship. **Remarks:** In the event of ties, companies are listed alphabetically. Also notes headquarters, rank for previous year, score for each criterion, and rank among the *Fortune 1000*and *AmLaw 200*. **Number listed:** 33

1. AAA Northern California, Nevada, & Utah Insurance Exchange, with 100 points
1. The Chubb Corp., 100
1. ING North America Insurance Corp., 100

1. MetLife Inc., 100
1. Nationwide, 100
1. Prudential Financial Inc., 100
1. Sun Life Financial Inc., 100
8. State Farm Insurance Companies, 95
9. Esurance Inc., 90
9. The Hartford Financial Services Group Inc., 90
9. Massachusetts Mutual Life Insurance Co., 90
9. The Progressive Corp., 90
9. The Travelers Cos., Inc., 90

Source: *Human Rights Campaign*, Corporate Equality Index (annual), 2011, p. 78.

3030 ■ BEST INTERNET SERVICES AND RETAILING COMPANIES FOR GAY AND LESBIAN EMPLOYEES, 2011

Ranked by: Score, on a scale of 100, based on how lesbian, gay, bisexual, and transgender (LGBT) employees are treated. Criteria include the equal employment opportunity policy, employment benefits, organizational LGBT competency, public engagement, and responsible citizenship. **Remarks:** In the event of ties, companies are listed alphabetically. Also notes headquarters, rank for previous year, score for each criterion, and rank among the *Fortune 1000* and *AmLaw 200*. **Number listed:** 7

1. eBay Inc., with 100 points
1. Google Inc., 100
1. Yahoo! Inc., 100
4. Amazon.com Inc., 90
5. Classified Ventures LLC, 80
5. Expedia Inc., 80
7. Hanover Direct Inc., 70

Source: *Human Rights Campaign*, Corporate Equality Index (annual), 2011, p. 79.

3031 ■ BEST LAW FIRMS FOR GAY AND LESBIAN EMPLOYEES, 2011

Ranked by: Score, on a scale of 100, based on how lesbian, gay, bisexual, and transgender (LGBT) employees are treated. Criteria include the equal employment opportunity policy, employment benefits, organizational LGBT competency, public engagement, and responsible citizenship. **Remarks:** In the event of ties, companies are listed alphabetically. Also notes headquarters, rank for previous year, score for each criterion, and rank among the *Fortune 1000* and *AmLaw 200*. **Number listed:** 141

1. Akin, Gump, Strauss, Hauer & Feld LLP, with 100 points
1. Alston & Bird LLP, 100
1. Baker & McKenzie LLP, 100
1. Bingham McCutchen LLP, 100
1. Brown Rudnick LLP, 100
1. Bryan Cave LLP, 100
1. Carlton Fields PA, 100
1. Chapman & Cutler LLP, 100
1. Choate, Hall & Stewart LLP, 100
1. Clifford Chance U.S. LLP, 100
1. Covington & Burling LLP, 100
1. Crowell & Moring LLP, 100
1. Debevoise & Plimpton LLP, 100

Source: *Human Rights Campaign*, Corporate Equality Index (annual), 2011, p. 79-82.

3032 ■ BEST MAIL AND FREIGHT DELIVERY COMPANIES FOR GAY AND LESBIAN EMPLOYEES, 2011

Ranked by: Score, on a scale of 100, based on how lesbian, gay, bisexual, and transgender (LGBT) employees are treated. Criteria include the equal employment opportunity policy, employment benefits, organizational LGBT competency, public engagement, and responsible citizenship. **Remarks:** In the event of ties, companies are listed alphabetically. Also notes headquarters, rank for previous year, score for each criterion, and rank among the *Fortune 1000* and *AmLaw 200*. **Number listed:** 5

1. United Parcel Service Inc. (UPS), with 100 points
2. FedEx Corp., 75
3. Union Pacific Corp., 65
4. Burlington Northern Santa Fe Corp., 20
4. YRC Worldwide Inc., 20

Source: *Human Rights Campaign*, Corporate Equality Index (annual), 2011, p. 82.

3033 ■ BEST MANUFACTURING COMPANIES FOR GAY AND LESBIAN EMPLOYEES, 2011

Ranked by: Score, on a scale of 100, based on how lesbian, gay, bisexual, and transgender (LGBT) employees are treated. Criteria include the equal employment opportunity policy, employment benefits, organizational LGBT competency, public engagement, and responsible citizenship. **Remarks:** In the event of ties, companies are listed alphabetically. Also notes headquarters, rank for previous year, score for each criterion, and rank among the *Fortune 1000* and *AmLaw 200*. **Number listed:** 18

1. Corning Inc., with 100 points
1. Cummins Inc., 100
1. Herman Miller Inc., 100
1. Owens Corning, 100
1. United Technologies Corp., 100
1. Whirlpool Corp., 100
7. Steelcase Inc., 90
8. Freescale Semiconductor Inc., 80
8. R. R. Donnelley & Sons Co., 80
10. Caterpillar Inc., 70

Source: *Human Rights Campaign*, Corporate Equality Index (annual), 2011, p. 82-83.

3034 ■ BEST OIL AND GAS COMPANIES FOR GAY AND LESBIAN EMPLOYEES, 2011

Ranked by: Score, on a scale of 100, based on how lesbian, gay, bisexual, and transgender (LGBT) employees are treated. Criteria include the equal employment opportunity policy, employment benefits, organizational LGBT competency, public engagement, and responsible citizenship. **Remarks:** In the event of ties, companies are listed alphabetically. Also notes headquarters, rank for previous year, score for each criterion, and rank among the *Fortune 1000* and *AmLaw 200*. **Number listed:** 7

1. Chevron Corp., with 100 points
2. BP America Inc., 85
2. Shell Oil Co., 85
2. Spectra Energy Corp., 85
5. ConocoPhillips, 55
6. Marathon Oil Corp., 15
7. Exxon Mobil Corp., -25

Source: *Human Rights Campaign*, Corporate Equality Index (annual), 2011, p. 83-84.

3035 ■ BEST PHARMACEUTICALS COMPANIES FOR GAY AND LESBIAN EMPLOYEES, 2011

Ranked by: Score, on a scale of 100, based on how lesbian, gay, bisexual, and transgender (LGBT) employees are treated. Criteria include the equal employment opportunity policy, employment benefits, organizational LGBT competency, public engagement, and responsible citizenship. **Remarks:** In the event of ties, companies are listed alphabetically. Also notes headquarters, rank for previous year, score for each criterion, and rank among the *Fortune 1000* and *AmLaw 200*. **Number listed:** 15

1. Bristol-Myers Squibb Co., with 100 points
1. Eli Lilly & Co., 100
1. GlaxoSmithKline plc, 100
1. Johnson & Johnson, 100
1. Pfizer Inc., 100
6. Boehringer Ingelheim USA Corp., 90
6. Merck & Co., Inc., 90
8. CVS Caremark Corp., 75
8. Hospira Inc., 75
8. Novartis Pharmaceuticals Corp., 75

Source: *Human Rights Campaign*, Corporate Equality Index (annual), 2011, p. 84.

3036 ■ BEST PUBLISHING AND PRINTING COMPANIES FOR GAY AND LESBIAN EMPLOYEES, 2011

Ranked by: Score, on a scale of 100, based on how lesbian, gay, bisexual, and transgender (LGBT) employees are treated. Criteria include the equal employment opportunity policy, employment benefits, organizational LGBT competency, public engagement, and responsible citizenship. **Remarks:** In the event of ties, companies are listed alphabetically. Also notes headquarters, rank for previous year, score for each criterion, and rank among the *Fortune 1000* and *AmLaw 200*. **Number listed:** 6

1. The McGraw-Hill Companies Inc., with 100 points
1. New York Times Co., 100
1. Pearson Inc., 100
4. UBM plc, 60
5. Gannett Co., Inc., 45
6. Houghton Mifflin Harcourt Publishing Co., 25

Source: *Human Rights Campaign*, Corporate Equality Index (annual), 2011, p. 84-85.

3037 ■ BEST RESIDENTIAL REAL ESTATE COMPANIES FOR GAY AND LESBIAN EMPLOYEES, 2011

Ranked by: Score, on a scale of 100, based on how lesbian, gay, bisexual, and transgender (LGBT) employees are treated. Criteria include the equal employment opportunity policy, employment benefits, organizational LGBT competency, public engagement, and responsible citizenship. **Remarks:** In the event of ties, companies are listed alphabetically. Also notes headquarters, rank for previous year, score for each criterion, and rank among the *Fortune 1000* and *AmLaw 200*. **Number listed:** 2

1. CB Richard Ellis Group Inc., with 85 points
2. Realogy Corp., 45

Source: *Human Rights Campaign*, Corporate Equality Index (annual), 2011, p. 85.

3038 ■ BEST RETAIL AND CONSUMER PRODUCTS COMPANIES FOR GAY AND LESBIAN EMPLOYEES, 2011

Ranked by: Score, on a scale of 100, based on how lesbian, gay, bisexual, and transgender (LGBT) employees are treated. Criteria include the equal employment opportunity policy, employment benefits, organizational LGBT competency, public engagement, and responsible citizenship. **Remarks:** In the event of ties, companies are listed alphabetically. Also notes headquarters, rank for previous year, score for each criterion, and rank among the *Fortune 1000* and *AmLaw 200*. **Number listed:** 48

1. Abercrombie & Fitch Co., with 100 points
1. Avon Products Inc., 100
1. Barnes & Noble Inc., 100
1. Best Buy Co., Inc., 100
1. The Clorox Co., 100
1. The Gap Inc., 100
1. Limited Brands Inc., 100
1. Nordstrom Inc., 100
1. Office Depot Inc., 100
1. Replacements Ltd., 100
1. Sears Holdings Corp., 100
1. Staples Inc., 100
1. The TJX Companies Inc., 100

Source: *Human Rights Campaign*, Corporate Equality Index (annual), 2011, p. 85-86.

3039 ■ BEST TELECOMMUNICATIONS COMPANIES FOR GAY AND LESBIAN EMPLOYEES, 2011

Ranked by: Score, on a scale of 100, based on how lesbian, gay, bisexual, and transgender (LGBT) employees are treated. Criteria include the equal employment opportunity policy, employment benefits, organizational LGBT competency, public engagement, and responsible citizenship. **Remarks:** In the event of ties, companies are listed alphabetically. Also notes headquarters, rank for previous year, score for each criterion, and rank among the *Fortune 1000* and *AmLaw 200*. **Number listed:** 12

1. Alcatel-Lucent, with 100 points
1. AT&T Inc., 100
1. Sprint Nextel Corp., 100
4. Motorola Solutions Inc., 90
4. QUALCOMM Inc., 90
4. Time Warner Cable Inc., 90
7. Avaya Inc., 80
8. The DirecTV Group Inc., 75
9. Nortel Networks Corp., 60
10. EarthLink Inc., 55
10. T-Mobile USA Inc., 55

Source: *Human Rights Campaign*, Corporate Equality Index (annual), 2011, p. 86.

3040 ■ BEST TRANSPORTATION AND TRAVEL COMPANIES FOR GAY AND LESBIAN EMPLOYEES, 2011

Ranked by: Score, on a scale of 100, based on how lesbian, gay, bisexual, and transgender (LGBT) employees are treated. Criteria include the equal employment opportunity policy, employment benefits, organizational LGBT competency, public engagement, and responsible citizenship. **Remarks:** In the event of ties, companies are listed alphabetically. Also notes headquarters, rank for previous year, score for each criterion, and rank among the *Fortune 1000* and *AmLaw 200*. **Number listed:** 11

1. Orbitz Worldwide Inc., with 100 points
2. CSX Corp., 85
3. Dollar Thrifty Automotive Group Inc., 80
3. Ryder System Inc., 80
3. Travel Impressions Ltd., 80

6. Sabre Holdings Inc., 75
7. Travelport Inc., 65
8. Avis Budget Group Inc., 60
8. Royal Caribbean Cruises Ltd., 60
10. Enterprise Holdings Inc., 50
10. Norfolk Southern Corp., 50

Source: *Human Rights Campaign*, Corporate Equality Index (annual), 2011, p. 87.

3041 ■ TOP U.S. COMPANIES FOR LESBIAN/GAY/ BISEXUAL/TRANSGENDER EMPLOYEES, 2011

Ranked by: Score based on employee-resource groups, recruitment practices, and same-sex domestic-partner benefits offered. **Remarks:** Specific scores not provided. To qualify, companies must have more than 1,000 U.S. employees. **Number listed:** 10

1. KPMG LLP
2. Wells Fargo & Co.
3. International Business Machines Corp. (IBM)
4. Aetna Inc.
5. Ernst & Young LLP
6. PricewaterhouseCoopers LLP
7. Sodexo
8. Bank of America Corp.
9. Merck & Co., Inc.
10. American Express Co.

Source: *DiversityInc*, Top 50 (annual), 2011, p. 98.

Hospitality

3042 ■ BEST HOSPITALITY COMPANIES TO WORK FOR IN BRITISH COLUMBIA, 2010

Ranked by: Editorial determination. **Remarks:** Specific scores not provided. **Number listed:** 5

1. Tourism Victoria
2. Adrena Line Adventure Tours Ltd.
3. Daniel Hospitality Group
4. Cactus Restaurants Ltd.
5. Joe Fortes & Goldfish Restaurants

Source: *BCBusiness*, Best Companies (annual), http:// www.bcbusinessonline.ca, December 2011.

3043 ■ STATES WITH THE HIGHEST RATE OF EMPLOYEES IN LEISURE AND HOSPITALITY, 2010

Ranked by: Percentage of nonfarm employees in the leisure and hospitality industry. **Number listed:** 51

1. Nevada, with 27.2%
2. Hawaii, 17.7%
3. Montana, 13.3%
4. Florida, 12.9%
5. Colorado, 12%
6. South Carolina, 11.3%
7. Wyoming, 11.1%
8. Mississippi, 11%
9. California, 10.8%
9. South Dakota, 10.8%
9. Vermont, 10.8%

Source: *State Rankings*, (annual), CQ Press, 2011, p. 199.

3044 ■ STATES WITH THE LOWEST RATE OF EMPLOYEES IN LEISURE AND HOSPITALITY, 2010

Ranked by: Percentage of nonfarm employees in the leisure and hospitality industry. **Number listed:** 51

1. Washington DC, with 8.2%
2. Kansas, 8.3%
3. Arkansas, 8.5%
3. Connecticut, 8.5%
3. New York, 8.5%
6. Nebraska, 8.6%
7. New Jersey, 8.7%
8. Pennsylvania, 8.9%
9. Illinois, 9%
9. Iowa, 9%

Source: *State Rankings*, (annual), CQ Press, 2011, p. 199.

Hospitals
See also: **Multihospital Systems; Nursing Homes; Psychiatric Hospitals**

3045 ■ BEST CARDIOVASCULAR COMMUNITY HOSPITALS, 2011

Ranked by: Score based on seven measures of clinical quality and efficiency of operations: volume, medical mortality, surgical mortality, complications, length of stay, cost, and percentage of heart bypass patients in which the mammary artery was used. **Remarks:** Specific scores not provided; hospitals are listed alphabetically by state/city, not ranked. Also notes number of years on list. **Number listed:** 15

1. St. Francis Medical Center (Lynwood, CA)
2. French Hospital Medical Center (San Luis Obispo, CA)
3. Martin Memorial Medical Center (Stuart, FL)
4. Provena Covenant Medical Center (Urbana, IL)
5. St. Vincent Heart Center of Indiana (Indianapolis, IN)
6. Heart Hospital of Lafayette (Lafayette, LA)
7. Nebraska Heart institute & Heart Hospital (Lincoln, NE)
8. Gaston Memorial Hospital (Gastonia, NC)
9. Chester County Hospital & Health System (West Chester, PA)
10. Doylestown Hospital (Doylestown, PA)

Source: *Modern Healthcare*, Thomson Reuters' Top Cardiovascular Hospitals (annual), November 14, 2011, p. 31.

3046 ■ BEST CHILDREN'S HOSPITALS FOR CANCER TREATMENT, 2012

Ranked by: Score based on reputation, mortality rate, and other care-related factors. **Remarks:** Scores not provided. **Number listed:** 52

1. Children's Hospital of Philadelphia
2. Dana-Farber Cancer Center/Boston Children's Hospital
3. Cincinnati Children's Hospital Medical Center
4. Texas Children's Hospital
5. Children's Hospital Los Angeles
6. St. Jude Children's Research Hospital (Memphis, TN)

7. Seattle Children's Hospital
8. Children's Hospital Colorado
9. Children's National Medical Center (Wash. DC)
10. Ann and Robert H. Lurie Children's Hospital of Chicago

Source: *U.S. News & World Report*, Best Children's Hospitals (annual), June 5, 2012.

3047 ■ BEST CHILDREN'S HOSPITALS FOR CARDIOLOGY AND HEART SURGERY, 2012

Ranked by: Score based on reputation, mortality rate, and other care-related factors. **Remarks:** Scores not provided. **Number listed:** 50

1. Boston Children's Hospital
2. Children's Hospital of Philadelphia
3. Texas Children's Hospital (Houston, TX)
4. University of Michigan C. S. Mott Children's Hospital
5. Nationwide Children's Hospital
6. Children's Healthcare of Atlanta
7. New York-Presbyterian Morgan Stanley-Komansky Children's Hospital
8. Cincinnati Children's Hospital Medical Center
9. Children's Hospital Los Angeles
10. Lucile Packard Children's Hospital (Palo Alto, CA)

Source: *U.S. News & World Report*, Best Children's Hospitals (annual), June 5, 2012.

3048 ■ BEST CHILDREN'S HOSPITALS FOR DIABETES AND ENDOCRINOLOGY, 2012

Ranked by: Score based on reputation, mortality rate, and other care-related factors. **Remarks:** Scores not provided. **Number listed:** 50

1. Children's Hospital of Philadelphia
2. Boston Children's Hospital
3. Yale-New Haven Children's Hospital
4. Children's Hospital Colorado
5. Cincinnati Children's Hospital Medical Center
6. Children's Hospital of Pittsburgh
7. Children's Hospital Los Angeles
8. Johns Hopkins Children's Center
9. Mattel Children's Hospital
10. New York-Presbyterian Morgan Stanley-Komansky Children's Hospital

Source: *U.S. News & World Report*, Best Children's Hospitals (annual), June 5, 2012.

3049 ■ BEST CHILDREN'S HOSPITALS FOR GASTROENTEROLOGY, 2012

Ranked by: Score based on reputation, mortality rate, and other care-related factors. **Remarks:** Scores not provided. **Number listed:** 52

1. Children's Hospital of Philadelphia
2. Boston Children's Hospital
3. Cincinnati Children's Hospital Medical Center
4. Texas Children's Hospital (Houston, TX)
5. Nationwide Children's Hospital (Columbus, OH)
6. Children's Hospital of Pittsburgh

7. Children's Hospital Los Angeles
8. Ann and Robert H. Lurie Children's Hospital of Chicago
9. Children's Hospital Cleveland Clinic
10. Children's Hospital Colorado

Source: *U.S. News & World Report*, Best Children's Hospitals (annual), June 5, 2012.

3050 ■ BEST CHILDREN'S HOSPITALS FOR NEONATOLOGY, 2012

Ranked by: Score based on reputation, mortality rate, and other care-related factors. **Remarks:** Scores not provided. **Number listed:** 51

1. Cincinnati Children's Hospital Medical Center
2. Texas Children's Hospital (Houston, TX)
3. Boston Children's Hospital
4. Children's Hospital of Philadelphia
5. Rainbow Babies & Children's Hospital
6. Children's National Medical Center (Washington DC)
7. Children's Hospital Los Angeles
8. Monroe Carell Jr. Children's Hospital at Vanderbilt
9. Children's Hospital of Pittsburgh
10. Johns Hopkins Children's Center (Baltimore, MD)

Source: *U.S. News & World Report*, Best Children's Hospitals (annual), June 5, 2012.

3051 ■ BEST CHILDREN'S HOSPITALS FOR NEPHROLOGY, 2012

Ranked by: Score based on reputation, mortality rate, and other care-related factors. **Remarks:** Scores not provided. **Number listed:** 51

1. Boston Children's Hospital
2. Children's Hospital of Philadelphia
3. Cincinnati Children's Hospital Medical Center
4. Seattle Children's Hospital
5. Texas Children's Hospital
6. Children's Mercy Hospitals & Clinics (Kansas City, MO)
7. Ann and Robert H. Lurie Children's Hospital of Chicago
8. Children's Medical Center Dallas
9. Nationwide Children's Hospital
10. Mattel Children's Hospital (Los Angeles, CA)

Source: *U.S. News & World Report*, Best Children's Hospitals (annual), June 5, 2012.

3052 ■ BEST CHILDREN'S HOSPITALS FOR NEUROLOGY AND NEUROSURGERY, 2012

Ranked by: Score based on reputation, mortality rate, and other care-related factors. **Remarks:** Scores not provided. **Number listed:** 50

1. Boston Children's Hospital
2. Children's Hospital of Philadelphia
3. Children's Hospital Cleveland Clinic
4. Cincinnati Children's Hospital Medical Center
5. Johns Hopkins Children's Center

5. Texas Children's Hospital (Houston, TX)
7. St. Louis Children's Hospital/Washington University
8. Seattle Children's Hospital
9. Children's National Medical Center
10. Nationwide Children's Hospital

Source: *U.S. News & World Report*, Best Children's Hospitals (annual), June 5, 2012.

3053 ■ BEST CHILDREN'S HOSPITALS FOR ORTHOPEDICS, 2012

Ranked by: Score based on reputation, mortality rate, and other care-related factors. Remarks: Scores not provided. Number listed: 50

1. Children's Hospital of Philadelphia
2. Rady Children's Hospital
3. Boston Children's Hospital
4. Cincinnati Children's Hospital Medical Center
5. Children's Medical Center/Texas Scottish Rite Hospital for Children
6. Children's Hospital Los Angeles
7. Alfred I. duPont Hospital for Children
8. St. Louis Children's Hospital/Washington University
9. Children's Hospital Colorado
10. Ann and Robert H. Lurie Children's Hospital of Chicago

Source: *U.S. News & World Report*, Best Children's Hospitals (annual), June 5, 2012.

3054 ■ BEST CHILDREN'S HOSPITALS OVERALL, 2012

Ranked by: Appearance on each of the 10 specialty rankings, placements that are based on reputation among specialists, death rate, and care-related factors. Number listed: 12

1. Boston Children's Hospital, with 20 points
1. Children's Hospital of Philadelphia, 20
3. Cincinnati Children's Hospital Medical Center, 19
4. Texas Children's Hospital (Houston, TX), 13
5. Children's Hospital Los Angeles, 6
6. Seattle Children's Hospital, 5
7. Children's Hospital Colorado, 4
7. Nationwide Children's Hospital, 4
9. Ann and Robert H. Lurie Children's Hospital of Chicago, 3
9. Children's Hospital of Pittsburgh, 3
9. Johns Hopkins Children's Center, 3
9. St. Louis Children's Hospital/Washington University, 3

Source: *U.S. News & World Report*, Best Children's Hospitals (annual), June 5, 2012.

3055 ■ BEST CHILDREN'S HOSPITALS FOR PULMONOL-OGY, 2012

Ranked by: Score based on reputation, mortality rate, and other care-related factors. Remarks: Scores not provided. Number listed: 51

1. Children's Hospital of Philadelphia
2. Cincinnati Children's Hospital Medical Center

3. Texas Children's Hospital
4. Boston Children's Hospital
5. Rainbow Babies & Children's Hospital
6. Nationwide Children's Hospital
7. Children's Hospital Colorado
8. North Carolina Children's Hospital
9. St. Louis Children's Hospital/Washington University
10. Riley Hospital for Children, Indiana University Health

Source: *U.S. News & World Report*, Best Children's Hospitals (annual), June 5, 2012.

3056 ■ BEST CHILDREN'S HOSPITALS FOR UROLOGY, 2012

Ranked by: Score based on reputation, mortality rate, and other care-related factors. Remarks: Scores not provided. Number listed: 50

1. Children's Hospital of Philadelphia
2. Boston Children's Hospital
3. Riley Hospital for Children, Indiana University Health
4. Cincinnati Children's Hospital Medical Center
5. Seattle Children's Hospital
6. Ann and Robert H. Lurie Children's Hospital of Chicago
7. Texas Children's Hospital (Houston, TX)
8. Monroe Carell Jr. Children's Hospital at Vanderbilt
9. Rady Children's Hospital
10. Children's Healthcare of Pittsburgh

Source: *U.S. News & World Report*, Best Children's Hospitals (annual), June 5, 2012.

3057 ■ BEST HOSPITALS FOR CANCER TREATMENT, 2011

Ranked by: Score based on reputation, mortality rate, and other care-related factors. Remarks: Scores not provided. Number listed: 870

1. University of Texas, M. D. Anderson Cancer Center (Houston, TX)
2. Memorial Sloan-Kettering Cancer Center (New York, NY)
3. Johns Hopkins Hospital (Baltimore, MD)
4. Mayo Clinic (Rochester, MN)
5. Dana-Farber/Brigham & Women's Cancer Center (Boston, MA)
6. University of Washington Medical Center (Seattle, WA)
7. Massachusetts General Hospital (Boston, MA)
8. University of California, San Francisco Medical Center
9. Cleveland Clinic
10. Ronald Reagan UCLA Medical Center (Los Angeles, CA)

Source: *U.S. News & World Report*, America's Best Hospitals (annual), http://www.usnews.com, July 18, 2011.

3058 ■ BEST HOSPITALS FOR CARDIOLOGY AND HEART SURGERY, 2011

Ranked by: Score based on reputation, mortality rate, and other care-related factors. Remarks: Scores not provided. Number listed: 685

1. Cleveland Clinic
2. Mayo Clinic (Rochester, MN)
3. Johns Hopkins Hospital (Baltimore, MD)
4. Texas Heart Institute at St. Luke's Episcopal Hospital (Houston, TX)
5. Massachusetts General Hospital (Boston, MA)
6. New York-Presbyterian University Hospital of Columbia & Cornell
7. Duke University Medical Center (Durham, NC)
8. Brigham & Women's Hospital (Boston, MA)
9. Ronald Reagan UCLA Medical Center (Los Angeles, CA)
10. Hospital of the University of Pennsylvania (Philadelphia, PA)

Source: *U.S. News & World Report*, America's Best Hospitals (annual), http://www.usnews.com, July 18, 2011.

3059 ■ BEST HOSPITALS FOR DIABETES AND ENDOCRINOLOGY, 2011

Ranked by: Score based on reputation, mortality rate, and other care-related factors. **Remarks:** Scores not provided. **Number listed:** 1084

1. Mayo Clinic (Rochester, MN)
2. Massachusetts General Hospital (Boston, MA)
3. Johns Hopkins Hospital (Baltimore, MD)
4. University of California, San Francisco Medical Center
5. Cleveland Clinic
6. New York-Presbyterian University Hospital of Columbia & Cornell
7. Ronald Reagan UCLA Medical Center (Los Angeles, CA)
8. Yale-New Haven Hospital (New Haven, CT)
9. Brigham & Women's Hospital (Boston, MA)
10. University of Washington Medical Center (Seattle, WA)

Source: *U.S. News & World Report*, America's Best Hospitals (annual), http://www.usnews.com, July 18, 2011.

3060 ■ BEST HOSPITALS FOR GASTROENTEROLOGY, 2011

Ranked by: Score based on reputation, mortality rate, and other care-related factors. **Remarks:** Scores not provided. **Number listed:** 1516

1. Mayo Clinic (Rochester, MN)
2. Cleveland Clinic
3. Johns Hopkins Hospital (Baltimore, MD)
4. Massachusetts General Hospital (Boston, MA)
5. Mount Sinai Medical Center (New York)
6. Ronald Reagan UCLA Medical Center (Los Angeles, CA)
7. Hospital of the University of Pennsylvania (Philadelphia, PA)
8. New York-Presbyterian University Hospital of Columbia & Cornell
9. University of Chicago Medical Center
10. University of Pittsburgh Medical Center

Source: *U.S. News & World Report*, America's Best Hospitals (annual), http://www.usnews.com, July 18, 2011.

3061 ■ BEST HOSPITALS FOR GERIATRICS, 2011

Ranked by: Score based on reputation, mortality rate, and other care-related factors. **Remarks:** Scores not provided. **Number listed:** 1489

1. Mount Sinai Medical Center (New York)
2. Ronald Reagan UCLA Medical Center (Los Angeles, CA)
3. Johns Hopkins Hospital (Baltimore, MD)
4. Massachusetts General Hospital (Boston, MA)
5. Duke University Medical Center (Durham, NC)
6. Mayo Clinic (Rochester, MN)
7. Cleveland Clinic
8. New York-Presbyterian University Hospital of Columbia & Cornell
9. University of Pittsburgh Medical Center
10. Yale-New Haven Hospital (New Haven, CT)

Source: *U.S. News & World Report*, America's Best Hospitals (annual), http://www.usnews.com, July 18, 2011.

3062 ■ BEST HOSPITALS FOR GYNECOLOGY, 2011

Ranked by: Score based on reputation, mortality rate, and other care-related factors. **Remarks:** Scores not provided. **Number listed:** 1447

1. Mayo Clinic (Rochester, MN)
2. Johns Hopkins Hospital (Baltimore, MD)
3. Brigham & Women's Hospital (Boston, MA)
4. Cleveland Clinic
5. Massachusetts General Hospital (Boston, MA)
6. University of Texas, M.D. Anderson Cancer Center
7. Magee-Women's Hospital of the University of Pittsburgh Medical Center
8. Memorial Sloan-Kettering Cancer Center (New York)
9. Duke University Medical Center (Durham, NC)
10. New York-Presbyterian University Hospital of Columbia & Cornell

Source: *U.S. News & World Report*, America's Best Hospitals (annual), http://www.usnews.com, July 18, 2011.

3063 ■ BEST HOSPITALS FOR NEPHROLOGY, 2011

Ranked by: Score based on reputation, mortality rate, and other care-related factors. **Remarks:** Scores not provided. **Number listed:** 1614

1. Mayo Clinic (Rochester, MN)
2. Cleveland Clinic
3. Johns Hopkins Hospital (Baltimore, MD)
4. Massachusetts General Hospital (Boston, MA)
5. New York-Presbyterian University Hospital of Columbia & Cornell
6. Brigham & Women's Hospital (Boston, MA)
7. Ronald Reagan UCLA Medical Center (Los Angeles, CA)
8. University of California, San Francisco Medical Center
9. Barnes-Jewish Hospital/Washington University (St. Louis, MO)
10. Duke University Medical Center (Durham, NC)

Source: *U.S. News & World Report*, America's Best Hospitals (annual), http://www.usnews.com, July 18, 2011.

3064 ■ BEST HOSPITALS FOR NEUROLOGY AND NEU-ROSURGERY, 2011

Ranked by: Score based on reputation, mortality rate, and other care-related factors. **Remarks:** Scores not provided. **Number listed:** 1300

1. Johns Hopkins Hospital (Baltimore, MD)
2. Mayo Clinic (Rochester, MN)
3. Massachusetts General Hospital (Boston, MA)
4. New York-Presbyterian University Hospital of Columbia & Cornell
5. University of California, San Francisco Medical Center
6. Cleveland Clinic
7. Ronald Reagan UCLA Medical Center (Los Angeles, CA)
8. Duke University Medical Center (Durham, NC)
9. St. Joseph's Hospital & Medical Center (Phoenix, AZ)
10. University of Pittsburgh Medical Center

Source: *U.S. News & World Report*, America's Best Hospitals (annual), http://www.usnews.com, July 18, 2011.

3065 ■ BEST HOSPITALS FOR OPHTHALMOLOGY, 2011

Ranked by: Score based on reputation among specialists, in percent. **Remarks:** Scores not provided. **Number listed:** 104

1. Bascom Palmer Eye Institute (Miami, FL)
2. Johns Hopkins Hospital, Wilmer Eye Institute (Baltimore, MD)
3. Wills Eye Hospital (Philadelphia, PA)
4. Massachusetts Eye & Ear Infirmary (Boston, MA)
5. UCLA Medical Center, Jules Stein Eye Institute (Los Angeles, CA)
6. University of Iowa Hospitals & Clinics (Iowa City, IA)
7. Duke University Medical Center (Durham, NC)
8. New York Eye & Ear Infirmary (New York, NY)
9. USC University Hospital, Doheny Eye Institute (Los Angeles, CA)
10. University of California, San Francisco Medical Center

Source: *U.S. News & World Report*, America's Best Hospitals (annual), http://www.usnews.com, July 18, 2011.

3066 ■ BEST HOSPITALS FOR ORTHOPEDICS, 2011

Ranked by: Score based on reputation, mortality rate, and other care-related factors. **Remarks:** Scores not provided. **Number listed:** 1586

1. Hospital for Special Surgery (New York)
2. Mayo Clinic (Rochester, MN)
3. Massachusetts General Hospital (Boston, MA)
4. Cleveland Clinic
5. Johns Hopkins Hospital (Baltimore, MD)
6. Duke University Medical Center (Durham, NC)
7. University of Pittsburgh Medical Center
8. Rush University Medical Center (Chicago, IL)
9. Barnes-Jewish Hospital/Washington University (St. Louis, MO)
10. Hospital for Joint Diseases, NYU Langone Medical Center

Source: *U.S. News & World Report*, America's Best Hospitals (annual), http://www.usnews.com, July 18, 2011.

3067 ■ BEST HOSPITALS OVERALL, 2011

Ranked by: Score based on appearance at the top of six or more of the 16 specialty rankings. **Remarks:** Scores not provided. Also notes number of specialities ranked upon. **Number listed:** 17

1. Johns Hopkins Hospital (Baltimore, MD), with 30 points
2. Massachusetts General Hospital (Boston, MA), 29
3. Mayo Clinic (Rochester, MN), 28
4. Cleveland Clinic, 26
5. Ronald Reagan UCLA Medical Center (Los Angeles, CA), 25
6. New York-Presbyterian University Hospital of Columbia & Cornell, 22
7. University of California, San Francisco Medical Center, 20
8. Brigham & Women's Hospital (Boston, MA), 18
8. Duke University Medical Center (Durham, NC), 18
9. Hospital of the University of Pennsylvania (Philadelphia, PA), 17

Source: *U.S. News & World Report*, America's Best Hospitals (annual), http://www.usnews.com, July 18, 2011.

3068 ■ BEST HOSPITALS FOR PULMONOLOGY, 2011

Ranked by: Score based on reputation, mortality rate, and other care-related factors. **Remarks:** Scores not provided. **Number listed:** 1622

1. National Jewish Health (Aurora, CO)
2. Mayo Clinic (Rochester, MN)
3. Cleveland Clinic
4. Johns Hopkins Hospital (Baltimore, MD)
5. Duke University Medical Center (Durham, NC)
6. University of Pittsburgh Medical Center
7. Massachusetts General Hospital (Boston, MA)
8. Barnes-Jewish Hospital/Washington University
9. Hospital of the University of Pennsylvania (Philadelphia, PA)
10. New York-Presbyterian University Hospital of Columbia & Cornell

Source: *U.S. News & World Report*, America's Best Hospitals (annual), http://www.usnews.com, July 18, 2011.

3069 ■ BEST HOSPITALS FOR REHABILITATION, 2011

Ranked by: Score based on reputation among specialists, in percent. **Remarks:** Scores not provided. **Number listed:** 147

1. Rehabilitation Institute of Chicago
2. Kessler Institute for Rehabilitation (West Orange, NJ)
3. University of Washington Medical Center (Seattle, WA)
4. Memorial Hermann TIRR, The Institute for Rehabilitation & Research (Houston, TX)
5. Spaulding Rehabilitation Hospital (Boston, MA)
6. Mayo Clinic (Rochester, MN)
7. Craig Hospital (Englewood, CO)
8. New York University Langone Medical Center, Rusk Institute (New York, NY)

9. Moss Rehabilitation (Elkins Park, PA)

10. Shepherd Center (Atlanta, GA)

Source: *U.S. News & World Report*, America's Best Hospitals (annual), http://www.usnews.com, July 18, 2011.

3070 ■ BEST HOSPITALS FOR RHEUMATOLOGY, 2011

Ranked by: Score based on reputation among specialists, in percent. **Remarks:** Scores not provided. **Number listed:** 111

1. Johns Hopkins Hospital (Baltimore, MD)

2. Hospital for Special Surgery (New York)

3. Cleveland Clinic

4. Mayo Clinic (Rochester, MN)

5. Brigham & Women's Hospital (Boston, MA)

6. Ronald Reagan UCLA Medical Center (Los Angeles, CA)

7. Massachusetts General Hospital (Boston, MA)

8. Hospital for Joint Diseases/New York University Langone Medical Center (New York)

9. University of California, San Francisco Medical Center

10. University of Pittsburgh Medical Center

Source: *U.S. News & World Report*, America's Best Hospitals (annual), http://www.usnews.com, July 18, 2011.

3071 ■ BEST HOSPITALS FOR THE TREATMENT OF THE EAR, NOSE, AND THROAT, 2011

Ranked by: Score based on reputation, mortality rate, and other care-related factors. **Remarks:** Scores not provided. **Number listed:** 1409

1. Johns Hopkins Hospital (Baltimore, MD)

2. Massachusetts Eye & Ear Infirmary (Boston, MA)

3. University of Pittsburgh Medical Center

4. Mayo Clinic (Rochester, MN)

5. University of Iowa Hospitals & Clinics (Iowa City, IA)

6. University of Texas, M. D. Anderson Cancer Center (Houston, TX)

7. Hospital of the University of Pennsylvania (Philadelphia, PA)

8. Cleveland Clinic

9. University of Michigan Hospitals & Health Centers (Ann Arbor, MI)

10. Barnes-Jewish Hospital/Washington University (St. Louis, MO)

Source: *U.S. News & World Report*, America's Best Hospitals (annual), http://www.usnews.com, July 18, 2011.

3072 ■ BEST HOSPITALS FOR UROLOGY, 2011

Ranked by: Score based on reputation, mortality rate, and other care-related factors. **Remarks:** Scores not provided. **Number listed:** 1458

1. Johns Hopkins Hospital (Baltimore, MD)

2. Cleveland Clinic

3. Mayo Clinic (Rochester, MN)

4. Ronald Reagan UCLA Medical Center (Los Angeles, CA)

5. Memorial Sloan-Kettering Cancer Center (New York)

6. University of California, San Francisco Medical Center

7. New York-Presbyterian University Hospital of Columbia & Cornell

8. Duke University Medical Center (Durham, NC)

9. Vanderbilt University Medical Center (Nashville, TX)

10. University of Texas, M. D. Anderson Cancer Center (Houston, TX)

Source: *U.S. News & World Report*, America's Best Hospitals (annual), http://www.usnews.com, July 18, 2011.

3073 ■ BEST LARGE COMMUNITY HOSPITALS, 2011

Ranked by: Score based on nine financial, clinical, and operating efficiency measures, including mortality and infection rates, average length of stay, operating profit margins, and expenses per discharge. **Remarks:** Specific scores not provided; hospitals are listed alphabetically by state, not ranked. Ranking includes teaching hospitals with 250 or more acute-care beds. **Number listed:** 20

1. Martin Memorial Medical Center (Stuart, FL)

2. Advocate Good Samaritan Hospital (Downers Grove, IL)

3. Silver Cross Hospital (Joliet, IL)

4. Edward Hospital (Naperville, IL)

5. Trinity Rock Island (Rock Island, IL)

6. Central DuPage Hospital (Winfield, IL)

7. Community Hospital (Munster, IN)

8. Beverly Hospital (Beverly, MA)

9. Allegiance Health (Jackson, MI)

10. Boone Hospital Center (Columbia, MO)

Source: *Modern Healthcare*, Thomson Reuters' Top 100 Hospitals (annual), September 12, 2011, p. 18.

3074 ■ BEST MAJOR TEACHING HOSPITALS, 2011

Ranked by: Score based on nine financial, clinical, and operating efficiency measures, including mortality and infection rates, average length of stay, operating profit margins, and expenses per discharge. **Remarks:** Specific scores not provided; hospitals are listed alphabetically by state, not ranked. Also notes number of years on list. **Number listed:** 15

1. Advocate Illinois Masonic Medical Center (Chicago, IL)

2. Northwestern Memorial Hospital (Chicago, IL)

3. NorthShore University HealthSystem (Evanston, IL)

4. Advocate Lutheran General Hospital (Park Ridge, IL)

5. Ochsner Medical Center (New Orleans, LA)

6. Beth Israel Deaconess Medical Center (Boston, MA)

7. Brigham & Women's Hospital (Boston, MA)

8. Caritas St. Elizabeth's Medical Center (Boston, MA)

9. Massachusetts General Hospital (Boston, MA)

10. Baystate Medical Center (Springfield, MA)

Source: *Modern Healthcare*, Thomson Reuters' Top 100 Hospitals (annual), September 12, 2011, p. 16.

3075 ■ BEST MID-SIZED COMMUNITY HOSPITALS, 2011

Ranked by: Score based on nine financial, clinical, and operating efficiency measures, including mortality and infection rates, average length of stay, operating profit margins, and expenses per discharge. **Remarks:** Specific scores not provided; hospitals are listed alphabetically by state, not ranked. Ranking includes teaching hospitals with 100 to 249 acute-care beds. **Number listed:** 20

1. Thomas Hospital (Fairhope, AL)
2. West Anaheim Medical Center (Anaheim, CA)
3. Middlesex Hospital (Middletown, CT)
4. Cleveland Clinic Florida (Weston, FL)
5. Columbus Regional Hospital (Columbus, IN)
6. Reid Hospital & Health Care Services (Richmond, IN)
7. St. Joseph East (Lexington, KY)
8. Minden Medical Center (Minden, LA)
9. Winchester Hospital (Winchester, MA)
10. Holland Hospital (Holland, MI)

Source: *Modern Healthcare*, Thomson Reuters' Top 100 Hospitals (annual), September 12, 2011, p. 18-20.

3076 ■ BEST SMALL COMMUNITY HOSPITALS, 2011

Ranked by: Score based on nine financial, clinical, and operating efficiency measures, including mortality and infection rates, average length of stay, operating profit margins, and expenses per discharge. **Remarks:** Specific scores not provided; hospitals are listed alphabetically by state, not ranked. Ranking includes teaching hospitals with 25 to 99 acute-care beds. **Number listed:** 20

1. Russell Medical Center (Alexander City, AL)
2. Andalusia Regional Hospital (Andalusia, AL)
3. Payson Regional Medical Center (Payson, AZ)
4. Sutter Davis Hospital (Davis, CA)
5. St. Elizabeth Community Hospital (Red Bluff, CA)
6. Kosciusko Community Hospital (Warsaw, IN)
7. Flaget Memorial Hospital (Bardstown, KY)
8. Harlan ARH Hospital (Harlan, KY)
9. Mercy Hospital Cadillac (Cadillac, MI)
10. Spectrum Health United Memorial (Greenville, MI)

Source: *Modern Healthcare*, Thomson Reuters' Top 100 Hospitals (annual), September 12, 2011, p. 20.

3077 ■ BEST TEACHING HOSPITALS WITH AT LEAST 200 BEDS, 2011

Ranked by: Score based on nine financial, clinical, and operating efficiency measures, including mortality and infection rates, average length of stay, operating profit margins, and expenses per discharge. **Remarks:** Specific scores not provided; hospitals are listed alphabetically by state, not ranked. Ranking includes teaching hospitals with 200 or more acute-care beds. **Number listed:** 25

1. Scripps Green Hospital (La Jolla, CA)
2. Decatur Memorial Hospital (Decatur, IL)
3. Riverside Medical Center (Kankakee, IL)
4. Carle Foundation Hospital (Urbana, IL)
5. St. Vincent Indianapolis Hospital (Indianapolis, IN)
6. Memorial Hospital & Health System (S. Bend, IN)
7. Mercy Medical Center North Iowa (Mason City, IA)
8. St. Elizabeth Healthcare (Edgewood, KY)
9. St. Vincent Hospital (Worcester, MA)

10. Spectrum Health Hospital Group (Grand Rapids, MI)

Source: *Modern Healthcare*, Thomson Reuters' Top 100 Hospitals (annual), September 12, 2011, p. 16-18.

3078 ■ BEST TEACHING HOSPITALS WITH CARDIOVASCULAR RESIDENCIES, 2011

Ranked by: Score based on seven measures of clinical quality and efficiency of operations: volume, medical mortality, surgical mortality, complications, length of stay, cost, and percentage of heart bypass patients in which the mammary artery was used. **Remarks:** Specific scores not provided; hospitals are listed alphabetically by state/city, not ranked. Also notes number of years on list. **Number listed:** 15

1. Mayo Clinic Hospital (Phoenix, AZ)
2. University of Kansas Hospital (Kansas City, KS)
3. Lahey Clinic (Burlington, MA)
4. St. Vincent Hospital (Worcester, MA)
5. Park Nicolett-Methodist Hospital (St. Louis Park, MN)
6. Deborah Heart & Lung Center (Browns Mills, NJ)
7. Hackensack University Medical Center (Hackensack, NJ)
8. New York University Longone Medical Center (New York, NY)
9. Doctors Hospital (Columbus, OH)
10. Kettering Medical Center (Bryn Mawr, PA)

Source: *Modern Healthcare*, Thomson Reuters' Top Cardiovascular Hospitals (annual), November 14, 2011, p. 30.

3079 ■ BEST TEACHING HOSPITALS WITHOUT CARDIOVASCULAR RESIDENCIES, 2011

Ranked by: Score based on seven measures of clinical quality and efficiency of operations: volume, medical mortality, surgical mortality, complications, length of stay, cost, and percentage of heart bypass patients in which the mammary artery was used. **Remarks:** Specific scores not provided; hospitals are listed alphabetically by state/city, not ranked. Also notes number of years on list. **Number listed:** 20

1. Morton Plant Hospital (Clearwater, FL)
2. St. Luke's Boise Medical Center (Boise, ID)
3. Decatur Memorial Hospital (Decatur, IL)
4. St. John's Hospital (Springfield, IL)
5. St. Jospeh Mercy Hospital (Ann Arbor, MI)
6. Marquette General Hospital (Marquette, MI)
7. Aultman Hospital (Canton, OH)
8. Mercy Medical Center (Canton, OH)
9. Bethesda North Hospital (Cincinnati, OH)
10. St. Luke's Hospital (Bethlehem, PA)

Source: *Modern Healthcare*, Thomson Reuters' Top Cardiovascular Hospitals (annual), November 14, 2011, p. 30-31.

3080 ■ LARGEST MILITARY HOSPITALS, 2011

Ranked by: Total number of staffed beds. **Remarks:** Also notes location, type of operation, and Web site. **Number listed:** 26

1. Walter Reed National Military Medical Center, with 350 beds
2. Naval Medical Center San Diego, 285
3. Naval Medical Center Portsmouth, 274

4. Madigan Healthcare System, 243
5. Brooke Army Medical Center, 226
6. Tripler Army Medical Center, 220
7. William Beaumont Army Medical Center, 209
8. U.S. Air Force Medical Center Keesler, 185
9. Womack Army Medical Center, 156
10. Dwight D. Eisenhower Army Medical Center, 125

Source: *Modern Healthcare*, Largest Military Hospitals (annual), February 13, 2012, p. 34.

3081 ■ MOST PROFITABLE CRITICAL-ACCESS HOSPITALS, 2011

Ranked by: Net income, in dollars. **Remarks:** Also notes location and website. **Number listed:** 25

1. Doctors Hospital of Tattnall, with $21,138,428
2. Defiance Regional Medical Center, $19,827,967
3. Mercy Walworth Hospital & Medical Center, $17,586,158
4. Riverside Medical Center, $13,501,011
5. St. Mary's Hospital-Superior, $13,301,875
6. Advocate Eureka Hospital, $12,948,418
7. St. Anthony Hospital, $12,717,736
8. Lourdes Medical Center, $12,704,475
9. Good Shepherd Medical Center, $12,536,965
10. Clinton Memorial Hospital, $12,352,630

Source: *Modern Healthcare*, Most Profitable Critical-Access Hospitals (annual), December 19, 2011, p. 32.

3082 ■ TOP HOSPITAL SYSTEMS FOR DIVERSITY, 2011

Ranked by: Score based on strength in four areas: CEO commitment to diversity, human capital, corporate and organizational communications, and supplier diversity. **Remarks:** Specific scores not provided. To qualify, companies must have more than 1,000 U.S. employees. **Number listed:** 5

1. Henry Ford Health System
2. Brigham & Women's Hospital
3. Massachusetts General Hospital
4. Cleveland Clinic
5. University Hospitals Health System

Source: *DiversityInc*, Top 50 (annual), 2011, p. 100.

Hotel Management Companies

3083 ■ LARGEST THIRD-PARTY HOTEL MANAGEMENT COMPANIES, 2010

Ranked by: Total number of rooms managed. **Remarks:** Also notes rank for previous year, properties owned and managed, and properties managed for other owners. **Number listed:** 50

1. Interstate Hotels & Resorts, with 56,483 rooms
2. White Lodging Services Corp., 23,208
3. GF Management, 18,890
4. TPG Hospitality, 16,823
5. Pyramid Hotel Group, 15,691
6. Aimbridge Hospitality, 14,932
7. Sage Hospitality, 13,675

8. Crescent Hotels & Resorts, 13,642
9. Davidson Hotel Co., 13,333
10. Remington, 13,259

Source: *Lodging Hospitality*, Top Third-Party Management Companies (annual), June 1, 2011, p. 30.

3084 ■ TOP HOTEL BRANDS, 2010

Ranked by: Total number of U.S. rooms. **Remarks:** Also notes rank for previous year, parent company, number of U.S. properties, breakdown by type of property, and number of foreign rooms and properties. **Number listed:** 50

1. Best Western, with 182,630 rooms
2. Hampton, 171,783
3. Holiday Inn Express, 144,493
4. Marriott Hotels & Resorts, 143,876
5. Magnuson Hotels, 131,423
6. Days Inn, 129,437
7. Holiday Inn Hotels & Resorts, 121,456
8. Courtyard by Marriott, 112,041
9. Super 8, 111,403
10. Comfort Inn, 110,932

Source: *Lodging Hospitality*, Top Hotel Brands (annual), June 1, 2011, p. 28.

3085 ■ TOP THIRD-PARTY HOTEL MANAGEMENT COMPANIES, 2011

Ranked by: Total number of rooms managed. **Remarks:** Also notes rank for previous year, figures for previous year, number of properties managed, revenue, and contact. **Number listed:** 171

1. Interstate Hotels & Resorts, with 61,984 rooms
2. Pillar Hotels & Resorts, 23,167
3. GF Management, 21,006
4. White Lodging Services Corp., 20,092
5. Pyramid Hotel Group, 17,318
6. TPG Hospitality, 16,709
7. Crescent Hotels & Resorts, 14,574
8. Remington, 14,196
9. Davidson Hotels & Resorts, 13,464
10. Island Hospitality Management, 10,847

Source: *Hotel Management*, Top Third-Party Management Companies (annual), March 2012, p. 42+.

Hotels and Motels

3086 ■ AMERICA'S LARGEST PRIVATE HOTEL, RESTAURANT, AND LEISURE COMPANIES, 2010

Ranked by: Revenue, in billions of dollars. **Remarks:** Also notes headquarters, number of employees, and overall rank in the *America's Largest Private Companies* list. Ranking is available online only, not in print. **Number listed:** 6

1. Caesars Entertainment Corp., with $8.82 billion
2. Hilton Worldwide Inc., $8
3. Carlson Cos., Inc., $4.13
4. OSI Restaurant Partners LLC, $3.63
5. AMC Entertainment Inc., $2.42
6. Burger King Holdings Inc., $2.33

Source: *Forbes*, America's Largest Private Companies (annual), http://www.forbes.com, December 5, 2011.

3087 ■ BRITAIN'S MOST ADMIRED LEISURE AND HOTEL COMPANIES, 2011

Ranked by: Survey of peers and investment analysts based on nine criteria: quality of management, financial soundness, quality of goods/services, ability to attract and retain talent, value as long-term investment, innovation, marketing, community and environmental responsibility, and use of corporate assets. **Number listed:** 5

1. InterContinental Hotels Group plc, with 65 points
2. Carnival plc, 58.3
3. Holidaybreak, 56.7
4. Whitbread plc, 53.8
5. Tui Travel, 51.5

Source: *Management Today*, Britain's Most Admired Companies (annual), December 2011, p. 45.

3088 ■ LARGEST HOTEL AND LODGING COMPANIES BY EMPLOYEES, 2010

Ranked by: Total number of employees. **Remarks:** Also notes contact information for headquarters, number of employees at headquarters, revenue, rank by revenue, and primary SIC code. **Number listed:** 89

1. Carlson Holdings Inc., with 191,838 employees
2. Carlson Inc., 166,718
3. Sheraton Corp., 145,000
3. Starwood Hotels & Resorts Worldwide Inc., 145,000
5. Marriott International Inc., 137,000
6. Hilton Hotels Holdings Corp., 135,000
7. Hilton Worldwide Inc., 105,000
8. Caesars Entertainment Corp., 69,000
9. MGM Resorts International, 62,000
10. Intercontinental Hotels Group Resources Inc., 60,000

Source: *Business Rankings*, (annual), Dun & Bradstreet Inc., 2011, p. VI.202-VI.203.

3089 ■ LARGEST HOTEL AND LODGING COMPANIES BY SALES, 2010

Ranked by: Total revenue, in dollars. **Remarks:** Also notes contact information for headquarters, number of employees at headquarters and overall, rank by employees, and primary SIC code. **Number listed:** 90

1. Marriott International Inc., with $11,691,000,000
2. North Bethesda Hotel LLC, $9,000,000,000
3. Caesars Entertainment Corp., $8,818,600,000
4. Las Vegas Sands Corp., $6,853,182,000
5. MGM Resorts International, $6,019,233,000
6. Starwood Hotels & Resorts Worldwide Inc., $5,071,000,000
7. Wynn Resorts Ltd., $4,184,698,000
8. Wyndham Worldwide Corp., $3,851,000,000
9. Hyatt Hotels Corp., $3,527,000,000
10. Boyd Gaming Corp., $2,140,899,000

Source: *Business Rankings*, (annual), Dun & Bradstreet Inc., 2011, p. V.176-V.177.

3090 ■ LARGEST U.S. HOTEL AND MOTEL COMPANIES OVERALL, 2011

Ranked by: Score based on revenue, profits, assets, and market capitalization. **Remarks:** Specific scores not provided. Also notes overall rank in the *Forbes 2000* and figures for each criterion. **Number listed:** 3

1. Starwood Hotels & Resorts Worldwide Inc.
2. Marriott International Inc.
3. Wyndham Worldwide Corp.

Source: *Forbes*, Forbes 2000 (annual), http://www.forbes.com, May 7, 2012.

3091 ■ TOP *FORTUNE 500* HOTELS, CASINOS, AND RESORTS, 2011

Ranked by: Revenue, in millions of dollars. **Remarks:** Also notes overall rank in the *Fortune 500;* profits; profits as a percentage of revenue; stockholders' equity; and rank by each criterion. **Number listed:** 6

1. Marriott International Inc., with $12,317 million
2. Las Vegas Sands Corp., $9,411
3. Caesars Entertainment Corp., $8,835
4. MGM Resorts International, $7,849
5. Starwood Hotels & Resorts Worldwide Inc., $5,624
6. Wynn Resorts, $5,270

Source: *Fortune*, Fortune 500 (annual), May 21, 2012, p. F-36.

3092 ■ TOP HOTEL CHAINS BY SALES PER UNIT, 2010

Ranked by: Sales per unit, in thousands of dollars. **Remarks:** Also notes rank for previous year, fiscal year-end, and figures for previous two years. **Number listed:** 5

1. Sheraton Hotels, with $4,732.3 thousand
2. Hilton Hotels, $4,688.3
3. Hyatt Hotels, $4,373
4. Marriott Hotels & Resorts, $3,920.2
5. Holiday Inn, $349.9

Source: *Nation's Restaurant News*, Top 100 (annual), June 27, 2011, p. 38.

3093 ■ TOP HOTEL CHAINS BY U.S. UNITS, 2010

Ranked by: Total number of U.S. units. **Remarks:** Also notes rank for previous year, fiscal year-end, and figures for previous two years. **Number listed:** 5

1. Holiday Inn, with 2,044 units
2. Marriott Hotels & Resorts, 326
3. Hilton Hotels, 253
4. Sheraton Hotels, 186
5. Hyatt Hotels, 122

Source: *Nation's Restaurant News*, Top 100 (annual), June 27, 2011, p. 68.

3094 ■ TOP HOTEL AND MOTEL FRANCHISES, 2012

Ranked by: Cumulative score based on financial strength and stability, growth rate, size of the system, number of years in business, the length of time franchising, start-up costs, litigation, percentage of terminations, and whether the company provides financing. **Remarks:** Specific scores not provided. Also notes overall rank within the *Franchise 500*, contact information, description, year founded, year started franchising, states where registered, available U.S. regions, where seeking foreign expansion, number of franchised and company-owned units for past three years, start-up costs, franchise fees, royalty fees, and type of financing available. **Number listed:** 26

1. Hampton Hotels
2. Days Inn
3. Super 8 Motels Inc.

4. InterContinental Hotels Group plc

5. Motel 6

6. Choice Hotels International Inc.

7. Hilton Garden Inn

8. Ramada

9. Hilton Hotels & Resorts

10. Knights Inn

Source: *Entrepreneur*, Franchise 500 (annual), January 2012, p. 180-181.

3095 ■ TOP HOTEL OWNERS, 2010

Ranked by: Total number of hotel rooms owned globally. **Remarks:** Also notes contact information. **Number listed:** 25

1. The Blackstone Group, with 232,938 rooms

2. Accor North America, 112,644

3. Host Hotels & Resorts Inc., 65,000

4. LQ Management LLC, 48,469

5. Hospitality Properties Trust, 42,880

6. Apple REIT Cos., 29,927

7. ING Clarion Partners, 27,844

8. Ashford Hospitality Trust, 26,257

9. JER Partners, 24,701

10. FelCor Lodging Trust Inc., 23,500

Source: *National Real Estate Investor*, Best of the Best (annual), 2011, p. 59-61.

3096 ■ TOP HOTELS CHAINS BY GROWTH IN UNITS, 2009-2010

Ranked by: Annual growth in number of U.S. units, in percent. **Remarks:** Also notes rank for previous year, fiscal year-end, and figures for previous year. **Number listed:** 5

1. Hilton Hotels, with 4.98%

2. Marriott Hotels & Resorts, 0%

3. Holiday Inn, -2.67%

4. Hyatt Hotels, -6.15%

5. Sheraton Hotels, -11.43%

Source: *Nation's Restaurant News*, Top 100 (annual), June 27, 2011, p. 68.

3097 ■ TOP U.S. HOTEL BRANDS, 2011

Ranked by: Total number of guestrooms. **Remarks:** Also notes rank for previous year, website, parent company, contact, number of U.S. properties, number of properties and guestrooms under development, and franchise availability. **Number listed:** 111

1. Best Western International, with 182,352 guestrooms

2. Hampton Hotels, 173,391

3. Holiday Inn Express, 147,070

4. Marriott Hotels & Resorts, 136,683

5. Days Inn, 127,993

6. Holiday Inn Hotels & Resorts, 119,580

7. Courtyard by Marriott, 115,507

8. Comfort Inn, 110,652

9. Super 8, 110,382

10. Hilton Hotels & Resorts, 104,299

Source: *Hotel Management*, Hotel Brands Survey (annual), February 2012, p. 20+.

3098 ■ TOP U.S. HOTEL COMPANIES, 2011

Ranked by: Total number of guestrooms in the U.S. **Remarks:** Also notes rank for previous year, contact information, type of company, number of properties in the U.S. and worldwide, and number of guestrooms worldwide. **Number listed:** 182

1. Marriott International Inc., with 497,812 guestrooms

2. Hilton Worldwide Inc., 489,040

3. Wyndham Hotel Group, 453,705

4. Choice Hotels International Inc., 390,407

5. InterContinental Hotels Group plc, 388,255

6. Best Western International Inc., 182,308

7. Starwood Hotels & Resorts Worldwide Inc., 156,000

8. Magnuson Hotels, 136,756

9. Accor, 107,690

10. Hyatt Hotels Corp., 87,955

Source: *Hotel Management*, Top Hotel Companies (annual), September 2011, p. 30-36.

3099 ■ WORLD'S LARGEST HOTEL AND MOTEL COMPANIES OVERALL, 2011

Ranked by: Score based on revenue, profits, assets, and market capitalization. **Remarks:** Specific scores not provided. Also notes country, overall rank in the *Forbes 2000,* and figures for each criterion. **Number listed:** 10

1. Carnival plc

2. Royal Caribbean Cruises Ltd.

3. Starwood Hotels & Resorts Worldwide Inc.

4. Marriott International Inc.

5. Accor

6. Wyndham Worldwide Corp.

7. InterContinental Hotels Group plc

8. Oriental Land Co., Ltd.

9. Shenzhen Overseas Chinese Town Co., Ltd.

10. Shangri-La Asia Ltd.

Source: *Forbes*, Forbes 2000 (annual), http://www.forbes.com, May 7, 2012.

3100 ■ WORLD'S MOST ADMIRED HOTEL, CASINO, AND RESORT COMPANIES, 2012

Ranked by: Score, on a scale of 10, based on a survey of executives, directors, and securities analysts of companies within their own industry on eight criteria: innovation, financial soundness, employee talent, use of corporate assets, long-term investment value, social responsibility, quality of management, and quality of products/services. **Remarks:** Specific scores not provided. Also notes rank for previous year. **Number listed:** 5

1. Wyndham Worldwide Corp.

2. Wynn Resorts Ltd.

3. Starwood Hotels & Resorts Worldwide Inc.

4. Hyatt Hotels Corp.

5. Marriott International Inc.

Source: *Fortune*, World's Most Admired Companies (annual), March 19, 2012, p. 148.

3101 ■ WORLD'S MOST ETHICAL LEISURE AND HOSPITALITY COMPANIES, 2012

Ranked by: Score based on five criteria: ethics and compliance program; reputation, leadership, and innovation; governance;

corporate citizenship and responsibility; and culture of ethics. **Remarks:** Specific scores not provided; companies are listed alphabetically, not ranked. **Number listed:** 5

1. Holland America Line (U.S.)
2. Kimpton Hotel & Restaurant Group LLC (U.S.)
3. Marriott International Inc. (U.S.)
4. The Rezidor Hotel Group (Belgium)
5. Seabourn (U.S.)

Source: *Ethisphere Magazine*, World's Most Ethical Companies (annual), http://www.ethisphere.com, 2012.

3102 ■ WORLD'S MOST VALUABLE LODGING BRANDS, 2011

Ranked by: Brand value, in millions of U.S. dollars. **Remarks:** Also notes rank within the *Global 500* for current and previous year, figures for current and previous year, country, and brand rating. Ranking is available online only. **Number listed:** 2

1. Genting, with $2,825 million
2. Marriott, $2,539

Source: *Global 500*, (annual), Brand Finance plc, March 2012.

3103 ■ WORLD'S TOP HOTEL SPAS, 2011

Ranked by: Score, on a scale of 100, based on consumer survey regarding ambience, treatments, service, and value. **Number listed:** 10

1. Sofitel Queenstown Hotel and Spa (New Zealand), with 98.93 points
2. Ritz-Carlton (New Orleans), 98
3. Couples Tower Isle (Jamaica), 97.67
4. Rome Cavalieri, A Waldorf Astoria Hotel (Italy), 96.92
5. Omni Bedford Springs Resort (Pennsylvania), 96.50
6. Couples Sans Souci (Jamaica), 95.86
7. Discovery Shores (Phillippines), 95.63
8. Mandarin Oriental (Thailand), 95.35
9. Four Seasons Hotel George V (France), 95.33
10. St. Regis Hotel (Singapore), 95.23

Source: *Travel + Leisure*, World's Best Awards (annual), August 2011.

3104 ■ WORLD'S TOP HOTELS, 2011

Ranked by: Score, on a scale of 100, based on consumer survey regarding rooms/facilities, location, service, restaurant/food, and value. **Number listed:** 100

1. Singita Grumeti Reserves (Tanzania), with 98.44 points
2. Singita Sabi Sand (South Africa), 97.95
3. Royal Malewane (South Africa), 97.88
4. ol Donyo Lodge (Kenya), 97.71
5. Oberoi Udaivilas (India), 97.70
6. Triple Creek Ranch (Montana), 97.10
7. Mandarin Oriental Dhara Dhevi (Thailand), 97
8. Oberoi Rajvilas (India), 96.92
9. Kirawira Luxury Tented Camp (Tanzania), 96.71
10. Serengeti Migration Camp (Tanzania), 96.50

Source: *Travel + Leisure*, World's Best Awards (annual), August 2011.

Hotels and Motels—Design and Construction

3105 ■ LARGEST HOTEL DESIGN FIRMS, 2011

Ranked by: Fees from lodging projects, in dollars. **Remarks:** Also notes rank for previous year, Web site, total revenue, number of lodging projects, total number of projects, projected number of projects, and type of company. **Number listed:** 66

1. 1. Hirsch Bedner Associates, with $85,442,000
2. 2. CWL Hospitality, $80,000,000
3. 3. M. Arthur Gensler Jr. & Associates Inc., $52,000,000
4. 4. HFS Concepts 4, $35,000,000
5. 4. Wilson Associates, $35,000,000
6. 6. Level 3 Design Group, $34,000,000
7. 7. HKS, $32,336,523
8. 8. Aedas, $25,300,000
9. 9. American Hotel Register Co., $25,000,000
10. 9. Innvision Design, $25,000,000

Source: *Hotel Management*, Top Design Firms (annual), May 2012, p. 24-28.

Hotels and Motels—Food Service

3106 ■ TOP HOTEL CHAINS BY GROWTH IN FOODSERVICE SALES, 2009-2010

Ranked by: Annual growth in systemwide foodservice sales, in percent. **Remarks:** Also notes rank for previous year, fiscal year-end, and figures for previous year. **Number listed:** 5

1. Hilton Hotels, with 6.24%
2. Marriott Hotels & Resorts, 4.33%
3. Holiday Inn, 2.84%
4. Hyatt Hotels, 0.92%
5. Sheraton Hotels, 0.21%

Source: *Nation's Restaurant News*, Top 100 (annual), June 27, 2011, p. 68.

3107 ■ TOP HOTEL CHAINS BY U.S. FOODSERVICE SALES, 2010

Ranked by: U.S. systemwide foodservice sales, in millions of dollars. **Remarks:** Also notes rank for previous year, fiscal year-end, and figures for previous two years. **Number listed:** 5

1. Marriott Hotels & Resorts, with $1,278 million
2. Hilton Hotels, $1,158
3. Sheraton Hotels, $937
4. Holiday Inn, $725
5. Hyatt Hotels, $551

Source: *Nation's Restaurant News*, Top 100 (annual), June 27, 2011, p. 68.

Hours of Labor

3108 ■ BEST COMPANIES FOR HOURLY WORKERS, 2011

Ranked by: Score based on such criteria as workforce, benefits, training, flexibility, and paid time-off. **Remarks:** Specific scores not provided; companies are ranked alphabetically, not ranked. Also notes headquarters, percentage of workforce that is hourly staff, top executive, human resources director, and comments. **Number listed:** 12

1. Best Buy Co., Inc.
2. Bon Secours Virginia
3. Capital One Financial Corp.
4. Cricket Communications Inc.
5. Hilton Worldwide
6. Marriott International Inc.
7. PETsMART Inc.
8. Sodexo
9. Target Corp.
10. University of Wisconsin Hospitals

Source: *Working Mother*, Best Companies for Hourly Workers (annual), 2012, p. 48+.

Household Appliances

3109 ■ CHINA'S LARGEST HOUSEHOLD APPLIANCE COMPANIES OVERALL, 2011

Ranked by: Score based on revenue, profits, assets, and market capitalization. **Remarks:** Specific scores not provided. Also notes overall rank in the *Forbes 2000* and figures for each criterion. **Number listed:** 3

1. Gree Electrical Appliances Inc.
2. GD Midea Holding Co., Ltd.
3. Qingdao Haier

Source: *Forbes*, Forbes 2000 (annual), http://www.forbes.com, May 7, 2012.

3110 ■ WORLD'S LARGEST HOUSEHOLD APPLIANCE COMPANIES OVERALL, 2011

Ranked by: Score based on revenue, profits, assets, and market capitalization. **Remarks:** Specific scores not provided. Also notes country, overall rank in the *Forbes 2000,* and figures for each criterion. **Number listed:** 6

1. Gree Electrical Appliances Inc.
2. LG Corp.
3. GD Midea Holding Co., Ltd.
4. Whirlpool Corp.
5. AB Electrolux
6. Qingdao Haier Co., Ltd.

Source: *Forbes*, Forbes 2000 (annual), http://www.forbes.com, May 7, 2012.

Household Income
See: **Income**

Household Products
See: **Housewares**

Houses—Maintenance and Repair

3111 ■ TOP CARPET, UPHOLSTERY, AND DRAPERY SERVICE FRANCHISES, 2012

Ranked by: Cumulative score based on financial strength and stability, growth rate, size of the system, number of years in busi-

ness, the length of time franchising, start-up costs, litigation, percentage of terminations, and whether the company provides financing. **Remarks:** Specific scores not provided. Also notes overall rank within the *Franchise 500,* contact information, description, year founded, year started franchising, states where registered, available U.S. regions, where seeking foreign expansion, number of franchised and company-owned units for past three years, start-up costs, franchise fees, royalty fees, and type of financing available. **Number listed:** 17

1. Chem-Dry Carpet, Drapery, & Upholstery Cleaning
2. Heaven's Best Carpet & Upholstery Cleaning
3. Oxi Fresh Franchising Co.
4. Sears Home & Business Franchises Inc.
5. Stratus Building Solutions
6. CleanNet USA
7. System4
8. Vanguard Cleaning Systems
9. ServiceMaster Clean
10. Anago Cleaning Systems

Source: *Entrepreneur*, Franchise 500 (annual), January 2012, p. 180-183.

3112 ■ TOP HANDYMAN FRANCHISES, 2012

Ranked by: Cumulative score based on financial strength and stability, growth rate, size of the system, number of years in business, the length of time franchising, start-up costs, litigation, percentage of terminations, and whether the company provides financing. **Remarks:** Specific scores not provided. Also notes overall rank within the *Franchise 500,* contact information, description, year founded, year started franchising, available U.S. regions, where seeking foreign expansion, number of franchised and company-owned units for past three years, start-up costs, franchise fees, royalty fees, and type of financing available. **Number listed:** 2

1. Handyman Connection
2. Mr. Handyman International LLC

Source: *Entrepreneur*, Franchise 500 (annual), January 2012, p. 182-183.

3113 ■ TOP HOME RESTORATION SERVICE FRANCHISES, 2012

Ranked by: Cumulative score based on financial strength and stability, growth rate, size of the system, number of years in business, the length of time franchising, start-up costs, litigation, percentage of terminations, and whether the company provides financing. **Remarks:** Specific scores not provided. Also notes overall rank within the *Franchise 500,* contact information, description, year founded, year started franchising, states where registered, available U.S. regions, where seeking foreign expansion, number of franchised and company-owned units for past three years, start-up costs, franchise fees, royalty fees, and type of financing available. **Number listed:** 7

1. Servpro
2. Rainbow Internnational Restoration & Cleaning
3. Disaster Kleenup International
4. Paul Davis Restoration
5. PuroClean
6. Steamatic
7. 1-800-Water Damage

Source: *Entrepreneur*, Franchise 500 (annual), January 2012, p. 186-187.

3114 ■ TOP MISCELLANEOUS HOME REPAIR FRANCHISES, 2012

Ranked by: Cumulative score based on financial strength and stability, growth rate, size of the system, number of years in business, the length of time franchising, start-up costs, litigation, percentage of terminations, and whether the company provides financing. **Remarks:** Specific scores not provided. Also notes overall rank within the *Franchise 500,* contact information, description, year founded, year started franchising, states where registered, available U.S. regions, where seeking foreign expansion, number of franchised and company-owned units for past three years, start-up costs, franchise fees, royalty fees, and type of financing available. **Number listed:** 6

1. Glass Doctor
2. Mr. Appliance Corp.
3. The Glass Guru
4. Furniture Medic
5. The Screenmobile
6. Precision Door Service

Source: *Entrepreneur,* Franchise 500 (annual), January 2012, p. 184-185.

Houses—Remodeling

3115 ■ LARGEST INDEPENDENT REMODELING FIRMS, 2010

Ranked by: Remodeling volume, in dollars. **Remarks:** Also notes headquarters, executive, website, projected volume, number of employees, and number of years in business. **Number listed:** 500

1. Belfor USA Group Inc., with $762,333,000
2. Champion Window Manufacturing & Supply Co., $316,970,124
3. U.S. Home Systems Inc., $145,873,000
4. Power Home Remodeling Group, $129,279,367
5. Bath Fitter, $63,298,876
6. Castle, the Window People Inc., $55,627,852
7. American Technologies Inc., $52,054,000
8. Thompson Creek Window Co., $47,885,820
9. Aspire Design Inc., $46,848,682
10. 1-800-Hansons, $46,159,920

Source: *Qualified Remodeler,* Top 500 (annual), August 2011, p. 34+.

3116 ■ TOP BUILDING AND REMODELING FRANCHISES, 2012

Ranked by: Cumulative score based on financial strength and stability, growth rate, size of the system, number of years in business, the length of time franchising, start-up costs, litigation, percentage of terminations, and whether the company provides financing. **Remarks:** Specific scores not provided. Also notes overall rank within the *Franchise 500,* contact information, description, year founded, year started franchising, states where registered, available U.S. regions, where seeking foreign expansion, number of franchised and company-owned units for past three years, start-up costs, franchise fees, royalty fees, and type of financing available. **Number listed:** 4

1. Solar Universe
2. Kitchen Tune-Up
3. A-1 Concrete Leveling Inc.
4. Precision Concrete Cutting

Source: *Entrepreneur,* Franchise 500 (annual), January 2012, p. 176-177.

3117 ■ TOP HOME PAINTING FRANCHISES, 2012

Ranked by: Cumulative score based on financial strength and stability, growth rate, size of the system, number of years in business, the length of time franchising, start-up costs, litigation, percentage of terminations, and whether the company provides financing. **Remarks:** Specific scores not provided. Also notes overall rank within the *Franchise 500,* contact information, description, year founded, year started franchising, states where registered, available U.S. regions, where seeking foreign expansion, number of franchised and company-owned units for past three years, start-up costs, franchise fees, royalty fees, and type of financing available. **Number listed:** 3

1. CertaPro Painters Ltd.
2. Fresh Coat
3. Five Star Painting

Source: *Entrepreneur,* Franchise 500 (annual), January 2012, p. 178-179.

3118 ■ TOP HOME SURFACE REFINISHING/ RESTORATION FRANCHISES, 2012

Ranked by: Cumulative score based on financial strength and stability, growth rate, size of the system, number of years in business, the length of time franchising, start-up costs, litigation, percentage of terminations, and whether the company provides financing. **Remarks:** Specific scores not provided. Also notes overall rank within the *Franchise 500,* contact information, description, year founded, year started franchising, states where registered, available U.S. regions, where seeking foreign expansion, number of franchised and company-owned units for past three years, start-up costs, franchise fees, royalty fees, and type of financing available. **Number listed:** 4

1. Miracle Method Surface Refinishing
2. Get A Grip Franchising LLC
3. Granite Transformations
4. Re-Bath LLC

Source: *Entrepreneur,* Franchise 500 (annual), January 2012, p. 178-179.

Housewares

3119 ■ EUROPE'S MOST VALUABLE HOUSEHOLD GOODS COMPANIES, 2011

Ranked by: Market value as of March 2011, in millions of U.S. dollars. **Remarks:** Also notes rank within the *FT Europe 500,* rank for previous year, country, revenue, net income, assets, number of employees, share price, price-to-earning ratio, dividend yield, and fiscal yearend. **Number listed:** 5

1. Reckitt Benckiser plc, with $37,269.2 million
2. Henkel KgaA, $24,642.3
3. AB Electrolux, $8,032.9
4. Groupe SEB, $4,928
5. Bic, $4,322

Source: *Financial Times,* FT 500 (annual), http://www.ft.com, June 24, 2011.

3120 ■ LARGEST NON-U.S. HOUSEHOLD AND PERSONAL PRODUCTS COMPANIES, 2010

Ranked by: Sales, in billions of U.S. dollars. **Remarks:** Also notes country. **Number listed:** 30

1. Unilever, with $28.5 billion
2. L'Oreal SA, $25.8
3. Reckitt Benckiser plc, $13
4. Henkel KgaA, $10
5. Kao Corp., $9.5
6. Shiseido Co., Ltd., $7.5
7. Beiersdorf AG, $7
8. LVMH Moet Hennessy Louis Vuitton SA, $4
9. Lion Corp., $2.9
9. Natura Cosmeticos SA, $2.9

Source: *Happi: Household & Personal Products Industry*, International Top 30 (annual), http://www.happi.com, August 2011.

3121 ■ MOST VALUABLE U.S. HOUSEHOLD GOODS COMPANIES, 2011

Ranked by: Market value as of March 2011, in millions of U.S. dollars. **Remarks:** Also notes rank within the *FT U.S. 500*, rank for previous year, country, revenue, net income, assets, number of employees, share price, price-to-earning ratio, dividend yield, and fiscal yearend. **Number listed:** 4

1. Procter & Gamble Co., with $172,528.2 million
2. Stanley Black & Decker Inc., $12,808.1
3. The Clorox Co., $9,642.4
4. Whirlpool Corp., $5,491.4

Source: *Financial Times*, FT 500 (annual), http://www.ft.com, June 24, 2011.

3122 ■ TOP HOUSEHOLD PRODUCT BRANDS BY ADVERTISING EXPENDITURES, 2010

Ranked by: Share of U.S. household product measured media spending, in percent. **Remarks:** Also notes parent company, measured media expenditures, and figures for previous year. **Number listed:** 10

1. Tide, with 7.5%
2. Clorox, 7.3%
3. Glade, 5.6
3. Febreze, 5.6%
3. Swiffer, 5.6%
6. Lysol, 4.1%
7. Charmin, 3%
8. Oxiclean, 2.8%
9. Energizer, 2.6%
10. Duracell, 2.5%

Source: *Advertising Age*, Leading National Advertisers (annual), June 20, 2011, p. 21.

3123 ■ WORLD'S LARGEST HOUSEWARES AND APPLIANCES COMPANIES, 2010

Ranked by: Sales, in millions of U.S. dollars. **Remarks:** Also notes brands and annual sales growth. **Number listed:** 10

1. Whirlpool Corp., with $18,400 million
2. AB Electrolux, $16,159
3. Bosch und Siemens Hausgerate GmbH, $12,536
4. GE Home & Business Solutions, $8,600
5. Stanley Black & Decker Inc., $8,400
6. Jarden Corp., $6,023
7. Groupe SEB SA, $5,046

8. Indesit Co. SpA, $3,978
9. Arcelik AS, $3,891
10. Makita Corp., $3,235

Source: *Consumer Goods Technology*, Consumer Goods Registry (annual), http://www.consumergoods.com, December 2011.

3124 ■ WORLD'S MOST VALUABLE HOUSEHOLD GOODS COMPANIES, 2011

Ranked by: Market value as of March 2011, in millions of U.S. dollars. **Remarks:** Also notes rank within the *FT 500*, rank for previous year, country, revenue, net income, assets, number of employees, share price, price-to-earning ratio, dividend yield, and fiscal year-end. **Number listed:** 3

1. Procter & Gamble Co., with $172,528.2 million
2. Reckitt Benckiser plc, $37,259.2
3. Henkel KgaA, $24,642.3

Source: *Financial Times*, FT 500 (annual), http://www.ft.com, June 24, 2011.

Housing—Costs

3125 ■ MOST EXPENSIVE ZIP CODES, 2011

Ranked by: Median home sale price, in millions of dollars. **Remarks:** Also notes annual percent change, average number of days on the market, inventory, median household income, and population density. Only the top 10 are available in print; the remainder is available online. **Number listed:** 500

1. 07620, Alpine, NJ, with $4.5 million
2. 94027, Atherton, CA, $4.3
3. 11962, Sagaponack, NY, $3.6
4. 94010, Hillsborough, CA, $3.5
4. 90210, Beverly Hills, CA, $3.5
6. 10012, New York, NY, $3.4
7. 10013, New York, NY, $3.3
7. 11976, Water Mill, NY, $3.3
9. 93108, Montecito, CA, $3.1
9. 11568, Old Westbury, NY, $3.1

Source: *Forbes*, Most Expensive Zip Codes (annual), November 7, 2011, p. 26.

Human Resource Managers

3126 ■ FASTEST-GROWING PRIVATE HUMAN RESOURCES COMPANIES IN THE U.S., 2007-2010

Ranked by: Average annual sales growth over three years, in percent. **Remarks:** Also notes headquarters, revenue, and rank in the overall *Inc. 500*. To qualify, private companies must have had annual revenues of at least $100,000 in 2007 and $2 million in 2010. **Number listed:** 7

1. Nextaff, with 1,167.5%
2. Optimum Outsourcing, 1,085.4%
3. Jobfox, 962.5%
4. M Force Staffing, 960.8%
5. BountyJobs, 881.1%
6. ROCS Entry Level Staffing, 862.4%
7. oDesk, 792.4%

Source: *Inc.*, Inc. 500 (annual), September 2011, p. 156.

Hypermarkets

3127 ■ LARGEST ASIA-PACIFIC HYPERMARKET COMPANIES, 2010

Ranked by: Sales, in millions of U.S. dollars. **Remarks:** Also notes country, fascias/brands, number of outlets, sales in national currency, sales area, sales per square meter, and figures for previous year. **Number listed:** 10

1. Shinsegae, with $9,422 million
2. Samsung Tesco, $7,931
3. Auchan China, $7,633
4. Wal-Mart (China) Investment, $7,150
5. China Resources Enterprise, $6,271
6. Carrefour (China) Hypermarket, $5,192
7. Lotte Shopping Co., Ltd., $5,170
8. Ek-Chai Distribution System, $3,629
9. Shenzhen A-Best Supermarket, $2,570
10. Brilliance Group, $2,491

Source: *Retail Asia*, Retail Asia-Pacific Top 500 (annual), July 2011, p. 65-65a.

Ice Cream Shops

3128 ■ TOP ICE CREAM AND FROZEN DESSERTS FRANCHISES, 2012

Ranked by: Cumulative score based on financial strength and stability, growth rate, size of the system, number of years in business, the length of time franchising, start-up costs, litigation, percentage of terminations, and whether the company provides financing. **Remarks:** Specific scores not provided. Also notes overall rank within the *Franchise 500,* contact information, description, year founded, year started franchising, states where registered, available U.S. regions, where seeking foreign expansion, number of franchised and company-owned units for past three years, start-up costs, franchise fees, royalty fees, and type of financing available. **Number listed:** 18

1. Dairy Queen
2. Baskin-Robbins USA Co.
3. Cold Stone Creamery
4. Culver Franchising System Inc.
5. Rita's Italian Ice
6. Carvel
7. Yogurtland Franchising Inc.
8. Yogen Fruz
9. Ben & Jerry's
10. Menchie's

Source: *Entrepreneur*, Franchise 500 (annual), January 2012, p. 166-169.

Income

3129 ■ STATES WITH THE HIGHEST MEDIAN HOUSEHOLD INCOME, 2009

Ranked by: Median household income, in dollars. **Number listed:** 51

1. New Hampshire, with $66,654
2. Connecticut, $65,213
3. Maryland, $65,183
4. New Jersey, $64,143
5. Alaska, $63,505
6. Virginia, $61,151
7. Hawaii, $61,055
8. Massachusetts, $59,981
9. Colorado, $59,964
10. Washington, $58,964

Source: *State Rankings*, (annual), CQ Press, 2011, p. 103.

3130 ■ STATES WITH THE HIGHEST PERSONAL INCOME, 2009

Ranked by: Personal income, in dollars. **Remarks:** Also notes share of national total **Number listed:** 51

1. California, with $1,572,650,187,000
2. Texas, $955,264,348,000
3. New York, $907,885,800,000
4. Florida, $720,949,106,000
5. Illinois, $540,994,727,000
6. Pennsylvania, $506,215,135,000
7. New Jersey, $435,465,803,000
8. Ohio, $410,799,065,000
9. Virginia, $347,849,874,000
10. Michigan, $342,302,212,000

Source: *State Rankings*, (annual), CQ Press, 2011, p. 98.

3131 ■ STATES WITH THE LOWEST MEDIAN HOUSEHOLD INCOME, 2009

Ranked by: Median household income, in dollars. **Number listed:** 51

1. Mississippi, with $36,650
2. Arkansas, $39,392
3. West Virginia, $40,627
4. Tennessee, $40,895
5. Kentucky, $41,489
6. Louisiana, $42,528
7. Alabama, $42,652
8. Montana, $42,778
9. South Carolina, $42,945
10. North Carolina, $43,229

Source: *State Rankings*, (annual), CQ Press, 2011, p. 103.

3132 ■ STATES WITH THE LOWEST PERSONAL INCOME, 2009

Ranked by: Personal income, in dollars. **Remarks:** Also notes share of national total. **Number listed:** 51

1. Vermont, with $24,261,430,000
2. Wyoming, $26,221,601,000
3. North Dakota, $26,343,904,000
4. Alaska, $30,180,493,000
5. South Dakota, $31,039,584,000
6. Montana, $33,923,301,000
7. Delaware, $35,359,927,000
8. Washington DC, $40,784,749,000
9. Rhode Island, $43,522,321,000
10. Maine, $48,089,690,000

Source: *State Rankings*, (annual), CQ Press, 2011, p. 98.

Income Tax
See also: **Taxation**

3133 ■ STATES WITH THE HIGHEST TOP CORPORATE INCOME TAX RATES, 2011

Ranked by: Top corporate income tax rate, in percent. **Remarks:** In the event of a tie, states are ranked alphabetically. **Number listed:** 51

1. Pennsylvania, with 9.99%
2. Washington DC, 9.97%
3. Iowa, 9.9%
4. Minnesota, 9.8%
5. Illinois, 9.5%
6. Alaska, 9.4%
7. Connecticut, 9%
7. New Jersey, 9%
7. Rhode Island, 9%
10. Maine, 8.93%

Source: *Small Business Survival Index*, (annual), Small Business & Entrepreneurship Council, November 2011, p. 41.

3134 ■ STATES WITH THE HIGHEST TOP PERSONAL INCOME TAX RATES, 2011

Ranked by: Top personal income tax rate, in percent. **Remarks:** In the event of a tie, states are ranked alphabetically. **Number listed:** 51

1. Hawaii, with 11%
1. Oregon, 11%
3. California, 10.3%
4. New Jersey, 8.97%
4. New York, 8.97%
6. Vermont, 8.95%
7. Maine, 8.5%
7. Washington DC, 8.5%
9. Minnesota, 7.85%
10. Idaho, 7.8%

Source: *Small Business Survival Index*, (annual), Small Business & Entrepreneurship Council, November 2011, p. 39.

3135 ■ STATES WITH THE LOWEST TOP CORPORATE INCOME TAX RATES, 2011

Ranked by: Top corporate income tax rate, in percent. **Remarks:** In the event of a tie, states are ranked alphabetically. **Number listed:** 51

1. Nevada, with 0%
1. Ohio, 0%
1. South Dakota, 0%
1. Texas, 0%
1. Washington, 0%
1. Wyoming, 0%
7. Alabama, 4.225%
8. Colorado, 4.63%
9 . Mississippi, 5%
9. South Carolina, 5%
9. Utah, 5%

Source: *Small Business Survival Index*, (annual), Small Business & Entrepreneurship Council, November 2011, p. 41.

3136 ■ STATES WITH THE LOWEST TOP PERSONAL INCOME TAX RATES, 2011

Ranked by: Top personal income tax rate, in percent. **Remarks:** In the event of a tie, states are ranked alphabetically. **Number listed:** 51

1. Alaska, with 0%
1. Florida, 0%
1. Nevada, 0%
1. New Hampshire, 0%
1. South Dakota, 0%
1. Tennessee, 0%
1. Texas, 0%
1. Washington, 0%
1. Wyoming, 0%
10. Pennsylvania, 3.07%

Source: *Small Business Survival Index*, (annual), Small Business & Entrepreneurship Council, November 2011, p. 39.

Individual Retirement Accounts (IRA's)

3137 ■ LARGEST S & LS BY IRA DEPOSITS, 2011

Ranked by: Total IRA deposits, in thousands of dollars. **Remarks:** Also notes city, state, association type, and dollar and percent change from previous year. **Number listed:** 25

1. Charles Schwab Bank, with $28,716,704 thousand
2. Scottrade Bank, $5,583,908
3. Raymond James Bank, FSB, $3,967,415
4. USAA FSB, $3,339,255
5. Hudson City Savings Bank, $2,256,003
6. Principal Bank, $1,822,957
7. Third Federal Savings & Loan Association of Cleveland, $1,479,993
8. Astoria Federal Savings & Loan Association, $1,444,764
9. American Express Bank, FSB, $1,350,043
10. Sovereign Bank NA, $1,270,357

Source: *Highline Bank and S&L Quarterly, Dec. ed.*, 2011, p. V.63.

3138 ■ LARGEST U.S. BANKS BY IRA DEPOSITS, 2011

Ranked by: Total IRA deposits, in thousands of dollars. **Remarks:** Also notes city, state, and dollar and percent change from previous year. **Number listed:** 25

1. Wells Fargo Bank NA, with $40,068,000 thousand
2. FIA Card Services NA, $25,170,292
3. TD Bank NA, $23,103,614
4. Citibank NA Inc., $19,016,000
5. Bank of America NA, $18,699,799
6. J. P. Morgan Chase Bank NA, $10,562,000
7. Morgan Stanley Bank NA, $8,392,000
8. UBS Bank USA, $7,789,294
9. PNC Bank NA, $6,706,275
10. RBS Citizens NA, $4,611,664

Source: *Highline Bank and S&L Quarterly, Dec. ed.*, 2011, p. I.50.

Industrial Distributors

3139 ■ WORLD'S LARGEST INDUSTRIAL DISTRIBU-TORS, 2010

Ranked by: Sales, in billions of U.S. dollars. **Remarks:** Specific figures not provided. Also notes top executive, headquarters, website, number of locations and employees, stock exchange, ticker symbol, and comments. **Number listed:** 50

1. Wolseley plc, with $20.9 billion
2. Sonepar, $19.3
3. Rexel, $15.7
4. Wurth Group, $12.3
5. HD Supply Inc., $7.5
6. W. W. Grainger Inc., $7.2
7. Anixter International Inc., $5.4
8. WESCO International Inc., $5.1
9. Graybar Electric Co., Inc., $4.6
10. Airgas Inc., $3.9

Source: *Industrial Distribution*, The Big 50 (annual), 2011, p. 20+.

Industrial Durable Goods

3140 ■ MOST PROFITABLE CANADIAN INDUSTRIAL COMPANIES, 2011

Ranked by: Profits, in millions of Canadian dollars. **Number listed:** 6

1. Canadian National Railway Co., with C$2,457 million
2. Bombardier Inc., C$837
3. Canadian Pacific Railway Ltd., C$570
4. SNC-Lavalin Group Inc., C$379
5. Finning International Inc., C$259
6. Toromont Industries Ltd., C$247

Source: *Canadian Business*, Investor 500 (annual), 2012, p. 55.

3141 ■ MOST VALUABLE U.S. GENERAL INDUSTRIAL COMPANIES, 2011

Ranked by: Market value as of March 2011, in millions of U.S. dollars. **Remarks:** Also notes rank within the *FT U.S. 500*, rank for previous year, country, revenue, net income, assets, number of employees, share price, price-to-earning ratio, dividend yield, and fiscal yearend. **Number listed:** 8

1. General Electric Co., with $212,917.8 million
2. 3M Co., $55,553.7
3. Honeywell International Inc., $46,876.9
4. Tyco International Ltd., $21,209.9
5. Eaton Corp., $18,871.8
6. ITT Corp., $11,035.1
7. Ball Corp., $5,069.9
8. Crown Holdings Inc., $5,008.6

Source: *Financial Times*, FT 500 (annual), http://www.ft.com, June 24, 2011.

Industrial Equipment Industry

3142 ■ CHINA'S LARGEST HEAVY EQUIPMENT COMPANIES OVERALL, 2011

Ranked by: Score based on revenue, profits, assets, and market capitalization. **Remarks:** Specific scores not provided. Also notes overall rank in the *Forbes 2000* and figures for each criterion. **Number listed:** 10

1. Zoomlion Heavy Industry
2. Shanghai Electric Group
3. Weichai Power
4. Sany Heavy Industry
5. CSR
6. China CNR
7. China International Marine
8. China CSSC Holdings
9. China Shipbuilding Industry
10. Yangzijiang Shipbuilding

Source: *Forbes*, Forbes 2000 (annual), http://www.forbes.com, May 7, 2012.

3143 ■ EUROPE'S MOST VALUABLE GENERAL INDUSTRIAL COMPANIES, 2011

Ranked by: Market value as of March 2011, in millions of U.S. dollars. **Remarks:** Also notes rank within the *FT Europe 500*, rank for previous year, country, revenue, net income, assets, number of employees, share price, price-to-earning ratio, dividend yield, and fiscal yearend. **Number listed:** 5

1. Siemens AG, with $125,465.5 million
2. ThyssenKrupp AG, $21,049
3. Smiths Group plc, $8,151.4
4. Bekaert NV, $6,840.2
5. Rexam plc, $5,107.9

Source: *Financial Times*, FT 500 (annual), http://www.ft.com, June 24, 2011.

3144 ■ EUROPE'S MOST VALUABLE INDUSTRIAL ENGINEERING COMPANIES, 2011

Ranked by: Market value as of March 2011, in millions of U.S. dollars. **Remarks:** Also notes rank within the *FT Europe 500*, rank for previous year, country, revenue, net income, assets, number of employees, share price, price-to-earning ratio, dividend yield, and fiscal yearend. **Number listed:** 22

1. ABB Ltd., with $55,670.6 million
2. AB Volvo, $37,407.8
3. Atlas Copco AB, $31,766.8
4. Sandvik AB, $22,396.6
5. Scania AB, $18,438.9
6. MAN SE, $18,248.7
7. Alstom, $17,430.4
8. Fiat Industrial SpA, $17,346.1
9. Schindler Holding Ltd., $14,566.5
10. SKF AB, $13,267

Source: *Financial Times*, FT 500 (annual), http://www.ft.com, June 24, 2011.

3145 ■ FASTEST-GROWING INDUSTRIAL COMPANIES, 2008-2011

Ranked by: Score based on three-year growth in revenue and earnings, and three-year total return to investors. **Remarks:** Specific scores not provided. To qualify for list, companies must have revenues of at least $50 million, net income of at least $10 million, market capitalization of at least $250 million, and stock price of at least $5. Int'l companies are eligible if they trade on a U.S. exchange and file quarterly reports. **Number listed:** 5

1. Sturm, Ruger & Co.
2. KapStone Paper & Packaging Corp.

3. Coinstar Inc.

4. Harbin Electric

5. Insituform Technologies

Source: *Fortune*, 100 Fastest-Growing Companies (annual), http://www.fortune.com, September 26, 2011.

3146 ■ ILLINOIS'S LARGEST HEAVY EQUIPMENT COMPANIES OVERALL, 2011

Ranked by: Score based on revenue, profits, assets, and market capitalization. **Remarks:** Specific scores not provided. Also notes overall rank in the *Forbes 2000* and figures for each criterion. **Number listed:** 3

1. Caterpillar Inc.

2. Deere & Co.

3. Navistar International

Source: *Forbes*, Forbes 2000 (annual), http://www.forbes.com, May 7, 2012.

3147 ■ JAPAN'S LARGEST HEAVY EQUIPMENT COMPANIES OVERALL, 2011

Ranked by: Score based on revenue, profits, assets, and market capitalization. **Remarks:** Specific scores not provided. Also notes overall rank in the *Forbes 2000* and figures for each criterion. **Number listed:** 5

1. Komatsu Ltd.

2. Mitsubishi Heavy Industries Ltd.

3. Kubota Corp.

4. Kawasaki Heavy Industries Ltd.

5. IHI

Source: *Forbes*, Forbes 2000 (annual), http://www.forbes.com, May 7, 2012.

3148 ■ JAPAN'S LARGEST MISCELLANEOUS INDUSTRIAL EQUIPMENT COMPANIES OVERALL, 2011

Ranked by: Score based on revenue, profits, assets, and market capitalization. **Remarks:** Specific scores not provided. Also notes overall rank in the *Forbes 2000* and figures for each criterion. **Number listed:** 4

1. Fanuc Ltd.

2. SMC

3. NSK

4. Sumitomo Heavy Industries

Source: *Forbes*, Forbes 2000 (annual), http://www.forbes.com, May 7, 2012.

3149 ■ LARGEST COMPANIES IN THE INDUSTRIAL/ COMMERCIAL MACHINERY AND COMPUTER EQUIP- MENT INDUSTRY BY EMPLOYEES, 2010

Ranked by: Total number of employees. **Remarks:** Also notes contact information for headquarters, number of employees at headquarters, revenue, rank by revenue, and primary SIC code. **Number listed:** 116

1. Hewlett-Packard Co., with 324,600 employees

2. Xerox Corp., 131,185

3. IBM World Trade Corp., 113,000

4. Dell Inc., 96,387

5. Caterpillar Inc., 93,813

6. Cisco Systems Inc., 70,700

7. Otis Elevator Co., 63,000

8. Western Digital Corp., 62,500

9. Deere & Co., 55,700

10. Parker Hannifin Corp., 54,800

Source: *Business Rankings*, (annual), Dun & Bradstreet Inc., 2011, p. VI.77-VI.79.

3150 ■ LARGEST COMPANIES IN THE INDUSTRIAL/ COMMERCIAL MACHINERY AND COMPUTER EQUIP- MENT INDUSTRY BY SALES, 2010

Ranked by: Total revenue, in dollars. **Remarks:** Also notes contact information for headquarters, number of employees at headquarters and overall, rank by employees, and primary SIC code. **Number listed:** 118

1. Hewlett-Packard Co., with $126,033,000,000

2. Apple Inc., $65,225,000,000

3. Dell Inc., $61,494,000,000

4. Caterpillar Inc., $42,588,000,000

5. Cisco Systems Inc., $40,040,000,000

6. Deere & Co., $26,004,600,000

7. Xerox Corp., $21,633,000,000

8. EMC Corp., $17,015,126,000

9. Baker Hughes Inc., $14,414,000,000

10. Cummins Inc., $13,226,000,000

Source: *Business Rankings*, (annual), Dun & Bradstreet Inc., 2011, p. V.77-V.79.

3151 ■ LARGEST U.S. HEAVY EQUIPMENT COMPANIES OVERALL, 2011

Ranked by: Score based on revenue, profits, assets, and market capitalization. **Remarks:** Specific scores not provided. Also notes overall rank in the *Forbes 2000* and figures for each criterion. **Number listed:** 7

1. Caterpillar Inc.

2. Deere & Co.

3. Cummins Inc.

4. Paccar Inc.

5. Navistar International Corp.

6. AGCO Corp.

7. Joy Global Inc.

Source: *Forbes*, Forbes 2000 (annual), http://www.forbes.com, May 7, 2012.

3152 ■ LARGEST U.S. MISCELLANEOUS INDUSTRIAL EQUIPMENT COMPANIES OVERALL, 2011

Ranked by: Score based on revenue, profits, assets, and market capitalization. **Remarks:** Specific scores not provided. Also notes overall rank in the *Forbes 2000* and figures for each criterion. **Number listed:** 7

1. Illinois Tool Works Inc.

2. Eaton Corp.

3. Parker Hannifin Corp.

4. Rockwell Automation Inc.

5. Roper Industries Inc.

6. The Timken Co.

7. Flowserve Corp.

Source: *Forbes*, Forbes 2000 (annual), http://www.forbes.com, May 7, 2012.

3153 ■ MOST VALUABLE U.S. INDUSTRIAL ENGINEER- ING COMPANIES, 2011

Ranked by: Market value as of March 2011, in millions of U.S. dollars. **Remarks:** Also notes rank within the *FT U.S. 500*, rank for previous year, country, revenue, net income, assets, number of employees, share price, price-to-earning ratio, dividend yield, and fiscal yearend. **Number listed:** 13

1. Caterpillar Inc., with $71,132.8 million
2. Deere & Co., $40,794.7
3. Illinois Tool Works Inc., $25,788.3
4. Cummins Inc., $21,575.3
5. Paccar Inc., $19,134.5
6. Ingersoll-Rand Co., $15,921.9
7. Parker Hannifin Corp., $15,327
8. Rockwell Automation Inc., $13,473.1
9. Dover Corp., $12,273.1
10. Joy Global Inc., $10,354

Source: *Financial Times*, FT 500 (annual), http://www.ft.com, June 24, 2011.

3154 ■ OHIO'S LARGEST MISCELLANEOUS INDUSTRIAL EQUIPMENT COMPANIES OVERALL, 2011

Ranked by: Score based on revenue, profits, assets, and market capitalization. **Remarks:** Specific scores not provided. Also notes overall rank in the *Forbes 2000* and figures for each criterion. **Number listed:** 3

1. Eaton Corp.
2. Parker Hannifin Corp.
3. The Timken Co.

Source: *Forbes*, Forbes 2000 (annual), http://www.forbes.com, May 7, 2012.

3155 ■ SOUTH KOREA'S LARGEST HEAVY EQUIPMENT COMPANIES OVERALL, 2011

Ranked by: Score based on revenue, profits, assets, and market capitalization. **Remarks:** Specific scores not provided. Also notes overall rank in the *Forbes 2000* and figures for each criterion. **Number listed:** 6

1. Hyundai Heavy Industries Co., Ltd.
2. Samsung Heavy Industries Co., Ltd.
3. Daewoo Shipbuilding & Marine Engineering Co., Ltd.
4. STX Corp.
5. Doosan Heavy Industries & Construction Co., Ltd.
6. STX Offshore

Source: *Forbes*, Forbes 2000 (annual), http://www.forbes.com, May 7, 2012.

3156 ■ SWEDEN'S LARGEST MISCELLANEOUS INDUSTRIAL EQUIPMENT COMPANIES OVERALL, 2011

Ranked by: Score based on revenue, profits, assets, and market capitalization. **Remarks:** Specific scores not provided. Also notes overall rank in the *Forbes 2000* and figures for each criterion. **Number listed:** 6

1. Atlas Copco AB
2. Sandvik AB
3. SKF AB
4. Assa Abloy
5. Alfa Laval AB
6. Hexagon

Source: *Forbes*, Forbes 2000 (annual), http://www.forbes.com, May 7, 2012.

3157 ■ TOP *FORTUNE 500* COMPANIES IN INDUSTRIAL MACHINERY, 2011

Ranked by: Revenue, in millions of dollars. **Remarks:** Also notes overall rank in the *Fortune 500;* profits; profits as a percentage of revenue; stockholders' equity; and rank by each criterion. **Number listed:** 6

1. Illinois Tool Works Inc., with $18,257 million
2. Eaton Corp., $16,049
3. Parker Hannifin Corp., $12,346
4. Dover Corp., $8,502
5. SPX Corp., $5,462
6. Timken Co., $5,170

Source: *Fortune*, Fortune 500 (annual), May 21, 2012, p. F-36.

3158 ■ WORLD'S LARGEST HEAVY EQUIPMENT COMPANIES OVERALL, 2011

Ranked by: Score based on revenue, profits, assets, and market capitalization. **Remarks:** Specific scores not provided. Also notes country, overall rank in the *Forbes 2000,* and figures for each criterion. **Number listed:** 31

1. Caterpillar Inc.
2. AB Volvo
3. Deere & Co.
4. Hyundai Heavy Industries Co., Ltd.
5. Komatsu Ltd.
6. Fiat Industrial SpA
7. Cummins Inc.
8. Paccar Inc.
9. Mitsubishi Heavy Industries Ltd.
10. Kubota Corp.

Source: *Forbes*, Forbes 2000 (annual), http://www.forbes.com, May 7, 2012.

3159 ■ WORLD'S LARGEST MISCELLANEOUS INDUSTRIAL EQUIPMENT COMPANIES OVERALL, 2011

Ranked by: Score based on revenue, profits, assets, and market capitalization. **Remarks:** Specific scores not provided. Also notes country, overall rank in the *Forbes 2000,* and figures for each criterion. **Number listed:** 24

1. Illinois Tool Works Inc.
2. Eaton Corp.
3. Atlas Copco AB
4. Sandvik AB
5. Parker Hannifin Corp.
6. Fanuc Ltd.
7. SKF AB
8. Schindler Holding Ltd.
9. Vallourec SA
10. Rockwell Automation Inc.

Source: *Forbes*, Forbes 2000 (annual), http://www.forbes.com, May 7, 2012.

3160 ■ WORLD'S MOST ADMIRED INDUSTRIAL AND FARM EQUIPMENT COMPANIES, 2012

Ranked by: Score, on a scale of 10, based on a survey of executives, directors, and securities analysts of companies within their own industry on eight criteria: innovation, financial soundness, employee talent, use of corporate assets, long-term investment value, social responsibility, quality of management, and quality of products/services. **Remarks:** Specific scores not provided. Also notes rank for previous year. **Number listed:** 8

1. Caterpillar Inc.
2. Deere & Co.
3. Illinois Tool Works Inc.
4. Cummins Inc.
5. Parker Hannifin Corp.
6. ABB Ltd.
6. Eaton Corp.
8. Komatsu Ltd.

Source: *Fortune*, World's Most Admired Companies (annual), March 19, 2012, p. 150.

3161 ■ WORLD'S MOST ETHICAL INDUSTRIAL MANUFACTURING COMPANIES, 2012

Ranked by: Score based on five criteria: ethics and compliance program; reputation, leadership, and innovation; governance; corporate citizenship and responsibility; and culture of ethics. **Remarks:** Specific scores not provided; companies are listed alphabetically, not ranked. **Number listed:** 7

1. Deere & Co. (U.S.)
2. Eaton Corp. (U.S.)
3. Honeywell International Inc. (U.S.)
4. Kennametal Inc. (U.S.)
5. Milliken & Co. (U.S.)
6. Schneider Electric SA (France)
7. The Timken Co. (U.S.)

Source: *Ethisphere Magazine*, World's Most Ethical Companies (annual), http://www.ethisphere.com, 2012.

3162 ■ WORLD'S MOST VALUABLE GENERAL INDUSTRIAL COMPANIES, 2011

Ranked by: Market value as of March 2011, in millions of U.S. dollars. **Remarks:** Also notes rank within the *FT 500*, rank for previous year, country, revenue, net income, assets, number of employees, share price, price-to-earning ratio, dividend yield, and fiscal year-end. **Number listed:** 12

1. General Electric Co., with $212,917.8 million
2. Siemens AG, $125,465.5
3. 3M Co., $66,553.7
4. Hutchison Whampoa Ltd., $50,481.7
5. Honeywell International Inc., $46,876.9
6. Jardine Strategic Holdings Ltd., $29,767.2
7. Jardine Matheson Holdings Ltd., $28,416.7
8. Swire Pacific Ltd., $21,532.4
9. Tyco International Ltd., $21,209.9
10. ThyssenKrupp AG, $21,049

Source: *Financial Times*, FT 500 (annual), http://www.ft.com, June 24, 2011.

3163 ■ WORLD'S MOST VALUABLE INDUSTRIAL ENGINEERING COMPANIES, 2011

Ranked by: Market value as of March 2011, in millions of U.S. dollars. **Remarks:** Also notes rank within the *FT 500*, rank for previous year, country, revenue, net income, assets, number of employees, share price, price-to-earning ratio, dividend yield, and fiscal year-end. **Number listed:** 14

1. Caterpillar Inc., with $71,132.8 million
2. ABB Ltd., $55,670.6

3. Deere & Co., $40,794.7
4. AB Volvo, $37,407.8
5. Fanuc Ltd., $36,382.8
6. Hyundai Heavy Industries Co., Ltd., $35,888.6
7. Komatsu Ltd., $34,042.6
8. Atlas Copco AB, $31,766.8
9. Illinois Tool Works Inc., $26,788.3
10. Mitsubishi Electric Corp., $25,441

Source: *Financial Times*, FT 500 (annual), http://www.ft.com, June 24, 2011.

Industrial Parks

3164 ■ TOP INDUSTRIAL DEVELOPERS, 2010

Ranked by: Total industrial space developed (includes completed development and construction underway), in millions of square feet. **Remarks:** Also notes contact information and officers. **Number listed:** 20

1. ProLogis, with 8.5 million sq.ft.
2. USAA Real Estate Co., 6.5
3. AMB Property Corp., 4.7
4. Panattoni Development Co., 4.69
5. Hines Interests LP, 4
6. McDonald Development Co., 3.5
7. Industrial Developments International, 2.9
8. CenterPoint Properties, 2.7
9. The Rockefeller Group, 2.6
10. McShane Development Co., 2.3

Source: *National Real Estate Investor*, Best of the Best (annual), 2011, p. 38+.

3165 ■ TOP INDUSTRIAL OWNERS, 2010

Ranked by: Total industrial space owned, in millions of square feet. **Remarks:** Also notes contact information and officers. **Number listed:** 25

1. ProLogis, with 438.4 million sq.ft.
2. AMB Property Corp., 156.6
3. RREEF, 117.4
4. Duke Realty Corp., 100.4
5. ING Clarion Partners, 98.4
6. CB Richard Ellis Investors LLC, 83.9
7. DCT Industrial Trust, 75.8
8. First Industrial Realty Trust, 73.5
9. LaSalle Investment Management, 72.3
10. Majestic Realty Co., 66

Source: *National Real Estate Investor*, Best of the Best (annual), 2011, p. 37.

Industrial Relations

3166 ■ COUNTRIES WITH THE BEST LABOR-EMPLOYER RELATIONS, 2010

Ranked by: Score, on a scale of seven, based on the level of cooperation between workers and management. **Number listed:** 142

1. Singapore, with 6.1 points

1. Switzerland, 6.1
3. Denmark, 5.9
4. Norway, 5.8
5. Netherlands, 5.7
5. Japan, 5.7
5. Sweden, 5.7
8. Iceland, 5.6
8. Austria, 5.6
10. Luxembourg, 5.5
10. Costa Rica, 5.5

Source: *Global Competitiveness Report*, (annual), World Economic Forum, 2011, p. 470.

3167 ■ COUNTRIES WITH THE WORST LABOR-EMPLOYER RELATIONS, 2010

Ranked by: Score, on a scale of seven, based on the level of cooperation between workers and management. **Number listed:** 142

1. Mauritania, with 3 points
2. Venezuela, 3.2
2. South Korea, 3.2
4. Nepal, 3.3
4. South Africa, 3.3
4. Romania, 3.3
4. Serbia, 3.3
4. Argentina, 3.3
9. Croatia, 3.4
9. France, 3.4

Source: *Global Competitiveness Report*, (annual), World Economic Forum, 2011, p. 470.

Industrials
See: **Mutual Funds**

Industry, Manufacturing
See: **Manufacturing Industry**

Inflation

3168 ■ COUNTRIES WITH THE HIGHEST INFLATION, 2010

Ranked by: Annual percent change in consumer price index. **Number listed:** 142

1. Venezuela, with 28.2%
2. Angola, 14.5%
3. Nigeria, 13.7%
4. India, 13.2%
5. Mozambique, 12.7%
6. Jamaica, 12.6%
7. Iran, 12.5%
8. Yemen, 12.1%
9. Pakistan, 11.7%
9. Egypt, 11.7%

Source: *Global Competitiveness Report*, (annual), World Economic Forum, 2011, p. 424.

3169 ■ COUNTRIES WITH THE LOWEST INFLATION, 2010

Ranked by: Annual percent change in consumer price index. **Number listed:** 142

1. Qatar, with -2.4%
2. Ireland, -1.6%
3. Latvia, -1.2%
4. Japan, -0.7%
5. Burkina Faso, 0.4%
6. Belize, 0.5%
6. Brunei Darussalam, 0.5%
6. Montenegro, 0.5%
9. Slovak Republic, 0.7%
9. Switzerland, 0.7%

Source: *Global Competitiveness Report*, (annual), World Economic Forum, 2011, p. 424.

Information Technology
See also: **High Technology Industry**

3170 ■ BEST U.S. PLACES TO WORK IN INFORMATION TECHNOLOGY, 2011

Ranked by: Score based on employee survey based on training and development programs, base salary, bonuses, health benefits, and work/life balance. **Remarks:** Specific scores not provided. To qualify, companies must be headquartered in the U.S. and must have at least 50 information technology (IT) employees. Also notes comments. **Number listed:** 100

1. USAA
2. Securian Financial Group Inc.
3. General Mills Inc.
4. Genentech Inc.
5. Verizon Wireless
6. University of Pennsylvania
7. Chesapeake Energy Corp.
8. Salesforce.com Inc.
9. Booz Allen Hamilton Inc.
10. Quicken Loans Inc.

Source: *Computerworld*, 100 Best Places to Work in IT (annual), June 20, 2011, p. 16+.

3171 ■ FASTEST-GROWING PRIVATE INFORMATION TECHNOLOGY SERVICE COMPANIES IN THE U.S., 2007-2010

Ranked by: Average annual sales growth over three years, in percent. **Remarks:** Also notes headquarters, revenue, and rank in the overall *Inc. 500*. To qualify, private companies must have had annual revenues of at least $100,000 in 2007 and $2 million in 2010. **Number listed:** 42

1. Advantis Global Services, with 8,972.2%
2. SingleHop, 7,304.7%
3. TekScape, 3,135.2%
4. Saxon-Global, 2,948%
5. LCS Technologies, 2,798.7%
6. The Portal Group, 2,580.4%
7. Cetan Corp., 2,275.4%
8. Soft Tech Consulting, 2,138%
9. Enstoa, 1,848.3%

10. Triad Web Design, 1,835.7%

Source: *Inc.*, Inc. 500 (annual), September 2011, p. 160-172.

3172 ■ LEADING INFORMATION TECHNOLOGY INNOVATORS, 2011

Ranked by: Score for U.S. companies with at least $1 billion in annual revenues based on technological, procedural, and organizational innovation. Criteria include application development, e-business, customer-relationship management, and business process/enterprise resource planning. **Remarks:** Specific scores not provided. Also notes headquarters, website, revenue, highest-ranking information technology executive, and industrial classification. **Number listed:** 250

1. PACCAR Inc.
2. Levi Strauss & Co.
3. Waste Management Inc.
4. Quintiles
5. Catalina Marketing Group
6. Associated Press
7. Automatic Data Processing Inc.
8. Procter & Gamble Co.
9. United Stationers Supply Co.
10. Vail Resorts Inc.

Source: *InformationWeek*, InformationWeek 250 (annual), September 19, 2011, p. 45-47.

3173 ■ LEADING INFORMATION TECHNOLOGY INNOVATORS IN THE AUTOMOTIVE INDUSTRY, 2011

Ranked by: Score for U.S. companies with at least $1 billion in annual revenues based on technological, procedural, and organizational innovation. Criteria include application development, e-business, customer-relationship management, and business process/enterprise resource planning. **Remarks:** Specific scores not provided; companies are listed alphabetically, not ranked. Also notes highest-ranking information technology executive. **Number listed:** 4

1. Emkay Inc.
2. Mitsubishi Motors North America Inc.
3. PACCAR Inc.
4. Toyota Motor Sales USA Inc.

Source: *InformationWeek*, InformationWeek 250 (annual), http://www.informationweek.com, September 19, 2011.

3174 ■ LEADING INFORMATION TECHNOLOGY INNOVATORS IN THE BANKING AND FINANCIAL SERVICES INDUSTRY, 2011

Ranked by: Score for U.S. companies with at least $1 billion in annual revenues based on technological, procedural, and organizational innovation. Criteria include application development, e-business, customer-relationship management, and business process/enterprise resource planning. **Remarks:** Specific scores not provided; companies are listed alphabetically, not ranked. Also notes highest-ranking information technology executive. **Number listed:** 26

1. BDO USA LLP
2. BNY Mellon
3. Capital Access Network Inc.
4. CME Group Inc.
5. Commonwealth Financial Network
6. Equifax Inc.
7. Fair Isaac Corp.

8. Fifth Third Bancorp.
9. First Data Corp.
10. First Horizon National Corp.

Source: *InformationWeek*, InformationWeek 250 (annual), http://www.informationweek.com, September 19, 2011.

3175 ■ LEADING INFORMATION TECHNOLOGY INNOVATORS IN THE BIOTECHNOLOGY AND PHARMACEUTICALS INDUSTRY, 2011

Ranked by: Score for U.S. companies with at least $1 billion in annual revenues based on technological, procedural, and organizational innovation. Criteria include application development, e-business, customer-relationship management, and business process/enterprise resource planning. **Remarks:** Specific scores not provided; companies are listed alphabetically, not ranked. Also notes highest-ranking information technology executive. **Number listed:** 7

1. Amgen Inc.
2. Eli Lilly & Co.
3. Merck & Co., Inc.
4. Pfizer Inc.
5. Pharmaceutical Product Development Inc.
6. Quintiles Transnational Corp.
7. Teva Pharmaceuticals USA Inc.

Source: *InformationWeek*, InformationWeek 250 (annual), http://www.informationweek.com, September 19, 2011.

3176 ■ LEADING INFORMATION TECHNOLOGY INNOVATORS IN THE CHEMICAL INDUSTRY, 2011

Ranked by: Score for U.S. companies with at least $1 billion in annual revenues based on technological, procedural, and organizational innovation. Criteria include application development, e-business, customer-relationship management, and business process/enterprise resource planning. **Remarks:** Specific scores not provided; companies are listed alphabetically, not ranked. Also notes highest-ranking information technology executive. **Number listed:** 2

1. Nalco Co.
2. Solutia Inc.

Source: *InformationWeek*, InformationWeek 250 (annual), http://www.informationweek.com, September 19, 2011.

3177 ■ LEADING INFORMATION TECHNOLOGY INNOVATORS IN THE CONSTRUCTION AND ENGINEERING INDUSTRY, 2011

Ranked by: Score for U.S. companies with at least $1 billion in annual revenues based on technological, procedural, and organizational innovation. Criteria include application development, e-business, customer-relationship management, and business process/enterprise resource planning. **Remarks:** Specific scores not provided; companies are listed alphabetically, not ranked. Also notes highest-ranking information technology executive. **Number listed:** 3

1. CH2M Hill Cos., Ltd.
2. Hovnanian Enterprises Inc.
3. Parsons Corp.

Source: *InformationWeek*, InformationWeek 250 (annual), http://www.informationweek.com, September 19, 2011.

3178 ■ LEADING INFORMATION TECHNOLOGY INNOVATORS IN THE CONSULTING AND BUSINESS SERVICES INDUSTRY, 2011

Ranked by: Score for U.S. companies with at least $1 billion in annual revenues based on technological, procedural, and organizational innovation. Criteria include application development, e-business, customer-relationship management, and business process/enterprise resource planning. **Remarks:** Specific scores not provided; companies are listed alphabetically, not ranked. Also notes highest-ranking information technology executive. **Number listed:** 35

1. Accenture Ltd.
2. Acxiom Corp.
3. Automatic Data Processing Inc.
4. Automotive Resources International
5. Capgemini SA
6. Catalina Marketing Corp.
7. CB Richard Ellis Group inc.
8. CenterPoint Properties
9. Cognizant Technology Solutions Corp.
10. Convergys Corp.

Source: *InformationWeek*, InformationWeek 250 (annual), http://www.informationweek.com, September 19, 2011.

3179 ■ LEADING INFORMATION TECHNOLOGY INNOVATORS IN THE CONSUMER GOODS INDUSTRY, 2011

Ranked by: Score for U.S. companies with at least $1 billion in annual revenues based on technological, procedural, and organizational innovation. Criteria include application development, e-business, customer-relationship management, and business process/enterprise resource planning. **Remarks:** Specific scores not provided; companies are listed alphabetically, not ranked. Also notes highest-ranking information technology executive. **Number listed:** 11

1. Avon Products Inc.
2. Beachbody LLC
3. Carhartt Inc.
4. Coca-Cola Enterprises Inc.
5. Colgate-Palmolive Co.
6. Levi Strauss & Co.
7. Movado Group Inc.
8. Polo Ralph Lauren Corp.
9. The Jones Group
10. Procter & Gamble Co.

Source: *InformationWeek*, InformationWeek 250 (annual), http://www.informationweek.com, September 19, 2011.

3180 ■ LEADING INFORMATION TECHNOLOGY INNOVATORS IN THE DISTRIBUTION INDUSTRY, 2011

Ranked by: Score for U.S. companies with at least $1 billion in annual revenues based on technological, procedural, and organizational innovation. Criteria include application development, e-business, customer-relationship management, and business process/enterprise resource planning. **Remarks:** Specific scores not provided; companies are listed alphabetically, not ranked. Also notes highest-ranking information technology executive. **Number listed:** 8

1. Arrow Electronics Inc.
2. Avnet Inc.
3. Do It Best Corp.
4. Genuine Parts Co.
5. HD Supply Inc.
6. McKesson Corp.
7. Tech Data Corp.
8. United Stationers Supply Co.

Source: *InformationWeek*, InformationWeek 250 (annual), http://www.informationweek.com, September 19, 2011.

3181 ■ LEADING INFORMATION TECHNOLOGY INNOVATORS IN THE ELECTRONICS INDUSTRY, 2011

Ranked by: Score for U.S. companies with at least $1 billion in annual revenues based on technological, procedural, and organizational innovation. Criteria include application development, e-business, customer-relationship management, and business process/enterprise resource planning. **Remarks:** Specific scores not provided; companies are listed alphabetically, not ranked. Also notes highest-ranking information technology executive. **Number listed:** 3

1. Cadence Design Systems Inc.
2. Celestica Inc.
3. Freescale Semiconductor Inc.

Source: *InformationWeek*, InformationWeek 250 (annual), http://www.informationweek.com, September 19, 2011.

3182 ■ LEADING INFORMATION TECHNOLOGY INNOVATORS IN THE ENERGY AND UTILITIES INDUSTRY, 2011

Ranked by: Score for U.S. companies with at least $1 billion in annual revenues based on technological, procedural, and organizational innovation. Criteria include application development, e-business, customer-relationship management, and business process/enterprise resource planning. **Remarks:** Specific scores not provided; companies are listed alphabetically, not ranked. Also notes highest-ranking information technology executive. **Number listed:** 10

1. The AES Corp.
2. Ameren Corp.
3. Atmos Energy Corp.
4. BP plc
5. Chevron Corp.
6. DTE Energy Co.
7. Kansas City Power & Light Co.
8. Republic Services Inc.
9. Sempra Energy
10. Southern Co.

Source: *InformationWeek*, InformationWeek 250 (annual), http://www.informationweek.com, September 19, 2011.

3183 ■ LEADING INFORMATION TECHNOLOGY INNOVATORS IN THE GENERAL MERCHANDISE RETAILING INDUSTRY, 2011

Ranked by: Score for U.S. companies with at least $1 billion in annual revenues based on technological, procedural, and organizational innovation. Criteria include application development, e-business, customer-relationship management, and business process/enterprise resource planning. **Remarks:** Specific scores not provided; companies are listed alphabetically, not ranked. Also notes highest-ranking information technology executive. **Number listed:** 3

1. J. C. Penney Co., Inc.
2. Wal-Mart Stores Inc.
3. Walgreen Co.

Source: *InformationWeek*, InformationWeek 250 (annual), http://www.informationweek.com, September 19, 2011.

3184 ■ LEADING INFORMATION TECHNOLOGY INNOVATORS IN THE HEALTHCARE AND MEDICAL INDUSTRY, 2011

Ranked by: Score for U.S. companies with at least $1 billion in annual revenues based on technological, procedural, and organizational innovation. Criteria include application development, e-business, customer-relationship management, and business process/enterprise resource planning. **Remarks:** Specific scores not provided; companies are listed alphabetically, not ranked. Also notes highest-ranking information technology executive. **Number listed:** 28

1. Advocate Health Care
2. Atlantic Health System
3. Banner Health
4. Baptist Health
5. Baylor Health Care System
6. Beaumont Health System
7. Beth Israel Deaconess Medical Center
8. Centene Corp.
9. Children's Hospital & Medical Center
10. Children's National Medical Center

Source: *InformationWeek*, InformationWeek 250 (annual), http://www.informationweek.com, September 19, 2011.

3185 ■ LEADING INFORMATION TECHNOLOGY INNOVATORS IN THE HOSPITALITY AND TRAVEL INDUSTRY, 2011

Ranked by: Score for U.S. companies with at least $1 billion in annual revenues based on technological, procedural, and organizational innovation. Criteria include application development, e-business, customer-relationship management, and business process/enterprise resource planning. **Remarks:** Specific scores not provided; companies are listed alphabetically, not ranked. Also notes highest-ranking information technology executive. **Number listed:** 7

1. Caesars Entertainment Corp.
2. Hyatt Hotels Corp.
3. InterContinental Hotels Group plc
4. Kimpton Hotel & Restaurant Group LLC
5. Marriott International Inc.
6. Sabre Holdings
7. Vail Resorts Inc.

Source: *InformationWeek*, InformationWeek 250 (annual), http://www.informationweek.com, September 19, 2011.

3186 ■ LEADING INFORMATION TECHNOLOGY INNOVATORS IN THE INFORMATION TECHNOLOGY INDUSTRY, 2011

Ranked by: Score for U.S. companies with at least $1 billion in annual revenues based on technological, procedural, and organizational innovation. Criteria include application development, e-business, customer-relationship management, and business process/enterprise resource planning. **Remarks:** Specific scores not provided; companies are listed alphabetically, not ranked. Also notes highest-ranking information technology executive. **Number listed:** 19

1. Advanced Health Media LLC
2. Blackbaud Inc.
3. BMC Software Inc.
4. Collabera Inc.
5. Dell Inc.
6. GXS Worldwide Inc.
7. HCL Technologies Ltd.
8. Hewlett-Packard Co.
9. Hitachi Data Systems Corp.
10. International Business Machines Corp.

Source: *InformationWeek*, InformationWeek 250 (annual), http://www.informationweek.com, September 19, 2011.

3187 ■ LEADING INFORMATION TECHNOLOGY INNOVATORS IN THE INSURANCE INDUSTRY, 2011

Ranked by: Score for U.S. companies with at least $1 billion in annual revenues based on technological, procedural, and organizational innovation. Criteria include application development, e-business, customer-relationship management, and business process/enterprise resource planning. **Remarks:** Specific scores not provided; companies are listed alphabetically, not ranked. Also notes highest-ranking information technology executive. **Number listed:** 19

1. Acuity, A Mutual Insurance Co.
2. Aetna Inc.
3. Aon Corp.
4. Arkansas Blue Cross & Blue Shield
5. Asurion Insurance Services
6. Aviva plc
7. Crawford & Co.
8. Group Health Cooperative of South Central Wisconsin
9. Harleysville Group Inc.
10. Hastings Mutual Insurance Co.

Source: *InformationWeek*, InformationWeek 250 (annual), http://www.informationweek.com, September 19, 2011.

3188 ■ LEADING INFORMATION TECHNOLOGY INNOVATORS IN THE LOGISTICS AND TRANSPORTATION INDUSTRY, 2011

Ranked by: Score for U.S. companies with at least $1 billion in annual revenues based on technological, procedural, and organizational innovation. Criteria include application development, e-business, customer-relationship management, and business process/enterprise resource planning. **Remarks:** Specific scores not provided; companies are listed alphabetically, not ranked. Also notes highest-ranking information technology executive. **Number listed:** 17

1. ABF Freight System Inc.
2. American Airlines Inc.
3. Amtrak
4. CRST International Inc.
5. Echo Global Logistics Inc.
6. England Logistics Inc.
7. FedEx Corp.
8. FFE Transportation Services Inc.
9. J. B. Hunt Transport Services inc.
10. Knight Transportation inc.

Source: *InformationWeek*, InformationWeek 250 (annual), http://www.informationweek.com, September 19, 2011.

3189 ■ LEADING INFORMATION TECHNOLOGY INNOVATORS IN THE MANUFACTURING INDUSTRY, 2011

Ranked by: Score for U.S. companies with at least $1 billion in annual revenues based on technological, procedural, and organizational innovation. Criteria include application development, e-business, customer-relationship management, and business process/enterprise resource planning. **Remarks:** Specific scores not provided; companies are listed alphabetically, not ranked. Also notes highest-ranking information technology executive. **Number listed:** 15

1. Baker Hughes Inc.
2. Boeing Co.
3. Brady Corp.

4. DST Output

5. Eaton Corp.

6. Emerson

7. GE Energy

8. Krueger International Inc.

9. Mitsubishi Power Systems Americas Inc.

10. Newpont Corp.

Source: *InformationWeek*, InformationWeek 250 (annual), http://www.informationweek.com, September 19, 2011.

3190 ■ LEADING INFORMATION TECHNOLOGY INNOVATORS IN THE MEDIA AND ENTERTAINMENT INDUSTRY, 2011

Ranked by: Score for U.S. companies with at least $1 billion in annual revenues based on technological, procedural, and organizational innovation. Criteria include application development, e-business, customer-relationship management, and business process/enterprise resource planning. **Remarks:** Specific scores not provided; companies are listed alphabetically, not ranked. Also notes highest-ranking information technology executive. **Number listed:** 6

1. American Greetings Interactive

2. Associated Press

3. Broadcast Music Inc.

4. Cox Enterprises Inc.

5. The Harry Fox Agency Inc.

6. Yahoo! Inc.

Source: *InformationWeek*, InformationWeek 250 (annual), http://www.informationweek.com, September 19, 2011.

3191 ■ LEADING INFORMATION TECHNOLOGY INNOVATORS IN THE METALS AND NATURAL RESOURCES INDUSTRY, 2011

Ranked by: Score for U.S. companies with at least $1 billion in annual revenues based on technological, procedural, and organizational innovation. Criteria include application development, e-business, customer-relationship management, and business process/enterprise resource planning. **Remarks:** Specific scores not provided; companies are listed alphabetically, not ranked. Also notes highest-ranking information technology executive. **Number listed:** 3

1. Arch Coal Inc.

2. Irving Materials Inc.

3. Peabody Energy

Source: *InformationWeek*, InformationWeek 250 (annual), http://www.informationweek.com, September 19, 2011.

3192 ■ LEADING INFORMATION TECHNOLOGY INNOVATORS IN THE SPECIALTY RETAILING INDUSTRY, 2011

Ranked by: Score for U.S. companies with at least $1 billion in annual revenues based on technological, procedural, and organizational innovation. Criteria include application development, e-business, customer-relationship management, and business process/enterprise resource planning. **Remarks:** Specific scores not provided; companies are listed alphabetically, not ranked. Also notes highest-ranking information technology executive. **Number listed:** 8

1. AutoTrader.com Inc.

2. CDW LLC

3. Dunkin' Brands Inc.

4. Eurpac Information Services

5. Lowe's Companies Inc.

6. Recreational Equipment Inc.

7. Rent-A-Center Inc.

8. Ross Stores Inc.

Source: *InformationWeek*, InformationWeek 250 (annual), http://www.informationweek.com, September 19, 2011.

3193 ■ LEADING INFORMATION TECHNOLOGY INNOVATORS IN THE TELECOMMUNICATIONS INDUSTRY, 2011

Ranked by: Score for U.S. companies with at least $1 billion in annual revenues based on technological, procedural, and organizational innovation. Criteria include application development, e-business, customer-relationship management, and business process/enterprise resource planning. **Remarks:** Specific scores not provided; companies are listed alphabetically, not ranked. Also notes highest-ranking information technology executive. **Number listed:** 6

1. AT&T Inc.

2. Broadview Networks Inc.

3. Global Crossing Ltd.

4. Sprint Nextel Corp.

5. Verizon Wireless

6. XO Communications

Source: *InformationWeek*, InformationWeek 250 (annual), http://www.informationweek.com, September 19, 2011.

3194 ■ MOST PROFITABLE CANADIAN INFORMATION TECHNOLOGY COMPANIES, 2011

Ranked by: Profits, in millions of Canadian dollars. **Number listed:** 6

1. Research in Motion Ltd., with C$1,164 million

2. CGI Group Inc., C$435

3. Celestica Inc., C$195

4. MacDonald, Dettwiler & Associates Ltd., C$160

5. Constellation Software Inc., C$157

6. Open Text Corp., C$123

Source: *Canadian Business*, Investor 500 (annual), 2012, p. 55.

3195 ■ TOP COMPANIES IN THE DIGITAL CONTENT INDUSTRY, 2011

Ranked by: Editorial determination. **Remarks:** Companies are listed alphabetically, not ranked. Also notes website, business category, year founded, number of employees, chief officer, and key products. **Number listed:** 100

1. Adobe Systems Inc.

2. Alacra Inc.

3. Alexander Street Press LLC

4. Alfresco Software Inc.

5. Amazon.com Inc.

6. AOL Inc.

7. Apple Inc.

8. Attributor Corp.

9. Atypon Systems Inc.

10. Automattic Inc.

Source: *EContent Magazine*, EC 100 (annual), http://www.econtentmag.com, December 2011.

3196 ■ TOP COMPANIES IN KNOWLEDGE MANAGEMENT, 2012

Ranked by: Editorial determination of a company's impact to the field of knowledge management; i.e., those whose products/

services continuously transform its operations. **Remarks:** Specific score not provided; companies are listed alphabetically, not ranked. **Number listed:** 100

1. A2iA
2. ABBYY USA
3. Accellion
4. AccessData
5. Accusoft
6. Acquia
7. Alfresco
8. Altep
9. AnyDoc Software
10. Appian Corp.

Source: *KMWorld*, 100 Companies That Matter in Knowledge Management (annual), http://www.kmworld.com, March 2012.

3197 ■ TOP *FORTUNE 500* COMPANIES IN INFORMATION TECHNOLOGY SERVICES, 2011

Ranked by: Revenue, in millions of dollars. **Remarks:** Also notes overall rank in the *Fortune 500;* profits; profits as a percentage of revenue; stockholders' equity; and rank by each criterion. **Number listed:** 6

1. International Business Machines Corp. (IBM), with $106,916 million
2. Computer Sciences Corp., $16,144
3. SAIC Inc., $10,657
4. CDW Corp., $9,602
5. Cognizant Technology Solutions Corp., $6,121
6. Booz Allen Hamilton Inc., $5,591

Source: *Fortune*, Fortune 500 (annual), May 21, 2012, p. F-36.

3198 ■ U.S. COMPANIES THAT ARE THE BOLDEST IN INFORMATION TECHNOLOGY, 2011

Ranked by: Score based on technological boldness, i.e., technology innovations that advance business results. **Remarks:** Specific scores not provided; companies are listed alphabetically, not ranked. Also notes headquarters, revenue, project type, business function, business goal, and chief information officer. **Number listed:** 100

1. Advanced Micro Devices Inc.
2. Aflac Inc.
3. Alta Colleges
4. Apollo Group Inc.
5. ABF Freight System Inc.
6. Baker Hughes Inc.
7. Bayer HealthCare Pharmaceuticals USA
8. BendPak
9. BMO Financial Group
10. BNY Mellon

Source: *CIO Magazine*, CIO 100 (annual), http://www.cio.com, June 2011.

3199 ■ THE UNITED STATES' MOST VALUABLE INFORMATION TECHNOLOGY SERVICE BRANDS, 2011

Ranked by: Brand value, in millions of U.S. dollars. **Remarks:** Also notes rank within the *Global 500* for current and previous year, figures for current and previous year, and brand rating. Ranking is available online only. **Number listed:** 2

1. IBM, with $39,135 million
2. HP, $21,707

Source: *Global 500*, (annual), Brand Finance plc, March 2012.

3200 ■ WORLD'S MOST ADMIRED INFORMATION TECHNOLOGY SERVICES COMPANIES, 2012

Ranked by: Score, on a scale of 10, based on a survey of executives, directors, and securities analysts of companies within their own industry on eight criteria: innovation, financial soundness, employee talent, use of corporate assets, long-term investment value, social responsibility, quality of management, and quality of products/services. **Remarks:** Specific scores not provided. Also notes rank for previous year. **Number listed:** 5

1. International Business Machines Corp. (IBM)
2. Accenture Ltd.
3. Booz Allen Hamilton Holding
4. Cognizant Technology Solutions Corp.
5. CACI International Inc.

Source: *Fortune*, World's Most Admired Companies (annual), March 19, 2012, p. 147.

3201 ■ WORLD'S MOST VALUABLE INFORMATION TECHNOLOGY SERVICE BRANDS, 2011

Ranked by: Brand value, in millions of U.S. dollars. **Remarks:** Also notes rank within the *Global 500* for current and previous year, figures for current and previous year, country, and brand rating. Ranking is available online only. **Number listed:** 5

1. IBM, with $39,135 million
2. HP, $21,707
3. Accenture, $6,853
4. Infosys, $3,628
5. Cap Gemini, $2,845

Source: *Global 500*, (annual), Brand Finance plc, March 2012.

3202 ■ WORLD'S TOP INFORMATION TECHNOLOGY COMPANIES IN CLIMATE SOLUTIONS, 2011

Ranked by: Score based on solutions to reduce greenhouse gases as measured by current savings calculations, public metrics, investment, and future savings goal. **Number listed:** 21

1. Fujitsu Ltd., with 28 points
2. Telefonaktiebolaget LM Ericsson, 24
3. Cisco Systems Inc., 22
4. Vodafone Group plc, 21
5. International Business Machines Corp. (IBM), 19
5. Sharp Corp., 19
5. Nippon Telegraph & Telephone Corp. (NTT), 19
8. NEC Corp., 17
9. Hewlett-Packard Co., 16
10. Alcatel-Lucent, 15

Source: *Cool IT*, (annual), Greenpeace, February 2012.

3203 ■ WORLD'S TOP INFORMATION TECHNOLOGY COMPANIES IN ENERGY IMPACT, 2011

Ranked by: Score based on solutions to reduce greenhouse gases as measured by absolute emissions reduction target, mitigation strategies, infrastructure siting policy, and product efficiency and supply chain footprint. **Number listed:** 21

1. International Business Machines Corp. (IBM), with 20 points

2. Alcatel-Lucent, 18

3. Cisco Systems Inc., 17

3. Google Inc., 17

3. Dell Inc., 17

3. Wipro Ltd., 17

7. SAP AG, 14

8. Telefonaktiebolaget LM Ericsson, 13

8. Hewlett-Packard Co., 13

10. Vodafone Group plc, 11

10. Microsoft Corp., 11

Source: *Cool IT*, (annual), Greenpeace, February 2012.

3204 ■ WORLD'S TOP INFORMATION TECHNOLOGY COMPANIES IN ENVIRONMENTAL POLITICAL ADVOCACY, 2011

Ranked by: Score based on solutions to reduce greenhouse gases as measured by political speeches, political policy, and repetition. Points are subtracted for negative lobbying. **Number listed:** 21

1. Softbank Corp., with 33 points

2. Google Inc., 23

3. Vodafone Group plc, 13

4. Wipro Ltd., 11

4. Telefonaktiebolaget LM Ericsson, 11

4. Fujitsu Ltd., 11

7. Cisco Systems Inc., 10

8. Sharp Corp., 9

9. Alcatel-Lucent, 7

10. HCL Technologies Ltd., 6

Source: *Cool IT*, (annual), Greenpeace, February 2012.

3205 ■ WORLD'S TOP INFORMATION TECHNOLOGY COMPANIES IN GREENHOUSE GAS REDUCTION, 2011

Ranked by: Score based on climate solutions, energy impact, and political advocacy. **Number listed:** 21

1. Google Inc., with 53 points

2. Cisco Systems Inc., 49

3. Telefonaktiebolaget LM Ericsson, 48

3. Fujitsu Ltd., 48

5. Vodafone Group plc, 45

6. Alcatel-Lucent, 40

7. Sharp Corp., 38

7. Softbank Corp., 38

9. International Business Machines Corp. (IBM), 35

10. Hewlett-Packard Co., 34

Source: *Cool IT*, (annual), Greenpeace, February 2012.

Injection Molders

3206 ■ LARGEST INJECTION MOLDERS IN NORTH AMERICA, 2011

Ranked by: Injection molding sales, in millions of U.S. dollars. **Remarks:** Also notes headquarters and top injection molding official. **Number listed:** 565

1. Magna International Inc., with $1,525 million

2. Berry Plastics Corp., $1,493

3. International Automotive Components Group LLC, $1,440

4. Automotive Components Holdings LLC, $1,000

5. SRG Global Inc., $848

6. Newell Rubbermaid Inc., $675

7. Nypro Inc., $644

8. AptarGroup Inc., $640

9. Rexam plc, $530

10. Closure Systems International Inc., $480

Source: *Plastics News*, North American Injection Molders (annual), http://www.plasticsnews.com, June 18, 2012.

Ink

3207 ■ LARGEST INK MANUFACTURERS IN NORTH AMERICA, 2011

Ranked by: North American ink revenue, in millions of U.S. dollars. **Remarks:** Figures not provided. Also notes global ink revenue, parent company, contact information, major products, key personnel, number of employees, operating facilities, and comments. **Number listed:** 20

1. Sun Chemical Corp.

2. Flink Ink Corp.

3. INX International Ink Co.

4. Siegwerk NAFTA

5. CR/T

6. DuPont Ink Jet

7. Wikoff Color Corp.

8. Hostmann-Steinberg

9. Sanchez SA de CV

10. Toyo Ink America LLC

Source: *Ink World*, North American Top 20 (annual), http://www.inkworldmagazine.com, 2012.

3208 ■ WORLD'S LARGEST INK MANUFACTURERS, 2010

Ranked by: Ink and graphic arts revenue, in millions of U.S. dollars. **Remarks:** Also notes contact information, major products, key personnel, number of employees, and comments. **Number listed:** 18

1. Dainippon Ink & Chemicals Inc./Sun Chemical Corp., with $4,880 million

2. Flint Ink Corp., $2,900

3. Toyo Ink, $1,580

4. Sakata INX, $1,280

5. Siegwerk Druckfarben AG, $1,160

6. Huber Group, $995

7. Tokyo Printing Ink, $563

8. SICPA, $400

9. T & K Toka, $386

10. Fujifilm North America, $350

Source: *Ink World*, Top International Ink Companies (annual), http://www.inkworldmagazine.com, 2011.

Instrument Industry

3209 ■ LARGEST COMPANIES IN THE MEASURING, ANALYZING, AND CONTROLLING INSTRUMENTS INDUSTRY BY EMPLOYEES, 2010

Ranked by: Total number of employees. **Remarks:** Also notes contact information for headquarters, number of employees at headquarters, revenue, rank by revenue, and primary SIC code. **Number listed:** 48

1. Emerson Electric Co., with 127,728 employees
2. Raytheon Co., 87,030
3. 3M Co., 75,214
4. BAE Systems Inc., 51,499
5. Honeywell Inc., 50,143
6. Danaher Corp., 46,600
7. Medtronic Inc., 43,000
8. Thermo Fisher Scientific Inc., 35,400
9. Fresenius Medical Care Holdings Inc., 31,261
10. Becton, Dickinson & Co., 28,803

Source: *Business Rankings*, (annual), Dun & Bradstreet Inc., 2011, p. VI.84-VI.85.

3210 ■ LARGEST COMPANIES IN THE MEASURING, ANALYZING, AND CONTROLLING INSTRUMENTS INDUSTRY BY SALES, 2010

Ranked by: Total revenue, in dollars. **Remarks:** Also notes contact information for headquarters, number of employees at headquarters and overall, rank by employees, and primary SIC code. **Number listed:** 49

1. 3M Co., with $26,662,000,000
2. Raytheon Co., $25,183,000,000
3. Emerson Electric Co., $21,039,000,000
4. Medtronic Inc., $15,817,000,000
5. Danaher Corp., $13,202,602,000
6. Thermo Fisher Scientific Inc., $10,788,700,000
7. Boston Scientific Corp., $7,806,000,000
8. Fresenius Medical Care Holdings Inc., $7,515,711,000
9. Becton, Dickinson & Co., $7,372,333,000
10. Stryker Corp., $7,320,000,000

Source: *Business Rankings*, (annual), Dun & Bradstreet Inc., 2011, p. V.84-V.85.

3211 ■ LARGEST U.S. INSTRUMENT MANUFACTURERS, 2010

Ranked by: Revenue, in millions of dollars. **Remarks:** Also notes overall rank within the *IW 500*, revenue growth, and profit margin. **Number listed:** 13

1. Thermo Fisher Scientific Inc., with $10,789 million
2. Agilent Technologies Inc., $5,444
3. Beckman Coulter Inc., $3,663
4. Snap-On Inc., $2,682
5. Ametek Inc., $2,471
6. Inverness Medical Innovations Inc., $2,155
7. Hologic Inc., $1,680
8. Waters Corp., $1,643
9. Teradyne Inc., $1,609
10. Bruker Corp., $1,305

Source: *IndustryWeek*, IW 500 (annual), http://www.industryweek.com, July 2011.

3212 ■ WORLD'S LARGEST INSTRUMENT MANUFACTURERS, 2010

Ranked by: Revenue, in millions of dollars. **Remarks:** Also notes rank for previous year, overall rank within the *IW 1000*, country, and revenue growth. **Number listed:** 14

1. Thales SA, with $17,556 million
2. Fresenius Medical Care AG, $12,053
3. Olympus Corp., $10,862
4. Thermo Fisher Scientific Inc., $10,789
5. Swatch Group AG, $6,899
6. Compagnie Financiere Richemont SA, $6,879
7. Agilent Technologies Inc., $5,444
8. Casio Computer Co., Ltd., $5,264
9. Husqvarna AB, $4,791
10. Yokogawa Electric Corp., $3,894

Source: *IndustryWeek*, IW 1000 (annual), http://www.industryweek.com, August 2011.

Insurance

3213 ■ THE UNITED STATES' MOST VALUABLE INSURANCE BRANDS, 2011

Ranked by: Brand value, in millions of U.S. dollars. **Remarks:** Also notes rank within the *Global 500* for current and previous year, figures for current and previous year, and brand rating. Ranking is available online only. **Number listed:** 6

1. MetLife, with $6,109 million
2. Prudential (U.S.), $6,788
3. Allstate, $3,763
4. Travelers, $3,018
5. Berkshire Hathaway, $2,770
6. Aflac, $2,737

Source: *Global 500*, (annual), Brand Finance plc, March 2012.

Insurance, Automobile

3214 ■ TOP U.S. WRITERS COMMERCIAL AUTO INSURANCE, 2010

Ranked by: Direct premiums written, in thousands of dollars. **Remarks:** Also notes market share. **Number listed:** 10

1. The Travelers Cos., Inc., with $1,976,227 thousand
2. Liberty Mutual Holding Co., $1,598,403
3. Zurich Financial Services Ltd., $1,585,895
4. Progressive Corp., $1,458,727
5. American International Group Inc., $1,111,197
6. Nationwide Mutual Group, $914,355
7. Old Republic International Corp., $731,981
8. Auto-Owners Insurance Co., $540,825
9. The Hartford Financial Services Group Inc., $523,736
10. American Financial Group Inc., $471,237

Source: *The I.I.I. Insurance Fact Book*, (annual), Insurance Information Institute, 2012, p. 63.

3215 ■ TOP U.S. WRITERS OF PRIVATE PASSENGER AUTO INSURANCE, 2010

Ranked by: Direct premiums written, in thousands of dollars. **Remarks:** Also notes market share. **Number listed:** 10

1. State Farm Mutual Automobile Insurance Co., with $31,132,669 thousand
2. Allstate Corp., $16,987,898
3. Berkshire Hathaway Inc., $14,179,673
4. Progressive Corp., $12,845,461
5. Zurich Financial Services Ltd., $9,943,802
6. Liberty Mutual Holding Co., $7,500,758
7. USAA Insurance Group, $7,268,980
8. Nationwide Mutual Group, $7,037,229
9. The Travelers Cos., Inc., $3,512,489
10. American Family Mutual Insurance Co., $3,227,718

Source: *The I.I.I. Insurance Fact Book*, (annual), Insurance Information Institute, 2012, p. 62.

3216 ■ TOP WRITERS OF AUTO INSURANCE IN CANADA, 2010

Ranked by: Direct premiums written, in thousands of Canadian dollars. **Remarks:** Also notes rank for previous year, AM Best number, percent change from previous year, net loss ratios for current and previous year, auto as a percentage of total company premiums, and net premiums written and earned. **Number listed:** 25

1. Intact Insurance Co., with C$1,805,584 thousand
2. State Farm Mutual Automobile Insurance Co., C$1,440,923
3. Wawanesa Mutual Insurance Co., C$1,163,881
4. Security National Insurance Co., C$1,017,904
5. Aviva Insurance Co. of Canada, C$851,155
6. Dominion of Canada General Insurance Co., C$787,969
7. Co-operators General Insurance Co., C$784,524
8. Economical Mutual Insurance Co., C$686,312
9. Unifund Assurance Co., C$659,428
10. Allstate Insurance Co. of Canada, C$453,688

Source: *Best's Review*, Top Auto Writers (annual), October 2011, p. 48.

3217 ■ TOP WRITERS OF AUTO INSURANCE IN THE U.S., 2010

Ranked by: Direct premiums written, in thousands of dollars. **Remarks:** Also notes rank for previous year, AM Best number, percent change from previous year, market share and adjusted loss ratios for current and two previous years, and auto as a percentage of total company premiums. **Number listed:** 25

1. State Farm Insurance Companies, with $30,177,999 thousand
2. Allstate Insurance Co., $17,354,605
3. Berkshire Hathaway Inc., $14,366,958
4. Progressive Insurance Group, $14,302,540
5. Farmers Insurance Group, $10,267,943
6. Liberty Mutual Insurance Companies, $9,066,368

7. Nationwide, $7,951,584
8. USAA, $7,202,821
9. Travelers Group, $5,435,255
10. American Family Insurance Group, $3,285,454

Source: *Best's Review*, Top Auto Writers (annual), October 2011, p. 48.

3218 ■ TOP WRITERS OF AUTO LIABILITY INSURANCE, 2010

Ranked by: Direct premiums written, in thousands of dollars. **Remarks:** Also notes rank for previous year, AM Best number, percent change from previous year, market share and adjusted loss ratios for current and two previous years, and auto liability as a percentage of total company premiums. **Number listed:** 25

1. State Farm Insurance Companies, with $18,313,356 thousand
2. Allstate Insurance Co., $10,138,719
3. Progressive Insurance Group, $9,410,734
4. Berkshire Hathaway Inc., $9,067,594
5. Farmers Insurance Group, $6,287,772
6. Liberty Mutual Insurance Companies, $5,784,336
7. Nationwide, $5,022,509
8. USAA, $3,966,654
9. Travelers Group, $3,743,261
10. Hartford Insurance Group, $2,056,257

Source: *Best's Review*, Top Auto Writers (annual), October 2011, p. 46.

3219 ■ TOP WRITERS OF AUTO PHYSICAL DAMAGE INSURANCE, 2010

Ranked by: Direct premiums written, in thousands of dollars. **Remarks:** Also notes rank for previous year, AM Best number, percent change from previous year, market share and adjusted loss ratios for current and two previous years, and auto physical damage as a percentage of total company premiums. **Number listed:** 25

1. State Farm Insurance Companies, with $11,864,643 thousand
2. Allstate Insurance Co., $7,215,886
3. Berkshire Hathaway Inc., $5,299,364
4. Progressive Insurance Group, $4,891,806
5. Farmers Insurance Group, $3,980,171
6. Liberty Mutual Insurance Companies, $3,282,031
7. USAA, $3,236,167
8. Nationwide, $2,929,074
9. Travelers Group, $1,691,994
10. American Family Insurance Group, $1,393,472

Source: *Best's Review*, Top Auto Writers (annual), October 2011, p. 47.

3220 ■ TOP WRITERS OF COMMERCIAL AUTO INSURANCE, 2010

Ranked by: Direct premiums written, in thousands of dollars. **Remarks:** Also notes rank for previous year, AM Best number, percent change from previous year, market share and adjusted loss ratios for current and two previous years, and commercial auto as a percentage of total company premiums. **Number listed:** 25

1. Travelers Group, with $1,922,765 thousand

2. Liberty Mutual Insurance Companies, $1,565,610
3. Progressive Insurance Group, $1,458,727
4. Zurich Financial Services North America Group, $1,259,649
5. American International Group Inc., $964,212
6. Nationwide, $914,355
7. Old Republic Insurance Group, $731,972
8. Auto-Owners Insurance Group, $540,825
9. Hartford Insurance Group, $523,093
10. Great American P & C Insurance Group, $471,237

Source: *Best's Review*, Top Auto Writers (annual), October 2011, p. 46.

3221 ■ TOP WRITERS OF PRIVATE PASSENGER AUTO INSURANCE, 2010

Ranked by: Direct premiums written, in thousands of dollars. **Remarks:** Also notes rank for previous year, AM Best number, percent change from previous year, market share and adjusted loss ratios for current and two previous years, and private-passenger auto as a percentage of total company premiums. **Number listed:** 25

1. State Farm Insurance Companies, with $29,725,743 thousand
2. Allstate Insurance Co., $16,987,898
3. Berkshire Hathaway Inc., $14,180,533
4. Progressive Insurance Group, $12,843,813
5. Farmers Insurance Group, $9,943,772
6. Liberty Mutual Insurance Companies, $7,500,758
7. USAA, $7,202,840
8. Nationwide, $7,037,229
9. Travelers Group, $3,512,489
10. American Family Insurance Group, $3,227,718

Source: *Best's Review*, Top Auto Writers (annual), October 2011, p. 47.

Insurance, Automobile—Rates

3222 ■ LEAST EXPENSIVE STATES FOR AUTO INSURANCE, 2008

Ranked by: Average expenditure, in dollars. **Number listed:** 10

1. North Dakota, with $503
2. Iowa, $519
3. South Dakota, $520
4. Nebraska, $547
5. Idaho, $562
6. Kansas, $576
7. Wisconsin, $581
8. North Carolina, $595
9. Maine, $600
10. Indiana, $612

Source: *The I.I.I. Insurance Fact Book*, (annual), Insurance Information Institute, 2012, p. 65.

3223 ■ LEAST EXPENSIVE U.S. CITIES FOR AUTO INSURANCE, 2011

Ranked by: Average annual auto premiums, in dollars. **Number listed:** 10

1. Roanoke, VA, with $937
2. Green Bay, WI, $999
3. Wapakoneta, OH, $1,008
4. Portland, ME, $1,053
5. Boise, ID, $1,065
6. Richmond, VA, $1,109
7. Fairfield, OH, $1,111
8. Charlotte, NC, $1,134
9. Lafayette, IN, $1,140
10. Pocatello, ID, $1,143

Source: *The I.I.I. Insurance Fact Book*, (annual), Insurance Information Institute, 2012, p. 65.

3224 ■ MOST EXPENSIVE STATES FOR AUTO INSURANCE, 2008

Ranked by: Average expenditure, in dollars. **Number listed:** 10

1. Washington DC, with $1,126
2. Louisiana, $1,105
3. New Jersey, $1,081
4. Florida, $1,055
5. New York, $1,044
6. Delaware, $1,007
7. Rhode Island, $986
8. Nevada, $970
9. Connecticut, $950
10. Maryland, $922

Source: *The I.I.I. Insurance Fact Book*, (annual), Insurance Information Institute, 2012, p. 65.

3225 ■ MOST EXPENSIVE U.S. CITIES FOR AUTO INSURANCE, 2011

Ranked by: Average annual auto premiums, in dollars. **Number listed:** 10

1. Detroit, MI, with $5,941
2. Philadelphia, PA, $4,076
3. New Orleans, LA, $3,599
4. Miami, FL, $3,388
5. Newark, NJ, $2,867
6. Baltimore, MD, $2,851
7. Tampa, FL, $2,796
8. Providence, RI, $2,711
9. Los Angeles, CA, $2,664
10. Las Vegas, NV, $2,651

Source: *The I.I.I. Insurance Fact Book*, (annual), Insurance Information Institute, 2012, p. 65.

Insurance Brokers

3226 ■ LARGEST GLOBAL INSURANCE BROKERS, 2010

Ranked by: Total brokerage revenue, in millions of U.S. dollars. **Number listed:** 20

1. Marsh & McLennan Cos., with $10,500 million
2. Aon Corp., $8,512
3. Willis Group Holdings Ltd., $3,340
4. Wells Fargo Insurance Services, $2,130
5. Arthur J. Gallagher & Co., $1,864

6. Jardine Lloyd Thompson Group plc, $1,164

7. BB & T Insurance Services Inc., $1,161

8. National Financial Partners Corp., $981.9

9. Brown & Brown Inc., $973.49

10. Lockton Cos., $836.12

Source: *Best's Review*, Top Global Insurance Brokers (annual), July 2011, p. 41.

3227 ■ LARGEST INSURANCE AGENTS, BROKERS, AND SERVICES BY EMPLOYEES, 2010

Ranked by: Total number of employees. **Remarks:** Also notes contact information for headquarters, number of employees at headquarters, revenue, rank by revenue, and primary SIC code. **Number listed:** 196

1. Marsh & McLennan Companies Inc., with 52,307 employees

2. James Sedgwick Inc., 52,306

3. Metropolitan Life Insurance Co., 46,000

4. Marsh USA Inc., 38,000

5. Aon Corp., 36,200

6. Farmers Group Inc., 28,975

7. Arthur J. Gallagher & Co., 10,700

8. Government Employees Insurance Co., 10,000

9. CNA Financial Corp., 8,900

10. Crawford & Co., 8,852

Source: *Business Rankings*, (annual), Dun & Bradstreet Inc., 2011, p. VI.184-VI.188.

3228 ■ LARGEST U.S. INSURANCE BROKERS OVERALL, 2011

Ranked by: Score based on revenue, profits, assets, and market capitalization. **Remarks:** Specific scores not provided. Also notes overall rank in the *Forbes 2000* and figures for each criterion. **Number listed:** 2

1. Aon Corp.

2. Marsh & McLennan Companies Inc.

Source: *Forbes*, Forbes 2000 (annual), http://www.forbes.com, May 7, 2012.

3229 ■ LARGEST U.S. WHOLESALE INSURANCE BROKERS BY TOTAL VOLUME, 2010

Ranked by: Wholesale premium volume, including employee benefits and from property/casualty placements, in dollars. **Number listed:** 10

1. AmWINS Group Inc., with $5,724,931,711

2. Crump Group Inc., $5,568816,901

3. CRC Insurance Services Inc., $2,145,000,000

4. Swett & Crawford Group Inc., $2,100,000,000

5. All Risks Ltd., $620,000,000

6. ARC Express & Surplus LLC, $480,000,000

7. Westrope, $401,434,900

8. Partners Specialty Group LLC, $322,000,000

9. U.S. Risk Insurance Group Inc., $307,000,000

10. Bliss & Glennon Inc., $223,000,000

Source: *Business Insurance*, Wholesale Insurance Brokers (annual), October 10, 2011, p. 20.

3230 ■ WORLD'S LARGEST BANK-OWNED INSURANCE BROKERS, 2010

Ranked by: Total brokerage revenue, in U.S. dollars. **Remarks:** Also notes parent company. **Number listed:** 10

1. Wells Fargo Insurance Services USA Inc., with $1,649,538,000

2. BB & T Insurance Services Inc., $1,078,576,900

3. Regions Insurance Group Inc., $99,594,000

4. BancorpSouth Insurance Services Inc., $81,611,594

5. Huntington Insurance Inc., $59,255,000

6. Eastern Insurance Group LLC, $55,817,80.3

7. Associated Financial Group LLC, $51,259,900

8. First Niagara Risk Management Inc., $45,953,038

9. BBVA Compass Insurance Agency Inc., $36,648,121

10. Old National Insurance, $35,737,161

Source: *Business Insurance*, World's Largest Brokers (annual), July 18, 2011, p. 20.

3231 ■ WORLD'S LARGEST INSURANCE BROKERS OVERALL, 2011

Ranked by: Score based on revenue, profits, assets, and market capitalization. **Remarks:** Specific scores not provided. Also notes country, overall rank in the *Forbes 2000,* and figures for each criterion. **Number listed:** 3

1. Aon Corp.

2. Marsh & McLennan Companies Inc.

3. Willis Group Holdings Ltd.

Source: *Forbes*, Forbes 2000 (annual), http://www.forbes.com, May 7, 2012.

3232 ■ WORLD'S LARGEST INSURANCE BROKERS BY REVENUE, 2010

Ranked by: Total brokerage revenue, in U.S. dollars. **Remarks:** Also notes contact information, CEO, percent change from previous year, number of employees and offices, and breakdown of revenue by type. **Number listed:** 10

1. Aon Corp., with $10,606,000,000

2. Marsh & McLennan Companies Inc., $10,596,000,000

3. Willis Group Holdings PLC, $3,300,000,000

4. Arthur J. Gallagher & Co., $1,789,884,000

5. Wells Fargo Insurance Services USA Inc., $1,649,538,000

6. Jardine Lloyd Thompson Group plc, $1,137,730,760

7. BB & T Insurance Services Inc., $1,078,576,900

8. Brown & Brown Inc., $966,917,112

9. Lockton Cos., $826,857,000

10. Hub International Ltd., $761,577,000

Source: *Business Insurance*, World's Largest Brokers (annual), July 18, 2011, p. 10.

3233 ■ WORLD'S LARGEST INSURANCE BROKERS BY U.S. BUSINESS, 2010

Ranked by: Brokerage revenue generated by U.S.-based clients, in U.S. dollars. **Remarks:** Also notes rank for previous year and percent change from previous year. **Number listed:** 100

1. Marsh & McLennan Companies Inc., with $4,662,240,000

2. Aon Corp., $4,242,400,000
3. Willis Group Holdings PLC, $1,650,000,000
4. Wells Fargo Insurance Services USA Inc., $1,649,538,000
5. Arthur J. Gallagher & Co., $1,557,199,080
6. BB & T Insurance Services Inc., $1,078,576,900
7. Brown & Brown Inc., $964,016,361
8. USI Holdings Corp., $632,249,000
9. Lockton Cos., $578,799,900
10. Hub International Ltd., $510,256,590

Source: *Business Insurance*, World's Largest Brokers (annual), July 18, 2011, p. 12.

3234 ■ WORLD'S LARGEST PRIVATELY-OWNED INSURANCE BROKERS, 2010

Ranked by: Total brokerage revenue, in U.S. dollars. **Remarks:** Ranking covers brokers that are not owned by banks or private equity firms. **Number listed:** 10

1. Lockton Cos., with $826,857,000
2. Leavitt Group, $191,062,000
3. Frank Crystal & Co., $131,530,000
4. Hays Group Inc., dba Hays Cos., $118,200,000
5. Bollinger Inc., $116,836,278
6. J. Smith Lanier & Co., $105,324,257
7. John L. Wortham & Son LP, $97,563,070
8. Beecher Carlson Holdings Inc., $94,684,300
9. Holmes Murphy & Associates Inc., $92,750,756
10. Hylant Group Inc., $88,242,480

Source: *Business Insurance*, World's Largest Brokers (annual), July 18, 2011, p. 16.

3235 ■ WORLD'S TOP INSURANCE BROKERS BY REVENUE, 2010

Ranked by: Brokerage revenue, in millions of U.S. dollars. **Remarks:** Also notes country. **Number listed:** 10

1. Aon Corp., with $10,606 million
2. Marsh & McLennan Companies Inc., $10,596
3. Willis Group Holdings plc, $3,300
4. Arthur J. Gallagher & Co., $1,790
5. Wells Fargo Insurance Services USA Inc., $1,650
6. Jardine Lloyd Thompson Group plc, $1,138
7. BB & T Insurance Services Inc., $1,079
8. Brown & Brown Inc., $967
9. Lockton Cos. LLC, $827
10. Hub International Ltd., $762

Source: *The I.I.I. Insurance Fact Book*, (annual), Insurance Information Institute, 2012, p. 6.

Insurance, Commercial

3236 ■ TOP U.S. BROKERS OF COMMERCIAL INSURANCE, 2010

Ranked by: Brokerage revenue, in millions of dollars. **Number listed:** 10

1. Marsh & McLennan Companies Inc., with $4,662.2 million

2. Aon Corp., $4,242.4
3. Willis Group Holdings plc, $1,650
4. Wells Fargo Insurance Services USA Inc., $1,649.5
5. Arthur J. Gallagher & Co., $1,557.2
6. BB & T Insurance Services Inc., $1,078.6
7. Brown & Brown Inc., $964
8. USI Holdings Corp., $632.2
9. Lockton Cos. LLC, $578.8
10. Hub International Ltd., $510.3

Source: *The I.I.I. Insurance Fact Book*, (annual), Insurance Information Institute, 2012, p. 108.

3237 ■ TOP U.S. WRITERS OF COMMERCIAL INSURANCE, 2010

Ranked by: Direct premiums written, in thousands of dollars. **Remarks:** Also notes market share. **Number listed:** 10

1. American International Group Inc., with $20,151,570 thousand
2. The Travelers Cos., Inc., $14,580,352
3. Liberty Mutual Holding Co., $14,005,460
4. Zurich Financial Services Ltd., $12,495,405
5. ACE Ltd., $7,470,050
6. CNA Financial Corp., $7,286,157
7. Chubb Corp., $6,909,680
8. The Hartford Financial Services Group Inc., $6,710,789
9. Nationwide Mutual Group, $4,746,593
10. Allianz SE, $4,528,084

Source: *The I.I.I. Insurance Fact Book*, (annual), Insurance Information Institute, 2012, p. 108.

3238 ■ TOP WRITERS OF COMMERCIAL MULTIPLE PERIL INSURANCE, 2010

Ranked by: Direct premiums written, in thousands of dollars. **Remarks:** Also notes A. M. Best number, percent change from previous year, market share and adjusted loss ratios for current and two previous years, and commercial multiple peril as a percentage of total company premiums. **Number listed:** 25

1. Travelers Group, with $3,059,335 thousand
2. Liberty Mutual Insurance Companies, $2,169,605
3. Hartford Insurance Group, $1,757,647
4. Chubb Group of Insurance Cos., $1,505,258
5. State Farm Insurance Companies, $1,498,615
6. Nationwide, $1,375,297
7. Farmers Insurance Group, $1,299,064
8. Tokio Marine U.S. Group, $1,172,084
9. Zurich Financial Services North America Group, $925,193
10. CNA Insurance Cos., $905,569

Source: *Best's Review*, Top P/C Writers by Line (annual), August 2011, p. 57.

Insurance Companies

3239 ■ FASTEST-GROWING PRIVATE INSURANCE COMPANIES IN THE U.S., 2007-2010

Ranked by: Average annual sales growth over three years, in percent. **Remarks:** Also notes headquarters, revenue, and rank in

the overall *Inc. 500*. To qualify, private companies must have had annual revenues of at least $100,000 in 2007 and $2 million in 2010. **Number listed:** 6

1. BrokersWeb.com, with 8,127.5%
2. HomeInsurance.com, 3,458%
3. Petplan, 2,206.7%
4. Health Plan One, 1,601.8%
5. Medigap360, 1,578.5%
6. Homeland HealthCare, 750.1%

Source: *Inc.*, Inc. 500 (annual), September 2011, p. 156-160.

3240 ■ ILLINOIS'S LARGEST DIVERSIFIED INSURANCE COMPANIES OVERALL, 2011

Ranked by: Score based on revenue, profits, assets, and market capitalization. **Remarks:** Specific scores not provided. Also notes overall rank in the *Forbes 2000* and figures for each criterion. **Number listed:** 2

1. The Allstate Corp.
2. Old Republic International Corp.

Source: *Forbes*, Forbes 2000 (annual), http://www.forbes.com, May 7, 2012.

3241 ■ LARGEST INSURANCE CARRIERS BY EMPLOYEES, 2010

Ranked by: Total number of employees. **Remarks:** Also notes contact information for headquarters, number of employees at headquarters, revenue, rank by revenue, and primary SIC code. **Number listed:** 50

1. Berkshire Hathaway Inc., with 257,000 employees
2. American International Group Inc., 96,000
3. UnitedHealth Group Inc., 80,000
4. State Farm Mutual Automobile Insurance Co., 68,000
5. MetLife Inc., 57,000
6. Liberty Mutual Holding Co., 45,000
7. Prudential Financial Inc., 41,943
8. LMHC Massachusetts Holdings Inc., 41,208
9. Liberty Mutual Group Inc., 41,165
10. WellPoint Inc., 40,500

Source: *Business Rankings*, (annual), Dun & Bradstreet Inc., 2011, p. VI.182-VI.183.

3242 ■ LARGEST U.S. DIVERSIFIED INSURANCE COMPANIES OVERALL, 2011

Ranked by: Score based on revenue, profits, assets, and market capitalization. **Remarks:** Specific scores not provided. Also notes overall rank in the *Forbes 2000* and figures for each criterion. **Number listed:** 13

1. American International Group Inc.
2. MetLife Inc.
3. The Allstate Corp.
4. Loews Corp.
5. The Hartford Financial Services Group Inc.
6. Reinsurance Group of America Inc.
7. Assurant Inc.
8. Genworth Financial Inc.
9. American Financial Group Inc.
10. Cincinnati Financial Corp.

Source: *Forbes*, Forbes 2000 (annual), http://www.forbes.com, May 7, 2012.

3243 ■ MOST VALUABLE U.S. NONLIFE INSURANCE COMPANIES, 2011

Ranked by: Market value as of March 2011, in millions of U.S. dollars. **Remarks:** Also notes rank within the *FT U.S. 500*, rank for previous year, country, revenue, net income, assets, number of employees, share price, price-to-earning ratio, dividend yield, and fiscal yearend. **Number listed:** 14

1. Berkshire Hathaway Inc., with $205,671.3 million
2. American International Group Inc., $53,093.9
3. The Travelers Cos., Inc., $25,639
4. ACE Ltd., $21,709.6
5. Chubb Group of Insurance Cos., $17,999.9
6. Loews Corp., $17,748.6
7. Aon Corp., $17,640.3
8. The Allstate Corp., $16,836.1
9. Marsh & McLennan Companies Inc., $15,219.3
10. Progressive Ohio, $13,914.2

Source: *Financial Times*, FT 500 (annual), http://www.ft.com, June 24, 2011.

3244 ■ NEW YORK'S LARGEST DIVERSIFIED INSURANCE COMPANIES OVERALL, 2011

Ranked by: Score based on revenue, profits, assets, and market capitalization. **Remarks:** Specific scores not provided. Also notes overall rank in the *Forbes 2000* and figures for each criterion. **Number listed:** 6

1. American International Group Inc.
2. MetLife Inc.
3. Loews Corp.
4. Assurant Inc.
5. Ambac Financial Group Inc.
6. MBIA Inc.

Source: *Forbes*, Forbes 2000 (annual), http://www.forbes.com, May 7, 2012.

3245 ■ OHIO'S LARGEST DIVERSIFIED INSURANCE COMPANIES OVERALL, 2011

Ranked by: Score based on revenue, profits, assets, and market capitalization. **Remarks:** Specific scores not provided. Also notes overall rank in the *Forbes 2000* and figures for each criterion. **Number listed:** 2

1. American Financial Group Inc.
2. Cincinnati Financial Corp.

Source: *Forbes*, Forbes 2000 (annual), http://www.forbes.com, May 7, 2012.

Insurance Companies, International

3246 ■ AUSTRIA'S LARGEST DIVERSIFIED INSURANCE COMPANIES OVERALL, 2011

Ranked by: Score based on revenue, profits, assets, and market capitalization. **Remarks:** Specific scores not provided. Also notes overall rank in the *Forbes 2000* and figures for each criterion. **Number listed:** 2

1. Vienna Insurance Group
2. UNIQA Versicherungen AG

Source: *Forbes*, Forbes 2000 (annual), http://www.forbes.com, May 7, 2012.

3247 ■ EUROPE'S MOST VALUABLE NONLIFE INSURANCE COMPANIES, 2011

Ranked by: Market value as of March 2011, in millions of U.S. dollars. **Remarks:** Also notes rank within the *FT Europe 500*, rank for previous year, country, revenue, net income, assets, number of employees, share price, price-to-earning ratio, dividend yield, and fiscal yearend. **Number listed:** 16

1. Allianz AG, with $63,872 million
2. AXA, $48,547
3. Zurich Financial Services Ltd., $41,202.8
4. Assicurazioni Generali SpA, $33,758.8
5. Munchener Ruckversicherungs-Gesellschaft AG (Munich Re), $29,687.4
6. Swiss Reinsurance Co., $21,293.1
7. Sampo Oyj, $17,891.1
8. MAPFRE SA, $11,365.9
9. PZU Group, $10,825.9
10. RSA Insurance Group, $7,372.9

Source: *Financial Times*, FT 500 (annual), http://www.ft.com, June 24, 2011.

3248 ■ FRANCE'S LARGEST DIVERSIFIED INSURANCE COMPANIES OVERALL, 2011

Ranked by: Score based on revenue, profits, assets, and market capitalization. **Remarks:** Specific scores not provided. Also notes overall rank in the *Forbes 2000* and figures for each criterion. **Number listed:** 3

1. AXA
2. CNP Assurances SA
3. SCOR

Source: *Forbes*, Forbes 2000 (annual), http://www.forbes.com, May 7, 2012.

3249 ■ GERMANY'S LARGEST DIVERSIFIED INSURANCE COMPANIES OVERALL, 2011

Ranked by: Score based on revenue, profits, assets, and market capitalization. **Remarks:** Specific scores not provided. Also notes overall rank in the *Forbes 2000* and figures for each criterion. **Number listed:** 4

1. Allianz AG
2. Munchener Ruckversicherungs-Gesellschaft AG (Munich Re)
3. Hannover Reinsurance Corp.
4. Nurnberger

Source: *Forbes*, Forbes 2000 (annual), http://www.forbes.com, May 7, 2012.

3250 ■ ITALY'S LARGEST DIVERSIFIED INSURANCE COMPANIES OVERALL, 2011

Ranked by: Score based on revenue, profits, assets, and market capitalization. **Remarks:** Specific scores not provided. Also notes overall rank in the *Forbes 2000* and figures for each criterion. **Number listed:** 4

1. Assicurazioni Generali SpA
2. Fondiaria-SAI
3. Unipol
4. Cattolica Assicurazioni

Source: *Forbes*, Forbes 2000 (annual), http://www.forbes.com, May 7, 2012.

3251 ■ LARGEST EUROPEAN INSURERS BY ASSETS, 2009

Ranked by: Total non-banking assets, in billions of euros. **Remarks:** Also notes A.M. Best number. **Number listed:** 20

1. AXA SA (France), with €672.54 billion
2. Allianz SE (Germany), €562.96
3. Assicurazioni Generali SpA (Italy), €423.82
4. Aviva plc (U.K.), €393.53
5. Legal & General Group plc (U.K.), €330.1
6. CNP Assurances (France), €298.63
7. AEGON NV (Netherlands), €298.63
8. ING Verzekeringen NV (Netherlands), €290.41
9. Zurich Financial Services Ltd. (Switzerland), €257.59
10. Prudential plc (U.K.), €253.1

Source: *Best's Review*, Top European Insurers, July 2011, p. 35.

3252 ■ LARGEST EUROPEAN INSURERS BY NET PREMIUMS, 2009

Ranked by: Net premiums written, in billions of euros. **Remarks:** Also notes A.M. Best number. **Number listed:** 20

1. AXA SA (France), with €81.26 billion
2. Assicurazioni Generali SpA (Italy), €63.94
3. Allianz SE (Germany), €59.96
4. Aviva plc (U.K.), €35.69
5. Zurich Financial Services Ltd. (Switzerland), €33.47
6. CNP Assurances (France), €31.58
7. ING Verzekeringen NV (Netherlands), €28.56
8. Prudential plc (U.K.), €22.2
9. Eureko BV (Netherlands), €19.01
10. PREDICA (France), €18.93

Source: *Best's Review*, Top European Insurers, July 2011, p. 35.

3253 ■ LARGEST INSURANCE COMPANIES IN EUROPE, 2010

Ranked by: Sales, in millions of U.S. dollars. **Remarks:** Also notes rank within country. **Number listed:** 100

1. Zurich Financial Services AG (Switzerland), with $70,270 million
2. ING Groep NV (Netherlands), $68,030.4
3. Munchener Ruckversicherungs-Gesellschaft AG (Munich Re, Germany), $65,016
4. Aviva plc (U.K.), $52,035
5. CNP Assurances SA (France), $37,057.2
6. Hannover Ruckversicherung AG (Germany), $36,407.4
7. Schweizerische Ruckversicherung GmbH (Germany), $32,869.3
8. Swiss Reinsurance Co. (Switzerland), $32,618.7
9. Prudential plc (U.K.), $30,448.5
10. Standard Life plc (U.K.), $26,152.5

Source: *Europe's 15,000 Largest Companies*, (annual), ELC International, 2011, p. 44.

3254 ■ NORWAY'S LARGEST DIVERSIFIED INSURANCE COMPANIES OVERALL, 2011

Ranked by: Score based on revenue, profits, assets, and market capitalization. **Remarks:** Specific scores not provided. Also notes overall rank in the *Forbes 2000* and figures for each criterion. **Number listed:** 2

1. Storebrand ASA
2. Gjensidige Forsikring ASA

Source: *Forbes*, Forbes 2000 (annual), http://www.forbes.com, May 7, 2012.

3255 ■ SWITZERLAND'S LARGEST DIVERSIFIED INSURANCE COMPANIES OVERALL, 2011

Ranked by: Score based on revenue, profits, assets, and market capitalization. Remarks: Specific scores not provided. Also notes overall rank in the *Forbes 2000* and figures for each criterion. Number listed: 5

1. Zurich Financial Services AG
2. Swiss Reinsurance Co.
3. ACE Ltd.
4. Baloise Group
5. Helvetia Group

Source: *Forbes*, Forbes 2000 (annual), http://www.forbes.com, May 7, 2012.

3256 ■ WORLD'S LARGEST DIVERSIFIED INSURANCE COMPANIES OVERALL, 2011

Ranked by: Score based on revenue, profits, assets, and market capitalization. Remarks: Specific scores not provided. Also notes country, overall rank in the *Forbes 2000,* and figures for each criterion. Number listed: 44

1. American International Group Inc.
2. AXA
3. Allianz AG
4. MetLife Inc.
5. Zurich Financial Services
6. Ping An Insurance (Group) Company of China Ltd.
7. Assicurazioni Generali SpA
8. Swiss Re AG
9. Munchener Ruckversicherungs-Gesellschaft AG (Munich Re)
10. ACE Ltd.

Source: *Forbes*, Forbes 2000 (annual), http://www.forbes.com, May 7, 2012.

3257 ■ WORLD'S MOST VALUABLE NONLIFE INSURANCE COMPANIES, 2011

Ranked by: Market value as of March 2011, in millions of U.S. dollars. Remarks: Also notes rank within the *FT 500*, rank for previous year, country, revenue, net income, assets, number of employees, share price, price-to-earning ratio, dividend yield, and fiscal year-end. Number listed: 12

1. Berkshire Hathaway Inc., with $206,671.3 million
2. Allianz AG, $63,872
3. American International Group Inc., $63,093.9
4. AXA, $48,547
5. Zurich Financial Services Ltd., $41,202.8
6. Assicurazioni Generali SpA, $33,758.8
7. Munchener Ruckversicherungs-Gesellschaft AG (Munich Re), $29,687.4
8. The Travelers Cos., Inc., $25,639
9. ACE Ltd., $21,709.6
10. Tokio Marine Holdings Inc., $21,588.6

Source: *Financial Times*, FT 500 (annual), http://www.ft.com, June 24, 2011.

3258 ■ WORLD'S TOP INSURANCE COMPANIES BY REVENUE, 2010

Ranked by: Revenue, in millions of U.S. dollars. Remarks: Also notes country and type of insurer. Number listed: 10

1. Japan Post Holdings Co., Ltd., with $203,958 million
2. AXA, $162,236
3. Berkshire Hathaway Inc., $136,185
4. Allianz AG, $127,379
5. Assicurazioni Generali SpA, $120,234
6. American International Group Inc., $104,417
7. Aviva plc, $90,211
8. Nippon Life Insurance Co., $78,571
9. Munchener Ruckversicherungs-Gesellschaft AG (Munich Re), $76,220
10. Prudential plc, $73,598

Source: *The I.I.I. Insurance Fact Book*, (annual), Insurance Information Institute, 2012, p. 4.

Insurance, Earthquake

3259 ■ TOP U.S. WRITERS OF EARTHQUAKE INSURANCE, 2010

Ranked by: Direct premiums written, in thousands of dollars. Remarks: Also notes market share. Number listed: 10

1. California Earthquake Authority, with $602,412 thousand
2. State Farm Mutual Automobile Insurance, $236,892
3. Zurich Financial Services Ltd., $195,520
4. American International Group Inc., $190,563
5. The Travelers Cos., Inc., $133,775
6. GeoVera Insurance Holdings Ltd., $125,772
7. AXIS Capital Holdings Ltd., $111,114
8. Liberty Mutual Holding Co., $76,936
9. ACE Ltd., $75,143
10. Endurance Specialty Holdings, $65,428

Source: *The I.I.I. Insurance Fact Book*, (annual), Insurance Information Institute, 2012, p. 107.

Insurance—Excess and Surplus Lines

3260 ■ LARGEST U.S. SURPLUS LINES INSURERS, 2010

Ranked by: Nonadmitted direct premiums written, in dollars. Remarks: Also notes contact information, principal officer, parent company, gross premiums, percent change from previous year, net written volume, and net income. Number listed: 10

1. Lexington Insurance Co., with $4,605,79,515
2. Steadfast Insurance Co., $1,073,451,439
3. Scottsdale Insurance Co., $1,004,147,047
4. Chartis Specialty Insurance Co., $784,795,135
5. Columbia Casualty Co., $718,064,491
6. Illinois Union Insurance Co., $532,554,380
7. Landmark American Insurance Co., $509,470,668
8. Evanston Insurance Co., $470,571,621

9. Westchester Surplus Lines Insurance Co., $409,449,256

10. Arch Specialty Insurance Co., $402,861,503

Source: *Business Insurance*, Surplus Lines Market Report (annual), October 10, 2011, p. 16.

3261 ■ TOP U.S. WRITERS OF SURPLUS LINES INSURANCE, 2010

Ranked by: Nonadmitted direct premiums written, in dollars. **Remarks:** Also notes parent company. **Number listed:** 10

1. Lexington Insurance Co., with $4,605,795,515
2. Steadfast Insurance Co., $1,03,451,439
3. Scottsdale Insurance Co., $1,004,147,047
4. Chartis Specialty Insurance Co., $784,795,135
5. Columbia Casualty Co., $718,064,491
6. Illinois Union Insurance Co., $532,554,380
7. Landmark American Insurance Co., $509,470,668
8. Evanston Insurance Co., $470,571,621
9. Westchester Surplus Lines Insurance Co., $409,449,256
10. Arch Specialty Insurance Co., $402,861,503

Source: *The I.I.I. Insurance Fact Book*, (annual), Insurance Information Institute, 2012, p. 47.

3262 ■ U.S. SURPLUS LINES INSURERS WITH THE HIGHEST STATUTORY COMBINED RATIO, 2010

Ranked by: Statutory combined ratio, in percent. **Number listed:** 5

1. Chartis Specialty Insurance Co., with 139.1%
2. General Star National Insurance Co., 136.7%
3. Lexington Insurance Co., 103.9%
4. Tudor Insurance Co., 103.6%
4. Western World Insurance Co., 103.6%

Source: *Business Insurance*, Surplus Lines Market Report (annual), October 10, 2011, p. 16.

3263 ■ U.S. SURPLUS LINES INSURERS WITH THE LOWEST STATUTORY COMBINED RATIO, 2010

Ranked by: Statutory combined ratio, in percent. **Number listed:** 5

1. Landmark American Insurance Co., with 62.7%
2. General Star Indemnity Co., 67.3%
3. Mt. Hawley Insurance Co., 72.2%
4. National Fire & Marine Insurance Co., 72.5%
5. Penn-America Insurance Co., 74.3%

Source: *Business Insurance*, Surplus Lines Market Report (annual), October 10, 2011, p. 16.

Insurance, Financial Guaranty

3264 ■ TOP U.S. WRITERS OF FINANCIAL GUARANTY INSURANCE, 2010

Ranked by: Direct premiums written, in thousands of dollars. **Remarks:** Also notes market share. **Number listed:** 10

1. Assured Guaranty Ltd., with $636,860 thousand
2. MBIA Inc., $352,363

3. Ambac Financial Group Inc., $243,002
4. Financial Guaranty Insurance Co., $71,567
5. Syncora Holdings Ltd., $69,600
6. Radian Group Inc., $49,350
7. CIFG Assurance North America Inc., $20,249
8. Stonebridge Casualty Insurance Co., $3,000
9. ACA Financial Guaranty Corp., $487
10. Century Insurance Co. (Guam) Ltd., $32

Source: *The I.I.I. Insurance Fact Book*, (annual), Insurance Information Institute, 2012, p. 119.

Insurance, Fire

3265 ■ TOP FIRE AND ALLIED INSURANCE COMPANIES, 2010

Ranked by: Direct premiums written, in thousands of dollars. **Remarks:** Also notes AM Best number, annual percent change in premiums, fire and allied as a percentage of total company premiums, and market share and adjusted loss ratio for current and previous two years. **Number listed:** 25

1. American International Group Inc., with $2,926,128 thousand
2. Ace INA Group, $2,113,846
3. Assurant P & C Group, $2,104,765
4. Balboa Insurance Group, $1,575,673
5. Travelers Group, $1,496,727
6. FM Global, $1,467,593
7. Citizens Property Insurance Corp., $1,447,618
8. Allianz of America Inc., $1,254,081
9. Wells Fargo Insurance Group, $1,139,018
10. QBE Americas Group, $1,074,224

Source: *Best's Review*, Top Marine, Fire, & Allied Writers (annual), December 2011, p. 28.

Insurance, Health

3266 ■ TOP FORTUNE 500 COMPANIES IN HEALTHCARE INSURANCE AND MANAGED CARE, 2011

Ranked by: Revenue, in millions of dollars. **Remarks:** Also notes overall rank in the *Fortune 500;* profits; profits as a percentage of revenue; stockholders' equity; and rank by each criterion. **Number listed:** 11

1. UnitedHealth Group Inc., with $101,862 million
2. WellPoint Inc., $60,711
3. Humana Inc., $36,832
4. Aetna Inc., $33,780
5. CIGNA Corp., $21,998
6. Coventry Health Care Inc., $12,187
7. Health Net Inc., $11,901
8. Amerigroup Corp., $6,318
9. WellCare Health Plans Inc., $6,107
10. Centene Corp., $5,341

Source: *Fortune*, Fortune 500 (annual), May 21, 2012, p. F-36.

3267 ■ TOP U.S. HEALTH INSURANCE GROUPS BY DIRECT PREMIUMS, 2010

Ranked by: Direct premiums written, in billions of dollars. **Remarks:** Also notes market share. **Number listed:** 10

1. WellPoint Inc., with $42.2 billion
2. UnitedHealth Group Inc., $41.1
3. Health Care Services Corp., $20.2
4. Humana Inc., $13.2
5. Highmark Inc., $11.6
6. Aetna Inc., $10
7. Coventry Health Care Inc., $9.8
8. EmblemHealth Inc., $9.7
9. Kaiser Foundation Health Plan Inc., $9.5
10. Independence Blue Cross, $9.3

Source: *The I.I.I. Insurance Fact Book*, (annual), Insurance Information Institute, 2012, p. 31.

3268 ■ WORLD'S MOST ADMIRED HEALTH CARE INSURANCE/MANAGED CARE COMPANIES, 2012

Ranked by: Score, on a scale of 10, based on a survey of executives, directors, and securities analysts of companies within their own industry on eight criteria: innovation, financial soundness, employee talent, use of corporate assets, long-term investment value, social responsibility, quality of management, and quality of products/services. **Remarks:** Specific scores not provided. Also notes rank for previous year. **Number listed:** 5

1. UnitedHealth Group Inc.
2. Aetna Inc.
3. Humana Inc.
4. WellPoint Inc.
5. CIGNA Corp.

Source: *Fortune*, World's Most Admired Companies (annual), March 19, 2012, p. 148.

3269 ■ WORLD'S MOST ETHICAL HEALTH INSURANCE COMPANIES, 2012

Ranked by: Score based on five criteria: ethics and compliance program; reputation, leadership, and innovation; governance; corporate citizenship and responsibility; and culture of ethics. **Remarks:** Specific scores not provided; companies are listed alphabetically, not ranked. **Number listed:** 4

1. AFLAC Inc. (U.S.)
2. Blue Cross Blue Shield of North Carolina (U.S.)
3. Blue Shield of California (U.S.)
4. Wisconsin Physicians Service Insurance Corp. (U.S.)

Source: *Ethisphere Magazine*, World's Most Ethical Companies (annual), http://www.ethisphere.com, 2012.

Insurance, Health—Costs

3270 ■ STATES WITH THE FEWEST HEALTH INSURANCE MANDATES, 2011

Ranked by: Score based on 0.05 points for each mandate imposed. **Remarks:** Health insurance mandates are requirements that insurers cover certain types of health care providers and benefits. **Number listed:** 51

1. Idaho, with 0.65 points
2. Alabama, 0.95
3. Hawaii, 1.15
4. Michigan, 1.25
4. Utah, 1.25
6. Washington DC, 1.35

6. Iowa, 1.35
8. Mississippi, 1.45
8. Ohio, 1.45
8. South Carolina, 1.45
8. South Dakota, 1.45

Source: *Small Business Survival Index*, (annual), Small Business & Entrepreneurship Council, November 2011, p. 49.

3271 ■ STATES WITH THE MOST HEALTH INSURANCE MANDATES, 2011

Ranked by: Score based on 0.05 points for each mandate imposed. **Remarks:** Health insurance mandates are requirements that insurers cover certain types of health care providers and benefits. **Number listed:** 51

1. Rhode Island, with 3.45 points
2. Maryland, 3.35
3. Minnesota, 3.20
4. Texas, 3
5. Connecticut, 2.95
6. New Mexico, 2.85
6. Pennsylvania, 2.85
6. Virginia, 2.85
6. Washington, 2.85
10. California, 2.80

Source: *Small Business Survival Index*, (annual), Small Business & Entrepreneurship Council, November 2011, p. 49.

Insurance, Homeowners

3272 ■ TOP U.S. WRITERS OF HOMEOWNERS INSURANCE, 2010

Ranked by: Direct premiums written, in thousands of dollars. **Remarks:** Also notes market share. **Number listed:** 10

1. State Farm Mutual Automobile Insurance, with $15,672,281 thousand
2. Allstate Corp., $6,865,832
3. Zurich Financial Services Ltd., $4,703,100
4. Liberty Mutual Holding Co., $3,729,987
5. The Travelers Cos., Inc., $3,295,031
6. USAA Insurance Group, $3,175,416
7. Nationwide Mutual Group, $2,832,201
8. Chubb Corp., $1,763,926
9. American Family Mutual Insurance Co., $1,514,843
10. Citizens Property Insurance Corp., $1,156,647

Source: *The I.I.I. Insurance Fact Book*, (annual), Insurance Information Institute, 2012, p. 90.

3273 ■ TOP WRITERS OF HOMEOWNERS MULTIPLE PERIL INSURANCE, 2010

Ranked by: Direct premiums written, in thousands of dollars. **Remarks:** Also notes A. M. Best number, percent change from previous year, market share and adjusted loss ratios for current and two previous years, and homeowners multiple peril as a percentage of total company premiums. **Number listed:** 25

1. State Farm Insurance Companies, with $15,272,031 thousand
2. Allstate Insurance Co., $6,865,832

3. Farmers Insurance Group, $4,633,471
4. Liberty Mutual Insurance Companies, $3,729,987
5. Travelers Group, $3,295,031
6. USAA, $3,174,410
7. Nationwide, $2,832,201
8. Chubb Group of Insurance Cos., $1,756,090
9. American Family Insurance Group, $1,514,843
10. Citizens Property Insurance Corp., $1,156,647

Source: *Best's Review*, Top P/C Writers by Line (annual), August 2011, p. 57.

Insurance, International

3274 ■ CHINA'S MOST VALUABLE INSURANCE BRANDS, 2011

Ranked by: Brand value, in millions of U.S. dollars. **Remarks:** Also notes rank within the *Global 500* for current and previous year, figures for current and previous year, and brand rating. Ranking is available online only. **Number listed:** 4

1. China Life Insurance, with $8,600 million
2. Ping An, $5,085
3. CPIC, $3,115
4. PICC, $2,763

Source: *Global 500*, (annual), Brand Finance plc, March 2012.

3275 ■ FRANCE'S MOST VALUABLE INSURANCE BRANDS, 2011

Ranked by: Brand value, in millions of U.S. dollars. **Remarks:** Also notes rank within the *Global 500* for current and previous year, figures for current and previous year, and brand rating. Ranking is available online only. **Number listed:** 2

1. AXA, with $13,406 million
2. CNP Assurances, $3,601

Source: *Global 500*, (annual), Brand Finance plc, March 2012.

3276 ■ GERMANY'S MOST VALUABLE INSURANCE BRANDS, 2011

Ranked by: Brand value, in millions of U.S. dollars. **Remarks:** Also notes rank within the *Global 500* for current and previous year, figures for current and previous year, and brand rating. Ranking is available online only. **Number listed:** 3

1. Allianz, with $10,951 million
2. Munich Re, $5,064
3. Ergo, $2,860

Source: *Global 500*, (annual), Brand Finance plc, March 2012.

3277 ■ THE NETHERLANDS' MOST VALUABLE INSURANCE BRANDS, 2011

Ranked by: Brand value, in millions of U.S. dollars. **Remarks:** Also notes rank within the *Global 500* for current and previous year, figures for current and previous year, and brand rating. Ranking is available online only. **Number listed:** 2

1. ING, with $7,054 million
2. Aegon, $3,460

Source: *Global 500*, (annual), Brand Finance plc, March 2012.

3278 ■ SWITZERLAND'S MOST VALUABLE INSURANCE BRANDS, 2011

Ranked by: Brand value, in millions of U.S. dollars. **Remarks:** Also notes rank within the *Global 500* for current and previous

year, figures for current and previous year, and brand rating. Ranking is available online only. **Number listed:** 3

1. Zurich, with $5,381 million
2. Swiss Re, $3,661
3. ACE, $2,449

Source: *Global 500*, (annual), Brand Finance plc, March 2012.

3279 ■ TOP NORTH AMERICAN PUBLIC INSURERES BY ASSETS, 2010

Ranked by: Assets, in thousands of dollars. **Remarks:** Also notes AM Best number, figures for previous year, and percent change from previous year. **Number listed:** 75

1. MetLife Inc., with $730,906,000 thousand
2. American International Group Inc., $683,443,000
3. Prudential Financial Inc., $539,854,000
4. Manulife Financial Corp., $417,770,773
5. Berkshire Hathaway Inc., $372,229,000
6. Hartford Financial Services Group Inc., $318,346,000
7. Sun Life Financial Inc., $209,790,977
8. Lincoln National Corp., $193,824,000
9. Principal Financial Group Inc., $145,631,100
10. Great-West Lifeco Inc., $131,527,151

Source: *Best's Review*, Top North American Insurers, July 2011, p. 37-38.

3280 ■ TOP NORTH AMERICAN PUBLIC INSURERES BY REVENUE, 2010

Ranked by: Revenue, in thousands of dollars. **Remarks:** Also notes AM Best number, figures for previous year, and percent change from previous year. **Number listed:** 75

1. Berkshire Hathaway Inc., with $136,185,000 thousand
2. UnitedHealth Group Inc., $94,155,000
3. American International Group Inc., $77,301,000
4. WellPoint Inc., $58,801,800
5. MetLife Inc., $52,717,000
6. Prudential Financial Inc., $38,414,000
7. Manulife Financial Corp., $37,636,763
8. Aetna Inc., $34,246,000
9. Humana Inc., $33,868,208
10. Allstate Corp., $31,400,000

Source: *Best's Review*, Top North American Insurers, July 2011, p. 39-40.

3281 ■ THE UNITED KINGDOM'S MOST VALUABLE INSURANCE BRANDS, 2011

Ranked by: Brand value, in millions of U.S. dollars. **Remarks:** Also notes rank within the *Global 500* for current and previous year, figures for current and previous year, and brand rating. Ranking is available online only. **Number listed:** 2

1. Prudential (U.K.), with $6,788 million
2. Aviva, $4,532

Source: *Global 500*, (annual), Brand Finance plc, March 2012.

3282 ■ WORLD'S LARGEST INSURERS BY TOTAL PREMIUMS, 2010

Ranked by: Total premiums written, in millions of U.S. dollars. **Remarks:** Also notes country, rank for previous year, company type, and annual revenue growth. **Number listed:** 100

1. Banco Bradesco SA, with $14,728.6 million
2. Investimentos Itau SA (Itausa), $7,820.3
3. Principal Life Insurance Co., $7,067
4. MAPFRE SA, $6,133.5
5. ING Groep NV, $4,974
6. MetLife Inc., $4,741.9
7. Porto, $4,530.6
8. Banco Santander SA, $4,509.2
9. Liberty Mutual Insurance Companies, $3,142.4
10. CNP Assurances SA, $2,940.8

Source: *Latin Trade*, Top 100 Insurers (annual), 2011, p. 44-45.

3283 ■ WORLD'S MOST VALUABLE INSURANCE BRANDS, 2011

Ranked by: Brand value, in millions of U.S. dollars. **Remarks:** Also notes rank within the *Global 500* for current and previous year, figures for current and previous year, country, and brand rating. Ranking is available online only. **Number listed:** 26

1. AXA, with $13,406 million
2. Generali, $11,168
3. Allianz, $10,951
4. China Life Insurance, $8,600
5. ING, $7,054
6. Prudential (U.K.), $6,788
7. MetLife, $6,109
8. Zurich, $5,381
9. Ping An, $5,085
10. Munich Re, $5,064

Source: *Global 500*, (annual), Brand Finance plc, March 2012.

3284 ■ WORLD'S MOST VALUABLE INSURANCE BRANDS, 2012

Ranked by: Brand value, a measure of a brand's earnings and contribution, in millions of U.S. dollars. **Remarks:** Also notes annual growth in brand value and rank by brand contribution and brand momentum. **Number listed:** 10

1. China Life Insurance, with $14,587 million
2. Ping An, $10,174
3. State Farm, $7,813
4. China Pacific Insurance, $3,387
5. AXA, $3,333
6. Allianz, $2,866
7. Geico, $2,733
8. Zurich, $1,891
9. MetLife, $1,858
10. Allstate, $1,496

Source: *Financial Times*, Global Brands (annual), http://www.ft.com, May 22, 2012.

Insurance, Life

3285 ■ BRITAIN'S MOST ADMIRED LIFE ASSURANCE AND INSURANCE COMPANIES, 2011

Ranked by: Survey of peers and investment analysts based on nine criteria: quality of management, financial soundness, quality of goods/services, ability to attract and retain talent, value as long-term investment, innovation, marketing, community and environmental responsibility, and use of corporate assets. **Number listed:** 5

1. Admiral Group plc, with 61 points
2. St. James's Place Wealth Management, 58.4
3. RSA Insurance, 57.9
4. Prudential plc, 57.2
5. Legal & General Group plc, 55.6

Source: *Management Today*, Britain's Most Admired Companies (annual), December 2011, p. 45.

3286 ■ CANADA'S LARGEST LIFE AND HEALTH INSURANCE COMPANIES OVERALL, 2011

Ranked by: Score based on revenue, profits, assets, and market capitalization. **Remarks:** Specific scores not provided. Also notes overall rank in the *Forbes 2000* and figures for each criterion. **Number listed:** 4

1. Power Corporation of Canada
2. Manulife Financial Corp.
3. Sun Life Financial Inc.
4. Industrial Alliance Insurance & Financial Services

Source: *Forbes*, Forbes 2000 (annual), http://www.forbes.com, May 7, 2012.

3287 ■ CHINA'S LARGEST LIFE AND HEALTH INSURANCE COMPANIES OVERALL, 2011

Ranked by: Score based on revenue, profits, assets, and market capitalization. **Remarks:** Specific scores not provided. Also notes overall rank in the *Forbes 2000* and figures for each criterion. **Number listed:** 3

1. China Life Insurance Co., Ltd.
2. China Pacific Insurance (Group) Co., Ltd.
3. New China Life Insurance Co., Ltd.

Source: *Forbes*, Forbes 2000 (annual), http://www.forbes.com, May 7, 2012.

3288 ■ EUROPE'S MOST VALUABLE LIFE INSURANCE COMPANIES, 2011

Ranked by: Market value as of March 2011, in millions of U.S. dollars. **Remarks:** Also notes rank within the *FT Europe 500*, rank for previous year, country, revenue, net income, assets, number of employees, share price, price-to-earning ratio, dividend yield, and fiscal yearend. **Number listed:** 12

1. ING Groep NV, with $48,543.9 million
2. Prudential plc, $28,828.5
3. Aviva plc, $19,565.7
4. AEGON NV, $14,319.5
5. CNP Assurances SA, $12,630.5
6. Old Mutual plc, $11,896
7. Legal & General Group plc, $10,833.8
8. Standard Life plc, $7,568.3
9. Ageas NV, $6,994.8
10. Resolution plc, $5,889.7

Source: *Financial Times*, FT 500 (annual), http://www.ft.com, June 24, 2011.

3289 ■ JAPAN'S LARGEST LIFE AND HEALTH INSURANCE COMPANIES OVERALL, 2011

Ranked by: Score based on revenue, profits, assets, and market capitalization. **Remarks:** Specific scores not provided. Also notes overall rank in the *Forbes 2000* and figures for each criterion. **Number listed:** 2

1. Dai-Ichi Life Insurance Co., Ltd.
2. T & D Holdings

Source: *Forbes*, Forbes 2000 (annual), http://www.forbes.com, May 7, 2012.

3290 ■ LARGEST U.S. LIFE AND HEALTH INSURANCE COMPANIES OVERALL, 2011

Ranked by: Score based on revenue, profits, assets, and market capitalization. **Remarks:** Specific scores not provided. Also notes overall rank in the *Forbes 2000* and figures for each criterion. **Number listed:** 9

1. Prudential Financial Inc.
2. AFLAC Inc.
3. Lincoln National Corp.
4. Unum Group
5. Torchmark Corp.
6. CNO Financial Group Inc.
7. Protective Life Corp.
8. American Equity Investment Life Holding Co.
9. Symetra Financial Corp.

Source: *Forbes*, Forbes 2000 (annual), http://www.forbes.com, May 7, 2012.

3291 ■ MOST VALUABLE U.S. LIFE INSURANCE COMPANIES, 2011

Ranked by: Market value as of March 2011, in millions of U.S. dollars. **Remarks:** Also notes rank within the *FT U.S. 500*, rank for previous year, country, revenue, net income, assets, number of employees, share price, price-to-earning ratio, dividend yield, and fiscal yearend. **Number listed:** 7

1. MetLife Inc., with $47,197.1 million
2. Prudential Financial Inc., $30,016.5
3. AFLAC Inc., $24,817.8
4. Principal Financial Group Inc., $10,301.3
5. Lincoln National Corp., $9,486.6
6. Unum Group, $8,129.1
7. Genworth Financial Inc., $6,593.9

Source: *Financial Times*, FT 500 (annual), http://www.ft.com, June 24, 2011.

3292 ■ SOUTH AFRICA'S LARGEST LIFE AND HEALTH INSURANCE COMPANIES OVERALL, 2011

Ranked by: Score based on revenue, profits, assets, and market capitalization. **Remarks:** Specific scores not provided. Also notes overall rank in the *Forbes 2000* and figures for each criterion. **Number listed:** 2

1. Sanlam Ltd.
2. MMI Holdings

Source: *Forbes*, Forbes 2000 (annual), http://www.forbes.com, May 7, 2012.

3293 ■ SOUTH KOREA'S LARGEST LIFE AND HEALTH INSURANCE COMPANIES OVERALL, 2011

Ranked by: Score based on revenue, profits, assets, and market capitalization. **Remarks:** Specific scores not provided. Also notes overall rank in the *Forbes 2000* and figures for each criterion. **Number listed:** 2

1. Samsung Life Insurance Co., Ltd.
2. Korea Life Insurance Co., Ltd.

Source: *Forbes*, Forbes 2000 (annual), http://www.forbes.com, May 7, 2012.

3294 ■ TAIWAN'S LARGEST LIFE AND HEALTH INSURANCE COMPANIES OVERALL, 2011

Ranked by: Score based on revenue, profits, assets, and market capitalization. **Remarks:** Specific scores not provided. Also notes country, overall rank in the *Forbes 2000,* and figures for each criterion. **Number listed:** 2

1. Cathay Financial Holding Co., Ltd.
2. Shin Kong Financial Holding Co., Ltd.

Source: *Forbes*, Forbes 2000 (annual), http://www.forbes.com, May 7, 2012.

3295 ■ TOP CANADIAN INSURERS OF GROUP LIFE INSURANCE, 2010

Ranked by: Net premiums written, in thousands of Canadian dollars. **Remarks:** Also notes rank for previous year, A.M. Best number, and total assets. **Number listed:** 48

1. Sun Life Assurance Co. of Canada, with C$1,326,006 thousand
2. Munich Reinsurance Co., Canadian Branch, C$632,040
3. Great-West Life Assurance Co., C$476,802
4. Cumis Life Insurance Co., C$171,540
5. CA Life Insurance Co. of Canada, C$148,624
6. London Life Insurance Co., C$144,327
7. Manufacturers Life Insurance Co., C$135,988
8. Industrial Alliance Insurance & Financial Services Inc., C$92,177
9. Canada Life Assurance Co., C$84,492
10. Industrial Alliance Pacific Insurance & Financial Services, C$76,807

Source: *Best's Review*, Top Canadian Writers, September 2011, p. 38.

3296 ■ TOP CANADIAN INSURERS OF INDIVIDUAL LIFE INSURANCE, 2010

Ranked by: Net premiums written, in thousands of Canadian dollars. **Remarks:** Also notes rank for previous year, A.M. Best number, and total assets. **Number listed:** 64

1. Sun Life Assurance Co. of Canada, with C$3,266,977 thousand
2. Manufacturers Life Insurance Co., C$3,080,966
3. London Life Insurance Co., C$1,814,361
4. Industrial Alliance Insurance & Financial Services Inc., C$816,513
5. Swiss Reinsurance Co., Canadian Branch, C$560,141
6. Canada Life Assurance Co., C$518,168
7. RBC Life Insurance Co., C$451,063
8. Great-West Life Assurance Co., C$446,153
9. CA Life Insurance Co. of Canada, C$419,150
10. Munich Reinsurance Co., Canadian Branch, C$407,987

Source: *Best's Review*, Top Canadian Writers, September 2011, p. 37.

3297 ■ TOP CANADIAN LIFE INSURANCE COMPANIES, 2010

Ranked by: Revenue, in thousands of Canadian dollars (unless otherwise noted). **Remarks:** Also notes percent change from previous year. **Number listed:** 10

1. Manulife Financial, with C$37,856,000 thousand
2. Great-West Lifeco Inc., C$30,000,000
3. Sun Life Financial Inc., C$24,686,000
4. Canada Life Financial, C$10,373,000
5. Industrial Alliance Insurance & Financial Services, C$3,844,000
6. Desjardins Financial Security Life, C$4,340,000
7. Standard Life Financial, C$3,114,284
8. SSQ Life Insurance, C$2,095,200
9. RBC Life Insurance, C$1,923,185
10. Capitale Civil Service Mutual, C$1,515,105

Source: *Report on Business Magazine*, Top 1000 Companies (annual), http://www.reportonbusiness.com, June 2011.

3298 ■ TOP CANADIAN LIFE INSURERS BY ASSETS, 2010

Ranked by: Total assets, in thousands of Canadian dollars. **Remarks:** Also notes rank for previous year, A.M. Best number, and total capital and surplus. **Number listed:** 81

1. Manufacturers Life Insurance Co., with C$80,785,757 thousand
2. Sun Life Assurance Co. of Canada, C$75,789,831
3. Great-West Life Assurance Co., C$28,003,291
4. London Life Insurance Co., C$26,810,673
5. Canada Life Assurance Co., C$22,785,351
6. Standard Life Assurance Co. of Canada, C$17,678,455
7. Industrial Alliance Insurance & Financial Services Inc., C$16,541,603
8. Sun Life Insurance (Canada) Ltd., C$11,582,511
9. CA Life Insurance Co. of Canada, C$9,411,898
10. RBC Life Insurance Co., C$7,099,433

Source: *Best's Review*, Top Canadian Writers, September 2011, p. 36.

3299 ■ TOP CREDIT LIFE/HEALTH INSURANCE WRITERS BY INSURANCE IN FORCE, 2010

Ranked by: Credit life insurance in force, in thousands of dollars. **Remarks:** Also notes A.M. Best number, rank for previous year, and percent change from previous year. **Number listed:** 25

1. Metropolitan Life & Affiliated Cos., with $27,575,115 thousand
2. CUNA Mutual Group, $26,180,306
3. Assurant Inc., $16,124,599
4. Aegon USA Inc., $11,144,613
5. HSBC Insurance Group, $8,887,041
6. Securian Financial Group Inc., $8,454,800
7. Citi Assurance Services Group, $7,253,009
8. RGA Group, $5,795,093
9. Central States Health & Life Group, $5,673,363
10. American National Group, $3,279,486

Source: *Best's Review*, Leading Writers: Life/Health (annual), September 2011, p. 34.

3300 ■ TOP CREDIT LIFE/HEALTH INSURANCE WRITERS BY INSURANCE ISSUED, 2010

Ranked by: Credit life insurance issued, in thousands of dollars. **Remarks:** Also notes A.M. Best number, rank for previous year, and percent change from previous year. **Number listed:** 25

1. CUNA Mutual Group, with $12,939,729 thousand
2. Life of the South Group, $5,880,006
3. Assurant Inc., $5,324,438
4. Independence Holding Co., $5,039,708
5. Citi Assurance Services Group, $4,392,676
6. American Enterprise Group, $4,218,608
7. Protective Life Corp., $3,709,336
8. Securian Financial Group Inc., $3,578,700
9. Aegon USA Inc., $3,107,560
10. Central States Health & Life Group, $3,071,317

Source: *Best's Review*, Leading Writers: Life/Health (annual), September 2011, p. 34.

3301 ■ TOP GROUP LIFE/HEALTH INSURANCE WRITERS BY INSURANCE IN FORCE, 2010

Ranked by: Group life insurance in force, in thousands of dollars. **Remarks:** Also notes A.M. Best number, rank for previous year, and percent change from previous year. **Number listed:** 25

1. Metropolitan Life & Affiliated Cos., with $2,862,223,079 thousand
2. Prudential of America Group, $1,885,558,990
3. Great-West Lifeco Inc., $1,161,287,302
4. Hartford Life Inc., $773,053,945
5. Securian Financial Group Inc., $561,440,033
6. Unum Insurance Group, $494,174,344
7. Aetna Life Group, $470,262,978
8. CIGNA Corp., $418,403,755
9. ING USA Life Group, $390,587,035
10. New York Life Group, $377,753,028

Source: *Best's Review*, Leading Writers: Life/Health (annual), September 2011, p. 34.

3302 ■ TOP GROUP LIFE/HEALTH INSURANCE WRITERS BY INSURANCE ISSUED, 2010

Ranked by: Group life insurance issued, in thousands of dollars. **Remarks:** Also notes A.M. Best number, rank for previous year, and percent change from previous year. **Number listed:** 25

1. Metropolitan Life & Affiliated Cos., with $166,571,640 thousand
2. Prudential of America Group, $126,876,016
3. Hartford Life Inc., $83,785,960
4. Securian Financial Group Inc., $74,231,418
5. CIGNA Corp., $73,424,299
6. Standard Insurance Group, $68,123,173
7. Unum Insurance Group, $65,901,821
8. Aetna Life Group, $62,749,136
9. Lincoln Financial Group, $56,395,464
10. UnitedHealth Group, $46,525,982

Source: *Best's Review*, Leading Writers: Life/Health (annual), September 2011, p. 34.

3303 ■ TOP MUTUAL *FORTUNE 500* COMPANIES IN LIFE/HEALTH INSURANCE, 2011

Ranked by: Revenue, in millions of dollars. **Remarks:** Also notes overall rank in the *Fortune 500;* profits; profits as a percentage of revenue; stockholders' equity; and rank by each criterion. **Number listed:** 7

1. New York Life Insurance Co., with $34,394 million

2. Teachers Insurance & Annuity Association-College Retirement Equities Fund (TIAA-CREF), $34,079

3. Northwestern Mutual Life Insurance Co., $24,861

4. Massachusetts Mutual Life Insurance Co., $24,226

5. Guardian Life Insurance Co. of America, $10,571

6. Thrivent Financial for Lutherans, $7,843

7. Western & Southern Financial Group, $4,986

Source: *Fortune*, Fortune 500 (annual), May 21, 2012, p. F-36-F-37.

3304 ■ TOP ORDINARY LIFE/HEALTH INSURANCE WRITERS BY INSURANCE IN FORCE, 2010

Ranked by: Ordinary life insurance in force, in thousands of dollars. Remarks: Also notes A.M. Best number, rank for previous year, and percent change from previous year. Number listed: 25

1. Aegon USA Inc., with $1,682,083,824 thousand

2. RGA Group, $1,579,036,800

3. Metropolitan Life & Affiliated Cos., $1,549,545,473

4. Swiss Reinsurance Co., $1,415,670,633

5. Prudential of America Group, $1,296,999,928

6. Northwestern Mutual Life Insurance Co., $1,242,136,395

7. ING USA Life Group, $1,065,033,537

8. Lincoln Financial Group, $947,273,768

9. Genworth Financial Group, $863,481,188

10. SunAmerica Financial Group, $833,351,468

Source: *Best's Review*, Leading Writers: Life/Health (annual), September 2011, p. 35.

3305 ■ TOP ORDINARY LIFE/HEALTH INSURANCE WRITERS BY INSURANCE ISSUED, 2010

Ranked by: Ordinary life insurance issued, in thousands of dollars. Remarks: Also notes A.M. Best number, rank for previous year, and percent change from previous year. Number listed: 25

1. Northwestern Mutual Group, with $123,902,931 thousand

2. Metropolitan Life & Affiliated Cos., $120,428,544

3. ING USA Life Group, $93,201,122

4. New York Life Group, $91,448,473

5. State Farm Life Group, $80,148,735

6. Aegon USA Inc., $66,912,646

7. Primerica Group, $65,280,601

8. Prudential of America Group, $59,465,925

9. Genworth Financial Group, $56,896,345

10. Lincoln Financial Group, $53,036,559

Source: *Best's Review*, Leading Writers: Life/Health (annual), September 2011, p. 35.

3306 ■ TOP STOCK *FORTUNE 500* COMPANIES IN LIFE/HEALTH INSURANCE, 2011

Ranked by: Revenue, in millions of dollars. Remarks: Also notes overall rank in the *Fortune 500;* profits; profits as a percentage of revenue; stockholders' equity; and rank by each criterion. Number listed: 10

1. MetLife Inc., with $70,641 million

2. Prudential Financial Inc., $49,045

3. AFLAC Inc., $22,171

4. Lincoln National Corp., $10,636

5. Genworth Financial Inc., $10,344

6. Unum Group, $10,278

7. Reinsurance Group of America Inc., $8,830

8. Principal Financial Group Inc., $8,710

9. Mutual of Omaha, $5,974

10. Pacific Life Insurance Co., $5,879

Source: *Fortune*, Fortune 500 (annual), May 21, 2012, p. F-37.

3307 ■ TOP TERM LIFE/HEALTH INSURANCE WRITERS BY INSURANCE IN FORCE, 2010

Ranked by: Term life insurance in force, in thousands of dollars. Remarks: Also notes A.M. Best number, rank for previous year, and percent change from previous year. Number listed: 25

1. RGA Group, with $1,522,897,986 thousand

2. Aegon USA Inc., $1,385,368,401

3. Swiss Reinsurance Co., $1,354,102,348

4. Prudential of America Group, $966,331,508

5. Metropolitan Life & Affiliated Cos., $931,059,999

6. ING USA Life Group, $886,667,849

7. Munich American Reassurance Co., $737,169,920

8. Northwestern Mutual Group, $714,869,453

9. Genworth Financial Group, $708,049,456

10. SunAmerica Financial Group, $657,839,965

Source: *Best's Review*, Leading Writers: Life/Health (annual), September 2011, p. 35.

3308 ■ TOP TERM LIFE/HEALTH INSURANCE WRITERS BY INSURANCE ISSUED, 2010

Ranked by: Term life insurance issued, in thousands of dollars. Remarks: Also notes A.M. Best number, rank for previous year, and percent change from previous year. Number listed: 25

1. ING USA Life Group, with $87,007,767 thousand

2. Northwestern Mutual Life Insurance Co., $86,438,585

3. Metropolitan Life & Affiliated Cos., $81,526,493

4. State Farm Life Group, $65,878,257

5. Primerica Group, $64,955,079

6. New York Life Group, $55,807,875

7. Prudential of America Group, $53,336,104

8. Aegon USA Inc., $50,878,605

9. SunAmerica Financial Group, $40,852,125

10. Legal & General America Group, $39,543,526

Source: *Best's Review*, Leading Writers: Life/Health (annual), September 2011, p. 35.

3309 ■ TOP TOTAL LIFE/HEALTH INSURANCE WRITERS BY INSURANCE IN FORCE, 2010

Ranked by: Total life insurance in force, in thousands of dollars. Remarks: Also notes A.M. Best number. rank for previous year, and percent change from previous year. Number listed: 25

1. Metropolitan Life & Affiliated Cos., with $4,441,743,743 thousand

2. Prudential of America Group, $3,185,572,581
3. Aegon USA Inc., $1,726,892,400
4. Great-West Lifeco Inc., $1,642,833,644
5. RGA Group, $1,628,358,624
6. Swiss Reinsurance Co., $1,505,593,206
7. ING USA Life Group, $1,455,779,858
8. Northwestern Mutual Group, $1,243,309,160
9. Lincoln Financial Group, $1,218,990,049
10. New York Life Group, $1,177,539,664

Source: *Best's Review*, Leading Writers: Life/Health (annual), September 2011, p. 33.

3310 ■ TOP TOTAL LIFE/HEALTH INSURANCE WRITERS BY INSURANCE ISSUED, 2010

Ranked by: Total life insurance issued, in thousands of dollars. **Remarks:** Also notes A.M. Best number, rank for previous year, and percent change from previous year. **Number listed:** 25

1. Metropolitan Life & Affiliated Cos., with $288,762,170 thousand
2. Prudential of America Group, $186,342,412
3. Northwestern Mutual Life Insurance Co., $123,902,931
4. ING USA Life Group, $118,146,096
5. Lincoln Financial Group, $109,432,023
6. New York Life Group, $105,104,468
7. Hartford Life Inc., $104,299,991
8. Securian Financial Group Inc., $97,445,618
9. State Farm Life Group, $80,263,338
10. Unum Insurance Group, $78,724,388

Source: *Best's Review*, Leading Writers: Life/Health (annual), September 2011, p. 33.

3311 ■ TOP U.S. LIFE AND HEALTH INSURANCE COMPANIES BY ASSETS, 2010

Ranked by: Admitted assets, in dollars. **Remarks:** Also notes figures for previous year. **Number listed:** 200

1. Metropolitan Life Insurance Co., with $316,204,246,915
2. Prudential Insurance Company of America, $233,140,797,926
3. Teachers Insurance & Annuity Association of America (TIAA), $214,544,169,119
4. John Hancock Life Insurance Co., $214,163,190,328
5. Northwestern Mutual Life Insurance Co., $179,209,385,990
6. Lincoln National Life Insurance Co., $158,433,198,169
7. Hartford Life Insurance Co., $148,900,298,076
8. AXA Equitable Life Insurance Co., $135,726,109,289
9. Massachusetts Mutual Life Insurance, $129,290,315,834
10. New York Life Insurance Co., $122,007,530,370

Source: *National Underwriter, Life & Health*, The NU 200 Industry Leaders (annual), September 19, 2011, p. 41.

3312 ■ TOP U.S. LIFE AND HEALTH INSURANCE COMPANIES BY GROUP LIFE PREMIUMS, 2010

Ranked by: Group life premiums, in dollars. **Remarks:** Also notes figures for previous year. **Number listed:** 200

1. Metropolitan Life Insurance Co., with $5,021,918,097
2. Prudential Insurance Company of America, $3,577,61,890
3. New York Life Insurance Co., $1,738,775,442
4. Minnesota Life Insurance Co., $1,200,236,964
5. Life Insurance Co. of North America, $1,059,817,311
6. Standard Insurance Co., $730,867,970
7. SunLife Assurance Co. of Canada (U.S. branch), $608,023,544
8. UNUM Life Assurance Co. of America, $603,160,580
9. Hartford Life & Accident Insurance Co., $593,661,409
10. Lincoln National Life Insurance Co., $558,099,899

Source: *National Underwriter, Life & Health*, The NU 200 Industry Leaders (annual), September 19, 2011, p. 28.

3313 ■ TOP U.S. LIFE AND HEALTH INSURANCE COMPANIES BY INDIVIDUAL ANNUITY PREMIUMS, 2010

Ranked by: Individual annuity premiums, in dollars. **Remarks:** Also notes figures for previous year. **Number listed:** 200

1. Jackson National Life Insurance Co., with $14,661,371,809
2. Pruco Life Insurance Co., $14,592,359,298
3. Lincoln National Life Insurance Co., $10,494,384,499
4. Medlife Investors USA Insurance Co., $9,550,780,780
5. Allianz Life Insurance Co. of North America, $9,315,317,715
6. New York Life Insurance & Annuity Co., $7,709,717,471
7. Teachers Insurance & Annuity Association of America (TIAA), $6,923,917,035
8. Riversource Life Insurance Co., $6,266,606,110
9. American Life Insurance Co., $6,087,251,227
10. Nationwide Life Insurance Co., $5,966,230,005

Source: *National Underwriter, Life & Health*, The NU 200 Industry Leaders (annual), September 19, 2011, p. 44.

3314 ■ TOP U.S. LIFE AND HEALTH INSURANCE COMPANIES BY INVESTMENT INCOME, 2010

Ranked by: Net investment income, in dollars. **Remarks:** Also notes figures for previous year. **Number listed:** 200

1. Metropolitan Life Insurance Co., with $10,795,994,836
2. Teachers Insurance & Annuity Association of America (TIAA), $10,458,511,468
3. Northwestern Mutual Life Insurance Co., $8,242,630,467
4. Prudential Insurance Company of America, $7,116,504,628
5. New York Life Insurance Co., $4,860,580,178
6. John Hancock Life Insurance Co., $4,397,322,303
7. Massachusetts Mutual Life Insurance Co., $4,359,124,304

8. Lincoln National Life Insurance Co., $3,653,205,323

9. New York Life Insurance & Annuity Co., $3,367,296,712

10. Allianz Life Insurance Co. of North America, $3,282,699,935

Source: *National Underwriter, Life & Health*, The NU 200 Industry Leaders (annual), September 19, 2011, p. 45.

3315 ■ TOP U.S. LIFE AND HEALTH INSURANCE COMPANIES BY PREMIUM INCOME, 2010

Ranked by: Premium income, in dollars. **Remarks:** Also notes figures for previous year. **Number listed:** 200

1. United Healthcare Insurance Co., with $39,966,180,565
2. Metropolitan Life Insurance Co., $31,363,583,525
3. American Family Life Assurance Co. Columbus, $18,324,800,317
4. Lincoln National Life Insurance Co., $18,052,689,164
5. Jackson National Life Insurance Co., $16,949,898,332
6. American Life Insurance Co., $16,504,523,801
7. Prudential Insurance Company of America, $16,370,778,677
8. Humana Insurance Co., $16,151,866,807
9. Pruco Life Insurance Co., $15,207,354,641
10. Aetna Life Insurance Co., $13,896,291,271

Source: *National Underwriter, Life & Health*, The NU 200 Industry Leaders (annual), September 19, 2011, p. 42.

3316 ■ TOP U.S. LIFE AND HEALTH INSURANCE COMPANIES BY TOTAL LIFE IN-FORCE, 2010

Ranked by: Total life in-force, in thousands of dollars. **Remarks:** Also notes figures for previous year. **Number listed:** 200

1. Metropolitan Life Insurance Co., with $3,480,121,972 thousand
2. Prudential Insurance Company of America, $2,643,742,207
3. RGA Reinsurance Co., $1,593,954,691
4. The Canada Life Assurance Co. (U.S. business), $1,313,331,720
5. Northwestern Mutual Life Insurance Co., $1,243,309,160
6. Swiss Re Life & Health America Inc., $1,242,795,681
7. Transamerica Life Insurance Co., $1,218,917,213
8. Lincoln National Life Insurance Co., $1,042,167,915
9. New York Life Insurance Co., $974,183,673
10. Munich American Reassurance Co., $775,896,341

Source: *National Underwriter, Life & Health*, The NU 200 Industry Leaders (annual), September 19, 2011, p. 43.

3317 ■ TOP U.S. WRITERS OF GROUP LIFE INSURANCE, 2010

Ranked by: Net premiums written, in thousands of dollars. **Remarks:** Also notes market share. **Number listed:** 10

1. MetLife Inc., with $5,296,037 thousand
2. Prudential Financial Inc., $3,087,212
3. New York Life Insurance Co., $1,501,053
4. The Hartford Financial Services Group Inc., $1,500,012
5. CIGNA Corp., $1,391,434
6. Minnesota Mutual Cos., Inc., $1,369,818
7. Unum Group, $1,119,006
8. Aetna Inc., $996,898
9. Sun Life Financial Inc., $801,404
10. StanCorp Financial Group Inc., $760,669

Source: *The I.I.I. Insurance Fact Book*, (annual), Insurance Information Institute, 2012, p. 35.

3318 ■ TOP U.S. WRITERS OF INDIVIDUAL LIFE INSURANCE, 2010

Ranked by: Net premiums written, in thousands of dollars. **Remarks:** Also notes market share. **Number listed:** 10

1. MetLife Inc., with $11,529,741 thousand
2. Northwestern Mutual Life Insurance Co., $8,542,955
3. New York Life Insurance Co., $6,719,673
4. Manulife Financial Corp., $5,108,587
5. Liberty National Corp., $5,024,163
6. AEGON NV, $4,099,350
7. Prudential Financial Inc., $3,864,795
8. Massachusetts Mutual Life Insurance Co., $3,547,826
9. State Farm Mutual Automobile Insurance Co., $3,541,387
10. AFLAC Inc., $3,333,383

Source: *The I.I.I. Insurance Fact Book*, (annual), Insurance Information Institute, 2012, p. 35.

3319 ■ TOP U.S. WRITERS OF LIFE/HEALTH ANNUITIES, 2010

Ranked by: Direct premiums written, in thousands of dollars. **Remarks:** Also notes market share. **Number listed:** 10

1. MetLife Inc., with $24,367,159 thousand
2. Prudential Financial Inc., $18,047,805
3. Jackson National Life Insurance Co., $15,732,654
4. Lincoln National Corp., $11,180,832
5. Allianz SE, $10,285,600
6. American International Group Inc., $8,557,339
7. New York Life Insurance Co., $8,133,126
8. Teachers Insurance & Annuity Association-College Retirement Equities Fund (TIAA-CREF), $7,021,041
9. Ameriprise Financial Inc., $6,625,530
10. Aviva plc, $5,796,478

Source: *The I.I.I. Insurance Fact Book*, (annual), Insurance Information Institute, 2012, p. 36.

3320 ■ TOP WRITERS OF LIFE/HEALTH INSURANCE BY ASSETS, 2010

Ranked by: Admitted assets, in thousands of dollars. **Remarks:** Also notes AM Best number and percent change from previous year. **Number listed:** 200

1. Metropolitan Life & Affiliated Cos., with $575,062,104 thousand
2. Prudential of America Group, $403,755,468
3. Manulife Financial Corp., $237,477,486
4. SunAmerica Financial Group, $230,206,221
5. Hartford Life Inc., $228,628,548
6. Teachers Insurance & Annuity Association-College Retirement Equities Fund (TIAA-CREF), $217,744,582
7. New York Life Group, $214,437,508
8. Aegon USA Inc., $187,622,590
9. ING USA Life Group, $185,172,540
10. Northwestern Mutual Group, $180,065,915

Source: *Best's Review*, Leading Writers: Life & Health (annual), July 2011, p. 28+.

3321 ■ TOP WRITERS OF U.S. LIFE/HEALTH INSURANCE BY DIRECT PREMIUMS, 2010

Ranked by: Direct premiums written, in thousands of dollars. Remarks: Also notes market share. Number listed: 10

1. MetLife Inc., with $100,537,632 thousand
2. Prudential Financial Inc., $46,600,755
3. New York Life Insurance Co., $25,490,993
4. Manulife Financial Corp., $21,925,761
5. Lincoln National Corp., $19,449,441
6. ING Groep NV, $18,222,110
7. Jackson National Life Insurance Co., $18,206,802
8. AEGON NV, $17,052,511
9. American International Group Inc., $16,631,038
10. Principal Financial Group Inc., $13,804,217

Source: *The I.I.I. Insurance Fact Book*, (annual), Insurance Information Institute, 2012, p. 15.

3322 ■ UNITED KINGDOM'S LARGEST LIFE AND HEALTH INSURANCE COMPANIES OVERALL, 2011

Ranked by: Score based on revenue, profits, assets, and market capitalization. Remarks: Specific scores not provided. Also notes overall rank in the *Forbes 2000* and figures for each criterion. Number listed: 5

1. Prudential plc
2. Legal & General Group plc
3. Aviva plc
4. Standard Life plc
5. Phoenix Group Holdings

Source: *Forbes*, Forbes 2000 (annual), http://www.forbes.com, May 7, 2012.

3323 ■ WORLD'S LARGEST LIFE AND HEALTH INSURANCE COMPANIES OVERALL, 2011

Ranked by: Score based on revenue, profits, assets, and market capitalization. Remarks: Specific scores not provided. Also notes country, overall rank in the *Forbes 2000,* and figures for each criterion. Number listed: 33

1. ING Groep NV
2. China Life Insurance Co., Ltd.
3. Prudential Financial Inc.
4. Prudential plc
5. AFLAC Inc.

6. Samsung Life Insurance Co., Ltd.
7. AIA Group Ltd.
8. China Pacific Insurance (Group) Co., Ltd.
9. Legal & General Group plc
10. Power Corporation of Canada

Source: *Forbes*, Forbes 2000 (annual), http://www.forbes.com, May 7, 2012.

3324 ■ WORLD'S MOST ADMIRED LIFE AND HEALTH INSURANCE COMPANIES, 2012

Ranked by: Score, on a scale of 10, based on a survey of executives, directors, and securities analysts of companies within their own industry on eight criteria: innovation, financial soundness, employee talent, use of corporate assets, long-term investment value, social responsibility, quality of management, and quality of products/services. Remarks: Specific scores not provided. Also notes rank for previous year. Number listed: 8

1. Prudential Financial Inc.
2. AFLAC Inc.
3. New York Life Insurance Co.
4. Northwestern Mutual Life Insurance Co.
5. Teachers Insurance & Annuity Association-College Retirement Equities Fund (TIAA-CREF)
6. MetLife Inc.
7. AXA
8. Massachusetts Mutual Life Insurance Co.

Source: *Fortune*, World's Most Admired Companies (annual), March 19, 2012, p. 148.

3325 ■ WORLD'S MOST VALUABLE LIFE INSURANCE COMPANIES, 2011

Ranked by: Market value as of March 2011, in millions of U.S. dollars. Remarks: Also notes rank within the *FT 500*, rank for previous year, country, revenue, net income, assets, number of employees, share price, price-to-earning ratio, dividend yield, and fiscal year-end. Number listed: 13

1. China Life Insurance Co., Ltd., with $94,680.5 million
2. Ping An Insurance (Group) Company of China Ltd., $65,120.7
3. ING Groep NV, $48,543.9
4. MetLife Inc., $47,197.1
5. AIA Group Ltd., $37,084.9
6. Manulife Financial Corp., $31,401.4
7. China Pacific Insurance, $30,960.8
8. Prudential Financial Inc., $30,016.5
9. Prudential plc, $28,828.5
10. Great-West Lifeco Inc., $26,244.2

Source: *Financial Times*, FT 500 (annual), http://www.ft.com, June 24, 2011.

3326 ■ WORLD'S TOP LIFE/HEALTH INSURANCE COMPANIES BY REVENUE, 2010

Ranked by: Revenue, in millions of U.S. dollars. Remarks: Also notes country. Number listed: 10

1. Japan Post Holdings Co., Ltd., with $203,958 million
2. AXA, $162,236
3. Assicurazioni Generali SpA, $120,234

4. Aviva plc, $90,211
5. Nippon Life Insurance Co., $78,571
6. Prudential plc, $73,598
7. AEGON NV, $65,136
8. China Life Insurance Co., Ltd., $64,635
9. Legal & General Group plc, $59,377
10. CNP Assurances SA, $59,320

Source: *The I.I.I. Insurance Fact Book*, (annual), Insurance Information Institute, 2012, p. 5.

Insurance, Malpractice

3327 ■ LARGEST MEDICAL PROFESSIONAL LIABILITY CARRIERS, 2010

Ranked by: Direct premiums written, in millions of dollars. Remarks: Also notes location, market share, and Web site. Number listed: 25

1. MLMIC Group, with $760.2 million
2. Berkshire Hathaway Insurance, $714.9
3. Doctors Co. Insurance Group, $694.6
4. ProAssurance Corp., $561.1
5. CNA Insurance Cos., $496.5
6. American International Group Inc., $466
7. Physicians' Reciprocal Insurers, $389.5
8. Coverys, $382.7
9. ISMIE Mutual Insurance Co., $306.9
10. MAG Mutual Insurance Co., $287.7

Source: *Modern Healthcare*, Largest Professional Liability Carriers (annual), February 6, 2012, p. 32.

3328 ■ TOP WRITERS OF MEDICAL PROFESSIONAL LIABILITY INSURANCE, 2010

Ranked by: Direct premiums written, in thousands of dollars. Remarks: Also notes A. M. Best number, percent change from previous year, market share and adjusted loss ratios for current and two previous years, and medical malpractice as a percentage of total company premiums. Number listed: 25

1. MLMIC Group, with $760,199 thousand
2. Berkshire Hathaway Insurance, $714,932
3. Doctors Co. Insurance Group, $694,567
4. ProAssurance Corp., $561,121
5. CNA Insurance Cos., $496,454
6. American International Group Inc., $465,970
7. Physicians' Reciprocal Insurers, $389,503
8. ProMutual Group, $382,721
9. ISMIE Mutual Insurance Co., $306,930
10. Mag Mutual Group, $287,724

Source: *Best's Review*, Top P/C Writers by Line (annual), August 2011, p. 58.

Insurance, Marine

3329 ■ TOP INLAND MARINE INSURANCE COMPANIES, 2010

Ranked by: Direct premiums written, in thousands of dollars. Remarks: Also notes AM Best number, annual percent change in premiums, inland marine as a percentage of total company premiums, and market share and adjusted loss ratio for current and previous two years. Number listed: 25

1. Liberty Mutual Insurance Companies, with $2,078,188 thousand
2. CNA Insurance Cos., $1,147,123
3. FM Global, $702,953
4. Travelers Group, $673,274
5. Chubb Group of Insurance Cos., $619,990
6. Allianz of America Inc., $617,826
7. State Farm Insurance Companies, $608,085
8. American International Group Inc., $536,539
9. Assurant P & C Group, $336,742
10. Zurich Financial Services North America Group, $328,621

Source: *Best's Review*, Top Marine, Fire, & Allied Writers (annual), December 2011, p. 28.

3330 ■ TOP OCEAN MARINE INSURANCE COMPANIES, 2010

Ranked by: Direct premiums written, in thousands of dollars. Remarks: Also notes AM Best number, annual percent change in premiums, ocean marine as a percentage of total company premiums, and market share and adjusted loss ratio for current and previous two years. Number listed: 25

1. Travelers Group, with $273,135 thousand
2. American International Group Inc., $270,155
3. CNA Insurance Cos., $199,782
4. Allianz of America Inc., $199,686
5. Starr International Group, $193,712
6. White Mountains Insurance Group Ltd., $134,902
7. Ace INA Group, $132,711
8. Chubb Group of Insurance Cos., $132,404
9. American Steamship Owners Mutual Protection & Indemnity Association, $115,337
10. HCC Insurance Group, $94,208

Source: *Best's Review*, Top Marine, Fire, & Allied Writers (annual), December 2011, p. 25.

Insurance, Mortgage Guaranty

3331 ■ TOP U.S. WRITERS OF MORTGAGE GUARANTY INSURANCE, 2010

Ranked by: Direct premiums written, in thousands of dollars. Remarks: Also notes market share. Number listed: 10

1. MGIC Investment Corp., with $1,079,369 thousand
2. Radian Group Inc., $789,593
3. American International Group Inc., $727,227
4. PMI Group Inc., $707,685
5. Genworth Financial Inc., $655,122
6. Old Republic International Corp., $518,898
7. Triad Guaranty Inc., $216,016
8. CMG Mortgage Insurance Group, $91,491
9. Essent U.S. Holdings Inc., $219
10. Southern Pioneer Property & Casualty Insurance Co., $170

Source: *The I.I.I. Insurance Fact Book*, (annual), Insurance Information Institute, 2012, p. 118.

Insurance, Property and Casualty

3332 ■ AUSTRALIA'S LARGEST PROPERTY AND CASUALTY INSURANCE COMPANIES OVERALL, 2011

Ranked by: Score based on revenue, profits, assets, and market capitalization. **Remarks:** Specific scores not provided. Also notes overall rank in the *Forbes 2000* and figures for each criterion. **Number listed:** 2

1. QBE Insurance Group Ltd.
2. Insurance Australia Group

Source: *Forbes*, Forbes 2000 (annual), http://www.forbes.com, May 7, 2012.

3333 ■ CANADA'S LARGEST PROPERTY AND CASUALTY INSURANCE COMPANIES OVERALL, 2011

Ranked by: Score based on revenue, profits, assets, and market capitalization. **Remarks:** Specific scores not provided. Also notes overall rank in the *Forbes 2000* and figures for each criterion. **Number listed:** 2

1. Fairfax Financial
2. Intact Financial

Source: *Forbes*, Forbes 2000 (annual), http://www.forbes.com, May 7, 2012.

3334 ■ FASTEST-GROWING PROPERTY AND CASUALTY INSURANCE GROUPS, 2009-2010

Ranked by: Annual net premium growth, in percent. **Remarks:** Also notes rank in the overall *Top 100* for current and previous year. **Number listed:** 10

1. MAPFRE Insurance Group, with 1,327.9%
2. Tokio Marine Holding Group, 547.9
3. AmTrust GMACI Maiden Group, 456.9%
4. QBE Insurance Group, 27.2%
5. Endurance Group, 25.7%
6. MBIA Group, 25.1%
7. ACE Ltd. Group, 22.7%
8. Meadowbrook Insurance Group, 19.6%
9. Utica National Insurance Group, 18.8%
10. Hanover Insurance Group, 16.7%

Source: *National Underwriter, Property & Casualty*, Top 100 (annual), July 25, 2011, p. 13.

3335 ■ JAPAN'S LARGEST PROPERTY AND CASUALTY INSURANCE COMPANIES OVERALL, 2011

Ranked by: Score based on revenue, profits, assets, and market capitalization. **Remarks:** Specific scores not provided. Also notes overall rank in the *Forbes 2000* and figures for each criterion. **Number listed:** 3

1. Tokio Marine Holdings Inc.
2. MS & AD Insurance Group Holdings Inc.
3. NKSJ Holdings Inc.

Source: *Forbes*, Forbes 2000 (annual), http://www.forbes.com, May 7, 2012.

3336 ■ LARGEST U.S. PROPERTY AND CASUALTY INSURANCE COMPANIES OVERALL, 2011

Ranked by: Score based on revenue, profits, assets, and market capitalization. **Remarks:** Specific scores not provided. Also notes overall rank in the *Forbes 2000* and figures for each criterion. **Number listed:** 4

1. The Travelers Cos., Inc.
2. The Chubb Corp.
3. The Progressive Corp.
4. W. R. Berkley Corp.

Source: *Forbes*, Forbes 2000 (annual), http://www.forbes.com, May 7, 2012.

3337 ■ LARGEST U.S. WHOLESALE INSURANCE BROKERS BY PROPERTY/CASUALTY VOLUME, 2010

Ranked by: Wholesale premium volume from property/casualty placements, in dollars. **Remarks:** Also notes contact information, gross revenue, percent change from previous year, principal officer, number of employees, and breakdown by type. **Number listed:** 10

1. AmWINS Group Inc., with $4,072,220,761
2. CRC Insurance Services Inc., $2,145,000,000
3. Swett & Crawford Group Inc., $2,100,000,000
4. Crump Group Inc., $1,383,291,903
5. All Risks Ltd., $620,000,000
6. ARC Express & Surplus LLC, $480,000,000
7. Westrope, $401,434,900
8. Partners Specialty Group LLC, $322,000,000
9. U.S. Risk Insurance Group Inc., $307,000,000
10. Bliss & Glennon Inc., $223,000,000

Source: *Business Insurance*, Wholesale Insurance Brokers (annual), October 10, 2011, p. 20.

3338 ■ SOUTH KOREA'S LARGEST PROPERTY AND CASUALTY INSURANCE COMPANIES OVERALL, 2011

Ranked by: Score based on revenue, profits, assets, and market capitalization. **Remarks:** Specific scores not provided. Also notes overall rank in the *Forbes 2000* and figures for each criterion. **Number listed:** 4

1. Samsung Fire & Marine Insurance Co., Ltd.
2. Dongbu Insurance
3. Hyundai Marine & Fire Insurance
4. LIG Insurance

Source: *Forbes*, Forbes 2000 (annual), http://www.forbes.com, May 7, 2012.

3339 ■ TOP MUTUAL *FORTUNE 500* COMPANIES IN PROPERTY/CASUALTY INSURANCE, 2011

Ranked by: Revenue, in millions of dollars. **Remarks:** Also notes overall rank in the *Fortune 500;* profits; profits as a percentage of revenue; stockholders' equity; and rank by each criterion. **Number listed:** 3

1. State Farm Insurance Companies, with $64,305 million
2. Nationwide, $30,698
3. Auto-Owners Insurance Group, $5,709

Source: *Fortune*, Fortune 500 (annual), May 21, 2012, p. F-37.

3340 ■ TOP PROPERTY AND CASUALTY INSURANCE COMPANIES BY COMBINED RATIO, 2010

Ranked by: Combined ratio. **Remarks:** Also notes rank in the overall *Top 100* for current and previous year, and annual increase or decrease. **Number listed:** 10

1. Bankamerica Corp. Group, with 47.9
2. Doctors Co. Group, 48.6

3. ProAssurance Corp. Group, 64.4
4. FM Global Group, 78.4
5. Assurant Inc. Group, 79.3
6. RLI Insurance Group, 81.3
7. HCC Insurance Holdings Group, 85.6
8. American Financial Insurance Group, 88.1
9. Munich American Holding Group, 89.1
10. AmTrust GMACI Maiden Group, 89.5

Source: *National Underwriter, Property & Casualty*, Top 100 (annual), July 25, 2011, p. 13.

3341 ■ TOP PROPERTY AND CASUALTY INSURANCE COMPANIES BY NET PREMIUMS, 2010

Ranked by: Net premiums written, in thousands of dollars. **Remarks:** Also notes rank for previous year, growth in net premiums, and combined ratio for current and previous year. **Number listed:** 100

1. State Farm Mutual Auto Insurance Co., with $32,527,559 thousand
2. Allstate Insurance Co., $23,483,377
3. State Farm Fire & Casualty Co., $13,613,006
4. Nationwide Mutual Insurance Co., $11,960,210
5. Government Employees Insurance Co., $9,958,568
6. Liberty Mutual Insurance Co., $7,740,795
7. Farmers Insurance Exchange, $6,594,806
8. Federal Insurance Co., $6,309,090
9. Continental Casualty Co., $5,636,928
10. United Service Automobile Association, $5,455,478

Source: *National Underwriter, Property & Casualty*, Top 100 (annual), July 25, 2011, p. 21.

3342 ■ TOP PROPERTY AND CASUALTY INSURANCE GROUPS BY NET PREMIUMS, 2010

Ranked by: Net premiums written, in thousands of dollars. **Remarks:** Also notes rank for previous year, growth in net premiums, and combined ratio for current and previous year. **Number listed:** 10

1. State Farm IL Group, with $50,808,635 thousand
2. Allstate Insurance Group, $24,796,656
3. Liberty Mutual Insurance Group, $21,483,996
4. Berkshire Hathaway Insurance Group, $21,358,714
5. Travelers Group, $20,594,458
6. Chartis/American International Group, $19,715,432
7. Zurich Insurance Group, $18,529,635
8. Nationwide Group, $14,489,531
9. Progressive Group, $14,476,676
10. USAA Group, $10,679,414

Source: *National Underwriter, Property & Casualty*, Top 100 (annual), July 25, 2011, p. 16.

3343 ■ TOP STOCK *FORTUNE 500* COMPANIES IN PROPERTY/CASUALTY INSURANCE, 2011

Ranked by: Revenue, in millions of dollars. **Remarks:** Also notes overall rank in the *Fortune 500;* profits; profits as a percentage of revenue; stockholders' equity; and rank by each criterion. **Number listed:** 15

1. Berkshire Hathaway Inc., with $143,688 million
2. American International Group Inc., $71,730
3. Liberty Mutual Group, $34,671
4. The Allstate Corp., $32,654
5. The Travelers Cos., Inc., $25,446
6. The Hartford Financial Services Group Inc., $21,918
7. United Services Automobile Association, $19,036
8. The Progressive Corp., $15,508
9. Loews Corp., $14,127
10. Chubb Group of Insurance Cos., $3,585

Source: *Fortune*, Fortune 500 (annual), May 21, 2012, p. F-37.

3344 ■ TOP WRITERS OF PROPERTY/CASUALTY INSURANCE BY NET PREMIUMS WRITTEN, 2010

Ranked by: Net premiums written, in thousands of dollars. **Remarks:** Also notes AM Best number and percent change from previous year. **Number listed:** 200

1. State Farm Insurance Companies, with $50,808,635 thousand
2. The Allstate Corp., $24,796,656
3. Liberty Mutual Insurance Companies, $21,483,996
4. Berkshire Hathaway Insurance, $21,358,316
5. Travelers Group, $20,594,458
6. American International Group Inc., $19,715,432
7. Nationwide, $14,489,531
8. Progressive Insurance Group, $14,476,676
9. Farmers Insurance Group, $14,129,512
10. USAA, $10,679,414

Source: *Best's Review*, Leading Writers: P & C (annual), July 2011, p. 23+.

3345 ■ TOP WRITERS OF U.S. PROPERTY/CASUALTY INSURANCE BY DIRECT PREMIUMS, 2010

Ranked by: Direct premiums written, in thousands of dollars. **Remarks:** Also notes market share. **Number listed:** 10

1. State Farm Mutual Automobile Insurance Co., with $52,378,166 thousand
2. Zurich Financial Services Ltd., $27,442,024
3. Allstate Corp., $25,863,277
4. American International Group Inc., $25,569,346
5. Liberty Mutual Holding Co., $25,318,187
6. The Travelers Cos., Inc., $21,541,289
7. Berkshire Hathaway Inc., $16,560,344
8. Nationwide Mutual Group, $14,875,572
9. Progressive Corp., $14,699,901
10. USAA Insurance Group, $11,235,772

Source: *The I.I.I. Insurance Fact Book*, (annual), Insurance Information Institute, 2012, p. 15.

3346 ■ WORLD'S LARGEST PROPERTY AND CASUALTY INSURANCE COMPANIES OVERALL, 2011

Ranked by: Score based on revenue, profits, assets, and market capitalization. **Remarks:** Specific scores not provided. Also notes country, overall rank in the *Forbes 2000,* and figures for each criterion. **Number listed:** 20

1. The Travelers Cos., Inc.

2. Tokio Marine Holdings Inc.

3. The Chubb Corp.

4. PICC Property & Casualty Co., Ltd.

5. QBE Insurance Group Ltd.

6. The Progressive Corp.

7. MS & AD Insurance Group Holdings Inc.

8. Samsung Fire & Marine Insurance Co., Ltd.

9. NKSJ Holdings Inc.

10. RSA Insurance Group plc

Source: *Forbes*, Forbes 2000 (annual), http://www.forbes.com, May 7, 2012.

3347 ■ WORLD'S LARGEST PROPERTY/CASUALTY INSURERS BY ASSETS, 2010

Ranked by: Total non-banking assets, in thousands of U.S. dollars. **Remarks:** Also notes rank for previous year, A.M. Best number, and percent change from previous year. **Number listed:** 25

1. Japan Post Insurance Co., Ltd. (Japan), with $1,089,463,948 thousand

2. AXA SA (France), $920,476,513

3. Allianz SE (Germany), $807,486,736

4. MetLife Inc. (U.S.), $730,906,000

5. American International Group Inc. (U.S.), $683,443,000

6. Aviva plc (U.K.), $572,208,859

7. Assicurazioni Generali SpA (Italy), $559,858,937

8. Prudential Financial Inc. (U.S.), $539,854,000

9. Nippon Life Insurance Co. (Japan), $527,095,201

10. Legal & General Group plc (U.K.), $501,063,918

Source: *Best's Review*, World's Largest P & C Insurers (annual), January 2012, p. 58.

3348 ■ WORLD'S LARGEST PROPERTY/CASUALTY INSURERS BY PREMIUMS WRITTEN, 2010

Ranked by: Net premiums written, in thousands of U.S. dollars. **Remarks:** Also notes rank for previous year, A.M. Best number, and percent change from previous year. **Number listed:** 25

1. AXA SA (France), with $107,912,553 thousand

2. Assicurazioni Generali SpA (Italy), $87,166,306

3. UnitedHealth Group Inc. (U.S.), $85,405,000

4. Allianz SE (Germany), $84,433,538

5. Japan Post Insurance Co., Ltd. (Japan), $80,985,521

6. National Mutual Insurance Federal Agricultural Cooperative (Japan), $63,643,779

7. Munich Reinsurance Co. (Germany), $57,841,393

8. WellPoint Inc. (U.S.), $54,109,700

9. Aviva plc (U.K.), $53,237,258

10. China Life Insurance (Group) Co. (China), $52,873,923

Source: *Best's Review*, World's Largest P & C Insurers (annual), January 2012, p. 58.

3349 ■ WORLD'S MOST ADMIRED PROPERTY AND CASUALTY INSURANCE COMPANIES, 2012

Ranked by: Score, on a scale of 10, based on a survey of executives, directors, and securities analysts of companies within their own industry on eight criteria: innovation, financial soundness, employee talent, use of corporate assets, long-term investment value, social responsibility, quality of management, and quality of products/services. **Remarks:** Specific scores not provided. Also notes rank for previous year. **Number listed:** 8

1. Berkshire Hathaway Inc.

2. Zurich Financial Services

3. The Travelers Cos., Inc.

4. Munchener Ruckversicherungs-Gesellschaft AG (Munich Re)

5. Allianz SE

6. Tokio Marine Holdings Inc.

7. State Farm Insurance Companies

8. Liberty Mutual Insurance Companies

Source: *Fortune*, World's Most Admired Companies (annual), March 19, 2012, p. 148.

3350 ■ WORLD'S MOST ETHICAL PROPERTY AND CASUALTY INSURANCE COMPANIES, 2012

Ranked by: Score based on five criteria: ethics and compliance program; reputation, leadership, and innovation; governance; corporate citizenship and responsibility; and culture of ethics. **Remarks:** Specific scores not provided; companies are listed alphabetically, not ranked. **Number listed:** 3

1. Sompo Japan Insurance Inc. (Japan)

2. The Progressive Group of Insurance Cos. (U.S.)

3. Tokio Marine Holdings Inc. (Japan)

Source: *Ethisphere Magazine*, World's Most Ethical Companies (annual), http://www.ethisphere.com, 2012.

3351 ■ WORLD'S TOP PROPERTY/CASUALTY INSURANCE COMPANIES BY REVENUE, 2010

Ranked by: Revenue, in millions of U.S. dollars. **Remarks:** Also notes country. **Number listed:** 10

1. Berkshire Hathaway Inc., with $136,185 million

2. Allianz AG, $127,379

3. American International Group Inc., $104,417

4. Munchener Ruckversicherungs-Gesellschaft AG (Munich Re), $76,220

5. Zurich Financial Services Ltd., $67,850

6. State Farm Insurance Companies, $63,177

7. MS & AD Insurance Group Holdings, $39,754

8. Tokio Marine Holdings Inc., $38,396

9. Liberty Mutual Insurance Companies, $33,193

10. People's Insurance Co. of China, $32,579

Source: *The I.I.I. Insurance Fact Book*, (annual), Insurance Information Institute, 2012, p. 4.

Insurance—Reinsurance

3352 ■ WORLD'S LARGEST REINSURANCE BROKERS, 2010

Ranked by: Reinsurance gross revenues, in U.S. dollars. **Remarks:** Also notes contact information, figures for previous year, percent change, number of employees, and principal officer. **Number listed:** 10

1. Aon Blenfield, with $1,444,000,000

2. Guy Carpenter & Co., $975,000,000

3. Willis Re, $664,000,000
4. JLT Reinsurance Brokers Ltd., $198,712,720
5. Towers Watson & Co., $172,289,000
6. Cooper Gay Swett & Crawford Ltd., $120,400,000
7. BMS Group Ltd., $77,569,040
8. Miller Insurance Services Ltd., $68,158,258
9. UIB Holdings Ltd., $49,446,400
10. Lockton Cos. International Ltd., $35,556,000

Source: *Business Insurance*, Reinsurance Brokers (annual), October 24, 2011, p. 12.

3353 ■ WORLD'S LARGEST REINSURANCE GROUPS, 2010

Ranked by: Gross premiums written, in millions of U.S. dollars. **Remarks:** Also notes net premiums written, non-life figures, and total shareholder funds. **Number listed:** 50

1. Munchener Rueckversicherungs-Gesellschaft AG (Munich Re), with $31,280 million
2. Swiss Reinsurance Co., $24,756
3. Hannover Rueckversicherung AG, $15,147
4. Berkshire Hathaway Inc., $14,374
5. Lloyd's of London, $12,977
6. SCOR SE, $8,872
7. Reinsurance Group of America Inc., $7,201
8. Allianz SE, $5,736
9. PartnerRe Ltd., $4,881
10. Everest Re Group Ltd., $4,201

Source: *Best's Review*, Top Global Reinsurance Groups (annual), September 2011, p. 54-55.

3354 ■ WORLD'S LARGEST REINSURERS BY PREMIUMS WRITTEN, 2010

Ranked by: Net premiums written, in U.S. dollars. **Remarks:** Also notes contact information, net premiums earned, annual growth, combined ratio, number of employees, and principal officer. **Number listed:** 10

1. Munchener Rueckversicherungs-Gesellschaft AG (Munich Re), with $29,149,859,435
2. Swiss Reinsurance Ltd., $19,433,000,000
3. Berkshire Hathaway Reinsurance Group/ General Re Corp., $14,669,000,000
4. Hannover Reinsurance Corp., $14,034,105,614
5. Lloyd's of London, $9,728,579,200
6. Scor SE, $8,146,232,300
7. PartnerRe Ltd., $4,705,116,000
8. Everest Re Group Ltd., $3,945,600,000
9. Transatlantic Holdings Inc., $3,881,693,000
10. Korean Reinsurance Co., $2,653,783,000

Source: *Business Insurance*, World's Largest Reinsurers (annual), September 26, 2011, p. 12.

3355 ■ WORLD'S REINSURERS WITH THE HIGHEST COMBINED RATIO, 2010

Ranked by: Combined ratio, in percent. **Number listed:** 5

1. American Agricultural Insurance Co., with 105.5%
2. Arab Insurance Group BSC, 104.1%

3. Everest Re Group Ltd., 102.8%
3. Greenlight Capital Re Ltd., 102.8%
5. Munchener Ruckversicherungs Gesellschaft AG (Munich Re), 100.5%

Source: *Business Insurance*, World's Largest Reinsurers (annual), September 26, 2011, p. 12.

3356 ■ WORLD'S REINSURERS WITH THE LOWEST COMBINED RATIO, 2010

Ranked by: Combined ratio, in percent. **Number listed:** 3

1. RenaissanceRe Holdings Ltd., with 38.4%
2. ACE Tempest Reinsurance Ltd., 72.5%
3. Argo Reinsurance, 72.8%

Source: *Business Insurance*, World's Largest Reinsurers (annual), September 26, 2011, p. 12.

3357 ■ WORLD'S TOP REINSURANCE BROKERS BY REVENUE, 2010

Ranked by: Reinsurance revenue, in thousands of U.S. dollars. **Remarks:** Also notes country. **Number listed:** 10

1. Aon Benfield, with $1,444,000 thousand
2. Guy Carpenter & Co., $975,000
3. Willis Re, $664,000
4. JLT Reinsurance Brokers Ltd., $198,713
5. Towers Watson & Co., $172,289
6. Cooper Gay Swett & Crawford Ltd., $120,400
7. BMS Group, $77,569
8. Miller Insurance Services Ltd., $68,158
9. UIB Holdings Ltd., $49,446
10. Lockton Cos. International Ltd., $35,556

Source: *The I.I.I. Insurance Fact Book*, (annual), Insurance Information Institute, 2012, p. 6.

3358 ■ WORLD'S TOP REINSURANCE COMPANIES BY PREMIUMS WRITTEN, 2010

Ranked by: Net premiums written, in millions of U.S. dollars. **Remarks:** Also notes country. **Number listed:** 10

1. Munchener Ruckversicherungs-Gesellschaft AG (Munich Re), with $29,149.9 million
2. Swiss Reinsurance Co., $19,433
3. Berkshire Hathaway Reinsurance Group/ General Re Corp., $14,669
4. Hannover Reinsurance Corp., $14,034.1
5. Lloyd's of London, $9,728.6
6. SCOR SE, $8,146.2
7. PartnerRe Ltd., $4,705.1
8. Everest Re Group Ltd., $3,945.6
9. Transatlantic Holdings Inc., $3,881.7
10. Korean Reinsurance, $2,653.8

Source: *The I.I.I. Insurance Fact Book*, (annual), Insurance Information Institute, 2012, p. 5.

Insurance, Warranty

3359 ■ TOP U.S. WRITERS OF WARRANTY INSURANCE, 2010

Ranked by: Direct premiums written, in thousands of dollars. **Remarks:** Also notes market share. **Number listed:** 10

1. American International Group Inc., with $885,551 thousand
2. GMAC Insurance Group, $470,999
3. Virginia Surety Co., $283,739
4. Zurich Financial Services Ltd., $226,415
5. AmTrust Financial Services Inc., $151,323
6. Courtesy Insurance Co., $125,879
7. American Road Insurance Co., $91,319
8. Wells Fargo & Co., $82,357
9. Dealers Assurance Co., $78,599
10. Old United Casualty Co., $74,915

Source: *The I.I.I. Insurance Fact Book*, (annual), Insurance Information Institute, 2012, p. 122.

Insurance, Workers' Compensation
See: **Workers' Compensation**

Interior Decoration

3360 ■ TOP DECORATING SERVICE FRANCHISES, 2012

Ranked by: Cumulative score based on financial strength and stability, growth rate, size of the system, number of years in business, the length of time franchising, start-up costs, litigation, percentage of terminations, and whether the company provides financing. **Remarks:** Specific scores not provided. Also notes overall rank within the *Franchise 500,* contact information, description, year founded, year started franchising, states where registered, available U.S. regions, where seeking foreign expansion, number of franchised and company-owned units for past three years, start-up costs, franchise fees, royalty fees, and type of financing available. **Number listed:** 2

1. Christmas Decor Inc.
2. Decor & You Inc.

Source: *Entrepreneur*, Franchise 500 (annual), January 2012, p. 178-179.

Interior Designers

3361 ■ FASTEST-GROWING INTERIOR DESIGN FIRMS, 2010-2011

Ranked by: Growth in interior design fees, in percent. **Remarks:** Also notes design fees for current and previous year, and overall rank in the *Top 100.* **Number listed:** 10

1. Corgan Associates, with 166%
2. Cooper Carry, 100%
3. Stonehill & Taylor Architects, 70%
4. AECOM, 66%
5. Array Healthcare Facilities Solutions, 60%
6. Design Duncan Miller Ullmann, 50%
7. Rapt Studio, 48%
8. FRCH Design Worldwide, 43%
9. BBG-BBGM, 41%
9. Callison, 41%

Source: *Interior Design*, Top 100 Design Giants (annual), http://www.interiordesign.net, January 2012.

3362 ■ LARGEST INTERIOR DESIGN FIRMS, 2011

Ranked by: Interior design fees, in millions of dollars. **Remarks:** Also notes headquarters, website, total value and square footage of work installed, number of design employees, and rank for previous year. **Number listed:** 100

1. M. Arthur Gensler Jr. & Associates Inc., with $398 million
2. HOK Group Inc., $105
3. Perkins & Will Inc., $96.203
4. Hirsch Bedner Associates, $80.478
5. Leo A. Daly Co., $79.4
6. Stantec Architecture, $69.821
7. Jacobs Engineering Group Inc., $69.507
8. Cannon Design Inc., $67.5
9. Callison, $56.25
10. IA Interior Architects Inc., $53.191

Source: *Interior Design*, Top 100 Design Giants (annual), http://www.interiordesign.net, January 2012.

3363 ■ TOP INTERIOR DESIGN FIRMS IN CORPORATE/OFFICE DESIGN, 2011

Ranked by: Corporate/office interior design fees, in dollars. **Remarks:** Also notes rank in the overall *Top 100 Design Giants.* **Number listed:** 10

1. M. Arthur Gensler Jr. & Associates Inc., with $199,000,000
2. HOK Group Inc., $55,650,000
3. Nelson, $50,925,000
4. IA Interior Architects Inc., $45,212,350
5. Perkins & Will Inc., $38,481,200
6. KlingStubbins, $35,530,000
7. M. Moser Associates, $24,426,000
8. Skidmore, Owings & Merrill, $22,818,710
9. Space Matrix, $22,680,000
10. Ted Moudis Associates, $20,250,000

Source: *Interior Design*, Top 100 Design Giants (annual), http://www.interiordesign.net, January 2012.

3364 ■ TOP INTERIOR DESIGN FIRMS IN CULTURAL DESIGN, 2011

Ranked by: Cultural interior design fees, in dollars. **Remarks:** Also notes rank in the overall *Top 100 Design Giants*. **Number listed:** 10

1. M. Arthur Gensler Jr. & Associates Inc., with $7,960,000
2. EwingCole, $2,560,000
3. Stantec, $2,094,620
4. SmithGroup, $2,057,200
5. tvsdesign, $1,603,800
6. Roger Ferris + Partners, $1,400,000
7. Rockwell Group, $1,383,900
8. AECOM, $1,380,000
9. Rapt Studio, $1,081,300
10. Perkins & Will Inc., $962,030

Source: *Interior Design*, Top 100 Design Giants (annual), http://www.interiordesign.net, January 2012.

3365 ■ TOP INTERIOR DESIGN FIRMS IN EDUCATIONAL DESIGN, 2011

Ranked by: Educational interior design fees, in dollars. **Remarks:** Also notes rank in the overall *Top 100 Design Giants*. **Number listed:** 10

1. M. Arthur Gensler Jr. & Associates Inc., with $27,860,000

2. Cannon Design Inc., $21,600,000
3. DLR Group, $13,915,000
4. Shepley Bulfinch Richardson & Abbott, $10,385,170
5. HOK Group Inc., $9,450,000
6. IA Interior Architects Inc., $7,978,650
7. Perkins & Will Inc., $7,696,240
8. Stantec Architecture, $5,585,653
9. Leo A. Daly Co., $5,557,974
10. SmithGroup, $4,937,280

Source: *Interior Design*, Top 100 Design Giants (annual), http://www.interiordesign.net, January 2012.

3366 ■ TOP INTERIOR DESIGN FIRMS IN FOREIGN WORK, 2011

Ranked by: Volume of projects that are overseas, in percent. Remarks: Also notes rank in the overall *Top 100 Design Giants*. Number listed: 15

1. Space Matrix, with 100%
1. Bilkey Llinas Design Associates, 100%
3. DiLeonardo International, 99%
4. M. Moser Associates, 96%
5. Hirsch Bedner Associates, 95%
6. Wilson Associates, 90%
7. KNA Design, 85%
8. Smallwood, Reynolds, Stewart, Stewart & Associates, 76%
9. Steelman Partners, 75%
10. Peter Marino Architect, 73%

Source: *Interior Design*, Top 100 Design Giants (annual), http://www.interiordesign.net, January 2012.

3367 ■ TOP INTERIOR DESIGN FIRMS IN GOVERNMENT DESIGN, 2011

Ranked by: Government institution interior design fees, in dollars. Remarks: Also notes rank in the overall *Top 100 Design Giants*. Number listed: 10

1. M. Arthur Gensler Jr. & Associates Inc., with $59,700,000
2. Jacobs Engineering Group Inc., $46,569,945
3. Leo A. Daly Co., $18,261,916
4. AECOM, $13,340,000
5. Fentress Architects, $12,448,800
6. HOK Group Inc., $11,550,000
7. PageSoutherlandPage, $7,200,000
8. Ewing Cole, $5,632,000
9. DLR Group, $5,313,000
10. Perkins & Will Inc., $4,810,150

Source: *Interior Design*, Top 100 Design Giants (annual), http://www.interiordesign.net, January 2012.

3368 ■ TOP INTERIOR DESIGN FIRMS IN HEALTHCARE/ ASSISTED-LIVING DESIGN, 2011

Ranked by: Healthcare/assisted-living interior design fees, in dollars. Remarks: Also notes rank in the overall *Top 100 Design Giants*. Number listed: 10

1. Perkins & Will Inc., with $38,481,200
2. Cannon Design Inc., $35,775,000

3. HDR Architecture, $24,500,000
4. Leo A. Daly Co., $23,025,894
5. NBBJ, $22,047,480
6. Perkins Eastman, $21,417,000
7. AECOM, $20,240,000
8. Stantec Architecture, $18,153,373
9. PageSoutherlandPage, $18,000,000
10. SmithGroup, $16,046,160

Source: *Interior Design*, Top 100 Design Giants (annual), http://www.interiordesign.net, January 2012.

3369 ■ TOP INTERIOR DESIGN FIRMS IN HOSPITALITY DESIGN, 2011

Ranked by: Hospitality interior design fees, in dollars. Remarks: Also notes rank in the overall *Top 100 Design Giants*. Number listed: 10

1. Hirsch Bedner Associates, with $80,478,000
2. M. Arthur Gensler Jr. & Associates Inc., $43,780,000
3. Wilson Associates, $42,570,000
4. Bilkey Llinas Design Associates, $23,580,000
5. Leo A. Daly Co., $20,643,905
6. Rockwell Group, $13,608,350
7. Daroff Design Inc. & DDI Architects, $13,319,800
8. Callison Architecture Inc., $11,250,000
9. DiLeonardo International, $10,028,000
10. Design Duncan Miller Ullmann, $8,930,790

Source: *Interior Design*, Top 100 Design Giants (annual), http://www.interiordesign.net, January 2012.

3370 ■ TOP INTERIOR DESIGN FIRMS IN RESIDENTIAL DESIGN, 2011

Ranked by: Residential interior design fees, in dollars. Remarks: Also notes rank in the overall *Top 100 Design Giants*. Number listed: 10

1. Marc-Michaels Interior Design, with $12,555,000
2. Creative Design Consultants, $9,500,000
3. Peter Marino Architect, $6,930,000
4. Robert A.M. Stern Architects, $6,248,000
5. Callison Architecture Inc., $5,625,000
6. Roger Ferris + Partners, $2,800,000
7. CBT Architects, $2,250,000
8. Skidmore, Owings & Merrill LLP, $2,106,342
9. Perkins Eastman Rockwell Group, $1,815,000
10. BraytonHughes Design Studios, $1,206,500

Source: *Interior Design*, Top 100 Design Giants (annual), http://www.interiordesign.net, January 2012.

3371 ■ TOP INTERIOR DESIGN FIRMS IN RETAIL DESIGN, 2011

Ranked by: Retail interior design fees, in dollars. Remarks: Also notes rank in the overall *Top 100 Design Giants*. Number listed: 10

1. M. Arthur Gensler Jr. & Associates Inc., with $39,800,000
2. Jacobs Engineering Group Inc., $14,596,550

3. FRCH Design Worldwide, $12,444,000
4. Peter Marino Architect, $11,682,000
5. Callison Architecture Inc., $11,250,000
6. JGA, $6,700,000
7. Tricarico Architecture & Design, $6,596,000
8. Vocon, $6,280,803
9. Little, $4,346,720
10. Aedifica, $4,260,000

Source: *Interior Design*, Top 100 Design Giants (annual), http://www.interiordesign.net, January 2012.

3372 ■ TOP INTERIOR DESIGN FIRMS IN TRANSPORTATION DESIGN, 2011

Ranked by: Transportation interior design fees, in dollars. **Remarks:** Also notes rank in the overall *Top 100 Design Giants*. **Number listed:** 10

1. M. Arthur Gensler Jr. & Associates Inc., with $15,920,000
2. HOK Group Inc., $9,450,000
3. Corgan Associates, $8,516,200
4. Fentress Architects, $6,669,000
5. Stantec, $4,189,240
6. Leo A. Daly Co., $3,969,982
7. Perkins & Will Inc., $1,924,060
8. LS3P Associates, $1,653,000
9. Gresham, Smith & Partners, $993,600
10. Jacobs Engineering Group Inc., $695,074

Source: *Interior Design*, Top 100 Design Giants (annual), http://www.interiordesign.net, January 2012.

Internet

3373 ■ CHINA'S MOST VALUABLE INTERNET BRANDS, 2011

Ranked by: Brand value, in millions of U.S. dollars. **Remarks:** Also notes rank within the *Global 500* for current and previous year, figures for current and previous year, and brand rating. Ranking is available online only. **Number listed:** 2

1. QQ, with $3,822 million
2. Baidu, $2,427

Source: *Global 500*, (annual), Brand Finance plc, March 2012.

3374 ■ LARGEST U.S. WEB PROPERTIES, 2011

Ranked by: Number of unique visitors during the month of December, in millions. **Remarks:** Also notes average numbers of minutes spent per visitor. **Number listed:** 25

1. Google sites, with 187.1 million visitors
2. Microsoft sites, 177.3
3. Yahoo! sites, 176.5
4. Facebook, 162.5
5. Amazon sites, 114.7
6. AOL, 107.1
7. Ask Network, 89.2
8. Glam Media, 86.6
9. Turner Digital, 84.2
10. Wikimedia Foundation sites, 83
10. Apple Inc., 83

Source: *Advertising Age*, Digital Issue (annual), February 27, 2012, p. 8.

3375 ■ TOP *FORTUNE 500* COMPANIES IN INTERNET SERVICES AND RETAILING, 2011

Ranked by: Revenue, in millions of dollars. **Remarks:** Also notes overall rank in the *Fortune 500;* profits; profits as a percentage of revenue; stockholders' equity; and rank by each criterion. **Number listed:** 5

1. Amazon.com Inc., with $48,077 million
2. Google Inc., $37,905
3. eBay Inc., $11,652
4. Liberty Interactive Corp., $11,624
5. Yahoo! Inc., $4,984

Source: *Fortune*, Fortune 500 (annual), May 21, 2012, p. F-37.

3376 ■ THE UNITED STATES' MOST VALUABLE INTERNET BRANDS, 2011

Ranked by: Brand value, in millions of U.S. dollars. **Remarks:** Also notes rank within the *Global 500* for current and previous year, figures for current and previous year, and brand rating. Ranking is available online only. **Number listed:** 10

1. Google, with $47,463 million
2. Amazon, $28,665
3. eBay, $8,959
4. Facebook, $8,792
5. Yahoo!, $4,550
6. Priceline, $4,001
7. QVC, $3,536
8. Paypall, $2,792
9. Expedia, $2,702
10. Symantec, $2,606

Source: *Global 500*, (annual), Brand Finance plc, March 2012.

3377 ■ WORLD'S MOST ADMIRED INTERNET SERVICES AND RETAILING COMPANIES, 2012

Ranked by: Score, on a scale of 10, based on a survey of executives, directors, and securities analysts of companies within their own industry on eight criteria: innovation, financial soundness, employee talent, use of corporate assets, long-term investment value, social responsibility, quality of management, and quality of products/services. **Remarks:** Specific scores not provided. Also notes rank for previous year. **Number listed:** 5

1. Google Inc.
2. Amazon.com Inc.
3. eBay Inc.
4. IAC/InterActiveCorp
5. Expedia Inc.

Source: *Fortune*, World's Most Admired Companies (annual), March 19, 2012, p. 147.

3378 ■ WORLD'S MOST TECHNOLOGICALLY INNOVATIVE WEB AND DIGITAL MEDIA COMPANIES - PRIVATE, 2012

Ranked by: Editorial determination. **Remarks:** Companies are listed alphabetically, not ranked. Also notes comments. **Number listed:** 6

1. Bluefin Laboratories
2. Dropbox
3. Facebook Inc.

4. OnLive
5. Spotify
6. Twitter Inc.

Source: *Technology Review*, TR 50 (annual), http://www.technologyreview.com, 2012.

3379 ■ WORLD'S MOST TECHNOLOGICALLY INNOVATIVE WEB AND DIGITAL MEDIA COMPANIES - PUBLIC, 2012

Ranked by: Editorial determination. **Remarks:** Companies are listed alphabetically, not ranked. Also notes comments. **Number listed:** 3

1. Google Inc.
2. Safaricom
3. Zynga

Source: *Technology Review*, TR 50 (annual), http://www.technologyreview.com, 2012.

3380 ■ WORLD'S MOST VALUABLE INTERNET BRANDS, 2011

Ranked by: Brand value, in millions of U.S. dollars. **Remarks:** Also notes rank within the *Global 500* for current and previous year, figures for current and previous year, country, and brand rating. Ranking is available online only. **Number listed:** 12

1. Google, with $47,463 million
2. Amazon, $28,665
3. eBay, $8,959
4. Facebook, $8,792
5. Yahoo!, $4,550
6. Priceline, $4,001
7. QQ, $3,822
8. QVC, $3,536
9. Paypal, $2,792
10. Expedia, $2,702

Source: *Global 500*, (annual), Brand Finance plc, March 2012.

Internet Retailers
See: **Electronic Commerce**

Internet Search Engines

3381 ■ TOP SEARCH ENGINES IN THE U.S., 2011

Ranked by: Number of searches during the month of December, in millions. **Remarks:** Also notes market share. **Number listed:** 5

1. Google, with 12,020 million searches
2. Microsoft/Bing, 2,750
3. Yahoo!, 2,650
4. Ask Network, 531
5. AOL, 287

Source: *Advertising Age*, Digital Issue (annual), February 27, 2012, p. 16.

3382 ■ TOP SEARCH ENGINES WORLDWIDE, 2011

Ranked by: Number of searches during the month of December, in millions. **Remarks:** Also notes market share. **Number listed:** 10

1. Google, with 127,195 million searches
2. Baidu, 12.829
3. Yahoo!, 10,709
4. Microsoft, 5,001
5. Yandex, 3,789
6. NHN, 3,013
7. eBay, 2,903
8. Facebook, 2,414
9. Alibaba, 2,212
10. Amazon, 1,600

Source: *Advertising Age*, Digital Issue (annual), February 27, 2012, p. 16.

Internet Shopping
See: **Electronic Commerce**

Internet Sites
See also: **Blogs**

3383 ■ TOP SOCIAL NETWORKING SITES, 2011

Ranked by: Number of unique viewers, in thousands. **Number listed:** 10

1. Facebook, with 162,486 thousand visitors
2. Twitter, 37,461
3. LinkedIn, 33,523
4. MySpace, 24,049
5. Google+, 20,674
6. Tumblr, 18,762
7. DeviantArt, 12,747
8. MyLife, 10,664
9. Windows Live, 8,320
10. Pinterest, 7,516

Source: *Advertising Age*, Digital Issue (annual), February 27, 2012, p. 16.

3384 ■ TOP SOCIAL NETWORKS, 2011

Ranked by: Market share, in percent. **Remarks:** Also notes site address. **Number listed:** 20

1. Facebook, with 64.45%
2. YouTube, 19.23%
3. Twitter, 1.66%
4. Yahoo! Answers, 1.05%
5. Tagged, 1.02%
6. LinkedIn, 0.83%
7. MySpace, 0.42%
8. myYearbook, 0.38%
9. Pinterest, 0.37%
10. Google+, 0.26%

Source: *Top Media Outlets*, (annual), BurrellesLuce, January 2012.

Internet Users

3385 ■ COUNTRIES WITH THE HIGHEST CONCENTRATIONS OF BROADBAND INTERNET SUBSCRIBERS, 2010

Ranked by: Number of broadband Internet subscribers per 100 population. **Number listed:** 142

1. Switzerland, with 38.2 subscribers
2. Netherlands, 38.0
3. Denmark, 37.4
4. South Korea, 36.6
5. Iceland, 34.6
5. Norway, 34.6
7. France, 33.9
8. Luxembourg, 32.8
9. Germany, 31.6
9. Sweden, 31.6

Source: *Global Competitiveness Report*, (annual), World Economic Forum, 2011, p. 494.

3386 ■ COUNTRIES WITH THE HIGHEST CONCENTRATIONS OF INTERNET USERS, 2010

Ranked by: Number of Internet users per 100 population. **Number listed:** 142

1. Iceland, with 96 users
2. Norway, 93.4
3. Netherlands, 90.7
4. Luxembourg, 90.6
5. Sweden, 90
6. Denmark, 88.7
7. Finland, 86.9
8. United Kingdom, 85
9. Switzerland, 83.9
10. South Korea, 83.7

Source: *Global Competitiveness Report*, (annual), World Economic Forum, 2011, p. 493.

3387 ■ COUNTRIES WITH THE LOWEST CONCENTRATIONS OF INTERNET USERS, 2010

Ranked by: Number of Internet users per 100 population. **Number listed:** 142

1. Timor-Leste, with 0.2 users
2. Ethiopia, 0.8
3. Cambodia, 1.3
4. Burkina Faso, 1.4
5. Madagascar, 1.7
5. Chad, 1.7
7. Burundi, 2.1
8. Malawi, 2.3
9. Cote d'Ivoire, 2.6
10. Mali, 2.7

Source: *Global Competitiveness Report*, (annual), World Economic Forum, 2011, p. 493.

Investment Advisors

3388 ■ AMERICA'S BEST INDEPENDENT FINANCIAL ADVISORS, 2011

Ranked by: Score based on assets under management, revenue and profits generated, and quality of service. **Remarks:** Also notes rank for previous year, location, firm assets, typical account size, typical net worth, and breakdown of customers by type. **Number listed:** 100

1. Steve Lockshin (Convergent Wealth Adv.), with 100 points

2. Ric Edelman (Edelman Financial), 99.999
3. David Zier (Convergent Wealth Adv.), 99.217
4. Robert A. Clarfeld (Clarfield Financial), 98.805
5. Fred Fern (Churchill Mgmt.), 98.457
6. Martin Bicknell (Mariner Wealth Adv.), 97.922
7. Howard Sontag (Sontag Advisory), 97.91
8. Ron Carson (Carson Wealth Mgmt.), 97.907
9. Richard Saperstein (HighTower), 97.592
10. Peter Mallouk (Creative Planning), 97.052

Source: *Barron's*, Top 100 Independent Financial Advisors (annual), August 29, 2011, p. S6+.

3389 ■ TOP FEMALE FINANCIAL ADVISERS IN THE U.S., 2011

Ranked by: Score, on a scale of 100, based on such criteria as assets, revenue, and customer satisfaction. **Remarks:** Also notes rank for previous year, location, breakdown of customers by size and type, total assets, typical account size, and typical net worth. **Number listed:** 100

1. Ami Forte (Morgan Stanley Smith Barney), with 100 points
2. Rebecca Rothstein (Morgan Stanley PWM), 99.598
3. Lori Van Dusen (Convergent), 99.006
4. Lorna Meyer (Merrill Lynch), 98.923
5. Susan Kaplan (Kaplan Financial), 98.613
6. Elaine Meyers (Credit Suisse Securities), 98.592
7. Karen McDonald (Morgan Stanley Smith Barney), 98.496
8. Jeanette Garretty (Wells Fargo Private Bank), 98.2
9. Melissa Corrado-Harrison (Merrill Lynch), 97.588
10. Theresa Chacopuios (Wells Fargo Investments), 97.496

Source: *Barron's*, Top 100 Women Financial Advisers (annual), June 6, 2011, p. S17+.

3390 ■ TOP REGISTERED INVESTMENT ADVISORS IN ASSET MANAGEMENT, 2011

Ranked by: Total assets under management, in millions of dollars. **Remarks:** Also notes city, website, number of employees that perform advisory functions, number of clients, discretionary and nondiscretionary assets, and total number of accounts. **Number listed:** 50

1. Veritable LP, with $10,058 million
2. Gilder Gagnon Howe & Co., $5,562
3. Curian Capital LLC, $5,383
4. Litman/Gregory Asset Management LLC, $4,859
5. Bel Air Investment Advisors LLC, $4,921
6. Windhaven Investment Management Inc., $4,693
7. Rothschild Asset Management Inc., $4,331
8. Wasmer Schroeder & Co., $3,756
9. R. H. Bluestein & Co., $3,394
10. Symmetry Partners, $3,343

Source: *Registered Rep.*, Top 100 RIAs (annual), http://www.registeredrep.com, July 2011.

3391 ■ TOP REGISTERED INVESTMENT ADVISORS IN WEALTH MANAGEMENT, 2011

Ranked by: Total assets under management, in millions of dollars. **Remarks:** Also notes city, website, number of employees that perform advisory functions, number of clients, discretionary and nondiscretionary assets, and total number of accounts. **Number listed:** 50

1. M & I Investment Management Corp., with $24,089 million
2. Genspring Family Offices LLC, $17,453
3. StanCorp Investment Advisers Inc., $17,220
4. Arnerich Massena Inc., $15,328
5. Canterbury Consulting Inc., $12,315
6. Oxford Financial Group Ltd., $10,441
7. Convergent Wealth Advisors LLC, $10,392
8. Sageview Advisory Group LLC, $10,210
9. Moneta Group Investment Advisors LLC, $10,187
10. Chevy Chase Trust Co., $9,250

Source: *Registered Rep.*, Top 100 RIAs (annual), http://www.registeredrep.com, July 2011.

3392 ■ TOP WIREHOUSE ADVISORS, 2011

Ranked by: Estimated assets under management, in millions of dollars. **Remarks:** Also notes city, number of years in the industry, and business description/specialty. **Number listed:** 100

1. Roger V. Coleman (Morgan Stanley Smith Barney), with $28,000 million
2. Mark T. Curtis (Morgan Stanley Smith Barney), $22,500
3. Joseph W. Montgomery (Morgan Stanley Smith Barney), $17,500
4. Karen A. McDonald (Morgan Stanley Smith Barney), $8,500
5. John Glotzbach (Morgan Stanley Smith Barney), $7,700
6. J. Dorian McKelvy (Morgan Stanley Private Wealth Mgmt.), $6,500
7. Ronald C. Hart (Morgan Stanley Smith Barney), $6,462
8. James Ryan (Merrill Lynch), $6,278
9. Brian C. Pfeifler (Morgan Stanley Private Wealth Mgmt.), $6,000
10. Todd DiScala (Merrill Lynch), $5,234

Source: *Registered Rep.*, America's Top 100 Wirehouse Advisors (annual), http://www.registeredrep.com, September 1, 2011.

Investment Management Firms

3393 ■ AUSTRALIA'S LARGEST INVESTMENT SERVICE COMPANIES OVERALL, 2011

Ranked by: Score based on revenue, profits, assets, and market capitalization. **Remarks:** Specific scores not provided. Also notes overall rank in the *Forbes 2000* and figures for each criterion. **Number listed:** 3

1. Macquarie Group Ltd.
2. AMP
3. Challenger Ltd.

Source: *Forbes*, Forbes 2000 (annual), http://www.forbes.com, May 7, 2012.

3394 ■ BRAZIL'S LARGEST INVESTMENT SERVICE COMPANIES OVERALL, 2011

Ranked by: Score based on revenue, profits, assets, and market capitalization. **Remarks:** Specific scores not provided. Also notes overall rank in the *Forbes 2000* and figures for each criterion. **Number listed:** 2

1. BM & F Bovespa
2. Bradespar

Source: *Forbes*, Forbes 2000 (annual), http://www.forbes.com, May 7, 2012.

3395 ■ CALIFORNIA'S LARGEST INVESTMENT SERVICE COMPANIES OVERALL, 2011

Ranked by: Score based on revenue, profits, assets, and market capitalization. **Remarks:** Specific scores not provided. Also notes overall rank in the *Forbes 2000* and figures for each criterion. **Number listed:** 2

1. The Charles Schwab Corp.
2. Franklin Resources Inc.

Source: *Forbes*, Forbes 2000 (annual), http://www.forbes.com, May 7, 2012.

3396 ■ CANADA'S LARGEST INVESTMENT SERVICE COMPANIES OVERALL, 2011

Ranked by: Score based on revenue, profits, assets, and market capitalization. **Remarks:** Specific scores not provided. Also notes overall rank in the *Forbes 2000* and figures for each criterion. **Number listed:** 2

1. Onex Corp.
2. Dundee Corp.

Source: *Forbes*, Forbes 2000 (annual), http://www.forbes.com, May 7, 2012.

3397 ■ CHINA'S LARGEST INVESTMENT SERVICE COMPANIES OVERALL, 2011

Ranked by: Score based on revenue, profits, assets, and market capitalization. **Remarks:** Specific scores not provided. Also notes overall rank in the *Forbes 2000* and figures for each criterion. **Number listed:** 6

1. CITIC Securities International Co., Ltd.
2. GF Securities
3. Haitong Securities
4. Huatai Securities
5. China Merchants Securities
6. Everbright Securities

Source: *Forbes*, Forbes 2000 (annual), http://www.forbes.com, May 7, 2012.

3398 ■ FRANCE'S LARGEST INVESTMENT SERVICE COMPANIES OVERALL, 2011

Ranked by: Score based on revenue, profits, assets, and market capitalization. **Remarks:** Specific scores not provided. Also notes overall rank in the *Forbes 2000* and figures for each criterion. **Number listed:** 2

1. Wendel
2. Eurazeo

Source: *Forbes*, Forbes 2000 (annual), http://www.forbes.com, May 7, 2012.

3399 ■ GERMANY'S LARGEST INVESTMENT SERVICE COMPANIES OVERALL, 2011

Ranked by: Score based on revenue, profits, assets, and market capitalization. **Remarks:** Specific scores not provided. Also notes overall rank in the *Forbes 2000* and figures for each criterion. **Number listed:** 2

1. Deutsche Boerse Systems Inc.
2. W & W - Wustenrot

Source: *Forbes*, Forbes 2000 (annual), http://www.forbes.com, May 7, 2012.

3400 ■ HONG KONG'S LARGEST INVESTMENT SERVICE COMPANIES OVERALL, 2011

Ranked by: Score based on revenue, profits, assets, and market capitalization. **Remarks:** Specific scores not provided. Also notes overall rank in the *Forbes 2000* and figures for each criterion. **Number listed:** 2

1. HK Exchanges & Clearing
2. First Pacific

Source: *Forbes*, Forbes 2000 (annual), http://www.forbes.com, May 7, 2012.

3401 ■ ISRAEL'S LARGEST INVESTMENT SERVICE COMPANIES OVERALL, 2011

Ranked by: Score based on revenue, profits, assets, and market capitalization. **Remarks:** Specific scores not provided. Also notes overall rank in the *Forbes 2000* and figures for each criterion. **Number listed:** 3

1. Delek Group Ltd.
2. Israel Corp.
3. IDB Holding Corp., Ltd.

Source: *Forbes*, Forbes 2000 (annual), http://www.forbes.com, May 7, 2012.

3402 ■ JAPAN'S LARGEST INVESTMENT SERVICE COMPANIES OVERALL, 2011

Ranked by: Score based on revenue, profits, assets, and market capitalization. **Remarks:** Specific scores not provided. Also notes overall rank in the *Forbes 2000* and figures for each criterion. **Number listed:** 3

1. Nomura Holdings Inc.
2. Daiwa Securities Group Inc.
3. Japan Securities Finance Co., Ltd.

Source: *Forbes*, Forbes 2000 (annual), http://www.forbes.com, May 7, 2012.

3403 ■ LARGEST COLORADO-BASED INVESTMENT MANAGERS AND FINANCIAL ADVISORS, 2010

Ranked by: Assets managed, in millions of dollars. **Remarks:** Also notes contact information. **Number listed:** 14

1. Denver Investment Advisors LLC, with $8,737 million
2. Cambiar Investors LLC, $6,000
3. First National Wealth Management, $4,500
4. Innovest Portfolio Solutions LLC, $3,500
5. First Western Trust Bank & Affiliates, $3,100
6. Strategic Capital Advisers, $2,462
7. AMG National Trust Bank, $2,434
8. ICON Advisers, $2,017
9. Capital Investment Counsel Inc., $1,890
10. The Milestone Group Inc., $1,200

Source: *ColoradoBiz*, Top Professional Services (annual), December 2011, p. 48.

3404 ■ LARGEST U.S. INVESTMENT SERVICE COMPANIES OVERALL, 2011

Ranked by: Score based on revenue, profits, assets, and market capitalization. **Remarks:** Specific scores not provided. Also notes overall rank in the *Forbes 2000* and figures for each criterion. **Number listed:** 21

1. Berkshire Hathaway Inc.
2. Goldman Sachs Group Inc.
3. Morgan Stanley
4. BlackRock Inc.
5. State Street Corp.
6. Ameriprise Financial Inc.
7. The Charles Schwab Corp.
8. Principal Financial Group Inc.
9. Franklin Resources Inc.
10. CME Group Inc.

Source: *Forbes*, Forbes 2000 (annual), http://www.forbes.com, May 7, 2012.

3405 ■ NEBRASKA'S LARGEST INVESTMENT SERVICE COMPANIES OVERALL, 2011

Ranked by: Score based on revenue, profits, assets, and market capitalization. **Remarks:** Specific scores not provided. Also notes overall rank in the *Forbes 2000* and figures for each criterion. **Number listed:** 2

1. Berkshire Hathaway Inc.
2. TD Ameritrade Holding Corp.

Source: *Forbes*, Forbes 2000 (annual), http://www.forbes.com, May 7, 2012.

3406 ■ THE NETHERLANDS' LARGEST INVESTMENT SERVICE COMPANIES OVERALL, 2011

Ranked by: Score based on revenue, profits, assets, and market capitalization. **Remarks:** Specific scores not provided. Also notes overall rank in the *Forbes 2000* and figures for each criterion. **Number listed:** 2

1. HAL Trust
2. Van Lanschot

Source: *Forbes*, Forbes 2000 (annual), http://www.forbes.com, May 7, 2012.

3407 ■ NEW YORK'S LARGEST INVESTMENT SERVICE COMPANIES OVERALL, 2011

Ranked by: Score based on revenue, profits, assets, and market capitalization. **Remarks:** Specific scores not provided. Also notes overall rank in the *Forbes 2000* and figures for each criterion. **Number listed:** 7

1. Goldman Sachs Group Inc.
2. Morgan Stanley
3. BlackRock Inc.
4. NYSE Euronext Inc.
5. Jefferies Group Inc.
6. The NASDAQ OMX Group Inc.
7. E*Trade Financial Corp.

Source: *Forbes*, Forbes 2000 (annual), http://www.forbes.com, May 7, 2012.

3408 ■ SOUTH AFRICA'S LARGEST INVESTMENT SERVICES COMPANIES OVERALL, 2011

Ranked by: Score based on revenue, profits, assets, and market capitalization. **Remarks:** Specific scores not provided. Also notes overall rank in the *Forbes 2000* and figures for each criterion. **Number listed:** 2

1. RMB Holdings

2. Hosken Consolidated

Source: *Forbes*, Forbes 2000 (annual), http://www.forbes.com, May 7, 2012.

3409 ■ SOUTH KOREA'S LARGEST INVESTMENT SERVICE COMPANIES OVERALL, 2011

Ranked by: Score based on revenue, profits, assets, and market capitalization. **Remarks:** Specific scores not provided. Also notes overall rank in the *Forbes 2000* and figures for each criterion. **Number listed:** 3

1. Shinhan Financial Group Co., Ltd.
2. KB Financial Group
3. Woori Finance Holdings Co., Ltd.

Source: *Forbes*, Forbes 2000 (annual), http://www.forbes.com, May 7, 2012.

3410 ■ SWEDEN'S LARGEST INVESTMENT SERVICE COMPANIES OVERALL, 2011

Ranked by: Score based on revenue, profits, assets, and market capitalization. **Remarks:** Specific scores not provided. Also notes overall rank in the *Forbes 2000* and figures for each criterion. **Number listed:** 2

1. Investor AB
2. Investment AB Kinnevik

Source: *Forbes*, Forbes 2000 (annual), http://www.forbes.com, May 7, 2012.

3411 ■ SWITZERLAND'S LARGEST INVESTMENT SERVICE COMPANIES OVERALL, 2011

Ranked by: Score based on revenue, profits, assets, and market capitalization. **Remarks:** Specific scores not provided. Also notes overall rank in the *Forbes 2000* and figures for each criterion. **Number listed:** 2

1. UBS AG
2. Credit Suisse Group AG

Source: *Forbes*, Forbes 2000 (annual), http://www.forbes.com, May 7, 2012.

3412 ■ TAIWAN'S LARGEST INVESTMENT SERVICE COMPANIES OVERALL, 2011

Ranked by: Score based on revenue, profits, assets, and market capitalization. **Remarks:** Specific scores not provided. Also notes overall rank in the *Forbes 2000* and figures for each criterion. **Number listed:** 4

1. Fubon Financial
2. Mega Financial Holding
3. Taishin Financial Holdings
4. Yuanta Financial Holding

Source: *Forbes*, Forbes 2000 (annual), http://www.forbes.com, May 7, 2012.

3413 ■ TOP CANADIAN INVESTMENT DEALERS, 2010

Ranked by: Revenue, in thousands of Canadian dollars (unless otherwise noted). **Remarks:** Also notes percent change from previous year. **Number listed:** 9

1. RBC Capital Markets, with C$5,887,000 thousand
2. BMO Nesbitt Burns, C$3,279,000
3. Scotia Capital, C$3,179,000
4. TD Securities, C$2,874,000

5. CIBC World Markets, C$1,714,000
6. National Bank Financial & Co., C$1,384,000
7. Canaccord Financial, C$577,537
8. GMP Capital, C$440,736
9. Desjardins Securities, C$340,000

Source: *Report on Business Magazine*, Top 1000 Companies (annual), http://www.reportonbusiness.com, June 2011.

3414 ■ UNITED KINGDOM'S LARGEST INVESTMENT SERVICE COMPANIES OVERALL, 2011

Ranked by: Score based on revenue, profits, assets, and market capitalization. **Remarks:** Specific scores not provided. Also notes overall rank in the *Forbes 2000* and figures for each criterion. **Number listed:** 6

1. Old Mutual plc
2. Investec plc
3. Resolution Ltd.
4. Schroders plc
5. ICAP plc
6. London Stock Exchange Group plc

Source: *Forbes*, Forbes 2000 (annual), http://www.forbes.com, May 7, 2012.

3415 ■ WORLD'S LARGEST INVESTMENT MANAGERS, 2010

Ranked by: Total assets under management, in millions of U.S. dollars. **Number listed:** 500

1. BlackRock (U.S.), with $3,560,968 million
2. State Street Global Advisors Inc. (U.S.), $2,010,447
3. Allianz AG (Germany), $2,009,949
4. Fidelity Investments (U.S.), $1,811,901
5. The Vanguard Group Inc. (U.S.), $1,764,960
6. Deutsche Bank AG (Germany), $1,562,352
7. AXA Group (France), $1,462,966
8. BNP Paribas (France), $1,313,882
9. J. P. Morgan Chase & Co. (U.S.), $1,303,372
10. Capital Group Companies Inc. (U.S.), $1,223,412

Source: *Pensions & Investments*, P&I/Towers Watson World 500 (annual), http://www.pionline.com, October 31, 2011.

3416 ■ WORLD'S LARGEST INVESTMENT SERVICE COMPANIES OVERALL, 2011

Ranked by: Score based on revenue, profits, assets, and market capitalization. **Remarks:** Specific scores not provided. Also notes country, overall rank in the *Forbes 2000,* and figures for each criterion. **Number listed:** 78

1. Berkshire Hathaway Inc.
2. UBS AG
3. Goldman Sachs Group Inc.
4. Morgan Stanley
5. Credit Suisse
6. Shinhan Financial Group Co., Ltd.
7. KB Financial Group Inc.
8. BlackRock Inc.
9. State Street Corp.
10. Woori Finance Holdings Co., Ltd.

Source: *Forbes*, Forbes 2000 (annual), http://www.forbes.com, May 7, 2012.

Investment Trusts
See: **Mutual Funds**

Investors

3417 ■ COUNTRIES WITH THE BEST PROTECTION OF MINORITY SHAREHOLDERS' INTERESTS, 2010

Ranked by: Score, on a scale of seven, based on the level of protection and enforcement of laws to protect the interests of minority shareholders. **Number listed:** 142

1. Sweden, with 6 points
2. Finland, 5.9
3. South Africa, 5.8
4. Norway, 5.7
5. Puerto Rico, 5.6
5. Singapore, 5.6
5. Bahrain, 5.6
8. New Zealand, 5.5
8. Saudi Arabia, 5.5
8. Canada, 5.5
8. Denmark, 5.5

Source: *Global Competitiveness Report*, (annual), World Economic Forum, 2011, p. 409.

3418 ■ COUNTRIES WITH THE WORST PROTECTION OF MINORITY SHAREHOLDERS' INTERESTS, 2010

Ranked by: Score, on a scale of seven, based on the level of protection and enforcement of laws to protect the interests of minority shareholders. **Number listed:** 142

1. Haiti, with 2.5 points
2. Kyrgyz Republic, 2.8
2. Serbia, 2.8
2. Bosnia & Herzegovina, 2.8
5. Ukraine, 2.9
5. Mongolia, 2.9
7. Timor-Leste, 3.0
8. Russian Federation, 3.1
8. Burundi, 3.1
8. Yemen, 3.1

Source: *Global Competitiveness Report*, (annual), World Economic Forum, 2011, p. 409.

Iron

3419 ■ AUSTRALIA'S LARGEST IRON AND STEEL COMPANIES OVERALL, 2011

Ranked by: Score based on revenue, profits, assets, and market capitalization. **Remarks:** Specific scores not provided. Also notes overall rank in the *Forbes 2000* and figures for each criterion. **Number listed:** 2

1. Fortescue Metals Group
2. Bluescope Steel

Source: *Forbes*, Forbes 2000 (annual), http://www.forbes.com, May 7, 2012.

3420 ■ BRAZIL'S LARGEST IRON AND STEEL COMPANIES OVERALL, 2011

Ranked by: Score based on revenue, profits, assets, and market capitalization. **Remarks:** Specific scores not provided. Also notes overall rank in the *Forbes 2000* and figures for each criterion. **Number listed:** 3

1. Companhia Siderurgica Nacional (CSN)
2. Metalurgica Gerdau SA
3. Usiminas Siderurgicas de Minas Gerais SA

Source: *Forbes*, Forbes 2000 (annual), http://www.forbes.com, May 7, 2012.

3421 ■ CHINA'S LARGEST IRON AND STEEL COMPANIES OVERALL, 2011

Ranked by: Score based on revenue, profits, assets, and market capitalization. **Remarks:** Specific scores not provided. Also notes overall rank in the *Forbes 2000* and figures for each criterion. **Number listed:** 10

1. Baoshan Iron & Steel Co., Ltd.
2. Angang Steel Co., Ltd.
3. Fosun International Ltd.
4. Hebei Iron & Steel
5. Wuhan Iron & Steel (Group) Corp.
6. Shanxi Taigang Stainless
7. Panzhihua New Steel & Vanadium Co., Ltd.
8. Hunan Valin Steel
9. Maanshan Iron & Steel
10. Inner Mongolia Baotou Steel

Source: *Forbes*, Forbes 2000 (annual), http://www.forbes.com, May 7, 2012.

3422 ■ INDIA'S LARGEST IRON AND STEEL COMPANIES OVERALL, 2011

Ranked by: Score based on revenue, profits, assets, and market capitalization. **Remarks:** Specific scores not provided. Also notes overall rank in the *Forbes 2000* and figures for each criterion. **Number listed:** 4

1. Tata Steel Ltd.
2. Steel Authority of India Ltd.
3. Jindal Steel & Power
4. JSW Steel

Source: *Forbes*, Forbes 2000 (annual), http://www.forbes.com, May 7, 2012.

3423 ■ JAPAN'S LARGEST IRON AND STEEL COMPANIES OVERALL, 2011

Ranked by: Score based on revenue, profits, assets, and market capitalization. **Remarks:** Specific scores not provided. Also notes overall rank in the *Forbes 2000* and figures for each criterion. **Number listed:** 4

1. Nippon Steel Corp.
2. JFE Holdings Inc.
3. Kobe Steel
4. Sumitomo Metal Industries

Source: *Forbes*, Forbes 2000 (annual), http://www.forbes.com, May 7, 2012.

3424 ■ LARGEST U.S. IRON AND STEEL COMPANIES OVERALL, 2011

Ranked by: Score based on revenue, profits, assets, and market capitalization. **Remarks:** Specific scores not provided. Also notes overall rank in the *Forbes 2000* and figures for each criterion. **Number listed:** 4

1. Nucor Corp.
2. Cliffs Natural Resources Inc.

3. United States Steel Corp.

4. Reliance Steel & Aluminum Co.

Source: *Forbes*, Forbes 2000 (annual), http://www.forbes.com, May 7, 2012.

3425 ■ LUXEMBOURG'S LARGEST IRON AND STEEL COMPANIES OVERALL, 2011

Ranked by: Score based on revenue, profits, assets, and market capitalization. **Remarks:** Specific scores not provided. Also notes overall rank in the *Forbes 2000* and figures for each criterion. **Number listed:** 2

1. ArcelorMittal

2. Ternium

Source: *Forbes*, Forbes 2000 (annual), http://www.forbes.com, May 7, 2012.

3426 ■ RUSSIA'S LARGEST IRON AND STEEL COMPANIES OVERALL, 2011

Ranked by: Score based on revenue, profits, assets, and market capitalization. **Remarks:** Specific scores not provided. Also notes overall rank in the *Forbes 2000* and figures for each criterion. **Number listed:** 5

1. Novolipetsk Steel

2. OAO Severstal

3. Mechel

4. Magnitogorsk Iron & Steel

5. TMK

Source: *Forbes*, Forbes 2000 (annual), http://www.forbes.com, May 7, 2012.

3427 ■ SOUTH KOREA'S LARGEST IRON AND STEEL COMPANIES OVERALL, 2011

Ranked by: Score based on revenue, profits, assets, and market capitalization. **Remarks:** Specific scores not provided. Also notes overall rank in the *Forbes 2000* and figures for each criterion. **Number listed:** 2

1. Pohang Iron & Steel Co., Ltd. (POSCO)

2. Hyundai Steel Co.

Source: *Forbes*, Forbes 2000 (annual), http://www.forbes.com, May 7, 2012.

3428 ■ WORLD'S LARGEST IRON AND STEEL COMPANIES OVERALL, 2011

Ranked by: Score based on revenue, profits, assets, and market capitalization. **Remarks:** Specific scores not provided. Also notes country, overall rank in the *Forbes 2000,* and figures for each criterion. **Number listed:** 43

1. ArcelorMittal

2. Pohang Iron & Steel Co., Ltd. (POSCO)

3. Nippon Steel Corp.

4. Baoshan Iron & Steel Co., Ltd.

5. JFE Holdings Inc.

6. Tata Steel Ltd.

7. China Steel Corp.

8. Companhia Siderurgica Nacional (CSN)

9. Nucor Corp.

10. CITIC Pacific Ltd.

Source: *Forbes*, Forbes 2000 (annual), http://www.forbes.com, May 7, 2012.

3429 ■ WORLD'S MOST VALUABLE IRON/STEEL BRANDS, 2011

Ranked by: Brand value, in millions of U.S. dollars. **Remarks:** Also notes rank within the *Global 500* for current and previous year, figures for current and previous year, country, and brand rating. Ranking is available online only. **Number listed:** 4

1. ArcelorMittal, with $4,027 million

2. Nippon Steel, $3,367

3. ThyssenKrupp, $3,320

4. POSCO, $2,490

Source: *Global 500*, (annual), Brand Finance plc, March 2012.

Juice Bars

3430 ■ TOP JUICE BAR FRANCHISES, 2012

Ranked by: Cumulative score based on financial strength and stability, growth rate, size of the system, number of years in business, the length of time franchising, start-up costs, litigation, percentage of terminations, and whether the company provides financing. **Remarks:** Specific scores not provided. Also notes overall rank within the *Franchise 500,* contact information, description, year founded, year started franchising, states where registered, available U.S. regions, where seeking foreign expansion, number of franchised and company-owned units for past three years, start-up costs, franchise fees, royalty fees, and type of financing available. **Number listed:** 5

1. Smoothie King

2. Nrgize Lifestyle Cafe

3. MixStirs

4. Robeks Premium Fruit Smoothies

5. Surf City Squeeze

Source: *Entrepreneur*, Franchise 500 (annual), January 2012, p. 168-169.

Junk Bonds
See also: **Bond Funds**

3431 ■ TOP MANAGERS OF GLOBAL INVESTMENT-GRADE BONDS, 2011

Ranked by: Proceeds, in billions of dollars. **Remarks:** Also notes market share for current and previous year. **Number listed:** 10

1. J. P. Morgan Chase & Co., with $141.8 billion

2. Bank of America Corp./Merrill Lynch, $130.6

3. Citigroup Inc., $106.5

4. Morgan Stanley, $105

5. Goldman Sachs Group Inc., $92.2

6. Deutsche Bank AG, $92.1

7. Barclays Capital Inc., $90.5

8. HSBC Holdings plc, $81.1

9. BNP Paribas SA, $72.4

10. The Royal Bank of Scotland Group plc, $70

Source: *The Wall Street Journal*, Year-End Review (annual), January 3, 2012, p. R9.

Labor Unions

3432 ■ LARGEST HEALTHCARE UNIONS, 2011

Ranked by: National membership within the healthcare industry. **Remarks:** Also notes headquarters, figures for previous year, and Web site. **Number listed:** 13

1. SEIU Healthcare, with 1,200,000 members
2. American Federation of State, County & Municipal Employees, 360,000
3. National Nurses United, 170,000
4. National Union of Hospital & Health Care Employees, 72,500
5. National Federation of Nurses, 71,000
6. American Federation of Teachers, 70,000
7. United Steelworkers, 45,000
8. International Brotherhood of Teamsters, 39,000
9. Office & Professional Employees International Union, 30,000
10. United Auto Workers, 13,600

Source: *Modern Healthcare*, Largest Healthcare Unions (annual), November 28, 2011, p. 32.

Labor-Management Relations
See: **Industrial Relations**

Landscape Architecture
See: **Lawn Care Services**

Law Firms

3433 ■ BEST U.S. LAW FIRMS, 2011

Ranked by: Score based on revenue per lawyer, pro bono work, associate satisfaction, and diversity. **Remarks:** Also notes location and score for each criterion. **Number listed:** 20

1. Hughes Hubbard & Reed LLP, with 1,141 points
2. Munger, Tolles & Olson LLP, 1,138
3. Paul Hastings Janofsky & Walker LLP, 1,124
4. Gibson, Dunn & Crutcher LLP, 1,079
5. Debevoise & Plimpton LLP, 1,065
6. Latham & Watkins LLP, 1,064
7. Milbank, Tweed, Hadley & McCloy, 1,062
7. Skadden, Arps, Slate, Meagher & Flom LLP, 1,062
9. Davis, Polk & Wardwell LLP, 1,050
9. Paul, Weiss, Rifkind, Wharton & Garrison LLP, 1,050

Source: *American Lawyer*, The A-List (annual), July 2011.

3434 ■ LARGEST COLORADO-BASED LAW FIRMS, 2010

Ranked by: Number of Colorado employees. **Remarks:** Also notes contact information and total number of employees. **Number listed:** 10

1. Holland & Hart LLP, with 477 employees
2. Sherman & Howard LLC, 322
3. Davis Graham & Stubbs LLP, 285
4. Brownstein Hyatt Farber Schreck LLP, 261
5. Holme Roberts & Owen LLP, 258
6. Faegre & Benson LLP, 184
7. Rothgerber Johnson & Lyons LLP, 149
8. Kutak Rock, 126
9. Hogan Lovells U.S. LLP, 118

10. Patton Boggs LLP, 76

Source: *ColoradoBiz*, Top Professional Services (annual), December 2011, p. 48.

3435 ■ LARGEST DENVER-AREA LAW FIRMS, 2011

Ranked by: Number of area lawyers as of February. **Remarks:** Also notes contact information, rank for previous year, areas of specialty, top local executive, and total number of employees and offices. **Number listed:** 50

1. Holland & Hart LLP, with 195 lawyers
2. Davis Graham & Stubbs LLP, 135
3. Sherman & Howard LLC, 134
4. Brownstein Hyatt Farber Schreck LLP, 113
4. Holme Roberts & Owen LLP, 113
6. Faegre & Benson LLP, 101
7. Hogan Lovells U.S. LLP, 70
8. Kutak Rock LLP, 68
9. Hall & Evans LLC, 64
10. Wheeler Trigg O'Donnell LLP, 62

Source: *Denver Business Journal*, Book of Lists (annual), December 16, 2011, p. 22+.

3436 ■ LARGEST LAW FIRMS IN CALIFORNIA, 2010

Ranked by: Number of lawyers in California. **Remarks:** Also notes rank and figures for previous year, number of lawyers firmwide, number of partners, number of female partners, and number of minority partners. **Number listed:** 50

1. Latham & Watkins LLP, with 625 lawyers
2. Morrison & Foerster LLP, 543
3. Lewis Brisbois Bisgaard & Smith LLP, 501
4. Sheppard, Mullin, Richter & Hampton LLP, 458
5. O'Melveny & Myers LLP, 445
6. Gibson, Dunn & Crutcher LLP, 424
7. Wilson Sonsini Goodrich & Rosati, 410
8. Orrick Herrington & Sutcliffe LLP, 398
9. DLA Piper, 355
10. Cooley Godward Kronish, 346

Source: *California Lawyer*, CA 50 (annual), September 2011.

3437 ■ LARGEST LAW FIRMS IN FLORIDA, 2011

Ranked by: Number of lawyers in Florida. **Remarks:** Also notes rank for previous year, contact information, total number of lawyers and employees, number of offices in Florida, specialty practice areas, and top executive in Florida. **Number listed:** 25

1. Akerman Senterfitt, with 408 lawyers
2. Greenberg Traurig PA, 357
3. Holland & Knight LLP, 340
4. Carlton Fields PA, 279
5. GrayRobinson PA, 253

Source: *Florida Trend*, Largest Law Firms (annual), http://www.floridatrend.com, February 2012.

3438 ■ LARGEST LAW FIRMS IN LOS ANGELES COUNTY, 2012

Ranked by: Number of Los Angeles County attorneys. **Remarks:** Also notes contact information, number of partners and equity partners, revenue, profits per partner, practice areas, headquarters, year established, number of offices, executive director, and managing partner. **Number listed:** 50

1. Gibson, Dunn & Crutcher LLP, with 262 attorneys
2. O'Melveny & Myers LLP, 259
3. Lewis Brisbois Bisgaard & Smith LLP, 257
4. Latham & Watkins LLP, 249
5. Sheppard Mullin Richter & Hampton LLP, 208
6. Quinn Emanuel Urquhart & Sullivan LLP, 192
7. Manatt Phelps & Phillips LLP, 150
8. Sidley Austin LLP, 149
9. Munger Tolles & Olson LLP, 147
10. Paul Hastings LLP, 140

Source: *Los Angeles Business Journal*, Largest Law Firms (annual), http://www.labusinessjournal.com, March 2012.

3439 ■ LARGEST LAW FIRMS IN ORANGE COUNTY, CALIFORNIA, 2010

Ranked by: Number of county attorneys. **Remarks:** Also notes rank for previous year, contact information, number of attorneys firmwide, number of partners, number of county employees, areas of practice, partial list of clients, number of offices firmwide, and top local official. **Number listed:** 51

1. Knobbe, Martens, Olson & Bear LLP, with 163 attorneys
2. Rutan & Tucker LLP, 146
3. Stradling Yocca Carlson & Rauth, 89
4. Gibson, Dunn & Crutcher LLP, 73
5. Latham & Watkins LLP, 70
6. Snell & Wilmer LLP, 67
7. O'Melveny & Myers LLP, 62
8. Sheppard, Mullin, Richter & Hampton LLP, 59
9. Jones Day, 58
10. Lewis Brisbois Bisgaard & Smith LLP, 54

Source: *Orange County Business Journal*, Largest Law Firms (annual), January 23, 2012, p. 36-40.

3440 ■ LARGEST LAW FIRMS IN SOUTH CAROLINA, 2011

Ranked by: Number of attorneys statewide. **Remarks:** Also notes contact information, number of employees, managing partner, other office locations, and year founded. **Number listed:** 23

1. Nelson Mulling Riley & Scarborough LLP, with 286 attorneys
2. Haynsworth Sinkler Boyd PA, 132
3. Nexsen Pruet LLC, 127
4. McNair Law Firm PA, 112
5. Turner Padget Graham & Laney PA, 90
6. McAngus Goudelock & Courie LLC, 70
7. Womble Carlyle Sandridge & Rice PLLC, 65
8. Ogletree Deakings Nash Smoak & Stewart PC, 61
9. Rogers Townsend & Thomas PC, 58
10. Parker Poe Adams & Bernstein LLP, 54

Source: *South Carolina Business*, Book of Lists (annual), 2011, p. 26.

3441 ■ LARGEST MINORITY-OWNED LAW FIRMS IN NEW YORK, 2011

Ranked by: Number of permanent full-time attorneys. **Remarks:** Ranking includes only firms based in New York. Also notes contact information and managing partner or principal. **Number listed:** 28

1. Morris Duffy Alonso & Faley, with 43 attorneys
2. Brown & Hutchinson, 12
3. Dai & Associates, 10
4. Wong, Wong & Associates, 9
5. Wilson & Chan, 8
6. Cannon & Acosta, 6
6. DeSimone, Aviles, Shorter & Oxamendi, 6
6. Krez & Flores, 6
9. Rosado, Chechanover & Bayrasli, 5
10. The Law Firm of Ravi Batra, 4
10. Law Offices of David J. Hernandez & Associates, 4
10. Maduegbuna Cooper, 4
10. Pettus & Williams, 4

Source: *New York Law Journal*, NYLJ 100 (annual), http://www.law.com, June 6, 2011.

3442 ■ LARGEST PRIVATE LAW OFFICES IN NEW YORK, 2011

Ranked by: Number of lawyers in the largest New York office. **Remarks:** Also notes location and total firm size. **Number listed:** 100

1. Skadden, Arps, Slate, Meagher & Flom LLP, with 756 lawyers
2. Paul, Weiss, Rifkind, Wharton & Garrison LLP, 619
3. Simpson Thacher & Bartlett LLP, 585
4. Davis, Polk & Wardwell LLP, 575
5. Weil, Gotshal & Manges LLP, 567
6. Sullivan & Cromwell LLP, 505
7. Cleary, Gottlieb, Steen & Hamilton LLP, 482
8. Dewey & LeBoeuf, 479
9. Cravath, Swaine & Moore LLP, 473
10. Debevoise & Plimpton LLP, 471

Source: *New York Law Journal*, NYLJ 100 (annual), http://www.law.com, June 6, 2011.

3443 ■ LARGEST U.S. LAW FIRMS BY NUMBER OF ATTORNEYS, 2011

Ranked by: Total number of full-type equivalent attorneys. **Remarks:** Also notes rank and figures for previous year, percent change, largest U.S. office, and breakdown of partners and attorneys by type. **Number listed:** 250

1. Baker & McKenzie LLP, with 3,805 attorneys
2. DLA Piper, 3,746
3. Jones Day, 2,407
4. Hogan Lovells International LLP, 2,253
5. Latham & Watkins LLP, 2,014
6. White & Case LLP, 1,906
7. Skadden, Arps, Slate, Meagher & Flom LLP, 1,832
8. K & L Gates LLP, 1,762
9. Greenberg Traurig PA, 1,699
10. Sidley Austin, 1,592

Source: *National Law Journal*, NLJ 250 (annual), http://www.nlj.com, April 2012.

3444 ■ TOP LAW FIRMS IN CONTRACTS LITIGATION, 2010

Ranked by: Number of mentions in a survey regarding corporate legal representation. **Number listed:** 17

1. Nilan Johnson, with 8 mentions
2. Morgan, Lewis & Bockius LLP, 5
2. Morrison & Foerster LLP, 5
4. Nelson Mullins, 4
4. Perkins Cole LLP, 4
4. Sedgwick, 4
7. Alston & Bird LLP, 3
7. Baker Hostetler, 3
7. Barger & Wolen, 3
7. Bryan Cave LLP, 3
7. Foley & Lardner LLP, 3
7. Goodwin Procter LLP, 3
7. Gordon & Rees, 3

Source: *Corporate Counsel*, Who Represents America's Biggest Companies (annual), http://www.law.com, October 2011.

3445 ■ TOP LAW FIRMS IN CORPORATE INTELLECTUAL PROPERTY LAW, 2010

Ranked by: Number of mentions in a survey regarding corporate legal representation. **Number listed:** 24

1. Fish & Richardson PC, with 13 mentions
2. DLA Piper, 9
3. Fulbright & Jaworski LLP, 8
3. Williams, Morgan, 8
5. Alston & Bird LLP, 7
5. Fenwick & West, 7
7. Duane Morris, 6
7. Howrey LLP, 6
7. Kilpatrick Townsend & Stockton, 6
7. Morris, Nichols, 6
7. Winston & Strawn LLP, 6

Source: *Corporate Counsel*, Who Represents America's Biggest Companies (annual), http://www.law.com, October 2011.

3446 ■ TOP LAW FIRMS IN CORPORATE LABOR LAW, 2010

Ranked by: Number of mentions in a survey regarding corporate legal representation. **Number listed:** 17

1. Ogletree Deakins, with 12 mentions
2. Littler Mendelson PC, 11
3. Jackson Lewis LLP, 8
3. Paul Hastings Janofsky & Walker LLP, 8
5. Morgan, Lewis & Bockius LLP, 7
6. Ford & Harrison LLP, 6
7. Hunton & Williams, 4
7. Jones Day, 4
7. Orrick Herrington & Sutcliffe LLP, 4
7. Sedgwick, 4

Source: *Corporate Counsel*, Who Represents America's Biggest Companies (annual), http://www.law.com, October 2011.

3447 ■ TOP LAW FIRMS IN CORPORATE LAW, 2010

Ranked by: Number of mentions in a survey regarding corporate legal representation. **Number listed:** 48

1. Morgan, Lewis & Bockius LLP, with 17 mentions
2. DLA Piper, 13

2. Fish & Richardson PC, 13
2. Fulbright & Jaworski LLP, 13
2. Littler Mendelson PC, 13
2. Perkins Cole LLP, 13
7. Alston & Bird LLP, 12
7. Jones Day, 12
7. Morrison & Foerster LLP, 12
7. Ogletree Deakins, 12

Source: *Corporate Counsel*, Who Represents America's Biggest Companies (annual), http://www.law.com, October 2011.

3448 ■ TOP LAW FIRMS IN TORTS LITIGATION, 2010

Ranked by: Number of mentions in a survey regarding corporate legal representation. **Number listed:** 25

1. Campbell, Campbell, Edwards, with 6 mentions
1. Lightfoot, Franklin, 6
1. Shook, Hardy, 6
4. Lewis Brisbois Bisgaard & Smith LLP, 5
5. Baker, Donelson, Bearman, Caldwell & Berkowitz PC, 4
5. Bryan Cave LLP, 4
5. Reed Smith, 4
5. Snell & Wilmer LLP, 4
9. Bowman & Brooke, 3
9. Butler, Snow, 3
9. Carlton Fields PA, 3
9. Dinsmore & Shohl, 3
9. Drinker Biddle & Reath LLP, 3

Source: *Corporate Counsel*, Who Represents America's Biggest Companies (annual), http://www.law.com, October 2011.

3449 ■ TOP PRO BONO LAW FIRMS, 2011

Ranked by: Score based on average pro bono house per lawyer and the percentage of lawyers who perform more than 20 hours of pro bono work. **Remarks:** Also notes figures for each criterion. **Number listed:** 200

1. Covington & Burling LLP, with 122 points
2. Hughes Hubbard & Reed LLP, 113.2
2. Paul Hastings Janofsky & Walker LLP, 113.2
4. Jenner & Block LLP, 109.4
5. Dewey & LeBoeuf, 108.8
6. Milbank, Tweed, Hadley & McCloy, 107
7. Holland & Hart, 102.8
8. Foley Hoag, 98.4
9. Robins, Kaplan, Miller & Ciresi LLP, 97
10. Gibson, Dunn & Crutcher LLP, 96.2

Source: *American Lawyer*, Pro Bono Report (annual), July 2011.

3450 ■ WORLD'S TOP LAW FIRMS BY LAWYER, 2011

Ranked by: Number of lawyers. **Remarks:** Also notes location, countries in which the firm has offices, and percentage of lawyers outside home country. **Number listed:** 100

1. Baker & McKenzie LLP, with 3,805 lawyers
2. DLA Piper, 3,348
3. Jones Day, 2,502
4. Clifford Chance LLP, 2,466
5. Hogan Lovells International LLP, 2,363

6. Linklaters LLP, 2,134
7. Allen & Overy LLP, 2,112
8. Garrigues, 2,037
9. Freshfields Bruckhaus Deringer, 2,034
10. Latham & Watkins LLP, 1,931

Source: *American Lawyer*, Global 100 (annual), October 2011.

3451 ■ WORLD'S TOP LAW FIRMS BY PROFITS PER PARTNER, 2011

Ranked by: Profits per equity partner, in U.S. dollars. **Remarks:** Also notes number of equity partners and gross revenue. **Number listed:** 10

1. Wachtell, Lipton, Rosen & Katz, with $4,345,000
2. Quinn Emanuel Urquhart & Sullivan LLP, $3,620,000
3. Sullivan & Cromwell LLP, $3,250,000
4. Cravath, Swaine & Moore LLP, $3,170,000
5. Kirkland & Ellis LLP, $3,075,000
6. Paul, Weiss, Rifkind, Wharton & Garrison LLP, $3,050,000
7. Simpson Thacher & Bartlett LLP, $2,640,000
8. Slaughter & May, $2,625,000
9. Cleary, Gottlieb, Steen & Hamilton LLP, $2,605,000
10. Milbank, Tweed, Hadley & McCloy, $2,490,000

Source: *American Lawyer*, Global 100 (annual), October 2011.

3452 ■ WORLD'S TOP LAW FIRMS BY REVENUE, 2011

Ranked by: Gross revenue, in U.S. dollars. **Remarks:** Also notes rank for previous year, number of lawyers, and revenue per lawyer. **Number listed:** 100

1. Baker & McKenzie LLP, with $2,265,000,000
2. Skadden, Arps, Slate, Meagher & Flom LLP, $2,100,000,000
3. DLA Piper, $1,961,000,000
4. Latham & Watkins LLP, $1,929,000,000
5. Clifford Chance LLP, $1,883,500,000
6. Linklaters LLP, $1,854,000,000
7. Freshfields Bruckhaus Deringer, $1,761,500,000
8. Allen & Overy LLP, $1,730,500,000
9. Hogan Lovells, $1,664,500,000
10. Kirkland & Ellis LLP, $1,625,000,000

Source: *American Lawyer*, Global 100 (annual), October 2011.

3453 ■ WORLD'S TOP LAW FIRMS BY REVENUE PER PARTNER, 2011

Ranked by: Revenue per equity partner, in U.S. dollars. **Number listed:** 10

1. Wachtell, Lipton, Rosen & Katz, with $2,290,000
2. Sullivan & Cromwell LLP, $1,440,000
3. Slaughter & May, $1,280,000
4. Quinn Emanuel Urquhart & Sullivan LLP, $1,205,000
5. Cravath, Swaine & Moore LLP, $1,195,000
6. Kirkland & Ellis LLP, $1,180,000

7. Davis, Polk & Wardwell LLP, $1,175,000
8. Simpson Thacher & Bartlett LLP, $1,140,000
9. Skadden, Arps, Slate, Meagher & Flom LLP, $1,130,000
10. Milbank, Tweed, Hadley & McCloy, $1,085,000

Source: *American Lawyer*, Global 100 (annual), October 2011.

Lawn Care Services

3454 ■ FASTEST-GROWING LANDSCAPING COMPANIES BY EMPLOYEES, 2009-2010

Ranked by: Annual growth in number of employees, in percent. **Number listed:** 25

1. RCI, with 91.8%
2. Maldonaldo Nursery & Landscaping, 55.5%
3. Schultz Industries, 52.1%
4. Cornerstone Solutions Group, 51.9%
5. Denison Landscaping Group, 42%
6. Heads Up Landscape, 36.2%
7. Dixie Landscape Co., 34.5%
8. Fairco, 33.3%
9. Earthworks Inc., 27.9%
10. Reliable Property Services, 26.1%

Source: *Landscape Management*, LM 150 (annual), June 2011, p. S14.

3455 ■ FASTEST-GROWING LANDSCAPING COMPANIES BY REVENUE, 2009-2010

Ranked by: Annual revenue growth, in percent. **Number listed:** 25

1. Earthworks, with 37.4%
2. RCI, 30.1%
3. The Highbridge Corp., 25%
4. Lucas Tree Expert Co., 23.9%
5. Mainscape, 22.4%
6. PROscape, 21.9%
7. Hoffman Landscapes, 21.8%
8. Grant & Power Landscapes, 20.3%
9. James River Grounds Management, 20%
10. Ryan Lawn & Tree, 18.5%

Source: *Landscape Management*, LM 150 (annual), June 2011, p. S16.

3456 ■ FASTEST-GROWING LANDSCAPING COMPANIES BY REVENUE PER EMPLOYEE, 2009-2010

Ranked by: Annual growth in revenue per employee, in percent. **Number listed:** 26

1. Ryan Lawn & Tree, with 89%
2. Precision Landscape Management, 71.7%
3. Shearon Environmental Design Co., 65.1%
4. Russell Landscape Group, 64.1%
5. Meadows Farms, 61.9%
6. Parker Interior Plantscape, 60.4%
7. Fairco, 50%
8. HighGrove Partners, 40.2%

9. Dixie Landscape Co., 37.4%
10. ArtisTree Landscape Maintenance & Design, 35.3%

Source: *Landscape Management*, LM 150 (annual), June 2011, p. S14.

3457 ■ LARGEST COMMERCIAL LANDSCAPING COMPANIES, 2010

Ranked by: Revenue, in U.S. dollars. **Number listed:** 25

1. ValleyCrest Landscape Cos., with $835,000,000
2. The Brickman Group Ltd., $565,255,600
3. USM Inc., $133,305,900
4. U.S. Lawns, $102,000,000
5. Ambius, $95,314,572
6. ISS Grounds Control, $68,485,320
7. Ruppert Landscape, $65,338,681
8. Vila & Son Landscaping Corp., $60,786,000
9. OneSource Landscape & Golf Services Inc., $60,000,000
10. Gothic Landscape Inc., $58,225,000

Source: *Landscape Management*, LM 150 (annual), June 2011, p. S14.

3458 ■ LARGEST LANDSCAPING COMPANIES, 2010

Ranked by: Revenue, in U.S. dollars. **Remarks:** Also notes headquarters, number of employees, annual growth, revenue per employee, and breakdown by commercial and residential business. **Number listed:** 150

1. TruGreen Lawncare & Landcare, with $1,335,175,000
2. ValleyCrest Landscape Cos., $835,000,000
3. The Brickman Group Ltd., $807,508,000
4. Davey Tree Expert Co., $591,732,000
5. ISS Grounds Control, $380,474,000
6. Scotts Lawn Service, $290,000,000
7. The F. A. Bartlett Tree Expert Co., $158,000,000
8. USM Inc., $133,305,900
9. Massey Services Inc., $129,011,218
10. Weed Man, $105,000,000

Source: *Landscape Management*, LM 150 (annual), June 2011, p. S4-S9.

3459 ■ LARGEST LANDSCAPING COMPANIES IN THE MIDWESTERN U.S., 2010

Ranked by: Revenue, in U.S. dollars. **Number listed:** 25

1. The Brickman Group Ltd., with $242,252,400
2. Scotts Lawn Service, $87,000,000
3. Acres Group, $41,151,872
4. Mariani Landscape, $35,000,000
5. The Bruce Co. of Wisconsin, $32,126,000
6. Ambius, $27,920,430
7. Spring-Green Lawn Care Corp., $23,950,500
8. Landscape Concepts Management, $23,656,000
9. Chalet, $23,100,000
10. Scott Byron & Co., $22,148,000

Source: *Landscape Management*, LM 150 (annual), June 2011, p. S11.

3460 ■ LARGEST LANDSCAPING COMPANIES IN THE NORTHEASTERN U.S., 2010

Ranked by: Revenue, in U.S. dollars. **Number listed:** 25

1. The Brickman Group Ltd., with $282,627,800
2. Scotts Lawn Service, $87,000,000
3. The F. A. Bartlett Tree Expert Co., $83,740,000
4. Lawn Doctor, $56,440,000
5. SavATree, $50,139,180
6. Ruppert Landscape, $39,203,209
7. Denison Landscaping Group, $36,000,000
8. Lipinski Outdoor Services, $32,067,163
9. NaturaLawn of America, $28,690,000
10. Shearon Environmental Design Co., $22,701,518

Source: *Landscape Management*, LM 150 (annual), June 2011, p. S10.

3461 ■ LARGEST LANDSCAPING COMPANIES IN THE SOUTHEASTERN U.S., 2010

Ranked by: Revenue, in U.S. dollars. **Number listed:** 25

1. The Brickman Group Ltd., with $169,56,680
2. Massey Services, $129,011,218
3. Scotts Lawn Service, $87,000,000
4. Vila & Son Landscaping Corp., $61,400,000
5. Yellowstone Landscape Group, $44,400,000
6. Nanak's Landscaping, $34,500,000
7. Bartlett Tree Experts, $26,860,000
8. Ruppert Landscape, $26,135,472
9. The Greenery, $25,200,000
10. James River Grounds Management, $23,721,283

Source: *Landscape Management*, LM 150 (annual), June 2011, p. S11.

3462 ■ LARGEST LANDSCAPING COMPANIES IN THE SOUTHWESTERN U.S., 2010

Ranked by: Revenue, in U.S. dollars. **Number listed:** 25

1. The Brickman Group Ltd., with $32,300,320
2. ISS Grounds Control, $30,437,920
3. The Groundskeeper, $29,826,925
4. Yellowstone Landscape Group, $29,600,000
5. AAA Landscape, $22,275,000
6. Maldonado Nursery & Landscaping, $21,000,000
7. DLC Resources, $20,372,200
8. Scotts Lawn Service, $20,300,000
9. Heads Up Landscape, $18,500,000
10. Clean Scapes, $18,226,000

Source: *Landscape Management*, LM 150 (annual), June 2011, p. S10.

3463 ■ LARGEST LANDSCAPING COMPANIES IN THE WESTERN U.S., 2010

Ranked by: Revenue, in U.S. dollars. **Number listed:** 25

1. The Brickman Group Ltd., with $80,750,800

2. Gothic Landscape, $48,635,000
3. Marina Landscape Inc., $43,000,000
4. Jensen Corp., $41,000,000
5. Sierra Landscape Co., $32,000,000
6. Cagwin & Dorward, $27,464,594
7. Mission Landscape Cos., $25,000,000
8. Terracare Associates, $24,500,000
9. Ambius, $21,181,015
10. Bemus Landscape, $19,300,000

Source: *Landscape Management*, LM 150 (annual), June 2011, p. S10.

3464 ■ LARGEST LAWN AND LANDSCAPE COMPANIES, 2011

Ranked by: Revenue, in dollars. **Remarks:** Also nots headquarters, percent change from previous year, and number of full-time and seasonal employees. **Number listed:** 100

1. The TruGreen Cos., with $1,100,000,000
2. ValleyCrest Landscape Cos., $850,000,000
3. The Brickman Group, $844,300,000
4. The Davey Tree Expert Co., $646,034,000
5. USM Services, $363,246,000
6. Scotts LawnService, $278,500,000
7. TruGreen LandCare, $248,000,000
8. Bartlett Tree Experts, $167,000,000
9. U.S. Lawns, $117,200,000
10. Weed Man, $110,000,000

Source: *Lawn & Landscape*, Top 100 (annual), May 2012, p. 52-53.

3465 ■ LARGEST RESIDENTIAL LANDSCAPING COMPANIES, 2010

Ranked by: Revenue, in U.S. dollars. **Number listed:** 25

1. Davey Tree Expert Co., with $591,732,000
2. Scotts Lawn Service, $281,300,000
3. The Brickman Group Ltd., $242,252,400
4. The F. A. Bartlett Tree Expert Co., $126,400,000
5. Massey Services Inc., $117,400,208
6. Weed Man, $99,750,000
7. Lawn Doctor Inc., $82,170,000
8. SavATree, $46,833,300
9. NaturaLawn of America, $33,975,000
10. Mariani Landscape Management, $31,500,000

Source: *Landscape Management*, LM 150 (annual), June 2011, p. S14.

3466 ■ TOP LAWN CARE FRANCHISES, 2012

Ranked by: Cumulative score based on financial strength and stability, growth rate, size of the system, number of years in business, the length of time franchising, start-up costs, litigation, percentage of terminations, and whether the company provides financing. **Remarks:** Specific scores not provided. Also notes overall rank within the *Franchise 500,* contact information, description, year founded, year started franchising, states where registered, available U.S. regions, where seeking foreign expansion, number of franchised and company-owned units for past three years, start-up costs, franchise fees, royalty fees, and type of financing available. **Number listed:** 5

1. Weed Man
2. Lawn Doctor Inc.
3. U.S. Lawns
4. Spring-Green Lawn Care
5. NaturaLawn of America

Source: *Entrepreneur*, Franchise 500 (annual), January 2012, p. 184-185.

Layoffs

3467 ■ AMERICA'S BEST COMPANIES WITH THE FEWEST LAYOFFS, 2012

Ranked by: Companies among the 100 Best Companies to Work For that have never laid off an employee. **Remarks:** Also notes number of employees and overall rank in the *100 Best Companies to Work For.* **Number listed:** 19

1. SAS Institute Inc.
2. Wegmans Food Markets Inc.
3. NuStar Energy LP
4. The Container Store
5. Ultimate Software
6. Scottrade Inc.
7. Nugget Market Inc.
8. St. Jude Children's Research Hospital
9. Baptist Health South Florida Inc.
10. Children's Healthcare of Atlanta

Source: *Fortune*, 100 Best Companies to Work For (annual), http://www.fortune.com, February 6, 2012.

Leadership

3468 ■ AMERICA'S WORST BOSSES, 2011

Ranked by: Score determined by a panel of workplace experts. **Remarks:** Specific scores not provided. Also notes location. **Number listed:** 100

1. Jon Peters (movie producer)
2. Rev. Jesse Jackson (Rainbow PUSH Coalition)
3. Ted Abrams (Tucson City Court)
4. Dr. Barry Lefkovitch (Arroyo Oaks Medical Group)
5. John Burgess (Int'l Profit Associates)
6. Jay Severin (WTKK-FM)
7. James Schwartz (El Camino College)
8. John Bibler (Frenchtown, MT, Fire District)
9. Ken Seaton (Family Inns)
10. Richard Moore (Aaron's Inc.)

Source: *eBoss Watch*, America's Worst Bosses (annual), http://www.ebosswatch.com, December 19, 2011.

3469 ■ ASIA PACIFIC'S TOP COMPANIES FOR LEADERS, 2011

Ranked by: Score based on leadership development programs, leadership strategy, succession planning, techniques for identifying high-potential junior employees, and more. **Remarks:** Scores not provided. Also notes industry. **Number listed:** 20

1. Aditya Birla Group
2. Hindustan Unilever

3. ICICI Bank
4. China Vanke
5. Infosys Technologies Ltd.
6. Wipro Ltd.
7. Mahindra & Mahindra
8. Bharti Airtel Ltd.
9. Whirlpool of India
10. Kotak Mahindra Bank

Source: *Fortune*, Top Companies for Leaders, November 21, 2011, p. 175.

3470 ■ EUROPE'S TOP COMPANIES FOR LEADERS, 2011

Ranked by: Score based on leadership development programs, leadership strategy, succession planning, techniques for identifying high-potential junior employees, and more. **Remarks:** Scores not provided. Also notes industry. **Number listed:** 7

1. Banco Bilbao Vizcaya Argentaria SA (BBVA)
2. L'Oreal SA
3. Unilever
4. ArcelorMittal
5. Siemens AG
6. Raiffeisen Bank International
7. Novartis AG

Source: *Fortune*, Top Companies for Leaders, November 21, 2011, p. 175.

3471 ■ LATIN AMERICA'S TOP COMPANIES FOR LEADERS, 2011

Ranked by: Score based on leadership development programs, leadership strategy, succession planning, techniques for identifying high-potential junior employees, and more. **Remarks:** Scores not provided. Also notes industry. **Number listed:** 5

1. Natura Cosmeticos SA
2. Companhia de Bebidas das Americas (AmBev)
3. Bancolombia
4. Wal-Mart de Mexico, SAB de CV
5. WEG Equipamentos Eletricos

Source: *Fortune*, Top Companies for Leaders, November 21, 2011, p. 175.

3472 ■ MOST POWERFUL ARAB WOMEN, 2012

Ranked by: Score based on scope of influence. **Remarks:** Specific scores not provided. Ranking excludes royalty and politicians, unless their influence extends into the business sector or other wider works. **Number listed:** 105

1. Reem Asaad
2. Sheikha Lubna Al Qasimi
3. Tawakkul Karman
4. Fairouz
5. Lubna Olayan
6. Leila El Solh
7. Nadine Labaki
8. Raja Easa Al Gurg
9. Lama Sulaiman
10. Dr. Ilham Al Qaradawi

Source: *Arab Business*, Power 500 (annual), June 4, 2012.

3473 ■ MOST POWERFUL ARABS IN ALGERIA, 2012

Ranked by: Score based on scope of influence. **Remarks:** Specific scores not provided. Also notes rank in the overall *Power 500*. **Number listed:** 9

1. Yazid Sabeg
2. Issad Rebrab
3. Rachid Bouchareb
4. Ahlam Mosteghanemi
5. Elias Zerhouni
6. Khadija Ben Ganna
7. Majid Bougherra
8. Lotfi Double Kanon
9. Karim Ziani

Source: *Arabian Business*, Power 500 (annual), June 4, 2012.

3474 ■ MOST POWERFUL ARABS IN BAHRAIN, 2012

Ranked by: Score based on scope of influence. **Remarks:** Specific scores not provided. Also notes rank in the overall *Power 500*. **Number listed:** 14

1. Rula Saffar
2. Adel Ali
3. Mona Almoayyed
4. Rasheed Al Maraj
5. Afnan Rashid Al Zayani
6. Adnan Ahmed Yousif
7. Abullah Ahmed Nass
8. Atif Abdulmalik
9. Fahad Al Rajaan
10. Talal Al Zain

Source: *Arabian Business*, Power 500 (annual), June 4, 2012.

3475 ■ MOST POWERFUL ARABS IN EGYPT, 2012

Ranked by: Score based on scope of influence. **Remarks:** Specific scores not provided. Also notes rank in the overall *Power 500*. **Number listed:** 58

1. Morsi Arab
2. Amr Diab
3. Mohammed El Erian
4. Sherife AbdelMessih
5. Ahmed Mohamed El Tayeb
6. Farouk El Baz
7. Yusuf Al Qaradawi
8. Hesham El Sahatry
9. Magdi Yacoub
10. Mohammed Hassanein Heikal

Source: *Arabian Business*, Power 500 (annual), June 4, 2012.

3476 ■ MOST POWERFUL ARABS IN IRAQ, 2012

Ranked by: Score based on scope of influence. **Remarks:** Specific scores not provided. Also notes rank in the overall *Power 500*. **Number listed:** 16

1. Zaha Hadid
2. Zainab Salbi
3. Selim Zilka
4. Kazim Al Saher
5. Nadhmi Auchi
6. Lihadh Al Ghazali
7. Emad Makiya
8. Sinan Al Shabibi
9. Madeeha Hasan Odhaib

10. Sinaan Antoon

Source: *Arabian Business*, Power 500 (annual), June 4, 2012.

3477 ■ MOST POWERFUL ARABS IN JORDAN, 2012

Ranked by: Score based on scope of influence. **Remarks:** Specific scores not provided. Also notes rank in the overall *Power 500*. **Number listed:** 27

1. Soraya Salti
2. Abdel Hamid Shoman
3. Fadi Ghandour
4. Naseer Homoud
5. Khaldoun Tabari
6. Nisreen Shocair
7. Usama Fayyad
8. Dr. Amin Amin
9. Nasser Sunnaa
10. Salah Oqbi

Source: *Arabian Business*, Power 500 (annual), June 4, 2012.

3478 ■ MOST POWERFUL ARABS IN KUWAIT, 2012

Ranked by: Score based on scope of influence. **Remarks:** Specific scores not provided. Also notes rank in the overall *Power 500*. **Number listed:** 26

1. Mohamed Alshaya
2. Badr Al Kharafi
3. Saad Al Barrak
4. Faisal Al Ayyar
5. Hosnia Hashem
6. Sheikha Al Bahar
7. Ghayda & Ghosson Al Khaled
8. Nabeel Bin Salamah
9. Marwan Boodai
10. Farouq Al Zanki

Source: *Arabian Business*, Power 500 (annual), June 4, 2012.

3479 ■ MOST POWERFUL ARABS IN LEBANON, 2012

Ranked by: Score based on scope of influence. **Remarks:** Specific scores not provided. Also notes rank in the overall *Power 500*. **Number listed:** 81

1. Matty Moroun
2. Charles Elachi
3. Elie Saab
4. Elie Khouri
5. Fairouz
6. Leila El Solh
7. Nadine Labaki
8. Joseph Ghossoub
9. Ghassan Bin Jiddu
10. Dani Richa

Source: *Arabian Business*, Power 500 (annual), June 4, 2012.

3480 ■ MOST POWERFUL ARABS IN LIBYA, 2012

Ranked by: Score based on scope of influence. **Remarks:** Specific scores not provided. Also notes rank in the overall *Power 500*. **Number listed:** 5

1. Mohammed Nabbous

2. Ibrahim Al Koni
3. Khaled Mattawa
4. Maher Zain
5. Aref Ali Nayed

Source: *Arabian Business*, Power 500 (annual), June 4, 2012.

3481 ■ MOST POWERFUL ARABS IN MOROCCO, 2012

Ranked by: Score based on scope of influence. **Remarks:** Specific scores not provided. Also notes rank in the overall *Power 500*. **Number listed:** 17

1. Mohamed Benselah
2. Miloud Chaabi
3. Alami Lazraq
4. Abdelatif Jouahri
5. Fatima Mernissi
6. Hynd Bouhia
7. Adel Taraabt
8. Hicham El Guerrouj
9. Rajaa Naji Al Makkawi
10. Mustafa Cherif

Source: *Arabian Business*, Power 500 (annual), June 4, 2012.

3482 ■ MOST POWERFUL ARABS IN OMAN, 2012

Ranked by: Score based on scope of influence. **Remarks:** Specific scores not provided. Also notes rank in the overall *Power 500*. **Number listed:** 4

1. Ali Al Habsi
2. Abdulrazak Al Issa
3. Sultan Bin Hamdoon Al Harthy
4. Assila Zaher Al Harthy

Source: *Arabian Business*, Power 500 (annual), June 4, 2012.

3483 ■ MOST POWERFUL ARABS OVERALL, 2012

Ranked by: Score based on scope of influence. **Remarks:** Specific scores not provided. Ranking excludes royalty and politicians, unless their influence extends into the business sector or other wider works. **Number listed:** 500

1. Prince Alwaleed bin Talal Al Saud
2. Sheikh Ahmed bin Saeed Al Maktoum
3. Reem Asaad
4. Mohamed Alabbar
5. Mohammed Nabbous
6. Mohamed Al Jaber
7. Morsi Arab
8. Khalid Al Falih
9. Khawla Al Kuraya
10. Sheikha Lubna Al Qasimi

Source: *Arab Business*, Power 500 (annual), June 4, 2012.

3484 ■ MOST POWERFUL ARABS IN PALESTINE, 2012

Ranked by: Score based on scope of influence. **Remarks:** Specific scores not provided. Also notes rank in the overall *Power 500*. **Number listed:** 36

1. Ibrahim Dabdoub
2. Munib Al Masri
3. Riad Kamal
4. Said Khoury

5. Samih Darwazah
6. Azmi Bishara
7. Wadah Khanfar
8. Khaled Sabawi
9. Suzanne Al Houby
10. Kholoud Faqih

Source: *Arabian Business*, Power 500 (annual), June 4, 2012.

3485 ■ MOST POWERFUL ARABS IN QATAR, 2012

Ranked by: Score based on scope of influence. **Remarks:** Specific scores not provided. Also notes rank in the overall *Power 500*. **Number listed:** 33

1. Ahmad Al Sayed
2. Sheikh Ahmed bin Jassim Al Thani
3. Akbar Al Baker
4. Ali Shareef Al Emadi
5. Saif Al Hajeri
6. Hassan Al Thawadi
7. Dr. Ilham Al Qaradawi
8. Dr. Ibrahim Al Ibrahim
9. Sheikh Khalid bin Khalifa Al Thani
10. Bader Al Darwish

Source: *Arabian Business*, Power 500 (annual), June 4, 2012.

3486 ■ MOST POWERFUL ARABS IN SAUDI ARABIA, 2012

Ranked by: Score based on scope of influence. **Remarks:** Specific scores not provided. Also notes rank in the overall *Power 500*. **Number listed:** 70

1. Prince Alwaleed bin Talal Al Saud
2. Reem Asaad
3. Mohamed Al Jaber
4. Khalid Al Falih
5. Khawla Al Kuraya
6. Fahad Al Mubarak
7. Hayat Sindi
8. Walid Al Ibrahim
9. Fahd Al Rasheed
10. Adel Aujan

Source: *Arabian Business*, Power 500 (annual), June 4, 2012.

3487 ■ MOST POWERFUL ARABS IN SUDAN, 2012

Ranked by: Score based on scope of influence. **Remarks:** Specific scores not provided. Also notes rank in the overall *Power 500*. **Number listed:** 4

1. Mo Ibrahim
2. Leila Aboulela
3. Ismail Ahmed Ismail
4. Mohammed Baloola

Source: *Arabian Business*, Power 500 (annual), June 4, 2012.

3488 ■ MOST POWERFUL ARABS IN SYRIA, 2012

Ranked by: Score based on scope of influence. **Remarks:** Specific scores not provided. Also notes rank in the overall *Power 500*. **Number listed:** 23

1. Moafaq Al Gaddah
2. Khaled Samawi

3. Sheikha Munira Qubeysi
4. Anas Kouzbari
5. Bassam Kousa
6. Al Laith Hajo
7. Safwan Dahoul
8. Mustafa Ali
9. Patrick Chalhoub
10. Ayman Asfari

Source: *Arabian Business*, Power 500 (annual), June 4, 2012.

3489 ■ MOST POWERFUL ARABS IN TUNISIA, 2012

Ranked by: Score based on scope of influence. **Remarks:** Specific scores not provided. Also notes rank in the overall *Power 500*. **Number listed:** 7

1. Amira Yahyaoui
2. Lina Ben Mhenni
3. Habib Selmi
4. Saber Rebai
5. Brahim Dargouthi
6. Azzedine Alaia
7. Hend Sabri

Source: *Arabian Business*, Power 500 (annual), June 4, 2012.

3490 ■ MOST POWERFUL ARABS IN THE UNITED ARAB EMIRATES, 2012

Ranked by: Score based on scope of influence. **Remarks:** Specific scores not provided. Also notes rank in the overall *Power 500*. **Number listed:** 61

1. Sheikh Ahmed bin Saeed Al Maktoum
2. Mohamed Alabbar
3. Sheikha Lubna Al Qasimi
4. Lieutenant General Dahi Khalfan Tamim
5. Khaldoon Al Mubarak
6. Sultan Ahmed Bin Sulayem
7. Mohammed Al Marri
8. Abdulaziz Al Ghurair
9. Sultan bin Nasser Al Suwaidi
10. Marwan Bin Bayat

Source: *Arabian Business*, Power 500 (annual), June 4, 2012.

3491 ■ MOST POWERFUL ARABS IN YEMEN, 2012

Ranked by: Score based on scope of influence. **Remarks:** Specific scores not provided. Also notes rank in the overall *Power 500*. **Number listed:** 6

1. Tawakkul Karman
2. Nujood Ali
3. Syed Mokhtar Al Bukhary
4. Khadeja Al Sallami
5. Bader Ben Hirsi
6. Mohammed Baobaid

Source: *Arabian Business*, Power 500 (annual), June 4, 2012.

3492 ■ NORTH AMERICA'S TOP COMPANIES FOR LEADERS, 2011

Ranked by: Score based on leadership development programs, leadership strategy, succession planning, techniques for identifying high-potential junior employees, and more. **Remarks:** Scores not provided. Also notes industry. **Number listed:** 25

1. International Business Machines Corp. (IBM)
2. General Mills Inc.
3. Procter & Gamble Co.
4. Colgate-Palmolive Co.
5. McDonald's Corp.
6. Whirlpool Corp.
7. PepsiCo Inc.
8. General Electric Co.
9. Deere & Co.
10. Target Corp.

Source: *Fortune*, Top Companies for Leaders, November 21, 2011, p. 175.

3493 ■ WORLD'S MOST POWERFUL PEOPLE, 2011

Ranked by: Score based on number of people influenced, financial resources, influence in multiple arenas, and extent to which power is actively wielded. **Remarks:** Specific scores not provided. Also notes age and comments. **Number listed:** 70

1. Barack Obama (President, U.S.)
2. Vladimir Putin (Prime Minister, Russia)
3. Hu Jintao (President, China)
4. Angela Merkel (Chancellor, Germany)
5. William H. Gates III (Co-chair, Bill & Melinda Gates Fnd.)
6. Abdullah bin Abdul Aziz al Saud (King, Saudi Arabia)
7. Benedict XVI (Pope)
8. Ben S. Bernanke (Chairman, U.S. Fed. Reserve)
9. Mark Zuckerberg (CEO, Facebook)
10. David Cameron (Prime Minister, U.K.)

Source: *Forbes*, The Most Powerful People on Earth (annual), November 21, 2011, p. 99+.

3494 ■ WORLD'S TOP COMPANIES FOR LEADERS, 2011

Ranked by: Score based on leadership development programs, leadership strategy, succession planning, techniques for identifying high-potential junior employees, and more. **Remarks:** Scores not provided. Also notes headquarters, revenue, number of employees, and comments. **Number listed:** 25

1. International Business Machines Corp. (IBM, U.S.)
2. General Mills Inc. (U.S.)
3. Procter & Gamble Co. (U.S.)
4. Aditya Birla (India)
5. Colgate-Palmolive Co. (U.S.)
6. Hindustan Unilever (India)
7. Icici Bank (India)
8. McDonald's Corp. (U.S.)
9. Whirlpool Corp. (U.S.)
10. PepsiCo Inc. (U.S.)

Source: *Fortune*, Top Companies for Leaders, November 21, 2011, p. 170-171.

Leasing and Renting of Equipment

3495 ■ JAPAN'S LARGEST RENTAL AND LEASING COMPANIES OVERALL, 2011

Ranked by: Score based on revenue, profits, assets, and market capitalization. **Remarks:** Specific scores not provided. Also notes overall rank in the *Forbes 2000* and figures for each criterion. **Number listed:** 3

1. Mitsubishi UFJ Lease & Finance Co., Ltd.
2. Century Tokyo Leasing Corp.
3. Fuyo General Lease Co., Ltd.

Source: *Forbes*, Forbes 2000 (annual), http://www.forbes.com, May 7, 2012.

3496 ■ WORLD'S LARGEST RENTAL AND LEASING COMPANIES OVERALL, 2011

Ranked by: Score based on revenue, profits, assets, and market capitalization. **Remarks:** Specific scores not provided. Also notes country, overall rank in the *Forbes 2000,* and figures for each criterion. **Number listed:** 5

1. Mitsubishi UFJ Lease & Finance Co., Ltd.
2. Hertz Global Holdings Inc.
3. Century Tokyo Leasing Corp.
4. Fuyo General Lease Co., Ltd.
5. Avis Budget Group Inc.

Source: *Forbes*, Forbes 2000 (annual), http://www.forbes.com, May 7, 2012.

Leather Industry

3497 ■ LARGEST LEATHER COMPANIES BY EMPLOYEES, 2010

Ranked by: Total number of employees. **Remarks:** Also notes contact information for headquarters, number of employees at headquarters, revenue, rank by revenue, and primary SIC code. **Number listed:** 49

1. Coach Inc., with 13,000 employees
2. Everett Smith Group Ltd., 6,020
3. Nine West Footwear Corp., 6,000
4. The Timberland Co., 5,600
5. Albert Trostel & Sons Co., 5,197
6. Samsonite LLC, 5,000
7. Eagle Ottawa LLC, 4,434
8. G. H. Bass & Co., 4,100
9. Wolverine World Wide Inc., 4,018
10. Kenneth Cole Productions Inc., 3,000

Source: *Business Rankings*, (annual), Dun & Bradstreet Inc., 2011, p. VI.69-VI.70.

3498 ■ LARGEST LEATHER COMPANIES BY SALES, 2010

Ranked by: Total revenue, in dollars. **Remarks:** Also notes contact information for headquarters, number of employees at headquarters and overall, rank by employees, and primary SIC code. **Number listed:** 50

1. Coach Inc., with $3,607,636,000
2. New Balance Athletic Shoe Inc., $1,500,000,000
3. The Timberland Co., $1,429,484,000
4. Wolverine World Wide Inc., $1,248,517,000
5. Steven Madden Ltd., $635,418,000
6. Kenneth Cole Productions Inc., $457,328,000
7. Rocky Brands Inc., $252,792,263
8. Tandy Brands Accessories Inc., $141,887,000
9. R. G. Barry Corp., $123,787,000
10. Rocket Dog Brands LLC, $100,000,000

Source: *Business Rankings*, (annual), Dun & Bradstreet Inc., 2011, p. V.69-V.70.

Legal Services

3499 ■ LARGEST LEGAL SERVICES COMPANIES BY EMPLOYEES, 2010

Ranked by: Total number of employees. **Remarks:** Also notes contact information for headquarters, number of employees at headquarters, revenue, rank by revenue, and primary SIC code. **Number listed:** 220

1. Baker & McKenzie LLP, with 8,000 employees
2. Clifford Chance U.S. LLP, 6,700
3. California State Department of Justice, 6,000
4. Mayer Brown LLP, 5,334
5. Jones Day, 4,600
6. Latham & Watkins LLP, 4,100
7. Skadden, Arps, Slate, Meagher & Flom LLP, 4,000
8. White & Case LLP, 3,662
9. Greenberg Traurig LLP, 3,500
9. Greenberg Traurig PA, 3,500

Source: *Business Rankings*, (annual), Dun & Bradstreet Inc., 2011, p. VI.249-VI.253.

3500 ■ LARGEST LEGAL SERVICES COMPANIES BY SALES, 2010

Ranked by: Total revenue, in dollars. **Remarks:** Also notes contact information for headquarters, number of employees at headquarters and overall, rank by employees, and primary SIC code. **Number listed:** 220

1. Greenberg Traurig PA, with $1,200,000,000
2. Cramer & Anderson, $597,513,175
3. Alston & Bird LLP, $550,000,000
4. H. Moffitt Lee Inc., $509,687,581
5. Seyfarth Shaw LLP, $462,988,628
6. Pre-Paid Legal Services Inc., $453,936,000
7. Patton Boggs LLP, $338,670,508
8. Town of Brookhaven, $318,192,160
9. Ballard Spahr LLP, $271,000,000
10. Snell & Wilmer LLP, $200,000,000

Source: *Business Rankings*, (annual), Dun & Bradstreet Inc., 2011, p. V.223-V.227.

Leisure

3501 ■ BRITAIN'S MOST ADMIRED LEISURE AND HOTEL COMPANIES, 2011

Ranked by: Survey of peers and investment analysts based on nine criteria: quality of management, financial soundness, quality of goods/services, ability to attract and retain talent, value as long-term investment, innovation, marketing, community and environmental responsibility, and use of corporate assets. **Number listed:** 5

1. InterContinental Hotels Group plc, with 65 points
2. Carnival plc, 58.3
3. Holidaybreak, 56.7

4. Whitbread plc, 53.8
5. Tui Travel, 51.5

Source: *Management Today*, Britain's Most Admired Companies (annual), December 2011, p. 45.

3502 ■ EUROPE'S MOST VALUABLE TRAVEL AND LEISURE COMPANIES, 2011

Ranked by: Market value as of March 2011, in millions of U.S. dollars. **Remarks:** Also notes rank within the *FT Europe 500*, rank for previous year, country, revenue, net income, assets, number of employees, share price, price-to-earning ratio, dividend yield, and fiscal yearend. **Number listed:** 11

1. Compass Group plc, with $17,003.2 million
2. Sodexo, $11,490.4
3. Accor SA, $10,204
4. Deutsche Lufthansa AG, $9,773.8
5. Carnival plc, $7,200.2
6. Ryanair Holdings plc, $7,085.8
7. OPAP SA, $6,840.1
8. International Airlines Group, $6,751.1
9. International Hotels Group, $5,941.3
10. Air France-KLM SA, $5,006

Source: *Financial Times*, FT 500 (annual), http://www.ft.com, June 24, 2011.

3503 ■ LARGEST LEISURE AND CONSUMER SERVICES COMPANIES IN EUROPE, 2010

Ranked by: Sales, in millions of U.S. dollars. **Remarks:** Also notes rank within country. **Number listed:** 100

1. NST Travel Group Holdings Ltd. (U.K.), with $59,705.8 million
2. TUI AG (Germany), $23,989.9
3. William Hill Organization Ltd. (U.K.), $20,220.4
4. Thomas Cook Group plc (U.K.), $13,903.2
5. Exel Ltd. (U.K.), $9,359.4
6. CEVA Group plc (U.K.), $7,416.9
7. Pari Mutuel Urbain (France), $6,395.5
8. Tanjong plc (U.K.), $5,847.2
9. TUI UK Ltd. (U.K.), $4,993.5
10. Arriva plc (U.K.), $4,721.7

Source: *Europe's 15,000 Largest Companies*, (annual), ELC International, 2011, p. 45.

3504 ■ MOST VALUABLE U.S. LEISURE GOODS COMPANIES, 2011

Ranked by: Market value as of March 2011, in millions of U.S. dollars. **Remarks:** Also notes rank within the *FT U.S. 500*, rank for previous year, country, revenue, net income, assets, number of employees, share price, price-to-earning ratio, dividend yield, and fiscal yearend. **Number listed:** 4

1. Activision Blizzard Inc., with $12,969.3 million
2. Mattel Inc., $8,663.7
3. Electronic Arts Inc., $5,529.2
4. Hasbro Inc., $5,419

Source: *Financial Times*, FT 500 (annual), http://www.ft.com, June 24, 2011.

3505 ■ MOST VALUABLE U.S. TRAVEL AND LEISURE COMPANIES, 2011

Ranked by: Market value as of March 2011, in millions of U.S. dollars. **Remarks:** Also notes rank within the *FT U.S. 500*, rank for previous year, country, revenue, net income, assets, number of employees, share price, price-to-earning ratio, dividend yield, and fiscal yearend. **Number listed:** 17

1. McDonald's Corp., with $79,384.6 million
2. Las Vegas Sands Corp., $30,671.6
3. Starbucks Corp., $27,564.7
4. Priceline.com Inc., $24,892.3
5. Yum! Brands Inc., $24,017.4
6. Carnival Corp., $23,316.7
7. Wynn Resorts Ltd., $15,846.7
8. Marriott International Inc., $13,091.2
9. Starwood Hotels & Resorts Worldwide Inc., $11,340.5
10. Southwest Airlines Co., $9,441.7

Source: *Financial Times*, FT 500 (annual), http://www.ft.com, June 24, 2011.

3506 ■ WORLD'S MOST ETHICAL LEISURE AND HOSPITALITY COMPANIES, 2012

Ranked by: Score based on five criteria: ethics and compliance program; reputation, leadership, and innovation; governance; corporate citizenship and responsibility; and culture of ethics. **Remarks:** Specific scores not provided; companies are listed alphabetically, not ranked. **Number listed:** 5

1. Holland America Line (U.S.)
2. Kimpton Hotel & Restaurant Group LLC (U.S.)
3. Marriott International Inc. (U.S.)
4. The Rezidor Hotel Group (Belgium)
5. Seabourn (U.S.)

Source: *Ethisphere Magazine*, World's Most Ethical Companies (annual), http://www.ethisphere.com, 2012.

3507 ■ WORLD'S MOST VALUABLE LEISURE BRANDS, 2011

Ranked by: Brand value, in millions of U.S. dollars. **Remarks:** Also notes rank within the *Global 500* for current and previous year, figures for current and previous year, country, and brand rating. Ranking is available online only. **Number listed:** 2

1. TUI Travel, with $2,791 million
2. Harley-Davidson, $2,617

Source: *Global 500*, (annual), Brand Finance plc, March 2012.

3508 ■ WORLD'S MOST VALUABLE LEISURE GOODS COMPANIES, 2011

Ranked by: Market value as of March 2011, in millions of U.S. dollars. **Remarks:** Also notes rank within the *FT 500*, rank for previous year, country, revenue, net income, assets, number of employees, share price, price-to-earning ratio, dividend yield, and fiscal year-end. **Number listed:** 4

1. Nintendo Co., Ltd., with $38,887.2 million
2. Sony Corp., $32,291.6
3. Koninklijke Philips Electronics NV (Royal Philips Electronics NV), $31,562
4. Panasonic Corp., $31,314.3

Source: *Financial Times*, FT 500 (annual), http://www.ft.com, June 24, 2011.

3509 ■ WORLD'S MOST VALUABLE TRAVEL AND LEISURE COMPANIES, 2011

Ranked by: Market value as of March 2011, in millions of U.S. dollars. **Remarks:** Also notes rank within the *FT 500*, rank for

previous year, country, revenue, net income, assets, number of employees, share price, price-to-earning ratio, dividend yield, and fiscal year-end. **Number listed:** 9

1. McDonald's Corp., with $79,384.6 million
2. Las Vegas Sands Corp., $30,671.6
3. Carnival plc, $30,516.9
4. Starbucks Corp., $27,564.7
5. Priceline.com Inc., $24,892.3
6. Yum! Brands Inc., $24,017.4
7. East Japan Railway Co., $22,321.4
8. MTR Gaming Group Inc., $21,374.9
9. Genting Singapore plc, $19,827.4

Source: *Financial Times*, FT 500 (annual), http://www.ft.com, June 24, 2011.

Licensed Product Merchandising

3510 ■ WORLD'S LARGEST LICENSING AGENTS, 2011

Ranked by: Retail sales of licensed merchandise for brands represented, in billions of U.S. dollars. **Remarks:** Also notes key clients and brands. **Number listed:** 30

1. IMG, with $8 billion
2. Equity Management, $5.4
3. LMCA, $5.3
4. IBML, $4
5. The Licensing Co., $3.5
6. The Beanstalk Group, $3.2
7. The Joester Loria Group, $2.1
8. Brand Central Group, $1.8
8. CPLG, $1.8
10. Exim, $1.6

Source: *License! Global*, Top 125 (annual), May 2012, p. T31.

3511 ■ WORLD'S LARGEST LICENSING COMPANIES, 2011

Ranked by: Annual retail sales of licensed products, in billions of U.S. dollars. **Remarks:** Also notes key executive, website, and comments. **Number listed:** 125

1. Disney Consumer Products, with $37.5 billion
2. Iconix Brand Group, $12
3. Phillips-Van Heusen Corp., $10
4. Mattel Inc., $7
5. Warner Bros. Consumer Products, $6
6. Nickelodeon Consumer Products, $5.5
7. Hasbro Inc., $5.2
8. Sanrio, $5
8. Major League Baseball, $5
10. The Collegiate Licensing Co., $4.6

Source: *License! Global*, Top 125 (annual), May 2012, p. T4-T30.

Lighting

3512 ■ TOP BRANDS OF LIGHTING CONTROL SYSTEMS, 2010

Ranked by: Popularity among *CE Pro 100* companies, in percent. **Number listed:** 5

1. Lutron, with 67%
2. Crestron, 51%
3. Control4, 39%
4. Vantage, 14%
5. URC, 9%

Source: *CE Pro*, Brand Analysis (annual), June 2011, p. 59.

Liquor Industry
See also: **Alcoholic Beverages**

3513 ■ WORLD'S TOP SPIRITS BRANDS, 2010

Ranked by: Volume, in thousands of nine-liter cases. **Remarks:** Also notes rank for previous year, type of spirit, and annual growth. **Number listed:** 50

1. Smirnoff, with 24,413.5 thousand cases
2. Bacardi, 18,748.6
3. Johnnie Walker, 15,543.1
4. Green Mark, 11,190.9
5. Absolut, 11,003.7
6. Jack Daniel's, 10,147.9
7. Nemiroff, 9,118.6
8. Captain Morgan, 8,898
9. Khlibniy Dar, 8,129.4
10. Baileys, 6,604.1

Source: *The IWSR Magazine*, Top 50 International Spirits Brands (annual), August 2011, p. 8-10.

Livestock
See also: **Agriculture**

3514 ■ LARGEST COMPANIES IN THE LIVESTOCK AND ANIMAL SPECIALTIES INDUSTRY BY EMPLOYEES, 2010

Ranked by: Total number of employees. **Remarks:** Also notes contact information for headquarters, number of employees at headquarters, revenue, rank by revenue, and primary SIC code. **Number listed:** 68

1. Foster Poultry Farms Inc., with 10,500 employees
2. Farm Credit Services of America PCA/FLCA, 10,000
3. Sanderson Farms Inc., 9,859
4. Sanderson Farms Inc. Production Division, 9,000
5. Tyson Chicken Inc., 7,800
6. Murphy-Brown LLC, 4,500
7. Premium Standard Farms Inc., 4,300
8. Michael Foods Group Inc., 3,800
8. Michael Foods Investors LLC, 3,800
8. Peco Foods Inc., 3,800

Source: *Business Rankings*, (annual), Dun & Bradstreet Inc., 2011, p. VI.5-VI.6.

3515 ■ LARGEST COMPANIES IN THE LIVESTOCK AND ANIMAL SPECIALTIES INDUSTRY BY SALES, 2010

Ranked by: Total revenue, in dollars. **Remarks:** Also notes contact information for headquarters, number of employees at headquarters and overall, rank by employees, and primary SIC code. **Number listed:** 69

1. Foster Poultry Farms Inc., with $2,200,000,000
2. Sanderson Farms Inc., $1,925,445,000
3. Michael Foods Inc., $1,542,779,000
4. Cal-Maine Foods Inc., $910,143,000
5. Mar-Jac Poultry Inc., $262,859,966
6. Claxton Poultry Farms Inc., $200,000,000
7. Anderson-Erickson Dairy Co., $147,239,039
8. Taconic Farms Inc., $142,581,841
9. Maple Leaf Farms Inc., $130,000,000
10. Austin Jack DeCoster, $114,000,000

Source: *Business Rankings*, (annual), Dun & Bradstreet Inc., 2011, p. V.5-V.6.

3516 ■ STATES WITH THE HIGHEST FARM INCOME IN LIVESTOCK, 2009

Ranked by: Farm income from livestock, in dollars. **Remarks:** Also notes share of national total. **Number listed:** 50

1. Texas, with $10,640,865,000
2. Iowa, $8,520,920,000
3. California, $7,814,006,000
4. Nebraska, $7,283,326,000
5. Kansas, $6,352,141,000
6. North Carolina, $5,709,940,000
7. Minnesota, $4,902,357,000
8. Wisconsin, $4,778,867,000
9. Georgia, $4,290,815,000
10. Arkansas, $3,964,065,000

Source: *State Rankings*, (annual), CQ Press, 2011, p. 13.

Local Taxation
See: **Taxation**

Local Transit

3517 ■ LARGEST LOCAL/SUBURBAN TRANSIT AND INTERURBAN PASSENGER TRANSPORTATION COMPANIES BY EMPLOYEES, 2010

Ranked by: Total number of employees. **Remarks:** Also notes contact information for headquarters, number of employees at headquarters, revenue, rank by revenue, and primary SIC code. **Number listed:** 48

1. FirstGroup America Inc., with 96,000 employees
2. First Student Inc., 68,000
3. Metropolitan Transportation Authority (New York City), 67,457
4. New York City Transit Authority, 47,956
5. American Medical Response Inc., 18,030
6. American Medical Response of Southern California, 18,000
7. Veolia Transportation Inc., 16,470
8. Durham School Services LP, 14,250
9. MV Transportation Inc., 12,389
10. Chicago Transit Authority, 12,000

Source: *Business Rankings*, (annual), Dun & Bradstreet Inc., 2011, p. VI.90-VI.91.

3518 ■ LARGEST LOCAL/SUBURBAN TRANSIT AND INTERURBAN PASSENGER TRANSPORTATION COMPANIES BY SALES, 2010

Ranked by: Total revenue, in dollars. **Remarks:** Also notes contact information for headquarters, number of employees at headquarters and overall, rank by employees, and primary SIC code. **Number listed:** 49

1. New York City Transit Authority, with $3,320,896,000
2. Kansas Department of Transportation, $1,136,131,000
3. MV Transportation Inc., $706,478,000
4. Jacobson Cos., $700,000,000
5. Rural/Metro Corp., $530,754,000
6. Durham School Services LP, $525,000,000
7. Regional Transportation Authority (Chicago), $503,461,000
8. Rural/Metro of Central Colorado Inc., $487,000,000
9. Rural Metro Transportation Corp., $444,155,094
10. Wheatland Enterprises Inc., $444,000,000

Source: *Business Rankings*, (annual), Dun & Bradstreet Inc., 2011, p. V.90-V.91.

Location of Industry

3519 ■ BEST COUNTRIES FOR BUSINESS, 2011

Ranked by: Score based on the ability of countries to attract entrepreneurs, investors, and workers. **Remarks:** Specific scores not provided. Also notes growth in gross domestic product (GDP), GDP per capita, trade balance and a percentage of GDP, and population. **Number listed:** 134

1. Canada
2. New Zealand
3. Hong Kong
4. Ireland
5. Denmark
6. Singapore
7. Sweden
8. Norway
9. United Kingdom
10. United States

Source: *Forbes*, Best Countries for Business (annual), http://www.forbes.com, October 03, 2011.

3520 ■ BEST LARGE METROS FOR BUSINESS AND CAREERS, 2011

Ranked by: Score based on 12 criteria related to job growth, costs, income growth, educational attainment, and projected economic growth, as well as quality of life issues and the number of highly ranked colleges in the area. **Remarks:** Scores not provided. Also notes population, projected annual job growth through 2013, and comments. **Number listed:** 25

1. Raleigh, NC
2. Des Moines, IA
3. Provo, UT
4. Lexington, KY
5. Fort Collins, CO

6. Nashville, TN
7. Austin, TX
8. San Antonio, TX
9. Denver, CO
10. Dallas, TX

Source: *Forbes*, Best Places for Business and Careers (annual), July 18, 2011, p. 68-71.

3521 ■ BEST SMALL METROS FOR BUSINESS AND CAREERS, 2011

Ranked by: Score based on 12 criteria related to job growth, costs, income growth, educational attainment, and projected economic growth, as well as quality of life issues and the number of highly ranked colleges in the area. **Remarks:** Ranking includes metropolitan areas with populations below 250,000. Scores not provided. Also notes population, projected annual job growth through 2013, and comments. **Number listed:** 25

1. Manhattan, KS
2. Sioux Falls, SD
3. Bismarck, ND
4. Logan, UT
5. Bowling Green, KY
6. Fargo, ND
7. Dubuque, IA
8. Columbia, MO
9. College Station, TX
10. Waterloo, IA

Source: *Forbes*, Best Places for Business and Careers (annual), July 18, 2011, p. 72-74.

3522 ■ BEST STATES FOR BUSINESS, 2012

Ranked by: Score based on a survey of chief executives of their perception of states in three general categories: taxation and regulation, quality of workforce, and living environment. **Remarks:** Specific scores not provided. Also notes rank for previous year and annual change in rank. **Number listed:** 10

1. Texas
2. Florida
3. North Carolina
4. Tennessee
5. Indiana
6. Virginia
7. South Carolina
8. Georgia
9. Utah
10. Arizona

Source: *Chief Executive*, Best and Worst States for Business (annual), http://www.chiefexecutive.net, 2012.

3523 ■ BEST STATES FOR BUSINESS AND CAREERS, 2011

Ranked by: Score based on cost of doing business, qualifications of the available labor pool, economic climate, regulatory climate, growth prospects, quality of life, gross state product, and five-year growth. **Remarks:** Specific scores not provided. Also notes rank for previous year, rank/figures for each criterion, population, and governor. **Number listed:** 50

1. Utah
2. Virginia
3. North Carolina

4. North Dakota
5. Colorado
6. Texas
7. Washington
8. Nebraska
9. Oregon
10. Iowa

Source: *Forbes*, Best States for Business and Careers (annual), http://www.forbes.com, November 22, 2011.

3524 ■ CANADIAN METRO AREAS WITH THE MOST NEW AND EXPANDED CORPORATE FACILITIES, 2011

Ranked by: Number of new and expanded facilities. **Number listed:** 6

1. Toronto, Ontario, with 61 facilities
2. Hamilton, Ontario, 21
3. Quebec City, Quebec, 17
3. Montreal, Quebec, 17
5. Windsor, Ontario, 8
5. London, Ontario, 8

Source: *Site Selection*, Canadian Rankings (annual), September 2011, p. 736.

3525 ■ MOST COMPETITIVE STATES FOR SITE SELECTION, 2011

Ranked by: Score based on number of and capital investment in new and expanded facilities, number of new jobs created, and growth in facilities. **Number listed:** 10

1. Virginia, with 420.5 points
2. Texas, 395
3. Ohio, 387.5
4. Louisiana, 382.5
5. North Carolina, 381.5
6. Utah, 362.5
7. Tennessee, 361
8. Pennsylvania, 360.5
9. Georgia, 359
10. Alabama, 354.5

Source: *Site Selection*, Top Competitive States (annual), May 2012, p. 79.

3526 ■ STATES WITH THE BEST BUSINESS CLIMATE ACCORDING TO EXECUTIVES, 2011

Ranked by: Score based on a survey of corporate site selectors. **Remarks:** Specific scores not provided. **Number listed:** 10

1. Texas
2. North Carolina
3. Georgia
4. Florida
5. Tennessee
5. Virginia
7. South Carolina
8. Ohio
9. Indiana
10. Alabama

Source: *Site Selection*, Business Climate Rankings (annual), November 2011, p. 909.

3527 ■ STATES WITH THE BEST BUSINESS CLIMATE OVERALL, 2011

Ranked by: Score based on a survey of corporate site selectors as well as number of new plants per one million in population and per 1000 square miles. **Remarks:** Also notes rank for each criterion. **Number listed:** 25

1. Texas, with 463 points
2. Georgia, 446.5
3. North Carolina, 437
4. Virginia, 432
5. South Carolina, 428.5
6. Indiana, 426
7. Louisiana, 408.5
8. Tennessee, 398.5
9. Ohio, 395
10. Florida, 379

Source: *Site Selection*, Business Climate Rankings (annual), November 2011, p. 907.

3528 ■ STATES WITH THE MOST *FORTUNE 500* HEADQUARTERS, 2011

Ranked by: Number of Fortune 500 companies headquartered in the state. **Number listed:** 51

1. California, with 53 headquarters
2. Texas, 52
3. New York, 50
4. Illinois, 32
5. Ohio, 28
6. Virginia, 24
7. Pennsylvania, 23
8. New Jersey, 21
9. Michigan, 20
10. Minnesota, 19

Source: *Fortune*, Fortune 500 (annual), http://www.fortune.com, May 21, 2012.

3529 ■ TOP ECONOMIC DEVELOPMENT GROUPS IN CANADA, 2011

Ranked by: Editorial ranking of the most successful groups in bringing large-scale corporate expansion projects to their respective communities; score is based on total capital investment, jobs created, investment per capita, jobs per capita, overall economic vitality, economic strength, diversity of industry, and ability to generate deals. **Remarks:** Specific scores not provided; groups are listed alphabetically by city, not ranked. Also notes CEO, Web site, and comments. **Number listed:** 10

1. Canada's Technology Triangle
2. Edmonton Economic Development Corp.
3. Greater Halifax Partnership
4. City of Hamilton Economic Development & Real Estate Division
5. London Economic Development Corp.
6. City of Mississauga Economic Development Office
7. Montreal International
8. Quebec International
9. Regina Regional Opportunities Commission
10. Windsor Essex Economic Development Corp.

Source: *Site Selection*, Canadian Rankings (annual), September 2011, p. 735-740.

3530 ■ TOP ECONOMIC DEVELOPMENT GROUPS IN THE U.S., 2011

Ranked by: Editorial ranking of the most successful groups in bringing large-scale corporate expansion projects to their respective communities; score is based on total capital investment, jobs created, investment per capita, jobs per capita, overall economic vitality, economic strength, diversity of industry, and ability to generate deals. **Remarks:** Specific scores not provided; groups are listed alphabetically by city, not ranked. Also notes website, statistics, and comments. **Number listed:** 10

1. Baton Rouge Area Chamber of Commerce (Baton Rouge, LA)
2. Dallas Regional Chamber (Dallas-Fort Worth-Arlington, TX)
3. Greater Houston Partnership (Houston, TX)
4. Greater Statesville Development Corp./Mooresville-South Iredell Economic Development Corp. (Iredell Cty., NC)
5. Kansas City Area Development Council (Kansas City, KS-MO)
6. Nashville Area Chamber of Commerce (Nashville, TN)
7. New York City Economic Development Corp. (New York, NY)
8. Pittsburgh Regional Alliance (Pittsburgh, PA)
9. Select Greater Philadelphia (Philadelphia, PA)
10. World Business Chicago (Chicago, IL)

Source: *Site Selection*, Top Groups (annual), May 2012, p. 68-73.

3531 ■ TOP NATIONAL INVESTMENT PROMOTION AGENCIES IN AFRICA AND THE MIDDLE EAST, 2011

Ranked by: Editorial determination. **Remarks:** Specific scores not provided. Also notes website. **Number listed:** 5

1. TradeInvestSA (South Africa)
2. Bahrain Economic Development Board
3. Dubai Development & Investment Authority
4. Saudi Arabian General Investment Authority
5. Qatar Investment Promotion Departent

Source: *Site Selection*, Global Best to Invest Rankings (annual), May 2012, p. 30.

3532 ■ TOP NATIONAL INVESTMENT PROMOTION AGENCIES IN ASIA PACIFIC, 2011

Ranked by: Editorial determination. **Remarks:** Specific scores not provided. Also notes website. **Number listed:** 5

1. Singapore Economic Development Board
2. Austrade (Australia)
3. Malaysia Industrial Development Authority
3. Korea Trade Investment Promotion Agency
5. Ministry of Planning & Investment (Vietnam)

Source: *Site Selection*, Global Best to Invest Rankings (annual), May 2012, p. 29.

3533 ■ TOP NATIONAL INVESTMENT PROMOTION AGENCIES IN EASTERN EUROPE, 2011

Ranked by: Editorial determination. **Remarks:** Specific scores not provided. Also notes website and top regions. **Number listed:** 5

1. ITD Hungary
2. Invest in Poland

2. Slovak Investment & Trade Development Agency
4. Estonian Investment & Trade Agency
4. CzechInvest

Source: *Site Selection*, Global Best to Invest Rankings (annual), May 2012, p. 29.

3534 ■ TOP NATIONAL INVESTMENT PROMOTION AGENCIES IN WESTERN EUROPE, 2011

Ranked by: Editorial determination. **Remarks:** Specific scores not provided. Also notes website and top regions. **Number listed:** 6

1. IDA Ireland
2. UK Trade & Investment
3. Germany Trade & Invest
4. ABA - Invest in Austria
5. Switzerland Trade & Investment Promotion
5. Italian Trade Commission

Source: *Site Selection*, Global Best to Invest Rankings (annual), May 2012, p. 29.

3535 ■ TOP NATIONAL LATIN AMERICAN INVESTMENT PROMOTION AGENCIES, 2011

Ranked by: Editorial determination. **Remarks:** Specific scores not provided. Also notes website. **Number listed:** 5

1. ProMexico Trade & Investment
2. APEX-Brazil
3. Costa Rican Investment Board
4. Chilean Economic Development Agency
5. Invest in Argentina

Source: *Site Selection*, Global Best to Invest Rankings (annual), May 2012, p. 30.

3536 ■ WORLD'S BEST CITIES FOR NEW BUSINESS, 2011

Ranked by: Score based on survey of corporate and economic development executives as to the best locations to launch a business. **Remarks:** Scores not provided; cities are listed alphabetically. **Number listed:** 15

1. Ahmedabad, India
2. Austin, TX
3. Bogota, Colombia
4. Chengdu, China
5. Chongqing, China
6. Doha, Qatar
7. Gurgaon, India
8. Lagos, Nigeria
9. Melbourne, Australia
10. San Jose, Costa Rica

Source: *Fortune*, Best New Cities for Business, July 25, 2011, p. 153.

3537 ■ WORST STATES FOR BUSINESS, 2012

Ranked by: Score based on a survey of chief executives of their perception of states in three general categories: taxation and regulation, quality of workforce, and living environment. **Remarks:** Specific scores not provided. Also notes rank for previous year and annual change in rank. **Number listed:** 10

1. California

2. New York

3. Illinois

4. Massachusetts

5. Michigan

6. New Jersey

7. Connecticut

8. Pennsylvania

9. Oregon

10. Hawaii

Source: *Chief Executive*, Best and Worst States for Business (annual), http://www.chiefexecutive.net, 2012.

Location of Industry—Growth

3538 ■ COMPANIES WITH THE BIGGEST CAPITAL INVESTMENT IN U.S. CORPORATE FACILITIES, 2011

Ranked by: Total capital investment in new and expanded facilities located in the U.S., in millions of dollars. **Remarks:** Also notes city, state, type of facility, and product line. **Number listed:** 5

1. Sasol Ltd., with $10,000 million

2. Cheniere/Sabine Pass, $6,500

3. Intel Corp., $5,000

4. Chevron Corp., $2,005

5. Mercedes Benz, $2,000

Source: *Site Selection*, Top Global Projects (annual), March 2012, p. 122.

3539 ■ COMPANIES GENERATING THE MOST JOBS IN CORPORATE FACILITY PROJECTS IN THE U.S., 2011

Ranked by: Total number of new jobs created in new and expanded facilities located in the U.S. **Remarks:** Also notes city, state, type of facility, and product line. **Number listed:** 5

1. Windkits LLC, with 4,000 jobs

2. G4 Synergetics, 2,498

3. eBay Inc., 2,200

4. General Motors Co., 1,900

5. Continental Tire the Americas, 1,700

Source: *Site Selection*, Top Global Projects (annual), March 2012, p. 122.

3540 ■ COMPANIES WITH THE LARGEST CORPORATE FACILITY PROJECTS IN THE U.S., 2011

Ranked by: Total size of new and expanded facilities located in the U.S., in thousands of square feet. **Remarks:** Also notes city, state, type of facility, and product line. **Number listed:** 5

1. Dell Inc., with 3,485 thousand sq.ft.

2. Integrated Water Technologies Inc., 2,000

3. Texas Specialty Sands, 1,742

4. Unilever, 1,500

4. Bridgestone Americas, 1,500

Source: *Site Selection*, Top Global Projects (annual), March 2012, p. 122.

3541 ■ LARGE METRO AREAS WITH THE MOST NEW AND EXPANDED CORPORATE FACILITIES, 2011

Ranked by: Number of new and expanded facilities. **Remarks:** Ranking includes metropolitan areas with populations over 1 million. **Number listed:** 10

1. Houston-Baytown-Sugar Land, TX, with 195 facilities

2. Chicago-Naperville-Joliet, IL-IN-WI, 167

3. Pittsburgh, PA, 141

4. Dallas-Fort Worth-Arlington, TX, 140

5. New York-Newark-Edison, NY-NJ-PA, 129

6. Cincinnati-Middletown, OH-KY-IN, 114

7. Philadelphia-Camden-Wilmington, PA-NJ-DE-MD, 113

8. Washington-Arlington-Alexandria, DC-VA-MD, 112

9. Atlanta-Sandy Springs-Marietta, GA, 105

10. Tampa-St. Petersburg-Clearwater, FL, 95

Source: *Site Selection*, Top Metros (annual), March 2012, p. 98.

3542 ■ MICROPOLITANS WITH THE MOST NEW AND EXPANDED CORPORATE FACILITIES, 2011

Ranked by: Number of new and expanded facilities. **Remarks:** Micropolitans are defined as having at least 10,000 people but less than 50,000. **Number listed:** 143

1. Statesville-Mooresville, NC, with 28 facilities

2. Wooster, OH, 21

3. Cullman, AL, 20

4. Lexington-Thomasville, NC, 18

5. Shelby, NC, 13

6. Batavia, NY, 10

6. Findlay, OH, 10

8. Daphne-Fairhope-Foley, AL, 9

8. Morgan City, LA, 9

8. Pottsville, PA, 9

Source: *Site Selection*, Top Micropolitans (annual), March 2012, p. 114.

3543 ■ MID-SIZED METRO AREAS WITH THE MOST NEW AND EXPANDED CORPORATE FACILITIES, 2011

Ranked by: Number of new and expanded facilities. **Remarks:** Ranking includes metropolitan areas with populations between 200,000 and 1 million. **Number listed:** 10

1. Baton Rouge, LA, with 38 facilities

2. Dayton, OH, 34

2. Tulsa, OK, 34

4. Allentown-Bethlehem-Easton, PA-NJ, 28

5. Harrisburg-Carlisle, PA, 27

6. Akro, OH, 26

7. Toledo, OH, 24

7. Greensboro-High Point, NC, 24

9. Shreveport-Bossier City, LA, 23

9. Hickory-Morganton-Lenoir, NC, 23

9. Scranton-Wilkes-Barre, PA, 23

Source: *Site Selection*, Top Metros (annual), March 2012, p. 98.

3544 ■ SMALL METRO AREAS WITH THE MOST NEW AND EXPANDED CORPORATE FACILITIES, 2011

Ranked by: Number of new and expanded facilities. **Remarks:** Ranking includes metropolitan areas with populations less than 200,000. **Number listed:** 10

1. Decatur, AL, with 13 facilities

2. Springfield, OH, 12

3. Williamsport, PA, 10

4. Lake Charles, LA, 9

4. Altoona, PA, 9

4. Blacksburg-Christiansburg-Radford, VA, 9

4. Wheeling, VA, 9

8. Johnstown, PA, 8

8. Charlottesville, VA, 8

8. Danville, VA, 8

Source: *Site Selection*, Top Metros (annual), March 2012, p. 98.

3545 ■ STATES WITH THE MOST NEW AND EXPANDED CORPORATE FACILITIES, 2011

Ranked by: Number of new and expanded facilities. **Number listed:** 10

1. Ohio, with 498 facilities

2. Texas, 464

3. Pennsylvania, 453

4. North Carolina, 310

5. Virginia, 273

6. Georgia, 234

7. Illinois, 216

8. Kentucky, 198

9. Tennessee, 190

10. Louisiana, 181

Source: *Site Selection*, The Governor's Cup (annual), March 3012, p. 83.

3546 ■ TOP METRO AREAS FOR JOB GROWTH, 2011

Ranked by: Score based on projected total employment in 2016. **Remarks:** Scores not provided. Also notes current employment and population. **Number listed:** 5

1. New York, NY

2. Atlanta, GA

3. Houston, TX

4. Los Angeles, CA

5. Dallas, TX

Source: *Forbes*, Where the Jobs Are, September 26, 2011, p. 107.

Logistics

3547 ■ FASTEST-GROWING PRIVATE LOGISTICS AND TRANSPORTATION COMPANIES IN THE U.S., 2007-2010

Ranked by: Average annual sales growth over three years, in percent. **Remarks:** Also notes headquarters, revenue, and rank in the overall *Inc. 500*. To qualify, private companies must have had annual revenues of at least $100,000 in 2007 and $2 million in 2010. **Number listed:** 10

1. Shipito.com, with 5,253.7%

2. American Group, 3,883.6%

3. SNS Logistics, 1,535%

4. Coyote Logistics, 1,436.6%

5. Desert Jet, 1,101.7%

6. Argent Associates, 969.3%

7. Kavoo, 969.3%

8. LogFire, 774.7%

9. IntegraCore, 752.4%

10. Source Consulting, 743.5%

Source: *Inc.*, Inc. 500 (annual), September 2011, p. 172-178.

Losses, Business
See: **Business Losses**

Luxury Goods

3548 ■ WORLD'S MOST VALUABLE LUXURY BRANDS, 2012

Ranked by: Brand value, a measure of a brand's earnings and contribution, in millions of U.S. dollars. **Remarks:** Also notes annual growth in brand value and rank by brand contribution and brand momentum. **Number listed:** 10

1. Louis Vuitton, with $25,920 million

2. Hermes, $19,161

3. Rolex, $7,171

4. Chanel, $6,677

5. Gucci, $6,420

6. Prada, $5,788

7. Cartier, $4,843

8. Hennessy, $4,596

9. Moet & Chandon, $4,217

10. Burberry, $4,090

Source: *Financial Times*, Global Brands (annual), http://www.ft.com, May 22, 2012.

Machinery

3549 ■ LARGEST U.S. MACHINERY MANUFACTURERS, 2010

Ranked by: Revenue, in millions of dollars. **Remarks:** Also notes overall rank within the *IW 500*, revenue growth, and profit margin. **Number listed:** 41

1. Caterpillar Inc., with $42,588 million

2. Deere & Co., $26,005

3. Xerox Corp., $21,633

4. Baker Hughes Inc., $14,414

5. National Oilwell Varco Inc., $12,156

6. ITT Corp., $10,995

7. Parker Hannifin Corp., $9,993

8. Dover Corp., $7,133

9. Agco Corp., $6,897

10. Cameron International Corp., $6,135

Source: *IndustryWeek*, IW 500 (annual), http://www.industryweek.com, July 2011.

3550 ■ TOP MACHINERY COMPANIES IN CORPORATE FACILITY PROJECTS, 2011

Ranked by: Investment in new or expanded facilities, in millions of dollars. **Remarks:** Also notes location, product line, and whether facility is new or expanded. **Number listed:** 10

1. Daikin Airconditioning India, with $506 million

2. Ford Motor Co., $500

3. Hitachi Ltd., $450

4. A. O. Smith, $418

5. Canon Inc., $382
6. Caterpillar Inc. (E. Peoria, IL), $340
7. Renault Nissan, $333
8. Caterpillar Inc. (Decatur, IL), $300
9. Rolls-Royce plc, $225
10. Caterpillar Inc. (Belgium), $213

Source: *Site Selection*, Top Industries (annual), March 2012, p. 121.

3551 ■ THE UNITED STATES' MOST VALUABLE DIVERSIFIED MACHINERY BRANDS, 2011

Ranked by: Brand value, in millions of U.S. dollars. **Remarks:** Also notes rank within the *Global 500* for current and previous year, figures for current and previous year, and brand rating. Ranking is available online only. **Number listed:** 2

1. John Deere, with $3,636 million
2. Cummins, $2,499

Source: *Global 500*, (annual), Brand Finance plc, March 2012.

3552 ■ WORLD'S LARGEST MACHINERY MANUFACTURERS, 2010

Ranked by: Revenue, in millions of dollars. **Remarks:** Also notes rank for previous year, overall rank within the *IW 1000*, country, and revenue growth. **Number listed:** 56

1. Caterpillar Inc., with $42,588 million
2. ABB Ltd., $31,589
3. Alstom, $26,285
4. Deere & Co., $26,005
5. Xerox Corp., $21,633
6. Wolseley plc, $20,632
7. Komatsu Ltd., $17,608
8. Linde AG, $17,472
9. CNH Global NV, $15,608
10. IHI Corp., $15,285

Source: *IndustryWeek*, IW 1000 (annual), http://www.industryweek.com, August 2011.

3553 ■ WORLD'S MOST VALUABLE DIVERSIFIED MACHINERY BRANDS, 2011

Ranked by: Brand value, in millions of U.S. dollars. **Remarks:** Also notes rank within the *Global 500* for current and previous year, figures for current and previous year, country, and brand rating. Ranking is available online only. **Number listed:** 3

1. John Deere, with $3,636 million
2. MAN, $2,783
3. Cummins, $2,499

Source: *Global 500*, (annual), Brand Finance plc, March 2012.

Magazine Advertising
See: **Advertising, Magazine**

Magazine Publishers and Publishing

3554 ■ TOP MAGAZINE COMPANIES IN THE U.S., 2010

Ranked by: Net U.S. magazine revenue, in millions of dollars. **Remarks:** Also notes rank and figures for previous year, annual growth, and top magazine. **Number listed:** 10

1. Advance Publications Inc., with $2,961 million
2. Time Warner Inc., $2,690
3. Hearst Corp., $2,269
4. Meredith Corp., $763
5. RDA Holding Co., $665
6. Wenner Media LLC, $603
7. Rodale Inc., $376
8. American Media Operations Inc., $369
9. Source Interlink Cos., $335
10. Bauer Publishing, $326

Source: *Advertising Age*, 100 Leading Media Companies (annual), October 3, 2011, p. 52.

Magazines

3555 ■ TOP CONSUMER MAGAZINES IN THE UNITED STATES, 2011

Ranked by: Total paid and verified circulation. **Number listed:** 25

1. *AARP the Magazine*, with 22,395,670 readers
2. *AARP Bulletin*, 22,236,761
3. *Better Homes & Gardens*, 7,648,900
4. *Game Informer*, 5,954,884
5. *Reader's Digest*, 5,653,440
6. *National Geographic*, 4,445,603
7. *Good Housekeeping*, 4,336,711
8. *Woman's Day*, 3,863,710
9. *Family Circle*, 3,816,958
10. *People*, 3,556,753

Source: *Top Media Outlets*, (annual), BurrellesLuce, January 2012.

3556 ■ TOP MAGAZINES IN THE U.S., 2011

Ranked by: Score based on how well a magazine operates as a brand. **Remarks:** Specific scores not provided. Also notes editor-in-chief and comments. **Number listed:** 10

1. *Vogue*
2. *Time*
3. *Food Network Magazine*
4. *Garden & Gun*
5. *Vanity Fair*
6. *Monocle*
7. *National Geographic*
8. *The New Yorker*
9. *This Old House*
10. *The Economist*

Source: *Advertising Age*, Magazine A-List (annual), October 10, 2011, p. 14-20.

Magazines—Advertising
See: **Advertising, Magazine**

Managed Health Care Plans

3557 ■ CONNECTICUT'S LARGEST MANAGED HEALTH-CARE COMPANIES OVERALL, 2011

Ranked by: Score based on revenue, profits, assets, and market capitalization. **Remarks:** Specific scores not provided. Also notes overall rank in the *Forbes 2000* and figures for each criterion. **Number listed:** 2

1. Aetna Inc.
2. Cigna Corp.

Source: *Forbes*, Forbes 2000 (annual), http://www.forbes.com, May 7, 2012.

3558 ■ LARGEST U.S. MANAGED HEALTHCARE COMPANIES OVERALL, 2011

Ranked by: Score based on revenue, profits, assets, and market capitalization. **Remarks:** Specific scores not provided. Also notes overall rank in the *Forbes 2000* and figures for each criterion. **Number listed:** 7

1. UnitedHealth Group Inc.
2. WellPoint Inc.
3. Aetna Inc.
4. CIGNA Corp.
5. Humana Inc.
6. Coventry Health Care Inc.
7. Health Net Inc.

Source: *Forbes*, Forbes 2000 (annual), http://www.forbes.com, May 7, 2012.

3559 ■ WORLD'S LARGEST MANAGED HEALTHCARE COMPANIES OVERALL, 2011

Ranked by: Score based on revenue, profits, assets, and market capitalization. **Remarks:** Specific scores not provided. Also notes country, overall rank in the *Forbes 2000,* and figures for each criterion. **Number listed:** 7

1. UnitedHealth Group Inc.
2. WellPoint Inc.
3. Aetna Inc.
4. CIGNA Corp.
5. Humana Inc.
6. Coventry Health Care Inc.
7. Health Net Inc.

Source: *Forbes*, Forbes 2000 (annual), http://www.forbes.com, May 7, 2012.

Management Consultants
See: **Business Consultants**

Manufacturing Industry

3560 ■ BEST U.S. MANUFACTURING COMPANIES, 2008-2010

Ranked by: Three-year performance in revenue growth, return on equity, profit margin, asset turnover, inventory turnover, and return on assets. **Remarks:** Specific scores not provided. Also notes revenue, revenue growth, and profit margin. **Number listed:** 50

1. Western Digital Corp.
2. Apple Inc.
3. Lorillard Inc.
4. Philip Morris International Inc.
5. Tempur-Pedic International Inc.

6. Microsoft Corp.
7. Polaris Industries Inc.
8. Deckers Outdoor Corp.
9. PepsiCo Inc.
10. Exxon Mobil Corp.

Source: *IndustryWeek*, 50 Best Manufacturing Companies (annual), http://www.industryweek.com, July 2011.

3561 ■ FASTEST-GROWING PRIVATE MANUFACTURING COMPANIES IN THE U.S., 2007-2010

Ranked by: Average annual sales growth over three years, in percent. **Remarks:** Also notes headquarters, revenue, and rank in the overall *Inc. 500.* To qualify, private companies must have had annual revenues of at least $100,000 in 2007 and $2 million in 2010. **Number listed:** 12

1. Solazyme, with 20,424.3%
2. KG Technologies, 3,919.7%
3. Product Movers, 2,659.4%
4. Aromatic Fusion, 1,455.3%
5. Legacy Converting, 1,289.2%
6. Simpak International, 1,186%
7. E Systems Technology, 936.2%
8. RSL Fiber Systems, 839.8%
9. MetroSpec Technology, 794.6%
10. Albeo Technologies, 776%

Source: *Inc.*, Inc. 500 (annual), September 2011, p. 178.

3562 ■ LARGEST COMPANIES IN MISCELLANEOUS MANUFACTURING INDUSTRIES BY EMPLOYEES, 2010

Ranked by: Total number of employees. **Remarks:** Also notes contact information for headquarters, number of employees at headquarters, revenue, rank by revenue, and primary SIC code. **Number listed:** 59

1. Tyco International (U.S.) Inc., with 106,000 employees
2. Mattel Inc., 27,000
3. Armstrong World Industries Inc., 10,800
4. AMF Bowling Worldwide Inc., 8,841
5. Brady Corp., 6,710
6. Bic Corp., 5,985
7. Hasbro Inc., 5,800
8. Jostens Inc., 5,645
9. Visant Corp., 5,250
10. YCC Holdings LLC, 5,110

Source: *Business Rankings*, (annual), Dun & Bradstreet Inc., 2011, p. VI.86-VI.87.

3563 ■ LARGEST COMPANIES IN MISCELLANEOUS MANUFACTURING INDUSTRIES BY SALES, 2010

Ranked by: Total revenue, in dollars. **Remarks:** Also notes contact information for headquarters, number of employees at headquarters and overall, rank by employees, and primary SIC code. **Number listed:** 58

1. Mattel Inc., with $5,856,195,000
2. Hasbro Inc., $4,002,161,000
3. Armstrong World Industries Inc., $2,766,400,000
4. International Game Technology Inc., $1,987,200,000

5. Edwards Lifesciences Financing LLC, $1,321,400,000
6. Brady Corp., $1,259,096,000
7. Visant Corp., $1,255,325,000
8. Callaway Golf Co., $967,656,000
9. Blyth Inc., $958,077,000
10. Bally Technologies Inc., $778,191,000

Source: *Business Rankings*, (annual), Dun & Bradstreet Inc., 2011, p. V.86-V.87.

3564 ■ LARGEST MANUFACTURERS IN WESTERN MASSACHUSETTS, 2011

Ranked by: Number of employees. **Remarks:** Also notes contact information, top local officer, and business description. **Number listed:** 26

1. Yankee Candle Co., with 3,000 employees
2. Hasbro Inc., 1,200
3. General Dynamics Advanced Information Systems, 1,000
4. Friendly Ice Cream Corp., 900
5. Smith & Wesson Corp., 885
6. Lenox Industrial Tools, 800
7. Callaway Golf Ball Operations Inc., 600
8. Kollmorgen Electro-Optical, 550
9. Berry Plastics Corp., 515
10. Solutia Inc., 514

Source: *BusinessWest*, Largest Manufacturers, February 27, 2012, p. 23.

3565 ■ LARGEST U.S. MANUFACTURING COMPANIES, 2010

Ranked by: Revenue, in millions of dollars. **Remarks:** Also notes rank for previous year, industry, and revenue growth. **Number listed:** 500

1. Exxon Mobil Corp., with $372,544 million
2. Chevron Corp., $199,291
3. ConocoPhilips, $195,522
4. General Electric Co., $150,211
5. General Motors Co., $135,592
6. Ford Motor Co., $128,954
7. Hewlett-Packard Co., $126,033
8. International Business Machines Corp. (IBM), $99,870
9. Valero Energy Corp., $82,233
10. Proctor & Gamble Co., $78,938

Source: *IndustryWeek*, IW 500 (annual), http://www.industryweek.com, July 2011.

3566 ■ LARGEST U.S. MISCELLANEOUS MANUFACTURERS, 2010

Ranked by: Revenue, in millions of dollars. **Remarks:** Also notes overall rank within the *IW 500,* revenue growth, and profit margin. **Number listed:** 20

1. Honeywell International Inc., with $33,370 million
2. Danaher Corp., $13,203
3. Fortune Brands Inc., $7,142
4. Jarden Corp., $6,023

5. Mattel Inc., $5,856
6. Newell Rubbermaid Inc., $5,759
7. Bemis Co., Inc., $4,835
8. Hasbro Inc., $4,002
9. MDU Resources Group Inc., $3,910
10. Life Technologies Corp., $3,588

Source: *IndustryWeek*, IW 500 (annual), http://www.industryweek.com, July 2011.

3567 ■ STATES WITH THE HIGHEST RATE OF EMPLOYEES IN MANUFACTURING, 2010

Ranked by: Percentage of nonfarm employees in the manufacturing industry. **Number listed:** 47

1. Indiana, with 15.8%
1. Wisconsin, 15.8%
3. Arkansas, 14.1%
4. Iowa, 14%
5. Ohio, 12.4%
6. Mississippi, 12.3%
7. Kansas, 12.1%
7. Kentucky, 12.1%
9. Michigan, 12%
10. South Carolina, 11.6%
10. Tennessee, 11.6%

Source: *State Rankings*, (annual), CQ Press, 2011, p. 201.

3568 ■ STATES WITH THE LOWEST RATE OF EMPLOYEES IN MANUFACTURING, 2010

Ranked by: Percentage of nonfarm employees in the manufacturing industry. **Number listed:** 47

1. Wyoming, with 3.2%
2. Nevada, 3.4%
3. New Mexico, 3.8%
4. Alaska, 4%
5. Florida, 4.2%
5. Montana, 4.2%
7. Maryland, 4.4%
8. New York, 5.4%
9. Colorado, 5.5%
10. Arizona, 6.2%

Source: *State Rankings*, (annual), CQ Press, 2011, p. 201.

3569 ■ THE UNITED STATES' MOST VALUABLE MISCELLANEOUS MANUFACTURING BRANDS, 2011

Ranked by: Brand value, in millions of U.S. dollars. **Remarks:** Also notes rank within the *Global 500* for current and previous year, figures for current and previous year, and brand rating. Ranking is available online only. **Number listed:** 5

1. GE, with $33,214 million
2. 3M, $10,717
3. Honeywell, $6,539
4. NBC International, $5,161
5. Danaher, $3,029

Source: *Global 500*, (annual), Brand Finance plc, March 2012.

Manufacturing Industry, International

3570 ■ BEST MANUFACTURING, CONSTRUCTION, AND DISTRIBUTION COMPANIES TO WORK FOR IN BRITISH COLUMBIA, 2010

Ranked by: Editorial determination. **Remarks:** Specific scores not provided. **Number listed:** 5

1. Kryton International Inc.
2. Waterplay Solutions Corp.
3. Great Little Box Co., Ltd.
4. Sequel Natural Ltd.
5. Maxem Eyewear Corp.

Source: *BCBusiness*, Best Companies (annual), http://www.bcbusinessonline.ca, December 2011.

3571 ■ INDIA'S LARGEST MANUFACTURING COMPANIES, 2010

Ranked by: Revenue, in millions of U.S. dollars. **Remarks:** Also notes rank for previous year, overall rank within the *IW 1000*, industry, and revenue growth. **Number listed:** 12

1. Indian Oil Corp., with $58,901 million
2. Reliance Industries Ltd., $49,408
3. Bharat Petroleum Corp., $29,408
4. Hindustan Petroleum Corp., $25,380
5. Oil & Natural Gas Corp., Ltd., $23,975
6. Tata Steel Ltd., $23,202
7. Tata Motors Ltd., $21,126
8. Steel Authority of India Ltd., $9,712
9. Gail India Ltd., $6,190
10. Chennai Petroleum Corp., $5,794

Source: *IndustryWeek*, IW 1000 (annual), http://www.industryweek.com, August 2011.

3572 ■ ISRAEL'S LARGEST MANUFACTURING COMPANIES, 2010

Ranked by: Revenue, in millions of U.S. dollars. **Remarks:** Also notes rank for previous year, overall rank within the *IW 1000*, industry, and revenue growth. **Number listed:** 2

1. Teva Pharmaceutical Industries Ltd., with $16,121 million
2. Israel Chemicals Ltd., $5,703

Source: *IndustryWeek*, IW 1000 (annual), http://www.industryweek.com, August 2011.

3573 ■ LARGEST AUSTRALIAN MANUFACTURING COMPANIES, 2010

Ranked by: Revenue, in millions of U.S. dollars. **Remarks:** Also notes rank for previous year, overall rank within the *IW 1000*, industry, and revenue growth. **Number listed:** 15

1. BHP Billiton Ltd., with $53,326 million
2. Wesfarmers Ltd., $53,155
3. Caltex Australia Ltd., $19,365
4. Amcor Ltd., $10,133
5. Bluescope Steel Ltd., $8,832
6. Origin Energy Ltd., $8,787
7. OneSteel Ltd., $6,399
8. Orica Ltd., $5,977

9. Paperlinx Ltd., $5,192
10. CSL Ltd., $4,733

Source: *IndustryWeek*, IW 1000 (annual), http://www.industryweek.com, August 2011.

3574 ■ LARGEST AUSTRIAN MANUFACTURING COMPANIES, 2010

Ranked by: Revenue, in millions of U.S. dollars. **Remarks:** Also notes rank for previous year, overall rank within the *IW 1000*, industry, and revenue growth. **Number listed:** 3

1. OMV AG, with $31,211 million
2. Voest-Alpine AG, $11,910
3. Andritz AG, $4,740

Source: *IndustryWeek*, IW 1000 (annual), http://www.industryweek.com, August 2011.

3575 ■ LARGEST BELGIAN MANUFACTURING COMPANIES, 2010

Ranked by: Revenue, in millions of U.S. dollars. **Remarks:** Also notes rank for previous year, overall rank within the *IW 1000*, industry, and revenue growth. **Number listed:** 7

1. Anheuser-Busch InBev SA/NV, with $36,782 million
2. Umicore SA, $13,054
3. Solvay SA, $9,509
4. AGFA-Gevaert NV, $4,393
5. Bekaert NV, $4,382
6. UCB SA, $4,302
7. Tessenderlo Chemie SA, $3,247

Source: *IndustryWeek*, IW 1000 (annual), http://www.industryweek.com, August 2011.

3576 ■ LARGEST BERMUDAN MANUFACTURING COMPANIES, 2010

Ranked by: Revenue, in millions of U.S. dollars. **Remarks:** Also notes rank for previous year, overall rank within the *IW 1000*, industry, and revenue growth. **Number listed:** 3

1. Yue Yuen Industrial Holdings Ltd., with $5,912 million
2. First Pacific Co., Ltd., $4,640
3. Marvell Technology Group Ltd., $3,612

Source: *IndustryWeek*, IW 1000 (annual), http://www.industryweek.com, August 2011.

3577 ■ LARGEST BRAZILIAN MANUFACTURING COMPANIES, 2010

Ranked by: Revenue, in millions of U.S. dollars. **Remarks:** Also notes rank for previous year, overall rank within the *IW 1000*, industry, and revenue growth. **Number listed:** 10

1. Petroleo Brasileiro SA (Petrobras), with $120,052 million
2. Vale SA, $45,293
3. Metalurgica Gerdau SA, $16,083
4. Braskem SA, $15,875
5. Companhia de Bebidas das Americas (Am-Bev), $15,564
6. Brasil Foods SA, $13,652
7. Companhia Siderurgica Nacional, $6,608

8. Usinas Siderurgicas de Minas Gerais SA, $6,575

9. Empresa Brasileira de Aeronautica SA (Embraer), $5,374

10. Fibria Celulose SA, $3,777

Source: *IndustryWeek*, IW 1000 (annual), http://www.industryweek.com, August 2011.

3578 ■ LARGEST CANADIAN MANUFACTURING COMPANIES, 2010

Ranked by: Revenue, in millions of U.S. dollars. **Remarks:** Also notes rank for previous year, overall rank within the *IW 1000*, industry, and revenue growth. **Number listed:** 26

1. Suncor Energy Inc., with $34,575 million

2. George Weston Ltd., $32,217

3. Imperial Oil Ltd., $25,256

4. Onex Corp., $24,525

5. Magna International Inc., $24,102

6. Research in Motion Ltd., $19,907

7. Husky Energy Inc., $18,297

8. Bombardier Inc., $17,681

9. Canadian Natural Resources Ltd., $12,985

10. Cenovus Energy Inc., $12,973

Source: *IndustryWeek*, IW 1000 (annual), http://www.industryweek.com, August 2011.

3579 ■ LARGEST CHILEAN MANUFACTURING COMPANIES, 2010

Ranked by: Revenue, in millions of U.S. dollars. **Remarks:** Also notes rank for previous year, overall rank within the *IW 1000*, industry, and revenue growth. **Number listed:** 2

1. Empresas COPEC SA, with $12,150 million

2. Empresas CMPC SA, $4,450

Source: *IndustryWeek*, IW 1000 (annual), http://www.industryweek.com, August 2011.

3580 ■ LARGEST CHINESE MANUFACTURING COMPANIES, 2010

Ranked by: Revenue, in millions of U.S. dollars. **Remarks:** Also notes rank for previous year, overall rank within the *IW 1000*, industry, and revenue growth. **Number listed:** 55

1. China Petroleum & Chemical Corp. (Sinopec), with $290,039 million

2. PetroChina Co., Ltd., $222,157

3. SAIC Motor Corp., Ltd., $49,526

4. Baoshan Iron & Steel Co., Ltd., $22,645

5. Great Wall Technology Co., Ltd., $16,008

6. Angang Steel Co., Ltd., $14,013

7. Sinopec Shanghai Petrochemical Co., Ltd., $10,946

8. Aluminum Corp. of China Ltd., $10,741

9. China Coal Energy Co., Ltd., $10,732

10. Shanghai Electric Group Co., Ltd., $9,717

Source: *IndustryWeek*, IW 1000 (annual), http://www.industryweek.com, August 2011.

3581 ■ LARGEST DANISH MANUFACTURING COMPANIES, 2010

Ranked by: Revenue, in millions of U.S. dollars. **Remarks:** Also notes rank for previous year, overall rank within the *IW 1000*, industry, and revenue growth. **Number listed:** 5

1. A. P. Moller-Maersk A/S, with $56,614 million

2. Novo Nordisk A/S, $11,027

3. Carlsberg A/S, $10,862

4. Vestas Wind Systems A/S, $9,258

5. FL Smidth & Co., $3,623

Source: *IndustryWeek*, IW 1000 (annual), http://www.industryweek.com, August 2011.

3582 ■ LARGEST DUTCH MANUFACTURING COMPANIES, 2010

Ranked by: Revenue, in millions of U.S. dollars. **Remarks:** Also notes rank for previous year, overall rank within the *IW 1000*, industry, and revenue growth. **Number listed:** 13

1. Royal Dutch Shell plc, with $372,199 million

2. EADS NV, $61,217

3. Koninklijke Philips Electronics NV (Royal Philips Electronics NV), $34,135

4. LyondellBasell Industries NV, $30,828

5. Heineken NV, $21,899

6. Akzo Nobel NV, $19,583

7. CNH Global NV, $15,608

8. Koninklijke DSM NV (Royal DSM NV), $12,286

9. Nutreco Holding NV, $6,607

10. ASML Holding NV, $6,030

Source: *IndustryWeek*, IW 1000 (annual), http://www.industryweek.com, August 2011.

3583 ■ LARGEST FINNISH MANUFACTURING COMPANIES, 2010

Ranked by: Revenue, in millions of U.S. dollars. **Remarks:** Also notes rank for previous year, overall rank within the *IW 1000*, industry, and revenue growth. **Number listed:** 12

1. Nokia Corp., with $57,413 million

2. Neste Oil Oyj, $16,015

3. Stora Enso Oyj, $13,986

4. UPM-Kymmene Oyj, $12,039

5. Fortum Oyj, $8,558

6. Metso Corp., $7,492

7. Kone Corp., $6,734

8. Wartsila Corp., $5,950

9. Outokumpu Corp., $5,717

10. Rautaruukki Corp., $3,250

Source: *IndustryWeek*, IW 1000 (annual), http://www.industryweek.com, August 2011.

3584 ■ LARGEST FRENCH MANUFACTURING COMPANIES, 2010

Ranked by: Revenue, in millions of U.S. dollars. **Remarks:** Also notes rank for previous year, overall rank within the *IW 1000*, industry, and revenue growth. **Number listed:** 44

1. Total SA, with $187,903 million

2. Peugeot SA, $75,413

3. France Telecom SA, $62,063

4. Cie. de Saint Gobain SA, $53,780

5. Renault SA, $52,392

6. Sanofi SA, $43,146

7. Vivendi SA, $38,628

8. Christian Dior SA, $28,254

9. Alstom, $26,285
10. Schneider Electric SA, $26,201

Source: *IndustryWeek*, IW 1000 (annual), http://www.industryweek.com, August 2011.

3585 ■ LARGEST GERMAN MANUFACTURING COMPANIES, 2010

Ranked by: Revenue, in millions of U.S. dollars. **Remarks:** Also notes rank for previous year, overall rank within the *IW 1000*, industry, and revenue growth. **Number listed:** 38

1. Volkswagen AG, with $169,710 million
2. Daimler AG, $130,766
3. E.On AG, $124,215
4. Siemens AG, $102,211
5. BASF SE, $86,726
6. Bayerische Motoren Werke AG (BMW), $81,168
7. RWE AG, $69,819
8. ThyssenKrupp AG, $57,377
9. Audi AG, $49,191
10. Bayer AG, $47,671

Source: *IndustryWeek*, IW 1000 (annual), http://www.industryweek.com, August 2011.

3586 ■ LARGEST GREEK MANUFACTURING COMPANIES, 2010

Ranked by: Revenue, in millions of U.S. dollars. **Remarks:** Also notes rank for previous year, overall rank within the *IW 1000*, industry, and revenue growth. **Number listed:** 4

1. Hellenic Petroleum SA, with $11,386 million
2. Coca-Cola Hellenic Bottling Co. SA, $9,087
3. Motor Oil (Hellas) SA, $8,331
4. Viohalco SA, $3,980

Source: *IndustryWeek*, IW 1000 (annual), http://www.industryweek.com, August 2011.

3587 ■ LARGEST HONG KONG MANUFACTURING COMPANIES, 2010

Ranked by: Revenue, in millions of U.S. dollars. **Remarks:** Also notes rank for previous year, overall rank within the *IW 1000*, industry, and revenue growth. **Number listed:** 6

1. CNOOC Ltd., with $27,751 million
2. Lenovo Group Ltd., $16,606
3. China Resources Enterprise Ltd., $11,508
4. China Agri-Industries Holdings Ltd., $7,004
5. Fosun International Ltd., $6,872
6. Techtronic Industries Co., Ltd., $3,385

Source: *IndustryWeek*, IW 1000 (annual), http://www.industryweek.com, August 2011.

3588 ■ LARGEST INDONESIAN MANUFACTURING COMPANIES, 2010

Ranked by: Revenue, in millions of U.S. dollars. **Remarks:** Also notes rank for previous year, overall rank within the *IW 1000*, industry, and revenue growth. **Number listed:** 3

1. PT Bumi Resources TBK, with $4,370 million
2. PT Gudang Garam TBK, $3,769
3. Indofood Sukses Makmur TBK PT, $3,714

Source: *IndustryWeek*, IW 1000 (annual), http://www.industryweek.com, August 2001.

3589 ■ LARGEST INDUSTRIAL MANUFACTURING COMPANIES IN EUROPE, 2010

Ranked by: Sales, in millions of U.S. dollars. **Remarks:** Also notes rank within country. **Number listed:** 100

1. CRH plc (Ireland), with $25,837.1 million
2. Compagnie Generale des Etablissements Michelin (France), $23,127.1
3. HeidelbergCement AG (Germany), $16,533.2
4. Svenska Cellulosa AB (SCA, Sweden), $15,808.2
5. Rolls-Royce plc (U.K.), $15,621
6. Voestalpine AG (Austria), $14,940.8
7. ZF Friedrichshafen AG (Germany), $13,936.6
8. Makespace Mezzanine Floors Ltd. (U.K.), $11,943.8
9. Nokia Siemens Networks Oy (Finland), $10,376.4
10. Sandvik AB (Sweden), $10,258.2

Source: *Europe's 15,000 Largest Companies*, (annual), ELC International, 2011, p. 43.

3590 ■ LARGEST IRISH MANUFACTURING COMPANIES, 2010

Ranked by: Revenue, in millions of U.S. dollars. **Remarks:** Also notes rank for previous year, overall rank within the *IW 1000*, industry, and revenue growth. **Number listed:** 10

1. CRH plc, with $22,999 million
2. Ingersoll-Rand plc, $14,079
3. Seagate Technology plc, $11,395
4. Covidien plc, $10,429
5. Smurfit Kappa Group plc, $8,961
6. Kerry Group plc, $6,635
7. Cooper Industries plc, $5,066
8. Shire plc, $3,471
9. Warner Chilcott plc, $2,974
10. Glanbia plc, $2,912

Source: *IndustryWeek*, IW 1000 (annual), http://www.industryweek.com, August 2011.

3591 ■ LARGEST ITALIAN MANUFACTURING COMPANIES, 2010

Ranked by: Revenue, in millions of U.S. dollars. **Remarks:** Also notes rank for previous year, overall rank within the *IW 1000*, industry, and revenue growth. **Number listed:** 15

1. ENI SpA, with $133,064 million
2. Fiat SpA, $47,994
3. Finmeccanica SpA, $25,610
4. Saipem SpA, $14,951
5. Edison SpA, $12,552
6. Luxottica Group SpA, $7,756
7. ERG SpA, $7,304
8. Italmobiliare SpA, $7,058
9. Pirelli SpA, $6,738
10. Italcementi SpA, $6,567

Source: *IndustryWeek*, IW 1000 (annual), http://www.industryweek.com, August 2011.

3592 ■ LARGEST JAPANESE MANUFACTURING COMPANIES, 2010

Ranked by: Revenue, in millions of U.S. dollars. **Remarks:** Also notes rank for previous year, overall rank within the *IW 1000*, industry, and revenue growth. **Number listed:** 211

1. Toyota Motor Corp., with $233,099 million
2. Hitachi Ltd., $110,314
3. Honda Motor Co., Ltd., $105,525
4. Nissan Motor Co., Ltd., $92,463
5. Panasonic Corp., $91,242
6. Nippon Oil Corp., $90,888
7. Sony Corp., $88,733
8. Toshiba Corp., $78,494
9. Japan Tobacco Inc., $75,458
10. Fujitsu Ltd., $57,559

Source: *IndustryWeek*, IW 1000 (annual), http://www.industryweek.com, August 2011.

3593 ■ LARGEST MALAYSIAN MANUFACTURING COMPANIES, 2010

Ranked by: Revenue, in millions of U.S. dollars. **Remarks:** Also notes rank for previous year, overall rank within the *IW 1000*, industry, and revenue growth. **Number listed:** 3

1. IOI Corp. Berhad, with $4,105 million
2. Shell Refining Co. Berhad, $3,379
3. UMW Holdings Berhad, $3,279

Source: *IndustryWeek*, IW 1000 (annual), http://www.industryweek.com, August 2011.

3594 ■ LARGEST MANUFACTURING COMPANIES IN THE CAYMAN ISLANDS, 2010

Ranked by: Revenue, in millions of U.S. dollars. **Remarks:** Also notes rank for previous year, overall rank within the *IW 1000*, industry, and revenue growth. **Number listed:** 6

1. Foxcomm International Holdings Ltd., with $6,779 million
2. Tingyi (Cayman) Islands Holdings Corp., $6,769
3. China Mengniu Dairy Co., Ltd., $4,608
4. Kingboard Chemical Holdings Ltd., $4,376
5. Belle International Holdings Ltd., $3,594
6. Fresh Del Monte Produce Inc., $3,553

Source: *IndustryWeek*, IW 1000 (annual), http://www.industryweek.com, August 2011.

3595 ■ LARGEST MEXICAN MANUFACTURING COMPANIES, 2010

Ranked by: Revenue, in millions of U.S. dollars. **Remarks:** Also notes rank for previous year, overall rank within the *IW 1000*, industry, and revenue growth. **Number listed:** 10

1. Cemex, SA de CV, with $14,440 million
2. Fomento Economico Mexicano, SA de CV (FEMSA), $13,747
3. Alfa SA de CV, $11,049
4. Grupo Bimbo SA de CV, $9,491
5. Coca-Cola FEMSA, SA de CV, $8,380
6. Grupo Modelo SA de CV, $6,887
7. Grupo Carso SA de CV, $5,200
8. Grupo Mexico SA de CV, $4,827

9. Gruma SA de CV, $3,775
10. Industrias Penoles SA de CV, $3,630

Source: *IndustryWeek*, IW 1000 (annual), http://www.industryweek.com, August 2011.

3596 ■ LARGEST NORWEGIAN MANUFACTURING COMPANIES, 2010

Ranked by: Revenue, in millions of U.S. dollars. **Remarks:** Also notes rank for previous year, overall rank within the *IW 1000*, industry, and revenue growth. **Number listed:** 4

1. Statoil ASA, with $90,888 million
2. Norsk Hydro ASA, $12,986
3. Yara International ASA, $11,218
4. Norske Skogindustrier ASA, $3,258

Source: *IndustryWeek*, IW 1000 (annual), http://www.industryweek.com, August 2011.

3597 ■ LARGEST POLISH MANUFACTURING COMPANIES, 2010

Ranked by: Revenue, in millions of U.S. dollars. **Remarks:** Also notes rank for previous year, overall rank within the *IW 1000*, industry, and revenue growth. **Number listed:** 4

1. Polski Koncern Naftowy Orlen SA (PKN Orlen), with $23,153 million
2. Grupa Lotos SA, $6,660
3. PGNIG SA, $6,528
4. KGHM Polska Miedz SA, $5,852

Source: *IndustryWeek*, IW 1000 (annual), http://www.industryweek.com, August 2011.

3598 ■ LARGEST PORTUGUESE MANUFACTURING COMPANIES, 2010

Ranked by: Revenue, in millions of U.S. dollars. **Remarks:** Also notes rank for previous year, overall rank within the *IW 1000*, industry, and revenue growth. **Number listed:** 2

1. Jeronimo Martins SGPS SA, with $12,171 million
2. Cimentos de Portugal SGPS SA (CIMPOR), $3,098

Source: *IndustryWeek*, IW 1000 (annual), http://www.industryweek.com, August 2011.

3599 ■ LARGEST RUSSIAN MANUFACTURING COMPANIES, 2010

Ranked by: Revenue, in millions of U.S. dollars. **Remarks:** Also notes rank for previous year, overall rank within the *IW 1000*, industry, and revenue growth. **Number listed:** 9

1. OAO Gazprom, with $117,828 million
2. Lukoil Oil Co., $104,956
3. OAO Neft Gazprom, $32,772
4. OAO Surgutneftegaz, $16,458
5. OAO Tatneft, $15,305
6. OAO Severstal, $13,469
7. OJSC Mining & Metallurgical Company Norilsk Nickel, $10,155
8. OAO Mechel, $9,746
9. OAO TMK, $5,580

Source: *IndustryWeek*, IW 1000 (annual), http://www.industryweek.com, August 2011.

3600 ■ LARGEST SOUTH AFRICAN MANUFACTURING COMPANIES, 2010

Ranked by: Revenue, in millions of U.S. dollars. **Remarks:** Also notes rank for previous year, overall rank within the *IW 1000*, industry, and revenue growth. **Number listed:** 10

1. Sasol Ltd., with $18,688 million
2. Steinhoff International Holdings Ltd., $7,452
3. Anglo American Platinum Ltd., $7,036
4. Sappi Ltd., $6,572
5. Barloworld Ltd., $6,253
6. Anglogold Ashanti Ltd., $5,895
7. Aveng Ltd., $5,158
8. ArcelorMittal South Africa Ltd., $4,588
9. Tiger Brands Ltd., $2,968
10. Nampak Ltd., $2,850

Source: *IndustryWeek*, IW 1000 (annual), http://www.industryweek.com, August 2011.

3601 ■ LARGEST SOUTH KOREAN MANUFACTURING COMPANIES, 2010

Ranked by: Revenue, in millions of U.S. dollars. **Remarks:** Also notes rank for previous year, overall rank within the *IW 1000*, industry, and revenue growth. **Number listed:** 38

1. Samsung Electronics Co., Ltd., with $139,169 million
2. Hyundai Motor Co., $101,332
3. SK Holdings Co., Ltd., $81,594
4. Pohang Iron & Steel Co., Ltd. (POSCO), $54,575
5. LG Electronics Inc., $51,988
6. SK Innovation Co., Ltd., $48,336
7. Hyundai Heavy Industries Co., Ltd., $40,567
8. Kia Motors Corp., $38,062
9. GS Holdings Co., Ltd., $38,043
10. LG Display Co.,Ltd., $24,296

Source: *IndustryWeek*, IW 1000 (annual), http://www.industryweek.com, August 2011.

3602 ■ LARGEST SPANISH MANUFACTURING COMPANIES, 2010

Ranked by: Revenue, in millions of U.S. dollars. **Remarks:** Also notes rank for previous year, overall rank within the *IW 1000*, industry, and revenue growth. **Number listed:** 4

1. Repsol YPF, SA, with $76,568 million
2. Compania Espanola de Petroleos SA (Cepsa), $29,955
3. Industria de Diseno Textil SA, $16,751
4. Gamesa Corporacion Tecnologica SA, $3,992

Source: *IndustryWeek*, IW 1000 (annual), http://www.industryweek.com, August 2011.

3603 ■ LARGEST SWEDISH MANUFACTURING COMPANIES, 2010

Ranked by: Revenue, in millions of U.S. dollars. **Remarks:** Also notes rank for previous year, overall rank within the *IW 1000*, industry, and revenue growth. **Number listed:** 17

1. AB Volvo, with $39,292 million
2. Telefonaktiebolaget LM Ericsson, $30,480
3. Svenska Cellulosa AB (SCA), $16,219
4. AB Electrolux, $15,800
5. Sandvik AB, $12,296
6. Atlas Copco AB, $10,409
7. Scania AB, $9,840
8. SKF AB, $9,143
9. SSAB AB, $5,946
10. Assa Abloy AB, $5,475

Source: *IndustryWeek*, IW 1000 (annual), http://www.industryweek.com, August 2011.

3604 ■ LARGEST SWISS MANUFACTURING COMPANIES, 2010

Ranked by: Revenue, in millions of U.S. dollars. **Remarks:** Also notes rank for previous year, overall rank within the *IW 1000*, industry, and revenue growth. **Number listed:** 25

1. Nestle SA, with $117,463 million
2. Novartis AG, $52,795
3. Roche Holding Ltd., $52,636
4. ABB Ltd., $31,589
5. Holcim Ltd., $23,181
6. Petroplus Holding AG, $20,735
7. Tyco International Ltd., $17,016
8. TE Connectivity Ltd., $12,070
9. Syngenta AG, $11,641
10. STMicroelectronics NV, $10,346

Source: *IndustryWeek*, IW 1000 (annual), http://www.industryweek.com, August 2011.

3605 ■ LARGEST THAI MANUFACTURING COMPANIES, 2010

Ranked by: Revenue, in millions of U.S. dollars. **Remarks:** Also notes rank for previous year, overall rank within the *IW 1000*, industry, and revenue growth. **Number listed:** 5

1. PTT Public Co., Ltd., with $63,703 million
2. The Siam Cement Public Co., Ltd., $10,247
3. IRPC Public Co., Ltd., $7,380
4. Charoen Pokphand Foods Public Co., Ltd., $6,412
5. PTT Exploration & Production Public Co., Ltd., $4,914

Source: *IndustryWeek*, IW 1000 (annual), http://www.industryweek.com, August 2011.

3606 ■ LARGEST TURKISH MANUFACTURING COMPANIES, 2010

Ranked by: Revenue, in millions of U.S. dollars. **Remarks:** Also notes rank for previous year, overall rank within the *IW 1000*, industry, and revenue growth. **Number listed:** 4

1. Turkiye Petrol Rafinerileri AS, with $17,164 million
2. Arcelik AS, $4,578
3. Eregli Demir Ve Celik Fabrikalari TAS, $4,395
4. Vestel Elektronok Sanayi ve Ticaret AS, $3,482

Source: *IndustryWeek*, IW 1000 (annual), http://www.industryweek.com, August 2011.

3607 ■ LARGEST U.K. MANUFACTURING COMPANIES, 2010

Ranked by: Revenue, in millions of U.S. dollars. **Remarks:** Also notes rank for previous year, overall rank within the *IW 1000*, industry, and revenue growth. **Number listed:** 35

1. BP plc, with $302,545 million
2. Unilever, $59,205
3. Rio Tinto Ltd., $54,646
4. GlaxoSmithKline plc, $44,710
5. Imperial Tobacco Group plc, $43,979
6. AstraZeneca plc, $34,098
7. BAE Systems plc, $33,160
8. Xstrata plc, $30,499
9. Anglo American plc, $27,960
10. British American Tobacco plc, $23,556

Source: *IndustryWeek*, IW 1000 (annual), http://www.industryweek.com, August 2011.

3608 ■ LUXEMBOURG'S LARGEST MANUFACTURING COMPANIES, 2010

Ranked by: Revenue, in millions of U.S. dollars. **Remarks:** Also notes rank for previous year, overall rank within the *IW 1000*, industry, and revenue growth. **Number listed:** 5

1. ArcelorMittal SA, with $78,025 million
2. Evraz Group SA, $13,394
3. Tenaris SA, $7,797
4. Ternium SA, $7,384
5. Aperam, $5,604

Source: *IndustryWeek*, IW 1000 (annual), http://www.industryweek.com, August 2011.

3609 ■ THE PHILIPPINES'S LARGEST MANUFACTURING COMPANIES, 2010

Ranked by: Revenue, in millions of U.S. dollars. **Remarks:** Also notes rank for previous year, overall rank within the *IW 1000*, industry, and revenue growth. **Number listed:** 2

1. San Miguel Corp., with $5,649 million
2. Petron Corp., $4,043

Source: *IndustryWeek*, IW 1000 (annual), http://www.industryweek.com, August 2011.

3610 ■ SINGAPORE'S LARGEST MANUFACTURING COMPANIES, 2010

Ranked by: Revenue, in millions of U.S. dollars. **Remarks:** Also notes rank for previous year, overall rank within the *IW 1000*, industry, and revenue growth. **Number listed:** 3

1. Flextronics International Ltd., with $28,680 million
2. Keppel Corp., Ltd., $7,622
3. Fraser & Neave Ltd., $4,449

Source: *IndustryWeek*, IW 1000 (annual), http://www.industryweek.com, August 2011.

3611 ■ TAIWAN'S LARGEST MANUFACTURING COMPANIES, 2010

Ranked by: Revenue, in millions of U.S. dollars. **Remarks:** Also notes rank for previous year, overall rank within the *IW 1000*, industry, and revenue growth. **Number listed:** 31

1. Hon Hai Precision Industry Co., Ltd., with $102,806 million
2. Quanta Computer Inc., $38,579
3. Compal Electronics Inc., $30,425
4. Formosa Petrochemical Corp., $21,801
5. Acer Inc., $21,577

6. Wistron Corp., $21,101
7. AU Optronics Corp., $16,024
8. Asustek Computer Inc., $14,743
9. Taiwan Semiconductor Manufacturing Co., Ltd., $14,737
10. Formosa Chemicals & Fibre Corp., $13,160

Source: *IndustryWeek*, IW 1000 (annual), http://www.industryweek.com, August 2011.

3612 ■ WORLD'S BEST MANUFACTURING PLANTS, 2011

Ranked by: Score based on quality, customer and supplier relations, employee involvement, application of technology, productivity, cost reductions, manufacturing flexibility and responsiveness, inventory management, environmental and safety performance, new product development, and overall market results. **Remarks:** Scores not provided; companies are listed alphabetically, not ranked. Also notes plant location. **Number listed:** 10

1. Carrier
2. Ethicon Inc.
3. General Cable Corp. (Lawrenceburg plant)
4. General Cable Corp. (Lincoln plant)
5. Klein Steel Service
6. L. B. Foster Co.
7. Life Technologies
8. Lockheed Martin Corp.
9. Swagelok Co.
10. Toyota Industrial Equipment Manufacturing Inc.

Source: *IndustryWeek*, Best Plants (annual), http://www.industryweek.com, January 2012.

3613 ■ WORLD'S LARGEST MANUFACTURERS BY GROSS REVENUE, 2010

Ranked by: Gross revenue, in millions of U.S. dollars. **Remarks:** Also notes rank for previous year, net income, figures for previous year, percent change, income as a percentage of revenue, revenue from assemblies, and assemblies as a percentage of revenue. **Number listed:** 50

1. Toyota Motor Corp., with $228,427 million
2. General Electric Co., $150,211
3. General Motors Co., $135,592
4. Daimler AG, $130,628
5. Ford Motor Co., $128,954
6. Hewlett-Packard Co., $126,033
7. Honda Motor Co., Ltd., $107,479
8. Nissan Motor Co., Ltd., $105,977
9. Siemens AG, $103,694
10. International Business Machines Corp. (IBM), $99,870

Source: *Assembly*, Top 50 (annual), November 2011, p. 32.

3614 ■ WORLD'S LARGEST MANUFACTURERS BY INCOME AS A PERCENTAGE OF REVENUE, 2010

Ranked by: Income as a percentage of gross revenue. **Remarks:** Also notes rank for previous year, net income, and gross revenue. **Number listed:** 30

1. QUALCOMM Inc., with 30%
2. Texas Instruments Inc., 23%
3. Johnson & Johnson, 22%

4. Apple Inc., 21%
5. Medtronic Inc., 19%
5. C. R. Bard inc., 19%
7. Becton, Dickinson & Co., 18%
7. St. Jude Medical Inc., 18%
9. Stryker Corp., 17%
9. Research in Motion Ltd., 17%

Source: *Assembly*, Top 50 (annual), November 2011, p. 40.

3615 ■ WORLD'S LARGEST MANUFACTURERS BY NET INCOME, 2010

Ranked by: Net income, in millions of U.S. dollars. **Remarks:** Also notes rank for previous year and net income for previous two years. **Number listed:** 30

1. International Business Machines Corp. (IBM), with $14,833 million
2. Apple Inc., $14,013
3. Johnson & Johnson, $13,334
4. General Electric Co., $11,644
5. Hewlett-Packard Co., $8,761
6. Ford Motor Co., $6,561
7. Cisco Systems Inc., $6,490
8. Honda Motor Co., Ltd., $6,423
9. Daimler AG, $6,245
10. General Motors Co., $6,172

Source: *Assembly*, Top 50 (annual), November 2011, p. 34.

3616 ■ WORLD'S LARGEST MANUFACTURERS BY REVENUE FROM ASSEMBLIES, 2010

Ranked by: Revenue from assemblies, in millions of U.S. dollars. **Remarks:** Also notes rank for previous year, rank in the overall *Top 50*, gross revenue, and assemblies as a percentage of revenue. **Number listed:** 30

1. Toyota Motor Corp., with $214,318 million
2. General Motors Co., $135,142
3. Ford Motor Co., $119,280
4. Daimler AG, $114,348
5. Honda Motor Co., Ltd., $100,708
6. Nissan Motor Co., Ltd., $99,830
7. Siemens AG, $99,293
8. Hewlett-Packard Co., $84,799
9. Robert Bosch GmbH, $63,147
10. General Electric Co., $60,812

Source: *Assembly*, Top 50 (annual), November 2011, p. 38.

3617 ■ WORLD'S LARGEST MANUFACTURING COMPANIES, 2010

Ranked by: Revenue, in millions of U.S. dollars. **Remarks:** Also notes rank for previous year, industry, and revenue growth. **Number listed:** 1000

1. Exxon Mobil Corp. (U.S.), with $372,544 million
2. Royal Dutch Shell plc (Netherlands), $372,199
3. BP plc (U.K.), $302,545
4. China Petroleum & Chemical Corp. (Sinopec, China), $290,039
5. Toyota Motor Corp. (Japan), $233,099
6. PetroChina Co., Ltd. (China), $222,157

7. Chevron Corp. (U.S.), $199,291
8. ConocoPhillips (U.S.), $195,522
9. Total SA (France), $187,903
10. Volkswagen AG (Germany), $169,710

Source: *IndustryWeek*, IW 1000 (annual), http://www.industryweek.com, August 2011.

3618 ■ WORLD'S LARGEST MISCELLANEOUS MANUFACTURERS, 2010

Ranked by: Revenue, in millions of dollars. **Remarks:** Also notes rank for previous year, overall rank within the *IW 1000*, country, and revenue growth. **Number listed:** 40

1. E.On AG, with $124,215 million
2. Vivendi SA, $38,628
3. Mitsubishi Heavy Industries Ltd., $36,173
4. Honeywell International Inc., $33,370
5. Hyundai Mobis, $19,930
6. Nintendo Co., Ltd., $17,643
7. Danaher Corp., $13,203
8. Alfa SA de CV, $11,049
9. Bollore SA, $9,377
10. Wendel, $7,346

Source: *IndustryWeek*, IW 1000 (annual), http://www.industryweek.com, August 2011.

3619 ■ WORLD'S MOST VALUABLE MISCELLANEOUS MANUFACTURING BRANDS, 2011

Ranked by: Brand value, in millions of U.S. dollars. **Remarks:** Also notes rank within the *Global 500* for current and previous year, figures for current and previous year, country, and brand rating. Ranking is available online only. **Number listed:** 11

1. GE, with $33,214 million
2. Tata, $16,343
3. Siemens, $16,320
4. 3M, $10,717
5. Honeywell, $6,539
6. NBC International, $5,161
7. Bombardier, $4,199
8. Fujifilm, $3,287
9. Wilmar, $3,206
10. Danaher, $3,029

Source: *Global 500*, (annual), Brand Finance plc, March 2012.

Marketing

3620 ■ BEST PLACES TO WORK IN MARKETING AND MEDIA, 2011

Ranked by: Score based on employee evaluation and company benefits, policies, practices, and other general information. **Remarks:** Scores not provided. Also notes location, number of employees, top executives, and comments. **Number listed:** 30

1. Allen & Gerritsen
2. BGT Partners
3. Digitas
4. IProspect
5. Dataxu
6. Ubermind

7. Mr. Youth
8. Airfoil Public Relations
9. Archer Malmo
10. Orion Trading

Source: *Advertising Age*, Best Places to Work (annual), August 22, 2011, p. 6-18.

3621 ■ TOP PROMOTION AGENCIES BY REVENUE, 2010

Ranked by: U.S. net revenue, in dollars. **Remarks:** Also notes headquarters, telephone number, principal executive, primary services, two-year growth in revenue, and agency age. **Number listed:** 100

1. DraftFCB, with $644,000,000
2. Digitas, $502,000,000
3. Wunderman, $446,000,000
4. Aspen Marketing Services, $284,917,600
5. BDA, $253,352,000
6. Integrated Marketing Services, $236,000,000
7. Momentum Worldwide, $189,000,000
8. Euro RSCG Worldwide, $185,000,000
9. MarketStar Corp., $148,000,000
10. The Integer Group, $145,000,000

Source: *PROMO Magazine*, PROMO 100 (annual), 2011.

3622 ■ TOP PROMOTION AGENCIES WITH A SPECIALTY IN AUTOMOTIVE, 2010

Ranked by: U.S. net revenue, in dollars. **Number listed:** 5

1. Aspen Marketing Services, with $284,917,600
2. Next Marketing, $8,500,000
3. Automotive Events Inc., $8,136,075
4. Sage Collective, $5,250,000
5. All Terrain, $3,250,216

Source: *PROMO Magazine*, PROMO 100 (annual), 2011.

3623 ■ TOP PROMOTION AGENCIES WITH A SPECIALTY IN CONSUMER PACKAGED GOODS, 2010

Ranked by: U.S. net revenue, in dollars. **Number listed:** 10

1. DraftFCB, with $644,000,000
2. Euro RSCG Worldwide, $185,000,000
3. The Integer Group, $145,000,000
4. TracyLocke, $122,400,000
5. G2 Worldwide, $121,000,000
6. The Marketing Arm, $108,200,000
7. Marketing Drive LLC, $78,700,00
8. Arc Worldwide, $65,600,000
9. Alcone Marketing Group, $65,500,000
10. Ryan Partnership, $61,063,000

Source: *PROMO Magazine*, PROMO 100 (annual), 2011.

3624 ■ TOP PROMOTION AGENCIES WITH A SPECIALTY IN EVENTS/EXPERIENTIALS, 2010

Ranked by: U.S. net revenue, in dollars. **Number listed:** 10

1. Momentum Worldwide, with $189,000,000
2. George P. Johnson, $134,528,766
3. Live Nation Network, $113,350,000
4. Arnold Brand Experience, $99,000,000

5. GMR Marketing, $91,100,000
6. Jack Morton Worldwide, $82,500,000
7. TBA Global, $45,000,000
8. TEAM Enterprises, $39,000,000
9. Marketing Werks, $34,457,998
10. Pierce, $26,500,000

Source: *PROMO Magazine*, PROMO 100 (annual), 2011.

3625 ■ TOP PROMOTION AGENCIES WITH A SPECIALTY IN INTERACTIVES, 2010

Ranked by: U.S. net revenue, in dollars. **Number listed:** 10

1. Digitas, with $502,000,000
2. Wunderman, $446,000,000
3. Aspen Marketing Services, $284,917,600
4. Euro RSCG Worldwide, $185,000,000
5. hawkeye, $72,570,000
6. AMP Agency, $55,673,000
7. ePrize, $40,356,127
8. Isobar, $27,000,000
9. Mr. Youth, $20,000,000
10. Gage Marketing Group LLC, $15,023,000

Source: *PROMO Magazine*, PROMO 100 (annual), 2011.

3626 ■ TOP PROMOTION AGENCIES WITH A SPECIALTY IN PROMOTIONAL PRODUCTS, 2010

Ranked by: U.S. net revenue, in dollars. **Number listed:** 5

1. BDA, with $253,352,000
2. PromoShop Inc., $11,800,000
3. Shumsky Enterprises, $6,507,222
4. Specialized Marketing Group Inc., $2,905,106
5. Brand Fuel Inc., $2,085,904

Source: *PROMO Magazine*, PROMO 100 (annual), 2011.

3627 ■ TOP PROMOTION AGENCIES WITH A SPECIALTY IN RETAIL, 2010

Ranked by: U.S. net revenue, in dollars. **Number listed:** 10

1. Integrated Marketing Services, with $236,000,000
2. MarketStar Corp., $148,000,000
3. The Integer Group, $145,000,000
4. TracyLocke, $122,400,000
5. G2 Worldwide, $121,000,000
6. The Marketing Arm, $108,200,000
7. Marketing Drive LLC, $78,700,000
8. Alcone Marketing Group, $65,500,000
9. MARS Advertising Inc., $39,000,000
10. Moroch Partners, $38,308,510

Source: *PROMO Magazine*, PROMO 100 (annual), 2011.

3628 ■ TOP PROMOTION AGENCIES WITH A SPECIALTY IN RETAILERS, 2010

Ranked by: U.S. net revenue, in dollars. **Number listed:** 5

1. Integrated Marketing Services, with $236,000,000
2. MarketStar Corp., $148,000,000
3. Moroch Partners, $38,308,510

4. PromoShop Inc., $11,800,000
5. Promotional Alliance International Inc.,
   $2,243,223

Source: *PROMO Magazine*, PROMO 100 (annual), 2011.

3629 ■ TOP PROMOTION AGENCIES WITH A SPECIALTY IN SOCIAL MARKETING, 2010

Ranked by: U.S. net revenue, in dollars. **Number listed:** 10

1. Digitas, with $502,000,000
2. Euro RSCG Worldwide, $185,000,000
3. hawkeye, $72,570,000
4. ePrize, $40,356,127
5. Mr. Youth, $20,000,000
6. Switch Liberate Your Brand, $14,400,000
7. Mastermind Marketing, $11,925,000
8. Shumsky Enterprises, $6,507,222
9. Media Logic, $5,781,655
10. Don Jagoda Associates, $5,089,016

Source: *PROMO Magazine*, PROMO 100 (annual), 2011.

3630 ■ TOP PROMOTION AGENCIES WITH A SPECIALTY IN SPORTS/ENTERTAINMENT, 2010

Ranked by: U.S. net revenue, in dollars. **Number listed:** 5

1. GMR Marketing (sports), with $91,100,000
2. Allied Integrated Marketing (entertainment),
   $26,000,000
3. CSE (sports), $19,860,000
4. Mastermind Marketing (entertainment),
   $11,925,000
5. JHE Production Group (sports), $11,502,706

Source: *PROMO Magazine*, PROMO 100 (annual), 2011.

Material Handling

3631 ■ WORLD'S LARGEST MATERIALS HANDLING SYSTEM SUPPLIERS, 2011

Ranked by: Total sales, in millions of U.S. dollars. **Remarks:** Also notes headquarters, website, and rank and figures for previous year. **Number listed:** 20

1. Daifuku Co., Ltd. (Japan), with $2,500 million
1. Schaefer Holding International GmbH
   (Germany), $2,500
3. Dematic GmbH (Germany), $1,300
4. Murata Machinery Ltd. (Japan), $1,050
5. Mecalux SA (Spain), $952
6. Vanderlande Industries BV (Netherlands), $747
7. Swisslog AG (Switzerland), $654
8. Kardex AG (Switzerland), $596
9. Beumer Group GmbH (Germany), $592
10. Fives Group (France), $508

Source: *Modern Materials Handling*, Top 20 Materials Handling System Suppliers (annual), April 2012, p. 29.

Materials

3632 ■ AMERICA'S LARGEST PRIVATE MATERIALS COMPANIES, 2010

Ranked by: Revenue, in billions of dollars. **Remarks:** Also notes headquarters, number of employees, and overall rank in the *Ameri-*

ca's Largest Private Companies list. Ranking is available online only, not in print. **Number listed:** 9

1. The Renco Group Inc., with $7.75 billion
2. Berry Plastics Corp., $4.44
3. Unisource Worldwide Inc., $4.2
4. Aleris International Inc., $4.12
5. NewPage Holding Corp., $3.6
6. Central National-Gottesman Inc., $3.4
7. W. L. Gore & Associates Inc., $3
8. American Tire Distributors Holdings Inc., $2.46
9. Boise Cascade LLC, $2.24

Source: *Forbes*, America's Largest Private Companies (annual), http://www.forbes.com, December 5, 2011.

3633 ■ BEST SMALL MATERIALS COMPANIES IN AMERICA, 2011

Ranked by: Score based on revenue, profits, and return on equity for the past 12 months and five years. **Remarks:** Specific scores not provided. Also notes rank in the overall *100 Best Small Companies in America*. To qualify, companies must have revenues between $5 million and $1 billion, a net margin above five percent, and share price above $5. List is available online only. **Number listed:** 3

1. KapStone Paper & Packaging
2. Royal Gold
3. UFP Technologies

Source: *Forbes*, Best Small Companies in America (annual), November 7, 2011.

Mattress Industry

3634 ■ LARGEST BEDDING STORES, 2011

Ranked by: Estimated sales of furniture, bedding, and accessories, in millions of dollars. **Remarks:** Also notes rank in the overall *Top 100*, figures for previous year, percent change, and number of units. **Number listed:** 10

1. Sleepy's, with $846 million
2. Mattress Firm, $831.2
3. Select Comfort, $713.5
4. Sleep Train, $371.8
5. America's Mattress, $275.5
6. Mattress Giant, $190.3
7. Back to Bed/Bedding Experts/Mattress Barn,
   $100
8. Sit 'n Sleep, $90.6
9. Innovative Mattress Solutions, $80
10. American Mattress, $63

Source: *Furniture Today*, Top 100 (annual), May 21, 2012, p. 32.

Meat Industry

3635 ■ LARGEST BEEF PROCESSORS, 2011

Ranked by: Beef sales, in millions of dollars. **Remarks:** Also notes total revenue. **Number listed:** 10

1. Tyson Foods Inc., with $13,243 million
2. National Beef Packing Co., $6,800
3. OSI Group LLC, $1,300

4. Greater Omaha Packing Co., $1,100
5. Agri Beef Co., $735
6. AdvancePierre Foods, $728
7. Kenosha Beef International, $677.2
8. Creekstone Farms Premium Beef LLC, $600
9. Caviness Beef Packers Ltd., $455
10. Harris Ranch Beef Co., $426

Source: *The National Provisioner*, Top 100 (annual), May 2012, p. 60.

3636 ■ LARGEST CHICKEN PROCESSORS, 2011

Ranked by: Chicken sales, in millions of dollars. **Remarks:** Also notes total revenue. **Number listed:** 10

1. Tyson Foods Inc., with $10,982 million
2. Perdue Farms, $2,745
3. Sanderson Farms Inc., $1,970
4. Wayne Farms LLC, $1,490
5. Mountaire Farms Inc., $1,390
6. Fieldale Farms Corp., $710
7. Simmons Foods Inc., $700
8. Case Foods Inc., $599
9. Bar-S Foods, $445
10. AdvancePierre Foods, $351

Source: *The National Provisioner*, Top 100 (annual), May 2012, p. 60.

3637 ■ LARGEST LAMB AND VEAL PROCESSORS, 2011

Ranked by: Lamb and veal sales, in millions of dollars. **Remarks:** Also notes total revenue. **Number listed:** 6

1. Superior Farms, with $300 million
2. Mountain States Rosen LLC, $172.1
3. Strauss Brands, $134.1
4. Halperns' Purveyors of Steak & Seafood, $26.6
5. AdvancePierre Foods, $13
6. Natural Food Holdings, $3

Source: *The National Provisioner*, Top 100 (annual), May 2012, p. 60.

3638 ■ LARGEST MEAT PROCESSORS, 2011

Ranked by: Net sales, in millions of dollars. **Remarks:** Also notes rank for previous year, location, chief officer, fiscal year-end, number of plants and employees, and description of operations. **Number listed:** 100

1. Tyson Foods Inc., with $32,300 million
2. JBS USA Holdings Inc., $19,973
3. Cargill Meat Solutions Corp., $15,000
4. Smithfield Foods Inc., $12,203
5. Hormel Foods Corp., $7,900
6. Pilgrim's Pride Corp., $7,500
7. National Beef Packing Co., $6,800
8. Keystone Foods LLC, $6,430
9. Kraft Foods Inc./Oscar Mayer, $5,000
10. Golden State Foods, $4,600

Source: *The National Provisioner*, Top 100 (annual), May 2012, p. 49-59.

3639 ■ LARGEST PORK PROCESSORS, 2011

Ranked by: Pork sales, in millions of dollars. **Remarks:** Also notes total revenue and overall rank within the *Top 100*. **Number listed:** 10

1. Smithfield Foods Inc., with $12,203 million
2. Tyson Foods Inc., $4,522
3. Seaboard Foods, $1,745
4. Fresh Mark Inc., $828.9
5. Clemens Food Group LLC, $680
6. OSI Group LLC, $600
7. Fair Oaks Farms LlC, $289
8. Natural Food Holdings, $279
9. Bar-S Foods, $172.2
10. J. H. Routh Packing Co., $166

Source: *The National Provisioner*, Top 100 (annual), May 2012, p. 60.

3640 ■ LARGEST PROCESSORS OF NATURAL/ORGANIC MEAT, 2011

Ranked by: Natural and organic meat sales, in millions of dollars. **Remarks:** Also notes total revenue. **Number listed:** 12

1. Sanderson Farms Inc., with $1,970 million
2. Bell & Evans, $207
3. Strauss Brands, $149
4. Creekstone Farms Premium Beef LLC, $120
5. Natural Food Holdings, $90
6. OSI Group LLC, $80
7. Rocky Mountain Natural Meats Inc., $60.4
8. Superior Farms, $30
9. Mountain States Rosen LLC, $22.2
10. Peer Foods Group, $20

Source: *The National Provisioner*, Top 100 (annual), May 2012, p. 61.

3641 ■ LARGEST TURKEY PROCESSORS, 2011

Ranked by: Turkey and duck sales, in millions of dollars. **Remarks:** Also notes total revenue. **Number listed:** 10

1. Butterball LLC, with $1,470 million
2. West Liberty Foods LLC, $399
3. Perdue Farms, $305
4. Cooper Farms, $292.5
5. Dakota Provisions, $187
6. Land O'Frost Inc., $132
7. Bar-S Foods, $65
8. AdvancePierre Foods, $26
9. Stampede Meat Inc., $16.3
10. Abbyland Foods Inc., $11.9

Source: *The National Provisioner*, Top 100 (annual), May 2012, p. 60.

3642 ■ TOP SMALL AND MID-SIZED BEEF PROCESSORS, 2010

Ranked by: Segment sales, in millions of dollars. **Remarks:** Ranking covers companies with up to $250 million in annual sales. Also notes total revenue and overall rank within the *Top 75*. **Number listed:** 6

1. FPL Food LLC, with $240 million
2. Stampede Meat Inc., $187.5
3. Halperns' Steak & Seafood Co., $109.7
4. Custom Food Products LLC, $104
5. Lincoln Provision Inc., $100.5

6. Vincent Giordano Corp., $84

Source: *Independent Processor*, Top 75 (annual), http://www.provisioneronline.com, June 2011.

3643 ■ TOP SMALL AND MID-SIZED CHICKEN PROCESSORS, 2010

Ranked by: Segment sales, in millions of dollars. **Remarks:** Ranking covers companies with up to $250 million in annual sales. Also notes total revenue and overall rank within the *Top 75*. **Number listed:** 6

1. John Soules Foods Inc., with $70 million
2. Peer Foods Group, $30
3. Stampede Meat Inc., $25
4. Custom Food Products LLC, $20.6
5. Lincoln Provision Inc., $13.4
6. Sunset Farm Foods Inc., $4.3

Source: *Independent Processor*, Top 75 (annual), http://www.provisioneronline.com, June 2011.

3644 ■ TOP SMALL AND MID-SIZED LAMB AND VEAL PROCESSORS, 2010

Ranked by: Segment sales, in millions of dollars. **Remarks:** Ranking covers companies with up to $250 million in annual sales. Also notes total revenue and overall rank within the *Top 75*. **Number listed:** 6

1. Mountain States Rosen LLC, with $156.8 million
2. Marcho Farms/Provimi Foods, $120
3. Halperns' Steak & Seafood Co., $26.6
4. Brown Packing Co., $26.1
5. Natural Food Holdings, $2.5
6. Bush Brothers' Provision Co., $2.3

Source: *Independent Processor*, Top 75 (annual), http://www.provisioneronline.com, June 2011.

3645 ■ TOP SMALL AND MID-SIZED MEAT PROCESSORS, 2010

Ranked by: Net sales, in millions of dollars. **Remarks:** Ranking covers companies with up to $250 million in annual sales. Also notes rank for previous year, location, chief officer, fiscal year-end, number of plants and employees, and description of operations. **Number listed:** 75

1. Natural Food Holdings, with $250 million
1. Stampede Meat Inc., $250
3. FPL Food LLC, $240
4. Abbyland Foods Inc., $225
4. Superior Farms, $225
6. Carl Buddig & Co., $220
7. Agri Beef Co., $212
8. Overhill Farms, $209
9. Fair Oaks Farms LLC, $205
10. Land O' Frost, $195

Source: *Independent Processor*, Top 75 (annual), http://www.provisioneronline.com, June 2011.

3646 ■ TOP SMALL AND MID-SIZED PORK PROCESSORS, 2010

Ranked by: Segment sales, in millions of dollars. **Remarks:** Ranking covers companies with up to $250 million in annual sales. Also notes total revenue and overall rank within the *Top 75*. **Number listed:** 6

1. Natural Food Holdings, with $197.5 million
2. J. H. Routh Packing Co., $130
3. Abbyland Foods Inc., $101.3
4. ALL Holding Co., $99.9
5. Atlantic Premium Brands Ltd., $84
6. Chicago Meat Authority, $72.5

Source: *Independent Processor*, Top 75 (annual), http://www.provisioneronline.com, June 2011.

3647 ■ TOP SMALL AND MID-SIZED PREPARED MEAT PROCESSORS, 2010

Ranked by: Segment sales, in millions of dollars. **Remarks:** Ranking covers companies with up to $250 million in annual sales. Also notes total revenue and overall rank within the *Top 75*. **Number listed:** 6

1. Abbyland Foods Inc., with $105.8 million
2. RMH Foods LLC, $30
3. Natural Food Holdings, $25
4. Atlantic Premium Brands Ltd., $15.8
5. Lincoln Provision Inc., $6.7
6. Farmington Foods Inc., $6

Source: *Independent Processor*, Top 75 (annual), http://www.provisioneronline.com, June 2011.

3648 ■ TOP SMALL AND MID-SIZED PROCESSORS OF NATURAL/ORGANIC MEAT, 2010

Ranked by: Segment sales, in millions of dollars. **Remarks:** Ranking covers companies with up to $250 million in annual sales. Also notes total revenue and overall rank within the *Top 75*. **Number listed:** 6

1. Natural Food Holdings, with $87.5 million
2. Rocky Mountain Natural Meats Inc., $47.6
3. Broadleaf (USA) Inc., $33.6
4. Peer Foods Group, $25
5. Farmington Foods Inc., $18
5. Carlton Packing Co., $18

Source: *Independent Processor*, Top 75 (annual), http://www.provisioneronline.com, June 2011.

3649 ■ TOP SMALL AND MID-SIZED TURKEY PROCESSORS, 2010

Ranked by: Segment sales, in millions of dollars. **Remarks:** Ranking covers companies with up to $250 million in annual sales. Also notes total revenue and overall rank within the *Top 75*. **Number listed:** 6

1. Godshall's Quality Meats Inc., with $28.8 million
2. Peer Foods Group, $15
3. Stampede Meat Inc., $12.5
4. Charlie's Pride Meats, $8.2
5. Burgers' Smokehouse, $5.9
6. Broadleaf (USA) Inc., $4.2

Source: *Independent Processor*, Top 75 (annual), http://www.provisioneronline.com, June 2011.

Meat Industry—Export/Import Trade

3650 ■ LARGEST MEAT EXPORTERS, 2011

Ranked by: Meat exports, in millions of dollars. **Remarks:** Also notes total revenue. **Number listed:** 23

1. Tyson Foods Inc., with $5,500 million
2. Smithfield Foods Inc., $1,586
3. Sanderson Farms Inc., $493
4. Greater Omaha Packing Co., $330
5. Hormel Foods Corp., $316
6. Mountaire Farms Inc., $278
7. Simmons Foods Inc., $273
8. Fieldale Farms Corp., $248.5
9. Butterball LLC, $225
10. OSI Group LIC, $160

Source: *The National Provisioner*, Top 100 (annual), May 2012, p. 61.

Meat Packing Industry
See: **Meat Industry**

Mechanical Contractors
See: **Contractors**

Media

3651 ■ LARGEST ASIA-PACIFIC MEDIA PRODUCTS RETAILERS, 2010

Ranked by: Sales, in millions of U.S. dollars. **Remarks:** Also notes country, fascias/brands, number of outlets, sales in national currency, sales area, sales per square meter, and figures for previous year. **Number listed:** 10

1. Culture Convenience Club, with $2,036 million
2. Book Off, $1,442
3. Zhenjiang Xinhua Bookstore, $1,098
4. Kinokuniya, $870
5. Electronics Boutique Australia, $596
6. Yurindo, $588
7. Tower Records Japan, $555
8. Junkudo, $495
9. Aeon Group, $466
10. Bunkyodo Group Holdings, $417

Source: *Retail Asia*, Retail Asia-Pacific Top 500 (annual), July 2011, p. 66-66a.

3652 ■ MOST POWERFUL ARABS IN MEDIA AND MARKETING, 2012

Ranked by: Score based on scope of influence. **Remarks:** Specific scores not provided. Also notes rank in the overall *Power 500*. **Number listed:** 47

1. Walid Al Ibrahim
2. Elie Khouri
3. Sheikh Ahmed bin Jassim Al Thani
4. Joseph Ghossoub
5. Dani Richa
6. Nart Bouran
7. Dr. Amina Al Rustamani
8. Alex Saber
9. Turki bin Abdullah Al Dakhil
10. Nezar Nagro

Source: *Arab Business*, Power 500 (annual), June 4, 2012.

Media Companies

3653 ■ AMERICA'S LARGEST PRIVATE MEDIA COMPANIES, 2010

Ranked by: Revenue, in billions of dollars. **Remarks:** Also notes headquarters, number of employees, and overall rank in the *America's Largest Private Companies* list. Ranking is available online only, not in print. **Number listed:** 7

1. Cox Enterprises Inc., with $14.6 billion
2. Advance Publications Inc., $6.55
3. Hallmark Cards Inc., $3.81
4. Hearst Corp., $3.80
5. International Data Group Inc., $3.24
6. Tribune Co., $3.22
7. Univision Communications, $2.25

Source: *Forbes*, America's Largest Private Companies (annual), http://www.forbes.com, December 5, 2011.

3654 ■ BEST SMALL MEDIA COMPANIES IN AMERICA, 2011

Ranked by: Score based on revenue, profits, and return on equity for the past 12 months and five years. **Remarks:** Specific scores not provided. Also notes rank in the overall *100 Best Small Companies in America*. To qualify, companies must have revenues between $5 million and $1 billion, a net margin above five percent, and share price above $5. List is available online only. **Number listed:** 4

1. DG
2. Dolby Laboratories
3. Rovi
4. DreamWorks Animation

Source: *Forbes*, Best Small Companies in America (annual), November 7, 2011.

3655 ■ BRITAIN'S MOST ADMIRED MEDIA COMPANIES, 2011

Ranked by: Survey of peers and investment analysts based on nine criteria: quality of management, financial soundness, quality of goods/services, ability to attract and retain talent, value as long-term investment, innovation, marketing, community and environmental responsibility, and use of corporate assets. **Number listed:** 5

1. British Sky Broadcasting Group plc (BSkyB), with 67.2 points
2. Pearson plc, 61.7
3. British Broadcasting Corp. (BBC), 55.4
4. Reed Elsevier plc, 53.2
5. Euromoney Institutional Investor, 52.7

Source: *Management Today*, Britain's Most Admired Companies (annual), December 2011, p. 47.

3656 ■ EUROPE'S MOST VALUABLE MEDIA COMPANIES, 2011

Ranked by: Market value as of March 2011, in millions of U.S. dollars. **Remarks:** Also notes rank within the *FT Europe 500*, rank for previous year, country, revenue, net income, assets, number of employees, share price, price-to-earning ratio, dividend yield, and fiscal yearend. **Number listed:** 18

1. Vivendi SA, with $35,381.2 million

2. British Sky Broadcasting Group plc (BSkyB), $23,180.2

3. Reed Elsevier plc, $19,850.9

4. WPP Group plc, $15,559.4

5. Pearson plc, $14,350.5

6. Publicis Groupe SA, $10,762.9

7. Eutelsat Communications, $8,803.9

8. SES SA, $8,588.3

9. Mediaset SpA, $7,516.4

10. JCDecaux SA, $7,446.7

Source: *Financial Times*, FT 500 (annual), http://www.ft.com, June 24, 2011.

3657 ■ FASTEST-GROWING PRIVATE MEDIA COMPANIES IN THE U.S., 2007-2010

Ranked by: Average annual sales growth over three years, in percent. Remarks: Also notes headquarters, revenue, and rank in the overall *Inc. 500*. To qualify, private companies must have had annual revenues of at least $100,000 in 2007 and $2 million in 2010. Number listed: 16

1. GoLive! Mobile, with 4,526.4%

2. Cellufun, 2,347.6%

3. MyDailyMoment.com, 1,951.7%

4. Gravitas Ventures, 1,499.8%

5. ChaCha, 1,441.1%

6. Thrillist.com, 1,266.2%

7. Welathpire, 1,184.7%

8. OkCupid.com, 1,128.7%

9. blip.tv, 1,037.8%

10. Integrated Media Solutions, 953.8%

Source: *Inc.*, Inc. 500 (annual), September 2011, p. 178-182.

3658 ■ LARGEST MEDIA AND ADVERTISING FIRMS IN EUROPE, 2010

Ranked by: Sales, in millions of U.S. dollars. Remarks: Also notes rank within country. Number listed: 100

1. Bertelsmann AG (Germany), with $22,849.3 million

2. Data Media & Research Ltd. (U.K.), $13,984.3

3. WPP plc (U.K.), $13,026.5

4. Lagardere SCA (France), $11,577.6

5. Reed Elsevier plc (U.K.), $9,106.5

6. British Sky Broadcasting Group plc (BSkyB, U.K.), $8,868

7. Pearson plc (U.K.), $8,436

8. British Sky Broadcasting Ltd. (U.K.), $6,721.5

9. Publicis Groupe SA (France), $6,630.3

10. Mediaset SpA (Italy), $5,992.9

Source: *Europe's 15,000 Largest Companies*, (annual), ELC International, 2011, p. 46.

3659 ■ MOST VALUABLE U.S. MEDIA COMPANIES, 2011

Ranked by: Market value as of March 2011, in millions of U.S. dollars. Remarks: Also notes rank within the *FT U.S. 500*, rank for previous year, country, revenue, net income, assets, number of employees, share price, price-to-earning ratio, dividend yield, and fiscal yearend. Number listed: 19

1. Walt Disney Co., with $81,830.8 million

2. Comcast Corp., $57,358.7

3. News Corp., $45,977.5

4. Time Warner Inc., $39,014.1

5. The DirecTV Group Inc., $37,045.7

6. Viacom Inc., $28,329.1

7. Time Warner Cable Inc., $24,497.1

8. Liberty Media Corp., $19,676.9

9. CBS Corp., $15,840.4

10. Omnicom Group Inc., $13,934.8

Source: *Financial Times*, FT 500 (annual), http://www.ft.com, June 24, 2011.

3660 ■ TOP CANADIAN MEDIA, BROADCASTING, AND CABLE COMPANIES, 2010

Ranked by: Revenue, in thousands of Canadian dollars (unless otherwise noted). Remarks: Also notes percent change from previous year. Number listed: 10

1. Rogers Communications Inc., with C$12,190,000 thousand

2. Quebecor Media, C$4,071,800

3. Shaw Communications Inc., C$3,858,946

4. Bell Media (U.S. Dollars), C$1,752,150

5. Videotron Ltee., C$2,209,000

6. Bell ExpressVu, C$1,749,000

7. Cogeco Inc., C$1,322,682

8. Canadian Broadcasting Corp., C$589,247

9. TVA Group, C$448,381

10. Newfoundland Capital Corp., C$117,836

Source: *Report on Business Magazine*, Top 1000 Companies (annual), http://www.reportonbusiness.com, June 2011.

3661 ■ TOP DIGITAL MEDIA COMPANIES, 2010

Ranked by: Revenue, in millions of dollars. Remarks: Also notes rank and figures for previous year, annual growth, and selected properties. Number listed: 10

1. Google Inc., with $9,297 million

2. Yahoo! Inc., $3,315

3. Microsoft Corp., $1,583

4. IAC/InterActiveCorp, $1,211

5. Facebook, $1,210

6. AOL Inc., $876

7. Cox Enterprises, $720

8. Gannett Co., $618

9. Monster Worldwide, $553

10. CBS Corp., $506

Source: *Advertising Age*, 100 Leading Media Companies (annual), October 3, 2011, p. 52.

3662 ■ TOP MEDIA COMPANIES, 2010

Ranked by: Total net U.S. media revenue, in millions of dollars. Remarks: Also notes headquarters, rank for previous year, percent change, and breakdown of U.S. revenue by medium. Number listed: 100

1. Comcast Corp., with $44,544 million

2. The DirecTV Group Inc., $20,676

3. Walt Disney Co., $18,596

4. Time Warner Inc., $18,208

5. Time Warner Cable Inc., $16,836

6. News Corp., $16,822

7. AT&T Inc., $12,712
8. Dish Network Corp., $12,544
9. Cox Enterprises Inc., $11,585
10. CBS Corp., $11,310

Source: *Advertising Age*, 100 Leading Media Companies (annual), October 3, 2011, p. 46-50.

3663 ■ TOP U.K. MEDIA AGENCIES, 2011

Ranked by: Billings, in millions of pounds sterling. **Remarks:** Also notes rank and figures for previous year, percent change, and top clients. **Number listed:** 50

1. MediaCom, with £1,255.77 million
2. Carat, £839.57
3. OMD, £760.3
4. Mindshare, £719.65
5. ZenithOptimedia, £713.47
6. MEC UK, £687
7. Starcom MediaVest Group, £418.39
8. Walker Media, £297.28
9. PHD, £288.93
10. Vizeum, £260.71

Source: *Campaign*, Top 100 Agencies (annual), March 16, 2012, p. 19.

3664 ■ TOP U.K. MEDIA HOLDING COMPANIES, 2011

Ranked by: Media billings, in millions of pounds sterling. **Remarks:** Also notes rank and figures for previous year, key media assets, and central buying unit. **Number listed:** 6

1. WPP, with £2,902.7 million
2. Publicis Groupe, £1,154
3. Omnicom, £1,119.5
4. Aegis, £1,100.3
5. Interpublic, £365.7
6. Havas, £325

Source: *Campaign*, Top 100 Agencies (annual), March 16, 2012, p. 20.

3665 ■ THE UNITED KINGDOM'S MOST VALUABLE MEDIA BRANDS, 2011

Ranked by: Brand value, in millions of U.S. dollars. **Remarks:** Also notes rank within the *Global 500* for current and previous year, figures for current and previous year, and brand rating. Ranking is available online only. **Number listed:** 4

1. Sky, with $6,414 million
2. Thomson Reuters, $5,843
3. BBC, $3,869
4. Pearson, $2,653

Source: *Global 500*, (annual), Brand Finance plc, March 2012.

3666 ■ THE UNITED STATES' MOST VALUABLE MEDIA BRANDS, 2011

Ranked by: Brand value, in millions of U.S. dollars. **Remarks:** Also notes rank within the *Global 500* for current and previous year, figures for current and previous year, and brand rating. Ranking is available online only. **Number listed:** 13

1. Walt Disney, with $15,392 million
2. Comcast, $12,473
3. Time Warner Cable, $9,140

4. Time Warner, $8,453
5. DirecTV, $8,212
6. FOX, $7,280
7. CBS, $4,960
8. Warner Bros., $4,844
9. Echostar, $3,774
10. MTV, $3,675

Source: *Global 500*, (annual), Brand Finance plc, March 2012.

3667 ■ WORLD'S MOST ETHICAL MEDIA COMPANIES, 2012

Ranked by: Score based on five criteria: ethics and compliance program; reputation, leadership, and innovation; governance; corporate citizenship and responsibility; and culture of ethics. **Remarks:** Specific scores not provided; companies are listed alphabetically, not ranked. **Number listed:** 2

1. Thomson Reuters (U.S./U.K.)
2. Time Warner Inc. (U.S.)

Source: *Ethisphere Magazine*, World's Most Ethical Companies (annual), http://www.ethisphere.com, 2012.

3668 ■ WORLD'S MOST VALUABLE MEDIA BRANDS, 2011

Ranked by: Brand value, in millions of U.S. dollars. **Remarks:** Also notes rank within the *Global 500* for current and previous year, figures for current and previous year, country, and brand rating. Ranking is available online only. **Number listed:** 19

1. Walt Disney, with $15,392 million
2. Comcast, $12,473
3. Time Warner Cable, $9,140
4. Time Warner, $8,453
5. DirecTV, $8,212
6. Fox, $7,280
7. Sky, $6,414
8. Thomson Reuters, $5,843
9. CBS, $4,960
10. Warner Bros., $4,844

Source: *Global 500*, (annual), Brand Finance plc, March 2012.

3669 ■ WORLD'S MOST VALUABLE MEDIA COMPANIES, 2011

Ranked by: Market value as of March 2011, in millions of U.S. dollars. **Remarks:** Also notes rank within the *FT 500*, rank for previous year, country, revenue, net income, assets, number of employees, share price, price-to-earning ratio, dividend yield, and fiscal year-end. **Number listed:** 13

1. Walt Disney Co., with $81,830.8 million
2. Comcast Corp., $67,358.7
3. News Corp., $46,977.5
4. Time Warner Inc., $39,014.1
5. The DirecTV Group Inc., $37,045.7
6. Vivendi SA, $35,381.2
7. Thomson Reuters Corp., $32,620.4
8. Viacom Inc., $28,329.1
9. Time Warner Cable Inc., $24,497.1
10. British Sky Broadcasting Group plc (BSkyB), $23,180.2

Source: *Financial Times*, FT 500 (annual), http://www.ft.com, June 24, 2011.

Medical Care

3670 ■ WORLD'S MOST ADMIRED MEDICAL FACILITIES, 2012

Ranked by: Score, on a scale of 10, based on a survey of executives, directors, and securities analysts of companies within their own industry on eight criteria: innovation, financial soundness, employee talent, use of corporate assets, long-term investment value, social responsibility, quality of management, and quality of products/services. **Remarks:** Specific scores not provided. Also notes rank for previous year. **Number listed:** 5

1. HCA Inc.
2. Health Management Associates Inc.
3. DaVita Inc.
4. Universal Health Services Inc.
5. Kindred Healthcare Inc.

Source: *Fortune*, World's Most Admired Companies (annual), March 19, 2012, p. 148.

Medical Equipment and Supplies

3671 ■ CALIFORNIA'S LARGEST MEDICAL EQUIPMENT AND SUPPLY COMPANIES OVERALL, 2011

Ranked by: Score based on revenue, profits, assets, and market capitalization. **Remarks:** Specific scores not provided. Also notes overall rank in the *Forbes 2000* and figures for each criterion. **Number listed:** 2

1. Intuitive Surgical Inc.
2. Varian Medical Systems Inc.

Source: *Forbes*, Forbes 2000 (annual), http://www.forbes.com, May 7, 2012.

3672 ■ LARGEST U.S. MEDICAL EQUIPMENT AND SUPPLY COMPANIES OVERALL, 2011

Ranked by: Score based on revenue, profits, assets, and market capitalization. **Remarks:** Specific scores not provided. Also notes overall rank in the *Forbes 2000* and figures for each criterion. **Number listed:** 12

1. Johnson & Johnson
2. Medtronic Inc.
3. Baxter International Inc.
4. Stryker Corp.
5. Becton, Dickinson & Co.
6. Boston Scientific Corp.
7. St. Jude Medical Inc.
8. Zimmer Holdings Inc.
9. Intuitive Surgical Inc.
10. Henry Schein Inc.

Source: *Forbes*, Forbes 2000 (annual), http://www.forbes.com, May 7, 2012.

3673 ■ LARGEST U.S. MEDICAL INSTRUMENTS AND EQUIPMENT MANUFACTURERS, 2010

Ranked by: Revenue, in millions of dollars. **Remarks:** Also notes overall rank within the *IW 500,* revenue growth, and profit margin. **Number listed:** 20

1. Medtronic Inc., with $15,817 million
2. Baxter International Inc., $12,843

3. Boston Scientific Corp., $7,806
4. Becton, Dickinson & Co., $7,372
5. Stryker Corp., $7,320
6. St. Jude Medical Inc., $5,165
7. Zimmer Holdings Inc., $4,220
8. Hospira Inc., $3,917
9. C. R. Bard Inc., $2,720
10. Dentsply International Inc., $2,221

Source: *IndustryWeek*, IW 500 (annual), http://www.industryweek.com, July 2011.

3674 ■ MINNESOTA'S LARGEST MEDICAL EQUIPMENT AND SUPPLY COMPANIES OVERALL, 2011

Ranked by: Score based on revenue, profits, assets, and market capitalization. **Remarks:** Specific scores not provided. Also notes overall rank in the *Forbes 2000* and figures for each criterion. **Number listed:** 2

1. Medtronic Inc.
2. St. Jude Medical Inc.

Source: *Forbes*, Forbes 2000 (annual), http://www.forbes.com, May 7, 2012.

3675 ■ NEW JERSEY'S LARGEST MEDICAL EQUIPMENT AND SUPPLY COMPANIES OVERALL, 2011

Ranked by: Score based on revenue, profits, assets, and market capitalization. **Remarks:** Specific scores not provided. Also notes overall rank in the *Forbes 2000* and figures for each criterion. **Number listed:** 3

1. Johnson & Johnson
2. Becton, Dickinson & Co.
3. C. R. Bard Inc.

Source: *Forbes*, Forbes 2000 (annual), http://www.forbes.com, May 7, 2012.

3676 ■ TOP BRANDS OF HOME ELECTRONIC HEALTH-CARE SYSTEMS, 2010

Ranked by: Popularity among *CE Pro 100* companies, in percent. **Number listed:** 7

1. Control4, with 3%
1. Life Control, 3%
3. GrandCare, 2%
4. Alarm.com, 1%
4. CloseBy, 1%
4. GE, 1%
4. LifeLink, 1%

Source: *CE Pro*, Brand Analysis (annual), June 2011, p. 60.

3677 ■ TOP *FORTUNE 500* COMPANIES IN MEDICAL PRODUCTS AND EQUIPMENT, 2011

Ranked by: Revenue, in millions of dollars. **Remarks:** Also notes overall rank in the *Fortune 500;* profits; profits as a percentage of revenue; stockholders' equity; and rank by each criterion. **Number listed:** 6

1. Medtronic Inc., with $15,933 million
2. Baxter International Inc., $13,893
3. Stryker Corp., $8,307
4. Becton, Dickinson & Co., $7,832
5. Boston Scientific Corp., $7,622

6. St. Jude Medical Inc., $5,612

Source: *Fortune*, Fortune 500 (annual), May 21, 2012, p. F-37.

3678 ■ WORLD'S LARGEST MEDICAL EQUIPMENT AND SUPPLY COMPANIES OVERALL, 2011

Ranked by: Score based on revenue, profits, assets, and market capitalization. **Remarks:** Specific scores not provided. Also notes country, overall rank in the *Forbes 2000,* and figures for each criterion. **Number listed:** 20

1. Johnson & Johnson
2. Medtronic Inc.
3. Baxter International Inc.
4. Fresenius SE
5. Covidien plc
6. Stryker Corp.
7. Becton, Dickinson & Co.
8. Boston Scientific Corp.
9. St. Jude Medical Inc.
10. Essilor International SA

Source: *Forbes*, Forbes 2000 (annual), http://www.forbes.com, May 7, 2012.

3679 ■ WORLD'S LARGEST MEDICAL INSTRUMENTS AND EQUIPMENT MANUFACTURERS, 2010

Ranked by: Revenue, in millions of dollars. **Remarks:** Also notes rank for previous year, overall rank within the *IW 1000,* country, and revenue growth. **Number listed:** 16

1. Fresenius SE, with $21,364 million
2. Medtronic Inc., $15,817
3. Baxter International Inc., $12,843
4. Covidien plc, $10,429
5. Boston Scientific Corp., $7,806
6. Luxottica Group SpA, $7,756
7. Becton, Dickinson & Co., $7,372
8. Stryker Corp., $7,320
9. Essilor International SA, $5,208
10. St. Jude Medical Inc., $5,165

Source: *IndustryWeek*, IW 1000 (annual), http://www.industryweek.com, August 2011.

Medical Instruments and Apparatus

3680 ■ LARGEST U.S. PRECISION HEALTHCARE EQUIPMENT COMPANIES OVERALL, 2011

Ranked by: Score based on revenue, profits, assets, and market capitalization. **Remarks:** Specific scores not provided. Also notes overall rank in the *Forbes 2000* and figures for each criterion. **Number listed:** 3

1. Thermo Fisher Scientific Inc.
2. Waters Corp.
3. Pall Corp.

Source: *Forbes*, Forbes 2000 (annual), http://www.forbes.com, May 7, 2012.

3681 ■ MASSACHUSETTS'S LARGEST PRECISION HEALTHCARE EQUIPMENT COMPANIES OVERALL, 2011

Ranked by: Score based on revenue, profits, assets, and market capitalization. **Remarks:** Specific scores not provided. Also notes overall rank in the *Forbes 2000* and figures for each criterion. **Number listed:** 2

1. Thermo Fisher Scientific Inc.
2. Waters Corp.

Source: *Forbes*, Forbes 2000 (annual), http://www.forbes.com, May 7, 2012.

3682 ■ TOP MEDICAL DEVICE MANUFACTURERS, 2010

Ranked by: Revenue, in billions of dollars. **Number listed:** 30

1. Johnson & Johnson, with $24.6 billion
2. GE Healthcare, $16.9
3. Siemens Healthcare, $16.7
4. Medtronic Inc., $15.8
5. Baxter International Inc., $12.8
6. Philips Healthcare, $11.4
7. Abbott Laboratories Inc., $9.3
8. Cardinal Health, $8.8
9. Covidien Ltd., $8.4
10. Boston Scientific Corp., $7.8

Source: *Medical Product Outsourcing*, Top Medical Device Manufacturers (annual), http://www.mpo-mag.com, 2011.

3683 ■ WORLD'S LARGEST PRECISION HEALTHCARE EQUIPMENT COMPANIES OVERALL, 2011

Ranked by: Score based on revenue, profits, assets, and market capitalization. **Remarks:** Specific scores not provided. Also notes country, overall rank in the *Forbes 2000,* and figures for each criterion. **Number listed:** 3

1. Thermo Fisher Scientific Inc.
2. Waters Corp.
3. Pall Corp.

Source: *Forbes*, Forbes 2000 (annual), http://www.forbes.com, May 7, 2012.

3684 ■ WORLD'S MOST ADMIRED MEDICAL EQUIPMENT COMPANIES, 2012

Ranked by: Score, on a scale of 10, based on a survey of executives, directors, and securities analysts of companies within their own industry on eight criteria: innovation, financial soundness, employee talent, use of corporate assets, long-term investment value, social responsibility, quality of management, and quality of products/services. **Remarks:** Specific scores not provided. Also notes rank for previous year. **Number listed:** 5

1. St. Jude Medical Inc.
1. Stryker Corp.
3. Baxter International Inc.
4. Becton, Dickinson & Co.
5. Medtronic Inc.

Source: *Fortune*, World's Most Admired Companies (annual), March 19, 2012, p. 149.

3685 ■ WORLD'S MOST ETHICAL MEDICAL DEVICES COMPANIES, 2012

Ranked by: Score based on five criteria: ethics and compliance program; reputation, leadership, and innovation; governance; corporate citizenship and responsibility; and culture of ethics. **Remarks:** Specific scores not provided; companies are listed alphabetically, not ranked. **Number listed:** 4

1. Becton, Dickinson & Co. (U.S.)
2. Coloplast (Denmark)
3. Henry Schein Inc. (U.S.)

4. Koninklijke Philips Electronics NV (Netherlands)

Source: *Ethisphere Magazine*, World's Most Ethical Companies (annual), http://www.ethisphere.com, 2012.

Metal Industry

3686 ■ AUSTRALIA'S LARGEST DIVERSIFIED METALS AND MINING COMPANIES OVERALL, 2011

Ranked by: Score based on revenue, profits, assets, and market capitalization. **Remarks:** Specific scores not provided. Also notes overall rank in the *Forbes 2000* and figures for each criterion. **Number listed:** 4

1. BHP Billiton Ltd.
2. Newcrest Mining Ltd.
3. Orica Ltd.
4. Iluka Resources Ltd.

Source: *Forbes*, Forbes 2000 (annual), http://www.forbes.com, May 7, 2012.

3687 ■ CANADA'S LARGEST DIVERSIFIED METALS AND MINING COMPANIES OVERALL, 2011

Ranked by: Score based on revenue, profits, assets, and market capitalization. **Remarks:** Specific scores not provided. Also notes overall rank in the *Forbes 2000* and figures for each criterion. **Number listed:** 10

1. Barrick Gold Corp.
2. Teck Resources Ltd.
3. Goldcorp Inc.
4. Yamana Gold
5. Kinross Gold
6. Silver Wheaton Corp.
7. First Quantum Minerals
8. Cameco
9. Iamgold
10. Eldorado Gold

Source: *Forbes*, Forbes 2000 (annual), http://www.forbes.com, May 7, 2012.

3688 ■ CHINA'S LARGEST DIVERSIFIED METALS AND MINING COMPANIES OVERALL, 2011

Ranked by: Score based on revenue, profits, assets, and market capitalization. **Remarks:** Specific scores not provided. Also notes overall rank in the *Forbes 2000* and figures for each criterion. **Number listed:** 13

1. China Shenhua Energy Co., Ltd.
2. China Coal Energy
3. Yanzhou Coal Mining
4. Jiangxi Copper
5. Zigin Mining Group
6. Inner Mongolia Yitai
7. Xishan Coal & Electricity
8. Shanxi Lu'an Environmental
9. Jizhong Energy Resources
10. Yang Quan Coal Industry

Source: *Forbes*, Forbes 2000 (annual), http://www.forbes.com, May 7, 2012.

3689 ■ EUROPE'S MOST VALUABLE INDUSTRIAL METALS AND MINING COMPANIES, 2011

Ranked by: Market value as of March 2011, in millions of U.S. dollars. **Remarks:** Also notes rank within the *FT Europe 500*, rank for previous year, country, revenue, net income, assets, number of employees, share price, price-to-earning ratio, dividend yield, and fiscal yearend. **Number listed:** 14

1. ArcelorMittal, with $56,539.9 million
2. Mining & Metallurgical Company Norilsk Nickel, $50,058.2
3. Novolipetsk Steel, $25,381.1
4. OAO Severstal, $19,764
5. Norsk Hydro, $16,965.7
6. Mechel, $13,021.3
7. KGHM, $12,691.9
8. Eramet, $9,812.6
9. Voestalpine, $7,947.8
10. Eregli Demir Celik, $5,765.6

Source: *Financial Times*, FT 500 (annual), http://www.ft.com, June 24, 2011.

3690 ■ INDIA'S LARGEST DIVERSIFIED METALS AND MINING COMPANIES OVERALL, 2011

Ranked by: Score based on revenue, profits, assets, and market capitalization. **Remarks:** Specific scores not provided. Also notes overall rank in the *Forbes 2000* and figures for each criterion. **Number listed:** 2

1. Coal India Ltd.
2. NMDC Ltd.

Source: *Forbes*, Forbes 2000 (annual), http://www.forbes.com, May 7, 2012.

3691 ■ JAPAN'S LARGEST DIVERSIFIED METALS AND MINING COMPANIES OVERALL, 2011

Ranked by: Score based on revenue, profits, assets, and market capitalization. **Remarks:** Specific scores not provided. Also notes overall rank in the *Forbes 2000* and figures for each criterion. **Number listed:** 4

1. Sumitomo Metal Mining Co., Ltd.
2. Mitsubishi Materials Corp.
3. Hanwa Co., Ltd.
4. Nippon Steel Trading Co., Ltd.

Source: *Forbes*, Forbes 2000 (annual), http://www.forbes.com, May 7, 2012.

3692 ■ LARGEST COMPANIES IN PRIMARY METAL INDUSTRIES BY EMPLOYEES, 2010

Ranked by: Total number of employees. **Remarks:** Also notes contact information for headquarters, number of employees at headquarters, revenue, rank by revenue, and primary SIC code. **Number listed:** 48

1. Alcoa Inc., with 59,000 employees
2. United States Steel Corp., 42,000
3. Corning Inc., 26,200
4. ArcelorMittal USA Inc., 20,500
5. Nucor Corp., 20,400
6. Precision Castparts Corp., 18,100
7. Alumax Inc., 14,400
8. Commscope Inc., 12,500

9. Commercial Metals Co., 11,558
10. General Cable Corp., 11,300

Source: *Business Rankings*, (annual), Dun & Bradstreet Inc., 2011, p. VI.73-VI.74.

3693 ■ LARGEST COMPANIES IN PRIMARY METAL INDUSTRIES BY SALES, 2010

Ranked by: Total revenue, in dollars. **Remarks:** Also notes contact information for headquarters, number of employees at headquarters and overall, rank by employees, and primary SIC code. **Number listed:** 48

1. Alcoa Inc., with $21,013,000,000
2. United States Steel Corp., $17,374,000,000
3. Nucor Corp., $15,844,627,000
4. Novelis Corp., $8,673,000,000
5. Corning Inc., $6,632,000,000
6. AK Steel Corp., $6,536,600,000
7. Commercial Metals Co., $6,306,102,000
8. Steel Dynamics Inc., $6,300,887,000
9. AK Steel Holding Corp., $5,968,300,000
10. Precision Castparts Corp., $5,486,600,000

Source: *Business Rankings*, (annual), Dun & Bradstreet Inc., 2011, p. V.73-V.74.

3694 ■ LARGEST METAL MINING COMPANIES BY EMPLOYEES, 2010

Ranked by: Total number of employees. **Remarks:** Also notes contact information for headquarters, number of employees at headquarters, revenue, rank by revenue, and primary SIC code. **Number listed:** 49

1. Freeport-McMoRan Copper & Gold Inc., with 28,400 employees
2. Freeport-McMoRan Corp., 15,600
3. Newmont Mining Corp., 14,500
4. Americas Mining Corp., 12,878
5. Southern Copper Corp., 11,523
6. PT Freeport Indonesia Co., 7,488
7. Cliffs Natural Resources Inc., 5,404
8. Kennecott Corp., 3,065
9. USEC Inc., 2,908
10. Compagnie des Bauxites de Guinee, 2,400
10. Nalco (Mining) Inc., 2,400

Source: *Business Rankings*, (annual), Dun & Bradstreet Inc., 2011, p. VI.15-VI.16.

3695 ■ LARGEST METAL MINING COMPANIES BY SALES, 2010

Ranked by: Total revenue, in dollars. **Remarks:** Also notes contact information for headquarters, number of employees at headquarters and overall, rank by employees, and primary SIC code. **Number listed:** 49

1. Freeport-McMoRan Copper & Gold Inc., with $18,982,000,000
2. Newmont Mining Corp., $9,540,000,000
3. Southern Copper Corp., $5,149,500,000
4. Cliffs Natural Resources Inc., $4,682,200,000
5. PT Freeport Indonesia Co., $3,412,281,000
6. USEC Inc., $2,035,400,000

7. Iamgold Purchasing Services Inc., $914,339,000
8. Doe Run Resources Corp., $800,000,000
9. Stillwater Mining Co., $555,878,000
10. Coeur D'Alene Mines Corp., $515,457,000

Source: *Business Rankings*, (annual), Dun & Bradstreet Inc., 2011, p. V.15-V.16.

3696 ■ LARGEST U.S. DIVERSIFIED METALS AND MINING COMPANIES OVERALL, 2011

Ranked by: Score based on revenue, profits, assets, and market capitalization. **Remarks:** Specific scores not provided. Also notes overall rank in the *Forbes 2000* and figures for each criterion. **Number listed:** 5

1. Freeport-McMoRan Copper & Gold Inc.
2. Newmont Mining Corp.
3. Peabody Energy Corp.
4. Consol Energy Inc.
5. Alpha Natural Resources Inc.

Source: *Forbes*, Forbes 2000 (annual), http://www.forbes.com, May 7, 2012.

3697 ■ LARGEST U.S. FABRICATED METAL PRODUCT MANUFACTURERS, 2010

Ranked by: Revenue, in millions of dollars. **Remarks:** Also notes overall rank within the *IW 500,* revenue growth, and profit margin. **Number listed:** 16

1. United States Steel Corp., with $17,374 million
2. Illinois Tool Works Inc., $15,870
3. Stanley Black & Decker Inc., $8,410
4. Crown Holdings Inc., $7,941
5. Ball Corp., $7,630
6. General Cable Corp., $4,865
7. Timken Co., $4,056
8. Silgan Holdings Inc., $3,072
9. Harsco Corp., $3,039
10. Crane Co., $2,218

Source: *IndustryWeek*, IW 500 (annual), http://www.industryweek.com, July 2011.

3698 ■ LARGEST U.S. PRIMARY METAL PRODUCT MANUFACTURERS, 2010

Ranked by: Revenue, in millions of dollars. **Remarks:** Also notes overall rank within the *IW 500,* revenue growth, and profit margin. **Number listed:** 16

1. Alcoa Inc., with $21,013 million
2. Freeport-McMoRan Copper & Gold Inc., $18,982
3. Nucor Corp., $15,845
4. Reliance Steel & Aluminum Co., $6,313
5. Commercial Metals Co., $6,306
6. Steel Dynamics Inc., $6,301
7. AK Steel Holding Corp., $5,968
8. Precision Castparts Corp., $5,487
9. Southern Copper Corp., $5,150
10. Schnitzer Steel Industries Inc., $2,301

Source: *IndustryWeek*, IW 500 (annual), http://www.industryweek.com, July 2011.

3699 ■ MEXICO'S LARGEST DIVERSIFIED METALS AND MINING COMPANIES OVERALL, 2011

Ranked by: Score based on revenue, profits, assets, and market capitalization. **Remarks:** Specific scores not provided. Also notes overall rank in the *Forbes 2000* and figures for each criterion. **Number listed:** 4

1. Grupo Mexico, SA de CV
2. Industrias Penoles, SAB de CV
3. Fresnillo
4. Minera Frisco

Source: *Forbes*, Forbes 2000 (annual), http://www.forbes.com, May 7, 2012.

3700 ■ MOST PROFITABLE CANADIAN METALS AND MINING COMPANIES, 2011

Ranked by: Profits, in millions of Canadian dollars. **Number listed:** 6

1. Barrick Gold Corp., with C$4,484 million
2. Teck Resources Ltd., C$2,668
3. GoldCorp Inc., C$1,881
4. Iamgold Corp., C$807
5. Silver Wheaton Corp., C$550
6. Yamana Gold Inc., C$548

Source: *Canadian Business*, Investor 500 (annual), 2012, p. 55.

3701 ■ MOST VALUABLE U.S. INDUSTRIAL METALS AND MINING COMPANIES, 2011

Ranked by: Market value as of March 2011, in millions of U.S. dollars. **Remarks:** Also notes rank within the *FT U.S. 500*, rank for previous year, country, revenue, net income, assets, number of employees, share price, price-to-earning ratio, dividend yield, and fiscal yearend. **Number listed:** 7

1. Freeport-McMoRan Copper & Gold Inc., with $52,577.9 million
2. Southern Copper Corp., $34,229.5
3. Alcoa Inc., $18,767.1
4. Nucor Corp., $14,544.2
5. Cliffs Natural Resources Inc., $13,313.3
6. United States Steel Corp., $7,754.6
7. Allegheny Technologies Inc., $5,699.8

Source: *Financial Times*, FT 500 (annual), http://www.ft.com, June 24, 2011.

3702 ■ POLAND'S LARGEST DIVERSIFIED METALS AND MINING COMPANIES OVERALL, 2011

Ranked by: Score based on revenue, profits, assets, and market capitalization. **Remarks:** Specific scores not provided. Also notes overall rank in the *Forbes 2000* and figures for each criterion. **Number listed:** 2

1. KGMH Polska Miedz
2. JSW Group

Source: *Forbes*, Forbes 2000 (annual), http://www.forbes.com, May 7, 2012.

3703 ■ RUSSIA'S LARGEST DIVERSIFIED METALS AND MINING COMPANIES OVERALL, 2011

Ranked by: Score based on revenue, profits, assets, and market capitalization. **Remarks:** Specific scores not provided. Also notes overall rank in the *Forbes 2000* and figures for each criterion. **Number listed:** 2

1. OJSC Mining & Metallurgical Company Norilsk Nickel
2. Polyus Gold

Source: *Forbes*, Forbes 2000 (annual), http://www.forbes.com, May 7, 2012.

3704 ■ SOUTH AFRICA'S LARGEST DIVERSIFIED METALS AND MINING COMPANIES OVERALL, 2011

Ranked by: Score based on revenue, profits, assets, and market capitalization. **Remarks:** Specific scores not provided. Also notes overall rank in the *Forbes 2000* and figures for each criterion. **Number listed:** 5

1. AngloGold Ashanti
2. Impala Platinum Holdings Ltd.
3. Gold Fields Ltd.
4. Exxaro Resources
5. African Rainbow

Source: *Forbes*, Forbes 2000 (annual), http://www.forbes.com, May 7, 2012.

3705 ■ SOUTH KOREA'S LARGEST DIVERSIFIED METALS AND MINING COMPANIES OVERALL, 2011

Ranked by: Score based on revenue, profits, assets, and market capitalization. **Remarks:** Specific scores not provided. Also notes overall rank in the *Forbes 2000* and figures for each criterion. **Number listed:** 2

1. Korea Zinc
2. Hyosung

Source: *Forbes*, Forbes 2000 (annual), http://www.forbes.com, May 7, 2012.

3706 ■ SWITZERLAND'S LARGEST DIVERSIFIED METALS AND MINING COMPANIES OVERALL, 2011

Ranked by: Score based on revenue, profits, assets, and market capitalization. **Remarks:** Specific scores not provided. Also notes overall rank in the *Forbes 2000* and figures for each criterion. **Number listed:** 2

1. Glencore International plc
2. Xstrata plc

Source: *Forbes*, Forbes 2000 (annual), http://www.forbes.com, May 7, 2012.

3707 ■ TOP FABRICATED METAL COMPANIES IN CORPORATE FACILITY PROJECTS, 2011

Ranked by: Investment in new or expanded facilities, in millions of dollars. **Remarks:** Also notes location, product line, and whether facility is new or expanded. **Number listed:** 10

1. MBA Building Supplies, with $775 million
2. NTN Bower Corp., $750
3. Hitachi Ltd., $136
4. Winkhaus GmbH, $128
5. Villacero, $107
5. Rexam plc, $107
7. Prime Flexible Steel, $104
8. SKF, $98
9. Stanley Black & Decker, $90
10. Firth Rixson Forgings LLC, $80

Source: *Site Selection*, Top Industries (annual), March 2012, p. 121.

3708 ■ TOP *FORTUNE 500* COMPANIES IN METALS, 2011

Ranked by: Revenue, in millions of dollars. **Remarks:** Also notes overall rank in the *Fortune 500;* profits; profits as a percentage of revenue; stockholders' equity; and rank by each criterion. **Number listed:** 9

1. Alcoa Inc., with $24,951 million
2. Nucor Corp., $20,024
3. United States Steel Corp., $19,884
4. Reliance Steel & Aluminum, $8,135
5. Steel Dynamics Inc., $7,998
6. Commercial Metals Co., $7,920
7. AK Steel Holding Corp., $6,468
8. Allegheny Technologies, $5,183
9. Aleris, $4,826

Source: *Fortune*, Fortune 500 (annual), May 21, 2012, p. F-37.

3709 ■ UNITED KINGDOM'S LARGEST DIVERSIFIED METALS AND MINING COMPANIES OVERALL, 2011

Ranked by: Score based on revenue, profits, assets, and market capitalization. **Remarks:** Specific scores not provided. Also notes overall rank in the *Forbes 2000* and figures for each criterion. **Number listed:** 6

1. Rio Tinto Ltd.
2. Anglo American plc
3. Eurasian Natural Resources Corp. plc
4. Vedanta Resources plc
5. Antofagasta
6. Kazakhmys

Source: *Forbes*, Forbes 2000 (annual), http://www.forbes.com, May 7, 2012.

3710 ■ WORLD'S LARGEST DIVERSIFIED METALS AND MINING COMPANIES OVERALL, 2011

Ranked by: Score based on revenue, profits, assets, and market capitalization. **Remarks:** Specific scores not provided. Also notes country, overall rank in the *Forbes 2000,* and figures for each criterion. **Number listed:** 70

1. BHP Billiton Ltd.
2. Vale SA
3. Rio Tinto Ltd.
4. Glencore International plc
5. China Shenhua Energy Co., Ltd.
6. Xstrata plc
7. Anglo American plc
8. Barrick Gold Corp.
9. Freeport-McMoRan Copper & Gold Inc.
10. OJSC Mining & Metallurgical Company Norilsk Nickel

Source: *Forbes*, Forbes 2000 (annual), http://www.forbes.com, May 7, 2012.

3711 ■ WORLD'S LARGEST FABRICATED METAL PRODUCT MANUFACTURERS, 2010

Ranked by: Revenue, in millions of dollars. **Remarks:** Also notes rank for previous year, overall rank within the *IW 1000,* country, and revenue growth. **Number listed:** 56

1. Nippon Steel Corp., with $42,899 million
2. JFE Holdings Inc., $34,986

3. Baoshan Iron & Steel Co., Ltd., $22,645
4. Sumitomo Electric Industries Ltd., $22,587
5. United States Steel Corp., $17,374
6. Illinois Tool Works Inc., $15,870
7. Angang Steel Co., Ltd., $14,013
8. OAO Severstal, $13,469
9. Norsk Hydro ASA, $12,986
10. Sandvik AB, $12,296

Source: *IndustryWeek*, IW 1000 (annual), http://www.industryweek.com, August 2011.

3712 ■ WORLD'S LARGEST PRIMARY METAL PRODUCT MANUFACTURERS, 2010

Ranked by: Revenue, in millions of dollars. **Remarks:** Also notes rank for previous year, overall rank within the *IW 1000,* country, and revenue growth. **Number listed:** 69

1. ArcelorMittal, with $78,025 million
2. ThyssenKrupp AG, $57,377
3. Rio Tinto Ltd., $54,646
4. Pohang Iron & Steel Co., Ltd. (POSCO), $54,575
5. BHP Billiton Ltd., $53,326
6. Vale SA, $45,293
7. Anglo American plc, $27,960
8. Tata Steel Ltd., $23,202
9. Alcoa Inc., $21,013
10. Kobe Steel Ltd., $20,554

Source: *IndustryWeek*, IW 1000 (annual), http://www.industryweek.com, August 2011.

3713 ■ WORLD'S MOST ADMIRED METALS COMPANIES, 2012

Ranked by: Score, on a scale of 10, based on a survey of executives, directors, and securities analysts of companies within their own industry on eight criteria: innovation, financial soundness, employee talent, use of corporate assets, long-term investment value, social responsibility, quality of management, and quality of products/services. **Remarks:** Specific scores not provided. Also notes rank for previous year. **Number listed:** 8

1. Alcoa Inc.
1. ArcelorMittal
3. Pohang Iron & Steel Co., Ltd. (POSCO)
4. Nippon Steel Corp.
5. ThyssenKrupp AG
6. Nucor Corp.
7. Tata Steel Ltd.
8. Baosteel Group Corp.

Source: *Fortune*, World's Most Admired Companies (annual), March 19, 2012, p. 149.

3714 ■ WORLD'S MOST ETHICAL METALS AND MINING COMPANIES, 2012

Ranked by: Score based on five criteria: ethics and compliance program; reputation, leadership, and innovation; governance; corporate citizenship and responsibility; and culture of ethics. **Remarks:** Specific scores not provided; companies are listed alphabetically, not ranked. **Number listed:** 4

1. Alcoa (U.S.)
2. The Mosaic Co. (U.S.)

3. Tata Steel Ltd. (India)

4. Umicore (Belgium)

Source: *Ethisphere Magazine*, World's Most Ethical Companies (annual), http://www.ethisphere.com, 2012.

3715 ■ WORLD'S MOST VALUABLE INDUSTRIAL METALS AND MINING COMPANIES, 2011

Ranked by: Market value as of March 2011, in millions of U.S. dollars. **Remarks:** Also notes rank within the *FT 500*, rank for previous year, country, revenue, net income, assets, number of employees, share price, price-to-earning ratio, dividend yield, and fiscal year-end. **Number listed:** 15

1. ArcelorMittal, with $56,539.9 million
2. Freeport-McMoRan Copper & Gold Inc., $52,577.9
3. Mining & Metallurgical Company Norilsk Nickel, $50,058.2
4. Pohang Iron & Steel Co., Ltd. (POSCO), $40,137.9
5. Southern Copper Corp., $34,229.5
6. Teck Resources Ltd., $31,215.2
7. Grupo Mexico SA de CV, $29,074.7
8. Tenaris SA, $29,032.7
9. Novolipetsk Steel, $25,381.1
10. Companhia Siderurgica Nacional, $24,322.9

Source: *Financial Times*, FT 500 (annual), http://www.ft.com, June 24, 2011.

Metal Products

3716 ■ LARGEST COMPANIES IN THE FABRICATED METAL PRODUCTS INDUSTRY BY EMPLOYEES, 2010

Ranked by: Total number of employees. **Remarks:** Also notes contact information for headquarters, number of employees at headquarters, revenue, rank by revenue, and primary SIC code. **Number listed:** 68

1. Masco Building Products Corp., with 35,000 employees
2. Kohler Co., 28,000
3. ThyssenKrupp USA Inc., 25,000
4. Fortune Brands Inc., 24,600
5. Crown Holdings Inc., 20,510
6. Reynolds Metals Co., 18,000
7. SPX Corp., 15,500
8. Weatherford U.S. LP, 15,000
9. Ball Corp., 14,500
10. ITT Fluid Technology Corp., 13,600

Source: *Business Rankings*, (annual), Dun & Bradstreet Inc., 2011, p. VI.75-VI.76.

3717 ■ LARGEST COMPANIES IN THE FABRICATED METAL PRODUCTS INDUSTRY BY SALES, 2010

Ranked by: Total revenue, in dollars, for companies outside of the machinery and transportation equipment industry. **Remarks:** Also notes contact information for headquarters, number of employees at headquarters and overall, rank by employees, and primary SIC code. **Number listed:** 70

1. Crown Holdings Inc., with $7,941,000,000
2. Ball Corp., $7,630,000,000

3. Fortune Brands Inc., $7,141,500,000
4. Federal Mogul Corp., $6,219,000,000
5. SPX Corp., $4,886,800,000
6. Rexam Inc., $3,268,924,000
7. Silgan Holdings Inc., $3,071,545,000
8. American Axle & Manufacturing Holdings Inc., $2,283,000,000
9. Crane Co., $2,217,825,000
10. Crown Cork & Seal Co., $2,102,000,000

Source: *Business Rankings*, (annual), Dun & Bradstreet Inc., 2011, p. V.75-V.76.

Metal Service Centers

3718 ■ TOP METAL SERVICE CENTERS, 2010

Ranked by: Revenue, in billions of dollars. **Remarks:** Also notes website, revenue projected for upcoming year, headquarters, number of stocking locations and employees, types of products and services, and market areas. **Number listed:** 50

1. Reliance Steel & Aluminum Co., with $6.31 billion
2. Ryerson Inc., $3.89
3. McJunkin Red Man Holding Corp., $3.85
4. Kloeckner Metals, $2.5
5. Samuel, Son & Co., Ltd., $2.49
6. ThyssenKrupp Materials North America Inc., $2.40
7. Russel Metals Inc., $2.11
8. O'Neal Steel Inc., $1.94
9. Carpenter Technology Corp., $1.7
10. Steel Technologies Inc., $1.52

Source: *Metal Center News*, Top 50 (annual), September 2011, p. 18+.

Microcomputers
See: **Personal Computers**

Military Contractors
See: **Defense Contracts**

Milk Products
See also: **Dairy Products**

3719 ■ TOP REFRIGERATED MILKSHAKE BRANDS IN THE U.S., 2011

Ranked by: Sales, in dollars. **Remarks:** Also notes percent change from previous year and market share. **Number listed:** 10

1. Hershey's, with $18,964,440
2. Rice Dream, $15,293,070
3. Chug, $9,039,167
4. Kern's Aguas Frescas, $3,821,458
5. Yoo Hoo, $3,476,931
6. private label, $3,430,964
7. Nestle Nesquick, $3,371,353
8. Dean's Choco Riffic, $1,568,026

9. Don Jose, $1,342,993

10. Odwalla Super Protein, $729,151

Source: *Beverage Industry*, State of the Industry Report (annual), July 2011, p. SIO-18.

Millionaires
See: **Wealth**

Mineral Industry
See: **Mining Industry**

Minimum Wage

3720 ■ STATES WITH THE HIGHEST MINIMUM WAGE RATE, 2011

Ranked by: Minimum wage rate, in dollars. **Number listed:** 46

1. Washington, with $8.67
2. Oregon, $8.50
3. Connecticut, $8.25
3. Illinois, $8.25
3. Nevada, $8.25
3. Washington DC, $8.25
7. Vermont, $8.15
8. California, $8
8. Massachusetts, $8
10. Alaska, $7.75

Source: *State Rankings*, (annual), CQ Press, 2011, p. 171.

3721 ■ STATES WITH THE LOWEST MINIMUM WAGE RATE, 2011

Ranked by: State minimum wage rate, in dollars. **Number listed:** 46

1. Georgia, with $5.15
1. Wyoming, $5.15
3. Minnesota, $6.15
4. Arkansas, $6.25
5. Delaware, $7.25
5. Florida, $7.25
5. Hawaii, $7.25
5. Idaho, $7.25
5. Indiana, $7.25
5. Iowa, $7.25
5. Kansas, $7.25
5. Kentucky, $7.25
5. Maryland, $7.25

Source: *State Rankings*, (annual), CQ Press, 2011, p. 171.

Mining Industry

3722 ■ EUROPE'S MOST VALUABLE MINING COMPANIES, 2011

Ranked by: Market value as of March 2011, in millions of U.S. dollars. **Remarks:** Also notes rank within the *FT Europe 500*, rank for previous year, country, revenue, net income, assets, number of employees, share price, price-to-earning ratio, dividend yield, and fiscal yearend. **Number listed:** 17

1. Rio Tinto Ltd., with $106,255.3 million
2. BHP Billiton Ltd., $85,482.4
3. Xstrata plc, $69,240.3
4. Anglo American plc, $67,950
5. Antofagasta, $21,507.6
6. Eurasian Natural Resources Corp. plc, $19,331.2
7. Fresnillo, $17,737.9
8. Kazakhmys, $11,960
9. Polyus Gold, $11,416.9
10. Vedanta Resources, $10,133.5

Source: *Financial Times*, FT 500 (annual), http://www.ft.com, June 24, 2011.

3723 ■ FASTEST-GROWING CANADIAN MINING COMPANIES, 2009-2010

Ranked by: Annual growth in revenue, in percent. **Remarks:** Also notes figures for current and previous year. **Number listed:** 15

1. Agrico-Eagle Mines, with 132%
2. Eldorado Gold, 121%
3. Uranium One, 115%
4. Mercator Minerals, 106%
5. Quadra FNX Mining, 100%
6. Equinox Minerals, 97%
7. Suncor Energy Inc., 70%
8. Breakwater, 64%
8. Potash Corp. of Saskatchewan Inc., 64%
8. New Gold, 64%

Source: *Canadian Mining Journal*, Canada's Top 40 (annual), August 2011, p. 16.

3724 ■ FASTEST-GROWING MINING COMPANIES, 2008-2011

Ranked by: Score based on three-year growth in revenue and earnings, and three-year total return to investors. **Remarks:** Specific scores not provided. To qualify for list, companies must have revenues of at least $50 million, net income of at least $10 million, market capitalization of at least $250 million, and stock price of at least $5. Int'l companies are eligible if they trade on a U.S. exchange and file quarterly reports. **Number listed:** 4

1. Silver Wheaton
2. IAMGOLD Corp.
3. Eldorado Gold
4. Newmont Mining

Source: *Fortune*, 100 Fastest-Growing Companies (annual), http://www.fortune.com, September 26, 2011.

3725 ■ LARGEST CANADIAN MINING COMPANIES BY ASSETS, 2010

Ranked by: Assets, in millions of Canadian dollars. **Remarks:** Also notes figures for previous year and percent change. **Number listed:** 14

1. Barrick Gold Corp., with C$34,321,660 million
2. Goldcorp Inc., C$29,673,373
3. Teck Resources Ltd., C$29,209,000
4. Kinross Gold, C$16,889,013

5. Potash Corp. of Saskatchewan Inc., C$16,087,879

6. Agrium Inc., C$13,098,510

7. Sherritt International, C$10,721,500

8. Yamana Gold, C$10,608,218

9. Cameco Corp., C$7,671,368

10. Canadian Oil Sands Ltd., C$7,016,000

Source: *Canadian Mining Journal*, Canada's Top 40 (annual), August 2011, p. 17.

3726 ■ LARGEST CANADIAN MINING COMPANIES BY REVENUE, 2010

Ranked by: Revenue, in millions of Canadian dollars. **Remarks:** Also notes year-end date, industry, net earnings, assets, and figures for previous year. **Number listed:** 40

1. Barrick Gold Corp., with C$11,251,720 million

2. Agrium Inc., C$11,065,290

3. Teck Resources Ltd., C$9,339,000

4. Suncor Energy Inc., C$7,028,000

5. Potash Corp. of Saskatchewan Inc., C$6,734,758

6. Goldcorp Inc., C$3,913,794

7. Canadian Oil Sands Ltd., C$3,460,000

8. Kinross Gold, C$3,100,403

9. First Quantum Minerals, C$2,449,546

10. Cameco Corp., C$2,123,655

Source: *Canadian Mining Journal*, Canada's Top 40 (annual), August 2011, p. 15.

3727 ■ LARGEST COMPANIES IN THE NON-METALLIC MINERAL MINING (EXCEPT FUELS) INDUSTRY BY EMPLOYEES, 2010

Ranked by: Total number of employees. **Remarks:** Also notes contact information for headquarters, number of employees at headquarters, revenue, rank by revenue, and primary SIC code. **Number listed:** 48

1. Longyear Holdings Inc., with 9,500 employees

2. Boart Longyear Co., 9,464

3. Vulcan Materials Co., 8,479

4. Legacy Vulcan Corp., 7,983

5. J. M. Huber Corp., 5,460

6. Martin Marietta Materials Inc., 4,554

7. Lehigh Hanson Inc., 4,000

7. Michels Corp., 4,000

9. Imerys USA Inc., 3,900

10. Carmeuse Lime Inc., 3,500

Source: *Business Rankings*, (annual), Dun & Bradstreet Inc., 2011, p. VI.21-VI.22.

3728 ■ LARGEST COMPANIES IN THE NON-METALLIC MINERAL MINING (EXCEPT FUELS) INDUSTRY BY SALES, 2010

Ranked by: Total revenue, in dollars. **Remarks:** Also notes contact information for headquarters, number of employees at headquarters and overall, rank by employees, and primary SIC code. **Number listed:** 50

1. Triangle Aggregates LLC, with $3,000,000,000

2. Vulcan Materials Co., $2,558,862,000

3. Martin Marietta Materials Inc., $1,782,857,000

4. J. M. Huber Corp., $1,392,755,000

5. Compass Minerals International Inc., $1,068,900,000

6. Amcol International Corp., $852,538,000

7. FML Holdings Inc., $398,660,000

8. Intrepid Potash Inc., $359,304,000

9. APAC Mid-South Inc., $300,000,000

10. TechniSand Inc., $247,813,542

Source: *Business Rankings*, (annual), Dun & Bradstreet Inc., 2011, p. V.21-V.22.

3729 ■ LARGEST MINING COMPANIES IN BRITISH COLUMBIA, 2010

Ranked by: Revenue, in thousands of Canadian dollars. **Remarks:** Also notes figures for previous year. **Number listed:** 10

1. Teck Resources Ltd., with $9,300,000 thousand

2. Goldcorp Inc., $3,913,562

3. First Quantum Minerals Ltd., $2,449,401

4. Quadra FNX Mining Ltd., $986,330

5. Eldorado Gold Corp., $814,862

6. Pan American Silver Corp., $650,907

7. New Gold Inc., $546,331

8. Northgate Minerals Corp., $499,569

9. Western Coal Corp., $438,568

10. Silver Wheaton Corp., $436,028

Source: *BCBusiness*, Top 100 (annual), July 2011, p. 135.

3730 ■ MOST PROFITABLE CANADIAN MINING COMPANIES, 2010

Ranked by: Net income, in millions of Canadian dollars. **Remarks:** Also notes figures for previous year and percent change. **Number listed:** 14

1. Barrick Gold, with C$3,372,220 million

2. Teck Resources Ltd., C$1,975,000

3. Potash Corp. of Saskatchewan Inc., C$1,860,386

4. Goldcorp, C$1,613,083

5. Suncor Energy Inc., C$1,492,000

6. Canadian Oil Sands Ltd., C$886,000

7. Kinross Gold, C$794,748

8. Agrium Inc., C$752,930

9. Cameco Corp., C$514,749

10. Yamana Gold, C$464,987

Source: *Canadian Mining Journal*, Canada's Top 40 (annual), August 2011, p. 16.

3731 ■ MOST VALUABLE U.S. MINING COMPANIES, 2011

Ranked by: Market value as of March 2011, in millions of U.S. dollars. **Remarks:** Also notes rank within the *FT U.S. 500*, rank for previous year, country, revenue, net income, assets, number of employees, share price, price-to-earning ratio, dividend yield, and fiscal yearend. **Number listed:** 7

1. Newmont Mining Corp., with $25,922.6 million

2. Peabody Energy Corp., $19,472.4

3. Consol Energy Inc., $12,152.1

4. Walter Energy Inc., $7,205.3

5. Alpha Natural Resources Inc., $7,153.1

6. Massey Energy Co., $7,072.2

7. Arch Coal Inc., $5,863.3

Source: *Financial Times*, FT 500 (annual), http://www.ft.com, June 24, 2011.

3732 ■ STATES WITH THE HIGHEST RATE OF EMPLOYEES IN MINING AND LOGGING, 2010

Ranked by: Percentage of employees in the mining and logging industries. **Number listed:** 41

1. Wyoming, with 9.7%

2. Alaska, 4.4%

3. West Virginia, 4.1%

4. Oklahoma, 3.1%

5. Louisiana, 2.6%

6. North Dakota, 2.5%

7. New Mexico, 2.2%

7. Texas, 2.2%

9. Montana, 1.8%

10. Kentucky, 1.3%

Source: *State Rankings*, (annual), CQ Press, 2011, p. 203.

3733 ■ SWITZERLAND'S MOST VALUABLE MINING BRANDS, 2011

Ranked by: Brand value, in millions of U.S. dollars. **Remarks:** Also notes rank within the *Global 500* for current and previous year, figures for current and previous year, and brand rating. Ranking is available online only. **Number listed:** 2

1. Glencore, with $2,870 million

2. Xstrata, $2,530

Source: *Global 500*, (annual), Brand Finance plc, March 2012.

3734 ■ TOP CANADIAN MINING COMPANIES, 2010

Ranked by: Revenue, in thousands of Canadian dollars (unless otherwise noted). **Remarks:** Also notes percent change from previous year. **Number listed:** 10

1. Rio Tinto Alcan Inc. (U.S. dollars), with C$15,206,000 thousand

2. Teck Resources Ltd., C$10,450,000

3. Vale Canada, C$4,712,000

4. First Quantum Minerals Ltd. (U.S. dollars), C$2,899,500

5. Cameco Corp., C$2,142,828

6. Sherritt International, C$1,835,900

7. Inmet Mining, C$1,109,494

8. Lundin Mining (U.S. dollars), C$983,786

9. Equinox Minerals (U.S. dollars), C$942,769

10. Quadra FNX Mining (U.S. dollars), C$924,626

Source: *Report on Business Magazine*, Top 1000 Companies (annual), http://www.reportonbusiness.com, June 2011.

3735 ■ TOP *FORTUNE 500* COMPANIES IN MINING AND CRUDE OIL PRODUCTION, 2011

Ranked by: Revenue, in millions of dollars. **Remarks:** Also notes overall rank in the *Fortune 500;* profits; profits as a percentage of revenue; stockholders' equity; and rank by each criterion. **Number listed:** 13

1. Occidental Petroleum Corp., with $24,216 million

2. Freeport-McMoRan Copper & Gold Inc., $20,880

3. Apache Corp., $16,888

4. Marathon Oil Co., $15,282

5. Anadarko Petroleum Corp., $13,967

6. Chesapeake Energy Corp., $11,635

7. Devon Energy Corp., $11,497

8. Newmont Mining Corp., $10,358

9. EOG Resources Inc., $10,126

10. Peabody Energy Corp., $8,096

Source: *Fortune*, Fortune 500 (annual), May 21, 2012, p. F-37.

3736 ■ THE UNITED KINGDOM'S MOST VALUABLE BRANDS, 2011

Ranked by: Brand value, in millions of U.S. dollars. **Remarks:** Also notes rank within the *Global 500* for current and previous year, figures for current and previous year, and brand rating. Ranking is available online only. **Number listed:** 2

1. BHP Billiton, with $6,139 million

2. Rio Tinto, $3,971

Source: *Global 500*, (annual), Brand Finance plc, March 2012.

3737 ■ WORLD'S MOST VALUABLE MINING BRANDS, 2011

Ranked by: Brand value, in millions of U.S. dollars. **Remarks:** Also notes rank within the *Global 500* for current and previous year, figures for current and previous year, country, and brand rating. Ranking is available online only. **Number listed:** 5

1. BHP Billiton, with $6,139 million

2. Rio Tinto, $3,971

3. Vale, $3,942

4. Glencore, $2,870

5. Xstrata, $2,530

Source: *Global 500*, (annual), Brand Finance plc, March 2012.

3738 ■ WORLD'S MOST VALUABLE MINING COMPANIES, 2011

Ranked by: Market value as of March 2011, in millions of U.S. dollars. **Remarks:** Also notes rank within the *FT 500*, rank for previous year, country, revenue, net income, assets, number of employees, share price, price-to-earning ratio, dividend yield, and fiscal year-end. **Number listed:** 16

1. BHP Billiton Ltd., with $247,079.5 million

2. Vale SA, $168,232.1

3. Rio Tinto Ltd., $144,447.4

4. China Shenhua Energy Co., $89,270.6

5. Xstrata plc, $69,240.3

6. Anglo American plc, $67,950

7. Barrick Gold Corp., $51,742.6

8. Goldcorp Inc., $39,677.6

9. Newcrest Mining Ltd., $31,502.9

10. Anglo Platinum Ltd., $27,159.6

Source: *Financial Times*, FT 500 (annual), http://www.ft.com, June 24, 2011.

Minorities—Employment

3739 ■ BEST EMPLOYERS FOR MINORITY ENGINEERS, 2012

Ranked by: Survey based on work environment for engineers who are members of minority groups. **Remarks:** Specific scores not provided. **Number listed:** 50

1. General Electric Co.
2. Raytheon Co.
3. Intel Corp.
4. Boeing Co.
5. CH2M Hill Cos., Ltd.
6. General Dynamics Corp.
7. Microsoft Corp.
8. Google Inc.
9. Procter & Gamble Co.
10. Siemens AG

Source: *Minority Engineer*, Top Employers (annual), http://www.eop.com/mags-ME.php, 2011.

3740 ■ BEST EMPLOYERS FOR MINORITY ENGINEERS AND IT PROFESSIONALS, 2011

Ranked by: Survey based on work environment for engineering and technical professionals who are women, minorities, and people with disabilities. **Remarks:** Specific scores not provided. **Number listed:** 50

1. Apple Inc.
2. Google Inc.
3. Microsoft Corp.
4. Eli Lilly & Co.
5. Verizon Communications Inc.
6. PricewaterhouseCoopers LLP
7. BAE Systems plc
8. International Business Machines Corp. (IBM)
9. Cisco Systems Inc.
10. Accenture Ltd.

Source: *Workforce Diversity for Engineering and IT Professionals*, Top Employers (annual), http://www.eop.com/mags-WD.php, 2011.

3741 ■ BEST EQUAL OPPORTUNITY EMPLOYERS, 2011

Ranked by: Survey based on work environment for members of minority groups. **Remarks:** Specific scores not provided. **Number listed:** 50

1. PricewaterhouseCoopers LLP
2. Microsoft Corp.
3. Google Inc.
4. American Express Co.
5. Verizon Communications Inc.
6. Goldman Sachs Group Inc.
7. The Coca-Cola Co.
8. PepsiCo Inc.
9. Oracle Corp.
10. CenturyLink Inc.

Source: *Equal Opportunity*, Top Employers (annual), http://www.eop.com/mags-EO.php, 2011.

3742 ■ BEST EQUAL OPPORTUNITY GOVERNMENT AGENCIES, 2011

Ranked by: Survey based on work environment for members of minority groups. **Remarks:** Specific scores not provided. **Number listed:** 20

1. U.S. Department of Labor
2. U.S. Department of State
3. Equal Employment Opportunity Commission
4. Internal Revenue Service

5. U.S. Department of Education
6. National Science Foundation
7. National Aeronautics & Space Administration (NASA)
8. U.S. Postal Service
9. U.S. Department of Veterans Affairs
10. Federal Drug Administration

Source: *Equal Opportunity*, Top Employers (annual), http://www.eop.com/mags-EO.php, 2011.

3743 ■ BEST GOVERNMENT AGENCIES FOR MINORITY ENGINEERS, 2012

Ranked by: Survey based on work environment for engineers who are members of minority groups. **Remarks:** Specific scores not provided. **Number listed:** 20

1. U.S. Army Corps of Engineers
2. U.S. Navy
3. U.S. Department of Defense
4. General Services Administration
5. National Aeronautics & Space Administration (NASA)
6. U.S. Air Force
7. National Security Agency
8. U.S. Department of Transportation
9. Federal Bureau of Investigation (FBI)
10. U.S. Department of Commerce

Source: *Minority Engineer*, Top Employers (annual), http://www.eop.com/mags-ME.php, 2011.

3744 ■ BEST GOVERNMENT AGENCIES FOR MINORITY ENGINEERS AND IT PROFESSIONALS, 2011

Ranked by: Survey based on work environment for engineering and technical professionals who are women, minorities, and people with disabilities. **Remarks:** Specific scores not provided. **Number listed:** 20

1. National Aeronautics & Space Administration (NASA)
2. U.S. Department of Homeland Security
3. Federal Aviation Administration
4. U.S. Navy
5. U.S. Environmental Protection Agency
6. U.S. Air Force
7. U.S. Department of Labor
8. Nuclear Regulatory Commission
9. U.S. Department of Housing & Urban Development
10. U.S. Coast Guard

Source: *Workforce Diversity for Engineering and IT Professionals*, Top Employers (annual), http://www.eop.com/mags-WD.php, 2011.

3745 ■ BEST PLACES FOR DIVERSE MANAGERS TO WORK, 2012

Ranked by: Score based on strategies for accountability, inclusion practices, and ongoing evaluation of retention/recruitment activities that allow and encourage managers of diverse backgrounds to excel and develop into leadership roles. **Remarks:** Specific scores not provided. **Number listed:** 50

1. Accenture Ltd.
2. Bank of America Corp.

3. CSX Corp.

4. Sprint Corp.

5. Blue Cross Blue Shield of Michigan

6. Capital One Corp.

7. Allstate Insurance Co.

8. Colgate-Palmolive Co.

9. Verizon Communications Inc.

10. Wal-Mart Stores Inc.

Source: *DiversityMBA Magazine*, 50 Out Front for Diversity Leadership (annual), http://www.diversitymbamagazine.com, 2012.

3746 ■ TOP COMPANIES FOR MULTICULTURAL BUSINESS OPPORTUNITIES, 2011

Ranked by: Score based on survey of minority-owned companies as to the corporations that offer the best business opportunities, in terms of volume, consistency, and quality. **Remarks:** Specific scores not provided. **Number listed:** 50

1. AT&T Inc.

2. Wal-Mart Stores Inc.

3. Dell Inc.

4. Office Depot Inc.

5. Northrop Grumman Corp.

6. Altria Group Inc.

7. Raytheon Co.

8. Verizon Communications Inc.

9. The Coca-Cola Co.

10. International Business Machines Corp. (IBM)

Source: *DiversityBusiness.com*, Div50 (annual), http://www.diversitybusiness.com, January 16, 2012.

3747 ■ TOP GOVERNMENT AGENCIES FOR MULTICULTURAL BUSINESS OPPORTUNITIES, 2011

Ranked by: Score based on survey of minority-owned companies as to the government agencies that offer the best business opportunities, in terms of volume, consistency, and quality. **Remarks:** Specific scores not provided. **Number listed:** 25

1. U.S. Postal Service

2. U.S. Department of Homeland Security

3. National Aeronautics & Space Administration (NASA)

4. U.S. Department of Transportation

5. U.S. Department of Defense

6. U.S. Air Force

7. U.S. Department of Energy

8. Small Business Administration

9. U.S. Department of the Treasury

10. U.S. Navy

Source: *DiversityBusiness.com*, Div50 (annual), http://www.diversitybusiness.com, February 1, 2012.

Minority Business Enterprises

3748 ■ CHICAGO'S LARGEST MINORITY-OWNED FIRMS, 2010

Ranked by: Revenue, in millions of dollars. **Remarks:** Also notes contact information, top executive, percent change in revenue from previous year, number of employees, year founded, minority group of ownership, and type of business. **Number listed:** 25

1. MAT Holdings Inc., with $660.6 million

2. Flying Food Group LLC, $333

3. Harpo Inc., $289

4. Raja Foods LLC, $220

5. Vmark Inc., $200

Source: *Crain's Chicago Business*, Chicago's Largest Minority-Owned Firms (annual), http://www.chicagobusiness.com, November 18, 2011.

3749 ■ FASTEST-GROWING AMERICAN INDIAN-RUN COMPANIES IN THE U.S., 2007-2010

Ranked by: Average annual sales growth over three years, in percent. **Remarks:** Also notes overall rank in the *Inc. 5,000*, state, and revenue for current year. To qualify, private companies must have had annual revenues of at least $100,000 in 2007 and $2 million in 2010. **Number listed:** 19

1. Cetan Corp., with 2,275%

2. New West Technologies, 1,297%

3. Ishpi, 1,081%

4. CSI, 996%

5. TeraThink Corp., 331%

6. Climate Control Mechanical Services, 318%

7. RFIP, 314%

8. AQIWO, 190%

9. P3I, 150%

10. Arrow Strategies, 94%

Source: *Inc.*, Inc. 500 (annual), http://www.inc.com, September 2011.

3750 ■ IDAHO'S LARGEST MINORITY-OWNED BUSINESSES, 2011

Ranked by: Number of employees. **Remarks:** Also notes contact information, key executive, year founded, and business description. **Number listed:** 5

1. North Wind Inc., with 410 employees

2. PromoShop Inc., 84

3. Paige Mechanical Group, 80

3. Silverhawk Realty, 80

5. MarCon Inc., 45

Source: *Idaho Business Review*, Largest Minority-Owned Businesses (annual), February 24, 2012.

3751 ■ LARGEST DENVER-AREA MINORITY-OWNED BUSINESSES, 2010

Ranked by: Total revenue, in dollars. **Remarks:** Also notes contact information, rank and figures for previous year, total number of employees, number of offices, business description, top local executive, owner, and headquarters. **Number listed:** 25

1. Mike Shaw Automotive, with $217,198,539

2. Shortline Automotive Inc., $80,898,277

3. E2 Consulting Engineers Inc., $51,000,000

4. New West Technologies LLC, $47,539,737

5. Alpine Buick Pontiac GMC, $39,998,930

6. AMI Mechanical Inc., $37,175,362

7. SofTec Solutions Inc., $19,344,155

8. Rocky Mountain Instrument Co., $19,000,000

9. All American Seasonings Inc., $15,000,000

10. RTL Networks Inc., $12,520,104

Source: *Denver Business Journal*, Book of Lists (annual), December 16, 2011, p. 56.

3752 ■ LARGEST INDIANAPOLIS-AREA MINORITY-OWNED BUSINESSES, 2011

Ranked by: Number of local employees. **Remarks:** Also notes rank for previous year, contact information, number of employees that are minority, revenue, and percentage minority-owned. **Number listed:** 5

1. DSS Consulting Inc., with 588 employees
2. BCForward, 446
3. Telamon Corp., 211
4. SmartIT Staffing Inc., 121
5. Mays Chemical Co., 118

Source: *Indianapolis Business Journal*, Largest Minority-Owned Businesses (annual), http://www.ibj.com, July 4, 2011.

3753 ■ LARGEST MINORITY-OWNED BUSINESSES IN HARTFORD, CONNECTICUT, 2011

Ranked by: Number of employees in the Hartford region. **Remarks:** Also notes contact information, total number of employees, sales, minority group, company description, key executive, and year founded. **Number listed:** 3

1. Charter Oak Building Maintenance Inc., with 250 employees
2. AI Engineers Inc., 75
3. Beverly Hills Limousine Inc. of Connecticut, 30

Source: *Hartford Business Journal*, Largest Minority-Owned Businesses (annual), http://www.hartfordbusiness.com, October 17, 2011.

3754 ■ LARGEST MINORITY-OWNED BUSINESSES IN NEW JERSEY, 2010

Ranked by: Revenue, in millions of dollars. **Remarks:** Also notes rank for previous year, contact information, year founded, senior executive, minority category, and industry. **Number listed:** 66

1. SHI International Corp., with $3,040 million
2. Collabera, $375
3. Compas Inc., $200.2
4. Foremost Groups Inc., $166
5. Quality Packaging Specialists International LLC, $153
6. Deep Foods Inc., $130
7. Marlabs Inc., $100.22
8. Officemate International Corp., $100
9. York Telecom Corp., $97.3
10. Global Business Dimensions Inc., $78

Source: *NJBiz*, Top Minority-Owned Businesses (annual), http://www.njbiz.com, July 11, 2011.

3755 ■ LARGEST MINORITY-OWNED BUSINESSES IN ORANGE COUNTY, CALIFORNIA, 2010

Ranked by: Revenue, in millions of dollars. **Remarks:** Also notes rank for previous year, contact information, annual revenue growth, number of employees, name and ethnicity of minority owner(s), business description, and top local official. **Number listed:** 32

1. Kingston Technology Co., with $5,800 million
2. Vizio Inc., $2,500
3. MS International Inc., $390
4. Northgate Gonzalez Market, $350

5. Tawa Supermarket Inc., $310
6. Angels Baseball LP, $240
7. Bascom Group, $224
8. Pacific Rim Capital Inc., $143.8
9. Express Manufacturing Inc., $103.5
10. Aeronet Logistics Inc., $70

Source: *Orange County Business Journal*, Minority-Owned Businesses (annual), March 12, 2012, p. 12-14.

3756 ■ LARGEST MINORITY-OWNED COMPANIES IN THE NEW YORK AREA, 2011

Ranked by: Revenue, in millions of dollars. **Remarks:** Also notes contact information, top executive, figures for previous year, number of New York City employees, total number of employees, year founded, percentage minority owned, and nature of business. **Number listed:** 25

1. Palladium Equity Partners, with $2,014.1 million
2. Goya Foods Inc., $1,700
3. Rush Communications, $600

Source: *Crain's New York Business*, Largest Minority-Owned Companies (annual), http://www.crainsnewyork.com, April 30, 2012.

3757 ■ LARGEST NATIVE AMERICAN-OWNED BUSINESSES IN DETROIT, 2010

Ranked by: Revenue, in millions of dollars. **Remarks:** Also notes contact information, majority owner, figures for previous year, percent change, number of local employees for current and previous year, percent Native American-owned, and type of business. **Number listed:** 5

1. Rush Trucking Corp., with $100 million
2. Systrand Manufacturing Corp., $40
3. Arrow Strategies, $25
4. Human Capital Staffing LLC, $8
5. R. B. Construction Co., $1.4

Source: *Crain's Detroit Business*, Book of Lists (annual), December 26, 2011, p. 41.

3758 ■ TOP MINORITY-OWNED COMPANIES IN COLORADO, 2010

Ranked by: Gross revenue, in thousands of dollars. **Remarks:** Also notes business description, rank and figures for previous year, percent change, number of employees, and number of years in business. **Number listed:** 50

1. Mike Shaw Automotive Group, with $252,088 thousand
2. Alpine Buick Pontiac GMC, $39,999
3. Ayuda Management Corp., $24,369
4. Rocky Mountain Instrument Co., $19,500
5. Softec Solutions Inc., $19,412
6. Managed Business Solutions LLC, $18,790
7. InLine Media Inc., $15,069
8. Protech Sales Inc., $14,800
9. Gallegos Sanitation Inc., $14,663
10. Pacific Western Technologies Ltd., $14,224

Source: *ColoradoBiz*, Top Minority-Owned Businesses (annual), July 2011, p. 42.

Mobile Communication Industry

3759 ■ TOP FREE IPAD APPS, 2011

Ranked by: Number of days each app was ranked first in its category in the App Store's top 20 categories. **Remarks:** Specific figures not provided. **Number listed:** 3

1. Temple Run
2. Sherlock Holmes & the Hound of the Baskervilles Collector's Edition
3. Snappers HD

Source: *Advertising Age*, Digital Issue (annual), February 27, 2012, p. 16.

3760 ■ TOP PAID IPAD APPS, 2011

Ranked by: Number of days each app was ranked first in its category in the App Store's top 20 categories. **Remarks:** Specific figures not provided. **Number listed:** 3

1. Where's My Water?
2. Ragdoll Blaster 3 HD
3. Pages

Source: *Advertising Age*, Digital Issue (annual), February 27, 2012, p. 16.

Models (Persons)

3761 ■ MOST POWERFUL MODELS, 2011

Ranked by: Score based on earnings and such measures of popularity as Internet presence, press clippings, magazine cover stories, and mentions on television and radio. **Remarks:** Specific scores not provided. Also notes overall rank in the *Celebrity 100*. **Number listed:** 3

1. Gisele Bundchen
2. Heidi Klum
3. Kate Moss

Source: *Forbes*, The Celebrity 100 (annual), http://www.forbes.com, June 6, 2011.

Money Managers
See: **Investment Management Firms**

Mortgage Bonds and Notes

3762 ■ LARGEST S & LS BY MORTGAGE POOL SECURITIES, 2011

Ranked by: Total mortgage pool securities, in thousands of dollars. **Remarks:** Also notes city, state, association type, and dollar and percent change from previous year. **Number listed:** 25

1. Charles Schwab Bank, with $36,874,312 thousand
2. ING Bank, FSB, $20,833,125
3. E*Trade Bank, $19,281,051
4. Hudson City Savings Bank, $13,285,913
5. Sovereign Bank NA, $9,039,881
6. State Farm Bank, FSB, $3,703,968
7. Nationwide Bank, $2,785,962
8. People's United Bank, $2,457,290

9. Ameriprise Bank, FSB, $2,414,222
10. Astoria Federal Savings & Loan Association, $2,409,566

Source: *Highline Bank and S&L Quarterly, Dec. ed.*, 2011, p. V.56.

Mortgage Loans
See: **Mortgages**

Mortgages

3763 ■ LARGEST S & LS BY HOME MORTGAGE LOANS, 2011

Ranked by: Total home mortgage loans, in thousands of dollars. **Remarks:** Also notes city, state, association type, and dollar and percent change from previous year. **Number listed:** 25

1. ING Bank, FSB, with $40,888,456 thousand
2. Hudson City Savings Bank, $29,345,457
3. Sovereign Bank NA, $18,918,447
4. E*Trade Bank, $11,720,859
5. USAA FSB, $11,303,157
6. Astoria Federal Savings & Loan Association, $10,903,469
7. OneWest Bank FSB, $10,237,603
8. Third Federal Savings & Loan Association of Cleveland, $10,045,483
9. Citicorp Trust Bank, FSB, $9,902,803
10. Charles Schwab Bank, $9,121,835

Source: *Highline Bank and S&L Quarterly, Dec. ed.*, 2011, p. V.56.

3764 ■ LARGEST S & LS BY NONRESIDENTIAL MORTGAGE LOANS, 2011

Ranked by: Total nonresidential mortgage loans, in thousands of dollars. **Remarks:** Also notes city, state, association type, and dollar and percent change from previous year. **Number listed:** 25

1. Sovereign Bank NA, with $9,771,234 thousand
2. People's United Bank, $5,436,865
3. Raymond James Bank, FSB, $4,351,214
4. Midfirst Bank, $2,424,468
5. OneWest Bank FSB, $1,460,131
6. Wilmington Savings Fund Society, $1,261,855
7. Columbia Bank, $912,712
8. State Farm Bank, FSB, $880,034
9. Flagstar Bank, FSB, $866,709
10. Everbank, $752,898

Source: *Highline Bank and S&L Quarterly, Dec. ed.*, 2011, p. V.57.

Motion Picture Distribution

3765 ■ LARGEST MOTION PICTURE DISTRIBUTORS IN LOS ANGELES COUNTY, 2011

Ranked by: Box office receipts, in millions of dollars. **Remarks:** Also notes contact information, number of films distributed, market share, top grossing film of the year, parent company, distribution partners, and top distribution executive. **Number listed:** 12

1. Paramount Domestic Distribution, with $1,957 million
2. Warner Bros. Domestic Theatrical Distribution, $1,826
3. Sony Pictures Releasing, $1,274

Source: *Los Angeles Business Journal*, Motion Picture Distributors (annual), http://www.labusinessjournal.com, January 30, 2012.

Motion Picture Industry

3766 ■ LARGEST MOTION PICTURE COMPANIES BY EMPLOYEES, 2010

Ranked by: Total number of employees. **Remarks:** Also notes contact information for headquarters, number of employees at headquarters, revenue, rank by revenue, and primary SIC code. **Number listed:** 57

1. National Amusements Inc., with 133,269 employees
2. Disney Enterprises Inc., 133,000
3. Anschutz Co., 112,634
4. News Corp., 51,000
5. Blockbuster Inc., 48,000
6. Movie Gallery Inc., 36,250
7. Regal Entertainment Group, 25,226
8. Regal Cinemas Corp., 23,000
9. AMC Entertainment Holdings Inc., 22,000
10. Cinemark Holdings Inc., 20,700

Source: *Business Rankings*, (annual), Dun & Bradstreet Inc., 2011, p. VI.233-VI.234.

3767 ■ LARGEST MOTION PICTURE COMPANIES BY SALES, 2010

Ranked by: Total revenue, in dollars. **Remarks:** Also notes contact information for headquarters, number of employees at headquarters and overall, rank by employees, and primary SIC code. **Number listed:** 60

1. News Corp., with $32,778,000,000
2. Blockbuster Inc., $4,062,400,000
3. Regal Entertainment Group, $2,807,900,000
4. AMC Entertainment Inc., $2,417,739,000
5. Netflix Inc., $2,162,625,000
6. Cinemark Holdings Inc., $2,141,144,000
7. Cinemark USA Inc., $1,976,500,000
8. Cinemark Inc., $1,742,287,000
9. DreamWorks Animation SKG Inc., $784,791,000
10. Carmike Cinemas Inc., $491,262,000

Source: *Business Rankings*, (annual), Dun & Bradstreet Inc., 2011, p. V.207-V.208.

3768 ■ TOP MOVIE STUDIOS BY MARKET SHARE, 2010

Ranked by: Market share of U.S. box-office gross sales, in percent. **Remarks:** Also notes measured media expenditures and figures for previous year. **Number listed:** 10

1. Time Warner, with 18.2%
2. Viacom, 16.4%
3. News Corp., 15.5%
4. Walt Disney Co., 14%

5. Sony Corp., 12.7%
6. Comcast Corp., 9.1%
7. Summit Entertainment, 5%
8. Lions Gate, 4.9%
9. Overture Films, 0.8%
9. Weinstein Co., 0.8%

Source: *Advertising Age*, Leading National Advertisers (annual), June 20, 2011, p. 22.

Motion Picture Theaters

3769 ■ LARGEST MOVIE THEATER CHAINS, 2011

Ranked by: Total number of movie screens. **Remarks:** Also notes contact information, executives, year founded, total number of sites, number of screens and sites for previous year, rank for previous year, number of corporate employees, and locations. **Number listed:** 50

1. Regal Entertainment Group, with 6,620 screens
2. AMC Entertainment Inc., 5,138
3. Cinemark USA, 5,096
4. Carmike Cinemas, 2,215
5. Cineplex Entertainment, 1,352
6. National Amusements, 960
7. Rave Motion Pictures, 918
8. Marcus Theatres Corp., 696
9. Hollywood Theaters, 540
10. Harkins Theatres, 428

Source: *Boxoffice Pro*, Giants of Exhibition (annual), January 2012, p. 24-34.

Motion Pictures

3770 ■ TOP FILMS IN THE U.S., 2011

Ranked by: Domestic box office, in dollars. **Number listed:** 250

1. *Harry Potter & the Deathly Hallows, Part 2*, with $381,011,219
2. *Transformers: Dark of the Moon*, $352,390,543
3. *The Twilight Saga: Breaking Dawn, Part 1*, $275,530,738
4. *The Hangover Part II*, $254,464,305
5. *Pirates of the Caribbean: On Stranger Tides*, $241,071,802
6. *Fast Five*, $209,837,675
7. *Cars 2*, $191,452,396
8. *Thor*, $181,030,624
9. *Rise of the Planet of the Apes*, $176,760,185
10. *Captain America: The First Avenger*, $176,654,505

Source: *Variety*, Domestic Top 250 (annual), January 9, 2012, p. 22-23.

3771 ■ TOP-GROSSING MOVIES OF THE YEAR, 2011

Ranked by: Total gross, in millions of dollars. **Number listed:** 15

1. *Harry Potter & the Deathly Hallows, Part 2*, with $381 million
2. *Transformers: Dark of the Moon*, $352

3. *The Twilight Saga: Breaking Dawn, Part 1*, $259

4. *The Hangover Part II*, $254

5. *Pirates of the Caribbean: On Stranger Tides*, $241

6. *Fast Five*, $210

7. *Cars 2*, $191

8. *Thor*, $181

9. *Rise of the Planet of the Apes*, $177

9. *Captain America: The First Avenger*, $177

Source: *Entertainment Weekly*, The Year in Charts (annual), December 2011, p. 118.

3772 ■ TOP MOVIES AT THE BOX OFFICE, 2011

Ranked by: Box office receipts, in dollars. **Number listed:** 10

1. *Harry Potter & the Deathly Hallows, Part 2*, with $381,011,219

2. *Transformers: Dark of the Moon*, $352,390,543

3. *The Hangover, Part II*, $254,464,305

4. *The Twilight Saga: Breaking Dawn, Part 1*, $250,457,900

5. *Pirates of the Caribbean: On Stranger Tides*, $241,071,802

6. *Fast Five*, $209,837,675

7. *Cars 2*, $191,446,625

8. *Thor*, $181,030,624

9. *Captain America: The First Avenger*, $176,658,003

10. *Rise of the Planet of the Apes*, $176,653,744

Source: *People*, Tops of 2011, December 26, 2011, p. 52.

Motor Vehicles
See: **Automobile Industry**

Motorcycle Industry

3773 ■ TOP POWERSPORTS DEALERSHIPS, 2012

Ranked by: Editorial determination. **Remarks:** Dealerships are listed alphabetically, not ranked. Also notes owners, location, store size, vehicle brands, and website. **Number listed:** 100

1. Advantage Powersports

2. Adventure Harley-Davidson

3. Al Lamb's Dallas Honda

4. Babbitts Sports Center

5. Barney's of Brandon

6. Bayside Harley-Davidson

7. Big St. Charles Motorsports

8. Bill & Eddy's Motorsports

9. Bob Weaver Motorsports & Marine

10. Bud's Harley-Davidson

Source: *Dealer News*, Top 100 Dealers (annual), March 2012, p. 28-45.

Multihospital Systems

3774 ■ LARGEST FOR-PROFIT HOSPITAL CHAINS, 2010

Ranked by: Total hospital operating revenue, in millions of dollars. **Remarks:** Also notes headquarters, number of hospitals, and total staffed beds. **Number listed:** 14

1. HCA, with $30,683 million

2. Community Health Systems, $12,986.5

3. Tenet Healthcare Corp., $9,205

4. Universal Health Services, $5,568.2

5. Health Management Associates, $5,115

6. Kindred Healthcare, $4,359.7

7. Vanguard Health Systems, $3,376.9

8. LifePoint Hospitals, $3,262.4

9. Iasis Healthcare, $2,521.4

10. Ardent Health Services, $1,814.6

Source: *Modern Healthcare*, Largest For-Profit Hospital Chains (annual), September 5, 2011, p. 40.

Music Industry

3775 ■ FASTEST-DECLINING MARKETS FOR MUSIC PRODUCTS, 2009-2010

Ranked by: Annual growth in sales of music products, in percent. **Number listed:** 5

1. Ireland, with -19.1%

2. Spain, -13.6%

3. Greece, -12%

4. Portugal, -9.1%

5. United Kingdom, -7.9%

Source: *Music Trades*, Global 225 (annual), December 2011, p. 59.

3776 ■ FASTEST-GROWING MARKETS FOR MUSIC PRODUCTS, 2009-2010

Ranked by: Annual growth in sales of music products, in percent. **Number listed:** 5

1. Brazil, with 19.6%

2. India, 16.7%

3. Israel, 15.9%

4. Argentina, 11%

5. Australia, 9.4%

Source: *Music Trades*, Global 225 (annual), December 2011, p. 59.

3777 ■ LARGEST NORTH AMERICAN MUSIC PRODUCT SUPPLIERS, 2011

Ranked by: Estimated revenue, in U.S. dollars. **Remarks:** Also notes CEO and number of employees. **Number listed:** 100

1. Fender Musical Instruments, with $700,554,000

2. Harman Professional, $613,282,000

3. Yamaha Corp. of America, $538,860,000

4. Shure Inc., $427,000,000

5. Steinway Musical Instruments, $346,200,000

6. Jam Industries, $290,000,000

7. Gibson Guitar Corp., $285,000,000

8. Avid Pro Audio, $275,000,000

9. Numark Industries, $251,450,000

10. Peavey Electronics Corp., $185,500,000

Source: *Music Trades*, Top 100 (annual), April 2012, p. 104-106.

3778 ■ TOP MARKETS FOR MUSIC PRODUCTS, 2010

Ranked by: Music products value, in millions of U.S. dollars. **Remarks:** Also notes figures for previous year, percent change, and per capita spending. **Number listed:** 15

1. United States, with $6,390 million
2. Japan, $2,150
3. Germany, $980
4. China, $977
5. France, $755
6. Canada, $690
7. United Kingdom, $578
8. Australia, $360
9. Italy, $275
10. Korea, $273

Source: *Music Trades*, Global 225 (annual), December 2011, p. 59.

3779 ■ TOP RECORDING IMPRINTS IN THE U.S., 2011

Ranked by: Score based on aggregate sales of physical and digital products, as well as radio airplay and digital streams. **Remarks:** Specific scores not provided. Also notes number of charted titles. **Number listed:** 10

1. Columbia
2. Capitol
3. Jive
4. Capitol Nashville
5. Def Jam
6. Atlantic
7. Cash Money
8. XL
9. Elektra
10. Interscope

Source: *Billboard*, The Year in Music & Touring (annual), December 17, 2011, p. 54.

3780 ■ TOP RECORDING LABELS IN THE U.S., 2011

Ranked by: Score based on aggregate sales of physical and digital products, as well as radio airplay and digital streams. **Remarks:** Specific scores not provided. Also notes number of charted titles. **Number listed:** 10

1. Sony Music
2. RCA Music Group
3. Interscope Geffen A & M
4. Universal Republic
5. Island Def Jam Music Group
6. Atlantic Group
7. Capitol
8. Warner Bros.
9. Sony Music Nashville
10. Capitol Nashville

Source: *Billboard*, The Year in Music & Touring (annual), December 17, 2011, p. 54.

3781 ■ WORLD'S LARGEST MUSIC PRODUCT COMPANIES, 2010

Ranked by: Estimated revenues, in U.S. dollars. **Remarks:** Also notes rank for previous year, number of employees, company type, CEO, headquarters, and website. **Number listed:** 225

1. Yamaha Corp., with $4,496,280,000
2. Roland Corp., $1,020,140,000
3. Kawai Musical Instruments Manufacturing Co., Ltd., $762,753,000

4. Sennheiser Electronic, $637,454,000
5. Fender Musical Instruments, $625,000,000
6. Harman Professional, $522,736,000
7. Shure Inc., $425,000,000
8. Steinway Musical Instruments, $318,000,000
9. Audio-Technica Corp., $295,000,000
10. KHS/Musix Co., Ltd., $293,000,000

Source: *Music Trades*, Global 225 (annual), December 2011, p. 80-88.

Music Industry—Artists

3782 ■ BEST-SELLING MUSIC ARTISTS IN THE U.S., 2011

Ranked by: Score based on aggregate sales of physical and digital products. **Remarks:** Specific scores not provided. Also notes number of charted titles, imprint, and label. **Number listed:** 50

1. Adele
2. Rihanna
3. Katy Perry
4. Lady Gaga
5. Lil Wayne
6. Bruno Mars
7. Nicki Minaj
8. Taylor Swift
9. Justin Bieber
10. Chris Brown

Source: *Billboard*, The Year in Music & Touring (annual), December 17, 2011, p. 54.

3783 ■ TOP FEMALE MUSIC ARTISTS IN THE U.S., 2011

Ranked by: Score based on aggregate sales of physical and digital products, as well as radio airplay and digital streams. **Remarks:** Specific scores not provided. Also notes number of charted titles, imprint, and label. **Number listed:** 10

1. Adele
2. Rihanna
3. Katy Perry
4. Lady Gaga
5. Nicki Minaj
6. Taylor Swift
7. Britney Spears
8. Pink
9. Ke$ha
10. Beyonce

Source: *Billboard*, The Year in Music & Touring (annual), December 17, 2011, p. 54.

3784 ■ TOP MALE MUSIC ARTISTS IN THE U.S., 2011

Ranked by: Score based on aggregate sales of physical and digital products, as well as radio airplay and digital streams. **Remarks:** Specific scores not provided. Also notes number of charted titles, imprint, and label. **Number listed:** 10

1. Lil Wayne
2. Bruno Mars
3. Justin Bieber

4. Chris Brown

5. Eninem

6. Jason Aldean

7. Wiz Khalifa

8. Pitbull

9. Kanye West

10. Usher

Source: *Billboard*, The Year in Music & Touring (annual), December 17, 2011, p. 54.

3785 ■ TOP MUSIC DUOS/GROUPS IN THE U.S., 2011

Ranked by: Score based on aggregate sales of physical and digital products, as well as radio airplay and digital streams. **Remarks:** Specific scores not provided. Also notes number of charted titles, imprint, and label. **Number listed:** 10

1. The Black Eyed Peas

2. Lady Antebellum

3. U2

4. LMFAO

5. Bon Jovi

6. Selena Gomez & the Scene

7. Zac Brown Band

8. The Band Perry

9. Take That

10. Rascal Flatts

Source: *Billboard*, The Year in Music & Touring (annual), December 17, 2011, p. 54.

Music Retailers

3786 ■ ARGENTINA'S LARGEST RETAILERS IN THE MUSIC INDUSTRY, 2011

Ranked by: Revenue, in U.S. dollars. **Remarks:** Also notes number of employees and locations. **Number listed:** 2

1. Daiam Musica, with $3,000,000

1. DMX SRL, $3,000,000

Source: *Music Trades*, Global Retail Report (annual), May 2012, p. 60.

3787 ■ AUSTRALIA'S LARGEST RETAILERS IN THE MUSIC INDUSTRY, 2011

Ranked by: Revenue, in U.S. dollars. **Remarks:** Also notes number of employees and locations. **Number listed:** 37

1. Allans Music & Billy Hyde, with $110,000,000

2. Kosmic Electronic, $16,500,000

3. Soundcorp, $12,500,000

4. Ellaways, $12,000,000

5. Pro Audio Supplies/Better Music, $10,500,000

5. Brisbane Sound Group, $10,500,000

7. Gallins Pro Musicians Store, $8,550,000

8. Turramurra Music, $8,500,000

9. Muso's Corner, $7,550,000

10. Derringers, $6,550,000

Source: *Music Trades*, Global Retail Report (annual), May 2012, p. 60.

3788 ■ BRAZIL'S LARGEST RETAILERS IN THE MUSIC INDUSTRY, 2011

Ranked by: Revenue, in U.S. dollars. **Remarks:** Also notes website and number of employees and locations. **Number listed:** 6

1. Musical Grellmann, with $15,367,390

2. Mil Sons Instrumentos, $15,000,000

3. Playtech Audio Video e Musicais Ltd., $12,000,000

4. Made in Brazil, $9,000,000

5. Reference Music Center, $6,000,000

6. Serenata Musico, $5,000,000

Source: *Music Trades*, Global Retail Report (annual), May 2012, p. 62.

3789 ■ CANADA'S LARGEST MUSIC PRODUCTS RETAILERS BY REVENUE, 2010

Ranked by: Estimated revenue, in U.S. dollars. **Remarks:** Also notes rank and figures for previous year, percent change, number of employees and store fronts, and types of products carried. **Number listed:** 10

1. Long & McQuade Ltd., with $210,000,000

2. Axe Music, $26,000,000

3. Tom Lee Music Co., $24,000,000

3. Steve's Music Store, $24,000,000

5. St. John's Music, $21,295,000

6. Cosmo Music Co., Ltd., $18,000,000

7. Italmelodie Inc., $15,500,000

8. I Tell Melody, $15,000,000

9. Guitar Works, $6,000,000

10. L. A. Music, $4,900,000

Source: *Music Trades*, Top 200 (annual), August 2011, p. 74.

3790 ■ CANADA'S LARGEST RETAILERS IN THE MUSIC INDUSTRY, 2011

Ranked by: Revenue, in U.S. dollars. **Remarks:** Also notes number of employees and locations. **Number listed:** 17

1. Long & McQuade Ltd., with $245,000,000

2. St. John's Music, $37,000,000

3. Axe Music, $26,000,000

4. Steve's Music Store, $24,000,000

4. Tom Lee Music Co., $24,000,000

6. Cosmo Music Co., Ltd., $18,000,000

7. Italmelodie Inc., $15,500,000

8. Guitar Works, $6,000,000

9. L. A. Music, $4,900,000

10. Arts Music Store, $4,855,000

Source: *Music Trades*, Global Retail Report (annual), May 2012, p. 62.

3791 ■ CHINA'S LARGEST RETAILERS IN THE MUSIC INDUSTRY, 2011

Ranked by: Revenue, in U.S. dollars. **Remarks:** Also notes number of employees and locations. **Number listed:** 10

1. Best Friend Music Co., Ltd., with $43,500,000

2. Yuebo Music, $28,570,000

3. Zhengzhou Yuhua Qinhang, $25,400,000

4. Hefei Haizhiyin, $17,480,000

5. Beijin Jiangjie Instrument, $12,700,000

6. Beijin Yuepeng Instrument Co., Ltd., $11,100,000

7. Chengdu Ouya Music, $9,520,000

8. Shijiazhuang Qinchuan Instruments, $5,560,000
9. Wuhan Yinkeke Music, $4,760,000
10. Shenyang Wangzu Music, $4,750,000

Source: *Music Trades*, Global Retail Report (annual), May 2012, p. 62.

3792 ■ COLOMBIA'S LARGEST RETAILERS IN THE MUSIC INDUSTRY, 2011

Ranked by: Revenue, in U.S. dollars. **Remarks:** Also notes number of employees and locations. **Number listed:** 2

1. Ortizo Instrumentos Musicales, with $8,000,000
2. Invermusic GE SA, $7,000,000

Source: *Music Trades*, Global Retail Report (annual), May 2012, p. 62.

3793 ■ FASTEST-GROWING MUSIC PRODUCTS RETAILERS, 2009-2010

Ranked by: Annual sales growth, in percent. **Remarks:** Also notes sales for current year, score in the overall *Top 200*, types of products carried, headquarters, and comments. **Number listed:** 7

1. Austin Bazaar, with 60%
2. Pro Audio Star, 59%
3. The Music Zoo, 48.6%
4. Pro Guitar Shop, 45.7%
5. I DJ Now, 33.4%
6. Nova Musik, 20%
7. Meyer Music, 16.6%

Source: *Music Trades*, Top 200 (annual), August 2011, p. 102-114.

3794 ■ FRANCE'S LARGEST RETAILERS IN THE MUSIC INDUSTRY, 2011

Ranked by: Revenue, in U.S. dollars. **Remarks:** Also notes number of employees and locations. **Number listed:** 18

1. Woodbrass.com, with $42,000,000
2. Milonga SA Siege, $24,874,808
3. Sonovente, $23,900,000
4. Star's Music, $16,757,765
5. Musikia, $15,989,199
6. Euroguitar, $13,012,000
7. La Baguetterie Paris, $9,886,956
8. Rhythmes & Sons, $7,350,038
9. Univers-Sons.com, $7,069,682
10. Michenaud & Co., $6,838,403

Source: *Music Trades*, Global Retail Report (annual), May 2012, p. 64.

3795 ■ GERMANY'S LARGEST RETAILERS IN THE MUSIC INDUSTRY, 2011

Ranked by: Revenue, in U.S. dollars. **Remarks:** Also notes number of employees and locations. **Number listed:** 13

1. Musikhaus Thomann, with $750,000,000
2. Music Store Professional, $132,794,000
3. Just Music GmbH, $85,533,000
4. Session Musik, $65,795,000
5. Hieber Lindberg, $39,477,000
6. Musikhaus Korn, $33,500,000

7. Musik Produktiv, $32,895,000
8. PPC Music Group, $27,500,000
9. Musik Klier, $26,500,000
10. Music World - Musik Kahrig, $26,000,000

Source: *Music Trades*, Global Retail Report (annual), May 2012, p. 64.

3796 ■ HONG KONG'S LARGEST RETAILERS IN THE MUSIC INDUSTRY, 2011

Ranked by: Revenue, in U.S. dollars. **Remarks:** Also notes number of employees and locations. **Number listed:** 2

1. Parsons Music Ltd., with $158,730,000
2. Tom Lee Music Co., Ltd., $135,000,000

Source: *Music Trades*, Global Retail Report (annual), May 2012, p. 64.

3797 ■ INDIA'S LARGEST RETAILERS IN THE MUSIC INDUSTRY, 2011

Ranked by: Revenue, in U.S. dollars. **Remarks:** Also notes number of employees and locations. **Number listed:** 2

1. Onstage Music, with $13,000,000
2. Bajaao Music Pvt. Ltd., $9,500,000

Source: *Music Trades*, Global Retail Report (annual), May 2012, p. 64.

3798 ■ JAPAN'S LARGEST RETAILERS IN THE MUSIC INDUSTRY, 2011

Ranked by: Revenue, in U.S. dollars. **Remarks:** Also notes number of employees and locations. **Number listed:** 9

1. Shimamura Music Co., Ltd., with $360,000,000
2. Shinseido Co., Ltd., $325,000,000
3. Yamano Music Co., Ltd., $236,000,000
4. Ishibashi Music Store Ltd., $142,500,000
5. Sound House, $131,000,000
6. Jeugia, $119,000,000
7. Ikebe Musical Instruments Store, $112,190,000
8. T. Kurosawa & Co., Ltd., $84,497,000
9. Miyaji Musical Instrument Co., Ltd., $64,042,800

Source: *Music Trades*, Global Retail Report (annual), May 2012, p. 66.

3799 ■ LARGEST MUSIC PRODUCTS RETAILERS BY EMPLOYEES, 2010

Ranked by: Number of employees. **Number listed:** 9

1. Guitar Center Inc., with 8,790 employees
2. Sam Ash Music Corp., 1,355
3. Sweetwater, 430
4. J. W. Pepper, 214
5. Schmitt Music Co., 182
6. Full Compass Systems Ltd., 178
7. West Music Co., 177
8. Daddy's Junky Music, 161
9. American Musical Supply, 125

Source: *Music Trades*, Top 200 (annual), August 2011, p. 76.

3800 ■ LARGEST MUSIC PRODUCTS RETAILERS BY INTERNET SALES, 2010

Ranked by: Estimated Internet revenue, in U.S. dollars. **Remarks:** Also notes number of employees, website, country, and web traffic rank. **Number listed:** 40

1. Musikhaus Thomann, with $752,400,000
2. Musician's Friend, $708,000,000
3. Sweetwater, $200,000,000
4. American Musical Supply, $175,032,000
5. Sound House, $118,000,000
6. Full Compass Systems Ltd., $105,051,000
7. Music Store Professional, $75,500,000
8. B & H Photo & Video, $60,000,000
9. J. W. Pepper, $59,000,000
10. DV247.com, $47,000,000

Source: *Music Trades*, Top 200 (annual), August 2011, p. 130.

3801 ■ LARGEST MUSIC PRODUCTS RETAILERS BY LOCATIONS, 2010

Ranked by: Number of locations. **Number listed:** 10

1. Guitar Center Inc., with 318 locations
2. Best Buy Co., Inc., 103
3. Sam Ash Music Corp., 46
4. Music Go Round, 33
5. Fletcher Music Center, 19
5. Daddy's Junky Music, 19
7. Piano & Organ Distributors, 16
8. J. W. Pepper, 14
9. George's Music, 10
10. Mills Music Inc., 9

Source: *Music Trades*, Top 200 (annual), August 2011, p. 76.

3802 ■ LARGEST MUSIC PRODUCTS RETAILERS BY SALES PER EMPLOYEE, 2010

Ranked by: Sales per employee, in dollars. **Remarks:** Also notes percent change and number of employees. **Number listed:** 10

1. American Musical Supply, with $1,400,256
2. Rondo Music, $1,151,000
3. Pro Audio Star, $908,864
4. Unique Squared, $888,899
5. Washington Music Center, $758,065
6. Piano Gallery - Dallas, $748,750
7. We Buy Guitars, $711,500
8. Fields Piano & Organ, $708,333
9. Daynes Music, $704,167
10. Steinway Piano Gallery, $666,667

Source: *Music Trades*, Top 200 (annual), August 2011, p. 76.

3803 ■ LARGEST MUSIC PRODUCTS RETAILERS BY SALES PER LOCATION, 2010

Ranked by: Sales per location, in dollars. **Remarks:** Also notes percent change. **Number listed:** 10

1. Sweetwater, with $200,000,000
2. American Musical Supply, $175,032,000
3. Full Compass Systems Ltd., $105,051,000
4. Washington Music Center, $70,500,000
5. B & H Photo & Video, $60,000,000
6. Unique Squared, $40,000,000
7. Pro Music Group, $29,800,000
8. Cascio Interstate Music, $27,407,000
9. Sheet Music Plus, $24,950,000

10. Pro Audio Star, $19,995,000

Source: *Music Trades*, Top 200 (annual), August 2011.

3804 ■ LARGEST U.S. MUSIC PRODUCTS RETAILERS BY REVENUE, 2010

Ranked by: Estimated revenue, in dollars. **Remarks:** Also notes rank and figures for previous year, percent change, number of employees and store fronts, and types of products carried. **Number listed:** 200

1. Guitar Center Inc., with $2,000,000,000
2. Sam Ash Music Corp., $410,000,000
3. Sweetwater, $200,000,000
4. American Musical Supply, $175,032,000
5. Full Compass Systems Ltd., $105,051,000
6. Best Buy Co., Inc., $75,000,000
7. Washington Music Center, $70,500,000
8. B & H Photo & Video, $60,000,000
9. J. W. Pepper, $59,000,000
10. Schmitt Music Co., $44,000,000

Source: *Music Trades*, Top 200 (annual), August 2011, p. 66-74.

3805 ■ MEXICO'S LARGEST RETAILERS IN THE MUSIC INDUSTRY, 2011

Ranked by: Revenue, in U.S. dollars. **Remarks:** Also notes number of employees and locations. **Number listed:** 9

1. Top Music, with $15,000,000
2. Faly Music, $8,500,000
3. Veerkamp Palacio de La Musica, $8,000,000
4. Veerkamp Mesones, $7,500,000
5. Music Club, $7,000,000
6. Metropoli Music Center, $3,500,000
6. Mr. CD, $3,500,000
8. Backstage, $3,400,000
9. Gama Music, $3,200,000

Source: *Music Trades*, Global Retail Report (annual), May 2012, p. 66.

3806 ■ THE NETHERLANDS' LARGEST RETAILERS IN THE MUSIC INDUSTRY, 2011

Ranked by: Revenue, in U.S. dollars. **Remarks:** Also notes number of employees and locations. **Number listed:** 2

1. Feedback, with $27,000,000
2. Tonika Music BV, $3,600,000

Source: *Music Trades*, Global Retail Report (annual), May 2012, p. 66.

3807 ■ RUSSIA'S LARGEST RETAILERS IN THE MUSIC INDUSTRY, 2011

Ranked by: Revenue, in U.S. dollars. **Remarks:** Also notes number of employees and locations. **Number listed:** 7

1. Muztorg Retail Chain, with $40,000,000
2. Pop Music, $20,000,000
3. Arsenal Music, $16,000,000
4. Svet I Zvuk, Russia, $15,000,000
5. Mir Muzuki, $12,500,000
6. World Music, $9,275,000
7. Avallon, $6,000,000

Source: *Music Trades*, Global Retail Report (annual), May 2012, p. 68.

3808 ■ SOUTH KOREA'S LARGEST RETAILERS IN THE MUSIC INDUSTRY, 2011

Ranked by: Revenue, in U.S. dollars. **Remarks:** Also notes number of employees and locations. **Number listed:** 2

1. Cosmos Corp., with $20,000,000
1. School Music, $20,000,000

Source: *Music Trades*, Global Retail Report (annual), May 2012, p. 66.

3809 ■ SPAIN'S LARGEST RETAILERS IN THE MUSIC INDUSTRY, 2011

Ranked by: Revenue, in U.S. dollars. **Remarks:** Also notes number of employees and locations. **Number listed:** 15

1. Adagio, with $13,500,000
2. Alfasoni, $6,920,015
3. Picholi, $5,990,320
4. Rock & Classics, $5,773,530
5. Madrid Musical, $4,000,000
6. Rivera Mota, $3,979,770
6. Clemente Pianos, $3,979,770
8. Salom y Pormar, $3,827,740
9. Sunomarket, $3,577,000
10. Tam Tam Percusion SL, $3,174,138

Source: *Music Trades*, Global Retail Report (annual), May 2012, p. 68.

3810 ■ SWEDEN'S LARGEST RETAILERS IN THE MUSIC INDUSTRY, 2011

Ranked by: Revenue, in U.S. dollars. **Remarks:** Also notes number of employees and locations. **Number listed:** 4

1. 4Sound/Music Retail Sweden, with $46,867,000
2. Order Music Sweden, $15,000,000
3. DLX Music, $5,090,361
4. Jam Stockholm, $5,000,000

Source: *Music Trades*, Global Retail Report (annual), May 2012, p. 68.

3811 ■ TAIWAN'S LARGEST RETAILERS IN THE MUSIC INDUSTRY, 2011

Ranked by: Revenue, in U.S. dollars. **Remarks:** Also notes number of employees and locations. **Number listed:** 4

1. K. H. S. Musical Co., Ltd., with $15,000,000
2. Aeolus Music Corp., $5,000,000
3. Supply Music, $3,000,000
4. Allinone Music, $2,500,000

Source: *Music Trades*, Global Retail Report (annual), May 2012, p. 68.

3812 ■ THE UNITED KINGDOM'S LARGEST RETAILERS IN THE MUSIC INDUSTRY, 2011

Ranked by: Revenue, in U.S. dollars. **Remarks:** Also notes number of employees and locations. **Number listed:** 11

1. DV247.com, with $58,000,000
2. Professional Music Technology, $48,000,000

3. Dawsons Music, $23,500,000
4. Guitar Amp & Keyboard, $19,000,000
5. Music Room, $18,000,000
6. Gear 4 Music, $16,000,000
7. Guitar Guitar UK, $12,500,000
8. Rimmers Music, $11,500,000
9. Decks, $9,750,000
10. Absolute Music, $9,500,000

Source: *Music Trades*, Global Retail Report (annual), May 2012, p. 70.

3813 ■ WORLD'S LARGEST RETAILERS IN THE MUSIC INDUSTRY, 2011

Ranked by: Revenue, in U.S. dollars. **Remarks:** Also notes number of employees and locations. **Number listed:** 10

1. Guitar Center Inc. (U.S.), with $2,000,000,000
2. Musikhaus Thomann (Germany), $750,000,000
3. Sam Ash Music Corp. (U.S.), $410,000,000
4. Shimamura Music Co., Ltd. (Japan), $360,000,000
5. Shinseido Co., Ltd. (Japan), $325,000,000
6. Long & McQuade Ltd. (Canada), $245,000,000
7. Yamano Music Co., Ltd. (Japan), $236,000,000
8. Sweetwater Sound (U.S.), $200,000,000
9. American Musical Supply (U.S.), $175,000,000
10. Parsons Music Ltd. (Hong Kong), $158,730,000

Source: *Music Trades*, Global Retail Report (annual), May 2012, p. 55.

Mutual Funds
See also: **Bond Funds; Equity Funds; Hedge Funds; Stock Funds**

3814 ■ BEST MUTUAL FUND FAMILIES, 2011

Ranked by: Score based on asset size and relative importance in the Lipper fund universe. **Remarks:** Also notes total assets, phone number, and funds rankings within the categories of U.S. equity, world equity, mixed equity, taxable bonds, and tax-exempt bonds. **Number listed:** 58

1. Delaware Management, with 75.03 points
2. Vanguard Group, 70.17
3. Neuberger Berman Management, 69.31
4. First Investors Management, 67.53
5. State Farm Investment Management, 67.50
6. State Street Bank & Trust, 67.48
7. MainStay Funds, 67.26
8. Charles Schwab Investment Management, 65.71
9. American Century Investment Management, 64.85
10. MFS Investment Management, 64.2

Source: *Barron's*, Best Mutual Fund Families (annual), February 6, 2012, p. 30.

3815 ■ BEST MUTUAL FUNDS, 2011

Ranked by: Score based on performance over three market cycles. **Remarks:** Scores not provided. Also notes performance during up and down markets, lead manager, maximum cumulative loss, annual total return, hypothetical investment results, maximum sales charge, and annual expenses. **Number listed:** 10

1. Turner Emerging Growth Investment
2. Bernstein Emerging Markets
3. CGM Focus
4. Bruce Fund
5. Blackrock International Opportunities-A
6. Wasatch Micro Cap
7. Rydex/SGI Mid Cap Value-A
8. Wells Fargo Small Cap Value-A
9. Royce Opportunity Investment
10. MFS International New Discovery-A

Source: *Forbes*, The Honor Roll (annual), August 08, 2011, p. 51.

3816 ■ BEST WORLD-EQUITY FUND FAMILIES, 2011

Ranked by: Score based on asset size and relative importance in the Lipper fund universe. **Number listed:** 5

1. Virtus Investment Partners , with 12.65 points
2. Aberdeen Asset Management, 12.18
3. Waddell & Reed Investment Management, 11.9
4. Delaware Management, 11.21
5. MFS Investment Management, 10.64

Source: *Barron's*, Best Mutual Fund Families (annual), February 6, 2012, p. 30.

3817 ■ TOP INTERNATIONAL STOCK FUNDS, 2012

Ranked by: Score based on long-term performance, management experience, risk, expenses, assets, and integrity. **Remarks:** Specific scores not provided; funds are listed alphabetically, not ranked. Also notes ticker symbol, expense ratio, toll-free number, and one-, three-, five, and 10-year return. **Number listed:** 4

1. Dodge & Cox International
2. Harbor International
3. Matthews Asia Dividend
4. T. Rowe Price Emerging Markets Stock

Source: *Kiplinger's Personal Finance*, Kiplinger 25 (annual), May 2012, p. 31.

3818 ■ TOP SPECIALIZED/COMMODITY/GO ANYWHERE FUNDS, 2012

Ranked by: Score based on long-term performance, management experience, risk, expenses, assets, and integrity. **Remarks:** Specific scores not provided; funds are listed alphabetically, not ranked. Also notes ticker symbol, expense ratio, toll-free number, and one-, three-, five, and 10-year return. **Number listed:** 3

1. FPA Crescent
2. Harbor Commodity Real Return Strategy
3. Merger Fund

Source: *Kiplinger's Personal Finance*, Kiplinger 25 (annual), May 2012, p. 31.

3819 ■ WORST WORLD-EQUITY FUND FAMILIES, 2011

Ranked by: Score based on asset size and relative importance in the Lipper fund universe. **Number listed:** 5

1. AllianceBernstein, with 1.42 points
2. Pyxis Capital, 1.87
3. GE Asset Management, 2.57

4. Manning & Napier Advisors, 2.79
5. Federated Investors, 3.1

Source: *Barron's*, Best Mutual Fund Families (annual), February 6, 2012, p. 30.

Nationalization of Industry
See: **Government Ownership**

Natural Gas

3820 ■ HONG KONG'S LARGEST NATURAL GAS UTILITIES OVERALL, 2011

Ranked by: Score based on revenue, profits, assets, and market capitalization. **Remarks:** Specific scores not provided. Also notes overall rank in the *Forbes 2000* and figures for each criterion. **Number listed:** 2

1. Hong Kong & China Gas
2. Beijing Enterprises

Source: *Forbes*, Forbes 2000 (annual), http://www.forbes.com, May 7, 2012.

3821 ■ WORLD'S MOST ETHICAL NATURAL GAS COMPANIES, 2012

Ranked by: Score based on five criteria: ethics and compliance program; reputation, leadership, and innovation; governance; corporate citizenship and responsibility; and culture of ethics. **Remarks:** Specific scores not provided; companies are listed alphabetically, not ranked. **Number listed:** 4

1. EnCana Corp. (Canada)
2. NiSource Inc. (U.S.)
3. Sempra Energy (U.S.)
4. Spectra Energy Corp. (U.S.)

Source: *Ethisphere Magazine*, World's Most Ethical Companies (annual), http://www.ethisphere.com, 2012.

Networks

3822 ■ WORLD'S MOST ADMIRED NETWORK AND OTHER COMMUNICATIONS EQUIPMENT COMPANIES, 2012

Ranked by: Score, on a scale of 10, based on a survey of executives, directors, and securities analysts of companies within their own industry on eight criteria: innovation, financial soundness, employee talent, use of corporate assets, long-term investment value, social responsibility, quality of management, and quality of products/services. **Remarks:** Specific scores not provided. Also notes rank for previous year. **Number listed:** 6

1. QUALCOMM Inc.
2. Cisco Systems Inc.
3. Telefonaktiebolaget LM Ericsson
4. Juniper Networks Inc.
5. Corning Inc.
6. Harris Corp.

Source: *Fortune*, World's Most Admired Companies (annual), March 19, 2012, p. 147.

New Business Enterprises

3823 ■ COUNTRIES WITH THE FEWEST PROCEDURES FOR BUSINESS LAUNCH, 2010

Ranked by: Total number of procedures required to start a business. **Number listed:** 140

1. Canada, with 1 procedures
1. New Zealand, 1
3. Australia, 2
3. Kyrgyz Republic, 2
3. Madagascar, 2
3. Rwanda, 2
3. Slovenia, 2
8. Finland, 3
8. Georgia, 3
8. Hong Kong, 3
8. Macedonia, 3

Source: *Global Competitiveness Report*, (annual), World Economic Forum, 2011, p. 457.

3824 ■ COUNTRIES WITH THE LEAST TIME REQUIRED FOR BUSINESS LAUNCH, 2010

Ranked by: Total number of days required to start a business. **Number listed:** 140

1. New Zealand, with 1 days
2. Australia, 2
3. Georgia, 3
3. Macedonia, 3
3. Rwanda, 3
3. Singapore, 3
7. Belgium, 4
7. Hungary, 4
9. Albania, 5
9. Canada, 5
9. Iceland, 5
9. Saudi Arabia, 5

Source: *Global Competitiveness Report*, (annual), World Economic Forum, 2011, p. 458.

3825 ■ COUNTRIES WITH THE MOST PROCEDURES FOR BUSINESS LAUNCH, 2010

Ranked by: Total number of procedures required to start a business. **Number listed:** 140

1. Uganda, with 18 procedures
2. Venezuela, 17
3. Philippines, 15
3. Greece, 15
3. Brunei Darussalam, 15
3. Brazil, 15
3. Bolivia, 15
8. China, 14
8. Argentina, 14
8. Algeria, 14

Source: *Global Competitiveness Report*, (annual), World Economic Forum, 2011, p. 457.

3826 ■ COUNTRIES WITH THE MOST TIME REQUIRED FOR BUSINESS LAUNCH, 2010

Ranked by: Total number of days required to start a business. **Number listed:** 140

1. Suriname, with 694 days
2. Venezuela, 141
3. Brazil, 120

4. Haiti, 105
4. Brunei Darussalam, 105
6. Zimbabwe, 90
7. Cambodia, 85
8. Timor-Leste, 83
9. Chad, 75
10. Angola, 68

Source: *Global Competitiveness Report*, (annual), World Economic Forum, 2011, p. 458.

3827 ■ STATES WITH THE FEWEST NEW FIRMS, 2008

Ranked by: Number of new employer firms. **Remarks:** Also notes share of national total. **Number listed:** 51

1. North Dakota, with 1,842 new firms
2. Alaska, 1,922
3. South Dakota, 2,127
4. Vermont, 2,146
5. Wyoming, 2,593
6. Delaware, 2,980
7. Rhode Island, 3,310
8. West Virginia, 3,363
9. Hawaii, 3,475
10. Washington DC, 3,939

Source: *State Rankings*, (annual), CQ Press, 2011, p. 111.

3828 ■ STATES WITH THE HIGHEST RATE OF FIRM LAUNCH, 2008

Ranked by: Firms launching operations during the year as a percentage of total firms in existence. **Number listed:** 51

1. Nevada, with 17%
2. Washington, 16.6%
3. Utah, 15.9%
4. Tennessee, 14.9%
5. Florida, 14.3%
6. Washington DC, 14.2%
7. Colorado, 13.7%
8. Virginia, 13.6%
9. Georgia, 13.4%
9. Idaho, 13.4%

Source: *State Rankings*, (annual), CQ Press, 2011, p. 112.

3829 ■ STATES WITH THE LOWEST RATE OF FIRM LAUNCH, 2008

Ranked by: Firms launching operations during the year as a percentage of total firms in existence. **Number listed:** 51

1. Iowa, with 8.2%
2. South Dakota, 8.5%
3. Minnesota, 8.7%
4. California, 8.8%
5. Ohio, 9%
6. North Dakota, 9.1%
7. Connecticut, 9.2%
7. West Virginia, 9.2%
9. Louisiana, 9.3%
10. Nebraska, 9.6%

Source: *State Rankings*, (annual), CQ Press, 2011, p. 112.

3830 ■ STATES WITH THE MOST NEW FIRMS, 2008

Ranked by: Number of new employer firms. **Remarks:** Also notes share of national total. **Number listed:** 51

1. California, with 103,572 new firms
2. Florida, 72,203
3. New York, 65,624
4. Texas, 55,214
5. Pennsylvania, 35,587
6. Washington, 33,701
7. Illinois, 31,493
8. Georgia, 28,980
9. New Jersey, 26,774
10. Virginia, 25,517

Source: *State Rankings*, (annual), CQ Press, 2011, p. 111.

New Products

3831 ■ TOP NEW FOOD PRODUCTS, 2011

Ranked by: Sales, in millions of dollars. **Remarks:** Ranking covers products that were launched during the year. **Number listed:** 10

1. P. F. Chang's Home Menu, with $101.6 million
2. Thomas' Bagel Thins, $73.6
3. Oscar Mayer Selects, $69.2
4. Folgers Gourmet Selections K-Cups, $58.4
4. M&M's Pretzel, $58.4
6. Sun Drop, $55.8
7. Kellogg's Special K Cracker Chips, $50.6
8. Lean Cuisine Market Creations, $48.6
9. Gold Peak Chilled Tea, $44.3
10. Bailey's Coffee Creamer, $44.2

Source: *Food Processing*, Pacesetters (annual), May 2012, p. 38.

Newspaper Publishers and Publishing

3832 ■ TOP NEWSPAPER COMPANIES IN THE U.S., 2010

Ranked by: Net U.S. newspaper revenue, in millions of dollars. **Remarks:** Also notes rank and figures for previous year, annual growth, and top newspaper. **Number listed:** 10

1. Gannett Co., Inc., with $2,968 million
2. New York Times Co., $2,103
3. Tribune Co., $2,096
4. Advance Publications Inc., $1,241
5. News Corp., $1,188
6. McClatchy Co., $1,133
7. MediaNews Group Inc., $1,132
8. Cox Enterprises Inc., $792
9. Hearst Corp., $744
10. Lee Enterprises Inc., $740

Source: *Advertising Age*, 100 Leading Media Companies (annual), October 3, 2011, p. 52.

Newspapers

3833 ■ TOP DAILY NEWSPAPERS IN THE UNITED STATES, 2011

Ranked by: Daily circulation. **Remarks:** Also notes Sunday circulation. **Number listed:** 100

1. *The Wall Street Journal*, with 2,096,169 readers
2. *USA Today*, 1,784,242
3. *The New York Times*, 1,150,589
4. *The Daily News* (NY, NY), 605,677
5. *Los Angeles Times*, 572,998
6. *San Jose Mercury News*, 527,568
7. *The New York Post*, 512,067
8. *Washington Post*, 507,465
9. *Chicago Tribune*, 425,370
10. *Dallas Morning News*, 409,642

Source: *Top Media Outlets*, (annual), BurrellesLuce, January 2012.

Newspapers—Advertising
See: **Advertising, Newspaper**

Nonwoven Fabrics Industry

3834 ■ WORLD'S LARGEST ROLL GOODS MANUFACTURERS, 2010

Ranked by: Worldwide nonwovens sales, in millions of U.S. dollars. **Number listed:** 40

1. Freudenberg & Co., with $1,500 million
2. E. I. du Pont de Nemours & Co., $1,400
3. Ahlstrom Corp., $1,350
4. Kimberly-Clark Corp., $1,200
5. Polymer Group Inc., $1,150
6. Fiberweb, $850
7. Johns Manville Corp., $670
8. Glatfelter, $350
9. Companhia Providencia, $326
10. Sandler, $288

Source: *Nonwovens Industry*, Top 40 (annual), September 2011, p. 31.

Nursing

3835 ■ LARGEST LOCUM TENENS NURSE STAFFING FIRMS, 2010

Ranked by: U.S. temporary staffing revenue, in millions of dollars. **Remarks:** Also notes market share and Web site. **Number listed:** 6

1. CHG Healthcare Services, with $421 million
2. AMN Healthcare, $284
3. Jackson Healthcare, $194
4. Cross Country Healthcare, $122
5. TeamHealth, $98
6. On Assignment, $66

Source: *Modern Healthcare*, Largest Nurse Staffing Firms (annual), May 14, 2012, p. 34.

3836 ■ LARGEST NURSING SCHOOLS, 2009-2010

Ranked by: Total graduates. **Remarks:** Also notes location, types of programs offered, and Web site. **Number listed:** 20

1. Excelsior College School of Nursing, with 2,229 graduates
2. Maricopa Community Colleges District Nursing Program, 1,115
3. Galen College of Nursing, 1,042
4. St. Petersburg College Department of Nursing, 685
5. Baptist Health Schools Little Rock School of Nursing, 664
6. Kent State University College of Nursing, 610
7. Indiana University of Pennsylvania Department of Nursing & Allied Health, 580
8. University of South Dakota School of Health Sciences, 497
9. University of Massachusetts Boston College of Nursing & Health Sciences, 467
10. Lansing Community College Community Health & Nursing Department, 404

Source: *Modern Healthcare*, Largest Nursing Schools (annual), July 4, 2011, p. 33.

3837 ■ LARGEST PER DIEM NURSE STAFFING FIRMS, 2010

Ranked by: U.S. temporary staffing revenue, in millions of dollars. **Remarks:** Also notes market share and Web site. **Number listed:** 5

1. Maxim Healthcare Services, with $226 million
2. Medical Staffing Network Healthcare, $203
3. AMN Healthcare, $90
4. ATC Healthcare Services, $55
5. Supplemental Health Care, $50

Source: *Modern Healthcare*, Largest Nurse Staffing Firms (annual), May 14, 2012, p. 34.

3838 ■ LARGEST TRAVEL NURSE STAFFING FIRMS, 2010

Ranked by: U.S. temporary staffing revenue, in millions of dollars. **Remarks:** Also notes market share and Web site. **Number listed:** 4

1. AMN Healthcare, with $275 million
2. Cross Country Healthcare, $180
3. C & A Industries, $53
4. Reliant Healthcare Professionals, $50

Source: *Modern Healthcare*, Largest Nurse Staffing Firms (annual), May 14, 2012, p. 34.

3839 ■ STATES WITH THE HIGHEST RATE OF NURSES, 2009

Ranked by: Number of registered nurses per 100,000 in population. **Number listed:** 51

1. Washington DC, with 1,483 nurses
2. South Dakota, 1,296
3. Massachusetts, 1,260
4. Delaware, 1,155
5. Rhode Island, 1,104
6. Maine, 1,093
6. Minnesota, 1,093
8. Nebraska, 1,054
9. Missouri, 1,038

10. Pennsylvania, 1,030

Source: *State Rankings*, (annual), CQ Press, 2011, p. 388.

3840 ■ STATES WITH THE LOWEST RATE OF NURSES, 2009

Ranked by: Number of registered nurses per 100,000 in population. **Number listed:** 51

1. Arizona, with 585 nurses
2. Nevada, 609
3. New Mexico, 614
4. California, 630
5. Utah, 635
6. Georgia, 665
7. Texas, 678
8. Idaho, 682
9. Hawaii, 689
10. Alaska, 717

Source: *State Rankings*, (annual), CQ Press, 2011, p. 388.

Nursing Homes

3841 ■ LARGEST SKILLED-NURSING COMPANIES, 2010

Ranked by: Number of skilled-nursing facilities. **Remarks:** Also notes type of ownership, number of staffed beds, figures for previous year, and Web site. **Number listed:** 32

1. Golden Living, with 305 facilities
2. HCR ManorCare, 278
3. Kindred Healthcare Inc., 226
4. Genesis HealthCare, 211
5. Sun Healthcare Group, 180
6. Extendicare Health Services, 163
7. National HealthCare Corp., 76
8. Evangelical Lutheran Good Samaritan Society, 67
9. Covenant Care, 51
10. Advocat, 46

Source: *Modern Healthcare*, Largest Skilled-Nursing Companies (annual), October 31, 2011, p. 33.

Nuts

3842 ■ TOP BRANDS OF NUTS AND TRAIL MIX, 2011

Ranked by: Sales for the 52 weeks ending March 20, 2011, in millions of dollars. **Remarks:** Also notes annual growth, dollar share, and unit sales. **Number listed:** 10

1. Private label, with $665.1 million
2. Planter's, $503.7
3. Blue Diamond, $175.5
4. Emerald, $127.3
5. Frito-Lay, $122.7
6. Wonderful Pistachios, $105.8
7. Wonderful Snack, $41.4
8. Planter's Nutrition, $40.5
9. Lance, $27
10. Nature Valley Nut Clusters, $22.2

Occupational Health and Safety

3843 ■ TOP OCCUPATIONS FOR INJURIES AND ILL-NESSES, 2009

Ranked by: Number of occupational injuries and illnesses, in thousands. Remarks: Also notes share of total. Number listed: 10

1. Laborers (nonconstruction), with 61,440 thousand
2. Truck drivers, heavy, 45,610
3. Nursing aides, Orderlies, 42,570
4. Truck drivers, light, 31,600
5. Salespersons, retail, 28,180
6. Janitors & cleaners, 26,980
7. Production workers, 24,400
8. Laborers (construction), 23,860
9. Nurses, registered, 20,270
10. Stock clerks and order fillers, 17,390

Source: *The I.I.I. Insurance Fact Book*, (annual), Insurance Information Institute, 2012, p. 169.

Office Developers

3844 ■ TOP OFFICE DEVELOPERS, 2010

Ranked by: Total office space developed or under construction, in millions of square feet. Remarks: Also notes contact information and officers. Number listed: 25

1. Hines Interests LP, with 11.6 million sq.ft.
2. Trammell Crow Co., 4.2
3. Carter, 4
4. The Alter Group, 3.3
5. Hillwood, 2.6
6. Boston Properties Inc., 2.2
7. Brandywine Realty Trust, 1.9
8. CenterPoint Properties, 1.8
9. Corporate Office Properties Trust, 1.2
10. USAA Real Estate Co., 0.96

Source: *National Real Estate Investor*, Best of the Best (annual), 2011, p. 34.

Office Equipment Industry

3845 ■ JAPAN'S MOST VALUABLE OFFICE AND BUSINESS EQUIPMENT BRANDS, 2011

Ranked by: Brand value, in millions of U.S. dollars. Remarks: Also notes rank within the *Global 500* for current and previous year, figures for current and previous year, and brand rating. Ranking is available online only. Number listed: 2

1. Canon, with $9,293 million
2. Ricoh, $2,535

Source: *Global 500*, (annual), Brand Finance plc, March 2012.

3846 ■ WORLD'S MOST VALUABLE OFFICE/BUSINESS EQUIPMENT BRANDS, 2011

Ranked by: Brand value, in millions of U.S. dollars. Remarks: Also notes rank within the *Global 500* for current and previous year, figures for current and previous year, country, and brand rating. Ranking is available online only. Number listed: 3

1. Canon, with $9,293 million
2. Xerox, $3,485
3. Ricoh, $2,535

Source: *Global 500*, (annual), Brand Finance plc, March 2012.

Office Supply Stores

3847 ■ TOP TONER REPLACEMENT FRANCHISES, 2012

Ranked by: Cumulative score based on financial strength and stability, growth rate, size of the system, number of years in business, the length of time franchising, start-up costs, litigation, percentage of terminations, and whether the company provides financing. Remarks: Specific scores not provided. Also notes overall rank within the *Franchise 500*, contact information, description, year founded, year started franchising, states where registered, available U.S. regions, where seeking foreign expansion, number of franchised and company-owned units for past three years, start-up costs, franchise fees, royalty fees, and type of financing available. Number listed: 2

1. Cartridge World
2. Cartridge Depot

Source: *Entrepreneur*, Franchise 500 (annual), January 2012, p. 152-153.

3848 ■ TOP U.S. OFFICE SUPPLY RETAILERS BY SALES, 2010

Ranked by: Sales volume, in thousands of dollars. Remarks: Also notes comparable-store sales and sales per store. Number listed: 3

1. Staples Inc., with $9,204,000 thousand
2. Office Depot Inc., $7,557,000
3. OfficeMax Inc., $5,655,000

Source: *Stores*, Top 100 Retailers (annual), July 2011, p. s4.

Off-Price Stores
See: **Discount Stores**

Oil and Gas Field Services
See: **Petroleum Drilling**

Oil and Gas Well Drilling Contractors
See: **Petroleum Drilling**

Oil Companies
See: **Petroleum Industry**

Oil Field Service Industry
See: **Petroleum Equipment Industry**

Oil Wells, Offshore Drilling
See: **Petroleum Drilling**

Optical Stores

3849 ■ LARGEST MASS MERCHANTS/CLUBS WITH OPTICAL DEPARTMENTS, 2011

Ranked by: Retail sales, in millions of dollars. **Remarks:** Also notes rank and figures for previous year, number of units, type of store, and operator. **Number listed:** 7

1. Wal-Mart Stores Inc., with $1,532.6 million
2. Costco Wholesale Corp., $628
3. Sam's Club, $136.2
4. ShopKo Stores Operating Co., LLC, $86
5. Target Corp./SuperTarget, $70.5
6. BJ's Wholesale Club Inc., $56.8
7. Fred Meyer Stores Inc., $9.6

Source: *Vision Monday*, Top 50 (annual), May 14, 2012, p. 50.

3850 ■ LARGEST OPTICAL RETAILERS, 2011

Ranked by: U.S. sales, in millions of dollars. **Remarks:** Also notes rank and figures for previous year, number of units, and comments. **Number listed:** 50

1. Luxottica Retail, with $2,520 million
2. Wal-Mart Stores Inc., $1,506.7
3. HVHC Retail, $729.2
4. National Vision, $685
5. Costco Wholesale Corp., $628
6. Refac Optical Group, $225
7. Eyemart Express, $180
8. Cohen's Fashion Optical, $137
9. For Eyes/Insight Optical Manufacturing, $110
10. Texas State Optical, $98.3

Source: *Vision Monday*, Top 50 (annual), May 14, 2012, p. 44-45.

Orange Juice

3851 ■ TOP REFRIGERATED ORANGE JUICE BRANDS IN THE U.S., 2011

Ranked by: Sales, in dollars. **Remarks:** Also notes percent change from previous year and market share. **Number listed:** 10

1. Tropicana Pure Premium, with $892,869,800
2. Simply Orange, $490,647,200
3. private label, $470,612,100
4. Florida's Natural, $292,125,900
5. Minute Maid Premium, $247,666,700
6. Minute Maid, $27,513,650
7. Minute Maid Premium Kids Plus, $24,979,700
8. Citrus World Donald Duck, $16,933,870
9. Tree Ripe, $15,262,640
10. Odwalla, $14,633,870

Source: *Beverage Industry*, State of the Industry Report (annual), July 2011, p. SIO-16.

Orthopedic Products

3852 ■ TOP ORTHOPEDIC DEVICE MANUFACTURERS, 2010

Ranked by: Revenue, in millions of dollars. **Number listed:** 10

1. Stryker Corp., with $7,300 million
2. DePuy Orthopaedics, $5,600
3. Zimmer Holdings Inc., $4,200
4. Smith & Nephew plc, $4,000
5. Synthes, $3,700
6. Medtronic Spinal & Biologics, $3,500
7. Biomet, $2,700
8. DJO Inc., $966
9. Orthofix, $564
10. Wright Medical Technologies, $519

Source: *Orthopedic Design & Technology*, Top 10 Orthopedic Device Manufacturers (annual), http://www.odtmag.com, 2011.

Outsourcing

3853 ■ TOP *FORTUNE 500* COMPANIES IN DIVERSIFIED OUTSOURCING SERVICE COMPANIES, 2011

Ranked by: Revenue, in millions of dollars. **Remarks:** Also notes overall rank in the *Fortune 500;* profits; profits as a percentage of revenue; stockholders' equity; and rank by each criterion. **Number listed:** 2

1. ARAMARK Corp., with $13,245 million
2. Automatic Data Processing Inc., $9,880

Source: *Fortune*, Fortune 500 (annual), May 21, 2012, p. F-34.

3854 ■ WORLD'S MOST ADMIRED DIVERSIFIED OUT-SOURCING COMPANIES, 2012

Ranked by: Score, on a scale of 10, based on a survey of executives, directors, and securities analysts of companies within their own industry on eight criteria: innovation, financial soundness, employee talent, use of corporate assets, long-term investment value, social responsibility, quality of management, and quality of products/services. **Remarks:** Specific scores not provided. Also notes rank for previous year. **Number listed:** 6

1. Towers Watson & Co.
2. ARAMARK Corp.
3. Iron Mountain Inc.
4. Sodexo
5. The ServiceMaster Co.
6. Cintas Corp.

Source: *Fortune*, World's Most Admired Companies (annual), March 19, 2012, p. 148.

Package Express Service
See also: **Air Freight Service**

3855 ■ TOP *FORTUNE 500* COMPANIES IN MAIL, PACKAGE, AND FREIGHT DELIVERY, 2011

Ranked by: Revenue, in millions of dollars. **Remarks:** Also notes overall rank in the *Fortune 500;* profits; profits as a percentage of revenue; stockholders' equity; and rank by each criterion. **Number listed:** 2

1. United Parcel Service Inc. (UPS), with $53,105 million
2. FedEx Corp., $39,304

Source: *Fortune*, Fortune 500 (annual), May 21, 2012, p. F-37.

3856 ■ TOP SHIPPING SERVICES FRANCHISES, 2012

Ranked by: Cumulative score based on financial strength and stability, growth rate, size of the system, number of years in business, the length of time franchising, start-up costs, litigation, percentage of terminations, and whether the company provides financing. Remarks: Specific scores not provided. Also notes overall rank within the *Franchise 500*, contact information, description, year founded, year started franchising, states where registered, available U.S. regions, where seeking foreign expansion, number of franchised and company-owned units for past three years, start-up costs, franchise fees, royalty fees, and type of financing available. Number listed: 2

1. Unishippers Global Logistics LLC
2. Worldwide Express

Source: *Entrepreneur*, Franchise 500 (annual), January 2012, p. 152-153.

3857 ■ WORLD'S MOST ADMIRED DELIVERY COMPANIES, 2012

Ranked by: Score, on a scale of 10, based on a survey of executives, directors, and securities analysts of companies within their own industry on eight criteria: innovation, financial soundness, employee talent, use of corporate assets, long-term investment value, social responsibility, quality of management, and quality of products/services. Remarks: Specific scores not provided. Also notes rank for previous year. Number listed: 6

1. United Parcel Service Inc. (UPS)
2. FedEx Corp.
3. Deutsche Post AG (DHL)
4. Poste Italiane
5. Nippon Express Co., Ltd.
6. La Poste

Source: *Fortune*, World's Most Admired Companies (annual), March 19, 2012, p. 150.

Packaging Industry
See: **Container Industry**

Paint Industry
See also: **Coatings**

3858 ■ NORTH AMERICA'S LARGEST PAINT AND COATINGS MANUFACTURERS, 2010

Ranked by: North American paint and coatings sales figures, in millions of U.S. dollars. Remarks: Also notes headquarters, CEO/president, parent company, and comments. Number listed: 25

1. PPG Industries Inc., with $9,860 million
2. The Sherwin-Williams Co., $5,830
3. DuPont Coatings & Color Technologies Group, $3,800
4. Valspar Corp., $2,990
5. RPM International Inc., $2,300
6. Behr Process Corp., $1,690
7. Comex Group, $1,360

8. Ennis Paint Inc., $387
9. Kelly-Moore Paint Co., $245
10. TIGER Drylac USA Inc., $235

Source: *Paint & Coatings Industry*, PCI 25 (annual), July 2011, p. 26+.

3859 ■ WORLD'S LARGEST PAINT AND COATINGS MANUFACTURERS, 2010

Ranked by: Global paint and coatings sales figures, in billions of U.S. dollars. Remarks: Also notes headquarters, key executive, parent company, and comments. Number listed: 10

1. Akzo Nobel NV, with $13.1 billion
2. PPG Industries Inc., $9.86
3. The Sherwin-Williams Co., $5.83
4. DuPont Performance Coatings, $3.8
5. BASF Coatings AG, $3.5
6. Valspar Corp., $2.99
7. Nippon Paint Co., Ltd., $2.4
8. Kansai Paint Co., Ltd., $2.38
9. RPM International Inc., $2.30
10. Jotun, $2

Source: *Paint & Coatings Industry*, PCI 25 (annual), July 2011, p. 24-25.

Paper Industry
See also: **Forest Products Industry**

3860 ■ JAPAN'S LARGEST PAPER AND PAPER PRODUCTS COMPANIES OVERALL, 2011

Ranked by: Score based on revenue, profits, assets, and market capitalization. Remarks: Specific scores not provided. Also notes overall rank in the *Forbes 2000* and figures for each criterion. Number listed: 2

1. Oji Paper Co., Ltd.
2. Nippon Paper Group Inc.

Source: *Forbes*, Forbes 2000 (annual), http://www.forbes.com, May 7, 2012.

3861 ■ LARGEST PAPER COMPANIES BY EMPLOYEES, 2010

Ranked by: Total number of employees. Remarks: Also notes contact information for headquarters, number of employees at headquarters, revenue, rank by revenue, and primary SIC code. Number listed: 48

1. Procter & Gamble Co., with 127,000 employees
2. Johnson & Johnson, 115,500
3. Kimberly-Clark Corp., 57,000
4. International Paper Co., 56,100
5. Georgia-Pacific LLC, 45,000
6. Avery Dennison Corp., 32,000
7. Mead Corp., 20,000
8. MeadWestvaco Corp., 19,960
9. Smurfit-Stone Container Corp., 19,000
10. Sealed Air Corp., 17,000

Source: *Business Rankings*, (annual), Dun & Bradstreet Inc., 2011, p. VI.58-VI.59.

3862 ■ LARGEST PAPER COMPANIES BY SALES, 2010

Ranked by: Total revenue, in dollars. **Remarks:** Also notes contact information for headquarters, number of employees at headquarters and overall, rank by employees, and primary SIC code. **Number listed:** 50

1. Procter & Gamble Co., with $78,938,000,000
2. Johnson & Johnson, $61,587,000,000
3. International Paper Co., $25,179,000,000
4. Kimberly-Clark Corp., $19,746,000,000
5. Avery Dennison Corp., $6,512,700,000
6. MeadWestvaco Corp., $5,693,000,000
7. Sealed Air Corp., $4,490,100,000
8. Sonoco Products Co., $4,124,121,000
9. Graphic Packaging Holding Co., $4,095,000,000
10. Temple-Inland Inc., $3,799,000,000

Source: *Business Rankings*, (annual), Dun & Bradstreet Inc., 2011, p. V.58-V.59.

3863 ■ LARGEST U.S. PAPER MANUFACTURERS, 2010

Ranked by: Revenue, in millions of dollars. **Remarks:** Also notes overall rank within the *IW 500*, revenue growth, and profit margin. **Number listed:** 16

1. International Paper Co., with $25,179 million
2. Kimberly-Clark Corp., $19,746
3. OfficeMax Inc., $7,150
4. Avery Dennison Corp., $6,513
5. MeadWestvaco Corp., $5,693
6. Smurfit-Stone Container Corp., $5,574
7. Sonoco Products Co., $4,124
8. Graphic Packaging Holding Co., $4,095
9. Temple-Inland Inc., $3,799
10. Greif Inc., $3,462

Source: *IndustryWeek*, IW 500 (annual), http://www.industryweek.com, July 2011.

3864 ■ LARGEST U.S. PAPER AND PAPER PRODUCTS COMPANIES OVERALL, 2011

Ranked by: Score based on revenue, profits, assets, and market capitalization. **Remarks:** Specific scores not provided. Also notes overall rank in the *Forbes 2000* and figures for each criterion. **Number listed:** 2

1. International Paper Co.
2. MeadWestvaco Corp.

Source: *Forbes*, Forbes 2000 (annual), http://www.forbes.com, May 7, 2012.

3865 ■ MOST PROFITABLE CANADIAN PAPER AND FOREST COMPANIES, 2011

Ranked by: Profits, in millions of Canadian dollars. **Number listed:** 6

1. West Fraser Timber Co., Ltd., with C$72.7 million
2. Canfor Pulp Products Inc., C$72.6
3. Stella-Jones Inc., C$55.7
4. Western Forest Products Inc., C$24
5. Tembec Inc., C$-3
6. Norbord Inc., C$-11

Source: *Canadian Business*, Investor 500 (annual), 2012, p. 55.

3866 ■ TOP *FORTUNE 500* COMPANIES IN FOREST AND PAPER PRODUCTS, 2011

Ranked by: Revenue, in millions of dollars. **Remarks:** Also notes overall rank in the *Fortune 500;* profits; profits as a percentage of revenue; stockholders' equity; and rank by each criterion. **Number listed:** 3

1. International Paper Co., with $26,034 million
2. Weyerhaeuser Co., $6,618
3. Domtar Inc., $5,612

Source: *Fortune*, Fortune 500 (annual), May 21, 2012, p. F-35.

3867 ■ WORLD'S LARGEST PAPER MANUFACTURERS, 2010

Ranked by: Revenue, in millions of dollars. **Remarks:** Also notes rank for previous year, overall rank within the *IW 1000*, country, and revenue growth. **Number listed:** 37

1. International Paper Co., with $25,179 million
2. Kimberly-Clark Corp., $19,746
3. Svenska Cellulosa AB (SCA), $16,219
4. Oji Paper Co., Ltd., $14,112
5. Stora Enso Oyj, $13,986
6. Nippon Paper Group Inc., $13,472
7. UPM-Kymmene Oyj, $12,039
8. Amcor Ltd., $10,133
9. Smurfit Kappa Group plc, $8,961
10. Mondi plc, $8,331

Source: *IndustryWeek*, IW 1000 (annual), http://www.industryweek.com, August 2011.

3868 ■ WORLD'S LARGEST PAPER AND PAPER PRODUCTS COMPANIES OVERALL, 2011

Ranked by: Score based on revenue, profits, assets, and market capitalization. **Remarks:** Specific scores not provided. Also notes country, overall rank in the *Forbes 2000*, and figures for each criterion. **Number listed:** 10

1. International Paper Co.
2. UPM-Kymmene Oyj
3. Stora Enso Oyj
4. Oji Paper Co., Ltd.
5. Empresas CMPC SA
6. Nippon Paper Group Inc.
7. Mondi
8. Smurfit Kappa Group plc
9. MeadWestvaco Corp.
10. Suzano Papel e Celulose SA

Source: *Forbes*, Forbes 2000 (annual), http://www.forbes.com, May 7, 2012.

3869 ■ WORLD'S LARGEST PULP AND PAPER COMPANIES BY OUTPUT, 2010

Ranked by: Paper and board output, in thousands of tons. **Remarks:** Also notes overall rank in the *Top 100*. **Number listed:** 57

1. International Paper Co., with 11,922 thousand tons
2. Stora Enso Oyj, 10,812
3. UPM-Kymmene Oyj, 9,914
4. Svenska Cellulosa AB (SCA), 8,948

5. Smurfit Kappa Group plc, 7,650
6. Nippon Paper Group Inc., 7,292
7. Nine Dragons Paper (Holdings) Ltd., 7,280
8. Sappi Ltd., 6,900
9. Oji Paper Co., Ltd., 6,861
10. Smurfit-Stone Container Corp., 5,896

Source: *Pulp and Paper International*, Top 100 (annual), September 2011, p. 13.

3870 ■ WORLD'S LARGEST PULP AND PAPER COMPANIES BY REVENUE, 2010

Ranked by: Revenue from pulp, paper, and converting operations, in millions of dollars. **Remarks:** Also notes rank for previous year, annual percent change, headquarters, figures from consolidated operations, breakdown of production by type, number of employees, and chief executive officer. **Number listed:** 100

1. International Paper Co., with $24,959 million
2. Procter & Gamble Co., $14,736
3. Stora Enso Oyj, $11,532.6
4. Oji Paper Co., Ltd., $11,503
5. Nippon Paper Group Inc., $11,089.8
6. Svenska Cellulosa AB (SCA), $10,823.2
7. UPM-Kymmene Oyj, $10,073.1
8. Kimberly-Clark Corp., $9,607
9. Smurfit Kappa Group plc, $8,842.5
10. Mondi plc, $8,101.9

Source: *Pulp and Paper International*, Top 100 (annual), September 2011, p. 16-19.

3871 ■ WORLD'S MOST ADMIRED FOREST AND PAPER PRODUCTS COMPANIES, 2012

Ranked by: Score, on a scale of 10, based on a survey of executives, directors, and securities analysts of companies within their own industry on eight criteria: innovation, financial soundness, employee talent, use of corporate assets, long-term investment value, social responsibility, quality of management, and quality of products/services. **Remarks:** Specific scores not provided. Also notes rank for previous year. **Number listed:** 5

1. International Paper Co.
2. Svenska Cellulosa AB (SCA)
3. Weyerhaeuser Co.
4. Stora Enso Oyj
5. Domtar Inc.

Source: *Fortune*, World's Most Admired Companies (annual), March 19, 2012, p. 149.

3872 ■ WORLD'S MOST ETHICAL FORESTRY, PAPER, AND PACKAGING COMPANIES, 2012

Ranked by: Score based on five criteria: ethics and compliance program; reputation, leadership, and innovation; governance; corporate citizenship and responsibility; and culture of ethics. **Remarks:** Specific scores not provided; companies are listed alphabetically, not ranked. **Number listed:** 4

1. International Paper Co. (U.S.)
2. Svenska Cellulosa AB (SCA, Sweden)
3. Stora Enso Oyj (Finland)
4. Weyerhaeuser Co. (U.S.)

Source: *Ethisphere Magazine*, World's Most Ethical Companies (annual), http://www.ethisphere.com, 2012.

Patents

3873 ■ COUNTRIES WITH THE HIGHEST INTELLECTUAL PROPERTY PROTECTION, 2010

Ranked by: Score, on a scale of seven, based on intellectual property protection and anti-counterfeiting measures. **Number listed:** 142

1. Finland, with 6.2 points
2. Singapore, 6.1
2. Switzerland, 6.1
4. Sweden, 6.0
5. Luxembourg, 5.9
6. Denmark, 5.9
7. France, 5.8
7. New Zealand, 5.8
7. Netherlands, 5.8
10. Ireland, 5.7
10. United Kingdom, 5.7

Source: *Global Competitiveness Report*, (annual), World Economic Forum, 2011, p. 391.

3874 ■ COUNTRIES WITH THE LOWEST INTELLECTUAL PROPERTY PROTECTION, 2010

Ranked by: Score, on a scale of seven, based on intellectual property protection and anti-counterfeiting measures. **Number listed:** 142

1. Haiti, with 1.6 points
2. Yemen, 1.7
2. Venezuela, 1.8
4. Burundi, 1.9
5. Kyrgyz Republic, 2.0
6. Madagascar, 2.1
7. Mongolia, 2.2
7. Algeria, 2.2
7. Suriname, 2.2
10. Paraguay, 2.3
10. Chad, 2.3
10. Cote d'Ivoire, 2.3

Source: *Global Competitiveness Report*, (annual), World Economic Forum, 2011, p. 391.

3875 ■ COUNTRIES PRODUCING THE MOST PATENTS, 2010

Ranked by: Number of utility patents (i.e., patents for an invention) granted during the year, per million population. **Number listed:** 142

1. Taiwan, with 355.7 patents
2. Japan, 252.9
3. United States, 339.4
4. Israel, 249.2
5. South Korea, 240.6
6. Finland, 215.7
7. Switzerland, 211.6
8. Sweden, 154.2
9. Germany, 150.6
10. Canada, 143.1

Source: *Global Competitiveness Report*, (annual), World Economic Forum, 2011, p. 520.

3876 ■ TOP COMPANIES RECEIVING U.S. PATENTS, 2010

Ranked by: Number of utility and statutory patents received. **Number listed:** 25

1. International Business Machines Corp. (IBM), with 5,895 patents
2. Samsung Electronics Co., Ltd., 4,551
3. Microsoft Corp., 3,091
4. Canon KK, 2,552
5. Panasonic Corp., 2,482
6. Toshiba Corp., 2,247
7. Sony Corp., 2,150
8. Intel Corp., 1,653
9. LG Electronics Inc., 1,490
10. Hewlett-Packard Development Co., 1,480

Source: *Intellectual Property Today*, Corporate Patent Scoreboard (annual), http://www.iptoday.com, July 2011.

3877 ■ TOP LAW FIRMS IN UTILITY PATENTS, 2011

Ranked by: Number of utility patents (i.e., patents for a new and useful process or item) issued during the year where the law firm or individual is listed as the legal representative on the face of the registration. **Remarks:** Also notes number of design and plant patents, total patents for current and previous two years, three-year average, number of attorneys and agents, and website. **Number listed:** 272

1. Oblon, Spivak, McClelland, Maier & Neustadt LLP, with 5,601 patents
2. Sughrue Mion PLLC, 3,413
3. Birch, Stewart, Kolasch & Birch LLP, 3,060
4. Oliff & Berridge plc, 2,855
5. Harness Dickey & Pierce plc, 2,475
6. Fish & Richardson PC, 2,232
7. Kilpatrick Townsend & Stockton, 2,060
8. Cantor Colburn LLP, 2,059
9. Knobbe, Martens, Olson & Bear LLP, 1,999
10. McDermott Will & Emery LLP, 1,823

Source: *Intellectual Property Today*, Top Patent Firms (annual), http://www.iptoday.com, March 2012.

Pension Fund Investments

3878 ■ WORLD'S LARGEST RETIREMENT PLANS, 2010

Ranked by: Total assets, in millions of U.S. dollars. **Number listed:** 300

1. Government Pension Investment (Japan), with $1,432,122 million
2. Government Pension Fund Global (Norway), $550,858
3. ABP (Netherlands), $318,807
4. National Pension (Korea), $289,418
5. Federal Retirement Thrift (U.S.), $264,013
6. California Public Employees (U.S.), $214,387
7. Local Government Officials (Japan), $189,633
8. Canada Pension (Canada), $149,142
9. Employees Provident Fund (Malaysia), $145,570
10. Central Provident Fund (Singapore), $144.844

Source: *Pensions & Investments*, P&I/Towers Watson World 300 (annual), http://www.pionline.com, September 5, 2011.

Periodicals
See: **Magazines**

Personal Care Products

3879 ■ AMERICA'S LARGEST PRIVATE HOUSEHOLD AND PERSONAL PRODUCT COMPANIES, 2010

Ranked by: Revenue, in billions of dollars. **Remarks:** Also notes headquarters, number of employees, and overall rank in the *America's Largest Private Companies* list. Ranking is available online only, not in print. **Number listed:** 5

1. Amway Corp., with $9.2 billion
2. S. C. Johnson & Son Inc., $9
3. Mary Kay Inc., $2.5
4. Conair Corp., $2.01
5. The Sun Products Corp., $2

Source: *Forbes*, America's Largest Private Companies (annual), http://www.forbes.com, December 5, 2011.

3880 ■ BEST SMALL HOUSEHOLD AND PERSONAL PRODUCT COMPANIES IN AMERICA, 2011

Ranked by: Score based on revenue, profits, and return on equity for the past 12 months and five years. **Remarks:** Specific scores not provided. Also notes rank in the overall *100 Best Small Companies in America*. To qualify, companies must have revenues between $5 million and $1 billion, a net margin above five percent, and share price above $5. List is available online only. **Number listed:** 4

1. Sturm, Ruger & Co., Inc.
2. True Religion Apparel
3. Steven Madden Ltd.
4. Iconix Brand Group

Source: *Forbes*, Best Small Companies in America (annual), November 7, 2011.

3881 ■ CALIFORNIA'S LARGEST HOUSEHOLD AND PERSONAL PRODUCTS COMPANIES OVERALL, 2011

Ranked by: Score based on revenue, profits, assets, and market capitalization. **Remarks:** Specific scores not provided. Also notes overall rank in the *Forbes 2000* and figures for each criterion. **Number listed:** 2

1. Mattel Inc.
2. The Clorox Co.

Source: *Forbes*, Forbes 2000 (annual), http://www.forbes.com, May 7, 2012.

3882 ■ EUROPE'S MOST VALUABLE PERSONAL GOODS COMPANIES, 2011

Ranked by: Market value as of March 2011, in millions of U.S. dollars. **Remarks:** Also notes rank within the *FT Europe 500*, rank for previous year, country, revenue, net income, assets, number of employees, share price, price-to-earning ratio, dividend yield, and fiscal yearend. **Number listed:** 15

1. LVMH Moet Hennessy Louis Vuitton SA, with $77,612.9 million
2. L'Oreal SA, $69,898.3
3. Richemont, $30,268.7
4. Christian Dior SA, $25,615.9
5. The Swatch Group Ltd., $23,587.3
6. Hermes International, $23,176
7. Beiersdorf AG, $15,404.1
8. Luxottica Group SpA, $15,248.4
9. adidas AG, $13,207.4
10. Svenska Cellulosa AB (SCA), $11,348.2

Source: *Financial Times*, FT 500 (annual), http://www.ft.com, June 24, 2011.

3883 ■ FRANCE'S MOST VALUABLE COSMETICS/PERSONAL CARE BRANDS, 2011

Ranked by: Brand value, in millions of U.S. dollars. **Remarks:** Also notes rank within the *Global 500* for current and previous year, figures for current and previous year, and brand rating. Ranking is available online only. **Number listed:** 2

1. L'Oreal, with $7,744 million
2. Lancome, $5,095

Source: *Global 500*, (annual), Brand Finance plc, March 2012.

3884 ■ GERMANY'S LARGEST HOUSEHOLD AND PERSONAL PRODUCTS COMPANIES OVERALL, 2011

Ranked by: Score based on revenue, profits, assets, and market capitalization. **Remarks:** Specific scores not provided. Also notes overall rank in the *Forbes 2000* and figures for each criterion. **Number listed:** 2

1. Henkel KgaA
2. Beiersdorf AG

Source: *Forbes*, Forbes 2000 (annual), http://www.forbes.com, May 7, 2012.

3885 ■ GERMANY'S MOST VALUABLE COSMETICS/PERSONAL CARE BRANDS, 2011

Ranked by: Brand value, in millions of U.S. dollars. **Remarks:** Also notes rank within the *Global 500* for current and previous year, figures for current and previous year, and brand rating. Ranking is available online only. **Number listed:** 2

1. Nivea, with $5,574 million
2. Schwarzkopf, $2,682

Source: *Global 500*, (annual), Brand Finance plc, March 2012.

3886 ■ JAPAN'S LARGEST HOUSEHOLD AND PERSONAL PRODUCTS COMPANIES OVERALL, 2011

Ranked by: Score based on revenue, profits, assets, and market capitalization. **Remarks:** Specific scores not provided. Also notes overall rank in the *Forbes 2000* and figures for each criterion. **Number listed:** 3

1. Kao Corp.
2. Uni-Charm
3. Shiseido Co., Ltd.

Source: *Forbes*, Forbes 2000 (annual), http://www.forbes.com, May 7, 2012.

3887 ■ JAPAN'S MOST VALUABLE COSMETICS/PERSONAL CARE BRANDS, 2011

Ranked by: Brand value, in millions of U.S. dollars. **Remarks:** Also notes rank within the *Global 500* for current and previous

year, figures for current and previous year, and brand rating. Ranking is available online only. **Number listed:** 2

1. Biore, with $3,336 million
2. Shiseido, $2,907

Source: *Global 500*, (annual), Brand Finance plc, March 2012.

3888 ■ LARGEST ASIA-PACIFIC HEALTH AND BEAUTY RETAILERS, 2010

Ranked by: Sales, in millions of U.S. dollars. **Remarks:** Also notes country, fascias/brands, number of outlets, sales in national currency, sales area, sales per square meter, and figures for previous year. **Number listed:** 10

1. Aeon Group, with $6,099 million
2. Matsumotokiyoshi Holdings, $4,100
3. Sundrug, $3,335
4. Cawachi, $2,640
5. Sugi Pharmacy, $2,384
6. Fiji Yakuhin, $1,946
7. Australian Pharmaceutical Industries, $1,789
8. Create Super Drugstore, $1,651
9. Mercury Drug Corp., $1,614
10. Sigma Pharmaceuticals, $1,383

Source: *Retail Asia*, Retail Asia-Pacific Top 500 (annual), July 2011, p. 65-65a.

3889 ■ LARGEST U.S. HOUSEHOLD AND PERSONAL PRODUCTS COMPANIES, 2010

Ranked by: Sales, in billions of dollars. **Remarks:** Also notes headquarters. **Number listed:** 50

1. Procter & Gamble Co., with $64.6 billion
2. Colgate-Palmolive Co., $13.3
3. S. C. Johnson & Son Inc., $8.8
4. Avon Products Inc., $7.7
4. The Estee Lauder Companies Inc., $7.7
6. Johnson & Johnson, $7.2
7. Amway Corp., $5.7
7. Ecolab Inc., $5.7
9. Coty Inc., $3.8
10. Diversey Inc., $3.1

Source: *Happi: Household & Personal Products Industry*, Top 50 (annual), http://www.happi.com, July 2011.

3890 ■ LARGEST U.S. HOUSEHOLD AND PERSONAL PRODUCTS COMPANIES OVERALL, 2011

Ranked by: Score based on revenue, profits, assets, and market capitalization. **Remarks:** Specific scores not provided. Also notes overall rank in the *Forbes 2000* and figures for each criterion. **Number listed:** 11

1. Procter & Gamble Co.
2. Kimberly-Clark Corp.
3. Colgate-Palmolive Co.
4. Stanley Black & Decker Inc.
5. The Estee Lauder Companies Inc.
6. Mattel Inc.
7. Avon Products Inc.
8. The Clorox Co.
9. Mead Johnson Nutrition Co.

10. Harbinger Group Inc.

Source: *Forbes*, Forbes 2000 (annual), http://www.forbes.com, May 7, 2012.

3891 ■ MOST VALUABLE U.S. PERSONAL GOODS COMPANIES, 2011

Ranked by: Market value as of March 2011, in millions of U.S. dollars. **Remarks:** Also notes rank within the *FT U.S. 500*, rank for previous year, country, revenue, net income, assets, number of employees, share price, price-to-earning ratio, dividend yield, and fiscal yearend. **Number listed:** 9

1. Colgate-Palmolive Co., with $39,609.4 million
2. Nike Inc., $29,409.8
3. Kimberly-Clark Corp., $25,307.7
4. Coach Inc., $15,392.1
5. Avon Products Inc., $11,804.5
6. The Estee Lauder Companies Inc., $11,678.3
7. VF Corp., $10,710
8. Polo Ralph Lauren Corp., $8,081.2
9. Fossil Inc., $5,994.4

Source: *Financial Times*, FT 500 (annual), http://www.ft.com, June 24, 2011.

3892 ■ NEW YORK'S LARGEST HOUSEHOLD AND PERSONAL PRODUCTS COMPANIES OVERALL, 2011

Ranked by: Score based on revenue, profits, assets, and market capitalization. **Remarks:** Specific scores not provided. Also notes overall rank in the *Forbes 2000* and figures for each criterion. **Number listed:** 4

1. Colgate-Palmolive Co.
2. The Estee Lauder Companies Inc.
3. Avon Products Inc.
4. Harbinger Group

Source: *Forbes*, Forbes 2000 (annual), http://www.forbes.com, May 7, 2012.

3893 ■ TEXAS'S LARGEST HOUSEHOLD AND PERSONAL CARE COMPANIES OVERALL, 2011

Ranked by: Score based on revenue, profits, assets, and market capitalization. **Remarks:** Specific scores not provided. Also notes overall rank in the *Forbes 2000* and figures for each criterion. **Number listed:** 2

1. Kimberly-Clark Corp.
2. Fossil Inc.

Source: *Forbes*, Forbes 2000 (annual), http://www.forbes.com, May 7, 2012.

3894 ■ TOP DRUG STORE NICHE BRANDS, 2011

Ranked by: Sales, in thousands of dollars. **Remarks:** Also notes breakdown by product and percent change from previous year. **Number listed:** 150

1. Monistat, with $100,994.3 thousand
2. Aussie, $100,393.4
3. Plan B One Step, $99,621.5
4. Abreva, $94,432.5
5. Next Choice, $87,883.3
6. Matrix, $87,146.9
7. Gold Bond, $86,468
8. Allergan, $83,746.4

9. St. Ives, $82,528.8
10. Fixodent, $82,013.4

Source: *Drug Store News*, Niche Brands, May 2012.

3895 ■ TOP *FORTUNE 500* COMPANIES IN HOUSEHOLD AND PERSONAL PRODUCTS, 2011

Ranked by: Revenue, in millions of dollars. **Remarks:** Also notes overall rank in the *Fortune 500;* profits; profits as a percentage of revenue; stockholders' equity; and rank by each criterion. **Number listed:** 6

1. Procter & Gamble Co., with $82,559 million
2. Kimberly-Clark Corp., $20,846
3. Colgate-Palmolive Co., $16,734
4. Avon Products Inc., $11,292
5. The Estee Lauder Companies Inc., $8,810
6. The Clorox Co., $5,326

Source: *Fortune*, Fortune 500 (annual), May 21, 2012, p. F-36.

3896 ■ TOP HEALTH PRODUCTS FRANCHISES, 2012

Ranked by: Cumulative score based on financial strength and stability, growth rate, size of the system, number of years in business, the length of time franchising, start-up costs, litigation, percentage of terminations, and whether the company provides financing. **Remarks:** Specific scores not provided. Also notes overall rank within the *Franchise 500*, contact information, description, year founded, year started franchising, states where registered, available U.S. regions, where seeking foreign expansion, number of franchised and company-owned units for past three years, start-up costs, franchise fees, royalty fees, and type of financing available. **Number listed:** 5

1. Miracle-Ear Inc.
2. Pearle Vision Inc.
3. Foot Solutions Inc.
4. Relax the Back Corp.
5. Amramp

Source: *Entrepreneur*, Franchise 500 (annual), January 2012, p. 176-177.

3897 ■ THE UNITED STATES' MOST VALUABLE COSMETICS/PERSONAL CARE BRANDS, 2011

Ranked by: Brand value, in millions of U.S. dollars. **Remarks:** Also notes rank within the *Global 500* for current and previous year, figures for current and previous year, and brand rating. Ranking is available online only. **Number listed:** 8

1. Olay, with $11,756 million
2. Avon, $7,901
3. Gillette, $7,806
4. Neutrogena, $6,248
5. Colgate, $4,415
6. Estee Lauder, $3,716
7. Pantene, $2,643
8. Aveeno, $2,384

Source: *Global 500*, (annual), Brand Finance plc, March 2012.

3898 ■ WORLD'S LARGEST BEAUTY COMPANIES, 2010

Ranked by: Sales, in billions of U.S. dollars. **Number listed:** 20

1. Procter & Gamble Co., with $28.2 billion
2. L'Oreal SA, $25.8
3. Unilever, $18.2

4. The Estee Lauder Companies Inc., $8.8
5. Shiseido Co., Ltd., $8
6. Avon Products Inc., $7.7
7. Johnson & Johnson, $7.2
8. Beiersdorf AG, $7
9. Kao Corp., $6.4
10. Alticor, $5.7

Source: *Beauty Packaging*, Top 20 (annual), http://www.beautypackaging.com, 2011.

3899 ■ WORLD'S LARGEST CONSUMER HEALTH AND BEAUTY AIDS COMPANIES, 2010

Ranked by: Sales, in millions of U.S. dollars. **Remarks:** Also notes brands and annual sales growth. **Number listed:** 10

1. L'Oreal SA, with $27,765 million
2. Avon Products Inc., $10,862
3. Biersdorf AG, $8,629
4. The Estee Lauder Companies Inc., $7,796
5. Shiseido Co., Ltd., $6,924
6. Natura Cosmeticos SA, $2,890
7. KOSE Corp., $1,856
8. Alberto-Culver Co., $1,600
9. Nu Skin Enterprises Inc., $1,540
10. Revlon Inc., $1,321

Source: *Consumer Goods Technology*, Consumer Goods Registry (annual), http://www.consumergoods.com, December 2011.

3900 ■ WORLD'S LARGEST HOUSEHOLD AND PERSONAL PRODUCTS COMPANIES OVERALL, 2011

Ranked by: Score based on revenue, profits, assets, and market capitalization. **Remarks:** Specific scores not provided. Also notes country, overall rank in the *Forbes 2000*, and figures for each criterion. **Number listed:** 22

1. Procter & Gamble Co.
2. L'Oreal SA
3. Henkel KgaA
4. Reckitt Benckiser plc
5. Kimberly-Clark Corp.
6. Colgate-Palmolive Co.
7. Stanley Black & Decker Inc.
8. Kao Corp.
9. Estee Lauder Cos.
10. Svenska Cellulosa AB (SCA)

Source: *Forbes*, Forbes 2000 (annual), http://www.forbes.com, May 7, 2012.

3901 ■ WORLD'S MOST ADMIRED SOAPS AND COSMETICS COMPANIES, 2012

Ranked by: Score, on a scale of 10, based on a survey of executives, directors, and securities analysts of companies within their own industry on eight criteria: innovation, financial soundness, employee talent, use of corporate assets, long-term investment value, social responsibility, quality of management, and quality of products/services. **Remarks:** Specific scores not provided. Also notes rank for previous year. **Number listed:** 6

1. Procter & Gamble Co.
2. Colgate-Palmolive Co.
3. L'Oreal SA

4. The Estee Lauder Companies Inc.
5. Reckitt Benckiser plc
6. Kimberly-Clark Corp.

Source: *Fortune*, World's Most Admired Companies (annual), March 19, 2012, p. 148.

3902 ■ WORLD'S MOST ETHICAL HEALTH AND BEAUTY COMPANIES, 2012

Ranked by: Score based on five criteria: ethics and compliance program; reputation, leadership, and innovation; governance; corporate citizenship and responsibility; and culture of ethics. **Remarks:** Specific scores not provided; companies are listed alphabetically, not ranked. **Number listed:** 3

1. L'Oreal SA (France)
2. Natura Cosmeticos (Brazil)
3. Shiseido Co. (Japan)

Source: *Ethisphere Magazine*, World's Most Ethical Companies (annual), http://www.ethisphere.com, 2012.

3903 ■ WORLD'S MOST VALUABLE PERSONAL CARE BRANDS, 2012

Ranked by: Brand value, a measure of a brand's earnings and contribution, in millions of U.S. dollars. **Remarks:** Also notes annual growth in brand value and rank by brand contribution and brand momentum. **Number listed:** 15

1. Gillette, with $19,055 million
2. Colgate, $14,948
3. L'Oreal, $13,773
4. Dove, $4,696
5. Nivea, $4,643
6. Garnier, $4,441
7. Lancome, $4,154
8. Clinique, $3,418
9. Crest, $3,379
10. Olay, $3,377

Source: *Financial Times*, Global Brands (annual), http://www.ft.com, May 22, 2012.

3904 ■ WORLD'S MOST VALUABLE PERSONAL GOODS COMPANIES, 2011

Ranked by: Market value as of March 2011, in millions of U.S. dollars. **Remarks:** Also notes rank within the *FT 500*, rank for previous year, country, revenue, net income, assets, number of employees, share price, price-to-earning ratio, dividend yield, and fiscal year-end. **Number listed:** 10

1. LVMH Moet Hennessy Louis Vuitton SA, with $77,612.9 million
2. L'Oreal SA, $69,898.3
3. Colgate-Palmolive Co., $39,609.4
4. Richemont, $30,268.7
5. Nike Inc., $29,409.8
6. Kimberly-Clark Corp., $26,307.7
7. Christian Dior SA, $25,615.9
8. The Swatch Group Ltd., $23,587.3
9. Hermes International, $23,176
10. Li & Fung Ltd., $20,690.5

Source: *Financial Times*, FT 500 (annual), http://www.ft.com, June 24, 2011.

Personal Care Products—Advertising

3905 ■ TOP PERSONAL CARE BRANDS BY ADVERTIS-ING EXPENDITURES, 2010

Ranked by: Share of U.S. personal care measured media spending, in percent. **Remarks:** Also notes parent company, measured media expenditures, and figures for previous year. **Number listed:** 10

1. L'Oreal Paris, with 6.9%
2. Olay, 5.2%
3. Maybelline New York, 4%
4. Cover Girl, 3.8%
5. Garnier, 3.6%
6. Proactiv, 3.4%
7. Dove, 3.3%
8. Gillette, 3.2%
9. Neutrogena, 2.8%
10. Crest, 2.7%

Source: *Advertising Age*, Leading National Advertisers (annual), June 20, 2011, p. 21.

Personal Computers
See also: **Computer Industry**

3906 ■ TOP BRANDS OF HOME COMPUTERS, 2010

Ranked by: Popularity among *CE Pro 100* companies, in percent. **Number listed:** 5

1. Dell, with 28%
2. Apple, 20%
3. HP, 5%
4. Sony, 3%
5. Toshiba, 2%

Source: *CE Pro*, Brand Analysis (annual), June 2011, p. 60.

Personal Income
See: **Income**

Personal Services

3907 ■ AMERICA'S LARGEST PRIVATE SERVICES COMPANIES, 2010

Ranked by: Revenue, in billions of dollars. **Remarks:** Also notes headquarters, number of employees, and overall rank in the *America's Largest Private Companies* list. Ranking is available online only, not in print. **Number listed:** 2

1. Enterprise Rent-A-Car Co., with $14.1 billion
2. Skadden, Arps, Slate, Meagher & Flom LLP, $2.1

Source: *Forbes*, America's Largest Private Companies (annual), http://www.forbes.com, December 5, 2011.

3908 ■ LARGEST PERSONAL SERVICE COMPANIES BY EMPLOYEES, 2010

Ranked by: Total number of employees. **Remarks:** Also notes contact information for headquarters, number of employees at headquarters, revenue, rank by revenue, and primary SIC code. **Number listed:** 458

1. Weight Watchers International Inc., with 50,000 employees
2. Cintas Corp., 30,120
3. Cintas Corp. No. 1, 27,000
4. Lifetouch Inc., 22,175
5. Service Corp. International, 20,725
6. SCI Funeral & Cemetery Purchasing Cooperative Inc., 20,000
7. Alsco Inc., 13,585
8. ARAMARK Uniform & Career Apparel LLC, 12,000
9. CPI Corp., 11,000
10. Ratner Cos., 10,000
10. UniFirst Corp., 10,000

Source: *Business Rankings*, (annual), Dun & Bradstreet Inc., 2011, p. VI.204-VI.213.

3909 ■ LARGEST PERSONAL SERVICE COMPANIES BY SALES, 2010

Ranked by: Total revenue, in dollars. **Remarks:** Also notes contact information for headquarters, number of employees at headquarters and overall, rank by employees, and primary SIC code. **Number listed:** 460

1. H & R Block Inc., with $3,874,332,000
2. Cintas Corp., $3,547,339,000
3. Service Corp. International, $2,190,552,000
4. Weight Watchers International Inc., $1,452,037,000
5. Coinstar Inc., $1,436,421,000
6. UniFirst Corp., $1,025,939,000
7. G & K Services Inc., $833,592,000
8. Jenniges Enterprises Inc., $614,385,000
9. Alsco Inc., $551,558,645
10. Stewart Enterprises Inc., $499,907,000

Source: *Business Rankings*, (annual), Dun & Bradstreet Inc., 2011, p. V.178-V.187.

3910 ■ TOP MISCELLANEOUS PERSONAL CARE FRANCHISES, 2012

Ranked by: Cumulative score based on financial strength and stability, growth rate, size of the system, number of years in business, the length of time franchising, start-up costs, litigation, percentage of terminations, and whether the company provides financing. **Remarks:** Specific scores not provided. Also notes overall rank within the *Franchise 500*, contact information, description, year founded, year started franchising, states where registered, available U.S. regions, where seeking foreign expansion, number of franchised and company-owned units for past three years, start-up costs, franchise fees, royalty fees, and type of financing available. **Number listed:** 2

1. No Mas Vello
2. Palm Beach Tan

Source: *Entrepreneur*, Franchise 500 (annual), January 2012, p. 196-197.

Pests—Control

3911 ■ LARGEST PEST CONTROL COMPANIES, 2011

Ranked by: Revenue, in dollars. **Remarks:** Also notes rank for previous year, headquarters, annual growth, and breakdown by type of service. **Number listed:** 100

1. Rollins, with $1,205,064,000
2. Terminix International LP, $1,193,075,000
3. Ecolab Inc., $329,040,000
4. Rentokil/Ehrlich/Presto-X, $246,200,000
5. Massey Services, $136,346,547
6. The Steritech Group, $114,014,000
7. Cook's Pest Control, $112,400,000
8. Arrow Exterminators, $110,100,000
9. Terminix Service, $105,133,441
10. Clark Pest Control, $102,501,000

Source: *Pest Control Technology*, Top 100 (annual), May 2012, p. 39-41.

Pet Shops

3912 ■ TOP PET STORE FRANCHISES, 2012

Ranked by: Cumulative score based on financial strength and stability, growth rate, size of the system, number of years in business, the length of time franchising, start-up costs, litigation, percentage of terminations, and whether the company provides financing. **Remarks:** Specific scores not provided. Also notes overall rank within the *Franchise 500,* contact information, description, year founded, year started franchising, states where registered, available U.S. regions, where seeking foreign expansion, number of franchised and company-owned units for past three years, start-up costs, franchise fees, royalty fees, and type of financing available. **Number listed:** 3

1. Wild Birds Unlimited
2. Nature's Pet Market
3. Petland

Source: *Entrepreneur*, Franchise 500 (annual), January 2012, p. 196-197.

Petroleum Drilling

3913 ■ LARGEST OIL AND GAS EXTRACTION COMPANIES BY EMPLOYEES, 2010

Ranked by: Total number of employees. **Remarks:** Also notes contact information for headquarters, number of employees at headquarters, revenue, rank by revenue, and primary SIC code. **Number listed:** 48

1. Schlumberger Ltd., with 60,000 employees
2. Halliburton Co., 51,672
3. Halliburton Energy Services Inc., 50,000
4. Marathon Oil Corp., 28,855
5. Transocean Inc., 21,100
6. Nabors Industries Inc., 16,847
7. Schlumberger Technology Corp., 16,800
8. BJ Services Co., 14,400
9. Hess Corp., 13,317
10. Total Holdings USA Inc., 13,000

Source: *Business Rankings*, (annual), Dun & Bradstreet Inc., 2011, p. VI.19-VI.20.

3914 ■ LARGEST OIL AND GAS EXTRACTION COMPANIES BY SALES, 2010

Ranked by: Total revenue, in dollars. **Remarks:** Also notes contact information for headquarters, number of employees at headquarters and overall, rank by employees, and primary SIC code. **Number listed:** 50

1. Marathon Oil Corp., with $73,621,000,000
2. Hess Corp., $34,613,000,000
3. Murphy Oil Corp., $23,345,071,000
4. Tesoro Corp., $20,583,000,000
5. Occidental Petroleum Corp., $19,157,000,000
6. Halliburton Co., $17,973,000,000
7. Transocean Inc., $12,674,000,000
8. Apache Corp., $12,092,000,000
9. Global Marine Inc., $11,556,000,000
10. Anadarko Petroleum Corp., $10,984,000,000

Source: *Business Rankings*, (annual), Dun & Bradstreet Inc., 2011, p. V.19-V.20.

Petroleum Equipment Industry

3915 ■ CANADA'S LARGEST OIL SERVICES AND EQUIPMENT COMPANIES OVERALL, 2011

Ranked by: Score based on revenue, profits, assets, and market capitalization. **Remarks:** Specific scores not provided. Also notes rank in the overall *Forbes 2000* and figures for each criterion. **Number listed:** 2

1. Enbridge Inc.
2. TransCanada Corp.

Source: *Forbes*, Forbes 2000 (annual), http://www.forbes.com, May 7, 2012.

3916 ■ EUROPE'S MOST VALUABLE OIL EQUIPMENT AND SERVICES COMPANIES, 2011

Ranked by: Market value as of March 2011, in millions of U.S. dollars. **Remarks:** Also notes rank within the *FT Europe 500*, rank for previous year, country, revenue, net income, assets, number of employees, share price, price-to-earning ratio, dividend yield, and fiscal yearend. **Number listed:** 12

1. Transocean Inc., with $25,182.7 million
2. Saipem SpA, $23,488.9
3. Seadrill, $13,769.9
4. Technip, $11,773.1
5. Subsea 7, $8,884.3
6. Petrofac, $8,251.5
7. Fugro, $7,082.9
8. Amec, $6,363.7
9. Aker Solutions ASA, $6,295.6
10. CGG Veritas, $5,470.7

Source: *Financial Times*, FT 500 (annual), http://www.ft.com, June 24, 2011.

3917 ■ LARGEST U.S. OIL SERVICES AND EQUIPMENT COMPANIES OVERALL, 2011

Ranked by: Score based on revenue, profits, assets, and market capitalization. **Remarks:** Specific scores not provided. Also notes overall rank in the *Forbes 2000* and figures for each criterion. **Number listed:** 12

1. Halliburton Co.
2. National Oilwell Varco Inc.
3. Baker Hughes Inc.
4. Kinder Morgan Inc.
5. Spectra Energy Corp.
6. The Williams Companies Inc.

7. Oneok Inc.
8. Cameron International Corp.
9. El Paso Corp.
10. FMC Technologies Inc.

Source: *Forbes*, Forbes 2000 (annual), http://www.forbes.com, May 7, 2012.

3918 ■ MOST VALUABLE U.S. OIL EQUIPMENT AND SERVICES COMPANIES, 2011

Ranked by: Market value as of March 2011, in millions of U.S. dollars. **Remarks:** Also notes rank within the *FT U.S. 500*, rank for previous year, country, revenue, net income, assets, number of employees, share price, price-to-earning ratio, dividend yield, and fiscal yearend. **Number listed:** 15

1. Schlumberger Ltd., with $126,818.6 million
2. Halliburton Co., $45,521.7
3. National Oilwell Varco Inc., $33,378.3
4. Baker Hughes Inc., $31,887.7
5. The Williams Companies Inc., $18,276
6. Weatherford International Ltd., $15,771.9
7. Cameron International Corp., $13,986.9
8. El Paso Corp., $13,778.7
9. Noble Corp., $11,499.9
10. FMC Technologies Inc., $11,351

Source: *Financial Times*, FT 500 (annual), http://www.ft.com, June 24, 2011.

3919 ■ OKLAHOMA'S LARGEST OIL SERVICES AND EQUIPMENT COMPANIES OVERALL, 2011

Ranked by: Score based on revenue, profits, assets, and market capitalization. **Remarks:** Specific scores not provided. Also notes overall rank in the *Forbes 2000* and figures for each criterion. **Number listed:** 3

1. The Williams Companies Inc.
2. ONEOK Inc.
3. Helmerich & Payne Inc.

Source: *Forbes*, Forbes 2000 (annual), http://www.forbes.com, May 7, 2012.

3920 ■ TEXAS'S LARGEST OIL SERVICES AND EQUIP-MENT COMPANIES OVERALL, 2011

Ranked by: Score based on revenue, profits, assets, and market capitalization. **Remarks:** Specific scores not provided. Also notes overall rank in the *Forbes 2000* and figures for each criterion. **Number listed:** 8

1. Halliburton Co.
2. National Oilwell Varco Inc.
3. Baker Hughes Inc.
4. Kinder Morgan Inc.
5. Spectra Energy Corp.
6. Cameron International Corp.
7. El Paso Corp.
8. FMC Technologies Inc.

Source: *Forbes*, Forbes 2000 (annual), http://www.forbes.com, May 7, 2012.

3921 ■ TOP *FORTUNE 500* COMPANIES IN OIL AND GAS EQUIPMENT/SERVICES, 2011

Ranked by: Revenue, in millions of dollars. **Remarks:** Also notes overall rank in the *Fortune 500;* profits; profits as a percentage of revenue; stockholders' equity; and rank by each criterion. **Number listed:** 6

1. Halliburton Co., with $24,829 million
2. Baker Hughes Inc., $19,831
3. National Oilwell Varco Inc., $14,658
4. Cameron International Corp., $6,959
5. FMC Technologies, $5,099
6. MRC Global, $4,832

Source: *Fortune*, Fortune 500 (annual), May 21, 2012, p. F-38.

3922 ■ UNITED KINGDOM'S LARGEST OIL SERVICES AND EQUIPMENT COMPANIES OVERALL, 2011

Ranked by: Score based on revenue, profits, assets, and market capitalization. **Remarks:** Specific scores not provided. Also notes overall rank in the *Forbes 2000* and figures for each criterion. **Number listed:** 5

1. Ensco plc
2. Petrofac Ltd.
3. Subsea 7 SA
4. John Wood Group plc
5. AMEC plc

Source: *Forbes*, Forbes 2000 (annual), http://www.forbes.com, May 7, 2012.

3923 ■ WORLD'S LARGEST OIL SERVICES AND EQUIP-MENT COMPANIES OVERALL, 2011

Ranked by: Score based on revenue, profits, assets, and market capitalization. **Remarks:** Specific scores not provided. Also notes country, overall rank in the *Forbes 2000,* and figures for each criterion. **Number listed:** 30

1. Schlumberger Ltd.
2. Halliburton Co.
3. National Oilwell Varco Inc.
4. Enbridge Inc.
5. Baker Hughes Inc.
6. TransCanada Corp.
7. Kinder Morgan Inc.
8. Tenaris SA
9. AK Transneft OAO (Transneft OJSC)
10. Spectra Energy Corp.

Source: *Forbes*, Forbes 2000 (annual), http://www.forbes.com, May 7, 2012.

3924 ■ WORLD'S MOST ADMIRED OIL AND GAS EQUIP-MENT AND SERVICES COMPANIES, 2012

Ranked by: Score, on a scale of 10, based on a survey of executives, directors, and securities analysts of companies within their own industry on eight criteria: innovation, financial soundness, employee talent, use of corporate assets, long-term investment value, social responsibility, quality of management, and quality of products/services. **Remarks:** Specific scores not provided. Also notes rank for previous year. **Number listed:** 5

1. FMC Technologies Inc.
2. Schlumberger Ltd.
3. National Oilwell Varco Inc.
4. Halliburton Co.
5. Cameron International Corp.

Source: *Fortune*, World's Most Admired Companies (annual), March 19, 2012, p. 149.

3925 ■ WORLD'S MOST VALUABLE OIL EQUIPMENT AND SERVICES COMPANIES, 2011

Ranked by: Market value as of March 2011, in millions of U.S. dollars. **Remarks:** Also notes rank within the *FT 500*, rank for previous year, country, revenue, net income, assets, number of employees, share price, price-to-earning ratio, dividend yield, and fiscal year-end. **Number listed:** 8

1. Schlumberger Ltd., with $126,818.6 million
2. Halliburton Co., $45,521.7
3. National Oilwell Varco Inc., $33,378.3
4. Baker Hughes Inc., $31,887.7
5. TransCanada Corp., $28,267.6
6. Transocean Inc., $25,182.7
7. Enbridge Energy Partners LP, $23,556.1
8. Saipem SpA, $23,488.9

Source: *Financial Times*, FT 500 (annual), http://www.ft.com, June 24, 2011.

Petroleum Industry

3926 ■ AMERICA'S LARGEST PRIVATE OIL AND GAS OPERATIONS COMPANIES, 2010

Ranked by: Revenue, in billions of dollars. **Remarks:** Also notes headquarters, number of employees, and overall rank in the *America's Largest Private Companies* list. Ranking is available online only, not in print. **Number listed:** 8

1. TransMontaigne Inc., with $12 billion
2. Sinclair Oil Co., $7
3. Mansfield Oil Co., Inc., $6.5
4. Colonial Group Inc., $5.2
5. Apex Oil Co., $4.26
6. Hunt Consolidated Inc./Hunt Oil Co., $4
7. Red Apple Group Inc., $3.8
8. Truman Arnold Cos., $2.6

Source: *Forbes*, America's Largest Private Companies (annual), http://www.forbes.com, December 5, 2011.

3927 ■ BEST SMALL OIL AND GAS OPERATIONS COMPANIES IN AMERICA, 2011

Ranked by: Score based on revenue, profits, and return on equity for the past 12 months and five years. **Remarks:** Specific scores not provided. Also notes rank in the overall *100 Best Small Companies in America*. To qualify, companies must have revenues between $5 million and $1 billion, a net margin above five percent, and share price above $5. List is available online only. **Number listed:** 2

1. Atwood Oceanics
2. GeoResources

Source: *Forbes*, Best Small Companies in America (annual), November 7, 2011.

3928 ■ CALIFORNIA'S LARGEST OIL AND GAS OPERATIONS COMPANIES OVERALL, 2011

Ranked by: Score based on revenue, profits, assets, and market capitalization. **Remarks:** Specific scores not provided. Also notes overall rank in the *Forbes 2000* and figures for each criterion. **Number listed:** 2

1. Chevron Corp.
2. Occidental Petroleum Corp.

Source: *Forbes*, Forbes 2000 (annual), http://www.forbes.com, May 7, 2012.

3929 ■ COLORADO'S LARGEST OIL AND GAS OPERATIONS COMPANIES OVERALL, 2011

Ranked by: Score based on revenue, profits, assets, and market capitalization. **Remarks:** Specific scores not provided. Also notes overall rank in the *Forbes 2000* and figures for each criterion. **Number listed:** 2

1. Cimarex Energy Co.
2. Whiting Petroleum Corp.

Source: *Forbes*, Forbes 2000 (annual), http://www.forbes.com, May 7, 2012.

3930 ■ LARGEST U.S. OIL AND GAS OPERATIONS COMPANIES OVERALL, 2011

Ranked by: Score based on revenue, profits, assets, and market capitalization. **Remarks:** Specific scores not provided. Also notes overall rank in the *Forbes 2000* and figures for each criterion. **Number listed:** 28

1. Exxon Mobil Corp.
2. Chevron Corp.
3. ConocoPhillips
4. Occidental Petroleum Corp.
5. Apache Corp.
6. Valero Energy Corp.
7. Hess Corp.
8. Devon Energy Corp.
9. Marathon Petroleum Corp.
10. Marathon Oil Corp.

Source: *Forbes*, Forbes 2000 (annual), http://www.forbes.com, May 7, 2012.

3931 ■ LARGEST U.S. PETROLEUM AND COAL PRODUCT MANUFACTURERS, 2010

Ranked by: Revenue, in millions of dollars. **Remarks:** Also notes overall rank within the *IW 500,* revenue growth, and profit margin. **Number listed:** 52

1. Exxon Mobil Corp., with $372,544 million
2. Chevron Corp., $199,291
3. ConocoPhillips, $195,522
4. Valero Energy Corp., $82,233
5. Marathon Oil Corp., $73,207
6. Sunoco Inc., $37,461
7. Hess Corp., $35,135
8. Enterprise Products Partners LP, $33,739
9. Murphy Oil Corp., $23,345
10. Tesoro Corp., $20,583

Source: *IndustryWeek*, IW 500 (annual), http://www.industryweek.com, July 2011.

3932 ■ MOST VALUABLE U.S. OIL AND GAS PRODUCERS, 2011

Ranked by: Market value as of March 2011, in millions of U.S. dollars. **Remarks:** Also notes rank within the *FT U.S. 500*, rank for previous year, country, revenue, net income, assets, number of employees, share price, price-to-earning ratio, dividend yield, and fiscal yearend. **Number listed:** 29

1. Exxon Mobil Corp., with $417,166.7 million
2. Chevron Corp., $215,780.6
3. ConocoPhillips, $114,171.6
4. Occidental Petroleum Corp., $84,936.8
5. Apache Corp., $50,109.9
6. Anadarko Petroleum Corp., $41,217.6
7. Devon Energy Corp., $39,185.8
8. Marathon Oil Corp., $37,898.3
9. EOG Resources Inc., $31,783.2

10. Hess Corp., $28,916.7

Source: *Financial Times*, FT 500 (annual), http://www.ft.com, June 24, 2011.

3933 ■ OKLAHOMA'S LARGEST OIL AND GAS OPERATIONS COMPANIES OVERALL, 2011

Ranked by: Score based on revenue, profits, assets, and market capitalization. **Remarks:** Specific scores not provided. Also notes overall rank in the *Forbes 2000* and figures for each criterion. **Number listed:** 3

1. Devon Energy Corp.
2. Chesapeake Energy Corp.
3. Continental Resources Inc.

Source: *Forbes*, Forbes 2000 (annual), http://www.forbes.com, May 7, 2012.

3934 ■ TEXAS'S LARGEST OIL AND GAS OPERATIONS COMPANIES OVERALL, 2011

Ranked by: Score based on revenue, profits, assets, and market capitalization. **Remarks:** Specific scores not provided. Also notes overall rank in the *Forbes 2000* and figures for each criterion. **Number listed:** 17

1. Exxon Mobil Corp.
2. ConocoPhillips
3. Apache Corp.
4. Valero Energy Corp.
5. Marathon Oil Corp.
6. EOG Resources Inc.
7. Anadarko Petroleum Corp.
8. Holly Corp.
9. Noble Energy Inc.
10. Pioneer Natural Resources Co.

Source: *Forbes*, Forbes 2000 (annual), http://www.forbes.com, May 7, 2012.

3935 ■ TOP *FORTUNE 500* COMPANIES IN MINING AND CRUDE OIL PRODUCTION, 2011

Ranked by: Revenue, in millions of dollars. **Remarks:** Also notes overall rank in the *Fortune 500;* profits; profits as a percentage of revenue; stockholders' equity; and rank by each criterion. **Number listed:** 13

1. Occidental Petroleum Corp., with $24,216 million
2. Freeport-McMoRan Copper & Gold Inc., $20,880
3. Apache Corp., $16,888
4. Marathon Oil Co., $15,282
5. Anadarko Petroleum Corp., $13,967
6. Chesapeake Energy Corp., $11,635
7. Devon Energy Corp., $11,497
8. Newmont Mining Corp., $10,358
9. EOG Resources Inc., $10,126
10. Peabody Energy Corp., $8,096

Source: *Fortune*, Fortune 500 (annual), May 21, 2012, p. F-37.

3936 ■ TOP U.S. OIL COMPANIES BY ASSETS, 2010

Ranked by: Total assets, in thousands of U.S. dollars. **Remarks:** Also notes rank for previous year, revenue, net income, stockholders' equity, capital and exploratory spending, worldwide and U.S. liquids production, worldwide and U.S. natural gas production, worldwide and U.S. liquids reserves, worldwide and U.S. natural gas reserves, net wells drilled in the U.S., and rank by each criterion. **Number listed:** 137

1. Exxon Mobil Corp., with $302,510,000 thousand
2. Chevron Corp., $184,769,000
3. ConocoPhillips, $156,314,000
4. Occidental Petroleum Corp., $52,432,000
5. Anadarko Petroleum Corp., $51,559,000
6. Marathon Oil Corp., $50,014,000
7. Apache Corp., $43,425,000
8. Chesapeake Energy Corp., $37,179,000
9. Hess Corp., $35,396,000
10. Devon Energy Corp., $32,927,000

Source: *Oil & Gas Journal*, OGJ 150 (annual), October 3, 2011, p. 38-39.

3937 ■ TOP U.S. OIL COMPANIES BY CAPITAL AND EXPLORATORY SPENDING, 2010

Ranked by: Capital and exploratory spending, in thousands of dollars. **Number listed:** 20

1. Exxon Mobil Corp., with $29,015,000 thousand
2. Chevron Corp., $19,612,000
3. ConocoPhillips, $9,761,000
4. Devon Energy Corp., $6,476,000
5. EOG Resources Inc., $5,581,382
6. Hess Corp., $5,492,000
7. Chesapeake Energy Corp., $5,242,000
8. Anadarko Petroleum Corp., $5,008,000
9. Marathon Oil Corp., $4,762,000
10. Apache Corp., $4,407,000

Source: *Oil & Gas Journal*, OGJ 150 (annual), October 3, 2011, p. 32.

3938 ■ TOP U.S. OIL COMPANIES BY NET INCOME, 2010

Ranked by: Net income, in thousands of dollars. **Number listed:** 20

1. Exxon Mobil Corp., with $31,398,000 thousand
2. Chevron Corp., $19,136,000
3. ConocoPhillips, $11,417,000
4. Occidental Petroleum Corp., $4,602,000
5. Devon Energy Corp., $4,550,000
6. Apache Corp., $3,032,000
7. Marathon Oil Corp., $2,568,000
8. Hess Corp., $2,138,000
9. Chesapeake Energy Corp., $1,774,000
10. Kinder Morgan CO2 Co. LP, $1,018,200

Source: *Oil & Gas Journal*, OGJ 150 (annual), October 3, 2011, p. 30.

3939 ■ TOP U.S. OIL COMPANIES BY RETURN ON ASSETS, 2010

Ranked by: Return on total assets, in percent. **Remarks:** Also notes overall rank in the *OGJ 150*. **Number listed:** 10

1. Houston American Energy Corp., with 37.9%
2. Dorchester Minerals LP, 22.8%
3. Wexpro, 20%

4. Reserve Petroleum Co., 18.4%

5. Gulfport Energy Corp., 14.8%

6. Apache Offshore Investment Partnership, 14.1%

7. Cimarex Energy Co., 13.2%

8. Ultra Petroleum, 12.9%

9. Quicksilver Resources Inc., 12.7%

9. Gasco Energy Inc., 12.7%

Source: *Oil & Gas Journal*, OGJ 150 (annual), October 3, 2011, p. 28.

3940 ■ TOP U.S. OIL COMPANIES BY RETURN ON REVENUE, 2010

Ranked by: Return on total revenue, in percent. **Remarks:** Also notes overall rank in the *OGJ 150*. **Number listed:** 10

1. Houston American Energy Corp., with 107.4%

2. EV Energy Partners LP, 61.8%

3. Belden & Blake Corp., 60.5%

4. Dorchester Minerals LP, 57.1%

5. Wexpro, 50.5%

6. Gasco Energy Inc., 49.9%

7. Quicksilver Resources Inc., 47.9%

8. Ultra Petroleum, 47.4%

9. EQT Production, 41.6%

10. Reserve Petroleum Co., 38%

Source: *Oil & Gas Journal*, OGJ 150 (annual), October 3, 2011, p. 28.

3941 ■ TOP U.S. OIL COMPANIES BY RETURN ON STOCKHOLDERS' EQUITY, 2010

Ranked by: Return on total stockholders' equity, in percent. **Remarks:** Also notes overall rank in the *OGJ 150*. **Number listed:** 10

1. RAM Energy Resources Inc., with 58%

2. Callon Petroleum Co., 53%

3. Quicksilver Resources Inc., 42%

4. Houston American Energy Corp., 41.8%

5. Ultra Petroleum, 40.8%

6. W & T Offshore Inc., 28%

7. Belden & Blake Corp., 27.1%

8. Gasco Energy Inc., 24.1%

9. Dorchester Minerals LP, 22.9%

10. PetroQuest Energy Inc., 22.6%

Source: *Oil & Gas Journal*, OGJ 150 (annual), October 3, 2011, p. 28.

3942 ■ TOP U.S. OIL COMPANIES BY REVENUE, 2010

Ranked by: Total revenue, in thousands of dollars. **Number listed:** 20

1. Exxon Mobil Corp., with $383,221,000 thousand

2. Chevron Corp., $204,928,000

3. ConocoPhillips, $198,655,000

4. Marathon Oil Corp., $73,621,000

5. Hess Corp., $34,613,000

6. Murphy Oil Corp., $23,345,071

7. Occidental Petroleum Corp., $19,157,000

8. Apache Corp., $12,092,000

9. Anadarko Petroleum Corp., $10,984,000

10. Devon Energy Corp., $9,940,00

Source: *Oil & Gas Journal*, OGJ 150 (annual), October 3, 2011, p. 28.

3943 ■ TOP U.S. OIL COMPANIES BY STOCKHOLDERS' EQUITY, 2010

Ranked by: Stockholders' equity, in thousands of dollars. **Number listed:** 20

1. Exxon Mobil Corp., with $152,679,000 thousand

2. Chevron Corp., $105,811,000

3. ConocoPhillips, $69,109,000

4. Occidental Petroleum Corp., $32,484,000

5. Apache Corp., $24,377,000

6. Marathon Oil Corp., $23,771,000

7. Anadarko Petroleum Corp., $21,439,000

8. Devon Energy Corp., $19,253,000

9. Hess Corp., $16,809,000

10. Chesapeake Energy Corp., $15,264,000

Source: *Oil & Gas Journal*, OGJ 150 (annual), October 3, 2011, p. 30.

3944 ■ TOP U.S. OIL COMPANIES BY U.S. LIQUIDS PRODUCTION, 2010

Ranked by: U.S. liquids production, in millions of barrels (bbl). **Number listed:** 20

1. Chevron Corp., with 178 million bbl

2. ConocoPhillips, 139

3. Exxon Mobil Corp., 123

4. Occidental Petroleum Corp., 99

5. Anadarko Petroleum Corp., 47

6. Devon Energy Corp., 44

7. Apache Corp., 40.3

8. EOG Resources Inc., 33.9

9. Hess Corp., 32

10. Marathon Oil Corp., 25

Source: *Oil & Gas Journal*, OGJ 150 (annual), October 3, 2011, p. 34.

3945 ■ TOP U.S. OIL COMPANIES BY WELLS DRILLED IN THE U.S., 2010

Ranked by: Net number of wells drilled in the U.S. **Number listed:** 20

1. Chesapeake Energy Corp., with 1,149 wells

2. Anadarko Petroleum Corp., 1,117

3. EOG Resources Inc., 895

4. Devon Energy Corp., 885.9

5. Chevron Corp., 672

6. The Williams Companies Inc., 661

7. Exxon Mobil Corp., 625

8. Sandridge Energy Inc., 481

9. Occidental Petroleum Corp., 535.6

10. Noble Energy Inc., 525

Source: *Oil & Gas Journal*, OGJ 150 (annual), October 3, 2011, p. 32.

3946 ■ TOP U.S. OIL COMPANIES BY WORLDWIDE LIQUIDS PRODUCTION, 2010

Ranked by: Worldwide liquids production, in millions of barrels (bbl). **Number listed:** 20

1. Exxon Mobil Corp., with 709 million bbl
2. Chevron Corp., 702
3. ConocoPhillips, 318
4. Occidental Petroleum Corp., 201
5. Apache Corp., 125.1
6. Hess Corp., 112
7. Marathon Oil Corp., 89
8. Anadarko Petroleum Corp., 73
8. Devon Energy Corp., 73
10. Murphy Oil Corp., 46.3

Source: *Oil & Gas Journal*, OGJ 150 (annual), October 3, 2011, p. 34.

3947 ■ THE UNITED STATES' MOST VALUABLE OIL AND GAS BRANDS, 2011

Ranked by: Brand value, in millions of U.S. dollars. **Remarks:** Also notes rank within the *Global 500* for current and previous year, figures for current and previous year, and brand rating. Ranking is available online only. **Number listed:** 4

1. Chevron, with $17,511 million
2. ExxonMobil, $16,419
3. ConocoPhillips, $6,690
4. Marathon, $2,405

Source: *Global 500*, (annual), Brand Finance plc, March 2012.

Petroleum Industry, Foreign

3948 ■ AFRICA'S LARGEST OIL AND GAS COMPANIES, 2010

Ranked by: Total assets, in millions of U.S. dollars. **Remarks:** Specific figures for most companies not provided; companies are listed alphabetically by country, not ranked. Also notes revenue, net income, capital and exploratory expenditures, worldwide oil and natural gas production, worldwide oil and natural gas reserves, and figures for previous year. **Number listed:** 7

1. Sasol Ltd. (S. Africa), with $20,402 million
2. Sonatrach (Algeria), $n/a
3. Sonangol (Angola), $n/a
4. Egyptian General Petroleum Corp. (Egypt), $n/a
5. National Oil Corp. (Libya), $n/a
6. L'Office National des Hydrocarbons & des Mines (ONHYM, Morocco), $n/a
7. Nigerian National Petroleum Corp. (Nigeria), $n/a

Source: *Oil & Gas Journal*, OGJ 100 (annual), October 3, 2011, p. 48-49.

3949 ■ ASIA PACIFIC'S LARGEST OIL AND GAS COMPANIES, 2010

Ranked by: Total assets, in millions of U.S. dollars. **Remarks:** Also notes country, revenue, net income, capital and exploratory expenditures, worldwide oil and natural gas production, worldwide oil and natural gas reserves, and figures for previous year. **Number listed:** 20

1. PetroChina Co., Ltd., with $198,749.4 million
2. Petroliam Nasional Berhad (Petronas), $125,691
3. BHP Billiton Petroleum Ltd., $88,852
4. China National Offshore Oil Corp., $48,041.2
5. Oil & Natural Gas Corp., Ltd., $32,659.5
6. Oil India Ltd., $32,464.7
7. Chinese Petroleum Corp., $22,579.1
8. Woodside Petroleum Ltd., $20,196
9. Santos Ltd., $14,099.5
10. PTT Exploration & Production Public Co., Ltd., $10,693.7

Source: *Oil & Gas Journal*, OGJ 100 (annual), October 3, 2011, p. 48-49.

3950 ■ AUSTRALIA'S LARGEST OIL AND GAS OPERATIONS COMPANIES OVERALL, 2011

Ranked by: Score based on revenue, profits, assets, and market capitalization. **Remarks:** Specific scores not provided. Also notes overall rank in the *Forbes 2000* and figures for each criterion. **Number listed:** 3

1. Woodside Petroleum
2. Santos
3. Caltex Australia

Source: *Forbes*, Forbes 2000 (annual), http://www.forbes.com, May 7, 2012.

3951 ■ BRAZIL'S LARGEST OIL AND GAS OPERATIONS COMPANIES OVERALL, 2011

Ranked by: Score based on revenue, profits, assets, and market capitalization. **Remarks:** Specific scores not provided. Also notes overall rank in the *Forbes 2000* and figures for each criterion. **Number listed:** 2

1. Petroleo Brasileiro SA (Petrobras)
2. OGX

Source: *Forbes*, Forbes 2000 (annual), http://www.forbes.com, May 7, 2012.

3952 ■ BRITAIN'S MOST ADMIRED OIL AND GAS EXTRACTION COMPANIES, 2011

Ranked by: Survey of peers and investment analysts based on nine criteria: quality of management, financial soundness, quality of goods/services, ability to attract and retain talent, value as long-term investment, innovation, marketing, community and environmental responsibility, and use of corporate assets. **Number listed:** 5

1. Royal Dutch Shell plc, with 70.2 points
2. BG Group plc, 67.1
3. Amec plc, 60.8
4. Petrofac, 60.7
5. Tullow Oil plc, 56.4

Source: *Management Today*, Britain's Most Admired Companies (annual), December 2011, p. 47.

3953 ■ CANADA'S LARGEST OIL AND GAS COMPANIES, 2010

Ranked by: Total assets, in millions of U.S. dollars. **Remarks:** Also notes revenue, net income, capital and exploratory expenditures, worldwide oil and natural gas production, worldwide oil and natural gas reserves, and figures for previous year. **Number listed:** 24

1. Suncor Energy Inc., with $70,519.5 million
2. Canadian Natural Resources Ltd., $42,882.3
3. EnCana Corp., $34,020
4. Husky Energy Inc., $29,278.7
5. Talisman Energy Inc., $24,314
6. Nexen Inc., $22,016.5
7. Imperial Oil Ltd., $20,682.9
8. Penn West Exploration, $13,434.8
9. Sherritt International Corp., $10,775.1
10. Canadian Oil Sands Ltd., $7,051.1

Source: *Oil & Gas Journal*, OGJ 100 (annual), October 3, 2011, p. 46-47.

3954 ■ CANADA'S LARGEST OIL AND GAS OPERATIONS COMPANIES OVERALL, 2011

Ranked by: Score based on revenue, profits, assets, and market capitalization. **Remarks:** Specific scores not provided. Also notes overall rank in the *Forbes 2000* and figures for each criterion. **Number listed:** 11

1. Suncor Energy Inc.
2. Canadian Natural Resources Ltd.
3. Husky Energy Inc.
4. Cenovus Energy
5. Talisman Energy
6. Nexen Inc.
7. EnCana Corp.
8. Penn West Petroleum Ltd.
9. Canadian Oil Sands Trust
10. Pacific Rubiales Energy Corp.

Source: *Forbes*, Forbes 2000 (annual), http://www.forbes.com, May 7, 2012.

3955 ■ CHINA'S LARGEST OIL AND GAS OPERATIONS COMPANIES OVERALL, 2011

Ranked by: Score based on revenue, profits, assets, and market capitalization. **Remarks:** Specific scores not provided. Also notes overall rank in the *Forbes 2000* and figures for each criterion. **Number listed:** 2

1. PetroChina Co., Ltd.
2. China Petroleum & Chemical Corp. (Sinopec)

Source: *Forbes*, Forbes 2000 (annual), http://www.forbes.com, May 7, 2012.

3956 ■ CHINA'S MOST VALUABLE OIL AND GAS BRANDS, 2011

Ranked by: Brand value, in millions of U.S. dollars. **Remarks:** Also notes rank within the *Global 500* for current and previous year, figures for current and previous year, and brand rating. Ranking is available online only. **Number listed:** 3

1. PetroChina, with $10,491 million
2. Sinopec, $8,127
3. SPC, $3,729

Source: *Global 500*, (annual), Brand Finance plc, March 2012.

3957 ■ EUROPE'S MOST VALUABLE OIL AND GAS PRODUCERS, 2011

Ranked by: Market value as of March 2011, in millions of U.S. dollars. **Remarks:** Also notes rank within the *FT Europe 500*, rank for previous year, country, revenue, net income, assets, number of

employees, share price, price-to-earning ratio, dividend yield, and fiscal yearend. **Number listed:** 27

1. Royal Dutch Shell plc, with $228,128.7 million
2. OAO Gazprom, $190,829.1
3. Total SA, $143,227.1
4. BP plc, $136,848
5. ENI SpA, $98,502.9
6. OAO Rosneft Oil Co., $96,953.5
7. StatoilHydro ASA, $88,366.3
8. BG Group plc, $84,230
9. OAO Lukoil, $60,835.3
10. OJSC Surgutneftegas, $43,418.2

Source: *Financial Times*, FT 500 (annual), http://www.ft.com, June 24, 2011.

3958 ■ INDIA'S LARGEST OIL AND GAS OPERATIONS COMPANIES OVERALL, 2011

Ranked by: Score based on revenue, profits, assets, and market capitalization. **Remarks:** Specific scores not provided. Also notes overall rank in the *Forbes 2000* and figures for each criterion. **Number listed:** 7

1. Reliance Industries Ltd.
2. Oil & Natural Gas Corp., Ltd.
3. Indian Oil Corp.
4. Bharat Petroleum Corp.
5. Hindustan Petroleum Corp.
6. Oil India
7. Essar Oil

Source: *Forbes*, Forbes 2000 (annual), http://www.forbes.com, May 7, 2012.

3959 ■ INDIA'S MOST VALUABLE OIL AND GAS BRANDS, 2011

Ranked by: Brand value, in millions of U.S. dollars. **Remarks:** Also notes rank within the *Global 500* for current and previous year, figures for current and previous year, and brand rating. Ranking is available online only. **Number listed:** 2

1. Reliance, with $4,367 million
2. Indian Oil, $3,666

Source: *Global 500*, (annual), Brand Finance plc, March 2012.

3960 ■ ITALY'S LARGEST OIL AND GAS OPERATIONS COMPANIES OVERALL, 2011

Ranked by: Score based on revenue, profits, assets, and market capitalization. **Remarks:** Specific scores not provided. Also notes overall rank in the *Forbes 2000* and figures for each criterion. **Number listed:** 2

1. ENI SpA
2. Saras

Source: *Forbes*, Forbes 2000 (annual), http://www.forbes.com, May 7, 2012.

3961 ■ JAPAN'S LARGEST OIL AND GAS OPERATIONS COMPANIES OVERALL, 2011

Ranked by: Score based on revenue, profits, assets, and market capitalization. **Remarks:** Specific scores not provided. Also notes overall rank in the *Forbes 2000* and figures for each criterion. **Number listed:** 6

1. JX Holdings Inc.

2. Inpex
3. Idemitsu Kosan
4. Cosmo Oil
5. Showa Shell Sekiyu
6. San-Ai Oil

Source: *Forbes*, Forbes 2000 (annual), http://www.forbes.com, May 7, 2012.

3962 ■ LARGEST AGRICULTURE, MINING, AND PETROLEUM COMPANIES IN EUROPE, 2010

Ranked by: Sales, in millions of U.S. dollars. **Remarks:** Also notes rank within country. **Number listed:** 100

1. BP plc (U.K.), with $358,908 million
2. Royal Dutch Shell plc (Netherlands), $278,190
3. BHP Billiton plc (U.K.), $79,197
4. Rio Tinto plc (U.K.), $62,737.5
5. Statoil ASA (Norway), $60,024.4
6. ENI SpA (Italy), $48,798.6
7. Total Raffinage Marketing (France), $45,114.1
8. Centrica Resources Petroleum UK Ltd. (U.K.), $44,950.1
9. Shell Deutschland Oil GmbH (Germany), $43,383.1
10. ConocoPhillips (U.K.) Ltd. (U.K.), $34,232.7

Source: *Europe's 15,000 Largest Companies*, (annual), ELC International, 2011, p. 35.

3963 ■ LARGEST OIL COMPANIES OUTSIDE THE U.S. BY PRODUCTION, 2010

Ranked by: Production, in millions of barrels (bbl). **Number listed:** 20

1. Saudi Arabian Oil Co. (Aramco), with 2,920 million bbl
2. National Iranian Oil Co., 1,350.5
3. Petroleos Mexicanos (PEMEX), 957
4. BP plc, 866
5. Iraq National Oil Co., 861.4
6. PetroChina Co., Ltd., 858
7. OAO Rosneft Oil Co., 847.4
8. Petroleos de Venezuela SA (PDVSA), 814
9. Abu Dhabi National Oil Co., 789.1
10. Petroleo Brasileiro SA (Petrobras), 783.3

Source: *Oil & Gas Journal*, OGJ 100 (annual), October 3, 2011, p. 44.

3964 ■ LARGEST OIL AND GAS COMPANIES IN EUROPE, 2010

Ranked by: Total assets, in millions of U.S. dollars. **Remarks:** Also notes country, revenue, net income, capital and exploratory expenditures, worldwide oil and natural gas production, worldwide oil and natural gas reserves, and figures for previous year. **Number listed:** 28

1. OAO Gazprom, with $349,349.9 million
2. Royal Dutch Shell plc, $322,560
3. BP plc, $272,262
4. Total SA, $192,036
5. ENI SpA, $176,586.9
6. Statoil, $110,404.5

7. OAO Rosneft Oil Co., $93,829
8. Repsol YPF, SA, $90,571.4
9. OAO Lukoil, $84,017
10. BG Group plc, $78,456.4

Source: *Oil & Gas Journal*, OGJ 100 (annual), October 3, 2011, p. 46-49.

3965 ■ LATIN AMERICA'S LARGEST OIL AND GAS COMPANIES, 2010

Ranked by: Total assets, in millions of U.S. dollars. **Remarks:** Also notes country, revenue, net income, capital and exploratory expenditures, worldwide oil and natural gas production, worldwide oil and natural gas reserves, and figures for previous year. **Number listed:** 11

1. Petroleo Brasileiro SA (Petrobras), with $308,683 million
2. Petroleos Mexicanos (PEMEX), $112,706
3. Empresa Colombiana de Petroleos SA (Ecopetrol SA), $34,384.7
4. Techint Tecpetrol SA, $28,039
5. YPF SA, $13,506
6. State Oil Co. Suriname Ltd., $814.1
7. Barbados National Oil Co. Ltd., $151.4
8. Petroleos del Ecuador, $n/a
8. Petroleos de Venezuela SA (PDVSA), $n/a
8. Cubapetroleo, $n/a
8. Petroleum Co. of Trinidad & Tobago Ltd., $n/a

Source: *Oil & Gas Journal*, OGJ 100 (annual), October 3, 2011, p. 46-47.

3966 ■ THE MIDDLE EAST'S LARGEST OIL AND GAS COMPANIES, 2010

Ranked by: Total assets, in millions of U.S. dollars. **Remarks:** Specific figures not provided; companies are listed alphabetically by country, not ranked. Also notes revenue, net income, capital and exploratory expenditures, worldwide oil and natural gas production, worldwide oil and natural gas reserves, and figures for previous year. **Number listed:** 10

1. Abu Dhabi National Oil Co. (Abu Dhabi)
2. Bahrain National Oil Co. (Bahrain)
3. Dubai Petroleum Co. (Dubai)
4. National Iranian Oil Co. (Iran)
5. Iraq National Oil Co. (Iraq)
6. Ministry of Energy & Infrastructure (Israel)
7. Kuwait Petroleum Corp. (Kuwait)
8. Petroleum Development Oman LLC (Oman)
9. Qatar Petroleum Corp. (Qatar)
10. Saudi Arabian Oil Co. (Aramco, Saudi Arabia)

Source: *Oil & Gas Journal*, OGJ 100 (annual), October 3, 2011, p. 48-49.

3967 ■ POLAND'S LARGEST OIL AND GAS OPERATIONS COMPANIES OVERALL, 2011

Ranked by: Score based on revenue, profits, assets, and market capitalization. **Remarks:** Specific scores not provided. Also notes overall rank in the *Forbes 2000* and figures for each criterion. **Number listed:** 2

1. Polski Koncern Naftowy Orlen SA (PKN Orlen)
2. Polskie Gornictwo Naftowe i Gazownictwo SA (PGNiG SA)

Source: *Forbes*, Forbes 2000 (annual), http://www.forbes.com, May 7, 2012.

3968 ■ THE RUSSIAN FEDERATION'S MOST VALUABLE OIL AND GAS BRANDS, 2011

Ranked by: Brand value, in millions of U.S. dollars. **Remarks:** Also notes rank within the *Global 500* for current and previous year, figures for current and previous year, and brand rating. Ranking is available online only. **Number listed:** 3

1. Gazprom, with $6,407 million
2. Lukoil, $3,809
3. Rosneft, $3,324

Source: *Global 500*, (annual), Brand Finance plc, March 2012.

3969 ■ RUSSIA'S LARGEST OIL AND GAS OPERATIONS COMPANIES OVERALL, 2011

Ranked by: Score based on revenue, profits, assets, and market capitalization. **Remarks:** Specific scores not provided. Also notes overall rank in the *Forbes 2000* and figures for each criterion. **Number listed:** 7

1. OAO Gazprom
2. OAO Lukoil
3. OAO Rosneft Oil Co.
4. TNK-BP Holding
5. Surgutneftegas
6. OAO Tatneft
7. Novatek

Source: *Forbes*, Forbes 2000 (annual), http://www.forbes.com, May 7, 2012.

3970 ■ SOUTH KOREA'S LARGEST OIL AND GAS OPERATIONS COMPANIES OVERALL, 2011

Ranked by: Score based on revenue, profits, assets, and market capitalization. **Remarks:** Specific scores not provided. Also notes overall rank in the *Forbes 2000* and figures for each criterion. **Number listed:** 4

1. SK Innovation
2. SK Holdings
3. S-Oil
4. GS Holdings

Source: *Forbes*, Forbes 2000 (annual), http://www.forbes.com, May 7, 2012.

3971 ■ SWITZERLAND'S LARGEST OIL SERVICES AND EQUIPMENT COMPANIES OVERALL, 2011

Ranked by: Score based on revenue, profits, assets, and market capitalization. **Remarks:** Specific scores not provided. Also notes overall rank in the *Forbes 2000* and figures for each criterion. **Number listed:** 3

1. Transocean Inc.
2. Weatherford International Ltd.
3. Noble Corp.

Source: *Forbes*, Forbes 2000 (annual), http://www.forbes.com, May 7, 2012.

3972 ■ THAILAND'S LARGEST OIL AND GAS OPERATIONS COMPANIES OVERALL, 2011

Ranked by: Score based on revenue, profits, assets, and market capitalization. **Remarks:** Specific scores not provided. Also notes overall rank in the *Forbes 2000* and figures for each criterion. **Number listed:** 2

1. PTT Public Co., Ltd.

2. Thai Oil Public Co., Ltd.

Source: *Forbes*, Forbes 2000 (annual), http://www.forbes.com, May 7, 2012.

3973 ■ TOP CANADIAN OIL AND GAS COMPANIES, 2010

Ranked by: Revenue, in thousands of Canadian dollars (unless otherwise noted). **Remarks:** Also notes percent change from previous year. **Number listed:** 10

1. Suncor Energy Inc., with C$36,820,000 thousand
2. Imperial Oil Ltd., C$25,092,000
3. Husky Energy Inc., C$18,261,000
4. Canadian Natural Resources Ltd., C$14,625,000
5. Cenovus Energy, C$13,621,000
6. Syncrude Canada, C$9,390,000
7. EnCana Corp. (U.S. dollars), C$9,097,000
8. Ultramar Ltd., C$8,411,012
9. Talisman Energy Inc., C$8,347,000
10. ConocoPhillips Canada Resource (U.S. dollars), C$5,841,000

Source: *Report on Business Magazine*, Top 1000 Companies (annual), http://www.reportonbusiness.com, June 2011.

3974 ■ UNITED KINGDOM'S LARGEST OIL AND GAS OPERATIONS COMPANIES OVERALL, 2011

Ranked by: Score based on revenue, profits, assets, and market capitalization. **Remarks:** Specific scores not provided. Also notes overall rank in the *Forbes 2000* and figures for each criterion. **Number listed:** 5

1. BP plc
2. BG Group plc
3. Tullow Oil plc
4. Essar Energy plc
5. Cairn Energy plc

Source: *Forbes*, Forbes 2000 (annual), http://www.forbes.com, May 7, 2012.

Petroleum Industry, International

3975 ■ TOP ENERGY EXPLORATION AND PRODUCTION COMPANIES, 2010

Ranked by: Score based on asset worth, revenue, profits, earnings per share, and return on invested capital. **Remarks:** Specific scores not provided. Also notes rank in the overall *Top 250*. **Number listed:** 28

1. CNOOC Ltd.
2. Oil & Natural Gas Corp., Ltd.
3. Apache Corp.
4. Devon Energy Corp.
5. OAO Tatneft
6. Bashneft OJSC
7. Chesapeake Energy Corp.
8. Canadian Natural Resources Ltd.
9. Inpex Holdings Inc.
10. EnCana Corp.

Source: *Platts*, Top 250 Global Energy Company Rankings (annual), http://www.platts.com/top250, November 2, 2011.

3976 ■ TOP INTEGRATED OIL AND GAS COMPANIES, 2010

Ranked by: Score based on asset worth, revenue, profits, earnings per share, and return on invested capital. **Remarks:** Specific scores not provided. Also notes rank in the overall *Top 250*. **Number listed:** 38

1. Exxon Mobil Corp.
2. Chevron Corp.
3. OAO Gazprom
4. PetroChina Co., Ltd.
5. Total SA
6. Royal Dutch Shell plc
7. ConocoPhillips
8. China Petroleum & Chemical Corp. (Sinopec)
9. OJSC Rosneft
10. OAO Lukoil

Source: *Platts*, Top 250 Global Energy Company Rankings (annual), http://www.platts.com/top250, November 2, 2011.

3977 ■ TOP PETROLEUM STORAGE AND TRANSFER COMPANIES, 2010

Ranked by: Score based on asset worth, revenue, profits, earnings per share, and return on invested capital. **Remarks:** Specific scores not provided. Also notes rank in the overall *Top 250*. **Number listed:** 11

1. AK Transneft OAO
2. Enbridge Inc.
3. TransCanada Corp.
4. Spectra Energy Corp.
5. Plains All American Pipeline LP
6. Ultrapar Participacoes SA
7. El Paso Corp.
8. Energy Transfer Partners LP
9. ONEOK Partners LP
10. Kinder Morgan Inc.

Source: *Platts*, Top 250 Global Energy Company Rankings (annual), http://www.platts.com/top250, November 2, 2011.

3978 ■ WORLD'S LARGEST OIL AND GAS OPERATIONS COMPANIES OVERALL, 2011

Ranked by: Score based on revenue, profits, assets, and market capitalization. **Remarks:** Specific scores not provided. Also notes country, overall rank in the *Forbes 2000,* and figures for each criterion. **Number listed:** 101

1. Exxon Mobil Corp.
2. Royal Dutch Shell plc
3. PetroChina Co., Ltd.
4. Petroleo Brasileiro SA (Petrobras)
5. BP plc
6. Chevron Corp.
7. OAO Gazprom
8. Total SA
8. China Petroleum & Chemical Corp. (Sinopec)
10. ConocoPhillips

Source: *Forbes*, Forbes 2000 (annual), http://www.forbes.com, May 7, 2012.

3979 ■ WORLD'S MOST ADMIRED MINING AND CRUDE OIL PRODUCTION COMPANIES, 2012

Ranked by: Score, on a scale of 10, based on a survey of executives, directors, and securities analysts of companies within their own industry on eight criteria: innovation, financial soundness, employee talent, use of corporate assets, long-term investment value, social responsibility, quality of management, and quality of products/services. **Remarks:** Specific scores not provided. Also notes rank for previous year. **Number listed:** 8

1. Occidental Petroleum Corp.
2. Apache Corp.
3. Devon Energy Corp.
4. BHP Billiton Ltd.
5. Oil & Natural Gas Corp., Ltd.
6. China National Offshore Oil Corp.
7. EnCana Corp.
8. BG Group plc

Source: *Fortune*, World's Most Admired Companies (annual), March 19, 2012, p. 149.

3980 ■ WORLD'S MOST ETHICAL OIL COMPANIES, 2012

Ranked by: Score based on five criteria: ethics and compliance program; reputation, leadership, and innovation; governance; corporate citizenship and responsibility; and culture of ethics. **Remarks:** Specific scores not provided; companies are listed alphabetically, not ranked. **Number listed:** 2

1. Alyeska Pipeline Service Co. (U.S.)
2. Statoil (Norway)

Source: *Ethisphere Magazine*, World's Most Ethical Companies (annual), http://www.ethisphere.com, 2012.

3981 ■ WORLD'S MOST VALUABLE OIL AND GAS BRANDS, 2011

Ranked by: Brand value, in millions of U.S. dollars. **Remarks:** Also notes rank within the *Global 500* for current and previous year, figures for current and previous year, country, and brand rating. Ranking is available online only. **Number listed:** 21

1. Shell, with $22,021 million
2. Chevron, $17,511
3. ExxonMobil, $16,419
4. Total, $12,968
5. PetroChina, $10,491
6. BP, $10,222
7. Sinopec, $8,127
8. ConocoPhillips, $6,690
9. Gazprom, $6,407
10. Eni, $6,295

Source: *Global 500*, (annual), Brand Finance plc, March 2012.

3982 ■ WORLD'S MOST VALUABLE OIL AND GAS BRANDS, 2012

Ranked by: Brand value, a measure of a brand's earnings and contribution, in millions of U.S. dollars. **Remarks:** Also notes rank by brand contribution and brand momentum. **Number listed:** 10

1. Exxon Mobil, with $18,315 million
2. Shell, $17,781
3. Sinopec, $13,940
4. PetroChina, $12,105
5. Petrobras, $10,560
6. BP, $10,424
7. Chevron, $8,599
8. Gazprom, $6,698
9. ConocoPhillips, $6,012

10. Total, $5,653

Source: *Financial Times*, Global Brands (annual), http://www.ft.com, May 22, 2012.

3983 ■ WORLD'S MOST VALUABLE OIL AND GAS PRODUCERS, 2011

Ranked by: Market value as of March 2011, in millions of U.S. dollars. **Remarks:** Also notes rank within the *FT 500*, rank for previous year, country, revenue, net income, assets, number of employees, share price, price-to-earning ratio, dividend yield, and fiscal year-end. **Number listed:** 46

1. Exxon Mobil Corp., with $417,166.7 million
2. PetroChina Co., Ltd., $326,199.2
3. Petroleo Brasileiro SA (Petrobras), $247,417.6
4. Royal Dutch Shell plc, $228,128.7
5. Chevron Corp., $215,780.6
6. OAO Gazprom, $190,829.1
7. Total SA, $143,227.1
8. BP plc, $136,848
9. ConocoPhillips, $114,171.6
10. CNOOC Ltd., $112,560.2

Source: *Financial Times*, FT 500 (annual), http://www.ft.com, June 24, 2011.

Petroleum Pipelines
See also: **Pipeline Companies**

3984 ■ TOP *FORTUNE 500* COMPANIES IN PIPELINES, 2011

Ranked by: Revenue, in millions of dollars. **Remarks:** Also notes overall rank in the *Fortune 500;* profits; profits as a percentage of revenue; stockholders' equity; and rank by each criterion. **Number listed:** 10

1. Enterprise Products Partners LP, with $44,313 million
2. Plains All American Pipeline LP, $34,275
3. ONEOK Partners LP, $15,119
4. Enbridge Energy Partners LP, $9,110
5. Kinder Morgan Inc., $8,265
6. Energy Transfer Equity LP, $8,241
7. Targa Resources Partners LP, $6,995
8. NuStar Energy LP, $6,575
9. Spectra Energy Corp., $5,602
10. El Paso Corp., $4,860

Source: *Fortune*, Fortune 500 (annual), May 21, 2012, p. F-38.

Petroleum Refineries

3985 ■ LARGEST PETROLEUM REFINING COMPANIES BY EMPLOYEES, 2010

Ranked by: Total number of employees. **Remarks:** Also notes contact information for headquarters, number of employees at headquarters, revenue, rank by revenue, and primary SIC code. **Number listed:** 50

1. Exxon Mobil Corp., with 106,035 employees
2. Koch Industries Inc., 70,000
3. Chevron Corp., 62,000

4. ConocoPhillips, 30,000
5. Shell Petroleum Inc., 26,888
6. BP America Inc., 22,800
7. BP Corp. North America Inc., 22,000
8. Valero Energy Corp., 20,920
9. ConocoPhillips Holding Co., 20,000
10. Carlisle Companies Inc., 10,953

Source: *Business Rankings*, (annual), Dun & Bradstreet Inc., 2011, p. VI.65-VI.66.

3986 ■ LARGEST PETROLEUM REFINING COMPANIES BY SALES, 2010

Ranked by: Total revenue, in dollars. **Remarks:** Also notes contact information for headquarters, number of employees at headquarters and overall, rank by employees, and primary SIC code. **Number listed:** 49

1. Chevron Corp., with $204,928,000,000
2. ConocoPhillips, $198,655,000,000
3. BP America Inc., $83,982,000,000
4. Valero Energy Corp., $82,233,000,000
5. Murphy Oil USA Inc., $13,292,055,000
6. Holly Corp., $8,322,929,000
7. Western Refining Inc., $7,965,053,000
8. Sinclair Cos., $7,753,458,000
9. Frontier Oil Corp., $5,884,906,000
10. Chalmette Refining LLC, $5,647,787,000

Source: *Business Rankings*, (annual), Dun & Bradstreet Inc., 2011, p. V.65-V.66.

3987 ■ TOP *FORTUNE 500* COMPANIES IN PETROLEUM REFINING, 2011

Ranked by: Revenue, in millions of dollars. **Remarks:** Also notes overall rank in the *Fortune 500;* profits; profits as a percentage of revenue; stockholders' equity; and rank by each criterion. **Number listed:** 12

1. Exxon Mobil Corp., with $452,926 million
2. Chevron Corp., $245,621
3. ConocoPhillips, $237,272
4. Valero Energy Corp., $125,095
5. Marathon Petroleum, $73,645
6. Sunoco Inc., $45,765
7. Hess Corp., $37,871
8. Murphy Oil Corp., $31,446
9. Tesoro Corp., $29,927
10. HollyFrontier, $15,440

Source: *Fortune*, Fortune 500 (annual), May 21, 2012, p. F-38.

3988 ■ TOP PETROLEUM REFINING AND MARKETING COMPANIES, 2010

Ranked by: Score based on asset worth, revenue, profits, earnings per share, and return on invested capital. **Remarks:** Specific scores not provided. Also notes rank in the overall *Top 250*. **Number listed:** 26

1. JX Holdings Inc.
2. Reliance Industries Ltd.
3. Indian Oil Corp.
4. Formosa Petrochemical Corp.
5. SK Innovation

6. Valero Energy Corp.

7. Idemitsu

8. Polski Koncern Naftowy Orlen SA (PKN Orlen)

9. Tonen General Sekiyu

10. S-Oil Corp.

Source: *Platts*, Top 250 Global Energy Company Rankings (annual), http://www.platts.com/top250, November 2, 2011.

3989 ■ WORLD'S MOST ADMIRED PETROLEUM REFINING COMPANIES, 2012

Ranked by: Score, on a scale of 10, based on a survey of executives, directors, and securities analysts of companies within their own industry on eight criteria: innovation, financial soundness, employee talent, use of corporate assets, long-term investment value, social responsibility, quality of management, and quality of products/services. **Remarks:** Specific scores not provided. Also notes rank for previous year. **Number listed:** 8

1. Chevron Corp.

2. Exxon Mobil Corp.

3. Royal Dutch Shell plc

4. Statoil ASA

5. Petroleo Brasileiro SA (Petrobras)

6. Total SA

7. Valero Energy Corp.

8. ENI SpA

Source: *Fortune*, World's Most Admired Companies (annual), March 19, 2012, p. 149.

Petroleum—Reserves

3990 ■ LARGEST OIL COMPANIES OUTSIDE THE U.S. BY RESERVES, 2010

Ranked by: Reserves, in millions of barrels (bbl). **Number listed:** 20

1. Saudi Arabian Oil Co. (Aramco), with 260,100 million bbl

2. Petroleos de Venezuela SA (PDVSA), 211,170

3. National Iranian Oil Co., 137,010

4. Iraq National Oil Co., 115,000

5. Kuwait Petroleum Corp., 101,500

6. Abu Dhabi National Oil Co., 92,200

7. National Oil Corp. (Libya), 46,420

8. Nigerian National Petroleum Corp., 37,200

9. Qatar Petroleum Corp., 25,380

10. OAO Rosneft Oil Co., 18,110

Source: *Oil & Gas Journal*, OGJ 100 (annual), October 3, 2011, p. 44.

3991 ■ TOP U.S. OIL COMPANIES BY U.S. GAS RESERVES, 2010

Ranked by: U.S. gas reserves, in billions of cubic feet (bcf). **Number listed:** 20

1. Exxon Mobil Corp., with 25,994 bcf

2. Chesapeake Energy Corp., 11,327

3. ConocoPhillips, 10,479

4. Devon Energy Corp., 9,065

5. Anadarko Petroleum Corp., 8,117

6. EOG Resources Inc., 6,491.5

7. EQT Production, 5,205.7

8. Southwestern Energy Co., 4,930

9. The Williams Companies Inc., 4,272

10. Ultra Petroleum Corp., 4,200.2

Source: *Oil & Gas Journal*, OGJ 150 (annual), October 3, 2011, p. 36.

3992 ■ TOP U.S. OIL COMPANIES BY U.S. LIQUIDS RESERVES, 2010

Ranked by: U.S. liquids reserves, in millions of barrels (bbl). **Number listed:** 20

1. Exxon Mobil Corp., with 1,952 million bbl

2. ConocoPhillips, 1,934

3. Occidental Petroleum Corp., 1,697

4. Chevron Corp., 1,275

5. Apache Corp., 759

6. Devon Energy Corp., 597

7. Pioneer Natural Resources Co., 544.9

8. EOG Resources Inc., 505.9

9. Anadarko Petroleum Corp., 498

10. Denbury Resources Inc., 338.3

Source: *Oil & Gas Journal*, OGJ 150 (annual), October 3, 2011, p. 32.

3993 ■ TOP U.S. OIL COMPANIES BY WORLDWIDE GAS RESERVES, 2010

Ranked by: Worldwide gas reserves, in billions of cubic feet (bcf). **Number listed:** 20

1. Exxon Mobil Corp., with 46,813 bcf

2. Chevron Corp., 24,251

3. ConocoPhillips, 18,235

4. Chesapeake Energy Corp., 11,327

5. Devon Energy Corp., 10,283

6. Apache Corp., 9,867.2

7. EOG Resources Inc., 8,470.2

8. Anadarko Petroleum Corp., 8,117

9. Occidental Petroleum Corp., 5,320

10. EQT Production, 5,205.7

Source: *Oil & Gas Journal*, OGJ 150 (annual), October 3, 2011, p. 36.

3994 ■ TOP U.S. OIL COMPANIES BY WORLDWIDE LIQUIDS RESERVES, 2010

Ranked by: Worldwide liquids reserves, in millions of barrels (bbl). **Number listed:** 20

1. Exxon Mobil Corp., with 9,418 million bbl

2. Chevron Corp., 6,503

3. ConocoPhillips, 3,616

4. Occidental Petroleum Corp., 2,476

5. Apache Corp., 1,308.7

6. Devon Energy Corp., 1,160

7. Hess Corp., 1,104

8. Anadarko Petroleum Corp., 749

9. Marathon Oil Corp., 630

10. Pioneer Natural Resources Co., 565

Source: *Oil & Gas Journal*, OGJ 150 (annual), October 3, 2011, p. 32.

Pets

3995 ■ TOP PET SERVICES FRANCHISES, 2012

Ranked by: Cumulative score based on financial strength and stability, growth rate, size of the system, number of years in business, the length of time franchising, start-up costs, litigation, percentage of terminations, and whether the company provides financing. **Remarks:** Specific scores not provided. Also notes overall rank within the *Franchise 500,* contact information, description, year founded, year started franchising, states where registered, available U.S. regions, where seeking foreign expansion, number of franchised and company-owned units for past three years, start-up costs, franchise fees, royalty fees, and type of financing available. **Number listed:** 4

1. Aussie Pet Mobile
2. Sit Means Sit Dog Training
3. Camp Bow Wow/Home Buddies
4. Snaggle Foot Dog Walks & Pet Care

Source: *Entrepreneur*, Franchise 500 (annual), January 2012, p. 196-197.

Pharmaceutical Industry
See also: **Drugs**

3996 ■ BEST SMALL DRUG AND BIOTECHNOLOGY COMPANIES IN AMERICA, 2011

Ranked by: Score based on revenue, profits, and return on equity for the past 12 months and five years. **Remarks:** Specific scores not provided. Also notes rank in the overall *100 Best Small Companies in America*. To qualify, companies must have revenues between $5 million and $1 billion, a net margin above five percent, and share price above $5. List is available online only. **Number listed:** 3

1. Questcor Pharmaceuticals
2. Medifast
3. Emergent Biosolutions

Source: *Forbes*, Best Small Companies in America (annual), November 7, 2011.

3997 ■ CALIFORNIA'S LARGEST PHARMACEUTICAL COMPANIES OVERALL, 2011

Ranked by: Score based on revenue, profits, assets, and market capitalization. **Remarks:** Specific scores not provided. Also notes overall rank in the *Forbes 2000* and figures for each criterion. **Number listed:** 2

1. McKesson Corp.
2. Allergan Inc.

Source: *Forbes*, Forbes 2000 (annual), http://www.forbes.com, May 7, 2012.

3998 ■ LARGEST U.S. PHARMACEUTICAL COMPANIES OVERALL, 2011

Ranked by: Score based on revenue, profits, assets, and market capitalization. **Remarks:** Specific scores not provided. Also notes overall rank in the *Forbes 2000* and figures for each criterion. **Number listed:** 13

1. Pfizer Inc.
2. Merck & Co., Inc.
3. Abbott Laboratories Inc.
4. Eli Lilly & Co.

5. Bristol-Myers Squibb Co.
6. McKesson Corp.
7. Cardinal Health Inc.
8. AmerisourceBergen Corp.
9. Allergan Inc.
10. Mylan Inc.

Source: *Forbes*, Forbes 2000 (annual), http://www.forbes.com, May 7, 2012.

3999 ■ LARGEST U.S. PHARMACEUTICAL PRODUCT MANUFACTURERS, 2010

Ranked by: Revenue, in millions of dollars. **Remarks:** Also notes overall rank within the *IW 500*, revenue growth, and profit margin. **Number listed:** 19

1. Pfizer Inc., with $67,809 million
2. Johnson & Johnson, $61,587
3. Merck & Co., Inc., $45,987
4. Abbott Laboratories Inc., $35,167
5. Eli Lilly & Co., $23,076
6. Bristol-Myers Squibb Co., $19,484
7. Amgen Inc., $15,053
8. Gilead Sciences Inc., $7,949
9. Allergan Inc., $4,919
10. Forest Laboratories Inc., $4,193

Source: *IndustryWeek*, IW 500 (annual), http://www.industryweek.com, July 2011.

4000 ■ MOST VALUABLE U.S. PHARMACEUTICALS AND BIOTECHNOLOGY COMPANIES, 2011

Ranked by: Market value as of March 2011, in millions of U.S. dollars. **Remarks:** Also notes rank within the *FT U.S. 500*, rank for previous year, country, revenue, net income, assets, number of employees, share price, price-to-earning ratio, dividend yield, and fiscal yearend. **Number listed:** 23

1. Johnson & Johnson, with $162,361.8 million
2. Pfizer Inc., $162,301.4
3. Merck & Co., Inc., $101,772.4
4. Abbott Laboratories Inc., $75,908.8
5. Amgen Inc., $49,839.6
6. Bristol-Myers Squibb Co., $45,054.7
7. Eli Lilly & Co., $40,715.1
8. Gilead Sciences Inc., $33,677.5
9. Celgene Corp., $25,766.6
10. Allergan Inc., $21,714.6

Source: *Financial Times*, FT 500 (annual), http://www.ft.com, June 24, 2011.

4001 ■ NEW JERSEY'S LARGEST PHARMACEUTICAL COMPANIES OVERALL, 2011

Ranked by: Score based on revenue, profits, assets, and market capitalization. **Remarks:** Specific scores not provided. Also notes overall rank in the *Forbes 2000* and figures for each criterion. **Number listed:** 2

1. Merck & Co., Inc.
2. Watson Pharmaceuticals

Source: *Forbes*, Forbes 2000 (annual), http://www.forbes.com, May 7, 2012.

4002 ■ NEW YORK'S LARGEST PHARMACEUTICAL COMPANIES OVERALL, 2011

Ranked by: Score based on revenue, profits, assets, and market capitalization. **Remarks:** Specific scores not provided. Also notes overall rank in the *Forbes 2000* and figures for each criterion. **Number listed:** 3

1. Pfizer Inc.
2. Bristol-Myers Squibb Co.
3. Forest Laboratories Inc.

Source: *Forbes*, Forbes 2000 (annual), http://www.forbes.com, May 7, 2012.

4003 ■ PENNSYLVANIA'S LARGEST PHARMACEUTICAL COMPANIES OVERALL, 2011

Ranked by: Score based on revenue, profits, assets, and market capitalization. **Remarks:** Specific scores not provided. Also notes overall rank in the *Forbes 2000* and figures for each criterion. **Number listed:** 2

1. AmerisourceBergen Corp.
2. Mylan Inc.

Source: *Forbes*, Forbes 2000 (annual), http://www.forbes.com, May 7, 2012.

4004 ■ TOP *FORTUNE 500* COMPANIES IN PHARMACEUTICALS, 2011

Ranked by: Revenue, in millions of dollars. **Remarks:** Also notes overall rank in the *Fortune 500;* profits; profits as a percentage of revenue; stockholders' equity; and rank by each criterion. **Number listed:** 12

1. Pfizer Inc., with $67,932 million
2. Johnson & Johnson, $65,030
3. Merck & Co., Inc., $48,047
4. Abbott Laboratories Inc., $38,851
5. Eli Lilly & Co., $24,287
6. Bristol-Myers Squibb Co., $21,244
7. Amgen Inc., $15,582
8. Gilead Sciences Inc., $8,385
9. Mylan Inc., $6,130
10. Allergan Inc., $5,419

Source: *Fortune*, Fortune 500 (annual), May 21, 2012, p. F-38.

4005 ■ WORLD'S LARGEST PHARMACEUTICAL COMPANIES BY U.S. PRESCRIPTIONS, 2011

Ranked by: Total number of U.S. prescriptions, in millions. **Remarks:** Also notes figures for previous year and annual sales growth. **Number listed:** 25

1. Teva Pharmaceutical Industries Ltd., with 558.3 million prescriptions
2. Mylan Inc., 366.3
3. Novartis AG, 289.7
4. Watson Pharmaceuticals Inc., 264.1
5. Pfizer Inc., 220.2
6. Endo Pharmaceuticals Holdings Inc., 176.1
7. Lupin Laboratories, 156.1
8. Amneal Pharmaceuticals Co. (India) Pvt. Ltd., 113.8
9. Boehringer Ingelheim, 88.9
10. Merck & Co., Inc., 88.1

Source: *Pharmaceutical Executive*, Pharm Exec 50 (annual), May 2012, p. 26.

4006 ■ WORLD'S LARGEST PHARMACEUTICAL COMPANIES BY U.S. REVENUE, 2011

Ranked by: U.S. pharmaceutical sales, in billions of U.S. dollars. **Remarks:** Also notes figures for previous year and annual sales growth. **Number listed:** 25

1. Pfizer Inc., with $25.1 billion
2. AstraZeneca plc, $19.9
3. Merck & Co., Inc., $19.3
4. Novartis AG, $19.2
5. Teva Pharmaceutical Industries Ltd., $15.1
6. Eli Lilly & Co., $14.9
7. Roche Group, $14.5
8. GlaxoSmithKline plc, $14.2
9. Amgen Inc., $13.1
10. Johnson & Johnson, $12.1

Source: *Pharmaceutical Executive*, Pharm Exec 50 (annual), May 2012, p. 28.

Pharmaceutical Industry, International

4007 ■ EUROPE'S MOST VALUABLE PHARMACEUTICALS AND BIOTECHNOLOGY COMPANIES, 2011

Ranked by: Market value as of March 2011, in millions of U.S. dollars. **Remarks:** Also notes rank within the *FT Europe 500*, rank for previous year, country, revenue, net income, assets, number of employees, share price, price-to-earning ratio, dividend yield, and fiscal yearend. **Number listed:** 14

1. Novartis AG, with $143,633 million
2. Roche Group, $127,055.6
3. GlaxoSmithKline plc, $98,600.1
4. Sanofi-Aventis SA, $92,044.4
5. AstraZeneca plc, $63,514.2
6. Novo Nordisk A/S, $61,961.4
7. Shire plc, $16,321.2
8. Novozymes A/S, $8,317.2
9. Actelion, $7,508.7
10. UCB SA, $6,972.4

Source: *Financial Times*, FT 500 (annual), http://www.ft.com, June 24, 2011.

4008 ■ INDIA'S LARGEST PHARMACEUTICAL COMPANIES, 2011

Ranked by: Score based on revenue, profits, assets, and market capitalization. **Remarks:** Specific scores not provided. Also notes overall rank in the *Forbes 2000* and figures for each criterion. **Number listed:** 2

1. Sun Pharma Industries
2. Piramal Healthcare

Source: *Forbes*, Forbes 2000 (annual), http://www.forbes.com, May 7, 2012.

4009 ■ IRELAND'S LARGEST PHARMACEUTICAL COMPANIES OVERALL, 2011

Ranked by: Score based on revenue, profits, assets, and market capitalization. **Remarks:** Specific scores not provided. Also notes overall rank in the *Forbes 2000* and figures for each criterion. **Number listed:** 2

1. Shire plc
2. Elan Corp. plc

Source: *Forbes*, Forbes 2000 (annual), http://www.forbes.com, May 7, 2012.

4010 ■ JAPAN'S LARGEST PHARMACEUTICAL COMPANIES OVERALL, 2011

Ranked by: Score based on revenue, profits, assets, and market capitalization. **Remarks:** Specific scores not provided. Also notes overall rank in the *Forbes 2000* and figures for each criterion. **Number listed:** 10

1. Takeda Pharmaceutical Co., Ltd.
2. Otsuka Holding
3. Astellas Pharmaceutical
4. Daiichi Sankyo
5. Eisai
6. Medipal Holdings
7. Alfresa Holdings
8. Suzuken
9. Taisho Pharmaceutical
10. Toho Holdings

Source: *Forbes*, Forbes 2000 (annual), http://www.forbes.com, May 7, 2012.

4011 ■ LARGEST CHEMICALS AND PHARMACEUTICALS COMPANIES IN EUROPE, 2010

Ranked by: Sales, in millions of U.S. dollars. **Remarks:** Also notes rank within country. **Number listed:** 100

1. BASF SE (Germany), with $75,390.6 million
2. AstraZeneca plc (U.K.), $49,206
3. Roche Holding AG (Switzerland), $48,299.5
4. Bayer AG (Germany), $46,353
5. Novartis AG (Switzerland), $44,270
6. GlaxoSmithKline plc (U.K.), $42,552
7. Ineos Group Ltd. (U.K.), $41,337.3
8. CP Pharmaceuticals International CV (Netherlands), $31,755.2
9. Laleham Health & Beauty Solutions Ltd. (U.K.), $28,720.4
10. Novartis Pharma AG (Switzerland), $28,540

Source: *Europe's 15,000 Largest Companies*, (annual), ELC International, 2011, p. 38.

4012 ■ SWITZERLAND'S LARGEST PHARMACEUTICAL COMPANIES OVERALL, 2011

Ranked by: Score based on revenue, profits, assets, and market capitalization. **Remarks:** Specific scores not provided. Also notes overall rank in the *Forbes 2000* and figures for each criterion. **Number listed:** 2

1. Novartis AG
2. Roche Holding Ltd.

Source: *Forbes*, Forbes 2000 (annual), http://www.forbes.com, May 7, 2012.

4013 ■ SWITZERLAND'S MOST VALUABLE PHARMACEUTICAL BRANDS, 2011

Ranked by: Brand value, in millions of U.S. dollars. **Remarks:** Also notes rank within the *Global 500* for current and previous year, figures for current and previous year, and brand rating. Ranking is available online only. **Number listed:** 2

1. Novartis, with $3,070 million
2. Roche, $2,388

Source: *Global 500*, (annual), Brand Finance plc, March 2012.

4014 ■ TOP PHARMACEUTICAL COMPANIES BY REVENUE, 2010

Ranked by: Pharmaceutical revenue, in millions of dollars. **Number listed:** 20

1. Pfizer Inc., with $58,523 million
2. Novartis AG, $44,420
3. Merck & Co., Inc., $39,811
4. Sanofi SA, $37,403
5. GlaxoSmithKline plc, $36,156
6. AstraZeneca plc, $32,515
7. Johnson & Johnson, $22,396
8. Eli Lilly & Co., $21,685
9. Abbott Laboratories Inc., $19,894
10. Bristol-Myers Squibb Co., $19,484

Source: *Contract Pharma*, Top 20 Pharmaceutical Companies (annual), http://www.contractpharma.com, 2011.

4015 ■ UNITED KINGDOM'S LARGEST PHARMACEUTICAL COMPANIES OVERALL, 2011

Ranked by: Score based on revenue, profits, assets, and market capitalization. **Remarks:** Specific scores not provided. Also notes overall rank in the *Forbes 2000* and figures for each criterion. **Number listed:** 2

1. GlaxoSmithKline plc
2. AstraZeneca plc

Source: *Forbes*, Forbes 2000 (annual), http://www.forbes.com, May 7, 2012.

4016 ■ WORLD'S LARGEST OVER-THE-COUNTER PHARMACEUTICAL COMPANIES, 2010

Ranked by: Sales, in millions of U.S. dollars. **Remarks:** Also notes brands and annual sales growth. **Number listed:** 5

1. Johnson & Johnson, with $14,600 million
2. Bayer Healthcare, $8,366
3. GlaxoSmithKline plc, $8,000
4. Novartis AG, $6,204
5. Pfizer Inc., $2,778

Source: *Consumer Goods Technology*, Consumer Goods Registry (annual), http://www.consumergoods.com, December 2011.

4017 ■ WORLD'S LARGEST PHARMACEUTICAL COMPANIES, 2011

Ranked by: Total U.S. sales, in billions of dollars. **Remarks:** Also notes headquarters, market share, and Web site. **Number listed:** 20

1. Pfizer Inc., with $25.12 billion
2. AstraZeneca plc, $19.89
3. Merck & Co., Inc., $19.34
4. Novartis AG, $19.24
5. Teva Pharmaceutical Industries Ltd., $15.06
6. Eli Lilly & Co., $14.86
7. F. Hoffmann-La Roche, $14.46
8. Amgen Inc., $13.07
9. GlaxoSmithKline plc, $12.86

10. Johnson & Johnson, $11.94

Source: *Modern Healthcare*, Largest Pharmaceutical Companies (annual), May 21, 2012, p. 34.

4018 ■ WORLD'S LARGEST PHARMACEUTICAL COMPANIES BY GLOBAL REVENUE, 2011

Ranked by: Global pharmaceutical sales, in billions of U.S. dollars. **Remarks:** Also notes headquarters, website, annual revenue growth, research and development expenditures, and three top-selling drugs. **Number listed:** 50

1. Pfizer Inc., with $57.7 billion
2. Novartis AG, $54
3. Merck & Co., Inc., $41.3
4. Sanofi SA, $37
5. Roche Group, $34.9
6. GlaxoSmithKline plc, $34.4
7. AstraZeneca plc, $33.6
8. Johnson & Johnson, $24.4
9. Abbott Laboratories Inc., $22.4
10. Eli Lilly & Co., $21.9

Source: *Pharmaceutical Executive*, Pharm Exec 50 (annual), May 2012, p. 26-32.

4019 ■ WORLD'S LARGEST PHARMACEUTICAL COMPANIES OVERALL, 2011

Ranked by: Score based on revenue, profits, assets, and market capitalization. **Remarks:** Specific scores not provided. Also notes country, overall rank in the *Forbes 2000,* and figures for each criterion. **Number listed:** 39

1. Pfizer Inc.
2. Novartis AG
3. Sanofi SA
4. Merck & Co., Inc.
5. Roche Holding Ltd.
6. GlaxoSmithKline plc
7. Abbott Laboratories Inc.
8. AstraZeneca plc
9. Eli Lilly & Co.
10. Bristol-Myers Squibb Co.

Source: *Forbes*, Forbes 2000 (annual), http://www.forbes.com, May 7, 2012.

4020 ■ WORLD'S LARGEST PHARMACEUTICAL PRODUCT MANUFACTURERS, 2010

Ranked by: Revenue, in millions of dollars. **Remarks:** Also notes rank for previous year, overall rank within the *IW 1000,* country, and revenue growth. **Number listed:** 40

1. Pfizer Inc., with $67,809 million
2. Johnson & Johnson, $61,587
3. Novartis AG, $52,795
4. Roche Holding Ltd., $46,845
5. Merck & Co., Inc., $45,987
6. GlaxoSmithKline plc, $44,710
7. Sanofi SA, $43,146
8. Abbott Laboratories Inc., $35,167
9. AstraZeneca plc, $34,098
10. Alfresa Holding Corp., $25,329

Source: *IndustryWeek*, IW 1000 (annual), http://www.industryweek.com, August 2011.

4021 ■ WORLD'S MOST ADMIRED PHARMACEUTICALS COMPANIES, 2012

Ranked by: Score, on a scale of 10, based on a survey of executives, directors, and securities analysts of companies within their own industry on eight criteria: innovation, financial soundness, employee talent, use of corporate assets, long-term investment value, social responsibility, quality of management, and quality of products/services. **Remarks:** Specific scores not provided. Also notes rank for previous year. **Number listed:** 7

1. Novartis AG
2. Abbott Laboratories Inc.
3. Bristol-Myers Squibb Co.
4. Merck & Co., Inc.
5. Johnson & Johnson
6. Roche Group
7. GlaxoSmithKline plc

Source: *Fortune*, World's Most Admired Companies (annual), March 19, 2012, p. 149.

4022 ■ WORLD'S MOST ADMIRED PHARMACY AND OTHER HEALTH SERVICES COMPANIES, 2012

Ranked by: Score, on a scale of 10, based on a survey of executives, directors, and securities analysts of companies within their own industry on eight criteria: innovation, financial soundness, employee talent, use of corporate assets, long-term investment value, social responsibility, quality of management, and quality of products/services. **Remarks:** Specific scores not provided. Also notes rank for previous year. **Number listed:** 5

1. Medco Health Solutions Inc.
2. Express Scripts Inc.
3. Catalyst Health Solutions Inc.
4. Covance Inc.
5. Cerner Corp.

Source: *Fortune*, World's Most Admired Companies (annual), March 19, 2012, p. 148.

4023 ■ WORLD'S MOST PROFITABLE PHARMACEUTICAL COMPANIES, 2010

Ranked by: Net income, in billions of U.S. dollars. **Remarks:** Also notes rank for previous year, figures for previous year, and percent change. **Number listed:** 23

1. Johnson & Johnson, with $13.3 billion
2. Novartis AG, $9.97
3. Pfizer Inc., $8.26
4. AstraZeneca plc, $8.08
5. Sanofi-Aventis SA, $7.33
6. Eli Lilly & Co., $5.07
7. Abbott Laboratories Inc., $4.63
7. Amgen Inc., $4.63
9. Teva Pharmaceutical Industries Ltd., $3.33
10. Bristol-Myers Squibb Co., $3.1

Source: *Pharmaceutical Executive*, Industry Audit (annual), http://www.pharmexec.com, September 2011.

4024 ■ WORLD'S MOST VALUABLE PHARMACEUTICAL BRANDS, 2011

Ranked by: Brand value, in millions of U.S. dollars. **Remarks:** Also notes rank within the *Global 500* for current and previous year, figures for current and previous year, country, and brand rating. Ranking is available online only. **Number listed:** 4

1. Pfizer, with $3,433 million
2. Novartis, $3,070
3. GlaxoSmithKline, $2,592
4. Roche, $2,388

Source: *Global 500*, (annual), Brand Finance plc, March 2012.

4025 ■ WORLD'S MOST VALUABLE PHARMACEUTICALS AND BIOTECHNOLOGY COMPANIES, 2011

Ranked by: Market value as of March 2011, in millions of U.S. dollars. **Remarks:** Also notes rank within the *FT 500*, rank for previous year, country, revenue, net income, assets, number of employees, share price, price-to-earning ratio, dividend yield, and fiscal year-end. **Number listed:** 20

1. Johnson & Johnson, with $162,361.8 million
2. Pfizer Inc., $162,301.4
3. Novartis AG, $143,633
4. Roche Group, $127,055.6
5. Merck & Co., Inc., $101,772.4
6. GlaxoSmithKline plc, $98,600.1
7. Sanofi-Aventis SA, $92,044.4
8. Abbott Laboratories Inc., $75,908.8
9. AstraZeneca plc, $63,514.2
10. Novo Nordisk Inc., $61,961.4

Source: *Financial Times*, FT 500 (annual), http://www.ft.com, June 24, 2011.

4026 ■ WORLD'S PHARMACEUTICAL COMPANIES WITH THE HIGHEST ENTERPRISE VALUE, 2010

Ranked by: Enterprise value (market capitalization plus cash minus debt), in billions of U.S. dollars. **Remarks:** Also notes rank for previous year, figures for previous year, and percent change. **Number listed:** 23

1. Pfizer Inc., with $171.32 billion
2. Johnson & Johnson, $155.83
3. Novartis AG, $146
4. Sanofi-Aventis SA, $130.89
5. GlaxoSmithKline plc, $111.57
6. Merck & Co., Inc., $106.39
7. Abbott Laboratories Inc., $92.45
8. AstraZeneca plc, $69.05
9. Novo Nordisk A/S, $68.63
10. Teva Pharmaceutical Industries Ltd., $51.1

Source: *Pharmaceutical Executive*, Industry Audit (annual), http://www.pharmexec.com, September 2011.

4027 ■ WORLD'S TOP PHARMACEUTICAL COMPANIES BY ENTERPRISE VALUE TO SALES RATIO, 2010

Ranked by: Enterprise value (market capitalization plus cash minus debt) divided by sales, in billions of dollars. **Remarks:** Also notes rank and figures for previous year. **Number listed:** 23

1. Celgene Corp., with $7.33 billion
2. Novo Nordisk A/S, $6.27
3. Allergan Inc., $5
4. Biogen Idec Inc., $4.76
5. Genzyme Corp., $4.36
6. Gilead Sciences Inc., $4.27
7. Amgen Inc., $3.37

8. Teva Pharmaceutical Industries Ltd., $3.17
9. Sanofi-Aventis SA, $3.04
10. Novartis AG, $2.83

Source: *Pharmaceutical Executive*, Industry Audit (annual), http://www.pharmexec.com, September 2011.

4028 ■ WORLD'S TOP PHARMACEUTICAL COMPANIES BY GROSS MARGIN, 2010

Ranked by: Sales minus the cost of goods sold, in percent. **Remarks:** Also notes rank and figures for previous year. **Number listed:** 23

1. Biogen Idec Inc., with 40.73%
2. Mylan Inc., 43.97%
3. Amgen Inc., 56.2%
4. Merck & Co., Inc., 58.28%
5. Novartis AG, 59.99%
6. Pfizer Inc., 69.47%
7. Cephalon Inc., 69.61%
8. Celgene Corp., 70.09%
9. Endo Pharmaceuticals Holdings Inc., 70.34%
10. GlaxoSmithKline plc, 71.89%

Source: *Pharmaceutical Executive*, Industry Audit (annual), http://www.pharmexec.com, September 2011.

4029 ■ WORLD'S TOP PHARMACEUTICAL COMPANIES BY INCOME TO ASSETS, 2010

Ranked by: Net income to assets ratio. **Remarks:** Also notes rank for previous year, figures for previous year, and percent change. **Number listed:** 23

1. Merck & Co., Inc., with 0.008
2. Mylan Inc., 0.030
3. Watson Pharmaceuticals Inc., 0.031
4. GlaxoSmithKline plc, 0.039
5. Pfizer Inc., 0.042
6. Sanofi-Aventis SA, 0.064
7. Endo Pharmaceuticals Holdings Inc., 0.066
8. Allergan Inc., 0.072
9. Abbott Laboratories Inc., 0.077
10. Novartis AG, 0.081

Source: *Pharmaceutical Executive*, Industry Audit (annual), http://www.pharmexec.com, September 2011.

4030 ■ WORLD'S TOP PHARMACEUTICAL COMPANIES OVERALL, 2010

Ranked by: Score based on financials. **Number listed:** 23

1. Novo Nordisk A/S, with 543 points
2. Biogen Idec Inc., 541
3. Gilead Sciences Inc., 502
4. Celgene Corp., 489
5. AstraZeneca plc, 412
6. Amgen Inc., 410
7. Eli Lilly & Co., 405
8. Bristol Myers Squibb Co., 378
9. Allergan Inc., 377
10. Pfizer Inc., 362

Source: *Pharmaceutical Executive*, Industry Audit (annual), http://www.pharmexec.com, September 2011.

4031 ■ WORLD'S TOP PHARMACEUTICAL COMPANIES BY PROFITS TO SALES, 2010

Ranked by: Net income to sales, in percent. **Remarks:** Also notes rank for previous year, figures for previous year, and percent change. **Number listed:** 23

1. Merck & Co., Inc., with 0.019
2. Watson Pharmaceuticals Inc., 0.051
3. GlaxoSmithKline plc, 0.057
4. Mylan Inc., 0.063
5. Genzyme Corp., 0.103
6. Allergan Inc., 0.122
6. Pfizer Inc., 0.122
8. Abbott Laboratories Inc., 0.131
9. Endo Pharmaceuticals Holdings Inc., 0.150
10. Cephalon Inc., 0.152

Source: *Pharmaceutical Executive*, Industry Audit (annual), http://www.pharmexec.com, September 2011.

4032 ■ WORLD'S TOP PHARMACEUTICAL COMPANIES BY SALES, 2010

Ranked by: Sales of prescription drugs and vaccines, in billions of U.S. dollars. **Remarks:** Also notes rank for previous year, figures for previous year, and percent change. **Number listed:** 23

1. Pfizer Inc., with $67.81 billion
2. Johnson & Johnson, $61.59
3. Novartis AG, $51.56
4. Merck & Co., Inc., $45.99
5. GlaxoSmithKline plc, $44.45
6. Sanofi-Aventis SA, $42.98
7. Abbott Laboratories Inc., $35.17
8. AstraZeneca plc, $33.27
9. Eli Lilly & Co., $23.08
10. Bristol-Myers Squibb Co., $19.48

Source: *Pharmaceutical Executive*, Industry Audit (annual), http://www.pharmexec.com, September 2011.

4033 ■ WORLD'S TOP PHARMACEUTICAL COMPANIES BY SALES TO ASSETS RATIO, 2010

Ranked by: Sales to assets ratio. **Remarks:** Also notes rank for previous year, figures for previous year, and percent change. **Number listed:** 23

1. Novo Nordisk A/S, with 0.901
2. Eli Lilly & Co., 0.744
3. Gilead Sciences Inc., 0.686
4. GlaxoSmithKline plc, 0.672
5. Bristol-Myers Squibb Co., 0.627
6. Watson Pharmaceuticals Inc., 0.612
7. Johnson & Johnson, 0.598
8. AstraZeneca plc, 0.593
9. Allergan Inc., 0.592
10. Abbott Laboratories Inc., 0.591

Source: *Pharmaceutical Executive*, Industry Audit (annual), http://www.pharmexec.com, September 2011.

4034 ■ WORLD'S TOP PHARMACEUTICAL COMPANIES BY SALES PER EMPLOYEE, 2010

Ranked by: Sales per employee, in thousands of U.S. dollars. **Remarks:** Also notes rank for previous year, figures for previous year, and percent change. **Number listed:** 23

1. Gilead Sciences Inc., with $1,987 thousand
2. Biogen Idec Inc., $972
3. Amgen Inc., $880
4. Celgene Corp., $867
5. Cephalon Inc., $754
6. Forest Laboratories Inc., $730
7. Bristol-Myers Squibb Co., $722
8. Pfizer Inc., $603
9. Eli Lilly & Co., $602
10. Watson Pharmaceuticals Inc., $592

Source: *Pharmaceutical Executive*, Industry Audit (annual), http://www.pharmexec.com, September 2011.

4035 ■ WORLD'S TOP PHARMACEUTICAL COMPANIES BY SELLING, GENERAL, & ADMINISTRATIVE COSTS, 2010

Ranked by: Selling, general, and administrative expenses, in billions of U.S. dollars. **Remarks:** Also notes figures for previous year, percent change, and annual growth in sales. **Number listed:** 23

1. Pfizer Inc., with $23.95 billion
2. GlaxoSmithKline plc, $20.44
3. Johnson & Johnson, $19.42
4. Novartis AG, $16.48
5. Merck & Co., Inc., $14.55
6. Abbott Laboratories Inc., $10.38
7. AstraZeneca plc, $10.07
8. Sanofi-Aventis SA, $10.04
9. Eli Lilly & Co., $7.06
10. Bristol-Myers Squibb Co., $4.79

Source: *Pharmaceutical Executive*, Industry Audit (annual), http://www.pharmexec.com, September 2011.

Photography Studios

4036 ■ TOP PHOTOGRAPHY AND VIDEO SERVICES FRANCHISES, 2012

Ranked by: Cumulative score based on financial strength and stability, growth rate, size of the system, number of years in business, the length of time franchising, start-up costs, litigation, percentage of terminations, and whether the company provides financing. **Remarks:** Specific scores not provided. Also notes overall rank within the *Franchise 500,* contact information, description, year founded, year started franchising, states where registered, available U.S. regions, where seeking foreign expansion, number of franchised and company-owned units for past three years, start-up costs, franchise fees, royalty fees, and type of financing available. **Number listed:** 2

1. Home Video Studio
2. Lil' Angels Photography

Source: *Entrepreneur*, Franchise 500 (annual), January 2012, p. 204-205.

Physical Fitness

4037 ■ TOP CHILDREN'S FITNESS FRANCHISES, 2012

Ranked by: Cumulative score based on financial strength and stability, growth rate, size of the system, number of years in business, the length of time franchising, start-up costs, litigation, percentage of terminations, and whether the company provides financing. **Remarks:** Specific scores not provided. Also notes overall rank within the *Franchise 500,* contact information, description, year founded, year started franchising, states where registered, available U.S. regions, where seeking foreign expansion, number of franchised and company-owned units for past three years, start-up costs, franchise fees, royalty fees, and type of financing available. **Number listed:** 8

1. Soccer Shots Franchising
2. Kinderdance International Inc.
3. i9 Sports
4. Gymboree Play & Music
5. HappyFeet Legends International
6. TGA Premier Junior Golf
7. The Little Gym
8. My Gym Children's Fitness Center

Source: *Entrepreneur*, Franchise 500 (annual), January 2012, p. 156-157.

4038 ■ TOP FITNESS FRANCHISES, 2012

Ranked by: Cumulative score based on financial strength and stability, growth rate, size of the system, number of years in business, the length of time franchising, start-up costs, litigation, percentage of terminations, and whether the company provides financing. **Remarks:** Specific scores not provided. Also notes overall rank within the *Franchise 500,* contact information, description, year founded, year started franchising, states where registered, available U.S. regions, where seeking foreign expansion, number of franchised and company-owned units for past three years, start-up costs, franchise fees, royalty fees, and type of financing available. **Number listed:** 10

1. Anytime Fitness
2. Jazzercise Inc.
3. Snap Fitness Inc.
4. Planet Fitness
5. Gold's Gym Franchising Inc.
6. Retro Fitness LLC
7. Get In Shape For Women
8. Tiger-Rock Martial Arts International
9. CKO Kickboxing
10. Koko FitClub

Source: *Entrepreneur*, Franchise 500 (annual), January 2012, p. 190-191.

Physicians

4039 ■ STATES WITH THE HIGHEST RATE OF PHYSICIANS, 2009

Ranked by: Number of physicians per 100,000 in population. **Number listed:** 51

1. Washington DC, with 896 physicians
2. Massachusetts, 525
3. Maryland, 476
4. New York, 443
5. Vermont, 442
6. Connecticut, 431
7. Rhode Island, 430
8. Hawaii, 371
9. New Jersey, 357

10. Pennsylvania, 352

Source: *State Rankings*, (annual), CQ Press, 2011, p. 387.

4040 ■ STATES WITH THE LOWEST RATE OF PHYSICIANS, 2009

Ranked by: Number of physicians per 100,000 in population. **Number listed:** 51

1. Oklahoma, with 203 physicians
2. Idaho, 204
3. Mississippi, 206
4. Iowa, 219
5. Nevada, 221
6. Wyoming, 227
7. Arkansas, 234
8. Texas, 240
9. Utah, 241
10. Alabama, 244

Source: *State Rankings*, (annual), CQ Press, 2011, p. 387.

Pipeline Companies
See also: **Petroleum Pipelines**

4041 ■ LARGEST PIPELINE (EXCEPT NATURAL GAS) COMPANIES BY EMPLOYEES, 2010

Ranked by: Total number of employees. **Remarks:** Also notes contact information for headquarters, number of employees at headquarters, revenue, rank by revenue, and primary SIC code. **Number listed:** 49

1. Kinder Morgan Energy Partners LP, with 7,931 employees
2. Plains All American Pipeline LP, 3,400
3. BP Oil Pipeline Co., 3,000
4. Tampa Pipeline Corp., 2,500
5. SemGroup Corp., 2,201
6. NuStar Energy LP, 1,753
7. NuStar GP Holdings LLC, 1,379
8. Sunoco Logistics Partners LP, 1,340
9. Exxon Pipeline Holdings Inc., 1,200
10. Magellan Midstream Holdings LP, 1,127

Source: *Business Rankings*, (annual), Dun & Bradstreet Inc., 2011, p. VI.100-VI.101.

4042 ■ LARGEST PIPELINE (EXCEPT NATURAL GAS) COMPANIES BY SALES, 2010

Ranked by: Total revenue, in dollars. **Remarks:** Also notes contact information for headquarters, number of employees at headquarters and overall, rank by employees, and primary SIC code. **Number listed:** 50

1. Plains All American Pipeline LP, with $25,893,000,000
2. Kinder Morgan Energy Partners LP, $8,077,700,000
3. Sunoco Logistics Partners LP, $7,838,000,000
4. Enbridge Energy Partners LP, $7,736,100,000
5. NuStar Energy LP, $4,403,061,000
6. Genesis Energy LP, $2,101,324,000
7. Magellan Midstream Holdings LP, $1,213,638,000

8. Colonial Pipeline Co., $824,064,000
9. Explorer Pipeline Services Co., $219,879,892
10. BlueKnight Energy Partners LP, $156,776,000

Source: *Business Rankings*, (annual), Dun & Bradstreet Inc., 2011, p. V.100-V.101.

Pipes

4043 ■ TOP COMPANIES IN PIPE, PROFILE, AND TUBING EXTRUDERS, 2010

Ranked by: Pipe, profile, and tubing sales, in millions of dollars. **Remarks:** Also notes headquarters and top extrusion official. **Number listed:** 218

1. JM Eagle, with $1,800 million
2. Royal Group Inc., $895
3. Advanced Drainage Systems Inc., $840
4. CertainTeed Corp., $675
5. Ply Gem Industries Inc., $575
6. North American Pipe Corp., $545
7. Performance Pipe, $400
8. Associated Materials LLC, $335
8. Ipex Inc., $335
10. Trex Co., $317.69

Source: *Plastics News*, Top Pipe, Profile, and Tubing Extruders (annual), http://www.plasticsnews.com, July 4, 2011.

Pizza
See also: **Frozen Pizza**

4044 ■ LARGEST INDEPENDENT PIZZA COMPANIES BY SALES, 2010

Ranked by: Gross sales, in dollars. **Remarks:** Also notes rank for previous year, owner/manager, headquarters, website, and number of restaurants. **Number listed:** 100

1. Buddy's Pizza, with $20,000,000
2. Marion's Piazza, $13,900,000
3. Frankie, Johnnie & Luigi, Too, $12,500,000
4. Glass Nickel Pizza Co., $12,000,000
4. Woodstock's Pizza, $12,000,000
4. Smoky Mountain Pizzeria, $12,000,000
7. Wick's Pizza Parlor & Pub, $10,600,000
8. Pitfire Pizza, $10,200,000
9. Reginelli's Pizzeria, $9,916,017
10. Borriello Bros. Real NY Pizza, $9,800,000

Source: *Pizza Today*, Hot 100 Independents (annual), October 2011, p. 54-55.

4045 ■ LARGEST PIZZA COMPANIES BY SALES, 2011

Ranked by: Gross sales, in dollars. **Remarks:** Also notes rank for previous year, headquarters, principal executive, website, and total number of units. **Number listed:** 100

1. Pizza Hut Inc., with $11,000,000,000
2. Domino's Pizza LLC, $6,000,000,000
3. Papa John's International Inc., $2,390,172,000
4. Little Caesars Pizza, $1,345,000,000
5. California Pizza Kitchen Inc., $710,000,000

6. Papa Murphy's Take 'N' Bake Pizza, $653,300,000
7. Sbarro Inc., $620,000,000
8. CiCi's Pizza, $560,000,000
9. Chuck E. Cheese's, $436,000,000
10. Round Table Pizza Inc., $410,000,000

Source: *Pizza Today*, Top 100 Pizza Companies (annual), November 2011, p. 54-55.

4046 ■ LARGEST U.S. PIZZA CHAINS BY SALES, 2010

Ranked by: U.S. pizza sales, in thousands. **Remarks:** Also notes figures for previous year and percent change. **Number listed:** 50

1. Pizza Hut, with $5,390,000 thousand
2. Domino's Pizza, $3,305,636
3. Papa John's Pizza, $2,097,272
4. Little Caesars Pizza, $1,253,000
5. Papa Murphy's Take 'N' Bake Pizza, $655,000
6. CiCi's Pizza, $545,000
7. Sbarro's Italian Eatery, $501,500
8. Chuck E. Cheese's, $425,941
9. Round Table Pizza, $369,000
10. Godfather's Pizza, $330,000

Source: *Pizza Marketing Quarterly*, Pizza Power (annual), September 2011, p. 58.

4047 ■ LARGEST U.S. PIZZA CHAINS BY UNITS, 2010

Ranked by: Number of U.S. units. **Remarks:** Also notes figures for previous year and percent change. **Number listed:** 50

1. Pizza Hut, with 7,542 units
2. Domino's Pizza, 4,929
3. Papa John's Pizza, 2,871
4. Little Caesars Pizza, 2,800
5. Papa Murphy's Take 'N' Bake Pizza, 1,239
6. Sbarro's Italian Eatery, 778
7. Godfather's Pizza, 647
8. CiCi's Pizza, 594
9. Hungry Howie's Pizza & Subs, 570
10. Chuck E. Cheese's, 529

Source: *Pizza Marketing Quarterly*, Pizza Power (annual), September 2011, p. 59.

4048 ■ TOP PIZZA FRANCHISES, 2012

Ranked by: Cumulative score based on financial strength and stability, growth rate, size of the system, number of years in business, the length of time franchising, start-up costs, litigation, percentage of terminations, and whether the company provides financing. **Remarks:** Specific scores not provided. Also notes overall rank within the *Franchise 500*, contact information, description, year founded, year started franchising, states where registered, available U.S. regions, where seeking foreign expansion, number of franchised and company-owned units for past three years, start-up costs, franchise fees, royalty fees, and type of financing available. **Number listed:** 13

1. Pizza Hut Inc.
2. Papa John's International Inc.
3. Hungry Howie's Pizza & Subs
4. Marco's Franchising LLC
5. Jet's Pizza
6. Villa Enterprises

7. The Pizza Ranch
8. Ledo Pizza System Inc.
9. Donatos Pizza
10. Straw Hat Pizza

Source: *Entrepreneur*, Franchise 500 (annual), January 2012, p. 168-171.

4049 ■ TOP TAKE AND BAKE PIZZA FRANCHISES, 2012

Ranked by: Cumulative score based on financial strength and stability, growth rate, size of the system, number of years in business, the length of time franchising, start-up costs, litigation, percentage of terminations, and whether the company provides financing. **Remarks:** Specific scores not provided. Also notes overall rank within the *Franchise 500*, contact information, description, year founded, year started franchising, states where registered, available U.S. regions, where seeking foreign expansion, number of franchised and company-owned units for past three years, start-up costs, franchise fees, royalty fees, and type of financing available. **Number listed:** 2

1. Papa Murphy's
2. Figaro's Pizza

Source: *Entrepreneur*, Franchise 500 (annual), January 2012, p. 170-171.

Plastic Films

4050 ■ LARGEST FILM AND SHEET MANUFACTURERS IN NORTH AMERICA, 2010

Ranked by: Film and sheet sales, in millions of dollars. **Remarks:** Also notes headquarters and top film and sheet official. **Number listed:** 181

1. Bemis Co., Inc., with $3,300 million
2. Sigma Plastics Group, $2,450
3. Berry Plastics Corp., $1,700
4. Sealed Air Corp., $1,300
5. E. I. du Pont de Nemours & Co., $1,260
6. Inteplast Group Ltd., $1,090
7. Printpack Inc., $950
8. AEP Industries Inc., $800.57
9. Glad Products Co., $700
10. Spartech Corp., $685

Source: *Plastics News*, North American Film and Sheet Manufacturers (annual), http://www.plasticsnews.com, September 19, 2011.

Plastics Industry

4051 ■ HIGHEST-PAID PLASTICS INDUSTRY EXECUTIVES IN NORTH AMERICA, 2010

Ranked by: Total compensation, in U.S. dollars. **Remarks:** Also notes title and business type. **Number listed:** 150

1. Frank Stronach (Magna Int'l), with $57,715,280
2. Belinda Stronach (Magna Int'l), $20,368,180
3. Donald J. Walker (Magna Int'l), $15,723,860
4. Siegfried Wolf (Magna Int'l), $15,581,600
5. Mark D. Ketchum (Newell Rubbermaid), $9,329,447
6. Vincent J. Galifi (Magna Int'l), $8,917,790
7. Ronald J. Kramer (Griffon), $8,021,057

8. E. V. (Rick) Goings (Tupperware), $7,868,516
9. Stephen D. Newlin (PolyOne), $6,972,145
10. Jeffrey O. Palmer (Magna Int'l), $6,931,800

Source: *Plastics News*, Highest-Paid Plastics Industry Executives (annual), http://www.plasticsnews.com, September 12, 2011.

4052 ■ LARGEST U.S. PLASTIC PRODUCT MANUFACTURERS, 2010

Ranked by: Revenue, in millions of dollars. **Remarks:** Also notes overall rank within the *IW 500*, revenue growth, and profit margin. **Number listed:** 7

1. Sealed Air Corp., with $4,490 million
2. PolyOne Corp., $2,622
3. Graham Packaging Co., $2,513
4. Tupperware Brands Corp., $2,300
5. AptarGroup Inc., $2,077
6. Kraton Performance Polymers Inc., $1,228
7. Spartech Corp., $1,023

Source: *IndustryWeek*, IW 500 (annual), http://www.industryweek.com, July 2011.

4053 ■ WORLD'S LARGEST PLASTIC PRODUCT MANUFACTURERS, 2010

Ranked by: Revenue, in millions of dollars. **Remarks:** Also notes rank for previous year, overall rank within the *IW 1000*, country, and revenue growth. **Number listed:** 3

1. Sealed Air Corp., with $4,490 million
2. Burelle SA, $4,399
3. Ibiden Co., Ltd., $3,373

Source: *IndustryWeek*, IW 1000 (annual), http://www.industryweek.com, August 2011.

Plastics—Molding

4054 ■ LARGEST ROTATIONAL MOLDERS IN NORTH AMERICA, 2010

Ranked by: Sales of rotomolded products, in millions of dollars. **Remarks:** Also notes headquarters and top rotational molding official. **Number listed:** 124

1. Step2 Co., with $145 million
1. Toter Inc., $145
3. Little Tikes Co., $121
4. Snyder Industries Inc., $107
5. Centro Inc., $102
6. Norwesco Inc., $96
7. Pelican Products Inc., $88.9
8. Indiana Rotomolding Inc., $60.5
9. Confluence Watersports Co., $45
10. Rotonics Manufacturing Inc., $42

Source: *Plastics News*, North American Rotational Molders (annual), http://www.plasticsnews.com, August 8, 2011.

4055 ■ TOP NORTH AMERICAN MOLD MAKERS, 2010

Ranked by: North American tooling sales, in millions of dollars. **Remarks:** Also notes headquarters and key executive. **Number listed:** 64

1. Husky Injection Molding Systems Ltd., with $113 million

2. Concours Mold Inc., $60
3. Active Burgess Mould & Design, $59
4. Hi-Tech Mold & Engineering Inc., $57
5. H. S. Die & Engineering Inc., $54
5. Proper Group International Inc., $54
7. Omega Tool Corp., $50
8. Triangle Tool Corp., $48.5
9. Integrity Tool & Mold Inc., $47.5
10. NyproMold Inc., $45
10. Wentworth Technologies Co., Ltd., $45

Source: *Plastics News*, Top Mold Makers (annual), http://www.plasticsnews.com, October 24, 2011.

Plumbing Industry

4056 ■ LARGEST COMPANIES IN THE PIPE TRADES, 2010

Ranked by: Pipe trades volume, in millions of dollars. **Remarks:** Also notes rank for previous year, headquarters, total revenue, and breakdown of revenue by plumbing, piping, hydronics, fire protection, waste water treatment, and other services. **Number listed:** 100

1. EMCOR Group Inc., with $4,199.46 million
2. Kinetics Group, $330
3. John E. Green Co., $250
4. American Residential Services LLC/Rescue Rooter, $210
5. Mr. Rooter Corp., $209.28
6. Comfort Systems USA, $188.41
7. BMW Constructors, $157.5
8. Harder Mechanical Contractors Inc., $150
9. P1 Group, $147.2
10. U.S. Engineering Co., $147.03

Source: *Plumbing & Mechanical*, Pipe Trades Giants (annual), August 2011, p. 38+.

4057 ■ LARGEST FIRE PROTECTION COMPANIES, 2010

Ranked by: Fire protection revenue, in millions of dollars. **Remarks:** Also notes headquarters and rank in the overall Top 100. **Number listed:** 10

1. EMCOR Group Inc., with $870.62 million
2. Fire & Life Safety America, $122.15
3. VSC Fire & Security, $100.1
4. Wayne Automatic Fire Sprinklers, $69
5. J. F. Ahern Co., $67.73
6. John E. Green Co., $25
7. Grunau Co., $19.78
8. E. M. Duggan, $13.6
9. Great Lakes Pluming & Heating Co., $12.24
10. J. C. Cannistraro, $11.75

Source: *Plumbing & Mechanical*, Pipe Trades Giants (annual), August 2011, p. 36.

4058 ■ LARGEST HYDRONICS COMPANIES, 2010

Ranked by: Hydronics revenue, in millions of dollars. **Remarks:** Also notes headquarters and rank in the overall Top 100. **Number listed:** 10

1. P1 Group, with $82.8 million
2. Mechanical Inc., $73.48
3. Hill Mechanical Group, $60.55
4. Murray Co., $54.47
5. John W. Danforth Co., $44.1
6. RK Mechanical, $38.52
7. Pierce Associates, $36.96
8. Durr Mechanical Construction, $35.43
9. Harris Cos., $35.2
10. R. W. Warner Inc., $29.88

Source: *Plumbing & Mechanical*, Pipe Trades Giants (annual), August 2011, p. 36.

4059 ■ LARGEST PIPING COMPANIES, 2010

Ranked by: Piping revenue, in millions of dollars. **Remarks:** Also notes headquarters and rank in the overall Top 100. **Number listed:** 10

1. EMCOR Group Inc., with $1,536.39 million
2. Kinetic Systems, $280.5
3. John E. Green Co., $150
4. BMW Constructors, $136.5
5. Murphy Co. Mechanical Contractors & Engineers, $130.01
6. U.S. Engineering Co., $110.71
7. Harder Mechanical Contractors Inc., $100
8. McKinstry Co., $95.63
9. AZCO, $30.58
10. Service Experts, $11.81

Source: *Plumbing & Mechanical*, Pipe Trades Giants (annual), August 2011, p. 36.

4060 ■ LARGEST PLUMBING COMPANIES, 2010

Ranked by: Plumbing revenue, in millions of dollars. **Remarks:** Also notes headquarters and rank in the overall Top 100. **Number listed:** 10

1. EMCOR Group Inc., with $1,024.26 million
2. American Residential Services LLC/Rescue Rooter, $210
3. Mr. Rooter Corp., $198.38
4. Comfort Systems USA, $177.33
5. Benjamin Franklin Plumbing, $134
6. Pan-Pacific Plumbing & Mechanical, $88
7. TDIndustries Ltd., $87
8. John E. Green Co., $75
9. ColonialWebb Contractors, $65.4
10. MMC Contractors, $62.96

Source: *Plumbing & Mechanical*, Pipe Trades Giants (annual), August 2011, p. 36.

4061 ■ LARGEST PLUMBING CONTRACTORS, 2011

Ranked by: Plumbing revenue, in millions of dollars. **Remarks:** Also notes headquarters and rank in the overall *Top 100*. **Number listed:** 10

1. EMCOR Group Inc., with $574.2 million
2. Roto-Rooter Services Co., $369.7
3. ARS/Rescue Rooter, $346.7
4. APi Group Inc., $206.45

5. Comfort Systems USA Inc., $198.4
6. Southland Industries, $145
7. TDIndustries Ltd., $78.78
8. John E. Green Co., $75
9. Direct Energy U.S. Home Services Inc., $62.15
10. BMW Contractors, $53.8

Source: *Contractor*, Book of Giants (annual), May 2012, p. 22.

4062 ■ TOP PLUMBING FRANCHISES, 2012

Ranked by: Cumulative score based on financial strength and stability, growth rate, size of the system, number of years in business, the length of time franchising, start-up costs, litigation, percentage of terminations, and whether the company provides financing. **Remarks:** Specific scores not provided. Also notes overall rank within the *Franchise 500,* contact information, description, year founded, year started franchising, states where registered, available U.S. regions, where seeking foreign expansion, number of franchised and company-owned units for past three years, start-up costs, franchise fees, royalty fees, and type of financing available. **Number listed:** 3

1. Rooter-Man
2. Mr. Rooter Corp.
3. Ace DuraFlo Systems

Source: *Entrepreneur*, Franchise 500 (annual), January 2012, p. 184-187.

Popcorn

4063 ■ TOP BRANDS OF POPCORN, 2011

Ranked by: Sales for the 52 weeks ending March 20, 2011, in millions of dollars. **Remarks:** Also notes annual growth, dollar share, and unit sales. **Number listed:** 10

1. Smartfood, with $118.8 million
2. Cracker Jack, $39.1
3. Popcorn, Indiana, $26.1
4. Crunch 'n Munch, $24.7
5. Private label, $24.6
6. Orville Redenbacher's Poppycock, $22.5
7. Popcorn Expressions, $17.5
8. Jay's O-Ke-Doke, $12.6
9. Wise, $11.4
10. Lance, $9.7

Source: *Snack Food & Wholesale Bakery*, State of the Industry (annual), July 2011, p. 44.

Pork Industry

4064 ■ LARGEST PORK PRODUCERS IN THE U.S., 2011

Ranked by: Total number of sows owned. **Remarks:** Also notes rank and figures for previous year, headquarters, and comments. **Number listed:** 25

1. Smithfield Foods Inc., with 837,951 sows
2. Triumph Foods, 377,000
3. Seaboard Foods, 213,600
4. The Maschhoffs Inc., 192,000
5. Prestage Farms, 165,000
6. Iowa Select Farms, 160,000

7. The Pipestone System, 140,000
8. Cargill Inc., 123,431
9. The Carthage System, 92,000
10. AMVC Management Services, 82,000

Source: *Successful Farming*, Pork Powerhouses (annual), http://www.agriculture.com/ag/sfonline, October 2011.

4065 ■ LARGEST PORK PRODUCERS IN WESTERN CANADA, 2011

Ranked by: Total number of sows owned. **Remarks:** Also notes rank and figures for previous year, headquarters, and comments. **Number listed:** 5

1. HyLife, with 60,000 sows
2. Big Sky Farms, 42,000
3. Maple Leaf Agri-Farms, 35,000
4. The Puratone Corp., 28,000
4. ProVista Agriculture, 28,000

Source: *Successful Farming*, Pork Powerhouses (annual), http://www.agriculture.com/ag/sfonline, October 2011.

Ports

4066 ■ TOP U.S. OCEAN CARGO PORTS, 2012

Ranked by: Shipments, in twenty-foot equivalent units (TEUs), for the first quarter of the year. **Remarks:** Also notes figures for previous year and percent change. **Number listed:** 30

1. Los Angeles, CA, with 949,063 TEUs
2. Newark, NJ/New York, NY, 673,723
3. Long Beach, CA, 673,172
4. Savannah, GA, 271,526
5. Seattle, WA, 195,326
6. Norfolk, VA, 188,802
7. Oakland, CA, 180,445
8. Houston, TX, 156,326
9. Charleston, SC, 155,951
10. Tacoma, WA, 118,188

Source: *Logistics Management*, Top U.S. Ports (annual), May 2012, p. 52A.

Postal Service

4067 ■ TOP POSTAL AND BUSINESS SERVICE FRANCHISES, 2012

Ranked by: Cumulative score based on financial strength and stability, growth rate, size of the system, number of years in business, the length of time franchising, start-up costs, litigation, percentage of terminations, and whether the company provides financing. **Remarks:** Specific scores not provided. Also notes overall rank within the *Franchise 500,* contact information, description, year founded, year started franchising, states where registered, available U.S. regions, where seeking foreign expansion, number of franchised and company-owned units for past three years, start-up costs, franchise fees, royalty fees, and type of financing available. **Number listed:** 5

1. The UPS Store/Mail Boxes Etc.
2. PostNet Neighborhood Business Centers
3. Postal Annex+
4. Pak Mail Centers of America Inc.

5. Handle With Care Packaging Store

Source: *Entrepreneur*, Franchise 500 (annual), January 2012, p. 204-205.

Potato Chips

4068 ■ TOP BRANDS OF POTATO CHIPS, 2011

Ranked by: Sales for the 52 weeks ending March 20, 2011, in millions of dollars. **Remarks:** Also notes annual growth, dollar share, and unit sales. **Number listed:** 10

1. Lay's, with $1,270.1 million
2. Ruffles, $547.6
3. Wavy Lay's, $327.8
4. Pringles, $320.6
5. Private label, $270.9
6. Lay's Natural, $207.8
7. Utz, $173.5
8. Lay's Kettle Cooked, $146.6
9. Baked Lay's, $131
10. Kettle, $124.8

Source: *Snack Food & Wholesale Bakery*, State of the Industry (annual), July 2011, p. 18.

Prescriptions
See: **Drugs, Prescription**

Printing Industry

4069 ■ FASTEST-GROWING NORTH AMERICAN PRINTING DISTRIBUTORS, 2009-2010

Ranked by: Annual growth in sales, in percent. **Remarks:** Also notes headquarters, sales for current year, and sales for previous year. **Number listed:** 25

1. Regency Office Products, with 100%
2. Peerless, 63%
3. Smart Source LLC, 45%
4. Golden Pacific Systems Inc., 44%
5. Exalt Printing Solutions LLC, 42%
6. Harris Media Group, 41%
7. The Venture Corp., 39%
8. PrintTek Inc., 36%
9. Integrated Print Solutions, 35%
10. WebbMason Inc., 34%

Source: *Print Solutions*, Top 100 Distributors (annual), August 2011, p. 48.

4070 ■ FASTEST-GROWING NORTH AMERICAN TRADE PRINTERS, 2009-2010

Ranked by: Annual growth in sales, in percent. **Remarks:** Also notes headquarters, sales for current year, and sales for previous year. **Number listed:** 25

1. CFC Print Solutions, with 58%
2. Hayes Graphics, 50%
3. Commercial Print & Imaging, 33%
4. ID Images, 29%

5. TLF Graphics Inc., 26%
5. Gill Studios Inc., 26%
5. Badger Tag & Label Corp., 26%
8. Luminer Converting Group, 23%
9. Adcraft Decals, 20%
10. Western Tag & Printing, 20%

Source: *Print Solutions*, Top Trade Printers (annual), July 2011, p. 36.

4071 ■ JAPAN'S LARGEST PRINTING AND PUBLISHING COMPANIES OVERALL, 2011

Ranked by: Score based on revenue, profits, assets, and market capitalization. **Remarks:** Specific scores not provided. Also notes overall rank in the *Forbes 2000* and figures for each criterion. **Number listed:** 2

1. Dai Nippon Printing Co., Ltd.
2. Toppan Printing Co., Ltd.

Source: *Forbes*, Forbes 2000 (annual), http://www.forbes.com, May 7, 2012.

4072 ■ LARGEST IN-PLANT PRINTERS BY EMPLOYEES, 2010

Ranked by: Number of full-time-equivalent employees. **Number listed:** 75

1. U.S. Government Printing Office, with 779 employees
2. The Church of Jesus Christ of Latter-day Saints, 323
3. Amway Corp., 190.5
4. Allstate Insurance Co., 147
4. Brigham Young University, 147
6. University of Oklahoma, 97.5
7. University of Washington, 96
8. Washington State Department of Printing, 92
9. State of Oregon Publishing & Distribution, 91
10. University of Missouri, 75.5

Source: *In-Plant Graphics*, Industry Giants (annual), December 2011, p. 30.

4073 ■ LARGEST IN-PLANT PRINTERS BY REVENUE, 2010

Ranked by: Revenue, in dollars. **Remarks:** Also notes operating budget. **Number listed:** 70

1. U.S. Government Printing Office, with $150,000,000
2. Allstate Insurance Co., $93,000,000
3. Amway Corp., $64,200,000
4. Washington State Department of Printing, $22,000,000
5. CVS Caremark, $n/a
6. State of Colorado, $16,985,895
7. University of Oklahoma, $15,100,000
8. State of Oregon Publishing & Distribution, $15,033,000
9. State of Missouri, $14,800,000
10. Spartan Stores, $14,067,515

Source: *In-Plant Graphics*, Industry Giants (annual), December 2011, p. 31.

4074 ■ LARGEST NON-PSDA-MEMBER NORTH AMERICAN PRINTING DISTRIBUTORS, 2010

Ranked by: Sales, in U.S. dollars. **Remarks:** Ranking covers companies that are not members of the Print Services and Distribution Association (PSDA). Also notes headquarters. **Number listed:** 20

1. WorkflowOne, with $580,693,000
2. InnerWorkings Inc., $482,212,101
3. Proforma, $358,800,000
4. USFI, $22,980,000
5. Tray, $17,196,236
6. Voluforms, $16,582,437
7. Bradley Marketing Group, $14,000,000
8. Midwest Single Source Inc., $13,338,896
9. Southern Imaging Group Inc., $12,350,000
10. Data Forms Inc., $9,167,711

Source: *Print Solutions*, Top 100 Distributors (annual), August 2011, p. 64.

4075 ■ LARGEST NON-PSDA-MEMBER NORTH AMERICAN TRADE PRINTERS, 2010

Ranked by: Sales, in dollars. **Remarks:** Ranking covers companies that are not members of the Print Services and Distribution Association (PSDA). Also notes headquarters. **Number listed:** 20

1. BCT Inc., with $100,000,000
2. 4over Inc., $81,370,000
3. Label Art, $42,148,480
4. Stouse Inc., $40,916,000
5. Diversified Labeling Solutions Inc., $35,205,285
6. Edison Lithograph & Printing Co., $30,000,000
7. USFI, $23,100,000
8. Direct Impressions, $23,000,000
9. 5 Day Business Forms, $12,047,000
10. AELitho Offset Printers Inc., $12,001,203

Source: *Print Solutions*, Top Trade Printers (annual), July 2011, p. 42.

4076 ■ LARGEST NORTH AMERICAN PRINTERS, 2011

Ranked by: Revenue, in millions of U.S. dollars. **Remarks:** Also notes headquarters, rank and figures for previous year, percent change, principal officer, number of employees, breakdown of revenue by primary specialty, type of ownership, number of plants, and number of web offset press, sheetfed press, and other press units. **Number listed:** 400

1. R. R. Donnelley & Sons Co., with $10,018.9 million
2. Quad/Graphics Inc., $4,765
3. Valassis Communications Inc., $2,333.5
4. Transcontinental Inc., $2,058.08
5. Cenveo Inc., $2,050
6. Deluxe Corp., $1,402.24
7. Vertis Communications, $1,200
8. Consolidated Graphics Inc., $1,054
9. VistaPrint Ltd., $817
10. The Standard Register Co., $668

Source: *Printing Impressions*, PI 400 (annual), December 2011, p. 37+.

4077 ■ LARGEST PSDA-MEMBER NORTH AMERICAN PRINTING DISTRIBUTORS, 2010

Ranked by: Sales, in U.S. dollars. **Remarks:** Ranking covers companies that are members of the Print Services and Distribution Association (PSDA). Also notes headquarters. **Number listed:** 50

1. American Solutions for Business, with $180,768,776
2. WebbMason Inc., $90,000,000
3. Data Supplies Inc., $67,045,000
4. DataSource Inc., $49,000,000
5. Smart Source LLC, $48,500,000
6. Vanguard Direct, $46,901,000
7. Fontis Solutions, $32,100,000
8. MHC Associates Inc., $26,000,000
9. Quality Resource Group Inc., $23,337,511
10. Prime Business Solutions, $21,840,000

Source: *Print Solutions*, Top 100 Distributors (annual), August 2011, p. 44-46.

4078 ■ LARGEST PSDA-MEMBER NORTH AMERICAN TRADE PRINTERS, 2010

Ranked by: Sales, in U.S. dollars. **Remarks:** Ranking covers companies that are members of the Print Services and Distribution Association (PSDA). Also notes headquarters. **Number listed:** 50

1. Ennis Inc., with $549,999,000
2. Western States Envelope & Label, $98,000,000
3. PRINTSouth Corp., $85,000,000
4. Wright Enterprises, a Holding Co., $52,443,807
5. NPC Inc., $52,000,000
6. Gill Studios Inc., $50,000,000
7. Sovereign Business Forms Inc., $30,501,109
8. Data Label Inc., $29,809,104
9. Universal Manufacturing, $29,500,000
10. Highland Computer Forms Inc., $29,150,000

Source: *Print Solutions*, Top Trade Printers (annual), July 2011, p. 32-34.

4079 ■ TOP NORTH AMERICAN COMMERCIAL PRINTERS, 2010

Ranked by: Commercial printing sales, in dollars. **Remarks:** Also notes headquarters. **Number listed:** 10

1. NPC Inc., with $40,000,000
2. Ennis Inc., $31,632,058
3. Universal Manufacturing, $29,000,000
4. GrowII.com, $15,000,000
5. Corporate Disk Co., $12,300,000
6. PRINTSouth, $8,500,000
7. Thorn Hill Printing, $8,113,677
8. Team Concept Printing & Thermography, $7,440,155
9. B & W Press Inc., $7,200,000
10. Hagg Press, $7,000,000

Source: *Print Solutions*, Top Trade Printers (annual), July 2011, p. 38.

4080 ■ TOP NORTH AMERICAN COMMERCIAL PRINTING DISTRIBUTORS, 2010

Ranked by: Commercial printing sales, in dollars. **Remarks:** Also notes headquarters. **Number listed:** 10

1. WebbMason Inc., with $47,000,000
2. Data Supplies Inc., $26,788,000
3. American Solutions for Business, $25,623,974
4. Vanguard Direct, $25,500,000
5. Innovative Print & Media Group Inc., $12,722,000
6. Smart Source LLC, $12,610,000
7. Quality Resource Group Inc., $10,268,504
8. Northern Printing Network Inc., $9,041,000
9. MHC Associates Inc., $7,000,000
10. DocuSource Print Management, $6,225,500

Source: *Print Solutions*, Top 100 Distributors (annual), August 8011, p. 50.

4081 ■ TOP NORTH AMERICAN ENVELOPE DISTRIBUTORS, 2010

Ranked by: Envelope sales, in dollars. **Remarks:** Also notes headquarters. **Number listed:** 10

1. American Solutions for Business, with $14,821,232
2. Data Supplies Inc., $4,406,000
3. Smart Source LLC, $2,425,000
4. Consolidated Graphic Communications, $2,200,000
5. American Diversity Business Solutions, $2,054,375
6. B & B Solutions, $1,683,000
7. Meridian/Rockford Forms, $1,650,000
8. Quality Resource Group Inc., $1,470,263
9. Vanguard Direct, $1,100,000
10. DocuSource Print Management, $1,055,000

Source: *Print Solutions*, Top 100 Distributors (annual), August 2011, p. 56.

4082 ■ TOP NORTH AMERICAN ENVELOPE PRINTERS, 2010

Ranked by: Envelope sales, in dollars. **Remarks:** Also notes headquarters and overall rank in the *Top 100*. **Number listed:** 10

1. Western States Envelope & Label, with $90,000,000
2. Ennis Inc., $21,680,577
3. CE Printed Products, $11,420,436
4. PRINTSouth, $8,500,000
5. EM Print Group, $7,000,000
6. Maggio Data, $3,400,000
7. Identity Group | Business Stationery, $2,500,000
8. Wright Enterprises, a Holding Co., $2,202,243
9. Team Concept Printing & Thermography, $1,825,070
10. Quick Tab II Inc., $672,336

Source: *Print Solutions*, Top Trade Printers (annual), July 2011, p. 41.

4083 ■ TOP NORTH AMERICAN LABELS AND TAGS DISTRIBUTORS, 2010

Ranked by: Labels and tags sales, in dollars. **Remarks:** Also notes headquarters. **Number listed:** 10

1. American Solutions for Business, with $16,675,919

2. WebbMason Inc., $10,200,000
3. The Venture Corp., $7,500,000
4. Data Supplies Inc., $4,409,000
5. DFI, $3,955,755
6. DocuSource Print Management, $2,800,000
7. Northern Printing Network Inc., $2,670,000
8. Consolidated Graphic Communications, $2,400,000
9. RBO PrintLogistix Inc., $2,374,000
10. American Diversity Business Solutions, $2,370,433

Source: *Print Solutions*, Top 100 Distributors (annual), August 2011, p. 54.

4084 ■ TOP NORTH AMERICAN LABELS AND TAGS PRINTERS, 2010

Ranked by: Labels and tags sales, in dollars. **Remarks:** Also notes headquarters. **Number listed:** 10

1. Data Label Inc., with $29,809,104
2. Gill Studios Inc., $27,800,000
3. ID Images, $27,208,404
4. Ennis Inc., $25,047,870
5. Repacorp Inc., $19,125,000
6. TLF Graphics Inc., $15,424,500
7. Allen-Bailey Tag & Label Inc., $10,918,971
8. AmeriCAL Inc., $10,429,413
9. McCourt Label Co., $10,001,898
10. Labels West Inc., $9,983,260

Source: *Print Solutions*, Top Trade Printers (annual), July 2011, p. 40.

4085 ■ TOP NORTH AMERICAN MAILING AND FULFILLMENT SERVICE SELLERS, 2010

Ranked by: Sales of list acquisition, data cleansing, warehousing, fulfillment, and related services, in dollars. **Remarks:** Also notes headquarters. **Number listed:** 10

1. American Solutions for Business, with $13,439,305
2. WebbMason Inc., $6,800,000
2. CTP Solutions, $6,800,000
4. MPX, $6,600,000
5. Northern Printing Network Inc., $4,500,000
6. Elite Print Services Inc., $3,572,786
7. Vanguard Direct, $2,750,000
8. Smart Source LLC, $2,425,000
9. Innovative Print & Media Group Inc., $2,205,000
10. MHC Associates Inc., $2,000,000

Source: *Print Solutions*, Top 100 Distributors (annual), August 2011, p. 62.

4086 ■ TOP NORTH AMERICAN PAPER-BASED FORMS PRINTERS, 2010

Ranked by: Sales of paper-based forms, such as stock and custom forms, checks, and letterhead, in dollars. **Remarks:** Also notes headquarters. **Number listed:** 10

1. Ennis Inc., with $168,355,159
2. PRINTSouth Corp., $68,000,000

3. Wright Enterprises, a Holding Co., $44,747,889
4. Sovereign Business Forms Inc., $30,185,617
5. Highland Computer Forms Inc., $29,150,000
6. KDM Enterprises LLC, $24,700,000
7. Maggio Data, $19,400,000
8. The Flesh Co., $19,200,000
9. Central States Business Forms, $15,020,000
10. Datatel Resources Corp., $15,000,000

Source: *Print Solutions*, Top Trade Printers (annual), July 2011, p. 39.

4087 ■ TOP NORTH AMERICAN PAPER-BASED PRODUCTS DISTRIBUTORS, 2010

Ranked by: Sales of paper-based forms, including stock and custom forms, checks, letterhead, cut sheets, and mailers, in dollars. **Remarks:** Also notes headquarters. **Number listed:** 10

1. Independent Forms Services Inc., with $38,142,213
2. American Solutions for Business, $29,374,926
3. Data Supplies Inc., $22,689,000
4. WebbMason Inc., $13,700,000
5. Prime Business Solutions, $12,600,000
6. RBO PrintLogistix Inc., $6,785,000
7. B & B Solutions, $6,335,000
8. Vanguard Direct, $6,000,000
9. Consolidated Graphic Communications, $5,700,000
10. Smart Source LLC, $5,335,000

Source: *Print Solutions*, Top 100 Distributors (annual), August 2011, p. 52.

4088 ■ TOP NORTH AMERICAN PLASTIC PRINTED PRODUCT DISTRIBUTORS, 2010

Ranked by: Sales of printed plastic products, including plastic cards, signs, point-of-purchase materials, and related products, in dollars. **Remarks:** Also notes headquarters. **Number listed:** 10

1. Smart Source LLC, with $7,275,000
2. American Solutions for Business, $3,976,913
3. American Diversity Business Solutions, $1,422,260
4. Data Supplies Inc., $713,000
5. Vanguard Direct, $520,000
6. CTP Solutions, $500,000
7. MPX, $350,000
8. Consolidated Graphic Communications, $300,000
9. DocuSource Print Management, $260,000
10. One Source Inc., $250,450

Source: *Print Solutions*, Top 100 Distributors (annual), August 2011, p. 58.

4089 ■ TOP NORTH AMERICAN PRINTED PROMOTIONAL PRODUCT DISTRIBUTORS, 2010

Ranked by: Sales of printed promotional products, in dollars. **Remarks:** Also notes headquarters. **Number listed:** 10

1. American Solutions for Business, with $61,485,787
2. Smart Source LLC, $12,125,000

3. WebbMason Inc., $10,000,000
4. Quality Resource Group Inc., $7,234,628
5. Prime Business Solutions, $7,000,000
6. Data Supplies Inc., $5,796,000
7. MHC Associates Inc., $5,500,000
8. Golden Pacific Systems Inc., $4,440,614
9. Vanguard Direct, $3,850,000
10. B & B Solutions, $3,385,000

Source: *Print Solutions*, Top 100 Distributors (annual), August 2011, p. 60.

4090 ■ TOP NORTH AMERICAN PRINTING MARKETING SERVICE SELLERS, 2010

Ranked by: Sales of marketing plan creation, ROI analytics, and design services, in dollars. **Remarks:** Also notes headquarters. **Number listed:** 10

1. American Solutions for Business, with $6,517,567
2. Elite Print Services Inc., $1,360,901
3. Consolidated Graphic Communications, $900,000
4. Vanguard Direct, $880,000
5. WebbMason Inc., $450,000
6. Innovative Print & Media Group Inc., $367,000
7. RBO PrintLogistix Inc., $299,000
8. MPX, $222,500
9. Peerless, $100,000
10. IBF, $68,204

Source: *Print Solutions*, Top 100 Distributors (annual), August 2011, p. 63.

4091 ■ TOP PRINTING FRANCHISES, 2012

Ranked by: Cumulative score based on financial strength and stability, growth rate, size of the system, number of years in business, the length of time franchising, start-up costs, litigation, percentage of terminations, and whether the company provides financing. **Remarks:** Specific scores not provided. Also notes overall rank within the *Franchise 500*, contact information, description, year founded, year started franchising, states where registered, available U.S. regions, where seeking foreign expansion, number of franchised and company-owned units for past three years, start-up costs, franchise fees, royalty fees, and type of financing available. **Number listed:** 5

1. Minuteman Press International Inc.
2. AlphaGraphics Printshops Of The Future
3. Allegra Marketing-Print-Mail
4. Sir Speedy Inc.
5. PIP Printing & Marketing Services

Source: *Entrepreneur*, Franchise 500 (annual), January 2012, p. 204-205.

4092 ■ TOP WIDE-FORMAT IMAGING PRINTERS IN NORTH AMERICA, 2012

Ranked by: Revenue. **Remarks:** Specific figures not provided. Also notes owner/president, location, and website. **Number listed:** 40

1. Coloredge New York/Los Angeles
2. Thomas Reprographics Inc.
3. Duggal Vision Solutions
4. Graphic Systems Group LLC

5. Ferrari Color
6. Big Mountain Imaging
7. Source One Digital
8. Vision Graphics
9. Firehouse Image Center
10. PacBlue Printing

Source: *Wide-Format Imaging*, Top Shops (annual), March 2012, p. 10.

Printing Industry, Commercial

4093 ■ LARGEST QUICK AND SMALL COMMERCIAL PRINTERS BY SALES, 2010

Ranked by: Sales, in millions of dollars. **Remarks:** Also notes location, owner/CEO, growth in sales, number of shops and new shops planned, number of employees, sales per employee, sales per shop, and year founded. **Number listed:** 100

1. CCI/CoakleyTech, with $34.72 million
2. Balmar/HBP Inc., $32
3. ColorNet/Rockville Printing & Graphics, $15.3
4. ASAP Printing Corp., $14.79
5. Frank Gumpert Printing of Annapolis, $11.8
6. EconoPrint, $11.45
7. Landmark Print, $10.86
8. Western Graphics, $10.68
9. Hatteras Inc., $10.15
10. Copy Central, $9.56

Source: *Quick Printing*, Top 100 (annual), June 2011, p. 20+.

Private Companies

4094 ■ AMERICA'S FASTEST-GROWING PRIVATE COMPANIES, 2007-2010

Ranked by: Average annual sales growth over three years, in percent. **Remarks:** To qualify, private companies must have had annual revenues of at least $100,000 in 2007 and $2 million in 2010. **Number listed:** 500

1. ideeli, with 40,882.2%
2. Solazyme, 20,424.3%
3. C2C Outdoor, 17,744.3%
4. Big Night Entertainment Group, 16,093.4%
5. Crystal Clear Technologies, 16,048.1%
6. Show Media, 11,748.5%
7. Contour, 11,662.7%
8. Gold & Silver Buyers, 11,430.3%
9. One Source Networks, 10,305.5%
10. Connected Logistics, 10,112.3%

Source: *Inc.*, Inc. 500 (annual), September 2011, p. 71-74.

4095 ■ AMERICA'S LARGEST PRIVATE COMPANIES, 2010

Ranked by: Revenue, in billions of dollars. **Remarks:** Also notes industry, CEO, and headquarters. Only the top 20 are featured in print; the full list is available online. **Number listed:** 212

1. Cargill Inc., with $109.6 billion
2. Koch Industries Inc., $100

3. Mars Inc., $30
4. PricewaterhouseCoopers LLP, $29.2
5. Bechtel Group Inc., $27.9
6. Publix Super Markets Inc., $25.1
7. Love's Travel Stops & Country Stores Inc., $24.4
8. Ernst & Young LLP, $22.9
9. C & S Wholesale Grocers Inc., $20.4
10. U.S. Foods Inc., $18.9

Source: *Forbes*, America's Largest Private Companies (annual), December 5, 2011, p. 82+.

4096 ■ LARGEST *INC. 500* COMPANIES BY REVENUE, 2010

Ranked by: Revenue, in billions of dollars. **Remarks:** Also notes headquarters, three-year growth rate, and rank in the overall *Inc 500*. To qualify, private companies must have had annual revenues of at least $100,000 in 2007 and $2 million in 2010. **Number listed:** 5000

1. HCA Inc., with $30.7 billion
2. Publix Supermarkets, $25.1
3. CDW Corp., $8.8
4. Kingston Technology Co., $6.5
5. CH2M Hill, $5.4
6. Sungard, $5
7. Brightstar, $4.6
8. Michael's, $4
9. Momentive Performance Materials Holdings, $3.8
10. Burlington Coat Factory, $3.7

Source: *Inc.*, Inc. 500 (annual), http://www.inc.com, September 2011.

4097 ■ LARGEST PRIVATE OR FOREIGN-OWNED COMPANIES IN THE U.S. BY EMPLOYEES, 2010

Ranked by: Total number of employees. **Remarks:** Also notes contact information for headquarters, number of employees at headquarters, revenue, rank by revenue, and primary SIC code. **Number listed:** 5000

1. Compass Group USA Investments Inc., with 360,000 employees
2. Express Services Inc., 357,735
3. ARAMARK Holdings Corp., 260,000
4. ARAMARK Intermediate Holdco Corp., 255,000
5. Securitas Holdings Inc., 250,000
6. General Motors Co., 244,500
6. General Motors Holdings LLC, 244,500
6. General Motors LLC, 244,500
9. American Drug Stores Inc., 200,000
10. Hercules Holding II LLC, 194,100

Source: *Business Rankings*, (annual), Dun & Bradstreet Inc., 2011, p. X.1+.

4098 ■ LARGEST PRIVATE OR FOREIGN-OWNED COMPANIES IN THE U.S. BY SALES, 2010

Ranked by: Revenue, in dollars. **Remarks:** Also notes contact information for headquarters, number of employees at headquarters and overall, rank by employees, and primary SIC code. **Number listed:** 5000

1. General Motors Co., with $135,592,000,000
2. BP America Inc., $83,982,000,000
3. NotionT Inc., $50,000,000,000
4. HCA Holdings Inc., $30,683,000,000
4. HCA Inc., $30,683,000,000
6. Methodist Healthcare Memphis Hospitals, $27,000,000,000
7. Veolia Water North America Northeast LLC, $23,000,000,000
8. Atlantic Trading & Marketing Inc., $19,000,000,000
9. DPH Holdings Corp., $18,060,000,000
10. Roche Holdings Inc., $17,098,000,000

Source: *Business Rankings*, (annual), Dun & Bradstreet Inc., 2011, p. IX.1+.

4099 ■ LARGEST PRIVATE U.S. COMPANIES BY EMPLOYEES, 2011

Ranked by: Total number of employees. **Number listed:** 300

1. U.S. Postal Service, with 583,908 employees
2. USAF, 475,323
3. Express Employment Professionals, 350,000
4. ARAMARK Corp., 255,000
5. Deloitte LLP, 169,587
6. Kaiser Permanente, 164,098
7. Carlson Cos., Inc., 160,000
8. Publix Super Markets Inc., 148,000
9. FedEx Express, 140,000
10. University of California, 134,644

Source: *Hoover's Handbook of Private Companies*, (annual), Hoover's Inc., 2012, p. 4a-5a.

4100 ■ LARGEST PRIVATE U.S. COMPANIES BY SALES, 2011

Ranked by: Sales, in millions of dollars. **Number listed:** 300

1. USAF, with $182,015 million
2. Cargill Inc., $107,882
3. Koch Industries Inc., $100,000
4. Shell Oil Co., $77,660
5. U.S. Postal Service, $67,052
6. Medco Health Solutions Inc., $65,968
7. Cellco Partnership, $63,400
8. U.S. Department of State, $52,581
9. DHS, $52,482
10. Kaiser Permanente, $42,100

Source: *Hoover's Handbook of Private Companies*, (annual), Hoover's Inc., 2012, p. 2a-3a.

4101 ■ METRO AREAS WITH THE MOST *INC. 5,000* COMPANIES, 2011

Ranked by: Number of Inc. 5,000 companies headquartered in the city/metro area. **Number listed:** 10

1. Washington DC, with 50 companies
2. New York, NY, 43
3. Los Angeles, CA, 42
4. San Francisco, CA, 19
5. Philadelphia, PA, 18

6. Atlanta, GA, 16
7. Chicago, IL, 15
8. Boston, MA, 13
8. Miami, FL, 13
8. Seattle, WA, 13

Source: *Inc.*, Inc. 500 (annual), September 2011, p. 90.

4102 ■ TOP *INC. 5,000* COMPANIES BY EMPLOYMENT GROWTH, 2007-2010

Ranked by: Number of jobs added in three years. **Remarks:** To qualify, private companies must have had annual revenues of at least $100,000 in 2007 and $2 million in 2010. **Number listed:** 4202

1. SeatonCorp, with 14,680 jobs added
2. Sutherland Global Services Inc., 12,500
3. Senior Helpers, 7,560
4. Universal Services of America, 7,393
5. Integrity Staffing Solutions Inc., 6,796
6. iQor, 6,000
7. Mission Essential Personnel, 5,100
8. Rose International, 3,900
9. CornerStone Staffing Solutions, 3,889
10. Insight Global, 3,342

Source: *Inc.*, Inc. 500 (annual), http://www.inc.com, September 2011.

4103 ■ TOP *INC. 5,000* EMPLOYERS, 2009

Ranked by: Total number of employees. **Remarks:** Also notes overall rank in the *Inc. 5,000*, state, and revenue for current year. To qualify, private companies must have had annual revenues of at least $100,000 in 2007 and $2 million in 2010. **Number listed:** 5000

1. HCA Inc., with 194,000 employees
2. Publix Supermarkets, 148,000
3. Michael's, 38,000
4. West Corp., 33,400
5. NCO Group, 32,900
6. Sutherland Global Services Inc., 30,000
7. SeatonCorp, 28,177
8. Burlington Coat Factory, 27,260
9. CH2M Hill, 23,500
10. AMC Entertainment, 20,600

Source: *Inc.*, Inc. 500 (annual), http://www.inc.com, September 2011.

Private Trucking Fleets

4104 ■ AMERICA'S TOP PRIVATE FLEETS, 2011

Ranked by: Total number of power vehicles in fleet. **Remarks:** Also notes headquarters, industry group, and breakdown by trucks, tractors, and trailers. **Number listed:** 500

1. AT&T Inc., with 62,507 vehicles
2. PepsiCo Inc., 60,851
3. Comcast Corp., 35,500
4. Verizon Communications Inc., 32,191
5. Waste Management Inc., 28,600
6. CenturyLink Inc., 22,350

7. Time Warner Cable Inc., 18,974
8. Republic Services Inc., 17,969
9. Coca-Cola Refreshments Inc., 15,860
10. Cintas Corp., 14,198

Source: *Fleet Owner*, Fleet Owner 500 (annual), February 2012, p. 37+.

4105 ■ COMPANIES WITH THE MOST STRAIGHT TRUCKS IN FLEET, 2011

Ranked by: Total number of straight trucks in fleet. **Remarks:** Specific figures not provided. Also notes overall rank in the *Fleet Owner 500*. **Number listed:** 10

1. AT&T Inc.
2. PepsiCo Inc.
3. Comcast Corp.
4. Verizon Communications Inc.
5. Waste Management Inc.
6. CenturyLink Corp.
7. Time Warner Cable Inc.
8. Republic Services Inc.
9. Cintas Corp.
10. The ServiceMaster Co.

Source: *Fleet Owner*, Fleet Owner 500 (annual), February 2012, p. 47.

4106 ■ COMPANIES WITH THE MOST TRACTOR-TRAILERS IN FLEET, 2011

Ranked by: Total number of tractor-trailers in fleet. **Remarks:** Specific figures not provided. Also notes overall rank in the *Fleet Owner 500*. **Number listed:** 10

1. PepsiCo Inc.
2. Coca-Cola Refershments Inc.
3. Sysco Corp.
4. Wal-Mart Stores Inc.
5. Peter Kiewit Sons' Inc.
6. U.S. Foodservice Inc.
7. Halliburton Energy Services Inc.
8. Crop Production Services
9. Tyson Foods Inc.
10. Schlumberger Ltd.

Source: *Fleet Owner*, Fleet Owner 500 (annual), February 2012, p. 47.

4107 ■ CONCRETE/CEMENT COMPANIES WITH THE LARGEST PRIVATE FLEETS, 2011

Ranked by: Total number of vehicles in fleet. **Remarks:** Specific figures not provided. Also notes overall rank in the *Fleet Owner 500*. **Number listed:** 5

1. Lafarge North America Inc.
2. Cemex, SA de CV (U.S. operating cos.)
3. Aggregate Industries
4. Ready Mix USA
5. CalPortland Co.

Source: *Fleet Owner*, Fleet Owner 500 (annual), February 2012, p. 47.

4108 ■ CONSTRUCTION COMPANIES WITH THE LARGEST PRIVATE FLEETS, 2011

Ranked by: Total number of vehicles in fleet. **Remarks:** Specific figures not provided. Also notes overall rank in the *Fleet Owner 500*. **Number listed:** 5

1. Oldcastle Inc.
2. Peter Kiewit Sons' Inc.
3. Quanta Services Inc.
4. MasTec North America
5. Dycom Industries Inc.

Source: *Fleet Owner*, Fleet Owner 500 (annual), February 2012, p. 47.

4109 ■ FOOD AND BEVERAGE COMPANIES WITH THE LARGEST PRIVATE FLEETS, 2011

Ranked by: Total number of vehicles in fleet. **Remarks:** Specific figures not provided. Also notes overall rank in the *Fleet Owner 500*. **Number listed:** 5

1. PepsiCo Inc.
2. Coca-Cola Refreshments Inc.
3. Sysco Corp.
4. ARAMARK Corp.
5. Hostess Brands Inc.

Source: *Fleet Owner*, Fleet Owner 500 (annual), February 2012, p. 47.

4110 ■ LARGEST COMMERCIAL TRUCKING FLEETS, 2011

Ranked by: Total number of trucks in fleet. **Remarks:** Also notes location, type of business, number of straight trucks, number of vans and pick-ups, fuel types, and maintenance services. **Number listed:** 100

1. United Parcel Service Inc. (UPS), with 85,050 trucks
2. AT&T Inc., 62,153
3. PepsiCo Inc., 49,654
4. Comcast Corp., 38,733
5. Verizon Communications, 34,850
6. FedEx Corp., 34,850
7. Waste Management Inc., 24,338
8. Republic Services Inc., 21,277
9. CenturyLink Inc., 18,752
10. Time Warner Cable, 18,000

Source: *Light & Medium Truck*, Top 100 Commercial Fleets (annual), July 2011, p. 16-19.

4111 ■ LARGEST PRIVATE CARRIERS IN THE U.S., 2010

Ranked by: Total number of tractors in fleet. **Remarks:** Also notes rank for previous year, location, stock exchange, ticker symbol, chief executive, website, annual sales, number of straight trucks and trailers, and comments. **Number listed:** 100

1. PepsiCo Inc., with 11,286 tractors
2. The Coca-Cola Co., 8,057
3. Sysco Corp., 7,576
4. Wal-Mart Stores Inc., 6,543
5. U.S. Foodservice Inc., 4,949
6. Halliburton Co., 3,563
7. Baker Hughes Inc., 2,856
8. Tyson Foods Inc., 2,510
9. Schlumberger Ltd., 2,465
10. Dr Pepper Snapple Group Inc., 2,424

Source: *Transport Topics*, Top 100 Private Carriers (annual), 2011, p. 4+.

4112 ■ LARGEST UTILITY FLEETS, 2011

Ranked by: Total number of vehicles in fleet. **Remarks:** Also notes location, utility services, type of fuel, and maintenance services. **Number listed:** 50

1. Pacific Gas & Electric Co., with 9,345 vehicles
2. National Grid plc, 7,233
3. Southern Co., 6,870
4. MDU Resources Group Inc., 6,480
5. American Electric Power, 6,275
6. Sempra Energy, 5,705
7. Dominion Resources Inc., 5,500
8. Southern California Edison, 4,886
9. Public Service Enterprise Group, 4,875
10. Duke Energy Corp., 4,756

Source: *Light & Medium Truck*, Top 50 Utility Fleets (annual), August 2011, p. 20+.

4113 ■ MANUFACTURING/PROCESSING COMPANIES WITH THE LARGEST PRIVATE FLEETS, 2011

Ranked by: Total number of vehicles in fleet. **Remarks:** Specific figures not provided. Also notes overall rank in the *Fleet Owner 500*. **Number listed:** 5

1. Tyco International (US) Inc.
2. Siemens AG
3. Weatherford U.S. LP
4. Otis Elevator Co.
5. Diebold Inc.

Source: *Fleet Owner*, Fleet Owner 500 (annual), February 2012, p. 47.

4114 ■ PETROLEUM/GAS COMPANIES WITH THE LARGEST PRIVATE FLEETS, 2011

Ranked by: Total number of vehicles in fleet. **Remarks:** Specific figures not provided. Also notes overall rank in the *Fleet Owner 500*. **Number listed:** 5

1. Energy Transfer Partners LP
2. AmeriGas Propane LP
3. Schlumberger Ltd.
4. Airgas Inc.
5. Halliburton Energy Services Inc.

Source: *Fleet Owner*, Fleet Owner 500 (annual), February 2012, p. 47.

4115 ■ RETAIL/WHOLESALE COMPANIES WITH THE LARGEST PRIVATE FLEETS, 2011

Ranked by: Total number of vehicles in fleet. **Remarks:** Specific figures not provided. Also notes overall rank in the *Fleet Owner 500*. **Number listed:** 5

1. Sears Holding Corp.
2. Crop Production Services
3. Wal-Mart Stores Inc.
4. Genuine Parts Co./NAPA Auto Parts
5. AutoZone Inc.

Source: *Fleet Owner*, Fleet Owner 500 (annual), February 2012, p. 47.

4116 ■ SANITATION COMPANIES WITH THE LARGEST PRIVATE FLEETS, 2011

Ranked by: Total number of vehicles in fleet. **Remarks:** Specific figures not provided. Also notes overall rank in the *Fleet Owner 500*. **Number listed:** 5

1. Waste Management Inc.
2. Republic Services Inc.
3. Waste Connections Inc.
4. Clean Harbors Inc.
5. Veolia Environmental Services North America Corp.

Source: *Fleet Owner*, Fleet Owner 500 (annual), February 2012, p. 47.

4117 ■ SERVICE COMPANIES WITH THE LARGEST PRIVATE FLEETS, 2011

Ranked by: Total number of vehicles in fleet. **Remarks:** Specific figures not provided. Also notes overall rank in the *Fleet Owner 500*. **Number listed:** 5

1. Comcast Corp.
2. Time Warner Cable Inc.
3. Cintas Corp.
4. The ServiceMaster Co.
5. Cox Enterprises Inc.

Source: *Fleet Owner*, Fleet Owner 500 (annual), February 2012, p. 47.

4118 ■ UTILITY COMPANIES WITH THE LARGEST PRIVATE FLEETS, 2011

Ranked by: Total number of vehicles in fleet. **Remarks:** Specific figures not provided. Also notes overall rank in the *Fleet Owner 500*. **Number listed:** 5

1. AT&T Inc.
2. Verizon Communications Inc.
3. CenturyLink Corp.
4. MDU Resources Group Inc.
5. American Electric Power Co., Inc.

Source: *Fleet Owner*, Fleet Owner 500 (annual), February 2012, p. 47.

Process Controls

4119 ■ TOP SUPPLIERS OF PROCESS AUTOMATION SYSTEMS AND SERVICES IN NORTH AMERICA, 2010

Ranked by: North American process control revenue, in millions of U.S. dollars. **Number listed:** 50

1. Emerson Process Management, with $3,337.1 million
2. Rockwell Automation Inc., $2,237.2
3. ABB Process Automation/ABB Automation Products, $1,621
4. Danaher Industrial Technologies, $1,584.2
5. Siemens AG, $1,416.8
6. General Electric Co., $1,156.8
7. Schneider Electric SA, $910
8. Honeywell Process Solutions/Sensing & Control, $718.9
9. Ametek EIG, $671
10. Flowservice Corp., Flow Control Division, $606.1

Source: *Control*, Top 50 (annual), December 2011, p. 30.

4120 ■ WORLD'S TOP SUPPLIERS OF PROCESS AUTOMATION SYSTEMS AND SERVICES, 2010

Ranked by: Process control revenue, in millions of U.S. dollars. **Number listed:** 50

1. Siemens AG, with $12,896.4 million
2. ABB Process Automation/ABB Automation Products, $10,945.6
3. Emerson Process Management, $6,533.3
4. Rockwell Automation Inc., $4,424
5. Schneider Electric SA, $4,415
6. Mitsubishi Electric Corp., $3,473.6
7. Danaher Industrial Technologies, $3,168.4
8. Yokogawa Electric Corp., $2,979.3
9. Honeywell Process Solutions/Sensing & Control, $2,775.1
10. General Electric Co., $2,200.1

Source: *Control*, Top 50 (annual), December 2011, p. 29.

Products, New
See: **New Products**

Professional Sports Clubs
See: **Sports Clubs**

Propane

4121 ■ TOP PROPANE RETAILERS, 2011

Ranked by: Number of retail gallons sold. **Remarks:** Also notes contact information, year founded, owners, fiscal year-end, and number of outlets, states in operation, customers, wholesale gallons sold, employees, bobtails, transports, and acquisitions. **Number listed:** 50

1. AmeriGas Propane, with 874,200,000 gallons
2. Ferrellgas Partners LP, 823,564,000
3. Heritage Propane Partners LP, 539,000,000
4. Inergy LP, 326,800,000
5. Suburban Propane Partners LP, 298,900,000
6. Growmark Inc., 214,956,000
7. CHS Inc., 204,000,000
8. NGL Energy Partners LP, 110,000,000
9. MFA Oil Co., 89,600,000
10. Blossman Gas Inc., 76,500,000

Source: *LP/Gas Magazine*, Top 50 Propane Retailers (annual), February 2012, p. 29+.

Property Tax
See also: **Taxation**

4122 ■ STATES WITH THE HIGHEST STATE AND LOCAL PROPERTY TAX RATES, 2011

Ranked by: Property taxes as a percentage of personal income. **Remarks:** In the event of a tie, states are ranked alphabetically. **Number listed:** 51

1. New Hampshire, with 5.75%
2. New Jersey, 5.36%
3. Vermont, 5.29%
4. Wyoming, 5.19%
5. Rhode Island, 4.96%
6. Connecticut, 4.61%

7. New York, 4.56%
8. Maine, 4.55%
9. Washington DC, 4.46%
10. Wisconsin, 4.41%

Source: *Small Business Survival Index*, (annual), Small Business & Entrepreneurship Council, November 2011, p. 43.

4123 ■ STATES WITH THE LOWEST STATE AND LOCAL PROPERTY TAX RATES, 2011

Ranked by: Property taxes as a percentage of personal income. **Remarks:** In the event of a tie, states are ranked alphabetically. **Number listed:** 51

1. Alabama, with 1.53%
2. Arkansas, 1.71%
3. Oklahoma, 1.74%
4. Delaware, 1.83%
5. New Mexico, 1.86%
6. Louisiana, 1.93%
7. Kentucky, 2.07%
8. Tennessee, 2.20%
9. West Virginia, 2.28%
10. Hawaii, 2.40%

Source: *Small Business Survival Index*, (annual), Small Business & Entrepreneurship Council, November 2011, p. 43.

Psychiatric Hospitals

4124 ■ BEST HOSPITALS FOR PSYCHIATRY, 2011

Ranked by: Score based on reputation among specialists, in percent. **Remarks:** Scores not provided. **Number listed:** 167

1. Johns Hopkins Hospital (Baltimore, MD)
2. Massachusetts General Hospital (Boston, MA)
3. McLean Hospital (Belmont, MA)
4. New York-Presbyterian University Hospital of Columbia & Cornell
5. The Menninger Clinic (Houston, TX)
6. Sheppard & Enoch Pratt Hospital (Baltimore, MD)
7. Resnick Neuropsychiatric Hospital (Los Angeles, CA)
8. University of Pittsburgh Medical Center
9. Mayo Clinic (Rochester, MN)
10. Yale-New Haven Hospital (New Haven, CT)

Source: *U.S. News & World Report*, America's Best Hospitals (annual), http://www.usnews.com, July 18, 2011.

Public Relations Firms

4125 ■ TOP INDEPENDENT PUBLIC RELATIONS FIRMS BY NET FEES, 2011

Ranked by: Net fees, in dollars. **Remarks:** Also notes percent change from previous year, number of employees, and headquarters. **Number listed:** 122

1. Edelman, with $604,740,732
2. APCO Worldwide, $120,701,000
3. Waggener Edstrom, $115,832,000

4. Ruder Finn, $81,281,000
5. Text 100 Global Public Relations, $50,425,771
6. WCG, $47,577,000
7. MWW Group, $38,626,000
8. ICR, $32,030,483
9. Qorvis Communications, $29,500,000
10. DKC Public Relations, $26,800,000

Source: *J. R. O'Dwyer Co.*, Top 100 Independent Firms (annual), http://www.odwyerpr.com, May 2012.

4126 ■ TOP PUBLIC RELATIONS FIRMS IN AGRICULTURE WORK, 2011

Ranked by: Net fees, in dollars. **Remarks:** Also notes headquarters. **Number listed:** 9

1. Edelman, with $39,843,916
2. Gibbs & Soell, $7,674,914
3. Morgan & Myers, $4,934,650
4. Padilla Speer Beardsley, $4,008,110
5. Standing Partnership, $703,353
6. French/West/Vaughn, $212,000
7. Levick Strategic Communications, $199,366
8. Guthrie/Mayes & Associates, $90,687
9. Feintuch Communications, $34,650

Source: *J. R. O'Dwyer Co.*, Top 100 Independent Firms (annual), http://www.odwyerpr.com, May 2012.

4127 ■ TOP PUBLIC RELATIONS FIRMS IN BEAUTY AND FASHION WORK, 2011

Ranked by: Net fees, in dollars. **Remarks:** Also notes headquarters. **Number listed:** 25

1. Edelman, with $40,204,778
2. Ruder Finn, $4,504,799
3. Kaplow, $4,200,000
4. M Booth, $3,723,290
5. French/West/Vaughan, $3,138,178
6. 5W Public Relations, $2,800,000
7. Black Twig Communications, $1,350,000
8. Hunter Public Relations, $1,230,436
9. Coyne Public Relations, $1,154,000
10. O'Malley Hansen Communications, $1,100,000

Source: *J. R. O'Dwyer Co.*, Top 100 Independent Firms (annual), http://www.odwyerpr.com, May 2012.

4128 ■ TOP PUBLIC RELATIONS FIRMS IN BOSTON, 2011

Ranked by: Net fees, in dollars. **Remarks:** Also notes headquarters and number of employees. **Number listed:** 10

1. Regan Communications Group, with $17,883,715
2. Rasky Baerlein, $9,862,286
3. Davies Murphy Group, $8,873,415
4. Matter Communications, $5,750,000
5. Schneider Associates, $3,394,599
6. ICR, $2,911,185
7. LaVoie Group, $2,385,063
8. Text 100 Global Public Relations, $2,162,000
9. RF | Binder Partners, $2,075,000

10. LaunchSquad, $695,767

Source: *J. R. O'Dwyer Co.*, Top 100 Independent Firms (annual), http://www.odwyerpr.com, May 2012.

4129 ■ TOP PUBLIC RELATIONS FIRMS IN CHICAGO, 2011

Ranked by: Net fees, in dollars. **Remarks:** Also notes number of employees. **Number listed:** 13

1. Edelman, with $90,366,909
2. Jasculca Terman & Associates, $6,107,628
3. Zeno Group, $5,873,918
4. Public Communications Inc., $4,788,597
5. L. C. Williams & Associates, $4,387,355
6. Gibbs & Soell, Hoffman Estates, $3,567,608
7. FoodMinds, $3,515,753
8. O'Malley Hansen Communications, $2,950,000
9. APCO Worldwide, $2,314,000
10. Finn Partners, $2,211,000

Source: *J. R. O'Dwyer Co.*, Top 100 Independent Firms (annual), http://www.odwyerpr.com, May 2012.

4130 ■ TOP PUBLIC RELATIONS FIRMS IN CONNECTICUT, 2011

Ranked by: Net fees, in dollars. **Remarks:** Also notes headquarters and number of employees. **Number listed:** 4

1. ICR, with $19,444,744
2. Cashman & Katz, $1,485,000
3. CJ Public Relations, $801,636
4. Regan Communications Group, $770,375

Source: *J. R. O'Dwyer Co.*, Top 100 Independent Firms (annual), http://www.odwyerpr.com, May 2012.

4131 ■ TOP PUBLIC RELATIONS FIRMS IN ENTERTAINMENT WORK, 2011

Ranked by: Net fees, in dollars. **Remarks:** Also notes headquarters. **Number listed:** 29

1. Edelman, with $10,939,284
2. Finn Partners, $5,539,000
3. MWW Group, $4,827,000
4. Allison & Partners, $3,200,000
5. Taylor, $3,145,000
6. Bender/Helper Impact, $2,725,946
7. APCO Worldwide, $1,589,900
8. Jackson Spalding, $1,494,013
9. 5W Public Relations, $1,400,000
10. Hunter Public Relations, $1,377,192

Source: *J. R. O'Dwyer Co.*, Top 100 Independent Firms (annual), http://www.odwyerpr.com, May 2012.

4132 ■ TOP PUBLIC RELATIONS FIRMS IN ENVIRONMENTAL WORK AND PUBLIC AFFAIRS, 2011

Ranked by: Net fees, in dollars. **Remarks:** Also notes headquarters. **Number listed:** 38

1. Edelman, with $55,391,301
2. APCO Worldwide, $30,360,000
3. Davies, $8,253,463
4. Cerrell Associates, $4,467,127

5. MWW Group, $4,395,000
6. Levick Strategic Communications, $3,393,489
7. Rasky Baerlein, $2,944,355
8. Finn Partners, $2,254,000
9. Singer Associates, $2,004,948
10. Moore Consulting, $1,560,000

Source: *J. R. O'Dwyer Co.*, Top 100 Independent Firms (annual), http://www.odwyerpr.com, May 2012.

4133 ■ TOP PUBLIC RELATIONS FIRMS IN FINANCIAL WORK AND INVESTOR RELATIONS, 2011

Ranked by: Net fees, in dollars. **Remarks:** Also notes headquarters. **Number listed:** 44

1. Edelman, with $30,032,105
2. ICR, $29,950,681
3. APCO Worldwide, $13,396,680
4. Ruder Finn, $12,818,018
5. CJP Communications, $8,173,359
6. MWW Group, $5,967,000
7. Intermarket Communications, $4,837,425
8. Makovsky & Co., $4,000,000
9. RF | Binder Partners, $3,800,000
10. Atomic Public Relations, $3,000,000

Source: *J. R. O'Dwyer Co.*, Top 100 Independent Firms (annual), http://www.odwyerpr.com, May 2012.

4134 ■ TOP PUBLIC RELATIONS FIRMS IN FLORIDA, 2011

Ranked by: Net fees, in dollars. **Remarks:** Also notes headquarters and number of employees. **Number listed:** 5

1. Zimmerman Agency, with $9,400,000
2. rbb Public Relations, $5,407,254
3. Moore Consulting Group, $3,432,644
4. Edelman, $1,094,039
5. TransMedia Group, $1,039,000

Source: *J. R. O'Dwyer Co.*, Top 100 Independent Firms (annual), http://www.odwyerpr.com, May 2012.

4135 ■ TOP PUBLIC RELATIONS FIRMS IN FOOD AND BEVERAGE WORK, 2011

Ranked by: Net fees, in dollars. **Remarks:** Also notes headquarters. **Number listed:** 58

1. Edelman, with $75,465,749
2. APCO Worldwide, $10,217,420
3. Hunter Public Relations, $7,593,065
4. MWW Group, $6,179,000
5. Taylor, $5,605,000
6. Formula Public Relations, $5,115,780
7. RF | Binder Partners, $4,700,000
8. CRT/tanaka, $4,627,546
9. Coyne Public Relations, $4,382,000
10. Regan Communications Group, $4,110,000

Source: *J. R. O'Dwyer Co.*, Top 100 Independent Firms (annual), http://www.odwyerpr.com, May 2012.

4136 ■ TOP PUBLIC RELATIONS FIRMS IN HEALTH-CARE WORK, 2011

Ranked by: Net fees, in dollars. **Remarks:** Also notes headquarters. **Number listed:** 65

1. Edelman, with $114,588,421
2. WCG, $43,350,100
3. Ruder Finn, $30,401,000
4. APCO Worldwide, $22,741,000
5. Cooney/Waters Group, $20,433,000
6. Waggener Edstrom, $7,935,000
7. GYMR, $5,969,294
8. Spectrum, $5,728,753
9. Makovsky & Co., $5,000,000
10. Hager Sharp, $4,796,177

Source: *J. R. O'Dwyer Co.*, Top 100 Independent Firms (annual), http://www.odwyerpr.com, May 2012.

4137 ■ TOP PUBLIC RELATIONS FIRMS IN HOME FURNISHINGS WORK, 2011

Ranked by: Net fees, in dollars. **Remarks:** Also notes headquarters. **Number listed:** 20

1. Edelman, with $39,725,514
2. Zeno Group, $4,968,942
3. L. C. Williams & Associates, $3,078,632
4. Gibbs & Soell, $2,798,969
5. Kaplow Communications, $1,431,000
6. Luckie Strategic Public Relations, $1,322,417
7. Hunter Public Relations, $1,054,478
8. Lou Hammond & Associates, $829,928
9. CRT/tanaka, $702,005
10. Formula PR, $679,462

Source: *J. R. O'Dwyer Co.*, Top 100 Independent Firms (annual), http://www.odwyerpr.com, May 2012.

4138 ■ TOP PUBLIC RELATIONS FIRMS IN LOS ANGELES, 2011

Ranked by: Net fees, in dollars. **Remarks:** Also notes number of employees. **Number listed:** 21

1. Edelman, with $17,129,392
2. Davies, $8,767,164
3. Formula Public Relations (San Diego), $5,132,708
4. Finn Partners, $4,884,000
5. Revive Public Relations, $4,600,000
6. Cerrell Associates, $4,467,127
7. Zeno Group, $4,461,062
8. Formula Public Relations (Los Angeles), $4,001,700
9. Bender/Helper Impact, $3,562,622
10. Phelps Group, $3,545,693

Source: *J. R. O'Dwyer Co.*, Top 100 Independent Firms (annual), http://www.odwyerpr.com, May 2012.

4139 ■ TOP PUBLIC RELATIONS FIRMS IN THE MIDWESTERN U.S., 2011

Ranked by: Net fees, in dollars. **Remarks:** Also notes headquarters and number of employees. **Number listed:** 13

1. Padilla Speer Beardsley, with $9,467,627
2. Fahlgren Mortine, $7,860,000
3. Black Twig Communications, $6,810,000
4. Airfoil Public Relations, $5,656,600

5. Lambert, Edwards & Associates, $3,866,266
6. Standing Partnership, $3,325,966
7. Morgan & Myers (Waterloo, IA), $2,410,326
8. Morgan & Myers (Waukesha, WI), $1,990,812
9. Kohnstamm Communications, $1,612,303
10. Beehive Public Relations, $1,322,096

Source: *J. R. O'Dwyer Co.*, Top 100 Independent Firms (annual), http://www.odwyerpr.com, May 2012.

4140 ■ TOP PUBLIC RELATIONS FIRMS IN NEW JERSEY, 2011

Ranked by: Net fees, in dollars. Remarks: Also notes headquarters and number of employees. Number listed: 4

1. Coyne Public Relations, with $15,950,000
2. MCS Healthcare Public Relations, $3,771,495
3. Communications Strategies, $3,446,709
4. Rosica Public Relations, $2,208,755

Source: *J. R. O'Dwyer Co.*, Top 100 Independent Firms (annual), http://www.odwyerpr.com, May 2012.

4141 ■ TOP PUBLIC RELATIONS FIRMS IN NEW YORK, 2011

Ranked by: Net fees, in dollars. Remarks: Also notes number of employees. Number listed: 49

1. Edelman, with $118,659,974
2. Ruder Finn, $37,790,000
3. MWW Group, $25,750,000
4. WCG, $22,985,000
5. Cooney/Waters Group, $20,433,000
6. M Booth, $13,892,873
7. CJP, $12,574,399
8. 5W Public Relations, $12,455,065
9. Finn Partners, $12,347,000
10. Hunter Public Relations, $12,031,691

Source: *J. R. O'Dwyer Co.*, Top 100 Independent Firms (annual), http://www.odwyerpr.com, May 2012.

4142 ■ TOP PUBLIC RELATIONS FIRMS IN PENNSYLVANIA, 2011

Ranked by: Net fees, in dollars. Remarks: Also notes number of employees. Number listed: 2

1. Gregory FCA, with $8,122,836
2. Furia Rubel Communications, $783,025

Source: *J. R. O'Dwyer Co.*, Top 100 Independent Firms (annual), http://www.odwyerpr.com, May 2012.

4143 ■ TOP PUBLIC RELATIONS FIRMS IN PROFESSIONAL SERVICES WORK, 2011

Ranked by: Net fees, in dollars. Remarks: Also notes headquarters. Number listed: 48

1. Edelman, with $44,467,185
2. MWW Group, $3,963,000
3. Hager Sharp, $3,834,486
4. 5W Public Relations, $2,600,000
5. CJP, $2,514,880
6. Allison & Partners, $2,500,000
6. Black Twig Communications, $2,500,000

8. APCO Worldwide, $2,466,000
9. Quinn & Co., $2,385,701
10. Rasky Baerlein, $2,273,082

Source: *J. R. O'Dwyer Co.*, Top 100 Independent Firms (annual), http://www.odwyerpr.com, May 2012.

4144 ■ TOP PUBLIC RELATIONS FIRMS IN SAN FRANCISCO AND NORTHERN CALIFORNIA, 2011

Ranked by: Net fees, in dollars. Remarks: Also notes number of employees. Number listed: 20

1. Edelman (Mountain View), with $24,767,054
2. Atomic Public Relations, $15,008,254
3. WCG, $13,240,000
4. Sparkpr, $10,396,043
5. The Hoffman Agency, $9,150,000
6. Edelman (San Francisco), $8,495,856
7. LaunchSquad, $5,573,586
8. Text 100 Global Public Relations, $5,224,000
9. Allison & Partners, $4,300,000
10. Singer Associates, $4,265,847

Source: *J. R. O'Dwyer Co.*, Top 100 Independent Firms (annual), http://www.odwyerpr.com, May 2012.

4145 ■ TOP PUBLIC RELATIONS FIRMS IN THE SOUTHEASTERN U.S., 2011

Ranked by: Net fees, in dollars. Remarks: Also notes headquarters and number of employees. Number listed: 19

1. French | West | Vaughan, with $13,325,710
2. Edelman, $12,309,345
3. Jackson Spalding, $10,465,757
4. Taylor, $6,200,100
5. Gibbs & Soell, $6,077,167
6. McNeely Pigott & Fox, $5,989,743
7. CRT/tanaka, $5,898,544
8. Dye, Van Mol & Lawrence Public Relations, $5,357,245
9. Jarrard Phillips Cate & Hancock, $3,828,297
10. Dodge Communications, $3,602,980

Source: *J. R. O'Dwyer Co.*, Top 100 Independent Firms (annual), http://www.odwyerpr.com, May 2012.

4146 ■ TOP PUBLIC RELATIONS FIRMS IN SPORTS WORK, 2011

Ranked by: Net fees, in dollars. Remarks: Also notes headquarters. Number listed: 28

1. Taylor, with $10,350,000
2. Catalyst Public Relations, $5,094,633
3. Edelman, $5,041,504
4. French/West/Vaughan, $3,512,446
5. Coyne Public Relations, $2,899,000
6. Formula Public Relations, $1,266,872
7. Regan Communications Group, $1,057,300
8. Ruder Finn, $984,620
9. Maloney & Fox, $493,600
10. rbb Public Relations, $484,833

Source: *J. R. O'Dwyer Co.*, Top 100 Independent Firms (annual), http://www.odwyerpr.com, May 2012.

4147 ■ TOP PUBLIC RELATIONS FIRMS IN TECHNOLOGY/INDUSTRIAL WORK, 2011

Ranked by: Net fees, in dollars. **Remarks:** Also notes headquarters. **Number listed:** 74

1. Edelman, with $126,752,418
2. Waggener Edstrom, $59,305,000
3. Text 100 Global Public Relations, $50,425,771
4. APCO Worldwide, $31,080,000
5. Atomic Public Relations, $12,006,603
6. Qorvis Communications, $10,458,650
7. Sparkpr, $10,396,043
8. The Hoffman Agency, $9,150,000
9. Davies Murphy Group, $8,883,415
10. Finn Partners, $8,700,000

Source: *J. R. O'Dwyer Co.*, Top 100 Independent Firms (annual), http://www.odwyerpr.com, May 2012.

4148 ■ TOP PUBLIC RELATIONS FIRMS IN TEXAS, 2011

Ranked by: Net fees, in dollars. **Remarks:** Also notes headquarters and number of employees. **Number listed:** 8

1. Edelman, with $7,301,551
2. Pierpont Communications, $4,428,399
3. Shelton Group, $3,502,354
4. MWW Group, $2,267,000
5. Allison + Partners, $1,300,000
6. Open Channels Group, $1,271,243
7. Phillips & Co., $713,351
8. The Harrell Group, $639,767

Source: *J. R. O'Dwyer Co.*, Top 100 Independent Firms (annual), http://www.odwyerpr.com, May 2012.

4149 ■ TOP PUBLIC RELATIONS FIRMS IN TRAVEL WORK, 2011

Ranked by: Net fees, in dollars. **Remarks:** Also notes headquarters. **Number listed:** 38

1. Edelman, with $22,288,557
2. The Zimmerman Agency, $6,950,000
3. Lou Hammond & Associates, $5,059,922
4. MMGY, $2,924,704
5. Development Counsellors International, $2,910,765
6. Allison & Partners, $2,700,000
7. Quinn & Co., $2,650,202
8. Coyne Public Relations, $1,520,000
9. Finn Partners, $1,372,000
10. Lane Public Relations, $1,258,452

Source: *J. R. O'Dwyer Co.*, Top 100 Independent Firms (annual), http://www.odwyerpr.com, May 2012.

4150 ■ TOP PUBLIC RELATIONS FIRMS IN THE WASHINGTON DC AREA, 2011

Ranked by: Net fees, in dollars. **Remarks:** Also notes headquarters and number of employees. **Number listed:** 15

1. Edelman, with $58,229,617
2. APCO Worldwide, $55,952,600
3. Qorvis Communications, $29,500,000
4. Levick Strategic Communications, $12,459,523

5. Hager Sharp, $8,630,663
6. Crosby Marketing Communications, $7,305,583
7. Merritt Group, $7,169,638
8. GYMR, $5,969,294
9. Spectrum, $5,728,753
10. Gibraltar Associates, $4,918,650

Source: *J. R. O'Dwyer Co.*, Top 100 Independent Firms (annual), http://www.odwyerpr.com, May 2012.

4151 ■ TOP PUBLIC RELATIONS FIRMS IN THE WESTERN U.S., 2011

Ranked by: Net fees, in dollars. **Remarks:** Also notes headquarters and number of employees. **Number listed:** 12

1. Edelman (Seattle), with $30,329,509
2. Edelman (Portland), $5,945,445
3. Linhart Public Relations, $4,599,067
4. Lane Public Relations, $4,144,943
5. Nyhus Communications, $3,321,305
6. Ground Floor Media, $2,913,159
7. APCO Worldwide, $2,538,900
8. Allison & Partners, $1,500,000
9. Catapult PR/IR, $1,044,924
10. Richmond Public Relations, $1,006,790

Source: *J. R. O'Dwyer Co.*, Top 100 Independent Firms (annual), http://www.odwyerpr.com, May 2012.

Public Transit

4152 ■ STATES WITH THE FEWEST WORKERS WHO USE PUBLIC TRANSIT, 2009

Ranked by: Percentage of workers who use public transportation to and from work. **Number listed:** 51

1. North Dakota, with 0.3%
2. Alabama, 0.4%
2. Arkansas, 0.4%
2. Kansas, 0.4%
2. Mississippi, 0.4%
2. Oklahoma, 0.4%
7. South Dakota, 0.5%
8. Nebraska, 0.6%
8. New Hampshire, 0.6%
8. South Carolina, 0.6%

Source: *State Rankings*, (annual), CQ Press, 2011, p. 590.

4153 ■ STATES WITH THE MOST WORKERS WHO USE PUBLIC TRANSIT, 2009

Ranked by: Percentage of workers who use public transportation to and from work. **Remarks:** Also notes figure for U.S. **Number listed:** 51

1. Washington DC, with 37.1%
2. New York, 26.6%
3. New Jersey, 10.6%
4. Massachusetts, 9.4%
5. Illinois, 8.8%
5. Maryland, 8.8%
7. Hawaii, 6%

8. Washington, 5.9%
9. Pennsylvania, 5.3%
10. California, 5.2%

Source: *State Rankings*, (annual), CQ Press, 2011, p. 590.

Publishers and Publishing

4154 ■ JAPAN'S LARGEST PRINTING AND PUBLISHING COMPANIES OVERALL, 2011

Ranked by: Score based on revenue, profits, assets, and market capitalization. **Remarks:** Specific scores not provided. Also notes overall rank in the *Forbes 2000* and figures for each criterion. **Number listed:** 2

1. Dai Nippon Printing Co., Ltd.
2. Toppan Printing Co., Ltd.

Source: *Forbes*, Forbes 2000 (annual), http://www.forbes.com, May 7, 2012.

4155 ■ LARGEST PRINTING AND PUBLISHING COMPANIES BY EMPLOYEES, 2010

Ranked by: Total number of employees. **Remarks:** Also notes contact information for headquarters, number of employees at headquarters, revenue, rank by revenue, and primary SIC code. **Number listed:** 137

1. R. R. Donnelley & Sons Co., with 56,853 employees
2. Thomson Reuters Corp., 55,000
3. Advance Publications Inc., 37,200
4. Gannett Co., Inc., 35,000
5. American Greetings Corp., 26,000
6. Washington Post Co., 21,500
7. The McGraw-Hill Companies Inc., 21,077
8. Tribune Co., 21,000
9. Reed Elsevier U.S. Holdings Inc., 20,840
10. Hearst Corp., 20,039

Source: *Business Rankings*, (annual), Dun & Bradstreet Inc., 2011, p. VI.60-VI.62.

4156 ■ LARGEST PRINTING AND PUBLISHING COMPANIES BY SALES, 2010

Ranked by: Total revenue, in dollars. **Remarks:** Also notes contact information for headquarters, number of employees at headquarters and overall, rank by employees, and primary SIC code. **Number listed:** 138

1. Thomson Reuters Corp., with $13,070,000,000
2. R. R. Donnelley & Sons Co., $9,857,400,000
3. The McGraw-Hill Companies Inc., $6,168,331,000
4. Gannett Co., Inc., $5,438,678,000
5. Tribune Co., $5,062,984,000
6. Reed Elsevier Inc., $5,000,000,000
7. Washington Post Co., $4,723,573,000
8. WMG Acquisition Corp., $2,984,000,000
9. New York Times Co., $2,393,463,000
10. Scholastic Corp., $1,912,900,000

Source: *Business Rankings*, (annual), Dun & Bradstreet Inc., 2011, p. V.60-V.62.

4157 ■ LARGEST U.S. PRINTING AND PUBLISHING COMPANIES OVERALL, 2011

Ranked by: Score based on revenue, profits, assets, and market capitalization. **Remarks:** Specific scores not provided. Also notes overall rank in the *Forbes 2000* and figures for each criterion. **Number listed:** 3

1. The McGraw-Hill Companies Inc.
2. R. R. Donnelley & Sons Co.
3. Gannett Co., Inc.

Source: *Forbes*, Forbes 2000 (annual), http://www.forbes.com, May 7, 2012.

4158 ■ TOP *FORTUNE 500* COMPANIES IN PUBLISHING AND PRINTING, 2011

Ranked by: Revenue, in millions of dollars. **Remarks:** Also notes overall rank in the *Fortune 500;* profits; profits as a percentage of revenue; stockholders' equity; and rank by each criterion. **Number listed:** 3

1. R. R. Donnelley & Sons Co., with $10,611 million
2. The McGraw-Hill Companies Inc., $6,336
3. Gannett Co., Inc., $5,240

Source: *Fortune*, Fortune 500 (annual), May 21, 2012, p. F-38.

4159 ■ UNITED KINGDOM'S LARGEST PRINTING AND PUBLISHING COMPANIES OVERALL, 2011

Ranked by: Score based on revenue, profits, assets, and market capitalization. **Remarks:** Specific scores not provided. Also notes overall rank in the *Forbes 2000* and figures for each criterion. **Number listed:** 2

1. Reed Elsevier plc
2. Pearson plc

Source: *Forbes*, Forbes 2000 (annual), http://www.forbes.com, May 7, 2012.

4160 ■ WORLD'S LARGEST PRINTING AND PUBLISHING COMPANIES OVERALL, 2011

Ranked by: Score based on revenue, profits, assets, and market capitalization. **Remarks:** Specific scores not provided. Also notes country, overall rank in the *Forbes 2000,* and figures for each criterion. **Number listed:** 10

1. Reed Elsevier plc
2. Thomson Reuters Corp.
3. Dai Nippon Printing Co., Ltd.
4. Pearson plc
5. The McGraw-Hill Companies Inc.
6. Toppan Printing Co., Ltd.
7. Nielsen Holdings BV
8. Lagardere SCA
9. R. R. Donnelley & Sons Co.
10. Gannett Co., Inc.

Source: *Forbes*, Forbes 2000 (annual), http://www.forbes.com, May 7, 2012.

Radio Advertising

4161 ■ TOP ADVERTISERS ON RADIO, 2010

Ranked by: Measured advertising spending, in millions of dollars. **Remarks:** Also notes percent change from previous year. **Number listed:** 10

1. Comcast Corp., with $211.9 million
2. Verizon Communications Inc., $154.3
3. AT&T Inc., $144.4
4. Safeway Inc., $103.4
5. Berkshire Hathaway Inc., $102.8
6. The Home Depot Inc., $99.6
7. News Corp., $84.4
8. Wal-Mart Stores Inc., $80.6
9. McDonald's Corp., $64.8
10. J. P. Morgan Chase & Co., $62.1

Source: *Advertising Age*, Leading National Advertisers (annual), June 20, 2011, p. 16-17.

Railroads
See also: **Commuter Railroads**

4162 ■ CANADA'S LARGEST RAILROAD COMPANIES OVERALL, 2011

Ranked by: Score based on revenue, profits, assets, and market capitalization. **Remarks:** Specific scores not provided. Also notes overall rank in the *Forbes 2000* and figures for each criterion. **Number listed:** 2

1. Canadian National Railway Co.
2. Canadian Pacific Railway Ltd.

Source: *Forbes*, Forbes 2000 (annual), http://www.forbes.com, May 7, 2012.

4163 ■ JAPAN'S LARGEST RAILROAD COMPANIES OVERALL, 2011

Ranked by: Score based on revenue, profits, assets, and market capitalization. **Remarks:** Specific scores not provided. Also notes overall rank in the *Forbes 2000* and figures for each criterion. **Number listed:** 9

1. East Japan Railway Co.
2. Central Japan Railway Co.
3. West Japan Railway Co.
4. Tokyu
5. Kintetsu
6. Hankyu Hanshin
7. Odakyu Electric Railway
8. Tobu Railway
9. Nagoya Railroad

Source: *Forbes*, Forbes 2000 (annual), http://www.forbes.com, May 7, 2012.

4164 ■ LARGEST RAILROADS BY EMPLOYEES, 2010

Ranked by: Total number of employees. **Remarks:** Also notes contact information for headquarters, number of employees at headquarters, revenue, rank by revenue, and primary SIC code. **Number listed:** 47

1. Union Pacific Railroad Co., with 43,531 employees
2. Union Pacific Corp., 42,884
3. BNSF Railway Co., 35,000
4. CSX Corp., 30,088
5. CSX Transportation Inc., 30,087
6. Norfolk Southern Corp., 28,593
7. Norfolk Southern Railway Co., 28,057

8. National Railroad Passenger Corp., 18,650
9. Norfolk & Western Railway Co., 13,000
10. CRR Holdings LLC, 7,435

Source: *Business Rankings*, (annual), Dun & Bradstreet Inc., 2011, p. VI.88-VI.89.

4165 ■ LARGEST RAILROADS BY SALES, 2010

Ranked by: Total revenue, in dollars. **Remarks:** Also notes contact information for headquarters, number of employees at headquarters and overall, rank by employees, and primary SIC code. **Number listed:** 50

1. Union Pacific Corp., with $16,965,000,000
2. BNSF Railway Co., $13,848,000,000
3. CSX Corp., $10,636,000,000
4. Norfolk Southern Corp., $9,516,000,000
5. Norfolk & Western Railway Co., $2,024,000,000
6. Norfolk Southern Railway Co., $2,009,642,000
7. Kansas City Southern, $1,814,800,000
8. Genesee & Wyoming Inc., $630,195,000
9. Metro-North Commuter Railroad Co., $538,589,000
10. RailAmerica Inc., $490,291,000

Source: *Business Rankings*, (annual), Dun & Bradstreet Inc., 2011, p. V.88-V.89.

4166 ■ LARGEST U.S. RAILROAD COMPANIES OVERALL, 2011

Ranked by: Score based on revenue, profits, assets, and market capitalization. **Remarks:** Specific scores not provided. Also notes overall rank in the *Forbes 2000* and figures for each criterion. **Number listed:** 4

1. Union Pacific Corp.
2. CSX Corp.
3. Norfolk Southern Corp.
4. Kansas City Southern

Source: *Forbes*, Forbes 2000 (annual), http://www.forbes.com, May 7, 2012.

4167 ■ TOP *FORTUNE 500* RAILROADS, 2011

Ranked by: Revenue, in millions of dollars. **Remarks:** Also notes overall rank in the *Fortune 500;* profits; profits as a percentage of revenue; stockholders' equity; and rank by each criterion. **Number listed:** 3

1. Union Pacific Corp., with $19,557 million
2. CSX Corp., $11,743
3. Norfolk Southern Corp., $11,172

Source: *Fortune*, Fortune 500 (annual), May 21, 2012, p. F-39.

4168 ■ WORLD'S LARGEST RAILROAD COMPANIES OVERALL, 2011

Ranked by: Score based on revenue, profits, assets, and market capitalization. **Remarks:** Specific scores not provided. Also notes country, overall rank in the *Forbes 2000,* and figures for each criterion. **Number listed:** 18

1. Union Pacific Corp.
2. East Japan Railway Co.
3. Central Japan Railway Co.
4. CSX Corp.

5. Norfolk Southern Corp.
6. Canadian National Railway Co.
7. MTR Corp.
8. Daqin Railway Co., Ltd.
9. West Japan Railway Co.
10. Tokyu Corp.

Source: *Forbes*, Forbes 2000 (annual), http://www.forbes.com, May 7, 2012.

Real Estate Brokers

4169 ■ TOP REAL ESTATE BROKERAGE COMPANIES, 2010

Ranked by: Total amount of leasing transactions and investment sales, in billions of dollars. **Remarks:** Also notes contact information and officers. **Number listed:** 25

1. CB Richard Ellis Group Inc., with $128.1 billion
2. Jones Lang LaSalle Inc., $67.2
3. Cushman & Wakefield Inc., $66.8
4. Colliers International, $59.6
5. NAI Global, $45
6. Studley, $43.7
7. Newmark Knight Frank, $41.6
8. Eastdil Secured, $22
9. TCN Worldwide, $21.6
10. Cassidy Turley, $17

Source: *National Real Estate Investor*, Best of the Best (annual), 2011, p. 31.

4170 ■ TOP REAL ESTATE FRANCHISES, 2012

Ranked by: Cumulative score based on financial strength and stability, growth rate, size of the system, number of years in business, the length of time franchising, start-up costs, litigation, percentage of terminations, and whether the company provides financing. **Remarks:** Specific scores not provided. Also notes overall rank within the *Franchise 500,* contact information, description, year founded, year started franchising, states where registered, available U.S. regions, where seeking foreign expansion, number of franchised and company-owned units for past three years, start-up costs, franchise fees, royalty fees, and type of financing available. **Number listed:** 4

1. Keller Williams Realty
2. Weichert Real Estate Affiliates Inc.
3. Re/Max LLC
4. Better Homes & Gardens Real Estate

Source: *Entrepreneur*, Franchise 500 (annual), January 2012, p. 204-207.

Real Estate Business

4171 ■ AUSTRALIA'S LARGEST REAL ESTATE COMPANIES OVERALL, 2011

Ranked by: Score based on revenue, profits, assets, and market capitalization. **Remarks:** Specific scores not provided. Also notes overall rank in the *Forbes 2000* and figures for each criterion. **Number listed:** 6

1. Westfield Group
2. Stockland Australia

3. Westfield Retail Trust
4. Lend Lease
5. CFS Retail Property Trust
6. Goodman Group

Source: *Forbes*, Forbes 2000 (annual), http://www.forbes.com, May 7, 2012.

4172 ■ BRITAIN'S MOST ADMIRED PROPERTY COMPANIES, 2011

Ranked by: Survey of peers and investment analysts based on nine criteria: quality of management, financial soundness, quality of goods/services, ability to attract and retain talent, value as long-term investment, innovation, marketing, community and environmental responsibility, and use of corporate assets. **Number listed:** 5

1. Derwent London, with 70.9 points
2. Shaftesbury, 68.2
3. Great Portland Estates, 66.6
4. Land Securities plc, 65.8
5. Hammerson, 61.5

Source: *Management Today*, Britain's Most Admired Companies (annual), December 2011, p. 47.

4173 ■ CALIFORNIA'S LARGEST REAL ESTATE COMPANIES OVERALL, 2011

Ranked by: Score based on revenue, profits, assets, and market capitalization. **Remarks:** Specific scores not provided. Also notes overall rank in the *Forbes 2000* and figures for each criterion. **Number listed:** 4

1. HCP Inc.
2. Public Storage Inc.
3. Prologis
4. CB Richard Ellis Group Inc.

Source: *Forbes*, Forbes 2000 (annual), http://www.forbes.com, May 7, 2012.

4174 ■ CANADA'S LARGEST REAL ESTATE COMPANIES OVERALL, 2011

Ranked by: Score based on revenue, profits, assets, and market capitalization. **Remarks:** Specific scores not provided. Also notes rank in the overall *Forbes 2000* and figures for each criterion. **Number listed:** 2

1. Brookfield Asset Management Inc.
2. Boardwalk Real Estate

Source: *Forbes*, Forbes 2000 (annual), http://www.forbes.com, May 7, 2012.

4175 ■ CHINA'S LARGEST REAL ESTATE COMPANIES OVERALL, 2011

Ranked by: Score based on revenue, profits, assets, and market capitalization. **Remarks:** Specific scores not provided. Also notes overall rank in the *Forbes 2000* and figures for each criterion. **Number listed:** 11

1. China Vanke Co., Ltd.
2. Evergrande Real Estate
3. Poly Real Estate Group
4. Country Garden Holdings Co., Ltd.
5. Longfor Properties
6. Guangzhou R & F
7. Shimao Property Holdings

8. Agile Property Holdings
9. Sino-Ocean Land Holdings
10. Soho China Ltd.

Source: *Forbes*, Forbes 2000 (annual), http://www.forbes.com, May 7, 2012.

4176 ■ EUROPE'S MOST VALUABLE REAL ESTATE COMPANIES, 2011

Ranked by: Market value as of March 2011, in millions of U.S. dollars. **Remarks:** Also notes rank within the *FT Europe 500*, rank for previous year, country, revenue, net income, assets, number of employees, share price, price-to-earning ratio, dividend yield, and fiscal yearend. **Number listed:** 2

1. Immofinanz, with $4,721.8 million
2. Emlak Konut Gayrimenkul, $4,307.4

Source: *Financial Times*, FT 500 (annual), http://www.ft.com, June 24, 2011.

4177 ■ FASTEST-GROWING PRIVATE REAL ESTATE COMPANIES IN THE U.S., 2007-2010

Ranked by: Average annual sales growth over three years, in percent. **Remarks:** Also notes headquarters, revenue, and rank in the overall *Inc. 500*. To qualify, private companies must have had annual revenues of at least $100,000 in 2007 and $2 million in 2010. **Number listed:** 12

1. Valuation Management Group, with 7,909.8%
2. Pointe Vista Development, 3,067.5%
3. Renters Warehouse, 2,085.2%
4. PalmerHouse Properties, 1,726.4%
5. Innotion Enterprises, 1,563.8%
6. US Appraisal Group, 1,432.5%
7. Real Property Management, 1,252.3%
8. Campus Habitat, 1,148.8%
9. The Menkiti Group, 988.1%
10. PayLease, 974%

Source: *Inc.*, Inc. 500 (annual), September 2011, p. 182-186.

4178 ■ FRANCE'S LARGEST REAL ESTATE COMPANIES OVERALL, 2011

Ranked by: Score based on revenue, profits, assets, and market capitalization. **Remarks:** Specific scores not provided. Also notes overall rank in the *Forbes 2000* and figures for each criterion. **Number listed:** 3

1. Unibail-Rodamco
2. Gecina
3. Fonciere des Regions

Source: *Forbes*, Forbes 2000 (annual), http://www.forbes.com, May 7, 2012.

4179 ■ HONG KONG'S LARGEST REAL ESTATE COMPANIES OVERALL, 2011

Ranked by: Score based on revenue, profits, assets, and market capitalization. **Remarks:** Specific scores not provided. Also notes overall rank in the *Forbes 2000* and figures for each criterion. **Number listed:** 14

1. Sun Hung Kai Properties Ltd.
2. Cheung Kong (Holdings) Ltd.
3. Henderson Land
4. China Resources Land

5. Wheelock & Co.
6. New World Development
7. Link REIT
8. Hang Lung Group
9. Sino Land
10. Hopson Development

Source: *Forbes*, Forbes 2000 (annual), http://www.forbes.com, May 7, 2012.

4180 ■ ILLINOIS'S LARGEST REAL ESTATE COMPANIES OVERALL, 2011

Ranked by: Score based on revenue, profits, assets, and market capitalization. **Remarks:** Specific scores not provided. Also notes overall rank in the *Forbes 2000* and figures for each criterion. **Number listed:** 3

1. Equity Residential
2. Ventas Inc.
3. General Growth Properties Inc.

Source: *Forbes*, Forbes 2000 (annual), http://www.forbes.com, May 7, 2012.

4181 ■ JAPAN'S LARGEST REAL ESTATE COMPANIES OVERALL, 2011

Ranked by: Score based on revenue, profits, assets, and market capitalization. **Remarks:** Specific scores not provided. Also notes overall rank in the *Forbes 2000* and figures for each criterion. **Number listed:** 4

1. Mitsubishi Estate Co., Ltd.
2. Mitsui Fudosan Co., Ltd.
3. Sumitomo Realty & Development Co., Ltd.
4. Tokyu Land

Source: *Forbes*, Forbes 2000 (annual), http://www.forbes.com, May 7, 2012.

4182 ■ LARGEST REAL ESTATE COMPANIES BY EMPLOYEES, 2010

Ranked by: Total number of employees. **Remarks:** Also notes contact information for headquarters, number of employees at headquarters, revenue, rank by revenue, and primary SIC code. **Number listed:** 433

1. Icahn Enterprises Holdings LP, with 39,002 employees
2. Jones Lang LaSalle Inc., 36,600
3. Ford Holdings Inc., 31,400
4. CB Richard Ellis Group Inc., 29,000
5. Related Companies LP, 20,000
6. CB Richard Ellis Inc., 12,617
7. Cushman & Wakefield Holdings Inc., 12,035
7. Cushman & Wakefield Inc., 12,035
9. Rockefeller Group Inc., 11,000
9. Domus Holdings Corp., 10,800

Source: *Business Rankings*, (annual), Dun & Bradstreet Inc., 2011, p. VI.189-VI.198.

4183 ■ LARGEST REAL ESTATE/CONSTRUCTION COMPANIES IN BRITISH COLUMBIA, 2010

Ranked by: Revenue, in thousands of Canadian dollars. **Remarks:** Also notes figures for previous year. **Number listed:** 10

1. Ledcor Group of Cos., with C$2,300,000 thousand

2. Colliers Macaulay Nicolls, C$861,916
3. Charlwood Pacific Group, C$700,000
4. Northland Properties Corp., C$611,000
5. Polygon Homes Ltd., C$450,000
6. Shato Holdings Ltd., C$425,000
7. Bosa Properties Inc., C$300,000
8. Aquilini Investment Group, C$250,000
9. Whistler Blackcomb Holdings Inc., C$224,673
10. ITC Construction Group, C$224,000

Source: *BCBusiness*, Top 100 (annual), July 2011, p. 135.

4184 ■ LARGEST U.S. REAL ESTATE COMPANIES OVERALL, 2011

Ranked by: Score based on revenue, profits, assets, and market capitalization. **Remarks:** Specific scores not provided. Also notes overall rank in the *Forbes 2000* and figures for each criterion. **Number listed:** 21

1. Simon Property Group Inc.
2. American Capital Agency Corp.
3. Equity Residential
4. Annaly Capital Management Inc.
5. Vornado Realty Trust
6. HCP Inc.
7. Public Storage Inc.
8. Weyerhaeuser Co.
9. Ventas Inc.
10. American Tower Corp.

Source: *Forbes*, Forbes 2000 (annual), http://www.forbes.com, May 7, 2012.

4185 ■ MARYLAND'S LARGEST REAL ESTATE COMPANIES OVERALL, 2011

Ranked by: Score based on revenue, profits, assets, and market capitalization. **Remarks:** Specific scores not provided. Also notes overall rank in the *Forbes 2000* and figures for each criterion. **Number listed:** 2

1. American Capital Agency Corp.
2. Host Hotels & Resorts Inc.

Source: *Forbes*, Forbes 2000 (annual), http://www.forbes.com, May 7, 2012.

4186 ■ MASSACHUSETTS'S LARGEST REAL ESTATE COMPANIES OVERALL, 2011

Ranked by: Score based on revenue, profits, assets, and market capitalization. **Remarks:** Specific scores not provided. Also notes overall rank in the *Forbes 2000* and figures for each criterion. **Number listed:** 2

1. American Tower Corp.
2. Boston Properties

Source: *Forbes*, Forbes 2000 (annual), http://www.forbes.com, May 7, 2012.

4187 ■ MOST PROFITABLE CANADIAN REAL ESTATE COMPANIES, 2011

Ranked by: Profits, in millions of Canadian dollars. **Number listed:** 6

1. Brookfield Asset Management Inc., with C$1,957 million
2. Brookfield Office Properties Inc., C$1,690

3. Boardwalk REIT, C$1,225
4. RioCan REIT, C$873
5. First Capital Realty Inc., C$502
6. Dundee REIT, C$401

Source: *Canadian Business*, Investor 500 (annual), 2012, p. 55.

4188 ■ NEW YORK'S LARGEST REAL ESTATE COMPANIES OVERALL, 2011

Ranked by: Score based on revenue, profits, assets, and market capitalization. **Remarks:** Specific scores not provided. Also notes overall rank in the *Forbes 2000* and figures for each criterion. **Number listed:** 5

1. Annaly Capital Management Inc.
2. Vornado Realty Trust
3. SL Green Realty Corp.
4. Chimera Investment Corp.
5. Kimco Realty Corp.

Source: *Forbes*, Forbes 2000 (annual), http://www.forbes.com, May 7, 2012.

4189 ■ QATAR'S LARGEST REAL ESTATE COMPANIES OVERALL, 2011

Ranked by: Score based on revenue, profits, assets, and market capitalization. **Remarks:** Specific scores not provided. Also notes overall rank in the *Forbes 2000* and figures for each criterion. **Number listed:** 3

1. Ezdan Real Estate
2. Barwa Real Estate
3. United Develpment Co. PSC

Source: *Forbes*, Forbes 2000 (annual), http://www.forbes.com, May 7, 2012.

4190 ■ SINGAPORE'S LARGEST REAL ESTATE COMPANIES OVERALL, 2011

Ranked by: Score based on revenue, profits, assets, and market capitalization. **Remarks:** Specific scores not provided. Also notes overall rank in the *Forbes 2000* and figures for each criterion. **Number listed:** 3

1. CapitaLand Ltd.
2. Global Logistic Properties
3. City Developments

Source: *Forbes*, Forbes 2000 (annual), http://www.forbes.com, May 7, 2012.

4191 ■ TOP *FORTUNE 500* COMPANIES IN REAL ESTATE, 2011

Ranked by: Revenue, in millions of dollars. **Remarks:** Also notes overall rank in the *Fortune 500;* profits; profits as a percentage of revenue; stockholders' equity; and rank by each criterion. **Number listed:** 2

1. CBRE Group, with $5,912 million
2. Host Hotels & Resorts Inc., $5,003

Source: *Fortune*, Fortune 500 (annual), May 21, 2012, p. F-39.

4192 ■ UNITED KINGDOM'S LARGEST REAL ESTATE COMPANIES OVERALL, 2011

Ranked by: Score based on revenue, profits, assets, and market capitalization. **Remarks:** Specific scores not provided. Also notes overall rank in the *Forbes 2000* and figures for each criterion. **Number listed:** 4

1. Land Securities Group plc
2. British Land plc
3. Hammerson plc
4. Songbird Estates

Source: *Forbes*, Forbes 2000 (annual), http://www.forbes.com, May 7, 2012.

4193 ■ WORLD'S LARGEST REAL ESTATE COMPANIES OVERALL, 2011

Ranked by: Score based on revenue, profits, assets, and market capitalization. **Remarks:** Specific scores not provided. Also notes country, overall rank in the *Forbes 2000,* and figures for each criterion. **Number listed:** 76

1. Brookfield Asset Management Inc.
2. Sun Hung Kai Properties Ltd.
3. Mitsubishi Estate Co., Ltd.
4. China Vanke Co., Ltd.
5. Mitsui Fudosan Co., Ltd.
6. Cheung Kong (Holdings) Ltd.
7. Westfield Group
8. Sumitomo Realty & Development Co., Ltd.
9. Simon Property Group Inc.
10. Unibail-Rodamco

Source: *Forbes*, Forbes 2000 (annual), http://www.forbes.com, May 7, 2012.

4194 ■ WORLD'S MOST ADMIRED REAL ESTATE COMPANIES, 2012

Ranked by: Score, on a scale of 10, based on a survey of executives, directors, and securities analysts of companies within their own industry on eight criteria: innovation, financial soundness, employee talent, use of corporate assets, long-term investment value, social responsibility, quality of management, and quality of products/services. **Remarks:** Specific scores not provided. Also notes rank for previous year. **Number listed:** 4

1. Vornado Realty Trust
2. Simon Property Group Inc.
3. Host Hotels & Resorts Inc.
4. Equity Residential

Source: *Fortune*, World's Most Admired Companies (annual), March 19, 2012, p. 149-150.

4195 ■ WORLD'S MOST ETHICAL REAL ESTATE COMPANIES, 2012

Ranked by: Score based on five criteria: ethics and compliance program; reputation, leadership, and innovation; governance; corporate citizenship and responsibility; and culture of ethics. **Remarks:** Specific scores not provided; companies are listed alphabetically, not ranked. **Number listed:** 3

1. British Land plc (U.K.)
2. Jones Lang LaSalle Inc. (U.S.)
3. Realogy Corp. (U.S.)

Source: *Ethisphere Magazine*, World's Most Ethical Companies (annual), http://www.ethisphere.com, 2012.

4196 ■ WORLD'S MOST VALUABLE REAL ESTATE COMPANIES, 2011

Ranked by: Market value as of March 2011, in millions of U.S. dollars. **Remarks:** Also notes rank within the *FT 500*, rank for previous year, country, revenue, net income, assets, number of

employees, share price, price-to-earning ratio, dividend yield, and fiscal year-end. **Number listed:** 5

1. Sun Hung Kai Properties Ltd., with $40,707.2 million
2. Cheung Kong (Holdings) Ltd., $37,758.1
3. Mitsubishi Estate Co., Ltd., $23,603.9
4. Brookfield Asset Management Inc., $20,215.3
5. Hang Lung Properties Ltd., $19,567.3

Source: *Financial Times*, FT 500 (annual), http://www.ft.com, June 24, 2011.

Real Estate Financing

4197 ■ TOP DIRECT LENDERS IN REAL ESTATE, 2010

Ranked by: Total amount financed, in billions of dollars. **Remarks:** Also notes contact information and officers. **Number listed:** 20

1. Wells Fargo & Co., with $36.9 billion
2. Prudential Mortgage Capital Co., $8.81
3. Deutsche Bank Commercial Real Estate, $8.80
4. MetLife Real Estate Investments, $8.4
5. PNC Real Estate, $4.4
6. CBRE Capital Markets Inc., $4.2
7. Berkadia Commercial Mortgage, $4.1
8. Northwestern Mutual, $3.5
9. CWCapital, $2.8
10. Strategic Alliance Mortgage, $2.7

Source: *National Real Estate Investor*, Best of the Best (annual), 2011, p. 43-45.

4198 ■ TOP FINANCIAL INTERMEDIARIES IN REAL ESTATE, 2010

Ranked by: Total amount arranged, in billions of dollars. **Remarks:** Also notes contact information and officers. **Number listed:** 20

1. HFF LP, with $11.9 billion
2. CBRE Capital Markets Inc., $11.3
3. Meridian Capital Group LLC, $9.8
4. Eastdil Secured, $8
5. Jones Lang LaSalle Inc., $7.6
6. Strategic Alliance Mortgage LLC, $5.4
7. NorthMarq Capital LLC, $4.7
8. Q10 Capital LLC, $1.7
9. Cushman & Wakefield Sonnenblick Goldman, $1.61
10. Grandbridge Real Estate Capital, $1.60

Source: *National Real Estate Investor*, Best of the Best (annual), 2011, p. 47.

Real Estate Investment Trusts

4199 ■ EUROPE'S MOST VALUABLE REAL ESTATE INVESTMENT TRUSTS, 2011

Ranked by: Market value as of March 2011, in millions of U.S. dollars. **Remarks:** Also notes rank within the *FT Europe 500*, rank for previous year, country, revenue, net income, assets, number of employees, share price, price-to-earning ratio, dividend yield, and fiscal yearend. **Number listed:** 10

1. Unibail-Rodamco, with $19,900.4 million
2. Land Securities, $9,052.9
3. Gecina, $8,647.6
4. British Land, $7,844.7
5. Klepierre, $7,707.8
6. Icade, $6,707.8
7. Corio, $6,374.4
8. Fonciere des Regions, $5,860.6
9. Capital Shopping Centres, $5,273.9
10. Hammerson, $5,063.1

Source: *Financial Times*, FT 500 (annual), http://www.ft.com, June 24, 2011.

4200 ■ MOST VALUABLE U.S. REAL ESTATE INVESTMENT TRUSTS, 2011

Ranked by: Market value as of March 2011, in millions of U.S. dollars. **Remarks:** Also notes rank within the *FT U.S. 500*, rank for previous year, country, revenue, net income, assets, number of employees, share price, price-to-earning ratio, dividend yield, and fiscal yearend. **Number listed:** 19

1. Simon Property Group Inc., with $31,393.9 million
2. Public Storage Inc., $18,913.3
3. Equity Residential Trust, $16,583.5
4. Vornado Realty Trust, $16,070.4
5. HCP Inc., $15,233.2
6. General Growth Properties Inc., $14,924.9
7. Annaly Capital Management Inc., $14,032.7
8. Boston Properties Inc., $13,455.8
9. Weyerhaeuser Co., $13,214.7
10. Host Hotels & Resorts Inc., $11,727.1

Source: *Financial Times*, FT 500 (annual), http://www.ft.com, June 24, 2011.

4201 ■ WORLD'S MOST VALUABLE REAL ESTATE INVESTMENT TRUSTS, 2011

Ranked by: Market value as of March 2011, in millions of U.S. dollars. **Remarks:** Also notes rank within the *FT 500*, rank for previous year, country, revenue, net income, assets, number of employees, share price, price-to-earning ratio, dividend yield, and fiscal year-end. **Number listed:** 3

1. Simon Property Group Inc., with $31,393.9 million
2. Westfield Group, $22,302.7
3. Unibail-Rodamco, $19,900.4

Source: *Financial Times*, FT 500 (annual), http://www.ft.com, June 24, 2011.

Real Estate Management

4202 ■ TOP PROPERTY MANAGERS, 2010

Ranked by: Total amount of space under management, in millions of square feet. **Remarks:** Also notes contact information and officers. **Number listed:** 25

1. CB Richard Ellis Group Inc., with 2,900 million sq.ft.
2. Colliers International, 2,000
3. Jones Lang LaSalle Inc., 1,800

4. Cushman & Wakefield Inc., 723.2
5. Newmark Knight Frank, 444.9
6. Cassidy Turley, 430
7. NAI Global, 315
8. Grubb & Ellis Co., 302
9. Lincoln Property Co., 271
10. ProLogis Simon Property Group Inc., 265

Source: *National Real Estate Investor*, Best of the Best (annual), 2011, p. 41.

Real Estate Managers
See: **Real Estate Management**

Real Estate Owners

4203 ■ TOP OFFICE OWNERS, 2010

Ranked by: Total office area in portfolio, in millions of square feet. **Remarks:** Also notes contact information and officers. **Number listed:** 25

1. RREEF Americas, with 71.9 million sq.ft.
2. Brookfield Office Properties, 69.3
3. The Blackstone Group, 65.6
4. CB Richard Ellis Investors LLC, 62.7
5. Hines Interests LP, 59.2
6. LaSalle Investment Management, 42.8
7. TIAA-CREF Asset Management, 42.1
8. Boston Properties Inc., 38.4
9. Vornado Realty Trust, 35.2
10. Duke Realty Corp., 34.7

Source: *National Real Estate Investor*, Best of the Best (annual), 2011, p. 33.

4204 ■ TOP SHOPPING CENTER OWNERS, 2010

Ranked by: Total U.S. shopping center/freestanding retail gross leaseable area (GLA), in millions of square feet. **Remarks:** Also notes contact information and international GLA owned. **Number listed:** 25

1. Simon Property Group Inc., with 251 million sq.ft.
2. General Growth Properties Inc., 164.1
3. Developers Diversified Realty Corp., 121
4. Kimco Realty Corp., 112.9
5. Centro Properties Group, 96
6. The Inland Real Estate Group of Cos., 83.1
7. CBL & Associates Properties Inc., 82.1
8. The Macerich Co., 72.5
9. Westfield LLC, 63
10. Weingarten Realty, 54.3

Source: *National Real Estate Investor*, Best of the Best (annual), 2011, p. 55.

Record Stores
See: **Music Retailers**

Recreation

4205 ■ BEST CHRISTIAN PLACES TO WORK AMONG U.S. CAMPS AND CONFERENCE CENTERS, 2012

Ranked by: Determination by judges who are Christian business professionals and leaders. **Remarks:** Specific scores not provided; organizations are listed alphabetically, not ranked. Also notes location. To qualify, an organization must be based in the U.S., have at least 10 employees, and have a publicly stated Christian mission and vision. **Number listed:** 2

1. Lake Ann Camp
2. SpringHill Camps

Source: *Best Christian Workplaces Institute*, Best Christian Workplaces (annual), http://www.bcwinstitute.com, January 2012.

Recreation Industry

4206 ■ INDIA'S LARGEST RECREATIONAL PRODUCTS COMPANIES OVERALL, 2011

Ranked by: Score based on revenue, profits, assets, and market capitalization. **Remarks:** Specific scores not provided. Also notes overall rank in the *Forbes 2000* and figures for each criterion. **Number listed:** 2

1. Bajaj Auto Ltd.
2. Hero Honda Motors Ltd.

Source: *Forbes*, Forbes 2000 (annual), http://www.forbes.com, May 7, 2012.

4207 ■ JAPAN'S LARGEST RECREATIONAL PRODUCTS COMPANIES OVERALL, 2011

Ranked by: Score based on revenue, profits, assets, and market capitalization. **Remarks:** Specific scores not provided. Also notes overall rank in the *Forbes 2000* and figures for each criterion. **Number listed:** 2

1. Yamaha Motor Co., Ltd.
2. Sega Sammy Holdings Inc.

Source: *Forbes*, Forbes 2000 (annual), http://www.forbes.com, May 7, 2012.

4208 ■ WORLD'S LARGEST RECREATIONAL PRODUCTS COMPANIES OVERALL, 2011

Ranked by: Score based on revenue, profits, assets, and market capitalization. **Remarks:** Specific scores not provided. Also notes country, overall rank in the *Forbes 2000,* and figures for each criterion. **Number listed:** 5

1. Yamaha Motor Co., Ltd.
2. Harley-Davidson Inc.
3. Bajaj Auto Ltd.
4. Hero Honda Motors Ltd.
5. Sega Sammy Holdings Inc.

Source: *Forbes*, Forbes 2000 (annual), http://www.forbes.com, May 7, 2012.

Recycling

4209 ■ LARGEST PLASTICS RECYCLERS AND BROKERS IN NORTH AMERICA, 2011

Ranked by: Reprocessed volume, in millions of pounds. **Remarks:** Also notes headquarters and top recycling official. **Number listed:** 224

1. Waste Management Recycle America LLC, with 520 million lbs.
2. KW Plastics Recycling, 515
3. B & B Plastics Inc., 321.6
4. Clean Tech Inc., 250
5. B. Schoenberg & Co., 230.4
6. Joe's Plastics Inc., 214
7. Custom Polymers Inc., 180
8. Custom Resins, 165
9. Omni Resource Recovery Inc., 157.3
10. MBA Polymers Inc., 155

Source: *Plastics News*, North American Plastics Recyclers and Brokers (annual), http://www.plasticsnews.com, May2012.

Refrigerated Trucks

4210 ■ LARGEST FOR-HIRE REFRIGERATED TRUCKING COMPANIES, 2010

Ranked by: Revenue, in thousands of dollars. **Remarks:** Also notes figures for previous year and percent change. **Number listed:** 14

1. C. R. England Inc., with $943,555 thousand
2. Prime Inc., $652,251
3. Stevens Transport, $508,930
4. Marten Transport, $392,764
5. Frozen Food Express Industries, $368,822
6. Central Refrigerated Services Inc., $346,472
7. TransAm Trucking, $269,660
8. KLLM Inc., $252,376
9. Navajo Express, $225,000
10. John Christner Trucking, $217,000

Source: *Transport Topics*, Top 100 For-Hire Carriers (annual), 2011, p. 26.

4211 ■ TOP REFRIGERATED FREIGHT CARRIERS, 2010

Ranked by: Score based on revenue, operating ratio, and other financial figures. **Remarks:** Specific scores not provided. Also notes rank in the overall *Top 250*. **Number listed:** 23

1. Prime Inc.
2. C. R. England Inc.
3. Marten Transport Ltd.
4. Stevens Transport Inc.
5. Central Refrigerated Service Inc.
6. FFE Transportation Services Inc.
7. KLLM Transport Services Inc.
8. TransAm Trucking Inc.
9. Navajo Express Inc.
10. Watkins Associated Industries

Source: *Commercial Carrier Journal*, The Top 250 (annual), August 2011, p. 88.

Regional Airlines
See: **Airlines**

Rehabilitation Services

4212 ■ LARGEST REHABILITATION PROVIDERS, 2010

Ranked by: Number of free-standing and hospital-based rehabilitation facilities. **Remarks:** Also notes type of ownership, number of staffed beds, figures for previous years, and Web site. **Number listed:** 15

1. Vibra Healthcare, with 8 facilities
2. UPMC Community Provider Services, 7
3. Select Medical Holdings Corp., 6
4. Good Shepherd Rehabilitation Network, 5
5. Carolinas Rehabilitation, 4
6. Meridian Health System, 2
7. Baylor Institute for Rehabilitation, 1
7. Brooks Rehabilitation, 1
7. Casa Colina Centers for Rehabilitation, 1
7. Children's Specialized Hospital, 1
7. Extendicare Health Services, 1
7. Faxton St. Luke's Healthcare, 1

Source: *Modern Healthcare*, Largest Rehabilitation Providers (annual), December 12, 2011, p. 33.

Research

4213 ■ TOP GLOBAL MARKET RESEARCH ORGANIZATIONS, 2010

Ranked by: Global research revenue, in millions of U.S. dollars. **Remarks:** Also notes rank for previous year, headquarters, parent country, website, number of countries with subsidiaries or branch offices, number of full-time research employees, annual percent change in revenues, and breakdown of revenue by domestic and foreign sources. **Number listed:** 25

1. The Nielsen Co., with $4,958 million
2. The Kantar Group, $3,183.6
3. IMS Health Inc., $2,211.6
4. GfK SE, $1,716.2
5. Ipsos SA, $1,512.8
6. Synovate, $884.8
7. SymphonyIRI Group, $727
8. Westat Inc., $455.3
9. INTAGE Inc., $416.2
10. Arbitron Inc., $395.4

Source: *Marketing News*, Honomichl Global 25 (annual), August 30, 2011, p. 16.

4214 ■ TOP U.S. MARKET RESEARCH ORGANIZATIONS, 2010

Ranked by: U.S. research revenue, in millions of dollars. **Remarks:** Also notes rank for previous year, headquarters, website, annual percent change in revenue, worldwide research revenue, non-U.S. research revenue, number of employees, and non-U.S. research revenue percent of total. **Number listed:** 50

1. The Nielsen Co., with $2,407 million
2. The Kantar Group, $914.7
3. IMS Health Inc., $801
4. SymphonyIRI Group, $457
5. Westat Inc., $455.3

6. Arbitron Inc., $390.4
7. Ipsos, $379.6
8. GfK USA, $290.9
9. Synovate, $235.8
10. The NPD Group Inc., $173.7

Source: *Marketing News*, Honomichl Top 50 (annual), June 30, 2011, p. 17+.

Research and Development

4215 ■ COUNTRIES WITH THE HIGHEST SPENDING ON RESEARCH AND DEVELOPMENT, 2010

Ranked by: Score, on a scale of seven, based on the level of companies' research and development expenditures. **Number listed:** 142

1. Japan, with 5.9 points
2. Sweden, 5.8
2. Switzerland, 5.8
4. Finland, 5.7
5. Germany, 5.5
6. United States, 5.3
7. Denmark, 5.1
7. Israel, 5.1
9. Taiwan, 5.0
10. Singapore, 4.9

Source: *Global Competitiveness Report*, (annual), World Economic Forum, 2011, p. 516.

4216 ■ COUNTRIES WITH THE LOWEST SPENDING ON RESEARCH AND DEVELOPMENT, 2010

Ranked by: Score, on a scale of seven, based on the level of companies' research and development expenditures. **Number listed:** 142

1. Yemen, with 1.6 points
2. Kyrgyz Republic, 1.8
3. Belize, 1.9
4. Algeria, 2.0
4. Cape Verde, 2.0
6. Moldova, 2.1
6. Syria, 2.1
8. Timor-Leste, 2.2
8. Angola, 2.2
8. Ethiopia, 2.2
8. Swaziland, 2.2

Source: *Global Competitiveness Report*, (annual), World Economic Forum, 2011, p. 516.

4217 ■ TOP COMPANIES IN RESEARCH AND DEVELOPMENT, 2011

Ranked by: Score based on importance, uniqueness, and usefulness of products. **Remarks:** Specific scores not provided; companies are listed alphabetically, not ranked. Also notes country, co-developers, and winning technology. **Number listed:** 100

1. A123 Systems Inc.
2. Agilent Technologies
3. Argonne National Laboratory
4. Battelle Memorial Institute

5. Black Box Network Services
6. Brookfield Engineering Labs Inc.
7. Brookhaven National Laboratory
8. Brooks Automation Inc.
9. Bruker Nano Surfaces Division
10. Calabazas Creek Research Inc.

Source: *R & D Magazine*, R & D 100 (annual), http://www.rdmag.com, September 2011.

4218 ■ TOP COMPANIES IN RESEARCH AND DEVELOPMENT, 2011

Ranked by: Research and development expenditures, in thousands of dollars. **Number listed:** 85

1. Merck & Co., Inc., with $12,821,606 thousand
2. Roche Holding Ltd., $12,260,987
3. Pfizer Inc., $10,491,496
4. Novartis AG, $9,817,596
5. Microsoft Corp., $9,691,540
6. Volkswagen AG, $9,401,453
7. GlaxoSmithKline plc, $7,666,183
8. Panasonic Corp., $7,437,305
9. Nokia Corp., $7,066,639
10. Intel Corp., $6,851,497

Source: *U.S. Sourcebook of R & D Spenders*, (annual), June 2011.

4219 ■ TOP U.S. AEROSPACE AND DEFENSE COMPANIES IN R & D SPENDING, 2010

Ranked by: Research and development expenditures, in millions of dollars. **Remarks:** Also notes figures for previous year. **Number listed:** 10

1. Boeing Co., with $4,121 million
2. General Electric Co., Aviation Division, $817.8
3. United Technologies Corp., Aviation Division, $715.9
4. Lockheed Martin Corp., $638
5. Raytheon Co., $625
6. General Dynamics Co., $508
7. Honeywell Inc., Aviation Division, $469.3
8. Northrop Grumman, $459.7
9. Textron, $403
10. Rockwell Collins, $347.5

Source: *R & D Magazine*, R & D Funding Forecast, December 2011, p. 50.

4220 ■ TOP U.S. CHEMICALS AND ADVANCED MATERIALS COMPANIES IN R & D SPENDING, 2010

Ranked by: Research and development expenditures, in millions of dollars. **Remarks:** Also notes figures for previous year. **Number listed:** 10

1. Dow Chemical, with $1,660 million
2. E. I. du Pont de Nemours & Co., $1,651
3. 3M Co., $1,434
4. PPG Industries, $394
5. Goodyear Tire & Rubber, $342
6. Honeywell Inc., Advanced Materials Division, $207.6
7. Alcoa Inc., $174

8. Huntsman International LLC, $151
9. Eastman Chemical Co., $145
10. Air Products & Chemicals, $116.7

Source: *R & D Magazine*, R & D Funding Forecast, December 2011, p. 54.

4221 ■ TOP U.S. ENERGY COMPANIES IN R & D SPENDING, 2010

Ranked by: Research and development expenditures, in millions of dollars. **Remarks:** Also notes figures for previous year. **Number listed:** 10

1. General Electric Co., Energy Infrastructure Division, with $1,741.3 million
2. Exxon Mobil Corp., $1,012
3. Chevron Corp., $526
4. ConocoPhillips, $230
5. Itron, $140.2
6. USEC Inc., $110.2
7. Cree, $95.9
8. First Solar, $94.8
9. Babcock & Wilcox, $69.2
10. A123 Systems Inc., $60.7

Source: *R & D Magazine*, R & D Funding Forecast, December 2011, p. 52.

4222 ■ TOP U.S. INFORMATION & COMMUNICATION TECHNOLOGY COMPANIES IN R & D SPENDING, 2010

Ranked by: Research and development expenditures, in millions of dollars. **Remarks:** Also notes figures for previous year. **Number listed:** 10

1. Microsoft Corp., with $8,951 million
2. Intel Corp., $6,576
3. International Business Machines Corp. (IBM), $6,026
4. Cisco Systems, $5,711
5. Oracle, $4,108
6. Google Inc., $3,762
7. Hewlett-Packard Co., $3,076
8. QUALCOMM Inc., $2,624
9. Apple Inc., $1,959
10. EMC Corp., $1,888

Source: *R & D Magazine*, R & D Funding Forecast, December 2011, p. 48.

4223 ■ TOP U.S. LIFE SCIENCES COMPANIES IN R & D SPENDING, 2010

Ranked by: Research and development expenditures, in millions of dollars. **Remarks:** Also notes figures for previous year. **Number listed:** 10

1. Pfizer Inc., with $9,402 million
2. Merck & Co., Inc., $8,669
3. Johnson & Johnson, $6,844
4. Eli Lilly & Co., $4,884.2
5. Abbott Laboratories, $3,724.4
6. Bristol-Myers Squibb Co., $3,566
7. Amgen, $2,894
8. Medtronic, $1,491
9. Biogen Idec Inc., $1,248.6

10. Monsanto Co., $1,241

Source: *R & D Magazine*, R & D Funding Forecast, December 2011, p. 46.

4224 ■ TOP U.S. MANUFACTURERS IN R & D SPENDING, 2010

Ranked by: Research and development expenditures, in millions of dollars. **Remarks:** Also notes figures for previous year. **Number listed:** 10

1. General Motors Co., with $6,962 million
2. Ford Motor Co., $5,000
3. Procter & Gamble Co., $1,975.5
4. Caterpillar, $1,905
5. Deere & Co., $1,085.7
6. Kraft Foods, $583
7. Whirlpool Corp., $516
8. PepsiCo, $488
9. Navistar International, $484
10. Eaton Corp., $425

Source: *R & D Magazine*, R & D Funding Forecast, December 2011, p. 44.

Restaurants

4225 ■ AMERICA'S LARGEST PRIVATE HOTEL, RESTAURANT, AND LEISURE COMPANIES, 2010

Ranked by: Revenue, in billions of dollars. **Remarks:** Also notes headquarters, number of employees, and overall rank in the *America's Largest Private Companies* list. Ranking is available online only, not in print. **Number listed:** 6

1. Caesars Entertainment Corp., with $8.82 billion
2. Hilton Worldwide Inc., $8
3. Carlson Cos., Inc., $4.13
4. OSI Restaurant Partners LLC, $3.63
5. AMC Entertainment Inc., $2.42
6. Burger King Holdings Inc., $2.33

Source: *Forbes*, America's Largest Private Companies (annual), http://www.forbes.com, December 5, 2011.

4226 ■ BEST PLACES IN THE U.S. TO OPEN A NEW RESTAURANT, 2012

Ranked by: Restaurant growth index, a measure that compares restaurant sales per capita in the market to the national average. **Remarks:** Also notes population, income per capita, sales per capita, sales as a percentage of income, total number of restaurants, sales per restaurant, and persons per establishment. **Number listed:** 150

1. Corbin, KY, with 692 points
2. Key West, FL, 670
3. Sevierville, TN, 540
4. Valdosta, GA, 341
5. Gallup, NM, 332
6. Ocean Pines, MD, 316
7. Kahului-Wailuku, HI, 303
8. Crestview, FL, 292
9. Kingsville, TX, 287
10. Kill Devil Hills, NC, 282

Source: *Restaurant Business*, Restaurant Growth Index (annual), April 2012, p. 24-30.

4227 ■ BEST SMALL HOTEL, RESTAURANT, AND LEISURE COMPANIES IN AMERICA, 2011

Ranked by: Score based on revenue, profits, and return on equity for the past 12 months and five years. **Remarks:** Specific scores not provided. Also notes rank in the overall *100 Best Small Companies in America*. To qualify, companies must have revenues between $5 million and $1 billion, a net margin above five percent, and share price above $5. List is available online only. **Number listed:** 2

1. Buffalo Wild Wings
2. BJ's Restaurants

Source: *Forbes*, Best Small Companies in America (annual), November 7, 2011.

4228 ■ BRITAIN'S MOST ADMIRED RESTAURANT AND PUB COMPANIES, 2011

Ranked by: Survey of peers and investment analysts based on nine criteria: quality of management, financial soundness, quality of goods/services, ability to attract and retain talent, value as long-term investment, innovation, marketing, community and environmental responsibility, and use of corporate assets. **Number listed:** 5

1. McDonald's Restaurants U.K., with 67.1 points
2. J. D. Wetherspoon plc, 62.9
3. Domino's Pizza (U.K.), 58
4. Marston's, 56.9
5. Greene King, 53.9

Source: *Management Today*, Britain's Most Admired Companies (annual), December 2011, p. 47.

4229 ■ FASTEST-GROWING CASUAL DINING CHAINS, 2009-2010

Ranked by: Annual revenue growth, in percent. **Remarks:** To qualify, chains must have annual revenues of at least $100 million. Also notes headquarters, sales, operating income, and number of stores. **Number listed:** 15

1. Five Guys, with 38%
2. Jimmy John's, 22%
3. Chipotle Mexican Grill, 20.9%
4. BJ's Restaurants, 20.4%
4. Wingstop Restaurants, 20.4%
6. Panda Restaurant Group, 17%
7. Bojangles Restaurants, 15.3%
8. Buffalo Wild Wings Grill & Bar, 15%
9. Cheddar's Casual Cafe, 14%
10. Focus Brands, 13.2%

Source: *Stores*, Hot 100 (annual), August 2011, p. s12.

4230 ■ FASTEST-GROWING LARGE U.S. RESTAURANT CHAINS, 2010-2011

Ranked by: Annual growth in sales, in percent. **Remarks:** Ranking includes chains with annual sales over $200 million. **Number listed:** 10

1. Five Guys Burgers & Fries, with 32.8%
2. Chipotle Mexican Grill, 23.4%
3. Jimmy John's Gourmet Sandwich Shop, 21.8%
4. Yard House, 21.5%

5. Firehouse Subs, 21.1%

6. BJ's Restaurant & Brewhouse, 20.9%

7. Buffalo Wild Wings Grill & Bar, 20.1%

8. Raising Cane's Chicken Fingers, 18.2%

9. Noodles & Co., 14.9%

10. Wingstop, 14.7%

Source: *Top 500*, (annual), Technomic Inc., March 19, 2012.

4231 ■ FASTEST-GROWING RESTAURANT CHAINS BY SALES GROWTH, 2009-2010

Ranked by: Annual growth in systemwide sales, in percent. **Remarks:** Also notes systemwide sales, total number of units, growth in units, and average unit volume. **Number listed:** 50

1. Brick House Tavern + Tap, with 209.1%

2. Menchie's Frozen Yogurt, 88.7%

3. American Deli, 73.3%

4. Anthony's Coal Fired Pizza, 64.4%

5. Lazy Dog Cafe, 55.5%

6. Crumbs Bake Shop, 55%

7. The Habit Burger Grill, 49.3%

8. Zoes Kitchen, 46.2%

9. The Chop House, 46%

10. Happy's Pizza, 38%

Source: *Restaurant Business*, Future 50 (annual), July 2011, p. F22.

4232 ■ LARGEST EATING AND DRINKING PLACES BY EMPLOYEES, 2010

Ranked by: Total number of employees. **Remarks:** Also notes contact information for headquarters, number of employees at headquarters, revenue, rank by revenue, and primary SIC code. **Number listed:** 466

1. McDonald's Restaurant Operations Inc., with 390,000 employees

1. McDonald's USA LLC, 390,000

3. McDonald's Corp., 385,000

4. Yum! Brands Inc., 378,000

5. Compass Group USA Investments Inc., 360,000

6. Pizza Hut Inc., 300,000

7. ARAMARK Holdings Corp., 260,000

8. ARAMARK Intermediate Holdco Corp., 255,000

9. Compass Group USA Inc., 180,000

10. Taco Bell Corp., 175,000

Source: *Business Rankings*, (annual), Dun & Bradstreet Inc., 2011, p. VI.155-VI.164.

4233 ■ LARGEST EATING AND DRINKING PLACES BY SALES, 2010

Ranked by: Total revenue, in dollars. **Remarks:** Also notes contact information for headquarters, number of employees at headquarters and overall, rank by employees, and primary SIC code. **Number listed:** 470

1. McDonald's Corp., with $24,074,600,000

2. McDonald's Restaurants of Pennsylvania Inc., $20,460,200,000

3. Yum! Brands Inc., $11,343,000,000

4. Starbucks Corp., $10,707,400,000

5. Darden Restaurants Inc., $7,113,100,000

6. OSI Restaurant Partners LLC, $3,601,827,000

7. Wendy's/Arby's Group Inc., $3,580,835,000

8. Wendy's/Arby's Restaurants LLC, $3,416,414,000

9. Brinker International Inc., $2,858,498,000

10. Wendy's International Inc., $2,437,095,000

Source: *Business Rankings*, (annual), Dun & Bradstreet Inc., 2011, p. V.155-V.164.

4234 ■ LARGEST U.S. RESTAURANT COMPANIES OVERALL, 2011

Ranked by: Score based on revenue, profits, assets, and market capitalization. **Remarks:** Specific scores not provided. Also notes overall rank in the *Forbes 2000* and figures for each criterion. **Number listed:** 5

1. McDonald's Corp.

2. Yum! Brands Inc.

3. Starbucks Corp.

4. Darden Restaurants Inc.

5. Chipotle Mexican Grill Inc.

Source: *Forbes*, Forbes 2000 (annual), http://www.forbes.com, May 7, 2012.

4235 ■ TOP BUFFET RESTAURANT FRANCHISES, 2012

Ranked by: Cumulative score based on financial strength and stability, growth rate, size of the system, number of years in business, the length of time franchising, start-up costs, litigation, percentage of terminations, and whether the company provides financing. **Remarks:** Specific scores not provided. Also notes overall rank within the *Franchise 500*, contact information, description, year founded, year started franchising, states where registered, available U.S. regions, where seeking foreign expansion, number of franchised and company-owned units for past three years, start-up costs, franchise fees, royalty fees, and type of financing available. **Number listed:** 3

1. Golden Corral Franchising Systems Inc.

2. CiCi's Pizza

3. Stevi B's Pizza

Source: *Entrepreneur*, Franchise 500 (annual), January 2012, p. 174-175.

4236 ■ TOP CASUAL DINING CHAINS BY GROWTH IN SALES, 2009-2010

Ranked by: Annual growth in systemwide sales, in percent. **Remarks:** Also notes rank for previous year, fiscal year-end, and figures for previous year. **Number listed:** 20

1. BJ's Restaurant & Brewery/Brewhouse/Pizza & Grill, with 19.79%

2. Buffalo Wild Wings Grill & Bar, 15.01%

3. LongHorn Steakhouse, 10%

4. Texas Roadhouse, 5.84%

5. Olive Garden, 5.82%

6. The Cheesecake Factory, 3.5%

7. Carrabba's Italian Grill, 3.3%

8. Logan's Roadhouse, 2.99%

9. Red Robin Gourmet Burgers & Spirits, 2.19%

10. P. F. Chang's China Bistro, 0.41%

Source: *Nation's Restaurant News*, Top 100 (annual), June 27, 2011, p. 52.

4237 ■ TOP CASUAL DINING CHAINS BY GROWTH IN UNITS, 2009-2010

Ranked by: Annual growth in number of U.S. units, in percent. **Remarks:** Also notes rank for previous year, fiscal year-end, and figures for previous year. **Number listed:** 20

1. Buffalo Wild Wings Grill & Bar, with 12.27%
2. BJ's Restaurant & Brewery/Brewhouse/Pizza & Grill, 10.87%
3. LongHorn Steakhouse, 6.34%
4. Olive Garden, 4.46%
5. Logan's Roadhouse, 4.43%
6. Texas Roadhouse, 4.23%
7. Red Robin Gourmet Burgers & Spirits, 2.62%
8. The Cheesecake Factory, 2.05%
9. P. F. Chang's China Bistro, 2.01%
10. California Pizza Kitchen, 1.81%

Source: *Nation's Restaurant News*, Top 100 (annual), June 27, 2011, p. 52.

4238 ■ TOP CASUAL DINING CHAINS BY SALES PER UNIT, 2010

Ranked by: Sales per unit, in thousands of dollars. **Remarks:** Also notes rank for previous year, fiscal year-end, and figures for previous two years. **Number listed:** 20

1. The Cheesecake Factory, with $9,823.1 thousand
2. BJ's Restaurant & Brewery/Brewhouse/Pizza & Grill, $5,297.7
3. Olive Garden, $4,765.3
4. P. F. Chang's China Bistro, $4,669.7
5. Texas Roadhouse, $3,698.2
6. Red Lobster, $3,628.2
7. Romano's Macaroni Grill, $3,233.4
8. T. G. I. Friday's, $3,093.1
9. California Pizza Kitchen, $3,044.8
10. Logan's Roadhouse, $3,003.4

Source: *Nation's Restaurant News*, Top 100 (annual), June 27, 2011, p. 38.

4239 ■ TOP CASUAL DINING CHAINS BY U.S. SYSTEM-WIDE SALES, 2010

Ranked by: U.S. systemwide foodservice sales, in millions of dollars. **Remarks:** Also notes rank for previous year, fiscal year-end, and figures for previous two years. **Number listed:** 20

1. Applebee's Neighborhood Grill & Bar, with $4,319.5 million
2. Chili's Grill & Bar, $3,785
3. Olive Garden, $3,493
4. Red Lobster, $2,420
5. Outback Steakhouse, $2,256
6. T. G. I. Friday's, $1,794
7. Buffalo Wild Wings Grill & Bar, $1,703
8. The Cheesecake Factory, $1,448.9
9. Ruby Tuesday, $1,439
10. Texas Roadhouse, $1,250

Source: *Nation's Restaurant News*, Top 100 (annual), June 27, 2011, p. 52.

4240 ■ TOP CASUAL DINING CHAINS BY U.S. UNITS, 2010

Ranked by: Total number of U.S. units. **Remarks:** Also notes rank for previous year, fiscal year-end, and figures for previous two years. **Number listed:** 20

1. Applebee's Neighborhood Grill & Bar, with 1,862 units
2. Chili's Grill & Bar, 1,300
3. Ruby Tuesday, 802
4. Outback Steakhouse, 778
5. Olive Garden, 749
6. Buffalo Wild Wings Grill & Bar, 732
7. Red Lobster, 668
8. T. G. I. Friday's, 568
9. Red Robin Gourmet Burgers & Spirits, 431
10. Hooters, 386

Source: *Nation's Restaurant News*, Top 100 (annual), June 27, 2011, p. 52.

4241 ■ TOP CHICKEN CHAINS BY GROWTH IN SALES, 2009-2010

Ranked by: Annual growth in systemwide sales, in percent. **Remarks:** Also notes rank for previous year, fiscal year-end, and figures for previous year. **Number listed:** 8

1. Chick-fil-A, with 11.45%
2. Bojangle's Famous Chicken 'n Biscuits, 8.44%
3. Zaxby's, 8.27%
4. Popeyes Louisiana Kitchen, 4.08%
5. Church's Chicken, 1.7%
6. KFC, -4.08%
7. El Pollo Loco, -4.31%
8. Boston Market, -5.43%

Source: *Nation's Restaurant News*, Top 100 (annual), June 27, 2011, p. 62.

4242 ■ TOP CHICKEN CHAINS BY GROWTH IN UNITS, 2009-2010

Ranked by: Annual growth in number of U.S. units, in percent. **Remarks:** Also notes rank for previous year, fiscal year-end, and figures for previous year. **Number listed:** 8

1. Bojangle's Famous Chicken 'n Biscuits, with 5.45%
2. Zaxby's, 4.05%
3. Chick-fil-A, 3.89%
4. Popeyes Louisiana Kitchen, 0.25%
5. Church's Chicken, -0.24%
6. El Pollo Loco, -0.72%
7. KFC, -2.07%
8. Boston Market, -3.87%

Source: *Nation's Restaurant News*, Top 100 (annual), June 27, 2011, p. 62.

4243 ■ TOP CHICKEN CHAINS BY SALES PER UNIT, 2010

Ranked by: Sales per unit, in thousands of dollars. **Remarks:** Also notes rank for previous year, fiscal year-end, and figures for previous two years. **Number listed:** 8

1. Chick-fil-A, with $2,359.9 thousand

2. Zaxby's, $1,542.9
3. Bojangle's Famous Chicken 'n Biscuits, $1,511.8
4. El Pollo Loco, $1,347
5. Popeyes Louisiana Kitchen, $1,018.4
6. Boston Market, $1,009.1
7. KFC, $920
8. Church's Chicken, $696.5

Source: *Nation's Restaurant News*, Top 100 (annual), June 27, 2011, p. 38.

4244 ■ TOP CHICKEN CHAINS BY U.S. SYSTEMWIDE SALES, 2010

Ranked by: U.S. systemwide foodservice sales, in millions of dollars. **Remarks:** Also notes rank for previous year, fiscal year-end, and figures for previous two years. **Number listed:** 8

1. KFC, with $4,700 million
2. Chick-fil-A, $3,526.9
3. Popeyes Louisiana Kitchen, $1,607
4. Church's Chicken, $872.4
5. Zaxby's, $777.6
6. Bojangle's Famous Chicken 'n Biscuits, $712.8
7. El Pollo Loco, $557
8. Boston Market, $511.6

Source: *Nation's Restaurant News*, Top 100 (annual), June 27, 2011, p. 62.

4245 ■ TOP CHICKEN CHAINS BY U.S. UNITS, 2010

Ranked by: Total number of U.S. units. **Remarks:** Also notes rank for previous year, fiscal year-end, and figures for previous two years. **Number listed:** 8

1. KFC, with 5,055 units
2. Popeyes Louisiana Kitchen, 1,580
3. Chick-fil-A, 1,523
4. Church's Chicken, 1,251
5. Zaxby's, 514
6. Boston Market, 497
7. Bojangle's Famous Chicken 'n Biscuits, 484
8. El Pollo Loco, 412

Source: *Nation's Restaurant News*, Top 100 (annual), June 27, 2011, p. 62.

4246 ■ TOP FAMILY CHAINS BY GROWTH IN SALES, 2009-2010

Ranked by: Annual growth in systemwide sales, in percent. **Remarks:** Also notes rank for previous year, fiscal year-end, and figures for previous year. **Number listed:** 8

1. Steak 'n Shake, with 5.52%
2. Cracker Barrel Old Country Store, 1.92%
3. International House of Pancakes/IHOP Restaurants, 1.82%
4. Waffle House, 0.85%
5. Denny's, -0.36%
6. Bob Evans Restaurants, -1.42%
7. Perkins Restaurant & Bakery, -2.85%
8. Friendly's Ice Cream, -5.87%

Source: *Nation's Restaurant News*, Top 100 (annual), June 27, 2011, p. 64.

4247 ■ TOP FAMILY CHAINS BY GROWTH IN UNITS, 2009-2010

Ranked by: Annual growth in number of U.S. units, in percent. **Remarks:** Also notes rank for previous year, fiscal year-end, and figures for previous year. **Number listed:** 8

1. Denny's, with 6.58%
2. International House of Pancakes/IHOP Restaurants, 3%
3. Cracker Barrel Old Country Store, 0.85%
4. Perkins Restaurant & Bakery, 0.65%
5. Waffle House, 0.44%
6. Bob Evans Restaurants, 0.35%
7. Steak 'n Shake, -0.41%
8. Friendly's Ice Cream, -1.38%

Source: *Nation's Restaurant News*, Top 100 (annual), June 27, 2011, p. 64.

4248 ■ TOP FAMILY CHAINS BY SALES PER UNIT, 2010

Ranked by: Sales per unit, in thousands of dollars. **Remarks:** Also notes rank for previous year, fiscal year-end, and figures for previous two years. **Number listed:** 8

1. Cracker Barrel Old Country Store, with $3,237.4 thousand
2. International House of Pancakes/IHOP Restaurants, $1,769
3. Bob Evans Restaurants, $1,701.8
4. Steak 'n Shake, $1,578.5
5. Perkins Restaurant & Bakery, $1,551.5
6. Denny's, $1,435.8
7. Friendly's Ice Cream, $1,187.9
8. Waffle House, $592.2

Source: *Nation's Restaurant News*, Top 100 (annual), June 27, 2011, p. 38.

4249 ■ TOP FAMILY CHAINS BY U.S. SYSTEMWIDE SALES, 2010

Ranked by: U.S. systemwide foodservice sales, in millions of dollars. **Remarks:** Also notes rank for previous year, fiscal year-end, and figures for previous two years. **Number listed:** 8

1. International House of Pancakes/IHOP Restaurants, with $2,573 million
2. Denny's, $2,186
3. Cracker Barrel Old Country Store, $1,911.7
4. Bob Evans Restaurants, $970
5. Waffle House, $946
6. Steak 'n Shake, $764
7. Perkins Restaurant & Bakery, $716
8. Friendly's Ice Cream, $596.9

Source: *Nation's Restaurant News*, Top 100 (annual), June 27, 2011, p. 64.

4250 ■ TOP FAMILY CHAINS BY U.S. UNITS, 2010

Ranked by: Total number of U.S. units. **Remarks:** Also notes rank for previous year, fiscal year-end, and figures for previous two years. **Number listed:** 8

1. Waffle House, with 1,601 units
2. Denny's, 1,571
3. International House of Pancakes/IHOP Restaurants, 1,476

4. Cracker Barrel Old Country Store, 593

5. Bob Evans Restaurants, 571

6. Friendly's Ice Cream, 499

7. Steak 'n Shake, 483

8. Perkins Restaurant & Bakery, 463

Source: *Nation's Restaurant News*, Top 100 (annual), June 27, 2011, p. 64.

4251 ■ TOP FAMILY RESTAURANT FRANCHISES, 2012

Ranked by: Cumulative score based on financial strength and stability, growth rate, size of the system, number of years in business, the length of time franchising, start-up costs, litigation, percentage of terminations, and whether the company provides financing. **Remarks:** Specific scores not provided. Also notes overall rank within the *Franchise 500,* contact information, description, year founded, year started franchising, states where registered, available U.S. regions, where seeking foreign expansion, number of franchised and company-owned units for past three years, start-up costs, franchise fees, royalty fees, and type of financing available. **Number listed:** 2

1. Denny's Inc.

2. Big Boy Restaurants International

Source: *Entrepreneur*, Franchise 500 (annual), January 2012, p. 174-175.

4252 ■ TOP MISCELLANEOUS FULL-SERVICE RESTAURANT FRANCHISES, 2012

Ranked by: Cumulative score based on financial strength and stability, growth rate, size of the system, number of years in business, the length of time franchising, start-up costs, litigation, percentage of terminations, and whether the company provides financing. **Remarks:** Specific scores not provided. Also notes overall rank within the *Franchise 500,* contact information, description, year founded, year started franchising, states where registered, available U.S. regions, where seeking foreign expansion, number of franchised and company-owned units for past three years, start-up costs, franchise fees, royalty fees, and type of financing available. **Number listed:** 4

1. Famous Dave's

2. Genghis Grill, the Mongolian Stir Fry

3. The Melting Pot Restaurants Inc.

4. HuHot Mongolian Grill

Source: *Entrepreneur*, Franchise 500 (annual), January 2012, p. 174-175.

4253 ■ TOP PIZZA CHAINS BY GROWTH IN SALES, 2009-2010

Ranked by: Annual growth in systemwide sales, in percent. **Remarks:** Also notes rank for previous year, fiscal year-end, and figures for previous year. **Number listed:** 6

1. Little Caesars Pizza , with 13.61%

2. Pizza Hut, 8%

3. Domino's Pizza, 7.2%

4. Papa Murphy Take 'N Bake Pizza, 3.59%

5. Papa John's Pizza, 1.45%

6. CiCi's Pizza, -3.26%

Source: *Nation's Restaurant News*, Top 100 (annual), June 27, 2011, p. 56.

4254 ■ TOP PIZZA CHAINS BY GROWTH IN UNITS, 2009-2010

Ranked by: Annual growth in number of U.S. units, in percent. **Remarks:** Also notes rank for previous year, fiscal year-end, and figures for previous year. **Number listed:** 6

1. Little Caesars Pizza, with 12.82%

2. Papa Murphy Take 'N Bake Pizza, 5.98%

3. Papa John's Pizza, 3.25%

4. Domino's Pizza, 0.04%

5. Pizza Hut, -0.32%

6. CiCi's Pizza, -4.96%

Source: *Nation's Restaurant News*, Top 100 (annual), June 27, 2011, p. 56.

4255 ■ TOP PIZZA CHAINS BY SALES PER UNIT, 2010

Ranked by: Sales per unit, in thousands of dollars. **Remarks:** Also notes rank for previous year, fiscal year-end, and figures for previous two years. **Number listed:** 6

1. CiCi's Pizza, with $894.5 thousand

2. Papa John's Pizza, $737

3. Pizza Hut, $714.9

4. Domino's Pizza, $673.7

5. Papa Murphy Take 'N Bake Pizza, $538

6. Little Caesars Pizza, $418.7

Source: *Nation's Restaurant News*, Top 100 (annual), June 27, 2011, p. 38.

4256 ■ TOP PIZZA CHAINS BY U.S. SYSTEMWIDE SALES, 2010

Ranked by: U.S. systemwide foodservice sales, in millions of dollars. **Remarks:** Also notes rank for previous year, fiscal year-end, and figures for previous two years. **Number listed:** 6

1. Pizza Hut, with $5,400 million

2. Domino's Pizza, $3,320.1

3. Papa John's Pizza, $2,097

4. Little Caesars Pizza, $1,269

5. Papa Murphy Take 'N Bake Pizza, $648.8

6. CiCi's Pizza, $545.2

Source: *Nation's Restaurant News*, Top 100 (annual), June 27, 2011, p. 56.

4257 ■ TOP PIZZA CHAINS BY U.S. UNITS, 2010

Ranked by: Total number of U.S. units. **Remarks:** Also notes rank for previous year, fiscal year-end, and figures for previous two years. **Number listed:** 6

1. Pizza Hut, with 7,542 units

2. Domino's Pizza, 4,929

3. Little Caesars Pizza, 3,213

4. Papa John's Pizza, 2,891

5. Papa Murphy Take 'N Bake Pizza, 1,241

6. CiCi's Pizza, 594

Source: *Nation's Restaurant News*, Top 100 (annual), June 27, 2011, p. 56.

4258 ■ TOP RESTAURANT CHAINS BY GROWTH IN FRANCHISED UNITS, 2009-2010

Ranked by: Annual growth in total number of franchised units, in percent. **Remarks:** Also notes rank for previous year, fiscal year-end, and figures for previous year. **Number listed:** 66

1. Five Guys Burgers & Fries, with 36.11%

2. Jack in the Box, 22.31%

3. Jimmy John's, 16.67%

3. Panda Express, 16.67%

5. Little Caesars Pizza, 15.91%

6. Waffle House, 13.71%

7. Buffalo Wild Wings Grill & Bar, 12.62%

8. California Pizza Kitchen, 11.11%

9. 7-Eleven, 9.06%

10. Denny's, 7.9%

Source: *Nation's Restaurant News*, Top 100 (annual), June 27, 2011, p. 40.

4259 ■ TOP RESTAURANT CHAINS BY GROWTH IN NUMBER OF UNITS, 2009-2010

Ranked by: Annual growth in total number of units, in percent. **Remarks:** Also notes rank for previous year, fiscal year-end, and figures for previous year. **Number listed:** 100

1. Centerplate, with 80.45%

2. Five Guys Burgers & Fries, 34.31%

3. Jimmy John's, 16.62%

4. Chipotle Mexican Grill, 13.19%

5. Little Caesars Pizza, 12.82%

6. Buffalo Wild Wings Grill & Bar, 12.27%

7. BJ's Restaurant & Brewery/Brewhouse/Pizza & Grill, 10.87%

8. HMSHost, 8.33%

9. Delaware North Cos. Sportservice, 8%

10. Aramark Healthcare, 7.02%

Source: *Nation's Restaurant News*, Top 100 (annual), June 27, 2011, p. 44.

4260 ■ TOP RESTAURANT CHAINS BY GROWTH IN SALES PER UNIT, 2009-2010

Ranked by: Annual growth in sales per unit, in percent. **Remarks:** Also notes rank for previous year, fiscal year-end, and figures for previous year. **Number listed:** 79

1. Starbucks Coffee, with 9.37%

2. Jimmy John's, 9.32%

3. Domino's Pizza, 8.48%

4. Pizza Hut, 8.16%

5. BJ's Restaurant & Brewery/Brewhouse/Pizza & Grill, 8.06%

6. Chick-fil-A, 7.2%

7. Hardee's, 6.74%

8. Panera Bread, 6.68%

9. Steak 'n Shake, 6.4%

10. Chipotle Mexican Grill, 6.25%

Source: *Nation's Restaurant News*, Top 100 (annual), June 27, 2011, p. 36.

4261 ■ TOP RESTAURANT CHAINS BY GROWTH IN U.S. REVENUE, 2009-2010

Ranked by: Annual growth in U.S. foodservice revenue, in percent. **Remarks:** Also notes rank for previous year, fiscal year-end, and figures for previous year. **Number listed:** 100

1. Five Guys Burgers & Fries, with 44.49%

2. Delaware North Cos., Sportservice, 32.53%

3. Jimmy John's, 29.35%

4. Chipotle Mexican Grill/Chipotle, 20.79%

5. BJ's Restaurant & Brewery/Brewhouse/Pizza & Grill, 19.79%

6. Levy Restaurants, 18.85%

7. Buffalo Wild Wings Grill & Bar, 15.01%

8. Bon Appetit Management Co., 14.52%

9. Little Caesars Pizza, 13.61%

10. Chartwells, 13.19%

Source: *Nation's Restaurant News*, Top 100 (annual), June 27, 2011, p. 34.

4262 ■ TOP RESTAURANT CHAINS BY MARKET SHARE, 2010

Ranked by: Market share, in percent. **Remarks:** Also notes parent company, figures for previous year, and advertising expenditures for current and previous year. **Number listed:** 10

1. McDonald's, with 8.97%

2. Subway, 2.94%

3. Starbucks, 2.51%

4. Burger King, 2.41%

5. Wendy's, 2.31%

6. Taco Bell, 1.92%

7. Dunkin' Donuts, 1.56%

8. Pizza Hut, 1.49%

9. KFC, 1.3%

10. Applebee's, 1.2%

Source: *Advertising Age*, Leading National Advertisers (annual), June 20, 2011, p. 22.

4263 ■ TOP RESTAURANT CHAINS BY SALES PER UNIT, 2010

Ranked by: Sales per unit, in thousands of dollars. **Remarks:** Also notes rank for previous year, fiscal year-end, and figures for previous two years. **Number listed:** 79

1. The Cheesecake Factory, with $9,823.1 thousand

2. BJ's Restaurant & Brewery/Brewhouse/Pizza & Grill, $5,297.9

3. Olive Garden, $4,765.3

4. Sheraton Hotels, $4,732.3

5. Hilton Hotels, $4,688.3

6. P. F. Chang's China Bistro, $4,669.7

7. Hyatt Hotels , $4,373

8. Marriott Hotels & Resorts, $3,920.2

9. Texas Roadhouse, $3,698.2

10. Red Lobster, $3,628.2

Source: *Nation's Restaurant News*, Top 100 (annual), June 27, 2011, p. 36.

4264 ■ TOP RESTAURANT CHAINS BY U.S. SALES, 2010

Ranked by: U.S. systemwide foodservice sales, in millions of dollars. **Remarks:** Also notes rank for previous year, type of chain, parent company, fiscal year-end, and sales for previous two years. **Number listed:** 100

1. McDonald's, with $32,395.4 million

2. Subway, $10,633

3. Burger King, $8,368

4. Starbucks Coffee, $7,955

5. Wendy's, $7,943

6. Taco Bell, $6,900

7. Dunkin' Donuts, $5,435

8. Pizza Hut, $5,400

9. KFC, $4,700

10. Applebee's Neighborhood Grill & Bar, $4,319.5

Source: *Nation's Restaurant News*, Top 100 (annual), June 27, 2011, p. 26+.

4265 ■ TOP RESTAURANT CHAINS BY U.S. UNITS, 2010

Ranked by: Total number of U.S. units. **Remarks:** Also notes rank for previous year, fiscal year-end, figures for previous two years, and breakdown by company and franchised units. **Number listed:** 100

1. Subway, with 23,850 units
2. Canteen Services, 18,125
3. McDonald's, 14,027
4. Starbucks Coffee, 10,580
5. Pizza Hut, 7,542
6. Burger King, 7,251
7. Dunkin' Donuts, 6,772
8. 7-Eleven, 6,137
9. Wendy's, 5,883
10. Taco Bell, 5,634

Source: *Nation's Restaurant News*, Top 100 (annual), June 27, 2011, p. 42.

4266 ■ TOP SPORTS BAR FRANCHISES, 2012

Ranked by: Cumulative score based on financial strength and stability, growth rate, size of the system, number of years in business, the length of time franchising, start-up costs, litigation, percentage of terminations, and whether the company provides financing. **Remarks:** Specific scores not provided. Also notes overall rank within the *Franchise 500,* contact information, description, year founded, year started franchising, states where registered, available U.S. regions, where seeking foreign expansion, number of franchised and company-owned units for past three years, start-up costs, franchise fees, royalty fees, and type of financing available. **Number listed:** 2

1. Beef 'O' Brady's
2. The Greene Turtle Sports Bar & Grille

Source: *Entrepreneur*, Franchise 500 (annual), January 2012, p. 174-175.

4267 ■ TOP U.S. RESTAURANT CHAINS BY SALES, 2010

Ranked by: Sales volume, in thousands of dollars. **Remarks:** Also notes comparable-store sales and sales per store. **Number listed:** 10

1. McDonald's Corp., with $23,130,000 thousand
2. Yum! Brands Inc., $17,306,000
3. Wendy's/Arby's Restaurants LLC, $10,026,000
4. Subway, $10,373,000
5. Burger King Holdings, $8,437,000
6. Darden Restaurants Inc., $7,603,000
7. Starbucks Corp., $7,560,000
8. DineEquity Inc., $5,884,000
9. OSI Restaurant Partners LLC, $3,314,000
10. Brinker International Inc., $3,090,000

Source: *Stores*, Top 100 Retailers (annual), July 2011, p. s14.

4268 ■ WORLD'S LARGEST RESTAURANT COMPANIES OVERALL, 2011

Ranked by: Score based on revenue, profits, assets, and market capitalization. **Remarks:** Specific scores not provided. Also notes country, overall rank in the *Forbes 2000,* and figures for each criterion. **Number listed:** 7

1. McDonald's Corp.
2. Compass Group plc
3. Yum! Brands Inc.
4. Starbucks Corp.
5. Darden Restaurants Inc.
6. Tim Hortons Inc.
7. Chipotle Mexican Grill Inc.

Source: *Forbes*, Forbes 2000 (annual), http://www.forbes.com, May 7, 2012.

Retail Industry
See also: **Chain Stores; Department Stores**

4269 ■ AMERICA'S LARGEST PRIVATE RETAILERS, 2010

Ranked by: Revenue, in billions of dollars. **Remarks:** Also notes headquarters, number of employees, and overall rank in the *America's Largest Private Companies* list. Ranking is available online only, not in print. **Number listed:** 19

1. Toys "R" Us Inc., with $13.86 billion
2. Menard Inc., $7.17
3. Levi Strauss & Co., $4.41
4. Michaels Stores Inc., $4.03
5. Neiman Marcus Group Inc., $4
6. Bass Pro Shops Inc., $3.83
7. Burlington Coat Factory Warehouse Corp., $3.67
8. Belk Inc., $3.51
9. The Sports Authority Inc., $3.2
10. Discount Tire Co., $3

Source: *Forbes*, America's Largest Private Companies (annual), http://www.forbes.com, December 5, 2011.

4270 ■ BEST RETAIL COMPANIES TO WORK FOR IN BRITISH COLUMBIA, 2010

Ranked by: Editorial determination. **Remarks:** Specific scores not provided. **Number listed:** 5

1. Pharmasave Drugs (Pacific) Ltd.
2. Flight Centre Canada
3. Tom Harris Cellular Ltd.
4. La-Z-Boy Vancouver
5. Mr. Lube Canada Inc.

Source: *BCBusiness*, Best Companies (annual), http://www.bcbusinessonline.ca, December 2011.

4271 ■ BEST SMALL RETAILING COMPANIES IN AMERICA, 2011

Ranked by: Score based on revenue, profits, and return on equity for the past 12 months and five years. **Remarks:** Specific scores not provided. Also notes rank in the overall *100 Best Small Companies in America.* To qualify, companies must have revenues between $5 million and $1 billion, a net margin above five percent, and share price above $5. List is available online only. **Number listed:** 7

1. Winmark
2. Rue21
3. Buckle
4. Liquidity Services

5. Hibbett Sporting Goods
6. Jos. A. Bank Clothiers
7. Copart

Source: *Forbes*, Best Small Companies in America (annual), November 7, 2011.

4272 ■ EUROPE'S MOST VALUABLE GENERAL RETAILERS, 2011

Ranked by: Market value as of March 2011, in millions of U.S. dollars. **Remarks:** Also notes rank within the *FT Europe 500*, rank for previous year, country, revenue, net income, assets, number of employees, share price, price-to-earning ratio, dividend yield, and fiscal yearend. **Number listed:** 6

1. Industria de Diseno Textil SA (Inditex), with $50,083.9 million
2. Hennes & Mauritz AB, $48,531.6
3. PPR SA, $19,465.1
4. Kingfisher plc, $9,317.8
5. Marks & Spencer plc, $8,553.3
6. Next Inc., $5,699.3

Source: *Financial Times*, FT 500 (annual), http://www.ft.com, June 24, 2011.

4273 ■ FASTEST-GROWING PRIVATE RETAIL COMPANIES IN THE U.S., 2007-2010

Ranked by: Average annual sales growth over three years, in percent. **Remarks:** Also notes headquarters, revenue, and rank in the overall *Inc. 500*. To qualify, private companies must have had annual revenues of at least $100,000 in 2007 and $2 million in 2010. **Number listed:** 18

1. ideeli, with 40,882.2%
2. UniqueSquared.com, 2,461.4%
3. Savings.com, 2,076.7%
4. 3tailer, 1,346.1%
5. BulkReefSupply.com, 1,248.1%
6. Wild Creations, 1,242.6%
7. VetDepot.com, 1,235.3%
8. Alligator Diesel Performance, 1,213.2%
9. The Ticket Experience, 1,027.3%
10. BeautyChoice.com, 884.4%

Source: *Inc.*, Inc. 500 (annual), September 2011, p. 186-188.

4274 ■ FASTEST-GROWING RETAIL COMPANIES, 2008-2011

Ranked by: Score based on three-year growth in revenue and earnings, and three-year total return to investors. **Remarks:** Specific scores not provided. To qualify for list, companies must have revenues of at least $50 million, net income of at least $10 million, market capitalization of at least $250 million, and stock price of at least $5. Int'l companies are eligible if they trade on a U.S. exchange and file quarterly reports. **Number listed:** 9

1. Lululemon Athletica
2. Amazon.com Inc.
3. Steven Madden Ltd.
4. O'Reilly Automotive Inc.
5. Chipotle Mexican Grill Inc.
6. Ulta Salon, Cosmetics & Fragrance
7. BJ's Restaurant & Brewhouse
8. First Cash Financial Services

9. Buffalo Wild Wings Grill & Bar

Source: *Fortune*, 100 Fastest-Growing Companies (annual), http://www.fortune.com, September 26, 2011.

4275 ■ FRANCE'S MOST VALUABLE RETAIL BRANDS, 2011

Ranked by: Brand value, in millions of U.S. dollars. **Remarks:** Also notes rank within the *Global 500* for current and previous year, figures for current and previous year, and brand rating. Ranking is available online only. **Number listed:** 2

1. Gucci, with $2,755 million
2. FNAC, $2,620

Source: *Global 500*, (annual), Brand Finance plc, March 2012.

4276 ■ JAPAN'S MOST VALUABLE RETAIL BRANDS, 2011

Ranked by: Brand value, in millions of U.S. dollars. **Remarks:** Also notes rank within the *Global 500* for current and previous year, figures for current and previous year, and brand rating. Ranking is available online only. **Number listed:** 3

1. Aeon, with $3,346 million
2. 7-Eleven, $4,549
3. Yamada, $2,647

Source: *Global 500*, (annual), Brand Finance plc, March 2012.

4277 ■ LARGEST ASIA-PACIFIC RETAIL COMPANIES, 2010

Ranked by: Sales, in millions of U.S. dollars. **Remarks:** Also notes outlet type, fascias/brands, number of outlets, sales in national currency, sales area, sales per square meter, and figures for previous year. **Number listed:** 500

1. Seven & I Holdings Co., Ltd. (convenience store, Japan), with $31,064 million
2. Aeon Group (Japan), $26,501
3. Woolworths Ltd. (Australia), $25,857
4. Seven & I Holdings (dept. store, Japan), $24,426
5. Lawson Inc. (Japan), $20,974
6. Wesfarmers Ltd. (Australia), $19,116
7. Family Mart (Japan), $15,992
8. Yamada Denki Co., Ltd. (Japan), $13,668
9. Uny (Japan), $12,651
10. Gome Electrical Appliances Holding (China), $11,674

Source: *Retail Asia*, Retail Asia-Pacific Top 500 (annual), July 2011, p. 46+.

4278 ■ LARGEST AUSTRALIAN RETAIL COMPANIES, 2010

Ranked by: Sales, in millions of U.S. dollars. **Remarks:** Also notes outlet type, fascias/brands, number of outlets, sales in national currency, sales area, sales per square meter, and figures for previous year. **Number listed:** 10

1. Woolworths Ltd., with $37,961 million
2. Wesfarmers Ltd., $34,785
3. Metcash Trading Australasia, $13,202
4. Harvey Norman Holdings, $5,047
5. Myer, $2,945
6. JB Hi-Fi, $2,426

7. David Jones, $1,834
8. Australian Pharmaceutical Industries, $1,789
9. Sigma Pharmaceuticals, $1,383
10. Zuellig Australia Pharmacy Services, $1,306

Source: *Retail Asia*, Retail Asia-Pacific Top 500 (annual), July 2011, p. 59-59a.

4279 ■ LARGEST CHINESE RETAIL COMPANIES, 2010

Ranked by: Sales, in millions of U.S. dollars. **Remarks:** Also notes outlet type, fascias/brands, number of outlets, sales in national currency, sales area, sales per square meter, and figures for previous year. **Number listed:** 10

1. Gome Electrical Appliances Holding, with $11,674 million
2. Suning Appliance, $10,467
3. China Resources Enterprise, $10,207
4. Brilliance Group, $9,317
5. Auchan China, $7,633
6. Wal-Mart (China) Investment, $7,180
7. Carrefour (China) Hypermarket, $5,192
8. Dashang Group, $4,575
9. Shanghai Nong Gong Shang Supermarket, $3,919
10. Belle International Holdings, $3,156

Source: *Retail Asia*, Retail Asia-Pacific Top 500 (annual), July 2011, p. 59-59a.

4280 ■ LARGEST GENERAL MERCHANDISE STORES BY EMPLOYEES, 2010

Ranked by: Total number of employees. **Remarks:** Also notes contact information for headquarters, number of employees at headquarters, revenue, rank by revenue, and primary SIC code. **Number listed:** 49

1. Wal-Mart Stores Inc., with 2,100,000 employees
2. Target Corp., 351,000
3. Sears Holdings Corp., 290,000
4. Sears, Roebuck & Co., 249,000
5. Macy's Inc., 161,000
6. J. C. Penney Co., Inc., 154,000
7. Costco Wholesale Corp., 147,000
8. Kohl's Corp., 133,000
9. Kohl's Department Stores Inc., 126,000
10. Macy's Retail Holdings Inc., 111,000

Source: *Business Rankings*, (annual), Dun & Bradstreet Inc., 2011, p. VI.129-VI.130.

4281 ■ LARGEST GENERAL MERCHANDISE STORES BY SALES, 2010

Ranked by: Total revenue, in dollars. **Remarks:** Also notes contact information for headquarters, number of employees at headquarters and overall, rank by employees, and primary SIC code. **Number listed:** 49

1. Wal-Mart Stores Inc., with $408,214,000,000
2. Costco Wholesale Corp., $77,946,000,000
3. Target Corp., $67,390,000,000
4. Sears Holdings Corp., $43,326,000,000
5. Macy's Inc., $23,489,000,000
6. J. C. Penney Co., Inc., $17,556,000,000

7. Kohl's Corp., $17,178,000,000
8. Dollar General Corp., $11,796,380,000
9. BJ's Wholesale Club Inc., $10,186,981,000
10. Family Dollar Stores Inc., $7,866,971,000

Source: *Business Rankings*, (annual), Dun & Bradstreet Inc., 2011, p. V.129-V.130.

4282 ■ LARGEST HONG KONG RETAIL COMPANIES, 2010

Ranked by: Sales, in millions of U.S. dollars. **Remarks:** Also notes outlet type, fascias/brands, number of outlets, sales in national currency, sales area, sales per square meter, and figures for previous year. **Number listed:** 10

1. Dairy Farm International Holdings, with $2,653 million
2. AS Watson Group, $1,845
3. Lifestyle International Holdings, $934
4. Chow Sang Sang Holdings International, $539
5. Lane Crawford International, $496
6. Aeon Stores (Hong Kong), $486
7. Luk Fook Holdings (International), $416
8. China Resources Enterprise, $377
9. Sa Sa International Holdings, $358
10. Marks & Spencer (Hong Kong), $312

Source: *Retail Asia*, Retail Asia-Pacific Top 500 (annual), July 2011, p. 59-59a.

4283 ■ LARGEST INDIAN RETAIL COMPANIES, 2010

Ranked by: Sales, in millions of U.S. dollars. **Remarks:** Also notes outlet type, fascias/brands, number of outlets, sales in national currency, sales area, sales per square meter, and figures for previous year. **Number listed:** 10

1. Future Value Retail, with $1,157 million
2. Titan Industries, $1,001
3. Reliance Retail, $793
4. Tata Group, $484
5. Pantaloon Retail India, $463
6. LG Electronics India, $456
7. Birla Group, $436
8. Shopper's Stop, $389
9. Next India Retail, $305
10. Godrej & Boyce Manufacturing, $269

Source: *Retail Asia*, Retail Asia-Pacific Top 500 (annual), July 2011, p. 60-60a.

4284 ■ LARGEST INDONESIAN RETAIL COMPANIES, 2010

Ranked by: Sales, in millions of U.S. dollars. **Remarks:** Also notes outlet type, fascias/brands, number of outlets, sales in national currency, sales area, sales per square meter, and figures for previous year. **Number listed:** 10

1. Matahari Putra Prima, with $1,763 million
2. Sumber Alfaria Trijaya, $1,394
3. Carrefour Indonesia/Alfa Retailindo, $1,342
4. Indomarco Prismatama, $1,064
5. Hero Supermarket, $880
6. Ramayana Lestari Sentosa, $657
7. Mitra Adi Perkasa, $635

8. Gramedia Asri Media, $309

9. Lion Superindo - Gelael, $210

10. Ace Hardware Indonesia, $173

Source: *Retail Asia*, Retail Asia-Pacific Top 500 (annual), July 2011, p. 60-60a.

4285 ■ LARGEST JAPANESE RETAIL COMPANIES, 2010

Ranked by: Sales, in millions of U.S. dollars. **Remarks:** Also notes outlet type, fascias/brands, number of outlets, sales in national currency, sales area, sales per square meter, and figures for previous year. **Number listed:** 10

1. Seven & I Holdings Co., Ltd., with $61,442 million

2. Aeon Group, $50,946

3. Uny, $23,012

4. Lawson Inc., $21,201

5. Family Mart, $15,992

6. Yamada Denki Co., Ltd., $13,668

7. Isetan Mitsukoshi Holdings, $11,066

8. Edion Corp., $9,316

9. J Front Retailing, $8,977

10. Daily Yamazaki, $8,446

Source: *Retail Asia*, Retail Asia-Pacific Top 500 (annual), July 2011, p. 60-60a.

4286 ■ LARGEST MALAYSIAN RETAIL COMPANIES, 2010

Ranked by: Sales, in millions of U.S. dollars. **Remarks:** Also notes outlet type, fascias/brands, number of outlets, sales in national currency, sales area, sales per square meter, and figures for previous year. **Number listed:** 10

1. GCH Retail, with $1,893 million

2. Tesco Stores, $1,140

3. Aeon, $1,040

4. Carrefour Magnificent Diagraph, $583

5. The Store Corp., $551

6. Parkson Corp., $469

7. 7-Eleven Malaysia, $381

8. Econsave Cash & Carry, $363

9. Watson's Personal Care Stores, $205

10. Senheng Electric, $190

Source: *Retail Asia*, Retail Asia-Pacific Top 500 (annual), July 2011, p. 61-61a.

4287 ■ LARGEST MISCELLANEOUS ASIA-PACIFIC RETAILERS, 2010

Ranked by: Sales, in millions of U.S. dollars. **Remarks:** Also notes country, fascias/brands, number of outlets, sales in national currency, sales area, sales per square meter, and figures for previous year. **Number listed:** 10

1. Woolworths Ltd., with $5,106 million

2. Metcash Trading Australasia, $4,900

3. Don Quijote, $4,159

4. Daiso Sangyo, $3,783

5. Wesfarmers Ltd., $2,307

6. Uny, $1,974

7. Ryohin Keikaku, $1,876

8. Toys "R" Us Japan, $1,575

9. Aeon Group, $1,451

10. Mr. Max Corp., $1,151

Source: *Retail Asia*, Retail Asia-Pacific Top 500 (annual), July 2011, p. 67-67a.

4288 ■ LARGEST MISCELLANEOUS RETAILERS BY EMPLOYEES, 2010

Ranked by: Total number of employees. **Remarks:** Also notes contact information for headquarters, number of employees at headquarters, revenue, rank by revenue, and primary SIC code. **Number listed:** 493

1. Walgreen Co., with 244,144 employees

2. CVS Caremark Corp., 211,000

3. American Drug Stores Inc., 200,000

4. Rite Aid Corp., 97,500

5. Staples Inc., 91,095

6. Bond Drug Co. of Illinois LLC, 90,000

7. Toys "R" Us Inc., 68,000

8. Toys "R" Us Delaware Inc., 57,900

9. Regis Corp., 56,000

10. CVS Pharmacy Inc., 54,332

Source: *Business Rankings*, (annual), Dun & Bradstreet Inc., 2011, p. VI.165-VI.175.

4289 ■ LARGEST MISCELLANEOUS RETAILERS BY SALES, 2010

Ranked by: Total revenue, in dollars. **Remarks:** Also notes contact information for headquarters, number of employees at headquarters and overall, rank by employees, and primary SIC code. **Number listed:** 497

1. CVS Caremark Corp., with $96,413,000,000

2. Walgreen Co., $67,420,000,000

3. Medco Health Solutions Inc., $65,968,300,000

4. Express Scripts Inc., $44,973,200,000

5. Amazon.com Inc., $34,204,000,000

6. Rite Aid Corp., $25,669,117,000

7. Staples Inc., $24,545,113,000

8. Toys "R" Us Inc., $13,568,000,000

9. Office Depot Inc., $11,633,094,000

10. Liberty Media Corp., $10,982,000,000

Source: *Business Rankings*, (annual), Dun & Bradstreet Inc., 2011, p. V.165-V.175.

4290 ■ LARGEST NEW ZEALAND RETAIL COMPANIES, 2010

Ranked by: Sales, in millions of U.S. dollars. **Remarks:** Also notes outlet type, fascias/brands, number of outlets, sales in national currency, sales area, sales per square meter, and figures for previous year. **Number listed:** 10

1. Foodstuffs, with $5,956 million

2. Woolworths, $3,493

3. The Warehouse Group, $1,059

4. Fletcher Building, $782

5. Harvey Norman Holdings, $625

6. The Farmers' Trading, $588

7. Wesfarmers Ltd., $421

8. Pharmacybrands, $364

9. Mitre 10 New Zealand, $317

10. Briscoe Group, $302

Source: *Retail Asia*, Retail Asia-Pacific Top 500 (annual), July 2011, p. 61-61a.

4291 ■ LARGEST PHILIPPINE RETAIL COMPANIES, 2010

Ranked by: Sales, in millions of U.S. dollars. **Remarks:** Also notes outlet type, fascias/brands, number of outlets, sales in national currency, sales area, sales per square meter, and figures for previous year. **Number listed:** 10

1. SM Investments Corp., with $3,606 million
2. Mercury Drug Corp., $1,614
3. Rustan Group of Cos., $707
4. Puregold Price Club, $597
5. Robinsons Retail Group, $459
6. Watson's Personal Care Store Philippines, $284
7. Sam Miguel Corp., $235
8. Philippine Seven Corp., $160
9. Abenson, $152
10. Ace Hardware Philippines, $106

Source: *Retail Asia*, Retail Asia-Pacific Top 500 (annual), July 2011, p. 61-61a.

4292 ■ LARGEST RETAILERS IN EUROPE, 2010

Ranked by: Sales, in millions of U.S. dollars. **Remarks:** Also notes rank within country. **Number listed:** 100

1. Carrefour SA (France), with $125,360 million
2. Tesco plc (U.K.), $8,5365
3. The Chef & Brewer Group Ltd. (U.K.), $7,7632.2
4. Spirit Group Retail Ltd. (U.K.), $6,0541.9
5. Finatis (France), $4,1020
6. Koninklijke Ahold NV (Royal Ahold NV, Netherlands), $4,0921.3
7. REWE Deutscher Supermarkt KG (Germany), $3,0772.4
8. J Sainsbury plc (U.K.), $2,9946
9. Wal-Mart Stores (U.K.) Ltd. (U.K.), $2,9754.6
9. ASDA Group Ltd. (U.K.), $2,9754.6

Source: *Europe's 15,000 Largest Companies*, (annual), ELC International, 2011, p. 47.

4293 ■ LARGEST SINGAPORE RETAIL COMPANIES, 2010

Ranked by: Sales, in millions of U.S. dollars. **Remarks:** Also notes outlet type, fascias/brands, number of outlets, sales in national currency, sales area, sales per square meter, and figures for previous year. **Number listed:** 10

1. NTUC Fairprice Co-operative, with $1,381 million
2. Dairy Farm International Holdings, $1,343
3. Sheng Siong Supermarket, $443
4. Takashimaya (Singapore), $338
5. Robinson & Co., $313
6. Mustafa Holdings, $300
7. Courts (Singapore), $286
8. Isetan (Singapore), $242
9. Best Denki (Singapore), $238
10. Pertama Holdings, $217

Source: *Retail Asia*, Retail Asia-Pacific Top 500 (annual), July 2011, p. 62-62a.

4294 ■ LARGEST SOUTH KOREAN RETAIL COMPANIES, 2010

Ranked by: Sales, in millions of U.S. dollars. **Remarks:** Also notes outlet type, fascias/brands, number of outlets, sales in national currency, sales area, sales per square meter, and figures for previous year. **Number listed:** 10

1. Lotte Shopping Co., Ltd., with $14,513 million
2. Shinsegae, $12,027
3. Samsung Tesco, $8,468
4. Hyundai Department Store, $3,566
5. GS Holdings Corp., $2,801
6. Hi-Mart, $2,093
7. Bokwang Family Mart, $1,868
8. LG Corp., $1,698
9. E Land Group, $1,658
10. Living Plaza, $1,197

Source: *Retail Asia*, Retail Asia-Pacific Top 500 (annual), July 2011, p. 62-62a.

4295 ■ LARGEST TAIWANESE RETAIL COMPANIES, 2010

Ranked by: Sales, in millions of U.S. dollars. **Remarks:** Also notes outlet type, fascias/brands, number of outlets, sales in national currency, sales area, sales per square meter, and figures for previous year. **Number listed:** 10

1. President Chain Store Corp., with $2,994 million
2. Shin Kong Mitsukoshi Department Store, $2,222
3. PresiCarre, $1,842
4. Chyuan Lien Enterprise, $1,565
5. Far Eastern Group, $1,367
6. Taiwan Family Mart, $1,119
7. Pacific Sogo Department Store, $1,074
8. Tsann Kuen Enterprise, $952
9. Dairy Farm International Holdings, $744
10. RT Mart Taiwan, $727

Source: *Retail Asia*, Retail Asia-Pacific Top 500 (annual), July 2011, p. 62-62a.

4296 ■ LARGEST THAI RETAIL COMPANIES, 2010

Ranked by: Sales, in millions of U.S. dollars. **Remarks:** Also notes outlet type, fascias/brands, number of outlets, sales in national currency, sales area, sales per square meter, and figures for previous year. **Number listed:** 10

1. CP All, with $5,076 million
2. Ek-Chai Distribution System, $4,192
3. Central Retail Corp., $2,971
4. Big C Supercenter, $2,120
5. Cencar, $982
6. Home Product Center, $689
7. The Mall Group, $610
8. Fresh Mart International, $292
9. Samart I-Mobile, $250
10. Siam Family Mart, $224

Source: *Retail Asia*, Retail Asia-Pacific Top 500 (annual), July 2011, p. 63-63a.

4297 ■ LARGEST VIETNAMESE RETAIL COMPANIES, 2010

Ranked by: Sales, in millions of U.S. dollars. **Remarks:** Also notes outlet type, fascias/brands, number of outlets, sales in national currency, sales area, sales per square meter, and figures for previous year. **Number listed:** 10

1. Saigon Jewellery Holding, with $844 million
2. Saigon Union of Trading Cooperatives, $630
3. Phu Nhuan Jewelry, $576
4. Nguyen Kim Trading, $341
5. Casino Guichard-Perrachon, $292
6. The Lion Group, $162
7. Mobile World, $160
8. Vien Thong A Import-Export Trading Production Corp., $120
9. G7 Trading & Service, $78
10. International Business Center Corp., $72

Source: *Retail Asia*, Retail Asia-Pacific Top 500 (annual), July 2011, p. 63-63a.

4298 ■ MOST POWERFUL ARABS IN RETAIL, 2012

Ranked by: Score based on scope of influence. **Remarks:** Specific scores not provided. Also notes rank in the overall *Power 500*. **Number listed:** 28

1. Mohamed Alshaya
2. Badr Al Kharafi
3. Adel Aujan
4. Aldaba Saif Al Darmaki
5. Bader Al Darwish
6. Mohammed Jameel
7. Sulaiman Al Muhaidib
8. Robert Mouawad
9. Patrick Chalhoub
10. Jameel Cheaib

Source: *Arabian Business*, Power 500 (annual), June 4, 2012.

4299 ■ MOST VALUABLE U.S. GENERAL RETAILERS, 2011

Ranked by: Market value as of March 2011, in millions of U.S. dollars. **Remarks:** Also notes rank within the *FT U.S. 500*, rank for previous year, country, revenue, net income, assets, number of employees, share price, price-to-earning ratio, dividend yield, and fiscal yearend. **Number listed:** 28

1. Wal-Mart Stores Inc., with $181,716.7 million
2. Amazon.com Inc., $81,239.3
3. The Home Depot Inc., $50,113.9
4. eBay Inc., $40,276.5
5. Lowe's Companies Inc., $34,843.2
6. Target Corp., $34,660.1
7. Costco Wholesale Corp., $32,030.5
8. The TJX Companies Inc., $19,377.7
9. Kohl's Corp., $15,403.8
10. Staples Inc., $13,972

Source: *Financial Times*, FT 500 (annual), http://www.ft.com, June 24, 2011.

4300 ■ SWEDEN'S MOST VALUABLE RETAIL BRANDS, 2011

Ranked by: Brand value, in millions of U.S. dollars. **Remarks:** Also notes rank within the *Global 500* for current and previous year, figures for current and previous year, and brand rating. Ranking is available online only. **Number listed:** 2

1. IKEA, with $15,211 million

2. H & M, $8,596

Source: *Global 500*, (annual), Brand Finance plc, March 2012.

4301 ■ TOP CANADIAN RETAILERS, 2010

Ranked by: Revenue, in thousands of Canadian dollars (unless otherwise noted). **Remarks:** Also notes percent change from previous year. **Number listed:** 10

1. Costco Wholesale Canada, with C$12,026,668 thousand
2. Shoppers Drug Mart, C$10,376,067
3. Canadian Tire Corp., C$8,988,700
4. Home Depot of Canada, C$6,560,000
5. Best Buy Canada, C$5,551,843
6. Sears Canada, C$4,957,800
7. Home Hardware Stores, C$4,850,000
8. Rona Inc., C$4,799,865
9. Parkland Fuel, C$2,916,539
10. Jean Coutu Group, C$2,599,700

Source: *Report on Business Magazine*, Top 1000 Companies (annual), http://www.reportonbusiness.com, June 2011.

4302 ■ TOP *FORTUNE 500* GENERAL MERCHANDISERS, 2011

Ranked by: Revenue, in millions of dollars. **Remarks:** Also notes overall rank in the *Fortune 500;* profits; profits as a percentage of revenue; stockholders' equity; and rank by each criterion. **Number listed:** 10

1. Wal-Mart Stores Inc., with $446,950 million
2. Target Corp., $69,865
3. Sears Holdings Corp., $41,567
4. Macy's Inc., $26,405
5. Kohl's Corp., $18,804
6. J. C. Penney Co., Inc., $17,260
7. Dollar General Corp., $14,807
8. Nordstrom Inc., $10,877
9. Family Dollar Stores Inc., $8,548
10. Dillard's Inc., $6,400

Source: *Fortune*, Fortune 500 (annual), May 21, 2012, p. F-36.

4303 ■ TOP MISCELLANEOUS RETAIL FRANCHISES, 2012

Ranked by: Cumulative score based on financial strength and stability, growth rate, size of the system, number of years in business, the length of time franchising, start-up costs, litigation, percentage of terminations, and whether the company provides financing. **Remarks:** Specific scores not provided. Also notes overall rank within the *Franchise 500*, contact information, description, year founded, year started franchising, states where registered, available U.S. regions, where seeking foreign expansion, number of franchised and company-owned units for past three years, start-up costs, franchise fees, royalty fees, and type of financing available. **Number listed:** 10

1. Aaron's Sales & Lease Ownership
2. Ace Hardware Corp.
3. Gateway Cigar Store/Newsstands
4. Crown Trophy Inc.
5. Color Me Mine Enterprises Inc.
6. Slumberland Franchising Inc.
7. Real Deals on Home Decor

8. ColorTyme
9. HobbyTown USA
10. Music Go Round

Source: *Entrepreneur*, Franchise 500 (annual), January 2012, p. 200-201.

4304 ■ TOP U.S. LARGE-FORMAT RETAILERS BY SALES, 2010

Ranked by: Sales volume, in thousands of dollars. **Remarks:** Also notes comparable-store sales and sales per store. **Number listed:** 6

1. Wal-Mart Stores Inc., with $303,894,000 thousand
2. Target Corp., $65,815,000
3. Costco Wholesale Corp., $58,983,000
4. Kmart/Sears Holdings Corp., $17,065,000
5. Meijer, $15,319,000
6. BJ's Wholesale Club, $10,876,000

Source: *Stores*, Top 100 Retailers (annual), July 2011, p. s8.

4305 ■ TOP U.S. RETAILERS BY SALES, 2010

Ranked by: Sales volume, in thousands of dollars. **Remarks:** Also notes headquarters, operating income, number of stores, number of stores, percent change from previous year, and comments. **Number listed:** 100

1. Wal-Mart Stores Inc., with $307,736,000 thousand
2. The Kroger Co., $78,326,000
3. Target Corp., $65,815,000
4. Walgreen Co., $61,240,000
5. The Home Depot Inc., $60,194,000
6. Costco Wholesale Corp., $58,983,000
7. CVS Caremark Corp., $57,464,000
8. Lowe's Companies Inc., $48,175,000
9. Best Buy Co., Inc., $37,110,000
10. Sears Holdings Corp., $35,362,000

Source: *Stores*, Top 100 Retailers (annual), July 2011, p. s7-s13.

4306 ■ TOP U.S. SMALL-FORMAT VALUE RETAILERS BY SALES, 2010

Ranked by: Sales volume, in thousands of dollars. **Remarks:** Also notes comparable-store sales and sales per store. **Number listed:** 6

1. Dollar General Corp., with $13,035,000 thousand
2. Family Dollar Stores Inc., $7,867,000
3. Dollar Tree Stores Inc., $5,801,000
4. Big Lots Inc., $4,903,000
5. Fred's Inc., $1,842,000
6. 99 Cents Only Stores, $1,380,000

Source: *Stores*, Top 100 Retailers (annual), July 2011, p. s10.

4307 ■ THE UNITED KINGDOM'S MOST VALUABLE RETAIL BRANDS, 2011

Ranked by: Brand value, in millions of U.S. dollars. **Remarks:** Also notes rank within the *Global 500* for current and previous year, figures for current and previous year, and brand rating. Ranking is available online only. **Number listed:** 4

1. Co-operative, with $5,435 million
2. Marks & Spencer, $4,575
3. Burberry, $3,050
4. Next, $2,568

Source: *Global 500*, (annual), Brand Finance plc, March 2012.

4308 ■ THE UNITED STATES' MOST VALUABLE RETAIL BRANDS, 2011

Ranked by: Brand value, in millions of U.S. dollars. **Remarks:** Also notes rank within the *Global 500* for current and previous year, figures for current and previous year, and brand rating. Ranking is available online only. **Number listed:** 25

1. Wal-Mart, with $38,320 million
2. McDonald's, $22,230
3. The Home Depot, $20,902
4. Target, $15,267
5. Walgreens, $11,564
6. Sam's Club, $11,517
7. CVS, $9,421
8. ASDA, $9,406
9. Lowe's, $8,882
10. Costco, $7,598

Source: *Global 500*, (annual), Brand Finance plc, March 2012.

4309 ■ WORLD'S LARGEST RETAIL COMPANIES, 2010

Ranked by: Sales, in millions of U.S. dollars. **Remarks:** Also notes brands and annual sales growth. **Number listed:** 10

1. Wal-Mart Stores Inc., with $405,000 million
2. Carrefour SA, $143,060
3. Tesco plc, $100,833
4. CVS Caremark Corp., $96,413
5. Metro AG, $95,325
6. The Kroger Co., $82,189
7. Costco Wholesale Corp., $76,300
8. The Home Depot Inc., $68,000
9. Walgreen Co., $67,420
10. Target Corp., $65,786

Source: *Consumer Goods Technology*, Consumer Goods Registry (annual), http://www.consumergoods.com, December 2011.

4310 ■ WORLD'S MOST ADMIRED GENERAL MERCHANDISERS, 2012

Ranked by: Score, on a scale of 10, based on a survey of executives, directors, and securities analysts of companies within their own industry on eight criteria: innovation, financial soundness, employee talent, use of corporate assets, long-term investment value, social responsibility, quality of management, and quality of products/services. **Remarks:** Specific scores not provided. Also notes rank for previous year. **Number listed:** 5

1. Target Corp.
2. Nordstrom Inc.
3. Wal-Mart Stores Inc.
4. Macy's Inc.
5. Kohl's Corp.

Source: *Fortune*, World's Most Admired Companies (annual), March 19, 2012, p. 149-150.

4311 ■ WORLD'S MOST ETHICAL GENERAL RETAILERS, 2012

Ranked by: Score based on five criteria: ethics and compliance program; reputation, leadership, and innovation; governance;

corporate citizenship and responsibility; and culture of ethics. **Remarks:** Specific scores not provided; companies are listed alphabetically, not ranked. **Number listed:** 3

1. Costco (U.S.)
2. Marks & Spencer plc (U.K.)
3. Target Corp. (U.S.)

Source: *Ethisphere Magazine*, World's Most Ethical Companies (annual), http://www.ethisphere.com, 2012.

4312 ■ WORLD'S MOST VALUABLE GENERAL RETAIL-ERS, 2011

Ranked by: Market value as of March 2011, in millions of U.S. dollars. **Remarks:** Also notes rank within the *FT 500*, rank for previous year, country, revenue, net income, assets, number of employees, share price, price-to-earning ratio, dividend yield, and fiscal year-end. **Number listed:** 15

1. Wal-Mart Stores Inc., with $181,716.7 million
2. Amazon.com Inc., $81,239.3
3. The Home Depot Inc., $60,113.9
4. Wal-Mart de Mexico, SAB de CV, $53,400.3
5. Industria de Diseno Textil SA (Inditex), $50,083.9
6. Hennes & Mauritz AB, $48,531.6
7. eBay Inc., $40,276.5
8. Wesfarmers Ltd., $38,092.3
9. Lowe's Companies Inc., $34,843.2
10. Target Corp., $34,660.1

Source: *Financial Times*, FT 500 (annual), http://www.ft.com, June 24, 2011.

4313 ■ WORLD'S MOST VALUABLE RETAIL BRANDS, 2011

Ranked by: Brand value, in millions of U.S. dollars. **Remarks:** Also notes rank within the *Global 500* for current and previous year, figures for current and previous year, country, and brand rating. Ranking is available online only. **Number listed:** 43

1. Wal-Mart, with $38,320 million
2. McDonald's, $22,230
3. The Home Depot, $20,902
4. Target, $15,267
5. IKEA, $15,211
6. Walgreens, $11,564
7. Sam's Club, $11,517
8. CVS, $9,421
9. Asda, $9,406
10. Lowe's, $8,882

Source: *Global 500*, (annual), Brand Finance plc, March 2012.

4314 ■ WORLD'S MOST VALUABLE RETAILER BRANDS, 2012

Ranked by: Brand value, a measure of a brand's earnings and contribution, in millions of U.S. dollars. **Remarks:** Also notes annual growth in brand value and rank by brand contribution and brand momentum. **Number listed:** 20

1. Walmart, with $34,436 million
2. Amazon, $34,077
3. Tesco, $18,007
4. The Home Depot, $12,968
5. eBay, $12,662

6. Target, $10,506
7. Aldi, $9,310
8. Ikea, $9,206
9. Carrefour, $7,836
10. Auchan, $6,799

Source: *Financial Times*, Global Brands (annual), http://www.ft.com, May 22, 2012.

Retail Industry—Advertising

4315 ■ TOP RETAIL COMPANIES BY TOTAL ADVERTISING EXPENDITURES, 2010

Ranked by: Measured advertising spending, in millions of dollars. **Remarks:** Also notes ad expenditures for previous year, and market share for current and previous year. **Number listed:** 10

1. Wal-Mart Stores Inc., with $903 million
2. Macy's Inc., $890
3. Sears Holdings Corp., $702
4. Target Corp., $650
5. The Home Depot Inc., $448
6. J. C. Penney Co., Inc., $414
7. Lowe's Companies Inc., $390
8. Kohl's Corp., $340
9. The Gap Inc., $322
10. Best Buy Co., Inc., $267

Source: *Advertising Age*, Leading National Advertisers (annual), June 20, 2011, p. 20.

Retail Industry—Food

4316 ■ TOP MISCELLANEOUS FOOD RETAIL FRANCHISES, 2012

Ranked by: Cumulative score based on financial strength and stability, growth rate, size of the system, number of years in business, the length of time franchising, start-up costs, litigation, percentage of terminations, and whether the company provides financing. **Remarks:** Specific scores not provided. Also notes overall rank within the *Franchise 500*, contact information, description, year founded, year started franchising, states where registered, available U.S. regions, where seeking foreign expansion, number of franchised and company-owned units for past three years, start-up costs, franchise fees, royalty fees, and type of financing available. **Number listed:** 2

1. Edible Arrangements International Inc.
2. The HoneyBaked Ham Co. & Cafe

Source: *Entrepreneur*, Franchise 500 (annual), January 2012, p. 174-175.

Retail Industry—Massagers

4317 ■ TOP MASSAGE SERVICES FRANCHISES, 2012

Ranked by: Cumulative score based on financial strength and stability, growth rate, size of the system, number of years in business, the length of time franchising, start-up costs, litigation, percentage of terminations, and whether the company provides financing. **Remarks:** Specific scores not provided. Also notes overall rank within the *Franchise 500*, contact information, description, year founded, year started franchising, states where registered, available U.S. regions, where seeking foreign expansion, number of franchised and company-owned units for past three years, start-up costs, franchise fees, royalty fees, and type of financing available. **Number listed:** 3

1. Massage Envy
2. LaVida Massage
3. Massage Heights

Source: *Entrepreneur*, Franchise 500 (annual, January 2012, p. 192-193.

Retail Stores

4318 ■ AUSTRALIA'S TOP RETAILERS BY REVENUE, 2010

Ranked by: Retail sales, in millions of U.S. dollars. **Remarks:** Ranking is available online only. Also notes rank in the overall *Top 250*, group sales (including non-retail), profits, dominant operational formats, countries of operation, and five-year retail revenue growth rates. **Number listed:** 2

1. Woolworths Ltd., with $51,771 million
2. Wesfarmers Ltd., $47,631

Source: *Stores*, Top Global Retailers (annual), January 2012.

4319 ■ AUSTRIA'S TOP RETAILERS BY REVENUE, 2010

Ranked by: Retail sales, in millions of U.S. dollars. **Remarks:** Ranking is available online only. Also notes rank in the overall *Top 250*, group sales (including non-retail), profits, dominant operational formats, countries of operation, and five-year retail revenue growth rates. **Number listed:** 2

1. SPAR, with $12,011 million
2. XXXLutz Group, $3,718

Source: *Stores*, Top Global Retailers (annual), January 2012.

4320 ■ BELGIUM'S TOP RETAILERS BY REVENUE, 2010

Ranked by: Retail sales, in millions of U.S. dollars. **Remarks:** Ranking is available online only. Also notes rank in the overall *Top 250*, group sales (including non-retail), profits, dominant operational formats, countries of operation, and five-year retail revenue growth rates. **Number listed:** 3

1. Delhaize Group SA, with $24,918 million
2. Louis Delhaize SA, $14,100
3. Groep Colruyt, $7,428

Source: *Stores*, Top Global Retailers (annual), January 2012.

4321 ■ BRAZIL'S TOP RETAILERS BY REVENUE, 2010

Ranked by: Retail sales, in millions of U.S. dollars. **Remarks:** Ranking is available online only. Also notes rank in the overall *Top 250*, group sales (including non-retail), profits, dominant operational formats, countries of operation, and five-year retail revenue growth rates. **Number listed:** 2

1. Grupo P, with $18,318 million
2. Lojas Americanas SA, $5,359

Source: *Stores*, Top Global Retailers (annual), January 2012.

4322 ■ BRITAIN'S MOST ADMIRED BROADLINE/HOME RETAILERS, 2011

Ranked by: Survey of peers and investment analysts based on nine criteria: quality of management, financial soundness, quality of goods/services, ability to attract and retain talent, value as long-

term investment, innovation, marketing, community and environmental responsibility, and use of corporate assets. **Number listed:** 5

1. John Lewis Partnership plc, with 67.8 points
2. Marks & Spencer plc, 64.9
3. Kingfisher plc, 61.5
4. Debenhams, 54.8
5. Dunelm, 54

Source: *Management Today*, Britain's Most Admired Companies (annual), December 2011, p. 47.

4323 ■ CANADA'S TOP RETAILERS BY REVENUE, 2010

Ranked by: Retail sales, in millions of U.S. dollars. **Remarks:** Ranking is available online only. Also notes rank in the overall *Top 250*, group sales (including non-retail), profits, dominant operational formats, countries of operation, and five-year retail revenue growth rates. **Number listed:** 10

1. Loblaw Cos. Ltd., with $21,782 million
2. Alimentation Couche-Tard Inc., $18,966
3. Empire Co., Ltd./Sobeys, $15,575
4. Metro Inc., $10,896
5. Shoppers Drug Mart Corp., $10,075
6. Canadian Tire Corp., $7,921
7. Katz Group Inc., $6,020
8. Jim Pattison Group, $4,123
9. Liquor Control Board of Ontario, $3,569
10. RONA Inc., $3,519

Source: *Stores*, Top Global Retailers (annual), January 2012.

4324 ■ CHILE'S TOP RETAILERS BY REVENUE, 2010

Ranked by: Retail sales, in millions of U.S. dollars. **Remarks:** Ranking is available online only. Also notes rank in the overall *Top 250*, group sales (including non-retail), profits, dominant operational formats, countries of operation, and five-year retail revenue growth rates. **Number listed:** 2

1. Cencosud SA, with $11,791 million
2. SACI Falabella, $7,473

Source: *Stores*, Top Global Retailers (annual), January 2012.

4325 ■ CHINA'S TOP RETAILERS BY REVENUE, 2010

Ranked by: Retail sales, in millions of U.S. dollars. **Remarks:** Ranking is available online only. Also notes rank in the overall *Top 250*, group sales (including non-retail), profits, dominant operational formats, countries of operation, and five-year retail revenue growth rates. **Number listed:** 5

1. Suning Appliance Co., Ltd., with $11,170 million
2. Bailian (Brilliance) Group, $13,344
3. Gome Home Appliance Group, $12,042
4. Dalian Dashang Group, $6,613
5. Nonggongshang Supermarket Group Co., Ltd., $3,684

Source: *Stores*, Top Global Retailers (annual), January 2012.

4326 ■ DENMARK'S TOP RETAILERS BY REVENUE, 2010

Ranked by: Retail sales, in millions of U.S. dollars. **Remarks:** Ranking is available online only. Also notes rank in the overall *Top 250*, group sales (including non-retail), profits, dominant operational formats, countries of operation, and five-year retail revenue growth rates. **Number listed:** 2

1. Dansk Supermarked A/S, with $10,563 million
2. FDB (Coop Danmark A/S), $6,822

Source: *Stores*, Top Global Retailers (annual), January 2012.

4327 ■ FASTEST-GROWING GLOBAL RETAILERS BY REVENUE, 2005-2010

Ranked by: Five-year compound annual growth rate of revenue, in percent. **Remarks:** Also notes country of origin, store formats, total retail sales, net profit margin, and overall rank in the *Top Global Retailers*. **Number listed:** 50

1. Wesfarmers Ltd., with 62.3%
2. OJSC Magnit, 38%
3. Suning Appliance Co., Ltd., 36.5%
4. Jumbo Supermarkten BV, 34.1%
5. Apple Inc./Apple Stores, 33%
6. Amazon.com Inc., 32.1%
7. Birlesik Magazalar AS, 31.2%
8. China Resources Enterprise Ltd., 27.9%
9. Lojas Americanas SA, 27.7%
10. GameStop Corp., 25.1%

Source: *Stores*, Top Global Retailers (annual), January 2012, p. G27-G29.

4328 ■ FINLAND'S TOP RETAILERS BY REVENUE, 2010

Ranked by: Retail sales, in millions of U.S. dollars. **Remarks:** Ranking is available online only. Also notes rank in the overall *Top 250*, group sales (including non-retail), profits, dominant operational formats, countries of operation, and five-year retail revenue growth rates. **Number listed:** 2

1. S Group, with $11,007 million
2. Kesko Corp., $10,356

Source: *Stores*, Top Global Retailers (annual), January 2012.

4329 ■ FRANCE'S TOP RETAILERS BY REVENUE, 2010

Ranked by: Retail sales, in millions of U.S. dollars. **Remarks:** Ranking is available online only. Also notes rank in the overall *Top 250*, group sales (including non-retail), profits, dominant operational formats, countries of operation, and five-year retail revenue growth rates. **Number listed:** 13

1. Carrefour SA, with $119,642 million
2. Groupe Auchan SA, $55,212
3. Centres Distributeurs E. Leclerc, $41,165
4. Casino Guichard-Perrachon SA, $37,875
5. ITM D, $33,994
6. Syst, $20,423
7. LVMH, $15,085
8. Groupe Adeo SA, $15,005
9. PPR SA, $14,803
10. Oxylane Groupe, $7,938

Source: *Stores*, Top Global Retailers (annual), January 2012.

4330 ■ GERMANY'S TOP RETAILERS BY REVENUE, 2010

Ranked by: Retail sales, in millions of U.S. dollars. **Remarks:** Ranking is available online only. Also notes rank in the overall *Top 250*, group sales (including non-retail), profits, dominant operational formats, countries of operation, and five-year retail revenue growth rates. **Number listed:** 19

1. Metro AG, with $88,931 million

2. Schwarz Unternehmens Treuhand KG, $79,119
3. Aldi Einkauf GmbH, $67,112
4. Rewe Group, $61,134
5. Edeka Zentrale AG, $54,072
6. Otto GmbH, $13,203
7. Tengelmann Warenhandelsgesellschaft KG, $10,599
8. Globus Holding GmbH, $7,270
9. drogerie markt GmbH, $6,922
10. Fa. Anton Schlecker, $6,580

Source: *Stores*, Top Global Retailers (annual), January 2012.

4331 ■ GLOBAL RETAILERS WITH THE HIGHEST "Q RATIO," 2010

Ranked by: Ratio of market value to asset value, or "Q ratio." **Remarks:** Also notes country. **Number listed:** 30

1. Coach Inc., with 7.15
2. Birlesik Magazalar AS, 5.81
3. Hennes & Mauritz AB, 5.67
4. Amazon.com Inc., 5.3
5. Apple Inc./Apple Stores, 4.69
6. CP All plc, 4.5
7. Inditex SA, 4.15
8. Dollar Tree Inc., 4.05
9. Woolworths Holdings Ltd., 3.69
10. Tractor Supply Co., 3.61

Source: *Stores*, Top Global Retailers (annual), January 2012, p. G30.

4332 ■ HONG KONG'S TOP RETAILERS BY REVENUE, 2010

Ranked by: Retail sales, in millions of U.S. dollars. **Remarks:** Ranking is available online only. Also notes rank in the overall *Top 250*, group sales (including non-retail), profits, dominant operational formats, countries of operation, and five-year retail revenue growth rates. **Number listed:** 3

1. AS Watson & Co., with $15,857 million
2. Dairy Farm International Holdings Ltd., $7,971
3. China Resources Enterprise Ltd., $7,089

Source: *Stores*, Top Global Retailers (annual), January 2012.

4333 ■ ITALY'S TOP RETAILERS BY REVENUE, 2010

Ranked by: Retail sales, in millions of U.S. dollars. **Remarks:** Ranking is available online only. Also notes rank in the overall *Top 250*, group sales (including non-retail), profits, dominant operational formats, countries of operation, and five-year retail revenue growth rates. **Number listed:** 4

1. Coop Italia, with $15,845 million
2. Conad Consorzio Nazionale, Dettaglianti Societe Coop ARL, $12,170
3. Esselunga SpA, $7,741
4. Luxottica Group SpA, $4,729

Source: *Stores*, Top Global Retailers (annual), January 2012.

4334 ■ JAPAN'S TOP RETAILERS BY REVENUE, 2010

Ranked by: Retail sales, in millions of U.S. dollars. **Remarks:** Ranking is available online only. Also notes rank in the overall *Top 250*, group sales (including non-retail), profits, dominant operational formats, countries of operation, and five-year retail revenue growth rates. **Number listed:** 38

1. Seven & I Holdings Co., Ltd., with $57,055 million
2. Aeon Co., Ltd., $53,458
3. Yamada Denki Co., Ltd., $25,193
4. Isetan Mitsukoshi Holdings Ltd., $13,933
5. UNY Co., Ltd., $12,635
6. The Daiei Inc., $10,415
7. J Front Retailing Co., Ltd., $9,866
8. Takashimaya Co., Ltd., $9,398
9. Fast Retailing Co., Ltd., $9,027
10. K's Holdings Corp., $9,020

Source: *Stores*, Top Global Retailers (annual), January 2012.

4335 ■ MEXICO'S TOP RETAILERS BY REVENUE, 2010

Ranked by: Retail sales, in millions of U.S. dollars. **Remarks:** Ranking is available online only. Also notes rank in the overall *Top 250*, group sales (including non-retail), profits, dominant operational formats, countries of operation, and five-year retail revenue growth rates. **Number listed:** 5

1. Organizaci, with $7,425 million
2. FEMSA Comercio, SA de CV, $4,933
3. Controladora Comercial Mexicana, SAB de CV, $4,348
4. Grupo Comercial Chedraui, SAB de CV, $4,142
5. El Puerto de Liverpool, SAB de CV, $3,845

Source: *Stores*, Top Global Retailers (annual), January 2012.

4336 ■ THE NETHERLANDS' TOP RETAILERS BY REVENUE, 2010

Ranked by: Retail sales, in millions of U.S. dollars. **Remarks:** Ranking is available online only. Also notes rank in the overall *Top 250*, group sales (including non-retail), profits, dominant operational formats, countries of operation, and five-year retail revenue growth rates. **Number listed:** 4

1. Koninklijke Ahold NV (Royal Ahold NV), with $39,213 million
2. SHV Holdings NV/Makro, $7,870
3. Jumbo Supermarkten BV, $4,665
4. Blokker Holding NV, $3,656

Source: *Stores*, Top Global Retailers (annual), January 2012.

4337 ■ NORWAY'S TOP RETAILERS BY REVENUE, 2010

Ranked by: Retail sales, in millions of U.S. dollars. **Remarks:** Ranking is available online only. Also notes rank in the overall *Top 250*, group sales (including non-retail), profits, dominant operational formats, countries of operation, and five-year retail revenue growth rates. **Number listed:** 3

1. Reitan Group, with $9,420 million
2. NorgesGruppen ASA, $5,062
3. Coop Norge, the Group, $4,581

Source: *Stores*, Top Global Retailers (annual), January 2012.

4338 ■ PORTUGAL'S TOP RETAILERS BY REVENUE, 2010

Ranked by: Retail sales, in millions of U.S. dollars. **Remarks:** Ranking is available online only. Also notes rank in the overall *Top 250*, group sales (including non-retail), profits, dominant operational formats, countries of operation, and five-year retail revenue growth rates. **Number listed:** 2

1. Jer, with $11,317 million
2. Sonae SGPS SA, $6,144

Source: *Stores*, Top Global Retailers (annual), January 2012.

4339 ■ RUSSIA'S TOP RETAILERS BY REVENUE, 2010

Ranked by: Retail sales, in millions of U.S. dollars. **Remarks:** Ranking is available online only. Also notes rank in the overall *Top 250*, group sales (including non-retail), profits, dominant operational formats, countries of operation, and five-year retail revenue growth rates. **Number listed:** 2

1. X5 Retail Group NV, with $11,264 million
2. OJSC Magnit, $7,776

Source: *Stores*, Top Global Retailers (annual), January 2012.

4340 ■ SOUTH AFRICA'S TOP RETAILERS BY REVENUE, 2010

Ranked by: Retail sales, in millions of U.S. dollars. **Remarks:** Ranking is available online only. Also notes rank in the overall *Top 250*, group sales (including non-retail), profits, dominant operational formats, countries of operation, and five-year retail revenue growth rates. **Number listed:** 6

1. Shoprite Holdings Ltd., with $10,279 million
2. Massmart Holdings Ltd., $7,589
3. Pick n Pay Stores Ltd., $7,140
4. The SPAR Group Ltd., $4,722
5. Steinhoff International Holdings Ltd., $3,701
6. Woolworths Holdings Ltd., $3,666

Source: *Stores*, Top Global Retailers (annual), January 2012.

4341 ■ SOUTH KOREA'S TOP RETAILERS BY REVENUE, 2010

Ranked by: Retail sales, in millions of U.S. dollars. **Remarks:** Ranking is available online only. Also notes rank in the overall *Top 250*, group sales (including non-retail), profits, dominant operational formats, countries of operation, and five-year retail revenue growth rates. **Number listed:** 3

1. Lotte Shopping Co., Ltd., with $11,487 million
2. Shinsegae Co., Ltd., $11,314
3. GS Holdings Co., Ltd., $3,614

Source: *Stores*, Top Global Retailers (annual), January 2012.

4342 ■ SPAIN'S TOP RETAILERS BY REVENUE, 2010

Ranked by: Retail sales, in millions of U.S. dollars. **Remarks:** Ranking is available online only. Also notes rank in the overall *Top 250*, group sales (including non-retail), profits, dominant operational formats, countries of operation, and five-year retail revenue growth rates. **Number listed:** 4

1. Mercadona SA, with $20,241 million
2. El Corte Ingles, $17,336
3. Inditex SA, $16,343
4. Grupo Eroski, $9,437

Source: *Stores*, Top Global Retailers (annual), January 2012.

4343 ■ SWEDEN'S TOP RETAILERS BY REVENUE, 2010

Ranked by: Retail sales, in millions of U.S. dollars. **Remarks:** Ranking is available online only. Also notes rank in the overall *Top 250*, group sales (including non-retail), profits, dominant operational formats, countries of operation, and five-year retail revenue growth rates. **Number listed:** 6

1. The IKEA Group (INGKA Holding BV), with $31,642 million
2. Hennes & Mauritz AB, $15,051
3. ICA AB, $12,818
4. KF Gruppen, $4,723
5. Axfood AB, $3,373
6. Systembolaget AB, $3,357

Source: *Stores*, Top Global Retailers (annual), January 2012.

4344 ■ SWITZERLAND'S TOP RETAILERS BY REVENUE, 2010

Ranked by: Retail sales, in millions of U.S. dollars. **Remarks:** Ranking is available online only. Also notes rank in the overall *Top 250*, group sales (including non-retail), profits, dominant operational formats, countries of operation, and five-year retail revenue growth rates. **Number listed:** 4

1. Migros-Genossenschafts Bund, with $20,937 million
2. Coop Group, $16,684
3. Alliance Boots GmbH, $11,859
4. Compagnie Financi, $4,591

Source: *Stores*, Top Global Retailers (annual), January 2012.

4345 ■ TOP GLOBAL RETAILERS BY REVENUE, 2010

Ranked by: Retail sales, in millions of U.S. dollars. **Remarks:** Also notes country of origin, group sales (including non-retail), profits, dominant operational formats, countries of operation, and five-year retail revenue growth rates. **Number listed:** 250

1. Wal-Mart Stores Inc., with $418,952 million
2. Carrefour SA, $119,642
3. Tesco plc, $92,171
4. Metro AG, $88,931
5. The Kroger Co., $82,189
6. Schwarz Unternehmens Treuhand KG, $79,119
7. Costco Wholesale Corp., $76,255
8. The Home Depot Inc., $67,997
9. Walgreen Co., $67,420
10. Aldi Einkauf GmbH, $67,112

Source: *Stores*, Top Global Retailers (annual), January 2012, p. G11-G17.

4346 ■ TURKEY'S TOP RETAILERS BY REVENUE, 2010

Ranked by: Retail sales, in millions of U.S. dollars. **Remarks:** Ranking is available online only. Also notes rank in the overall *Top 250*, group sales (including non-retail), profits, dominant operational formats, countries of operation, and five-year retail revenue growth rates. **Number listed:** 2

1. BIM Birlesik Magazalar A.S., with $4,371 million
2. Migros Ticaret A.S., $4,232

Source: *Stores*, Top Global Retailers (annual), January 2012.

4347 ■ THE UNITED KINGDOM'S TOP RETAILERS BY REVENUE, 2010

Ranked by: Retail sales, in millions of U.S. dollars. **Remarks:** Ranking is available online only. Also notes rank in the overall *Top 250*, group sales (including non-retail), profits, dominant operational formats, countries of operation, and five-year retail revenue growth rates. **Number listed:** 15

1. Tesco plc, with $92,171 million

2. J Sainsbury plc, $32,837
3. Wm. Morrison Supermarkets plc, $25,248
4. Marks & Spencer plc, $15,157
5. Kingfisher plc, $14,846
6. The Co-Operative Group Ltd., $12,957
7. Dixons Retail plc, $12,738
8. John Lewis Partnership plc, $11,359
9. Home Retail Group plc, $8,886
10. Kesa Electricals plc, $7,879

Source: *Stores*, Top Global Retailers (annual), January 2012.

4348 ■ THE UNITED STATES' TOP RETAILERS BY REVENUE, 2010

Ranked by: Retail sales, in millions of U.S. dollars. **Remarks:** Ranking is available online only. Also notes rank in the overall *Top 250*, group sales (including non-retail), profits, dominant operational formats, countries of operation, and five-year retail revenue growth rates. **Number listed:** 81

1. Wal-Mart Stores Inc., with $418,952 million
2. The Kroger Co., $82,189
3. Costco Wholesale Corp., $76,255
4. The Home Depot Inc., $67,997
5. Walgreen Co., $67,420
6. Target Corp., $65,786
7. CVS Caremark Corp., $57,345
8. Best Buy Co., Inc., $50,272
9. Lowe's Companies Inc., $48,815
10. Sears Holdings Corp., $43,326

Source: *Stores*, Top Global Retailers (annual), January 2012.

Roofing

4349 ■ TOP METAL ROOFERS, 2010

Ranked by: Total square footage. **Remarks:** Also notes headquarters, year founded, tonnage, and figures for previous year. **Number listed:** 13

1. A-Lert Roof Systems, a division of Centurion Industries Inc., with 1,507,238 sq.ft.
2. Advanced Metal Roofing, 1,217,025
3. Champion Metal Inc., 565,000
4. Cincinnati Commercial Contracting, 229,480
5. AARA Construction Inc., 227,518
6. The Sheridan Corp., 194,509
7. Crossland Construction Co., Inc., 187,456
8. Septagon Industries, 159,885
9. LaFave's Construction Co., 137,600
10. Coleman Adams Construction Inc., 30,000

Source: *Metal Construction News*, Top Metal Roofers (annual), July 2011, p. 20.

4350 ■ TOP ROOFING CONTRACTORS, 2010

Ranked by: Roofing revenue, in millions of dollars. **Remarks:** Also notes percentage change from previous year. **Number listed:** 20

1. Tecta America Corp., with $410 million
2. Centimark Corp., $363.6
3. Kalkreuth Roofing & Sheet Metal Inc., $74.1

4. Nations Roof LLC, $68
5. The Campbell Cos., $61
6. Best Contracting Services Inc., $49.2
7. Birdair Inc., $46
8. Schreiber Roofing, $44.1
9. Latite Roofing & Sheet Metal Co., Inc., $40
10. Douglass Colony Group, $30.1

Source: *ENR: Engineering News-Record*, Top 600 Specialty Contractors (annual), October 17, 2011, p. 63.

Rubber Industry

4351 ■ LARGEST RUBBER AND PLASTICS COMPANIES BY EMPLOYEES, 2010

Ranked by: Total number of employees. **Remarks:** Also notes contact information for headquarters, number of employees at headquarters, revenue, rank by revenue, and primary SIC code. **Number listed:** 48

1. Goodyear Tire & Rubber Co., with 72,000 employees
2. Illinois Tool Works Inc., 59,000
3. Bridgestone Americas Inc., 45,000
4. Nike Inc., 34,400
5. International Automotive Components Group North America LLC, 28,425
6. Michelin North America Inc., 23,500
7. Jarden Corp., 20,640
8. Bemis Co., Inc., 20,400
9. SCC Holding Co., 19,500
10. Berry Plastics Group Inc., 16,020

Source: *Business Rankings*, (annual), Dun & Bradstreet Inc., 2011, p. VI.67-VI.68.

4352 ■ LARGEST RUBBER AND PLASTICS COMPANIES BY SALES, 2010

Ranked by: Total revenue, in dollars. **Remarks:** Also notes contact information for headquarters, number of employees at headquarters and overall, rank by employees, and primary SIC code. **Number listed:** 49

1. Nike Inc., with $19,014,000,000
2. Goodyear Tire & Rubber Co., $18,832,000,000
3. Illinois Tool Works Inc., $15,870,376,000
4. Jarden Corp., $6,022,700,000
5. Bemis Co., Inc., $4,835,042,000
6. Berry Plastics Corp., $4,257,000,000
7. Cooper Tire & Rubber Co., $3,360,984,000
8. Graham Packaging Co., $2,512,733,000
8. Graham Packaging Holdings Co., $2,512,733,000
10. Oil States International Inc., $2,411,984,000

Source: *Business Rankings*, (annual), Dun & Bradstreet Inc., 2011, p. V.67-V.68.

4353 ■ LARGEST U.S. RUBBER PRODUCT MANUFACTURERS, 2010

Ranked by: Revenue, in millions of dollars. **Remarks:** Also notes overall rank within the *IW 500*, revenue growth, and profit margin. **Number listed:** 4

1. Goodyear Tire & Rubber Co., with $18,832 million
2. Cooper Tire & Rubber Co., $3,361
3. Armstrong World Industry Inc., $2,766
4. West Pharmaceutical Services Inc., $1,105

Source: *IndustryWeek*, IW 500 (annual), http://www.industryweek.com, July 2011.

4354 ■ WORLD'S LARGEST RUBBER PRODUCT MANUFACTURERS, 2010

Ranked by: Revenue, in millions of dollars. **Remarks:** Also notes rank for previous year, overall rank within the *IW 1000*, country, and revenue growth. **Number listed:** 13

1. Bridgestone Corp., with $35,198 million
2. Continental AG, $34,991
3. Goodyear Tire & Rubber Co., $18,832
4. Sumitomo Rubber Industries Ltd., $7,436
5. Sinochem International Co., Ltd., $6,076
6. Yokohama Rubber Co., Ltd., $5,736
7. Hankook Tire Co., Ltd., $5,232
8. Korea Kumho Petrochemical Co., Ltd., $5,147
9. NOK Corp., $5,102
10. Trelleborg AB, $4,056

Source: *IndustryWeek*, IW 1000 (annual), http://www.industryweek.com, August 2011.

Salads

4355 ■ TOP BRANDS OF FRESH-CUT SALADS, 2011

Ranked by: Sales, in millions of dollars. **Remarks:** Also notes unit sales and annual growth. **Number listed:** 5

1. Fresh Express, with $1,033.6 million
2. Private label, $711.3
3. Dole, $617.1
4. Earthbound Farm, $140.9
5. Ready Pac, $123.9

Source: *Refrigerated & Frozen Foods*, State of the Industry (annual), July 2011, p. 48.

Salaries
See: **Compensation**

Sand and Gravel Industry

4356 ■ LARGEST SAND AND GRAVEL PRODUCERS, 2011

Ranked by: Total production. **Remarks:** Specific figures not provided. **Number listed:** 50

1. Oldcastle Materials Inc.
2. Cemex SAB de CV
3. Vulcan Materials Co.
4. Lehigh Hanson Inc.
5. MDU Resources Group Inc.
6. U.S. Bureau of Land Management

7. Holcim Group/Aggregate Industries Management Inc.
8. Martin Marietta Aggregates
9. Lafarge North America Inc.
10. Granite Construction Inc.

Source: *Pit & Quarry*, MegaProducers (annual), June 2012, p. 32.

4357 ■ OWNERS OF THE LARGEST SAND AND GRAVEL PLANTS, 2011

Ranked by: Total output. **Remarks:** Specific figures not provided. Also notes location. **Number listed:** 5

1. Trinity Industries Inc.
2. CalPortland Co.
3. All American Asphalt Co.
4. Vulcan Materials Co.
5. Lehigh Hanson Inc.

Source: *Pit & Quarry*, MegaProducers (annual), June 2012, p. 32.

Sandwiches

4358 ■ LARGEST SANDWICH FAST-FOOD CHAINS BY SALES, 2010

Ranked by: Systemwide sales, in millions of dollars. **Remarks:** Also notes average sales per unit, number of franchised and company-owned units, total number of units, and overall rank in the *The QSR 50*. **Number listed:** 7

1. Subway, with $10,600 million
2. Panera Bread, $3,100
3. Arby's, $3,010
4. Quizno's Classic Subs, $1,430
5. Jimmy John's Gourmet Sandwiches, $735
6. Jason's Deli, $503.2
7. Einstein Brothers Bagels, $400.4

Source: *QSR Magazine*, The QSR 50 (annual), http://www.qsrmagazine.com, August 2011.

4359 ■ TOP MISCELLANEOUS SANDWICH FRANCHISES, 2012

Ranked by: Cumulative score based on financial strength and stability, growth rate, size of the system, number of years in business, the length of time franchising, start-up costs, litigation, percentage of terminations, and whether the company provides financing. **Remarks:** Specific scores not provided. Also notes overall rank within the *Franchise 500*, contact information, description, year founded, year started franchising, states where registered, available U.S. regions, where seeking foreign expansion, number of franchised and company-owned units for past three years, start-up costs, franchise fees, royalty fees, and type of financing available. **Number listed:** 6

1. Jimmy John's Gourmet Sandwich Shops
2. Arby's Restaurant Group
3. Pita Pit
4. Togo's Franchisor LLC
5. Which Wich? Superior Sandwiches
6. Great Wraps

Source: *Entrepreneur*, Franchise 500 (annual), January 2012, p. 172-173.

4360 ■ TOP PHILLY CHEESESTEAK SANDWICH FRANCHISES, 2012

Ranked by: Cumulative score based on financial strength and stability, growth rate, size of the system, number of years in busi-

ness, the length of time franchising, start-up costs, litigation, percentage of terminations, and whether the company provides financing. **Remarks:** Specific scores not provided. Also notes overall rank within the *Franchise 500*, contact information, description, year founded, year started franchising, states where registered, available U.S. regions, where seeking foreign expansion, number of franchised and company-owned units for past three years, start-up costs, franchise fees, royalty fees, and type of financing available. **Number listed:** 4

1. Charley's Grilled Subs
2. Penn Station East Coast Subs
3. The Great Steak & Potato Co.
4. The Steak Escape

Source: *Entrepreneur*, Franchise 500 (annual), January 2012, p. 170-171.

4361 ■ TOP SANDWICH CHAINS BY GROWTH IN SALES, 2009-2010

Ranked by: Annual growth in systemwide sales, in percent. **Remarks:** Also notes rank for previous year, fiscal year-end, and figures for previous year. **Number listed:** 21

1. Five Guys Burgers & Fries, with 44.49%
2. Jimmy John's, 29.35%
3. Chipotle Mexican Grill, 20.79%
4. In-N-Out Burger, 7.38%
5. Jason's Deli, 6.7%
6. Subway, 6.34%
7. Hardee's, 6.08%
8. Culver's, 5.03%
9. McDonald's, 4.39%
10. Whataburger, 3.97%

Source: *Nation's Restaurant News*, Top 100 (annual), June 27, 2011, p. 48.

4362 ■ TOP SANDWICH CHAINS BY GROWTH IN UNITS, 2009-2010

Ranked by: Annual growth in number of U.S. units, in percent. **Remarks:** Also notes rank for previous year, fiscal year-end, and figures for previous year. **Number listed:** 21

1. Five Guys Burgers & Fries, with 34.31%
2. Jimmy John's, 16.62%
3. Chipotle Mexican Grill, 13.19%
4. In-N-Out Burger, 5.02%
5. Subway, 3.54%
6. Culver's, 2.66%
7. Whataburger, 2.14%
8. Jason's Deli , 1.86%
9. Carl's Jr., 0.83%
10. Sonic Drive-In, 0.79%

Source: *Nation's Restaurant News*, Top 100 (annual), June 27, 2011, p. 48.

4363 ■ TOP SANDWICH CHAINS BY SALES PER UNIT, 2010

Ranked by: Sales per unit, in thousands of dollars. **Remarks:** Also notes rank for previous year, fiscal year-end, and figures for previous two years. **Number listed:** 21

1. Jason's Deli, with $2,318.9 thousand
2. McDonald's, $2,313.4

3. In-N-Out Burger, $2,257.1
4. Chipotle Mexican Grill, $1,800.3
5. Whataburger, $1,727.6
6. Culver's, $1,646.6
7. Wendy's, $1,350.9
8. Jack in the Box, $1,328.6
9. Carl's Jr., $1,259.5
10. White Castle, $1,249.7

Source: *Nation's Restaurant News*, Top 100 (annual), June 27, 2011, p. 38.

4364 ■ TOP SANDWICH CHAINS BY U.S. SYSTEMWIDE SALES, 2010

Ranked by: U.S. systemwide foodservice sales, in millions of dollars. **Remarks:** Also notes rank for previous year, fiscal year-end, and figures for previous two years. **Number listed:** 21

1. McDonald's, with $32,395.4 million
2. Subway, $10,633
3. Burger King, $8,368
4. Wendy's, $7,943
5. Taco Bell, $6,900
6. Sonic Drive-In, $3,619.9
7. Jack in the Box, $2,934.8
8. Arby's, $2,757
9. Dairy Queen, $2,660
10. Chipotle Mexican Grill, $1,832.7

Source: *Nation's Restaurant News*, Top 100 (annual), June 27, 2011, p. 48.

4365 ■ TOP SANDWICH CHAINS BY U.S. UNITS, 2010

Ranked by: Total number of U.S. units. **Remarks:** Also notes rank for previous year, fiscal year-end, and figures for previous two years. **Number listed:** 21

1. Subway, with 23,850 units
2. McDonald's, 14,027
3. Burger King, 7,251
4. Wendy's, 5,883
5. Taco Bell, 5,634
6. Dairy Queen, 4,514
7. Sonic Drive-In, 3,572
8. Arby's, 3,523
9. Quizno's Sub, 3,440
10. Jack in the Box, 2,206

Source: *Nation's Restaurant News*, Top 100 (annual), June 27, 2011, p. 48.

4366 ■ TOP SUBMARINE SANDWICH FRANCHISES, 2012

Ranked by: Cumulative score based on financial strength and stability, growth rate, size of the system, number of years in business, the length of time franchising, start-up costs, litigation, percentage of terminations, and whether the company provides financing. **Remarks:** Specific scores not provided. Also notes overall rank within the *Franchise 500,* contact information, description, year founded, year started franchising, states where registered, available U.S. regions, where seeking foreign expansion, number of franchised and company-owned units for past three years, start-up costs, franchise fees, royalty fees, and type of financing available. **Number listed:** 7

1. Subway

2. Jersey Mike's Subs
3. Firehouse Subs
4. Blimpie Subs & Salads
5. Capriotti's Sandwich Shop Inc.
6. Cousins Subs
7. Port of Subs

Source: *Entrepreneur*, Franchise 500 (annual), January 2012, p. 170-171.

Sausage

4367 ■ TOP BRANDS OF BREAKFAST SAUSAGE/HAM, 2011

Ranked by: Sales in supermarkets, drug stores, and mass merchandisers (excluding Wal-Mart), in dollars. **Remarks:** Also notes percent change from previous year, unit sales, and market share. **Number listed:** 10

1. Jimmy Dean, with $269,025,900
2. Bob Evans, $115,045,900
3. Private label, $101,802,100
4. Johnsonville, $94,707,340
5. Tennessee Pride, $52,171,270
6. Farmer John, $29,096,560
7. Jennie-O Turkey Store, $17,813,290
8. Eckrich Smoky Links, $17,064,850
9. Taylor, $16,953,360
10. Hatfield, $16,920,820

Source: *The National Provisioner*, State of the Industry (annual), October 2011, p. 49.

4368 ■ TOP BRANDS OF DINNER SAUSAGE, 2011

Ranked by: Sales in supermarkets, drug stores, and mass merchandisers (excluding Wal-Mart), in dollars. **Remarks:** Also notes percent change from previous year, unit sales, and market share. **Number listed:** 10

1. Johnsonville, with $400,070,400
2. Hillshire Farm, $330,075,500
3. Private label, $192,480,600
4. Eckrich, $114,724,300
5. Aidells, $45,698,950
6. Premio, $39,885,410
7. Shady Brook Farms, $36,865,030
8. Bar S, $35,035,060
9. Al Fresco, $33,252,320
10. Jennie-O Turkey Store, $25,188,350

Source: *The National Provisioner*, State of the Industry (annual), October 2011, p. 36.

Savings Banks

4369 ■ TOP SAVINGS INSTITUTIONS BY TOTAL ASSETS, 2011

Ranked by: Total assets, in dollars. **Remarks:** Also notes location. **Number listed:** 501

1. ING Bank FSB, with $91,413,704,000
2. Sovereign Bank, $76,586,967,000

3. Charles Schwab Bank, $56,866,447,000
4. Hudson City Savings Bank, $51,780,521,000
5. USAA FSB, $48,783,813,000
6. E*Trade Bank, $44,883,561,000
7. American Express Bank FSB, $38,983,622,000
8. New York Community Bank, $38,055,567,000
9. Citizens Bank of Pennsylvania, $32,561,811,000
10. OneWest Bank FSB, $26,432,928,000

Source: *The Savings Directory*, (annual), 2011, p. R.10-R.16.

4370 ■ TOP SAVINGS INSTITUTIONS BY TOTAL DEPOSITS, 2011

Ranked by: Total deposits, in dollars. **Remarks:** Also notes location. **Number listed:** 500

1. ING Bank FSB, with $82,102,302,000
2. Charles Schwab Bank, $52,360,748,000
3. Sovereign Bank, $46,821,365,000
4. USAA FSB, $43,814,098,000
5. E*Trade Bank, $31,464,232,000
6. Hudson City Savings Bank, $25,582,105,000
7. Citizens Bank of Pennsylvania, $25,278,075,000
8. American Express Bank FSB, $20,916,955,000
9. New York Community Bank, $20,132,498,000
10. People's United Bank, $18,231,836,000

Source: *The Savings Directory*, (annual), 2011, p. R.17-R.23.

4371 ■ TOP SAVINGS INSTITUTIONS BY TOTAL LOANS, 2011

Ranked by: Total loans, in dollars. **Remarks:** Also notes location. **Number listed:** 500

1. Sovereign Bank, with $49,904,773,000
2. ING Bank FSB, $41,187,815,000
3. USAA FSB, $34,818,813,000
4. Hudson City Savings Bank, $30,289,683,000
5. New York Community Bank, $27,965,946,000
6. American Express Bank FSB, $25,955,965,000
7. GE Money Bank, $19,540,787,000
8. E*Trade Bank, $19,208,046,000
9. People's United Bank, $17,627,418,000
10. OneWest Bank FSB, $15,348,036,000

Source: *The Savings Directory*, (annual), 2011, p. R.24-R.30.

Savings and Loan Association Loans

4372 ■ LARGEST S & LS BY CONSTRUCTION LOANS, 2011

Ranked by: Total construction loans, in thousands of dollars. **Remarks:** Also notes city, state, association type, and dollar and percent change from previous year. **Number listed:** 25

1. Sovereign Bank NA, with $607,654 thousand
2. People's United Bank, $561,589
3. Columbia Bank, $209,511
4. Flagstar Bank, FSB, $140,644
5. First Place Bank, $138,681

6. State Farm Bank, FSB, $91,062
7. Provident Bank, $86,494
8. Dollar Bank, FSB, $74,605
9. OneWest Bank FSB, $70,627
10. Midfirst Bank, $67,025

Source: *Highline Bank and S&L Quarterly, Dec. ed.*, 2011, p. V.58.

4373 ■ LARGEST S & LS BY CONSUMER LOANS, 2011

Ranked by: Total consumer loans, in thousands of dollars. **Remarks:** Also notes city, state, association type, and dollar and percent change from previous year. **Number listed:** 25

1. USAA FSB, with $26,492,988 thousand
2. GE Capital Retail Bank, $22,287,071
3. American Express Bank, FSB, $13,668,745
4. E*Trade Bank, $5,748,661
5. State Farm Bank, FSB, $5,600,694
6. Sovereign Bank NA, $3,306,360
7. John Deere Financial, FSB, $1,861,695
8. Charles Schwab Bank, $748,939
9. Brookline Bank, $578,532
10. Farm Bureau Bank, FSB, $405,760

Source: *Highline Bank and S&L Quarterly, Dec. ed.*, 2011, p. V.59.

4374 ■ LARGEST S & LS BY CREDIT CARD AND OTHER UNSECURED LOANS, 2011

Ranked by: Total credit card and other unsecured loans, in thousands of dollars. **Remarks:** Also notes city, state, association type, and dollar and percent change from previous year. **Number listed:** 25

1. GE Capital Retail Bank, with $20,954,401 thousand
2. USAA FSB, $14,944,206
3. American Express Bank, FSB, $13,660,794
4. John Deere Financial, FSB, $1,861,695
5. State Farm Bank, FSB, $1,464,511
6. Ameriprise Bank, FSB, $202,917
7. Sovereign Bank NA, $187,995
8. Nordstrom FSB, $156,200
9. Farm Bureau Bank, FSB, $135,169
10. Nationwide Bank, $112,235

Source: *Highline Bank and S&L Quarterly, Dec. ed.*, 2011, p. V.60.

4375 ■ LARGEST S & LS BY LAND LOANS, 2011

Ranked by: Total land loans, in thousands of dollars. **Remarks:** Also notes city, state, association type, and dollar and percent change from previous year. **Number listed:** 25

1. Sovereign Bank NA, with $220,106 thousand
2. Everbank, $149,846
3. AnchorBank, FSB, $129,364
4. BankAtlantic, $112,614
5. Midfirst Bank, $105,493
6. OneWest Bank FSB, $105,094
7. Severn Savings Bank, FSB, $102,899
8. First Federal Savings & Loan Association of Charleston, $102,440

9. USAA FSB, $99,817

10. North American Savings Bank, FSB, $95,577

Source: *Highline Bank and S&L Quarterly, Dec. ed.*, 2011, p. V.58.

4376 ■ LARGEST S & LS BY LOANS ON MULTIPLE-PERSON DWELLING UNITS, 2011

Ranked by: Total loans for five-plus dwelling units, in thousands of dollars. **Remarks:** Also notes city, state, association type, and dollar and percent change from previous year. **Number listed:** 25

1. Sovereign Bank NA, with $7,026,062 thousand
2. Dime Savings Bank of Williamsburg, $2,603,057
3. OneWest Bank FSB, $2,562,032
4. Luther Burbank Savings, $2,264,534
5. Astoria Federal Savings & Loan Association, $1,702,942
6. Flushing Savings Bank, FSB, $1,393,601
7. People's United Bank, $1,018,392
8. BOFI Federal Bank, $681,799
9. Malaga Bank FSB, $561,335
10. Brookline Bank, $464,264

Source: *Highline Bank and S&L Quarterly, Dec. ed.*, 2011, p. V.57.

4377 ■ LARGEST S & LS BY NONPERFORMING CONSUMER LOANS, 2011

Ranked by: Nonperforming consumer loans, in thousands of dollars. **Remarks:** Also notes city, state, association type, and dollar and percent change from previous year. **Number listed:** 25

1. GE Capital Retail Bank, with $423,256 thousand
2. American Express Bank, FSB, $166,314
3. USAA FSB, $134,407
4. State Farm Bank, FSB, $29,267
5. AnchorBank, FSB, $29,105
6. Sovereign Bank NA, $16,580
7. E*Trade Bank, $4,531
8. First Federal Savings & Loan Association of Charleston, $4,071
9. John Deere Financial, FSB, $3,869
10. Farm Bureau Bank, FSB, $1,928

Source: *Highline Bank and S&L Quarterly, Dec. ed.*, 2011, p. V.55.

4378 ■ LARGEST S & LS BY NONPERFORMING LOANS, 2011

Ranked by: Total nonperforming loans, in thousands of dollars. **Remarks:** Also notes city, state, association type, and dollar and percent change from previous year. **Number listed:** 25

1. Midfirst Bank, with $2,069,689 thousand
2. Everbank, $1,920,375
3. OneWest Bank FSB, $1,885,986
4. Flagstar Bank, FSB, $1,871,649
5. Sovereign Bank NA, $1,364,374
6. ING Bank, FSB, $1,219,589
7. E*Trade Bank, $1,073,056
8. Hudson City Savings Bank, $1,022,686

9. People's United Bank, $554,947

10. Citicorp Trust Bank, FSB, $485,953

Source: *Highline Bank and S&L Quarterly, Dec. ed.*, 2011, p. V.53.

4379 ■ LARGEST S & LS BY NONPERFORMING REAL ESTATE LOANS, 2011

Ranked by: Nonperforming real estate loans, in thousands of dollars. **Remarks:** Also notes city, state, association type, and dollar and percent change from previous year. **Number listed:** 25

1. Midfirst Bank, with $2,063,024 thousand
2. Everbank, $1,896,964
3. OneWest Bank FSB, $1,878,556
4. Flagstar Bank, FSB, $1,870,827
5. ING Bank, FSB, $1,219,423
6. Sovereign Bank NA, $1,101,820
7. E*Trade Bank, $1,068,525
8. Hudson City Savings Bank, $1,022,666
9. Citicorp Trust Bank, FSB, $485,615
10. People's United Bank, $402,294

Source: *Highline Bank and S&L Quarterly, Dec. ed.*, 2011, p. V.54.

4380 ■ LARGEST S & LS BY TOTAL LOANS, 2011

Ranked by: Total loans, in thousands of dollars. **Remarks:** Also notes city, state, association type, and dollar and percent change from previous year. **Number listed:** 25

1. Sovereign Bank NA, with $51,823,209 thousand
2. ING Bank, FSB, $41,604,961
3. USAA FSB, $38,028,229
4. Hudson City Savings Bank, $29,486,594
5. American Express Bank, FSB, $29,379,946
6. GE Capital Retail Bank, $23,519,623
7. People's United Bank, $20,573,514
8. E*Trade Bank, $17,584,899
9. OneWest Bank FSB, $15,031,179
10. Astoria Federal Savings & Loan Association, $13,347,475

Source: *Highline Bank and S&L Quarterly, Dec. ed.*, 2011, p. V.52.

Savings and Loan Associations
See also: **Thrift Institutions**

4381 ■ LARGEST S & LS BY ASSETS, 2011

Ranked by: Assets, in millions of dollars. **Remarks:** Also notes city, state, percent change from previous year, ratings, and measures of loan exposure, capital adequacy, asset quality, earnings, and liquidity. **Number listed:** 100

1. ING Bank, FSB, with $92,212 million
2. Sovereign Bank NA, $78,147
3. Charles Schwab Bank, $68,084
4. USAA FSB, $52,182
5. E*Trade Bank, $45,806
6. Hudson City Savings Bank, $45,374
7. American Express Bank, FSB, $35,402

8. People's United Bank, $27,319

9. OneWest Bank FSB, $26,181

10. GE Capital Retail Bank, $25,101

Source: *Highline Bank and S&L Quarterly, Dec. ed.*, 2011, p. V.47-V.50.

4382 ■ LARGEST S & LS BY BROKERED DEPOSITS, 2011

Ranked by: Total brokered deposits, in thousands of dollars. **Remarks:** Also notes city, state, total assets, brokered deposits as a percentage of assets, core capital as a percentage of assets, liquid assets as a percentage of total liability, and nonperforming loans as a percentage of total loans. **Number listed:** 186

1. GE Capital Retail Bank, with $17,086,685 thousand

2. E*Trade Bank, $11,014,202

3. Scottrade Bank, $7,078,111

4. USAA FSB, $4,875,400

5. American Express Bank, FSB, $4,838,526

6. State Farm Bank, FSB, $4,609,362

7. Ameriprise Bank, FSB, $4,232,502

8. Everbank, $2,589,458

9. Aurora Bank FSB, $1,983,073

10. Midfirst Bank, $1,188,784

Source: *Highline Bank and S&L Quarterly, Dec. ed.*, 2011, p. V.41-V.44.

4383 ■ LARGEST S & LS BY DEPOSITS, 2011

Ranked by: Total deposits, in thousands of dollars. **Remarks:** Also notes city, state, association type, and dollar and percent change from previous year. **Number listed:** 25

1. ING Bank, FSB, with $82,984,186 thousand

2. Charles Schwab Bank, $60,880,111

3. Sovereign Bank NA, $48,049,815

4. USAA FSB, $46,613,888

5. E*Trade Bank, $32,017,680

6. Hudson City Savings Bank, $25,645,582

7. American Express Bank, FSB, $21,418,106

8. People's United Bank, $20,824,983

9. GE Capital Retail Bank, $17,978,885

10. OneWest Bank FSB, $15,408,202

Source: *Highline Bank and S&L Quarterly, Dec. ed.*, 2011, p. V.52.

4384 ■ LARGEST S & LS BY FEE INCOME, 2011

Ranked by: Total fee income, in thousands of dollars. **Remarks:** Also notes city, state, association type, and dollar and percent change from previous year. **Number listed:** 25

1. American Express Bank, FSB, with $5,299,819 thousand

2. USAA FSB, $1,351,060

3. FDS Bank, $733,975

4. GE Capital Retail Bank, $619,145

5. E*Trade Bank, $563,830

6. Sovereign Bank NA, $496,788

7. OneWest Bank FSB, $487,030

8. Nationwide Bank, $285,312

9. Aurora Bank FSB, $282,189

10. Flagstar Bank, FSB, $277,213

Source: *Highline Bank and S&L Quarterly, Dec. ed.*, 2011, p. V.62.

4385 ■ LARGEST S & LS BY INCOME, 2011

Ranked by: Income before extraordinary items, in thousands of dollars. **Remarks:** Also notes city, state, association type, and dollar and percent change from previous year. **Number listed:** 25

1. American Express Bank, FSB, with $1,348,350 thousand

2. GE Capital Retail Bank, $1,110,950

3. USAA FSB, $646,874

4. Charles Schwab Bank, $626,725

5. Sovereign Bank NA, $337,813

6. FDS Bank, $332,556

7. E*Trade Bank, $301,773

8. Midfirst Bank, $256,534

9. People's United Bank, $206,318

10. ING Bank, FSB, $155,844

Source: *Highline Bank and S&L Quarterly, Dec. ed.*, 2011, p. V.51.

4386 ■ LARGEST S & LS BY LEGAL EXPENSE, 2011

Ranked by: Total legal expenses, in thousands of dollars. **Remarks:** Also notes city, state, association type, and dollar and percent change from previous year. **Number listed:** 25

1. OneWest Bank FSB, with $29,253 thousand

2. Aurora Bank FSB, $22,678

3. Everbank, $20,710

4. ING Bank, FSB, $17,382

5. USAA FSB, $17,251

6. Flagstar Bank, FSB, $17,197

7. Sovereign Bank NA, $15,013

8. BankAtlantic, $11,657

9. E*Trade Bank, $11,166

10. People's United Bank, $7,201

Source: *Highline Bank and S&L Quarterly, Dec. ed.*, 2011, p. V.62.

4387 ■ LARGEST S & LS BY NET CHARGE-OFFS, 2011

Ranked by: Net charge-offs, in thousands of dollars. **Remarks:** Also notes city, state, association type, and dollar and percent change from previous year. **Number listed:** 25

1. GE Capital Retail Bank, with $960,747 thousand

2. American Express Bank, FSB, $878,819

3. USAA FSB, $651,497

4. E*Trade Bank, $612,142

5. ING Bank, FSB, $408,209

6. Sovereign Bank NA, $205,995

7. Citicorp Trust Bank, FSB, $205,050

8. State Farm Bank, FSB, $166,835

9. Flagstar Bank, FSB, $157,591

10. First Federal Savings & Loan Association of Charleston, $130,142

Source: *Highline Bank and S&L Quarterly, Dec. ed.*, 2011, p. V.53.

4388 ■ LARGEST S & LS BY OCCUPANCY EXPENSE, 2011

Ranked by: Total occupancy expenses, in thousands of dollars. **Remarks:** Also notes city, state, association type, and dollar and percent change from previous year. **Number listed:** 25

1. Sovereign Bank NA, with $374,988 thousand
2. USAA FSB, $333,935
3. People's United Bank, $133,171
4. ING Bank, FSB, $72,466
5. OneWest Bank FSB, $71,315
6. Flagstar Bank, FSB, $67,880
7. Astoria Federal Savings & Loan Association, $62,842
8. Everbank, $56,724
9. GE Capital Retail Bank, $54,554
10. Midfirst Bank, $46,744

Source: *Highline Bank and S&L Quarterly, Dec. ed.*, 2011, p. V.61.

4389 ■ LARGEST S & LS BY REPOSSESSED ASSETS, 2011

Ranked by: Total repossessed assets, in thousands of dollars. **Remarks:** Also notes city, state, association type, and dollar and percent change from previous year. **Number listed:** 25

1. Flagstar Bank, FSB, with $657,833 thousand
2. OneWest Bank FSB, $274,186
3. ING Bank, FSB, $210,780
4. Sovereign Bank NA, $118,964
5. Everbank, $118,281
6. Eastern Savings Bank, FSB, $116,146
7. E*Trade Bank, $87,615
8. AnchorBank, FSB, $86,925
9. BankAtlantic, $77,171
10. Midfirst Bank, $57,148

Source: *Highline Bank and S&L Quarterly, Dec. ed.*, 2011, p. V.55.

4390 ■ LARGEST S & LS BY SALARY AND BENEFIT EXPENSE, 2011

Ranked by: Total salary and benefit expenses, in thousands of dollars. **Remarks:** Also notes city, state, association type, and dollar and percent change from previous year. **Number listed:** 25

1. Sovereign Bank NA, with $617,446 thousand
2. USAA FSB, $596,061
3. People's United Bank, $447,509
4. OneWest Bank FSB, $306,456
5. Flagstar Bank, FSB, $261,301
6. ING Bank, FSB, $246,795
7. Everbank, $238,861
8. GE Capital Retail Bank, $220,489
9. Aurora Bank FSB, $189,155
10. Astoria Federal Savings & Loan Association, $144,948

Source: *Highline Bank and S&L Quarterly, Dec. ed.*, 2011, p. V.61.

Science Parks
See: **Industrial Parks**

Scientific Instruments and Apparatus

4391 ■ TOP *FORTUNE 500* COMPANIES IN SCIENTIFIC, PHOTOGRAPHIC, AND CONTROL EQUIPMENT, 2011

Ranked by: Revenue, in millions of dollars. **Remarks:** Also notes overall rank in the *Fortune 500;* profits; profits as a percentage of revenue; stockholders' equity; and rank by each criterion. **Number listed:** 4

1. Danaher Corp., with $16,476 million
2. Thermo Fisher Scientific Inc., $11,780
3. Agilent Technologies Inc., $6,615
4. Eastman Kodak Co., $6,022

Source: *Fortune*, Fortune 500 (annual), May 21, 2012, p. F-39.

Seafood

4392 ■ NORTH AMERICA'S TOP SEAFOOD SUPPLIERS, 2011

Ranked by: Revenue, in millions of dollars. **Remarks:** Also notes rank and figures for previous year, Web site, and headquarters. **Number listed:** 20

1. Tri-Marine International, with $1,200 million
2. Bumble Bee Foods, $960
3. Thai Union International, $900
4. Nippon Suisan USA, $790
5. High Liner Foods, $668.5
6. StarKist, $630
7. Cooke Aquaculture, $570
8. The Mazzetta Co., $502
9. American Seafoods Group, $490
10. Icicle Seafoods, $475

Source: *SeaFood Business*, North America's Top 20 Seafood Suppliers (annual), May 2012, p. 21.

Seaports
See: **Ports**

Securities Firms

4393 ■ TOP *FORTUNE 500* COMPANIES IN SECURITIES, 2011

Ranked by: Revenue, in millions of dollars. **Remarks:** Also notes overall rank in the *Fortune 500;* profits; profits as a percentage of revenue; stockholders' equity; and rank by each criterion. **Number listed:** 3

1. BlackRock Inc., with $9,081 million
2. Franklin Resources Inc., $7,140
3. The Charles Schwab Corp., $4,884

Source: *Fortune*, Fortune 500 (annual), May 21, 2012, p. F-39.

4394 ■ WORLD'S MOST ADMIRED SECURITIES FIRMS, 2012

Ranked by: Score, on a scale of 10, based on a survey of executives, directors, and securities analysts of companies within their own industry on eight criteria: innovation, financial soundness, employee talent, use of corporate assets, long-term investment value, social responsibility, quality of management, and quality of products/services. **Remarks:** Specific scores not provided. Also notes rank for previous year. **Number listed:** 6

1. The Charles Schwab Corp.
2. T. Rowe Price Group Inc.
3. Franklin Resources Inc.
4. Raymond James Financial Inc.
5. TD Ameritrade
6. Jones Financial Cos. LLLP

Source: *Fortune*, World's Most Admired Companies (annual), March 19, 2012, p. 148.

Securities—Initial Public Offerings

4395 ■ TOP BOOKRUNNERS OF AFRICAN INITIAL PUBLIC OFFERINGS, 2011

Ranked by: Total value of deals, in millions of U.S. dollars. **Remarks:** Also notes number of deals. **Number listed:** 3

1. Java Capital (Pty.), with $330 million
2. UBS, $125
3. FirstRand, $123

Source: *The Banker*, Top International Finance Centres, April 2012, p. 101.

4396 ■ TOP BOOKRUNNERS OF ASIA-PACIFIC INITIAL PUBLIC OFFERINGS, 2011

Ranked by: Total value of deals, in millions of U.S. dollars. **Remarks:** Also notes number of deals. **Number listed:** 3

1. Deutsche Bank AG, with $4,665 million
2. Ping An Securities, $4,459
3. Guosen Securities, $4,003

Source: *The Banker*, Top International Finance Centres, April 2012, p. 101.

4397 ■ TOP BOOKRUNNERS OF EUROPEAN INITIAL PUBLIC OFFERINGS, 2011

Ranked by: Total value of deals, in millions of U.S. dollars. **Remarks:** Also notes number of deals. **Number listed:** 3

1. Credit Suisse Group AG, with $4,078 million
2. Citi, $3,442
3. Morgan Stanley, $3,072

Source: *The Banker*, Top International Finance Centres, April 2012, p. 101.

4398 ■ TOP BOOKRUNNERS OF LATIN AMERICAN INITIAL PUBLIC OFFERINGS, 2011

Ranked by: Total value of deals, in millions of U.S. dollars. **Remarks:** Also notes number of deals. **Number listed:** 3

1. Itau BBA, with $1,351 million
2. Bank of America Corp./Merrill Lynch, $870
3. Credit Suisse Group AG, $849

Source: *The Banker*, Top International Finance Centres, April 2012, p. 101.

4399 ■ TOP BOOKRUNNERS OF MIDDLE EASTERN INITIAL PUBLIC OFFERINGS, 2011

Ranked by: Total value of deals, in millions of U.S. dollars. **Remarks:** Also notes number of deals. **Number listed:** 3

1. Gulf International Bank BSC, with $131 million
2. HSBC Holdings plc, $106
3. Falcom Financial Services, $88

Source: *The Banker*, Top International Finance Centres, April 2012, p. 101.

4400 ■ TOP BOOKRUNNERS OF NORTH AMERICAN INITIAL PUBLIC OFFERINGS, 2011

Ranked by: Total value of deals, in millions of U.S. dollars. **Remarks:** Also notes number of deals. **Number listed:** 3

1. Goldman Sachs Group Inc., with $5,564 million
2. Morgan Stanley, $4,792
3. Barclays Capital Inc., $4,196

Source: *The Banker*, Top International Finance Centres, April 2012, p. 101.

4401 ■ TOP INTERNATIONAL FINANCE CENTRES FOR INITIAL PUBLIC OFFERINGS, 2011

Ranked by: Volume of initial public offerings, in million of U.S. dollars. **Remarks:** Also notes number of deals and rank for previous year. **Number listed:** 50

1. New York, NY, with $43,536.02 million
2. Hong Kong, $31,524.54
3. Shenzhen, China, $25,973.22
4. London, England, $18,768.45
5. Shanghai, China, $15,648.08
6. Singapore, $7,331.85
7. Madrid, Spain, $5,300.2
8. Sao Paulo, Brazil, $4,411.83
9. Busan, South Korea, $3,443.34
10. Warsaw, Poland, $2,887.64

Source: *The Banker*, Top International Finance Centres, April 2012, p. 101.

4402 ■ TOP UNDERWRITERS OF INITIAL PUBLIC OFFERINGS (IPOS), 2011

Ranked by: Proceeds from global offerings by U.S. issuers, in billions of dollars. **Remarks:** Also notes market share, number of issues, and rank and figures for previous year. **Number listed:** 10

1. Goldman Sachs Group Inc., with $11.3 billion
2. Morgan Stanley, $10.1
3. Deutsche Bank AG, $9
4. Citigroup Inc., $8.7
5. Credit Suisse Group, $8.5
6. J. P. Morgan Chase & Co., $8.2
7. Bank of America Corp./Merrill Lynch, $7.5
8. Barclays Capital Inc., $5.7
9. UBS AG, $4.7
10. Ping An Securities, $4.5

Source: *The Wall Street Journal*, Year-End Review (annual), January 3, 2012, p. R9.

4403 ■ WORLD'S BEST-PERFORMING INITIAL PUBLIC OFFERINGS (IPOS), 2011

Ranked by: Gain from offer price to year-end price, in percent. **Remarks:** Also notes country, business description, issue date, offer price, U.S. proceeds, and percent change in first-day trading. **Number listed:** 10

1. Korea Aerospace Industries, with 155.2%
2. Derby Cycle, 124.8%
3. Hyundai Wia, 119.2%
4. Imperva, 92.8%
5. Beijing TRS Information Technology, 86.5%
6. GNC Holdings, 80.9%
7. Calbee, 79.3%
8. Henan Billions Chemicals, 77.4%
9. Shinsegae International, 75.4%
10. Qingdao Eastsoft, 64.7%

Source: *The Wall Street Journal*, Year-End Review (annual), January 3, 2012, p. R18.

4404 ■ WORLD'S LARGEST INITIAL PUBLIC OFFERINGS (IPOS), 2011

Ranked by: Proceeds, in millions of U.S. dollars. **Remarks:** Also notes country, business description, issue date, managers, and percent change in first-day trading and through the year-end. **Number listed:** 10

1. Glencore International, with $10,045.7 million
2. Hutchison Port Holdings Trust, $5,453.5
3. Bankia, $4,424
4. HCA Holdings, $4,353.9
5. Kinder Morgan, $3,293.6
6. Prada, $2,469.3
7. Vallares, $2,127.1
8. Sinohydro Group, $2,116.8
9. Chow Tai Fook Jewellery, $2,025.8
10. JSW SA, $1,923.2

Source: *The Wall Street Journal*, Year-End Review (annual), January 3, 2012, p. R18.

4405 ■ WORLD'S WORST-PERFORMING INITIAL PUBLIC OFFERINGS (IPOS), 2011

Ranked by: Decline from offer price to year-end price, in percent. **Remarks:** Also notes country, business description, issue date, offer price, U.S. proceeds, and percent change in first- day trading. **Number listed:** 10

1. FriendFinder, with -92.5%
2. Pang Da Automobile Trade, -86.3%
3. Sinovel Wind Group, -82.6%
4. Imperial Holdings, -82.4%
5. Renren, -74.4%
6. Sequans Communications, -72.4%
7. Shindoo Chemical Industry, -69%
8. Wuhu Shunrong Auto Parts, -68.1%
9. Jiangsu Skyray Instrument, -68%
10. Whenzhen Dvsion Video, -66%

Source: *The Wall Street Journal*, Year-End Review (annual), January 3, 2012, p. R18.

Security Dealers

4406 ■ LARGEST SECURITY/COMMODITY BROKERS, DEALERS, EXCHANGES, AND SERVICES BY EMPLOYEES, 2010

Ranked by: Total number of employees. **Remarks:** Also notes contact information for headquarters, number of employees at headquarters, revenue, rank by revenue, and primary SIC code. **Number listed:** 50

1. Merrill Lynch & Co., Inc., with 64,200 employees
2. Caxton-Iseman Investments LP, 52,800
3. Merrill Lynch Pierce Fenner & Smith Inc., 46,000
4. FMR LLC, 41,050
5. Jones Financial Cos. LLLP, 40,500
6. Citigroup Global Markets Holding Inc., 39,000
7. Edward D. Jones & Co., 36,000
7. National Financial Services LLC, 36,000
9. Oppenheimer Holdings Inc., 35,000
10. State Street Corp., 28,925

Source: *Business Rankings*, (annual), Dun & Bradstreet Inc., 2011, p. VI.180-VI.181.

Security Services

4407 ■ FASTEST-GROWING PRIVATE SECURITY COMPANIES IN THE U.S., 2007-2010

Ranked by: Average annual sales growth over three years, in percent. **Remarks:** Also notes headquarters, revenue, and rank in the overall *Inc. 500*. To qualify, private companies must have had annual revenues of at least $100,000 in 2007 and $2 million in 2010. **Number listed:** 7

1. Foreground Security, with 3,543.7%
2. MFS Supply, 2,060.3%
3. Easy Solutions, 1,479.9%
4. Global Strategies, 1,470.4%
5. Ciphent, 1,442%
6. Exacq Technologies, 850.6%
7. LifeLock, 759.8%

Source: *Inc.*, Inc. 500 (annual), September 2011, p. 188.

Security Systems

4408 ■ NORTH AMERICA'S TOP SECURITY SYSTEMS INTEGRATORS, 2010

Ranked by: Revenue, in U.S. dollars. **Remarks:** Also notes rank for previous year, headquarters, number of new systems installed, largest and smallest new projects of the year, number of full-time employees, number of business locations, and key markets. **Number listed:** 130

1. ADT Security Services Inc., with $1,800,000,000
2. Siemens Industry Inc., $1,400,000,000
3. SimplexGrinnell LP, $925,000,000
4. Diebold Security, $567,850,000
5. Stanley Convergent Security Solutions Inc., $352,000,000
6. Johnson Controls Inc., $255,200,000
7. Convergint Technologies LLC, $202,699,302
8. Niscayah Inc., $200,000,000
9. HBE, a Kratos Co., $93,000,000
10. Schneider Electric, $83,400,000

Source: *Security Distributing & Marketing*, Top Systems Integrators (annual), July 2011.

4409 ■ TOP BRANDS OF CLOSED-CIRCUIT TELEVISION (CCTV) CAMERAS, 2010

Ranked by: Popularity among *CE Pro 100* companies, in percent. **Number listed:** 5

1. Panasonic, with 31%
2. IC Realtime, 28%
3. Axis Communication, 19%
4. Speco, 13%
5. GE, 10%

Source: *CE Pro*, Brand Analysis (annual), June 2011, p. 60.

4410 ■ TOP BRANDS OF HOME SECURITY SYSTEMS, 2010

Ranked by: Popularity among *CE Pro 100* companies, in percent. **Number listed:** 5

1. GE Security, with 39%
2. Honeywell, 25%
3. DSC, 20%
4. HAI, 11%
5. Bosch, 6%

Source: *CE Pro*, Brand Analysis (annual), June 2011, p. 60.

4411 ■ TOP SECURITY/STRUCTURED WIRING-BASED ELECTRONICS INTEGRATORS, 2011

Ranked by: Revenue. **Remarks:** Specific figures not provided. **Number listed:** 5

1. ADT Security Services
2. Vivint
3. Guardian Protection
4. Accent Electronic Systems Integrators
5. Crime Prevention Security Systems & Custom Home Entertainment

Source: *CE Pro*, CE Pro 100 (annual), May 2012, p. 42.

4412 ■ TOP SECURITY SYSTEMS COMPANIES BY NON-RESIDENTIAL REVENUE, 2011

Ranked by: Revenue from non-residential systems installation, in dollars. **Remarks:** Also notes number of installations and rank in the overall *SDM 100*. **Number listed:** 57

1. Vector Security Inc., with $63,135,000
2. AFA Protective Systems Inc., $31,200,000
3. Slomin's Inc., $28,469,760
4. Tri-Signal Integration Inc., $26,000,000
5. ASG Security, $24,340,345
6. Allied Fire & Security, $19,600,000
7. Interface Security Systems Holdings Inc., $19,506,041
8. Per Mar Security Services, $14,085,323
9. Intelligent Access Systems, $13,305,797
10. Intertech Security, $10,900,000

Source: *Security Distributing & Marketing*, SDM 100 (annual), May 2012, p. 74.

4413 ■ TOP SECURITY SYSTEMS COMPANIES BY RECURRING MONTHLY REVENUE, 2011

Ranked by: Recurring monthly revenue, in dollars. **Remarks:** Also notes headquarters, gross revenue, number of subscribers, number of employees and locations, and breakdown by residential and non-residential installations. **Number listed:** 100

1. ADT, with $299,900,000
2. Stanley Convergent Security Solutions Inc., $35,749,000

3. Vivint Inc., $27,800,000
4. Protection 1, $25,200,000
5. Monitronics International Inc., $22,342,047
6. Slomin's Inc., $14,693,590
7. Vector Security Inc., $10,200,000
8. Guardian Protection Services Inc., $9,104,531
9. ASG Security, $7,026,924
10. Bay Alarm Co., $6,680,600

Source: *Security Distributing & Marketing*, SDM 100 (annual), May 2012, p. 63-76.

4414 ■ TOP SECURITY SYSTEMS COMPANIES BY RESIDENTIAL CUSTOMERS, 2011

Ranked by: Number of residential subscribers. **Remarks:** Also notes total number of subscribers and rank in the overall *SDM 100*. **Number listed:** 61

1. Vivint Inc., with 572,897 subscribers
2. Monitronics International Inc., 550,000
3. Protection 1, 402,000
4. Slomin's Inc., 263,113
5. Guardian Protection Services Inc., 228,802
6. Vector Security Inc., 211,466
7. Central Security Group Inc., 140,053
8. Protect America Inc., 131,010
9. ASG Security, 121,755
10. Security Networks, 120,000

Source: *Security Distributing & Marketing*, SDM 100 (annual), May 2012, p. 68.

4415 ■ TOP SECURITY SYSTEMS COMPANIES BY TOTAL REVENUE, 2011

Ranked by: Gross revenue, in millions of dollars. **Remarks:** Also notes figures for previous year and rank in the overall *SDM 100*. **Number listed:** 99

1. ADT, with $5,100 million
2. Stanley Convergent Security Solutions Inc., $798.4
3. Protection 1, $345.6
4. Monitronics International Inc., $313
5. Vivint Inc., $312.9
6. Slomin's Inc., $257
7. Vector Security Inc., $212.1
8. Guardian Protection Services Inc., $136.4
9. ASG Security, $106.2
10. Bay Alarm Co., $96.5

Source: *Security Distributing & Marketing*, SDM 100 (annual), May 2012, p. 78.

4416 ■ WORLD'S LARGEST SECURITY SYSTEMS COMPANIES OVERALL, 2011

Ranked by: Score based on revenue, profits, assets, and market capitalization. **Remarks:** Specific scores not provided. Also notes country, overall rank in the *Forbes 2000*, and figures for each criterion. **Number listed:** 2

1. Tyco International Ltd.
2. G4S plc

Source: *Forbes*, Forbes 2000 (annual), http://www.forbes.com, May 7, 2012.

Security Underwriting

4417 ■ TOP UNDERWRITERS OF GLOBAL EQUITY, 2011

Ranked by: Amount, in billions of U.S. dollars. **Remarks:** Also notes market share for current and previous year. **Number listed:** 10

1. Goldman Sachs Group Inc., with $54.3 billion
2. Morgan Stanley, $46.8
3. J. P. Morgan Chase & Co., $42.8
4. Bank of America Corp./Merrill Lynch, $42.3
5. Credit Suisse Group, $37.5
6. Deutsche Bank AG, $35.3
7. Citigroup Inc., $35.2
8. UBS AG, $30.7
9. Barclays Capital Inc., $22.7
10. Nomura, $10.5

Source: *The Wall Street Journal*, Year-End Review (annual), January 3, 2012, p. R9.

4418 ■ TOP UNDERWRITERS OF GLOBAL STOCKS AND BONDS, 2011

Ranked by: Proceeds, in billions of U.S. dollars. **Remarks:** Also notes number of issues for current year, market share, and rank and figures for previous year. **Number listed:** 10

1. J. P. Morgan Chase & Co., with $430.4 billion
2. Deutsche Bank AG, $400.9
3. Barclays Capital Inc., $399.2
4. Bank of America Corp./Merrill Lynch, $356.3
5. Citigroup Inc., $345.9
6. Goldman Sachs Group Inc., $305.1
7. Morgan Stanley, $284
8. UBS AG, $283.8
9. Credit Suisse Group, $265.6
10. BNP Paribas SA, $242.1

Source: *The Wall Street Journal*, Year-End Review (annual), January 3, 2012, p. R9.

Seed Industry

4419 ■ LARGEST U.S. RETAILERS IN SEED, 2010

Ranked by: Seed as a percentage of total revenue. **Number listed:** 100

1. East Kansas Chemical Co., with 44%
2. Jimmy Sanders Inc., 32%
3. Home Oil Co., 31%
3. Ritter Crop Services, 31%
3. G & H Seed Co., 31%
6. United Cooperative, 28%
7. Hefty Seed Co., 27%
7. MRM Ag Services Inc., 27%
9. Baltz Feed Co., 26%
10. North Central Farmers Elevator, 24%

Source: *CropLife*, CropLife 100 (annual), http://www.croplife.com, December 2011.

Semiconductor Industry

4420 ■ BEST SMALL SEMICONDUCTOR COMPANIES IN AMERICA, 2011

Ranked by: Score based on revenue, profits, and return on equity for the past 12 months and five years. **Remarks:** Specific scores not provided. Also notes rank in the overall *100 Best Small Companies in America*. To qualify, companies must have revenues between $5 million and $1 billion, a net margin above five percent, and share price above $5. List is available online only. **Number listed:** 7

1. IPG Photonics
2. NVE
3. Hittite Microwave
4. Cirrus Logic
5. Alliance Fiber Optic Products
6. Volterra Semiconductor
7. FEI

Source: *Forbes*, Best Small Companies in America (annual), November 7, 2011.

4421 ■ CALIFORNIA'S LARGEST SEMICONDUCTOR COMPANIES OVERALL, 2011

Ranked by: Score based on revenue, profits, assets, and market capitalization. **Remarks:** Specific scores not provided. Also notes overall rank in the *Forbes 2000* and figures for each criterion. **Number listed:** 10

1. Intel Corp.
2. Applied Materials Inc.
3. Broadcom Corp.
4. Altera Corp.
5. KLA-Tencor Corp.
6. NVIDIA Corp.
7. Advanced Micro Devices Inc.
8. Xilinx Inc.
9. Maxim Integrated Products
10. Linear Technology Corp.

Source: *Forbes*, Forbes 2000 (annual), http://www.forbes.com, May 7, 2012.

4422 ■ JAPAN'S LARGEST SEMICONDUCTOR COMPANIES OVERALL, 2011

Ranked by: Score based on revenue, profits, assets, and market capitalization. **Remarks:** Specific scores not provided. Also notes overall rank in the *Forbes 2000* and figures for each criterion. **Number listed:** 2

1. Tokyo Electron Ltd.
2. Renesas Electronics Corp.

Source: *Forbes*, Forbes 2000 (annual), http://www.forbes.com, May 7, 2012.

4423 ■ LARGEST U.S. SEMICONDUCTOR COMPANIES OVERALL, 2011

Ranked by: Score based on revenue, profits, assets, and market capitalization. **Remarks:** Specific scores not provided. Also notes overall rank in the *Forbes 2000* and figures for each criterion. **Number listed:** 14

1. Intel Corp.
2. Texas Instruments Inc.

3. Applied Materials Inc.
4. Broadcom Corp.
5. Micron Technology Inc.
6. Altera Corp.
7. Analog Devices Inc.
8. KLA-Tencor Corp.
9. Nvidia Corp.
10. Advanced Micro Devices Inc.

Source: *Forbes*, Forbes 2000 (annual), http://www.forbes.com, May 7, 2012.

4424 ■ THE NETHERLANDS' LARGEST SEMICONDUCTOR COMPANIES OVERALL, 2011

Ranked by: Score based on revenue, profits, assets, and market capitalization. **Remarks:** Specific scores not provided. Also notes overall rank in the *Forbes 2000* and figures for each criterion. **Number listed:** 2

1. ASML Holding NV
2. NXP Semiconductors

Source: *Forbes*, Forbes 2000 (annual), http://www.forbes.com, May 7, 2012.

4425 ■ SOUTH KOREA'S LARGEST SEMICONDUCTOR COMPANIES OVERALL, 2011

Ranked by: Score based on revenue, profits, assets, and market capitalization. **Remarks:** Specific scores not provided. Also notes overall rank in the *Forbes 2000* and figures for each criterion. **Number listed:** 2

1. Samsung Electronics Co., Ltd.
2. Hynix Semiconductor Inc.

Source: *Forbes*, Forbes 2000 (annual), http://www.forbes.com, May 7, 2012.

4426 ■ TAIWAN'S LARGEST SEMICONDUCTOR COMPANIES OVERALL, 2011

Ranked by: Score based on revenue, profits, assets, and market capitalization. **Remarks:** Specific scores not provided. Also notes overall rank in the *Forbes 2000* and figures for each criterion. **Number listed:** 4

1. Taiwan Semiconductor Manufacturing Co., Ltd.
2. United Microelectronics Corp.
3. Advanced Semiconductor Engineering Inc.
4. MediaTek Inc.

Source: *Forbes*, Forbes 2000 (annual), http://www.forbes.com, May 7, 2012.

4427 ■ TOP *FORTUNE 500* COMPANIES IN SEMICONDUCTORS AND OTHER ELECTRONIC COMPONENTS, 2011

Ranked by: Revenue, in millions of dollars. **Remarks:** Also notes overall rank in the *Fortune 500;* profits; profits as a percentage of revenue; stockholders' equity; and rank by each criterion. **Number listed:** 9

1. Intel Corp., with $53,999 million
2. Jabil Circuit Inc., $16,519
3. Texas Instruments Inc., $13,735
4. Applied Materials Inc., $10,517
5. Micron Technology Inc., $8,788
6. Broadcom Corp., $7,389

7. Sanmina-SCI Corp., $6,602
8. Advanced Micro Devices Inc., $6,568
9. SanDisk Corp., $5,662

Source: *Fortune*, Fortune 500 (annual), May 21, 2012, p. F-39.

4428 ■ THE UNITED STATES' MOST VALUABLE SEMICONDUCTOR BRANDS, 2011

Ranked by: Brand value, in millions of U.S. dollars. **Remarks:** Also notes rank within the *Global 500* for current and previous year, figures for current and previous year, and brand rating. Ranking is available online only. **Number listed:** 2

1. Intel, with $21,908 million
2. Texas Instruments, $3,283

Source: *Global 500*, (annual), Brand Finance plc, March 2012.

4429 ■ WORLD'S LARGEST SEMICONDUCTOR COMPANIES OVERALL, 2011

Ranked by: Score based on revenue, profits, assets, and market capitalization. **Remarks:** Specific scores not provided. Also notes country, overall rank in the *Forbes 2000,* and figures for each criterion. **Number listed:** 29

1. Samsung Electronics Co., Ltd.
2. Intel Corp.
3. Taiwan Semiconductor Manufacturing Co., Ltd.
4. Texas Instruments Inc.
5. Applied Materials Inc.
6. ASML Holding NV
7. Broadcom Corp.
8. Tokyo Electron Ltd.
9. Hynix Semiconductor Inc.
10. STMicroelectronics NV

Source: *Forbes*, Forbes 2000 (annual), http://www.forbes.com, May 7, 2012.

4430 ■ WORLD'S MOST ADMIRED SEMICONDUCTORS COMPANIES, 2012

Ranked by: Score, on a scale of 10, based on a survey of executives, directors, and securities analysts of companies within their own industry on eight criteria: innovation, financial soundness, employee talent, use of corporate assets, long-term investment value, social responsibility, quality of management, and quality of products/services. **Remarks:** Specific scores not provided. Also notes rank for previous year. **Number listed:** 8

1. Intel Corp.
2. Texas Instruments Inc.
3. Broadcom Corp.
4. Taiwan Semiconductor Manufacturing Co., Ltd.
5. Applied Materials Inc.
6. Micron Technology Inc.
7. Jabil Circuit Inc.
8. Infineon Technologies AG

Source: *Fortune*, World's Most Admired Companies (annual), March 19, 2012, p. 149.

4431 ■ WORLD'S MOST VALUABLE SEMICONDUCTOR BRANDS, 2011

Ranked by: Brand value, in millions of U.S. dollars. **Remarks:** Also notes rank within the *Global 500* for current and previous year, figures for current and previous year, country, and brand rating. Ranking is available online only. **Number listed:** 3

1. Samsung, with $38,197 million
2. Intel, $21,908
3. Texas Instruments, $3,283

Source: *Global 500*, (annual), Brand Finance plc, March 2012.

Service Industry

4432 ■ EUROPE'S MOST VALUABLE SUPPORT SERVICES COMPANIES, 2011

Ranked by: Market value as of March 2011, in millions of U.S. dollars. **Remarks:** Also notes rank within the *FT Europe 500*, rank for previous year, country, revenue, net income, assets, number of employees, share price, price-to-earning ratio, dividend yield, and fiscal yearend. **Number listed:** 13

1. SGS SA, with $13,979.6 million
2. Adecco SA, $12,495.2
3. Experian plc, $12,339.1
4. Wolseley plc, $9,573.8
5. Randstad Holding NV, $9,483.7
6. Bureau Veritas, $8,593.5
7. Amadeus IT, $8,574.7
8. The Capita Group plc, $7,297.7
9. Aggreko, $6,935
10. Edenred, $6,826.5

Source: *Financial Times*, FT 500 (annual), http://www.ft.com, June 24, 2011.

4433 ■ MOST VALUABLE U.S. SUPPORT SERVICES COMPANIES, 2011

Ranked by: Market value as of March 2011, in millions of U.S. dollars. **Remarks:** Also notes rank within the *FT U.S. 500*, rank for previous year, country, revenue, net income, assets, number of employees, share price, price-to-earning ratio, dividend yield, and fiscal yearend. **Number listed:** 11

1. Accenture Ltd., with $35,691 million
2. Automatic Data Processing Inc., $25,471.1
3. Waste Management Inc., $17,741.9
4. Republic Services Inc., $11,537.2
5. Paychex Inc., $11,356.6
6. Fidelity National Information Services Inc., $9,890.3
7. W. W. Grainger Inc., $9,561.1
8. Fastenal Co., $9,557.9
9. Fiserv Inc., $9,162
10. Stericycle Inc., $7,572.1

Source: *Financial Times*, FT 500 (annual), http://www.ft.com, June 24, 2011.

4434 ■ STATES WITH THE HIGHEST RATE OF EMPLOYEES IN PROFESSIONAL AND BUSINESS SERVICES, 2010

Ranked by: Percentage of employees in professional and business services. **Number listed:** 51

1. Washington DC, with 21.7%
2. Virginia, 18.1%
3. Maryland, 15.6%
4. New Jersey, 15.3%
5. California, 15%

6. Colorado, 14.8%
7. Arizona, 14.7%
7. Massachusetts, 14.7%
9. Florida, 14.4%
10. Illinois, 13.9%

Source: *State Rankings*, (annual), CQ Press, 2011, p. 205.

4435 ■ STATES WITH THE LOWEST RATE OF EMPLOYEES IN PROFESSIONAL AND BUSINESS SERVICES, 2010

Ranked by: Percentage of employees in the professional and business service industry. **Number listed:** 51

1. Wyoming, with 6%
2. South Dakota, 6.7%
3. Vermont, 7.6%
4. North Dakota, 8%
4. West Virginia, 8%
6. Alaska, 8.1%
7. Mississippi, 8.3%
8. Iowa, 8.5%
9. Montana, 9%
10. Maine, 9.4%
10. Wisconsin, 9.4%

Source: *State Rankings*, (annual), CQ Press, 2011, p. 205.

4436 ■ TOP MISCELLANEOUS SERVICE FRANCHISES, 2012

Ranked by: Cumulative score based on financial strength and stability, growth rate, size of the system, number of years in business, the length of time franchising, start-up costs, litigation, percentage of terminations, and whether the company provides financing. **Remarks:** Specific scores not provided. Also notes overall rank within the *Franchise 500,* contact information, description, year founded, year started franchising, states where registered, available U.S. regions, where seeking foreign expansion, number of franchised and company-owned units for past three years, start-up costs, franchise fees, royalty fees, and type of financing available. **Number listed:** 13

1. Pop-A-Lock Franchise System
2. Two Men & a Truck International Inc.
3. Caring Transitions
4. Speedpro USA Inc.
5. Complete Music
6. Signal 88 Security
7. Showhomes
8. Plan Ahead Events
9. EmbroidMe
10. College Hunks Hauling Junk

Source: *Entrepreneur*, Franchise 500 (annual), January 2012, p. 206-209.

4437 ■ WORLD'S MOST VALUABLE SUPPORT SERVICES COMPANIES, 2011

Ranked by: Market value as of March 2011, in millions of U.S. dollars. **Remarks:** Also notes rank within the *FT 500*, rank for previous year, country, revenue, net income, assets, number of employees, share price, price-to-earning ratio, dividend yield, and fiscal year-end. **Number listed:** 4

1. Mitsubishi Corp., with $47,282.3 million

2. Accenture Ltd., $35,691

3. Mitsui & Co., Ltd., $32,906.2

4. Automatic Data Processing Inc., $25,471.1

Source: *Financial Times*, FT 500 (annual), http://www.ft.com, June 24, 2011.

Service Stations
See: **Automobile Service Stations**

Shipping

4438 ■ WORLD'S TOP GLOBAL SHIPPING COMPANIES, 2011

Ranked by: Editorial determination. **Remarks:** Scores not provided. Also notes headquarters and comments. **Number listed:** 10

1. United Parcel Service Inc. (UPS, U.S.)

2. DHL Express (Germany)

3. FedEx Corp. (U.S.)

4. U.S. Postal Service

5. Schenker AG (Germany)

6. TNT NV (Netherlands)

7. YRC Worldwide (U.S.)

8. Parcelforce Worldwide (U.K.)

9. Royal Mail (U.K.)

10. Japan Post Service

Source: *Supply Chain*, World's Top 10 Shipping Companies, June 2011, p. 98-107.

Shoe Industry

4439 ■ WORLD'S LARGEST CONSUMER FOOTWEAR, APPAREL, AND ACCESSORY COMPANIES, 2010

Ranked by: Sales, in millions of U.S. dollars. **Remarks:** Also notes brands and annual sales growth. **Number listed:** 20

1. LVMH Moet Hennessy Louis Vuitton SA, with $28,210 million

2. PPR SA, $20,049

3. Nike Inc., $19,014

4. adidas AG, $16,646

5. VF Corp., $7,703

6. Compagnie Financiere Richemont SA, $7,186

7. Polo Ralph Lauren Corp., $5,000

8. PVH Corp., $4,636

9. Esprit Co., $4,335

10. Hanesbrands Inc., $4,327

Source: *Consumer Goods Technology*, Consumer Goods Registry (annual), http://www.consumergoods.com, December 2011.

Siding Materials

4440 ■ TOP HOME SIDING SYSTEMS FRANCHISES, 2012

Ranked by: Cumulative score based on financial strength and stability, growth rate, size of the system, number of years in busi-

ness, the length of time franchising, start-up costs, litigation, percentage of terminations, and whether the company provides financing. **Remarks:** Specific scores not provided. Also notes overall rank within the *Franchise 500,* contact information, description, year founded, year started franchising, states where registered, available U.S. regions, where seeking foreign expansion, number of franchised and company-owned units for past three years, start-up costs, franchise fees, royalty fees, and type of financing available. **Number listed:** 2

1. ABC Inc.

2. United States Seamless Inc.

Source: *Entrepreneur*, Franchise 500 (annual), January 2012, p. 178-179.

Signs

4441 ■ TOP BUSINESS SIGN FRANCHISES, 2012

Ranked by: Cumulative score based on financial strength and stability, growth rate, size of the system, number of years in business, the length of time franchising, start-up costs, litigation, percentage of terminations, and whether the company provides financing. **Remarks:** Specific scores not provided. Also notes overall rank within the *Franchise 500,* contact information, description, year founded, year started franchising, states where registered, available U.S. regions, where seeking foreign expansion, number of franchised and company-owned units for past three years, start-up costs, franchise fees, royalty fees, and type of financing available. **Number listed:** 4

1. FastSigns International Inc.

2. Sign-A-Rama Inc.

3. Signs Now Corp.

4. Signs By Tomorrow

Source: *Entrepreneur*, Franchise 500 (annual), January 2012, p. 152-153.

Ski Resorts

4442 ■ IDAHO'S LARGEST SKI AREAS, 2010-2011

Ranked by: Number of skier visits. **Remarks:** Also notes contact information, key executive, price for full-day and half-day lift tickets, number of lifts and trails, year opened, and average annual snowfall. **Number listed:** 3

1. Bogus Basin Mountain Recreation Area, with 356,080 skier visits

2. Lookout Pass Ski Area, 65,000

3. Pomerelle Mountain Resort, 49,000

Source: *Idaho Business Review*, Largest Ski Areas (annual), September 16, 2011.

4443 ■ LARGEST COLORADO SKI AREAS BY SKIABLE AREA, 2011

Ranked by: Total skiable area, in acres. **Remarks:** Also notes contact information, vertical rise, number of lifts and trails, skier visits, types of trals, top local executive, owner, ticker symbol, and headquarters **Number listed:** 25

1. Vail Mountain, with 5,289 acres

2. Keystone Resort, 3,148

3. Snowmass, 3,132

4. Winter Park Resort/Mary Jane, 3,078

5. Steamboat Ski & Resort Corp., 2,965

6. Copper Mountain Resort, 2,465

7. Breckenridge Ski Resort, 2,358
8. Telluride Ski Resort, 2,000
9. Silverton Mountain, 1,819
10. Beaver Creek Resort, 1,815

Source: *Denver Business Journal*, Book of Lists (annual), December 16, 2011, p. 139.

4444 ■ LARGEST COLORADO SKI AREAS BY VISITORS, 2010-2011

Ranked by: Number of skier visits. **Remarks:** Also notes contact information. **Number listed:** 7

1. Keystone Resort, with 1,000,000 skier visits
2. Beaver Creek Resort, 899,728
3. Telluride Ski Resort, 420,621
4. Arapahoe Basin Ski Area, 400,000
5. Eldora Mountain Resort, 268,000
6. Wolf Creek Ski Area, 192,022
7. Monarch Mountain, 175,000

Source: *Denver Business Journal*, Book of Lists (annual), December 16, 2011, p. 139.

Small Business

4445 ■ BEST SMALL COMPANIES IN AMERICA, 2011

Ranked by: Score based on revenue, profits, and return on equity for the past 12 months and five years. **Remarks:** Specific scores not provided. To qualify, companies must have revenues between $5 million and $1 billion, a net margin above five percent, and share price above $5; banks and other financial institutions are not considered. Also notes type of business and sales. **Number listed:** 100

1. Questcor Pharmaceuticals
2. American Public Education Inc.
3. IEC Electronics
4. Grand Canyon Education
5. SolarWinds
6. IPG Photonics
7. LSB Industries
8. Interactive Intelligence
9. Allegiant Travel
10. KapStone Paper & Packaging

Source: *Forbes*, Best Small Companies in America (annual), November 7, 2011, p. 98+.

4446 ■ BEST STATES FOR SMALL BUSINESS, 2011

Ranked by: Small business survival index, a measure of the climate for entrepreneurship that considers 23 criteria, including tax rates, health care costs, electricity costs, workers' compensation premiums, crime rate, right-to-work status, number of bureaucrats, tax limitation status, minimum wage, and liability score. **Remarks:** The lower the score, the better the small business climate. **Number listed:** 51

1. South Dakota, with 32.292 points
2. Nevada, 38.531
3. Texas, 39.076
4. Wyoming, 46.049
5. South Carolina, 47.047
6. Alabama, 48.765

7. Ohio, 49.538
8. Florida, 50.81
9. Colorado, 51.317
10. Virginia, 51.697

Source: *Small Business Survival Index*, (annual), Small Business & Entrepreneurship Council, November 2011, p. 2.

4447 ■ WORST STATES FOR SMALL BUSINESS, 2011

Ranked by: Small business survival index, a measure of the climate for entrepreneurship that considers 23 criteria, including tax rates, health care costs, electricity costs, workers' compensation premiums, crime rate, right-to-work status, number of bureaucrats, tax limitation status, minimum wage, and liability score. **Remarks:** The lower the score, the better the small business climate. **Number listed:** 51

1. Washington DC, with 84.354 points
2. New York, 82.787
3. New Jersey, 82.625
4. Vermont, 78.291
5. Rhode Island, 77.250
6. California, 76.357
7. Maine, 75.876
8. Connecticut, 75.587
9. Minnesota, 75.308
10. Massachusetts, 73.976

Source: *Small Business Survival Index*, (annual), Small Business & Entrepreneurship Council, November 2011, p. 2.

Smokeless Tobacco
See: **Tobacco Industry**

Snack Food Industry

4448 ■ TOP BEVERAGE/SNACK CHAINS BY GROWTH IN SALES, 2009-2010

Ranked by: Annual growth in systemwide sales, in percent. **Remarks:** Also notes rank for previous year, fiscal year-end, and figures for previous year. **Number listed:** 3

1. Starbucks Coffee, with 7.28%
2. Dunkin' Donuts, 5.33%
3. Krispy Kreme Doughnuts, 4.14%

Source: *Nation's Restaurant News*, Top 100 (annual), June 27, 2011, p. 58.

4449 ■ TOP BEVERAGE/SNACK CHAINS BY GROWTH IN UNITS, 2009-2010

Ranked by: Annual growth in number of U.S. units, in percent. **Remarks:** Also notes rank for previous year, fiscal year-end, and figures for previous year. **Number listed:** 3

1. Dunkin' Donuts, with 3.14%
2. Krispy Kreme Doughnuts, 2.23%
3. Starbucks Coffee, 0.13%

Source: *Nation's Restaurant News*, Top 100 (annual), June 27, 2011, p. 58.

4450 ■ TOP BEVERAGE/SNACK CHAINS BY SALES PER UNIT, 2010

Ranked by: Sales per unit, in thousands of dollars. **Remarks:** Also notes rank for previous year, fiscal year-end, and figures for previous two years. **Number listed:** 2

1. Krispy Kreme Doughnuts, with $2,133.3 thousand
2. Dunkin' Donuts, $815

Source: *Nation's Restaurant News*, Top 100 (annual), June 27, 2011, p. 38.

4451 ■ TOP BEVERAGE/SNACK CHAINS BY U.S. SYSTEMWIDE SALES, 2010

Ranked by: U.S. systemwide foodservice sales, in millions of dollars. Remarks: Also notes rank for previous year, fiscal year-end, and figures for previous two years. Number listed: 3

1. Starbucks Coffee, with $7,955 million
2. Dunkin' Donuts, $5,435
3. Krispy Kreme Doughnuts, $483.2

Source: *Nation's Restaurant News*, Top 100 (annual), June 27, 2011, p. 58.

4452 ■ TOP BEVERAGE/SNACK CHAINS BY U.S. UNITS, 2010

Ranked by: Total number of U.S. units. Remarks: Also notes rank for previous year, fiscal year-end, and figures for previous two years. Number listed: 3

1. Starbucks Coffee, with 10,580 units
2. Dunkin' Donuts, 6,772
3. Krispy Kreme Doughnuts, 229

Source: *Nation's Restaurant News*, Top 100 (annual), June 27, 2011, p. 58.

Snacks

4453 ■ TOP BRANDS OF JERKY AND MEAT SNACKS, 2011

Ranked by: Sales for the 52 weeks ending March 20, 2011, in millions of dollars. Remarks: Also notes annual growth, dollar share, and unit sales. Number listed: 10

1. Jack Link's, with $403.1 million
2. Private label, $46.7
3. Jack Link's Matador, $41.9
4. Slim Jim, $22.3
5. Oh Boy! Oberto, $18.6
5. World Kitchens, $18.6
7. Tillamook Country Smoker, $12
8. Old Trapper, $11.1
9. Pemmican, $11
10. Love's, $10.7

Source: *Snack Food & Wholesale Bakery*, State of the Industry (annual), July 2011, p. 54.

4454 ■ TOP BRANDS OF PORK RINDS, 2011

Ranked by: Sales for the 52 weeks ending March 20, 2011, in millions of dollars. Remarks: Also notes annual growth, dollar share, and unit sales. Number listed: 10

1. Baken-Ets, with $71 million
2. Tom's, $21.1
3. Turkey Creek Snacks, $19.2
4. Golden Flake, $16.5
5. Private label, $13.9
6. Mac's, $8.7

7. Carolina Country Snacks, $6.3
8. Lee's, $5.6
9. Wallace's, $5.5
10. Guerrero, $5.3

Source: *Snack Food & Wholesale Bakery*, State of the Industry (annual), July 2011, p. 58.

4455 ■ TOP BRANDS OF PRETZELS, 2011

Ranked by: Sales for the 52 weeks ending March 20, 2011, in millions of dollars. Remarks: Also notes annual growth, dollar share, and unit sales. Number listed: 9

1. Snyder's of Hanover, with $286.2 million
2. Rold Gold, $187.6
3. Private label, $115.9
4. Combos, $79.4
5. Utz, $43.2
6. Herr's, $20.5
7. Rold Gold Natural, $16.4
8. Snyder's of Hanover 100-Calorie Pack, $12.1
9. Bechman, $11.7

Source: *Snack Food & Wholesale Bakery*, State of the Industry (annual), July 2011, p. 32.

Snow Removal Companies

4456 ■ LARGEST SNOW REMOVAL CONTRACTORS, 2010-2011

Ranked by: Snow removal revenue during the winter of 2010 and 2011, in dollars. Remarks: Also notes headquarters. Number listed: 100

1. The Brickman Group, with $192,500,000
2. ValleyCrest Landscape Cos., $35,400,000
3. Lipinski Snow Services, $32,000,000
4. Clintar Landscape Management, $30,000,000
5. Ferrandino & Son, $26,750,000
6. Reliable Property Services, $18,750,000
7. TruGreen LandCare, $14,865,518
8. Arctic Snow & Ice Control, $14,000,000
9. Acres Group, $12,700,000
10. Yardworx, $7,900,000

Source: *Snow Magazine*, Top 100 Contractors (annual), October 2011, p. 42+.

Soccer

4457 ■ TOP EUROPEAN FOOTBALL CLUB BRANDS, 2011

Ranked by: Brand vaulue, in millions of pounds sterling. Remarks: Also notes rank and figures for previous year, percent change, brand rating, and comments. Number listed: 30

1. Manchester United, with £412 million
2. Real Madrid, £401
3. Barcelona, £392
4. Bayern Munich, £308
5. Chelsea, £196
6. Arsenal, £188

7. AC Milan, £170

8. Internazionale Milano, £164

9. Liverpool, £156

10. Juventus, £115

Source: *European Football Brands*, (annual), Brand Finance plc, September 2011.

4458 ■ WORLD'S MOST VALUABLE SOCCER TEAMS, 2011

Ranked by: Value, in revenue and operating income, in millions of U.S. dollars. **Remarks:** Also notes owner/majority shareholder, annual growth in value, revenue, operating income, and debt-tovalue ratio. **Number listed:** 20

1. Manchester United (England), with $2,235 million

2. Real Madrid (Spain), $1,877

3. Barcelona (Spain), $1,307

4. Arsenal (England), $1,292

5. Bayern Munich (Germany), $1,235

6. AC Milan (Italy), $989

7. Chelsea (England), $761

8. Liverpool (England), $619

9. Juventus (Italy), $591

10. Schalke 04 (Germany), $587

Source: *Forbes*, Soccer Team Valuations (annual), May 7, 2012, p. 42.

Soft Drink Industry

4459 ■ TOP CARBONATED SOFT DRINK COMPANIES, 2011

Ranked by: Market share, in percent. **Number listed:** 8

1. The Coca-Cola Co., with 43.1%

2. PepsiCo Inc., 29.2%

3. Dr Pepper Snapple Group Inc., 17.1%

4. Cott Corp., 3.5%

5. National Beverage Corp., 2.9%

6. Big Red Inc., 0.4%

7. Carolina Beverage Corp., 0.1%

8. Others, 3.7%

Source: *Beverage World*, State of the Industry Report (annual), May 2012, p. 27.

4460 ■ TOP SOFT DRINK BRANDS, 2011

Ranked by: Market share, in percent. **Remarks:** Also notes figures for previous year and percent change. **Number listed:** 10

1. Coca-Cola, with 11.6%

2. Diet Coke, 6.7%

3. Pepsi-Cola, 6.6%

4. Mountain Dew, 4.7%

5. Dr Pepper, 4.4%

6. Sprite, 3.9%

7. Diet Pepsi, 3.2%

8. Coke Zero, 1.5%

9. Diet Mountain Dew, 1.3%

9. Diet Dr Pepper, 1.3%

Source: *Beverage World*, State of the Industry Report (annual), May 2012, p. 28.

4461 ■ WORLD'S MOST VALUABLE SOFT DRINK BRANDS, 2012

Ranked by: Brand value, a measure of a brand's earnings and contribution, in millions of U.S. dollars. **Remarks:** Also notes annual growth in brand value and rank by brand contribution and brand momentum. **Number listed:** 10

1. Coca-Cola, with $60,286 million

2. Diet Coke/Coca-Cola Light/Coca-Cola Zero, $14,000

3. Pepsi, $10,313

4. Red Bull, $9,984

5. Fanta, $3,998

6. Sprite, $3,793

7. Gatorade, $3,456

8. Mountain Dew, $2,577

9. Diet Pepsi, $2,285

10. Dr Pepper, $2,138

Source: *Financial Times*, Global Brands (annual), http://www.ft.com, May 22, 2012.

Software
See: **Computer Software Industry**

Soymilk

4462 ■ TOP REFRIGERATED KEFIR/SOYMILK BRANDS IN THE U.S., 2011

Ranked by: Sales, in dollars. **Remarks:** Also notes percent change from previous year and market share. **Number listed:** 10

1. Silk, with $205,900,300

2. Blue Diamond Almond Breeze, $76,350,130

3. Silk Light, $70,589,620

4. Silk Pure Almond, $66,011,890

5. private label, $58,185,870

6. Lifeway Kefir, $30,237,810

7. 8th Continent, $20,535,870

8. Odwalla Protein Monster, $15,686,430

9. Silk Plus, $14,825,530

10. Meyenberg, $10,236,120

Source: *Beverage Industry*, State of the Industry Report (annual), July 2011, p. SIO-18.

Spanish-Speaking Market
See: **Hispanic Market**

Specialty Stores

4463 ■ BRITAIN'S MOST ADMIRED SPECIALTY RETAILERS, 2011

Ranked by: Survey of peers and investment analysts based on nine criteria: quality of management, financial soundness, quality of goods/services, ability to attract and retain talent, value as long-term investment, innovation, marketing, community and environmental responsibility, and use of corporate assets. **Number listed:** 5

1. Carphone Warehouse, with 65.2 points
2. Inchcape, 57.9
3. Pets at Home, 56.3
4. WH Smith, 56.1
5. Wickes, 55.8

Source: *Management Today*, Britain's Most Admired Companies (annual), December 2011, p. 49.

4464 ■ FLORIDA'S LARGEST SPECIALTY RETAILERS OVERALL, 2011

Ranked by: Score based on revenue, profits, assets, and market capitalization. **Remarks:** Specific scores not provided. Also notes overall rank in the *Forbes 2000* and figures for each criterion. **Number listed:** 2

1. AutoNation Inc.
2. Office Depot Inc.

Source: *Forbes*, Forbes 2000 (annual), http://www.forbes.com, May 7, 2012.

4465 ■ LARGEST U.S. SPECIALTY RETAILERS OVERALL, 2011

Ranked by: Score based on revenue, profits, assets, and market capitalization. **Remarks:** Specific scores not provided. Also notes overall rank in the *Forbes 2000* and figures for each criterion. **Number listed:** 12

1. Staples Inc.
2. Bed Bath & Beyond Inc.
3. AutoZone Inc.
4. Genuine Parts Co.
5. CarMax Inc.
6. O'Reilly Automotive Inc.
7. Advance Auto Parts Inc.
8. AutoNation Inc.
9. Tiffany & Co.
10. PETsMART Inc.

Source: *Forbes*, Forbes 2000 (annual), http://www.forbes.com, May 7, 2012.

4466 ■ SPECIALTY HARD LINES RETAILERS ADDING THE MOST NEW STORES, 2011

Ranked by: Total number of new stores added during the year. **Remarks:** Also notes figures for previous year. **Number listed:** 11

1. GameStop Corp., with 300 new stores
2. Best Buy Co., Inc., 175
3. Tractor Supply Co., 85
4. Jo-Ann Fabric & Craft Stores, 70
5. PETsMART Inc., 60
6. Hibbett Sporting Goods Inc., 55
7. Bed Bath & Beyond Inc., 45
8. Michaels Stores Inc., 40
8. HHGregg Inc., 40
8. Staples Inc., 40

Source: *Chain Store Age*, Big Builders (annual), December 2011, p. 38.

4467 ■ SPECIALTY SOFT LINES RETAILERS ADDING THE MOST NEW STORES, 2011

Ranked by: Total number of new stores added during the year. **Remarks:** Also notes figures for previous year. **Number listed:** 14

1. The Gap Inc., with 115 new stores
2. rue21 Inc., 110
3. Genesco Inc., 104
4. The Children's Place Retail Stores Inc., 85
5. Forever 21, 70
6. Brown Shoe Co., Inc., 59
7. Jos. A. Bank Clothiers Inc., 50
8. Aeropostale Inc., 48
9. Abercrombie & Fitch Co., 47
10. Collective Brands Inc., 45

Source: *Chain Store Age*, Big Builders (annual), December 2011, p. 38.

4468 ■ TOP *FORTUNE 500* APPAREL SPECIALTY RETAILERS, 2011

Ranked by: Revenue, in millions of dollars. **Remarks:** Also notes overall rank in the *Fortune 500;* profits; profits as a percentage of revenue; stockholders' equity; and rank by each criterion. **Number listed:** 5

1. The TJX Companies Inc., with $23,191 million
2. The Gap Inc., $14,549
3. Limited Brands Inc., $10,364
4. Ross Stores Inc., $8,608
5. Foot Locker Inc., $5,623

Source: *Fortune*, Fortune 500 (annual), May 21, 2012, p. F-39.

4469 ■ TOP MISCELLANEOUS *FORTUNE 500* SPECIALTY RETAILERS, 2011

Ranked by: Revenue, in millions of dollars. **Remarks:** Also notes overall rank in the *Fortune 500;* profits; profits as a percentage of revenue; stockholders' equity; and rank by each criterion. **Number listed:** 22

1. Costco Wholesale Corp., with $88,915 million
2. The Home Depot Inc., $70,395
3. Best Buy Co., Inc., $50,272
4. Lowe's Companies Inc., $50,208
5. Staples Inc., $25,022
6. Toys "R" Us Inc., $13,909
7. Office Depot Inc., $11,490
8. GameStop Corp., $9,551
9. Bed Bath & Beyond Inc., $8,759
10. AutoZone Inc., $8,073

Source: *Fortune*, Fortune 500 (annual), May 21, 2012, p. F-39.

4470 ■ VIRGINIA'S LARGEST SPECIALTY RETAILERS OVERALL, 2011

Ranked by: Score based on revenue, profits, assets, and market capitalization. **Remarks:** Specific scores not provided. Also notes overall rank in the *Forbes 2000* and figures for each criterion. **Number listed:** 2

1. CarMax Inc.
2. Advance Auto Parts Inc.

Source: *Forbes*, Forbes 2000 (annual), http://www.forbes.com, May 7, 2012.

4471 ■ WORLD'S LARGEST SPECIALTY RETAILERS OVERALL, 2011

Ranked by: Score based on revenue, profits, assets, and market capitalization. **Remarks:** Specific scores not provided. Also notes country, overall rank in the *Forbes 2000,* and figures for each criterion. **Number listed:** 19

1. Compagnie Financiere Richemont SA
2. Staples Inc.
3. Luxottica Group SpA
4. Bed Bath & Beyond Inc.
5. AutoZone Inc.
6. Genuine Parts Co.
7. Canadian Tire Corp.
8. CarMax Inc.
9. O'Reilly Automotive Inc.
10. Advance Auto Parts Inc.

Source: *Forbes*, Forbes 2000 (annual), http://www.forbes.com, May 7, 2012.

4472 ■ WORLD'S MOST ADMIRED APPAREL SPECIALTY RETAILERS, 2012

Ranked by: Score, on a scale of 10, based on a survey of executives, directors, and securities analysts of companies within their own industry on eight criteria: innovation, financial soundness, employee talent, use of corporate assets, long-term investment value, social responsibility, quality of management, and quality of products/services. **Remarks:** Specific scores not provided. Also notes rank for previous year. **Number listed:** 5

1. Limited Brands Inc.
2. The TJX Companies Inc.
3. Neiman Marcus Group Inc.
4. Abercrombie & Fitch Co.
5. Ross Stores Inc.

Source: *Fortune*, World's Most Admired Companies (annual), March 19, 2012, p. 149-150.

4473 ■ WORLD'S MOST ADMIRED DIVERSIFIED SPECIALTY RETAILERS, 2012

Ranked by: Score, on a scale of 10, based on a survey of executives, directors, and securities analysts of companies within their own industry on eight criteria: innovation, financial soundness, employee talent, use of corporate assets, long-term investment value, social responsibility, quality of management, and quality of products/services. **Remarks:** Specific scores not provided. Also notes rank for previous year. **Number listed:** 6

1. Costco Wholesale Corp.
2. Staples Inc.
3. The Home Depot Inc.
4. Lowe's Companies Inc.
5. Toys "R" Us Inc.
6. Bed Bath & Beyond Inc.

Source: *Fortune*, World's Most Admired Companies (annual), March 19, 2012, p. 150.

4474 ■ WORLD'S MOST ETHICAL SPECIALTY RETAILERS, 2012

Ranked by: Score based on five criteria: ethics and compliance program; reputation, leadership, and innovation; governance; corporate citizenship and responsibility; and culture of ethics. **Remarks:** Specific scores not provided; companies are listed alphabetically, not ranked. **Number listed:** 4

1. Best Buy Co., Inc. (U.S.)
2. OfficeMax (U.S.)
3. Petco (U.S.)
4. Ten Thousand Villages (U.S.)

Source: *Ethisphere Magazine*, World's Most Ethical Companies (annual), http://www.ethisphere.com, 2012.

Sporting Events

4475 ■ WORLD'S MOST VALUABLE SPORTS BRANDS: EVENTS

Ranked by: Brand value, in millions of dollars. **Number listed:** 10

1. Super Bowl, with $425 million
2. Summer Olympic Games, $230
3. FIFA World Cup, $147
4. MLB World Series, $140
5. UEFA Champions League, $132
6. Winter Olympic Games, $123
7. Daytona 500, $112
8. NCAA Men's Final Four, $92
9. MLB All-Star Week, $76
10. Kentucky Derby, $70

Source: *Forbes*, Fab 40, http://www.forbes.com, October 03, 2011.

Sporting Goods Stores

4476 ■ LARGEST ASIA-PACIFIC SPORTING GOODS RETAILERS, 2010

Ranked by: Sales, in millions of U.S. dollars. **Remarks:** Also notes country, fascias/brands, number of outlets, sales in national currency, sales area, sales per square meter, and figures for previous year. **Number listed:** 10

1. Alpen, with $2,097 million
2. Xebio, $1,739
3. Aeon Group, $1,042
4. Himaraya, $521
5. Rebel Sports, $479
6. Decathlon China, $376
7. Nikki Golf, $332
8. Murasaki Sports, $316
9. Super Cheap Auto Group, $245
10. Tsuruya Golf, $244

Source: *Retail Asia*, Retail Asia-Pacific Top 500 (annual), July 2011, p. 66-66a.

4477 ■ TOP SPORTS EQUIPMENT AND APPAREL FRANCHISES, 2012

Ranked by: Cumulative score based on financial strength and stability, growth rate, size of the system, number of years in business, the length of time franchising, start-up costs, litigation, percentage of terminations, and whether the company provides financing. **Remarks:** Specific scores not provided. Also notes overall rank within the *Franchise 500,* contact information, description, year founded, year started franchising, states where registered, available U.S. regions, where seeking foreign expansion, number of franchised and company-owned units for past three years, start-up costs, franchise fees, royalty fees, and type of financing available. **Number listed:** 3

1. Play It Again Sports
2. The Athlete's Food
3. Fleet Feet Sports

Source: *Entrepreneur*, Franchise 500 (annual), January 2012, p. 196-197.

Sports

4478 ■ TOP SPORTS BUSINESS FRANCHISES, 2012

Ranked by: Cumulative score based on financial strength and stability, growth rate, size of the system, number of years in business, the length of time franchising, start-up costs, litigation, percentage of terminations, and whether the company provides financing. **Remarks:** Specific scores not provided. Also notes overall rank within the *Franchise 500*, contact information, description, year founded, year started franchising, states where registered, available U.S. regions, where seeking foreign expansion, number of franchised and company-owned units for past three years, start-up costs, franchise fees, royalty fees, and type of financing available. **Number listed:** 2

1. American Poolplayers Association
2. GolfTEC

Source: *Entrepreneur*, Franchise 500 (annual), January 2012, p. 196-197.

4479 ■ WORLD'S MOST VALUABLE SPORTS BRANDS: BUSINESSES

Ranked by: Brand value, in millions of dollars. **Number listed:** 10

1. Nike, with $15,000 million
2. ESPN, $11,500
3. Adidas, $5,000
4. Sky Sports, $3,000
5. Gatorade, $2,500
6. Reebok, $1,500
7. Under Armour, $1,000
8. EA Sports, $625
9. YES Network, $600
10. MSG Network, $500

Source: *Forbes*, Fab 40, http://www.forbes.com, October 03, 2011.

Sports Clubs

4480 ■ MOST EFFICIENT PROFESSIONAL SPORTS TEAMS, 2011

Ranked by: Efficiency index, a score based on deviation from the league norm in average cost per win compared to number of wins and losses over the last five completed seasons. **Remarks:** Also notes sport, average wins per season, and average cost per win. **Number listed:** 122

1. Nashville Predators, with -1.67 points
2. Florida Marlins, -1.61
3. Tampa Bay Rays, -1.47
4. New England Patriots, -1.35
5. San Antonio Spurs, -1.24
6. San Jose Sharks, -1.23
7. Indianapolis Colts, -1.20
8. Pittsburgh Pirates, -1.19
9. San Diego Padres, -1.18
10. New York Islanders, -1.15

Source: *Bloomberg Businessweek*, The Smartest Spenders in Sports, October 24, 2011, p. 100-101.

4481 ■ WORLD'S MOST VALUABLE SPORTS BRANDS: TEAMS

Ranked by: Brand value, in millions of dollars. **Number listed:** 10

1. New York Yankees, with $340 million
2. Manchester United, $269
3. Real Madrid, $264
4. Dallas Cowboys, $193
5. Bayern Munich, $179
6. Boston Red Sox, $173
7. Barcelona, $172
8. Arsenal, $158
9. AC Milan, $147
10. New England Patriots, $146

Source: *Forbes*, Fab 40, http://www.forbes.com, October 3, 2011.

Sports Drink Industry

4482 ■ TOP NON-ASEPTIC SPORTS DRINKS BRANDS IN THE U.S., 2011

Ranked by: Sales, in dollars. **Remarks:** Also notes percent change from previous year and market share. **Number listed:** 10

1. Gatorade Perform, with $1,935,655,000
2. Powerade Ion4, $655,768,800
3. Gatorade, $398,168,800
4. G2 Perform, $383,604,600
5. Powerade Zero, $188,279,100
6. G2, $55,917,140
7. Gatorade Frost, $52,173,870
8. Gatorade Cool Blue, $45,198,730
9. Powerade, $37,716,640
10. Gatorade Recover, $33,205,430

Source: *Beverage Industry*, State of the Industry Report (annual), July 2011, p. SOI-4.

4483 ■ TOP SPORTS DRINK MIX BRANDS IN THE U.S., 2011

Ranked by: Sales, in dollars. **Remarks:** Also notes percent change from previous year and market share. **Number listed:** 10

1. Propel, with $22,380,100
2. Gatorade, $18,339,710
3. G2 Perform, $7,073,522
4. Gatorade Perform, $5,405,275
5. Propel Calcium, $4,059,769
6. Gatorade Frost, $2,851,208
7. Propel Zero, $1,960,120
8. Powerade Ion4, $629,265
9. private label, $314,359
10. G2 Stick Packs, $250,865

Source: *Beverage Industry*, State of the Industry Report (annual), July 2011, p. SIO-4.

4484 ■ TOP U.S. ENERGY DRINK BRANDS BY SALES, 2011

Ranked by: Sales, in millions of dollars. **Remarks:** Also notes annual growth. **Number listed:** 20

1. Red Bull, with $2,602.2 million

2. Monster Energy, $1,380.9

3. Rockstar Energy, $472.2

4. NOS Energy, $237

5. Java Monster, $196.7

6. Monster Mega, $196.6

7. Amp Energy, $142.7

8. Rockstar Recovery, $137.8

9. Monster Rehab, $125.8

10. Full Throttle, $97.3

Source: *Beverage World*, State of the Industry Report (annual), May 2012, p. 25.

4485 ■ TOP U.S. ENERGY SHOT BRANDS BY SALES, 2011

Ranked by: Sales, in millions of dollars. **Remarks:** Also notes annual growth. **Number listed:** 10

1. 5-Hour Energy, with $928.4 million

2. 5-Hour Energy Extra, $54.3

3. Stacker 26-Hour Power, $28.7

4. Worx Energy, $13

5. Private label, $12.6

6. Red Bull, $11.4

7. E6, $4.9

8. Stacker 2, $4.4

9. Spike Double Shot, $3.6

10. VPX Redline Power Rush, $3.3

Source: *Beverage World*, State of the Industry Report (annual), May 2012, p. 25.

4486 ■ TOP U.S. SPORTS DRINK BRANDS BY SALES, 2011

Ranked by: Sales, in millions of dollars. **Remarks:** Also notes annual growth. **Number listed:** 10

1. Gatorade G Series Perform, with $2,023.5 million

2. Powerade Ion 4, $659.3

3. Gatorade, $421.3

4. Gatorade G2 Perform, $421.2

5. Powerade Zero, $184.2

6. Gatorade Frost, $56.3

7. Gatorade Cool Blue, $54.7

8. G2, $47.5

9. Powerade, $38.7

10. Gatorade Recover, $30.2

Source: *Beverage World*, State of the Industry Report (annual), May 2012, p. 33.

Stadiums
See also: **Amphitheaters**

4487 ■ WORLD'S TOP CONCERT STADIUMS, 2011

Ranked by: Gross sales, in U.S. dollars. **Remarks:** Also notes venue capacity, total attendance, total capacity, number of shows, and number of sellouts. **Number listed:** 10

1. Wembley Stadium (London), with $61,713,184

2. Estadio do Morumbi (Sao Paulo, Brazil), $53,077,965

3. City of Manchester Stadium (Manchester, England), $44,183,145

4. MetLife Stadium (E. Rutherford, NJ), $32,727,380

5. Estadio Unico Ciudad de la Plata (Buenos Aires, Argentina), $26,524,292

6. Estadio Azteca (Mexico City), $22,866,542

7. Stadium of Light (Sunderland, England), $21,600,077

8. Etihad Stadium (Melbourne, Australia), $21,599,592

9. Patersons Stadium (Perth, Australia), $18,531,167

10. Croke Park (Dublin, Ireland), $18,217,500

Source: *Billboard*, The Year in Music & Touring (annual), December 17, 2011, p. 100.

Staffing Services

4488 ■ TOP STAFFING SERVICES FRANCHISES, 2012

Ranked by: Cumulative score based on financial strength and stability, growth rate, size of the system, number of years in business, the length of time franchising, start-up costs, litigation, percentage of terminations, and whether the company provides financing. **Remarks:** Specific scores not provided. Also notes overall rank within the *Franchise 500,* contact information, description, year founded, year started franchising, states where registered, available U.S. regions, where seeking foreign expansion, number of franchised and company-owned units for past three years, start-up costs, franchise fees, royalty fees, and type of financing available. **Number listed:** 4

1. Express Employment Professionals

2. Remedy Intelligent Staffing

3. Spherion Staffing

4. Labor Finders

Source: *Entrepreneur*, Franchise 500 (annual), January 2012, p. 152-153.

Standard and Poor's—Stock Price Index

4489 ■ TOP COMPANIES ON THE S & P 500, 2011

Ranked by: Score based on one- and five-year risk-adjusted returns, consensus analyst recommendations, and projected earnings growth. **Remarks:** Scores not provided. **Number listed:** 50

1. MasterCard Inc.

2. Priceline.com Inc.

3. American Tower Corp.

4. Dollar Tree Stores Inc.

5. Union Pacific Corp.

6. Apple Inc.

7. Cabot Oil & Gas

8. Precision Castparts Corp.

9. Airgas Inc.

10. The TJX Companies Inc.

Source: *Bloomberg Businessweek*, Bloomberg Businessweek 50 (annual), January 23, 2012, p. 51-54.

State Data (for individual states)

4490 ■ STATES WITH THE HIGHEST GROSS DOMESTIC PRODUCT, 2009

Ranked by: Gross domestic product, in dollars. **Remarks:** Also notes share of national total. **Number listed:** 51

1. California, with $1,891,363,000,000
2. Texas, $1,144,695,000,000
3. New York, $1,093,219,000,000
4. Florida, $737,038,000,000
5. Illinois, $630,398,000,000
6. Pennsylvania, $554,774,000,000
7. New Jersey, $482,967,000,000
8. Ohio, $471,264,000,000
9. Virginia, $408,443,000,000
10. North Carolina, $398,042,000,000

Source: *State Rankings*, (annual), CQ Press, 2011, p. 93.

4491 ■ STATES WITH THE LOWEST GROSS DOMESTIC PRODUCT, 2009

Ranked by: Gross domestic product, in dollars. **Remarks:** Also notes share of national total. **Number listed:** 51

1. Vermont, with $25,438,000,000
2. North Dakota, $31,872,000,000
3. Montana, $35,954,000,000
4. Wyoming, $37,544,000,000
5. South Dakota, $38,308,000,000
6. Alaska, $45,709,000,000
7. Rhode Island, $47,837,000,000
8. Maine, $51,293,000,000
9. Idaho, $54,005,000,000
10. New Hampshire, $59,400,000,000

Source: *State Rankings*, (annual), CQ Press, 2011, p. 93.

State Taxation
See: **Taxation**

Steel Industry

4492 ■ AUSTRALIA'S LARGEST IRON AND STEEL COMPANIES OVERALL, 2011

Ranked by: Score based on revenue, profits, assets, and market capitalization. **Remarks:** Specific scores not provided. Also notes overall rank in the *Forbes 2000* and figures for each criterion. **Number listed:** 2

1. Fortescue Metals Group
2. Bluescope Steel

Source: *Forbes*, Forbes 2000 (annual), http://www.forbes.com, May 7, 2012.

4493 ■ BRAZIL'S LARGEST IRON AND STEEL COMPANIES OVERALL, 2011

Ranked by: Score based on revenue, profits, assets, and market capitalization. **Remarks:** Specific scores not provided. Also notes overall rank in the *Forbes 2000* and figures for each criterion. **Number listed:** 3

1. Companhia Siderurgica Nacional (CSN)
2. Metalurgica Gerdau SA
3. Usiminas Siderurgicas de Minas Gerais SA

Source: *Forbes*, Forbes 2000 (annual), http://www.forbes.com, May 7, 2012.

4494 ■ CHINA'S LARGEST IRON AND STEEL COMPANIES OVERALL, 2011

Ranked by: Score based on revenue, profits, assets, and market capitalization. **Remarks:** Specific scores not provided. Also notes overall rank in the *Forbes 2000* and figures for each criterion. **Number listed:** 10

1. Baoshan Iron & Steel Co., Ltd.
2. Angang Steel Co., Ltd.
3. Fosun International Ltd.
4. Hebei Iron & Steel
5. Wuhan Iron & Steel (Group) Corp.
6. Shanxi Taigang Stainless
7. Panzhihua New Steel & Vanadium Co., Ltd.
8. Hunan Valin Steel
9. Maanshan Iron & Steel
10. Inner Mongolia Baotou Steel

Source: *Forbes*, Forbes 2000 (annual), http://www.forbes.com, May 7, 2012.

4495 ■ INDIA'S LARGEST IRON AND STEEL COMPANIES OVERALL, 2011

Ranked by: Score based on revenue, profits, assets, and market capitalization. **Remarks:** Specific scores not provided. Also notes overall rank in the *Forbes 2000* and figures for each criterion. **Number listed:** 4

1. Tata Steel Ltd.
2. Steel Authority of India Ltd.
3. Jindal Steel & Power
4. JSW Steel

Source: *Forbes*, Forbes 2000 (annual), http://www.forbes.com, May 7, 2012.

4496 ■ JAPAN'S LARGEST IRON AND STEEL COMPANIES OVERALL, 2011

Ranked by: Score based on revenue, profits, assets, and market capitalization. **Remarks:** Specific scores not provided. Also notes overall rank in the *Forbes 2000* and figures for each criterion. **Number listed:** 4

1. Nippon Steel Corp.
2. JFE Holdings Inc.
3. Kobe Steel
4. Sumitomo Metal Industries

Source: *Forbes*, Forbes 2000 (annual), http://www.forbes.com, May 7, 2012.

4497 ■ LARGEST U.S. IRON AND STEEL COMPANIES OVERALL, 2011

Ranked by: Score based on revenue, profits, assets, and market capitalization. **Remarks:** Specific scores not provided. Also notes overall rank in the *Forbes 2000* and figures for each criterion. **Number listed:** 4

1. Nucor Corp.
2. Cliffs Natural Resources Inc.

3. United States Steel Corp.

4. Reliance Steel & Aluminum Co.

Source: Forbes, Forbes 2000 (annual), http://www.forbes.com, May 7, 2012.

4498 ■ LUXEMBOURG'S LARGEST IRON AND STEEL COMPANIES OVERALL, 2011

Ranked by: Score based on revenue, profits, assets, and market capitalization. **Remarks:** Specific scores not provided. Also notes overall rank in the *Forbes 2000* and figures for each criterion. **Number listed:** 2

1. ArcelorMittal

2. Ternium

Source: Forbes, Forbes 2000 (annual), http://www.forbes.com, May 7, 2012.

4499 ■ RUSSIA'S LARGEST IRON AND STEEL COMPANIES OVERALL, 2011

Ranked by: Score based on revenue, profits, assets, and market capitalization. **Remarks:** Specific scores not provided. Also notes overall rank in the *Forbes 2000* and figures for each criterion. **Number listed:** 5

1. Novolipetsk Steel

2. OAO Severstal

3. Mechel

4. Magnitogorsk Iron & Steel

5. TMK

Source: Forbes, Forbes 2000 (annual), http://www.forbes.com, May 7, 2012.

4500 ■ SOUTH KOREA'S LARGEST IRON AND STEEL COMPANIES OVERALL, 2011

Ranked by: Score based on revenue, profits, assets, and market capitalization. **Remarks:** Specific scores not provided. Also notes overall rank in the *Forbes 2000* and figures for each criterion. **Number listed:** 2

1. Pohang Iron & Steel Co., Ltd. (POSCO)

2. Hyundai Steel Co.

Source: Forbes, Forbes 2000 (annual), http://www.forbes.com, May 7, 2012.

4501 ■ WORLD'S LARGEST IRON AND STEEL COMPANIES OVERALL, 2011

Ranked by: Score based on revenue, profits, assets, and market capitalization. **Remarks:** Specific scores not provided. Also notes country, overall rank in the *Forbes 2000,* and figures for each criterion. **Number listed:** 43

1. ArcelorMittal

2. Pohang Iron & Steel Co., Ltd. (POSCO)

3. Nippon Steel Corp.

4. Baoshan Iron & Steel Co., Ltd.

5. JFE Holdings Inc.

6. Tata Steel Ltd.

7. China Steel Corp.

8. Companhia Siderurgica Nacional (CSN)

9. Nucor Corp.

10. CITIC Pacific Ltd.

Source: Forbes, Forbes 2000 (annual), http://www.forbes.com, May 7, 2012.

4502 ■ WORLD'S MOST VALUABLE IRON/STEEL BRANDS, 2011

Ranked by: Brand value, in millions of U.S. dollars. **Remarks:** Also notes rank within the *Global 500* for current and previous year, figures for current and previous year, country, and brand rating. Ranking is available online only. **Number listed:** 4

1. ArcelorMittal, with $4,027 million

2. Nippon Steel, $3,367

3. ThyssenKrupp, $3,320

4. POSCO, $2,490

Source: Global 500, (annual), Brand Finance plc, March 2012.

Stock Exchanges

4503 ■ COUNTRIES WITH THE LEAST EFFECTIVE REGULATION OF SECURITIES EXCHANGES, 2011

Ranked by: Score, on a scale of seven, based on the level of effective regulation and supervision of securities exchanges. **Number listed:** 142

1. Yemen, with 1.4 points

2. Haiti, 2.0

2. Burundi, 2.0

2. Mauritania, 2.0

5. Angola, 2.1

6. Madagascar, 2.4

6. Algeria, 2.4

8. Chad, 2.5

9. Kyrgyz Republic, 2.6

9. Timor-Leste, 2.6

9. Albania, 2.6

Source: Global Competitiveness Report, (annual), World Economic Forum, 2011, p. 486.

4504 ■ COUNTRIES WITH THE MOST EFFECTIVE REGULATION OF SECURITIES EXCHANGES, 2011

Ranked by: Score, on a scale of seven, based on the level of effective regulation and supervision of securities exchanges. **Number listed:** 142

1. South Africa, with 6.4 points

2. Singapore, 6.0

3. Sweden, 5.9

3. Finland, 5.9

3. Norway, 5.9

6. Luxembourg, 5.8

6. Qatar, 5.8

6. Bahrain, 5.8

9. Brazil, 5.7

9. Australia, 5.7

Source: Global Competitiveness Report, (annual), World Economic Forum, 2011, p. 486.

Stock Funds
See also: **Mutual Funds**

4505 ■ TOP LARGE COMPANY STOCK FUNDS, 2012

Ranked by: Score based on long-term performance, management experience, risk, expenses, assets, and integrity. **Remarks:** Specific scores not provided; funds are listed alphabetically, not ranked. Also notes ticker symbol, expense ratio, toll-free number, and one-, three-, five-, and 10-year return. **Number listed:** 5

1. Artisan Value
2. BBH Core Select
3. Dodge & Cox Stock
4. Fidelity Contrafund
5. Vanguard Dividend Growth

Source: *Kiplinger's Personal Finance*, Kiplinger 25 (annual), May 2012, p. 30.

4506 ■ TOP PERFORMING STOCK FUNDS, 2010-2011

Ranked by: Annual change in share price, in percent. **Remarks:** Also notes ticker symbol, 36-month performance rating, three-month share price change, five-year average share price change, and 10-year average share price change. **Number listed:** 50

1. PIMCO StockPLUS Long Duration Institutional, with 21.31%
2. Virtus Small-Cap Sustainable Growth - A, 19.46%
3. Touchstone Premium Yield Equity - A, 15.4%
4. Delaware Pooled Select 20, 15.04%
5. Payden Value Leaders, 14.78%
6. Federated Strategic Value Dividend - A, 14.72%
7. Sequoia, 13.61%
8. Copley, 13.45%
9. Pear Tree Quality Ordinary, 13.21%
10. ING Corporate Leaders Trust Series B, 12.67%

Source: *Investor's Business Daily*, The Year in Review (annual), January 3, 2012, p. A15.

4507 ■ TOP SMALL AND MIDSIZED COMPANY STOCK FUNDS, 2012

Ranked by: Score based on long-term performance, management experience, risk, expenses, assets, and integrity. **Remarks:** Specific scores not provided; funds are listed alphabetically, not ranked. Also notes ticker symbol, expense ratio, toll-free number, and one-, three-, five-, and 10-year return. **Number listed:** 7

1. Akre Focus
2. Baron Small Cap
3. Fidelity Low-Priced Stock
4. Homestead Small-Company Stock
5. T. Rowe Price Small-Cap Value
6. Vanguard Selected Value
7. Wells Fargo Advantage Discovery

Source: *Kiplinger's Personal Finance*, Kiplinger 25 (annual), May 2012, p. 30.

Stocks

4508 ■ BEST CANADIAN DEFENSIVE STOCKS, 2012

Ranked by: Score based on market capitalization, debt rating, dividend yield, return on equity, and beta. **Remarks:** Specific scores not provided; companies are listed alphabetically, not ranked. Also notes ticker symbol, figures for each criterion, and year-to-date stock performance. **Number listed:** 8

1. Bank of Montreal
2. Bank of Nova Scotia

3. Canadian Imperial Bank of Commerce
4. Great-West Lifeco Inc.
5. IGM Financial Inc.
6. Power Financial Corp.
7. Royal Bank of Canada
8. Toronto-Dominion Bank

Source: *Canadian Business*, Investor 500 (annual), 2012, p. 40.

4509 ■ BEST CANADIAN DIVIDEND STOCKS, 2012

Ranked by: Score based on dividend yield, payout ratio, and five-year dividend growth. **Remarks:** Specific scores not provided. Also notes ticker symbol, figures for each criterion, and year-to-date stock performance. **Number listed:** 5

1. Black Diamond Group Ltd.
2. Enbridge Inc.
3. Killam Properties Inc.
4. Rogers Communications Inc.
5. Shaw Communications Inc.

Source: *Canadian Business*, Investor 500 (annual), 2012, p. 39.

4510 ■ BEST CANADIAN GROWTH STOCKS, 2012

Ranked by: Score based on projected price-to-earnings growth ratio and annual earnings per share growth rate. **Remarks:** Specific scores not provided; companies are listed alphabetically, not ranked. Also notes ticker symbol, one-year revenue growth, figures for each criterion, and year-to-date stock performance. **Number listed:** 9

1. Cameco Corp.
2. Canadian Natural Resources Ltd.
3. Celestica Inc.
4. Eldorado Gold Corp.
5. Goldcorp Inc.
6. High Liner Foods Inc.
7. Iamgold Corp.
8. Progressive Waste Solutions Ltd.
9. Yamana Gold Inc.

Source: *Canadian Business*, Investor 500 (annual), 2012, p. 35.

4511 ■ BEST CANADIAN VALUE STOCKS, 2012

Ranked by: Score based on price-to-book and price-to-earnings values. **Remarks:** Specific scores not provided; companies are listed alphabetically, not ranked. Also notes ticker symbol, figures for each criterion, five-year average return on equity, and year-to-date stock performance. **Number listed:** 10

1. Brookfield Office Properties Inc.
2. Dundee REIT
3. High River Gold Mines Ltd.
4. HudBay Minerals Inc.
5. Melcor Developments Ltd.
6. Pan American Silver Corp.
7. Research in Motion Ltd.
8. Thompson Creek Metals Co.
9. Torstar Corp.
10. Trican Well Service Ltd.

Source: *Canadian Business*, Investor 500 (annual), 2012, p. 36.

4512 ■ BEST MANAGED CANADIAN STOCKS, 2012

Ranked by: Score based on three-year net sales and net income growth rates, trading price, and three-year total return. **Remarks:**

Specific scores not provided; companies are listed alphabetically, not ranked. Also notes ticker symbol, figures for each criterion, and year-to-date stock performance. **Number listed:** 10

1. Calfrac Well Service Ltd.
2. Centerra Gold Inc.
3. Dundee Precious Metals Inc.
4. Dundee REIT
5. Inmet Mining Corp.
6. Lundin Mining Corp.
7. OceanaGold Corp.
8. SEMAFO Inc.
9. Taseko Mines Ltd.
10. Teck Resources Ltd.

Source: *Canadian Business*, Investor 500 (annual), 2012, p. 43.

4513 ■ LARGE COMPANIES WITH THE BEST STOCK, 2011

Ranked by: Score, on a scale of four, based on performance compared to the S&P 500, three-year median cash flow return on investment (CFROI), actual CFROI return compared to the median CFROI return, and annual sales growth. **Remarks:** Also notes ticker symbol, rank for previous year, and score for each criterion. **Number listed:** 500

1. CF Industries Holdings Inc., with 4 points
1. Apple Inc., 4
1. Southern Copper Corp., 4
1. QUALCOMM Inc., 4
5. Visa Inc., 3.67
5. Intel Corp., 3.67
5. Philip Morris International, 3.67
5. MasterCard Inc., 3.67
5. MetLife Inc., 3.67
5. Henry Schein Inc., 3.67
5. Potash Corp. of Saskatchewan Inc., 3.67
5. EMC Corp., 3.67
5. Coca-Cola Enterprises Inc., 3.67

Source: *Barron's*, Barron's 500 (annual), May 7, 2012, p. S10-S18.

4514 ■ MOST ACTIVE STOCKS, 2011

Ranked by: Number of traded issues, in millions. **Remarks:** Also notes ticker symbol, closing price, annual percent change, high and low prices, and stock exchange. **Number listed:** 24

1. SPDR S & P 500, with 55,003 million issues
2. Bank of America Corp., 53,652
3. Select Sector SPDR Financial, 23,072
4. Ford Motor Co., 17,829
5. Cisco Systems Inc., 17,215
6. iShares Russell 2000, 17,097
7. PowerShares QQQ Tr. Series 1, 16,680
8. iShares MSCI Emerging Markets, 16,640
9. General Electric Co., 16,135
10. Intel Corp., 15,481

Source: *The Wall Street Journal*, Year-End Review (annual), January 3, 2012, p. R6.

4515 ■ MOST POPULAR STOCKS FOR INVESTMENT CLUBS, 2011

Ranked by: Number of investment clubs holding stock. **Remarks:** Also notes ticker symbol, number of shares held by National As-

sociation of Investors Corp. (NAIC) members, total value of shares held by NAIC members, and rank by total shares held and by total value of shares held. **Number listed:** 100

1. Apple Inc., with 1,653 clubs
2. General Electric Co., 1,640
3. Johnson & Johnson, 1,336
4. Ford Motor Co., 1,171
5. Stryker Corp., 1,096
6. Microsoft Corp., 999
7. Procter & Gamble Co., 973
8. PepsiCo Inc., 966
9. ExxonMobil Corp., 913
10. Intel Corp., 909

Source: *Better Investing*, Top 100 Companies (annual), April 4012, p. 36-37.

4516 ■ TOP CANADIAN DIVIDEND STOCKS FOR RETIREMENT, 2011

Ranked by: Letter grade based on yield, reliability, and value. **Remarks:** Also notes ticker symbol, industry, market capitalization, share price, dividend growth, price-to-earnings, dividend earnings, debt to equity, price-to-cash flow, price-to-book, and one- and five-year returns. **Number listed:** 100

1. Great-West Lifeco, with A
1. Husky Energy Inc., A
1. Power Corp. of Canada, A
1. Power Financial, A
1. Sun Life Financial, A
1. Toronto-Dominion Bank, A
7. ATCO Ltd., B
7. Bank of Montreal, B
7. Scotiabank--Bank of Nova Scotia, B
7. Brookfield Asset Management, B

Source: *MoneySense*, Retirement 100 (annual), http://www.moneysense.ca, November 2011.

4517 ■ TOP GLOBAL STOCK ISSUES, 2011

Ranked by: Amount, in billions of dollars. **Remarks:** Also notes issue date. **Number listed:** 10

1. Glencore International, with $10 billion
2. American International Group, $8.7
3. Commerzbank (June), $7.8
4. The Mosaic Co., $7.5
5. Porsche Automobil, $7.2
5. Intesa Sanpaolo, $7.2
7. Resona Holdings, $6.9
8. MetLife, $6.3
9. Commerzbank (April), $6.2
10. Hutchison Port Holdings, $5.5

Source: *The Wall Street Journal*, Year-End Review (annual), January 3, 2012, p. R9.

4518 ■ TOP STOCKS BY PRICE CHANGE, 2010-2011

Ranked by: Annual change in share price, in percent. **Remarks:** Company shares must be priced $12 or higher at beginning of year. Also notes ticker symbol, industry, and other financial data. **Number listed:** 100

1. Pharmasset, with 489%

2. Medivation, 204%
3. Golar LNG Ltd., 196%
4. Questcor Pharmaceutical, 182%
5. Valhi, 174%
6. Liquidity Services, 163%
7. Sturm Ruger, 119%
8. Dominos Pizza, 113%
9. HealthSpring, 106%
10. Cabot Oil & Gas, 101%

Source: *Investor's Business Daily*, The Year in Review (annual), January 3, 2012, p. A11.

Stocks—Price Indexes and Averages

4519 ■ TOP U.S. INDEXES, 2012

Ranked by: Score based on long-term performance, management experience, risk, expenses, assets, and integrity. **Remarks:** Specific scores not provided; funds are listed alphabetically, not ranked. Also notes ticker symbol, expense ratio, toll-free number, and one-, three-, and five-year return. **Number listed:** 5

1. S & P 500 Stock Index
2. Russell 2000 Index
3. MSCI EAFE Index
4. Merrill Lynch U.S. Broad Market Index
5. Dow Jones UBS Commodity Index

Source: *Kiplinger's Personal Finance*, Kiplinger 25 (annual), May 2012, p. 30.

Stocks—Prices

4520 ■ BEST PERFORMING STOCKS, 2010-2011

Ranked by: Annual growth in price, in percent. **Remarks:** Also notes ticker symbol, closing price, low and high prices, and stock exchange. **Number listed:** 18

1. Pharmasset, with 488.6%
2. Silicon Motion Technology, 381.9%
3. Medivation, 204%
4. Golar LNG, 196.1%
5. Questcor Pharmaceutical, 182.3%
6. Valhi Inc., 173.5%
7. Parkvale Financial, 167.6%
8. Liquidity Services, 162.6%
9. Ariad Pharmaceutical, 140.2%
10. Elan Corp., 139.8%

Source: *The Wall Street Journal*, Year-End Review (annual), January 3, 2012, p. R6.

4521 ■ WORST PERFORMING STOCKS, 2010-2011

Ranked by: Annual decline in price, in percent. **Remarks:** Also notes ticker symbol, closing price, high and low prices, and stock exchange. **Number listed:** 18

1. YRC Worldwide, with -99.1%
2. Tennessee Commerce, -98.4%
3. Energy Conversion Devices, -95.6%
4. AMR Corp., -95.5%
5. FiberTower, -95.4%

6. Motricity, -95.2%
7. TBS International, -94.8%
8. Marina Biotechnology, -94.2%
9. IFM Investments (ADS), -94%
10. SmartHeat, -93.9%

Source: *The Wall Street Journal*, Year-End Review (annual), January 3, 2012, p. R6.

Stone

4522 ■ LARGEST COMPANIES IN THE STONE, CLAY, GLASS, AND CONCRETE PRODUCTS INDUSTRY BY EMPLOYEES, 2010

Ranked by: Total number of employees. **Remarks:** Also notes contact information for headquarters, number of employees at headquarters, revenue, rank by revenue, and primary SIC code. **Number listed:** 48

1. St. Gobain Corp., with 25,836 employees
2. Owens-Illinois Inc., 24,000
3. Guardian Industries Corp., 19,000
3. Owens Corning Sales LLC, 19,000
5. Lafarge North America Inc., 16,600
6. Owens Corning, 16,000
7. St.-Gobain Delaware Corp., 11,474
8. St.-Gobain Abrasives Inc., 11,446
9. USG Corp., 10,100
10. Cemex Inc., 10,000

Source: *Business Rankings*, (annual), Dun & Bradstreet Inc., 2011, p. VI.71-VI.72.

4523 ■ LARGEST COMPANIES IN THE STONE, CLAY, GLASS, AND CONCRETE PRODUCTS INDUSTRY BY SALES, 2010

Ranked by: Total revenue, in dollars. **Remarks:** Also notes contact information for headquarters, number of employees at headquarters and overall, rank by employees, and primary SIC code. **Number listed:** 49

1. Owens-Illinois Inc., with $6,633,000,000
2. Owens Corning, $4,997,000,000
3. Polymicro Technologies LLC, $4,000,000,000
4. USG Corp., $2,939,000,000
5. Minerals Technologies Inc., $1,002,354,000
6. Pilkington North America Inc., $967,896,000
7. Ash Grove Cement Co., $884,651,000
8. Centex Corp., $816,263,414
9. Libbey Inc., $801,584,000
10. Quanex Building Products Corp., $798,314,000

Source: *Business Rankings*, (annual), Dun & Bradstreet Inc., 2011, p. V.71-V.72.

4524 ■ LARGEST NORTH AMERICAN CONCRETE PRODUCERS, 2010

Ranked by: Revenue. **Remarks:** Specific figures not provided. Companies are broken down by revenue range; the top 11 companies have revenue of at least $1 billion. Also notes North American headquarters and comments. **Number listed:** 100

1. Oldcastle Inc.
2. Cemex, SA de CV

3. Lafarge North America Inc.

4. Holcim Inc.

5. Colas SA

6. HeidelbergCement AG

7. Vulcan Materials Co.

8. Trinity Construction Products Group

9. Martin Marietta Materials Inc.

10. Knife River Corp.

Source: *The Concrete Producer*, TCP 100 (annual), http://www.theconcreteproducer.com, August 2011.

4525 ■ LARGEST U.S. MANUFACTURERS OF STONE, CLAY, AND CONCRETE PRODUCTS, 2010

Ranked by: Revenue, in millions of dollars. **Remarks:** Also notes overall rank within the *IW 500,* revenue growth, and profit margin. **Number listed:** 5

1. Owens-Illinois Inc., with $6,633 million

2. Owens Corning, $4,997

3. USG Corp., $2,939

4. Vulcan Materials Co., $2,559

5. Martin Marietta Materials Inc., $1,783

Source: *IndustryWeek*, IW 500 (annual), http://www.industryweek.com, July 2011.

Stone Mining and Quarrying

4526 ■ LARGEST CRUSHED-STONE PRODUCERS, 2011

Ranked by: Total production. **Remarks:** Specific figures not provided. **Number listed:** 50

1. Vulcan Materials Co.

2. Martin Marietta Aggregates

3. Lehigh Hanson Inc.

4. Oldcastle Materials Inc.

5. Lafarge North America Inc.

6. Cemex SAB de CV

7. Carmeuse Lime & Stone

8. Rogers Group Inc.

9. Holcim Group/Aggregate Industries Management Inc.

10. New Enterprise Stone & Lime Co.

Source: *Pit & Quarry*, MegaProducers (annual), June 2012, p. 28-30.

4527 ■ OWNERS OF THE LARGEST CRUSHED STONE PLANTS, 2011

Ranked by: Total output. **Remarks:** Specific figures not provided. Also notes location. **Number listed:** 5

1. Martin Marietta Aggregates

2. Cemex SAB de CV

3. Tower Rock Stone Co.

4. Vecellio & Grogan Inc.

5. Texas Crushed Stone Co.

Source: *Pit & Quarry*, MegaProducers (annual), June 2012, p. 30.

Store Fixtures

4528 ■ NORTH AMERICA'S LARGEST WOOD STORE FIXTURES COMPANIES, 2010

Ranked by: Revenue, in dollars. **Remarks:** Also notes headquarters and percent change from previous year. **Number listed:** 19

1. Leggett & Platt Inc., with $550,000,000

2. idX Corp., $180,000,000

3. L. A. Darling Co., $150,000,000

4. Colony Inc., $80,000,000

4. Impressions Marketing Group, $80,000,000

6. Aritalia Group Inc., $65,000,000

7. Fetzer Architectural Woodwork, $49,000,000

8. Hamilton Fixture Co., $40,000,000

9. EMI Industries Inc., $36,000,000

10. CSC Worldwide, $35,000,000

Source: *Wood & Wood Products*, Wood 100 (annual), September 2011, p. 52.

Stores, Chain
See: **Chain Stores**

Stores, Retail
See: **Retail Industry**

Supermarkets
See also: **Convenience Stores**

4529 ■ AMERICA'S LARGEST PRIVATE FOOD MARKETS, 2010

Ranked by: Revenue, in billions of dollars. **Remarks:** Also notes headquarters, number of employees, and overall rank in the *America's Largest Private Companies* list. Ranking is available online only, not in print. **Number listed:** 18

1. Publix Super Markets Inc., with $25.13 billion

2. H. E. Butt Grocery Co., $15.6

3. Meijer Inc., $14.63

4. Giant Eagle Inc., $8.2

5. Hy-Vee Inc., $6.9

6. Wegmans Food Markets Inc., $5.6

7. Save Mart Supermarkets Inc., $4.8

8. WinCo Foods Inc., $4.73

9. Roundys Supermarkets Inc., $3.8

10. Stater Bros. Holdings Inc., $3.67

Source: *Forbes*, America's Largest Private Companies (annual), http://www.forbes.com, December 5, 2011.

4530 ■ AMERICA'S LARGEST SUPERMARKET CHAINS BY REVENUE, 2011

Ranked by: Estimated annual all-commodity volume, in thousands of dollars. **Remarks:** Also notes rank for previous year, headquarters, website, number of supermarkets, square feet of selling area, number of checkouts, number of store employees, number of stores, top banner names, and chief trading areas. **Number listed:** 50

1. Wal-Mart Stores Inc., with $118,725,880 thousand

2. The Kroger Co., $61,128,860

3. Safeway Inc., $35,504,560

4. SuperValu Inc., $28,229,188

5. Ahold USA Inc., $26,162,500

6. Publix Super Markets Inc., $22,770,800

7. Delhaize America Inc., $18,624,840
8. H. E. Butt Grocery Co., $12,983,100
9. Lone Star Funds, $10,449,920
10. Meijer Inc., $9,217,000

Source: *Progressive Grocer*, The Super 50 (annual), May 2012, p. 38-42.

4531 ■ AUSTRALIA'S LARGEST FOOD RETAILERS OVERALL, 2011

Ranked by: Score based on revenue, profits, assets, and market capitalization. **Remarks:** Specific scores not provided. Also notes overall rank in the *Forbes 2000* and figures for each criterion. **Number listed:** 3

1. Wesfarmers Ltd.
2. Woolworths Ltd.
3. Metcash Ltd.

Source: *Forbes*, Forbes 2000 (annual), http://www.forbes.com, May 7, 2012.

4532 ■ BELGIUM'S LARGEST FOOD RETAILING COMPANIES OVERALL, 2011

Ranked by: Score based on revenue, profits, assets, and market capitalization. **Remarks:** Specific scores not provided. Also notes overall rank in the *Forbes 2000* and figures for each criterion. **Number listed:** 2

1. Delhaize Group
2. Groep Colruyt

Source: *Forbes*, Forbes 2000 (annual), http://www.forbes.com, May 7, 2012.

4533 ■ BRITAIN'S MOST ADMIRED FOOD AND PERSONAL PRODUCTS RETAILERS, 2011

Ranked by: Survey of peers and investment analysts based on nine criteria: quality of management, financial soundness, quality of goods/services, ability to attract and retain talent, value as long-term investment, innovation, marketing, community and environmental responsibility, and use of corporate assets. **Number listed:** 5

1. Wm. Morrison Supermarkets plc, with 67.3 points
2. Alliance Boots, 64.5
3. Tesco plc, 64.3
4. Asda, 60.9
5. J Sainsbury plc, 60.8

Source: *Management Today*, Britain's Most Admired Companies (annual), December 2011, p. 47.

4534 ■ CANADA'S LARGEST FOOD RETAILERS OVERALL, 2011

Ranked by: Score based on revenue, profits, assets, and market capitalization. **Remarks:** Specific scores not provided. Also notes overall rank in the *Forbes 2000* and figures for each criterion. **Number listed:** 4

1. George Weston Ltd.
2. Alimentation Couche-Tard Inc.
3. Metro Inc.
4. Empire

Source: *Forbes*, Forbes 2000 (annual), http://www.forbes.com, May 7, 2012.

4535 ■ EUROPE'S MOST VALUABLE FOOD AND DRUG RETAILERS, 2011

Ranked by: Market value as of March 2011, in millions of U.S. dollars. **Remarks:** Also notes rank within the *FT Europe 500*, rank for previous year, country, revenue, net income, assets, number of employees, share price, price-to-earning ratio, dividend yield, and fiscal yearend. **Number listed:** 13

1. Tesco plc, with $49,141.7 million
2. Carrefour SA, $30,116.6
3. Metro AG, $22,176.1
4. Koninklijke Ahold NV (Royal Ahold NV), $16,014.1
5. Magnit, $12,470.9
6. Wm. Morrison Supermarkets plc, $11,679.6
7. Casino Guichard-Perrachon, $10,489.3
8. Jeronimo Martins SGPS SA, $10,135.8
9. J Sainsbury plc, $10,029.6
10. Groep Colruyt, $8,874.8

Source: *Financial Times*, FT 500 (annual), http://www.ft.com, June 24, 2011.

4536 ■ FASTEST-GROWING FOOD/DRUG/MASS MERCHANDISE STORE CHAINS, 2009-2010

Ranked by: Annual gain in basis points. **Remarks:** To qualify, chains must have annual revenues of at least $100 million. Also notes sales and market share for current and previous year. **Number listed:** 25

1. Kroger, with 223 points
2. Walgreen, 166
3. Dollar General, 78
4. Whole Foods Market, 61
5. Aldi, 60
6. Tops Markets, 45
7. H. E. Butt, 36
8. Target, 33
9. Trader Joe's, 31
10. Dollar Tree, 28

Source: *Stores*, Hot 100 (annual), August 2011, p. s4.

4537 ■ FOOD RETAILERS ADDING THE MOST NEW STORES, 2011

Ranked by: Total number of new stores added during the year. **Remarks:** Also notes figures for previous year. **Number listed:** 10

1. SuperValu Inc., with 90 new stores
2. Aldi Group, 80
3. Publix Super Markets Inc., 26
3. Safeway Inc., 26
5. Delhaize America Inc., 21
6. The Kroger Co., 20
7. Fresh & Easy, 18
7. Whole Foods Market Inc., 18
9. The Fresh Market Inc., 14
10. Harris Teeter Inc., 7

Source: *Chain Store Age*, Big Builders (annual), December 2011, p. 37.

4538 ■ FRANCE'S LARGEST FOOD RETAILERS OVERALL, 2011

Ranked by: Score based on revenue, profits, assets, and market capitalization. **Remarks:** Specific scores not provided. Also notes overall rank in the *Forbes 2000* and figures for each criterion. **Number listed:** 2

1. Carrefour SA
2. Finatis

Source: *Forbes*, Forbes 2000 (annual), http://www.forbes.com, May 7, 2012.

4539 ■ JAPAN'S LARGEST FOOD RETAILERS OVERALL, 2011

Ranked by: Score based on revenue, profits, assets, and market capitalization. **Remarks:** Specific scores not provided. Also notes overall rank in the *Forbes 2000* and figures for each criterion. **Number listed:** 2

1. Seven & I Holdings Co., Ltd.
2. Lawson Inc.

Source: *Forbes*, Forbes 2000 (annual), http://www.forbes.com, May 7, 2012.

4540 ■ LARGEST ASIA-PACIFIC SUPERMARKET COMPANIES, 2010

Ranked by: Sales, in millions of U.S. dollars. **Remarks:** Also notes country, fascias/brands, number of outlets, sales in national currency, sales area, sales per square meter, and figures for previous year. **Number listed:** 10

1. Woolworths Ltd., with $25,857 million
2. Wesfarmers Ltd., $19,116
3. Aeon Group, $10,337
4. Metcash Trading Ltd. Australasia, $8,067
5. Foodstuffs (NZ), $5,477
6. Life Corp., $5,150
7. Seven & I Holdings Co., Ltd., $5,109
8. Brilliance Group, $4,310
9. China Resources Enterprise, $3,853
10. The Maruetsu, $3,737

Source: *Retail Asia*, Retail Asia-Pacific Top 500 (annual), July 2011, p. 66-66a.

4541 ■ LARGEST FOOD STORES BY EMPLOYEES, 2010

Ranked by: Total number of employees. **Remarks:** Also notes contact information for headquarters, number of employees at headquarters, revenue, rank by revenue, and primary SIC code. **Number listed:** 256

1. The Kroger Co., with 334,000 employees
2. Safeway Inc., 186,000
3. Ahold USA Inc., 169,835
4. SuperValu Inc., 160,000
5. Publix Super Markets Inc., 142,000
6. New Albertson's Inc., 140,000
7. American Stores Co., 127,000
8. Delhaize America Inc., 109,000
9. Jewel Cos., Inc., 82,000
10. H. E. Butt Grocery Co., 70,000

Source: *Business Rankings*, (annual), Dun & Bradstreet Inc., 2011, p. VI.131-VI.136.

4542 ■ LARGEST FOOD STORES BY SALES, 2010

Ranked by: Total revenue, in dollars. **Remarks:** Also notes contact information for headquarters, number of employees at headquarters and overall, rank by employees, and primary SIC code. **Number listed:** 260

1. The Kroger Co., with $76,733,000,000

2. Safeway Inc., $41,050,000,000
3. SuperValu Inc., $40,597,000,000
4. Publix Super Markets Inc., $25,328,054,000
5. H. E. Butt Grocery Co., $14,752,321,000
6. Whole Foods Market Inc., $9,005,794,000
7. The Great Atlantic & Pacific Tea Co., Inc., $8,813,568,000
8. Winn-Dixie Stores Inc., $7,247,804,000
9. Hy-Vee Inc., $6,894,397,000
10. Wegmans Food Markets Inc., $5,193,210,000

Source: *Business Rankings*, (annual), Dun & Bradstreet Inc., 2011, p. V.131-V.136.

4543 ■ LARGEST U.S. FOOD RETAILERS OVERALL, 2011

Ranked by: Score based on revenue, profits, assets, and market capitalization. **Remarks:** Specific scores not provided. Also notes overall rank in the *Forbes 2000* and figures for each criterion. **Number listed:** 5

1. The Kroger Co.
2. Sysco Corp.
3. Safeway Inc.
4. Whole Foods Market Inc.
5. SuperValu Inc.

Source: *Forbes*, Forbes 2000 (annual), http://www.forbes.com, May 7, 2012.

4544 ■ MOST VALUABLE U.S. FOOD AND DRUG RETAILERS, 2011

Ranked by: Market value as of March 2011, in millions of U.S. dollars. **Remarks:** Also notes rank within the *FT U.S. 500*, rank for previous year, country, revenue, net income, assets, number of employees, share price, price-to-earning ratio, dividend yield, and fiscal yearend. **Number listed:** 9

1. CVS Caremark Corp., with $46,886.8 million
2. Walgreen Co., $37,025.8
3. McKesson Corp., $20,099.3
4. Sysco Corp., $15,141
5. The Kroger Co., $14,876.6
6. Cardinal Health Inc., $14,385.2
7. Whole Foods Market Inc., $11,437.9
8. AmerisourceBergen Corp., $10,843.2
9. Safeway Inc., $8,667.4

Source: *Financial Times*, FT 500 (annual), http://www.ft.com, June 24, 2011.

4545 ■ NORTH AMERICA'S TOP SUPERMARKET RETAILERS AND WHOLESALERS, 2011

Ranked by: Sales, in billions of dollars. **Number listed:** 75

1. Wal Mart Stores Inc., with $264.2 billion
2. The Kroger Co., $90.4
3. Costco Wholesale Corp., $88.9
4. Target Corp., $70
5. Safeway Inc., $43.6
6. SuperValu Inc., $36.1
7. Loblaw Cos. Ltd., $30.6
8. Publix Super Markets Inc., $29.9
9. Ahold USA Inc., $25.1

10. C & S Wholesale Grocers Inc., $20.4

Source: *Supermarket News*, Top 75 (annual), January 30, 2012.

4546 ■ PORTUGAL'S LARGEST FOOD RETAILERS OVERALL, 2011

Ranked by: Score based on revenue, profits, assets, and market capitalization. **Remarks:** Specific scores not provided. Also notes overall rank in the *Forbes 2000* and figures for each criterion. **Number listed:** 2

1. Jeronimo Martins
2. Sonae

Source: *Forbes*, Forbes 2000 (annual), http://www.forbes.com, May 7, 2012.

4547 ■ RUSSIA'S LARGEST FOOD RETAILERS OVERALL, 2011

Ranked by: Score based on revenue, profits, assets, and market capitalization. **Remarks:** Specific scores not provided. Also notes overall rank in the *Forbes 2000* and figures for each criterion. **Number listed:** 2

1. Magnit
2. X5 Retail Group

Source: *Forbes*, Forbes 2000 (annual), http://www.forbes.com, May 7, 2012.

4548 ■ TEXAS'S LARGEST FOOD RETAILERS OVERALL, 2011

Ranked by: Score based on revenue, profits, assets, and market capitalization. **Remarks:** Specific scores not provided. Also notes overall rank in the *Forbes 2000* and figures for each criterion. **Number listed:** 2

1. Sysco Corp.
2. Whole Foods Market Inc.

Source: *Forbes*, Forbes 2000 (annual), http://www.forbes.com, May 7, 2012.

4549 ■ TOP *FORTUNE 500* FOOD AND DRUG STORES, 2011

Ranked by: Revenue, in millions of dollars. **Remarks:** Also notes overall rank in the *Fortune 500;* profits; profits as a percentage of revenue; stockholders' equity; and rank by each criterion. **Number listed:** 10

1. CVS Caremark Corp., with $107,750 million
2. The Kroger Co., $90,374
3. Walgreen Co., $72,184
4. Safeway Inc., $43,630
5. SuperValu Inc., $37,534
6. Publix Super Markets Inc., $27,179
7. Rite Aid Corp., $25,216
8. Whole Foods Market Inc., $10,108
9. The Great Atlantic & Pacific Tea Co., Inc., $8,078
10. Winn-Dixie Stores Inc., $6,930

Source: *Fortune*, Fortune 500 (annual), May 21, 2012, p. F-35.

4550 ■ TOP SMALL CHAIN AND INDEPENDENT SUPERMARKETS, 2011

Ranked by: Sales, in millions of dollars. **Remarks:** Also notes headquarters, top executives, number of stores, supplier, and website. **Number listed:** 50

1. The Fresh Market, with $1,100 million
1. Grocery Outlet, $1,100
3. Fareway Stores, $1,000
3. Woodman's Markets, $1,000
5. Lowe's Market, $975
6. Bodega Latina, $950
7. Redner's Market, $859
8. King Kullen Grocery Co., $828
9. Northgate Gonzalez Market, $825
10. Rouses Enterprises, $820

Source: *Supermarket News*, Top 50 (annual), February 13, 2012.

4551 ■ TOP U.S. SUPERMARKET CHAINS BY SALES, 2010

Ranked by: Sales volume, in thousands of dollars. **Remarks:** Also notes comparable-store sales and sales per store. **Number listed:** 15

1. The Kroger Co., with $71,120,000 thousand
2. Safeway Inc., $33,262,000
3. SuperValu Inc., $30,398,000
4. Publix Super Markets Inc., $25,072,000
5. Ahold USA Inc., $23,515,000
6. Delhaize America Inc., $18,799,000
7. H. E. Butt Grocery Co., $14,947,000
8. ShopRite, $11,800,000
9. Whole Foods Market Inc., $8,736,000
10. Aldi, $8,362,000

Source: *Stores*, Top 100 Retailers (annual), July 2011, p. s10.

4552 ■ UNITED KINGDOM'S LARGEST FOOD RETAILERS OVERALL, 2011

Ranked by: Score based on revenue, profits, assets, and market capitalization. **Remarks:** Specific scores not provided. Also notes country, overall rank in the *Forbes 2000,* and figures for each criterion. **Number listed:** 3

1. Tesco plc
2. Wm. Morrison Supermarkets plc
3. J Sainsbury plc

Source: *Forbes*, Forbes 2000 (annual), http://www.forbes.com, May 7, 2012.

4553 ■ WORLD'S LARGEST FOOD RETAILERS OVERALL, 2011

Ranked by: Score based on revenue, profits, assets, and market capitalization. **Remarks:** Specific scores not provided. Also notes country, overall rank in the *Forbes 2000,* and figures for each criterion. **Number listed:** 34

1. Tesco plc
2. Wesfarmers Ltd.
3. Seven & I Holdings Co., Ltd.
4. Woolworths Ltd.
5. Metro AG
6. Carrefour SA
7. Koninklijke Ahold NV (Royal Ahold NV)
8. The Kroger Co.
9. Sysco Corp.
10. Wm. Morrison Supermarkets plc

Source: *Forbes*, Forbes 2000 (annual), http://www.forbes.com, May 7, 2012.

4554 ■ WORLD'S MOST ADMIRED FOOD AND DRUG STORES, 2012

Ranked by: Score, on a scale of 10, based on a survey of executives, directors, and securities analysts of companies within their own industry on eight criteria: innovation, financial soundness, employee talent, use of corporate assets, long-term investment value, social responsibility, quality of management, and quality of products/services. **Remarks:** Specific scores not provided. Also notes rank for previous year. **Number listed:** 5

1. Whole Foods Market Inc.
2. Publix Super Markets Inc.
3. The Kroger Co.
4. Walgreen Co.
5. CVS Caremark Corp.

Source: *Fortune*, World's Most Admired Companies (annual), March 19, 2012, p. 149-150.

4555 ■ WORLD'S MOST ETHICAL FOOD RETAILING COMPANIES, 2012

Ranked by: Score based on five criteria: ethics and compliance program; reputation, leadership, and innovation; governance; corporate citizenship and responsibility; and culture of ethics. **Remarks:** Specific scores not provided; companies are listed alphabetically, not ranked. **Number listed:** 6

1. Kesko Oyj (Finland)
2. The Co-Operative Group Ltd. (U.K.)
3. Safeway Inc. (U.S.)
4. SONAE (Portugal)
5. Wegmans Food Markets Inc. (U.S.)
6. Whole Foods Market Inc. (U.S.)

Source: *Ethisphere Magazine*, World's Most Ethical Companies (annual), http://www.ethisphere.com, 2012.

4556 ■ WORLD'S MOST VALUABLE FOOD AND DRUG RETAILERS, 2011

Ranked by: Market value as of March 2011, in millions of U.S. dollars. **Remarks:** Also notes rank within the *FT 500*, rank for previous year, country, revenue, net income, assets, number of employees, share price, price-to-earning ratio, dividend yield, and fiscal year-end. **Number listed:** 7

1. Tesco plc, with $49,141.7 million
2. CVS Caremark Corp., $46,886.8
3. Walgreen Co., $37,025.8
4. Woolworths Ltd., $33,716.2
5. Carrefour SA, $30,116.6
6. Metro AG, $22,176.1
7. McKesson Corp., $20,099.3

Source: *Financial Times*, FT 500 (annual), http://www.ft.com, June 24, 2011.

Supply Chain

4557 ■ TOP SUPPLY CHAIN MANAGEMENT SOFTWARE SUPPLIERS, 2010

Ranked by: Revenue, in millions of dollars. **Remarks:** Also notes website and types of software and services provided. **Number listed:** 20

1. SAP AG, with $1,317 million
2. Oracle Corp., $1,210

3. JDA Software Group Inc., $362
4. Manhattan Associates Inc., $136
5. RedPrairie Corp., $94
6. IBS, $83
7. Lawson Software, $80
8. Descartes Systems Group, $75
9. Kewill Solutions, $64
10. Retailix, $58.5

Source: *Modern Materials Handling*, Top 20 Supply Chain Management Software Suppliers (annual), July 2011, p. 29.

4558 ■ TOP SUPPLY CHAIN PARTNERS, 2011

Ranked by: Score based on peer opinion, research opinion, return on assets, inventory turns, and revenue growth. **Remarks:** Specific scores not provided; companies are listed alphabetically, not ranked. Also notes website and user testimonial. **Number listed:** 100

1. 4Sight Supply Chain Group
2. Access America Transportation
3. Acuitive Solutions
4. Airgroup
5. APICS
6. APL Logistics
7. Ariba Inc.
8. ASAP Automation
9. Avercast
10. Averitt Express

Source: *SupplyChainBrain*, Supply Chain Top 100 (annual), 2011, p. 82-83.

4559 ■ WORLD'S MOST INNOVATIVE SUPPLY CHAIN COMPANIES, 2011

Ranked by: Score, on a scale of 10, based on supply chain innovation, as well as inventory turns, three-year return on assets, and three-year revenue growth. **Remarks:** Also notes figures for each criterion. **Number listed:** 25

1. Apple Inc., with 8.5 points
2. Dell Inc., 5.14
3. Procter & Gamble Co., 5.13
4. Research in Motion Ltd., 5.10
5. Amazon.com Inc., 5.07
6. Cisco Systems Inc., 4.82
7. Wal-Mart Stores Inc., 4.4
8. McDonald's Corp., 4.35
9. PepsiCo Inc., 4.11
10. Samsung Electronics Co., Ltd., 3.98

Source: *World Trade 100*, Gartner Supply Chain Top 25 (annual), September 2011, p. 23.

Swimming Pools

4560 ■ TOP BUILDERS OF RESIDENTIAL POOLS BY REVENUE, 2010

Ranked by: Total residential construction revenue, in dollars. **Remarks:** Also notes rank for previous year, breakdown of revenue by new and renovation, number of pools built, average pool price, average renovation price, and gross revenue. **Number listed:** 50

1. Blue Haven Pools & Spas, with $100,585,069
2. Anthony & Sylvan Pools Corp., $67,000,000
3. Premier Pools & Spas Inc., $38,368,115
4. California Pools & Spas, $25,471,814
5. Shasta Industries, $25,400,000
6. Platinum Pools, $21,800,000
7. Cody Pools Inc., $21,790,125
8. Adams Pool Solutions, $21,648,476
9. Paddock Pools & Spas, $21,619,500
10. Keith Zars Pools Ltd., $20,681,100

Source: *Pool & Spa News*, Top 50 Builders (annual), http://www.poolspanews.com, September 2011.

Syndicated Loans

4561 ■ TOP SYNDICATED LOAN MANAGERS, 2011

Ranked by: Proceeds from syndicated loans in the U.S., in billions of dollars. **Remarks:** Also notes market share for current and previous year. **Number listed:** 10

1. J. P. Morgan Chase & Co., with $409.3 billion
2. Bank of America Corp./Merrill Lynch, $355.5
3. Citigroup Inc., $190.5
4. Wells Fargo Securities, $179.9
5. Barclays Capital Inc., $83.3
6. Credit Suisse Group, $63.7
7. The Royal Bank of Scotland Group plc, $52.5
8. BNP Paribas SA, $51.2
9. Deutsche Bank AG, $49
10. Morgan Stanley, $47.4

Source: *The Wall Street Journal*, Year-End Review (annual), January 3, 2012, p. R9.

Synthetic Fibers Industry
See: **Textile Industry**

Tank Trucks

4562 ■ LARGEST FOR-HIRE TANK/BULK TRUCK COMPANIES, 2010

Ranked by: Revenue, in thousands of dollars. **Remarks:** Also notes figures for previous year and percent change. **Number listed:** 13

1. Kenan Advantage Group, with $772,447 thousand
2. Quality Distribution Inc., $686,598
3. Trimac Group, $579,551
4. A & R Logistics, $212,000
5. Superior Bulk Logistics, $207,060
6. Groendyke Transport Inc., $191,050
7. Schneider National Bulk Carriers, $175,949
8. Ruan Transport Corp., $172,139
9. Foodliner Inc./Quest Logistics, $166,885
10. Enterprise Transportation Co., $151,341

Source: *Transport Topics*, Top 100 For-Hire Carriers (annual), 2011, p. 24.

Tax Services

4563 ■ TOP TAX FIRMS, 2011

Ranked by: Revenue from tax services, in millions of dollars. **Remarks:** Also notes headquarters, chief executive, total revenue, tax services as a percentage of total revenue, annual growth in total revenue, number of offices, and number of staff. **Number listed:** 16

1. H & R Block Inc., with $2,912.36 million
2. PricewaterhouseCoopers LLP, $2,564.76
3. Deloitte LLP, $2,387.8
4. Ernst & Young LLP, $2,325
5. KPMG LLP, $1,393.86
6. McGladrey & Pullen, $491.84
7. Liberty Tax Service, $333.51
8. Grant Thornton LLP, $332.37
9. Ryan, $233.5
10. CBIZ/Mayer Hoffman McCann, $161.33

Source: *Accounting Today*, Top 100 (annual), March 2012, p. 10.

4564 ■ TOP TAX SERVICE FRANCHISES, 2012

Ranked by: Cumulative score based on financial strength and stability, growth rate, size of the system, number of years in business, the length of time franchising, start-up costs, litigation, percentage of terminations, and whether the company provides financing. **Remarks:** Specific scores not provided. Also notes overall rank within the *Franchise 500,* contact information, description, year founded, year started franchising, states where registered, available U.S. regions, where seeking foreign expansion, number of franchised and company-owned units for past three years, start-up costs, franchise fees, royalty fees, and type of financing available. **Number listed:** 5

1. H & R Block Inc.
2. Liberty Tax Service
3. Tax Centers of America
4. Express Tax
5. Eagle Tax

Source: *Entrepreneur*, Franchise 500 (annual), January 2012, p. 162-163.

Taxation
See also: **Income Tax; Property Tax**

4565 ■ COUNTRIES WITH THE HIGHEST IMPACT OF TAXATION, 2010

Ranked by: Score, on a scale of seven, based on the level in which taxation significantly limits the incentives to work or invest. **Number listed:** 142

1. Brazil, with 2.1 points
2. Ukraine, 2.2
2. Croatia, 2.2
2. Italy, 2.2
5. Argentina, 2.3
5. Belgium, 2.3
7. Burundi, 2.5
7. Romania, 2.5
7. Portugal, 2.5

7. Yemen, 2.5

7. Belize, 2.5

7. Hungary, 2.5

Source: *Global Competitiveness Report*, (annual), World Economic Forum, 2011, p. 455.

4566 ■ COUNTRIES WITH THE HIGHEST TAX RATE, 2010

Ranked by: Profit tax, labor tax and contribution, and other taxes, in percent. **Number listed:** 140

1. Gambia, with 292.3%

2. Burundi, 153.4%

3. Argentina, 108.2%

4. Tajikistan, 86%

5. Bolivia, 80%

6. Colombia, 78.7%

7. Algeria, 72%

8. Brazil, 69%

9. Italy, 68.6%

10. Mauritania, 68.4%

Source: *Global Competitiveness Report*, (annual), World Economic Forum, 2011, p. 456.

4567 ■ COUNTRIES WITH THE LOWEST IMPACT OF TAXATION, 2010

Ranked by: Score, on a scale of seven, based on the level in which taxation significantly limits the incentives to work or invest. **Number listed:** 142

1. Bahrain, with 6.1 points

2. Kuwait, 5.7

2. United Arab Emirates, 5.7

2. Hong Kong, 5.7

5. Oman, 5.5

6. Singapore, 5.4

7. Saudi Arabia, 5.3

8. Luxembourg, 5.1

8. Mauritius, 5.1

8. Switzerland, 5.1

Source: *Global Competitiveness Report*, (annual), World Economic Forum, 2011, p. 455.

4568 ■ COUNTRIES WITH THE LOWEST TAX RATE, 2010

Ranked by: Profit tax, labor tax and contribution, and other taxes, in percent. **Number listed:** 140

1. Timor-Leste, with 0.2%

2. Namibia, 9.6%

3. Macedonia, 10.6%

4. Qatar, 11.3%

5. United Arab Emirates, 14.1%

6. Saudi Arabia, 14.5%

7. Bahrain, 15.0%

8. Georgia, 15.3%

9. Kuwait, 15.5%

10. Zambia, 16.1%

Source: *Global Competitiveness Report*, (annual), World Economic Forum, 2011, p. 456.

4569 ■ STATES WITH THE HIGHEST STATE DIESEL TAX RATES, 2011

Ranked by: State diesel tax rates, in dollars per gallon of gasoline. **Number listed:** 51

1. California, with $0.525

2. Indiana, $0.499

3. Hawaii, $0.497

4. New York, $0.484

5. Connecticut, $0.462

6. Illinois, $0.444

7. Pennsylvania, $0.392

8. Michigan, $0.386

9. Washington, $0.375

10. North Carolina, $0.353

Source: *Small Business Survival Index*, (annual), Small Business & Entrepreneurship Council, November 2011, p. 47.

4570 ■ STATES WITH THE HIGHEST STATE GAS TAX RATES, 2011

Ranked by: State gas tax rates, in dollars per gallon of gasoline. **Number listed:** 51

1. Connecticut, with $0.496

2. New York, $0.495

3. California, $0.491

4. Hawaii, $0.474

5. Illinois, $0.412

6. Michigan, $0.408

7. Indiana, $0.397

8. Washington, $0.375

9. North Carolina, $0.353

10. Florida, $0.345

Source: *Small Business Survival Index*, (annual), Small Business & Entrepreneurship Council, November 2011, p. 46.

4571 ■ STATES WITH THE HIGHEST STATE AND LOCAL SALES, GROSS RECEIPTS, AND EXCISE TAXES, 2011

Ranked by: Sales, gross receipts, and excise taxes as a percentage of personal income. **Number listed:** 51

1. Hawaii, with 5.78%

2. Washington, 5.49%

3. Wyoming, 5.40%

4. Louisiana, 5.31%

5. Nevada, 4.98%

6. New Mexico, 4.88%

7. Arkansas, 4.71%

8. Tennessee, 4.48%

9. Mississippi, 4.29%

10. Florida, 4.15%

Source: *Small Business Survival Index*, (annual), Small Business & Entrepreneurship Council, November 2011, p. 44.

4572 ■ STATES WITH THE HIGHEST TOP CAPITAL GAINS TAX RATES, 2011

Ranked by: Top capital gains tax rate, in percent. **Remarks:** In the event of a tie, states are ranked alphabetically. **Number listed:** 51

1. Oregon, with 11%

2. California, 10.3%

3. New Jersey, 8.97%

3. New Jersey, 8.97%

5. Vermont, 8.95%

6. Maine, 8.5%

6. Washington DC, 8.5%

8. Minnesota, 7.85%

9. Idaho, 7.8%

10. North Carolina, 7.75%

Source: *Small Business Survival Index*, (annual), Small Business & Entrepreneurship Council, November 2011, p. 40.

4573 ■ STATES WITH THE HIGHEST TOP CORPORATE CAPITAL GAINS TAX RATES, 2011

Ranked by: Top corporate capital gains tax rate, in percent. **Remarks:** In the event of a tie, states are ranked alphabetically. **Number listed:** 51

1. Pennsylvania, with 9.99%

2. Washington DC, 9.97%

3. Iowa, 9.90%

4. Minnesota, 9.8%

5. Illinois, 9.5%

6. Connecticut, 9%

6. New Jersey, 9%

6. Rhode Island, 9%

9. Maine, 8.93%

10. California, 8.84%

Source: *Small Business Survival Index*, (annual), Small Business & Entrepreneurship Council, November 2011, p. 42.

4574 ■ STATES WITH THE HIGHEST UNEMPLOYMENT TAX RATES, 2011

Ranked by: Maximum state tax rate applied to state wage base as a percentage of state average annual pay. **Remarks:** In the event of a tie, states are ranked alphabetically. **Number listed:** 51

1. North Dakota, with 6.67%

2. Utah, 6.49%

3. Minnesota, 6.43%

4. Iowa, 5.89%

5. Idaho, 5.87%

6. Wyoming, 5.49%

7. Washington, 4.59%

8. Montana, 4.41%

9. Hawaii, 4.31%

10. Rhode Island, 4.05%

Source: *Small Business Survival Index*, (annual), Small Business & Entrepreneurship Council, November 2011, p. 45.

4575 ■ STATES WITH THE LOWEST STATE DIESEL TAX RATES, 2011

Ranked by: State diesel tax rates, in dollars per gallon of gasoline. **Number listed:** 51

1. Alaska, with $0.080

2. Oklahoma, $0.140

2. Wyoming, $0.140

4. South Carolina, $0.168

5. Missouri, $0.173

6. New Jersey, $0.175

7. Tennessee, $0.184

8. Mississippi, $0.188

9. Arizona, $0.190

10. Kentucky, $0.195

Source: *Small Business Survival Index*, (annual), Small Business & Entrepreneurship Council, November 2011, p. 47.

4576 ■ STATES WITH THE LOWEST STATE GAS TAX RATES, 2011

Ranked by: State gas tax rates, in dollars per gallon of gasoline. **Number listed:** 51

1. Alaska, with $0.080

2. Wyoming, $0.140

3. New Jersey, $0.145

4. South Carolina, $0.168

5. Oklahoma, $0.170

6. Missouri, $0.173

7. Mississippi, $0.188

8. New Mexico, $0.189

9. Arizona, $0.190

10. New Hampshire, $0.196

Source: *Small Business Survival Index*, (annual), Small Business & Entrepreneurship Council, November 2011, p. 46.

4577 ■ STATES WITH THE LOWEST STATE AND LOCAL SALES, GROSS RECEIPTS, AND EXCISE TAXES, 2011

Ranked by: Sales, gross receipts, and excise taxes as a percentage of personal income. **Number listed:** 51

1. Oregon, with 0.59%

2. Montana, 1.03%

3. Delaware, 1.08%

4. New Hampshire, 1.25%

5. Alaska, 1.72%

6. Massachusetts, 1.74%

7. Virginia, 2.08%

8. Maryland, 2.20%

9. Connecticut, 2.59%

10. New Jersey, 2.61%

Source: *Small Business Survival Index*, (annual), Small Business & Entrepreneurship Council, November 2011, p. 44.

4578 ■ STATES WITH THE LOWEST TOP CAPITAL GAINS TAX RATES, 2011

Ranked by: Top capital gains tax rate, in percent. **Remarks:** In the event of a tie, states are ranked alphabetically. **Number listed:** 51

1. Alaska, with 0%

1. Florida, 0%

1. Nevada, 0%

1. New Hampshire, 0%

1. South Dakota, 0%

1. Tennessee, 0%

1. Texas, 0%

1. Washington, 0%

1. Wyoming, 0%

10. New Mexico, 2.45%

Source: *Small Business Survival Index*, (annual), Small Business & Entrepreneurship Council, November 2011, p. 40.

4579 ■ STATES WITH THE LOWEST TOP CORPORATE CAPITAL GAINS TAX RATES, 2011

Ranked by: Top corporate capital gains tax rate, in percent. **Remarks:** In the event of a tie, states are ranked alphabetically. **Number listed:** 51

1. Nevada, with 0%
1. Ohio, 0%
1. South Dakota, 0%
1. Texas, 0%
1. Washington, 0%
1. Wyoming, 0%
7. Hawaii, 4%
8. Alabama, 4.225%
9. Alaska, 4.5%
10. Colorado, 4.63%

Source: *Small Business Survival Index*, (annual), Small Business & Entrepreneurship Council, November 2011, p. 42.

4580 ■ STATES WITH THE LOWEST UNEMPLOYMENT TAX RATES, 2011

Ranked by: Maximum state tax rate applied to state wage base as a percentage of state average annual pay. Remarks: In the event of a tie, states are ranked alphabetically. Number listed: 51

1. California, with 0.86%
1. Washington DC, 0.86%
3. Florida, 0.94%
4. Arizona, 0.97%
5. Indiana, 1.00%
6. Virginia, 1.04%
7. Georgia, 1.09%
8. Mississippi, 1.11%
9. South Carolina, 1.13%
10. Colorado, 1.15%

Source: *Small Business Survival Index*, (annual), Small Business & Entrepreneurship Council, November 2011, p. 45.

Tea Industry

4581 ■ TOP BAGGED/LOOSE LEAF TEA BRANDS IN THE U.S., 2011

Ranked by: Sales, in dollars. Remarks: Also notes percent change from previous year and market share. Number listed: 10

1. Lipton, with $167,523,100
2. Bigelow, $89,397,590
3. private label, $57,623,860
4. Twinings, $46,366,850
5. Celestial Seasonings, $37,763,840
6. Luzianne, $36,217,100
7. Stash, $29,411,980
8. Tetley, $24,983,640
9. Tazo, $23,196,950
10. Yogi, $15,469,430

Source: *Beverage Industry*, State of the Industry Report (annual), July 2011, p. SIO-10.

4582 ■ TOP READY-TO-DRINK TEA BRANDS BY SALES, 2011

Ranked by: Sales, in millions of dollars. Remarks: Also notes annual growth. Number listed: 20

1. AriZona, with $614.4 million
2. Lipton Brisk, $286.2

3. Lipton, $257.4
4. Snapple, $188.2
5. Lipton Pureleaf, $148.6
6. AriZona Arnold Palmer, $146
7. Diet Snapple, $143
8. Nestea, $99.7
9. Gold Peak, $84.8
10. Lipton Diet, $75.4

Source: *Beverage World*, State of the Industry Report (annual), May 2012, p. 30.

4583 ■ TOP READY-TO-DRINK TEA BRANDS IN THE U.S., 2011

Ranked by: Sales, in dollars. Remarks: Also notes percent change from previous year and market share. Number listed: 10

1. Arizona, with $623,292,800
2. Lipton Brisk, $283,352,800
3. Lipton, $280,079,300
4. Snapple, $186,867,500
5. Lipton Pureleaf, $158,616,700
6. Diet Snapple, $135,520,100
7. Arizona Arnold Palmer, $113,732,600
8. Nestea, $105,450,900
9. Gold Peak, $81,087,740
10. Lipton Diet, $59,055,310

Source: *Beverage Industry*, State of the Industry Report (annual), July 2011, p. SIO-10.

Teachers

4584 ■ STATES WITH THE HIGHEST-PAID COLLEGE PROFESSORS, 2009

Ranked by: Average annual salary for faculty at institutions of higher education, in dollars. Number listed: 51

1. Massachusetts, with $91,612
2. Connecticut, $90,314
3. New Jersey, $89,013
4. Washington DC, $88,635
5. California, $87,736
6. Delaware, $85,476
7. New York, $82,642
8. Rhode Island, $82,332
9. New Hampshire, $80,335
10. Nevada, $79,794

Source: *State Rankings*, (annual), CQ Press, 2011, p. 146.

4585 ■ STATES WITH THE HIGHEST-PAID PUBLIC SCHOOL TEACHERS, 2010-2011

Ranked by: Average public school teachers' salaries, in dollars. Number listed: 51

1. New York, with $72,708
2. Massachusetts, $71,017
3. California, $69,434
4. New Jersey, $66,985
5. Washington DC, $66,601
6. Connecticut, $65,571

7. Maryland, $65,113
8. Illinois, $63,005
9. Alaska, $61,093
10. Rhode Island, $60,923

Source: *State Rankings*, (annual), CQ Press, 2011, p. 125.

4586 ■ STATES WITH THE LOWEST-PAID COLLEGE PROFESSORS, 2009

Ranked by: Average annual salary of faculty at institutions of higher education, in dollars. **Number listed:** 51

1. North Dakota, with $54,551
2. Arkansas, $54,600
3. Mississippi, $55,302
4. South Dakota, $55,667
5. Montana, $56,689
6. West Virginia, $57,440
7. Idaho, $57,786
8. South Carolina, $59,920
9. Kentucky, $60,003
10. Oklahoma, $61,106

Source: *State Rankings*, (annual), CQ Press, 2011, p. 146.

4587 ■ STATES WITH THE LOWEST-PAID PUBLIC SCHOOL TEACHERS, 2010-2011

Ranked by: Average public school teachers' salaries, in dollars. **Number listed:** 51

1. South Dakota, with $35,201
2. North Dakota, $44,266
3. Missouri, $46,411
4. Utah, $46,571
5. Florida, $46,702
6. Mississippi, $46,818
7. North Carolina, $46,850
8. New Mexico, $46,950
9. Tennessee, $47,043
10. Kansas, $47,080

Source: *State Rankings*, (annual), CQ Press, 2011, p. 125.

Technology
See also: **High Technology Industry; Information Technology**

4588 ■ AMERICA'S LARGEST PRIVATE TECHNOLOGY HARDWARE AND EQUIPMENT COMPANIES, 2010

Ranked by: Revenue, in billions of dollars. **Remarks:** Also notes headquarters, number of employees, and overall rank in the *America's Largest Private Companies* list. Ranking is available online only, not in print. **Number listed:** 7

1. CDW Corp., with $8.8 billion
2. Kingston Technology Co., $6.48
3. SHI International Corp., $3
3. World Wide Technology Inc., $3
5. Vizio Inc., $2.9
6. D & H Distributing Co., $2.61
7. Bose Corp., $2.28

Source: *Forbes*, America's Largest Private Companies (annual), http://www.forbes.com, December 5, 2011.

4589 ■ FASTEST-GROWING TECHNOLOGY COMPANIES, 2008-2011

Ranked by: Score based on three-year growth in revenue and earnings, and three-year total return to investors. **Remarks:** Specific scores not provided. To qualify for list, companies must have revenues of at least $50 million, net income of at least $10 million, market capitalization of at least $250 million, and stock price of at least $5. Int'l companies are eligible if they trade on a U.S. exchange and file quarterly reports. **Number listed:** 28

1. Baidu
2. Cirrus Logic
3. Priceline.com Inc.
4. Ebix Inc.
5. Apple Inc.
6. Acme Packet
7. Riverbed Technology
8. VanceInfo Technologies
9. AboveNet
10. Cree Inc.

Source: *Fortune*, 100 Fastest-Growing Companies (annual), http://www.fortune.com, September 26, 2011.

4590 ■ FASTEST-GROWING TECHNOLOGY COMPANIES, 2008-2011

Ranked by: Three-year growth in sales, in percent. **Remarks:** Also notes type of business, stock price, estimated price-to-earnings ratio, growth in earnings per share, annual revenue, and one-year growth in sales. To qualify for ranking, company must have a 10 percent growth in sales for each year, $150 million in revenue, a minimum market value of $500 million, a positive annual net income, and be free of large litigation or other liabilities. **Number listed:** 25

1. LinkedIn, with 89%
2. Apple Inc., 43%
3. Qlik Technologies, 40%
4. AthenaHealth, 33%
5. Equinix, 32%
5. Ebix, 32%
7. Aruba Networks, 31%
7. Riverbed Technology, 31%
7. Cognizant Technology Solutions, 31%
10. Shutterfly, 30%

Source: *Forbes*, The Fast Tech List (annual), May 21, 2012, p. 88.

4591 ■ TOP MISCELLANEOUS TECHNOLOGY FRANCHISES, 2012

Ranked by: Cumulative score based on financial strength and stability, growth rate, size of the system, number of years in business, the length of time franchising, start-up costs, litigation, percentage of terminations, and whether the company provides financing. **Remarks:** Specific scores not provided. Also notes overall rank within the *Franchise 500,* contact information, description, year founded, year started franchising, states where registered, available U.S. regions, where seeking foreign expansion, number of franchised and company-owned units for past three years, start-up costs, franchise fees, royalty fees, and type of financing available. **Number listed:** 6

1. Fast-teks On-site Computer Services
2. WSI Internet
3. Cell Phone Repair

4. CMIT Solutions Inc.
5. Computer Troubleshooters
6. The Utility Co.

Source: *Entrepreneur*, Franchise 500 (annual), January 2012, p. 208-209.

4592 ■ THE WORLD'S "GREENEST" BIG TECHNOLOGY COMPANIES, 2011

Ranked by: Score based on environmental impact, policies, and reputation. **Remarks:** Scores not provided. **Number listed:** 30

1. International Business Machines Corp. (IBM)
2. Tata Consultancy Services
3. Infosys
4. Fujitsu
5. Hewlett-Packard Co.
6. SAP AG
7. Nokia Corp.
8. Samsung Electronics
9. Dell Inc.
10. Toshiba Corp.

Source: *Newsweek*, The Greenest Big Companies (annual), http://www.newsweek.com, October 16, 2011.

4593 ■ WORLD'S MOST INNOVATIVE TECHNOLOGY COMPANIES, 2012

Ranked by: Editorial determination. **Remarks:** Companies are listed alphabetically, not ranked. Also notes comments. **Number listed:** 50

1. Alcatel-Lucent
2. Alta Devices
3. Apple Inc.
4. Applied Materials Inc.
5. ARM Holdings plc
6. Athenahealth
7. Babcock & Wilcox
8. Better Place
9. Bluefin Laboratories
10. Cellular Dynamics International

Source: *Technology Review*, TR 50 (annual), http://www.technologyreview.com, 2012.

4594 ■ WORLD'S MOST INNOVATIVE TECHNOLOGY MATERIALS COMPANIES - PRIVATE, 2012

Ranked by: Editorial determination. **Remarks:** Companies are listed alphabetically, not ranked. Also notes comments. **Number listed:** 2

1. Siluria
2. Wildcat Discovery

Source: *Technology Review*, TR 50 (annual), http://www.technologyreview.com, 2012.

4595 ■ WORLD'S MOST INNOVATIVE TECHNOLOGY MATERIALS COMPANIES - PUBLIC, 2012

Ranked by: Editorial determination. **Remarks:** Companies are listed alphabetically, not ranked. Also notes comments. **Number listed:** 3

1. Applied Materials Inc.

2. European Aeronautic Defense & Space Co. (EADS)
3. Intel Corp.

Source: *Technology Review*, TR 50 (annual), http://www.technologyreview.com, 2012.

Telecommunications Industry
See also: **Telephone; Wireless Telephones**

4596 ■ AUSTRALIA'S MOST VALUABLE TELECOMMUNICATION BRANDS, 2011

Ranked by: Brand value, in millions of U.S. dollars. **Remarks:** Also notes rank within the *Global 500* for current and previous year, figures for current and previous year, and brand rating. Ranking is available online only. **Number listed:** 2

1. Telstra, with $5,283 million
2. Optus, $2,529

Source: *Global 500*, (annual), Brand Finance plc, March 2012.

4597 ■ BRAZIL'S MOST VALUABLE TELECOMMUNICATION BRANDS, 2011

Ranked by: Brand value, in millions of U.S. dollars. **Remarks:** Also notes rank within the *Global 500* for current and previous year, figures for current and previous year, and brand rating. Ranking is available online only. **Number listed:** 3

1. TIM, with $7,859 million
2. Vivo, $4,316
3. Oi, $2,782

Source: *Global 500*, (annual), Brand Finance plc, March 2012.

4598 ■ BRITAIN'S MOST ADMIRED TELECOMMUNICATIONS COMPANIES, 2011

Ranked by: Survey of peers and investment analysts based on nine criteria: quality of management, financial soundness, quality of goods/services, ability to attract and retain talent, value as long-term investment, innovation, marketing, community and environmental responsibility, and use of corporate assets. **Number listed:** 5

1. Telefonica O2, with 66.2 points
2. Vodafone Group plc, 66
3. Virgin Media, 61.7
4. Inmarsat plc, 59.3
5. BT Group plc, 58.9

Source: *Management Today*, Britain's Most Admired Companies (annual), December 2011, p. 49.

4599 ■ CANADA'S LARGEST TELECOMMUNICATIONS SERVICES COMPANIES OVERALL, 2011

Ranked by: Score based on revenue, profits, assets, and market capitalization. **Remarks:** Specific scores not provided. Also notes overall rank in the *Forbes 2000* and figures for each criterion. **Number listed:** 3

1. BCE Inc.
2. Rogers Communications Inc.
3. TELUS Corp.

Source: *Forbes*, Forbes 2000 (annual), http://www.forbes.com, May 7, 2012.

4600 ■ CANADA'S MOST VALUABLE TELECOMMUNICATION BRANDS, 2011

Ranked by: Brand value, in millions of U.S. dollars. **Remarks:** Also notes rank within the *Global 500* for current and previous

year, figures for current and previous year, and brand rating. Ranking is available online only. **Number listed:** 3

1. Bell, with $5,258 million
2. Rogers, $4,087
3. Telus, $3,019

Source: *Global 500*, (annual), Brand Finance plc, March 2012.

4601 ■ CHINA'S MOST VALUABLE TELECOMMUNICATION BRANDS, 2011

Ranked by: Brand value, in millions of U.S. dollars. **Remarks:** Also notes rank within the *Global 500* for current and previous year, figures for current and previous year, and brand rating. Ranking is available online only. **Number listed:** 2

1. China Telecom, with $7,357 million
2. Huawei, $4,832

Source: *Global 500*, (annual), Brand Finance plc, March 2012.

4602 ■ EUROPE'S MOST VALUABLE FIXED-LINE TELECOMMUNICATIONS COMPANIES, 2011

Ranked by: Market value as of March 2011, in millions of U.S. dollars. **Remarks:** Also notes rank within the *FT Europe 500*, rank for previous year, country, revenue, net income, assets, number of employees, share price, price-to-earning ratio, dividend yield, and fiscal yearend. **Number listed:** 15

1. Telefonica SA, with $114,411.3 million
2. France Telecom SA, $59,428.3
3. Telecom Italia SpA, $28,759.9
4. Koninklijke KPN NV (Royal KPN NV), $26,068.1
5. Swisscom AG, $23,186.6
6. BT Group plc, $23,094.5
7. Turk Telekomunikasyon, $17,592.1
8. Belgacom SA, $13,112.3
9. Portugal Telecom SA, $10,361.1
10. Telekomunikacja Polska, $8,278.4

Source: *Financial Times*, FT 500 (annual), http://www.ft.com, June 24, 2011.

4603 ■ EUROPE'S MOST VALUABLE MOBILE TELECOMMUNICATIONS COMPANIES, 2011

Ranked by: Market value as of March 2011, in millions of U.S. dollars. **Remarks:** Also notes rank within the *FT Europe 500*, rank for previous year, country, revenue, net income, assets, number of employees, share price, price-to-earning ratio, dividend yield, and fiscal yearend. **Number listed:** 9

1. Vodafone Group plc, with $145,923.3 million
2. Deutsche Telekom AG, $66,658.6
3. TeliaSonera AB, $37,443
4. Telenor ASA, $27,273.1
5. Mobile Telesystems OJSC, $18,199.4
6. Turkcell Iletisim Hizmetleri AS, $13,024.4
7. JSFC Sistema, $11,544.7
8. Tele2 AB, $10,341.3
9. Inmarsat plc, $4,459.5

Source: *Financial Times*, FT 500 (annual), http://www.ft.com, June 24, 2011.

4604 ■ FRANCE'S MOST VALUABLE TELECOMMUNICATION BRANDS, 2011

Ranked by: Brand value, in millions of U.S. dollars. **Remarks:** Also notes rank within the *Global 500* for current and previous

year, figures for current and previous year, and brand rating. Ranking is available online only. **Number listed:** 3

1. Orange, with $18,557 million
2. Alcatel-Lucent, $3,349
3. Cannal+, $2,727

Source: *Global 500*, (annual), Brand Finance plc, March 2011.

4605 ■ GERMANY'S MOST VALUABLE TELECOMMUNICATION BRANDS, 2011

Ranked by: Brand value, in millions of U.S. dollars. **Remarks:** Also notes rank within the *Global 500* for current and previous year, figures for current and previous year, and brand rating. Ranking is available online only. **Number listed:** 2

1. T-Mobile, with $12,046 million
2. T (Deutsche Telekom), $5,867

Source: *Global 500*, (annual), Brand Finance plc, March 2012.

4606 ■ HONG KONG'S LARGEST TELECOMMUNICATIONS SERVICES COMPANIES OVERALL, 2011

Ranked by: Score based on revenue, profits, assets, and market capitalization. **Remarks:** Specific scores not provided. Also notes overall rank in the *Forbes 2000* and figures for each criterion. **Number listed:** 2

1. China Mobile Ltd.
2. China Unicom Ltd.

Source: *Forbes*, Forbes 2000 (annual), http://www.forbes.com, May 7, 2012.

4607 ■ HONG KONG'S MOST VALUABLE TELECOMMUNICATION BRANDS, 2011

Ranked by: Brand value, in millions of U.S. dollars. **Remarks:** Also notes rank within the *Global 500* for current and previous year, figures for current and previous year, and brand rating. Ranking is available online only. **Number listed:** 2

1. China Mobile, with $17,919 million
2. China Unicom, $7,944

Source: *Global 500*, (annual), Brand Finance plc, March 2012.

4608 ■ INDIA'S LARGEST TELECOMMUNICATIONS SERVICES COMPANIES OVERALL, 2011

Ranked by: Score based on revenue, profits, assets, and market capitalization. **Remarks:** Specific scores not provided. Also notes overall rank in the *Forbes 2000* and figures for each criterion. **Number listed:** 2

1. Bharti Airtel Ltd.
2. Reliance Communications

Source: *Forbes*, Forbes 2000 (annual), http://www.forbes.com, May 7, 2012.

4609 ■ JAPAN'S LARGEST TELECOMMUNICATIONS SERVICES COMPANIES OVERALL, 2011

Ranked by: Score based on revenue, profits, assets, and market capitalization. **Remarks:** Specific scores not provided. Also notes overall rank in the *Forbes 2000* and figures for each criterion. **Number listed:** 3

1. Nippon Telegraph & Telephone Corp. (NTT)
2. Softbank Corp.
3. KDDI Corp.

Source: *Forbes*, Forbes 2000 (annual), http://www.forbes.com, May 7, 2012.

4610 ■ JAPAN'S MOST VALUABLE TELECOMMUNICATION BRANDS, 2011

Ranked by: Brand value, in millions of U.S. dollars. **Remarks:** Also notes rank within the *Global 500* for current and previous year, figures for current and previous year, and brand rating. Ranking is available online only. **Number listed:** 3

1. NTT Group, with $26,324 million
2. SoftBank, $6,841
3. au, $5,072

Source: *Global 500*, (annual), Brand Finance plc, March 2012.

4611 ■ LARGEST TELECOMMUNICATIONS COMPANIES IN EUROPE, 2010

Ranked by: Sales, in millions of U.S. dollars. **Remarks:** Also notes rank within country. **Number listed:** 100

1. Deutsche Telekom AG (Germany), with $96,076.1 million
2. Vodafone Group plc (U.K.), $66,708
3. Vivendi SA (France), $35,790
4. France Telecom SA (France), $33,462
5. Telecom Italia SpA (Italy), $31,423
6. BT Group plc (U.K.), $31,288.5
7. Koninklijke KPN NV (Royal KPN NV, Netherlands), $20,004.3
8. Telefonica de Espana SA (Spain), $16,727.5
9. TeliaSonera AB (Sweden), $15,566.4
10. Orange France (France), $15,449

Source: *Europe's 15,000 Largest Companies*, (annual), ELC International, 2011, p. 48.

4612 ■ LARGEST U.S. TELECOMMUNICATIONS SERVICES COMPANIES OVERALL, 2011

Ranked by: Score based on revenue, profits, assets, and market capitalization. **Remarks:** Specific scores not provided. Also notes overall rank in the *Forbes 2000* and figures for each criterion. **Number listed:** 9

1. AT&T Inc.
2. Verizon Communications Inc.
3. CenturyLink Inc.
4. Sprint Nextel Corp.
5. Virgin Media Inc.
6. Crown Castle International Corp.
7. Windstream Corp.
8. Frontier Communications Corp.
9. Level 3 Communications Inc.

Source: *Forbes*, Forbes 2000 (annual), http://www.forbes.com, May 7, 2012.

4613 ■ MEXICO'S MOST VALUABLE TELECOMMUNICATION BRANDS, 2011

Ranked by: Brand value, in millions of U.S. dollars. **Remarks:** Also notes rank within the *Global 500* for current and previous year, figures for current and previous year, and brand rating. Ranking is available online only. **Number listed:** 2

1. Claro, with $5,721 million
2. Telcel, $3,756

Source: *Global 500*, (annual), Brand Finance plc, March 2012.

4614 ■ MOST POWERFUL ARABS IN TELECOMMUNICATION, 2012

Ranked by: Score based on scope of influence. **Remarks:** Specific scores not provided. Also notes rank in the overall *Power 500*. **Number listed:** 16

1. Mohammed Omran
2. Saad Al Barrak
3. Osman Sultan
4. Nasser Marafih
5. Habib Haddad
6. Nabeel Bin Salamah
7. Fawaz Zu'bi
8. Hessa Al Jaber
9. Ahmad Julfar
10. Khalid Al Kaf

Source: *Arabian Business*, Power 500 (annual), June 4, 2012.

4615 ■ MOST PROFITABLE CANADIAN TELECOMMUNICATIONS COMPANIES, 2011

Ranked by: Profits, in millions of Canadian dollars. **Number listed:** 6

1. BCE Inc., with C$2,340 million
2. Rogers Communications Inc., C$1,563
3. Telus Corp., C$1,219
4. Bell Aliant Inc., C$323
5. Manitoba Telecom Services Inc., C$167
6. Phonetime Inc., C$3

Source: *Canadian Business*, Investor 500 (annual), 2012, p. 55.

4616 ■ MOST VALUABLE U.S. FIXED-LINE TELECOMMUNICATIONS COMPANIES, 2011

Ranked by: Market value as of March 2011, in millions of U.S. dollars. **Remarks:** Also notes rank within the *FT U.S. 500*, rank for previous year, country, revenue, net income, assets, number of employees, share price, price-to-earning ratio, dividend yield, and fiscal yearend. **Number listed:** 8

1. AT&T Inc., with $180,948.8 million
2. Verizon Communications Inc., $107,911.9
3. CenturyTel Inc., $12,698.1
4. Qwest Communications International Inc., $12,065.4
5. Leucadia National Corp., $9,152.6
6. Virgin Media Inc., $8,948.7
7. Frontier Communications Corp., $8,180.8
8. Windstream Corp., $5,568.6

Source: *Financial Times*, FT 500 (annual), http://www.ft.com, June 24, 2011.

4617 ■ MOST VALUABLE U.S. MOBILE TELECOMMUNICATIONS COMPANIES, 2011

Ranked by: Market value as of March 2011, in millions of U.S. dollars. **Remarks:** Also notes rank within the *FT U.S. 500*, rank for previous year, country, revenue, net income, assets, number of employees, share price, price-to-earning ratio, dividend yield, and fiscal yearend. **Number listed:** 6

1. American Tower Corp., with $20,604.3 million
2. Sprint Nextel Corp., $13,875.5
3. Crown Castle International Corp., $12,377.3
4. Millicom International Cellular SA, $10,487.6
5. NII Holdings Inc., $7,072.2
6. MetroPCS Communications Inc., $5,791.6

Source: *Financial Times*, FT 500 (annual), http://www.ft.com, June 24, 2011.

4618 ■ THE NETHERLANDS' LARGEST TELECOMMUNICATIONS SERVICES COMPANIES OVERALL, 2011

Ranked by: Score based on revenue, profits, assets, and market capitalization. **Remarks:** Specific scores not provided. Also notes overall rank in the *Forbes 2000* and figures for each criterion. **Number listed:** 2

1. Koninklijke KPN NV (Royal KPN NV)
2. VimpelCom Ltd.

Source: *Forbes*, Forbes 2000 (annual), http://www.forbes.com, May 7, 2012.

4619 ■ THE RUSSIAN FEDERATION'S MOST VALUABLE TELECOMMUNICATION BRANDS, 2011

Ranked by: Brand value, in millions of U.S. dollars. **Remarks:** Also notes rank within the *Global 500* for current and previous year, figures for current and previous year, and brand rating. Ranking is available online only. **Number listed:** 3

1. Beeline, with $4,707 million
2. Rostelecom, $4,510
3. MTS, $3,491

Source: *Global 500*, (annual), Brand Finance plc, March 2012.

4620 ■ RUSSIA'S LARGEST TELECOMMUNICATIONS SERVICES COMPANIES OVERALL, 2011

Ranked by: Score based on revenue, profits, assets, and market capitalization. **Remarks:** Specific scores not provided. Also notes overall rank in the *Forbes 2000* and figures for each criterion. **Number listed:** 2

1. Sistema JSFC
2. Rostelecom

Source: *Forbes*, Forbes 2000 (annual), http://www.forbes.com, May 7, 2012.

4621 ■ SAUDI ARABIA'S LARGEST TELECOMMUNICATIONS SERVICES COMPANIES OVERALL, 2011

Ranked by: Score based on revenue, profits, assets, and market capitalization. **Remarks:** Specific scores not provided. Also notes overall rank in the *Forbes 2000* and figures for each criterion. **Number listed:** 2

1. Saudi Telecom Co.
2. Mobily

Source: *Forbes*, Forbes 2000 (annual), http://www.forbes.com, May 7, 2012.

4622 ■ SOUTH KOREA'S LARGEST TELECOMMUNICATIONS SERVICES COMPANIES OVERALL, 2011

Ranked by: Score based on revenue, profits, assets, and market capitalization. **Remarks:** Specific scores not provided. Also notes overall rank in the *Forbes 2000* and figures for each criterion. **Number listed:** 3

1. SK Telecom Co., Ltd.
2. KT Corp.
3. LG Uplus Corp.

Source: *Forbes*, Forbes 2000 (annual), http://www.forbes.com, May 7, 2012.

4623 ■ SPAIN'S MOST VALUABLE TELECOMMUNICATION BRANDS, 2011

Ranked by: Brand value, in millions of U.S. dollars. **Remarks:** Also notes rank within the *Global 500* for current and previous

year, figures for current and previous year, and brand rating. Ranking is available online only. **Number listed:** 2

1. Movistar, with $14,412 million
2. O2, $6,773

Source: *Global 500*, (annual), Brand Finance plc, March 2012.

4624 ■ SWEDEN'S LARGEST TELECOMMUNICATIONS SERVICES COMPANIES OVERALL, 2011

Ranked by: Score based on revenue, profits, assets, and market capitalization. **Remarks:** Specific scores not provided. Also notes overall rank in the *Forbes 2000* and figures for each criterion. **Number listed:** 2

1. TeliaSonera AB
2. Tele2 AB

Source: *Forbes*, Forbes 2000 (annual), http://www.forbes.com, May 7, 2012.

4625 ■ SWEDEN'S MOST VALUABLE TELECOMMUNICATION BRANDS, 2011

Ranked by: Brand value, in millions of U.S. dollars. **Remarks:** Also notes rank within the *Global 500* for current and previous year, figures for current and previous year, and brand rating. Ranking is available online only. **Number listed:** 2

1. Ericsson, with $6,735 million
2. Telia, $2,648

Source: *Global 500*, (annual), Brand Finance plc, March 2012.

4626 ■ TAIWAN'S LARGEST TELECOMMUNICATIONS SERVICES COMPANIES OVERALL, 2011

Ranked by: Score based on revenue, profits, assets, and market capitalization. **Remarks:** Specific scores not provided. Also notes overall rank in the *Forbes 2000* and figures for each criterion. **Number listed:** 2

1. Chunghwa Telecom Co.
2. Taiwan Mobile Co., Ltd.

Source: *Forbes*, Forbes 2000 (annual), http://www.forbes.com, May 7, 2012.

4627 ■ TAIWAN'S MOST VALUABLE TELECOMMUNICATION BRANDS, 2011

Ranked by: Brand value, in millions of U.S. dollars. **Remarks:** Also notes rank within the *Global 500* for current and previous year, figures for current and previous year, and brand rating. Ranking is available online only. **Number listed:** 2

1. HTC, with $4,106 million
2. Chunghwa Telecom, $2,418

Source: *Global 500*, (annual), Brand Finance plc, March 2012.

4628 ■ TEXAS'S LARGEST TELECOMMUNICATIONS SERVICES COMPANIES OVERALL, 2011

Ranked by: Score based on revenue, profits, assets, and market capitalization. **Remarks:** Specific scores not provided. Also notes overall rank in the *Forbes 2000* and figures for each criterion. **Number listed:** 2

1. AT&T Inc.
2. Crown Castle International Corp.

Source: *Forbes*, Forbes 2000 (annual), http://www.forbes.com, May 7, 2012.

4629 ■ TOP *FORTUNE 500* COMPANIES IN TELECOMMUNICATIONS, 2011

Ranked by: Revenue, in millions of dollars. **Remarks:** Also notes overall rank in the *Fortune 500;* profits; profits as a percentage of revenue; stockholders' equity; and rank by each criterion. **Number listed:** 15

1. AT&T Inc., with $126,723 million
2. Verizon Communications Inc., $110,875
3. Comcast Corp., $55,842
4. Sprint Nextel Corp., $33,679
5. The DirecTV Group Inc., $27,226
6. Time Warner Cable Inc., $19,675
7. CenturyLink, $15,351
8. Dish Network Corp., $14,048
9. Liberty Global Inc., $10,247
10. Cablevision Systems Corp., $7,252

Source: *Fortune*, Fortune 500 (annual), May 21, 2012, p. F-39.

4630 ■ TURKEY'S LARGEST TELECOMMUNICATIONS SERVICES COMPANIES OVERALL, 2011

Ranked by: Score based on revenue, profits, assets, and market capitalization. Remarks: Specific scores not provided. Also notes overall rank in the *Forbes 2000* and figures for each criterion. Number listed: 2

1. Turk Telekomunikasyon AS
2. Turkcell Iletisim Hizmetleri AS

Source: *Forbes*, Forbes 2000 (annual), http://www.forbes.com, May 7, 2012.

4631 ■ UNITED KINGDOM'S LARGEST TELECOMMUNICATIONS SERVICES COMPANIES OVERALL, 2011

Ranked by: Score based on revenue, profits, assets, and market capitalization. Remarks: Specific scores not provided. Also notes overall rank in the *Forbes 2000* and figures for each criterion. Number listed: 2

1. Vodafone Group plc
2. BT Group plc

Source: *Forbes*, Forbes 2000 (annual), http://www.forbes.com, May 7, 2012.

4632 ■ THE UNITED KINGDOM'S MOST VALUABLE TELECOMMUNICATION BRANDS, 2011

Ranked by: Brand value, in millions of U.S. dollars. Remarks: Also notes rank within the *Global 500* for current and previous year, figures for current and previous year, and brand rating. Ranking is available online only. Number listed: 2

1. Vodafone, with $30,044 million
2. BT, $9,820

Source: *Global 500*, (annual), Brand Finance plc, March 2012.

4633 ■ THE UNITED STATES' MOST VALUABLE TELECOMMUNICATION BRANDS, 2011

Ranked by: Brand value, in millions of U.S. dollars. Remarks: Also notes rank within the *Global 500* for current and previous year, figures for current and previous year, and brand rating. Ranking is available online only. Number listed: 8

1. AT&T, with $28,379 million
2. Verizon, $27,616
3. Cisco, $12,865
4. CenturyLink, $5,181
5. Virgin Media, $4,764
6. Sprint (Nextel), $3,680
7. Motorola, $2,940
8. Qualcomm, $2,397

Source: *Global 500*, (annual), Brand Finance plc, March 2012.

4634 ■ WORLD'S LARGEST TELECOMMUNICATIONS SERVICES COMPANIES OVERALL, 2011

Ranked by: Score based on revenue, profits, assets, and market capitalization. Remarks: Specific scores not provided. Also notes country, overall rank in the *Forbes 2000,* and figures for each criterion. Number listed: 62

1. Vodafone Group plc
2. China Mobile Ltd.
3. AT&T Inc.
4. Nippon Telegraph & Telephone Corp. (NTT)
5. Telefonica SA
6. Verizon Communications Inc.
7. France Telecom SA
8. America Movil, SA de CV
9. China Telecom Corp., Ltd.
10. Telecom Italia SpA

Source: *Forbes*, Forbes 2000 (annual), http://www.forbes.com, May 7, 2012.

4635 ■ WORLD'S MOST ADMIRED TELECOMMUNICATIONS COMPANIES, 2012

Ranked by: Score, on a scale of 10, based on a survey of executives, directors, and securities analysts of companies within their own industry on eight criteria: innovation, financial soundness, employee talent, use of corporate assets, long-term investment value, social responsibility, quality of management, and quality of products/services. Remarks: Specific scores not provided. Also notes rank for previous year. Number listed: 9

1. Verizon Communications Inc.
2. AT&T Inc.
3. Telefonica SA
4. Vodafone Group plc
5. Nippon Telegraph & Telephone Corp. (NTT)
6. Comcast Corp.
7. America Movil, SA de CV
8. Deutsche Telekom AG
9. KDDI Corp.

Source: *Fortune*, World's Most Admired Companies (annual), March 19, 2012, p. 147.

4636 ■ WORLD'S MOST ETHICAL TELECOMMUNICATION EQUIPMENT COMPANIES, 2012

Ranked by: Score based on five criteria: ethics and compliance program; reputation, leadership, and innovation; governance; corporate citizenship and responsibility; and culture of ethics. Remarks: Specific scores not provided; companies are listed alphabetically, not ranked. Number listed: 2

1. Cisco Systems Inc. (U.S.)
2. Juniper Networks Inc. (U.S.)

Source: *Ethisphere Magazine*, World's Most Ethical Companies (annual), http://www.ethisphere.com, 2012.

4637 ■ WORLD'S MOST ETHICAL TELECOMMUNICATION SERVICES COMPANIES, 2012

Ranked by: Score based on five criteria: ethics and compliance program; reputation, leadership, and innovation; governance; corporate citizenship and responsibility; and culture of ethics. Remarks: Specific scores not provided; companies are listed alphabetically, not ranked. Number listed: 3

1. Portugal Telecom (Portugal)

2. Singapore Telecommunications Ltd. (Singapore)

3. T-Mobile USA Inc. (U.S.)

Source: *Ethisphere Magazine*, World's Most Ethical Companies (annual), http://www.ethisphere.com, 2012.

4638 ■ WORLD'S MOST VALUABLE FIXED-LINE TELECOMMUNICATIONS COMPANIES, 2011

Ranked by: Market value as of March 2011, in millions of U.S. dollars. **Remarks:** Also notes rank within the *FT 500*, rank for previous year, country, revenue, net income, assets, number of employees, share price, price-to-earning ratio, dividend yield, and fiscal year-end. **Number listed:** 13

1. AT&T Inc., with $180,948.8 million

2. Telefonica SA, $114,411.3

3. Verizon Communications Inc., $107,911.9

4. Nippon Telegraph & Telephone Corp. (NTT), $65,284

5. France Telecom SA, $59,428.3

6. Telstra Corp., Ltd., $36,288.2

7. Telecom Italia SpA, $28,759.9

8. BCE Inc., $27,245.4

9. Koninklijke KPN NV (Royal KPN NV), $26,068.1

10. Chunghwa Telecom Co., $24,154.1

Source: *Financial Times*, FT 500 (annual), http://www.ft.com, June 24, 2011.

4639 ■ WORLD'S MOST VALUABLE MOBILE TELECOMMUNICATIONS COMPANIES, 2011

Ranked by: Market value as of March 2011, in millions of U.S. dollars. **Remarks:** Also notes rank within the *FT 500*, rank for previous year, country, revenue, net income, assets, number of employees, share price, price-to-earning ratio, dividend yield, and fiscal year-end. **Number listed:** 16

1. China Mobile (Hong Kong) Ltd., with $184,842.3 million

2. Vodafone Group plc, $145,923.3

3. America Movil, SAB de CV, $81,595.4

4. NTT DoCoMo Inc., $76,998.4

5. Deutsche Telekom AG, $66,658.6

6. Softbank Corp., $43,363.8

7. China Unicom Ltd., $39,138.1

8. Singapore Telecommunications Ltd., $38,179.9

9. MTN Group Ltd., $38,075.7

10. TeliaSonera AB, $37,443

Source: *Financial Times*, FT 500 (annual), http://www.ft.com, June 24, 2011.

4640 ■ WORLD'S MOST VALUABLE TELECOMMUNICATION PROVIDER BRANDS, 2012

Ranked by: Brand value, a measure of a brand's earnings and contribution, in millions of U.S. dollars. **Remarks:** Also notes annual growth in brand value and rank by brand contribution and brand momentum. **Number listed:** 10

1. AT&T, with $68,870 million

2. Verizon, $49,151

3. China Mobile, $47,041

4. Vodafone, $43,033

5. Deutsche Telekom, $26,837

6. Movistar, $17,113

7. NTT DoCoMo, $15,981

8. Orange, $15,351

9. Airtel, $11,531

10. Telecom Italia, $9,572

Source: *Financial Times*, Global Brands (annual), http://www.ft.com, May 22, 2012.

4641 ■ WORLD'S TOP TELECOM BRANDS, 2011

Ranked by: Brand value, in millions of U.S dollars. **Remarks:** Also notes rank and figures for previous year, country, and brand rating. **Number listed:** 500

1. Vodafone, with $30,674 million

2. AT & T, $28,884

3. Verizon, $27,293

4. NTT Group, $26,927

5. China Mobile, $19,317

6. Orange, $18,622

7. Movistar, $14,935

8. Cisco, $11,667

9. NTT DoCoMo, $9,801

10. Nokia, $9,658

Source: *Top 500 Telecom Brands*, (annual), Brand Finance plc, 2011.

Telecommunications Services

4642 ■ AMERICA'S LARGEST PRIVATE TELECOMMUNICATIONS SERVICE COMPANIES, 2010

Ranked by: Revenue, in billions of dollars. **Remarks:** Also notes headquarters, number of employees, and overall rank in the *America's Largest Private Companies* list. Ranking is available online only, not in print. **Number listed:** 2

1. Avaya Inc., with $5.3 billion

2. Brightstar Corp., $4.61

Source: *Forbes*, America's Largest Private Companies (annual), http://www.forbes.com, December 5, 2011.

4643 ■ BEST SMALL TELECOMMUNICATIONS SERVICE COMPANIES IN AMERICA, 2011

Ranked by: Score based on revenue, profits, and return on equity for the past 12 months and five years. **Remarks:** Specific scores not provided. Also notes rank in the overall *100 Best Small Companies in America*. To qualify, companies must have revenues between $5 million and $1 billion, a net margin above five percent, and share price above $5. List is available online only. **Number listed:** 5

1. Neutral Tandem

2. AboveNet

3. j2 Global Communications

4. Hickory Tech

5. Atlantic Tele-Network

Source: *Forbes*, Best Small Companies in America (annual), November 7, 2011.

4644 ■ FASTEST-GROWING PRIVATE TELECOMMUNICATIONS COMPANIES IN THE U.S., 2007-2010

Ranked by: Average annual sales growth over three years, in percent. **Remarks:** Also notes headquarters, revenue, and rank in

the overall *Inc. 500*. To qualify, private companies must have had annual revenues of at least $100,000 in 2007 and $2 million in 2010. **Number listed:** 17

1. One Source Networks, with 10,305.5%
2. Phone Power, 6,337.1%
3. Link America, 3,224.4%
4. Star2Star Communications, 1,555.9%
5. CFN Services, 1,517.8%
6. CallingMart, 1,473.5%
7. TeleQuality Communications, 1,376.9%
8. Network Solutions Provider, 1,101.7%
9. Access Media 3, 1,068.9%
10. QuadGen Wireless Solutions, 1,006.4%

Source: *Inc.*, Inc. 500 (annual), September 2011, p. 198-200.

4645 ■ NEW YORK'S LARGEST TELECOMMUNICATION SERVICES COMPANIES OVERALL, 2011

Ranked by: Score based on revenue, profits, assets, and market capitalization. **Remarks:** Specific scores not provided. Also notes overall rank in the *Forbes 2000* and figures for each criterion. **Number listed:** 2

1. Verizon Communications Inc.
2. Virgin Media

Source: *Forbes*, Forbes 2000 (annual), http://www.forbes.com, May 7, 2012.

Telecommuting

4646 ■ AMERICA'S BEST COMPANIES IN TELECOMMUTING, 2012

Ranked by: Percentage of employees who regularly telecommute. **Remarks:** Also notes overall rank in the *100 Best Companies to Work For*. **Number listed:** 85

1. Cisco Systems Inc., with 90%
2. Baptist Health South Florida, 88%
3. Accenture Ltd., 81%
4. Teach For America Inc., 80%
4. Intel Corp., 80%
6. World Wide Technology, 70%
6. PricewaterhouseCoopers LLP, 70%
8. Ultimate Software, 50%
9. Perkins Cole, 45%
10. American Fidelity Assurance Co., 40%

Source: *Fortune*, 100 Best Companies to Work For (annual), http://www.fortune.com, February 6, 2012.

Telephone
See also: **Telecommunications Industry**

4647 ■ TOP BRANDS OF HOME TELEPHONE SYSTEMS, 2010

Ranked by: Popularity among *CE Pro 100* companies, in percent. **Number listed:** 3

1. Panasonic, with 66%
2. NEC, 6%
3. Cisco, 5%

Source: *CE Pro*, Brand Analysis (annual), June 2011, p. 58.

Television Advertising

4648 ■ TOP ADVERTISERS ON NETWORK TELEVISION, 2010

Ranked by: Measured advertising spending, in millions of dollars. **Remarks:** Also notes percent change from previous year. **Number listed:** 10

1. AT&T Inc., with $869.8 million
2. Procter & Gamble Co., $708.5
3. General Motors Co., $679.4
4. Verizon Communications Inc., $603.6
5. Ford Motor Co., $575.2
6. Pfizer Inc., $505
7. Sprint Nextel Corp., $453.1
8. Toyota Motor Corp., $447.7
9. Time Warner Inc., $411
10. McDonald's Corp., $380.6

Source: *Advertising Age*, Leading National Advertisers (annual), June 20, 2011, p. 16.

4649 ■ TOP ADVERTISERS ON SPOT TELEVISION, 2010

Ranked by: Measured advertising spending, in millions of dollars. **Remarks:** Also notes percent change from previous year. **Number listed:** 10

1. Fiat, with $371.3 million
2. AT&T Inc., $334.8
3. Honda Motor Co., Ltd., $274
4. Comcast Corp., $265.1
5. Verizon Communications Inc., $254.5
6. General Mills Inc., $222.4
7. General Motors Co., $188
8. Time Warner Cable Inc., $142
9. McDonald's Corp., $139.2
10. Toyota Motor Corp., $135.4

Source: *Advertising Age*, Leading National Advertisers (annual), June 20, 2011, p. 16-17.

Television Broadcasting

4650 ■ TOP BROADCAST TELEVISION COMPANIES IN THE U.S., 2010

Ranked by: Net U.S. broadcast television revenue, in millions of dollars. **Remarks:** Also notes rank and figures for previous year, percent change, and top broadcast property. **Number listed:** 10

1. CBS Corp., with $5,815 million
2. Comcast Corp., $4,813
3. News Corp., $4,778
4. Walt Disney Co., $4,000
5. Univision Communications Inc., $1,769
6. Gannett Co., Inc., $770
7. Tribune Co., $767
8. Sinclair Broadcast Group Inc., $731
9. Hearst Corp., $711
10. Belo Corp., $649

Source: *Advertising Age*, 100 Leading Media Companies (annual), October 3, 2011, p. 52.

Television Networks

4651 ■ LARGEST TV STATION GROUPS, 2011

Ranked by: Revenue, in thousands of dollars. **Remarks:** Also notes headquarters, coverage, ownership, portfolio, programming on main channels, affiliations on subchannels, key executives, and comments. **Number listed:** 30

1. Fox Television Stations, with $1,611,700 thousand
2. CBS Television Stations, $1,466,425
3. NBC Universal, $1,224,013
4. ABC, $1,019,875
5. Tribune Broadcasting, $792,750
6. Sinclair Broadcast Group, $732,300
7. Gannett Broadcasting, $727,025
8. Hearst Television, $678,250
9. Belo Corp., $661,425
10. Univision Communications, $655,025

Source: *TVNewsCheck*, BIA/Kelsey Top 30 (annual), NewsCheck-Media LLC, April 15, 2012.

Television Programs

4652 ■ TOP REGULARLY SCHEDULED TV SERIES OF THE YEAR, 2011

Ranked by: Number of viewers. **Remarks:** Also notes network. **Number listed:** 15

1. "American Idol" (Wed.), with 23.9 million
2. "American Idol" (Thurs.), 22
3. "Dancing with the Stars," 19.7
4. "Dancing with the Stars" Results Show, 16.7
5. "NCIS," 15
6. "America's Got Talent" (Tues.), 12.6
7. "NCIS: Los Angeles," 12.5
8. "2 Broke Girls," 12.1
9. "The Voice," 11.9
9. "America's Got Talent" (Wed.), 11.9

Source: *Entertainment Weekly*, The Year in Charts (annual), December 2011, p. 119.

Temporary Help Service Agencies

4653 ■ TOP *FORTUNE 500* COMPANIES IN TEMPORARY HELP, 2011

Ranked by: Revenue, in millions of dollars. **Remarks:** Also notes overall rank in the *Fortune 500;* profits; profits as a percentage of revenue; stockholders' equity; and rank by each criterion. **Number listed:** 2

1. Manpower Inc., with $22,006 million
2. Kelly Services Inc., $5,551

Source: *Fortune*, Fortune 500 (annual), May 21, 2012, p. F-39.

4654 ■ WORLD'S MOST ADMIRED TEMPORARY HELP COMPANIES, 2012

Ranked by: Score, on a scale of 10, based on a survey of executives, directors, and securities analysts of companies within their own industry on eight criteria: innovation, financial soundness, employee talent, use of corporate assets, long-term investment value, social responsibility, quality of management, and quality of products/services. **Remarks:** Specific scores not provided. Also notes rank for previous year. **Number listed:** 3

1. Robert Half International Inc.
2. Manpower Inc.
3. Randstad Holding NV

Source: *Fortune*, World's Most Admired Companies (annual), March 19, 2012, p. 148.

Terrorism

4655 ■ COUNTRIES WITH THE HIGHEST BUSINESS COSTS OF TERRORISM, 2011

Ranked by: Score, on a scale of seven, based on the level of business costs associated with the threat of terrorism. **Number listed:** 142

1. Colombia, with 2.9 points
2. Pakistan, 3.0
3. Nepal, 3.6
3. Yemen, 3.6
5. Uganda, 3.7
6. Lebanon, 3.8
6. Egypt, 3.8
8. Algeria, 3.9
9. Turkey, 4.0
9. Kenya, 4.0
9. El Salvador, 4.0

Source: *Global Competitiveness Report*, (annual), World Economic Forum, 2011, p. 402.

4656 ■ COUNTRIES WITH THE LOWEST BUSINESS COSTS OF TERRORISM, 2011

Ranked by: Score, on a scale of seven, based on the level of business costs associated with the threat of terrorism. **Number listed:** 142

1. Slovenia, with 6.8 points
2. Syria, 6.7
2. Iceland, 6.7
2. Finland, 6.7
2. Uruguay, 6.7
6. Austria, 6.5
6. Montenegro, 6.5
8. Saudi Arabia, 6.4
8. Mongolia, 6.4
8. Brunei Darussalam, 6.4
8. Estonia, 6.4
8. Oman, 6.4
8. Bosnia & Herzegovina, 6.4

Source: *Global Competitiveness Report*, (annual), World Economic Forum, 2011, p. 402.

Textile Industry

4657 ■ LARGEST TEXTILE MILL COMPANIES BY EMPLOYEES, 2010

Ranked by: Total number of employees. **Remarks:** Also notes contact information for headquarters, number of employees at headquarters, revenue, rank by revenue, and primary SIC code. **Number listed:** 49

1. Hanesbrands Inc., with 55,500 employees
2. Mohawk Industries Inc., 27,400
3. Shaw Industries Inc., 26,000
4. Fruit of the Loom Inc., 23,000
4. Union Underwear Co., 23,000
6. Mohawk Carpet LLC, 20,431
7. Aladdin Manufacturing Corp., 17,000
8. TK Holdings Inc., 16,900
9. BP Amoco Chemical Co., 14,700
10. Russell Brands LLC, 14,288

Source: *Business Rankings*, (annual), Dun & Bradstreet Inc., 2011, p. VI.50-VI.51.

4658 ■ LARGEST TEXTILE MILL COMPANIES BY SALES, 2010

Ranked by: Total revenue, in dollars. **Remarks:** Also notes contact information for headquarters, number of employees at headquarters and overall, rank by employees, and primary SIC code. **Number listed:** 50

1. Mohawk Industries Inc., with $5,319,072,000
2. Hanesbrands Inc., $4,326,713,000
3. Federal Prison Industries Inc., $983,227,000
4. Interface Inc., $961,827,000
5. Albany International Corp., $914,356,000
6. Unifi Inc., $616,753,000
7. Royal Ten Cate USA Inc., $566,660,000
8. Xerium Technologies Inc., $548,334,000
9. National Presto Industries Inc., $479,000,000
10. Propex Operating Co., $400,000,000

Source: *Business Rankings*, (annual), Dun & Bradstreet Inc., 2011, p. V.50-V.51.

4659 ■ LARGEST U.S. TEXTILE MANUFACTURERS, 2010

Ranked by: Revenue, in millions of dollars. **Remarks:** Also notes overall rank within the *IW 500,* revenue growth, and profit margin. **Number listed:** 4

1. Mohawk Industries Inc., with $5,319 million
2. Hanesbrands Inc., $4,327
3. Interface Inc., $962
4. Albany International Corp., $914

Source: *IndustryWeek*, IW 500 (annual), http://www.industryweek.com, July 2011.

4660 ■ WORLD'S LARGEST TEXTILE PRODUCT MANUFACTURERS, 2010

Ranked by: Revenue, in millions of dollars. **Remarks:** Also notes rank for previous year, overall rank within the *IW 1000,* country, and revenue growth. **Number listed:** 10

1. Reliance Industries Ltd., with $49,408 million
2. Formosa Chemicals & Fiber Corp., $13,160
3. Hyosung Corp., $10,432
4. Far Eastern New Century Corp., $6,867
5. Kolon Corp., $6,580

6. Daiwabo Holdings Co., Ltd., $5,522
7. Mohawk Industries Inc., $5,319
8. Cheil Industries Inc., $4,609
9. Hanesbrands Inc., $4,327
10. Toyobo Co., Ltd., $3,921

Source: *IndustryWeek*, IW 1000 (annual), http://www.industryweek.com, August 2011.

Thermoformers

4661 ■ LARGEST THERMOFORMERS IN NORTH AMERICA, 2011

Ranked by: Thermoforming sales, in millions of dollars. **Remarks:** Also notes headquarters and top thermoforming official. **Number listed:** 227

1. Pactiv Foodservice, with $3,200 million
2. Solo Cup Co., $790
3. Dart Container Corp., $480
4. Genpak LLC, $455
5. Berry Plastics Corp., $450
6. Sonoco Plastics Thermoforming, $330
7. D & W Fine Pack LLC, $310
8. Fabri-Kal Corp., $300
9. Anchor Packaging Inc., $211
10. Tekni-Plex Inc., $205

Source: *Plastics News*, North American Thermoformers (annual), http://www.plasticsnews.com, March 5, 2012.

Third-Party Logistics Services
See: **Contract Logistics Services**

Thrift Institutions
See also: **Savings and Loan Associations**

4662 ■ LARGEST U.S. THRIFTS AND MORTGAGE FINANCE COMPANIES OVERALL, 2011

Ranked by: Score based on revenue, profits, assets, and market capitalization. **Remarks:** Specific scores not provided. Also notes overall rank in the *Forbes 2000* and figures for each criterion. **Number listed:** 4

1. New York Community Bancorp Inc.
2. Hudson City Bancorp Inc.
3. People's United Financial Inc.
4. First Niagara Financial Group Inc.

Source: *Forbes*, Forbes 2000 (annual), http://www.forbes.com, May 7, 2012.

4663 ■ NEW YORK'S LARGEST THRIFTS AND MORTGAGE FINANCE COMPANIES OVERALL, 2011

Ranked by: Score based on revenue, profits, assets, and market capitalization. **Remarks:** Specific scores not provided. Also notes overall rank in the *Forbes 2000* and figures for each criterion. **Number listed:** 2

1. New York Community Bancorp Inc.
2. First Niagara Financial Group Inc.

Source: *Forbes*, Forbes 2000 (annual), http://www.forbes.com, May 7, 2012.

4664 ■ WORLD'S LARGEST THRIFTS AND MORTGAGE FINANCE COMPANIES OVERALL, 2011

Ranked by: Score based on revenue, profits, assets, and market capitalization. **Remarks:** Specific scores not provided. Also notes country, overall rank in the *Forbes 2000,* and figures for each criterion. **Number listed:** 4

1. New York Community Bancorp Inc.
2. Hudson City Bancorp Inc.
3. People's United Financial Inc.
4. First Niagara Financial Group Inc.

Source: *Forbes*, Forbes 2000 (annual), http://www.forbes.com, May 7, 2012.

Tire Industry

4665 ■ LARGEST U.S. AND CANADIAN TIRE MANUFACTURERS, 2011

Ranked by: New tire sales, in billions of U.S. dollars. **Remarks:** Also notes figures for previous year. **Number listed:** 11

1. Bridgestone/Firestone, with $11.1 billion
2. Goodyear Tire & Rubber Co., $9.3
3. Michelin North America Inc., $8.5
4. Cooper Tire & Rubber Co., $2.7
5. Continental Tire, the Americas, $2.6
6. Yokohama Tire Corp., $1.5
7. Sumitomo Rubber Industries Ltd., $1.3
8. Hankook Tire America Corp., $1.2
9. Toyo Tire Holdings of Americas Inc., $1
10. Kumho Tire U.S.A. Inc., $0.81

Source: *Modern Tire Dealer*, Facts Issue (annual), January 2012, p. 34.

4666 ■ TOP CANADIAN REPLACEMENT TIRE BRANDS FOR LIGHT TRUCKS, 2011

Ranked by: Market share, in percent. **Number listed:** 20

1. Goodyear, with 16%
2. Michelin, 12%
3. Motomaster, 10%
4. BFGoodrich, 9%
5. Bridgestone, 8.5%
6. Firestone, 5.5%
6. Yokohama, 5.5%
8. Hankook, 5%
9. General, 4.5%
10. Toyo, 4%

Source: *Modern Tire Dealer*, Facts Issue (annual), January 2011, p. 32.

4667 ■ TOP CANADIAN REPLACEMENT TIRE BRANDS FOR PASSENGER VEHICLES, 2011

Ranked by: Market share, in percent. **Number listed:** 24

1. Motomaster, with 13%

2. Michelin, 12%
3. Goodyear, 10%
4. Bridgestone, 8%
5. BFGoodrich, 6%
5. Hankook, 6%
7. General, 4%
8. Firestone, 3.5%
8. Nexen, 3.5%
8. Toyo, 3.5%
8. Yokohama, 3.5%

Source: *Modern Tire Dealer*, Facts Issue (annual), January 2012, p. 32.

4668 ■ TOP INDEPENDENT TIRE STORE CHAINS, 2010

Ranked by: Total number of outlets. **Remarks:** Also notes headquarters, website, tire brands, chief officer, and breakdown by outlets by type. **Number listed:** 100

1. TBC Corp., with 837 outlets
2. Discount Tire Co., 800
3. Les Schwab Tire Centers, 430
4. Monro Muffler Brake Inc., 291
5. Mavis Discount Tire, 120
6. Somerset Tire Service Inc., 118
7. Town Fair Tire Centers Inc., 84
8. Belle Tire Distributors Inc., 81
9. Rent-A-Wheel/Rent-A-Tire Inc., 80
10. Pomp's Tire Service, 71

Source: *Modern Tire Dealer*, MTD 100 (annual), July 2011, p. 19+.

4669 ■ TOP U.S. REPLACEMENT FARM TIRE BRANDS - REAR BIAS, 2011

Ranked by: Market share, in percent. **Number listed:** 10

1. BKT, with 31%
2. Firestone, 26%
3. Goodyear, 18%
4. Titan, 13%
5. Harvest King, 2.5%
6. Alliance, 2%
6. American Farmer, 2%
6. Trelleborg, 2%
6. Others, 1.5%
10. Akuret, 2%

Source: *Modern Tire Dealer*, Facts Issue (annual), January 2012, p. 44.

4670 ■ TOP U.S. REPLACEMENT FARM TIRE BRANDS - REAR RADIAL, 2011

Ranked by: Market share, in percent. **Number listed:** 8

1. Goodyear, with 29%
2. Firestone, 27%
3. BKT, 19.5%
4. Michelin, 10.5%
5. Titan, 7%
6. Alliance, 3%
7. Trelleborg, 2.5%

8. Others, 1.5%

Source: *Modern Tire Dealer*, Facts Issue (annual), January 2012, p. 44.

4671 ■ TOP U.S. REPLACEMENT FARM TIRE BRANDS - SMALL FARM, 2011

Ranked by: Market share, in percent. **Number listed:** 11

1. Firestone, with 28.5%
2. Goodyear, 19%
3. BKT, 15.5%
3. Titan, 15.5%
5. American Farmer, 6%
6. Harvest King, 4.5%
7. Alliance, 3%
7. Carlisle, 3%
9. Trelleborg, 2%
10. Akuret, 1%

Source: *Modern Tire Dealer*, Facts Issue (annual), January 2012, p. 44.

4672 ■ TOP U.S. REPLACEMENT TIRE BRANDS FOR LIGHT TRUCKS, 2011

Ranked by: Market share, in percent. **Number listed:** 30

1. Goodyear, with 11.5%
2. BFGoodrich, 9%
3. Bridgestone, 8%
4. Michelin, 7%
5. Firestone, 6.5%
6. Cooper, 6%
7. Multi-Mile, 4.5%
8. General, 4%
8. Yokohama, 4%
10. Hankook, 3.5%
10. Toyo, 3.5%

Source: *Modern Tire Dealer*, Facts Issue (annual), January 2012, p. 28.

4673 ■ TOP U.S. REPLACEMENT TIRE BRANDS FOR MEDIUM/HEAVY TRUCKS, 2011

Ranked by: Market share, in percent. **Number listed:** 20

1. Michelin, with 18%
2. Bridgestone, 17%
3. Goodyear, 14%
4. Yokohama, 9%
5. Firestone, 7.5%
6. Continental, 5.5%
7. General, 4%
8. Double Coin, 3.5%
9. Hankook, 3%
10. Dunlop, 2.5%

Source: *Modern Tire Dealer*, Facts Issue (annual), January 2011, p. 42.

4674 ■ TOP U.S. REPLACEMENT TIRE BRANDS FOR PASSENGER VEHICLES, 2011

Ranked by: Market share, in percent. **Number listed:** 30

1. Goodyear, with 14%

2. Michelin, 8.5%
3. Bridgestone, 8%
4. Firestone, 7%
5. BFGoodrich, 5%
5. Cooper, 5%
5. Hankook, 5%
8. General, 3.5%
8. Yokohama, 3.5%
10. Falken, 3%
10. Kumho, 3%

Source: *Modern Tire Dealer*, Facts Issue (annual), January 2012, p. 28.

4675 ■ WORLD'S LARGEST TIRE MANUFACTURERS, 2011

Ranked by: New tire sales, in billions of U.S. dollars. **Remarks:** Also notes figures for previous year. **Number listed:** 12

1. Bridgestone Corp., with $31.2 billion
2. Compagnie Generale des Etablissements Michelin, $28.3
3. Goodyear Tire & Rubber Co., $22.3
4. Continental AG, $11.9
5. Pirelli & C. SpA, $7.8
6. Sumitomo Rubber Industries Ltd., $7.3
7. Hankook Tire Co., $5.9
8. Yokohama Rubber Co., Ltd., $5.7
9. Cooper Tire & Rubber Co., $4
10. Cheng Shin Rubber Industry Co., Ltd., $3.9

Source: *Modern Tire Dealer*, Facts Issue (annual), January 2012, p. 34.

Tire Repair

4676 ■ TOP U.S. TIRE RETREADERS, 2011

Ranked by: Score based on the amount of tread rubber used to retread a variety of types of tires. **Remarks:** Also notes headquarters, number of shops, pounds of rubber used, processes, and daily output. **Number listed:** 50

1. Wingfoot Commercial Tire Systems LLC/ Goodyear Tire & Rubber Co., with 22,276 points
2. Bridgestone Americas Tire Operations, 12,642
3. Southern Tire Mart, 12,497
4. Purcell Tire & Rubber Co., 12,165
5. Snider Tire Inc., 7,515
6. Best One Tire Group, 7,070
7. TCI Tire Centers, 6,650
8. McCarthy Tire Service Co., 5,608
9. Northwest Retreaders Inc./Hudson-Odom, 5,354
10. Pomp's Tire Service, 5,110

Source: *Modern Tire Dealer*, Top 50 Tire Retreaders (annual), April 2012, p. 35-36.

Tobacco Industry

4677 ■ EUROPE'S MOST VALUABLE TOBACCO COMPANIES, 2011

Ranked by: Market value as of March 2011, in millions of U.S. dollars. **Remarks:** Also notes rank within the *FT Europe 500*, rank for previous year, country, revenue, net income, assets, number of employees, share price, price-to-earning ratio, dividend yield, and fiscal yearend. **Number listed:** 3

1. British American Tobacco plc, with $79,904 million
2. Imperial Tobacco Group plc, $31,456.3
3. Swedish Match AB, $7,686.1

Source: *Financial Times*, FT 500 (annual), http://www.ft.com, June 24, 2011.

4678 ■ JAPAN'S MOST VALUABLE TOBACCO BRANDS, 2011

Ranked by: Brand value, in millions of U.S. dollars. **Remarks:** Also notes rank within the *Global 500* for current and previous year, figures for current and previous year, and brand rating. Ranking is available online only. **Number listed:** 2

1. Camel, with $3,296 million
2. Mild Seven, $2,893

Source: *Global 500*, (annual), Brand Finance plc, March 2012.

4679 ■ LARGEST FOOD, BEVERAGE, AND TOBACCO COMPANIES IN EUROPE, 2010

Ranked by: Sales, in millions of U.S. dollars. **Remarks:** Also notes rank within country. **Number listed:** 100

1. Nestle SA (Switzerland), with $105,973.4 million
2. Unilever NV (Netherlands), $59,224.8
3. Imperial Tobacco Group plc (U.K.), $39,775.5
4. Anheuser-Busch InBev SA/NV (Belgium), $36,758
5. SABMiller plc (U.K.), $27,030
6. Heineken NV (Netherlands), $21,863.3
7. British American Tobacco plc (U.K.), $21,312
8. Groupe Danone SA (France), $21,452.6
9. Caledonian Brewery Ltd. (U.K.), $18,000
10. Diageo plc (U.K.), $14,670

Source: *Europe's 15,000 Largest Companies*, (annual), ELC International, 2011, p. 42.

4680 ■ LARGEST TOBACCO COMPANIES BY EMPLOYEES, 2010

Ranked by: Total number of employees. **Remarks:** Also notes contact information for headquarters, number of employees at headquarters, revenue, rank by revenue, and primary SIC code. **Number listed:** 48

1. Philip Morris International Inc., with 77,300 employees
2. Danville Leaf Tobacco Co., 24,000
3. Altria Group Inc., 10,000
4. Philip Morris USA Inc., 7,300
5. R. J. Reynolds Tobacco Holdings Inc., 6,800
6. Reynolds American Inc., 6,550
7. UST LLC, 4,610
8. Mafco Consolidated Group Inc., 4,500
9. Schweitzer-Mauduit International Inc., 2,900
10. Lorillard Tobacco Co., 2,700

Source: *Business Rankings*, (annual), Dun & Bradstreet Inc., 2011, p. VI.48-VI.49.

4681 ■ LARGEST TOBACCO COMPANIES BY SALES, 2010

Ranked by: Total revenue, in dollars. **Remarks:** Also notes contact information for headquarters, number of employees at headquarters and overall, rank by employees, and primary SIC code. **Number listed:** 50

1. Philip Morris International Inc., with $67,713,000,000
2. Altria Group Inc., $24,363,000,000
3. Reynolds American Inc., $8,551,000,000
4. Lorillard Tobacco Co., $5,000,000,000
5. Danville Leaf Tobacco Co., $2,500,000,000
6. Vector Group Ltd., $1,063,289,000
7. Schweitzer-Mauduit International Inc., $740,200,000
8. Commonwealth Brands Inc., $200,000,000
9. North Atlantic Trading Co., $117,627,000
10. S & M Brands Inc., $100,000,000

Source: *Business Rankings*, (annual), Dun & Bradstreet Inc., 2011, p. V.48-V.49.

4682 ■ LARGEST U.S. TOBACCO COMPANIES OVERALL, 2011

Ranked by: Score based on revenue, profits, assets, and market capitalization. **Remarks:** Specific scores not provided. Also notes overall rank in the *Forbes 2000* and figures for each criterion. **Number listed:** 4

1. Philip Morris International Inc.
2. Altria Group Inc.
3. Reynolds American Inc.
4. Lorillard Inc.

Source: *Forbes*, Forbes 2000 (annual), http://www.forbes.com, May 7, 2012.

4683 ■ LARGEST U.S. TOBACCO MANUFACTURERS, 2010

Ranked by: Revenue, in millions of dollars. **Remarks:** Also notes overall rank within the *IW 500,* revenue growth, and profit margin. **Number listed:** 6

1. Philip Morris International Inc., with $67,713 million
2. Altria Group Inc., $24,363
3. Reynolds American Inc., $8,551
4. Lorillard Inc., $5,932
5. Alliance One International Inc., $2,308
6. Vector Group Ltd., $1,063

Source: *IndustryWeek*, IW 500 (annual), http://www.industryweek.com, July 2011.

4684 ■ MOST VALUABLE U.S. TOBACCO COMPANIES, 2011

Ranked by: Market value as of March 2011, in millions of U.S. dollars. **Remarks:** Also notes rank within the *FT U.S. 500*, rank for previous year, country, revenue, net income, assets, number of employees, share price, price-to-earning ratio, dividend yield, and fiscal yearend. **Number listed:** 4

1. Philip Morris International Inc., with $117,945.6 million
2. Altria Group Inc., $54,454.4
3. Reynolds American Inc., $20,710

4. Lorillard Inc., $13,829

Source: *Financial Times*, FT 500 (annual), http://www.ft.com, June 24, 2011.

4685 ■ NORTH CAROLINA'S LARGEST TOBACCO COMPANIES OVERALL, 2011

Ranked by: Score based on revenue, profits, assets, and market capitalization. **Remarks:** Specific scores not provided. Also notes overall rank in the *Forbes 2000* and figures for each criterion. **Number listed:** 2

1. Reynolds American Inc.
2. Lorillard Inc.

Source: *Forbes*, Forbes 2000 (annual), http://www.forbes.com, May 7, 2012.

4686 ■ TOP *FORTUNE 500* COMPANIES IN TOBACCO, 2011

Ranked by: Revenue, in millions of dollars. **Remarks:** Also notes overall rank in the *Fortune 500;* profits; profits as a percentage of revenue; stockholders' equity; and rank by each criterion. **Number listed:** 3

1. Philip Morris International Inc., with $31,097 million
2. Altria Group Inc., $16,619
3. Reynolds American Inc., $8,541

Source: *Fortune*, Fortune 500 (annual), May 21, 2012, p. F-40.

4687 ■ UNITED KINGDOM'S LARGEST TOBACCO COMPANIES OVERALL, 2011

Ranked by: Score based on revenue, profits, assets, and market capitalization. **Remarks:** Specific scores not provided. Also notes overall rank in the *Forbes 2000* and figures for each criterion. **Number listed:** 2

1. British American Tobacco plc
2. Imperial Tobacco Group plc

Source: *Forbes*, Forbes 2000 (annual), http://www.forbes.com, May 7, 2012.

4688 ■ THE UNITED STATES' MOST VALUABLE TOBACCO BRANDS, 2011

Ranked by: Brand value, in millions of U.S. dollars. **Remarks:** Also notes rank within the *Global 500* for current and previous year, figures for current and previous year, and brand rating. Ranking is available online only. **Number listed:** 3

1. Marlboro, with $15,171 million
2. Winston, $3,728
3. Newport, $2,517

Source: *Global 500*, (annual), Brand Finance plc, March 2012.

4689 ■ WORLD'S LARGEST TOBACCO COMPANIES, 2010

Ranked by: Sales, in millions of U.S. dollars. **Remarks:** Also notes brands and annual sales growth. **Number listed:** 7

1. British American Tobacco plc, with $70,609 million
2. Philip Morris International Inc., $67,713
3. Japan Tobacco Inc., $65,936
4. Imperial Tobacco Group plc, $45,360
5. Altria Group Inc., $24,363
6. Reynolds American Inc., $8,551

7. Lorillard Inc., $5,932

Source: *Consumer Goods Technology*, Consumer Goods Registry (annual), http://www.consumergoods.com, December 2011.

4690 ■ WORLD'S LARGEST TOBACCO COMPANIES OVERALL, 2011

Ranked by: Score based on revenue, profits, assets, and market capitalization. **Remarks:** Specific scores not provided. Also notes country, overall rank in the *Forbes 2000,* and figures for each criterion. **Number listed:** 11

1. Philip Morris International Inc.
2. British American Tobacco plc
3. Imperial Tobacco Group plc
4. Japan Tobacco Inc.
5. Altria Group Inc.
6. Reynolds American Inc.
7. ITC Ltd.
8. Lorillard Inc.
9. KT & G Corp.
10. PT Gudang Garam TBK

Source: *Forbes*, Forbes 2000 (annual), http://www.forbes.com, May 7, 2012.

4691 ■ WORLD'S LARGEST TOBACCO PRODUCT MANUFACTURERS, 2010

Ranked by: Revenue, in millions of dollars. **Remarks:** Also notes rank for previous year, overall rank within the *IW 1000*, country, and revenue growth. **Number listed:** 10

1. Japan Tobacco Inc., with $75,458 million
2. Philip Morris International Inc., $67,713
3. Imperial Tobacco Group plc, $43,979
4. Altria Group Inc., $24,363
5. British American Tobacco plc, $23,556
6. Reynolds American Inc., $8,551
7. Lorillard Inc., $5,932
8. Grupo Carso SA de CV, $5,200
9. PT Gudang Garam TBK, $3,769
10. KT & G Corp., $3,241

Source: *IndustryWeek*, IW 1000 (annual), http://www.industryweek.com, August 2011.

4692 ■ WORLD'S MOST ADMIRED TOBACCO COMPANIES, 2012

Ranked by: Score, on a scale of 10, based on a survey of executives, directors, and securities analysts of companies within their own industry on eight criteria: innovation, financial soundness, employee talent, use of corporate assets, long-term investment value, social responsibility, quality of management, and quality of products/services. **Remarks:** Specific scores not provided. Also notes rank for previous year. **Number listed:** 5

1. Philip Morris International Inc.
2. British American Tobacco plc
3. Altria Group Inc.
4. Universal Corp.
5. Imperial Tobacco Group plc

Source: *Fortune*, World's Most Admired Companies (annual), March 19, 2012, p. 148.

4693 ■ WORLD'S MOST VALUABLE TOBACCO BRANDS, 2011

Ranked by: Brand value, in millions of U.S. dollars. **Remarks:** Also notes rank within the *Global 500* for current and previous

year, figures for current and previous year, country, and brand rating. Ranking is available online only. **Number listed:** 6

1. Marlboro, with $15,171 million
2. Winston, $3,728
3. Camel, $3,296
4. Pall Mall, $3,087
5. Mild Seven, $2,893
6. Newport, $2,517

Source: *Global 500*, (annual), Brand Finance plc, March 2012.

4694 ■ WORLD'S MOST VALUABLE TOBACCO COMPANIES, 2011

Ranked by: Market value as of March 2011, in millions of U.S. dollars. **Remarks:** Also notes rank within the *FT 500*, rank for previous year, country, revenue, net income, assets, number of employees, share price, price-to-earning ratio, dividend yield, and fiscal year-end. **Number listed:** 7

1. Philip Morris International Inc., with $117,945.6 million
2. British American Tobacco plc, $79,904
3. Altria Group Inc., $54,454.4
4. Japan Tobacco Inc., $36,257.2
5. ITC Holdings Corp., $31,485.3
6. Imperial Tobacco Group plc, $31,456.3
7. Reynolds American Inc., $20,710

Source: *Financial Times*, FT 500 (annual), http://www.ft.com, June 24, 2011.

Tortilla Chips

4695 ■ TOP BRANDS OF TORTILLA CHIPS, 2011

Ranked by: Sales for the 52 weeks ending March 20, 2011, in millions of dollars. **Remarks:** Also notes annual growth, dollar share, and unit sales. **Number listed:** 10

1. Doritos, with $1,158.3 million
2. Tostitos, $372.3
3. Tostitos Natural, $240.5
4. Tostitos Scoops, $204.3
5. Santitas, $168.2
6. Private label, $155
7. Mission, $81.3
8. Barcel Takis, $33.5
9. Baked Tostitos Scoops, $31.5
10. On the Border, $27.1

Source: *Snack Food & Wholesale Bakery*, State of the Industry (annual), July 2011, p. 26.

Tourist Industry

4696 ■ LARGEST TOURISM/HOSPITALITY COMPANIES IN BRITISH COLUMBIA, 2010

Ranked by: Revenue, in thousands of Canadian dollars. **Remarks:** Also notes figures for previous year. **Number listed:** 10

1. British Columbia Ferry Services Inc., with C$732,305 thousand
2. Charlwood Pacific Group, C$700,000
3. Flight Shops Inc., C$657,777

4. Northland Properties Corp., C$611,000
5. Vancouver Airport Authority, C$368,653
6. Coast Hotels Ltd., C$245,000
6. Gateway Casinos & Entertainment Inc., C$245,000
8. Whistler Blackcomb Holdings Inc., C$224,673
9. Armstrong Hospitality Group Ltd., C$200,000
10. British Columbia Pavilion Corp., C$41,603

Source: *BCBusiness*, Top 100 (annual), July 2011, p. 135.

4697 ■ WORLD'S TOP TOUR OPERATORS AND SAFARI OUTFITTERS, 2011

Ranked by: Score, on a scale of 100, based on consumer survey regarding staff/guides, itineraries/destinations, activities, accommodations, food, and value. **Number listed:** 25

1. Micato Safaris, with 97.04 points
2. Ker & Downey, 96.85
3. Explore Inc., 96.33
4. Wilderness Safaris, 95.05
5. Austin-Lehman Adventures, 94.85
6. Cox & Kings, 94.24
7. Costa Rica Expeditions, 93.84
8. Travcoa, 93.62
9. andBeyond, 93.56
10. Asia Transpacific Journeys, 93.33

Source: *Travel + Leisure*, World's Best Awards (annual), August 2011.

Toys

4698 ■ WORLD'S LARGEST TOYS AND GAMES COMPANIES, 2010

Ranked by: Sales, in millions of U.S. dollars. **Remarks:** Also notes brands and annual sales growth. **Number listed:** 10

1. Nintendo Co., Ltd., with $18,877 million
2. Mattel Inc., $5,856
3. Namco Bandai Holdings Inc., $4,950
4. Hasbro Inc., $4,000
5. Electronic Arts Inc., $3,654
6. TOMY Group Ltd., $2,289
7. Take-Two Interactive Software Inc., $1,160
8. Sanrio Co., Ltd., $1,011
9. Jakks Pacific Inc., $747
10. LeapFrog Enterprises Inc., $433

Source: *Consumer Goods Technology*, Consumer Goods Registry (annual), http://www.consumergoods.com, December 2011.

Trade Journals
See: **Trade Magazines**

Trade Magazines

4699 ■ TOP SMALL-BUSINESS TRADE PUBLICATIONS, 2011

Ranked by: Circulation. **Remarks:** Also notes publisher, URL, auditor, and audit date. **Number listed:** 11

1. *The Wall Street Journal*, with 2,117,796 copies
2. *Forbes*, 928,900
3. *Bloomberg Businessweek*, 921,839
4. *Fast Company*, 738,950
5. *Entrepreneur*, 615,411
6. *Black Enterprise*, 507,765
7. *Hispanic Business*, 241,588
8. *Crain's New York Business*, 49,075
9. *Crain's Chicago Business*, 45,702
10. *Crain's Detroit Business*, 25,494

Source: *BtoB*, Marketing to Small Business, November 7, 2011, p. 26.

Trade Shows

4700 ■ TOP U.S. TRADESHOWS, 2011

Ranked by: Total exhibition space, in net square feet. **Remarks:** Also notes organizer, number of exhibitors and attendees, event dates, and venue. **Number listed:** 250

1. CONEXPO-CON/AGG, with 2,400,000 sq. ft.
2. International CES, 1,600,000
3. Atlanta International Gift & Home Furnishings Market (January), 1,168,605
4. International Construction & Utility Equipment Exposition, 1,111,908
5. Atlanta International Gift & Home Furnishings Market (July), 1,105,533
6. Las Vegas Market (Winter), 1,084,975
7. Specialty Equipment Market Association Show, 935,000
7. National Business Aviation Association Annual Meeting & Convention, 935,000
9. RECon, the Global Retail Real Estate Convention, 900,000
10. MAGIC Marketplace, 873,140

Source: *Top 250 Trade Shows*, (annual), Trade Show News Network, May 2, 2012.

Trademarks

4701 ■ TOP TRADEMARK LAW FIRMS, 2011

Ranked by: Number of trademarks secured during the year. **Remarks:** Also notes figures for previous two years, three-year average, annual percent change, headquarters, and website. **Number listed:** 142

1. Fross Zelnick Lehrman & Zissu PC, with 951 trademarks
2. DLA Piper, 755
3. Kilpatrick Townsend & Stockton, 662
4. Knobbe Martens Olson & Bear LLP, 648
5. Brinks Hofer Gilson & Lione, 639
6. Arent Fox LLP, 592
7. Cozen O'Connor, 563
8. Venable LLP, 516
9. Dorsey & Whitney LLP, 511
10. Ladas & Parry LLP, 508

Source: *Intellectual Property Today*, Top Trademark Firms (annual), http://www.iptoday.com, May 2012.

Trading Companies

4702 ■ CHINA'S LARGEST TRADING COMPANIES OVERALL, 2011

Ranked by: Score based on revenue, profits, assets, and market capitalization. **Remarks:** Specific scores not provided. Also notes overall rank in the *Forbes 2000* and figures for each criterion. **Number listed:** 3

1. Minmetals Development Co., Ltd.
2. Shanghai Material Trading Co., Ltd.
3. Xiamen C & D Inc.

Source: *Forbes*, Forbes 2000 (annual), http://www.forbes.com, May 7, 2012.

4703 ■ JAPAN'S LARGEST TRADING COMPANIES OVERALL, 2011

Ranked by: Score based on revenue, profits, assets, and market capitalization. **Remarks:** Specific scores not provided. Also notes overall rank in the *Forbes 2000* and figures for each criterion. **Number listed:** 8

1. Mitsubishi Corp.
2. Mitsui & Co., Ltd.
3. Sumitomo Corp.
4. Itochu Corp.
5. Marubeni Corp.
6. Toyota Tsusho Corp.
7. Sojitz
8. Kanematsu

Source: *Forbes*, Forbes 2000 (annual), http://www.forbes.com, May 7, 2012.

4704 ■ SOUTH KOREA'S LARGEST TRADING COMPANIES OVERALL, 2011

Ranked by: Score based on revenue, profits, assets, and market capitalization. **Remarks:** Specific scores not provided. Also notes overall rank in the *Forbes 2000* and figures for each criterion. **Number listed:** 4

1. Samsung C & T Corp.
2. SK Networks
3. Hanwha Corp.
4. LG International

Source: *Forbes*, Forbes 2000 (annual), http://www.forbes.com, May 7, 2012.

4705 ■ WORLD'S LARGEST TRADING COMPANIES OVERALL, 2011

Ranked by: Score based on revenue, profits, assets, and market capitalization. **Remarks:** Specific scores not provided. Also notes country, overall rank in the *Forbes 2000,* and figures for each criterion. **Number listed:** 17

1. Mitsubishi Corp.
2. Mitsui & Co., Ltd.
3. Sumitomo Corp.
4. Itochu Corp.
5. Marubeni Corp.
6. Toyota Tsusho Corp.
7. Li & Fung Ltd.
8. Samsung C & T Corp.

9. Sojitz Corp.

10. Adani Enterprises Ltd.

Source: *Forbes*, Forbes 2000 (annual), http://www.forbes.com, May 7, 2012.

Training

4706 ■ COMPANIES WITH THE BEST TRAINING PROGRAMS, 2011

Ranked by: Score based on the connection of learning to business strategies, a culture that encourages and instills learning across all levels of the organization, and development of learning initiatives that promote teamwork, leadership, and growth. **Remarks:** Specific scores not provided. Also notes headquarters, number of employees, and industry. **Number listed:** 32

1. Shell Oil Co./Jiffy Lube International
2. Grant Thornton LLP
3. U.S. Navy, Naval Education & Training Command
4. United Overseas Bank Ltd.
5. CaridianBCT
6. BJC HealthCare
7. Cbeyond Inc.
8. Summit Credit Union
9. Reliance Industries Ltd., Refinery Division
10. Steelcase Inc.

Source: *T + D Magazine*, Very Best Companies (annual), October 2011, p. 30+.

4707 ■ TOP BUSINESS TRAINING FRANCHISES, 2012

Ranked by: Cumulative score based on financial strength and stability, growth rate, size of the system, number of years in business, the length of time franchising, start-up costs, litigation, percentage of terminations, and whether the company provides financing. **Remarks:** Specific scores not provided. Also notes overall rank within the *Franchise 500,* contact information, description, year founded, year started franchising, states where registered, available U.S. regions, where seeking foreign expansion, number of franchised and company-owned units for past three years, start-up costs, franchise fees, royalty fees, and type of financing available. **Number listed:** 2

1. Leadership Management Inc.
2. Sandler Training

Source: *Entrepreneur*, Franchise 500 (annual), January 2012, p. 154-155.

4708 ■ U.S. AND CANADIAN COMPANIES WITH THE BEST TRAINING PROGRAMS, 2011

Ranked by: Score based on questionnaires and interviews. **Remarks:** Specific scores not provided. To be considered, training and development services cannot be a company's primary business. Also notes rank for previous year, headquarters, primary business, annual revenue, number of employees, number of trainers, total training budget, training budget as a percentage of payroll, tuition reimbursement, and training infrastructure. **Number listed:** 125

1. Verizon Communications
2. Farmers Insurance
3. Miami Children's Hospital
4. Mohawk Industries Inc.
5. McDonald's USA LLC

6. The Economical Insurance Group
7. ABF Freight System Inc.
8. BB & T Corp.
9. Coldwell Banker Real Estate
10. McCarthy Building Cos.

Source: *Training*, Top 125 (annual), 2012, p. 66+.

Transportation

4709 ■ AUSTRALIA'S LARGEST MISCELLANEOUS TRANSPORTATION COMPANIES OVERALL, 2011

Ranked by: Score based on revenue, profits, assets, and market capitalization. **Remarks:** Specific scores not provided. Also notes overall rank in the *Forbes 2000* and figures for each criterion. **Number listed:** 2

1. Toll Holdings Ltd.
2. Transurban Group

Source: *Forbes*, Forbes 2000 (annual), http://www.forbes.com, May 7, 2012.

4710 ■ BEST SMALL TRANSPORTATION COMPANIES IN AMERICA, 2011

Ranked by: Score based on revenue, profits, and return on equity for the past 12 months and five years. **Remarks:** Specific scores not provided. Also notes rank in the overall *100 Best Small Companies in America*. To qualify, companies must have revenues between $5 million and $1 billion, a net margin above five percent, and share price above $5. List is available online only. **Number listed:** 2

1. Allegiant Travel
2. Air Methods

Source: *Forbes*, Best Small Companies in America (annual), November 7, 2011.

4711 ■ BRITAIN'S MOST ADMIRED TRANSPORTATION COMPANIES, 2011

Ranked by: Survey of peers and investment analysts based on nine criteria: quality of management, financial soundness, quality of goods/services, ability to attract and retain talent, value as long-term investment, innovation, marketing, community and environmental responsibility, and use of corporate assets. **Number listed:** 5

1. Stagecoach Group plc, with 68.1 points
2. Ryanair Holdings plc, 56.8
3. Arriva plc, 56.7
4. Go-Ahead Group, 56.3
5. EasyJet plc, 55.9

Source: *Management Today*, Britain's Most Admired Companies (annual), December 2011, p. 49.

4712 ■ BRITAIN'S MOST ADMIRED TRANSPORTATION SERVICES COMPANIES, 2011

Ranked by: Survey of peers and investment analysts based on nine criteria: quality of management, financial soundness, quality of goods/services, ability to attract and retain talent, value as long-term investment, innovation, marketing, community and environmental responsibility, and use of corporate assets. **Number listed:** 5

1. UPS (U.K.), with 64.6 points
2. Kuehne + Nagel (U.K.), 62.1

3. DHL (U.K.), 55.9

4. Ceva Logistics U.K., 54.6

5. Wincanton, 53

Source: *Management Today*, Britain's Most Admired Companies (annual), December 2011, p. 49.

4713 ■ CHINA'S LARGEST MISCELLANEOUS TRANSPORTATION COMPANIES OVERALL, 2011

Ranked by: Score based on revenue, profits, assets, and market capitalization. **Remarks:** Specific scores not provided. Also notes overall rank in the *Forbes 2000* and figures for each criterion. **Number listed:** 3

1. China COSCO Holdings Co., Ltd.

2. Shanghai International Port (Group) Co., Ltd.

3. China Shipping Container Lines Co., Ltd.

Source: *Forbes*, Forbes 2000 (annual), http://www.forbes.com, May 7, 2012.

4714 ■ EUROPE'S MOST VALUABLE INDUSTRIAL TRANSPORTATION COMPANIES, 2011

Ranked by: Market value as of March 2011, in millions of U.S. dollars. **Remarks:** Also notes rank within the *FT Europe 500*, rank for previous year, country, revenue, net income, assets, number of employees, share price, price-to-earning ratio, dividend yield, and fiscal yearend. **Number listed:** 12

1. A. P. Moller-Maersk A/S, with $40,926.7 million

2. Deutsche Post AG, $21,823.7

3. Kuhne + Nagel International, $16,854.8

4. Abertis, $16,077.5

5. Atlantia, $13,774.8

6. TNT, $9,759.6

7. ADP, $9,128.2

8. Fraport, $6,718.8

9. Vopak, $6,158.9

10. Bollore, $5,747

Source: *Financial Times*, FT 500 (annual), http://www.ft.com, June 24, 2011.

4715 ■ JAPAN'S LARGEST MISCELLANEOUS TRANSPORTATION COMPANIES OVERALL, 2011

Ranked by: Score based on revenue, profits, assets, and market capitalization. **Remarks:** Specific scores not provided. Also notes overall rank in the *Forbes 2000* and figures for each criterion. **Number listed:** 3

1. Nippon Yusen Kabushiki Kaisha

2. Mitsui OSK Lines Ltd.

3. Kawasaki Kisen Kaisha

Source: *Forbes*, Forbes 2000 (annual), http://www.forbes.com, May 7, 2012.

4716 ■ LARGEST TRANSPORTATION COMPANIES IN EUROPE, 2010

Ranked by: Sales, in millions of U.S. dollars. **Remarks:** Also notes rank within country. **Number listed:** 100

1. Deutsche Lufthansa AG (Germany), with $33,139.3 million

2. Societe Nationale des Chemins (France), $23,739.5

3. Carnival plc (U.K.), $19,735.5

4. Air France SA (France), $18,647

5. TNT NV (Netherlands), $14,079.1

6. Societe Air France (Italy), $12,987.2

7. British Airways plc (U.K.), $11,991

8. Deutsche Lufthansa AG (Italy), $10,481.2

9. Financiere de l'Odet SA (France), $10,325.4

10. Nedlloyd Container Line Ltd. (U.K.), $10,071

Source: *Europe's 15,000 Largest Companies*, (annual), ELC International, 2011, p. 49.

4717 ■ LARGEST TRANSPORTATION SERVICES COMPANIES BY EMPLOYEES, 2010

Ranked by: Total number of employees. **Remarks:** Also notes contact information for headquarters, number of employees at headquarters, revenue, rank by revenue, and primary SIC code. **Number listed:** 69

1. Burlington Northern Santa Fe LLC, with 39,985 employees

2. Carlson Wagonlit Travel Inc., 22,000

3. Schneider National Carriers Inc., 20,000

4. UTI Worldwide Inc., 19,514

5. Lockheed Martin Space Operations Co., 19,000

6. Expeditors International of Washington Inc., 12,010

7. Ceva Logistics LLC, 11,500

8. Arkansas Best Corp., 10,750

9. Sabre Holdings Corp., 9,000

9. Sovereign Holdings Inc., 9,000

Source: *Business Rankings*, (annual), Dun & Bradstreet Inc., 2011, p. VI.102-VI.103.

4718 ■ LARGEST TRANSPORTATION SERVICES COMPANIES BY SALES, 2010

Ranked by: Total revenue, in dollars. **Remarks:** Also notes contact information for headquarters, number of employees at headquarters and overall, rank by employees, and primary SIC code. **Number listed:** 67

1. C. H. Robinson Worldwide Inc., with $9,274,305,000

2. Expeditors International of Washington Inc., $5,967,573,000

3. C. H. Robinson Co., $3,651,420,000

4. UTI (U.S.) Holdings Inc., $3,567,522,000

4. UTI Worldwide Inc., $3,567,522,000

6. Expedia Inc., $3,348,109,000

7. Buckeye Partners LP, $3,151,268,000

8. Priceline.com Inc., $3,084,905,000

9. Hub Group Inc., $1,833,737,000

10. DB U.S. Holding Corp., $1,773,372,446

Source: *Business Rankings*, (annual), Dun & Bradstreet Inc., 2011, p. V.102-V.103.

4719 ■ MOST POWERFUL ARABS IN TRANSPORTATION, 2012

Ranked by: Score based on scope of influence. **Remarks:** Specific scores not provided. Also notes rank in the overall *Power 500*. **Number listed:** 19

1. Sheikh Ahmed bin Saeed Al Maktoum

2. Sultan Ahmed Bin Sulayem
3. Akbar Al Baker
4. Fadi Ghandour
5. Adel Ali
6. Carlos Ghosn
7. Mattar Al Tayer
8. Samer Majali
9. Marwan Boodai
10. Salma Ali Saif bin Hareb

Source: *Arabian Business*, Power 500 (annual), June 4, 2012.

4720 ■ MOST VALUABLE U.S. INDUSTRIAL TRANSPORTATION COMPANIES, 2011

Ranked by: Market value as of March 2011, in millions of U.S. dollars. **Remarks:** Also notes rank within the *FT U.S. 500*, rank for previous year, country, revenue, net income, assets, number of employees, share price, price-to-earning ratio, dividend yield, and fiscal yearend. **Number listed:** 7

1. United Parcel Service Inc. (UPS), with $54,644.4 million
2. Union Pacific Corp., $48,280.1
3. FedEx Corp., $29,529.8
4. CSX Corp., $28,973.5
5. Norfolk Southern Corp., $25,955.5
6. C. H. Robinson Worldwide Inc., $12,081.3
7. Expeditors International of Washington Inc., $10,633.6

Source: *Financial Times*, FT 500 (annual), http://www.ft.com, June 24, 2011.

4721 ■ SOUTH KOREA'S LARGEST MISCELLANEOUS TRANSPORTATION COMPANIES OVERALL, 2011

Ranked by: Score based on revenue, profits, assets, and market capitalization. **Remarks:** Specific scores not provided. Also notes overall rank in the *Forbes 2000* and figures for each criterion. **Number listed:** 3

1. Hyundai Glovis
2. Hanjin Shipping
3. Hanjin Shipping Holdings

Source: *Forbes*, Forbes 2000 (annual), http://www.forbes.com, May 7, 2012.

4722 ■ SPAIN'S LARGEST MISCELLANEOUS TRANSPORTATION COMPANIES OVERALL, 2011

Ranked by: Score based on revenue, profits, assets, and market capitalization. **Remarks:** Specific scores not provided. Also notes overall rank in the *Forbes 2000* and figures for each criterion. **Number listed:** 2

1. Grupo Ferrovial SA
2. Abertis Infraestructuras SA

Source: *Forbes*, Forbes 2000 (annual), http://www.forbes.com, May 7, 2012.

4723 ■ STATES WITH THE HIGHEST RATE OF EMPLOYEES IN TRADE, TRANSPORTATION, AND PUBLIC UTILITIES, 2010

Ranked by: Percentage of employees in the trade industry, transportation industry, and public utilities. **Number listed:** 51

1. New Hampshire, with 21.2%

1. Tennessee, 21.2%
3. Montana, 21.1%
3. New Jersey, 21.1%
3. North Dakota, 21.1%
6. Georgia, 21%
7. Nebraska, 20.8%
8. Kentucky, 20.6%
9. Florida, 20.3%
9. South Dakota, 20.3%

Source: *State Rankings*, (annual), CQ Press, 2011, p. 207.

4724 ■ STATES WITH THE LOWEST RATE OF EMPLOYEES IN TRADE, TRANSPORTATION, AND PUBLIC UTILITIES, 2010

Ranked by: Percentage of employees in the trade industry, transportation industy, and public utilities. **Number listed:** 51

1. Washington DC, with 3.6%
2. Rhode Island, 15.9%
3. New Mexico, 16%
4. Massachusetts, 16.9%
4. New York, 16.9%
6. Virginia, 17.2%
7. Maryland, 17.3%
8. Delaware, 17.7%
9. Connecticut, 17.8%
10. Colorado, 17.9%
10. West Virginia, 17.9%

Source: *State Rankings*, (annual), CQ Press, 2011, p. 207.

4725 ■ TOP CANADIAN TRANSPORTATION COMPANIES, 2010

Ranked by: Revenue, in thousands of Canadian dollars (unless otherwise noted). **Remarks:** Also notes percent change from previous year. **Number listed:** 10

1. Air Canada, with C$10,950,000 thousand
2. Canadian National Railway Co., C$8,515,000
3. Canadian Pacific Railway Ltd., C$5,013,300
4. Transat A.T., C$3,517,678
5. WestJet Airlines, C$2,619,171
6. TransForce Inc., C$2,044,192
7. Chorus Aviation, C$1,486,789
8. NAV Canada, C$1,240,000
9. Mullen Group, C$1,059,186
10. Vitran Corp., C$672,708

Source: *Report on Business Magazine*, Top 1000 Companies (annual), http://www.reportonbusiness.com, June 2011.

4726 ■ TOP *FORTUNE 500* COMPANIES IN TRANSPORTATION AND LOGISTICS, 2011

Ranked by: Revenue, in millions of dollars. **Remarks:** Also notes overall rank in the *Fortune 500;* profits; profits as a percentage of revenue; stockholders' equity; and rank by each criterion. **Number listed:** 3

1. C. H. Robinson Worldwide Inc., with $10,336 million
2. Expeditors International of Washington Inc., $6,150

3. Con-Way Inc., $5,290

Source: *Fortune*, Fortune 500 (annual), May 21, 2012, p. F-40.

4727 ■ WORLD'S LARGEST MISCELLANEOUS TRANSPORTATION COMPANIES OVERALL, 2011

Ranked by: Score based on revenue, profits, assets, and market capitalization. **Remarks:** Specific scores not provided. Also notes country, overall rank in the *Forbes 2000,* and figures for each criterion. **Number listed:** 26

1. A. P. Moller-Maersk A/S
2. Grupo Ferrovial SA
3. China COSCO Holdings Co., Ltd.
4. Nippon Yusen Kabushiki Kaisha
5. Abertis Infraestructuras SA
6. Mitsui OSK Lines Ltd.
7. Atlantia SpA
8. Kuehne & Nagel International AG
9. C. H. Robinson Worldwide Inc.
10. Shanghai International Port (Group) Co., Ltd.

Source: *Forbes*, Forbes 2000 (annual), http://www.forbes.com, May 7, 2012.

4728 ■ WORLD'S MOST ADMIRED TRUCKING, TRANSPORTATION, AND LOGISTICS COMPANIES, 2012

Ranked by: Score, on a scale of 10, based on a survey of executives, directors, and securities analysts of companies within their own industry on eight criteria: innovation, financial soundness, employee talent, use of corporate assets, long-term investment value, social responsibility, quality of management, and quality of products/services. **Remarks:** Specific scores not provided. Also notes rank for previous year. **Number listed:** 5

1. Union Pacific Corp.
2. C. H. Robinson Worldwide Inc.
3. Norfolk Southern Corp.
3. CSX Corp.
5. Expeditors International of Washington Inc.

Source: *Fortune*, World's Most Admired Companies (annual), March 19, 2012, p. 150.

4729 ■ WORLD'S MOST ETHICAL TRANSPORTATION AND LOGISTICS COMPANIES, 2012

Ranked by: Score based on five criteria: ethics and compliance program; reputation, leadership, and innovation; governance; corporate citizenship and responsibility; and culture of ethics. **Remarks:** Specific scores not provided; companies are listed alphabetically, not ranked. **Number listed:** 3

1. Nippon Yusen Kabushiki Kaisha (Japan)
2. Autoridad del Canal de Panama (Panama)
3. United Parcel Service Inc. (UPS, U.S.)

Source: *Ethisphere Magazine*, World's Most Ethical Companies (annual), http://www.ethisphere.com, 2012.

4730 ■ WORLD'S MOST TECHNOLOGICALLY INNOVATIVE TRANSPORTATION COMPANIES, 2011

Ranked by: Editorial determination. **Remarks:** Companies are listed alphabetically, not ranked. Also notes comments. **Number listed:** 3

1. Better Place
2. SpaceX
3. WiTricity

Source: *Technology Review*, TR 50 (annual), http://www.technologyreview.com, 2012.

4731 ■ WORLD'S MOST VALUABLE INDUSTRIAL TRANSPORTATION COMPANIES, 2011

Ranked by: Market value as of March 2011, in millions of U.S. dollars. **Remarks:** Also notes rank within the *FT 500*, rank for previous year, country, revenue, net income, assets, number of employees, share price, price-to-earning ratio, dividend yield, and fiscal year-end. **Number listed:** 9

1. United Parcel Service Inc. (UPS), with $54,644.4 million
2. Union Pacific Corp., $48,280.1
3. A. P. Moller-Maersk A/S, $40,926.7
4. Canadian National Railway Co., $34,497.2
5. FedEx Corp., $29,529.8
6. CSX Corp., $28,973.5
7. Norfolk Southern Corp., $25,955.5
8. Deutsche Post AG, $21,823.7
9. Daqin Railway Co., Ltd., $19,433.3

Source: *Financial Times*, FT 500 (annual), http://www.ft.com, June 24, 2011.

4732 ■ WORLD'S MOST VALUABLE TRANSPORTATION BRANDS, 2011

Ranked by: Brand value, in millions of U.S. dollars. **Remarks:** Also notes rank within the *Global 500* for current and previous year, figures for current and previous year, country, and brand rating. Ranking is available online only. **Number listed:** 14

1. UPS, with $18,083 million
2. FedEx, $10,072
3. DHL, $8,169
4. Union Pacific, $5,670
5. JR-East, $3,459
6. C. H. Robinson, $3,241
7. NYK, $3,147
8. CSX, $3,029
9. Norfolk, $2,819
10. JR-Central, $2,802

Source: *Global 500*, (annual), Brand Finance plc, 2012.

Transportation—Equipment and Supplies

4733 ■ LARGEST TRANSPORTATION EQUIPMENT COMPANIES BY EMPLOYEES, 2010

Ranked by: Total number of employees. **Remarks:** Also notes contact information for headquarters, number of employees at headquarters, revenue, rank by revenue, and primary SIC code. **Number listed:** 47

1. General Motors Co., with 244,500 employees
1. General Motors Holdings LLC, 244,500
1. General Motors LLC, 244,500
4. United Technologies Corp., 206,700
5. Ford Motor Co., 198,000
6. Boeing Co., 157,100
7. Lockheed Martin Corp., 140,000
8. Honeywell International Inc., 122,047
9. Northrop Grumman Corp., 120,322

10. Northrop Grumman Systems Corp., 120,000

Source: *Business Rankings*, (annual), Dun & Bradstreet Inc., 2011, p. VI.82-VI.83.

4734 ■ LARGEST TRANSPORTATION EQUIPMENT COMPANIES BY SALES, 2010

Ranked by: Total revenue, in dollars. **Remarks:** Also notes contact information for headquarters, number of employees at headquarters and overall, rank by employees, and primary SIC code. **Number listed:** 49

1. General Motors Co., with $135,592,000,000
2. Ford Motor Co., $128,954,000,000
3. Boeing Co., $64,306,000,000
4. United Technologies Corp., $54,326,000,000
5. Lockheed Martin Corp., $45,803,000,000
6. Northrop Grumman Corp., $34,757,000,000
7. Honeywell International Inc., $33,370,000,000
8. General Dynamics Corp., $32,466,000,000
9. DPH Holdings Corp., $18,060,000,000
10. TRW Automotive Holdings Corp., $14,383,000,000

Source: *Business Rankings*, (annual), Dun & Bradstreet Inc., 2011, p. V.82-V.83.

4735 ■ LARGEST U.S. MANUFACTURERS OF RAILCARS, SHIPS, AND OTHER TRANSPORTATION EQUIPMENT, 2010

Ranked by: Revenue, in millions of dollars. **Remarks:** Also notes overall rank within the *IW 500*, revenue growth, and profit margin. **Number listed:** 4

1. General Dynamics Corp., with $32,466 million
2. Trinity Industries Inc., $2,189
3. Polaris Industries Inc., $1,991
4. Wabtec Corp., $1,507

Source: *IndustryWeek*, IW 500 (annual), http://www.industryweek.com, July 2011.

4736 ■ TOP TRANSPORTATION EQUIPMENT COMPANIES IN CORPORATE FACILITY PROJECTS, 2011

Ranked by: Investment in new or expanded facilities, in millions of dollars. **Remarks:** Also notes location, product line, and whether facility is new or expanded. **Number listed:** 10

1. Daimler AG/Beijing Automotive Industry Corp., with $2,700 million
2. Mercedes Benz, $2,000
2. Nissan Motor Co., Ltd. (Mexico), $2,000
4. Shanghai Volkswagen, $1,850
5. Nissan Motor Co., Ltd. (Brazil), $1,500
6. Fiat SpA, $1,436
7. Daimler AG, $1,300
7. Audi, $1,300
9. Ford Motor Co. (China), $1,100
9. Ford Motor Co. (U.S.), $1,100

Source: *Site Selection*, Top Industries (annual), March 2012, p. 120.

4737 ■ WORLD'S LARGEST MANUFACTURERS OF RAIL-CARS, SHIPS, AND OTHER TRANSPORTATION EQUIP-MENT, 2010

Ranked by: Revenue, in millions of dollars. **Remarks:** Also notes rank for previous year, overall rank within the *IW 1000*, country, and revenue growth. **Number listed:** 13

1. Hyundai Heavy Industries Co., Ltd., with $40,567 million
2. General Dynamics Corp., $32,466
3. Bombardier Inc., $17,681
4. Kawasaki Heavy Industries Ltd., $14,434
5. Samsung Heavy Industries Co., Ltd., $11,781
6. Daewoo Shipbuilding & Marine Engineering Co., Ltd., $11,724
7. Mitsui Engineering & Shipbuilding Co., Ltd., $9,422
8. STX Offshore & Shipbuilding Co., Ltd., $8,020
9. China International Marine Containers Group Ltd., $7,673
10. Keppel Corp., $7,622

Source: *IndustryWeek*, IW 1000 (annual), http://www.industryweek.com, August 2011.

Transportation—Marine

4738 ■ WORLD'S TOP OCEAN CARRIERS, 2011

Ranked by: Shipments, in twenty-foot equivalent units (TEUs). **Remarks:** Also notes market share. **Number listed:** 30

1. A. P. Moller-Maersk A/S, with 2,455,014 TEUs
2. Mediterranean Shipping Co., 2,029,482
3. CMA CGM Group, 1,324,174
4. COSCO Container Lines, 650,840
5. Hapag-Lloyd, 627,725
6. Evergreen Line, 611,678
7. APL Ltd., 586,364
8. China Shipping Container Lines Co., Ltd. (CSCL), 505,913
9. Hanjin Shipping, 494,654
10. CSAV Group, 468,562

Source: *Logistics Management*, Top 30 Ocean Carriers (annual), October 2011, p. 54s.

Travel

4739 ■ EUROPE'S MOST VALUABLE TRAVEL AND LEISURE COMPANIES, 2011

Ranked by: Market value as of March 2011, in millions of U.S. dollars. **Remarks:** Also notes rank within the *FT Europe 500*, rank for previous year, country, revenue, net income, assets, number of employees, share price, price-to-earning ratio, dividend yield, and fiscal yearend. **Number listed:** 11

1. Compass Group plc, with $17,003.2 million
2. Sodexo, $11,490.4
3. Accor SA, $10,204
4. Deutsche Lufthansa AG, $9,773.8
5. Carnival plc, $7,200.2
6. Ryanair Holdings plc, $7,085.8
7. OPAP SA, $6,840.1
8. International Airlines Group, $6,751.1
9. International Hotels Group, $5,941.3
10. Air France-KLM SA, $5,006

Source: *Financial Times*, FT 500 (annual), http://www.ft.com, June 24, 2011.

4740 ■ FASTEST-GROWING PRIVATE TRAVEL COMPANIES IN THE U.S., 2007-2010

Ranked by: Average annual sales growth over three years, in percent. **Remarks:** Also notes headquarters, revenue, and rank in the overall *Inc. 500*. To qualify, private companies must have had annual revenues of at least $100,000 in 2007 and $2 million in 2010. **Number listed:** 4

1. Sixthman, with 2,861.1%
2. Ludus Sports, 1,252.9%
3. Mammoth Property Reservations, 825.5%
4. ElJet Aviation Services, 823.4%

Source: *Inc.*, Inc. 500 (annual), September 2011, p. 200.

4741 ■ MOST VALUABLE U.S. TRAVEL AND LEISURE COMPANIES, 2011

Ranked by: Market value as of March 2011, in millions of U.S. dollars. **Remarks:** Also notes rank within the *FT U.S. 500*, rank for previous year, country, revenue, net income, assets, number of employees, share price, price-to-earning ratio, dividend yield, and fiscal yearend. **Number listed:** 17

1. McDonald's Corp., with $79,384.6 million
2. Las Vegas Sands Corp., $30,671.6
3. Starbucks Corp., $27,564.7
4. Priceline.com Inc., $24,892.3
5. Yum! Brands Inc., $24,017.4
6. Carnival Corp., $23,316.7
7. Wynn Resorts Ltd., $15,846.7
8. Marriott International Inc., $13,091.2
9. Starwood Hotels & Resorts Worldwide Inc., $11,340.5
10. Southwest Airlines Co., $9,441.7

Source: *Financial Times*, FT 500 (annual), http://www.ft.com, June 24, 2011.

4742 ■ WORLD'S MOST VALUABLE TRAVEL AND LEISURE COMPANIES, 2011

Ranked by: Market value as of March 2011, in millions of U.S. dollars. **Remarks:** Also notes rank within the *FT 500*, rank for previous year, country, revenue, net income, assets, number of employees, share price, price-to-earning ratio, dividend yield, and fiscal year-end. **Number listed:** 9

1. McDonald's Corp., with $79,384.6 million
2. Las Vegas Sands Corp., $30,671.6
3. Carnival plc, $30,516.9
4. Starbucks Corp., $27,564.7
5. Priceline.com Inc., $24,892.3
6. Yum! Brands Inc., $24,017.4
7. East Japan Railway Co., $22,321.4
8. MTR Gaming Group Inc., $21,374.9
9. Genting Singapore plc, $19,827.4

Source: *Financial Times*, FT 500 (annual), http://www.ft.com, June 24, 2011.

Travel Agencies

4743 ■ TOP CRUISE-ONLY TRAVEL AGENCY FRANCHISES, 2012

Ranked by: Cumulative score based on financial strength and stability, growth rate, size of the system, number of years in busi-

ness, the length of time franchising, start-up costs, litigation, percentage of terminations, and whether the company provides financing. **Remarks:** Specific scores not provided. Also notes overall rank within the *Franchise 500,* contact information, description, year founded, year started franchising, states where registered, available U.S. regions, where seeking foreign expansion, number of franchised and company-owned units for past three years, start-up costs, franchise fees, royalty fees, and type of financing available. **Number listed:** 3

1. Cruise Planners Franchising LLC/American Express Co.
2. CruiseOne Inc.
3. Cruise Holidays

Source: *Entrepreneur*, Franchise 500 (annual), January 2012, p. 198-199.

4744 ■ TOP MISCELLANEOUS TRAVEL AGENCY FRANCHISES, 2012

Ranked by: Cumulative score based on financial strength and stability, growth rate, size of the system, number of years in business, the length of time franchising, start-up costs, litigation, percentage of terminations, and whether the company provides financing. **Remarks:** Specific scores not provided. Also notes overall rank within the *Franchise 500,* contact information, description, year founded, year started franchising, states where registered, available U.S. regions, where seeking foreign expansion, number of franchised and company-owned units for past three years, start-up costs, franchise fees, royalty fees, and type of financing available. **Number listed:** 2

1. Results! Travel
2. Travel Leaders

Source: *Entrepreneur*, Franchise 500 (annual), January 2012, p. 198-199.

Truck Freight Service
See: **Trucking Industry**

Trucking Industry
See also: **Refrigerated Trucks; Tank Trucks**

4745 ■ CANADA'S LARGEST FOR-HIRE CARRIERS, 2011

Ranked by: Total number of vehicles in fleet. **Remarks:** Also notes rank for previous year, headquarters, number of employees, and breakdown of fleet by type of vehicle. **Number listed:** 100

1. TransForce Inc., with 22,100 vehicles
2. Mullen Group Inc., 11,595
3. Vitran Corp., 11,375
4. Day & Ross Transportation Group, 6,295
5. TransX, 5,718
6. Groupe Robert, 5,399
7. Challenger Motor Freight Inc., 5,010
8. Bison Transport Inc., 4,446
9. Canada Cartage Diversified Income Fund, 4,382
10. Armour Transportation Systems, 4,000

Source: *Today's Trucking*, TT 100 (annual), March 2012, p. 25+.

4746 ■ JAPAN'S LARGEST TRUCKING COMPANIES OVERALL, 2011

Ranked by: Score based on revenue, profits, assets, and market capitalization. **Remarks:** Specific scores not provided. Also notes overall rank in the *Forbes 2000* and figures for each criterion. **Number listed:** 2

1. Yamato Holdings Co., Ltd.
2. Nippon Express Co., Ltd.

Source: *Forbes*, Forbes 2000 (annual), http://www.forbes.com, May 7, 2012.

4747 ■ LARGEST FOR-HIRE DEDICATED CONTRACT CARRIAGE COMPANIES, 2010

Ranked by: Revenue, in thousands of dollars. **Remarks:** Also notes figures for previous year and percent change. **Number listed:** 6

1. J. B. Hunt Dedicated Contract Services, with $906,760 thousand
2. Greatwide Dedicated Transport, $655,368
3. Ryder Supply Chain Solutions, $482,583
4. Canada Cartage System, $470,645
5. Ruan Transport Corp., $418,985
6. Cardinal Logistics Management, $274,100

Source: *Transport Topics*, Top 100 For-Hire Carriers (annual), 2011, p. 25.

4748 ■ LARGEST FOR-HIRE FLATBED/HEAVY SPECIAL-IZED TRUCKING COMPANIES, 2010

Ranked by: Revenue, in thousands of dollars. **Remarks:** Also notes figures for previous year and percent change. **Number listed:** 18

1. Landstar System Inc., with $744,053 thousand
2. TransForce Inc., $425,036
3. United Vision Logistics, $373,491
4. Mercer Transportation, $363,695
5. Contrans Group, $347,918
6. TMC, $347,000
7. Anderson Trucking Services, $332,563
8. Greatwide Logistics Services, $216,872
9. Maverick USA, $200,09
10. Lone Star Transportation, $198,000

Source: *Transport Topics*, Top 100 For-Hire Carriers (annual), 2011, p. 26.

4749 ■ LARGEST FOR-HIRE HOUSEHOLD GOODS/COMMERCIAL DELIVERY TRUCKING COMPANIES, 2010

Ranked by: Revenue, in thousands of dollars. **Remarks:** Also notes figures for previous year and percent change. **Number listed:** 10

1. SIRVA Inc., with $1,731,900 thousand
2. UniGroup Inc., $1,520,000
3. Atlas World Group, $759,998
4. Graebel Cos., $266,000
5. Suddath Cos., $281,515
6. Specialized Transportation Inc., $230,700
7. Arpin Van Lines, $180,706
8. Wheaton Van Lines, $160,000
9. Bekins Holding Corp., $91,271
10. Furniture Transportation Group, $82,757

Source: *Transport Topics*, Top 100 For-Hire Carriers (annual), 2011, p. 26.

4750 ■ LARGEST FOR-HIRE INTERMODAL/DRAYAGE TRANSPORTATION COMPANIES, 2010

Ranked by: Revenue, in thousands of dollars. **Remarks:** Also notes figures for previous year and percent change. **Number listed:** 12

1. J. B. Hunt Intermodal, with $2,141,200 thousand
2. Hub Group, $1,285,163
3. Pacer International Inc., $1,081,500
4. RoadLink USA, $297,000
5. U.S. 1 Industries, $210,751
6. Consolidated Fastfrate Inc., $196,021
7. Bridge Terminal Transport, $192,567
8. Evans Network of Cos., $178,730
9. Trailer Bridge Inc., $118,186
10. Universal Truckload Services Inc., $87,877

Source: *Transport Topics*, Top 100 For-Hire Carriers (annual), 2011, p. 24.

4751 ■ LARGEST FOR-HIRE LESS-THAN-TRUCKLOAD TRANSPORTATION COMPANIES, 2010

Ranked by: Revenue, in thousands of dollars. **Remarks:** Also notes figures for previous year and percent change. **Number listed:** 31

1. FedEx Freight, with $4,833,000 thousand
2. YRC Worldwide, $4,238,700
3. Con-Way Freight, $3,075,064
4. UPS Freight, $2,208,000
5. ABF Freight System Inc., $1,533,242
6. Estes Express Lines, $1,322,600
7. Old Dominion Freight Line, $1,318,088
8. R + L Carriers, $1,077,000
9. Saia Inc., $836,195
10. Averitt Express, $824,000

Source: *Transport Topics*, Top 100 For-Hire Carriers (annual), 2011, p. 24.

4752 ■ LARGEST FOR-HIRE MOTOR VEHICLE TRANSPORTATION COMPANIES, 2010

Ranked by: Revenue, in thousands of dollars. **Remarks:** Also notes figures for previous year and percent change. **Number listed:** 5

1. Allied Systems Holdings, with $528,000 thousand
2. United Road Services Inc., $285,000
3. Jack Cooper Transport, $275,000
4. Cassens Transport Co., $177,714
5. The Waggoners Trucking, $162,000

Source: *Transport Topics*, Top 100 For-Hire Carriers (annual), 2011, p. 26.

4753 ■ LARGEST FOR-HIRE PACKAGE/COURIER TRUCKING COMPANIES, 2010

Ranked by: Revenue, in thousands of dollars. **Remarks:** Also notes figures for previous year and percent change. **Number listed:** 5

1. United Parcel Service Inc. (UPS), with $29,742,000 thousand
2. FedEx Corp., $18,614,000
3. Purolator Inc., $1,448,777
4. TransForce Inc., $384,279
5. OnTrac, $198,000

Source: *Transport Topics*, Top 100 For-Hire Carriers (annual), 2011, p. 25.

4754 ■ LARGEST FOR-HIRE TRANSPORTATION COMPANIES IN THE U.S., 2010

Ranked by: Revenue, in thousands of dollars. **Remarks:** Also notes rank for previous year, location, stock exchange, ticker symbol, chief executive, website, net income, number of employees, figures for previous year, percent change, operating units, and number and types of equipment. **Number listed:** 100

1. United Parcel Service Inc. (UPS), with $49,600,000 thousand
2. FedEx Corp., $38,180,000
3. Con-Way Inc., $4,952,000
4. YRC Worldwide Inc., $4,334,640
5. J. B. Hunt Transport Services Inc., $3,793,485
6. Schneider National Inc., $3,100,000
7. Swift Transportation Co., Inc., $2,929,723
8. Landstar System, $2,400,170
9. Penske Logistics, $2,400,000
10. TransForce Inc., $1,942,746

Source: *Transport Topics*, Top 100 For-Hire Carriers (annual), 2011, p. 4-23.

4755 ■ LARGEST FOR-HIRE TRUCKLOAD TRANSPORTATION COMPANIES, 2010

Ranked by: Revenue, in thousands of dollars. **Remarks:** Also notes figures for previous year and percent change. **Number listed:** 44

1. Swift Transportation Co., Inc., with $2,631,000 thousand
2. Schneider National Truckload Services, $2,350,000
3. U.S. Xpress Enterprises, $1,585,283
4. Werner Enterprises Inc., $1,550,601
5. Landstar System Inc., $1,248,088
6. Knight Transportation Inc., $730,709
7. Crete Carrier Corp., $655,558
8. TransForce Inc., $623,969
9. Con-Way Truckload, $569,741
10. Celadon Group, $541,841

Source: *Transport Topics*, Top 100 For-Hire Carriers (annual), 2011, p. 25.

4756 ■ TOP DEDICATED CONTRACT CARRIERS, 2010

Ranked by: Score based on revenue, operating ratio, and other financial figures. **Remarks:** Specific scores not provided. Also notes rank in the overall *Top 250*. **Number listed:** 9

1. Greatwide Logistics Services
2. Ryder Supply Chain Solutions
3. Penske Logistics LLC
4. Ruan Transportation Management Systems
5. FirstFleet Inc.
6. Estenson Logistics LLC
7. Black Horse Carriers Inc.
8. Webster Trucking Corp.
9. Salem Carriers Inc.

Source: *Commercial Carrier Journal*, The Top 250 (annual), August 2011, p. 86.

4757 ■ TOP FLATBED, SPECIALIZED, AND HEAVY HAUL CARRIERS, 2010

Ranked by: Score based on revenue, operating ratio, and other financial figures. **Remarks:** Specific scores not provided. Also notes rank in the overall *Top 250*. **Number listed:** 25

1. United Vision Logistics
2. TMC Transportation Inc./Annett Holdings
3. Mercer Transportation Co.
4. Anderson Trucking Service Inc.
5. Acme Truck Line Inc.
6. Maverick USA Inc.
7. Boyd Bros. Transportation Inc.
8. Specialized Transportation Inc.
9. PGT Trucking Inc.
10. Melton Truck Lines Inc.

Source: *Commercial Carrier Journal*, The Top 250 (annual), August 2011, p. 86.

4758 ■ TOP *FORTUNE 500* COMPANIES IN TRUCKING AND TRUCK LEASING, 2011

Ranked by: Revenue, in millions of dollars. **Remarks:** Also notes overall rank in the *Fortune 500;* profits; profits as a percentage of revenue; stockholders' equity; and rank by each criterion. **Number listed:** 2

1. Ryder System Inc., with $6,051 million
2. YRC Worldwide Inc., $4,869

Source: *Fortune*, Fortune 500 (annual), May 21, 2012, p. F-40.

4759 ■ TOP HOUSEHOLD GOODS CARRIERS, 2010

Ranked by: Score based on revenue, operating ratio, and other financial figures. **Remarks:** Specific scores not provided. Also notes rank in the overall *Top 250*. **Number listed:** 10

1. UniGroup Inc.
2. Sirva Inc.
3. Atlas Van Lines Inc.
4. Coleman World Group
5. Bekins Van Lines LLC
6. Wheaton Van Lines Inc.
7. Arpin Group Inc.
8. Graebel Van Lines Inc.
9. Stevens Worldwide Van Lines
10. The Suddath Companies

Source: *Commercial Carrier Journal*, The Top 250 (annual), August 2011, p. 86.

4760 ■ TOP INTERMODAL CARRIERS, 2010

Ranked by: Score based on revenue, operating ratio, and other financial figures. **Remarks:** Specific scores not provided. Also notes rank in the overall *Top 250*. **Number listed:** 7

1. Pacer International Trucking Operations
2. RoadLink LLC
3. Bridge Terminal Transport Inc.
4. Kaplan Trucking Co./Horizon Freight System Inc.
5. California Multimodal LLC
6. C & K Trucking LLC
7. First Coast Logistics Services

Source: *Commercial Carrier Journal*, The Top 250 (annual), August 2011, p. 86.

4761 ■ TOP LESS-THAN-TRUCKLOAD FOR-HIRE CARRIERS, 2011

Ranked by: Revenue, in millions of dollars. **Remarks:** Also notes comments. **Number listed:** 25

1. FedEx Freight, with $4,710 million
2. Con-Way Freight, $3,197
3. YRC Freight, $3,183
4. UPS Freight, $2,299
5. Old Dominion Freight Line Inc., $1,732
6. ABF Freight Systems Inc., $1,681
7. Estes Express Lines Inc., $1,636
8. YRC Regional, $1,554
9. R + L Carriers, $1,207
10. SAIA Motor Freight Line Inc., $1,030

Source: *Logistics Management*, Top 50 Trucking Companies (annual), April 2012, p. 54s.

4762 ■ TOP MOTOR VEHICLE CARRIERS, 2010

Ranked by: Score based on revenue, operating ratio, and other financial figures. **Remarks:** Specific scores not provided. Also notes rank in the overall *Top 250*. **Number listed:** 9

1. Allied Systems Holdings
2. Jack Cooper Transport Co., Inc.
3. United Road Services Inc.
4. Quality Drive Away Inc.
5. Cassens Transport Co.
6. JHT Holdings
7. The Waggoners Trucking
8. Star Fleet Trucking Inc.
9. Fleet-Car Lease Inc.

Source: *Commercial Carrier Journal*, The Top 250 (annual), August 2011, p. 86.

4763 ■ TOP PARCEL AND SMALL SHIPMENT CARRIERS, 2010

Ranked by: Score based on revenue, operating ratio, and other financial figures. **Remarks:** Specific scores not provided. Also notes rank in the overall *Top 250*. **Number listed:** 5

1. United Parcel Service Inc. (UPS)
2. FedEx Corp.
3. DHL Americas
4. Tricor America
5. Spee Dee Delivery Service Inc.

Source: *Commercial Carrier Journal*, The Top 250 (annual), August 2011, p. 86-88.

4764 ■ TOP TANK TRUCK AND BULK COMMODITIES CARRIERS, 2010

Ranked by: Score based on revenue, operating ratio, and other financial figures. **Remarks:** Specific scores not provided. Also notes rank in the overall *Top 250*. **Number listed:** 28

1. Kenan Advantage Group
2. Quality Distribution Inc.
3. Trimac Transportation System
4. Groendyke Transport Inc.
5. Superior Bulk Logistics
6. The Dana Cos.
7. McCoy Group Transportation Div.
8. A & R Logistics Inc.
9. Enterprise Transportation Co.
10. Venezia Inc.

Source: *Commercial Carrier Journal*, The Top 250 (annual), August 2011, p. 88.

4765 ■ TOP TRUCKLOAD FOR-HIRE CARRIERS, 2011

Ranked by: Revenue, in millions of dollars. **Remarks:** Also notes subsidiary portfolio and comments. **Number listed:** 25

1. Swift Transportation Co., with $3,021 million
2. Schneider National Inc., $2,600
3. Werner Enterprises Inc., $1,684
4. Landstar System, $1,660
5. U.S. Xpress Enterprises Inc., $1,570
6. J. B. Hunt Transport Services Inc., $1,536
7. Prime Inc., $1,206
8. C. R. England Inc., $1,007
9. Crete Carrier Corp., $942
10. Greatwide Logistics, $907

Source: *Logistics Management*, Top 50 Trucking Companies (annual), April 2012, p. 56s.

4766 ■ TOP TRUCKLOAD AND LESS-THAN-TRUCKLOAD GENERAL FREIGHT CARRIERS, 2010

Ranked by: Score based on revenue, operating ratio, and other financial figures. **Remarks:** Specific scores not provided. Also notes rank in the overall *Top 250*. **Number listed:** 134

1. YRC Worldwide Inc.
2. Con-Way Inc.
3. Swift Transportation Co.
4. Schneider National Carriers Inc.
5. J. B. Hunt Transport Inc.
6. Landstar System Inc.
7. Werner Enterprises Inc.
8. U.S. Xpress Enterprises Inc.
9. Estes Express Lines Inc.
10. Old Dominion Freight Line Inc.

Source: *Commercial Carrier Journal*, The Top 250 (annual), August 2011, p. 84-86.

4767 ■ TOP U.S. CARRIERS OVERALL, 2010

Ranked by: Score based on revenue, operating ratio, and other financial figures. **Remarks:** Specific scores not provided. Also notes rank for previous year, headquarters, carrier type, revenue for current and previous year, percent change, and breakdown by type of equipment. **Number listed:** 250

1. United Parcel Service Inc. (UPS)
2. FedEx Corp.
3. YRC Worldwide Inc.
4. Con-Way Inc.
5. Swift Transportation Co.
6. Schneider National Carriers Inc.
7. J. B. Hunt Transport Inc.
8. Landstar System Inc.
9. Werner Enterprises Inc.
10. U.S. Xpress Enterprises Inc.

Source: *Commercial Carrier Journal*, The Top 250 (annual), August 2011, p. 63+.

4768 ■ WORLD'S LARGEST TRUCKING COMPANIES OVERALL, 2011

Ranked by: Score based on revenue, profits, assets, and market capitalization. **Remarks:** Specific scores not provided. Also notes country, overall rank in the *Forbes 2000,* and figures for each criterion. **Number listed:** 3

1. Yamato Holdings Co., Ltd.
2. Nippon Express Co., Ltd.
3. Imperial Holdings Ltd.

Source: *Forbes*, Forbes 2000 (annual), http://www.forbes.com, May 7, 2012.

4769 ■ WORLD'S TOP INDUSTRIAL LIFT TRUCK SUPPLIERS, 2010

Ranked by: Global revenue, in millions of U.S. dollars. **Remarks:** Also notes rank for previous year, headquarters, and North American brands. **Number listed:** 20

1. Toyota Industries Corp., with $5,900 million
2. Kion Group, $4,700
3. Jungheinrich Lift Truck Corp., $2,400
4. Crown Equipment Co., $1,800
5. Nacco Industries Inc., $1,800
6. Mitsubishi Caterpillar Forklift, $1,200
7. Komatsu Utility Co., $1,000
8. Nissan Forklift Corp., $900
9. TCM Corp., $889
10. Anhui Forklift Group, $777

Source: *Modern Materials Handling*, World's Top 20 Lift Truck Suppliers (annual), August 2011, p. 34.

Trucks

4770 ■ TOP-SELLING LIGHT TRUCKS IN CANADA, 2010

Ranked by: Number of trucks sold. **Number listed:** 10

1. Ford F-Series, with 95,446 trucks
2. Dodge Caravan, 55,306
3. Ram Pickup, 53,386
4. GMC Sierra, 45,457
5. Ford Escape, 43,038
6. Chevrolet Silverado, 41,737
7. Hyundai Santa Fe, 27,882
8. Honda CR-V, 24,930
9. Dodge Journey, 23,785
10. Toyota RAV4, 22,810

Source: *Ward's Automotive Yearbook*, (annual), 2011, p. 113.

4771 ■ TOP-SELLING LIGHT TRUCKS IN MEXICO, 2010

Ranked by: Number of trucks sold. **Number listed:** 10

1. Nissan PN300, with 21,044 trucks
2. Ford F-Series, 20,733
3. Chevrolet Silverado, 16,634
4. Nissan Pickup, 14,837
5. Ram Pickup, 13,884
6. Ford Ranger, 13,049
7. Dodge Journey, 12,879
8. Honda CR-V, 12,650
9. Ford Escape, 8,916
10. Chevrolet Tornado, 8,727

Source: *Ward's Automotive Yearbook*, (annual), 2011, p. 129.

4772 ■ TOP-SELLING LIGHT TRUCKS IN THE U.S., 2010

Ranked by: Number of trucks sold. **Number listed:** 10

1. Ford F-Series, with 502,125 trucks
2. Chevrolet Silverado, 370,135
3. Honda CR-V, 203,714
4. Ram Pickup, 194,175
5. Ford Escape, 191,026
6. Toyota RAV4, 170,877
7. Chevrolet Equinox, 149,979
8. GMC Sierra, 129,794
9. Ford Edge, 118,637
10. Chrysler Town & Country, 112,275

Source: *Ward's Automotive Yearbook*, (annual), 2011, p. 212.

Underwriting of Securities
See: **Security Underwriting**

Unemployment

4773 ■ STATES WITH THE HIGHEST UNEMPLOYMENT BENEFIT, 2010

Ranked by: Average weekly unemployment benefit, in dollars. **Number listed:** 51

1. Hawaii, with $416.16
2. New Jersey, $397.39
3. Massachusetts, $390.74
4. Washington, $381.04
5. Rhode Island, $379.40
6. Ohio, $366.01
7. Minnesota, $354.76
8. Colorado, $345.69
9. Pennsylvania, $337.40
10. Wyoming, $335.56

Source: *State Rankings*, (annual), CQ Press, 2011, p. 175.

4774 ■ STATES WITH THE HIGHEST UNEMPLOYMENT RATE, 2010

Ranked by: Unemployment rate, in percent. **Number listed:** 51

1. Nevada, with 14.5%
2. California, 12.5%
3. Florida, 12%
4. Michigan, 11.7%
5. Rhode Island, 11.5%
6. South Carolina, 10.7%
7. Oregon, 10.6%
8. Kentucky, 10.3%
9. Georgia, 10.2%
10. Mississippi, 10.1%

Source: *State Rankings*, (annual), CQ Press, 2011, p. 83.

4775 ■ STATES WITH THE LOWEST UNEMPLOYMENT BENEFIT, 2010

Ranked by: Average weekly unemployment benefit, in dollars. **Number listed:** 51

1. Mississippi, with $189.78
2. Alabama, $205.50
3. Louisiana, $207.50
4. Arizona, $213.85
5. Tennessee, $224.07
6. Florida, $230.81
7. South Carolina, $236.12
8. Alaska, $238.49
9. Missouri, $243.31
10. Delaware, $246.57

Source: *State Rankings*, (annual), CQ Press, 2011, p. 175.

4776 ■ STATES WITH THE LOWEST UNEMPLOYMENT RATE, 2010

Ranked by: Unemployment rate, in percent. **Remarks:** Also notes figure for U.S. **Number listed:** 51

1. North Dakota, with 3.8%
2. Nebraska, 4.4%
3. South Dakota, 4.6%
4. New Hampshire, 5.5%
5. Vermont, 5.8%
6. Iowa, 6.3%
7. Wyoming, 6.4%
7. Hawaii, 6.4%
9. Virginia, 6.7%
10. Oklahoma, 6.8%
10. Kansas, 6.8%

Source: *State Rankings*, (annual), CQ Press, 2011, p. 183.

Unit Trusts
See: **Mutual Funds**

Vacuum Cleaners

4777 ■ TOP BRANDS OF CENTRAL VACUUMS, 2010

Ranked by: Popularity among *CE Pro 100* companies, in percent. **Number listed:** 3

1. HP Products, with 15%
2. Beam, 14%
3. Honeywell, 3%

Source: *CE Pro*, Brand Analysis (annual), June 2011, p. 58.

Value-Added Resellers (Computers)

4778 ■ FASTEST-GROWING COMPUTER RESELLERS, 2008-2010

Ranked by: Growth in revenue, in percent. **Remarks:** Also notes headquarters and net sales for current year. **Number listed:** 100

1. Edge Solutions, with 2,633.33%
2. Ahead, 1,949.07%
3. Transcend United Technologies, 956.05%
4. MicroTechnologies LLC, 748.8%
5. Genesis Networks Enterprises LLC, 651.32%
6. Universal Understanding, 585.59%

7. OpenSky, 553.46%
8. Sovereign Systems, 518.49%
9. Emergent, 451.86%
10. Technology Support International, 420.73%

Source: *CRN*, Fast Growth 100 (annual), http://www.crn.com, September 2011.

4779 ■ TOP COMPUTER RESELLERS FOR THE ACCOUNTING INDUSTRY, 2010

Ranked by: Revenue, in millions of dollars. **Remarks:** Also notes location, number of offices and staff members, top executive, and accounting software. **Number listed:** 100

1. Tectura, with $300 million
2. Columbus IT Partners, $168
3. RSM McGladrey, $104.5
4. Tribridge, $65
5. Professional Advantage, $40
6. Crowe Horwath, $38.1
7. ePartners, $35
8. Net@Work, $27
9. Wipfli, $25
10. Fullscope, $23.65

Source: *Accounting Today*, VAR 100 (annual), August 2011, p. 32-34.

4780 ■ TOP COMPUTER RESELLERS IN TECHNOLOGY INVESTMENT, 2012

Ranked by: Score based on investments in information technology certifications and technical training in a wide range of technologies and vendor programs. **Remarks:** Specific scores not provided; companies are listed alphabetically, not ranked. Also notes location, top executive, and description. **Number listed:** 250

1. AdvizeX Technologies
2. Alexander Open Systems
3. Bluewater Communications Group
4. Cincinnati Bell Technology Solutions
5. CompuCom Systems
6. Compugen
7. CompuNet
8. Computer Design & Integration
9. Computex
10. Continental Resources

Source: *CRN*, Tech Elite 250 (annual), http://www.crn.com, February 2012.

Venture Capital

4781 ■ COUNTRIES WITH THE LEAST VENTURE CAPITAL AVAILABILITY, 2011

Ranked by: Score, on a scale of seven, based on the level of ease for entrepreneurs to locate venture capital. **Number listed:** 142

1. Burundi, with 1.4 points
1. Haiti, 1.4
3. Angola, 1.5
3. Cote d'Ivoire, 1.5
5. Burkina Faso, 1.6

6. Mongolia , 1.8

6. Kyrgyz Republic, 1.8

6. Mauritania, 1.8

6. Belize, 1.8

6. Iran, 1.8

6. Zimbabwe, 1.8

6. Malawi, 1.8

Source: *Global Competitiveness Report*, (annual), World Economic Forum, 2011, p. 484.

4782 ■ COUNTRIES WITH THE MOST VENTURE CAPITAL AVAILABILITY, 2011

Ranked by: Score, on a scale of seven, based on the level of ease for entrepreneurs to locate venture capital. **Number listed:** 142

1. Qatar, with 5.4 points

2. Israel, 4.5

3. Norway, 4.4

3. Singapore, 4.4

3. Hong Kong, 4.4

6. Sweden, 4.3

7. Saudi Arabia, 4.2

7. Bahrain, 4.2

7. Finland, 4.2

10. Malaysia, 4.1

10. Luxembourg, 4.1

Source: *Global Competitiveness Report*, (annual), World Economic Forum, 2011, p. 484.

4783 ■ MOST POWERFUL VENTURE CAPITALISTS IN TECHNOLOGY/LIFE SCIENCE, 2012

Ranked by: Score based on history of building both valuable and efficient businesses, measured in terms of market capitalization, change in value since going public or being sold, length of involvement, and depth of influence. **Remarks:** Specific scores not provided. Also notes rank for previous year, company name, notable deals, and comments. Only technology and life science companies that have gone public or been acquired in the past five years in a deal worth at least $200 million qualify for list. **Number listed:** 100

1. Jim Breyer

2. Marc Andreessen

3. Reid Hoffman

4. David Sze

5. Peter Fenton

6. Josh Kopelman

7. Paul Madera

8. Peter Thiel

9. Kevin Efrusy

10. Jeremy Levine

Source: *Forbes*, The Midas List (annual), May 21, 2012, p. 78-86.

4784 ■ TOP VENTURE CAPITAL COMPANIES, 2012

Ranked by: Number of partners on the Midas List. **Number listed:** 7

1. Accel Partners, with 10 partners

2. Bessemer Venture Partners, 5

2. Greylock Partners, 5

2. Sequoia Capital, 5

5. Benchmark Capital, 4

5. Kleiner Perkins Caufield & Byers, 4

5. New Enterprise Associates, 4

Source: *Forbes*, The Midas List (annual), May 21, 2012, p. 85.

Veterans—Employment

4785 ■ BEST MEDIUM-SIZED METROPOLITAN AREAS FOR MILITARY RETIREES TO LAUNCH SECOND CAREERS, 2011

Ranked by: Score based on employment opportunities and sectors that align with military skill sets; overall job climate; number of small businesses; proximity to a military installation and a VA hospital/clinic; and general quality of life and financial criteria. **Remarks:** Specific scores not provided. Medium-sized metros are defined as having a population between 175,000 and 500,000. **Number listed:** 10

1. Manchester, NH

2. Anchorage, AK

3. Killeen, TX

4. Huntsville, AL

5. Ann Arbor, MI

6. Rockingham County, NH

7. York, PA

8. Roanoke, VA

9. Topeka, KS

10. Lexington, KY

Source: *Best Places for Military Retirement: Second Careers*, (annual), USAA, November 9, 2011.

4786 ■ BEST METROPOLITAN AREAS FOR MILITARY RETIREES TO LAUNCH SECOND CAREERS, 2011

Ranked by: Score based on employment opportunities and sectors that align with military skill sets; overall job climate; number of small businesses; proximity to a military installation and a VA hospital/clinic; and general quality of life and financial criteria. **Remarks:** Specific scores not provided. **Number listed:** 10

1. Oklahoma City, OK

2. Norfolk, VA

3. Richmond, VA

4. Austin, TX

5. San Antonio, TX

6. Madison, WI

7. Philadelphia, PA

8. Raleigh, NC

9. Omaha, NE

10. Manchester, NH

Source: *Best Places for Military Retirement: Second Careers*, (annual), USAA, November 9, 2011.

4787 ■ BEST PREMIUM METROPOLITAN AREAS FOR MILITARY RETIREES TO LAUNCH SECOND CAREERS, 2011

Ranked by: Score based on employment opportunities and sectors that align with military skill sets; overall job climate; number of small businesses; proximity to a military installation and a VA hospital/clinic; and general quality of life and financial criteria. **Remarks:** Specific scores not provided. Premium metros are defined as having housing costs that are 40 percent or more above the national median. **Number listed:** 10

1. Nassau, NY
2. Washington DC
3. Cambridge, MA
4. Honolulu, HI
5. Bethesda, MD
6. Baltimore, MD
7. Edison, NJ
8. Boston, MA
9. New York, NY
10. Seattle, WA

Source: *Best Places for Military Retirement: Second Careers*, (annual), USAA, November 9, 2011.

4788 ■ BEST SMALL METROPOLITAN AREAS FOR MILITARY RETIREES TO LAUNCH SECOND CAREERS, 2011

Ranked by: Score based on employment opportunties and sectors that align with military skill sets; overall job climate; number of small businesses; proximity to a military installation and a VA hospital/clinic; and general quality of life and financial criteria. **Remarks:** Specific scores not provided. Small metros are defined as having a population less than 175,000. **Number listed:** 10

1. Cheyenne, WY
2. La Crosse, WI
3. Rapid City, SD
4. Columbia, MO
5. Lebanon, PA
6. State College, PA
7. Wichita Falls, TX
8. Warner Robins, GA
9. Jefferson City, MO
10. Lawton, OK

Source: *Best Places for Military Retirement: Second Careers*, (annual), USAA, November 9, 2011.

4789 ■ COMPANIES WITH THE BEST RESERVE AND GUARD POLICIES, 2011

Ranked by: Score based on policies for National Reserve and Guards. **Remarks:** Scores not provided. **Number listed:** 10

1. USAA
2. Citizens Financial Group
3. BAE Systems Inc.
4. URS Corp.
5. Bank of America Corp.
6. Johnson Controls Inc.
7. BNSF Railway
8. Amazon.com Inc.
9. AT&T Inc.
10. Dyncorp International

Source: *G.I. Jobs*, Top 100 Military Friendly Employers (annual), December 2011, p. 122.

4790 ■ COMPANIES HIRING THE HIGHEST PERCENTAGE OF MILITARY VETERANS, 2011

Ranked by: Percentage of new veteran hires. **Remarks:** Figures not provided. **Number listed:** 10

1. Aerotek Inc.
2. AAR Corp.
3. Dyncorp International
4. Cubic Mission Support Services
5. Wyle
6. ManTech International Corp.
7. American Eurocopter
8. IAP Worldwide Services Inc.
9. URS Corp.
10. Booz Allen Hamilton Inc.

Source: *G.I. Jobs*, Top 100 Military Friendly Employers (annual), December 2011, p. 122.

4791 ■ COMPANIES WITH THE MOST ASSETS COMMITTED TO RECRUITING MILITARY VETERANS, 2011

Ranked by: Assets devoted to the hiring of military veterans. **Remarks:** Specific figures not provided. **Number listed:** 10

1. Brink's U.S.
2. CACI International Inc.
3. Cubic Mission Support Services
4. Wyle
5. American Eurocopter
6. AlliedBarton Security Services
7. URS Corp.
8. Fluor Corp.
9. Johnson Controls Inc.
10. U-Haul International Inc.

Source: *G.I. Jobs*, Top 100 Military Friendly Employers (annual), December 2011, p. 122.

4792 ■ TOP ARIZONA EMPLOYERS FOR MILITARY VETERANS, 2011

Ranked by: Score based on long-term commitment to hiring military veterans, recruiting and hiring efforts and results, policies for Reserve/Guard members called to active duty, and the presence of special recruitment military programs. **Remarks:** Scores not provided. Also notes headquarters and rank in the overall *Top 100*. To qualify, companies must have at least $500 million in annual revenue. Ranking does not include government agencies, non-profit organizations, and universities. **Number listed:** 3

1. U-Haul International Inc.
2. Freeport-McMoRan Copper & Gold Inc.
3. Triwest Healthcare Alliance

Source: *G.I. Jobs*, Top 100 Military Friendly Employers (annual), December 2011, p. 124.

4793 ■ TOP ARKANSAS EMPLOYERS FOR MILITARY VETERANS, 2011

Ranked by: Score based on long-term commitment to hiring military veterans, recruiting and hiring efforts and results, policies for Reserve/Guard members called to active duty, and the presence of special recruitment military programs. **Remarks:** Scores not provided. Also notes headquarters and rank in the overall *Top 100*. To qualify, companies must have at least $500 million in annual revenue. Ranking does not include government agencies, non-profit organizations, and universities. **Number listed:** 2

1. J. B. Hunt Transport Inc.
2. Wal-Mart Stores Inc.

Source: *G.I. Jobs*, Top 100 Military Friendly Employers (annual), December 2011, p. 124.

4794 ■ TOP CALIFORNIA EMPLOYERS FOR MILITARY VETERANS, 2011

Ranked by: Score based on long-term commitment to hiring military veterans, recruiting and hiring efforts and results, policies for Reserve/Guard members called to active duty, and the presence of special recruitment military programs. **Remarks:** Scores not provided. Also notes headquarters and rank in the overall *Top 100*. To qualify, companies must have at least $500 million in annual revenue. Ranking does not include government agencies, non-profit organizations, and universities. **Number listed:** 7

1. Wyle Corp.
2. Southern California Edison
3. QUALCOMM Inc.
4. CB Richard Ellis Group Inc.
5. Intuit Corp.
6. 24 Hour Fitness Worldwide Inc.
7. Applied Materials Inc.

Source: *G.I. Jobs*, Top 100 Military Friendly Employers (annual), December 2011, p. 124.

4795 ■ TOP CONNECTICUT EMPLOYERS FOR MILITARY VETERANS, 2011

Ranked by: Score based on long-term commitment to hiring military veterans, recruiting and hiring efforts and results, policies for Reserve/Guard members called to active duty, and the presence of special recruitment military programs. **Remarks:** Scores not provided. Also notes headquarters and rank in the overall *Top 100*. To qualify, companies must have at least $500 million in annual revenue. Ranking does not include government agencies, non-profit organizations, and universities. **Number listed:** 3

1. General Electric Co.
2. United Rentals Inc.
3. The Hartford Financial Services Group Inc.

Source: *G.I. Jobs*, Top 100 Military Friendly Employers (annual), December 2011, p. 125.

4796 ■ TOP EMPLOYERS FOR MILITARY VETERANS, 2011

Ranked by: Score based on long-term commitment to hiring military veterans, recruiting and hiring efforts and results, policies for Reserve/Guard members called to active duty, and the presence of special recruitment military programs. **Remarks:** Scores not provided. Also notes industry, headquarters, number of employees, revenue, corporate Web site, employment Web Site, and comments. To qualify, companies must have at least $500 million in annual revenue. Ranking does not include government agencies, non-profit organizations, and universities. **Number listed:** 100

1. Amazon.com Inc.
2. Southern Co.
3. CSX Corp.
4. BNSF Railway
5. URS Corp.
6. ManTech International Corp.
7. Johnson Controls Inc.
8. Booz Allen Hamilton Inc.
9. USAA
10. T-Mobile USA Inc.

Source: *G.I. Jobs*, Top 100 Military Friendly Employers (annual), December 2011, p. 28+.

4797 ■ TOP FLORIDA EMPLOYERS FOR MILITARY VETERANS, 2011

Ranked by: Score based on long-term commitment to hiring military veterans, recruiting and hiring efforts and results, policies

for Reserve/Guard members called to active duty, and the presence of special recruitment military programs. **Remarks:** Scores not provided. Also notes headquarters and rank in the overall *Top 100*. To qualify, companies must have at least $500 million in annual revenue. Ranking does not include government agencies, non-profit organizations, and universities. **Number listed:** 4

1. CSX Corp.
2. Harris Corp.
3. G4S Secure Solutions (USA)
4. IAP Worldwide Services Inc.

Source: *G.I. Jobs*, Top 100 Military Friendly Employers (annual), December 2011, p. 125.

4798 ■ TOP FRANCHISES FOR VETERANS, 2011

Ranked by: Score based on incentives for veterans and number of veteran-owned franchises. **Remarks:** Scores not provided. Also notes rank in the *Franchise 500*, contact information, start-up costs, incentives, start year of veteran incentives, veteran leadership, and ways the company supports the troops. **Number listed:** 10

1. Matco Tools
2. The UPS Store/Mail Boxes Etc.
3. Sport Clips
4. Dunkin' Donuts
5. CruiseOne Inc.
6. Meineke Car Care Centers
7. WIN Home Inspection
8. Aire Serv Heating & Air Conditioning Inc.
9. Mr. Handyman International LLC
10. Snap-on Tools

Source: *Entrepreneur*, Veteran Franchises, July 2011, p. 102-104.

4799 ■ TOP GEORGIA EMPLOYERS FOR MILITARY VETERANS, 2011

Ranked by: Score based on long-term commitment to hiring military veterans, recruiting and hiring efforts and results, policies for Reserve/Guard members called to active duty, and the presence of special recruitment military programs. **Remarks:** Scores not provided. Also notes headquarters and rank in the overall *Top 100*. To qualify, companies must have at least $500 million in annual revenue. Ranking does not include government agencies, non-profit organizations, and universities. **Number listed:** 2

1. Southern Co.
2. The Home Depot Inc.

Source: *G.I. Jobs*, Top 100 Military Friendly Employers (annual), December 2011, p. 125.

4800 ■ TOP ILLINOIS EMPLOYERS FOR MILITARY VETERANS, 2011

Ranked by: Score based on long-term commitment to hiring military veterans, recruiting and hiring efforts and results, policies for Reserve/Guard members called to active duty, and the presence of special recruitment military programs. **Remarks:** Scores not provided. Also notes headquarters and rank in the overall *Top 100*. To qualify, companies must have at least $500 million in annual revenue. Ranking does not include government agencies, non-profit organizations, and universities. **Number listed:** 8

1. Combined Insurance Co. of America
2. AAR Corp.
3. CN
4. Sears Holdings Corp.
5. Exelon Corp.

6. State Farm Insurance Companies

7. CDW Corp.

8. U.S. Cellular Corp.

Source: *G.I. Jobs*, Top 100 Military Friendly Employers (annual), December 2011, p. 124.

4801 ■ TOP IOWA EMPLOYERS FOR MILITARY VETERANS, 2011

Ranked by: Score based on long-term commitment to hiring military veterans, recruiting and hiring efforts and results, policies for Reserve/Guard members called to active duty, and the presence of special recruitment military programs. **Remarks:** Scores not provided. Also notes headquarters and rank in the overall *Top 100*. To qualify, companies must have at least $500 million in annual revenue. Ranking does not include government agencies, non-profit organizations, and universities. **Number listed:** 2

1. MidAmerican Energy

2. Rockwell Collins Inc.

Source: *G.I. Jobs*, Top 100 Military Friendly Employers (annual), December 2011, p. 124.

4802 ■ TOP MARYLAND EMPLOYERS FOR MILITARY VETERANS, 2011

Ranked by: Score based on long-term commitment to hiring military veterans, recruiting and hiring efforts and results, policies for Reserve/Guard members called to active duty, and the presence of special recruitment military programs. **Remarks:** Scores not provided. Also notes headquarters and rank in the overall *Top 100*. To qualify, companies must have at least $500 million in annual revenue. Ranking does not include government agencies, non-profit organizations, and universities. **Number listed:** 4

1. URS Corp.

2. Lockheed Martin Corp.

3. Sodexo

4. Aerotek Inc.

Source: *G.I. Jobs*, Top 100 Military Friendly Employers (annual), December 2011, p. 125.

4803 ■ TOP MINNESOTA EMPLOYERS FOR MILITARY VETERANS, 2011

Ranked by: Score based on long-term commitment to hiring military veterans, recruiting and hiring efforts and results, policies for Reserve/Guard members called to active duty, and the presence of special recruitment military programs. **Remarks:** Scores not provided. Also notes headquarters and rank in the overall *Top 100*. To qualify, companies must have at least $500 million in annual revenue. Ranking does not include government agencies, non-profit organizations, and universities. **Number listed:** 2

1. U.S. Bank

2. Xcel Energy Inc.

Source: *G.I. Jobs*, Top 100 Military Friendly Employers (annual), December 2011, p. 124.

4804 ■ TOP NEBRASKA EMPLOYERS FOR MILITARY VETERANS, 2011

Ranked by: Score based on long-term commitment to hiring military veterans, recruiting and hiring efforts and results, policies for Reserve/Guard members called to active duty, and the presence of special recruitment military programs. **Remarks:** Scores not provided. Also notes headquarters and rank in the overall *Top 100*. To qualify, companies must have at least $500 million in annual revenue. Ranking does not include government agencies, non-profit organizations, and universities. **Number listed:** 2

1. Union Pacific Corp.

2. Werner Enterprises Inc.

Source: *G.I. Jobs*, Top 100 Military Friendly Employers (annual), December 2011, p. 124.

4805 ■ TOP NEW JERSEY EMPLOYERS FOR MILITARY VETERANS, 2011

Ranked by: Score based on long-term commitment to hiring military veterans, recruiting and hiring efforts and results, policies for Reserve/Guard members called to active duty, and the presence of special recruitment military programs. **Remarks:** Scores not provided. Also notes headquarters and rank in the overall *Top 100*. To qualify, companies must have at least $500 million in annual revenue. Ranking does not include government agencies, non-profit organizations, and universities. **Number listed:** 5

1. Prudential Financial Inc.

2. Public Service Enterprise Group Inc.

3. Merck & Co., Inc.

4. Novartis Pharmaceuticals Corp.

5. DRS Technologies Inc.

Source: *G.I. Jobs*, Top 100 Military Friendly Employers (annual), December 2011, p. 125.

4806 ■ TOP NEW YORK EMPLOYERS FOR MILITARY VETERANS, 2011

Ranked by: Score based on long-term commitment to hiring military veterans, recruiting and hiring efforts and results, policies for Reserve/Guard members called to active duty, and the presence of special recruitment military programs. **Remarks:** Scores not provided. Also notes headquarters and rank in the overall *Top 100*. To qualify, companies must have at least $500 million in annual revenue. Ranking does not include government agencies, non-profit organizations, and universities. **Number listed:** 4

1. J. P. Morgan Chase & Co.

2. Verizon Communications Inc.

3. The Travelers Cos., Inc.

4. ITT Corp.

Source: *G.I. Jobs*, Top 100 Military Friendly Employers (annual), December 2011, p. 125.

4807 ■ TOP NORTH CAROLINA EMPLOYERS FOR MILITARY VETERANS, 2011

Ranked by: Score based on long-term commitment to hiring military veterans, recruiting and hiring efforts and results, policies for Reserve/Guard members called to active duty, and the presence of special recruitment military programs. **Remarks:** Scores not provided. Also notes headquarters and rank in the overall *Top 100*. To qualify, companies must have at least $500 million in annual revenue. Ranking does not include government agencies, non-profit organizations, and universities. **Number listed:** 2

1. Lowe's Companies Inc.

2. Bank of America Corp.

Source: *G.I. Jobs*, Top 100 Military Friendly Employers (annual), December 2011, p. 125.

4808 ■ TOP OHIO EMPLOYERS FOR MILITARY VETERANS, 2011

Ranked by: Score based on long-term commitment to hiring military veterans, recruiting and hiring efforts and results, policies for Reserve/Guard members called to active duty, and the presence of special recruitment military programs. **Remarks:** Scores not provided. Also notes headquarters and rank in the overall *Top 100*. To qualify, companies must have at least $500 million in annual revenue. Ranking does not include government agencies, non-profit organizations, and universities. **Number listed:** 5

1. FirstEnergy Corp.
2. Cintas Corp.
3. Progressive Insurance Group
4. Eaton Corp.
5. American Electric Power Co., Inc.

Source: *G.I. Jobs*, Top 100 Military Friendly Employers (annual), December 2011, p. 124.

4809 ■ TOP PENNSYLVANIA EMPLOYERS FOR MILITARY VETERANS, 2011

Ranked by: Score based on long-term commitment to hiring military veterans, recruiting and hiring efforts and results, policies for Reserve/Guard members called to active duty, and the presence of special recruitment military programs. **Remarks:** Scores not provided. Also notes headquarters and rank in the overall *Top 100*. To qualify, companies must have at least $500 million in annual revenue. Ranking does not include government agencies, non-profit organizations, and universities. **Number listed:** 3

1. Sunoco Logistics
2. AlliedBarton Security Services
3. PPL Corp.

Source: *G.I. Jobs*, Top 100 Military Friendly Employers (annual), December 2011, p. 125.

4810 ■ TOP TENNESSEE EMPLOYERS FOR MILITARY VETERANS, 2011

Ranked by: Score based on long-term commitment to hiring military veterans, recruiting and hiring efforts and results, policies for Reserve/Guard members called to active duty, and the presence of special recruitment military programs. **Remarks:** Scores not provided. Also notes headquarters and rank in the overall *Top 100*. To qualify, companies must have at least $500 million in annual revenue. Ranking does not include government agencies, non-profit organizations, and universities. **Number listed:** 2

1. Eastman Chemical Co.
2. Corrections Corp. of America

Source: *G.I. Jobs*, Top 100 Military Friendly Employers (annual), December 2011, p. 125.

4811 ■ TOP TEXAS EMPLOYERS FOR MILITARY VETERANS, 2011

Ranked by: Score based on long-term commitment to hiring military veterans, recruiting and hiring efforts and results, policies for Reserve/Guard members called to active duty, and the presence of special recruitment military programs. **Remarks:** Scores not provided. Also notes headquarters and rank in the overall *Top 100*. To qualify, companies must have at least $500 million in annual revenue. Ranking does not include government agencies, non-profit organizations, and universities. **Number listed:** 11

1. BNSF Railway
2. USAA
3. Fluor Corp.
4. Fugro
5. West Corp.
6. Waste Management Inc.
7. 7-Eleven Inc.
8. AT&T Inc.
9. Brink's U.S.
10. Southwest Airlines Co.

Source: *G.I. Jobs*, Top 100 Military Friendly Employers (annual), December 2011, p. 125.

4812 ■ TOP VIRGINIA EMPLOYERS FOR MILITARY VETERANS, 2011

Ranked by: Score based on long-term commitment to hiring military veterans, recruiting and hiring efforts and results, policies for Reserve/Guard members called to active duty, and the presence of special recruitment military programs. **Remarks:** Scores not provided. Also notes headquarters and rank in the overall *Top 100*. To qualify, companies must have at least $500 million in annual revenue. Ranking does not include government agencies, non-profit organizations, and universities. **Number listed:** 13

1. ManTech International Corp.
2. Booz Allen Hamilton Inc.
3. Northrop Grumman Corp.
4. Dyncorp International
5. CACI International Inc.
6. BAE Systems Inc.
7. Computer Sciences Corp.
8. Deloitte LLP
9. Science Applications International Corp. (SAIC)
10. PricewaterhouseCoopers LLP

Source: *G.I. Jobs*, Top 100 Military Friendly Employers (annual), December 2011, p. 125.

4813 ■ TOP WASHINGTON EMPLOYERS FOR MILITARY VETERANS, 2011

Ranked by: Score based on long-term commitment to hiring military veterans, recruiting and hiring efforts and results, policies for Reserve/Guard members called to active duty, and the presence of special recruitment military programs. **Remarks:** Scores not provided. Also notes headquarters and rank in the overall *Top 100*. To qualify, companies must have at least $500 million in annual revenue. Ranking does not include government agencies, non-profit organizations, and universities. **Number listed:** 3

1. Amazon.com Inc.
2. T-Mobile USA Inc.
3. Cubic Mission Support Services

Source: *G.I. Jobs*, Top 100 Military Friendly Employers (annual), December 2011, p. 124.

4814 ■ TOP WISCONSIN EMPLOYERS FOR MILITARY VETERANS, 2011

Ranked by: Score based on long-term commitment to hiring military veterans, recruiting and hiring efforts and results, policies for Reserve/Guard members called to active duty, and the presence of special recruitment military programs. **Remarks:** Scores not provided. Also notes headquarters and rank in the overall *Top 100*. To qualify, companies must have at least $500 million in annual revenue. Ranking does not include government agencies, non-profit organizations, and universities. **Number listed:** 3

1. Johnson Controls Inc.
2. Oshkosh Corp.
3. Schneider National Inc.

Source: *G.I. Jobs*, Top 100 Military Friendly Employers (annual), December 2011, p. 124.

Video

4815 ■ TOP SITES FOR VIDEO STREAMING, 2011

Ranked by: Total number of streams during the month of December, in millions. **Number listed:** 5

1. YouTube, with 13,783 million streams
2. Hulu, 757
3. Vevo, 435
4. AOL Media Network, 359
5. Yahoo!, 339

Source: *Advertising Age*, Digital Issue (annual), February 27, 2012, p. 16.

Video Games

4816 ■ TOP BRANDS OF HOME GAMING SYSTEMS, 2010

Ranked by: Popularity among *CE Pro 100* companies, in percent. **Number listed:** 3

1. Sony, with 34%
2. Microsoft, 26%
3. Nintendo, 22%

Source: *CE Pro*, Brand Analysis (annual), June 2011, p. 60.

4817 ■ TOP-SELLING VIDEO GAMES SOLD ON AMAZON.COM, 2011

Ranked by: Sales. **Remarks:** Specific figures not provided. **Number listed:** 10

1. Call of Duty: Modern Warfare 3
2. Just Dance 3
3. The Elder Scrolls V: Skyrim
4. Battlefield 3
5. Portal 2
6. Batman: Arkham City
7. Just Dance 2
8. Madden NFL 12
9. Gears of War 3
10. Call of Duty: Black Ops

Source: *Entertainment Weekly*, The Year in Charts (annual), December 2011, p. 119.

4818 ■ TOP VIDEO GAMES, 2012

Ranked by: Number of units sold in the month of January, in thousands. **Number listed:** 5

1. Call of Duty: Modern Warfare 3, with 377 thousand units
2. Just Dance 3, 367
3. Elder Scrolls V: Skyrim, 329
4. NBA 2K12, n/a
5. Battlefield 3, n/a

Source: *Advertising Age*, Digital Issue (annual), February 27, 2012, p. 16.

Vitamins

4819 ■ TOP VITAMIN FRANCHISES, 2012

Ranked by: Cumulative score based on financial strength and stability, growth rate, size of the system, number of years in business, the length of time franchising, start-up costs, litigation, percentage of terminations, and whether the company provides financing. **Remarks:** Specific scores not provided. Also notes

overall rank within the *Franchise 500,* contact information, description, year founded, year started franchising, states where registered, available U.S. regions, where seeking foreign expansion, number of franchised and company-owned units for past three years, start-up costs, franchise fees, royalty fees, and type of financing available. **Number listed:** 3

1. GNC Franchising Inc.
2. Complete Nutrition
3. Max Muscle Sports Nutrition

Source: *Entrepreneur*, Franchise 500 (annual), January 2012, p. 200-201.

Wages and Salaries
See: **Compensation**

Warehousing

4820 ■ LARGEST NORTH AMERICAN THIRD-PARTY WAREHOUSE OPERATORS, 2010

Ranked by: Total warehouse area, in millions of square feet. **Remarks:** Also notes headquarters and website. **Number listed:** 20

1. DHL Exel Supply Chain, with 95 million sq.ft.
2. GENCO Supply Chain Solutions, 37
3. Jacobson Cos., 35
4. AmeriCold Logistics Inc., 34.5
5. CEVA Logistics, 33
6. OHL, 30.2
7. Ryder Supply Chain Solutions, 30
8. Caterpillar Logistics Services Inc., 29
9. Kenco Logistic Services, 25
10. APL Logistics, 24.7

Source: *Modern Materials Handling*, Warehouse Operators (annual), December 2011, p. 38.

Waste Management Industry

4821 ■ LARGEST ELECTRIC, GAS, AND SANITARY SERVICES COMPANIES BY EMPLOYEES, 2010

Ranked by: Total number of employees. **Remarks:** Also notes contact information for headquarters, number of employees at headquarters, revenue, rank by revenue, and primary SIC code. **Number listed:** 49

1. Waste Management Inc., with 43,530 employees
2. Republic Services Inc., 31,000
3. AES Corp., 27,000
4. Southern Co., 26,112
5. Puget Holding Co., 22,860
6. American Electric Power Co., Inc., 21,673
7. Progress Energy Inc., 20,500
8. PG & E Corp., 19,425
9. Pacific Gas & Electric Co., 19,401
10. Edison International, 19,244

Source: *Business Rankings*, (annual), Dun & Bradstreet Inc., 2011, p. VI.106-VI.107.

4822 ■ LARGEST ELECTRIC, GAS, AND SANITARY SERVICES COMPANIES BY SALES, 2010

Ranked by: Total revenue, in dollars. **Remarks:** Also notes contact information for headquarters, number of employees at headquarters and overall, rank by employees, and primary SIC code. **Number listed:** 50

1. Enterprise Products Partners LP, with $33,739,300,000
2. Veolia Water North America Northeast LLC, $23,000,000,000
3. Exelon Corp., $18,644,000,000
4. Southern Co., $17,456,000,000
5. Nextera Energy Inc., $15,317,000,000
6. Dominion Resources Inc., $15,197,000,000
7. American Electric Power Co., Inc., $14,427,000,000
8. Constellation Energy Group Inc., $14,340,000,000
9. Duke Energy Corp., $14,272,000,000
10. AES Corp., $14,119,000,000

Source: *Business Rankings*, (annual), Dun & Bradstreet Inc., 2011, p. V.106-V.107.

4823 ■ LARGEST U.S. ENVIRONMENTAL AND WASTE COMPANIES OVERALL, 2011

Ranked by: Score based on revenue, profits, assets, and market capitalization. **Remarks:** Specific scores not provided. Also notes overall rank in the *Forbes 2000* and figures for each criterion. **Number listed:** 2

1. Waste Management Inc.
2. Republic Services Inc.

Source: *Forbes*, Forbes 2000 (annual), http://www.forbes.com, May 7, 2012.

4824 ■ LARGEST WASTE MANAGEMENT COMPANIES, 2010

Ranked by: Revenue, in millions of dollars. **Remarks:** Also notes headquarters, CEO, rank for previous year, whether company is public or private, types of customers, number of employees, and types of services. **Number listed:** 100

1. Waste Management Inc., with $12,500 million
2. Republic Services Inc., $8,100
3. Veolia Environmental Services North America Corp., $1,900
4. Clean Harbors Inc., $1,700
5. Covanta Energy Corp., $1,600
6. Stericycle Inc., $1,440
7. Progressive Waste Solutions Ltd., $1,430
8. Waste Connections Inc., $1,320
9. Newpark Resources Inc., $716
10. Recology Inc., $539

Source: *Waste Age*, Waste Age 100 (annual), June 2011, p. 38+.

4825 ■ TOP *FORTUNE 500* COMPANIES IN WASTE MANAGEMENT, 2011

Ranked by: Revenue, in millions of dollars. **Remarks:** Also notes overall rank in the *Fortune 500;* profits; profits as a percentage of revenue; stockholders' equity; and rank by each criterion. **Number listed:** 2

1. Waste Management Inc., with $13,378 million

2. Republic Services Inc., $8,193

Source: *Fortune*, Fortune 500 (annual), May 21, 2012, p. F-40.

4826 ■ WORLD'S LARGEST ENVIRONMENTAL AND WASTE COMPANIES OVERALL, 2011

Ranked by: Score based on revenue, profits, assets, and market capitalization. **Remarks:** Specific scores not provided. Also notes country, overall rank in the *Forbes 2000,* and figures for each criterion. **Number listed:** 2

1. Waste Management Inc.
2. Republic Services Inc.

Source: *Forbes*, Forbes 2000 (annual), http://www.forbes.com, May 7, 2012.

Water, Bottled
See: **Bottled Water**

Water Companies

4827 ■ EUROPE'S MOST VALUABLE GAS, WATER, AND MULTIUTILITIES COMPANIES, 2011

Ranked by: Market value as of March 2011, in millions of U.S. dollars. **Remarks:** Also notes rank within the *FT Europe 500*, rank for previous year, country, revenue, net income, assets, number of employees, share price, price-to-earning ratio, dividend yield, and fiscal yearend. **Number listed:** 13

1. GDF Suez, with $91,809.4 million
2. E.On AG, $61,193.3
3. RWE AG, $35,754.8
4. National Grid Transco plc, $33,402.3
5. Centrica plc, $26,876
6. International Power plc, $25,143.2
7. Snam Rete Gas SpA, $20,097.9
8. Gas Natural SDG SA, $17,338.3
9. Veolia Environnement SA, $15,540.2
10. Suez Environnement, $10,145.9

Source: *Financial Times*, FT 500 (annual), http://www.ft.com, June 24, 2011.

4828 ■ WORLD'S MOST VALUABLE WATER UTILITIES BRANDS, 2011

Ranked by: Brand value, in millions of U.S. dollars. **Remarks:** Also notes rank within the *Global 500* for current and previous year, figures for current and previous year, country, and brand rating. Ranking is available online only. **Number listed:** 2

1. Veolia, with $4,077 million
2. Suez Environnement, $2,700

Source: *Global 500*, (annual), Brand Finance plc, March 2012.

Water Transportation Services

4829 ■ LARGEST WATER TRANSPORTATION COMPANIES BY EMPLOYEES, 2010

Ranked by: Total number of employees. **Remarks:** Also notes contact information for headquarters, number of employees at headquarters, revenue, rank by revenue, and primary SIC code. **Number listed:** 46

1. Carnival Corp., with 89,200 employees
2. Royal Caribbean Cruises Ltd., 60,300
3. FRS Capital Corp., 12,002
4. NCL Corp., 12,000
5. Carrix Inc., 11,000
6. SSA Marine Inc., 10,000
7. Tidewater Inc., 7,900
8. Seacor Holdings Inc., 5,648
9. Princess Cruise Lines Ltd., 5,000
9. SSA International Inc., 5,000

Source: *Business Rankings*, (annual), Dun & Bradstreet Inc., 2011, p. VI.96-VI.97.

4830 ■ LARGEST WATER TRANSPORTATION COMPANIES BY SALES, 2010

Ranked by: Total revenue, in dollars. **Remarks:** Also notes contact information for headquarters, number of employees at headquarters and overall, rank by employees, and primary SIC code. **Number listed:** 50

1. Carnival Corp., with $14,469,000,000
2. Royal Caribbean Cruises Ltd., $6,752,504,000
3. Seacor Holdings Inc., $2,649,368,000
4. Crowley Maritime Corp., $1,955,826,000
5. NCL Corp., $1,855,204,000
6. Crowley Holdings Inc., $1,531,953,000
7. Tidewater Inc., $1,168,634,000
8. Horizon Lines Inc., $1,158,481,000
9. Kirby Corp., $1,109,557,000
10. Overseas Shipholding Group Inc., $1,045,610,000

Source: *Business Rankings*, (annual), Dun & Bradstreet Inc., 2011, p. V.96-V.97.

Water Treatment

4831 ■ LARGEST WATER/WASTE-WATER TREATMENT COMPANIES, 2010

Ranked by: Water/waste-water treatment revenue, in millions of dollars. **Remarks:** Also notes headquarters and rank in the overall Top 100. **Number listed:** 10

1. EMCOR Group Inc., with $768.19 million
2. Monterey Mechanical Co., $55.06
3. Durr Mechanical Construction, $39.68
4. J. F. Ahern Co., $35.86
5. Foley Co., $32.45
6. Corval Constructors Inc., $27.6
7. John W. Danforth Co., $25.2
8. Kinetic Systems, $16.5
9. Murray Co., $13.62
10. IPS, $9.75

Source: *Plumbing & Mechanical*, Pipe Trades Giants (annual), August 2011, p. 36.

Wealth

4832 ■ AMERICA'S RICHEST INVESTORS, 2011

Ranked by: Net worth, in billions of dollars. **Remarks:** Also notes biographical information and comments. **Number listed:** 95

1. Warren Edward Buffett, with $39 billion
2. George Soros, $22
3. John Paulson, $15.5
4. Carl Icahn, $13
5. Ronald Perelman, $12
5. Abigail Johnson, $11.7
7. James Simons, $10.6
8. Harols Simmons, $9.3
9. Steven Cohen , $8.3
10. Philip Anschutz, $7
10. Andrew Beal, $7

Source: *Forbes*, Forbes 400 Richest in America (annual), http://www.forbes.com, October 10, 2011.

4833 ■ AMERICA'S RICHEST PEOPLE, 2011

Ranked by: Net worth, in billions of dollars. **Remarks:** Also notes biographical information and comments. **Number listed:** 400

1. William H. Gates III (Microsoft), with $59 billion
2. Warren Edward Buffett, $39
3. Lawrence Joseph Ellison (Oracle), $33
4. Charles Koch, $25
4. David Koch, $25
6. Christy Walton and family (Walmart), $24.5
7. George Soros, $22
8. Sheldon Adelson, $21.5
9. Jim. C. Walton (Walmart), $21.1
10. Alice Walton (Walmart), $20.9

Source: *Forbes*, Forbes 400 Richest in America (annual), October 10, 2011, p. 210-261.

4834 ■ AMERICA'S RICHEST PEOPLE IN THE AUTOMOTIVE INDUSTRY, 2011

Ranked by: Net worth, in billions of dollars. **Remarks:** Also notes biographical information and comments. **Number listed:** 3

1. Bruce Halle, with $3.4 billion
2. Thomas Friedkin, $1.6
2. Norman Braman, $1.6

Source: *Forbes*, Forbes 400 Richest in America (annual), http://www.forbes.com, October 10, 2011.

4835 ■ AMERICA'S RICHEST PEOPLE IN THE CONSTRUCTION AND ENGINEERING INDUSTRY, 2011

Ranked by: Net worth, in billions of dollars. **Remarks:** Also notes biographical information and comments. **Number listed:** 3

1. Riley P. Bechtel, with $3 billion
1. Stephen D.Bechtel Jr., $3
3. Alfred James Clark, $1.8

Source: *Forbes*, Forbes 400 Richest in America (annual), http://www.forbes.com, October 10, 2011.

4836 ■ AMERICA'S RICHEST PEOPLE IN DIVERSIFIED INDUSTRIES, 2011

Ranked by: Net worth, in billions of dollars. **Remarks:** Also notes age, residence, and source of wealth. **Number listed:** 3

1. Charles Koch, with $25 billion
1. David Koch, $25
3. Phillip Ruffin, $2.4

Source: *Forbes*, Forbes 400 Richest in America (annual), http://www.forbes.com, October 10, 2011.

4837 ■ AMERICA'S RICHEST PEOPLE IN ENERGY, 2011

Ranked by: Net worth, in billions of dollars. **Remarks:** Also notes biographical information and comments. **Number listed:** 35

1. George Kaiser, with $10 billion
2. Len Blavatnik, $9.5
3. Harold Hamm, $7.5
4. Richard Kinder, $6.4
5. Jeffrey Hildebrand, $5.3
6. Robert Rowling, $4.7
7. Ray Lee Hunt, $4.3
8. William Koch, $4
9. Robert Bass, $3.6
9. Trevor Rees-Jones, $3.6

Source: *Forbes*, Forbes 400 Richest in America (annual), http://www.forbes.com, October 10, 2011.

4838 ■ AMERICA'S RICHEST PEOPLE IN FASHION AND RETAIL, 2011

Ranked by: Net worth, in billions of dollars. **Remarks:** Also notes biographical information and comments. **Number listed:** 24

1. Christy Walton and family, with $24.5 billion
2. Jim C. Walton, $21.1
3. Alice Walton, $20.9
4. S. Robson Walton, $20.5
5. Phil Knight, $13.1
6. Ralph Lauren, $6.1
7. Charles Butt, $5.7
8. Frederik Meijer, $5
9. John Menard, $4.5
10. John Paul DeJoria, $4
10. David Green, $4
10. Roger Wang, $4

Source: *Forbes*, Forbes 400 Richest in America (annual), http://www.forbes.com, October 10, 2011.

4839 ■ AMERICA'S RICHEST PEOPLE IN FOOD AND BEVERAGE, 2011

Ranked by: Net worth, in billions of dollars. **Remarks:** Also notes biographical information and comments. **Number listed:** 30

1. Forrest Edward Mars, with $13.8 billion
1. Jacqueline Mars, $13.8
1. John Franklyn Mars, $13.8
4. James Leprino, $2.7
4. David Murdock, $2.7
6. Pauline MacMillan Keinath, $2.6
6. Cargill MacMillan, $2.6
6. Whitney MacMillan, $2.6
6. Marion MacMillan Pictet, $2.6
10. Peter Buck, $2.2
10. Fred DeLuca, $2.2
10. Mary Alice Dorrance Malone, $2.2
10. William Wrigley, $2.2

Source: *Forbes*, Forbes 400 Richest in America (annual), http://www.forbes.com, October 10, 2011.

4840 ■ AMERICA'S RICHEST PEOPLE IN THE GAMING INDUSTRY, 2011

Ranked by: Net worth, in billions of dollars. **Remarks:** Also notes biographical information and comments. **Number listed:** 3

1. Sheldon Adelson, with $21.5 billion
2. Kirk Kerkorian, $3
3. Stephen Wynn, $2.8

Source: *Forbes*, Forbes 400 Richest in America (annual), http://www.forbes.com, October 10, 2011.

4841 ■ AMERICA'S RICHEST PEOPLE IN HEALTH CARE, 2011

Ranked by: Net worth, in billions of dollars. **Remarks:** Also notes biographical information and comments. **Number listed:** 12

1. Patrick Soon-Shiong, with $7 billion
2. Barbara (Basia) Piasecka Johnson, $3.1
3. Thomas Frist Jr., $2.8
4. Randal J. Kirk, $2.4
5. Ronda Stryker, $2.3
6. Phillip Frost, $2.1
7. Michael Jaharis, $1.9
8. Gary Michelson, $1.4
9. Stewart Rahr, $1.3
9. Pat Stryker, $1.3

Source: *Forbes*, Forbes 400 Richest in America (annual), http://www.forbes.com, October 10, 2011.

4842 ■ AMERICA'S RICHEST PEOPLE IN LOGISTICS, 2011

Ranked by: Net worth, in billions of dollars. **Remarks:** Also notes biographical information and comments. **Number listed:** 8

1. Dennis Washington, with $5 billion
2. Victor Fung, $2.8
3. Donald Schneider, $2.5
4. Frederick Smith, $1.7
5. Manuel Moroun, $1.5
6. Johnelle Hunt, $1.4
7. William Connor, $1.2
8. Peter Lewis, $1.05

Source: *Forbes*, Forbes 400 Richest in America (annual), http://www.forbes.com, October 10, 2011.

4843 ■ AMERICA'S RICHEST PEOPLE IN MANUFACTURING, 2011

Ranked by: Net worth, in billions of dollars. **Remarks:** Also notes biographical information and comments. **Number listed:** 17

1. Mitchell Rales, with $3 billion
2. Archie Aldis Emmerson, $2.6
3. H. Fisk Johnson, $2.3
3. Imogene Powers Johnson, $2.3
3. S. Curtis Johnson, $2.3
3. Helen Johnson-Leipold, $2.3
3. Winnie Johnson-Marquart, $2.3
8. Diane Hendricks, $2.2
9. Jim Davis, $1.8
9. Min Kao, $1.8
9. Herbert Kohler, $1.8

9. Leandro Rizzuto, $1.8

Source: *Forbes*, Forbes 400 Richest in America (annual), http://www.forbes.com, October 10, 2011.

4844 ■ AMERICA'S RICHEST PEOPLE IN MEDIA, 2011

Ranked by: Net worth, in billions of dollars. **Remarks:** Also notes biographical information and comments. **Number listed:** 36

1. Anne Cox Chambers, with $12 billion
2. Rupert Murdoch, $7.4
3. Samuel I. Newhouse Jr., $6.6
4. Charles Ergen, $6.4
5. James C. Kennedy, $6
5. Blair Parry-Okedon, $6
7. Donald Newhouse, $5.9
8. David Geffen, $5.5
9. John Malone, $4.5
10. Sumner Redstone, $4.1

Source: *Forbes*, Forbes 400 Richest in America (annual), http://www.forbes.com, October 10, 2011.

4845 ■ AMERICA'S RICHEST PEOPLE IN THE METALS AND MINING INDUSTRY, 2011

Ranked by: Net worth, in billions of dollars. **Remarks:** Also notes age, residence, and source of wealth. **Number listed:** 2

1. Robert Friedland, with $2.8 billion
2. Jim Justice, $1.1

Source: *Forbes*, Forbes 400 Richest in America (annual), http://www.forbes.com, October 10, 2011.

4846 ■ AMERICA'S RICHEST PEOPLE IN THE OIL INDUSTRY, 2011

Ranked by: Net worth, in billions of dollars. **Remarks:** Also notes age, residence, and source of wealth. **Number listed:** 2

1. Dan Wilks, with $1.4 billion
1. Farris Wilks, $1.4

Source: *Forbes*, Forbes 400 Richest in America (annual), http://www.forbes.com, October 10, 2011.

4847 ■ AMERICA'S RICHEST PEOPLE IN REAL ESTATE, 2011

Ranked by: Net worth, in billions of dollars. **Remarks:** Also notes biographical information and comments. **Number listed:** 27

1. Donald Bren, with $12 billion
2. Richard LeFrak, $5
3. Samuel Zell, $4.7
4. Leonard N. Stern, $4.2
5. Theodore Lerner, $3.3
6. John A. Sobrato, $3.2
7. Stephen Ross, $3.1
8. Donald J. Trump, $2.9
9. Igor Olenicoff, $2.6
10. Alfred Taubman, $2.5

Source: *Forbes*, Forbes 400 Richest in America (annual), http://www.forbes.com, October 10, 2011.

4848 ■ AMERICA'S RICHEST PEOPLE IN THE SERVICE INDUSTRY, 2011

Ranked by: Net worth, in billions of dollars. **Remarks:** Also notes biographical information and comments. **Number listed:** 28

1. Jack Taylor, with $9 billion
2. Leonard Lauder, $6.3
3. Richard DeVos, $5
4. Micky Arison, $4.2
5. Steven Udvar-Hazy, $3.2
6. Barbara Carlson Gage, $3
6. Marilyn Carlson Nelson, $3
8. Steven Rales, $2.7
9. Anthony Pritzker, $2.5
10. Tamara Gustavson, $2.3

Source: *Forbes*, Forbes 400 Richest in America (annual), http://www.forbes.com, October 10, 2011.

4849 ■ AMERICA'S RICHEST PEOPLE IN THE SPORTS INDUSTRY, 2011

Ranked by: Net worth, in billions of dollars. **Remarks:** Also notes biographical information and comments. **Number listed:** 16

1. E. Stanley Kroenke, with $3.2 billion
2. Malcolm Glazer, $2.7
3. Jerry Jones, $1.9
4. Robert Kraft, $1.7
5. Robert McNair, $1.5
6. James Irsay, $1.4
7. Stephen Bisciotti, $1.3
7. Arthur Blank, $1.3
9. Frank Fertitta, $1.25
10. Lorenzo Fertitta, $1.20

Source: *Forbes*, Forbes 400 Richest in America (annual), http://www.forbes.com, October 10, 2011.

4850 ■ AMERICA'S RICHEST PEOPLE IN TECHNOLOGY, 2011

Ranked by: Net worth, in billions of dollars. **Remarks:** Also notes biographical information and comments. **Number listed:** 48

1. William H. Gates III, with $59 billion
2. Lawrence Joseph Ellison, $33
3. Jeffrey P. Bezos, $19.1
4. Mark Zuckerberg, $17.5
5. Sergey Brin, $16.7
5. Larry Page, $16.7
7. Michael Dell, $15
8. Steven Ballmer , $13.9
9. Paul Allen, $13.2
10. James Goodnight, $7.1

Source: *Forbes*, Forbes 400 Richest in America (annual), http://www.forbes.com, October 10, 2011.

4851 ■ TOP BILLIONAIRES IN THE AMERICAS (EXCLUDING THE U.S.), 2012

Ranked by: Net worth, in billions of U.S. dollars. **Remarks:** Also notes rank in the overall *Global Billionaires*, country of citizenship, and source of wealth. **Number listed:** 10

1. Carlos Slim Helu and family, with $69 billion
2. Eike Batista, $30
3. Iris Fontbona and family, $17.8
4. David Thomson and family, $17.5
5. Ricardo Salinas Pliego and family, $17.4

6. Alberto Bailleres Gonzalez and family, $16.5

7. German Larrea Mota Velasco and family, $14.2

8. Joseph Safra, $13.8

9. Luis Carlos Sarmiento, $12.4

10. Antonio Ermirio de Moraes and family, $12.2

Source: *Forbes*, The Global Billionaires (annual), March 26, 2012, p. 78+.

4852 ■ TOP BILLIONAIRES IN THE U.S., 2012

Ranked by: Net worth, in billions of U.S. dollars. Remarks: Also notes rank in the overall *Global Billionaires*, age, and state of residence. Number listed: 425

1. William H. Gates III, with $61 billion

2. Warren E. Buffett, $44

3. Lawrence J. Ellison, $36

4. Christy Walton and family, $25.3

5. Charles Koch, $25

5. David Koch, $25

7. Sheldon Adelson, $24.9

8. Jim C. Walton, $23.7

9. Alice L. Walton, $23.3

10. S. Robson Walton, $23.1

Source: *Forbes*, The Global Billionaires (annual), March 26, 2012, p. 166+.

4853 ■ TOP-EARNING FICTIONAL CHARACTERS, 2011

Ranked by: Net worth, in billions of dollars. Remarks: Also notes residence, source of wealth, and comments. Number listed: 15

1. Smaug (dragon in "The Hobbit"), with $62 billion

2. Flintheart Glomgold (character in "Uncle Scrooge"), $51.9

3. Carlisle Cullen ("Twilight" doctor), $36.3

4. Jed Clampett (oil tycoon), $9.8

5. Anthony Stark (Iron Man's alter ego), $9.3

6. Richie Rich (comics' richest kid in the world), $8.9

7. Charles Foster Kane (lead character in "Citizen Kane"), $8.3

8. Bruce Wayne (Batman's alter ego), $6.9

9. Forrest Gump (lead character in "Forrest Gump"), $5.7

10. Mr. Monopoly (boardgame real estate tycoon), $2.5

Source: *Forbes*, Fictional 15 (annual), May 7, 2012, p. 138-144.

Wealth, Foreign

4854 ■ ARGENTINA'S TOP BILLIONAIRES, 2012

Ranked by: Net worth, in billions of U.S. dollars, of Argentinian citizens. Remarks: Also notes rank in the overall *Global Billionaires*, age, and source of wealth. Number listed: 4

1. Carlos and Alejandro Bulgheroni, with $5.1 billion

2. Eduardo Eurnekian, $1.8

3. Gregorio Perez Companc and family, $1.5

4. Maria Ines de Lafuente Lacroze, $1.2

Source: *Forbes*, The Global Billionaires (annual), http://www.forbes.com, March 26, 2012.

4855 ■ AUSTRALIA'S RICHEST PEOPLE, 2012

Ranked by: Worth, in billions of U.S. dollars. Remarks: Also notes age. Number listed: 40

1. Georgina Rinehart, with $18 billion

2. Ivan Glasenberg, $7.2

3. Andrew Forrest, $5.3

4. James Packer, $4.5

5. Frank Lowy, $4.4

6. Harry Triguboff, $4

7. Anthony Pratt, $3.4

8. John Gandel, $3.2

9. Angela Bennett & Michael Wright, $2.3

10. Kerr Neilson, $2.1

Source: *Forbes*, Australia's 40 Richest (annual), http://www.forbes.com, February 1, 2012.

4856 ■ AUSTRALIA'S TOP BILLIONAIRES, 2012

Ranked by: Net worth, in billions of U.S. dollars, of Australian citizens. Remarks: Also notes rank in the overall *Global Billionaires*, age, and source of wealth. Number listed: 18

1. Georgina Rinehart, with $18 billion

2. Ivan Glasenberg, $7.3

3. Andrew Forrest, $5.8

4. James Packer, $4.7

5. Frank Lowy and family, $4.4

6. Harry Triguboff, $4

7. John Gandel, $3.2

8. Angela Bennett & Michael Wright, $2.3

9. Kerr Neilson, $2.1

10. David Hains, $2

10. Kerry Stokes, $2

Source: *Forbes*, The Global Billionaires (annual), http://www.forbes.com, March 26, 2012.

4857 ■ AUSTRIA'S TOP BILLIONAIRES, 2012

Ranked by: Net worth, in billions of U.S. dollars, of Austrian citizens. Remarks: Also notes rank in the overall *Global Billionaires*, age, and source of wealth. Number listed: 6

1. Johann Graf, with $5.3 billion

1. Dietrich Mateschitz, $5.3

3. Karl Wlaschek, $4.7

4. Heidi Horten, $3.2

5. Helmut Sohmen, $1.4

6. Reinold Geiger, $1.3

Source: *Forbes*, The Global Billionaires (annual), http://www.forbes.com, March 26, 2012.

4858 ■ BELGIUM'S TOP BILLIONAIRES, 2012

Ranked by: Net worth, in billions of U.S. dollars, of Belgian citizens. Remarks: Also notes rank in the overall *Global Billionaires*, age, and source of wealth. Number listed: 2

1. Albert Frere, with $3.6 billion

2. Patokh Chodiev, $2.8

Source: *Forbes*, The Global Billionaires (annual), http://www.forbes.com, March 26, 2012.

4859 ■ BRAZIL'S TOP BILLIONAIRES, 2012

Ranked by: Net worth, in billions of U.S. dollars, of Brazilian citizens. **Remarks:** Also notes rank in the overall *Global Billionaires*, age, and source of wealth. **Number listed:** 36

1. Eike Batista, with $30 billion
2. Joseph Safra, $13.8
3. Antonio Ermirio de Moraes and family, $12.2
4. Jorge Paulo Lemann, $12
5. Marcel Herrmann Telles, $5.7
6. Carlos Alberto Sicupira, $5.2
7. Dorothea Steinbruch and family, $4.5
8. Aloysio de Andrade Faria, $4.2
9. Francisco Ivens de Sa Dias Branco, $3.8
10. Ana Lucia de Mattos Barretto Villela, $3.6
10. Abilio dos Santos Diniz, $3.6

Source: *Forbes*, The Global Billionaires (annual), http://www.forbes.com, March 26, 2012.

4860 ■ CANADA'S RICHEST PEOPLE, 2011

Ranked by: Net worth, in billions of Canadian dollars. **Remarks:** Also notes location, age, rank for previous year, and comments. **Number listed:** 100

1. Thomson family, with C$21.34 billion
2. Galen Weston, C$8
3. James Irving, Arthur Irving, estate of John Irving, C$7.8
4. Rogers family, C$5.94
5. James Pattison, C$5.73
6. Saputo family, C$4.34
7. Paul Desmarais Sr., C$4.27
8. Jeffrey Skoll, C$3.75
9. Fred Mannix and Ron Mannix, C$3.44
10. Bernard Sherman, C$3.31

Source: *Canadian Business*, Rich 100 (annual), October 24, 2011, p. 30+.

4861 ■ CANADA'S TOP BILLIONAIRES, 2012

Ranked by: Net worth, in billions of U.S. dollars, of Canadian citizens. **Remarks:** Also notes rank in the overall *Global Billionaires*, age, and source of wealth. **Number listed:** 26

1. David Thomson and family, with $17.5 billion
2. Galen Weston and family, $7.6
3. James Irving and Arthur Irving, $5
4. Paul Desmarais, $4.3
4. Jim Pattison, $4.3
6. Emanuele Saputo, $3.7
6. Bernard Sherman Jeffrey Skoll, $3.7
8. Clayton Riddell, $3
9. David Azrieli and family, $2.9
9. Chip Wilson, $2.9

Source: *Forbes*, The Global Billionaires (annual), http://www.forbes.com, March 26, 2012.

4862 ■ CHILE'S TOP BILLIONAIRES, 2012

Ranked by: Net worth, in billions of U.S. dollars, of Chilean citizens. **Remarks:** Also notes rank in the overall *Global Billionaires*, age, and source of wealth. **Number listed:** 5

1. Iris Fontbona and family, with $17.8 billion
2. Eliodoro, Bernardo, and Patricia Matte, $10.2
3. Horst Paulmann and family, $9.3
4. Sebastian Pinera, $2.4
5. Roberto Angelini Rossi, $1.2

Source: *Forbes*, The Global Billionaires (annual), http://www.forbes.com, March 26, 2012.

4863 ■ CHINA'S RICHEST PEOPLE, 2011

Ranked by: Net worth, in millions of U.S. dollars. **Remarks:** Also notes age and origin of wealth. **Number listed:** 400

1. Liang Wengen, with $9,300 million
2. Robin Li, $9,200
3. Liu Yongxing, $6,800
4. Liu Yonghao & family, $6,600
5. Zong Qinghou, $6,500
6. Hui Ka Yan, $6,200
7. Wu Yajun & family, $5,900
8. Zhang Jindong, $5,600
9. He Xiangjian, $5,500
10. Qiu Guanghe & family, $4,800

Source: *Forbes*, The 400 Richest Chinese (annual), http://www.forbes.com, September 13, 2011.

4864 ■ CHINA'S TOP BILLIONAIRES, 2012

Ranked by: Net worth, in billions of U.S. dollars, of Chilean citizens. **Remarks:** Also notes rank in the overall *Global Billionaires*, age, and source of wealth. **Number listed:** 105

1. Robin Li, with $10.2 billion
2. Liang Wengen, $8.1
3. Zong Qinghou, $6.5
4. He Xiangjian, $6.2
5. Hui Ka Yan, $5.8
5. Liu Yongxing, $5.8
7. Wu Yajun and family, $5.7
8. Ma Huateng, $4.7
8. Yang Huiyan, $4.7
10. Zhang Jindong, $4.5

Source: *Forbes*, The Global Billionaires (annual), http://www.forbes.com, March 26, 2012.

4865 ■ COLOMBIA'S TOP BILLIONAIRES, 2012

Ranked by: Net worth, in billions of U.S. dollars, of Colombian citizens. **Remarks:** Also notes rank in the overall *Global Billionaires*, age, and source of wealth. **Number listed:** 3

1. Luis Carlos Sarmiento, with $12.4 billion
2. Alejandro Santo Domingo Davila, $9.5
3. Woods Staton, $1.7

Source: *Forbes*, The Global Billionaires (annual), http://www.forbes.com, March 26, 2012.

4866 ■ CYPRUS'S TOP BILLIONAIRES, 2012

Ranked by: Net worth, in billions of U.S. dollars, of Cyrpus citizens. **Remarks:** Also notes rank in the overall *Global Billionaires*, age, and source of wealth. **Number listed:** 2

1. John Fredriksen, with $11.3 billion
2. Suat Gunsel, $1

Source: *Forbes*, The Global Billionaires (annual), http://www.forbes.com, March 26, 2012.

4867 ■ THE CZECH REPUBLIC'S TOP BILLIONAIRES, 2012

Ranked by: Net worth, in billions of U.S. dollars, of Czech citizens. **Remarks:** Also notes rank in the overall *Global Billionaires*, age, and source of wealth. **Number listed:** 3

1. Petr Kellner, with $8.2 billion
2. Zdenek Bakala, $1.9
3. Andrej Babis, $1.4

Source: *Forbes*, The Global Billionaires (annual), http://www.forbes.com, March 26, 2012.

4868 ■ DENMARK'S TOP BILLIONAIRES, 2012

Ranked by: Net worth, in billions of U.S. dollars, of Colombian citizens. **Remarks:** Also notes rank in the overall *Global Billionaires*, age, and source of wealth. **Number listed:** 3

1. Kjeld Kirk Kristiansen, with $6 billion
2. Lars Larsen, $3.6
3. Niels Peter Louis-Hansen, $1.5

Source: *Forbes*, The Global Billionaires (annual), http://www.forbes.com, March 26, 2012.

4869 ■ EGYPT'S TOP BILLIONAIRES, 2012

Ranked by: Net worth, in billions of U.S. dollars, of Egyptian citizens. **Remarks:** Also notes rank in the overall *Global Billionaires*, age, and source of wealth. **Number listed:** 7

1. Nassef Sawiris, with $5.1 billion
2. Naguib Sawiris, $3.1
3. Onsi Sawiris, $2.9
4. Mohamed Mansour, $1.7
5. Yasseen Mansour, $1.6
6. Youssef Mansour, $1.5
7. Mohamed Al Fayed and family, $1.3

Source: *Forbes*, The Global Billionaires (annual), http://www.forbes.com, March 26, 2012.

4870 ■ FRANCE'S TOP BILLIONAIRES, 2012

Ranked by: Net worth, in billions of U.S. dollars, of French citizens. **Remarks:** Also notes rank in the overall *Global Billionaires*, age, and source of wealth. **Number listed:** 15

1. Bernard Arnault, with $41 billion
2. Liliane Bettencourt, $24
3. Francois Pinault and family, $13
4. Serge Dassault and family, $9.9
5. Alain and Gerard Wertheimer, $7.5
6. Jean-Claude Decaux and family, $4.9
7. Xavier Niel, $4.5
8. Alain Merieux and family, $3.7
9. Pierre Bellon and family, $3.4
10. Martin and Olivier Bouygues, $3

Source: *Forbes*, The Global Billionaires (annual), http://www.forbes.com, March 26, 2012.

4871 ■ GERMANY'S TOP BILLIONAIRES, 2012

Ranked by: Net worth, in billions of U.S. dollars, of German citizens. **Remarks:** Also notes rank in the overall *Global Billionaires*, age, and source of wealth. **Number listed:** 55

1. Karl Albrecht, with $25.4 billion
2. Berthold and Theo Albrecht Jr., $17.8
3. Michael Otto and family, $17.6
4. Susanne Klatten, $13
5. Stefan Quandt, $11.2
6. Johanna Quandt, $10
7. Klaus-Michael Kuhne, $9.8
8. August von Finck, $7.8
9. Hasso Plattner, $7.2
10. Curt Engelhorn, $6.6

Source: *Forbes*, The Global Billionaires (annual), http://www.forbes.com, March 26, 2012.

4872 ■ GREECE'S TOP BILLIONAIRES, 2012

Ranked by: Net worth, in billions of U.S. dollars, of Greek citizens. **Remarks:** Also notes rank in the overall *Global Billionaires*, age, and source of wealth. **Number listed:** 3

1. Aristotelis Mistakidis, with $2.8 billion
2. Spiro Latsis and family, $2.6
3. Philip Niarchos, $2.5

Source: *Forbes*, The Global Billionaires (annual), http://www.forbes.com, March 26, 2012.

4873 ■ HONG KONG'S RICHEST PEOPLE, 2012

Ranked by: Worth, in billions of U.S. dollars. **Remarks:** Also notes age. **Number listed:** 40

1. Li Ka-Shing, with $22 billion
2. Lee Shau Kee, $17
3. Kwok family, $15.4
4. Cheng Yu-Tung, $15
5. Joseph Lau, $6.5
6. Michael Kadoorie, $6.4
7. Victor & William Fung, $6.2
8. Lui Che Woo, $4.6
9. Tang Yiu, $4.2
10. Chee Chen Tung, $3.9

Source: *Forbes*, Hong Kong's 40 Richest (annual), http://www.forbes.com, January 5, 2012.

4874 ■ HONG KONG'S TOP BILLIONAIRES, 2012

Ranked by: Net worth, in billions of U.S. dollars, of Hong Kong citizens. **Remarks:** Also notes rank in the overall *Global Billionaires*, age, and source of wealth. **Number listed:** 38

1. Li Ka-Shing, with $25.5 billion
2. Thomas Kwok, Raymond Kwok, and family, $18.3
3. Lee Shau Kee, $18
4. Cheng Yu-Tung, $16
5. Michael Kadoorie and family, $6.6
6. Joseph Lau, $6.5
7. Lui Che Woo, $5.7
8. Peter Woo and family, $4.5
9. Tang Yiu and family, $4
10. William Fung, $3.8

Source: *Forbes*, The Global Billionaires (annual), http://www.forbes.com, March 26, 2012.

4875 ■ INDIA'S RICHEST PEOPLE, 2011

Ranked by: Worth, in millions of U.S. dollars. **Remarks:** Also notes source of wealth, age, marital status, and residence. **Number listed:** 100

1. Mukesh Ambani, with $22,600 million
2. Lakshmi Mittal, $19,200
3. Azim Premji, $13,000
4. Shashi & Ravi Ruia, $10,200
5. Savitri Jindal, $9,500
6. Sunil Mittal, $8,800
7. Gautam Adani, $8,200
8. Kumar Birla, $7,700
9. Pallonji Mistry, $7,600
10. Adi Godrej, $6,800

Source: *Forbes*, India's Richest (annual), http://www.forbes.com, October 26, 2011.

4876 ■ INDIA'S TOP BILLIONAIRES, 2012

Ranked by: Net worth, in billions of U.S. dollars, of Indian citizens. **Remarks:** Also notes rank in the overall *Global Billionaires*, age, and source of wealth. **Number listed:** 48

1. Mukesh Ambani, with $22.3 billion
2. Lakshmi Mittal, $20.7
3. Azim Premji, $15.9
4. Savitri Jindal and family, $10.9
5. Sunil Mittal and family, $8.1
6. Kumar Birla, $8
7. Anil Ambani, $7.8
8. Dilip Shanghvi, $7.4
9. Shashi & Ravi Ruia, $7
10. Kushal Pal Singh, $6.4

Source: *Forbes*, The Global Billionaires (annual), http://www.forbes.com, March 26, 2012.

4877 ■ INDONESIA'S RICHEST PEOPLE, 2011

Ranked by: Net worth, in millions of U.S. dollars. **Remarks:** Also notes age. **Number listed:** 40

1. R. Budi Hartono & Michael Hartono, with $14,000 million
2. Susilo Wonowidjojo, $10,500
3. Eka Tjipta Widjaja, $8,000
4. Low Truck Kwong, $3,700
5. Anthoni Salim, $3,600
6. Sukanto Tanoto, $2,800
7. Martua Sitorus, $2,700
8. Peter Sondakh, $2,600
9. Putera Sampoerna, $2,400
10. Achmad Hamami, $2,200

Source: *Forbes*, Indonesia's 40 Richest (annual), http://www.forbes.com, November 23, 2011.

4878 ■ INDONESIA'S TOP BILLIONAIRES, 2012

Ranked by: Net worth, in billions of U.S. dollars, of Indonesian citizens. **Remarks:** Also notes rank in the overall *Global Billionaires*, age, and source of wealth. **Number listed:** 17

1. R. Budi Hartono, with $6.5 billion
2. Michael Hartono, $6.3
3. Low Tuck Kwong, $3.6
4. Martua Sitorus, $3
5. Sukanto Tanoto, $2.8
6. Peter Sondakh, $2.6

7. Achmad Hamami and family, $2.2
8. Sri Prakash Lohia, $2
8. Chairul Tanjung, $2
10. Kiki Barki, $1.7

Source: *Forbes*, The Global Billionaires (annual), http://www.forbes.com, March 26, 2012.

4879 ■ IRELAND'S RICHEST PEOPLE, 2011

Ranked by: Wealth, in millions of pounds sterling. **Remarks:** Also notes overall rank in the *Rich List*, annual rise or fall in wealth, and source of wealth. **Number listed:** 10

1. Hilary Weston and family, with £5,900 million
2. Denis O'Brien, £2,169
3. John Dorrance, £1,516
4. Dermot Desmond, £1,389
5. Earl of Iveagh and Guinness family, £850
6. Pearse Lyons and family, £720
7. Martin Naughton, £699
8. Lord Ballyedmond, £650
9. Paddy McNally, £515
10. U2, £514

Source: *The Sunday Times*, Rich List (annual), http://www.timesonline.co.uk, April 29, 2012.

4880 ■ IRELAND'S TOP BILLIONAIRES, 2012

Ranked by: Net worth, in billions of U.S. dollars, of Irish citizens. **Remarks:** Also notes rank in the overall *Global Billionaires*, age, and source of wealth. **Number listed:** 5

1. Pallonji Mistry, with $9.7 billion
2. Denis O'Brien, $5
3. John Dorrance III, $2.4
4. Martin Naughton, $2
5. Dermot Desmond, $1.5

Source: *Forbes*, The Global Billionaires (annual), http://www.forbes.com, March 26, 2012.

4881 ■ ISRAEL'S TOP BILLIONAIRES, 2012

Ranked by: Net worth, in billions of U.S. dollars, of Israeli citizens. **Remarks:** Also notes rank in the overall *Global Billionaires*, age, and source of wealth. **Number listed:** 13

1. Idan Ofer, with $6.2 billion
2. Beny Steinmetz, $5.9
3. Eyal Ofer, $5.8
4. Stef Wertheimer and family, $4.2
5. Shari Arison, $3.9
6. Arnon Milchan, $3.8
7. Alexander Machkevich, $2.8
8. Gil Shwed, $1.9
8. Yitzhak Tshuva, $1.9
10. Lev Leviev, $1.7

Source: *Forbes*, The Global Billionaires (annual), http://www.forbes.com, March 26, 2012.

4882 ■ ITALY'S TOP BILLIONAIRES, 2012

Ranked by: Net worth, in billions of U.S. dollars, of Italian citizens. **Remarks:** Also notes rank in the overall *Global Billionaires*, age, and source of wealth. **Number listed:** 16

1. Michele Ferrero and family, with $19 billion
2. Leonardo Del Vecchio, $11.5
3. Giorgio Armani, $7.2
4. Miuccia Prada, $6.8
5. Paolo & Gianfelice Mario Rocca, $6
6. Silvio Berlusconi and family , $5.9
7. Patrizio Bertelli, $3.7
8. Stefano Pessina, $2.6
9. Carlo Benetton, $2.1
9. Gilberto Benetton, $2.1
9. Giuliana Benetton, $2.1
9. Luciano Benetton, $2.1

Source: *Forbes*, The Global Billionaires (annual), http://www.forbes.com, March 26, 2012.

4883 ■ JAPAN'S TOP BILLIONAIRES, 2012

Ranked by: Net worth, in billions of U.S. dollars, of Japanese citizens. **Remarks:** Also notes rank in the overall *Global Billionaires*, age, and source of wealth. **Number listed:** 24

1. Tadashi Yanai and family, with $10 billion
2. Masayoshi Son, $7.2
3. Hiroshi Mikitani, $6.2
4. Kunio Busujima and family, $5.9
5. Yoshikazu Tanaka, $4.3
6. Akira Mori and family, $3.5
6. Takemitsu Takizaki, $3.5
8. Han Chang-Woo and family, $3.1
8. Keiichiro Takahara, $3.1
10. Eitaro Itoyama, $2.9

Source: *Forbes*, The Global Billionaires (annual), http://www.forbes.com, March 26, 2012.

4884 ■ KAZAKHSTAN'S TOP BILLIONAIRES, 2012

Ranked by: Net worth, in billions of U.S. dollars, of Kazakhstan's citizens. **Remarks:** Also notes rank in the overall *Global Billionaires*, age, and source of wealth. **Number listed:** 3

1. Vladimir Kim, with $3.5 billion
2. Alijan Ibragimov, $2.8
3. Bulat Utemuratov, $1.5

Source: *Forbes*, The Global Billionaires (annual), http://www.forbes.com, March 26, 2012.

4885 ■ KUWAIT'S TOP BILLIONAIRES, 2012

Ranked by: Net worth, in billions of U.S. dollars, of Kuwaiti citizens. **Remarks:** Also notes rank in the overall *Global Billionaires*, age, and source of wealth. **Number listed:** 5

1. Bassam Alghanim, with $1.6 billion
1. Kutayba Alghanim, $1.6
3. Fawzi Al-Kharafi, $1.2
3. Jassim Al-Kharafi, $1.2
3. Mohannad Al-Kharafi, $1.2

Source: *Forbes*, The Global Billionaires (annual), http://www.forbes.com, March 26, 2012.

4886 ■ LEBANON'S TOP BILLIONAIRES, 2012

Ranked by: Net worth, in billions of U.S. dollars, of Lebanese citizens. **Remarks:** Also notes rank in the overall *Global Billionaires*, age, and source of wealth. **Number listed:** 6

1. Najib Mikati, with $3 billion
1. Taha Mikati, $3
3. Bahaa Hariri, $2.5
4. Saad Hariri, $1.7
5. Ayman Hariri, $1.3
5. Fahd Hariri, $1.3

Source: *Forbes*, The Global Billionaires (annual), http://www.forbes.com, March 26, 2012.

4887 ■ MALAYSIA'S TOP BILLIONAIRES, 2012

Ranked by: Net worth, in billions of U.S. dollars, of Malaysian citizens. **Remarks:** Also notes rank in the overall *Global Billionaires*, age, and source of wealth. **Number listed:** 9

1. Robert Kuok, with $12.4 billion
2. Ananda Krishnan, $9.9
3. Lee Shin Cheng, $5.2
4. Teh Hong Piow, $5
5. Quek Leng Chan, $4.2
6. Syed Mokhtar Al Bukhary, $3.3
7. Yeoh Tiong Lay and family, $2.6
8. Tiong Hiew King, $1.5
9. Vincent Tan, $1.2

Source: *Forbes*, The Global Billionaires (annual), http://www.forbes.com, March 26, 2012.

4888 ■ MEXICO'S TOP BILLIONAIRES, 2012

Ranked by: Net worth, in billions of U.S. dollars, of Mexican citizens. **Remarks:** Also notes rank in the overall *Global Billionaires*, age, and source of wealth. **Number listed:** 11

1. Carlos Slim Helu and family, with $69 billion
2. Ricardo Salinas Pliego and family, $17.4
3. Alberto Bailleres Gonzalez and family, $16.5
4. German Larrea Mota-Velasco and family, $14.2
5. Jeronimo Arango and family, $4
6. Emilio Azcarraga Jean, $2
7. Roberto Gonzalez Barrera and family, $1.9
8. Carlos Hank Rhon and family, $1.4
9. Roberto Hernandez Ramirez, $1.3
10. Joaquin Guzman Loera, $1
10. Alfredo Harp Helu and family, $1

Source: *Forbes*, The Global Billionaires (annual), http://www.forbes.com, March 26, 2012.

4889 ■ MONACO'S TOP BILLIONAIRES, 2012

Ranked by: Net worth, in billions of U.S. dollars, of Monaco citizens. **Remarks:** Also notes rank in the overall *Global Billionaires*, age, and source of wealth. **Number listed:** 2

1. David Nahmad and family, with $3 billion
2. Lily Safra, $1.2

Source: *Forbes*, The Global Billionaires (annual), http://www.forbes.com, March 26, 2012.

4890 ■ MOROCCO'S TOP BILLIONAIRES, 2012

Ranked by: Net worth, in billions of U.S. dollars, of Moroccan citizens. **Remarks:** Also notes rank in the overall *Global Billionaires*, age, and source of wealth. **Number listed:** 3

1. Miloud Chaabi, with $2.9 billion

2. Othman Benjelloun, $2.3

3. Anas Sefrioui, $1.6

Source: *Forbes*, The Global Billionaires (annual), http://www.forbes.com, March 26, 2012.

4891 ■ THE NETHERLANDS' TOP BILLIONAIRES, 2012

Ranked by: Net worth, in billions of U.S. dollars, of Dutch citizens. **Remarks:** Also notes rank in the overall *Global Billionaires*, age, and source of wealth. **Number listed:** 6

1. Charlene de Carvalho-Heineken, with $7.7 billion
2. Frits Goldschmeding, $2.8
3. John de Mol, $2
4. Hans Melchers, $1.5
5. Ralph Sonnenberg, $1.4
6. Joop van den Ende, $1.3

Source: *Forbes*, The Global Billionaires (annual), http://www.forbes.com, March 26, 2012.

4892 ■ NEW ZEALAND'S TOP BILLIONAIRES, 2012

Ranked by: Net worth, in billions of U.S. dollars, of New Zealand citizens. **Remarks:** Also notes rank in the overall *Global Billionaires*, age, and source of wealth. **Number listed:** 3

1. Graeme Hart, with $5.7 billion
2. Richard Chandler, $4.6
3. Christopher Chandler, $1

Source: *Forbes*, The Global Billionaires (annual), http://www.forbes.com, March 26, 2012.

4893 ■ NIGERIA'S TOP BILLIONAIRES, 2012

Ranked by: Net worth, in billions of U.S. dollars, of Nigerian citizens. **Remarks:** Also notes rank in the overall *Global Billionaires*, age, and source of wealth. **Number listed:** 2

1. Aliko Dangote, with $11.2 billion
2. Mike Adenuga, $4.3

Source: *Forbes*, The Global Billionaires (annual), http://www.forbes.com, March 26, 2012.

4894 ■ NORTHERN IRELAND'S RICHEST PEOPLE, 2011

Ranked by: Wealth, in millions of pounds sterling. **Remarks:** Also notes comments and source of wealth. **Number listed:** 40

1. Eddie Haughey, with £386 million
2. Sam Morrison, £208
3. Roma Downey, £202
4. William Creighton and Frank Boyd, £193
5. John King, £161
6. Danny Hill, £151
7. Tim Martin, £143
8. Michael and Kevin Lagan, £123
9. Maureen Wheeler, £116
10. Joe Sloan, £109
10. Bil McCabe, £109

Source: *Belfast Telegraph*, Northern Ireland's Richest People (annual), http://www.belfasttelegraph.co.uk, March 13, 2012.

4895 ■ NORWAY'S TOP BILLIONAIRES, 2012

Ranked by: Net worth, in billions of U.S. dollars, of Norwegian citizens. **Remarks:** Also notes rank in the overall *Global Billionaires*, age, and source of wealth. **Number listed:** 5

1. Olav Thon, with $5 billion
2. Stein Erik Hagen and family, $2.7
3. Kjell Inge Rokke, $2.1
4. Arne Wilhelmsen and family, $1.6
5. Petter Stordalen, $1.2

Source: *Forbes*, The Global Billionaires (annual), http://www.forbes.com, March 26, 2012.

4896 ■ PERU'S TOP BILLIONAIRES, 2012

Ranked by: Net worth, in billions of U.S. dollars, of Peruvian citizens. **Remarks:** Also notes rank in the overall *Global Billionaires*, age, and source of wealth. **Number listed:** 2

1. Eduardo Hochschild, with $2.2 billion
2. Carlos Rodriguez-Paster, $2

Source: *Forbes*, The Global Billionaires (annual), http://www.forbes.com, March 26, 2012.

4897 ■ THE PHILIPPINES' RICHEST PEOPLE, 2011

Ranked by: Net worth, in millions of U.S. dollars. **Remarks:** Also notes age. **Number listed:** 40

1. Henry Sy, with $7,200 million
2. Lucio Tan, $2,800
3. John Gokongwei Jr., $2,400
4. Andrew Tan, $2,000
5. David Consunji, $1,900
6. Jaime Zobel de Ayala, $1,700
7. Enrique Razon Jr., $1,600
8. Eduardo Cojuangco Jr., $1,400
9. Roberto Ongpin, $1,300
10. George Ty, $1,100

Source: *Forbes*, The Philippines' 40 Richest (annual), http://www.forbes.com, June 22, 2011.

4898 ■ THE PHILIPPINES' TOP BILLIONAIRES, 2012

Ranked by: Net worth, in billions of U.S. dollars, of Philippine citizens. **Remarks:** Also notes rank in the overall *Global Billionaires*, age, and source of wealth. **Number listed:** 6

1. Henry Sy and family, with $8 billion
2. Lucio Tan and family, $3.5
3. Andrew Tan, $2.1
4. Enrique Razon Jr., $1.9
5. Eduardo Cojuangco, $1.3
6. Roberto Ongpin, $1

Source: *Forbes*, The Global Billionaires (annual), http://www.forbes.com, March 26, 2012.

4899 ■ POLAND'S TOP BILLIONAIRES, 2012

Ranked by: Net worth, in billions of U.S. dollars, of Polish citizens. **Remarks:** Also notes rank in the overall *Global Billionaires*, age, and source of wealth. **Number listed:** 4

1. Jan Kulczyk, with $2.7 billion
2. Zygunt Solorz-Zak, $2.5
3. Michal Solowow, $1.8
4. Leszek Czarnecki, $1.3

Source: *Forbes*, The Global Billionaires (annual), http://www.forbes.com, March 26, 2012.

4900 ■ PORTUGAL'S TOP BILLIONAIRES, 2012

Ranked by: Net worth, in billions of U.S. dollars, of Portuguese citizens. **Remarks:** Also notes rank in the overall *Global Billionaires*, age, and source of wealth. **Number listed:** 3

1. Americo Amorim, with $4.4 billion
2. Eliseo Alexandre Soares dos Santos and family, $2.5
3. Belmiro de Azevedo, $1

Source: *Forbes*, The Global Billionaires (annual), http://www.forbes.com, March 26, 2012.

4901 ■ RICHEST PEOPLE IN THE U.K., 2011

Ranked by: Wealth, in millions of pounds sterling. **Remarks:** Also notes rank for previous year, annual rise or fall in wealth, and source of wealth. **Number listed:** 1000

1. Lakshmi Mittal and family, with £12,700 million
2. Alisher Usmanov, £12,315
3. Roman Abramovich, £9,500
4. Sri & Gopi Hinduja, £8,600
5. Leonard Blavatnik, £7,580
6. Ernesto & Kirsty Bertarelli, £7,400
7. Duke of Westminster, £7,350
8. David & Simon Reuben, £7,083
9. John Fredriksen & family, £6,600
10. Galen & George Weston, £5,900

Source: *The Sunday Times*, Rich List (annual), http://www.timesonline.co.uk, April 29, 2012.

4902 ■ RICHEST WOMEN IN THE U.K., 2011

Ranked by: Wealth, in millions of pounds sterling. **Remarks:** Also notes overall rank in the *Rich List*, annual rise or fall in wealth, and source of wealth. **Number listed:** 15

1. Kirsty Bertarelli, with £7,400 million
2. Charlene de Carvalho, £5,400
3. Kirsten Rausing, £3,900
4. Lady Green, £3,300
5. Baroness Howard de Walden and family, £2,200
6. Anita Zabludowicz, £1,500
7. Christina Ong and family, £1,200
8. Dame Mary Perkins, £870
9. Xiuli Hawken, £819
10. Denise Coates, £800

Source: *The Sunday Times*, Rich List (annual), http://www.timesonline.co.uk, April 29, 2012.

4903 ■ RUSSIA'S TOP BILLIONAIRES, 2012

Ranked by: Net worth, in billions of U.S. dollars, of Russian citizens. **Remarks:** Also notes rank in the overall *Global Billionaires*, age, and source of wealth. **Number listed:** 96

1. Alisher Usmanov, with $18.1 billion
2. Vladimir Lisin, $15.9
3. Alexei Mordashov, $15.3
4. Vladimir Potanin, $14.5
5. Vagit Alekperov, $13.5
6. Mikhail Fridman, $13.4
7. Mikhail Prokhorov, $13.2
8. Viktor Vekselberg, $12.4
9. Roman Abramovich, $12.1
10. Leonid Mikhelson, $11.9

Source: *Forbes*, The Global Billionaires (annual), http://www.forbes.com, March 26, 2012.

4904 ■ SAUDI ARABIA'S TOP BILLIONAIRES, 2012

Ranked by: Net worth, in billions of U.S. dollars, of Saudi Arabian citizens. **Remarks:** Also notes rank in the overall *Global Billionaires*, age, and source of wealth. **Number listed:** 8

1. Prince Alwaleed Bin Talal Alsaud, with $18 billion
2. Mohammed Al Amoudi, $12.5
3. Mohamed Bin Issa Al Jaber, $7
4. Sulaiman Al Rajhi, $5.9
5. Mohamed Al Issa, $2.2
5. Abdullah Al Rajhi, $2.2
7. Saleh Kamel, $1.7
8. Mohamed Al Rajhi, $1.5

Source: *Forbes*, The Global Billionaires (annual), http://www.forbes.com, March 26, 2012.

4905 ■ SCOTLAND'S RICHEST PEOPLE, 2011

Ranked by: Wealth, in millions of pounds sterling. **Remarks:** Also notes overall rank in the *Rich List*, annual rise or fall in wealth, and source of wealth. **Number listed:** 10

1. Mahdi al-Tajir, with £1,600 million
2. The Grant and Gordon family, £1,400
3. Alastair Salvesen and family, £1,300
4. Sir Ian Wood and family, £1,187
5. Jim McColl, £1,000
6. Lord Laidlaw, £745
7. Thomson family, £700
8. Sir Brian Souter and Ann Gloag, £665
9. J. K. Rowling, £560
10. Duke of Sutherland, £525

Source: *The Sunday Times*, Rich List (annual), http://www.timesonline.co.uk, April 29, 2012.

4906 ■ SINGAPORE'S RICHEST PEOPLE, 2011

Ranked by: Net worth, in millions of U.S. dollars. **Remarks:** Also notes age. **Number listed:** 40

1. Ng family, with $8,900 million
2. Khoo family, $6,700
3. Wee Cho Yaw, $4,200
4. Richard Chandler, $4,000
5. Kwee brothers, $3,900
6. Kuok Khoon Hong, $3,500
7. Ong Beng Seng & Christina Ong, $1,900
8. Peter Lim, $1,800
9. Kwek Leng Beng, $1,700
10. Lee Seng Wee, $1,400

Source: *Forbes*, Singapore's 40 Richest (annual), http://www.forbes.com, July 27, 2011.

4907 ■ SINGAPORE'S TOP BILLIONAIRES, 2012

Ranked by: Net worth, in billions of U.S. dollars, of Singapore citizens. **Remarks:** Also notes rank in the overall *Global Billionaires*, age, and source of wealth. **Number listed:** 5

1. Wee Cho Yaw and family, with $3.8 billion
2. Kuok Khoon Hong, $3.5
3. Peter Lim, $1.7
4. Zhong Sheng Jian, $1.4

5. Sam Goi, $1.2

Source: *Forbes*, The Global Billionaires (annual), http://www.forbes.com, March 26, 2012.

4908 ■ SOUTH AFRICA'S TOP BILLIONAIRES, 2012

Ranked by: Net worth, in billions of U.S. dollars, of South African citizens. **Remarks:** Also notes rank in the overall *Global Billionaires*, age, and source of wealth. **Number listed:** 4

1. Nicky Oppenheimer and family, with $6.8 billion
2. Johann Rupert and family, $5.1
3. Christoffel Wiese, $3.1
4. Patrice Motsepe, $2.7

Source: *Forbes*, The Global Billionaires (annual), http://www.forbes.com, March 26, 2012.

4909 ■ SOUTH KOREA'S TOP BILLIONAIRES, 2012

Ranked by: Net worth, in billions of U.S. dollars, of South Korean citizens. **Remarks:** Also notes rank in the overall *Global Billionaires*, age, and source of wealth. **Number listed:** 20

1. Lee Kun-Hee, with $8.3 billion
2. Chung Mong-Koo, $6.2
3. Jay Y. Lee, $3.6
4. Kim Jung-Ju and family, $3.3
5. Chung Eui-Sun, $2.8
6. Chung Mong-Joon, $2.5
7. Chey Tae-Won, $2.1
8. Shin Chang-Jae, $1.9
9. Koo Bon-Moo, $1.8
9. Shin Dong-Bin, $1.8

Source: *Forbes*, The Global Billionaires (annual), http://www.forbes.com, March 26, 2012.

4910 ■ SPAIN'S TOP BILLIONAIRES, 2012

Ranked by: Net worth, in billions of U.S. dollars, of South Korean citizens. **Remarks:** Also notes rank in the overall *Global Billionaires*, age, and source of wealth. **Number listed:** 16

1. Amancio Ortega, with $37.5 billion
2. Isak Andic and family, $4.8
3. Juan Roig, $4.7
4. Rosalia Mera, $4.5
5. Daniel Mate, $2.8
6. Manuel Jove, $2.6
7. Alicia Koplowitz, $2.1
8. Juan Abello, $2
9. Esther Koplowitz, $1.6
9. Florentino Perez, $1.6

Source: *Forbes*, The Global Billionaires (annual), http://www.forbes.com, March 26, 2012.

4911 ■ SWEDEN'S TOP BILLIONAIRES, 2012

Ranked by: Net worth, in billions of U.S. dollars, of Swedish citizens. **Remarks:** Also notes rank in the overall *Global Billionaires*, age, and source of wealth. **Number listed:** 11

1. Stefan Persson, with $26 billion
2. Birgit Rausing and family, $14
3. Hans Rausing, $10
4. Antonia Johnson, $6.

5. Liselott Persson, $3.6
6. Bertil Hult, $3
6. Ingvar Kamprad and family, $3
6. Melker Schorling, $3
9. Gustaf Douglas, $2.8
10. Fredrik Lundberg, $2.7

Source: *Forbes*, The Global Billionaires (annual), http://www.forbes.com, March 26, 2012.

4912 ■ SWITZERLAND'S TOP BILLIONAIRES, 2012

Ranked by: Net worth, in billions of U.S. dollars, of Swiss citizens. **Remarks:** Also notes rank in the overall *Global Billionaires*, age, and source of wealth. **Number listed:** 9

1. Ernesto Bertarelli and family, with $10.6 billion
2. Hansjorg Wyss, $8.1
3. Walter Haefner, $4.3
4. Thomas Schmidheiny, $4.2
5. Stephan Schmidheiny, $2.7
5. Sergio Mantegazza, $2.3
7. Jean-Claude Gandur, $2
7. Esther Grether and family, $2
9. Thomas Straumann, $1

Source: *Forbes*, The Global Billionaires (annual), http://www.forbes.com, March 26, 2012.

4913 ■ TAIWAN'S TOP BILLIONAIRES, 2012

Ranked by: Net worth, in billions of U.S. dollars, of Taiwanese citizens. **Remarks:** Also notes rank in the overall *Global Billionaires*, age, and source of wealth. **Number listed:** 24

1. Tsai Wan-Tsai and family, with $6.5 billion
2. Tsai Eng-Meng, $6.2
3. Terry Gou, $5.5
4. Cher Wang and Wenchi Chen, $4
5. Barry Lam, $3.7
6. Wang Yung-tsai, $3.2
7. Lin Yu-lin, $3
7. Luo Jye and family, $3
9. Lin Rong San, $2.8
10. T. Y. Tsai, $2.2

Source: *Forbes*, The Global Billionaires (annual), http://www.forbes.com, March 26, 2012.

4914 ■ THAILAND'S RICHEST PEOPLE, 2011

Ranked by: Net worth, in millions of U.S. dollars. **Remarks:** Also notes age. **Number listed:** 40

1. Dhanin Chearavanont, with $7,400 million
2. Chaleo Yoovidhya, $5,000
3. Charoen Sirivadhanabhakdi, $4,800
4. Chirathivat family, $4,300
5. Krit Ratanarak, $2,500
6. Aloke Lohia, $2,100
7. Chamnong Bhirombhakdi, $2,000
8. Vichai Maleenont, $1,500
9. Isara Vongkusolkit, $1,400
10. Praneetsilpa Vacharaphol, $1,050

Source: *Forbes*, Thailand's 40 Richest (annual), http://www.forbes.com, August 30, 2011.

4915 ■ THAILAND'S TOP BILLIONAIRES, 2012

Ranked by: Net worth, in billions of U.S. dollars, of Thai citizens. **Remarks:** Also notes rank in the overall *Global Billionaires*, age, and source of wealth. **Number listed:** 5

1. Dhanin Chearavanont and family, with $7 billion
2. Charoen Sirivadhanabhakdi, $5.5
3. Chaleo Yoovidhya, $5
4. Aloke Lohia, $1.9
5. Krit Ratanarak, $1.2

Source: *Forbes*, The Global Billionaires (annual), http://www.forbes.com, March 26, 2012.

4916 ■ TOP BILLIONAIRES IN THE ASIA-PACIFIC, 2012

Ranked by: Net worth, in billions of U.S. dollars. **Remarks:** Also notes rank in the overall *Global Billionaires*, country of citizenship, and source of wealth. **Number listed:** 20

1. Li Ka-shing, with $25.5 billion
2. Mukesh Ambani, $22.3
3. Lakshmi Mittal, $20.7
4. Raymond and Thomas Kwok and family, $18.3
5. Lee Shau Kee, $18
5. Georgina Rinehart, $18
7. Cheng Yu-Tung, $16
8. Azim Premji, $15.9
9. Robert Kuok, $12.4
10. Savitri Jindal and family, $10.9

Source: *Forbes*, The Global Billionaires (annual), March 26, 2012, p. 94+.

4917 ■ TOP BILLIONAIRES IN EUROPE, 2012

Ranked by: Net worth, in billions of U.S. dollars. **Remarks:** Also notes rank in the overall *Global Billionaires*, country of citizenship, and source of wealth. **Number listed:** 20

1. Bernard Arnault, with $41 billion
2. Amancio Ortega, $37.5
3. Stefan Persson, $26
4. Karl Albrecht, $25.4
5. Liliane Bettencourt, $24
6. Michele Ferrero and family, $19
7. Alisher Usmanov, $18.1
8. Berthold & Theo Jr. Albrecht, $17.8
9. Michael Otto and family, $17.6
10. Rinat Akhmetov, $16

Source: *Forbes*, The Global Billionaires (annual), March 26, 2012, p. 118+.

4918 ■ TOP BILLIONAIRES IN THE MIDDLE EAST AND AFRICA, 2012

Ranked by: Net worth, in billions of U.S. dollars. **Remarks:** Also notes rank in the overall *Global Billionaires*, country of citizenship, and source of wealth. **Number listed:** 10

1. Prince Alwaleed Bin Talal Alsaud, with $18 billion
2. Mohammed Al Amoudi, $12.5
3. Aliko Dangote, $11.2
4. Mohamed Bin Issa Al Jaber, $7
5. Nicky Oppenheimer and family, $6.8

6. Idan Ofer, $6.2
7. Beny Steinmetz, $5.9
7. Sulaiman Al Rajhi, $5.9
9. Eyal Ofer, $5.8
10. Johann Rupert, $5.1
10. Nassef Sawiris, $5.1

Source: *Forbes*, The Global Billionaires (annual), March 26, 2012, p. 152+.

4919 ■ TURKEY'S TOP BILLIONAIRES, 2012

Ranked by: Net worth, in billions of U.S. dollars, of Turkish citizens. **Remarks:** Also notes rank in the overall *Global Billionaires*, age, and source of wealth. **Number listed:** 34

1. Husnu Ozyegin, with $3 billion
2. Mehmet Emin Karamehmet, $2.9
3. Murat Ulker, $2.8
4. Semahat Sevim Arsel, $2.6
4. Ferit Faik Sahenk, $2.6
6. Mustafa Rahmi Koc, $2.5
7. Filiz Sahenk, $2.4
8. Sarik Tara, $2.3
9. Suna Kirac, $2.2
10. Ali Ibrahim Agaoglu, $2.1

Source: *Forbes*, The Global Billionaires (annual), http://www.forbes.com, March 26, 2012.

4920 ■ THE UKRAINE'S TOP BILLIONAIRES, 2012

Ranked by: Net worth, in billions of U.S. dollars, of Ukraine citizens. **Remarks:** Also notes rank in the overall *Global Billionaires*, age, and source of wealth. **Number listed:** 8

1. Rinat Akhmetov, with $16 billion
2. Victor Pinchuk, $4.2
3. Ihor Kolomoyskyy, $3
4. Henadiy Boholyubov, $2.8
5. Kostyantin Zhevago, $1.8
6. Yuriy Kosiuk, $1.3
7. Petro Poroshenko, $1
7. Andrey Verevskiy, $1

Source: *Forbes*, The Global Billionaires (annual), http://www.forbes.com, March 26, 2012.

4921 ■ THE UNITED ARAB EMIRATES' TOP BILLIONAIRES, 2012

Ranked by: Net worth, in billions of U.S. dollars, of UAE citizens. **Remarks:** Also notes rank in the overall *Global Billionaires*, age, and source of wealth. **Number listed:** 4

1. Abdul Aziz Al Ghurair and family, with $2.9 billion
2. Saif Al Ghurair and family, $2
3. Abdulla Al Futtaim, $1.6
4. Majid Al Futtaim, $1.1

Source: *Forbes*, The Global Billionaires (annual), http://www.forbes.com, March 26, 2012.

4922 ■ THE UNITED KINGDOM'S TOP BILLIONAIRES, 2012

Ranked by: Net worth, in billions of U.S. dollars, of U.K. citizens. **Remarks:** Also notes rank in the overall *Global Billionaires*, age, and source of wealth. **Number listed:** 36

1. Gerald Cavendish Grosvenor and family, with $11 billion
2. David & Simon Reuben, $9
3. Charles Cadogan and family, $4.6
4. Richard Branson, $4.2
4. James Dyson, $4.2
4. Philip & Cristina Green, $4.2
7. Joseph Lewis, $3.8
8. Bruno Schroder and family, $3.4
9. David and Frederick Barclay, $3.2
10. Ian and Richard Livingstone, $3
10. Eddie and Sol Zakay, $3

Source: *Forbes*, The Global Billionaires (annual), http://www.forbes.com, March 26, 2012.

4923 ■ VENEZUELA'S TOP BILLIONAIRES, 2012

Ranked by: Net worth, in billions of U.S. dollars, of Venezuelan citizens. **Remarks:** Also notes rank in the overall *Global Billionaires*, age, and source of wealth. **Number listed:** 2

1. Gustavo Cisneros and family, with $4.2 billion
2. Lorenzo Mendoza and family, $3.4

Source: *Forbes*, The Global Billionaires (annual), http://www.forbes.com, March 26, 2012.

Wealth, International

4924 ■ WORLD'S TOP BILLIONAIRES, 2012

Ranked by: Net worth, in billions of U.S. dollars. **Remarks:** Also notes rank for previous year, country, and source of wealth. **Number listed:** 1226

1. Carlos Slim Helu and family, with $69 billion
2. William H. Gates III, $61
3. Warren E. Buffett, $44
4. Bernard Arnault, $41
5. Amancio Ortega, $37.5
6. Lawrence J. Ellison, $36
7. Eike Batista, $30
8. Stefan Persson, $26
9. Li Ka-shing, $25.5
10. Karl Albrecht, $25.4

Source: *Forbes*, The Global Billionaires (annual), March 26, 2012, p. 50+.

Web Sites
See: **Internet Sites**

Wholesale Trade

4925 ■ LARGEST WHOLESALE COMPANIES IN EUROPE, 2010

Ranked by: Sales, in millions of U.S. dollars. **Remarks:** Also notes rank within country. **Number listed:** 100

1. REWE-Zentalfinanz EG (Germany), with $53,227.5 million
2. Louis Dreyfus Holding BV (Netherlands), $50,441.7

3. Trafigura Beheer BV (Netherlands), $47,269.4
4. Shell Nederland BV (Netherlands), $36,620.8
5. Celesio AG (Germany), $31,970.6
6. PetroFina SA (Italy), $30,448.8
7. Acacia Foods Ltd. (U.K.), $26,250
8. Compuware Europe BV (Netherlands), $24,585.5
9. ConocoPhillips Ltd. (U.K.), $23,949
10. Weyerhaeuser International Inc. (Switzerland), $22,629

Source: *Europe's 15,000 Largest Companies*, (annual), ELC International, 2011, p. 50.

4926 ■ TOP *FORTUNE 500* DIVERSIFIED WHOLESALERS, 2011

Ranked by: Revenue, in millions of dollars. **Remarks:** Also notes overall rank in the *Fortune 500;* profits; profits as a percentage of revenue; stockholders' equity; and rank by each criterion. **Number listed:** 7

1. World Fuel Services Corp., with $34,623 million
2. Global Partners, $14,836
3. Genuine Parts Co., $12,459
4. W. W. Grainger Inc., $8,078
5. Anixter International Inc., $6,270
6. WESCO International Inc., $6,126
7. Graybar Electric Co., Inc., $5,375

Source: *Fortune*, Fortune 500 (annual), May 21, 2012, p. F-40.

4927 ■ WORLD'S MOST ADMIRED DIVERSIFIED WHOLESALERS, 2012

Ranked by: Score, on a scale of 10, based on a survey of executives, directors, and securities analysts of companies within their own industry on eight criteria: innovation, financial soundness, employee talent, use of corporate assets, long-term investment value, social responsibility, quality of management, and quality of products/services. **Remarks:** Specific scores not provided. Also notes rank for previous year. **Number listed:** 6

1. W. W. Grainger Inc.
2. Graybar Electric Co., Inc.
3. Airgas Inc.
4. Rexel
5. Anixter International Inc.
5. Reliance Steel & Aluminum Co.

Source: *Fortune*, World's Most Admired Companies (annual), March 19, 2012, p. 150.

Wholesale Trade—Durable Goods

4928 ■ LARGEST DURABLE GOODS WHOLESALERS BY EMPLOYEES, 2010

Ranked by: Total number of employees. **Remarks:** Also notes contact information for headquarters, number of employees at headquarters, revenue, rank by revenue, and primary SIC code. **Number listed:** 481

1. Ricoh Americas Corp., with 36,400 employees
2. Luxottica US Holdings Corp., 35,000
3. Wolseley Investments Inc., 32,986
4. Shaw Industries Group Inc., 30,000
5. American Honda Motor Co., Inc., 26,000

6. IKON Office Solutions Inc., 25,000

6. Philips Holding USA Inc., 25,000

8. Marmon Holdings Inc., 20,881

9. Gores Group LLC, 19,800

10. Newell Rubbermaid Inc., 19,500

Source: *Business Rankings*, (annual), Dun & Bradstreet Inc., 2011, p. VI.108-VI.118.

4929 ■ LARGEST DURABLE GOODS WHOLESALERS BY SALES, 2010

Ranked by: Total revenue, in dollars. **Remarks:** Also notes contact information for headquarters, number of employees at headquarters and overall, rank by employees, and primary SIC code. **Number listed:** 485

1. Ingram Micro Inc., with $34,588,984,000

2. Tech Data Corp., $22,099,876,000

3. Avnet Inc., $19,160,172,000

4. Arrow Electronics Inc., $18,744,676,000

5. Mitsui & Co. USA Inc., $10,742,694,000

6. LG Electronics USA Inc., $10,365,966,717

7. Hyundai Motor America, $10,156,527,000

8. Canon USA Inc., $9,700,000,000

9. Synnex Corp., $8,614,141,000

10. Owens & Minor Inc., $8,123,608,000

Source: *Business Rankings*, (annual), Dun & Bradstreet Inc., 2011, p. V.108-V.118.

Wholesale Trade—Electronics

4930 ■ TOP *FORTUNE 500* ELECTRONICS AND OFFICE EQUIPMENT WHOLESALERS, 2011

Ranked by: Revenue, in millions of dollars. **Remarks:** Also notes overall rank in the *Fortune 500;* profits; profits as a percentage of revenue; stockholders' equity; and rank by each criterion. **Number listed:** 8

1. Ingram Micro Inc., with $36,329 million

2. Avnet Inc., $26,534

3. Tech Data Corp., $26,488

4. Arrow Electronics Inc., $21,390

5. SYNNEX Corp., $10,410

6. Insight Enterprises Inc., $5,287

7. Brightpoint Inc., $5,244

8. United Stationers Inc., $5,006

Source: *Fortune*, Fortune 500 (annual), May 21, 2012, p. F-40.

4931 ■ WORLD'S MOST ADMIRED OFFICE EQUIPMENT AND ELECTRONICS WHOLESALERS, 2012

Ranked by: Score, on a scale of 10, based on a survey of executives, directors, and securities analysts of companies within their own industry on eight criteria: innovation, financial soundness, employee talent, use of corporate assets, long-term investment value, social responsibility, quality of management, and quality of products/services. **Remarks:** Specific scores not provided. Also notes rank for previous year. **Number listed:** 5

1. Avnet Inc.

2. Arrow Electronics Inc.

2. Tech Data Corp.

4. Ingram Micro Inc.

5. SYNNEX Corp.

Source: *Fortune*, World's Most Admired Companies (annual), March 19, 2012, p. 150.

Wholesale Trade—Food

4932 ■ TOP *FORTUNE 500* FOOD AND GROCERY WHOLESALERS, 2011

Ranked by: Revenue, in millions of dollars. **Remarks:** Also notes overall rank in the *Fortune 500;* profits; profits as a percentage of revenue; stockholders' equity; and rank by each criterion. **Number listed:** 4

•

1. Sysco Corp., with $39,323 million

2. CHS Inc., $36,916

3. Core-Mark Holding Co., $6,163

4. Nash Finch Co., $4,807

Source: *Fortune*, Fortune 500 (annual), May 21, 2012, p. F-40.

4933 ■ WORLD'S MOST ADMIRED FOOD AND GROCERY WHOLESALERS, 2012

Ranked by: Score, on a scale of 10, based on a survey of executives, directors, and securities analysts of companies within their own industry on eight criteria: innovation, financial soundness, employee talent, use of corporate assets, long-term investment value, social responsibility, quality of management, and quality of products/services. **Remarks:** Specific scores not provided. Also notes rank for previous year. **Number listed:** 4

1. Sysco Corp.

2. United Natural Foods Inc.

3. Unified Grocers Inc.

4. Spartan Stores Inc.

Source: *Fortune*, World's Most Admired Companies (annual), March 19, 2012, p. 150.

Wholesale Trade—Health Care

4934 ■ TOP *FORTUNE 500* HEALTHCARE WHOLESALERS, 2011

Ranked by: Revenue, in millions of dollars. **Remarks:** Also notes overall rank in the *Fortune 500;* profits; profits as a percentage of revenue; stockholders' equity; and rank by each criterion. **Number listed:** 5

1. McKesson Corp., with $112,084 million

2. Cardinal Health Inc., $102,644

3. AmerisourceBergen Corp., $80,218

4. Owens & Minor Inc., $8,628

5. Henry Schein Inc., $8,530

Source: *Fortune*, Fortune 500 (annual), May 21, 2012, p. F-40.

4935 ■ WORLD'S MOST ADMIRED HEALTHCARE WHOLESALERS, 2012

Ranked by: Score, on a scale of 10, based on a survey of executives, directors, and securities analysts of companies within their own industry on eight criteria: innovation, financial soundness, employee talent, use of corporate assets, long-term investment value, social responsibility, quality of management, and quality of products/services. **Remarks:** Specific scores not provided. Also notes rank for previous year. **Number listed:** 4

1. Henry Schein Inc.

2. McKesson Corp.
3. AmerisourceBergen Corp.
4. Cardinal Health Inc.

Source: *Fortune*, World's Most Admired Companies (annual), March 19, 2012, p. 150.

Wholesale Trade—Non-Durable Goods

4936 ■ LARGEST NONDURABLE GOODS WHOLESALERS BY EMPLOYEES, 2010

Ranked by: Total number of employees. **Remarks:** Also notes contact information for headquarters, number of employees at headquarters, revenue, rank by revenue, and primary SIC code. **Number listed:** 291

1. Cardinal Health Inc., with 46,600 employees
2. Sysco Corp., 46,000
3. Fresh Del Monte Produce Inc., 44,000
4. McKesson Corp., 37,300
5. OfficeMax Inc., 31,000
6. Universal Corp., 28,000
7. Marathon Petroleum Co., 25,000
7. US Foodservice Inc., 25,000
7. Universal Corp. (subsidiary), 25,000
7. USF Holding Corp., 25,000

Source: *Business Rankings*, (annual), Dun & Bradstreet Inc., 2011, p. VI.119-VI.125.

4937 ■ LARGEST NONDURABLE GOODS WHOLESALERS BY SALES, 2010

Ranked by: Total revenue, in dollars. **Remarks:** Also notes contact information for headquarters, number of employees at headquarters and overall, rank by employees, and primary SIC code. **Number listed:** 297

1. McKesson Corp., with $108,702,000,000
2. Cardinal Health Inc., $98,502,800,000
3. AmerisourceBergen Corp., $77,953,979,000
4. Sysco Corp., $37,243,495,000
5. McLane Co., $31,133,614,952
6. CHS Inc., $25,267,931,000
7. World Fuel Services Corp., $19,131,147,000
8. Atlantic Trading & Marketing Inc., $19,000,000,000
9. McKesson Corp. (Maryland), $12,428,200,000
10. Enterprise Crude Oil LLC, $12,000,000,000

Source: *Business Rankings*, (annual), Dun & Bradstreet Inc., 2011, p. V.119-V.125.

Window Cleaning

4938 ■ TOP WINDOW CLEANING FRANCHISES, 2012

Ranked by: Cumulative score based on financial strength and stability, growth rate, size of the system, number of years in business, the length of time franchising, start-up costs, litigation, percentage of terminations, and whether the company provides financing. **Remarks:** Specific scores not provided. Also notes overall rank within the *Franchise 500*, contact information, description, year founded, year started franchising, states where registered, available U.S. regions, where seeking foreign expansion, number of franchised and company-owned units for past

three years, start-up costs, franchise fees, royalty fees, and type of financing available. **Number listed:** 3

1. Fish Window Cleaning Services Inc.
2. Window Gang
3. Window Genie

Source: *Entrepreneur*, Franchise 500 (annual), January 2012, p. 188-189.

Window Treatments

4939 ■ TOP BRANDS OF AUTOMATIC SHADE CONTROL/WINDOW COVERING SYSTEMS, 2010

Ranked by: Popularity among *CE Pro 100* companies, in percent. **Number listed:** 5

1. Lutron, with 59%
2. Somfy, 12%
3. Mechoshade, 10%
4. Crestron, 4%
4. Draper, 4%

Source: *CE Pro*, Brand Analysis (annual), June 2011, p. 59.

Windows and Doors

4940 ■ LARGEST MANUFACTURERS OF WINDOWS AND DOORS, 2011

Ranked by: Revenue, in millions of dollars. **Remarks:** Companies are listed alphabetically within a revenue range. Also notes headquarters, product lines, number of employees, and website. **Number listed:** 100

1. Andersen Corp., with $1,000+ million
1. Formosa Plastics Corp., $1,000+
1. Jeld-Wen Inc., $1,000+
1. Masonite International Corp., $1,000+
1. Pella Corp., $1,000+
1. VKR Holdings A/S, $1,000+
1. YKK AP Inc., $1,000+
8. Atrium Windows & Doors, $500-1,000
8. Fortune Brands Inc., $500-1,000
8. The Marvin Cos., $500-1,000
8. Ply Gem, $500-1,000

Source: *Window & Door*, Top 100 Manufacturers (annual), http://www.windowanddoor.net, 2012.

Wine Industry

4941 ■ HOTTEST SMALL WINE BRANDS, 2011

Ranked by: Score based on representation of market trends or innovation, as well as leadership in region. **Remarks:** Scores not provided. Also notes location of winery. **Number listed:** 30

1. Wine by Joe
2. Cecchitti Wine
3. JC Cellars
4. Turett Hurst
5. Barnard Griffin
6. Bennett Valley Cellars

7. Talbott Vineyards
8. Veritas Vineyard & Winery
9. Barrister Winery
10. Lone Madrone

Source: *Wine Business Monthly*, Hot Small Brands (annual), February 2012, p. 67.

4942 ■ LARGEST U.S. WINE COMPANIES, 2011

Ranked by: Number of cases sold in the U.S. **Number listed:** 30

1. E & J Gallo Winery, with 75,000,000 cases
2. The Wine Group, 62,000,000
3. Constellation Wines, 47,000,000
4. Treasury Wine Estates, 18,000,000
5. Trinchero Family Estates, 16,500,000
6. Bronco Wine Co., 12,000,000
7. Ste. Michelle Wine Estates, 7,300,000
8. Diageo Chateau & Estates Wines, 6,000,000
9. Jackson Family Wines, 5,500,000
10. DFV Wines, 4,500,000

Source: *Wine Business Monthly*, WBM 30 (annual), February 2012, p. 24.

4943 ■ TOP TABLE WINES BRANDS IN THE U.S., 2011

Ranked by: Sales, in dollars. **Remarks:** Also notes percent change from previous year and case sales. **Number listed:** 10

1. Barefoot, with $315,955,800
2. Sutter Home, $265,944,800
3. Yellow Tail, $224,029,900
4. Franzia Box, $195,198,200
5. Woodbridge by Robert Mondavi, $193,920,600
6. Kendall Jackson Vintners Reserve, $151,439,400
7. Beringer California Collection, $131,718,200
8. Carlo Rossi, $117,135,300
9. Gallo Family Vineyards, $116,542,400
10. Chateau Ste. Michelle, $98,377,910

Source: *Beverage Industry*, State of the Industry Report (annual), July 2011, p. SOI-22.

Wireless Communications System

4944 ■ TOP BRANDS OF HOME WIRELESS EQUIPMENT, 2010

Ranked by: Popularity among *CE Pro 100* companies, in percent. **Number listed:** 5

1. Sonos, with 26%
2. Control4, 16%
3. Cisco/Linksys, 9%
4. Ruckus, 7%
5. Netgear, 6%

Source: *CE Pro*, Brand Analysis (annual), June 2011, p. 60.

Wireless Telephones
See also: **Telecommunications Industry**

4945 ■ TOP FREE IPHONE APPS, 2011

Ranked by: Number of days each app was ranked first in its category in the App Store's top 20 categories. **Remarks:** Specific figures not provided. **Number listed:** 3

1. Egg Punch
2. Temple Run
3. Ski on Neon

Source: *Advertising Age*, Digital Issue (annual), February 27, 2012, p. 16.

4946 ■ TOP PAID IPHONE APPS, 2011

Ranked by: Number of days each app was ranked first in its category in the App Store's top 20 categories. **Remarks:** Specific figures not provided. **Number listed:** 3

1. Where's My Water?
2. Ragdoll Blaster 3
3. Clear

Source: *Advertising Age*, Digital Issue (annual), February 27, 2012, p. 16.

4947 ■ TOP WIRELESS PROVIDERS, 2010

Ranked by: Market share, in percent. **Remarks:** Also notes figures for previous year and advertising expenditures for current and previous year. **Number listed:** 4

1. Verizon Wireless, with 31.3%
2. AT&T, 26.6%
3. Sprint Nextel Corp., 16.1%
4. T-Mobile USA Inc., 12.2%

Source: *Advertising Age*, Leading National Advertisers (annual), June 20, 2011, p. 20.

4948 ■ WORLD'S TOP MOBILE HANDSET MANUFACTURERS, 2011

Ranked by: Number of units, in millions. **Remarks:** Also notes market share. **Number listed:** 8

1. Nokia Corp., with 417 million units
2. Samsung Electronics Co., Ltd., 327
3. Apple Inc., 93
4. LG Electronics Inc., 88
5. ZTE Corp., 78
6. Huawei, 54
7. Research in Motion Ltd., 52
8. HTC Corp., 45

Source: *Advertising Age*, Digital Issue (annual), February 27, 2012, p. 16.

4949 ■ WORLD'S TOP SMARTPHONE MANUFACTURERS, 2011

Ranked by: Number of units, in millions. **Remarks:** Also notes market share. **Number listed:** 8

1. Samsung Electronics Co., Ltd., with 97 million units
2. Apple Inc., 93
3. Nokia Corp., 77
4. Research in Motion Ltd., 52
5. HTC Corp., 44
6. Sony Mobile, 21
7. LG Electronics Inc., 20
8. Motorola, 19

Source: *Advertising Age*, Digital Issue (annual), February 27, 2012, p. 16.

Wiring

4950 ■ TOP BRANDS OF CONSUMER ELECTRONICS WIRING/CABLE, 2010

Ranked by: Popularity among *CE Pro 100* companies, in percent. **Number listed:** 7

1. Liberty, with 47%
2. AudioQuest, 17%
2. Monster, 17%
4. Tributaries, 14%
5. Honeywell, 8%
5. Perfect Path, 8%
5. Planet Waves, 8%

Source: *CE Pro*, Brand Analysis (annual), June 2011, p. 57.

4951 ■ TOP BRANDS OF STRUCTURED CABLING, 2010

Ranked by: Popularity among *CE Pro 100* companies, in percent. **Number listed:** 5

1. Legrand, with 30%
2. Liberty, 16%
3. Channel Vision, 12%
4. Leviton, 11%
5. Linear, 8%

Source: *CE Pro*, Brand Analysis (annual), June 2011.

Women

4952 ■ AMERICA'S MOST POWERFUL WOMEN IN THE UNITED KINGDOM, 2011

Ranked by: Score of women in politics, business, and social causes based on current position, past accomplishments, economic size of her arena, and visibility. **Remarks:** Specific scores not provided. Also notes title, occupation, and rank in the overall *Top 100*. Ranking is available online only, not in print. **Number listed:** 3

1. Queen Elizabeth II
2. Helen Boaden (BBC News Group)
3. Joanne (J.K.) Rowling (author)

Source: *Forbes*, World's Most Powerful Women (annual), http://www.forbes.com, September 12, 2011.

4953 ■ MOST POWERFUL WOMEN IN AUSTRALIA, 2011

Ranked by: Score of women in politics, business, and social causes based on current position, past accomplishments, economic size of her arena, and visibility. **Remarks:** Specific scores not provided. Also notes title, occupation, and rank in the overall *Top 100*. Ranking is available online only, not in print. **Number listed:** 3

1. Georgina Rinehart
2. Julia Gillard (Prime Minister)
3. Gail Kelly (Westpac)

Source: *Forbes*, World's Most Powerful Women (annual), http://www.forbes.com, September 12, 2011.

4954 ■ MOST POWERFUL WOMEN IN BRAZIL, 2011

Ranked by: Score of women in politics, business, and social causes based on current position, past accomplishments, economic size of her arena, and visibility. **Remarks:** Specific

scores not provided. Also notes title, occupation, and rank in the overall *Top 100*. Ranking is available online only, not in print. **Number listed:** 2

1. Dilma Rousseff (President)
2. Gisele Bundchen (model/fashion designer)

Source: *Forbes*, World's Most Powerful Women (annual), http://www.forbes.com, September 12, 2011.

4955 ■ MOST POWERFUL WOMEN IN CHINA, 2011

Ranked by: Score of women in politics, business, and social causes based on current position, past accomplishments, economic size of her arena, and visibility. **Remarks:** Specific scores not provided. Also notes title, occupation, and rank in the overall *Top 100*. Ranking is available online only, not in print. **Number listed:** 3

1. Cha Laiwa & family
2. Zhang Xin & family
3. Margaret Chan

Source: *Forbes*, World's Most Powerful Women (annual), http://www.forbes.com, September 12, 2011.

4956 ■ MOST POWERFUL WOMEN IN FRANCE, 2011

Ranked by: Score of women in politics, business, and social causes based on current position, past accomplishments, economic size of her arena, and visibility. **Remarks:** Specific scores not provided. Also notes title, occupation, and rank in the overall *Top 100*. Ranking is available online only, not in print. **Number listed:** 2

1. Christine Lagarde (Int'l Monetary Fund)
2. Dominique Senequier (AXA Private Equity)

Source: *Forbes*, World's Most Powerful Women (annual), http://www.forbes.com, September 12, 2011.

4957 ■ MOST POWERFUL WOMEN IN INDIA, 2011

Ranked by: Score of women in politics, business, and social causes based on current position, past accomplishments, economic size of her arena, and visibility. **Remarks:** Specific scores not provided. Also notes title, occupation, and rank in the overall *Top 100*. Ranking is available online only, not in print. **Number listed:** 3

1. Sonia Gandhi (President)
2. Chanda Kochhar (ICICI Bank)
3. Kiran Mazumdar-Shaw

Source: *Forbes*, World's Most Powerful Women (annual), http://www.forbes.com, September 12, 2011.

4958 ■ MOST POWERFUL WOMEN IN SOUTH AFRICA, 2011

Ranked by: Score of women in politics, business, and social causes based on current position, past accomplishments, economic size of her arena, and visibility. **Remarks:** Specific scores not provided. Also notes title, occupation, and rank in the overall *Top 100*. Ranking is available online only, not in print. **Number listed:** 2

1. Maria Ramos (Absa Group Banks)
2. Nonkululeko Nyembezi-Heitz

Source: *Forbes*, World's Most Powerful Women (annual), http://www.forbes.com, September 12, 2011.

4959 ■ MOST POWERFUL WOMEN IN THE UNITED STATES, 2011

Ranked by: Score of women in politics, business, and social causes based on current position, past accomplishments, economic size of her arena, and visibility. **Remarks:** Specific scores not provided. Also notes title, occupation, and rank in the overall *Top 100*. Ranking is available online only, not in print. **Number listed:** 65

1. Hillary Rodham Clinton
2. Indra Nooyi (PepsiCo)
3. Sheryl Sandberg (Facebook)
4. Melinda Gates
5. Michelle Obama
6. Irene Rosenfeld (Kraft Foods)
7. Lady Gaga
8. Jill Abramson (NY Times)
9. Kathleen Sebelius (Sec. of Health & Human Svcs.)
10. Oprah Winfrey

Source: *Forbes*, World's Most Powerful Women (annual), http://www.forbes.com, September 12, 2011.

4960 ■ WORLD'S MOST POWERFUL WOMEN, 2011

Ranked by: Score of women in politics, business, and social causes based on current position, past accomplishments, economic size of her arena, and visibility. **Remarks:** Specific scores not provided. **Number listed:** 100

1. Angela Merkel (Chancellor, Germany)
2. Hillary Rodham Clinton
3. Dilma Rousseff (President, Brazil)
4. Indra Nooyi (PepsiCo)
5. Sheryl Sandberg (Facebook)
6. Melinda Gates
7. Sonia Gandhi (President, Indian Nat'l Congress Party)
8. Michelle Obama
9. Christine Lagarde (Int'l Monetary Fund)
10. Irene Rosenfeld (Kraft)

Source: *Forbes*, World's Most Powerful Women (annual), September 12, 2011, p. 98+.

Women in Banking

4961 ■ MOST POWERFUL WOMEN IN BANKING, 2011

Ranked by: Score based on performance and personal accomplishments, including position and responsibility, financial performance, length of time in banking, management style, ties to the community, and influence wielded in industry and community. **Remarks:** Specific scores not provided. **Number listed:** 25

1. Karen Peetz (Bank of NY Mellon)
2. Carrie Tolstedt (Wells Fargo)
3. Ellen Costello (Harris Financial)
4. Irene Dorner (HSBC Bank USA)
5. Ellen Alemany (Citizens Financial Group)
6. Pamela Joseph (US Bancorp)
7. Mary Callahan Erdoes (JPMorgan Chase)
8. Avid Modjtabai (Wells Fargo)
9. Barbara Desoer (Bank of America)
10. Melissa Moore (JPMorgan Chase)

Source: *American Banker Magazine*, 25 Most Powerful Women in Banking (annual), October 2011, p. 44+.

Women in Business

4962 ■ BEST COMPANIES FOR MULTICULTURAL WOMEN, 2011

Ranked by: Score based on diversity efforts and the hiring, pay, and promotion practices for women of color. **Remarks:** Specific scores not provided; companies are listed alphabetically, not ranked. Also notes location, type of business, number of employees, number of women of color in overall employment pool and among leaders, key executives, and comments. **Number listed:** 23

1. Allstate Insurance Co.
2. American Express Co.
3. CA Technologies
4. Chubb Group of Insurance Cos.
5. Cisco Systems Inc.
6. Citigroup Inc.
7. Colgate-Palmolive Co.
8. Deloitte LLP
9. General Mills Inc.
10. Goldman Sachs Group Inc.

Source: *Working Mother*, Best Companies for Multicultural Women (annual), 2011, p. 49.

4963 ■ BEST COMPANIES FOR WORKING MOTHERS, 2011

Ranked by: Score based on flexibility, opportunities for advancement, and equitable distribution of benefits, including types of benefits offered, how widely available they are, and usage rates. **Remarks:** Specific scores not provided; companies are ranked alphabetically within the top ten. Also notes number of years appearing on list, total number of employees, percentage of employees that is female, and scores/figures for each criterion. **Number listed:** 100

1. Bank of America Corp.
2. Dell Inc.
3. Deloitte LLP
4. Discovery Communications Inc.
5. Ernst & Young LLP
6. General Mills Inc.
7. KPMG LLP
8. Prudential Financial Inc.
9. PricewaterhouseCoopers LLP
10. TriHealth

Source: *Working Mother*, 100 Best Companies for Working Mothers (annual), October 2011, p. 54-60.

4964 ■ MOST POWERFUL BUSINESS WOMEN OUTSIDE THE U.S., 2011

Ranked by: Score based on the size and importance of her business in the global economy, her clout inside the company, the arc of her career, and her influence on mass culture and society. **Remarks:** Specific scores not provided. Also notes rank for previous year, title, and country. **Number listed:** 50

1. Cynthia Carroll (Anglo American)
2. Gail Kelly (Westpac)
3. Marjorie Scardino (Pearson)
4. Barbara Kux (Siemens)
5. Chandra Kochhar (ICICI Bank)

6. Guler Sabanci (Sabanci Holding)
7. Maria Ramos (ABSA)
8. Sock Koong Chua (Singapore Telecom)
9. Ornella Barra (Alliance Boots)
10. Annika Falkengren (SEB)

Source: *Fortune*, 50 Most Powerful Women in Business (annual), October 17, 2011, p. 136.

4965 ■ MOST POWERFUL NONBANK WOMEN IN FINANCE, 2011

Ranked by: Score based on performance and personal accomplishments, including position and responsibility, financial performance, length of time in banking, management style, ties to the community, and influence wielded in industry and community. **Remarks:** Specific scores not provided. Ranking considers women in securities, asset management, insurance, private equity, and exchange businesses. **Number listed:** 25

1. Abigail P. Johnson (Fidelity)
2. Barbara Byrne (Barclays Capital)
3. Ruth Porat (Morgan Stanley)
4. Val Soranno Keating (Barclaycard)
5. Nicole S. Arnaboldi (Credit Suisse)
6. Teresa Ressel (UBS Securities)
7. Candace Browning (Banc of America Securities)
8. Diana Offereins (Discover Fin'l)
9. Elizabeth Robinson (Goldman Sachs)
10. Stacy Bash-Polley (Goldman Sachs)

Source: *American Banker Magazine*, 25 Most Powerful Women in Banking (annual), October 2011, p. 81+.

4966 ■ MOST POWERFUL WOMEN IN U.S. BUSINESS, 2011

Ranked by: Score based on the size and importance of her business in the global economy, her clout inside the company, the arc of her career, and her influence on mass culture and society. **Remarks:** Specific scores not provided. Also notes title, age, rank for previous year, and comments. **Number listed:** 50

1. Irene Rosenfeld (Kraft Foods)
2. Indra Nooyi (PepsiCo)
3. Patricia Woertz (Archer Daniels Midland)
4. Ellen Kullman (DuPont)
5. Angela Braly (WellPoint)
6. Andrea Jung (Avon)
7. Ginni Rometty (IBM)
8. Ursula Burns (Xerox)
9. Meg Whitman (H-P)
10. Sherilyn McCoy (Johnson & Johnson)

Source: *Fortune*, 50 Most Powerful Women in Business (annual), October 17, 2011, p. 127+.

Women—Compensation

4967 ■ HIGHEST-PAID WOMEN IN U.S. BUSINESS, 2011

Ranked by: Total compensation, in dollars. **Remarks:** Ranking covers U.S. companies with more than $1 billion in revenue. Also notes title and overall rank in the *50 Most Powerful Women in Business*. **Number listed:** 25

1. Safra Catz (Oracle), with $42,095,887

2. Wellington Denahan-Norris (Annaly Capital), $23,634,800
3. Carol Meyrowitz (TJX), $19,252,740
4. Susan Ivey (Reynolds American), $16,823,00
5. Marina Armstrong (Gymboree), $16,426,365
6. Shona Brown (Google), $16,268,742
7. Martine Rothblatt (United Therapeutics), $16,094,652
8. Ina Drew (JPMorgan Chase), $15,545,000
9. Indra Nooyi (PepsiCo), $14,032,298
10. Laura Alber (Williams-Sonoma), $13,555,412

Source: *Fortune*, 50 Most Powerful Women in Business (annual), http://www.fortune.com, October 17, 2011.

Women—Employment

4968 ■ AMERICA'S BEST COMPANIES WITH THE MOST WOMEN, 2012

Ranked by: Percentage of employees that are women. **Remarks:** Also notes number of employees and overall rank in the *100 Best Companies to Work For*. **Number listed:** 100

1. Bright Horizons Family Solutions Inc., with 96%
2. Build-A-Bear Workshop Inc., 85%
3. Children's Healthcare of Atlanta, 83%
4. Meridian Health, 80%
5. Southern Ohio Medical Center, 79%
6. The Everett Clinic, 78%
7. OhioHealth, 77%
7. Scripps Health, 77%
9. Atlantic Health System Inc., 76%
10. Methodist Hospital, 74%
10. Baptist Health South Florida, 74%

Source: *Fortune*, 100 Best Companies to Work For (annual), http://www.fortune.com, February 6, 2012.

4969 ■ COUNTRIES WITH THE HIGHEST FEMALE PARTICIPATION IN THE LABOR FORCE, 2009

Ranked by: Female-to-male participation ratio in the labor force. **Number listed:** 142

1. Burundi, with 1.04
2. Rwanda, 1.03
3. Ghana, 0.99
3. Mozambique, 0.99
5. Tanzania, 0.97
6. Madagascar, 0.96
6. Finland, 0.96
6. Malawi, 0.96
9. Sweden, 0.94
9. Norway, 0.94

Source: *Global Competitiveness Report*, (annual), World Economic Forum, 2011, p. 478.

4970 ■ COUNTRIES WITH THE LOWEST FEMALE PARTICIPATION IN THE LABOR FORCE, 2009

Ranked by: Female-to-male participation ratio in the labor force. **Number listed:** 142

1. Pakistan, with 0.26

2. Syria, 0.27

2. Saudi Arabia, 0.27

4. Yemen, 0.28

5. Egypt, 0.30

6. Jordan, 0.32

7. Lebanon, 0.33

8. Oman, 0.34

8. Morocco, 0.34

10. Turkey, 0.35

Source: *Global Competitiveness Report*, (annual), World Economic Forum, 2011, p. 478.

4971 ■ STATES WITH THE FEWEST WOMEN IN THE LABOR FORCE, 2009

Ranked by: Number of women in the civilian labor force. **Remarks:** Also notes share of national total. **Number listed:** 51

1. Wyoming, with 133,000 women

2. Alaska, 167,000

3. Washington DC, 169,000

4. North Dakota, 171,000

5. Vermont, 178,000

6. Delaware, 213,000

7. South Dakota, 214,000

8. Montana, 235,000

9. Rhode Island, 274,000

10. Hawaii, 297,000

Source: *State Rankings*, (annual), CQ Press, 2011, p. 184.

4972 ■ STATES WITH THE HIGHEST RATE OF FEMALE EMPLOYMENT, 2009

Ranked by: Percentage of women who are employed in the civilian labor force. **Number listed:** 51

1. Vermont, with 68.8%

2. South Dakota, 68.3%

3. Iowa, 68%

4. North Dakota, 67.7%

5. Nebraska, 67.6%

6. Minnesota, 67.4%

7. Wisconsin, 66.5%

8. Kansas, 65.9%

9. Alaska, 65.6%

10. New Hampshire, 65.5%

Source: *State Rankings*, (annual), CQ Press, 2011, p. 185.

4973 ■ STATES WITH THE LOWEST RATE OF FEMALE EMPLOYMENT, 2009

Ranked by: Percentage of women who are employed in the civilian labor force. **Number listed:** 51

1. West Virginia, with 49.2%

2. Mississippi, 52.1%

3. Alabama, 53.1%

4. Louisiana, 54.7%

5. Kentucky, 55.8%

6. Arkansas, 55.9%

7. Arizona, 56.2%

7. New Mexico, 56.2%

7. Tennessee, 56.2%

10. South Carolina, 56.5%

Source: *State Rankings*, (annual), CQ Press, 2011, p. 185.

4974 ■ STATES WITH THE MOST WOMEN IN THE LABOR FORCE, 2009

Ranked by: Number of women in the civilian labor force. **Remarks:** Also notes share of national total. **Number listed:** 51

1. California, with 8,218,000 women

2. Texas, 5,271,000

3. New York, 4,607,000

4. Florida, 4,303,000

5. Illinois, 3,083,000

6. Pennsylvania, 3,036,000

7. Ohio, 2,851,000

8. Michigan, 2,306,000

9. Georgia, 2,219,000

10. North Carolina, 2,162,000

Source: *State Rankings*, (annual), CQ Press, 2011, p. 184.

Women Engineers

4975 ■ BEST EMPLOYERS FOR FEMALE ENGINEERS, 2012

Ranked by: Survey based on work environment for engineers who are women. **Remarks:** Specific scores not provided. **Number listed:** 50

1. General Electric Co.

2. Boeing Co.

3. Google Inc.

4. Lockheed Martin Corp.

5. Cisco Systems Inc.

6. International Business Machines Corp. (IBM)

7. Hewlett-Packard Co.

8. Microsoft Corp.

9. E. I. du Pont de Nemours & Co.

10. Raytheon Co.

Source: *Woman Engineer*, Top Employers (annual), http://www.eop.com/mags-WE.php, 2012.

4976 ■ BEST GOVERNMENT AGENCIES FOR FEMALE ENGINEERS, 2012

Ranked by: Survey based on work environment for engineers who are women. **Remarks:** Specific scores not provided. **Number listed:** 20

1. U.S. Navy

2. National Aeronautics & Space Administration (NASA)

3. U.S. Environmental Protection Agency (EPA)

4. U.S. Army Corps of Engineers

5. U.S. Department of Energy

6. Federal Bureau of Investigation (FBI)

7. U.S. Patent Office

8. Highway Traffic Safety Administration

9. National Institute of Standards & Technology (NIST)

10. Nuclear Regulatory Commission

Source: *Woman Engineer*, Top Employers (annual), http://www.eop.com/mags-WE.php, 2012.

Women Executives

4977 ■ FASTEST-GROWING PRIVATE WOMAN-RUN COMPANIES IN THE U.S., 2007-2010

Ranked by: Average annual sales growth over three years, in percent. **Remarks:** Also notes overall rank in the *Inc. 5,000*, state, and revenue for current year. To qualify, private companies must have had annual revenues of at least $100,000 in 2007 and $2 million in 2010. **Number listed:** 375

1. Crystal Clear Technologies, with 16,048%
2. Valuation Management Group, 7,910%
3. JMA Solutions, 4,317%
4. Simplicity Consulting, 3,727%
5. Cask, 3,714%
6. PetRays, 3,249%
7. HappyBaby, 3,207%
8. Petplan, 2,207%
9. InGenesis Diversified Healthcare Solutions, 2,177%
10. Soft Tech Consulting, 2,138%

Source: *Inc.*, Inc. 500 (annual), http://www.inc.com, September 2011.

4978 ■ TOP U.S. COMPANIES FOR EXECUTIVE WOMEN, 2011

Ranked by: Score based on mentoring, employee-resource groups, work/life benefits, and commitment from top leadership in promoting women to the highest levels. **Remarks:** Specific scores not provided. To qualify, companies must have more than 1,000 U.S. employees. **Number listed:** 10

1. Kraft Foods Inc.
2. PricewaterhouseCoopers LLP
3. Sodexo
4. Kaiser Permanente
5. Procter & Gamble Co.
6. Johnson & Johnson
7. Ernst & Young LLP
8. Deloitte LLP
9. Bank of America Corp.
10. American Express Co.

Source: *DiversityInc*, Top 50 (annual), 2011, p. 96.

4979 ■ TOP WOMEN IN WORLD BUSINESS, 2011

Ranked by: Score based on biographical data; size, scope, and complexity of the company; and competitive landscape. **Remarks:** Specific scores not provided. Ranking covers only executives managing a group's controlling company. **Number listed:** 50

1. Irene Rosenfeld (Kraft Foods)
2. Guler Sabanci (Sabanci Holding)
3. Indra Nooyi (PepsiCo)
4. Ursula Burns (Xerox)
5. Andrea Jung (Avon)
6. Ellen Kullman (DuPont)
7. Dong Mingzhu (Gree Electric)
8. Angela Ahrendts (Burberry)

9. Yoshiko Shinohara (Temp Holdings)
10. Chanda Kochhar (ICICI Bank)

Source: *Financial Times*, Top 50 Women in World Business (annual), http://www.ft.com, November 15, 2011.

Women-Owned Business Enterprises

4980 ■ CHICAGO'S LARGEST WOMEN-OWNED FIRMS, 2011

Ranked by: Revenue, in millions of dollars. **Remarks:** Also notes contact information, top executive, figures for previous year, percent change, number of Chicago employees, year founded, number of years of female-majority ownership, percent woman-owned, and type of business. **Number listed:** 25

1. Shure Inc., with $465 million
2. Flying Food Group LLC, $369
3. Harpo Inc., $309
4. United Scrap Metal Inc., $268
5. DSC Logistics Inc., $265

Source: *Crain's Chicago Business*, Largest Women-Owned Firms (annual), http://www.chicagobusiness.com, May 7, 2012.

4981 ■ IDAHO'S LARGEST WOMEN-OWNED BUSINESSES, 2011

Ranked by: Number of employees. **Remarks:** Also notes contact information, key executive, year founded, and business description. **Number listed:** 10

1. Paige Mechanical Group, with 80 employees
1. Silverhawk Realty, 80
3. MarCon Inc., 45
4. Alarmco Inc., 26
5. Keller Williams Realty Boise, 14
6. Prosperity Organic Foods Inc., 7
6. Silver Bridge CPA, 7
8. Handyman Connection, 5
8. QB Solutions inc., 5
10. IDAHO Magazine, 4

Source: *Idaho Business Review*, Largest Women-Owned Businesses (annual), February 24, 2012.

4982 ■ LARGEST DENVER-AREA WOMEN-OWNED BUSINESSES BY REVENUE, 2010

Ranked by: Revenue, in dollars. **Remarks:** Also notes contact information, rank and figures for previous year, number of local employees and offices, business description, top local executive, owners, and percentage women-owned. **Number listed:** 25

1. Ralph Schomp Automotive Inc., with $250,599,315
2. The Cain Travel Group Inc., $94,178,000
3. Alpine Buick GMC, $39,998,930
4. Craters & Freighters, $39,380,580
5. HB Management Group Inc., $36,915,431
6. PrimeSource Staffing LLC, $26,100,000
7. Birko Corp., $22,425,000
8. Greiner Electric, $18,000,000
9. ISYS Technologies Inc., $17,000,000
10. PayReel, $16,800,000

Source: *Denver Business Journal*, Book of Lists (annual), December 16, 2011, p. 59.

4983 ■ LARGEST WOMAN-OWNED BUSINESSES IN DETROIT, 2010

Ranked by: Revenue, in millions of dollars. **Remarks:** Also notes contact information, majority owner, figures for previous year, and percent woman-owned. **Number listed:** 20

1. RKA Petroleum Cos., with $492.6 million
2. MotorCity Casino-Hotel, $446.4
3. Troy Motors Inc., $376.6
4. Strategic Staffing Solutions Inc., $205
5. Rush Trucking Corp., $100
6. Vendor Managed Solutions Inc., $89.5
7. Iconma LLC, $88.6
8. BlueWater Technologies Group Inc., $65
9. Technical Training Inc., $63.5
10. Unibar Services Inc., $60

Source: *Crain's Detroit Business*, Book of Lists (annual), December 26, 2011, p. 42.

4984 ■ LARGEST WOMEN-OWNED BUSINESSES IN LOS ANGELES COUNTY, 2010

Ranked by: Revenue, in millions of dollars. **Remarks:** Also notes figures for previous year, contact information, number of offices and employees, percentage women-owned, year founded, company description, and top local executive. **Number listed:** 100

1. Forever 21 Inc., with $2,664.7 million
2. Roll Global LLC, $2,400
3. America Chung Nam Inc., $1,812

Source: *Los Angeles Business Journal*, Women-Owned Businesses (annual), http://www.labusinessjournal.com, August 15, 2011.

4985 ■ LARGEST WOMEN-OWNED BUSINESSES IN NEW JERSEY, 2010

Ranked by: Revenue, in millions of dollars. **Remarks:** Also notes rank for previous year, contact information, year founded, owner, and industry. **Number listed:** 139

1. SHI International Corp., with $3,040 million
2. Turtle & Hughes Inc., $400
3. Officemate International Corp., $100
4. Atrium Staffing, $90
5. The Star Group, $80.1
6. Stillwell-Hansen Inc., $52
7. D'Artagnan Inc., $50
8. ACCU Staffing Services, $46.16
9. Champion Container Corp., $40
10. Crystal Springs Resort, $36

Source: *NJBiz*, Top Women-Owned Businesses (annual), http://www.njbiz.com, August 15, 2011.

4986 ■ LARGEST WOMEN-OWNED COMPANIES IN THE NEW YORK AREA, 2010

Ranked by: Revenue, in millions of dollars. **Remarks:** Also notes contact information, top female executive, figures for previous year, number of New York City employees, total number of employees, year founded, and nature of business. **Number listed:** 25

1. J & R Music & Computer World, with $425 million

2. Turtle & Hughes Inc., $397
3. Eileen Fisher Inc., $310

Source: *Crain's New York Business*, Largest Women-Owned Companies (annual), http://www.crainsnewyork.com, September 19, 2011.

4987 ■ TOP WOMEN BUSINESS OWNERS IN CANADA, 2011

Ranked by: Gross revenue, in Canadian dollars. **Remarks:** Specific figures not provided. Also notes company, revenue range, three-year revenue growth, number of employees, and export revenue. **Number listed:** 100

1. Shannon Rogers
2. Sally Daub
3. Susan Niczowski
4. Madeleine Paquin
5. Elana Rosenfeld
6. Dawna Henderson
7. Lynne Fafard
8. Marion Witz
9. Victoria Sopik & Jennifer Nashmi
10. Alice Reimer

Source: *Profit*, W 100 (annual), http://www.profitguide.com, November 2011.

4988 ■ TOP WOMEN-OWNED COMPANIES IN COLORADO, 2011

Ranked by: Gross revenue, in thousands of dollars. **Remarks:** Also notes rank and figures for previous year, percent change, business description, number of years in business, and number of employees. **Number listed:** 100

1. Ralph Schomp Automotive Inc., with $286,425 thousand
2. Mile High Specialty Foods, $160,256
3. Prudential Rocky Mountain Realtors, $103,000
4. Vladimir Jones, $69,733
5. Alpine Buick Pontiac GMC, $41,499
6. C & D Enterprises Inc., $38,500
7. Stellar Solutions, $36,186
8. GlobalLinks LLC, $33,900
9. PrimeSource Staffing LLC, $29,000
10. Good Day Pharmacy, $28,000
10. Houg Special Services Inc., $28,000

Source: *ColoradoBiz*, Top 100 Women-Owned Businesses (annual), May 2012, p. 14-15.

Women's Apparel Industry
See: **Clothing Industry**

Wood Products

4989 ■ LARGEST COMPANIES IN THE LUMBER AND WOOD PRODUCTS (EXCEPT FURNITURE) INDUSTRY BY EMPLOYEES, 2010

Ranked by: Total number of employees. **Remarks:** Also notes contact information for headquarters, number of employees at headquarters, revenue, rank by revenue, and primary SIC code. **Number listed:** 60

1. Masco Corp., with 35,400 employees
2. Jeld-Wen Inc., 20,000
3. Clayton Homes Inc., 14,000
4. Andersen Corp., 12,050
5. Masterbrand Cabinets Inc., 11,000
6. Forest Products Holdings LLC, 10,191
7. Pella Corp., 8,600
8. Armstrong Wood Products Inc., 6,300
9. CMH Manufacturing Inc., 5,292
10. UFP Eastern Division Inc., 4,900
10. Universal Forest Products Inc., 4,900

Source: *Business Rankings*, (annual), Dun & Bradstreet Inc., 2011, p. VI.54-VI.55.

4990 ■ LARGEST COMPANIES IN THE LUMBER AND WOOD PRODUCTS (EXCEPT FURNITURE) INDUSTRY BY SALES, 2010

Ranked by: Total revenue, in dollars. **Remarks:** Also notes contact information for headquarters, number of employees at headquarters and overall, rank by employees, and primary SIC code. **Number listed:** 60

1. Masco Corp., with $7,592,000,000
2. Building Materials Corp. of America, $2,748,909,000
3. Universal Forest Products Inc., $1,890,851,000
4. Louisiana-Pacific Corp., $1,383,600,000
5. Roseburg Forest Products Co., $1,200,000,000
6. RLC Industries Co., $1,000,000,000
7. CMH Manufacturing Inc., $950,000,000
8. Builders FirstSource Inc., $700,343,000
9. Mid South Lumber Inc., $600,000,000
10. McCord Treated Wood Inc., $468,105,000

Source: *Business Rankings*, (annual), Dun & Bradstreet Inc., 2011, p. V.54-V.55.

4991 ■ LARGEST U.S. WOOD PRODUCT MANUFACTURERS, 2010

Ranked by: Revenue, in millions of dollars. **Remarks:** Also notes overall rank within the *IW 500*, revenue growth, and profit margin. **Number listed:** 6

1. Weyerhaeuser Co., with $6,552 million
2. Universal Forest Products Inc., $1,891
3. Louisiana-Pacific Corp., $1,384
4. Rayonier Inc., $1,315
5. Plum Creek Timber Co., $1,190
6. Wausau Paper Corp., $1,056

Source: *IndustryWeek*, IW 500 (annual), http://www.industryweek.com, July 2011.

4992 ■ NORTH AMERICA'S FASTEST-GROWING WOOD PRODUCTS COMPANIES, 2009-2010

Ranked by: Annual growth in revenue, in percent. **Remarks:** Also notes headquarters and revenue for current year. **Number listed:** 100

1. Acacia Originals LLC, with 166.3%
2. Advanced Cabinet Systems, 120.1%
3. Centorbi LLC, 109.1%
4. Custom Source Woodworking Inc., 106.7%

5. Casework Solutions LLC, 90%
6. Pinnacle Furnishings, 88.1%
7. BriMar Wood Innovations Inc., 62.1%
8. PIN, 57.6%
9. Triple A Custom Wood Design LLC, 55%
10. Closet America, 50.7%

Source: *Wood & Wood Products*, Wood 100 (annual), September 2011, p. 50-51.

4993 ■ NORTH AMERICA'S LARGEST WOOD CABINET COMPANIES, 2010

Ranked by: Revenue, in dollars. **Remarks:** Also notes headquarters and percent change from previous year. **Number listed:** 22

1. Masco Corp., with $1,464,000,000
2. Master Brand Cabinets Inc., $1,200,000,000
3. American Woodmark Corp., $452,589,000
4. RSI Home Products, $400,000,000
5. Elkay Cabinetry Group, $300,000,000
6. Norcraft Cos., $265,000,000
7. VT Industries Inc., $175,000,000
8. Cardell Kitchen & Bath Cabinetry, $152,000,000
9. Woodcraft Industries Inc., $150,000,000
10. U.S. Home Systems Inc., $145,000,000

Source: *Wood & Wood Products*, Wood 100 (annual), September 2011, p. 52.

4994 ■ WORLD'S LARGEST WOOD PRODUCT MANUFACTURERS, 2010

Ranked by: Revenue, in millions of dollars. **Remarks:** Also notes rank for previous year, overall rank within the *IW 1000*, country, and revenue growth. **Number listed:** 2

1. Sumitomo Forestry Co., Ltd., with $8,904 million
2. Weyerhaeuser Co., $6,552

Source: *IndustryWeek*, IW 1000 (annual), http://www.industryweek.com, August 2011.

Workers' Compensation

4995 ■ STATES WITH THE HIGHEST WORKERS' COMPENSATION PAYMENT PER WORKER, 2008

Ranked by: Workers' compensation benefit payment per covered worker, in dollars. **Number listed:** 51

1. West Virginia, with $901
2. Washington, $778
3. Alaska, $689
4. California, $618
5. Montana, $596
6. Pennsylvania, $524
7. Illinois, $522
7. Oklahoma, $522
9. South Carolina, $514
10. Delaware, $501

Source: *State Rankings*, (annual), CQ Press, 2011, p. 177.

4996 ■ STATES WITH THE HIGHEST WORKER'S COMPENSATION PAYMENTS, 2008

Ranked by: Total workers' compensation benefit payments, in dollars. **Remarks:** Also notes share of national total. **Number listed:** 51

1. California, with $9,426,019,000
2. New York, $3,536,944,000
3. Illinois, $2,994,420,000
4. Pennsylvania, $2,902,243,000
5. Florida, $2,787,022,000
6. Ohio, $2,490,080,000
7. Washington, $2,192,885,000
8. New Jersey, $1,916,466,000
9. Georgia, $1,601,644,000
10. North Carolina, $1,526,320,000

Source: *State Rankings*, (annual), CQ Press, 2011, p. 176.

4997 ■ STATES WITH THE HIGHEST WORKERS' COMPENSATION PREMIUMS, 2011

Ranked by: Score based on workers' compensation benefits per $100 of covered wages. **Number listed:** 10

1. West Virginia, with 2.1 points
2. Montana, 1.89
3. Washington, 1.82
4. Oklahoma, 1.57
5. Alaska, 1.56
6. South Carolina, 1.47
7. Vermont, 1.33
8. Idaho, 1.32
9. Maine, 1.30
10. Wyoming, 1.27

Source: *Small Business Survival Index*, (annual), Small Business & Entrepreneurship Council, November 2011, p. 51.

4998 ■ STATES WITH THE LOWEST WORKERS' COMPENSATION PAYMENT PER WORKER, 2008

Ranked by: Workers' compensation benefit payment per covered worker, in dollars. **Remarks:** Also notes figure for U.S. **Number listed:** 51

1. Washington DC, with $166
2. Arkansas, $193
3. Texas, $198
4. Indiana, $221
5. Utah, $255
6. Arizona, $256
7. Massachusetts, $264
8. South Dakota, $296
9. Kansas, $311
10. North Dakota, $313

Source: *State Rankings*, (annual), CQ Press, 2011, p. 177.

4999 ■ STATES WITH THE LOWEST WORKERS' COMPENSATION PAYMENTS, 2008

Ranked by: Workers' compensation benefit payments, in dollars. **Remarks:** Also notes share of national total. **Number listed:** 51

1. Washington DC, with $81,263,000
2. North Dakota, $105,837,000
3. South Dakota, $113,555,000
4. Vermont, $127,204,000

5. Wyoming, $137,133,000
6. Rhode Island, $158,006,000
7. Alaska, $205,363,000
8. Delaware, $208,562,000
9. Arkansas, $215,404,000
10. New Hampshire, $239,290,000

Source: *State Rankings*, (annual), CQ Press, 2011, p. 176.

5000 ■ STATES WITH THE LOWEST WORKERS' COMPENSATION PREMIUMS, 2011

Ranked by: Score based on workers' compensation benefits per $100 of covered wages. **Number listed:** 51

1. Washington DC, with 0.27 points
2. Texas, 0.47
3. Massachusetts, 0.55
4. Arkansas, 0.57
4. Virginia, 0.57
6. Indiana, 0.61
7. Arizona, 0.66
8. Utah, 0.70
9. South Dakota, 0.76
10. Maryland, 0.79

Source: *Small Business Survival Index*, (annual), Small Business & Entrepreneurship Council, November 2011, p. 51.

5001 ■ TOP WRITERS OF WORKERS' COMPENSATION INSURANCE, 2010

Ranked by: Direct premiums written, in thousands of dollars. **Remarks:** Also notes A. M. Best number, percent change from previous year, market share and adjusted loss ratios for current and two previous years, and workers' compensation as a percentage of total company premiums. **Number listed:** 25

1. Liberty Mutual Insurance Companies, with $4,073,327 thousand
2. American International Group Inc., $3,129,570
3. Travelers Group, $2,819,879
4. Hartford Insurance Group, $2,643,316
5. Zurich Financial Services North America Group, $2,023,964
6. State Insurance Fund of New York, $1,309,759
7. State Compensation Insurance Fund of California, $1,140,203
8. Ace INA Group, $952,074
9. Old Republic Insurance Group, $852,764
10. Accident Fund Group, $742,608

Source: *Best's Review*, Top P/C Writers by Line (annual), August 2011, p. 59.

World Wide Web (Computer Network)
See: **Internet**

Writers
See: **Authors**

AF AB
Engineering Design, International 2585
AFA Forest Products (USA) Inc.
Forestry 2772, 2773
AFA Protective Systems Inc.
Security Systems 4412
Affiliated Computer Services Inc.
Homosexuals--Employment 3017
Affiliated Engineers Inc.
Engineering Firms 2593
Affiliated Managers Group
Bond Funds 612
Affinia Group Inc.
Corporations--Michigan 1856
Affinity Credit Union
Credit Unions 2248
Affinity Plus Credit Union
Credit Unions 2241
Affinity Plus Federal Credit Union
Credit Unions 2204
AFL Telecommunications LLC
Broadband Communication Systems 699
Aflac
Insurance 3213
Aflac Credit Union
Credit Unions 2239
AFLAC Inc.
Child Care 990
Corporations--Georgia 1650, 1651, 1655, 1656
Diversity 2359
Insurance, Health 3269
Insurance, Life 3290, 3291, 3306, 3318, 3323, 3324
Aflac Inc.
Information Technology 3198
Afnan Rashid Al Zayani
Leadership 3474
AFP Crecer El Salvador
Corporations--El Salvador 1596
Africa Oil Corp.
Corporations--Canada 1532
African Bank
Banks and Banking--Africa 340
African Cats: A Lion's Pride
Best Sellers 564
African Export-Import Bank
Banks and Banking--Arab 362
African Rainbow
Metal Industry 3704
Afriland First Bank
Banks and Banking--Africa 329
Ag Processing Inc.
Agricultural Cooperative Associations 95
Agaoglu; Ali Ibrahim
Wealth, Foreign 4919
AGCO Corp.
Agricultural Machinery Industry 107
Construction Machinery 1188
Corporations--Georgia 1656
Industrial Equipment Industry 3151
Agco Corp.
Machinery 3549
Ageas NV
Corporations--Belgium 1435
Insurance, Life 3288
Agee's Bicycle
Bicycles 599
Agency of Credit Control Inc.
Collection Agencies 1034
AGFA-Gevaert NV
Manufacturing Industry, International 3575
Agfa HealthCare Inc.
Corporations--Canada 1502
Aggregate Industries
Private Trucking Fleets 4107
Aggregate Industries Management Inc.
Sand and Gravel Industry 4356
Stone Mining and Quarrying 4526
Aggreko

Corporations--United Kingdom 2111, 2114
Service Industry 4432
Aggreko plc
Business Services 775, 785
Carbon 826, 868
Corporations--United Kingdom 2115, 2116, 2117, 2119, 2125
AgigA Tech Inc.
Communication Industry 1057
Agile Alliance
Computer Software Industry, International 1125
Agile Property Holdings
Corporations--Asia 1423
Corporations--China 1544
Real Estate Business 4175
Agilent Technologies
Corporations--California 1474, 1477
Corporations--India 1715
Research and Development 4217
Agilent Technologies Inc.
Electronic Industry 2482, 2490, 2491, 2496
Homosexuals--Employment 3027
Instrument Industry 3211, 3212
Scientific Instruments and Apparatus 4391
AgileThought Inc.
Corporations--Florida 1614
Agiliance
Computer Software Industry 1097
Agility
Brand Name Products, International 681
Chemical Industry--Distributors 939
AGL Energy Ltd.
Electric Utilities, International 2428
Agnico-Eagle Mines
Gold Mines and Mining 2825
Agnico-Eagle Mines Ltd.
Corporations--Canada 1502
Agosto; Benny Jr.
Hispanics 2962
Agrani Bank
Banks and Banking--Asia 375
Agri Beef Co.
Meat Industry 3635, 3645
AgriBank FCB
Corporations--Minnesota 1871
Agribank FCB
Cooperatives 1345
Agrico-Eagle Mines
Mining Industry 3723
Agricultural Bank of China
Banks and Banking--Asia 379, 380, 390
Banks and Banking, International 491, 495, 497
Brand Name Products, International 658, 660, 687
Corporations--China 1541, 1542
Corporations, International 1760
Financial Institutions 2685
Agricultural Bank of Greece
Banks and Banking--Europe 431
Agricultural Limestone Ltd.
Corporations--Ireland 1776
Agriculture Financial Services Corp.
Corporations--Canada 1482, 1497, 1524
Agrium Inc.
Chemical Industry, International 951, 956
Chemicals, Specialty 972, 982
Corporations--Canada 1482, 1497, 1509
Diversity 2360
Mining Industry 3725, 3726, 3730
Agrium U.S. Retail
Agricultural Organizations 108
Agro Power Development Inc.
Crops 2282

Agroindustrijsko Komercijalna Banka
Banks and Banking--Europe 457
Agromepa SRO
Corporations--Slovakia 2042
Agropur Cooperative
Cooperatives 1344
Dairy Industry 2290
Aguirre; Fernando
Hispanics 2957, 2962
Ahead
Value-Added Resellers (Computers) 4778
Ahimsa Development Ltd.
Corporations--Cyprus 1583
Ahlam Mosteghanemi
Leadership 3473
Ahlers
Chemical Industry--Distributors 939
Ahli Bank
Banks and Banking--Arab 370
Ahli United Bank
Banks and Banking--Middle East 521
Brand Name Products, International 680
Ahli United Bank KSC
Banks and Banking--Middle East 527
Ahlstrom Corp.
Nonwoven Fabrics Industry 3834
Ahmad Al Sayed
Banks and Banking--Arab 367
Leadership 3485
Ahmad Julfar
Telecommunications Industry 4614
Ahmed Mohamed El Tayeb
Leadership 3475
Ahmedabad, India
Location of Industry 3536
Ahold NV; Koninklijke
Carbon 845
Corporations--Netherlands 1907, 1909
Environmental Protection 2614
Retail Industry 4292
Retail Stores 4336
Supermarkets 4535, 4553
Ahold NV; Royal
Carbon 845
Corporations--Netherlands 1907, 1909
Environmental Protection 2614
Retail Industry 4292
Retail Stores 4336
Supermarkets 4535, 4553
Ahold USA Inc.
Supermarkets 4530, 4541, 4545, 4551
Ahrendts; Angela
Women Executives 4979
AI Engineers Inc.
Minority Business Enterprises 3753
AIA Group Ltd.
Corporations--Hong Kong 1692
Insurance, Life 3323, 3325
Aida Alvarez
Hispanics 2957
Aidells
Sausage 4368
Aim High Academy of Martial Arts
Corporations--Oregon 1987
Aimbridge Hospitality
Hotel Management Companies 3083
AIMCO
Apartment Houses 174, 175
AIPSO
Corporations--Rhode Island 2024
Air Academy Credit Union
Credit Unions 2217
Air Arabia PJSC
Airlines, International 132, 143, 144
Air Berlin plc
Airlines, International 136
Air Canada

Airlines, International 140, 141
Transportation 4725
Air Canada Centre
Concerts 1140
Air China
Airlines, Cargo 126, 127
Airlines, International 130, 151
Air China Ltd.
Airlines, International 133, 134, 154, 155
Air Force; U.S.
Minorities--Employment 3743, 3744, 3747
Air France
Airlines, International 151
Air France-KLM
Airlines, International 154
Air France-KLM SA
Airlines, International 135, 136, 142, 150, 152, 153, 156, 157, 158
Corporations--France 1646
Leisure 3502
Travel 4739
Air France SA
Transportation 4716
Air France; Societe
Transportation 4716
Air Hydro Power
Corporations--Kentucky 1802
Air Line Pilots Association Credit Union
Credit Unions 2211
Air Liquide Electronics U.S. LP
Chemical Industry 926
Air Malta plc
Corporations--Malta 1830
Air Methods
Corporations--Colorado 1553
Transportation 4710
Air Methods Corp.
Corporations--Colorado 1555
Air New Zealand
Airlines, International 139
Air Products
Chemical Industry, International 950
Air Products & Chemicals
Research and Development 4220
Air Products & Chemicals Inc.
Chemical Industry 928, 930, 932
Chemical Industry, International 957
Chemicals, Specialty 974, 977, 982
Corporations--Pennsylvania 1999, 2004
Homosexuals--Employment 3014
AirAsia Berhad
Airlines, International 144, 146, 148, 149
Airbus
Brand Name Products, International 671
Defense Industry 2312
Aircastle Ltd.
Growth Companies 2845
Airclic
Communication Industry 1057
Aire-Master of America Inc.
Building Cleaning Industry 722
Aire Serv Heating & Air Conditioning
Building Cleaning Industry 720
Aire Serv Heating & Air Conditioning Inc.
Veterans--Employment 4798
Airfoil Public Relations
Marketing 3620
Public Relations Firms 4139
airG Inc.
Corporations--Canada 1489
Airgas Inc.
Chemicals, Specialty 977
Corporations--Pennsylvania 2003
Industrial Distributors 3139
Private Trucking Fleets 4114

Computer Software Industry, International 1116
Corporations 1363, 1367, 1388, 1390
Corporations, International 1737, 1738, 1741, 1761, 1762
Corporations--Washington 2160, 2162, 2169, 2170, 2171, 2173, 2174, 2175, 2177, 2178, 2179, 2180, 2181, 2183
Economic Development 2380, 2381
Electronic Commerce 2461, 2462, 2463, 2464, 2465, 2478
Electronics Stores 2506
Home Electronics 2981, 2984
Homosexuals--Employment 3030
Information Technology 3195
Internet 3375, 3377
Retail Industry 4274, 4289, 4299, 4312
Retail Stores 4327, 4331
Supply Chain 4559
Veterans--Employment 4789, 4796, 4813
AMB Property Corp.
Industrial Parks 3164, 3165
Amba Research Costa Rica
Corporations--Costa Rica 1582
Ambac Financial Group Inc.
Insurance Companies 3244
Insurance, Financial Guaranty 3264
Ambani; Anil
Wealth, Foreign 4876
Ambani; Mukesh
Wealth, Foreign 4875, 4876, 4916
AmBev
Beverage Industry 588
Leadership 3471
Manufacturing Industry, International 3577
Ambit Energy
Direct Selling 2335, 2336
Ambius
Lawn Care Services 3457, 3459, 3463
Ambrose Employer Group LLC
Corporations--New York 1934
Ambulatory Services Inc.
Corporations--Hawaii 1677
AMC Entertainment
Private Companies 4103
AMC Entertainment Holdings Inc.
Motion Picture Industry 3766
AMC Entertainment Inc.
Corporations--Missouri 1893
Homosexuals--Employment 3023
Hotels and Motels 3086
Motion Picture Industry 3767
Motion Picture Theaters 3769
Restaurants 4225
Amco Insurance Co.
Corporations--Iowa 1769
Amcol International Corp.
Mining Industry 3728
Amcon Distributing Co.
Convenience Stores 1332, 1333, 1334, 1340
Amcor Ltd.
Container Industry 1223
Manufacturing Industry, International 3573
Paper Industry 3867
Amcor Rigid Plastics
Blow Molders 611
AMEC
Engineering Design 2560
Amec
Petroleum Equipment Industry 3916
AMEC Americas Ltd.
Corporations--Canada 1497, 1502
AMEC plc
Construction Project Management 1197
Engineering Design 2556, 2562, 2563, 2568, 2569

Engineering Design, International 2572, 2573, 2574, 2576, 2579, 2580, 2581, 2584, 2585, 2589
Petroleum Equipment Industry 3922
Amec plc
Petroleum Industry, Foreign 3952
Amedisys
Health Care Industry 2872
Amen Bank
Banks and Banking--Africa 356
Banks and Banking--Arab 366
Amerco Inc.
Automobiles--Maintenance and Repair 279
Corporations--Nevada 1911
Ameren
Electric Utilities 2425
Environmental Protection 2612
Ameren Corp.
Corporations--Missouri 1890, 1892, 1895
Electric Utilities 2424
Gas Utilities 2807, 2813
Information Technology 3182
Ameresco
Construction Industry 1145
Corporations--Massachusetts 1839
America Air Liquide Holdings Inc.
Chemical Industry 926
America Chung Nam Inc.
Women-Owned Business Enterprises 4984
America First Credit Union
Credit Unions 2268, 2270
America Movil
Corporations--Mexico 1854
America Movil, SA de CV
Carbon 843
Corporations, Foreign 1638
Corporations--Mexico 1852, 1853
Telecommunications Industry 4634, 4635
America Movil, SAB de CV
Telecommunications Industry 4639
AmeriCAL Inc.
Printing Industry 4084
American Academy of Pediatrics
Adoption 32
American Agricultural Insurance Co.
Insurance--Reinsurance 3355
American Airlines Credit Union
Credit Unions 2266, 2267
American Airlines Inc.
Air Transport 118, 119
Airlines 120
Airlines, International 141, 152, 157, 158
Information Technology 3188
American Apparel
Growth Companies 2840
American Apparel Inc.
Clothing Industry 994
American Associated Pharmacies
Drug Stores 2367
American Axle & Manufacturing Holdings Inc.
Automobile Parts 257
Metal Products 3717
American Bank of the North
Banks and Banking 304
American Banker
Business-to-Business Advertising 803
American Beacon Advisors
African American Business Enterprises 82
American Cancer Socity Mid-South Division Inc.
Corporations--Alabama 1404
American Capital Agency
Corporations 1368
American Capital Agency Corp.
Corporations--Maryland 1835

Real Estate Business 4184, 4185
American Century Investment Management
Mutual Funds 3814
American Century Zero Coupon
Bond Funds 615
American Coradius International LLC
Collection Agencies 1033
American Deli
Restaurants 4231
American Diversity Business Solutions
Printing Industry 4081, 4083, 4088
American Drug Stores Inc.
Corporations, Foreign 1636
Corporations--Idaho 1698
Private Companies 4097
Retail Industry 4288
American Eagle Credit Union
Credit Unions 2218
American Eagle Federal Credit Union
Corporations--Connecticut 1570
American Eagle Outfitters
Clothing Industry 998
American Eagle Outfitters Inc.
Clothing Stores 1015, 1016, 1021
American Electric Power
Private Trucking Fleets 4112
American Electric Power Co., Inc.
Corporations--Ohio 1967, 1970
Electric Utilities 2413, 2414, 2415, 2417, 2420
Energy Industry 2536
Gas Utilities 2803, 2804
Private Trucking Fleets 4118
Veterans--Employment 4808
Waste Management Industry 4821, 4822
American Engineering Testing Inc.
Corporations--Minnesota 1883
American Enterprise Group
Insurance, Life 3300
American Equity Investment Life Holding
Corporations--Iowa 1766
Financial Services 2692
American Equity Investment Life Holding Co.
Corporations--Iowa 1767
Insurance, Life 3290
American Eurocopter
Veterans--Employment 4790, 4791
American Express
Banks and Banking, International 496, 498
Financial Institutions 2685
Financial Services 2708, 2712
American Express Bank FSB
Savings Banks 4369, 4370, 4371
American Express Bank, FSB
Commercial Loans 1039, 1040
Individual Retirement Accounts (IRA's) 3137
Savings and Loan Association Loans 4373, 4374, 4377, 4380
Savings and Loan Associations 4381, 4382, 4383, 4384, 4385, 4387
American Express Centurion
Bank Deposits 287
Banks and Banking 310
American Express Co.
Advertisers 35
Asian Americans in Business 184
Banks and Banking 322
Corporations--Japan 1785
Corporations--New York 1937, 1943
Credit Cards 2200, 2201
Diversity 2359, 2365
Financial Services 2699, 2700, 2701, 2709, 2711, 2713
Homosexuals--Employment 3013, 3015, 3041

Minorities--Employment 3741
Travel Agencies 4743
Women in Business 4962
Women Executives 4978
American Express India Pvt. Ltd.
Corporations--India 1715
American Family Insurance Group
Corporations--Wisconsin 2194
Insurance, Automobile 3217, 3219, 3221
Insurance, Homeowners 3273
American Family Life Assurance Co.
Insurance, Life 3315
American Family Mutual Insurance Co.
Insurance, Automobile 3215
Insurance, Homeowners 3272
American Farmer
Tire Industry 4669, 4671
American Federation of State, County & Municipal Employees
Labor Unions 3432
American Federation of Teachers
Labor Unions 3432
American Fidelity Assurance Co.
Corporations--Oklahoma 1980
Telecommuting 4646
American Financial Group Inc.
Insurance, Automobile 3214
Insurance Companies 3242, 3245
American Financial Inc.
Homosexuals--Employment 3015
American Financial Insurance Group
Insurance, Property and Casualty 3340
American Funds
Equity Funds 2632
American Furniture Warehouse Co.
Corporations--Colorado 1562, 1565
Family-Owned Corporations 2653
American Greetings Corp.
Corporations--Ohio 1966
Publishers and Publishing 4155
American Greetings Interactive
Information Technology 3190
American Group
Logistics 3547
American Heritage Credit Union
Credit Unions 2258
American Honda Motor Co., Inc.
Corporations, Foreign 1632
Wholesale Trade--Durable Goods 4928
American Hotel Register Co.
Hotels and Motels--Design and Construction 3105
"American Idol"
Hispanic Market 2946
Television Programs 4652
American International Group
Corporations 1382, 1393
Stocks 4517
American International Group Inc.
Corporations--New York 1944, 1946
Insurance, Automobile 3214, 3220
Insurance, Commercial 3237
Insurance Companies 3241, 3242, 3243, 3244
Insurance Companies, International 3256, 3257, 3258
Insurance, Earthquake 3259
Insurance, Fire 3265
Insurance, International 3279, 3280
Insurance, Life 3319, 3321
Insurance, Malpractice 3327, 3328
Insurance, Marine 3329, 3330
Insurance, Mortgage Guaranty 3331
Insurance, Property and Casualty 3343, 3344, 3345, 3347, 3351
Insurance, Warranty 3359
Workers' Compensation 5001

Index

Housewares 3123
Manufacturing Industry, International 3606
ArcelorMittal
Carbon 845
Corporations, International 1753
Corporations--Luxembourg 1822
Iron 3425, 3428, 3429
Leadership 3470
Metal Industry 3689, 3712, 3713, 3715
Steel Industry 4498, 4501, 4502
ArcelorMittal Fiat Carbon Europe SA
Corporations--Luxembourg 1821
ArcelorMittal SA
Manufacturing Industry, International 3608
ArcelorMittal Sourcing SCA
Corporations--Luxembourg 1821
ArcelorMittal South Africa Ltd.
Manufacturing Industry, International 3600
ArcelorMittal USA Inc.
Metal Industry 3692
Arch Capital Group Ltd.
Corporations--Caribbean 1533
Arch Coal Inc.
Coal Mines and Mining 1026, 1027
Information Technology 3191
Mining Industry 3731
Arch Specialty Insurance Co.
Insurance--Excess and Surplus Lines 3260, 3261
Arch Western Resources LLC
Coal Mines and Mining 1027
Archbishop Bergan Mercy Hospital
Corporations--Nebraska 1900
Archer Daniels Midland Co.
Corporations--Illinois 1705, 1707, 1710, 1712, 1713
Environmental Protection 2612
Food Industry 2719, 2720, 2721, 2723
Food Industry, International 2736, 2738, 2741, 2742
Food Processing 2747, 2750, 2756
Archer Malmo
Marketing 3620
Archer Western Contractors Ltd.
Contractors 1233, 1234
Archie Aldis Emmerson
Wealth 4843
Archipelago Learning
Growth Companies 2848
Architech
High Technology Industry 2895
Architectural Glass & Aluminum Co.
Glazing 2824
Architectural Record
Business-to-Business Advertising 803
Archstone
Apartment Houses 174
Arcilia C. Acosta
Hispanics 2957
Arcos Dorados
Corporations--Central America 1536
Arcos Dorados Argentina
Corporations--Argentina 1407
Arcos Dorados de Colombia SA
Corporations--Colombia 1545
Arcos Dorados Panama
Corporations--Central America 1535
Corporations--Panama 1993
ArcTeryx Equipment Inc.
Corporations--Canada 1489
Arctic Slope Regional Corp.
Contracts, Government 1308, 1322
Diversified Corporations 2347
Arctic Snow & Ice Control
Snow Removal Companies 4456
ArcusIT

Communication Industry 1053
Ardent Health Services
Multihospital Systems 3774
Area Erectors Inc.
Contractors 1281
Aref Ali Nayed
Leadership 3480
Arent Fox LLP
Trademarks 4701
Ares Capital
Corporations--New York 1935
Financial Services 2692
AREVA
Electric Utilities, International 2435, 2454
Gas Utilities 2816
AREVA Group
Corporations, International 1744
Argent Associates
Logistics 3547
Argentina
Business Loans 743
Crime and Criminals 2278
Economy 2386
Export/Import Trade 2640, 2641
Industrial Relations 3167
Music Industry 3776
New Business Enterprises 3825
Taxation 4565, 4566
ARGI Financial Group
Corporations--Kentucky 1802
Argo Reinsurance
Insurance--Reinsurance 3356
Argonne National Laboratory
Research and Development 4217
Argos
Brand Name Products, International 670
Argy, Wiltse & Robinson
Accounting Firms 5, 15
Ariad Pharmaceutical
Stocks--Prices 4520
ARIAD Pharmaceuticals Inc.
High Technology Industry 2911
Arias; Maria
Hispanics 2959
Ariat.com
Electronic Commerce 2466
Ariba Inc.
Supply Chain 4558
Ariel Investments LLC
African American Business Enterprises 82
Arihant Capital Markets
Corporations--India 1716
ARISE Technologies
High Technology Industry 2900
Arison; Micky
Basketball 547
Wealth 4848
Arison; Shari
Wealth, Foreign 4881
Aristeo Construction Co.
Corporations--Michigan 1855
Aristotelis Mistakidis
Wealth, Foreign 4872
Aritalia Group Inc.
Store Fixtures 4528
AriZona
Tea Industry 4582
Arizona
Bankruptcy 299
Business Failures 737
Farms 2657
Financial Services 2703
Location of Industry 3522
Manufacturing Industry 3568
Nursing 3840
Service Industry 4434
Taxation 4575, 4576, 4580
Tea Industry 4583
Unemployment 4775
Women--Employment 4973
Workers' Compensation 4998, 5000
AriZona Arnold Palmer

Tea Industry 4582
Arizona Arnold Palmer
Tea Industry 4583
Arizona Central Credit Union
Credit Unions 2209
Arizona Credit Union
Credit Unions 2209
Arizona State Savings & Credit Union
Credit Unions 2209
Arizona Tea
Brand Name Products 636
Arkansas
Compensation 1066
Dental Clinics 2316
Electric Utilities 2422
Employment 2520
Financial Services 2704
Gross Domestic Product 2835
Hospitality 3044
Income 3131
Livestock 3516
Manufacturing Industry 3567
Minimum Wage 3721
Physicians 4040
Property Tax 4123
Public Transit 4152
Taxation 4571
Teachers 4586
Women--Employment 4973
Workers' Compensation 4998, 4999, 5000
Arkansas Best Corp.
Transportation 4717
Arkansas Best Credit Union
Credit Unions 2210
Arkansas Blue Cross & Blue Shield
Corporations--Arkansas 1415
Information Technology 3187
Arkansas Children's Hospital Research Institute Inc.
Corporations--Arkansas 1417
Arkansas Credit Union
Credit Unions 2210
Arkansas Superior Credit Union
Credit Unions 2210
Arlene Gonzalez-Sanchez
Hispanics 2963
ARM Holdings plc
Computer Industry 1091
High Technology Industry 2897
Technology 4593
The Armando Montelongo Co.
Education 2395
Hispanic American Business Enterprises 2926
Armando Olivera
Hispanics 2958
Armani; Giorgio
Wealth, Foreign 4882
Armanio; Jose
Hispanics 2962
Armanio McKenna LLP
Accounting Firms 24
Armenia
Competition, International 1067, 1068
Armetta; Jim
Consultants 1211
Armour Transportation Systems
Trucking Industry 4745
Armstrong Garden Centers
Garden Centers 2797
Armstrong Hospitality Group Ltd.
Tourist Industry 4696
Armstrong; Marina
Women--Compensation 4967
Armstrong Wood Products Inc.
Wood Products 4989
Armstrong World Industries Inc.
Corporations--Pennsylvania 2002
Manufacturing Industry 3562, 3563
Armstrong World Industry Inc.
Rubber Industry 4353
Army Aviation Center Credit Union

Credit Unions 2207
Army Corps of Engineers; U.S.
Minorities--Employment 3743
Women Engineers 4976
Arnaboldi; Nicole S.
Women in Business 4965
Arnault; Bernard
Wealth, Foreign 4870, 4917
Wealth, International 4924
Arne Glimcher
Art Dealers 180
Arne Wilhelmsen
Wealth, Foreign 4895
Arnerich Massena Inc.
Investment Advisors 3391
Arnold
Advertising Agencies 48
Arnold Brand Experience
Marketing 3624
Arnold; John
Business Leaders 740
Hedge Funds 2891
Arnon Milchan
Wealth, Foreign 4881
Aromatic Fusion
Manufacturing Industry 3561
Aronson
Accounting Firms 15
Arpadis Chemicals
Chemical Industry--Distributors 935
Arpin Group Inc.
Trucking Industry 4759
Arpin Van Lines
Trucking Industry 4749
Array Healthcare Facilities Solutions
Interior Designers 3361
ArrayShield Technologies Private Ltd.
Communication Industry 1053
Arriva plc
Leisure 3503
Transportation 4711
Arrow Electronics
Corporations--Colorado 1556, 1568, 1569
Arrow Electronics Inc.
Electronic Industry 2490
Information Technology 3180
Wholesale Trade--Durable Goods 4929
Wholesale Trade--Electronics 4930, 4931
Arrow Exterminators
Pests--Control 3911
Arrow Financial Corp.
Banks and Banking--Independent Banks 484
Arrow S3
Corporations--New York 1932
Arrow Stage Lines
Buses 728
Arrow Strategies
Minority Business Enterprises 3749, 3757
Arrowhead
Bottled Water 631, 632
ArrowStream Inc.
Food Industry 2724
Arroyo; Raymond
Hispanics 2959
Arroyos; Adam
Hispanics 2962
Arryve
Corporations--Washington 2159
ARS Investment Holdings LLC
Corporations--Tennessee 2083
Arsalon Technologies LLC
Corporations--Kansas 1791
Arsel; Semahat Sevim
Wealth, Foreign 4919
Arsenal
Soccer 4457, 4458
Sports Clubs 4481
Arsenal Music
Music Retailers 3807

Index

Barrett Business Services
Corporations--Washington 2170
Barrett Developments
Construction Industry, International 1162
Barrett Distribution Centers
Chemical Industry--Distributors 939
Barrick Gaming Operations LLC
Corporations--Nevada 1910
Barrick Gold
Corporations--Canada 1503, 1518
Mining Industry 3730
Barrick Gold Corp.
Carbon 821
Corporations--Canada 1492, 1500, 1519
Gold Mines and Mining 2825
Metal Industry 3687, 3700, 3710
Mining Industry 3725, 3726, 3738
Barristrer Winery
Wine Industry 4941
Barron's
Business-to-Business Advertising 795
Barry Corp.; R. G.
Leather Industry 3498
Barry Lam
Wealth, Foreign 4913
The Bartech Group Inc.
African American Business Enterprises 85
Bartle Bogle Hegarty
Advertising Agencies, International 56
Bartlett Dairy Inc.
Hispanic American Business Enterprises 2940
Bartlett Tree Experts
Lawn Care Services 3461, 3464
Barton Malow Co.
Family-Owned Corporations 2651
Baruch College, Zicklin School of Business
Business Schools and Colleges 755
Barum Continental spol sro
Corporations--Czech Republic 1584
Barwa Real Estate
Corporations--Qatar 2023
Real Estate Business 4189
Bascom Group
Minority Business Enterprises 3755
The Bascom Group
Corporations--California 1455
Bascom Palmer Eye Institute
Hospitals 3065
Basden Steel Corp.
Contractors 1281
Base Productions
Film Production 2679
Base Technologies
Corporations--Virginia 2142
BASF
Chemicals 970, 971
BASF AG
Chemical Industry, International 940, 941, 947, 948, 960, 961, 968, 969
Coatings 1028
BASF Canada
Chemical Industry, International 956
BASF Coatings AG
Paint Industry 3859
BASF Corp.
Homosexuals--Employment 3014
BASF SE
Carbon 825, 829, 869, 870
Chemical Industry 931
Chemical Industry, International 942, 962, 963, 964
Corporations--Europe 1605
Corporations--Germany 1661, 1662, 1663, 1664
Manufacturing Industry, International 3585

Pharmaceutical Industry, International 4011
BASF (U.K.)
Corporations--United Kingdom 2113, 2114
Bash-Polley; Stacy
Women in Business 4965
Bashneft OJSC
Energy Industry 2528, 2538
Petroleum Industry, International 3975
Basin Electric Power Cooperative
Corporations--North Dakota 1960
Baskin-Robbins
Fast Food Restaurants 2667
Baskin-Robbins USA Co.
Ice Cream Shops 3128
Basler Kantonalbank
Banks and Banking--Europe 466, 467
Bass & Co.; G. H.
Leather Industry 3497
Bass; Carl
Executives--Compensation 2638
Bass Pro Shops
Catalogs 902
Bass Pro Shops Inc.
Corporations--Missouri 1893
Retail Industry 4269
Bass; Robert
Wealth 4837
Bassam Alghanim
Wealth, Foreign 4885
Bassam Kousa
Celebrities 906
Leadership 3488
Bassett Home Furnishings
Furniture Stores 2791
Bassford Remele
Corporations--Minnesota 1884
Batanga
Hispanic Market 2956
Batavia, NY
Location of Industry--Growth 3542
Batelco
Brand Name Products, International 680
Bath Fitter
Houses--Remodeling 3115
Batista; Eike
Wealth 4851
Wealth, Foreign 4859
Wealth, International 4924
Batman: Arkham City
Video Games 4817
Baton Rouge Area Chamber of Commerce
Location of Industry 3530
Baton Rouge, LA
Location of Industry--Growth 3543
Batra; Law Firm of Ravi
Law Firms 3441
BATS Exchange
Commodities Exchanges 1045
Battelle Memorial Institute
Contracts, Government 1309, 1318, 1319
Corporations--Washington 2161
Environmental Services Firms 2621, 2622, 2624, 2626
Research and Development 4217
Batteries Plus
Batteries 548
Battlefield 3
Video Games 4817, 4818
BaubleBar.com
Electronic Commerce 2474
Bauer Publishing
Magazine Publishers and Publishing 3554
Bauerie & Co.
Accounting Firms 8
Bauknight, Pietras & Stormer PA
Accounting Firms 6
Bausch & Lomb Inc.
Health Care Industry 2860

Baxter
Corporations--Spain 2059
Baxter BioScience
Biopharmaceutics 600
Baxter Credit Union
Credit Unions 2229
Baxter International
Corporations--Illinois 1712
Baxter International Inc.
Carbon 818, 846, 870, 874
Chemical Industry 926
Health Care Industry 2876, 2885
Medical Equipment and Supplies 3672, 3673, 3677, 3678, 3679
Medical Instruments and Apparatus 3682, 3684
Bay Alarm Co.
Security Systems 4413, 4415
Bay Area Bicycles
Bicycles 599
Bay Cities Paving & Grading Inc.
Hispanic American Business Enterprises 2929
Bayada Home Health Care
Family-Owned Corporations 2652
Bayat; Marwan Bin
Leadership 3490
Bayer
Brand Name Products 637
Chemicals 970, 971
Corporations--Pennsylvania 2007, 2008, 2010
Bayer AG
Chemical Industry, International 941, 942, 947, 948, 962, 963, 967, 968
Corporations--Germany 1661
Manufacturing Industry, International 3585
Pharmaceutical Industry, International 4011
Bayer Corp.
Chemical Industry, International 964
Homosexuals--Employment 3014
Bayer CropScience Canada Inc.
Corporations--Canada 1482, 1527
Bayer Healthcare
Pharmaceutical Industry, International 4016
Bayer HealthCare Pharmaceuticals USA
Information Technology 3198
Bayer Heritage Credit Union
Credit Unions 2274
Bayer Inc.
Corporations--Canada 1491, 1497, 1502, 1527
Bayerische Landesbank
Banks and Banking--Europe 427
Bayerische Motoren Werke AG
Aged--Employment 93
Automobile Industry 225
Automobile Industry, International 231, 234, 239, 243, 244, 245, 248
Corporations--Europe 1605
Corporations--Germany 1661, 1662, 1663, 1664
Corporations, International 1753
Manufacturing Industry, International 3585
Bayern Munich
Soccer 4457, 4458
Sports Clubs 4481
Baylor Health Care System
Information Technology 3184
Baylor Institute for Rehabilitation
Rehabilitation Services 4212
Bayport Credit Union
Credit Unions 2272
Bayside Harley-Davidson
Motorcycle Industry 3773
Baystate Health Systems Health Services Inc.

Corporations--Massachusetts 1841
Baystate Medical Center
Hospitals 3074
Baystate Medical Center Inc.
Corporations--Massachusetts 1841
Baz; Farouk El
Leadership 3475
BB & T
Banks and Banking 303
BB & T Corp.
Banks and Banking 317, 318
Corporations--North Carolina 1954, 1956, 1957
Training 4708
BB & T Insurance Services Inc.
Insurance Brokers 3226, 3230, 3232, 3233, 3235
Insurance, Commercial 3236
BBA Inc.
Corporations--Canada 1484
BBC
College Graduates 1035
Corporations--United Kingdom 2116
Media Companies 3655, 3665
BBDO
Advertising Agencies 48
BBDO Worldwide
Advertising Agencies, International 60
Advertising, International 72
BBG-BBGM
Interior Designers 3361
BBH Core Select
Stock Funds 4505
BBMG
Construction Materials 1190
BBVA
Banks and Banking--Europe 422, 441, 460, 461, 463
Brand Name Products, International 675
Carbon 858
Corporations--Spain 2063, 2064, 2066
Leadership 3470
BBVA Banco Continental
Banks and Banking--Latin America 519
BBVA Banco Frances
Banks and Banking--Latin America 501
BBVA Banco Provincial
Banks and Banking--Latin America 520
BBVA Bancomer Mexico
Corporations--Mexico 1849
BBVA Chile
Banks and Banking--Latin America 506
BBVA Colombia
Banks and Banking--Latin America 507
BBVA Compass Insurance Agency Inc.
Insurance Brokers 3230
BBVA PR Holding Corp.
Banks and Banking 321
BC Assessment
Corporations--Canada 1489
BC Biomedical Laboratories Ltd.
Corporations--Canada 1484
BC Housing Management Commission
Corporations--Canada 1489
BC Hydro
Corporate Directors 1349
Corporations--Canada 1485, 1489, 1491
Diversity 2360
BC Hydro & Power Authority
Corporations--Canada 1498, 1513
BC Public Service
Corporations--Canada 1491, 1497
BCB Holdings
Banks and Banking--Latin America 510

C. C. Sabathia
Athletes--Compensation 187
C. H. James Restaurant Holdings LLC
African American Business Enterprises 78
C. H. Robinson
Transportation 4732
C. H. Robinson Co.
Transportation 4718
C. H. Robinson Worldwide
Corporations 1395
C. H. Robinson Worldwide Inc.
Contract Logistics Services 1225, 1226
Corporations--Minnesota 1869, 1881
Transportation 4718, 4720, 4726, 4727, 4728
C. J. Hughes Construction Co., Inc.
Contractors 1282
C. R. Bard Inc.
Manufacturing Industry, International 3614
Medical Equipment and Supplies 3673, 3675
C. R. England Inc.
Refrigerated Trucks 4210, 4211
Trucking Industry 4765
C. S. E. Credit Union
Credit Unions 2234
C2 Exchange
Commodities Exchanges 1045
C2 Solutions Group Inc.
Corporations--Virginia 2144
C2C Outdoor
Advertising Agencies 49
Private Companies 4094
CA Inc.
Computer Software Industry 1098
Computer Software Industry, International 1114
Homosexuals--Employment 3019
CA Life Insurance Co. of Canada
Insurance, Life 3295, 3296, 3298
CA Technologies
Environmental Protection 2611
Women in Business 4962
Cabanas; Alex
Hispanics 2962
Cabela's
Catalogs 902
Cabela's Inc.
Corporations--Nebraska 1900, 1901
Cabelas.com
Electronic Commerce 2477
Cabin Fever
Best Sellers 555
Cable & Wireless Communications
Corporations--United Kingdom 2124
Cable-Dahmer Chevrolet Inc.
Hispanic American Business Enterprises 2927
Cablevision Systems Corp.
Broadband Communication Systems 700
Telecommunications Industry 4629
Cabot Creamery Cooperative Inc.
Corporations--Vermont 2139
Cabot Oil & Gas
Standard and Poor's--Stock Price Index 4489
Stocks 4518
cacaFly International Media
Communication Industry 1053
Cache Valley Electric Co.
Contractors 1264
CACI International
Corporations--Virginia 2148
CACI International Inc.
Contracts, Government 1312, 1323
Information Technology 3200
Veterans--Employment 4791, 4812

Cactus Marketing Communications
Advertising Agencies 50
Cactus Restaurants Ltd.
Corporations--Canada 1486, 1527
Hospitality 3042
Cadbury
Food Industry 2725
Caddell Construction Co.
Corporations--Alabama 1404
Cadence Design Systems Inc.
Computer Software Industry, International 1130
Information Technology 3181
Cadet Holding Corp.
Corporations--Iowa 1769
Cadillac Stone Works
Construction Industry 1146
Cadogan; Charles
Wealth, Foreign 4922
CAE Inc.
High Technology Industry 2896, 2916
Caesars Entertainment
Casinos 887
Corporations--Nevada 1912
Caesars Entertainment Corp.
Casinos 886, 888, 889
Corporations--Nevada 1911, 1913
Homosexuals--Employment 3028
Hotels and Motels 3086, 3088, 3089, 3091
Information Technology 3185
Restaurants 4225
Caforio; Jon
Consultants 1211
Cagwin & Dorward
Corporations--California 1449
Lawn Care Services 3463
The Cain Travel Group Inc.
Women-Owned Business Enterprises 4982
Cain Watters & Associates
Accounting Firms 23
Cainz
Electronics Stores 2503
Cairn Energy plc
Petroleum Industry, Foreign 3974
Cairn India Ltd.
Energy Industry 2525, 2538
Cairo Amman Bank
Banks and Banking--Middle East 526
Caisse de depot et placement
Government Ownership 2827
Caisse de depot et placement du Quebec
Corporations--Canada 1506
Caixa Economica Federal
Banks and Banking--Latin America 502, 516
Caixa Geral de Depositos
Banks and Banking--Europe 452
CaixaBank SA
Banks and Banking--Europe 462
Corporations--Spain 2066
Caja de Ahorros y Monte de Piedad
Banks and Banking--Europe 475
Banks and Banking, International 500
Caja de Ahorros y Pensiones de Barcelona - la Caixa
Banks and Banking--Europe 460
Caja Espana de Inversiones, Salamanca y Soria
Banks and Banking, International 499
Cakrawala Andalas Televisi
Advertisers, International 40
Cal-Maine Foods
Eggs 2400
Cal-Maine Foods Inc.
Corporations--Mississippi 1887
Livestock 3515
Calabazas Creek Research Inc.
Research and Development 4217

Calavo Growers
Food Industry 2716
Calbee
Securities--Initial Public Offerings 4403
Calcon Constructors Inc.
Contractors 1227
Calculated Risk
Blogs 608, 610
Caldic
Chemical Industry--Distributors 933, 934
Caledonian Brewery Ltd.
Beverage Industry 576
Food Industry, International 2731
Tobacco Industry 4679
Calfrac Well Service Ltd.
Stocks 4512
Calgary Co-operative Association
Cooperatives 1344
Calgary Laboratory Services
Corporations--Canada 1491
Calian Technologies
High Technology Industry 2920
California
Business Failures 739
Compensation 1064
Construction Industry 1158
Corporations 1387
Crops 2284
Dental Clinics 2315
Education 2397
Electric Utilities 2421
Employment 2518, 2519, 2523
Farms 2654, 2655, 2656, 2658
Hospitality 3043
Income 3130
Income Tax 3134
Insurance, Health--Costs 3271
Livestock 3516
Location of Industry 3528, 3537
Minimum Wage 3720
New Business Enterprises 3829, 3830
Nursing 3840
Public Transit 4153
Service Industry 4434
Small Business 4447
State Data (for individual states) 4490
Taxation 4569, 4570, 4572, 4573, 4580
Teachers 4584, 4585
Unemployment 4774
Women--Employment 4974
Workers' Compensation 4995, 4996
California Adventist Credit Union
Credit Unions 2212
California-Berkeley, Haas School of Business; University of
Business Schools and Colleges 750
California Closets
Home Improvement Industry 3006
California Dairies Inc.
Agricultural Cooperative Associations 95
California Drywall Co.
Contractors 1283
California Earthquake Authority
Insurance, Earthquake 3259
California-Irvine; University of
Corporations--California 1466
California Lithuanian Credit Union
Credit Unions 2213
California-Los Angeles, Anderson School of Management; University of
Business Schools and Colleges 748, 750, 752
California, Los Angeles; University of
Business Schools and Colleges, International 770
California Multimodal LLC

Trucking Industry 4760
California Pizza Kitchen
Restaurants 4237, 4238, 4258
California Pizza Kitchen Inc.
Pizza 4045
California Pools & Spas
Swimming Pools 4560
California Public Employees
Pension Fund Investments 3878
California, San Francisco Medical Center; University of
Hospitals 3057, 3059, 3063, 3064, 3065, 3067, 3070, 3072
California Square LP
Corporations--Kentucky 1805
California State Department of Justice
Legal Services 3499
California State University, Fullerton
Corporations--California 1466
California; University of
Private Companies 4099
Calix Inc.
Corporations--California 1467
Call of Duty: Black Ops
Video Games 4817
Call of Duty: Modern Warfare 3
Video Games 4817, 4818
Callaway Golf Ball Operations Inc.
Manufacturing Industry 3564
Callaway Golf Co.
Manufacturing Industry 3563
Callinan Mining Ltd.
Corporations--Canada 1520
CallingMart
Telecommunications Services 4644
Callison
Interior Designers 3361, 3362
Callison Architecture Inc.
Architectural Firms 176
Interior Designers 3369, 3370, 3371
Callon Petroleum Co.
Petroleum Industry 3941
Calloway's Nursery
Garden Centers 2797
Calm Air International LP
Corporations--Canada 1515
Calpine Corp.
Bankruptcy 298
Energy Industry 2536
CalPortland Co.
Private Trucking Fleets 4107
Sand and Gravel Industry 4357
Caltex Australia
Petroleum Industry, Foreign 3950
Caltex Australia Ltd.
Manufacturing Industry, International 3573
Calvert Funds
Bond Funds 616, 617
Equity Funds 2632
Calvin Klein
Clothing Industry, International 1012
CAMAC International Corp.
African American Business Enterprises 86
Camara de Comercio de Medellin para Antioquia
Corporations--Colombia 1545
Cambiar Investors LLC
Investment Management Firms 3403
Cambodia
Internet Users 3387
New Business Enterprises 3826
Cambodian Public Bank
Banks and Banking--Asia 377
Cambridge, MA
Business Conditions 730
Veterans--Employment 4787
Cambridge; University of, Judge Business School

Index

Index

Index

Index

Cox Communications Inc.
African Americans--Employment 90
Diversity 2366
Cox; Courteney
Entertainers 2606
Cox Enterprises
Media Companies 3661
Cox Enterprises Inc.
Broadband Communication Systems 700
Communication Industry 1055
Corporations--Georgia 1652, 1654
Homosexuals--Employment 3023
Information Technology 3190
Media Companies 3653, 3662
Newspaper Publishers and Publishing 3832
Private Trucking Fleets 4117
Cox Health Systems
Corporations--Missouri 1889
Cox School of Business; Southwest Methodist University
Business Schools and Colleges 748, 750
Coyne Public Relations
Public Relations Firms 4127, 4135, 4140, 4146, 4149
Coyote Logistics
Logistics 3547
Cozen O'Connor
Trademarks 4701
CP All
Convenience Stores 1328
Corporations--Thailand 2106
Retail Industry 4296
CP All plc
Retail Stores 4331
CP Pharmaceuticals International CV
Pharmaceutical Industry, International 4011
CPAlead
Advertising Agencies 49
CPFL Energia
Electric Utilities, International 2429
CPI
Agriculture 109
CPI Corp.
Personal Services 3908
CPIC
Brand Name Products, International 646
Insurance, International 3274
CPLG
Licensed Product Merchandising 3510
CR-V; Honda
Trucks 4770, 4771, 4772
Cracker Barrel Old Country Store
Corporations, International 1745
Restaurants 4246, 4247, 4248, 4249, 4250
Cracker Jack
Popcorn 4063
Craig Hospital
Hospitals 3069
Craig Wireless Systems
Corporations--Canada 1504
Crain's Chicago Business
Trade Magazines 4699
Crain's Detroit Business
Trade Magazines 4699
Crain's New York Business
Trade Magazines 4699
Cramer & Anderson
Legal Services 3500
Crane Bank
Banks and Banking--Africa 357
Crane Co.
Metal Industry 3697
Metal Products 3717
Cranfield School of Management
Business Schools and Colleges, Foreign 766
Crate & Barrel
Catalogs 896

Furniture Stores 2792
Craters & Freighters
Women-Owned Business Enterprises 4982
Cravath, Swaine & Moore LLP
Law Firms 3442, 3451, 3453
Cravens Advertising
Advertising Agencies, International 57
Crawford & Co.
Information Technology 3187
Insurance Brokers 3227
Crawford & Company (Canada) Inc.
Corporations--Canada 1526
Crawford Group Inc.
Automobiles--Maintenance and Repair 278
CRC Insurance Services Inc.
Insurance Brokers 3229
Insurance, Property and Casualty 3337
CRDB Bank plc
Banks and Banking--Africa 355
Cream Productions
Film Production 2676
Create Super Drugstore
Personal Care Products 3888
Creativ Co.
Corporations--Europe 1600
Creative Artists Agency
Agents 94
Creative Associates International Inc.
Contracts, Government 1315
Creative Design Consultants
Interior Designers 3370
Creative Lodging Solutions
Adoption 33
Corporations--Kentucky 1802
Credential Direct
Brokers--Internet 715
Credicard Hall
Concerts 1143
Credicorp
Corporations--Peru 2015
Credit Acceptance Corp.
Corporations--Michigan 1858
Financial Services 2692
Credit Agricole
Banks and Banking--Europe 426
Credit Agricole SA
Banks and Banking--Europe 424, 425, 442, 476
Corporations--France 1645
Corporations, International 1755
Credit Andorra
Banks and Banking--Europe 408
Credit du Maroc
Banks and Banking--Arab 364
Credit Europe Bank
Banks and Banking--Europe 449
Credit Libanais
Banks and Banking--Arab 363
Credit Management Services Inc.
Collection Agencies 1033
Credit Mutuel
Banks and Banking--Europe 424
Credit Populaire d'Algerie
Banks and Banking--Africa 334
Credit Saison
Financial Services 2694
Credit Suisse
Banks and Banking--Europe 468
Brand Name Products, International 677
Investment Management Firms 3416
Credit Suisse Group
Banks and Banking--Europe 466
Banks and Banking, International 492
Corporate Acquisition and Merger Services 1346
Corporations--Switzerland 2077, 2078

Debt Financing 2293
Health Care Financing 2859
Securities--Initial Public Offerings 4402
Security Underwriting 4417, 4418
Syndicated Loans 4561
Credit Suisse Group AG
Corporations--Switzerland 2076, 2079
Investment Management Firms 3411
Securities--Initial Public Offerings 4397, 4398
Credit Suisse Securities (USA) LLC
Futures Contracts 2795
Credit Suisse USA Inc.
Homosexuals--Employment 3013
Credit Union 1
Credit Unions 2208, 2229
Credit Union Central Sasketchawan
Cooperatives 1343
Credit Union of America
Credit Unions 2232
Credit Union of Colorado
Credit Unions 2217
Credit Union of Denver
Credit Unions 2217
Credit Union of New Jersey
Credit Unions 2248
Credit Union One
Credit Unions 2240
Credit Union West
Credit Unions 2209
Credito Emiliano
Banks and Banking--Europe 439
Credito Hipotecario Nacional de Guatemala
Banks and Banking--Latin America 513
Credito Valtellinese
Banks and Banking--Europe 439
Cree
Research and Development 4221
Cree Inc.
Growth Companies 2847
Technology 4589
Creekstone Farms Premium Beef LLC
Meat Industry 3635, 3640
Creighton; William
Wealth, Foreign 4894
Creme Software Ltd.
High Technology Industry 2908
CresaPartners
Corporations--California 1447
Crescent Electric Supply Co.
Electronic Industry--Distributors 2501
Crescent Hotels & Resorts
Hotel Management Companies 3083, 3085
Crescent Point Energy
Carbon 822
Crest
Personal Care Products 3903
Personal Care Products--Advertising 3905
Crestmark Bank
Banks and Banking--Independent Banks 482
Crestone Capital Advisors LLC
Corporations--Colorado 1552
Crestor
Drugs 2376, 2377
Drugs, Prescription 2378
Crestron
Air Conditioning Industry 114
Audio and Video Equipment 196, 202, 205, 206, 207
Home Automation 2971
Home Electronics 2977, 2979, 2980
Lighting 3512
Window Treatments 4939
Crestview, FL

Restaurants 4226
Crete Carrier Corp.
Trucking Industry 4755, 4765
Crevier BMW
Automobile Dealers 215, 218
CRH plc
Building Materials Industry 726
Construction Industry, International 1165, 1179
Construction Materials 1194
Corporations--Ireland 1775, 1776, 1777
Manufacturing Industry, International 3589, 3590
Cricket Communications Inc.
Hours of Labor 3108
Crime Prevention Security Systems & Custom Home Entertainment
Security Systems 4411
Cristacurva Glass
Glass 2822
Cristiano Ronaldo
Athletes 185, 186
Athletes--Compensation 190
Cristina Green
Wealth, Foreign 4922
Critchfield Mechanical Inc.
Contractors 1254
Criteria CaixaCorp
Financial Services 2691
CriticalControl Solutions
Computer Software Industry, International 1111
Critter Control Inc.
Building Cleaning Industry 720
CRN
Business-to-Business Advertising 797
Croatia
Corporate Directors 1348
Economy 2388
Industrial Relations 3167
Taxation 4565
Croda International
Corporations--United Kingdom 2113, 2116
Croda International plc
Chemical Industry, International 940
Croke Park
Stadiums 4487
Crop Production Services
Private Trucking Fleets 4106, 4115
Crosby Marketing Communications
Public Relations Firms 4150
Cross Country Healthcare
Nursing 3835, 3838
Cross, Fernandez & Riley LLP
Corporations--Florida 1613
Crossfit
Brand Name Products 636
Crossland Construction Co.
Hispanic American Business Enterprises 2929
Crossland Construction Co., Inc.
Roofing 4349
Crossroads Properties
Corporations--Minnesota 1885
Crowe Clark Whitehill LLP
Accounting Firms, International 28
Crowe Haworth
Consultants 1204
Crowe Horwath
Accounting Firms 11, 12, 13
Consultants 1203
Value-Added Resellers (Computers) 4779
Crowe Horwath LLP
Accounting Firms 7
Corporations--Kentucky 1801
Crowell & Moring LLP
Homosexuals--Employment 3031
Crowley Holdings Inc.
Water Transportation Services 4830

Index

Index

Digimo Media
High Technology Industry 2910
DiGiorno
Frozen Pizza 2779
Digital Broadcasting Group
Growth Companies 2837
Digital China Holdings
Corporations--China 1544
Digital Credit Union
Credit Unions 2215, 2223, 2237
Digital Management Inc.
Contracts, Government 1316
Digital Projection
Audio and Video Equipment 200
Digitas
Corporations--Connecticut 1570
Corporations--Illinois 1700
Marketing 3620, 3621, 3625, 3629
DiLeonardo International
Interior Designers 3366, 3369
Dilip Shanghvi
Wealth, Foreign 4876
Dillard's
Corporations--Arkansas 1416
Dillards
Clothing Stores 1020
Dillard's Inc.
Corporations--Arkansas 1418, 1419
Department Stores 2320, 2321
Retail Industry 4302
Dilma Rousseff
Women 4954, 4960
Dime Savings Bank of Williamsburg
Savings and Loan Association
Loans 4376
Dimensional Fund Advisors
Equity Funds 2634
Dimon; Jamie
Chief Executive Officers 984
DineEquity Inc.
Chain and Franchise Operations 911
Growth Companies 2843, 2851
Restaurants 4267
Dinh Vu Port Investment & Development
Corporations--Vietnam 2140
Diniz; Abilio dos Santos
Wealth, Foreign 4859
Dinsmore & Shohl
Law Firms 3448
Diodes Inc.
Corporations--Texas 2095
Dior
Holding Companies 2967, 2970
Direct Credit Union
Credit Unions 2238
Direct Energy Marketing Ltd.
Corporations--Canada 1495
Electric Utilities, International 2448
Gas Utilities 2809
Direct Energy U.S. Home Services Inc.
Plumbing Industry 4061
Direct Impressions
Printing Industry 4075
Direct Link
Aged--Care 91
Directech of Kentucky Inc.
Corporations--Kentucky 1805
Directions Credit Union
Credit Unions 2253
Directors' Choice
Corporations--Canada 1487
DirecTV
Communication Industry 1056
Media Companies 3666, 3668
The DirecTV Group Inc.
Advertising--Appeal to Hispanics 64, 65, 68
Broadband Communication Systems 700
Broadcasting Industry 701, 704, 708
Homosexuals--Employment 3039

Media Companies 3659, 3662, 3669
Telecommunications Industry 4629
DirecTV Holdings LLC
Communication Industry 1056
Direxion Monthly 10-Year Note
Bond Funds 615
DIS AG
Corporations--Germany 1659
DiS AG
Corporations--Europe 1598
Disaster Kleenup International
Houses--Maintenance and Repair 3113
DiScala; Todd
Investment Advisors 3392
Disco Corp.
Corporations--Japan 1785
Discount Tire Co.
Corporations--Arizona 1410
Retail Industry 4269
Tire Industry 4668
Discover Bank
Bank Credit Cards 286
Bank Deposits 287
Bank Loans 291
Banks and Banking 312
Discover Financial Services
Credit Cards 2201
Financial Services 2699, 2709
DiscoverOrg
Asian Americans in Business 181
Discovery Communications
Corporations--Maryland 1832
Corporations--New York 1932
Entertainment Industry 2608
Growth Companies 2842
Discovery Communications Inc.
Cable Networks 805
Corporations--Maryland 1834, 1835, 1837
Entertainment Industry 2610
Women in Business 4963
Discovery en Espanol
Hispanic Market 2953
Discovery Point Franchising Inc.
Child Care Centers 992
Discovery Shores
Hotels and Motels 3103
Dish DBS Corp.
Corporations--Colorado 1567
Dish Network
Corporations 1389
Dish Network Corp.
Advertising--Appeal to Hispanics 65, 69
Broadband Communication Systems 700
Broadcasting Industry 702, 704, 708
Corporations--Colorado 1556, 1564, 1566, 1567, 1569
Media Companies 3662
Telecommunications Industry 4629
Dish Network LLC
Corporations--Colorado 1558, 1559, 1560, 1561
Employment 2515
Disnat
Brokers--Internet 715
Disney
Brand Name Products, International 694
Disney Co.; Walt
Advertising, Outdoor 75
Broadcasting Industry 701, 704, 708
Cable Networks 805
Cable Television Industry--Advertising 806
Communication Industry 1055, 1056
Corporations 1379
Corporations--California 1458, 1463, 1464, 1466, 1476, 1479, 1480

Corporations, International 1738, 1739, 1740, 1741, 1742
Electronic Commerce--Advertising 2479
Entertainment Industry 2609, 2610
Homosexuals--Employment 3023
Media Companies 3659, 3662, 3669
Motion Picture Industry 3768
Television Broadcasting 4650
Disney Consumer Products
Licensed Product Merchandising 3511
Disney Cruise Line
Cruise Lines 2285
Disney Enterprises Inc.
Corporations--California 1463
Motion Picture Industry 3766
Disney Parks
Brand Choice 635
Disney Parks & Resorts U.S. Inc.; Walt
Amusement Industry 172
Disney; Walt
Media Companies 3666, 3668
Disney/Pixar Cars 2: Race Around the World
Best Sellers 564
Distefano; John
Consultants 1211
Distribuidora Internacional de Alimentacion SA
Discount Stores 2342
Diversey Inc.
Personal Care Products 3889
Diversified Labeling Solutions Inc.
Printing Industry 4075
Diversify Consulting Group AB
Corporations--Sweden 2069
Diversinet Corp.
Computer Software Industry, International 1130
Dixie Landscape Co.
Lawn Care Services 3454, 3456
Dixon Hughes Goodman
Accounting Firms 22
Dixon Hughes Goodman LLP
Accounting Firms 6
Dixon; T. Troy
Financial Executives 2683
Dixons Retail plc
Electronics Stores 2507
Retail Stores 4347
DJ Orthopedics de Mexico
Corporations--Mexico 1850
Django
Computer Software Industry, International 1122
DJO Inc.
Orthopedic Products 3852
Djokovic; Novak
Athletes--Compensation 191
DKC Public Relations
Public Relations Firms 4125
DKSH
Chemical Industry--Distributors 938
DKV Seguros
Corporations--Spain 2059
DLA Piper
Law Firms 3436, 3443, 3445, 3447, 3450, 3452
Trademarks 4701
DLC Resources
Lawn Care Services 3462
DLKW Lowe
Advertising Agencies, International 56
DLR Group
Architectural Firms 176
Interior Designers 3365, 3367
DLT Solutions Inc.
Contracts, Government 1325
Dlubak Corp.
Glass 2822
DLX Music
Music Retailers 3810

dm
Brand Name Products, International 663
DMX SRL
Music Retailers 3786
DnB
Brand Name Products, International 672
DnB NOR
Banks and Banking--Europe 450
DnB NOR ASA
Corporations--Norway 1962
DnB Nord Bankas
Banks and Banking--Europe 446
Do It Best Corp.
Corporations--Indiana 1728
Information Technology 3180
Doan Xa Port
Corporations--Vietnam 2140
Doc Rivers
Basketball 545
Doctors Co. Group
Insurance, Property and Casualty 3340
Doctors Co. Insurance Group
Insurance, Malpractice 3327, 3328
Doctors Foster and Smith
Catalogs 899
Doctors Hospital
Hospitals 3078
Doctors Hospital of Sarasota
Health Care Industry 2862, 2863
Doctors Hospital of Tattnall
Hospitals 3081
DocuSource Print Management
Printing Industry 4080, 4081, 4083, 4088
Dodge
Automobiles 272
Dodge & Cox International
Mutual Funds 3817
Dodge & Cox Stock
Stock Funds 4505
Dodge Attitude
Automobiles 276
Dodge Caravan
Trucks 4770
Dodge Communications
Public Relations Firms 4145
Dodge Journey
Trucks 4770, 4771
Dodgers; Los Angeles
Baseball 544
Doe Run Resources Corp.
Metal Industry 3695
Doha Bank
Banks and Banking--Arab 370
Banks and Banking--Middle East 531
Brand Name Products, International 683
Corporations--Qatar 2023
Doha, Qatar
Location of Industry 3536
Doheny Eye Institute
Hospitals 3065
Dolby Laboratories
Corporations--California 1453
Media Companies 3654
Dole
Salads 4355
Dole Food Co., Inc.
Crops 2281, 2282
Dole Holding Co., LLC
Crops 2281
Dollar Bank, FSB
Savings and Loan Association
Loans 4372
Dollar General
Supermarkets 4536
Dollar General Corp.
Chain Stores 917, 918, 922
Corporations--Tennessee 2084, 2087, 2089
Discount Stores 2340, 2341, 2342
Retail Industry 4281, 4302, 4306

Index

Index

Index

Index

Index

Index

Great Circle Works Inc.
 Growth Companies 2839
Great Clips Inc.
 Hair Salons 2852
Great Eastern
 Brand Name Products, International 690
Great Harvest Franchising Inc.
 Baked Goods 284
Great Lakes Aviation
 Growth Companies 2841
Great Lakes Aviation Ltd.
 Corporations--Wyoming 2198
Great Lakes Plumbing & Mechanical Co.
 Contractors 1239
Great Lakes Pluming & Heating Co.
 Plumbing Industry 4057
Great Little Box Co., Ltd.
 Construction Industry, International 1160
 Corporations--Canada 1486
 Manufacturing Industry, International 3570
Great Plains Credit Union
 Credit Unions 2243
Great Portland Estates
 Corporations--United Kingdom 2117
 Real Estate Business 4172
The Great Steak & Potato Co.
 Sandwiches 4360
Great Wall Motor
 Automobile Industry, International 230
Great Wall Technology
 Home Electronics 2973
Great Wall Technology Co., Ltd.
 Manufacturing Industry, International 3580
Great West Life & Annuity Insurance Co.
 Corporations, Foreign 1633
Great-West Life Assurance Co.
 Insurance, Life 3295, 3296, 3298
Great-West Lifeco
 Stocks 4516
Great-West Lifeco Inc.
 Corporations--Canada 1501, 1507
 Finance Companies 2682
 Insurance, International 3279
 Insurance, Life 3297, 3301, 3309, 3325
 Stocks 4508
Great Western Bank
 Agricultural Loans 105
Great Wraps
 Sandwiches 4359
Greater Baltimore Medical Center Inc.
 Corporations--Maryland 1833
Greater Halifax Partnership
 Location of Industry 3529
Greater Houston Partnership
 Location of Industry 3530
Greater Iowa Credit Union
 Credit Unions 2231
The Greater Journey
 Best Sellers 558
Greater Nevada Credit Union
 Credit Unions 2246
Greater Omaha Packing Co.
 Meat Industry 3635
 Meat Industry--Export/Import Trade 3650
Greater Statesville Development Corp.
 Location of Industry 3530
Greatwide Dedicated Transport
 Trucking Industry 4747
Greatwide Logistics
 Trucking Industry 4765
Greatwide Logistics Services
 Trucking Industry 4748, 4756
Gree Electrical Appliances Inc.
 Household Appliances 3109, 3110

Greece
 Corporate Directors 1348
 Debt 2291
 Economy 2388
 Music Industry 3775
 New Business Enterprises 3825
Greek Theatre
 Amphitheaters 171
Green Bay Packers
 Football 2767
Green Bay, WI
 Insurance, Automobile--Rates 3223
Green; Cristina
 Wealth, Foreign 4922
Green; David
 Wealth 4838
Green Earth
 Asian Americans in Business 182
 Business Services 776
Green Eggs & Ham
 Best Sellers 561
Green; Lady
 Wealth, Foreign 4902
Green Mark
 Liquor Industry 3513
Green Mountain Coffee
 Beverages 596
Green Mountain Coffee Roasters
 Catalogs 893
Green Mountain Coffee Roasters Inc.
 Beverage Industry 573, 577
 Corporations--Vermont 2136, 2139
 Growth Companies 2842, 2846
Green; Philip
 Wealth, Foreign 4922
Green Plains Renewable Energy
 Energy Industry 2526
 Growth Companies 2842, 2843, 2849
Green Plains Renewable Energy Inc.
 Corporations--Nebraska 1901
Green Street Advisors
 Corporations--California 1451
Green Thumb-Green Arrow
 Garden Centers 2797
Green Valley Oil LLC
 Corporations--Rhode Island 2028
Greenberg Traurig LLP
 Legal Services 3499
Greenberg Traurig PA
 Law Firms 3437, 3443
 Legal Services 3499, 3500
Greene King
 Restaurants 4228
The Greene Turtle Sports Bar & Grille
 Restaurants 4266
The Greenery
 Lawn Care Services 3461
Greenlight Capital Re Ltd.
 Insurance--Reinsurance 3355
Greenman-Pedersen
 Engineering Design 2554
GreenRubino
 Corporations--Washington 2159
Greensboro-High Point, NC
 Location of Industry--Growth 3543
Greensboro, NC
 Business Conditions 731
Greenspring Energy
 Energy Industry 2529
GreenStar Services Corp.
 Contractors 1261
Greenstar Services Corp.
 Contractors 1269
Greenville Hospital System Inc.
 Corporations--South Carolina 2046
Greenway Ford Inc.
 Hispanic American Business Enterprises 2927, 2928
Greenwood Credit Union
 Credit Unions 2238, 2261
Greenwood Industries Inc.
 Contractors 1279

Greg Jensen
 Business Leaders 740
Greg Weishar
 Executives--Compensation 2637
Gregg Popovich
 Basketball 545
Gregorio Perez Companc
 Wealth, Foreign 4854
Gregory Boyce
 Chief Executive Officers 985
Gregory FCA
 Public Relations Firms 4142
Gregory Henslee
 Chief Executive Officers 983
Gregory House Programs
 Corporations--Hawaii 1687
Gregory Kenny
 Executives--Compensation 2637
Greif Inc.
 Paper Industry 3863
Greiner Electric
 Women-Owned Business Enterprises 4982
Greis Sia
 Corporations--Latvia 1812
Grenadines
 Economy 2387
Grenoble Graduate School of Business
 Business Schools and Colleges, International 771
Gresham, Smith & Partners
 Interior Designers 3372
Grether; Esther
 Wealth, Foreign 4912
Grey
 Advertising Agencies 48
Greylock Credit Union
 Credit Unions 2237, 2262
Greylock Partners
 Venture Capital 4784
"Grey's Anatomy"
 Hispanic Market 2946
Greystar Real Estate Partners LLC
 Apartment Houses 174
Greystone Masonry
 Contractors 1237
Griffin
 Booksellers and Bookselling 630
Griffin Cement LLC
 Contractors 1230, 1237
Griffin Fertilizer Co.
 Fertilizer Industry 2674
Griffin; Kenneth
 Hedge Funds 2891
Grigsby & Associates Inc.
 African American Business Enterprises 87
Griswold Special Care
 Aged--Care 91
Grizzley Industrial
 Corporations--Washington 2166
Grocers Supply Co.
 Corporations--Texas 2102
Grocery Outlet
 Supermarkets 4550
Groendyke Transport Inc.
 Tank Trucks 4562
 Trucking Industry 4764
Groep Colruyt
 Corporations--Belgium 1435
 Retail Stores 4320
 Supermarkets 4532, 4535
Groninger Construction
 Contractors 1237
Grontimij NV
 Engineering Design, International 2577, 2588
Grontmij NV
 Engineering Design, International 2578
Grosvenor; Gerald Cavendish
 Wealth, Foreign 4922
Ground Floor Media
 Public Relations Firms 4151
GroundFloor Media Inc.

 Corporations--Colorado 1554
The Groundskeeper
 Lawn Care Services 3462
Group 1 Automotive Inc.
 Automobile Dealers 214
 Automobile Industry 226
Group Banco Mare Nostrum
 Banks and Banking--Europe 460
Group Builders Inc.
 Contractors 1283
Group Excellence
 Education 2395
Group Health Cooperative
 Homosexuals--Employment 3026
Group Health Cooperative of South Central Wisconsin
 Information Technology 3187
Group Health Permanente
 Homosexuals--Employment 3026
Group Medical Services
 Corporations--Canada 1522
Group O Inc.
 Hispanic American Business Enterprises 2928, 2934, 2940
Groupe Adeo SA
 Retail Stores 4329
Groupe Auchan SA
 Retail Stores 4329
Groupe Banques Populaire
 Banks and Banking--Africa 333
 Banks and Banking--Arab 364
Groupe BPCE
 Banks and Banking--Europe 424, 442, 476
 Corporations--France 1645
Groupe Consoursmania
 High Technology Industry 2905
Groupe Credit Agricole
 Banks and Banking--Europe 412
Groupe Danone
 Beverage Industry 589, 590
 Corporations--France 1646
 Food Industry, International 2728, 2735, 2736, 2737, 2741
 Food Packages 2743
 Food Processing 2756
Groupe Danone SA
 Beverage Industry 576
 Food Industry, International 2731
 Tobacco Industry 4679
Groupe Promutuel
 Cooperatives 1343
Groupe Robert
 Trucking Industry 4745
Groupe SEB
 Housewares 3119
Groupe SEB SA
 Housewares 3123
Groupo Modelo SA
 Beverage Industry 589
Groupon Inc.
 Electronic Commerce 2461, 2478
Groupon.com
 Electronic Commerce 2471
Grow Financial Credit Union
 Credit Unions 2224
Growers Fertilizer Corp.
 Fertilizer Industry 2674
Growll.com
 Printing Industry 4079
GROWMARK Inc.
 Agricultural Cooperative Associations 95
 Agricultural Organizations 108
 Cooperatives 1345
Growmark Inc.
 Propane 4121
The Growth Coach
 Business Consultants 732
Grubb & Ellis Co.
 Real Estate Management 4202
GrubHub
 Food Industry 2717
Gruma Corp.
 Agriculture--Services 110, 111
Gruma Mexico

Index

Wealth, Foreign 4922

James Gallogly
Chemical Industry, International 966
Executives--Compensation 2636

James Goodnight
Wealth 4850

James Irsay
Wealth 4849

James Irving
Wealth, Foreign 4860, 4861

James; LeBron
Athletes 185, 186
Athletes--Compensation 188
Entertainers 2599

James Leprino
Wealth 4839

James O'Brien
Executives--Compensation 2637

James Packer
Wealth, Foreign 4855, 4856

James Patterson
Authors 211
Entertainers--Compensation 2607

James Pattison
Wealth, Foreign 4860

James River Grounds Management
Lawn Care Services 3455, 3461

James Ryan
Investment Advisors 3392

James Schwartz
Leadership 3468

James Sedgwick Inc.
Insurance Brokers 3227

James Simons
Hedge Funds 2891
Wealth 4832

James Skinner
Business Leaders 741

Jamie Dimon
Chief Executive Officers 984

Jan Kulczyk
Wealth, Foreign 4899

Jan-Pro Franchising International Inc.
Home-Based Businesses 2972

Janata Bank
Banks and Banking--Asia 375

Janicki Machines
Corporations--Washington 2164

Janitors
Occupational Health and Safety 3843

Janssen
Corporations--Spain 2059

Japan
Brand Name Products, International 666
Competition, International 1069, 1070, 1072
Customer Service 2288
Debt 2291
Economy 2383
Employee Training 2513
Export/Import Trade 2640, 2643
Gross Domestic Product 2828
Industrial Relations 3166
Inflation 3169
Music Industry 3778
Patents 3875
Research and Development 4215

Japan Airlines
Airlines, Cargo 127

Japan Airlines Corp.
Airlines, International 134

Japan Airlines International Co.
Corporations--Hawaii 1683

Japan Post Holdings Co., Ltd.
Corporations--Asia 1420
Corporations, International 1759
Corporations--Japan 1788
Insurance Companies, International 3258
Insurance, Life 3326

Japan Post Insurance Co., Ltd.

Insurance, Property and Casualty 3347, 3348

Japan Post Service
Shipping 4438

Japan Securities Finance Co., Ltd.
Investment Management Firms 3402

Japan Tobacco Inc.
Consumer Goods 1218
Manufacturing Industry, International 3592
Tobacco Industry 4689, 4690, 4691, 4694

Jarden Corp.
Home Furnishings Industry 2992, 2993
Housewares 3123
Manufacturing Industry 3566
Rubber Industry 4351, 4352

Jardine Lloyd Thompson Group plc
Insurance Brokers 3226, 3232, 3235

Jardine Matheson Holdings Ltd.
Carbon 852, 880
Corporations--Hong Kong 1692
Diversified Corporations 2350, 2357
Industrial Equipment Industry 3162

Jardine Strategic Holdings Ltd.
Carbon 852, 880
Industrial Equipment Industry 3162

Jardines
Brand Name Products, International 650
Holding Companies 2970

Jarrard Phillips Cate & Hancock
Public Relations Firms 4145

Jasculca Terman & Associates
Public Relations Firms 4129

Jason Aldean
Music Industry--Artists 3784

Jason's Deli
Sandwiches 4358, 4361, 4362, 4363

Jassim Al-Kharafi
Wealth, Foreign 4885

Jasuindo Tiga Perkasa
Corporations--Indonesia 1732

Java Capital (Pty.)
Securities--Initial Public Offerings 4395

Java Monster
Beverages 595
Sports Drink Industry 4484

Jay-Mar Inc.
Agriculture 109

Jay Severin
Leadership 3468

Jay Y. Lee
Wealth, Foreign 4909

Jay-Z
Entertainers 2602

JayBirdGear.com
Electronic Commerce 2473

Jaynes Corp.
Corporations--New Mexico 1930

Jay's O-Ke-Doke
Popcorn 4063

Jazz Aviation LP
Corporations--Canada 1521

Jazzercise Inc.
Home-Based Businesses 2972
Physical Fitness 4038

JB Hi-Fi
Retail Industry 4278

JBM
Corporations--Virginia 2142

JBS
Corporations, International 1754
Food Processing 2744

JBS SA
Corporations--Brazil 1443
Food Industry, International 2735, 2742

JBS USA

Food Packages 2743

JBS USA Holdings Inc.
Food Processing 2749
Meat Industry 3638

JC Cellars
Wine Industry 4941

JC Decaux
Advertising Agencies, International 60

JCDecaux SA
Media Companies 3656

JCP.com
Electronic Commerce 2470

JCPenney.com
Electronic Commerce 2462

JD Williams & Co.
Direct Mail Advertising 2324

JDA Software Group Inc.
Computer Software Industry, International 1110
Supply Chain 4557

JDS Professional Group LLC
Accounting Firms 8

J.E. Dunn Construction Group
Contractors 1240

Jean-Claude Decaux
Wealth, Foreign 4870

Jean-Claude Gandur
Wealth, Foreign 4912

Jean Coutu Group
Brand Name Products, International 686
Retail Industry 4301

Jean Coutu Group Inc.
Corporate Directors 1349

Jean Coutu Group PJC Inc.
Corporations--Canada 1529

Jean; Emilio Azcarraga
Wealth, Foreign 4888

Jean-Jacques Bienaime
Executives--Compensation 2638

Jeanette Garretty
Investment Advisors 3389

Jeanne d'Arc Credit Union
Credit Unions 2237

Jed Clampett
Wealth 4853

Jed Rakoff
Business Ethics 735

Jeep
Automobiles 272

Jeff Dunham
Entertainers 2600

Jeff George
Business Leaders 740

Jeff Gordon
Automobile Racing 267

Jeffer Mangels Butler & Mitchell LLP
Corporations--California 1448

Jefferies Group Inc.
Investment Management Firms 3407

Jeffers
Catalogs 899

Jefferson Bank
Banks and Banking--Independent Banks 485

Jefferson City, MO
Veterans--Employment 4788

Jefferson County, CO
Employment 2516

Jefferson Financial Credit Union
Credit Unions 2234

Jeffery H. Boyd
Chief Executive Officers--Compensation 989

Jeffrey Bezos
Business Leaders 741

Jeffrey Boyd
Chief Executive Officers 984

Jeffrey Hildebrand
Wealth 4837

Jeffrey O. Palmer
Plastics Industry 4051

Jeffrey P. Bezos

Chief Executive Officers 983, 984
Wealth 4850

Jeffrey Skoll
Wealth, Foreign 4860

Jeld-Wen Inc.
Windows and Doors 4940
Wood Products 4989

Jena-Optronik GmbH
Aged--Employment 93

Jenkins Living Center Inc.
Corporations--South Dakota 2050

Jenner & Block LLP
Law Firms 3449

Jennie-O Turkey Store
Sausage 4367, 4368

Jennifer Aniston
Entertainers 2598

Jennifer Nashmi
Women-Owned Business Enterprises 4987

Jenniges Enterprises Inc.
Personal Services 3909

Jensen Corp.
Lawn Care Services 3463

Jensen; Greg
Business Leaders 740

Jer
Retail Stores 4338

JER Partners
Hotels and Motels 3095

Jeremy Levine
Venture Capital 4783

Jeronimo Arango
Wealth, Foreign 4888

Jeronimo Martins
Supermarkets 4546

Jeronimo Martins Dystrybucja SA
Corporations--Poland 2018

Jeronimo Martins SGPS SA
Corporations--Portugal 2020, 2021
Manufacturing Industry, International 3598
Supermarkets 4535

Jerry Bruckheimer
Entertainers 2601
Entertainers--Compensation 2607

Jerry Jones
Football 2768
Wealth 4849

Jerry Seinfeld
Entertainers 2600

Jersey Mike's Subs
Sandwiches 4366

Jersey Trades Credit Union
Credit Unions 2239

Jess Diaz Trucking Inc.
Hispanic American Business Enterprises 2939

Jet-Black International
Building Cleaning Industry 720

Jet2
Airlines, International 143

JetBlue Airways
Airlines 124
Airlines, International 144

JetBlue Airways Corp.
Airlines 120
Airlines, International 141, 145, 146, 147, 148, 149
Homosexuals--Employment 3010

Jeter; Derek
Athletes--Compensation 187

Jets Manufacturing Co.
Asian Americans in Business 183

Jets; New York
Football 2767

Jet's Pizza
Pizza 4048

Jetstar
Airlines, International 145, 146

JetStar Inc.
Airlines, International 147, 149

Jetta; Volkswagen
Automobiles 276

Jeugia
Music Retailers 3798

Index

Index

Mattress Industry 3634
Mattson Resources
Corporations--California 1455
Matty Moroun
Construction Industry, International 1173
Leadership 3479
Mauer; Joe
Athletes--Compensation 187
Maui Family Support Services Inc.
Corporations--Hawaii 1687
Maui Land & Pineapple Co., Inc.
Corporations--Hawaii 1680
Maui Medical Group Inc.
Corporations--Hawaii 1680
Maui Petroleum Inc.
Corporations--Hawaii 1680
Maui Wowi Hawaiian Coffees & Smoothies
Chain and Franchise Operations 910
Coffee Shops 1031
Mauldin & Jenkins
Accounting Firms 22
Mauna Lani Resort (Operation) Inc.
Corporations--Hawaii 1678, 1683
Maureen Wheeler
Wealth, Foreign 4894
Mauritania
Auditing 209
Banks and Banking, International 487
Business Ethics 734
Business Loans 743
Business Schools and Colleges, International 768
Competition, International 1068, 1071
Corporate Directors 1348
Corporations, Foreign 1626
Customer Service 2289
Employee Training 2514
Financial Services 2688, 2689
Gross Domestic Product 2830
Industrial Relations 3167
Stock Exchanges 4503
Taxation 4566
Venture Capital 4781
Mauritius
Economy 2385, 2393
Taxation 4567
Mauritius Commercial Bank
Banks and Banking--Africa 344
Mauritius Post & Cooperative Bank
Banks and Banking--Africa 344
Maverick USA
Trucking Industry 4748
Maverick USA Inc.
Trucking Industry 4757
Mavericks; Dallas
Basketball 546
Maverik Inc.
Corporations--Wyoming 2198
Mavis Discount Tire
Tire Industry 4668
Max Muscle Sports Nutrition
Vitamins 4819
Max, Your Community Credit Union
Credit Unions 2207
Maxem Eyewear Corp.
Construction Industry, International 1160
Manufacturing Industry, International 3570
Maxim Healthcare Services
Nursing 3837
Maxim Integrated Products
Semiconductor Industry 4421
Maxima Lt UAB
Corporations--Lithuania 1814
Maximum Ride No. 6: Fang
Best Sellers 564
MaxLinear Inc.
Growth Companies 2845
Maxwell House
Coffee 1029

Maxxis
Brand Name Products, International 678
Mayan Resorts Los Cabos
Corporations--Mexico 1851
Mayan Resorts Puerto Penasco
Corporations--Mexico 1851
Mayan Resorts Riviera Maya
Corporations--Mexico 1850
Maybank
Corporations--Malaysia 1829
Maybelline New York
Personal Care Products--Advertising 3905
Mayer Brown LLP
Legal Services 3499
Mayer Hoffman McCann PC
Accounting Firms 7
Mayo Clinic
Corporations--Minnesota 1870, 1873
Group Medical Practice 2836
Health Care Industry 2869
Hospitals 3057, 3058, 3059, 3060, 3061, 3062, 3063, 3064, 3066, 3067, 3068, 3069, 3070, 3071, 3072
Psychiatric Hospitals 4124
Mayo Clinic Hospital
Hospitals 3078
Mayo Clinic Jacksonville Corp.
Corporations--Florida 1619
Mayo Employees Credit Union
Credit Unions 2241
Mayo Employees Federal Credit Union
Credit Unions 2204
Mayo Foundation for Medical Education & Research
Accounting Firms 9
Corporations--Minnesota 1868
Engineering Services 2595
Mayra Alvarez
Hispanics 2963
Mays Chemical Co.
Minority Business Enterprises 3752
Maytag Corp.
Electronic Industry 2488
Mazars
Accounting Firms, International 26
Mazda
Automobile Industry, International 238
Capital Spending 812
Mazda Motor Corp.
Automobile Industry, International 237
Mazda3
Automobiles 275, 276
Mazeikiu Nafta Trading House Ou
Corporations--Estonia 1597
Mazor Robotics
High Technology Industry 2909
Mazuma Credit Union
Credit Unions 2243
Mazumdar-Shaw; Kiran
Women 4957
The Mazzetta Co.
Seafood 4392
MB Financial Bank NA
Banks and Banking 301
MB Trading
Brokers--Internet 710, 711, 714
MBA Building Supplies
Metal Industry 3707
MBA Polymers Inc.
Recycling 4209
MBA Preferred
Books 618
MBAF CPAs
Accounting Firms 17
MBIA Group
Insurance, Property and Casualty 3334
MBIA Inc.
Insurance Companies 3244

Insurance, Financial Guaranty 3264
MBM Corp.
Corporations--North Carolina 1955
Food Industry 2715
MBMS Inc.
Corporations--New York 1934
MBNA America Delaware NA
Corporations--Delaware 1586
MBNA Canada Bank
Banks and Banking--North America 543
MBNA Consumer Services Inc.
Corporations--Delaware 1586
MBNA Europe Bank
Direct Mail Advertising 2324
MBP
Corporations--Virginia 2141
McAbee Talbert Holliday & Co.
Accounting Firms 6
McAngus Goudelock & Courie LLC
Law Firms 3440
MCB Bank
Banks and Banking--Middle East 530
McCabe; Bill
Wealth, Foreign 4894
McCallister; Michael
Executives--Compensation 2637
McCann Erickson
Advertising Agencies, International 56
McCann Erickson Worldwide
Advertising Agencies, International 60
McCann Worldgroup
Advertising, International 72
McCarl's
Contractors 1251
McCarl's Inc.
Contractors 1266
McCarthy; Anna Duarte
Hispanics 2959
McCarthy Building Cos.
Contractors 1231, 1270
Corporations--California 1448
Training 4708
McCarthy Holdings
Contractors 1230
McCarthy Holdings Inc.
Contractors 1235, 1240
Corporations--Missouri 1893
McCarthy Tire Service Co.
Tire Repair 4676
McCartney; Paul
Entertainers 2603
McClatchy Co.
Newspaper Publishers and Publishing 3832
McColl; Jim
Wealth, Foreign 4905
McCombs School of Business; University of Texas-Austin
Business Schools and Colleges 754
McCord Treated Wood Inc.
Wood Products 4990
McCormick & Co.
Corporations--Maryland 1835
McCormick Co.
Agricultural Industry--Advertising 96, 97, 99, 104
McCourt Label Co.
Printing Industry 4084
McCoy Group
Trucking Industry 4764
McCoy; Sherilyn
Women in Business 4966
McCoy's Building Supply
Building Materials Industry 725
MCD
Concerts 1136
MCD Telekom
High Technology Industry 2912
McDermott Inc.
Construction Industry, Nonresidential 1182

McDermott International Inc.
Construction Industry, Nonresidential 1182, 1183
Contractors 1241, 1245
McDermott Will & Emery LLP
Patents 3877
McDonald Development Co.
Industrial Parks 3164
McDonald; Karen
Investment Advisors 3389
McDonald; Karen A.
Investment Advisors 3392
McDonald's
Advertising Expenditures 70
Brand Name Products, International 667, 694, 696
Fast Food 2659
Fast Food Restaurants 2660, 2662, 2663
Restaurants 4262, 4264, 4265
Retail Industry 4308, 4313
Sandwiches 4361, 4363, 4364, 4365
McDonald's Belgium
Corporations--Belgium 1436
McDonald's Corp.
Advertising--Appeal to Hispanics 64, 65, 67, 68
Advertising, International 71
Advertising, Outdoor 75
African Americans--Employment 90
Chain and Franchise Operations 908, 912
Corporations 1369, 1372, 1375, 1379, 1392
Corporations--Arizona 1409
Corporations--Europe 1599
Corporations--Illinois 1707, 1710, 1712
Corporations, International 1735, 1736, 1738, 1739, 1740, 1743
Corporations--Peru 2013
Corporations--Uruguay 2129
Corporations--Washington DC 2186
Fast Food Restaurants 2669
Food Service Industry 2760, 2765, 2766
Leadership 3492, 3494
Leisure 3505, 3509
Radio Advertising 4161
Restaurants 4232, 4233, 4234, 4267, 4268
Supply Chain 4559
Television Advertising 4648, 4649
Travel 4741, 4742
McDonald's Danmark
Corporations--Denmark 1589
McDonald's de Venezuela SA
Corporations--Venezuela 2135
McDonald's France
Corporations--France 1641
McDonald's Italia
Corporations--Italy 1779
McDonald's Mexico
Corporations--Mexico 1849
McDonald's Restaurant Operations Inc.
Corporations 1369
Restaurants 4232
McDonald's Restaurants of Ireland
Corporations--Ireland 1772
McDonald's Restaurants of Pennsylvania Inc.
Restaurants 4233
McDonald's Restaurants U.K.
Corporations--United Kingdom 2118
Restaurants 4228
McDonald's Sweden
Corporations--Sweden 2068
McDonald's USA LLC
Corporations 1369
Restaurants 4232
Training 4708
McDonnell; Thomas A.
Chief Executive Officers--Compensation 988

Index

Nivea
Cosmetics Industry 2199
Personal Care Products 3885, 3903
NKSJ Holdings Inc.
Insurance, Property and Casualty 3335, 3346
NLV Financial Corp.
Corporations--Vermont 2138
NMDC Ltd.
Metal Industry 3690
NMHG Holding Co.
Corporations--Oregon 1989
No Mas Vello
Personal Services 3910
NOAH Indoor Stage
Corporations--Japan 1786
Nobel Group
Carbon 852
Noble Corp.
Energy Industry 2546
Petroleum Equipment Industry 3918
Petroleum Industry, Foreign 3971
Noble Energy Inc.
Petroleum Industry 3934, 3945
Noble Group
Corporations, International 1754
Noble Group Ltd.
Diversified Corporations 2350
Noblis Inc.
Business Services 788
NOK Corp.
Rubber Industry 4354
Nokia
Telecommunications Industry 4641
Nokia Corp.
Carbon 877
Communication Equipment Industry 1051, 1052
Corporations--Finland 1610
High Technology Industry 2897
Homosexuals--Employment 3027
Manufacturing Industry, International 3583
Research and Development 4218
Technology 4592
Wireless Telephones 4948, 4949
Nokia Komarom Kft
Corporations--Hungary 1694
Nokia Nederland BV
Corporations--Netherlands 1906
Nokia Oyj
Aerospace Industry 76
Corporations--Finland 1611
Electronic Industry 2487
Nokia Siemens Networks Oy
Corporations--Finland 1611
Manufacturing Industry, International 3589
Nokia Theatre L.A. Live
Concerts 1143
Nokian Renkaat Holding Oy
Automobile Industry, International 231
Nolan; Christopher
Entertainers 2601
Nomos Bank
Banks and Banking--Europe 455
Banks and Banking, International 499
Nomos-Bank
Banks and Banking--Europe 443
Nomura
Financial Services 2695, 2712
Security Underwriting 4417
Nomura Holdings
Banks and Banking--Asia 387, 391
Nomura Holdings Inc.
Investment Management Firms 3402
Nomura Research Institute
Financial Services 2698
Nonggongshang Supermarket Group Co., Ltd.
Retail Stores 4325

Nonkululeko Nyembezi-Heitz
Women 4958
Noodles & Co.
Chain and Franchise Operations 910
Corporations--Colorado 1566
Restaurants 4230
Nooter Construction
Contractors 1251, 1255
Nooter Construction Co.
Contractors 1277
Nooyi; Indra
Women 4959, 4960
Women in Business 4966
Women--Compensation 4967
Women Executives 4979
Norasia Container Lines Ltd.
Corporations--Malta 1830
Norbord Inc.
Paper Industry 3865
Norcraft Cos.
Wood Products 4993
Norddeutsche Landesbank Luxembourg
Banks and Banking--Europe 447
Nordea
Brand Name Products, International 676
Corporations--Denmark 1592
Nordea Bank
Banks and Banking, International 491
Nordea Bank AB
Corporations, Foreign 1640
Corporations--Sweden 2071, 2074
Nordea Bank Danmark
Banks and Banking--Europe 419
Nordea Bank Finland
Banks and Banking--Europe 423
Nordea Bank Norge
Banks and Banking--Europe 450
Nordea Group
Banks and Banking--Europe 464
Nordea Liv & Pension
Corporations--Denmark 1589
Nordea Live & Pension
Corporations--Europe 1598
Nordic PCL Construction Inc.
Corporations--Hawaii 1677, 1682
Nord/LB Norddeutsche Landesbank
Banks and Banking--Europe 427
Nordstrom
Catalogs 898
Clothing Stores 1014
Nordstrom FSB
Savings and Loan Association Loans 4374
Nordstrom Inc.
Chain Stores 915
Clothing Stores 1015, 1016
Corporations, International 1741
Corporations--Washington 2162, 2169, 2171, 2174, 2177, 2178, 2179, 2180, 2181, 2182, 2183
Department Stores 2317, 2320, 2321, 2323
Homosexuals--Employment 3038
Retail Industry 4302, 4310
Norfolk
Transportation 4732
Norfolk & Western Railway Co.
Railroads 4164, 4165
Norfolk Southern Corp.
Corporations--Virginia 2146, 2148, 2149, 2151
Homosexuals--Employment 3040
Railroads 4164, 4165, 4166, 4167, 4168
Transportation 4720, 4728, 4731
Norfolk Southern Railway Co.
Railroads 4164, 4165
Norfolk, VA
Ports 4066

Veterans--Employment 4786
Norfos Mazmena UAB
Corporations--Lithuania 1814
NorgesGruppen ASA
Retail Stores 4337
Norgren USA
Corporations, Foreign 1633
Noridian Mutual Insurance Co.
Corporations--North Dakota 1959
Norilsk Nickel (Cyprus) Ltd.
Corporations--Cyprus 1583
Norilsk Nickel; Mining & Metallurgical Company
Metal Industry 3689, 3715
Norilsk Nickel; OJSC Mining & Metallurgical Company
Corporations--Russia 2036
Manufacturing Industry, International 3599
Metal Industry 3703, 3710
Norinchukin Bank
Banks and Banking--Asia 387, 391
Norman Braman
Wealth 4834
Norsan Group
Hispanic American Business Enterprises 2937
Norsk Hydro
Metal Industry 3689
Norsk Hydro ASA
Aluminum Industry 170
Corporate Social Responsibility 1355
Corporations--Norway 1962
Manufacturing Industry, International 3596
Metal Industry 3711
Norske Skogindustrier ASA
Manufacturing Industry, International 3596
Nortel Networks Corp.
Homosexuals--Employment 3039
North American Breweries
Beer 550
North American Coatings LLC
Contractors 1278
North American Dismantling Corp.
Contractors 1271
North American Pipe Corp.
Pipes 4043
North American Savings Bank, FSB
Savings and Loan Association Loans 4375
North Atlantic Trading Co.
Tobacco Industry 4681
North Bay Health Care
Corporations--California 1473
North Bethesda Hotel LLC
Corporations--Maryland 1834
Hotels and Motels 3089
North Carolina
Compensation 1066
Construction Industry 1158
Dental Clinics 2316
Employment 2520, 2523
Farms 2654, 2655, 2656
Income 3131
Insurance, Automobile--Rates 3222
Livestock 3516
Location of Industry 3522, 3523, 3525, 3526, 3527
Location of Industry--Growth 3545
State Data (for individual states) 4490
Taxation 4569, 4570, 4572
Teachers 4587
Women--Employment 4974
Workers' Compensation 4996
North Carolina Children's Hospital
Hospitals 3055
North Central Farmers Elevator
Corporations--South Dakota 2050
Seed Industry 4419
North Dakota
Business Failures 736

Compensation 1066
Construction Industry 1155, 1156
Corporations 1386
Crops 2284
Electric Utilities 2422
Employment 2517, 2521, 2522
Farms 2656, 2657
Gross Domestic Product 2832
Income 3132
Insurance, Automobile--Rates 3222
Location of Industry 3523
Mining Industry 3732
New Business Enterprises 3827, 3829
Public Transit 4152
Service Industry 4435
State Data (for individual states) 4491
Taxation 4574
Teachers 4586, 4587
Transportation 4723
Unemployment 4776
Women--Employment 4971, 4972
Workers' Compensation 4998, 4999
North Hawaii Community Hospital
Corporations--Hawaii 1678
North Highland
Consultants 1198, 1199, 1200, 1201, 1202, 1203, 1208, 1209
Corporations--California 1447
Corporations--Florida 1612
Corporations--New York 1931
The North Highland Co.
Corporations--New Jersey 1916
North Highland Consulting
Corporations--Texas 2090
North Jersey Media Group
Family-Owned Corporations 2652
North Kansas City Hospital
Corporations--Missouri 1889
North Korea
Economy 2382, 2384
North Mississippi Health Services Inc.
Corporations--Mississippi 1886
North Mississippi Medical Center Inc.
Corporations--Mississippi 1886
North Point Ministries
Corporations--Georgia 1648
North Shore Bank, FSB
Commercial Loans 1040
North Star Community Credit Union
Credit Unions 2252
North Wind Inc.
Minority Business Enterprises 3750
Northcountry Credit Union
Credit Unions 2271
Northeast Arkansas Credit Union
Credit Unions 2210, 2255
Northeast Bancorp
Banks and Banking--Independent Banks 482
Northeast Credit Union
Credit Unions 2247
Northeast Remsco Construction Inc.
Contractors 1261
Hispanic American Business Enterprises 2929
Northeast Utilities
Corporations--Massachusetts 1842
Northern Arizona Healthcare Corp.
Corporations--Arizona 1411
Northern Hills Credit Union
Credit Unions 2264
Northern Lights Casino, Hotel & Event Center
Casinos 885
Northern Printing Network Inc.
Printing Industry 4080, 4083, 4085
Northern Skies Credit Union
Credit Unions 2208
Northern Tier Credit Union

Index

Index

Panasonic Corp.
Carbon 839
Computer Industry 1086
Corporations--Asia Pacific 1427
Corporations--Japan 1788, 1789
Debt Financing 2292
Electronic Industry 2494, 2497
Home Electronics 2974, 2986
Leisure 3508
Manufacturing Industry, International 3592
Patents 3876
Research and Development 4218
Panasonic Electric Works Co., Ltd.
Electric Equipment 2407
Panattoni Development Co.
Industrial Parks 3164
Panda Express
Restaurants 4258
Panda Restaurant Group
Restaurants 4229
Panera Bread
Restaurants 4260
Sandwiches 4358
Panera Bread Co.
Chain and Franchise Operations 908
Pang Da Automobile Trade
Securities--Initial Public Offerings 4405
Panin Bank
Banks and Banking--Asia 385
Panin Sekuritas
Corporations--Indonesia 1732
Pantaloon Retail India
Retail Industry 4283
Pantene
Personal Care Products 3897
Pantheon Enterprises
Chemical Industry, International 965
Panther Expedited Services
Air Freight Service 115
Pantry Inc.
Automobile Dealers 213
The Pantry Inc.
Convenience Stores 1329
Corporations--North Carolina 1952
Panzhihua New Steel & Vanadium Co., Ltd.
Iron 3421
Steel Industry 4494
Pao de Acucar
Brand Name Products, International 644
Food Industry, International 2726
Paolo Rocca
Wealth, Foreign 4882
Papa John's International
Corporations--Kentucky 1803
Papa John's International Inc.
Pizza 4045, 4048
Papa John's Pizza
Fast Food Restaurants 2665
Pizza 4046, 4047
Restaurants 4253, 4254, 4255, 4256, 4257
Papa Murphy Take 'N Bake Pizza
Restaurants 4253, 4254, 4255, 4256, 4257
Papa Murphy's
Pizza 4049
Papa Murphy's Pizza
Fast Food Restaurants 2665
Papa Murphy's Take 'N' Bake Pizza
Pizza 4045, 4046, 4047
Paper Flow
Books 618
Paperlinx Ltd.
Manufacturing Industry, International 3573
Paquin; Madeleine
Women-Owned Business Enterprises 4987
Par Plumbing Co.
Contractors 1239, 1251

Para Space Landscaping Inc.
Corporations--Canada 1486
The Paradies Shops
Corporations--California 1448
Paradigm
Audio and Video Equipment 199
ParadisePen.com
Electronic Commerce 2476
Paragon Credit Union
Credit Unions 2248
Paraguay
Business Ethics 734
Patents 3874
Parametric Technology Corp.
Computer Software Industry 1099
Corporations--Massachusetts 1848
Paramount Building Solutions LLC
Corporations--Arizona 1411
Paramount Communications Acquisition Corp.
Corporations--New York 1937
Paramount Domestic Distribution
Motion Picture Distribution 3765
Parasoft
Computer Software Industry, International 1121
Parcelforce Worldwide
Shipping 4438
Pardot
Corporations--Georgia 1649
ParenteBeard
Accounting Firms 18
Pargesa
Financial Services 2691
Pargon Technology Group Inc.
Contracts, Government 1316
Pari Mutuel Urbain
Leisure 3503
Paris, France
Airports 160, 161
Airports, Cargo 163, 167
Paris Hotel Casino Resort
Corporations--Nevada 1910
The Paris Wife
Best Sellers 556
Pariveda Solutions Inc.
Corporations--Texas 2091
Park City Group Inc.
Computer Software Industry, International 1109
Park Community Credit Union
Credit Unions 2233
Park Nicolett Methodist Hospital
Hospitals 3078
Park Seed
Catalogs 900
Park Side Credit Union
Credit Unions 2244
Parker Hannifin Corp.
Corporations--Ohio 1967, 1968
Industrial Equipment Industry 3149, 3152, 3153, 3154, 3157, 3159, 3160
Machinery 3549
Parker Interior Plantscape
Lawn Care Services 3456
Parker Poe Adams & Bernstein LLP
Law Firms 3440
Parker; Sarah Jessica
Entertainers 2598
Parkland Fuel
Retail Industry 4301
Parkland Health & Hospital System
Corporations--Texas 2096
Parkson Corp.
Retail Industry 4286
Parkvale Financial
Stocks--Prices 4520
Parkview Hospital Inc.
Corporations--Indiana 1725
Parmalat
Food Industry, International 2728
Parry-Okedon; Blair
Wealth 4844
Parsian Bank

Banks and Banking--Middle East 522
Parsons Brinckerhoff
Construction Industry 1152
Parsons Brinckerhoff Inc.
Construction Industry 1147
Construction Project Management 1196, 1197
Engineering Design 2553, 2554, 2555, 2556, 2557, 2559, 2560, 2564, 2567, 2568
Engineering Design, International 2589
Engineering Firms 2592
Environmental Services Firms 2619
Parsons Corp.
Construction Project Management 1196
Contractors 1242
Engineering Design 2561, 2566, 2567
Engineering Design, International 2590
Environmental Services Firms 2616, 2620, 2623, 2629
Information Technology 3177
Parsons Music Ltd.
Music Retailers 3796, 3813
Partena Ziekenfonds & Partners
Corporations--Belgium 1436
Partner Credit Union
Corporations--Colorado 1550
Partnerre
Corporations, Foreign 1627
PartnerRe Ltd.
Corporations--Caribbean 1533
Insurance--Reinsurance 3353, 3354, 3358
Partners HealthCare System
Group Medical Practice 2836
Partners Specialty Group LLC
Insurance Brokers 3229
Insurance, Property and Casualty 3337
Partridge Snow & Hahn LLP
Corporations--Rhode Island 2025
Partstripe Ltd.
Corporations--United Kingdom 2121
PartyLite
Direct Selling 2337
Pason Systems
High Technology Industry 2916
Passport Health
Health Care Industry 2879
Pat Stryker
Wealth 4841
Patagonia Inc.
Clothing Industry, International 1009
Patelco Credit Union
Credit Unions 2216
Patent Office; U.S.
Women Engineers 4976
Patersons Stadium
Stadiums 3487
Patient Safety Technologies Inc.
Corporations--California 1462
PatientsLikeMe
Biotechnology Industry 606
Patokh Chodiev
Wealth, Foreign 4858
Patriarch Partners LLC
Corporations--New York 1937
Patrice Motsepe
Wealth, Foreign 4908
Patricia Gandara
Hispanics 2960
Patricia Matte
Wealth, Foreign 4862
Patricia Woertz
Women in Business 4966
Patrick Apodaca
Hispanics 2958
Patrick Chalhoub
Leadership 3488

Retail Industry 4298
Patrick; Danica
Automobile Racing 267
Patrick Henry Creative Promotions
Corporations--Texas 2093
Patrick Industries Inc.
Corporations--Indiana 1731
Patrick Soon-Shiong
Wealth 4841
Patriots; New England
Football 2767
Sports Clubs 4480, 4481
Patrizio Bertelli
Wealth, Foreign 4882
Patterson Cos.
Catalogs 897
Patterson; James
Authors 211
Entertainers--Compensation 2607
Patterson; Neal
Chief Executive Officers 983
Patterson; Neal L.
Chief Executive Officers--Compensation 988
Pattinson; Robert
Entertainers 2597
Pattison; James
Wealth, Foreign 4860
Pattison; Jim
Wealth, Foreign 4861
Patton Boggs LLP
Corporations--New Jersey 1916
Law Firms 3434
Legal Services 3500
Paul Allen
Basketball 547
Football 2768
Wealth 4850
Paul; Chris
Athletes--Compensation 188
Paul Davis Restoration Inc.
Houses--Maintenance and Repair 3113
Paul Desmarais
Wealth, Foreign 4861
Paul Desmarais Sr.
Wealth, Foreign 4860
Paul Diaz
Executives--Compensation 2637
Paul Hastings Janofsky & Walker LLP
Law Firms 3433, 3446, 3449
Paul Hastings LLP
Law Firms 3438
Paul Madera
Venture Capital 4783
Paul McCartney
Entertainers 2603
Paul Rooke
Executives--Compensation 2637
Paul Varga
Executives--Compensation 2637
Paul, Weiss, Rifkind, Wharton & Garrison LLP
Law Firms 3433, 3442, 3451
Paul Young Co.
Hispanic American Business Enterprises 2927
Paula Cooper
Art Dealers 180
Pauline MacMillan Keinath
Wealth 4839
Paulmann; Horst
Wealth, Foreign 4862
Paulsen Marketing Communications
Agricultural Industry--Advertising 103
Paulson; John
Wealth 4832
Pawtucket Credit Union
Corporations--Rhode Island 2024
Credit Unions 2261
Paychex Inc.
Business Services 780, 782, 788
Financial Services 2710

Index

Taxation 4573, 4574
Teachers 4584, 4585
Transportation 4724
Unemployment 4773, 4774
Women--Employment 4971
Workers' Compensation 4999
Rhode Island Credit Union
Credit Unions 2261
Rhode Island Hospital
Corporations--Rhode Island 2028
Rhode Island Hospital Inc.
Corporations--Rhode Island 2027
Rhodes III; William
Chief Executive Officers 983
Rhon; Carlos Hank
Wealth, Foreign 4888
Rhumbline Advisers
African American Business Enterprises 82
Rhythm Engineering
Contracts, Government 1304
Corporations--Kansas 1791
Rhythmes & Sons
Music Retailers 3794
Riad Kamal
Construction Industry, International 1173
Leadership 3484
Rib-X Pharmaceuticals
Corporations--Connecticut 1572
Ric Edelman
Investment Advisors 3388
Ricardo Salinas Pliego
Wealth 4851
Wealth, Foreign 4888
Rice Dream
Milk Products 3719
Rice Financial Products Co.
African American Business Enterprises 87
Rice University, Jones Graduate School of Business
Business Schools and Colleges 750
Riceland Foods Inc.
Corporations--Arkansas 1415
Rich; Richie
Wealth 4853
Richa; Dani
Leadership 3479
Media 3652
Richard Alderman
Business Ethics 735
Richard & Sons Inc.; A. J.
Home Furnishings Stores 2997
Richard Branson
Wealth, Foreign 4922
Richard Chandler
Wealth, Foreign 4892, 4906
Richard Childress Racing
Automobile Racing 268
Richard DeVos
Wealth 4848
Richard Devos
Basketball 547
Richard Gray's
Home Electronics 2977
Richard Kinder
Chief Executive Officers--Compensation 989
Wealth 4837
Richard LeFrak
Wealth 4847
Richard Livingstone
Wealth, Foreign 4922
Richard M. Weil
Chief Executive Officers--Compensation 986
Richard Moore
Leadership 3468
Richard Petty Motorsports
Automobile Racing 268
Richard Rodgers
Celebrities 907
Richard Saperstein
Investment Advisors 3388

Richard T. O'Brien
Chief Executive Officers--Compensation 986
Richardson Projects Holdings Ltd.
Corporations--United Kingdom 2121
Richemont
Personal Care Products 3882, 3904
Richemont SA; Compagnie Financiere
Carbon 861
Clothing Industry, International 1007, 1008
Consumer Goods 1215
Corporations--Switzerland 2078
Instrument Industry 3212
Shoe Industry 4439
Specialty Stores 4471
Richie Rich
Wealth 4853
The Richman Group Affordable Housing Corp.
Apartment Houses 175
Richmond-Master Distributors Inc.
Convenience Stores 1337
Richmond Public Relations
Public Relations Firms 4151
Richmond, VA
Insurance, Automobile--Rates 3223
Veterans--Employment 4786
Rick Adelman
Basketball 545
Rick Carlisle
Basketball 545
Rick Case Honda
Automobile Dealers 217, 220
Ricoh
Office Equipment Industry 3845, 3846
Ricoh Americas Corp.
Wholesale Trade--Durable Goods 4928
Ricoh Co., Ltd.
Business Supplies 792, 794
Ricoh Corp.
Home Electronics 2987
Riddell; Clayton
Wealth, Foreign 4861
RidgeWorth Funds
Equity Funds 2635
Rietumu Banka AS
Corporations--Latvia 1812
Rieu; Andre
Concerts 1137
Right at Home Inc.
Aged--Care 91
The Right-Brain Business Plan
Books 623
Right-On Inc.
Clothing Stores 1017
RightsFlow
Corporations--New York 1931
Rihanna
Music Industry--Artists 3782, 3783
Riley Hospital for Children
Hospitals 3055, 3056
Riley P. Bechtel
Wealth 4835
Rimi Eesti Food AS
Corporations--Estonia 1597
Rimmers Music
Music Retailers 3812
RimTyme
Automobile Industry 228
Rinat Akhmetov
Wealth, Foreign 4917, 4920
Rinehart; Georgina
Wealth, Foreign 4855, 4856, 4916
Women 4953
Ringkjobing Landbobank
Banks and Banking--Europe 419
Rio Alto Mining Ltd.
Corporations--Canada 1499, 1532
Rio Tinto
Mining Industry 3736, 3737

Rio Tinto Alcan
Capital Spending 811
Rio Tinto Alcan Inc.
Corporations--Canada 1512
Mining Industry 3734
Rio Tinto Ltd.
Corporations, Foreign 1639
Corporations--United Kingdom 2127, 2128
Manufacturing Industry, International 3607
Metal Industry 3709, 3710, 3712
Mining Industry 3722, 3738
Rio Tinto plc
Petroleum Industry, Foreign 3962
RioCan REIT
Real Estate Business 4187
Rise of the Planet of the Apes
Motion Pictures 3770, 3771, 3772
Rita's Italian Ice
Ice Cream Shops 3128
Rite Aid Corp.
Corporations--Pennsylvania 1999, 2002, 2009
Drug Stores 2367, 2369, 2371, 2372, 2373
Retail Industry 4288, 4289
Supermarkets 4549
Ritter & Co.; E.
Crops 2282
Ritter Crop Services
Seed Industry 4419
Ritz
Cookies and Crackers 1341
Ritz Camera & Image LLC
Corporations--Maryland 1833
Ritz-Carlton
Hotels and Motels 3103
River City Credit Union
Credit Unions 2255
River Valley Credit Union
Credit Unions 2271
Rivera Mota
Music Retailers 3809
Riverbed Technology
Growth Companies 2840
Technology 4589, 4590
Rivermark Community Credit Union
Credit Unions 2257
Rivers; Doc
Basketball 545
Rivers; Philip
Athletes--Compensation 189
Riverside Bank
Banks and Banking--Independent Banks 486
Riverside, CA
Fast Food Restaurants 2670
Riverside Medical Center
Hospitals 3077, 3081
Riversource Life Insurance Co.
Insurance, Life 3313
Riverstone Residential Group
Apartment Houses 174
Rivet Software
Computer Software Industry 1097
Riyad Bank
Banks and Banking--Arab 361, 365, 368
Banks and Banking--Middle East 533
Brand Name Products, International 684
Corporations--Saudi Arabia 2037
Rizal Commercial Banking Corp.
Banks and Banking--Asia 394
Rizzuto; Leandro
Wealth 4843
RK Mechanical
Plumbing Industry 4058
RK Mechanical Inc.
Contractors 1228
Corporations--Colorado 1548
Family-Owned Corporations 2653
RKA Petroleum Cos.

Women-Owned Business Enterprises 4983
RLC Industries Co.
Wood Products 4990
RLI Insurance Group
Insurance, Property and Casualty 3340
RLJ Development LLC
African American Business Enterprises 86
RLJ Equity Partners LLC
African American Business Enterprises 89
RLJ McLarty Landers Automotive Group
African American Business Enterprises 83
RLJ McLarty Landers Automotive Holdings LLC
Corporations--Arkansas 1415
RMB Holdings
Corporations, Foreign 1630
Investment Management Firms 3408
RMB Inc.
Collection Agencies 1033
RMH Foods LLC
Meat Industry 3647
RNL
Engineering Design 2552
RNL Design Inc.
Architectural Firms 178
Road Runner Sports
Catalogs 902
RoadLink LLC
Trucking Industry 4760
RoadLink USA
Trucking Industry 4750
Roadnet Technologies
Computer Software Industry, International 1107, 1111
Roadway LLC
Freight and Freightage 2775
Roanoke, VA
Insurance, Automobile--Rates 3223
Veterans--Employment 4785
Robeks Premium Fruit Smoothies
Juice Bars 3430
Robert A. Clarfeld
Investment Advisors 3388
Robert A.M. Stern Architects
Interior Designers 3370
Robert Bass
Wealth 4837
Robert Bosch
Corporations--Germany 1664
Robert Bosch GmbH
Automobile Industry, International 239
Automobile Parts 265
Corporations--Europe 1603
Electronic Industry 2494
Manufacturing Industry, International 3616
Robert Bosch LLC
Automobile Parts 260
Robert Downey Jr.
Entertainers 2597
Robert Friedland
Wealth 4845
Robert; Groupe
Trucking Industry 4745
Robert Half International
Corporations--California 1476
Robert Half International Inc.
Temporary Help Service Agencies 4654
Robert Kraft
Wealth 4849
Robert Kuok
Wealth, Foreign 4887, 4916
Robert McNair
Wealth 4849
Robert Mnuchin
Art Dealers 180
Robert Mouawad

Corporations--Oregon 1984, 1987
Rose International
Private Companies 4102
Roseburg Forest Products Co.
Wood Products 4990
Rosemount-Apple Valley & Eagan
Corporations--Minnesota 1868
Rosendin Electric Inc.
Construction Industry 1151
Contractors 1272, 1273
Rosenfeld; Elana
Women-Owned Business Enter-
prises 4987
Rosenfeld; Irene
Business Leaders 741
Women 4959, 4960
Women in Business 4966
Women Executives 4979
Rosen's Diversified Inc.
Corporations--Minnesota 1871,
1875
Roses Southwest Papers Inc.
Hispanic American Business Enter-
prises 2932, 2935
Roseville Toyota
Automobile Dealers 219, 220
Rosica Public Relations
Public Relations Firms 4140
Rosneft
Brand Name Products, Interna-
tional 673
Petroleum Industry, Foreign 3968
Rosneft Oil Co.; OAO
Corporations--Russia 2035, 2036
Petroleum Industry, Foreign 3957,
3963, 3964, 3969
Petroleum--Reserves 3990
Rosneft; OJSC
Energy Industry 2535, 2549
Petroleum Industry, Interna-
tional 3976
Ross Dress for Less
Discount Stores 2340
**Ross School of Business; Univer-
sity of Michigan**
Business Schools and Col-
leges 748, 750
Ross-Simons
Catalogs 895
Ross; Stephen
Wealth 4847
Ross; Stephen M.
Football 2768
Ross Stores
Clothing Stores 1014
Corporations 1388
Ross Stores Inc.
Clothing Stores 1013, 1015, 1016,
1018, 1021, 1022
Information Technology 3192
Specialty Stores 4468, 4472
Rossi; Roberto Angelini
Wealth, Foreign 4862
Rostelecom
Brand Name Products, Interna-
tional 673
Telecommunications Industry 4619,
4620
Rotel
Audio and Video Equipment 194
Rothblatt; Martine
Women--Compensation 4967
Rothgerber Johnson & Lyons LLP
Law Firms 3434
Rothschild Asset Management Inc.
Investment Advisors 3390
Rothstein Kass
Corporations--Colorado 1552
Corporations--New York 1932
Corporations--Texas 2090
Rothstein, Kass & Co.
Accounting Firms 18
Rothstein; Rebecca
Investment Advisors 3389
**Rotman School of Business; Uni-
versity of Toronto**

Business Schools and Colleges,
Foreign 758
Roto-Rooter Services Co.
Contractors 1250
Plumbing Industry 4061
Rotonics Manufacturing Inc.
Plastics--Molding 4054
Rotork
Corporations--United King-
dom 2112, 2115, 2116, 2117,
2125
Engineering 2550
Rotterdam School of Management
Business Schools and Colleges,
Foreign 760
Business Schools and Colleges,
International 771
Round Rock Honda
Automobile Dealers 216
Round Table Pizza
Pizza 4046
Round Table Pizza Inc.
Pizza 4045
Roundbank
Banks and Banking--Independent
Banks 483
Roundys Supermarkets Inc.
Corporations--Wisconsin 2196
Supermarkets 4529
Rouses Enterprises
Supermarkets 4550
Roush Fenway Racing
Automobile Racing 268
Rousseff; Dilma
Women 4954, 4960
Route1 Inc.
Computer Software Industry, Inter-
national 1108
Rovi
Media Companies 3654
Rowling; J. K.
Wealth, Foreign 4905
Rowling; J.K.
Women 4952
Rowling; Joanne
Women 4952
Rowling; Robert
Wealth 4837
Roxul Inc.
Corporations--Canada 1525
Roy O. Martin Lumber Co.
Forestry 2772
Roy Smith Co.
Asian Americans in Business 183
Royal Ahold NV
Carbon 845
Corporations--Netherlands 1907,
1909
Environmental Protection 2614
Retail Industry 4292
Retail Stores 4336
Supermarkets 4535, 4553
Royal Air Maroc
Airlines, International 132
Royal Bam Groep NV
Contractors, Foreign 1287
Contractors, International 1295
Royal Bank of Canada
Banks and Banking--North
America 537, 538, 542, 543
Corporations--Canada 1492, 1493,
1494, 1500, 1503, 1505, 1511,
1518, 1519
Finance Companies 2682
Stocks 4508
Royal Bank of Scotland
Banks and Banking--Europe 474
Corporations--Pennsylvania 2008,
2010
**The Royal Bank of Scotland Group
plc**
Banks and Banking--Europe 441,
442, 472, 473
Banks and Banking, Interna-
tional 489
Corporations, International 1755

Corporations--United King-
dom 2122
Junk Bonds 3431
Syndicated Loans 4561
Royal Bank of Scotland plc
Banks and Banking--Europe 476
Royal Canin
Corporations--Spain 2062
Royal Caribbean Cruises Ltd.
Homosexuals--Employment 3040
Hotels and Motels 3099
Water Transportation Ser-
vices 4829, 4830
Royal Caribbean International
Cruise Lines 2285
Royal Credit Union
Credit Unions 2215, 2275
Royal DSM NV
Carbon 845
Chemical Industry, Interna-
tional 952
Manufacturing Industry, Interna-
tional 3582
Royal Dutch Shell plc
Carbon 844, 876
Chemical Industry, Interna-
tional 948, 961, 969
Coal Industry 1025
Corporations--Europe 1602, 1604,
1606
Corporations, Foreign 1635, 1639,
1640
Corporations, International 1756,
1757, 1758, 1759, 1763, 1764,
1765
Corporations--Netherlands 1906,
1907, 1908, 1909
Corporations--United King-
dom 2112, 2114, 2115, 2116,
2117, 2125, 2127
Energy Industry 2535, 2547, 2549
Manufacturing Industry, Interna-
tional 3582, 3617
Petroleum Industry, Foreign 3952,
3957, 3962, 3964
Petroleum Industry, Interna-
tional 3976, 3978, 3983
Petroleum Refineries 3989
Royal Gold
Corporations--Colorado 1553
Materials 3633
Royal Group Inc.
Pipes 4043
Royal Hyway Tours Inc.
Buses 728
Royal Jordanian Airlines Co., plc
Airlines, International 131
Royal KPN NV
Carbon 844, 878
Corporations--Netherlands 1909
Telecommunications Industry 4602,
4611, 4618, 4638
Royal Mail
Shipping 4438
Royal Mail Group
Corporations--United King-
dom 2123
Royal Malewane
Hotels and Motels 3104
Royal Mall Group
Corporations--United King-
dom 2124
Royal Oak Ford Sales Inc.
African American Business Enter-
prises 83
Royal Palm Toyota/Scion
Automobile Dealers 216
Royal Philips Electronics NV
Aerospace Industry 76
Carbon 844
Corporations--Netherlands 1907,
1908
Corporations--Pennsylvania 2008
Electronic Industry 2487, 2497
Environmental Protection 2613
Leisure 3508

Manufacturing Industry, Interna-
tional 3582
Royal Ten Cate USA Inc.
Textile Industry 4658
Royce Opportunity Investment
Mutual Funds 3815
RPG
Audio and Video Equipment 192
RPM International Inc.
Coatings 1028
Paint Industry 3858, 3859
RREEF
Industrial Parks 3165
RREEF Americas
Real Estate Owners 4203
RSA Insurance
Insurance, Life 3285
RSA Insurance Group
Insurance Companies, Interna-
tional 3247
RSA Insurance Group plc
Insurance, Property and Casu-
alty 3346
RSI Home Products
Wood Products 4993
RSL Fiber Systems
Manufacturing Industry 3561
RSM McGladrey
Accounting Firms 14
Value-Added Resellers (Comput-
ers) 4779
RSM Tenon
Accounting Firms, International 25,
26, 27, 28, 29
RSVP Publications
Advertising 45
RT Mart Taiwan
Retail Industry 4295
RTI
Audio and Video Equipment 205
RTI Cryogenics
High Technology Industry 2900
RTI Cryogenics Inc.
High Technology Industry 2911
RTI International
Contracts, Government 1321
RTKL
Architectural Firms 179
RTKL Associates Inc.
Architectural Firms 177
RTL Group
Broadcasting Industry 705
Corporations--Luxembourg 1821,
1822
RTL Networks Inc.
Minority Business Enterprises 3751
RTN Credit Union
Credit Unions 2237
Ruan Transport Corp.
Tank Trucks 4562
Trucking Industry 4747
**Ruan Transportation Management
Systems**
Trucking Industry 4756
Rubel; Matthew E.
Chief Executive Officers--Compen-
sation 988
RubinBrown
Accounting Firms 19
RubinBrown LLP
Accounting Firms 5
Ruby Receptionists
Corporations--Oregon 1986
Ruby Tuesday
Restaurants 4239, 4240
Ruckus
Broadband Communication Sys-
tems 698
Wireless Communications Sys-
tem 4944
Ruder Finn
Public Relations Firms 4125, 4127,
4133, 4136, 4141, 4146
Rudolph & Sletten Inc.
Contractors 1231
Rue Insurance

Electric Utilities, International 2430, 2434, 2450
Energy Industry 2530
Scottrade
Electronic Commerce--Advertising 2479
Scottrade Bank
Individual Retirement Accounts (IRA's) 3137
Savings and Loan Associations 4382
Scottrade Inc.
Brokers--Internet 716
Corporations--Missouri 1891
Discount Brokers 2339
Layoffs 3467
Scotts Lawn Service
Lawn Care Services 3458, 3459, 3460, 3461, 3462, 3465
Scotts LawnService
Lawn Care Services 3464
Scottsdale Healthcare Corp.
Corporations--Arizona 1411
Scottsdale Insurance Co.
Insurance--Excess and Surplus Lines 3260, 3261
The Scoular Co.
Corporations--Nebraska 1904
Food Industry 2715
SCRA
Corporations--South Carolina 2045
Scranton-Wilkes-Barre, PA
Location of Industry--Growth 3543
The Screenmobile
Houses--Maintenance and Repair 3114
Scribner
Booksellers and Bookselling 630
Scripps Green Hospital
Hospitals 3077
Scripps Health
Aged--Employment 92
Compensation 1062
Diversity 2358
Women--Employment 4968
Scripps Networks Interactive
Cable Networks 805
SDA Bocconi
Business Schools and Colleges, Foreign 760
SDI International Corp.
Hispanic American Business Enterprises 2938
SEA Corp.
Corporations--Rhode Island 2024
Seaboard Corp.
Corporations--Kansas 1793, 1794, 1797, 1798, 1799
Food Industry 2723
Seaboard Foods
Meat Industry 3639
Pork Industry 4064
Seabourn
Cruise Lines 2287
Hotels and Motels 3101
Leisure 3506
SeaBright Insurance Holdings
Corporations--Washington 2170
SeaComm Federal Credit Union
Corporations--New York 1934
Seacor Holdings Inc.
Water Transportation Services 4829, 4830
Seacrest; Ryan
Entertainers 2604
SeaDream Yacht Club
Cruise Lines 2287
Seadrill
Petroleum Equipment Industry 3916
Seadrill Ltd.
Corporations--Caribbean 1533
Energy Industry 2546
Seagate Technology Inc.
Computer Industry 1088
Computer Storage Devices 1133

Corporations, Foreign 1638
Corporations--Ireland 1775
Seagate Technology plc
Manufacturing Industry, International 3590
Sealed Air
Corporations, International 1737
Sealed Air Corp.
Container Industry 1222, 1224
Corporations, International 1742
Corporations--New Jersey 1922
Paper Industry 3861, 3862
Plastic Films 4050
Plastics Industry 4052, 4053
Sealy Corp.
Furniture Industry 2783
Home Furnishings Industry 2993
Sean (Diddy) Combs
Entertainers 2602
The Search
Best Sellers 568
Searcy Living Magazine
Adoption 33
Sears Canada
Corporate Directors 1350
Retail Industry 4301
Sears Hardware Stores
Home Improvement Centers 3000
Sears Holding Corp.
Private Trucking Fleets 4115
Sears Holdings
Clothing Stores 1020
Corporations, International 1744, 1746, 1747, 1749, 1752
Sears Holdings Corp.
Advertising--Appeal to Hispanics 66
Advertising, Newspaper 74
Catalogs 894
Chain Stores 921
Corporations 1392
Corporations--Illinois 1710, 1713
Department Stores 2320, 2321, 2323
Electronic Commerce 2465
Home Electronics 2984
Home Furnishings Stores 2998
Homosexuals--Employment 3038
Retail Industry 4280, 4281, 4302, 4304, 4305
Retail Industry--Advertising 4315
Retail Stores 4348
Veterans--Employment 4800
Sears Home & Business Franchises Inc.
Houses--Maintenance and Repair 3111
Sears, Roebuck & Co.
Retail Industry 4280
Sears.com
Electronic Commerce 2462
SEAT Ibiza
Automobiles 276
Seaton; Ken
Leadership 3468
SeatonCorp
Private Companies 4102, 4103
Seattle Children's Hospital
Hospitals 3046, 3051, 3052, 3054, 3056
Seattle, WA
Fast Food Restaurants 2670
Ports 4066
Private Companies 4101
Veterans--Employment 4787
Seattle's Best
Coffee 1029, 1030
Seaway Bank & Trust Co.
African American Business Enterprises 84
SEB banka
Banks and Banking--Europe 444
SEB Bankas
Banks and Banking--Europe 446
SEB; Groupe
Housewares 3119
SEB Pank

Banks and Banking--Europe 421
SEB SA; Groupe
Housewares 3123
Sebastian Pinera
Wealth, Foreign 4862
Sebelius; Kathleen
Women 4959
Secom
Carbon 840
SECOM Co., Ltd.
Business Services 787
SecondMarket
Growth Companies 2837
Securian Financial Group Inc.
Corporations--Minnesota 1871
Information Technology 3170
Insurance, Life 3299, 3300, 3301, 3302, 3310
Securitas Holdings Inc.
Business Services 778
Corporations, Foreign 1636
Private Companies 4097
Securitas Security Services USA Inc.
Business Services 778
Security Bank Corp.
Banks and Banking--Asia 373, 394
Security National Insurance Co.
Insurance, Automobile 3216
Security Networks
Security Systems 4414
Security Service Credit Union
Credit Unions 2266, 2267, 2268
Security State Bank
Banks and Banking--Independent Banks 486
Sedgwick
Law Firms 3444, 3446
Sedro-Woolley School District
Corporations--Washington 2164
Seedorff Masonry Inc.
Contractors 1276
SeekingSitters Franchise System Inc.
Child Care Centers 992
Sefrioui; Anas
Wealth, Foreign 4890
Sega Sammy Holdings Inc.
Recreation Industry 4207, 4208
Seguridad Atlas Ltda.
Corporations--Colombia 1545
Seguros Bolivar
Corporations--Latin America 1810
Seguros Bolivar SA
Corporations--Colombia 1545
Seguros de Riesgos Profesionales Suramericana SA
Corporations--Colombia 1545
Seguros de Vida Suramericana SA
Corporations--Colombia 1545
Seguros Generales Suramericana SA
Corporations--Colombia 1545
Seifi Ghasemi
Executives--Compensation 2636
Seiko Epson Corp.
Business Supplies 792, 794
Seinfeld; Jerry
Entertainers 2600
SEIU Healthcare
Labor Unions 3432
Sekisui Chemical
Construction Industry, International 1170
Sekisui House
Construction Industry, International 1170
Selco Community Credit Union
Credit Unions 2257
Select Comfort
Furniture Stores 2791, 2792
Mattress Industry 3634
Select Greater Philadelphia
Location of Industry 3530
Select Health of South Carolina
Corporations--South Carolina 2045

Select Medical Holdings Corp.
Corporations--Pennsylvania 2002
Health Care Industry 2872
Rehabilitation Services 4212
Select Sector SPDR Financial
Stocks 4514
Selectbuild Construction Inc.
Construction Industry 1148
Selena Gomez & the Scene
Music Industry--Artists 3785
Self-Help Credit Union
Credit Unions 2251
Self Reliance New York Credit Union
Credit Unions 2213
Selim Zilka
Leadership 3476
Sellers, Richardson, Holman & West
Accounting Firms 17
Selmi; Habib
Leadership 3489
SEMAFO Inc.
Stocks 4512
Semahat Sevim Arsel
Wealth, Foreign 4919
Semen Gresik
Corporations--Indonesia 1733
SemGroup Corp.
Pipeline Companies 4041
Sempra Energy
Electric Utilities 2424
Gas Utilities 2805, 2807, 2813, 2817, 2820
Homosexuals--Employment 3021
Information Technology 3182
Natural Gas 3821
Private Trucking Fleets 4112
Senequier; Dominique
Women 4956
Seng; Ong Beng
Wealth, Foreign 4906
Senheng Electric
Retail Industry 4286
Senior Helpers
Aged--Care 91
Private Companies 4102
Senior plc
Defense Industry 2297
Sennheiser Electronic
Music Industry 3781
Sentinel Credit Union
Credit Unions 2264
Sentra; Nissan
Automobiles 276
Senuku Prekybos Centras UAB
Corporations--Lithuania 1814
SEOmoz Daily SEO Blog
Blogs 608, 610
SEP
Corporations--Indiana 1722
SEPCO Electric Power Construction Corp.
Contractors, International 1300
Sephora
Brand Name Products, International 662
Sephora.com
Electronic Commerce 2470
Septagon Industries
Roofing 4349
Sequans Communications
Securities--Initial Public Offerings 4405
Sequel Natural Ltd.
Construction Industry, International 1160
Manufacturing Industry, International 3570
Sequoia
Stock Funds 4506
Sequoia Capital
Venture Capital 4784
Sequoia Senior Solutions
Corporations--California 1452
Ser Padres

St. Gobain Corp.
Stone 4522
St.-Gobain Delaware Corp.
Stone 4522
St. Helena Hospital
Corporations--California 1472
St. Ives
Personal Care Products 3894
St. James's Place Wealth Management
Insurance, Life 3285
St. John Health System Inc.
Amusement Industry 173
Corporations--Oklahoma 1978
St. John Providence Health System
Corporations--Michigan 1861
St. John's Health System Inc.
Corporations--Missouri 1889
St. John's Hospital
Hospitals 3079
St. John's Mercy Health System
Corporations--Missouri 1889
St. John's Music
Music Retailers 3789, 3790
St. John's Regional Health Center
Corporations--Missouri 1889
St. Joseph East
Hospitals 3075
St. Joseph Health System
Corporations--California 1466, 1474
St. Joseph Medical Center Inc.
Corporations--Maryland 1833
St. Joseph Mercy Hospital
Hospitals 3079
St. Joseph Mercy Oakland Foundation
Corporations--Michigan 1859
St. Joseph's Healthcare Hamilton
Corporations--Canada 1525
St. Joseph's Hospital & Medical Center
Hospitals 3064
St. Jude Children's Research Hospital
Corporations--Tennessee 2086
Employee Benefits 2509
Hospitals 3046
Layoffs 3467
St. Jude Medical Inc.
Corporations--Minnesota 1881
Manufacturing Industry, International 3614
Medical Equipment and Supplies 3672, 3673, 3674, 3677, 3678, 3679
Medical Instruments and Apparatus 3684
St. Louis Children's Hospital
Hospitals 3052, 3053, 3054, 3055
St. Louis Community Credit Union
Credit Unions 2243
St. Lucia
Economy 2387
St. Luke's Boise Medical Center
Hospitals 3079
St. Luke's Episcopal Hospital; Texas Heart Institute
Hospitals 3058
St. Luke's Health System
Corporations--Idaho 1696
St. Lukes Health System Ltd.
Corporations--Idaho 1698
St. Luke's Hospital
Hospitals 3079
St. Luke's Hospital & Health Network
Corporations--Pennsylvania 1998
St. Lukes Regional Medical Center Ltd.
Corporations--Idaho 1698
St. Margaret Mercy Healthcare Center
Corporations--Indiana 1725
St. Martin's

Booksellers and Bookselling 626, 628, 630
St. Mary's Bank Credit Union
Credit Unions 2247
St. Mary's Duluth Clinic Health System Hospice & Palliative Care
Corporations--Minnesota 1868
St. Marys Health System
Corporations--Maine 1825
St. Mary's Hospital-Superior
Hospitals 3081
St. Mary's Medical Center Inc.
Corporations--West Virginia 2189
St. Mary's University of Minnesota
Business Schools and Colleges 753
St. Patrick Hospital & Health Sciences Center
Corporations--Montana 1896
St. Patrick Hospital Corp.
Corporations--Montana 1896, 1897
St. Paul Fire & Marine Insurance Co.
Corporations--Minnesota 1868
St. Peters Hospital
Corporations--Montana 1896
St. Petersburg College
Nursing 3836
St. Regis Hotel
Hotels and Motels 3103
St. Thomas Credit Union
Credit Unions 2269
St. Thomas, Opus College of Business; University of
Business Schools and Colleges 753
St. Vincent
Economy 2387
St. Vincent Health Services Inc.
Corporations--Arkansas 1417
St. Vincent Health System
Corporations--Arkansas 1417
St. Vincent Healthcare Foundation Inc.
Corporations--Montana 1896
St. Vincent Heart Center of Indiana
Hospitals 3045
St. Vincent Hospital
Corporations--New Mexico 1929
Hospitals 3077, 3078
St. Vincent Hospital & Health Care Center Inc.
Corporations--Indiana 1725
St. Vincent Indianapolis Hospital
Hospitals 3077
Stacker 2
Sports Drink Industry 4485
Stacker 26-Hour Power
Sports Drink Industry 4485
Stacker2
Beverages 593
Stacker2 6 Hour Power
Beverages 593
Stacy Bash-Polley
Women in Business 4965
Stacy's Pita Chips
Cookies and Crackers 1341
Stadium of Light
Stadiums 4487
Stafford-Smith Inc.
Food Distribution 2714
Stagecoach: California's Country Music Festival
Concerts 1142
Stagecoach Group plc
Corporations--United Kingdom 2117
Transportation 4711
Staker Parsons Cos.
Contractors 1236
Staluppi Auto Group
Automobile Dealers 214
Stampede Meat Inc.
Meat Industry 3641, 3642, 3643, 3645, 3649
Stan Kroenke

Hockey 2966
Stan Van Gundy
Basketball 545
Stanbank
Banks and Banking--Africa 352
Corporations--South Africa 2044
Stanbic Bank Botswana
Banks and Banking--Africa 336
Stanbic Bank Ghana
Banks and Banking--Africa 332
Stanbic Bank Tanzania
Banks and Banking--Africa 355
Stanbic Bank Uganda
Banks and Banking--Africa 357
Stanbic Bank Zambia
Banks and Banking--Africa 358
Stanbic Bank Zimbabwe
Banks and Banking--Africa 359
Stanbic IBTC Bank
Banks and Banking--Africa 348
StanCorp Financial Group Inc.
Corporations--Washington 2170
Insurance, Life 3317
StanCorp Investment Advisers Inc.
Investment Advisors 3391
Standard Bank Group
Banks and Banking--Africa 333, 340, 352
Carbon 853
Corporations--South Africa 2044
Standard Bank Malawi
Banks and Banking--Africa 342
Standard Bank Mauritius
Banks and Banking--Africa 344
Standard Bank Mozambique
Banks and Banking--Africa 346
Standard Bank Namibia
Banks and Banking--Africa 347
Standard Bank Swaziland
Banks and Banking--Africa 354
Standard Chartered
Banks and Banking--Europe 474
Standard Chartered Bank
Brand Name Products, International 669
Standard Chartered Bank Botswana
Banks and Banking--Africa 336
Standard Chartered Bank Ghana
Banks and Banking--Africa 332
Standard Chartered Bank Hong Kong
Banks and Banking--Asia 381
Standard Chartered Bank Kenya
Banks and Banking--Africa 338
Brand Name Products, International 688
Standard Chartered Bank Korea
Banks and Banking--Asia 398
Standard Chartered Bank Mauritius
Banks and Banking--Africa 344
Standard Chartered Bank plc
Banks and Banking--Europe 414, 422, 472, 473, 475
Banks and Banking, International 494
Corporations--United Kingdom 2128
Standard Chartered Bank Thailand
Banks and Banking--Asia 402
Standard Drywall Inc.
Contractors 1283
Standard Insurance Co.
Insurance, Life 3312
Standard Insurance Group
Insurance, Life 3302
Standard Life Assurance Co. of Canada
Insurance, Life 3298
Standard Life Financial
Insurance, Life 3297
Standard Life plc
Insurance Companies, International 3253
Insurance, Life 3288, 3322
Standard Pacific Corp.

Construction Industry, Residential 1184
Standard Parking Corp.
Automobiles--Maintenance and Repair 279
The Standard Register Co.
Printing Industry 4076
Standard Solar
Energy Industry 2529
Standex International Corp.
Corporations--New Hampshire 1915
Standing Partnership
Public Relations Firms 4126, 4139
Standing Stone Brewing Co.
Corporations--Oregon 1984
Stanford Hospital & Clinics
Corporations--California 1463
Stanford University
Business Schools and Colleges 749, 754, 756
Business Schools and Colleges, International 769
Stanley Black & Decker
Metal Industry 3707
Stanley Black & Decker Inc.
Corporations--Connecticut 1573, 1577, 1580
Home Furnishings Industry 2992, 2995
Housewares 3121, 3123
Metal Industry 3697
Personal Care Products 3890, 3900
Stanley Consultants
Engineering Design 2557
Stanley Convergent Security Solutions Inc.
Security Systems 4408, 4413, 4415
Stanley Kroenke
Basketball 547
Football 2768
Stantec
Engineering Design 2558
Interior Designers 3364, 3372
Stantec Architecture
Interior Designers 3362, 3365, 3368
Stantec Consulting Services Inc.
Engineering Design 2556
Stantec Inc.
Engineering Design 2554, 2559, 2571
Engineering Design, International 2579, 2586, 2588
Engineering Firms 2592
Environmental Services Firms 2618, 2621
Staples Center
Concerts 1140
Staples Inc.
Catalogs 903
Corporations--Massachusetts 1842, 1844, 1846, 1847
Electronic Commerce 2463, 2465
Home Electronics 2981
Homosexuals--Employment 3038
Office Supply Stores 3848
Retail Industry 4288, 4289, 4299
Specialty Stores 4465, 4466, 4469, 4471, 4473
Staples.com
Electronic Commerce 2476
Star Fleet Trucking Inc.
Trucking Industry 4762
The Star Group
Women-Owned Business Enterprises 4985
Star Nursery
Garden Centers 2797
Star One
Communications Satellites 1059
Star One Credit Union
Credit Unions 2211, 2216, 2260, 2267
Star Paving Co.

Corporations--California 1465
Wholesale Trade--Electronics 4930,
4931
Synnex Corp.
Wholesale Trade--Durable
Goods 4929
Synova Inc.
Asian Americans in Business 183
Synovate
Research 4213, 4214
Synovus Bank
Bank Loans 289
Synovus Financial Corp.
Banks and Banking 302
Synta Pharmaceuticals
Growth Companies 2841, 2849
Syntel
Computer Software Industry 1095
Syntel Inc.
Computer Software Industry, Inter-
national 1110
Synthes
Orthopedic Products 3852
Synthes Inc.
Carbon 862
Health Care Industry 2866
Synthon Hispania
Corporations--Spain 2060
Syntroleum Corp.
Growth Companies 2849
Syria
Auditing 209
Corporations, Foreign 1626
Crime and Criminals 2279, 2280
Employee Training 2514
Research and Development 4216
Terrorism 4656
Women--Employment 4970
Sysco
Corporations, International 1739,
1740
Sysco Corp.
Corporations--Texas 2097, 2098,
2103
Drug Stores 2370
Private Trucking Fleets 4106, 4109,
4111
Supermarkets 4543, 4544, 4548,
4553
Wholesale Trade--Food 4932, 4933
Wholesale Trade--Non-durable
Goods 4936, 4937
Sysgtems Electro Coating
African American Business Enter-
prises 79
Syska Hennessy Group
Engineering Design 2566
Engineering Firms 2593
Syst
Retail Stores 4329
System4
Home-Based Businesses 2972
Houses--Maintenance and Re-
pair 3111
Systemax
Catalogs 891
Systembolaget AB
Retail Stores 4343
**Systems Management/Planning
Inc.**
Corporations--New York 1947
SYSTRA
Engineering Design, Interna-
tional 2587
Systrand Manufacturing Corp.
Minority Business Enterprises 3757
Szatmar Butorgyar Kft
Corporations--Hungary 1694
Sze; David
Venture Capital 4783

T

T
Telecommunications Industry 4605
T & D Holdings

Insurance, Life 3289
T & K Toka
Ink 3208
T. B. Penich & Sons
Contractors 1237
T-Bonds
Futures Contracts 2794
T. G. I. Friday's
Restaurants 4238, 4239, 4240
T. H. Agri-Chemicals Inc.
Crops 2283
T. Kurosawa & Co., Ltd.
Music Retailers 3798
T-Mobile
Brand Name Products, Interna-
tional 649
Telecommunications Industry 4605
T-Mobile USA Inc.
Corporations--Washington 2161
Homosexuals--Employment 3039
Telecommunications Industry 4637
Veterans--Employment 4796, 4813
Wireless Telephones 4947
T-Notes
Futures Contracts 2794
**T. Rowe Price Emerging Markets
Stock**
Mutual Funds 3817
T. Rowe Price Group
Environmental Protection 2612
T. Rowe Price Group Inc.
Corporations--Maryland 1835, 1837
Securities Firms 4394
T. Rowe Price Small-Cap Value
Stock Funds 4507
T. Troy Dixon
Financial Executives 2683
T. Y. Tsai
Wealth, Foreign 4913
T. Z. Group
Chemical Industry--Distributors 936
T4F: Time For Fun
Concerts 1136
Tabari; Khaldoun
Leadership 3477
Tableau Software
Computer Software Industry, Inter-
national 1107, 1111
Tabula
Computer Industry 1090
Taco Bell
Fast Food 2659
Fast Food Restaurants 2662, 2663,
2664
Restaurants 4262, 4264, 4265
Sandwiches 4364, 4365
Taco Bell Corp.
Restaurants 4232
Tacoma, WA
Ports 4066
Taconic Farms Inc.
Livestock 3515
TacoTime
Fast Food Restaurants 2671
Tadamon Islamic Bank
Banks and Banking--Africa 353
Tadashi Yanai
Wealth, Foreign 4883
Tae-Won; Chey
Wealth, Foreign 4909
Taff Housing Association
Corporations--United Kingdom 2110
TAG Holdings LLC
African American Business Enter-
prises 85, 86
Tag Oil Ltd.
Corporations--Canada 1499
Tagged
Internet Sites 3384
Taha Mikati
Wealth, Foreign 4886
Taiga Building Products Ltd.
Corporations--Canada 1530
Forest Products Industry 2770
Taiheiyo Cement
Construction Materials 1192

Taiheiyo Cement Corp.
Building Materials Industry 726
Taikisha Ltd.
Contractors, International 1297,
1298
Taipei Fubon Bank
Banks and Banking--Asia 400
Taipei, Taiwan
Airports, Cargo 162
Taisei
Construction Industry, Interna-
tional 1170
Taishin Financial Holdings
Investment Management
Firms 3412
Taisho Pharmaceutical
Pharmaceutical Industry, Interna-
tional 4010
Taiwan
Competition, International 1070
Customer Service 2288
Economy 2383
Export/Import Trade 2643
Financial Services 2690
Patents 3875
Research and Development 4215
Taiwan Business Bank
Banks and Banking--Asia 401
Taiwan Cement Co., Ltd.
Carbon 864, 881
Taiwan Cooperative Bank
Banks and Banking--Asia 400
Financial Services 2705
Taiwan Family Mart
Retail Industry 4295
Taiwan Mobile Co., Ltd.
Telecommunications Industry 4626
Taiwan Semiconductor
Computer Industry 1091
**Taiwan Semiconductor Manufac-
turing Co., Ltd.**
Carbon 863
Corporations--Taiwan 2082
High Technology Industry 2922
Manufacturing Industry, Interna-
tional 3611
Semiconductor Industry 4426,
4429, 4430
Tajikistan
Taxation 4566
Takahara; Keiichiro
Wealth, Foreign 4883
Takashimaya
Department Stores 2318, 2319
Takashimaya Co., Ltd.
Retail Stores 4334
Takashimaya (Singapore)
Retail Industry 4293
Take That
Concerts 1137, 1138
Music Industry--Artists 3785
Take-Two Interactive Software Inc.
Toys 4698
Takeda Pharmaceutical Co., Ltd.
Pharmaceutical Industry, Interna-
tional 4010
Takemitsu Takizaki
Wealth, Foreign 4883
Takenaka Corp.
Contractors, International 1298
Takizaki; Takemitsu
Wealth, Foreign 4883
Takkt America
Catalogs 897
Talal Al Zain
Leadership 3474
Talbots
Catalogs 905
Talbott Vineyards
Wine Industry 4941
Taleo Corp.
Growth Companies 2840
Talisman Energy
Petroleum Industry, Foreign 3954
Talisman Energy Inc.

Petroleum Industry, Foreign 3953,
3973
Talisman Engineering
Carbon 821
Tallink Grupp AS
Corporations--Estonia 1597
TAM Linhas Aereas SA
Airlines, International 137, 138
Tam Tam Percusion SL
Music Retailers 3809
Tamara Gustavson
Wealth 4848
**Tamim; Lieutenant General Dahi
Khalfan**
Leadership 3490
Tamoil Overseas Ltd.
Corporations--Cyprus 1583
Tampa Bay Rays
Sports Clubs 4480
Tampa, FL
Insurance, Automobile--Rates 3225
Tampa Pipeline Corp.
Pipeline Companies 4041
**Tampa-St. Petersburg-Clearwater,
FL**
Location of Industry--Growth 3541
Tampico
Fruit Drinks 2780
Tamro Oyj
Corporations--Finland 1611
Tan; Andrew
Wealth, Foreign 4897, 4898
Tan; Lucio
Wealth, Foreign 4897, 4898
Tan; Vincent
Wealth, Foreign 4887
Tanaka; Yoshikazu
Wealth, Foreign 4883
Tandy Brands Accessories Inc.
Leather Industry 3498
Tang-Martinez; Zuleyma
Hispanics 2960
Tang Yiu
Wealth, Foreign 4873, 4874
Tangible
Direct Marketing Agencies 2325
Tanjong plc
Leisure 3503
Tanjung; Chairul
Wealth, Foreign 4878
Tanner
Accounting Firms 20
Tanoto; Sukanto
Wealth, Foreign 4877, 4878
Tanzania
Diseases 2343
Gross Domestic Product 2831
Women--Employment 4969
Tapestry
Hispanic American Business Enter-
prises 2944
TAQA
Brand Name Products, Interna-
tional 685
Corporations--United Arab Emir-
ates 2109
Tara; Sarik
Wealth, Foreign 4919
Taraabt; Adel
Leadership 3481
Targa Resources
Corporations 1389
Targa Resources Partners LP
Petroleum Pipelines 3984
Target
Brand Name Products 638
Electronic Commerce 2460
Retail Industry 4308, 4313, 4314
Supermarkets 4536
Target Corp.
Advertising--Appeal to Hispanics 66
Advertising, Newspaper 74
Chain Stores 915, 917, 919, 920,
921
College Graduates 1036, 1037,
1038

Index

Index

Zhenjiang Xinhua Bookstore
Media 3651
Zhevago; Kostyantin
Wealth, Foreign 4920
Zhong Sheng Jian
Wealth, Foreign 4907
Ziad Rahbani
Celebrities 906
Ziani; Karim
Leadership 3473
Zicklin School of Business;
Baruch College
Business Schools and Colleges 755
Ziebart
Automobiles 273
Zier; David
Investment Advisors 3388
ZIGEXN Co., Ltd.
Corporations--Japan 1786
Zigin Mining Group
Metal Industry 3688
Zilka; Selim
Leadership 3476
Zimbabwe
AIDS (Disease) 112
Diseases 2344
Economy 2384, 2392
Export/Import Trade 2642
New Business Enterprises 3826
Venture Capital 4781
Zimmer Holdings Inc.
Corporations--Indiana 1723, 1726
Medical Equipment and Supplies 3672, 3673
Orthopedic Products 3852

The Zimmerman Agency
Public Relations Firms 4149
Zimmerman Agency
Public Relations Firms 4134
Zions Bancorp
Corporations--Utah 2134
ZipCar
Automobile Leasing and Renting 252
Zipfy Inc.
Growth Companies 2839
Zips Dry Cleaners
Dry Cleaning 2379
Zix Corp.
Corporations--Texas 2095
ZocDoc
Health Care Industry 2862, 2863
ZocDoc Inc.
Corporations--New York 1931
Zoes Kitchen
Restaurants 4231
Zoll Medical
Corporations--Massachusetts 1839
Health Care Industry 2864
Zondervan
Booksellers and Bookselling 630
Zong Qinghou
Wealth, Foreign 4863, 4864
Zongshen PEM Power Systems
Automobile Industry, International 242
Zoomlion Heavy Industry
Corporations--Asia Pacific 1426
Industrial Equipment Industry 3142
Zoup! Systems LLC
Fast Food Restaurants 2673

ZTE Corp.
Communication Equipment Industry 1051
Wireless Telephones 4948
Zubi Advertising Services
Hispanic American Business Enterprises 2943
Zu'bi; Fawaz
Telecommunications Industry 4614
Zuckerberg; Mark
Business Leaders 740, 741
Leadership 3493
Wealth 4850
Zuellig Australia Pharmacy Services
Retail Industry 4278
Zuleyma Tang-Martinez
Hispanics 2960
Zumiez
Corporations--Washington 2172
Zurcher Kantonalbank
Banks and Banking--Europe 466
Zurich
Brand Name Products, International 677
Insurance, International 3278, 3283, 3284
Zurich Financial Services
Corporations--Switzerland 2077, 2078
Insurance Companies, International 3256
Insurance, Property and Casualty 3349
Zurich Financial Services AG

Corporations--Switzerland 2076, 2079
Insurance Companies, International 3253, 3255
Zurich Financial Services Ltd.
Insurance, Automobile 3214, 3215
Insurance, Commercial 3237
Insurance Companies, International 3247, 3251, 3252, 3257
Insurance, Earthquake 3259
Insurance, Homeowners 3272
Insurance, Property and Casualty 3345, 3351
Insurance, Warranty 3359
Zurich Financial Services North America Group
Insurance, Automobile 3220
Insurance, Commercial 3238
Insurance, Marine 3329
Workers' Compensation 5001
Zurich Insurance Group
Insurance, Property and Casualty 3342
Zurich Services Corp.
Business Losses 746
Zwirner; David
Art Dealers 180
Zygunt Solorz-Zak
Wealth, Foreign 4899
Zylog Systems Ltd.
Computer Software Industry, International 1130
Zynex Inc.
Corporations--Colorado 1555
Zynga
Internet 3379